Phonetic symbols

Symbol	*Pronounced as in Standard English words (as spoken by Scottish speakers)*

Consonants

j	**y**ard
x	lo**ch**
hw	**wh**en
ʃ	**sh**e
ʒ	trea**s**ure
tʃ	**ch**ild
dʒ	**j**am
ŋ	si**ng**
θ	**th**in
ð	**th**ese

Vowels

a	m**a**n
ɑ	s**a**w: *see* p. xxv
e	g**a**te, p**ay**
ɛ	p**e**n
ĕ	s**e**ven: *see* p. xxii
i	m**ee**t, s**ea**
ɪ	b**i**t
o	c**oa**t
u	l**oo**se, sh**oe**
ʌ	b**u**d
ø	*see* p. xxii
ə	b**u**tter, **a**bout

Diphthongs

aɪ	**eye**
əi	b**i**te
oi	*see* p. xxiii
ʌu	h**ou**se
ju	d**u**ty

in Scottish Standard English only

ɔ	c**o**t
ɔɪ	**boy**

Other symbols

~	stands for headword: *see* p. xli
&c	stands for other spellings: *see* p. xx

THE CONCISE SCOTS DICTIONARY

THE CONCISE SCOTS DICTIONARY

Editor-in-chief
MAIRI ROBINSON

ABERDEEN
UNIVERSITY
PRESS

© *The Scottish National Dictionary Association Ltd* 1985
First published August 1985
Reprinted (with corrections) September 1985

Aberdeen University Press, Aberdeen, Scotland
A member of the Pergamon Group
Distributors Pergamon Press Ltd
Headington Hill Hall, Oxford OX3 0BW

The Concise Scots dictionary
1. English language—Dialects—Scotland
—Dictionaries
I. Robinson, Mairi
427′.9411′03   PE2106

ISBN 0-08-028491-4
ISBN 0-08-032447-9 Leather

Printed and bound in Great Britain by
A. Wheaton & Co. Ltd, Exeter

CONTENTS

DEDICATION

To the memory of Sir Harald Leslie, K.T., Q.C.,
the Hon. Lord Birsay,
in gratitude for his lifelong devotion to the Scots language
and for his many years of service
to the Scottish National Dictionary Association
as its President

ACKNOWLEDGMENTS

Very many people have helped to make this dictionary possible. The editors of CSD are conscious first of all of their debt to all those whose labours brought into being the great 'source dictionaries' on which CSD especially depends, the *Scottish National Dictionary*, the *Dictionary of the Older Scottish Tongue*, the *Oxford English Dictionary*. If one name is to be singled out from all of these, it must be that of David Murison, Editor of the *Scottish National Dictionary* from 1946 till its completion in 1976, whose work underlies so much that follows and who has always been an enthusiast for the making of CSD.

Secondly, Professor A. J. Aitken, Editor of the *Dictionary of the Older Scottish Tongue*, has given invaluable help throughout as general adviser to the editorial team. His main contributions have been his work on the pronunciation, much of it original, and the section 'A History of Scots' (p. ix).

Professor Aitken was also responsible, along with Mairi Robinson, for the initial planning of CSD, which first arose from a suggestion by Professor Angus McIntosh.

Another person who has earned special gratitude is Mr J. W. Mort, Secretary and Treasurer of the Scottish National Dictionary Association. It is difficult to imagine how CSD could have been produced without his constant encouragement and his unstinting hard work on the administration of the project.

Initially CSD was funded entirely by the Scottish National Dictionary Association but, as a result of inflation, further funding had to be sought from other sources. The editors and the Council of the SNDA express their great gratitude to all those whose financial contributions, large and small, allowed the work to continue. Space is unfortunately lacking to mention all of these individually but special thanks for very substantial financial support are due to:

The Scottish Arts Council
An anonymous donor
Mary Ringsleben
Col. Gayre of Gayre and Nigg
The late Helen B. Cruikshank
The late Catherine J. Hogg
The James Wood Trust.

Equally thanks are due to all those whose expert knowledge and advice has helped to fill gaps in the information provided by the parent dictionaries, especially in bringing the information up to date. In particular:

Professor Robert Black, Department of Scots Law, University of Edinburgh, has, with unfailing friendliness and patience, given many hours to answering innumerable queries on legal terminology and its pronunciation.

Others who have given substantial help include:
The Staff of the Dictionary of the Older Scottish Tongue
Professor G. W. S. Barrow, Department of Scottish History, University of Edinburgh
Ian Begg (architecture)
W. G. F. Boag, Assistant Keeper, Scottish United Services Museum
Professor E. K. Borthwick, Department of Greek, Univ. of Edinburgh (football, golf)
Dr Alan Bruford, School of Scottish Studies, University of Edinburgh
Dr R. G. Cant, University of St Andrews
Rev. Professor A. C. Cheyne, Department of Ecclesiastical History, Univ. of Edinburgh
Peter Cooke, School of Scottish Studies, University of Edinburgh
Margaret Duguid (pronunciation)
Alexis Easson (land measures)
Dr Alexander Fenton, National Museum of Antiquities, Edinburgh
Dr W. Ferguson, Department of Scottish History, University of Edinburgh
Ray Footman, Director of Information Services, University of Edinburgh
Ian A. Fraser, Place-name Survey, School of Scottish Studies, University of Edinburgh
Dr Alexander Grant, Department of History, University of Lancaster
Robin L. C. Lorimer (piping)
Dr Michael Lynch, Department of Scottish History, University of Edinburgh
Dr John MacInnes, School of Scottish Studies, University of Edinburgh
R. W. Munro (history)
Dr Jean Munro (history)
Iain K. Murray, Convention of Scottish Local Authorities
David North (Standard English)
J. I. D. Pottinger, Lyon Clerk and Keeper of the Records, Edinburgh
Dr Anna Ritchie (archaeology)
Dr Graham Ritchie, Royal Commission on the Ancient Monuments of Scotland
The Scottish Brewing Archive, Heriot-Watt University
David Sellar, Department of Scots Law, University of Edinburgh
Robert N. Smart, Keeper of the Muniments, University of St Andrews
Professor Sir Thomas Smith, former Chairman, Her Majesty's Law Commission in Scotland
Dr Hans H. Speitel, Linguistic Survey of Scotland
Dr David Tulloch (golf)
Mrs J. S. Wilson, Law Department, Church of Scotland

CSD STAFF

Editor-in-chief: Mairi Robinson

Editorial Consultant and pronunciation editor:
Professor A. J. Aitken

Senior editor: Iseabail Macleod

Editors: Marace Dareau
      Ruth Martin
      Lorna Pike
      Patricia Wilson

Secretary and keyboarder: Elizabeth Glass

Secretary: Hilda Jack

Proof-readers: Pauline Cairns
      Dr Sheila Hearn
      Alexander Watson

THE SCOTTISH NATIONAL DICTIONARY
ASSOCIATION

President: Sir Kenneth Alexander

Vice-President: Sir Kenneth Dover

Hon. Vice-President: Professor W. S. Watt

Chairman of Executive Council:
    Professor John MacQueen

Secretary and Treasurer: J. W. Mort

Members of Council
(a) *Present*
    Mrs K. Ann Aikman Smith
    Professor A. J. Aitken
    Professor R. Black
    Dr Kenneth Buthlay
    Professor David Daiches
    Dr A. Fenton
    Professor A. D. S. Fowler
    James Gilchrist
    Professor W. Gillies
    Deirdre Keaney
    R. L. C. Lorimer
    J. Derrick McClure
    M. P. McDiarmid
    Ruari McLean
    Felicity Riddy
    Trevor Royle
    Lorna Smith
(b) *Former*
    Captain L. Gellatly
    (*Chairman of Executive Council*)
    Professor J. W. L. Adams
    Hon. Lord Birsay (*President*)
    G. D. Cheyne
    Professor G. P. Henderson
    Hester L. D. Henderson
    Edna Jackson
    Professor Angus McIntosh
    Alexander MacMillan
    J. R. Peddie
    Professor Sir Thomas Smith

INTRODUCTION

A HISTORY OF SCOTS

I   A general outline

The Concise Scots Dictionary is concerned mainly with Scots, the language of Lowland Scotland, the area delimited by the regions listed on pp. xxxiv–xxxv and mapped on pp. xxxi and xxxii. Roughly this is the area lying to the north, east and south of the Scottish Highlands and it includes Scotland's great cities and industrial centres. To some degree it is the native language of virtually all locally-educated people in this area and it has also influenced the English speech of the Highlands and Islands, where the first language once was, and for many people, especially in the Outer Isles, still is, Gaelic. Furthermore a variety of Scots is spoken in large enclaves in Northern Ireland, as a result of settlements there, especially from the west and south-west of Scotland in the seventeenth century and later.

The first speakers of the Old English ancestor of this language arrived in what is now southern Scotland early in the seventh century, as a northern offshoot of the Anglian peoples then comprising the Anglo-Saxon kingdom of Bernicia or northern Northumbria. The areas which these first Old English speakers occupied, as defined by place-names containing early Old English place-name elements, consisted of a wide swathe of what is now south-eastern and southern Scotland, with less extensive settlements along the Solway and, perhaps rather later, in Kyle in mid-Ayrshire.

Before the twelfth century the English-speaking part of Scotland was limited to these south-eastern and southern areas (except perhaps for the royal court of King Malcolm III and his queen, Margaret, a princess of the ancient royal house of Wessex, whom he married about 1070). There is also chronicle and place-name evidence that by the tenth and eleventh centuries the Gaelic language was in use throughout the whole of Scotland, including the English-speaking south-east, though no doubt the longer-established Northern English continued to be the dominant language there. In origin Gaelic was the native language of the Scots of Alba or Scotland, the kingdom centred north of the Forth and Clyde, whose kings in the tenth and eleventh centuries also gained dominion of the more southerly parts of what then became an expanded Scottish kingdom.

Until the late eleventh century the trend was towards the linguistic dominance of Scotland by Gaelic but this was reversed with the accession of the Normanized kings of Scotland, particularly King David I (1124–53) and his immediate successors. Thereafter place-names and other indications show a spread of the English-speaking area beyond the south-east, first to other parts of southern Scotland, then in the late twelfth and thirteenth centuries to eastern Scotland north of the Forth.

This expansion of English-speaking in Scotland was brought about by several important groups of immigrants to Scotland at this time: English-speaking servants and retainers of the new Anglo-Norman and Flemish landowners and of the monks from England and France who now arrived in Scotland at the invitation of the King; and English-speaking pioneer burgesses, chiefly from south-east Scotland and from England, who settled in the new royal and baronial burghs of eastern and southern Scotland. Though the language of the royal court and the baronage of Scotland was now Norman French, the native tongue of many of these immigrants of lesser rank was a variety of Northern English heavily influenced in pronunciation, vocabulary and grammar by the Scandinavian language of the former Viking settlers in northern and midland England whence these immigrants came. This Scandinavianized Northern English — or Anglo-Danish — was certainly the principal, though probably not the only, language of the early Scottish burghs and its contribution to the formation of the language later known as Scots is probably even greater than that of the original Old English of south-eastern and southern Scotland.

By the fourteenth century this language had become the dominant spoken tongue of all ranks of Scots east and south of the Highland Line, except in Galloway where a form of Gaelic appears to have survived down to the seventeenth century. In some areas the country folk had by now abandoned their former Gaelic for the Northern English of the burghs, the local centres of government, law and trade. And the barons had also abandoned their minority tongue, French, for the Northern English of the majority of the Lowland population, perhaps in part influenced by an impulse towards national solidarity when the nation was beleaguered in the War of Independence by English barons and knights who were still French-speaking. From about this time, too, the same Northern English tongue was beginning to be used in Caithness, Orkney and Shetland; so began the long process of the supplanting by Scots of the old Norse or Norn speech formerly spoken under the Norse earls of these territories.

Until the latter decades of the fourteenth century, written records of Early Scots consist of no more than a few vernacular words and phrases and some descriptive place-names and surnames which crop up sporadically in early Latin documents from the twelfth century onwards. From these fragmentary written records and by extrapolation from later evidence we do however learn something of how medieval Scots was developing internally as a language, and some account of this is given below.

Continuous written records of Early Scots begin in 1376 with John Barbour's great poem *Brus* — an account of the exploits of the heroes Robert Brus and James Douglas in the War of Independence. Other verse and prose writings in Scots follow, including (from 1424) the statutes of the Scottish Parliament. Gradually an ever wider range of prose and verse genres was written in Scots, so that, by the second half of the fifteenth century, Older Scots became the principal literary and record language of the Scottish nation, having successfully competed in this function with Latin. Hence in the later fifteenth and the sixteenth centuries there were two national languages in use in Britain, metropolitan Tudor English in the kingdom of England, and metropolitan Older Scots in the kingdom of Scotland. Though these were politically or socially separate languages, linguistically they were distinct but quite closely related dialects, much as is the case with the Scandinavian languages today. Because of this close relationship, elements originally English could be infiltrated into Scots writings and, later, speech without appearing particularly incongruous. This is indeed what now began to take place.

Traditionally, the anglicization of Scots at this stage is attributed to influences resulting from the Reformation of 1560, in particular the adoption by the Scots Reformers of the English Geneva Bible and a mainly English Psalter instead of a Bible and a Psalter in Scots, and from the much closer political and social contacts between the two nations which followed the Reformation and, still more, after the Union of the Crowns in 1603. Unquestionably these events, and the huge prestige of Elizabethan English literature, strongly reinforced the impulse to anglicization. But they did not initiate the process.

Literary influence of English writings on Scots writers long predated the Reformation.

Readers of Sir David Lyndesay will recall his allusions to 'Inglis bukis' and to New Testaments in English and printed in England, which were being read by Scots of Protestant leanings before the Reformation. And of course English poetry and prose circulated in Scotland from the fourteenth century or earlier, and the writings of Chaucer and his successors, in particular, were admired and emulated by Scottish poets.

Indeed, what may have triggered the anglicization process was the practice of the Scottish fifteenth- and sixteenth-century makars of including in their grandest and most pretentious poetry occasional imitations of the English spellings of Chaucer and their other English mentors, as alternatives to the corresponding native Scots forms: such as *quho* (Scots *quha*), *moste* (Scots *maist*), English words like *frome* (Scots *fra*), *tho* (Scots *than*) and *twane* (Scots *twa*), and English verbal inflexions such as the ending *-n* in *seyn* (Scots *se*, to see) and the ending *-ith* (corresponding to English *-eth*, Scots *-is*). By 1540 similar spellings were appearing, though still quite rarely, in Scots prose, but after 1560 the phenomenon was much more pervasive. By now Scots writing was in a mixed dialect, in which pairs of spellings and spelling-symbols like *aith* and *oath*, *ony* and *any*, *gude* and *good*, *quh-* and *wh-*, *sch-* and *sh-*, co-existed as options, with the English-derived options gradually increasing in popularity.

Until the seventeenth century, few Scots seem to have had any strong feeling for the linguistic identity of the Scots language (though there were certainly some who did so). One indication of this is the tardiness with which the Scots adopted a separate name for their language. Not until 1494 did any Scottish writer apply the name *Scots* to his own tongue. Before that it was always called *Inglis* (i.e. English), as no doubt befitted a tongue which shared with the English of England a dialect relationship and a common Anglo-Saxon origin. And even after 1494 and indeed until the end of the Older Scots period both names continued in use, with no obvious predominance of either.

From early in the sixteenth century there are occasional hints that, even though Scots was now the national language, it was felt to be somewhat less elegant than literary English. As early as 1513 the poet Gavin Douglas thought of his own vernacular as 'braid and plane' alongside 'sudron' (i.e. English). In 1603 this feeling was stated quite explicitly (see p. xi below) and from time to time thereafter.

The progressive anglicization of writings in manuscript (records, diaries, manuscript histories, and others) proceeded through the seventeenth century and into the eighteenth, until finally virtually every trace of Scottishness had disappeared from Scottish writing. In print, partly or largely as a result of commercial considerations by publishers and printers, the demise of literary Older Scots is far earlier and more sudden. After 1610, except for a few legal texts and one or two comic or satiric *tours-de-force*, all Scots writings in prose, whether printed in Scotland or, as often, in London, are in what can only be called English — with an occasional Scots locution only every dozen pages or so.

There was however one exception to the general trend towards anglicization. The tradition of printing popular heroic and comic poems of the classical Early and Middle Scots periods continued through the seventeenth century (albeit in somewhat anglicized spelling). A few new comic and satiric pieces such as Robert Sempill's *Habbie Simson* were also composed at this time, mostly in up-to-date popular Scots. These served as a springboard for the eighteenth-century revival of Scots writing launched by Allan Ramsay and his contemporaries in lyric, comic and descriptive verse, in balladry and, a little later, in humorous tales and ghost stories in prose, and prose dialogue and monologue. This however was in a more colloquial Scots than the formal style of most Older Scots writing. Some of the new features of spelling and grammar of this Modern literary Scots are mentioned below.

While Scottish writing was becoming anglicized in these ways from the sixteenth century or earlier, the indications are that, except for a very few Scotsmen of unusual personal histories like John Knox, the *speech* of all Scotsmen continued fully Scots into the seventeenth century. Following the Reformation in 1560, however, Scotsmen of all classes were coming for the first time into regular visual and aural contact with writings in southern English: aural in that at least once a week, and in the case of devout people several times a week, they heard readings from the English Bible, and sermons in a language partly modelled on Biblical English. In the course of the seventeenth century there was also a considerable increase in meetings between Scotsmen and Englishmen. No doubt most important of all these anglicizing influences was the great increase during this century in contacts of all sorts between the upper classes of the two countries. Intermarriage between the Scottish and English aristocracies was becoming common, a trend almost unknown before 1603. After the Restoration in 1660, every Scotsman of the nobility was likely to spend part of his time in southern England, at court or residing in the Home Counties, and nearly all other eminent Scots visited London for longer or shorter periods. And the practice of well-to-do Scots of sending their sons to school in England — pioneered by John Knox in the sixteenth century — was not entirely unknown at this time (though it does not seem to have become common until the late eighteenth century). Under these circumstances it is not surprising that the Scottish upper classes gradually gave up their native Scots speech for what had long been regarded as the more 'elegant and perfect' English of the south, as it was called by one Scottish writer in 1603.

It is doubtless possible to exaggerate the length things had gone by the late seventeenth century, and individuals no doubt varied, as they do today. But the overall impression must be that, in contrast with the sixteenth century, when all Scots (with very rare exceptions like John Knox) simply spoke native Older Scots, by this time the formal or, in the language of the period, 'polite' speech of the social élite of Scotland was now expected to approximate to the southern English dialect. This was now the language of social pretension, of intellectual discussion and of formal speech. For some it must also already have become the usual informal or fully vernacular style. From this time onwards, forms of speech which mostly favoured traditional Scots usages were identified with conservatives, eccentrics and, especially, with the common people.

This is not to deny that some upper- and middle-class Scots still used occasional Scotticisms, though uneasily aware that these were regarded as undignified, and that they spoke their English with a noticeable Scottish accent. But this was also the time when the Augustan culture of eighteenth-century England began strongly influencing the Scottish cultural scene. Augustanism was a fashion which laid great emphasis on 'propriety' and prohibited in 'polite' usage anything 'unrefined', 'vulgar' or 'provincial'.

These prescriptions were swallowed by nearly all educated Scots of the eighteenth century, though there were some dissentient voices like those of the poets Allan Ramsay and Alexander Ross. A notable result was a greatly increased self-consciousness on the part of the Scots intellectuals and middle classes about the provinciality of their English speech. Residual Scottish features were now regarded as sullying what might otherwise have been exemplary refined English, and it was all but universally accepted as desirable for anyone with pretensions to being 'polite' that he should write and speak English with 'propriety' — that is, according to the standards of London society. This is already in evidence in the records of the Fair Intellectual Club, founded in 1719 for educated young ladies of Edinburgh, in which the first president complimented her members on the propriety of their English 'considering how difficult it is for our country people to acquire it'. The well-known consequences of these notions include the publication, from 1752 onwards, of several alphabetical lists of Scottish words and expressions, compiled expressly so that Scots people could learn to avoid them in their writing and speech, and also the descent on Edinburgh, from 1748 onwards, of a long line of English, Irish and anglicized Scottish lecturers on elocution, who spearheaded the attack on the Scots accent.

Though some continued, and no doubt continue today, to hold that the total extinction of vernacular Scots is desirable, this seems to have ceased to be the establishment position early in the nineteenth century. We may perhaps associate this change of heart with the publication of John Jamieson's *Etymological Dictionary of the Scottish Language* in 1808, with the new wave of Scots Romantic writers, with the burgeoning of nineteenth-century antiquarianism, and with the sturdy Scots patriotism of people like Lord Cockburn (1779–1854), the celebrated Edinburgh judge and raconteur. It was now accepted that Scots was 'going out as a spoken tongue every year', as Cockburn put it in 1838, but for some, such as Cockburn himself, this was a matter for nostalgic regret at the incipient demise of a rich and expressive old tongue, and no longer, as it had been, for universal congratulation.

As the nineteenth century progressed, there arose a further distinction between traditional, usually equated with rural, dialects of Scots, which were widely approved, and 'slovenly perversions of dialect', usually equated with urban dialects, which were not. And this threefold division into English, 'good Scots' and 'bad Scots' continues to the present day, colouring social and educational attitudes.

II   The position today

The language of contemporary Lowland Scotland can fairly be described as fluid. It is marked by a wide and almost infinitely variable range of speech-styles, ranging from the full Scots of some fisher-folk and farming people in the North-East, through various intermediate 'mixtures of Scots and English', to a variety of Standard English spoken in a Scottish accent. Even the last of these retains obvious affiliations with the more fully Scottish speech-styles — in the accent with which it is pronounced, in its speakers' frequent recourse to a repertory of ostentatious Scotticisms like *keep a calm souch* or *let that flee stick tae the wa*, in their unstudied use of some other Scotticisms like *pinkie, to swither, to miss yourself*, and in the peculiarly Scottish pronunciations of certain words such as *length* (with *n* not *ng*), of *Wednesday* (with three clear syllables), of *fifth* and *sixth* (as *fift* and *sixt*), and of *loch, patriarch* and *technical* (with *ch* not *k*).

The speech of an individual will vary according to region (some regions being strikingly more 'Scottish' than others), social class, age, sex, circumstance (for example, the well-known contrast between classroom and playground speech), and the national and local loyalties of the speaker.

This mixed and variable speech is the country's everyday vernacular, but now no more than that. Though the terminology of law, church, education and administration is still strongly Scottish, nearly all conversation beyond local and intimate settings is in Standard English. The sixteenth century situation in which the Scottish language was the universal language of Scotland has long disappeared.

It may therefore reasonably be asked if there is any sense in which Scots is entitled to the designation of a language any more than any of the regional dialects of English in England? This is not at all a new question. It has been a preoccupation of many Scots writers from the sixteenth century to the present day.

In reply one may point out that the Scots tongue possesses several attributes not shared by any regional English dialect. In its linguistic characteristics it is more strongly differentiated from Standard English than any English dialect. The dictionary which follows displays a far larger number of words, meanings of words and expressions not current in Standard English than any of the English dialects could muster, and many of its pronunciations are strikingly different from their Standard English equivalents.

As yet no means has been devised of measuring how frequently individuals or whole communities actually use dialect expressions in the course of their conversation. But anyone who scans the dictionary or listens to a modern Scots play might reasonably suppose that the Scots are in general more broad-spoken and more loyal to their vernacular than many of their English cousins are. One illustration of this is the fact that a fair number of dialect words — such as *aye* always, *pooch* a pocket, *shune* shoes, *een* eyes, and *nicht* night — have very recently died out in northern England but remain in vigorous use throughout Scotland right down to the Border.

It is of course true that Scots shares many words with dialects of northern England. Words such as *hame, stane, doon, lass, bairn, bonny, loon* and *glaur*, which many Scots think of as purely Scots words, are indeed very much northern English words as well. But it is also true that a large number of Scotticisms are now confined within the Border, and many of them perhaps always were. A number of the features of Scots described in IV below are of this class. Indeed, easily the most definite dialect-boundary in the English-speaking world is the Scottish-English Border.

In England the only dialect which can match Scots in possessing its own separate and well-documented history is Standard English itself. And only England as a whole can compare with Lowland Scotland as a whole for dialect variety, as briefly described at IV (e) below.

But what most of all distinguishes Scots is its literature. Nowhere in the English-speaking world is there a dialect literature which remotely compares with Scottish literature for antiquity, for extent and variety, and for distinction. This embraces writings in mainstream or standard literary Scots (in a language based on Central Scots dialect speech), in which we may include the great medieval makars and the writers of Older Scots literary prose as well as distinguished modern performers such as Burns, Scott, Hogg, Hugh MacDiarmid, Lewis Grassic Gibbon, and innumerable others. In addition to this, several regional dialects have developed substantial and distinguished literatures in their own regional standards — notably North-Eastern Scots since the early eighteenth century, Shetland since the nineteenth century, Glasgow from early in the present century. Beyond this art-literature in Scots, and the large body of Scots folksong, the truly popular literature of newspaper comic strips and cartoons in diluted mainstream Scots and of the Scots pantomime comic reaches a very wide audience.

Though Scottish literature has had only limited official recognition from government bodies, and Scottish language until very recently almost none at all, both have for centuries been subjects of academic study. Important recent contributions to this have been made by the two great dictionaries on which the present work is based and the three-volume *Linguistic Atlas of Scotland* (1975, 1977, and forthcoming).

All of the phenomena just described have reinforced and in turn been reinforced by the ancient loyalty of some, and in more recent times of many, Scots to their own language. Though this has from time to time encountered opposition, it has never been wholly extinguished between the sixteenth century and the present day.

From at least the first half of the eighteenth century, Scots has always been thought to be 'dying out' as a spoken language. From time to time suggestions have been made for 'restoring' or 'reviving' it — from the solid base of literary Scots, where its permanence has been less often in doubt. As a first step it has sometimes been suggested that Scots needs a body of writing in prose beyond the spheres of dialogue and monologue to which, since the Older Scots period, it has been all but confined. The 1970s and 80s especially have produced some important contributions to this end, not least the superb translation of the *New Testament* into Scots by W. L. Lorimer (1983).

The unique characteristics of Scots which we have just surveyed — its linguistic distinctiveness, its occupation of its own 'dialect-island' bounded by the Border, its individual history, its own dialect variation, its varied use in a remarkable literature, the ancient loyalty of the Scottish people to the notion of the Scots language, as well as the fact that since the sixteenth century Scots has adopted the nation's name — all of these are attributes of a language rather than a dialect. Manifestly Scots is to be seen as much more than simply another dialect of English. The present dictionary is intended not only as a record of the copiousness and variety of the resources of the Scots language, but also as a contribution to the self-assurance of the Scottish people about that language, which enshrines their past and lives in their daily speech.

III   The principal chronological periods in the history of Scots and English

The main periods in the history of Scots

Old English:	to 1100
Older Scots:	to 1700
Pre-literary Scots:	to 1375
Early Scots:	to 1450
Middle Scots:	1450 to 1700
Early Middle Scots:	1450 to 1550
Late Middle Scots:	1550 to 1700
Modern Scots:	1700 onwards

A corresponding list of the periods for English

Old English:	to 1100
Middle English:	1100 to 1475
Early Middle English:	1100 to 1250
Late Middle English:	1400 to 1475
Early Modern English:	1475 to 1650
Modern English:	1650 onwards

IV   Internal history: some important changes in the language itself

IV (a)   Sound changes: vowels and diphthongs

In the Early and Middle Scots periods, some important sound-changes resulted in differences in the pronunciation of vowels and diphthongs between Scots and Standard English (including Scottish Standard English). These include the following contrasts:

(1)   Scots *stane, gae* — (Sc)StEng *stone, go*

This results from the twelfth century rounding of Early Middle English $\bar{a}$ (e.g. in *stān* and *gān*) in midland and southern England to a sound of *o*-like quality, whereas no such rounding occurred in the north. The different sounds which resulted had different subsequent developments, leading ultimately to the modern contrast.

(2) Scots *buit, muin,* — (Sc)StEng *boot,*
       puir   *moon, poor*
    (with front vowel) (with back vowel)

This results from a fronting of an original long
ō-sound in these words in the thirteenth century
in Northern Middle English and, especially,
Early Scots, yielding a sound of *ü*-like quality
in the ancestor of Scots, but leaving *ō* (which
later became the modern *oo*) in the ancestor of
(Sc)StEng. Further development brought about
dialect variations within Scots (*ee* in Northern,
ai or *i* in Central, *ü* remaining in Shetland,
Orkney, Angus, Perthshire and Southern).

(3) Scots *aw, au* [ɑ], — (Sc)StEng *al* (*l*),
     ow [ʌu], *ou, u* [u]   *ol* (*l*), *ul* (*l*)
     in *baw, saut, sowder,*   in *ball, salt, solder,*
     row, mouter, fou   *roll, multure, full*

This results from an early fifteenth century
Scots replacement of *l* by *u* in this position —
the so-called vocalization of *l*.

(4)   Scots   — (Sc)StEng
     (and Northern English) *cow, house, down*
       coo, house, doon

This results from an important difference in the
direction taken by the fifteenth century Great
Vowel Shift in the north from that taken in the
midlands and south of England. Scots and
Northern English retain the original Old and
Middle English and Early Scots monophthong,
which became a diphthong in the fifteenth century only in more southerly dialects of English.
The main effects of the Great Vowel Shift on
Scots itself can be seen by following through
the later developments of the Early Scots
vowels i:, e:, ɛ:, a: and the diphthong ai, in the
Table at 5.5.3.

Note: The Scottish system of vowel-length
described at 5.4.2 below first arose at this time,
partly as a result of the Great Vowel Shift.

IV (b) Spellings

The spelling-system of Older Scots was exceptionally variable. Some features which distinguished it from the spelling of midland and
southern English of the time are:

(1) Among the spellings of consonants, Scots
quh-, qwh- corresponding to *wh-*, e.g. in Scots
quhat, quhite; Scots *sch-* corresponding to *sh-*;
Scots *-ch* corresponding to *-gh*, e.g. in *lauch,*
nicht, dochter; Scots ʒ corresponding to *y*, e.g. in
ʒ*ere* (year), ʒ*ing* (young). Common variations
within Scots in spellings of consonants included:
for *-ch* as in *lauch* or *laich* (low), also *-cht;* for *-th*
as in *baith* (both) or *mouth,* also *-tht;* and for
either of these, superscript *ᵗ; v* and *w* interchanged, and *-v-* interchanged with *-u-, -w-* or
-f (*f*)-.

(2) Among the vowels, the device of adding *-i*
or *-y* to distinguish certain Early Scots long
vowels from similarly spelled short vowels, e.g.
hait (hot) from *hat* (hat); *meit* (meet or meat)
from *met, coit* (coat) from *cot, buit* (boot) from
but; and some writers even use *yi* as in *byit*
(bite) to distinguish this vowel from that in *bit*
in the same way.

As a consequence of the sound-change
mentioned at IV(a) (3) above, the following
sets of spellings became interchangeable:

al, aul with *au, aw* e.g. in *halk, haulk, hawk*
(hawk), or *walter, wawter, water* (water);

ol, oul, owl, with *ou, ow* e.g. in *nolt, noult,*
nowlt, nowt, nout (cattle);

ul, oul, owl with *ou, ow* e.g. in *pulder, poulder,*
powlder, pouder, powder.

As well as introducing new alternative
English word-forms such as *oath* beside *aith, most*
beside *maist, quhich* beside *quhilk, church* beside
kirk, any beside *ony, if* beside *gif,* the anglicization process (see I above) also resulted in
massive changes in ways of spelling Scots words
themselves. By the eighteenth century many
characteristic Older Scots spellings had been
discarded: *quh-, sch-,* the letter ʒ (though this
did survive as *z* — see ʒ in the Dictionary), the
alternative spelling of *o-e* as *oi, oy,* e.g. in *cote,*
coit (coat) and such spellings as *walter* (water),
nolt (cattle) and *pulder* (powder); and many
others of the alternative spelling options just
illustrated. New symbols of mainly southern
English origin were introduced: *wh, sh, gh, ee,*
oo, ea and *oa,* and word-final *-ae* and *-oe.* Where
a Scots word differed from a corresponding
English word in the apparent omission of a
letter, this was acknowledged with an intruded
apostrophe, as *ha'e* beside *have, fu'* beside *full.*

Some Older Scots spellings did, however,
survive, notably *ch* as in *lauch, nicht,* and *ai, ei*
and *ui.*

Though still much more variable than Standard English, this new hybrid spelling system of
Modern Scots was much less variable than that
of Older Scots. It continues in use in Scottish
literature to this day (alongside some recent,
highly innovative systems to represent localized
varieties of spoken Scots). Attempts to make it
more consistent and less subservient to the
Standard English system, notably the *Scots Style*
Sheet of the Makars' Club in 1947, have had at
best only limited success.

IV (c) Grammar

Modern Scots inherits from Early Scots a
number of characteristic Northern English
grammatical features, of which the following is
a small sample:

(1) irregular plurals: *een* (eyes), *shune* (shoes), *kye*
(cows), *hors* (horses), *caur* (calves), and *thir* (pl.
of *this*), *thae* (pl. of *that*).

(2) distinction between present participle in -*an* (*He's aye gutteran aboot*) and verbal noun in -*in* (*He's fond o gutterin aboot*). This distinction is still found in extreme Northern and Southern dialects.

(3) past tense and past participle forms: *greet* (weep), pt *grat*, ptp *grutten*; *lauch* (laugh), pt *leuch*, ptp *lauchen*; *gae* (go), pt *gaed* (Older Scots *3eid*), ptp *gane*; *hing* (hang), pt *hang*, ptp *hungin*.

(4) distinction in present-tense verb forms according to whether a personal pronoun is or is not immediately adjacent to the verb (e.g. *they say he's owre auld* but *them that says he's owre auld* or *thir laddies says he's owre auld*).

Modern Scots also has a number of features which have arisen since the Early Middle Scots period:

(1) reduced forms of the negative adverb: Older Scots *nocht*, Modern Scots *no* or *nae* and -*na* or -*ny*;

(2) new rules for negative and interrogative constructions: Older Scots *He gais nocht, Gais he nocht?*, Modern Scots *He's no gaun, Is he no gaun?*;

(3) new usages of auxiliary verbs such as *may* (common in Older Scots, little used in Modern Scots, where *can* and constructions with *maybe* take its place); similarly *sall* (and its reduced form '*se*) is almost obsolete.

IV (d)   Vocabulary

Early Scots shared much of its word-stock with contemporary Northern Middle English. This included virtually all its word-borrowings from Scandinavian, since these had originally reached Scotland as part of the Northern English speech of the Anglo-Danish immigrants mentioned on p. ix. Among the hundreds of characteristic expressions of this source in Modern Scots are such well-known items as *bairn*, *brae*, *gate* (road), *graith* (equipment), *nieve* (fist), *kirk*, *lass*, *big* (build), *flit* (remove), *hing* (hang), *dreich* (dry), *lowse* (loose), and several of the grammatical features mentioned in the preceding section. (But the history of the still more numerous Scandinavian borrowings into the dialects of Shetland, Orkney and Caithness is quite different. These derive directly from the former Norn or Norwegian language of the inhabitants of these regions, following their colonization by Norwegian Vikings after c. 800 A.D.)

All the other sources of Early Scots vocabulary contributed many words and expressions exclusive to Scots as well as others shared with the English of England. From French, both the Norman French of the original twelfth century Norman settlers and the Central French which later superseded this, came many words originally shared with English but which have survived only in Scots, such as *leal*, *ashet*, *aumry*, *coup*, *douce*, *houlat* and *tassie*, and others, perhaps resulting from direct Scots-French contact in the Franco-Scottish Alliance (1296–1560), such as *deval* (stop), *disjune* (breakfast), *fash* (bother), *spairge* (spatter), *vennel*, *vivers* (rations), and *gardyloo* and *Hogmanay*.

Other borrowings originally special to Scots include many from Gaelic, beginning at least as early as the 12th century, such as *cairn*, *cranreuch*, *glen*, *loch*, *strath* and *capercailzie*, *ingle*, *messan*, *oe*, *quaich*, *sonse*, *tocher*, *car* (left(-hand)) and *crine* (shrink), along with more recent borrowings such as *claymore*, *gillie*, *pibroch*, *spleuchan*, *sporran*, *whisky*, and, still more recently, *ceilidh*.

Between the twelfth and the eighteenth centuries contacts between Scotland and the Low Countries were constant and close, with, for example, Flemish craftsmen settling in the Scottish burghs and Scottish traders settling at the Scottish staple ports in the Netherlands. One result was the many Scots words of Dutch or Flemish origin, such as *bucht*, *callan*, *croon*, *cuit*, *mutch*, *pinkie*, *golf* and *scone*, the past tense *coft* (bought), and the names of measures such as *mutchkin* and coins such as *doit* and *plack*.

Other important elements of the distinctive vocabulary of Scots come from Anglo-Saxon itself, whence, for example, *bannock*, *but and ben*, *eldritch*, *gloamin*, *haffet*, *haugh*, *heuch*, *lanimer*, *wee*, *weird*, and from the continuing processes of word-formation and word-coinage, which produced *bogle*, *bonny*, *canny* and *uncanny*, *glower*, *gomerel*, *gove* (to stare), *gully*, *limmer*, *pawk*, *scunner*.

Borrowing from Latin was in Older Scots carried out virtually independently of English. Many words of Latin origin were borrowed into the two languages at widely different dates and often in strikingly different meanings: *liquid*, *liquidate*, *local*, *locality*, *narrative* is only a small sample of these. Besides this, Scots law has a large and distinctive vocabulary of Latin origin, such as *executor-dative*, *homologate*, *hypothec*, *nimious*, *sederunt*. Scots often prefers a different form of the same word (often a verb) from that preferred by English: *dispone* (beside *dispose*), *promove* (beside *promote*), and others; and Scots often prefers ending-less (and thus more 'etymological') forms of Latin past participles, like (*weel*) *educate*, *depute*, and *habit and repute*. School Latin, partly borrowed in the modern period, has yielded such characteristic Scotticisms as *dominie*, *dux*, *fugie*, *pandie*, *vaig*, *vaik* and *vacance*.

From the foregoing it is evident that by, say, the 16th century, Scots differed strikingly in vocabulary as well as in all other ways from all its contemporary dialects of English, not excluding Northern English. Since the 17th century the process of direct borrowing of vocabulary from foreign sources has largely, though not entirely, ceased, but the processes of coinage and word-formation appear to continue apace, and indeed down to the present day: recent expressions of the latter origin include *scheme* (local-authority housing estate), *high-heid-yin, henner, fantoosh, to miss oneself, to put* (someone's) *gas at a peep, to be up to high doh,* and many others. Even so, the many apparently new words which first appear in Modern Scots are by no means all of recent origin: many, such as *boorach, golach, gumption, gyte, slaister, theevil,* are doubtless older words which have emerged into record only in the modern period, as a result of the rather different pre-occupations of most writers of Older Scots, primarily an official and record language, and of Modern Scots, primarily a folk-tongue. Many words which (approximately) coincide in form with Standard English words have very different meanings in Scots: this is true of some of the words of Latin origin mentioned above; others of diverse sources include *divider, find, flit, hold, hurl, mind, outcast, outcome, policy, sober, sort, travel, want, weave, word* and the definite article *the.*

IV (e) The spoken dialects

As a broad generalization the traditional division of Scots into four major dialects, Insular (i.e. of Shetland and Orkney), Northern, Central and Southern, as delineated by the map on p. xxxi, is acceptable, though of course the detail is not as straightforward or clear-cut as that might suggest. The best and fullest description of the major dialects and their subdivisions is still William Grant's 'Phonetic Description of Scottish Language and Dialects' which occupies pp. ix-xli of Volume 1 of SND. A few characteristic features of certain dialects are mentioned incidentally at IV (a) above and at 5.3.3, 5.3.4 and 5.4 below. Some others are:

A well-known Northern feature is *f*- where other dialects have *wh*- as in *fa* (who), *fite* (white). A well-known characteristic of Southern Scots is the occurrence at the ends of words of *-ow* [-ʌu] where other dialects have *-oo* [-u] and *-ey* [-ɔi] where other dialects have *-ee* [-i], making this the so-called 'yow and mey dialect', e.g. 'Yow and mey'll gang oot and

pow a pey' — 'You and me will go out and pull a pea'.

Grammatical variations include the distinction between singular *thou, thee* and plural *ye* in Sh, Ork and eRoss (cf *tu* and *vous* in French), and that between the present participle and the verbal noun (see IV (c) above). As a result of their special histories certain localities favour words of a particular etymological source: words of Scandinavian origin in Shetland, Orkney and Caithness; a special group of words of Dutch origin in Shetland; Gaelic in the Northern dialect and in Kintyre; Romany in parts of the South-East and South; and some words special to particular occupations (notably fishing and coal-mining) are localized to particular places and regions. Beyond this it is as yet not possible to offer further generalizations on the regional distributions of different classes of word within Scotland, except to point to the very numerous variations between dialects in their terms for common notions: for 'little finger' *peerie finger* and variants in Shetland, Orkney and Caithness, North-Eastern *crannie,* Fife and neighbouring countries *curnie,* and *pinkie* everywhere; for 'to rinse' the mainly East Central *synd* and West Central *syne,* the North-Eastern *sweel* and the scattered *reenge* and variants; for 'mud' *dubs, gutter, glabber, clabber* and *glaur* are scattered around the country, with *dubs* favoured in the North-East, *gutters* in northern East Central, *glabber and clabber* in West Central, *glaur* in Central and Southern. One could multiply these examples many times. The dictionary provides copious information on the present regional distributions both of words and of individual meanings of words.

Further Reading

A. J. Aitken, ed. *Lowland Scots,* Association for Scottish Literary Studies, Occasional Papers No. 2, Edinburgh 1973.

David Murison *The Guid Scots Tongue,* Blackwood, Edinburgh 1977.

A. J. Aitken, Tom McArthur, eds. *Languages of Scotland,* W. & R. Chambers, Edinburgh 1979.

Peter Trudgill, ed. *Language in the British Isles,* Cambridge University Press 1984.

HOW TO USE CSD

The Concise Scots Dictionary contains a great deal of information, and considerable care has been taken to present it as clearly as possible. Many readers will find that the lists on the endpapers are all that they need in order to use the dictionary successfully. But for those who want more detail, additional guidance has been given on all aspects of CSD in sections 1 to 15 below. The contents of these are listed on p. v.

1 What does CSD contain and what are its sources?

CSD is a dictionary of *Scots*, that is, the language of Lowland Scotland. See 'A History of Scots' p. ix.

1.1 Sources
CSD is based mainly on two major dictionaries, the Scottish National Dictionary (SND) for the modern period from 1700 to the present day, and the Dictionary of the Older Scottish Tongue (DOST) for the centuries up to 1700.

The main difference between these two works is that whereas DOST covers the whole of the Scots language of the period, including what is shared with English, SND concentrates on what is different from Standard English in the modern language (but including items found also in English dialects, especially Northern English).

For the latter part of the alphabet (Pr–Z) in CSD, where DOST was not yet available, Older Scots material was identified from the Oxford English Dictionary (OED) and included in CSD according to the criteria set out below. In order to supplement this sparser amount of material, other sources were used where possible, e.g. the information in SND's etymologies and the glossaries of selected texts (both of major authors and of less literary material). Occasionally information has been drawn from DOST files, more frequently in letters P (latter part) and R, which were edited though not published when CSD was being prepared.

In addition to the above, the editors have in many entries amplified the information in the main sources, frequently with the help of expert colleagues. (*See also* 1.2. *below* and *Acknowledgments* p. vii.)

1.2 Inclusions
CSD aims to include what is (or was) wholly or mainly Scots (including the Scottish elements in Scottish Standard English), and in addition words and usages which, according to the evidence available, were used at least 100 years earlier or later in Scots than in the English of England. Thus:

earliest evidence

Sc	Eng	therefore
1485	1605	in CSD
1500	1556	not in CSD
1500	1460	not in CSD

latest evidence

Sc	Eng	
1560	1420	in CSD
1560	1485	not in CSD
present day	1760	in CSD

Meanings shared with the English of Southern England (referred to as 'Common British English') are however frequently included, often as the first definition of an entry or part-of-speech section, e.g. **man** *n* **1** = man *1a14–*.

This indicates that Scots has been using the word in the same senses as English since the late 14th century. (*See also* 7 *below*.)

CSD, like its sources, contains a considerable amount of encyclopaedic information, e.g. names of Scottish regiments, religious sects, legal and educational institutions. This will add greatly to its usefulness as a general reference book.

Efforts have been made to include new words and usages where possible. One area where vast changes have come about is local government, following the reorganization of 1975. Many words, especially titles of local government officials, were still current when the relevant part of SND went to press but are now obsolete, e.g. **Dean of Guild**. Some however are still used but in a different, usually more restricted way, e.g. **provost**. Other words have acquired new meanings, e.g. **region** and **district**.

NB For inclusion of rare items in major authors see 1.3.3 below.

1.3 Exclusions
1.3.1 The **quotations**, which provide such a rich source of information and pleasure in the parent dictionaries, cannot be included in a dictionary such as CSD, which aims at compression of information. Therefore they are included only very rarely (and without identification) in order to help to clarify a meaning or usage. (*See* 7.10 *below*.)

In addition the following categories of material have been omitted:

1.3.2 Shetland, Orkney and Caithness
Material from these areas which belongs not to

Scots but to Norn, the Norse language formerly spoken there. (*See* 'A History of Scots', p. xv.)

1.3.3 Rarities

Most items for which there are only one or two pieces of evidence altogether in the parent dictionaries are omitted. In other words, normally a total of three quotations and/or references is required to justify inclusion.

There are certain exceptions to this rule:

(1) In the latter part of the alphabet where OED is the main source for Older Scots an item may be included in CSD even if it has only a single attestation in OED or two attestations in the glossaries, (*see* 1.1 *above*) *e.g.* **spycarie**.

(2) Many items from the following major authors have been included, even if there is only one occurrence, especially if it is thought that inclusion would be helpful to a reader of their works. The authors are:

Barbour, Henryson, Dunbar, Douglas, Ramsay, Fergusson, Burns.

(3) Many legal terms from the modern period have been included, even if there is only one reference.

(4) Sometimes a meaning etc. with sparse evidence has been included in order to clarify another meaning for which the evidence is more plentiful.

(5) In some cases one entry may be reinforced by another, *e.g.* where there are two attestations of a noun + one of a verb, the noun will be included.

1.3.4 Letters of the alphabet, prefixes, suffixes

SND in particular does include entries for these (*e.g.* **M, ma-**), but they are normally omitted from CSD.

A few prefixes and suffixes, *e.g.* **un-, -some**, have however been included and the letter **ȝ** has its own entry.

1.3.5 Reference-book material

Material found only in dictionaries and other reference books is omitted even if there are more than two occurrences. Words and meanings are often copied indiscriminately from one reference book to another and appearance in a dictionary cannot be taken as evidence of the item's actual existence without some other supporting evidence.

1.3.6 Transparent derivatives etc.

Derivatives, compounds etc. whose meaning

and form can easily be worked out from that of the base word(s) are often omitted, *e.g.* adverbs ending in *-ly*, nouns in *-ness*. (*See also* 10 *below*.)

2 How to find a word in CSD

2.1 Order of entries

Material is entered in alphabetical order of the first headword. Words which have the same spelling but different etymological sources are entered separately with consecutive superscript numbers attached to the first headword, *e.g.* **gab¹**, **gab²**, **gab³**. Words with initial capital letters are entered after any non-capitalized words with the same spelling.

2.2 Spelling variants

Scots has always had so many spelling variants that it would be impossible for a one-volume dictionary to list them all. Most CSD entries do however contain several variants, many of them representing other variants. (*See* 3 and 4 *below*.)

2.3 How to find a word

(1) Look in the obvious alphabetical position. If the word is not found:

(2) Glance above and below for a similar spelling. If the word is not found:

(3) Could it be a compound or derivative form (*e.g.* **backman** or **backfu** from **back**), a past tense or past participle of a verb, or a plural of a noun? Look under a likely base form: in the case of compounds try the first element first; in the case of past tenses or plurals, what might a normal English spelling of the present tense or singular be? Repeat stages (1) and (2).

If the word is still not found:

(4) Consult the lists of variants (*see* 3 *below*). Vowel variation is more likely than consonant; try vowel lists first. Look up words with double consonants under single consonants and vice versa, *e.g.* *defforce* under **deforce**.

3 Variants

Certain variants are regarded as predictable, *i.e.* they regularly interchange with one another and if a word is not found under one spelling it is likely to be found under one of the variants.

Variants list

In the following list the entries in bold type consist of sets of variants, as far as possible in descending order of the spellings most likely to be found as headwords in CSD. For example, suppose you meet a word containing the sequence *-cht-*. On looking this up in the list below you are referred to the sets under **ch**.

Therefore try the dictionary for an entry containing -*ch*-. If there is no entry which fits, try -*th*-, and so on down the list.

a	*see*	AI *or* AU *or* O
ae	*see*	AI
a-e	*see*	AI *or* UI
ai, ae, a-e, ay, a, ea, i, y, ii, yi, oi, oy, ei,		
ey, o, oa, o-e;		
ai, e;		
ai	*also see*	EI *or* UI
al	*see*	AU
au, aw, al, aul, a		
aul	*see*	AU
aw	*see*	AU
ay	*see*	AI *or* EI
b, bb		
c, s, t;		
c	*also see*	CK
ch, th, cht, tht, chtht, tch;		
ch, gh, ght;		
ch	*also see*	SH
cht	*see*	CH
chtht	*see*	CH
ck, c, k, kk, ct		
cks, x, ks		
ct	*see*	CK
d, dd, ld, t, tt, th		
dd	*see*	D
dg	*see*	G
e	*see*	EI *or* AI *or* I-E
é	*see*	EI
ea	*see*	EI *or* AI
ee	*see*	EI *or* UI
e-e	*see*	EI
ei, ee, e-e, ey, e, é, ea, i, ie, y;		
ei, ai, ay;		
ei	*also see*	AI *or* UI
eu, ew, ou, u, ui, ue, ow, yow		
ew	*see*	EU
ey	*see*	AI *or* EI *or* UI
f, ff, ph, v;		
f, th;		
f	*also see*	WH
g, gg;		
g, dg, j		
gg	*see*	G
gh	*see*	CH
ght	*see*	CH
i	*see*	AI, EI, I-E *or* UI
ie	*see*	EI *or* I-E
i-e, i, e, ie, ii, iy, y, y-e, yi		
ii	*see*	AI *or* I-E
iy	*see*	I-E
j	*see*	G
k	*see*	CK
kk	*see*	CK
l, ll		
ld	*see*	D
ll	*see*	L
m, mm, mb;		
m, n		

n, nn, nd, nt, ng;		
n, m		
nd	*see*	N
ng, nzie, ngie, nȝ(i)e, ny(i)e;		
ng	*also see*	N
ngie	*see*	NG
ngth	*see*	NTH
nn	*see*	N
nt	*see*	N
nth, ngth		
ny(ie), nȝ(i)e, nzie *see* NG		
o, a;		
o	*also see*	AI, O-e, OU *or* U
oa	*see*	AI *or* O-E
oe	*see*	O-E *or* UI
o-e, o, oe, oi, oy, oa;		
o-e	*also see*	AI *or* UI
oi	*see*	AI, O-E *or* UI
ol	*see*	OU
oo	*see*	OU *or* UI
ou, ow, ol, oul, oo, u, o, ue, u-e;		
ou	*also see*	EU *or* UI
oul	*see*	OU
ow	*see*	EU, OU *or* UI
oy	*see*	ai, O-E *or* UI
p, pp, pt		
ph	*see*	F
pp	*see*	P
pt	*see*	P
qu, qw, quh;		
qu	*also see*	WH
quh	*see*	QU *or* WH
qw	*see*	QU *or* WH
r, rr, rh		
s, sc, ss, z;		
s	*also see*	C *or* SH
sc	*see*	S *or* SK
sch	*see*	SH *or* SK
scl, skl, sl		
sh, sch, ch, sk, s		
sk, sc, sch;		
sk	*also see*	SH
skl	*see*	SCL
sl	*see*	SCL
ss	*see*	S
t	*see*	C *or* D
tch	*see*	CH
th, tht;		
th, y;		
th	*also see*	CH, D *or* F
tht	*see*	CH *or* TH
tt	*see*	D
u, o, v, w;		
u	*also see*	EU, OU *or* UI
ue	*see*	EU, OU *or* UI
u-e	*see*	OU *or* UI
uee	*see*	UI
ui, uy, ue, u-e, u, oo, oi, oy, oe, o-e, ou,		
ow, ee, ei, ey, wee, uee, i, ai, a-e;		
ui	*also see*	EU
uy	*see*	UI
v	*see*	F *or* U

w	*see*	U
wee	*see*	UI
wh, quh, qu, qw;		
wh, f		
x	*see*	CKS
y, yh, ꝫ, ꝫh, z;		
y	*also see*	AI, EI, I-E *or* TH
yh	*see*	Y
yi	*see*	AI *or* I-E
yow	*see*	EU
ꝫ	*see*	Y
ꝫh	*see*	Y
z	*see*	S, Y

Word beginnings and endings

Many word beginnings and endings in Scots vary considerably and the following lists give just a few examples of these.

Word beginnings

en-, an-, in-
in-, on-, un-, wn-
ower-, over-, our-, ouer-, ovir-, owir-,
   owyr-, ovyr-
per-, par-
re-, ra-

Word endings

Note that many words may also have a final 'e'.

-er, -eir, -eyr, -eur, -ar, -air, -ayr, -ir, -yr,
   -or, -oir, -oyr, -our, -ur
-ie, -y, -ye, -e, -é, -ee, -ey, -ay, -ae
-ing, -yng, -and, -an, -ant
-in, -yn, -en, -ein, -eyn, -eng, eing, -eyng
-ed, it(t), -yt(t), -et(t)
-le, -il(l), -yl(l), -el(l), -al(l), ol(l)
-ion, -ioun, -tio(u)n, -cio(u)n, -sio(u)n,
   -shio(u)n, -shun, -zhun

What does a typical CSD entry contain?

4 Headwords

4.1 How are CSD headwords chosen?

Headwords (printed in bold type) are normally selected from the numerous variants for which there is evidence in the parent dictionaries. Those which also represent other variants are followed by &c.

For the convenience of the user who may want to consult the parent dictionaries, *all* first headwords in the parent dictionaries are normally given in CSD. These are the **reference headwords** and they are separated from each other by commas; a semi-colon separates these from any other variants (the **non-reference headwords**), which are also separated from each other by commas.

The main SND headword, where there is one, is given first, followed by DOST and/or other SND headwords or, in the latter part of the alphabet, OED headword(s).

The non-reference headwords have been selected on various criteria, the most important being frequency and lack of predictability.

In some cases the parent-dictionary headword of the entry which provided the information is not included as a CSD headword. This happens most frequently in the latter part of the alphabet where the OED headword has no Scottish usages. The parent-dictionary headword is then included at the end of the etymology.

4.2 A typical long entry may have headwords as follows:
   haud &c *16-*, **hald** &c *1a14-e20*, **hold** &c *1a15-*; **hauld** &c *1a14-e20*, **had** &c *1a16-*, **haul** &c *19-* etc.
haud is an SND main headword; **hald** is a DOST main headword;
hold is a headword in DOST Supplement;
hauld, had and the rest of the CSD headwords are subsidiary headwords in either or both parent dictionaries.

4.3 Cross-references

Every CSD headword, whether reference or non-reference, also appears in its own alphabetical place, with a cross-reference to the first headword of the CSD article in which it appears, except where it is alphabetically adjacent to that article. (*See* 12 *below*.)

4.4 Predictable variants as headwords (*see also* 3 *above*)

Only a single representative from any group of variants (*see* 3 *above*) will normally be given as a CSD headword, followed by &c to represent the others.
   The sign &c after a Standard English spelling represents forms current at any time in Standard English.

A predictable variant is however given as a CSD headword when it also happens to be a headword in one of the parent dictionaries. (*See* 4.1 *above*).

5. Pronunciation

Contents

5.1   **Introduction**
5.1.1 How are the pronunciations given?
5.1.2 What are the stress-patterns of words without phonetic transcriptions?
5.1.3 How should a native speaker of Scots use CSD as a guide to pronunciation?

5.1 Introduction

5.1.1 **How are the pronunciations given?**

The pronunciations of nearly all[1] words in CSD are shown in one or other of the following ways. Where the headword spellings clearly indicate the word's pronunciations by normal English conventions, these spellings are left to serve in place of a phonetic transcription. But where any of the principal headword spellings seems ambiguous or misleading or the stress-pattern is unclear, a broad phonetic transcription is supplied, in the symbols of the International Phonetic Alphabet (IPA). These symbols are explained below (5.2).

5.1.2 **What are the stress-patterns of words without phonetic transcriptions?**

In words of more than one syllable which are left untranscribed, either:
(1) the stress-pattern is that of the same English word, e.g. certi**fi**cate;
(2) the stress-pattern is according to general English practice, as in, e.g., asse**da**tion, discon**tig**uous, ex**cresce**;
(3) in all other cases, the stress falls on the first syllable, e.g. **can**trip.

5.1.3 **How should a native speaker of Scots use CSD as a guide to pronunciation?**

A native speaker of Scots should have no difficulty in interpreting either the spellings or the phonetic symbols in terms of the precise qualities of each sound in his own dialect. (*See also* 5.4.)

5.1.4 **Can anyone learn to pronounce Scots from CSD?**

Yes. Anyone who is not a native speaker of Scots will achieve a plausible Scots pronunciation if he interprets the phonetic transcriptions by giving the symbols their usual IPA values as given at 5.2, or, when no transcription is provided, if he pronounces the spellings with the sounds listed there.

5.1.5 **Which words and variants are treated as current and which as obsolete?**

Words or variants are treated as current if they have been definitely attested within this century. Otherwise they are regarded as obsolete and their phonetic transcriptions are preceded by an asterisk. (*See* 5.2.5 *and* 5.5.)

5.1.6 **On what evidence do the phonetic transcriptions depend?**

The pronunciations of current forms represented in the phonetic transcriptions are derived from the transcriptions in SND and other authorities on the pronunciation of Scots, from indications of spelling and rhyme in SND and writings in Scots, from personal knowledge of members of the editorial staff, and by consultation with local speakers.

---

[1] The exceptions are a small number of relatively rare words, now obsolete, the pronunciations of which are more than usually uncertain.

The pronunciations of obsolete words and forms are deduced from spelling and rhyme evidence and from the examination or words in context in verse, supported by current knowledge of earlier Scots and English pronunciation, as this has been established by scholars.

5.1.7 Correspondence of headword spellings and pronunciations

There is not always an exact correspondence between the lists of pronunciations given in the phonetic transcriptions and the (more selective) lists of headword spellings. For instance, it sometimes happens that evidence exists for a pronunciation of which the parent dictionaries provide no corresponding spelling of the same date and/or region.

5.1.8 How exhaustive is CSD as a pronouncing dictionary of Scots?

For various reasons some words which have or had specially Scottish pronunciations have not qualified for inclusion in CSD (*see* p. 1.3). Hence such pronunciations as [dʒɪs] *juice*, [*ha'bit] *habit*, [pə'zɪʃən] *position*, ['pʌŋktər] *puncture* do not appear in it. Nevertheless, CSD's account of the pronunciation of Scots words remains by far the most complete available today.

5.2 The phonetic transcriptions

5.2.1 Consonant symbols

For the most part the IPA consonant symbols have the same values as in ordinary English, e.g. [b] is as in *butter* or *club*, [h] is as in *house* or *hand*. Symbols of this kind are: [b], [d], [f], [g], [h], [k], [l], [m], [n], [p], [r][1], [s], [t], [v], [w], [z]. There are also special symbols or symbol-combinations. In this Dictionary we have made use of the following:

----

[1] *See also 5.3.5 below*

Phonetic symbols	typical spellings	as in Scots words	as in Standard English words (as spoken by Scottish speakers)
j	*y*	*yaird, tailye, Spainyie, nyaff*	*yard, million, William, onion*
x	*ch*	*dreich, lauch, loch, nicht, dochter*	*loch, Brechin, Buchan, Bach*
hw	*wh*	*wha, wheech*	*when, wheel*
ʃ	*sh*	*shilpit, snash, ashet*	*she, ash, bishop*
ʒ	*s(h)i, su*	*fushion* ['fuʒən], *pleasure* ['pliʒər]	*evasion, closure, treasure*
tʃ	*ch, tch*	*chield, fleech, wratch*	*child, beech, catch*
dʒ	*j, dg, g*	*jeelie, fadge, fugie*	*jam, lodge, magic*
ŋ	*ng*	*hing, ingan, fank*	*sing, bank*
θ	*th*	*thole, thrawn, graith*	*thin, three, cloth*
ð	*th*	*thir, kythe, gether*	*these, bathe, gather*

5.2.2 Vowel and diphthong symbols

Phonetic symbols	typical spellings	as in Scots words	as in Standard English words (as spoken by Scottish speakers)
Vowels			
a	*a*	*cran, plat*	*man, cat*
ɑ	*au, aw, a'*	*fause, saut, ba*	*cause, caught, saw*
e	*ai, ay, a-e*	*graith, gate, tae*	*faith, gate, pay*
ɛ	*e*	*ken, hecht*	*pen, get*
ë	*i, e*	*birky, yird*	*devil, seven, earth, next*[1]
i	*ee, ei, ea*	*deif, dee*	*leaf, meet, sea*
ɪ	*i*	*lit, birl, nixt*	*bit, whirl, fix*
o	*o, oa, o-e*	*boss, cot, loch, thole*	*close (adj), close (v), coat, coal*
u	*oo, ou, ow*	*crouse, doo*	*loose, shoe*
ʌ	*u*	*buss, bud*	*bus, bud*
ø	*ui, u-e, oo, o*	*cuit, muin, fluir, do*[2]	
ə	*a, e, o, u*	*bannock* ['banək], *smeddum* ['smɛdəm] *stotter* ['stotər], *aboot* [ə'but]	*cassock* ['kasək], *autumn* ['ɔtəm], *butter* ['bʌtər], *about* [ə'bʌut]

Phonetic symbols	typical spellings	as in Scots words	as in Standard English words (as spoken by Scottish speakers)
Diphthongs			
aɪ	*i-e, y-e*	*kye, ay* (yes), *guise, rive*[3]	*eye, rise, hive, die*
əɪ	*i-e, y-e, oi, ey, ay*	*gyte, oil, join, aye* (always)	*bite, mile, line*
oi	*oi, oy*	*Boyd, noise, boy*[4]	
ʌu	*ou, ow*	*louse, owre, know*	*house, hour, cow*
ju	*eu, ew, ue*	*teuch, ewest*	*feud, duty, few*[5]

[1] The quality of vowel is that of a phonetically 'centralized' variant of 'Cardinal Vowel' [ɛ].
[2] Chiefly Shetland, Orkney, Angus, Perthshire and Southern Scots dialects, as a more or less rounded front vowel, ranging in quality from the vowels in French *lune*, German *über* to those in French *peu*, German *schön*.
[3] But some dialects have [əɪ] not [aɪ] in the last two words.
[4] In dialect Scots, this diphthong has a phonetically higher or closer quality throughout than its Standard English equivalent [ɔɪ]: compare the qualities shown here for [o] and [i] and for [ɔ] (in the next paragraph) and [ɪ], as the respective starting and final points of the two diphthongs.
[5] Though this sequence [j] + [u] is no longer strictly a diphthong, it is included here for comparison with its equivalent [iu] in Older Scots and in Modern Southern Scots (*see* 5.5.3 and 5.2.4).

5.2.3 Scottish Standard English vowel and diphthong symbols

For those words, such as Scots law terms, which are chiefly rendered with Scottish Standard English rather than dialect Scots pronunciations, the following additional symbols are used:

Vowel or diphthong	typical spellings	as in Scottish Standard English words
ɔ	*o, au, aw*	*cot, cause, loch, caught, saw*
ɔɪ	*oi, oy*	*Boyd, noise, boy, joint, royal*

5.2.4 Additional vowel and diphthong symbols

Conservative Southern Scots retains the falling diphthong [iu], that is, with the emphasis on the first element of the diphthong, in words which are elsewhere rendered with [ju], e.g. [briu] **brew**, [hiux] **heuch**, [riul] **rule**. A few Southern Scots words have been so transcribed.

Some local Northern Scots dialects (chiefly of Caithness and Easter Ross) have a diphthong [ei] in words which elsewhere have [i] or [e], such as *aince, bread, claes, ease, sweat, wait*. A few localized words and forms containing this diphthong have been so transcribed, including **cair, het, kebbock**.

5.2.5 Other symbols used

[:] the preceding vowel is long, e.g.: [li:d] *pt* of **lee** (to lie), [*Sh* mi:d] **meith**.

['] the following syllable is stressed, e.g.: [ka'hutʃɪ] **cahoochy**, ['kepər'keljɪ] **capercailzie**, ['kle'mor] **claymore**.

[*] the following pronunciation is believed to be no longer current.

[*?] this obsolete pronunciation is especially conjectural or uncertain.

[?] this pronunciation may still be current but it has not been possible to confirm it.

[&c] there are or were additional pronunciations which have not been transcribed.

5.2.6 The glottal stop

Many Scots speakers today substitute the glottal stop [ʔ], a sound made by momentarily closing the glottis, for the consonants [t], [p], or [k], especially [t], in certain positions in the word, as ['bʌʔər] *butter*, ['boʔl] *bottle*, [hwɔʔ] *what*. CSD does not record such variants, giving only the more conservative forms with [t] etc. But a few pronunciations with the glottal stop have been shown in special cases, such as the optional pronunciation [wɪ'ʔut] **without** (also [wɪ'ut]).

5.2.7 Other conventions of the phonetic transcriptions

These are illustrated by the following examples:
1. **weet**[1] [wit; *sEC, WC, SW Rox Uls* wat; *Per Fif also* wat; *Dmf* wʌt; *wet]
   (1) The General Scots form is [wit], but
   (2) in *sEC..Uls* it is replaced by [wat], and in *Dmf* by [wʌt],
   (3) in *Per* and *Fif*, beside [wit], [wat] also occurs;

(4) in addition to the earlier pronunciations corresponding to [wit], [wat] and [wʌt], a form [wɛt] or its antecedent also formerly occurred (*see* 5.5.2). In a few cases regional labels or a regional label followed by *also* have been used for obsolete pronunciations, with the same meanings as in (2) and (3) above, but usually localization of obsolete pronunciations has not been attempted.

2. **round** [run(d); . .]
Both [rund] and [run] occur widely.

3. **roup**[2] [rup; *local also* rʌup]
Beside [rup], the form [rʌup] occurs here and there over a wide area.

4. **row**[1] [rʌu; *also* rʌul]
Both [rʌu] and [rʌul] occur widely, but [rʌul] is much the less common.

5. **powk**[1] [pʌuk; *chf Sh Ork* puk]
[pʌuk] is the widespread form; [puk] also occurs, but is chiefly confined to Shetland and Orkney, where it is the common form.

5.3 Which pronunciations are and are not included in the phonetic transcriptions?

5.3.1 Are all the principal Scottish pronunciations included?
Yes. If a transcription is given at all, all the principal current and former Scottish pronunciations of the word are included, even though some of these may be adequately indicated by headword spellings, e.g.

banyel &c, bengle &c; bangyal &c [ˈbanjəl, ˈbaɲjəl, ˈbɛnjəl, ˈbɛɲjəl, ˈbɛɲl]

The only exceptions to this are:
(1) words which have a plethora of variants, where some more or less predictable variants may be subsumed under *&c* (*see* 5.2.5), e.g. **coachbell** where the variants [ˈkotʃb(ə)l, ˈswɪtʃp(ə)l, ˈskotʃb(ə)l, ˈskotʃʃɪbl, ˈskodʒɪbl. .] are given, but some others on the same lines are represented simply by [*&c*].
(2) obsolete words with numerous variants, some of which may similarly be replaced by *&c*.

5.3.2 Are (Scottish) Standard English pronunciations included in the phonetic transcriptions?
Often CSD gives only the vernacular Scots pronunciations, and it is taken for granted that the reader is aware that (Scottish) Standard English ((Sc)StEng) pronunciations also exist, e.g. the following (Sc)StEng pronunciations: [brek] for *break* (**brak**), [hʌus] for *house* (**hoose**), [rɛd] for *red* (**reid**), [sol] for *soul* (**saul**).

But (Sc)StEng pronunciations may be given in certain circumstances:
(1) if any of the headword spellings seem misleading and only the (Sc)StEng pronunciations exists, such as for **cut, cute, cowt,** pronounced only [kʌt], or
(2) if the (Sc)StEng rather than the Scots pronunciation is the commonest one, either generally or in some regions, as **leaf** [lif; *Sh Ork nEC* lef], **powl** [pʌul, pol],
(3) if the (Sc)StEng pronunciation is the only or the principal current form, though more typically Scottish pronunciation(s) formerly existed, e.g. **prison** [ˈprɪzən; *ˈprizun, &c], **ring** [rɪŋ; *rɪŋ],
(4) for words which have special Scottish pronunciations of their Standard English forms, e.g. **seeven** . . [ˈsiv(ə)n; . .; *St* ˈsëvn; . .]
(5) where the Standard English pronunciation is the only one used in some of the word's meanings, e.g. **pruif** . . [prøf, . . *St* pruf; . .], **croon** . . [krun] . . **Crown Agent** [(*St*) ˈkrʌun ˈedʒənt].
In (4) and (5) the label *St*(andard) is normally given.
(6) for expressions of Scots law as pronounced by Scots lawyers today, e.g. **homologate** [hɔˈmɔloget], **interlocutor** . . [ɪntərˈlɔkətər, *also* -ˈlɔk(j)utər].

5.3.3 Localized vowel and diphthong sounds omitted from CSD
CSD's system of phonetic symbols accounts for all the distinctive sounds of Scots which are shared widely between the dialects. There are however four vowel or diphthong sounds which are limited to particular districts:

(1) [iu] and [ei], the diphthongs described in 5.2.4.

(2) [eː] or [e·ə], the long vowel or diphthong found in Angus, East Fife and elsewhere in such words at *bait*, *hail*; and [oː] with long-vowel pronunciation, found in Angus, Perthshire and elsewhere in such words as *coat*, *thole*.

As information on the occurrence of these sounds in particular words is at present quite incomplete, localized pronunciations containing these sounds are not included in CSD's phonetic transcriptions, except for [iu] and [ei] as described in 5.2.4.

5.3.4 Predictable variations between consonants
The following predictable or regular variations in consonant sounds in certain districts are not usually shown in CSD's phonetic transcriptions:

(1) word-initial consonant sequences, formerly general in both Scots and English, but now surviving only in dialects north of the Tay:

[kn-], in Angus and East Perthshire commonly changed to [tn-], elsewhere now [n-], in e.g. **knife, knit**.

[wr-], in the North-East now [vr-], elsewhere now [r-], in e.g. **wrang, writ**.

These consonant sequences are normally indicated by the corresponding spellings, **kn-** (for Angus, sometimes also **tn-**) and **wr-** (for the North-East, sometimes also **vr-**) respectively.

But the few words containing the similar sequence [gn-], elsewhere now [n-], have all been given transcriptions, e.g. **gnap** [(g)nap; *Mry Bnf* gnɛp].

(2) the simplification of word-initial [tʃ] to [ʃ] in Shetland, Caithness, Easter Ross and Berwickshire, in e.g. **chaft**[1] [tʃaft; *Sh Bwk* ʃaft], **cheese, chimley**.

(3) the change of word-initial [dʒ] to [tʃ] in Orkney and Caithness, in e.g. **jabble** ['dʒabl, 'dʒebl; *Ork* 'tʃabl], **jealous, jupe** [dʒøp, dʒup; *Ork Cai* tʃup; . .].

(4) the alternation of [hw] with [kw] in parts of Shetland and Orkney, in e.g. **queer, quern, white, whitrat**.

(5) the replacement of [θ] with [t], and [ð] with [d], in Shetland and Orkney in e.g. **thee** [θi; *Sh Ork* ti], **tho** [θo; *Sh Ork* to], **thrapple** ['θrapl; *Sh Ork* 'tr-], **there** [ðer; *Sh Ork* der], **thou** [ðu; *Sh Ork* du].

(6) the omission of initial [ð] in Caithness and Buchan in e.g. **the** [(ð)ɪ], **this** [(ð)ɪs], **there** [(ð)er], **thestreen** [(ð)ɪ'strin].

(7) the change of [-ək] (**-ock** etc) to [-əg] (**-ag**) in Caithness, in e.g. **bannock, puddock**.

(8) the change of [-ət] (**-et**) to [-əd] (**-ad**) in Caithness, in e.g. **latchet**.

The variants (1) to (8) listed above have only been included in the transcriptions when they were needed to clarify other aspects of the pronunciations of the words in question.

(9) for the ending of the gerund, e.g. **leasing**, Scottish Standard English favours **-ing** [-ɪŋ], vernacular Scots **-in** [-ɪn]; only one of these is normally transcribed.

(10) the occasional pronunciation of **thr-** in Central and Southern Scots as [ʈr-] or the like in place of [θr-], in e.g. **thrash, threat, three**, has not been shown in the transcriptions.

5.3.5 Vowel + r

In Scots and in some accents of Scottish Standard English, r is always pronounced, unlike in some parts of England, where it is pronounced only before a vowel. Equally, in Scots the vowel before r does not alter in quality, e.g.

serve	[sɛrv]	**set**	[sɛt]
bird	[bɪrd]	**bid**	[bɪd]
hurl	[hʌrl]	**hut**	[hʌt]
corbie	['korbɪ]	**cot**	[kot]

For the majority of such words, no transcription is given.

5.4 How precise are the phonetic transcriptions?

5.4.1 CSD's transcriptions are intentionally broad

Many of CSD's phonetic symbols cover a range of sound-qualities, ignoring local variations, e.g. [ɛ] as in *get, ken, hecht* ranges from a fairly close pronunciation in the North-east (verging on [e] as in *gate*) to a much more open pronunciation in the South (rather like the vowel [æ] in *cat* in South-east English middle-class speech). CSD [ɛ] represents both of these sounds as well as Central Scots [ɛ].

[ɑ] as in *saut* (salt), *cause, saw* ranges from the sound of the vowel in Northern English *hat*, through that of the first vowel in South-east English *father*, to that of the vowel in *bought* in most varieties of British Standard English. The Northern and Southern Scots dialects favour one or other of the first two of these sounds, the Central Scots dialects the last. CSD [ɑ] represents all three.

In the same way, local variants are not given for the unstressed vowels, such as [ɪ] as in **cairry, peerie, blessin**.

CSD does not normally provide more than one transcription for alternative pronunciations such as [pro'pon, prə'pon] for **propone**, in which, if the fuller unstressed vowel pronunciation is given, the alternative pronunciation with a reduced vowel [ə] or [ɪ] is taken for granted.

Equally, for pairs of alternatives such as ['θivl] (['θivəl]) **theevle**, ['stødən] (['stødn]) **stuiden**, past participle of **stand**, [ʌur] (['ʌuər]) **owre**, [erm] (['erəm]) **airm**, ['larɪk] (['larək]) **larick**, CSD normally gives only the first of each pair.

5.4.2 How does CSD treat vowel-length?

Scots and Scottish Standard English have their own system of vowel-length, which is different from that of all other parts of the English-speaking world.

1. Certain vowels, i.e. [ɪ] and [ʌ], are always pronounced short.
2. Certain other vowels, i.e. [ɑ] in most dialects, and the vowels discussed at 5.3.3 (2), are always pronounced long.
3. The remaining vowels are normally pronounced long
   (1) before the consonants [v], [ð], [z], [ʒ] and, for many dialects, [r], and,
   (2) when the vowel is final (in a word or in the first part of a compound word),
   (3) when the vowel is followed by an ending such as the past-tense ending [-d].
   In all other positions these vowels are in some dialects pronounced short, e.g. before [f], [θ], [t], [d], [l], [m], etc. But other dialects vary as to whether they make par-

ticular vowels of this group short or long in particular positions,

e.g. [e] is short before [l] in some dialects but long in others,

[a] is short before [d] in some dialects but long in others.

In these circumstances it is clearly impossible for a dictionary such as CSD to record the precise vowel-length for each word in every dialect, and this has not been attempted. Consequently, vowels are not normally marked for length in the transcriptions, and it is left to the reader to pronounce the vowel in each case either with the length appropriate to his own dialect or according to the general indications set out above.

A long vowel is however marked long

(1) when it occurs in a position in the word where the dialect or dialects in question normally have a short vowel, e.g. Shetland [mi:d] **meith** (a landmark), compare [nid] **need**,

(2) when it is necessary to mark a contrast with a short-vowel pronunciation, e.g. the two forms of the *pt* of **gae** *v*, [ge:d] and [ged], or ['ga:lık] beside ['galık] **Gaelic**.

5.5 Pronunciation of obsolete words

5.5.1 Pronunciations given for obsolete as well as current words

A unique feature of this Dictionary is the application of the broad principles stated at 5.1.1 to obsolete as well as current words or variants, including many which have been obsolete since the Middle Scots period of the 16th century. (For CSD's criteria for distinguishing current and obsolete words, *see* 5.1.5.) The Dictionary thus serves as a guide not only to attested pronunciations of Modern Scots but also to those in use in Early and Middle Scots (*see* p. xiii for the periods covered by these terms). For the evidence from which obsolete pronunciations are deduced, *see* 5.1.6.

5.5.2 **Mode of transcription of obsolete words**

CSD does not attempt to transcribe obsolete words or variants with the exact sound-qualities which they had in earlier times. Instead, it transcribes them with the pronunciations they would have had if they had survived to the present day, except that it follows the earlier stress-patterns when these appear to have been different from those of today. In the following paragraph there is a Table of the approximate sound-qualities of the vowels and diphthongs of Early and Middle Scots corresponding to each of the Modern Scots sounds used in CSD's transcriptions. (Since the qualities of the consonants have not significantly changed since Early Scots, no similar Table is required for these.) As stated at 5.2.5, obsolete pronunciations are preceded by *, or in especially doubtful cases by *?.

5.5.3 **Vowel and diphthong systems of Early, Middle and Modern Scots** (*see* p. xiii)

Modern Scots	Middle Scots	Early Scots	Scots and (Scottish) Standard English words with these vowels and diphthongs
a (as in *cat*)	a	a	*cran*, *lass*
ɑ (as in *caught*)	a:	au al	*saw*, *cause*, *chaumer* (chamber) *salt* (Sc *saut*), *ball* (Sc *ba*)
e (as in *gate*)	e:	a: ɛ: ai	*gate*, *baith* (both), *gae* *deaf*, *dead* *bait*, *day*
ɛ (as in *get*)	ɛ	ɛ	*pen*, *hecht*
ë	ɪ	ɪ	*bird*, *next*, *earth*
ɪ (as in *bit*)	ɪ	ɪ	*mill*, *sit*
i (as in *meet*)	i:	e: ɛ: ei	*meet*, *see* *deaf*, *dead* *dee* (die)
o (as in *coat*)	o o:	o o:	*cot*, *loch*, *boss* (hollow) *coat*, *before*, *close* [klos *n*, kloz *v*]

Modern Scots	Middle Scots	Early Scots	Scots and (Scottish) Standard English words with these vowels and diphthongs
u (as in *rook*)	u:	u: ul	*crouse* (jaunty), *house*, *doo* (dove) *multure*, *pull* (Sc *pou*)
ʌ (as in *cut*)	u	u	*butt*, *fur*
ø (quality between those of the vowels of French *lune* and *peu*)	ø:	ø:	*use* [(Sc) *n* øs; *v* øz], *fruit*, *mune*, *do* [(Sc) dø] (*see* **dae**[1])
ə (as in *better* [ˈbɛtər])	ə	various vowels	*bannock* [ˈbanək], *above* [əˈbʌv], *abune* [əˈbøn] (above)
aɪ (as in *buy*)	ei	i:	*rise*, *byre*, *ay* (yes)
əi (as in *bite*)	ei ui ei (word-final)	i: ui ai (word-final)	*bite*, *bide*, *wice* (wise) *doit*, *oil*, *poison* (*see* **pushion**) *May*, *aye* (always)
oi (as in *boy*)	oi	oi	*noise*, *Boyd*, *boy*
ʌu (as in *cow*)	ou	ou ol	*nowt* (cattle), *grow* *solder* (*see* **sowther**), *roll* (*see* **row**)
ju (as in *few*)	iu	eu iu	*beauty*, *few* *teuch* (tough), *new*
ei (see 5.2.4)	ʔɛi	a: ai ɛ:	*hate* (hot) (*see* **het**), *aince* *wait* *sweat* (*see* **sweet**), *ease*

As the preceding paragraph explains, it is only the symbols for the Modern Scots vowels and diphthongs in the above Table that are used in the phonetic transcriptions in the Dictionary itself. See 5.2.2 for the full key to the phonetic values of these symbols.

5.5.4 Early and Middle Scots long vowels
The Modern Scots system of vowel-length briefly described at 5.4.2 has emerged only since the Middle Scots period (probably since *c* 1550). Prior to this Scots had a much larger number of invariably long vowels than it now has. These are the vowels marked in the preceding Table with the symbol for length [:]. Strictly these vowels should be pronounced fully long in all positions in the word by anyone attempting a restored pronunciation of Early or Middle Scots.

5.5.5 Early and Middle Scots diphthongs
As the Table at 5.5.3 also shows, Early and Middle Scots also had a number of diphthongs of qualities different from those now found in Scots. These Early and Middle Scots diphthongs therefore do not appear in the list of sounds at 5.2.2. Approximate pronunciations of these diphthongs may however be obtained by

pronouncing the starting and final points of the diphthongs as these are individually identified in the Table at 5.2.2 and in the Modern Scots column of the Table at 5.5.3: e.g. the diphthong [ei] begins at [e] as in *gate*, and moves towards [i] as in *meet*.

5.5.6 Restoring Early and Middle Scots pronunciation
Readers seeking further guidance on restoring Middle and Early Scots pronunciation should however consult 'How to Pronounce Older Scots' by Adam J. Aitken, in *Bards and Makars*, edited by Adam J. Aitken et al., University of Glasgow Press, 1977, pp. 1–21.

5.5.7 Which obsolete words and forms have been left untranscribed?
As with modern words (*see* 5.1.1), transcriptions are in general not given if the headword spellings clearly and unambiguously represent the

pronunciations by (modern) English conventions. Nor have transcriptions normally been given in the following cases:

(1) for the many Early and Middle Scots word-suffixes, chiefly of French or Latin origin, such as those often spelled *-tioun, -sioun, -cial, -ciar*, etc, which were then pronounced with two syllables, so that the word *natioun*, e.g., was a trisyllabic word [*'nesɪun]. These suffixes have now commonly been reduced to single syllables, as in ['neʃən] *nation*.

(2) for the many Early and Middle Scots prefixes and suffixes which probably had fuller vowel pronunciations than are now usual, though perhaps only optionally, e.g. prefixes in [*a-], now [ə-], as in **adduce**, or suffixes in [*-sɪun] or [*-ur], now [-ʃ(ə)n] or [-ər], as in **assedatioun** or **dyvour**.

(3) for the Early and Middle Scots word-endings in *-é, -ive, -y*, which were then pronounced, though in Middle Scots only optionally, as [*-i], [*-aɪv], [*-aɪ], now [-ɪ], [-ɪv], [-ɪ], respectively, as in **ceté, daynté, motive, succudry, trinity** or the adverbial ending *-ly*.

(4) for the Early and Middle Scots ending [*-at] as an alternative to [-et] for the suffix *-ate, -att*, of Latin origin, in such words as **educate, registrate**.

(5) the spellings *u-(e), -u(e)*, in words of French or Latin origin, represented one or other of two different sounds in Older Scots.

1. When *u(e)* was followed by a second vowel as in **cruet** or **patruell**, or was final in the word, as in **due** or **virtue**, the sound represented was [iu] or, later, [(j)u], as [*'kriuət], [*'patriuəl], [*diu], [*'vɛrtiu].

2. But when a consonant followed, as in **adduce, dissimulate, desuetude, figurate, gratitude, illumine, mature, matutine, obscure**, the sound represented by the *u-(e)* spelling was in Older Scots [ø]. By influence from Standard English it has now mainly become [(j)u], as e.g. [*a'døs] (**adduce**), now [ə'djus] or [ə'dʒus], [*'r'ləmɪn] (**illumine**), now [ɪ'l(j)umɪn].

CSD does not normally provide transcriptions in any of the above cases, unless there is some other aspect of the word's pronunciation to be shown.

6 Grammar and word-formation

6.1 Parts of speech
Most headwords are given a part-of-speech label or labels, with a very few exceptions, chiefly proper names, *e.g.* **Cameron**.

The first part-of-speech label follows the pronunciation information, if this is included; otherwise it immediately follows the headword(s). Later part-of-speech sections each form a new paragraph. The order of the parts of speech is usually etymological.

6.2 noun (*n*)
Plural forms of nouns are not given if they are the same as the Standard English plural or if they conform to one of the regular patterns of plurals in Scots. For example **leaves** and **leiffis** as plurals of **leaf** are regarded as regular plurals and are not specified in CSD. (*See 7.8 below*).

6.3 verb (*v*)
Verbs are usually labelled with the following:
>   *vt* verb transitive
>   *vi* verb intransitive
>   *vr* verb reflexive
>   or in any combination, *e.g. vti*.

Where a verb has more than one meaning division (*See 7.6 below*), these are given separate verb labels where necessary. When a division does not have such a label it means that it belongs to the same category as its predecessor(s). In other words any verb label continues to operate throughout a series of meaning divisions until it is cancelled by another label.

present participle (*presp*)/**verbal noun** (not abbreviated)
Regular Scots forms of the present participle (*e.g.* in **-and, -an**) and the verbal noun (*e.g.* in **-in, -en**) are not normally given in CSD. (*See also* 'A History of Scots' p. *xv*.) These are included only where a Scots meaning or usage is treated, usually in the derivatives section. (*See* 10.1.)

6.3.1 past tense (*pt*) and past participle (*ptp*)
These forms are not normally given when they follow the regular patterns of Scots and/or English. But where the standard 'common British English' form is earlier in Scots than in English, it is included according to the rules set out in 1.2 above.

Where a standard form exists but is not given, other forms are introduced with *also*, as follows:
   lowp[1] ... *ptp* also **lowpen** 1*a*17-
This implies that the predictable past participle **lowpit** or **lowped** is found as well as **lowpen**.

Note: Certain past tenses using the past-participle form, *e.g.* **seen, done,** though not Standard English, are in world-wide use, and have therefore been omitted from CSD (though some will be found in SND).

6.4 **adjective** *(adj)*/**adverb** *(adv)*

Comparatives and superlatives are given in the fairly rare cases where these differ from the normal 'common British English' pattern, *e.g.*

> **dear** ... *comparative also* **derrar &c** *1a15-e16*, **darrer** *15-e17. superlative also* **derrast &c** *15-16*, **darrest** *15-e17.*

> **least &c** ... ~**est** *double superlative adj, 1a19-, now Sh.*

7 Definitions

7.1 Definitions (in roman type) are based on those in the parent dictionaries. However every definition and indeed every quotation in the parent dictionaries has been examined afresh, and often their definitions have been modified in the light of the more comprehensive information available to CSD editors.

7.2 The wording of CSD definitions has been kept as simple as possible. Definitions from the parent dictionaries have therefore been simplified where necessary. But it is not always possible to avoid complicated or technical language. Sometimes the concept is complicated in itself. In other cases the evidence in the parent dictionaries is insufficient to allow accurate re-wording of their definitions.

7.3 Synonyms used in definitions are normally separated by commas; where a semi-colon is used, this indicates a slight shift in meaning, *e.g.* **nip** ... **8** seize, catch; snatch, make off with ...

7.4 **'Umbrella' definitions** See also 1.2 above. Many words share a common history with English for some of their meanings and usages, at least for part of their history, and this is indicated by means of an 'umbrella' or 'covering' definition, *e.g.* **man** ... *n* **1** = man *1a14-.*

This indicates that this word has been present in both English and Scots since the late 14th century both in the modern Standard English meanings and possibly in others which were common to both English and Scots at other periods.

> **stane &c** ... *n* **1** = stone *1a14-.*

indicates that the Scots spelling *stane* and its predictable variants, have been used with at least some of the same meanings as English *stone* since the late fourteenth century.

Such 'umbrella' definitions are usually given as the first meaning, but there are cases where they are given later in the entry for historical reasons, *e.g.*

> **clatter &c** *n* **1** *freq in pl* noisy idle chatter, gossip, scandal; rumours *lal6-.* **2** a chatterer, a gossip *20-, NE.* **3** = clatter.

Sometimes, and quite frequently in the latter part of the alphabet where DOST was not available, such definitions are given without a date, because of lack of evidence for their early use.

Note (1) An entry which contains such an 'umbrella' definition is not normally given an etymology. (*See* 11.1 *below.*)

(2) Sometimes 'umbrella' definitions are given additional definitions, *e.g.*

1. because the word has more than one meaning in modern English, *e.g.* **flag²** *&c n* **1** = flag, a flagstone *16-.*

2. because the word is obsolete and may not be understood by many users, *e.g.* **barrace** ... **1** = barrace, a barrier in front of a castle etc *1a14-16.*

3. because the particular meaning is obsolete and may be misunderstood, *e.g.* **flaur** ... = flavour, smell ...

(3) 'Umbrella' definitions are also used where Scots uses a different word from English, but uses it over a similar range of meanings, *e.g.* **ken** *vti* **1** = know *1a14-.*

This indicates that *ken* has been used in Scots in similar ways to English *know* since the late 14th century.

7.5 The ordering of meanings within an entry, part-of-speech or sub-entry on the whole follows historical order, but the system is not rigid and sometimes a meaning for which the evidence is later may come first, especially if such ordering makes for a clearer presentation of the development of the meanings, *e.g.* **cavel¹**.

7.6 **Division of meanings**

Where necessary, entries, parts of speech or sub-entries are separated into meaning divisions, introduced by a number in bold type, *e.g.*

> **gae** ... **1** *vi* = go *1a14-.* **2** *vt* cover on foot *1a18-, local Abd-Rox.* **3** ...

In some cases further sub-division is thought to be helpful and numbers in brackets are used, *e.g.*

> **gae thegither 1** ... **2** (1) get married *1a18-19, local.* (2) *of lovers* court *1a19-.*

These sub-categories are normally separated by full stops, but if part of the definition applies to all sub-divisions, a semi-colon is used.

Occasionally there is further sub-division, using letters in brackets, *e.g.*

> **neb**...**3** any projecting tip or point: (1) on a person's body, as (a) of fingers or toes *1a16-*; (b) of the tongue *1a16-19*...

Rarely a fourth layer is used, introduced by roman numerals in brackets, *e.g.*

> **pretty**...**3** (1) (a)...(b) *specif* (i) *of men* courageous...

In *very* rare cases there is a different kind of division of the entry, using capital letters in bold type, *e.g.* the entry **Scots** is divided into:

> **A**—detailed notes on the use of the different forms, and
> **B**—the meanings.

7.7 Dating and geographical distribution

Most definitions are followed by a date indicating the period during which they were used, to the nearest half-century. (*See* 8 *below.*) Some are also followed by a label or labels indicating the counties or area(s) in which they are found, especially when their use is restricted in the modern period. (*See* 9 *below.*)

7.8 Information on constructions

Such information is given in definitions in several ways. For example, if prepositions etc. in the definition are printed in bold type, this means that the same prepositions are used with the Scots word, *e.g.* **ca**[1]...**7** *vt* drive **in** (nails etc.); ...

Where a definition begins with a label such as *in negative, in pl* or *chf in negative, chf in pl*, the definition is worded in the negative or plural, *e.g.* **cheese**[2] *n* **say** ∼ *in negative* not mention, ...

7.9 Field labels

Labels (such as *mining, law*), are occasionally used to indicate which field of knowledge the item belongs to. They are placed before the definition, *e.g.* **box**[1]...**3** *law* a box in the corner of *Parliament House* ...

7.10 Illustrative phrases

Illustrative phrases, where possible culled from the quotations in the parent dictionaries, are included occasionally to clarify a meaning or usage. They are given at the end of the item which they illustrate, *e.g.* **gane &c 1** (1) past, ago *18-*: 'Sunday gane a week'.

8 Dating

8.1 Dates (in italic type) are given in half-centuries, as far as available evidence allows, both for forms (see below) and meanings. Thus:

> *e16* means that there is evidence (normally a quotation or quotations in one or more of the sources) between 1500 and 1550;
> *1a16*: between 1550 and 1600;
> *16*: for the whole of the 16th century;
> *1a14-16*: from the second half of the 14th century to the end of the 16th century;
> *15-19*: from the beginning of the 15th to the end of the 19th century;
> *1a16-e19*: from the second half of the 16th to the first half of the 19th century;
> *16-20*: from the beginning of 16th century onwards but recently obsolete or known to be obsolescent;
> *1a14-*: from the second half of the 14th century to the present day.

Occasionally where there is a long gap in the evidence, two date ranges are given, *e.g.*

> *e16, 19-* means that there is early 16th century evidence but nothing more until the early 19th century.

8.2 Certain authors have not been included for the calculation of date range, as they are known to have been deliberate users of archaic language, *e.g.* H. P. Cameron, P. H. Waddell.

Prominent authors such as Sir Walter Scott and Hugh MacDiarmid have however been included, even if they are obviously using deliberate archaisms. Such instances are normally marked *arch* (for Scott) or *literary* (for MacDiarmid).

8.3 Place-names

Place-name dating evidence is not normally used, but it is sometimes stated separately, alongside other dates, *e.g.* **new**...**1** = new *1a14-*, *in place-names 12-*.

8.4 Dating of forms

Forms which are not dated are found over the whole date-range of the entry, *e.g.*

> **barra &c** *20-*, **barrow &c, borrow** *17-e18*, **borra &c** *19- n* = (hand- etc) barrow *1a14-*.

This indicates that there is evidence of the form **barrow** and/or its predictable variants from the late 14th century onwards.

9 Geographical distribution

9.1 The maps of Scotland on pages xxxi–xxxii show:

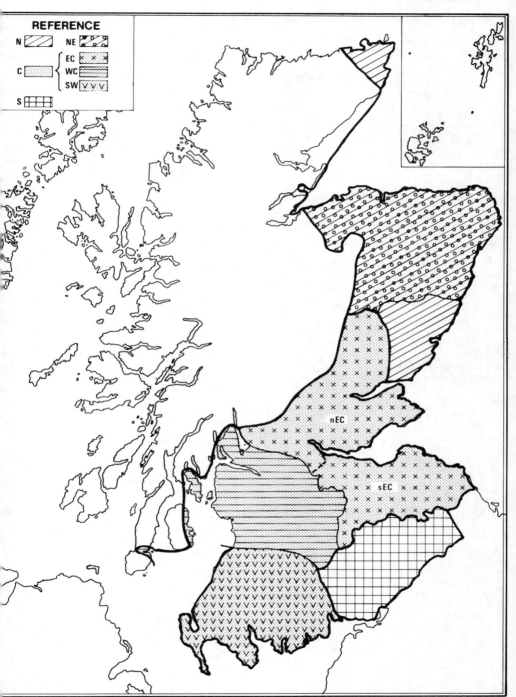

Map 1 Scotland: the main dialect divisions of Scots — *see* 9.3

Map 2   Scotland: pre-1975 counties — *see* 9.3

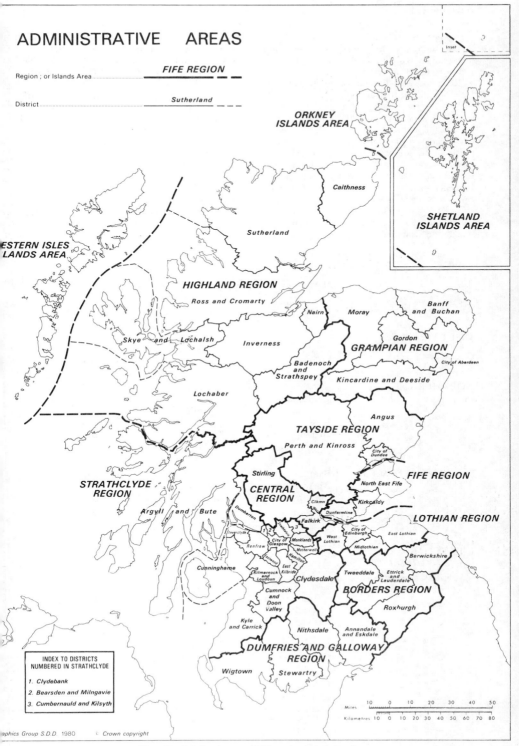

Map 3 Scotland: post-1975 regions and districts
(reproduced by permission of Graphics Group Scottish Development Department)

(1) the extent of the main Scots-speaking area in the east and south of the country and its boundary with the Highlands and the Hebrides to the north and west;

(2) various sub-divisions of the Scots area, based on shared dialect features.

CSD deals mainly with the Scots-speaking area to the east and south, as well as Shetland and Orkney to the north. The Highlands and the Hebrides are or recently were Gaelic-speaking and so use Highland or Hebridean English, *i.e.* varieties of Standard English influenced mainly by Gaelic rather than Scots. (*See* 9.9 Note (2) *below*.)

9.2 Where a form, meaning, usage or pronunciation is limited to an area or areas, and especially where it is thus limited at the present time, this is indicated by means of CSD's system of abbreviations as set out below. This system is based on that of SND except that some abbreviations have been altered for greater clarity (*e.g. Kcdn* rather than *Kcd, SW* rather than *sm.Sc.*). Although the counties as administrative units were abolished in 1975, all SND's research had by that time already been done on the basis of these demarcations. Therefore county names continue to be used with their pre-1975 significance.

The abbreviations (in italic type) normally follow the spellings, meanings etc to which they refer, except in the pronunciations, where they are placed before the transcriptions to which they refer.

9.3 **DIALECT DISTRICTS OF SCOTS**

SND Area name	County	SND abbreviation	CSD abbreviation
INSULAR SCOTS		I.Sc.	Sh Ork
	Shetland	Sh.	Sh
	Orkney	Ork.	Ork
NORTHERN SCOTS		n.Sc.	N
	Caithness	Cai.	Cai
	Sutherland	Sth.	Suth
	Ross	Rs.	Ross
	Inverness	Inv.	Inv
NORTH-EAST SCOTS (ne.Sc.)	Nairn	Nai.	Nai
	Moray	Mry.	Mry
	Banff	Bnff. (NE)	Bnf
	Aberdeen	Abd.	Abd
	Buchan	Bch.	Buchan
	Kincardine	Kcd.	Kcdn
	east Angus	e.Ags.	Ags
MID SCOTS		m.Sc.	C (Central)
EAST MID SCOTS		em.Sc.	EC (East Central)
east mid Scots (a)		em.Sc.(a)	nEC
	west Angus	w.Ags.	Ags
	east and south-east Perthshire	e. and se. Per.	Per
	Stirling	Slg.	Stlg
	Fife	Fif.	Fif
	Kinross	Knr.	Kinr
	Clackmannan	Clc.	Clcm
east mid Scots (b)		em.Sc. (b)	sEC
	West Lothian	w.Lth.	wLoth
	Edinburgh	Edb.	Edb
	Midlothian	m.Lth.	midLoth
	East Lothian	e.Lth.	eLoth
	Berwick	Bwk.	Bwk
	Peebles	Peb.	Pbls

SND Area name	County	SND abbreviation	CSD abbreviation
WEST MID SCOTS		wm.Sc.	WC (West Central)
	Dunbarton	Dmb.	Dnbt
	Argyll	Arg.	Arg
	Bute	Bte.	Bute
	Renfrew	Rnf.	Renfr
	Glasgow	Gsw.	Gsw
	Lanark	Lnk.	Lnk
	north Ayr	n.Ayr.	Ayr
SOUTH MID SCOTS		sm.Sc.	SW (South-West)
	south Ayr	s.Ayr.	Ayr
	Wigtown	Wgt.	Wgt
	Kirkcudbright	Kcb.	Kcb
	Galloway	Gall.	Gall
	west Dumfries	w.Dmf.	Dmf
SOUTHERN SCOTS		s.Sc.	S
	Roxburgh	Rxb.	Rox
	Selkirk	Slk.	Slk
	east and mid Dumfries	e. and m. Dmf.	Dmf
ULSTER SCOTS		Uls.	Uls

9.4 The order of the list is roughly north to south, *i.e.* from *Sh* down the east coast to *Bwk*, and then down the west coast of the mainland to *Wgt* and *Kcb*, followed by *S* (*i.e.* Southern Scots—*Rox*, *Slk* and part of *Dmf*), and finally *Uls*. The abbreviations are given in CSD, as in SND, strictly in the order of the list in 9.3, *e.g.*

Bnf Abd Kcdn Ags
Bnf Abd Ags Fif
sEC Lnk

9.5 Normally where an item is found in more than two consecutive counties or areas on the list, only the first and last are given, with a dash to show continuity, *e.g.*

Bnf-Per means that the item is found in *Bnf*, *Abd*, *Kcdn*, *Ags* and *Per*.
Fif-Wgt means that the item is found in *Fif*, *Kinr*, *Clcm*, *sEC*, *WC*, *Ayr* and *Wgt*.
sEC-S means that the item is found in *sEC*, *WC*, *SW* and *S*.
local Bnf-Per means that it is found throughout this area but only sporadically.
local NE means that it is found sporadically from *Mry* to just south of the River Dee.
local without any qualification means that it is found sporadically throughout the whole country.
E is also used to cover *Sh*, *Ork*, *N* and *EC*.
ECoast is occasionally used, *esp* for fisher communities of the East Coast.

9.6 Where SND labels Gen.Sc., meaning that the item is in general use throughout the whole country, this is indicated in CSD by giving a current date (*e.g. la14-*) with no restricting label.

The label *Gen* is used as a distribution label in CSD only in cases such as the following:

Gen except Sh Ork, meaning that it is used throughout the whole country except for Shetland and Orkney.

9.7 **use of** *now*
now NE means that the usage is now confined to the North-East, although it was formerly more (or, in rare cases, less) widespread.

9.8 **use of** *chf*
chf SW means that the item is found chiefly, but not exclusively, in the South-West.

9.9 Note (1) In CSD (as in SND) the label *N* includes that part of Angus which is included in SND's Northern division, and *NE* includes the northern edge of *Kcdn*.
(2) (*See also* 9.1 *above*) *Cai-Inv* is used as a label not only for Scots words which are used on the east coast of these counties, but also for words, chiefly of Gaelic origin, used throughout these counties, *e.g. stroupach* (STROUP).
Highl labels words, chiefly of Gaelic origin, used in the Gaelic-speaking (or recently Gaelic-speaking) parts of *Cai*, *Suth*, *Ross*, *Inv*, *Per*, *Dnbt* and *Arg*. *Hebrides* is similarly used for words from the Western Isles. The Highland and Hebridean English of these regions are varieties

of Standard English influenced mainly by Gaelic rather than Scots.

9.10 Occasionally information about distribution is given in parentheses, indicating that it applies to the immediately preceding date only and not to the whole date range, *e.g.* *1a14-16, 1a19-(NE)*. This means that the evidence from the late 19th century onwards is confined to the North-East, but that the restriction does not apply to the medieval period.

10 Derivatives, compounds, phrases

10.1 **Derivatives**, *e.g.* **flesher, fleshing, fleshlyk** from **flesh**, form a new paragraph, following all of the definitions of the headword on its own. They are in alphabetical order of the suffix, *e.g.*

> **flesh** *n* 1 ... 2 ...
> 3 ...
> ~**er** ... ~**ing** ... ~**lyk**

10.2 **Compounds** which have the headword as first element form another new paragraph, following the derivatives (where there are any). They are in alphabetical order of the second element, *e.g.* **maister**[1] ... ~ **man** ... ~ **tree** ...

The presence or absence of the possessive **s** has been ignored in the alphabetization as its presence or absence is frequently inconsistent in Scots.

10.3 **Phrases** follow in another new paragraph in alphabetical order of the first significant element (whether or not this is the headword). Function-words such as pronouns, prepositions, the definite or indefinite article are normally ignored. It is not however possible to make rigid rules about the order in which phrases appear. In some cases a preposition may be a significant part of a phrase, *e.g.*, **cut**[1] ... **cut before the point** while in other cases it may not be significant, *e.g.* **crack**[1] ... ~ **like a pen-gun**.

Also, the first word of a phrase may vary in different versions; *see* 10.5 *below*.

The phrase section also contains:

(1) phrasal verbs (i.e. verbs + preposition or adverb), *e.g.*

> **gae** ... ~ **aboot** ... ~ **awa** ... ~ **back** ...

It also contains nouns, adjectives etc formed from a phrasal verb, even if the phrasal verb itself is not in fact included, *e.g.* **gae** ... **go-between** ...

(2) compounds which do not have the headword as first element. (*See* 10.5 *below*).

10.4 Occasionally a derivative, compound or phrase is included in one of the main sections of the article, *e.g.* where it is identical in meaning with one of the parts of speech or with one of the meaning divisions, or when it is the chief illustration of one of these, *e.g.* **pug**[1] ... **2** *chf* ~**ie**.

10.5 Most compounds and phrases will be found under the first element. Thus **Lord Advocate** will be found under LORD and not under ADVOCATE. But there are exceptions to this, *e.g.* where there is a CSD headword for the second element and not for the first, or where the first element is not constant; it is then usually inserted under the next significant word, *e.g.* **haud** *or* **steek one's gab** is under GAB[2].

Compounds appearing under the second element are inserted in the phrase section of the article.

As there is not enough space in the Dictionary to allow an item to be included more than once, users may not always find the item they are looking for at the first attempt. In such cases they should then try one of the other elements.

Except in very rare instances, no cross-reference is given from one element of a phrase or compound to another.

10.6 Derivatives, compounds and, rarely, phrases may form self-contained **sub-entries**. For example, they may be found in more than one part-of-speech; only in such cases are they given a part-of-speech label. They may also have meaning divisions and they may have other derivatives, compounds and phrases dependent on them.

In such cases, all these are given immediately following the base derivative etc., in the same order as such items would have in the main part of the entry, but without the separate paragraphs. The most frequent example of this is the compound or phrase based on a derivative, which will therefore be found in the *derivatives* paragraph, not among the compounds, *e.g.*

> **stour** ...
>> **stourie** ... **stourie drink**
> **lay** ...
>> **laid** ... **laid drain** ... **laid walk**

11 Etymologies

See list of abbreviations on p. xxxix–xli.

11.1 Etymologies are included for most entries, within square brackets, usually at the end (after the last full stop). The main type of entry for which no etymology is given is that which contains an 'umbrella' definition—*see 7.4 above*. Such a definition shows the word's relationship to English and if further etymological information is desired, it can be found in any English dictionary which contains etymologies.

11.2 Etymologies in CSD are, broadly, of two types:

    1. a simple etymology, usually based on that of the parent dictionary or dictionaries

or 2. a direct cross-reference to one or more of these in the form: [see SND], [see DOST], [see OED], [see SND and DOST] etc.

Type 2 is used when the etymologies in the parent dictionaries are too long and/or complicated for CSD use and also where the parent-dictionary etymologies contain references to entries which are not included in CSD.

11.3 In some cases etymologies are also included for a single item within an entry or for part of an entry. These are placed before the full stop at the end of the item to make it clear that they refer only to that item or section, *e.g.*

    ream...**raemikle**... [REAM + Norw dial *kolla*...]. ~**pig**...

11.4 English in etymologies

Where relevant, the first information given in CSD's etymologies is the immediately previous history of the word in English, before its appearance in Scots. This may include various periods of English and/or various dialects.

Datings for periods of English used in CSD are as follows:

ModEng	1650–
eModEng	1475–1650
ME	1100–1475
with the	sub-divisions
eME	1100–1250
laME	1400–1475
OE	up to 1100

The most frequently-occurring dialects of English in CSD are:
northern, usually abbreviated as 'n', as in 'nME' (northern Middle English);
midland, abbreviated as 'midl'.

Others, such as southern (abbreviated 's') and West Saxon (abbreviated 'WSaxon') appear only occasionally. All dialects used are given in the list of abbreviations on p. xxxix.

Comments such as 'only Sc', 'chf Sc', 'earlier in Sc' frequently appear as the first item in a CSD etymology. These refer to the word's history in Scots in relation to other varieties of English, *e.g.* 'only Sc' means that the word is found only in Scots and not in any other variety of English since the Old English period. Information about the word's relationship to languages other than English then usually follows.

11.5 Latin in etymologies

Vowel quantities (*e.g.* $\bar{a}$, $\bar{e}$) are given for classical and late Latin but not for medieval Latin, including Scottish medieval Latin.

Nouns, adjectives and pronouns are normally given in the nominative case and verbs in the infinitive, where necessary with other parts in addition, *e.g.*

    [L *regȳrāre* turn about]
    [L *substract-*, ptp stem of *substrahere*...]

Scottish medieval Latin is not used for dating purposes within a CSD entry but is included in the etymology with the label ScL.

    e.g. **craig**[1]... [ScL *cragga e12*;...]

11.6 French in etymologies

Datings for periods of French used in CSD are:

OF	up to 1600
F	1600–.

11.7 Where the etymology of an item is problematical, the following have sometimes been used:
[obscure] indicating that there are some ideas about parts of the origin, but they do not make a convincing whole.
[uncertain] indicating that there are theories about the origin but that no one theory stands out as better than another.
[unknown] no theories have so far been put forward.

11.8 The following are also used:
[onomat] where the meaning of the word is suggested by its sound, *e.g.* **skrauch**.
[imit] where the sound of the word mimics the sound described, *e.g.* **cockieleerie**.

11.9 The etymology may also contain a reference to a parent-dictionary headword whose entry is used in CSD but whose headword does not appear as a CSD headword, *e.g.*

    [obscure. OED *shonk*]

This happens more frequently in the second half of the alphabet—*see 4.1 above*.

12 Cross-references

NB In all cross-references the first headword of the entry referred to is given in SMALL CAPITALS.

12.1 Every variant form given in an entry also appears as a main-entry cross-reference in its own alphabetical place, *e.g.*

gabbart ..., **gabar ...**, **gabert**

Therefore:

gabar *see* GABBART

gabert *see* GABBART

The only exceptions to this are:

(1) where the variant form would be alphabetically adjacent to the first headword, *e.g.*

gallant[1] **&c, galland ...**

(2) a derivative or compound is not cross-referred unless it is difficult to recognize as coming from one of the headwords which have already been given.

12.2 In order to save space, lists of cross-references have been conflated where possible, *e.g.*

gall *see* GA, GAW

gaain, gan *see* GAE

12.3 Reference to other entries may also be made as part or all of a definition, or to add comparative information after a definition, *e.g.* **ratchell ...** a gravelly TILL[2] ...

12.4 Where reference is made in definitions etc. to other entries or to other parts of the same entry, the reference may be

(1) to a headword: this is given in SMALL CAPITALS as above.

(2) to a subsidiary headword or to a sub-entry: in such cases, *italic* is used followed by the first headword in parentheses in SMALL CAPITALS, *e.g.* ... = *town guard* (TOUN) ...

(3) to a particular part of an entry: in this case numbers are given in roman type, rather than bold, *e.g.*

factorship the office of FACTOR (*n* 1) ...

13 Typefaces

CSD uses four typefaces:
(1) **bold**
(2) roman
(3) *italic*
(4) SMALL CAPITALS

as follows:

(1) **bold** for:
all headwords (printed in larger type)
grammatical forms (such as plurals of nouns, past tenses and participles of verbs etc.)
sub-entries (derivatives, compounds, phrases)
variant spellings found within the entry (*e.g.* **gaup &c, gowp &c ... 1** *only* **gaup &c**)
sub-entry material found within a definition (*e.g.* **ride ... 6** ... *freq* **~ out ...**)
prepositions etc. where the Scots construction coincides with the wording of the definition (*e.g.* **row**[1] **... 9** wind **up** (a clock etc ...))
numbers separating main meaning divisions, (*e.g.* **gab**[1] **... 1 ... 2**)

(2) roman for:
definitions (which thus stand out from surrounding information in bold and italic)
numbers and letters separating sub-divisions of meanings
numbers in cross-references (*e.g.* = *n* 4, *1a* 16-18.)
phonetic symbols (see note at 'definitions' above)
explanatory words and most abbreviations in etymologies.

(3) *italic* for:
abbreviations and other labels
• (including those indicating geographical distribution)
dates
other explanatory words
illustrative phrases (in inverted commas)
citations of words in etymologies
cross-reference material—*see* 12.4 *above.*

NB Sometimes where two separate uses of a typeface come together, *e.g.* an explanatory word followed by a cross-reference in italic, the desired distinction would be lost. In such cases the former appears exceptionally in roman, *e.g.* **eviction ...** ; cf *action of* ~

(4) SMALL CAPITALS for:
cross-references—*see* note at 12 *above*)

14 Punctuation

Throughout CSD, in order to achieve an uncluttered page, as little punctuation as possible has been used. For example full stops have been omitted from most abbreviations. In cases where consecutive abbreviations etc. might cause confusion, a comma has been inserted, *e.g. . . . vi, law.*

A colon is also occasionally used to separate one category of information from another, *e.g.* **gain-: gain-call**

15 Abbreviations, labels and symbols

CSD contains a wide variety of different types of information and this has made it necessary to use a large number of abbreviations and other labels. Efforts have been made to keep these as simple and as easily understood as possible. Therefore some of the parent dictionaries' abbreviations have been simplified (*see*, for example, 9.3 *above*) or left unabbreviated (especially if they are rarely used).

The abbreviations are listed below. Unabbreviated labels (not listed) include those indicating the fields of knowledge (*e.g. mining, law, weaving*) and those indicating levels of language (*e.g. formal, informal, slang*). Some of the less common grammatical labels are also left unabbreviated (*e.g. genitive, gerund*).

abbrev	abbreviated, abbreviation
Abd	Aberdeenshire
absol	absolute(ly)
adj	adjective, adjectival
adv	adverb(ial)
AF	Anglo-French
agric	agriculture
Ags	Angus
AN	Anglo-Norman
Anglo-Ir	Anglo-Irish
Anglo-L	Anglo-Latin
appar	apparent(ly)
arch	archaic
archaeol	archaeology
Arg	Argyll
attrib	attributive(ly)
aux	auxiliary
Ayr	Ayrshire
Bnf	Banffshire
Bwk	Berwickshire
c	*circa*, about
C	Central Scots (= EC + WC + SW)
Cai	Caithness
cf	compare
chf	chiefly
Clcm	Clackmannanshire
colloq	colloquial(ly)
comb	combination
conj	conjunction
Crom	Cromarty
Cumb	Cumberland
Dan	Danish
def art	definite article

deriv	derivative
derog	derogatory
dial	dialect(al)
dim	diminutive
Dmf	Dumfriesshire
Dnbt	Dunbartonshire
DOST	*Dictionary of the Older Scottish Tongue*
Du	Dutch
e	early (as in *e16* = early 16th century, eModEng = early Modern English); east
E	East: (1) in general; (2) = Sh Ork N + EC dialects (*see* 9 *above*)
EC	East Central Scots (*see* 9 *above*)
eccl	ecclesiastic(al)
EcclL	ecclesiastical Latin
ECoast	East Coast, applied (usually) to fishing terminology used in several dialect areas on the east coast
ed	editor, edition
Edb	Edinburgh
eds	editors, editions
eg	for example
eLoth	East Lothian
eModEng	early Modern English
Eng	English
equiv	equivalent
erron	erroneous(ly)
esp	especially
etc	et cetera (in compounds, phrases and definitions)
&c	et cetera (after spelling variants—*see* 2 *above*, and pronunciations—*see* 5 *above*)
exclam	exclamation, exclamator(il)y
f	from
F	French
fem	feminine
Fif	Fife
fig	figurative(ly)
Flem	Flemish
freq	frequent(ly)
Gael	Gaelic
Gall	Galloway
gen	general(ly)
Gen	General Scots
geol	geology
Ger	German
Gk	Greek
Goth	Gothic
Gsw	Glasgow
HighGer	High German
Highl	Highland
hist	historical
Icel	Icelandic
ie	that is
IE	Indo-European
imit	imitative (see 11 above)
imperf	imperfect

indef art	indefinite article	OED	*Oxford English Dictionary*
infin	infinitive	OF	Old French
infl	influence(d)	OFrisian	Old Frisian
interj	interjection	OHighGer	Old High German
interrog	interrogative(ly)	OIcel	Old Icelandic
intrans	intransitive(ly)	OIr	Old Irish
Inv	Inverness-shire	ON	Old Norse
Ir	Irish	onomat	onomatopoeic(ally)
IrGael	Irish Gael	ONorthumb	Old Northumbrian
irreg	irregular(ly)	orig	original(l)y, origin
Ital	Italian	Ork	Orkney
joc	jocular(ly)	OSax	Old Saxon
Kcb	Kirkcudbright (county)	OSc	Older Scots
Kcdn	Kincardineshire	OT	Old Testament
Kinr	Kinross	Pbls	Peeblesshire
L	Latin	Per	Perthshire
la	late (as in *la16* = late 16th century, laME = late Middle English)	perh	perhaps
		pers	person
		phonol	phonology
lang	language	phr(s)	phrase(s)
lit	literal(ly)	pl	plural
Lnk	Lanarkshire	Port	Portuguese
Loth	Lothian	ppl	participial
LowGer	LowGerman	prec	preceding
M	Middle (of languages)	predic	predicative, predicated
masc	masculine	prep	preposition
MDan	Middle Danish	pres	present, present tense
MDu	Middle Dutch	presp	present participle
ME	Middle English	presum	presumably
Med	medieval	prob	probably
MedL	medieval Latin	pronunc	pronunciation
metath	metathetic(ally), metathesiz(ed)	pt	past, past tense
		ptp	past participle
MHighGer	Middle High German	qv	*quod vide*, which see
MIr	Middle Irish	ref	reference
midl	midland	Renfr	Renfrewshire
midLoth	Midlothian	Ross	Ross and Cromarty
MLowGer	Middle Low German	Rox	Roxburghshire
Mod	modern	s	southern
ModEngdial	modern English dialect	S	Southern Scots (*see 9 above*); South
ModIrdial	modern Irish dialect (i.e. of English)		
		Sc	Scots
Mry	Morayshire	Scand	Scandinavia(n)
ms(s)	manuscript(s)	Sc and IrGael	Scottish and Irish Gaelic
MSw	Middle Swedish	ScGael	Scottish Gaelic
n	noun; northern	ScL	Scottish medieval Latin (*see 11 above*)
N	Northern Scots; North	Sc Univs	Scottish Universities
		sEC	southern East Central Scots (*see 9 above*)
Nai	the county of Nairn		
naut	nautical	Sh	Shetland
NE	North-East Scots (*see 9 above*)	sing	singular
nEC	northern East Central Scots (*see 9 above*)	Slk	Selkirkshire
		SND	*Scottish National Dictionary*
Northumb	Northumbrian	Span	Spanish
Norw	Norwegian	specif	specific(ally)
NT	New Testament	St	standard (*see 5 above*)
O	Old(er) (of languages)	StEng	Standard English
obs	obsolete	Stlg	Stirlingshire
occas	occasional(ly)	Suppl	Supplement
ODan	Old Danish	Suth	Sutherland
OE	Old English	Sw	Swedish

SW	South-West Scots (*see* 9 *above*)	W	West
synon	synonym(ous)	WC	West Central Scots (*see* 9
tech	technical(ly)		*above*)
theol	theology, theological	Wgt	Wigtownshire
trans	transitive(ly)	wLoth	West Lothian
transf	transferred use	WSaxon	West Saxon
Uls	Ulster Scots		
US	United States		
usu	usually		
v	verb		
var(s)	variant(s)		

Symbols (*see also* Pronunciation Key *in* 5 *above*)

vi	verb intransitive	
vir	verb intransitive and reflexive	* in etymologies, indicates a hypothetical form; in pronunciations, indicates a reconstructed form. (*See also* 5 *above*)
vr	verb reflexive	
vt	verb transitive	
vti	verb transitive and intransitive	= *see* 7 *above*
vtir	verb transitive, intransitive and reflexive	~ used to replace the headword throughout one article, *e.g.* in derivatives, compounds and phrases.
vtr	verb transitive and reflexive	
vulgarL	vulgar Latin	> in etymologies, leads to, becomes
w	with (only in etymologies); west	< in etymologies, comes from
		&c see *etc* in list above

A

a¹ [*unstressed* ə, *stressed* a] *indef art* = a, an: **1** *before vowels and consonants*, la14-. **2** *with numbers*, 16-: '*a twenty chosyn men*'. [ME, reduced f ANE²; *cf* AN]

a² [ə; *C also* ı] *prep, before an infin, freq suffixed to the prec word* (*chf* **gaunna** &c) *to* la19-. [see SND]

a³ [ə] *prep* **1** = a la15-: '*a coming*'; '*a west*'. **2** *with verbal noun, forming passive*, la16-19: '*her dress is a-making*'. [reduced f Eng *on*]

a *see* AE, O¹

A *see* ı

a', all &c; **ale** 15-e16, **aw** 15-19, **aa** 20-, *Sh Abd* [ɑ; *Sh Ork Cai Arg Uls also* al] *adj* **1** = all la14-. **2** every la14-.
n (15-), *adv* (la14-), *conj* (la14-15) = all.
~ **bedene** *only verse* at once la14-16. **a' body** everybody 19-. **a' body's body** a general favourite la18-. **a' gait** 19-, **a' gates** 19, **algate** la14-16, **algatis** 16 **1** = always; at all events la14-16. **2** everywhere 19-. **alhale** &c complete(ly), entire(ly) la14-16. **alhalely** &c = *alhale* (*adv*) la14-16. **alkin** *adj* of every kind: **1** *with sing n, freq* **alkin thing, alkinwise** la14-16; **2** *with pl n* every kind of la14-16. ~**kin kind** *n* every kind (**of**) 15-. **alkind** *adj* every kind of la14-16, *only Sc. n* every kind of 15-. **a' thing**(**s**) &c 19-, **all thing** 15-16, **althing** la14-15 everything la14-. ~ **time** at all times, always 15-16.
~ **and haill** &c *law* entire 15-18. **like a' that** with the utmost speed, energy etc la19-.

ab *see* ALB

aback, abak [ə'bak] *adv* **1** = aback 15-. **2** back; away, aloof, off 16-. **3** behind, in the rear la18-.
~ **o** behind, to the rear of 19-e20. ~**written** written on the back (of a document) la16-e17.

abade &c [*ə'bed] *n* = abode, the action of waiting; a stay la14-16. [eME *abad*]

abade *see* ABIDE

abais [*ə'bes] *vt, chf* ~**it** = abashed la14-e17. ~**itness** alarm; discouragement la14-16.

abaise *see* ABUISE

abak *see* ABACK

abandoun la14-16; **abandon** *v* **1** *vt* = abandon la14-. **2** subdue, conquer la14-16, *only Sc.* **3** *vr* risk oneself, rush headlong la14-e15.
n, only **in** *or* **at** ~ impetuously la14-e15.
~**ly** impetuously, recklessly la14-15, *only Sc.*

abatement *n* **1** = abatement la17-. **2** relaxation, recreation, amusement 16, *only Sc.*

abbacy, abbasy [*'abası, -əsı] *n* **1** the office or dignity of an abbot 15-17. **2** an abbey la15-19, *only Sc.* [MedL *abbacia, abbatia*]

abbey &c la16-, **abbay** &c la14-16 *n* **1** = abbey la14-. **2 the A**~ *specif* Holyrood Abbey, Edinburgh, the precincts of which were formerly used as a sanctuary by debtors 18-; *cf* A~ *laird* and *laird in the Abbey* (LAIRD).
~ **croun** a coin minted at Holyrood la16. **A**~ **laird** *joc* a debtor 18-e19.

abbot *n* = abbot 14-.
A~ **of Na rent** &c 15-16, **A**~ (**of**) **Unreason** &c la15-16 the leader of the revels in a BURGH festival which burlesqued religious institutions etc and was suppressed at the Reformation.

abbreviate &c *n, law* an abstract, abridgement, *latterly specif* of a DECREE of ADJUDICATION or, in bankruptcy, of the petition of *sequestration* (SEQUESTRATE) 17-.
vt = abbreviate.

A B C *n* **1** ABC 15-. **2** an alphabetical list or table la16-17.

abeen *see* ABUNE

abeese *see* ABUISE

abefore *see* OF-BEFORE

abeich &c 18-e20; **on beich** la16 [*ə'bix, *on'bix] *adv* aloof, aside, away, apart from others. [obscure]

abeoufe *see* ABOVE

Aberdeen, Aiberdeen ['ebər'din, *St* 'ab-]: **Aberdeen Angus** la18-, **Aberdeen and Angus** la18-19 name of a breed of black hornless beef-cattle, *orig* from Abd and Ags la18-.
~ **awa** &c Aberdeen and its neighbourhood or dialect 19-e20. [the NE city]

Aberdonian ['ebər'donıən, *St* 'ab-] a native or citizen of Aberdeen la18-. [f MedL *Aberdonia* Aberdeen]

abetwix [*ə'bı'twıks] *prep* between 16, *only Sc.*

abhor &c *v* **1** *vt* = abhor la15-. **2** *vi* ~ **with** feel repugnance for la15-16. **3** shrink, draw away, deviate **from** la16, *only Sc.* **4** *vt* shrink back from, regard with repugnance 16-e17, *only Sc.*

abide *vti, pt* **abade** &c la14-19 **1** = abide la14-. **2** *vi* stay behind la14-19. **3** ~ **fra** stay away from (a person, place etc) la16-e17, *only Sc.* **4** ~ **at** stand by, adhere to 15-e17, *only Sc.* **5** *vt* remain faithful to; adhere to la15-e16, *only Sc.*

abies [*ʔə'baız, ə'biz] *prep* in comparison with; in addition to; except 19-e20. [appar *a-* + *by's* (BY)]

abill *see* ABLE

abilʒeit; abulʒeit 16 [*ə'bıljıt, *-'biljıt, *-'bøl-, *-'bʌl-] *ptp* arrayed, dressed; equipped la15-e17. [var of ptp of HABILLIʒE]

abilʒement *see* ABUILYIEMENT

abirioun *see* HABERSCHOUN

abit &c ['a:'bıt, 'abət; *Rox* 'ɛbıt] ah, but ..; aye, but .. la19-e20, *only Sc.*

ablach &c 18-, *N*; **ablack** 19 ['abləx; *Buchan also* 'ebləx; *Abd Ags also* *'ablək] *n* **1** a mangled carcass 18-19. **2** an insignificant or contemptible person: (1) through lack of size la18-; (2) through lack of will or intellect la19-. [Sc and IrGael *ablach* carrion; a useless person or thing etc]

able &c la15-, **abill** &c la14-17, **ebill** &c la16-e17, **yable** &c 18-, *now S*; **yibble** &c la19-, *S adj* **1** = able la14-. **2** *with infin* ready,

prepared; on the point of *16*. **3** possible *la16-e17*. **4** physically fit, strong *20-*. **5** having an appetite **for** *la20-*.
adv perhaps *la15-19*. [*cf* ABLES, AIBLINS and HABILE]

ableeze [ə'bliz] *adv*, *adj* = ablaze *19-*, *only Sc*.

ablens *see* AIBLINS

ables; yibbles *la19-e20*, *Bwk S adv* = ABLE *adv*, *la18-e20*.

ablow [ə'blo] *prep* under, below, *freq* **in** ∼ *la19-*. *adv* below, beneath, lower down *la19-e20*. [for *a-below*, by analogy w *above* etc]

abody *see* A'

aboif *see* ABOVE

aboil [ə'bɔil] *adv* at or to boiling point *19-e20*. [*a* + Eng *boil*]

abolis &c [*a'bɒlɪs, -ɪs] *vt* = abolish *16-e17*, *only Sc*.

abone, aboon *see* ABUNE

aboord, aburde [*ə'bɔrd, *ə'burd] *adv* = aboard *16-19*. [*cf* BUIRD¹]

aboot, about [ə'but] *adv* **1** = about *la14-*. **2** on the move, going about (*esp* after an illness) *20-*: '*Tam's aboot again*'.
prep = about *14-*.
about spech a circumlocution *e16* [translating L *circumlocutio*].
∼ **it** about the same *la19-*: '*hoo are ye? muckle aboot it*'. **be** ∼ **wi** be even with, avenged on *18-19*. **hae mair** ∼ **one nor** have more sense than *20-*, *NE*.

aboun *see* ABUNE

about *see* ABOOT

above &c, **abufe &c** *la14-16*; **abeoufe &c** *la14*, **aboif &c** *la15-e17* [*ə'bøv, *ə'buv &c] *adv* = above *la14-*.
prep **1** = above *la14-*. **2** beyond, more than, in addition to *la14-e18*. [*cf* ABOVIN, ABUNE]

abovin; abufin &c [*ə'bøvən] *adv*, *prep* = above *la14-15*.
∼**-writtin** above-written *la14-16*. [nME; *cf* ABOVE, ABUNE]

abraird, abreird &c [*ə'brerd, *ə'brird] *adv* sprouted *la15-e20*, *latterly chf arch or verse*. [only Sc; reduced f *on brerd* (see BREARD)]

abreed *19-e20*, **abrede &c** [ə'brid] *adv* **1** on or in breadth, widely, far and wide, abroad *la16-e20*. **2** wide, apart, open *19-e20*. [ME *on brede*, OE *on bræde* in breadth]

abrege &c [*a'bredʒ] *vt* = abridge *15-e17*.

abreird *see* ABRAIRD

abreist [ə'brist] *adv* = abreast *la19-*.

abrico &c [*'abrıko] *n* an apricot *la16-e17*. [only Sc; F *abricot*]

absence *16-*; **absens** ['absɛns, *ab'sɛns] *la14-17 n* **1** = absence *la14-*. **2** = *absents* (ABSENT *n*) *la15-17*.

absent [*ab'sɛnt] *adj* = absent *15-*.
n, *chf in pl* absentees *chf* from a court of justice *15-e18*.

absolvitor *17-*, **absolvitour &c** *16-17* [ab'zɔlvɪtɔr] *n*, *law* a decision by a court in favour of the *defender* (DEFEND) *16-*.
adj, *following its noun*, *law* in favour of the *defender* (DEFEND) *17*. [only Sc; see DOST]

absolʒe *vt* absolve *15-16*. [conflation of ASSOILZIE w *absolve*]

absteen &c *la16-e20*, *latterly N*, **abstene &c** *la15-e17*, **obstene** *la15-16 vtir* = abstain.

abstract; abstrak *la15-17* [ab'strak(t)] *vtir* = abstract *la15-*.

abthan *n*, *explained as* 'father or superior of the THANES' *la15-16*. [only Sc; ScL *abthanus*, wrongly inferred f *abthania*, Gael *abdhaine* abbacy]

abufe *see* ABOVE

abufin *see* ABOVIN

abuilyiement &c, abilʒement &c; bullament &c *18-e20*, **bulyament &c** *19-e20* [*Sh NE* 'bʌl(j)ımənts, *NE also* 'bul-; *Uls* 'bɔil-; *ə'bıl-, *ə'bøl-, *ə'bʌl-] *n*, *freq in pl* **1** garments, attire *la15-e18*. **2** equipment, arms *la15-e19*. **3** *in pl*, *only* **b∼s** outer garments, *usu* of a ragged or ridiculous type *e20*, *local*. [var of HABILʒEMENT]

abuise, abuse &c; abaise &c *la19-e20*, *Bwk SW*, **abeese &c** *17-e20* [*n ə'bøs; v ə'bøz, ə'bez, N ə'biz] *n* = abuse *la16-e20*.
v **1** *vt* = abuse *15-e20*. **2** *vr* behave in a disorderly or licentious way *la16*. **3** disuse, discontinue the use of *la15-16*, *only Sc*.

abuit &c [ə'bøt; *NE* ə'bit] *adv* into the bargain *19-e20*. [BUIT²]

abulʒeit *see* ABILʒEIT

abund *vi* = abound *la16*.

abune &c *la15-*, **abone &c** *la14-17*, **aboun &c; aboon** *18-*, **abeen** *19-e20*, *N* [ə'bøn; *N* ə'bin; *nEC* ə'ben; *C* əbın; *ə'bun] *adv* **1** = above *la14-*. **2** in good cheer, in or into better condition *la18-*.
prep = above *la14-*.
∼**-writtin** above-written *la15-17*. ∼ **the breath** above the nostrils or the windpipe *19-*, *now Cai Fif*. **get** ∼ recover from, get over (an illness, a disappointment) *19-*, *now NE Ags*. [shortened f ABOVIN; *cf* ABOVE]

aburde *see* ABOORD

abuse *see* ABUISE

academy, academie *n* **1** = academy *16-*. **2** *orig* a public or private secondary school in a BURGH, *freq* replacing a grammar school or providing a more modern curriculum, *later* applied to many state secondary schools irrespective of their origins *la18-*.

acause [ə'kɑz] *conj* because *la19-e20*, *SW, S Uls*. [prob f nEng and Ir dial]

accavite *see* AQUAVITA

accep &c, accept &c [ak'sɛp(t), ək-] *vt* = accept *la15-*. [*cf* EXCEPT]

accep(t) *see* EXCEP

acceptilation [ak'sɛptıleʃn, ək-] *n*, *law* the

extinction of a debt by an arrangement other than by full payment *la17-*. [L *acceptilātio* an accounting of a thing as received]

accesse &c [*ək'sɛs] *n* = excess *15-16*.

accession *n* **1** = accession. **2** *law* complicity, concurrence or assent in some action *17-*.

deed of ~ a deed executed by the creditors of an insolvent, approving and accepting an arrangement by him for settling his affairs *19-*.

accessor &c [*ʔak'sɛsur, -or] *n* **1** one who, or that which, is additional or accessory *la15-e17*. **2** accessory **to** (a crime) *17*. [only Sc; L *accessōrius*; *cf* Eng *accessory*]

accident &c *n* **1** = accident, a fortuitous occurrence, chance *la15-*. **2** a casual sum *la15-e17*, *only Sc*.

Accies ['akız] *n pl* **1** nickname for pupils or former pupils of an ACADEMY, *esp* when organized as a team *20-*. **2** nickname for Hamilton Academicals football team *20-*.

acclame &c [*ə'klem] *vt* claim, lay claim to *16-17*.

n a claim *16-17*. [chf Sc; MedL *acclāmāre*]

accomie *see* ALCOMY

accomplis, accomple(i)s [*a'kʌmplıs, -ıs] *vt* = accomplish *la15-e17*.

accountant *n* **1** = accountant. **2** *banking* the chief clerk in a bank branch, the deputy of the manager or *latterly* of the assistant manager *20-*. **A~ of Court** *law* an officer of court who supervises the conduct of *judicial factors* (JUDICIAL) etc *19-*.

accress &c; accresce [*a'krɛs] *vi* **1** (1) increase *la16-18*. (2) be added, united *la16-e17*. **2** accrue or fall **to** (a person) *la16-18*. [only Sc; L *accrescere*]

accur *see* OCCUR

accusabil *16*; **accusable** *la15-* [*a'køzəbl] *adj* liable to be accused.

accusatour &c [*a'køzatur] *n* an accuser *15-16*. [ME; OF *accusateur*, L *accūsātor*]

ace, ess &c; (e)yiss &c *la19-e20*, **eace** *e20*, *chf NE* [es, ɛs; *Abd* is; *Bwk S* jıs] *n* **1** = ace *16-*. **2** *only* **ace** the smallest possible amount *16-e20*.

ach; auch [ax] *interj* expressing impatience, disappointment, contempt, remonstrance etc *16-*. [*cf* AICH[1], AY[1], ECH, HECH, HOCH[2], OCH, OUCH]

achan *see* AUCHAN

achen *see* AUCHTEEN

acherspyre &c, acherspire ['axərspaır, *Bnf* 'akıspəır] *vi*, *of grain* sprout during malting *17-e20*.

n the sprouting of grain during malting; a sprout of such grain *19-e20*. [see SND]

achesone *see* ATCHESON

achet *see* ESCHEAT

acht *see* AUCHT[1], AUCHT[2], AWE[2]

ack *see* ACT

acker &c *n* **in** ~ in fragments, in bits *la19-e20*, *Sh NE*. [prob related to AICHER]

acker *see* ACRE

acknawlege &c [*ə'knalɛdʒ] *vt* = acknowledge *la16-17*.

ackwa &c, aqua [*'akwə] *n* WHISKY *19-e20*. [reduced f AQUAVITA]

ackwally *see* ACTUAL

ackwart *see* AWKWARD

acquant[1] &c *la17-*, **acquent &c; acquaint** *la16-*, **acquynt &c** *la14-15* [ə'kwant, *Kcdn Ags C S also* ə'kwɛnt; *a'kwəint] *ptp, adj* acquaint, acquainted (**with**) *la14-*.

acquant[2] *17-*, **acquent &c; acquaint &c** *17-* [ə'kwant, -'kwɛnt; *a'kwəint] *vt*, *ptp also* **acquyntit** *16* = acquaint *15-*.

~ance, aquyntance &c *la14-e16* = acquaintance *la14-*.

acquart *see* AWKWARD

acquent *see* ACQUANT[1], ACQUANT[2]

acquiet &c [*a'kwaıɛt] *vt* guarantee undisturbed possession of (land), *usu with* **warrand and defend** *la15-16*. [MedL *acquietare*, in charters as *warrantizabimus acquietabimus et defendemus*]

acquynt *see* ACQUANT[1]

acquyntance, acquyntit *see* ACQUANT[2]

acre &c; acker &c *16-e20*, **aiker &c** *16-17*, **akir &c** *14-16* ['ekər; *N* 'akər] *n*, *uninflected in pl after numerals etc* = acre, the measure of land *la12-*.

vti harvest grain crops at a stated rate per acre *la19-e20*, *NE*.

act, ack &c *n* = act *15-*.

vt **1** enact, decree *15-e18*. **2** enter (an agreement, obligation etc) in a record-book *la15-16*. **3** (1) **be** *or* **become actit** have one's name recorded as being under some bond or obligation *la15-17*. (2) *vr* enter oneself as being under a bond or obligation *la16-17*. **4** = act. [*cf* ENACT]

actentik *see* AUTENTIK

action &c, actioun &c *15-17* *n* **1** = action *15-*. **2** *law* a charge against a person; a civil or criminal offence *15-e16*, *only Sc*. **3** a matter concerning a person or his interests; one's 'cause' *15-e17*, *only Sc*. **4** the celebration of the sacrament of the Lord's Supper or the Mass *la16-17*.

~ sermon the sermon preceding the celebration of the sacrament of Holy Communion *18-19*, *only Sc*.

actitate *ptp* = actit (ACT *v* 3) *16*. [only Sc; MedL *actitatus*]

actor &c *n* **1** = actor *la15-*. **2** an agent, *esp law* one who acts on behalf of another *la15-17*. **3** an author, originator *16*, *only Sc*.

actorney &c *la14-e18*, *only Sc*, **atto(u)rnay &c** *15-16* [*a'turne, *-'tʌrn-, *ak-] *n* = attorney. [see DOST, SND]

actual &c *adj* **1** = actual *la15-*. **2** sexual *la15-16*, *only Sc*.

~ly *la15-*, **ackwally &c** *la19-e20* = actually.

adae *20-*, **ado &c** *16-*, **adow &c** *la15-e20*; **adee &c** *la18-*, *chf Abd* [ə'dø; *N* ə'di; *C* ə'de; *S* *also* ə'de] *v*, *infin* **1** = to do *la14*-: '*quhat is the best ado?*'; '*I hae naething ado*'; '*I widna hae naething adee wi ye*'. **2** going on, being done *17*-: '*what's adee?*' **3** the matter **with** *la19*-: '*fat's adee wi ye?*' *n* **1** = ado, fuss, commotion *16*-. **2** *freq in pl* trouble, difficulty, *eg* **have one's ain** ~(**s**) *la15*-. **3** business, occupation; *chf in pl* concerns, affairs *la16-e19*. [nME *at do* to do, of Scand orig]

Adam: Adam-an-Eves the tubers of the orchis *la20*-, *local*. ~'**s wine** water *18*-.

add *vti* **1** = add *la15*-. **2** *vi* make an *addition* (*n* 2) to the *exercise* (EXERCEESE *n* 4 (1, 2)) at a meeting of the PRESBYTERY *la16-e17*.
~**er** a person who makes the *addition* to the *exercise* (as in *v* 2) *17*.
~**ition** &c **1** = addition *16*-. **2** a discourse made after the *exercise* (EXERCEESE) (as in *v* 2) *la16-e17*.

addebted, addettit [*ə'dɛtɪt, a-] *ptp* **1** = indebted *16-e19*. **2** owed, due *la16-e19*. [only Sc]

adder *see* ETHER

addiscence *see* AUDISCENCE

addle, adill; adle &c *la18-e19* ['adl, 'edl] *n* foul putrid liquid, *esp* from dung *16-e20*. [*cf* Eng]

address *vti* **1** = address *15*-. **2** *vr* prepare oneself, put oneself in good order *la14-16*. **3** *vt* (1) put in order, arrange, prepare *la14-16*. (2) *golf* position oneself properly relative to (the ball) *la19*-. **4** *vi* proceed, go; set about, prepare (to do etc) *la15-16*.

adduce *vt* **1** = adduce *la16*-. **2** *law* bring forward or produce (a person) in proof *la17*-.

adee *see* ADAE

adest *see* ADIST

adew &c [*a'dju] *interj* = adieu, farewell *la15-17*.
adv (*adj*) gone, departed *la15-e16*. [ME]

adge *see* AGE

adherde [*əd'(h)ɛrd] *vi* adhere **to** *16*. [var of ANHERD, w infl f ADHERE]

adhere &c *vi* **1** = adhere *16*-. **2** *law* (1) *of a husband or wife* remain with and be faithful (to the other) *16*-; (2) confirm or sustain the judgment of a lower court *17*-.
adherence &c **1** *law* the fulfilment of the legal obligation of residing with one's spouse *16*-. **2** = adherence. **adherent** &c **1** = adherent *la16*-. **2** *Presbyterian Church* a (*usu* young) person who attends the services but is not in full communion *la19*-.

adhibit &c *vt* **1** = adhibit *la16*-. **2** put (one's signature or seal) to a document *la18*-.

adill *see* ADDLE

adione *see* ADJUNE

adir *see* AITHER

adist, adest *la17*; **athist** &c *19-e20* [*ə'ðɪst, *ə'dɪst] *prep* on this side of, *usu contrasted with* AYONT *17-e20*. [see SND]

adjoin *see* ADJUNE

adjourn &c *vti* = adjourn *la16*-.
~**al** &c *law* = act of adjournal, book of adjournal, *la15-16*. **act of adjournal** &c **1** a decision of court requiring one person to give satisfaction to another within a specified time *la15-17*. **2** *in pl* the records and regulations of the *High Court of Justiciary* (JUSTICIARY) *18*-. **book of adjournal** &c **1** a register containing the *acts of adjournal*, *16-17*. **2** *in pl* = act of ~al, 2, *la18*-.

adjournay &c [*ə'dʒurne, *ə'dʒʌrne] *vt* **1** summon for trial *15-e17*. **2** adjourn, put off *la15-17*. [only Sc; laL *adjornāre*]

adjudication, adjudicatioun *17* *n* **1** *law* the seizure of land or other HERITABLE estate in satisfaction of debt *17*-. **2** = adjudication.

adjuge *la15-16*; **adjudge** *vt* **1** = adjudge *15*-. **2** ~ **to** *or* **in** sentence judicially to (a certain fine) *la15-e17*. **3** ~ **to** assign (property) by ADJUDICATION to (the creditor) *17*-.

adjune *la15-16*; **adione** &c *la15-e17*, **adjoin** &c *la16*- [*ə'dʒøn, *ə'dʒəin] *vti* **1** = adjoin *la15*-. **2** *vt* join, unite **with** (another person etc) *16*. **3** join together *16*.

adjutorie &c [*ə'adʒøtorɪ] *n* help; a helper *16*. [L *adjūtōrius*]

adle *see* ADDLE

admeir &c [*ad'mir] *vti* = admire *17*.
admiration &c **1** = admiration *16*-. **2** wonder; astonishment *16*-, *now Sh*.

adminicle *n* **1** *law* a piece of supporting or corroborative evidence *la16*-. **2** = adminicle, something which helps.
adminiculate &c *la17*; **adminiculated** *18-e19* *ptp*, *law* supported by evidence. [only Sc; L *adminiculāt*-, ptp stem of *adminiculāre* prop up]

administrate &c *ptp* = administered *la16-e18*. *vt* **1** = administer (a sacrament or oath) *la16-e18*. **2** = administrate. [L *administrāt*-, ptp stem of *administrāre*]

admiral &c *la15*-, **amerale** &c *e15*; **ammiral** &c *la15-16* ['admɪral; *'am(ə)ral] *n* = admiral *la15*-.
~**ity** &c **1** = admiralty *la15*-. **2** *law* (**High**) **Court of Admiral(i)ty** the court in which the *High Admiral* of Scotland exercised extensive jurisdiction (civil and criminal) *la17-e19*. **Great** ~ *la15-17*, **High** ~ *17-19*, **lord** (**high** *etc*) ~ *la16-e17* the commander-in-chief of the navy.

admiration *see* ADMEIR

admit &c *vti* **1** = admit *15*-. **2** allow (a person) to enter; permit (a person) to proceed in some act etc *15*-.

admoneis &c *la16-e17*; **admonis** &c *la15-e17* [*ad'monɪs, -is] *vt* = admonish.

admove *vt* appoint *16-e17*. [ME; L *admovēre*]

adneir *see* ANHERD

ado *see* ADAE

adoun &c; adoon *la19-e20*, **adown** *18* [ə'dun] *adv* (*la15-e20*), *prep* (*17-e20*), *chf verse* down. [ME]

adow *see* ADAE

adown *see* ADOUN

adreich &c [*ə'drix] *adv* afar, at a distance *16-19*. [reduced f *on dreich* (DREICH)]

adune [*a'døn] *vt* unite *la15-16*. [only Sc; L *adūnāre*]

advancear &c *n* a person who advances money *la16-17*.

adveece *la19*, **advise &c** *la15-17*, **avise &c** *la14-e17*; **avis &c** *la14-16*, **advice &c** *la16-* [əd'vəis, əd'vis, *a'vəis, *a'vis] *n* **1** = advice *la14-*. **2** a piece of advice *la18-19*.
be mine *etc* **avis(e)** in my opinion *la15-16*.
by the ~ **of** without or against the advice of *16*. [*cf* ADVISE]

adventur &c [*advɛn'tør &c] *n* = adventure *la15-e17*.

adversare &c [*'advɛrsar] *n*, *also* **adversour** *la14-16*, *only Sc* [*'advɛrsur] = adversary *15-e17*.
adj adverse, opposing *15-e17*.

adverteese *la19*, **advertise &c; adverteis &c** *16-e17*, **advertish** *17-e18* [advər'tiz; *ad'vɛrtɪs, -ɪʃ, -ɪs &c] *vti*, *pt*, *ptp also* **advertist &c** *la15-16* = advertise *la15-*.
~**ment** [*sometimes* advər'taɪzmənt] = advertisement *16-*.

advice *see* ADVEECE

advise &c *la16-*, **avise &c** *la14-e17*; **avis &c** *la14-16* [əd'vaɪz, *a'vaɪz, *a'vəis, *ə'vis] *vti* **1** = advise *la14-*. **2** *vt* give advice to (a person) *la14-*. **3** *only* **avis(e)** take into consideration *la15-16*. **4** *only* **advise**, *law* reserve for further consideration; review, reconsider *17-*, *only Sc*; *cf* AVISANDUM.
avised = advised, informed, aware of *19-e20*.
be ~it take counsel (with oneself *or* others); come to a decision or conclusion after reflection; attain a clear understanding *la14-16*.
~**ment 1** deliberation, consideration; *only* **advisement** consultation *la14-17*. **2** *only* **avisement** counsel, advice *la14-e19*. [*cf* ADVEECE]

advise *see* ADVEECE

advocate, advocat &c *n* **1** *law* a professional pleader in a court of justice, a barrister *la14-*; *cf* *Lord A*~ (LORD). **2** = advocate *15-*. **3** *law* a solicitor *18-*, *Abd*.
ptp called as an action from a lower to a higher court *16-17*, *only Sc*.
vti, *law* appeal from a lower court to a higher one, *now* only in criminal cases; *of the higher court* call (a case) before itself *la16-*.
advocation &c 1 = advocation *la15-e17*. **2** *law* the calling of an action before a superior court *la16-19*.
~**-depute** a salaried ADVOCATE appointed by the *Lord Advocate* (LORD) to prosecute under his directions *19-*.

ae *17-*, **a** *la14-e19*, **yae &c** *la18-*, *now WC, S*; **ya** *la17-19*, **yee &c** *18-e20* [*Sh-nEC* e; *sEC-SW* je; *S* jɛ] *adj* **1** *numeral* = one (1) *in gen*, *la14-*; (2) *emphatic* **the** ~, **this** ~ *la19-*, *now Ork NE*. **2** *usu* **the** ~ one of two, one as opposed to another or others *19-*; *cf the tae* (TAE[3]). **3** the same *19-*: '*bapteezed oot o ae water*'. **4** only (son etc) *19-*. **5** before a superlative, adding emphasis, *now chf verse*, *la18-*: '*the ae warst woman*'. **6** a certain (person or thing) *la19-*. **7** about, approximately *la19-e20*: '*ae twenty cheese*'.
~**some** single, solitary *la19-e20*.
~**-fur-land** land which can only be ploughed in one direction because of its steepness *19-e20*.
~**-pointed-gairss** name for various single-pointed grasses *19-*, *local*. [nME *a*, reduced f *an* (ANE[1])]

ae *see* AY[1]

aefauld &c *17-*, **afald &c** *la14-17*; **afauld &c** *la15-e17* [*Sh-N* 'e'fal; *nEC* 'e'fald; *sEC, WC* 'je'fal(d); *SW* 'je'fal; *S* 'jɛ'fal(d)] *adj* **1** single *la14-*. **2** *also* **anefald &c** *la15-e17*, **aufauld &c** *la15-16*, **efauld &c** *la16-e17*, *only Sc*, **ewfall** *e17*, **ewfauld &c** *la16* [*'en'fald, *'a'fald, *?'ɛ'fald, *'jufal(d)] simple, sincere; honest, faithful; single-minded *la15-*.
~**ly &c** sincerely, honestly, faithfully *la15-e17*. [nME *anfald*, WSaxon *ānfeald* single, sincere]

aeger *n* an auger *20-*, *Sh Abd Fif Ayr*. [Du dial *egger*]

ae noo *see* EENOO

aequall *see* EQUAL

aequie *see* EQUE

aet *see* EAT

af *see* AFF

afa(u)ld *see* AEFAULD

afeard &c *17-*, **aferde &c** *15-16*; **afferit** *16* [ə'fird, ə'firt] *adj* alarmed, afraid *15-*. [*ptp* of AFERE]

afeild *see* AFIEL

afen *see* AFTEN

aferde *see* AFEARD

afere &c, affeir, effere *only Sc*, **effeir** *only Sc* [*ə'fir] *v* **1** *vi* be afraid *16*. **2** *vt* fear, be afraid of (someone) *16*.
n fear *16*. [Eng *afear* frighten; see AFEARD]

aff &c *la16-*, **af &c** *16-17*, **off &c**, **of &c** *adv* **1** = of, off *la14-*. **2** *with ellipsis of verb*: '*I'll aff and see the session clerk*'. **3** *of the ages of horses and cattle* less than one year past the number of years specified *la19-e20*: '*he's three aff*'.
prep **1** = off *la14-*. **2** away from (a place) *la15-*. **3** opening out from *18-*.
adj = off *la19-*.
affin &c *prep* off *19-e20*, *NE*. **affin(g)** *n* = offing *19-*.
affcome *n* **1** the way something turns out, the way a person comes out of an encounter or enterprise; outcome, result; (good *or* bad) reception; escape *19-*. **2** a strange saying; a smart or witty remark *e20* [*cf* OFFCOME]. ~ **fa'in, off-falling &c 1** *in pl*, *lit and fig* scraps,

remnants *17-e20, only Sc.* **2** *only* **off-falling &c** a decline or lapse in morals *17-e19.* ~**go** *n* start, outset *la19-.* ~**gaun, offgoing** departure; withering; death *18-e20.* ~-**lat &c** an outlet *18-19, NE.* ~-**loof** offhand *18-.* ~-**pit 1** excuse, evasion, reason for delay *18-.* **2** a delay, waste of time *la19-e20.* **3** one who or that which delays *la19-e20, NE, SW, S.* **4** a makeshift, *specif* a hasty meal *la19-, now Loth S.* ~-**pittin,** ~-**putting** *n* postponement, evasion, excuse *la15-.* *adj* delaying, trifling, dilatory *19-.* ~**set** *n* **1** an ornament *17-.* **2** a delay, an excuse *la18-e20.* **3** an outset, a start *la19-.* **4** a hindrance, stoppage; anything causing this; a loss of time (and pay) *la19-e20.* ~**tak &c 1** a mocking remark, a jeer *19-.* **2** a person who ridicules others, a mimic *la19-.* **3** a deduction (of wages) *la19-e20.* ~**taking** *n* **1** *only* **offtaking &c** taking off, removal *la15-e18.* **2** mockery *19-.* *adj* waggish, jeering *la19-.*
~ **an on** *adv* **1** = off and on, intermittently *20-.* **2** *also* ~ **an on aboot** approximately *19-e20.* *adj* **1** vacillating, undecided, changeable, unsettled *la19-.* **2** *of a (sick) person's health* sometimes better, sometimes worse *19-.* ~ **o,** ~ **of** off, from, away from *17-.* ~ **or on** *of a decision etc* one way or another, settled *la16-.* **be** ~ **wi** have done with, disengage oneself from *18-e19.*

affect &c; affeck &c *n* = effect *15-17.*

affeir *la16-e20,* **affere &c** *la14-e16,* **effeir &c** *la15-,* **effere &c** *la14-e17* [ə'fir] *v* **1** *vi* (1) belong, pertain **to;** be appropriate **to,** be fitting or proper **for** (a person) *la14-.* (2) *with infin, la14-16.* **2** appertain, belong properly or naturally **to** (a thing); be convenient **for** *la14-16.* **3** be suitable, fitting *la14-17.* **4** *vt* concern (a person) *15-16.*
~**and** *la15-17,* **effeiring &c** *la15-, now law* pertaining, appropriate (**to**); corresponding (**to**). ~**andly** appropriately, suitably *16.* **affeirin ti** relative or proportionate to *e20, Rox.*
(**in form**) **as** ~**s** *law* in the proper way, in due form *la14-.* [ME (rare); OF *af(f)erir* belong, pertain; *cf* FERE³]

affeir *see* AFERE

affere &c *la14-16,* **effere &c** *la14-17* [*ə'fir] *n* **1** (1) manner of bearing, appearance, deportment *la14-16.* (2) *in pl* manners, ways, actions *15-e16.* **2** state, condition *la14-15.* **3** equipment, outfit; an array or display of armed force *la14-e16.* **4** *also* **effair &c** *16-17* [*ə'fer] an affair, a matter of business or concern *15-e17.*
gret ~ pomp, ceremony, display *la14-15.* [eME *affere,* OF *afere* var of *afaire,* Eng *affair; cf* FEIR]

affere *see* AFFEIR
afferit *see* AFEARD

affirm &c *15-,* **afferme &c** *la14-17,* **efferme** *15-16 vti* **1** = affirm *la14-.* **2** *vt* = FENCE *v* 1, *la15-17.*

---

affirmative affirmatively *la15-e17.* [eMod Eng *affirme,* ME *afferme,* F *affirmer,* OF *afermer*]

affix &c; effix &c *la15-16 vt* **1** attach (a seal) to a document *la15-.* **2** fix, fasten; fix up *16-.* **3** assign, appoint *16-e17.* [orig only in *ptp;* L *affixus,* ptp of *affigere*]

afflick, afflict *vt* = afflict, *freq in ptp* ~**it** *la16-.*

affoord *la18-19,* **affuird &c** [ə'førd; *N* ə'furd; *C* ə'ferd] *vt* = afford *17-e20.*

afforrow *see* AFORROW

affrayitly; affraitly [*ə'freıtlı] *adv* in alarm, in panic *la14-16.* [only Sc; f OSc *affrayit (ptp),* ME *affray(e)t, affrayed* (> Mod Eng *afraid*); cf *effrayitly* (EFFRAY)]

affuird *see* AFFOORD

afiel &c *la16-18,* **afeild &c** [ə'fil] *adv* = afield *16-.*

afit [ə'fıt] *adv* = afoot; on foot *18-.*

afleyd &c [*ə'fləıd] *adj* dismayed, afraid *la18-19.* [*cf* FLEY; see SND]

aflocht &c; aflought [ə'floxt] *adv* agitated, in a flutter *16-e20.* [f *on flocht* (FLOCHT)]

afordell *see* FORDEL

afore &c, effore &c *la15-16, only Sc* [ə'for] *adv* **1** *of time* before, previously *la15-.* **2** *of place* before, in front; in advance *la16-.* **3** at an earlier point in a piece of writing or document, above *la15-17.* **4** *of a clock* fast *20-.*
prep **1** *of time* before, previous to, earlier than *16-.* **2** *of place* before, in front of; in advance of; into the presence of *16-.* **3** *of what is to come* confronting, in store for *19-.* **4** *of rank or consequence* above, before; in preference to *16-.*
conj **1** *of time* before *16-.* **2** rather than *la19-.*
~-**hand** in advance, beforehand *la16-.* [*cf* BEFORE and ANEATH, ATWEEN]

aforenens &c *15-e16;* **aforenent &c** *la15-16* [*ə'fornɛn(t)s, *-nɛnt] *prep* over against. [AFORE + FORENENT]

aforrow; afforrow [*ə'forʌu, *-o] *adv* before, previously *16.* [only Sc; f FOROW, after AFORE]

afouth *see* FOUTH

aft *adv, now arch and verse* = oft *la15-.*
~**times** *chf verse* = oft-times *la16-.*

aften, afen &c *la19-e20* ['af(ə)n] *adv, comparative* ~**er** *la17-* = often *18-, Gen except S.*
~**times &c** *chf verse* = oftentimes *la16-e20.*

after *see* EFTER

again &c; agane &c *la14-e19,* **agen** *19-e20,* **agin** *la19* [ə'gen] *adv* **1** = again *la14-.* **2** *with verb of motion* back *la14-.* **3** in return *la15-e20.* **4** *in questions, asking for a reminder, la19-, now local:* 'what was I at again?'
prep **1** = again, facing *la14-e16.* **2** towards, so as to meet or greet *15-16.* **3** in hostility or opposition to: in defiance of; to the hurt or disadvantage of; unfavourable to; not in accordance with *la14-.* **4** against, into collision with *la18-.* **5** leaning or resting against; close to or

touching *la19-e20*. **6** in anticipation of, in preparation for (a particular time etc) *la15-*. **7** *of time* towards, by *18-e20*: '*pay the bills again Michalmass*'.

conj in anticipation of or in preparation for a particular time etc when; until *16-*.

~-call recall, call back; annul, revoke, repeal *la14-e17*. **~-cuming** return, returning *la14-16*.

haud &c again hold back *15-*, *now NE Ags.*

nocht againstandand notwithstanding, despite *la14-15*. [*cf* next and AGANIST, GAIN-, GIN³]

against *la18-*, **againis &c** *la14-e17*; **aganis &c** *la14-e17* [ə'genst; *ə'genz] *prep* **1** = against *la14-e17*. **2** *of time* towards, near *la18-e20*. [*cf* AGANIST]

agait &c, agate [ə'get] *adv* **1** in motion *la16-e17*. **2** on the road, going about, *esp* after illness *19-e20*. **3** away *19-e20*.

~ward *la16-e17*, **~wards** *16-17*, *only Sc* on the road or way. [chf northern in Eng]

a'gait *see* A'

agane *see* AGAIN

aganis *see* AGAINST

aganist *16-17* [*ə'genst] *prep* **1** = AGAIN. **2** = AGAINST.

agate *see* AGAIT

a'gates *see* A'

age &c; aige &c *16-17*, **adge** *la16-17*, **eage &c** *la16-e17* *n* = age *15-*.

be ~s with &c be of the same age as (someone else) *la19-*.

agee *see* AJEE

agen *see* AGAIN

agent &c ['edʒənt; *N, C also* 'adʒənt] *n* **1** = agent, a person who acts for another *la16-*. **2** *law* = law agent (LAW¹) *la16-*. **3** a part-time representative of a firm etc, *eg* a country bank manager or stationmaster *la18-e20*.

v, only Sc **1** *vt* act as an agent in *17*. **2** *vti, specif* act as legal representative (in a cause) *18-e19*. **~rie &c** the office or function of agent *la16-e17*, *only Sc*.

aggrage &c [*a'gredʒ] *vt* **1** make greater, aggravate *17*. **2** exaggerate *la16-17*. [only Sc; OF *aggragier &c*, var of *agregier* (> AGGREGE)]

aggre *see* AGREE

aggrege &c [*a'gredʒ] *vt* **1** = aggrege, exaggerate *16-17*. **2** increase the gravity of (a misdeed, penalty etc); aggravate *16-17*. [*cf* AGGRAGE]

agile &c; agill *16* *adj* agile, able to move or act quickly, nimble *15-*.

agilité &c *n* **1** = agility *la15-16*. **2** quickness of intellect; cleverness, skill *la15-e16*.

agill *see* AGILE

agin *see* AGAIN

agitat¹ &c *ptp, adj* **1** tossed about; perturbed *la16-e17*. **2** debated, discussed *17*. [only Sc; L *agitāt-*, ptp stem of *agitāre*]

agitat² &c *vt* perturb, disturb *la16-17*. [*cf* Eng *agitate*]

agley; aglee *adv, adj* [ə'gli, ə'gləi; *N, only* ə'gləi] **1** off the straight, awry, oblique(ly) *19-*. **2** *fig* wrong, awry *la18-*.

aglied squintingly *e17*. [*cf* GLEY, *gleyed &c*]

agmentation *see* AUGMENTATION

agnamed [*'agnemd] *adj* named, nicknamed *la17-e19*. [by analogy w L *agnōmen*]

agnat &c *la15-e17*; **agnate &c** ['agnet, *'agnat] *n* a relative on the father's side *la15-*. [F *agnat*, L *agnātus*]

agnosce [*'agnos] *vt* **1** acknowledge, confess; avow *la16*. **2** investigate, establish by proof *la16*. [only Sc; L *agnōscere*]

agree &c, agré *la15-16*; **aggre &c** *la15-e17* *v* = agree *la15-*.

~ with agree to, consent to *19-e20*.

agrouf &c [ə'gruf] *adv* face downwards, prone *16-e20*. [reduced f *on grouf* (GROOF)]

Agust *see* AUGUST

Ahallomes *see* ALHALLOW

ahame [ə'hem] *adv* at home *la18-e20*. [*a* at + HAME]

ahaud &c [ə'had] *adv* on fire *e20*, *S*. [*a* + HAUD in the grip (*ie* of fire)]

aheat [ə'hit] *adv* in(to) a hot or warm condition *la19-e20*. [eModEng (once)]

ahint &c; ahin *la19-*, **ahent &c** *la19-e20* [ə'hɪnt, ə'hɪn] *adv* **1** *of place* behind, remaining, left behind, in or to the rear, at the back, following *la19-*. **2** *of time* in one's past life, in time past *19-*. **3** at a later time, late, too late *la18-*. **4** *of a clock* slow *la19-e20*. **5** *fig* = behind *la19-*.

prep **1** *of place, also fig* behind *la18-*. **2** *of time* later than, after (a person) *la19-*. **3** after (a circumstance or point of time); too late for; in view of; in spite of *la19-e20*, chf NE.

~ (the) hand 1 late, after the event *la18-e20*. **2** in reserve *e20*, *NE*. **come** *etc* **in ~ one** take the advantage of one *19-e20*. [only Sc; *cf* eME *at-hind*, OE *æt-hindan*]

Aiberdeen *see* ABERDEEN

aiblins &c *18-*, **ablens &c** ['eblɪnz; *S* 'jɪb-] *adv* perhaps, possibly *la16-*, *now chf literary*. [ABLE *adv* + -*lin(g)s*]

aich¹ &c [ex] *interj* expressing surprise, sorrow etc *19*. [*cf* ACH]

aicher *19-e20, Ork Cai*, **echer &c** *16*, **icker** *la18-19, SW* [*Ork Cai* 'exər; *SW* 'ɪkər; *&c*] *n* an ear of corn. [ONorthumb *eher*, OE *ēar; cf* ACKER]

aicht *see* AUCHT¹, AUCHT³

aider *see* EDDER

aidge *see* EDGE

aiell *see* ALE

aifter *see* EFTER

aigars *n pl* **aigar-meal** meal from well-dried grain, ground in a hand-mill and *usu* mixed with peasemeal *19*. [*cf* AICHER]

aige *see* AGE, EDGE

aigle &c *n* = eagle *la16-19*. [OF; *cf* EGILL]

aik, ake &c; **eak** &c *la16-17*, **yik** *e20*, *S n*, *now almost obs or verse* = oak *15-*.

aiker *see* ACRE

ail &c *v* **1** = ail *la14-*. **2** *impersonal* **what ails ye** *etc* **at** what objection have you etc to?, what grounds for complaint have you etc against? *la15-*, *only Sc.* **3** *with infin* hinder, prevent *19-*: 'What suld ail me to ken it?' *n* an illness *la15-*.

ailay *see* ALLAY

aild *see* AULD

aile *see* AISLE

Ailsa cock *n* the puffin *19*. [f as next]

Ailsa Craig *n* a *curling stone* (CURL) made from the volcanic rock of Ailsa Craig *la19-*. [the island off the Ayrshire coast]

ain &c *la16-*, **awin** &c *la14-17*; **awn** &c *la14-e18*, **awing** &c *16 adj* **1** = (one's) own *la14-*. **2 the** proper or natural *16*. **my** *etc* ~**sel** *emphatic* myself etc *19-e20*. **o my** *etc* ~**s** = of my etc own *la19-e20*. [for phonol see DOST, SND]

aince *la18-*, **anis** &c *la14-e19*, **once** &c *la16-*, **onis** &c *15-e17*, **wance** &c *la19-*; **ance** &c *la16-e20*, **anes** *la16-e20*, **eence** *e20*, **yince** &c *la18-*, **yinst** *la19-e20*, *WC SW* [*Nai Mry Bnf nEC* ens; *Sh Ork NE Ags* ins; *Sh Ork Cai WC Uls* wans(t); *C, S Uls* jıns(t); **ons*] *adv* (*la14-*), *conj* (*18-*) = once.

~ **errand** &c, ~ **e(e)ran(d)** *e20*, **end's errand** *19-e20*, **yince yirrant** &c *e20*, *Rox* ['ens &c, *also* 'enz, 'jınz, 'ɛnz; 'ɛrən(d), 'ırən(d), *S* 'jırən(d); -ənt] *adv* for the express purpose, as a special errand *la16-e20*. **ane** *etc* **end's errand** = prec *19-e20*: 'He went wan end's errand to see him.' **at** ~, **attanis** *la14-e17* = at once *la14-*. ~ **in** *etc* **a day** once upon a time *18-*, *now NE*.

aipple &c *la16-*, **appil** &c, **epple** *la19-e20*; **apill** &c *la14-17*, **aple** *la15-17 n* = apple *la14-*.

~ **garnet** a pomegranate *16-17*. ~ **orange** &c an orange *la15-16*.

aippleringie &c, **overeengie** &c *NE* ['epl'rıŋı, -'rıŋı, -'rɛnı, 'apl-; *Abd* 'ovə'rıŋı, 'ıvə'rıŋı; &c] *n* southernwood *19-e20*. [see SND]

air[1] &c; **are** *la14-e16 n* = air, atmosphere etc *la14-*.

~**el** a flute *e19*, *S.* ~**ish** cool, chilly *19-e20*. **take the** ~ **off** take the chill off *la18-e20*.

air[2] *n* a small quantity, a particle, morsel, taste etc *la16-e20*, *chf Sh-N.* [prob f AIR[1]; *cf* AIR[4]]

air[3] &c *la15-e20*, **are** *15-16*; **ar** *la14-16 n* an oar. [nME *are*; OE, ON *ār*]

air[4] *vt* taste; sniff, smell *19-*, *chf Ork.* [prob f AIR[2]]

air[5], **are** *adv* = ERE *adv* 1 (*la14-e16*), 2 (*15-*). *adj* early *16-e20*.

~ **yestreen** *19-e20*, **eidi-streen** *e20*, *Cai* ['eidəstrin &c] = erethestreen (ERE) *19-e20*. [nME *are*, ONorthumb *ār*, ON *ár* early; *cf* OR]

air *see* HEIR

airand *see* EERANT

airch &c [ertʃ] *n* an aim *19-e20*, *chf N.* *vi*, *also* **erch** *e20*, *Cai Bnf* [ɛrtʃ] take aim *19-e20*, *N Rox.* [OF *archer* (*v*) arch, curve, OF *arc*, L *arcus* a bow]

aire &c; **are**, **ay(e)r** *n* a circuit court held by itinerant judges or officers *15-e17*. [ModEng *eyre*, ME *eire*, OF *eire*]

airgument ['ergjumənt &c] *n* = argument *la19-*, *NE Ags.*

airie; **arrie** *n* a *shieling* (SHIEL[1]) *la18-e20*. [Gael *àirigh*]

airk *see* ARK[1]

airm &c *la16-*, **arm** &c *la14-*, **erm** *la19- n*, *lit and fig* = arm.

airmour &c *la16-*, *now local Sh-Ags*, **armour** &c *la14- n* = armour.

airmy &c *16-*, *now NE Ags*, **armie** &c *16- n* = army.

airn *see* EARN, IRON

airnest *see* EERNEST

airra *n* = arrow *la19-*, *now NE Ags.*

airt[1] *16-*, **art** &c, **ert** *la19-*, *now Sh Arg n* = art, skill *la14-*.

~ **and part** &c *law* denoting participation in a crime *15-*.

airt[2] &c *16-*, **art** &c *15-*, **airth** &c *la16-*, **arth** *15-16* [ert; *Sh Ork* ɛrt; *N, EC* erθ; *Uls also* art] **1** a point of the compass, a quarter *15-*. **2** a direction, way, manner *la16-*.

v **1** *vt* (1) direct, guide (a person) to a place; set (something) facing or moving in a certain direction *la17-*. (2) incite, urge forward *la18-*. (3) *also* ~ **out** discover by search *19-e20*, *Rox.* **2** *vi* direct one's way (**to, towards**); make (**for**), take the road (**to**) etc *19-*.

airtan(s) ['ertın(z)] *direction; tendency *la19-e20*. [nME *art* (*n*); obscure; *v* 1 (2) may be derived f OSc, ME *art* constrain, force]

ais *see* EASE[1]

aise *see* ASS, EASE[1]

aish *see* ESH

aishan *see* ETION

aisiament *see* EASEMENT

aislar &c *16-e20*, **aslar** &c *16-17*, **ezlar** *19-e20*, *chf Rox*, **eslar** &c *16-17*, **estlair** &c *16-e18*; **astler** &c *la14-16*, **aistlar** *16-e17*, **eastler** &c *17* ['eslər, 'eʃ-, ***'ɛs-, &c; *Ayr Rox* ɛz-] *n*, *also* ~ **stane** *16* ashlar, square-hewn stone *la14-e19*.

~ **wark** &c masonry constructed of such stone *16-e20*. [OF *aiseler* plank, board, L *axillaris*, f *axilla* dim of *axis* axle, plank]

aisle *la18-*, **ile** &c *la15-17*, **aile** &c *e17*, *la19* [əil] *n* **1** = aisle *la14-*. **2** an enclosed and covered burial place, adjoining a church, though not a part of it *la18-19*.

aisle *see* AIZLE

aisle-tuith &c,   assle-tuith &c ['esl'tøθ, 'ezl-, 'asl-, 'azl-] *n* a molar tooth; a bicuspid tooth *la19-e20, SW, S.* [only Sc; ON *jaxl* grinder + Eng *tooth*]

aisment *see* EASEMENT

aist *see* EAST

aistlar *see* AISLAR

aisy *see* EASY

ait &c, ate *la15-e20,* **oat &c** *17-,* **ote &c** *17,* **yit &c** *19-, EC, S;* **eat &c** *la16-17,* **eit** *la16-e17,* **yett &c** *19-* [et; *EC, SW, S* jɪt] *n, chf in pl =* oat *la15-.*
  aiten *adj* oaten *la18-e20.*
  ~**cake** a thin flat crisp biscuit made of oatmeal *la16-.* ~-**laif &c** *16-17* a loaf of oat bread. ~-**seed &c 1** the seed of the oat *16-e20.* **2** the sowing of oats, the season for sowing oats *la16-19.* **ait-seed time,** ~**sen &c tyme** the time for sowing oats *la16-17.*

ait *see* EAT

aiten[1] *n* a partridge *e19.* [obscure; *cf* AITHEHEN]

aiten[2] *la19,* **eaten** *la18 n* juniper *Abd.* [Gael *aitionn; cf* ETNACH]

aiten *see* AIT

aith *see* OATH

aithehen &c [*'eθ'hɛn] *n = gray hen* (GRAY[1]) *la16-e17.* [obscure; *cf* AITEN[1]]

aither &c, ayther &c, ether &c, eather *la16-17;* **ather &c** *la14-e18,* **adir** *e16,* **edder &c** *la19-, Sh NE* ['eðər; *Sh* 'ɛd-; *NE also* 'ed-, 'ɛd-; *C also* ɛð-] *adj =* either *la14-e20.*
  adv, also **aithers** *19-, now local =* either *la14-.*
  pronoun, conj = either *la14-.*
  etherin; eitherins &c, edderin(s *Sh Abd adv,* in negative not either, not any more than another *19-e20.* [*cf* OWTHER and NAITHER]

aither *see* ITHER

aitnach *see* ETNACH

aiven *see* EVEN[2]

aiver[1] *18-e20,* **aver &c** *16-e19* ['evər] *n, sometimes disparaging* a workhorse, carthorse; an old or worthless horse *16-e20.*
  averill = *n, e16.* [ME, OF *aver* property, estate; MedL *averum* property, *specif* a beast of burden]

aiver[2]; **yivver** [*Rox* *'evər; *Ork* 'jɪv-] *adj* eager, ardent *la19-e20.*
  aiverie &c *la18-19,* **yivvery &c** *16-e20* [*'evərɪ; *Ork Abd* 'jɪv-; *Ayr S* *'iv-] *adj* desirous, anxious; *specif* hungry *16-e20.* **yivverin** in a state of great excitement, very eager or agitated *la19-e20, Abd.* [OE *gīfre* greedy, desirous; *cf* northern ModEng dial *givour* greedy]

aivis &c ['evɪs] *n* a silly or useless occupation; a trick *e20, NE.* [see SND]

aiwal *see* AWALD[1]

aix &c *16-,* **ax** *la14-;* **ex** *16* [ɛks, eks] *n =* axe.

aixies &c *la16-la19,* **axes** *la17-e19* [*'eksɪz, *'ɛksɪz] *n* an attack of ague. [var of Eng *access*]

aixle *n =* axle *20-.*

aix-tree &c *16-e20,*   **axtré &c** *la15-16,* **extrie &c** *la16-e20,* **extré &c** *16;* **axetree &c** *la15-e18 n* an axle of a wheel. [ME *axtré, extre,* OE *eax* an axle + *trēow* a beam; *cf* ASSLE-TREE]

aizle &c *19-,* **isill &c** *e16, 19;* **aisle** *la19, WC,* **eizel &c** *19-e20, chf NE,* **izal &c** *19-e20* ['ezl, 'ɪzl; *NE also* əizl] *n* **1** an ember; a spark *16-e20.* **2** a burnt-out cinder *19.*
  vi, only **aisle** glow *la19.* [ME *isyl,* OE *ysel* ashes]

ajee; agee [ə'dʒi] *adv (adj)* **1** to one side, aside, off the straight *18-.* **2** *of a door etc* ajar, partly open *la18-.* **3** *fig* aside, off the straight; *esp of the mind* in or into a disturbed or disordered state *18-.* [*a* + JEE]

a-jour &c [*a'dʒur] *adj,* needlework of openwork *la16:* '*pasimentis .. plane or ajower*'. [F *à jour* (open) to the day]

ake *see* AIK

akir *see* ACRE

aknawin &c [*ə'knɑ(ə)n] *ptp* known to *or* til (a person) *la14-e15.* [ME *aknowen,* ptp of *aknowe(n)* recognize, confess, OE *oncnāwan* know, acknowledge]

alabast [*'aləbast] *n =* alabaster *la14-e17.* [only Sc; OF *alabastre,* L *alabaster*]

alacampine *see* ALLICOMPAIN

alace &c *la16-e19,*   **allace &c** *la14-16;* **al(1)eace** *16* [*a'les] *interj* **1** = alas *la14-e19.* **2** *used as n* an 'alas' *16:* '*thai grat with mony saire allace*'. [*cf* ALISS]

alackanie *see* ALAKE

alaft &c *la16-e20,* **aloft &c** [ə'laft, ə'loft] *adv =* aloft *la16-.*

alage *see* ALLEGE

alagrugous &c [*alə'grugəs] *adj* grim, ghastly; sour; woebegone *la18-e20.* [uncertain; *cf* GRUGOUS]

alagust &c [*?alə'gʌst] *n* suspicion, disgust *18-e20, NE.* [obscure]

alairm [ə'ler(ə)m] *vt, n =* alarm *20-, now local Sh-Ags.*

alake &c *16-,* **allake &c** *la15-16* [ə'lek] *interj =* alack *la15-, now arch or verse.*
  alakanee, alackanie [*ə'lakəni] = prec *18-e19, only Sc.*

Alan &c; Aulin ['alən] *n* the Arctic skua *19-e20, Sh Ork.*
  Allan-hawk name given to several sea birds, *eg* **1** = prec *la19;* **2** the great northern diver *19-e20.* [uncertain]

alandward &c,   alandwart &c [*ə'land-ward, *-wart &c] *adv* in or into the country *la16-18.* [f *upaland* (UPONLAND); *cf* LANDWARD]

alane &c,   allane &c *la14-e17,* **allone &c** *15-e17;* **aleen &c** *16-e20* [ə'len; *Sh Ork NE* ə'lin] *adj (la14-),* *adv (16-) =* alone.
  him *etc* ~ (*la14-18*), **his** *etc* ~ (*16-e17*) by or of himself.

alanerallie *see* ALLENARLY

alang [ə'laŋ] *prep* (*la16-*), *adv* (*18-*) = along. [*cf*
ENDLANG]
alangis, alangs, alangst *see* ALONGST
alasant [*'aləsant] *n* a striped silk made in
Egypt *la17-e18*. [ME *alisaundre*, OF *Alisandrie*
Alexandria]
alaw [*ə'la] *adv* down, low down *15-19*. [Eng
alow]
alb &c; **ab** &c *16 n* = alb, the vestment *15-*.
Albany ['albənı, 'ɑl-] ~ **herald** one of the Scottish heralds *la15-*. [MedL *Albania* Scotland
north of Forth and Clyde]
albeit &c; **albeid** &c *la15-16* ['al'biɪt, *-'bi:d,
*'ɑ'biɪt] *conj* = albeit, although, even if *la15-*.
albuist &c; **apiece** &c [*'al'bist, *('ɑ)'pis(t)
&c] *conj* although *la18, Abd*. [appar f *all beis it*
= all be it]
alcomy &c; **accomie** &c *la16-e19* [*'akəmɪ] *n*
a mixed metal (*latterly only* applied to cutlery)
16-e19. [Eng *alchemy*]
ald *see* AULD
alderman &c [*'aldərman] *n* the chief officer of
a GUILD; a MAGISTRATE in a BURGH *la14-e17*.
[ScL *aldirmannus 14*, ME *alderman*, ONorthumb
aldorman, f *aldor* elder, chief; cf *elderman* (ELDER)]
ale &c, **eel** *la19-, Sh Ork*, **ile** *18-, Cai-Ross*, **yill**
&c *18-, now C, S*; **aiell** &c *16-17*, **eill** &c
la16-17, **yeal** *la17-e18*, **yell** &c *18-19*, **yuill**
&c *la19* [el; *Sh Ork* il; *Cai-Ross* əil; *C, S* jɪl] *n* 1
= ale *la14-*. 2 lemonade, ginger beer etc
la20-, NE Ags.
vt treat to ale *19*.
~**berry** &c 1 = aleberry, ale boiled with
bread, sugar, and spice *17-e18*. 2 ale boiled
with oatmeal and sugar *la19-e20, NE*. ~**cap**
&c, ~**cop** a wooden ale-cup *16-e19*. ~**-cun-
nare** *la15-16*, ~**-tastare** *15*, an official inspector of ale offered for sale. ~**-wand** a WAND
indicating that ale is for sale *15-16*. **yill-wife**
a woman who sold ale, *usu* of her own brewing
la18-19.
ale *see* A'
aleace *see* ALACE
aleen *see* ALANE
alenth &c [ə'lɛnθ] *adv, chf fig* onward, forward
19-, Sh NE-Per: 'far alenth'. [*a-* + LENTH]
alevin *see* ELEEVEN
algate, alhale *see* A'
Alhallow &c [*'al'halʌu, *'ɑ'halʌu, *-'halo,
*-ə] *n* 1 all the saints, *only in* **be** ~ *e16*. 2 *attrib*
Allhallowtide *la15-16*.
~**day** All Saints Day *la14-17*. ~ **evin** = *Halloween* (HALLOW²) *la15-16*. ~**mes**, **A(ll)-
hallomes** &c *la16-e17* the feast of All Saints
15-e17. [ONorthumb *alle hālga(n)*; cf Eng *all
hallows*]
aliament *n* = ALIMENT *17*.
alicht &c [ə'lɪxt] *vi* = alight, dismount etc
16-19, only Sc.
alicreesh; alicrees &c [*'alɪ'kriʃ, *-'kris,

*'alə-] *n* liquorice *19-e20*. [prob f Du *lakkeri*
&c; *cf* LICKERY and *sucker alacreishe, sugaralli*
(SUCCAR)]
alienar &c [*'eliənar] *n* alien, stranger *la15-e16*
[only Sc; f Eng *alien*]
alikeways [*ə'ləikwez] *adv* likewise *16*. [c
elikewise (ELIKE)]
aliment *n, law* maintenance or support claimed
from another; alimony *la17-*. [F *aliment*, L *ali-
mentum* food]
alishunners *see* ALSHINDER(S)
aliss &c [ə'lɪs] *interj* (*chf* as cry of pain) stop!
stop hurting me!; oh! *la19-e20, NE*. [var o
ALACE]
alist [ə'lɪst] *adv* **come** ~ recover consciousnes
la18-e20. [see SND]
alkin(d), all *see* A'
allacay *see* ALLEKAY
allace *see* ALACE
allage *see* ALLEGE
allake *see* ALAKE
allane *see* ALANE
allanerly *see* ALLENARLY
Allan-hawk *see* ALAN
alla-volie *see* ALLEVOLIE
allay; ailay &c *la16-e17 n* = alley, a garde
walk or path *la15-e17*.
~ **bowlis** the game of bowls *la16-e17*.
allay(a) *see* ALLYE
alleace *see* ALACE
alleadgeance &c, **allegeance** &
[*'a'lɛdʒans] *n* 1 an allegation, an assertio
la15-e18. 2 *specif* (*with sing form sometimes use*
as pl) an allegation of right or title advanced i
a court of law, or one implying a charge o
accusation against a person *la15-17*. [
ALLEGE; form *allegance* may be directly f OF *alle*
gance or MedL *allegantia*]
allegance *see* ALLEGEANCE
allege &c; **al(l)age** &c *16*, **alleage** &
la16-e17 vti 1 = allege *la14-*. 2 appeal **to** *o*
till (something) *la15*.
~**it** alleged, asserted *16-*.
allegeance &c; **allegance** &c *la15-el*
[*'a'lidʒ(ɪ)əns] *n* = allegiance *15-17*.
allegeance *see* ALLEADGANCE
allekay &c *16-e19*, **allacay** &c *16-e1*
[*'aləke] *n* 1 a footman, lackey *16-e17*. 2 th
best man, the bridegroom's attendant *la18-e19*
Ags. [OF *alacays*; *cf* LECKIE]
allenarly &c *la15-*, **allanerly** &c *15-e18*
alanerallie &c *16-17* [ə'lɛnərlɪ, *a'len-] *ad*
1 singly, solitarily *la14-e15*. 2 *now law* only
solely, exclusively *la14-*.
adj sole, single, only *la15-16*. [*all* (A') +
ANERLIE]
aller &c ['alər] *n* = alder (tree) *16-e20*
[eModEng *aller*, OE *aler*; *cf* ARN]
allering *see* ALLOURING
alleris &c [*'alərz] *adj, only* **our** *or* **thair** ~ of u

all, of all of them *la14-e16*. [ME *aller*, ONorthumb *alra*, genitive pl of *all* + possessive *-is*]

allevolie &c *e19*, **alla-volie** *e17* [*'alə'volɪ] *adv* at random. [F *à la volée*]

allicompain &c *19*, **alacampine &c** *la16-e20* [*'alɪkəm'pen &c*] *n* = elecampane, the plant or the extract from it.

allocate, allocat [*'aloket, -at] *ptp* assigned *la16-e18*.
vt assign (something) **to** (someone) *17-e18*. [MedL *allocat-*, ptp stem of *allocāre*]

allone *see* ALANE

allongs *see* ALONGST

alloo *see* ALLOW

allouring &c; allering &c *16*, **alrin &c** *16-17* [*'al(ə)rɪŋ, -ɪn] *n* the stone pavement placed behind the battlements of a hall etc; the material of which it is built *16-17*. [ME *aluring*, f OF *alure* a place to walk in]

allow &c; alloo &c *la19-* [ə'lu] *vti* **1** = allow *15-*. **2** omitting verb of motion *20-*: '*he was allowed ashore*'.
at (the rate o) nae ∼ance without stint, with the utmost vigour *la18-*, *now local Ork-Per*.

alluterly &c, allutraly &c *la14-16* [*'al'ʌtərlɪ] *adv* completely, entirely, absolutely *la14-17*. [*all* (A') + Eng *utterly*]

allwhair *see* A WHERE

allya *see* ALLYE

allyat &c [*'a'laɪat] *ptp* allied *16*. [Latinized form of *allyit*, ptp of *ally*]

allye &c *la14-16*, **allya &c** *15-e17* [*'alaɪ, *a'laɪe &c*] *n*, *also* **allay(a)** *la16-e17* **1** *collective* allies *la14-16*. **2** an ally, associate *15-e17*. **3** alliance, association; kinship *15-e17*. [ModEng *ally*, ME *alye*, OF *alié*]

alma(i)st *see* ALMOST

alme *see* AUM

almeral &c *15-16*; **awmerale &c** *e15* [*'alməral, *'ɑ-] *n* = admiral. [var of *amerale* (ADMIRAL), w infl f MedL *almirallus*]

almery *see* AUMRY

almessar *see* AWMOUS

almicht &c [*'al'mɪxt] *adj*, *verse* = almight, almighty *15-16*.

almichty &c *15-*, **a'michty** *20-* [al'mɪxtɪ, ɑ'mɪxtɪ] *adj*, *also* **almichtine &c** *16*; **almichting &c** *16* = almighty *15-*.
n = Almighty *16-*.

almorie *see* AUMRY

almosar *see* AWMOUS

almost &c *16-*, **amaist &c** *15-e20*, **almast &c** *e16*, **amast** *e16*; **almaist &c** *la15-18*, **amest** *la16-e20* ['ɑ'mest; a'mest, ə'mest; *'al'most, *'al'mest, *al'mest] *adv* = almost *16-*.
almost never seldom or never *la18-*.
almaist nocht *etc* scarcely any *la15-16*.
almost nothing *etc* little or nothing *la18-*.

almous, almoussare, alms *see* AWMOUS

aloft *see* ALAFT

alongst *la17-*, **alongest** *la16-17*, **alongis &c** *la16-17*; **allongs &c** *la17-e18* [ə'loŋs(t)] *prep*, *also* **alangst &c** *la18-e20*, **alangis &c** *16-e17*, **alangs** *17-e20* [ə'laŋs(t)] along *la16-*.
adv along *17-e18*. [laME, eModEng *alongest* &c]

alow¹ [ə'lo] *adv, prep* below *la19-e20*. [prob f Eng *below*; cf AFORE for *before*]

alow² &c [ə'lʌu] *adv* on fire, ablaze *19-e20*. [a- + LOW¹]

alquhare *see* A WHERE

alrady, alreddy *see* A'READY

alrin *see* ALLOURING

alrische *see* ELDRITCH

alrone *see* ARN

alsa [*'alse, *al'se] *adv* **1** = also, as well *la14-e16*. **2** as *la14-15*. [reduced f ALSWA]

alsammyn [*'al'samən, *-'sem-] *adv* all together *la14-e16*. [only Sc; *all* (A') + ME *samen* together]

alse, als &c [*'als] *adv* **1** = also, as well *la14-e18*. **2** as (1) **als .. as** = as .. as *la14-e18*; (2) *without* **as** following, *la15-e18*: '*a mat of xx fut lang, and alls brad*'.
alsmekill &c *n, adj, adv* = as much *15-e17*.
alsmony as many *15-e16*. **alssone &c** immediately, at once *la14-e16*.
als(s)one as as soon as *15-e17*. **∼weill &c, alswele, alswell &c** *(15-17)* **as 1** as well (..) as, as much (..) as, to the same extent (..) as *la14-e18*: '*he day allsweill as nichtlie*'; '*alswele beyhond the see as on this side*'. **2** both .. and *la14-17*: '*aswele vndir erde as abone*'. **alsswyth &c** *only verse* at once, immediately *la14-16*. **alsswyth as** as soon as *e16*. [reduced f ALSA; also nME]

alset &c [*'al'sɛt] *conj* although *la14-15*. [only Sc; *all* (A') + SET¹ *conj*]

alshin *see* ELSHIN

alshinders &c; alishunners &c ['al(ɪ)ʃɪn(d)ər(z), -ʃʌn-] *n* = Alexanders, horseparsley; *bishopweed* (BISHOP) *19-e20*. [see SND]

also &c [*'al'so, *'also] *adv* **1** = also, as well *la15-*. **2** *(sometimes combined with the following word)* as *15-16*. [cf ALSA]

alssone, alsswyth *see* ALSE

alswa &c *la14-16*; **alsway &c** *la15-e16* [*'alswe, *al'swe] *adv* = also, in the same way, in addition etc *la14-16*. [ME *al swa*, OE *eall swā*; cf ALSA, ALSO, ALSE]

alswele, alswell *see* ALSE

alter &c *vti* **1** = alter *la15-*. **2** *law* change the judgment of a lower court *la18-*; *cf* ADHERE.

alteratioun &c *n* **1** = alteration *16-e17*. **2** *erron for* altercation *la16*.

althing *see* A'

although &c, althoch &c *la14-16* [əl'θo, *al'θox] *conj* **1** = although *la14-*. **2** *with omission of clause* although it be so *la19-*: '*an what altho?*'
adv though, all the same, however *e20*: '*I wisna invitet but I'm gaun although*'.

altime &c [*'al'təim] *adv* always *la14-15, only Sc*.

alunt [ə'lʌnt] *adv, chf* set ~ set on fire *19-e20, chf S*. [*a-* + LUNT¹]

always &c, **alwayis** &c *la14-17*; **awayis** *16-e17* [*'al'wez, *a(l)'wez &c] *adv* **1** = always *la14-*. **2** still *19-*: '*he is always living*'.

alwhair *see* A WHERE

alwise [*'al'waız &c] *adv* **1** = alwise, in every way *la16*. **2** = always *la16-18*. [ME]

amagger &c [ə'magər] *adv* in spite of *19-e20, N*. [*cf* MAUGRE; also *cf* laME *amaugrey* f OF *à mal gré*]

amains *see* AMENDS

amaist *see* ALMOST

amal *vt* enamel *16*. [laME *amall*, AF **amal*]

amand &c [*a'mand] *n, chf law* a fine *la16-e19*. [OF *amande*, var of *amende* > AMENDS]

amang &c, **among** &c *la16-, imang* &c *la14-15, la19*; **amon** *la19-e20, Abd Ags*, **amo** *la18-e20* [ə'maŋ; *NE* ə'mo(n), ə'mʌ(n)] *prep* **1** = among *la14-*. **2** *with sing or collective noun* in or into the midst of, amid *16-*: '*I stuck among the snow*'.

amangst &c *la16-*, **amongst** &c *17-*, ~**is** &c *15-e17* [ə'maŋst, *ə'maŋs, *ə'maŋz] *prep* **1** = amongst *la15-*. **2** = AMANG 2, *15-*.

~ **my** *etc* **feet** at or beside my *etc* feet *19-*. ~ **you** *etc* **be it** settle it among yourselves *19-*. [*chf* nME *amang* &c, nME *imang* &c, sME *among* &c, OE *amang, on mang, (on) gemang*]

amast *see* ALMOST

ambaxiatour *n* an ambassador *la15-e16*. [only Sc; MedL *ambaxiator*]

ambland; amland &c *adj, chf of a horse* = ambling *16-e17*.

ambrie *see* AUMRY

ame *see* BE, EEM

amedon &c *n* = amydon, a preparation of wheat-flour; starch *la16*.

ameise &c; **ames** [*ə'miz] *vt* **1** appease, placate, soothe (a person) *la14-e16*. **2** mitigate, moderate, assuage *la14-e16*. [chf Sc; OF *ameisier* calm, appease]

amend *vti* **1** = amend *la14-*. **2** make amends *la15-16*.

amends, amendis; amens &c *18-e20, chf NE*; **amains** *e20, NE* [ə'mɛn(d)z] *n* **1** = amends *la14-*. **2** *chf* ~ **o** advantage of, upper hand of *19-e20*. [*cf* MENDS, AMAND]

amene &c [*ə'min] *adj, verse* agreeable, pleasing, pleasant *la15-16*. [ME; L *amoenus*]

amens *see* AMENDS

amerale *see* ADMIRAL

amerant &c, **amerot** &c *n* = emerald *16*. [OF *amiraude, amerade; cf* EMERANT]

amerciat &c [*a'mɛrsıat &c] *ptp* subjected to or punished by a fine, fined *la15-e18*. *vt* amerce, fine *16-e19*. [only Sc; MedL *amerciatus*, ptp of *amerciare*]

amerot *see* AMERANT

amers &c *16-e17, e20*, **emmers** *17-*, now Sh

Abd Bwk; **ammers** *e16, e20* ['ɛmərz; Ork Ros 'am-] *n pl* = embers. [ME *aymer, emer*, O] *æmerge* or ON *eimyrja*]

amery *see* AUMRY

ames *see* AMEISE

amest *see* ALMOST

amichty *see* ALMICHTY

amids &c *la19*, **amiddis** &c *e16* [*ə'mıdz] *a* in the midst of (something). [ME *amiddes* &c]

amidwart &c *adv, prep* = amid *e16*. [M] *amydward*]

amind [ə'məind] *adv (adj)* in mind, disposed (t do something) *la18-19*.

amissing &c *adj* missing, wanting *la16-1* [chf Sc; *cf* AWANTING]

amitan &c ['amıtən] *n, disparaging* a person wh plays the fool; a person lacking common sens *19-e20, Cai Gall*. [Gael *amadan* a fool]

amland *see* AMBLAND

ammers *see* AMERS

ammiral *see* ADMIRAL

amna *see* BE

amo, amon, among *see* AMANG

amonitioune &c *n* = ammunition *17*. [onl Sc; F *amonition* popular form of *a(m)munition*]

amour &c [*'amur, *a'mur] *n* **1** *pl* love, love making; love affairs *la14-16*. **2** = amou love, affection *la15-16*.

amove¹ &c; **amuff** *15* [*a'møv] *vti* **1** affec with strong emotion, excite; annoy, ange *la14-e16*. **2** move to action, influence *la14-e16* **3** set in motion, cause *15*. **4** *vi* be excited *la15* [eME; OF *amover*, L *admovēre*]

amove² &c [*a'møv] *vt* remove; put or tak away *la15-e16*. [L *āmovēre*]

ampersyand &c; **eppershand** &c *N* ['ampərsıand, 'abərzıant, 'ɛpərsıand, -ʃand &c] *n* = ampersand *la19-e20*. [corruptions c *and per se and, et per se and*]

ample &c *vt* amplify *16*. [*cf* ME *amplye*]

amplefeyst *n* a sulky humour *e19*. [obscure]

amshach &c *NE*, **hamshoch** &c ['(n)amʃəx 'ham-] *n* an accident, misfortune; an injur *la18-e20, NE*. [prob Gael *amsith* mischance + -*ach*]

amuff *see* AMOVE¹

an *indef art* = an, a: **1** *before vowels, la15-*; **2** *befor consonants, la14-e18*; **3** *before h-, la14-*. [rare i OSc, in place of ANE²; *cf* A¹]

an *see* AND, ANE¹, THAN

ana &c; **annay** &c ['anı, 'anə] *n* a river islan *la18-19, Rox*. [obscure]

ana *see* AND

anale, analy *see* ANNALZIE

anamal &c [*ə'naml] *vt* = enamel *la14-16*.

anarmit &c [*ən'armıt, *-'ermıt] *ptp* enarmed, armed *15-e16*.

anawin &c, **inawing** &c *la16-e17* [ın'ɑ(ə)n ən-] *presp* **1** *of persons* owing, indebted *la16-e20* latterly *chf SW*. **2** *of the sum owed* due to b paid, constituting a debt *la16-e17*. [f AWE²]

ance *see* AINCE

anchor-stock; ankerstock &c *n* a large, long loaf of (*usu*) rye-bread *19-e20*. [f supposed resemblance to an *anchor-stock*]

ancien &c [*'ansɪən, *'anʃ(ɪ)ən] *adj* = ancient *la15-e17*. [OF *ancien*; ME *auncyen*; *cf* ANCIENT]

ancienitie *see* ANCIENTÉ

ancient &c; **auncient** &c *16-e20*, **anshent** &c *la17-e20* ['anʃənt; *'ansɪənt, &c] *adj* **1** = ancient *la15-*. **2** *of children* precocious; having the ways or intelligence of an adult *la19-*. [*cf* ANCIEN]

ancienté &c *la14-16*; **ancietie** &c *la16-17*, *only Sc*, **ancienitie** &c *la15-16*, *only Sc* [*'ansɪə(n)tɪ, &c] *n* = ancienty, antiquity.

and &c, **an** *conj* **1** (1) = and *14-*. (2) used before the last number in making compound ordinal numbers where ordinals are used throughout *la18*: '*the hundredth fortieth and fifth psalm*'. **2** *with object* (*chf* ModSc) *or subject* (*chf* OSc) *personal pronoun, but without finite verb* expressing a contrast or objection to the preceding *la15-*: '*an me wi a bad leg tae*'; '*How can ye chant, ye little birds, And I sae weary, fu o care!*' **3** *chf* **an** *la14-*, **in** *19-*, *now Bnf-Ags* if. **4** even if, although *la16-19*.

an a', ana' [ən'ɑ] **1** and all besides, and everything *or* everyone else connected therewith *19-*: '*to see them bedded an a'*'. **2** besides, as well *la19-*: '*I want a piece ana'*'. **3** *giving emphasis to adjs*, *la19-*: '*big an' strong an' a' as she is*'.

ande *see* AYND

Andermess &c, **Androsmes; Andersmes** &c *16-19*, **Andromes** &c *la16* St Andrew's Day, 30 Nov *la15-19*. [*Andro* &c Sc form of *Andrew* + MESS[2]]

Andrew Ferrary &c *n* a Scottish broadsword *e19, hist*. [traditionally f the names *Andrea dei Ferrari, Andrew Ferars* or *Ferrier* a swordsmith]

Andro(s)mes *see* ANDERMESS

ane[1] &c, **one** &c *15-*, **yin** *la18-*, *chf sEC-S*; **an** *la15-e18*, **yane** *la16-19* [en; *sEC, WC, SW, S* jɪn] *numeral adj* = one *la14-*.
numeral pronoun **1** *also* **een** &c *la18-*, *local Sh-Ags* = one *15-*. **2** a certain person, someone (= F *quelqu'un*) *la14-19*: '*ane telt me to gae up by*'. **3** **een** &c *specif* a woman *20-*, *now Sh Ags*: '*a braa een*'. **4** *in pl, freq* **yins**, *after us, you, them* used to emphasize a distinction or contrast *la19-*, *chf WC, S*: '*I'll tak them yins*': '*youse yins'll have tae hurry*'.
n = one *la14-*.
indef pronoun = one (= F *on*) *la18-* [f Eng or Ir; the Sc idiom is *a body* (BODY)].
een(ick)ie = *indef pronoun, 20-, NE*. **aning** &c [*'enɪŋ] union, agreement, alliance *la14-e15*. **~rie, eenrie** &c *la19-*, *local Sh-N*, *in children's counting rhyme* one *19-*, *now local*.
.. of ~ *usu with superlatives* of all, beyond all *la14-e16*: '*the best of ane*'. **in** ~ **1** = in one, unanimously; together *la15-16*. **2** continuously *la14-16*. **121** [St 'wʌn'tu'wʌn] informal name for the offices of the *Church of Scotland*

(CHURCH), since 1929 situated at 121 George Street, Edinburgh *20-*. [nME *an(e)*, OE *ān; cf* AE, WAN[1] and next]

ane[2] [*unstressed* *ən, *stressed* *an; *before consonants, unstressed* *ə, *stressed* *a; *also* *en] *indef art* = a, an: **1** *before vowels, la14-e18*; **2** *before consonants, la15-18*; **3** *before h-, 15-e17*. [ME *an*, unstressed form of eME *an*, OE *ān*, OE *ān* > ANE[1]; *cf* AN and A[1]]

ane[3]; awn [*ɑn] *n, lit and fig* an ass *la15-16*. [only Sc; OF *ane*, L *asinus* ass]

aneath &c *18-*, **aneth** *16-e20* [ə'nɛθ; ə'niθ] *prep* **1** under, below, beneath *16-*. **2** *specif* under the authority, control or influence of *19-e20*.
~ **the breath** in a whisper *la19-*. [f *beneath* with prefix *a-* replacing *be-*; *cf* AFORE, ATWEEN]

anee [ə'ni] *interj* a cry of lamentation *19-e20*; *more freq in combs*, eg *alakanee* (ALAKE). [? termination of *ochanee* (OCH), ? f Gael *ochanaich* sighing]

anefald *see* AEFAULD

aneist, aniest; anist *la16-e20*, **anext** &c *la15-16* [ə'nist, ə'nɪst; *ə'nɪkst, &c] *prep* **1** nearest or next to, adjoining, adjacent to *la15-e20*. **2** on this side of; *fig* short of *18-e20*.
adv next *la15-e20*. [*a-* + NEIST]

ane-levin *numeral* = *alevin* (ELEEVEN) *16-e17*. [wrong expansion by analogy w A[1], ANE[2]]

anely; anly *adv, adj* = only *la14-16*. [nME]

anent &c [ə'nɛnt] *prep* **1** over against, opposite, in front of, before *la14-20*. **2** in a line with; on a level with, alongside of *19-e20*. **3** concerning, about *la14-*. **4** in the sight or opinion of (someone); before; in the presence of *la15-20*.
anentis &c *la14-e17*; **anenst** *la16, e20*, **anens** &c *la14-16* [*ə'nɛn(t)s, ə'nɛnst] = *prep* 1 (*la14-e20*), 3 (*la14-e17*), 4 (*la14-15*). [ME; OE *on efen* on even ground, near]

anerd *see* ANHERD

anerlie &c, **anerly** &c [*'enərlɪ] *adj* (*la14-16*), *adv* (*la14-e16, e19* (*arch*)) = only. [chf Sc; var of ANELY; *cf* ALLENARLY]

anes *see* AINCE, ANE[1]

aneth *see* ANEATH

aneuch *see* ENEUCH

anew *see* ENEW

anext *see* ANEIST

angel &c; **angill** &c *la14-e17* ['endʒl] *n* = angel *la14-*.

angeller *see* ANGULAR

anger &c ['aŋər] *n* **1** a cause of grief or vexation; distress, grief *la14-e20*. **2** = anger *la14-*. **3** a fit or spell of rage *la16-e19*.
vt **1** = anger *la14-*. **2** *vi* become angry *la15-e19*.
~**some** provoking, vexatious *la19-*.

angill *see* ANGEL

anglar *see* ANGULAR

angleberry *la16-e20*, **angilberry** *la16*, **ingleberry** *19-*, *Fif Loth SW* ['aŋlbɛrɪ, 'ɪŋl-] *n* a fleshy growth on horses, cattle or sheep. [see SND]

angular; angeller &c, **anglar** &c

[*'aŋ(ø)lər] *n* a brace-piece or tie in the interior angle of a wooden frame *16-e17*. [only Sc; L *angulāris (adj)* angular]

Angus 1 ~ **herald** one of the former Scottish heralds *la15*. **2** name of a breed of cattle *19-*; *cf* ABERDEEN. [the former county]

anherd &c *la14-16*, **enherde &c** *la14-e16*, **inherd** *15-e16*; **anerd** *la14-e16*, **adneir &c** *la16*, **annere &c** *16* [*'ən'(h)ɛrd; *ə(d)'nir] *vi* **1** adhere **to**, join **with** (a person or party) *la14-16*. **2** hold firmly **to**; consent, assent **to** (some purpose etc) *15-e16*.

~**ance &c** adherence; *collective* adherents *15-e16*. ~**and** *la15-e16*, **anerdar** *15-e16* an adherent. [only Sc; OF *enherdre*]

anidder *see* ANITHER

aniest *see* ANEIST

anis *see* AINCE

anist *see* ANEIST

anither; anidder &c [ə'nɪðər; *Sh Abd* ə'nɪdər; *Abd* ə'nʌdər] *adj, pronoun* = another *19-*.

anker *n* a liquid or dry measure *18-e20*, *chf Sh N*. [Du, Dan]

ankersaidil &c; hankersaidil *e16 n* an anchorite, hermit *16-e17*. [OE *ancersetl* a hermit's cell]

ankerstock *see* ANCHOR-STOCK

anklet *19*, **ankleth &c** *15-16* [*'aŋklɛt, *'aŋklɛθ] *n* the ankle. [only Sc; ME *ankle* + LITH a limb; *cf* ON *ökla-liðr*, Dan *ankel-led*]

anly *see* ANELY

ann¹ &c *n* = awn, beard of barley etc *e20*, *local*. [see SND]

ann² *n* = ANNAT 1, *17-18*. [only Sc; short for ANNAT or next]

anna; annay *n* = ANNAT 1, *la15-e16*. [only Sc; F *année*, laL *annāta*]

annalzie *la16-e18*, **analy** *15-16*; **an(n)ale** *la15-16* [*ə'nel(j)ɪ] *vt* transfer to the ownership of another; alienate *15-e18*. [unexplained var of Eng *alien*, but see DOST *aly*]

annat &c *n* **1** *law* the first half-year's (*or orig* year's) income of a benefice legally due to the executors of the deceased previous incumbent *16-18*. **2** *also in pl* = annates, the first year's revenue of a see etc paid to the Pope *la16*. [laL *annāta*; *cf* ANN², ANNA]

annay *see* ANA, ANNA

annere *see* ANHERD

annex *n* **1** *law, of property* an appurtenance, *freq* ~ **and connex** *16*, *only Sc*. **2** = annex.

anniversar &c [*anɪ'vɛrsar &*c*] *adj* yearly, annual *15-16*.

n a mass said annually on the anniversary of a person's death; payment for this *15*. [only Sc; L *anniversārius*]

annual *adj* = annual *18-*.

n, law an annual payment of rent, quit-rent, duty or interest *la14-19*.

~ **rent 1** = annual rent *15-*. **2** interest on money *17-20*, *only Sc*. [ME; laL *annuālis*; *cf* ANNUEL]

annuel &c *adj* see comb below.

n **1** = ANNUAL *n*, *15-e17*. **2** interest on money *la16-e17*, *only Sc*.

~**lar** one who receives an annual rent *la16*.

~ **rent** = annual rent (ANNUAL) 1 (*15-16*), 2 (*17*). [ME, OF; laL *annuālis*]

anonder *see* ANUNDER

anouch *see* ENEUCH

anower *see* INOWER

anse *see* ENSE

ansenȝe; anseinȝie &c *la16-e17*, **ansinyie &c** *16-e17*, **anscheinȝe &c** *la16-e17* [*an'sinjɪ, *-'sɪnjɪ, *-'sɪnjɪ, *-'senjɪ, *-'ʃinjɪ, *-'ʃɪnjɪ, &*c*] *n* = ENSENȝE 1 (*16-e17*), 2 (*la14-16*). [only Sc; OF *ansigne*, var of *enseigne*; *cf* HANDSENȝE]

anshent *see* ANCIENT

ansinyie *see* ANSENȝE

answer &c; answeir &c *la14-e17*, **awnswer &c** *15-e17* [*'answir, *'ansur, *an'swir, *-'swer &*c*] *n* = answer *la14-*.

vti **1** = answer *la14-*. **2** obey, respond to the commands of (an authority): (1) *vt, la14-*, *now Sh Ork NE*; (2) *vi*, ~ **to** (a person) *la15-16*. **3** *vt* requite, compensate (a person) *16*. **4** *vt* = SUIT¹ *v* 7, *e20*: 'I always answered pink'.

ant *see* AUNT

antecestor &c *n* = ancestor *16-17*, *only Sc*. [conflation of Eng *antecessour* and *ancestor*]

antefit &c *n* some item of clothing, *prob* part of a hat etc *e17*.

antepend *n, church* a veil or covering for the front of the altar *16*. [only Sc, MedL *antependium*]

anter &c, **aunter &c** *vtir* = adventure *la14-e19*.

antrin &c *la19-e20 adj* **1** occasional, chance, single, odd *la18-*. **2** odd, peculiar, strange *20-*, *literary*. *n* an occasional one *la19-e20*.

~**cast** a misfortune, a mischance *la18-e19*, *chf N*.

Antiburgher *n* a member of that section of the Secession Church (SECEDE) which separated *e18* from the rest of the membership over the question of taking the *burgess oath* (BURGESS) *la18-e19*; *cf Burgher* (BURGH).

antle *vti, also* ~ **on** keep on repeating a complaint, nag, grumble *20*, *Cai Dmf*. [*cf* ON *annt* eager, anxious; pressing]

antrin *see* ANTER

antrum &c *n* the afternoon, early evening; the meal taken at that time *19-e20*. [see SND]

anunder &c *19-e20*, **anonder &c** *la16-e19* [ən'ʌn(d)ər] *prep* under, beneath. [eME *an under*; perh also *in* + *under*]

anxeeity *n* = anxiety *19-*, *now Ags*.

apairt, apart [ə'pert] *adv* = apart *16-*.

apane *see* APAYN

apardon &c; aperdon &c *16* [*a'pardun, *a'pɛrd-, *-ən] *vt* **1** pardon, forgive (a person)

16-e17. **2** make allowances for, excuse *16-e17.*
3 forgive (a person) for (some offence) *la16-e17.*
[only Sc; *a-* + Eng *pardon*]
apart *see* APAIRT
apayn; apane [*a'pen] *adv* by chance, possibly
la14-e16.
~ **of** on pain of, under the penalty of *15.*
[only Sc; OF *a peine* in or with difficulty]
apen *see* OPEN
aperdon *see* APARDON
Aperell *see* APRILE
apert [*a'pɛrt] *adj* **1** = apert, open; bold
la14-16. **2** *of actions* performed openly and
boldly *la14-e15.*
apiece *see* ALBUIST
apill *see* AIPPLE
apin *see* OPEN
apirsmart &c [*apər'smart, *-'smɛrt] *adj*
sharp, severe *e16.* [F *âpre*, OF *aspre* + *smart*
(SMAIRT)]
aple *see* AIPPLE
apo, apon *see* UPON
aporte &c; apport &c *15-16* [*a'port] *n* bearing, demeanour *la14-e16.* [F *aport*]
apostol &c *la14-e17*; **apostil &c** *la14-16* *n* =
apostle.
apotheck *see* HYPOTHEC
apothicar &c *la16-e18,* **apothecar &c** *15-17,*
ipothecar &c *16-e17*; **apotecar &c**
la16-e17, **ipoticar &c** *16-e17* [*a'poθɪkər,
*-'pot-, *ə-, &c] *n* = apothecary. [OF
apot(h)ecaire, laME *apotiquare,* laL *apothēcārius; cf*
HIPOTHECAR, *pothecar* (POTICARY)]
appail *see* APPELL
apparaling &c; **apperrelling &c**
[*a'parəlɪŋ] *n* **1** = apparelling *la15-e17.* **2**
equipment; attire *la14-e17.*
appearance, apperance &c *15-17* *n* =
appearance *15-.*
be ~ seemingly, in appearance *la15-16, only Sc.*
enter ~ signify one's intention of defending an
action in the *Court of Session* (SESSION) or the
Sheriff Court (SHERIFF) *20-.*
appearingly *see* APPERAND
appell &c *15-e19,* **appele &c** *la14-e17*; **appail**
&c *la16, la19* [ə'pil, *ə'pɛl, *ə'pel] *vti* = appeal
la14-19.
n = appeal *la15, 19.*
append &c [*a'pɛnd] *vt* attach (a seal) to a document *la15-16.* [earlier in Sc; L *appendere; cf*
next]
appense [*a'pɛns] *vt* = APPEND *la15-16.* [OF
appenser, or L *appens-,* ptp stem of *appendere*]
apperance *see* APPEARANCE
apperand &c *la14-17,* **apperant &c** *la15-17,*
appering &c [ə'pirənt, -ən; *a'pirand]
16-e20 presp, adj = apparent *la14-18.*
~**ly** [*Abd* ə'pirəntlɪ], **appearingly &c** *adv* =
apparently, evidently, obviously *la15-, now NE.*
~ **air** heir apparent *la14-17.* [SND *apparand*]
apperrelling *see* APPARALING

appeteet &c *17-19,* **appety &c** *19-e20,* **appe-**
tite &c [*'apətit, 'apətɪ] *n* = appetite *la14-.*
appetized &c *adj* having an appetite, hungry
la18-e19. [F *appétissant*]
appety *see* APPETEET
appil *see* AIPPLE
appin *see* OPEN, HAPPEN
applese &c; apples &c *la15* [*a'pliz] *vt*
please, gratify, propitiate; content, satisfy
la15-e17. [ME (rare) *apleyse;* see OED]
apply &c *vti* **1** = apply *la15-.* **2** *vt* attach (*esp*
oneself) **to** (a person, party etc) *15-16.* **3** *vi*
incline, be inclined *la15-16.*
apponct *see* APPUNCT
appoint &c *ptp, adj* = appointed *la16-e17.*
appone *see* OPPONE
apport *see* APORTE
appose *see* OPPOSE
appraiser *n, law* a person appointed to value
goods which are the subject of a *poinding*
(POIND) *19-.*
appreciate *see* APPRETIATE
appreciation *see* APPRETIATION
apprehend &c *vt* **1** = apprehend *la15-.* **2**
come upon, find (a person) *la15-e17, only Sc.* **3**
find and seize (goods etc); get or lay hold of as a
legal act *la15-17.*
appreiff *see* APPREVE
appretiate *18,* **appreciate** [ə'prisɪet,
ə'priʃɪet] *vt, ptp also* **appreciate** *e16* **1** *law*
appraise, value *16-18.* **2** = appreciate.
appretiation, appreciation *law* the valuing
of *poinded* (POIND) goods *la18-e20.*
appreve &c *la14-16;* **apprive &c** *15-16,*
appreiff &c *la15-16* [*a'priv] *vti, ptp*
approven &c *16-19* [ə'prov(ə)n] = approve.
[ME *apreve,* OF *appreuve; cf* APPRUVE]
apprise &c [ə'praɪz] *vt* **1** *lit and fig* appraise, estimate the worth of, value, appreciate *16-.* **2**
law value and sell (a debtor's land) to pay off
the debt *16-e19, only Sc.* [ME (rare); OF
apriser]
apprive *see* APPREVE
approbate &c ['aprobet] *ptp* = approbate,
approved *16.*
vt, see phrase below.
~ **and reprobate** ['rɛprobet] assent to part of
a deed and object to the rest (a course disal-
lowed by law) *la18-.*
appropir &c; **appropry** [*a'propər,
*a'propraɪ, *a'proprɪ] *vt* assign or make over in
possession or property **to** (a person etc); appropriate *la15-16.*
approprit proper or peculiar **to**, appropriate
to *la15-16.* [ME *appropre,* OF *approprier*]
approve *see* APPRUVE
approven *see* APPREVE
appruve &c *15-, now Sh,* **approve &c** *la14-*
[ə'prøv] *vti* = approve. [*cf* APPREVE]
appunct &c *15-16,* **apponct &c** *la15-e17;*
appunt &c *la15-16* [*a'pʌn(k)t] *vt* =
appoint.

~(ua)ment an appointment *la15-16.* [only Sc; MedL *appunctuare; cf* next]

appunctuat *ptp* fixed by agreement, appointed *la15-16.* [only Sc; MedL *appunctuat-,* ptp stem of *appunctuare; cf* prec]

appunt *see* APPUNCT

appurvay [*apʌr've] *vt* provide, supply *la14.* [OF *apourveir*]

Aprile &c, Aprill &c, Aperell &c *la15-16;* **Apreill &c** *17-e18* [ə'prəil; *a'prɪl, *apə'rɪl, *-'rəil] *n* = April *la14-.*
April(e) errand an errand on which an April fool is sent *18-, Sh-Fif WC.* [ME; L *aprīlis; cf* AVERIL]

aprin *19-e20, NE,* **aproun &c** *16;* **apron &c** *16-,* **awpron &c** *la19-e20, N* ['epron; *N* 'aprən] *n* **1** = apron *16-.* **2** *plumbing* a strip of lead folded over the edge of a gutter etc to conduct rain-water into it *19-.*

apud acta ['apʌd 'akta] *law, of notices etc given in open court* during the proceedings *la15-.* [L]

aqua *see* ACKWA

aqual *see* EQUAL

aquavita *e18,* **aquavite &c** *la15-e18;* **aquavitae** *la16-* **accavite &c** *e17* ['akwa'vite, 'akwə-, ak(w)a'vɪtɪ, -'vəitɪ] *n* = aquavitae, spirits; *specif* WHISKY *la15-.*

ar *see* AIR[3]

arace; arrace, arrais &c [*a'res] *vt* = arace, pull up or out, snatch away, tear down *15-16.*

arage *see* AVERAGE

araise *see* ARISE

arbiter[1] **&c** *n, law* a person chosen or appointed to decide in a dispute between parties, an arbitrator *la15-.* [L]

arbiter[2] *n* will, pleasure; arbitration *la15-16.* [ME, OF *arbitre,* L *arbitrium*]

arbitral &c, arbitrale *adj, law* of, belonging to, made or pronounced by an ARBITER[1], *chf* **decreet &c** *or (latterly)* **decree** ~ *la15-.* [F; laL *arbitralis*]

arbitrar *adj* = ARBITRAL *la16-17.* [only Sc; OF *arbitraire,* L *arbitrārius*]

arch [*artʃ] *n* = ARK[1] *la15-16.* [eME; OF *arche,* L *arca*]

archedene &c, archidene &c, ersedene &c *la14-e16* [*'artʃ(ɪ)'din, *-'den, *ars-, *ɛrs-] *n* = archdeacon *15-e17, only Sc.*

archibischop &c [*'artʃɪ'bɪʃəp &c*] *n* = archbishop *la15-e17.*

archidiacone [*'artʃɪ'daɪakon] *n* = archdeacon *15-16.* [only Sc; L *archidiaconus̜*]

archidene *see* ARCHEDENE

archly *see* ERGH

archpriestrie &c *n* the office of head priest (at Dunbar) *la16-e17, only Sc.*

are [*er] *vti* = EAR[2] *16-e19.* [perh after L *arāre*]

are *see* AIR[1], AIR[3], AIR[5], AIRE

a'ready *la19-,* **alreddy** *la16-e17;* **alrady** *la16-e17* [ɑ'rɛdɪ, ə'rɛdɪ; *'al-; *-'radɪ] *adv* = already.
alreadies, areddies &c = *adv, 20-.*

arear, arere &c *la15-16* [*a'rir, *ə-] *adv* **1** *freq fig* backwards *la15-16.* **2** *orig fig* behind, in the rear or background *la15-19.* [ME *arear* behind, OF *arere*]

areddies *see* A'READY

areke [*a'rik] *vti* reach *e16.* [ME *areche,* OE *arǣcan*]

arer *see* HEIR

arere *see* AREAR

aret [*a'rɛt] *vt* accuse *la14-15.* [OF *aretter; cf* ME *arette* reckon]

argentar &c; argenteir &c *n* a royal officer having charge of money belonging to the king or queen *16.* [L *argentārius,* F *argentier*]

argentie &c *n, chf attrib* a kind of fabric *la16-e17.* [only Sc; appar F *argenté* silvered, or *argentif* silvery]

argh *see* ERGH

argie &c *20-,* **argu &c** *la14-16;* **argue &c** *15-* ['argɪ; 'arg(j)u] *vti* **1** = argue *(in form* **argie** *usu implying contention) la14-.* **2** *vt* accuse (a person) *la14-16.* **3** call in question *15.*
n an assertion *19-.*

argie-bargie ['argɪ'bargɪ] *n* a quarrel, haggling *20-.* *vi* dispute, haggle *la19-.* **argifee, argufy** ['argɪfi, 'argɪfaɪ] argue *la18-e20.* **argle-bargain &c** [*'argl'bargən] *vi* dispute *18-19.* **argle-bargle** ['argl'bargl] *n* contention, dispute *la19-.* *vi* dispute *la19-.* **argle-barglous** quarrelsome *19-e20.* **argue-bargue** ['argjə'bargjə &c] *vi, orig inflected in both parts, now only in second element* = argue *la19-.* [*cf* ARGUN]

argown *see* ARGUN

argu(e), argufy *see* ARGIE

argun; argown [*'argun, *-ən] *vti* = argue (ARGIE) *la15-e17.* [only Sc; *-n* as in MINNON]

Argyll [ər'gəil, ar-] **the ~shire Highlanders** a Scottish regiment raised in 1794; linked in 1881 with *The Sutherland Highlanders* (SUTHERLAND) to form the ~ **and Sutherland Highlanders (Princess Louise's).** [the former county]

aricht &c [ə'rɪxt] *adv, chf verse* = aright, rightly *16-19.*

arise &c *vi, pt also* **araise &c** *16-e17* [*a'rez] = arise *16-.*

ark[1]**; airk** *la16-e20 n* **1** = ark *15-.* **2** a chest, *esp* a large one for storing grain etc *15-.* **3** an enclosure for confining or catching fish *18-19.*

ark[2] *n* the curved structure which carries the water off from a breast-shot mill-wheel; the waterway under a mill-wheel *la18-e20.* [prob f L *arcus* a bow > ModEng *arc*]

arle &c, arl, erle &c [arl; *WC* *ɛrl; *S* jɪrl] *n* **1** *in pl* earnest money *la15-e20.* **2** an earnest, a foretaste of something more to come *15-19.* *vt* **1** engage for service by payment of a sum of money *la14-19.* **2** secure a right to (something) by some preliminary action or service *la19.*

~ **penny** *etc 18-e19,* **arles &c penny** *la16-17* = *n* 1. [ME *erles,* appar f OF *erles*]

arm *see* AIRM
armie *see* AIRMY
armour *see* AIRMOUR
arn &c *la17-e20*, **alrone &c** *la15-e17* [arn; *alrən]* *n* = alder (tree). [ME *alloren*, OE *ælren* f *aler*; *cf* ALLER]
arnit; arnut &c *18-19*, **earnit &c** *19-e20* ['arnɪt; *Ayr Rox* ɛr-; *&c*] *n* an edible plant root, earth-nut *18-e20*, *in place-names 16-*.
swine ~ *see* SWINE. [OE *eorð-hnutu*; *cf* MDu *erde-noot*]
arr &c; aur &c *n* a scar, the mark left by a wound *19-e20*.
~(e)d marked with scars *la19-e20*. [ME *arre, erre*; ON *ørr*]
arrace *see* ARACE
arrage *see* AVERAGE
arrais *see* ARACE
arras &c *n* = arris, the sharp edge at the angle between two surfaces *19-e20*. [*cf* AWRIGE]
array &c *vt* **1** = array *la14-*. **2** adorn *la14-16*: 'my palace arayd with gold'.
arreenge [ə'rindʒ] *vti* = arrange *la19-*, *Sh N*.
arreist &c, arrest &c [ə'rist, *St* ə'rɛst] *n* = *la14-*.
vti **1** = arrest *la14-*. **2** *vt* cause to stop *la14-e17*. **3** *law* seize (property), apprehend (a person) by legal warrant *15-*.
~ee [arɛ'sti] *law* the person in whose hands the *arrestment* is laid *18-*. ~er *law* a person who arrests, *specif* one who under legal authority arrests MOVEABLE property belonging to his debtor which is in the hands of a third party *la15-e18*. ~ment *law* **1** the action of arresting, apprehending or seizing by legal authority *la15-*. **2** the seizing of a debt which is in the hands of a third party *19-*.
arriage *sĕe* AVERAGE
arridge *see* AWRIGE
arrie *see* AIRIE
arrour *see* ERROUR
arscap &c *la15*; **heirskap &c** *19-e20* ['erskap, -skɪp] *n* = *heirship* (HEIR). [appar MLowGer *arfskap*]
arschip *see* HEIR
arselins ['arslɪnz, 'ɛrs-] *adv* backwards *18-e19*. [see SND]
arset [*'arsət] *adv* backwards *19*. [reduced f obs Eng *arseward*; *cf ersit* (ERSE)]
art *see* AIRT[1], AIRT[2]
artaillery, artailliarie, artailʒe *see* ARTILʒERIE
artailʒeit [*ar'teljɪt] *adj* provided with artillery *16*. [OF *arteillé*, ptp of *artiller* provide with war-engines; *cf* ARTILʒERIE]
artailʒerie, artalʒerie *see* ARTILʒERIE
artation &c [*ar'tesɪun, *-teʃɪun, *-ɪən] *n* instigation, incitement *la15-e16*. [only Sc; L *artātio*]
artelʒerie *see* ARTILʒERIE
arth *see* AIRT[2]
Arthuris hufe &c *15-e17*, **Arthur's Oon**

17-, *now hist* [*'arθərz 'høv, *- 'øn] an ancient monument near the Roman Wall at Falkirk, demolished 1743, traditionally associated with King Arthur, so called because of its oven-like shape. [see DOST]
article &c; artikil &c *la14-16 n* **1** = article *la14-*. **2** a thing, iota, small portion of anything *la19-e20*.
Lords of (the) A~s *see* LORD.
articulat *ptp* expressed in words *la16*. [L *articulāt-*, ptp stem of *articulāre* articulate, utter distinctly]
artilʒerie *la15-e17*, **artaillery** *16-e17*, **artilʒere** *la15-16*, **artailʒe** *la15-e16*; **arta(i)lʒerie** *la15-e17*, **artailliarie** *la16-e17*, **artelʒerie &c** *16-17*, **artilʒie** *16* [*ar'tɪljərɪ, *al-, *-'tɛl-, *-'tɛl-, *-'til-; *'artɪljɪ, &c] *n* = artillery. [only Sc]
as[1] &c, is &c *16-*, *now Sh-EC* [az; *weak forms* əz, z, s] *adv, conj* **1** *also* **has &c** *la14-e17, only Sc* = as *la14-*. **2** as if *la14-e20*. **3** than *la16-20, Gen except N*. **4** (see etc) how *la16-e19*. **5** (so ..) that *17-18*: 'she sung sae loud as I might hear'. **6** such as *16*: 'except beneficis as ar at the gift of Sanctandris'.
relative pronoun that *la19-e20*: 'this is the man as told me'.
~sone = als(s)one (ALSE) *la16*.
~ of as regards, in respect or consideration of *la14-15*.
as[2] &c [as] *n* = ass *15-16*.
as *see* ASK[2], ASS
aschame &c *15-17*, **eschame &c** *la14-e17*; **ashame** *15-*, **escheme &c** *la14-16* [*a'ʃem, *-ə-] *v* **1** *vt, chf in ptp* = ashamed *15-*. **2** *vi* feel shame *15-e17*.
asche *see* ESH
Asch Wedinisday *see* ASK WEDINSDAY
aschaet *see* ESCHEAT
ascrive &c [*a'skraɪv] *vt* = ascribe *la15-17*.
aseth *see* ASSYTH
ashame *see* ASCHAME
asheer *see* ASSURE
ashet *n* **1** an oval serving plate, *esp* for a joint *18-*. **2** a pie-dish *20-*, *WC*. [only Sc; F *assiette* a plate]
ashypet *see* ASSIEPET
aside &c *adv* **1** = aside *16-*. **2** close by *la18-*.
prep beside; close to, in comparison with *la18-*.
asides *adv, prep* besides *20-*, *EC, SW, S*. [only Sc]
asine &c [*'asɪn] *n* an ass *16-e17*. [only Sc; OF *asine*, L *asina*]
ask[1]; awsk *el5*, **esk** *la16-e20* *n* a newt, eft *15-*. [nME *arske* (rare), OE *aðexe*]
ask[2] &c, as &c *la15-16*, **ax** *16* *vti, pt also* **ast** *15-16* **1** = ask *la14-*. **2** ~ **at** ask (a person) *15-*.
asklent &c; aslent *18* [ə'sklɛnt] *adv* aslant; aside, astray; askew *la16-e20*. [nME *on slent*; *cf* SKLENT[1]]

Ask-Wedinsday *16*; **As Wodinsday &c** *la16*, **Asch Wedinisday &c** *16-e17* *n* = Ash Wednesday.

aslar *see* AISLAR

asleep, asleip &c *la16* *adv* **1** = asleep *la16-*. **2** *law* of a civil action where no further step in procedure has been taken within a year and a day after it was first lodged *18-*; *cf* SLEEP, WAUKEN.

aslent *see* ASKLENT

asoond *la19-e20*, *Sh*, **asound** *17* [ə'sund; **ə's(w)un] *adv* = aswoon, in a faint. [var after SOUND³]

aspar &c [**ə'spar, **ə'spɛr] *adv* apart, with legs apart *17-e19*. [*a-* + Eng *spar* a crossbar]

asperans &c [**'aspərans] *n* = esperance, hope *la15-16*.

asposit [**a'spozɪt] *adj* disposed *la15-16*, *only Sc*.

aspy &c [**ə'spaɪ] *vti* = espy *la14-16*.

aspyne &c *n* a ship's boat *la14*. [only Sc; ON *espingr*. DOST *espyne*]

ass &c *15-e20*, **as &c** *la15-e17*, **ess &c** *17-*, now *Sh*; **aise &c** *la16-e20* [as, es] *n* **1** = ash, ashes *la15-*. **2** *specif* wood ash, potash *15-e17*.

~ **hole, assole** *e20*, *local* a place below or in front of the grate, or a hole outside the house, for ashes *19-e20*. ~ **midden** an ash-heap *19-*, now *NE*.

assaill &c [**a'sel] *n* assault, attack *la14-16*. [earlier in Sc; OF *assaille*]

assailʒe; assalʒe &c *la14-e16*, **asseilʒe** *16* [**a'sel(j)ɪ] *vti* = assail *la14-e17*.

assailʒeour &c assailant *la14-16*. [only Sc; OF *asaillir*]

assalt &c; **assaut &c** *la14-45* [**a'sɑt] *n* = assault *la14-16*.

assalʒe *see* ASSAILʒE

assassor *see* ASSESSOUR

assay &c *la14-17*, **essay &c** *la16-17* [**a'se, **ə-] *n* **1** = assay *la14-*. **2** a demonstration of ability, capacity or acquired skill *16-e17*.

assedat *see* ASSIDAT

assedation &c, assedatioun &c *la15-16* *n*, *law* the act of letting or assigning on lease; a lease *15-e19*. [only Sc; MedL *assedatio*, f *assedare* > ASSIDAT]

asseer *see* ASSURE

asseilʒe *see* ASSAILʒE

assembly &c, assemblé &c *la14-e17* [a'sɛm(b)lɪ, **asɛm'bli] *n* **1** = assembly *la14-*. **2** *church* (1) a meeting of a congregation or *kirk session* (KIRK) *la16*. (2) = *General Assembly* (GENERAL) *la16-*. **3** a muster of armed men *la15-16*, *only Sc*.

Asserian *see* ASSIRIEN

assessour &c; assassor &c *la16* *n* = assessor *la15-17*.

asseth *see* ASSYTH

asseur *see* ASSURE

assidat, assedat *vt*, *freq in ptp*, *law* let, leased *16-e17*. [only Sc; MedL *assedat-*, ptp stem of *assedare* assign; *cf* ASSEDATION]

assiepet; ashypet ['asɪ'pɛt, 'aʃɪ-] *n*, *usu attrib* a scullery-maid *19-e20*. [see SND and *cf* Dan *askepot* a Cinderella]

assigna &c; assignay &c [**?a'sɪgne, **a'sɪ(ŋ)ne] *n* = assignee *15-17*.

assignation &c *n* **1** *law* an assignment of a right or rights; the INSTRUMENT by which this is done *la15-*. **2** = assignation.

assilag *n* the stormy petrel *la17-19*. [Gael *asaileag*]

assiltree *see* ASSLE-TREE

Assirien; Asserian &c [**a'sɪrɪən &c] *n* = Assyrian *16*.

assise *see* ASSIZE

assist *vti* **1** = assist *15-*. **2** *vi* assent, agree **to** (an opinion etc) *16*. **3** take sides **with**, agree **with** *16-e17*.

assith *see* ASSYTH

assize *18-*, **assise &c** *la14-e18*; **asyse &c** *la14-e18*, **essyis** *la16-e17* *n*, *chf law* **1** = assize *15-*. **2** a trial by jury; a jury *la14-*, *only Sc*. **3** *attrib* of articles or payments subject to some regulation, tax etc *16-*.

assizer &c *e18*, **assisour &c** *15-e18* a juryman.

~ **herring** a royalty of herring due to the king from boats engaged in the herring fishing *16-e18*, *only Sc*.

grete ~ an assize consisting of 25 nobles or gentlemen appointed to try charges against an ordinary assize *15-16*.

assle-tree &c *18-e20*, **assiltre &c** *16-e17* *n* = axle-tree, an axle. [ME *axeltree*; *cf* AIX-TREE]

assle-tuith *see* AISLE-TUITH

associate, associat &c *la16-17* *adj* **1** = associate *16-*. **2** *specif* in titles of various sects of the *Secession Church* (SECEDE), *eg* **A~ Presbytery, General A~ Church** *18-e19*.

assoilzie &c *18-e20*, **assoilʒe &c** *la14-17*; **assolʒe &c** *la14-e18*, **assoly &c** *15-e18* [ə'soil(j)ɪ; **?a'søl(j)ɪ] *vtir* **1** = assoil, absolve *la14-16*. **2** *law* decide in favour of (the *defender* (DEFEND)) in an action, acquit of a charge *la15-*. **3** *vr*, *law* absolve oneself *16-19*.

assole *see* ASS

assoly, assolʒe *see* ASSOILZIE

assonʒe *see* ESSONʒE

assover &c [**a'sʌvər] *vti* = ASSURE *la14-e16*. **~ance &c** = assurance **2** (ASSURE) *la14-e16*. [only Sc; *cf* SOVER]

assume &c *vt* **1** = assume *la15-*. **2** levy, collect as a due (from ecclesiastical property) *la16*, *only Sc*.

assumption &c 1 = assumption (into heaven) *la14-16*. **2** the action of assuming or taking on *la15-*. **3** the collecting **of** (the *thirds of benefices* (THIRD)) *la16*, *only Sc*.

assure &c, asseer *la19-*, *NE* **asseur &c** *la15-16*, **asheer** *la19-*, *NE* [**a'sør &c; NE ə'sir, -ʃir] *vti* = assure *la14-*.

assurance &c 1 = assurance *la16-*. **2** a guarantee of safety or immunity; a safe-conduct *la14-e17*. **3** certification; guarantee by act or statement *la16*. [*cf* ASSOVER]

assyth &c, assith &c; as(s)eth &c *la14* [*n* *a'sɛθ, *a'sɪθ, *a'sɔiθ; *v* ə'saɪð; *a'sɛθ &c] *n* satisfaction, reparation, compensation *la14-15*.

v **1** *vt* (1) satisfy; compensate (a person) *la14-*, now only hist. (2) *freq* ~ **of** (the amount at issue) *la14-e16*: '*fullely assythit of the said fowrty pond*'. (3) *with double object*, *la14-e15*: '*till assytht thame thare yharnyng*'. **2** pay, make payment of (a sum) *15-e16*. **3** *vi* pay compensation *15*.

~**ment** [ə'sɔiθm(ə)nt] **1** compensation for loss or injury by payment; reparation, indemnification *la15-*, now only hist. **2** satisfaction other than financial *16*. [nME *asith*, ME *aseth*; OF *aset* (*n*), var of *asez* enough, f laL *ad satis*]

ast *see* ASK²

astabill &c [*ə'stebl] *vt* = estable, establish *e16, only Sc*.

astarn *19-*, **astern &c** *la16-* *adv* **1** = astern *la16-*. **2** *fig* in debt, insolvent *la20-*, local *Sh-Ayr*.

asteep [ə'stip] *adv* lay *or* set one's brain(s) ~ make a mental effort, think hard *la19-*. [only Sc; *a-* + STEEP]

asteer *la18-*, **asteir** *16*; **astir** *19-* [ə'stir, *St* ə'stɪr] *adv* in a commotion, up and about, stirring *16-*. [*a-* + STEER¹; *cf* Eng *astir 19-*]

astent *see* EXTENT

astern *see* ASTARN

astir *see* ASTEER

astler *see* AISLAR

astonait &c [*ə'stʌneɪt] *ptp* = astonied, astounded, astonished *15-16*.

astonist &c, estonist &c; astonisit &c [*ə'stʌnɪst] *ptp* = astonished *16, only Sc*.

astragal &c *n* a glazing bar in a window *19-*. [*cf* Eng = a moulding on a column]

astrenʒe [*a'strinʒɪ] *vt* = astrain *la15-e16*.

astrict *la16-*, **astrick &c** *16-e17* *vt* **1** = astrict, restrict *la16-*. **2** bind legally, *orig also* by a moral obligation *16-*.

~**ion** *law* a bond, obligation *16-e20*. ~(**it**) **multures** MULTURES to which a mill is entitled from the tenants of certain lands *la16-17*. [L *astrict-*, ptp stem of *astringere* bind]

astrolog &c [*'astrolog] *n* an astronomer, an astrologer *la14-16*. [F *astrologue*, L *astrologus*]

astuce [*a'støs] *adj* astute *e16*. [only Sc; OF *astuce*, L *astūtus*]

As Wodinsday *see* ASK WEDINSDAY

asyse *see* ASSIZE

at¹ &c *prep* **1** = at *14-*. **2** *with verb of asking* (*cf* ASK²) from *la14-*. **3** (1) beside, with, in the presence of (a person) *15-17*. (2) within reach of (so as to thrash etc); meddling with, hurting *19-*: '*Who was at ye?*' (3) be ~ someone about something talk to a person about a thing; try to get someone's support or consent with regard to something; keep finding fault with, tease someone *20-*. **4** in the direction of,

towards, against, in contact with *la14-16*. **5** *used after nouns expressing anger, ill-will, objection(s) etc* *la18-*: '*few can keep anger at a bairn*'. **6** *used after vt* implying continued or repeated action *19-*; *cf* AT²: '*so a' the lads are wooing at her!*'

~ **onesel 1** in one's right mind; in a calm state *la17-*, now *NE SW Uls*. **2** healthy, flourishing *19-e20*. **what are ye at?** *etc* what do you mean? *19-*.

at² *adv*, *used after verbs* expressing **1** continuance of action = on *e20*, S: '*lauch at!*'; **2** energetic action *e20, Sh Ork*: '*he was layan at for a he was worth*'. [perh w infl f ON, *eg* ON *leggja at* attack; *cf* AT¹ 6]

at³, *unstressed* **it** *19-*, now *NE Ags*, *relative pronoun* = that: **1** *in gen*, *la14-*; **2** *with possessive expressed by various circumlocutions*: (1) *followed by possessive adj*, *la19-*: '*the crew at thir boat wis vrackit*'; (2) ~ o't &c *la19-*: '*the scheip at the tail o't was cuttit off*'. *conj* = that *la14-*. [nME, appar reduced f ME *that*, perh w infl f ON *at*; *cf* THAT]

at *see* THAT

atcheson &c, achesone &c [*'atʃəsən, *'etʃ-] *n* a silver-coated copper coin of low value *17*. [f surname of Thomas Achesoun, master of the mint 1581-1611]

ate *see* AIT

aten *see* EAT

athe *see* OATH

atheen [ə'θin] *prep* above *e20, NE*.

athegither &c ['αðɪ'gɪðər &c] *adv* = altogether *19-*. [*cf* THEGITHER]

ather *see* AITHER, ITHER

athill &c *adj* noble *la15*. [ME *athel*, OE *æðele*]

athin *e20, Sh Ork; ithin* *la19-*, now *Sh* [ə'θɪn] = within. [*cf* WITHIN]

athist *see* ADIST

Athole &c brose *etc* ['aθəl 'broz] *n* honey (or meal) mixed with WHISKY *la18-*, *chf Highl*. [see SND]

Atholl Crescent ['aθəl &c 'krɛsənt] informal name for the Edinburgh College of Domestic Science *20*. [sited in Atholl Crescent 1891-1970]

athoot *la19-* *prep*, *also* **ithoot** *la19-*, *Sh-nEC*, **thout &c** *19-*, now *C* [(ə)'θut] = without *19-*. *adv* outside *20-*. *conj* unless *20-*. [*cf* WITHOOT]

athort &c; athourt &c *la15-e16* [ə'θort; *ə'θurt; &c] *prep* **1** across; from one side of (a place or thing) to the other *la15-*. **2** (1) across in various directions; to and fro over; all over *16-*. (2) abroad through, among *la16-*. *adv* across in various directions, all over, about *16-*. [*a* + THORT]

athraw [ə'θrα] *adv* awry *la18-e20*. [*a-* + THRAW]

atour &c; attouir &c *la15-16*, **attower &c** *18-e20* [ə'tʌur; *law* (*erron*) ə'tur] *prep* **1** across; (down) over; out of; above; beyond *la14-*, now *law*. **2** *of degree, number etc* (1) above, more

than *la14-17*; (2) besides, in addition to *la15-e19*; (3) beyond (a certain time); after (a date) *la14-e17*. **3** in violation of *la14-e17*. *adv* **1** all over, everywhere *15-e16*. **2** farther off or out; back; away; across; over; out; apart *la16-e20*. **3** besides, over and above *15-e20*. **4** *introducing a further statement* (**and**) besides, (**and**) moreover *15-16*.
by and ~ *see* BY. [only Sc; appar f AT[1] + OWER or *out* + OWER; *cf* OUT OWER]

attachiament &c [*a'tatʃɪəmənt, *ə'tetʃ-] *n* = attachment, apprehension, seizure *15-e17*. [MedL *attachiamentum*]

attane *see* ATTEEN

attanis *see* AINCE

atteal &c, **atteil** &c [*?a'til, *?ɑ-] *n* a species of wild duck *la16-19*. [only Sc; obscure]

atteche &c [*a'titʃ] *vt* = attach, accuse, arrest *la15-e17*.
~**ment** attachment, summons, arrest *16-e17*. [only Sc; OF *atiech-*, var of *atach-*, attach]

atteen *la16-*, *now Sh*, **attene** &c *la14-17*, **attane** &c *la15-16* [ə'tin] *vti* = attain *la14-*, *now Sh*.

atteil *see* ATTEAL

attemp &c, **attempt** &c *n*, *vti* = attempt *16-*.

attemptat &c [*?a'tɛm(p)tat, *?a'tɛnt-] *n* an attempt involving violence or wrong; an outrage *la14-e17*. [OF; MedL *attemptatus*]

attene *see* ATTEEN

attent [*a'tɛnt] *adj* = attentive *16*.
n attention *la15*.
attentfully *e16*, **attentlie** attentively *la15-16*.

attentik *see* AUTENTIK

attenuat *ptp* made thin or weak *e16*. [L *attenuāt-*, ptp stem of *attenuāre* make thin]

atter, attir *n* corrupt matter, pus *16-19*.
attery, attry &c **1** venomous, malignant *16*. **2** purulent, containing or exuding matter *la16-e20*. **3** (1) bad-tempered, spiteful, quarrelsome *e20*, *Cai*. (2) *of looks or appearance* grim, angry, forbidding *18-e20*. **4** *of weather etc* stormy, bitter *19-e20*. [eModEng, ME *atter*, OE *ātor* poison; *cf* ETTER]

attercap &c *la16-e20*, **attircop** &c *15-16*, **ettercap** &c *18-*, **ettercope** &c *la15-e16* *n* **1** a spider *15-*, *now local Sh-wLoth*. **2** a spiteful or venomous person *16-*, *now local Sh-Ags*. [ME *attercop*, OE *āttorcoppe*; *cf* NETTERCAP]

attingent [*a'tɪndʒənt] *adj* touching, being near or close in age or relationship *la16-e17*. [L *attingent-*, presp stem of *attingere* touch]

attir *see* ATTER

attircop *see* ATTERCAP

attolerance [*a'tolərəns] *n* toleration; permission *la16-17*. [only Sc; irreg f Eng *tolerance*]

attornay *see* ACTORNEY, ATTOURNAY

attouir *see* ATOUR

atto(u)rnay &c [*a'turne, *-'tʌrn-, *ak-] *n* the appointment of a legal representative or agent *15-e17*. [ME *atorné*, OF *atournée*]

attournay *see* ACTORNEY

attower *see* ATOUR

attrack [ə'trak] *vt* = attract *la19-*.

attry *see* ATTER

atwae; atwa *e19* [Dmf S ə'twe] *adv* in two *19-e20*. [OE *on twā*; *cf* ME *atuo*]

atweel [(ə)'twil] *adv* assuredly, certainly, indeed *la18-*. [prob orig short for *I wat weel*]

atween [(ə)'twin] *prep* (*la18-*), *adv* (*la19-*) = between.
~ **and** .. between this place or time, and that indicated *18-e20*: 'you'll be back this way atween and three months'. ~ **the een** before one's eyes; with one's own eyes; in the face *la18-e20*. ~ **hands** in the intervals of regular occupation; at intervals; in the meantime *19-*. ~ **whiles** between times *la19-*. [*cf* BETWEEN and AFORE, ANEATH]

atweesh; (**a**)**tweest,** (**a**)**tweesh**(**t**) [ə'twiʃ; Sh Kcb ə'twist; Ayr *also* twiʃ(t), ə'kwiʃ; Kcb twist] *prep* = betwixt, between *la18-*. [appar var of BETWEESH; *cf* ATWIXT]

atwixt [ə'twikst] *prep*, *adv* = betwixt, between *18-e20*. [*cf* ATWEESH, BETWIX]

aubirchoun *see* HABERSCHOUN

auch *see* ACH, AUCHT[1]

auchan; achan ['ɑxən] *n* a variety of pear *la17-19*. [f *Auchans House* (Ayr)]

auchen *see* AUCHTEEN

auchful [*'ɑxfəl] *adj* = awful *la14*. [irreg var; *cf* AWFU]

auchlet *see* AUCHT[1]

aucht[1] &c, **echt** *la16-*, **eght** &c *16-e18*, **eicht** &c *16-*; **acht** *la14-e16*, **auch** &c *la15-17*, **aicht** *20-*, **eight** *la18-* [ɑxt, ɛxt; Bwk Rox *also* əit] *numeral adj* **1** *also n* = eight *la14-*. **2** = eighth *la15-*.
~**een** &c **1** = eighteen *la14-*. **2** eighteenth *la15-17*. ~**eent,** ~**ent** &c eighteenth *16-*, *now Ork NE*. **auchlet** &c, **auchlot** [*'ɑxlət] a measure (of meal), one eighth of a BOLL, half of a FIRLOT *la16-18*. ~**some** &c, *chf* **eightsome** a group of eight persons or things, *freq attrib* of a dance, *esp* a REEL[1]; *latterly* the REEL[1] itself *16-*.
~**day** *adj* ordinary, everyday, typical of its kind *20-*, *chf NE*. *n* a common daily occurrence *20-*, *chf NE*. ~ **days** *freq treated as a sing* a week *16-*, *now local*: 'I'll be back again gin an aucht days'. **this** *or* **that day** ~ **days** this or that day week *la15-*, *now local Ork-Stlg*. **was** ~ **days** a week ago *18-*, *now local Ork-Stlg*. **echt-pairt** the eighth part of an inch *20-*, *local Abd-Kcb*.
a (**common**) **five aicht**(**s**) &c an average or ordinary person or thing *la19-*, *local*. [nME *acht* &c, ME *eyȝte* &c, OE *eahta*]

aucht[2]; acht *15-e20* [ɑxt; Rox ʌuxt] *n* **1** (1) property *la14-e18*. (2) applied to persons, with adjs of blame or (ironic) praise *la18-e19*: 'a bad aucht'. **2** possession, ownership, *chf* **in your** *etc* ~ *e15-e20*. [nME *auht* &c, eME *ahte*, OE *æht*]

aucht[3] &c, **aicht** &c *19-e20*, *Ork NE*, **aich** &c *19-e20*, *N*, **ya(u)cht** *la19-e20*, *NE*; **echt** &c

19-e20, NE [ɑxt; *NE* jɑxt; *Sh S* ʌuxt; *WC Pbls S* oxt; *Ork NE* ɛxt, ex(t)] *v* **1** *vt* owe, be owing *16-e20*. **2** *vi* be incumbent upon or due to a person; be owing **to** one *16*. **3** *also* **ought** &c (*la16-e20*), *3 pers sing pres freq without inflexion* own, possess *la16-e20*: '*fa aicht this?*' (cf *wha's aucht* (AWE²)).

~**and** *la16-17*, ~**in** &c *16-19 presp, adj* **1** *of money etc* owing, due *16-19*. **2** *of persons* owing, indebted in, having to pay *la16-17*. ~**ing** *n, only in pl* debts *la16*.

~ due and customary *la15-e16, only Sc.* [pt of AWE² used as pres; *cf* OCHT²]

aucht *see* AWE², OCHT¹

auchteen &c *la17-18*, **auchtand** &c *15-16*, **auchtad** *la15-e16*; **auchtane** *la15-16*, **a(u)chen** *la15-16* [*ˈɑx(t)and, -ˈən] *numeral adj* eighth, *esp* ~ **part** (of land etc) *15-18*. [nME *aghten*, ON **ahtande*; *cf* AUCHT¹]

auchteen *see* AUCHT¹

auctenty *see* AUTENTYFE

audiscence; addiscence [ˈɑdɪsəns] *n* attention, encouragement to speak *la19-e20, NE:* '*a gied her nae addiscence*'. [altered f *audience*]

auditour¹ &c; **auditor** *la16-* *n* **1** = auditor *15-*. **2** a judicial hearer **of** (complaints or suits) *15*.

A~ of the Court of Session *or* **of the Sheriff Court** an auditor who examines the accounts of EXPENSES (*n* 3) incurred in the respective courts *19-*. **lordis ~is** *see* LORD.

auditour² *n* an auditory; an audience *16*. [only Sc; L *audītōrium* > Eng *auditory*]

aufald *see* AEFAULD

augmentation &c, **augmentatioun** &c *la15-e17*; **agmentatioun** &c *la16-e17* *n* **1** = augmentation *15-*. **2** *specif, law* an increase in the amount of a periodical payment, *eg* a MINISTER's *stipend* (STEEPEND), rent *17-*.

augurian &c *adj* augural *e16*.

n an augur *e16*. [only Sc; f L *augurius* augural]

August &c; **Agust** &c *la16-17* *n* = August *la14-*.

Auhallomes *see* ALHALLOW

auld &c, **old** &c, **owld** &c *16-*, **ald** *la14-*, *in place-names la11-*; **aild** *16*, **aul** &c *la19-e20, chf NE* [ɑld; *N also* ɑl; *Sh Ork Cai Ross Arg* ʌuld; *Uls* ʌul(d)] *adj* **1** = old *la14-*. **2** *specif of persons of* olden times *15-16*: '*the ald Hebrew David*'. **3** (1) *of styles of dating* Old Style *15-*; see eg *Auld Yule* (YULE). (2) *in titles of civic officials* former, previous, ex- *la15-e19*: '*the office of old provost*'. **4** the same, usual *18-*: '*Pate will still be the auld man*'. **5** *indicating family relationships:* (1) great-*19*: '*auld uncle*'; (2) grand- *19-e20*: '*auld mither*'; (3) oldest *18-, now local:* '*auld brither*', '*auld son*'. **6** *in names for the Devil, 19-*: '*Auld Nick*', '*The Auld Ane*'. **7** *of bread* stale *la18-*.

n = old *la14-*.

~ **day** the day after a celebration, market etc, when only essential work is done *la19-e20, NE*. **auld-farrant** &c, **auldfarran** &c *la18-e20 adj*

1 old-fashioned; quaint *la18-e20; freq blended with 3*. **2** *of children or young people* having the ways or shrewdness of older persons; precocious *18-*. **3** (1) *of persons, their ways, sayings etc* sagacious, prudent, witty, ingenious *18-; freq blended with 1*. (2) *of proverbs etc* old and wise *la18-e20*. ~**-fashioned 1** = old-fashioned *20-*. **2** *of children or young people* = ~- *farrant 2, la19-*. **the Old Firm** Rangers and Celtic football teams considered together *20-*. **auld-gabbit** speaking an ancient tongue; ancient looking *e18*. **Auld Kirk** the established *Church of Scotland* (CHURCH), as distinguished from the *Free Church* (FREE) *19-e20*. **auld licht** *see* LICHT¹. **old man** southernwood *20-, Fif Edb Slk*. ~ **man's milk** a drink, a kind of egg-flip *18-e20*. **auld-mou'd** wise, wily, crafty *18-e19, chf NE*. **Auld Reekie** nickname for Edinburgh *18-*. ~**-tasted** musty *19-, now local Sh-Per*. **Old Town** name for the part of Edinburgh along the Castle ridge, so called since the building of the *New Town* (NEW) in the late 18th century. **auld warld** belonging to past time, old, antique; old-fashioned *18-*. **auld wife** *etc* **1** a rotating chimney-cowl *19-e20; cf* GRANNIE. **2** a fussy, gossipy man, an 'old woman' *20-*. **Auld Year** (always in contrast with NEW-YEAR) the previous year; the year that is about to end; the last few days of the year *19-*. **A~ Year's Day** *or* **Night** = HOGMANAY 1, *la19-*. ~ **young** middle-aged, mature *19-, now Sh*.

auld lang syne *see* LANG¹. **auld marriet** &c **man** a married man from the day after his marriage *la20-, local*. **A~ New Year's Day** New Years's Day (Old Style) *19-, now Sh Ork*. **in** (**the**) ~ *la16-e20*, **of the** ~ *la15-, now Ags* of old, formerly.

Aulin *see* ALAN

aum &c *la19-e20*, **alme** &c *la15-e18* *n* = alum *la15-e20*.

vt treat with alum, *esp* to cure (skins) *17-19*.

aumeril *n* an awkward stupid fellow *19-e20*. [unknown]

aumos *see* AWMOUS

aumry &c, **almery** &c; **amery** &c *16-e20*, **almorie** &c *16-e19*, **ambrie** *17-18* [ˈɑm(b)rɪ, *ˈalm(ə)rɪ] *n* **1** a cupboard, pantry, *usu* a separate piece of furniture made of wood *la15-e20*. **2** *fig* a clumsy, stupid person *19*. [ME *almary*, ultimately f L *armārium* a repository for *arma* utensils]

auncient *see* ANCIENT

aunt; ant *16-17*, **aynt** &c *la16-e17* [ant; **ant] *n* = aunt *15-*.

auntie 1 *familiar* = aunt *la18-*. **2** an unmarried woman who kept an inn etc; drink obtained in such an establishment *19*.

Auntie Beenie a rather old-fashioned looking woman *la20-, local C*.

aunter *see* ANTER

auntie *see* AUNT

aur *see* ARR

aurea *e20*; **aurrie** *19-e20* ['ɑrɪə, 'ɑrɪ] *n* = area, an open space.

austern &c [*'ɑstərn, *'ɑstrən; *Wgt* *'ʌustərən] *adj* = austere *15-e20*. [ME]

autentik &c; **attentik** &c *15-16*, **actentik** &c *15-e16* [*ɑ(k)'tɛntɪk, *a(k)-] *adj* = authentic *15-e17*. [ME; *cf* AUTENTYFE]

autentyfe &c, **auctenty** *e16* [*'ɑtɛntaɪv, *'ɑ(k)tɛntaɪ, *-ɪ] *adj* authentic *la15-e16*. [OF *autentif* &c, var of *autentique*]

authir *see* OWTHER

author, **owthor** &c *19-20*, **authour** &c *16-e17* ['ɑθər; *NE* 'ʌuθər] *n* **1** = author *16-*. **2** an informant, authority; instigator *16-e20*. **3** *law* a person from whom another derives his title, *eg* by sale or gift *18*.

autorise &c *vt* = authorize *la15-16*.

ava; awa *la18-e20* [ə'vɑ] *adv phr* **1** at all *la19-*. **2** of all *la18-e19*: 'warst ava'. [only Sc; *av* of + A'; *cf* F *du tout*]

avail &c *vti* = avail *la14-*.
n **1** = avail *15-*. **2** worth, value *la15-e19*. **3** an equivalent in value *16-17*: 'the saidis guidis or the availl thairof'.
to *etc* **the maist** *etc* ∼ at the highest possible price or rate *16-17*. **within the** ∼ within or below the proper value *la16-17*.

availlour *see* AVALOUR

availȝe &c; **avalȝe** &c [*'ə'veljɪ] *vti* = avail *la14-16*.
avalȝe que valȝe whatever might happen, come what may *la14*. [not in F; var of AVAIL corresponding to *vailȝe* (VAILL)]

avald *see* AWALD¹, AWALD²

avalour &c, **availlour** &c [*ʔə'valur, *-ər] *n* avail, value *16*. [only Sc; var of Eng *valour*]

avalȝe *see* AVAILȜE, VAILL

avance &c [*a'vans] *v* **1** = advance *la14-16*. **2** provide beforehand, advance (money) *16-e17*.

avantage &c [*avan'tedȝ, *a'vantedȝ] *n* = advantage *la14-16*.
at (**his** *etc*) ∼ in a position of superiority; having the upper hand *la14-16*.

avareis &c [*'avərɪs] *n* a duty on goods; a charge additional to the freight *16-e17*. [only Sc; OF *avaries*]

avay &c [*a've] *law*, *vi* speak or plead at law, present evidence *15*.
n an argument or plea advanced in court *15*, *only Sc*.
∼**ment** a legal declaration *15*. [ME *avay* &c, OF *avier* &c direct, instruct]

ave¹ &c [ɑv] *n* a small net used *chf* in herring-fishing *e20*. [obscure]

ave² &c [ev] *n* **in** *etc* **the** ∼ **o** on the point of *e20*, *Bnf Abd*. [Eng *eve*]

ave *see* AWE¹

avedent *see* EVIDENT

avenand &c; **avenant** &c *15-16* [*'avənand,

*-ant] *adj* convenient, agreeable; handsome *la14-16*. [nME; OF *avenant* presp of *avenir* befit]

aventure &c *la14-16*, **eventure** &c *16-e17*, *only Sc* [*'avəntər &c, *'ɛvənt-] *n* = aventure, adventure *la14-16*.
the wild aventuris &c dues levied on hazardous commercial undertakings *la15-16*. [*cf* ANTER, ADVENTUR]

aver *see* AIVER¹

average &c *la15-16*, **arage** &c *16-e20*, **arrage** &c *16-18*, **harrage** &c *la15-18*; **arriage** &c *la16-e17*, **harriage** &c *la15-18* [*'avəredȝ, *'aredȝ] *n* a feudal service of uncertain nature, *chf* ∼ **and carriage** &c. [OF *average*; MedL *averagium*]

Averil &c, **Averill** &c [*'avərɪl &c] *n* = April *la14-e20*. [ME, OF *Averil*; *cf* APRILE]

averill *see* AIVER¹

averin &c; **avern** &c *la19-e20* ['ev(ə)rən] *n* the cloudberry *la18-e20*, *chf NE*. [obscure]

avis *see* ADVEECE, ADVISE

avisandum; avizandum [avɪ'zandʌm] *n*, *law* further consideration *17-*. [gerund of MedL *avizare* consider; *cf* ADVISE *v* 4]

avise [*ə'vaɪz] *n* manner, fashion, style *16*. [appar alteration of Eng *wise* (*n*)]

avise *see* ADVEECE, ADVISE

avizandum *see* AVISANDUM

avow &c [*a'vu] *vti* **1** *vi* make a vow (to do .., or that ..) *la14-e19*. **2** *vt* undertake or promise (something) with a vow *la14-e17*.
n a vow *la14-e19*. [ME *avowe*, OF *avouer*, laL *votāre*]

aw *interj* = oh! *19-*.

aw *see* A', AWE¹, AWE²

Aw *see* I

awa &c, **away** &c [ə'wɑ; *sEC*, *S* ə'we] *adv* **1** = away: (1) *in gen*, *la14-*; (2) *freq in verbal combs*, *chf with verbal noun or ptp*, *la14-e18*; see below. **2** *with verb of motion* = on, along *la19-*: 'come awa to your bed'. **3** (1) dead *17-*. (2) wasted, reduced in flesh *la19-*: 'he's awa to skin and bane'.
interj expressing incredulity, surprise or (contemptuous) dismissal (of a person or concept) *19-*: 'awa wi ye!'
∼**biding** staying away *16-e17*. ∼ **cuming** &c departure *la16-17*. ∼**had** removed *15*: 'our gudis to be tane and away had'. ∼**led** &c carried off *la14-17*. ∼**-passing** departure *la16-e17*. ∼ **put** set aside, removed *15-16*. ∼**-putting** &c removal, suppression, abstraction *la15-17*. ∼**take** &c take away, carry off *la15-e18*. ∼ **frae** *followed by gerund* past; unable to *la19-*, *Sh N*: 'he wis awa fae speakin'. ∼ **i the heid** deranged, lunatic *19-*, *now Edb*. ∼ **wi 't** done for; broken in health; ruined; out of one's senses; lost; dead *19-*. **here**∼ hereabouts *la18-*. **there**∼ thereabouts *19-*. **where**∼ whereabouts *19-*. [*cf* WA²]

awa *see* AVA

awach [*'ə'watʃ] *vi* keep watch *e16*.

a wait; a wat &c *NE*, **awite** &c *chf NE* [ə'wat; *NE also* ə'wəit; *S also* ə'wet] assuredly, indeed, in truth, I'm sure *19-e20*. [*a* = I + WAT; *cf* ATWEEL]

awake *vti* 1 = awake, awaken *la15-*. 2 *vt* keep watch over *e16, only Sc.*

awal *see* AWALD²

awald¹ &c, **avald** &c, **yaval** &c *NE*; **awalt, aiwal** &c ['awəlt, 'awəl(d), 'avəl(d); *NE* 'javəl, 'ewəl, 'evəl; *Dmf* 'a(w)ul, jʌul] *adj (adv)* lying on one's back and unable to rise: 1 *chf of sheep, la18-e20*; 2 *of humans (also fig) esp when drunk or unconscious, la18-e20.*
vi, of a sheep tumble down backwards, fall and lie on its back *19-e20*. [see SND *awald²*]

awald² &c, **avald** &c, **yaval** &c *19-, Ork NE*; **awal** &c *17-18*, **awat** &c *la16-e20* ['awəl(d), 'awəlt, 'avəl(d), *'award; Ork NE* 'javəl; *Ags* 'awat, 'ewət; *Abd Lnk* *'ewəl] *adj, of a crop of grain, esp oats* grown for the second year on the same land: 1 *of the* INFIELD *16-18*; 2 *of the* OUTFIELD *and in gen, 16-e20.*
yaval broth second day's broth *la19-, NE.* [see SND]

awalk *see* AWAUK
awalt *see* AWALD¹
awan, awand *see* AWE²
awant [ə'want, ə'wɑnt] *adv* ~ **o** for want of *la19-, Abd sEC, WC.*
awanting *la19-e20*, **awantand** *la16* [ə'wantən, -'wɑnt-] *adj* lacking, missing: '*three letters are awanting*'. [chf Sc; *cf* AMISSING]
awar *see* AWAUR
a-wastle *e19, literary*, **awestill** &c *la15-16* [*ə'wastl, *ə'wɛstl] *prep* to the west of. [*a- + wastle* (WAST)]
awat *see* A WAIT, AWALD²
awauk &c, **awalk** &c *16-e17* [ə'wak] *vti* = awake, awaken *16-.*
~en = awaken *16-18.* [only Sc; see WAUK]
awaur *la19*, **awar** &c [ə'wɑr] *adj* = aware *17-e20.*
away *see* AWA
awayis *see* ALWAYS
awband *see* AWEBAND
awblaster &c *n* = alblastre, arbalest, a crossbow *15-e16.*
awe¹, **aw; ave** &c [ɑ; *NE* ɑv, ɑf; *Abd* jɑ] *n* a float-board on an undershot water-wheel *la16-e20.*
start-an-~ (wheel), startin ~ an undershot wheel *la19-e20, N.* [eModEng *awe* &c, F *aube; cf* YAAVE]
awe² &c, **aw** &c, **owe** *la17-*, **ow** *la17*, **yaw** &c *la19-, NE, only Sc* [ɑ; *N also* jɑ; *St* o] *vti, pt, ptp also* **aucht** &c *la14-17*, **acht** &c *la14-16*, **ocht** *la16-17*, [*ɑxt] 1 = owe *la14-.* 2 *vt* own, possess *la14-.* 3 *vi* have a claim or right, be entitled (to do or be something) *la14-17; cf* Eng *ought.*
adj, only **owe** [o] owing, due *19-, Gen except Sh Ork*: '*I'm owe 'im a shilling*'.

awan &c *16*, **awand** &c *15-17*, **awing** &c *la15-e20*, **awn** &c *19-e20*, **awnd** &c *la19-e20, S*, **owand** *la17*, **owne** &c *la17* ['ɑən, ɑn; *NE also* jɑn; *Rox also* ɑnd; &c] 1 *of persons* owing *15-e20.* 2 *of money* etc owing, due *15-e20.* **wha** *etc* **is, was** *etc* **aucht** &c *la16-e20 or* **awe** &c *la19-e20, local* who owns ..? [nME *aw*, OE *āgan*; see AUCHT³; *cf* AWN]
aweband, awband &c [*'a'band, *'abən] *n* a check, curb, restraint, deterrent *16-19.* [Eng *awe* + BAND¹ a bond]
awee [ə'wi] *adv* 1 a little while *la18-.* 2 to a small extent or degree, somewhat *19.* [A¹ + WEE]
aweel [ə'wil, ə'wɛl] *adv, used to introduce a remark, sometimes expressing agreement, resignation or submission* well *19-*: '*Aweel, Jamie, what think ye?*'
~ **a wat** &c assuredly *la18-19.*
aweers [ə'wirz] *adv (adj)* ~ **o** + *gerund* on the point of *19-e20, NE*: '*aweers o thinkin*'. [f on or in *weers* (WEER)]
awestill *see* A-WASTLE
awfu &c, **awfull** &c, **yafu** *19-e20, NE*; **awfy** *20-* ['ɑfə; *C* 'ɑfɪ; *N also* jɑfə; *C also* 'afɪ] *adj* 1 = awful *la14-.* 2 *as intensive epithet* shocking; lamentable; ugly; remarkable; difficult; very great *la18-.*
adv, chf with adj or adv, rare with verb very, extremely; very much *19-.*
awfully &c causing awe or dread *la14-16.* **an** ~ .. a great many .. *20-.* [*cf* AUCHFUL]
a'where *la19-*, **alquhare** &c *la14-e17*; **al(l)whair** &c *la14-e17* ['a'hwer; *'al'hwer] *adv* = all where, everywhere *la14-.*
our ~ over all, everywhere *la14-16.*
awid [ə'wɪd] *adj* eager, longing *la19-e20.* [f WUID²]
awin, awing *see* AIN
awite *see* A WAIT
awkward *19-*, **awkwart** &c *la15*, **ackwart** &c *16-*; **acquart** *e16 adv* = awkward, with a backward stroke *la15.*
adj 1 = awkward, ill-natured, hostile, oblique etc *la15-.* 2 *only* **awkward** obstinate *la19-, chf NE.*
awmerale *see* ALMERAL
awmous &c, **almous** &c, **alms** &c *15-*; **aumos** &c *19-e20* ['ɑməs; *'almus, *'alməs] *n* 1 = alms *la14-.* 2 a good deed; *ironic* one's just deserts *la15-19.*
almosar &c *la15-e17*, **almessar** &c *e16*, **almoussar** &c *la16-e17* = almoner. [nME *almus*, ON *almusa* = OE *ælmysse* alms; *cf* ALMS]
awn &c *n* = awn *la14-.*
~y *of grain* bearded *la18-e20, only Sc.*
awn *see* AIN, ANE³, AWE², OWN
awnd *see* AWE²
awnswer *see* ANSWER
awonder *v* 1 *vi* wonder, marvel *e16.* 2 *vt* astonish, surprise *e16.* [prob f ME]
awp *n* a bullfinch *e16.* [ME *alpe*]
awpron *see* APRIN

awrige; arridge ['arıdʒ] *n* the sharp angle of the ridge made by ploughing *19-e20, Gall.* [OF *areste* an edge, ridge; the backbone of a fish; L *arista* bones of a fish; *cf* ARRAS]

awsk *see* ASK[1]

awte &c *n* the grain of wood, rock etc; a flaw *19-e20, chf NE.* [perh f Gael *alt* a seam, joining]

ax *see* ASK[2], AIX

axes *see* AIXIES

axetree, axtré *see* AIX-TREE

ay[1]; ae [e] *interj* expressing surprise or wonder *19-e20.* [ME *ey*; *cf* ACH]

ay[2]; aye [aı] *interj (adv)* **1** = yes *la19-.* **2** *freq followed by a rebutting, strengthening or sarcastic statement 19-*: '*ay, it's a lang time*'. **3** *introducing a statement as a form of greeting, sometimes sarcastic* = hello, well there you are etc *19-*: '*Ay ay Souter!*' **4** *usu* ~ ~ just so, that's it *19-*. [Eng *aye*]

aye, ay; ey *17-e20* [əi] *adv* **1** always, continually; at all times *la14-.* **2** still; all the same *19-*.

~-**lestand** everlasting *la14-15.* ~ **and while** *law* until, during the time that *la15-19.* [ME *ay*, ON *ei*; *cf* ModEng *ay*]

ayer *see* AIRE, HEIR

aynd &c *la14-e20*, **ande &c** *la14-e15*, **end &c** *la16-e20, only Sc* [end] *n* breath *la14-e20, latterly chf Sh.*
vti breathe (on) *la14-16.* [nME *ande*, ON *ande (n), anda (v)*]

aynt *see* AUNT

ayont; ayon *20* [ə'jont; *Abd also* ə'jon] *prep (adv)* = BEYONT 1, 2, *la18-*.

ayr *see* AIRE

Ayrshire *n, also attrib* (one of) a breed of *chf* dairy cattle with reddish-brown and white colouring and turned-up horns *19-*.
~ **Lassie** *draughts* a set opening *la19.* ~ **needlework** fine needlework on muslin *19-, orig chf Ayr.* [the former county]

ayther *see* AITHER

B

ba¹ &c *17-*, **ball &c; baw** [bɑ; *bal] *n* **1** = ball *16-*. **2** football; *specif* **the** ~ the annual game of football *formerly* played in some areas on Shrove Tuesday *la19-*. **3** *chf* **the Ba** a game of handball (HAND) played on certain annual holidays in the BORDERS and in Ork *20-*.
ba'ing &c a game of football *la18-19, Abd.*
~**-cod** the scrotum *la15-e17.* ~**-grene** a GREEN¹ on which ball games are played *17.*

ba² &c *20-*; **baw** [bɑ] *vt* lull, hush (a child) to sleep *la16-.*
baw baw(s) *or* **beddie ba(s)** *child's word* bed; the act of going to sleep *la19-.* [prob imit of the lips in kissing]

baa &c, bae *16-18* [ba, *be, *bɛ] *vi* **1** = baa *la18-.* **2** speak in a bellowing or bleating tone, like a cow, sheep etc *la19-.*
n = baa *16-.*

bab *see* BOB¹, BOB²

babanquaw *see* BOB²

bab at *etc* **the bowster, babbity bowster** ['bab ət ðɪ 'bʌustər, 'bab o ðɪ ~, 'babətɪ ~] *n* **1** *also* **bob-at-the-bowster &c** an old country dance, finishing off a ball etc *19-, now Abd.* **2** a children's game differing according to district *e20.* [var of Eng *bob* + BOWSTER]

babby &c *n* = baby *16-e20.*

babie *see* BAWBEE

babord *17-e19*, **baburd** *16* [*'babørd, *-bərt] *n* larboard, port. [F *bâbord; cf* OE *bæcbord*, ON *bakborði*]

bachelor &c, bacheleer *19-e20*, **bachelere** *15-16* ['batʃə'lir, *'batʃlir, 'batʃ(ə)lər] *n* **1** = bachelor *la14-.* **2** *only* **bachelor** a third-year student at St Andrews or Glasgow University *18-19.*
bachelor's buttons *pan drops* (PAN¹) *20-, now local.*

bachle *see* BAUCHLE

back¹ *la15-*, **bak** *la14-e17* *n* **1** = back *la14-.* **2** the outermost boards from a sawn tree *la17-, now Bnf Ags.* **3** a backer, backing; support *la16-19.* **4** *mining and quarrying* a fault in a seam; a main, (almost) vertical joint by which strata are intersected *e19.*
v **1** *vt* put or force back; repress, harm *la15-16.* **2** *vti* = back *16-.* **3** address (a letter) *18-e20.* **4** *also* ~ **up** endorse (a folded document) *19-.* **5** *mining, also* ~ **out** throw coal along the face to the *roadhead* (ROAD) to be filled into TUBS *la19-, now Fif.*
adj late, behindhand; *fig* on the way down *19-.*
~**art(s) &c**, ~**wart(is)** = backward(s) *la14-, only Sc.* ~**fu** as much as can be carried on one's back, a back-load *19-e20.* ~**ie** *n* a hoist on the back; a piggy-back *la19-, local.* ~**in(g) 1** providing with a back; material for this *la16-e17.* **2** the address (on a letter) *la19-.* **3** *in pl* refuse of wool, tow etc *la18-19.*
~**in(g)rock** a distaff for spinning *backings,*
la19-e20, Fif. ~**in(g) turf &c** a turf laid on a low fire to keep it alive through the night *19-, now Bnf.* ~**lin(g)s &c** backwards *15-e20.* ~**-birn** a burden carried on the back *la18-e20.* ~**-bond,** ~**-band** *law* an INSTRUMENT (*n* 2) which qualifies another unqualified INSTRUMENT *la16-.* ~**-breed** a fall or throw on the back *la19.* ~**-calver** a cow which calves towards the end of the year *la19-.* ~**-cast** *freq fig* an unexpected blow *18-e20.* ~ **chap** a back stroke; a retort; a helping hand *la19-, now Ags.* ~**-come 1** recrimination; an expression of regret or disappointment *la20-, Sh Ork Per midLoth.* **2** *also* ~**-coming &c** a return *la16-e19.* ~**-door trot(t)** diarrhoea *la18-.* ~**draucht** the drawing in of the breath, *eg* the gasp in whooping cough *19-.* ~ **dyke** a back wall *16-17.* ~ **end &c** the end of harvest, late autumn *19-.* ~**-fa** the outlet of a *mill lade* (MILL) *la19-e20.* ~**-friend** a supporter; one who does his best for another *e19.* ~**-gaein &c** *adj, of persons and animals* not thriving *la18-e20.* *n, also* ~**-gangin** a relapse *19-, now local N-SW.* **go the** ~**gate** or deceitfully *19-, now Abd Per.* ~ **hand &c** rent *law* rent payable by agreement later than at the legal term *20-.* ~**hash, baghash** ['~'haʃ, 'bag'haʃ] abuse, scold vigorously *19, Ags Per.* ~**-jar** a setback in health or circumstances *la19-, now Bnf.* ~**-jaw** impudence, abusive language *20-, Bnf Abd Lnk.* ~**land** ['bak'lan(d)] the back of a piece of ground; the building on it; a house built behind another *la15-e20.* ~ **letter** = *back-bond, la18-.* ~**-man** a follower (in war) *la16-e19.* **2** a person who carries loads on his back *17-e19.* ~**-rape &c** the rope which goes over a horse's back *17-e20.* ~**-roup** *vi* bid at an auction merely to raise the price *la18-19.* ~**set** [*n* 'bakset; *v* 'bak'sɛt] *n* something which hinders or causes a relapse *18-, now Bnf.* *vt* weary; worry; disgust *la19-, Bnf Abd.* ~**sey** ['bak'saɪ] *butchering* name for various parts of the loin of beef etc *18-, local.* ~**side** ['bak'səid] **1** the back part of a house or building; the space, yard or fields adjoining it *la15-e20.* **2** = backside *16-.* **3** *in pl* the parts of a town off the main streets *19-e20.* **on** *etc* **the** ~**side** on the side facing the back, behind *la15-17.* ~**spang 1** a legal flaw or loophole *19.* **2** (the taking of) an underhand advantage *19-, now Arg.* ~**speir &c** ['bak'spir] question, cross-examine *la16-e20.* ~**sprent** [*'bak'sprɛnt] a spring or catch used as a hold or check *la16.* ~**stair** ['bak'ster] backstairs *16-.* ~**stane** ['bak'sten] a broad stone, or projection of a wall, at the back of a fireplace *19-e20.* ~ **ta(c)k** a TACK² connected with WADSETS, whereby the actual possession of the WADSET lands was continued, or returned, to the proprietor or *reverser* (REVERSE), on payment of a rent corresponding to the interest of

the loan *17-19*. ~-**water** excess water in a *mill lade* (MILL) *la16-19*. **gar someone's ee**(n) **stan** (in) ~-**water** &c reduce someone to a state of helplessness *la17-e20*. ~ **widdie** the band over a cart saddle, supporting the shafts *19*. ~ ȝet, ~ **yett** a back gate or door *15-e17*. **at a** ~ at a loss *e20*, *Bnf Abd*. **at the** ~ **of** not long after *19-*: '*at the back of six*'. ~ **and bed** possession or provision of clothing and bedding *la14-16*. ~ **and fore** 1 *esp designating a whole property* (in) back and front *la16-17*. 2 backwards and forwards *la17-*. ~ **of** less than (a certain amount) *19-*, now *NE*. **the** ~ **of beyond** &c a remote, inaccessible place *19-*. ~ **o my hand** contemptuous term of farewell or dismissal **to** *la18-e20*. ~ **out owre** &c *adv* backwards *la19-e20*. *prep* back, away from, out of *la19-*, now *NE*. ~ **owre** *adv* behind, backwards *17-19*. *adj* back- *e20*. **come up one's** ~ come into one's mind, fit in with one's own inclination (to do something) *la19-*. **go up one's** ~ be beyond one's power *la19-*, now *Abd*. **on the** ~ **of** = *at the* ~ *of*, *19-*. **with** *etc* **one's** ~ **to** *or* **at the wall** hard-pressed, facing desperate odds *16-*.
back² &c *n* an instrument for toasting; a GIRDLE *19-e20*, *chf Ags*. [perh f BAUK¹ (*n* 6) because it resembled the scale of a balance]
back *see* BAUK²
backet &c *la17-e20*, **bakkat** *15-e16 n* 1 a shallow wooden receptacle for lime, salt etc *15-19*. 2 a wooden box for fuel, ashes etc *la17-e20*. 3 a dustbin *e20*, *Abd*; *cf* BUCKET. [only Sc; F *baquet*, dim of *bac* a trough, basin]
backie; bawkie &c *n* the bat, the animal *la19-*. ~ **bird** = *n*, *la18-e20*. [dim of OSc *bak*, ME *bakke*, of Scand orig]
backlin(g)s *see* BACK¹
bad &c *adj* 1 = bad *16-*. 2 unwell, in pain, physically ill *la19-*.
adv badly *20-*.
~**ly** *adj* ill, ailing *la18-e20*.
the ~ **man** *child's word* the devil *la19-e20*. **the** ~ **place** hell *la19-e20* [*cf* Gael *droch àite*]. ~**use** ill-treat; misuse; abuse *la19-*, now *Sh NE Ags*. **no** *or* **nae** ~ pretty well *20-*: '*How are you gettin on? - No bad ata*'.
bad *see* BED, BID
badder *see* BATHER
badderlock &c *n*, *chf in pl* a kind of edible seaweed *la18-*, now *Ags*. [see SND]
baddock *n* the (young of the) coal-fish *la18-*, now *NE Bwk*. [perh Gael *bodach* (*ruadh*) a codfish, *bodach* an old man]
bade &c *n* waiting; delay, pause *15-16*.
but *or* **forout**(in) *etc* (**langer** *etc*) ~ without (more) delay *la14-16*.
bade *see* BID, BIDE
badkin *see* BAUDKIN
bad-money &c; **bald-money** &c *n* = bald-money, the gentian; the spignel (used medicinally in the *Highlands* (HIELAND)) *19-e20*. [see SND]
badrans *see* BAUDRONS
badrie *see* BAWDRY
bae *see* BAA
baeshin &c *n* = ˈbasin *19-e20*, *SW*.
baet *see* BATE
baff¹ &c *n* a blow, *esp* with something soft *la16*, *19-*.
~**ie** &c a kind of golf club *20-*. [only Sc; *cf* OF *baffe* a blow with the back of the hand and BUFF²]
baff² *n*, *chf in pl* carpet slippers *e20*.
~**ie** = *n*, *la20-*, *local*. [perh connected w BAUCHLE]
bafuff, ballfuff &c [balˈfʌf, bə(l)ˈfʌf] *n* **the back o** ~ a remote, unspecified, fictitious place *la19-*, *Bnf Ags*.
bag &c *n* 1 = bag *15-*. 2 the stomach; the paunch *18-e20*.
vti 1 = bag. 2 *vt* stuff, cram, cause to swell like a bag *la20-*, *local Stlg-Slk*.
~**gage** 1 = baggage. 2 anything worthless *la19-*, *Bnf Abd Ags*. ~**get** &c the coal-fish *la19-e20*, *NE*. ~**gie** &c 1 the belly, stomach *la18-e19*. 2 also ~**gie mennen** &c *19-*, now *Ayr* a kind of large minnow *19-*, *local Renfr-Rox*. ~**git** &c *adj* 1 big with young; full of spawn *15-e20*. 2 *of a stallion* testicled *e16*. 3 bulging, swelled out *19-*, now *local*. 4 corpulent, big-bellied *la19-e20*. *n*, also **bag**(g)**ot** a fish full of spawn *19-*.
~**cheke** &c the Henry VIII groat *e16* [so called from the King's face on the coin]. ~ **irnis** the metal mountings of a bag *la15*. ~ **raip** the thick double straw rope round the eaves of a thatched stack *19-e20*, *N*.
bage &c [*bedȝ] *n* a heraldic badge *16-17*. [ME, OF; Anglo-L *bagea*, *bagia*]
bagening &c [*ˈbedȝənɪn] *n* rough horseplay at harvest time *la19-e20*. [obscure]
bagget *see* BAG
baggie &c [ˈbagɪ; *Bwk Rox* ˈbegɪ] *n* the swede *la19-e20*, *SE, S*. [prob f second element of Eng *rutabaga*, Sw dial *rotabagge*]
baggit, baggot *see* BAG
baghash *see* BACK¹
bagie [*ˈbadȝɪ, *?ˈbedȝɪ] *n* = BAGE *16*. [eModEng]
bagnet &c *la19*, **bagonet** &c *la17-e20*; **baig**(o)**net** *la18-e20* [ˈbag(ə)nɛt, ˈbeg-] *n* = bayonet.
bagot *see* BAG
bahookie *see* BEHOUCHIE
bahuif &c, **bahuis** &c; **balhuif** &c [*ˈbɑˈhø(v), *-ˈhøz] *n* a chest, coffer, or trunk *16-e17*. [only Sc; OF *bahu*, var of *bahud*, *bahut* a large trunk with an arched lid]
baible *vi* drink carelessly *19-e20*. [var of obs Eng *bibble* (*v*) drink; dabble]

baigle; beegle &c *n* **1** = beagle, the dog etc. **2** a disagreeable dirty person; a 'sight' *19-, now Arg Uls.*

baiglet *see* BAIKLET

baig(o)net *see* BAGNET

baik *see* BAUK[1], BECK

baikie[1] **&c, bakie** *n* a square wooden container for ashes, coal, rubbish etc *17-, C.* [perh dim of Eng *back* a trough, or F *baquet*; *cf* BACKET]

baikie[2] **&c** ['bekɪ; *NE also* 'bjɑkɪ] *n* **1** an iron or wooden peg to which a tether was fastened *19-e20, Bnf Abd.* **2** the stake to which a cow etc was tied in the stall *la19-e20.* [see SND]

baiklet &c, baiglet *n* a child's under-vest *la17-e20.*

bailie, baillie, bailʒe &c *la14-e20,* **bylie &c** *la19-;* **ballie &c** *la14-17,* **balʒe &c** *15-17,* **belʒe &c** *la15-e20* ['belɪ; 'bɔilɪ; *** 'beljɪ] *n* **1** an officer of a *barony* (BARON) or REGALITY *la14-19.* **2** a town MAGISTRATE next in rank to the PROVOST, since 1975 used only as a courtesy title by certain local authorities *la14-.* **3** *also* cow ~ the person in charge of the cows on a farm *la19-, now Bnf Abd Ags Lnk.*

bail(i)ery &c, bailʒery &c [*'bel(j)ərɪ] the jurisdiction of a BAILIE or the district under him *la15-19.*

~ **court** a local court held by a BAILIE *16-18.*

~ **work** work to be done by tenants as prescribed by the landlord's BAILIE *la16-18.* [ME *baili,* OF *bailli,* f as Eng *bailiff*]

bailiff, bailive *17-e18 n* **1** a BAILIE (*n* 2) *la16-e18.* **2** = bailiff *la16-.*

baill *see* BALE

baillie *see* BAILIE

bailʒe &c *la15-16,* **baillie** *la16-e17* [*'bel(j)ɪ] *n* = bailey, the (upper or lower) court of a castle. [ME, OF *baile*]

bailʒe *see* BAILIE

ba'ing *see* BA[1]

bair *see* BEAR[1]

baird *see* BARD, BEARD

bairge[1] *vi* walk with a jerk or spring upwards; strut *19-e20.* [obscure]

bairge[2] **&c, barge** *la19-e20, Ayr Uls* [berdʒ; *Ayr Uls* bardʒ] *vi* speak loudly and angrily; scold or taunt loudly *19-, now Bnf.* [obscure]

bairge[3] *vi* (threaten to) collide violently; move clumsily and noisily *19-, now Bnf.* [see SND]

bairge *see* BARGE[1], BARGE[2]

bairn &c *la15-,* **barne** *la14-e17;* **bern &c** *la14-e18* [bern] *n* **1** *expressing relationship* someone's child; offspring of any age *la14-.* **2** a child as conceived or born *15-16.* **3** *expressing age* a child or infant (1) *in gen, la14-;* (2) *specif* a child at school or in a choir; a schoolboy or chorister *15-e17;* (3) a youth, young person *15-16.* **4** *in pl* **the B~s** nickname for Falkirk football team *20-* [f the town's motto 'Better meddle wi' the deil than the bairns o' Falkirk']. *vt* make pregnant *19-e20.*

barnage &c [*'bɛrnedʒ] childhood; youth

15-e17. ~**heid &c** childhood, infancy *la14-e20.* ~**ie** a little child *la17-.* ~**lie &c** *adj* childish; childlike *16-e20. adv* childishly *16-e17.* ~**liness &c** childishness *16-19.*

~**-bed** the womb or a condition affecting it *16.* ~'s **bargain** a bargain that can be easily broken *19-, now Bnf Fif.* ~'s **part** (of gear *etc*) a child's portion of HERITABLE property *la15-19; cf* LEGITIM. ~**time &c** **1** *also* ~**teme** *15-e17* a brood of children; offspring (of persons or animals) *15-19* [nME; OE *bearntēam* begetting children]. **2** childhood *19-e20* [BAIRN + Eng *time*]. [ME; OE *bearn*; ON *barn*]

bairne *see* BERN

bais *see* BAISS[1]

baise &c [*bez] *vt, chf in ptp* ~**d &c** dismayed, confused, bewildered *la14-e20. n* confusion, bewilderment *19.* [nME; reduced f *abaise* (ABUISE)]

baisies &c [*'beziz] *n* rounders *la19-e20.* [dim of Eng *base*]

baiss[1] **&c** *19-e20,* **bais** *16-e17,* **bess** *la19-, now Sh vt* = baste, sew loosely *only Sc.*

baiss[2] *19-,* **base &c** *16 vt* = baste, beat soundly, *orig only in pt, ptp* **baist &c** *16-, now Bnf.*

bait *see* BATE, BITE, BOAT[1]

baitchel &c *vt* beat; break *19-e20, S.* [*cf* BATE]

baith &c *la15-,* **bathe &c** *la14-16;* **both &c** *15-,* **beith &c** *16-e17* [beθ; *Sh* bed] *adj, pronoun, adv* = both *la14-.*

~ **as ane and ane as** ~ **&c** *law* jointly and equally *15-16.* ~ (**the**) **two** (**of them** *etc*) both (of them etc) *16-.*

baith *see* BATHE

baitten *see* BATE

baittle *19, S,* **battill &c** *e16 adj, of grass, pasturage* rich, fattening for cattle. [see SND]

baiver *vi* gad about *19, WC.* [perh extension of BEVER[2]]

baivie; baivis &c ['bevɪs, 'bɪvɪs, *'bevɪ] *n* a large fire *19-e20.* [uncertain]

bajan, bajone *see* BEJAN

bak *see* BACK[1], BAUK[1]

bake &c, byaak &c *la19-, NE* [bek; *NE* b(j)ɑk] *vt, pt also* **beuk &c** *16-e20* [*NE* bjuk; *bøk]. *ptp also* **baken &c** *15-e20* **1** = bake *15-.* **2** knead (dough) *19.*

n **1** a (*usu* thick or soft) biscuit *16-.* **2** a PEAT[1] kneaded from wet PEAT[1] dust *la18, Rox.*

bakie = *n* 2, *19-e20, Gall.*

~**-board &c** *16-, now local,* ~**breid &c** *16-, now Abd,* **bakbred &c** *la15-e16* ['bek'bord, *local Abd-Ayr* -'brod, *NE* -'brid, *EC* -'brɛd, *Rox* -'børd; *Rox also* 'bɑ'brid; *'bek'bred; *'bak'brɛd; *'bɑ'brɛt] a baking board. ~ **stule &c, bakstule &c** [*'bek'støl, *'bak-] a stool used in bread-making *la14-16.*

bakie *see* BAIKIE[1]

bakin *see* BAUDKIN

bakkat *see* BACKET

bakkin(g)s *see* BACK[1]

bakon *n* some animal *la15*. [prob erron]

bakster *see* BAXTER

bakstule *see* BAKE

Balaam *n, printing and publishing* second-rate copy kept in reserve to fill a gap in a newspaper etc *19-*. [see SND Suppl]

balbie *see* BAWBEE

bald *see* BAULD

balderry &c, **beldairy** &c, **bulldairy** &c ['baldırı, -erı; 'bɛldɛrı; *Sh* 'bʌldɪrı; *bɑdrı] *n* any of several types of wild orchid (sometimes thought to have aphrodisiac powers) *19-e20*. [obscure]

baldie ['baldı] *n* a kind of fishing boat *la19-, now Bnf*. [perh contracted f *Garibaldi*]

bald-money *see* BAD-MONEY

baldy *see* BELD¹

bale *la15-e19*; **baill** &c *la14-e19*, **bele** &c *16-19 n* a large fire; a bonfire or beacon-fire *la14-19*. [(chf n)ME; ON *bál*, OE *bǽl*]

bale *see* BEAL

balhuif *see* BAHUIF

balk *see* BAUK¹

ball¹ [bal] *n* **1** (1) = ball, a gathering for dancing. (2) any kind of social gathering *la18-, now Sh*. **2** bustle, disturbance; a spree *19-, now Sh Bnf*.
on the ~ constantly drinking *la19-, now Ags*.

ball² [bal] *vt* roll together; put in disorder *la18-, now Sh*. [*cf* ON *ballrast* (*vr*) crowd together in a confused throng]

ball³ [*?bal] *n* boot-blacking *18-19*. [contracted f Eng *blacking ball*]

ball *see* BA¹

ballance &c [*'baləns] *n* **1** *also* **ballandis** *15-16* = balance (for weighing) *15-e17*. **2** a plate, flat dish *e16*.

ballane &c *16-17*; **balling** &c *17* [*'balən, -ın] *n* = baleen, whalebone.

ballant &c *19-, only Sc*, **ballat** &c *la15-e20*; **ballett** &c *la15-e19* ['balənt, -ət] *n* = ballad *la15-*. **a hole in the** ~ any blank or omission *la19-* [orig the ballad-singer's excuse when his broadside was torn].

ballfuff *see* BAFUFF

ballie *see* BAILIE

balling &c ['balın] *n* dancing; holding or frequenting of balls *la16-, now Bnf*. [f F *baller* (*v*) dance]

balling *see* BALLANE

balloch *see* BEALACH

ballop &c *19-, now local C*, **ballope** *la16* ['baləp] *n* a trouser-flap; trouser-flies. [eModEng *ballup*]

bally ['balı] *n, also* ~ **cog** a milk pail *19-e20, Bnf*. [*cf* Dan *balje* a tub]

bally *see* BELLY¹

Balmoral [bal'morəl] *n, also* ~ **bonnet** a kind of bonnet (like a KILMARNOCK *n* 1) with a *toorie* (TOUR¹) on the crown and a (usu *diced* (DICE)) band, worn to one side *la19-*.

~**ity** enthusiasm for the superficial elements of Scottish culture rather than real concern for Scotland's problems *20-*. [the royal castle on Deeside]

baloo &c, **baloue**, **balulalow** &c [ba'lu; *ba'lula'lu] *n* a lullaby *la16-e20*.
interj used to hush a child to sleep *18-e20*. [only Sc]

balʒe *see* BAILIE

bambaize *see* BUMBAZE

bambor *see* BAOMBE

Bamff *see* BANFF

bamling *see* BUMMLE

ban &c *v* **1** *vt* curse *la14-e20*. **2** *vi* swear, utter curses *la15-e20*. [ME; ON *banna* prohibit, interdict, curse]

ban *see* BAND¹, BAND²

bancat *see* BANKET

bancour &c [*'baŋkər] *n* = banker, a covering for a seat or bench *la15-16*. [*cf* BUNKER]

band¹ &c; **ban** *la19-, now Bnf Abd* [ban(d); bɑn(d)] *n* **1** = band, something which binds *la14-*. **2** a hinge, fastening for a door etc *la14-, now Bnf*. **3** a rope, straw-twist etc used to bind corn etc *la15-, now Abd*. **4** a promise, agreement, contract (1) *in gen, la14-19*; (2) the marriage bond *la14-e20*; (3) an alliance of mutual interest; a covenant, league *15-e17*; (4) a formal or documentary bond or contract entered into by an individual *15-19*. **5** a range (of hills); a ridge (of a hill) *e16, e19*. **6** *now in pl* the two short white linen strips hanging from the collar, worn as part of the pulpit or officiating dress of an ordained MINISTER *18-*.
v **1** *vt, chf in ptp* ~**it** secured or strengthened with (metal) bands *la15-e17*. **2** *vti* = band *la16-*.
~**er** a person who enters into, or signs, a bond or covenant *17*. ~**ster** the member of a party of harvesters who binds the sheaves *19-*.
~ **stane** = bondstone *la15-, now Sh*.

band²; **ban** [ban(d); bɑn(d)] *n* **1** = band, a company, group *16-*. **2** a (church) choir *19-*.
bandwin the band of three to eight reapers who work together and are served by one *bandster* (BAND¹) *17-e20*.

band *see* BIND

banderoll &c [*'band(ə)rol, &c] *n* a bandoleer *la16-17*. [Sc misuse of Eng *banderole*]

bandie &c ['bandı; *Bnf* 'banı] *n* a minnow or stickleback *la19-, now Bnf*. [prob contracted f BANSTICKLE]

bandis; **bands** *n pl* = banns of marriage *la16-17, only Sc*. [var of *banns*, prob w infl f BAND¹ 4 (2)]

bandwin *see* BAND²

bane &c, **bone** &c *16-*; **been** &c *16-* [ben; *Ork N* bin] *n* **1** = bone *la14-*. **2** *chf* **bone** *fig* pith, marrow, life *la19-, local Bnf-Kcb*.
banefire &c = bonfire *la16-19* [orig made with animal bones]. ~ **kaim** a bone comb; a

small fine-toothed comb *la19-e20*. ~**schaw**
sciatica; hip gout *la16-17*. **banwart**
[*'banwərt] = bonewort, the daisy *e16*.
bane *see* BAYNE, BENE
banere &c; benner *16* [*ba'nir, *'benər,
*'bɛnər, 'banər] *n* = banner *la14-e17*.
banerman, bannerman a banner-bearer
la15-16, only Sc, as personal name la14-.
banesoun *see* BENNISON
banestikkill *see* BANSTICKLE
Banff; Bamff [bamf] **go to** ~**!** 'get lost!', 'go to
blazes!' *e19*.
~ **bailies** large white snowy clouds rising
along the horizon, regarded as a sign of bad
weather *la19-, NE*. [the North-East town]
bang[1] *v* **1** *vt* surpass, excel, beat, overcome,
thrash *la16-*. **2** *vi* hurry, dash *la16-e19*. **3** *vti*
= bang.
n **1** = bang *la16-*. **2** a throbbing pain *la18-e19*.
adj **1** fierce, violent, strong *la18-e20*. **2** agile
and powerful *19-e20*.
~**ie** *n* a man (*occas* a policeman) specially
appointed to watch the Solway and Annan for
salmon poachers *la19-e20, Dmf. adj* impetuous; quarrelsome *19*. ~**ster &c** a violent or
lawless person; a bully *la16-e20, only Sc*.
~**strie &c** violence (to person or property);
bullying behaviour *la16-e20, only Sc*.
~ **out** rush out, fall out violently *18-19*. ~
up jump, rise hastily *18-*. **in** *etc* **a** ~ in haste
18-e19. [see also BUNG[1]]
bang[2] *n* a crowd *18-, now Abd*.
the whole ~**-dollop** *or* ~**-jing** the whole lot
la19-e20. [*cf* JING-BANG]
bang[3] *n, also* ~ **chain** a chain for fastening a
load of heavy logs *20-, now Ags*. [unknown]
bangyal *see* BANYEL
banis[1] **&c** *la14-e17*; **bannis &c** *15-e16*, **beneis**
&c *la16-17* [*'banɪs, *'bɛn-, *-ɪʃ] *vt* = banish
la14-17.
~**ment** = banishment *la16-17*. [only Sc]
banis[2] **&c; benis &c** *n* some kind of fur
la15-e16. [perh misreading of *baueris*
(BEVER[1])]
bank[1] *n* **1** = bank (of a river etc) *la14-*. **2** the
place in a *peat moss* (PEAT[1]) where PEATS[1] are cut
la19-.
the Bankies nickname for Clydebank football
team *20-*.
bank[2] *n* the beat of a drum, *esp* as used in making
a public proclamation, *chf as* **beat a** ~ *17-e18*.
[only Sc; Sw *banka*, Dan *banke*, ON *banga* (*v*)
beat]
bank[3] *n* **1** = bank, a bench. **2** a basket of bobbins of yarn used in making up the warp in a
loom; a section of the warping frame in which
the bobbins are set up *19-, now Ayr*.
banket *16-e17*; **bancat &c** *16-e17 n, vti* = banquet. [eModEng]
bannerman *see* BANERE
bannet *see* BONNET
bannie *see* BANNOCK

bannis *see* BANIS[1]
bannock &c *17-*, **bannok &c** *la16-e17*; **bon-**
nock &c *la16-*, **bannie &c** *19-e20* ['banək;
sEC, WC 'banək; *Ork* 'bano; *sEC also* 'banɪ; *S*
'banɪ, -ə] *n* **1** a round flat cake, *usu* of oat-,
barley- or pease-meal, baked on a GIRDLE *la16-*.
2 a quantity of meal sufficient to make a BAN-
NOCK, due to the servant of a mill from each of
those using it *la16-18*. **3** a flat cake (of tallow
or wax) *la16-e19*.
~ **hive** *joc and derog* a gastric upset caused by
overeating *la16, e20*. **B**~ **Day** *or* **Night**
Shrove Tuesday *la19-e20*. **bonnock &c iron**
an iron for baking BANNOCKS *la17*. ~ **stane** a
stone placed in the fire, on which BANNOCKS
were baked *la18-e20*. [nME *bannok*, OE *bannuc*
(once); *cf* Gael *bonnach, bannach*, prob f Sc]
banrent &c *n* = banneret *la14-e17, only Sc*.
banshee *la18-*; **benshie &c** *la18-e19* ['ban'ʃi]
n a female spirit, *freq* connected with a family,
whose wail was thought to forecast death or disaster *la18-*. [ScGael *ban-sìth*, IrGael *bean-sìdhe*
a fairy-woman]
banstickle &c *18-e20*, **banestikkill &c**
15-e17 ['ban'stɪkl; *Ork* 'bran-; *Rox* 'benɪ'tɪkl,
'benɪ'tɪkl; *'ben'stɪkl] *n* a stickleback.
[northern eModEng *baynstikille*, prob f BANE +
stickle as in Eng *stickleback*]
banter *vti* **1** = banter. **2** *vt* scold, drive away
by scolding *18-e19*.
bantim; bantin(g) &c *n* = bantam *19-e20*,
only Sc.
banwart *see* BANE
banyel &c, bengle &c; bangyal &c ['banjəl,
'banjəl, 'bɛnjəl, 'bɛnjəl, 'bɛŋl] *n* a bundle; a
heap; a crowd *19-e20*. [perh f F *ballon* a small
pack, w infl f BANG[2]]
baombe (*sheep-counting*), **bambor** (*children's*
rhymes) *numeral* five *la19-e20*. [see ZEENDI]
bap *n* a bread roll, varying locally in shape, size
and texture *16-*.
vi walk in a plodding, flat-footed way *20-, now*
Abd.
be bappin on *or* **in** be getting on with something, not waste time over something *20-, NE*.
~**-faced** having a face like a BAP, soft and stupid-looking *la20-, local*. ~ **fit &c** a flat foot
la19-, NE. [obscure]
bapteese &c *e20*, **baptise &c** *la14-*; **baptese**
&c *la16-e17, only Sc* [bap'tiz] *vt* = baptize.
baptime &c *la14-e17*; **bapteme &c** *la15-e17*
[*'baptɪm, -ɪm] *n* = baptism.
baptise *see* BAPTEESE
bar[1] **&c** [bar; *sEC, WC* bɑr] *n* **1** = bar (of wood
etc) *15-*. **2** *in pl* = bars, the game of prisoner's
base *la15-16*.
vt = bar, secure, exclude *la14-*.
burrie, ~**rie** = ~**-the-door**, *la19, Bnf Abd*.
barrit, bard = barred *16*. **barrit** *or* **bard**
grote a kind of groat *la16*.
~**-the-door, barley-door** the game of LEAVE-
o *20-, local*.

like the ~(s) o Ayr *19-*, *now Loth Ayr* [f the sea bars formerly at the mouth of the River Ayr] *or* **Hell** *20-*, *Loth* (moving etc) fast and noisily.
bar²; bawr &c [bar; *sEC, WC* bɑr] *n* a joke, humorous situation, practical joke *la19-.* [obscure]
bar *see* BEAR¹
barat *see* BARRAT
barbar &c *adj* barbarous, barbarian *16-17.*
n a barbarian *16-e18.* [ME (once) as *n*; OF *barbare (n, adj)*]
barbarize &c *vti* act as a barber, shave *17-e18, only Sc.*
barber *n* a freezing coastal mist in calm frosty weather *20-*, *now Bnf Kcdn.* [obscure]
barbulyie *e19*, **barbulȝe &c** *la16* [*bar'bøljɪ] *vt* disorder, confuse; besmear. [only Sc; F *barbouiller* smear; stammer]
barcatt &c *n* a kind of wooden trestle or support *la16.* [obscure]
bard &c, baird &c *16-19* [bard; *berd] *n* **1** *orig* (*15-18*) *freq derog* a poet; a strolling singer or player; a vagabond minstrel, buffoon; a scurrilous person *15-*, *as personal name 14-.* **2** a scold, a noisy woman *16-e20.*
~**ach** [*'bardəx] stout, fearless *la18-e19.* ~**ie** *n* a minor poet, humble BARD *18-e19.* *adj* bold, impudent, quarrelsome *18-19.* ~**rie** scurrility; scurrilous language *16.* [Sc and IrGael]
bard *see* BAR¹
barding &c [*'bardɪŋ, *'berd-] *n* horse armour *16.* [OF *barde*]
bare¹ &c *adj* **1** = bare *la14-.* **2** *of weapons* unsheathed *la14-.*
~**fute**, ~**fut(it) &c** *la14-e17*, ~**fit(ted) &c** *la18-* [*N* 'barfɪt; *Sh Ork C, S* 'berfɪt, 'bɛr-; 'ber'fɪtɪt; *N also* 'ber'fɪtɪt; *'berføt, *'ber'føtɪt] = barefoot(ed) *la14-.* ~**fit broth** *or* **kail** BROTH¹ made with a little butter but no meat *la18-e20, NE.* ~**-leg** bare-legged *la16-e17.*
~**man** a destitute person; a debtor, bankrupt *15-17.*
bare² &c *n* = boar *la14-e17.* [nME; OE *bār*]
bare *see* BEAR²
bargain *la16-*, **bargane &c** *la14-19*; **bergan &c** *16-19* *n* **1** contention, conflict, struggle *la14-19.* **2** = bargain *la16-.*
v **1** *vi* = bargain *la17-.* **2** *vti* contend, fight (with) *la14-18.*
barganour &c [*'barganər] a quarreller, wrangler *15-e16.*
barge¹; bairge *n* **1** a kind of shutter similar to a venetian blind, used in drying-sheds *la18-e20.* **2** a slat of wood etc to protect windows, doors etc from rain or flood-water *18-19.* [see SND]
barge² la14-; bairge *16-e17, only Sc n* = barge, the boat.
barge *see* BAIRGE²
bargle *vi* wrangle, bandy words *la19-*, *now Abd.* [short for *argle-bargle* (ARGIE)]

barisdall &c [*'barɪsdəl] *vt, n* (subject to) an instrument of torture invented and used only by MacDonald of Barisdale *e18.*
bark¹; berk *15-16* [bark; *sEC* bɑrk; *Rox* bɛrk] *vi* (*la14-*), *n* (*la19-*), *of dogs etc* = bark.
bark² [bark; *sEC* bɑrk; *Rox* bɛrk] *n* **1** = bark (of a tree) *15-.* **2** tanner's bark, tan *15-.* **3** the skin *18-*, *now Sh.*
vt = bark, tan (leather) *15-.*
~**en** *vti* encrust, plaster over, blacken *la18-.* ~**ened &c 1** dried into a crust, encrusted *16-.* **2** *of leather* tanned *la18-.* ~**er &c** a tanner *15-17.* ~**it 1** = barked, tanned *15-17.* **2** dried into a crust, encrusted (*freq* with dirt); *hence* dirty *16-*, *now Mry.*
~ **hole &c** a tanner's bark-pit *la16-17.* ~ **pot** a pot or pit for tanner's bark *la16-e17.*
barking and fleeing *presp* spending wastefully and over-extravagantly; on the verge of ruin *19-*, *now Fif.* [see SND]
barlaw *see* BIRLIE
barleke *see* BARLIE
barley *see* BARLIE, BIRLIE
barley-door *see* BAR¹
barlie *la15-e17*, **barleke &c** *15-16*; **barley** *17-* ['barlɪ, *C* 'bɑr-; *-lɪk] *n* = barley *15-.*
~**hood** violent ill-temper, obstinacy resulting from drunkenness *18-19.*
~**-bree &c** malt liquor, WHISKY *18-.* ~ **fever, barrel-fever** intoxication, drunkenness *la18-19.* ~**-pickle** a grain of barley *19-e20.* ~**-sick, barrel-sick** drunk *la18-e19.* [rare in early sources; *cf* BEAR¹]
barm [barm; *'bɛrm] *n* **1** = barm, yeast *15-.* **2** an insult; blame *20-*, *Mry.*
v **1** *vt* mix with yeast *la19-*, *now Sh.* **2** *vi, lit and fig* ferment, come to a head, 'fume' *19-*, *now Sh Abd wLoth.*
~**y 1** yeasty; frothy *la14-.* **2** *colloq* flighty, foolish *19.* **3** *colloq* = barmy, crazy.
barme horse &c *n* ? a pack-horse *15-e17, e19.*
barmekin &c; barnekin &c *n, also fig* a battlement, battlemented wall; a wall of defence *la15-e19.* [perh altered f Eng *barbican*]
barn &c *16-*, **bern &c** *la14-17*, **born &c** *16-17, chf WC n* = barn *la14-.*
barnman a thresher *la16-e20.* **barns-breaking** an idle frolic; a mischievous action *19.* ~**yard &c** = barnyard *15-.*
barnage *see* BAIRN
barne *see* BAIRN
barné &c [*'barni, *-ɪ] *n* the baronage *la14-e15.* [only Sc; OF]
barnekin *see* BARMEKIN
baron *la15-*, **baroun &c** *la14-e17*; **barron &c** *16-e18 n* = baron; one who holds land directly of the Crown, in Scotland until a later date than in England including commoners (and *freq* lesser landowners); *also* a member of the lowest rank of the nobility *la14-.*
~**ial 1** = baronial. **2** *also* **Scottish** ~**ial**

applied to an ornate style of architecture characterized by numerous turrets, crow-stepped (CRAW) gables etc, used *esp* for 19th century country-houses and Edinburgh *Old Town* (AULD) TENEMENTS *19-*.

~**y**, *also* ~**ry** the lands etc held by or the tenure appropriate to a BARON *la14-*. **in** ~**y** by baronial tenure *15-e16*; *cf burgh of* ~*y* (BURGH).

~ **bailie &c** a BARON's deputy with both civil and criminal jurisdiction in the *Baron Court*, *la16-19*. ~ **court** a court held by a BARON or his deputy in his *barony*, *la16-e19*. ~ **officer** an estate official *la17-e19*.

B~s of (the) Exchequer title of the judges of the Scottish Court of Exchequer *18-19*; *cf Lord Chief Baron (of Exchequer)* (LORD).

barp *n* a chambered cairn *19-e20*, *Hebrides*. [Gael *barpa*]

barra *&c 20-*, **barrow &c**, **borrow** *17-e18*, **borra** *&c 19-* ['barə; *C* 'barɪ, 'barɪ; *local* 'borə, -ɪ] *n =* (hand- *etc*) barrow *la14-*.

~**man** a person who helps to carry a handbarrow; a person who carries building materials on a barrow *la15-*, *now Bnf*, *as personal name la14-*. ~**-steel &c**, **barrow-tram** a barrowshaft *16-e20*.

set (doun) the ~ go bankrupt *la19-*, *now NE Kcb*.

barrace *la15-e19*, **barras &c** *la14-18*; **barres &c** *15-e19* *n* **1** = barrace, a barrier in front of a castle etc *la14-16*. **2** an enclosure for judicial combats, tournaments etc *la15-e19*. **3** a barrier or barricade *16-e17*.

barras ʒet *16* or **gate** *18-*, *Abd*, *now only as place-name* a gate in or beside a barrier.

barrane &c, **barrand &c** *adj =* barren *la14-e17*, *only Sc*.

barras *see* BARRACE

barrat &c *la15-18*; **barat &c** *15-19* *n* **1** = barrat, fraud; contention *15-16*. **2** distress, trouble, vexation *la15-e17*.

~**our &c** a person who obtained benefices by underhand means *15-16*. ~**ry** *law* the crime **1** by an ecclesiastic, of corrupt purchase of benefices *15*; **2** by a judge, of pronouncing a particular judgment in return for a bribe *la18-19*.

barrekin *see* BARRIKIN

barrel &c, **barrell &c** *la15-17* *n* **1** = barrel, *esp* as a quantity or measure **of** (some commodity) *15-*. **2** a dry measure of varying amount *la19-*, *now Bnf Ags*.

vt = barrel *la15-*.

barrel-fever *see* BARLIE

barrell *see* BARREL

barrel-sick *see* BARLIE

barrere &c *15-e16*; **barrier** ['barɪər; *ba'rir; *'barir] *n* = barrier *la15-*.

Barrier Act an act passed by the *General Assembly* (GENERAL) of the *Church of Scotland* (CHURCH) in 1697, which provided that acts

involving an important change in church law must be approved by the PRESBYTERIES as well as by the *General Assembly*.

barres *see* BARRACE

barrie[1] **&c** *n* a baby's flannel coat; a binder *la18-e20*. [perh connected w OE *beorgan* protect; *cf* Eng dial *barrow(-coat)*]

barrie[2] **&c** *adj* fine; big; smart in appearance *20-*, *Rox*, *now also EC*. [gipsy]

barrikin &c; **barrekin &c** *n* a small cask or barrel *la16-e17*. [only Sc; F *barrique*; source of *-kin* ending not clear]

barron *see* BARON

barrow *see* BARRA, BORROW[1]

barse *see* BERS

Bartane *see* BERTANE

Bartanʒe *see* BRETANʒE

barteshing *e18*, **bartising &c** *la16-17*; **bartisan &c** *17-e18*, **barty** *la19-e20*, *Edb* [*'bartɪsɪn, *-ən, *-an, *-ɪʃ-; 'bartɪ] *n* a battlement, parapet. [metath f ME *bretasynge*]

Bartle *17-e20*, **Bartill &c** *la15-e17*; **Barthol &c** *la16-e18*: ~ **day** St Bartholomew's day, 24 Aug *la15-e20*. ~ **fair** a fair held on that day, *esp* that at Kincardine O'Neil, Abd *la16-e20*. [only Sc; reduced f OSc *Bartilmo (e16)*]

barty *see* BARTESHING

bas *see* BERS

basan &c [*'basan, *-ən] *n*, *usu* ~ **skin** sheepskin tanned with bark *la15-16*. [only Sc; F *basane*]

basar &c [*'besər] *n* an executioner *la14-15*. [obscure; perh *cf* BAISS[2]]

base &c *adj* = base *la15-*.

~ **holding** *etc* a SUBFEU *la16-*.

base *see* BAISS[2]

bash[1] *vt* beat, smash (**in** *etc*) *la18-*.

n a heavy blow, *usu* so as to smash on something *19-*, *only Sc*.

on the ~ having a drinking bout, on the spree *20-*. [*v chf* Sc and nEng; prob onomat, but *cf* also Sw *basa*, Dan *baske* whip, lash]

bash[2] *vi* be abashed or confused *la18*. [aphetic f Eng *abash*]

basin &c, **basson &c** *17-e18* ['besən] *n* = basin *la14-*.

~ **silver &c** a gratuity to certain royal servants at special seasons *la15-e16*.

bask *adj* **1** unpleasant, distasteful *la16*. **2** *of weather* dry, withering *la19-e20*. [ME *bask*, *baisk*, ON *beisk* acrid, bitter]

baslar &c [*'bezlər] *n* a dagger or short sword worn at the girdle *la15-e16*. [only Sc; OF *baselaire*; *cf* ME *baselard &c*]

bason(ed) *see* BAWSANT

bass *n* **1** *also* ~ **mat** a mat of bast, coarse straw, rushes etc, *esp* a doormat *18-*. **2** (1) a workman's tool-basket or bag *20-*, *local*. (2) a fishbasket *20-*, *local Bnf-Loth*.

~**-bottomed** *of chairs* with a BASS seat *20-*, *now Bnf*. [var of Eng *bast*]

bassie¹, bawsey &c ['basɪ, 'bɑsɪ] *adj* = BAW-SANT *la17-e18*.
n pet name for a horse; an old horse *la18-e20*.
bassie² 18-19, bossie &c *la19-, Bnf Abd* [*NE* 'bosɪ; *'basɪ; *Kcb* *'besɪ] *n* a wooden basin or bowl for carrying meal to the baking board or in which meal is mixed and kneaded *18-19*. [perh reduced f Eng *basin*]
basson *see* BASIN
bastailȝe *see* BASTILE
bastant &c *adj* sufficient(ly strong) *la16-17*. [only Sc; obs F]
bastard *see* BYSTART
bastardry &c *n* = bastardy *la15-e17*. [nME (rare)]
bastart *see* BYSTART
baste *see* BEAST
bastile *la18-19, hist,* **bastailȝe &c** *la15-16, only Sc;* **bastle &c** *16-e20, latterly hist* ['bastl, *'basteljɪ, &c] *n* = bastille, a fortified tower; a siege-tower.
bastion &c *17-e18,* **baston &c** *15-e18 n* = baston, a cudgel, truncheon *la15-e18*.
staf *etc* **and baston** the symbols by which the possession of land was resigned *15-17* [translating L *per fustem et baculum*].
bastle *see* BASTILE
baston *see* BASTION
bat¹, batt *n* **1** = bat, a blow; an implement for hitting a ball etc *la15-*. **2** an iron batten or bar; a staple or loop of iron *17-19*. **3** a lead wedge for securing lead flashings in masonry joints *19-*.
vt **1** = bat *la17-*. **2** fasten or secure with BATS¹ (*n* 2 and 3) *17-*.
aboot a ~ equal in ability *19-e20*.
bat² &c [*bet] *n* a small extra amount given free to a buyer *la15-e16*. [only Sc; MDu *baet, bate* profit, advantage]
bat³ *n* a drove (of sheep) *20-, Bwk S.* [Gael *bad* a cluster; a flock; prob borrowed f Highl drovers]
batailȝe &c [*ba'teljɪ] *n* = battle *la14-15, only Sc.*
batalrus *see* BATTALOUS
batchie *n* a baker; a baker's man *19-e20*. [deriv of Eng *batch* (of bread)]
bate *19-,* **bete &c** *la14-e15,* **baet** *la16, 20-,* **bet &c** [bit; bet] *vt, ptp also* **bet &c** *15-, now local,* **bait &c** *la17-, now local,* **baitten &c** *17-, now local* = beat *la14-*.
n, only **bate** something which surpasses something else *la19-*.
bate *see* BOAT¹
bath &c *n* = bath *la14-*.
~ **fat** a bath-tub *la15-16*.
bathe &c *15-;* **baith** *la15-17, only Sc vti* = bathe.
bathe *see* BAITH
bather &c, budder *20-, Sh N;* **badder** *20-, Sh N vti, n* = bother *la19-*.
batie; bawtie [*'betɪ, *'bɑtɪ] *adj* round, plump *19*.

~**-bum &c** a feckless person *la16*. [perh OE *batian* prosper, grow fat]
batie *see* BAWTIE
batoun &c *16-e17;* **baton &c** ['batən] *n* a baton *16-*.
vt strike with a baton *e17*.
bats *see* BATTS
batt *see* BAT¹
battalous &c *la15-e16;* **batalrus** *e16 adj* = battailous, bellicose.
battard &c; battart &c *n* a kind of small cannon *16-e17*. [only Sc; F *bâtard*, later form of *bastard*]
batter &c *vt* **1** = batter, beat *la15-*. **2** paste, fasten (to a wall, together), stiffen as with paste *la16-19*.
n **1** *cookery* = batter. **2** a paste or glue *la19-*. **3** a medicinal plaster *la19-, now NE Ags.* **4** *in pl* the covers of a book *la19-*.
~ **horn** a horn for holding shoemakers' paste *la18-20*.
on the ~ on the spree *19-*.
battill *see* BAITTLE
battis *see* BATTS
battle *see* BOTTLE¹
batts *18-e20,* **battis &c** *la16;* **bats** *la17-e19 n pl* **1** the bots, *esp* in horses *la17-e20*. **2** colic etc in human beings *la16-e20*. [obscure]
bauch &c [bɑx; *also* *bex] poor, sorry; ineffective *16-*. **2** *of blows* inflicted with a cudgel etc as opposed to a sharp weapon *16-e17*. **3** *of a cutting implement* blunt, dull, turned on edge *19-*. **4** *of ice* affected by thaw; not slippery *19-*. **5** backward, timid, sheepish, foolish *18-*. **6** weak, exhausted, seedy *18-e20*. [perh ON *bagr* awkward, clumsy, or *bágr* uneasy; hard up]
bauchle &c, bauchill &c *la15-16;* **bachle &c** ['bɑxl; *eLoth also* 'bexl] *v* **1** *vt* denounce openly; disgrace, discredit (publicly) *la15-16*. **2** treat contemptuously, cause trouble or harm to *19*. **3** *vti* shamble; wear (*esp* shoes) out of shape; distort, spoil *la19-*.
n **1** an old shoe, *esp* one worn down at the heel; a loose slipper *la18-*. **2** an old, useless, worn-out person or thing *19-*. **3** an untidy or clumsy person *20-*.
mak a ~ **o** make a laughing-stock *or* botch of *17-e20*. [perh connected w BAUCH]
baudkin &c *la14-e15;* **badkin &c** *16, only Sc,* **bakin &c** *16, only Sc* [*'badkɪn] *n* = baudkin, a richly embroidered cloth; a baldachin, canopy.
baudrons &c; badrans &c *la18-e19,* **bauldrins &c** *la15, 19* ['badrənz, 'ba-ŏ-] *n* **1** affectionate name for a cat *la15-*. **2** a hare *20-, local; cf* Eng *puss.* [perh BAWD w extended meaning + *-ron* imit of a cat's purr]
bauk¹ &c *la15-,* **balk &c** *la14-19;* **bak &c** *16-,* **baik &c** *16-e17* [bɑk; *balk] *n* **1** = balk, an unploughed ridge; a wooden beam *la14-*. **2** a ridge still apparent in a field after the BAUKS¹ (*n* 1) were tilled *18-e20*. **3** a (garden) path *20-,*

now Fif. **4** a crossbeam, rafter *16-.* **5** the beam of a pair of scales etc *15-.* **6** a hen roost *la15-e20.* **7** *in pl* a church gallery *la19-,* now *Loth.* **8** a seat in a boat, *esp* a fishing boat *e20.* *vt* leave small strips of (land) inadvertently unploughed *19-e20.*
~ **hicht** &c *adv* as high as the rafters *18-e20.* ~(**s**) **and brade**(**s**) a beam with scales for weighing large articles *15-e20.* **balk** &c **and burrel** &c *rig and fur* (RIG[1]) in ploughing *la19.*
bauk[2]; **back** &c *n* a rope, *esp* the head rope in fishing lines and nets *la19-,* now *Cai.* [see SND]
baul *see* BELD[1]
bauld &c, **bald** &c *la14-e18* [bal(d)] *adj* **1** = bold *la14-.* **2** *of animals* bold, fierce *la15-16.* **3** *of things, orig of fire* strong, fierce *la15-e16, e19.* *adv, chf of fire or wind* boldly, strongly, fiercely *la14-e19.* *vt* kindle or blow up (a fire) *e15, 19-e20.*
bauldrins *see* BAUDRONS
bauldy *see* BELD[1]
baurley *see* BIRLIE
bausond, bausoun *see* BAWSANT
bausy &c [*?'basɪ] *adj* large, fat, coarse *la15-e16, 19.* [*cf* Norw dial *basse* a big, well-fed animal; a big, strong man]
bauthles *n pl* ? contracts *e16.* [prob erron]
bavary &c [*bə'varə, *-ɪ] *n* a greatcoat or cloak *la18-e20.* [prob F *bavarois* Bavarian; *cf* obs Eng *bavaroy*]
baver *see* BEVER[1]
baw *see* BA[1], BA[2]
bawaw &c ['ba'wɑ] *n* a sideways glance *19-e20.*
bawbee &c *la17-,* **bawbé** &c *la16-17;* **balbie** *la16-17,* **babie** &c *16-18* ['ba'bi] *n* **1** a billon or *later* a copper coin, *orig* valued at six pennies SCOTS, equivalent to a halfpenny sterling *16-18.* **2** a halfpenny *18-.* **3** *chf in pl* money *la19-.* [prob f *Sillebawbe* the land and territorial designation of Alexander Orrock, a 16th century master of the mint]
bawbrek &c ['ba'brɛk, -'brɪk] *n* a kneading trough or board *19-e20.* [prob altered f *bakbread* &c (BAKE)]
bawcan ['bakən] *n* a BOGLE, ghost *20-,* now *Arg.* [prob Gael *bòcan* a hobgoblin; a ghost; *cf* Ork Sh *bawkie* a ghost etc, f ON *bokki*]
bawd &c *n* a hare *la18-.* [*cf* BAWTIE, BAUDRONS]
bawdry &c *16-;* **badrie** *la16-e17,* only *Sc* ['badrɪ] *n* = bawdry.
bawkie *see* BACKIE
bawr *see* BAR[2]
bawsant &c *16-19,* **bausond** &c *15-18,* **bausoun** &c *15-e19;* **bason** &c *la16-e18,* **basoned** &c *la16-e20* ['basənt, -ən(d)] *adj, of an animal, orig a horse* having a white mark or streak on the face. [nME *bausand,* OF *bausant, bausan* white-spotted, piebald]
bawsey *see* BASSIE[1]

bawtie &c *la16-e20,* **bawté** &c *e16;* **batie** *18-19* ['batɪ] *n* (name for) **1** a dog *16-19;* **2** a hare; a rabbit *19-e20, Rox.* [*cf* BAWD]
bawtie *see* BATIE
baxter &c *15-e19, as personal name 14-;* **bakster** &c *la15-17* *n* a baker *15-e19.*
baxtarie, baxtrey &c (the craft of) baking *16-e18.* [ME; OE *bæcestre,* fem of *bæcere* a baker]
bay *n* the singing of birds *e16.* [perh f Eng *bay* baying of hounds]
bayne *la15;* **bane** *la15-16 adj* = bain, ready, willing *la15-16.*
adv readily, willingly *la15-e16.*
be &c; **bey** *19-,* S [bi; *S* bəi] *v, pres indicative all pers also* **be** *la14-e19;* 1, 2 *pers sing, 1-3 pers pl (where personal pronoun is not immediately preceding) also* **is** *la14-;* 2, 3 *pers sing, 1-3 pers pl also* **beis, bees** *la14-,* now *Sh* [biz]; *1, 3 pers sing also* **bene** &c *la15-e17; 1 pers sing also* **ame** *la15-16; 3 pers sing also* **his** *la14-16; pl also* **ir**(**r**) *19-; negative 1 pers* **amna** &c *20-, local Sh-SW,* **immen** &c *20-, local Sh-SW* ['ʌmn(ə); *negative interrog, Abd* 'ʌmnən]. *pres subjunctive negative also* **binna** &c *la18-e20* ['bɪnə, 'binə]. *imperative also* **beis** *la14-e16* [*biz]; *negative imperative also* **binna** *la18-e19.*
pt indicative 1, 3 pers sing also **wes** *la14-e20,* **wis** &c *la18-,* now *Ork NE,* **wus** *20-,* now *C,* **wur** *la19-; pl also* **war** *la14-,* now *NE,* **ware** *la14-e20,* **wur** *19-,* now *Sh; (where personal pronoun is not immediately preceding)* **was** *la14-,* **wis** &c *la19-e20; pt subjunctive also* **war**(**e**) *la14-e20,* **was** &c *18-e20; pt indicative and subjunctive negative also* **wasna** &c *la19-,* **wiznan** &c *la19-, Abd* [*sing* waz, wɛz; *unstressed* wəz, wɪz; *pl etc* war, wʌr, wɪr; *negative* 'wɪznə, &c; *negative interrog, Abd* 'wɪznən].
ptp also **bein** &c *la14-e17* [bin].
A 1 beis &c [biz] in subordinate clauses after **gif, till** etc, *la14-,* now *Sh: 'if need bees'.* **2 was** introducing a past date *la15-e17: 'the beginning of July was a year';* *cf gane* (GAE). **3 bene** &c [bin] as perfect or pluperfect without *have, had* etc, *la14-: 'I been consulting with a lawyer'; 'the Church wad been dark';* see also *wad* (WILL[1]). **4 being** &c followed by another presp *16-e17: 'Margaret being doing her necessar adois'.*
B 1 = be *la14-.* **2** have as followers, *esp* in fighting *la14-16.* **3** serve as material for (a garment etc) *la15-e17.*
beid [*bi:d] = be it *la15-16.* **sae beins** ['se 'biənz] that being so *la18-, NE* [ie *sae bein* as].
binna ['bɪnə, 'binə; *Edb* 'bɪnɪ] *prep (19-e20), conj (la19-e20)* unless. **twar** [twar] = it were *19-,* now *NE Ags.* **ward** [*ward] = were it *la16,* only *Sc.*
be *see* BEE[1], BEHOVE, BY
bead &c *la17-,* **bede** &c *la14-e20* [bid; *nEC* bed] *n* **1** = bead *la14-.* **2** a glass or quantity of spirits *19-: 'he had a good bead in him yesterday'.* **3** (a measure of) the strength of spirits *19-e20.*

bedhous, bede-house &c an almshouse, hospital *la16-e20*. ~ **lam**(**b**)**s** part of the mounting of a silk-loom *19*. **bede**(**s**)**man** &c **1** = beadsman *15-19*. **2** a pauper, a beggar *la18-19*.

beadle *see* BEDDAL

beal &c *17-*, **bele** &c *15-16*; **bale** &c *e20* [bil; *Sh Ork nEC* bel; *local NE also* bel] *vti* **1** fester *la15-*. **2** *fig* swell with rage, fill with rancour, pain, remorse etc *15-*.
~**in** a festering sore, boil, pimple etc *19-*. [obscure]

bealach *20-*, *esp mountaineering*, **balloch** *la18-*, *esp in place-names* ['bɛləx, 'baləx; *Gael* 'bjalax] *n* a narrow mountain pass. [Sc and IrGael *bealach*]

beall *n* = bail *la17*.

beam &c; **been** &c *vt* steep (a barrel, tub etc) to make it tight *19-e20*. [obscure]

beam *see* BEME[1]

bear[1] *16-e20*, **bere** &c *la14-e20*; **bair** &c *16-e20*, **bar** *17*, *e20* [bir; *Sh Ork N also* ber] *n* = bear, barley; *specif* four- or six-row barley, hardier and coarser than ordinary two-row barley *la14-e20*.
~**-root** (**crop**) &c the first crop after BEAR *18-19*. ~**-sawing** the sowing of barley; seed barley *16-17*. ~**-seed** &c **1** the seed of the barley; barley for sowing *16*. **2** the (time for) sowing of barley or BEAR *16-e19*. [*cf* BARLIE]

bear[2] *la16-*, **bere** &c, **beir** &c *la14-*, *now Cai*; **bare** &c *la14-e16* [ber; *sEC, WC Kcb S* bir; *NE also* bir] *v*, *pt* **bare** &c *la14-16*, **bure** &c *la15-19* [bur; *Sh Ork C, S* bør; ***ber] **1** *vt* = bear *la14-*. **2** *law* ~ **fra** *etc* dispossess (a person) of land etc; take (something) away from a person *la15*. **3** *vi* carry oneself; act, behave *16*. **4** signify, mean, imply *la15-e20*.
~**er** *mining* a person, *usu* a woman or girl, who carried coal in baskets from the workings to the shaft *la19*. **bore breiff** &c a birth certificate *la16-e18*. **borne man** *etc* **of** *or* **in** .. a native of (a place) *la16-e17*.

beard *la16-*, **berde** &c *la14-17*, **baird** *16-* [*chf* berd; *also* bird] *n* = beard *la14-*.
~**ie** *n* **1** *also* **chinney** ~**ie** *20-* the rubbing of a man's rough chin against another person's chin or cheek, the squeezing of another's chin with the hand *la19-*. **2** a large jar (with the figure of a bearded old man on it) *la19*. **3** the three-spined stickleback *19-e20*. **4** *chf* ~**ie lotchie** &c the loach *19-e20*. *adj*, *of cheese* mouldy, hair-moulded *la20-*, *Loth SW*.

beas *see* BEAST

bease *see* BOOSE[1]

beast *17-*, **beste** &c *la14-e17*; **baste** &c *la18-e20* [bist; *Ork NE nEC Uls also* best] *n*, *pl* *also* **bes** &c *la14-15*, **beas** &c *la18-*, **bease** &c *la19-* [bis; *Sh Ork NE nEC also* bes] **1** = beast *la14-*. **2** *pl freq* **beas** a cow, any bovine animal *17-*, *local*. **3** a creature of any sort, a bird, fish, insect etc, a (body- and head-)louse etc *la18-*. **4** a skin of a fur-bearing animal *la15-e16*.

vt overcome, vanquish *19-*, *now Bnf*.
~**ie 1** familiar and affectionate form of BEAST *la18-*. **2** *fishermen's taboo* a pig *20-*, *Ags Bwk*.

beat &c [bit, bet] *vti* = bet *la18-*, *now local N*.

becam(**e**), **become** *see* BECUM

beck *16-*, **bek** *la15-e17*, **baik** *19-e20* *n* **1** a bow, a curtsy *la15-e20*. **2** = beck. *vi* make a gesture of respect, bow, curtsy *la15-e20*.

becum &c *15-17*; **become** &c *la16-* *vti*, *pt* **become** *la14-17*, **became** &c *16-*, **becam** *17-19*. *ptp* *also* **becummin** &c *15-16*, **becum** &c *16-e17*, **becummit** *la15-17* **1** = become *la14-*. **2** *vt* succeed in getting; acquire *15-17*.
~ **in** come into, enter into (a state or situation) *la15-17*.

bed &c; **bede** &c *la14-17*, **bad** &c *la14-e17* [bɛd] *n* **1** = bed *la14-*. **2** a flat base or foundation; a level structure *16-*. **3** a bank in the sea *la16-e17*. **4** *in pl* the spaces chalked on the ground for playing PEEVER[1]; the game itself *la19-*.
v **1** *vi* = bed, go to bed (**with** another) *la14-18*. **2** retire for the night *19-e20*. **3** *vt* put (*esp* children) to bed *la18-e20*.
~**ding** &c **1** = bedding *15-*. **2** the ceremony of putting a bride to bed *19*. ~**ding of clathis** a supply of bedclothes for one bed *la16-17*. ~**dit up** confined to bed through illness *la20-*, *NE*. ~**lar** &c *la15-19*, ~**rall** &c *16-*, *now Bnf*, ~**el** &c *la16-*, *now Kcdn*, ~**al** &c *la16-*, *now NE Kcdn adj* confined to bed, bedridden *la15-e17*. *n* a bedridden person, *formerly esp* as an inmate of a hospital or almshouse *16-*, *now NE Kcdn*.
~ **evil** an illness confining one to bed *15-e17*, *only Sc*. ~**fast** bedridden *la16-*. ~ **mat** = MAT 2, *20-*, *C*. ~ **pan**(**d**) the valance of a bed *la17*, *20-*, *now Bnf*. ~ **plaid** a PLAID (*n* 3) *la16-*, *now C*, *only Sc*.

bed *see* BIDE

bedal *see* BED

beddal &c *15-e19*, **bedel** &c *la14-e17*, **bedler** &c *la17-19*, **bedrall** &c *la16-19*; **beth**(**er**)**el** &c *la17-19*, **beadle** *la18-* ['bidl; ***'bɛdl, ***'bɛðl, ***'bɛdlər, ***'bɛdrəl, ***'bɛð(ə)rəl] *n* **1** = beadle, a herald etc *la14-e17*. **2** *also* **pedell** &c an officer in the service of an ecclesiastical organization, university etc *la16-17*. **3** *also* **peddell** &c *17*, *specif*: a kirk officer (KIRK) *la16-*. **4** a gravedigger, *prob usu* the same person as *n* 3, *19-e20*. [see SND]

beddie ba *see* BA[2]

bede *see* BEAD, BED

bedeen *la18-e20*, **bedene** &c *la14-16* [bɪ'din] *adv*, *usu as rhyme* **1** = bedene, altogether, entirely *la14-16*. **2** at once, quickly, soon *15-e20*.

bedel *see* BED, BEDDAL

bedellus &c [bɪ'dɛlʌs] *n* the chief porter and macebearer in the Universities of St Andrews, Glasgow and Edinburgh *18-*. [MedL]

bedene *see* BEDEEN
bedettit &c [*bɪˈdɛtɪt] *adj* indebted *e16*.
bedhous *see* BEAD
bedink [bɪˈdɪŋk] *vt* bedeck *19-e20*. [*be* + DINK]
bedirten *see* BEDRITE
bedlar *see* BED
bedler *see* BEDDAL
bedovin &c [*bɪˈdovn] *ptp* immersed *15-e16*.
[only Sc; OE *bedofen*, ptp of *bedūfan* submerge]
bedraigle [bɪˈdregl] *v*, *ptp* ~**d** = bedraggled
la19-e20.
bedrait *see* BEDRITE
bedrall *see* BED, BEDDAL
bedrite [bɪˈdrəit] *vt*, *pt* **bedrait &c** *16-e18*
[bɪˈdret]. *ptp also* **bedirten &c** *16-e18*
[bɪˈdɪrtən] foul **1** with excrement *16-e20*; **2**
with dirt *16-e18*. [*be-* + Eng *dirt*]
bedrucken [bɪˈdrʌkn] *adj* drunken *la19-*, *now*
Sh Ags. [*be* + DRUCKEN]
bee[1] **&c** *la15-*, **be** *la14-16* [bi; *S* bəi] *n* **1** = bee
la14-. **2** a whim, fanciful idea *16-e19*.
~**-headed &c** harebrained, unsettled *19-e20*.
~ **skep** a beehive *la16-17*.
busy &c ~ a very busy person *la14-*. **head in**
the ~**s** confused, light-headed *la18-19*.
bee[2] **&c** [*wDmf* bi; *eDmf Rox* bəi] *n* a metal ring
or ferrule *19-e20*, *Dmf Rox*. [OE *bēah* a ring]
be-east *17-e19*, **be-est &c** *15-17* [*bɪˈist &c*]
adv to(wards) the east; on the east side *la15-17*.
prep to the east of, eastward from *15-17*. [only
Sc; OE *be ēastan*]
bee-baw-babbety &c *n* a (kissing) game or
dance *20-*, *C*. [var of BAB AT THE BOWSTER]
beef *la18-*, **beif &c** *la14-17* [bif] *n* **1** = beef
la14-. **2** human flesh; the body *la16-18*. **3** an
ox or cow intended for slaughter *17-19*. **4** any
butcher's meat *20-*.
be-eft &c [*bɪˈɛft] *prep* after, behind *15-17*.
[only Sc; OE *beæftan*; *cf* ME *bafte &c*]
beegle *see* BAIGLE
beek &c *la15-*, **beke &c** *la14-18* *vti* **1** warm
(oneself); bask *la14-*. **2** *vi*, *of the sun* shine
brightly *19-*. **3** *vt* add fuel to (a fire) *la19-e20*.
n an act of warming (oneself etc) *18-e20*.
[uncertain]
been *see* BANE, BEAM
beenge &c *la18-e20*, **binge &c** *la15-19*;
beinge &c *16-18* [bindʒ, bɪndʒ] *vi* bow (humbly or servilely); cringe, fawn. [only Sc;
obscure]
beerach *see* BOURACH
beeran &c *n* a small trout *la19-*, *Suth Inv*.
[Gael *bioran* a little stick]
beerial *see* BURIAL
beerie &c *la19-e20*, **bury &c** *16-* [*N* ˈbirɪ; *C*, *S*
ˈbørɪ; *St* ˈbɛrɪ] *vt* = bury *la19-e20*. [*cf* BURIAL]
bees *see* BE
beest &c, **beist &c** [bist] *n* the first milk of a
cow after calving *la16-*, *now Cai*.
~**in** *19-*, *now Abd*, **beesenin &c** *la19-*, *now Kcb*,
~**y** *la18-e20*, all *chf attrib* = *n*. [OE *bēost*; *cf*
eModEng]

be-est *see* BE-EAST
beet[1] **&c** *18-19*, **beit** *la15* [bit] *n* a sheaf or bundle of flax. [eModEng *bete*, perh f OE *bēatan*
beat]
beet[2] **&c** *la16-e20*, **bete &c** *la14-17*; **bet &c**
la14 [bit] *vt*, *pt*, *ptp also* **bet** *la14-e19* **1** relieve,
lessen (distress, need etc) *la14-16*. **2** amend,
correct *la14-16*. **3** relieve (a person) **of** (something); assist, help, comfort *la14-e19*. **4** repair,
mend *la15-e20*. **5** *only in ptp* **bet &c** made, constituted *e16*. **6** supply something missing to
(something): (1) replace hooks on (a fishing
line) *19-*, *now Kcdn*; (2) *forestry* plant (trees) to
replace others *la18-*. **7** *also fig* kindle or add
fuel to (a fire) *la14-e19*.
n material for mending or for adding to a garment *e16*.
beitment &c repair(ing), making up, mending
16-e17.
~ **a mister** see MISTER. [ME *beete &c*,
ONorthumb *bæta*, OE *bētan*, ON *bǽta*]
beet *see* BEHOVE, BUIT[1], BUIT[2]
beetle *see* BITTLE
beetyach *e20*; **bittock &c** *19-e20* [ˈbitjəx,
*ˈbitək] *n* a sword, dagger, small knife. [only
Sc; see SND]
beezer &c *n*, *child's word* a thing or person bigger
or better than usual *20-*. [obscure]
befa *19*, **befall**, **befaw** *la15-16* [bɪˈfɑ] *vti* **1** =
befall *la14-*. **2** *vt* get as one's lot or share *16*. **3**
vi become; happen (to be etc) *la15-e17*.
beff *la19*; **beft** *la19* *v*, *pt*, *ptp* **beft &c** *la14-19* **1**
vt, *chf in pt*, *ptp* struck, beat(en) *la14-19*. **2** *vi*, *chf*
in pt delivered blows *15-e16*. [nME *beft*,
ONorthumb *beafton (pl)*]
beffan &c *n* a stupid, often fat and flabby, person *la19-*, *chf Bnf*. [see SND]
before &c, **beforn &c** *la14-e19*, *chf in rhymes*;
beforrow *la16*, *only in rhymes* [bɪˈfor, *-ˈforn,
*-ˈforʌu] *adv*, *prep*, *conj* = before *la14-*.
of ~ before in time; formerly *15-e17*, *only Sc*.
[*cf* AFORE]
beft *see* BEFF
befyle &c [bɪˈfəil] *vt* soil, defile *16-e20*.
[eModEng]
beg *see* BIG[1]
begar *see* BEGGAR
begary &c *16-17*, **begare &c** *la15-16* [*v*, *n*
*ˈbɪˈgerɪ, *v* *-ˈger] *vt* **1** *freq in ptp* ornamented
with stripes or trimmings of another material or
colour *la15-e17*. **2** variegate with streaks of
colour *16-17*.
n a trimming, facing, or stripe of different material on a garment *la16-e17*. [only Sc; F *bigarrer*
variegate, diversify with colours]
begeck; begeik &c [*Ross-Per* bɪˈgɛk, -ˈgəik; *Bnf*
also -ˈgɪk; *Ags also* -ˈgik] *vt* deceive, disappoint
la16-e20.
n a trick, disappointment *la18-e20*, *chf N*.
[prob *be-* + GECK; *cf* MDu, MLowGer *begecken*
deride; *cf* eModEng *begeck (n)* (once). DOST
bejaip]

be ges *see* BEGUESS
beggar &c; begar &c *la14-e17* ['bɛgər] *n, vt* = beggar *la14-*.
~tie &c = beggary *16, only Sc.*
~-man a fish, *usu* a flounder *e20, Mry.*
~'s bed *in a farm or country house* a bed made up for beggars, *usu* in the barn *la18-19.*

begin &c *vti, pt also* **begouth &c** *only Sc,* **begud** *&c only Sc,* **begood** *la18-* [bɪ'gud; *Bwk Rox also* -'gød; **-*'guθ; *NE* **-*'gʌd] = begin *la14-.*
~ to start (on) *19-, now Mry Ags.*

beglamour &c [*bɪ'glamər] *vt* bewitch *19.* [*be-* + GLAMOUR]
begood *see* BEGIN
begotted &c; bigotit &c [bɪ'gotɪt, 'bigətɪt] *adj*
1 = bigoted *la19-.* **2** infatuated *19-e20.*
begouth *see* BEGIN
begowk &c [bɪ'gʌuk] *vt* befool *la19-e20.* [*be-* + GOWK¹]
begoyt; begyte [bɪ'gɔit] *adj* foolish, mad *la18-e20.* [*be-* + GYTE]
begrutten &c *17-e20,* **begrett &c** *e16, la19* [bɪ'grʌt(ə)n, **-*'grat, **-*'grɛt, *&c*] *adj* tear-stained, sorrowful. [*be-* + grutten (GREET¹)]
begud *see* BEGIN
beguess &c *18-, now Bnf;* **be ges &c** *15-16* [bɪ'gɛs] *adv* by guessing; at random. [*orig* prep phr *be* (BY) + GUESS]
begunk &c [bɪ'gʌŋk] *vt* **1** cheat, deceive, jilt *19-e20.* **2** befool *la19-e20.*
n **1** a disappointment, misfortune *la18-e20.* **2** a trick *18-e20.* [*be-* + GUNK]
begyte *see* BEGOYT
beha(l)d *see* BEHAUD
behalf &c *la15-,* **behalve** *15;* **behaw** *la15-16* [*bɪ'half, **-*'halv, **-*'ha, *&c*] *n* = behalf.
behangt &c [bɪ'haŋ(t)] *interj* expressing impatience *la19-.* [*be-* + ptp of HING]
behaud &c *la16-,* **behald &c** *la14-17;* **behad &c** *18-* [bɪ'had; -'had; **-*'hald; **-*'hald] *v, ptp also* **behudden &c** **1** *vt* = behold *la14-.* **2** contemplate, consider, regard *la15-16.* **3** *vi* suspend action, hold back, wait *17-e20.* **4** *vt* eye (a person) watchfully, keep an eye on *19-, now Bnf.*
behaw *see* BEHALVE
behear &c [bɪ'hir] *interj* expressing surprise *20-, now Ags.* [*perh* contraction of Eng *God behear us* but *cf* Eng *God be here!*]
behecht *la15-e16, only Sc,* **behight &c** *la15, e18* [*bɪ'hɛxt; **-*'hɪxt] *vti* = behight, vow, promise *la15-e18.*
n, only **behecht** = behight, a promise *e16.*
beheef &c *la19-e20, N,* **behufe &c** *la14-e17,* **behove &c** *la14-17;* **behuve &c** *15-17* [*N* bɪ'hif, -'hiv; **bɪ'høf, **-*'høv] *n* = behoof *la14-e20.*
behuffull &c = behoveful, necessary; advantageous *15-e16.* [*cf* BEHOVE]
behight *see* BEHECHT

behin &c *la18-,* **behind &c** *la14-;* **behint &c** *la19-* [bɪ'hɪn(t); *Uls also* -'hain; **-*'hɪnd] *adv, prep* = behind.
behouchie &c; bahookie &c [bə'huxɪ, *&c*] *n, freq to children* the behind, backside *20-, Gen except Sh Ork.* [conflation of Eng *behind* w *houch* (HOCH¹)]
behove &c, behufe &c *la14-e17,* **boost** *19-e20;* **behuve &c** *15-19* [bɪ'huv; *NE* bɪ'hiv; *C also* bɪ'hʌv; **bɪhøv; bust, bøst, bɪst; *N* bist] *v, 3 pers sing pres also* **behus &c** *la15-16* [**bɪ'høz] *pt forms also sometimes used as pres. pt also* **behud &c** *la15-16,* **bude &c** *19-,* **bute &c** *16-19,* **bit &c** *la17-e20,* **bood &c** *19-e20,* **bud &c** *19-e20,* **beet &c** *la19-e20, chf NE,* **be** (*followed by* t(ae), *by wrong division*) *19-* [**bɪ'hø:d, *&c*; bud, bod, bød, bid, bʌd; *N* bid; **but, bɪt, bʌt; *N Uls* bit; **bøt; 'bi:t(ɪ)] **1** *vi* = behove *la14-.* **2** *with personal subject* be under an obligation or necessity *la14-.*
beet- *or* **bude-(tae)-be** something which one was obliged to do *19-e20.* [*cf* BEHEEF]
behove *see* BEHEEF
behss &c [*NE-Ags* bes; *Ags also* bez] *n* bustle, hurry *la19-, now Ags.* [onomat]
behud *see* BEHOVE
behudden *see* BEHAUD
behufe *see* BEHEEF, BEHOVE
behuffull *see* BEHEEF
behus *see* BEHOVE
behuve *see* BEHEEF, BEHOVE
beid *see* BE
beif *see* BEEF
beig *see* BIG²
beil *see* BIELD
beild *see* BIELD, BUILD
bein &c *see* BE, BIEN
being *see* BE
beinge *see* BEENGE
beir &c *la15-19,* **bere** *la14-16* [*bir] *n* an outcry, shouting; noise, din *la14-19.*
vi cry, roar *la14-16.* [ME *bere &c*]
beir *see* BEAR²
beirn *see* BERN
beis *see* BE, BY
beist *see* BEEST
beit *see* BEET¹
beith *see* BAITH
beitment *see* BEET²
bejan &c *la19-20,* **bajan &c** *17-e20;* **bajone &c** *17,* **bejant &c** *19-* ['bedʒən; *St Andrews* 'bidʒənt] *n* a first-year student at a Scottish university *17-, now only St Andrews.*
bejanella *la19-20, Aberdeen Univ* [bedʒə'nɛlə], **bejantine** *la19-, St Andrews Univ* [bidʒən'təin(ə)] a female first-year student. [F *béjaune, bec jaune* a young bird; an inexperienced youth]
bek *see* BECK
beke *see* BEEK
beken &c [*bɪ'kɛn] *vt, law* admit as possessor *e16.* [*be* + KEN; *cf* ME]

bekin &c ['bik(ə)n] *n* **1** = beacon *16-*. **2** a sign, a signal *la15-e16*.
vti = beckon, give a sign *la14-e17*.
bekis [*biks] *n pl* ? corner teeth (of a horse) *e16*. [perh OF *bec*]
belang [bə'laŋ] *vi* **1** = belong *15-*. **2** *with indirect object* belong to *16-*. **3** own, possess *la19-*, now *Ork C*. **4** belong to (a place), be a native of *la19-*, now *C*: 'he belangs Glesca'.
as ∼**and** as concerning *la15-e16*.
belaubir [bə'labər] *vt* = belabour, thrash *20-*, now *Sh Bnf Ags*.
belaw *see* BELOW
belch¹ &c *e15*, *la18-19*, **belge** *19-*; **bilch &c** *la18-* [bɛlx, bɪlx; *NE* bɛldʒ; *Kcb* bɪldʒ; *Dmf* bɪltʃ; *S* bɪlʃ; *Lnk* *bɛlʃ] *n* **1** the belly *e15*. **2** *freq contemptuous* a stout, *usu* short person *la18-*, now *Kcb*. **3** contemptuous term for a person, *esp* a child *19-e20*.
∼**y** short, plump and thriving *18-*, now *Dmf*. [only *Sc*; *ON belgr* a bag; *cf* BILGET²]
belch² [*bɛlx] *n* a deep pool, an abyss *e17*. [obscure]
beld¹ &c *la15-*, now *Abd*, only *Sc*, **bellit** *15-e17*; **bell &c** *la16-e20*, **baul &c** *la18-e19* [bɛld; *NE* bɛlt; *C, S also* bɛl; *Abd Kcb* bal; *bɛlɪt] *adj* **1** = bald *15-*. **2** *of horses or cattle* having a white spot or mark on the forehead *16-e18*.
vt make bald *la19-*, *Bnf Abd*.
n, *only* **bell** a white mark on a horse's face *la16*, *19*.
bauldy &c, **baldy** ['baldɪ] bald *20-*: 'bauldy-heidit'.
bell-kite &c, **bel-poot &c** the bald coot *la19-e20*.
beld² *adj* bold *la15*, *e19*. [see SND]
beld *see* BUILD
beldairy *see* BALDERRY
belde *see* BIELD
bele *see* BALE, BEAL
belechere &c [*'bil'tʃir, *?bɛl-] *n* good cheer; entertainment *e16*. [ME *beele chere*, OF *bele chere*]
beleve¹ &c *la14-16*; **beleif &c** *la15-16*, only *Sc*, **belief** *17-* [*bɪ'liv] *n* **1** = belief *la14-*. **2** expectation, anticipation *e16*, only *Sc*.
beleve² &c *16-e17*; **beleif &c** *la14-16* [bɪ'liv] *vti* **1** = believe *la14-e17*. **2** *vt*, *chf with infin* expect *16*: 'he belevis to lerne'.
belfert *see* BILF²
belge *see* BELCH¹
belgh [*bɛlx] *n* an outburst *e17*. [*fig* var of Eng *belch*; *cf* BILSH]
be-licket *chf* deil *etc* ∼ devil a bit, absolutely nothing *18-e19*.
belief *see* BELEVE¹
beligger [*bɪ'lɪgər] *vt* = beleaguer *e17*, only *Sc*.
belike *la18-e19*, **belyke &c** *la16-e17* [bɪ'ləik] *adv* to all appearances, surely; presumably, probably. [eModEng]
belive *see* BELYVE
bell¹ &c *n* = bell *la14-*.

∼**cast** *building* a decrease in the pitch of a roof near the eaves; *fig* a taper, slant *la20-*. ∼ **custome** *prob* a custom-due for the upkeep of a bell *la16-e17*, only *Sc*. ∼-**heidit** *of nails* with a bell-shaped head *e17*, only *Sc*. ∼-**house &c** a tower etc to hold a bell or set of bells *15-e19*. ∼-**penny** money set aside to pay for one's funeral *19*. ∼-**string** *la16-e17*, ∼-**tow** *la16-*, now *Bwk*, only *Sc* a bell rope. ∼ **ware, belliwar &c** a coarse seaweed *la18-*, now *Abd*, only *Sc*. ∼**waver &c** *vi*, *also fig* straggle, stroll; move about aimlessly *la18-19*, only *Sc*.
bell the cat *vi* **1** undertake a hazardous action *la16-e17*. **2** dispute, contend, *esp* with a superior *18-e19*. **Bell the Cat** nickname given to Archibald Douglas, fifth Earl of Angus, who daringly offered to remove James III's favourite in 1482, *la18-*, *hist* [f the fable, 'The Cat and the Mice'].
bell² *n* a bubble *16-e20*.
vi bubble up *e19*. [ME, Flem *belle*; *cf* Du *bel*]
bell *see* BELD¹
bellamy &c *n* a fellow; an unpleasant or rough person *la15-16*. [only *Sc*; eModEng, ME *belamy &c*, OF *bel ami* fair friend]
bellibucht &c ['bɛlɪbʌxt, 'bɪlɪ-] *n* a hollow in a hill, running across the slope *19-*, *SW*. [prob *biely*, Kcb form of BIELD + *bucht* (BOUCHT²) (*n* 1)]
bellies &c *la16-*, now *Sh*, **bellis &c** *la14-17* ['bɛlɪz] *n pl*, *also as double pl* **bellises &c** *16-e20*, **bellowses** *la19-e20* ['bɛlɪsɪz] = bellows.
belli-hooin &c ['bɛlɪ'hu(x)ɪn] *n*, *adj* riotous(ness) *la19-*, *Fif*.
bellis [*'bɛlɪs] *vt* embellish *15-e17*.
∼**ant** serving to embellish; beautiful *la15-e17*. [F *bellissant*, presp of *bellir* make beautiful]
bellis(es) *see* BELLIES
bellit *see* BELD¹
belliwar *see* BELL¹
belloch ['bɛlox,-əx] *vi*, *of cattle* bellow *la19-e20*. [only *Sc*; altered f Eng dial *bellock*; *cf* BELLY²]
bellox *n pl* = ballocks, testicles *la16*.
bellowses *see* BELLIES
bellum &c *n* noise, din; a blow; force *18-*, now *Fif*. [only *Sc*; perh L *bellum* war]
belly¹ *la15-*; **bally &c** *la14-16* ['bɛlɪ; *balɪ] *n* = belly *la14-*.
vi eat or drink voraciously *19-*, now *Bnf*.
∼-**blind** blind man's buff; the blindfolded person in it *la15-e20*. ∼ **brace** a girth for a horse *la15-e17*, only *Sc*. ∼ **flaught** *17-*, ∼ **flaucht &c** *la14-* **1** flat on one's face or stomach *18-*, now *Abd Kcb*. **2** in full flight, headlong, like a bird descending on its prey *18-e19*. **flay** ∼ **flaught** skin (a rabbit etc) by pulling the skin over the head *la14-e19*. ∼ **god** *la16*, *e19*, ∼ **gut** *la19-*, *NE adj*, *n* gluttonous; a glutton. ∼ **rive(r)** [-'raiv(ər)] a great feast, eating to repletion *20-*, *Bnf Abd*; *cf* RIVE *v* 13, 15. ∼**thraw** colic, belly-ache *16-e20*. ∼-**timber &c** food, provisions *la18-19*.

over the ~ of in spite of *18*.

belly[2] &c *la18-*, now *Mry*; **bully** *20-*, now *Ags vi* = bellow. [*cf* BELLOCH]

belovit &c *15-e17*; **belufit** &c *15-16* [*bɪ'løvɪt] *adj* = beloved *15-16*.

n, chf in pl beloved subjects *la15-e17*.

below *19-*, **belaw** *la16-19* [bə'lo, *bə'lɑ] *adv*,

prep = below *la16-*.

vr lower oneself *19-e20*.

in ~ under *la19-*.

bel-poot *see* BELD[1]

belt &c *n* **1** = belt *la14-*. **2 the** ~ the *tawse* (TAW[1]) *20-*. **3** a blow, a hit *19-*.

vt **1** surround, encircle *15-16*. **2** put a belt on (a person), *specif* as part of the insignia of an earl *15-*. **3** fasten on (a sword etc) with a belt *16-*. **4** beat or thrash (with or without a belt) *la15-*.

~**ed plaid(y)** *see* PLAID. ~**in** a clump or line of trees *20-*. ~**ing**, *chf* ~**ing silk** ? silk cord *la16*.

Beltane &c, **Beltyme** &c *la16*; **Beltan** &c *la15-* **1** 1 or 3 May; an old Scottish quarter-day (which may also have been on other days in May) *15-*. **2** a pagan fire festival on these days (and sometimes also on 21 June); identified by the Church as the feast of the Invention of the Cross (3 May) *la15-*. ~ **buke** an account book in which the reckoning was made annually at BELTANE *la16-e17*. ~ **day** the day of the BELTANE festival or fair *16-17*. [ScGael *bealltainn* &c, IrGael *bealltaine*, OIr *belltaine* &c]

belufit *see* BELOVIT

belyf *see* BELYVE

belyke *see* BELIKE

belyve &c *la14-e20*, **belive** &c *16-19*; **belyf** &c *la14-16* [bə'laɪv] *adv* quickly, at once; soon. [ME]

belȝe *see* BAILIE

bemang [bɪ'maŋ] *vt* ~'**d** &c hurt, injured *19-e20*. [see SND]

beme[1] &c *la14-e17*; **beam** &c *la16-* [bim; *nEC* bem] *n* = beam *la14-*.

~**fill** *building, also fig* = beamfill, fill the space between the wall-plate and the roof *16-*. **beamfill't**, **beamfoo** filled to overflowing; indulged; intoxicated *19-*, now *Abd Bnf*.

beme[2] *n* = beme, a trumpet *la15*.

vi sound loudly; ring or resound *e16*.

bemean [bɪ'min] *vt* disparage, humiliate *19-e20*. [*be-* + Eng *mean*]

ben[1] &c *adv* **1** in or towards the inner part of a house etc; in or to the best room; inside *15-*. **2** *specif, mining* inwards, towards the workings *la19-*, now *Fif*.

prep through (a house) towards the inner part; in or to the best room, *freq* ~ **the hoose** *la16-*.

adj inner, interior *19-e20*.

n **1** the inner room, the best room *la18-e20*. **2** (1) *mining* a miner's right to enter the pit, *freq*

claim one's ~ *la19-*, now *Fif*. (2) one's place in a queue, *freq* **keep, stand** *etc* one's ~ *la19-*, now *Fif Lnk Ayr*.

~**ner** inner *la16-e20*. ~**most** &c furthest in, in the second, inner room *la18-e20*. ~**ward** &c inward(s) *la15*, *19-e20*. [ME *byn(ne)*, *binne*, ONorthumb *binna* &c, OE *binnan* within; *cf* BUT]

ben[2] *la19-*, **bin(n)** *la18-*, latterly only place-names *n* a mountain, hill, **ben** *usu* being applied to the higher Scottish mountains. [Gael *beann, beinn*]

ben *see* BEND[1]

bench *see* BINK[1]

bend[1] *n* **1** *heraldry* = bend *la15-*. **2** *also* **benn** &c *la17-19* a band, sash, ribbon worn on clothing, on the hair etc *16-19*. **3** *also* **ben**, *chf* ~ **leather** toughened ox leather used for boot soles *18-19*.

bend[2] *v* **1** *vt* = bend *la14-*. **2** *vi* spring, leap *16-e19*. **3** drink hard *18-e19*.

n **1** = bend, curve etc *15-*. **2** a spring, leap *16-18*.

~**er** a hard drinker *18* [*cf* Eng slang = a drinking bout]. ~**it** *of a gun etc* cocked, made ready for firing *16-17*. **bentnes** &c inclination, intentness *la16-17*, only *Sc*.

~ **the bicker** &c = *v* 3, *la18-e20*.

bene &c *15-16*, **bane** &c *16-e17* *n* = bean *15-e17*.

King *or* **Queen of B**~ the person in whose portion of Twelfth-Night cake the bean was found *la15-16*.

bene *see* BE, BIEN

benefit &c, **benefite** &c *la16-e17* *n* **1** = benefit *la16-*. **2** payment in kind as part of a farmworker's wages, *freq* ~ **man** a farmworker who receives such *la18-*, *SW*.

beneis *see* BANIS[1]

beneth &c [*bɪ'nɛθ, *-'niθ, *-'neθ] *prep, adj* = beneath *la14-e17*.

benevolence &c *n* **1** = benevolence *15-*. **2** free will, voluntary action *16*, only *Sc*.

bengle *see* BANYEL

benicht [bɪ'nɪxt] *v, ptp, adj* ~**ed** *lit and fig* = benighted *19-*, now *Abd*.

bening &c [*bɪ'nɪŋ] *adj* = benign *15-16*, only *Sc*.

benis *see* BANIS[2]

beniso(u)n *see* BENNISON

benk *see* BINK[1]

benmost *see* BEN[1]

benn *see* BEND[1]

bennel &c *n, freq in pl* **1** any long reedy grass *19-e20*. **2** a reed or rush mat used in poorer houses to line the ceiling rafters etc *19-e20*, *Bwk Rox*. [uncertain]

benner *see* BANERE, BEN[1]

bennison &c *la16-e19*, only *Sc*, **benisoun** &c *la14-16*; **benison** &c *la14-*, **banesoun** *e16* ['bɛnɪsən, *-un; *'ban-] *n*, now *arch or verse* = benison, blessing.

benok &c [*'binok, *'bɪn-] *n* a kind of skin or hide *la16-e17*. [only *Sc*; *appar dim* of Gael *bian* skin, hide]

benorth &c [bɪˈnorθ, *Sh* -ˈnort] *prep* to the north of *la14-*, *now Sh.*
adv to or in the north *la16-e20*. [OE *benorðan*; *cf* ME *bynorth* (rare)]
bense &c [bɛns] *vi* walk or move with great energy; bounce *19-e20*.
bensin bouncing, vigorous *la19-e20*, *Bnf.* [only Sc; prob back-formation f next]
bensell &c [ˈbɛnsl, *also* ˈbɛnzl] *n* **1** bending, straining *e16*. **2** a state of excitement; a strong inclination *17*. **3** vigorous action; force; violence (of a storm, fire etc) *la17-e20*. **4** a place exposed to storm *19-*, *now Per Fif.*
vt beat or thrash soundly *19-*, *now Bnf.* [northern ModEng dial; ON *benzl* (*npl*) bent state of a bow]
benshie *see* BANSHEE
bensin *see* BENSE
bent &c *n* **1** = bent, coarse grass *15-*. **2** (1) *also in pl* a stretch of open ground (covered with bent); a moor *la15-17*. (2) *chf in pl* a sandy hillock covered with bent *la19-e20*.
~y covered with bent *la16-19*.
~ silver money paid by schoolchildren to provide bent for the schoolroom floor *la16-e18*.
go *or* **take to the ~** flee (from danger or from one's creditors) *18-e19*.
bentnes *see* BEND²
benweed, benwod *see* BUNWEED
bequeyst [bɪˈkwəist] *n* = bequest *20-*, *NE.*
berde *see* BEARD
bere *see* BEAR¹, BEAR², BEIR
Bereans *n pl* a Protestant sect *la18*. [the people of Berea, in Acts xvii 10, 11]
bergan *see* BARGAIN
bergell &c *n* a species of wrasse *la18-e20*, *Sh Ork Mry.* [Scand *berggylta* &c, *lit* rock-pig, ON *gyltr* a young sow]
beriall &c *la14-16*; **buriall** &c *la16-e17* [*?ˈbɪrıal, *?ˈbɛrıal, *ˈbɪrəl, *ˈbʌrıəl] *n* = beryl, the precious stone; fine crystal. [-*u*- form by analogy w *beriall* (BURIAL)]
beriall *see* BURIAL
beris &c [*ˈbirɪs] *n* a burying place; a burial *la15-e16*.
vt bury *la15-16*. [only Sc; perh ME *berieles* &c, OE *byrgels*]
berk *see* BARK¹
bern &c *la15-16*; **beirn** &c *15-e17*, *only Sc*, **bairne** *16-e17*, *only Sc* [*bɛrn, *birn] *n*, *only verse* = bern, a warrior.
bern *see* BAIRN, BARN
berrick *n* = barrack *19-*, *local*, *only Sc.*
berry¹ &c *16-*, **bery** &c *la15-16* [ˈbɛrɪ] *n* = berry *la15-*.
no the ~ not the thing; not to be trusted *la19-e20*, *Bnf Abd.*
berry² &c [ˈbɛrı; *WC, SW* ˈbarı] *vti* thresh (corn); thrash (*esp* a child) *19-e20*, *chf SW, S.* [ME *berien* &c; ON *berja* beat]

bers *only Sc*, **bas; barse** &c *only Sc* [*bɛrs, *ba(r)s] *n* the smallest kind of cannon *16-e17*. [OF *berce*; *cf* laME *base*]
Bertane &c *la15-e16*; **Bartane** &c *la15-16* *n* **1** = Britain *la15-16*. **2** = Brittany *la15-e16*.
~ claith *etc* cloth etc from Brittany *la15-16*.
Bertanʒe *see* BRETANʒE
berthy *see* BIRTH¹
bertisse &c *n* = brattice, a breastwork or parapet *15-17*. [metath]
Bertonar &c *n* a man or ship of Brittany *e16*.
bertyn *see* BRITTIN
bervie *n* a kind of split dried haddock *18-e20*. [only Sc; f Inverbervie, Kcdn]
bery *see* BERRY¹
bes *see* BEAST
beschop *see* BISHOP
beseek *la19*, **beseke** &c *15-e16*; **beseik** *15-e20*, *only Sc* [bɪˈsik] *vti*, *pt*, *ptp* **besocht** &c [bɪˈsoxt] = beseech. [northern and nmidl ME]
besom *18-*, **bisom** &c *la16-e20*, **bussom** &c *16-e20*, *only Sc*, **boosome** &c *la16-e20*, *only Sc* [ˈbɪz(ə)m, ˈbɪz(ə)m, *also* bɪs(ə)m; *ˈbʌz(ə)m] *n* **1** = besom; *more gen* any broom *16-*. **2** a bunch of twigs used as a scourge *16*, *only Sc.* **3** *transf* a comet or its tail *la16-e17*, *only Sc.* **4** term of contempt for a person, *esp* a woman *19-*. [see SND]
bess *see* BAISS¹
bessie¹ &c *n* an ill-mannered, boisterous, bad-tempered woman or girl *la19-e20*. [only Sc; dim of *Bess*, short for *Elizabeth*]
bessie² *n*, *also* **~ bairdie** &c, **~ lotchie** &c the loach *19-e20*, *Rox.* [unknown]
best &c *adj*, *n* **1** = best *la14-*. **2** *chf* **the B~** Providence, God *la19-e20*, *chf Ork.*
~ aucht the most valuable article or animal owned by a person, claimed by a SUPERIOR on the death of a tenant *16-e17*. **~ cheip** &c cheapest *16*, *only Sc.* **~-lyk** &c [*~-ˈləik] of best appearance *16*, *only Sc.* **~ maid** a bridesmaid *la18-*, *only Sc.* **~ man** the chief attendant on a bridegroom *la18-*.
beste *see* BEAST
bestial, bestiale &c *n* **1** domestic animals, livestock *la14-e20*. **2** (wild) animals in general *15-e17*. [ME *bestyall* &c, OF *bestaille*, laL *bestiālia*]
beswakkit [*bɪˈswakɪt] *ptp* soaked, drenched *e16*. [*be-* + SWACK¹ *v*]
besy *see* BISSY
bet *see* BATE, BEET²
betak &c [bɪˈtak] *v* **1** *vt* hand over; deliver (goods, a blow) *la14-*, *now Abd.* **2** overtake *la16-19*. **3** *vr* recover *la19-*, *Bnf Abd.* [ME]
betaken &c [*bɪˈtekən] *vt* = betoken *la14-e19*.
bete *see* BATE, BEET²
beteach *la16-e18*, **beteche** &c *la14-e17* [*bɪˈtitʃ] *vt* **1** commit, hand over; give up,

entrust *la14-e17*. **2** commit, commend, *esp* **to** (God or the Devil) *la14-e18*. [ME; OE *betæcan*]

bethankit [bɪˈθaŋkɪt] *interj* God be thanked! *la18-19, only Sc.*

beth(er)el *see* BEDDAL

betide *see* BETYDE

betill *see* BITTLE

betimes &c *adv* **1** = betimes *la16-*. **2** occasionally; at (certain) times *la15, la19.*

betraise &c *la14-16*; **betrese** &c *la14-e17* [*bɪˈtrez, *-ˈtriz] *vt* betray. [ME; OF *traiss-, trahiss-*, lengthened stem of *traïr*]

betrump [*bɪˈtrʌmp] *vt* deceive *e16*.

betteis *n pl* ? remedies *e16*. [*cf* BEET²]

better &c *adj* = better *la14-*.
n better fortune; advantage *15-*.
adv **1** = better *la14-*. **2** completely recovered from an illness *19-*. **3** *as intensifier with repeated verb, 17-:* 'ran and better ran'.
∼-**mais**(t) better-class *e20*. ∼**ness** recovery *20-, local.*
∼ **chepe** &c cheaper; more cheaply *la15-e17.*
∼-**faured** better-featured, better-looking *20-.*
∼-**like** better-looking *20-.* (**on the**) ∼ **side** (of) older or younger than *20-, Bnf Abd.*
I *etc* **am** ∼ **to** *19-*, I *etc* ∼ *la19-* or I *etc* **will** ∼ *la18-* I *etc* had better .. **the** ∼ **of** the better for *la18-.*

betuxe *see* BETWIX

between &c *16-*, **betwene** &c *la14-16*; **betwine** &c *la16 prep, adv* = between *la14-.*
∼ **the** (**two**) **lichts** twilight *20*. [*cf* ATWEEN]

betweesh &c *la18-e20, Bnf Abd*, **betwis** &c *15-e20* [bɪˈtwiʃ, -ˈtwis, *-ˈtwɪs, *-twɪʃ] *prep* = BETWIX. [only *Sc; cf* ATWEESH]

betwene *see* BETWEEN

betwex *see* BETWIX

betwine *see* BETWEEN

betwis *see* BETWEESH

betwix &c *la14-e17*, **betwixt** &c *15-*; **betwex** &c *15-16*, **betuxe** &c *la14-e17* [bɪˈtwɪks(t), *-ˈtwiks, *-ˈtuks, *-ˈtʌks(t), *-ˈtwɪʃt] *prep* = betwixt, between *la14-.*
∼ **and** .. between now and .. *la15-18*; cf *atween and* (ATWEEN). [*cf* ATWIXT]

betyde &c, **betide** [bɪˈtəid] *vi* **1** = betide *la14-*. **2** succeed, fare (well) *la16, e20 (Abd).*

beuch &c [bjux] *n* **1** *pl also* **bewis** &c *la15-e17* [*bju(i)z] = bough, a branch of a tree *la15-19.* **2** the shoulder or limb of an animal or person *la16-19, only Sc.* **3** the bow of a ship etc *e17, la19-e20 (NE).*

beuk *see* BAKE, BUIK

beune &c [*bɪˈøn] *adv, prep* above *la14-16.* [only *Sc*; reduced f OE *beufan; cf* ABUNE and eME *buven*]

beust [bɪst] *n* withered grass from the previous year *19-, SW.* [unknown]

beuté *see* BEWTÉ

bevel *18-e19*, **bevell** *e17* [*ˈbɛvl] *n* a staggering blow. [only *Sc*; perh Eng *bevel*]

bever¹ &c *15-e17*; **baver** &c *la15-17, only Sc* [*ˈbivər, *ˈbevər] *n* = beaver.

bever² &c [ˈbɛvər, ˈbevər] *n* shaking; a trembling (fever) *la17.*
vi shake, tremble *la19-e20, S.*
∼ **hair** a trembling old man *la15.* [ME *v*]

beverage *n* **1** = beverage. **2** a fine in the form of money, drink, or a kiss demanded from a person wearing something new, *chf* **gie, get** *etc* **the** ∼ **o** (the new garment) *19-e20.*

bew *see* BLUE

bewar(e) *see* BEWAUR

bewast &c *16-19*, **bewest** *15-e18* [bɪˈwast, -ˈwɛst] *prep* to the west of; on the west side of *la15-19.* [ME *biwesten (adv)*, OE *be westan (adv, prep)*]

bewaur &c *19-e20*, **beware** &c *la14-*; **bewar** &c *16-17* [bɪˈwar] *vtir* = beware.

bewave &c [bɪˈwev] *vt, ptp also* **bewave** toss about; blow or sweep away *e16.* [only *Sc*; f Eng *wave*]

bewest *see* BEWAST

bewis *see* BEUCH

bewté &c *la14-e17*; **beuté** &c *la14-16* *n* = beauty.

bey *see* BE

beyont *18-*, **be3ond** &c *la14-e17*; **beyon** &c *la19*, **beyond** *la15-*, **be3ound** &c *15-16* [bəˈjon(t); &c] *prep, adv* **1** = beyond *la14-.* **2** *of time, number, degree* above, more than etc *la15-.* [*cf* AYONT]

bhoy *see* BOY

bi *see* BY

biach &c; **byauch** [bjɑx] *n* colloq form of address *e20, Cai Ross.* [only *Sc; cf* Gael *beadach* impertinent]

bibble *see* BUBBLE

bibliothecar &c *n* a librarian *la16-e18.* [L *bibliothecārius*, F *bibliothécaire; cf* eModEng *bibliothecarie*]

biche *see* BITCH

bick¹ *18-20*, **bik** &c *e16, e20 n* = bitch, a female dog. [ON *bikkja*; cognate w OE *bicce* > BITCH]

bick² &c *n, chf* (∼) ∼ **birr** imitation of the call of the grouse *la19-, chf Abd.*

bicker¹ *16-*, **bikker** &c *la14-e17 v* **1** *vt* attack with arrows, stones etc *la14-e17.* **2** *vi* fight with arrows, stones, or other weapons; make skirmishing attacks; engage in (street) fights *15-19.* **3** (1) *of water in gen* move quickly and noisily; *of rain* pelt, patter; *of boiling water* bubble quickly *la18-, now Abd.* (2) *of living creatures* move quickly and noisily, rush *19-e20.* **4** *of light, fire etc* gleam, flicker, sparkle *e19.* **5** laugh heartily *20-, NE.*
n **1** a fight with missiles; a skirmish; a street- or school-fight; a quarrel *la15-e20.* **2** a rapid, noisy movement, a short run *la18-e20, only Sc.* [ME *biker(e)*]

bicker², **bikker &c** *n* = beaker, a drinking vessel, *esp* of wood; a (porridge) bowl, *formerly* one made of staves *16-*.

bid &c *vt, pt* **bad(e)** [bad, bed; *bɑd] **1** = bid *la14-*. **2** offer, desire, seek (to do something) *15-16*. **3** invite (to a wedding etc) *16-*.

biddable &c obedient, amenable to discipline *19-*. **bidding 1** a command *la14-*. **2** an invitation (to do something)*19-*.

bide &c *v, pt, ptp* **bade &c, bed &c** *la16-e20* [bed, bɪd; *Ork NE* bid; *bad], **bided** *19*. *pt also* **bode** *la19-, ptp also* **bidden &c** *15-* **1** *vi* remain, stay (*esp* temporarily), dwell, reside *la14-*. **2** remain in a certain state or condition *la14-16*. **3** await, delay departure or action (until..) *la14-16*. **4** *vt* await, stay for *la14-*. **5** await the effect of; tolerate, endure *15-*. *n* pain *19-, now NE, only Sc*.

lawful *etc* **time bidden** at the time appointed by law *la15-16*. **bidie-in** a person who lives with another of the opposite sex without marriage *20-, Abd*.

~ at *la15-e16* or **by &c** *17-e19* stand by, adhere to, submit to. **~-in &c** = *bidie-in, 20-, Abd*. [ME; ONorthumb *bīda*, OE *bīdan*]

bield *la18-*, **belde &c** *la14-e16*; **beild** *15-e20*, **beil &c** *la16-, now Bnf* [bil(d)] *n* **1** *chf literary* protection; relief, succour; refuge, shelter *15-, now Bnf*. **2** a person acting as a protector, comforter etc *la14-18*. **3** something which gives protection, aid etc *15-16*. **4** a place giving refuge or shelter *la15-e20*.

vt, pt, ptp **beild &c, beildit &c 1** succour, help; protect *la15-19, only Sc*. **2** cover over; shelter *la15-19*. **3** place securely (in a certain state etc) *la15-16*.

beild *la18-19*, **beildy** *la18-, now S* sheltered, cosy. [nME *belde*; OE (Anglian) *beldo* boldness, courage, *beldan* embolden]

bien *18-*, **bene** *la14-16*; **bein &c** *la15-e20* [bin] *adj* **1** in good condition *la14, 19-*. **2** comfortable(-looking), pleasant, cosy *la15-*. **3** well-to-do, well-off *18-*. **4** *of a house etc* well-stocked *18-*.

adv handsomely; liberally; comfortably *la15-19*. **~ly** pleasantly; comfortably; cosily *15-e19*. **~ness** prosperity *19*. [ME *bene*]

bier(d)ly *see* BUIRDLY

big¹ &c; **bigg** *la16-e20*, **bige &c** *la14-15*, **beg &c** *la15-16* [bɪg; *ECoast* bəig] *vti, pt also* **bug** *la18-, now Loth* [by analogy with Eng *dig, dug*] **1** build, construct, erect *la14-*. **2** *of birds* build nests *15-*. **3** *vt, also* **~ on** *la16-17* build, make (a fire) *16-*. **4** occupy (land), *esp* by building on it; build on (land or ground) *15-16*. **5** stack (hay, corn etc) *la19-*.

~gin(g) &c 1 (the act of) building *15-*. **2** a building *14-*. **3** *in pl* subsidiary buildings on an estate, *later specif (perh also orig)* cottages *15-*. **4** a collection or cluster of houses *19-e20*. **~git 1** *also* **ill** *etc* **-biggit** (badly etc) built, constructed

la14-. **2** *of land* occupied, inhabited; cultivated; built on *la14-*. **~ly** pleasant to live in, habitable; handsomely made *la15, 19-e20*.

~ up 1 (re)build, repair *la14-e19*. **2** close or block up by building *16-e17*. [chf nME *big(ge) &c*, ON *byggja* inhabit, dwell in; build]

big², **beig** *20-*, *ECoast Rox* [bɪg; *ECoast* bəig] *adj* **1** = big *la15-, orig (la15-16) only verse*. **2** conceited, swollen-headed; of consequence *la19-*. **3** friendly, intimate *la19-, now Mry Abd*.

biggen swell, grow larger; be pregnant *18-e19*. **~sie** ['bɪgsɪ] proud, conceited *e20, Ork NE*. **~ coat** a greatcoat, an overcoat *19-e20*. **~ house** the principal dwelling house of the LAIRD etc on an estate *la18-*. **~ miss** a great loss by death, or by the departure of a friend *20-, local*. **~ sma faimily** a large family of young children *la19-, local*. **~ yins** older children *la19-, local*.

bige *see* BIG¹

bigg &c *n* a variety of barley *la18-*; see SND. [ON *bygg* barley]

bigg *see* BIG¹

biggin &c *n* a linen cap *e19*. **biggonet** = *n, 18-e19*. [eModEng; F *béguin* a cap]

bightsom [*?'bɪxtsəm] *adj* easy, relaxed *la18-19*. [OE *byht* a bend]

bigotit *see* BEGOTTED

bik *see* BICK¹

bikker *see* BICKER¹, BICKER²

bilbie *n* shelter; freedom *19-, Ags*. [only Sc; prob ON *bøl* a resting-place]

bilch *see* BELCH¹

bild *see* BUILD

bile¹ *20-*, **boil &c** *la16-*, **builʒe &c** *15-16* [bəil; *'bølji] *vti, n* = boil *15-*.

boiling a boiled sweet *20-*. **~ house** a building with a boiler for animal food *20-, local Abd-Fif*.

(awa an) bile yer heid! *very familiar* get lost! *la20-*.

bile² &c *la14-*, **byle &c** *15-*; **byll** *la15-17* [bəil] *n* = boil, a suppuration.

bilf¹ &c; bulf *n* a blow *19*. [prob onomat]

bilf² &c; bulf *n* a sturdy, growing young man *20-, Bnf Abd Ags*.

~ert, belfert a bigger than usual thing or person *20-, now Bnf*. **bulfie** *of persons* fat *20, Bnf Abd Ayr*. [perh altered f *bilch* (BELCH)]

bilge *n, also fig* the lower part of a ship's hull *16-*. **~it** large-hulled *e16*. [earlier in Sc; obscure]

bilget¹ *18-e20*, **billiet &c** *17*, **billgate &c** *18-e20* [*'bɪlget, *-get; *'bɪljɛt] *n* = billet, a document, *specif and chf* one containing a military order.

bilget² &c *19-e20*, **bilʒet &c** *la16* ['bɪldʒet; *'bɪljɛt] *n, carpentry* a piece of wood prepared for various purposes, *latterly esp* as a support for shelves. [ME *bylet &c*; F *billette* a chunk of wood; *cf* Eng *billet*]

bill &c *n* **1** (1) = bill, a document *la14-*. (2)

specif, law the document used to initiate proceedings in the *Bill Chamber, la17-e20.* **2** a decorative scroll containing a motto or other writing *la15-16.*

B~ Chamber a court separate from, but staffed by judges of, the *Court of Session* (SESSION) *la17-e20.*

burn one's ~ perform an act of recantation *16.* **in ~** in a written document, in writing *15-16.*

bill *see* BULL
billet *see* BULLET
billgate *see* BILGET[1]
billie *see* BILLY
billiet *see* BILGET[1]
billy *la18-*, **billie** *n* **1** a lover *16-e20.* **2** a (close) friend, comrade *la16-e20.* **3** a brother, actual or as a fellow member of a craft etc *19-e20.* **4** a fellow, lad *la18-e20.* **5** *usu* **the ~** a person etc particularly suited to, good at or characterized by something *la19-e20.* **6** *in pl, freq* **grand** *etc* **billies** on very friendly terms *la18-*, *now Mry.*
~ blin &c a *brownie* (BROON), a benevolent spirit *19-e20.* [prob Eng *bully &c* now obs as term of endearment]
Billy *n, slang* a Protestant, Orangeman *la20-, Gsw.* [as being a supporter of King William III against King James in *la17* Irish history]
bilsh *vi* speak loudly or angrily *19-e20.* [*fig* var of Eng *belch; cf* BELGH]
bilʒard &c *la16-e17*, **bulʒard &c** *17* ['bɪlʒərd, *-jə(r)t, *'bʌl-] *n* = billiard.
bilʒett *see* BILGET[2]
bin *see* BEN[2], BIND
binage &c [*'bɪnedʒ] *n* = BONDAGE 2, *18-e19, Abd.* [var of **beenage*, NE form of eModEng *boonage*, with additional confusion w BONDAGE]
bind &c, bin &c *15-* [bɪn(d)] *v, pt also* **band &c** *ptp also* **bundin &c** *la14-e17* [*'bʌndən *'bundən], **bun(d) &c** *la15-* [bʌn(d), bun(d))] **1** *vt* = bind *la14-.* **2** unite in alliance or attachment *la14-.* **3** *also ~* **up** make (a compact etc) firm or sure *la14-16.* **4** *vi* agree, pledge oneself *15-e19.* **5** *vt* tether *la19-.*
n **1** a bundle of hides *15-e16.* **2** a standard measure for the barrels in which certain commodities were packed, *freq* with name of the authorizing town *etc, eg* **the ~ of Banff, Burdeaux ~:** (1) of salmon etc *15-e18;* (2) of wine *la16-e17;* (3) of tar *la16-e17.* **3** the capacity (of a person etc), *chf* in drinking *la18-e20.* **4** *only* **bin** humour, mood *19-, NE.*
binnen &c a tether, *eg* for cattle *la19-e20.* **binner** = *n* 4, *20-, NE.* **~le** = *binnen*, *19-, now NE Ags.* **bun** *19-*, **bund** [bʌn(d), bun(d)] *ptp, adj* **1** = bound, tied etc *15-.* **2** joined or fitted together, *perh esp* by mortise-and-tenon joints; *also* referring to the covering of a join with beading, *orig freq* **bundwark** *16-, now Lnk Kcb.*
bun(d)-bed a *box-bed* (BOX[1]), *la17-, now Bnf Abd Ags* [from its panelled construction].
bun(d) breest &c a *box-bed* with a cupboard or

cupboards in the panelling *la19-*, *NE.* **bun(d) shafe &c** someone engaged to be married *20-, Abd.* **~wood &c** ['bɪn(d)'wʌd, -'wɪd] ivy; woodbine, honeysuckle, convolvulus *19-e20.*
be neither *etc* **to haud nor ~** be beyond control *19-.* **of the grete(st)** *etc*, **myddill** *or* **lest ~** of the largest etc size *16.*
bine *see* BOYNE
bing &c *n* **1** a heap or pile *16-.* **2** *specif* a funeral pile *e16.* **3** *now chf* a slag-heap *18-.* *vt* heap or pile up *16-19.* [ON *bingr* a heap; *cf* ME *bing* a bin]
binge *see* BEENGE
bink[1] **&c** *la15-*, **benk** *now Sh*, **bench** *la18-* *n* **1** = bench *la14-.* **2** a wall rack or shelf for dishes etc; a kitchen dresser *la18-e20.* **3** a bank, *freq* a *peat bank* (PEAT[1]) *la18-*, *now Arg.* **4** a hob on a fireplace; a shelf, ledge etc at the side of such *la18-e20.* **5** a hive (of bees etc) *19-e20.* [nME *bynk &c*, *benk*]
bink[2] *n* a bending movement, crease, fold *e19.* *vi* bend, bow *19-*, *now Fif.* [see SND]
binn *see* BEN[2]
binna *see* BE
binnen *see* BIND
binner *vti* **1** move noisily *19-e20.* **2** *vi* run, gallop *la18-*, *Abd.*
n a noise *e20, NE.* [uncertain]
binner *see* BIND
bir *see* BIRR[1]
bird &c, burd &c *16-* [bɪrd, bërd, bʌrd] *n* **1** = bird *15-.* **2** a young bird, nestling *15-e20.* **3** the young, offspring (1) of an animal *16-e20;* (2) of a person, *usu derog as* **Deil's bird** *16-e19.* **4** *orig only in verse, latterly* (*la18-*) *chf familiar or disparaging* a lady, woman; a girl *la15-* [ME *bird, burd*, perh f OE *byrde* well-born]. **5** term of endearment, *esp* to children *19-e20.*
~ie a young halibut *la19-, Mry Abd.*
~-alane *adj, adv* quite alone; single, solitary *la16-*, *now local.* *n* an only child, the only child left in a family *la16-e20.* **~-mouthed** unwilling to speak out *18-*, *now Gsw.*
birding *see* BURDEN[1]
birges &c *la15-e17*, **birge &c** *16-e17*; **burge &c** *16-e17*, **birdis &c** *la16* [*'bɪrdʒɪz, *-ɪs, *'bʌrdʒ-, *'bɪrdɪz, &c*, *bɪrdʒ, *bʌrdʒ] *n ~* **satin, ~ threid** satin or thread from Bruges in Flanders. [metath var]
birk[1] **&c** [bɪrk; *also* bërk, bʌrk] *n* **1** = birch *14-.* **2** *in pl* birch twigs, *esp* as used for decoration *la15-e17.* **3** *in pl* a small wood consisting mainly of birches *la18-.*
~en &c *adj* = birchen *la15-*, *in place-names la12-.* *n* a birch tree *la19-e20.* **as bare as ~ie** *la19-e20*, **as bare as da ~ o Yule een** *20-, Sh* completely bare.
birk[2] *vi* move energetically or restlessly *la18-e20.* [perh var of BIRR[1]]
birk[3] [bɪrk, bʌrk] *n* a BIRKIE[1] (*n* 1), a stout, well-built boy or lad *20-, Bnf Abd.* [perh shortened f next, w infl f GURK]

birkie¹ &c ['bɪrkɪ, 'bërkɪ, 'bʌrkɪ] *n* **1** a smart (*usu* young) fellow *la18-*. **2** a conceited fellow *la18-e20*. **3** a sharp-tongued, quick-tempered person, *usu* a woman *20-, Edb. adj* **1** lively, spirited *19-, WC.* **2** sharp-tongued, tart; huffy *19-, now Per.*
auld ~ *colloq* old boy *18-e19.* [only Sc; see SND]
birkie² *n* the card game beggar-my-neighbour *19.*
birl¹, burl &c *la19-* [bɪrl, bërl, bʌrl] *vti* **1** revolve rapidly, whirl round, dance; make a rattling or whirring sound *la18-.* **2** move rapidly, hurry along *la18-e20.* **3** toss a coin *19-e20.* **4** whistle *la19-e20.*
n **1** a turn, twist, revolving movement *la19-.* **2** a whistle, *esp* a policeman's or a school's; the sound made by a whistle *20-, C.* **3** *piping* a grace-note introducing the note A, produced by two rapid touches on G, the lowest note on the CHANTER *20-.*
~ quheil a spinning wheel *e17.* [prob onomat]
birl² &c *v* **1** *vt, orig also* ~ (**up**)**on** pour out, serve (wine etc) to (a person) *la15-e20.* **2** *vi, also* ~ **at ale** *etc* drink, carouse *la16-e19.*
birlie &c *17-e20,* **birlaw &c** *la15-e20,* **burlaw &c** *15-e17,* **burley &c** *la17-,* **bourlaw** *la17-e18,* **barley** *17-,* **barlaw &c** *la16-19* [*'bʌrlɑ]* *n* **1** = byrlaw, local customary law, *chf* ~ **court,** ~ **man** *la16.* **2** *only* **barley** *la18-, now local Sh-WC,* **baurley &c** *20, C, chf children's games* a truce, pause.
barley-bracks, -breikis &c ['barlɪ'braks, -'briks] a children's chasing game *la16-e20.* ~ **court** a neighbourhood court for the settlement of local disputes or complaints *la16-e17.*
barlafummil &c [*'barlɪ'fʌml,* *'barlə-]* a cry for truce in fighting or play *la16-19.*
~-man one of the group of persons elected or appointed to act as judges or ARBITERS in local disputes *la15-e20.* **barley play** a cry for truce in games *la15-19, now Sh Ork.*
cry (a) ~ call for a truce *la18-, now Ags Per.*
crying (of) the burley the proclamation of the town's charter at the annual *Riding of the Marches* (RIDE) *20-, Slk.*
birling &c; birlin *n* a large rowing boat or galley used in the West *Highlands* (HIELAND) *la16-e18.* [only Sc; Gael *birlinn*]
birn *see* BURDEN¹, BURN²
birny &c; byrne [*'bɪrnɪ]* *n, also in pl la15-e16* = brinie, a mail-coat; a cuirass or breastplate *la14-16.* [metath var]
birr¹ *18-,* **bir &c** *15-e20 n* **1** force, energy, an onrush; bustling activity *15-.* **2** enthusiasm, verve *18-.* **3** a whirring sound *19-.*
vti (cause to) whirr or vibrate *16-, now local.* [nME *bir, byrre,* ON *byrr* a breeze]
birr² *n* **in a** ~ *etc, of hair etc* standing up on end,

tousled; brushed so as to stand out from the head *20-, now Abd.* [*cf* Eng *bur* a prickly flower-head etc]
birrat *see* BURRAT
birs *see* BIRSE
birsall *see* BRISSELL
birse, birs *16-e17* [bɪrs, *also* bʌrs; *Ork* bɪs] *n* **1** (1) bristles, (a) bristle *16-.* (2) the bristle fixed on a shoemaker's thread *19-e20.* **2** a brush *la16-e17.* **3** a sheaf or plume of bristles *la19-e20.* **4** anger, temper, *chf* **his** *etc* ~ **is up** *etc 17-e20.*
vt, of shoemakers attach a bristle to a thread *la19-e20; cf birsit* 2.
birsie &c 1 bristly; hairy *16-19.* **2** hot-tempered, passionate *la19-e20.* **birsit 1** *of animals* bristly *e16.* **2** *of thread* supplied with a bristle *la16.* [OE *byrst*]
birse *see* BRIZZ
birse-cup, birse tea *n* a final cup of tea with WHISKY or other spirit instead of milk *e20, Bnf Abd.* [see SND and Suppl]
birsell foul *see* BRISSELL-COCK
birsil *see* BIRSLE
birsket &c *16-17,* **briscat &c** *la15-17 n, only Sc* = biscuit, *freq* ~ **breid.**
birsket *see* BRISKET
birsle &c *19-,* **birsil &c** *16-19,* **bristle** *la19-, now Abd Kcb;* **brissill** *e16* ['bɪrsl; *also* 'bʌrsl; 'brɪsl] *vt* **1** scorch *16-.* **2** broil; toast; warm thoroughly *19-.*
(**weel-**)**birsled** well-cooked, fried until crisp *20-, local.* **birsling 1** scorching *20-.* **2** completely dry *la19-.* [eModEng *burstle,* metath var of *brystylle,* of uncertain orig]
birst &c *la15-20,* **burst &c** *la16-,* **brust** *la16-, now local Abd-Arg,* **brist** *la14-e17 vti, pt also* ~**it &c,** *now local,* **brast** *la14-e15. ptp also* **bursen** *la15-, now local,* **bursten** *18-, now local* = burst *la14-.*
n **1** *only* **birst** *la19,* **burst** *la19-, now Bnf Fif* an injury caused by over-exertion. **2** *only* **burst** (1) a bout of drunkenness *20-, local Bnf-Kcb;* (2) a big feed, *freq* **a hunger or a burst** a feast or a famine *la19-, now local Cai-Arg.*
burs(t)en &c *ptp, adj* **1** = burst *la15-.* **2** filled to bursting *20-, now local Bnf-Lnk.* **3** breathless from over-exertion *19-, now Bnf Fif.* **4** fat, corpulent *la18-, now Bnf.* **bursen grease** lubricating grease which has become thin through friction *20-, Bnf Abd.* **burster** *mining* a blast into a seam without previous cutting or boring *la19-, now Fif.*
birstle *n* = bristle, the stubble on an unshaved chin *la20-, Sh Ork N.* [metath var]
birth¹ &c [bɪrθ, bërθ] *n* **1** = birth *la14-.* **2** produce of the soil; a crop *15-16, only Sc.*
~ful &c *la16,* **~y** *la15-19,* **berthy** *la15-19, only Sc* prolific, fertile.
birth² **&c** *n* the burden or carrying capacity (of a ship) *la15-e17.* [only Sc; ON *byrðr*]
birthing, birthinsake *see* BURDEN¹

birze *see* BRIZZ

bis *see* BIZZ[1]

bishop &c *15-*, **bischop** &c *la14-17*; **bischape** &c *la14-e16*, **bischep** &c *la14-16*, **beschop** &c *la14-e17*, **biscop** &c *la14-e16* *n* **1** = bishop *la14-*. **2** an instrument for ramming down stones and earth *19-*, *now Abd.* ~**rie** &c = bishopric *16-e17*, *only Sc.* ~ **sattin** &c satin of some sort *17-18.* ~('**s**) **weed** common gout-weed, ground elder, *Aegopodium podagraria 19-.* **the ~'s foot has been in the broth** *etc* the BROTH etc is burnt *18-e19.*

bisket *see* BRISKET

bismere &c [*'bɪsmər] *n* a disreputable woman *16.* [ME *bismer* &c shame, disgrace; reproach]

bisom *see* BESOM

bissart *see* BIZZARD

bisset &c *n, usu in pl* a narrow lace, a trimming or edging *la16.* [only Sc; F *bisette* a gold, silver, or copper trimming for cloth]

bissy &c *15-e18*, **bussie** &c *16-17*, **besy** &c *la14-16* [*'bɪzɪ, *'bʌzɪ, *'bɪsɪ] *adj, vtr* = busy.

bit &c *n* **1** *of food*: (1) a bite, a mouthful *16-19*; (2) = bit, a small piece (of food) *16-.* **2** *in gen* a small piece (of something) *la15-.* **3** (1) *specif* a small piece of ground; a spot, place *la16-*, *now Lnk S.* (2) one's place of residence or employment; one's situation, job *la19-*, *now WC-S.* (3) *chf* **the** ~ a person's original position, the same place, *freq* **can't** *etc* **get out** *etc* **of the** ~ be unable to make any progress, be stuck *19-*, *local.* **4** distance *la19-*, *local Ork-Per.* **5** *with omission of 'of'* indicating smallness, endearment or contempt *18-*: '*a bit stick; twa bit lassies*'. ~**tie** *n* **1** a small piece; a short distance or time *la19-.* **2** *with omission of 'of'* a small bit, portion *20-.* *adv* **a** ~**tie** somewhat *la19-.* ~**tock** &c = ~**tie**, *la18-.* **aff the** ~ off the mark, wrong, 'out' *20-*, *SW, S.* **at the** ~ at the critical point *la16-19.* ~ **and brat** &c food and board *19.* (**the**) ~ **and the buffet** *fig* food and blows, the good with the bad *la16-e19.* ~**s o ..** term of disparagement *19-*, *now Bnf*: '*my ~s o things*'. **come to the** ~ come to the point of decision *19-.* **nae a ~!** *interj* expressing surprise or incredulity *20-*, *NE.*

bit *see* BEHOVE

bitch &c, **biche** &c *16 n* **1** = bitch *16-.* **2** term of contempt for (1) a woman *la16-*; (2) a man *19-e20.* [*cf* BICK[1]]

bite *la15-*; **byt** &c *la14-e17 v, pt also* **bait** &c *la14-*, *now local vti* = bite. **no be able** *etc* **to** ~ **one's fingers** *or* **thoum** be very drunk *la18-*, *now N-Per.*

bittle &c *la15-*, **betill** *la15-16*; **beetle** *19-* ['bɪtl, 'bɪtl] *n* **1** = beetle, a mallet *la15-.* **2** a kitchen implement for bruising barley, mashing potatoes etc *18-e20.* *vt* **1** beat (linen, cloth etc) *19-e20.* **2** thrash *la19-e20.*

bittock *see* BEETYACH, BIT

bizz[1] &c *18-*, **bis** &c *16*, *la19* [bɪz] *vi* **1** = buzz *16-*, *now Abd.* **2** *of liquids* hiss, fizz *16-e20.* *n* a state of commotion, bustle *la19-*, *now local NE-S.* **cry** *or* **play** ~ **aff o** rebound from *la19-*, *Bnf Abd Ags.*

bizz[2] *interj* shame!, tut-tut! *20-*, *now Abd.*

bizzard *la18-19*, **bussard** &c *la15-e17*; **bissart** &c *la16* ['bɪzərd, 'bʌz-, -ə(r)t] *n* = buzzard.

bla *see* BLAE

blab &c [blab, blɛb] *vi* drink excessively *19-e20*, *NE.* [prob onomat; *cf* BLIB, BLYBE]

blab *see* BLOB

blabber &c *16-e20*, **blaber** *15-e16* ['blabər] *vi* speak inarticulately; babble. [ME *blaberen*]

blacht *see* BLECHE

black *16-*, *in place-names 13-*, **blak** &c *13-17*, **blake** *16-e17*, *in place-names la12-* *n* **1** = black *la15-.* **2** *usu in pl* mourning clothes *la19-*, *chf NE.* **3** *in pl, mining*: coaly blaes (BLAE *n* 2) *la19-*, *now Fif.* *adj* **1** = black *la13-.* **2** *of persons, their complexion, hair etc, freq attached to a personal name* dark *14-e17*: '*Blac Annes*', '*blak Archibald of Douglas*'. **3** *fig* dark, dismal, unfortunate, shameful *16-.* **4** *as an intensifier* utter, downright, out-and-out *19-*: '*ye micht think black burnin' shame*'. *adv* **1** completely, utterly *la16, 20-.* **2** intensely, extremely *18-*, *now Dmf.* ~**en**, *also* **blekin** *la16* [*blɛkən] *vti* = blacken *15-.* ~**en someone's door** darken someone's door *la19-*, *now Ork Ags.* ~**ie** the blackbird *20-.* ~**-a-viced**, ~**-a-vised** &c [~ ə'vɔist, ~ ə'vaɪzd] dark-complexioned *18-e20.* ~**-back** nickname for a miner *la20*, *Fif Ayr.* ~**-baised** &c depressed *e19, S.* ~**-berry** the blackcurrant *la18-*, *now Abd.* ~ **bitch** **1** a bag for fraudulently catching meal from the mill spout *19-*, *now Kcb.* **2** a native of Linlithgow *la20-*, *Stlg wLoth* [f the dog on the town's coat of arms]. ~ **broun** dark brown *la16-e17.* ~ **bun** a very rich spiced fruit cake, baked in a pastry crust and eaten at HOGMANAY *20-.* ~ **byde** &c *la19*, ~ **boyd** &c *19* the berry of the *bramble* (BRAMMLE). ~ **coal** coal which has been slightly burned by igneous rock *la19-*, *now Fif.* ~ **coat** taboo term for a clergyman, MINISTER *20-*, *ECoast.* ~ **cock** &c the (male of the) black grouse *15-.* **mak a** ~ **cock of** shoot (a person) *la18-e19.* ~ **crap** &c (a crop of) peas and/or beans *la17-e19.* ~ **fish** &c a recently-spawned fish, *chf* salmon *la16-*, *now Fif.* ~**-fisher** a night poacher of fish *19.* ~**-fishing** night salmon-fishing with torches *la18-e19.* ~**-foot** [~ 'fɪt] a lovers' go-between *19-e20.* ~ **gate** the road to ruin *19-*, *now Mry Bnf.* ~**-gray** *adj, n* (a) dark grey (colour or cloth) *la15-e19.* ~ **guaird** &c [*n* 'bla(k)gerd, 'blakjərt, 'blagjərd; *Per* 'blɛ-; *v* blə(k)'gerd] = blackguard *e20.* ~ **house** *la19-*, *now hist*, ~

hut *la18* a Hebridean or West *Highland* (HIE-
LAND) house of turf and rough stones with a
thatched roof and a central fireplace on an
earthen floor. ~ **mail &c** a payment exacted
or made in return for protection from plunder
or injury; an illegal exaction *16-18*. ~ **man 1**
in threats to children, the bogy-man *la19-, local.* **2**
a kind of toffee; *also* name for other kinds of
dark-coloured sweets *19-, now Fif Loth.* **3 a**
~**man** an ice-cream with a plain wafer on one
side and a marshmallow-filled wafer with choc-
olate edges on the other *la20-, Fif Edb Gsw.* **4 a**
~**man** a piece of black matter in the nose *20-,*
C. ~ **mone(y) &c** copper or billon coins
la15-17. ~**-neb &c** a person with democratic
or anti-government sympathies *la18-e20.* ~ **ox**
an imaginary black ox said to trample on someone who has suffered a bereavement or other
severe calamity *18-e19.* **Black Parliament**
name given to various parliaments *16, hist.* ~
pudding &c a savoury type of sausage made of
oatmeal or flour, suet, seasoning and blood, *usu*
of a pig *18-.* **B~ Sattirday &c** the day of the
Battle of Pinkie, 10 Sept 1547, *la16-e18, only Sc.*
~**smith &c 1** = blacksmith *la15-.* **2** the halibut *la19-, Mry Abd.* ~ **sole** = ~*-foot, 18-e19.*
~**-spaul &c** a cattle disease, a kind of pleurisy
characterized by black colour on the skin *e19.*
~**-spit** a lung disease formerly common among
miners *19-, now local.* ~ **stone,** ~ **stane** *Sc*
Univs a dark-coloured stone (*later* part of a
chair) on which students sat during an annual
public examination *la16-19.* ~**-strippit ba** a
bull's eye, the sweet *20-, local C.* ~ **sugar &c**
liquorice (juice) *la18-.* ~**-tang** a kind of seaweed, *Fucus vesiculosus, la18-e19.* ~ **victual** =
~ **crap,** *la18-, now Stlg.* ~ **ward** *law* holding
in WARD by a SUBVASSAL of another VASSAL who
also held in WARD of his SUPERIOR *la17-e18.*
the B~ Watch a Scottish regiment, raised
from the INDEPENDENT COMPANIES in 1739, *18-*
[so called f their dark green and black TARTAN].
~ **weet** rain *la19-, now Ork.* ~**yirt &c** =
~*guaird, la19-e20.*

blad *n* ~ **haet** absolutely nothing *19-e20.* [poss
an intensifier]

blad *see* BLADE, BLAUD¹, BLAUD²

bladarie *see* BLADRY

bladder *see* BLETHER¹

bladdoch &c *la18-19,* **bledoch &c** *la16-e20;*
blatho &c *19-e20* ['blado(x), -ə(x), 'blɛdəx; *Sh*
'blɛdɪk; *Ork* 'blaðo, 'blaðɪk] *n* buttermilk.
[only Sc; Gael *blàthach*]

bladds, bladdy *see* BLAUD¹

blade &c *la15-,* **blad &c** *la14, 19-;* **bleed &c**
la16-e17, **bled** *la16-e20 n* **1** = blade *la14-.* **2**
(1) a leaf of cabbage, turnip, tobacco etc
17-e20. (2) a tea-leaf *19-, now Ork Abd Ags.*
3 *only* **blad &c** (1) a portfolio *19-, now Edb;* (2)
a blotting or writing pad *20-, now Stlg Edb.*
vt strip the leaves from (a plant) *19-.*

bladry &c *18-e20,* **bladarie** *la16;* **blaidrie**
la16-e18 n **1** filth(iness) *la16-17.* **2** foolishness,
ostentation, harm *18-e20.* [only Sc; obscure]

bladʒean [*'bladjən] *n* term of abuse for a person *e16.* [obscure]

blae *la16-,* **bla &c** *13-17;* **blay &c** *la16-18,*
blea &c *17-18 adj* **1** blue; bluish; dark bluish
grey, livid *la14-.* **2** (1) *formerly* (*13-e17*) *freq*
with **bludy** livid or bluish from a blow *13-.*
(2) *of a blow* making a livid mark or bruise
16-e17. **3** livid or bluish from cold, bloodless-
ness etc *la15-.* **4** *of skin* black, *chf* **bla man** *la15.*
n **1** a bruise, contusion *la16-17 (Sh N), e19.* **2**
blae *e17,* **blaes &c** *18-* a bluish-grey hardened
clay, soft slate or shale.
~**ness** lividness *20-.* **blairdie &c** *chf child's*
word the bilberry *la19-, Bnf Abd.*
~**-beds** layers of BLAES (*n* 2) *la18-, now Fif.*
~**berry** the bilberry *la15-.* ~ **wing** *angling* an
artificial fly tied with a bluish-grey wing *20-.*

blawort &c, **blaver &c** *19-e20,* *NE,* *S*
['blawərt; *Abd Rox* 'ble-; *NE, S* 'blavər(t)] one
of several blue plants: **1** the harebell *19-e20;* **2**
the cornflower *la18-e20;* **3** the germander
speedwell *19;* **4** *only* **blivert** ['blɪvərt] the bilberry *20-, Abd.*

blaes and balls BLAES (*n* 2) with ironstone
nodules embedded *la19-, now Fif.* [nME *bla &c,*
ON *blár* (dark) blue, livid, black]

blaeflum *see* BLAFLUM

blaff *n* a blast, bang, crash *la19-e20.* [perh
onomat]

blaffart *see* BLUFFART

blaflum &c *la16-e20;* **bleflum &c** *e17,*
blaeflum *e19,* **blafum &c** *17-e20* [*n*
'blaf(l)ʌm, 'ble-; blə'f(l)ʌm; *v* blə'flʌm] *n* a
deception; a hoax, illusion; nonsense, idle talk
la16-19.
vt cajole, deceive *18-e20.* [only Sc; obscure]

blaid *see* BLAUD¹, BLAUD²

blaidrie *see* BLADRY

blaiken; **blakyn &c** *la15-e16* ['blekən] *vi* **1**
become pale *la15-16.* **2** *chf in ptp* made pale or
pallid *la15-, now Abd.* [nME *blake,* OE *blācian*
become pale, corresponding to ME *bleyken;* ON
bleikr shining, white and Eng *bleach*]

blaiker *see* BLECK¹

blain¹ *la18-, now Bnf Abd,* **blane** *e16 n, also fig* a
scar from a sore or wound; a weal. [Eng *blain*
an inflamed swelling, sore etc]

blain² *n* a bare patch in a field of crops *19-e20.*
[perh f prec]

blaink *see* BLINK

blairdie *see* BLAE

blait *la15-e20,* **blate** *16,* **blete &c** *15-* [blet,
blit] *vi* = bleat.
bleater, blitter, bluiter ['blitər, 'blɪt-, 'bløt-]
the cock snipe; the bittern *la18-, now Kcb.*

blak(e) *see* BLACK

blakyn *see* BLAIKEN

blame **&c** *n* **1** = blame *la14-.* **2** *with possessive*
pronoun fault *19-:* '*it's not my blame*'.

vt = blame *la14-*.

~ (**something**) **on** (**a person**) ascribe the blame to (a person) for (something) *19-*.

blan *see* BLIN[1]

blancheferme &c *la14-17*, **blencheferme &c** *la16-e18*, **blanche &c** *16-*, **blench &c** *la16-* ['blanʃ(-'fɛrm), 'blɛnʃ] *n, law* a small or nominal quit-rent paid in money or otherwise *la14-17*.

adj, of lands held in BLANCHEFERME *la15-*.

adv by the payment or on the tenure of BLANCHEFERME *la15-*.

blench-duty &c = *n, 17*. **blench-holding** the holding of (land) as in *n, 17-18*.

in ~ = *adv, 15-e18*. [only Sc; OF *blanche ferme* white rent, rent paid in silver]

bland[1] *vt* mix, mingle *la15-e20*.

~**ed** *or* **blendit bear** BEAR[1] mixed with barley *la18-e19*, Fif. [ME *blande &c* (rare), ON *blanda*; *perh also* Eng *blend*]

bland[2] *adj* flattering, pleasant *la15-*. [*cf* ModEng]

blander *vt* diffuse, disperse scantily or over-thinly *la17-19*. [obscure]

blane *see* BLAIN[1]

blansht *20-*, Bnf Abd, **blenched** *19-*, *now Bnf adj, of* (skimmed) *milk* slightly sour. [*cf* BLINK *v* 4 (2)]

blanter *n* food made from oats, *eg* bread, porridge *la18-19*. [obscure; *cf* BLANDER]

blare &c *la18-e20*, **blere &c** *la16* [bler; *blir] *vi* 1 = blare *la16-*. 2 *of a sheep or goat* bleat *la18-e20*.

blare *see* BLEAR

blase &c [blez, bliz] *vt, chf in ptp, of milk* slightly soured *19-*, *now Bnf Ags*. [*cf* BLANSHT and *fired* (FIRE)]

blase *see* BLEEZE[1], BLEEZE[2]

blash *n* 1 a splash of liquid etc *la18-*. 2 a heavy or drenching shower of rain etc *19-*. 3 a weak mixture of drink, soup etc *la19-*. 4 a semi-liquid or soft slimy mass, a dirty mess *19-*, *now Bnf*. 5 *usu contemptuous* a large draught (of liquor) *19-*, *now Bnf Abd Ags*. 6 a torrent of words *la19-*, *now Bnf Ags Lnk*.

vi 1 pour down with a splashing noise *20-*, *now Abd Ags*. 2 *esp of rain, sleet, snow* batter (against a person or thing) *19-*, *now Bnf*.

~**y** 1 rainy, wet, gusty *18-*. 2 *of food or drink* weak *19-*, *now Abd*. [prob onomat]

blason &c; blazon *la18-* ['blezən] *n* 1 = blazon *15-*. 2 *law* the badge of office displayed by a King's messenger *la16-18*.

vt 1 = blazon, describe or proclaim with praise *la15-16*. 2 describe in heraldic terms *15*. 3 proclaim with reproach *la16-e17*.

blasphematioun &c *n* 1 evil-speaking, calumniation *la15-16*. 2 blaspheming; blasphemy *16*. [only Sc; L *blasphēmātio*]

blast *n* 1 *also* **blist &c** *15-e16* = blast *la14-*. 2 a smoke, a puff of a pipe *19-*, *only Sc*. 3 a stroke, a sudden attack of illness *18-*, *now Bnf*.

vti 1 = blast *la16-*. 2 shout loudly, declaim in violent language *la16-*, *now Bnf*. 3 smoke (tobacco) *19-e20*. 4 *vi* pant, breathe hard *la18-*, *now Bnf*.

~**er &c** *la15-e16*, **bleester** *20-* *vi, of wind* blow in blasts *la15-e16*, *20-*, Bnf Arg. *n, also fig* a blast of wind *20-*, *now Bnf Arg*. ~**ie** *n, contemptuous* a shrivelled dwarf; a bad-tempered, unmanageable child or animal *la18-*, *now Bnf Gsw*. *adj* gusty, boisterous *19-*, *now Bnf Abd*. ~**it** paralysed *la18-e20*.

blate &c; bleat &c *la16-19 adj* 1 bashful, timid, diffident, modest *la15-*. 2 dull, stupid, easily deceived *16-*, Bnf Ags C. 3 *of crops* backward in growth *20-*, *now Bnf Ags*. [obscure]

blate *see* BLAIT

blather *see* BLETHER[1]

blatho *see* BLADDOCH

blatter &c *vti* 1 talk volubly, noisily and fast; babble *16-*. 2 *freq of rain, hail etc* rattle, beat with violence *17-*. 3 *vi* run noisily with short steps *19-*, *now Bnf*.

n 1 a loud rattling or rustling noise *18-*. 2 a storm of rain, hail etc *19-*, *now local Bnf-Ayr*. 3 a blow; a heavy fall; a gunshot *la18-*, *now Bnf Kcb*. 4 an incoherent flow of words *19-*, *now Bnf*. [obs Eng chatter, babble]

blaud[1] **&c, blad** *16-e20*; **blaid &c** *la16-e18 vt* 1 damage, spoil by harsh or careless treatment, harm, injure *16-*. 2 defame *la16-*. 3 *of storms, rain etc* buffet, beat *19-*, *now Ags*. 4 make a violent thrusting motion; slap, strike *la18-19*. 5 spoil (a child etc) *e20*.

n 1 an injury; a blow *la16-e19*. 2 *in pl, also* **bladds** a disease causing pustules *la16*, *la19* (Sh). 3 a blast of wind, a downpour of rain *19-*, *now Ags*.

bladdy *of weather* unsettled *19-*, *now Cai Abd*. [prob onomat]

blaud[2] **&c, blad; blaid &c** *17-e18 n* 1 a piece, lump, portion, fragment *16-e19*. 2 *specif* a piece or strip of cloth *la16-e19*. 3 a portion of something written; a selection or specimen; a snatch *16-19*. [obscure]

blaugh *see* BLECHE

blaver &c *see* BLAE

blaw[1] **&c, blow** *19-*, **byauve** *20-*, NE Coast; **blyave &c** *19-e20*, NE [blɑ; NE *also* bl(j)ɑv, bjɑv] *vti* 1 = blow *la14-*. 2 (1) *vt* utter arrogantly, *chf* ~ (**a great**) **bost** *la14-16*. (2) *vi* brag, boast; exaggerate *la16-*. 3 *vt* inflate, cause (meat) to swell to improve its appearance *16-e18*. 4 smoke (a pipe) *la18-*, *now Lnk Dnbt*. 5 *draughts* take a piece from (one's opponent) *19-*, *now local Abd-Kcb*.

n 1 a blowing (of a horn etc) *la15-*. 2 *of wind etc* = blow, a blast, gust *19-*, *now Abd*. 3 a puff (of a pipe) *20-*. 4 a pull (of liquor) *la18-e19*. 5 (1) boasting, a boast *19-*. (2) a boaster *19-*, *now Lnk*.

~**in(g) horne** a horn sounded by blowing *15-e17*.

~**doon &c** a back-draught in a chimney or fireplace *20-*. ~ **grass** a hill-grass, a variety of bent *la18-, now Ayr Gall.*
at full blow at full cock *20-, now Abd.* ~ **a cauld coal** suffer failure, engage in a hopeless task *18-e19*. ~ **in someone's lug** flatter a person *19-e20.* ~ **lown** [lʌun] make little or no noise; avoid boasting *19-, now Abd.* ~ **out on** denounce formally or after blowing a horn to attract public attention *15-e16.* ~ **up 1** = blow up, explode *17-*. **2** flatter, hoax, make (a person) believe what is untrue *19-*.
blaw² &c *n* = blow, a stroke *la15-*.
blaw³ *vi* blossom *19-, now Abd.* [perh by confusion of OE *blāwan* blow w *blōwan* bloom]
blaw⁴ *n, (tinkers') cant* oatmeal *20-, now NE.* [unknown]
blawort, blay *see* BLAE
blaze *see* BLEEZE¹, BLEEZE²
blazon *see* BLASON
blea &c [blɛ, ble] *vi* bleat, as a lamb or kid *19-e20, S.* [prob onomat]
blea *see* BLAE
bleach &c [blitʃ] *vt* strike; beat *19-, now Abd.* *n* a blow, stroke *18-19.* [also northern ModEng dial; ME *blecen, blechen* hurt, wound, OF *blecier, blecher*]
bleach *see* BLECHE
blear &c *17-*, **blere &c** *15-16*; **blare &c** *la16-e20* [blir; *Mry Bnf also* bler] *v* **1** *vt* = blear, *usu* ~ **someone's ee** deceive someone *15-*. **2** *vi* shine dimly *la18-, now Abd.*
n, usu in pl something which obscures the sight; matter in the eye *17-, now Bnf.*
~**ed &c 1** *also* **blerit &c** = bleared *16-*. **2** debauched-looking *20-*. **3** *of writing* blotted *20-, now Loth Lnk.* **4** *only* **bleared** = ~**ie** *adj* 2, *19-, now Loth Lnk.* ~**ie** *adj* **1** watery-eyed *19-*. **2** *of liquid food* (too) thin *19.* *n* liquid food, *eg* gruel *19-, now local Cai-Kcb.*
draw the ~ **ower someone's eye &c** deceive someone *la18-e20.*
bleat *see* BLATE
bleater *see* BLAIT
bleatery *see* BLEETER
bleb *see* BLOB
bleche &c *16-17*; **bleach &c** *17-* [blitʃ] *vt* = bleach *16-*.
n = bleach.
blechit &c *16-17*, **blacht &c** *16-19*, **blaugh** *19* ['blitʃɪt; *blɑx(t)] **1** = bleached *16-19.* **2** pale, livid *19.*
bleachfield a bleaching works with its adjacent drying-ground *18-, now chf in place-names.*
bleck¹ &c *vt* **1** baffle; puzzle *19-e20, Bnf Abd.* **2** surpass, beat, excel *19-, now Ags.*
blaiker a puzzle, a challenge to a feat of daring *e19, Bnf Abd.* [obscure]
bleck² *la16-*, **blek &c *15-e20* *n* **1** blacking (for leather) *16-*. **2** *fig* a black mark; a spot or stain *16.* **3** (1) (a particle of) soot or smut *la19-e20.*

(2) smut, mildew on plants *la19-, now Bnf Ags Bwk.* **4** a Negro *la19-.* **5** *sometimes joc* a blackguard, scoundrel *la19-.*
vt **1** make black, blacken (*latterly esp* the face with soot etc); dirty; disfigure *la15-*. **2** *freq* blacken with ink, write on (paper) *16-, now Ags.* **3** *fig* (1) stain, blemish, defile *15-16*; (2) blacken in character etc, defame *16-, now Edb.*
blecknin &c blacking (for leather) *la19-* [but *cf* also *blekin* (BLACK)]. ~**it wheat &c** mildewed wheat *la17.* [ME *blek(e)*, ON *blek* ink]
bled *see* BLADE
bledder *see* BLETHER¹, BLETHER²
blede *see* BLEED
bledoch *see* BLADDOCH
bleed *19-*, **blede &c** *vi* **1** = bleed *la14-*. **2** ~ **weel** *etc, of grain etc* give a good yield *19-*.
~**-raing** become bloodshot *la19-, Bnf.* [*cf* BLUDE]
bleed *see* BLADE, BLUDE
bleem *see* BLUME
bleester *see* BLAST
bleeter &c *n, vi* rain *19-, now Abd.*
bleatery cold, raw, showery *20-, Abd.* [see SND]
bleeter *see* BLUITER
bleeze¹ &c *18-*, **blese &c** *la14-e19*, **blase &c** *la14-e18*; **blaze &c** *17-* [bliz; *Sh-Mry nEC, Wgt* blez] *n, also* **bles** *la14-e16* **1** = blaze *la14-*. **2** a blazing brand, a torch: (1) *in gen, 15-e16*; (2) *specif* as used when spearing fish *la16-, now Abd Ayr.* **3** a beacon fire, a bonfire *16-, now Ags.*
v **1** *vi* = blaze *16-*. **2** *vt* light up (water) to attract fish *18-, now Ayr.*
bleezed, bleezin (fou) very drunk *19-*.
bleezy *of the eyes* showing signs of intoxication *19.*
~ **money** *la19-, now Kcb*, ~ **silver** *la16* a gratuity given by pupils to their schoolmasters at Candlemas (CANLEMAS).
in a ~ *of a crop* suddenly ripe; ready to be thinned *20-, now Ags.*
bleeze² *19-*; **blase** *la16-e17*; **blaze** *19* *vi* **1** = blaze, proclaim *la16-*. **2** boast, brag *19-, now Abd Fif.*
~ **awa(y)** brag, exaggerate *19-, now Bnf.* [see SND]
bleflum *see* BLAFLUM
bleib *see* BLOB
blek *see* BLECK²
blekin *see* BLACK
blellum *n* an idle, ignorant, talkative man *la18-19.* [only Sc; perh conflation of BLABBER, BLAB w SKELLUM]
blemish *vt* **1** = blemish. **2** damage *la19-20.*
blench, blench-duty *see* BLANCHEFERME
blenched *see* BLANSHT
blencheferme *see* BLANCHEFERME
blendit *see* BLAND¹
blenk *see* BLINK

blenshaw &c *n* a drink made of oatmeal, sugar, milk, water, and nutmeg *19-e20*. [only Sc; F *blanche eau* white water]

blent *see* BLINK

blere *see* BLARE, BLEAR

bles(**e**) *see* BLEEZE[1]

blete *see* BLAIT

blether[1] *e15, 18-*, **bladder** *16-18*, **bledder** *16-e20*; **blather** *18-e20* ['blɛðər; *Abd also* 'blɛd-; ***'blað-, ***'blad-] *vi* **1** talk foolishly, loquaciously or idly; brag *15-*. **2** stammer, speak indistinctly *la16-e19*.

n **1** *freq in pl* foolish talk, nonsense; long-winded (boasting) talk *18-*. **2** a person who talks foolishly or too much *19-*. **3** *in pl as interj* nonsense!, rubbish! *19-*.

∼**ation** = ∼*ie*, *20-*. ∼**er** = *n 2, la18-*. ∼**ie** *n* foolish talk *la19-*, *now Bnf Abd*. ∼**ing Tam** the whitethroat *la19-e20*, *WC, SW*. ∼(**an**)**skate** &c *la17-*, ∼(**um**)**skite** &c *la19-* [∼(ən)'sket; ∼'skəit; *Kcb Uls* ∼əm'skəit; &c] **1** a silly foolish person; a babbler *la17-*. **2** a boaster *la19-*, *now Fif*. [also northern ModEng dial; ON *blaðra*; *cf* Norw *bladra*]

blether[2] &c *17-*, **bledder** &c *la14-e20 n* = bladder *la14-*.

∼ **an leather** a football *20-*, *now Ayr*.

blew *see* BLUE

blib &c [blɪb, blɛb, bləib] *n* a weak watery portion of tea, soup etc *20-*, *Bnf Abd*. [*cf* BLAB, BLYBE]

blibbans *n pl* strips of something soft and slimy, *esp* seaweed *19-*, *now Kcdn Gall*. [prob conflation of BLIB w Eng *ribbons*]

blibberin *see* BLUBBER

blichan &c ['blɪxən, -əm] *n* **1** contemptuous term for a person *19-*, *now Ags*. **2** a lean, worn-out, worthless animal or person *19-e20*, *SW*. [see SND]

blicht [blɪxt] *n, vt, literary* = blight *la19-e20*.

blicker *n* (the talk of) a boaster or stupid person *e20*. [uncertain]

blid *see* BLUDE

blide *see* BLITHE

bliffert *see* BLUFFERT

blin[1] &c *vi, pt also* **blan** *chf verse* cease, stop; come to an end *la14-*, *now Abd*. [ME; OE *blinnan*]

blin[2] *la18-*, **blind** *la14-*, *in place-names 13-* [blɪn(d)] *adj* **1** = blind *la14-*. **2** *of a transaction etc* executed without full knowledge *e17*. **3** *of mist etc* dense *20-*, *now Bnf Abd*. **4** *esp of a cow's teat* having no opening *20-*, *now Bnf Arg*.

v **1** *vt* blind *la14-*. **2** *vti* close (the eyes) as in sleep *19-*, *now Bnf Abd*. **3** *vt* pack (the large stones forming the bed of a road) with smaller material to give strength and firmness *19-*.

blindlingis *16-e17*, ∼**lins** *la16-*, *now Lnk* blindly; heedlessly; with eyes shut. **blinner** move the eyelids like a person with defective sight *20-*, *Cai Bnf*. **blinners** blinkers *20-*, *Bnf Abd Lnk*.

blin bargain a bargain made without care or

full knowledge, a pig in a poke *la18-*, *now Abd Kcb*. **blind coal** a kind of anthracite *la18-*, *now Fif*. **blin drift** drifting snow *19-*. ∼ **ee** &c the dogfish *19-e20*. ∼ **een**(**s**) with the eyes shut, without needing to look *19-*, *now Abd*. **blind fair** *freq of albinos* extremely fair *19-*, *local*. **blin fou** very drunk *la19-*. **blind Harrie** &c [∼ 'harɪ, ∼ 'hɛrɪ] blindman's buff *la18-*, *now Lnk*. **blin hooie** &c *vt* exchange *20-*, *now Lnk*. *n* an exchange *20-*, *now Loth Lnk Ayr*. ∼ **lump** a boil which does not come to a head *20-*. ∼ **men's baw** &c *la18-e19*, ∼ **man's buff** *20-*, *now Kcb* the common puffball. ∼ **nale** &c ? a blunt nail *16-e17*. ∼ **oors** the late hours of the night *la19-*, *now Bnf Kcdn*. **blind parables** communication by signs, whispers etc in order to conceal something from someone present *20-*, *Bnf-Kcdn*. ∼ **sieve** a basket or tray for carrying grain etc *19-*, *now Ork*. **blin swap** the exchange of articles by schoolboys with their eyes shut or with the articles in closed hands *20-*.

blind &c [*blɪn(d)] *n* a spritsail *16-e17*. [only Sc; Du]

blind, blindlingis, blindlins *see* BLIN[2]

blink &c *16-*, **blenk** *la14-17*, **blent** [from *pt, ptp*] *verse, la15-16, 19-*, *now Loth*; **blaink** &c *la17 v, pt, ptp, verse also* **blent** *la15-e17* **1** *vi* give a glance or sudden look *la14-16*. **2** = blink. **3** *vti* glance kindly, look fondly (at); ogle *18-19*. **4** *vt* glance at with the evil eye: (1) bewitch *19-e20*; (2) turn (milk etc) sour *18-*, *now Bnf*. **5** *vti, chf* **blent** (**up**) *of light, the sun etc* gleam, shine *16, 19-*, *now Lnk*. **6** *vt* give a spark to or of; light (a lamp) *la19-*, *now Sh*. **7** *vi* be drunk, under the influence of drink *19-*, *now Ayr*. **8** *vt* deceive, cheat *19-e20*.

n **1** = blink. **2** a (pleasant) glance, (brief) look *la15-*. **3** *of (a source of) light, esp the sun* a brief or bright gleam; a (short) period of shining, *now esp* of sunshine between clouds *16-*. **4** *fig* a gleam of comfort etc *e17*. **5** a short time, moment *19-*. **6** a wink of sleep *20-*, *now local Sh-Kcb*. **7** a momentary use of borrowed light *19-*, *now Sh Bnf*: *'gie me the blink o a candle'*.

blinker 1 the eye *la19-*, *now local Sh-Arg*. **2** a heavenly body *19-e20*. **3** *in pl* eyelashes *la19-*, *now Bnf Loth*. **4** a cheat, a spy *la18-e19*. **5** a person who is nearly blind or blind in one eye *19-*, *now Abd*. **6** a lively, attractive girl *la18-e20*. **blinter** *n, also* **blenter 1** a boisterous gusty wind *19-e20*. **2** a strong sharp blow or hit *19*. *v* **1** *vt, also* **blenter** strike *19-e20*. **2** *vi* glimmer, flicker *19-*, *now Abd*. **3** squint; blink *e19*. **blinterer** a short-sighted person *20-*, *now Bnf*. **blintrin** short-sighted *19-e20*, *NE*. ∼**in eed** weak-eyed *la19-*, *now Bnf Abd*.

blirt *vi* cry, weep, burst into tears *18-*, *now Bnf Abd Ags*.

n, only Sc **1** an outburst (of weeping) *la18-*, *now Bnf*. **2** a gust of wind with rain *19-*, *now Bnf*.

~**ie** *of weather* changeable and showery *19-*, *now Bnf Abd*. [prob onomat; *cf* Eng *blurt*]

bliss *la19-*, **blis &c** *la14-17 vt* = bless. [ME]

blist *see* BLAST

blithe &c *la15-*, **blith &c** *la14-18*; **blide &c** *19-*, *now Sh* [blaɪð, blaɪθ; *Sh Ork* blaɪd; *Bwk Rox* bləɪð; *Rox also* bləɪθ] *adj* **1** = blithe *la14-*. **2** joyous, cheerful, glad, in good spirits *la14-*. **3** happy because of **of**, glad **of** *la14-*, *now Ags*. **4** *of the face, bearing etc* happy, cheerful *la14-16*. *vt* = blithe, gladden *la15*.
adv happily, cheerfully, kindly *la18-*.
blithfull &c joyful, glad *la14-16*. **blithesome &c** cheerful, merry *18-*.
~**meat 1** a thanksgiving feast after the birth of a child *la17-*, *now Lnk*. **2** food given to people in a house at the time of a birth *19-*, *now Lnk*.

blitter *n* a thin watery mess *20-*, *Abd Edb Ayr*. [see SND]

blitter *see* BLAIT, BLUITER

blivert *see* BLAE

blob, blab *18-*, *now Mry*; **bleib &c** *19-*, *now Abd* [blob, blab, bleb, blɛb, bləɪb] *n* **1** a drop of moisture, a bubble *15-*. **2** a pimple or pustule; *in pl* a rash *16-*, *now Ork*. **3** the bag of a honey bee *19-e20*. **4** *only* **blob**, *also* **honey blob** a gooseberry *18-19*.
vt **1** *only* **blob** disfigure with blobs of ink, blot *15-19*. **2** *only* **blab, bleb** besmear *19-*, *now Abd*. [onomat; perh w infl f OE *blawan* > Eng *blow*]

blocher &c *19-*, *now Bnf Abd Per Uls*, **bloigh &c** *20-*, *Uls* ['bloxər; *Uls* 'bloix(ər)] *vi*, *only* **blocher &c** make a gurgling noise in coughing *19-*, *now Bnf Abd Per Uls*.
n a loose, catarrhal cough *20-*, *now Per Uls*. [prob onomat]

block[1] *la15-*, **blok &c** *15-e17 n* **1** = block (of wood) *16-*. **2** a quantity of goods sold at one time *la16-e17*. **3** a pulley or sheaf of pulleys *16-e17*. **4** contemptuous term for a person *16*, *20-*, *now Ags*. **5** the base in hide-and-seek etc *la20-*, *local Sh-Fif*.
vt **1** hinder, impede *15-*. **2** sketch or block out; draft *la16*.
~, **hammer, and nail** a children's game *la19-*, *now Abd*.
~ **the ice** *curling* (CURL) block the run of the stones with guards *19-*, *now Abd Kcb*.

block[2] **&c** *la16-*, **blok &c** *16-e17 n* **1** a scheme, plot *16*. **2** (1) a bargain or agreement in buying and selling; a commercial or business transaction, *freq* **mak blok** *16-e20*. (2) something bought or sold; a bargain *la16-e17*.
v **1** *vi* bargain; trade *16-17*. **2** *vt* acquire by bargaining *la16-e17*.
~**er** a trader, broker *e17*. ~**in ale &c** a drink taken by the parties to a bargain *19-*, *NE*. [only Sc; related to BLOCK[1] *v*]

block[3] *n* a cod *e20*, *Bnf*.

~**an** *la17-e20*, **bluchan** *19-* ['blʌxən] the young coalfish *chf SW*. ~**ie** a small cod *20-*, *now Cai*. [uncertain]

blod *see* BLUDE

bloigh *see* BLOCHER

bloit *see* BLOUT[2]

blok *see* BLOCK[1], BLOCK[2]

blome *see* BLUME

bloncat &c [*'blʌŋkət, *'blaŋkət] *adj*, *n* = blunket, grey, greyish blue; a cloth of this colour *15-e17*.

blondin *n* a cableway between two towers with a skip which can carry *eg* stone in a quarry backwards and forwards or up and down *la19-*, *chf Abd*. [f Charles *Blondin* (1824-97), the French tightrope walker]

blonk *n*, *only verse* a steed *la15-16*. [ME]

blood *see* BLUDE

bloom *see* BLUME

blost *see* BLOUST

bloster *see* BLOUSTER

blot &c *n*, *vt* = blot *la16-*.
~-**sheet** blotting-paper *la19-*.

blotch *vt* **1** = blotch. **2** blot, stain with ink *20-*, *now Bnf Abd Kcb*. **3** blot **out**, delete *la19-*, *now Abd Kcb*.

bloust &c, blost *20-*, *Cai*; **bluist** *e20* [blʌust; *Cai* blost; *Kcb Rox also* bløst] *n* a boast; boasting *19-*, *now Cai Ags*.
vi brag, boast *19-*, *now Cai Ags*. [reduced f next; *cf* also Eng *blast*]

blouster &c *17-*; **bluister &c** *19-* ['blʌustər; *SW Rox also* bløstər] *n* **1** *also* **bloster** *20-*, *now Ayr Kcb* ['blostər] a violent wind with squalls *20-*, *now Bnf*. **2** a boaster, braggart *17-e20*.
vi brag, boast *19-e20*. [onomat; *cf* Eng *bluster*]

blout[1] **&c** [*blʌut] *adj* barren, bare *e16*. [only Sc; *cf* Du *bloot* bare and ON *blautr* soft, wet]

blout[2] **&c** [blʌut] *n* **1** a sudden burst, *esp* of wind, rain etc *la18-*, *now Ayr*. **2** *only* **bloit** [bloit] a sudden bowel movement, diarrhoea *19-e20*, *SW*.
~**er** *n* a blast of wind *19-*, *now Abd*. [only Sc; perh ON *blautr* soft, wet or OE *blāwan* (*v*) blow; *cf* BLOWDER]

blow *see* BLAW[1]

blowder &c ['blʌudər; *Bnf also* *'blʌuðər] *n* a sudden gust of wind *la19-e20*, *NE*. [f the same root as OE *blāwan* (*v*) blow; *cf* BLOUT[2]]

bluachie &c ['bl(j)uəx(t)ɪ] *adj*, *freq in comb* bluish *20-*, *now Bnf*. [only Sc; Eng *blue* + Gael suffix *-ach* + Sc dim suffix *-ie*]

blubber &c *vti* = blubber *16-*.
blibberin slobbering; making a noise when drinking soup *20-*, *Abd*.
blubber-totum &c *n* name for any drink made too thin or weak, *eg* tea, gruel *20-*, *Abd*. [see SND]

bluchan *see* BLOCK[3]

bluchtan &c ['blʌxtən] *n* a piece of hollow stem used as a peashooter *19-*, *Gall Dmf*. [obscure]

blud *see* BLUDE

bludder *see* BLUTHER

blude &c, blood &c *17-,* **blid** *20-, C;* **blud &c** *la14-, now Sh,* **bluid &c** *16-,* **blod &c** *13-e17,* **bleed &c** *la18-, N* [blod; *NE* blid; *C* blɪd] *n* **1** = blood *la14-.* **2** an act of bloodshed; an assault causing bleeding *16-e18.* **3** a fine for bloodshed *e17.* **4** *with negative* not a single person or thing *la19-, now Sh Edb.*
v **1** *vt* cause to bleed *16-.* **2** *vi* bleed; have blood flowing *17-, now Ork.*
bludie &c = bloody *13-.* **bluidy fingers** the foxglove *la18-e20.* **bluidy &c puddin &c 1** = *black puddin* (BLACK) *la18-e20.* **2** nickname for an inhabitant of Stromness, Ork *20-, Ork Cai.*
~-drawing the drawing of blood by assault or wounding *15-e17.* **~-friend &c** a blood relation *17-, now Sh.* **~ puddin &c** = *black puddin* (BLACK) *18-19.* **~ roll &c** a roll of persons accused of bloodshed *16-.* **~ run** *18-, now Bnf Abd,* **~shed** *la19-, now local Cai-Ayr* bloodshot.
~wite &c *13-17,* **~weck &c** *la15-e17* [*'blod'wɔit, *-'wit, *-'wik, *-'wɪk, *&c*] **1** guiltiness of, or liability to a penalty for bloodshed; an action against a person for bloodshed *la13-17.* **2** a fine for bloodshed; the right of imposing or collecting this *15-17.*
of blude related by blood *15-e17.* [*cf* BLEED]
bluder *see* BLUTHER

blue *18-,* **blew &c** *15-17,* **bew &c** *la16, 20-, NE, WC* [blu; *Sh Ork NE, S also* blju; *NE, WC also* bju] *adj* = blue *15-.*
n **1** = blue *la15-.* **2** WHISKY or other spirits *la18-19.*
~bell 1 = *harebell* (HARE) *la18-.* **2** the English bluebell *20-.* **~ blanket** the banner of the craftsmen of Edinburgh *la16-e20, latterly hist.* **~ bonnet 1** a man's flat-topped round cap without a peak *la16-e19.* **2** the wearer of such a cap *e19.* **3** *in pl* name of several flowers, *specif* (1) the cornflower *la18-e20;* (2) knapweed *e20.* **4** the bluetit *19-e20.* **~ cap** *mining* the blue haze over the flame of a safety-lamp when firedamp is present in the air *la19-, now Fif.* **~ clue** a ball of blue worsted used in divining at *Halloween* (HALLOW²) *la18-e20.* **~ day 1** a very cold or frosty day *19-, now Abd.* **2** a day on which some disturbance takes place *19-, now Bnf.* **3** a day when one is very anxious or depressed *la19-, now Abd.* **~ do** *colloq* a poor performance, a failure, a black outlook *la20-.* **~ ee** a black eye *19-, NE nEC.* **~gown** a (licensed) beggar *la17-18* [so called because they wore blue cloaks]. **~ grass** any of the various sedge grasses *e19.* **~ grey** *of cattle* applied to a crossbreed of a Galloway cow and a shorthorn bull *20-.* **~ mogganer** a native of Peterhead, *esp* a fisherman *la19-, NE.* **~ nose** *contemptuous term used by Roman Catholics* a Protestant *la20-, Fif WC.* **~ threid** an indecent or smutty touch (in a story) *19-, now local Sh-Ayr.*

I've seen as licht a ~ I've seen as much *20-, Bnf Abd.*
bluff¹ *adj* = bluff *19-.*
n a credulous person *la18-, now Abd.*
bluff² *vt* blow (small objects) by means of a tube *la19-, now Abd.* [onomat]
bluffert; bliffert &c *n* **1** a squall (of wind and rain) *19-, NE Ags Ayr.* **2** *also* **blaffart** a blow, slap *19-, NE Ags.* [prob f BLUFF²]
bluid *see* BLUDE
bluist *see* BLOUST
bluister *see* BLOUSTER
bluiter &c, bleeter *20-, Bnf Abd* ['blotər; *N* 'blitər; *C* 'blɪtər; *NE also* 'bl(j)utər] *n* **1** term of abuse or contempt for a person *la16-: specif* (1) a big, clumsy, useless person *19-, now Bnf;* (2) a senseless talker *19-, now Edb wLoth Kcb.* **2** a rumbling noise *19-20.*
v **1** *vi* make a rumbling noise *la18-e20.* **2** do work in a bungling way *la19-e20.* **3** *vti, also* **blitter** *20-, Abd Kcb* talk foolishly; blurt out *la19-, now Bnf Abd Bwk.*
blitter blatter *adv phr* expressing a rattling irregular noise *19-, now Abd wLoth.* [obscure]
bluiter *see* BLAIT
blume &c, blome *la14-17,* **bleem** *20-, N;* **bloom** *la18-* [bløm; *N* blim; *C* blɪm] *vi* = bloom *la15-.*
n **1** = bloom *la14-.* **2** *in pl* potato tops *20-, now Ags.*
blumf &c *n* a dull, stupid person *19-, now Bnf Abd.* [perh Eng *bluff,* w infl f GRUMPH]
blunderbush [*'blʌndərbʌʃ] *n* = blunderbuss *18-, now Abd.*
blunk¹ [bl(j)ʌŋk] *n* **1** a small block of wood or stone *la19-, now Abd.* **2** a dull, lifeless person *19-, now Bnf.*
~art &c = *n, la19-e20.* [obscure]
blunk² &c *n* a cloth woven to be printed on *la18-19.* [perh short for BLONCAT or var of Eng *blank*]
blunk³ &c *vt* spoil, mismanage *19-e20.* [obscure]
blunochs &c ['blʌnəxs] *n pl* clothes *e20, Abd.* [obscure]
blunt &c *adj* = blunt *la15-.*
n a stupid fellow *19-, now Abd.*
~ie &c a sniveller; a stupid fellow, *chf* **look like ~ie** *la18-e19.*
blush *v* **1** *vi* = blush *la16-.* **2** *vti* (raise a) blister *19-e20, Bwk Rox.*
~in a blister; a pustule, as in smallpox *19-e20, SW Uls.*
bluther; bludder &c *16-e19 v* **1** *vi* be stained or disfigured with something wet *16-e18.* **2** *vt* soil, disfigure (the face, eyes, mouth) with tears etc *17-, now Ags.* [onomat; *cf* Eng *blubber*]
blyave *see* BLAW¹
blybe *n* a large quantity of liquid, *esp* of spirits *la19-, Bnf Abd.*
vi drink heavily *la19-, now Abd.* [*cf* BLIB, BLAB]

blype *n* a layer of skin as it peels or is rubbed off *la18-19.* [*cf* FLYPE]

bo *la16-*; **boo &c** *19-* [bo, bu] *interj* = boo! *la16-. vi* make a face *e16.*

~-**man** a bogyman *19-*, *now Bnf.*

not be able to say ~ **to your** *etc* **blanket** not be able to reproach you etc, not be able to injure your etc reputation *17-e20.*

boak *see* BOCK

boakie &c *n* a piece of hard matter in the nose *20-*, *now Abd.* [perh f BOCKIE; cf *black man* 4 (BLACK) and BOWSIE²]

boal *see* BOLE

boam &c *n* **1** a wooden framework on which yarn is hung to be shaken and dried *la19-*, *now Fif.* **2** *only* **bolm** [*bʌum] a boat-pole *e16.* **3** *only* **bome &c** a beam, bar; a boom to close a river etc *16-17.* [Du *boom* a tree; a punt-pole; boom; *cf* Eng *boom* a spar]

boast *la16-*, **bost &c** *14-e20 n* **1** = boast *la14-.* **2** a threatening, a menacing *la15-e17.*

v **1** *vi* = boast *16-.* **2** (1) *vti* utter threats, threaten; scold, reprove *la15-*, *now Sh-N.* (2) *vt* command or drive with threats *la15-e17, e20.* (3) announce with threats *la16.*

~**our &c** **1** = boaster *la16-.* **2** name of an engine of war *14-e15.*

boat¹ *17-*, **bait &c** *la14-e20*, **bate** *la14-16*, **bote &c** *la15-e17*; **boit &c** *la15-17* [bot; bo:t, &c; *bet] *n* **1** = boat *la14-.* **2** a ferry *la18-*, *now Bnf Abd.*

v **1** *vt* put into or carry in a boat *16-e17.* **2** *vi* go into a boat, embark *16-e19.*

boatic, bottick = boat-hook *20-*, *now Sh Bnf.* ~(**is**)**man** = boatman *la14-.* **baitschele &c** a boatshed, *esp* for a ferryboat *la15-17.* **bait wricht &c** a boatbuilder *16.*

boat² *19-*, **bote &c** *15-e17*; **bot(t)** *la15-e17 n* **1** a cask, butt (for wine etc) *15-e17.* **2** a barrel, tub *19.* [F, Ital *botte*, Span, Port *bota*; *cf* Eng *butt*]

bob¹, bab *la18-e20 n* **1** (1) = bob, a bunch; a knob *la15-16.* (2) a bunch of flowers *19-*, *now Abd.* **2** a small luxuriant patch of grass, corn etc *la19-*, *Bnf Kcb.* [ME]

bob² *vti, also* **bab** *18-e19* = bob, move up and down *la16-.*

n **1** a dance *la16-.* **2** *angling* any fly on a cast other than a tail-fly *19-e20.*

bobber = *n* 2, *e19.* **Bobbin John** a kind of hand-sower *la18-*, *now Abd.* **bobbin-quaw, babanquaw &c** ['bob(ən)'kwɑ, 'bab-] a quaking bog, quagmire *19-e20.* **bobantilter** ['bob(ə)n'tıltər] something dangling; an icicle *20-*, *Cai.*

bob³ *n* **1** a mark, butt *19-*, *now Arg.* **2** a taunt, scoff *la18-*, *now Sh.* [perh OF *bobe* deception, mocking]

bob *see* BUB

bobantilter *see* BOB²

bob-at-the-bowster *see* BAB AT THE BOWSTER

bobbie &c *la18-*, **bubba** *e20, Ross n* a grandfather *la18-e20.*

auld B~ the devil *la18-*, *now Abd.* [*cf* PAWPIE]

boch [box] *n* a child's toy, a knick-knack; contemptuous term for a person *20-*, *Cai.* [only Sc; *cf* Gael = ecstasy, great happiness]

bocht *see* BUY

bock *la16-*, **bowk** *19-*, *now Abd Ags Edb*, **bolk** *la15*, **bok &c** *15-e20*, **byock &c** *20-*, *NE*; **boak &c** *19-* [bok; *Mry Bnf Loth Bwk S* bʌuk; *NE also* bjok] *vti* belch; retch, vomit *la15-.*

n **1** a belch, a retch *15-.* **2** nausea; a feeling of disgust or revulsion *20-*, *Cai Ags Ayr.*

byochy-byochy ['bjoxı-] retch, vomit *la19-*, *Ags.*

gie (**someone**) *or* **get the** (**dry**) ~(**s**) *lit and fig* (cause to) feel sick, retch or vomit *20-*, *local C.* [eModEng *boke*, ME *bolk*, prob onomat]

bockie; bokie &c *n* a hobgoblin; a scarecrow *19-*, *Sh-N.* [*cf* ON *bokki* a he-goat; a man, fellow, posh f Eng *bogy*]

bod &c ? *n, proverb* **new shot, new** ~ in reference to making a fresh attempt at something *16-e19.* [perh BODE (*n*) or reduced f BODEN]

bod *see* BODE

bodach &c ['bodəx] *n* **1** *freq contemptuous* an old man *la19-*, *now Cai.* **2** a small and insignificant person *la19-*, *now Bnf.* **3** a spectre, bugbear *19.* **4** *only* **boddoch** a MUTCHKIN *e17.* [Gael = an old man; a bad-tempered old man; a MUTCHKIN]

boday &c [*?'bo'daı] *n* = bow-dye, a scarlet dye *la17.*

boddam *la19-*, *N*, **boddom &c** *15-*, **botham** *la19*, *Sh Ork NE*, **bothome &c** *la16-*, *now Abd*; **bottom &c** *la16-* ['bodəm, 'botəm; *Sh Ork NE* 'boðəm; *SW* 'bʌdəm] *n* (*15-*), *vt* (*la16-*) = bottom.

bottomer *mining* the person who loads and unloads the cages at the bottom or intermediate landings in a shaft *19-*, *now Fif.*

boddom breadth the amount of space necessary for a person to sit *la19-*, *now Bnf Abd Ags.* **bottom room** = *boddom breadth*, *esp* in a church pew *19-.*

boddened *see* BODEN

boddin *see* BODEN

boddle *see* BODLE

boddoch *see* BODACH

boddom *see* BODDAM

boddy *see* BODY

bode; bod *la16- n* **1** an offer, a bid (*esp* at an auction) *la15-.* **2** the price asked by a seller; the offer of goods at a certain rate *19-*, *now Bnf Abd Fif.* **3** an invitation, *esp* to a wedding *19-*, *now Sh.*

vt **1** = bode, portend. **2** expect, desire, aim at *la16-*, *now Bnf.* **3** offer with insistence, press (something) **on** (someone) *19-*, *now Bnf.*

bodement foreboding *19-*, *now Abd.*

bod penny the sum decided in advance to be the regular increase between each bid at an auction *18-*, *now NE.*

bode *see* BIDE

boden *18-*, **bodin** *la14-e19*; **boddin** *15-17 ptp*, *adj* **1** furnished with arms; equipped for fighting *la14-17.* **2** provided, prepared *15-*, *now Abd.* **weel** *etc* ~, **weel-boddened** well etc equipped or provided *15-*, *now Sh.* [only Sc; see DOST, SND]

bodilik &c *adj*, *adv* = bodilich, bodily *la14-15*, *only Sc.*

bodin *see* BODEN

bodle &c; boddle *19 n* **1** a small copper coin = two pence SCOTS, a TURNER *la17-19*, *latterly hist.* **2** *transf* something of little value, *chf* **not to care** *or* **not worth a** ~ *la18-.* ~ **preen** a pin of the value of a BODLE *19.* [only Sc; obscure]

bodsy *n* a little, dapper, or neat person *la18-*, *chf Abd.* [perh colloq Eng *bod* a person + *-sie*]

bodword &c *la14-*, *now Abd*; **bodwart** *16* ['bodwʌrd, *-wərt] *n* a message, announcement, report; an invitation. [nME; *cf* BODE]

body &c; boddy &c *15-e16* ['bodɪ] *n* **1** = body *la14-.* **2** *also* **bothie** *e16, 19*, **buddy** *la19-* ['bodɪ, 'bʌdɪ] a person, a human being: (1) *chf* **a** ~, *in gen*, *15-*; (2) **a** ~, *referring to the speaker himself or to another* someone, one, a person *la16-*: '*could you no leave a body in peace?*'; '*sorrow a body heiris us but ourselves*'; (3) *with adj or noun, freq* indicating contempt or sympathy *la14-*: '*a cantie body*'; '*a tailor body*'; (4) a puny or little person *19-*, *now Bnf Fif*; (5) *chf* **buddies** nickname for the inhabitants of Paisley and for St Mirren football team (*cf* SAINT *n* 2) *20-.* **3** a great number (of fish) *20-*, *now Bnf Fif.* **bodily &c** *adj* = bodily *15-.* *adv* **1** = bodily *la14-.* **2** by a corporal oath *la14-16*, *only Sc.* **bodily athe** *or* **faith** a corporal oath *la14-e17*, *only Sc.* **a** ~**'s sel** onself *20-*, *now NE.* **nae ither** ~ no one else *la18-.*

bog[1] *n* = bug *la19-*, *now Loth Lnk.*

bog[2] &c *n* a bog, mire *13-.* *v* **1** *vt* = bog *19-.* **2** *vi* work in wet, dirty surroundings; work slowly *19-e20.* **3** *esp of shoemakers working in a customer's house* work at a daily rate *la19.* ~**-bleater &c** the bittern *19-e20.* ~**-cotton** cotton-grass *20-.* ~**-hay** hay gathered from uncultivated or marshy ground *la18-.* ~**-hyacinth** a kind of wild orchid *la19-*, *now Abd.* ~**-stalker** an idle, bashful man *18-e20.* ~**-th(r)issle** the thistle, *Carduus palustris*, *20-*, *now Abd.*

bogentully ['bogən'tʌlɪ] *n* a heavy boot *20-*, *now Bnf.* [obscure]

boggle *vi*, *of the eyes* protrude, bulge with fear or pain *20-*, *now EC.* [perh f Eng = take fright]

boggle *see* BOGLE

bogie[1] ['bogɪ] *n*, *chf* ~ **roll &c** a kind of coarse black tobacco of a medium twist *19-e20.* [f the River Bogie, Abd, near which it was first manufactured]

bogie[2] ['bogɪ] *n* **the game's a** ~ *children's games* a call to cancel a game and start again when there has been a fault *20-*, *C.* [Eng *bogy* a goblin]

bogle *17-*, **bogill &c** *16-e19*; **boggle** *la16-e20* ['bogl] *n* **1** an ugly or terrifying ghost or phantom; a bugbear *16-.* **2** *also fig* a scarecrow *la19-.* **bogly** haunted by BOGLES *19-*, *now Abd.* ~**-bo &c** a hobgoblin, spectre *18-19.* ~ **about the stacks** *etc* a kind of hide-and-seek *19-e20.* [uncertain]

bogshaivelt &c [bog'ʃevlt, -'dʒevlt, bʌu-] *adj* knocked out of shape, distorted *20-*, *now Bnf.* [see SND]

boich &c [box, bjox] *vi* cough with difficulty *19-*, *now Abd.* [onomat]

boick &c *see* BYKE[1]

boikin &c *17-19*, **boitkin &c** *16-e17* [*'boi(t)kɪn] *n* = bodkin.

boil *see* BILE[1]

boist *see* BUIST[1]

boit *see* BOAT[1]

boitkin *see* BOIKIN

bok *see* BOCK

bokie *see* BOCKIE

boldin[1] &c *15-e17*; **bowdin &c** *16-e17* ['bʌudən; *'boldən] *vi* swell (up); *esp* rise in flood *15-e17.* ~**it &c** **1** swelled with pride, grief etc *la16-e17.* **2** *only* **bowdened &c** *of people or animals* swollen from overeating *19-*, *now Bnf.* [only Sc; var of obs Eng *bolne*; *cf* next]

boldin[2] &c *16-e17*; **bowdin &c** *16* [*'boldən, *'bʌudən] *adj* **1** physically swollen or distended *16-e17.* **2** affected by extreme grief, pride etc *16.* [only Sc; corresponding to ME *bollen*, f *bell* (*v*) or *bolned*, f *bolne* (*v*); *cf* prec]

bole &c *la17-*, **bowall &c** *16-e20*; **boal** *18-e20* [bol, 'bʌuəl] *n* **1** a recess in a wall, *later* one used as a cupboard; a small opening in a wall *16-.* **2** *specif* a pay-desk window *20-*, *Ags wLoth.* *vt*, *only* **bowal &c** build or join (a wall) with a recess *e16.* [obscure]

bolk *see* BOCK

boll &c; bow &c *la15-e20* [bol; bʌu] *n* **1** a dry measure of weight or capacity varying according to commodity and locality, *eg* a ~ **of meal** = 140 lbs (approx 63.5 kg) *la14-.* **2** a valuation of land according to the quantity of BOLLS it produced *18-e19.* **3** payment in food to a farm-worker *la18-e20.* [prob OE *bolla* or ON *bolle*, *bolli* a bowl]

boll *see* BOW[3]

bolm *see* BOAM

bolster *see* BOWSTER

bolt *see* BOWT

bomb *n* **1** *also* **boomb** *la20, Sh NE* [bum] = bomb. **2** a puff or belch of smoke *la20-, now Per.*

bombasie &c *16-e17;* **bumbasy &c** *la16-17* [*'bʌmbası, *-bəsı] *n* = bombasine.

bombaze *see* BUMBAZE

bome *see* BOAM

bon &c *n* humour, mood *20-, now Ags.* [*cf* Norw *bunsa* burst out, rush violently on]

Bonaccord &c ['bonə'kord] *n* **1** the motto of the city of Aberdeen; the city itself *la19-.* **2** concord; friendly agreement *17-e18.* **3** a toast *17, Abd.*

Abbot and Prior *15-16 or* **Lordis of** ~ *16* two persons elected annually by the town council of Aberdeen to organize public sports and entertainments *Abd.* [only Sc; OF *bone acorde* good accord, harmony]

bonage *see* BONE²

bonailie &c *17-e20,* **bonallay &c** *la15-e20* [bon'elɪ, -'alɪ] *n* a drink with or toast to a departing friend; a farewell greeting. [only Sc; F *bon* good + *aller* go(ing)]

bond *n* **1** = bond *la17-.* **2** *specif* a mortgage *la19.* [*cf* BAND¹]

bond *see* BOUN²

bondage &c, boundage &c *16-17;* **bonnage &c** *la17-e20* ['bon(d)edʒ, 'bʌn-; *'bund-, *'bʌnd-] *n* **1** = bondage *15-.* **2** service due from a tenant to his SUPERIOR or from a farmworker to a farmer *17-e20.*

bondager a person who performs BONDAGE service, *chf* a female field-worker supplied by a farm-tenant in accordance with the conditions of his tenancy *19-e20.*

bonday wark *see* BONE²

bondelesoure; bonelesew &c [*'bond'lisur; *'bøn'lisju; &c] *n* ? pasturage connected with bond- or boon-service *la15.* [ME *bond* a peasant or BONE² + *lesour* or *lesu* (LIZOUR)]

bone¹ [bon] *vt* dun, pester for money owed *la19-, now Bnf Ags Ayr.* [prob Eng *bone* remove bones from]

bone² &c [*bøn] *n* = boon, a prayer; the thing prayed for *la14-16.*

bonage &c [*'bønedʒ] service rendered by a tenant *la15-18* [*cf* BONDAGE].

bonday [*'bønde] **wark** work done without payment as part of tenant service *la16-e17.* ~**-plewis &c** ploughs used in unpaid tenant service *la15-16.* ~ **service** *etc = bonday wark, la16.* ~ **silver** money paid in lieu of service *e16.*

bone *see* BANE

bonegrace *see* BON-GRACE

bonelesew *see* BONDELESOURE

bonet *see* BONNET

bonevale &c [*bon'velɪ] *n* = BONAILIE *e17.* [appar by conflation w L *vale* farewell]

bon-grace &c *la16-e20,* **bonegrace** *16 n* **1** a

shade attached to a woman's bonnet *16-17.* **2** a coarse straw hat, *esp* as worn by countrywomen *la18-e20.* [eModEng]

bonker *see* BUNKER

bonnage *see* BONDAGE

bonnet &c *16-,* **bonet &c** *la14-e17;* **bannet &c** *la15-,* **bunnet** *20-, sEC, WC n* **1** a soft flat brimless cap worn by men and boys, *latterly usu* one with a peak *la14-.* **2** = bonnet, a woman's (brimmed) head-dress *la15-.* **3** a (metal) helmet *16-e17.* **4** an additional piece laced to a sail *la15-e17.* **5** *mining* a portion of a seam left as a roof *la19-, now Fif Lnk.*

vt put one's bonnet on the top of (a mast etc) as a feat of daring *la19-, now Bnf.*

~**ie &c** a boys' game played with bonnets and varying according to district *la19-.*

~ **fir** the Scots pine *la19, Ags.* ~ **fleuk &c** the brill *18-, now Fif.* ~ **laird** a small landowner who farmed his own land *19-, now hist.* ~ **mutch** a woman's bonnet-like cap *e17.* ~ **piece** a gold coin of James V, showing the King wearing a BONNET *la16-19, latterly hist.*

bonnilie *see* BONNY

bonnock *see* BANNOCK

bonny &c *la16-,* **bony &c** *la15-18 adj* **1** beautiful, pretty *la15-.* **2** *specif of boys or men* handsome, attractive *la16-.* **3** *transf, also ironic* good, excellent, fine *la15-.* **4** in terms of endearment *16-:* 'my bonnie bairn'. **5** *of a space of time, as intensifier, orig appar* short, *but latterly* considerable, *freq* **a ~ while &c** *la15-.* **6** *in gen* great, considerable *la16-.*

adv **1** in a BONNY way *19-.* **2** *also* ~ **and** *as intensifier* very *la19-, now Ork NE.*

bonnilie &c prettily; well, satisfactorily *la16-.* ~ **die** a trinket, toy *19-e20.* ~ **penny** a high price *20-, now local Cai-Kcb.* ~ **wallie** = ~ **die,** *18-e19.* [ME]

bonspiel &c *la16-,* **bonspell &c** *la16* ['bon-'spil; *-'spɛl] *n* a match or contest; *latterly (19-) only* a *curling* (CURL) match. [see SND]

bontath *see* BOUNTITH

bontay, bonté *see* BOUNTY

bonteth *see* BOUNTITH

bonty *see* BOUNTY

bony *see* BONNY

boo¹ *19-,* **bow &c** [bu; *S* bʌu] *vti* **1** = bow, stoop in respect etc *la14-.* **2** *vi* bend, curve; become bent or crooked *15-.* **3** *vt* cause to bend *la14-.*

n **1** = bow (in greeting etc) *19-.* **2** an arch; a bend or curve *e20, Abd.*

bowed rig a strip of land on a hillside ploughed in winding curves to prevent water from draining off directly and carrying top soil with it *la19-, WC.*

boo-backit hump-backed *la19-, local Cai-Kcb.*

boo an ee *in negative* not close one's eyes, fail to sleep *20-, local.*

boo² &c *n* a louse *la19-, now Cai.* [prob F *pou*]

boo³ &c 1 *vti* = boo. **2** *vi* speak loudly, monotonously and to little purpose *la19-*, *now local NE-EC, only Sc.*

boo *see* BO

bood *see* BEHOVE

boodie &c *n* **1** a ghost, hobgoblin *19-*, *now Bnf Abd.* **2** *chf* **tattie** ~ a scarecrow *19-*, *Bnf Abd.* [prob Gael *bodach* (as in *bodach rocais* a scarecrow), w infl f BO]

boof *see* BUFF²

boohoo *v* **1** *vi* = boohoo. **2** *vti* show contempt (for) by using this sound *19-*, *now Bnf.*

book *see* BUIK

bool¹ &c *16-*, **boull &c** *la15-e20* [bul] *n* **1** = bowl, the ball used in bowls; *in pl* the game itself *la15-*. **2** a ball or rounded object, *eg* a cannonball, a round stone, a round sweet *16-*. **3** a marble *19-*.
~ **maill** rent or hire of a bowling green *la17-e18*.
the ~**s row** (ROW¹) *etc* **smooth** *etc* things are going well *19-*. **have a** ~ **in one's mou &c** speak habitually in an affected way *la20-*.

bool² *19-*, **boull &c** *la15-e20* [bul] *n* a curved or semi-circular band, forming: **1** the handle of a pot, bucket etc *la15-20*; **2** the bow of a key *la16-19*; **3** the ring joining the blades of a pair of shears or the finger and thumb holes in scissors *la16-19*.
vt provide with a BOOL² (*n* 1) *17*.
n a bow-legged person *19-e20*.
~**ie, bowlie &c** ['bʌulɪ, *also* 'bulɪ] *adj* crooked, bent *19-*, *now Fif WC.* ~**ie-backit** hump-backed; round-shouldered *19-*, *now Bnf Fif wLoth.* **bowly-legged &c** bow-legged *20-*, *WC.* ~**-horned 1** with curved or twisted horns *18.* **2** *of persons* perverse, obstinate *la18-e20.* [nME *boule*, MDu *boghel*]

bool³ *n*, *freq with adj* contemptuous term for a man *19-*, *now Bnf*: 'auld bool'. [only Sc; perh Eng *bole* a tree trunk or BOOL¹]

bool⁴ &c [*?bøl] *vi* weep or sing with a long-drawn-out mournful sound *e19*, *S.* [only Sc; see SND]

boolder *n* = boulder *la19-*.

boomb *see* BOMB

boon¹ &c [*NE* bin; *bun, *bøn] *prep* above *la18-*, *now Abd.*
~**most &c** highest, uppermost *la18-*. [*cf* ABUNE]

boon² &c [bun] *n* a band of reapers, shearers etc *la18-*, *now Uls.* [f BONE²]

boon *see* BOUN¹

boons *see* BOUN²

boorach &c; boorock &c ['burəx, 'burək; *'bʌrəx] *n* **1** a mound, small hill *19-.* **2** a heap or mass *la19-e20.* **3** a crowd, group, cluster *18-*, *now NE Fif.* **4** a small, humble house *la18-*, *now Ags.* **5** a muddle, mess, state of confusion; a fuss *20-*, *Cai Mry Highl*; cf *v* 3.

v **1** *vt* heap up *20-*, *now Ags.* **2** *vi* crowd together *19-*, *now Bnf.* **3** mess or grub about *20-*, *Highl* [*cf* Gael *bùrach* dig, root up].
~**ie** = *n*, *la19-.* [only Sc; perh OE *būr* a dwelling + *-ock*, or OE *burg* a fort, earthwork]

boorag &c *n* a rough piece of turf used as a PEAT¹ (*n* 1) *la19-e20*, *Cai.* [only Sc; Gael *bùrach* a digging, Eng *burrow*]

boord *see* BUIRD¹

boordly *see* BUIRDLY

boorock *see* BOORACH

boosam *see* BOWSOME

boose¹ &c; bease *n* a stall for a horse or cow *la18-*, *now Arg.*
vi, ~ **up** command to a cow to take its place in a stall etc *19-e20.*
buisin stane &c the stone partition between BOOSES¹ *18-*, *now Arg.* [ME, ModEng dial *boos(e) &c*; *cf* ON *báss*]

boose² &c [bus] *vi* bustle or rush about *la19-*, *now Bnf.* [*cf* Norw *buse*, Sw *busa* dash, bound, EFrisian *bûsen* be violent, bluster]

boose *see* BUSS²

boosome *see* BESOM

boost &c *vt* drive off, shoo away *la19-e20.* [*cf* BOAST]

boost *see* BEHOVE

boot *see* BUIT¹

bootch; boutch &c [butʃ; *Ags* bʌutʃ] *n* a botch, bungle, muddle *la19-.*
vt botch, bungle, muddle *la19-e20.* [perh f MDu *butsen* (*v*) strike, patch up; *cf* Eng *botch*]

bootyer &c *n* a glutton *e19.* [see SND]

booyangs &c ['bu(ɪ)'jaŋz, 'boi'jaŋks, &c] *n pl* = NICKIE-TAMS *20-.* [see SND Suppl]

boozy *see* BOWSIE³

boral *see* BORE

borch(t) *see* BORROW¹

bord &c *n* **1** a ridge or rim of a hill *15-e17.* **2** an edging, border, hem on a garment, hat etc *la16-*, *now Kcb.* [ME *borde* edging]

bordel &c *16-*, **bordale &c** *la14-e17* ['bordl, *'bordɛl] *n* a brothel *la14-e19.*
~**er &c** a keeper or frequenter of brothels *la14-e19.*
~ **house** = *n*, *15-*, *now Abd.* [ME]

border &c *la16-*, **bordour &c** *15-e17 n* **1** = border *15-.* **2** *chf* **the B**~**s** the area lying between the Scottish-English border and Lothian; see also B~s (Region) *la15-.* **3** one's furthermost limit *la18-*, *now Abd Ags.*
B~**er &c** a dweller on the border between Scotland and England, *latterly chf specif in the Borders* (*n* 2) *15-.*
~**man** = B~er, *la16-e17.* **B**~**s** (**Region**) a REGION formed from the former counties of Peebles, Berwick, Roxburgh and Selkirk and part of the former county of Midlothian *la20-.*

bore &c *n* **1** = bore, a hole *16-.* **2** a hole, crevice, *freq* a shelter or hiding-place *la15-.* **3** *chf* **blue** ~ an opening in the clouds showing blue sky *17-*, *now Bnf Abd.* **4** *curling* (CURL) a passage between two *guards* (GAIRD) *la18-*, *now Bnf.* **5** a hole in a series, the space between holes, *eg* on a belt or the yarn beam of a loom *la18-*, *now Abd.*

v **1** *vt* = bore *la15-*. **2** *vi* press (against etc) *la19-*.

boral &c, **borell** &c *carpentry* a boring tool *la15-e20*. **borie** = *n* 3, *la19-*, *now Abd.*

~ **staff** the part of a loom which maintains tension on the warp *19-e20*. ~ **stone** &c, ~ **stane** &c **1** a stone bored to hold a flagstaff *la18-*, *now hist.* **2** a boundary stone *la19-*, *now in place-names.* ~ **at, in** *etc*, *usu contemptuous* study deeply or intently *la19-*, *now Ags.* **tak in** *or* **up a** ~ turn over a new leaf *19-*, *Bnf Abd.*

bore breiff *see* BEAR[2]

borell, borie *see* BORE

born *see* BARN

borne *see* BEAR[2]

born head *adv* straight and impetuously *e19*. [obscure]

borow *see* BORROW[1], BURGH

borra *see* BARRA

borrel &c *19*, *literary*, **burell** &c *la15-e16* [*'bor(ə)l, *'bʌr(ə)l] *adj* rough, rude. [ME]

borrow[1] &c *15-*, **borow** &c *la14-e17* *vt* **1** *also* **barrow** &c *17-e19* = borrow *la14-*. **2** *law* stand surety for, bail (a person) *15-e17*. **3** ransom, redeem, release (a person's life, soul etc) *la15-e20*.

n, *in sing* **borch**(t) &c *la14-e18* [*'borx], **broch** &c *15-16* [*'brox], *in pl* **borrowis** &c *la14-e18*, *only Sc* a surety, pledge.

borrowing *etc* **days** the last three days of March (Old Style) *16-* [from the fable that March borrowed three days from April].

bor(r)owgang the fact of becoming surety; suretyship *la14-e17*.

to borch as a pledge or security *la14-e16*. **draw in** (**to**) **borch** put in pledge *la14-15*. **lat** *etc* **to borch** allow security or pledge to be given for (a person or thing) *la14-e17*. **borch** &c *15-17*, **brogh** &c *la16-e19* *or* **burgh** *17-18* [*'bʌrx] **of** *or* **and hamehald** &c *law* a pledge that an animal sold is not stolen.

borrow[2] *n*, *curling* (CURL), *golf* the allowance made *eg* for unevenness of ice or ground *19-*. [prob f prec]

borrow *see* BARRA

bos &c [*'bos] *n* **1** a leather bottle for wine etc *la14-16*. **2** contemptuous term for a person, *freq* **old** ~ *16*. [only Sc; obscure]

bos *see* BOSS[1], BOSS[2]

bosie *see* BOSUM

boskill *see* BOSS[3]

bosom *see* BOSUM

boss[1] *la19-*, **bos** &c *16-e20* [bos] *n* **1** = boss, a rounded prominence *16-*. **2** a round mass; a tussock etc *la19-*, *now Abd Ayr.*

~**ie** a metal button used in the game of *buttony* (BUTTON) *20-*, *Abd.*

boss[2] *la16-*, **bos** &c *16-19* [bos] *adj* **1** hollow; concave; empty *16-*. **2** *fig* destitute (of means or brains) *la18-*.

n, *mining* the waste or exhausted workings of a mineral *la19-*, *now Fif.*

vt, *mining* undercut (a thick seam) *la19-*, *now Fif.*

bossing *building* the woodwork on the recessed part on the inside of a wall below a window *la20-*.

~**-heid** the piece of metal on a door frame into which the bolt of a lock fits *20-*, *local.* ~ **lok** a type of lock *16-e17*. ~ **window** a bow or bay window *16-17*. [perh BOS *or* BOSS[1]]

boss[3] *n* the wooden frame on which a cornstack is built *19-*, *now Abd Ags Lnk.*

bossin *now Arg*, **boskill** &c ['bos'kɪl] *now Abd* a ventilation hole in a cornstack *19-*. [perh f prec]

bossie *see* BASSIE[2]

bost *see* BOAST

boster *see* BOWSTER

bosum &c *la14-e17*; **bosom** &c *16-* ['bozəm; *NE* 'bʌuzəm] *n* **1** = bosom *la14-*. **2** the womb *la15-16*.

bosie &c ['bozɪ; *NE also* 'bʌuzɪ] = *n* 1, *la18-*.

bot &c *n* a bolt *la15-e17*. [obscure]

bot *see* BOAT[2], BUT

botano &c *n* a kind of bombazine or fustian *17*. [only Sc; Ital *bottana*]

bote *see* BOAT[1], BOAT[2], BUIT[1]

both *see* BAITH

botham *see* BODDAM

bothan ['boθən; *Gael* 'bɔhan] *n* an unlicensed drinking house or hut, a kind of shebeen *20-*, *Lewis Gsw.* [Gael = a hut, shack; *cf* BOTHY]

bothe *see* BUITH

botherer ['boðərər] *n* annoyance *19-*, *now Abd Fif.*

bothie *see* BODY

bothome *see* BODDAM

bothy &c *n* **1** a rough hut used as temporary accommodation *eg* by shepherds, salmon-fishers, mountaineers *la18-*. **2** permanent living quarters for workmen, *esp* a separate building on a farm used to house unmarried male farm-workers *la19-*.

vi live in a BOTHY *la19-*, *now local.*

~ **wife** *or* **woman** the woman who takes charge of the BOTHY (*n* 2) *la19-*, *now Bnf.* [prob Gael *bothan* a hut, with altered ending; *cf* BOTHAN]

bothyn *n* a *sheriffdom* (SHERIFF) *or* *lordship* 2 (LORD) *e15*. [only Sc; ScL *bothena*]

boting &c [*'botin] *n* a boot *16*. [only Sc; F *botine*, dim of *botte*]

bott *see* BOAT[2]

bottell *see* BOTTLE[1]

bottick *see* BOAT[1]

bottle[1] *18-*, **bottell** *e16*; **battle &c** *19-*, **buttle &c** *19-e20* ['botl; *WC Kcb* 'bʌtl; *Gall Uls also* 'batl] *n* = bottle, a bundle (of hay or straw); a sheaf *16-*, *now Kcb Uls*.
vt bundle up (hay or straw) for fodder *la17-*, *now Ags Lnk*.
gang tae Buckie *etc* **an** ~ **skate** 'get lost!', 'go to blazes!' *20-*, *now Bnf Abd*.

bottle[2] *n* a rounded piece of timber running along the ridge of a roof, over which a covering of lead or zinc is fixed *la20-*, *now WC*. [var of Eng *boltel* a rounded moulding]

bottom *see* BODDAM

botwand *n* meaning obscure *e16*.

bouch &c [bʌux; *Ags Rox also* bux] *n* a bark (of a dog) *19-*, *now Kcb*.
vi **1** bark *e20*. **2** cough *la19-*, *local Bnf-Rox*.
[prob onomat]

boucheour &c *la15-16*; **butcher &c** *la16-* ['butʃər, 'bʌtʃər; *?*'botʃər] *n* **1** = butcher, a slaughterer; an executioner, *freq* **bludy** ~ *la15-17*; *cf* FLESHER. **2** = butcher, a dealer in meat.
~ **meat** = butcher's meat *la18-*.

boucht[1] **&c**; **bought &c** *18-e20* [bʌxt] *n* a bend, fold; a knot; a coil of rope *19-*, *now Bnf*.
vt bend, fold *18-e19*. [see SND; *cf* BOUGHT]

boucht[2] **&c** *17-e20*, **bowcht &c** *15-e16*; **bucht &c** *la16-e20* [bʌxt, bʌuxt, boxt] *n* **1** a sheepfold; *specif* a small inner fold for milking ewes *15-e19*.
2 a square pew in a church *19*.
vt enclose (*esp* ewes for milking) in a fold *18-19*. [only Sc; Flem *bocht, bucht* an enclosure for swine, sheep etc]

bought *see* BOUGHT, BUY

bouet &c *18-*, **bowat &c** ['buət] *n* a (hand) lantern *la15-*.
MacFarlane's ~ **the moon** *19-e20* [because the moon's light guided the *Highland* (HIELAND) cattle-raiders]. [ME]

bouff[1] **&c** [bʌuf] *vi* **1** *esp of a large dog* bark; make a loud dull sound *19-*. **2** *freq* ~ **and host** cough loudly *19-*.
n **1** a bark; a loud, dull sound, *specif mining* the thud heard when a roof is cracking *la19-*, *now EC*. **2** *also* **bowfer** a dog *la19-*, *now Abd*.
boufing smelly *20-*, *C*. [onomat; *cf* BUFF[2]]

bouff[2] **&c** [bʌuf] *n* contemptuous term for a big person *la19-*, *Bnf Abd*. [obscure]

bouff *see* BUFF[2]

boug &c [bʌug] *n* the stomach, belly *esp* of a child *e20*, *Cai*. [Gael *balg, bolg* a bag; the belly]

bougar &c; **buggar &c** *19-e20* ['bugər, 'bʌgər, 'bogər] *n* a cross-beam in a roof; a rafter *16-e20*.
~ **stake** the lower part of the BOUGAR, that reached to the ground in old houses *la17-e19*, *S*. [obscure]

bought &c; **boucht &c** *la19-e20* [bʌxt] *n* **1** the

bend of the arm (or leg) *la18-*, *now Abd Fif*. **2** *freq* ~**y &c** a branch, twig; a fork of a tree *la18-e20*. [see SND; *cf* BOUCHT[1]]

bought *see* BOUCHT[1]

bouk[1] **&c** [buk; *Rox also* bʌuk] *vt* = buck, steep (dirty linen etc) in lye before bleaching *18-e20*.

bouk[2] **&c**; **buke &c** *la16-18*, **boulk &c** *la16-e17* [buk] *n* **1** the carcass of a slaughtered animal *15-*. **2** the body of a person (living or dead) *16-*. [ME *bouke &c*, ON *búkr* the body, OE *būc* the belly]

bouk[3] **&c**; **buik &c** *la17-e20* [buk] *n* **1** = bulk, size, quantity *16-*. **2** a quantity of some merchandise *la16-e17*.
vi **1** = bulk *18-*. **2** *of a rope* increase on a capstan as its coils are wound round *la19-*, *now NE-nEC*.
bouking *mining* segments of wood etc used for increasing the diameter of a drum *la19-*, *now Fif*. ~**it** -sized, in size, *freq* **little, muckle** *etc* ~**it** **1** bulky, swollen *16-e20*. **2** *also* ~**in** pregnant *18-e20*. ~**some** large, bulky *18-*, *NE*.
break &c ~ open up and unload a cargo; unpack merchandise *16-*. [conflation in ME of *prec* w ME *bolke* heap, ON *búlki* cargo]

bouk[4] **&c** *vt* stop up (the touch-hole of a cannon) *la16*. [only Sc; prob F **bouker*, dial var of *boucher* fill up an opening]

bould *see* BUILD

boulk *see* BOUK[2]

boull *see* BOOL[1], BOOL[2]

boult *see* BOWT

bouman *see* BOW[1]

boun[1] **&c** [bun] *adj* **1** *also* **boon** *19-e20* prepared, ready, *freq* ~ **to** *or* **to do** (something), **mak oneself** ~ *la14-e19*. **2** = bound, ready, prepared to set out (on a journey) *15-e20*. **3** *of things* made ready, put in order *la14-16*.
v, *also* **bound** *la16* [**bund*], *ptp* **bound, bun** *20-*, *local Bnf-Kcb*, **bounit &c** [bun, *also* bʌn; ***'bunɪt, **bund*] **1** *vi* get ready, prepare (to do something) *15-*, *now Abd*. **2** get ready to go; set out (*freq* **to** a place etc) *la14-e20*. **3** *vr* prepare, make oneself ready, betake oneself *la14-e19*. [chf verse; ME; ON *bún-, búenn*, ptp of *búa* make ready]

boun[2] *19-*, **bound &c**, **bond** *la14-e16*, **bund &c** *la15-e17* [bun(d); ***bʌnd] *n* **1** = bound, a boundary, limit *la14-*. **2** *in pl* (*sometimes treated as a sing la15-16*), *also* **boons** *e20*, *NE* a district or stretch of land within certain boundaries *15-*, *now Bnf Ayr*. **3** extent, width *la19-*, *now Abd Kcb*.
vti = bound *la15-*.
bounding &c specifying the bounds of property, *usu* **bounding charter &c** *16-*.
bound court a district court *la15*. **bound road &c** a boundary road or track; a boundary, *specif* that between Scotland and England near Berwick *la16-19*.

bound &c [**bun(d)] *n* a bundle (*esp* of flax) *16-17*. [ME *bonde &c*, Flem *bond*]

bound *see* BOUN¹, BOUN²

boundage *see* BONDAGE

boundance &c [*'bundəns] *n* = abundance *la15*.

boundand &c [*'bundand, *&c*] = abundant *la15*. [apheticl]

bountath *see* BOUNTITH

bountay, bounté, bountee *see* BOUNTY

bountith &c *18-e20*, **bonteth &c** *16-17*, **bounteth &c** *16-e19*; **bo(u)ntath &c** *la16*, **bounties &c** *18-e19* [*'buntəð, *'bʌnt-] *n* a bounty, gratuity, *latterly usu* a gift stipulated in a contract of employment in addition to money wages, *freq* **fee and ~**. [nME; OF *bontet*, *bonted*, earlier form of *bonté*; *cf* BOUNTY]

bountree *see* BOURTREE

bounty &c *n* **1** *also* **bontay** *e16*, **bountay &c** *16-e17*, **buntha &c** *16-e17* ['buntɪ, *'bʌntɪ] = bounty, a gratuity *16-*. **2** *also* **bounté &c** *la14-16*, **bountee** *la15*, **bonté &c** *16-e17*, **bonty &c** *16-e17* = bounty, goodness, generosity etc *la14-*. **3** a bonus paid to fishermen for the season's fishing in addition to the price for the fish caught *e20, Cai Mry Abd, hist.* [*cf* BOUNTITH]

bour &c [bur] *n* = bower *la14-, now arch.*

bourach *19*, **burroch** *19-e20*, **beerach** *20-*, *Cai* ['burəx; *Cai* 'birəx; *WC, SW* 'bʌrəx] *n* a rope etc tied round the hindlegs of a kicking cow during milking. [Gael *buarach* a cow fetter]

bourd &c [burd; *also* *bʌrd] *n* **1** = bourd, sport, jesting, fun *15-16*. **2** a cause of amusement, joke; a funny or mocking story etc *la15-e20*. *vi* sport or play, *esp* in words; jest, joke *la14-e20*. **na ~** no jest, no trivial matter *la15-e18*.

bourgh *see* BURGH

bourie &c ['burɪ] *n* a rabbit's burrow; an animal's lair *19-e20*. [perh reduced f Eng *burrow* or dim of BOUR w extended meaning]

Bourignonism &c [bu'rinjonɪzm] *n* the emotional and visionary religious doctrines of Antoinette Bourignon, a 17th century French mystic, popular among the Episcopalians and Jacobites of the North-East in the early 18th century *18-, now hist.*

bourlaw *see* BIRLIE

bourow- *see* BURGH

bourtree &c *la16-*, **bourtré &c** *la15-16*; **bountree &c** *19-* ['bur'tri, 'bor'tri, 'bun'tri] *n* the elder tree *la15-*.

~ gun a popgun *19-*. [see SND]

boushty &c ['buʃtɪ, 'bʌʃtɪ] *n* ~ **ba** *etc* a bed *la18-, now Bnf Abd.* [only Sc; OF *boiste* a box, receptacle made of wood]

bouster *see* BOWSTER

bousterous &c ['bʌust(ə)rəs] *adj* = boisterous, fierce; rowdy *20-, now local Cai-Kcb.*

bout¹ &c [bʌut] *n* a hank or skein of thread or worsted *19-, now Stlg.* [f as next]

bout² &c [bʌut, but] *n* **1** = bout, a spell of work

etc. **2** the extent of ground covered as a plough etc moves across a field (and sometimes the distance back again) *19-, now local.*

lying in the ~ *of corn or hay* lying in rows after being cut *19-, Bnf Abd Ags.* [also infl by Eng *bout*, aphetic f *about*; *cf* BOUTGATE]

bout³ &c *16-e20*, **bult &c** *14-e15* [but; *bʌlt] *vt* = bolt, sift (flour etc) *15-e20*.

~claith &c *14-e19*, **~claithing &c** *la16-e17* bolting cloth; cloth of a thin or open texture.

bouthous a building in which flour is bolted *la16-17*.

boutch *see* BOOTCH

boutgate &c ['but'get] *n* **1** a roundabout way or course; an evasion; an underhand means *la16-, now Abd.* **2** the doing of a round of work, *eg in ploughing* two furrows, outwards and back *la19-e20*. **3** *mining, in a shallow pit* a secondary access road to the mine, independent of the shaft *19-20, nEC Ayr.* [aphetic f Eng *about* + GATE¹]

bouth *see* BUITH

bouzy *see* BUSS¹

bow¹ &c [bu; *Rox* bʌu] *n* a stock or herd of cattle, *esp* of cows *15-e19*.

~er &c a tenant who hires cattle and grazing rights on land *18-, now Lnk Ayr Kcb.* **~in(g)** such a lease of stock and land *19-, now local WC-SW.*

~-hous(e) a cattle-shed, cowhouse *16-e17*.

~man *la15-e17*, **bouman** *la18-e20* the man who had charge of the cattle on a farm; a tenant with a BOW. [nME *bu*; ON *bú* a homestead; livestock]

bow² &c [bʌu] *n* = boll, the seed-pod of flax *17-e20*.

bow³ &c, boll *16* [bʌu] *n* **1** = bow, the weapon *la14-*. **2** an arch, *esp* of a bridge, an arched gateway, *freq* in names of town gateways, *eg* **Netherbow** [-'bʌu; *St* -'bo] *la15-, local.* **3** the curve of a street, furrow etc *19-, now Bnf.* **4** an ox-bow *16-, now Bnf.* **5** the semi-circular handle of a pail, pot etc *19-, now Bnf Abd Ags.*

bowar &c = **~maker**, *15-17*. **bowit** provided with a BOW (*n* 1, 5) *15-16*. **bowdy** ['bʌudɪ] (**-leggit**) bandy-legged *20-, now Edb.*

~backit &c hump-backed *la19*. **~ brig &c** an arched bridge *16-e20*. **~butts &c** ground for archery practice *la16-, now in place-names.* **~ draucht &c** the distance of a bow-shot *la14-e18*. **~-hand &c** style of fiddling, skill in fiddle-playing *19-, now local Bnf-Kcb.* **~-houghd &c** bandy-legged *la18-, now Ags Fif.* **~maker** a maker of bows, bowyer *14-16*. **~merkis &c** = **~butts**, *15*. **~-saw** a narrow-bladed saw on an arched frame *la16-e17*. **~-sting &c** a bowstaff, a stick suitable for making into a bow *la15-e17, only Sc.* **~ an ee** *in negative* not close one's eyes, fail to sleep *18-, now local Bnf-Ayr.* **gae &c owre the bows** *la19-, Abd Ags*, **be** *or* **gae through the bows** *la19-, Bnf Abd Ags* go beyond all bounds.

take a person throw the bows take a person severely to task *19-*, *Bnf Abd*. [there has been some confusion w *bow* (BOO¹)]

bow⁴ &c, buy &c *17-e18* [bʌu; bɔi; 'buɪ; *'bɒɪ] *n* = buoy *17-*, now *Mry Bnf*.

~ **rope &c**, *also* **boy rape &c** *16* ['bɔi'rep, *&c*] **burop &c** *17* [*'bʌrəp] a buoy rope *16-*, now *Mry*.

bow⁵ [*bu] *n* = bull, a papal seal or letter *16*, only *Sc*.

bow *see* BOLL, BOO¹

bowall *see* BOLE

bowat *see* BOUET

bowbart &c [*'bʌubərt, *-bərd] *n* a dull or sluggish person *e16*. [only *Sc*; OF *bobert* a fool, lout]

bowbraid &c *la19*, **bowbreid &c** *la16* [*'bʌu'brid, *-'bred] *butchery, n* a portion of the shoulder of a carcass *la16*.

vt **1** remove the *bowbreid* from *la16*. **2** prick or pierce (an animal), *chf* in the flanks before slaughter, to tenderize the meat *la19*. [*bow*, var of BEUCH (*n* 2) + *brede* (BREEDS)]

bowcaill *see* BOW-KAIL

bowcht *see* BOUCHT²

bowdened *see* BOLDIN¹

bowder ['bʌudər] *n* a heavy squall, a storm of wind and rain *20-*, now *Abd Kcb*. [see SND]

bowdin *see* BOLDIN¹, BOLDIN²

bowdy *see* BOW²

bowel &c ['buəl, 'bu(:)l, 'bʌu(ə)l] *n* = bowel *la14-*.

~ **hive(s)** enteritis etc in children *la17-*, now *Stlg Fif*.

bowen *see* BOYNE

bowfarts ['bʌufərts] *n pl* **in the** ~ in difficulty, implying inability to get up or free oneself *la19-*, now *Mry*. [only *Sc*; obscure]

bowfer *see* BOUFF¹

bowie, bowy &c ['bʌuɪ] *n* **1** a broad, shallow dish, bowl or small tub *16-*, now *Bnf Ags*. **2** a barrel for holding water or ale *la16-*. **3** a bucket *18-*, now *Kcb*. [only *Sc*; prob dim of **bow*, f OE *bolla* or ON *bolli* a bowl; cf *bow* (BOLL)]

bowk *see* BOCK

bow-kail &c *16-*, now *Bnf Abd Lnk*, **bowcaill &c** *16-17* ['bʌu'kel; *also* 'bu-] *n* cabbage. [only *Sc*; uncertain, but ? OE *bolla* a bowl or ? BOW³]

bowl¹ &c [bʌul] *vti* ~**and &c** bending, curving, twisting *16*, only *Sc*. ~**t &c** crooked, distorted *19-*, now *Fif wLoth*. [perh MDu *boghelen* (*v*) curve; *cf* BOOL²]

bowl² [bʌul; bol] *n* = bowl; *in Sc used also where Eng prefers* basin *la18-*: '*pudding bowl*'. ~**ie** = *n*, *20-*.

bowlie *see* BOOL²

bowl-money &c *n* money thrown to children at a wedding *la19-*, now *Kcb*. [perh f the idea of rolling the money out]

bowlocks &c [*?'bʌuləks] *n* ragweed *19-e20*, *Gall*. [only *Sc*; *cf* Gael *buaghallan* ragwort; ragweed]

bowse &c [bʌus] *v* **1** *vt* swing out (*eg* a boat) *19-*, now *Bnf Abd Ags*. **2** *vi* bounce *la19-*, *Bnf Ags*. [perh f as BOOSE²]

bowsh [bʌuʃ] *n* an errand, a message *20-*, *Inv*. ~**er &c** an errand-boy *e20*, *Inv*. [unknown]

bowsie¹ &c ['bʌuzɪ] *adj* crooked *19-e20*. [F *bosse* a hump, perh w infl f BOW⁵; *cf* Eng *bossy* swelling like a boss]

bowsie² &c ['bʌuzɪ,'buzɪ] *n*, *also* ~**-man** a bogeyman, an imaginary monster invoked to frighten children *la19-*, now *Kcb*. [only *Sc*; see SND]

bowsie³ &c; boozy &c ['bʌuzɪ, 'buzɪ] *adj* big, fat, corpulent, puffed up *19-*, now *Bnf Abd Kcb*. [Ger *bausen* (*v*) swell, MHighGer *bûs* inflation, swelling, *bausen* (*v*) swell]

bowsome, bowsum &c ['bu(:)səm; *Rox* 'bʌu-] *adj* **1** obedient, willing, obliging; amiable *la14-e20*. **2** *also* **boosam &c** *la19-e20*, *Sh Ork*: *chf of a woman* = buxom, handsome; pleasant, agreeable *la16-e20*.

bowsplit *la19-*, *Bnf Ayr*, **bowspleit &c** *16* ['bʌusplɪt] *n* = bowsprit.

bowster &c, bouster &c *la15-e20*, **boster &c** *la15-16*, **bolster &c** ['bʌustər; *'bostər] *n* **1** = bolster *la15-*. **2** a piece of timber used to prevent chafing, a bearing, *orig chf, later only* for a wheelshaft in a watermill *16-*, now *Bnf*.

bowstock ['bʌu'stok] *n* a cabbage with a properly-developed heart *18-*, now *Bnf Abd*. [*cf* BOW-KAIL]

bowsum *see* BOWSOME

bowt &c *15-*, **bolt &c** *14-*; **boult &c** *16* [bʌut] *n, vi* = bolt. ~**foot** a club-foot *la17-*, now *Ags*.

bowy *see* BOWIE

box¹ &c *n* **1** = box *la15-*. **2** *specif* a strong-box, *esp* of a GUILD or corporation; the GUILD etc treasury. **3** *law* a box in the corridor of *Parliament House* (PARLIAMENT¹), Edinburgh, containing an ADVOCATE's professional papers *20*. **4** *mining* = HUTCH 2, *la18-*, now *Fif*. **5** *colloq* a melodeon or accordion *20-*, *chf Highl*.

vt **1** = box. **2** wainscot, cover with boards *18-e19*. **3** *law*: LODGE (*v* 3) (papers required in a lawsuit by the *Court of Session* (SESSION)) with the clerk, who put them in the appropriate box for the judge or official concerned *19-20*.

~**ie** = *n* 5, *20-*, now *Cai Abd*. ~**in &c** wainscoting *la18-*, now *Ayr*.

~**-bed** a bed enclosed in wooden panelling, the front having either sliding panels, hinged doors, or curtains *la17-*. ~~**-day** *law* a day in the *Court of Session* (SESSION) vacation appointed for *boxing* (*v* 3) papers *18-e20*. ~~**-ladder** a narrow staircase, like a step-ladder but enclosed with wood behind and walls on both sides *la19-*, now *Stlg wLoth*. ~~**-master &c** a treasurer, *esp* of a GUILD or corporation *17-*, now *Abd Ags*.

box   59   braid

~-penny a market duty levied for the benefit of a BOX¹ (*n* 2) of a craft or BURGH *17*. **~-seat** a square pew in a church *20-*, now *Ags Lnk*.

on the ~ receiving weekly assistance from a poor fund, more recently from National Health Insurance benefit *18-20*. **the whole &c ~ an dice** the whole lot, everything or everybody *la19-*, now *Ags*.

box² *vti* **1** = box, fight.   **2** *of animals* attack with the horns, butt *la19-*, now *Cai Bnf*.

boy *n, possessive pl also* **~ses**, *20-*, now *Ayr* ['boiziz] **1** = boy *15-*.   **2** (1) a bachelor of any age still living with his parents *la19-*. (2) a man of any age; also used as a term of address [*cf* Gael *a' bhalaich*] *20-*, *Hebrides Highl*.   **3** *specif* an apprentice *20-*.   **4 the ~** term of commendation and praise *20-*.   **5** *in pl* **the Bhoys** nickname for Celtic football team *la19-* [the (mock-)Ir spelling reflects the club's origins].

~ackie &c, a little boy *la19-*, *Cai Abd*.

~s a day *exclam, freq* used as a greeting to a child *e20*.

boyart *n* a small one-masted vessel *16*.   [MDu, MLowGer *bojer(t) &c*; *cf* eModEng *boyer*]

boyis &c [*boiz] *n pl* leg-irons for the confinement of prisoners *la14-e17*.   [only Sc; OF *boie*, *buie*]

boyne &c *la17-*; **bowen &c** *17-e19*, **bine &c** *la18-e20* [boin, bəin; *bʌu(ə)n] *n* **1** a shallow tub, *latterly esp* a wash-tub *17-*, now *Bnf Kcb*.   **2** a broad shallow container in which to skim milk *19-e20*.   [*cf* Norw *bûna* a tub]

boy rape *see* BOW⁴

bra *see* BRAE, BRAW

brabanar *see* BRABONER

brabblach &c *19-*, now *Arg*, **brabble** *20-*, *Ags* ['brab(ə)l(ɔx)] *n* something small or worthless. [prob Gael *pràbar &c* little people; refuse of grain]

braboner &c *16-17*, **brabanar &c** *la15-e18*; **brebnar &c** *la16-e17* [*'brab(ə)nər, *'brɛb-] *n* a weaver.   [Du *Brabander* a native of Brabant; surviving in surnames *Brebner* and *Bremner*]

brace &c *la15-*, **brase &c; bras** *15-e16* [bres] *n* **1** = brace.   **2** *archery* a guard for the wrist *15-e17*.   **3** a strap, thong, belt *15-17*.   **4** *building* a band of stonework, wood etc used to strengthen a structure; *latterly esp* the breast or arch of a chimney *15-17*.   **5** a fireplace *19-*, now *Lnk*.   **6** a mantelpiece *18-*, now *Lnk*.   **7** a chimney made of straw and clay *19*.

brace *see* BRESS

bracelet &c *16-*; **braslat &c** *la15-17*, **breslet &c** *17* ['breslət] *n* = bracelet.

brachan &c *la18-e20*, **breckan &c** *18-*, now *Kcb*, **brakan &c** *la15-e16, in place-names la13-*; **brechan** *19-e20* ['braxən, 'brɛx-, 'brak-, 'brɛk-] *n* = bracken.

brachan *see* BROCHAN

brachton &c [*'braxtən] *n* a large, weighty, clumsy man or (*occas*) thing *la18-19*, *SW*. [uncertain]

brack, brak *adj* briny *e16*.   *n* brine *e19*.   [prob Du *brak*]

bracken *see* BRAK

brad &c *n* term of abuse for a thing or a person, *esp* an old man *18-e19*, *SW*.

brade, braid &c *v* **1** *vt* lift, throw up *etc*, draw out *etc* with a quick movement *la14-16*.   **2** *vi* make a sudden movement; start, spring *la15-e17, 19* (*literary*).

n = braid, a sudden movement, an attack *la14-16*.

at a *or* **the ~side** in a hurry, suddenly, unexpectedly *19-*, now *Bnf*.

~ of have the nature or qualities of (a person or thing) *15-16*.

brade *see* BRAID

brae *la16-*, **bra &c** *13-16*; **bray &c** *la14-e18*, **brea &c** *la16-e18* [bre] *n* **1** the (steep or sloping) bank of a river or lake or shore of the sea *13-*.   **2** (1) a bank or stretch of ground rising fairly steeply; a hillside *la14-*. (2) *freq in street names* a road with a steep gradient *19-*.   **3** the brow of a hill *la19-*.   **4** an upland, mountainous district, *freq* (*in pl*) in the name of the district *la15-*: '*the Braes o Balquhidder*'.   **5** a salmon trap consisting of an artificial gravel-and-stone bank across a river *18*, *Mry*.

~head ['bre'hid *&c*] the top of a BRAE *16-*.

~man an inhabitant of a hilly region, *specif* of the southern side of the Grampians *18-e19*.

~set situated on a slope; steep *19-e20*.

go *etc* **down the ~** go to ruin, cease to prosper; *of an old person* fail physically *17-*.   [ON *brá* an eyelash; *cf* OE *brū* an eyelash, eyebrow, brow; the brow of a hill; *cf* Gael *bràighe* the upper part (of places), *bruach* a bank, brink, represented in Sc by BRAE, *cf also* BROO², BREE³]

brag &c *la15-*; **braig &c** *15-e20 vti* **1** = brag *la15-*.   **2** *vt* (1) threaten, taunt *la16*. (2) challenge, defy *18-e19*.   **3** reproach, scold *18-e19*.

n **1** = brag *15-*.   **2** a defiant note (on a trumpet etc) *la15-e16*.   **3** a challenge *18-e20*.

braggal boastful, smug *e20*, *Inv*.   **~gie** ostentatious, boastful *19-*, *Ags*.

bragwort *see* BROGAT

braicham *see* BRECHAM

braid &c *la15-*, **brade &c** *la14-e17, in place-names 13-*; **bread &c** *16-18*, **bred &c** *16-e19*, **broad &c** *la16-* [bred, brɛd; *Abd Coast also* brəid] *adj* = broad *la14-*.

adv **1** *chf* **~ out** unrestrainedly, indiscreetly *la18-*.   **2** in an extended manner, laid or squeezed flat *la19-*, *NE*.

~lingis &c 1 = broadling, broadwise *e17*.   **2** flat (on the ground); with the limbs extended *la16*.

in ~ band *of corn* lying unbound on the harvest field *la18-19*.   **~ benisoun** *or* **malisoun**

full blessing or curse *la15-e16*. ~ **bonnet** = *Kilmarnock bonnet* (KILMARNOCK) *19-e20*. ~ **Scots** = SCOTS *n* 1, *18-*.

in *etc* ~ **Scotland** in the whole (breadth) of Scotland *la17-*. **look** *etc* **someone** ~ **in the face** look someone straight or squarely in the face *19*.

braid *see* BRADE, BRED[1], BREED[1], BREID

braig *n, also* ~ **knife** a large knife *16-e17*. [obscure]

braig *see* BRAG

braiggle &c *n* something useless or unsafe because of age or condition *19-e20, SW*.

braik *see* BRAK

brain[1] **&c** *n* a loud noise *19-e20, NE*.
vi roar, bellow *la18-, now Abd*. [see SND]

brain[2] **&c** *n* = brain *la15-*.
vt **1** = brain *16-*. **2** hurt, *esp* by a blow to the head, wound, beat severely, *freq* as a threat to children *18-, now local Abd-S*.
adj mad, enraged, furious *15-19* [perh shortened f *brainwode*].
~**ish** wandering in the mind *la19-, Ags Fif*.
~**y** **1** = brainy. **2** (high-)spirited, lively *19-, now Fif*.
~**wode &c** [*'bren'wød, &c*] mad *la14-e16*.

brainch &c *la16-e20*, **branch &c**; **brench &c** *16-17* [brenʃ, brɛnʃ] *n* **1** = branch *la14-*. **2** *heraldry* an addition or attachment to an escutcheon *la17*.

brainge *see* BREENGE

braingel *see* BRANGLE

brainyell &c *vi* break out, rush violently *19-e20*. *n* an uproar; outburst *e19*. [*cf* Norw dial *brengja* wriggle, twist]

braisant *see* BRESS

braise &c [brez] *n* the roach *la18-e20*. [*cf* OE *bærs* the perch, Norw *brasen* the bream]

braissle *see* BRASTLE

braith *see* BRATH[1], BREATH

brak &c, brek &c, braik &c *16-18*, **brik &c** *la15-19*, **break** *la16-*; **breke &c** *15-e17* [brak, brɛk; *S also* brɪk; **brik] v, pt also* **brak &c, bruk &c** *17-19* [brak; *Sh Ork N* bruk; *Sh Ork* brøk, brʌk; **brek]. ptp also* **bracken &c** *la17-e20*, **brock &c** *17-e19* ['brak(ən), 'brʌk(ən), 'brok(ən)] **1** *vti* = break *la14-*. **2** *vt* break (up) into separate portions, parts or lots *15-*. **3** apportion a tax on (a person) *la16-e17*. **4** break up, disband (a company) *la15-17*. **5** throw into disorder; scatter *la14-e16*. **6** overcome by persuasion, force etc *16*. **7** *vi, of milk* curdle, coagulate, either by its becoming sour or in the process of churning *la20-, now Sh NE Kcb*. **8** *vt* cause a change in (the weather) *19-, now Cai*.
n **1** = break *16-*. **2** a breach of friendly relations etc; an outbreak of contention or disorder *la15-e17*. **3** a breach or breaking of a promise, obligation etc *la15-17*. **4** ground broken up for cultivation; a division of land under the old system of rotation of crops *la18-, now local Bnf-Kcb*.

5 a fall of snow or rain; a layer or deposit of snow *19-e20, S*. **6** the breaking up of (1) a storm, frost, ice etc *19-, now Abd Ags Fif*; (2) a market *la19-, Bnf Ags*. **7** a hollow in a hill *la19-e20*. **8** failure, bankruptcy *la19-, local Bnf-Fif*.

broken &c, brokken &c *16-* **1** = broken *la14-*. **2** *of persons, esp in the Highlands* (HIELAND) *and* BORDERS outlawed for some crime; having no feudal SUPERIOR or chief; ruined, impoverished, and living irregularly or lawlessly, *usu* **broken men** *16-e18*. **3** ruined, bankrupt *la19-*. **4** *of a ship* stranded or wrecked *la14-e17*. **5** *of milk* curdled, *esp* of cream in the churn *19-, now local Cai-Kcb*. **brakins &c** ['brakɪnz] the remains of a meal *19-e20, Abd*. ~**er &c** **1** = breaker *16-*. **2** *specif* a breaker (**of** laws, peace, faith etc) *la14-*.

~**fast** *16-*, ~**wast &c** *la19-, now Cai* ['brakfəst, -wəs(t), 'brɛk-, 'brek-] = breakfast. **brak-fur &c** *vt* plough (land) lightly *la19-, Bnf. n* a kind of light ploughing *la19-, now Abd*.

~ **a bottle** open a new bottle *19-*. ~ **an egg** *curling* (CURL) a command to strike a stone with another with a force such as would break an egg *19-, now Abd Fif*. ~ **in** prepare (a field) for seed by harrowing *19-, now Fif*. ~ **on** *or* **o 1** begin to use (stored food or drink) *la19-e20*. **2** change (a banknote or coin) for smaller money *la19-, now local Ags-Kcb*. ~ **up** break out; burst forth; appear suddenly *15-e17*. ~ **wi a or the fu han** make a fraudulent bankruptcy *la19-*. **ye've pu'd a stick tae brak yer ain back** you will suffer from the consequences of your own actions *20-, Bnf Ags Stlg*.

brak *see* BRACK

brakan *see* BRACHAN

brakane *see* BRECHAN

brake &c *n* **1** = brake, a flax-harrow *la16-17*. **2** a heavy harrow for soil *la18-, now Bnf Abd Ags*.

brall [**bral] vi* soar, fly *la16*. [perh F *branler* move from side to side; *cf* OSc, ME *brawl* waver, quiver]

bramble *see* BRAMMLE

brammel &c; bramlin &c *n, also* **brammel worm** a striped worm found in old dunghills and leaf-heaps, used as bait for freshwater fish, *esp* trout *19-*. [*cf* Eng *brandling*]

brammle &c *19-*, **brymyll &c** *16-e19*, **brummle &c** *la19-, local Abd-Dmf*; **bramble** ['bram(b)l, 'brʌml; **briml] n* the blackberry; its bush. [in Eng only = the bush]

bran &c *16-e20*, **brawn &c** *n* **1** = brawn (as food) *la14-*. **2** a fleshy part of the body; a rounded muscle of the arm or leg, *latterly* the calf *15-e20*. **3** *only* **brawn &c** (1) a boar for the table *la14*; (2) a boar *19-, SW, S*.

branch *see* BRAINCH

Brandane 1 *in pl* **Brandanis &c** the followers of Stewart of Bute *15-e17, latterly hist*. **2** a

native of the island of Bute *la19-*, *now Bute*.
[prob f St Brandan or Brendan of Clonfert, who
had a foundation in Bute]
brander *see* BRANDRETH
brandered, brandie *see* BRANDIT
brandis &c [*'brandɪs] *v* **1** *vt* = brandish (a
weapon) *la14-e15*. **2** *vi* act showily, swagger
15-e16.
brandit &c, brandered *e20*, *N*; **brannet &c**
la18-e20 ['bran(d)ɪt; *N* 'brandərd; *'brɑn(d)ɪt]
adj of a reddish-brown colour with darker
stripes or markings, brindled *la14-*, *now Abd
Ags*.
   brandie &c name for a brindled cow *19-*, *now
Abd*. [Norw *brandet &c*, Icel *bröndóttr*; *cf*
eModEng *branded*]
brandreth &c *la14-18*, **brander &c** *la15-*
['bran(d)ər; *'brandrɛð] *n* **1** a gridiron *la14-*. **2**
also **brandrie &c** *16-e17* [*'brandrɪ], **bran-
draucht &c** *16* [*?'brandrɛð] a framework of
metal or *freq* wood, wooden supports as used in
the construction of buildings, bridges etc or in
the foundations of structures etc; a trestle *la15-*.
3 the iron grating over an entrance to a drain
etc *19-*.
vt, only **brander 1** support with a BRANDER (*n*
2) *16-18*. **2** *joinery* fix cross-strips of wood to
ceiling joists to support (the ceiling) *la19-*, *now
Ayr Kcb*. **3** broil on a gridiron, grill *la18-*.
   brandering the material or structure forming
a BRANDER (*n* 2) *la16-19*.
   brander bannock a thick *oatcake* (AIT) baked
on a gridiron *19-e20*. [nME; ON *brandreið*; *cf*
OE *brandrād &c*]
brang *see* BRING
brangle; brangil &c *16-e17* ['braŋl] *v* **1** *vi*
shake, move unsteadily *e16*. **2** *vt* shake, brandish (a weapon) *16-e17*. **3** cause to shake, batter down *la16-e20*. **4** shake the firmness or
steadiness of (beliefs etc); throw into confusion
la16-e18.
n, also **braingel** ['breŋl] **1** a lively dance
16-e19. **2** a state of confusion; a tangle; a disturbance *16-e19*. **3** a motion, movement; an
impulse *17*. **4** a confused crowd *19-e20*. [F
branler, branle; *cf* eModEng *branle &c*]
brank *vi* **1** behave violently or without restraint
e15. **2** bear oneself proudly, prance, strut *16-*,
now Abd Fif. **3** dress up in finery *16-*, *now Fif*.
~ie finely or showily dressed *la18-e19*. [see
SND]
branks¹ &c *la16-*, **brankis** *16-17* *n*, *chf in pl*,
also used as sing **1** a kind of bridle or halter, *orig*
with wooden side-pieces *16-*. **2** an instrument
of public punishment, an iron bridle and gag
used to punish breaches of the peace or abusive
language *la16-*, *now hist*.
vt **brank** *la16-*, **branks** *la19-e20* **1** put the
BRANKS¹ (*n* 2) on; punish with the BRANKS¹
la16-e17. **2** bridle, halter *la19-*, *now Fif*.

put the ~ on restrain, cut (a person) down to
size, checkmate *20-*, *local Ork-WC*. [only Sc;
see DOST, SND]
branks² *n pl* the mumps *la18-*, *now Fif Loth Lnk*.
[perh f prec, f an association with the neck]
brannet *see* BRANDIT
branny &c *n* = brandy *18-e19*.
bras *see* BRACE, BRESS
brase *see* BRACE
brash &c, brasche *la16-17* *n* **1** an attack,
assault in battle *la16*. **2** *fig* an onset; a bout; an
extra effort *17-e20*. **3** a short bout of illness; an
illness *17-*. **4** a sudden gust of wind or burst of
rain *19-*, *now local Bnf-wLoth*. **5** *freq in churning*
a short turn of work *19-e20*.
v **1** *vt* break through or down by assault; bash,
batter *la16-e19*. **2** *vi* bring up liquid into the
mouth by belching *19-*, *now Bnf Kcb*.
~y &c 1 delicate in constitution, subject to illness *19-*, *now Bnf Stlg Fif*. **2** stormy, wet and
windy *19-*, *now Stlg*. [chf Sc and nEng dial; *cf*
F *brèche* a breach, MLowGer *brasch* a crash]
brashloch &c [*'braʃlox] *n* a mixed crop of rye
with oats or barley *17-e19*, *SW*. [obscure]
braslat *see* BRACELET
brass *see* BRESS
brast *see* BIRSE
brastle &c; braissle &c *vi* work hurriedly;
struggle, exert oneself *19-e20*, *S*.
   brastling noisy and menacing *la17*. [perh
onomat; *cf* BREESHLE]
brat &c *n* **1** a (poor or ragged) garment
la15-e20. **2** (1) a bib, pinafore *19-*, *now Bnf Stlg
Lnk*. (2) a (worker's) coarse apron *19-*, *now local
Arg-Slk*. **3** a cloth put on a *tup-hog* (TUIP) to
prevent mating *19-*, *now Loth*. *cf* BREEK 2. **4** the
thick(er) surface on a liquid etc, *eg* curdled
cream on milk, skin on porridge *la17-e20*, *only
Sc*. [eModEng *bratte* a rag, OE, ONorthumb
bratt a cloak; *cf* Gael *brat* a mantle]
brath¹; braith [*breθ] *adj* fierce, violent,
strong *la14-e16*. [nME *brath*, ON *bráðr*]
brath² &c [*breð] *vt* weave (straw-ropes) round
a stack *la18-e20*. [ON *bregða* (*v*) bind, pass a
rope round; OE *bregdan* (*v*) weave]
brattle *la16-*, **brattill &c** *16* *n* **1** a loud clatter,
a rattle, *eg* of horses' hooves *16-*. **2** a peal of
thunder *la19-*. **3** a sharp assault; a fight, struggle *17-e19*. **4** a short rush; a sudden bound *18-*,
now Bnf. **5** a sudden blast of wind and rain, a
spell of bad weather *la19-*, *now Bnf*.
vi **1** clatter, clash, rattle *16-*, *now local Bnf-Kcb*.
2 rush noisily *e19*. [onomat]
brave &c [brev; *brɑv, &c] *adj* **1** = brave. **2**
latterly freq ironic splendid, excellent, fine *16-*,
now Abd Fif.
~ly &c 1 = bravely *17-*. **2** splendidly, very
well, *latterly freq as intensifier*, *16-*, *now local Bnf-
Lnk*. **bravity &c, bravetie** splendour, ele-
gance, *esp* in dress *la16-e20*.
~ and .. = braw and .. (BRAW) *la19-e20*. [*cf*
next]

braw &c; **bra** [brɑ] *adj* **1** = BRAVE, fine, splendid: (1) *of persons, also* **brow** *19-*, *NE* [brʌu] (a) *latterly specif* handsome, of fine physique *17-*; (b) *slightly familiar* worthy *19-*; (2) *of things, also ironic, 17-*. **2** splendid in dress; well-, prettily- or gaily-dressed *17-*. **3** very good, excellent *17-*. **4** *specif of weather* fine, pleasant *19-*. **5** *of sums of money etc* considerable *18-*, now *Fif*.

adv **1** well, finely *la19-*. **2** *as intensifier* very *la19-*.

~**ly** &c *adv* **1** finely; elegantly *17*. **2** *also* **browly** *NE* ['brʌulɪ] very well, excellently *la18-*. **3** *predic adj* well, in good health *19-*. ~**s** **1** good clothes, one's best clothes *la18-*: '*Sunday braws*'. **2** beautiful or good things *19-*, now *Abd Lnk*.

B~ **Lad, B**~ **Lass** the young man and girl chosen annually by the people of Galashiels to represent the BURGH at the Braw Lads' Gathering on 29 June; *in pl also* the young people of Galashiels *20-*.

~ **an(d)** .. *as intensifier or superlative, eg* ~ **and weel** in good health; ~ **and soon** in full time *19-*, now *Kcb*. **in** ~ **time** in very good time *la19-*, *local NE-EC*. [only Sc; var of prec, from which it is not clearly separable in early examples with *-w-* for *-v-*]

brawlins &c ['brɑlǝns] *n pl* the berries of the cowberry or cranberry *la18-e20*. [Gael *braoileagan*, pl of *braoileag* a whortleberry]

brawn *see* BRAN

braxy &c ['braksɪ] *n* **1** *also* **breakshugh** &c *la18-e19* [***'brekʃǝx, **'brɛkʃɑ, &c] a *usu* fatal intestinal disease of sheep *la18-*. **2** the salted flesh of a sheep that has died of BRAXY *20-*, *local Bnf-Lnk*.

~ **bree** soup made from BRAXY (*n* 2) *20-*, *Bnf Arg*. ~ **ham** the ham of a BRAXY sheep *19-*, now *Bnf Lnk*. [only Sc; uncertain]

bray *vt* push, shove *20-*, *NE*. [*cf* ON *bregða* cause to move quickly, OE *bregdan* drag, pull]

bray *see* BRAE

braze &c *n* any of several species of fish, *eg* bream, roach *la18-*, now *wLoth*.

bre &c [bri] *vt* terrify, frighten *15-e16*. [nME; OE *brēgan*]

bre *see* BREE³

brea *see* BRAE

bread *see* BRAID, BREED³, BREID

break *see* BRAK

breakshugh *see* BRAXY

breard &c *la17-*, **brerd** *la15-e19*; **breird** &c *la15-e19*, **breer** &c *la18-e20* [*N nEC* brir(d); *C, S* brerd; *Cai* 'briðǝr] *n* **1** the top surface; the brim *la15-e19*. **2** the first shoots of grain etc *la15-*. **3** *spinning* the short flax obtained from a second hackling of the first tow *18-19*.

vi sprout above the ground, germinate *la15-*. [ME *brerd* the top surface, OE *brerd* a brim, margin]

breast *see* BREIST

breath *la16-*, **breth** *la15-16*; **breith** &c *la15-16*, **braith** &c *16-*, [breθ; *briθ] *n* **1** = breath *la15-*. **2** an opinion, a line of thought *la18-*, now *local Bnf-Lnk*.

brebnar *see* BRABONER

brecham &c *16-*; **braicham** &c *17-e20* ['brɛxǝm, *-ǝn; *Bnf* 'brɛxǝm; *Mry also* 'brɑxǝn] *n* **1** a collar for a draught-horse or ox *16-*. **2** a bulky scarf etc *20-*, now *Fif wLoth*. [only Sc; nME *bargham* &c, ME *berhom*]

brechan &c *la16-18*, **brakane** &c *16-e19*, **brochan** *la16-19* [*'brɛxǝn; *'brakǝn, *'braxǝn, &c; *'broxǝn] *n* a PLAID; TARTAN. [Gael *breacan*, f *breac* spotted]

brechan, breckan *see* BRACHAN

bred¹ &c *la15-e20*, *WC-S*; **braid** &c *16-18* [brɛd] *n, vt* = BROD² *n* 2 (*la19-e20*), 3 (*la15-e20*), 4 (*la16-e17*), 5 (*16-e20*), 6 (*la16*), 8 (*16-e19*), 9 (*19-e20*), *v* (*15-e16*). [ME *brede*, OE *bred*, cognate w OE *bord* (see BROD², BUIRD¹)]

bred² &c *n* a unit of quantity (of budge, a kind of lambskin) *la15-e16*. [perh prec or *brede* (BREED¹)]

bred *see* BRAID

brede *see* BREED¹, BREED⁴, BREID

breder, bredren *see* BRITHER

bredthe *see* BREED¹

bree¹ &c *n* **1** liquid in which something has been steeped or boiled to extract the essence, stock; soup, gravy *la18-*. **2** WHISKY *18-*, now *local Bnf-Lnk*; *cf barley bree* (BARLIE). **3** juice *20-*, *local Bnf-Lnk*. **4** liquid or moisture of any kind *la19-*, now *local Cai-Lnk*.

vt drain the water from (vegetables etc that have been boiled) *la19-*, now *Bnf Abd*. [ME *bre*; obscure; *cf* BROO¹]

bree² *n* the consequences, the brunt *la19-*, now *Bnf wLoth*. [perh fig f prec]

bree³ *la16-*, **bre** *la15* *n* **1** the eyebrow *la15-e19*. **2** the brow, the forehead *18-*, now *Fif*.

~**rs** &c **1** the eyelashes *la18-*, now *Abd*. **2** the eyebrows *e20*, *Sh Abd*. **hing by the** ~**rs o the ee(n)** be in a very precarious position, *esp* on the verge of bankruptcy *la19-e20*, *Bnf Abd Ags*. **move neither ee nor** ~ remain absolutely motionless *la18-e19*. [ME *bre*; OE *brēg*; *cf* BROO²]

bree⁴ *n, chf* **nae** &c ~ an unfavourable opinion *la19-e20*. [uncertain; *cf* BROO³]

breechin *see* BRITCHIN

breed¹ &c *17-*, **brede** &c *la14-e17*, **bredthe** &c *la16*, **braid** *la16-19*, **breedth** &c *la16*, *e20*, **breeth** *e20*, *NE* [brid, bred, bridθ; *NE* briθ] *n* = breadth: **1** *in gen*, *la14-*; **2** *with specification of measurement, 15-16*: '*of fourty fute brede*'.

i the ~ **o someone's face** *etc* to someone's face, in the face *19-e20*. **on** ~ abroad *16*. **on the** ~ **o one's back** flat on one's back *la19-e20*.

breed² *vi* ~ **of** resemble, *esp* in manners *17-*, now *Bnf Fif*. [OE *bregdan*, *brēdan on* turn into; *cf* ON *bregða til* resemble]

breed[3], **breid; bread** [brid] *n* **in bad ∼ 1** in disfavour, on bad terms (**with**) *la19-*, now *Ork NE.* **2** in a bad way *19.* [obscure]

breed[4] **&c, brede** *n, chf in pl* **1** = brede, a piece of meat for roasting *e16.* **2** the innards of an animal, *usu* as food, *chf* the pancreas, *esp* of a sheep *16-*, now *Abd.*

breed *see* BROD[3]

breedth *see* BREED[1]

breek *17-*, **breke &c** *la14-e17* [brik; *Abd also* brɪk] *n* **1** (1) = breech, trousers *in sing la14-19*, *in pl la15-*. (2) *in sing and pl* underpants, knickers *20-*. **2** a cloth put on a ewe to prevent mating *20-*, now *Bnf; cf* BRAT 3. **3** *in pl* a forked stick such as is used for a catapult; a fork in a tree *20-*, *Ags nEC.* **4** *in pl, draughts* the position when a king lies between two opposite men and can thus take either of them *20-*, now *Bnf Arg Lnk.*
v **1** *vt* put into trousers *la19-*. **2** tuck up (a dress etc) to the knees, *esp* for farm work *19-*, now *Bnf.* **3** *vi* set to work *20-*, now *Bnf.*
∼**less** wearing a KILT[1] *20-*, now *Bnf.* ∼**lums** affectionate term for a small child *la19-*, *Bnf Ags.* ∼**ums &c** *n pl* **1** *occas in sing* (very) short trousers; knee-breeches *19-*, now *Abd Fif.* **2** *sing or pl* a small person; affectionate term for a little boy *la19-*, now *Bnf.* ∼**umstoich** [*?'brɪkəm'stoix] a small stout child in breeches *19.*
∼**band** (**heid**) (the top of) a trouser waistband *20-*, now *Bnf Abd Kcb.* ∼ **brother &c** a rival in love *la16-e20.*
it's no(t) in your ∼**s** you won't be able to do something or get something *18-*, now *Abd Fif Stlg.* **pull up one's** ∼**s** pull up one's socks *la19-*. **wear the** ∼**s** *of a wife* wear the trousers *la19-*.

breel *vi, usu of a carriage* move quickly and noisily *19-e20.* [perh metath f BIRL[1]]

breem[1] **&c** *19-*, now *Fif;* **brim &c** *la16-*, now *Kcb vi, esp of a sow* be in heat. [laME, eModEng *brim &c*]

breem[2] *e19*, **breme** *15-16*, **brim &c** *adj* **1** = breme, bright, clear *e15.* **2** furious, fierce, violent *la15-e19.*

breem *see* BROOM

breenge &c *19-*; **brainge &c** [brindʒ; *Fif WC, SW* brendʒ] *v* **1** *vi* rush forward recklessly or carelessly; plunge; make a violent effort *la18-*. **2** *vt* drive with a rush; batter, bang *la19-*, now *Abd Ags.*
n a violent or clumsy rush, a dash, a plunge *la18-*.
breengin &c wilful, pushing, sharp-tongued; bustling *19-*, now *local.*
let &c ∼ aim a blow *20-*. [obscure; *cf* BRAIN-YELL, BRANGLE]

breer &c *la16-*, **brere &c** *15-e17* *n* = brier *15-*.
∼**ie &c** *19-e20*, **brery** *la14-e16*, *only in place-names adj* = briery. *n* a place covered with briers *e19.*

breer *see* BREARD

breers *see* BREE[3]

breese [briz] *n* crushed rock, *esp* sandstone or limestone *e20*, *Ayr.* [prob f BRIZZ; *cf* Eng *breeze* small cinders etc]

breeshle &c ['briʃl; *'brisl] *vi* hurry, rush *19-*, now *Abd Ags Lnk.*
n the act of rushing; a rush *19-*, *local Cai-Lnk.* [*cf* BRASTLE]

breet *see* BRUIT

breeth *see* BREED[1]

brefe *see* BRIEF

bregwort *see* BROGAT

breid &c *15-*, **brede &c** *la14-e19*; **bread** *la16-*, **braid &c** *la16-e17* [brid; *nEC* bred] *n* **1** = bread *la14-*. **2** *freq uninflected in pl after numerals etc* a loaf or roll of bread *15-e19.* **3** an oatcake (AIT) *20-*, *Cai Bnf Abd.*
∼**-berry** small pieces of bread with hot milk poured over *la19-*, *local Abd-Ayr.* ∼**hous** [*'brid'hus, &c] a store-room for bread; a pantry *la15-e16.*
bread-and-cheese 1 = *cheese-an-breid* (CHEESE[1]) *20-*, now *Fif Kcb.* **2** the inside of a thistle head *20-*, now *local Cai-Ags.* **he** *etc* **disna aet the** ∼ **o idleseat** he etc works hard for his living *20-*, *local Bnf-Lnk.* [for the vowel *cf* SHREED]

breid *see* BREED[3]

breif &c *adj* = brief *15-16.*

breird *see* BREARD

breist &c *la15-*, **brest &c** *la14-17*; **breast** *la18-*, **brist** *la14-e17* [brist] *n* **1** = breast *la14-*. **2** a perpendicular cut in PEAT[1] *19-*. **3** the desk board of a pew *19-*, *Abd Ags.* **4** the front or projecting part of something, *eg* a cart *la16-*, now *Cai Bnf.*
vi spring up or forward; press forward; climb *la16-*, now *Abd Ags Stlg.*
∼ **bore** an instrument for boring *19-*, now *Fif.* ∼**-curch &c** a kerchief for covering the breast *la15-e16.* ∼**-seat** the front seat in the gallery of a church *la18-*, *Bnf Abd.*
∼ **o the laft** the front of the gallery in a church *20-*. ∼ **to** ∼ face to face *20-*, now *Abd Ags.* **in a** ∼ abreast *20-*, *local Bnf-Lnk.*

breith *see* BREATH

brek *see* BRAK

brekanetyne *see* BRIGANTINE

breke *see* BRAK, BREEK

breme *see* BREEM[2]

brench *see* BRAINCH

brenn *see* BURN[2]

brent[1] *vi* spring forward *la19-*, now *Bnf.*
adv with a sudden bound or spring; directly, fairly and squarely *19-*, now *Bnf.* [*cf* ON *bruna* advance quickly]

brent[2] *adj* **1** upright, *freq* browis ∼ *la14-e17.* **2** *freq of the brow* smooth, unwrinkled *18-*. **3** steep, precipitous *19-e20.* [ME *brent*, var of *brant* high, steep]

brent *see* BURN[2]

brenth &c [brenθ] *n* = breadth *20-, now Kcb.*
[w infl f LENTH, STRENTH; *cf* WEENTH]
brerd *see* BREARD
brere, brery *see* BREER
brese *see* BRIZZ
breslet *see* BRACELET
bress &c *la16-,* **bras &c; brace &c** *la15-17,*
brass &c [brɛs, bras; *bres] *n* = brass *la14-.*
braisant &c ['brez(ə)nt] brazen-faced *la18-,*
now Bnf Abd Fif. **brassy &c coal** *mining* coal
with veins of iron pyrites *20-, now Fif.*
bressie &c *n* a fish, the bib or pout *18-, now Fif.*
[perh Eng *wrasse*]
brest *see* BREIST
Bret *see* BRIT
Bretane &c [*brɛ'ten, *'brɛten] = Britain
la14-e17.
Bretanʒe &c *la14,* **Bertanʒe** *e16;* **Bartanʒe**
&c *16-e17* [*brɛ'tenjɪ; *'bɛrtənjɪ, *'bart-] =
Britanny.
breth *see* BREATH
brether(ing) *see* BRITHER
Brettowne &c, Brettane &c [*'brɛtun, *-ən]
= Briton *15.*
breuk *see* BRUIK
breve *see* BRIEF
brew &c [br(j)u] *vti, ptp also* **browin &c**
la15-e19, **brewine &c** *la17* [*'brʌu(ə)n;
*'br(j)u(ə)n] = brew *15-.*
~**ing lume &c** a brewing vessel *16-e18.*
browst &c *la16-,* **brewst &c** *19-20* [brʌust,
brust] a brewing. **brewster &c** *15-20,* **brow-**
ster &c *la14-, now Bnf Abd,* **brostar &c**
la15-e17 ['brʌustər, 'brustər; *?'brostər] a
brewer. **browster &c house** a brewhouse,
brewery *la16-e17.* **Browster &c land** =
~*land, la14, in place-names.* **brewster wife**
18-20, **browster &c wife** *la18-, now Abd Fif* a
woman who brews or sells ale; a landlady.
~ **caldron &c** a brewing vessel *la15-e17.* ~
croft a CROFT ranking as ~*land, 17.* ~**land**
land connected with the brewing on an estate
14-16. ~**seat** a piece of ~*land, la18-e19.*
~**-tak &c** a TACK[2] of ~*land, la16-17.* ~ **tal-**
loun &c tallow paid as a tax for the privilege of
brewing *17-e18.*
brewis *e19,* **bruise &c** *16-19;* **browis &c**
la16-e20 [bruz; *also* *?brøz] *n* broth, stock made
from meat and vegetables. [eModEng *brues,*
ME *browes &c,* OF *brouetz,* f *bro* > BROO[1]]
brewine, brewst, brewster *see* BREW
bricht &c; bright &c *15-* [brɪxt] *adj* **1** =
bright *la14-.* **2** *of colour, la14-.*
n a beautiful woman *la15-16.*
~**ie** the chaffinch *la19-, now Kcb;* cf BRISKIE.
brick *n* **1** = brick. **2** a loaf of bread, *freq with an*
indication of its price or size, la18-e20: 'penny brick'.
bride &c *16-,* **bryd &c** *la14-e17 n* = bride
la14-.
brithal &c *la17-e19,* **brithell &c** *17,* **brydale**
&c *la14-17,* **bridell &c** *16-17,* **bridal &c** *15-*
['brəid(ə)l; *'brəið-, *'brɪd-, *'brɪð-; *'brəid'el]

= bridal. **bridie &c** ['brəidɪ], *also* **Forfar**
bridie a kind of pie made of a circle of pastry
folded over, with a filling of meat, onions etc,
orig made in Forfar *19-* [appar f ~*'s pie*].
~**scake** = bridecake, wedding cake, *orig* a
homemade one which was broken over the
head of the bride *20-.* ~**'s pie** a pie made by
the bride's friends and distributed among the
company at a wedding *la18.*
bridle &c *16-,* **bridill &c** *la14-e17* ['brəidl] *n* **1**
= bridle *la14-.* **2** a retaining band or beam; a
crossbeam supporting the ends of joists *la16-20.*
vt **1** = bridle *15-.* **2** punish or ill-treat (a person) by the application of a bridle or BRANKS[1] (*n*
2) *la16-e17.* **3** rope (a stack) *19-, now Bnf.*
~ **silver** a gratuity given to a servant for leading a horse *la15-e16.*
keep a ~ **hand** keep in control *18-, now Ags*
Stlg.
brie &c [*Arg* brəi; *Kcb* bri] *n* sandstone etc
pounded down to use for rubbing on doorsteps
etc *e20, Arg.*
~**-stone** sandstone *20-, now Loth Lnk.* [*prob*
OSc, ME *bray &c* pound, grind small, but *cf*
BREESE]
brief &c *la15-,* **brefe &c** *la14-18,* **breve &c**
15-; **brieve &c** *la16-* [brif; *law chf* briv] *n* **1**
law an official document; a summons, legal writ
la14-. **2** *latterly chf* **brieve &c** *specif* a warrant
from CHANCERY authorizing an inquest or
inquiry by a jury, *latterly* in such questions as
the appointment of a TUTOR to a PUPIL (*n* 2)
17-20.
vt **1** = brief. **2** write, express in writing
15-e17. **3** write, compose (a letter, book etc)
e16.
adj, adv = brief *la15-.*
~ **of division &c** *law* a BRIEF of CHANCERY
providing for the dividing of lands between
heirs-portioners (HEIR) *la15-.* ~ **of inquest** *law*
a *retourable* (RETOUR) BRIEF directing the SHER-
IFF or (in a BURGH) BAILIES to try the validity of
a claimant's title *la15-e16.* ~ **of lining** *law* a
non-*retourable* BRIEF out of CHANCERY, directed
to the PROVOST and BAILIES of a BURGH for settling the boundaries of holdings by *lining*
(LINE[1]) *la15-17.* ~ **of mortancestry &c**
15-18 [*'mortan'sɛstrɪ, *-'ansɛstrɪ] *or*
mortancestor &c *14-e15* [*'mortan'sɛstər,
*-'ansɛstər] *law* a BRIEF out of CHANCERY
directing an inquest into a claim that the raiser
is heir to certain property formerly possessed by
an ancestor and now wrongfully held by
another.
brig &c *n* **1** = bridge *la14-, in place-names la12-.*
2 a drawbridge *la14-15.* **3** a gangway for a
boat *la14-e17.* **4** a connecting part of a mechanism or implement *16-17.* **5** a reef, a long
low ridge of sea-rocks *la19-, now in ECoast place-*
names. **6** *freq in pl* the division between flues in
a chimney *la19-, now local.*

~ **penny** a tax or toll for the upkeep of a bridge *17-19, latterly hist.* ~-**wark &c** the work of building or maintaining a bridge *la15-16*

brigand &c; brigane &c *16-e17* [*'brɪgən(d)] *n* = brigand *la15-*.
brigancy &c brigandage; robbery with violence *la16-e17, only Sc.* **brigan(n)er &c** a brigand, thief, robber *17-, now Bnf.*

brigantine &c; brekanetyne &c [*'brɪgə(n)-təin, *'brɪk-, &c] *n* = brigandine, a kind of armour *la15-e16.*

brigdie &c *n* the basking shark *19-e20, Sh Ork N.* [ON *bregða*, OE *bregdan* move quickly]

bright *see* BRICHT

brigue &c *vi* intrigue, use underhand means; canvass *la16-e19.* [chf Sc; F *briguer*]

brik *see* BRAK

bril3eane *n* meaning obscure *e16.* [prob nonsense word]

brim &c *n* a brook, stream *la14-15.* [ME *brimme &c* the sea; water]

brim *see* BREEM[1], BREEM[2], BRIME[2], BURN[2]

brime[1] &c *n* = brine; pickle *17-, now Bnf Abd Ags.*

brime[2] *e20, Bnf Ags;* **brim** *e20, Cai Ross Mry vt* fill (a boat) with salt water to swell and close the timbers after it has been lying ashore. [see SND]

brin *see* BURN[2]

brindle &c *n, slang* money, cash *19-, now Bnf Abd.* [cf *brint silver* (BURN[2])]

bring &c *vt, pt also* **brang** *18-.* ptp also **brocht &c, broucht &c** [broxt; *Sh Ork S also* brʌuxt; *S also* brʌuxt], **brung** *la18-, Gen except Cai Bnf* = bring *la14-.*

brinkie-brow ['brɪŋkɪ-'bru] *n, used to children* the forehead *la19-, now Bnf Abd Ags.* [perh alteration of *brentie* deriv of BRENT[2]]

brint *see* BURN[2]

bris *see* BRIZZ

briscat *see* BIRSKET, BRISKET

brisken *vt* ~ **up** freshen, stimulate; smarten *la19-, local Fif-Kcb.* [Eng *brisk* + *-en*]

brisket &c *la18-,* **bisket** *la18-, now Bnf,* **briscat** *16,* **birsket &c** *la16-17 n* **1** = brisket *la16-.* **2** the breast of a person *la16-, now local Abd-Fif.*

briskie &c *n* the chaffinch *la19-.* [perh Eng *brisk* + *-ie;* cf *brichtie* (BRICHT)]

brissel-cock &c *e19,* **brissill cok** *la16,* **birsell foul** *e17;* **brissell fowl** *la16 n* a kind of (?game-)bird. [perh Eng *bristle* f the puffing out of the feathers]

brissell &c *16-e19,* **birsall &c** *16-e18* [*'brɪsl, *'bɪrsl, &c] *n* = brazil, the wood or the dye-stuff obtained from it.

brissill *see* BIRSLE

brissill cok *see* BRISSEL-COCK

brist *see* BIRST, BREIST

bristle *see* BIRSLE

Brit *e16,* **Bret** *e15* a Briton, *esp* of *Strathclyde* (STRATH) *hist.* [OE]

Britane &c [*brɪ'ten, *'brɪtən] *n* = BRETANE *la15-e16.*
adj of Britain; British *16-e17.*

britchin &c; breechin &c ['brɪtʃɪn; *also* 'britʃ-] *n* = breeching, a strap round the hindquarters of a shaft horse to let it push backwards *19-.*
hing in *or* **on the** ~ hang back, hesitate *20-, now Bnf Ags Kcb.* **sit in the** ~(**s**) refuse to move; not do one's fair share of work *19-, now local Ork-Kcb.*

brithal, brithell *see* BRIDE

brither &c *la18-,* **brother &c, broder &c** *15-e18;* **bruther &c** *la14-e20* ['brɪðər; *Sh* 'brɪd-; *NE* 'brid-, 'brɪd-, 'briə-; *brøð-, *'brød-] *n, pl also* **brether &c** *now Fif,* **brethering &c** *la16-e17,* **brither** *16-e17,* **breder** *Sc 15-19,* **bredren &c** *16-e17* ['brɛðər, 'brɛd-, 'briə-; *bridər, *'briðrɪn, &c] = brother *la14-.*
vt **1** *chf* **brother** admit or initiate into a trade, corporation or society *la17-, now WC.* **2** accustom; inure *la19-, now Bnf.*
~-**barn** a brother's child *la16.* **brether-barnis &c** the children of brothers *16-e17.* ~-**dochter &c** a niece on one's brother's side *la16-e20.* ~-**son &c** a nephew on one's brother's side *16-e20.*

british ['brɪtɪʃ] *n, mining* a wall, block of mineral etc which supports the roof of a working *la19-, now Fif.* [var of Eng *brattice*]

Britoner *n* a Britoner, a Breton *16.* [ME]

brittin &c, bertyn &c, *only Sc* [*'brɪtən, *'bɛrt-, *'bart-] *vt, only verse* hack or hew to pieces; slaughter *la15-16.* [ME *britten;* OE *brytnian* divide]

brittle *adj* **1** = brittle. **2** difficult, KITTLE[1] *19-, now Abd Fif.*

brizz &c *15-,* **bris &c** *la15-e20,* **birse &c** *la14-e20,* **brese &c** *la15-e20,* **birze** *la18-e20* [brɪz, briz, bɪrz; *braiz, *bɪrs] *v* **1** *vt* = bruise, crush; *freq* break (bones etc) by crushing etc *la14-.* **2** *vti* push, press *la18-e20.*
n **1** a bruise *19-, now Lnk Kcb.* **2** pressure; struggle *19-, now Fif.*

bro *see* BROO[1]

broach &c *la17-,* **broche &c** *la15-e19* [brotʃ] *n* **1** = broach *la15-.* **2** *also* **bruche &c** [*brʌtʃ] = brooch *la14-18.* **3** *also* **brutch** [brʌtʃ] the spindle on which newly-spun yarn is wound *16-, now Abd.*
vt = broach *la15-.*
broach someone on something open discussion with someone on something *la18-, now Bnf Abd Ags.*

broad *see* BRAID, BROD[2]

broath *see* BROTH[1]

brob *n* a prick, jab *la20-, Bnf Abd.* [prob chf onomat, w infl f BROD[1], BROGUE[1]]

broch &c *16-,* **brouch &c** *16-e20,* **bruch &c**

16-e20; **brugh &c** *la15-e20* [brox, brʌx] *n* **1** =
BURGH; *latterly also* **the Broch** used as a proper
name for the nearest town, *now only*
Fraserburgh in Abd or Burghhead in Bnf *la15-*.
2 a late prehistoric structure (dating *chf* from
the first century BC and the first two centuries
AD), found *chf* in Ork and Sh, the *Western Isles*
(ILE) and the adjacent Scottish mainland, consisting of a large round tower with hollow
stone-built walls; popularly but erroneously
supposed to have been built by the *Picts*
(PECHT); *now* in general use as an archaeological term *la17-*. **3** a halo: (1) *in gen, e17, la19*; (2)
specif one round the sun or *esp* the moon, the
latter indicating bad weather *la18-*. **4** *curling*
(CURL) a circle round the TEE[1] *19-, now Abd.*
[metath var of BURGH; ON *borg* a castle]
brochan &c; brachan &c *e18* ['broxən] *n* **1**
thick or thin gruel (with butter, honey etc);
sometimes (esp Arg Uls) porridge *18-e20*. **2** a
mixture of cereals for feeding young calves *19-,
now Abd.* [only Sc; ScGael *brochan*, IrGael
brochán gruel; porridge]
brochan *see* BRECHAN
broche *see* BROACH, BROTH[2]
brochle &c ['broxl] *n* a lazy, indolent person
19-, now Cai Kcb. [obscure; *cf* BROCK[1] *n* 2]
brocht *see* BRING
brock[1] &c *la16-*, **brok** *la15-16 n* **1** the
badger *la15-*. **2** contemptuous term for a person *19-*. [ME *brok &c*, OE, Gael *broc*]
brock[2] *18-*, **brok** *16-19*; **broke &c** *18-e20*
[brok; *Sh Ork* brʌk] *n, in sing as collective* **1** broken or small pieces; rubbish *16-*. **2** (1) scraps of
bread, meat etc; leftovers *18-, now Fif Arg Kcb.*
(2) kitchen refuse used for feeding pigs *e20, local
C.* **3** the rakings of straw from a harvested
field *20-, now Bnf Abd Ags.* **4** small potatoes
20-, now Abd Kcb.
vt handle carelessly or unskilfully; spoil
la17-e20. [ME *broke &c*, OE *broc*, f *brecan* (*v*)
break; *cf* BRAK]
brock *see* BRAK, BROK
brock-faced *see* BROCKY
brockit &c *19-*, **brokit &c** *la16-e17*; **brocked**
la17-, **brucket &c** *la18-e20 adj* having black
and white stripes or spots: **1** *of an animal, esp a
cow or sheep* having a white streak down its face
la16-e20; **2** *of oats* black and white growing
together *la16-e20*; **3** *of persons* streaked with dirt;
filthy; disfigured *la19-*; **4** *of things* marked *eg*
with soot or mud, streaky, lined *la19-e20.*
brockle a cross-bred sheep, from a Leicester
ram and a blackface ewe *19-, now SW.* [*cf*
Norw dial *brokutt*, Dan *broget* flecked, streaked;
cf BROOK[1]]
brocklie *see* BRUCKLE
brocky &c ['broki, *'brʌki] *n* name for a cow
with a BROCKIT face *la18-, now Bnf Abd.*
brock(ie) &c-faced *of an animal* having a
BROCKIT face *la18-, now Cai.* [back-formation f
BROCKIT; prob not connected w BROCK[1]]

brod[1] &c *n* **1** something with a point, a goad, a
spur *la14-, now Bnf Abd Fif.* **2** a prod or prick
with a goad etc *15-, now Bnf Stlg.* **3** *fig* a stimulus, strong influence *la14-e16.*
vt goad, prick, pierce, jab *la15-, now Abd wLoth.*
[eModEng, nME *brod*, ON *broddr*]
brod[2]; broad &c *16- n* **1** = board: (1) *in gen,
la16-*; (2) *chf in pl* the boards or cover of a book
16-; (3) a table spread for a meal *la16-, now Bnf
Lnk*; (4) a games board, *now esp* a draughtboard *la16-*; (5) a committee etc *20-, now Bnf
Fif.* **2** *usu in pl* the scales of a weighing-machine
15-17. **3** a (church) offertory or collection
plate *16-, now local NE-nEC.* **4** a panel painted
with a picture or a coat of arms; the dial of a
clock *la16-17.* **5** a (window) shutter *17-e20.* **6**
a pot-lid *la19-e20.*
vt fit with a board or boards, *esp* shutters
la16-e17. [metath var of ME and OE *bord* (see
BUIRD[1]); *cf* BRED[1]]
brod[3] &c *la15-e20*, **brude &c** *la15-e19*; **brood**
[brod, brud, brød] *n* **1** *also* **breed** *19-e20*, *NE*
[brid] = brood *la15-*. **2** a young child, the
youngest of a family *19.*
   brudy &c *16*, **breedy &c** *la16, 19-, now Bnf Fif
Kcb*, **broody &c** *la17-e19* ['bridi; *'brødi] prolific; able or apt to breed.
   brodmell *e16*, **brodmal &c** *19*, *NE* a brood.
broder *see* BRITHER
brodstar *see* BROWD
brog [brog, *also* brʌg; *Cai* brʌug] *n* **1** a spike
la15-e16. **2** a bradawl; a goad *19-.*
vt prick, pierce *19-, now Abd Stlg.*
   ~(g)it staff a staff with an iron point, a pike
15-e19. **~gle &c** botch, bungle *19-e20.*
[obscure]
brog *see* BROGUE[1]
brogat &c *la16-e17*, **bragwort &c** *19-e20*;
brogac &c *la16*, **bregwort** *19-e20 n* =
bragget, a drink made of ale and honey.
broggit staff, broggle *see* BROG
brogh *see* BORROW[1]
brogue[1]; brog &c *n, orig a Highlander's* (HIE-
LAND) shoe of untanned hide stitched with
leather thongs; *now* a heavy shoe, *esp* decorated
with a distinctive pierced pattern along the
seams *18-.* [ScGael *bròg*, IrGael *bróg* a shoe]
brogue[2] *n* a trick, hoax *la18-e20.* [eModEng]
broigh *see* BROTH[2]
brok &c *n* the profit or interest on capital; usufruct *15-e17.*
   stock and brock principal and interest *17-e18.*
   [OE *broc* use, advantage; cf *broke* (BRUIK)]
brok *see* BROCK[1], BROCK[2]
broke *see* BROCK[2], BRUIK
broken *see* BRAK
brokill *see* BRUCKLE
brokit *see* BROCKIT
brokken *see* BRAK
brolach ['broləx] *n* **1** a mess; confusion; ruin;

rubbish *19-*, *Cai Bnf.* **2** an old, weak or effete person *la19-*, *now Bnf.* [ScGael *brollach* a mess; IrGael *brothlach* the cooking pit of the Fiann]

brome *see* BROOM

brone &c *n* a twig *e16.* [obscure]

bront *la15-e16;* **brunt &c** *la16-*, **brount** *16* [brʌnt] *n* **1** = brunt *la15-.* **2** the front rank(s) of an army *16.*

broo¹ *la16-*, **bro &c** *16-19;* **brue &c** *la16-e20* [bru; brø; *C* bre] *n* **1** liquid, *esp* that in which something has been boiled *16-*, *now Fif Lnk.* **2** liquid or moisture of any kind, *esp* **snow ~** *la19-*, *now Ags Lnk.* [nME *bro*, prob OF *bro*, *breu* soup; *cf* BREE¹]

broo² &c *la19-*, **brow &c** [bru] *n* **1** = brow, the eyebrow *la14-.* **2** = brow, the forehead *la15-.* **3** the brow of a hill *15-.* **4** the overhanging bank of a river *20-*, *now Lnk.*

browband [*'bru'band] a band for the front of a hat *la16-e17.* [*cf* BREE³]

lat *or* **put doon a ~** show displeasure *la19-*, *now local Ork-Ags.*

broo³; brow *18-e20* [bru; *S* brʌu] *n*, *chf in negative* an unfavourable opinion *18-*, *now local Abd-Lnk*: '*I've nae broo o him*'. [uncertain; *cf* BREE⁴]

broo *see* BUROO

brood *see* BROD³

brook¹ *19-*, **bruke &c** *15-e16* [bruk; brøk] *vt* make black or dirty, streak or smear with dirt, soot, *chf in ptp* **~it &c** *15-*, *now Bnf Abd Ags.* *n* soot on pots, kettles etc *20-*, *now local Cai-Fif.* **~ie** *adj* grimy, dirty *20-*, *now Bnf Abd.* *n* name for a blacksmith *18-*, *now Abd.* [northern eModEng *brouked; cf* BROCKIT]

brook² &c [bruk] *n* a deep layer of seaweed cast ashore by stormy weather, *freq* **~ o ware &c** *la18-e20*, *Sh Ork N.* [ON *brúk* a heap, *esp* of seaweed; *cf* BROOK⁴]

brook³ *n* a game of marbles *e20*, *Arg.* [see SND]

brook⁴ *la19-e20*, **bruke &c** *15-19* [bruk, brøk] *n* a kind of boil, ulcer or sore. [*cf* Icel *brúk* a swelling, rising (of yeast), ON *brúk* a heap; *cf* BROOK²]

brook *see* BRUIK

broom &c *18-*, **broum &c** *la14-17*, **brome &c** *14-17*, **brume &c** *la15-*, *now local Ags-Kcb*, **breem &c** *19-*, *NE;* **broume &c** *15-e17* [brum, brøm; *NE* brim; *C* brɪm] *n* **1** = broom *15-.* **2** *usu in pl* bushes, a stretch or expanse of broom *14-17.* **~ cow &c** a branch of broom *la19-*, *local.* **brume &c park** a park or enclosure grown with broom *la15-e17.*

sing the ~ cry out because of punishment inflicted *20-*, *Bnf Abd.*

broon &c *17-*, **broun &c** *15-*; **brun** *13*, **brown** *la16-* [brun] *adj* = brown *13-.* *n* **1** = brown *la15-.* **2** a brown horse *e15*, *20-*, *local Abd-wLoth.* **3** porter, ale *19-*, *now Bnf Abd.*

~ie &c a *chf* benevolent sprite, supposed to perform household tasks in the night; *latterly also* a more malevolent goblin *16-.*

broon pig an earthenware jar for WHISKY *la19-*, *Abd Ags.* **broon robin** home-brewed ale *la19-*, *Ags Loth.*

broonchadis &c; **broonkaties &c** [brun'ketɪs; *Sh Ags* -'kedis; *Stlg* -'kɪtɪs] *n* = bronchitis *20-*, *local Sh-wLoth.*

broose &c [bruz; brøz; *Abd* briz; *C* brez] *n* a race at a country wedding from the church or the bride's home to the bridegroom's home, *freq* **ride, rin &c** *or* **win the ~** *la18-e20.* [see SND and Suppl]

broostle &c; brussel &c [*Rox* 'brʌsl, 'brʌzl; *Ayr Slk* *'*brusl] *vi* be in a great hurry, bustle *19-e20.*

n bustling; hard exertion *19-e20*, *chf S.* [prob onomat]

broozle &c *vt* bruise, crush, smash *19-e20.* [prob frequentative of Eng *bruise*]

brose &c [broz] *n* **1** a dish of oat- or pease-meal (PEASE¹) mixed with boiling water or milk, with salt and butter etc added *la17-.* **2** a meal of which BROSE was the chief ingredient; *transf* one's living, livelihood *la19-*, *now Bnf Ags.*

brosie &c ['brozɪ; *Rox also* *'*brøzɪ] **1** bedaubed or fed with BROSE *19-*, *now local Abd-Lnk.* **2** stout, bloated with too much food or drink; soft, inactive *19-.* **3** coarse, clumsy *20-*, *now Bnf wLoth.* **brosie &c-faced** having a fat, flaccid face *19-*, *now Abd.* **brosie-headit** very stupid, fat and inactive *la19-*, *Bnf Ags.* **brosing-time** *mining* a meal-time *la19-*, *now Fif.*

~-bicker *19-*, *now Bnf Abd*, **~-cap &c** *20-*, *now Bnf Ags* a wooden dish for BROSE. **~-meal** parched *pease-meal* (PEASE¹) for making BROSE *19-*, *now Bnf.* **~-time** a meal-time *19-*, *now NE.*

brostar *see* BREW

brot¹ *n* **1** a rag *la19-e20*, *Cai.* **2** an apron *19-*, *Abd Ags.* [Gael *brot* a veil; an upper garment, var of *brat; cf* BRAT]

brot² *n* a tangle, muddle *la19-*, *now Abd.* [obscure]

brotekin &c [*'*brotɪkɪn] *n* = brodekin, a high boot *16-e18*, *only Sc.*

broth¹ &c; **broath &c** *17-19 n*, *la18-*, *freq treated as pl* = broth; in Scotland however *usu* a thick soup made from mutton, barley and vegetables, Scotch broth *16-.*

broth² &c, broche *e17*, **broigh &c** *19* [broθ; *brox, *broix] *vi* sweat profusely *la16-*, *now Kcb.* *n*, *freq* **~ o sweat** a heavy sweat *19-*, *now Stlg.* [*cf* Gael *bruich, bruith* boil, cook, and prec]

brother *see* BRITHER

brottlet *la18-e20*, **brotlet** *e17 n* **1** ? a table-cloth *e17.* **2** a small coverlet *la18-e20.* [*cf* BROT¹, BRAT]

brouch *see* BROCH

broucht *see* BRING

brouk *see* BRUIK

broulery &c [*'brulərɪ] *n* struggle, disturbance *la17-e19*. [only Sc; F *brouillerie*; *cf* BRULZIE]

broum(e) *see* BROOM

broun *see* BROON

brount *see* BRONT

brow *see* BRAW, BROO², BROO³

browd [*brʌud] *vt* embroider *la15-e16*.

~**stare &c** *15-e17*, ~**ister &c** *16-e17*, **brodstar &c** *e16*, ~**instare &c** *la15-e17*, **browstar &c** *la15-e16* [*'brʌud(ɪ)stər, *'brʌudɪnstər, *'brod-; *'brʌustər] an embroiderer. [ME *broude*, OF *brouder*, *broder* embroider, w infl f next]

browden &c *17-*, **browdin &c** *la14-16* ['brʌudən; *Ork* 'brod-] *adj* **1** embroidered *la14-16*. **2** stained (with blood) *e16*, *e19*. **3** *chf* ~ **on** *etc* enamoured, extremely fond of; intent on, insistent for *la16-*, *now Bnf*.

vti be fond (of), be intent (on); pet, pamper *la17-*, *now Bnf Abd Fif*. [appar for *browdit* (BROWD), w infl f ME *browden* twisted, plaited, woven, OE *brogden*, ptp of *bregdan*]

browdinstare, browdister, browdstare *see* BROWD

browin *see* BREW

browis *see* BREWIS

browl [brʌul] *n*, *usu in pl* dry pieces of firewood *e20*, *local Abd-Stlg*. [see SND]

brown *see* BROON

browst *see* BREW

browstar *see* BROWD

browster *see* BREW

broynd *see* BRUIND

bruch *see* BROCH

bruche *see* BROACH

brucket *see* BROCKET

bruckle &c *la15-*, **brukill &c** *la14-e20*; **brokill &c** *la14-15* ['brʌkl] *adj* **1** easily broken, brittle; crumbling *la14-*. **2** morally weak; readily yielding to temptation *la14-16*. **3** unstable, uncertain; hazardous *la15-*.

brucklie &c 1 *of persons* in a weak state of health; *of weather* unsettled *la19-*, *now Bnf Abd*. **2** *also* **brocklie** *20-* friable *la18-*, *now Bnf Ags*. [chf Sc; nME *brukel*, OE *-brucol*, f *bruc-*, var stem of *brecan*; *cf* BRAK]

bruckles *n pl* the prickly-headed carex, a sedge *la19*, *NE*. [see SND]

brude, brudy *see* BROD³

brue *see* BROO¹

brugh *see* BROCH

bruik &c *la15-19*, **bruke &c** *la14-e19*, **broke &c**, **brouk &c** *la14-16*; **brook &c** *la16-*, **breuk &c** *la15-e18* [bruk; *brøk] *vt* **1** have or enjoy the use or possession of (lands, property, office etc) *la14-19*. **2** = brook, put up with. **3** used to wish someone well when wearing something for the first time *18-19*: '*weel may he brook it*'.

brookable bearable *19*, *chf Sc*.

bruind *e19*, **brund** *la14-15*; **broynd** *16-17* [*brʌnd, *brønd] *n* = brand, a burning or burnt piece of wood etc *la14-17*.

vi emit sparks, blaze *e19*.

bruise *see* BREWIS

bruit &c, brute, breet *la18-*, *NE* [brøt; *NE* brit; *C* brɪt] *n* **1** = brute *la16-*. **2** *only* **breet** *indicating pity, affection, tolerance etc* a (poor etc) fellow, creature *la18-*, *NE*.

adj = brute *la16-*.

bruk *see* BRAK

bruke *see* BROOK¹, BROOK⁴, BRUIK

brukill *see* BRUCKLE

brulie *see* BRULZIE

brulyie &c *15-e19*, **brulʒe &c** *la14-16* [*'brøljɪ] *vti* = broil, burn.

brulzie &c *la18-e20*, **brulʒe &c** *16*; **brulie &c** *la18-e20* [*'brul(j)ɪ, *'brʌl(j)ɪ] *n* = broil, a turmoil, commotion, quarrel etc *16-e20*.

~**ment &c** = *n*, *18-e20*.

brumaill [*brø'mel] *adj* wintry *e16*. [L *brūmālis*; *cf* eModEng *brumal &c*]

brume *see* BROOM

brummle *see* BRAMMLE

brumstane *see* BURN²

brun *see* BROON

brund *see* BRUIND

brung *see* BRING

brunt *see* BRONT, BURN²

brusery [*'brøzərɪ] *n* embroidery *e16*. [*cf* BRUSIT]

brush¹ &c *18-e19*, **brusche &c** *15-16*; **brus &c** *e15*, *e18* [*brʌʃ, *brʌs] *n* a violent impetus, onrush or onset *la15-e19*.

v **1** *vi* burst or spring out; rush, gush *15-e16*. **2** *vt* force or drive violently; cause to rush or gush *15-e16*. [ME *brusche &c*]

brush², brusche &c *e17* *n* = brush *17-*.

vt **1** = brush. **2** *mining* remove part of the roof or pavement of a working to heighten the roadway *la19-*, *now Fif Edb Lnk*.

~**ing** the part removed as in *v* 2, *la19-*, *now Fif*.

brusit &c [*'brøzɪt] *adj* embroidered *la15-e16*.

brusoure &c [*'brøzur, *-ər] an embroiderer *la15-e16*. [MedL *brusdus &c*; *cf* BRUSERY]

brussel *see* BROOSTLE

brust *see* BIRST

brutal &c [*'brøtl] *adj* **1** of or like an animal, *usu* ~ **beste** *la15-16*. **2** = brutal *16-*.

brutch *see* BROACH

brute &c [*brøt] *n* **1** = bruit, noise, din; rumour, report *la15-17*. **2** a rumour involving praise or blame of a person, good or bad report *la15-17*.

vt **1** = bruit, rumour *la16-e19*. **2** accuse or credit (a person) by rumour *la16-e17*.

brute *see* BRUIT

bruther *see* BRITHER

bryd(ale) *see* BRIDE

brymyll *see* BRAMMLE

bub *16*, **bob &c** *la16* *n* a blast, sudden squall. [only Sc; perh onomat]

bubba *see* BOBBIE

bubble *18-*, **bubbil &c** *e16*; **bibble** *la18-*, *chf NE n* **1** = bubble *16-*. **2** mucus from the nose *19-*.
vi **1** = bubble. **2** *usu of children* weep in a snivelling, blubbering way *18-*.
bub(b)ly &c 1 = bubbly *la16-*. **2** snotty, dirty with nasal mucus *19-*. **3** tearful, blubbering *la19-*. **4** *usu* **bubbly jock** a turkey cock *la18-* [prob imit, but *cf* SND].
sair hauden &c doun by the bubbly jock overwhelmed with too much to do *la19-*, *now Bnf Kcb.*

bubby &c *n*, *chf in pl* the breasts *18-e20*. [prob imit f baby language; *cf* Ger dial *bübbi* a teat]

bubly *see* BUBBLE

buccar &c; **bucker &c** *n* a fast-sailing boat used in smuggling *la18-e20*. [perh altered f Eng *buccaneer*]

buccassy *see* BUCKASIE

Buchan humlie *see* HUMMEL

Buchanite [*'bʌxənəit] *n* one of a fanatical religious sect, founded by Mrs Buchan, the wife of a Glasgow dyer *la18*, *SW.*

bucher &c ['bʌxər, 'bjuxər] *n* a fit of uncontrollable coughing; a cough which causes this *la19-*, *Bnf Abd.* [onomat; *cf* BOICH, BOUCH]

bucht *see* BOUGHT²

buck¹ *vi* pour or gush out; make a gurgling noise *19-*, *now Bnf Abd.* [prob onomat; *cf* BOCK]

buck² *vti* **1** push, butt; batter; fight *la16-e20*. **2** *vi* walk to and fro *la19-*, *now Kcb.*
~ie &c *n* a smart blow, *esp* on the jaw *19-*, *Abd Ags.* *vti* strike or push roughly *la19-*, *Bnf Abd.* [perh f Eng *buck* a he-goat]

buck *see* BUK

buckartie-boo *vi* coo as a pigeon *la19-*, *Bnf Abd.* [imit]

buckasie &c; **buckesie &c**, **buccassy &c** *16-e17* [*'bʌkəsɪ] *n* = bocasin, a kind of fine buckram *la15-17*, *only Sc.*

bucker¹ &c *v* **1** *vi* fuss, move or work aimlessly, awkwardly, yet fussily *la19-*, *Bnf Abd.* **2** *vt* make a mess of, bungle *20-*, *Bnf Abd.*
n **1** a mess, bungling *20-*, *Bnf Abd.* **2** vexation, annoyance; a nuisance *20-*, *now Bnf Abd.* [prob frequentative of BUCK²]

bucker² *n* a species of whale; a porpoise *la18-*, *now Arg.*

bucker *see* BUCCAR

buckesie *see* BUCKASIE

bucket &c *la16-*, **bukket &c** *la15-e17*; **buket** *la13-17* ['bʌkət] *n* **1** = bucket *la13-*. **2** a glass of spirits; a quantity of drink, *freq* **he can take a fair, good** *etc* ~ *la19-*. **3** a dustbin; a wastepaper basket *20-*.

buckie¹ &c *n* **1** the whelk, edible or otherwise; its shell; sometimes applied to other molluscs *la16-*. **2** *fig* a protuberance on the cheek *16-e17*. **3** a snail-shell *20-*, *now wLoth.* **4** something of

little value, *chf* **not care a** ~, **not worth a** ~ *la19-*, *now Abd Fif wLoth.* [perh L *buccinum* a shellfish used in dyeing purple]

buckie² &c *n* a hip, the fruit of the wild rose *la19-*, *now Abd Arg.*
~ **breer &c** a wild-rose bush *la19-e20*, *Dmf Uls.* [obscure, but *cf* BUCKIE-FAULIE]

buckie³ *n* a child's rattle made of plaited rushes and dried peas *la18-*, *Abd.* [obscure]

buckie⁴ *n* a perverse, obstinate person, *freq* **Deil's &c** ~ *18-*. [perh f BOCKIE or Eng *buck* a he-goat or BUCKIE¹]

buckie-faulie &c *n* the fruit or flower of the briar; the primrose *e20*, *Cai.* [Gael *bocaidh-fhàileag* the hip, the fruit of the wild rose, f *bòc* (*v*) swell; *cf* BUCKIE²]

buckle &c *18-*, **bukkill &c** *16*; **bukle** *15-17 n* = buckle *15-*.
vti **1** = buckle *16-*. **2** join or be joined in marriage *18-20*. **3** *vt* partner, *eg* in a dance *19-20*. **4** dress *la18-*, *NE.* **5** wrap up; fasten up *la18-e20*.
~-**(the)-beggar(s)** a person who performs irregular marriage ceremonies *18-e20*.
up in the ~ **1** elated *19-*, *now Fif Lnk.* **2** conceited *la19-e20*.

bucksturdie [?'bʌk'stʌrdɪ] *adj* obstinate *19-*, *Ags.* [perh Eng *buck* a he-goat + *sturdy*]

bud &c *n* a bribe; a private reward for services rendered *15-e18*.
vt bribe *la16-17*. [perh f *bud-*, var stem of OE *bēodan*]

bud *see* BEHOVE

budder *see* BATHER

buddies, buddy *see* BODY

bude *see* BEHOVE

budgell &c; **budʒell &c** [*'bʌdʒəl, *'bʌdʒəl] *n* a bottle *la16-e17*. [only Sc; Gael *buideal*]

buff¹ *v* **1** *vt* (1) puff out (*eg* breeches) *la16*, *e19*: '*buffit hois*'. (2) stuff (furniture) *e18*. **2** *vi* laugh aloud *19-e20*. **3** *vt* toast, *eg* on a gridiron (a salt herring which has been steeped in fresh water) *18-19*.
n, *freq in pl* the lungs *la18-*, *local C.*
~**ie &c** *freq of the face* fat, chubby *19-*, *now Bnf Abd.* ~**ing &c** a puffed part of a pair of breeches *la16-e17*. [prob OF *buffer*, F *bouffer* puff out; onomat]

buff² &c, **bouff &c** *18-*, *now Bnf Abd*, **boof** *19-*, *now Abd* [bʌf; bʌuf; buf] *n* a blow, *esp* one making a dull sound *19-*, *now Bnf Abd Lnk.*
v **1** *vi* make a soft or puffing sound *e16*. **2** *vt* strike, beat, buffet *18-*, *now Bnf Abd Lnk.* **3** *vt* only **buff** thresh (grain) without untying the sheaf *19-e20*. **4** *only* **buff**, *of a storm* beat down, flatten (grain) *19-*, *NE.*
the best of him *etc* **is buffed &c** he etc is in decline, his etc strength is going *19*. **play** ~ strike (**on** something) making a dull sound *la19-*, *now local Sh-WC.* **not** *etc* **play buff** make no impression *la19-e20*. [prob onomat, but *cf* OF *buffe*, LowGer *buff* a blow and BAFF¹]

buff³ *n* silly or irrelevant talk, *freq* ~ **and styte** *la18-*, *local Bnf-Lnk*.

neither ~ **nor stye** neither one thing nor the other; nothing at all *19-*, *now Abd Fif Dnbt*. [prob onomat]

buff⁴ *adj* = buff *19-*.

AB ~ the alphabet, so called from the colour of the school primer; *hence* something very simple or elementary *la19-20*; *cf penny-buff* (PENNY).

buffate stule *see* BUFFET STOOL

buffets &c *n pl* a swelling in the glands of the throat; mumps *19-*, *now Ags Fif*. [*cf* BUFF¹ and SND]

buffet stool &c *la16-e20*, **buffate stule &c** *la15-17*, **buffy stool** *20-*, *Ags Stlg Lnk* ['bʌfɪt 'støl &c; 'bʌufɪt '-; 'bʌfɪ '-] *n* a kind of square stool. [ME]

bug *see* BIG¹

bugdalin &c *18-e20*, **buk denning &c** *16-17* ['bʌgdəlɪn; *'bʌg'dɛnɪn; *'bʌk'dɛnɪn] *n* **1** the inside planking of a ship *16-e18*. **2** anything used to line the hold of a ship before putting the cargo in; any loose material, *esp* for packing, filling in *18-*, *now Sh Cai*. [Du dial *buikdenning, -delling*]

buge &c [*'bʌdʒ] *n* a kind of (hooked) weapon, *freq* ~ **staff** *la15-e16*. [only Sc; OF *bouge*]

buggar *see* BOUGAR

bugrist *n* a person who practises buggery *e16*.

buik &c *16-*, **buke &c**, **book &c** *la16-*; **beuk &c** *16-*, **byeuk &c** *19-* [bjuk, buk; *Ork S* bøk; *WC* *bjʌk] *n* **1** = book *la14-*. **2** a record book or register *la15-*. **3** (1) the Bible *15-*. (2) the reading of the Bible, family worship *la19-*, *now local*. **4** a packet (of gold leaf) *la15-17*.

vt **1** = book, record, register *la16-*. **2** *specif* record the names of (a betrothed couple) in the register of the *session clerk* (SESSION) before marriage *la19-*, *Bnf Abd Ags*.

~**ing &c** the act of entering (a name) in a book or register *16-*. **tenure of booking** *law* a system of land tenure in the BURGH of Paisley requiring registration in the BURGH register *la19*; *cf infeftment* (INFEFT).

~ **buird &c** a bookshelf in a pew, pulpit etc *la19-*, *now local NE-Lnk*. ~**-lare &c** learning, education *19-*, *local NE-C*.

at one's ~ reading, studying *la19-*, *now local NE-C*. **be i the gudeman's** ~**s** be in favour, in a person's good books *19-*, *now Bnf Abd Ags*. **far i the** ~ well-read, learned, clever *la19-*, *now Ork*. **tak the B**~(**s**) hold family worship *19-*, *now local*.

buik *see* BOUK³

build &c *16-*, **beild** *la15-e17*; **beld** *la15-e16*, **bild &c** *16*, **buld** *la16-17*, **bould &c** *la16-17* [*Loth Bwk S* bøld, *ptp* bølt; *bild] *vti* = build *la15-*.

be built up on be wrapped up in, devoted to (someone) *la19-*, *NE, C*. [*cf* BIG¹]

builʒe *see* BILE¹

buird¹ **&c** *la15-*, **burd &c** *la14-e17*; **boord &c** *17-* [burd; børd; *N also* bjurd; *C also* berd, bɪrd] *n* **1** = board *la14-*. **2** a table, *freq* one spread for a meal *la14-*, *now Bnf Abd*. **3** a board for laying out a corpse; a bier *la19-*, *now Bnf Abd*. **4** the net closest to the side of the boat *e20*, *N*.

vt = board *la16-*.

burdin &c made of boards *15-16*.

~ **bed** boards used as a bed *la16*. ~**cla**(**i**)**th &c** a tablecloth *15-e20*. ~**heid &c** the head of a table *la16-e18*.

bed ~**s** = ~ *bed*, *19-*, *now Bnf Lnk*. **on** ~ *of a ship* alongside *e16*. [nME *burd*(*e*), ME and OE *bord*; *cf* BROD², BRED¹]

buird² [*børd] *adj* strong, of sturdy build *la19-e20*. [reduced f next]

buirdly &c *la18-*, **burely &c** *la14-e16, e20* (*literary*), **burly &c** *la14-15, 19-*; **boor**(**d**)**ly &c** *19-e20*, **bier**(**d**)**ly** *la18-e19* ['bør(d)lɪ, 'bʌrlɪ; *Sh Ork Kcdn Ags* 'bur(d)lɪ; *NE* 'bɪrlɪ, 'bjurlɪ; *Loth* 'bɪrdlɪ] *adj* **1** = burly *la14-e16, la18-*. **2** rough *19-*, *now Abd*. [perh w infl f BUIRD¹]

buirk &c [børk, bɪrk] *vi* belch *20-*, *now Fif*.

buisin stane *see* BOOSE¹

buist¹ **&c** *la15-*, **boist &c** *la14-e17*; **bust &c** *la15-17* [bust; bøst; *NE also* bjust; *Abd also* buʃt; *Fif* best] *n* **1** a box or chest *la14-*, *now Sh Fif*. **2** *specif* (1) a small box for ointment, spices, sweets etc *la14-17*; (2) a small box for documents, money etc *la15-17*. **3** a pad etc placed under a garment *la16-e17*. [ME; OF *boiste*; *cf* F *boîte*]

buist² **&c** [bust; bøst; *N* bjust; *Loth* bɪst] *n* **1** an identification mark branded or painted on sheep *19-e20*. **2** an iron stamp for marking sheep *e20*, *SW*.

vt mark (cattle or sheep) with their owner's mark *18*, *now Kcb*.

~**er 1** a person who marks sheep thus *19-*, *now Cai*. **2** *also* ~**in**(**g**) **iron** *19-e20* the instrument used for marking sheep *20-*, *SW*. [perh f prec, f the box in which the branding tar etc was kept]

buit¹ **&c** *16-*, **bute &c** *15-*, **boot** *la16-*; **bote &c** *la14-16*, **butt &c** *16-17*, **beet** *la19-*, *now N* [bøt; *N* bit; *C* bɪt; *Fif* bet; *bʌt] *n* **1** = boot *la14-*. **2** *chf in pl* an instrument of torture *la16-17*.

vt torture with the BUITS (*n* 2) *la16-17*.

~**catcher** a servant who removes and cleans boots *la17*.

buit² **&c** *16-*, **bute &c** *la14-19*; **beet &c** *e20*, *N* [bøt; *N* bit; *C* bɪt] *n* **1** = boot, help, remedy, relief *la14-e17*. **2** *chf in negative, freq* **na** ~ no alternative or choice *la14-e19*. **3** *in compounds* a compensation, payment, reparation, eg *kinbutte* (KIN). **4** an amount added to one side of a bargain to make up a deficiency of value, something thrown in *la16-*, *now Bnf Abd Ags*.

vti **1** = boot, help *16-17*. **2** complete (a bargain) as *n* 4, *20-*, *now Abd*.

to the ~ in addition, into the bargain, to boot *la18-*, now *local Bnf-Stlg.* **to the beet of the bargain** in addition *20-*, now *Cai Abd.*
buith &c *la15-17, e19* (*literary*), **buth** *15-e17*; **bothe &c, bouth &c** *la15-16* [*bøð; *?buθ; &c] n = booth *14-*.
~ **haldar,** ~**man** a shopkeeper *la15-16.*
the ~ **raw** a row of shops or stalls, *esp* that in Edinburgh *15-17.*
buk &c, buck &c *n* = buck *15-*.
~**-hid, -hud &c** [*bʌk'həd, &c] blindman's buff; peep-bo *la15-16* [*cf* Sw *blindbock*, Dan *blindebuk*]. ~ **tooth &c** a large projecting tooth *la15-*.
buk denning *see* BUGDALIN
buke *see* BOUK², BUIK
buk(k)et *see* BUCKET
bukkill, bukle *see* BUCKLE
buld *see* BUILD
bulder *see* BULLER¹
bule *see* BULL
bulf *see* BILF¹, BILF²
Bulgan's Day *see* BULLION'S DAY
bulger [*'bʌldʒər] *n, golf* a golf-club *la19.* [prob f Eng *bulge*]
bulget *see* BULLGIT
bulister *see* BULLISTER
bulkie &c *n* a policeman *19-*, now *Abd.* [perh Eng *bulky*]
bull &c *15-*, **bill &c** *la16-*, **bule &c** *la14-16* [bʌl; bɪl] *n* **1** = bull *la14-*. **2** *only* **bill** a kind of fish *la19-*, *Dmf.*
bullie &c the bullfinch *la19-*, now *Fif.* **bully-horn** a kind of hide-and-seek *la19-*, *Ags.* **bullock-yellow** a kind of swede *20-*, *Bnf Abd.*
bulls-bags the green-veined or purple orchid *19-*, now *Ags.* **as prood as** ~ **beef** very proud or conceited *la19-*, *Bnf Abd Ags.* **bull-grass &c** the brome grass *la19-*, now *Abd.* **bull's head &c** a symbol of condemnation to death, warning of immediate execution *la16-19.* **bull-reel** a REEL¹ danced by men only *19-*, now *Abd.* **bull-seg(g)** a bull which has been castrated when fully grown *19-*, now *Abd.* **bull-o-the-bog** the bittern *19-e20.*
bullament *see* ABUILYIEMENT
bullax &c ['bʌl'aks; *Mry* '-as; *Wgt* *'bɪl-] *n* an axe, hatchet *16-e20*, *chf N.* [Dan *buløkse*, ON *bol-øx*, f *bolr* a tree trunk]
bulldairy *see* BALDERRY
buller &c, bulder *la19-*, *Sh Ork Cai* ['bʌlər, 'bular; *Sh Ork Cai* 'bʌldər] *n* **1** a bubble; a whirlpool; a bubbling or boiling up of water *la15-*, now *in place-name* **the Bullers of Buchan.** **2** a roar, bellow *19-*, now *Abd Ags.* **3** blustering talk, nonsense *la19-e20.*
vi **1** *of water* boil or bubble up; rush noisily; make a loud gurgling sound *la15-*, now *Abd Ags.* **2** roar, bellow like a bull *16-*, now *Bnf Abd Ags Fif.*
~**and** (**in his** *etc* **blude**) with blood issuing

from the body, bleeding *15-e17.* [only Sc; *cf* OF *bullir*, Icel *bulla* boil, Sw *bullra*, Dan *buldre* rumble]
bullet &c, billet *la16-e19* ['bʌlət, 'bɪl-] *n* **1** = bullet *16-*. **2** the game of bowls or something similar *18-e20.* **3** a rounded stone *19-*, now *Cai Bnf Arg.*
~**-gun** a pop-gun made from a branch of elder *19-e20*, *SW-S.* ~ **stane &c 1** a round stone, used *eg* as a missile *17-e19.* **2** a hailstone *20-*, now *Bnf.*
bullgit *20-*, **bulget &c** *la15-e17* ['bʌldʒɪt] *n* **1** a pouch, bag, sack *la15-e17.* **2** a large, shapeless, untidy bundle *20-*, *Bnf Abd Ags.* [only Sc; OF *boulgette*, dim of *boulge* a leather bag; *cf* Eng *budget*]
bullie ['bʌlɪ] *n, vi* = bellow, howl *19-*, *NE.*
bullie *see* BULL
Bullion's Day *la19*, **Bulgan's &c Day** *e20*, *Cai* [*'bʌlɪənz, *'bʌlgənz, *'bʌulgənz-] = *Martin Bullion's Day* (MARTIN BULLION).
bullister &c *19*, *SW*, **bulister** *e16* *n* a wild plum (tree or bush). [eModEng *bullester*, prob f *bullace tre*]
bullox ['bʌloks] *vt* spoil, make a mess of *20-*. *n* a mess *20-*. [perh conflation of form of BULLAX w meaning of Eng *ballocks*]
bully ['bʌlɪ] *n* the game of conkers *20-*, now *Abd.* [see SND]
bully *see* BELLY²
Bully Wee: the ~ nickname for Clyde football team *20-*. [colloq Eng *bully* 'jolly', first-rate + WEE f their not being a major team]
bult *see* BOUT³
bulyament *see* ABUILYIEMENT
bulȝard *see* BILȝARD
bum¹ &c *vi* **1** make a humming or buzzing noise *la16-*. **2** *esp of bagpipes or of a person singing or reading indistinctly* make a droning sound *18-*. **3** cry, weep *la19-*, now *Bnf Abd Gsw.* **4** brag, boast *19-*, *local.* **5** go on vigorously *20-*, *NE Ags.*
n **1** a humming or droning sound *la19-*. **2** a person who reads, sings or plays badly *la19-*, *Bnf.* **3** a musical note *la19-*, *Bnf Ags.*
~**mer &c 1** an insect that makes a humming noise, *esp* a bumblebee or bluebottle *la19-*, now *local Bnf-Fif.* **2** (1) a humming toy *19.* (2) a humming top *20-*, *local Bnf-Ayr.* **3** a factory siren *20-*, *local Abd-Lnk.* **4** = n 2, *19-*, now *Ags.* **5** a thing or person (or animal) which is very large or wonderful of its kind *20-*, now *local Bnf-Kcb.* **6** = heid bummer (HEID) *e20.* ~**mie &c 1** a bumblebee *la19-*, now *Abd Ags Lnk.* **2** a stupid person, a fool *19-*, now *Ags.* ~**min** very good, worth boasting about *20-*, *Bnf Ags.*
~**bee** ['bʌm'bi] a bumblebee *18-*. ~**-bummin(g)** a continuous humming sound *la19-*, now *Bnf Abd Fif.* ~**-clock** a humming beetle *la18-*, now *Kcb.* [ME *bummyn, bumben &c* (*v*) hum; onomat]
bum² *vt* **1** strike, knock *19-*, now *Fif wLoth.* **2**

throw away carelessly or noisily; dismiss without ceremony *20-, now Loth Lnk.* [perh onomat]

bum³ *n* a kind of Dutch fishing boat *20-, now Bnf Abd.* [Du *bom, bomschuit,* LowGer *boomschip, bumboot* a broad rowing boat > Eng *bumboat*]

bumbard &c *n* **1** a lazy or stupid person *e16.* **2** a bumblebee *la16.* [prob f BUM¹]

bumbase *see* BUMBAZE

bumbasy *see* BOMBASIE

bumbaze &c *la17-,* **bumbase** *la17,* **bambaize** &c *la19;* **bombaze** &c *19-e20* ['bʌm'bez, bəm'bez] *vt, chf in ptp* perplexed, confused, stupefied. [prob conflation of Eng *bamboozle* w BAISE]

bumble *see* BUMMEL

bumfle &c, **bumple** *vt, chf in ptp* **1** puffed out, bulging *la19-e20.* **2** rolled up untidily; rumpled up *20-, now local Abd-Kcb.*
n an untidy bundle; a pucker, ruffle, untidy fold, *esp* in cloth *20-, now Ags C.*
bumfly &c ['bʌmflɪ, 'bamflɪ] bundled up, rumpled; untidily put on *la19-, local C.* [prob frequentative of BUMPH]

bumfy *see* BUMPH

bumlack &c *n* **1** a stone on which one might trip; a stumbling-block *19-, Bnf Abd.* **2** a large clumsy thing or person *20-, Bnf Abd.* [perh f BUMMLE]

bumlie &c; **bumler** *n* something which is larger than usual *20-, Bnf Abd.* [perh reduced f prec or direct f BUMMLE]

bummasal &c [bəmə'sal, bɪ-, baɪ-] *interj* by my soul! *20-, Bnf Abd Ags.*

bummel &c; **bumble** &c *vi* boil up, bubble; tumble *19-e20.* [see SND]

bummle &c *vi* **1** *of a bee* hum *20-, local Bnf-Ayr.* **2** (1) read, play or sing badly *18-, now Bnf Abd.* (2) stutter, stammer; speak carelessly *20-, now Lnk.* **3** weep *la19-, Bnf Abd.* **4** bustle about, work noisily but ineffectively, blunder about *19-, now Lnk.*
n **1** a wild bee *la18-, now Abd Lnk Kcb.* **2** indistinct blundering reading *la19-, Bnf Abd Lnk.* **3** a person who reads, sings or plays badly *la18-, now Bnf.* **4** a bungle, mess *19-, now local Bnf-Kcb.*
bummler &c a blundering person, a bungler *la16-, now Cai.* **bamling** &c, **bummlin** clumsy, careless *19-e20.* [frequentative of BUM¹; cf Eng *bumble, bungle*]

bumph [bʌmf] *n* **1** a lump, bundle *e19.* **2** a stupid person *19-, now Kcb.*
bumfy *of a person* lumpy in shape *20-, now Abd Edb.* [var of Eng *bump; cf* BUMFLE]

bumple *see* BUMFLE

bumpy *n* the buttocks *la19-e20.* [f Eng *bump*]

bun¹ &c *n* **1** = bun; in Sc now *usu* less sweet than in StEng *la16-.* **2** = *black bun* (BLACK) *18-.*

bun² &c *n* **1** the buttocks *16-e19.* **2** the tail of a hare or rabbit *18-e20.* [cf Gael *bun* a root, base, and colloq Eng *bum*]

bun³ &c *n* a small cask *la16-e19.* [obscure; cf BOYNE]

bun *see* BIND, BOUN¹

bunce¹ &c *n, vti* share *19-, Edb.* [Eng slang = money, profit]

bunce² *vti* = bounce *la19-, Bnf Abd Fif.*

bunch &c *n* a small stout girl or young woman *19-, now Lnk.* [prob onomat]

bund *see* BIND, BOUN²

bundin *see* BIND

bundling *n* a form of courtship in which the partners lie in bed together with their clothes on *la19-e20, Sh Hebrides* [also US and elsewhere].

bundwark *see* BIND

bune [bøn] *adj* = ABUNE *20-, SW.* [aphetic]

bunewand, bunwand &c [*'bøn'wand, *'bʌn-] *n* a hollow plant stem, *eg* of the dock plant or cow parsnip *la16-e19.* [eModEng, ME *bunne*]

bung¹ *vt* throw violently, hurl, 'chuck' *19-.*
n **1** the act of throwing forcibly *19-, now Bnf Abd Fif.* **2** a violent rush *la19-, Bnf Abd.*
adv with sudden impetus or impact *la19-, now local Bnf-Arg.*
~y huffy *19-, now Bnf.*
in a *or* **the ~(s)** in a temper or the sulks *la19-, now Bnf Abd.* **tak the** *or* **a ~** go into a huff *19-, now Bnf Abd.* [var of BANG¹]

bung² *vi* make a booming or twanging sound *19-, now Abd Fif.*

bung³ *n, slang* an old worn-out horse *19-, now Stlg.*

bung⁴ &c *n* = bung *16-.*
~-fu &c **1** completely full *19-.* **2** very drunk *la18-, now local Bnf Arg.*

bunk *n* **1** a chest which is used as a seat *20-, local NE-EC.* **2** the lodgings of a St Andrews student *la19-, Fif.*
vi lodge *20-, Bnf Fif.*
~wife a landlady of *n* 2, *20-, Fif.* [cf BUNKER, BINK¹ and Eng *bunk(-bed)*]

bunker &c *17-,* **bonker** &c *16-17;* **bunkart** &c *19-e20, NE n* **1** a chest or box, *freq* one used also as a seat *16-, now Abd Lnk.* **2** a rough outdoor seat; a bank of earth etc at the roadside *19-, now Abd Ags.* **3** a large heap, *eg* of stones, clay *la19-, Bnf Abd.* **4** a small sandpit, *now esp* on a golf-course *19-.* **5** a storage receptacle for household coal, inside or outside the house *18-, now local Abd-WC.* [obscure]

bunnel &c *n* the cow parsnip *19-, Lnk.* [cf BUNEWAND]

bunnet *see* BONNET

bunsucken &c ['bʌn'sʌkən] *adj* **1** *of a farm: thirled* (THIRL²) to a certain mill *la19-e20, Bnf Abd.* **2** under an obligation, beholden *20-, NE.* [*bun* ptp of BIND + SUCKEN¹, used attrib]

bunt¹ *n* = BUN² 2, *19-e20, Rox.* [perh w infl f RUNT¹]

bunt² *n, also* **~ie** &c **1** a hen without a rump

18-e19. **2** a short plump person *20-, now local Abd-Lnk.* [perh reduced f BUNTIN[1] and BUNTIN[2]]

buntha *see* BOUNTY

buntin[1] *adj* plump, short and stout *19-e20.* [perh next, but *cf* Eng (*baby*) *bunting*]

buntin[2] *n* a bantam *20-, Bnf Abd wLoth.* [prob var of *bantin* (BANTIM)]

buntlin[1] *&c adj* short and thick *19.* [*cf* BUNTIN[1]]

buntlin[2] *&c n* the corn bunting *la18-19.* [prob f as prec]

bunwand *see* BUNEWAND

bunweed *19-, now Ayr,* **bunwede** *&c la15-e19,* **benwod** *la16,* **benweed** *19-e20* ['bʌn'wid, 'bɛn-] *n* (a stalk of) ragwort. [uncertain]

bur *&c n* the tongue or top edge of the upper of a shoe *la18-, now Bnf Abd.* [only Sc; ON *borð* a margin, rim]

bural *see* BURIAL

burble *&c n* a tangle; something in disorder, *eg* yarn *19-, Lnk SW.*

vt, chf in ptp tangled, disordered *19-, Lnk SW.* [altered f BARBULYIE]

burch *see* BURGH

burd *see* BIRD, BUIRD[1]

Burdeaulx *&c,* **Burdeous** *&c* [*'bʌrdɪɑ(l)s, *-ɪus, &c*] = Bordeaux *16.*

burden[1] *&c la16-,* **burdin** *&c 16-17,* **birding** *&c 15-16,* **burding** *&c 16-17,* **birthing** *&c 13-18,* **burthing** *&c la16-17,* **burthen** *&c la16-e19,* **birn** *&c la14-e20 n* **1** = burden *la14-.* **2** a load, an amount serving as a measure of quantity (*eg* of wood, fish) *15-, now Cai Bnf Kcb.* **3** *law* a restriction or encumbrance affecting property *la17-.* **4** *only* **birn** *&c* a crowd of people, things etc, a tribe of people etc *la18-e20.*

vt = burden *la16-.*

burdinabill *&c* burdensome *la16-17.*

burdiner = ∼-*taker, 17.*

birthinsake *&c 13-17,* **burdingseck** *&c 17* [*'bɪrðɪn'sek, *-sak, &c*] a theft of as much as could be carried on the back. **burdin-taker** one who undertakes (*esp* financial) responsibility for another, a guarantor *17.*

takand the burding on one assuming responsibility *la16-e17.*

burden[2] *&c n, piping* a drone *la18-e20.* [OF *bourdon* a buzzing > ME = a low-pitched accompaniment and ModEng = a low-pitched organ-stop or bell]

Burdeous *see* BURDEAULX

burdin *see* BUIRD[1]

burdin(g), burdingseck *see* BURDEN[1]

burdoun *&c* [*'bʌr'dun, *'bʌrdun] *n* a stout staff, a cudgel *15-e17.*

staff and ∼ = *staf and baston* (BASTION) *16.* [ME *burdoun,* OF *bourdon* a pilgrim's staff]

bure [*'bør] *n* a coarse woollen cloth *la16.* [OF *bure; cf* BURRAT]

bure *see* BEAR[2]

burell *see* BORREL

burely *see* BUIRDLY

burgage *&c n* **1** the form of tenure by which land within a *royal burgh* (ROYAL) is held of the king, *usu* **in** (**fre**) ∼ *16-, now hist.* **2** *also* ∼ **land** *la17-e19* land held in BURGAGE *la16-e17.* [MedL *burgāgium; cf* eModEng]

burgall *see* BURGH

burge *see* BIRGES

burgen [*'bʌrdʒɛn] *n* a burgess *15.* [only Sc; MedL *burgensis*]

burgess *la15-7,* **burges** *&c la14-17 n* = burgess, a citizen or freeman of a BURGH *la14-.*

vt make (a person) a burgess *la17-e19, latterly hist, only Sc.*

burgesry *&c* the status or privileges of a burgess *la15-16.*

burgess oath the oath required of anyone wishing to become a burgess in the major *royal burghs* (ROYAL); there was bitter dispute in the 18th century between the *Burgher* (BURGH) and ANTIBURGHER *Seceders* (SECEDE) as to whether or not it required the swearer to uphold the Established Church, and thus whether or not it could be sworn with good conscience. ∼ **ticket** a certificate of *burgesry, la17.*

burgh *&c la14-, in place-names 12-,* **burch** *&c la14-e17;* **bourgh** *&c la15-e17,* **borough** *&c la16-e20,* **burrow-** *&c la14-e20,* **bourow-** *&c la14-e17,* **borow-** *&c 15-e20* ['bʌrə; *'bʌrx; only in combs, derivs and pl* 'bʌrɔ,*'bʌrʌu,* 'boro, *-ʌu] *n, pl also* **burrowis** *&c la14-e18,* **burrois** *&c 16* **1** = borough, a town with special privileges conferred by charter and having a municipal corporation *la14-; cf royal burgh* (ROYAL), ∼ *of barony,* ∼ *of regality.* **2** town (*esp* as opposed to country), *freq* **in** *or* **to burgh** (**and land**) *15-17.* **3** *in pl* boroughs, towns; burgesses collectively *la14-17.*

burrowage *&c la15-e17,* **borowage** *&c 15-e16* = BURGAGE. **burghal** *la16-, now hist,* **burgall** *17* of a BURGH. **Burgher** a member of that section of the *Secession Church* (SECEDE) which upheld the lawfulness of the *burgess oath* (BURGESS) *la18-, latterly hist; cf* ANTIBURGHER. ∼ **acres** the land belonging to a BURGH *17-e19.* ∼ **clerk** *&c* a town clerk *la15-17.* ∼ **court** a court held within a BURGH *15-e17.* ∼ **dalis** = ∼ *acres, 16-18.* ∼ **greff** a MAGISTRATE of a BURGH *e15.* ∼ **land** land belonging to or situated within a BURGH *la15-e18.* ∼ **laws** *&c* the code of law governing the BURGHS, translated in the early 15th century from *Leges Quatuor Burgorum, 17-, now hist.* ∼ **mail** *&c* the annual duty payable by a BURGH to the Crown in return for its rights *15-e18.* ∼**mure** *&c* the moor belonging to a BURGH, *esp* that of Edinburgh *15-, now only in place-name.* ∼ **rudis** *&c* cultivated land belonging to a BURGH *16-e19.* ∼ **school** a school maintained by a BURGH *la19-e20.* ∼**(s)toun** *&c* a BURGH *15-e20.* **burgh in** *or* **of barony** a BURGH under the jurisdiction of a BARON *16-20*. ~ **of regality** a BURGH under the jurisdiction of a *Lord of Regality* (LORD) *la17-, now hist.* [*cf* BROCH]

burgh *see* BORROW[1]

Burgher *see* BURGH

burial &c, **buriall** &c *la16-18*, **bural** &c *la16, la19-e20*, **beriall** *16-17*, **beerial** &c *la19-e20*, NE ['bɪrɪəl, 'bɛrɪəl, 'bʌrɪəl; 'bʌr(ə)l; *Sh Ork Ags* 'bør(ə)l; *NE* 'bɪrɪəl; *['børɪəl] n* = burial: **1** a burying place *la16-17*; **2** an interment; a funeral; *latterly esp* the occasion accompanying the interment *la16-*. ~ **silver** money for a funeral *e17*. ~ **yard** &c burial ground *la16-e17*. [*cf* BEERIE]

buriall *see* BERIALL

burl *see* BIRL[1]

burlat &c *n* a pad, a padded portion of or addition to a garment etc *la15-16*. [F *bourlet; cf* BURR[2]]

burlaw, burley *see* BIRLIE

burly *19-e20*, **burlo** *la20-, Ork n* a crowd, cluster. [prob reduced f Eng *hurly-burly*]

burly *see* BUIRDLY

burn[1] &c *n* **1** a brook, stream *la14-, in place-names la12-*. **2** water drawn (1) for domestic etc use, *latterly esp* from a well or fountain *16-, now Abd wLoth Arg*; (2) *specif* for use in brewing *16-e20*. **3** urine, *freq* **mak one's** ~ *18-, now wLoth Lnk Kcb*.
~**becker** &c the dipper *19-, SW.* ~**ledar** [*-'lidər] *16*, ~**man** *la16-e17* a water-carrier.
~**stand** a large tub or barrel for holding water *la16-e18*. [ME, OE]

burn[2] &c *la15-*, **birn** &c *la14-e20*, **brin** &c *la14-16*, **brenn** *e15, 19-, now Fif Arg vti, ptp also* **brunt** *la15-*, **brint** *la14-e19* **1** = burn *la14-*. **2** *vt, only* **birn, brin** brand by burning *16*. **3** *in passive*: (1) *only* **be burnt** suffer *19-, now Abd Fif*; (2) be cheated or swindled in a bargain *19-, now local Cai-Fif*. **4** *vti, only* **burn**: *curling* (CURL), *bowling* spoil a game by improper interference with (a stone or bowl) *19-, now local Abd-Arg*. **5** *vt, only* **burn** light up (water) when fishing at night to attract and spear fish *la18-, now Bnf Abd Lnk*.
n **1** = burn. **2** *only* **birn** a brand of ownership on an animal, *usu* **skin and birn** *also fig* in its etc entirety, 'lock, stock and barrel' *16-e20*. **3** *only* **birn** the scorched stem of heather remaining after the small twigs are burnt *18-e20*. **4** *only* **birn** a pasture on dry heathy land *la18-e20*. **5** *only* **brin, brim** a flash, gleam *la18-19, N.*
birning branding as a punishment *la15-16*.
brent burned, branded *la16, la19*. **bruntie** a blacksmith *la19-, now Ags*. **burnt** (*la18*) *or* **brunt** (*la20-, Ork NE*) **ale** the refuse of a WHISKY still. **Brint** *or* **Brunt Candlemes** *hist* the Candlemas of 1355 when Edward III burnt much of south Scotland *la15-17*. **burnt coal** *mining* coal which has been altered and carbonized by the intrusion of igneous rock *la19-, now Fif.* **burnt end** *carpet bowls* a call to lift the

bowls and restart the end *la20-, WC, SW.*
bruntland &c [*'brʌnt'land, *'brʌntlən] rough mossy ground, *formerly* burnt periodically *18-, now Sh.* **burnt-nebbit** *of tawse* (TAW[1]) having had the ends hardened in the fire *la19-e20*. **brent new** brand new *la18-, now Abd Fif Lnk.* **brint silver** *etc* refined silver etc *la15-16.* **brintstane** *la15-16*, **bruntstane** *16-19 = brinstane.* **birny** consisting of, covered with or like *birns* (*n* 3); *fig* rough *la18-e20.*
brinstane *la14-17*, **brumstane** *19* = brimstone.
burne coill &c charcoal *la16-e17*. **birn** *or* **burn irne** a branding iron *16-17*. **burn wood** &c wood for burning *16-19.*
burn nits burn nuts at *Halloween* (HALLOW[2]) to foretell the marriages of the younger members of the party *la18-.* **burn-the-wind** &c ['bʌrn(ð)ə'wɪn(d)] *slang* a blacksmith *19-, now local Abd-Lnk.*
Burns: ~ **Night** 25 January, the anniversary of the birth of the poet Robert Burns. ~ **Supper** an annual celebration of the birthday of Robert Burns, with various traditional features such as the serving of HAGGIS, NEEPS *and* WHISKY, the reciting and singing of Burns' poems and songs, the making of various speeches (see *The Immortal Memory* (IMMORTAL)).

buroo &c, **broo** &c [bʌ'ru, bə'ru, bru] *n* the Labour Exchange, *now* the Unemployment Benefit Office; unemployment benefit received from it, *freq* **on the** ~ on the dole *20-*. [Eng *bureau*]

burop *see* BOW[4]

burr[1] &c *n* **1** a fircone *19-, now Bnf.* **2** a seaurchin *la19-, now Mry Bnf.* [see SND]

burr[2] *n* = BURLAT *16-e17*.
~**it,** ~**ed** padded *16-e17*. [F *bourre* fur, coarse wool used for stuffing]

burrat &c, **birrat** &c *n* a coarse woollen cloth *la16-e17*. [F *burat; cf* BURE]

burreau *see* BURRIO

burrel &c *n, ploughing* a ridge in the *balk and burrel* (BAUK[1]) method, *freq* ~ **rig** etc, *la18-19*. [uncertain; *cf* BORREL]

burreour *see* BURRIO

burrie &c *vti* push roughly, jostle *19-, now Abd.* [perh var of BERRY[2]]

burrie *see* BAR[1]

burrio &c *16-e19*, **burreau** &c *16-e17*, **burreour** &c *16-e18* [*'bʌrɪɑ, *'bʌrɪo, &c; *'bʌrɪur, *-ɪər] *n* an executioner. [only Sc; F *bourreau*]

burroch *see* BOURACH

burrois *see* BURGH

burrough duck, burrow duck *n* the sheldrake *19-e20*. [f its habit of nesting in rabbits' burrows]

burrow- *see* BURGH

burr-thistle &c; **burr-thristle** &c *n* the spear thistle *la18-*. [Eng *burr* a prickly seedbox + THRISSEL]

burry man *n* a public scapegoat, on whom was laid all the bad luck of the fishing and who was then chased out of a village; *later* a man dressed in wool and covered with burrs etc, paraded through a town to bring luck in the fishing season *la19-e20*, *chf NE*. [from ancient times ghosts and evil spirits were thought of as sticking like burrs to the skin of the living]

bursar &c *la16-*, **busser &c** *17*, **bursour &c** *la15-e17 n* **1** *only* **bursour &c** a treasurer *la15-e16*. **2** a holder of a BURSARY *la16-*.
~**y** a scholarship or endowment given to a student in a school, university etc *la17-*. ~**y competition**, *also informal* ~**y comp** a competitive examination for university BURSARIES held by each of the four older Scottish universities (and *latterly* the University of Dundee), *now only* in Aberdeen, Dundee and Glasgow *la19-*. [MedL *bursarius*, f *bursa* a purse]

burse &c *n* **1** = burse, a purse; a bourse, exchange *16-17*. **2** a *bursary* (BURSAR) *la16-18*. [eModEng; F *bourse*, L *bursa*]

bursen *see* BIRST

bursour *see* BURSAR

burst *see* BIRST

burth &c *n* the distance between fishing boats when setting lines *20-*, *now Ags Cai*. [see SND]

burthen, burthing *see* BURDEN[1]

bury *see* BEERIE

bus *see* BUSK, BUSS[1]

busch *see* BUSH[3]

buschbome; buschboun *n* boxwood *e16*. [Flem *busboom*]

busche &c [*bʌʃ] *n* = bouche, an allowance of food *15-16*.

busche *see* BUSH[2], BUSS[1]

bush[1] [bʌʃ] *vti, freq* ~ **up** move about or work nimbly; make clean and tidy *la19-*, *now Stlg Kcb*. [*cf* BUSH[3], *buss* (BUSK)]

bush[2] **&c** *17-*, **busche** *15-e17* [bʌʃ] *n* = bus, a kind of cargo- or fishing-boat *15-e18*.
~ **rope** *fishing* the rope to which the nets of a DRIFT are attached *la19-*, *now local Cai-Ags*. [ME, OF *busse* a broad cargo-boat, Du *buis* a herring boat]

bush[3] *la16*, *e19*, **busch** *15-16* [bʌʃ] *vi* rush or gush **out** *15-e19*.
interj expressing a gushing sound *e19*. [ME *buschen*]

bush[4] [*bʌʃ] *n, also* **timmer** ~ a warehouse or timberyard, *esp* in Leith *17-19*. [only Sc; perh f F *bourse* an exchange]

bush *see* BUSS[1]

bushle-breeks &c [?'bʌʃl 'briks] *n pl* wide baggy trousers *la19-*, *chf Ayr*. [perh Eng *bustle* (of a dress) + BREEKS]

bushock *see* BUSS[1]

busk &c *v* **1** prepare, get ready (*freq* to do something): (1) *vi*, *la14-19*; (2) *vr*, *la14-e15*. **2** *vi* set out, go, *chf* with implication of haste *la14-15*. **3** (1) *vt* prepare, make ready, equip *la14-*, *now Abd Ags Lnk*. (2) *also* **buss**, *specif* dress (hooks

or a fly) for fly-fishing *la17-*. **4** (1) *vi* dress oneself *16-e19*. (2) *vtr, also* **bus(s) &c** dress; adorn, deck, dress up *la15-*. (3) *vt* disguise, put on a disguise *16*. (4) *also* **buss** decorate with ribbons etc (*specif* the flags of various BORDER towns on the eve of the *Common Riding* (COMMON)) *18-*.
n a woman's head-dress *16-e17*.
~**in(g) &c** **1** attire, adornment *17-18*. **2** *also* **bussin(g)** = *n*, *17-e19*. [nME; ON *búask* (*vr*), f *búa-sek* prepare oneself]

buss[1] **&c** *16-*, **bus &c** *la15-*, **busk** *13-e20*, **bush** *18-*, **busche** *e16* [bʌs, bʌʃ; *bʌsk] *n* **1** = bush *13-*. **2** a thicket; a clump or stand of trees; a wood *la14-e20*. **3** a clump of some low-growing plant, *eg* heather, rushes, fern, grass *16-*, *now local Cai-Kcb*. **4** a mass of seaweed growing on sunken rocks and exposed at low tide, a ledge of rock covered with seaweed *19-*, *now Bnf Abd*.
bushock the hedge-sparrow *la19-*, *Stlg*.
bussy &c *17-*, *now Bnf Ags*, **bouzy &c** *la18-e20* ['bʌsɪ; *'buzɪ; *'bʌskɪ] = bushy.
~**sparrow** = *bushock*, *la19*.
wag as the bus wags *or* **wagged** agree sycophantically with someone *la16-e17*.

buss[2] **&c** *19-*, **boose &c** *la19-* [bʌs, bus] *n* the mouth, *esp* if pouting; a sulky, bad-tempered expression, *eg* **have a** ~ **on** *19-*, *now Cai Highl*. *vi* pout, sulk *la19-e20*. [Gael *bus* a mouth, *esp* that of an animal or one with protruding lips etc; *cf* Eng *buss* a kiss]

buss *see* BUSK

bussard *see* BIZZARD

busser *see* BURSAR

bussie *see* BISSY

bussom *see* BESOM

bussy *see* BUSS[1]

bust *see* BUIST[1]

busteous &c *16-e19*, **bustuous &c** *15-16* [*'bʌstwɪs, *-wəs, *'bʌst(ɪ)əs, &c] *adj* = boistous, boisterous.

bustine &c *17-18*, **bustiane &c** *la14-e17 n* = bustian, a cotton fabric.

but &c [bʌt] *conj, also* **bot** *la14-e17* = but *la14-*. *prep* **1** *also* **bot** *la14-e17* = but *la14-*. **2** *also* **bot** *la14-e18* without, lacking; free from *la14-e20*. **3** excluding, not counting; in addition to *la14-15*. **4** out or away from the speaker or spectator; over; across, through (a house etc) towards the outer part *la16-*, *now local Bnf-Arg*.
adv **1** in or towards the outer part of a house etc; into the kitchen or outer room; out *15-*. **2** *rare* into the parlour or best room *la19-*, *now Bnf*.
adj **1** outer, outside; of the BUT *la19-*, *now Cai Abd Fif*. **2** of the parlour or best room *la19-*, *Bnf Abd*.
n the kitchen or outer room, *chf* of a *but and ben*, *19-*, *Gen except Edb Arg*.
bot (*la14-e17*) *or* **but** (*e18*) **and** besides, as well as, and also. ~ **and ben** *adv* **1** in (or to) both

the outer and inner parts, backwards and forwards, to and fro; everywhere *la14-e20*. **2** at opposite ends (of the same house, passage or landing) *la18-e20*. *n* a two-roomed cottage *la18-*. ~ **the hoose &c 1** the kitchen or outer end of a *but and ben, 19-*, now *Cai Bnf Ags*. **2** the best room *20-, NE*. [*cf* BEN[1]]

but *see* BUTT[1], BUTT[2]

butch [bʌtʃ] *vt* = butcher, slaughter (an animal) for meat *la18-*, now *Bnf*.
~**-hoose** a slaughterhouse *20*, now *Abd Fif*. [back-formation]

butcher *see* BOUCHEOUR

bute *see* BEHOVE, BUIT[1], BUIT[2]

Bute pursevant [*St* bjut; *bøt] one of the Scottish PURSUIVANTS *la16-19*. [f the island in the Firth of Clyde]

buth *see* BUITH

butt[1] **&c** *la17-*, now *Abd Ags*, in *place-names 13-*, **but &c** *16-17 n, ploughing* a ridge or strip of ploughed land; *later* an irregularly shaped ridge; a small piece of ground cut off in some way from adjacent land. [ME; Anglo-L *butta*]

butt[2] **&c** *la16-*, **but** *la15-17 n, chf in pl* **1** = butts, targets *la15-*. **2** a measure of distance, *freq* **a pair of** ~**lenths** *16* or ~**s** *la16-e19*. **3** ground for archery practice *19-*, now *Abd Fif*. **4** *games* a line drawn on the ground to indicate the starting point *19-*, now *Lnk Kcb*. **5** *grouse-shooting* a wall or bank of earth erected to hide the guns *20-*.

butt *see* BUIT[1]

butter &c *n* = butter *la14-*.
vt = butter.
~**ed 1** = buttered, spread with butter. **2** made with butter as an ingredient *la18-*, now *Abd*: '*buttered bannocks*'. ~**ie 1** a butter biscuit; a bread roll made of a high-fat, croissant-like dough *la19-*, *orig NE*. **2** = butterfly *la19-, Bnf Ags*. ~**y-lippit** *etc* smooth-tongued, flattering *20-, Ags Kcb*.
~ **bannock** a BANNOCK spread with butter *20-*, now *Abd Fif Lnk*. ~ **bap** a SCONE made with butter *20-*, now *Abd Fif*. ~ **blob** the globe-flower *la19-*, now *Abd Lnk Kcb*. ~**-brods** *20-, Bnf Abd Lnk*, ~**-clappers** *20-*, now *Lnk Kcb* a pair of wooden boards for working butter. ~**-kit** a container for butter *la19-*, *local Bnf-Lnk*. ~**man** a dealer in butter *la16*. ~**milk-an-meal** a bowl of buttermilk with oatmeal on top *la19-, Bnf Ags*. ~ **tron** the TRON for the weighing of butter *la15-16, Edb*.
~ **an breid &c** bread and butter *la18-*, now *local Cai-Kcb*.

buttereis, butterage &c [*bʌtərɛs, *-əredʒ, &c] *n* = buttress *la16-e17*.

buttle *see* BOTTLE[1]

buttock *16-*, **buttok &c** *15-16 n* = buttock *15-*.
~ **mail &c 1** *also* ~ **hire** *la18-e19* a fine for sexual immorality *16-e19*. **2** a spanking *20-*, *Abd*.

button &c *n* **1** = button *15-*. **2** *in pl* a boys' game rather like marbles, but played with buttons with distinctive names and values *la19-*, *Bnf Abd*.
~**y &c** = *n* 2, *20-, Abd Kcb*.

butts *n pl the* ~ the fire-engine *la19-e20*. [prob Eng *butt* a barrel, the first fire-engines being water barrels on carts]

buy *15-*, **by &c** *la14-e17 v, pt, ptp also* **bocht &c, boucht &c** [bɔxt; *Ork S* bʌu(x)t] **1** *vt* = buy *la14-*. **2** buy over, bribe (a person) *15-*.

buy *see* BOW[4]

buzzle *vi, of grain crops* rustle (indicating ripeness) *20-, Bnf Abd*. [perh var of BIRSLE (*v* 1)]

b'wye *see* BY

by; bi *15-e17*, **bye** *16-* [*chf stressed* baɪ] *prep* **1** *also* **be** [*chf unstressed* bɪ] = by *la14-*. **2** apart from, away from, out of *16-17*. **3** contrary to, at variance with, against *15-e17*. **4** *also* **be** *la16* [*bɪ] in comparison with, as distinct from *la14-*. **5** in addition to, besides *la15-e17*. **6** above, beyond; more than *16-*, now *local*. **7** *also* **be** [bɪ], except, besides *la16-*, *local*. **8** *of age, quality etc* past *20-*, *local*: '*by their best*'. **9** concerning, about *la18-*, now *Cai Mry Kcb*.
adv **1** = by *la14-*. **2** *after noun* nearby; present *la15-*, now *local N Ags Kcb*. **3** aside, *freq* **lay** *etc* ~ *16-*.
conj **be** *la14-e20*, **by** *18-* [bɪ; baɪ] **1** by the time that, as soon as *la14-*, now *Abd Fif*. **2** compared with (what); than *la18-*, now *local Bnf-Kcb*.
~**ous &c** [ˈbaɪəs] *adj* wonderful, extraordinary, exceptional *19-*, now *Ags*. *adv* exceedingly, very *19-*, now *Bnf Ags*. ~'**s** *20-*, **beis &c** *18-* [*stressed* baɪz, biz, bɪz] *prep* **1** except; instead of *20-, NE Lnk*. **2** compared with *19-*, now *local Bnf-Lnk*. *adv (conj)* compared with (what); *after comparatives* than *20-*, *local Bnf-Lnk*: '*ye're an auld man beis A thocht ye wus*'.
NB *The normal comb form is* **by-** [*stressed* baɪ-]:
~**-bit(e)** [ˈbaɪˈbəit, -ˈbɪt] a snack between meals *19-*, now *Abd Lnk*. ~**-burd &c** a side-table *la16-e18*. ~**-common** out of the ordinary, unusual *19-*; *cf* *by-ordinar*. ~**cumming** [*ˈbaɪˈkʌmɪŋ] the act of coming past a place *la16-e17*. **bygane &c** *15-*, **begane** *16* [ˈbaɪˈgen; *also* *bɪˈgen] **1** *of (a period of) time, orig following its noun* past; ago *15-*, now *local Abd-Lnk*: '*these seaven years bygaine*'. **2** *of actions, things* belonging to past time; done etc in the past *la15-*, now *local Abd-Lnk*. **3** *of payments* made or due for past periods of time *la15-e18*. **byganis &c** [ˈbaɪˈgenz] **1** things of the past or done in the past, *esp* past offences or injuries *la16-*. **2** payments for past periods; arrears *la16-18*. ~**gaun &c** *la18-*, ~**ganging &c** *17-e20*, ~**going** *17-* [ˈbaɪˈgɑ(ɪ)n, -ˈgaɲɪn, &c] passing by, *freq* **in the** ~**gaun &c** in the passing, incidentally. ~**-gate &c** an indirect way, a side-path; a byway *16-*, now *local Bnf-Lnk*. ~**gottin &c** [*ˈbaɪˈgotən] illegitimate *la15-16*. ~**-hand** *17-*, now *Abd Fif*, *only Sc*, **behan(d)** *la19-e20, NE* [ˈbaɪˈhand;

bɪ'han(d) &c] finished, over and done with, *esp*
of work. ~**-hours** time in addition to ordinary
work, overtime *19-*, *now Bnf.* **bye-job** *also fig* an
additional job on the side *la18-*, *now local Bnf-
Stlg.* ~**knife &c** [*'baɪ'knəif,   *also*
*'bəit'knəif] a knife carried beside a dagger
la15-17. ~**-ordinar &c,** ~**-ornar** *la19-e20 adj*
extraordinary, unusual *la17-.* *adv* extraordinarily, unusually *la19-.* ~**past &c** *la14-17*, ~**passit &c** *la14-e16* [*'baɪ'past, &c] **1** *of time, a
specific date etc* past, elapsed *la14-17: 'August last
by past'.* **2** *of events, actions etc* done in, belonging to past time *la15-17.* ~**-pit** *la19-*, ~**-put**
15- *ptp* set aside *15-e16.* *n* **1** a temporary substitute, a pretence *la19-*, *now Bnf Abd.* **2** a pro-
crastinator *la19-*, *now Bnf Abd.* ~**-place** an
out-of-the-way place *la18-*, *now Abd Kcb.* ~**run**
la15-17, ~**runnyn &c** *la15-16* [*'baɪ'rʌn(ən)] **1**
of time past; expired *la15-16.* **2** *of payments* due
for a period in the past *16-17.* ~**runnis &c**
la16-17, ~**rins &c** *la17-*, *now Abd*, ~**rinnins**
20-, *NE* ['baɪ'rɪn(ɪn)z, &c] arrears. ~**-sle(e)ve**
an additional or over-sleeve; *fig* a hanger-on,
nonentity *la16-e18.* ~**-south &c** [bɪ'suθ] *prep*
on or to the south of; below, beyond *15-*, *now
Bnf Abd.* *adv* in the south; on the south *16-e20.*
~**spel &c** ['baɪspɛl, -'spil] *n, adj, also ironic* an
extraordinary person; extraordinary, wonderful
19-e20 [ME *bispell* a parable, proverb].
~**-time** stand beside or near *15-16.* ~**-time**
spare time *la19-*, *now Abd Fif.* **at a** ~**-time**
occasionally *19-*, *now Bnf.* ~**-usual** = *by common*, *la19-.* ~**went** [*'baɪ'wɛnt] bygone, past
la15-e16.
~ **and aboon** over and above *la19-*, *now Abd
Fif.* ~ **and atour** *la16-e19*, ~ **an(d) out
owre** *la17-*, *now Abd Fif*, ~ **and besides**
la16-e17, *orig freq law etc* in addition to, besides.
~ **and gane** completely over, finished *20-*, *local
Bnf-Fif.* ~ **the common** *predicative* = *by common*, *19-.* ~ **my feggs** a mild oath *la18-*, *now
local Cai-Fif.* ~ **the hand** in reserve, at one's
disposal, available *19-*, *now Ork Abd.* ~ **one's
mind** *la15-16*, ~ **oneself** *16-* out of one's
mind, insane, beside oneself. ~ **one's ordinar**
out of one's usual health *20-*, *now local.* ~ **the
ordinar** = *by the common*, *la19-.* ~ **wi** over
and done with, finished *la19-.* **b'wye** [bwaɪ,
&c] as it were, by the way *20-*, *Abd Ags Fif.*
by *see* BUY

byaak *see* BAKE
byas bowl &c [*'baɪəs 'bul] *bowling* a bowl *17.*
   [*cf* Eng *biassed bowl*]
byauch *see* BIACH
byauve *see* BLAW[1]
bye(s) *see* BY
byeuk *see* BUIK
byke[1] **&c** *n* **1** *also* **boick** *la17-*, *NE* a bees',
   wasps' or ants' nest; a beehive *15-.* **2** a dwelling, habitation *la15-*, *now Abd Lnk.* **3** a bee-
   hive-shaped cornstack *la18-e20*, *Cai.* **4** a
   swarm, *esp* of persons *16-*, *now local Bnf-Abd.* **5**
   a collection, something acquired *19-*, *now Bnf.*
   vi, of bees swarm *la18-*, *now Bnf Abd Ags.*
   [nME]
byke[2] *n* the nose *la19-*, *now Ags.* [obscure; *cf*
   next, BECK and Eng *beak*]
byke[3] **&c** *n* the bend of a hook; the hook at the
   end of chain for holding a pot over a fire *la19-*,
   now Bnf. [obscure; *cf* prec]
byke[4] *vi* weep, whine, sob *19-e20*, *chf SW.*
   [uncertain]
byle *see* BILE[2]
bylie *see* BAILIE
byll *see* BILE[2]
byochy-byochy, byock *see* BOCK
byous *see* BY
byrd &c [*'bɪrd] *v* **1** *impersonal* = burde, it
   behoves (one) *la14-e15.* **2** *vi* (you etc) ought
   (to do etc) *la14-16.*
byre &c [baɪr, bəir] *n* a cowshed *15-.*
   ~**-claut** a CLAUT (*n* 3) for cleaning out a BYRE
   la19-, *now Ags Kcb.* ~**man** a cattleman *la16-*,
   now Bnf Kcb. ~**woman** a woman who looks
   after cows *20-*, *now Bnf Abd Kcb.* [northern
   eModEng, OE *bȳre* (rare), perh related to OE
   būr a dwelling]
byrne *see* BIRNY
bys *see* BY
bysning *see* BYSYN
bystart &c *la18-19*, **bastard** *15-*; **bastart**
   la15-16 ['bastərd, &c; *?'baɪ'start] *n, adj* = bastard. [see SND]
bystour [*?'baɪstər, *?'bəi-] *n* contemptuous
   term for a person *16.* [obscure]
bysyn &c *la14-e17* *n, also* **bysning &c** *la14-e16*
   [*'baɪz(ə)n, *'baɪznɪŋ, *'bɪz-] a monster. [ON
   bysn a marvel, portent]
byt *see* BITE

C

ca¹ &c *18-*, call &c; caw &c *16-* [kɑ; *kal] *v*, *ptp also* cald &c *15-e17*, ca'd &c *la17-* 1 = call *la14-*. 2 *specif* (1) summon before a court *15-*. (2) *in passive* be ~ed to a church be invited formally by a congregation to be its MINISTER *la16-*. 3 order (a drink) *18-*, *now local N-Lnk*. 4 abuse, miscall *la19-*, *now wLoth*. 5 (1) urge on (by calling), drive (animals) *la15-*. (2) drive (a vehicle, plough, load etc) *la14-*. (3) *specif* bring home (turnips etc) from the fields *20-*. 6 *vi, freq* ~ awa be driven; drive on one's way, proceed; keep going, plod on *19-*. 7 *vt* drive in (nails etc); fix on by hammering *16-*. 8 knock, push *la18-*. 9 set or keep in motion (*eg* a skipping rope) *la19-*. 10 ransack, search *19-*, *NE Ags*. 11 sell or hawk in a cart *la19-*, *NE Arg*.

n 1 = call *16-*. 2 *fig* a hurry *20-*, *NE*: '*fit's yer cau, the nicht's bit young*'. 3 a knock, blow *20-*, *local Abd-Loth*. 4 a search *la19-*, *NE Ags Fif*. 5 the motion of the waves *19-*, *Sh N*. 6 a turn, *eg* of a skipping rope *20-*.

~ aboot circulate, send round (a punch bowl etc) *la18-*. ~ again &c 1 recall, revoke, retract *la14-16*; *cf again-call* (AGAIN). 2 oppose, contradict *19-*, *now Ags Per*. ~ canny *chf in imperative* proceed warily; act *cannily* (CANNY) *20-*. ~ clashes *or* the clash, ~ (aboot) a story spread gossip *19-*, *NE Ags*. ~ the cows out o the kail-yard perform a very simple and reasonable act *19-*, *now Cai Ags*. ~ the crack converse, talk *la19-*, *now NE Lnk*. ca for someone call on, visit *la18-*. ~ someone for .. 1 abuse as being .., *chf* ~ someone for everything heap abuse on someone *la19-*. 2 name after *19-*, *now local*. ca one's *or* the girr &c proceed, carry on *20-*, *local Abd-SW*. ~ a nail to the head go to extremes, exaggerate *la18-*, *NE*. ~ on demand, ask for *la19-*, *now local Abd-Kcb*. ~ oot dislocate *20-*. ~ tae shut (a door) *la19-*. ~ through &c *v* 1 work with a will *la18-*, *now local Bnf-Lnk*. 2 pull through (an illness) *la19-*, *Bnf Ags Fif*. *n* ca-through &c 1 drive, energy *la19-*, *Bnf Abd Ags Fif*. 2 a disturbance *19-*, *Bnf Abd Ags Fif*. 3 *of clothes* a slight or preliminary wash *20-*, *local Bnf-Kcb*. 4 a search *20-*, *Abd Ags Fif*. have the ~ have the right to call upon the next performer *la19-*, *NE Fif*. no worth ~in oot o a kail-yard valueless *la19-*, *now Cai Ags*.

ca² [kɑ] *n* a cart road, a *loaning* (LOAN¹) *19-*, *chf Cai*. [prob Gael *cadha* a narrow pass]

ca³ [kɑ] *n, pl* caas &c a calf *19-*, *now Abd*. *vi, chf* new ca'd newly-calved *la18-20*, *SW*. [prob back-formation f CAUR calves]

ca(a) *see* KAE¹

caak [kɑk] *vi, n, of a hen etc* cackle *20-*, *Cai*. [imit]

cab &c *vt* pilfer, filch *19-*, *now Abd*. [contraction of Eng dial *cabbage*]

cabal &c [kə'bal, 'kabl] *n* 1 = cabal *17-*. 2 a group of people met together for gossip or drinking *18-*, *now Abd*. 3 a violent dispute *19-*, *chf Bnf*.
vi 1 quarrel, dispute *18-20*. 2 find fault *la19-*, *Bnf*.

cabar [*ka'bar, *'kabər] *n* = GABBART *la16-17*. [only Sc; OF *cabarre*]

cabbage, cabbitch *20-*, *NE Ags*, *n* ~ kail cabbage *la17-*, *NE Ags*. ~ runt, stock a cabbage stalk, a CASTOCK *20-*, *chf NE Fif Kcb*.

cabbiclaw &c *n* a dish of salt cod *18*. [see SND]

cabbitch *see* CABBAGE

cabbrach &c, cabroche &c ['kabrəx] *adj* lean, scraggy *16-e19*.
n a big, disagreeable, uncouth person *la18-*, *Bnf Kcb*. [see SND, OED]

cabby-labby &c; kebby-lebby &c *n* a quarrel, altercation, wrangle; hubbub *la18-e20*, *local*. *vi* wrangle *19*. [*cf* Eng *gabble*, MDu *kebbelen*, EFrisian *kabbeln*]

cabelew &c [*?'kabɪlʌu] *n* a young cod; salt cod or pike; a dish of this *18-e20*, *local Sh-Per*. [see SND, OED]

caber, kaber &c *16-19*; keaber &c *la16-19*, kebar &c *la16-e19*, kebber *la17-19* ['kebər, 'kɛb-, 'kab-] *n* 1 a heavy pole or spar, a long slender tree-trunk *16-*. 2 a rafter, beam *la16-*, *now chf NE*. 3 *specif* a side- or subsidiary rafter, one laid across the main beams and supporting the thatch *18-19*. 4 a large stick or staff *19-*, *Cai Abd*. 5 *fig* (1) a big coarse clumsy man *19-*, *chf NE*. (2) an old useless horse *20-*, *Cai Bnf*.
toss the ~ throw the heavy pole, as in *Highland Games* (GAME) *la19-*. [Gael *cabar* a pole, rafter]

cabil &c *15-e17*; cable &c ['kebl] *n, also* capill *16-e17* [*'kepl] = cable *la15-*.
~ stok a capstan *e16*, *only Sc*. ~ tow a cable-rope *la16-e17*, *only Sc*. ~ ȝarne yarn for making cables *la16*, *only Sc*.

cabin *see* CAIBIE

cabok *see* KEBBOCK

caboschoun &c *n* a precious stone polished but not cut or faceted *la16*. [F *cabochon*]

cabroche *see* CABBRACH

cace *see* CASE¹, CASE²

cache¹ &c [*katʃ, *ketʃ] *n* the game of hand-tennis *la15-e17*. [MDu *caetse*; *cf* CACHEPELL]

cache² &c; catch &c [*katʃ] *v, chf verse* 1 *vt* chase, drive *la15-e17*; 2 *vi* make one's way, go *la15-e17*. [ME; OF *cachier*, northern var of *chacier* > Eng *chase*]

cache *see* CATCH

cachepell, kachepele; keche- &c, -pule &c [*'katʃpɛl, *-pəl, *'ketʃ-] *n* 1 = CACHE¹ *la16*. 2 a ground or court for playing this *16-17*.
~er a keeper of or attendant at a tennis-court *la16-e17*. [MDu, Flem *caets-spel*, f *caetse* = CACHE¹]

cachet &c [*'katʃət] *n* a seal or stamp for impressing documents *17-18, only Sc.*

cack, cawk *e16;* **kach** &c *e20, Cai Bnf Ayr* [kak, kɑk, kax] *vi* void excrement *e16, 20-. n* human excrement *la18-.*
~**ie** = *v, 19-e20.* [ME *cakke,* L *cacāre,* MDu *cacken; cf* KICH]

cacker *see* CAUK²

ca'd *see* CA¹

cadda &c, **caddow** &c *n* a rough woollen covering or rug *la16-e17, la19 (Uls).* [eModEng *caddow*]

caddas *see* CADDIS

caddel &c ['kadl, 'kaðl] *n* **1** = caudle *17-e18.* **2** beaten eggs: (1) *specif* when scrambled *la20-, Sh NE;* (2) *only* **cathel** a kind of egg-nog *18-19. vt* stir or mix into a mess *20-, Bnf Kcb.*

cadden &c **nail, caddone nail** a large nail or iron pin *16-, now Abd.* [obscure; *cf* CADDLE]

caddie¹ &c, **cadie** &c ['kadɪ] *n* **1** a military cadet *17-e19.* **2** a messenger or errand-boy; *chf in pl* an organized corps of such in Edinburgh and other large towns *18.* **3** a ragamuffin, a rough lad or fellow *la18-, now Abd Fif Uls.* **4** *golf* an attendant who carries a player's clubs *19-.*
vi, golf act as a caddie (*n* 4) *20-.* [F *cadet*]

caddie² &c *la19-, Sh Ork,* **keddie** *la16, Abd n, freq attrib* a pet-lamb. [*cf* Eng *cade*]

caddie³ &c: ~ **nail** *or* **bolt** a bolt or iron pin used in fixing the body of a cart to its axle *19-, now Ags Per.* [*cf* CADDEN NAIL]

caddis &c, **caddas** &c *la15-e16 n* **1** cotton wool, flock, padding *la15-e17.* **2** (cotton- or wool-) fluff, ends of thread etc collected into bunches or knots *la19-, now local NE-Loth.* **3** shreds of material, rags *la19-, chf NE Ags.* **4** surgical lint *18-e19.* [ME, OF *cadas* &c]

caddle &c *n* = CADDEN NAIL *20-, NE.*
cathel nail ['kaθl-] = *n, 19-, Per Fif Ayr.*

caddone nail *see* CADDEN NAIL

caddow *see* CADDA

caddroun *see* CAUDRON

cadent [*'kadənt] *n* = cadet, a younger son *17.*

cadge¹ *vti* **1** peddle wares *18-.* **2** carry loads, parcels etc *19-.* **3** *vi* beg, sponge *la19-.* [uncertain; *cf* Eng and CADGER]

cadge² &c *vt* shake up, knock about, jostle *la18-, NE.*
n a shake, jolt; a nudge, hint *la18-, NE.* [uncertain; *cf* KEYTCH]

cadger &c *la16-,* **cadgear** *la15-e17;* **cagger** &c *la15-e16* ['kadʒər] *n* **1** an itinerant dealer, *esp* in fish, a hawker; a carrier of goods, a carter *la15-.* **2** an ill-tempered person *la19-, Bnf Abd.*
~**'s news** stale news *la19-, Abd Ags Fif.* ~**'s whips** *said by children learning to write* letters such as *r* which have a curve resembling a CADGER's whip *la19-, Ags.*
bolt *or* **cowp the** ~ vomit *la19-, Ags.* **the king will come in the** ~**'s road** a great man

may need the services of a humble one *la19-, local Bnf-Kcb.* [prob f CADGE¹; earlier in Sc; *cf* ModEng = a person who begs]

cadgy &c, **kidgie** &c *19-, chf NE;* **caigy** &c *la19-20 adj* cheerful, in good spirits; friendly, hospitable *18-.*
adv cheerfully *19-, Renfr Kcb.* [see SND]

cadie ['kedɪ] *n* a man's or boy's cap *la19-, now C.* [unknown]

cadie *see* CADDIE

caduac, cadouk &c [*ka'duk] *n* an accidental gain, a windfall *17-e19.* [MedL *caduca* transitory things; *cf* eModEng *caduke* transitory]

caduciar *la17;* **caduciary** *la18-19* [*kə'dʒusɪərɪ; *ka'dəsɪər] *adj, adv, law* = caducary, subject to or by way of ESCHEAT. [only Sc]

caff &c; **calf** &c *la15-e19,* **cauf** &c *17-,* **kaff** *20, Sh-Cai* [kaf; kɑf] *n* = chaff, *freq* used for stuffing mattresses *la15-.*
~ **bed** a bed-tick filled with chaff *la16-.* ~ **bouster** a chaff-filled bolster *la16-e17.* ~ **hoose** the compartment connected with a corn-threshing machine which receives the chaff as it leaves the fanners of the winnower *20-, N Fif Kcb.* [nME *caf; cf* OE *ceaf*]

caff *see* CAUF¹

caffunʒe *n* footwear of some sort *la15-e16.* [only Sc; obscure]

cag; kag &c *la16-19,* **caig** &c *17-18* [kag, kɑg; Kcb keg] *n* **1** a keg *la15-, now Bnf Fif.* **2** *fig* stomach, belly *20-, now Bnf Edb.* [nME *kag,* ON *kaggi*]

cageat &c [*'kadʒət] *n* a small box, casket *la14-16.* [only Sc; obscure]

cagger *see* CADGER

cahoochy &c [ka'hutʃɪ, kə-] *n, chf attrib* rubber *la19-, local Abd-Kcb.* [F *caoutchouc*]

cahow &c [ka'hu, kə-] *interj* a call in the game of hide-and-seek announcing the beginning of the search *19-, Bnf Abd.* [*cf* KEEHOY]

cahute &c [*kə'høt] *n* a ship's cabin; a separate room or space *e16.* [only Sc; F]

caib &c [keb] *n* the iron or cutting part of a spade etc *la18-, Suth Ross.* [Gael *ceaba*]

caibe [keb] *n* a cabinet-maker *20-, local Ags-Ayr.* [prob contracted f *caibinet(-maker)*]

caibie &c; **cabin** ['kebɪ, 'kebɪn] *n* a hen's crop or gizzard *20-, Cai Abd.* [Gael *geuban* &c]

caibin *n* = cabin *20-, NE Ags.*

caif &c *adj, of wild birds* tame *19-, Rox.* [ME *caf,* OE *cāf* swift, eager]

caif *see* CAVE¹

caig *see* CAG

caigy *see* CADGY

caikle *vi* = cackle *20-, NE EC.* [*cf* KECKLE]

cailleach ['keljəx, 'kal(j)əx] *n* **1** an old woman *19-, chf Highl N WC Uls.* **2** the last sheaf of corn cut at harvest *e20, local.* **3** the festival of harvest-home *20-, Abd Uls; cf* CLYACK 3. [Gael = 1 and 2]

caip, cape, kaip *16-e18*, **kape** *16-17*; **cap-** *19-* *n* **1** = cope *15-16*. **2** (1) a coping-stone *16-17*. (2) a coping *la17-, now Abd.*
vt furnish with a coping *la16-e20*.
   cape house *la16-e18*, **cap-house** *la19-e20*, *hist* a small erection on top of another building.
   ~ **stane** etc = *n* 2 (1), *la16-20*.
   a ~ **of leid** a lead coffin *la15-16, only Sc.*
caip *see* KEP¹
cair &c *vt* **1** stir *19-, N.* **2** scrape or rake up *19-, now Abd.* **3** *also* **keir** *20-, Cai* [keir] prepare (threshed corn) for winnowing by separating out the broken pieces of straw etc *la19-, N.* **4** mix together *la19-, Sh NE.* [Norw *kara* (*v*) rake, scrape]
cair *see* CAUR
cairban &c *n* the basking shark *la18-e19.* [Gael *cearban*]
caird¹ &c, kard &c *la16-e19* [kerd; *NE also* kjard] *n* **1** a tinker *la16-, specif* (1) the craftsman who mends pots etc *la16-17*; (2) a vagrant or rough person *18-.* **2** a person who scolds *19-, local N.*
vt abuse, scold *19-, NE Per.*
   kyaard-tung't given to loose talk *20-, Bnf Abd.* [Gael *ceàrd* a craftsman]
caird² &c, card &c *la15-17*, **kard &c** *16-17* [kerd; *NE also* kjard] *n* = card, the instrument for carding wool etc *16-, latterly chf N.*
vt = card (wool etc) *16-e20.*
caird³ &c *vt,* ~ **through ither** mix together *18-.* [CAIRD², perh w infl f CAIR *v* 4]
caird *see* CARD¹
cairie, kairy &c *n, only* **cairie** a breed of sheep *20, Cai.*
adj, only **kairy** *of the fleece* streaked, striped *20-, Cai.* [Gael *caora,* a sheep]
cairl *see* CARLE¹
cairn &c, carne &c *16-e18*; **kairn &c** *la16-e18* [kern; *NE also* kjarn] *n* **1** a pyramid of loose stones in *place-names* *15-, in personal names* *la14-*: (1) as a boundary-marker or other landmark, *freq* now on the tops of mountains *la15-*; (2) as a memorial, marking a grave *16-*; (3) *in gen* a heap of stones *la16-.* **2** a heap or quantity of anything *la18-, N.* **3** **C~** = **C~** *terrier, 20-.*
vt heap, pile (**up**) *la18-, Bnf Abd.*
   ~**it** furnished with CAIRNS as boundary marks *16, chf NE.*
   ~ **net** a small net for catching fish lying behind stone-piles in a river *la19-e20, S.* **C~ terrier** a particular type of small *West Highland* (WAST) terrier, now a separate breed *la19-.* [Gael *càrn*]
cairngorm &c *n* a yellowish semi-precious stone *la18-.* [f *Cairngorm,* the mountain, where the stone is found]
cairrage &c *la16-*, **carriage &c** *16-*, **cariage &c** *la14-17* *n* = carriage *la14-.*
   ~ **man** a man engaged in carriage or transport *la14-e17, only Sc.*
cairry &c *17-*, **cary &c** *la14-e18*; **carry &c**

la16- *vti* **1** = carry *la14-.* **2** *vt* conduct, escort, lead *16-19.* **3** *vi* make one's way, proceed, go *la15-e16.*
n **1** a (heavy) weight, burden *19-, now Abd Ags Fif Kcb.* **2** a 'lift' in a vehicle *la19-, now Cai Abd.* **3** the motion of the clouds; *in pl* the clouds in motion *19-.* **4** the sky *19-, now Bnf Abd.*
   carried &c *adj* **1** *fig* carried away, transported, elated *18-, local.* **2** conceited *19-, local.* **3** delirious, not rational *19-, local.* **cairrier, caryar** = carrier *17-.* **come (back) wi the blin cairrier** return only after a very long time or never *19-, now Ags Fif.* **have something carrying** carry something *la19-e20.*
   ~**-out &c** food or alcoholic drink bought in a restaurant, pub etc for consumption elsewhere *la20-.* [*cf* Eng *takeaway*].
cairt¹ *16-*, **cart &c**, **kart &c** *la14-17* *n* = cart *la14-.*
vt = cart *la15-.*
   ~**er &c** = carter *16-.* **kill the** ~**er** name for a very strong variety of WHISKY *20-, local Cai-Stlg.* **cairtle &c** a cart-load *16-, chf NE Ags* [prob for *cairt-full* or *-tale*].
   ~ **door** the tail-board of a cart *20-, local NE-S.* ~ **draught** a cart-load *la17-, now Abd Fif.* **gate &c** a cartroad, a road suitable for carts *16-17.* ~ **girden** a rope used to secure a load *20-, NE.* ~ **raik** the time taken to dispose of a cart-load *20-, now Bnf Kcb.* ~ **wheel** a large variety of daisy or marguerite *20-, now Abd Lnk.*
cairt² &c *la16-*, **cart &c**, **kart &c** *la15-18* [kert] *n* **1** = chart *la15-17.* **2** a playing card; *chf in pl, freq* **the** ~**s** a game of cards *la15-.*
   ~**er &c** a card-player *la16-e17.* ~**in** card-playing *20, Bnf Abd.*
   up by ~**s** *transf* 'up in the world', in an exalted position *la19-20, Abd Ags* [f the game of *catch the ten* (CATCH)]. [ME, F *carte; cf* CARD¹]
caition *see* CAUTION
cake &c, kake &c *15-19* [kek; *N also* kjak] *n* **1** = cake, *freq* an oatcake (AIT) *15-.* **2** *specif* cake, fruit loaf etc given to children or callers at New Year *la19-, now Fif.* **3** *transf* a sheet or slab of metal, *esp* lead *16-17.*
   C~ day HOGMANAY *19-e20, Fif Rox;* cf *singin cake* (SING¹). ~ **fidler** a parasite *e16.* ~ **of breid** an oatcake (AIT) *la17, 20-, Bnf.* **nocht (worth) ane** ~ worthless *15-16.*
caker *see* CAUKER²
calamy &c ['kaləmɪ] *n* calomel *19-, now local Bnf-Stlg.*
calchen *see* KILCHAN
calcul &c *n* reckoning, calculation *la16-18.*
vt calculate *16.* [ME]
calculat &c *ptp* calculated *la16-20.* [*cf* eModEng]
cald *see* CA¹, CAULD
caldron *see* CAUDRON
cale *see* KAIL

caleery [kə'lirī] *adj* frivolous; vain; full of mischief *la19*, Uls.

n a silly, light-hearted person, a harum-scarum *e20*, Uls. [f ModIr dial *caleer* (*v*) caper]

calendars *see* KALENDS

calf *see* CAFF, CAUF[1]

calfat &c [*'kalfat, *-ət] *vt* make watertight, caulk *la16-17*.

~**ar** a ship-caulker *16-e17*. ~**ing** caulking *16*. [only Sc; F *calfater*, Du *kalfaten*; *cf* Eng (once) *calfret e17* and COLF]

calfin *see* COLF

calk *see* CAUK[1]

call *n* origin and meaning obscure *17*.

call *see* CA[1]

callan[1] **&c, calland &c, cullan** *20-*, WC ['kalən, -ənt; *Cai* -ənd] *n* **1** a customer *16-e17*. **2** an associate; a youth, fellow *la16-*. **3** affectionate or familiar term for an older man *20-*, *now Abd Ags*. [northern F, Du *caland*]

callan[2] *n* a girl *la18-e19*, Gall. [prob Ir; *cf* Gael *caile* a girl, dim *cailin*]

calland *see* CALLAN[1]

caller &c *la17-*, **callour &c** *la14-17* ['kalər; *C* also 'kalər] *adj* **1** *of fish, vegetables etc* fresh, just caught or gathered *la14-*. **2** *of air, water etc* cool, fresh, refreshing *16-*. **3** healthy, vigorous *la18-*. *vt* freshen, cool *19-*, *chf* NE.

as ~ as a kail-blade very cool and fresh *19-*, *now* NE. [obscure; *cf* ME *calver*]

callet[1] *n* disparaging term for a girl *la18-19*. [see SND]

callet[2] **&c** *n* a MUTCH or cap *19*. [F *calotte; cf* Eng *calotte*]

callivan *see* KEELIVINE

callour *see* CALLER

calm &c; cam &c *la16-*, **caum &c** [kɑm] *n*, only in *pl*, sometimes treated as *sing* moulds, *esp* bullet-moulds *16-*. [obscure]

calm *see* CAM

calme; cam &c [kɑm] *n*, weaving, *chf in pl* heddles *19-*, Ags. [obscure]

calp; cawp &c *la15-16* [*kalp, *kɑp] *n* **1** = *best aucht* (BEST) *16-17*, *chf* Highl. **2** a gift made by a tenant to his SUPERIOR or CHIEF in return for his support and protection *la15-16*, SW. [Sc and IrGael *colpa* a full-grown cow or horse, taken as the unit for grazing animals; *cf* ScGael *colpach* duty payable by tenants to landlords; *cf* COLPINDACH]

calsay *see* CAUSEY

calshes &c ['kalʃɪz] *n pl* boys' trousers with jacket or vest attached *la19-e20*, *chf* WC, SW. [OSc, eModEng *calsouns &c* hose, trousers; *cf* F *calçons &c* underpants]

calshie &c ['kalʃ(ɪ), 'kalʃɪx] *adj* crabbed, surly *la18-*, *now* NE. [see SND]

calumpné &c [*'kalʌmnɪ; *ka'lʌm(p)nɪ] *n* calumny *la15-16*.

calumpniat &c *ptp, v* calumniate(d) *la16-e17*. [MedL *calumpnia* (*n*) and *calum(p)niat-*, ptp stem of *calum(p)niārī; cf* Eng *calumny*]

cal3e [*'keljɪ] *n* a scale, *chf* **cal3eit** *of a horse's trappings* embroidered with scales *la16*.

cam[1] **&c** *la18-*, **calm &c** *la15, 18-20*; **caum &c** *la19-* [kɑm] *n* **1** limestone *la15-19*. **2** pipeclay *la19-*, Gen except Sh Ork. **3** slate pencil *la19-e20*.

vt whiten with pipeclay *la19-*, *now Ags Fif Lnk*. ~ **stane &c 1** = *n* 1, *16-e19*. **2** = *n* 2, *19-*, *now local Abd-Kcb*. [obscure]

cam[2] *n* the tilt or angle given to a furrow as it falls over from the ploughshare, adjusted by the setting of the coulter, *chf* **gie a fur mair** *or* **less** ~ *la20-*, NE Fif; *cf* TWEEL[1]. [appar f Eng *camber*]

cam *see* CALM, CALME, COME

caman ['kamən; *Gael* 'kaman] *n* the club or stick used in the game of SHINTY *la19-*, Hebrides Highl. [Gael]

cambreche, cambrige *see* CAMRICK

camceil ['kam'sil] *n* a sloping ceiling or roof *20-*, Stlg WC.

camsiled ['kam'sɔild] *adj* having a sloping roof *la19-*, *now* WC. [? Gael *cam* bent + CIEL; *cf* COOM[2]]

came *see* KAME

camerage *see* CAMRICK

cameral &c *19-*, NE, **gamrel** *la19-e20* ['kam(ə)rəl, 'kɛm(ə)rəl] *n* a haddock after spawning *19-*, NE. [*cf* IrGael *camramhail* dirty]

Cameron ['kamərən] **1** *also* ~ **Highlander** a soldier in *The Queen's Own Cameron Highlanders* (QUEEN) *19-20*. **2 The** ~**s** informal name for *The Queen's Own Cameron Highlanders*, *la19-20*.

Cameronian [kamə'ronɪən] *n* **1** a follower of Richard Cameron, the *Covenanter* (COVENANT); a member of the *Reformed Presbyterian Church* (REFORM) *la17-19*. **2** a soldier in the Cameronian Regiment (Scottish Rifles) raised in 1689 among the CAMERONIANS (*n* 1) or WHIGS in the west of Scotland in support of William of Orange; *now* represented only in the Territorial Army; 1786 became 26th Cameronian Regiment; 1881, linked with 90th *Perthshire Light Infantry* (PERTHSHIRE) to form The Cameronians (Scottish Rifles) *la17-*.

cammas *see* CANNAS

cammavyne *see* CAMOVINE

cammock &c; cummock *la18* *n* **1** a crooked staff or stick *16-*, *now Abd*. **2** = SHINTY *n* 1, *e19*. [eModEng *camok*, ME *cambok*, laL *cambuca*]

camovine &c, cammavyne &c ['kamovəin, 'kaməvəin, -wəin] *n* = camomile *16-*, *now* NE Ags, only Sc.

camp *vi* exert oneself *la16*.

campy bold, brave *19-20*. [eModEng *camp &c* contend, ME *campyn*, OE *campian; cf* KEMP]

campioun &c *n* a champion *la14-e17*. [ME; northern OF *campiun*]

campstarie *see* CAMSTAIRY

camrick &c *la15-*, *now Abd Fif*, **camerage &c**

16-e17, **cambreche &c** *la16-e17;* **cam(b)rige &c** *la16-17* ['kamrɪk, *-rɪdʒ, *-rɪtʃ] *n* = cambric.

camschoch *see* CAMSHEUGH

camshachle &c; camshauchle &c ['kam-ˈʃaxl, -ˈʃaxl, kəmˈʃakl] *vt, chf in ptp* distorted, bent, twisted, disordered *19-, now local Abd-Edb.* [prob Gael *cam* crooked and SHAUCHLE]

camsheugh &c *la18-, now NE,* **camschoch &c** *16;* **camsho &c** *la16-e19* ['kamˈʃux, 'kamʃəx, 'kam(p)ʃo] *adj* **1** crooked, distorted, deformed *16-e19.* **2** *fig* surly, perverse *17-, now Bnf.* [prob Gael *cam* + Sc *sheuch,* var of SHAUCH]

camsiled *see* CAMCEIL

camstairy &c, campstarie *la16;* **camsteery &c** *la19-20* [kam(p)'sterɪ, -'stɪrɪ, -'strerɪ, kəm-] *adj* perverse, unruly, quarrelsome *17-20.*

n an uproar *la19-, now Fif.* [see SND]

can¹ &c, kan &c *16-e20 n* **1** = can, a container, made of wood, earthenware etc as well as metal *la14-.* **2** *specif* = a chimney-pot, *freq* **chimley ~, lum ~** *19-.*

can² *v, pt also* **c(o)uth &c** *la14-16,* **c(o)ud** *la15-,* **cuid &c** *la16-,* **culd** *la16-17,* **quid** *la20, NE* [kud, kʌd, *unstressed* kəd; *NE* kwɪd; *kuθ]. *negative, pres* **canna** *19-, interrog* **cannin** *20-, Abd; pt* **cudna &c** *20-, interrog* **cudnin &c** *la19-, Abd* **1** = can, be able *la14-.* **2** *pt, in negative with ptp of main verb* = could not have *19-; local Bnf-Fif:* '*it coudna been better*'. **3** *as infin in pres and pt forms:* (1) *with* WILL¹ = future tense, *freq* expressing doubt or possibility *la18-:* '*nae doot ye'll can ..*'; (2) with *micht* (MAY) *20-:* '*I thocht a micht cood ..*'; (3) with *would* (WILL¹) = conditional *20-:* '*he wouldna could dae't*' = he would not be able to do it; (4) with *use to* (USE) *20-, now wLoth Kcb:* '*I didn't use tae could tak them at aa*'.

n **1** skill, knowledge, ability *17-, chf N.* **2** supernatural power, witchcraft *la18-19.*

can³ *v pt, also double pt* **c(o)uth** *la14-e16,* **culd &c** *16-e17* [*kuθ, *kud] *verse* did *la14-18:* '*to Parys can he ga*'. [orig substitution for ME *gan,* pt of *gin* (*aux verb*)]

can, canage *see* KANE

canally &c *19-, now local Bnf-Lnk,* **canaille &c** *la16,* **kinallie** *20-, NE;* **canailly &c, -zie &c** *la18-19* [kə'nal(j)ɪ, kə'nel(j)ɪ] *n* = canaille, the rabble; a mob, unruly crowd.

cancellar *n* = CHANCELLOR *16-e17.* [L *cancellārius*]

cancellat &c *vt* cancel *16.* [*cf* eModEng *cancellate*]

candavaig *n* a variety of salmon *la18-e19, Abd.* [uncertain]

candill *see* CANNLE

Candillismes, Candilmes *see* CANLEMAS

candle *see* CANNLE

Candlemas, Candlesmes *see* CANLEMAS

candy *n* = candy.

vt, ptp also **candeit** *e17* = candy *17-.*

~ bob = ~ *man, la19-, NE.* **candibrod &c** sugarcandy *20-, Abd Ags Fif Rox.* **~ glue** candy made from treacle *la19-, now Ags.* **~ man** a hawker, ragman, because he gave candy in exchange for rags etc *la19-.* **~ rock** candy in blocks or sticks *20-, now Abd Fif.*

cane *see* KANE

cangle &c ['kaŋl] *vi* wrangle, dispute *17-.* [onomat; *cf* Norw *kjangle*]

canker &c *n* **1** = canker *la14-.* **2** ill-temper *la18-, local Bnf-WC.*

v **1** *vi* fret; become ill-tempered *19-, now Abd Ags.* **2** *vt* put into a bad temper *19-, now Bnf Abd.* **3** *vi, of plants* become infected with blight *20-, Bnf Abd Kcb.*

~(i)t &c **1** = cankered *la14-.* **2** cross, ill-natured *16-.* **3** *of weather* gusty, threatening, stormy *la18-, now Bnf Abd.* **4** bent, twisted *19-, now Abd.*

~some *la19-, SW,* **cankry &c** *la18-, WC* ill-natured.

Canlemas *19-e20,* **Candilmes &c** *15-17,* **Candillismes** *la16;* **Candlesmes &c** *la16-e18,* **Candlemas** *18-* ['kanlmas, -məs, *'kanlz-] *n* = Candlemas, 2 Feb, a Scottish quarter-day *15-.*

~ ba a football match played on 2 Feb *la19-, now Bnf Kcb.* **~ bleeze** a gift made by pupils to a schoolmaster at CANDLEMAS *19, SW, S.* **~ king** title given to the boy who gave the highest money present to the schoolmaster at CANDLEMAS *la18-e20, local.* **~ term** the second or spring term in the Universities of St Andrews and Glasgow *20-.*

canlie &c ['kanlɪ, 'kʌnlɪ] *n, game* a variety of tig; the player who is 'it' *19-, Abd.*

canna *see* CAN³, CANNACH

cannabie &c [*'kanəbɪ] *n* = canopy, *esp* for a bed *16-17.* [chf Sc]

cannach; canna [*'kanə(x)] *n, also* **canna down** cotton-grass *19-, now Abd Ags Fif Arg.* [Gael *canach*]

cannas &c *la18-, now NE Ags,* **canvas &c** *la15-,* **cammas &c** *la15-e19,* **cannowse &c** *e17 n* **1** = canvas *la15-.* **2** *only* **cannas &c** *specif, agric* a canvas sheet for catching grain etc *la19-, NE.* **3** *only* **canvas** linoleum *20-, NE.*

cannas braid &c a canvas-breadth; a small patch *la18-e20.*

cannel¹ &c *n* the sloping edge of an axe, chisel or plane after sharpening *20-, now Bnf Ags Kcb.* *vt* give the wrong bevel to (the edge of the tool being sharpened) *20-, NE.* [only Sc; F *canneler* (*v*), L *canālis* (*n*) groove]

cannel² &c *n* cinnamon *la15-18.*

~ water a drink flavoured with cinnamon *17.* [ME, OF *canele*]

cannellie &c *n* **tanny ~** a kind of cloth *la16-e17.* [? F *cannelé* fluted]

cannle &c, candill &c *la14-17,* **candle** *la16-*

['kanl; *C* 'kɑnl] *n* **1** = candle *la14-*. **2** *in sing as*
collective candles; tallow, wax *la15-*, *now Abd*. **3**
a corpse candle *la19-*, *NE*.
~ **doup** a candle-end *la19-*. **candle fir** split
fir-wood used instead of candles *la18-*, *chf NE*.
~ **scheris &c** candle snuffers *16-e17*.
neither dance nor haud the ~ take no part,
refuse to participate *18-*, *now Ags*. [*cf*
CANLEMAS]
Cannogait *see* CANONGATE
cannon *n* ~ **nail** *19-20*, *S*, ~ **pin** *20-*, *Abd Ayr*
the nail or pin which attaches the cart to its
axle. [*cf* CARRON-NAIL, *garron-nail* (GARRON²)]
cannonar &c, -er *n* a cannoneer *16-e17*, *only Sc*.
cannowse *see* CANNAS
canntaireachd &c ['kʌuntaraxk] *n* chanting
of pipe music in syllables, the vocables varying
in different piping traditions (generally the
vowels representing melody notes, the consonants grace-notes); *loosely also* a written representation of this *19-*. [Gael, *lit* = chanting]
canny &c; kanny &c *18* ['kanı; *C also* 'kɑnı]
adj **1** cautious, careful, prudent, astute *la16-*. **2**
skilful, dexterous *19-*. **3** (1) favourable, lucky,
of good omen *la17-*. (2) *in negative* unnatural,
supernatural *19-*, *now wLoth Stlg*: '*this is no
canny*'; *cf* UNCANNIE. **4** *chf* ~ **man**, ~ **wife**, ~
woman a person who deals in the supernatural
la18-, *now Abd Fif*. **5** frugal, sparing *19-*: '*be
canny wi the butter*'. **6** gentle, quiet, steady *la18-*.
7 pleasant; good, kind *la17-*. **8** comfortable,
easy *19-*.
adv cautiously, carefully *la18-*.
~ **ways** *la19-*, *NE Ags*, **wise** *19-*, *now Sh Ags*
cautiously, gently.
~**ca &c** the woodworm *19-e20*, *Fif*. ~
moment &c the moment of childbirth *18-*.
~ **nanny** a species of yellow stingless bumble-
bee *20-*, *C, S*. ~ **wife** a midwife *18-*, *now Abd
Fif*. [*chf Sc*; appar f CAN²; *cf* ON *kunnigr*
versed in magic, Norw *kunnig* knowing]
Canongait, Cannogait &c ['kanən'get;
'kanə'get, &c] *n* ~ **breeks** venereal disease
la16-e18. [the former BURGH, now part of
Edinburgh]
canous &c; canos &c [*'kenəs, *'kan-] *adj*
hoary; grey-haired *15-e16*. [L *cānus*]
canse &c *vi* speak pertly, saucily, in a self-
important way *19-e20*, *Dmf*. [see SND]
cant¹ *vti* sing; tell stories *18-e19*.
n a song; a story *16-e19*.
~**ation** talk, conversation *la18-e20*, *Ags*.
cant² *n* a trick; a habit, custom *19-*, *Abd*. [perh
connected with CANT¹; *cf* CANTRIP]
cant³ &c *adj* brisk, lively, smart *la14-e16*.
canty &c *adj* **1** lively, cheerful; pleasant *18-*. **2**
small and neat *19-*, *now local Bnf-Fif*. **3** comfortable *20-*, *now Ags*. [nME (and northern
ModEng dial); *cf* LowGer *kant* lively, Du *kant*
neat, clever]

cantail3e &c, cantrail3e &c [*'kən't(r)elʒɪ] *n*
some sort of trimming for garments, *prob* lace
la16. [only Sc; obs F *canetille* lace]
cantle¹, cantell &c *n* **1** a corner, projection,
ledge *15-*, *now Abd*. **2** (the crown of) the head
of a person or animal *19-*, *now Abd*. [ME,
northern OF *cantel*, MedL *cantellus*]
cantle² *v* **1** *vti* stand or set on high *la19-e20*. **2**
vt, fig stimulate, strengthen *20-*, *Abd*. **3** ~ **up**
(1) brighten *20-*, *Bnf Abd*; (2) *vi* recover one's
health or spirits *20-*, *Bnf Abd*; (3) bristle with
anger *la19-*, *Bnf Abd*. [*cf* CANTLE¹ and Eng *cant*
tilt]
cantrag *n* a festivity to celebrate a forthcoming
marriage *20-*, *Cai*. [specif use of *contrack*
(CONTRACT)]
cantrail3e *see* CANTAIL3E
cantrip &c *n* **1** a spell, charm; magic, *chf* **cast**
~**s** *la16-*. **2** a trick, antic, piece of mischief
19-. [perh f Gael *canntaireachd*; see SND
Suppl]
canvas *see* CANNAS
caochan, keechan &c ['kixən, *'kɛx-] *n* **1** a
stream, rivulet *la19-*, *N*. **2** *distilling* fermented
liquor before it goes through the still *19-e20*.
[Gael]
cap¹ &c *la16-*, **cop &c** *la14-17*, **cope** *la14-17*;
caup *18-* [kap; *C also* kɑp; *'kop] *n* **1** a
(wooden) cup or bowl *la14-*, *now local*. **2** *only*
cop a leper's alms-bowl, *freq* ~ **and clapper**
15-16. **3** a bowl used as a measure for liquor or
grain *16-18*.
~**per &c 1** a cupbearer; a keeper of cups *16-17*.
2 a maker of wooden bowls or other wooden
articles *la19-20*, *now Abd*. **3** nickname for a late
riser *20-*, *NE*; see SND. ~**fu(ll) 1** a dishful
la17-. **2** a quarter of a PECK² *19-*, *now NE Fif*.
cappie *adj* hollow, bowl-shaped *e20*, *Ayr*. **cappie hole** *marbles* a game involving hollows
made in the ground *18-e19*. **drink out o a
toom cappie** be in want *20-*, *Bnf Abd*.
cap ale a kind of beer *19*. ~ **almery &c** a
cupboard *la15-e17*. ~**burd &c** = cupboard
la15-17. **cophous(e)** a store-room for cups or
plates *e17*.
~ **out** *e16*, **clean** ~ (**out**) *19-*, *chf NE Ags*, *chf*
as noun phr denoting the emptying of the bowl in
drinking; *cf play cop out*. **cap(pie)** (**and**)
cog(gie) *appar* a contribution paid by
carpenters to the common fund of their INCOR-
PORATION *la18*, *Gsw*. **he's as fou's** ~ **or**
staup'll mack him he is completely drunk
la19-, *Bnf Abd*. **kiss** (**a** *or* **the**) ~(**s**) drink out
of the same vessel, *usu* as a token of friendship
la18-. **play cop out** empty the cup, carouse
16. [nME (rare) *cop*, ONorthumb *copp*, ON
koppr; MLowGer, MDu *cop*, MedL *coppa*; *cf*
COUP⁴]
cap² *vi* sail, keep a course; ? drift *e16*. [obscure]
cap³ &c *vti* bend, twist, warp *19-*, *chf Ayr*.
[obscure]

cap[4] *vt, of children* grab (another child's toy) *19.*
[see SND]

cap *see* CAIP, KEP[1]

cape *vt* **caper** a privateer *la17-e19.* **caping**
la17-18, **capering** *la17* privateering. [Du,
Flem *kapen* (*v*) plunder, *kaper* (*n*) a privateer]

cape *see* CAIP

capellane &c [*'kapələn] *n* a chaplain *16.* [laL
capellānus]

caper &c [*'kepər, *kap-] *n* a piece of bread or
oatcake (AIT) with butter and cheese *la18-19.*
[Gael *ceapaire*]

caper *see* CAPE

capercailzie &c *19-,* **capercail3e** *16-e17;*
-keily &c *17-* ['kapər'kel(j)ı, -'kəil(j)ı, -'kelzı,
'kepər-] *n* the wood-grouse. [Gael *capull coille*]

capernicious &c ['kapər'nıʃəs] *adj* short-tempered, fretful, fault-finding *la19-, NE.* [confla-
tion of Eng *capricious* w next]

capernoitie &c ['kapər'noitı] *adj* = *capernoited*
2 (*la18-, now Abd*), 3 (*19-, now Abd*).
capernoited &c 1 capricious, crazy *18-, now
Abd Lnk.* **2** intoxicated, giddy *19-, now Abd Fif.*
3 irritable *la18-, now Abd Fif.* [uncertain; *cf*
CAPPIT]

capes *n pl* grain retaining some part of the chaff
or husk *la18-e19.* [f as Eng *cap, cape, cope*]

capey-dykey &c ['kepı'dəikı, 'kapı-] *n* a game
played with marbles or a ball, involving throwing. at a wall *la19-, Ags.* [see SND]

cap-house *see* CAIP

capidosé [*'kapı'dosı] *n* a kind of cap, *chf* of
velvet *16.* [*cf* ME *capados*]

capill *see* CABIL, CAPPEL

capilowe &c *vt* outdistance *e19,* Rox.
[uncertain]

capitanry &c, captanery &c [*'kap(ı)tenrı]
n a captaincy *15-e17.* [eModEng *capteinry*
(*la16*), F *capitainerie*]

capitbirne &c *n* a hood for a cloak *la15.*
[obscure]

capoosh *e20,* **capusche &c** *la16-e17* [*kə'puʃ]
n a hood. [eModEng, F *capuche*]

cappel, capill &c [*'kapl] *n* a horse, *esp* a cart-
or work-horse *15-19.* [ME *capil,* Sc and Ir Gael
capull a horse; a mare; prob ultimately f L
caballus]

capper *n* = copper *la17-e19.*

capper *see* CAP[1]

cappit &c *adj* peevish, ill-humoured, crabbed
la16-e20. [ME (once) *coppid,* f *cop* head]

capprois &c [*'kaproz, *-əz] *n* = copperas
la16-17, only Sc.

capricht *n* ? part of the dress or armour of a
horse *e16.*

caprowsy *n* ? an undergarment *e16.* [obscure]

capstride *vt* anticipate; perform a task sooner
or better than (another) *la18-e20.* [see SND]

captanery *see* CAPITANERY

caption &c *n* **1** = caption *15-.* **2** *law* arrest; a

warrant for an arrest for debt *16-19.* **3** *fig* the
acquiring of something valuable or serviceable;
a lucky acquisition *19-, NE.*

captour &c *n* a person appointed to catch or
detect offenders *la16-17.* [L *captor; cf* Eng
captor]

capusche *see* CAPOOSH

car[1] **&c, kar** *la16-17,* **ker** *la15-17* [kar; *WC*
kɑr; *ker] *n* **1** = car *la15-.* **2** a sledge, latterly
for transporting PEATS[1] or hay *la15, la18-e20*
(*SW*).
kerfull a cart-load *la15-e16.*
~ **saddle &c** a saddle designed to take the
shafts of a cart *la15-e19.*

car[2] **&c** *la16-,* **ker &c; caur &c** *la19-20* [kar,
ker, kɑr] *adj* left (hand or side), left-handed
14-.
~**ry &c** = *adj, la19-.* **corrie-fisted** left-
handed *20-.* **corrie-fister** a left-handed person *la20-, WC.* ~**ry-handed &c** left-handed
la19-.
~**-handit &c** (*la16-*), ~**-pawed** (*la19-, chf Fif*)
left-handed; awkward. [Gael *cearr* wrong, awkward; left(-handed)]

car *see* CAUR

carb &c; *vi* wrangle, quarrel *19-, Bnf Abd Fif.*
n wrangling, an argument *la19-, Bnf Abd.*
carble &c = *v, n, 19-, now Bnf Abd Fif.* [prob f
Eng *carp*]

carcage &c; carcache &c *la16-e17,* **carcish
&c** *la19-, now Sh* ['karkıtʃ, -ıdʒ, -ıʃ] *n* **1** = a
carcase *la15-, now local Bnf-Fif.* **2** a corpse
la16-17. [only Sc; ScL *carcagium la13,* var of
MedL *carcosium*]

carcake *see* CARECAKE

carcansoun &c *n* a kind of cloth *e16.* [only
Sc; ? f *Carcassonne,* the town in France]

carcish *see* CARCAGE

card[1]**; caird &c** *n* **1** = card, *orig chf* a playing-
card (*cf* CAIRT[2]) *la16-.* **2** a chart, map *17-20.* **3**
a photograph *la19-, now Abd-Fif.*
~**er** a card-player *17-e18.*

card[2] *n* some kind of fabric *e16.* [obscure]

card *see* CAIRD[2]

cardow &c [*'kar'du, *kər'du] *vi* work at a
trade illegally without being a freeman, *chf* ~**er**
one who does this; a travelling tailor or tinker
la18-20. [see SND]

care &c *n* = care *la14-.*
v **1** *vi* = care (for) *16-.* **2** *vt* care, have regard
for *la16-e17, only Sc: 'he cairis ʒow nocht'.* **3** *chf in
negative* not be reluctant, have no objections
*la16-, now Bnf Ags: 'me to spulʒie sum not spairis; to
tak my geir no captane cairis'.*
~ **bed** a sick-bed *la14-20.*
~**'s my case** woeful is my plight *19-, Abd Ags.*
~**na by** be indifferent *la18-, now Ags.* **have a
~** o watch over, protect *la19-, NE Ags Fif.*
take ~ o be a match for *la19-, NE Ags.*

carecake &c; ca(u)r- &c [*'ker'kek, *'kɑr-; *S
also *ker-] *n* a kind of small cake eaten on
Shrove Tuesday *19.* [*cf* next]

Care Sonday &c *n* the fifth Sunday in Lent, Passion Sunday *16*. [*cf* ODan *kæresöndag*, ONorw *kærusunnudagr* and Eng *carling Sunday*]

carfuffle &c *19-*, **curfuffle** &c [kar'fʌfl, kə(r)-; *Bnf* -'fʌxl] *vt* disorder, throw into confusion *la16-*.

n **1** a disorder, mess *19-*. **2** a disagreement, quarrel *20-*, *Ags Fif SW*. **3** a state of excitement or agitation; a fuss *19-*. [*car-*, intensifier, f Gael *car* a twist, turn, and FUFFLE]

cariage *see* CAIRRAGE

caribald &c *n* term of abuse for a person *16*. [obscure]

cark *n* **1** = cark, a certain weight, a load *15-e16*. **2** care, anxiety, *chf* ~ **an care** *la18-*, now *Bnf*. *vi*, *also* **kerk** *la19-*, *Dmf* complain, grumble *20-*, *now Cai Bnf Dmf, only Sc*.

carl-doddie &c *n* = CURL-DODDY 3, *19-*, *Bnf Abd Ags Fif Lnk*. [conflation w CARLE[1] 4]

carle[1] &c, **kerl** &c *la16*, *la19-20*, **karle** &c *15-e16*, *e20*; **cairl** &c *la16-* *n* **1** = carl: (1) a man, fellow *la14-*, now local *Bnf-Lnk*; (2) a man of the common people, a peasant or labourer *la14-*, now *Bnf Abd Lnk*. **2** *derog*: (1) *freq* with descriptive adj, *15-*, now *NE Fif Lnk*: '*ilk crabbit auld carle*'; (2) in apposition to an abusive noun *16*: '*glutton carl*'. **3** *attrib* male; *hence* strong, large *la16-*. **4** *chf* **kerl** a tall candlestick *19-20*, *SW*.

carlie &c *humorous, sympathetic or depreciatory* = *n* 1, *la18-*, now local *Bnf-Fif*.

the auld ~ the Devil *la19-*, *Bnf Abd Ags Fif*. **play** ~ **again** give as good as one gets *18-19*. **a stalk of** ~ **hemp** &c *fig* a tough or stubborn element *17-18*.

carle[2] *n*, *chf in pl and as* ~ **scones** (*Ags*) small cakes given to carol-singers *la19-20*. [Eng *carol*]

carline &c *15-*, **carling**, **kerlying** &c *la14-e20* ['karlɪn, 'kɛrlɪn; *Bnf also* *'kjarlɪn] *n* **1** *freq derog* a (*usu* old) woman *la14-*, now *Bnf Abd Fif*. **2** a witch *la14-*, now *Bnf Abd Fif*. **3** the last sheaf of corn; the corn-dolly made with it *20-*, now *Abd*.

~ **heather** *bell-heather* (HEATHER) *19-*, *Ags*. ~ **spurs** furze *19-*, *N*. [nME *kerling*, ON *kerling*, fem of *karl*]

carlings &c *n pl* peas, variously prepared, *appar* eaten on Passion Sunday *18-e19*. [see SND]

carmagnole &c *n* a soldier in the French Revolutionary army; *fig* a rascal *la18-e19*. [see SND]

carmele &c [*'kar(ə)'mil, *-'məil, &c] *n* the heath-pea *18*. [Gael *carra-meille*]

carmudgel &c [kar'mʌdʒəl, kər-] *vt* bash, crush, damage *19-*, now *Abd*. [*car-*, depreciatory prefix + MUDGE]

carmusche &c *n* (*16-e17*), *vti* (*la16*) skirmish (**with**). [only Sc; OF *escarmusche*]

carnaptious &c [kar'napʃəs, kər-] *adj* irritable, quarrelsome *la19-*. [*car-*, intensifier + KNAP[2] *v* 3]

carne *see* CAIRN

carneed &c ['kar'nid, 'kʌr-] *n* the runt of the litter, *chf* of pigs *20*, *Mry*. [see SND]

Carnwath-like *adj*, *also* **Carnwath** awkward; odd-looking *19*, *C*. [see SND and SND Suppl]

carolus &c *n* a French coin of Charles VIII, worth 10 silver pence *16*. [L; *cf* eModEng]

carp &c *vti* **1** = carp *la14-*. **2** *vi* produce musical sounds; sing, recite, *freq* **harp and** ~ *la15*, *19*, *latterly chf ballad*.

carpet &c *n* **1** = carpet *la14-*. **2** *in pl* carpet slippers *20-*, *Bnf Abd Ags*.

~ **bowling** *or* **bowls** indoor bowls, played on a carpet *19-*.

carpoll *n* a pole or spar *16*. [obscure]

carrant &c [ka'rant, kə'rant, ku'rant] *n* **1** an expedition, a sudden journey *la19-*, now *Kcb*. **2** a revel; an escapade; an uproar *20-*, *now Bnf Fif*. [F *courante* a dance]

carriage *see* CAIRRAGE

carrick *n* = SHINTY *n* 1, *la19-*, *Fif*. [prob Gael *carraig* a knot of wood]

Carrik &c *la15*; **Carrick**: ~ **pursuivant** &c one of the Scottish PURSUIVANTS *la15-*. [the district in Ayr]

carried *see* CAIRRY

carritch &c *n*, *freq in pl*, *Presbyterian Church* the catechism *19-*, now local *Abd Kcb*.

mither's ~(**es**) a simplified form of the *Shorter Catechism* (SHORT) *la18-20*. [only Sc; var (as *carritches*) of CATECHIS, thought of as *pl* and new *sing* formed]

carron-nail &c the nail fixing a cart to its axle *la19-*, *Abd Rox*. [perh f *Carron*, the Iron Works; *cf* CADDENNAIL, *garron-nail* (GARRON[2]), CANNON]

carry *see* CAIRRY

carry *n* a weir *la18-19*. [Gael *caraidh*]

carsackie; **cur-**, **kerseckie** &c *la19-* [kar-, kɛr-, kɪr-, kʌr-, -'sakɪ, -'sɛkɪ] *n* an overall, pinafore; a labourer's smock *la19-20*, local *NE-S*. [see SND but *cf* also Eng *cassock*]

carse[1], **cars**, **kers**(**e**) [kars, kɛrs] *n* (*chf an* extensive stretch of) low alluvial land along the banks of a river *la14-*, *freq in place-names la13-*. [see SND]

carse[2] *la18-e19*, **kers**(**e**) *15-e16* [*kɛrs, *kars] *n*, *latterly only in pl* = cress. [metath; ME *kerse*, *carse*, OE *cærse*]

carsy &c *adj* ~ **coal** a kind of coal found near Bo'ness *19-20*, *wLoth*. [see SND]

cart *n* the crab-louse; the skin-disease it causes *20-*, *Abd*.

kartie &c the crab-louse *19-*, now *Sh*. [*cf* Eng dial *cart* the shell of a crab]

cart *see* CAIRT[1], CAIRT[2]

carter *n* = charter *e17*. [only Sc; after L *carta*]

cartoush &c [*'kartuʃ] *n* a woman's short jacket or gown *la18-e20*. [F *court* short and *housse* a short mantle of coarse cloth]

cartow &c [*'kartʌu] *n* a quarter-cannon, throwing a ball of a quarter of a hundredweight (12.7 kilos) *17*. [only Sc; OFlem *kartouwe*]

cartyke &c *n or adj* used to describe taffeta *la16*. [obscure]

carvey, carvie &c *n, freq attrib* **1** = caraway *16-, local N-WC*. **2** a sweet containing caraway seed *19-, now Fif Kcb*.
carvied *adj* flavoured with caraway *19-, now Abd*.
~ **sweetie** a sugar-coated caraway seed *la19-, local NE WC*. [only Sc; F *carvi*]

cary *see* CAIRRY

cas *see* CAUSE

casar *n* a board or box for displaying bread for sale *la16-e17, Fif Edb*. [obscure]

casay *see* CAUSEY

caschelaws *see* CASHIELAWS

caschie *see* CASSIE

caschielaws *see* CASHIELAWS

cas crom; cas-chrom ['kaʃ'krom; *Gael* kas'xrʌum] *n* a crook-handled spade, a kind of foot-plough *la19-20, chf Hebrides Highl*. [Gael]

case¹ &c, **cace** &c *la14-17*, **kess** &c *la15-17 n* = case, occurrence etc *la14-*.
~**able** &c natural or appropriate to a particular case *la16-20, only Sc*.
in a ~ in a state of excitement *20-, NE*. (**in**) ~ **be,** ~ **by** in case, lest; perhaps *19-, now Bnf Abd*.

case² &c, **cace** &c *la15-17*, **kace** &c *la15-17 n* **1** = case, receptacle *la14-*. **2** a window frame; a casing *16-17*.
casit fitted with a frame (*n* 2) *16-e17*.
~ **camb** a comb kept in a case *la16-17*. ~ **windo(k)** a casement window *16*.

caser &c [*'kezər, *-ərd] *n* an emperor *15-16*. [ME *kaser*, OE *caser; cf* eModEng *Caesar*]

cash¹ *n, banking* ~ **account,** ~ **credit** a loan-system allowing credit on the surety of two guarantors up to a specified maximum, interest being chargeable only on the amount on loan at any time *18-e20*.

cash² *n, also* ~**y blaes** *mining* soft coaly *blaes* (BLAE) *la19-, now Fif*. [see SND]

cashie *adj, of vegetation* luxuriant, succulent *19, chf Dmf*. [see SND]

cashielaws &c *la18-e20, hist,* **casch(i)elawis** *la16-e17 n* an instrument of torture. [obscure]

cashti &c *n, gipsy* a stick *e20, Gall Rox*. [Sanskrit *kāshtha*]

Cashub; cassup &c [*'kaʃub, *'kasup, *-əp] *n, chf* ~ **ash(es)** a kind of wood ash used in bleaching *18*. [Polish *kaszub*, f *Kaszubja* a province of Poland near Danzig]

casnat &c *n* = cassonade, unrefined cane-sugar, *chf* ~ **suggar** *la16-17*.

cassacioun &c *n* cassation, cancellation *15*. [earlier in Sc]

cassay *see* CAUSEY

cassie &c *la16-*, **caschie** *e17*; **kaisie** &c *e20* [Sh N 'kası, 'kazı; Ork N 'kezı; Sh also 'kesı, 'keʃı] *n* a straw-basket or pannier *la16-e20, orig only Sh Ork, 19-e20 Sh-Bnf*. [Icel *kassi, kass* a basket, box, ON *kass* a case, creel]

cassie *see* CAUSEY

cassin *see* CAST

cassup *see* CASHUB

cast &c, **kast** &c; **kiest** *20-, Abd Ags* [kast; *Abd Ags also* kəist] *vti, pt also* **kist** &c *la14-e17,* **kest** *la14-19,* **kiest** &c *la16-* [køst; *C, S* kıst; *NE* *kwist; *kɛst]. *ptp also* **casten** &c, **cassin** &c *la15-*, **cuisten** &c *la19-*, **cuist** &c *e20* ['kas(t)n; 'køs(t)n, *C* 'kıs(t)n; *køst]* **1** = cast *la14-*. **2** *vt* vomit (**up**) *la4-, now Fif*. **3** (1) dig, cut (PEATS¹ etc) *15-*. (2) dig, clear out (a ditch etc) *16-, now Cai-Abd*. **4** *of animals* give birth to, *latterly esp* prematurely *15-, now local*. **5** take **in**, store, stack (grain etc) *la15-16*. **6** turn over, dismantle (a stack of grain) for airing or threshing *16-, now Ags Bwk*. **7** *vi, of bees* swarm *la16-*. **8** *vt, of a horse* throw (its rider) *18-*. **9** toss (the head) *la18-, now local NE-WC*. **10** make fast (a rope) by means of a hitch *la18-, N Kcb*. **11** throw (**off**) clothes etc *19-, now local NE-WC*. **12** sow (seed) *la19-, now local NE-WC*. **13** drop (eggs) into water for the purpose of divination *19-, chf NE*. **14** estimate, reckon, assess *15-20*. **15** *chf law* reject or oppose as illegal or improper; annul *la16-e17*. **16** *in passive* be rejected, defeated *la19-, NE*.
n **1** = cast *la14-*. **2** *lit and fig* a turn or twist *la15-, now local NE-WC*. **3** (1) one's lot, fortune, fate *la14-, now Abd Lnk*. (2) a casting of lots, a random selection; a share thus apportioned *18*. **4** an opportunity, chance (of getting something) *19-, now Abd*. **5** (1) a particular quantity (of a certain thing) *17-, now Arg*. (2) *fig* a degree, amount *la19-, now Abd Fif*. **6** a friendly turn; help, assistance *18-, now Abd Ags Fif*. **7** aspect, demeanour; appearance *la15-e20*. **8** an assessment, rating *la17*. **9** a ditch, cutting; excavation *la16-17*.
casten &c *of colours* faded *20-, local N-WC*.
~**ing 1** = casting *la15-*. **2** *in pl* cast-off clothing *16-e19*.
~ **line** the thin casting-line attached to the reel-line of a fishing-rod *19-, now Fif*.
~ **aboot** &c manage, arrange, look after *19-, now Abd Ags*. ~ **aff** &c **1** ~ **aff wi** cut oneself off from *19-, Abd*. **2** recover from (an illness) *20-, now Abd Ags Fif*. ~ **at** spurn, condemn *18-20*. ~ **something at someone** reproach someone with something *la19-, Abd Ags Fif*. ~**-awa** a waste *la19-, local Bnf-Fif*. ~**-back** a setback, relapse *la19-, now Abd Fif Stlg*. ~ **a clod at** reproach *20-, N*. ~ **the colours** perform the flag-waving ceremony at Selkirk Common Riding (COMMON) *la19-, Slk*. ~ **the cup** tap the cup prior to 'reading' the tea-leaves *la19-, now Bnf Abd*. ~ **a dash** make a great show, cut a dash *la18-, now Abd*. ~ **of one's hand** a helping hand *19-, now Fif*. ~ **oot** &c disagree, quarrel *18-*. ~ **owre** consider *la19-, now local Bnf-Stlg*. ~ **up 1** *chf* ~ **something up to someone** reproach someone with something; cast something in someone's teeth *18-*. **2**

appear, 'turn up'; befall *18-*. **3** *of the weather, sky* clear up *19-*, *now Ags*. **4** *of storm-clouds* gather *19-*, *now Bnf Abd Fif*.

castellane &c *n* one of the garrison of a castle *15-e17*. [*cf* Eng *castellan* the governor of a castle]

castellaw &c *n* a measure of flour or cheese *16*, *Arg*. [? Gael]

castellward &c [*'kastl'ward, *-'werd] *n* castle-guard, a payment in commutation of the feudal service of guarding a castle *15-e17*. [earlier in Sc]

castock &c ['kastok, 'kastək; *eLoth Renfr Ayr Slk* 'kʌstək] *n* a stalk of KAIL or cabbage *17-*, *now local Bnf-Kcb*. [KAIL + STOCK; late nME *caustocke*, ON *kálstokkr*]

casual &c *adj* **1** accidental; liable to occur *la15*, *19-*, *now Bnf Abd*. **2** = casual.

casualty &c *16-*, **casualté &c** *la15-e18*, **casualité** *16-e18* *n* **1** the aggregate of incidental items of the royal revenue *e16*. **2** *law* an incidental item of income or revenue; *specif* that due from a tenant or VASSAL in certain contingencies *16-20*. **3** = casualty.

cat¹ &c, katt &c *la14-e17, e20* (*Sh Ork*) *n* = cat *la14-*.

cattie &c *n* **1** the game of tip-cat *19-*, *now Abd Fif*. **2** a catapult *20-*, *now Fif Lnk*. **lat the cattie dee** allow a swing to come gradually to rest *20-*, *local Abd-Lnk*.

~**'s carriage** a seat formed by two persons' crossed hands *19-*, *now Abd Fif*. ~**cluke** the bird's-foot trefoil *16*. ~**'s een** the germander speedwell *la19-*, *now Lnk Kcb*. ~**'s face** a round of six SCONES *la20-*, *Kcdn nEC*. ~**'s hair** cirrus or cirrostratus cloud *la19-*, *Bnf Abd*. ~**heather** a species of heath, varying according to district *19-*, *Abd Ags*. ~**kindness** cupboard love *19-*, *now Bnf Abd Lnk*. ~**'s lick** a hasty superficial wash *20-*. **catloup** a short distance or time *19-*, *now Abd Ags Fif*. **tumble** *or* **coup** (**the**) **catma** somersault *19-*, *chf Ags*. ~**-steps** crowsteps (CRAW¹) on a gable *19-e20*, *Rox*. ~**('s)** **tail(s)** cotton-grass *la18-*, *now Abd*. ~**wittit 1** hare-brained, unbalanced *19-*, *local Cai-Kcb*. **2** spiteful; savage; short-tempered *19-e20*.

atween you an me an the cat between ourselves, confidentially *la19-*, *NE*. ~ **and bat** *20-*, *now Cai Edb Lnk*, ~ **and dog** *la19-*, *now Ags Fif* the game of tip-cat. **meet the ~ in the morning** suffer a setback, have bad luck *la19-*, *Bnf Abd*.

cat² &c *n* **1** *chf* ~ **and clay** a handful of straw mixed with soft clay used in building or repairing walls *la16-e20*. **2** a handful of straw or reaped grain laid on the ground without being put into a sheaf *19-e20*, *S*.

vt build or repair with *cat and clay* (*n* 1), *la17-e20*, *S*. [obscure]

catale *see* CATTLE

catalogue &c, cataloge &c *la16-e17* *n* **1** a register *la16-e20*. **2** = catalogue.

catband &c *n* an iron strap or bar for securing a door or gate *16-e19*. [*cat-* (obscure) + BAND¹]

catch &c, cache &c *16* [katʃ] *v, pt also* **catchit &c** *la16-*, **caucht &c** *15-*, **cotch &c** *la19-*, *local* [katʃt, 'katʃɪt, kɑxt, kotʃ]. *infin also* **caucht** *la15-e16* [*kɑxt] [prob f pt] = catch *15-*.

n **1** a hold, grasp *la19-*, *local Cai-Kcb*. **2** a sharp pain, a 'stitch' *la19-*, *local Bnf-Kcb*. **3** a knack *la19-*, *now Abd Fif*.

~**ers** *n pl* a game played with a ball, or bat and ball *20-*, *Edb Kcb*. ~**y** ready to take advantage of another *19-*, *Abd Stlg Kcb*. ~**ie-hammer** one of the smallest of a stonemason's hammers *19-*, *now Bnf Per*.

~ **kow** ? a cow-catcher *e16*.

~ **the salmond** a boys' game *la19-*. ~ **the-ten,** ~ **lang tens** a card game *la19-*.

catecheese &c, -ise ['katə'kiz, 'katə'tʃiz, 'katə'dʒiz] *vt* = catechize *la16-*.

catechis &c ['katətʃɪs, 'katədʒɪz] *n* **1** a or the catechism *la16-*, *now Bnf Abd Stlg*; *cf* CARRITCH. **2** a catechizing; *latterly also* cross-questioning *la16-*, *now Bnf Abd*. [eModEng *catechise*, F *catéchèse*, L (f Gk) *catēchēsis*]

catechise *see* CATECHEESE

cateran &c, catherane &c, katherane &c, ketharan &c ['kat(ə)rən, *'kɛt-, *'kaθ-, *'kɛθ-] *n* a *Highland* (HIELAND) marauder; a band of these *16-20*, *latterly hist or literary*. [ScL *katheranus &c*, Gael *ceatharn* a troop]

caterve &c *n* catarrh *la16*. [appar irreg var]

caterwoul; -wail ['katər'wʌul, -'wel] *vi, only in presp* ~**ing** = caterwauling *la17-*, *now Bnf-Ags*.

cat-harrow &c *n* draw (**at** *or* **in**) **the** ~ pull in different directions, thwart each other *16-e19*. [? f CAT¹]

cathead *n* an inferior kind of ironstone *la18-19*, *chf Lnk*. [uncertain]

cathel *see* CADDEL

cathel nail *see* CADDLE

catholic &c, catholik &c *la15-e17* *adj, n* = catholic *la15-*.

~ **creditor** *law* one who holds security for his debt over more than one piece of property belonging to his debtor *la19-*.

catherane *see* CATERAN

cat-hud *n* the large stone used as a back to the fire on the hearth of a cottager's house *19-20*. [? CAT¹ + HUD]

catioun *see* CAUTION

catlill *vt* punish by pressing the finger into the hollow under a child's ear *19*, *SW*. [see SND]

catter¹ &c *n, chf attrib* some kind of cloth *la16-e17*.

catter² &c *la18-e20*, **cauder &c** *19-20*, *chf Abd* *n* money, cash. [f as Eng *cater*]

catterbatter &c *n* a quarrel, disagreement *19-e20*, *Fif Rox*.

vi wrangle *19-e20*, *S*. [see SND]

catter-wurr *n* an ill-tempered person *20-*, *Bnf Abd*. [see SND]

cattiewurrie *n* a violent dispute *la19-*, *Bnf*. *vi* wrangle violently *la19-*, *Bnf*. [*cf* prec]

cattill &c *n* = KETTLE 1 and 2, *16-e17*. (ON *katl-*, stem of *ketill*]

cattle &c *la15-*, **catale &c** *la14-e17* *n* **1** = cattle *la14-*. **2** lice etc *la18-*, *now Abd Lnk*. **3** birds and beasts *in gen*, *la19-*, *now Abd*. **4** term of contempt for persons *la19-*, *local Abd-Lnk*.

cattler, cattlie a cattleman on a farm *20-*, *NE*. **~ beas(ts) &c** livestock *la19-*, *local Bnf-Lnk*. **~ bucht** *20-*, *Abd Fif*, **~ court** *20-*, *Bnf-Ags*, **~ reed** *la19-*, *NE nEC* a cattle yard. **~ creep** a low arch or gangway for cattle under or over a railway *20-*, *now Bnf*. **~ raik** a road along which cattle are driven to fairs *20-*, *Ags*.

caucht *see* CATCH

cauder *see* CATTER[2]

caudron &c *la15-*, *now local Bnf-Lnk*, **caldron &c** *la14-*; **caddroun &c** *la15-18* ['kɑdrən, 'kaðrən, *'kad-] *n* a cauldron.

cauf¹ &c *15-*, **calf &c; caff &c** *15-* [kɑf; *Rox also* kav] *n* = calf *la14-*. *vi* [kɑf; *Kcb also* kav] = calve *la16-*. **~ie's cheese** a soft cheese or curd made with the milk of a newly-calved cow *la20-*, *Abd Per*. **~ grund &c** *la19-*, *now Ags Fif*, **~ kintra &c** *19-* the place of one's birth and early life. **~'s lick** a cow-lick *20-*, *local Cai-Kcb*. **~ ward** an enclosure for calves *la18-*, *now Bnf Abd*.

cauf² &c *n* = calf (of the leg) *19-*.

cauf *see* CAFF

cauk¹ &c *la15*, *18-*, **calk** *16-17*, **kalk** *20-*, *Abd Ags Per* [kak] *n* = chalk, lime *la15-*. *vt* **1** mark, treat or wash with chalk *la15-*. **2** (1) mark up with chalk (something to be remembered or paid), chalk up *20-*, *now Bnf Abd Fif*. (2) make (someone) pay dearly *20-*, *now Bnf Abd*. **~ and keel** chalk and ruddle, as used by fortune-tellers *18-e19*.

cauk² &c [kak] *vt* = calk (a horse), fix a guard on or sharpen (a horseshoe) to prevent slipping *19-*, *Abd Fif*. **~er, cacker &c** *la19-* a calkin: (1) a horseshoe treated as in *v*, *la18-*; (2) an iron rim fixed on a clog or shoe to minimize wear *20-*, *Abd SW*.

cauker¹ &c ['kakər] *n* a dram of liquor, a bumper *la18-*, *now local N Fif*. [see SND]

cauker² &c; caker [*NE Ags* 'kakər; *Abd Fif* 'kekər] *n* a stroke on the palm of the hand from a strap *la19-*, *now Abd Ags Fif*.

caul &c [kal(d)] *n* a weir or dam *la16-*, *chf SW*, *S*. [obscure]

cauld &c, cald &c, cowld &c *la19-*, *local*; **cold** *17-*, **caul** *la19-*, *NE* [kal(d); *Ork Cai Ross-Mry Arg Uls* kʌul(d)] *n* = cold *la14-*, in place-names *la12-*. *adj* **1** = cold *la14-*. **2** *of land* stiff, clayey *la19-*. **~it, ~ed** *adj* suffering from a cold *19-*, *now local NE-Lnk*. **~rif(e)** [' ~-rɪf, ' ~-rəif] *adj* **1** *lit*

cold, causing or susceptible to cold *18-*. **2** *fig* cold in manner; indifferent; lacking in cheerfulness *la17-*, *now NE Ags Fif*. **3** lacking in religious zeal *la17-e18*. **~ comfort** inhospitality *19-*, *now local NE-Kcb*. **~ gab** a period of stormy weather at the beginning of May *20-*, *Abd Fif*. **~ iron 1** *fishermen's* taboo, *exclam* used to ward off possible bad luck when one of the prohibited words has been uttered *19-*, *local Sh-Ags*. **2** used as a solemn pledge by schoolchildren *e20*, *Abd Ags Kcb*. **~ kail het again** re-heated BROTH or other food; *chf fig*, *of a stale story etc*, *19-*. **~ morality** a sermon lacking fervour *20-*. **~ seed** late oats or peas *la18-e20*. **~ steer** sour milk or water and oatmeal stirred together *19-*, *now Abd Ags*. **~ straik** neat WHISKY, as opposed to toddy *e19*. **~-warned** cold in manner, cold-blooded *la19-*, *now Fif*. **~-water** apathetic, indifferent *la19-*, *now Abd*.

caum *see* CALM, CAM

caup *see* CAP¹

caur &c *16-*, **cair &c** *la16-17*; **car &c** *la17-20* [kar] *n pl* calves *chf NE Ags*; for *sing see* CA³. [reduced f *calver*, laOE *calfur*, pl of *calf &c*]

caur *see* CAR²

caurcake *see* CARECAKE

causa, causais *see* CAUSEY

cause &c *n* = cause *la14-*. *vt* **1** = cause *la14-*. **2** *with infin*, *eg* **~ make something** = have something made *la16-e18*: 'cause build a loft'. *conj*, *also* **cas &c** *la19-*, **kis &c** *la19-* because *la16-*, *now local Bnf-Edb*. **in the hour of ~** at the time appointed for the trial *la15-e19*.

causey &c *17-*, **causa(y)** *la15-*, **causé** *la14-e15*, **calsay &c** *15-e18*, **cassie &c** *17-*, **cassay &c** *16-e19*, **casay &c** *la16-17* ['kazi, 'kasi] *n* **1** a paved area, a roadway, street, pavement, *latterly chf* cobblestones *la14-*. **2** the paved or hard-beaten area in front of or around a farmhouse *la19-*, *NE Lnk Uls*. **3** *only* **cassie &c** the cobbled part of a BYRE or stable *20-*, *Bnf Abd*. *vt* pave *16-*. **causyer, calsier** a road-maker *17-e19*. **~ clash** street-talk; gossip *19-*, *now Abd Fif*. **casey croon** = *crown of the ~*, *la19-*, *local Abd-S*. **~ paiker &c** a street-walker *16-e20*. **~ saint** a person who is well-behaved and pleasant when away from home *19-*, *now Ags Lnk*. **~ stane &c** a paving- or cobblestone *la16-*. **crown of the ~** the middle of the road, *freq fig* a public, conspicuous, creditable, respectable or dominant position, *eg* **keep the crown of the ~** *17-*. **kiss the ~** 'come a cropper', meet defeat *la18-*, *now Fif*. [obs or dial in Eng]

caution &c *15-*, **catioun &c** *16-17*; **caition &c** *la16-e20* ['keʃ(ə)n] *n* = caution: **1** *law* security; bail *la15-*; **2** one who stands surety *16-*.

vt **1** = caution *17-*. **2** guarantee; wager *la19-e20*.

~er &c = *n* 2, *16-*. **~ry, ~arie &c** suretyship; the obligation entered into by a *cautioner*, *la16-e20*.

cave¹ &c, caif &c *la14-e16* [kev] *n* **1** = cave *la14-*. **2** a cellar, dungeon; a wine-cellar *la15-17*. **3** a case for holding bottles of wine or spirits *16-e18, la19-e20* (*Sh*).

cave² &c *16-*, now *Bnf*, **keave &c** *17-*, now *Bwk Wgt* [kev] *v* **1** *vi* topple, fall **over** *16-e20*. **2** *vti* toss (*chf* the head, horns) *la17-*, now *Bnf Bwk Wgt*. **3** knock, push *19-e20*.

cavie &c *vi* **1** rear, prance *e19, NE*. **2** walk affectedly *18-e19*. [see DOST]

cave³ *vt* ~ **the corn** separate the grain from broken straw etc *19-*, now *Bnf*.

cavings &c broken straw as in *v, 19-*, now *Bnf*. [f CAFF]

cavel¹ &c, cavill, kavill &c, kevill ['kevl] *n* **1** a piece of wood used in casting lots *la15-e16*. **2** a lot cast *16-*, now *Mry Abd*. **3** division or assignment by lot *la12-e16*. **4** a division or share of property, *orig* assigned by lot *la15-e19*. **5** one's fate; chance *la16-18*.

vt divide or assign by lot *la15-e19*.

be ~is by lot *16-17*. **cast ~s &c** draw lots as in *n* 1 and 2, *la15-*, now *Mry Abd*. [nME *cavel*, MDu *cavele*, MLowGer *kavele*; *cf* ON *kafle*]

cavel² &c, kevel &c [*'kevl] *n* a low, rough fellow *16-e20*. [chf Sc; ME *kevell*]

cavell *see* KEVEL³

cavey *see* KEAVIE

cavie¹ &c ['kevi] *n* a hen-coop *16-*, now *Ags-Lnk*. [OFlem *kavie*]

cavie² ['kevi] *n* the game of prisoners' base *la19-*, now *Fif*. [see SND]

cavie *see* CAVE²

cavill *see* CAVEL¹

caw *see* CA¹

cawandar *n* some kind of entertainer *e16*.

ca waw, ca way *see* COME

cawk *see* CACK

cawp *see* CALP

cawpable *adj* = capable *19-*, *NE Ags Fif*.

cedar &c *n* = cider *la15-e18*.

cedent [*'sidənt] *n*, *law* a person who assigns property to another *la16-18*. [L *cēdent-*, presp stem of *cēdere* grant, concede]

ceeliehoo *see* SEIL

ceepher, seefer ['sifər] *n* a person of no significance, an impudent or empty-headed person *19-*, *local Abd-Rox*. [var and extension of Eng *cipher*]

ceevil *adj* = civil *19-*.

ceilidh *20-*, **kailie &c** *19-20, chf Uls* ['keli; *Uls* also 'kelji] *n* **1** *orig* an informal social gathering among neighbours, with or without singing, playing instruments, story-telling etc, spontaneously performed by some or all of those present; a visit, chat, gossip *19-*, *Highl*. **2** an organized

evening entertainment (in a hall, hotel etc) of Scottish music etc, with some at least of the performers engaged in advance *20-*.

vi visit, chat, gossip *20-*, *chf Highl N Uls*.

kailier a person who outstays his welcome *e20*, *Ross Inv Uls*. [Gael *céilidh*]

celdre *see* CHALDER

cellarie *see* SELLARIE

celsitude &c [*'sɛlsɪtød] *n*, *chf as title* **his** *etc* highness, majesty *la15-e17*.

censement *see* SENSEMENT

censor, censour *16 n* **1** = censor *16-*. **2** title of an official in a university or school, *usu* the person who called the roll or kept the attendance register (still used at George Heriot's School, Edinburgh) *la16-*.

centiner &c, sentiner [*'sɛnt(ɪ)nər] *n* a hundredweight *16-17*. [Ger *Centner &c*]

central *adj* = central.

C~ Region a REGION formed from the former county of Clackmannan and parts of the former counties of Perth, Stirling and West Lothian *la20-*.

centreis, sentrice &c; centries &c [*'sɛntriz, *-ɪz, *-ɪs] *n pl* the timbers used to support an arch in the process of building *16-e17*. [eModEng *centries*, *la17*; ME *cynter*, F *cintre*, MedL *cintrum*]

centrell &c, sentrell [*'sɛntrəl] *n* = CENTINER *e17*. [only Sc; altered form]

centries *see* CENTREIS

ceptna ['sɛptnə] *prep* = except, save *20-*, now *Bnf Abd*. [shortened f Eng *except* + NA²]

cerse *see* SEARCH¹

certain &c, certane &c *la14-e17*; **serten &c** *16 n* **1** certainty, truth *la14-e18*. **2** a definite but unspecified (1) number **of** (persons or things) *15-e17*; (2) quantity **of** (something) *la15-16*.

adj = certain *la14-*.

adv = certain, certainly *la15-e16*.

~ sure absolutely certain *la19-*, *local NE, EC*.

certaint &c *adj* = certain *17-*, *local Bnf-Fif*. [see SND]

certane *see* CERTAIN

certie &c *19-*, **certis &c** ['sɛrti, 'sɛrtiz] *adv*, *interj* = certes, assuredly *la14-*, now *local Abd-Lnk*.

(by) my &c ~ = prec, *esp* expressing surprise or emphasis *19-*, *Gen except Sh Ork*.

Certificate *n*, *secondary education* **~ of Sixth Year Studies**, *also colloq* **SYS** a state examination at a more advanced level than the Higher Grade examinations (*see* HIGHER); the certificate awarded to the successful candidates, introduced 1968. **(Higher) Leaving ~** a certificate awarded for proficiency in certain subjects or groups of subjects on the results of examinations conducted annually by the Scottish Education Department from 1888 to 1961 in secondary schools in Scotland at the end of the secondary course, replaced in 1962 by next *la19-20.* **Scottish Certificate of Education, SCE 1** the various examinations ie *Highers* (HEICH), *O Grades* (ORDINAR *adj* 4 (2)) and ~ *of Sixth Year Studies,* replacing prec since 1962. **2 the SCEs** *colloq* these examinations *la20-.* [see *Intermediate Certificate* (INTERMEDIATE), *Standard Grade* (STANDART)]

certification &c, certificatioun *la15-e17 n* **1** = certification *la15-.* **2** *law* a warning of the penalty to be inflicted for non-compliance with an order, *chf* **with** ~ (**that**) .. introducing the penalty clause *la15-.*

certify &c *vti* **1** = certify *la14-.* **2** warn *16-e17, only Sc.*

certiorat(e) ['sɛrʃərɛt; *'sɛrtɪorat] *ptp, vt, chf in ptp* certified *la16-19.* [L *certiōrāt-,* ptp stem of *certiōrāre*]

certis *see* CERTIE

cesnat *see* SESNIT

cess [sɛs] *n* **1** a tax: (1) the king's or land tax *la17-e20;* (2) a local tax *la18-, now Abd Ags Fif;* (3) *in pl* rates and taxes *in gen, la19-, now Bnf.* **2** an exaction of any kind; a tribute *18-, now Bnf.* **3** *of persons* a burden (to another) *19-, now Bnf. vt* tax *18-, now Bnf.* [*cf* Eng]

cessio bonorum ['sɛsɪo bɔ'noɪʌm] *law* a process whereby a debtor could escape imprisonment if he surrendered all his means and was innocent of fraud *la19-e20.* [L = the surrender of one's goods]

cessioner, cessionar &c [*'sɛsɪɔnər] *n* a person to whom a cession of property is made *la15-e18, only Sc.*

cessioun(e) *see* SESSION

cessone *see* SAISON

chack[1], chak *la15-16,* **check, chek** *16 n* **1** = check *la15-e18.* **2** a groove or notch cut to receive an edge or serving as a check, a rabbet *la16-.* **3** *only* **check** a door-key *la19-, now Stlg. vti* **1** = check *la15-.* **2** *vt* make a CHACK (*n* 2) on (a board etc) *19-.* **3** *only* **check** rebuke, reprove *la16-.*

chak reel &c a reel, *appar* with a check or catch for measuring the thread *17-e19.* **chakwache &c** a patrol *la14-e17, only Sc.*

chack[2], chak *v* **1** *vt* snap shut; bite *16-, now Lnk Kcb.* **2** *vi* make a clicking noise; *of the teeth* chatter *16-, now Abd.* **3** *vt, also* **check** catch (*eg* fingers in a door), hack, chop *19-, now Fif Edb. n* **1** *also* **check** a cut or hack; a bruise, nip *la19-, now Fif Lnk Kcb.* **2** a snack *19-.*

chackart &c *n* **1** the stonechat; the whinchat; the ring-ouzel *19-, Bnf Abd Lnk;* see also *stane chack* (STANE). **2** term of endearment or affectionate reproof *la19-, Bnf Abd.* **chackie mill &c** *n* the death-watch beetle *la19-, now Abd.* [onomat]

chack[3] &c *n* = check, checked fabric *la19-, now Bnf Abd Stlg Lnk.*

chackie *n* a striped cotton bag used by farm servants for carrying their clothes *20-, NE.* ~**it** = checked, TARTAN *19-, now Bnf Abd Fif.*

chackert &c, chakkerit &c *la16-e17 adj* = chequered *la16-, now NE.*

chack-purse &c *n* = SPORRAN *20-, NE.* [see SND]

chacks *see* CHUCK[2]

chad &c *n* gravel *18-, now NE.* [uncertain]

chadders *see* CHATTERS

chader *see* CHALDER

chafer *see* CHAFFER

chaff[1] *vt* **1** = chafe, rub, wear *18-, NE Fif.* **2** *baking* knead or mould (the individual loaves) *la19-, now Ayr.*

chaff[2] *vt* heat (wheat) by damp *e16.* [ME *chaffe,* var of *chauf &c* > ModEng *chafe*]

chaffer &c *16-e17, 19,* **chafer &c** *la15-e17,* **choffer &c** *la16-17, e20 n* **1** = chafer, a chafing-dish *la15-19.* **2** a portable grate or stove used in a corn-kiln, as a heater etc *18-e20.*

chaffie *n* a chaffinch *la19-, local.*

chafferon; schaffroun *n* an ornament worn by ladies *16.* [obscure. OED *shaffron*]

chaffery &c *n* merchandise *la15-e16.* [earlier in Sc]

chaft[1] &c *n, chf in pl* ~**s 1** *also* shaft *19-, Sh Bwk* jaws *15-.* **2** cheeks *18-, now NE Kcb.* **big-~ed** = big-jawed *la19-, now Bnf Abd.* ~ **blade 1** the jaw-bone *16-.* **2** the cheek-bone *19-.* ~ **tooth** a molar *19-, chf Fif.* [nME; OE *cēafl,* ON *kjaptr*]

chaft[2] *n* = shaft (of a spear etc) *16.*

chaip &c, chape &c *vti* = escape *la14-e19.* [chf Sc; nME *chape* (once), aphetic f ESCHAPE]

chaipel &c *la16-,* **chapel &c, cheppell &c** *16-17 n* **1** = chapel *la14-.* **2** the royal or an ecclesiastical chancellery *15-16.* **3** a Roman Catholic or (*local*) a Scottish Episcopal church *18-.*

chapell bed ? a canopied bed *17.*

chairge &c *16-,* **charge &c; cherge &c** *16 n* **1** = charge *la14-.* **2** an expense, a cost *la14-.* **3** *only* **charge,** *law* an injunction issued under warrant of the SIGNET to compel *specif* an heir to a debt-encumbered estate or other debtor to act in relation to the debt or to obey the DECREE of a court *18-, only Sc.*

vti **1** = charge *la14-.* **2** press heavily upon; charge in battle *la14-16.* **3** send with a commission or errand *la14-15.* **4** order or commit **to ward** *or* **prison** *la15-16.* **5** chaff (a person) *20-, SW, S.*

chargeand *adj* burdensome, oppressive *la14-e16.* **charger 1** an accuser, plaintiff *la16-17.* **2** a person who employs a CHARGE (*n* 3), *esp* a creditor in trying to recover his money *18-19.* **3 chargeour** an appliance for charging a gun *la15-e16.*

under all payne and ~ used *to emphasize a command, la15-e16.*

chairter *see* CHARTER

chaistifie *see* CHASTIFY

chak *see* CHACK[1], CHACK[2]

chakker *see* CHEKKER

chakkerit *see* CHACKERT

chakmait &c *n* = checkmate *16*.

chalance, chalange *see* CHALLENGE

chalder &c, celdre &c *15-e16*, **chelder &c** *15-e16*; **cha(w)der &c** *la15-19* ['tʃadər; ***'tʃald-, ***'tʃɛld-] *n* a dry measure of capacity **1** *in sing* (1) *of grain* = 16 BOLLS *la14-*, *now Bnf Abd Fif*; (2) *chf of salt, lime, coal etc* a variable quantity, *usu* between 20 and 64 imperial bushels *15-19*. **2** *uninflected in pl after numerals etc*, *la15-17*. [northern eModEng = 1 (2); ? OF *chaldere* a measure, L *caldāria*]

chalf *n* = CAFF *la17*. [anglicized var]

challance *see* CHALLENGE

challender &c *n* a maker of coverlets *la16-e17*. [only Sc; ME *chaloner*, F *chalon*]

challenge &c, **chalange** *la14-17*; **chal(l)ance &c** *la14-e17*, *only Sc n* **1** = challenge *la14-*. **2** a calling to account *la14-15*. **3** a summons by death *19-*, *Bnf Abd*. *vt* **1** = challenge *15-17*. **2** summon or invite defiantly *15-e16*. **3** reprove, find fault with *la19-*, *local Bnf-Kcb*.

challop &c *n* = shallop, a kind of large boat *16-e17*.

chalmer *see* CHAUMER

chalmerlane *see* CHAMBERLAIN

cham &c *vt* bite, chew *19-e20*, *SW, S*. [ME]

chamberlain &c, chalmerlane &c *16-e18*, **chamerlane &c** *15-e17*, **chawmerlane &c** *15-e16* [*'tʃemərlen, *'tʃamər-] *n* a steward: **1** *title* one of the chief officers of the royal household, *esp* ~ **of Scotland** *la14-e17*; *see also* LORD; **2** *in gen* the FACTOR of an estate etc *15-*, *now Arg*. ~**ry &c** the office of CHAMBERLAIN *la15-e18*. ~ **aire** *15-e16*, ~ **court** *16-e17* the circuit court held by the CHAMBERLAIN.

chamer *see* CHAUMER

chamerlane *see* CHAMBERLAIN

champ¹ &c *vt* trample; crush, pound, mash *la18-*, *now Bnf C, S*. *n* **1** a stretch of muddy trodden ground *19-e20*, *S*. **2** mashed potatoes *la19-e20*, *Uls*. ~**ers** *la19-*, *Edb Lnk Kcb*, ~**ies** *19-*, *now Bnf Kcb*, ~**it tatties** *19-*, *local* = *n* 2. [prob Eng *champ* munch]

champ² *n* **1** = champ, the field in a heraldic shield *la15*. **2** a raised or overlaid pattern on a rich cloth *16*. ~**it** *adj*, *of cloth* so patterned *la15-e17*.

champart &c *n*, *law* champerty *14-17*. [only Sc; OF]

chance &c *n* **1** = chance *la14-*. **2** a casual or fortuitous event or circumstance *la14-15*. **3** *chf in pl* tips, perquisites *la18-*, *local Bnf-Lnk*. *vti* = chance *16-*. **chancy &c** *adj* **1** *latterly chf in negative* unfortunate, unlucky *16-*, *only Sc*. **2** *in negative* not to be relied on, dangerous *19-*, *local Bnf-Lnk*.

chancellar &c *adj* belonging to the chancel of a church *15-16*. [only Sc; MedL *cancellarius*]

chancellor *18-*, **chancellar &c** *15-17*, **chanceller &c** *14-17*, **chancellour &c** *la16-e18*, **chanclar &c** *la15-17*, **chancler &c** *16-e18*, **chanslar &c** *15-17 n* **1** = chancellor *15-*. **2** the highest officer of the Crown and chief legal authority, *freq* ~ **of Scotland** *15-17*. **3** the foreman of a jury *la15-*.

chancery *n* **1** an office, *orig* issuing *brieves* (BRIEF) directing an inferior judge to try a specified issue with a jury; *latterly* dealing with the SERVICE of heirs or the recording of SERVICES etc *19-*. **2** = chancery.

chandler &c *16-*, **chandelare &c** *la15-e17*, **chandeler &c** *16-e17*, **shandeller** *e16*; **chanler &c** *16-e18 n* a candlestick, chandelier *la15-e18*. ~**-chafted** lantern-jawed *18-*, *Abd Fif*. [chf Sc and nME *chand(e)ler &c*, AF *chandeler*, OF *chandelier*]

chang *n*, *verse* a ringing sound *la18-e20*. [imit]

change &c, **chenge &c** *la14-e17*, **cheenge &c** *19-*, **chynge &c** *la16-* [Sh Abd-Fif tʃin(d)ʒ; *Cai Nai-Abd C* tʃəin(d)ʒ] *n* **1** = change *15-*. **2** (1) exchange, trade *la15-*. (2) custom, business, patronage *19-*, *now NE*. **3** = ~**-house** *17-19*. *vti*, *also* **chaunge &c** *15* **1** = change *la14-*. **2** exchange *la14-*, *now local NE-EC*. **3** *of food* deteriorate, go bad, go off *20-*, *N*. ~**ing &c** *adj* **1** undergoing or causing change *la15-17*. **2** *specif of fabric* showing different colours in different aspects or lights *la16-e17*. **chyngin ba** a sweet that changes colour as it is sucked *20-*, *Mry Ags*. ~**-house** an inn, alehouse *17-*, *local Abd-Lnk*. ~**-keeper** an innkeeper *18-e19*. ~ **one's breath** have a drink *20-*, *local Bnf-Kcb*. ~ **one's feet** put on dry shoes and stockings *la19-*, *local Bnf-Lnk*. ~ **oneself** change one's clothes *18-*, *Gen except Sh Ork*.

chanler *see* CHANDLER

channel &c ['tʃanl; *C* 'tʃanl] *n* **1** = channel *la15-*. **2** *specif* a gutter *16-*, *now Ags*. **3** *also* **channer** shingle, gravel *la16-*, *local Abd-Lnk*. *v*, *curling* (CURL) play at curling, *la19-e20*. ~ **stane** a curling-stone, *la18-*, *now Fif Lnk Kcb*.

channer &c *la14*, *la18-*, *now Kcb*; **chawner &c** *la18-*, **chunner &c** *la19- vi* grumble. [prob onomat]

channer *see* CHANNEL

channery *e17*, *la19*, **chanounrie &c** *la15-17*, **channorie &c** *la16-e17*, **chanré &c** *16-e17*; **chanonry** *20-*, *in place-names* ['tʃanənrɪ, *'tʃan(ə)rɪ] *n* = canonry.

chanslar *see* CHANCELLOR

chansoune &c *n* a song *la15-e17*. [F *chanson*; *cf* eModEng *chanson*]

chant &c *vti* **1** = chant *la15-*. **2** chatter pertly *19-e20*. **chanter &c** *n* **1** = chanter *15-17*. **2** (1) the double-reeded pipe on which a bagpipe melody is played *la18-*. (2) a separate pipe with a weaker reed used for learning and practising bagpipe fingering.

chanty *n, slang* a chamber-pot *la18-*. [unknown]

chan3e &c [*'tʃenjɪ, *'tʃenjɪ] *n (la16-17), vt (la16)* = chain. [var of CHEN3E, w vowel infl by Eng *chain*]

chap¹ *n* **1** = chap, a fellow *la18-*. **2** a lover *20-, N Fif Kcb*.

  chappie &c 1 a little boy *la19-*. **2** *affectionate, familiar* = *n* 1, *18-*.

chap² *n* the threshing-floor *20, NE*. [perh f CHAP³]

chap³ &c, shap *la17-, now Sh-Ross n* **1** a knock, blow *16-*. **2** *specif* a stroke of a clock or bell *la16-*. **3** a stroke, turn (of work) *la19-, Bnf Abd Ags*. **4** a swell, choppiness (of the sea) *la19-, now Sh Ags*.
  vti **1** knock, strike: (1) *in gen, la16-e20*; (2) *of a clock, la16-, Gen except Sh-Cai*; (3) with a hammer, as in a smithy *la19-, local Cai-Kcb*; (4) *curling* (CURL) strike away (a stone) *la19-, local Cai-Lnk*; (5) *dominoes or card games* tap on the table as an indication that one cannot play at one's turn *20-*. **2** *vi* tap at a door or window *la16-, now local Ork-Kcb*. **3** *mining* signal by means of a striking apparatus *la19-, now Fif*. **4** *vt* grind (sand) small *la19-, now Lnk Kcb*. **5** mash (vegetables) *18-*. **6** chop *la18-, now local Bnf-Lnk*. **7** choose, select; pick sides *la18-, now NE-Stlg*. **8** strike a bargain with; agree to or ratify (a bargain) *la19-, now Abd Ags Fif*.
  chapper *n* **1** a beetle for pounding *20-, Bnf Abd Ags*. **2** a door knocker *20-, Bnf Abd Arg*.
  chapper-up a person whose job is to wake people by banging on their doors *20-, chf Dundee Gsw*. **~ping-stick 1** a stick etc for striking with *18-, now local Bnf-Lnk*. **2** a potato-masher *la19-, Sh-Ross*. **~pit tatties** mashed potatoes *19-, now Sh Ork N*.
  ~ and chuse make a choice *18-, now Bnf Abd*. **~ hands** shake hands *17-, now Stlg*. **~ (someone) in aboot, ~ in (someone's) taes** take (a person) down a peg, snub *la19-, Bnf Abd*. [Sc var of CHOP]

chape &c *n (la15-e17), adj (17-)* = cheap.
  be chape *or* **cheap o** *or* **on** get off lightly with (something); serve (someone) right *19-*: '*ye've got your fairin, an I maun say I think ye're cheap o't*'.

chape *see* CHAIP
chapel *see* CHAIPEL
chapellanry *see* CHEPLANE
chapin *see* CHOPIN
chaplanry *see* CHEPLANE
chappie *see* CHAP¹
chappin *see* CHOPIN
chaps &c; chips *20-, NE vt* **1** pick out, choose *19-, Bnf Abd Stlg*. **2** *specif* choose (sides for a game) *la19-, local Bnf-Kcb*.
  ~ me I claim, I prefer *la19-, local Bnf-Kcb*. [prob f CHAP³]

chaptane *n* a captain *e16*. [only Sc; *cf* OF *chapitain*]
chapterly &c *adj* having or belonging to an ecclesiastical chapter *17.*
  adv, also **cheptourly &c** as a chapter, in full chapter, *freq* ~ **gadderit &c** *16-e17*. [only Sc]
char &c *n a or on* ~ = ajar *16-18*. [ME *char* a turn, return, OE *cerr*]
charbukyll *n* a fabric used for church vestments or cloths *e15*. [obscure]
charet *see* CHARRIT
charge *see* CHAIRGE
charity &c *16-*, **charité &c** *la15-e16*, **cherity &c** *15-*, **cherité &c** *la14-16*, **chirity &c** *la16-, now NE* ['tʃɛrɪtɪ; *NE* 'tʃɪrɪtɪ] *n* **1** = charity *la14-*. **2** a small additional amount given to a purchaser, *esp* of grain *la15-18*.
  cheriteit &c with a CHARITY (*n* 2) added or given in addition *la16-18*.
chark *see* CHIRK
charlie *n, joc* a chamber-pot *la20-, NE Ayr*. [*cf* Eng slang *jerry, mickey*]
charrit *la19-*, **charet** *la16*, **cherret &c** *17 n* a carriage. [ME *charett*, OF *charrette*]
charter &c, chartour &c *la15-17*; **chairter &c** *la16-e17 n* = charter *14-*.
  vt put in possession (**of** lands) by a charter *15-e16*.
  ~our &c a Carthusian *la15-e16*.
  ~ hous &c a room for the keeping of charters *la16, only Sc*. **~ kist, ~ chist** a chest for the keeping of charters *16-17, only Sc*.
chase &c *n* **1** = chase *la14-*. **2** haste, hurry *la19-, local Bnf-Fif*.
  vti **1** = chase *la14-*. **2** hurry, run at speed *20-, now Bnf Fif Stlg*.
  chaser &c 1 a pursuer (in battle) *la14-e15*. **2** a ram with imperfectly-developed genitals *la16-, now Cai Kcb*. **chasie 1** *marbles* a variety of the game *20-, local NE-Ags*. **2** the game of tig *20-, local*.
chassal *see* CHESWELL
chasteeze &c [tʃa'stiz] *vt* = chastise *la19-, now Ags*.
chastify; chaistifie &c *16* [*'tʃɛstɪfaɪ] *vt* chastise, castigate *16-20*. [OF *chastifier*, laL *castificāre*; eModEng (once) *la17*]
chasty &c; chestee &c *e16* [*'tʃɛstɪ, *'tʃɛstɪ] *vt* = chasty, reprove; chastise *la14-e16*.
chat¹ *n* **1** = chat. **2** impudence, impertinent talk *la19-*.
chat² &c *n* a snack; a morsel *19-, NE*.
  vt bite, chew *19-, NE*. [see SND]
  ~tle *vt* nibble *19-, now Abd*.
chat³ *n* a call to a pig *la19-, NE*. [*cf* CHATTIE and CHATTY-PUSS]
chat⁴ *n* **1** a small haddock *20-, now Bnf*. **2** a small potato *20-, now Bnf Ayr*. [see SND]
chat⁵ *vt* ~**tit &c** chafed, frayed *19-, now Bnf*. [see SND]
chat⁶: **ga ~ three** *etc* expression of contempt *e16*. [uncertain]

chate *see* CHEAT

chathers *see* CHATTERS

chatter[1] *vt* = shatter *la17-, chf NE.*

chatter[2] *vt, chf* ~**ed &c** nibbled; frayed, tattered *la18-, now NE.* [frequentative of CHAT[2] or CHAT[3]]

chattering-bite, -piece *etc n* = **chitterin bit** (CHITTER) *20-, local Abd-Kcb.*

chatters *e20, Bnf Abd eLoth,* **chathers** *e20, local Mry-Fif* ['tʃaðərz], **chadders** *e20, Bnf-Ags,* **shatters** *20-, chf Cai-Ross n pl* iron staples in a rudder-post into which the rudder is fixed.

chattie *n* a pig, boar *la19-, Bnf Abd.*

chatton &c *n* the collet of a ring *la16-e17.* [only *Sc; F chaton*]

chatty-puss *n* a call to a cat *19-, now Bnf Abd Fif.* [perh *F chat* + *Eng puss; cf* CHAT[3] and CHEET]

chaud mellé &c, -mella &c [*'tʃad 'mɛlɪ] *n, chf* **of** *or* **from** (**sudden**) ~ **of** a *murder* committed in the heat of the moment *la14-e20.* [only *Sc; OF* = heated affray]

chaudpis *see* JAWPISH

chaumer &c, chawmer &c, chalmer &c *la15-20,* **chamer &c** *15-20* ['tʃamər; *'tʃɛmər] *n* **1** = chamber *la14-.* **2** a private room, *orig* a bedroom, *latterly also* the parlour *la14-.* **3** *specif* a sleeping place for farm workers *19-, chf NE.*

~**it &c** closeted, shut up *16-19.* **chalmirleir** a chambermaid *e16* [perh *erron* for *chalmerer*].

~ **cheild &c** a young attendant; a valet *16-.* **chalmer glew** sexual activity *la15-16.*

chaunge *see* CHANGE

chaunt *n* = chant *19-.*

chauve *see* TYAUVE

chaveling *see* SHAVE

chaw[1] **&c** *vt* **1** *also* **chow** [tʃʌu] = chaw, chew *16-.* **2** provoke, vex; make jealous *19-, now local Ags-Kcb.*

n **1** *also* **chow** = chew *19-.* **2** a disappointment, snub; a cutting retort *20-, now Bnf Abd Fif.*

chawl &c *vi* eat noisily or listlessly *19-, SW.*

~**some** causing envious disappointment, galling *la19-, now Lnk.*

~**-throu** a toilsome attempt *20-, Bnf Abd.* ~ **one's words** mumble *20-, Bnf Abd.* **look like** *etc* **a chowed mouse &c** have a debauched or worn-out appearance *la19-e20, chf S.*

chaw[2] *n* = jaw, a lecture, reprimand *20-, N.*

chaw *see* HAW[1]

chawder *see* CHALDER

chawl *see* CHAW[1]

chawmer *see* CHAUMER

chawmerlane *see* CHAMBERLAIN

chawner *see* CHANNER

chay *interj* a call to cows to calm them *la19-e20, Uls.*

chean *see* CHEEN

cheap *see* CHAPE

chear *see* CHEER[1]

cheat &c *la17-,* **chete** *15-16,* **chate &c** *20-, chf NE,* **chet** *20-, local* [tʃit; *N nEC Kcb* tʃet] *vt* **1** = cheat *16-.* **2** *specif, in 1 pers* (*passive or impersonal*) = I'm very much mistaken *19-, local: 'he's a hamely chiel yon, or I'm cheated'; 'it cheats me gin the candidate dinna fin oot'.*

n = cheat *15-.*

~**ry &c** *n* **1** escheat(s) *la15-16, only Sc.* **2** cheating, deceit, fraud *la17-.* **3** *attrib* fraudulent, deceitful *e19.*

chate-the-belly *etc* an insubstantial kind of food, *eg* puff pastry *20-, now Bnf Fif.*

cheats &c *n pl* sweetbreads *18-e19.* [see SND]

check *see* CHACK[1], CHACK[2]

cheek *18-,* **cheke &c** *la14-17 n* **1** = cheek (of the face) *la14-.* **2** the side of anything, *esp* of a door, gate, fireplace *la14-.*

~**-warmer** a short-stemmed tobacco pipe *20-.* ~ **in wi** court the favour of *la19-, NE.* ~ **up** cheek, use insolent language to *20-, now Ags Stlg.* ~ **up till** make up to, make amorous approaches to *la19-, local Cai-Kcb.*

cheekaside &c *adj* askew *18-e20, NE.*

cheen *la19-,* **chene &c** *la14-16,* **cheyne &c** *la14-e17;* **chine &c** *17-, now NE,* **chean** *la16-e18* [tʃin; *NE also* tʃəin] *n* (*la14-*), *vt* (*20-*) = chain *Gen except Sh Ork.* [*cf* CHENƷE]

cheenge *see* CHANGE

cheeny *see* CHINA

cheep[1]**, chepe** *e16 vi* **1** *of a bird etc* = cheep, chirp *16-.* **2** speak softly, whisper; make a plaintive sound *la19-, now local.* **3** *of inanimate objects* squeak, creak *19-, chf N.*

n **1** *chf in negative* not a whisper, hint, word *19-, Gen except Ork Sh.* **2** a light kiss *la19-, local C.*

~**er** = *n* 2, *la19-, local C.*

keep a quiet ~ be silent *la19-, now Abd.* **play** *or* **say** ~ *chf in negative* not make a sound, remain silent *la18-, now Fif.*

cheep[2] *v* **cheepin shoppie** a shebeen *la19-, Ags Fif.* [see SND]

cheer[1]**, chear &c** *la14-17,* **chyar** *la15-e17,* **chyre** *16-;* **shire &c** *la16-e18,* **cheir &c** *la14-17,* **scheir &c** *la16-e18* [tʃir; *sEC, S* 'tʃəi(ə)r; *Bwk also* 'ʃəi(ə)r; *'tʃiər; *'tʃaɪ(ə)r, *ʃir] *n* = chair *la14-.*

draw, pull *or* **tack in one's** ~ **an sit down** acquire affluence without any effort of one's own *la19-, local Cai-Per.*

cheer[2]**, chere &c** *n* (*la14-*), *vt* (*la16-*) = cheer. **cheerer** *n* a glass of spirits; a toddy *la18-e19.* **cheerie pyke** a tasty morsel, a treat *20-, Bnf Abd.* **cheerisome** *adj* cheerful, merry *la19-, now Sh Loth WC.*

cheese[1] **&c, cheis &c** *la15-17 n* **1** = cheese *la15-.* **2** the receptacle of the thistle *20-, local Abd-Lnk.* **3** *spinning* a bobbin without flanges which when full resembles a cheese *la20-, Ork Fif Ayr.*

~ **bandages** wrappings for cheese while it is being cured *20-, now Kcb.* ~ **bauk** a board or rafter on which cheeses mature *19-, now Abd*

Lnk. ~ **cloots** wrappings for cheese while it is in the cheese-press *20-*, *now Abd Lnk Kcb.* ~ **stane** a stone worked with a screw for pressing cheese *20-*, *now Abd.*

~-an-breid the first green shoots on *esp* hawthorn hedges *20-*, *now Fif Kcb*; cf *bread-and-cheese* (BREID). **hung** ~ cheese made by suspending the curds in a cloth *la18-*, *now NE.*

cheese² *n* **say** ~ *in negative* not mention, keep quiet about something *20-*, *local Cai-Fif.* [see SND]

cheese *see* CHUSE

cheesie *adj* nonsense word applied to bats in a children's rhyme *la19-*, *Ags.*

cheet *n* a cat; a call to a cat *19-*.
cheetie-pussy = *n*, *20-*. [*cf* CHATTY-PUSS]

cheetle, chittle *vi* chirp, warble *19-*. [*cf* Eng dial *cheet* and eModEng *chit* chirp]

cheeve [ʃiv; *Ags also* tʃiv] *n* = sheave, a pulley-wheel *20-*, *N.*

chefe *see* CHIEF

chefftane *see* CHIFTANE

cheir *see* CHEER¹

cheis *see* CHEESE¹

chek *see* CHACK¹

cheke *see* CHEEK

chekker; chakker *n* **1** the annual audit of royal revenues; the royal exchequer or court of account *la14-17*, *chf Sc.* **2** = chequer *15-17.*
~ **compt** an account laid before the audit or exchequer *16-e17.* ~ **hous** the house occupied by the exchequer *16-e17.*
((the) **Lordis**) **auditouris of** (**the** (**king's**)) ~ those appointed by commission under the *Quarter Seal* (QUARTER) to hold the audit and constituting the court of exchequer to hear cases relating to the royal revenues *la15-e17.*

cheld *see* CHIELD

cheldbed lare *see* CHILDBEDLAIR

chelder *see* CHALDER

chelleis &c *n* = chalice *la14-16*, *only Sc.*

chemer [*tʃɪˈmir, *ˈtʃimər, *ˈtʃɪmər] *n* = chimer, a loose upper robe *la14-e17.*

chemis [*tʃɛˈmis, *ˈtʃɛmis] *n* the principal dwelling, manor, mansion of an estate *15-e17.* [OF *chemois* f *chef més* chief mansion; *cf* CHYMMIS]

chemlay *see* CHIMLEY

chene *see* CHEEN

chenge *see* CHANGE

chenʒe [*tʃinjɪ, *ˈtʃiŋ(j)ɪ; *also* *ˈʃinjɪ, &c] *n* (*la14-17*), *vt* (*la15-16*) = chain. [*cf* nME *cheny* and CHEEN]

chep *see* SHIP

chepe &c *n* = sheep *la15-e17.* [ME]

chepe *see* CHEEP¹

cheplane &c *n* = chaplain *la15-17.*
~**ry** *16-e17*, **chapellanry** *la15-e17*, **chaplanry** *15-17* a chaplaincy *only Sc.*

chepman *n* = chapman *la15-17*, *as personal name 14-e16.*

cheppell *see* CHAIPEL

cheptour &c *n* = chapter *la15-17.*

cheptourly *see* CHAPTERLY

cherarchy &c [*ˈtʃɛrartʃɪ] *n* = hierarchy *la15-16.*

chere *see* CHEER²

cherge *see* CHAIRGE

cheriot &c [*ˈtʃɛrɪot] *n* = chariot *16-e17.*

cheris *see* SHEAR²

cherité, cherity *see* CHARITY

cherk *see* CHIRK

cherret *see* CHARRIT

cherry-coal *n* a type of shiny, freely-burning coal *19-*, *now Fif.* [uncertain]

chese *see* CHUSE

cheseb *n* = chesabill, chasuble *e16.*

chesell *see* CHESWELL

chesin *see* CHUSE

cheson; chessoun &c [*tʃɛˈzun, *ˈtʃizən, *ˈtʃezən] *n* **1** = chesoun, occasion *la14-15.* **2** objection, exception, demur, *as* **without** *or* **but** ~ *15-16*, *only Sc.*
vt find fault with, blame, accuse *la15-16*, *only Sc.*

chess &c *n* a window-sash, -frame *18-*, *now Ags Stlg Lnk.* [eModEng *chasses* (*pl*), OF *chasse*]

chessart &c; chesser, chisset &c [ˈtʃɛsər(t), -ət, ˈtʃizə(r)t] *n* a cheese-vat, -press *18-*. [Eng *cheese* + *-art*; *cf* KAISART]

chessoun *see* CHESON

chestane *see* CHESTON

chestee *see* CHASTY

chester *n* ~ **barley** *or* **bere** a variety of barley *la18-*, *now Ags.* [obscure]

cheston, chestane &c *n* a chestnut *17-e18.* [ME; OF *chastaigne*]

cheswell *18-e19*, **chesell &c** *la17-19*, **chassal** *la19-*, *NE-Lnk*, **chisell &c** *19-20* [ˈtʃasl; *ˈtʃeswəl, *ˈtʃɛsl, *ˈtʃɪsl, *ˈtʃɪzl] *n* a cheese-mould, -press *la17-*.
the ~ **one was staned** *or* **made in** one's original social class *18-19.* [only Sc; Eng *cheese* + *well*]

chet, chete, chetry *see* CHEAT

cheuch *see* TEUCH

cheveron &c [*ˈtʃivrən, *ˈtʃɪvrən] *n* kid-skin; a kid-glove *la16-e19*, *latterly arch.* [see SND]

Cheviot [ˈtʃiviət] *n* a breed of sheep *la18-*. [f the *Cheviots*, the range of hills on the Scottish-English border]

chew &c *interj* a reprimand to a dog *19-e20.* [*cf* Eng *shoo*]

cheyne *see* CHEEN

chice *see* CHUSE

chick *n* a clicking noise, *esp* one made to encourage horses etc *20-*, *local Bnf-Kcb.*
vi click as in *n*, *19-*, *now Abd Fif.* [onomat]

chickenweed; chickenwort &c *n* = chickweed *19-*. [obs in Eng]

chickie-mellie &c [ˈtʃɪkɪˈmɛlɪ; *Ags* -ˈmɑlɪ] *n* a boys' game or trick *20-*, *chf Ags*; see SND. [prob CHICK + MELL²]

chief &c, chefe &c *la14-e17* *n* **1** = chief *la14-*. **2** *specif* the head of a CLAN, *kindred* (KIN) or feudal community *15-*; *cf* CHIFTANE.

adj **1** = chief *la14-*. **2** intimate, friendly, 'thick' *la19-*. [see SND]

chieftain *see* CHIFTANE

chield &c *la16-*, **cheld &c** *la14-e17*; **chiel &c** *18-* [tʃil(d); *Sh Cai* ʃild] *n, pl also* ~**er** *16*, ~**erin**(g) *la16-e17* **1** = child *la14-*, *now local*. **2** *also* **childe** *e20*, *literary* a lad, (young) man, fellow *la15-*. **3** a young woman *la18-*, *now Fif*.
the Auld C~ the Devil *20-*, *now Abd Fif*. [*cf* CHILD]

chiffer &c *n* = cipher, a secret mode of writing *la16-e17*. [only *Sc*; F *chiffre*]

chiffin &c *n* a particle, crumb, fragment *20-*, *Abd*. [see SND]

chiftane &c *la14-e17*, **chefftane &c** *15*; **chieftain &c** *16-* ['tʃiften; *'tʃıften, *'tʃɛf-] *n* **1** = chieftain *la14-*. **2** *specif* a CLAN chief *la16-*; *cf* CHIEF *n* 2.

child [tʃəil(d); *chf Abd* tʃıl; *tʃıld; *tʃild] *n, pl* **childer** *la14-*, *now Abd Stlg*, **childreine** *16-17*, *only Sc*, **child(e)ring** *16-17*, *only Sc* ['tʃıldər, 'tʃıldrın] **1** *also* **chile &c** *16-20*, *latterly chf Abd*, **tsill &c** *la19-e20*, *Bnf-Abd* = child *la14-*. **2** *in pl* the common sailors or hands on a ship *15-16*. **3** *in pl* fellows, people *la16*.
chillie &c = *n* 1, *e20*, *Abd*.
one's ~**-ill** the pains of childbirth *la14-e16*. [*cf* CHIELD]

childbedlair &c *16-e17*, **cheldbed lare &c** *la15-16* [*'tʃəild'bɛd'ler; *tʃild-, &c] *n* = childbed. [Eng *childbed* + LAIR[1]]

childe *see* CHIELD

childer, childering, childreine, childring, chile, chillie *see* CHILD

chilp *n* a chirp *20-*, *Bnf Abd*.
vi chirp, squeak; cry in distress or querulously *20-*, *Bnf Abd*. [onomat; see SND]

chilpy &c *adj* = chilly *la19-*, *Bnf Abd*. [altered form, perh w infl f prec]

chim *vt* make up to (a person) *20-*, *NE*.
~ **in wi** agree with fawningly *la19-*, *Bnf Abd*. [appar var of Eng *chum*; *cf* CHUM]

chimley &c, **chimlay** *16-*, **shimley &c** *la16-e17*, *e20* **chimbley &c** *la17-*, **chemlay &c** *17*, **chum-** *la19-* *n* **1** = chimney *16-*, *now local Cai-Stlg*. **2** a grate, hearth, fireplace *la16-*, *now Abd*.
~ **brace** a mantelpiece *17-*, *now Ayr*. ~ **cheek** the side of the fireplace or grate *19-*, *now Abd Fif*. ~ **heid 1** a chimneytop *la19-*, *local Bnf-Kcb*. **2** a mantelpiece *la19-*, *local Abd-Fif*. ~ **lug** the fireside *la18-*, *now chf NE*. ~ **neuk** the chimney corner *19-*, *now Cai-Fif*. ~ **rib** a bar of a grate *19-*, *Abd Ags Fif*.

china, cheeny &c *la19-*, *Gen except Sh Ork* *n* **1** = china. **2** a china marble *20-*, *now Abd Fif Kcb*.

chincough &c ['tʃınkox] *n* = kink cough (KINK[2]) *la18-*, *now Cai Fif Arg*. [eModEng; Eng dial *chink* catch the breath in laughing or coughing + *cough*]

chine *see* CHEEN

chingle *18-*, *chf Bnf Abd*, **chingill &c** *15-18*, **jingle** *la18-*, *now Gall Uls* ['tʃıŋl; 'dʒıŋl] *n* = shingle.

chingly &c gravelly, pebbly *la18-*, *Ork Bnf Abd*.

chinney beardie *see* BEARD

chip &c *vti* **1** = chip. **2** *vi, of buds or seeds* break open; germinate *la15-e19*. **3** *vt, chf curling* (CURL) knock, strike, *freq* ~ **the winner** avoid the guard stones and strike what can be seen of the winning stone *20-*.

chippit tipsy *20-*, *Bnf Abd*. **chippy &c** a marble; a variety of the game of marbles *20-*.

chips *see* CHAPS

chirawk [tʃı'rɑk] *n, vi* = squawk *20-*, *Abd Kcdn*. [onomat]

chirity *see* CHARITY

chirk &c; chark, cherk &c *v* **1** *vi* make a harsh strident noise *19-*, *now Abd Fif Kcb*. **2** *vti* gnash, rub (teeth, gums) **together** *19-*, *chf NE SW*. **3** *vi* chirrup *19-e20*.
~**er** the house-cricket *la19-e20*, *chf Dmf*. [ME *chirkin*, OE *cearcian*; *cf* CHORK]

chirl[1], **churl** *vi, n* chirp, warble, murmur *17-e20*. [onomat]

chirl[2] **&c; churl &c** *n, in pl* **1** kindling wood *la19-*, *now Bnf*. **2** small coal *la19-*, *now Fif-Edb*.

chirle &c [tʃʌrl] *n* = CHOLLER 1, *19-*, *now Ork*. [perh metath f *chuller* (CHOLLER)]

chirm &c *n* a bird's call, chirp *16-e20*.
vti **1** warble, murmur *16-e20*. **2** fret, complain *17-e20*. [ME *chirme*, OE *cirman*]

chirple *vti* twitter *19*, *N*. [frequentative of Eng *chirp*]

chirry &c *n* = cherry *16-*, *now Bnf*.

chirt &c *v* **1** *vt* squeeze, press, squirt *17-e20*. **2** *vi* squirt, spurt *16-e20*.
n **1** a squeeze, hug *19-*, *chf SW*. **2** a small quantity *19-e20*, *chf Rox*. [onomat]

chirurgian &c [*tʃı'rʌrdʒ(ı)en, *-(ı)ən, *tʃi-] *n* = surgeon *16-17*.
chirurgenair = *n, la16*. ~**rie** surgery *la16-17*, *only Sc*. [*cf* SURRIGINE]

chisell *see* CHESWELL

chisset *see* CHESSART

chit *n* a packed lunch *19-*, *now Arg Kcb*. [see SND]

chitter *vti* **1** chatter, shiver (with cold etc) *la16-*, *now local Abd-Kcb*. **2** *only verse* flicker, flutter *e20*. **3** *of birds* twitter *la18-*, *local Bnf-Kcb*.
chitterin bit *or* **bite** a snack eaten after bathing *19-*. ~**-chatter** = *v* 1, *la19-*, *now Abd*. [prob var of Eng *chatter*]

chittirlilling *n* term of abuse *e16*. [obscure]

chittle *vt* nibble, gnaw *19-*, *SW*.

chittle *see* CHEETLE

chitty wran &c *n* the common wren *la19-*, *now Arg*. [see SND]

chiver &c [*'tʃıvər] *vi* = shiver *16-19*.

chizors ['tʃızərz] *n pl* = scissors *17-e20*.

chock[1] *vti* = choke *la16-*.

~it suffering from quinsy *la19-*, *chf NE*; *cf*
CHOKIS. **~ roap** a flexible appliance for clearing an obstruction in an animal's throat *20-*, *N*.
chock² &c *n* = shock, a set of sixty pieces
17-e18.
choffer *see* CHAFFER
choice, choise *see* CHUSE
choke *see* CHOWK¹
chokis; chowkkis &c [*tʃoks, *tʃʌuks] *n pl* **1**
quinsy *e16*. **2** the JOUGS *la16*. [eModEng
chokes quinsy, f Eng *choke* (CHOCK¹)]
choll *n* = jowl *la15-e16*. [ME]
choller &c *19-*, **chollare** *e16*; **chuller**
la18-e19 *n*, *chf in pl* **1** the jowls, a double chin
e16, *la18-*, *now Abd Dmf*. **2** the gills of a fish
la18-e20, *SW*, *S*. **3** the wattles of a cock *20-*,
SW, *S*. [see SND]
chookie *see* CHUCK¹
choop &c *19-e20*, *SW*, *S*, **jupe** *19-*, *Dmf Rox* *n*
the hip of the wild rose. [Icel *hjupa*; OE *hēope*]
choose *see* CHUSE
chop *vti* **1** = chop, strike *la15-*. **2** = CHAP³ *v* 1
(*16-e18*, *chf Sc*), 2 (*16-17*).
n = chop *17-*.
~ handis = chap hands (CHAP³) *17*.
chop *see* SHOP
chopin, chap(p)in &c *la16-e20*; **choppin &c**
16-19 ['tʃopən, 'tʃapən] *n* **1** *liquid measure* a
SCOTS half-pint (approx = 0.85 litre) *15-*, *now*
Abd Stlg. **2** a container of this capacity *la15-16*.
~ stoup &c a drinking vessel holding a CHOPIN
16-17. [only Sc; ME *chopin*, of the French liquid measure, OF *chopine*]
chopman *n* = shopman (a shopkeeper) *or* chapman *la16-17*.
choppin *see* CHOPIN
chore *vti* steal *la19-*, *local E*, *S*. [gipsy]
chork [tʃork; Bwk ʃork] *vi* squelch *18-e20*. [var
of CHIRK]
chose *see* CHUSE
chouk *see* CHOWK¹
choup [tʃʌup] *n*, *in negative* not a cheep, not a
single word *20-*, *Abd*. [see SND]
chow &c [tʃʌu] *n* **1** SHINTY 1, *la16-19*, *NE*. **2**
SHINTY 3, *19-20*, *NE*. [? NF *choule* a ball]
chow *see* CHAW¹, CHOWL¹
chowk¹, chouk &c; choke &c [tʃʌuk; Ork
Arg Uls tʃok; Abd also tʃuk] *n*, *chf in pl* the
cheeks, jaws *la15-*.
~ band the jaw-strap of a bridle *16-*, *chf NE*.
[*cf* ON *kjálki* a jaw-bone, Norw *kjake* a cheek,
Norw dial *kôk* jaws, the neck]
chowk² &c [tʃʌuk] *vti* = choke *19-e20*, *SW*, *S*.
chowkkis *see* CHOKIS
chowl¹ &c, chow [tʃʌu(l)] *n* = jowl, *chf* **cheek
for ~** cheek by jowl, close together, very
friendly *18-*, *now local Cai-Kcb*.
chowl² &c [tʃʌul] *vt* **~ one's (chanler-)chafts**
make a face *19-*, *chf Ags*. [see SND]
chowp [*?tʃʌup] *vi* ? talk indistinctly *e16*, *only Sc*.
chows [tʃʌuz] *n pl* small coal, nuts *la18-*, *local*
Ork-Kcb. [uncertain]

chree *see* THREE
Chrissenmas,   Christinmes &c
['krɪsə(n)məs; *Abd also* 'kɪrsən-] *n* Christmas
la16-, *now Bnf-Ags*. [ME *Chrystenmasse*]
christen *see* KIRSTEN
Christmas ['krɪsməs] *n* a Christmas present,
Christmas box *la19-*: '*there's yer Christmas*'. [*cf*
NEW-YEAR]
chuck¹ *n* = chick, a chicken *19-*, *local Bnf-Fif*.
~ie &c *18-*, **chookie** *20-*, *C* = *n*.
chuck², juck *20-*, *now Fif* *n* **1** a pebble (or *occas*
a marble) *19-*. **2** *in pl*, *also* **chacks** *20-*, *local EC*
Kcb a game involving throwing and catching
pebbles etc *19-*; *cf five stanes* (FIVE).
~ie, *also* **~ie stane &c 1** = *n* 1, *19-*. **2** *in pl*
= *n* 2, *19-*. [prob f Eng *chuck* throw]
chuck³ *n* food *20-*, *local C*. [see SND]
chucken *n* = chicken *la18-*, *chf NE*. [*cf*
CHUCK¹]
chucks mei ['tʃʌks 'məi] = chaps me (CHAPS)
20-, *S*.
chuff *n* a churl, a rude, coarse person *la15-19*.
[ME]
chuffel *n* = shovel *la17-e18*. [eModEng *chofell*]
chuffie &c *adj* fat(-faced), portly *la18-19*.
~-cheeked &c *esp of a child* chubby-cheeked
18-20. [prob f CHUFF]
chug(gle) *see* TUG
chuller *see* CHOLLER
chum *vt* accompany as a friend *20-*. [*cf* colloq
Eng noun]
chumbley, chumlay, chumley *see* CHIMLEY
chump *n*, *esp of boys or children* a thickset person
la19-, *Bnf*. [*cf* Eng = a thick lump (of wood)]
chun &c *n* a sprout, *chf* of a potato *19-*, *chf SW*.
v **1** *vt* remove the sprouts from (potatoes) *19-*,
chf SW. **2** *vi*, *of potatoes* sprout *la19-*, *SW*.
[OE *cinu* a fissure, *cīnan* (*v*) crack]
chunner *see* CHANNER
church &c *n* = church *la16-*, *in place-names* *12-*
(see DOST *kirk*).
~ officer = kirk officer (KIRK) *la19-*.
C~ of Scotland title of the established
reformed church in Scotland, for most of its history presbyterian *17-*. [*cf* KIRK]
churl *see* CHIRL¹, CHIRL²
churr muffit &c *n* the whitethroat *la19*. [see
SND]
chuse &c (*v* (*16-e20*), *n* (*la16-17*)), **choise &c**
la15-e18; **choice &c** *la17-* [*v* tʃøz, tʃez; *Abd also*
tʃois; *n* tʃois; *tʃøz] *vt*, *also* **chese &c** *la14-e17*,
cheese &c *la19-*, *chf NE*, **chyse &c** *la19-*, *NE*,
EC [tʃiz; *NE*, *EC* tʃaiz], *ptp also* **chesin &c**
la15-16 [*'tʃizən], **josyne &c** *la15-16*
[*'dʒozən] = choose.
n, *also* **chose &c** *la14-16*, **chice &c** *la19-*, *Abd-*
Lnk, **choose** *17* [tʃois; *NE* tʃais; *tʃoz; *tʃøz;
Abd also *tʃaiz] = choice.
chyar *see* CHEER¹
chye &c *n* the chaffinch *20-*, *NE*.
chymmis &c [*tʃɪ'mis, *'tʃɪmɪs] *n* **1** = CHEMIS

la14-e16. **2** a chief town or city *15-e16.* **3** a mansion, house *e16.* [OF *chymois,* var of *chemois* (> CHEMIS)]

chynge *see* CHANGE

chyre *see* CHEER[1]

chyse *see* CHUSE

ciel [*?sil] *n* a ceiling *19, SW, S.* [F; *cf* Eng and SYLE]

cieté &c [*'sitɪ] *n* = cité, city *la15-e17.*

cietenar &c a citizen *16.* [only Sc]

ciete3an *see* CITE3AN

cinner &c *la17-,* now *NE Fif Ayr,* **shinner &c** *19-,* now *NE;* **shunner &c** *19-,* now *NE, SW,* **schinder** *la16,* **shunder** *la19-e20* ['sɪnər, 'ʃɪn(d)-, 'ʃʌn(d)-] *n* = cinder.

circuat [*'sɪrkjuat] *ptp* encircled *la16-e17.* [MedL *circuāt-,* ptp stem of *circuāre*]

circue [*'sɪrkju] *vt, chf in pt, ptp* **circuit** [*also* *'sɪrkwɪt]: **1** *pt and ptp* encircled *la15-16;* **2** *only ptp* encircled (**with**) *la15-e17.* [ME *sircuit* ptp; F *circuir* (v), L *circuīre,* ptp stem *circuit-*]

circuilie &c *adv* ~ **inquerit** asked in turn *e16.* [only Sc; f L *circu-; cf* CIRCUE]

circule [*sɪr'køl] *vt, chf in ptp* **circulit**: **1** encircled, surrounded (**with**) *15-16;* **2** placed round in a circle *16.* [ME has *vi*]

circumduce *vt* **1** = circumduce, carry round *e16.* **2** *law* declare or claim (the term for *leading* (LEAD) a proof) to have elapsed *la16-19.*

circumferat &c *ptp* surrounded, encircled *la16-.* [only Sc; irreg f L *circumferre*]

circumscriptioun &c *n* an encircling inscription *15-16.*

circumstance &c *n* **1** = circumstance *la15-.* **2** elaborateness of detail, *chf* **with** ~ *15-16.*

circumstantiate, circumstantiat *ptp, adj* = circumstantiated, circumstanced *la17-e19, chf Sc.*

circumvene &c *vt* circumvent *la15-18, chf Sc.*

Cistercien *n* Cistercian *16-e17.* [only Sc; F]

Cisteus &c; Systeus &c *n* Cistercian(s) *15-e16.* [OF *Cisteux* (now *Cîteaux*) the site of an abbey near Dijon, the mother-house of the order]

citat &c [*?'soitat] *ptp* cited, summoned *la16-e17.* [L *citāt-,* ptp stem of *citāre*]

cite3an &c, cite3en &c [*'sitɪjen, *-jən &c] *n* a citizen *15-16.* [only Sc; OF *citeyain*]

cite3our &c [*'sitɪjur, *-jər] *n* a citizen *la15-e16.* [only Sc; irreg var of OSc *cete3ener,* f CITE3AN]

citiner &c, citionar *16, only Sc* [*'sɪtɪnər, *'sitɪnər] *n* a citizen *la15-e17.* [nME *cyttenere,* OF *citien*]

citisinar &c *n* a citizen *la16-e17.* [only Sc; OSc, ME *citisain &c*]

cituate *see* SITUATE

city *n* **1** name for some of the (*esp* larger) BURGHS which were or had been episcopal seats (see OED) *15-.* **2** = city.

C~ Chambers the municipal offices of Edinburgh, Glasgow, Dundee and (*formerly*) Perth *20-.* ~ **guard** = *town guard* (TOUN) *la17-e19.*

The Four Cities collective name for Edinburgh, Glasgow, Dundee and Aberdeen *20-.*

clabber &c, glabber *n* mud, clay, mire *19-,* now *local Fif-Uls.*

~(**e**)**d** covered with mud or dirt *20-,* now *Kcb.* [Gael *clàbar*]

clabbydhu &c ['klabɪdu] *n* a large variety of mussel *la19-, WC.* [prob f Gael *clab* an enormous mouth + *dubh* black]

clachan &c; clauchan *la16-* ['klaxən] *n* **1** a hamlet, village *la16-, in place-names la15-.* **2** a village inn *la19.* [Gael]

clack[1] *la18-,* **clak** *la16 n* **1** (1) a sharp impact *la16.* (2) = clack, a sharp sound. **2** the clapper of a mill *19-,* now *Ags.* **3** *also* **cleck** gossip, chatter, insolence *19-.*

vi **1** = clack, make a sharp noise *la16-.* **2** *also* **cleck** gossip, talk loudly and idly *18-.*

clack[2] **&c** *n* a kind of treacle toffee *la19-e20.* [see SND]

clack *see* CLAIK[3], CLAIK[4]

clackan &c *la19-,* **clekane &c** ['klakən, *'klɛkən] *n* **1** a shuttlecock *la16-18.* **2** a wooden bat or racquet *la19-.*

cleckinbrod &c = *n* 2, *18-e19.* [obscure]

clackin *see* CLECK

clad *adj* **cladding &c** cladding boarding; lining with such *18-; cf cleeding* 3 (CLEED).

claddach ['kladəx] *n* the gravelly bed or edge of a river *la19-e20, Mry SW.* [Gael *cladach* a shore, beach]

claes &c *la15-,* **clothes &c** *16-;* **claise &c** *la16-e19,* **clathes &c** *la14-* [klez; *NE also* kləɪz] *n pl* = clothes *la14-.*

~ **beetle** a mallet for beating clothes when washing them *la19-, chf NE, SW.* ~ **pole 1** a clothes-prop *la19-.* **2** a fixed pole to which the clothes-line is attached *la19-.* ~ **rope** a clothes-line *20-.* ~ **screen** a clothes-horse *19-.*

claff; claft *n, curling* (CURL) a piece of iron studded into the ice and acting as a foot-grip *la19-, Lnk.*

tak the ~ *curling* come between the two *guards* (GAIRD) *20-, Lnk.* [f as Eng *cleft, cleave*]

clag &c, cleg &c *la19-e20, Sh Uls vt* **1** besmear (**with** mud, clay etc) *la15-,* now *chf NE.* **2** clog, clot, stop up *la15-, local N-C.*

n **1** *law* an encumbrance on or claim against property *la16-e19.* **2** a fault, cause for reproach *la16-e19.* **3** a lump or mass of clay, mud, snow etc *19-,* now *local NE-C.* **4** a quantity of any kind of soft (sticky) food *19-, local NE, C.*

claggum &c treacle toffee *la19-,* now *Bnf Abd.*

claggy, cleggy *e20, Sh Uls* sticky, glutinous; *also transf of weather* producing heavy sticky soil *19-.* **clyager, clagger &c** ['kl(j)agər] = *v* 1, *20-, chf Cai.* [(chf northern) eModEng]

claif *see* CLEAVE

claik[1] **&c, clake** [klek; *NE also* kljak] *n* **1** a shrill, raucous bird-cry *la15-,* now *chf NE.* **2** *also in pl* gossip *19-, Bnf-Fif.* **3** a gossip *19-, Bnf-Fif.*

vi **1** *of birds* cry *16-, chf NE.* **2** *freq of children* cry incessantly and impatiently *19-e20, chf NE.* **3** gossip, chatter *la18-,* now *Bnf-Fif.* [prob imit; *cf* ON *klaka*]

claik² *vt* besmear, dirty (**with** something sticky) *19-, NE.* [*cf* CLAG]

claik³ &c, **clack** *la17 n* the barnacle, the crustacean *la17-e20, Sh Ork Abd.* [obscure; *cf* next]

claik⁴ &c; **clack** *la16-e19 n* the barnacle-goose *la15-19.* [obscure; *cf* prec]

claikin see CLECK

clair¹ &c *adj* **1** = clear *la15-.* **2** prepared, ready *16-e20,* latterly *chf Sh,* only *Sc.*
adv completely, clearly *la15-,* now *chf NE.*
vt = clear *15-e19.* [OF *clair; cf* CLEAR]

clair² *vt* harm, injure *la16.* [obscure]

clairschow see CLARSACH

claise see CLAES

claisp see CLESP

claith &c, **clathe**, **cloth** &c *16-,* **cloith** *la16-17* [[kleθ] *n, pl* CLAES **1** = cloth *la14-.* **2** *in sing* as *collective* clothing *la14-,* now *local NE-C.*
cloth-brush a clothes-brush *la18-,* now *local.*
~ **of lede** a sheet of lead *la14-16.* [*cf* CLETH]

claitt *n* = cleat *17-e18.*

clak see CLACK¹

clam¹ &c *n* a scallop (shell) *18-.*
~ **shell** &c = *n, 16-.* [*cf* Eng, where it is applied to various other bivalve molluscs]

clam² &c *vi* grope, grasp *19-, chf SW.* [Norw *klemme* seize]

clam³, clamm *adj* sticky, damp, clammy *la16-,* now *Bnf Rox.* [ME]

clam see CLIM

clamant *adj* **1** = clamant, crying out, clamorous. **2** urgent, calling for redress *18-, chf Sc.*

clamb see CLIM

clame &c *la15-17,* **cleme** &c *la14-e17 n, vti* = claim. [ME *cleme* &c, OF *clame(r), claime(r)*]

clame see CLIM

clamersum &c ['klamərsʌm] *adj* noisily discontented, contentious *la19-,* now *Bnf Abd.*

clamihewit &c ['klamɪ'h(j)uɪt &c] *n* **1** a blow, a drubbing *la18-e20.* **2** a hubbub *la19-.* [obscure]

clamjamfry &c; **clan-** *19-e20* [klam'dʒamfrɪ, klan-] *n* **1** *chf disparaging* a company, crowd of people; rabble, riff-raff *19-.* **2** rubbish, junk *19-e20.*
vt crowd, clutter up *la19-e20.* [obscure]

clamm see CLAM³

clammer &c *vi* = clamber *la19-, chf NE.*

clammis see CLAMS

clamp¹ &c *vt* patch; make or mend clumsily *la15-,* now *NE.*
n a patch *la19, Sh Ork NE.*
~**er** &c *n* **1** a metal plate or patch *e17.* **2** *fig* a patched-up argument or charge *la17-e18.* *vt, fig* patch (**up**), put together *la15-e19.* [prob f Eng *clamp* a brace]

clamp² &c *v* **1** *vi* walk noisily or heavily, clump *19-, local NE-SW.* **2** *vt* move (something) noisily *19-.*

n a heavy footstep, tread *la18-,* now *local N.*
~**er** &c; **clumper** *v* **1** *vi* = *v* 1, *19-, local EC.* **2** *vt* crowd, clutter, litter *19-, chf SW.* *n* a stout heavy shoe, clog *19-e20, Sh Stlg.* [prob onomat; *cf* Eng *clump* and Norw *klamp*]

clamp³ &c *n* **1** a piece of spiked iron worn on the shoe by *curlers* (CURL) to prevent slipping *la19-,* now *Fif.* **2** a spiked iron protector for the toe or heel of a boot *la19-, Ags.* [Eng *clamp* something that clasps]

clamper *vi* quarrel, struggle *17-18.* [perh f CLAMP²]

clams *la18-,* now *NE,* **clammis** *la14,* **glaums** *19-, Cai SW n pl* = clam, clamp, pincers, vice.

clan *n* **1** a local or family group, *esp* in the Highlands (HIELAND) or BORDERS, bearing a common name (from a supposed joint ancestor) and united under a CHIEF *15-.* **2** *in gen* a tribe or race *16.* **3** a class or set of persons *16-.*
clannit &c *adj* belonging to a CLAN (*n* 1) *16-e17.*
~**sman** a man belonging to a CLAN *n* 1, *19-.* [Gael *clann* children; *esp in kin-names* descendants]

clang *v pt* = clung *19-,* now *local Bnf-Fif.* [prob by analogy w *eg* ring, rang]

clange see CLENGE

clanjamfry see CLAMJAMFRY

clank &c *n* a resounding blow *18-19.*
v **1** *vt* throw **down** *e17.* **2** snatch, clutch, seize *e19.* **3** *vir* sit, flop (**down**) *20-, local Bnf-Stlg.* [*cf* Eng *clank*, MDu *klank* a clinking sound and CLINK¹]

clap¹ &c *n* **1** = clap *la14-.* **2** a heavy blow, stroke *16-.* **3** an affectionate pat *la19-.* **4** a clapper (1) of a mill = *mill-clap* (MILL), *freq* ~ **and happer** the symbols used in the SASINE of mills *la16-e19;* (2) as used in making public proclamations *la17;* (3) *transf* the town-crier *18-e20.*
vti **1** = clap *la15-.* **2** *vt* pat affectionately *15-.* **3** (1) press down, flatten *19-;* (2) *specif* (a) compress (soil) *la18;* (b) *transf* bury (a person) *19-,* now *Sh.* **4** *vi* flop, crouch (**down**) *19-.* **5** adhere, cling, press (against) *19-.* **6** shrink, shrivel *19-,* now *Sh.*
clappers *n pl* = *butter clappers* (BUTTER) *20-, local Cai-Kcb.* **clappit** having the flesh clinging to the bones; shrunken *17-,* now *local Bnf-Fif.*
~ **dyke** a turf or earth wall *la18-e19.*
~ **o(f) the hass** or **throat** the uvula *la17-,* now *Ags Fif.* **in a** ~ **1** all of a sudden *17.* **2** in a moment *la18-.*

clap² *n* a rabbit burrow or hare's form *20-, local SW, S.* [*cf* next]

clappard &c *n* a rabbit burrow or hole *16.* [ME *claper*, F *clapier*, MedL *claperius* &c]

clapperdin &c ['klapər'dɪn] *n* a gossip *20-, NE.* [f colloq Eng *clapper* the tongue + *din*]

clare constat see PRECEPT

clareschaw see CLARSACH

clark &c *la16-*, **clerk &c** [klɛrk] *n* = clerk *la14-*.

vt **1** record in writing *la18-*. **2** write, compose *19-*, *NE*.

~ **play** a play composed or acted by clerics or scholars *la15-16*, *only Sc*.

C~ (**of the** *or* **his**) **Register** *see* REGISTER. **Clerk of Session** a clerk of court in the *Court of Session* (SESSION) *19-*. **Clerk of** *or* (*latterly*) **to the Signet** = *writer to the Signet* (WRITE) *la16-*, *now rare*.

clarsach *20-*, **clarschach &c** *15-e19*; **clareschaw &c** *la15-16*, **clairschow &c** *la16-e17*, **clersha &c** *15-e17* ['klarsax, -ʃax, *'kler-, *-ʃɑ] *n* **1** a *Highland* (HIELAND) harper *15-e16*. **2** a *Highland* or Irish harp, strung with wire *la15-*.

clarshocher &c = *n* 1, *16-e17*. [ScGael *clàrsach*, IrGael *cláirseach* = *n* 2]

clarschar &c [*'klarʃər &c*] *n* = CLARSACH 1, *16-e17*. [Gael *clàirsear*]

clart¹ &c; clort &c *la19-*, **klurt** *Sh Ork* [klart, klort, klert, klɛrt; *Sh Ork* klʌrt] *n* **1** mud, mire *la19-*. **2** a lump or clot of something unpleasant *19-*. **3** a big, dirty, untidy person *la19-*, *local*.

v **1** *vt* besmear, dirty *19-*. **2** *vi* act in a slovenly, dirty way; work with dirty or sticky substances *20-*, *local*.

~**y** **1** dirty, muddy; sticky *la16-*. **2** *of a painting etc* daubed, smudgy *20-*, *Sh Bnf Abd*. [*cf* eME *biclarten* defile]

clart² &c *vt* clear or scrape with a muck-rake *19-*, *local*. [prob conflation of CLAUT w prec]

clary &c ['klerı, 'kları, 'klɑrı] *n* a mess *la19-*, *local WC-SW*.

vt besmear *20-*, *local WC-Uls*. [perh f *glaurie* (GLAUR)]

clash, clasch &c *16* *n* **1** a resounding impact, a blow *16-*. **2** = clash. **3** a mass of something soft or moist; a downpour *la19-*. **4** a large amount *la19-*. **5** chatter, talk, gossip *la17-*. **6** a tale, story *19-*, *now Abd-Fif*. **7** a gossiping person *20-*, *now Fif wLoth*.

v **1** *vt* strike, slap *16-*. **2** *vti* = clash. **3** *vt* slam (a door) *la19-*. **4** (1) throw forcefully or noisily (*esp* anything wet or liquid) *19-*. (2) repair by throwing wet mortar into joints and crevices *18-*. **5** *vi, freq of rain* fall with a crash or splash *la19-*. **6** tell tales, gossip, chatter *la17-*.

adv with a crash, bump *la19-*: '*doon a fell clash in the glaur*'.

~**er** a tell-tale, gossip *la18-*, *now Bnf wLoth*. ~**ing** *adj* soaking, dripping *la18-e20*, *WC*. ~**y** given to gossip *20-*, *now Cai Bnf Fif*. ~**-bag** *la18-*, ~**-pyot** *la19-* a tell-tale.

clash-ma-claver ['klaʃmə'klevər] *n*, *chf in pl* gossip, idle tales *la19-*, *now Bnf Fif Lnk*. [f CLASH by analogy w *clishmaclaver* (CLISH)]

clasp *see* CLESP

class &c *n* **1** a division of the Roman people *e16*. **2** a class in a university etc *la16-*. **3** *Church of Scotland* (CHURCH): a PRESBYTERY, *specif* when

meeting for religious exercises and study *18-e19*, *Ayr*. **4** *also* **cless** *20-* = class. [earlier in Sc; OF *classe*, L *classis*]

clat &c *n* **1** a lump, clot, *esp* of something soft *la16-*. **2** a mess, muddle *la19-*, *now wLoth*.

vt besmear, dirty *19-*.

clatty muddy, dirty; disagreeable *17-*, *now wLoth Arg Lnk*. [*cf* Eng *clot* or MDu *clatte* (*n*)]

clat *see* CLAUT

clatch¹ &c; clotch *n* **1** a splashing sound *19-*. **2** *transf* a wet mass, clot *19-*, *chf Sh Bnf*. **3** a dirty, untidy person, a slut; a fat clumsy woman *19-*. **4** a badly built, clumsy structure, one unfit for use *19-*, *now Ags Kcb*.

vi move with a splashing or squelching sound *20-*.

~**y** muddy, sticky *20-*, *now Bnf*. ~ **on** spread thickly, besmear *19-*. ~ **up** **1** fill or stop up with mud etc *19-*, *now Kcb*. **2** build carelessly or clumsily *19-*, *now Ags Lnk Kcb*. [onomat; see SND]

clatch² &c *vi* sit lazily, lounge *19-*, *SW*. [see SND]

clatchin *n* a clutch (of chickens etc, eggs) *la19-*, *Ayr Uls*. [*cf cleckin* (CLECK)]

clathe *see* CLAITH

clathes *see* CLAES

clatter &c *n* **1** *freq in pl* noisy idle chatter, gossip, scandal; rumours *la16-*. **2** a chatterer, a gossip *20-*, *NE*. **3** = clatter.

vi **1** = clatter *16-*. **2** gossip, talk scandal *17-*. **3** *of birds* chatter, call *16-*.

~**er &c** a chatterer; a tale-bearer *la15-*.

~ **bag(s)** a tale-bearer *19-*, *now NE*. ~ **banes &c** **1** *only proverb* bones which rattle together *18-*, *now local*. **2** bones, pieces of bone etc used like castanets *19-e20*. ~**-traps** odds and ends *19-* [by analogy w Eng *rattle-traps*].

clauchan *see* CLACHAN

claucher &c [*'klɑxər*] *vi* move with difficulty, struggle *19-20*. [see SND]

claucht *see* CLEEK

claught &c [klɑxt] *vt* grasp, seize, clutch *18-*, *now NE*.

n **1** a clutch, grasp, grab *la18-*, *now NE Arg*. **2** *in pl* = clutches *19-*, *now Bnf*. **3** a handful *19-*, *chf NE*. **4** a blow *la19-*, *now Ags*. [*pt, ptp* of CLEEK]

claught *see* CLEEK

claut &c, clat &c *n* **1** a claw; *chf transf, in pl* grasping fingers *la17-*, *now Lnk*. **2** a clutch, grasp, hold *la18-*, *now Abd Ags*. **3** a hoe; an implement for scraping dung, dirt etc *la17-*, *now Ags wLoth Kcb*. **4** a handful; a lump *19-*, *local Bnf-Kcb*.

vt **1** claw, scrape, scratch *la16-*, *now wLoth*. **2** scrape, clean by scraping, rake *la17-*, *now local NE-C*. **3** ~ **oot** snatch *19-e20*. [obscure]

claut and clay &c *n* = *cat and clay* (CAT²) *la18-e20*. [but *cf* eModEng *clate* a hurdle]

clautch &c *n* a sudden grasp, a clutch *la19-*, *now Fif*. [see SND]

clautie-scone &c a kind of oat bread or SCONE *19-e20*. [prob f CLAUT *n* 4]

claver[1] &c *vti, also* **glaver** &c *19-, now midLoth* ['klevər, 'glev-] talk idly or foolishly; gossip *la16-.*
n **1** *now chf in pl* prating; gossip; nonsense *18-*. **2** a fuss, a murmur *19-, now Fif*. **3** *also* **glaver** *la20-, midLoth* a foolish idle talker *20-, SW, S.* [see SND]

claver[2] &c, **clever** &c *la16-17* ['klevər, *'kliv-; *Abd* 'klɪv-] *n* = clover *16-e20.*

clavie &c ['klevɪ] *n* a torch carried round the fishing boats on New Year's Eve to ensure a successful season *la17-e18, Mry*. [see SND and SND Suppl]

claw[1] &c *la15-*, **clow** &c *16-e20* [klɑ, *WC, SW, S* *klʌu] *n* **1** = claw *16-*. **2** a scratching, *freq* of the head as an indication of mild astonishment *la18-.*
vti **1** = claw *la15-e17*. **2** *vt* scratch gently so as to relieve irritation; scratch (the head) as an indication of astonishment or uncertainty *la15-*. **3** scrape; clean out, empty *la18-, now Abd Lnk*. **4** beat, strike *19-, N.*
clawin post a rubbing post for cattle *la19-, chf NE.*
~ **aff** *or* **awa** do (something) with speed or eagerness *la18-, NE*. ~ **an auld man's heid** *in negative* fail to live to a ripe old age *19-, local*. ~ **someone's back** flatter someone, ingratiate oneself with someone *16-*. ~ **someone's hide** *or* **skin** punish, beat *la18-, local Bnf-Fif*. **gar** (ane) ~ **whaur it's no yeuky** &c, **gar** (ane) ~ **without a youk** give (someone) a drubbing *18.*

claw[2] *n* **in a** ~ in an excited state of annoyance or anxiety *20-, NE.*

clay &c, **cley** &c *17-*, **kley** *17-, now WC Kcb* [kləi] *n* = clay *la14-.*
clayey *n* a clay marble *20-.*
~ **davie** an agricultural labourer or navvy *20-, now Abd.*
~ **up** close or seal up with or as with clay *19-.*

claymore &c ['kle'mor] *n* the Highlanders' (HIELAND) large two-edged sword; *also* the basket-hilted single-edged broad-sword *18-*. [Gael *claidheamh* a sword + *mór* great]

clean, clene &c *la14-17* [klin; *SW also* klen] *adj* **1** = clean *15-*. **2** *fig* pure, absolute, complete *15-19.*
vt **1** = clean *16-*. **2** clear, remove *19-, now Bnf Abd Ags.*
n, also **cleanin** the afterbirth of an animal, *esp* a cow *19-, N, S.*
~(**t**) **lan** land after a root crop has been grown on it *20-.*
mak a ~ **breast wi** speak one's mind to, have it out with *19-, now Bnf Ags Lnk*. **make a** ~ **house** *or* **toun** &c **o** *of servants, farm-workers* leave, *of the master etc* dismiss (the servants etc), all at one time *18-, chf NE.*
cleange *see* CLENGE

clear &c, **clere** &c *la14-17 adj* = clear *la14-.*
adv **1** = clear *la14-*. **2** fully, completely *15-16.*
vt = clear *la15-.*
n a fair lady *16-e17.*
clearance *n* **1** = clearance. **2** proof; revelation *la19-, now Abd*. **3** *in pl, marbles* a call requiring removal of an obstacle *20-, Abd Fif*. **4** *chf in pl* a series of mass removals of their tenants by Highland (HIELAND) landlords *chf* in order to introduce sheep-runs or, on the more fertile land, to enlarge and improve the farms *19-, now hist.*
the ~ (**stuff**) whisky *19-, now Abd Ags*. **luik** **wi** ~ **een** look long and earnestly *19-, chf NE*. [*cf* CLAIR[1]]

clearin &c *vbl n* a scolding, beating *19-*. [? *cf* CLAIR[2]]

cleathin &c *NE*; **cleeding** &c *Fif* [*NE* 'kliðın, 'kleð-, *Fif* 'klid- &c] *n* the mould-board of a plough *19-e20*. [perh f CLEED]

cleave *17-*, **cleve** &c *la14-16*; **cleif** *16 vt, pt also* **claif** &c *la14-e17*. *ptp also* **clo'en** *19-, chf NE*, **clowen** *19-, NE* ['kloən] **1** = cleave *la14-*. **2** *also* ~ **down** *or* **oot** (*Abd*) *ploughing* 'split' (a ridge) *la18-, Abd midLoth.*
n, mining a division of a seam, *usu* of ironstone *la19-, now Fif.*
cleaving &c *chf in pl* the crotch *16-, now Abd Ags.*
~ **cannles** &c make candles of fir roots *la19-, NE.*

cleck &c, **clek** *la15-e17 vt* **1** hatch *la15-*. **2** bring forth, give birth to *16-*. **3** *fig* invent; conceive *la16-, chf WC.*
cleckin &c; **clackin, claikin** *20- n* **1** the act of hatching or giving birth *19-, now Bnf*. **2** a brood, litter: (1) of animals *19-*; (2) *derog* of human beings *19-*. [ME *clekke* (rare), OE *klikja*]
cleck *see* CLACK[1]

cleckinbrod *see* CLACKAN

cleed *la18-*, **cleid** &c *16-17*, **clethe** &c [klid; *local also* kled, klið; *WC, S also* kleð] *vt, pt ptp* **clethit** &c *la15-*, **cleedet** *la19-*; **cled** &c, **cleed** &c *20-, local* [klɛd; *local also* kled, klid, kleðd, 'klidɪt]. **1** = clothe *la14-*. **2** *of a tailor* make a suit of clothes for *la19-*. **3** cover thickly; fill, throng *19-e20.*
cled &c *pt, ptp* **1** = clothed *la14-*. **2** *law* provided **with** (1) (a husband or wife) *la15-17*; (2) (some material object) *la15*. *adj, of a measure or weight* heaped, full *19-, SW, S*. **cled score** *chf of sheep* twenty-one in number *la19-, SW.*
~**in(g)** **1** = clothing *la14-*. **2** a garment, suit of clothes *la15-e20*. **3** a covering or facing applied to a framework etc; the act of making or fixing this *16-e17*; *cf cladding* (CLAD). **4** *mining* the wood of the box of a HUTCH etc *la19-, now Fif*. [ME *clethe*, OE *clæðan*, ON *klæða*; *cf* CLETH *n* and CLAD]

cleeding *see* CLEATHIN

cleek &c, **cleke** *la14-e17*; **click** &c *la17-* [klik;

chf SW klɪk] *n* **1** a hook: (1) a substantial metal hook for holding, pulling or suspending *15-*; (2) a salmon gaff *la19-*; (3) a latch, a catch *18-*; (4) a muck-rake *20-*; (5) a crochet-hook *19-*; (6) the hooked piece of iron used by children for guiding a GIRD¹ 4, *20-*, *Abd Edb Lnk*; (7) *mining* a hook attaching the HUTCHES to the pulley, *chf* **stop, taigle** *etc* **the ~** interrupt the output of coal *19-*. **2** *in pl* leg cramps in horses *la16-*, *now Bnf*. **3** an inclination to trickery, a trick *18-*, *NE*. **4** a golf-club corresponding to the No 4 iron *19-20*.

v, pt, ptp **claucht &c, claught** [klɑxt] **1** *vt* seize, snatch, catch so as to take for oneself *la15-*. **2** lay hold of, clutch *16-*. **3** hook, catch or fasten with a hook *19-*. **4** *vi* link arms, walk arm in arm **with** *la18-*. **5** *dancing* link arms and whirl round *la18-*, *local NE, C*. **6** *vt* ensnare, 'hook' (a man) *19-*, *Bnf Fif*. **7** *vi* find oneself a sweetheart *20-*, *midLoth*.

~ie *adj* cunning, astute *18-*, *now Mry*. *n* a walking stick with a crook *19*. **cleekit** *adj* **1** *of horses* having string-halt *20-*, *NE*. **2** *of gloves, etc* crocheted *la20-*.

~ anchor a small anchor *la19-*, *Cai Kcb*. **~s-man** *mining* the man in charge of the CLEEK *n* 1 (7), who unhooked the baskets of coal at the pithead *la18*.

~ in *or* **up wi(th)** associate, be intimate with *19-*, *now Abd Lnk*. **~ on** put, throw on (clothes etc) *16*. [nME *cleke* corresponding to midl and sME *cleche*, appar f OE **clǣcan*]

cleesh¹ &c *interj, marbles* (*Ags Fif*), *bowls* (*eLoth*) *etc* a call made by a player requiring a clear path for his shot *20-*.

n room to manoeuvre, elbow-room *20-*, *Ags*. [obscure]

cleesh² &c *vt* whip, lash with a whip *19-e20, S*. *n* a lash with a whip; a blow *e20, SW, S*. [*cf* CREESH *v* 2]

cleester; klister &c ['klɪstər, 'klɛst-, 'klest-; *NE* 'klɔɪst-] *vt* smear, bedaub, plaster *19-*.

n a glutinous mass *la19-*. [*cf* Dan *klistre* (*v*) paste]

cleg &c; gleg *20-, local E* *n* **1** *also* **gled** *19-, now Slk* a gadfly, horsefly *15-*. **2** a missile used by rioters against troops or police, *esp* during the Radical movement *e19, C*. [nME; ON *klegge*]

cleg *see* CLAG

cleid *see* CLEED

cleif *see* CLEAVE

cleinge *see* CLENGE

cleister &c *n* = clyster, an enema *la16-e17*.

cleit &c [klet] *n* a small dry-stone structure used for drying PEAT¹ and storing food on St Kilda *la19-, now hist*. [Gael]

clek *see* CLECK

clekane *see* CLACKAN

cleke *see* CLEEK

cleket *n* a catch, bolt or trigger *la14*. [ME *cleket &c, cliket &c* a latch, OF *cliquet*]

clem¹ &c [*klɛm; *klam] *adj, chf schoolboy's word, of persons* **1** mean, unprincipled *19-e20, Edb Rox*. **2** curious, queer *19-e20*. [see SND]

clem² &c *vt* stop (**up**) (a hole) *19-, N*. [OE *clǣman* clog, daub]

cleme *see* CLAME

clench *see* CLINCH

clene *see* CLEAN

clenge &c, clange &c *la15-e17*; **cleinge** *la16-17*, **cleange** *17* [*klɛndʒ, *klindʒ, *klendʒ] *vt* **1** = cleanse *la14-17*. **2** *law* (1) *vr* clear oneself; declare, prove oneself not guilty *15-17*; (2) *vt* clear by a judicial verdict; find not guilty *la16-17*.

~er a cleanser of infected persons or places, a disinfecter *16-e17*. **~ing &c** **1** = cleansing *15-e17*. **2** *specif* disinfecting *16-e17*. **3** clearing from a charge *15-e17*. [nME]

clenkett *see* CLINK²

clenʒe [*'klɪnjɪ] *vt* = CLEAN¹ *16-17*. [var by analogy w eg CHENʒE and CHEEN]

clep &c *19-*, **clip &c** *n* **1** = clip, a device for seizing or grasping *la15-*. **2** *specif, fishing* a gaff *18-*. **3** *in pl* (1) an adjustable iron handle for suspending a pot over the fire *17-e20*; (2) a wooden instrument for pulling thistles out of standing corn *la18-, now Arg*.

vt = clip *la15-*.

clepe *n* **~ and call** a legal summons *14*. [nME *clepe* (*n*), f ME *clepe* (*v*)]

clerk *see* CLARK

clere *see* CLEAR

clersha *see* CLARSACH

clesch *n, vt* abuse *la16*. [*cf* CLASH, *clish-clash* (CLISH)]

clesp *la16-*, **clasp; claisp &c** *la16- n, vt* = clasp *la15-*.

cless *see* CLASS

cleth &c [*kliθ] *n, pl also* **cleis** *la16-e17* [*kliz] = CLAITH, CLAES *la14-e17*. [nME *cleth*, ON *klæði*]

clethe *see* CLEED

cleugh &c, cleuch &c [kl(j)ux] *n, pl also* **clewis** *15-e16* [*'kl(j)u(ɪ)z] **1** a gorge, ravine *la14-, in place-names la12-*. **2** a cliff, crag *16-19*. [nME *cloghe*]

cleuk¹ &c *16-*, **cluke &c** *la14-16*; **clook** *17-e20* [kl(j)uk; *kløk] *n* **1** a claw *la14-, now Ags Fif wLoth*. **2** a hand *la18-, Abd Ags*. **3** *chf in pl* 'clutches' *la19-, now N*.

vt claw, scratch *19-, Abd*. [*n* and early sME *cloke*; *cf* Eng *clutch*]

cleuk² ** *la15-e19*; **cluik &c *la16-e17* [*kl(j)uk; *kløk; *Mry Per Ayr* kjʌk] *n* = cloak. [irreg var; *cf* CLOCK³]

clev &c [klɛv; klɪv] *vt* **~ the line(s)** protect the *tippin* (TIP¹) and hooks before treating a deep-sea fishing line with a preservative after use *20-, N*. [see SND]

cleve *see* CLEAVE

clever¹, cliver &c *la17-* ['klɛvər; 'klɪvər;

'klĕvər] *adj* **1** = clever *la17-*. **2** swift, quick
la18-. **3** handsome, well-made *19-*, now *Cai*. **4**
of persons or things good, nice *la19-*.
cleverality cleverness *19-*, now *Fif*.
clever² *vi* clamber, cling *16-18*. [var of ME
claver]
clever *see* CLAVER²
cleverus *adj* nimble, quick *e16*. [f ME *clever*]
clew *n* a claw *16-19*. [obscurely related to
CLAW¹]
clewis *see* CLEUGH
cley *see* CLAY
click *see* CLEEK
click-clack *n* loquacity *19-*, *NE*. [onomat]
clift¹ &c *n* = cliff *15-*, now *Arg*. [ME (rare)]
clift² &c *n* **1** a plank, board *la15-e20*. **2** a cleft,
fissure; a cave *16-*. **3** the crotch *16-*, now *Abd*; cf
cleaving (CLEAVE). [ME]
cliftie &c *adj* clever, active, nimble *la17-19*. [*cf*
eModEng *clifty*; MLowGer *kluftich* clever, MDu
cluchtich capable]
clim &c [klɪm] *vti, pt* **clam, clame** *la14-e16*,
clamb *17-e20*, **clum** *la19*; **climmed &c** *17-e20*
[klam; klʌm; klɪmt; &c]. *ptp* **clummyn &c**
la14-16, **clum** *la16-19* = climb *la14-*.
climp¹ *vt* snatch *19-e20*, chf *Fif*. [see SND]
climp² *vi* limp *19-*, *SW-Uls*. [perh conflation of
Eng *limp* w CLINCH]
clinch, clinsch &c; clench *18-19* [*WC, SW*
klɪnʃ; *NE* klɛnʃ] *vi* limp, halt *la15-*, now *NE,
SW*.
n a limp *la18-*, chf *NE*. [obscure]
cling &c *vi* dry up, shrink *la15-*, now *Kcb*.
n diarrhoea in sheep *e19*, *S*.
clung *ptp, adj* **1** dried up, contracted, shrivelled
16-, now *Bnf*. **2** *specif* shrunken with hunger,
hungry *la18-*, now *Bnf-Fif*. [ME; OE *clingan*]
clink¹ &c *n* **1** = clink, a clinking sound *16-*. **2**
money, cash *18-*. **3** a blow *la19-*. **4** a sudden
fall *19-*, *N*.
vti **1** = clink *15-*. **2** *vt* strike, slap, beat *19-*, now
Abd Fif. **3** snatch (**up**) *19-*, now *Fif*. **4** *vti, of
news or gossip* spread *19-*, now *Fif*. **5** move
quickly, hurry *19-*, chf *NE*.
clinker *n* **1** chf in *pl* coins, money *19-*, now *Ags*.
2 *in pl* broken pieces of rock *19-*, now *Cai Kcb*. **3**
fig a 'stunner', something astonishing, either
good or bad *19-*, now *Sh Ork N*. **clinkum &c** *n*
a bellman, town-crier, also functioning as
grave-digger *la18-e19*. **clinkum-clank** *n, of a
bell* a ringing sound *19-*, now *Abd Stlg*.
~ doun &c 1 *vi* flop, sit or fall suddenly *19-*,
now *Bnf Abd Stlg*. **2** *vt* dump, deposit *19-*, now
Bnf. **in a ~** in a flash *la19-*, now *Bnf Ags*. [*cf*
Norw *klinka*]
clink² &c *vt* **1** *freq fig* = clench, rivet *19-*. **2**
compose (verses) *18-19*.
n a rivet *19-*, *Bnf Dmf*.
clenkett rivetted *la16*. [nME *clynk*; cf LowGer,
Du *klinken*, Norw *klinke*]

clink³ &c *v*, chf ~**it** *adj* thin, emaciated *la19-*,
now *Kcb*. [prob LowGer *klinken* contract,
wither; *cf* CLING¹]
clinkand *adj* spangled, tinselled *la16*. [F *clin-
quant*, assimilated to CLINK¹; cf next]
clinkard &c; clinker *n* a spangle *la16-e17*.
adj = CLINKAND *e17*. [altered f prec w infl f
CLINK¹]
clinsch *see* CLINCH
clint &c *n* **1** a cliff, crag, precipice *16-*, latterly chf
SW, S. **2** *curling* (CURL) a rough stone thrown
first as being likely to keep its place on the ice
la18-e19, *WC-SW*.
~y stony, rocky *18-19*. [ME *clint*; cf Dan, Sw
klint a steep cliff]
clip¹ &c [klɪp; *Gall Uls* klɪb] *n* **1** a colt *la19-*, chf
NE. **2** a pert or mischievous child, chf a girl
la19-, now local *NE-SW*. [ScGael *cliobag* a filly,
IrGael *cliobóg* a filly, colt]
clip² &c *v* **1** = clip, cut *la15-*. **2** destroy (false
coin) by cutting in pieces *la15-16*.
clip- *or* ~**ping-hous** a place where false coin
was destroyed *la16*. **at the** *or* **in** ~**ping-time**
&c at the right moment, in the nick of time *19-*,
chf *Bnf*.
~shear &c *n* an earwig *la19-*, now local *EC*,
WC, S.
clip³ &c *vti* = clepe, call, name *la15-16*. [chf
Sc; ME *clyppe* (rare), OE *clipian*]
clip *see* CLEP
clippie &c *adj* pert *la19-*, now *Kcb*.
n a pert, sharp-tongued girl *19-*, now *Ayr*.
[prob f CLIP¹ 2, perh infl by CLIP²; cf *a tongue that
wad clip cloots* (CLOOT¹)]
clish &c *vi* repeat gossip *19-e20*.
clish-clash, clis-clas *la17*; **clishmaclash &c**
la19-e20 ['klɪʃmə'klaʃ] *n* idle talk, gossip *la17-*.
clishmaclaver &c *n* **1** idle talk, gossip; endless
talk *18-*. **2** a talkative busybody *19-*, now *Bnf
Abd*. *vi* gossip, chatter *19-*, now *NE*. [*cf* CLASH]
clitter *see* CLOITER
clitter-clatter &c *n* **1** a rattling, clattering
noise, a continuous sharp crackle *16-*. **2** noisy
animated talk, senseless chatter, meaningless
verbiage *16-e20*.
vi talk endlessly, chatter *19-*. [eModEng; reduplication of CLATTER]
cliv *see* CLUIF
cliver *n* a tether for a cow *18-e20*. [see SND]
cliver *see* CLEVER¹
clivvie &c *n* a cleft *19-*, *Bnf Abd*. [*cf* ON *klyf*]
cloak *17-18*, **cloke &c** *16-17* *n* = clock.
cloak *see* CLOCK¹
cloch &c [klox] *vi* cough *19-e20*, chf *Cai*.
~er &c *n* **1** bronchial mucus *19-*. **2** a rough or
wheezing cough *19-*. *vi* cough, expectorate *19-*,
now *Cai*. [prob onomat]
clocharet &c [*'klox(ə)rɪt] *n* the wheatear; the
stonechat *la18-19*. [*cf* Gael *clacharan*]
clock¹, clok &c; cloak &c *n* the clucking
sound made by a broody hen *19-*, now local *Cai-
Kcb*.

vti **1** = cluck *16*. **2** *of birds* brood, sit on, hatch (eggs) *la17-*. **3** *vi, also* **clook** *20-, Cai, fig* sit idly for a long time; crouch *19-, now Cai Abd.*

clocker *n* a broody hen *19-*. **clockin &c** *n* **1** the desire to brood; *of persons* the desire to marry *19-*. **2** freedom from disturbance, quiet *20-, now Mry.* **~ing hen 1** a broody hen *20-*. **2** a woman past the age of childbearing *19-, now Loth Kcb.* **3** a woman during the time of bearing and rearing a family *20-, now Bnf Stlg.* **4** a sum of money earning interest *20-, local NE-Kcb.* [ME *clokke*, OE *cloccian*; *cf* Du *klokken* and Eng *cluck*]

clock², clok &c *n* a beetle *la16-*.
~er = *n, esp* a large one; a cockroach *la19-, local.*
~ bee a flying beetle *19-, now Abd.* **~ leddy** the ladybird *19-, now Kcb.* [northern eModEng *clocke*]

clock³, clok *n* = cloak *la14-, now NE.*
vt = cloak *la16-17.* [*cf* CLEUK²]

clod &c *n* **1** = clod (of earth) *16-*. **2** a sod *20-*. **3** a PEAT¹ *20-, N.* **4** a (*usu* wheaten) loaf *la18-e20.*
vt **1** pelt with missiles *16-*. **2** throw *19-*. **3** free (land) from clods or stones *18-, now Arg.* **4** pile up (PEATS¹, turnips) *la19-, Gall.*

clo'en *see* CLEAVE

clof &c *n* a certain weight of iron *15-e17.* [obscure]

cloff¹ &c [klof; *S* kloft] *n* a cleft: **1** of the crotch *16*; **2** of branches in a tree *19-e20, chf S.* [ON *klof*]

cloff² &c *n, only in pl, in a mill* 'that which separates what are called the bridgeheads' *la16.* [obscure]

clog &c *n* **1** a log or block of wood *16-*. **2** = clog, a wooden shoe *la17-.*

clogbag, clogbog *n* a saddle-bag *16-18.* [obscure]

cloit¹ &c, clyte &c *19-* *n* a sudden heavy fall *19-, local.*
vi **1** fall heavily or suddenly *18-, local.* **2** sit down suddenly *19-, now Ags.*
adv, only **clyte** heavily, suddenly *la19-.*
clyter *vi* fall *la19-, NE.* [see SND]

cloit² &c *19-, now Abd Ags Kcb,* **gloit** *la18-, Wgt Kcb;* **clyte** *la19-e20* *n* a dull, heavy person, a stupid and inactive person *la19-, now Abd Ags Kcb.*
adj, only **gloit** soft, delicate *20-, Wgt Kcb.* [perh Eng *clot; cf* ModFlem *kluite*]

cloiter &c; clyter &c, clitter ['kloitər; *N also* 'klʌtər; *NE also* 'kləitər; *Ork Cai EC also* 'klʌutər; *S also* 'kløtər; *C also* 'klɪtər] *vi* **1** be engaged in dirty, *chf* wet, work *19-, local NE-C.* **2** work in a dirty, disgusting way, *esp* in liquids *19-, now Abd Ags wLoth.* **3** walk in a slovenly way, *esp* in wet or muddy conditions *la19-e20, chf N.*
n a disgusting, wet or sticky mass *la19-, local NE-C.*

cloitery &c *adj* wet, disagreeable, dirty *la19-, local NE-C.* [*cf* MDu *clāteren* (*v*) dirty, MLowGer *kladeren*]

cloith *see* CLAITH

clok *see* CLOCK¹, CLOCK², CLOCK³

cloke *see* CLOAK

clomph &c *vi* walk heavily *19-, now local C.* [*cf* Eng *clump*]

cloo; clue *n* a ball of straw-rope used in thatching stacks *la18-e20, only Sc.* [*cf* Eng *clew* a ball of yarn etc]

clood *vt* cart in small loads *e20, Bnf Abd.* [uncertain]

clood *see* CLUD

clook *see* CLEUK¹

clook *see* CLOCK¹

cloor *see* CLOUR

cloose *la19-,* **clous &c; cluse &c** *la16-* [klus] *n* a sluice *la15-*. [ME *clouse*; OE *clūse* confinement, laL *clūsa* an enclosed place]

clooster *n* a mass of something wet or sticky, mud etc *19-, chf Gall.* [*cf* CLEESTER]

cloot¹ &c *la18-,* **clout &c** *n* **1** a patch *16-*. **2** a patch of metal etc *18-, now Abd Fif.* **3** a piece of cloth, a rag, *freq* a dishcloth, duster *la14-*. **4** a baby's nappy *19-, now local Bnf-wLoth.* **5** *chf in pl, freq* contemptuous clothes *la18-, now local Bnf-wLoth.* **6** a patch (of land) *la15-17.* **7** *archery, specif by the Royal Company of Archers* (ROYAL) a target; a hit on the target *19-*.
vt patch, mend (clothes); repair (pots, pans, footwear etc) with a metal plate *la15-*.
~er a patcher, cobbler *16-19.* **~ie** made of cloths or rags *20-*: '*clooty rug*'. **~ie dumpling** a DUMPLING wrapped in a cloth and boiled *la19-, Gen except Sh Ork.*
a tongue like to *or* **that wad clip ~s** a sharp or voluble tongue *la20-.* [ME *clout*, OE *clūt(ian)*]

cloot² *20-,* **clout &c** *n* a blow *16-*.
vt strike, slap *la18-*. [ME *clout;* see SND]

cloot³, clute &c [klut; kløt; *C* klɪt] *n* **1** one of the divisions in the hoof of cloven-footed animals; the whole hoof *18-e20.* **2** *transf* a person's foot *la19-e20.* **3** *chf in pl, freq* **auld C~(s)** the Devil *19-.*
(**auld**) **C~ie** = *n* 3, *la18-*. [prob f as CLAUT]

clootie &c *n, also attrib* a left-handed person *la19-e20, Abd Uls.* [uncertain]

clorach &c ['klorəx; *Bnf also* 'klirəx] *vi* **1** work in a slovenly way *la19-, NE.* **2** clear the throat noisily, hawk *20-, NE.* **3** sit lazily by the fire as if ill *la19-, Bnf.*
n a disgusting mass of something *e20, chf NE.* [see SND]

clort *see* CLART¹

close¹ &c, clos *la15-e18* *adj* [klos], *also* **closse** *17-19* **1** = close *la15-*. **2** *of work etc* constant, unremitting *la18-*.
adv [klos] **1** = close *15-*. **2** completely *la16-17.*

vti [kloz] **1** = close *la14*-. **2** suffer from congestion of the respiratory system *la19*-, now *Abd Ags Fif*.

closer *n* an argument which shuts one up *19*-, now *NE*. **closing &c** respiratory congestion; croup *la18-e20*.
~ **bed** *la16*-, **closed-in bed** *la19*-, *NE* an enclosed bed, a *box-bed* (BOX[1]). ~ **cairt &c** a farm cart with fixed shafts *la18*-, now *Fif*. ~ **cap** an older or married woman's head-dress *19-e20*, *N*. ~**-eared**, ~**-luggit** *of a cap* fitting snugly round the ears *19*-, now *Bnf Fif*. ~**-fit** with feet close together *e20*. ~ **weather** *etc* a heavy snowfall *la18*-, now *Abd*.

close[2] **&c, clos** *la15-17*; **closse &c** *la16-e20* [klos] *n* **1** an enclosure, courtyard *la15*-, now *chf Edb*. **2** *specif* a farmyard *la19*-. **3** an ENTRY, passageway, alley *16*-, *orig Edb*. **4** *specif* the ENTRY to a TENEMENT, the passageway giving access to the *common stair* (COMMON) *la19*-, *chf WC, SW*.
~ **mou &c** the entrance to a CLOSE[2] *n* 3 and 4, *19*-.
it's a' up a closie (wi) it is a hopeless position, it is a poor outlook (for) *20*-, *local*. **in the wrang** ~ in an irretrievable predicament, in grievous error *18*-, now *NE, WC*.

close coort *n* the square yard round which a farm *steading* (STEID[1]) is built *20*-, *NE*. [CLOSE[1] *adj* 1 enclosed or CLOSE[2] 2]

closhach &c; clossach *19-e20*, *Bnf* ['kloʃəx, 'klos-] *n* **1** the carcase of a fowl *la19*-, *NE*. **2** a mass of something, *esp* semi-liquid *la19*-, *NE*. **3** a hoard of money *la19*-, *NE*.
the haill ~ the whole quantity or number *la19*-, *NE*. [Gael *closach* a carcase]

closse *see* CLOSE[1], CLOSE[2]

clotch *see* CLATCH[1]

cloth *see* CLAITH

clothes *see* CLAES

clotterd &c *adj* clotted, congealed, caked *19*-, now *local NE-C*. [frequentative of Eng *clot*]

cloud *see* CLUD

cloup &c [klup] *n* ~**ie** a walking stick with a curved handle *19*-, *SW*. [*cf* LowGer *kluppel*, MDu *cluppel* a club]

clour &c; cloor *19*- [klur] *n* **1** a blow *la18*-. **2** a lump, swelling caused by a blow *16*-, now *local NE-S*. **3** a hollow, dent, *esp* in metal *19*-, *local N-S*.
vt **1** deal a blow to, batter, thump; damage, disfigure *20*-. **2** dent *la16*-. **3** dress or chisel (stone) *la19-e20*.
~**er** a stone-dressing chisel *e20*. [obscure]

clous *see* CLOOSE

clout *see* CLOOT[1], CLOOT[2]

clove *vt* break or split (flax) fibres before heckling *la18-19*. [for vowel *cf* Eng *cloven* ptp of *cleave*]

clow [klʌu] *n* **1** = clove, the spice *la15*-, now *local Bnf-Fif*. **2** *also* ~ **gillie flower &c** the clove pink *18-e19*. [see SND]

clow *see* CLAW[1]

clowen *see* CLEAVE

club &c *n* a member of a trade, *esp* shoemaking, who has not gone through a full or formal apprenticeship *18-e19*. [perh *cf* Eng dial *club* a clumsy fellow]

clucane *n* ? a yokel *e16*. [obscure]

clud &c *15*-, **cloud &c; clood** *la16*- [Sh Ork NE, EC klud; Bwk S klʌd] *n* = cloud *la14*-. *vti* = cloud *19-e20*.
~ **of nicht** darkness of night *16-17*. **under** ~ **of nicht** under cover of darkness *16-e19*.

cludgie *n*, *slang* a W.C. *la20*-, *Fif Edb WC*. [perh conflation of Eng *closet* w *lodge*]

clue *see* CLOO

clufe *see* CLUIF

cluff &c *n* a cuff or slap *la19-e20*, *chf S*. [also in nEng dial; perh conflation of CLOOT[2] w Eng *cuff*]

cluif *la16-e19*, **clufe &c; cliv &c** *la19-e20*, *Sh Ork Cai* [*kløf, pl *klø(v)z; Sh Ork Cai kliv] *n* a hoof, *orig* cloven *16-e20*. [*cf* ON *klauf*, Dan *klov*]

cluik *see* CLEUK[2]

cluke *see* CLEUK[1]

clum, clummyn *see* CLIM

clump *n* **1** = clump. **2** a heavy, inactive person *19*-, now *NE*.

clumper *see* CLAMP[2]

clung *see* CLING[1]

clunk[1] **&c** [klʌŋk; Ork Cai also glʌŋk, Cai also glʌuŋk] *n* **1** a hollow, gurgling sound made by liquid in motion *19*-, now *local NE-WC*. **2** a plopping or popping sound *19*-, *NE, SW*.
vi make a hollow gurgling sound as of liquid being poured *la18*-, now *NE*. [onomat; *cf* Norw *klunk*, *klukke*]

clunk[2] *vi* walk heavily *20*-, *chf NE*. [see SND]

clunkart *n* a very large piece or lump of something *la19*-, *NE*. [f as next]

clunker *n* a lump, a bump *la18-e20*, *chf Ags*. [prob LowGer dial *klunker* a lump of dirt]

cluse *see* CLOOSE

clute *see* CLOOT[3]

cluther &c ['klʌθər, 'klʌð-, 'klʌd-] *n* a close group; a disordered crowd *la18*-. [*cf* Eng *clutter*]

clyack &c ['klaɪək; *NE also* 'glaɪək] *n* **1** the last sheaf of corn of the harvest dressed as a girl or decorated with ribbons, *chf* **tak, hae** ~ *la18-e20*, *NE*. **2** the end of harvest *la18-e20*, *NE*. **3** the harvest-home supper *19-e20*, *NE*. [Gael *caileag* a girl; *cf* MAIDEN and KIRN[2]]

clyager *see* CLAG

Clyde: I *etc* **didna** *etc* **come up the Clyde on a banana boat, skin** *etc* I'm no fool *la20*-, *local*. [the river]

clype[1] **&c** [kləip; Bwk S klep] *v* **1** *vi* be talkative, gossip *19*-, now *Bnf Kcb*. **2** *also* ~ **on** tell tales, inform against someone *20*-. **3** *vt* report, relate, tell *19*-, *local NE-WC*.
n **1** an idle tale, a lie, gossip *la18*-, *local NE-WC*.

2 a tell-tale *la19-*. **3** *rick-building* the person who passes hay or sheaves from the forker to the builder *e20, SW*.

clypach ['klǝipǝx] a gossip *la19-, Bnf*. *vi* gossip *la19-, now Abd*. **clypie** talkative, tattling *19-, now Abd*.

~**-clash** a tale-bearer *la19-, now Kcb*. [ME *clepe*, OE *cleopian* call, name; *cf* CLIP³]

clype² &c *n* **1** a big, uncouth, awkward or ugly person *la15-, now NE*. **2** a rather large piece *la19-e20, Uls*. **3** an unpleasant mass or clot of any liquid, semi-liquid or soft wet substance; a bedraggled mass *la19-, Bnf*.

clypach ['klǝipǝx] = *n* 3, *la19-, Bnf Abd*. *vi* work or walk in a slovenly way *la19-, NE*. [obscure]

clype³ &c *n* a heavy, noisy fall *19-, Bnf Abd*. *vi* fall *19-e20, NE*.

adv, of a fall suddenly and noisily *19-, NE*.

clypach ['klǝipǝx] = *n, v, adv, 19-, chf NE*. [uncertain]

clype⁴ *n* a blow *la19-, now Bnf Abd Fif*. [*cf* colloq Eng *clip* a slap]

clyre &c *n* **1** 'a gland in meat'; 'an unsound spot in the internal fat of *eg* cattle' *19-, now Cai Kcb*. **2** a source of grievance *19-, now Cai*. **3** *in pl* a disease in cattle similar to glanders in horses *19-e20*.

clyred *adj* affected with tumours *la17*. [MDu *cliere* a gland]

clytach &c ['klǝitǝx] *n* incomprehensible talk, *orig* in a foreign language, *esp* GAELIC, senseless chatter, balderdash *la18-e20, chf NE*.

vi talk in a strange language, *esp* GAELIC, chatter *19-e20, NE*. [obscure]

clyte &c *n* a smart blow *20-, local*.

vt strike; rap (one's knuckles) against a hard object *20-, local*. [? CLOIT¹ or CLOOT²]

clyte *see* CLOIT¹, CLOIT²

clyter *see* CLOIT¹, CLOITER

co *see* QUO

coach, coche &c *la16-e18 n* **1** = coach *la16-*. **2** *freq* ~**ie** a baby's pram *la19-, Abd Ags*.

coachbell &c *19-e20, chf Lnk*, **scodgebell** *20-, chf Bwk Rox*, **switchbell** &c *la19-, Lnk Rox* [*chf Lnk* 'kotʃb(ǝ)l, 'swɪtʃp(ǝ)l; *chf Rox* 'skotʃb(ǝ)l, 'skotʃɪbl, 'swɪtʃb(ǝ)l; *chf Bwk* 'skodʒɪbl; &c] *n* the earwig. [nEng dial *twitch-ballock* or *-bell*]

coad *see* COD¹

coal &c *la16-*, **cole** &c *la14-e17*, **coll** &c *la15-*, **quile** *la19-, NE n* = coal *la14-*.

coalie-back; colly buckie &c *n* a pickaback ride *la20-, Abd Edb* [child's alteration of Eng *coal-back* carry coals on one's back]. **col3ear** &c ['koljǝr] = collier *la15-17*.

~**bearer** the woman who carried the coal on her back from the workings to the surface *17-18*. ~ **coom** *20-, local*, ~ **gum** *la19-, now Stlg* coal dust. **coll-ever** a horse for carrying coal *e16*. ~ **heuch** &c a coal-working or -pit *15-19*. ~ **hill** ground occupied at a pit-head

for colliery purposes *la17-, chf Stlg*. ~ **hood** &c any of several species of black-headed birds *18-19*. ~ **neuk** &c a recess for keeping coal; a coal-cellar *la17-, now Bnf*. ~ **ree** a store from which coal is sold *18-, local*.

bring out o'er *or* **tak ower the** ~**s** = haul over the coals *18-*. **coal and candle-light, col-cannel-week** &c *n* the long-tailed duck *la19-* [imit of the bird's cry].

coam *see* COLMIE

coarse *see* COORSE¹

coarum *see* QUORUM

coast¹ &c, **cost** &c *la14-e17 n* **1** = coast *la14-*. **2** bodily girth or frame *19-, S*.

~ **side** = *n* 1, *15-e17*.

coast² *la17-18*, **cost** *la15-*; **coist** *la15-e17 n, v* = cost.

coat *la16-*, **cote** &c *la15-17*, **cot** &c *la15-e20*, **cwite** &c *la19-, NE*, **quite** *18-, NE* [kot; *NE* kwǝit; *Mry also* kwit] *n* **1** = coat *la15-*. **2** *chf in pl* a woman's or child's petticoat; a skirt *19-*.

on ane's ain ~ **tails(s)** forced to make or pay one's own way; independent(ly) *19-, now Abd*. **hae one's** ~ **kilted, gae** ~**s kilted** be pregnant *19-, local C*. [the short- and long-vowel forms come from similar variants in OF]

coatter *see* COTE

cob¹ &c *vt, also* **keb** *la19, Bnf* beat or strike, *usu* on the buttocks, *S*.

n **1** *also* **keb** *la18-e19, WC Gall* a blow *19-20*. **2** the game of tip-cat; the bat or stick used in the game *20-, Dmf*. [ME *cob* fight, give blows]

cob² *n* a pea-pod *19-e20*. [uncertain]

cobill *see* COBLE²

coble¹ &c *vti* rock *19-, now Bnf Abd Arg*. [perh Eng *cobble* a rounded stone or COBLE²]

coble² &c, **cobill** &c *la14-17*; **cowbill** &c *la15-e20* ['kobl; *'kʌubl] *n* **1** a short flat-bottomed rowing-boat, used *esp* in salmon-fishing or lake- or river-fishing *la14-*. **2** a ferry-boat *15-, now Bnf*.

~ **and net** *or* **net and** ~ *law* the symbols used in the transference of the ownership of fishing rights *la16-18*. [nME; ScL *cobellus* (*e14*), *cobella* (*la13*); *cf* ONorthumb *cuopil* a boat, Welsh *ceubal* a ferry-boat]

coble³ &c ['kobl; *'kʌubl] *n* **1** *brewing* a vat for steeping malt *16-e19, Ags Per Edb*. **2** a drainage cistern, cesspool *16-e17*. **3** a pond, a watering place *la19-, NE*. [prob f COBLE²]

cob-worm *n* the larva of the cockchafer *la18-, Fif*. [unknown]

coch &c [kox] *n* = cough *la16-, now Cai*.

coghle [*'koxl] *vi* cough weakly; gasp *19*. [see SND Suppl]

coche *see* COACH

cock¹ &c *la16-*, **cok** &c *la14-17*, **kok** &c *15-17 n* **1** = cock *la14-*. **2** *curling* (CURL) the circle at the end of the rink at which the stones are aimed *la18-, now Abd*.

cocked *of eggs* fertile *la18-19*. **cockie-bendie** &c **1** a small, bumptious or rather effeminate man; *affectionate* a small boy *la19-*, *local.* **2** a dance tune *la19-*, *local.* **cocky-breeky, cock-a-breeky** a small boy, *esp* one who has just been put into trousers *la19-*, *chf Bnf Abd.* **cockie leekie &c, cock-a-leekie** chicken and leek soup *18-*.

~'s eggs the small yolkless eggs laid by a hen about to stop laying *19-*, *now Bnf Abd Fif.* **~'s eye** a halo round the moon, thought to be a sign of stormy weather *la19-*, *Cai Bnf.* **~ fight** a boys' game in which the players hopping on one foot and with the arms folded try to knock their opponents off balance *la18-*. **~ laft** the gallery in a church *20-*. **~ laird** = *bonnet laird* (BONNET) *18-*, *now Abd Ags.* **~ paddle &c** the lumpfish *18-*, *now Bnf.*

cock-a-bendy boat a boat made by folding a sheet of paper *la19-*, *Abd.* **~s and hens** name for the buds, stems or seeds of various plants, and of games played with them, *eg* the stems of the ribwort plantain, the leaf-buds of the plane-tree, the flowers of the bird's foot trefoil *la19-*, *chf S.* **~ of the north** nickname for the Marquises of Huntly *la17-*. **~ and pail** spigot and faucet *17-*, *now Ork.*

cock² *v* **1** *vt* raise (a fist) in a threatening manner *la18-*, *Cai-Fif.* **2** *vi* revive; pick up (after an illness) *20-*, *now Abd wLoth.* **3** drink *18-*, *now Ags.* **cockit &c bonnet** a boat-shaped cap of thick cloth, with the points at the front and back *la19-*; *cf Glengarry* (GLEN¹). **cockit hat** a kind of three-cornered *curling stone* (CURL) *18.*

~ one's wee finger drink, tipple *la19-*. [*cf* Eng *cock* (*v*), ultimately f COCK¹]

cock³ *vt* indulge, pamper, *chf* ~ (**someone**) **up with** (**something**) *la19-*, *local Abd-Kcb.* [see SND]

cock-a-lorie *n*, *in a counting-out rhyme*, *la19-*, *Bnf Abd*: '*Eetum, peetum, penny pie, Cock-a-lorie, jinky jye*'. [*cf* Sussex shepherds' numeral *cocktherum &c*]

cockapentie &c ['kokə'pɛntɪ] *n* a snob *19-e20*. [see SND]

cocker *vi* rock, totter, walk unsteadily *19-*, *local.* **~ie** unsteady, shaky *la19-*, *local.* [eModEng; *cf* COCKLE]

cockerdecosie, cockertie-hooie &c ['kokerdɪ'kozɪ, 'kokə(r)tɪ'huɪ, -'hoɪ &c] *adv* (ride etc) on someone's shoulders *19-*, *N.* [*cf* COCKER *v*]

cockernony &c ['kokər'nonɪ] **1** *n* a women's hairstyle in which the hair is gathered up on top of the head *18-19.* **2** a woman's cap with starched crown *19.* [perh COCKER *v* or COCK¹; see also COCK-UP]

cockertie-hooie *see* COCKERDECOSIE

cockie-law &c *n* the Thursday preceding the spring Communion, kept as a fast day *la19-e20*, *chf Gsw.* [? Gael *cóigeamh là* fifth day]

cockieleerie &c ['kokɪ'lirɪ] *n* **1** the crowing of a cock *19-*, *local.* **2** the cock itself *la19-*, *local.* **~ law &c** = *n*, *19-*, *local.* [imit]

cockle *vi* totter *la19-e20*, *chf S.* [*cf* COCKER; see SND]

cockmaleerie &c ['kokmə'lirɪ] *n* name for the cock *19-*, *now Bnf Lnk.* [*cf* COCKIELEERIE]

cock-up *n* a pad of false hair used to heighten a coiffure; a coiffure thus arranged *19.* [*cf* COCKERNONY]

cocky-roosie; cocky-ridie-roosie &c ['kokɪ('rəɪdɪ)'ruzɪ, -'rozɪ] *n* a children's game of riding on each other's shoulders *19-e20*, *Lnk Rox.* [*cf* COCKERDECOSIE]

coclink *see* COWCLINK

cod¹ &c; coad &c *n* **1** a cushion, pillow *15-*. (1) a support or bearing for a bell *la16-17.* (2) *in gen* a bearing, *esp* an axle-bearing *la18-*, *local.* **codding** *n*, *building*: **1** stones acting as supports for various constructions *la19-*; **2** the last course of short slates below the roof ridge *la20-*. **~bere &c** *la15-e17*, **codware &c** *la15-19* a pillowcase. [nME; ON *kodde*]

cod² *n* a pod or husk (of peas, beans) *18-*, *now Cai Abd Lnk.* **~ pease** pilfer pea-pods *18*, *SW.* [ME *codde*, OE *codd*, ultimately f as prec]

codderar *see* CODROCH

coddoch, coddow *see* CUDDOCH

codgie *adj* comfortable, content *la19-*, *Bnf Abd.* [prob var of CADGY]

cod-needle *n* a curved needle with the eye in the point for binding BESOMS *20-*, *Abd.* [prob f COD¹]

codroch &c, codrach(t) [*'kodrəx, *'koð-] *n*, *also* **codderar** *e16*, *Abd* an idle low-class person *la15-17.* *adj* **1** low-class *17.* **2** having country manners, rough *18-e19.* [uncertain]

coer *see* COVER

cofe *n* an exchange *la15.* **coffing &c** = *n*, *la15-e16.* [appar misreading for COSE]

coff &c *vt* buy *la18-e20.* [back-formation from COFT]

coff *see* COOF

coffee *n* **gie** (**someone**) **his** ~ scold roundly, chastise *la19-*. [*cf* Eng slang *give (someone) beans*]

coft &c *pt, ptp* bought, purchased *15-*, *now arch.* [MDu *cofte* pt, *(ghe)coft* ptp of *copen* buy]

cog¹ &c [kog; *Cai* kʌug] *n* a wooden container made of staves, a pail or bowl *16-*. *vt* **1** empty into a COG *18-19.* **2** feed (*chf* calves) from a COG *20-*, *Bnf Abd.* **~ wame** a pot-belly *la18-*, *now Fif.* **coup the** ~ drink *19-*, *NE.* [*cf* ON *kaggi*, Eng *keg*]

cog² &c *n* **1** = cog (in machinery) *16-*. **2 a** wedge or support *la19-*, *Kcb Uls.* **3** a small iron wedge fixed in a horse's shoe to prevent it slipping on ice *20-*, *local Ork-Wgt.* *vt* steady by means of a wedge; wedge, scotch (a wheel) *17-*, *now Bnf Abd Kcb.*

coggle &c; cogle &c, kugl &c *Sh* ['kogl; *Sh*

'kʌgl] *v* **1** *vi* rock, totter, shake *la18-*. **2** *vt* cause to rock, so as to seem ready to overturn *19-*, *now Bnf Abd*.

coggly &c *adj* unsteady, easily overturned *la19-*. [see SND]

coghle *see* COCH

cognate *adj*, *also* **cognat** *e17* = cognate *17-*.
n a relative on the mother's side *la17-*.

cogneezance [*kog'nizəns] *n* = cognizance *la19-20*.

cognition, cognitioun &c *la15-e17* *n* **1** = cognition *la15-*. **2** *law* authoritative or judicial knowledge or the acquisition of this by inquiry or investigation, cognizance, *freq* **tak** ~; *latterly specif* a process to ascertain certain facts, *eg* to prove a person insane *la15-*.

cognosce; cognos &c *la16-e19*, **cognosche** *la16-e17* [*kog'nos, *-'noʃ] *v*, *law* **1** *vi* make judicial inquiry; take cognizance or jurisdiction (**upon**) *16-e18*. **2** *vt* declare or assign judicially; adjudicate *la16-e17*. **3** investigate, examine; inquire into *la16-e19*. [*chf Sc*; eModEng; L *cognōscere*]

cognossance &c [*kog'nosəns] *n* = cognoscence *16-e17*. [only Sc; OF *cognoissance*]

cogster *n* a person involved in the dressing of flax, the scutcher *19-e20*, *Rox*. [*cf* nEng dial *cog* beat]

coif *see* COVE

coil *see* QUILE

coin *see* QUEAN

coine-house *n* = *cunʒe-hous* (CUNYIE) *17*. [anglicized var]

coinʒie *see* CUNYIE

coist *see* COAST²

coit *see* QUOIT

coitter *see* COTE

cok *see* COCK¹

cokalane &c *n* a lampoon *la16-e17*. [only Sc; F *coq-à-l'âne*]

col-cannel-week *see* COAL

cold *see* CAULD

coldoch *see* CUDDOCH

cole &c *n* a haycock *18-*.
vt put up (hay) in cocks *e20*.
collar a maker of haycocks *la16*. [perh connected w ON *kollr* a top, head; a rick; *cf* QUILE]

cole *see* COAL, COLL²

colemoth *see* COLMIE

colf [kolf; *NE also* kʌlf] *vt* fill in, stop up *19-*, *chf NE*.
~**ing, calfin &c** ['kolfin; 'kalf-] *n* **1** *also* **cuffing &c** *16-e17* material for caulking or stopping *16-17*. **2** gun-wadding *17-*, *now NE*. *vt* caulk, stop up *la15-e19*. [reduced f CALFAT]

coll¹ *n*, curling (CURL), *chf* ~**ie 1** a line drawn across the rink *e19*. **2** a stone that fails to cross this line and so does not count in the game *19*. [obscure]

coll² &c; cole &c [kol; *Sh Ork also* koil] *vt* **1** cut;

cut obliquely, taper; shape *la17-*, *now Abd Kcb*. **2** clip, trim (*esp* hair) *la16-e20*. [nME; *cf* ON *kollr* a top, a shaven crown; *cf* COW²]

coll *see* COAL

collar *see* COLE

collate *vt* **1** = collate. **2** *law* pool (inheritances) as in next (*n* 2) *la17-*.

collation, collatioun &c *15-e17* *n* **1** = collation *15-*. **2** *law* the pooling of inheritances with a view to their equitable distribution amongst the heirs *la17-*.
vt = collation, collate *17*.

collationate &c *ptp* **1** collated, compared *16-e17*. **2** put in possession **of** or appointed **to** (a benefice) *16*. [only Sc; MedL *collationat-*, ptp stem of *collationare*]

colleague *la18-*, **colleg &c** *16* [ko'lig, ko'lɪg] *v* **1** *vti* = colleague, join as an ally *16*. **2** *vi*, *chf derog* associate, be friendly **with** *la19-*, *now Bnf Abd*. **3** associate **with** for purposes of crime or mischief, plot, conspire *la18-*, *now Abd*.
n partnership; alliance; collusion *16-19*. [*cf* COLLOGUE]

collectorie &c *n* **1** the office of collector (of tax etc) *la15-17*. **2** that part of the royal revenue derived from the collection of the *thirds of benefices* (THIRDS) *la16*. [only Sc; perh OF *collecterie* = 1]

colleg *see* COLLEAGUE

college &c *n* **1** = college *15-*. **2** *chf* **the** ~ a or the university *la16-*. **3** a course of lectures *18*.
vt educate at a university *19-*, *chf C*.
C~ of Justice collective name for the body of judges (*Lords of Council and Session* (LORD)) and others composing the supreme civil court *16-*; see also *Court of Session* (SESSION).

collegianer &c, collegiiner &c [ko'lidʒɪnər, ko'lɪdʒənər] *n* a student at a college or university *la17-*. [eModEng]

collep *n* some kind of drinking vessel *e16*. [obscure]

collerach *see* CULRACH

coll-ever *see* COAL

collie¹ &c *n* a sheepdog, *usu* black (and white) *la17-*.
he never asked *etc* ~ **wull ye lick** *or* **taste?** he never even invited me to have something to eat *19-*. [obscure; the word when used in Eng can refer either to the Scottish sheepdog type or to a larger, *usu* tan and white thoroughbred dog]

collie² *n* ~ **doug** (*Gsw*), **Buttery Wullie C~** (*Abd*) a university student *la19-e20*. [prob f COLLEGE, conflated w COLLIE¹]

colliebuction &c ['kolɪ'bʌkʃən] *n* a noisy squabble *19-*, *now Fif*. [*cf* COLLIESHANGIE; perh w infl f Eng slang *ruction*]

collie-fox &c *vt* tease *la19-*, *Uls*. [obscure]

collieshangie &c, killie- *19-*; **cullie-** *la18-* ['kolɪ'ʃaŋ(ɪ), 'kʌlɪ-] *n* **1** a noisy dispute, uproar

18-. **2** a dog-fight *la19-*, now *Bnf*. **3** a talk, animated conversation *la19-e20*, *NE*. [see SND]

collig &c; colligue [*'kolɪg] *n* = colleague *16-17*. [by association w L *colligāre*]

collitigant &c [*'ko'lɪtɪgənt] *n* an opponent in a lawsuit *16-e17*. [? MedL *collitigans*]

collogue &c [ko'log; *Uls* -'lʌug] *n* a whispered conversation, private interview *la19-*. *vi* **1** talk together, chat *la19-*. **2** be in league, have an understanding **with**, scheme *19-*, now *Bnf Fif*. [perh conflation of eModEng *colloque* w COLLEAGUE]

collop &c *n* a slice of meat *16-*. [ME]

collum *n* a ship *e16*. [obscure]

colly-buckie *see* COAL

colmie &c *19*, **colemoth** *15*, **colmouth &c** *16-19*; **coam &c** *19-e20*, *Bnf* *n* the mature coal-fish *15-e20*. [Eng *coal* + ?]

colour-de-roy &c *n* a purple or tawny dress material *16*. [F *couleur de roy*; *cf* ModEng = purple, tawny *e17*]

colpindach &c *11-e17*, **copnoche** *la16*, **coupnoch** *la16*, **cupno(w)** *la16*; **coupnay &c** *la16-17* [*'kolpɪndox &c, pl* *-dʌu(ɪ)z; *'ko(l)pnox, *'kʌup-, *'kʌp- &c, pl* *-nʌu(ɪ)z] *n* a young cow or ox. [obscurely related to Gael *colpach* a female calf, a heifer; *cf* also CALP and CUDDOCH]

colrach *see* CULRACH

columbie &c *adj*, *of cloth* dove-coloured *la16-e17*. [f OF *columbe*, L *columba* a dove]

columby &c *n* the columbine *la15-e16*.

colȝear *see* COAL

comb *see* KAME

come &c, cum &c [kʌm] *v*, *pt* **come &c, cum** *la16-*, **cam &c** *la15-*, **coyme** *15-16* [kam; *C also* kʌm]. *ptp also* **cum(m)yn &c** *la14-e20*, **cum &c** *16-*, **cumit &c** *la16-*, **cum(m)ed &c** *16-* ['kʌmən; kʌm; 'kʌmɪt, kʌmd] **1** *vi* (1) = come *14-*. (2) *impersonal* of the arrival of a particular time of the day *20-*, *Bnf Abd Ags*: '*it came four o'clock*'. (3) *in phrases indicating a future date, as* (a) **on Monday** *etc* ~ **eight days** *etc la15-17*, **eight days** *or* **a week** *etc* ~ **Monday** *etc la19-* a week *etc* on Monday *etc*; (b) **five** *etc* (**years** *etc*) ~ **the time** five etc on one's next birthday, five years etc on the anniversary (of an event) *19-*, now *Bnf Abd Ags*. **2** stretch, expand *la19-*, now *Bnf Stlg*. **3** *vt* equal, match *20-*, now *Abd Lnk*.

n **1** = come, arrival *la14-e16*. **2** the angle between a tool and its user *20-*, *Abd*. **3** a thaw; moisture in the air *20-*, *Lnk-S*.

cummins &c the rootlets of malt *la19-*, now *Abd*.

~-again *n* a scolding, reproof; a beating *la19-*, *NE*. ~ **aifter** court, seek in marriage *la19-*, *NE*. ~ **at** *of a misfortune* befall; affect, distress *20-*, *Sh NE*. **come ather** *call to a horse* turn to the left *19-*, *NE* [Eng *come hither*]. ~ **away 1** *of seeds*, *plants* germinate, grow rapidly *la19-*,

local Bnf-Loth. **2** *chf imperative* come along *19-*, *Bnf-Fif*. ~ **back an fore** visit regularly *20-*, *local*. ~ **back on a person** *of food* repeat *20-*. ~ **doon &c** *of a river* be in flood *la18-*, now *Fif*. ~ **doun with one's spirit** humble oneself *19-*, now *Abd Lnk*. ~ **forrit** make progress, *esp* in growth *20-*, *local*. ~ **and gang** (**a wee**) compromise *19-*, now *Abd Stlg Lnk*. ~ **guid for** be surety for; back up *19-*, *local*. ~ **hame** born *la19-*, now *Bnf Ags*. ~ **in** collapse *20-*, *Fif*. ~ **in by**(**e**) come in, draw near *la18-*. ~ **in to the fire** draw near to the fire *la18-*. ~ **o** *impersonal* become of (one), happen to *20-*. **~-o-will &c** an illegitimate child *19-*, now *Abd*. ~ **on 1** *chf imperative* come along *la19-*. **2** *imperative* = I don't believe a word of it! *la20-*. **3** be about (to do something) *la19-*, *local Sh-Per*. ~ **out &c** study (to be ..), qualify (for a particular profession) *20-*. ~ **a blow** *etc* **out ower** strike *19-*, now *local NE-C*. ~ **ower &c 1** *chf of misfortune* happen to befall (a person) *19-*. **2** repeat, make mention of *la19-*, now *Bnf Abd Fif*. ~ **paddy owre** get round (a person) *la19-*, now *Ags Lnk*. ~ **speed** make progress, get on quickly *la19-*. ~ **tae &c 1** regain one's composure after a time of mental stress *19-*, *local*. **2** become reconciled; comply *la18-*, *local*. **3** come near *la18-*, *Bnf Abd*. **4** grow up *la17-*, *chf Bnf Abd*. ~ **tee te** *or* ~ **tee wee** overtake *la19-*, *Bnf Abd*. ~ **to the door** *of a knock* sound on the door *la18-*, now *NE*. ~ **through** recover from an illness *19-*. **ca way** *20-*, **ca waw** *20-*, **c'way** *19-*, **quay** *19-* [kwɑ; *WC*, *S* kə'we, kwe] *imperative* = come away. ~ **your** *etc* **ways** *chf imperative* come along *19-*.

comman *la18-*, **command &c** [kə'man(d)] *vt* = command *la14-*.

n **1** a command, an order *la15-*. **2** *chf in pl* the ten commandments *16-*, now *local*.

commanding *of pain* severe, disabling *la19-*, *local*.

commandiment, commandement [*kə'mandɪmənt] *n* = commandment *la14-19*. [ME]

commend[1] [*'ko'mɛnd] *n* **1** = commendam, *chf in* ~ *of a benefice* to be held by a bishop etc (in addition to his own preferment) or by a layman *la15-e16*, *only Sc*. **2** commendation, praise *la15-e17*.

vt = commend *la14-*.

commend[2] [*'ko'mɛnd] *n* = comment, a commentary *la15-16*. [erron var]

commendatare &c [*?ko'mɛndətər] *n* a holder of a benefice *in commend* (COMMEND[1] *n* 1) *16-e17*. [only Sc; MedL *commendatarius*; *cf* eModEng *commendatary* and next]

commendatour &c [*?ko'mɛndətur] *n* = COMMENDATAR(E) *16*. [var after L nouns in *-ator*; earlier in Sc]

commentar &c [*'komɛntar] *n* = commentary *la16-e17*. [only Sc; F *commentaire*, L *commentārium*]

commere *see* CUMMER²
commie &c *Gsw*, **commonie** *Fif Rox n* an ordinary marble *e20*. [f COMMON]
commissar &c [*'komɪsar] *n*, *law* **1** = commissary *la14-17*. **2** = COMMISSIONER 2, *15-e17*. **3** a civil official taking the place of the former ecclesiastical diocesan commissary, *freq* C~ of Lanark, Edinburgh *etc*, *la16-e18*.
commissariat [*komɪ'serɪat, *-'sar-] *n*, *law* the office, jurisdiction or court of a COMMISSAR *n* 3; the district included in such jurisdiction *la16-e18*. [only Sc; F; *cf* Eng]
commissary ['kɔmɪsərɪ] *n*, *law* later name for a COMMISSAR *n* 3, *la18-e19*.
~ **clerk** the *sheriff clerk* (SHERIFF) when acting in relation to confirmation of executors *19-*. [see COMMISSAR *n* 3, COMMISSARIAT; *cf* Eng]
commissioner &c *la16-*, **commissionar** &c *la15-17 n* **1** = commissioner *la15-*. **2** a representative of a BURGH at the annual *convention of burghs* (CONVENTION) *la15-16*. **3** a member of the Scottish Parliament *la16-e18*. **4** a member of the *General Assembly* (GENERAL) of any of the Scottish Presbyterian Churches *18-*; for *n* 3 and 4 see also *Lord (High) Commissioner* (LORD). **5** a FACTOR, steward *la19-*, *now Bnf Abd*.
C~ **of Supply** *usu in pl* the group of landowners in each county which exercised various administrative functions, *orig* the assessors for the apportionment of the SUPPLY *n* 4, *18-19*; **Lord** C~ **of Justiciary** *see* LORD.
commixtion [kə'mɪkstɪən, kə'mɪkstʃən] *n*, *law* a mixture of property belonging to different people *18-*. [L *commixtio*; *cf* ME, eModEng = a mixing; a mixture]
commodate, **commodatum** ['kɔmodet, -etʌm] *n* a free loan of an article which must be returned exactly as lent *la17-*. [L, ptp of *commodāre* lend]
commodité &c *n* **1** = commodity *15-16*. **2** *in pl* advantages or benefits deriving from the possession or use of property *la14-e17*.
common &c, **commoun** &c, **cowmon** &c *16-*, *now NE* ['komən; *NE also* 'kʌumən] *adj* = common *la14-*.
n **1** = common *la14-*. **2** a debt, obligation *la16-e20*. **3** *in pl* the foot-soldiers in an army *15-16*.
vti **1** = common, commune *la14-17*. **2** discourse, discuss, negotiate (about) *la15-e18*.
~ **debtor** when A owes money to B which B recovers by taking from C a sum owed by C to A, A is known as the common debtor *la18-*. ~ **good** &c the property and revenues of the corporation of a *royal burgh* (ROYAL) (and now administered by their successors the *District Councils* (DESTRICK)), which are not held under special acts of parliament nor raised by taxation *15-*. ~ **head** *religion* an exercise or discourse on a general point *17*. ~ **law** the usual

civil law *15-e16*. ~ **mett** a public standard system or unit of measurement; a standard instrument for measuring *la15-e17*. **the** ~ **popular** &c the common people *la16*. C~ **Riding** name for the *Riding of the Marches* (RIDE) in certain towns, *eg* Selkirk, Hawick *20-*. ~ **stair** *in* a TENEMENT the communal staircase giving access to the flats etc *19-*.
for ~ commonly, generally *15-*, *now Per*. **in (someone's)** ~ in debt or under an obligation to someone *la16-e18*. **quit(e)** *or* **repay a** ~ repay a debt or injury *la16-e17*. **than** ~ than usual *la19-*, *now Sh Ags*.
commonaté *see* COMMONITÉ
commonie *see* COMMIE
commonité &c, **commonaté** &c [*ko'mɒnɪtɪ, *ko'mun-, *&c*] *n* **1** = community *15-e17*. **2** a common pasture *17*.
commonty &c, **commonté** &c *15-16 n* **1** = commonty, the community *la15-17*. **2** common possession or enjoyment of land *15-*, *only Sc*. **3** land possessed or used in common; a common *la15-*, *only Sc*.
in ~ in common, as common property *16-18*.
commoun *see* COMMON
commove &c [*ko'mɒv] *vt* **1** move to anger, excite to passion *la15-e19*. **2** = commove, set in motion or agitation *16*.
communing &c *n* a debate, discussion *18-*, *now Abd*.
communio bonorum [kɔ'munɪo bɔ'norəm] *n*, *law* the stock of MOVEABLE property owned jointly by a husband and wife *la19-*.
compaingen [kəm'peŋən] *n* = companion *la20-*, *Cai Bnf Abd*.
companionrie &c [*kəm'penjənrɪ] *n* companionship *la16-17*. [chf Sc; f Eng *companion*]
compare¹ &c *vti* = compare *16-*.
n comparison, resemblance *16-*, *now Abd Fif*.
in ~ **of** in comparison with *16*. [*cf* COMPERE]
compare² &c *adj* comparable, equal *e16*. [only Sc; L *compar*]
comparisoun &c *n* a caparison *e16*. [only Sc; irreg f F *caparasson*]
compartiner &c [*kəm'partɪnər] *n* a co-partner *la16-17*. [*cf* eModEng *comparcioner*]
compear &c *la16-*, **compere** &c [kəm'pir; *also* *kəm'per] *vi* **1** appear **before** (1) a court or other authority *15-*; (2) a congregation, *esp* for rebuke *17-e19*. **2** present oneself, appear *la15-e20*.
~**ance** &c appearance, as a formal act, *freq* **non-, nocht-** *la15-e18*. [chf Sc; laME *compere*, OF *comparoir*, L *comparēre*]
compeditour &c [*kəm'pɛdɪtur] *n* = competitor *16-e17*. [irreg var]
compell &c *vt* **1** = compel *15-e17*. **2** force (a person) by distraint of property; distrain (goods etc) *la15-18*.
compendize &c *vt* abridge, summarize *la17-e18*. [only Sc; f Eng *compend (n)*]
compensation *n* **1** = compensation. **2** *law*,

also **compensatio injuriarum** a plea that a *defender* (DEFEND) should not be compelled to pay damages to a *pursuer* (PURSUE) on the grounds that the *pursuer* is liable for as great or greater damages to the *defender*, *la19-*.

compere *v* = COMPARE[1] *v*, *la14-16*. [only Sc; OF *comperer*]

compere *see* COMPEAR

compesce &c [*kəm'pɛs] *vt* restrain, repress *17-19*. [ME *compesse*; L *compescere*]

competable &c [*?'kompɛtebl, *?'kʌm-] *adj* competent, suitable *la15-e16*. [only Sc; OF *competable*]

compleen *la17-*, **complene &c** *la15-17*, **complain &c** [kəm'plin] *vti* **1** = complain *15-*. **2** *vi* be ailing, unwell, *chf in adj* ~**in &c** unwell, ailing *19-*.

complener &c *16-17*, **complainer &c** *17-* *law* a plaintiff, *latterly* a victim of a crime who has reported it to the authorities.

complent &c [kom'plɛnt] *n* = complaint *16-e20*.

complenȝe [*kəm'plinjɪ] *vt* = COMPLEEN 1, *15-16, only Sc.*

complese &c [*kom'pliz] *vt* please, satisfy *la14-16*. [*cf* OF *complais-*, f *complaire* and eModEng *complease*]

complete &c *adj* = complete *la15-*.
vt, ptp also **complete &c** *la15-16* complete, finish *15-*.

compliment *n* **1** a gift *la19-*, now *Bnf Ags*. **2** = compliment.

compluther; complouter &c *19*, **comploiter** [kom'plʌθər, -'pluθər, -'plʌuθər, -'ploitər, *-'plutər] *vi* **1** agree, coincide, fit in (**with**) *19-e20*. **2** mix, associate **with** *la19-e20*.
n a mix-up; confusion *19-e20*. [only Sc; perh f F *complot* a crowd, mêlée]

compone &c [*kəm'pon] *v* **1** *vt* = compone, compose *la15-e17*. **2** *specif* compose in speech or writing *la15-16*. **3** compose, calm (oneself) *16*. **4** *vi* come to an agreement (**with** (another) **for** (something)); compound or settle by payment etc *la15-18*. **5** *vt* settle (disputes etc) *16-e17*. **6** compound (a payment) **for** (a certain sum) *16-e17*.

componitour[1] *n* = COMPOSITOR *la15-16*. [erron expansion of scribal *compõtour*]

componitour[2] **&c** [*kəm'ponɪtur] *n* = COMPOSITIOUN (*n* 1 and 2) *15-16*. [only Sc; appar L *componitur* it is settled]

compositioun &c *la14-e17*; **composition &c** *la15-* *n* **1** = composition, an agreement for the settlement of a dispute etc *la14-e17*. **2** a sum paid in settlement of a claim, dispute or obligation; the amount fixed by mutual agreement *la15-e17*. **3** = (literary etc) composition *la16-*.

compositor &c, **compositour &c** [*kəm-'pozɪtur, *-ər] *n* a person who settles disputes etc *la14-e18*. [only Sc; AF *compositour*, L *compositor*]

comprise &c *vt* **1** comprehend, grasp mentally *la14-16*. **2** = comprise *15-*. **3** attach, distrain (property) *16-17, only Sc*. **4** appraise, value *la16-e20, only Sc.*

compromit &c [*'kompromɪt] *vtr* = compromit, agree; settle; pledge oneself *la15-16*.
n a settlement, agreement *la15-e17, only Sc.*

compt &c *n* **1** = count, an account *15-17*. **2** *specif* a list, register, inventory *la15-17, only Sc.*
vti = count *15-17*.
~**ar**, ~**er** a person who keeps or renders accounts; a treasurer *la15-e18, only Sc.* ~**ar-wardane** = prec *16*.
(**to**) **gude** ~ (to) the full amount *la15-16*. [ME; re-spelling, after OF *compte*, of COONT and CONT]

compterfit *see* CONTRAFAIT

comptes &c [*'kuntɛs] *n* a countess *16-e17*. [only Sc; OF *comtesse*]

compulsitor, compulsatour &c *adj, law* compelling performance *e16*.
n a writ ordering the performance of some act; anything which compels *16-19*. [MedL *compulsatorius* in *litterae compulsatoriae*]

con *n* a squirrel *la15-16*. [obscure; also in northern ModEng dial]

conand, connand, cunnand &c [*'kʌnand] *n* = covenant *la14-16*. [ME]

conburges [*kon'bʌrdʒɛs] *n* = comburgess, a fellow burgess *la15-16*.

concait, conceat *see* CONCEIT

conceil *see* CONCELE

conceit &c, conceat &c, consait &c; concait *la19-*, *Bnf* [kon'sit, -'set] *n* **1** = conceit *15-*. **2** a scheme, stratagem *15-16*. **3** an idea, opinion, notion *16-*, now *Abd Ags*. **4** a good opinion **of** (oneself *la18-*, another *16-e17 or* a thing *la18-e19*). **5** interest, lively attention, concern, *chf* **tak a** ~ **in** *la18-*, now *Abd Fif*. **6** a fancy article, a quaint or dainty object or person *la16-*, now *Ags Lnk*.

conceity &c, conceaty &c *adj, chf Sc* **1** fanciful, flighty *la16-17*. **2** conceited, vain, proud *la17-*. **3** witty, apt *la19-*, *chf Kcb*. **4** neat, tidy, dainty *la18-*.

concele &c; conceil *only Sc vt* = conceal *la14-e17*.

conclusion &c *n* **1** = conclusion *la14-*. **2** *law* the clause in a *court of session* (SESSION) SUMMONS which states the precise relief sought *19-*.

concord &c [*n* 'konkord; *v* *kon'kord] *n* = concord *15-*.
vti agree; come to an agreement *la14-16*.

concourse *see* CONCURSE

concredit &c [*kon'krɛdɪt] *ptp* entrusted *la16-e17*. [only Sc; L *concrēdit-*, ptp stem of *concrēdere*; *cf* eModEng *concredit* (*v*)]

concreour &c [*'konkrɪur] *n* = conqueror *16*. [only Sc; irreg var]

concurse &c *17-e18*, **concourse** [*kon'kʌrs, *-'kurs] *n* **1** *law* (1) concurrence, *esp* of an authority whose consent is necessary to a legal process, *eg* of the public prosecutor in a private prosecution *17-*; (2) the simultaneous existence of two actions based on the same grounds *19-*. **2** = concourse.

condame, condamp *see* CONDAMPNE

condampnatioun &c *n* = condemnation *15-16*. [only Sc; OF *condampnation*, after *dampner*, L *damnāre*]

condampnatour &c [*kon'dampnatur] *adj* = condemnatory *16-e17*.
n a condemnatory sentence or decree *la16-e17*. [only Sc; OF *condamnatoire*; *cf* prec]

condampne &c; condamp &c *16*, **condame** *16* [*inflected* *kon'dampn-, *uninflected* *kon'dam(p)] *v* **1** = condemn *la14-e17*. **2** damage, *esp* with artillery fire *la16-e17*. **3** block, fill up (a door etc) *la16-e17*. [OF *condampner*; *cf* prec]

condempnatour [*kon'dɛmpnatur] *n* = CONDAMPNATOUR *la16-17*. [eModEng *condemnatorie*, MedL *condem(p)natorius*]

condescend &c *vti* **1** = condescend *16-*. **2** ~ **on** *or* **upon** enter into particulars about; specify, detail *16-*, *chf Sc*.
~**ence &c**, ~**ency** *la17* **1** agreement, acquiescence *17*. **2** a specification, statement of particulars, *freq* of legal statements of fact *17-*.

condie *see* CUNDY

conding &c, condigne &c [kon'dɪŋ] *adj* = condign *15-e17*.
~**ly** **1** = condignly *16-18*. **2** agreeably, lovingly *19-*, *N*.

conditionate &c [*kon'dɪsɪənat, *-et] *ptp* agreed in a bargain, stipulated *16-e17*. [MedL *conditionat-*, ptp stem of *conditionare*; *cf* eModEng *conditionate* (*v*)]

conduce &c [*kon'døs] *vti* **1** = conduce *la15-*. **2** *vt* engage the services of, hire *la15-17*. **3** *vi* bargain, deal **with** *la16-e18*.

conduck &c, conduct [*n* *'kondʌk(t), *kon'dʌk(t); *v* kon-'dʌkt] *n* **1** = conduit, a channel for water *16-e17*. **2** a safe-conduct *la15-*, *now Abd Fif*.
vti = conduct *16-*.

confabble &c [kon'fabl] *n* a confabulation, talk *19-*, *now Abd Fif*.
vi = confabulate *19-*, *now Abd Fif*. [laME *confable, confabuler* or L *confabulāri*]

confaise *see* CONFEESE

confeerance &c *17-*, **conference &c** [kon-'firəns] *n* **1** = conference *la16-*. **2** comparison, *latterly only* **in** ~ **to** *la16-*, *now Bnf Abd*.

confeerin *see* CONFERE

confeese &c; confaise &c [kon'fiz] *vt*, *chf in ptp* **confeesed &c** confused *19-*, *chf NE, EC*.

confer *v* **1** *vt* = confer *16-*. **2** *vi* talk together, hold conference *15-*.

confere [kon'fir] *vti* = confer *la16-*.

confeerin &c *adj* suitable, corresponding *la19-*, *NE*. *adv* considering, taking everything into consideration *la18-*, *NE*. **confeerin to** *or* **wi** in accordance with, according to *la18-*, *now Bnf*.

conference *see* CONFEERANCE

confidder *see* CONFIDER

confide &c *vti* confide *la15-*. [earlier in Sc]

confider; confidder &c [*kon'fɪdər] *vti* = confeder, confederate *16*, *only Sc*.

confiderat [*kon'fɪdərat] *n* = confederate *16-e17*, *only Sc*.

confideratioun &c [*konfɪdə'resɪun] *n* = confederation *la15-e17*, *only Sc*.

confirmation &c, confirmatioun &c *la14-e17* *n* **1** = confirmation *la14-*. **2** *law* a process whereby executors are judicially recognized or confirmed in their office and receive a title to the property of a deceased person *17-*.

conflummix [kon'flʌmɪks] *vt*, *n* confuse, bewilder; a shock *20-*, *Bnf Abd*. [*con-* + colloq Eng *flummox* bewilder]

confoon [kon'fun] *vt* = confound *la19-*, *Bnf Abd*.

confooter [kon'futər] *vt* confound *..! 20-*, *Bnf Abd*. [conflation of Eng *confound* w FOUTER]

conform &c *adj* **1** = conform *16-*. **2** *specif, of furnishings etc* matching, in keeping with the rest *la17*.
~ **to** in conformity or accordance with *16-*, *only Sc*. **non-conform** *adj* nonconformist (applied to dissenting MINISTERS of the Presbyterian party during the Restoration period) *la17*, *appar chf Sc*.
letters conform, conformand *see* LETTER.

confortable &c [*'konfortebl, *kon'fortəbl] *adj* = comfortable *15-19*.

confusion &c, confusioun &c *la14-16* [*kən'føzɪun] *n* **1** = confusion *la14-*. **2** *law, also* **confusio** (1) a mixture of liquids *la17-*; (2) a mode of extinguishing a debt, right or claim where either party acquires the title of the other by inheritance or otherwise *la17-*.

congregatioun &c *15-16*; **congregation &c** *n* **1** = congregation *la14-*. **2** the body of those forming the Protestant party at and after the Reformation *la16*.

coning *see* CUNING

conjoin &c, conjone *16-e17*; **conjune &c** *la15-16* [*law* kən'dʒɔɪn; *kon'dʒøn] *vti* **1** = conjoin *la15-*. **2** *law, specif* order a joint trial of (two processes involving the same subject and the same parties) *19-*.

conjunct &c [kon'dʒʌŋkt] *adj, of persons* **1** combined, united; associated; joint *16-17*. **2** *specif, latterly law* connected by blood *la15-19*. **3** *law* possessed or shared in jointly, *chf* ~ **feftment** *15-16* or **fee** *16-*.
~**ly and severally** *law* where each of the persons named is singly liable etc for the whole of the obligation etc *la15-*.
~ **fiar, fear** *law* a person who holds property jointly with another *16-18*.
conjunct and confident persons *law* persons related by blood and connected by interest, *eg* in a bankruptcy case where recent transfer of property is challengeable *17-*.

conjune see CONJOIN
connach &c *NE* ['konəx] *vt* **1** waste *la18-*. **2** spoil; devour *la18-*. **3** fuss over *la19-*. *n* a botch *la19-*. [obscure, but perh connected w CONNOCH]
connand see CONAND
conneck [kə'nɛk] *vti* = connect *la19-*. *n* = connection, link *la19*, *Ags*.
conneeve [ko'niv] *vi* = connive *19-*, *now NE*.
connex *n* an item of property connected with another, an appurtenance *16-e19*: 'annexis, connexis and pertinentis'. [*cf* eModEng]
connoch &c ['konəx] *n* a cattle-plague, murrain *15-e19*.
~ worm the caterpillar larva of the hawkmoth *19*, *local*. [Gael *conach*]
connotar &c [*'ko(n)'notər] *n* a notary acting conjointly with another *la16-17*. [MedL *connotarius*, obs F *connotaire*; *cf* NOTAR]
conqueis see CONQUIS
conqueist see CONQUEST
conques &c [*'konkwɛs, *'kʌn-] *n* = CONQUEST *n*, *16-17*. [var of CONQUIS or CONQUEST after CONQUESS]
conquess &c, conques &c; conquesh *17* [*'konkwɛs, *-kwɛʃ, also *kon'kwɛs] *vt* **1** conquer *la15-e20*. **2** acquire (land etc) otherwise than by inheritance *la15-e19*. **3** acquire, gain *la15-17*. [back-formation f *conquest*, pt, ptp of CONQUEST *v*]
conquest; conqueist *16-17* ['konkwɛst; *-kwist] *n* **1** = conquest *15-*. **2** *law* acquisition, *esp* of property; property acquired, not inherited *la15-19*.
vt, pt, ptp **conquest, conqueist 1** = conquest, conquer *15-e17*. **2** acquire, gain *la15-19*.
conquis &c, conqueis [*'konk(w)ɪs, *-kwis; *v* also *kon'kwɪs] *n* = CONQUEST *n* 1 *(16-e17)*, *n* 2 *(la16-e18)*.
vt = CONQUEST *v* 1 *(16-17)*, 2 *(16-17)*. [OF *conquis, conquise*, ptp of *conquerre*; *conqueis* forms perh partly back-formation f *conqueist*, pt, ptp of CONQUEST; *cf* CONQUES]
conray, cunray [*'kʌn're, *'kʌnre] *vt* handle or deal with severely *e15*. [only Sc; OF *conraier*; *cf* CUMRAY]
consait see CONCEIT
consanguinean [konsaŋ'gwɪnɪən] *adj*, *law* descended from the same father but not the same mother *18-*. [L *consanguineus*]
conserjary &c, consergerie &c [*'kon-'sɛrdʒərɪ] *n*, *chf* **~ hous** the house used as an inn by the Scottish merchants at Campvere, Holland *17-e18*. [only Sc; F *conciergerie*]
conservator, conservatour &c *15-e17* *n* **1** = conservator *la14-*. **2** an official defender of the privileges of an institution or corporate body *16*. **3** an officer of the STAPLE at Campvere, Holland, appointed to protect the rights of the Scottish merchants and settle their disputes *16-18*; see also LORD.

considerin [kon'sɪdərən] *adj* considerate *20-*, *local*. [f Eng *consider*]
consign &c; consing &c *la16-e17* [*kon'sɪŋ, inflected *-'sɪŋj-] *vt* **1** = consign *la16-*. **2** *law* consign, deposit (*specif* money) as a pledge or pending judicial action *la16-e18*.
~atioun &c the depositing of a sum of money as in *v*, *la16-17*.
consistoré &c [*'konsɪs'torɪ, *'kon'sɪstərɪ] *n*, *law* = consistory, *specif* a bishop's court or the later COMMISSAR court *la15-e17*.
consistorial *adj*, *orig* pertaining to or competent before a CONSISTORÉ, *latterly in any court* pertaining to actions between spouses involving status (*eg* for divorce, separation) *la15-*. [MedL *consistorialis*; *cf* eModEng]
consither [kon'sɪðər] *vt* = consider *19-*, *chf N*.
consolidat *la16-17*, **consolidate** *vt* **1** *law* combine the superiority (SUPERIOR) and ownership of (property) in one person *la16-*. **2** = consolidate.
consolidation 1 *law* the joining of the superiority (SUPERIOR) and ownership of property in one person *17-*. **2** = consolidation.
constabill &c *la14-e17*, **counstable** *la15-16*; **constable &c** [*'kʌnstebl, *'kun-, *'kon-] *n* = constable *la14-*.
~ry, constablerie [*kən'stɛblərɪ &c] *n* = CONSTABULARY 1 *(la14-e17)*, 2 *(la15-e16)*.
C~ of Scotland one of the chief officers of the royal household *15-16*. **High C~ 1** *also* **Lord High C~** = prec, the hereditary title, held by the Hays of Errol, being reserved by the Treaty of Union in 1707, *17-*. **2** a member of a society of special constables created 1611 in Edb, who assumed the title *High* in 1805, *19-*, *now Edb*.
constabulary &c [*kən'stɛbələrɪ &c] *n* **1** the district under the jurisdiction of a constable *la15-16*. **2** the rank or office of constable *16-17*. **3** = constabulary.
constancy *n* **for a ~** incessantly, always *19*. [*cf* Eng]
constant &c *adj* **1** = constant *la15-*. **2** steadfast in an attachment, *esp* **to** (a person or cause) *or* **in** (a belief) *15-16*. **3** evident, proved *17*.
adv constantly, always *19-*, *now Ork Abd Ags*.
consterie *e18*, **constrie &c** [*'konst(ə)rɪ] *n* = CONSISTORÉ *la15-e18*. [reduced form; *cf* eModEng *const(e)ry*]
constitute &c *ptp* constituted *16-e19*.
vt **1** = constitute *la15-*. **2** give legal or official form to (an assembly) *17-*, *19-* *chf church*. [eModEng; L *constitut-*, ptp stem of *constituere*]
constrene &c *la15-16*, **constryne** *la16* [*'kon'strin, *-'strain] *vt* = constrain *la15-16*. [nME]
constrenʒe &c [*kon'strinji] *vt* = CONSTRENE *la15-16*. [only Sc; OF *constreign-*, stem of *constreindre*]
constrie see CONSTERIE

construct &c *vt* **1** build, construct *16-*. **2** construe, interpret in a certain way *17*, *only Sc.* [earlier in Sc; L *construct-*, ptp stem of *construere*]

constryne *see* CONSTRENE

consuetude &c [*'konswitəd] *n* **1** = consuetude *la15-*. **2** custom, habit *la15-19*.

consul *vti* = counsel *la15-e16*, *only Sc.*

consumpt [ʔkon'sʌm(p)t] *n* consumption, amount consumed *18-*. [L *consumpt-*, ptp stem of *consumere*]

consumption dyke *n* a wall built to use up the stones cleared from a field *la19-*, *now Abd.* [Eng *consumption* + DYKE]

cont *n* (*15*), *also* **cunt** *la14-e16*, *vt* (*la14-16*) [*kʌnt] = COMPT *n* 1, *v.* [only Sc; OF *conte(r)*, *cunte*, var of *counte(r)*]

containow *see* CONTEENA

conteen &c *la16-*, **contene** &c *la14-17* [kon'tin] *vtir* **1** = contain *la14-*, *now NE, Fif.* **2** *vr* bear or conduct oneself *la14-16.*

~**ing** behaviour, bearing *la14-e15.*

conteena &c *19-*, *local*, **continue** &c; **continow** *la15-e18*, **containow** *la17-e18* [*kon-'tin(j)u; kon'tinə, -ɪ] *vti* **1** = continue *la14-*. **2** *law* (1) adjourn, prorogue, put off (a case etc) *15-*, *chf Sc*; (2) grant (a person) a delay or respite *16.*

continuation &c **1** = continuation *15-*. **2** adjournment, postponement *la15-*. **with continuation of days** &c *law* with provision or allowance for a case etc to be continued or adjourned to a later date *la14-17.*

contempn &c [*kon'tɛm(p)n] *vt* = contemn *la15-e17.*

~**andly** contemptuously, scornfully *la15-e17.*

contemporane &c [*kon'tɛmporen, *-ən] *adj* = contemporaneous *15-16*. [L *contemporāneus*]

contemptioun &c [*kon'tɛmp(t)ʃ(ɪ)un, *-ən] *n* **1** contempt; insolent disregard **of** (authority), *freq* **in** (**hie**) ~ **of** *la15-e17*. **2** the state of being scorned *16.*

~ **done to** a display of contempt shown to (an authority). [chf Sc; L *contemptio*; *cf* eModEng *contempcion* (rare)]

contemptiouslie &c [*kon'tɛmp(t)ɪəslɪ] *adv* = contemptuously *la16-e17*. [only Sc; irreg var]

contene &c; **contine** *la15-16* [*kon'tin] *vti* = continue *la14-16*. [ME; irreg var]

contene *see* CONTEEN

content[1] *adj* **1** = content *15-*. **2** pleased, happy *19-*, *now Fif Stlg.*

content[2] [kon'tɛnt] *n* **1** = content, satisfaction *la15-*. **2** a drink of hot water, milk and sugar *19-*, *Bnf Ags Fif Arg.*

conter &c ['kontər; *'kuntər, *'kʌnt-] *prep* against *la18-*, *now Edb.*

adj opposite, *freq* ~**gate**(**s**) *20-*, *now Ags.*

n **1** the contrary *20-*, *now Bnf Ags.* **2** a reverse, misfortune *la18-*, *now Ags.*

vt **1** = counter *la14-16*. **2** oppose, contradict, thwart *la18-.*

~**min't** contrary, perverse *la19-*, *Abd.* ~**-tree** a crossbar preventing a door being opened from the inside *e19*, *NE.*

gae ~ **to** go against (someone's wishes, expectations) *la19-*. [*cf* Eng *counter* and CONTRA]

conterm [*kon'tɛrm] *vt*, *only as ptp*, *adj* ~(**i**)**t** determined *la15-e20*. [obscure]

contermacious &c ['kontər'maʃəs, 'kontrə-, &c] *adj* perverse, self-willed, obstinate *19-*, *local Bnf-Fif.* [altered f Eng *contumacious* w infl f CONTER]

contermaister, **countermaister** [*'kuntər-'mestər] *n* the mate of a ship *la16-e17*. [only Sc; OF *contremaistre*]

contigue &c [*kon'tigju &c] *adj* contiguous, adjacent *la15-e18*. [only Sc; F *contigu*, L *contiguus*]

contine *see* CONTENE

continow, continue *see* CONTEENA

contra &c [*kon'tre, *'kontre] *prep* **1** = contra, *chf* **pro and** ~ *la15-*. **2** *in gen* against *la15-17*, *only Sc.* [*cf* CONTER]

contract; contrack &c *only Sc* [*n*, *v* *kon-'trak(t)] *n* = contract *la14-.*

v **1** *vt* bring together, collect *e16*. **2** *vti* = contract, agree *16-.*

contrafait &c, **compterfit** &c [*'kontrə'fet, *'kunter'fet, *-'fit, *-'fɪt, &c] *vt* = counterfeit *16*. [*cf* COUNTERFUTE[2]]

contrair &c, **contrare** &c, **contrer** *la14-16* [kon'trer, 'kontrər] *adj*, *adv*, *n* = contrary *la14-.*

prep **1** in opposition to, against *15-e19*. **2** contrary to, at variance with *la15-e17.*

vt go contrary to, oppose, contradict *la14-*. [chf Sc; ME (rare); F *contraire*]

contramand *vt* = countermand *16*. [var after L *contrā-*]

contrapart &c *n* = counterparty, the opposing party *16*. [var after L *contra-*]

contrare *see* CONTRAIR

contrary &c [*kon'trerɪ] *vti* **1** = contrary, oppose *la14-e16*. **2** *of the wind* be contrary *15-e17.*

contravaill &c *vt* countervail *la16*. [var after L *contrā-*]

contravene &c *v* **1** *vt* = contravene *16-*. **2** *vi* act contrary **to** (a statute etc) *la16-17.*

contray, contré *see* COUNTRA

contremandment *n* a counter-order *la14-e15*. [F *contremandment*; *cf* eModEng *countre-maundement*]

contrer *see* CONTRAIR

contreth *see* CUNTRETH

contryne &c [*kon'trəin] *vt* constrain *la16*. [var of CONSTRYNE after F *contraindre*]

contumax &c [*'kontəmaks] *adj* = contumax, contumacious *la15-17.*

~(**i**)**t**, ~**ed** declared guilty of contumacy *la16-17.*

convalesce &c; convales, convoles *la16-17*
vi **1** = convalesce *16-*. **2** become strong,
acquire or regain strength *16-e17, only Sc.*

conveen *see* CONVENE

conveevial [kon'vivɪəl] *adj* = convivial *la19-*.

convene &c; convine &c *la16-17*, **conveen**
&c *17-e19* [kon'vin] *vti* **1** = convene *15-*. **2** *vt*
summon before a tribunal *15-17*. **3** *vi* come to
an accord, agree *16-e17*. **4** *vt* agree upon,
arrange *16*. **5** *vi* suit, be fitting, pertain naturally **to** *la15-19*.

convener &c *n* **1** = convener, a person who
assembles along with others, a person who convenes a meeting *la16-*. **2** *specif* the president of
the *Incorporated Trades* (INCORPORATE) in a
BURGH, the *deacon convener* (DEACON) *17-*. **3** the
chairman of a committee, *esp* a county council
or a committee of a town or county council or
latterly of a *Regional* (REGION) or *Islands Council*
(ISLAND) *la17-*.

convenery *n* **1** a body met for official purposes,
a convention *la18-e19*. **2** *specif* the court presided over by CONVENER *n* 2, *la18-19*.

convention &c *n* **1** = convention *15-*. **2** an
extraordinary meeting of *the Estates* (ESTATE) to
deal with emergencies *16-e18*. **3** a meeting of
the commissioners of BURGHS *16-20, freq* **C~ of**
Burghs &c *la16-e18*, **C~ of Royal Burghs**
la18-20, now amalgamated with other local
government bodies to form the **C~ of Scottish**
Local Authorities (**COSLA**) *la20-*.

conversation &c *n* **1** = conversation *la14-*. **2**
specif, elliptical for **~ sweet** *or* **lozenge** a flat
sweet of varying shape inscribed with a motto
la19-, local.

convey &c *vt* **1** = convey *16-*. **2** escort, conduct
la16-, now Bnf Abd. [*cf* CONVOY]

convict &c *la16-* *vt, also* **convick &c** *15-* = convict *la15-*.
n a conviction, verdict of guilty *la16, only Sc.*

convine *see* CONVENE

convoles *see* CONVALESCE

convoy &c [*n, v* kon'voi; *Cai NE* kon'vəi] *vt* **1**
convey *la14-*. **2** escort, accompany, conduct
la14-, chf Sc. **3** pursue *la14-e15, only Sc.* **4** carry,
transport (goods etc) *16-*.
n **1** deportment, bearing *e16*. **2** the escorting or
accompanying of a person on his way; company
la16-. **3** an escort *la16-e17*. **4** the management
of affairs *la16*.
~ance &c **1** = conveyance *16-19*. **2** escort,
escorting *16, 20-* (*Ags*).
a Scots *or* **Hielan** (*la19-, now Ork Ags Per*) **~**
accompanying a person on his journey home:
(1) some of the way *19-*; (2) all the way and
being accompanied in return some of the way
back *20-, WC.* [ME *convoye* (*v*) (rare), OF *con-*
voyer (*v*), var of *conveyer*, and *convoi* (*n*); *cf*
CONVEY]

convyn &c [*'konvəin, *kən'vəin] *n* = covin,
an agreement; condition; a company *la15-e16*.
[only Sc; OF *convine*, var of *covine*]

conyngare *see* CUNIGAR

conȝe *see* CUNYIE

coo *la19-*, **kow &c, cow, quow** *la16-e17* [ku;
Bwk S kʌu] *n, pl* **kye &c** *la14-* [kaɪ], **~s &c**
la16- **1** = cow *la14-*. **2** a cow given as a payment to the clergy on the death and burial of a
householder *16*.
~ie a (baby's) teat *20-, now Edb Bwk.*
~-cakes the cow parsnip *la19-, now Fif.*
~-cracker the bladder campion *la19-, C, S.*
~'s drink hot treacle given to sick cows; a hot
drink of any sort to induce sweating *la19-, Ags*
Fif. **~-feeder** a dairy farmer *19-, chf Ags.* **~**
gang pasturage for a cow *19-e20, S.* **~(i)s** *or*
kyis (*la15-17*) **gress, girs** enough pasturage
for a cow *la15-, now Kcb Rox.* **~('s) quake &c**
a short spell of bad weather in May *17-, now*
Abd Fif. **kye-time** milking-time *la20-, NE Uls.*

cooard &c *19-*, **cowart &c** *la14-19*; **coord-**
la19- ['ku(ə)rd, 'ku(ə)rt] *n, adj* = coward *la14-*.
~iness = cowardliness *la19-, local Bnf-Fif.*
~ly = cowardly *la14-, now local Abd-Fif.* **~y**
= prec *la19-, now Fif Stlg.* **~y lick** a blow
given as a challenge to fight *la19-, now Fif Lnk.*

cooch *la19-*, **couch &c** [kutʃ, kʌtʃ] *n* **1** =
couch *16-*. **2** a cradle-cloth *la14-e16.*
vti **1** = couch *la15-*. **2** *specif* make, command
(a dog) to lie down *20, Abd.*
~er 1 a coward, poltroon *17-e20*. **2** a blow or
tap on the shoulder as a challenge to fight *19-,*
now local C, only Sc.
~ bed a couch used as a bed; a bed without
hangings or canopy *la15-e17.*
~ up *vi, of persons* go to bed *20, local NE, EC.*

cood¹ *la18-*, **cude, quid** *la19-, NE*; **cweed &c**
la19-, NE [kød; *Cai Uls* kid; *NE* kwid; *C* kɪd]
= cud *la16-*.

cood², **cude &c, cud, quid** *19-, NE*; **cweed**
&c *la19-, NE* [kød; *Sh* kʌd; *NE* kwid] *n* **1** a
shallow tub, a wooden dish or basin, *esp* for
holding milk *la16-, now Abd.* **2** a large tub for
washing, storage, transportation etc *17-, now*
Ags.
~ie, cootie [*'kødɪ &c, *'køtɪ] = *n, 17-.*
cuitty-boyne *n* a small tub used for
foot-washing *19-e20, SW.* [see SND Suppl]

coof &c, coff &c *la16* [kuf, køf, kɪf] *n* **1** a
rogue *la16*. **2** a fool, simpleton *18-*. **3** a useless,
incompetent person; a feckless person *la19-*. **4** a
lout, rustic *19-, now Fif.* **5** a coward *19-, now*
Ags. [*cf* eModEng *cofe* and Eng slang *cove*]

coo-heel *vi, imperative, esp to a dog* come away
la19-, Ags. [prob corruption of Eng *come to heel*]

cook &c [kuk, kug] *vi* disappear suddenly from
view; dart in and out of sight *la18-e20.*
n the game of hide-and-seek *la19-, now Fif.*
~erty, ~erty, I, I, I *exclam* in the game of
hide-and-seek *la20-, S.* [perh connected w
KEEK¹; *cf* LowGer *kucken* peep]

cook *see* CUIK

cookie &c, cukie &c ['kukɪ] *n* **1** a plain bun
18-. **2** a prostitute, 'tart' *20-, Fif WC.*

~ **shine** a tea party *19-*.
fruit *etc* ~ a bun with currants etc in *18-*.
[perh f Eng *cook*, but *cf* Du *koekje* a small cake > US *cookie*]
cool &c *19-*, **cowl, coule** &c [kul] *n* **1** *now only* **cowl** = cowl *la15-*. **2** a (*usu* woollen) close-fitting cap *18-*.
cool *see* CUIL
coom[1] &c, **cowm** [kum] *n* **1** soot; coal-dust; DROSS *16-*. **2** PEAT[1]-dust; fine turf mould *la19-e20, SW Uls*.
vt dirty, blacken, stain *la16-*.
~**y** *n* a miner *la19-*, *chf Ayr*. [appar var of Eng *culm*; *cf* ME *coame* and GUM[5]]
coom[2] &c, **cowm** &c [kum] *n* **1** the wooden frame on which an arch (*freq* of a bridge) is built; an arch or vault *16-19*. **2** the sloping part of an attic ceiling *20-*, *local*.
~**ed** vaulted, arched; *of a ceiling* sloping *18-*.
coomceil &c, **cumseil, -syle** &c ['kum'sil; 'kʌm-; -'səil] *vt* **1** furnish with an arched ceiling *la16-17*. **2** lath and plaster (a ceiling) *la18-e20*. **3** *only in adj* **coomceiled** &c having a sloping ceiling *19-*. *n* = CAMCEIL *la18-*, *rare*. [uncertain]
coont *la19-*, **count** &c, **cwint** *e20, Abd* [kunt; *Abd* kwɪnt] *vti* **1** = count *la14-*. **2** *vi* do arithmetic *19-*. **3** *vi* settle accounts **with** *18-*, *chf NE*.
n **1** an account (of money etc) *15-*, *now Abd Ags*. **2** = count *16-*. **3** *chf in pl* arithmetic, sums *20-*.
counter = comptar (COMPT) *la16-17*.
~ **kin wi** compare one's pedigree with that of, claim relationship with *19-*, *now Bnf Abd*.
coontenance *n* = countenance *20-*.
coonter-louper *n* a person who serves behind a counter, a shop-assistant *la19-*. [Eng *counter* + *loup* (LOWP[1])]
coonty *n* = county *la19-*.
coop[1] *n* a small heap of manure, hay etc *19-e20*. [*cf* Gael *coip* a heap of foam]
coop[2] *vt* make or repair (casks) *la18-e19*. [f Eng *cooper*]
coop *see* COUP[1]
Co-operative [kopə'retɪv] *n* = STORE 2, *20-*, *local*.
coor[1] *la19-*, **cour** &c; **curr** *la18-* [kur, kʌr] *v* **1** *vi* = cower *la15-*. **2** *vt* bend, lower, fold *la18-*, *local NE-Ayr*.
~**ie** &c *adj* timid, cringing *19-*, *C, S*. *vi* **1** stoop, bend, crouch **down**; cringe *18-*. **2** snuggle, nestle *20-*, *local*. ~**ie hunker** squat, crouch *20-*, *local*.
coor[2] *19-*, **cure** &c [kur] *vt* = cover *la15-*, *now Fif*.
coorag[1] *n* a woollen cap; a nightcap *20-*, *Cai*. [Gael *currachd*, appar f CURCH]
coorag[2] &c *n* the index finger *20-*, *Cai*. [Gael *corrag*]
coord- *see* COOARD
coordie &c *vi* be cowed, shrink *20-*, *now Bnf Abd Fif*. [prob conflation of COOARD w *coorie* (COOR[1])]

coorgy ['kurdʒɪ] *n* a blow or push given as a challenge to fight; a challenge *20-*, *Loth Lnk*. [see SND]
coorie [*'kørɪ] *n* the stables of the royal household *e17*. [only Sc; F *écurie*]
coorse[1] *la19-*, **cours** &c *16-17*; **coarse** *la18-* [kurs] *adj* **1** = coarse *16-*. **2** *of weather* foul, stormy *la18-*. **3** *of persons* (1) wicked, bad, naughty *la19-*, *chf NE*; (2) rough, awkward, over-direct in manner(s) *la19-*. **4** hard, trying; disagreeable *la19-*, *Bnf-Ags*.
coorse[2] &c, **cours**; **course** &c [kurs] *n* **1** = course *la14-*. **2** usual legal procedure, *usu* **be** ~ **of commoun law** *15-16*.
coursable *adj, law, appar* legal, fulfilling normal legal procedure, *esp* **coursable brevis of one's** *or* **the chapel** *la15-e16*.
in ~ **1** of course *la19-*, *now local Cai-Uls*. **2** in due course *la19-*, *N Per Ayr*.
coort *see* COURT
cooser &c; **cuisser** &c [*'kusər] *n* a stallion *18-e20*. [altered f CURSOUR]
coosie ['kuzɪ] *n* a challenge to a feat of dexterity or daring *la19-*, *Ags*. [? reduced f *that coos ye* (COW[2])]
coot; queet &c [kwit] *n* the guillemot *la17-*, *NE*. [see OED]
coot *see* CUIT
cooter *20-*, **culter** &c; **couter** &c *16-19* ['kutər; *Sh Ork* 'kultər] *n* **1** = coulter *la14-*. **2** ludicrous name for the nose *la19-*, *chf N*.
coothie *see* COUTH
cootie &c *adj, of fowls* having feathered legs *la18-e20, SW*. [prob f CUIT]
cootie *see* COOD[2]
cop &c [kop, kʌp] *interj, freq* ~ ~ call to a horse to approach *20-*, *local*. [Eng *come up*; *cf ca way* etc (COME)]
cop *see* CAP[1]
cope &c *vt, n* = COUP[2] *la16-e17*.
copar &c a person who buys and sells, a dealer *16-e17*. **coping-boit** = *couperboit* (COUP[2]) *la16*. [laME *cope*, MDu *copen*]
cope *see* CAP[1]
cope-carlie *see* COUP[1]
copnoche *see* COLPINDACH
copy &c; **coppé** &c *16* *n* **1** = copy *la14-*. **2** a copy-book *20-*.
vt **1** = copy *la15-*. **2** note, observe *la15-e16*, *only Sc*.
~ **wattie** copy, crib; take note of *20-*, *Abd*.
coram *n* = quorum *17-e18*. [conflation of Eng *quorum* w L *coram* in the presence of; *cf* QUORUM]
corbell &c *n* = corbel *15-17*.
~**sail3e** &c a series of corbels *e16*.
Corbett *n, mountaineering* name for a Scottish mountain of between 2500 and 3000 feet (761 - 914 metres approx) *la20-*. [f J R Corbett, who listed them; *cf* DONALD and MUNRO]
corbie &c, **corby** *n* **1** the raven *15-*. **2** *occas* the carrion crow or hooded crow *la19-*. **3** the rook *20-*, *local*.

~ **messenger** the raven sent out by Noah; *transf* a dilatory or unfaithful messenger *la15-, now Bnf Fif.* ~ **stanes** = *crawsteps* (CRAW¹) *20-, local.*

be a gone ~ be a 'goner', be done for *19-.* [chf Sc; OF *corbe*]

corcag &c ['korkəg] *n* a small knife *20-, Cai.* [Gael]

corchat [*'kortʃət] *n* = crotchet (in music) *e16, only Sc.*

corce *see* CROSS¹

cord¹ *vti* = accord *la14-, now Kcb.* [aphetic]

cord² &c *n* **1** = cord *la14-.* **2** *specif* one of the ropes (held by close relatives and friends of the deceased) by which a coffin is lowered into the grave *20-.* **3** a bundle **of** (skins) *la16-17.* **4** *in pl* an intestinal inflammation in calves *19-, now Lnk.*

cordale *see* CORDELL

cordecedron *see* CORDISIDRON

cordell; cordale &c *16 n* a rope, *esp* as part of a ship's tackle *16-e17.* [F *cordelle,* f *corde* a rope; *cf* US, Canadian and F = a towing rope]

cordiner &c, cordenar &c *la15-16,* **cordonar &c** *15-e17* ['kord(ə)nər] *n* = cordwainer, a shoemaker *15-, only Sc.*

cordisidron &c, cordecedron &c [*'kordɪ-'sɪdron, *-'sid-] *n* lemon peel *17-e18.* [only Sc; F *écorce de citron*]

cordonar *see* CORDINER

cordwall &c *n* = cordwain, Cordovan leather *la15-e16.* [only Sc; irreg var]

core &c *n* **1** *curling* (CURL) a team of *curlers la18-, now Abd Ags.* **2** a (*freq* convivial) party or company *la18-.* [eModEng *chore* a choir, company]

corenoch *see* CORONACH

corf &c *n* a basket *16-e17.* [eModEng]

corfhouse &c *n* a salmon-curing shed *la16-.* [see SND]

cork *n* **1** an overseer; a master tradesman; a small employer; name given by weavers to a manufacturer's agent *la19-, local.* **2** name for anyone in authority *19-, local.* [see SND]

corkir &c *n* a red lichen used in dyeing *18-e19.* [Gael *corcur* crimson]

corklit [*'kork(ə)'lɪt] *n* = prec *la17-e20, SW.* [appar obs Eng *cork* (f as CORKIR) + LIT]

corky *adj* of or like cork.

n a feather-brained person *18-.*

~**-heidit** feather-brained *la18-19.* ~ **noddle** = *n, 19.* [Eng colloq = light; lively; skittish]

cormundum [*'kor'mʌndəm] *v* = cry ~, *19.* **cry** ~ confess one's fault *16.* [L = a clean heart in Psalms li. 10 (*Vulgate* l. 12)]

corn &c *n* **1** = corn *la14-.* **2** *specif* oats *la18-.* **3** a single grain *la15-, now Kcb.* **4** *in pl* crops of grain *la14-.*

v **1** *vt* feed with oats or grain (1) (a horse) *la18-;* (2) (poultry) *la20-, NE Ags.* **2** *vi, of persons* take food etc *18-.*

~**ed** exhilarated with drink, tiddly *19-, chf Bnf.* ~**in time** meal-time *la19-, now Fif.*

~**-crake, -craik 1** the corncrake, the landrail *la15-.* **2** a toy rattle *la19-, local.* ~ **harp** an instrument for separating grain and weed seeds *19-, NE.* ~ **kist** a storage-bin for corn *17-.* ~ **kister** a type of song sung at farmworkers' gatherings *20-, Bnf Abd Fif.* ~ **pipe** a music-pipe made from an oat stem *16-e20.* ~ **yaird,** ~ **ȝard &c** a stack-yard *la15-.*

waur to water than (**to**) ~ addicted to drink *19-.*

corneill &c [*kor'nil] *n* = corneole, a cornelian *16-e17.*

cornel &c *n* = colonel *la17-19.*

cornet *n* **1** = cornet *16-.* **2** [*Hawick also* kor'nɛt] *specif in ceremonies of riding of the marches* (RIDE) the chief rider and standard-bearer of the BURGH *18-, chf S*; see also LORD.

cornicle &c *n* = chronicle *la14-e17, only Sc.*

coronach &c, corenoch &c, cronach &c *la18-19* ['korənəx, 'kronəx] *n* **1** a funeral lament or outcry; a dirge *16-.* **2** *chf* **the** ~ an outcry; a loud shout from a crowd *16-17.*

cronachin *presp* gossiping, tattling; grumbling *19-e20.* [only Sc; ScGael *corranach,* IrGael *coránach*]

coronell &c *n* = coroner *la16-e17.* [by conflation of form w Eng *coronell* a colonel]

corp &c *n, pl* **corps &c** *17-* **1** = corpse *la15-.* **2** **the** deceased *la19-, local Bnf-Lnk.*

~ **candle &c** a will-o'-the-wisp *la19-, WC, SW.* ~**-lifter** a body-snatcher *la19-, chf NE.* [prob erron sing f ME *corps*]

corpus *n* **1** = corpus. **2** the live body of a man or animal *19-, now Abd Fif.*

corrie &c *n* a hollow on the side of a mountain or between mountains *16-.* [Gael *coire* a cauldron or place resembling one; a kettle]

corrie *see* CAR²

corrieneuchin &c [korɪ'njuxɪn, -ən; -'njuk-] *presp* conversing intimately *19-, Bnf Ags Fif.* *n* a tête-à-tête *la19-, Bnf Ags.* [perh *coorie* (COOR¹) + NEUK]

corruption &c *n* **1** = corruption *la15-.* **2** temper, anger *la19-, now local Bnf-Fif.*

corrydander [korɪ'dandər] *n* = coriander *19-, now Abd Lnk.*

cors *vt* search for, seek out; visit *16.* [only Sc; obscure]

cors(e) *see* CROSS¹

cors-gard &c, **crose-gaird &c** [*?'kors'gard, *-'gerd; *?'kros-] *n* = corps de garde, a small body of soldiers on guard-duty; a guard-room *la16-e17.*

Corstorphine cream *n* a preparation of thickened milk and sugar *18-20.* [f the place-name [kor'storfɪn], now part of Edinburgh]

corsy-belly &c *n* a child's pleated shirt *la18-e20, chf Abd.* [uncertain]

corter *see* QUARTER

cortrik *n* cloth from Courtray *la14-15*. [only Sc; MFlem *Cortrik* Courtray in Flanders]

cose &c, **cosse** &c, **quoss** *e16* [*Sh Ork* koz; *sEC* *kos] *vt* exchange; barter *15-*, *now Sh Ork*. *n* an exchange (*esp* of lands) *la15-e17*. [chf Sc; eModEng *coase* (*la16*); *cf* Eng dial *corse, scorce*]

cosey *see* COSIE

cosh &c *adj* **1** snug, comfortable, cosy *la18-*. **2** friendly, intimate *la18-*, *local*. [perh conflation of TOSH w COSIE]

cosie &c ['kozɪ] *adj* **1** *of persons* warm and comfortable, well wrapped-up *la17-*. **2** *of places* sheltered, providing comfort and protection *la18-*.
n, *only* **cosey** a woollen scarf *la19-*, *local*. [see SND Suppl]

COSLA *see* CONVENTION

cosnant &c [*'kosnənt] *n* wages without board *la17-e19*.
adv **costanent** &c [*'kostənənt] working for wages without board *19-e20*, *chf Uls*.
~ **work** etc work unpaid either in money or board *e19*. [obscure]

cosse *see* COSE

cost &c *n* payment in kind for rent, dues or wages *16-*, *chf Ork*. [ON *kostr* food, ultimately f MedL *costa* food, victuals]

cost *see* COAST[1], COAST[2]

costanent *see* COSNANT

cot &c *n* = cot, a cottage *16-*.
cottar &c *n* a tenant occupying a cottage with or (*la18-19*) without land attached to it; a married farmworker who has a cottage as part of his contract *15-*. *vi* live as a *cottar* in a *cot-house*, *20-*, *NE*.
cottery &c a *cottar*'s holding *la15-e19*.
cottar &c ('s) **beer** &c barley grown as part of a *cottar*'s remuneration *18-e19*. **cottar house** = *cot house*, a tied cottage *la16-*. **cottar** &c **land** = *cot land*, *la16-e17*. **cottar town** &c = *cot to(u)n*, *17-*, *Ags*. **cottrall** &c = *cottar*, *la15-16*.
~**-folk** those who live in farm cottages *la18-*. ~ **house** a cottage; a farmworker's cottage *16-*. ~**land** land attached to a cottage *15-18*. ~**man** = *cottar*, *la16-*, *chf SW*. ~**-to(u)n** &c a hamlet *esp* of farm cottages *16-*, *now Ags Fif*.

cot *see* COAT, QUOT

cotch *see* CATCH

cote *n* = COT *la15-16*, in *place-names 14-*.
cotar &c *la15-e16*, **coitter** *16-e17*, **coatter** *17* [*'kotər] *n* = cottar (COT) *la15-17*.
~ **house** (*16-e18*), ~ **land** (*la14-17*) = COT-. [ME, OE]

cote *see* COAT, QUOT

cotonar &c *n* a piece of some small fur, used for lining *e16*. [only Sc; OF *cotoner*]

cottar *see* COT

cotter *vt* scramble (eggs) *la19-*, *Ags Fif*. [eModEng *cotter* clot, coagulate]

cotter, cottery, cottrall *see* COT

couch *see* COOCH

coud *see* CAN[2]

cougher ['koxər] *vi* cough continuously *19-*, *now Abd*. [frequentative of Eng *cough*]

couk *see* COWK

coukuddy &c [*ku'kʌdɪ, *ko-] *n* = CURCUDDIE *n*, *la18-19*. [perh COOK + CUDDY]

coule *see* COOL

coulichin *see* KILCHAN

coulie *see* COWLIE

coulter &c [*'kʌultər] *n* a cautery *la17-e18*. [eModEng *cauter* &c]

councell *see* COUNSAILL

council &c ['kunsl] *n* = council *17-*.
~ **house 1** = *counsail-hous* (COUNSAILL) *la17-19*. **2** = council house. [*cf* COUNSAIL]

counger &c ['kun(d)ʒər; *Rox also* 'kʌn(d)ʒər &c] *vt* **1** keep in order, scold *la19-*, *NE*, *WC*. **2** overawe, intimidate *19-*, *NE, S*. [see SND]

counsail &c, **councell** &c *la16-17*, **counsele** &c [*kun'sel, *'kunsel, *'kunsl] *n* **1** = counsel, council *15-17*. **2** a council of the realm; a CONVENTION of *the Estates* (ESTATE), taking the place of a parliament, *esp* **General C~** *15-16*. **3** the body of advisers to the king, queen or regent, *esp* **Privy C~**, **Secret C~**, **Lordis of ~** *15-e17*. **4** a town council *la15-17*. *vti* = counsel *15-e17*.
counsally &c *adv* as a town-council *16*, *Edb Peebles*. ~ **hous** the house where council (*esp* town-council) meetings were held *la15-17*. [*cf* COUNCIL and CUNSAIL]

counstable *see* CONSTABILL

count *see* COONT

counter &c [*'kuntər] *n* the part of a horse's breast immediately under the neck *16*. [earlier in Sc]

countercheck ['kuntər'tʃɛk] *n* a tool for cutting the groove which unites the two sashes of a window *19-*, *now Abd Kcb*.

counterfoot *see* COUNTERFUTE[2]

counterfute[1] &c [*'kuntər'føt, *'kʌntər-, *-'fɪt] *n* some kind of plate or dish *16*. [obscure]

counterfute[2] &c; **counterfoot** &c *17* [*'kuntərfɪt, *-føt] *adj*, *vt*, *n* = counterfeit *la15-17*. [irreg var, prob after prec; *cf* CONTRAFAIT]

countermaister *see* CONTERMAISTER

countra &c *la19-*, **countré** &c *15-16*, **contré** &c *15-e17*, **contray** *la15-16*, **cuntray** &c *15-17*, **cuntré** &c *la14-e17*, **kintra** &c *la18-*, **cwintry** &c *la18-*, *N*; **country** &c *la15-*, **quintra** &c *e16*, *19-*, (*N*) ['kʌntrə; *NE* 'kwɪntrə, 'kwintrɪ; *C*, *S* 'kɪntrə, -ɪ; *'kuntrə] *n* **1** = country *la14-*. **2** a district; its inhabitants; the territory of a CLAN *la14-*, *now local*.
countryfeed = countryfied *la19-*, *local NE*, *nEC*.
~ **clash** the gossip of the district *19-*, *local Bnf-Kcb*. ~ **Jock** *disparaging* a farmworker *20-*, *Abd Fif*. **country-side** a rural district or tract of country *18-*.

county of the city ['kuntɪ; *St* 'kʌuntɪ] *n, pl* **counties of cities** any of the county BURGHS of Edinburgh, Glasgow, Dundee and Aberdeen, now all altered into *districts* (DESTRICK) with extended boundaries and more limited responsibilities *20*.

counȝe *see* CUNYIE

counȝie *n* meaning obscure *e16*.

coup[1] **&c, cowp &c; coop &c** *20-, Sh Ork* [kʌup; *Sh Ork* kup, kʌp; *Arg Uls* kop] *n* **1** an upset, overturning; a fall *16-, Gen except Sh Ork.* **2** a rubbish tip *la19-, local.* **3** *mining* a sudden break in a stratum of coal *la18-, now Fif.* **4** *freq contemptuous* a company, group *18-19.*
v **1** *vt* upset, overturn; *fig* lay low, ruin *la16-.* **2** set (a church-bell) *17.* **3** (1) tilt up; empty by upturning *la17-, Gen except Ags.* (2) toss off (liquor), quaff *la18-, now Bnf Abd Fif.* **4** *vi* overbalance, fall over, capsize; go bankrupt *17-, local.* **5** bend, incline as if to fall, heel over *la19-e20.*
~**y** a sheep that has turned over on its back and is unable to get up *20-, SW, S.*
~ **facken** shallow autumn ploughing to let the frost into the ground *20-, NE.* ~ **fauch &c** plough up (the green strip between furrows after *brak-furring* (BRAK)) *20-, NE.*
cope-carlie &c turn head over heels *19-e20, chf Uls.* ~ **the creels** **1** turn a somersault, fall head over heels *18-, now Fif.* **2** *of a woman* have an illegitimate child *19-, now Fif.* **3** die *19-e20.* **4** foil the plans or get the better **of** *la19-, NE.* ~ **the laidle** play see-saw *19-, Bnf Abd Fif.* **free** ~ a place where rubbish may be dumped free of charge *la19-, local.* **the haill** ~ the whole lot *19-, now Fif Lnk.* [chf Sc; ME *cowp* (*v*) strike, F *couper* (*v*) cut, *coup* a blow]

coup[2] **&c, cowp &c** [kʌup] *vt* buy, trade (goods, horses); barter, exchange *16-, now Bnf Abd Fif.*
~**er &c** **1** a trader, dealer *16-.* **2** *specif* (1) a horse-dealer *la16-;* (2) a buyer of herring *17-e19.* **couper-boit** a herring-buyer's boat *la16-e17.* [nME *coupe* (rare); ON *kaupa; cf* COPE]

coup[3] **&c** [kup] *n* **1** a basket for catching salmon *la15-e17.* **2** a closed cart for carrying manure or earth *la15-18.* [Eng *coop*]

coup[4], **cupe &c** *la16-17,* **culpe &c** *15-e16* [*kup, *kop, *køp] *n* = cup *la14-e17.* [OF; *cf* CAP[1]]

coupar *see* CUPAR

coup-cairt &c ['kʌup'kert, *'kup-] *n* **1** = COUP[3] 2, *la18-.* **2** a tipping cart *18-.* [prob orig f COUP[3], later associated w COUP[1]]

couper &c, cupar *la16-e17* ['kupər] *n* = cooper, a maker of casks etc *15-e18, as personal name la13-.*

couple, coupill &c *la14-e17,* **cuppill &c** *la14-17,* **cupple, kipple &c** *la17-, now WC-S,* **kipill &c** *16-17* ['kʌpl, 'kɪpl, *'kupl] *n* **1** = couple *la15-.* **2** *also* **kepill &c** *16* (1) a pair of rafters, forming a V-shaped roof support; one of these, a principal rafter *15-;* (2) used as a standard of length (= 12 feet (3.65 metres)) in a building *la15-17.* **3** *only* **cuppil &c** a measure of butter and cheese sold together *la17-e18, local WC.*
vti **1** = couple *la14-.* **2** *latterly chf* **kipple,** *vtir* marry *16-19.*

coupling &c **1** = coupling *la14-.* **2** (1) the framing of a roof with COUPLES (*n* 2 (1)) *la15-e16.* (2) a rafter *19-, now Per Slk.* **3** *only* **cupplin** the bottom of the spine where it joins the sacrum *19-, Bnf Fif.*
~ **bauk &c** = BAUK[1] *n* 5, *la18-, now local Cai-Fif.* ~ **leg** one of the pair of rafters as in *n* 2 (1), *19-, now Cai Bnf Fif.*

coupnay, coupnocht *see* COLPINDACH

coupon &c, coupoun &c *16* ['kʌupən, 'kup-] *n* a small piece (cut off), a fragment *16-e20.* [ME *culpon,* OF *colpon, copon* > ModF *coupon* whence it has been re-introduced into Eng]

coupy *see* COUP[1]

cour *see* COOR[1], COWER

courchay *see* CURCHA(Y)

courche *see* CURCH

cours *see* COORSE[1], COORSE[2]

course *see* COORSE[2]

coursere, coursour *see* CURSOUR

court &c, coort *la19-* [kurt] *n* **1** = court *la14-.* **2** a (covered) enclosure for cattle *la19-, local.*
vti = court, *latterly freq* ~ **wi** *17-.*
court buke the book containing the records of a court of justice *la15-16.* **court-house** the building where law-courts are held *19-, now NE.* **court plaint** the feudal privilege of dealing with complaints made to a court of justice *la15-e17.*

Court of Session see SESSION.

courtasy, courtesy *see* CURTASSY

courtician &c [*'kurtɪsɪən, *'kʌrt-] *n* a courtier *16.* [only Sc; obs F *courtisien*]

couschein *see* CUSHIN

cousigne, cousinace *see* KIZZEN

cout *see* COWT

couter *see* COOTER

couth &c [kuθ] *adj* **1** = couth, known *la14-16.* **2** = *couthie* 1 (*18-19*), 2 (1) (*18-, now Rox*).
~**ie &c, coothie** *adj* **1** *of persons* agreeable, sociable, friendly, sympathetic *18-.* **2** *of places or things* comfortable, snug, neat; pleasant, agreeable *la18-, local.* [ME; OE *cūþ,* ptp of CAN[3]]

couth *see* CAN[2], CAN[3]

couther *see* CUITER

cove &c; coif &c *la15-e17* [kov] *n* a cave, cavern *15-, now Cai Ags.*
vt hollow, scoop out (*chf* earth) *18-, now Sh.*
~ **ceiling** an arched or vaulted ceiling *la19-, local.* [*cf* Eng = a small bay etc]

coven *see* COVINE

covenant &c ['kʌvənənt] *n* **1** = covenant *la14-.* **2** *specif* **the C**~ the National Covenant (1638) *or* the Solemn League and Covenant (1643).

vi, specif be a supporter of either of *n* 2, *chf as* **C~er** *(17-),* **C~ing** *(19-)* [kʌvəˈnantər, -ˈnɛntər; kʌvəˈnantɪŋ], *now hist.*

non-covenanter one who did not support the COVENANT (*n* 2) *el7.*

cover &c, cuver &c *15-17,* **kiver** *18-, now Abd Loth Bwk,* **coer** *la18-19, WC* [ˈkʌvər; ˈkɪvər; *WC* *?ˈkoər, *?ˈkʌur] *vt* = cover *la14-.*

n **1** = cover *la15-.* **2** *specif* the maximum livestock a farm will carry *la18-.* **3** *mining* the strata between the workings and the sea-bed *la19-, now Fif.*

~ **the table** lay the cloth on the table *la18-, now Bnf Abd.*

covetta [?kəˈvɛtə] *n* a plane for moulding framed work, a quarter-round *19-, local.* [*cf* Eng *cavetto* a hollow moulding whose profile is a quadrant]

covine &c, **covyne;** **coven &c** [ˈkʌvən; *?ˈkovən] *n* **1** = covin, a compact, agreement; plot *la14-16.* **2** a company, band; *specif* a group of witches *16-.*

covin tree a tree in front of a Scottish mansion at which guests were met and from which they were sent off *19-e20, hist.* [ultimately f as Eng *convent*]

cow[1] **&c** [kʌu, ku] *n* **1** a twig or branch; a tufted stem of heather etc *16-;* see also *broom cow* (BROOM) and *heather cow* (HEATHER). **2** a BESOM or broom, *specif* as used in *curling* (CURL), *19-.* **3** a birch used for whipping *19-e20, NE.* [only Sc; perh the same as next]

cow[2] **&c** [kʌu] *vt* **1** poll, crop; cut (hair) *16-.* **2** cut, cut short *16-e20.* **3** eat up, consume *18-e20.* **4** surpass, outdo *la19-, local.*

n a crop, a haircut *la19-, local.*

~**it &c** *of cattle* polled *la16, e20.*

~ **a',** ~ **a'thing,** ~ **a' green thing** *(20-, NE),* ~ **the cadger** *(local),* ~ **the cuddy** *(local),* ~ **the gowan** *(19-, local)* surpass or beat everything *la19-.* [var of COLL[2]]

cow[3] **&c** [kʌu] *n* a hobgoblin; an object of terror *16-e20.* [obscure; perh f as cow[4]]

cow[4] [*kʌu] *vt* upbraid, scold, rebuke (one's equal or superior) *la18-el9.* [*cf* Eng *cow* intimidate]

cow *see* COO

cowan &c [ˈkʌuən] *n* **1** (1) a builder of *dry-stane* dykes (DRY) *la16-.* (2) *disparaging* one not properly apprenticed and trained as a mason *19-.* **2** *freemasonry* one outside the brotherhood, *esp* one seeking to know its secrets *la18-e20, local.* **3** an unskilled or uninitiated person; an amateur *19-e20.* [obscure]

cowart *see* COOARD

cowbill *see* COBLE[2]

cowbrig &c [*ˈkuˈbrɪg] *n* the orlop-deck of a vessel *16-el7.*

~**ing** material for such a deck *e16.* [only Sc; Du *koe-brügg*]

cowclink &c; **coclink** [*?ˈkuˈklɪŋk] *n* a prostitute *16.* [obscure]

cowd &c [kʌud] *vi* float slowly, rock gently on waves *19-e20, chf WC.*

cowdle = *v, 19-e20.* [obscure]

cowda, cowdach *see* CUDDOCH

cowdeich *see* CUDEIGH

cowdow *see* CUDDOCH

cowdrum &c [ˈkʌudrəm] *n* **get** ~ get one's deserts; get a beating or severe scolding *19-, NE.* [Gael *cothrum* justice]

cower &c, **cover &c** *la14-el7,* **cuver &c** *15-16;* **cour &c** *la18-* [*NE* kʌur, kəˈʌur; *ˈkʌvər] *v* **1** *vi* recover, get well *la14-, now chf NE.* **2** *vt* restore, revive *la14-el7.* **3** get over, recover from (something) *la18-, NE.*

cowffyne *n* meaning unknown *la16.*

cowgrane &c *n* ~ **silk** *or* **taffeteis** some kind of fabric *la16.* [perh altered f GROWGRANE]

cowhuby &c [*ˈkuˈhøbɪ] *n* ? a weak or silly person *16.* [obscure]

cowie *see* COO

cowk &c; **couk &c** [kʌuk] *vi* retch; vomit *la18-, now Bnf Abd Stlg.*

n a retch *20-, NE.* [only Sc; *cf* Du *kolken* (*v*) belch, Ger dial *kölken* vomit and Eng dial *keck*]

cowkin *n* (*adj*) meaning obscure *e16.* [perh = KOKEN]

cowl *see* COOL

cow-lady-stane &c [*?ˈkʌuˈledɪˈsten, &c] *n* a variety of quartz *19-e20, S.* [perh f Eng *cow-lady* the ladybird + STANE, f the colouring of the quartz]

cowld *see* CAULD

cowlie &c, **coulie** [ˈkʌulɪ] *n* **1** contemptuous term for a man *la17-, now Cai.* **2** a boy *19-e20, Edb.* [*cf* Eng slang *cully*]

cowm *see* COOM[1], COOM[2]

cowmon *see* COMMON

cown &c [kʌun] *vi* weep, lament *la19-, now Cai.* [Gael *caoin*]

cowp *see* COUP[1], COUP[2]

cowshin &c [ˈkʌuʃən] *vti* pacify, quieten *la19-, chf NE Ags.* [*cf* CAUTION and see SND]

cowshus &c [ˈkʌuʃəs] *adj* **1** = cautious *la19-, now local Bnf-Fif.* **2** unassuming, kindly, considerate *la19-, now Abd.* [*cf* prec]

cowslem &c [*S* *?ˈkʌuzləm] *n* the evening star *19-e20, S.* [perh Eng *cow's* + LEAM[1], the gleam of the star when the cattle are being driven home; *cf* Eng *folding-star*]

cowstick [ˈkʌustɪk] *n, adj* = caustic *la19-, now Bnf Abd Fif.* [for vowel *cf* COWSHIN]

cowsy &c [ˈkʌuzi, ˈkʌusi] *n, mining* a self-acting incline on which one or more full descending HUTCHES pull up a corresponding number of empties *la19-, local.*

~ **wheel** the drum or pulley on a COWSY *la19-, now Fif.* [perh CAUSEY]

cowt &c; **cout &c** [kʌut] *n* **1** = colt *15-.* **2** *transf of persons*: (1) a rough, awkward person *19-, now Abd;* (2) an adolescent boy or girl *19-, now Bnf.*

~ **foal** a young horse when suckling *la18-*, *SW*, *S*. ~ **halter** &c a halter made of rope or straw *19-*, *local NE-C*.

cowt *see* CUT[1]

coy, cwe &c [*koi, *kwi] *n* a cabin-bed, berth, bunk *16-e17*. [only Sc; Du *kooi*]

coy *see* QUEY

coyd *see* CUDE[3]

coyme *see* COME

coygerach *see* QUIGRICH

coyn3he *see* CUNYIE

coyst *see* CUST

crab; craib &c *la16-e17* *v* **1** *vt* annoy, make angry *la15-19*. **2** *vi* become angry *la15-*, *now Kcb*. [nME (rare); prob f CRABBIT]

crabbit &c, **crabit** &c; **craibit** &c *la16*, **crabbed** &c *la17-* *adj* **1** = crabbed *la14-*. **2** *now only* **crabbit** in a bad temper, cross *la14-*.

crack[1], **crak** &c, **craik** &c *16-17* *vti* **1** = crack *15-*. **2** *vi* boast, brag *la15-e20*. **3** talk, converse, gossip *la16-*. **4** *vt* strike sharply *20-*, *NE*.

n **1** = crack *la14-*. **2** *chf in pl* loud boasts or brags *16-e20*. **3** (1) a talk, gossip, conversation *la16-*. (2) a story, tale *18-*. (3) an entertaining talker, a gossip *19-e20*. **4** a moment, a short space of time, *chf* **within** *or* **in a** ~ *18-*. **5** a 'go', a SHOT in a game etc *la19-*.

~**er** &c **1** a boaster, braggart *16-*. **2** a talker, gossip *la19-*, *now Bnf Fif Stlg*. **3** *chf in pl* pieces of bone or wood used as castanets *la19-*, *now local Bnf-Stlg*. **4** the lash of a whip *19-*, *now local Cai-Kcb*. **5** *in pl*, *also* ~**erheads** TANGLE, an edible seaweed *19*, *Ags*. ~**y** &c talkative, affable; loquacious *19-*, *local*.

~ **nut** &c a hazelnut *la19-e20*. ~**raip** a gallows-bird *la15*.

~ **one's credit** become bankrupt; lose one's reputation, trust etc *19*. ~ **a match** *etc* strike a match *20-*, *N Kcb*. ~ **like a (pen-)gun, pea guns** *or* **twa hand guns** talk in a lively way, chatter loudly *la18-*, *now Bnf Abd Fif*. ~ **looves** &c shake hands; seal a bargain *la18-e19*. **get on the** ~ start a conversation *20-*. **gie's yer** ~(**s**) give us your news *18-*.

crack[2] *adj* crack-brained, crazy *19-*, *Bnf Abd*. ~**-wittet** = *adj*, *20-*, *Bnf Abd*. [prob reduced f Eng *cracked*]

crackie &c; **crocky** &c *n*, *also* ~ **stool** a low three-legged stool *19-e20*, *Ags S*. [*cf* Norw and Sw dial *krakk*]

crackins &c, **crakkings** &c, **craklings**; **cracklings** *n pl and attrib in sing* **1** the residue from tallow-melting *la16-e20*. **2** the residue from any rendered fat or oil *e20*, *local*. **3** a dish of fried oatmeal *20-*, *now NE*. [ME *crakan*]

cradill, cradle *see* CRAIDLE

cradoun *see* CRAWDOUN

craft &c *n* = craft *la14-*. ~**y** &c **1** = crafty *la14-*. **2** skilful, ingenious, clever *la14-*, *now local*.

craft *see* CROFT

crag *see* CRAIG[1], CRAIG[2]

craib *see* CRAB

craibit *see* CRABBIT

craidle &c *17-*, **cradill** &c *la14-e17*, **credill** &c; **cradle** *la16-* ['kredl, 'krɛdl] *n* **1** = cradle *la14-*. **2** a crate (of glass) *16-e17*.

vt **1** = cradle. **2** *chf mining* line (a shaft) with stone *17-*, *now Fif Ayr*.

craif *see* CRAVE

craig[1] &c, **crag** &c *n* **1** a crag, rock; cliff *la13-*. **2** a projecting spur of rock *la18-*. **3** rock as a material *16-e19*.

~**leif** &c leave to dig coal from a HEUCH *16-18*. ~ **mail** &c rent or other charges levied for quarrying *17-18*, *WC*. ~ **stane** &c a detached rock; a large stone *15-17*.

~**-and-tail** *geol* a formation consisting of a hill with a steep rock-face at one end sloping towards the other in a mass of drift or moraine, caused by the obstruction and splitting of a glacier by hard rock *19-*. [ScL *cragga e12*; *cf* nME *crag*; obscurely related to Gael *creag*, Welsh *craig*]

craig[2] &c, **crag** &c [kreg; *krag; *Rox also* *krag] *n* **1** the neck: (1) of a person *15-*; (2) of an animal, *esp* as part of a carcass *16-e17*; (3) of a garment *la16-e17*. **2** the throat, gullet *la18-*. *vt* drink, swallow *la19*.

~**ed**, ~**it** &c **1** -necked, *chf* **lang** ~ etc *la16-*. (**lang-**)~**ed heron** the heron *la19-*, *NE*. ~**ie** &c = *n*, *18-*, *now local Bnf-Edb*.

~ **cloth** &c a cravat *la17-e19*. ~'**s close** &c *joc* = *n* 2, *19-*. ~ **piece** armour for the neck *17*.

pit ower one's ~ swallow *la19-*, *now Bnf Abd Fif*. [MDu *craghe*, MLowGer, MHighGer *krage*; also in northern eModEng]

craighle &c, **creachle** &c; **crechle** &c ['krexl, 'krixl, 'krɛxl, &c] *vi* cough drily or huskily; wheeze *19-*, *now local Abd-Kcb*. [prob onomat; *cf* CROICHLE]

craik &c *vi* **1** *of birds* utter a harsh cry, croak *15-*, *now local*. **2** *of things* creak *19-*, *now Bnf Fif*. **3** ask persistently, clamour *19-*, *now local Abd-Kcb*. **4** grumble, complain *19-*, *local*.

n **1** the harsh cry of a bird, *esp* the landrail *16-*, *now local*. **2** the landrail *la18-*, *now Abd Fif*. **3** ill-natured gossip; grumbling talk *la19-e20*, *S*. [ME *crake*; imit]

craik *see* CRACK[1]

Crail capon *n* a type of dried or smoked haddock *19*, *Fif*. [Crail, the Fife village]

crainroch *see* CRANREUCH

craip &c; **crape** &c, **creip** &c *la16-17* [krep; *krip] *n* **1** = crape *la16-*. **2** a band of crape on an article of dress *16-17*.

craishan &c *n* a withered shrunken person *la19-*, *Cai*. [unknown]

craive *see* CRUIVE

crak *see* CRACK[1]

crakkings, craklings *see* CRACKINS

cram *v* **1** *vt* = cram. **2** *vi* push, crowd **in**(**to**) *la18-*, *local*.

cramasie &c, crammasy &c [*'kram(ə)zɪ]
adj, chf of materials, esp satin, velvet crimson *15-19*.
n crimson cloth *la15-e18, e20, latterly literary, only
Sc*. [OF *cramoisi; cf* obs Eng *cramoisy &c*]
crambo *n* = crambo.
~ **clink**, ~ **jink**, ~ **jingle** doggerel *la18-e20*.
crame &c, creme &c *la15-17*; **creame &c**
la16-19 n **1** a merchant's booth, stall *la15-e20*.
2 a portable case of goods, a pack *la16-e18*.
cramer &c a person who sells goods from a
stall or pack *la15-18*. ~**ery &c** a stall-holder's
or pedlar's goods *16-e18*. [only Sc; MDu *kraem*
a stall]
cramp[1] *n* **1** = cramp, a tool for holding. **2**
curling (CURL) = CRAMPET *n* 5 (1) and (*also in
pl*) 5 (2), *19-*.
cramp[2] *vt* munch *e20, N*. [only Sc; prob onomat; *cf* CRUMP]
cramp[3] *vi* strut, swagger; prance *la15-e17*. [only
Sc; obscure]
crampet &c; crampit &c *n* **1** = crampet (on
a scabbard) *16-e18*. **2** a cramp-iron *16-e19*. **3**
the iron guard at the end of a staff *18-e19*. **4** a
roof-gutter bracket, a support *19-, Abd*. **5** *chf
curling* (CURL) (1) a spike fixed to the shoe *17-,
now Ags Fif Lnk*; (2) the iron foot-board from
which a player throws his stone *la19-, now Abd
Fif Kcb*.
cramsh &c *vti* grit (one's teeth); crunch *20-,
Bnf Abd*. [onomat]
cran[1] **&c, cren** *15-e16*; **crane** *la18- n* **1** =
crane, the bird *15-*. **2** the heron *la18-e20*. **3** the
swift *la19-e20, local C-S*.
vi eavesdrop *20-, NE*.
cran[2] **&c** *now local NE-C*; **crane &c** *n* **1** =
crane, the machine *la14-*. **2** a means of supporting a pot etc over a fire: (1) an iron frame
placed across the fire *la18-e20*; (2) a trivet *18-,
now Cai*; (3) an iron upright with projecting
arm *18-, now Fif Stlg*.
cran[3] *n, measure of fresh, uncleaned herrings* one barrel, *latterly* fixed at 37.5 gallons (170.48 litres)
18-20. [Gael *crann*; see SND]
cran[4] **&c** *n* a tap *19-, Gen except Sh Ork*. [only
Sc; Du *kraan*]
crance &c *n* **1** some object made of brass, *perh* a
candle-holder *la16-e17*. **2** = cranse, a wreath
la16. [Du *krans*, garland, wreath]
crane &c *n* the cranberry *la18-, chf S*.
crane *see* CRAN[1], CRAN[2]
crank[1] *n* **1** = crank, a twist etc. **2** a snare; a
wile; a difficulty *la18-19, SW-S*.
crank[2] *n* a harsh noise *la18*.
vi make a harsh noise *la19*. [prob onomat]
crank[3] **&c** *adj* difficult *la18-e20*.
~**ie &c 1** unsteady, insecure, unreliable *la19-*. **2**
= cranky, bad-tempered; eccentric. **crank-
ous** *adj* fretful, captious *la18-e20*. ~**um** *n, chf
in pl* something odd or difficult to understand,
esp a mechanism *19-, Rox*. [see SND]
crannak *see* CRANNOG

crannie[1] **&c** *n* **1** = cranny. **2** a recess in a wall
20-, NE.
crannie[2] **&c** *n* the little finger *20-, Bnf-Ags*.
~ **doodlie** *20-, NE*, ~ **wannie** *la18-, Abd* = *n*.
[prob f CRAN[4]]
crannog &c *la19-*, **crannak** *e17 n, now archaeol*
an ancient lake dwelling. [ScGael *crannag*,
IrGael *crannóg*]
cranreuch &c *la18-, now Fif-Ayr*, **crainroch
&c** *la17-e19*, **cranra** *e16, e19* ['kranrux, -rəx,
-rjʌx, *-rə, &c] *n* hoar-frost. [perh Gael *crann*
shrink, shrivel + *reotha* frost]
crap *see* CREEP, CROP
crape *see* CRAIP, CREEP
crasie &c ['krezɪ] *n* a sunbonnet *19-e20, C, S*.
[var of CRUISIE, from its shape]
crasit *see* CRAZE
crauch [krɑx] *interj, perh* expressing submission
e16. [unknown]
crave; craif &c *la14-e17*, **creve &c** *la16-18 vti*
1 = crave *la14-*. **2** *vt, law* ask for as of right;
demand or claim as properly or legally one's
due *15-*. **3** press or dun for payment of a debt
la15-, now local Cai-Edb.
n **1** *law* a request or petition as in *v* 2, *18-*. **2**
desire, hankering after *19-, now Bnf Ags*.
craw[1]; **crow** *18- n* **1** = crow, the bird, in Scotland *usu* applied to the rook *15-*. **2** *in pl* = ~
coal *la19-, now Fif*.
~(**s**) **aipple** the crab apple *la19-e20*. ~**berry**
the crowberry; the cranberry *19-, now Abd, in
place-names 16-*. ~ **bogle** a scarecrow *20-, now
Abd Lnk Fif*. ~ **coal** *mining* an inferior coal
la18-, local. ~**crooks &c 1** the crowberry *19*. **2**
the cranberry *la19-, now Ags*. ~ **court** a parliament of rooks *19-, now Fif*. ~ **iron &c** a crowbar, *esp* with a claw for drawing nails *la16-19*.
~ **mill** a child's rattle *19-, Ags*. ~ **nancy** =
~ *bogle 20-, now Lnk S*. ~ **pea**(**s**) the vetch
la19-, now Bnf. ~ **picker** *mining* a person who
picks stones from coal or shale at the pit-head
la19-, Fif Ayr. ~**step** step-like projections up
the sloping edge of a gable *19-*. ~**tae**(**s**) **1** *chf
in pl* crow's feet, wrinkles at the corner of the
eye *19-, now Bnf Abd Fif*. **2** crow's foot, a cal-
trop (for impeding cavalry etc) *la18-e19*. **3** (1)
the creeping crowfoot *18-, local*. (2) the
bird's-foot trefoil *la19-, local*. (3) the English
bluebell, wild hyacinth *la19-, now Kcb*. ~'s
weddin *etc* a large assembly of crows *19-, local*.
~ **widdie &c** a rookery *20-, local*.
be shot amo the ~s be involved in trouble
through bad associates *la20-, local Ork-Per*. **sit
like ~s in the mist** sit in the dark *19-, local
Bnf-Fif*.
craw[2] *n* **1** = crow, the crowing of a cock *la15-*.
2 a similar sound made by other birds, *esp* the
rook *la18-, Bnf Abd*.
v, ptp also **crawn** *18-, now Bnf Abd Fif* = crow
la14-.
~ **crouse, croose in the ~** *see* CROUSE.

craw³ *n* an enclosure for animals, *esp* a pigsty *la19-*, *now Cai Fif*. [*cf* CRUE; but the vowel is anomalous]

crawdoun &c; cradoun [*'krɑdun] *n* a coward *16-e17*. [*cf* eModEng and northern ModEng dial *craddon* and perh ME *crathon*]

Crawfordjohn *n* a dark granite, used to make curling stones (CURL) *la19-*. [the Lnk village ['krɑfərd 'dʒon] where the stone is quarried]

craws *n pl* **wae's my** ~! dear me! *e19*, *nEC*. [unknown]

cray *see* CRUE, CRY

craze *vt*, *chf in ptp and adj* **crazed, crasit &c 1** = crazed, damaged *16*. **2** *of persons* broken down in health, infirm *16-e20*.
n a crack *17-e19*.

cre [*kri] *vt* create *la15-e16*. [only Sc; L *creāre*]

creachle *see* CRAIGHLE

creagh [krex] *n* a *Highland* (HIELAND) foray, raid; the booty obtained *19-e20*, *hist*. [Gael *creach* plunder]

cream [krim; *Sh Ork nEC* krem] *n*, *vti* = cream. ~ (**of**) **the water** *or* **well** (draw) the first water from a well on New Year's morning *18-e20*, *now Abd Ags Fif*; *cf* FLOUR *n* 3.

creame *see* CRAME

crear &c [*'kriər] *n* = crayer, a small trading vessel *15-17*, *only Sc*.

crechle *see* CRAIGHLE

crede *see* CREED

credill *see* CRAIDLE

credit *n*, *vt* = credit *16-*. **earn someone's** ~ gain someone's approval or esteem *la19-*, *Bnf Abd Ags*.

creed &c, crede &c *n* **1** = creed *la14-*. **2** a severe rebuke *19-e20*, *local*.

creedit *n* = credit *la19-*, *now Sh Ags*. [perh w infl f CREED]

creek¹, **creik** [krik] *n* = creek *la16-*. ~**s and corners** nooks and crannies *19-*, *now Bnf Abd*.

creek² *n*, *also* ~ **o day** break of day, dawn *18-*, *now Bnf Ags*. [eModEng; MDu *krieke*, LowGer *krik*; *cf* GREEK and SKREEK]

creel &c, crele &c, kreill &c *la17* [kril] *n* **1** a deep basket for carrying PEATS¹, fish etc on the back, or one of a pair to be carried by a horse or donkey; a crate *15-*. **2** a basketful **of** (*chf* PEATS¹) *la15-e18*. **3** a fish-trap, lobster-pot *la15-*, *now local Cai-Arg*. **4** *fig* the stomach; the womb *19-*, *NE*.
vt put into a CREEL *16-e20*, *chf S*.
~**ing** any of various customs to which a newly-married man may be subject, *freq* involving carrying a CREEL *18-e20*, *local C*.
~**man** one who carries goods or brings them to market in a CREEL *16-e17*.
in a ~ in confusion or perplexity; mad *la18-*, *now local Abd-Kcb*. [earlier in Sc; obscure]

creenge *vi* = cringe *la19-*, *local Bnf-Kcb*.

creep &c *17-*, **crepe &c** *la14-17* *vi*, *pt also* **creepit &c** *la16-*; **crape** *la14-e17*, **crap** *la15-*,

now *Abd Ags*. *ptp also* **croppin &c** *16-e19*, **cruppin &c** *la16-* **1** = creep *la14-*. **2** *of rocks etc* move slowly, gradually *15-*. **3** *curling* (CURL), *of the stone* move slowly or gently *19-*, *now Lnk*.
n a contemptible fellow, a sneak *la20-*.
~**er &c** a grappling iron, grapnel *16-*, *now Arg*.
~**ie** *n* **1** a low stool *17-*. **2** a footstool *19-*, *now Bnf Fif Kcb*. **3** *specif* the stool of repentance (REPENT) *18-e19*. **4** any small chair *la18-19*.
~**ing crape** a variety of crape or grogram *la16-e17*, *only Sc*. **cruppen doun** shrunk or bent with age *la18-*, *now Fif*.
cattle ~ a passage for animals under (*usu*) a railway *la19-*, *local*. **cauld** ~(**s**) gooseflesh, the creeps *19-*, *local Bnf-Lnk*. ~ **afore ye gang** *proverb* = walk before you run *19-*. ~**-at-even** someone out late courting *la19-*, *Bnf Abd*. ~ **in 1** *of daylight hours* shorten *la19-*. **2** grow smaller, shrink *19-*. ~ **in 's ye crap oot** go to an unmade bed *20-*, *Abd Ags Kcb*. ~ **out** *of hours of darkness* lengthen *20-*, *now Bnf Abd Fif*. ~ **ower** swarm, be infested (with vermin) *la19-*, *now Bnf Abd Fif*. ~ **thegither** shrink, huddle up with cold or age *19-*.

creesh &c *la16-*, **cresche &c** *15-17*, **cres** *e15*; **creis &c** *16-e17* [kriʃ; *kris] *n* fat, grease, tallow *15-*.
vt **1** grease; oil; lubricate *la15-*. **2** beat, thrash *19-*, *now Abd Kcb*.
~**ie** greasy; fat; dirty *16-*. ~**ie mealie** oatmeal fried in fat *20-*, *Ags*; *cf mealy creeshie* etc (MEALIE). ~ **someone's loof &c** grease someone's palm, pay, tip, bribe someone *18-*, *local Bnf-Wgt*. [only Sc; OF *cresse, creisse*]

creest *la18-e20*, **creste** *e16*; **creist** *16-e17* [krist] *n* **1** = crest *16-17*. **2** a self-important or officious person *19-e20*, *local*.
vti brag; put on airs *19-e20*, *SW S*.

creik *see* CREEK¹

creip *see* CRAIP

creis *see* CREESH

creist *see* CREEST

crele *see* CREEL

creme *see* CRAME

cren *see* CRAN¹

crepe *see* CREEP

cres, cresche *see* CREESH

cress *n*, *vt* = crease, fold etc *la18-*, *now Bnf Abd*.

cressent; cressen *n* some sort of decoration (sometimes of satin) on harness or armour *e16*. [perh Eng *crescent*]

creste *see* CREEST

cretar &c [*'kritər] *n* a writing-case *la16-e17*. [only Sc; F *écritoire*]

creull *see* CROWL

creve *see* CRAVE

crewk *see* CRUIK

crib¹ *n* **1** = crib *15-*. **2** a hen-coop *19-*, *local Cai-Fif*.

crib² *n* a reel for yarn *e19*, *S*. [uncertain]

crib³ *n* = curb, kerb *18-*, *Fif Kcb*.

~-stane = *n*, *la19-*, *now Abd*. [metath; *cf* CRUB¹]
cricket *n* **1** = cricket, the insect. **2** a grasshopper *19-*, *now Rox*.
cricklet *n* the smallest of a litter, weakest of a brood *19-e20*, *WC*. [*cf* Eng dial *crick* a very small child, LowGer *kriik* small]
criffins &c *19-*, *now Bnf Gsw Kcb*, **crivens &c** *la19-*, *now local Bnf-Lnk* ['krɪfnz, 'krɪvnz, *'krɪftənz] *interj* expressing astonishment. [perh f *Christ fend us*]
crile &c, **cryll**, **croyll &c** *n* a dwarf, a dwarfish or deformed creature *la16-e20*. [perh f MDu *kriel* very small, dwarfish; see SND]
criminabill &c [*krɪmɪ'nebl, *?'krɪmɪnəbl] *adj* **1** capable of being regarded or indicted as a crime *la15-16*. **2** capable of being accused of a crime *16-e17*. [only Sc; ? f MedL *criminabilis* culpable]
crimpet *n* = crumpet *20-*, *Bnf Abd*.
crimple *vti* = crumple *la19-*, *now Abd*.
crimpson &c *adj* = crimson *17*, *only Sc*. [*cf* *Simpson/Simson* etc]
crinch &c; crunch *vt* = crunch *19-*, *now Fif*.
n a very small piece *19-e20*.
~ie = *n*, *20-*, *now Fif*.
crine &c, **cryne &c** [krəin; *Cai also* krin; *Ayr also* *kroin] *v* **1** *vi* shrink, shrivel *16-*, *Gen except Sh Ork*. **2** *vt* cause to grow smaller, shrink, shrivel *16-*, *now Abd Stlg*. [Gael *crion* little, withered]
cripple, **crippill &c** *la14-e17* ['krɪpl; *'kripl] *n* = cripple *la14-*.
adj lame *la16-*, *now Abd Stlg*.
vi walk lamely, hobble *19-*, *now local Bnf-Stlg*.
~ **Dick** a lame person *19-*.
crisp *vt* fold (cloth) lengthwise after weaving *la19-*, *Ags Uls*.
cristalline &c *adj* = crystalline *16*.
n crystal *16*, *only Sc*.
crit *see* CROOT
criticeese &c [krɪtɪ'siz, krit-] *vt* = criticise *la19-*, *local Bnf-Rox*.
crittle *see* CROTE
crive *see* CRUIVE
crivens *see* CRIFFINS
cro¹ &c [*krø] *n* compensation or satisfaction for a killing *e15*. [only Sc; IrGael *cró*]
cro² [*kro] *n*, *appar* = CROCHLE *n*, *e20*, *Cai*.
cro *see* CRUE
croce-present, **cros-presand** *n* = corse-present, a gift due to the clergy from the goods of a householder on his death and burial *la15-16*.
croce *see* CROSS¹, CROSS²
crochle ['krɔxl, *'kroixl] *vi* limp *la19-*, *Bnf Abd*.
n, *chf in pl* a disease of cattle causing lameness *19-*, *NE*.
~ **girs** a plant said to cause prec *la19-*, *Bnf*. [uncertain; *cf* CROICHIT]
crock¹, **crok &c** *n* an old ewe *la15-*, *now Bnf*. [obscure]

crock² &c *n* **1** = crock. **2** *specif* an earthenware container for foodstuffs, *eg* milk, salt, butter *20-*.
~anition &c [krokə'nɪʃən, krokɪ'niʃən, *&c*] smithereens *19-*, *local Ork-Fif*. ~er an earthenware marble *19-e20*, *local*. [*cf* Eng]
crock³ *vi* = croak, *specif slang* die *20-*, *local Ork-Stlg*.
crocky *see* CRACKIE
croft &c, **craft** *la16-*, *latterly chf NE n* = croft; *specif* a smallholding *15-*, *now chf Highl*, *in place-names 13-*.
~er a person who occupies a smallholding *18-*.
Crofters Commission a commission set up to administer the Crofting Acts *la19-*. ~ing the practice of croft-holding; the holding itself *la16-*. **crofting counties** those Scottish counties where *crofting* is important and which receive special treatment by government; *now* (since 1975) still used loosely of the former counties *20-*.
crog &c *n* a big hand, a paw *19-*, *e20* (*chf Cai*). [Gael *cròg*]
croichit *adj* ? lame *e17*. [*cf* CROCHLE]
croichle &c ['krɔxl; *Per WC Gall* *'kroixl] *vi* cough *19-*, *now Bnf*.
n a cough *19-*, *now Bnf*. [prob onomat; *cf* CRAIGHLE]
croinkle &c *vti*, *n* = crinkle *20-*, *chf Abd*.
croishtarich; crosstarrie &c [*'krɔʃ'tarɪx, *-'terɪ] *n* = fiery cros (FIRE) *18*. [Gael *croistarra &c* cross + ?]
croittoch &c [*'kroitəx, *'krut-, *&c] *n* lameness in cattle *19*, *SW*. [prob related to Gael *crotach* humpbacked, *crotachd* unevenness]
crok *see* CROCK¹
croke *see* CRUIK
crom *vt* bend (up *or* in) *la19-e20*, *NE*.
crum(m)et having crooked horns *17-e19*.
crommie &c, **crummie** *n* a cow with crooked horns, *freq* used as name for a pet cow *18-*, *now local Bnf-Fif*. [eModEng (once); *cf* MLowGer *krummen*, MDu *krommen* and Gael *crom* crooked, bent]
cronach *see* CORONACH
crone *see* CROON¹, CROON²
croo *vi*, *of doves etc* coo *la19-*, *now Ags*. [imit; *cf* CROOD¹]
croo *see* CRUE
crooch [krutʃ] *vi* = crouch *20-*.
crouchie &c hump-backed *la18-*, *Ayr Pbls*.
crood¹, **croude &c** [krud] *vi*, *of doves etc* coo *16-19*.
~lin doo *= v*, *la19-*, *now local Bnf-Fif*. ~lin doo **1** a wood-pigeon *20-*, *now Bnf Abd*. **2** term of endearment *19-*, *now Bnf Abd Fif*. [imit]
crood² &c *n*, *vti* = crowd *18-*.
crood *see* CRUD
croodie *see* CROWDIE²
croodle ['krudl; *Fif* *'krʌudl] *vi* cower; nestle *19-e20*. [prob frequentative of CROOD²]
crook *see* CRUIK

croon¹, croun &c, crone &c *la14-16;* **crown &c** [krun] *n* **1** = crown *la14-.* **2** the opening furrow in ploughing *20-, Cai SW.*
vt = crown *la14-.*
~**er** the crowning happening, the best or worst *la19-, Cai Ags Fif Kcb.*
Crown Agent [*(St)* 'krʌun 'edʒənt] *law* the chief Crown solicitor in criminal matters *la19-.*
croun as a superior kind of potash *la16, only Sc.*
croon² &c, crune &c, crone *16-19* [krøn; *also* krun; *N* krin; *C* krɪn] *v* **1** *vi* bellow, roar *16-, now Kcb.* **2** utter a lament, mourn; sing in a wailing voice *17-, now N.* **3** sing in a low tone; mutter, hum: (1) *vi, la16-;* (2) *vt, freq* ~ **ower** *la18-.*
n **1** = a bellow *16-19.* **2** a wail, lament, mournful song *la18-e20.* **3** a low murmuring tune, a song *18.*
crunan *e16,* ~**er** *18-e20, local,* ~**ick &c** *la19-, chf Bnf,* ~**yil &c** *la19-e20, chf Mry* the gurnard. [nME *croyne,* MDu *kronen*]
croonge *vi* crouch *la19-, Bnf Abd.* [prob conflation of CREENGE w CROOCH]
croose *see* CROUSE
croot; crute, crit [*C-S* krɪt; *S also* krøt] *n* **1** a puny child; a short misshapen person *19-e20, C-S.* **2** a small or puny creature; the youngest of a brood *19-e20, chf S.* [*cf* eModEng (once) *croot,* Welsh *crwt* a boy]
croove *see* CRUIVE
crop &c, cropt &c *la16-18,* **crap &c** *17-* *n* **1** = crop *15-.* **2** the top of a tree or plant; a head of corn *15-.* **3** *only* **crap** *specif* the substance which rises to the top of boiled whey *19-e20, SW.* **4** the stomach *15-, now Bnf-Fif.*
vti = crop *la15-.*
~**pin &c** *freq joc* = *n* **4**, *19-, now Kcb.* **crappit heids** *cookery* stuffed haddocks' heads *19-, now local Bnf-Stlg* [*cf* MDu, MLowGer *kroppen* stuff the crop].
clear one's crap get a piece of news off one's chest *la19-, Bnf Abd Ags.* **crop the causey &c** *freq fig* take or hold the crown of the road *la17-e20.* ~ **and rute &c** *n* the highest point or development of something *16.* *adv* completely, root and branch *17-, NE.* **crap o the wa** the space between the top of a wall and the roof of a building *19-, now Bnf Abd Ags.* **crop(t) and year &c** expressing an inclusive date *la16-18:* 'for and after cropt and year 1724'. **craw in someone's crap** irritate, annoy or henpeck someone; give cause for regret *la18-, now Ags Fif.* **get the crap on** = 'get the wind up' *20-, Bnf Abd Gsw.* **have a** ~ **for all corn** be greedy; *lit and fig* have a capacity for absolutely anything *18-.* **shake one's crap** give vent to grievances *la18-e20, NE.* **stick in one's crap** cause resentment, 'stick in one's gullet' *19-, now Abd Stlg Lnk.*
croppin *see* CREEP
cropt *see* CROP

crosat ducat &c *n* a variety of ducat *16.* [only Sc; obscure]
crose &c [kroz] *vi* talk in a fawning, whining way, flatter *la19-, now Bnf.* [onomat]
cros(e) *see* CROSS¹
crose-gaird *see* CORS GARD
cros-presand *see* CROCE-PRESENT
cross¹ &c, croce *la15-e17,* **crose** *15-17,* **cros** *la15-e17,* **corse &c, cors &c** *la14-e20,* **corce** *la14-16* [kros; kors] *n* **1** = cross *la14-.* **2** a market cross; a market-place *15-.* **3** a cross as a boundary marker *16-17.* **4** part of a sail; a cross-sail *16.* **5** *only* **cors &c** a coin with a cross on one side *16-18.*
vti **1** = cross *la14-.* **2** *vt, only* **cross** harrow (a field) across the ploughing *20-, Bnf Abd Arg.*
corsie (crown) a game like noughts and crosses *19-e20, SW.*
cross dollar a Spanish dollar with a cross on one side *la16-e17.* ~**-fit &c** the starfish *la18-, now Abd.* **corshous** [*'kors'hus] a house standing crossways to others *la16-e17.* ~ **kirk** **1** a transept *15-16.* **2** a church founded because of a cross *la15-.* **cross-road** *mining* a moderately-inclined main road *la19-, now Fif.* **cross tig** a variant of the game of TIG *la19-, now Kcb.* ~**-tailit band** a tie or connecting piece with a crossed end *la16-e17.*
cross², croce *prep, adv* = across *17-, now Cai.* ~**-speir** = cross-question *la19-, now Bnf Abd Fif.* [aphetic]
crosstarrie *see* CROISHTARICH
crotal *see* CROTTLE
crote *n* a particle, crumb *e15.*
crottle &c; crittel &c *la19-e20 n* a fragment, crumb *19-e20, chf SW.*
crotly &c fragmentary, crumbly *19-e20, chf SW.* [ME]
crottle; crotal &c *n* dye-producing lichen *19-, local.* [Gael *crotal*]
crottle *see* CROTE
crouchie *see* CROOCH
croude *see* CROOD¹
croun *see* CROON¹
croup¹ &c, crowp [krup, krʌup] *vi* **1** *of birds, esp crows* croak, caw *16-, now Bnf Abd Fif.* **2** speak hoarsely *19-, now Bnf Abd Fif.* **3** *also* **growp** *la19-, now Mry* [grʌup] grumble *20-, NE.*
~**ie** **1** the raven *19, chf Fif.* **2** the common street pigeon *la20-, Fif Edb.* ~**it** croaking, hoarse *la19-, now Cai Fif.* [imit; *cf* eModEng]
croup² [krup] *n* an inflammatory disease of the larynx and trachea in children *18-.* [earlier in Sc; prob imit]
croupert &c ['krʌupərt, 'krɑ-] *n* the crowberry *la19-, NE.*
crouse &c, crous; crowse &c *la15-e19,* **croose &c** *19-* [krus] *adj* **1** bold, courageous, spirited *la15-, now Bnf.* **2** confident,

self-satisfied; cheerful, merry *la15-*. **3** conceited, arrogant, proud *la16-*, *now Bnf Abd Ags*. **4** cosy, comfortable *19-*, *now Bnf Abd*. **5** touchy *la19-*, *local*.

crack ~ **1** = *craw* ~, *la17-18*. **2** talk in a lively, cheerful way *la18-e20*. **craw** ~ boast, talk loudly and confidently *la16-*. **croose i the craw** full of self-confident talk *20-*, *local Bnf-Lnk*. [nME *crous &c*; *cf* MHighGer, MLowGer *krus* crisp, Ger *kraus* crinkly, curly; sullen etc]

crout &c [*krut] *vi* croak *la17-19*. [imit]

crove *see* CRUIVE

crow *see* CRAW[1]

crowat *see* CRUET

crowdie[1] &c ['krʌudɪ] *n* oatmeal and water mixed and eaten raw *la17-*.
~ **mowdy &c** [*' ~ 'mʌudɪ] **1** ludicrous term of endearment *e16* [variant reading for *towdy-mowdy* (TOWDY)]. **2** = *n*, *18*. [uncertain]

crowdie[2] &c; croodie *e20*, *chf Cai* ['krudɪ; 'krʌudɪ] *n* a kind of soft cheese *19-*. [f CRUD, w formal infl f CROWDIE[1]]

crowl[1] *la18-*, *now local Bnf-Fif*, **creull &c** *la16-e17* [krʌul] *vi* crawl. [nME; uncertain]

crowl[2] &c [krʌul] *n* **1** term of contempt for a dwarf or very small person *la19-e20*, *SW*. **2** a (*freq* tiny) child *19-e20*. [uncertain]

crown *see* CROON[1]

crownell[1] &c [*'krunl] *n* = coronal *la15-e17*.

crownell[2] &c [*'krunl] *n* = coronel, colonel *la16-e17*. [only Sc; w infl f Eng *crown*]

crowner &c [*'krunər] *n* = CROWNELL[2] *la16-17*. [only Sc; formal conflation w Eng *crowner* a coroner]

crowp *see* CROUP[1]

crowse *see* CROUSE

croy *n* a tiny crustacean on which herring feed *la19-*, *Arg*. [reduced f Gael *crò-dhearg* crimson]

croy *see* CRUE

croyll *see* CRILE

crub[1] &c, crubb; crube *17-e18* *n* (*18*), *vt* (*17*) = curb *now local Bnf-EC*.
~ **in aboot** keep under strict discipline *20-*, *Bnf Abd*.

crub[2] *n* = crib (for cattle-fodder) *la19-e20*, *Sh Abd*.

cruban[1] &c ['krubən] *n* a crab *19-e20*, *chf Arg Uls*. [Gael *crùban*]

cruban[2] &c ['krubən, 'krup-] *n* a disease of the legs and feet of animals *19-e20*, *Cai Arg*. [Gael *crùban*, prob f as prec]

cruban[3] ['krʌbən] *n* a kind of wooden pannier fixed to a horse's back *la18-*, *Cai*. [*cf* Gael *crúbag*]

crubb, crube *see* CRUB[1]

cruchet [*'krʌtʃɛt] *n* = crochet, a little hook *la14*.

crud &c; crood &c *la18-e20* *n*, *chf in pl* **1** = curds *la15-e20*. **2** = CROWDIE[2], *20-*, *now Bnf*. **3** frog-spawn *20-*, *Bnf Fif*.

crudle &c *vti* = curdle *18-*, *now Bnf Kcb Rox*. ~**dy** curdled, full of curds *la18-e20*. ~**dy butter** = *n* 2, *20-*, *now Bnf Abd*.

crue &c, croy *la15-e20*, **cro** *la15-e17*; **croo** *la18-19*, **kro** *20-*, *Sh Ork* [krø; *Cai* kri; *C* kre, *also* kri] *n* **1** = CRUIVE *n* 1, *la14-e19*. **2** *only* **croy** a mound or quay to protect a riverbank *16-e20*, *chf Per*. **3** *also* **cray** *la19-*, *C* an animal pen or fold; *now chf* a pigsty *16-*. **4** a hovel *la16-19*. [only Sc; ScL *croa* *la13-15*; Gael *cró &c* a fold, hut, Icel *kró* a sheepfold (borrowed f Celtic); see *also* CRUIVE]

cruels &c, cruelles ['kruəlz] *n pl* scrofula, **the** king's evil *la16-*, *now Bnf Fif Kcb*. [only Sc; F *écrouelles*]

cruet, crowat &c *la14-e17* ['kruət] *n* **1** = cruet *la14-*. **2** a carafe; a decanter *la19-*, *now Bnf Abd*.

crufe *see* CRUIVE

cruik &c, cruke &c *la14-*, *in place-names la13-*; **crewk &c** *16-e19*, **croke &c** *16-17*, *in place-names 13-*, **crook &c** *la16-* [kr(j)uk; *Ork also* krøk; *nEC, WC also* krʌk] *n* **1** = crook *la15-*. **2** a hook, *esp* a pot-hook *la14-e20*. **3** a hook on which a door or gate is hung *la15-19*. **4** crookedness, lameness; a limp *16-e18*. **5** *fig* a misfortune, difficulty *la18-e19*.
v **1** *vi* = crook *la15-*. **2** be lame; limp *la15-e18*. **3** *vt* lame *la15-19*.
~**ie &c** a sixpence *e19*. ~**it &c** *adj* **1** = crooked *la15-*. **2** lame, *esp* of a horse *16-*, *now Cai*. **tak up wi the ~it stick** accept an inferior suitor *la19-*, *now Ags*.
~ **saidle &c** a saddle with hooks for supporting panniers *la16-e20*. ~ **study &c** a beaked anvil *la16-e17*. ~ **tree** a beam above the fire from which pot-hooks are hung *19-e20*.
as black as a *or* **the** ~ very black, dirty *la18-*, *now local Bnf Fif*. ~ **one's elbow** drink (alcohol), *esp* rather freely *19-*, *local*. ~ **one's mou 1** move the mouth so as to speak or whistle *la18-*, *now Abd Ags*. **2** distort the mouth as a sign of displeasure or ill temper *18-19*. **a ~ in one's or the lot** = *n* 5, *18-e19*. **not to ~ a finger** not to make the least exertion *19-*, *now local*. **as peer's** *or* **like the links o the** ~ very poor; very thin, meagre *20-*, *NE*.

cruise ['krøz &c] *n* = CRUISIE *la16-e20*, *only Sc*.

cruisie &c, crusie &c *la17-e20* ['kruzɪ; *wPer* 'krɪzɪ; *Fif Ayr* 'krɛzɪ; *'krøzɪ] *n* an open, boat-shaped lamp with a rush wick; a candleholder *16-e20*. [only Sc; OF *creuset &c* a crucible; OF *creuseul*, MDu *kruysel*, MLowGer *krusel* a lamp, *also* > ME *crusell*]

cruive *la17-*, **cruve** *16-17*, **crove** *14-e18*, **crufe &c** *15-17*; **croove** *17-e20*, **crive &c** *la17-e20*, **craive &c** *17-*, *EC* [krøv; *N Bwk* kriv; *NE* krɪv; *EC* krev] *n* **1** a fish-trap in the form of an enclosure or row of stakes (*orig* of wicker, *latterly chf* of wood) across a river or

estuary *la14-*; *cf* YAIR. **2** a pen, fold *chf NE, EC*; *specif* (1) a pigsty *16-*; (2) a hen-coop *18-*. **3** a hovel *16-*, *now Rox*.
vt shut up in a pen or stall *20-*, *Bnf Abd*.
~ **dyke** &c a rubble dyke extending across a river to hold CRUIVES (*n* 1) *19-*, *local*. [orig and chf Sc; var of CRUE with excrescent *-v-*]
cruke *see* CRUIK
crulge &c [krʌldʒ, kruldʒ] *vi* cower, crouch *la18-*, *now Bnf Abd Ags*. [conflation of CRULL w Eng *cringe*]
crull &c [*also* krʌul, **krul*] *vi* huddle, cower *19-e20*. [ME *crullen* (*v*) curl, *crull* (*adj*) curly]
crum &c; **crumb** *19- n* **1** = crumb *la14-*. **2** a small particle of something *16-*.
~**ch** &c = *n* 2, *la19-*, *NE*. ~**chick**(**ie**) &c, ~**chie** &c = (*la19-*, *NE*), ~**le** &c, ~**lick**(**ie**) (*la19-*, *chf NE*) = *n*.
crumet, crummet *see* CROM
crummie &c *n* = CRUMMOCK[1] *19*. [w substitution of Sc for Gael dim suffix]
crummie *see* CROM
crummle &c *vti* = crumble *20-*, *now Bnf Abd*.
crummock[1] &c ['krʌmək; *Arg Ayr also* 'kromək] *n* a stick with a crooked head, a shepherd's crook *la18-*, *local*. [only Sc; Gael *cromag* a hook, crook]
crummock[2] &c *n* the plant skirret *la17-e18*. [only Sc; Gael *cromag, crumag*]
crump &c *v* **1** *vt* crunch, munch *la18-*, *now local NE-C*. **2** *vi* crackle *la18-*, *now Bnf Abd*.
adj, esp of ice or snow crisp, brittle *e19*.
~**ie** &c *la19-*, *now Bnf Kcb*, **crumshy** *20-*, *Bnf Abd* = *adj*. [onomat; *cf* CRAMP[2]]
crunan *see* CROON[2]
crunch *see* CRINCH
crune *see* CROON[2]
crunkle &c *19-*, *local*, **grunkle** *20-*, *Bnf Abd Ags vti* = crinkle; wrinkle, crackle.
crunt *n* a heavy blow *la18-e20*, *Ayr*.
vt strike a blow on (the head) *la19-e20*. [prob onomat]
cruppin *see* CREEP
crupple *see* CURPLE
crusie *see* CRUISIE
crute *see* CROOT
cruve *see* CRUIVE
cry &c; **cray** *la16-17* [kraɪ] *v* **1** *vti* = cry *la14-*. **2** *vi* call **on** (a person) for help etc *la14-*. **3** *vt* summon *la15-*, *now local*. **4** call, give a name to *18-*, *chf WC*. **5** *in passive* have one's marriage banns proclaimed *18-*, *Gen except Sh Cai*. **6** *vi* be in labour *la17-*, *now Bnf Abd Fif*.
n **1** = cry *la14-*. **2** a call, summons *15-*. **3** *in pl* the proclamation of banns, *chf* **gie** *or* **pit in the cries** *la19-*, *now Cai-Fif Kcb*. **4** the distance a call can carry *17-e20*. **5** a short visit (in passing), *chf* **gie** (**someone**) **a** ~ (**in**) *la19-*, *local NE-C*.
~**ing** &c **1** = crying *la15-*. **2** labour; a confinement *19-*, *now NE*. ~**ing cheese** a cheese specially made at a birth *la19-*, *NE*. **a cryit** &c

fair a fair or market proclaimed in advance *16-e17*. **like a cried fair** in a state of bustle *19-*.
~ **at the cross** make public *la19-*, *local*. ~ **back** recall *19-*. ~ **by** = ~ **in** (**by**), *20-*, *Bnf Fif*. ~ **clap, clyte, dird** *etc* go thump etc, make the noise described *la18-*, *Bnf Abd*. ~ **down** &c **1** forbid, suppress, disown by proclamation *la15-17*. **2** reduce (money) in value by proclamation *la16-17*. ~ **in** (**by**) *vi* call in, visit *la19-*. ~ **names** = call (someone) names *20-*. ~ **tae** &c = ~ **in** (**by**), *la20-*, *NE*. ~ **up** raise (money) in value by proclamation *17*. ~ **upon** *20-*, *Bnf-Fif, Rox*, ~ **up to** *la19-*, *Bnf Ags* call in upon, visit. **a far** ~ *lit and fig* a very long distance, a long way (**from**) *la18-*.
crya *15*; **cryé** [***'kraɪe, -ɪ] *la14-e15 n* a proclamation; a hue and cry *la14-e16*. [only Sc; OF *criée*]
cryll *see* CRILE
cryne *vt* fear *e16*. [only Sc; *cf* F *craign-, craindre*]
cryne *see* CRINE
cubbart &c *n* = cupboard *19-*, *WC-S*.
cuckoo &c *n* = cuckoo.
~**'s-spittens** = cuckoo-spit *la19-*, *Bnf-Fif*.
cud[1] *n* **1** = cud. **2** the sound of cattle chewing the cud *19-e20*, *Mry Wgt*.
vi chew the cud *19-*, *SW*.
cud[2] *n* a cudgel *la18-e19*, *C*. [MDu *codde*]
cud *see* CAN[2], COOD[2]
cudbear &c *n* a purple dyestuff, prepared from lichens *la18-e20*. [f the name of the patentee, Dr Cuthbert Gordon]
cuddeich *see* CUDEIGH
cuddie &c; **cuddin** &c *la19-* ['kʌdɪ; *Mry also* 'kwid(ɪ)] *n* a young coalfish *la18-*, *now N Fif Arg*. [*cf* Gael *cudaig,cudainn*; *cf* CUITHE]
cuddle *v* **1** *vt* = cuddle *la18-*. **2** *vi* squat, sit close *19-*, *local*. **3** *vt, also vi* ~ **up tae** approach so as to coax or wheedle *20-*, *Bnf Abd Stlg*. **4** *vi, marbles* throw or place a marble close to the target *la19-*, *Bnf*.
cuddly(-**ba** *or* -**bye**) bed *la19-*, *Stlg Kcb*.
cuddoch &c *la18-e20*, **cowda** &c *la18-e20*, **coldoch** &c *16*, **cowdach** &c *la16-e17*, **coddoch** &c *16-e17*, **kowdoch** &c *la16-e17*; **cowdow** &c *la16-e17*, **coddow** *16* ['kʌdəx, 'kʌtəx; ***'ko(l)dǝ(x), ***'kʌudǝ(x)] *n* = COLPINDACH *16-e17*, *appar chf Edb Lnk*, *la18-e20*, *chf SW, S*. [perh reduced f COLPINDACH]
cuddum &c *vt* train, accustom *la18-e20*. [perh as *couthie* (COUTH)]
cuddy &c *n* **1** a donkey *19-*, *Gen except Sh Ork*. **2** a horse *20-*, *local*. **3** a joiner's (JOIN) trestle *20-*. **4** a gymnasium horse *20-*, *local Abd-Lnk*. **5** *mining* a loaded bogie used to counterbalance the HUTCH on a ~**-brae**, *la19-*, *now Fif*.
~ **ass** = *n* 1, *19-*, *local Bnf-Arg*. ~**-brae** *mining* an inclined roadway with a CUDDY on it *la19-*, *now Fif*. ~ **heel** an iron heel on a boot or shoe

la19-, now Stlg Lnk. **~-lowp** *la19-, Loth WC Slk,*
~-lowp-the-dyke *20-, S* the game of leapfrog;
cf *lowp the cuddy* (LOWP¹).
cude¹ &c [*kød] *n* a chrisom-cloth *la14-e17*.
[ME *code* (once), northern eModEng *cud*
(once); obscure]
cude² [*?kød] *n* the butler or storekeeper at
George Heriot's Hospital *19, Edb.*
cude³ &c, coyd &c [*kød] *adj* hare-brained
la16-e20, chf S. [obscure]
cude *see* COOD¹, COOD²
cudeigh &c *18-e19,* **cuddeich &c** *16-e18,*
cowdeich &c *16* [*'kʌdix, *-ɪx, &c] *n* **1** a
night's entertainment due from a tenant to his
SUPERIOR, or its equivalent in value *16-e17.* **2** a
gift, bribe; a premium for the use of money
18-e19. [Gael *cuid* a share + *oidhche* a night; *cf*
Anglo-Ir *cuddie* (*la15-16*)]
cudna *see* CAN²
cuff¹ *n* **~ of the neck** the nape or scruff of the
neck *18-.* [prob var of Eng *scuff, scruff*]
cuff² *vt* **1** winnow for the first time *la18-, Bnf Abd.*
2 remove a layer of soil with a rake from (a
piece of ground) before sowing, replacing it
afterwards *la18-e20.* [prob var of SCUFF¹]
cuffing *see* COLF
cuffock *n* a coil in a ball of wool, with the
strands wound in one direction *20-, Abd.* [prob
dim of Eng *cuff*]
cuid *see* CAN²
cuik &c *16-e20,* **cuke &c** *la14-16,* **kuke &c**
la15-e17, **kyeuk &c** *19-e20,* **cook &c** *la16-*
[*NE* kjuk; *C* *køk, *kjʌk] *n* = cook *la14-.*
vti **1** = cook *la16-.* **2** *vt, only* **cook** coax *19-, chf*
NE.
   maister cuke the head cook of the royal or
other large household *la15-e17, only Sc.*
cuil &c, cule, queel &c *la18-, NE;* **cool** [køl;
Cai kil; *NE* kwil; *C* kɪl; *nEC* kel] *vti, adj* = cool
la15-.
   ~ing stone a stone at or near a school, on
which boys who have been whipped were made
to sit *19, Abd Ags.*
   ~-the-loom a lazy worker *19-e20, chf S.*
   ~-an-sup live from hand to mouth *19-e20, chf*
S.
cuir *see* CURE
cuisser *see* COOSER
cuist &c [*køst] *n, only in pl* pieces of stone used
in building an oven *16-e17.* [obscure]
cuist *see* CAST, CUST
cuit &c, cute &c, queet &c *la18-, NE;* **kute**
&c *17-e20,* **coot** *la17-e19* [køt; *Cai* kit; *NE*
kwit; *C* kɪt; *nEC* ket] *n* **1** the ankle *16-.* **2** the
fetlock *17, e20 (Ayr).*
   ~ikins *n pl* cloth gaiters *19-20, local.*
   not a ~ = not a jot *16-e17.* [only Sc; MDu
cote]
cuiter &c; couther ['k(j)utər, 'kuθər] *vt, freq*
~ up 1 nurse; pamper *19-20.* **2** coax, wheedle
19-, now Bnf. **3** mend, patch up *19.* [*cf* nEng
dial *couther* comfort, cure]

cuithe &c *la18-, Ork;* **queeth &c** *19-, NE* [*Sh
Ork* køð;*Bnf* kwɪð] *n* the young coalfish. [*cf*
Norw dial *kod* and CUDDIE]
cuittle &c *19-,* **cuttle &c** ['kutl, 'kʌtl] *v* **1** *vi,*
only **cuttle** whisper *la15-17.* **2** *vt* coax, flatter
19-e20, SW, S. **3** cuddle, caress *la18-19, SW.* **4**
vi smile ingratiatingly *la18-e19, S.* [see SND]
cuittle *see* KITTLE¹
cuitty-boyne *see* COOD²
cuke *see* CUIK
cukie *see* COOKIE
culd *see* CAN², CAN³
Culdee &c *la17-,* **Kildé &c** *15-17* *n* a Culdee,
a member of an ascetic religious movement
(*8-e14*) in the Celtic Church *15-, hist.* [OIr *céle*
Dé a companion or servant of God; *cf* ScL
Keldei &c (pl) la12]
cule *see* CUIL
cullage *n* ? shape, markings *e16, only Sc.*
[unknown]
cullan *see* CALLAN¹
Cullen skink *n* a smoked-fish soup *20-.* [*Cullen*
the Bnf village + SKINK¹]
cullie *see* CULYIE
cullieshangie *see* COLLIESHANGIE
cullion, culyeon &c *n* term of abuse for a person *la17-, now Abd.* [eModEng; ME *coillon* a
testicle, F *couillon*]
cullour &c *n* **1** = colour *15-17.* **2** rhythm,
metre *16-e17, only Sc.*
   vt = colour *16-17.*
   ~ du roy *n* = COLOUR DE ROY *16-e17.*
culmas &c [*'kʌlməs, *-mɪʃ] *n* a curved sword;
a sabre *e16.* [obscure]
culpable &c *adj* = culpable *la14-.*
   ~ homicide *law* a killing caused by fault
which falls short of the evil intention required
to constitute murder, *corresponding to Eng* manslaughter *la18-, only Sc.*
culpe *see* COUP⁴
culrach &c, colrach &c *16;* **collerach &c**
16 [*?'kʌlreð, *-rax] *n* the surety given on
removing a case from one court to another; the
person acting as surety *15-17.* [prob Gael]
culroun &c *n* term of abuse for a person
la15-16. [obscure]
culsh *n* a big, disagreeable person *la19-, Bnf Abd.*
[*cf* GULCH]
cultellar &c *n* a cutler *16-17.* [MedL *cultel-*
larius; cf eModEng *cultelere* (rare) having the
form of a knife]
culter *see* COOTER
culum &c [*'køləm] *n* the buttocks; the anus
la15-16. [only Sc; L *cūlum*, accusative of *cūlus*]
culvering &c *n* **1** a hand-gun *la15-e17.* **2** =
culverin, a large cannon *16-e17.*
culyeon *see* CULLION
culyie &c, culȝe &c *la15-16;* **cullie &c** *17-e20*
['kʌl(j)ɪ; *Sh* *'k(j)øl ɪ; *Cai* 'kuljɪ; *Mry* 'kwilɪ] *vt* **1**
fondle *la15-e20.* **2** cherish *la18-e20.* **3** receive,
entertain kindly *la16-e17.* **4** coax, entice
17-e20. [*cf* eModEng *cully* (once), *cull*, ME *coll*]

cum *see* COME
cumber *see* CUMMER[1]
cumer *see* CUMMER[2]
cummen &c, cumming &c, kimming &c
n a tub, *esp* as used in brewing *16-e20*. [only Sc; obscure]
cummer[1] &c, cumber &c *n* **1** trouble, distress; difficulty *15-e17*. **2** *chf in pl* troubles, commotions *16-e17*. **3** a hindrance or encumbrance *16-e19*.
vt **1** = cumber *la14-e17*. **2** hamper, impede *la14-e16*.
~**sum &c 1** *of places* difficult to pass through, full of obstructions *la14-16*. **2** troublesome, causing trouble or difficulty *16-19*. **3** full of trouble *16*.
cummerwarld &c = cumber-world, a useless encumbrance *e16*.
mak *etc* ~ cause trouble or disturbance *16-e17*.
be quit of someone's ~ be free of trouble etc caused by the person mentioned *16-e19*.
cummer[2] &c *15-*, **commere &c** *la15-e17*; **cumer &c** *16-e17*, **kimmer &c** *17-* ['kʌmər, 'kɪmər] *n* **1** a godmother (*orig* in relation to the parents and other godparents) *la16-e20*. **2** *also* **gimmer** *la18-* ['gɪmər] *now Abd midLoth, freq as familiar mode of address* a female intimate or friend; a gossip *15-*. **3** a midwife *la16-e20*. **4** a married woman, a wife *18-e20*. **5** a girl, lass *la18-*, *now Bnf*. **6** a witch *18-e19*.
vi gossip *la17-e19*, S.
~ **fealls** an entertainment at the birth of a child *19*. [*cf* ME *commare* (once), OF *commere*]
cumming *see* CUMMEN
cummins *see* COME
cummock *see* CAMMOCK
cumper &c *n* the father-lasher *19-e20*, *Ork NE*. [obscure]
cumray &c [*kʌm're, *'kʌmre] *vt* = CONRAY *la14-e16*. [perh conflation of CONRAY w CUMMER[1] *v*]
cumseil *see* COOM[2]
cun &c *vt* **1** get to know; learn *la14-17*. **2** taste *16-e19*. **3** *specif* taste (ale); evaluate by tasting *la15-e17*.
cunnar &c *15-16*, **cunstar &c** *16-17*, *chf NE* a person appointed to test the quality of ale and fix its price.
~ **someone** (**nae** *etc*) **thanks** feel or express (no etc) gratitude to someone *la15-e20*. [eME *cunne*, OE *cunnian* inquire into, *cunnan* know > *can*, *con*]
cundy &c; condie &c *n* **1** a covered drain, the entrance to a drain *19-*, *Gen except Sh Ork*. **2** a tunnel, passage *20-*, *Gen except Sh Ork*. **3** a hole in a wall for the passage of sheep etc *19-e20*. [var of Eng *conduit*]
cunigar *see* CUNINGAR
cuning &c *15-16*, **coning &c** *la15-e17*, **kinnen &c** *17-e20*, **kinning** *17-19*; **cunning &c** *la15-e17*, *e20* (*Ork*), **kjunning** *la19-20*, *Sh*

[*'kʌnɪŋ, *-ɪn, *'kɪnɪn; *Sh* 'kjʌ-] *n* a rabbit, cony *la15-e20*. [ME *conyng*, *cunin*, OF *conyn*(*g*), L *cunīculus*]
cuningar &c, cunigar &c, conyngare *15* ['kʌnɪ(ŋ)gər] *n* a rabbit-warren *15-e19*, *in place-names la15-*. [ME *conynger &c*, OF *coniniere &c*]
cunnand *see* CONAND
cunner *vt* scold *19-e20*, *WC*. [? var of CHANNER]
cunning *see* CUNING
cunray *see* CONRAY
cunsail &c, cunsele &c [*kʌn'sel, *'kʌnsl] *n* = COUNSAIL *15-e17*. [laME (rare) *cunseil &c*, after OF *cunseil*]
cunstar *see* CUN
cunt *see* CONT
cuntbitten &c [*'kʌnt'bɪtən] *adj* poxed *e16*.
cuntray, cuntré *see* COUNTRA
cuntreth &c *15-e17*, **contreth &c** *16-e17* [*'kʌntrɪð, *-trɛð] *n* = country. [only Sc; early OF *cuntrede &c*, later *cuntrée* > Sc *cuntré* (COUNTRA)]
cunyie &c *19-e20*, **cunzie** *18-e20*, **conʒe &c** *15-17*, **cunʒe &c** *la14-17*, **coinʒie &c** *la16-19*, **coynʒhe &c** *la14-e17*, **counʒe** *la16-e17*, **quinie &c** *18-*, *now Cai*; **quinʒie &c** *la16*, **quinzie** *la16-e19* ['kʌnjɪ; *'kwɪn(j)ɪ, *'kwɪŋɪ, &c; *'kʌnzɪ; &c] *n* **1** = coin; quoin *la14-*. **2** *appar* a corner piece of ground *la15-17*. **3** coining (of money) *16-e17*.
vt = coin *15-18*.
~ **hous** the mint *la15-17*, *only Sc*. [OED *quinyie*]
cupar *see* COUPER
Cupar; coupar &c ['kupər] *n* ~ **justice** formal trial after summary punishment *la17-19*; *cf Jeddart Justice* (JETHART).
he that will to ~ **maun to** ~ a stubborn person will have his way *18-*, *local*. [*Cupar*, Fif or *Coupar-Angus*, *Per*]
cupe *see* COUP[4]
cupno(w) *see* COLPINDACH
cuppill, cupple *see* COUPLE
curale &c, currell &c *17*, **curle** *e17* [*'kʌr(ə)l] *n* **1** = coral, the substance and the colour *la15-17*. **2** coral-coloured cloth *17*.
curat &c [*'kɒrat, *-et; *NE* *'kir-] *n* **1** = curate *la15-e17*. **2** = CURATOR 1, *la15*.
~**ry** = CURATORY *la15*.
curator, curatour &c *15-17* ['kjurətər, kju'retər; *'kørətur] *n* **1** *law* a person either entitled by law or appointed by the Court or an individual to manage the affairs of a legally incapable person, *eg* a MINOR *15-*; *cf* DATIVE *adj* 1. **2** = curator *17-*. **3** *in pl*, *also* **C**~**s of Patronage** *Edb Univ* the seven persons, appointed by the Town Council (*now* Edinburgh *District Council* (DESTRICK)) and the University Court, who have the power of appointing to the office of PRINCIPAL and to some professorships *la19-*.

curatrix [*'køratrɪks] *n* a female CURATOR (*n* 1) *la16-17.*

~ bonis [~ 'bonis] the person appointed to manage the estate either of a MINOR (instead of his legal guardian), or of a person suffering from mental or, less commonly, physical infirmity 20-. [sometimes confused w TUTOR]

curatory &c [*'køratorɪ] *n*, *chf law* the office of a CURATOR *n* 1 and 2, *la15-19.* [only Sc; L *cūrātoria*]

curch &c, courche &c *la15-e17,* **querche** *la14* [kʌrtʃ, *kurtʃ, *kwɪrtʃ] *n* a kerchief, a woman's cap *la14-e20.* [reduced f CURCHEFFE, prob through the pl]

curchay &c, courchay &c [*'kʌr(t)ʃe, *'kur(t)ʃe, *-ɑ] = CURCH *16-e17.*

curcheffe &c [*'kʌrtʃɛf] *n* = kerchief *16-17.*

curchie &c ['kʌrtʃɪ] *n* (*19-, now Abd*), *vi* (*19*) = curtsy.

curcuddie &c [kʌr'kʌdɪ, kər-] *n* **dance** ~ perform a crouching dance *19-e20.* [prob *cur-,* intensifier + CUDDY; *cf* COUKUDDY]

curcuddoch &c [kʌr'kʌd(j)əx] *adj* **1** sitting close together or side by side *la18-e20.* **2** cordial, kindly *18-e19.* [prob f CURCUDDIE]

curd *n* = curd *16-.*

C~ Fair, C~ Saturday a holiday in Kilmarnock around the time of the old *hiring fair* (HIRE) in May *la19-, Ayr.*

curdie &c *n* a very small coin; a farthing *la19-, local.* [Sc gipsy (*e20*) = a halfpenny; perh f Span *cuarto* a small coin, or Romany *xurdo* little]

curdoo &c [kʌr'du] *vi* coo (as a pigeon); make love *19-, now Fif.* [prob Eng *curr* + DOO]

cure &c, cuir &c *16-, now Sh Ork C, S,* **kuir** *la16-17,* **kure** *la16,* **keer &c** *la18-, NE* [kør, ker; *Bwk* also kir; *NE* *kir] *n* **1** = cure *15-.* **2** care, attention, diligence, *freq* **set, do** (**one's**) **~, tak ~** *la14-e17.*

vti **1** = cure *la14-.* **2** *vi, in negative:* (1) have no anxiety or scruples in some regard *16*; (2) **~ of** have no care or concern for *la16.* **3** *vt, chf in negative* have no regard, heed or consideration for, fail entirely to value *16-e17.*

have ~ of *freq in negative* have no concern for or interest in *la15-16.* **in ~** in charge *la14-16.*

tak na ~ of fail to heed, take no account of *la16.*

cure *see* COOR[2]

curfuffle *see* CARFUFFLE

curie &c [*'kørɪ] *n* the royal stables *la16-e17.* [only Sc; F *écurie*]

curious &c, kerious &c *19-e20, Abd;* **kwerious** *la19-20, Bnf Abd* ['kørɪəs, 'ker-; *NE* 'k(w)ir-] *adj* **1** = curious *la14-.* **2** ready, desirous, eager *la16-e17.* **3** *of words or sounds* carefully or elaborately expressed or modulated; elegant, artificial *15-16.*

keeriosity &c [*NE* kɪrɪ'ozɪtɪ, *Abd* also kwir-] = curiosity *18-, now NE.*

curl &c *vi* play at *curling, 18-.*

n, curling the curving motion given to the stone *19.*

~er a person who plays at *curling, 17-.* **~er('s) word** = *curling word, la18-e19, Dmf.* **~ing** a game played by sliding heavy stones on ice *17-.* **~ing court** a mock court of *curlers* held after a *curling*-club supper *18-e20.* **~ing house** a hut near the pond for storing *curling-stones* etc *la19-.* **~ing-stone &c** the smooth rounded stone, now *freq* of polished granite, used in *curling, 17-.* **~ing word** a word or formula used as a password in *curling* societies *la18-e19, WC.* [prob Eng *curl (v)*]

curl-doddy &c, curl-dodie *n* name for various plants with a rounded flower-head including: **1** the devilsbit scabious *19-, now Bwk;* **2** the field scabious *la19-, now Rox;* **3** the ribwort and greater plantain *16, 20-, now Fif;* **4** clover *19-, chf Ork.* [prob Eng *curl* + DODDY]

curle *see* CURALE

curlie &c, curly *adj* = curly.

n, chf in pl = ~ **kail,** *19-, now Bnf Abd Fif.* **~ doddy** a kind of SWEETIE *19-e20.* **~ green** *n, chf in pl* = ~ **kail,** *la19-, local Bnf-Edb Rox.* **~ kail &c** *n* curly colewort *19-.* **~ murly** *n* a kind of SWEETIE *la19-, Ags.* **~-willie** *n* = ~ *murly, la19-, Fif.* **~wurlie** *n* an elaboration, an ornamentation *la18-19.*

curly-andra &c *n* a sugared coriander or caraway seed *la19-, Fif.* [altered f Eng *coriander*]

curmud &c [kʌr'mʌd, kər-] *adj* **1** close, near, intimate *19-e20, S.* **2** snug *19-e20, S.* [see SND]

curmur &c [kʌr'mʌr, kər-] *vi* make a low rumbling or murmuring sound; purr *19-.*

n flatulence, the rumbling sound associated with it *20-, local NE-Kcb.*

~ing &c 1 = *n, la18-, now Bnf-Fif.* **2** a murmur of talk *20-, now Abd Fif.* **3** a grumbling or complaining; a source of complaint *la19-e20, local.* [*cur-,* intensifier + MURR]

curn[1] &c; kurn &c *la15-, la19,* **curran &c** *19 n* **1** a single grain of corn, *freq* as **the third, the fourty** *etc* ~ indicating a proportion of a crop etc; *in pl* grain *la15-17.* **2** a grain or particle *la15-, now Bnf Ags Stlg.* **3** a (small) number or quantity; a few *la18-, now local Bnf-Per.*

~y coarse, grainy *19.* [obscurely related to OE *corn* > CORN; *cf* KIRN[2], QUERN[2]]

curn[2] a currant *la19-, chf Rox.*

curn *see* KIRN[1]

curnawin &c [kʌr'nɑɪn; *NE* also -'n(j)ɑvɪn] *n* a gnawing sensation of hunger *19-, now Bnf Abd.* [*cur-,* intensifier + Eng *gnawing*]

curnie *n*, *also* **~-wurnie** *child's word* the little finger *19-, Fif.*

curpall *see* CURPLE

curpin &c, curpon *n* **1** a horse's crupper, the strap *la16, 19-, now Bnf Abd.* **2** the behind or rump *18-e20.* [metath f ME, OF *croupon*]

curple &c, curpall &c *n* **1** *also* **crupple** *19-e20, SW, S* = crupper *la15-e20.* **2** the buttocks *la18, Ayr.* [only Sc]

curpon *see* CURPIN

curr *see* COOR[1]

currach[1] **&c, currok &c** *16* [*'kʌrəx, *-ok, *-ək] *n* a coracle *la15-e19.* [Gael *curach*]

currach[2] **&c, curreck &c** [*'kʌrəx, *-ək] *n* a wickerwork pannier *la17-19.* [*cf* Gael *curran*]

currack &c *n* tangle (TANG[1]), the seaweed *la19-, Bnf.* [Gael *corrag* a finger]

curran *n* = currant *la18-.*

~ **bun** = black bun (BLACK) *la18-.*

curran *see* CURN[1]

curreck *see* CURRACH[2]

currell *see* CURALE

currie &c *n* a small stool *19-, local.* [prob f COOR[1]]

currieboram &c ['kʌrɪ'borəm] *n* a confused, noisy or frightened crowd *la19-, Bnf Abd.* [see SND]

curriebuction ['kʌrɪ'bʌkʃən] *n* = prec *la19-, now Bnf Abd.* [see SND]

currieshang &c ['kʌrɪ'ʃaŋ] *n* a dispute, quarrel *20-, Cai.* [*cur(rie)-*, intensifier + back-formation f SHANGIE[2]]

currie-wurrie *n* a violent dispute *19-, now local Bnf-Lnk.*

vi dispute violently *la19-, Bnf.* [prob *cur(rie)-*, intensifier + *wurr* growl as in *gurry-wurry* 2 (GURR[1])]

currok *see* CURRACH[1]

curroo [kʌ'ru] *vi, of a male pigeon* coo *19-, chf Ags.* [imit; *cf* Eng *curr*]

currour &c *n* **1** a watcher or ranger of a forest *15-e16, only Sc, as proper name la13.* **2** = courier *la15-e16.*

curseckie *see* CARSACKIE

Curse of Scotland *n* the nine of diamonds *e18.* [several explanations are suggested; see SND]

cursit *see* CURST

curson &c *n* a fruiting spur *la18.* [only Sc; F *courçon*]

cursour, curser &c *15-e17*, **coursere &c** *la14-16*, **coursour** *15-e17* [*'kʌrsur, *-ər, *'kurs-] *n* **1** = courser, a charger *la14-16.* **2** a stallion *16-19, latterly proverb.*

~ **hors** = *n* 1, *la16.* [*cf* COOSER]

curst, cursit &c *adj* **1** = cursed, curst *la14-.* **2** very cross *la19-, now Abd Ags.*

curtassy &c *la14-e16*, **courtasy &c** *la15-e17*, **courtesy &c** *la16-* [*'kʌrtəzɪ, *'kurt-] *n* **1** = courtesy *la14-.* **2** *orig* the ~ of Scotland *law:* a *liferent* (LIFE) conferred on a widower, of the HERITAGE of his deceased wife *la15-20.*

cury [*?'kɔrɪ, *?'kju-] *n* a cooked dish, concoction *16-e17.* [ME *cury, kewery*, OF *keuerie, cueurie*]

cusa(i)n *see* KIZZEN

cuschen *see* CUSHIN

cuschet *see* CUSHAT

cusching *see* CUSHIN

cush &c *n* a soft, useless person *la19-, chf Rox.* [also in ModNorthumb dial]

cushat &c, cuschet &c *n* the ring-dove, wood-pigeon *la15-.*

cushie &c ['kʌʃɪ, 'kuʃɪ] = *n, 20-.* **cushie-doo &c 1** = *n, 19-, Gen except Sh Ork.* **2** term of endearment *la19-, local.* [nME *cowschote*, OE *cusceote*]

cushie-dreel *n* a trouser opening *20-, Ags.* [GUSHET + Eng *drill* a furrow]

cushin &c *17-, now local Cai-Stlg*, **cuschen &c** *16-e17*, **cushing** *la15-e17*, **couschein &c** *la16-17* ['kʌʃən, *'kʌs-] *n* = cushion.

cushle-mushle &c *n* a whispering, muttering *18, Abd.* [reduplicated f *mushle* (see MUSH[2])]

cusigne, cusine, cusines, cusing, cussin(g) *see* KIZZEN

cust &c, cuist, coyst [*kʌst, *køst] *n* term of abuse or contempt for a person *la15-16.* [*cf* CUSTRIL, CUSTRIN]

custom *see* CUSTUME

customer, customar *la15-e17* *n* = customer: a customs officer; a regular buyer *la15-.*

~ **wark &c** *weaving* orders carried out for a private customer as opposed to factory or speculative work *19.* ~ *or* **customary weaver** a weaver who works for private customers *19.* [*cf* CUSTUMAR]

custril [*'kʌstrəl, *'køst-, *'kəist-] *n* a fool *19-e20, S.* [eModEng *custrel, coistrel* a knave, ME = a groom]

custrin, custrone &c [*'kʌstrən, *'køst-, *'kwɪst-] *n* a wicked person, knave, rogue *16-19.* [eModEng *coystrowne*, ME *quystroun*, OF *coistron* a scullion]

custumar &c, custumer &c [*'kʌstəmər, *'kʌstəm-] *n* = customer, a customs officer *la14-e17.*

custumary &c the office of collector of customs *la15-16, only Sc.* [*cf* CUSTOMER]

custume &c *la14-17*, **custom &c** [*'kʌstəm, -əm] *n* **1** = custom *la14-.* **2** a customary right or privilege *e15.*

vt **1** = custom *16.* **2** impose a customs duty on *16.*

~ **fr(i)e** free of customs duty *la15-17.*

cut[1]; **cute &c** *la14-e17*, **cowt &c** *la15-16* [kʌt] *v, pt, ptp also* ~**tit &c** *la16-* = cut *la14-.*

n **1** = cut. **2** a piece of timber cut off a larger piece, beam or tree *16-17.* **3** a length **of** (cloth) *la16-17.* **4** a quantity of linen or woollen yarn, *usu* 120 rounds of a 93-inch reel, *ie* 300 ELLS or 310 yards (283.46 metres) *17-.* **5** temper, (bad) humour *20-, local: 'he's in bad cut'.* **6** a group of sheep divided from the rest *20-, now Bnf.* **7** a score in handball, less than a HAIL[4] *20-, Rox.* **8** *in pl* the clevis of a plough *19-, SW; cf cutwiddie.* NB *For combs with ptp, see below.* ~**ter &c 1** a person who cuts (*esp* wood) without permission *la16-17.* **2** a reaper, harvester *la19-, now Bnf Abd.* **3** a crack or crevice in a stratum of rock *la18-19.* ~**ting &c 1** = cutting *la15-.* **2** a piece (of wood, cloth etc) produced by cutting (*cf n* 1, 2) *la16-17*. **3** *piping* (the playing of) a single very brief grace-note, prefixed to a lower melody note *la18-*. ~**ting loaf** bread old enough to be easily cut *20-*, *local*. **cuttit &c, cut** *ptp, adj* **1** = cut *la15-*. **2** *only* ~**tit** curt, abrupt, snappish *19-*, *now Bnf Abd*. ~**titly &c** abruptly, curtly *17-e18*. ~**ty &c** *adj* short, stumpy *18-*, *now chf in combs*. *n* **1** (1) a short, dumpy girl *19-*, *now Ags*. (2) affectionate name for a child *19-*. (3) a mischievous or disobedient girl *19-*. (4) contemptuous term for a woman *19-*, *now Bnf Abd Fif*. **2** = ~*ty-pipe*, *18-*. **3** = ~*ty-spoon*, *la17-19*. **4** the hare *la18-19* [*cf* Gael *cutach* bobtailed]. **5** the black guillemot *19-e20*. *vi* sup greedily *la18-e20* [f ~*ty-spoon*]. ~**ty clay** *la19-*, *local Bnf-Lnk*, ~**ty gun** *18-19* = ~*ty pipe*. ~**ty mun** name of a dance *18-e19*. ~**ty pipe** a short, stumpy (clay) pipe *19-*. ~**ty quean &c** *chf* contemptuous term for a woman *la18-*, *now Bnf Abd*. ~**ty rung** a crupper for use with a pack-saddle *19-e20*, *N*. ~**ty sark** a short chemise or undergarment *la18-19*, *SW*. ~**ty spoon &c** a short-handled spoon, *usu* of horn *la17-20*. ~**ty stool &c** **1** a low, *usu* three-legged, stool *19-*, *now local*. **2** the *stool of repentance* (REPENT), the place in a church where those guilty of misconduct were obliged to sit *la18-e19*. ~**ty stoup** a pewter vessel holding ⅛ of a CHOPIN *la18-e19*, *local*. ~**ty wran &c** the wren *19-*, *chf SW*. ~ **coal** *mining*: in *stoup-and-room* (STOUP) working, coal cut on two sides where two ROOMS meet *la19-*, *now Fif*. ~**-luggit &c** crop-eared *17-e19*. **cut note** *piping* an accented short note preceding an unaccented long one; *occas* an unaccented short note following an accented long one *20-*. ~ **throat &c 1** = cut-throat *16-*. **2** a kind of light artillery or firearm *16-e17*. **3** a dark lantern *la17-e18*. ~**widdie**, ~**wuddie** the crossbeam attaching a plough or harrow to the traces; *in pl* the links connecting the mechanism of the implement to the crossbeam *la16-e19*. ~**-an-dry** cut-and-dried tobacco *la17-*, *now Bnf*

Abd. ~ **before the point** to anticipate *19-*, *now Kcb*. ~ **harrows** sever relations, stop being on speaking terms *20-*, *Rox*. **a** ~ **of a man** a sturdy, middle-sized man *20-*, *Cai Bnf*. ~ **out** to cut off *la18-*, *now Fif*.

cut[2] *n* an appetite *la19-*, *Bnf*. ~ **pock &c** the stomach *la18-e20*, *NE*. [var of Eng *gut*]

cutchack &c ['kʌtʃək, *'kut-] *n* a small, blazing, coal or PEAT[1] fire *18-*, *NE*. [Gael *cùilteag* a small corner]

cute *see* CUIT, CUT[1], QUOIT

cuth *see* CAN[2], CAN[3]

cuthill &c [*'kʌθl, *'køθl] *n, perh* a grove, small wood *15-e17*. [only Sc; obscure]

cutlack &c *n* impertinence, impudence *20-*, *Abd*. [*cf* CUT[1] *n* 5, *cuttit* 2]

cuttag *n* a sturdy, middle-sized woman *20-*, *Cai*. [Gael *cutag* a little dumpy woman, prob f *cutty* (CUT[1])]

cuttance &c *n* **1** an account; news *la18-*, *Abd*. **2** *in negative* no encouragement *la19-*, *local Abd-Stlg*. [Eng *quittance*]

cutter *n* a hip-flask holding half a MUTCHKIN of WHISKY *la19-*, *local Cai-Fif*. **rin the** ~ carry out liquor from a public house or brewery unobserved *20-*, *local*. [f Eng *cutter* a boat used for smuggling, or *revenue cutter* that which tries to prevent smuggling]

cuttle &c [*Sh Bwk Rox* 'køtl; *'kʌtl] *vt* sharpen, whet *19-e20*. [back-formation f OSc *cutelere*, *cutler* [*'kʌtlər, *'køt(ə)lər]]

cuttle *see* CUITTLE

cuvatise &c [*'kʌvətəis] *n* = covetise, covetousness *15-16*.

cuver *see* COVER, COWER

cuz *adv, adj* closely; close *la18-e20*, *Ags*. [appar altered f Eng *close*]

cwe *see* COY

cweed *see* COOD[1], COOD[2]

cwint *see* COONT

cwintry *see* COUNTRA

cwite *see* COAT

cyse *see* SITH

cythe *see* SYTH

D

'd *pronoun, chf in rhyme 15-16* = IT, used after vowels and continuant consonants and freq joined to preceding word, eg *dude* (DAE¹), FORD, *haid* (HAE¹), *herd* (HEAR) *15-e20.*

da *n* a canopy over a throne etc *la16.* [F *dais* (w silent *s*); *cf* DEAS]

da *see* DAE², DAW², DAY, THE

daak &c [dɑk] *vi* doze for a short time *20-, Cai.* *n* a lull in wet or windy weather *20-, Cai Bnf.* [Norw *daka* go slowly]

daaken &c ['dɑkən] *vi* dawn *20-, Cai.* [*cf* Norw dial *dagna*]

dab¹ *19-,* **dawb &c** *vt* **1** *of birds etc* peck *la16-, now local, Bnf-Kcb.* **2** = dab, strike lightly. **3** pierce slightly, stab *19-, now local Bnf-Kcb.* **4** aim (a marble etc) **at** *20-, EC, S.* **5** push, shove smartly *la19-, local N.*
n **1** a blow, slap *18-, now local N.* **2** = dab, a light stroke. **3** (a throw in) a children's game *la19-, Ags Clcm.* **4** melted fat, gravy etc in which potatoes are dipped *la19-, now local Ork-nEC;* cf *tatties and dab* (TATTIE).
dabach &c a stroke, blow *19-, Bnf Abd.* **dabber** (*NE*), **dabble** *vi* wrangle *19.* **dabbie** a game played with marbles or tops *20-, local C.*
dabbity *n* **1** *chf in pl* (small) ornaments *la19-20.* **2** a game of chance played with small cut-out pictures *la19-, Gsw-Ayr.*
∼-at-the-stool &c pepper (*now Stlg Ayr*) or potatoes (*Abd*) and salt *la19-.* **let ∼** *chf in negative* not to disclose information (that ..) *20-, Gen except Sh Ork.*

dab² *n* **common** *or* **plain ∼** a plain, ordinary or unpretentious person or thing *20-, NE Per.* [see SND Suppl]

dabble *v* **∼d &c** bemused, distraught *la19-, Bnf.* [perh frequentative of DAB¹]

daberlack &c ['dabərlok, -lək] *n, chf in pl* **1** = BADDERLOCK *19-, Mry Bnf.* **2** wet, dirty scraps of cloth or leather *19-, Mry Bnf.* **3** hair in lank, tangled, separate locks *19-, Mry Bnf.* **4** *chf disparaging* a tall uncomely person *la19-, Bnf.* [metath]

dacent &c *19-,* **decent** ['desənt] *adj* = decent *16-.*

dachle *see* DACKLE

dacker¹, daker; daiker &c ['dakər, 'dekər] *vi* **1** bargain *la17-e20.* **2** walk slowly, aimlessly or weakly *19-, now Bnf Abd Fif.* **3** grapple; interfere *18-, now Bnf.* **4** *chf* **∼ on** jog along (**with**) *la18-.* **5** be engaged in undemanding work *19-, now Sh Stlg.* [*cf* Eng dial = waver, totter, MDu *daeckeren* flutter, move about, shake]

dacker² &c, daker ['dakər, *'dekər] *vt* search (a house, person) for stolen goods etc (by official warrant) *la16-e20, NE.* [perh f as DACKER¹]

dackle &c; dachle &c ['dakl, 'daxl] *v* **1** *vi* hesitate, dawdle, go slowly *19-, Bnf Abd Ags.* **2** *vt* cause to hesitate, impede *20-, Bnf Abd.*

---

n **1** a lull, state of suspense *19.* **2** a hesitating step *20-, Bnf Abd.* [var of DACKER¹]

dad &c, dade *la16;* **daud &c** [dɑd, ? *also* dad] *v* **1** *vt* strike heavily, beat violently; jolt *la16-, now Cai midLoth.* **2** *vi* dash, bump about, thud *19-e20.* **3** *vt* PELT¹; bespatter *19-, now Sh.* **4** *vi, of wind, rain etc* blow in gusts, drive *la18-, now local Sh-Bwk.* **5** *vti, freq* **∼ to** bang, slam (a door) *18-, now local Bnf-Kcb.*
n **1** a heavy blow, thud *la16-20.* **2** a large piece, lump, quantity (knocked off) *18-, now local Bnf-Kcb.*
come *or* **play ∼** fall with a heavy thud *18-, local Bnf-Edb SW.* [prob imit]

daddy *16-,* **dadie &c** *16-e20,* **deddy** *la16-, now Cai* ['dadı, 'dedı, 'dɛdı] *n* = daddy *16-.*
be a their ∼s excel, be the best, be an extreme example *20-, local Bnf-Rox.*

dade &c [*ded] *n* = dad, father *16-e19.*

dade *see* DAD

dadgeon &c *n* **∼ wabster** *or* **weaver** a weaver of linen or woollen material for country neighbours *19, WC.* [see SND]

dadie *see* DADDY

dae¹ *la19-, only Sc,* **do &c; du(e) &c** *16-e20, only Sc,* **dow &c** *16-e19, only Sc,* **dee** *19-, only Sc* [dø, de; *NE* di] *vti, pres indicative all pers also* **dois &c** *la14-16; emphatic and interrog also* **div &c** *19-e20; 3 pers sing also* **dis &c** *la17-* [døz, dɪz]; *negative also* **disna &c** *18-* ['døzna, 'dɪz-, -nı, *Abd* -nɪn], **dinna &c** *19-* ['døna, 'dɪna, -nı, *Abd* -nın]. *pt negative also* **didna &c** *19-. presp also* **deand &c** *la14-e17,* **dowand &c** *la14-16. ptp also* **dune &c** *la14-e20,* **downe &c** *la14-e17,* **doun &c** *15-e18,* **doin &c** *la14-e17,* **deen &c** *la18-e20* [døn, dın; *N* din; *nEC* den] **1** = do *la14-.* **2** *vr, latterly ballad* proceed, betake oneself *15-e19.* **3** *in perfect, as aux with ptp etc,* *16:* 'thay have done brokin the dyk'.
doer a person who acts for another; a FACTOR, agent *la15-e20.*
be ∼in 1 be content, satisfied *19-, now Bnf-Stlg.* **2** *chf in negative* not be able to put up **with** *18-:* 'I can't be doing with their nonsense'. **daeinless &c** unprosperous, feckless; clumsy, awkward *19-, now Fif.* **daeless &c** helpless, feeble, useless *20-, now Stlg.* **doless &c** lazy, improvident *18-, now Stlg Dmf.* **be deen wi it** be dying *20-, Bnf-Stlg.* (**so &c** (*16-*) *or* **that** (*19-*)) **done** *16-e17,* **dune &c** *19-, now local* (so) very, extremely *16-:* 'I'm no that dune gleg i the hearin'. **deester** *often contemptuous* a person in a position of authority *la18-, now Bnf Abd.*
∼-nae-better a poor substitute *19-, now Kcb.* **∼-na-gude &c** a ne'er-do-well *19-, now Abd Fif.* **dude &c** *chf rhyme* = do it *la15-e17.*

dae² *&c la15-16, la18,* **da &c** *la14-16* [*de] *n* = doe, the female of the fallow deer.

daff &c *vi* act playfully or foolishly *16-, Gen except Sh Ork.*

daffery, dafrie &c *n* **1** folly, foolishness *la16-18*. **2** fun, merriment *la18-*, now *Bnf Fif*.
daffin &c **1** fun; foolish behaviour *16-e20*. **2** licentious behaviour; smutty language *18-e19*.
on the ~in out for fun, on holiday *la19-*, now *Bnf Abd*.
daffins *n pl* the cords used to fasten drift-nets to the rope from which they are hung *20-*, *Ork Cai Mry*. [unknown]
daft &c *adj* **1** foolish, stupid, lacking intelligence *15-*. **2** crazy, insane; lacking commonsense *la15-*. **3** frivolous, thoughtless *la16-*. **4** *chf* ~ **aboot, for, on** extremely fond of, crazy about *la18-*.
~ie an imbecile; a mentally handicapped person; a fool *la19-*. **~ish** somewhat deranged *19-*, now *Abd Fif*. **~ness** foolishness; wantonness *la16-*.
~ **days 1** a time of frivolity and fun; *hence* one's youth *19-*, now *Bnf Abd Edb*. **2** the period of festivity at Christmas and New Year *la18-e20*. [ME; OE *gedæfte* gentle, meek]
dag¹ &c *n* **1** a thin drizzling rain *19-e20*. **2** a heavy shower (of rain) *19-*, now *Cai Bnf Abd*. *vi* rain gently, drizzle *19*.
daggy &c *adj* drizzling, moist, misty *19-*, now *Abd*. [ON **dagg-*, orig stem of *dǫgg* dew, *dǫggva* bedew; cognate w OE *dēaw* dew]
dag² &c [*Sh* dag; *Abd* djag] *n*, *chf in pl*, *fishermen's taboo* woollen mittens or half-mittens worn to protect the hands; (pieces of) cloth used for this purpose *la19-e20*, *Sh Abd*. [uncertain]
dag³ &c, **dog** [dag, dog; *NE also* dɛg] *interj* confound it *etc la19-*, now *Cai Bnf Abd*.
~ **on it** *etc* confound it etc *la19-*, now local *Bnf-Kcb*. [perh corruption of *God damn, dang* etc, w confusion w *dog*]
daggle &c ['dagl, 'degl] *vi* move, act or work slowly or idly *19-*, *local NE-S*. [see SND]
dagone *n* a villain *e16*. [*Dagon* the Philistine god]
daible *vti, n* = dabble *19*.
daice *see* DEAS
daich *see* DAIGH
daichie; daikie [***dexɪ, 'dekɪ] *n* a bivalve smooth-shelled mollusc *la19-e20*, *Fif*.
daidle¹ &c *n* **1** a (child's) pinafore or bib *19-*. **2** an apron *19-*, *local*.
daidlie &c **1** = *n* 1, *19-*. **2** = *n* 2, *la19-*, *local*. **3** a doily *20-*, *WC*. [see SND]
daidle² &c *vi* **1** idle, waste time; potter about; saunter *la18-*, *local Abd-Kcb*. **2** waddle; stagger *19-e20*.
daidler a trifler *19-*, now *Fif*.
~ **and drink** wander from place to place drinking; tipple *19*. [*cf* Eng dial *daddle* go slowly, stagger and Eng *dawdle*]
daidle³ &c ['dedl; *chf Abd* 'dɑdl] *vt* **1** dirty, wet (one's clothes etc) *19-*, now *Abd*. **2** *of wind etc* buffet *20-*, *Abd*. [perh frequentative of DAD]
daidle⁴ *vti* dandle, fondle (a child); *of a child* be dandled, fondled *la19-*, now *Abd*.

daigh &c *18-*, now *Ags Arg Lnk*, **daich, dauch** &c *la16-e17*, **dewche** *la16*, *Fif*, **deuch** &c *19-*, now *Bwk Rox* [dex, djux, ***dɑx] *n* **1** = dough *16-*. **2** a mixture of meal and hot water for chicken food *19-e20*.
~ie &c **1** = doughy *19-e20*. **2** *of persons* inactive, lacking in spirit *19-e20*.
daigie &c ['degɪ] *n* a variety of the game of marbles *20-*, now *Bnf*. [? f DEG]
daik *la18-*, now *Bnf Abd*, **dek** &c [dek, ***dɛk] *vt* **1** = deck, adorn *16-*. **2** smooth down (the hair etc) *19-*, now *Abd Ags*.
n a smoothing down *la18-*, now *Abd*.
daiker &c *vt* decorate, deck (**out**) *19-e20*. [perh F *décorer* or frequentative of DAIK]
daiker *see* DACKER¹, DAKER
daikie *see* DAICHIE
dail(1) silver *see* DALE¹
daily *see* DAY
daim *see* DEM
daimen &c; **demmin** &c ['demən] *adj* rare, occasional *la18-*, now *Ags*. [see SND Suppl]
daimish *see* DAMISH
dainner *see* DENNER
dainshach &c; **denshag** &c ['denʃəx, 'dɛnʃəx] *adj* fastidious, particular; fussy about food *19-*, now *Cai*. [*cf* Eng dial *dainsh* &c dainty, fastidious and DANE]
daintess *see* DAINTY
daintith &c, **danteth** *la15* [***dentɛð] *n* a dainty *la15*, *18-19* (*literary*). [ME *daynteth*, OF *daintiet*]
dainty, daynté &c *la14-e16* ['dentɪ, ***'dɛntɪ] *n*, *pl also* **daintess** &c *19-*, **dentice** ['dentɪs, 'dɛnt-] *19-* = dainty *la14-*.
adj, also **den(n)ty** *19-* ['dentɪ, 'dɛntɪ] **1** = dainty *15-*. **2** pleasant, agreeable *la18-*, now *Bnf-Fif*. **3** large, fair-sized; *of time* considerable *la19-*, now *Stlg*.
dainty-lion *see* DENTYLION
dair *see* DEAR
dairk *see* DARG¹
dairt *see* DART, DERT
dais *see* DEAS
daise &c, **dase** &c; **dease** &c *la18-e20* [dez; *Ork* daz] *v* **1** *vt* = daze *la14-e20*. **2** *vi* become rotten, spoiled by age, damp etc, *chf* **daised** *19-*, now *Kcb*.
dazent &c damned *20-*, now *Abd*. [ME *dasen* grow dizzy, stupefy; *cf* ON *dasaðr* weary and exhausted]
daiss *see* DASS
daith &c *la15-*, **death** *la16-*, **deeth** *la19-*, *local*, **dethe** &c *15-e17*, **deith** *16-*, now *Cai Abd Kcdn Fif* [deθ, diθ] *n* = death *15-*.
(**law of**) **deathbed** the law by which an heir could annul deeds made to his disadvantage by a terminally-ill predecessor within 60 days before death, *chf* (**up**)**on the head of ~bed** *18-19*. **de**th candle** a will-o-the-wisp, thought to foretell death *19-*, now *Bnf Abd Fif*.

deathchap a knocking, thought to foretell death *19-*, *now local Cai-Fif*. **death dwam** a death-like faint *la19-*, *now Abd*. [*cf* DEID]

daizzle *vt* = dazzle *19-*, *now local Bnf Abd Fif*.

daker &c *15-17*; **daiker** &c *la16-17* *n* = dicker, a set of ten hides.

daker *see* DACKER¹, DACKER²

dale¹ &c *15-*, *now local Cai-Kcb*, **dele** &c; **deal** *16-* *n* **1** = deal *la14-*. **2** (1) a part, portion, share *15-*. (2) each share in a herring-fishermen's profit-sharing scheme *18-e20*. **3** (1) a share, portion or piece of land *la15-*, *now Abd*. (2) an ecclesiastical division of land *la16-e17*. **4** a certain quantity or measure (of coal) *la17-18*, *E*. **5** a dealing out, division or distribution, *eg* of land *15-e18*. **6** dealings with others, association *la15-16*. **7** sexual intercourse, *chf* **have** ~ **with** *la15-16*.
vti **1** = deal *la14-*. **2** divide, distribute *la14-19*.
~**sman** a sharer or partner in a ship, fishing boat etc *la16-e20*. **dail**(1) **silver** money given as dole or alms *la16-17*.

dale² &c, **dell** *la16-e17*, *Ags Per* *n* **1** = deal, a plank *la15-*. **2** a shelf *19-*, *now local Cai-Kcb*. **3** a diving-board at a swimming pool *e20*, *WC*. **4** a container (*orig* made of wood), *usu* for milk *18-*, *now Bwk*.

dale³ &c, **dell** *n*, *games* a goal, stopping place or base *19-*, *now local Abd-Kcb*. [*prob* extended f Eng *dale* a hollow, valley]

dalk &c *n* one of several types of clay found in coal *la18-e19*. [*prob* connected w Norw dial *dalk* a sticky lump]

dall [dal] *n* = doll, a pretty, silly woman *19-*, *now Bnf Abd Lnk*.

dallar &c [*'dalər] *n* = dollar *17*.

dalldrums &c *n pl* foolish fancies *19*. [var of Eng *doldrums*]

dalmes *see* DAMIS

dalphin &c [*'dalfɪn, *'daf-, *'dolf-] *n* = dauphin *la15-16*.

daly *see* DAY

dam¹ &c; **dame** &c *la15-17* *n* **1** = dam *15-*. **2** the amount of urine discharged at a time (*usu* by children) *19-*, *now Bnf Abd*.
vti = dam *la16-*.
~**-dike** &c the retaining wall of a dam *la16-*, *now SW*. ~**head** a weir *16-*, *now Cai*.
~**min**(g) **and lavin**(g) a method of removing water, used in mining and poaching *18-19*; *cf* *dem and lave* (DEM).

dam² *n*, *only in pl* **the** ~**s** the game of draughts *la17-*, *now Bnf Abd Fif*.
~**brod 1** a draughtboard *18-19*. **2 the** ~**brod** the game of draughts *19-*, *now Abd*. **3** *attrib* chequered *la18-*, *now local Bnf-Stlg*. ~**heid** the top or bottom of a dambrod, *20-*, *now Abd*. [eModEng *dammes*, F *dames* pl of *dame* > DAME]

dam³ *n* **1** (1) a lady, dame *15-e17*. (2) title prefixed to a woman's name *la14-e17*. **2** = dam, a female parent *16-*. [var of DAME]

damacella &c [*damə'sɛlə] *n* a type of cloth *e17*.

damas *see* DAMIS

dame &c *n* **1** = dame *la14-*. **2** a mother *la14-e19*. **3** a (farmer's) wife, housewife *la18-*, *now Bnf Abd Fif*. **4** a young (unmarried) woman *la18-*, *now Bnf Abd Ags*.
damie = *n* 4, *la18-*, *now Ags*. [*cf* DEEM and DAM³]

dame *see* DAM¹

dames *see* DAMIS

damicel *see* DAMISHELL

damis &c *la17-e18*, **damas** &c *la15-e17*, **dames** &c *16-17*, **dalmes** &c *la15-16*; **dammas** &c *la15-16* [*'daməs] *n* = damask.

damisel *see* DAMISHELL

damish &c, **daimish** ['damɪʃ, 'demɪʃ] *vti* = damage *19-*, *now Bnf Fif*.

damishell &c *18-*, *now Abd*, **damisel** &c *15-e17*; **damicel** &c *la14-e15* ['demɪʃəl, *'daməsɛl, &c] = damsel.

dammas *see* DAMIS

dammer *see* DAUMER

dammish &c *la16-*, *now Bnf*, **dammis** *la16-e17* *vt*, *chf in ptp*, *adj* ~**t** &c stunned, stupefied *la17-e20*. [perh var of Eng *damage*]

damnage &c, **dampnage** &c *n* damage *16-e18*. [*cf* Eng; MedL *dam*(*p*)*nagium*]

damnifé *see* DAMPNIFÉ

damnis &c *vt* damage *la16-17*. [only Sc; obscure; *cf* DAMISH, DAMMISH]

damnum fatale ['damnʌm fa'tale] *n*, *law* a loss due to an inevitable accident, such as an exceptional flood or storm *18-*. [L = a loss ordained by fate]

dampnage *see* DAMNAGE

dampnifé &c, **damnifé** &c [*'dam(p)nɪfaɪ, *-fi] *vt* damage or injure, *esp* by causing loss *la16*. [eModEng *dam*(*p*)*nify* &c, OF *dam*(*p*)*nifier*, L *dam*(*p*)*nificāre*]

dampnis [*'dam(p)nɪz] *n pl* damages *la15-e16*. [only Sc; L *dampna*, pl of *dam*(*p*)*num* loss]

damster *see* DEMPSTER

Dan, *also* ~**nie boy** nickname for a Roman Catholic *la20-*, *WC*. [familiar form of *Daniel*, a common name among Roman Catholic Irish]

dan *see* THAN

dance &c, **dans** &c *15-16* *vti* (*la14-*), *n* (*la15-*) = dance.
the (**Merry** *or* **Pretty**) **D**~**rs** the Northern Lights, Aurora Borealis *18-*, *chf N*. **dancie** a dancing master *la19-*, *now local Bnf-Lnk*. **dancin mad** in a towering rage *la19-*, *now local Cai-Kcb*.
~**-in-my-loof** a very small person *19-*, *now Ags*. ~ **one's lane** dance with joy or rage *18-*, *now Abd*.

dander¹ &c; **dauner** &c *19-* ['dan(d)ər, 'dɑn(d)ər] *vi* stroll, saunter *la16-*.
n a stroll, leisurely walk *19-*. [see SND]

dander² ['dan(d)ər; *Ayr also* 'danər] *n, chf in pl* the refuse of a smith's fire; clinker *la18-*. [obscure]

dander³ *n* a kind of sweet bun or biscuit, a rock-cake *20-, local C.* [perh f prec]

dandie &c *vi, chf herring fishing* keep moving a line up and down in the water *20-, Sh Bnf.*
n, only in pl = ~ **hanlin**, *la19-, now Bnf Abd.*
~ **hanlin** a type of fishing line *la19-, now Bnf*; see SND. ~ **line** a line used as in *v, la19, Sh NE.* [see SND]

dandiefechan &c *n* a slap; a stunning blow *e19.* [obscure]

dandilly, dandillie &c [*'dandılı] *n* a (spoilt) pet *16-e20.*
adj petted, pampered; fancy, over-ornamented *la18-19.* [cf Eng *dandle (v)* pet *la16-*]

dandrum *n* a whim; a freak *la19-, now Bnf Abd.* [var of TANTRUM]

dandy *n* a dandy-brush *20-, now Cai Kcb.*

dane &c *adj* haughty, reserved, dignified *16.* [ME *deyne*, var of DIGNE]

dane *see* DEAN

dang¹ *vt* strike, knock *la19-, now Kcb.* [pt of DING]

dang² &c *vt, n, euphemistic* damn *19-e20.*

dang *see* DING

danger &c *15-;* **daunger &c** *la14-16* ['dendʒər, *'dandʒər] *n* **1** = danger *la14-.* **2** power to harm *la14-, now Lnk.* **3** the state of being in debt *la16.* **4** disdain; displeasure, enmity *16.*

dank *see* DUNK

dans *see* DANCE

Danskin &c *la15-e17*; **Danskene &c** *la16-e17* *adj* connected with, made in, from Danzig *la15-e17.*
n the town of Danzig, Gdansk *la15-e17.* [Polish *Gdansk* + *adj* ending]

dant; daunt &c *vt* = daunt *la14-.*
n, only in pl **daunts** discouraging words *19-, now Lnk.*
dantar &c a subduer, controller *16.* ~**it 1** broken in, tamed *la14-e16.* **2** vanquished, subdued *e16.*

danteth *see* DAINTETH

dantoun *see* DAUNTON

daover; dover ['dovər] *numeral, sheep-counting and children's rhymes* nine *la19-e20, local.* [see ZEENDI]

dar *see* DAUR

dare &c; daur *v* **1** *vi* = dare, lurk, crouch *la14-15.* **2** *freq* ~ **at** be afraid of *19.* **3** *vt* terrify, intimidate *19-, now Abd.*
n (an instilling of) a feeling of awe or fear *19-, Fif Bwk.*

darett *vt* direct *e16.* [irreg or erron]

darf *see* DERF

darg¹ &c *16-, **dairk** *la16-e17*, **dark &c** *la16-*, **dawerk &c** *15-16* [darg, derg, dɑrg; *dark &c; *'dewərk, *'da-] *n* **1** a day's work *15-.* **2** work, *chf* **the** *etc* **day's darg** *19-.* **3** the result

or product of a day's work *la15-, now Edb.* **4** *chf* **darg** the amount (of meadow) which can be mowed in a day *la16-17.*
vi, only **darg 1** work, toil *la19-, now Bnf Abd Fif.* **2** *chf agric* work by the day *la19-e20.*
darger, darker a casual unskilled labourer *18-, now Bnf Abd Fif.* [cf Eng *daywork*]

darg² *n* a young whiting *la19-e20, NE.*
~**ie** the (fry of the) coal-fish *la19-e20.*

dark [dark, *dɛrk] *adj* = dark.
~**ening &c** ['darkənın, *Rox* *'dɛrk-] *n* twilight, GLOAMIN *19-.*
~**-avised &c** *adj* having dark hair and eyes *20-, now Ork Bnf Arg* [cf *black-a-viced* (BLACK)]. **the D~ Blues** nickname for Dundee football team *20-* [f the colour of their jerseys; cf DEE and TAYSIDERS].

dark *see* DARG¹

darle *see* DORLE

darloch *see* DORLACH

darn¹ &c *vti* **1** = darn. **2** thread one's way in and out (of) *e19.*

darn² &c *n* dry, soft *etc* ~ constipation, diarrhoea *etc* in cattle *la17-, now Bnf Abd.* [see SND]

darn *see* DERN¹

darra *see* DORRO

darrer, darrest *see* DEAR

dart; dairt *adj, of oxen and horses* meaning obscure *la15-16.*

dart *see* DERT

darth *see* DEARTH

dascant &c [*'daskən(t)] *vti* = descant, discourse (about) *la16-e17.* [eModEng *descant*]

dase *see* DAISE

daseyne [*de'zin] *n* = daisy *e16.* [var for rhyme]

dash, dasche &c *la16-e17* *vt* = dash *la16-.*
dashy showy *19-, now Bnf Abd.*
a dash of rain *etc* a sudden fall of rain *la18-, now Bnf Abd Lnk.*

dashle &c *chf ptp, adj* ~**d** soiled; battered, worn *19-e20, WC Kcb.* [perh Eng *dash* + *-le*]

dask &c, desk *n* **1** = desk *16-.* **2** a seat or pew in a church *16-, now local Ork-Lnk.* [see SND]

dass; daiss, dess *n* **1** a ledge on a hillside, cliff *etc* *la18-e20.* **2** a layer in a pile of hay, PEATS¹ *etc* *19-, now Bwk Kcb.* **3** a cut of hay, coal *etc* *19-e20.* [see SND]

dat *see* THAT

date *see* DAUT

dative *adj, after its noun, law, of an executor or* TUTOR: appointed by a court *la15-;* see also *tutor dative* (TUTOR) and *cf* NOMINATE.
n, law **1** (1) = *decree dative* (DECREE); (2) an executor DATIVE *la16-e17.* **2** = dative. [cf *testament dative* (TESTAMENT)]

dauble *vi* potter about, waste time *18-, now Bnf Abd.* [cf Eng *dabble*]

dauch *see* DAIGH, DAUGH, DAVACH

dauchie &c ['dɑxı] *adj, of ice in curling* (CURL) dull and sticky *19-e20.* [see SND]

dauchter *see* DOCHTER

daud *see* DAD

daugh; dauch [dɑx] *n* soft coaly fireclay, *esp* in a coal seam *la18-, now local.* ~**er** a long thin pick for use in a DAUGH band *20-, now Fif.* [see SND]

daugh *see* DAWK

dauk *adj* stupid; sluggish *la19-e20.* [see SND]

daumer; dammer ['dɑmər] *vt* stun, confuse *19-, now Bnf.* [obscure]

dauner *see* DANDER¹

daunger *see* DANGER

daunt *see* DANT

daunton &c, dantoun &c *16-e17 vt* **1** overcome, subdue; intimidate *16-, now Stlg Lnk.* **2** bring under control; suppress *la16-17.* **3** break in, tame *la16-17.* [only Sc; irreg f DANT]

daupit &c *adj* stupid, slow-witted *la18-19.* [obscure]

daur *18-,* **dar &c** *vti, negative chf* ~**na 1** = dare, venture *la14-.* **2** *pt* **durst** *used as pres, 18-.* **3** *imperative* = don't you dare! *la19-, now Bnf Abd Fif.*
n = dare, (an act of) daring.

daur *see* DARE

daut &c, date &c *la16-17* [dɑt, *dat] *vt* pet, fondle, make much of *16-, now local Cai-Lnk.*
n **1** a caress *la18-e20.* **2** a darling *20-, now Cai.*
~**ie** a pet, darling *la17-, now local Bnf-Lnk.* [obscure]

davach &c; dauch &c *16-e18* [*'davəx, *dɑx] *n* a measure of land, *prob* based *orig* on produce rather than area and varying from area to area; like the *ploughgate* (PLEUCH), used for assessment of tax etc *13-e19, chf N.* [Gael *dabhach* a vat; a measure of land]

dave *vi* = dive *e18, 20-* (*Ags*).

dave *see* DEAVE

davel *see* DEVEL

daver &c; dever &c *19-e20* ['devər] *v* **1** *vi* wander aimlessly or dazedly; stagger (*eg* from a blow) *la16, 19-, now Bnf Abd Kcb.* **2** dawdle *19-, now Abd.* **3** be stupid or in one's dotage *la18-, now Bnf.* **4** *vt* stun, stupefy, daze *19-, now Bnf Bwk.* **5** make numb, chill *la18-, now Bnf Abd.* **6** damn ..! *19-, now Loth Lnk Kcb.* [perh cognate w DEAVE, w infl f TAIVER]

daviely &c *adv* listlessly, languidly *19-e20.* [see SND]

daw¹ &c *vi, pt also* **dew** *la14-17. ptp also* **dawin &c** *la14-e16* dawn *la14-, now local Abd-Kcb.*
n dawn *la19-e20.*
~**ing &c** dawn, dawning *la15-18.* [ME]

daw²; da &c [dɑ] *n* **1** a lazy person *16-e19.* **2** a slattern *la17-e20.* [fig extension of Eng *daw* a jackdaw]

daw³ &c *n* a whit, a jot, *chf* **never a** ~ *e19.*

dawb *see* DAB¹

daweling &c *n* ? = DEVELLING *e16.*

dawerk *see* DARG¹

dawin *see* DAW¹

dawk &c; daugh &c [dɑk, dɑx] *n, vi* drizzle *19.*
~**ie &c** drizzly *la17-, now Fif.* [obscure]

dawlie &c *adj, n* (a person who is) physically or mentally slow *la18-e20.* [perh f DAW²]

day &c; da *la15-16 n* = day *la14-.*
daily &c, daly &c *la15-e17 adj, adv* = daily *la15-.* **daily day** every day, constantly *la17-, now local Bnf-Fif.*
~**-daw** dawn *la18-, now Abd Fif.* ~**-licht** *la15-,* ~**is &c licht** *15-e16, la19,* = daylight. **not be able to see daylicht til** *or* **for someone** be blind to someone's faults *la19-, now Bnf Abd.* ~**sman** an arbitrator, umpire *la16-19.* ~**-set &c** sunset; nightfall *17-, now Cai.* ~ **tale** the daily wage of a day labourer *la19-, now Bwk.*
all the ~**s of his** *etc* **life** all his etc life *la14-.*
~ **and daily** daily *la19-, now local Cai-Kcb.* ~ **and** ~ **about** on alternate days *19-, now Abd Ags Kcb.* **get** *or* **see** ~ **aboot wi** get one's own back on *la19-e20.* **not hear** ~ **nor door** be unable to distinguish sounds *la18-e20.*

dayamond *see* DIAMOND

dayell *see* DIAL

dayligaun &c *n* twilight *la19-e20.* [reduced f *daylicht* (DAY) + *gaun* (GAE) going]

day-nettle &c *n* **1** either of two types of hempnettle *19-, now Sh Bnf.* **2** the dead-nettle *19-, local.* [see SND]

daynté *see* DAINTY

dazent *see* DAISE

de *see* DEE, THE, THERE

deacon¹ &c *la16-,* **deakin &c** *la16-e17,* **decane &c** *la15-17,* **dekin &c** *15-17,* **decon &c** *la16-17* ['dikən; NE Per also 'dəikən] *n* **1** the chief official of a craft or trade; the president of one of the *Incorporated Trades* (INCORPORATE) of a town (formerly an *ex officio* member of the Town Council) *15-.* **2** a master of a craft; an expert *19-, now Fif, Kcb.*
~**heid** *17,* ~**rie** *la16-e18,* ~**ship** *la16-e17* (the holding of) the office of deacon; the right of having a deacon; the control of a deacon.
deacon convener the DEACON who convenes and presides over meetings of the *Incorporated Trades* (INCORPORATE) of a town *la16-.* [L *decānus* one in charge of ten]

deacon² *la16-,* **decane &c** *16,* **dekin &c** *la14-16,* **diacon &c** *la16-e17* ['dikən; *'daɪakon] *n* **1** *Church* = deacon *la14-.* **2** *Presbyterian Churches* one of the laymen or -women elected and ordained to manage the temporal affairs of a congregation *la16-.*
D~**s' Court** a committee which runs a congregation's temporal affairs, consisting of the MINISTER(s), ELDERS, and DEACONS *20-.* [L *diaconus* a deacon, Gk *diákonos* a servant]

dead *see* DEID

deaf *la16-,* **defe &c** [dif; Sh-Mry nEC Wgt def] *adj* **1** = deaf *la14-.* **2** *of soil etc* poor, unproductive, barren *la18-e20.*

~**ening** sound-proofing (of a building) by pugging *19-*. ~**ie &c** *n* a deaf person *la20-*, *Sh Ork Fif. adj*, also **diffy 1** *of sound* dull *20-*, *now Fif Loth Lnk*. **2** *of a ball etc* without bounce *la20-*, *local*.

~ **nut** a nut without a kernel *chf fig*, as **nae** ~ **nit(s) &c** no inconsiderable thing or person *e19*; **not fed on** *or* **wi** ~ **nuts** plump, well-fed, well-developed *18-e20*.

deakin *see* DEACON[1]

deal *see* DALE[1]

deam *see* DEEM

deambulatour [*di'ambølatur] *n* a place to walk in; a walk *16*. [only Sc; L *dēambulatōrium*; *cf* Eng *deambulatory*]

dean *la16-*, **dene &c, dane** *15-16* [din, *den] *n* **1** = dean *la14-*. **2** with local designation, as ~ **of Glasgow** *etc*, *la15-*.

denry &c = deanery *15-17*.

dean of (*16-18*) *or* **of the** (*18-*) **Faculty 1** *freq* **of Arts** *etc* the head of a faculty in a Scottish university *16-*. **2 D~ of Faculty** *Gsw Univ* a general officer of the University; *post-Reformation* an auditor of the accounts, *now* honorary *16-*. **3** the elected leader of the Bar, whether of the *Faculty of Advocates* (FACULTY) or of a local Bar of solicitors *18-*. **D~ of Guild** (*15-20*) *or* **the Guild** (*15*) *only Sc n* the head of the GUILD or merchant company of a *royal burgh* (ROYAL); *latterly* (*except Perth*) a member of the town council, who presided over the *Dean of Guild Court*, *15-20*. *vt* ~ **o guil(d)** test and stamp (weights) officially; investigate thoroughly *20-*, *now Abd*. **Dean of Guild Court** a court with jurisdiction over the buildings of a BURGH (some of them earlier having jurisdiction also over weights and measures) *19-20*. [OF *deien, dien*, L *decānus* one in charge of ten; *cf* DEACON[1]]

deand *see* DAE[1]

dear *la16-*, **dere &c** *la14-17*; **dair &c** *17 adj*, *comparative also* **derrar &c** *la15-e16*, **darrer** *15-e17. superlative also* **derrast &c** *15-16*, **darrest** *15-e17*. **1** = dear *la14-*. **2** *elliptical* = dear Lord *19-*, *local*.

adv = dear *la14-*.

vt make dear, expensive *15*.

~ **meal** a time of famine or high price of meal *la18-e19*.

(**the**) ~ **be here,** ~ **keep us** good gracious! *19-*, *now local Cai-Fif*. ~ **kens** *or* **knows** God knows .. *la19-*, *now local Cai-Kcb*.

dearth &c *la16-*, **derth &c** *15-17*, **darth** *16-e20* [dεrθ; *also* dirθ; *Sh Ork* *dart; *darθ] *n* **1** = dearth *15-*. **2** dearness, high price *17-*, *now Bnf Abd*.

vt make dear in price (in order to cause a scarcity) *la15-19*.

deas &c *la16-e20*, **dese &c** *15-17*, **dais &c** *la15-*; **daice** *la16-e19*, **deese** *18-e20*, **dice** *la16-19* [dis, des, *dεs] *n* **1** = dais *15-*. **2** a desk or pew in a church *la16-e20*. **3** a wooden seat

or settle, which could also be used as a table, or as a bed *19-*, *now Bnf Abd Lnk*. **4** a stone- or turf-seat outside a cottage *19-e20*.

vt provide with a dais, seats or benches *17-e18*.

chamber &c of ~ *orig* a private room (at the dais end of a hall); *latterly*, a best room *16-e19*.

dease *see* DAISE

deasil &c [*'d(ʒ)εsl] *n* the custom of walking sunwise round a person or thing to bring good fortune *la18-e20*. [Gael *deiseil* southward, sunward]

deassone *see* DIZZEN

death *see* DAITH

deave *17-*, **deve &c; dave** *la19-e20*, *Sh Ork*, **deif &c** *la16-e17* [div; *Sh Ork nEC* dev; *Cai Ags also* dev] *vt* **1** deafen *15-*, *now Cai Lnk*. **2** annoy with noise or talk; bore *15-*.

n an interminable talker *20-*, *now Abd*.

deavance &c annoyance, nuisance *19-*, *now Abd*. [ME *deve*, OE (*ā*)*dēafian*; *Sh Ork* forms perh f ON *deyfa* make deaf]

debar *vt* **1** = debar *la16-*. **2** *specif* exclude formally from Communion (those guilty of certain sins) *la16-19*.

debate &c *n* **1** = debate *14-*. **2** action in defence or aid of others *la16*. **3** a (matter of) dispute as to legal rights etc *la14-16*. **4** *law, court procedure* the legal argument submitted by the parties on the closed RECORD *la19-*. **5** a struggle, a defence *la19*, *Dmf Uls*.

v **1** = debate *la15-*. **2** *vtr* fight for; defend *la15-e17*. **3** *vt* maintain or support by action or argument *16-e17*. **4** fight against; stop by force; overcome *16-e17*.

debatable &c 1 admitting of debate or dispute *15-*. **2** *of lands, boundaries* subject to dispute *15-e17*. **debat(e)able land** *etc* the land on the Scottish-English border, *esp* between the Esk and the Sark *la15-16*.

mak ~ begin or maintain a fight, in attack or defence *la14-16*. **but** *or* **without &c** ~ without resistance; without effort; peacefully *la14-e17*.

deblat &c *n* a little devil, imp *la15-16*. [ME (*once*) *deblet*, OF *deablot*, dim of *deable, diable*]

debosh &c; debush &c [dɪ'boʃ, *-'bʌʃ] *vti* **1** = debauch *17-*, *now Bnf Abd Fif*. **2** *vt* **debuish &c** oust, get rid of *e19*, *WC*. [only Sc]

debowaill &c [*'dɪ'buəl] *vt* = disembowel *la14-e16*.

debt *see* DET

debuish *see* DEBOSH

deburse &c [*dɪ'bʌrs] *vt* = disburse *16-18*, *only Sc*.

debush *see* DEBOSH

decane *see* DEACON[1], DEACON[2]

decanter *n* **1** = decanter. **2** a table jug *la19-*, *now Abd*.

decart &c [*dɪ'kart, *-'kert] *vt* set aside; discard *la16-e17*. [only Sc; F *descarter*, f *carte* a card]

decay &c, dekey &c *16* [dɪ'ke, *dɪ'kəi, *dɪ'ki] *vi* = decay *16-*.

n **1** = decay *15-*. **2** a decline (in health), *esp* from tuberculosis *la17-e20*.

deceis *see* DECES

deceivenie *n* deceit *19-e20*.

December &c *15-*; **Discembar** &c *la14-16* [dɪ'zɛmbər] *n* = December.

decent *see* DACENT

deceptioun *see* DISCEPTIOUN

decern &c *15-17*, **discern** &c *la15-e17 vti* **1** = decern, decide *15-17*. **2** discern, distinguish *15-16*. **3** *law* pronounce judicially; decide judicially or formally; decree *15-*.
decerniture &c a DECREE (*n* 2) or sentence of a court *17-*.

deces &c *15-e17*, **decesse** *la14-16*, **deses** &c *la15-17*, **discese** &c *la14-16*, **dissesse** &c *la14-16*; **deceis** *la15-e17* [*dɪ'sɛs, *-'sis] *n, vi* = decease.

deces *see* DECIST

decesse *see* DECES

decest *see* DECIST

decht *see* DICHT

decide *la15-*, **dissyde** *la15-17*; **desyde** &c *16-17*, **discyde** &c *la16-e17 vti* = decide.

decisioun &c *la15-17*; **desicioun** &c *16-e17*, **dississioun** &c *la15-e17 n* = decision.

decist &c *15-16*; **decest** &c *la15-16*, **deces** &c *16* [*dɪ'sɪs(t)] *vi* = desist.

declaration, declaratioun &c *15-16 n* **1** = declaration *15-*. **2** *law* the statement made before his committal and in the presence of the SHERIFF by a person whom it is intended to try on indictment *18-*.

declarator &c [dɪ'klarətər] *n, law, also* **action of ~** *18-* an action brought by an interested party to have some legal right or status declared, but without claim on any person called as *defender* (DEFEND) to do anything *16-*. [F *déclaratoire*, MedL *declaratorius*]

declere &c *la14-15* [*dɪ'klir], **disclar** *la14* [*dɪs'kler] *vt* = declare.

declinature *17-*, **declinatour** *la15-e18*; **declinator** [*dɪ'klɪnatur, *-ər, *St* -jur] *n, law, also* **exception ~** *la15-e17* the refusal by a judge to exercise jurisdiction, appropriate to a case in which by reason of relationship to a party or pecuniary or other interest his decision might be thought affected; refusal to accept some office, appointment or benefit, *eg* as a trustee nominated by the truster *la16-*. [MedL (*exceptio*) *declinatoria*]

decline *vti* **1** = decline *la14-*. **2** *vt* reject formally the jurisdiction of *la15-*.

decon *see* DEACON[1]

decore[1] &c [*dɪ'kor] *adj* beautiful, comely *16*. [L *decōrus*]

decore[2] &c [dɪ'kor] *vt* **1** decorate, adorn *16-e20*. **2** invest with some honour or distinction *16-17*.
decorement &c **1** decoration, embellishment *la16-e19*. **2** a decoration, ornament *la16-e20*. [laME *decore*, OF *decorer*, L *decorāre*]

decourt [*dɪ'kurt] *vt* force out of, dismiss from Court *la16-17*, *chf Sc*.

decree, decré &c *la15-16* [dɪ'kri; *law* 'dikri, *'dɛkri] *n* **1** = decree *la15-*. **2** *law* a final judgment *la18-*; *cf* DECRETE *n* 2.
~ arbitral *see* ARBITRAL. **~ conform** *law* a judgment by one court to render effective the decree of another *19-*. **~ dative** *law* the judgment appointing a person executor *20-*.

decrepit *see* DECRIPPIT

decrete[1] &c [*dɪ'krit, *'dɛkrit, *'dikrit] *n* **1** a decision, decree, *esp* of an authority *15-16*. **2** a judgment, decree of a court or judge *la14-e20*.
~ arbitral *see* ARBITRAL. [ME, OF *decret*, L *dēcrētum*; *cf* DECREE]

decrete[2] &c [*dɪ'krit] *v* **1** *vt* order, decree, *esp* judicially *la15-e19*. **2** decide, determine (to do) *la15-16*. **3** *vi* make, pronounce a decree *la16-e17*. [eME; OF *decreter*, L *dēcrēt-*, ptp stem of *dēcernere* decern]

decrippit &c *la16-*, now *Bnf*, **decrepit** &c *la15-* [dɪ'krɪpɪt, *-'kripɪt] *adj* = decrepit.

deddy *see* DADDY

dede &c [did] *n* **1** = deed *la14-17*. **2** a kind or charitable act, *chf* **~ of alms, mercy** *etc la14-16*. **3** a criminal act; an act of violence *la14-e17*. **4** an act of legal import or consequence *16-e17*.
~-doer &c the doer of a deed of violence; a murderer *15-e17*.
into ~ in fact, indeed *15*.

dede *see* DEID

deden3e[1] &c, **dedeigne** &c [*dɪ'din(jɪ), *-'dɪŋ] *vt* deign *la14-16*. [*cf* DISDAINE]

deden3e[2], **dedigne** &c *la14* [*dɪ'din(jɪ), *-'dɪŋ(jɪ)] *n* (*la14-15*), *vt* (*e16*) = dedeyn, disdain. [*cf* DISDENE]

deduce [*dɪ'døs] *vt* **1** conduct, prosecute (a process or cause) *la15-17*. **2** deduct, subtract *16-18*. [eME; L *dēdūcere* deduct, subtract]

dee *la15-*, **de** *la14-16*; **dey** *la14-16* [di; *S also* dəi] *vi* = die, suffer death.

Dee nickname for Dundee football team *la20-*. [short for *Dundee*; *cf Dark Blues* (DARK) and TAYSIDERS]

dee *see* DAE[1], DEY[1], THOU, THY

deed[1] *adv* indeed *la18-*.
~ aye *or* **no** yes or no indeed *20-*. [aphetic]

deed[2] *n* **upon** *or* **by my ~** upon my word *la18-19*, *Ork Bnf Abd*.

deedle *see* DIDDLE[2]

deek &c *vt* catch sight of, see *la18-e20*, *chf S*.
n a peep; a look *19-e20*, *chf S*. [gipsy *dik* look, see]

deem *la19-*, *chf NE*, **deme** &c *la14-16*; **deam** &c *la16-e20 n* **1** = dame *la14-*. **2** an elderly woman *la19-*, *now Abd*. **3** a young woman; an unmarried woman *19-*, *now Ross Bnf Abd*. **4** a kitchenmaid on a farm *20-*, *now Bnf Abd*. [*cf* DAME]

deemis &c ['diməs] *adv* extremely, very *19-*, *now Abd Kcb*. [aphetic f UNDEEMOUS]

deem's day doomsday *la19-, NE.*
deen *see* DAE[1]
deep &c *adj* = deep.
~ **plate** a soup plate or similarly-shaped smaller dish *la18-*.
~**th** depth *20-, chf Abd.*
deer('s) hair name for various types of rush: **1** the scaly-stalked club rush *la18-e20;* **2** the scaly-stalked spike rush *19*.
deese *see* DEAS
deeth *see* DAITH
deevil *see* DEIL
deface &c *la16-;* **defase &c** *la15-e17 vt* = deface.
deface *see* DEFESE
defaik *see* DEFALK
defait &c *16-e19,* **defeat &c** *la16-,* **defett &c** *la16* [dɪ'fet] *ptp, adj* **1** defeated *16-, now local Bnf-Fif.* **2** exhausted, worn out *18-, now Bnf Abd.*
vt, n = defeat *la16-e17.* [ME *defet &c (adj),* OF *desfait &c,* ptp of *desfaire* undo]
defalk *la15-17,* **defaik &c** *la15-e16;* **defalc** *16-17* [*dɪ'falk, *-'fek] *vt* = defalk, deduct.
defalt &c *15-16,* **defaut &c** *la14-15;* **default** [*dɪ'falt, *dɪ'fɑt] *n, vti* = default *la14-*.
in his *etc* ~ through his etc fault, failure, or negligence *la15-17.*
defamatoir &c [*dɪ'famatur, *-or] *adj* defamatory *la15-16.* [only Sc; OF *diffamatoire,* MedL *diffamatorius*]
defamation &c *17-,* **defamatioun &c** *15-16* *n* **1** = defamation *15-.* **2** *law, corresponding to Eng* libel *or* slander *la17-.*
defame &c *n* **1** = defame, defamation *15-16.* **2** ill fame; disgrace, discredit *la14-e17.*
defase *see* DEFACE, DEFESE
defau(l)t *see* DEFALT
defe *see* DEAF
defease *see* DEFESE
defeat *see* DEFAIT
defection &c, defectioun &c *16 n* **1** = defection *16-.* **2** a defect, flaw; a failure *la16-, now Ags.*
defeeckwalt &c [dɪ'fikwəlt] *adj* = difficult *19-, now local Bnf-Kcb.*
defence &c, defens &c *la14-16 n* **1** = defence *la14-.* **2** defence against an accusation, claim etc, or in support of an opinion *la15-.* **3** *in pl, law* the pleading of a *defender* (DEFEND) in a civil action *la18-.*
mak defens (attempt to) defend oneself etc *la14-e16.*
defend &c; diffend &c *15 vt* **1** = defend *la14-.* **2** protect (property etc) against encroachment etc; maintain in a legal right *15-16.* **3** maintain or vindicate (one's fame etc) against attack etc *15-16.* **4** ward off, resist *la15-e19.*
~**er &c 1** = defender *la14-.* **2** *law* a defendant, *latterly only* in a civil case *15-.*
defens *see* DEFENCE

defer &c, differ *la15* [*dɪ'fɛr] *v* **1** *vi* agree or assent **to** (a legal exception etc) *la15.* **2** *vt* allot, assign, consign; refer for consideration *la15-16.* **3** refer (something) **to** (someone's oath) *la15.* **4** *vi* defer **to** (someone) *la15-.* [earlier in Sc; L *dēferre*]
defese &c *la15-16,* **defase &c** *16-e17;* **defease** *la16-17,* **deface &c** *la16* [*dɪ'fiz, *dɪ'fez, &c] *vt* **1** allow as a deduction, deduct *la15-17.* **2** acquit or discharge from an obligation or penalty *la15-16.* **3** expunge, cancel *e16.*
defesance &c, defaisance &c acquittance, discharge *la14-16.*
defett *see* DEFAIT[1]
deficient *adj* = deficient *17-.*
n a person who fails to comply with a requisition or demand; a defaulter *17.*
deficill *see* DIFFICIL
deficulté *see* DIFFEECULTY
de fideli [de fɪ'delaɪ] *n, law* an oath taken by persons appointed to perform certain public or other duties that they will faithfully carry them out (a breach of which does not amount to perjury) *18-.* [contraction of L *de fideli administratione officii* on the faithful performance of a duty]
define &c *vt* **1** = define *16-.* **2** decide, settle, arrange *16.*
defluxion &c; defluction *n* a running or discharge, *chf* from the nose or eyes; expectoration, phlegm *16-, now Stlg Fif.* [eModEng; F *défluxion,* L *dēfluxio*]
deforce *la15-,* **deforse &c** *la14-e17 v* **1** *vt* = deforce, keep (away) by force *15-e17.* **2** rape, violate (a woman) *la14-e17.* **3** *vti* impede, prevent by force (an officer of the law or body of officials) from the discharge of duty *la15-.*
n = deforcement, *la14-17.*
~**r &c** the committer of a *deforcement, 15-18.*
~**ment, deforsment** the crime of *deforcing, la15-.*
deforciament *n* = deforcement (DEFORCE) *e16.* [MedL *deforciamatum*]
deformate &c [*dɛfor'met] *adj* deformed, transformed *15-16.*
deforse *see* DEFORCE
defoul &c [*dɪ'ful] *vt* **1** = defoul, trample underfoot; make foul *la14-16.* **2** treat with scorn; disparage, despise *la14-e15.*
n = defoul *la14-15.*
defound *see* DEFUND
defoylȝe &c [*dɪ'fuljɪ &c] *vt* = defoul *16.* [ME *defoyle,* irreg var of DEFOUL]
defund, defound [*dɪ'fʌnd, *dɪ'fund] *vt* pour down, shed; diffuse *16.* [only Sc; L *dēfundere*]
deg &c *vt* strike (a sharp-pointed object) quickly into something *19-, now Bnf Abd.*
n a sharp stroke *19-, now Bnf.* [OSc, ME *dag* (*v*) stab; obscure]
degeist, degest *see* DIGEEST
degraduat &c [*dɪ'gradjuat] *adj* deposed, degraded *e17.* [*cf* eModEng *degraduate* (*v*) depose]

degré; degrie *la16-e17* [*dɪ'gri] *n* = degree
la14-e17.
in al ~ in all respects, in every way *la14-e16*.
in na ~ to no extent *15-16*.
deiching *see* DICHT
deid &c, dede *la14-e20*, **dead &c** *la16-*, **deyd**
20-, *Cai* [did; *nEC Wgt* ded] *adj* **1** = dead *la14-*.
2 *of a golf ball* so near the hole that a PUTT¹ (*n* 2
(1)) is 'dead' certain *19-*. **3** *of opponents' bowls etc*
equidistant from the TEE¹ *la19-*, *now Abd Stlg*.
n **1** = death *la14-*. **2** the cause of (someone's)
death *la17-e20*.
deadal *esp of funeral garments* connected with
death *19*. **~ly** = deadly *15-*. **against &c all
deadly &c** *law* against all persons *15-18*.
ded(e)like &c *adj* mortal, liable to death
la14-e15. *n pl, chf* **al ~likes** mortals *la14-e15*.
~-bed = deathbed *la15-e17*. **~-bell 1** a passing bell *la15-e20*. **2** a sudden sensation of deaf-
ness and a ringing in the ears, thought to
foretell death *19-*, *now Sh*. ~ **box** a coffin *20-*,
now Cai Fif Renfr. **~-chack &c 1** a dinner prepared for magistrates after a public execution
e19. **2** the ticking of the deathwatch beetle,
thought to foretell death *la17-e20*. ~ **chist** =
~-kist, *la17-e19*. **~-claes &c** a shroud *18-*, *now
Abd Ags Fif*. **~-deal** the board on which a
corpse is laid *la18-*, *now Fif*. **~-drap** a drop of
water dripping on the floor, thought to foretell
death *19-e20*. **~-house &c 1** a mortuary *19-*,
now Abd Fif. **2** a grave *e19*. **~-ill &c** a mortal
illness *15-e20*. **~-kist** a coffin *17-e20*.
~-licht(s) &c a strange light, thought to foretell death *la18-*, *now Abd*. **deid-man &c,** ~
man's bellows bugle, the plant *la19-*, *now Ayr*.
~ **man's bells** the foxglove *19-*, *now Abd*. **~'s
part (of gear)** (*la16-*) *or* **thrid** (*la16-17*) *law*
that part of a person's MOVEABLE estate which a
testator can freely dispose of by will. **~-rap** an
unexplained knocking, thought to foretell death
la19-e20. **~-ruckle** the death-rattle *19-e20*.
~-spail &c = SPAIL *n* 5, *19-e20*, *Bwk Rox*. ~
straik &c a death blow *17*. ~ **thraw &c**
death throe *15-*, *now Abd Kcb*. **in the ~ thraw
1** between hot and cold *19-*, *now Abd Ags*. **2**
between one state and another; undecided *19-*,
now Abd. ~ **watch** the deathwatch beetle; its
ticking sound *la18-e20*.
the ~ o .. the cause of (something bad) *20-*,
now Abd. **be like a ~ dog** be out of sorts *20-*,
now Bnf Abd. **tak (the) dede** die *la14-15*, *only
Sc*. [the noun is a *chf nME* var of *dethe* (see
DAITH) prob after the adj]
deificate &c [*di'ɪfɪkat, *-et] *adj* deified
la15-16. [laL *deificātus*]
deif *see* DEAVE
deigne *see* DENZIE
deik *see* DYKE
deil &c, deevil *19-*, **divil &c** *16-*, *now NE*,
devil &c; deivil &c *e17* [dil, 'divl; *N, SW*

also 'dɪvl; *Arg also* 'dʌvl; *St* 'dɛ̈vl] *n* **1** = devil
la14-. **2** *chf* **deil** *colloq* a shoemaker's last *la19-*,
now Abd.
deevilock &c a little devil, imp *19-*, *now Bnf
Abd*. **deviltry** ['divltrɪ, 'dɛ̈vl-] devilry *la19-*,
now local Bnf-Kcb.
~'s bairn a mischievous person, a rascal *18-*,
now Bnf. **~'s bird** the magpie *la19-*, *now Abd*.
~'s darning needle the dragonfly *19-e20*.
~'s dizzen &c thirteen *la18-e20*. **~'s fit** a
shoemaker's last *20-*, *now Abd Ayr*. **~'s luck**
bad luck *20-*, *now Fif Arg*. **~'s milk** the white
milky sap of many plants *19-e20*, *Gall*. **deil's
pictur buicks** playing cards *la20-*, *NE*. **~'s
snuffbox** the common puffball *19-*, *now Ayr*.
~ **a ..** no .., not a .., never a .. *la18-*. ~ **a
fear(s)** not likely, no fear *la19-*, *now Cai Abd
Fif*. ~ **all** nothing at all *20-*, *now Bnf*. ~ **ane**
not one; no one at all *la18-*, *now Fif Stlg*. ~ **ava**
= ~ *all*, *la20-*, *Abd Fif*. ~ **in a bush** the herb
Paris *la19-*, *now Abd*. ~ **kens** goodness knows
19-, *now local Bnf-Kcb*. ~ (**may**) **care** no matter; for all that *19-*, *now Bnf*. ~ **speed the
liars** a quarrel, dispute *18-*, *now Bnf*.
deing *see* DEE
deinʒe *see* DENZIE
deith *see* DAITH
deivil *see* DEIL
deject, dejeck *vt* deject, throw down *16*.
dek *sheep-counting*, *la19-e20*, *Lnk Dmf*, **dick,
dock &c** *children's rhymes*, *la19*, *N numeral* ten.
[see ZEENDI]
dek *see* DAIK
dekay, dekey *see* DECAY
dekin *see* DEACON¹, DEACON²
del *see* DELL
delait *see* DELETE
delapidat *see* DILAPIDAT
delasch; delash [*dɪ'laʃ] *vt* discharge, let fly
la16-e17. [obs F *delacher*]
delate¹ &c *16-e20*, **dilate &c** *la15-17 vt* **1** =
delate, accuse, inform against *la15-17*. **2** *specif*
accuse, denounce **for** *or* **of** (an offence) *or* **as**
(an offender), *later esp* to a *kirk session* (KIRK) *or*
PRESBYTERY *16-18*.
ptp delated, accused *17*.
delation &c *la16-e19*, **dilatioun** *16-17* (a)
denouncement, (an) accusation. **delator &c**
16-e18, **delater &c** *la16-17*, **dilatour &c** *17* an
accuser, informer.
delate² &c [*dɪ'let] *vt* = dilate, extend, report
16-e17. [eModEng (once) *e17*]
delatour *see* DILATOR
dele *see* DALE¹
delectus personae [dɪ'lɛktʌs pɛr'sone] *n*, *law*
the right of selection of a particular person to
occupy any specific position, *eg* as a tenant in a
lease or as partner in a firm; important in
preventing assignation or delegation of a duty
by that person *la18-*. [L = choice of the
person]
deleer &c; delire [dɪ'lir] *vi*, *chf in ptp* **~it &c**

delirious, mad; temporarily out of one's senses *la18-, now Fif Renfr Ayr.* [OF *delirer* dote, rave, L *dēlīrāre* be deranged, rave; *cf* eModEng *delire* rave]

delegat; deligat [*?'dɛlɪgat, *?'dɪ-] *ptp, adj* = delegate, delegated *la15-e17.*

delete &c; delait &c *la16-17 vt* = delete *16. ptp* deleted; destroyed *15-19.*

delf; delph *n* **1** a place dug out, *latterly esp* in turf; a hole or pit; a grave *14-, now Cai.* **2** what is removed by digging; a sod *19.* [ME *delf*, OE *dælf*]

delf *see* DELVE

deliberat [*dɪ'lɪbərat] *ptp, also* ~e determined, resolved *la16-e18.*
vi deliberate, consider, decide *la16-e17.* [L *dēlīberāt-*, ptp stem of *dēlīberāre*]

delicate &c, deligat &c *la15-e17*, **dilicat &c** *la16-e17*, **diligat &c** *la15-e17* ['dɛlɪket, *'dɪlɪket, *-get &c] *adj* = delicate *la14-. n* = delicate, a delicacy *16-e17.*

delicht [dɪ'lɪxt] *n, vti* = delight *17-.* [erron var by analogy w LICHT; *cf* DELYTE]

delict ['dɪlɪkt] *n, law* a wrong, now only a civil, but formerly also a criminal one *la18-.* [L *dēlictum* offence, crime]

deligat *see* DELEGAT, DELICATE

delire *see* DELEER

deliver[1] **&c** *v* **1** *vt* = deliver *la14-.* **2** allow or enable to leave on completion of business *15-16.* **3** *vi* give a decision or judgment (that ..) *15-16.* **4** *vt* decide, settle (an action etc) *la15.* **5** declare, state, utter *15-e17.*
~**ance &c 1** = deliverance *15-.* **2** the freedom or permission to leave; the completion of an errand entitling one to this *15-16.* **3** a formal decision or judgment, *later* a judicial decision; *now* used of the orders of the court in *sequestrations* (SEQUESTRATE), including any order, warrant, judgment, decision, INTERLOCUTOR or DECREE *la14-.* **4** the act of surrendering (a stronghold, hostage, prisoner etc) *15-16.* **5** activity, agility *e16.* **6** *Presbyterian Churches* the findings or decision of the *General Assembly* (GENERAL) or other Church court on a report from a committee or special commission *19-.*
~**it &c** deliberate, determined, resolved *la15-16.*

deliver[2] **&c** *adj* **1** = deliver, agile *la14-16.* **2** delivered (of a child) *la14-e17.*

dell; del *vi* = delve, dig *18-, Sh-Abd.* [*cf* DELVE]

dell *see* DALE[2], DALE[3]

delph *see* DELF

delt; dilt *v, chf* ~**it** petted, spoilt *19-, local NE.* [perh connected w Gael *dalta* a foster-child]

delve *la15-;* **delf &c** *la14-e17 v, ptp also* **dollin** *15-e16* **1** *vti* = delve *la14-.* **2** *specif* dig over a garden *la18-.* [*cf* DELL]

delyte &c [*dɪ'lɔit] *vti, n* = delight *la14-e18.*
~**able &c** delectable, delightful *la14-16.*
delytably &c delightfully, daintily *15.*
~(e)**sum** delightful *e16.*

tak *etc* in ~ take *etc* delight in *15-16.*

dem; daim &c *la19- vt* = dam *15-, now Bnf Abd.*
~ **and la(i)ve** an extravagant profusion *la19-, Bnf;* cf *dammin and lavin* (DAM[1]).

dem *see* THEM

demain *vt* injure, maim *la17-e18.* [conflation of next w Eng *maim*]

demain &c *la16-19,* **demayne** *la14-16;* **demane** *la14-e17,* **demean** *la17-* [dɪ'men] *vt* **1** = demean *la14-.* **2** treat or deal with in a particular way *la14-e18.* **3** deal with as traitors, thieves etc *16.* **4** treat with severity, harshness or cruelty; maltreat, injure (*formerly esp* criminals at execution) *la14-, now Bnf.*

demand &c *vt, n* = demand *la14-.*
without ony *etc* ~ without question or delay *e16.*

demane, demayne *see* DEMAIN

deme *see* DEEM

demean *see* DEMAIN

demember [*dɪ'mɛmbər] *vt* = dismember *15-e18.*

demembration *freq law* dismembering, mutilation *la16-19.* [only Sc; OF *demembrer*, MedL *dēmembrāre*]

dementit *adj* demented, *esp* highly excited *18-e20.*

demerit &c *vti, n* = demerit *la15-.*
for *or* **efter ones** ~**is** according to one's misdeeds *la15-e17.*

demi-bever &c [*'dɛmɪ 'bevər] *n* a demicastor (hat) *17, only Sc.*

demigrane &c; dimmegrane &c, domegrane &c [*'dɛmɪ'gren, *'dɪmɪ-, &c] *n* a type of woven fabric *16.* [only Sc; ? *demi-* + *graine* as in *grograine* grogram]

demi-ostage &c [*'dɛmɪ'ostedʒ, *'dɪmɪ-, &c] *n* a woven fabric, *prob* linsey-woolsey *16.* [OF *demie* + *ostade* worsted]

demit &c, dimit *16-e18* [dɪ'mɪt, di-] *v* **1** *vti* resign, give over (an office, possession etc) *16-.* **2** dismiss; allow to go, release *la16-e20.* [eModEng; laME *dymytte*, L *dīmittere*]

demmin *see* DAIMEN

demoleis &c; dimolische &c [*dɪ'molɪs, *-ɪʃ, *-ɪs &c] *vt* = demolish, pull down *la16-e17, only Sc.*

dempster *la15-18,* **dempstar &c** *15-16,* **demstar &c** *la14-e17,* **damstar &c** *la16-e17 n* the officer of a court who pronounced doom or sentence as directed by the clerk or judge *la14-18, as personal name la14-.* [nME *dempster, demester* a judge, *orig* fem of *demer &c* a judge]

demuired &c [*Cai* dɪ'mjurd; *S* dɪ'mørd] *adj* sad, downcast *e20, Cai S.* [*cf* eModEng *demured*, f *demure* (*vti*) look or make demure]

demy &c [*?'dɛmɪ, *?'dimɪ; *'dɪmɪ] *n* a gold coin of varying value *15-16.* [appar elliptical for OF *demi-couronne* a half-crown of gold]

den[1] **&c** *n* a narrow valley, *esp* one with trees *16-, Gen except Sh Ork.*

vt hide *19*. [var of ME, OE *dene*]

den[2] **&c** *n* **1** = den, lair *15-*. **2** *games* a base, place of safety *20-*. **3** the forecastle of a herring boat *20-*, *local*.

den[3] *n* a groove, *eg* for the blade in a scythe handle *18-*, *now Abd*. [perh f DEN[1]]

den[4] *vt* dam *la14*. [obscure; *cf* DEM]

dence *see* DENS

Dene &c [*din] *n* a Dane *16-e17*. [OE *Dene* pl; *cf* DENS]

dene *see* DEAN

dener *see* DENNER

denere &c *15-17*, **dinneir** *15-17* [*dɪˈnir; *ʔˈdɛnər, *ʔˈdinər] *n* a silver penny; *also* a French coin, the twelfth of a sou. [OF *dener*, later *denier*, L *dēnārius; cf* eModEng *deneere*, *denier*]

denk *see* DINK

denner &c, dennar &c *16-e19*, **dainner** *20-*, *Bnf Abd*; **dener** *16-18* [ˈdɛnər; *Abd also* ˈdinər] *n* = dinner *16-*.

v **1** *vi* dine, have dinner *la18-*, *now Bnf Abd*. **2** *vt* dine, supply with dinner *19-*, *now Abd Fif*.

dennty *see* DAINTY

denounce *see* DENUNCE

denry *see* DEAN

dens &c *la15-17*; **dence** *16* [*dɛns] *adj* Danish *la15-17*.

n the Danish language; a Dane *16*.

~ **ax(e)** a long-bladed axe *la15-e18*. ~**man &c** a Dane *la15-e17*. [ME *densh, denez*, OE *denisc; cf* DENE]

denschyre &c *n*, *freq* ~ **cairsay** Devonshire kersey *la16-e17*. [*cf* Eng *denshire* (*v*)]

denshag *see* DAINSHACH

dent *see* DINT[1]

dent-de-lyon *see* DENTYLION

dentice, denty *see* DAINTY

dentylion &c *la16*, **dent-de-lyon** *e16*; **dainty-lion &c** *la18-e20* [ˈdɛntɪˈlaɪən, ˈdentɪ-] *n* = dandelion.

denude[1] **&c** [*dɪˈnød] *v* **1** *vt* strip off; make naked; strip **of** (clothing etc) *16-*. **2** make empty or unoccupied; clear *e16*. **3** deprive **of** (some possession, right etc) *la15-17*. **4** *vi* divest oneself of a right etc *la17*. **5** *vt* deprive **of** (a quality); exclude **from** (a state) *16*. **6** *law, of a trustee* hand over the trust estate on giving up the office of trustee *18-*.

denude[2] **&c** [*dɪˈnød] *adj, chf fig* denuded *15-e16*. [f denudit (DENUDE[1]) by analogy w similar short forms]

denumb; denum &c [dɪˈnʌm] *vt* confound, perplex, stupefy *19-*, *now Abd, only Sc*.

denunce &c *15-e17*; **denounce &c** *la15-* [*dɪˈnʌns, *-ˈnuns] *vt* **1** proclaim as condemned by the church *15-e16*. **2** proclaim (**as**) **rebel** or **traitor** *16-e17*. **3** sentence, condemn; proclaim as condemned *16-17*. **4** = denounce *la15-*.

denunciation &c, denunciatioun &c *la16-e17* *n* **1** = denunciation *la16-*. **2** *also* ~ **to**

etc **the horn**, *law* the act by which a person who has disobeyed a charge was proclaimed a rebel *la16-19*.

deny &c *v* **1** *vt* = deny *la14-*. **2** *vti* refuse (to do something), *now esp* refuse to move etc *la14-*, *now Bnf Abd*.

denzie *la18*, **denȝe &c** *la14-e17*; **deinȝe** *la14-16*, **deigne** *la14-15* [*ˈdɛnjɪ, *ˈdenjɪ, *ˈdɪnjɪ, *ˈdɪnjɪ] *vi* = deign.

deochandorus &c; dochan doris &c [ˈd(j)ox(ə)nˈdorəs] *n* a stirrup cup *la17-*. [Gael *deoch an dorus* a drink at the door]

deochray &c [ˈdjoxre, -ri] *n* a kind of SOWANS *la18-e20, chf Cai*. [Gael *deoch-rèith*]

deow *see* DEW

depairt &c *la15-*, **depart &c** [dɪˈpert] *vti* **1** = depart *la14-*. **2** *vi, of a woman* give birth *16*.

departal &c [*ʔdɪˈpartl] *n* departure *18-e19*.

departising &c [*dɪˈpartɪsɪn] *n* division *la15*. [only Sc; perh f ME *departison*]

depauper [*dɪˈpɑpər] *vt* impoverish, reduce to poverty *la16-17*. [only Sc; OF *depauperer; cf* next]

depauperat &c *la16-e18*, **depuperet &c** *e18*, *la19-e20* (*Sh*) [*dɪˈpɑpərət; *Sh* *-ˈpupər-] *ptp, adj* impoverished, bankrupt. [L *dēpauperāt-*, ptp stem of *dēpauperāre; cf* prec]

depend &c *vi* = depend *la15-*.

~**and** being still in process or undecided; awaiting settlement *la15-e17*. ~**ar &c** a dependant, adherent *la16-e17, chf Sc*.

dependentis *n pl* amounts still owing *16-17*, *Ayr*.

depesche &c [*dɪˈpɛʃ] *vt, n* = depeach, dispatch *16*.

depin &c *16*, **dipin** *la17* [*ˈdipɪn, *ˈdɪpɪn] *n* a section of a fishing net, one fathom in depth *16*. [eModEng *deeping*, f eME *deopen* (*v*), perh w var also f OE *dyppan* dip]

depone &c [dɪˈpon] *v* **1** *vi* testify; give evidence on oath *la15-e19*. **2** *vt* declare on oath *la15-e20*. **3** take, swear (an oath) *e16*. **4** remove from office; depose *e16*. **5** resign, give up *16-e17*. **6** deposit *la16-17*.

deponar &c a person who DEPONES *la16-17*. [chf Sc; L *dēpōnere*]

depose &c *vt* = depose *16-e17*.

n a deposit; something entrusted to one; an accumulated amount; a store *la14-e16*.

in ~ on deposit, in trust *la14-16*.

deposit *n, law, also* **deposition** a contract under which a MOVEABLE is entrusted by one (the depositor) to another (the depository or depositary) to be kept either for payment or without reward *la18-*.

depositate &c [*dɪˈpozɪtat, -et] *ptp* deposited *la17-18*. [MedL *depositat-*, ptp stem of *depositare*]

depredation &c, depredatioun &c *e16* *n* **1** = depredation *16-*. **2** *law* the offence of driving away cattle etc with armed force *la18-19*.

deprise &c *vt* depreciate, despise *la15-16*. [only Sc; F *dépriser; cf* Eng *disprize*]

deprivat &c [*'dɛprɪvat] *adj* deprived, excluded *la16*. [only Sc; MedL *deprivatus*]

depulȝe &c [*dɪ'pʌljɪ] *vt* = despoil *e16*. [only Sc; F *dépouiller*]

depuperet *see* DEPAUPERAT

depurse &c [*dɪ'pʌrs] *vt* disburse *la16-18*. [only Sc; conflation of DEBURSE w Eng *purse*]

depute &c; deput &c *la14-e18*, **deputt** *la15-e17* [*adj, n* 'dɛpjut, *'dɛpøt, *'dɛpʌt; *v* dɪ'pjut, *dɪ'pøt, *dɪ'pʌt, *'dɛpøt &c] *adj, chf following the noun, now chf law* appointed or acting as deputy *15-*: 'advocate *depute*'.
n a deputy *la14-*.
vt **1** appoint, assign, ordain *la14-16*. **2** appoint as one's substitute or representative, or to act in some official capacity *la14-*.
deputrie &c the office of deputy *la14-e17*. [ME, *orig* as ptp; OF *député ⟨ptp⟩, deputer ⟨v⟩*]

der *see* THEIR, THERE

deray &c [dɪ're] *n* **1** = deray, disturbance, trouble *la14-16*. **2** disturbance, noise *15-e20*, *latterly arch*. **3** disorderly revelry or mirth *15-e20, latterly arch*.
at ~ impetuously *e15*.

derb &c *n* an ordinary marble *20-*, *Inv*. [f *darb* a game of marbles, var of DORB]

dere¹ &c [dir] *n* = deer *la14-e17*.

dere² &c [*dir] *vt* harm, hurt, injure *la14-16*.
n hurt, harm, injury *la15-e19*. [ME; OE *derian ⟨v⟩*]

dere *see* DEAR, THERE

dereck, derect *see* DIRECK

dereliction *n, law* abandonment of something owned *la19-*.

derenȝe &c [*dɪ'rɛnjɪ, *-'rinjɪ] *v, n* = deraign, challenge *la14-16*.

derf &c; darf *la15-e16 adj, verse* **1** = derf, difficult *la15-16*. **2** *of persons* bold, daring, hardy *la14-e20*. **3** unbending, sullenly taciturn *19-e20*. **4** *of things, lit and fig* hard, rough, violent *16-e19*.
~**ly** boldly, fiercely, roughly, violently *15-e19*. [ME; ON *djarfr* bold, daring]

dergie, derigé *see* DIRGIE

derk *adj* = dark *19-e20, chf S*.

dern¹, derne; darn &c *16-e20 adj* **1** secret, hidden *la14-e20*. **2** serving to hide or conceal *la15-e16*. **3** dark, dreary, desolate *la18-e19*.
vtir **1** hide, conceal; go into hiding *la16-e20*. **2** *vi* loiter; eavesdrop *19-e20*.
adv secretly; in secret or concealment *16-e17*.
in(to) ~ in(to) secrecy, darkness, obscurity *la14-e16, la19 ⟨literary⟩*. [ME; OE *derne*]

dern² &c *vti* = darn *la18-*, *now Rox*.

derne *see* DERN¹

deroub &c [*dɪ'rub, *-'rʌb] *vt* = derob, rob *la15-16*. [only Sc; OF *derouber*]

deroy &c [*dɪ'roi] *adj, freq* ~ **culourit** purple; tawny *17*. [f COLOUR-DE-ROY]

derrar, derrast *see* DEAR

derril &c *n* a broken piece of bread etc *19*. [var of *darb* ⟨DORB⟩]

dert &c *la16-*, **dairt** *la16-*, **dart &c** *n ⟨la14-⟩, vti ⟨17-⟩* = dart.

derth *see* DEARTH

desave &c *15-*, *now Ags*, **dissave &c** *la14-16*; **desaif &c** *la16*, **dissaif &c** *la14-e17, only Sc* [dɪ'sev] *vt* deceive.

descense &c, discens &c; discence [*dɪ'sɛns] *n* **1** = descence, descent *15-16*. **2** a downward course or movement *15-16*.

descrive &c *16-e19*, **discrive &c** *la14-e19* [*dɪ'skraɪv] *vt* = describe.

dese *see* DEAS

desert &c *v* **1** *vt* desert, abandon *la15-*. **2** *law* drop, cease to go on with, discontinue (a SUMMONS, action etc), *latterly chf* ~ **the diet** *la15-*, *only Sc*. **3** *vti* (cause to) come to an end, adjourn (a parliament etc) *la16-e17*.
adj, ptp **1** = desert, deserted *16-*. **2** given up; annulled; null and void *la15-e17, only Sc*.

deservice *n* = dew service ⟨DUE⟩ *la15-e16*. [? f L *dēservīre*]

deses *see* DECES

desicioun *see* DECISIOUN

design [dɪ'zəin, *dɪ'zɪŋ] *vti* **1** = design *17-*. **2** *vt, law* assign (something to someone); bestow, grant (*esp* MANSES and *glebes* ⟨GLEIB⟩) for the clergy) *la16-19*. **3** set forth a person's occupation and address *la17-*.
~**ation &c** **1** = designation. **2** *specif* assigning as in *v* 2, *la16-19*.

desing &c *la16-17*; **desseing &c** *la16-17* [*dɪ'sɪŋ, *-'sɪŋ, *-'sin &c] *n* = design. [only Sc; OF *desseing &c ⟨> ModF dessein⟩; cf* eModEng *deseigne*]

desire *la14-*; **dissyre &c** *la14-e17 v, n,* = desire.

desk *see* DASK

desolate &c *14-*; **dissolate &c** *la14-e17 adj* = desolate.

desperation &c *n* **1** = desperation *16-*. **2** a great rage *la19-*, *now Bnf Abd*.

despone *see* DISPONE

dess *see* DASS

desseing *see* DESING

destané, destenie *see* DESTINÉ

destinat &c *ptp, v* destine(d), ordain(ed), appoint(ed) *16-e18*. [ME; L *dēstināt-*, ptp stem of *dēstināre*]

destination *n* **1** = destination. **2** *law* a direction as to the persons who are to succeed to property, *chf* in a will etc affecting HERITABLE property *18-*.
~-**over** a DESTINATION to one person on failure of a precedent gift, usually by will, to another *20-*.

destiné *la14-e16*; **destané &c** *la14-e16*; **destenie** *la16 n* = destiny.

destrick *20-*, *Bnf Abd Ayr*, **district** [*Bnf Abd Ayr* 'dɛstrɪk] *n* **1** = district. **2** *only* **district** a division of a REGION *n* 2, *la20-*: '*District Council*'.

desuetude *n* **1** *law, of old statutes* disuse, *chf* **be, fall in(to)** ~ *17-*. **2** *in gen* = desuetude.

desy &c, dissy &c ['dɪzɪ, *'dizɪ] *adj* = dizzy *la14-16*.
vt make dizzy *e16*.
desyde *see* DECIDE
det &c *la14-e17*, **debt &c** *la16*- *n* = debt *la14*-.
~**ful**(1) *adj* **1** proper, due *15-17*. **2** owing, owed *e17*. **3** indebted, owing *la16-e17*, *chf Sc*.
~**fully &c** *only Sc* **1** dutifully *15*. **2** duly, properly *la15-16*. ~**tit &c** *adj* = debted *la14-e17*.
~**bund &c** *adj* = debtbound *la15-e17*. [ME (rare)]
deteen *17*-, *now local Bnf-Stlg*, **detene &c** *16-17* [dɪ'tin] *vt* = detain *16*-.
detenar &c detainer *la16-e17*.
deteriorat *adj* deteriorated, impaired *la16-17*. [only Sc; L *dēteriorāt*-, ptp stem of *dēteriorāre*]
determ [*dɪ'tɛrm] *vti* = determine *la14-e17*. [f L *dētermināre*, after Eng *term*; eModEng]
dethe *see* DAITH
detractour; detrakkar &c *n* = detractor *16-e17*.
deuch &c; dyoch [djux, djox] *n* a drink; drink, *esp* if intoxicating *19*. [Gael *deoch* a drink]
deuch *see* DAIGH
deugend &c ['djugən(d)] *adj* wilful, obstinate; litigious *19*-, *Cai*.
deuk &c *19*-, **jeuk** *20*-, **duke** *la15-e19*, **duck** *19*-; **juck** *19*-, *now local C*, **jouk &c** *la19-e20* [djuk, dʒuk; *C* dʒʌk; *Ork Loth Bwk S* døk] *n* **1** = duck *la15*-. **2** *only* **duck** a small stone used in a children's game; the game itself *19*.
duckie **1** *also* **dockie &c** = *n* **2**, *la19-e20*. **2** *only* **dockie &c** a rounded stone used in roadmaking etc *20*-, *Ags Fif*.
~**('s) &c dub** a duck pond *18*-, *now Fif Kcb Dmf*. ~**fittit** splay-footed *20*-, *chf SW*.
deval &c, devall &c, devale &c *la15-e17*; **dival &c** *17*-, **devald &c** *la19*-, **devolve &c** *la19*- [dɪ'val, -'valv, -'vald(ʒ); *Cai Mry* -'wald; *dɪ'vel] *vi* **1** move downwards; sink, fall *la15-e17*. **2** stop, cease, leave off *la16*-, *now Gen except Sh Ork*.
n **1** a sloping surface, a slope; the amount of downward slope required by a ditch etc *la17*-, *now Sh Abd*. **2** cessation, stop *19*-, *now Bnf Abd*. [chf Sc; laME *devale*, OF *devaler*]
devanter &c [*dɪ'vantər] *n* a dress-front; an apron *la16*. [only Sc; F *devantier*]
devat *see* DIVOT
devay &c [*dɪ've] *vi* go astray, wander *16*. [only Sc; AF *desveier*, OF *desvoier*]
deve *see* DEAVE
devel &c; davel [*'dɛvl, *'devl] *n* a severe and stunning blow *la18-e20*.
vt strike with violence; beat; dash *19-e20*. [perh var of DAVER]
develling &c *n* a covering of centres or COOMS[2] used in building arches *16-e17*. [only Sc; obscure]
dever *see* DAVER
device *see* DEVISE[1]
devide *see* DIVIDE

devil *see* DEIL
devise[1] *la14-e17*; **device &c** [dɪ'vəis, *dɪ'vaɪz] *n* **1** = device *la14*-. **2** disposition (of property etc); one's will *15-e17*.
efter one's ~ in accordance with one's plans etc *la15-e16*. **at all** ~ in all respects, completely *la14-16*.
devise[2] **&c** [dɪ'vaɪz] *vt* = devise *la14*-.
as I *etc* ~ as I *etc* relate, explain *la14-16*.
devise *see* DIVISE
devoid &c [*dɪ'void, *dɪ'vəid] *v* **1** *vt* = devoid, remove, clear *la14-e17*. **2** *vir* depart, withdraw *15-e17*. **3** *freq* ~ **and red** vacate (lands etc) *15-e16*.
devolution &c *n* **1** = devolution *la15*-. **2** *law* the referring of a decision to an *oversman* (OWERSMAN) by ARBITERS[1] who differ in opinion.
clause of ~ a clause devolving some office, obligation, or duty, on a person, *eg* to act as an ARBITER[1] *19*-.
devolve *v* **1** *vt* = devolve, transfer *la15*-. **2** *vi*, *law*, *of* ARBITERS[1] pass a decision over to an *oversman* (OWERSMAN) *20*-.
devolve *see* DEVAL
devoor *19*-, *now Bnf Abd Fif*, **devore &c** *la15-e19 vt* = devour.
devory [*dɛvo'raɪ, *'dɛvorɪ] *n*, *in pl* dues or duties payable *la15-16*. [MedL *devoria &c*; *cf* Eng *devoir*]
devote &c [*dɪ'vot, *'dɛvot] *adj* **1** devout, pious *la14-17*. **2** devoted **to** *la14-16*. [ME; OF *devot*, L *dēvōtus*]
dew &c; deow &c *la19-e20*, *NE* [dju; *NE* djʌu; *Cai Bwk also* djʌu] *n* **1** = dew *la14*-. **2** whisky *la19*-, *now Bnf Abd* [contracted f mountain dew (MOUNTAIN)].
vi rain gently, drizzle *19*-, *now Bnf Abd*.
dew *see* DAW[1], DUE
dewar *n*, *hist* the hereditary keeper of a relic of a (Celtic) saint, *esp* a bell or staff, *latterly also a personal name*. [Gael *deòradh* an alien, stranger; a pilgrim]
dewche *see* DAIGH
dewg &c *la17-e20*, **duig** *la16* [*djug, *døg] *n*, *in pl*, *also* **juggins &c** *19-e20* ['djʌgənz, 'dʒʌg-] small pieces, shreds. [obscure]
dewgard &c [*'djugar(d)] *interj* (*n*) God preserve you; a greeting in these words *la15-16*. [ME *dugarde*, F *dieu* (*vous*) *garde*]
dewité *see* DUTY
dewlie &c *adj* due, proper *la15-e16*, *only Sc*.
dewty *see* DUTY
dey[1] **&c; dee** *18-e19* [daɪ, dəi, *di] *n* a dairymaid *la16*-, *now Cai*. [ME *deye*, OE *dǣge*]
dey[2] *19*-, *now Fif Bnf*, **tae** *la20*-, *Fif Bwk* [de; *NE* dəi; *Fif Bwk also* te] *n* **1** *child's word* father *19*-, *now Fif Bwk*. **2** a grandfather, *usu* as respectful term of address for an old man *la19*-, *now Bnf Fif Bwk*. [shortened f *daidie* (DADDY)]
dey *see* DEE, THERE

deyd, deydie ['dəid(ɪ)] *n* a grandfather; a grandmother *20-, NE.*

deyd *see* DEID

diacle &c ['daɪ(ə)kl] *n* a small dial or compass, *latterly* in a fishing boat *la15-e17, 19-e20 (Sh Ork).* [only Sc; appar dim of DIAL]

diacon *see* DEACON[2]

dial &c *la19-,* **dyall &c** *16-e17;* **dayell &c** *17-e18 n* = dial *16-.*
~ **stane** a stone on which figures are inscribed *la19-, now Bnf Ags.*

dialectician &c *n* a person skilled in dialectics *la16-.* [earlier in Sc]

diamond &c, diamont &c *15-17,* **diamant &c** *la15-16;* **dayamond &c** *la16-17 n* **1** = diamond *la15-.* **2** a diamond-shaped piece of iron, *esp* a spearhead *la15-e16.* **3** *in pl* **the D~s** nickname for Airdrieonians football team *la20-* [f the red diamond design on their jerseys; *cf* WAYSIDERS].

dib *see* DUB

dibber-dabber &c *vi* wrangle, argue *la19-, Bnf Abd.*
n wrangling, argument *18-e20.* [only Sc; see SND]

dice *la15-,* **dyce &c** *15-18,* **dys &c** *15-e17 n* **1** = dice *15-.* **2** *only* **dys &c** a small cubical piece (of iron) *la15-16, only Sc.*
vti **1** = dice *16-.* **2** *vt* ornament or mark with a chequered pattern, *chf* ~**it,** ~**ed** *17-.* **3** *freq* ~ **aff, oot, up** make trim and neat *la18-, now midLoth Bwk.*
~**-board** a draught- or chess-board *la19-, now Cai.*

dice *see* DEAS

dichen *19-, chf S,* **dichel &c** *17-19* ['dɪxən, *'dɪxl] *n, in pl* a reproof, beating, *chf* **get one's** *or* **gie someone his** ~**s** *17-, now Rox.* [only Sc; ? vars of *dichting* (DICHT)]

dicht &c; dight; decht &c *16* [dɪx(t); *Ork* dəit; *Mry* dəixt; *Bwk Rox also* dəit] *v, pt, ptp* **dicht** *la14-e20,* **dight** *la15-, now arch, verse* [dɪxt, dəit]; ~**it &c** *la16-.* *verbal noun also* **deiching &c** *la15-16* **1** *vt* = dight *la14-.* **2** *vr* array, equip, dress oneself; make oneself ready *la14-18.* **3** put in good order, arrange, dress, make fit for use *la14-e19.* **4** finish off, decorate with *la14-e16.* **5** prepare, cook (food, a meal) *la14-18.* **6** prepare by a special process; *specif* dress or plane (wood) *15-17.* **7** wipe or rub clean or dry *16-.* **8** clean up, polish *16.* **9** clean (**up**) by sweeping, removing dust etc, make tidy *15-, now local Bnf-Edb.* **10** sift or winnow (grain); sift (meal) *la15-, now local Bnf-Rox.* **11** dress (a wound) *la14-e16.* **12** scold, reproach, thrash; strike *18-, now Abd Lnk.*
n, only Sc **1** a wipe, a cursory wash; a rub *la19-, Gen except Sh Ork.* **2** a blow, smack, swipe; a trouncing, heavy defeat *la19-, now Abd.*
he *etc* **may** ~ **his** *etc* **neb and flee up** he may as well 'get lost' *18-, now local Abd-Kcb.* ~ **yer**

etc **ain door steen** be sure that you etc are beyond reproach before criticizing others *20-, Bnf Abd.*

dichty ['dɪxtɪ] *adj* ~ **water** (**English**) the affected speech of a Scot trying to sound English *la19-, now Ags.* [only Sc; see SND]

dick *n* a schoolmaster *20-, Abd-Ags.* [only Sc; see SND]

dick *see* DEK, DYKE

dictat *pt, ptp* = dictated *17.* [only Sc; L *dictāt-,* ptp stem of *dictāre*]

dictay *see* DITTAY

dictionar &c *n* = dictionary *la16-, now local Bnf-Stlg.* [only Sc; F *dictionnaire,* MedL *dictionarium*]

dictum *n* a saying *la16-.* [earlier in Sc; L]

didder &c *vi* tremble; move jerkily *la14, la19-, now Sh.* [ME; onomat]

didderums *e20, Arg,* **dodrums** *19-e20, local C n pl* half-daft notions, 'bees in one's bonnet'. [see SND]

diddle[1] **&c** *v* **1** *vi, also fig* dance with a jigging movement *18-e20.* **2** *vti* move (the elbow) to and fro in fiddling; fiddle *la18-e20.* **3** dandle (a child) *19-.*
n a short, jerky, lively tune *19-e20.* [only Sc; *cf* DIDDER]

diddle[2] **&c; deedle** *vti* sing without words, *usu* in imitation of instrumental dance music *19-.*
n a wordless singing, as in *v, la19-20.*
diddler a person who accompanies dancing as in *v, 20-.* [onomat, perh w infl f DOUDLE]

diddle[3] *vi* busy oneself without getting much done; waste time; potter, dawdle *19-, now local Sh-EC, S.*
diddle-daddle *only Sc, vi* = *v, la19-, Bnf Abd. n* great activity with little result; trifling activity *la19-, Bnf Abd.* [prob extension of DIDDLE[1]; *cf* Eng *fiddle*]

didna *see* DAE[1]

die *n* a toy, trinket *19.* [only Sc; perh extension of Eng *die* a dice]

diet[1]**, dyet &c** *la15-e18 n* **1** = diet, food *la15-.* **2** a meal, repast *18-, now local Ork-Stlg, only Sc.*
~**-cake,** ~**-loaf** a kind of sponge cake *la18-19, only Sc.* ~**-hour** meal time *la19-, now local Cai-Fif, only Sc.*

diet[2] **&c, dyet** *la15-e18;* **dyat &c** *16-17 n* **1** = diet, a meeting *la15-.* **2** a meeting or session of a court, council or other (*usu* official) body *la15-19, only Sc.* **3** (1) a church meeting for worship or business *17, Inv Abd.* (2) a church service *la19-, now Abd Arg Kcb, only Sc.* **4** a day or date fixed for a meeting (*eg* of a court), or for a market *la16-, only Sc.* **5** a particular day or date *la16-17, only Sc.* **6** the list of summonses set down to come before the *Court of Session* (SESSION) from each quarter of the country *16-e17, only Sc.* **7** a journey or its date; the movements of a person travelling *la16-17, chf Sc.*

∼-**buke** a day-book; a journal; the book containing the deliberations of a DIET *n* 2, *la16-e17*, *only Sc.*

by ∼ beyond the proper time or measure *la16-e17, only Sc.* ∼ **of examination** a meeting held in a house by a MINISTER to examine the religious knowledge of the residents of a district *la18-e19, only Sc.* ∼ **of examinations** a group of university degree examinations at a particular time *20-.* ∼ **of worship** = *n* 3 (2), *la19-, now local Abd-Kcb, only Sc.* **keep** (**the, our** *etc*) ∼ appear (at a court or meeting) on the day appointed *la15-e18, only Sc.*

diffat *see* DIVOT

diffeeculty *19-,* **difficulté &c** *la14-e16;* **deficulté &c** *la15-16,* **diffeekwalty &c** *la17-* [dɪˈfik(w)əltɪ, *dɪˈfɪk-] *n* difficulty.

diffend *see* DEFEND

differ &c *vi* **1** = differ *la15-.* **2** quarrel; express disagreement, dispute *e16, la19-, now local Bnf-Fif Kcb.*
n **1** a difference of opinion; a disagreement or dispute *la16-, now Sh Ags Fif.* **2** a difference, dissimilarity *17.*
in ∼ in dispute *la16-e17.*

differ *see* DEFER

difficil &c; deficill &c *15-16* [*dɪˈfɪsl] *adj* **1** = difficile, difficult. **2** difficult to travel or pass over *16-17.* [laME, OF *difficile*, L *difficilis*]

difficle &c [*ˈdɪfɪkl] *adj* difficult *16-e17.* [eModEng *difficul*]

difficult *v, freq in ptp* ∼**ed**, placed in a difficulty *18-19.* [OSc *deficultat* (*ptp*), f ptp stem of MedL *difficultare*; *cf* OF *difficulter* make difficult]

difficulté *see* DIFFEECULTY

diffy *see* DEAF

digeest &c *19-, now local Bnf-Stlg,* **digest &c** *16-,* **disgest** *la16-, now Sh,* **degest** *15-16,* **disgeest &c** *18-, now Bnf Abd Fif;* **degeist** *16-e19* [dɪˈdʒist, dɪsˈdʒist, -ˈdʒɛst] *vti* = digest *15-.*
adj, only **degest, digest** composed, settled; mature, grave *la15-16.*
disgeester *la19-, now Fif,* **disgeestion &c** *la19-, now Bnf Ags* digestion. **degestlie,** dimaturely, carefully, with full deliberation *la15-e17, only Sc.*

dight *see* DICHT

digne &c; ding &c [*ˈdɪnj(ə), *dɪŋ] *adj* **1** = digne, worthy *la14-16.* **2** of great or exceptional worth or merit *la14-16.* [*cf* DANE]

dike *see* DYKE

dilapidat, delapidat [*dɪˈlapɪdat] *vt* dilapidate, squander *16-17.*
ptp dissipated, squander *16.*

dilate *see* DELATE¹

dilator &c, dilatour, delatour *la15-16* [*ˈdɪlatur &c] *adj* dilatory, causing delay, *esp* in a legal action, *freq* **exception** ∼ *la15-e18.*
n **1** a delay, *esp* in giving a legal decision; a dilatory plea etc *la15-17.* **2** *law* = dilatory defence, *la15-e18.*

dilatory defence *law* a defence which is purely technical, not touching the merits of the case *la19-.* [only Sc; L *dīlātōrius* etc]

dilce *see* DILSE

diled *see* DOILT

dilicat *see* DELICATE

dilgit; dulget [ˈdɪldʒɪt, ˈdʌldʒ-] *n* a lump; an untidy heap or bundle (*eg* of clothes); *in pl* lumpy odds and ends *19-, Bnf Abd.*

diligat *see* DELICATE

diligence &c *n* **1** = diligence *15-.* **2** *law* application of legal means against a person, *esp* for the enforcing of a payment or recovery of a debt; a warrant issued by a court to enforce the attendance of witnesses, or the production of writings *la16-.*

dill *v* **1** *vti* soothe, quieten down, die away *la15-e20.* **2** *vi, chf of a rumour etc* die **down,** be forgotten, pass out of mind *la18-, Sh Bnf Abd, only Sc.* [nME = make dull, *adj* = sluggish, dull]

dills *see* DILSE

dilly daw *n* a slow, slovenly person, a slattern *e19.* [only Sc; *dilly* as in Eng *dilly-dally* + DAW²]

dilmont *see* DINMONT

dilp &c *n* a trollop, a slovenly woman; a thriftless housewife *la18-19.*
vi stalk; stump, hobble *la19-, now Ags.* [only Sc; perh onomat]

dilse *17-, now local Cai-Ags;* **dilce** *17-e18,* **dills &c** *17-e20 n* = dulse *only Sc.*

dilt *see* DELT

diminew &c [*dɪˈmɪnju, *ˈdɪmɪnju] *vti* diminish *la15-16.* [OF *diminuer*, L *dēminuere*; *cf* ME (once) *dymynue* speak disparagingly]

diminis &c *vt* = diminish *la15-e17, only Sc.*

dimissioun &c [*dɪˈmɪsɪun &c] *n* the action of giving up or laying down (an office, possession etc), *freq* ∼ **and** *etc* **resignation** *16-e18.* [laME *dimission*]

dimit *see* DEMIT

dimmegrane *see* DEMIGRANE

dimolische *see* DEMOLEIS

dimple &c *n* (*18-*), *vt* (*la19-*) = dibble *now Bnf Abd.* [only Sc]

din¹ &c *n* **1** = din *15-.* **2** *chf of running water* a slight noise *18-19.* **3** loud talk or discussion; a fuss, disturbance *15-, now local Bnf-Kcb, only Sc.* **4** a report, rumour; a scandal *la19-, now Bnf Abd Ayr, only Sc.*
vi **1** make a loud noise or outcry *la15-16, only Sc.* **2** ring with sound or noise; resound, re-echo *16.*
∼**some** noisy, riotous, brawling *18-e20, only Sc.*
∼-**raisin** quarrelsome; *of a tale-bearer* deliberately causing trouble *la19-, Bnf Abd.*

din² &c *adj* **1** = dun *16-.* **2** *of persons* dark-complexioned, sallow *16-, Gen except Sh Ork.*
∼**ness** sallowness, darkness *19-, now Cai Bnf.*
nae ∼-**bonnets** *of persons and things* not to be despised, first-rate *la19-, Abd.* [only Sc]

dindee; dundee, dinniedeer &c *n* a noise, uproar; a fuss, disturbance *la19-*, *now Abd.* [only Sc; DIN¹ + *adee* (ADAE)]

dindill *see* DINNLE

dine *la16-*, **dyne &c** *la14-e17 vti* = dine *la14-*. *n* **1** dinner; dinnertime *16-e20*. **2** *in pl, also* **common ~s** *St Andrews University* the communal university dinners; the place where they are held *20*.

ding &c *v, pt* **dang, dung** *la16-e20. ptp* **dungin &c** *la14-e16*, **doungin &c** *la14-16* [*'duŋən]; **do(u)ng** *16-18* [*duŋ], **dung &c** *16-e20*, **dang** *19* **1** *vt* (1) *freq* ~ **aff, down** *etc* knock, beat or strike (with heavy blows) *la14-*. (2) beat with a rod or scourge as a punishment *la14-e17*. (3) defeat, overcome (with blows); attack violently *16-e18*. (4) beat, get the better of *18-, now local E, only Sc*. (5) batter, beat down with shot *16-e17, only Sc*. **2** *vi* (1) = ding, deal blows *la14-e17*. (2) *freq* ~ **on, down** *of rain, wind etc* descend with great force, fall heavily and continuously *16-, now Bnf-Fif*. **3** *vt* pierce with a violent thrust *e16*. **4** (1) drive, dash (with violence); push suddenly and forcibly *la14-*. (2) drive (nails etc) with force *16-e17, only Sc*. (3) drive into the mind, din into someone's ears *la16-19, only Sc*. (4) drive (mad etc) *18-, now Bnf Abd Stlg, only Sc*. (5) reduce to fragments by beating or smashing *la16-e17*. **5** strike, force, drive **from, out of, off &c** (a person, thing etc) *15-*. **6** *also fig* beat, cast, throw **down** *la14-*. **7** drive, force, beat **back, up** *etc 15-*. **8** *in imprecations* = dash! *19-, now Cai Bnf Abd*.
n a knock or blow, a smart push *19-, local Bnf-Kcb*.
go one's ~er go at something very vigorously or boisterously *20-, now local EC-WC, only Sc*.
~-dust *adv* very fast *e20, Uls*.
~ to dede *etc* kill by blows or strokes *la14-16*.

ding *see* DIGNE

ding dang *adv* speedily, in rapid succession; in confusion *18-, now Bnf Abd Fif*. [only Sc; *cf* Eng *ding-dong*]

dinge &c *vt* dent, bruise *la19-, Sh Dnbt SW Uls*. *n* a blow; a dent *19-, now Arg Kcb*. [eModEng (once); ModEng dial; perh connected w DINT²]

dingle ['dıŋl] *vi* **1** tingle (with cold or pain) *19-, now Sh Ayr Slk*. **2** vibrate, resound, jingle *la18-, now Bnf Abd*. [conflation of DINNLE w Eng *tingle*]

dingle-dousie &c ['dıŋl 'duzı] *n* **1** *child's toy* a lighted stick, PEAT¹ etc waved rapidly to form an arc of light *19-e20*. **2** *fig* an active bustling person *la19-e20*. [only Sc; Eng dial *dingle* + DOOZIE]

Dingwall: ~ **pursuivant** one of the Scottish PURSUIVANTS *la16-19, la20-*. [the town in Ross]

dink &c; denk *adj* **1** *latterly only of women* neat, trim, finely dressed, dainty *16-, now Abd Fif*. **2** prim, precise; haughty *18-e20*.
vti, freq ~ **up, out** dress neatly or sprucely, adorn *19-, now Bnf Abd Bwk Rox*.

dinkie &c neat, trim *la18-*. **dinkly** neatly, sprucely, trimly *la18-e20*. [obscure]

dinmont &c *15-*, **dunmont &c** *la15-18*, **dilmont &c** *16-17*, **dulmond** *la16-e17*, **dynmonth &c** *la15-16*, **dinmound &c** *14-e17* ['dınmont, -mənt, *-mund &c] *n* a wether between the first and second shearing, *ie* between one and a half and two and a half years old, *now esp* of the Cheviot breed. [obscure; perh pre-Celtic; also in northern eModEng and nEng dial]

dinna *see* DAE¹

dinneir *see* DENERE

dinnen skate *n* a kind of skate (the fish) *18-e20, local E*.

dinniedeer *see* DINDEE

dinnle &c *18-*, **dinnill &c** *16*, **dindill &c** *16-e18 v* **1** *vi* shake, vibrate *16-, now local Bnf-Kcb*. **2** *of bells, thunder etc* peal, roll, drone *la18-e20*. **3** *esp of the fingers* tingle with cold or pain; twinge *18-*. **4** *vt* cause to tremble, vibrate, tingle with pain; shake *16-, now Fif*. **5** *only* **dindill &c** *vti* (cause to) ring, resound, vibrate with sound *e16*.
n **1** a vibration, tremor *19-, now Ags*. **2** a vibrating or tingling sensation, *eg* as caused by a knock on the elbow; such a knock; *fig* a thrill (of emotion) *19-, now Bnf Abd Ags*. [ME *dyndel; cf* DINGLE]

dint¹ &c; dent &c, dinta &c *la18-e19* [*'dent(ə), *'dınt(ə)] *n, chf* ~ **of** affection, liking, regard for *la18-e20, Abd Ags*. [only Sc; OSc, ME *daynté &c* (DAINTY) esteem, regard, affection, OF *dainté* pleasure, joy, L *dignitas*]

dint² &c *n* **1** = dint, a blow etc *la14-*. **2** a chance, occasion, opportunity *18-e19, only Sc*. **3** a force comparable to a blow; a shock, assault; a deep impression, impact *la14-19*.
vt, in passive be pierced with an elf-arrow or Cupid's arrow *la18-e20, SW Uls, only Sc*.
steal a ~ seize an opportunity against a person *16-18, only Sc*. [*cf* DUNT]

diocesie &c [*'daıosızı] *n* a diocese *15-17*. [MedL *diocesis; cf* northern eModEng *diocoesie*]

diocie &c, diocy &c [*'daıosı] *n* **1** = diocese *la14-19*. **2** jurisdiction, a district *la16* [translating L *ditio*]. [only Sc]

dip &c *vti* **1** = dip *15-*. **2** *vi, chf* ~ **in** investigate; touch **upon** *la16-e17*.
n **1** = dip *la18-*. **2** melted fat in which potatoes are dipped *la19-, now local Bnf-WC, only Sc*.
dippin &c *n* a place by a river with steps leading down, where pails, clothes etc are dipped *la18-e20*.

dipin *see* DEPIN

dir *see* THERE

dird *n* **1** a hard blow, knock *18-, now Bnf Abd*. **2** a sharp or stunning fall, a bump; a bounce, romp *la18-, now Bnf Abd*. **3** *usu ironic* a mighty deed, an achievement *la18-e19*.

v **1** *vt* push or thrust violently, bump *la19-, now Bnf Abd*. **2** *vi* bump, bounce, jolt *19-, now Bnf Abd*. **3** act or walk conceitedly *20-, Cai*.
adv with a bang or bump *la19-, now Bnf Abd*.
dog-~er a dog-handler, kennel attendant *la19-, Bnf Abd Kcb*. [only Sc; onomat]

dirdum &c; durdum &c *18-e20 n* **1** tumultuous noise, altercation, uproar *16-*. **2** a quandary, problem *19-, now Ags Per, only Sc*. **3** a heavy stroke or blow *19-, now Bnf, only Sc*. **4** blame; punishment; a scolding; retribution *la17-*. **5** bad temper, ill humour; violent excitement *19-, now Lnk, only Sc*. **6** *usu ironic* an achievement, great deed *la18-e20, only Sc*.
dree the ~(s) bear the punishment, take the consequences *19-, now Fif, only Sc*. [prob onomat; *cf* DIRD]

dirdy-lochrag &c; -wachlag &c ['dɪrdɪ-'loxrag, -'waxlag, &c] *n* a lizard *20-, Cai*. [Gael *dearc-luachrach*]

direck &c *la15-*, **direct &c; dereck &c** *la15-17*, **derect** *16-17* [*dɪ'rɛk(t)] *adj, vt* = direct *15-*.
adv directly; in a direct course or manner *la15-*.
ptp = directed *15-17*.
~ar &c *16*, **directour** *la15-e17* director (*esp* of the chancellary) *only Sc*.

dirgie &c *la17-19*, **dirigé &c** *15-17*, **dregy** *16-*; **draidgy &c** *16-e19* [*'dɪr(ɪ)dʒɪ, *'dɛr-, *'dir-, *'der-, *'drɪdʒɪ, *'drɛdʒɪ, &c] *n* **1** *also* **derigé &c** *la15-16*, **dergie &c** *16-e17* = dirge *15-19*. **2** *also* **dredgie &c** *18-e20* a funeral feast, *esp* of drink *17-19, only Sc*.

dirk &c *adj* dark *la15-19*.
n darkness (of night) *la15-e16*.
vti go surreptitiously, slink *la18-e19*.
~in &c *vti* **1** (make) dark *e16*. **2** *vi* lurk, lie hidden *e16*. **~nes** darkness *la15-16*. [ME]
dirk *see* DURK[1]

dirken &c *n* a fir-cone (used in smoking fish) *e20, local Ross-Kcdn*. [Gael *duircean*, pl or dim of *duirc*]

dirl &c *v* **1** *vt* pierce or cause to tingle with emotion or pain *la16-, now Sh Fif Rox*. **2** cause to vibrate, shake *20-, now local Bnf-Fif*. **3** *vi* vibrate, rattle, reverberate; ring when struck; whirl, BIRL[1] *la16-*. **4** thrill, quiver or tingle with emotion, pain etc *18-*.
n **1** a knock or blow causing the person or thing struck to DIRL; a shock, jar, clatter *19-*. **2** the pain caused by such a blow; a tingling sensation *18-, now local*. **3** a tremulous or vibratory motion, *chf* accompanied by a sharp noise, a clatter or rattle *19-, now local Sh-WC*. **4** a gust (of wind) *20-, Sh Bnf Abd, only Sc*. **5** a hurry, bustle; *fig* a short space of time; an energetic movement *20-, Sh Abd, only Sc*.
adv with a clatter, crash, *chf* **come, fall, play ~** *la18-, now Sh Bnf Fif, only Sc*.
~er a chamber-pot *20-, Cai Bnf Abd*. **~ie-bane &c** the funny-bone *la19-, now local Bnf-WC*. **~ing** = *n* 2, *16-e19*.

~ aff *of an alarm clock* go off with a whirring noise *20-, Bnf Abd Fif, only Sc*. **~ to** shut with a bang *20-, Bnf Fif, only Sc*. **~ up** strike up (a song, tune), *esp* on the bagpipes, play vigorously *la18-, now Bnf Abd, only Sc*. [see SND]

dirr &c [dɪr; *Rox* dʌr] *n* a humming, buzzing sound *19-, now Rox, only Sc*. [onomat; *cf* Norw *dirre* quiver, vibrate, Sw dial *durra* buzz, hum]

dirry[1] *n* the ashes on top of a pipe *20-, now Bnf Abd, only Sc*.

dirry[2] *n* **haud on the ~** whip up (horses); speed (something) up *20-, Bnf Abd, only Sc*.

dirrydan, dirrye dantoun *n* name of a dance; sexual intercourse *e16*. [obscure]

dirt *n* **1** = dirt *16-*. **2** contemptuous (now *chf* offensive) term for a person, *esp* a troublesome child *19-, now local Bnf-Kcb*. **3** *mining* material produced other than coal, ore or mineral *20-, now Fif*.
vti, ptp **dirten** *18-* **~ on**, *also fig* defecate on, befoul *18-, now Bnf Abd*.
~en &c *adj* **1** dirtied, filthy, soiled with excrement *16-, now Abd Ags, only Sc*. **2** *fig* mean, contemptible; conceited, disdainful *la18-, now Abd, only Sc*. **3** *in superlative* **dirtenist &c** utmost *20-, Bnf Abd, only Sc*.
~en allen &c the skua *la18-, now Cai*. **~rie &c** *n* worthless people or things *19-e20, only Sc*. **~y** *adj* **1** = dirty. **2** *of land, crops* weed-infested *la19-*. *adv* very, completely, ignominiously, as **~y bate** ignominiously beaten *20-*. **~y coal** a coal seam with much BLAES or fireclay; a very ashy coal *la19-, now Fif*.
~ bee the common dung-beetle *la19-, Bnf Ags, only Sc*. **~ fear** extreme terror [such as would cause loss of control of the bowels] *e18, only Sc*. **~ flee** = **~** bee, *19-, now Abd Ags, only Sc*. **~ deen** extremely tired *20-, Bnf Abd, only Sc*. [*cf* DRITE]

dis &c [*dɪs] *n* some double interval in music *la15*. [L (f Gk) *dis-* as in *disdiapāsōn* a double octave]
dis *see* DAE[1], THIS

disabuse &c [*dɪsə'bøz; *Abd* dɪsə'biz] *vt* **1** = disabuse. **2** misuse, damage; spoil *17-, now Abd, only Sc*.
n damage, bad usage; disturbance *19-, Abd*.

disagreeance *20-, now Sh*, **disagrieance** *la16 n* disagreement. [eModEng *disagreaunce*; *cf* OF *desagreance*]

disagyse &c [*dɪsə'gaɪz] *vt* = disguise *15-e17, only Sc*.

disannul &c *vt* **1** = disannul. **2** do away with, obliterate, demolish (material objects) *20-, local Sh-Ags, only Sc*.

disassent &c *vi* **1** = disassent, refuse or withhold assent *la15-17*. **2** refuse to agree **that ..** *16-e17, only Sc*.

disays *see* DISEASE

disburden &c *la16-*; **disburding** *la16-e17 vt* = disburden.

Discembar *see* DECEMBER

discence, discens *see* DESCENSE
discentioun *see* DISSENSIOUN
disceptioun &c *la15-16*, **deceptioun &c** *la15-e17 n* = deception.
discern *see* DECERN
discese *see* DECES
disch *see* DISH
dischairge &c *16-*, **discharge &c** [dɪs'tʃerdʒ, -'tʃardʒ; *n also* 'dɪstʃardʒ] *v* **1** *vtr* = discharge *15-*. **2** *vt, latterly only* discharge, *chf law* forbid, prohibit from doing something: (1) ~ **from** *etc* doing .. *16-e19, only Sc*; (2) ~ **to do** .. *16-e18, only Sc*. **3** resign, give up *la15-e16, only Sc*. **4** *vr* declare oneself to have resigned all claim to something *la15-e16, only Sc*. *n* = discharge *16-*.
dischort *see* DISHORT
discipline &c [*dɪsɪ'pləin, *-'plin] *n* = discipline *la14-*.
  Book of D~ either of two books adopted in 1560 and 1581 respectively, laying down the constitution of the Reformed Church and also dealing with education *la16-, now hist*.
disclamation &c *16-19*, **disclamatioun** *la16-e17 n* **1** *law* the renunciation by a tenant or VASSAL of obligation to his SUPERIOR *16-19*. **2** repudiation *la18-19*. [MedL *disclamatio* a disclaimer, f *disclamare* disclaim]
disclar *see* DECLERE
discomfish *19*, **discomfis &c** *16-e17*; **discumfys &c** *la15-e16*, **disconfeis** *16* [*dɪ'skʌmfɪʃ, *-'skʌmfɪs, *-'skʌmfis &c] *vt* = discomfit, overcome, defeat *la15-19*. [only Sc; OF *desconfis-*, pres stem of *desconfire* > next; *cf* SCOMFISH]
discomfit &c [dɪskʌm'fɪt, *-'fit, *-'fəit] *vt* **1** = discomfit *la14-*. **2** put to inconvenience *la19-, now Abd*.
disconfeis *see* DISCOMFISH
disconformable *adj* = next *la16-17*. [earlier in Sc]
disconform &c *adj*, ~ **to** *or* **from** not conforming to, disagreeing with *la16-17, la19*. [only Sc; MedL *disconformis*]
discontigue *adj* not contiguous, disconnected *16-e18*. [only Sc; *dis-* + CONTIGUE]
discontiguous *adj* = prec *18-19*. [only Sc; *dis-* + Eng *contiguous*]
disconvenient &c *adj* inconvenient *la15, 19-, now Sh Bnf Fif*.
disconvenience *n, vt* inconvenience *19-, now Sh Bnf Abd Ags*. [ME]
discover &c *v* **1** *vt* = discover *la14-*. **2** *vti* reconnoitre *la14-e16*.
  discoverour &c *e15*, **discurr(i)our &c** *la14-16* a reconnoitrer, scout.
discreet *18-*, **discrete &c** *la14-16 adj* **1** = discreet *la14-*. **2** civil, polite, well-behaved *18-e20, only Sc*.
discrepance &c [*dɪskrɛ'pans] *n* = discrepance *15-*.

but *or* **without** ~ without difference, without divergence in opinion, without delay *16*.
discrete *see* DISCREET
discrive *see* DESCRIVE
discumfys *see* DISCOMFISH
discurr(i)our *see* DISCOVER
discuss &c, discus *la16-17 vt* **1** = discuss *15-*. **2** *law* proceed against one of two possible debtors such as a principal debtor and a *cautioner* (CAUTION), before proceeding against the other *la16-*.
discyde *see* DECIDE
disdaine &c [*dɪs'den] *vt* deign *la16*. [var of *dedeigne* (DEDEN3E[1]), w infl f Eng *disdain*]
disdene &c *e16*, **disden3e** *la14-e16* [*dɪs'din(jɪ)] *n* (*la14-e16*), *vti* (*16*) = disdain. [only Sc; *cf* DEDEN3E[2]]
disemal &c *15-19*, **dismall** *16*; **dysemell** *e17* [*'dəis(ə)mel, *'dəisməl] *n, adj* = dismal.
disese &c *la14-16*; **dises &c** *la14-e17*, **disays &c** *la16* [*dɪ'siz, *dɪ'sez] *n, vt* = disease.
disfigurate &c *adj* disfigured, deformed *la15-16*. [ME]
disgeest, disgest *see* DIGEEST
dish *18-*, **disch &c** *la14-e17 n* = dish *la14-*.
  vi, also ~ **on** rain heavily, pour with rain *19-, now Abd; cf* Eng *bucket*.
  ~**clout &c** a dish-cloth *18-*. ~**man** a hawker of crockery *19-e20*. ~ **washins** dishwater *19-, now Sh Ork*.
  get *etc* **a** ~ **o** want get no food at all *la19-, N*.
dishabilitate &c *vt, law* subject to legal disqualification *17*. [only Sc; f ptp stem of MedL *dishabilitare*; OF *dishabiliter*]
dishaunt *la16-18*, **dishant** *la16-17* [*dɪs'hant, *-'hɑnt] *vt* **1** cease to frequent, stay away from (*esp* a church or religious services) *la16-e18*. **2** give up, discontinue (a practice) *la16-e17*. [only Sc; OF *deshanter*]
dishealth *n* ill-health, illness *la18-e20*. [only Sc; *dis-* + Eng *health*]
disherish &c *la17-19*, **disheris &c** *la14-e17* [*dɪs'(h)erɪʃ, *-'(h)erɪs] *vt* disinherit *la14-19*. [only Sc; prob back-formation f Eng and Sc *disherison*]
disherten &c [dɪs'hertən] *vt* = dishearten *la19-, now local Bnf-Fif*.
dishilago *see* TUSHILAGO
dishort &c *la16-e19*, **dischort** *16-e17* [*dɪ'ʃort] *n* an injury, a mischief, hurt. [only Sc; obscure]
disjacket *see* DISJECKIT
disjaskit &c [dɪs'dʒaskɪt; *Rox also* -'dʒeskɪt] *adj* **1** dejected, downcast, depressed *19-, local*. **2** dilapidated, neglected, untidy *18-, local*. **3** exhausted, worn out; weary-looking *19-, local*. [see SND]
disjeckit, disjacket [dɪs'dʒɛkɪt, -'dʒakɪt] *adj* = dejected *la19-e20*.
disjoin &c *vt* **1** = disjoin *la16-*. **2** *law* detach or separate (one church or parish from another) *17-*.

disjone, disjoyne *see* DISJUNE

disjunction *n* **1** = disjunction. **2** *law* the disjoining or dividing up (of parishes) *19-*.

disjune &c *16-e19*, **disjone** &c *la15-el7*; **disjoyne** &c *la16-el7* [*dɪs'dʒøn, *dɪʃ'dʒøn, *'dɪ'ʃøn] *n* (*la15-e19*), *vi* (*16-el7*) breakfast. [only Sc; OF *desjuner, desjun*]

disloaden &c *vt* = disload, unload *17, e20* (*Cai*).

dislock *vt* dislocate (a joint) *19*. [eModEng]

disluge [*dɪs'lʌdʒ] *vti* = dislodge *la15-16, only Sc*.

dismall *see* DISEMAL

disna *see* DAE[1]

disobeyance &c *n* = disobeisance, disobedience *16, only Sc*.

disone *see* DIZZEN

dispare &c *v, n* = despair *la14-17*.

disparit &c *la14-el7*, **disperat** *la16-el7*, **dispert** &c *16-, now Ags* [*dɪ'sperɪt, *'dɪspərat, *'dɛ-; dɪ'spɛrt] *adj, ptp* despairing; desperate *la14-, now Ags*.

disparissing &c *n* = disparaging *la15-e16, only Sc*.

dispasche &c [*dɪ'spaʃ] *vt* = dispatch *16-el7*. [form w infl f DISPESCHE]

dispeace *n* dissension, enmity, disquiet *19*. [orig Sc; *dis-* + Eng *peace*]

disperat *see* DISPARE

disperne &c [*dɪ'spɛrn] *vt* disperse, drive away; despise *16*. [only Sc; L *dispernere*]

disperson &c *vt* treat with indignity, insult, abuse *15-el7*. [chf Sc; ME (rare); MedL *dispersonare*]

dispert *see* DISPARE

dispesche &c [*dɪ'spɛʃ] *vt* dispatch *16-el7*. [only Sc; OF *despechier; cf* DEPESCHE, DISPASCHE]

dispite &c *n* = despite *la14-el7*.
vt despite, regard with dislike or contempt *la14-16*.
~fully 1 spitefully, cruelly *la14-16*. **2** scornfully, contemptuously *la14-el7*.
speak ~(s) use contemptuous or malicious language *16*.

displeesure *la19-*, **displesour** &c *la15-17*, **displesere** &c *la15-16* [dɪs'plizər, *dɪsple'zur, *-ple'zir &c] *n* = displeasure.

displenish &c [dɪs'plɛnɪʃ] *vt* strip (*now chf* a farm) of furnishings or stock, sell off contents of *la16-, now local*.
n = next *19-, Sh Bnf Abd Ags*.
~ing sale a sale of the stock, implements etc on a farm *la19-, Gen except NE*. [only Sc; *dis-* + PLENISH]

displesere, displesour *see* DISPLEESURE

dispoilʒe &c, **dispulʒe** &c; **dispolʒe** &c [*dɪ'spʌljɪ, *-'spøl(jɪ) &c] *vt* = despoil *la14-16, only Sc*.

dispone &c, **dispoune** &c *16-el7*; **despone** *la16-el8* [*dɪs'pon] *v* **1** (1) *vt* set in order, arrange *la14-el8*. (2) *vr* make oneself ready, prepare oneself to do something *la14-16*. (3) *vt* put (a person) in a suitable frame of mind for something *la15-16*. **2** deal with, dispose of, hand over, *freq* as a gift *la14-el8*. **3** *law* deal over, convey (land) *la15-*. **4** *vi* dispose or make disposition **of** (a thing or person) *la14-el6*. **5** exercise disposition, authority or control **on** (something) *15-e19*.
~r &c a giver, donor, distributor; *latterly law* the person who conveys property *15-*. **disponee** *law* the person to whom property is conveyed *18-*. [chf Sc; ME; OF *disponer*, L *dispōnere* distribute, dispose; *cf* next]

dispose *vti* **1** = dispose *la15-*. **2** *vi, ~* **on** etc = DISPONE 5; dispose of *17-e19*.

disposition &c *16-*, **dispositioun** &c *la14-el7* *n* **1** = disposition *la14-*. **2** *law* a deed of conveyance, an assignation of property *la15-*.
bond and ~ in security a form of HERITABLE security consisting of obligation to pay debt and security as well as DISPOSITION of the property *20-*.

dispositive *adj* ~ **clause** *law* the operative clause of a deed by which property is conveyed *la18-*. [*cf* prec]

dispoune *see* DISPONE

disprese &c *vt* = dispraise, depreciate, undervalue *la16, only Sc*.

dispulʒe *see* DISPOILʒE

disremember *vt* fail to remember, forget *la17-, now Abd Ags Lnk*.

disrentell &c *vt* remove from a rent-roll *la16*. [*dis-* + RENTAL]

disrespeck &c *n, vt* = disrespect *la18-*.

disrig *vt* unrig (a ship etc) *17*. [*dis-* + Eng *rig*]

disruption *n* **1** = disruption. **2 the D~** the split which took place in the Established Church of Scotland in 1843 when 450 of its 1200 MINISTERS formed themselves into the *Free Church* (FREE) *19-*.

dissaif *see* DESAVE

dissasine &c [*dɪ'sezɪn, *dɪ'sizɪn] *n* = disseisin, dispossession *16-17*.

dissave *see* DESAVE

disseck *vt* = dissect *19-*.

dissensioun &c *la14-16*; **discentioun** &c *la15-el7* [*dɪ'sɛnsɪun] *n* = dissension.

dissesse *see* DECES

dissimilance &c; **dissimulance** &c *n* dissimulation *la15-e16*. [only Sc; L *dissimulantia*]

dissimulate &c *adj* dissembled, pretended; dissembling, deceitful *la15-el7*. [chf Sc; L *dissimulāt-*, ptp stem of *dissimulāre*]

dissipat &c *vti, ptp* = dissipate *la16-17*.

dississioun *see* DECISIOUN

dissle[1] *n* a slight shower, a drizzle *18-19*. [appar cognate w Norw *dysja* (*v*) drizzle]

dissle[2] &c *vi* struggle forward, push on *18-19*. [uncertain]

dissolate *see* DESOLATE

dissone *see* DIZZEN

dissy *see* DESY

dissyde *see* DECIDE

dissyre *see* DESIRE

dist *see* DUST

distell [*dɪ'stɛl] *vti* = distill *16, only Sc.*

distene &c; disteynȝe &c [*dɪ'stin(jɪ)] *vt* = distain, stain, discolour *la15-16.*

distingue, disting &c [*dɪ'stɪŋ] *vt* distinguish *la15-16.* [ME]

distrack &c *vt* = distract, *chf in adj* **distrackit &c** *la16-.*

district *see* DESTRICK

distrenzie &c *18-e19,* **distrenȝe &c** *la14-e17;* **distreinȝie &c** *15-e18,* **distrenȝie &c** *16-e17,* **distrinȝe &c** *la14-16* [*dɪ'strin(jɪ),* *-'strɪŋjɪ, *-'strɪnjɪ, *-'strɛnjɪ, &c]* *vti* = distrain; subject to constraint; seize (land or goods) by way of enforcing fulfilment of an obligation *la14-e19.*

~abill &c liable or subject to distraint *15-e16.* [only Sc]

distress &c *la15-,* **distres &c** *la14-16 n* **1** = distress *la14-.* **2** illness *la19-, now Ags Fif.* *vt* = distress *15-.*

distribulance *n* = distrublance (DISTROUBLE) *la15-16.* [only Sc; perh after L *tribulāre*]

distribute &c [*dɪ'strɪbøt, *'dɪstrɪbøt] *ptp* distributed *15-e20.* *vt* = distribute *16-.* [ME]

district *see* DESTRICK

distrinȝe *see* DISTRENZIE

distrouble &c *la14-15,* **distruble &c** *la14-16;* **distroble &c** *la14-15* [*dɪ'strubl, *dɪ'strʌbl] *vt* = distrouble, disturb, trouble *la14-e16.*

distroublance &c *n* = distroublance, disturbance *la14-16, chf Sc.*

distroy &c *v* **1** *vt* = destroy *la14-e17.* **2** *vi* commit destruction *la14-16.*

distruble *see* DISTROUBLE

disturs [*dɪs'tʌrs] *vt* = distruss, rob, strip (someone) **of** *la15-e17, only Sc.*

disuse &c [*dɪs'øz] *vt* **1** *only in ptp* **disusit** out of practice; disaccustomed *la14-e16.* **2** = disuse, discontinue *16-.*

dit &c *vt* **1** shut up, close *(chf* the mouth) *la14-, now Bnf.* **2** *freq* ~ **up** obstruct, block (the light etc) *19-e20.* **3** darken, dim *19-e20.* [ME *ditte(n),* OE *dyttan* shut (the ears), stop (the mouth)]

dite *17-e19,* **dyte &c** *15-17 vt* **1** compose, indite *15-e19.* **2** direct, instruct *15-e17.* **3** dictate *16-e19.* **4** = dite, indict, summon *la15-e16.* *n* **1** a composition, writing or written work *15-16.* **2** manner or style of composition, diction *15-16, only Sc.*

~ment 1 a written composition *la16-e17.* **2** dictation, direction, instruction *la16-e17.* **dyter** an inditer, writer *la16.* [ME; OF *diter* (v), *dit* (n), L *dictāre* (v), *dictum* (n)]

diton &c [*'dɪtun, -on, -ən] *n* a phrase or sentence, a motto *la16-e17.* [only Sc; F *dicton*]

dittay &c *15-e20;* **ditty &c** *la16-19,* **ditta &c** *15-e17* [*'dɪte, *'dɪtɪ] *n, law* **1** *also* **dictay,** *also fig* a statement of the charge(s) against an accused person; an indictment *15-e20.* **2** a body or list of indictments coming before a court for trial *15-16.* **3** formal accusation, indictment; information forming a basis of indictment *la15-19.*

point(s) of ~ = DITTAY 1, *la16-18.* **take (up)** ~ obtain information and proof with a view to prosecution *la15-19.* [only Sc; OF *ditté, dité*]

ditter *see* DOIT²

ditty *see* DITTAY

div *see* DAE¹

dival *see* DEVAL

divert [dɪ'vɛrt] *n* an entertainment, amusement; an amusing person or thing *19-.* [f Eng *v* = entertain, amuse; *cf* next]

divertishment *n* = divertisement, entertainment *la17.*

divett *see* DIVOT

divide &c, devide &c *15-17 vt* = divide *15-.* **devider &c** a person appointed to divide land etc *la16, Gsw.* **divider** a ladle, a serving spoon *la18-, local Cai-Dmf.* **deviding &c** formal division (of lands or property) *la15-16.* **dividing spoon** = divider, *la18-, local Bnf-Dmf.*

dividual &c *adj* particular, distinct *19.* [obs in Eng]

divil *see* DEIL

divise &c *la14-e17, only Sc,* **devise** *15* [*dɪ'vaɪz] *n* a bound, boundary between lands. [OF *divise, de-,* laL *dīvīsa,* MedL *devisa*]

division &c, divisioun &c *15-17 n* **1** = division *15-.* **2** formal partition (of land etc) *15-16.* **action of** ~ an action by which common property is divided *la18-.*

divortioun &c [*dɪ'vorsɪun] *n* a divorce *16.* [only Sc; MedL *divortio*]

divot &c *17-,* **devat &c** *16-18,* **divett &c** *la16-,* **dovat &c** *la15-e18,* **dowatt &c** *16-17,* **duvat &c** *15-e17,* **diffat &c** *16-18,* **duffat &c** *16-e17* ['dɪvət; *eRoss also* 'dɪfət; *'dʌvət, *'dɪvət, &c] *n* **1** a turf, sod; a piece of turf thinner than a FAIL *16-.* **2** turf, PEAT¹; turf in thin pieces *15-19.* **3** a thick clumsy piece or slice of bread, meat etc *la19-, now local Bnf-Arg.* *v* **1** *vt* thatch with turf *la17-19.* **2** *vi* cut DIVOTS *la18-19.* [uncertain]

dixie &c *n* a sharp scolding, *chf* **get one's** *or* **gie someone his** ~(s) *19-, now Ork Bnf Abd.* [uncertain; prob f L *dixi* I have said]

dizzen &c *18-,* **deassone &c** *la16-17,* **disone &c** *17,* **dissone &c** *la15-17,* **dosane &c** *la15-e17,* **dosoun &c** *la15-17,* **dousane &c** *la15-17,* **dousoun &c** *16-e17,* **dusane &c** *15-17,* **dussone &c** *la15-17;* **dossand &c** *16* ['dɪz(ə)n; *'duzən] *n* **1** = dozen *la15-.* **2** *chf* **the dusane, dousane &c** the body of ordinary councillors in a BURGH *15;* see DOST.

do *see* DAE¹

doach &c [dox] *n, in pl* name for a rocky stretch of the river Dee at Tongland; a salmon-trap or weir at this point *la18-, Kcb.* [Gael *dabhach* a vat, tub]

doaf *see* DOWF
dob *vt* prick *la19-*, *now Sh Ork Bnf*.
n a prick *19-*, *now Bnf*.
~**bie** &c having spikes, prickly *la19-*, *now Bnf*.
~**bing** pricking *e17*.
dobbie &c; **doobie** &c *e20* *n* a dull, stupid, clumsy person; the dunce of a class *19-*, *now Fif Stlg Edb Kcb*. [uncertain]
dochan doris *see* DEOCHANDORUS
docher &c ['doxər, 'dokər] *n* **1** injury; rough handling, wear and tear *la18-e20*. **2** *of material* strength, durability *la19-e20*. [Gael *dochair* hurt, damage, injury]
dochle ['doxl] *n* a dull, stupid person, a fool *19-e20*. [cf *dachle* (DACKLE)]
docht *see* DOW[1]
dochter &c, **dother** &c *la15-e20*, **dowter** *e20*, **dauchter** &c *la16-17*, **douchter** &c *la14-e20*; **dowchtir** *la14-e17*, **dowthir** *16* ['doxtər; *Sh Ork Bwk Rox also* 'dʌu(x)tər; *NE Ags* 'doθər; *Ork Cai sEC also* *'dɑxtər; *NE also* *'dɑθər] *n* = daughter *la14-*.
~**(is) son**, ~ ~ grandson or grand-daughter by one's daughter *15-16*.
dochtie *see* DOUCHTY
dock &c *la16-*, **dok** *16*; **dook** *20-*, *chf Rox n* **1** the buttocks *16-*, *now local Cai-Fif*. **2** the rear or butt of something *la16-19*. **3** a haircut *la19-*, *Bnf Ags Fif*.
vt **1** = dock, shorten (clothes); put (an infant) into short clothes *la19-*. **2** push (someone) **up** by placing one's head or shoulder to his buttocks and rising *20-*, *Rox*.
dockie &c neat, tidy *19-e20*, *SW*. ~**it** &c *of speech or temper* clipped, short *19-*, *now Bnf Abd Fif*. **docketie** short, round and jolly *19-*, *Rox*. ~**y-doon** *n* help in descending from a vehicle *20-*, *Rox*.
~**nail 1** the nail used to fix a blade or handle on a scythe, plough etc *e20*, *Abd*. **2** a ploughman *20-*, *Abd Kcdn*. **3** any person or part indispensable to the efficiency of a job, tool etc *20-*, *now Abd*.
dock *see* DEK, DOK
docken &c *17-*, **dokane** &c *la15-16 n* **1** = dock, the plant *la15-*. **2** *fig, in negative* something of no value or significance *la19-*: '*it disna maitter a doaken*'.
docket *see* DOCQUET
dockie *see* DUCK
docquet &c *17-*, **docket** &c *n* **1** = docket *la16-*. **2** *law* a statement appended to an *instrument of sasine* (INSTRUMENT) declaring its authenticity *17-19*.
vt = docket *17-*.
doctering *see* DOCTRINE
doctor &c *15-*, **doctour** &c *la14-17 n* **1** = doctor *la14-*. **2** an assistant-master in a school *la16-18*. **3** a large minnow; the red-breasted minnow *la19-*, *now Fif Edb Ayr*.
vt **1** = doctor. **2** do for, finish off, *eg* in a fight *19-*, *now Sh Lnk*: '*he fairly doctored Jock this time*'.

doctrix an assistant school-mistress *18*.
doctrine &c *la15-*; **doctering** &c *16*, **doctreine** &c *la16-e17* ['doktrɪn, *dok'traɪn, *-'trɪn] *n* = doctrine.
document *n* **1** = document *la15-*. **2** proof, evidence, testimony *la15-e16*. **3** written evidence, a written statement or record of a legal matter *la15-*.
docus &c [*'dokəs] *n* a stupid person *la18-*, *local C*. [unknown]
dod[1] &c *vi* move slowly and unsteadily, totter, dodder *19-*, *now Ayr*. [? onomat; *cf* DODDLE[3], DODGE]
dod[2] &c [dod; *NE also* djod] *n, interj, euphemistic* = God *la19-*, *Gen except Sh-Ross*.
dod[3] &c *n, chf in pl* the sulks *la18-e20*.
doddy sulky, bad-tempered *19-e20*.
tak the ~**s** take a fit of bad temper, sulk *19-*, *now Stlg Fif*. [Gael = a huff, tantrum]
doddie &c ['dodɪ; *Bnf* 'dʌudɪ] *n* **1** (1) a hornless bull or cow *la18-*, *now Bnf Abd Fif*. (2) a hornless sheep *19-*, *S*. **2** humorous or contemptuous term for a person *la19-e20*.
adj, of cattle hornless *19-*, *now Bnf*.
~**-mitten** a mitten, a worsted glove with a separate division for the thumb only *la18-*, *Bnf-Fif*. [f Eng *dod* poll; *cf* next]
doddit &c *adj, of cattle or sheep* hornless *17-e20*. [f as prec]
doddle[1] ['dodl] *n* a small lump of home-made toffee sold in little corner-shops *e20*, *Edb*. [prob f DAD *n* 2]
doddle[2] ['dodl] *n* **1** something attractive *e20*. **2** something which is easy to do *20-*, *local*. [appar Eng *dawdle* in specialized applications]
doddle[3] &c ['dodl] *vi* TODDLE, walk feebly or slowly *la16*, *la19-*, *now Bnf Abd*.
n, chf in pl the male genitals *18-*, *now Cai*. [? onomat; ? akin to Eng *dawdle*, northern eModEng *dadder*, ME *totere(n)*, *totter*; *cf* DOD[1]]
dodge *vi* jog, trudge along *19-*, *local Ork-Kcb*. [prob f DOD[1]; *cf* DAD]
dodgel &c *n* something large of its kind, a lump; *transf* a clumsy person *19-*, *now Ork Bnf*. [see SND]
Dodgill Reepan &c *n* the marsh orchis, the roots of which were used in a love potion *19*. [unknown]
dodrums *see* DIDDERUMS
dog &c, **dowg** &c *la17, 19-*, *now local Cai-nEC*, **dug** *19-*; **doig** *la16* [dog; *Sh C* dʌg; *Cai-Buchan* dʌug] *n* **1** = dog *15-*. **2** a kind of cannon *16-17*. **3** a lever used by blacksmiths in hooping cart-wheels etc *18-*, *now Abd*.
doggar &c a dog-keeper *e16*.
~ **afore his maister** the swell of the sea that often precedes a storm *la19-*, *now Bnf*. ~ **daisy** the ox-eye daisy *la19-*, *SW*. ~ **dollour** &c the Dutch lion dollar *e17*. ~ **drave** *etc* ruin, utter confusion *18-19*. ~**('s) flourish** one of various umbelliferous plants *20-*, *local C-S*. ~**-heather** heather, LING[2] *19-*, *Abd Ags*. ~ **hillock** &c a

small mound or hillock covered with long grass *la19-*, now *Cai Abd*. ~('s) **hip** the fruit of the dog-rose, the rosehip *18-*, now *local Abd-S*. ~ **hole** a hole left in the wall of a building as an entrance for a dog *la19-*, now *Bnf Ags*. ~ **ledder &c** leather made from dog-skin *la16-e17*. ~'s **wages** food given as the only wages for service *la18-*, now *Abd*.

dog *see* DAG³

doggar &c *n* a kind of coarse ironstone *usu* found in globular concretions; one of these concretions *la18-*, now *Edb*. [see SND]

doggit *adj* = dogged *15-16*.

dogone *n* contemptuous term for a man *e16*. [prob same as DAGONE]

doig *see* DOG

doilt &c *18-*, **doillit &c** *e16*; **diled &c** *19-e20*, **doyld &c** *la16-e19* [doilt, -d, dəilt, -d] *adj* **1** dazed, confused, stupid *16-*, now *Sh Dmf*. **2** wearied, fatigued; grief-stricken *la18-*, now *Abd*. [perh f as DOOL¹]

doin, dois *see* DAE¹

doist &c; doish(t) &c *la19-*, now *Abd*, **dyst** *la19-* [doist, dəist, doiʃ(t), dəiʃ(t)] *n*, *also* **dois** *e16* a heavy blow; a thud, bump, crash *la18-*, now *Abd-Kcdn*.
vti fall, sit or throw (**down**) with a thud, bump *19-*, now *Abd Kcdn*.
~**er** a stormy wind blowing in from the sea *19-*, now *Bnf Abd Ayr*. [*cf* DUSH]

doit¹ &c; dyte &c *la17-e19* [doit; NE *Ayr Rox* dəit] *n* **1** = doit, a small Dutch copper coin used in Scotland *la16-e18*. **2** something of little value, *chf* **not to care a ~, not worth a ~** *18-e20*.

doit² &c; dyte &c [doit; *Cai NE, C* dəit; *Fif* dʌut] *vi* **1** act foolishly, be crazed, enfeebled or confused in mind *16-*, now *Abd*. **2** walk with a stumbling or short step *la18-*, now *Bnf Abd*.
n a stupid person, a fool *19-e20*.
~**er &c** *19-*; **ditter &c** *20-* walk or move unsteadily, hang about *19-*, now *local Bnf-S*.
~**ered &c** witless, confused, *chf* from old age *19-*, now *Fif*. ~**it &c** *la15-*, **dowtit &c** *19-e20*, *Fif adj*, *of persons* not of sound mind, foolish, silly. **doitrified** stupefied, dazed, senseless *19-*, now *Bnf Ags Fif*. [only Sc; perh irreg var of Eng *dote* think or act foolishly]

dok; dock *17-* *n* = dock, a bed for a vessel *la15-*.
~ **maill &c** *17*, ~ **silver &c** *la16-e17* dock dues, the charges made for the use of a dock.

dok *see* DOCK

dokane *see* DOCKEN

dolder, doldie *see* DOLL

dole *n*, *law* the corrupt, malicious, or evil intention which is an essential constituent of a criminal act *la17-*. [obs Eng = deceit, fraud]

dolf *see* DOWF

doll &c [dol, *dul, *dʌul] *n* a portion, large piece of anything, *freq* of dung *la19-*, now *Bnf Abd*.

dolder &c something large of its kind *la19-*, now *Bnf Abd*. **doldie &c** *19-*, *Abd w*Loth, **toldie** *20-*, *Bnf Abd* a lump. ~**er** a large marble *la19-*, now *Bnf Abd Ags*. ~**icker, dollie (marble)** *la20-* a very large marble about six to eight times the normal size *la19-*, *Edb*. **tollie &c** a lump of excrement *19-*, *Gen except Sh Ork*. [see SND]

dollin *see* DELVE

dollop *n* **1** = dollop. **2** a slut, an untidy woman *20-*, *Bnf Abd*.

dollour &c, dolour &c *n* = dollar *la16-17*, *only Sc*.

dolly *n* an old-fashioned oil-lamp, a CRUISIE *e20*, *Bnf Abd*. [reduced f *eelie-dolly* (OIL)]

dolly *see* DOWIE¹

doly *see* DOOL¹

dom *n* = DOMINIE *20-*, *Bnf Abd*.
~**sie** = *n*, *la19-*, *Bnf Abd Stlg*.

dome *see* DOOM

domegrane *see* DEMIGRANE

domicile &c [*'domɪsəil, *-sil] *n* **1** *collective* household effects *la15-17*. **2** a household article *la16-17*. [only Sc; appar f L *domicilii*, genitive sing of *domicilium* a household > Eng *domicile*]

dominant tenement *n*, *law* a piece of land with the ownership of which goes a SERVITUDE right over adjoining land *18-*; *cf* SERVIENT.

domineer *vt* **1** = domineer. **2** deafen, stupefy with loud noise or too much talk *la19-*, *Bnf Abd*.

dominie &c *n* **1** a schoolmaster *18-*. **2** a clergyman *e18-*. [only Sc; L *domine* sir, vocative of *dominus* a master]

dominium [dɔ'mɪnɪʌm] *n*, *law* ~ **directum** [~ dai'rɛktʌm] the right in land enjoyed by the SUPERIOR *la18-*. ~ **utile** [~ 'jutɪle] the substantial right in land enjoyed by the VASSAL, ownership *la18-*. [L = (simple *or* advantageous) right of ownership]

dominus litis ['domɪnʌs 'laitɪs] *n*, *law* the person really though not nominally behind legal proceedings, liable to be ordered to pay EXPENSES *la19-*. [L = master of the lawsuit]

donal; donald *n* **1** a Highlander (HIELAND) *19-*, now *Cai*. **2** a measure of WHISKY, about half a gill *19-*, *local Bnf-WC*. [f the personal name *Donald*, common in the *Highlands*, Gael *Dòmhnall*]

Donald *n* a hill in the Scottish *Lowlands* (LAWLAND) of 2000 feet (610 m) or over *la20-*. [f Percy Donald, who listed them; *cf* CORBETT and MUNRO]

donatar *see* DONATOR

donatary *see* DONATORY

donator *17-19*, **donatour** *16-e17*, **donatar &c** *16-17* [*'donətur, -ər *n*, *law* the receiver of a donation, *esp* in cases of failure of succession, of a forfeiture or ward and marriage *16-19*.
donatrix [*'donətrɪks] a female donee *la16*. [only Sc; MedL *donatorius, -arius*, OF *donatoire, -aire*]

donatory; donatary ['donətərɪ] *n, law* = prec (*now* only from the Crown) *la18-*. [MedL *donatarius; cf* Eng *donatory*]

donatour *see* DONATOR

done *see* DAE¹, DOON¹

dongerees [doŋgə'riz] *n* = dungarees *20-*. [only Sc; uncertain]

donie &c [*'donɪ] *n, chf verse* a hare *19-e20*. [only Sc; uncertain]

donk *see* DUNK

donner &c *19-*; **donnar &c** *vti* daze, stun, stupefy, *chf* **donnert &c** dull, stupid *17-*. [see SND]

Dons *n pl* **the** ~ nickname for Aberdeen football team *20-*. [perh short for *Aberdonians or* (a folk etymology) f their founders having been teachers]

donsie &c *adj* **1** unfortunate, luckless *la18-e20*. **2** glum, dejected *18-19*. **3** *of persons and things* sickly, feeble, delicate *la18-*, *now Arg*. **4** dull, stupid *19-*, *S*. **5** badly behaved, ill-tempered *la18-e19*, *SW*. **6** neat, tidy (*freq* with the notion of self-importance) *18-19*. [Gael *donas* bad luck, mischief + suffix *-ie*]

doo *la18-*, **dow &c** [du; *S also* dʌu] *n* **1** = dove *la14-*. **2** familiar term of endearment, *esp* for a sweetheart or child *la15-*. **3** a kindly loving person *20*, *local E*.
~'**s cleckin** *or* **sitting** a family of two, *usu* a boy and a girl *la19-*, *local Bnf-Rox*. ~**cot** *15-*, ~**cat** *la15-e19*, **ducat** *la16-18* ['dukət, *'dʌ-] = dovecote *15-*. ~**cot hole** a pigeon-hole *19-e20*. ~**-docken** coltsfoot *19-*, *Cai*. ~**-talit** *joinery* dove-tailed *16-e17*.
flee the (**blue**) ~ send out a messenger surreptitiously for WHISKY *e20*, *Bnf Abd*. **not to care a** ~'**s ee** not to care a jot *20-*, *now Kcb*.

doobie *see* DOBBIE

dooble &c *e17*, *la19-*, **double &c**, **duble &c** *la14-17*, **dowle** *la16-e17* [perh misreading for *double*] ['dubl] *adj* (*adv*) = double *la14-*.
n **1** = double *la14-*. **2** a duplicate of a written document *16-*, *chf Sc*.
vti **1** = double *la14-*. **2** *vt* make a duplicate or copy of *17-e18*.
doubling 1 = doubling *la15-*. **2** *piping* (1) *in* PIBROCH the form in which a variation may be repeated, *usu* with more complete or perfect development *la18-*; (2) a kind of trill prefacing a note *20-*.
~ **cairt** a cart pulled by two horses, one in the shafts and one in the traces *20-*, *now Bnf Abd*. **double distress** *law* two or more claims on a single fund, an essential of a MULTIPLEPOINDING *la18-*. **double letter** a capital letter *19-*, *chf Bnf Abd*. **double poinding** = MULTIPLEPOINDING *la16-17*. **double raip** a straw rope twisted double *la15*, *20-* (*Bnf Abd*). **double-solit** having a double sole *la15-17*.

doobrack &c *n* the smelt or sparling *la18-e20*, *Bnf Abd*. [Gael *dubh bhreac*]

doodle &c *vt* dandle, lull (a child) to sleep *la18-*, *now Kcb*. [only Sc; prob onomat]

doof *see* DOWF

dook¹ *19-*, **douk &c** *la15-e19* [duk] *vti* **1** = duck *la15-*. **2** bathe *19-*. **3** *vt* baptize as a Baptist *20-*, *Ags Stlg*. **4** *vi*, *of the day or the sun, freq* ~ **doon** draw to a close, go down *19*.
n **1** = duck *la15-*. **2** a bathe *la19-*. **3** a drenching, a soaking *la18-*, *now Bnf Abd*. **4** liquid into which something is dipped *19-e20*. **5** *mining* an inclined roadway *la19-*, *now Fif Ayr*.
the ~**ing** bathing *e19*.
~ **workings** *mining* workings below the level of the pit bottom *la19-*, *now Fif*.
~ **for apples &c** *Halloween* (HALLOW²) *game* attempt to get hold of apples floating in a tub etc with one's teeth, by dipping one's head in the water and without using one's hands *la19-*.

dook² *n* **1** a wooden peg etc driven into a wall to hold a nail *18-*. **2** a plug, a bung of a cask, boat etc *19-*, *Bnf*.
vt insert such wooden pegs etc in (a wall) *20-*.
~ **hole 1** a hole cut in a wall for a DOOK² *20-*, *NE Ags Kcb*. **2** the plug hole of a cask (*now Kcb*) or boat (*Cai*), *20-*. [only Sc; see SND]

dook *see* DOCK

dool¹ *la16-*, **dule &c; duill &c** *15-18*, **doul &c** *la16-e17* [dul; *Sh Ork C, S* døl; *Loth Ayr* dɪl] *n* **1** *now verse* grief, distress *la14-*. **2** = dole, mourning clothes *16-17*. **3** *exclam* alas! *18-*, *now Sh*.
vti lament, mourn *16-19*.
adj sad, sorrowful *18-e20*.
~**ful &c** *la14-19*, ~**some** *16*, *la18-e20*, **doly** *la15-e17*, **duly** *la15-16* = doleful.
~ **habit** = ~ **weed**(s), *e16*, *only Sc*. ~ **string** a piece of black crepe worn round the hat as a sign of mourning *la18-19*. ~ **tree** a gallows tree *la18-e20*. ~ **weed**(s) **&c** mourning clothes *16-e19*.

dool² *la17-*, **dule &c** *la16-*; **dult** *20-*, *local WC* [dul; *døl; Ork C* dʌl; *WC also* dʌlt] *n* **1** = dool, a boundary mark *la16*, *19-*, *now Ork*. **2** *games* the goal or place of safety *la16-*, *now WC*.
dully prisoners' base; rounders *19-e20*.
the ~**s** = prec *19-e20*.

dool³ *19-*, **doule &c** *16-17* [dul] *n* = dowel *16-*.

doolie &c *n* **1** a hobgoblin, a spectre *19-*, *now Ags*. **2** a stupid, dithering, nervous person *20-*, *local C*.

doom *la17-*, **dome** *la14-e17*, **dume &c** *15-e17*; **doum &c** *la14-e16*, **doym &c** *15-e16*, **duyme &c** *la15-16* [St dum; *døm] *n, law* = doom, a law, a judgment, a sentence *la14-20*.
vt, law pronounce sentence against, condemn *18-*.
doomster *e17*, *19-e20*, **domster &c** *16-e17* = DEMPSTER.
but *or* **withoutin** ~ (**or law**) without proper (trial and) sentence *15-e17*. **give** (**for**) ~ give (as) judgment *la14-e17*.

dooms [dumz] *adv* (*adj*) extremely, very; 'dashed' *19-*, *now Abd Fif Ayr*. [uncertain]

doon[1] *la19-*, **doun** &c; **done** &c *la14-16* [dun]
adv (adj), *comparative* **douner** *la17-*, *now Ayr*,
superlative **doonmaist** &c *la19-*, *now local Bnf-
Stlg* ['dunməst] **1** = down *la14-*. **2** *of prices or
reckonings* (1) by way of reduction *la15-*, *now
local Bnf-Stlg*; (2) ~ **of** below *la18-*, *local Sh-Kcb*.
3 *of seed* sown *la19-*, *Cai Bnf Abd Fif*. **4** *of a river*
in flood *la19-*. **5** *mining, of a stratum* requiring
support from below *20-*, *now Fif*.

doonie *games* a member of the *hand-ball* (HAND)
team playing towards the downward goal, the
doonies usu coming from the lower part of the
town *20-*, *Ork Rox; cf* UPPIE. ~**lins** downwards
20-, *Bnf Abd*.

~**-by**(**e**) down there, in the neighbourhood *19-*.
~**-come 1** a downfall, descent *15-19*. **2** a
heavy fall of snow or rain *la19-*, *local Bnf-Kcb*.
3 *fig* a fall in status, humiliation *19-*, *local*.
~**-ding** *n* a heavy fall of rain or snow *19-*, *now
Abd Ags Fif*. *vt* beat down, defeat *la19*. ~**-drag**
&c a handicap *19-*, *Bnf Abd Ags*. ~**draught** &c
now Ags Stlg, ~**-draw** *now Ags* a depressing
influence, a heavy load, a handicap *19-*. ~**fa** a
downward slope *19-*, *local*. ~**-falling** *15-16*,
~**-ganging** *15* the setting (of the sun). ~**-get-
ting** the action of obtaining a reduction or
remission (of custom dues) *16-17*. ~**-going** =
~**-ganging**, *17*. ~**-haud** &c a handicap, something that prevents one rising in the world *19-*.
~**hadden** kept in subjection *la19-*. ~ **hame**
at home, *freq* applied to Dumfries by the locals
20-. ~**hamers** nickname for the inhabitants of
Dumfries, and for *Queen of the South* (QUEEN)
football team *20-*. ~**leuk** &c **1** a displeased
look, disapproval *la18*. **2** a hangdog expression
la19-, *Bnf Abd*. ~**-lookin** &c sullen, guilty
looking *18-e20*. ~**-lyin** confinement, lying in,
chf **at the** ~**-lyin** about to be confined *la16,
19-*. ~ **mouth** a sad expression *19-*, *local Bnf-
Stlg*. ~**-moued** &c depressed *la19-*, *now Abd*.
~**-passing** the setting (of the sun) *la15-e17*.
~**-pouring** the pouring down (of rain etc)
la19-, *now Sh Ags*. ~**raxter** *vt, n* knock down
e17, only Sc. ~**set**, ~**setting 1** a (good etc) settlement, *usu* that obtained on marriage *19-*, *now
Fif Arg Ayr*. **2** a scolding *19-*, *now Bnf*. **3** a
laying-low (*eg* from a heavy blow, misfortune
etc) *19-*, *now Bnf Stlg*. **4** *of food etc* a (grand etc)
'spread' *20-*, *now Ork Abd*. ~**-sitting 1** the
opening session of a deliberative body *la16-e18*.
2 the action of settling in a place *la16, la19-*
(*Bnf Abd*). **3** *also* ~**-sit** a settlement, *esp* one
obtained by marriage or inheritance *la19-*. **at a**
or **ae** ~**sittin** = at a or a single sitting *20-*, *local
Bnf-Stlg*. ~**-tak** a humiliation, a taunt *la19-*.
~**-thring** press or thrust down; suppress
la14-16, *only Sc*. ~ **through** &c in(to) the
lower-lying part of the country or the coastal
areas *19-*, *now Cai Bnf Abd*. **downthrow** *mining*

a fault which has displaced the strata downwards relative to the workings ahead *19-*, *now
Fif*. ~**with** downwards, downhill *la15-*, *now
Bnf Abd*.
be on the ~ **hand** *of prices* fall *20-*, *Bnf Abd*.
~ **the gate** down the road, yonder *la18-e20*.
~ **the hoose** in the best room *19-*, *SW Uls*. ~
the watter down the river, *specif* of pleasure
trips or resorts on the Clyde *la19-*. **gae** ~ **the
brae** *or* **hill** *fig* go downhill, deteriorate in
health, fortune etc *la18-*. **gang** ~ *of a school*
close for holidays *20-*, *Stlg Kcb*.

doon[2] *19-*, **doun** &c *n* **1** = down, soft plumage
16-. **2** in *pl* = prec *16-e18*, *only Sc*.

doon[3] *n* the goal or home in a game *la18-19*, *SW*.
[f DUN, w *infl* f DOOL[2]]

doons &c [*dunz] *adv*, *chf in negative* not very
(much) *18-19*. [only Sc; perh conflation of
DOON[1] w DOOMS]

door &c *16-*, **dure** &c *la14-e17*; **duir** &c
16-e20, **dorr** *la16-e18* [dor; *dør, *dʌr] *n*
= door *la14-*.
~**ie** *marbles* a game played against a door *20-*,
Abd.
~**-cheek** &c a door-post; a door, doorway *16-*.
~**-heid** &c the upper part of a door-case *la17-*,
now Bnf Abd Rox. ~ **neighbour** a next-door
neighbour *17-*, *now Bnf*. ~ **sole** the threshold
19-, *now Ork Cai*. ~**-stane** &c a flagstone in
front of the threshold of a door; the threshold
19-, *local Sh-Fif*. ~**-staple** &c an iron hook on
the door-post to secure the bar or bolt on the
inside of a door *la19-*, *now Bnf Ags*. ~**-thrashel**
the threshold *20-*, *NE*.
gie someone the ~ (**in his face**) show someone the door, slam the door in someone's face
la19-, *local*. **make open** ~**s** *law* force open a
locked door (under legal authority) *18-e19*. **he**
etc **hasn't been** *etc* **over** &c **the** ~ he etc hasn't
been outside or out of the house *18-*. **put
someone to the** ~ ruin someone *18-*, *now Bnf
Abd*. **tak the** ~ **on your** *etc* **back** go away,
clear out *19*. **tak the** ~ **wi ye** *etc* = prec; shut
the door as you etc go out *la19-*, *now Bnf Abd*.

doorie &c ['durɪ; *Uls* 'dʒorɪ] *n* a pig; the smallest pig of a litter *la19-e20*, *Arg SW Uls*. [Gael
durradh a pig, sow; *durrag* a little pig]

doose *la19-*, **dous** &c *e16, 18-19* [dus] *vt* strike,
knock, thrash *18-*, *local*.
n a heavy blow; a butt, push; a thud *e16, 19-*,
now Sh Ork Bnf Abd. [*cf* Eng *douse* and DUSH]

doosht &c [duʃt; *Sh Arg* dust] *n* a dull, heavy
blow, a push; a thud, a beat *la18-*, *Sh Cai Bnf
Abd*.
vt **1** strike with a dull, heavy blow, thump *la19-*,
now Bnf Abd. **2** throw (down) in a violent, careless way *la19-*, *Bnf Abd*. [onomat; *cf* DUSH]

doot *19-*, **dout** &c; **doubt** &c *la15-* *n* = doubt
la14-.
vti **1** = doubt *la14-*. **2** *vi*, ~ **for** *or* **to do** .. fear,

be afraid of (something) or of doing (something) *15-16*. **3** *vt* fear, be afraid, suspect (that ..) *la14-*. **4** expect, rather think *la18-*.

~sum &c *16-e17*, *la19-e20* **1** of doubtful or uncertain meaning, ambiguous, undecided *16-17*. **2** of uncertain issue or result *16*. **3** involving risk or danger, formidable *16*. **4** doubtful, undecided in opinion *16*, *la19-e20*.

~wise &c = doubtous, doubtful *la14-e16*.

I *etc* **hae my ~s** I etc am doubtful *la19-*.

doozie &c *n* **1** a light, a flame (of a candle, lamp etc) *la19-*, now *Ayr.* **2** = DINGLE-DOUSIE *1*, *19-*, *SW.* [uncertain]

dorb &c *n* a peck; a prod *20-*, now *Bnf*.
vti, of birds peck, grub *20-*, *Bnf.* [var of DOB]

dorbie¹ &c *n* a stonemason *19-*, now *Bnf Abd Rox*. [obscure]

dorbie² &c *adj* delicate, weak *la19-*, *Bnf Abd*. [uncertain]

dorche *see* DROICH

dorder-meat &c [*'dordər-, *'dortər-] *n* a snack between meals, *chf* one given to farmworkers between dinner and supper *la18-19*. [northern ModEng dial *downder*, ME, OE *undern*, *orig* the third hour of the day, later the sixth hour or midday, OE *undern-mete*]

dorlach &c, dorloch, darloch ['dorləx, 'darləx, -lək] *n* **1** a quiver (for arrows) *la16-17*. **2** a bundle used by *Highland* (HIELAND) soldiers instead of a knapsack *e19*, *hist*. **3** a large piece of something solid *la19-*, now *Bnf Abd*. [Gael = a handful, bundle; a quiver]

dorle, darle [dorl, *darl] *n* a small quantity, a piece of something, *esp* of something edible *la17-*, now *Bnf Abd*. [perh back-formation f prec]

dorloch *see* DORLACH

dormie &c *adj, golf, chf* **~ one** *etc* as many holes up on one's opponent as still remain to be played *19-*. [unknown]

dorneedy &c; dorneed &c ['dor'nid, dor'nidɪ] *n, chf of pigs* the runt of a litter *la19-*, now *NE.* [obscure]

dornell *n* = darnel, the weed *16*.

dorne werk *n* = DORNICK *16*. [only Sc; altered after *werk* (WARK)]

dornick &c *17-e19*, **dornik &c** *16* [*'dorn(w)ɪk] *n* a linen used for tablecloths etc *la15-e19*. [f *Doornik* (Tournai) in Flanders where the cloth was *orig* made; *cf* Eng = a fabric used for hangings etc; see prec]

dorr *see* DOOR

dorro &c *e20*; **darra &c** *la19-* ['darə; *'dorə; *Ork* daro; *Sh also* *'doro] *n* a trailing cord with hooked lines attached, used in catching cod, mackerel etc *la19-*, now *Bnf.* [Norw, ON *dorg*]

dort *n, chf in pl* the sulks, the huff, *freq* **tak the ~s** *17-*.
vi sulk, take offence *e17*, *19-*, now *Sh-Cai Fif*.

~y &c 1 bad-tempered, sulky *la16-*, now *Ork*. **2**

saucy; haughty *16-*, now *Ork Ags Kcb*. **3** fastidious, difficult to please *la18-*, *SW.* **4** feeble, delicate, sickly; *of plants or animals* difficult to rear *19-*, now *Bnf Abd*.

Meg D~s a sulky, bad-tempered woman *18-19*. [obscure]

dos *see* DOSS¹

dosane *see* DIZZEN

Do-School &c, Dough School [*St* 'do 'skul] familiar name for any of the Colleges of Domestic Science *20-*, *Abd Edb Gsw.* [perh short for *Domestic Science*, or (as popularly supposed) f Eng *dough*]

dose &c [doz; *Rox also* duz] *n* **1** = dose *18-*. **2** a large quantity or number *19-*.
a ~ of the cold a cold *la19-*.

dose *see* DOZE

do-service [*'dø 'sɛrvɪs] *n* = dew service (DUE) *la15-e17*. [f verbal phrase *do service*]

dosh *n* term of endearment for a girl *la19-*, now *Sh Abd*.

dosinnit &c *la14-16*; **dozened &c** *18-* ['doz(ə)nt, -d; *'dozɪnt] *adj* **1** stupefied, dazed, stupid, physically weakened (through age, drink etc) *la14-*, now *local Sh-Lnk.* **2** numb, stiff with cold *la18-19*. **3** *of wood, fruit etc* rotten *18*, *20-*, now *Ags Fif.* [obscure; *cf* DOZEN]

dosoun *see* DIZZEN

doss¹ *19-*, **dos &c** *15-e16 adj* spruce, neat, tidy *19-e20*.
vt dress (**up**); tidy, make neat *15-e16*, *19-*, now *Bnf Abd.* [only Sc; Du *dossen*]

doss² *n* a knot or bow (of ribbon, flowers etc) *19-*, now *Bnf Abd*.
~ie a small knob or heap *la19-*, *NE.* [only Sc; Gael *dos* a tuft; a bow; a bunch of hair]

doss³ *n* a box or pouch for tobacco or snuff *la18-e19*. [only Sc; Du *doos* a box]

doss⁴ *vt, chf* **~ doon** toss or pay down (money) *18-*, now *Abd*.
~ie *vt* = prec *la18-*, now *Abd*. [uncertain]

dossach &c ['dosəx; *Abd also* 'doʃ-] *vi, freq* **~ wi** fondle, pet, fuss over needlessly *19-*, *Bnf Abd*. [uncertain]

dossan &c *n* a forelock *la19-*, now *Cai Ross*. [Gael *dosan*, dim of *dos* (see DOSS²)]

dossand *see* DIZZEN

dossie *see* DOSS⁴

dot¹ *n* a nap, a short sleep *19-*, now *Cai.* [*cf* Icel *dotta* (*v*) nod from sleep]

dot² *n* **1** = dot, a spot. **2** a person of small stature *la19-*, *Bnf Abd Edb*.
v **1** *vt* = dot, mark with a dot. **2** *vi* walk (**about**) with short quick steps *la19-*, *local Bnf-Kcb*.
dottle = *n* 2, *19-*, *Bnf Abd*.

dotate &c *ptp* **1** *also pt* endowed *16*. **2** given as an endowment *la16*. [only Sc; L *dōtāt-*, ptp stem of *dōtāre; cf* next]

dote¹ &c *n* a dowry *16-17*, *19*.
vt **1** endow (**with** property, dignities, some quality etc) *16-e17*. **2** provide (a woman) with

a dowry *la16*. **3** give or grant (lands etc) as an endowment *16-19*. [OF *dote*, *doter*, L *dōt-*, stem of *dōs* (*n*), *dōtāre* (*v*); *cf* Eng]

dote² &c *vi* = dote *la14-*.
dottered stupid, enfeebled in mind, *chf* from old age *la19-* [*cf* Eng *dotard*]. **dotterel** &c a dotard, an imbecile *16*, *la19-*, *now Stlg*. **dotit** &c silly, stupid, *chf* from old age *la15-16*, *la19*. **dottle** *adj* in a state of dotage, witless *19*.
v **1** *vi* be in or fall into a state of dotage, become crazy *19-*, *Cai Bnf Abd Ags*. **2** *vt* make crazy or confused *19-*, *Bnf Abd*. [*cf* DOIT²]

dother *see* DOCHTER
dotter &c *vi* walk unsteadily, stagger *18-e20*. [*cf* *doiter* (DOIT²), DOT²]
dottered, dotterel *see* DOTE²
dottle &c *n* **1** a particle, a jot, something small *19-*, *Stlg eLoth Ayr*. **2** the plug of tobacco left at the bottom of a pipe after smoking *19-*. **3** a cigarette end *20-*, *Bnf Fif Ayr*. **4** the core of a boil *la19-*, *now Abd Fif*. [dim of Eng *dot* a small lump or spot]
dottle *see* DOT², DOTE²
doub *see* DUB
double *see* DOOBLE
doublet &c, **doublat** &c *15-e17*, **dublet** *la16-e17*, **dowlet** &c *la16*, *only Sc* [prob misreading] [*'dublət*] *n* **1** = doublet *15-*. **2** *in pl* clothes, garments *19-*, *now Bnf*.
doubt *see* DOOT
doucat *see* DOO
douce; douse &c *la16*, *19-e20* [dus] *adj* **1** sweet, pleasant, lovable *la16-*, *local Bnf-Lnk*. **2** sedate, sober, respectable *18-*. **3** neat, tidy, comfortable *19-*, *now Stlg*. [OF *dous*, *douce*; obs in Eng]
doucht &c [*doxt*, *dʌxt*] *n* power, strength, ability *la18-19*.
~less powerless, worthless *19-*, *now Fif*, *only Sc*. [back-formation f DOUGHTY]
doucht *see* DOW¹
douchter *see* DOCHTER
douchty &c; **duchtie** &c *16*, **dughtie** &c *e16*, *e19*, **dochtie** *la16*, *19-e20* [*doxtɪ*, *'dʌxtɪ*] *adj* = doughty *la14-e20*. [ME *douȝti* &c; laOE *dohtig*]
doudle &c [*'dudl*] *vti* **1** play (a wind instrument, *chf* a DOUDLE or the bagpipes) *19-e20*. **2** *vi* sing or hum over a tune as an accompaniment to dancers *20-*, *Fif Arg Ayr*.
n a musical instrument made from a reed *20*. [chf Sc; *cf* Ger *dudeln* play the bagpipes, f Polish *dudlić* play badly on a wind instrument]
douf *see* DOWF
Dough-School *see* DO-SCHOOL
Douglas grot &c *n* a groat coined during the domination of Archibald Douglas, Earl of Angus, early in the reign of James V, *16*.
douk *see* DOOK¹
doul *see* DOOL¹
doule *see* DOOL³

doull *see* DWALL
doum *see* DOOM
doun *see* DAE¹, DOON¹, DOON³
doung *see* DING
doup¹ &c [dʌup; *Ork* dup; *Dmf* *dop] *n* **1** the bottom of an eggshell *17-*, *now Cai Bnf Abd Fif*. **2** the buttocks (of a person or animal) *la17-*. **3** the seat of a pair of trousers *19-*, *now local Bnf-Fif*. **4** the bottom or end of anything *la18-19*. **5** *specif* (1) the end of a used candle *18-*; (2) the stub of a cigarette or cigar *20-*; (3) a loop or the set of loops of the short HEDDLE used in weaving gauze *19*.
v **1** *vt* dump (a person) down smartly on the buttocks, *eg* as in the initiation ceremony of burgesses *la18-*, *Abd Fif*. **2** *vi* sit or squat **down** *19-*, *now Bnf*.
~ end = *n* 5 (3), *20-*, *Sh Per Ayr*. **~ scour** a thump on the buttocks caused by falling *19-*, *Bnf Abd*. [only Sc; *cf* LowGer *dop* &c a shell; a fingertip, Du *dop* a shell; a knob; *cf* also *e-dolp* (EE¹)]
doup² [dup] *vi* **1** stoop, bend, duck *la17-*, *now Bnf Abd Stlg*. **2** *of the day* draw to a close; *of darkness* fall *la18-e19*.
~ o day or **een** *verse* the close of day *18-e20*. [*cf* Norw dial *duppa* (*v*) nod]
doup³ &c *vt* stab (a person); thrust (a weapon) into *la16-17*. [only Sc; obscure]
dour &c; **dure** *la14*, *la18-e19* [dur] *adj* **1** *of persons, actions or things* determined, hard, stern, severe *la14-*. **2** obstinate, stubborn, unyielding *la14-*. **3** *of persons* sullen, humourless, dull *la15*, *19-*, *local Bnf-Kcb*. **4** slow, sluggish, reluctant (to do something) *18-*, *now Fif WC*. **5** *of the weather* bleak, gloomy *la18-*, *now Fif Kcb*. **6** *of land* hard, barren *la18-*, *local Cai-Rox*.
adv severely, relentlessly, obstinately *15-e19*.
tak the dourles &c [*'dur(ə)lz*] take offence, take a huff *20-*, *now Ayr*. **~ly 1** resolutely, stubbornly *15-16*, *la19*. **2** sulkily, sullenly *la18-19*.
dour seed late-ripening oats *la18-e19*. [uncertain; appar F *dur* or L *dūrus* hard, though the vowel is not the normal development]
dous *see* DOOSE
dousane *see* DIZZEN
douse *see* DOUCE
dousoun *see* DIZZEN
dout *see* DOOT
douth [duθ; *S also* dʌuθ] *adj* **1** *of persons* dispirited, depressed *19-e20*, *chf S*. **2** *of places* gloomy, dreary, dark *19-e20*, *S*. [prob var of DOWF]
dovat *see* DIVOT
dove [dov] *vi* become drowsy, doze *19-*, *now Bnf Ags*.
dovie *adj* stupid *19-*, *Fif*. *n* a stupid-looking person *19-*, *now Fif*. [*cf* Norw *dova* (*v*) fall asleep, ON *dofinn* drowsy, OE *dofung* dotage, and *cf* DOVER]
dovekie &c [*?'dʌv(ə)kɪ*] *n* the black guillemot *19*. [only Sc; Eng *dove* + double dim *-ick*, *-ie*]

dover &c ['dovǝr] *vi* **1** *freq* ~ **ower &c** doze off, fall into a light sleep *19-*. **2** wander hesitatingly, walk unsteadily *19-e20*.
n a doze, a nap *19-*.
doverit &c sunk in light sleep *16*. [frequentative f as DOVE]
dover *see* DAOVER
dow¹ &c [dʌu] *vi, pt* **doucht &c** *la14-19*, **docht** *la15-e20* [doxt, *dʌxt] **1** *chf in negative* be of no value or use, not be worthwhile *la14-18*. **2** *chf in negative* be unable, not have the strength or ability (to do something) *la14-e20*. **3** *chf in negative* be unwilling, not have the strength of mind or courage (to do something), not to dare *18-e20*. **4** thrive, prosper *18-e19*.
~**less** feeble, lacking in strength or energy *la18-, now Stlg*. [ME]
dow² &c [dʌu] *vi* fade away, wither, become musty, *chf in adj* ~**it**, ~**ed** faded, withered, not fresh *17-, now Sh Abd*. [uncertain; cf eModEng *dowed* dulled]
dow³ [*dʌu] *adj* dismal, sad *19*. [prob shortened f DOWIE¹]
dow *see* DAE¹, DOO
dowand *see* DAE¹
dowariar &c *la16*, **dowarer &c** *16*, **dowriar &c** *la16*; **dowrier &c** *la16-17* [*du(ǝ)r(ɪ)ǝr] *n* a dowager *la16-17*. [only Sc; F *douairière*]
dowatt *see* DIVOT
dowbart *see* DULBERT
dowcat *see* DOO
dowchtir *see* DOCHTER
dowcot *see* DOO
dowf &c *18-, local Cai-Fif*, **dolf** *la15-e16*; **doof** *18-e20*, **douf &c** *la18-e20*, **doaf** *e19*, **duff** *la19-, now Sh Ork* [dʌuf; *Sh Ork* dʌf; *SW Uls* dof; *Arg* dɪf; *S* dǝf; *C also* *dǝf] *adj* **1** dull, spiritless; stupid; weary *la15-16, 18-, now local Bnf-Fif*. **2** sad, melancholy *18-, now Bnf Abd Fif*. **3** *of excuses* feeble, failing to carry conviction *la18-19*. **4** *of a sound* dull, hollow *la18-, now Bnf Abd Fif*. **5** *of ground* poor, infertile *19*. **6** *of a part of the body* numb, insensitive *19-, now Sh*.
n **1** a stupid or gloomy person *18-, now Ork Abd*. **2** a dull blow with something soft *19-, now Cai Bnf Abd*.
vti **1** strike with something soft, thump *19-, now Bnf Abd*. **2** *vt* bounce (a ball) *19-e20*.
dowfart &c *adj, verse* dull, spiritless; stupid *la18-e20*. *n* a dull stupid person *18-19*. **dowffie** *adj* dull, slow, stupid *19*; *n* a stupid person, a dolt *19-e20*. [see SND]
dowg *see* DOG
dowie¹ &c *la16-*, **dolly** *la15-16* ['dʌuɪ; *'dolɪ] *adj* **1** sad, dismal; dull, dispirited *la15-*. **2** ailing, weak, delicate *la19-, now local Bnf-Stlg*.
~**ly** sadly, mournfully *19-e20*. [obscure; cf DULLY]
dowie² *n* ~ **stane &c** name for one of the large granite stones deposited in the ice-age *e20, Dmf*. [obscure]

dowité *see* DUTY
dowle *see* DOOBLE
dowlet *see* DOUBLET
dowly &c [*'dʌulɪ] *adj* sad, doleful *la18-e20*. [ME; uncertain]
downe *see* DAE¹
dowriar, dowrier *see* DOWARIAR
dowt [dʌut, *Arg* dot] *n* a cigarette-end *20-, local C*. [Eng dial *dout* put out, extinguish (a fire), f *do + out*]
dowter, dowthir *see* DOCHTER
dowtit *see* DOIT²
doxie &c *n, verse* a sweetheart *19*. [obs or dial and chf disparaging in Eng]
doxy &c; duxy &c ['doksɪ, 'dʌksɪ] *adj, of persons and animals* lazy, slow *19-, Bnf Abd Ags*. [? f DOCK]
doyld *see* DOILT
doym *see* DOOM
doze; dose *19-e20 v* **1** *vi* = doze. **2** *vt* stupefy, stun *19-, now Ork Fif*. **3** *vti* spin (a top) so fast that it appears not to move; spin like a top *19-, now Fif; cf* SLEEP *v* 2.
dozed *of wood, cloth, rope etc* rotten *19-e20*.
dozen ['dozn] *vi* be or become cold or numb *18-19*. [back-formation f *dozened* (DOSINNIT)]
dozened *see* DOSINNIT
dozie *adj* stupid *20-, local Fif-Rox*.
n a stupid person *20-, Bwk SW Rox*. [reduced f *dozened* (DOSINNIT)]
drabble *19-, local Bnf-Arg*; **draible &c** *19-e20* ['drabl; *Fif Edb Dnbt Lnk* 'drebl] *vti* **1** = drabble. **2** *vt* dirty (one's clothes, boots etc) *19-, now Bnf Fif*. **3** *vti* spill *19-, now Bnf Abd Fif*. **4** *vi, of rain* drizzle *20-, Abd Ags*.
n **1** *chf in pl* spots of dirt, *esp* of liquid food spilt while eating *19-, local Bnf-Arg*. **2** *chf disparaging* a small quantity of liquid food *la19-, now Abd Fif*. **3** refuse, rubbish, *chf* anything too small for use *19-, now Ags*.
drabblich &c = *n, 19-e20*. **drabbly, drabblichy** *of the weather* showery, drizzly *20-, Bnf Abd*.
dracht *see* DRAUCHT
drack *see* DRAIK
draff &c *16-*, **draf &c** *la15-e17 n* = draff, dregs, the refuse of malt after brewing *la15-*.
~**ie &c** out of condition, unable to walk or run easily *20-, now Cai Ags*.
~ **pook &c** a sack for carrying DRAFF; *fig* an imperfection, a blemish *17-e19*.
draft *see* DRAUCHT
drag *n* **1** = drag. **2** a large heavy harrow *la19-*. **3** *also* **draig** the motion of the tide *la19-, now Sh Cai Fif*.
vti = drag.
never out (o) **the** ~ never finished *la19-, now Bnf Abd Fif*.
draggle, dragle *see* DRAIGLE
dragon, dragoun *see* DRAIGON
dragy &c [*'dredʒɪ, *'drɛdʒɪ] *n* = dragy, dredge, a kind of sweetmeat *14-16*.

~ **muskie** sweetmeats flavoured with musk *la16-e17*.

draible *see* DRABBLE

draidgy *see* DIRGIE

draif *see* DRAVE, DRIVE

draig *see* DRAG, DREG[1]

draigle *la16-*, *local*, **dragle** *e16*; **draggle** *19-e20 v* **1** *vt* = draggle, bedraggle (a garment etc) *16-*. **2** mix (flour, meal etc) with water *la19-*, *Bnf Abd*. **3** *vi* move slowly or wearily, *eg* through rain or mud *la16, 19-e20*.
n a dirty, untidy person *19-*, *now local Bnf-Edb*.
draigelt soaked through, drenched *20-*, *now Ork Ags Per*. **draggly** straggly, untidily dressed *e19*.

draigon *la19-*, **dragoun &c** *la14-16*; **dragon &c** *n* **1** = dragon *la14-*. **2** a paper kite *la18-*.
rais ~ commit devastation *la14*.

draik *la16-*, *now Bwk Arg*, **drake** *la16-19*, **drawk** *15-16, 20-*, *now S*; **drack** *e20 vt* drench, soak *15-*, *now Bwk Slk*.
drackie &c *of the weather* damp, wet, misty *19-e20*, *chf W*. [uncertain]

dram *n* = dram, the weight; a small drink of liquor *la16-*.
vi drink alcohol, tipple *19*.
be one's ~ pay one's share of the drinks *19-*, *now Ags Fif*.

dram *see* DRUM[1]

drame *see* DREAM

drammach *see* DRAMMOCK

drammlick *n*, *chf in pl* the small pieces of oatmeal dough which stick to the basin when making *oatcakes* (AIT) *la19-*, *now Abd*. [uncertain]

drammock &c *la16-*, *now local Abd-Kcb*; **drammach &c** *18-e20*, **drummock &c** *la18-e20* ['dramək, -əx; *WC, SW* 'drʌm-] *n* a mixture of raw oatmeal and cold water, CROWDIE[1] *la16-*, *local Abd-Kcb*. [Gael *dramag*]

drangle *see* DRING[2]

drant *see* DRAUNT

drap &c *la16-*, **drop &c** *n* **1** (1) = drop *la15-*; (2) *with omission of 'of'* = a drop of *19-*. **2** the dripping of water or the line down which it drops from the eaves of a house *16-*, *now Bnf-Ags Kcb*. **3** *in pl* small shot, pellets *17-*, *now local Bnf-Fif*. **4** ¹⁄₁₆th of an ounce *17-e19*. **5** a disappointment *20-*; *cf* DREEP *n* 6.
v **1** *vt* = drop *la15-*. **2** (1) *vti* stop (work) *19-*, *now Stlg SW*. (2) *impersonal* stop (raining) *20-*, *Bnf Abd Fif*. **3** *impersonal* rain slightly, drizzle *la19-*, *Bnf Abd Kcb*.
drop(ped) scone *see* SCONE. **a** ~**pie** a drink *19-*. **the** ~**pie** drink *19-*. **dropping** *n* dripping (from roasting meat), *chf* **dropping pan** a dripping pan *la16-17*. *adj* dripping; *of weather* showery *la18-*, *now local Cai-Fif*. **drappin drouth** a showery day during a dry spell *20-*, *now Ags Fif*. **drappit** rare, occasional *la19-*, *Bnf Abd*. **drappit egg** an egg poached in gravy

made from the liver of a fowl *la18-*, *now Abd*.
droppit *of material* spotted, speckled *16-17*.
~**py** showery, drizzly *19-*, *Bnf Abd*.
~**-ripe** *of fruit* ready to drop from ripeness *18-*, *now Ags*. ~ **wecht** = *n* 4, *la16-e17*.
have a ~ **at one's nose** have something waiting to be done of which one doesn't want to divulge details, *eg* the paying of a debt *20-*, *now Bnf Ags*. **no a** ~ **o his** *etc or* **no a drap's blude** ((a-)kin) not a blood-relation *19-*, *now local Bnf-Fif*.
~ **glasses** drop part of an egg-white into a glass of water in order to foretell the future *la19-*, *now Sh*.

dratch &c *19-*, *now Ags*, **drich &c** *la14-15* [dratʃ, *drɪtʃ, *drɛtʃ] *vti* delay, dawdle, move slowly and heavily. [ME *dreche*; obscure]

drate *see* DRITE

draucht &c; **dracht &c** *la15-17, 20-*, *now Cai*, **draft** *la18-*, *now Bnf Kcb Rox* [drɑxt; draft] *n* **1** = draught *15-*. **2** (1) a load *15-*, *local Sh-Ags*. (2) two or more cartloads brought at one time *la19-*, *now Bnf Abd*. **3** the process of drawing off water from a stream etc; a water channel or ditch *la15-e17, 19*. **4** a scheme, plot, plan *la15-e19*. **5** the entrails of an animal *la16-*, *now Mry Ags Kcb*. **6** *attrib*, *chf of sheep* withdrawn from the flock as being unfit for further breeding *la15-*, *now Bnf Kcb Rox*. **7** a convulsive gasping or choking *la19-*, *Bnf Abd Fif*.
vt **1** *chf* ~**it** *of a horse* broken in, harnessed for work *20-*, *Abd*. **2** line off (land) with the plough by means of straight furrows *20-*, *Cai Bnf Ags*.
deep-, far-, lang-drauchtit &c designing, crafty *19-e20*. ~**y** = prec *la18-19*.
~ **net** a net drawn to catch fish *15-16*. ~ **trumpet** a war trumpet or trumpeter *16*.

draunt &c; **drant** *vti* drawl, whine, drone *18-e20*.
n a slow, drawling way of speaking, a whine *18-e20*. [chf Sc; onomat]

drave &c; **draif &c** *la16-e17, la19*, **dreave &c** *la16-17 n* **1** = drove *16-*, *now Abd*. **2** the annual herring fishing *16-*, *now Fif Bwk*. **3** a shoal of fish; a catch *la16-e20*.
~ **boat &c** a herring boat *la16-e19*. [only Sc; OE *drāf* a drove, herd, crowd; *cf* DROVE]

drave *see* DRIVE

draw &c *v*, *pt also* **dreuch &c** *la14-e16* [*drjux; *Rox* driu] *ptp also* **drawin &c** *la14-17* [drɑn; *Bwk* dru(:)n] **1** *vti* = draw *la14-*. **2** *vt* ornament (a garment) with a different material *16*. **3** cart (a load) *19-*, *now Kcb*. **4** aim (a blow); raise (one's hand, foot etc) in attack *la18-*, *now Bnf Abd Kcb*. **5** *curling* (CURL) *and* bowls aim (a shot) carefully so as to land on a particular spot up at the TEE[1] *la18-*. **6** supply, produce *la18-*, *now Bnf*. **7** milk (a cow) *la19-*, *now Bnf Abd*. **8** *vi* ~ **to** (1) head for *19-*, *now Bnf Fif*; (2) come to like (someone) gradually *la19-*, *now Bnf Abd*

Fif. **9** *with pl subject* agree, get on together *19-*, now *Fif Lnk Kcb*. **10** *vti* infuse, become infused (1) *of tea* , *la18-*; (2) *of the teapot*, *19-*, *local*.
n 1 = draw. **2** a puff at a pipe, a smoke *la19-*. **3** *curling* (CURL) *and bowls* a shot played carefully so that it comes to rest on a particular spot *la19-*, now *local Bnf-Kcb*.
~**ing** a collection for charitable purposes *la20-*, *Fif.* ~**n length** *curling* (CURL) the force needed to bring a stone to the TEE[1] etc *la19-*, now *Kcb Lnk*. ~**n sheaf** a sheaf of straw selected by ~*ing strae* (see *draw strae*) *18-*, now *Sh Ork*.
~**-bed** a truckle bed, a low bed on wheels *la16-e18*. ~**-boord &c** ? an extending table *e17*. ~**-dyk** a ditch for drawing off water *la15-16*. ~**-kiln &c** a lime-kiln in which the burned lime is drawn at the bottom *la18-*, now *Edb*. ~ **moss** the harestail cotton-grass *la19-e20*.
~ **in borrowgang** *etc* put (land, oneself etc) in pledge, offer as security *la14-15*. ~ **a body's leg** pull someone's leg *la19-*, *N midLoth SW*. ~ **strae** *etc: thatching etc* pull straw through the hands so that pieces short of the required length fall to the ground *la18-*, now *Sh Abd SW*. ~ **straes** draw lots with straws; draw conclusions *20-*, *Ork Cai Abd*. ~ **straes** *or* **a strae afore someone's een** *etc* tease, make fun of someone; deceive someone *la15-*, now *Sh Cai*. ~ **the door on yer** *etc* **back** shut the door behind you etc *19-*, now *Abd Fif Stlg*. ~ **thegither** *of the eyes* close in sleep *19-*, now *Abd Fif*. ~ **to rain** be likely to rain *19-*. ~ **up** become friendly (**with**), get to know *18-*, now *Ags Fif*.
drawk *see* DRAIK
drawlie &c *adj* slow and slovenly *e19*. [*cf* obs Eng *drawl* move along at a loitering pace]
dray *see* DRY
dre *see* DREE[1]
dreaddour &c *la16-e17*, *e19*, **dredour &c** *la15-19*; **dridder &c** *la16-19* [*'dridur, -ər, *'drıdər, *nEC* *'drıðər] *n* **1** ~ **of** (1) fear or dread of *la15-e19*; (2) fear on account of or for *la15-e17*. **2** fear, dread, apprehension, distrust *la15-19*.
vti fear, dread; hesitate *la18-19*. [only Sc; DREID + *-our* after ME, OSc *horrour* etc]
dream &c *16-*, **dreme &c** *15-16*, **drame** *e16*, *la19-* (now *Ork nEC*) [drim; *Sh-Nai nEC Wgt* drem] *n*, *vti* = dream *15-*.
~**ing bread** wedding or christening cake, so-called because the recipients slept with a piece under their pillow *la18-19*.
dreary *adj* = dreary.
drearifu, ~**some** sad, dreary *la18-*, *local Bnf-Edb*.
dreave *see* DRAVE
dred(d), **drede** *see* DREID
dredge box *n* a flour-dredger *19*.
dredgie *see* DIRGIE
dredour *see* DREADDOUR
dree[1] *la16-*, **dre** *la14-e17*; **drey** *la14-e16*, **drie**

la16-e19 [dri] *v* **1** *vt* endure, suffer (pain, misfortune etc) *la14-*. **2** pass, spend (time) miserably, drag out (an existence) *18-19*. **3** *vi* endure, last or hold out, continue *la14-e16*, *19-e20*.
n trouble, misfortune *la18-e20*.
~ **one's** (**ain**) *or* **a sore** *etc* **weird** endure one's fate, suffer a hard etc fate; suffer the consequences of something *19-*. [ME *v* and (once) *n*; OE *drēogan* suffer, endure]
dree[2] *vt* suspect; fear *19-*, now *Ags*. [reduced f DREID]
dree *see* DREICH
dreeble *see* DRIBBLE
dreel, **dreill** *e17*, *la19* [dril] *vti* **1** = drill, exercise; bore *17-*. **2** *vi*, *of things* move rapidly *la18-*, *local Cai-Fif*. **3** *of persons* work quickly and smoothly *la18-*, now *Cai*. **4** *vt* drive with force, hustle *la18-*, now *Ork*. **5** scold, rebuke *19-*, *local*.
n **1** = drill, exercise; a boring tool. **2** energy, forcefulness *la18-*, now *Ags*. **3** a scolding, a dressing-down *19-*, *local Cai-Ags*.
dreep *la17-*, **drepe &c** *15-19* *vti* **1** = drip *15-*. **2** *vt* drain, strain (*chf* potatoes after boiling) *19-*. **3** *vti* descend from (a wall etc) by letting oneself down to the full stretch of the arms and dropping *la19-*.
n **1** = drip. **2** the line down which water drips from the eaves *la19-*, *Bnf Abd Ags Fif*. **3** a steady fall of light rain *20-*, *Abd Fif*. **4** a wet, dripping condition, *eg* with sweat *19-*, now *Bnf Abd Fif*. **5** a game of marbles in which each player tries to hit and win an opponent's marbles *e20*. **6** a disappointment *20-*, *Cai Fif*. **7** a channel or groove, *esp* one cut for drainage *la20-*, *local C*.
dreeper a sloping board etc used for draining in several different processes *la18-*. **dreepin** *n* a drink (of liquor etc) *19*. *adj* soaking wet *20-*.
~**in drought** a showery day during a spell of dry weather *20-*, *Abd Ags*. ~**ing roast, dripping roast** a constant source of income *19-*.
dreepit = *dreepin* (*adj*), *la19-*. **dreeple, dripple** *n* (*20-*, *Sh Ags*), *vi* (*19-*, now *Abd*) drip, trickle.
Sammy ~ a 'drip', a spiritless, ineffective person *20-*, *local Bnf-Kcb*.
dreetle *see* DRIDDLE
dreeve *see* DRIVE
dreg[1] **&c**; **draig** *19-* *n* **1** *also* **drig**, *chf* in *pl* = dregs *15-*. **2** *chf* ~ **wine** inferior wine made from the marc of grapes *la16-17*. **3** *distilling* the refuse of malt from the still *18-e20*. **4** a small quantity, a drop (*chf* of spirits) *19-*, now *Fif*.
~**gle &c** *19-e20*, ~**lin** *19-*, now *Fif* = *n* 4.
dreg[2] *vti* dredge (shellfish etc) *16-17*, *19-e20*.
~ **boat** a fishing-boat using a drag-net *la15-e18*. [only Sc; *cf* Eng *dredge* and perh *drag*]
dreg[3] *n* **1** haulage *la16*. **2** = drag *la17-*, now *Ayr*.
vti = drag *e20*.
dregy *see* DIRGIE
dreich &c; **dree** *la18-e20* [drix; *'dri] *adj* **1** dreary, long-lasting, persistent; tiresome, hard

to bear *15-*. **2** *of time, journeys etc* long, wearisome *18-*. **3** *of sermons, speeches etc* long-winded; dry, uninteresting *17-*. **4** *of the weather, scenery etc* dreary, bleak *la16-*. **5** *of persons* (1) slow; backward; tardy *la18-e20*; (2) slow to pay debts *18-*, *now Ags Per*; (3) depressed, doleful, dull, boring *19-*. **6** *of tasks etc* difficult, requiring close attention *19-*, *now Abd*.
~ **a** *or* **in drawin(g)** *etc* slow to move, slow in deciding *la18-*, *now Abd*. **on** ~ at or to a distance *15-16*. **the deid** ~ *of ground* the dead level *16-*. [ME *dregh*, *dre(i)ȝ*]
dreid *la15-16*, *la19-*, **drede** *la14-16* [drid] *vtir*, *pt also* **dred(d)** *&c la14-16, 19* **1** = dread *la14-*. **2** *vir* be in doubt *la15-e16*. **3** *vt* suspect, fear *la18-*.
n = dread *la14-*.
ill ~ grave suspicion, apprehension *19-*, *local Cai-Fif*.
dreill *see* DREEL
drekters *n* ? a drake's penis *la15*. [Eng *drake* + eModEng *terse, tarse* the penis]
dreme *see* DREAM
drenk *see* DRINK
drepe *see* DREEP
dress &c, dres *la14-e17*; **drese** *16 vtir* **1** = dress *la14-*. **2** *vt* arrange (affairs etc), bring to a satisfactory state or conclusion *la15-e17*. **3** cut and smooth (stone), prepare for building *16-*. **4** iron (linen) *19-*, *local Cai-Fif*. **5** prepare (a web) for the loom with a starch made from flour etc *18-e20*. **6** neuter (a cat) *20-*.
n **1** = dress *16-*. **2** settling, arranging, negotiating *la16*. **3** a settlement, an arrangement, steps towards settling or arranging *la16-e17*, *only Sc*.
~**ing iron** a smoothing iron *la17-19*. ~**ory &c** a room in which food is dressed *e16*, *only Sc*.
dreuch *see* DRAW
drevel &c [*'drivl] *vi* live miserably; feel feeble and wretched *e16*. [*cf* Eng *drivel*]
drevin *see* DRIVE
drey *see* DREE[1]
drib[1] *n* **1** a drop, a small quantity of liquid or semi-liquid *18-*, *now Bnf Abd Fif*. **2** *in pl* dregs *18-19*.
vt extract the last drops of milk from (a cow) *la19-*, *now Bnf Abd*. [chf dial in Eng]
drib[2] *vt* **1** beat, thrash *20-*, *Bnf Abd*. **2** scold *la19-*, *now Bnf*. [prob var of Eng *drub*; *cf* Norw dial *dribba* thump, strike against something]
dribble, dreeble *e20 vti* **1** = dribble. **2** tipple, drink *la18-*, *now Ags*. **3** *vi* drizzle *19-*, *local*.
n **1** a slight trickle; a drop, *chf* of alcohol *la17-*, *local*. **2** a drizzle *la18-*, *now Bnf Abd Fif*.
dribblach ['drıbləx] = *n* 1, *la19-*, *Bnf Abd*.
dribbly beards &c: curly *kail* (CURLIE) boiled in fat broth *18-e20*.
drich *see* DRATCH
dridder *see* DREADDOUR
driddle &c; druttle &c *19-e20*, **dreetle** *la19-e20* ['drıdl, 'drıtl; *Bnf Ags also* 'dritl; *local C also* 'dridl] *v* **1** *vi* walk slowly or uncertainly;

dawdle, saunter *la18-*, *now Sh*. **2** potter, idle, waste time *19-*, *now Abd Ayr*. **3** *vti* (1) spill, dribble, let fall through carelessness *19-e20*. (2) *specif* urinate in small quantities *19-*. **4** play the fiddle, strum *19-e20* [see SND].
n **1** an awkward, helpless person *19-e20*. **2** a small quantity of something *la19-*, *now Abd Ags*.
dridland suffering from diarrhoea *la16*. [onomat, w infl f DRIBBLE, DIDDLE[1]]
drie *see* DREE[1]
drien *see* DRIVE
drieshach ['driʃəx] *n* the glowing embers of a PEAT[1] fire *19-*, *now Abd*. [f Gael *griosach* burning embers]
drife *see* DRIVE
driffle &c *v* **1** *vi* drizzle, rain or snow lightly *e17*, *19-e20, Gall Rox*. **2** *vti* put off (time) *la16*. **3** *vt* scold *la19-*, *now Bnf Abd*.
n **1** a slight shower of rain or snow *19-*, *now Dmf*. **2** a scolding *la19-*, *Bnf Abd*. **3** a gale, a strong wind *20-*, *now Bnf Abd*. [*cf* eModEng *drifle* produce slowly, Norw dial *drivla* drizzle]
drift &c *n* **1** = drift *la15-*. **2** a drove, flock, herd *la15-e19*. **3** delay, procrastination *la16-e17*. **4** falling snow driven by the wind *la16-*. **5** a set of fishing-nets suspended from a cable and allowed to drift with the tide *19*.
vti **1** = drift. **2** *vt* subject (a person etc) to delay *la16-e17*. **3** delay (to do etc) *la16*.
~**y** snowy *18-e20*.
~ **time** delay, make delays *la16-17*.
drig *see* DREG[1]
dring[1] &c *vi* sing in a slow, droning way *18-19*. [prob onomat]
dring[2] *vi* loiter, delay *19-e20*.
n a lazy person *la18-e20*.
dringle *19-*, **drangle** *la18-19* ['drıŋl; *'draŋl] *vi* saunter, dawdle *la18-*, *now Ork* [*cf* Norw dial *drigla, drangla* drag oneself along]. [uncertain]
dring[3] *n* a poor or miserly person *16*. [only Sc; prob f OSc and ME *dreng* a free tenant]
drink &c; drenk *la15, la19-e20* [drıŋk; *Fif* drəıŋk] *n* = drink *la14-*.
vti, ptp **drunken &c** *15-17, 20-, Bnf Abd*, **drukken &c** *la15-e19* [ON *drukkin*, ptp of *drekka* drink; *cf* DRUCKEN and DRUNKEN] = drink *la14-*.
~ **siller &c** a gratuity given to be spent on drink *la15-*, *now Abd Stlg*.
~ **in** *of the day* draw in *20-*, *Cai Bnf Abd*.
drint &c *pt, ptp* drenched, drowned *e16*. [ME *drente, dreinte*, pt, ptp of *drench*]
dripping roast, dripple *see* DREEP
drite &c, dryte &c; drate &c *la19-* [drəit; *Sh Ork also* drıt; *Cai NE also* dret] *vti, pt* **drate &c** *la16-*. *ptp* **drate** *la18*, **dritten &c** *20-*, *local* defecate *16-*.
n, chf as term of abuse dirt, excrement *la19-*, *now Bnf Abd Kcdn Edb*. [ME *drite*, OE *drītan*; *cf* DIRT]
drive &c; drife &c *la14-16 vti, pt also* **draif &c** *15-16*, **drave &c** *15-*, **dreeve &c** *la19-*, *NE*

[drev; *NE* also driv; *Lnk Kcb* also drɪv; *Uls* also drʌv]. *ptp also* **drevin &c** *15-e17*; **drien &c** *la18-e20* [*'driv(ə)n, *'dri(ə)n] **1** = drive *la14-*.
2 *vt, freq* ~ **ower** pass (time) idly, live out (one's life, days etc), spend (time) *la14-e19*. **3** break or smash by force, burst open *la15-19*. **4** *vti, golf* strike (the ball) for a distance shot, *now esp* in playing off the TEE[1] *la15-*. **5** throw with force or speed *19*.
n **1** = drive. **2** a forceful blow (at a person) *19*.
driver 1 = driver. **2** *specif, curling* (CURL) *and bowls* the SKIP[2], *19*.
~ **swine** *or* **pigs** snore loudly *20-, now local Ork-Kcb*.

drizzen &c *vi, chf of cows* make a low plaintive sound *la18-, now Abd*. [only Sc; *cf* MDu *druysschen* emit a hollow, roaring sound]

drob *vt* prick with a sharp instrument *19*. [only Sc; onomat]

droch *see* DROICH

drocht *see* DROUTH

drod &c *n* a short, thickset person *19-, now Rox*. [obscure]

droddum &c *n* the buttocks *la18-, now Bnf Abd Ags*.

dress someone's ~ punish someone, give someone a thrashing *la18-e20*. [prob f DROD]

drog; droig &c *la16-e17*, **drogue** *la17, 20-, now Fif* [drog; *Cai* drʌug] *n* **1** = drug *la15-, now local Bnf-Kcdn*. **2** a kind of SWEETIE, made of spices etc *16-e17*.
droggie &c *la19-, Abd Fif*, **droggist** *la17, 19-, now Cai Abd Kcdn* (nickname for) a druggist.

drogget &c *17-19*, **drogat &c** *la16-17, e20*; **droggit &c** *la16-18*, **drugget &c** *la19-* *n* = drugget, a coarse woollen cloth *la16-*.
~ **scone** an oatmeal and potato SCONE *20-, now Dmf*.

droich, dorche *la15*; **droch &c** *la16, 19-* [droix; *NE Fif Loth Lnk* drox; *Per Rox* *drix; *dorx] *n* a dwarf, a person of stunted growth *16-, now local*.

drochle &c ['droxl; *Cai* 'droixl] *n* **1** a short dumpy person, a puny insignificant person *19-, now local Cai-Fif*. **2** a fat dumpy animal, small of its kind *la19-, Bnf Abd*. *vi* walk slowly and feebly taking small steps *la19-, Bnf Abd*. **drochlin &c 1** puny, dwarfish *la18-, now Bnf Abd*. **2** lazy *19-, now Bnf Abd*. [only Sc; perh metath f DWERCH; Gael also has *droich*]

droig *see* DROG

drokin *see* DRUCKEN

drone[1] &c *vi* talk in a monotonous tone, make a low, continuous, buzzing sound *16-*.
n **1** = drone, a monotonous buzzing; a bass pipe of a bagpipe *16-*. **2** a bagpipe *e16, la18-e19*.
droner a bumble-bee *la19-, Bnf Ags*.

drone[2] *n* the buttocks, the backside *la18-, now Ags*. [only Sc; Gael *dronn*]

dronkin *see* DRUNKEN

droog *v, chf* **droogled** drenched, soaked *20-, now Bnf Abd*. [var of DROUK]

drook *see* DROUK

drool[1] *vi* utter or sound mournfully *19-e20, S*. [Eng *droul* (*vt*) *la17*]

drool[2] &c *n* a lazy person *19-e20*. [uncertain]

droon *la19-*, **droun &c** *vti, ptp also* **droondit** *20-, local* = drown *la14-*.
~ **the miller 1** dilute *chf* alcohol with too much water *la19-*. **2** (cause to) go bankrupt *19-e20*.

droosy &c ['druzɪ] *adj* = drowsy *19-e20*.

drooth *see* DROUTH

drop *see* DRAP

dross &c *n* **1** = dross *16-*. **2** small coal, coaldust *la19-*. [*cf* DRUSH]

droucht *see* DROUTH

droud &c [drʌud] *n* a codfish, *chf* one of poor quality *19-, now Arg*. [unknown]

drouk &c; drook *la19-* [druk] *v* **1** *vt, chf* **droukit &c** drenched, soaked; steeped *16-*. **2** *vi, chf* **droukin &c** dripping with moisture *la19-, now Stlg*.
n a drenching, soaking *19-, now Ags Fif*.
~**it stour** mud *20-, now Ags*. **drookle** drench, soak *20-, Sh Bnf Fif*. [obscure; *cf* DROOG]

droun *see* DROON

drouth &c; drocht *la19-*; **drooth** *20-*, **droucht &c** *16-e17, e20* [druθ; *Cai Mry* droxt; *NE* drʌxt; *Kcb* druxt] *n* **1** = drought, prolonged or extreme dry weather; drying breezy weather *la15-e20*. **2** *chf* **drouth &c** thirst *16-*. **3** *only* **drouth &c** a drunk, a habitual drinker *la19-*.
drouchtit parched *20-, now Bnf Abd Kcb*. **drouchty** dry *20-, Bnf Abd*. **drouthy 1** *of the weather* dry *la16-e20*. **2** thirsty, addicted to drinking *la18-*.

drove *n* **1** *chf* ~ **road** a road or track used for driving cattle or sheep to markets *18-, latterly hist*. **2** a stonemasons' broad-faced chisel *19-, now Cai Bnf Abd*. **3** = drove, a flock, crowd.
vti **1** drive (cattle or sheep), be a drover *17-19*. **2** *vt* prepare stone for building using a DROVE *n* 2, *la18-, now Abd*.
droving driving (of cattle) *17-19*. [*cf* DRAVE]

drow[1] &c [drʌu] *n* a cold, wet mist, a drizzle *17-, now Bwk Rox*.
vi misty, drizzling, damp *19-e20*.
~**ie** misty, drizzling, damp *19-e20*.
Liddisdale ~ a wetting drizzle *19-e20, Rox*. [only Sc; obscure]

drow[2] &c [drʌu] *n* an attack of illness, a fainting fit; a spasm of anxiety *la16, 19-, now Abd Ags Fif*. [only Sc; obscure]

drowiar *see* DROWRIAR

drowlack &c [*'drʌulək] *n* a seat with a rope attached for letting a man down over a precipice *19-e20, Bnf*. [Gael *drolag* a swing]

drowriar &c, drowiar [*'drurɪər] *n* a dowager *16*. [only Sc; altered f DOWARIAR]

drowry &c [*'dru(ə)rɪ] *n* = druery, love, a love-token *la14-16*.

drowry *see* DRURIE

drub *vt* **1** = drub. **2** scold, abuse *la19-*, *Abd Ags Fif.*

drucken &c *17-*, **drukkin** &c *16-e17*; **drokin** &c *16-17 adj* drunken *16-*.

~**some** &c inclined to drink too much *la16, 19*. [only Sc; ON *drukkinn* (*ptp*) drunken; *cf* DRUNKEN and *drukken* (DRINK)]

drug &c [drʌg; *Cai* drug] *vti* pull forcibly, drag *15-16, 18-*, now *Cai Abd Kcb*.

n a rough pull, a tug *la18-*, now *Cai*.

adj, curling (CURL), *of slightly thawed ice* dragging, slow *19-*, *Fif SW*. [ME *drugge*]

drugget *see* DROGGET

drukkin *see* DRUCKEN

drum[1] *18-e20*, **dram** &c *16-19 adj* sad, dejected, sulky. [only Sc; obscure]

drum[2] &c *n* **1** = drum *la16-*. **2** the cylindrical part of a threshing machine *19-*.

~**-fu** as tight as a drum, full (of food) *la19-*, *Abd Ags Fif.*

~ **major** *n* a domineering woman *19-*. *vt* 'boss', order around *20-*, now *Abd Edb*.

drum[3] *n* **1** a long narrow ridge or knoll *la18-*, now *Per*, *freq in place-names*. **2** *in pl* an area of ridged land intersected by marshy hollows *19-*, *Gall.*

~**lin** = *n*, *esp* a long whaleback mound of glacial deposit, often occurring in groups in low-lying areas *la19-* [now geol term in St Eng].

drumeheid the head of a ridge *e17*. [Sc and IrGael *druim* the ridge of a hill]

drumble *see* DRUMLE

drumblie *see* DRUMLIE

drumle &c *17-*, now *Rox*, **drumble** *17-e19 vti*, *also fig* make or be muddy or disturbed *17-*, now *Rox.*

n mud raised when water is disturbed *19-e20*, *S*. [prob back-formation f DRUMLIE]

drumlie &c, **drumly** &c, **drumblie** &c *17-e19 adj* **1** (1) *of streams or water* troubled, clouded, muddy *16-*. (2) *of liquor* full of sediment *la18-19*. **2** *of the weather* cloudy, gloomy *16-*. **3** *fig* troubled, disturbed, muddled, confused *17-*, now *Rox*. [only Sc; var of OSc and ME *drubly*]

drummock *see* DRAMMOCK

drummoid &c [drʌ'moid] *adj* dull, dejected *20-*, *Cai Ross*. [altered f DRUMMURE and DEMUIRED]

drummure &c [*'drʌ'm(j)ur] *adj*, *of persons* serious, sad-looking, dejected *19-*, now *Cai*. [f Eng *demure* (*cf* DEMUIRED), perh w infl f DRUM[1]]

drumshorlin [*drʌm'ʃorlɪn] *adj* sulky; having an uncared-for or miserable appearance *19-e20*, *Lnk*. [obscure; prob DRUM[1] + ?]

drunkart &c *la15-e20*, **drunkat** &c *16-e17 n* = drunkard, *only Sc*.

drunken &c *17-*, **drunkin** &c *la14-e17*; **dronkin** &c *la15-e17 adj* = drunken, addicted to drink *la14-*.

~**some** given to drunkenness *la15-*, *e19*. [*cf* DRINK and DRUCKEN]

drunt &c *n*, *chf in pl* the sulks, a fit of ill-humour *19-*, now *Rox*.

take (**the**) ~(**s**) take the huff *19-e20*. [uncertain]

Druntin &c Trondheim, Norway *18-e20*, *only Sc.*

drurie &c *19* (*ballad*), **drowry** &c *la15-16* [*'dru(ə)rɪ] *n* a dowry. [altered f Eng *dowry*, w infl f DROWRY]

drush &c [drʌʃ] *n* powdery waste, *esp* of PEAT[1] *18-*, now *Bnf Abd*. [*cf* DROSS]

druttle *see* DRIDDLE

dry &c; **dray** *la16-17 adj* (*la14-*), *vti* (*15-*) = dry.

n a flaw or crack in a stone *19-*, now *Abd Edb*.

~**achty** *of the weather* inclined to be dry *20-*, *Bnf Abd*. ~**ster** the person in charge of the drying of grain in a kiln *la15-*, now *Cai Abd*.

~ **burrow** &c a BURGH not situated on the coast *la16-17*. ~ **drift** powdery snow *la19-*, now *Abd Ags Fif*. ~ **dyke** = ~**-stane dyke**, *19-*; ~ **dyker** = ~**-stane dyker**, *19-*. ~ **field** land above the flood level, *esp* in the Forth and Tay valleys *la18-e20*. ~**-haired** *of cattle which have been exposed to the weather* not sleek-coated, having a rough, dry coat *19-*, now *Bnf Abd*. ~ **keep** cattle feed consisting of turnips and straw *20-*, *Cai Abd*. ~ **lodging** lodging without board *la18-e19*. ~**-mou'd** not drinking, not having a glass of liquor *19-*, now *Bnf Abd Fif*. ~ **multure** *law* an annual duty of money or grain paid to a mill, whether the grain was ground there or not *18-e20*. ~ **seat** a commode *17-e19*. ~ **shave** the rubbing of another's cheek with an unshaven chin or with the fingers *20-*. ~ **siller** hard cash *la19-*, *Bnf Abd Fif*. ~ **stane(s)** &c (*16-*), ~ **stones** (*18-*) stones built up without mortar, now *chf* ~**-stane** &c **dyke** a stone wall built without mortar (*18-*), ~**-stane dyker** a person who builds such walls (*la19-*). ~ **stool** &c = ~ seat, *la16-e18*. ~ **tapstar** &c a retailer of ale who does not brew it *la15-e17*. ~ **time** a spell of dry weather *20-*, *Bnf Abd*. ~ **ware 1** goods packed in barrels for transport by sea *16-17*. **2** the cask into which the goods were packed *16-e17*.

dryte *see* DRITE

du *see* DAE[1], THOU

dub[1], **doub** &c *la16* [dʌb; *dɪb] *n* **1** a pool, *esp* of muddy or stagnant water; a pond *la15-e20*. **2** *also* **dib** &c *la18-e20* a small pool, *esp* of rain water, a puddle *la15-*. **3** *also* **dib** *la18-19*, *joc* the ocean *la18-*, now *Ags Fif*. **4** a sea pool (*esp* one only visible at low tide) *19-*, now *Fif Bwk*. **5** *chf in pl* mud *18-e20*, *N*.

vt cover with mud; bedaub *19-*, now *Bnf Abd*.

~**bie** muddy *19-*, now *Bnf Abd*.

~-**skelper** a person who travels rapidly regardless of the state of the roads *18-*, *now Bnf Fif.* ~-**water** dirty water *18-*, *now Fif.* [MLowGer, LowGer, WFrisian *dobbe*; also in northern ModEng dial]

dub² *vt* consign, condemn *e16.* [obscure]

duble *see* DOOBLE

dublet *see* DOUBLET

ducat *see* DOO

duchall &c [*'duxəl] ~ **quhite** *of hose* of some light-coloured material *e16.* [unknown]

duchas &c [*'duxəs] *n* the possession of land on which one's ancestors have lived *18-e19, Highl.* [Gael *dù(th)chas* place of one's birth; hereditary right]

duchtie *see* DOUCHTY

duck *see* DEUK

dud *n* **1** *chf in pl* ragged clothes, rags, tatters *16-.* **2** *chf in pl* = duds, clothes *18-.* **3** a coarse linen or cotton cloth used for domestic purposes, *eg* **daily dud** a dish-cloth, **hand dud** a coarse towel *la18-*, *chf Abd.* **4** *fig, contemptuous* a dull, spiritless person *19.*

duddie ragged, tattered *18-.* **Dudsday &c** applied to various *hiring markets* (HIRE) *19-e20, Ayr*; see SND.

dudderon &c *18-e19*, **duddroun** *e16* *n* a slut, a lazy, slovenly person. [only Sc; obscure]

dude *see* DAE¹

dudgit *n* a clumsy parcel or pack *20-, Bnf Abd.* [var of DILGIT and DULSHET prob conflated w Eng *budget*]

Dudsday *see* DUD

due *17-*, **dew** *la15-17* [dju, dʒu] *adj* (*la16-*), *n* (*la16-*) = due.

dew service &c service required from, or rendered by a tenant to a SUPERIOR *16-e17* [*cf* DESERVICE, DO-SERVICE]. ~ **sober** quite sober *la19-, now Kcb.*

be ~ *of persons* be indebted, owe *18-.*

due *see* DAE¹

duff¹ *vi* draw out of an undertaking *20-, Rox.* [*cf* colloq Eng = cheat]

duff² **&c** *n* a soft spongy substance, *chf* PEAT¹, moss etc *19-, now Sh.*

~**ie** **1** soft, spongy *19-, now Sh Fif.* **2** *of coal* soft, inferior *19-, now Edb.* ~**tin** a soft, crumbly, inferior PEAT¹ *la19-e20, Abd.*

~ **mould** = *n*, *19-, chf Sh.* [northern ModEng dial = coal-dust; Eng var of *dough*]

duffie *n* a W.C. *la19-, now eLoth Bwk S.*

duff *see* DOWF

duffat *see* DIVOT

dug *see* DOG

duggeoun &c [*'dʌdʒun, *-ən] *n* = dudgeon, a kind of wood *16-e17.*

dughtie *see* DOUCHTY

duig *see* DEWG

duik *see* DUKE

duill *see* DOOL¹

duir *see* DOOR

duist *see* JUIST

duité *see* DUTY

duke *la15-*; **duk &c** *la14-17*, **duik &c** *16-e17* [*'døk, *dʌk, *djuk, &c] *n* = duke.

duke *see* DEUK

dukerie &c [*'døk(ə)rɪ, &c] *n* a dukedom *la16.*

duk *see* DUKE

dulapse *n* a second offence against church discipline *la18.* [L *du-* two- + Eng *lapse*; *cf* TRILAPSE, QUADRULAPSE, RELAPSE]

dulbert &c *19-*, **dowbart** *e16* ['dʌlbərt, *'dubərt] *n* a stupid person, a fool *e16, 19-, SW.* [Eng *dull* (*adj*) + perh *beard*; *cf* colloq Ger *dummbart*]

dulcorate &c *adj, of the voice* endowed with sweetness *16.* [only Sc; L *dulcōrāt-*, ptp stem of *dulcōrāre* sweeten]

dule *see* DOOL¹, DOOL²

dulget *see* DILGIT

dull &c *adj* **1** = dull *la15-.* **2** *also* ~ **o hearing** *18-* deaf, hard of hearing *e16, 18-.* *vti* = dull *15-.*

dully *adj* doleful, gloomy, dismal *la15-16.* [only Sc; *cf doly* (DOOL¹) and *dolly* (DOWIE)]

dulmond *see* DINMONT

dulshet, dulshoch ['dʌlʃət, -ʃəx] *n* a small or untidy bundle *19-, Bnf Abd.* [only Sc; *cf* DILGIT and DUDGIT]

dult *n* **1** = dolt *la18-, now Renfr Lnk Kcb.* **2** the pupil at the bottom of the class *19-, now Gsw.*

dult *see* DOOL²

dumb *18-*, **dum** *la14-17 adj* = dumb *la14-.*

dummie &c a dumb person *la16-.*

~**fooner &c** [dʌm'funər] = dumbfounder, flabbergast, *chf* ~**t &c** *la19-.*

Dumbarton: D~ **youth** a person (*usu* a woman) over thirty-five years old *e19.* [the town on the Clyde]

dume *see* DOOM

Dumf familiar name for the Dunfermline College of Physical Education after it left Dunfermline *20-.* [orig sited in Dunfermline, Fife, later in Aberdeen, now in Edinburgh]

dumfooner *see* DUMB

dumfoutter &c [dʌm'futər] *vt* bewilder, nonplus, *chf* ~**t &c** *19-, Bnf Abd.* [conflation of *dumfooner* (DUMB) w FOUTER]

Dumfries and Galloway (Region) a REGION formed from the former counties of Dumfries, Kirkcudbright and Wigtown *la20-.*

dummie *see* DUMB

dump¹ *v* **1** *vt* beat, thump, kick *la16-, now local Ags-Kcb.* **2** *vi* walk with short, heavy steps, stump **about** *19-, now Kcb.*

n a blow, a thump, a thud *19-, now Abd.*

adv thump, thud *19-, now Bnf Stlg Kcb.*

~**er** **1** *mining* a tool for keeping a borehole circular *la19-.* **2** a tool used in paving roads, a rammer *la19-, C.*

gie someone his *or* **get one's dumps** give or get thumps on the back as a birthday ritual, the number of thumps corresponding to the age reached *20-*, *now Loth Dnbt*. [ME = throw or fall heavily]

dump² *n* a hole scooped in the ground for playing marbles; *in pl* the game of marbles *19-*, *Ags Rox*.
~y = *n*, *19-e20*. [*cf* Yorkshire dial = a deep hole, Norw = a depression in the ground]

dumpling *n* **1** a kind of rich, boiled or steamed fruit pudding *la19-*; cf *clootie dumpling* (CLOOT¹). **2** = dumpling.

dumpy &c *n* **1** = dumpy, a short thickset person *e19*. **2** one of a breed of short-legged fowl *la19*.

dun &c [dun] *n* a small stone-walled defensive homestead of the iron age, *freq* situated on an isolated site, found *chf* in western and central Scotland; in general use as an archaeological term *la18-*, *in place-names la17-*. [ScGael *dùn*, IrGael *dún* a fort, a fortification]

Dunbar [dʌn'bar] **weather &c** *n* a salted herring *la18-e20*. [the eLoth coastal town + Eng *wether*]

dunch *la18-e20*, **dunche &c** *la17*; **dunsh &c** *la17*, *19-e20* [dʌnʃ] *vti* **1** punch, thump, bump, nudge *la17*. **2** *of animals* butt *la18-*, *now Fif Kcb*. *n* **1** a blow, a bump, a nudge *19-*. **2** a butt from an animal *la19-*, *now Kcb*.
~ach ['dʌnʃəx] **1** a heavy blow, a thud *la19-*, *now Abd*. **2** a large, untidy bundle of rags etc *la19-*, *Bnf Abd*. [ME; uncertain]

dundee *see* DINDEE
dunder *see* DUNNER
dune *see* DAE¹
dung *see* DING

dungeon *la16-*, **dungeoun &c** *la14-16* *n* **1** = dungeon *la14-*. **2** *fig* a person of great knowledge, *chf* ~ **o learnin** *18-*, *local Bnf-Kcb*.

dungstead *n* a MIDDEN, dunghill *19-*, *now Kcb*. [only Sc; Eng *dung* + *-stead*]

duniwassal &c [*'dunɪˌwasl, *'dʌnɪ-] *n* a *clansman* (CLAN) of rank below the chief; a gentleman of secondary rank *la16-*, *latterly hist*. [Gael *duin(e)-uasal* a gentleman, f *duine* a man + *uasal* noble, well-born]

dunk &c *16-e20*, **donk &c** *la15-e19*; **dank** *19-* *adj* = dank, damp, moist *15-e20*.
n moisture, a mouldy dampness *16-e20*.
vt = dank, make damp or wet *16*.
~y &c damp, moist, wettish *16*, *19-e20*.

dunkle &c *vt* dent, make a slight depression in *19-*, *now Kcb*.
n a dent or slight depression *19-*, *now Ayr*. [dim and frequentative of DUNT]

Dunlop &c [dʌn'lop] ~ **cheese** a kind of *sweet-milk cheese* (SWEET²) *orig* made in west-central Scotland *la18-*. [the Ayrshire village]

dunmont *see* DINMONT

dunner &c; **dunder** *19-e20* ['dʌnər; *Abd also* 'dɪnər; *Sh Ork Cai Uls* 'dʌndər] *vi* **1** make a noise like thunder, rumble, thump, bang *la18-*. **2** move quickly and noisily *la18-e20*, *S*.

n **1** a loud rumbling noise; a commotion *la18-*, *now Abd*. **2** a violent, noisy blow *la18-e20* [only Sc; frequentative, f as DONNER]

dunny &c *n*, *chf in pl* the underground cellars and passages usual in old TENEMENT buildings; *in sing* a basement *19-*, *C*. [reduced f Eng *dungeon*]

dunsh *see* DUNCH

dunt &c *n* **1** a heavy, dull-sounding blow or stroke, knock *16-*. **2** the wound caused by such a blow *la19-*, *now Cai Bnf Ags*. **3** a dent *20-*, *now Abd*. **4** a heavy fall, thud, bump; the sound caused by such a fall *19-*. **5** a throb or quickened beat of the heart *la18-*, *now Bnf Abd Fif*. **6** a blow to fortunes, feelings; a shock, disappointment *19-*. **7** a dig, insult; a slanderous lie *19-e20*. **8** a chance, opportunity, occasion *19-*, *now Sh*. **9** a lump, large piece, *esp* of food *19-*, *now local Sh-Kcb*.
vti **1** beat, strike or stamp heavily, thump, bump, knock, so as to produce a dull sound *la15-*. **2** *vi* (1) *of the heart* throb, beat rapidly or violently, palpitate *la16-*, *now local*. (2) *of a sore* throb *la20-*, *Cai Abd Ags*. **3** stamp down (herrings) in a barrel *18-*, *now Bnf*. **4** *vt* shake together the contents of (*eg* a sack) by knocking on the ground *la19-*, *now local Bnf-Kcb*. **5** crush or dent by striking *la19-*, *now local Abd-Kcb*.
~er the common porpoise; the dolphin *19-*, *now Ork*. **~er duck** *etc* the eider duck *la17-*, *now Sh Ork Fif*. **~le**, *also* **~le doon** pay a forfeit in a game played with a teetotum *19-*, *Ags*.
~aboot a servant who is roughly shifted from one piece of work to another *20-*, *Per Kcb Rox*, *only Sc*. **~ out** settle (a quarrel or misunderstanding) by discussion, thrash out *la18-e20*. **the** (**very** *etc*) ~ the very thing *20-*, *Bnf Abd Kcb*, *only Sc*. [prob onomat; chf Sc; ME (once); cf DINT² and Norw dial *dunt* a blow, bump, thump]

duntibour &c [*'dʌntɪbur, *'duntɪ-] *n* term of abuse for a woman, *chf* an attendant at court *16*. [only Sc; obscure]

dunty *n* a mistress *18-e19*. [only Sc; contracted f DUNTIBOUR]

duplar &c *adj* = DUPLATE *la15*. [MedL *duplaris*]

duplate &c *adj*, *music* duple *la15-e16*. [L *duplāt-*, ptp stem of *duplāre*; cf prec]

duplicand &c [d(j)uplɪ'kand, dʒu-] *n*, *law* a doubling or doubled amount of *feu-duty* (FEU) for one year at certain specified intervals or on certain occasions *la18-e20*. [only Sc; L *duplicando* by doubling, f *duplicāre* (*v*) double]

duply &c [d(j)uplaɪ, 'dʒu-] *n*, *law* a second answer, *ie* the *defender's* (DEFEND) rejoinder to the *pursuer's* (PURSUE) REPLY *la16-e19*.
v **1** *vi*, *law* answer in a DUPLY *16-e19*. **2** *vt* allege in a DUPLY *17*. [only Sc; OF *duplique(r)* (*n*, *v*), MedL *duplicare* (*v*), w form by analogy w Eng *reply*; cf QUADRUPLY]

durand &c [*'dørənd] *prep* = during *la14-16*.
[nME]

durato &c *n* = duretto, a coarse durable cloth
e17.

durdum *see* DIRDUM

dure *see* DOOR, DOUR

durk[1] &c; **dirk** *19-* [dʌrk] *n* **1** a short dagger
worn in the belt by *Highlanders* (HIELAND) *la16-*.
2 a stab, a prod *la19-*, *now Sh Ork*.
vt stab with a DURK *la16-e20*. [obscure]

durk[2] &c *n* something big and clumsy; a large
clumsily-built person *la19-*, *local Sh-Abd*.
vt bungle, ruin (a job etc) *19-e20*.
~**y** thickset, squat *19-*, *now Ags*. [Norw dial
dorg a heap; a heavy, slovenly woman; *cf* Gael
dorc, durc a lump, a shapeless piece]

durkin &c *n* something short, thick and strong,
eg a club; a short, thickset person *la19-*, *Bnf*.
[Gael *durcan*, dim of *durc* (see prec)]

durst *see* DAUR

dusane *see* DIZZEN

dush &c *15, la18-*, **dusch** *la14-16* [dʌʃ; *Abd Ags*
duʃ; *WC Slk* *dıʃ] *v* **1** *vt* push or strike with
force, butt *la14-*, *now Ork Bnf Abd*. **2** *vi* fall
heavily *la14-16*. **3** beat or strike heavily *15-e16*.
4 rush or dash violently *15-e16*.
n a heavy blow, a violent jolt *la14-e16, 19-*, *now
Bnf*. [ME; obscure, prob onomat; *cf* DOOSE,
DOOSHT, DOIST]

dussone *see* DIZZEN

dust &c; **dist** *17-*, *chf Abd n* **1** = dust *la15-*. **2**
particles of meal and husk produced in grinding
corn *la16-*, *now Bnf Abd*.
~**y** *adj* = dusty *16-*. *n* name for a miller *19-*,
now Lnk. ~**y foot** &c a travelling merchant, a
pedlar *15-e20*. ~**y melder** &c the last milling
of a season's crop *la18-e20*. ~**y miller** &c **1**
auricula, a species of primula, so called because
of the white powdery appearance of the flowers
and leaves *la19-e20*. **2** a kind of bumble-bee
which deposits a light dust on the hand when
seized *20-*, *local Abd-Rox*.

dutch *n* = ditch *la18-*, *NE*.

duty *16-*, **dewty** &c *16-17*, **duité** &c *la15-16*,
dewité &c *la15-16*, **dowité** &c *la15-16*
['dju(ı)tı; *'du-] *n* **1** a service due to a feudal
SUPERIOR *la15-16*. **2** = duty *la15-*. **3** *law* a payment made to a feudal SUPERIOR; *feu duty* (FEU)
la15-19.

duvat *see* DIVOT

dux [dʌks] *n* the best pupil in a school, class or
subject *la18-*. [only Sc; L = a leader]

duxy *see* DOXY

duyme *see* DOOM

dwaam *see* DWAM

dwabble *see* DWAIBLE

dwadle ['dwadl] *vi* loiter, tarry *la19-*, *local Cai-
Kcb*. [var of Eng *dawdle*]

dwaffle &c *adj* limp, soft; weak, feeble *19-e20*,
chf NE.

dwaible *local* *Bnf-Fif*; **dwabble** &c,
dweeble ['dwebl, 'dwabl; *NE, EC also* 'dwibl;

NE Uls also 'dwəibl] *adj* **1** flexible, flabby *la19-*,
local Bnf-Fif. **2** *chf of the legs* weak, feeble, shaky
la18-, *now Bnf Abd Fif*.
n a weak, helpless person *la19*.
vi totter, walk feebly *la19*.
dwaibly &c shaky, wobbly, weak *la19-*, *now
local Abd-Ayr*. [see SND]

dwall &c *la16-e20*, **dwell** &c; **doull** &c *16*
[dwal, *dul &c] *vi* **1** = dwell *la14-*. **2** *of things*
remain in the possession of a specified person
la14.
dwelling &c **1** = dwelling *la14-*. **2** a person's
household or retinue *la14-e15*. **mak dwelling**
1 stay in a place *la14-15*. **2** take up or have
one's residence *la14-16*.

dwam *la16-*, **dwalm** *la16-e20*; **dwaum** &c
16-e20, **dwaam** *la19-e20* [dwam, *dwʌm] *n* **1**
a swoon, a fainting fit; a sudden attack of illness
16-. **2** a stupor; a daydream *19-*.
vi **1** faint, swoon *la16-*, *now Bnf Abd Fif*. **2** ail,
decline in health *19-*, *now Stlg*. **3** *fig* grow faint,
fade *la18-19*. **4** *chf* ~ **ower** fall asleep, take a
nap *20-*, *local*.
~**ie** *now local Abd-EC*, ~**ish** *now Abd Fif* sickly,
faint; dreamy *la19-*. **dwamle** &c *n* a sick or
faint turn *19-*, *now Abd Arg*. *vi* faint, appear
faint *la19-*, *now Abd*. [only Sc; see SND]

dwamfle &c ['dwamfl] *adj* flexible, loose, sagging *20-*, *Bnf*. [var of DWAFFLE]

dwamle *see* DWAM

dwang &c *n* **1** a transverse piece of wood
inserted between joists or posts to strengthen
them *la15-*. **2** a large iron lever used by blacksmiths; a tap-wrench *19-*, *now Gsw Rox*. **3** a bar
of wood used by carters for tightening ropes etc
la19-, *now Abd Kcdn*. **4** toil, labour; rough handling *la18-*, *now Ags*.
v **1** *vt* subject to pressure, harass, worry *la16-*,
now Ags. **2** *vi* toil, work hard *la18-e20*. [only
Sc; *cf* Du = compulsion, restraint, MLowGer
dwanc; OHighGer = bridle, curb; Du *dwingen*
(*v*) force, constrain]

dwaum *see* DWAM

dweeble *see* DWAIBLE

dwell *see* DWALL

dwerch &c [*d(w)ɛrx] *n* a dwarf *la15-e16*. [ME
dwergh, dwerʒe; OE *dweorh, dwerh*; *cf* DROICH]

dwine &c, **dwyne** &c [dwəin] *v* **1** *vi*, *of persons
or animals* pine, waste away, fail in health *la15-*.
2 *of things* fade, wither *16-e20*. **3** *vt* cause to
pine or wither *la16-19*. **4** *as exclam* confound..!,
damn..! *19-*, *now Sh*.
n a decline, a waning *19-*, *now local Ork-WC*.
dwiny &c sickly, pining *20-*, *now Fif*. [ME; OE
dwinan; ON *dvína* dwindle, pine away]

dwinnle &c *vti* = dwindle *19*.

dwyne *see* DWINE

dy *see* THY

dyall *see* DIAL

dyang *see* GAE

dyat *see* DIET[2]

dyaun *see* GAE

dyce see DICE

dyester *19-, now local Cai-S,* **dyster** *la17-18* [?'daɪstər] *n* a dyer. [laME *deyster*, eME *diestare*]

dyet see DIET[1], DIET[2]

dyke, deik &c, dick &c *la14-17, 20-, now Cai;* **dike** *la15-* [dəik; *Sh* dɛk; *Cai* dɪk; *Arg Wgt also* dek] *n* **1** = dyke, a ditch; a wall, mound *la14-*. **2** a (boundary) wall of stones, turf etc *15-*. **3** a hedge *20-, chf SW*. **4** *geol and mining* a vein of igneous rock in a vertical fissure in the earth's strata; now in general use as a geological term *la18-*.
v **1** *vt* surround with a DYKE *la14-*. **2** enclose, shut out etc with a DYKE *16-17*. **3** *vi* build or repair DYKES *la15-*. **4** *vir, chf* **deik** hide *e20*.

dyker a builder of DYKES *la14-*. **dykie** the hedge-sparrow *19-, SW*. **dykit** *mining, of a road* cut off by a fault *20-, now Fif*.

~-back the back of a wall *la18-e20*. **~-louper &c 1** an animal which leaps the DYKE sur-rounding its pasture *la18-, now Bnf Abd Fif*. **2** a person of immoral habits *19-e20, S*. **~-side** the ground alongside a DYKE *la16-*.

dyne see DINE

dynmonth see DINMONT

dyoch see DEUCH

dyour see DYVOUR

dyper &c ['dəipər] *vt* = diaper, adorn, deck up *la19-e20, Abd*.

dys see DICE

dysemell see DISEMAL

dyst see DOIST

dyster see DYESTER

dyte see DITE, DOIT[1], DOIT[2]

dyvour *16-20;* **dyour &c** *15-16,* **dyver &c** *la16-e18* [*'daɪvər, *'daɪur] *n* **1** a debtor, a bankrupt *15-e20*. **2** a rogue, a good-for-nothing *19-20*.
~ie &c debtorship, bankruptcy *la16-17*. [only Sc; obscure]

E

e; ee [i] *pronoun* **1** *chf unstressed, but also stressed NE,
S* = YE *la19-.* **2** = *thee* (THOU) *la19-e20, W.*

e *see* EE[1], HE

eace *see* ACE

eadwul *see* EEDOL

eage *see* AGE

eak *see* AIK

ear[1] &c *la16-*, er(e) &c *la14-e17 n* = ear *la14-.*
~iewig &c an earwig *20-, chf WC Uls.*

hear one's ~s hear oneself speak *la19-, local
mLoth-Uls.*

ear[2], ere *vti* plough *15-19.* [ME *eren*, OE *erian*;
cf ARE]

'ear *see* YEAR

eard *see* ERD

earl &c *la16-*, erle &c *la14-17*, yerl &c *la14-*,
now S; eryll &c *la14-17*, yirl *la19-e20* [ɛrl;
Mry S jɛrl, jɪrl] *n* = earl *la14-.*

~ o Hell **1** the Devil *19-, Sh C, S.* **2** name for
any wild lawless character *19.* as black as the
~ o Hell's waistcoat pitch black *20.*

ear-leather &c *la17-e20*, ere-ledder &c
la15-17 n = *neir leather* (NEIR[1]). [initial *n* lost
by wrong division after *a*]

earn *18-*, erne &c *la14-e20*; eirn &c *la14-e17*,
airn &c *la16-e17*, yirn &c *la18-* [ɛrn; *Ork*
jɪrn; *Ayr* *jɛrn] *n* **1** an eagle *la14-.* **2** *latterly
specif*: (1) the white-tailed or sea-eagle *la18-*,
now Ork; (2) the golden eagle *la18-, now Sh Cai.*

ernfern a kind of fern, *esp* polypody (found on
high rocks) *19.* [OE *earn*, OE *orn, ern-*]

earn *see* YIRN[1]

earn-bleater &c; yern-blit(t)er *n* the common snipe *la18-e20, NE.* [obscure; *cf heather-
bleater* (HEATHER)]

earnit *see* ARNIT

earock &c; er(r)ock &c *19-e20* ['irək, 'ɛr-] *n* a
young hen (*usu* in its first year), a pullet just
beginning to lay *la18-, now Abd WC.* [Gael
eirag]

Earse *see* ERSE

earth *see* ERD

ease[1] &c *16-*, es(e) *la14-e16*; eise &c *15-16*,
ais(e) &c *16-17* [iz; *ez] *n* **1** = ease *la14-.* **2** a
reduction or remission of an amount or service
due *la17-18.* **3** the act of relieving the bowels,
chf do one's ~ *15-e17.*

v **1** *vtr* = ease *la14-.* **2** *vr* take one's ease, enjoy
ease *la14-e15.* **3** *vt* provide, furnish (someone)
with (something) *la16-e18.*

~dom &c comfort, leisure, relief from anxiety
etc *19-, now Sh Abd, only Sc.* ~ful(l) giving ease
or comfort *la14-.*

put to (ane) ~ bring to a settlement, arrange
satisfactorily *e17.* stule *etc* of ~ a close-stool
16.

ease[2] *n* a children's ball-game *la19-e20, Mry.*
[uncertain]

easedrop *see* ESEDROP

easel *see* EAST

easement &c *la16-*, es(e)ment &c *la14-e17*,
aisment &c *la15-17*, aisiament &c
15-e17, esiament &c *15-16*; esiement &c
15-16 ['izmənt; *'ezmənt; *'ezɪəmənt; *'izɪ(ə)-]
n **1** a material convenience or advantage, *esp* in
connection with the occupation of land or
buildings, *latterly esp* an opening for entrance,
air or light *la14-e17*: '*fredomis, commoditeis, & ese-
mentis*'. **2** *chf in pl* accommodation, buildings,
lodgings etc *la18-e19.* **3** personal comfort etc;
relief from physical discomfort or inconvenience
la15-, now local. **4** the giving or having of ease
or convenience *la15-e17.* [ME *es(e)ment*, OF
aisement; *cf* MedL *aisiamentum*]

easin(s) &c *17-*, esing &c *la16-e20* ['iz(ɪ)n(z),
'ezin(z); *Sh also* 'eʒ-, 'eʃ-] *n*, *chf in pl* **1** the eaves
of a building *la16-.* **2** the corresponding part of
a haystack *la18-.* **3** the angular space between
the top of the side wall and the roof inside the
house *la19-, now local N-Arg.* **4** *transf* the edge of
the sky, the horizon *20-, NE.*

easing drop = ESEDROP *la16-19.* ~ gang a
course of sheaves projecting a little at the EASIN
2, to keep the rain out *19-, local.* [nME *esynge*
reduced f *evesing*, OE *efesung*]

easlins, eassel *see* EAST

east *18-*, est &c *la14-e17*; eist &c *la15-e17*,
aist &c *e20* [ist, est] *n* = east *la14-, in place-
names 13-.*

adj, *comparative* easter. *superlative* ~most,
~mest *la15-e17*, ~mast *15-* = east *la14-.*

adv **1** = east *la14-.* **2** *indicating direction* right;
left; *imprecisely* in one of two possible directions;
homewards *18-, local*: '*move that ashet a bittie east*'.
prep in an easterly direction along *la16-.*

eastart &c *la18-, now local Sh-Arg*, estwart &c
la16 adv (16-), *n (la18-)*, *adj (la19-)* = eastward. easten *e20*, estin &c *16-e20 adj* east,
eastern *only Sc.* easter *la16-*, ester &c *la15-16*,
eister &c *16-la17 adj* eastern, lying towards
the east, the more easterly of two places etc, *freq*
contrasted with *waster* (WAST) *la15-, in place-
names 13-.* *n* the east wind *la19-, chf NE.* *vi, of
wind* shift towards the east *20-, Sh NE.* the ~er
seas the Baltic *la16-e17.* Eastie familiar contraction of a farm name containing EAST *or
easter*, applied to the tenant or owner *la19-, now
NE*; *cf Wastie* (WAST). eastle *la18-e20*, eistell
&c *la16-e17*, estal(d) *la15-e16*; eas(s)el &c
19-e20, chf S ['isl, 'esl; *'is(t)l(d)] *adv* towards
the east, eastwards *19-e20.* *prep* to the east of
la18-e20, S. an estald *la15-16*, a(n) eistell
la16-e17 [*ə'nistl(d)] to the east of. ~lin eastern, easterly *18-19.* ~lins *la18-, now NE*, easlins *20-, NE* eastward.

Eastlan &c *la18-19*, Estland *14-16*, Eistland
16-e19 n Estonia, or another eastern Baltic
country *14-16.* *adj*, *also* e~ belonging to or of
the east, *orig specif* of or from the countries in

the eastern part of the Baltic, *esp* **Eastlan &c burdis** *15-16* boards from the region *15-19* [Dan, Sw *Estland*, ON *Eistland* Estonia].
~ **the road** *etc orig* in an easterly direction along the road etc, *latterly* eastwards *la16-*, *now local N, EC, S.* ~ **the toun** towards the east of the town *19-*, *local N, EC, S.*

eastler *see* AISLAR

easwas &c; eizewas &c ['izwɑz, 'ez-] *n pl* the top of the walls of a house, on which the rafters rest; the inner angle between the level top of a wall and the sloping edge of an unlined roof, often serving as a shelf *20-*, *chf Cai*. [Eng *eaves* + *walls*; *cf* EASIN(S)]

easy &c *la16-*, **esy &c** *15-17*, **aisy &c** *16-e20* *adj* **1** = easy *15-*. **2** *followed by the gerund* (*where Eng would have infin*) *19-*: '*It's easy speakin*.'
easy osy &c *adj, of persons* easy-going, inclined to be lazy; *of things* involving the minimum of effort *19-*. *n* an easy-going or lazy person *la19-*, *now Bwk*.

eat &c *la16-*, **ete &c** *la14-e20*; **et(t)** *la14-*, *now Bnf Abd Rox*, **aet** *18-*, *now Uls*, **ait &c** *19-e20*, *NE* [it; *Sh NE Bwk Rox also* ɛt; *NE nEC also* et] *vti, pt also* **ett** *20-*, *now C, S*, **eit &c** *la14-16*, **eet &c** *20-*, *now Uls*, **eated &c** *la16-e20* [ɛt, it; *Sh* øt; 'itɪt, 'ɛtɪt *&c*]. *ptp also* **etten &c** *la14-*, **eattin** *16-e17*, **aten &c** *19-e20*, *SW* ['ɛtn, 'etn] **1** = eat *la14-*. **2** cause or allow (grass etc) to be eaten by grazing animals, *freq* ~ **grass** *etc* **with one's horses** *etc 16-*, *now local Sh-Kcb*: '*he eats the herbage with his sheep*'.
n **1** the action of eating *19-*, *NE*. **2** what is eaten, a meal or feast *20-*, *Bnf Abd*.
aten out o ply *of an animal* that will not fatten however well-fed *19-e20*, *SW*. **etten &c and spued** *fig* unhealthy looking, 'washed out' *la18-*. ~**en corn** oats eaten by trespassing animals *la17-e20*. ~**ing 1** = eating *15-*. **2** the eating of grass, growing grain etc, by grazing animals *la14-*.
~ **in one's words** eat one's words, retract *18-e19*. ~**-meat** an idler, parasite *la19-e20*, *Bnf Abd*. ~ **oneself,** ~ **one's thumb(s)** be extremely annoyed or vexed *la18-*, *now Sh Abd Ags*.

eat *see* AIT

eath *see* OATH

eather *see* AITHER

eavesdrop *n*, *law* the SERVITUDE by which one has the right to shed roof-water on an adjoining property *la18-*. [*cf easing drop* (EASIN(S)), ESEDROP, STILLICIDE]

ebb, eb &c *15-16* [ɛb; *local Abd also* əib] *n* **1** = ebb *16-*. **2** the foreshore, sections of which might be assigned to individual fishermen *la15-*, *now local Sh-Abd*.
adj shallow, lacking in depth, scant: **1** *of low water*; *latterly of the contents of a vessel*, *15-*, *now*

local Bnf-Rox; **2** *of cloth etc*, *la17-e20*; **3** *fig, of the mind*, *17-e20*; **4** *of the ground*, *esp in ploughing or mining*, *18-e20*.
v **1** *vi* = ebb *la14-*. **2** *vti, of a boat* ground or be grounded at low tide *la14-17*, *only Sc*.
~**ness** *lit and fig* shallowness, scarcity *17*.

ebdomadare &c [**εb'domadar, **-'domɪtər &c*] *n* a member of a college or chapter taking a weekly turn in performing the services in the church *la15-e16*. [ME *ebdomadary*, MedL *hebdomadarius*; *cf* HEBDOMADER]

ebill *see* ABLE

ebraik *see* EEBREK

ebure &c [**'ibər*] *n* ivory *15-16*. [only Sc; L *ebur*]

ech [εx] *interj* expressing pity, surprise, disgust *20-*. [*cf* ACH]

eche *see* EETCH

echer *see* AICHER

echt *see* AUCHT[1], AUCHT[3]

economist, economus *see* OECONOMUS

edder &c; ether &c ['εdər, 'εðər] *n* a straw-rope used in thatching a haystack *e20*, *chf Abd*.
vt, *also* **aider &c** rope (a stack) in order to secure the thatch *18-*, *Bnf Abd*.
~**in &c** *freq in pl* a straw-rope used on stacks, loads etc, a cross-rope *la18-*, *chf NE*. [*cf* Eng *dial edders* plaited withes, Eng dial, ME *edder* (*v*) plait such, prob f OE *e(o)der* enclosure, fence etc]

edder *see* AITHER, UDDER

edderin(s) *see* AITHER

eddicate *see* EDUCATE

eddication &c *19-*, **educatioun** *la16 n* = education. [*cf* EDUCATE]

eddir, eddris *see* ETHER

edge &c *15-*, **ege &c** *15-16 n*, *also* **egge &c** *16-17*, **ai(d)ge &c** *16-e17* = edge *15-*.
vti = edge *16-*.
edgie &c quick, active, mentally and physically *la19-*, *now midLoth Rox*.
~ **coals** *or* **seams** (*mining*) seams lying at a very steep angle *la19-*, *now Fif*. ~ **lume &c** = edgelome, an edged tool or weapon *16-17*.
at *or* **in the** ~ **o a time** from time to time, occasionally *19-e20*. **at, i** *or* (**up)on** (**the**) ~ **o** almost, very nearly, on the verge of *la18-e20*. ~ **hame** proceed slowly homewards *la19-*.

edict; edick &c *16* ['idɪkt; **'idɪk] *n* **1** = edict *16-*. **2** *law* a proclamation made in a public place summoning persons to appear before the courts *16*. **3** *church* a legally authoritative public *intimation* (INTIMATE) from the pulpit *la16-*.
~**al citation** [i'dɪktl səi'teʃn] *law and church* a citation made by EDICT, *now* by sending copies of the summons to the **Keeper of E~al Citations** *la17-*. ~**ally** by means of an EDICT or edictal citation, *la17-19*.

Edinburgh ~ **rock** a stick-shaped sweet made of sugar, cream of tartar, water and various flavourings, *orig* made in Edinburgh *20-*.

edris *see* ETHER

educate, educat &c; eddicate *20-* ['ɛdɪkət, -et; *Sh Mry* 'id-] *ptp* educated *la16-*. [eModEng; L *ēducātus*; *cf* EDDICATION]

education *see* EDDICATION

ee¹, e &c *la14-16*, **eye &c** *15-* [i; *S also* əi] *n, pl* **een &c, ene** *la14-e17*, **eyne &c** *la14-19*, **ewine &c** *la14*, **eyes** *16-*, **ees &c** *la16-* [in; iz] *n* **1** = eye *la14-*. **2** an opening: (1) an eyelet *16-e17*; (2) *mining* an opening or entrance into a shaft *16-*; (3) an opening through which water passes *la16-*, *now Sh Ork*; (4) the hole in the centre of a millstone *la16-*, *now Sh Abd*; (5) the hole in the head of a pick or hammer into which the shaft is fitted *20-*, *WC, SW*; (6) the loop in a snare *19-*, *now Sh Abd*. **3** *in pl* globules of fat in soup etc *la19-e20*. **4** *fig* regard, liking, craving: '*you wi a lang ee till anither lad*'.
eenie &c *n* = *n* 1, *la19-*, *NE. adj* having the appearance of eyes; *specif of soup or rancid milk* full of *een* (*n* 3) *19-e20*. **~some** handsome, pleasing to the eye *19-e20*.
~-bree &c an eyebrow *16-e20*. **~-brier** an eyelash *e20*. **~-broo** = *ee-bree*, *la19-*. **e dolp** *e16*, **~hole** *18-e20* an eyesocket. **eelist &c** *la16-e19*, **elest &c** *16-17*, **eilest &c** *la16-e17*, **eyelist** *la16-e17*, **ilest** *la16-e17* [*'i:lɪst, *-ləst] *n* **1** a fault, flaw or defect *16-e19*. **2** a cause of offence, disagreement or ill-feeling; a grievance; a ground for a quarrel *la16-e17* [*-list* f ME *lest*, ON *lǫstr* a fault]. **~-wink(er)** **1** an eyelash *19-*, *now Bwk*. **2** an eyelid *19-e20*. **~ winkie &c** children's rhyme the eye *19-*, *local Sh-Ags*.
a person's ae *or* **tae &c** ~ a person's favourite, the apple of someone's eye *19-*, *now local NE-Kcb*. **a drap(pie) in the** ~ just enough drink to make one mildly intoxicated *la18-19*. ~ **o (the) day** midday *e19*. **have** ~ **to** have regard or consideration for, pay heed to (something) *la14-16*. **have one's ee** *or* **een in** covet *la19-*, *local*. **put out a person's** ~ obtain an advantage over, supplant *la19-*, *Gen except Sh Ork*. **say black is (the white of) a person's** ~ speak ill of a person *19-e20*.

ee² *interj* expressing *eg* dismay or foreboding *20-*, *Abd*. [prob a natural alarm call]

ee *see* E, THE

eean &c, ion ['iən] *n* a one-year-old horse or cow *19-*, *NE*. [obscure]

eebrek &c, ebraik *n, chf attrib* land ploughed the third year after being left fallow *la16-e19*. [unknown]

eechie (n)or ochie &c ['ix(ɪ) nər 'oxɪ], *always in negative* neither one thing nor another, not the smallest word or sound; absolutely nothing *la18-*, *now local*. [ECH + OCH, the second perh w infl f OCHT¹ and NOCHT]

eediot *la19-*, **idiot &c, idiwut &c** *19-*, *now Ayr*; **eedit &c** *la19-e20*, **eedyit &c** *20-*, *local*, **eediwat &c** *19-e20 n* = idiot *la14-*.
eediocy = idiocy *la19-*. **idiotical** foolish, senseless, stupid *la18-*, *NE, EC*. **idiotry &c** *law* = idiocy, the inability to conduct one's own affairs because of mental weakness *la15-19*, *only Sc*.

eedle-doddle &c *adj* easy-going, lacking initiative, muddle-headed *la19-e20*, *N*.
n a person with such a character *e20*, *N*. [reduplicated (cf *easy osy* (EASY)), w infl f Eng *idle*, and second element f DODDLE³ *v*]

eedol &c; eadwul &c *la19-* ['id(ə)l, 'idwəl] *n* = idol *19-*, *now Bnf Ags*.

eedyit *see* EEDIOT

eekfow *see* EQUAL

eeksie-peeksie &c; icksy-picksy &c *la19-*, *NE adj* much alike, six and half-a-dozen *19-*, *Gen except Sh Ork*. [reduplicated f EQUAL]

eel *18-*, **ele &c** *la14-17 n* = eel *la14-*.
eelat *n* an eel-like fish, *Myxine glutinosa la19-e20*, *N*.
~ **ark** eel trap *16-e20*. **~-backit &c** *of a horse* having a dark stripe along its back *la16-e19*.
~-drowner &c *usu ironic* a person who can do the impossible, an exceedingly clever person *19-e20*: '*he's nae eel-drowner*'. **eel-stab, ~-stob &c** a V-shaped incision in the ear of an animal as a mark of ownership *19-*, *now Arg Kcb*.
~-stabbed &c marked in this way *la17-19*.
nine-eed ~ the lesser lamprey *19-e20*.

eel *see* ALE, YELD, YULE

eelat *see* EEL

eelie *see* OIL, ELY

eelist *see* EE¹

eem &c *16-19*, **eme &c** *la14-e19*; **emm &c** *15-e18 n* **1** an uncle *la14-18*. **2** *also* **ame &c** *la16* applied to any near male relative, and *latterly* to a close friend *15-19*. [ME *eme &c*, OE *ēam*]

eemach *see* EEMOCK

eemage &c *19-*, **image &c** ['imɪdʒ] *n* **1** = image *la14-*. **2** a ghost of one's former self, a pitiful figure; a spectacle *19-*, *now local*, *Sh-Bwk*.

eemir *see* HUMOUR

eemis *see* IMMIS

eemock &c *la18-*, **emot &c; emmock &c** *la18-e20*, **immick &c** *la19-e20*, **eemach** *e20*, *NE* ['imək, -əx; 'ɛm-] *n* **1** = emmet, an ant *la14-*, *now local NE-S*. **2** a tiny person; a fairy *e20*, *Abd Ags*. [*cf* EMMERTEEN]

eemost *see* UMOST

een *see* ANE¹, EE¹

e'en *see* EVEN¹, EVEN²

eenach &c ['inəx] *n* the natural grease in sheep's wool *la19-e20*, *Abd*. [Gael *eanach* dandruff; down, wool]

eence *see* AINCE

eend *see* EVEN²

eendy; eenty *numeral, children's rhymes* one *la19*-. [deriv of *een* (ANE¹) w rhyme infl f TEENTY; *cf* ZEENDI]

eenickie *see* ANE¹

eenie *vti, of a ewe* give birth to (a lamb) *20*-, *Cai*. [prob var of INGY]

eenie *see* EE¹

eenil *e19*, **eindill &c** *la16*, *la19-e20*, *latterly Sh* [*'in(d)l, &c] *vi* be or become jealous. [obscure]

eenin(g) &c *la16*-, **evining** *la14*- ['inɪn] *n* = evening. [*cf* EVEN¹]

eenoo *19*-, **evenoo &c** *19-e20*; **enow &c** *la18-e20*, **ae noo** *19-e20* [i'nu, iv(ə)'nu; *NE also* əi'nu, e'nu; *C also* jə'nu; *S* i'nʌu, jɪ'nʌu; *N Fif Ayr also* ev(ə)'nu; *Abd also* əiv'nu] *adv* **1** just now, at the present time, a moment ago *la18*-. **2** in a short time, soon, at once *19*-, *now local*. [var of Eng *even now*]

eenrie *see* ANE¹

eens, eent *see* EVEN²

eenty *see* EENDY

eer *see* ERE, URE³, YOUR

eerant &c *19-e20*, **erand &c** *la14-17*, **herand** *15-e16*; **errand &c** *la15*-, **airand &c** *la16-19*, **erran &c** *la19-e20*, **yirran(t) &c** *19-e20* [*sEC, S* 'irənt, 'irənd; *N, WC* 'irən; *Ags Fif* 'erənt; *WC, SW, S* 'jɪrən] *n* **1** = errand *la14*-. **2** *in pl* purchases, parcels, shopping *la19*-.

eerie &c *18*-, **ery &c** *la14-18* ['iri] *adj (adv)* **1** *of persons* affected by fear or dread, *esp* by a fear of the supernatural which gives rise to uneasiness or loneliness; *less freq* apprehensive *in gen*, *la14*-, *Gen except Sh Ork*. **2** *chf of things* ghostly, strange *la18*-. **3** *of persons and things* gloomy, dismal, melancholy *18-19*.

eerily weirdly; drearily *la19*-. **eeriness &c** fear, dread *la14-19*. **~some** uncanny, gloomy *19*-, *now Abd*. [nME *eri*; obscure]

eerieoy *see* IEROE

eeriorums [irɪ'orəmz] *n pl* details; ornamentation *la19*-, *local Sh-Abd*. [prob f VARIORUM]

Eerish &c *la15-16*, *la19-e20*, *latterly chf WC, SW*, **Erische &c** *la14-e17*; **Eris** *la15-e17* ['irɪʃ, *'iris] *adj* **1** Irish *la14-e17*, *la19*. **2** *Highland* (HIELAND), GAELIC *la14-e17*.

n **1** the Irish language *16*, *la19*. **2** Scottish GAELIC *16*.

~man *la16-e17*, *la19*. **~ry** the native Irish, the *Highlanders* (HIELAND), *la14-15*. [var of IRISH; *cf* ERSE]

eernest &c *la15-19*, *latterly NE*, **ernist &c** *la14-e17*; **airnest** *la16-e17 n* (*la14-19*), *adj* (*la16-17*) = earnest.

eeroy *see* IEROE

ees *see* EE¹

eese *see* USE

eeshan &c ['iʃən] *n, freq derog or playful* a small

child; a small and puny person of any age *la19*-, *local Cai-Abd*. [Gael *isean* a chicken; a small person]

eeshogel *see* ICE

eeswal *see* USUAL

eet *see* EAT

eetch &c *la16*-, **eche &c** *la16-e18* [itʃ; *Uls also* ɛdʃ] *n* an adze. [ONorthumb *eadesa*, OE *adesa* adze]

eetim &c *n* **1** = item *19-e20*, *local Sh-Fif*. **2** a task *la19-e20*, *local Sh-Fif*.

eetle ottle *in counting-out rhymes*, *la19*-, *local Sh-Ayr*: 'eetle ottle black bottle, eetle ottle out'.

vt choose by counting out *20*-, *WC*. [*cf* next]

eettie-ottie *in counting-out rhyme and children's game*, *la19-e20*. [*cf* prec]

eevie &c *n* **creepin ~** convolvulus *la19*-, *NE*. [var of Eng *ivy*]

eezie-ozie *see* HEEZE

efauld *see* AEFAULD

effair *see* AFFERE

effeck &c *15*-, **effect &c** *n* **1** = effect *la14*-. **2** the essential part or substance of anything *15-16*.

~wal *19*-, *now Sh Ags*, **effectual &c** = effectual *la15*-. **Effectual &c Calling** name for and opening phrase in the answer to Question 31 in the *Shorter Catechism* (SHORT) *17*-.

in ~ *la15*-, **in gude ~** *16* so far as the effect or result is concerned, in fact, in reality. **of ~** of worth or importance *la15-16*.

effecteouslie *see* EFFECTUIS

effectionat &c *adj* = affectionate, well disposed; loving *la16-e17*, *only Sc*.

effectioun &c *n* = affection *15-e17*, *only Sc*.

effectuis *only Sc*, **effectuous &c** [*i'fɛktwus, -(w)ʌs &c] *adj* = effectuous, effectual *15-16*. **~lie** *15-16*, **effecteouslie &c** *la16-e17*, **effectuslie** *15-16 adv* **1** = effectuously, effectually *15-16*. **2** earnestly, urgently *15-e17*, *only Sc*.

effeir *see* AFERE

effere *see* AFERE, AFFEIR, AFFERE

efferme *see* AFFIRM

effix *see* AFFIX

effore *see* AFORE

effray [*'ɛ'fre] *n* **1** a state of alarm or fear; fright, terror *la14-e16*. **2** a cause, occasion or instance of alarm *15-16*.

vt alarm, scare, terrify *16-e17*.

~it &c *ptp, adj* = afraid *la14-e17*. **~itly** in alarm, in fear *la14-16*. [OF *effrei* (*n*), *effrayer* (*v*); *cf* Eng *affray* (*n, v*) and AFFRAYITLY]

effusion &c *la16*-, **effusioun &c** *15-e17 n* = effusion *15*-.

to the ~ of (one's) **blood** *law* applied to cases of assault where blood is shed *17*-.

eft *adv* **1** *nautical* = aft *17*-. **2** towards the rear of anything *20*-.

adj belonging to the after part; back, rear *19*-.

~ **castell**, ~ **schip** the poop or stern of a vessel *e16*.

efter &c, after &c; aifter *la19-* ['ɛftər] *prep* **1** = after *la14-*. **2** *in telling the time* past *la18-*, *now local Sh-Stlg*: 'half an hour after ten'. *adv* **1** = after *la14-*. **2** *in a document or narrative below* *la14-16*: 'we devyidis the said land as eftir followis'.

vt obtain the very last drops of milk from (a cow) by milking her twice *20-*, *EC Arg*.

~**in(g)s 1** the last drops of milk taken while milking *la18-*, *now midLoth*. **2** final results, consequences; remainder *19-e20*. **efterwairds** *18-20*, **efterwartis &c** *la14-e16 adv* = afterwards. **efterwarde, efterwart &c** *la14-16 adv* = afterward, subsequently *la14-e17*.

~ **cast** *19-e20*, ~ **clap(s)** *la16-e20*, ~**come &c** *la16-e20* an effect, consequence. ~**hin** *19-*, ~**hend &c** *15-*; ~**hand &c** *20-*, **afterin &c** *la19- adv* afterwards *15-*. *prep* after *la14-e20*. *adj, of a boat* port side *e20*, *ECoast*. ~**mes** a second course, dessert *la14*, *only Sc*. ~**nuin &c** *la15-*, ~**none &c** *15-e17*, ~**neen** *la19-*, *N* ['ɛftər'nøn, *C* -'nɪn, *N* -'nin] *prep phr* in the afternoon *15-e17*. *n* **1** = afternoon *la16-*. **2** a meal taken during the afternoon *la16-e17*, *la19-*, *now Sh*. ~ **schot &c** a supplementary or additional act or performance *17-e18*. ~ **specifeit** specified below *la16-17*.

be ~ **daein &c** .. have done .. *19-*: 'I am after telling him' [found in Gael districts, translating Gael *air + verbal n*]. ~ **ane** alike, uniform, unchangeable, the same *e16*, *19-*, *now NE*: 'he's aye efter-ane'. ~ **as** according as *15-16*. ~ **the back** back foremost, backwards, on the back *la19-*, *N*. ~ **the heid** headfirst *20-*, *Ork-Ags*.

eg *see* EGG[1], EGG[2]

egal *adj* = egall, equal *16-e18*. [OF *egal*]

ege *see* EDGE

egg[1], eg; ege &c *la15-17 n* = egg *15-*.

~**ler** a hawker who collects eggs from outlying farms and villages for sale at local markets *la18-19*.

~**-bed** an ovary *19-e20*. ~**-siller** money from selling eggs *20-*, *local Bnf-midLoth*.

aff (**o**) **one's** ~**s 1** mistaken *la18-*, *now Ork NE-S*. **2** nervous *20-*, *local Sh-Kcb*.

egg[2] &c, eg *la14*, **eig &c** *18-e20* [ɛg; *Sh Mry also* ɪg] *vt, also* ~ **up** *la19-* = egg, incite, urge on *la14-*.

~**le** incite, egg on, stir up; quarrel *la19-e20*, *Ork N*. [*cf* EIK[3]]

egge *see* EDGE

eght *see* AUCHT[1]

egill &c *15-e17*; **egle** *16* [*'*igl] *n* = eagle. [*cf* AIGLE]

Egiptian *see* EGYPTIAN

egle *see* EGILL

Egypt *n* an Egyptian *15*. [only Sc; L *Aegyptius*]

Egyptian, Egiptian &c *la15-e19 n* **1** = Egyptian *la15-*. **2** a gipsy *16-19*.

eh ['ɛ, 'e] *interj* ~ **aye** *la19-*, ~ **man** *20-*, ~ **sirs** *19- usu* expressing affirmation, surprise, dismay *now local NE-C*.

ei *see* HE

eicen *see* EISEN

eicht *see* AUCHT[1]

eickel *see* EIK[3]

eid *see* HEID

eident &c *18-*, **ithand &c** *la14-16*, **idand &c** *16-e17*; **yden &c** *la16-e17*, **ythen &c** *la14*, **ident &c** *la16-e19*, **ey(e)dant** *18-e20* ['əidənt; *Rox also* *'idiənt; *'ɪðən, *'ɪðənd; *'əiðənd; *'əidən] *adj* **1** assiduous, diligent, busy *la14-*. **2** *freq of rain etc* continuous, persistent *la14-e20*, *latterly NE*. **3** conscientious, careful, attentive *19-e20*. [nME *iþen*, ON *iðinn*]

eidi-streen *see.* AIR[5]

eig *see* EGG[2]

eight *see* AUCHT[1]

eik[1] &c [ik, *also* jik] *n* **1** the natural grease in sheep's wool *la15-*, *now Rox*. **2** human perspiration *19-e20*, *S*. [MDu *iecke*]

eik[2] &c, eke &c [ik] *n* **1** an addition, extension, increase; an additional part or piece *16-*. **2** *specif* (1) *law* an addition or supplement to a document, *latterly esp* an extension of the confirmation of an executor, to cover property not originally included *la16-*; (2) an addition or extension to a garment, a patch, a gusset *17-*; (3) an additional ring of plaited straw or wood used to enlarge a beehive *18-*, *now local Bnf-Kcb*; (4) an additional drink; a little drop more *la19-e20*.

vti **1** increase, add (**to**), supplement *la14-*. **2** *specif* (1) add (**to**) by way of repair; lengthen, patch *la15-*; (2) *law* make an addition to a document etc *la15-19*; (3) give an increase *eg* in payment to (a person etc) *la15-16*; (4) join, unite *la18-e19*.

~**ed &c** increased, extended, added *17-*.

~ **name** a nickname *e20*.

~ **up** fill up (a container) *la19-*, *local EC*. [ME; OE *ēaca* (*n*), *ēacian* (*v*)]

eik[3] &c [ik] *vt* stir **up**, urge **on**, incite *19-*, *Abd*. **eickel &c** ['ikl, 'əikl] = *v*, *20-*, *NE*. [f EIK[2] *v*, w semantic infl f EGG[2]]

eild &c, elde &c *la14-16*, **heild** *15-e16*, **yeild &c** *la16-e20* [ild; **jild] *n* **1** the age of a person *la14-19*. **2** old age *la14-*. **3** mature or legal age, full age *15-16*. **4** antiquity, long ago *la15-*.

vi grow old *la15-e16*.

(**be**) **eil(d)ins, yealin(g)s &c** *18-e20* [**'il(d)ɪnz, **'jil(d)ɪnz] (be) contemporaries, persons born in the same year *18-20*. ~**it** aged *16-e20*.

within ~ under age *15-*. [ME *elde &c*, OE *eldo*; *cf* AULD. OED *eld[2]*, *yeild*]

eild *see* YELD

eilest *see* EE[1]

eilins *see* EILD

eill *see* ALE

eill-stob *see* EEL-STAB

ein *see* EVEN[2]

eindill *see* EENIL

eine *see* EE[1]

eird *see* ERD

eirn *see* EARN

eise *see* EASE[1]

eisen &c *18-*, **eicen** *la17* ['isən; *'əisən] *vi, of a cow* desire the male *la17-, now Bwk.* [see SND]

eist *see* EAST

eistack &c [*'istək, *'istɪk,&c] *n* something rare, surprising, or eyecatching *la18-e19.* [appar EE[1] + Eng *stick (v)* fix]

eistell, eister, Eistland *see* EAST

eit *see* AIT, EAT

eith &c [iθ; *Dmf also* *eθ] *adj, also* **eth** *la14-16, chf verse or proverb* easy *la14-19.*
adv easily *la14-e19.*
~**ly** *adv la14-e20.* [ME *ethe,* OE *ēaþe* easily]

eitherins *see* AITHER

eizel *see* AIZLE

eizewas *see* EASWAS

ejection &c, ejectioun *16-e17 n* **1** = ejection. **2** *law* (1) unlawful and violent expulsion of a person from his HERITAGE, ejectment *16-*; *cf action of* ~; (2) eviction *18-.*
action of ~ *law* an action either to eject a person or to recover property lost as in *n* 2, *17-.*

eke *see* EIK[2]

elaskit [ɪ'laskɪt] *n* = elastic *20-.*

elba &c *la19-, now Ayr,* **elbo** *la14-e17;* **elby &c** *20-, now midLoth Bwk n* = elbow *la14-.*
elbow(it) grass foxtail grass *19-, now Uls.* [*cf* next]

elbuck &c *18-, now Fif,* **elbok &c** *16-e17;* **elbi(c)k** *e20, Sh Ork NE n* = elbow *16-e20.* [var of Eng *elbow* (f OE *el(n)boga*) with phonologically irregular *-k* as in WARLOCK and WINNOCK; *cf* prec]

elby *see* ELBA

elcruke &c [*'il'krøk, *'jul-, *'el- &c] *n* a hook for lifting meat out of a pot *la15-e17.* [ME *ewel, awel,* OE *āwel* flesh-hook + CRUIK *n*]

elde *see* EILD[1]

elder &c; el(y)er &c *la19-20, chf NE* ['ɛl(d)ər, 'ɛljər; *NE also* 'əiljər] *n* **1** = elder *la14-.* **2** *Presbyterian Churches* a person elected and ordained to take part in church government as a member of the ecclesiastical courts (*eg the kirk session* (KIRK)), who does not have the authority to teach, *freq* (*though less freq 20-*) called **ruling** ~ (RULE) in contrast to the MINISTER or **teaching** ~; only men up to 1966, thereafter also women *la16-.*
~**n, eldren; eld(e)rin(g)** *la16-e18* old, *specif* **1** *of persons, 16-20;* **2** *of things etc, la16-e17.* ~**ship** **1** the office of *n* 2, *la16-.* **2** the kirk session (KIRK)

of a church *la16-.* **3** an assembly composed of MINISTERS and ELDERS of a number of parishes *la16.*
~**s' hours** respectable hours, *usu* considered to be about 10 pm *la19-.* ~**man** a MAGISTRATE or councillor in a BURGH *la15-e17; cf* ALDERMAN.

eldin &c, elding &c ['ɛldɪn] *n* fuel *la15-e20.* [ME, ON]

eldnyng &c [*'ildnɪŋ] *n* jealousy *e16, only Sc.* [metath f *eindilling* (EENIL)]

eldren, eldring *see* ELDER

eldritch &c *la18-,* **elriche &c** *16-e19,* **erlish &c** *e19;* **elrage** *e16,* **elrisch &c** *la16,* **alrische &c** *la16-e17 adj* **1** belonging to or resembling the elves or similar beings *16.* **2** weird, ghostly, strange, unearthly *16-, now chf literary.* [poss representing OE **ælfrīce &c* fairy kingdom, used attrib]

ele *see* EEL

eleck &c, elect &c *la16-* [ɪ'lɛk(t)] *n* **1** = elect *16-.* **2** *only* **elect** a bishop elect *15-e16.*
vt = elect *16-.*

electuare &c [*'ɪlɛktju'er, *'ɪ'lɛktjuər] *n* = electuary, a medicinal syrup etc *15-e16.* [*cf* F *électuaire*]

eleeven &c *19-,* **ellevin &c** *la14-17,* **alevin &c** *la14-17,* **levin** *la14-16;* **eleven &c** *la15-,* **eleiven &c** *17-,* **le'en &c** *e19,* S [ə'livn; *Cai Per* ə'levn; *NE* ə'ləivn; *sEC also* *'livn; S also* *li:n; *St* i'lɛvn, ə'lɛvn] *numeral* = eleven *la14-.*
~**t** *15-, now local,* ~**th** *17-* = eleventh. [*cf* ANELEVIN]

eleid *see* ELIDE

eleiven *see* ELEEVEN

elementar &c *adj* = elementary *16.* [ME, F *élémentaire,* L *elementārius*]

elemosinar &c *n* an almoner *16-17.* [OF *elemosinaire,* MedL *elimosinarius*]

eler *see* ELDER

elest *see* EE[1]

eleven *see* ELEEVEN

elf &c; elph(e) *la16 n* = elf *16-.*
~**-arrow** a flint arrowhead, thought to be used by fairies *la16-e20.* ~**-candle** a spark or flash of light, thought to be of supernatural origin *la18-e19.* ~**-cup** a small stone 'perforated by friction at a waterfall' *19-, now Rox.* ~**-mill** the death-watch beetle *19-e20, N.* ~**-ring** a fairy ring *19-, now Uls.* ~**-shot** *n* **1** a sickness (*usu* of cattle) thought to be caused by fairies *16-19.* **2** = ~*-arrow, la18-19. adj* shot by an ~*-arrow*; bewitched *17-, now Uls.* [*cf* ELFIN, FAIRY]

Elfin &c *la18-e20,* **Elphyne** *la16 n* **1** fairyland, the land of the elves *la16, la18-e20.* **2** *euphemistic* Hell *19-e20.* [perh f eModEng *elvene land* or altered f OSc (once) *elfame* (*cf* ON *alfheimar*)]

elic passion &c ['ilɪk 'paʃən, 'pasən, 'ɛlɪk, 'əilɪk &c] *n, orig* appendicitis, *now* colic *19-20.* [corruption of Eng *iliac passion*]

elide &c; **eleid** &c *17* [i'ləid, *ı'lid] *vt* **1** *law* annul, quash, exclude *la16-*. **2** = elide.

elike &c; **elik** &c [*i'ləik, *i'lık, *ı-] *adj* **1** = alike *la14-16*. **2 the** like, **the** same *la16-e17*. *adv* = alike *la14-16*.

~**wis**(**e**) &c likewise; also *la15-16*; *cf* ALIKEWAYS. [chf Sc; nME (rare); *cf* IN LIKE]

ell &c, **elne** &c *15-17*; **ellin** &c *la15-e17* *n*, *pl* also **elvis** &c *17* **1** = ell, the measure of length, the SCOTS ELL = approx four fifths of the English *15-*, now *hist*. **2** *in square measure* a square ELL *1*, *la15-*. **3** *uninflected in pl after numerals etc*, *15-17*.

~**-braid** ELL-wide *16-e17*. ~ **coal** *mining* a type of coal normally found in seams averaging one ELL in thickness *la18-*, now *Lnk*. ~**wan**(**d**) &c, **elvan** &c *la16-e20* *n* **1** (1) a measuring rod, one ELL long; *latterly* a yardstick *16-20*. (2) *attrib* long and thin *e19*. **2** the group of stars known as the Belt of Orion *16-e20*. **the King's Ellwand 1** the foxglove *la19-e20*, *S*. **2** = ~*wand* 2, *19-e20*. **Our** or **the Lady's Ellwand** = ~*wand* 2, *18-*, now *Ork*.

like five *etc* ~(**s**) **o'** (**blue**) **wind** at great speed, like lightning *la19-*, now *Ags*.

eller *n* = elder, the elder tree *e20*, *S*. [ModEng dial, ME]

ellevin *see* ELEEVEN

ellin *see* ELL

ellis *see* ELSE

elne *see* ELL

elongate *ptp*, *pt* removed to a distance *e16*. [L *ēlongāt-*, ptp stem of *ēlongāre*]

elph(**e**) *see* ELF

Elphyne *see* ELFIN

elrage, elriche, elrisch *see* ELDRITCH

else &c *la16-*, **ellis** &c *la14-e17* *adv* **1** = else *la14-*. **2** otherwise *la14-*, now *local*. **3** already, previously *16-e20*.

or ~ **no** *ironic* I don't think! *19-*, now *Bwk*.

elshin &c *la16-e19*; **elsing** &c *la16*, **elsone** &c *16-e18*, **alshin** &c *la18-e20* ['ɛl(ı)ʃın, 'ɛl(ı)sın] *n* an awl *16-*, now *Ork Rox*. [ME *elsyn*, MDu *elsene*]

elvan, elvis, elwand *see* ELL

ely &c; **eelie** ['ilı; *Dmf* *'elı; *S* 'jılı] *vi*, *chf* ~ **away 1** disappear, vanish gradually *19-e20*, *chf S*. **2** *of a group dispersing* drop off one by one *19*, *S*. [obscure]

elyer *see* ELDER

em [ɛm] *vti* = aim, *esp* throw (a stone) *20-*, *chf EC*, *S*.

ember *see* IMMER

embezle &c, **imbazel** &c; **embazle** &c, **imbesil** &c *vt* = embezzle *la17-e18*.

embrace *see* ENBRACE

Embro; Embr(**o**)**ugh** &c *la18-e19* ['ɛmbro, 'ɛmbrə, 'ɛmbrı] *familiar* = Edinburgh *la18-*.

eme *see* EEM

emerant &c [*'ɛmərant &c] *n* = emerald *la15-16*. [ME; *cf* AMERANT]

emergent *n* an accidental or unforeseen event; an emergency *17-18*. [eModEng]

emm *see* EEM

emmers *see* AMERS

emmerteen &c *n* an ant *la19-*, *NE*. [prob f Eng *emmet*, w intrusive *r* + *-in*(*g*); *cf* EEMOCK]

emmledeug &c [*'ɛml'djug, -'djʌg, &c] *n* butcher's offal, scraps *19-e20*. [obscure; *cf* EMMLINS]

emmlins &c *n pl* scraps; entrails, giblets *e20*, *Abd*. [Norw dial *emmel* strip + dim suffix *-ing*; *cf* EMMLEDEUG]

emmock *see* EEMOCK

emoliment &c [*'ı'molımənt] *n* = emolument *la15-17*. [L *ēmolimentum*, *ēmolu-*]

emot *see* EEMOCK

empasche *see* IMPESCHE

emperiour *see* EMPRIOUR

emphiteose *n* a perpetual FEU *la16-e17*. [only Sc; OF *emphiteose*, MedL *emphiteosis*, L *emphyteusis*]

empire *see* IMPIRE

emplese &c, **enplese** *la14* [ɛm'pliz, &c] *v* **1** *vt* please or satisfy (a person) *la14-e16*. **2** *vi* give pleasure or satisfaction (**to** a person); fit suitably (**to** a thing) *la14-e15*. **3** *absol* be pleased; choose *16*.

emplesance *15*, **empleseir** *la15-e16*, **emplesour** *la15-16* pleasure, satisfaction. [only Sc; OF *emplais-*, *emplaire*]

emprice &c [*'ɛmp(ə)rəis, &c] *n* = empress *la14-16*.

empriour &c [*'ɛmprıur] *n* **1** also **empreour, emperiour, impriour, imperiour** [*'ımp-&c] = emperor *15-e17*. **2** a military commander *15-16*.

emprunt &c, **enprunt** *n* a loan *la16*. [only Sc; F *emprunt*]

emptive &c *adj* empty *la15-16*. [altered f *empty*, by analogy with adjs of F orig in *-i* and *-if*]

empy &c *la18*, **empty** &c *adj* (*16-*), *v* (*la18-*) = empty. [*adj* rare in OSc; *cf* TUME]

en &c *19-*, **end** &c [ɛn; *N* also əin] *n*, *also* **hend** *16-e17*, **ine** *la19-*, *Bnf Abd* **1** = end *la14-*. **2** a room, *orig* one room of a two-roomed cottage *19-*. **3** *shoemaking* the (*now* waxed) thread used in sewing leather *18-e19*. **4** *weaving* a warp thread of yarn or silk *la18-*, now *Fif WC Slk*. **5** *curling* (CURL) an end, a unit of play, as in bowls *la19-*, now *local Abd-Kcb*.

vti **1** = end *la14-*. **2** stand on end *la19-*, *local Sh-Kcb*. **3** (1) *vt* kill, despatch *la19-*. (2) *vi* die *15-e20*. **4** settle, come to an agreement *la15-e17*.

~**less 1** = endless *la14-*. **2** pertinacious; long-winded *19-e20*.

~**day** the last day of one's life *la14-e17*. ~**-gird** *20-*, now *Sh*, ~**-hooping** *e19* the end-hoop of a barrel etc. ~-**pickle** the grain of corn at the top of a stalk *la19-e20*. ~-**rig** the land at the end of the furrow on which the plough is turned *18-*. ~**ways** forward, straight ahead; successfully *19-*, *now midLoth Bwk*. ~**wye** progress *la19-*, *Sh Fif*.

~ **out** bring to completion *la16-e17*. **first** *or* **last** ~ the first or last instalment of money etc *16-18*. **single** ~ a one-roomed house or flat *la19-*, *Gen except NE*. **tak** ~ come to an end *la14-*, *now Sh*.

enache &c [*?'ɛnəx, *?'i-] *n* amends or satisfaction for a fault or trespass *15-16*. [Gael *eineach* a truce]

enact, inact *vtr* **1** = enact. **2** = ACT *v* 3 (1) *17*, 3 (2) *17-e18*.

enarm &c *15-e19*, **inarme &c** *16-e17 vtr* enarm, equip with weapons.

enbalden &c *vt* = embolden *16-e17*.

enbandown &c [*ɛn'bandun, *-ən] *vt* = ABANDOUN *la14-e15*. [OF *en bandon*, var of *a bandon*]

enbrace &c *vt* **1** *also* **inbrace &c** *16-e17* = embrace *la14-e16*. **2** *also* **embrace** *la16* put (a shield) on the arm *la14-16*.

enchape *see* ESCHAPE

encheif [*ɛn'tʃiv] *vt* = encheve, achieve, win *la16-17*. [*cf* ESCHEVE]

enchesone &c [*'ɛntʃezun, *ɛn'tʃizun, *-ən, &c] *n* **1** = encheason, reason, occasion *la14-16*. **2** objection, dissent *la15-e16*.

vt challenge, accuse, blame *15-16*, *only Sc*.

enchew *see* ESCHEW

encoonter *vt* = encounter *la19-*.

encourage &c *vt* = encourage *16-*.

~**ment 1** = encouragement *la16-*. **2** pay, salary *18*, *only Sc*.

end *see* AYND, EN

endaivour *20-*, *local*, **endevoir &c** *la16-e17*, **indevoir &c** *la16-17*; **ende(e)vour** *la19-*, *now NE* [ɪn'devər, -'divər; *also* *ɪndə'vor] *n*, *vti* = endeavour *la16-*.

do one's ~(**s**) do one's utmost *la16-*.

endent [*ɛn'dɛnt] *vt* **1** = indent *la14-15*. **2** state formally, specify *la14-15*.

endevoir, endevour *see* ENDAIVOUR

endew *see* ENDUE

endill scheit *see* ENEL SHEET

endite &c [*ɛn'dəit] *vti* = indite, express in words or writing; write *la15-16*.

n composition, style of writing *e16*.

endlang &c; enlang &c *18-e20* [*prep* *ɛn(d)'laŋ, *-'land, *ɪn-]; *adv*, *?adj*, *?v* 'ɛn(d)'laŋ] *prep*, *also* **endland** *16*, **in lang** *la16* along, by the side of, from end to end of *la14-e19*.

adv **1** right along, straight on *la14-*. **2** lengthwise, at full length *19-*, *now local Bnf-Rox*.

adj at full length *la18-e20*.

vi harrow a field along the furrows *19-e20*.

endlangis *16-e17*, **inlangis** *la16-e17* = *prep*. [ME *endelong*, OE *andlang* (*adj*, *prep*), ON *end(e)lang-r* (*adj*)]

endoo *vt* = endow *19-*, *now Ork NE*.

end's errand *see* AINCE

endue &c, endew; indew &c *la17* [*ɛn'dju, *ɪn-] *adj* **1** *of sums etc* due to be paid, owing *la17*. **2** *of persons etc* owing, indebted *la17-19*. [*only Sc*; f DUE *adj*]

endurand *15-e16*, *only Sc*, **enduring** *15-e17*, **indurand &c** *la15-16*, *only Sc*, **induring &c** *la15-e17*, *only Sc* [*ɛn'dørən(d), *ɪn-, &c] *prep* during. [*presp* of Eng *endure*]

ene *see* EE[1]

enel-sheet &c *la17-19*, **endill scheit &c** *la16-e17* [*'ɛn(d)l 'ʃit] *n* a winding sheet, shroud. [obscure]

enemy &c, inemy &c *la15-16*, *only Sc*, **inimy &c** *15-e17*, *only Sc* ['ɛnəmɪ; *also* *'ɪnəmɪ, *'ɪnɪmɪ] *n* **1** = enemy *la14-*. **2 the** Devil *la15-*. **the auld** ~ *la19-*, **our ald** ~**is** *15-16* the English. **Goddis inymyes** *etc usu* the Saracens *15-e16*.

eneuch &c *15-*, **ineuch &c** *la14-e17*, **aneuch &c** *la15-e20*; **enouch &c** *15-19*, **inouch &c** *la14-16*, **anouch &c** *17-e20* [ɪ'n(j)ux; *nEC, WC* ɪ'n(j)ʌx; *Cai eRoss* ɪ'njox; ə-; *ə'nøx] *adj*, *adv*, *n* = enough. [ME *enoghe &c, inogh &c, anough &c*]

enew &c *la15-*, *latterly NE*, **inew &c** *la14-e16*, **anew** *la15-*, *only Sc*; **enow** *18-19* [ɪ'n(j)u, ə-] *adj* sufficient in number or quantity *la15-*.

n a sufficient number or quantity *la15-e20*. [eModEng *enow(e)*, ME *enoghe &c, inew &c, anowe*, OE *genōge*, pl of *genōg* enough]

enefftment *see* INFEFT

enflambe *16*, **inflam &c** *la14-16*, **inflamb &c** *16-e17* [*ɛn'flam, *-'flɑm; *ɪn-] *vt* = inflame, fire with desire or passion. [ME *enflaumme*, OF *enflammer*]

engage &c *la16-e17*, **engadge** *17-e18*, **ingadge** *la16-e18*, **ingage &c** *16-17 vti* **1** = engage *la16-*. **2** *vi* pray, launch into prayer *la19-*, *NE*. **3** *only* **ingadge** enlist *la17-e18*.

enga(d)ger one who took part in the *engagement* of 1647-48, *17*. ~**ment 1** = engagement *17-*. **2** the undertaking of 1647-48 to send an army to England in support of Charles I, *17*.

engaigne [*ɛn'genj(ɪ)] *n* resentment *la14*. [*only Sc*; OF = deception; resentment]

engender &c *la15-*, **ingener &c** *15-e17*; **engener &c** *la15-16* [*ɛn'dʒɛn(d)ər, *ɪn-] *vt* = engender.

engill *see* INGILL

engine *see* INGINE

Englify ['ɪŋ(g)lɪfaɪ] *vt*, *v*, *chf in ptp* **Englified** anglicized (in speech or manner) *19-*. [only Sc; formed on analogy w eg *modify*]

English &c, Englis &c *15-16* ['ɪŋlɪʃ, *-ɪs, *'ɪŋlz] *adj* **1** = English *la16-*. **2** Episcopal, Episcopalian *18-*; see SND.

n **1** = INGLIS *n* 1, *15-*. **2** *in pl* ~**es** = INGLIS *n* 3, *17*.

~**er** *now usu derog* an Englishman *la17-*, *now nEC Rox*.

~ **blanket** a blanket with a thick nap *18-*, *now WC*; *cf Scots blanket* (SCOTS). ~ **pint** the Imperial pint, ⅓ *Scots pint* (SCOTS) *la18-*. ~ **School** a school where English was taught, as opposed to a grammar school (where Classics was taught) *18-19*.

~ **and Scots** a children's game imitating the old BORDER Raids, played in various ways locally *la18-e20*. [*cf* INGLIS]

engreve; ingreve &c; engreif &c [*ɛn'griv, *ɪn-] *vt* **1** do hurt or harm to, injure *la14-e17*. **2** annoy *la15-e16*. [ME *engreve*, OF *engrever*]

engyre *see* INGERE

enhaunse *see* INHANCE

enherde *see* ANHERD

enjose &c *16-e17*, **injoys &c** *la16-e17* [*ɛn'dʒoz, *ɪn-] *vt* enjoy. [laME *enjoyse*, OF *enjoiss-* f *enjoir*]

enlaike *see* INLAIK

enlairge *la16-*, **enlarge** *la16-*, **inlarge &c** *17*, **inlairge &c** *la16-17* [*ɛn'lerdʒ &c*] *vt* = enlarge.

enlang *see* ENDLANG

enlichten [ɛn'lɪxtən; *Abd also* ɛn'lɪxən] *vt* = enlighten *19-*, *now local Bnf-midLoth*.

enner *see* INNER

ennet seid *n* = anet seed, dill seed *16-e17*. [only Sc]

ennow *see* INWITH

ennoy [*ə'nɔi] *n* annoyance, vexation, trouble *la14-e16*. [laME *ennoye*, OF *enoi*]

enorm &c [*St* i'nɔrm; *i'nɔrm] *adj* **1** = enorm, enormous; unusual *16-19*. **2** *also* **inorme** *la16-e17* heinous *16-e18*. **3** *law* considerable, severe, *chf* ~ **lesioun** *etc* great detriment *16-*. **4** *of persons* acting irregularly or without regard for law *la16-e17*.

~**ity &c, inormité &c** *la14-e17* **1** = enormity, an outrageous act *15-*. **2** extreme wickedness *la14-*.

enouch *see* ENEUCH

enouth *see* INWITH

enow *see* EENOO, ENEW

enplese *see* EMPLESE

enprunt *see* EMPRUNT

enquire *see* INQUIRE

enrage, inrage &c *la16-17* *vti* **1** = enrage *16-*. **2** *vt* make furious *16-*.

enschew &c *17*, **insew &c** *la16-17*, **inschew &c** *la16-17* [*ɛn'ʃu, *-'sju, *ɪn-] *vti* = ensue.

enschew *see* ESCHEVE, ESCHEW

ense &c; anse &c *adv* else, otherwise *la18-*, *now local Abd-Slk*.

or ~ **no** *ironic* I don't think! *19-*, *now Ags midLoth*. [*an* (THAN) + *-se* f *else*; *cf* ELSE]

ensenʒe &c *la14-e17*; **enseignie &c** *la15-e17*,

ensignie &c *la15-16* [*ɛn'sinʒı, *-'sinʒı, *-'sɪnʒı, *-senʒı, &c*] *n* **1** a war cry, a rallying cry or signal *la14-16*. **2** a distinguishing emblem or symbol; *in pl* insignia of dignity or office *la15-e17*. **3** = ensign *la15-e17*. [ME *ensaigne*, OF *enseigne*; *cf* ANSENʒE, HANDSENʒE]

entechment [*ɛn'titʃmɛnt] *n* instruction *e16*. [only Sc; *en-* + *techment* (TEACH)]

enteece *vt* = entice *la19-e20, Bnf-Ags*.

enteetle *vt* = entitle *19-*, *now Ags Uls*.

entent &c *la14-16*, **intent** *15-* *n* = intent *la14-*.

set (**one's**) ~ set one's mind *la14-16*.

ententely [*ɛn'tɛntılı] *adv* attentively *la14-e15*. [only Sc; perh f ME *ententyfly*; *cf* Eng *intently*]

enter &c, inter &c *la14-*, *now NE Ags* ['ɛntər; *NE Ags* 'ɪntər] *vti* **1** = enter *la14-*. **2** *freq* ~ **in** *or* **to** obtain or assume possession of lands etc *la14-16*. **3** (1) *vi, also* ~ **in** *15-e16*, **to** *la15-e18*, *latterly esp of harvesting* engage in (a task), begin work *15-*, *now local Abd-Uls*. (2) *vt* cause to begin, put to work *la16-19*. **4** *vi* (1) appear or present oneself in a court *la15-16*. (2) return oneself in to prison *la15-16*. **5** *vt* produce, present (a person) to a court of justice; place in custody *15-17*. **6** put (a person) formally in possession or occupation of land, property, or an office *15-19*. **7** record or register as a member of a body, note by name *la15-*. **8** record (a vessel or cargo) in an official register *15-*.

enterin(g) *of weather* suitable for work, *esp* **enterin(g) morning** *la19-e20*.

enteray *see* ENTRY

enterchangeably *see* INTERCHANGE

enterdick *see* INTERDICT

enteres *see* ENTRESS, INTERES

enterie *see* ENTRY

entermiddill &c, **intermiddill** [*ɛntər'mɪdl, *ɪntər-] *vt* intermingle *e16*. [only Sc; ME *entermedle &c*]

enterpreeze *la19-*, *now Ags*, **enterprise &c** *la15-* *n* = enterprise.

enterteen *19-20*, **entertene &c** *la16-e18*, **enterteny &c** *16-e17*, **intertene &c** *16-e17*, **interteny &c** *16-e17*; **intertynie &c** *la16-e17* [ɛntər'tin, *-'tɛnı, *-'tinı, *ɪntər-, &c*] *vt* = entertain.

entertenyr [*ɛntərtə'nir] *vt, only as infin* entertain *e16*. [only Sc; OF *entretenir*]

entra *see* ENTRY

entrais *see* ENTRESS

entray, entré *see* ENTRY

entreis *see* ENTRESS

entres *see* INTERES

entress &c *la16-e18*, **entres &c** *la15-e17*, **enteres &c** *la15-17*, **interes** *15-16*, **intres &c** *16-e17*; **entrais &c** *la15-e16*, **entreis &c** *la16-e17* [*ɛn'trɛs, *-'tres, *-'trɪs, *ɛntər-, *ɪnt(ə)r-, &c*] *n* = ENTRY 1 (*la15-e18*), 5 (*16-17*), 6 (*la15-e16*).

~ **silver** = *entry silver* (ENTRY) *16-e17*.

non ~ *n, law* = NON-ENTRY 1 (*la15-17*), 2 (*la15-e16*). [? f ENTER + *-ess* after Eng *duress* etc]

entrie *see* ENTRY

entromet *v* = INTROMIT *15*.

entry *la16-*, **entré &c** *la14-16*, **entra** *15-e16*, **entrie &c** *la16-e18*, **intré** *la15-16, only Sc*, **intra &c** *la15*, **intery &c** *la16-17, only Sc*; **ent(e)ray &c** *15-e16*, **enterie &c** *17* ['ɛntrɪ, *'ɪntrɪ &c*] *n* **1** = entry *la14-*. **2** a place of entry *la14-*: (1) an alley or covered passage, *usu* public, in or between houses *18-*, *now Gen except Sh Ork Abd*; (2) the front doorway of a house; an entrance-lobby or porch, *latterly esp* in a block of flats *la18-*, *now local*; (3) the entrance to an avenue leading to a house; the avenue itself *18-*, *now local NE, EC*. **3** the coming in of goods to port; the note of this in official records *15-e16*. **4** an appearance or presentation in a court of justice; the return of a prisoner to custody *15-e17*. **5** *law* the establishment of an heir as a new VASSAL with his SUPERIOR, thereby making his ownership effective *15-19*; *see also* NON-ENTRY.
~ **silver** money paid on entering into the occupation of land, on being admitted as an apprentice, on bringing goods into port etc *16*.

enty *adj* ? empty *e16, only Sc.*

enunte *ptp* = enoynt, anointed *e16*.

enveron &c, inviroun &c [*ɛn'virun, *-ən, *-'vaɪrən, *ɪn-] *vt* = environ, encircle *la14-e17*.

envy &c, invy &c *la14-e17* [ən'vaɪ] *n, vt* = envy *la14-*.
invyar &c a person who envies *la16-e17*. **envyfu &c** *19-20*, **invyfu &c** full of malice or envy, envious **of** *or* **that**. **invious &c** = envious *15-e17*.

ephesian [ə'fiʒən] *n* a pheasant *19-e20*. [f *a pheesan*; see also FEESANT]

ephor ['ɛfər] *n* a prefect at the Edinburgh Academy *la19-*, *Ebd*. [Gk *éphoros* overseer]

Episcopaulian &c *n* = Episcopalian *19-e20*.

eppershand *see* AMPERSYAND

epple *see* AIPPLE

equal &c *16-*, **equale &c** *la15-16*, **aqual** *la19-20*, **eekfow &c** *la18-e19* [*'ikfu]; **aequall &c** *la16 adj* **1** = equal *la15-*. **2** in line or on a level with (something) *la16*.
equal-aqual ['ikwəl 'akwəl] *adj* equally balanced, alike, similar, quits *19-*, *local Cai-Bwk*.
adv, also **equals-aquals** *19-*, *now midLoth* equally, alike *19-e20*.

equate *ptp, pt* levelled; made equal *e16*. [ME; MedL *equatus*, L *aequātus*]

eque &c *16-e19*; **equie &c** *17-e18*, **aequie &c** *la17-18* [*'ɛkwɪ, *'ikwɪ] *adj, in full sic* ~ *of accounts* duly balanced *16*.
n **1** an acquittance or receipt for a properly balanced account, or for money paid *la16-17*. **2**

the contribution paid annually by each constituent BURGH to the *Convention of Royal Burghs* (CONVENTION), in effect the *burgh mails* (BURGH) or *feu duty* (FEU) payable to the crown *la17-e19*. [MedL; L *aequē* equally]

Equivalent *n* **the** sum of money which the English government guaranteed to pay to Scotland as compensation for Scotland's prospective share in the English public debt as part of the new United Kingdom *e18*.

er *see* EAR[1], ERE

erand *see* EERANT

erch *see* AIRCH, ERGH

erchin *see* HURCHEON

erd &c *la14-e20*, **erthe &c** *la14-e19*; **eird** *la15-e19*, **eard &c** *la16-e20*, **earth &c** *la16-* [*St* ërθ; *ird] *n* = earth *la14-*.
vt, latterly chf **eard** *la16-e20* bury *la14-20*.
erthlins &c earthwards; along or towards the ground *18-19*.
erd-dyn &c *e15*, **erdine &c** *la14-16* an earthquake; cf *yird din* (YIRD). ~**-fast** fixed in the ground *la15-*. ~**-house &c** a building with earthen walls; *latterly* an Iron-Age underground walled dwelling etc *la15-*. ~ **hun &c** a mysterious animal (actually a mole?) supposed to burrow in graveyards *la19-*, *NE*. ~**-silver** payment for burial-ground *la15-16, only Sc.*
earth-worm *fig* a money-grubber *19-*, *now Bnf Abd*.
at (**the**) ~ *of buildings* completely demolished *16-e17*. **by a the earth** for all the world, exactly *la19-e20*, *local Bnf-midLoth*. ~ **and stane** symbols used in the transference of landed property *15-17*. **let the** ~ **big** *or* **bear the dike** *proverb* let the cost of something be taken out of the profit that it yields later *18-*, *now Sh.* [*cf* YIRD]

ere &c; **er &c, eer &c** [ir; *unstressed also* ər] *adv* **1** = ere, before, formerly *la14-16*. **2** early, soon *la18-e20*.
prep, verse = ere *19*.
conj before, until *20-*, *Sh Abd Ags.*
erar &c *adv* sooner, rather, as a matter of preference or choice *la14-16*. **the erar** the sooner, all the more readily *la15-16*. **erast &c** *adj* first, earliest *15-16*. *adv* **1** = erst, in the first place, by choice or preference *15-16*. **2** earliest, first *la14-e16*.
erefernyear &c the year before last *la15-e20*, *latterly chf Sh.* **erethestreen, ere da streen &c** *20-*, *Sh Ork n* (*adv*) the night before last *18-*. **ereyesterday &c** the day before yesterday *19-e20*. [*cf* AIR[5], OR]

ere *see* EAR[1], EAR[2]

erection &c, erectioun &c *la15-16 n* **1** = erection *la15-*. **2** *law, after the Reformation* the creation of a temporal lordship out of a spiritual benefice; the lordship so created *17-18*; cf *Lord of E*~ (LORD).

ere-ledder *see* EAR-LEATHER
ergh &c *19-e20*, **erch &c** *la16-e20*, **argh &c**
15-e20; **erf** *19-e20* [ɛrx, erx; *NE also* arx; *Abd*
also ɛrf] *adj* **1** timorous *15-e20*. **2** hesitant,
reluctant *15-20*. **3** scanty, insufficient;
exhausted physically or in resources *19-e20*.
vi be timid, feel reluctant, hesitate *la16-e19*.
n doubt, fear, timidity *19-20*.
archly timidly; scarcely *la14-15*. **~ness** = *n*,
15-e20. [ONorthumb *arȝ* cowardly, OE *argian*
be slothful, lose heart, ON *argr* cowardly]
Eris, Erische *see* EERISH
eritabill *see* HERITABLE
eritage *see* HERITAGE
erle *see* ARLE, EARL, HERLE
erlish *see* ELDRITCH
erm *see* AIRM
ern *e19*, **urn &c** *la15-e19* *vt* pain, irritate. [only
Sc; obscure]
erne *see* EARN, IRON
ernist *see* ERNEST
erock *see* EAROCK
eroy *see* IEROE
erran, errand *see* EERANT
errasy &c *n* = heresy *15-e17*. [ME *eresie*, OF
eresie]
errock *see* EAROCK
errour &c, arrour &c *la15-e17* *n* **1** = error
la14-e17. **2** *law* a mistaken or wrongful decision
on a *brief of inquest* (BRIEF) *la15-e16*.
assise of ~ *law* an ASSIZE appointed to REDUCE
an erroneous service of *heirship* (HEIR) *la15-17*.
Ersche *see* ERSE
erse &c, ers *15-e17* *n* **1** = arse *15-*. **2** the hin-
terland, the interior *la19-*, *local Ork-Abd*.
ersie *adj* hinder *20-*, *chf Sh Ork*. **ersit, essart**
stubborn, perverse *la19-*, *chf SW*; *cf* ARSET.
esscock an inflamed pimple *18-20*, *chf NE*.
aa ~ an pooches describing the back view of
a stout dumpy man *20-*, *Abd*.
Erse *la16-*, **Ersche &c** *la15-e17*; **Earse &c**
17-19 [ɛrs, *ɛr*ʃ] *adj* **1** Irish; *Highland* (HIE-
LAND), GAELIC *la15-16*. **2** used by *Lowlanders*
(LAWLAND) to describe *Highlanders*, their language, customs etc *18-e19*. **3** = Erse.
n **1** Scottish GAELIC *16-19*. **2** = Erse.
Erschry = *Erischry* (EERISH) *15-e16*. [reduced
from EERISH; *cf* IRISH and GAELIC]
ersedene *see* ARCHEDENE
ersel *see* YOUR
ersit *see* ERSE[1]
ert *see* AIRT[1]
erthe *see* ERD
eruction *n* a violent outburst *19-*. [*cf* Eng *eruction* belching and colloq Eng *ruction*]
erumption [ɪˈrʌmpʃn] *n* an outburst, uproar
e20, *local EC-S*. [f Eng *eruption*]
ery *see* EERIE
eryll *see* EARL
es *see* EASE[1]

eschaet *see* ESCHEAT
eschame *see* ASCHAME
eschape &c [*ɛsˈtʃep] *n* = escape *la14-e17*.
vti, *also* **escheap &c** *la15-e17*, **enchape** *15*, *only*
Sc, **ethchape &c** *e15* [*ɛnˈtʃep, *ɛθ-] = escape
la14-e17.
esche *see* ESH, ISH
escheap *see* ESCHAPE
escheat &c *la16-*, **eschete &c** *la14-17*, **achet**
la15; **eschaet &c** *15-16*, **aschaet** *16-e17*
[ɛsˈtʃit; *ɛsˈtʃet, *ə(s)ˈtʃit] *n*, *also* **ethchete** *e15*
[*ɛθ-] *law* **1** property, possessions or goods
taken from a person by forfeiture or confiscation, *esp* that falling to the Crown thus *la14-17*.
2 the forfeiture of a person's property, HERITA-
BLE or MOVEABLE, on his conviction for certain
crimes, and until 1748 on denunciation for non-
payment of debts *15-e20*.
vt, *ptp also* **escheat &c** forfeit *15-19*. [ME; OF
eschete, f *escheoir* fall to one's share; *cf* Eng *escheat*
= the reverting of property to the overlord or
the state when there is no heir]
escheif *see* ESCHEVE
escheme *see* ASCHAME
eschete *see* ESCHEAT
escheve; escheif &c *la14-e16* [*ɛsˈtʃiv, *ɛˈʃiv,
&c] *v* **1** *vt* (1) *also* **enschew** *15-e16* [*?ɛnˈʃiv]
accomplish, bring to a successful issue, achieve
la14-15. (2) overcome, vanquish *la14-e15*, *only*
Sc. **2** *vi* succeed *la14-e16*. **3** *vti* succeed in
escaping (from) *15-16*; *cf* ESCHEW 2. [ME
escheffe; OF *eschever*, var of *achever*]
eschew [ɛsˈtʃ(j)u] *v* **1** *also* **enchew &c** *la15*,
enschew *15* [*ɛnˈtʃ(j)u, *ɛnˈʃ(j)u] = eschew
la14-. **2** get off or away, escape *la14-e17*. **3**
draw back, withdraw (**from** a person etc);
draw aside *15-16*, *only Sc*.
ese *see* EASE[1]
esedrop &c; easedrop &c [*ˈizdrop, *ˈez-] *n*
the dripping of water from the eaves of a house;
the space liable to receive this *la15-16*.
[eModEng *ese*, reduced f *eves*, OE *efes* eaves +
Eng *drop*; *cf* laOE *yfesdripe* and EAVESDROP]
eseikis gray *see* ESSEX GRAY
esement *see* EASEMENT
esh *20-*, *local WC-Uls*, **esche &c** *16-17*, **aish**
&c *la16-19*, **asche** *la16-17* *n* = ash(-tree or
-wood).
esiament, esiement *see* EASEMENT
esikis gray *see* ESSEX GRAY
esing *see* EASIN(S)
esk *see* ASK[1], YESK
eslar *see* AISLAR
esment *see* EASEMENT
esp *n* = asp, the aspen tree *la16-e20*.
ess[1] &c *n* a waterfall *19-*, *NE*, *chf in place-names*.
~cock the dipper *la19-e20*, *NE*. [Gael *eas*]
ess[2] &c *n* an S-shaped hook *19-e20*.
ess *see* ACE, ASS
essart *see* ERSE[1]

essay *see* ASSAY

esscock *see* ERSE[1], ESS[1]

Essex gray; es(e)ikis &c gray [*'ɛsɪks 'gre]
n ? a grey cloth made in Essex *e17*.

essonʒe &c, assonʒe &c *la14-16* [*ɛ'sʌnʒɪ,
*ʔɛ'səɪnʒɪ, *ə-] *n* an excuse, *esp* one offered as a
legal defence, a pretext *la14-17*.
vtr excuse *la14-e17*.

essonʒeour &c a person who offers an excuse
la14-e17. [ME *essoyn*, OF *essoyne*, MedL *essonia*;
cf SONYIE, Eng *essoin*]

essyis *see* ASSIZE

est *n* = nest *19-e20*, S. [wrong division of *a nest*]

est *see* EAST

estaiblish &c *la16-*, *now local*, **establis &c**
15-16; **establish &c, estabilish &c** *la16 vt*
= establish *la16-*.

E∼ed **Kirk** the *Church of Scotland* (CHURCH) *20-*.
∼**ment 1** = establishment *la19-*. **2** = E∼ed
Kirk, 18-19.

estal(d) *see* EAST

estate &c *n* = estate *15-*.

The E∼s *la16-*, **The Three** E∼s *la14-* the
three bodies composing the Scottish Parliament, *now hist*: (1) the archbishops and bishops,
and, before the reformation, all abbots and
mitred priors; (2) the barons, *ie* both the nobility and the COMMISSIONERS for shires and *stewar-
tries* (STEWART); (3) the COMMISSIONERS from the
royal burghs (ROYAL).

estent *see* EXTENT

ester *see* EAST

estimy &c [*'ɛstɪmɪ] *vt* = esteem *15-16*. [perh
after OF *estimé*, ptp of *estimer*]

estin *see* EAST

Estland *see* EAST

estlair *see* AISLAR

estonist *see* ASTONIST

estreen *see* YESTREEN

estwart *see* EAST

esy *see* EASY

et, ete *see* EAT

eth *see* EITH

ethchape *see* ESCHAPE

ethchete *see* ESCHEAT

ether, eddir; adder &c *la18-* ['ɛðər; *NE*
'ɛdər] *n, pl also* **ed(d)ris &c** *la14-e15* = adder
la14-.

∼**bell** the dragonfly *19*. ∼**stane &c** a small
perforated prehistoric stone or bead, used as an
amulet *la18-19*. **fleeing** ∼ = etherbell, *19-*, S.
[*cf* NETHER[1]]

ether *see* UDDER, AITHER, EDDER

etherin *see* AITHER

ethnik &c *n* a heathen, pagan *la14-16*. [laME;
laL (f Gk) *ethnicus*]

etin &c [*'ɪtɪn] *n* a giant *la15-*, *now arch*. [ME
etene &c, OE *eoten*]

etion; aishan &c *la19-* ['eʃən] *n, freq contemptuous* stock, kindred, breed *18-*, *chf NE*. [wrong
division of *a nation*]

etle *see* ETTLE

etnach ['ɛtnəx] *adj* of or belonging to the juniper; made of juniper wood *la18-e20*.
n, also **aitnach &c** *la19-e20*, N the juniper, the
juniper berry *la18-*, *now NE*. [Gael *aitionnach*
(*adj*), *aitionn* (*n*) juniper; *cf* AITEN[2]]

ett, etten *see* EAT

etter *n* = ATTER *19-e20*.
vi emit purulent matter, fester *19-e20*.
∼**some** *of persons* contentious, disagreeable *e20*,
Sh-Ags. ∼**y** = attery (ATTER) 3 (1), (2) (*19-e20*,
S), 4 (*19-e20*). [*cf* ON *eitr* (*n*), *eitra* (*v*)]

ettercap, ettercope *see* ATTERCAP

etterlin &c, etterlyne *la16 n* a two-year old
cow or heifer in calf *la16-e20*. [perh f Gael
atharla a heifer]

ettle &c, ettil &c; etle &c *15-e18* ['ɛtl; *Bnf also*
*'atl] *v* **1** *vi* purpose or intend **to do** *la14-*. **2** *vt*
intend, plan (something) *16-*. **3** (1) *vt* aim,
direct (a blow or missile) *la15-e20*. (2) *vi, chf* ∼
at, for take aim at, take as or make one's objective, try to reach *la15-*. **4** (1) *vt* attempt, venture *19-e20*. (2) *vi* try, make an attempt **at** *18-*.
5 *vi* direct one's efforts, give attention **to**
la16-e17. **6** (1) *vt* guide, direct the course of *20-*,
Ags. (2) *vir* ∼ **to, at** *etc* make for, direct one's
course towards *19-*, *now Ags*. **7** *vi, chf* ∼ **at** try
to express, 'get at' *19-*, *now midLoth*. **8** *vti* ∼
for, after *or* **to do** desire very much, be eager
for *la19-*, *chf N*. **9** *vi* ∼ **to do** be about to, on
the verge of *la19-e20*. **10** *vt* expect, anticipate,
guess *19-*, *chf WC*, S.
n **1** *chf verse* one's aim, purpose, design, object
la18-19. **2** an effort, attempt *19-*. **3** an ambi-
tion, desire *e20*.

in ∼ **earnest** in dead earnest *la19-*, S. [ME
ettil &c (*v*), ON *ætla*]

Ettrick Shepherd *nom de plume* James Hogg
la18-.

eucharist &c *n* **1** = eucharist *15-*. **2** the vessel
containing the consecrated bread *15-16*, *only Sc*.

euk *see* YEUK

euther *see* YOWDER

evade &c *v* **1** *vt* avoid, shun, escape from, elude
la15-. **2** *vi* get away, escape *16-*. [eModEng; F
évader, L *ēvādere*]

eveit *see* EVITE

even[1] &c *la16-*, **evin &c** *la14-16*; **e'en &c** *16-*
n = even, evening, *freq* the eve of a saint's day
etc *la14-*.
at ∼ in the evening *15-*. [*cf* EENING]

even[2] &c *15-*, **evin &c** *la14-e20*, **e'en &c** *la18-*;
ein *19-e20*, *SW*, **aiven** (*adj, adv*) *la19-*, *nEC*
['ivən; *N nEC Ayr* 'evən; *N also* 'əivən; *C, S also*
in; *SW* *əin] *adj* **1** = even *la14-*. **2** *of numbers*
not odd, exactly divisible by two *la14-*.
adv **1** = even *la14-*. **2** directly, in a straight

line, straight *la14-19*. **3** in a direct line of descent *la14-e15, only Sc.* **4** in a level position *la14-16, only Sc.* **5** no less *or* no other than; just *la14-e17.* **6** *only* **e'en &c**, *with verbs* just, simply *la18-*: '*I may een gae hang*'.

vtir **1** = even *15-*. **2** *vt* estimate, compare **with**, liken **to** *15-*. **3** ~ (**someone**) **to** (**someone**) talk of (someone) as a possible marriage match for (someone) *la18-19*. **4** bring to the same level or condition; *chf* lower, demean *19-, now Ags.* **5** (1) make (someone) out **to be** *etc la18-e20.* (2) impute (something) **to** (someone) *19-e20.* (3) *vr, in a good sense* think oneself entitled **to** *19-e20.*

~**ar** a person appointed to apportion lands *16.* ~**er &c** *weaving* an instrument for spreading out the yarn on the beam *19-, now Kinr.* **eend** *adj* straight, level, exact *e20, Rox.* **eend on** continuous(ly), incessant(ly) *20-, chf S.* **einins &c** *marbles* a call claiming the right to **tak einins,** *ie* to change to a more favourable position at an equal distance from the ring *20-, local.* ~**lik(e) &c** *adj* **1** equal *e15.* **2** just, equitable *e15. adv* equally, evenly *la14-e15.* ~**likly** exactly; directly *e15.* ~**ly** *adj* **1** smooth, even, level *la16-, now Ags Arg.* **2** (1) equal in amount *la14-16.* (2) equal in character, size, force *15-e17.* **3** (1) equitable, just *la14-e17.* (2) impartial *la15-16. adv* **1** = evenly *la14-.* **2** uniformly, without variation *la14-.* **3** in an even or level position *la15-16.* ~**lyness** equality; equanimity *15-19.* **eens &c** even as *19-e20.* **be ~s** (**with**) be even or quits (with) *la18-, now local EC.* **eent** indeed *19-, now Arg:* '*I am not. Ye are eent*' [contracted f *even it*].

~**doon &c** *adj* **1** *esp of very heavy and continuous rain* straight, perpendicular *la18-.* **2** sheer, absolute, downright *la18-e20.* **3** honest, frank, sincere *18-e20. adv* absolutely, completely, downright *19-e20.* ~ **forrit &c** straightforward *18-e20.* ~ **on** continuously, without ceasing, straight on *19-, Gen except Sh Ork.* ~ **out** forthright(ly), without restraint *19-, now Ags Fif.* ~ **up** *adj* straight, erect *la16-19. adv* straight up *la18-, now Sh Ags.*

~ **hands** *or* **heads wi** on an equal footing with *19-e20.* ~ **one's wit to** condescend to argue with *la19-e20.* [*cf* EENOO]

evenoo *see* EENOO

eventure *see* AVENTURE

ever &c, iver *la20-* ['ɪvər, 'ɛvər, *St* 'ɛ̈vər] *adv, also* **oor** *la19-e20, Cai* = ever *la14-.*

~**ly** constantly, perpetually *19-, now Gall.* ~**ilk &c** every, each *la14-19.* ~**ilkane &c** *la14-e17*, ~**ilkon(e)** *la16-e19* every one. ~**ilk dele** every whit, altogether *la14-16.* ~**lasting &c** *adj* = everlasting *la14-. n* **a** *or* **a guid** ~**lasting &c** a considerable or seemingly interminable while *19-e20.* **at the** ~**leevin** (**gallop**) as fast as possible, very fast *la19-, chf Abd.*

~ **now** just now *20-, chf Highl* [corruption of *evenoo* (EENOO)]. ~ **and on** continually *20-, local N-Ayr.*

ever *see* IVER

everé *see* EVERY

evert *vt* **1** = evert, overturn, destroy *16-e17.* **2** overthrow (a person) in an argument *18-19.*

every &c, ivery &c *20-*; **everé &c** *la14-e17* ['ɪv(ə)rɪ, 'ɛv(ə)rɪ, *St* 'ɛ̈vrɪ] *adj* **1** = every *la14-.* **2** each of two, both *la18-e20.*

interj, marbles a call for liberty to play in any position *20-, now midLoth.*

~**day** a weekday as opposed to Sunday *la19-, local EC-S.*

evident &c; avedent &c *la15-16* ['ɛvɪd(ə)nt, **?*'evɪdənt] *adj* = evident *la15-.*

n, law **1** a document establishing a legal right or title to anything, *freq* **writs and** ~**s** *la14-.* **2** a piece of evidence, a proof *15.*

evill &c *n, adj, adv* = evil *la14-.*

~**-avisit** disposed to wrong-doing *la15-16.* ~**-dedy** *adj* evil-doing *16.* ~**-disposit** **1** = evil-disposed *la15-e17.* **2** not in good health or condition *16.* ~**- gevin** inclined to do evil or cause trouble *16.* ~**-willy** malevolent *16.*

evin &c [**?*'ivən] *n* matter, subject-matter; substance, means *la15.* [ME *evene &c*, ON *efne*]

evin *see* EVEN¹, EVEN²

evining *see* EENIN(G)

evite &c; eveit *17* [ə'vit, ə'vəit; **ə'vɪt*; ɪ-] *vt* avoid, escape, shun *17-.* [eModEng; F *éviter*, L *ēvītāre*]

evor &c [**'ivor, *-ər*] *n* = ivory *la15-16.*

~ **bane &c** = *n, 16.*

ewder *see* YOWDER

ewe *see* YOWE

ewest &c; ewis &c *la15-e17*, **ewous &c** *16* [**'juist, *'juis, *-əs*] *prep* close to, next to (a place); beside *la15-e17.*

adj close, near, next **to** *la15-e20.* [appar wrong division of ME *anewest*, OE *on nēawast* in the vicinity]

ewfall, ewfauld *see* AEFAULD

ewin-drift *see* YOWDENDRIFT

ewine *see* EE¹

ewis, ewous *see* EWEST

ex *see* AIX

exack, exact [ɛg'zak(t)] *adj* (*adv*) = exact *la16-.*

exactly **1** = exactly *la16-.* **2** without more ado; just; positively *la19-, local Abd-Bwk.*

exaemen *see* EXAMIN

exalt &c [**ɛg'zalt*] *ptp* exalted *la15-16.*

exame *see* EXEM

examin &c, examine &c; exemin &c *16-19*, **exaemen &c** *la19-, NE* [ɛg'zemɪn; **ɛg'zɛmɪn*] *n* **1** examination *la15-, now Abd.* **2** *specif* an examination by a Presbyterian clergyman of the theological knowledge of his parishioners, in preparation for Communion *18-e20.*

vt = examine *15-*.

examinable persons those eligible for *n* 2, *18-e19*. **exeminatioun** *la16*, **exemination** *la19-*, *NE* = examination. [L *examen*; *cf* EXEM]

examinate &c [*ɛg'zemɪnat, *-et, *ɛg'zɛmɪn-] *ptp* examined *15-e19*.

vt = examine *la16-17*, *only Sc*.

examinator &c an examiner, interrogator *la16-19*. [L *examināt-*, ptp stem of *exāmināre*]

exauctorate &c *vt*, *chf in ptp* **exauctorate** deposed from office, relieved of authority *18-e19*. [L *exauctōrāt-*, ptp stem of *exauctōrāre* dismiss from service]

excaise &c *19-*, **excuse &c, exkeese &c** *19-*, *NE* [*n and v: NE* ɛk'skiz, *C* ɛk'skez; *ɛk'skøz] *n* (*la15-*), *vti* (*la14-*) = excuse.

excamb [ɛk'skam(b); ɪk-] *vt, law* exchange (land) *la15-*. [only Sc; MedL *excambiare*]

excambion &c [ɛk'skambɪɔn, -ɪən; ɪk-] *n, law* exchange of land or property *la15-*. [only Sc; var of next after words w -*io(u)n*]

excambium [*ɛk'skambɪʌm] *n, law* = EXCAM-BION *la15-e16*. [MedL; *cf* EXCAMB]

ex capite lecti [ɛks 'kapɪte 'lɛktaɪ] *law* = (*up*)*on the head of deathbed* (DAITH), *19*. [L]

excede &c [*ɛk'sid] *vti* **1** = exceed *la14-17*. **2** *vt* surpass, outdo (in excellence, rank etc) *la14-16*. **3** *vi* be in excess *la15-16*.

excedand exceeding, excessive *15*.

excellence &c *n* **1** = excellence *la15-*. **2** *as a title of honour*, *la14-16*.

excep &c, except [ɛk'sɛp(t), ək-] *v, also* **accept** *la15-16*, **accep** *la15-16*, *pt, ptp also* **excep(p)it** *la15-e19*, *ptp also* **excep(t) &c** *15-16* **1** *vt* = except *la15-*. **2** *vi, law* make an objection, protest *la15-e16*.

prep **1** = except *la15-*. **2** leaving out of account; in addition to, besides *la15-16*.

conj = except *la15-*.

~**and** *15-16*, **exceppin(s)** *19-*, *now Sh Ags midLoth* = *prep* 1.

except; excep(p) *16* [*ɛk'sɛp(t), *ək-] *vt* = accept *la15-e17*. [ME; L *except-*, ptp stem of *excipere* receive; *cf* ACCEP]

exception &c, exceptioun &c *la14-16 n* **1** = exception *la14-*. **2** *law* (1) a plea against a charge etc, a defence *15-*, *only Sc*; (2) an objection to a judge's charge to the jury in a civil case *19-*.

excers *see* EXERCE

exchequer,   exchak(k)er &c   *17*; **exchek(k)er &c** *17* [ɛks'tʃɛkər, *-'tʃakər] *n* = (the royal) exchequer *17-*.

Court of E~ a court having jurisdiction in revenue cases (merged since 1856 in the *Court of Session* (SESSION)) *18-19*. [*cf* CHEKKER]

excipient [*ɛk'sɪpɪənt] *n, law* a person who raises an EXCEPTION in law *la16-17*. [L *excipient-*, presp stem of *excipere* except]

exclaim *n* a shout, exclamation *19-e20*.

excresce *18-e19*, **excres(s)** *la16-17 n* increase; surplus *la16-e19*.

vti = excresce, increase, exceed *la16-e17*.

excrescence &c *n* **1** an excess amount, increase, surplus *la15-18*. **2** = excrescence.

excress *see* EXCRESCE

excuse *see* EXCAISE

exectour *see* EXECUTOR

execute &c *ptp* **1** carried out, performed *la15-19*. **2** made legally effective *la15-18*. **3** put to death *17*.

execution &c, executioun &c *la14-16 n* **1** = execution *la14-*. **2** *law* the writing in which an officer of the law narrates his fulfilment of duty *18-*.

put to ~ execute, perform *la15-16*.

executor, executour, exectour &c *15-16* [ɛg'zɛkɪtər; *ɛg'zɛkøtur, *-ər, *ɛg'zɛktur] *n, law* **1** = executor *15-*. **2** a person who serves a writ or executes a warrant *15-19*, *only Sc*.

~**y** *law* the office of an EXECUTOR *16-18*.

executry *law* the whole MOVEABLE property of a deceased person *17-*. [see also DATIVE, NOMINATE]

executorial &c *only in pl, adj* **letters** ~**is** (*la15-17*) *or as n* (*16-e18*) instructions or legal authority for executing a decree or sentence. [MedL *executorialis*]

exeem &c,   exeme *16*;   **exime** *17-e18* [*ɛg'zim] *vt* **1** free, exempt (*chf* **from** some obligation) *16-e19*. **2** set free, deliver *la16-e18*. **3** remove, exclude *e17*. [only Sc; L *eximere*]

exem &c *la15-e20*, **exame** *la14-e17*, **exeme** *la15-e16* [ɛg'zɛm, ɛg'zem] *vt* examine. [reduced f EXAMIN]

exeme *see* EXEEM

exemin *see* EXAMIN

exemp *vt* = exempt *la15-*.

exemple &c *n* = example *15-19*. [ME, OF; L *exemplum*]

exerce &c; exers &c *la15-16*, **excers** *la15-e16 v* **1** *vt* make use of, avail oneself of *la15-e17*. **2** discharge the duties of (an office) *la15-18*. **3** perform, do (an act etc) *la15-18*. **4** (1) practise (a virtue, vice etc) *16*. (2) carry on (a trade or calling) *la15-16*. (3) hold (a fair or market) *16-e17*. **5** exert, apply (strength etc) *la15-17*. **6** (1) occupy in or train by practice or exercise *16*. (2) *vr, chf* ~ **oneself in** occupy oneself in (an activity); practise (a virtue) *16*. **7** *vi* act (in a certain capacity) *16-e18*.

n exercise, function *16-e18*.

exercit &c exercised, made expert, experienced *16*. [ME (rare) *exerce*, OF *exercer*, L *exercēre*; commoner in OSc than EXERCEESE]

exerceese &c, exercise &c (*the commonest form in religious senses*) [ɛksər'siz, *ɛksər'siz] *n* **1** = exercise *la16-*. **2** *also* **family** ~ family worship, prayers *17-e20*. **3** practice or occupation in study or discussion, *esp* of religious themes

la16-e17. **4** (1) the exposition or discussion of a passage of Scripture, either as part of a church service or by the members of a PRESBYTERY *la16-17, only Sc.* (2) an exegetical sermon or discourse delivered to a PRESBYTERY by one of its members, or by a divinity student before ordination *18-e20, only Sc; cf* TRIAL. (3) a PRESBYTERY *la16-17, only Sc.*
vti **1** = exercise *la15-.* **2** *vi* perform the EXERCISE (*n* 4 (1)): (1) in PRESBYTERY *la16-e17;* (2) as part of public or private worship *18-e20.*
exerciser &c the MINISTER performing the EXERCISE (*n* 4 (1)) *17.* **make** ~ hold family worship *19.* **make the** ~ perform the EXERCISE (*n* 4 (1)) *e17.* [*cf* EXERCE]
exercitioun &c [*ɛksər'sɪsɪun, *'-sɪʃɪun &c] *n* **1** the exercise **of** (some pursuit, office etc) *la15-e17.* **2** occupation, application to work *la15-16.* **3** physical exercise *16.* **4** exercise or practice in something *16.* [only Sc; L *exercitio*]
exers *see* EXERCE
exhibition &c *n* **1** the presentation (of a person) in court *la16.* **2** *law* production or delivery of documents at the instance of a court *18.* **3** = exhibition.
exhoner *see* EXONER
exhorbitant *see* EXORBITANT
exhortar &c [*ɛg'zɔrtər] *n* a person appointed to give religious exhortation under a MINISTER *la16-e17.* [eModEng *exhorter &c* a person who exhorts]
exhoust *see* EXOWST
exime *see* EXEEM
exkeese *see* EXCAISE
exle ['ɛksl] *n* = axle *la19-.*
exoner &c; exhoner &c *la16-17* [ɛg'zonər, ɪk'sonər, *St* -'zɔnər, -'sɔnər] *v, law, chf* ~ **of 1** *vt* relieve of an obligation or responsibility *16-.* **2** *vr* free oneself by resigning an office etc *16-17.* **3** *vt* free from a burden, unload *e16.* **4** free from blame *17.*
~ation &c *law* the act of being legally disburdened of, or liberated from the performance of a duty or obligation *la16-.* [only Sc; F *exonérer,* L *exonerāre; cf* Eng *exonerate*]
exorbitant; exhorbitant &c *la15-e17 adj* **1** grossly or flagrantly excessive or unfair *la15-e17.* **2** *specif, of price etc* = exorbitant.
exowst &c *18-, now local Sh-Fif;* **exhoust &c** *19-, now Pbls* [ɛg'zʌust] *vt* = exhaust.
expairience &c *n* = experience *la19-e20, NE Ags.*
expawtiate [ɛk'spaʃɪet] *vi* = expatiate *19-20.*
expec(k) *vt* = expect *19-.*
expectant *n* the prospective occupier of a post, *esp church* a candidate for the *ministry* (MINISTER), a *probationer* (PROBATION) *17-e19.* [eModEng = one entitled to expect something to which he will succeed, L *expectans* expectant]
expede &c, exped *17* [ɛk'spid, *also* *-'spɛd] *vt,*

pt, ptp **exped** *la16-17,* **expede &c** *la16-* [-spid, *-spɛd] **1** accomplish, complete; deal promptly and effectively with *16-18.* **2** *law* complete and issue (a document) *la16-.* **3** send, expedite *la16-e17.* [only Sc; F *expédier* make out copies of (letters and writs), L *expedīre* make ready]
expense &c, expens *n, freq in pl* **1** money or means for spending *15.* **2** = expense *la15-.* **3** *law* costs *18-.*
(**up)on one's (awin) expens(is** at one's (own) expense *la15-e17.*
expensive *adj* **1** = expensive. **2** extravagant *19-, now local Sh-Pbls.*
expire &c *v* **1** *vt* render (a charter etc) void of further effect *15-e16.* **2** *vi* = expire *la15-.*
expiry *of time, contracts etc* termination *la18-* [*cf* Eng *expiration*].
expiscate *vt* examine; discover by investigation *la17-19.*
expiscation &c investigation *la17-18.* [eModEng (once); L *expiscārī* (*v*) fish out]
expone [*ɛk'spon] *vtr* **1** expose, lay open *15-e17.* **2** *vt* expound, explain *la14-e17.* **3** state, declare, make known *la15-e17.* [ME (rare); L *expōnere*]
expoond [ɛk'spun(d)] *vt* = expound, explain (*esp* Scripture) *la19-e20.*
export *n, adj* **1** = export. **2** applied to a superior-quality stronger beer, slightly darker in colour than HEAVY *20-.*
exposeetion [ɛkspo'ziʃ(ə)n] *n* = exposition, *chf* of a passage of Scripture *la19-e20.*
expreme &c; exprime [*ɛk'sprim] *vt* express in words; state, name *15-e17.* [ME *exprime,* OF *exprimer,* L *exprimere*]
expugnate *ptp* taken by storm *16.* [L *expugnātus*]
extend *v* **1** *vi* = extend *15-.* **2** (1) amount or come **to** (a specified sum, quantity etc) *la15-16.* (2) reach a certain limit *la15-e16: 'the man that spendis mar than his rent extendis'.* **3** *vt* (1) apply (a law) specially or more extensively *la15-e17.* (2) exert, apply *la16-e17: 'ʒe lykwyse ought ʒour ayde and help extend'.* **4** *law* make a final copy of (a legal document) for signature *19-e20.*
extensioun &c *n* **1** a holding out **of** (the hand) *la15-16.* **2** = extension.
extent &c [ɛk'stɛnt, *ɛ'stɛnt, *ə'stɛnt] *n, also* **estent** *la14-16,* **astent** *15* **1** the valuation or assessment of land; the value as fixed by assessment *15-, now hist, freq* **auld** ~ *la15-e19,* **new** ~ *la16-18.* **2** a levy, contribution or tax imposed by assessment *la15-e17.*
vt **1** assess the value of (lands) *15-16, only Sc.* **2** tax by assessment *16-e17, only Sc.*
~our &c an assessor *15-e17, only Sc.* [ME, AF *estente,* MedL *extenta; cf* STENT², Eng *extent*]
exterminioun &c [*ɛkstɛr'mɪnɪun, *-ən] *n* extermination, destruction; expulsion *16-17.* [eModEng (once) *extermynion,* L *exterminium*]

extirpit &c [? ɛk'stırpıt] *ptp* = extirpated *18-,
now Abd.* [L *extirpātus* with substitution of Sc
ptp suffix *-it*]

extors &c *vt* subject to extorsion or oppression
la16-17. [only Sc; L *extors-*, rare ptp stem of
extorquēre]

extract; extrack *la16-, now Sh* [*n* 'ɛkstrak(t);
vt, ptp ɛk'strak(t)] *n* **1** *law* an official certified
copy of a judgment of a court or of any other
publicly-recorded document *16-, only Sc; cf*
EXTRETE. **2** = extract.

vt, ptp also **extract** *la15-e20* **1** = extract *16-*. **2**
law make an official, properly-authenticated
copy of (any publicly-recorded document)
la15-, only Sc.

extranean [*ɛk'strenıən] *adj* = EXTRANEARE
la16-17.

n a boy from a country district attending Aberdeen Grammar School for a short time to study
intensively for the University *bursary competition*
(BURSAR) *19, Abd.* [only Sc; L *extrāneus*]

extraneare &c; extranier &c [*ɛk'strenıər]
n an outsider; one not belonging to the BURGH,
district etc; a stranger *16-17.*

adj foreign; coming from outside; not belonging
to the BURGH *16-17.* [only Sc; L *extrāneus*]

extraordinar &c; **extrornar** *18-19*
['ɛkstrə'ordnər, ɛk'stror(d)nər,
ɛkstər'ord(ə)nər] *adj* = extraordinary *la15-.*

extravage [*'ɛkstrə'veg] *vi* wander about, *chf
fig* digress, ramble in talking *la17-18.* [only Sc;
MedL *extravagari* wander, stray beyond limits;
cf Eng *extravagate* and STRAVAIG]

extré *see* AIX-TREE

extrec(t) &c [*ɛk'strɛk(t)] *n* = EXTRETE
la15-17. [conflation of EXTRETE w L *extracta*]

extrete &c [*ɛk'strit] *n* a certified copy of the
fines imposed at (*chf*) a *justice aire* (JUSTICE) or
other court; *in pl* the fines specified in this
la15-16. [AF *estrete*, L *extracta; cf* EXTRACT *n*,
EXTREC(T)]

extrie *see* AIX-TREE

extrinsic *adj, law,* of a fact or circumstance given
under oath not essentially qualifying the matter
attested, not inherent to the point immediately
at issue *18-; cf* INTRINSIC.

extrornar *see* EXTRAORDINAR

ey *pronoun* = they *la19-, N.*

ey *see* AYE

eydant *see* EIDENT

eye *see* EE[1]

eyedant *see* EIDENT

eyland; eyllane [*'ilən(d)] *n* = island *16-e17.*

eyelist *see* EE[1]

eyiss *see* ACE

eyllane *see* EYLAND

eyne *see* EE[1]

eyntment *la19-, local Bnf-Rox;* **intment** *20-,
local Bnf-Rox,* ['əintmənt] *n* = ointment. [*cf*
UNƷEMENT]

eyrisland *see* URE[5]

ezlar *see* AISLAR

F

fa¹ &c *la16-*, *now Bnf*, **fall** &c; **faw** *la15-16*, *19-e20* [fɑ, *fal] *v, ptp* also **fawin** *16*, **fa(e)n** &c *19-* ['fɑ(ə)n] **1** *vi* = fall *la14-*. **2** *of night* come on *la14-*. **3** *vt* befall, happen to, *chf in blessings or curses* **fair, foul, shame** *etc* **fa** *la14-*, *now Gen except WC*. **4** obtain, win, come by *la15-19*. **5** (1) venture to obtain, aspire or lay claim to, *chf* **canna** *etc* ~ *la18-e19*. (2) have a right to obtain, deserve *la18-*, *now Sh*. (3) *chf in negative* not be able to obtain or keep; be unable to afford *la18-*, *now Ork*. **6** (1) *freq impersonal with indirect object* fall (to one) as a duty or turn; be appropriate, suit *15-19*. (2) *personal* be under obligation or necessity, have **to be, do** *etc 18-*, *now Sh*. **7** *vi* diminish in bulk, crumble, fall to pieces: (1) *of limestone or clay*, *la18-*, *now Sh Arg*; (2) *of fruit in boiling*, *e20*.
n **1** = fall *la14-*. **2** the distance over which a measuring rod falls: (1) *lineal measure* 6 ELLS or 6.22 imperial yards, *latterly* used as an equivalent to the pole (5½ yards) *la14-*, *now local C*; (2) *square measure* the square measure corresponding to this, 36 square ELLS *la16-*. **3** (1) that which befalls one; one's fate, fortune, lot *la18-19*. (2) a share, portion, *specif* a sub-division of land *la18-e19*.
fall-brig a boarding-bridge on the side of a ship *la14*, *only Sc*.
~ **about** set about, fall to (a task) *17-e18*. ~ **aff ane's feet** tumble, fall down *la19-e20*. ~ **awa 1** waste away, decline in health *la19-*. **2** faint *la20-*, *Sh NE Ags*. ~ **by 1** go missing, be mislaid *18-e19*. **2** take to one's bed, through illness or childbirth *19-*, *NE*. ~ **in 1** *of the body* shrink, shrivel *la19*. **2** *of a river* subside, *esp* after a flood *19-*, *now Wgt*. ~ **in fancy wi** take a fancy to *la19*, *Sh Ork Gsw Lnk*. ~ **on** start courting (**with**) *la19-*, *now Bnf*. ~ **oot (up)on** lose one's temper with, speak angrily to *la19-*, *Abd Ags*. ~ **ower** fall asleep *la18-*. ~ **ower the brim** go to one's doom or destruction *20-*, *now Abd*. **fa tae** *v* = fall to. *n* **fa-tae 1** a lean-to building *20-*, *local NE-S*. **2** a set-to, quarrel, row *la19-*, *now Sh Ork*. ~ **through 1** make a botch of, mismanage (*esp* an attempt at formal speech beyond one's capabilities) *la18-*, *now Abd*. **2** abandon (a task) from negligence or laziness *19-*, *now Ags*. **fa wi bairn** *or* **child** become pregnant *18-e20*. **fair** ~ **masel(1)** who can compare with me? *e20*, *N*.
fa² &c, **fall** [fɑ, *fal] *n* a falling mouse- or rat-trap *la15-*, *now local*. [laME *falle*, OE (*mūs*) *fealle*]
fa *see* FAE, WHA
faa &c [fɑ] *n* the entrails of a slaughtered animal, used for sausages etc *la18-*, *chf Sh Ork*. [Norw dial, ON *fall* a slaughtered animal carcass]
faal *see* WHAAL
faap *see* WHAUP¹
fab¹ *n* = fob, a small pocket, pouch *la18-19*.

fab² *n* a truant *e20*, *Stlg*. [obscure]
fab *see* FOB
fabala *n* = falbala, a flounce, furbelow *19-e20*.
fabric *n* **1** = fabric. **2** an ungainly or ugly thing, animal or person *la19-*, *local Sh-Fif*.
Februar(y) *see* FEBRUAR
face &c, **feice** &c *20-*, *Cai*; **fais** &c *la15-e17* [fes] *n* = face *la14-*.
vti = face *la16-*.
facie &c *adj* **1** bold, ready to face danger *19-*, *now midLoth*. **2** impudent, cheeky *19-*, *midLoth Bwk Rox*. **facin** &c *n*, *also* **fasing** = facing *16-*. **facing iron** a smoothing iron with a polished surface *la20-*.
~ **caird** &c, ~ **cairt** a court card *19-*. ~ **claith** &c ? a cloth for wiping the face *17*. ~ **clout** a face-cloth *la20-*. ~ **dyke** a wall consisting of stones on one side and earth and turf on the other *la18-19*.
the ~ **of clay** any man alive *19-*, *now Bnf Abd*. **hold one's** ~ **to** vouch for *18-*, *now Abd*. **oot o' (the)** ~ without a break, in orderly sequence *20-*, *Arg Kcb Uls*. **put in a** ~, **put a** ~ **in** put in an appearance *20-*. **stare someone in the** ~ resemble someone closely *la19-*, *now Abd Stlg*.
facile &c *adj* **1** = facile *16-*. **2** *esp law* easily influenced by others, weak-minded *16-*.
facility &c **1** = facility. **2** *esp law* being FACILE (*adj* 2) *16-*.
facioun *see* FASHION
fack &c *la16-*, **fact** *n* = fact *la15-*.
fack! indeed!, really! *19*. (**as**) ~ **as** as sure(ly) as (death etc) *la19-*, *local N Kcb*.
faction, factioun *la16 n* **1** = faction *16-*. **2** *Aberdeen Grammar School* a section of a class; the bench at which each section sat *18-19*.
factor *17-*, **factour** &c *15-17 n* **1** a person appointed to manage property for its proprietor *15-*. **2** = factor, a business agent *16-*. **3** a person appointed by a court to manage forfeited etc property *18-e19*; *cf judicial factor* (JUDICIAL). *vt* act as FACTOR (*n* 1) for (an estate) *la19-*. **factorship** the office of FACTOR *n* 1, *la19-*. **factory** &c **1** *law* authority granted to a person to act on behalf of another; a deed conferring this *la16-*. **2** the office or jurisdiction of FACTOR *17-e19*. **factrix** a female *judicial factor* (JUDICIAL) *la16*, *la18*.
faculty &c *la16-*, **faculté** *la14-16 n* **1** = faculty *la14-*. **2** (1) permitted power to do something etc *15-*. (2) *law* a power given to do something at will *18-*. **3** social position, station *15-16*. **4** one's personal character, disposition *la15-e17*.
the F ~ **of Advocates** *collective* the members of the Scottish bar *18-*.
faddom &c *la16-*, **fadom** &c *la14-19*; **fawdom** &c *la15-e16*, **faldom** &c *16-e17*, **foddom** &c *la16-e20* ['fadəm, *'fɑdəm] *n* = fathom *la14-*.
vti = fathom *17-*.

fade &c *la14-;* **feid** *16, only Sc* [fed] *vti* = fade.

fader *see* FAITHER

faderils *see* FATTERALS

fadge &c *17-,* **fage &c** *15-17;* **faige &c** *15-17* [fadʒ] *n* **1** a flat round thick loaf or BANNOCK, formerly of barley meal *15-,* now *Bwk S.* **2** a kind of *tattie-scone* (TATTIE) *la19-, Uls.* [only *Sc*; obscure]

fadmel *n* a weight or quantity of lead *e16.* [only *Sc*; obscure]

fadom *see* FADDOM

fae &c *la16-,* **fa &c** *la14-e17;* **fay** *la14-16* [fe] *n* = foe *la14-,* now *verse.*

fae *see* FRAE

faem *la18-e20,* **fame &c** *15-19* [fem; *Ork* fim] *n* = foam *15-e20.*
vti **1** = foam *la15-e20.* **2** *vi* gush *la19-, chf Ork.*

faen *see* FA¹

fag¹ *n* a sheep-tick *la18-,* now *Ayr.* [unknown]

fag² *vi* fail from weariness *18-e20.* [obscure]

fage *see* FADGE

faggald &c *la14-e20,* **flaggat &c** *la14 n* = faggot.

faggot &c; **faggat &c** *la14-16 n* **1** = faggot *la14-.* **2** term of abuse for a woman or child implying (1) slatternliness *20-,* now *Arg Bwk;* (2) exasperating behaviour *19-.*
burn (**one's**) ~(**s**) renounce heresy *la16.*

faid *n* a company of hunters *16.* [Gael *faghaid,* OIr *faegaid*]

faider *see* FAITHER

faige *see* FADGE

faik¹ *vt* grasp, grip, get hold of *16.* [obscure; see next]

faik² **&c** [fek; *NE also* fjɑk] *n* **1** a fold of a garment *18-,* now *Abd.* **2** a PLAID, wrap, shawl *18-,* now *NE.* **3** a strand of rope *20-,* now *Cai Abd.* **4** *mining and quarrying, chf in pl* layers of shaly sandstone or limestone *19-e20.*
vti **1** *vt* (1) fold, tuck (cloth or a garment) around *18-e20.* (2) fold the mouth of (a sack etc) outwards and downwards *e20.* **2** fold, tuck (a limb) under one; *vi, of limbs* bend, give way under one *la18-e19.* **3** *vt* coil (a rope or line) *20-,* now *Sh Fif.* [perh f prec]

faik³ **&c,** **falk** *la15* [*fek, *falk] *vt* **1** lower, abate, remit (price, money) *la15, la18-19.* **2** spare, excuse, let (someone) go *la18-19.* [only *Sc*; aphetic f *defaik* (DEFALK)]

faikin &c *adj* deceitful *la15.* [eME *faken &c*; OE *fācne*]

faiks *see* FEGS

fail¹ &c *15-,* **fale** *15-16;* **feal** *la16-,* **feill &c** *la16-,* now *Sh Ork Cai* [fel; *Sh Ork Cai also* fil] *n* **1** turf as a material for building or roofing *15-,* now *chf N.* **2** a piece of turf, a sod *16-,* now *chf N.*
~**-dyke** *n* a field wall built or covered with sods *16-, Gen except Sh Ork Gall.*
~ [*chf* fil] **and divot** *law* a SERVITUDE giving the right to cut turf for building, thatching or fuel *18-.* [obscure; Gael *fàl* a sod is prob f Sc]

fail², **faill** *la14-19;* **fell** *la15-16,* **feal &c** *la16-19* [fel] *vi* **1** = fail *la14-.* **2** *of persons* give way under strain, flag, collapse from exhaustion *la14-19.*
n = fail *la14-.*
~**ed,** ~**it 1** *of persons* impaired in health, infirm *la14-.* **2** *of things* broken down, worn out by age, use etc *16-e18.* ~**er** = *failʒear* (FAILʒIE) *la16-17.*

failzie &c *17-e20,* **failʒe &c** *16-e17;* **falʒe** *la15-e16,* **faillie &c** *la14-20* [*'fel(j)ɪ] *vti* **1** = fail *la14-17.* **2** *law* default (**in**) *la15-e19.*
n **1** = fail *la14-e18.* **2** failure, non-performance of an obligation *la15-e20.* **3** a sum payable in case of failure, penalty *17-18.*

failʒeand *la14-e17,* **failʒeing** *la15-17 presp, adj* **1** = failing *la14-17.* **2** in the absence or lack **of** (a designated heir etc) *la14-17.* **failʒeand &c** **of** in the event of (something) not happening or not being obtainable *15-e17.* **failʒeand &c** **that..not** = prec *la15-16.* **failʒear, failyier &c** a person who fails to perform an obligation, a defaulter *la15-17.* **party failʒear &c** = prec *la16-e18.* **failʒeit 1** = *failed* (FAIL²) 1, *la14-e17.* **2** *chf of buildings* in bad condition, dilapidated *16.* **3** faded in colour *16.*
gif it ~(**s**) if it so mischance *la15.* **in case of** ~ in the event of failing to comply with a condition or fulfil an obligation *la16-17.* **under the ~ of** under the penalty of (a certain sum) *17-e18.*

failzure &c [*'fel(j)ər] *n* = failure *18.*

faimily &c *la17-,* **familie &c** *la16-* [*'fem(ə)lɪ] *n* = family *la16-.*

faimish &c *la19-e20,* **famis &c** *16-e17 vti* = famish.

fain &c; **fane** *15-e17 adj* **1** = fain *la14-.* **2** loving, affectionate, amorous *la18-e20.* **3** fond **of** *18-,* now *Sh Ork.*
adv = fain *la14-19.*
~**est** most gladly *15-16.* ~**ness 1** gladness, joy *16-19.* **2** liking, love *la18-,* now *Sh.* [*adj* 1 and *adv* are now *arch* or *verse* in Eng]

faint &c; **fant &c** *16-,* now *N,* **fent** *la16- adj* (*15-*), *vi* (*16-*) = faint.
n a fainting fit, a swoon *la18-,* only *Sc.*

faiple &c *n, of persons or animals* a loose drooping underlip *19-,* now *Fif Dmf.*
vi **fippill &c,** **feppill** put out the lower lip *la15-e16.*
hang a *or* **one's** ~ look glum or sour *19-e20.* [uncertain]

fair¹ &c *adj* **1** = fair *la14-.* **2** complete, absolute, utter *la19-:* '*ye're a fair disgrace*'.
adv **1** = fair *la14-.* **2** completely, absolutely, simply, quite *la18-.* **3** directly, without deviating *la18-.*
vi, of weather clear (**up**), become fine *19-.*
~**hede &c** = fairhead, beauty *la14-16.* ~**ly 1** = fairly *la14-.* **2** *emphatic* certainly!, of course!, yes indeed! *20-, Abd.*
~**-avised** fair-complexioned *20-,* now *Bnf Fif*

SW. ~-**ca'in** smooth-tongued, flattering *19-*, now *Fif.* **the F~** City Perth *19-*. ~ **daylight** broad daylight *16-*, now *Abd Ags Wgt.* ~-**faced** superficially polite, deceitful *la19-*, local *N-Uls.* ~-**farrand &c 1** handsome *la15-e17.* **2** plausible, specious, flattering, superficially attractive *la15-e20.* ~ **folk** fairy folk *16-e17.* ~-**gyaun** *of crops* fairish *20-*, *Bnf Abd.* ~-**spoken** frank, friendly *20-*, local *Bnf-Slk.* ~ **furth the gate** *adv (adj)* candid(ly), straightforward(ly) *la19-*, now *Abd.* ~ **oot** = *prec la19-*, now *NE Fif SW.* **a ~ strae death** death from natural causes *la18-e20.* **it was nae mair than** *etc* ~ **guid day and** ~ **guid een** *etc* they were barely on speaking terms *19.*

fair² **&c** *15-*; **fare** *la15-e19* *n* **1** = fair, the gathering for buying and selling *15-*. **2** a gift bought at a fair *la18-19.* **3 the F~** the annual summer holiday, *esp* **the Glasgow F~**, now the last two weeks in July; *also* the first Monday of this period, held as a public holiday; *cf* TRADES. ~**in(g)** *n* a present, *freq* food from a fair or at a festive season *18-20.* **get** *or* **tak one's ~ins** be punished, get one's deserts, **gie someone his ~ins** punish someone *la18-*, now local *Abd-Rox.* **be taken to the ~** *of an over-confident person* be taken aback, discomfited *la19-*, local.

fair *see* WHAR
fairce *adj* = fierce *19.*
faird *16-19*, **fard &c** *16* [*ferd] *n*, *also fig* a hasty movement, impetus, rush *16-19.*
  ferdy &c [*Sh* 'fɛrdɪ, 'fɪrdɪ; *ferdɪ] strong, active *la16-*, now *Sh.* [only *Sc*; obscurely related to FARE]
faird *see* FARD
fairly *see* FERLIE
fairnytickle *see* FERNTICKLE
fairnȝer *see* FERNYEAR
fairrie &c *vi* collapse from exhaustion or sudden illness *19-*, *Abd.* [obscure]
fairs *see* FARCE
fairsie *see* FIERCIE
fairy &c *17-*, **fary &c** *16-17*; **ferry &c** *la19-*, *Sh Ork* *n* **1** = fairy *la15-*. **2** a dazed or excited state of mind *la15-e16*, only *Sc.* ~ **raid &c** the ride of the fairies to their celebrations at BELTANE *e19.*
fais *see* FACE
faise *see* FAIZE¹
faisible &c *la19-*; **feasible** *la18-* ['fezəbl] *adj* **1** = feasible. **2** *of things* neat, tidily made; satisfactory *la18-*, now *midLoth Slk.* **3** *of persons* neat, tidy; respectable, decent *19-*, now *midLoth Slk.*
fait *see* FATE
faither &c *la17-*, **father &c** *la16-*, **fader &c** *la14-*, now *Sh NE*; **faider &c** *la15-e20* ['feðər; *Sh NE* 'fadər, 'fɛdər; *Sh also* 'fɑdər] *n* = father *la14-*.
  v **1** *vt* = father. **2** *vr* show who one's father is by resemblance etc *19-*, now *Ork N Kcb.*
  ~ **better** (*17*), ~ **war** (*la15-16*) better or

worse than one's father. ~ **broder &c**, ~ **sister** a paternal uncle or aunt *16-e17.* ~ **broder son** a paternal cousin *16-e17.* **father side** the paternal side of a family *17-e18.*
fathers and brethren *Presbyterian Churches* the members of the *General Assembly* (GENERAL) or of the SYNODS or PRESBYTERIES *19-*.
faizart &c, **fazart &c** *16-e19* ['fezərt, *-ərd] **1** a hermaphrodite fowl *la16-*, now *Sh.* **2** a puny effeminate man, a weakling *16-*, now *Sh.* [only *Sc*; obscure]
faize¹ &c, **faise &c** [fez] *vti* **1** *freq* ~ **oot**, *of something woven* unravel, fray *19-*, now *N nEC Bwk Rox.* **2** *vt* make (metal or wood) rough, splintered or jagged *la16-*, now *Bnf Abd.* [eModEng *feaze*, *faze* unravel, in some way related to OE *faes* a fringe > FAS]
faize² &c *vt* **1** annoy, inconvenience, ruffle *la19-*, now *Bnf.* **2** *also* ~ **on** make an impression on *19-*, now *Arg Kcb Uls.* [ME *feeze*, OE *fesian* drive; *cf* also US *faze* disturb]
faizle *see* PHRASE¹
falcon &c *16-*; **falcoun &c** *15-16* [*'falkən, *'fakən] *n* = falcon *15-*.
  falconar &c *la14-*, **fauconer &c** *la12-16* = falconer.
fald *see* FAULD¹, FAULD²
falderal &c ['faldə'ral] *n* **1** = falderal. **2** an idle fancy, a fuss about trifles *la19-e20.*
faldom *see* FADDOM
fale *see* FAIL¹
falk *see* FAIK³
Falkirk &c ['fɑkɪrk; *St* 'fɔlkɪrk; *'falkɪrk] ~ **Tryst** the cattle market held near Falkirk, the largest of its kind in Scotland *la18-e20.* [the town in Stlg]
Falkland &c [*'fɑklənd, now (St)* 'fɔlklənd] ~ **bred** well-mannered, as if bred at court *18-19.* [the village in Fif with a royal palace]
fall *see* FA¹, FA²
fallachan *n* a hoard, a concealed store *la19-*, *chf Arg.* [Gael *falachan* hidden treasure]
fallauge *see* VOLAGE
fallow &c, **follow &c** now *Sh Cai Abd Uls*, **fella** *20-*; **fallie &c** *20-* ['falə, 'fɛlə; *EC, S* 'falɪ; *Sh Cai Abd Uls also* 'folə, -o] *n* (*15-*), *vt* (*la15-16*) = fellow *la14-*.
fellow-craft *n*, *freemasonry* one who has taken the second degree *18-* [*orig* one who has passed his apprenticeship and is a full member of his craft].
fallow *see* FOLLOW
fals(e), **falsed(e)** *see* FAUSE
falset &c [*'falsɛt, *-ət, *'fasət] *n* **1** falsehood *la14-e20.* **2** *law* = falsehood **2** (FAUSE) *15-17.* [*chf Sc*; OF *falset*]
falshede, **falisifé** *see* FAUSE
falt *see* FAT², FAUT
falteis *see* FAUTISE
faltive [*'faltɪv, *'fat-] *adj* **1** *of persons* having

committed a fault, guilty of wrongdoing *la15-16*. **2** *of things* faulty, defective *la15-16*. [only Sc; OF *faultif &c*]

falȝe *see* FAILZIE

fama ['fama] *n* **1** *church law* a report of scandalous behaviour, *chf* against a MINISTER or *probationer* (PROBATION) *20-*. **2** *colloq* scandal *la20-*, *Ross Abd*. [f next]

fama clamosa ['fama kla'moza] *n*, *church law* a widely-circulating rumour of scandalous behaviour *usu* by a MINISTER or *probationer* (PROBATION) *18-*. [L = a noisy rumour; *cf* prec]

fame *see* FAEM

fameeliar &c *adj* = familiar *20-*.

famell &c [*?'feməl] *adj* female *la15-e17*. *n* females; a female *15-16*. [only Sc; MedL *famella*, var of *femella* > Eng *female*]

famell *see* FAMYLE

famh [fɑv] *n*, *folklore* a small animal somewhat like a mole *la18-e19*. [Gael = a mole]

familie *see* FAIMILY

famis *see* FAIMISH

famous &c *adj* **1** = famous *15-*. **2** *chf law*, *esp of witnesses* of good repute, of unexceptionable character *la15-e18*, *la20-*, *midLoth*.

famyle &c; famell &c [*fa'mɔil, *-'mil, *'feməl] *n* **1** a family *la14-16*. **2** a kindred (KIN) or lineage *15-e16*. [appar only Sc; OF *famille*]

fan *vi* = fawn *la16-e17*, *chf Sc*.

fan *see* FA¹, FIND, WHAN

fand *see* FIND

fand &c; faynd &c *only Sc* [*fend; *also* *fɑnd] *vt* **1** = fand, put to the test, make trial of *la14-16*. **2** test by exercise, exert *la14-15*.

fane *see* FAIN

fang &c *n* **1** = fang, a capture *la14-16*. **2** booty, plunder, stolen goods *la16-*, *now Abd*. **3** a heavy bundle *20-*, *Cai Abd*. **4** *of a pump* the capacity for suction, *chf* **aff the ~** (*local*), **oot o ~** (*Mry midLoth Wgt*) (1) having lost its suction *19-*; (2) *fig*, *of persons etc* without one's usual spirit or skill *20-*. **5** a rope for steadying the gaff of a sail *e16*. **6** a coil or bend of a rope *19-*, *now midLoth*; *cf* FANK¹.
vt **1** acquire, catch, seize, capture *la14-20*. **2** pull or draw **in** *e16*. **3** prime a pump in (a well etc) *19-*, *local NE-SW*.
lose *etc* **the ~ 1** lose the power of retaining water *19-*, *now Abd Stlg midLoth*. **2** *fig* fail, lose the knack or skill *la18-19*.
(**be taken**) **in** *etc* **a ~** (be caught) (1) in a predicament *la18-19*; (2) in the act of stealing *la17-e18*. (**be taken**) **with the ~** *law* (be caught) in possession of stolen goods *18-19*.

fang *see* WHANG

fangle *see* FANKLE

fank¹ *n*, *also fig* a coil of rope, noose, tangle *la18-*, *now midLoth*.
vt **1** tangle, twist *19-*, *now local*. **2** catch in a noose, snare *18-19*.
~it &c entangled *17-*.

~ o tows a coil of rope *la19-*, *now Sh*. [only Sc; var of FANG; *cf* FANKLE]

fank² *n* a sheepfold *19-*.
vt drive into a sheepfold *19-*. [only Sc; Sc and IrGael *fang* a sheepfold]

fankle; fangle *la19-*, *now NE Ags* ['faŋkl; *NE Ags* 'faŋl] *v* **1** *vt* trap, ensnare *18-e20*. **2** tangle, mix up *19-*, *now EC-S*. **3** *vi* become tangled *la19-*, *now Ayr Rox*. **4** stumble *la19-*, *now Ayr*.
n a tangle, muddle *19-*. [frequentative of FANK¹ and FANG]

fanner *n* **1** a blowing fan *la16*. **2** *chf in pl* a winnowing machine, grain-sifter *la18-*. [eModEng = one who fans; OE *fann* a fan]

fant *see* FAINT

fantise &c [*fan'təis, *-'tɪs] *n* fantasy, illusion, deceit *la14-16*. [only Sc; appar irreg alteration of Eng *fantasy*]

fanton &c [*fan'ton, *'fantən] *n* an unreal thing or state, a phantom *15-e16*. [ME, var of *fantome*]

fantoosh &c [fan'tuʃ] *adj* flashy, ultra-fashionable *20-*, *local*. [only Sc; see SND]

far &c, fer &c *la14-*, *now S*; **faur** *la19-*, *C adv*, *adj*, *comparative* **farrer &c** *la14-e20*, **ferrer** *la14-e16*, *20-*, *S*, **faurer** *la20-*, *N, C*, **farder** *16-*, *now local*, **fa(u)ther** *19-*, *now Fif midLoth Bwk*, **ferther** *15-e16*, *19-*, *S. superlative* **farrest** *la14-*, *now N, C*, **farmost** *la19-*, *local*, **ferrest** *la14-e16*, **fardest** *la16-*, *now local* = far *la14-*.
~ness &c amount of distance *la16*, *la20-*, *now local*.
~land *adj* foreign, connected with distant countries *la16-e17*.
~ and about from far and near *20-*, *Abd-Ags Uls*. **far aff** distant in relationship *19-*, *now Sh NE midLoth*. **~ awa** *of space, time or relationship* remote, distant *18-*. **farawa skreed** a letter or news from abroad *19-*, *now local*. **~ awa wi't** feeble; frail, seriously ill *la19-*, *Sh Ork NE Bwk*. **~ back** *adj* **1** backward as regards progress, ignorant *20-*, *Ross Abd Ags* [Gael *fada air ais*]. **2** in debt *la19-*, *nEC midLoth Rox*. *adv* long ago *la20-*. **~ ben 1** (1) intimate, friendly, in great favour *19-*, *local*. (2) *specif* in favour with God *17-*, *now local*. **2** *of the eyes* dreamy, abstracted *20-*, *now midLoth Bwk Uls*. **3** deeply versed, having deep or specialized knowledge *19-*, *now Ork Abd*. **~ in** = **~ ben 1** (1) *19-*. **~ kent &c** known far and wide, famous *la18-*, *local*. **~ north** astute, wide-awake *la19-*, *Abd WC Rox*. **~ oot &c 1** on bad terms, not friendly *20-*, *local Mry-Fif*. **2** distant in relationship *la19-*. **~ oot aboot** remote, out-of-the-way *20-*, *now Ork Abd Ags*. **~ seen** far-sighted; deeply-skilled *la18-*, *now Ags Uls*. **~ throu &c 1** *of clothes etc* finished, worn out *la19-*. **2** very ill, at death's door *la19-*.

far *see* WHAR

faran; farran, forin ['farən, 'for-] *n*, *chf attrib* the starboard side of a boat *la19-*, *chf NE*. [only Sc; reduced f FOREHAND; see SND]

farand *see* FARE

farce; fars *16,* **fairs** &c *16,* **ferse** &c *la16,* **phrais** &c *la16* *n* **1** = farce *16-.* **2** a funny story, a joke *20-, local N-EC.*

farcost &c *la14-e15;* **fercost** *15-e17 n* = farcost, a small cargo-vessel.

farcy *see* FIERCIE

fard; faird &c *only Sc vt* = fard, paint (the face); *fig* embellish *16-e19.*

fard *see* FAIRD

fardel[1] &c, **fardell** *n* **1** a fourth part, a quarter *la15.* **2** a three-cornered cake, *esp* oatcake (AIT), *usu* the fourth part of a round *17-,* now *NE Stlg Edb.* **3** a large slice or piece (*esp* of food) *19-,* now *Bnf Abd.* [OE *féorþa dǽl,* a fourth part]

fardel[2] &c, **fardell** &c *n* **1** = fardel, bundle *la14-e17.* **2** the third stomach of a ruminant, *chf* ~ **bound** a disease of cattle in which the contents of this stomach become impacted *19-e20.*

farden &c *la16-,* **farding** &c *15-17 n* = far-thing *15-.*
~ **land** a quarter of a *pennyland* (PENNY) *16-17, chf Ork Highl.*

farder, fardest *see* FAR

farding *see* FARDEN

fare &c *vi, pt also* **fure** &c *la14-e19* [*før]. *ptp also* **forn** *la18-,* now *Sh* = fare, go *la14-.* *n* **1** = fare *la14-.* **2** one's fortune(s) *la14, e18.*

farrant &c, **farand** &c ['farənt, -(ə)n(d); *'fer-] **1** comely *la14-e16.* **2** of a certain disposition, eg *auld-farrant* (AULD), *fair-farrand* (FAIR[1]) *la15-.* **farandman** a travelling person *15-16.*

farin ['ferɪn] *n* food, fare *19-, local NE-EC.*
sic *or* **sae** ~**s o** *or* **wi** that's just like, that's just what you would expect of, that's just what happened to (him *etc*) *18-e20.*

fare *see* FAIR[2]

farin *see* FARE

farkage &c ['farkedʒ, -ɪʃ; *Ork* 'fargɪs] *n* an untidy heap or bundle *19-,* now *Ork.*
ferkishin &c ['ferkɪʃɪn, 'ferk-] a large (untidy) amount, a crowd, seething mob *la19-e20, S.* [see SND]

farl &c, **farle** *n* = FARDEL[1] 1; *now also* of SCONES, rolls, *shortbread* (SHORT) *17-, Gen except N.* [reduced f FARDEL[1]]

farlan &c *n, fish-curing* a long box into which herrings are emptied for gutting *la19-, Sh N Fif Bwk.* [var, orig *Sh,* of FORELAND the foreshore, on which curing orig took place]

farle *see* FARL

farly *see* FERLIE

farm *see* FERM

farmorar *see* FERMORAR

farmost *see* FAR

farmourar *see* FERMORAR

farne *see* FERN

farnȝer *see* FERNYEAR

farrach &c ['farəx; *Abd also* fjar-] *n* **1** strength, energy *18-, NE.* **2** a bustle; a mix-up; a state of agitation *la19-,* now *Ags.* [Gael = force]

farran *see* FARAN

farrant *see* FARE

---

farrer, farrest *see* FAR

farrow *17-,* **fer(r)ow** &c *la15-,* **forrow** &c *16-* ['farə; *N Per* 'fɛrə, -ɪ; *local* 'forə; *WC* 'fʌrə] *adj, of a cow* not in calf; having missed a pregnancy, *locally* either still giving milk or not *la15-.* [chf *Sc;* MDu *verre-koe* &c a cow past bearing]

fars *see* FARCE

fary *see* FAIRY

fas &c [fas] *n* **1** a tassel *la15-e17.* **2** something of little value, *chf* **nocht worth a** ~ *la15-16.* *vt* provide with tassels *16-e17.* [only *Sc;* OE *fæs* a fringe; *cf* FAIZE[1]]

fasch *see* FASH

faschioun *see* FASHION

fash &c *17-,* **fasch** &c *16-e17 v* **1** *vt* trouble, annoy, anger, inconvenience *16-.* **2** *vr* vex or bother oneself *17-.* **3** *vt* afflict (with a disease) *18-e20.* **4** *vi* (1) trouble oneself, take pains *la16-.* (2) ~ **at, of** be impatient with, grow weary of *18-.* **5** make trouble *la16-17.*
n **1** trouble, pains; annoyance; bother *18-.* **2** a troublesome person *19-,* now *midLoth WC.*
~**erie** &c trouble, annoyance *la16-e20.* ~**ious** &c **1** troublesome, annoying; tricky *16-.* **2** fractious, peevish *18-.*
never *etc* ~ **yer heid, thumb** *etc* don't be put out; pay no heed *18-.* [OF *fascher* (*v*), *fascherie, fascheux; cf* ModF *fâcher*]

fashion *19-,* **faschioun** &c *16-17,* **fassoun** &c *la14-e17,* **fassioun** &c *16-e17,* **facioun** &c *15-16* ['faʃən; *'fason, *'fesən, *'fosən &c] *n* **1** = fashion *la14-.* **2** *in pl* social intercourse; manners, behaviour, *chf* **fair** *or* **ill** ~**s** *la16-,* now *local.*
vt, only **fashion, fassoun** = fashion *la14-.*
~**t** &c **1** of a specified appearance, manner etc, *eg* **auld, fair, ill** ~**t** *la15, 19; cf farrant* (FARE). **2** well-mannered, respectable *la18-19.* **ill** ~**t** rudely inquisitive *la19, Sh NE.*
make (a) ~ **(of doing)** pretend (to do) *19-,* now *Abd.*

fasiane *see* FEESANT

fasing *see* FACE

fassin *see* FEST

fassioun, fassoun *see* FASHION

fast *n* **1** = fast *la14-.* **2** *chf attrib, freq* **fast day** *Presbyterian Churches* a day in the week preceding the celebration of half-yearly Communion, treated as a holiday with a service of preparation for the SACRAMENT *18-,* now *chf Highl.*
vi = fast *la14-.*

fast *see* FEST

fastern's een &c *18-e20,* **fasternisevin** &c *15-17,* **fasterisevin** &c *la15-16,* **fas-ternevin** &c *la14-16,* **fastingeven** &c *la15-e20,* **fastingisevin** &c *la15-18* ['fastərn(z)'ivən, -'in, 'fastən(z)-, *'fastər(z)-; *NE also* 'fɛstərn(z)-; &c] *n* Shrove Tuesday. [ONorthumb *fæstern(es)* (nominative and genitive) fasting, a fast, WSaxon *fæsten,* applied to the fast of Lent + *e'en* (EVEN[1])]

fat¹ &c *adj* = fat *15*-.

~ **brose** BROSE made with hot stock or fat instead of boiling water *la18-19*.

fat²; fatt; falt *16*, *only Sc* [fat; *also* *fɑt] *n* a vat, a container for either liquid or dry goods *la14*-, *now Sh*. [ME; OE *fæt*, ON *fat*]

fat³ *adj*, *also* **fattie, fatum** *marbles* applied to marbles in a ring game which are disqualified if they come to rest inside the ring *20*-, *local*. [uncertain]

fat *see* WHAT¹

fatale &c *la15-16*; **fatell &c** *la15-e17*, *only Sc* *adj* = fatal.

fate *16-e19*, **fait &c** *15-e17* *n* = feat.

fatell *see* FATALE

faten *see* WHATTEN

father *see* FAITHER, FAR

fatt *see* FAT²

fatterals &c *la18-e19*; **faderils** *19* *n pl* ribbon ends, loose pieces of trimming; anything loose and trailing. [prob Eng *falderals*]

fatten *see* WHATTEN

fattie, fatum *see* FAT³

fatuous *adj* **1** *law* in a state of imbecility and therefore incapable of managing one's own affairs *18-e20*. **2** = fatuous.

fauch &c [fɑx; *NE also* fjɑx] *n* **1** a fallow field *14-e20*; *see* SND. **2** the breaking up of such land by light ploughing, harrowing or both *la18-e20*, *chf Abd*.
adj fallow, not sowed, untilled *la16-e18*.
v **1** *vt* plough or harrow (fallow ground) *16*-, *now local Sh-Bwk*. **2** (1) scratch, claw, rub, scrub hard *20*-, *Bnf Abd*. (2) *vi* toil away *la19*-, *now Abd*.
fauchinless weak, without energy *la19-e20*, *Mry Bnf*. [chf Sc; OE *fealh* fallow land]

fauch *see* FAUGH

fauchat ['fɑxət] *vt*, *lit and fig* throw or give up *la19*-, *Arg*. [see SND]

fauchle &c; fyachle &c *la19*-, **fouchle** *20*-, *Cai* ['f(j)ɑxl; *Cai also* 'fʌu-] *vi* **1** work lazily, listlessly or ineffectually *19-e20*, *Cai Bnf Gall*. **2** walk with difficulty due to lack of strength; trudge, plod *la19*-, *now Cai*.
n a slow inept worker, a bungler *la19*-, *now SW*.
fauchled &c tired, worn-out, harassed *20*-, *now C*, *S*. [see SND]

faucht &c [fɑxt] *n* = FECHT *16*-, *now WC Dmf*. [var f pt]

faucht *see* FECHT

faucon ['fɑkən] *n* a mock sun, a parhelion *20*-, *now Ross*. [obscure]

fauconer *see* FALCON

faugh, fauch &c [fɑx] *adj* pale; pale brown, yellowish *16*, *e19*.
~**ie &c** ['f(j)ɑxi] **1** = *adj*, *20*-, *N*. **2** *of persons* pasty-faced, sickly looking *20*-, *N*. [ME *falwe* (> Eng *fallow*) assimilated to FAUCH]

fauld¹ &c, fald &c [fɑld; *N*, *SW* fɑl; *Ags Per* fad] *n* **1** = fold (of cloth etc) *15*-. **2** a strand (of rope) *20*-, *local Sh-Ags*.

vti **1** = fold *la14*-. **2** *vt* shut, close (a door, a clasp-knife, the eyes, the fist etc) *la18-e20*. **3** *vi*, *of the limbs etc* double up, bend under one *la18*-, *now Sh Ags*.
~**it** *of the fists* clenched *la16-e17*.
~ **one's feet** *16-e18*, **fit** *la19*-, *Bnf Abd*, **hoch** *19*-, *now Ags Per* sit down, rest.

fauld² &c *15-e20*, **fald &c** *la14-18*, **fold** *16*- [fɑl(d)] *n* **1** = fold, a pen *la14*-. **2** (1) an enclosed piece of ground used for cultivation; a small field *la15-17*. (2) *chf in pl* the part of the OUTFIELD which was manured by folding cattle on it *18-19*. **3** the penning of cattle for milking; the milking *19*. **4** a halo round the moon, a warning of stormy weather *19*-, *now Ayr*. **5** *only* **fold** a herd of (*usu*) twelve *Highland* (HIELAND) cows used for breeding *19*-, *now Arg*.
vt = fold, enclose (animals) *la16*-.
~**in** a cattle- or sheepfold *la18-19*.
~**-dyke** a wall enclosing a fold *15-19*.
coal ~ a coal yard; a recess or cellar for keeping coal *18-19*. **lime** ~ a place for storing lime *e16*. **wauking o the** ~ the all-night watch at a sheepfold at weaning time to prevent the lambs returning to their mothers *18-19*.

fault *see* FAUT

faup *see* WHAUP¹

faur, faurer *see* FAR

fause &c *19*-, **fals &c** *la14-e17*; **false** *la15*- [fɑs; *fɑls] *adj* **1** = false *la14*-. **2** *of fortune, the world* deceitful, treacherous *15-e17*.
vt = false, break (an oath etc) *la15-e17*.
~**hood** *la17*-, **falshede &c** *la14-16*, **falsed(e)** *la14-16* **1** = falsehood *la14*-. **2** *only* **falsehood** *law* the crime of fraud or forgery; an instance of this *la17*-. **falser &c 1** a forger *la15-e17*. **2** a person who challenges a legal judgment *16-e17*.

falsifé &c = falsify *la16*. **falsifé a dome** *law* = ~ **a dome**, *la16-e17*. ~**ing** the act of questioning a legal judgment *la15-e17*.
~ **face** a face-shaped mask *19*-. ~ **hoose &c** a conical structure of wooden props built inside a corn stack to facilitate drying *la18*-, *local*.
~ **a dome** *law* deny the justice of a sentence and appeal to a superior court *15-e17*.

faut &c, falt &c *15-e17*, **fault &c** *la15*- [fɑt; *falt] *n* **1** = fault *la14*-. **2** a want, lack, *freq* of food *la15*-, *now Abd Fif Uls*. **3** harm, injury *la19*-, *Sh Abd*.
v **1** *vi* = fault, commit a fault *15-e17*. **2** *vt* find fault with, blame *la15*-, *local N-S*. **3** subject to a penalty *e16*.
~**er &c** *16-e20*, ~**our** *la15-e19*, ~**or** *la15-e19* a faulter, a wrongdoer, *specif* one who offends against Church discipline.
hae a *or* **nae** ~ **til** have a or no fault to find with *la18*-, *local*. **in** ~ **of** in the want or absence of *la14-e16*. **in a** *or* **the** ~ in the wrong, at fault *la16-e19*. (**it war**) **na(e)** ~ *contemptuous interj used of pretentious people*, *la18-19*.

fauther *see* FAR

fautise &c *15*, **falteis** *la16-e17* [*'fɑtəis, -ɪs]
adj faulty. [only Sc; appar OF **fautis*, nominative of *fautif*]
favour &c ['fevər; *Sh Ork NE* 'favər] *n* **1** =
favour *la14-*. **2** appearance, looks *la15-19*.
vt **1** = favour *15-*. **2** resemble, look like *la19-*.
but ∼(**is**) without favour *la15-e16*. **for any** ∼
for any sake, for goodness' sake *la19-*, *Gen except
Sh Ork*. **in** ∼**s of** in favour of *la15-*, now *Abd Fif
midLoth*.
faw *adj* variegated *la15-e16*, *in place-names 13-*.
[ME]
faw *see* FA[1]
fawdom *see* FADDOM
fawin *see* FA[1]
fawmous &c *adj* = famous *la19-*, *NE*.
fay &c [**fe*] *n* = fay, faith(fulness) *la14-16*.
 Inglis (**men's**) *or* **Scottis** ∼ allegiance to
England or Scotland *la14-15*.
fay *see* FAE
faynd *see* FAND
fazart *see* FAIZART
fe &c [**fi*] *n* = fee, cattle or sheep *la14-e16*.
 ∼ **master** &c a herdsman *e16*.
fe *see* FEE
fead *see* FEID
feal &c [**'fiəl*] *adj* loyal, faithful *la16-e19*. [only
Sc; OF]
feal *see* FAIL[1], FAIL[2], FIALL
fear *18-*, **fere** &c *15-17* [fir; *Sh Ork nEC* fer] *n* **1**
= fear *15-*. **2** a fright, a scare *19-*, now *Sh NE
Fif Dmf*.
v **1** *vt* = fear *16-*. **2** frighten, scare *18-*. **3** *also vi*
∼ **o** be afraid or fear for *19-*, now *Ags Fif*.
∼**ed** *la16-*, **ferd** *la15-17*, ∼**it** &c *la14-17*, **feart**
la18-: ∼**ed** &c **at, o, for** frightened or afraid of
la14-. **feardie** &c, **feardie gowk** *chf child's
word* a coward *20-*. **dinna be** ∼**t o** *humorous*
don't be so sparing with *20-*, *NE Fif Arg*. **ye're
nae** ∼**t** *ironic* you are pretty brazen-faced *20-*.
∼**some** &c frightening, terrifying *la18-*.
but ∼ without fear *la15-16*. **nae** ∼**s!** = no
fear! *la19-*.
fear *see* FEE, FIAR
fearsie *see* FIERCIE
feart [firt] *v* ∼**it** *adj* afraid *la20-*, *Renfr Gsw Ayr*.
[f *feart* (*adj*) (FEAR)]
feat *la16-*, **feit** *la16-e19* [fit; **fet*] *adj* **1** fitting;
clever, adroit *la16-19*. **2** *of persons or their dress*
neat, trim *18-*, now *Mry eLoth Gall*. [ME; OF
fait (*adj*) made]
feather *la18-*, **fether** &c *15-e18*, **fedder** &c
la15-, now *Sh Ork N* *n* **1** = feather *15-*. **2** the
projecting wing on the sock of a plough, which
cuts out the furrow *la18-*. **3** the lines and grain-
ing in polished wood *la19-*, now *Arg Ayr*.
v **1** *vt* = feather *16-*. **2** *vi, of a bird* get its feathers *la18-*, now *NE midLoth Bwk*. **3** *vt* beat, chastise *20-*, *Bnf Abd*. **4** smooth the top and sides of
(a rick) *la20-*, *Per Ayr Uls*.

fetherame &c, **feddrame** &c [**fɛð(ə)rəm,
'fɛd-] a coat of feathers, plumage *15-e17* [ME
fetherham &c, OE *feðerhama*].
 shak *etc* **one's** ∼**s** get out of bed, stir oneself
19-, now *Abd*.
featherfooly &c *n* = featherfew, feverfew, the
plant *19-*, now *Abd Ags*. [for second element *cf*
FOILZIE]
feasible *see* FAISIBLE
Februar &c *la14-19*, **Februer** &c *16*,
Fever3ere *la14-e16*; **Feberwar** &c *la16-19*,
Fabruar &c *la15-e17*, **Fabruary** &c
la15-e17, **Feberwerrie** &c *17-* ['fɛbruər; *Sh
NE, EC Ayr* 'fɛbərwər(ɪ); *Gall* -wir; **'fɛbr(j)uir*,
*'fabr(j)uər, **'fɛvərjir*, **'fɛbərjir*] *n* =
February.
fech *see* FESH
fecht &c, **ficht** *la14-18*; **feicht** &c *la14-e20*
[fɛxt; *Bwk also* faɪxt; **fɪxt*] *vti, pt also* **focht** &c
la19-, **faucht** &c *la14* [foxt; *Bwk also* faxt; *S*
fjuxt]. *ptp also* **focht**(**en**) &c ['foxtən, 'foxən,
foxt; *S* 'fjuxn, fjuxt; **'fʌux(t)ən, *'faxən*] **1** (1)
= fight *la14-*. (2) *vi, specif* struggle against misfortune *etc la18-*. **2** *vt, chf in ptp* harassed, worn
out *la18-*, now *NE*. **3** *vi* wrestle, kick or fling the
limbs about *la19-*, now *Abd Ags*.
 n a fight, struggle; exertion; pugnacity *15-*.
 a bonnie fechter an intrepid fighter (*freq fig*
for a cause) *la19-*. ∼**ie** &c courageous, ready to
fight *la19-*, now *local Bnf-Fif*.
 ∼ **wi one's ain taes** be excessively quarrelsome *20-*, *Sh Cai*.
feck &c, **fect** *16* *n* **1** = effect, force, value
la15-19. **2** the majority, the greater part *la15-*.
3 a (great etc) quantity, number, (any etc)
amount *17-*, now *local Abd-Slk*.
 ∼**fu** &c **1** effective, capable, efficient *16-e20*. **2**
sturdy, forceful, powerful *16-*, now *Fif*. ∼**less**
ineffective, weak, incompetent *la16-*. ∼**lessness** weakness, incompetence *17-*. ∼**ly** &c
mostly, almost *la18-*, now *NE Ags*. [aphetic]
fecket &c *n* a woollen garment with sleeves and
buttoned front *la18-*, *C, S*.
 fir ∼ a coffin *19*. [uncertain]
fect *see* FECK
fedder, feddrame *see* FEATHER
fede *see* FEED, FEID
fedill *see* FEEDLE
fee &c *15-*, **fe** *la14-16*, **fey** &c *15-17* [fi; *S* fəi] *n*
1 = fee *la14-*. **2** *also in pl* a servant's wages, *esp*
those paid half-yearly or for specific services
la14-e20. **3** an engagement as a servant
la19-e20.
v **1** *vt* engage, hire as a servant *15-e20*. **2** take
on hire (a carriage, horse etc) *la15-e17*. **3** *vi*
accept an engagement as a servant *17-e20*.
fiar *la15-*, **fear** *la15-e17* ['fiər] the owner of the
fee-simple of a property. ∼**in**(**g**) **fair** *midLoth
Bwk Ayr*, ∼**in**(**g**) **market** a fair or market, *usu*
held at WHITSUNDAY and MARTINMAS, where
farmers engaged servants for the coming TERM
19-e20.

~ **and heritage** a feudal holding with HERITA-BLE rights *la15*. **in ~ and heritage** in feudal possession with HERITABLE rights *la14-e16*.

feech[1] &c *18-, now NE, WC Rox,* **feuch** *19-, now local NE-SW* [fix, fjux] *interj* expressing disgust, pain or impatience *18-*.
  feechie foul, dirty, disgusting; *of the weather* rainy, puddly *la20-, Kcdn Ags Per*. [*cf* Gael *fuich*]

feech[2] &c [fix] *n* the projecting knob under the bowl of a clay pipe to hold it by when the bowl becomes hot *la19-, now Abd*. [uncertain]

feechie *see* FEECH[1]

feed *18-,* **fede** &c *la14-17 vti* **1** = feed *la14-*. **2** *vt* pasture (animals) *17-18*.
  ~**er** a bovine animal being fattened for market *la19-, local NE-SW*. ~**ing** (**sheep** *etc*) being fattened for market *19-*. ~**ing storm** *etc* a storm etc which adds more snow to that already lying *el7, 19-, now local NE-Gall*.

feedle &c *19-e20,* **fedill** &c *16 n* = field *NE*. [metath]

feegarie &c [fi'gɛrɪ] *n* finery in dress; frippery *19*. [altered and extended f Eng *vagary*; *cf* FLAGARIE]

feegur &c ['figər, 'fɪgər] *n, vti* = figure *19-, local Fif-S*.

feel[1] *18-,* **fele** *la14-16,* **feill** &c *la14-17* [fil] *vti* **1** = feel *la14-*. **2** *vt* perceive by smell (*la14-*) or taste (*la19-*).
  n **1** mental feeling, perception, knowledge *la15-e18*. **2** a feeling or idea; a shrewd suspicion *la15-16*. **3** = feel.
  ~**less** without feeling, numb *lɑl7-e19*.

feel[2] *adj* **1** *of things* cosy, neat *19-e20, S*. **2** *of persons* comfortable, cosy *19-e20, S*. **3** soft, smooth to the touch *la18-, now Bwk Dmf Rox*. [ME *fele* &c proper, of the right sort, OE *fǣle* faithful, good, pleasant]

feel *see* FUIL

feelimageery *see* WHIGMALEERIE

feem &c *NE n* **1** = fume. **2** a state of sudden heat, a sweat *19-*. **3** *fig* a state of agitation or rage *19-*.
  vi **1** = fume. **2** be in a state of great heat or perspiration *19-e20*.

feenal *adj* = final *19*.

feenich &c [*'fin(j)əx] *n* the knot grass, *esp* its flowerhead and seed *el8, e20* (*Bnf Abd*). [? *cf* Gael *fianach* matgrass]

feenish *la19-,* **finis** &c *15-e17, only Sc;* **finish** &c *la16-* ['fmɪʃ; *fmɪs] *vti* **1** = finish *15-*. **2** *ploughing* cut the final furrow in a RIG[1] *20-*.
  n **1** *ploughing* the final furrow which separates one RIG[1] from another *la19-*. **2** a mixture of alcohol and shellac used in varnishing, and as an intoxicant by meths-drinkers etc *la19-, now Ayr*.

feer &c *vt, ploughing* make the first guiding furrow on (the land) *18-*.
  ~**in** &c **1** the act of making the first furrow

18-e20. **2** the first furrow made *19-, now Renfr*.
  ~**in pole** one of the poles set up as a guide in drawing the first furrow *19-*. [nME *fere*, OE *fyrian*, cut a furrow, f OE *furh* furrow]

feerd *see* FUIRD

feerich &c ['firəx] *n* **1** ability, activity *19-, now Bnf Abd*. **2** a state of agitation, excitement, rage or panic *19-, now Bnf Abd*.
  feerichin *n, adj* bustling, fumbling because of excitement *19-, now Abd*. [only Sc; see SND]

feerie *see* FERE[1]

feerious *see* FURIOUS

Feersday *see* FUIRSDAY

feery-farry &c *18-e20,* **fery fary** &c *16-17* ['fɪrɪ'farɪ, -'fɛrɪ] *n* a bustle, a state of excitement or confusion *16-e20*. [only Sc; reduplicated f FAIRY 2]

feesant &c *19-,* **fasiane** &c *16-e20* ['fizən(t); *N Per Fif Loth Uls* 'feʒən, *Ayr S* 'fezn(t)] *n* = pheasant. [*cf* EPHESIAN]

feesick &c *19-,* **feisik** *la15 n* = physic.

feess *see* FESH

feeth *la18,* **feith** &c [*fiθ] *n, freq attrib* a salmon net fixed on stakes and stretched into the bed of a river *la15-19, NE*. [unknown]

feetie *see* FIT[1]

feetspur *see* FIT[1]

feeze &c *la18-,* **fize** *17* [fiz; *Ork* viz; *faɪz] *n* a screw; a screwing or twisting motion *17, e19*.
  v **1** *vt,* ~ **aff, on** *etc* twist, screw, cause to revolve (a spinning wheel etc) *la18-20*. **2** wriggle (the body), wag (the tail) *19-e20*. **3** *vi, also* ~ **up** work hard (at) *la19-e20, NE*. **4** *vir, fig* fawn, get oneself into another's favour *19-e20*. [only Sc; *cf* Flem, Du dial *vijze*, MDu *vise*; *cf* PHISE]

feff *n* a bad smell, a stench *20-, Cai Ross*. [only Sc; ON *þefr* a smell]

feftie *see* FIFTY

feg &c *n* = fig *la15-, now Bnf Fif*.

fegour *see* FIGOUR

fegs &c; **faiks** &c *19-, chf S Uls* [fɛgz, fegz, feks] *n,* see phrases below.
  interj, expressing emphatic assertion or surprise indeed!, goodness! *la18-*.
  by (**my**) ~ *19,* **guid** ~ *la18-, now Abd,* **my** ~ *19-* = *interj.* [reduced f obs Eng (*by my*) *faikings,* f *fay* or *faith* + *kins*]

fegur *see* FIGOUR

feice *see* FACE

feicht *see* FECHT

feid &c *la15-e19,* **fede** &c; **fead** *la16-18* [fid; *fed] *n* **1** *freq* **auld, dedely** *etc* ~, *or contrasted with* FAVOUR enmity, hostility; a feud *la14-e19*. **2** a continued state of hostility, an ongoing feud *la15-17*.
  bere (*la16-e17*), **hald** (*la15-e17*) *or* **have** (*la15-16*) **at** ~ be at enmity with, be hostile towards. [nME (once), OF *fede*; adopted into Eng *16* as *feud* &c]

feid *see* FADE

feifteen *19-20*, **fiftene &c** *la14-* ['fɪf'tin; *N* 'fəif-; *Fif Loth also* 'fɛf-, 'fɛ̈f-] *adj* **1** = fifteen *la14-*. **2** = fifteenth *la14-*, *now Abd Fif.*

fifteint &c = fifteenth *la16-17.*

the fifteen 1 the *Court of Session* (SESSION), then consisting of fifteen judges, *esp* when acting in a body as a court of appeal *la18-e19.* **2 the F∼** the Jacobite rising of 1715.

feik *see* FYKE

feilamort &c, philamort &c; feildamort &c [*'fil(ə)'mort, *&c*] *n* = filemot, the colour of a dead leaf *la16-17, only Sc.*

feill *see* FAIL¹, FEEL¹

feingie &c *la14, la19-* (*NE*), **fenȝe &c** *la14-16*; **feingȝie &c** *la16-17*, **fenzie &c** *la18*, **fenye &c** *la15-16*, **fenyhe** *la14-e15*, **fe-** *la14-19*, **fei-** *la14-*, **fi-** *la16-*, **-e** *la14-17*, **-ie** *16-* ['fɛŋ(j)ı, *NE* fɛŋ; *'finjı, *'finjı, *&c*] *v* **1** *vt* = feign *la14-*, *now Bnf Abd.* **2** *vi* make pretence, act deceptively *la14-*.

∼it &c 1 = feigned *la14-*. **2** (1) *of documents* forged, spurious *la15-e17.* (2) *of things* counterfeit, imitation *16.*

feir &c, fere [*fir] *n* **1** = AFFERE 1 (1), *15-16.* **2** *in pl* = AFFERE 1 (2), *15-e16.* **3** a band, host, following *e19.*

in ∼ of were &c in warlike array *la14-e18.* [reduced f AFFERE; *n* 3 may be arch revival of ME *fere*, OE *gefēre* company]

feir *see* FERE, FIAR

feird *see* FOURT

feisik *see* FEESIK

feist *see* FESTE

feit *see* FEAT

feith *see* FEETH

feitho *n* a polecat *la15.* [for *feicho* [*'fitʃu], var of ME *fecheu &c* > ModEng *fitchew*]

feld(e) *see* FIELD

feldifare *see* FELTIEFLIER

fele *see* FEEL¹

fell¹ &c *n* **1** = fell, hide, skin *la15-*. **2** the skin of a sheep, as distinguished from the wool *19-, S.*

fell² *n* a (*usu* steep, rocky) hill; a tract of hillmoor *la15-, freq in place-names.* [nME; ON *-fell, fjall*]

fell³ *vt* **1** = fell, cause to fall *la14-*. **2** slaughter, kill (*orig* animals) *17-*. **3** injure; thrash *la18-e20.* **4** *salmon fishing* cast (a net) from a boat into a river *la18-19.*

n a knock-down or stunning blow *20-, now Wgt Dmf.*

∼ed prostrate, *esp* with illness *la16-, C-S.* **∼ed sick** too ill to move *19-, now Ayr.*

∼ twa dogs wi ae bane (*now Sh Ork Abd Ags*) *or* **stane** (*now midLoth Kcb*) = kill two birds with one stone *18-.*

fell⁴ *vt* befall, be the lot of, *chf impersonal* **weel fells** .. lucky is etc .. *la18-19, Abd.*

n lot, fate *la18-e19, NE.* [see SND]

fell⁵ &c *adj* **1** (1) *of persons etc* fierce, of cruel disposition, ruthless *la14-e20.* (2) *of pain, misfortune etc* severe, acute, grievous *la14-, now Abd Fif*

Bwk. (3) *of the weather etc* severe, inclement *la14-*, *now Abd Fif Bwk.* **2** remarkable or considerable of its kind; extremely strong, big, loud etc *la14-*, *now NE Dmf Rox.* **3** energetic and capable, sturdy *18-*, *now sEC-S.* **4** clever, shrewd *18-*, *now local EC-S.* **5** *of cheese* strong-tasting, pungent; *of drink* potent *la18-19.*

adv **1** extremely, greatly, very *la14-*, *now NE, EC, S.* **2** vigorously, energetically; sternly *la18-e20.* [ME *fell*, OF *fel* cruel]

fell *see* FAIL²

fella *see* FALLOW

felloun &c *adj* **1** = felon, fierce, cruel *la14-e17.* **2** great, huge, loud, strong *la14-16.*

adv very, very much *la15-e18.* [*cf* FELL⁵]

fellow-craft *see* FALLOW

fellow deir &c *n* = fallow deer *la16-17.* [only Sc; prob erron anglicization]

felny *n* = felony *la14-15, only Sc.*

felt¹ *n* **1** = felt, the material *la16-*. **2** worn-out arable pasture consisting *chf* of fine bent-grass *19-, now Per.*

felt² *n, chf* **∼ gravel** the disease gravel *16-e18.* [obscure]

felter &c *vt* **1** tangle (hair etc) *la15-e19.* **2** *freq fig* entangle, encumber *la16-e19.*

n, chf weaving a defect, a mistake *19-e20, Fif.*

feltie *n* = FELTIEFLIER *n* 1, *la19-, now midLoth Dmf.*

feltieflier &c *19-*, *now midLoth*, **feldifare &c** *la15-16*; **feltifer** *18-*, *now Fif*, **feltifare** *19-*, *now Kcb* ['fɛltı'fliər, 'fɛltıfər] *n* **1** the fieldfare *la15-*, *now local.* **2** the missel-thrush *la19-e20.* [ME *feldefare &c*]

fen *see* FEND

fence, fens &c *la14-17* *n* **1** = fence *la14-*. **2** *law* an arrest of goods or lands *16.*

vt **1** *law* open the proceedings of (a court (*15-*) or parliament (*la16-17*)) by uttering a formula forbidding interruption *15-*. **2** put under arrest *16-e17.* **3** = fence *la15-*.

∼ment the formal opening of a court or of parliament *la16.*

∼-fed *of animals* fed with titbits brought to the side of the fence; pampered *19-, Abd Ags.*

∼ the tables *Presbyterian Church* at a communion service, explain the significance of the SACRAMENT and indicate those who may properly partake *18-*, *now chf Highl.*

fencible *18-e20*, **fensabill &c** *la15-16*; **fensible &c** *la16-17* *adj* **1** *of men* capable of and liable for defensive military service *la15-e19.* **2** *of arms etc* capable of serving for defence *la15-16, only Sc.* **3** capable of or actually serving for defence or protection *16-e19.*

n, freq attrib a soldier called up for home defence *18-19.* [chf Sc; ME, aphetic f *defensible*]

fend &c; fen *18-* *v* **1** *vt* defend, protect, shelter *la14-*, *now Cai NE.* **2** *vti* = fend *15-*. **3** *vtr* provide (oneself or another) with sustenance, maintain *la15-e20.* **4** *vi* support oneself; scrape an existence *la16-*.

fend *n* **1** a defence, resistance *17-e20*. **2** an effort, attempt, *esp* to maintain oneself, *chf* **make a ~** *18-, now local Ags-Kcb*. **3** fare, sustenance *19-e20, Abd*.

~fu able to fend for oneself, energetic *19-, now Ags*. **~ie &c 1** able to look after oneself, managing, thrifty *la18-, chf SW*. **2** active, lively, healthy *18-, chf Ayr*. **~less 1** lacking resource or energy *la19-, Sh Cai NE, SW*. **2** without flavour *la19-e20, NE*. **3** of corn, straw short, thin, without substance *la19-, NE*.

how do ye *etc* **~ ?** how goes it with you? *la18-e19*.

fend(e) *see* FIENT

fens *see* FENCE

fensabill, fensible *see* FENCIBLE

fensum *adj* ? loathsome *e16*. [prob misreading for *fowsum* (FOUSOME)]

fent &c *n* a slit or opening in a garment *la15-, now local Ork-Fif*. [ME; OF *fente*]

fent *see* FAINT

fenye, fenyhe, fenʒe, fenzie *see* FEINGIE

feppill *see* FAIPLE

fer *see* FAR

fercost *see* FARCOST

ferd *see* FEAR, FOURT

ferding *n* meaning unknown *la15-e16, Abd*.

ferdy *see* FAIRD

fere¹ *la14-e16, 19-e20*; **feir &c** *16-e20* [fir] *adj* **1** of persons and animals healthy, sturdy, *chf* **hale and ~** (HAIL¹) *la14-e20*. **2** of things sound, unimpaired *la14-16*.

feerie &c *la17-e20*, **fery &c** *15-16* active, nimble. [eME; OE *fēre*, f pt stem of *faran* go]

fere² &c, pheare *17-19*, **pheere** *e17* [fir] *n* = fere, companion, comrade *la14-e20, latterly arch or verse*.

~ for ~ equal in every respect *la18-e19, NE*.

fere³ &c *vi* belong, pertain, be appropriate *la14-16*. [ME *fēr*, reduced f *effeir* (AFFEIR)]

fere *see* FEAR, FEIR

ferekin &c *la16*, **firikin &c** *la15-e19* [*'fir(i)kin, *'fir(i)-] *n* = firkin, *only Sc*.

ferge [ferdʒ, *fɛrg] *vi, chf* **at** *or* **up** work with vigour, rub, beat hard, *esp* to little effect *la19-, now Abd*. [var of FERK]

feriale [*?'firiəl] *adj* **1** = ferial, pertaining to an ordinary week-day *la15-16*. **2** = FERIAT *la15-e18*.

feriat &c *la15-e19*; **feriot &c** *la16-e17* [*?'firiət] *adj, law*, **~ time** *etc* a time in which no legal proceedings can be taken *la15-e19*. [only Sc; L *fēriāt-*, ptp stem of *fēriāri* keep holiday]

Ferintosh &c ['fɛr(i)n'toʃ] *n* a kind of WHISKY formerly (18) distilled at Ferintosh, Ross; WHISKY *in gen, 18-e20*.

feriot *see* FERIAT

ferk &c *vti* jerk; poke, turn over *la19-, now Abd*. [ME *ferk* carry, drive, OE *fercian* (once) bring]

ferkishin *see* FARKAGE

ferlie, ferly &c, farly &c *la14-16*; **fairly &c** *la15-* ['fɛrli; *Cai Uls* 'farli] *n* **1** (1) a strange sight, a marvel, a curiosity *la14-*. (2) *disparaging, of a person or animal, la18-, now Abd*. **2** a piece of (surprising) news; *in pl* gossip; an object of gossip *19-*.

vti **1** wonder, marvel, be surprised (at) *la14-*. **2** *vt, chf impersonal* cause to wonder, surprise *la14-e15, e20 (Sh)*.

adj (adv) strange(ly), wonderful(ly) *la14-e20*.

ferlifull &c wonderful, marvellous *la14-16*.

have ~ marvel, wonder *la14-16*. **na, gret, sma** *etc* **~** no, great, small *etc* wonder *15-e20*.

spy ~s interfere in someone else's business, be inquisitive *la18-, local Cai-Kcb*. [ME *ferly (adj)*; ON *ferligr* monstrous, dreadful]

ferlot *see* FIRLOT

ferly *see* FERLIE

ferm &c, farm &c *la16- n* **1** = farm, *orig* the condition of (land) being let at a fixed rent etc, *latterly* land leased etc for cultivation etc *la14-*. **2** *also in pl* a fixed yearly amount, *freq* paid in kind, as rent for land *la15-19*. **3** grain paid as rent *17*.

vti = farm *17-*.

~ bear &c, corn *or* **meal** barley, grain or meal paid as rent *16-e19*. **~ onstead** (19) *or* **stead** (19-, now Fif) farm buildings, homestead. **~ steading** the farm buildings with or without the farmhouse *la16-*. **~ stockin** farm animals, *esp* cattle and sheep *19*. **~ toun &c** the homestead of a farm *17-*. **~ victual** grain paid as rent *la15-e19*.

let *or* **set for ~** let for a fixed amount *15-e16*.

fermance &c *la15-e17*, **firmance &c** *n* **1** close keeping, confinement, custody, *freq* **sure** *etc* **~** *la15-18*. **2** *only* **firmance** a stable state or condition; a means of stability or security *la15-e16*. [only Sc; OF *fermance* an enclosure, a guarantee]

fermorar &c *la15-17*, **firmorar &c** *16*, **farmo(u)rar &c** *la16-17 n* = farmer. [only Sc; MedL *fermarius*]

fern &c *18-19*, **farne &c** *la15-e18, only Sc n* **1** = fern, the plant *la15-*. **2** *specif* bracken *18-*. **~ owl** the nightjar *la18-e20*.

ferntickle &c; fairnytickle &c ['fɛrn'tɪkl; *C, S* 'fɛrni-; *Uls* 'farn-] *n* a freckle *18-*.

~ed freckled *18-*. [ME *farntikylle &c*]

fernyear &c *17-*, **fernʒere &c** *la15-17*, **farnʒer &c** *la15-18*; **fairnʒer &c** *la16-18* ['fɛrn'(j)ir, 'fɛrnir, 'fɛrn(j)ər; *'farn-, *'fɛrn-] *n* last year; the preceding year *la15-*.

auld ~s stories of long ago *la18-20, NE*.

ferow *see* FARROW

ferré *see* FERRY¹

ferrer, ferrest *see* FAR

ferrick &c *n* a parhelion, a mock sun *la19-e20*. [see SND]

ferrier *n* **1** = farrier *18-*. **2** a veterinary surgeon *20-, NE midLoth*.

ferrior, ferriour *see* FERRY¹

ferrow *see* FARROW

ferry[1] &c, **ferré** 16-17 vt, n = ferry 14-.
   ferryar &c 15-16, **ferrio(u)r** la16-e17 a ferry-
   man only Sc.
ferry[2] &c vi = farrow, bring forth young la14-,
   now local Sh-midLoth, only Sc.
ferry see FAIRY
ferse see FARCE
fersell &c [*?'fersl, *?'ferʃl] adj energetic,
   active la19-e20. [perh f FAIRCE]
fersie see FIERCIE
ferst see FIRST
ferter &c n 1 = fertre, feretory, a shrine, reli-
   quary la14-16. 2 a bier e16.
ferther see FAR
fery see FERE[1]
fery fary see FEERY-FARRY
fesch see FISH
fesh &c la16-19, **fech** &c la14-17 [fɛʃ, fɛtʃ] v,
   pres also **fess** la19-, now NE Ags Wgt [fɛs]. pt
   also **feess** &c 19-, NE, **fuish** &c la18-, now local
   Per-Ayr, **fotch** 19-, now Ags Fif Ayr [fis, føʃ,
   fotʃ, fuʃ, foʃ]. ptp also **fessen** la19-, now N,
   fu(i)shen 19-, now Bwk ['fɛsən, 'føʃən, 'fʌʃ-,
   'foʃ-, 'fuʃ-, 'fɛʃ-, 'fɛtʃ-, 'fotʃ-] 1 vt = fetch
   la14-. 2 ~ **up** bring up, rear, nurture la18-,
   now NE Ags. 3 ~ **on** bring forward, advance,
   bring to maturity la19-, now NE Ags. 4 vi
   breathe with difficulty, pant, gasp la18-, now Sh.
   fill an ~ **ben** (NE) or **mair** (now Abd Ags Kcb)
   extravagant living 19-.
fest &c la19-, **fast** adj 1 = fast 15-. 2 busy,
   occupied la19-, now Bnf.
   adv = fast la14-.
   festen &c la14-, **fessin** &c 15-, **fassin** &c
   16-e17, **festn-** la14-e17, **fesn-** 15-e17 vt =
   fasten.
   festinance &c custody, confinement 15-16, only
   Sc. **fessener** a puzzler, a baffling problem 20-,
   now midLoth.
   ~ **place** mining a working place in advance of
   the others la19-, now Fif.
   fast in the foot mining, of a pump choked la19-,
   now Fif.
feste la14-e16; **feist** &c la15-16, only Sc, **fest**
   la14-16 [*fist; *fɛst] n, vti = feast.
festinance see FEST
feth interj = faith! 19-.
fether see FEATHER
fetter &c n 1 = fetter la14-. 2 in pl, law the
   restrictions imposed by a deed of entail la18-19.
   vt = fetter la14-.
fettle &c, **fettill** e15 n strength, vigour, condition la18-.
   v 1 vi = fettle, make oneself ready e15. 2 vt put
   to rights, repair; settle 19-, now local NE-Bwk, S.
   3 attend to the needs of, feed and clothe
   la19-e20. 4 fall upon, 'go for' (a person) la19-,
   now Bwk. 5 vi ~ **to** or **wi** set about, tackle (a
   job) with vigour 19.
   adj neat, trim; exactly suited 19-, now SW.

what ~ ? how are you? la19-, local midLoth-Kcb.
how are ye fettlin? how are you keeping?
   la19-, now Bwk.
feu &c, **few** &c la15-e18 [fju] n, law 1 orig a
   feudal tenure of land where the VASSAL, in place
   of military service, made a return in grain or in
   money; latterly a holding in which a VASSAL has
   the exclusive possession and use of HERITABLE
   property in return for payment of a feu duty to a
   SUPERIOR la15-; see feu duty. 2 a piece of land
   held by this tenure 18-. 3 = feu duty, 16-.
   vt, also ~ **out** or **off** grant in feu, la16-.
   ~**ar** &c a person who holds land in FEU 16-.
   ~ **charter** &c the document granting a new
   FEU la16-. ~ **duty** &c the fixed annual payment for a FEU; since 1974 no new contracts
   may impose a feu duty and existing ones may be
   bought out (and must be on a change of ownership of the FEU) la16-. ~ **ferme** &c 1 now only
   in the formula of a feu charter = n 1, freq in ~
   ferme 15-. 2 = feu duty, 16-17. ~
   ferm(or)an &c the holder of a FEU 15-16. ~
   holding = feu ferme, 18-19. ~ **mail** &c = feu
   duty, 16-e18. ~ **right(s)** the right(s) established by feu charter, 18-e20.
   hold ~ chf in passive, of lands etc be held by this
   tenure 17-. (**have** etc or **set**) **in** ~ (hold or
   grant) by this tenure la15-. [only Sc; OF = a
   feudal holding; cognate w FEE]
feu see FEW[1]
feuach &c ['fjuəx] n a very sparse crop of grain
   or grass e20, NE. [perh connected w Gael fiadh
   wild]
feuch[1] &c [fjux] vti puff (**at** a pipe), smoke
   la18-, now Bnf Abd.
   n a draw, a puff (at a pipe) 20-, Bnf Abd Ags.
   [onomat]
feuch[2] &c [fjux] n a resounding blow 18-, NE.
   [uncertain]
feuch[3] &c [fjux] n a state of great excitement or
   rage; a commotion la18-, now Ags midLoth.
   [uncertain]
feuch see FEECH[1]
feuchter [*'fjuxtər] n a slight fall of snow
   la19-e20. [see SND]
feul see FUIL
Feverȝere see FEBRUAR
few[1] &c, **fyow** &c la19-, N; **feu** la16-e17 [fju;
   NE fjʌu] adj = few la14-.
   a ~ **nowmer** &c a small number 16. **a** ~
   broth, porridge, soup etc a little BROTH[1], porridge, soup etc la18-, now Stlg WC. **a good** ~ a
   good many, a considerable number (of) 19-.
few[2] &c vi show promise or aptitude la19-e20.
   [nEng dial]
few see FEU
fewale &c la14-e18, **fuaill** &c la14 [*'fjuəl] n
   = fuel.
fewlume [*?'føløm] n some kind of bird e16.
   [perh Gael faoileann a gull]
fewter &c vi close in combat e16. [perh var of
   FELTER]

fey[1] &c [fəi] *adj* **1** *of persons* fated to die, doomed, *esp* as portended by peculiar, *usu* elated behaviour; *more vaguely* other-wordly *la14-*. **2** leading to death; fatal *la15-e16*. **3** behaving in an excited or irresponsible way *19-*, *now local NE-Uls*.

~**dom** the state of being FEY; a portent, *chf* of death; doom *18-19*.

~ **token** &c a sign of approaching death *la18-e19*. [only Sc; OE *fǣge*, ON *feigr*]

fey[2] &c [fəi; *Abd also* faɪ] *n* = INFIELD *la17-e20*, *Gall.*

vt clean out, scour (a ditch, drain) *la19-*, *Abd Per.* [see SND]

fey *see* FEE, WHEY

feyall *see* FIALL

feyt *see* FIT[1]

fiall &c *la16-18*, **feal** &c *15-19*; **feyall** &c *la16-17* [*'fiəl] *n* **1** feudal tenure *la15-e17*. **2** payment for services, wages *la15-18*. **3** a feudal tenant; a paid servant or workman *16-e18*. [only Sc; ? OF *feal*; sense 2 w infl f FEE]

fiar *17-20*, **feir** &c *16-e18*; **fear** &c *la17-e20* ['fiər; *'fir] *n*, *chf in pl* the price(s) of grain for the year, used to determine MINISTERS' *stipends* (STEEPEND), *latterly* fixed in spring by the local SHERIFF in the **Fiars Court** *16-20*.

strike (**the**) ~**s** fix these amounts *la17-20*. [only Sc; OF *feor*, *feur* a fixed price, f L *forum* a market]

fiar *see* FEE

fiarter ['fjartər] *n* term of abuse for an insignificant or undersized person or animal *19-*, *Cai.* [Eng *fart*]

fiber &c *n* a beaver *la15*. [only Sc; L]

ficher &c ['fɪxər; *NE also* 'fʌxər] *vi* **1** fumble, fiddle nervously with the fingers *19-*, *Sh NE Ags*. **2** work in a bungling way *19-*, *now NE*. **3** ~ **wi** handle (a woman) indelicately, grope, 'touch up' *19-*, *local Sh-Ags*.

n a fiddling, inept way of working *19-*, *Bnf Abd*. [uncertain]

ficht *see* FECHT

fickle &c *la18-*, **fickill** &c *15-16 adj* **1** = fickle *15-*. **2** difficult, tricky *19-*, *local Ork-Renfr*.

vt puzzle, perplex *19-*, *local Inv-S*.

n a puzzle, a riddle *la19-e20*.

fickler a puzzle, a baffling problem *20-*, *midLoth Rox*. **ficklie** &c puzzling, difficult, tricky *19-*, *now Fif midLoth*.

ficks facks *see* FYKE-FACK

fidder *vi* flutter, be in a state of excitement *19-*, *now Kcb*. [frequentative of FUD *v*]

fidder *see* FUTHER

fiddle &c *17-*, **fidill** &c *la15-e17 n* **1** = fiddle *la15-*. **2** a hand-machine for sowing grain, worked by drawing a rod over an opening in the seed-container with a similar motion to a violin bow *20-*, *local NE-SW*.

fiddler &c **1** = fiddler *la15-*, *in place-names 13-*. **2** the sandpiper *19-e20*. **fiddler's biddin** a last-minute invitation *la19-*, *NE midLoth WC*.

fiddler's news stale news *la19-*, *local NE-Rox*.

fiddlie nickname for a fiddler *20-*, *Bnf Abd Ags*.

fiddltie-fa a fuss; a trifling excuse; hesitation *la19-e20*, *Bnf Abd*.

~ **diddle** *interj* describing the sound of a fiddle *19-*. ~ **face** a long face; a sad face *la19-*, *now midLoth Arg Ayr*.

look *etc* **like the far** (**awa**) **end of a** (**French**) ~ have a long face, look sour or disdainful *18-*, *local*. **find a** ~ come upon something rare or precious, get a pleasant surprise *la18-*, *now Abd*.

fidge &c *vi* fidget; move restlessly from excitement; twitch, itch *la16-*.

n a shrug, twitch, jerk *19-*, *local Sh-EC*.

be fidgin fain be restlessly or excitedly eager *la17-*, *now local Bnf-Fif*. [eModEng; *cf* FITCH[1]]

fidill *see* FIDDLE

field &c, **fiel** *la18-e20*, **felde** &c *la14-17*; **feld** *la14-17*, *in place-names 13-17* [fil(d)] *n* = field *la14-*, *in place-names 13-*.

v **1** *vt* sink a margin round (a wooden panel) *19-*, *local*. **2** *vti* = field.

~**y** &c the hedge-sparrow *e20*.

~ **conventicle** a meeting of *Covenanters* (COVENANT) in the open air *la17*, *Gall.* ~ **land** land consisting of a field or fields *15-16*. ~**land aitis** oats growing on such land *la16-e17*. ~ **meeting** *18-19*, ~ **preaching** *19-*, *local* a religious service held in the open air, a relic of *Covenanting* times, still surviving in special commemorative services.

fient &c *la17-*, **fende** &c *la14-17*; **fiend** &c *17-*, **fend** *la14-16* [fint] *n* **1** = fiend *la14-*. **2** *exclam* the devil..! *freq* ~ **nor**, ~ **that** would to the devil that.. *18-e19*.

(**the**) ~ (**a**) devil a, never a, not a blessed.. *16-*. ~ **all** nothing at all, not a thing *20-*, *local*. ~(**s**) **ma**(**y**) **care**(**s**) devil may care, who cares? *la18-e20*.

fiercelins *adv* hurriedly, impetuously, violently *la18-20*. [Eng *fierce* + *-lins*]

fiercie &c *18-e19*, *only Sc*, **farcy** &c *16-*, **fairsie** &c *la16*; **fe**(**a**)**rsie** &c *16*, *only Sc n* = farcy, the disease of horses.

fiery *see* FIRE

Fife *n* Fifan *chf verse* belonging to Fife *la17-19*. **Fifer 1** a native of Fife, *freq* with implication of cunning and unscrupulousness *la19-*. **2** a kind of soft, dull brown marble *20-*, *Bnf Abd*. **Fifie** a type of herring fishing boat, *prob* first built and used on the Fife coast *20-*, *ECoast*. **Fifish** eccentric, slightly deranged *19-*, *now Ags Fif*. **Fife** (**Region**) a REGION formed from the former county of Fife *la20-*. [the east-coast county (*now* REGION); see also KINGDOM]

fife *see* FIVE

fift &c *la14-*; **fyift** *la16*, *only Sc* [fɪft, fɛ̈ft; *'fəift] *adj* = fifth.

fifteint, **fiftene** *see* FEIFTEEN

fifty &c; **feftie** *e17 adj* = fifty *la14-*.

figmaleerie *see* WHIGMALEERIE

figorata &c [*?fɪgəˈrata, -o &c] *n* some figured fabric *e17*. [only Sc; Ital *figurata* or Span *figurada*; *cf* FIGURÉ]

figour &c *15-e17*; **feg(o)ur** *la16* [ˈfɪgər; *ˈfɪgør; *ˈfɪg- &c] *n* = figure.

figurate &c *ptp* figured, expressed or compared metaphorically *la15-16*.
adj figured (velvet etc) *16*; *cf* FIGURÉ.

figuré &c *adj* **sattin** ~ figured or patterned satin *la15*. [only Sc; F *figuré*; *cf* FIGURATE, FIGORATA]

fil *see* FILL

filbow &c [ˈfɪlbə] *n* a blow, thump *19-e20, Abd Kcdn*. [see SND]

file *see* WHILE

files *see* WHILES

filget &c [ˈfɪldʒɪt] *n* an untidy, disreputable-looking person *20-, Bnf Abd*. [uncertain]

filiate *vt, law* determine the paternity of (a child), *chf* **filiation** the act of or legal action for doing this *19-*.

filk *see* WHILK[2]

fill &c; **fil** *vti* **1** = fill *la14-*. **2** *vt* fill in with earth *la14-e17*. **3** *vi, of the sea* flow landward *15-16*. **4** *vt* pour out *16-, now N-C*. **5** *weaving* fill (the bobbins) with yarn *la19-, now Ags Fif*. **6** load (PEATS[1] etc) *la18-, Sh Abd*.
n **1** = fill *la14-*. **2** the action of filling, the amount necessary to fill (a container) *19-, now NE Ags*.
adj full *18-, Ork NE, only Sc*.
~er 1 = filler *16-*. **2** a funnel for pouring liquids through *17-*.
~ drunk *or* **fou** make drunk *19-*. **~ up** increase in bulk or girth *la19-, Abd Ags Arg SW*.

fillebeg &c; **philabeg** &c [ˈfɪləbɛg, *ˈfɪlɪ-, *ˈfɪlɪ-, &c] *n, chf literary* a KILT[1] *18-*. [Gael *féileadh-beag* little KILT[1], *féileadh* being orig the whole PLAID which, when belted, was a significant development towards the modern KILT[1]]

fillet &c *n* **1** *freq in pl* the loins or thighs (of a person) *la15-, now Cai Abd*. **2** = fillet *16-*.

fillie, filly &c *n* = felloe, (part of) the rim of a wheel *16-, only Sc*.

filsh[1] &c *n* a big, disagreeable person, a lout *19-, Bnf Abd*.
filschach [ˈfɪlʃəx] a dishonest, greedy person *20-, Bnf Abd*. [uncertain]

filsh[2] &c *adj* weak, faint *19-e20*. [uncertain]

fin *see* FIND

finance &c; **finans** &c *la15-e16* *n* **1** = finance *15-*. **2** fineness, metallic content (of gold or silver) *la15-16, only Sc*.

find &c; **fin** *la18-* [fɪnd; *N, WC, SW* fɪn] *vt, pt* **fand** &c *la14-19*, **fund** *la15-, now local*, **fan** *la19-, now Arg. ptp also* **foundin** &c *la14-e16*, **fundin** *la14-e17*, **fun(d)** *la15-, local* [fʌn(d); *ˈfundən, *fun(d), *ˈfʌndən] **1** = find *la14-*. **2** feel, be conscious of *la14-*. **3** feel with the fingers, grope (1) *in gen, la18-*; (2) *in an indecent sense, la18-, local Bnf-Arg*. **4** be aware of (a smell or taste) *19-*.

n **1** the feel (**of** something), the impression produced by touch *19-, Bnf Abd Kcb*. **2** indecent handling of a woman *20-, local NE-SW*.

Findram *see* FINNAN

fine[1] &c *adj* **1** = fine *la14-*. **2** comfortable, contented, having had enough, *eg* of food; in good health *la18-*. **3** *of persons* pleasant-mannered, likeable *la18-*.
adv very well, very much *la18-*: '*I like it fine*'.
vt sort out (wool) by separating the fine from the coarse parts *la17-19*.
finery *chf in pl, chf of food* delicacies *19-, now Sh*.
fining quhele &c a spinning wheel for making a fine woollen yarn *17*.
~ an(d).. very, properly, really... *la18-*; *cf* Eng *nice and...* ~ **day** *20-, local Sh-Ayr*, ~ **ham** *chf slang, 20-, Abd Fif Gsw Lnk exclam* 'go on!', nonsense! ~ **that** (very well) indeed, certainly *la19-*.

fine[2] &c *n* **1** = fine *la14-*. **2** final issue, settlement, result *15-e17*.
vti **1** = fine *la14-16*. **2** *vi, of a* MAGISTRATE compound **with** (an accused person) *16-e17, only Sc*.

fineer &c [fəˈnir] *vt* **1** *lit and fig* = veneer *19-20, local Ork-C*. **2** ornament fancifully *la19-20, local NE-S*.

finger &c [ˈfɪŋər] *n* = finger *la14-*.
~fu a pinch, a small quantity *la19-, now midLoth Bwk*.
~-fed pampered *la15-, now Abd*. ~ **neb** a fingertip *la18-, now Fif Ayr*. ~ **steel** &c *19-, now N Bwk*, ~ **stuil** &c *la19-, local Sh-Rox* a finger-stall.
turn up one's wee ~ be addicted to drink *la19-, local NE-Rox*.

fingering &c *17-*; **fingram** &c *17-18*, **finʒering** *e17* [ˈfɪŋ(ə)rɪn] *n* **1** a kind of worsted, *orig* spun from combed wool on the small wheel *17-*. **2** a kind of woollen cloth *17-e18*. [earlier in Sc; uncertain, but prob f FINGER, because of some process during the spinning]

fingie *see* FEINGIE

finick [ˈfɪnɪk] *n* a fussy, fastidious person *20-, local NE-C*.
~y fussy, fiddling *20-*. [back-formation f Eng *finical*]

finis, finish *see* FEENISH

finkle &c, **finkil** &c *n* fennel, the plant *16-e19*. [ME *fenkylle*]

finnak *see* FINNOCK

Finnan &c *18-*; **Findram** &c *la18-19* [ˈfɪnən; *also *ˈfɪndrəm, &c] **F~ haddock, F~ haddie** *etc* a haddock cured with the smoke of green wood, PEAT[1] or turf. [local name for Findon, a small Kcdn fishing village, noted for its smoke-cured fish; the alternative form is by confusion with Findhorn, Mry]

finner *n* a whale of the genus *Balaenoptera*, *la18-19, chf Sh*. [f its prominent dorsal fin]

finnie &c *adj, proverb, of corn etc* full of substance *18-e19*. [ME *findig* &c]

finnis &c *vi* **finnissin** &c fidgeting, anxious *20-, Per.* [uncertain]

finnock &c, **finnak** &c *n* a young sea-trout or salmon *17-,* now *N (except Cai) nEC Arg.* [Gael *fionnag* a sea-trout; a young salmon]

finster &c *n* meaning unknown *la17, Edb.*

finʒe *see* FEINGIE

finʒering *see* FINGERING

fippill *see* FAIPLE

fir &c [fɪr; *C* fʌr; *Cai-Mry also* fʌr] *n* = fir *15-.*

fyrne &c *la15-e17,* **firrin** &c *16-e17* made of fir-wood.

~ **candle** = *candle fir* (CANNLE) *19-,* now *Bnf.* ~ **gullie** &c a large broad-bladed knife used for splitting prec *la19-e20, Abd.* ~ **tap** &c *18-,* now *Fif,* ~ **yowe** &c *19-,* now *NE Ags* a fir-cone.

fir *see* FOR

firdoun *see* FRIDDON

fire &c *n* **1** = fire *la14-.* **2** fuel *la16-,* now *local Sh-EC.* **3** a foreign body (*usu* metallic) in the eye *la19-,* now *local Cai-Ayr.* **4** the phosphorescence of the sea *la19.*

vt **1** = fire *15-.* **2** *cookery* bake (*oatcakes* (AIT), SCONES, bread etc) by browning in an oven or over a flame *18-.* **3** inflame (a part of the body) by chafing *la18-.* **4** heat (a house etc), *chf* **keep** (**a house** *etc*) **fired** *20-, local.*

fired *of milk, meat etc* soured by hot weather *19-,* now *midLoth Kcb.* **fiery cross** = *fire cors, 18-, latterly hist.* **firies** &c *skipping* very fast turns of the rope *20-, Ags.*

~ **bitt** a crate containing combustible material to be set on fire as a beacon *17, only Sc.* ~ **burn** sea phosphorescence *la19-,* now *Fif Kcb.* ~ **coal** coal supplied to workmen connected with a colliery *la19-,* now *Fif.* ~ **cors,** ~ **cros** a wooden cross burnt at one end and dipped in blood at the other, carried from place to place by a succession of runners to summon the fighting men of the district to arms *16-17; cf* CROISHTARICH. ~ **edge 1** the sharp edge of a new tool *20-, NE Fif Arg.* **2** *fig* the first wave of enthusiasm *19-, Bnf Abd Kcb.* ~ **end** &c the fireside, the end of a house or room where the fireplace is *la18-, local C.* ~**fangit** &c *chf of* manure scorched, spoilt by excessive fermentation *la18-,* now *Ork.* ~**-flaucht** &c **1** lightning; flashes of lightning *15-17, la19-,* now *local Sh-Per.* **2** a flash of lightning, a thunderbolt *15-,* now *Fif.* **3** a shooting star *19-e20, WC, SW.* ~ **house** a house with a fireplace, a dwelling-house as opposed to out-buildings *15-,* now *Bnf Abd.* ~**-kinlin** a house-warming party *19-, Bnf Abd.* ~ **master 1** one of a group of citizens appointed to take charge of fire-fighting *e18, Edb.* **2** the chief officer of a fire-brigade *la19-.* ~ **new** brand new, as new as metal from the fire *la18-, NE Fif.* ~**-raising** &c *law* arson *la16-.* ~ **room** a room with a fireplace *la16-e19.* ~**slaucht** &c = *fireflaucht, la14-e16.* ~ **spere** &c a spear carrying fire with it *16-e17, only Sc.* ~ **stane** &c a hearth stone *20-,*

Ork Abd, only Sc. ~ **stink** *mining* the smell of coal burning spontaneously *la19-,* now *Fif.* ~ **vessel** &c vessels for use on a fire; cooking utensils *la16-17.* ~**werk** &c **1** fittings for guns *la16-e17.* **2** *chf in pl* firearms *la16-17.*

(**like**) ~ **and tow** rash(ly), impetuous(ly) *19-,* now *Bnf Ags.*

firikin *see* FEREKIN

firlot &c *15-20,* **ferlot** &c *la14-e16,* **furlot** &c *15-17,* **forlot** &c *la15-16,* **fourlet** &c *16;* **firlat** &c *la15-e18,* **furlet** &c *15-e18 n* **1** the fourth part of a BOLL *la14-20.* **2** a measure containing this amount *15-19.* [only *Sc;* ScL *firlota, ferthelota, firthelota;* ON *fiórþe* fourth + *hlotr* lot, portion]

firm *see* FURM

firmance *see* FERMANCE

firme &c *n* = FERM *16.* [MedL *firma*]

firmorar *see* FERMORAR

firr *n* a state of agitation or excitement *20-, Bnf Abd.* [onomat; *cf* Eng *whirr,* FIRRIS and VIRR]

firris &c *n* excitement, rage; a bother, a predicament *la19-e20, Abd.* [prob onomat w infl f FEERY-FARRY; *cf* FIRR]

firrin *see* FIR

firsle *vi* rustle *19-, SW Uls.* [var of FISSLE with intrusive *-r-*]

first &c, **ferst** *la14, 18-e19 adj (n), adv* = first *la14-.*

~**en** &c *ballad* first *la18-19.*

~ **fit** &c *n* **1** the first person (or animal) met on a journey, *esp* by a wedding or christening party on the way to church *18-,* now *Cai Abd Stlg.* **2** the first person to enter a house on New Year's morning, considered to bring good (or bad) luck for the year *la18-. vti* be the first to visit (a person) in the New Year; go on a round of such visits *19-.* ~ **fitter** &c a person who does this *la19-.* ~ **flat,** ~ **floor** the ground floor of a building *la18-, local.*

in the ~ in the first place *la14-e17, only Sc.* **Monday** *etc* ~ next Monday etc, Monday etc immediately following *la18-; cf* NEXT.

first *see* FRIST

firth[1] &c *la14-,* **frith** &c *14-17* [fɪrθ; *Cai-Mry, C also* fʌrθ; *frɪθ] n* a wide inlet of the sea; an estuary. [ON *firð,* stem of *fjörðr* a fjord]

firth[2] &c *n, verse, chf in alliterative phrases* a wood, wooded country *la14-18.* [ME *fyrthe,* but *usu frith,* OE *fyrþ*]

firtig *see* FORTIG

fiscale &c *e16;* **fiscal** &c *la17- adj* = fiscal *16-. n, also* **fischall** &c *la16-17,* **phiscall** &c *17-e18* = *procurator fiscal* (PROCURATOR) *la16-.*

fish *la17-,* **fush** *18-,* **fisch** &c *la14-e17;* **fesch** &c *la14-15 n* **1** = fish *la14-.* **2** the salmon *local.* **3** white fish, as opposed to herring *20-, Cai Ags Fif.*

vti **1** = fish *15-.* **2** endeavour, contrive *19-, Arg Ayr.* ~**er,** ~**ar** &c *15-e17* **1** = fisher, a fisherman *la14-.* **2** a member of a fishing community

19-, local N. ~**er toun &c** a fishing village *18-,
now Abd.* ~**ing wand &c** a fishing rod *18-, now
local Sh-Dmf.*

~ **boit &c** a fishing boat *16-e17, only Sc.*
~**-cadger** a fish hawker *19-.*

fisk &c *n, law* the public treasury, the revenue
falling to the Crown by ESCHEAT *17-e18.*
[eModEng *fiske* an exchequer; F *fisc*; L *fiscus*]

fiss *vi* make a hissing noise *la19-, NE.* [onomat;
cf Eng *fizz*]

fissle &c *la18-;* **fistle** *18-19,* **fussle &c**
la19-e20 v **1** *vi* make a rustling, scuffling noise
18-, now SW Rox Uls. **2** *vt* rustle *20-, now Uls.* **3**
vi fidget, bustle *la18-19.*

n **1** a rustling sound *19-, now SW Rox Uls.* **2** a
bustle, commotion, fuss *18-19.* [onomat; *cf* Eng
fizzle and FISS]

fit[1] **&c** *16-,* **fute &c** *la14-e20;* **fuit &c** *16-17,*
foot &c *17-* [fɪt; *Ork Cai-Mry* fit; *nEC* fʌt;
*føt] n, pl also **feyt &c** *15-e17* [fɪt] **1** = foot
la14-. **2** (1) *in sing, freq with local term preceding*
the lower end *chf* of a piece of ground, a stream,
street etc *16-: 'baillie Hopes land foot'.* (2) *in pl*
the foot of the class, the dunce *20-, now Ags Uls;
cf* HEID *n* 8. **3** a foothold, step, *chf* **lose, miss,
slip** *etc* **a, one's** *or* **the** ~ *18-.*

vti **1** = foot *16-.* **2** *of a horse* kick *19-, now Dmf.*
3 *vt* add up (an account) and insert the total
la15-19. **4** set (PEATS[1]) up on end to dry *la16-,
now local Ags-Uls.*

fitted account, futit compt &c *law* an
account rendered by one party and docqueted
as correct by the other without any express discharge; it is presumed that no other amounts
are outstanding *16-.* **fitter** *vi* **1** *chf of the feet*
patter, move restlessly *19-, now local NE-Dmf.* **2**
walk unsteadily, stumble *19-, now Cai.* **a left
fitter** name (used by Protestants) for a Roman
Catholic *20-, local.* **fittie** *n, pl* **feetie** *18-19* **1** =
foot *la18-19.* **2** the dunce of a class *20-, Ags
Rox. adj* nimble, agile *19-, now Dmf.* **fittininment** [ˈfɪtɪnˈɪnmənt] *n* concern, interference; a
footing in something *la18-e20, Abd.* ~**less** *adj* **1**
= footless. **2** unsteady on the feet, apt to stumble *la18-.* **fittock &c** *n* **1** the foot of an old
stocking cut off and worn as a shoe or as an
extra sock or drawn over a boot *la19-, Ork Cai
NE.* **2** a PEAT[1] cut with an ordinary spade from
the bottom of a *peat-bank* (PEAT[1]) when the
upper layers have been removed *20-, NE.*

~ **ale &c** a drink of ale to celebrate the completion of a sale of cattle *19-e20.* ~ **breed(th) &c**
the breadth of a foot *la14-, now Cai Abd Ags.* ~
brod &c a footboard, treadle, foot-rest *la16-,
now Abd.* ~ **eitch &c** a ship's carpenter's
long-handled adze held in place by the foot
la19-, now Sh Ork Cai Abd. ~ **fang** *NE,* ~
wang *Sh* a strap used by cobblers looped round
knee and foot and over the work to keep it
firmly in position *la18-.* ~ **fell &c** the skin of a
lamb dead soon after birth *15-17.* ~ **folk(s)**
pedestrians, *esp* those attending church, market

etc on foot *la18-, local NE-Kcb.* ~ **gang &c** **1** a
plank or planks for workmen to walk on while
engaged in building etc *16-17.* **2** a length of
plank flooring to walk on, *esp* between church
pews *la16-e19.* **3** a long footstool beside a bed
la16-e18. ~**ick &c** [ie *fit-huik*] the chain and
hook connecting the muzzle of the plough with
the *fit-tree, 20-, Arg SW Uls.* ~ **market** the
part of a fair or market where pedestrians can
move about freely *18-, now Abd.* ~ **pad** a foot-
path *la19-, SW.* ~ **pan** a bed valance *la19-,
NE Kcb.* ~ **road &c** = *fit pad, 16-.* ~ **side(s)**
&c even **with**, in line or step **with** *17-19.* ~
sok &c a short sock *la15-e17.* ~ **spade &c** an
ordinary digging spade *la15-17.* ~ **spar** *la19-,
Sh NE, C,* **feetspur** *20-, now Cai Ross* a bar of
wood across the floor of a boat for pressing the
feet against when rowing. ~ **stead &c** a foot-
print *16-19.* ~ **stuil &c** **1** = footstool *la16-.* **2**
fig the earth *la19-e20.* ~ **tree** the wooden spar
to which the traces are attached in ploughing
etc *e20. chf* **feet-washin(g)** the ceremony of
washing the feet of a bridegroom or bride, performed by friends on the eve of the wedding
18-, local NE-SW.

a' one's feet at full speed *la19-e20.* **aboon my**
etc ~ beyond my *etc* capacity or means *19.* **aff
one's** *or* **the fit** *or* **feet 1** unfit for work *19-, now
Cai.* **2** morally astray *la19-, now midLoth Bwk.*
at hir ~ *of a calf or* STIRK still going with the
cow *16.* **be** *or* **have a guid, ill, lucky** *etc* ~ be
a person who brings good *or* bad fortune *19-,
local Sh-EC.* **change one's feet** change one's
footwear *la19-.* ~ **an a half** (a call in) a kind
of leapfrog *la19-, now local NE-SW.* ~ **fair** *curling* (CURL) take up position for delivering the
shot at the proper distance from the far TEE[1]
19-. ~ **for** ~ step by step, side by side, closely
19-e20. ~ **the floor &c** dance *la18-, now Sh
Abd Ayr.* **gaither one's** *or* **the feet** lit *and fig*
recover from a fall, regain one's footing *la17-,
now Abd Stlg Rox.* **get up one's** ~ be scolded
la19-, now NE Ags Dmf. **gie (a stane) feet** *curling* accelerate the movement (of a stone) by
sweeping the ice before it *20-.* **gie (someone)
up his** *etc or* **the** ~ scold, rebuke *19-, now local.*
have a guid *etc* ~ see *be a guid etc* ~. **(ilka)** ~
and fur every detail *19.* **lift one's feet** *fig*
show great activity *la19-, now midLoth Rox.*
mak one's feet one's friend(s) go off at a
great pace, take to one's heels *la19-, NE Ags.*
pit in a ~ walk more quickly *19-, NE Ags Fif
Dmf.* **tak (one's)** ~ **in (one's) hand** start off,
take one's leave *la18-, now Sh Ork NE Ags.* **till
one's** ~ recovered from illness, up and about
la19-e20. **(up)on** ~ **1** well, in good health *19-,
Sh Ork NE Ags.* **2** alive *20-, midLoth Bwk.* **upon
the** ~ *of grain* standing, unthreshed *la18-e20.*

fit[2] *vti* **1** = fit. **2** *vt* suit, meet the requirements
of, *chf* **fittit** pleased, satisfied *la18-, now local
NE-Rox.*

fit *see* WHAT[1]

fitch[1] *vtir* move slightly or restlessly, edge along *la15-*, now *Sh Ork Cai*. [prob related to FIDGE; *cf* FOTCH]

fitch[2] &c *n* = vetch, the plant *la15-e20*.

fite *see* WHITE[1], WHITE[2]

fiteichtie *see* WHITE[1]

fither *see* WHETHER

fitick *see* FIT[1]

fitin *see* WHITIN

fitit broon *see* WHITE[1]

fittiefie &c [ˈfɪtɪˈfaɪ, -ˈfɑ] *n* a whim, fussy action; a quirk, quibble *19-*, *Abd*. [altered f WHITTIE-WHATTIE]

fittininment, fittock *see* FIT[1]

fittret *see* WHITRAT

five &c; **fife** &c *la14-17 numeral* 1 = five *la14-*. 2 *in pl* = five stanes, *la19-*, *local*.

fivesome &c five in all, a set or group of five *la14-15, 19-*, *only Sc*.

five stanes the game of CHUCKS[2] played with five stones or pebbles *la19-*, now *Fif*.

fivver *19-*, **fiver** &c *la16-* [ˈfɪvər] *n* = fever, *freq specif* scarlet fever.

fize *see* FEEZE

fizz &c *vi* 1 = fizz. 2 make a fuss, bustle; be in a great rage *la18-*.

n 1 = fizz. 2 a bustle, commotion, a state of great excitement or rage *19-*.

~in deevil a pellet of wet gunpowder set alight as a kind of firework *la19-e20*, *NE Ags*.

fla *see* FLAE[1], FLAE[2]

flacat *see* FLAKKET

flaccon *see* FLAGON

flacht *see* FLAUCHT[1]

flachter *see* FLAUCHTER

flad &c *n* a large piece, a slab *19*, *only Sc*.

flae[1] *la16*, *la18-e20*, **flay** [fle] *vt* 1 = flay, strip *la14-*. 2 strip (ground) of turf, *chf* before cutting PEAT[1] *la16-e20*; *cf* FLAW[1].

flae[2] &c *18-*, **fla** *la14-e17* [fli; *Ork sEC-S* fle] *n* 1 a fly *la14*. 2 a flea *16-*.

~-luggit &c harum-scarum, hare-brained *18-e19*. [the vowel is irreg; *cf* FLECH]

flaesock &c [ˈflɛzək] *n* 1 *chf in pl* wood shavings *la19-*, *NE*. 2 a small particle, *chf* of ash from burning wood *e20*, *NE*. [see SND]

flaff &c *v* 1 *vi* flap, flutter; palpitate *16-*. 2 *of the wind* blow in gusts *19-*, now *Sh Ags Fif*. 3 *vt* make unsteady, cause to flap or flutter *la15-*. 4 *also fig* fan (a flame) *19-*, now *Fif*.

n 1 a flapping movement *19-*. 2 a flick, a light blow with something flat *19-e20*. 3 (1) a gust or puff (of wind) *19-*. (2) *fig* a brief moment, an instant *19*. 4 a flash (of lightning etc) *19*.

adv with a sudden fluttering movement *la19-*, now *Bnf Abd*.

~er *vti* flutter, flap, palpitate *la18-*, now *NE Ags Fif*.

n 1 a fluttering, flapping motion *19-*, now *NE Ags Fif*. 2 a pound note *la19-*, now *NE Ags Fif*. [onomat; *cf* FLUFF]

flag[1] &c *n* a large, clumsy, slovenly woman *e16, 19-e20*. [uncertain]

flag[2] &c *n* 1 = flag, a flagstone *16-*. 2 a piece of turf cut or pared from the surface, a sod *18-e20*. [*cf* Icel *flag* a place where turf has been cut]

flag[3] *n* a blast or gust, a flash (of lightning) *16*. [only Sc; obscurely related to FLAW[2]]

flag[4] *n* a large snowflake *19-*, *N*.

vi, of snow fall in large flakes *19-e20*, *Bnf Abd*. [also nEng dial; cognate w Eng *flake*]

flag[5] *vt* = flog, whip *19-e20*.

flagarie &c *19-e20*; **fleegarie** &c *18-e19* [*flaˈgerɪ, *flɪ-] *n* 1 an ornament, something excessively fancy, *chf* in dress *18-19*. 2 a whim; a piece of frivolity *19-e20*. [altered f FEEGARIE perh w infl f FLEE[1] and FLING]

flaggat *see* FAGGALD

flaggert &c *n* a loose flapping garment *e20*, *Abd*. [see SND]

flagon *19-*, **flagoun** &c *17*, **flaccon** &c *la15-e17 n* 1 = flagon *la15-*. 2 a small metal can, *chf* used for carrying milk *19-*, *Abd Ags Per midLoth*.

flaich *see* FLECH

flail &c *n* 1 = flail *la14-*. 2 a tall, gawky person *la19-*, *Cai NE*.

vt = flail *16-*.

~ soople &c the part of a FLAIL which beats out the grain *la19-*, *Sh Ork Abd*.

flaip &c *n* a dull heavy unbroken fall, *chf* on something soft, a thud; the sound of such a fall *19-e20*, *S*. [var of FLAP; *cf* FLYPE[2]]

flair &c *vti* flatter; boast *la18-e20*. [see SND]

flair *see* FLUIR

flairdie *vt* flatter, cajole *la19-e20*, *Kcb*.

n 1 flattery; insincerity *20-*, *SW*. 2 a wheedling person, *esp* a child *20-*, *SW*. [prob f FLAIR]

flake[1] &c; **fleck** *la16-18 n* 1 a hurdle or framework of crossed slats, *usu* portable and used as a fence, gate etc *la15-*, *Gen except Sh Ork*. 2 *in pl* a temporary pen for sheep or cattle made of such a framework *18-*, *NE*, *SW*. 3 a kind of rack used *eg* for displaying goods for sale, feeding hay to animals *la16-19*. 4 a weir or lattice fence across a river *18-e20*. 5 *distilling, chf* **~ stand** a wooden box containing water through which the worm passes *18-e20*.

vt pen (sheep) by means of FLAKES *la18-*, now *Bwk Rox*. [ME; ON *flaki* a wicker hurdle]

flake[2] *n* a side of bacon *20-*, *midLoth Bwk S*. [Eng dial *flick*, ON *flikki* w formal infl f FLAKE[1]]

flakket &c *la15-17*, **flacat** &c *16-e17*, *only Sc* [*ˈflakət, *ˈflek-, *ˈflɛk-] *n* = flacket, a flask.

flam[1] *n* = flawn, name for various kinds of flat tart or cake *la16-e19*.

flam[2] &c *la15-18, e20* (*Rox*); **flamb** &c *15-16, e19*, **flame** *la16-* [flam now *Rox*; *flɑm] *n* = flame *15-*.

v 1 *vi* = flame *la14-*. 2 *vt* baste (meat etc) *16-e19*, *only Sc*.

flam(m)er *17-e18*, **flaming spoon** *la17-19* a basting ladle.

flam *see* FLAN

flamagaster [flamə'gastər] *n* a stunning shock of surprise or disappointment *e20, NE*. [nasalized var based on Eng *flabbergast*; cf *stammygaster* (STAMAGAST)]

flamb, flame *see* FLAM²

flan &c *18-*, **flam &c** *18-*, *now Cai*; **flann** *18-e20 n* **1** a blast, storm *la15*. **2** a gust of wind, *chf* one blowing smoke down a chimney, a back-draught *la18-, now Sh Ork N*. **3** a sudden squall of wind blowing from high land over the sea *18-, Sh Fif Arg*.
vi blow in sudden gusts; *of smoke* sweep down a chimney *19-, Sh Ork N Fif*.
flannie squally *19-, Sh Fif Ags*. [only Sc; *cf* Icel, Norw dial *flana* rush blindly, Icel *flan* a rush]

flanan *see* FLANNEN

Flanders baby *n* a Dutch doll *19-e20*.

flane &c *la15-16, 18-e20 (arch) n* an arrow. [ME *flone*, OE *flān*]

flann *see* FLAN

flannen &c *16-*; **flanan &c** *la17-e18*, **flannin(g)** *17-19 n* = flannel *16-*.
~ette flannelette *la19-, local Cai-Bwk*.
flannan broth milk-sops, sweetened with treacle or sugar *20-, Bnf Abd Ags*.

flap *n* **1** = flap *15-*. **2** the lair of a hare or other animal *20-, Bnf Ags Ayr*.
vti **1** = flap *16-*. **2** *vi* fall down flat suddenly, *esp* in order to hide, flop *la19-, local Sh-SW*.
flapper move in a loose, unsteady, flapping way, flutter noisily *19*.

flary *adj* gaudy, showy *la19-20, SW*. [f Eng *flare* (obs = display, flaunt)]

flas¹ [*flas] *n* a powder-flask *16-e17*. [only Sc; perh f Flem *flasch*, Du *flesch*, LowGer *fles, flesse*]

flas² *adj* = flat *la15-e17*. [obscure]

flash *n* **1** = flash. **2** *chf in pl* the tabs of cloth, *usu* scarlet, worn on the garter of a KILT¹ stocking and visible below the turndown *20-*.

flat¹ &c, **flet &c** *19- n* **1** = flat *14-*, *in placenames 13-*. **2** (1) a level part of a structure *17-18*. (2) a floor or storey of a house *18-*. (3) a set of self-contained apartments, occupied by one family, on one floor of a house of two or more storeys *18-*. **3** any flat plate etc for placing beneath some other dish etc; a saucer *18-, now Mry midLoth WC*.
adj = flat *15-*.
vti **1** = flat *17-*. **2** *vt, only* **flet** pour (tea) into one's saucer *20-, now Stlg midLoth*.
flatlin(g)s &c flat, prostrate *la14-, now Sh Abd*.
flattie = *n* 3, *e20, NE*.

flat² *vt* flatter *e16*. [only Sc; F *flatter*]

flate *see* FLYTE

flaucht¹ &c; **flacht** *17-19* [flaxt] *n* **1** a burst of flame, a flash of lightning *la15-, now Sh NE*. **2** a flake, *chf* of snow *la18-, now Sh*. **3** a lock or tuft of hair or wool *la18-e20*.
vi, chf of snow fall in flakes, *chf* **~in &c** a flake, fleck *19-, now Ags Per*.

flachtit *of wool* carded *la16*. [ME *flaʒt* = *n, also* a turf; OE *fl(e)aht*, f *flēan (v)* flay; cognate w Eng *flake* and FLAW¹]

flaucht² &c [*flaxt] *vt* weave, intertwine, link with *19*. [only Sc; appar OE *fleohtan* plait, weave]

flaucht *see* FLOCHT

flauchter &c *la15-*; **flachter &c** *la16-17, e20* ['flaxtər] *vt* pare (turf) from the ground *18-, now Arg SW Rox*.
n = flauchter-spade, *20-, SW*.
~ fail &c a piece of turf cut with next *la16-19*.
~ spade &c a two-handed spade with a broad heart-shaped blade used for cutting turf *la15-20*. [only Sc; ? frequentative of FLAUCHT¹]

flaunter &c *vi* **1** quiver, tremble with excitement or agitation *la18-19*. **2** waver, falter in speech; prevaricate *la18-e19*. [only Sc; see SND]

flauntie &c *adj* capricious, flighty *la18-e20*. [cf Eng *flaunty* showy]

flaur *e19*, **fleur &c** *la14-17*, **flevour &c** *15-16* [*'fleur,*-ər, *fljur, *'flivur, *-ər] *n* = flavour, smell *only Sc*.

flaw¹ &c *n* **1** = flaw, a flake; a crack, defect *15-*. **2** a flash or spark (of fire etc) *15-e16*. **3** a kind of nail; the point of a horseshoe nail *16-e20, only Sc*. **4** a falsehood, a lie *18-e20*.
v **1** *vt* remove turf from (a PEAT¹ bank) before cutting PEAT¹ *19-e20, chf Sh*. **2** *vti* boast, exaggerate, tell lies *la16-19*.
not a ~ nothing at all, not at all *la16, 19*.

flaw² *n* a gust or squall of wind, *chf* one bringing rain *e16, 19-e20*. [MDu, MLowGer *vlage*; cf eModEng *flawe*]

flaw *see* FLEE¹

flay *see* FLAE¹

fle *la14-16*; **flee** *la15-*, **fley** *15-16*, **flie** *16-e17* [fli] *vti, pt, ptp also* **fleid** *la14-e16* = flee *la14-*.
~ar &c a fugitive, a person who flees *la14-e17*.

fle *see* FLEE¹, FLEE², FLEY

Fleams *see* FLEMIS

flech &c; flaich *19-, Sh* [flɛx] *n* **1** = flea *17-, local Sh-Fif*. **2** a restless, active person *19-, NE Ags Per*.
vt rid (oneself or another) of fleas *19-, N Fif*.
~y covered or infested with fleas *19-, local Sh-Fif*. [OE *flēah*]

flech *see* FLESH

fleche, flechour *see* FLEECH

fleck *see* FLAKE¹

fleckie *adj* = fleckie, spotted *e17*.
n **F~ &c** name for a spotted cow *19-, now Ork Abd Arg*.

flee¹ *17-*, **fle** *la14-17*, **fly** *19-* [fli; *S* fləi] *v, pt* **flaw** *la14-16, 19*, **flew** *la16-*. *ptp also* **flowin &c** *la14-e16*, **floun &c** *la19-* [*NE Ayr S* 'flʌuən; *EC* 'flu(ə)n, *S* fljun] **1** *vi* = fly *la14-*. **2** be violently excited, *esp* by drink, *chf* **fleein** hilariously drunk *la19-, local*.
~in bent purple melic, the plant *19-e20*. **~in draigon** a paper kite *19-e20*. **fleein**

merchant a travelling salesman, a hawker *19-e20, Abd.* **~ing tailor** a travelling tailor *19-e20.*

~-about a gadabout; a person of fickle principles *la19-, now local Sh-Ags.* **~ intae** severely rebuke, scold *20-, NE midLoth Rox.* **flee-up-(i-the-air)** a frivolous or pretentious person *la19-, now NE Ags Fif Dmf.*

flee² &c *17-*, **fle** *la15-16*; **flie** *la16-e20* [fli] *n* **1** = fly, the insect *la15-.* **2** *in negative* not at all, not a whit, *chf* **not worth a ~, not to care a ~** *15-.* **let that ~ stick tae the wa** drop a particular (*usu* embarrassing) subject, say no more about a topic *la18-.*

flee *see* FLE, FLEY

fleece *see* FLEESH

fleech &c *18-*, **fleche** &c *la14-16*; **fleitch** &c *la16-e19* [flitʃ] *v* **1** *vt* coax, flatter, entreat *la14-, now local Bwk-Rox.* **2** *vi* use cajoling or flattering words (**with**) *15-17, la19.*

flechour &c *15-16*, **fleecher** *la18-e19* a flatterer, a wheedler. [uncertain]

fleed *n*, ploughing an *end-rig* (EN) *19-, NE.* [uncertain]

fleed *see* FLUDE

fleegarie *see* FLAGARIE

fleein *see* FLEE¹

fleem &c *19-, now Ags Bwk SW*, **fleume** &c *la15-e17, 19-, now Sh Ork* [*Ags Bwk SW* flim; *Sh Ork Bwk S* fløm; ***fljum] *n* = phlegm.

fleep &c [flip; *NE also* fləip] *n* a lazy lout, an oaf *la18-, Ork Cai NE.* [uncertain]

fleepie &c *n* a somersault *la19-, Ags.* [obscure]

fleer *see* FLUIR

fleerish &c *la19-e20*, **furisine** *e16*; **flourish** &c *19-e20* [*NE* 'flirɪʃ; *nEC* 'flʌr-; ***'førɪsən] *n* a short piece of steel curved to go round the knuckle, used for striking sparks from a flint-stone to ignite tinder or match-paper. [only Sc; MLowGer *vûrisern*, MHighGer *viurisen* (*lit*) fire-iron; *cf* FRIZZEL]

fleesh &c *la18-, now local Sh-EC*, **fleis** *la15-17*; **fleische** *la16-e17*, **fleece** &c *16-* [fliʃ] *n* **1** = fleece *la15-.* **2** a large number, a lot (of persons or things) *19-, now Abd Kcdn.*

fleet¹ &c *17-*, **flete** *la14-16*, **fleit** &c *la15-17* [flit] *vi* **1** float, rise to the surface of a liquid *la14-, now Sh.* **2** *of water etc* flow *15-e17, 19-e20.* *n* **1** = fleet (of ships) *la17-.* **2** *fishing* a set of nets or lines carried by a single boat *la17-.*

~ing *in pl or attrib* the thick curds formed on the top of boiling whey *20-, Abd.*

~ dyke a wall built to prevent flooding *19-, now Ayr.* **~ water** water which overflows ground *19-, now C.* [ME; OE *flēotan*]

fleet² *adj* **1** = fleet, swift: (1) *literary, as in Eng, la18-;* (2) *in gen use, la19-, local NE-EC.* **2** easy to deal with, manageable *20-, Bnf Abd.*

fleg¹ &c *v* **1** *vt* frighten, scare *17-, now local.* **2** dispel, drive away (illness, stormy weather etc) *la18-, now NE Ags.* **3** *vi* take fright, be scared *la18-, chf NE.*

n a fright, a scare *18-, Gen except WC, SW.*

get a ~ *or* **one's ~s** be scared; *of food, snow, a pile of work etc* diminish appreciably *la19-, now Ork NE Ags.* **tak ~** take fright *19-, now NE.* [only Sc; obscure; *cf* FLEY]

fleg² &c *n* a severe blow, a kick *18-e20.* *vi* **1** fly or rush from place to place, dash about *la18-, SW.* **2** *freq* **~ on** hurry, work hard *20-, SW.* [only Sc; obscure]

flegear &c [***'flɛdʒər] *n* = fletcher, an arrowmaker *la15-e17.*

fleggar *n* term of abuse for a person *e16.* [obscure]

fleid *see* FLE

fleis, fleische *see* FLEESH

fleit *see* FLEET¹, FLEY

fleitch *see* FLEECH

fleme &c [***flim] *vt* **1** banish, drive into exile *15-e17.* **2** put to flight, drive away, expel *la15-16, e19* (*arch*). **3** put away (anger etc) from oneself; refrain from *la15.* [ME; OE *flīeman*]

Flemis &c *la15-e17*; **Fleymes** &c *17*, **Fleams** &c *e17* [***'flimɪs, ***'flimz] *adj* = Flemish, *only Sc.*

flench¹ *now Sh Bnf Abd*; **flinch** [flɛnʃ, flɪnʃ] *vti* **1** = flinch *19-.* **2** *of weather* be unreliable, give a deceitful promise of improvement, *chf* **a flinchin Friday** *la19-, now Bnf.*

flench² *v*, *coopering* bevel the stave ends of a barrel *la19-, now Abd.* [uncertain]

flender *see* FLINDER

flesh &c *la16-*, **flesch** &c *la14-17*; **flech** &c *16-17* [flɛʃ; ***flɛs] *n* **1** = flesh *la14-.* **2** butcher's meat *la14-, now local Sh-SW.* **3** *in pl* carcases *18-19.*

~er *la16-*, **~ar** &c *15-17*, **~our** &c *la15-17* a butcher. **~ing** the trade of a butcher *20-.* **~lyk** &c fleshly *la14.*

~ crook &c a meat hook *la16-18.* **~ fatt** &c a beef-barrel *16-e17.* **~ meat** butcher's meat *19.* **~ pryssar** &c a fixer of meat prices *la15-e16.* **~ stock** &c a butcher's block *16-20.*

flet &c *n* **1** the inner part of a house *15-e19.* **2** = flet, house-room, in **fire and ~** *la16.* [ME, OE *flett*, ON *flet* floor, dwelling; house; *cf* FLAT]

flet *see* FLAT¹, FLYTE

flete *see* FLEET¹

flether &c [***'flɛðər] *vi* flatter, cajole *la18-e19.* *n*, *chf in pl* flattery *19.* [see SND]

fleuk &c *18-*, **fluke** *la15-e20* [fl(j)uk; *C* fløk] *n* the flounder *la15-.*

sole ~ the sole *la17-19.* [ME *fluke*, OE *flōc*]

fleume *see* FLEEM

fleur, flevour *see* FLAUR

flew *see* FLEE¹

flewit &c *n* a blow, a stroke, a slap *18-19.* [eModEng *flewet*; obscure]

fley &c, **fle** *la14-16*; **flee** &c *18-e20* [fləi; *WC, SW* fli] *vt* **1** frighten, scare *la14-, now local Ork-Dmf.* **2** *chf* **~ awa** put to flight, drive off by frightening *15-, now NE Fif Kcb.*

n **1** a fright, a scare *la18-*, *local NE-Dmf*. **2** a source of fear; a fearsome looking person *e20*. **fleit &c, fleyd &c** *ptp, adj* frightened, scared *la14-*. **fleyitnes &c** fear, fright, alarm *la15-16*. **~ed for** frightened of *19-*, *now C*. **~some** terrifying, terrible *la18-*, *now NE, SW, S*. [ME *fley*, *flay*; see SND]

fley *see* FLE

Fleymes *see* FLEMIS

flichan *see* FLICHT³

flicher &c, ['flɪxər] *vi* giggle, give a silly laugh *19-e20*. [extended f Eng *flicker* flutter, quiver, blink]

flicher *see* FLICHTER

flicht¹ &c; flight *la18-* [flɪxt] *n* **1** = flight, the act of flying *15-*. **2** *chf in pl* the fly of a spinning-wheel, which guides the thread to the spool *19-*, *Sh NE Ags*.

~ie &c flighty, capricious *19-*. **~rife &c** unsteady, fickle, changeable *19-e20*.

~ speid full speed *la16*.

at the ~ about to set out; in all haste *16*.

flicht² &c; flight &c *17-* [flɪxt; *Bwk also* flɛxt, flaɪxt] *n* = flight, the act of fleeing *la14-*. *vi* take to flight, fly, flee *la18-*, *now Cai Ags*.

flicht³ [flɪxt] *n* a flake, a small speck of soot, dust, snow etc *19-*, *now Bwk*.

flichan &c ['flɪx(t)ən] a flake of snow, a small particle or speck of something *19-*, *now local EC, SW*. [ME *flyghte* a flake of snow, perh f OE **fliht*, but prob confused w FLICHT¹]

flichter &c; flighter &c *16-18*, **flicher** *la19* ['flɪx(t)ər; *Ork* 'flaɪxtər] *v* **1** *vi, of birds* flutter, fly awkwardly; *of persons* rush about excitedly *la14-*, *now local Ork-Pbls*. **2** make fluttering movements or efforts *16-17*. **3** *chf of children* run with outspread arms to greet someone *la18-e20*. **4** *of the heart* flutter, quiver, palpitate *18-e20*. **5** *of light* flicker *19-*, *now Fif Pbls SW*. **6** *vt* startle, frighten *18-*, *now Ags*.

n **1** (1) a flutter(ing) *la19-*, *now Wgt*. (2) a state of excitement *19-*, *now Abd*. **2** a small particle or flake of snow, soot etc *la19-*, *now Cai Fif*. **3** a flicker, a glimmer (of light) *19-*, *now Fif*.

~some *la19-*, *now Bnf*, **~y** *20-*, *now Ags* changeable, full of whims.

~ lichtie a light-headed person unable to settle down to any employment *la19-*, *Bnf*. [uncertain; *cf* FLICHT¹ and FLICHT³]

flichter *see* FLIGHTER

flick *n* a glimmering, a streak of light etc *la19-*, *now midLoth*. [var of Eng *fleck*]

flie *see* FLE, FLEE²

flight *see* FLICHT¹, FLICHT²

flighter *17-18*, **flichter** *la16-e17* [***'flɪxtər] *vt* bind (the limbs) with cords. [obscure]

flighter *see* FLICHTER

flim *n* a haze, a mist rising from the ground; *fig* something unsubstantial or illusory *19-e20*. [metath f Eng *film*]

flinch *see* FLENCH¹

flinder &c *la16-*, **flender &c** *15-e20* ['flɪn(d)ər, 'flɛnd-] *n, in pl* fragments, splinters, pieces *15-*, *now Sh Abd Ags*. [Scand; *cf* Norw dial *flindra* a splinter, flake]

flindrikin &c ['flɪn(d)rɪkən, ***'flɪndərkən] *n* **1** term of contempt for a person *la16, 19*. **2** *chf of cloth or garments* something light, flimsy and unsubstantial *la19-*, *now NE*.

adj light, flimsy *la19-*, *now Abd*. [see SND]

fling &c *vti* **1** = fling *la14-*. **2** *vi, chf of animals* kick *la14-*. **3** dance *esp* a Scottish dance, caper *16-*, *now local NE-Ayr*. **4** jerk the head or body sideways as a gesture of displeasure, flounce *la18-*, *now local*. **5** *vt* jilt *la18-*, *now NE Fif*.

n **1** = fling. **2** the act of kicking, a kick from a horse *19-*, *now local*. **3** (name for) a dance *18-e20*; see also Highland *fling* (HIELAND).

~in tree the part of a flail which strikes the grain *la18-e19*.

get *or* **gie someone the ~** be jilted or jilt someone *19-*, *now NE midLoth Bwk*. **tak the ~s** go into the sulks *18-e20*.

flinty *adj* **1** = flinty. **2** *of persons* keen, sharp, lively *19-*, *now Ayr*.

flird &c *vi* **1** ? talk idly, flirt *e16*. **2** flutter; flounce; move restlessly or frivolously from place to place *19-e20*.

n **1** something thin, flimsy or tawdry *la18-e20*. **2** a vain, dressy or fickle person *la18-19*.

~ie = *n* 2, *la19-e20*. [see SND]

flirr *vt* stir, ruffle *e20*. [onomat]

flisk *v* **1** *vi* dart from place to place, frolic about, caper, frisk *la17-*, *now local Sh-Dmf*. **2** *vti* whisk, make an abrupt sweeping motion, swipe *19-e20*. *n* a sudden sweeping movement, a flick, whisk; a caper *19-*, *local Sh-Kcb*.

~ie &c **1** restless, flighty, skittish *la18-*, *now NE Wgt*. **2** *of a horse* apt to kick *19-*, *now NE*. [eModEng; onomat w infl f WHISK]

fliskmahaigo *19-e20*, **fliskmahoy** *19-*, *now Slk* [flɪskmə'hego, -mə'hoɪ] *n* a flighty or frivolous woman. [see SND]

flist *vi* **1** puff; whizz; explode with a sharp hiss or puff *la17-*, *Cai Abd Ags*. **2** fly into a rage *19-*, *now NE*. **3** boast, brag; exaggerate *la19-*, *Cai Bnf*.

n **1** an explosion *la16, la19-* (*Cai NE*). **2** a sudden outburst of rage, a fit of temper *19-*, *NE Ags*. **3** (1) a fib, a boast *la19-*, *now Abd*. (2) a boaster, a fibber *la19-*, *now Cai Abd*.

~y irascible, irritable *19-*, *NE Ags*.

let ~ let fly (a blow), hit out *20-*, *Cai NE*. [unknown]

flit &c *v* **1** *vt* (1) remove, transport from one place to another *la14-e20*. (2) *specif* remove (one's household etc) to another house *la16-*. (3) move (tethered animals) to fresh grazing *la18-*, *now Sh Abd Fif*. **2** *vi* (1) leave a place, go elsewhere *la14-*, *now midLoth*. (2) move house *la15-*. (3) die *la16-e20*. **3** = flit *16-*.

n = *flitting* 2, *19-*.

~ter a person who *flits* as in *v* 2 (2), one who is fond of *flitting*, *19-e20*. **flitting &c** *n* **1** the removal of a thing or person from one place to another *16-e17*. **2** the act of moving from one house to another *17-*. **3** goods, *esp* household goods, when being moved *15-*. **flitting Friday** the WHITSUNDAY removal day *16*. **moonlight flitting** removal of one's household at night to avoid paying debts *18-*.

F~ Friday the WHITSUNDAY or (*chf*) MARTINMAS removal day for farm-workers *19-20*, *Ags*.

~ and remove *etc* = *v* 1 (2) and *v* 2 (2) *16-17*. **moonlight ~** = *moonlight flitting, 20-*.

flit *see* FLYTE

flither *see* FLUTHER[1]

flitten *see* FLYTE

flitter &c *n, chf in pl* shreds, splinters *19-e20*. [uncertain]

floan &c [flon] *vi* **1** *chf of a woman towards men* show affection, *esp* in a sloppy way *la18-, Abd*. **2** lounge, loaf *la19-, NE*.

n a short rest, a lying down *20-, NE*. [prob Scand; *cf* Norw, Sw dial *flana*, Dan *flane* gad about, be flighty or frivolous; a coquette]

float[1] *19-*, **flott &c** *la16-19 n* grease, scum, *esp* on a boiling pot of soup, jam etc *la16-, now Ayr*. **~ whey &c** a dish made by boiling whey, often with meal and milk, to form a soft floating curd *16-e20*. [only Sc; ON *flot* floating fat]

float[2], **flote &c** *la14-e17 n* **1** = float *la14-*. **2** *mining* a sheet of intrusive rock lying roughly in the same plane as the surrounding strata *la19-, now Ayr*. **3** a flat spring cart without sides, for light transport *20-, local*.

vi = float *16-*.

flocht, **flaucht &c** *18-*; **flought &c** *17-19*, **flucht &c** *la19-, NE* [floxt, flɑxt; *NE also* flʌxt] *n* **1** a flutter, a state of excitement *la15-, now Sh Abd*. **2** the act of fleeing, flight *e16, la19*. **3** a flight or flock of birds *19-e20*. **4** a bustle, a flurry, a great hurry *19-e20*. **5** bustle, excitement, stress *19-, Abd*. **6** a sudden gust of wind *19-, now Abd*.

v **1** *vi* bustle, go off in a flurry *19-e20*. **2** shake, tremble, vibrate *la19-, now Sh*. **3** *vt* excite, flurry; startle, frighten *la19-, NE*.

~er *v* **1** *vi, esp of a bird's wings* flutter, flap *la18-, now local Sh-Fif*. **2** (1) spread open, sprawl *20-, now Sh*. (2) *vt* knock down, knock out *19-, now Abd*. **3** fluster *la19-e20*. *n* **1** a fluttering, flapping *la18-, now Sh Ork*. **2** a state of excitement *20-, Abd*. **~erous** hurried and confused, fluttering *la18-e19, Mry Abd Ags*.

flaucht braid with the limbs extended like a bird in flight; spread-eagled *18-19*.

at the (clean) flaucht at full speed *19-, Abd*. [only Sc; see DOST, SND]

flodder &c *vt* flood, overflow *e16*. [only Sc; related to FLUDE]

flodge &c [flodʒ; *Rox* flotʃ; *flʌtʃ] *vi* walk clumsily, waddle *19-20*.

n a fat, slovenly person, *esp* a woman *19-, now*

Bnf Dmf. [onomat; prob with infl f obs Eng *flod* walk slowly, and Sh Ork *flatch* flatten; anything large and flat]

flooer *see* FLOUR

floop-like *see* FLUP

flooster *see* FLUISTER

Florence &c *n, attrib, of silk and satin* of Florence, Florentine *la16-e17*.

florie &c *adj* vain, showy *la18-e19*.

vi swagger, strut about conceitedly *19-, now Cai*. [see SND]

floris *see* FLOURISH

flory &c *n* **~ boat** a boat carrying passengers to and from steamers which cannot get alongside the pier *la19, Fif*. [see SND]

flosh *see* FLUSH

flot &c *n* an area of land of varying breadth, ploughed at one turn *20-, Cai*. [Norw dial *flot* level ground, Icel *flöt*]

flote &c *vt* ? line or back (a garment) *la15*. [obscure]

flote *see* FLOAT[2]

flott *see* FLOAT[1]

flotter &c *vt* overflow, wet *e16*. [only Sc; *cf* FLODDER and Eng *float*]

flought *see* FLOCHT

floun *see* FLEE[1]

flour &c; flooer &c *20-*, **flower &c** *la15-* [flur] *n* **1** = flower *la14-*. **2** a bunch of flowers, a bouquet *la18-*. **3** the first water drawn from the well in the New Year *19-e20, local; cf* CREAM. **4** wheaten flour *la14-*.

vt **1** adorn with or as with flowers *15-17*. **2** embroider (flowers or similar designs) *19-*.

flour dammes [*flur 'damǝs] *n* auricula, the flower *e16*. [only Sc; OF (*flour*) *damas*]

flour *see* FLUIR

flourish &c *la16-*, **floris &c** *la14-16*, **flouris &c** *15-17*, **fluris &c** *la14-e17* ['flurɪʃ; *'flurɪs, *'flʌrɪs] *vi* **1** = flourish *la14-*. **2** blossom, be in flower *la14-, now local NE-S*. **3** embroider *20-, now Ork Abd Ags*.

n blossom, *esp* on fruit or hawthorn trees *la15-, Gen except Sh Ork*.

florist &c, flurist &c *adj* = flourished, flowery *15-16*.

flourish *see* FLEERISH

flow &c [flʌu] *vi* = flow *15-*.

n **1** a wet PEAT[1] bog, a morass *la18-, now Cai SW, S*. **2** a very small quantity (of a powdery substance, *eg* meal, dust) *19-, now NE Ags*.

~in(g) &c *adj* **1** = flowing *15-*. **2** *fig* unstable, changeable, fickle *la15-16*. *n* **1** = flowing *la15-*. **2** = *n* 2, *19-, now Bnf Abd*.

~ moss mossy, boggy ground; the spongy moss which grows there *18-e20*.

flower *see* FLOUR

flowin *see* FLEE[1]

flozen *vi, chf* **flozent** *of the body* swollen, puffed out *19-, Bnf Abd*. [see SND]

flucht *see* FLOCHT

fludder *see* FLUTHER[1], FLUTHER[2]

flude &c; fleed *19-e20*, N [flød, flɪd; N flid] *n*
(*la14-*), *vti* (*20-*) = flood.

fluff *vti* **1** puff, blow *la18-*. **2** *vi* flutter, move
lightly in a breeze *19-*, now *Sh*.
n a puff *19-e20*.
~**y &c** puffy, chubby *20-*, *Abd midLoth Gall*.
[only *Sc*; *cf* FLAFF, FUFF]

fluffer *v* **1** *vi* flutter, flap *la19-e20*. **2** *vt, fig* excite,
agitate *la19-e20*.
n a flapping, fluttering motion *la19-*, now *NE*.
[frequentative of prec]

fluir &c *16-*, now *Abd*, **flure &c** *15-19*; **flair &c**
19-, *C*, **fleer &c** *la18-*, *NE*, **flour &c** *la14-e19*
[flør; *C* fler; *NE* flir; *flur] *n* = floor *15-*.
vt = floor *16-*.
~**ing 1** = flooring *la15-*. **2** *also* ~**ing nail &c**
la16-e17 a floor-nail *17*.

fluise &c [flez; *'fløz] *vt* roughen, blunt (*chf*
tools) *19-e20*, *chf Kcb*. [see SND]

fluister &c; flooster &c [*Sh Ork S* 'fløstər;
Ags Ayr 'flɪstər; *Uls* 'flustər] *vti* **1** = fluster, hustle, bustle *la19-*, now *Sh Ork Rox Uls*. **2** *vt* coax,
flatter *20-*, *Uls*.

fluke &c [*fl(j)uk; *S* *fløk] *n* diarrhoea *18-e19*.
[only *Sc*; altered f Eng *flux*]

fluke *see* FLEUK

flumgummery &c [?flʌm'gʌm(ə)rɪ] *n* any
foolish or frivolous thing or action; fanciful
ornamentation or trimmings *19-*, *Bnf Abd*. [see
SND]

flunce &c *vti* = flounce *18-*, now *Sh Abd*.

flunkie &c *n*, *freq attrib*, *chf contemptuous* a manservant, *esp* in livery, a footman, lackey *la18-*.
[orig *Sc*; obscure]

flunner &c *n* = flounder, the fish *18-*, now *N*.

flup &c *n* a stupid, clumsy person *19-e20*.
floop-like stupid and awkward *la17*. [prob
onomat w infl f Eng *flap*, *flop*; *cf* FLEEP]

flure *see* FLUIR

fluris *see* FLOURISH

flush &c *16-*, **flosh &c** *15-19* *n* a piece of boggy
ground, *esp* one where water lies on the surface;
a pool of water *15-*, now *Arg Rox*.
~**an &c** a large shallow puddle *19*. [ME *flosche*;
cf Eng *flash*, *plash*]

fluther¹ &c *la18-e20*, **flither &c** *19-*, *chf Fif*;
fludder &c *la19-e20* ['flʌðər, 'flɪðər, 'flʌdər,
'flʌuðər &c] *vti* = flutter *la18-e20*.
n = flutter, confusion *19-*, now *Fif*.

fluther² &c *18-e20*, **fludder** *17-18* *n* **1** a boggy
piece of ground, a marsh *17-e20*. **2** a slight rise
or turbidity in a river *la18-e20*. [obscure]

fly *see* FLEE¹

flype¹ &c [fləip; *Ork Cai* flip] *v* **1** *vt, also fig* fold
back; turn wholly or partially inside out *16-*. **2**
tear off (the skin) in strips, peel *18-*, *local*. **3** *vi*,
of the tongue, lip, loose skin etc curl *19*.
n **1** a fold, brim etc of a garment *la17-*, now *Sh*.
2 the cutting of a strip of skin; a shred or loose
piece of skin *18-*, *Ork Cai Fif*. [ME]

flype² *vi* fall heavily, flop down for a short rest
la18-, *NE*. [onomat, w infl f Eng *flap*, *flop*, *flip*; *cf*
FLAIP]

flyre &c [*flaɪr, *fləir] *vti* = fleer, grimace,
mock *la15-19*.
~**dome** mockery; an object of scorn *la15-e17*.

flyrok *n* ? a deformed person *e16*. [obscure]

flyte &c *v*, *pt also* **flate &c** *la14*, *la18-19*, **flet &c**
16-e20, **flit** *19*. *ptp also* **flitten &c** *la14-*, now *Sh*
1 *vi*, *chf* ~ **wi** *la14-*, now *Ork Abd midLoth*, ~ **at**
19-, *local*, ~ (**up**)**on** *la19-*, *local* scold, chide,
rail at; altercate, wrangle violently with *la14-*.
2 *vt* scold, rail at *19-*, *local Abd-Rox*.
n **1** a scolding *18-*, now *Sh Arg Ayr*. **2** a scolding
match *19-*, now *Sh midLoth Bwk*.
flyter &c a scold; a person who engages in *flyting*, *la15-e20*. **flyting &c 1** scolding, quarrelling, employing abusive language *la15-*. **2** a
contest between poets in mutual abuse *16*. **flyting free** blameless *17-e18*.
~**pock &c** a double chin *19-*, now *Ags*. [ME,
OE *flītan* contend, argue]

foal &c, fole &c *15-19*; **foll &c** *15-e17* *n* =
foal *15-*.
vt **1** = foal *15-*. **2** *chf humorous, of a horse* throw
(its rider) *19-*, *NE Ags*.

fob; fab &c *la20-*, *Mry Bnf* *vi* pant with heat or
exertion, breathe hard *18-*, *NE*. [onomat]

foche [fotʃ] *vi* move away, depart *la16*. [ME
var of Eng *fetch*]

focht, fochten *see* FECHT

fock *see* FOWK

foddom *see* FADDOM

fodge &c [fodʒ, fʌdʒ] *n* **1** a fat, clumsy person
la18-e20, *sEC*, *S*. **2** a bundle (*chf* of sticks)
19-e20. [uncertain]

fodgel &c ['fodʒəl, 'fʌdʒəl] *adj* plump, buxom
18-, now *Abd*.
n a plump, good-humoured person *19-*, now *Uls*.
[prob f prec]

fog &c [fog; *Sh C* fʌg; *Cai* fʌug] *n* **1** = fog, grass
left in the field in winter *e16*. **2** moss, lichen (1)
in gen, *la15-*; (2) *freq* used as thatching material
or for packing walls *la15-e18*.
v **1** *vi* gather moss, become moss-grown *18-*, now
NE Ags. **2** *vt* thatch (a roof) or pack (a wall)
with moss *18*. **3** *vi, fig* save money, feather one's
nest *la19-*, now *NE Ags*.
foggage &c 1 winter grazing *15-19*. **2** the second crop of grass after hay *18-*. **foggie &c** *adj*
mossy *18-*. *n* the wild or moss bee *19-*, now *Ross*
NE Fif. **foggie bee** *19-*, *local NE-S*, **foggie
bummer** *19-*, now *Bnf Abd*, **foggie toddler**
la19-, *NE Ags Fif* the wild or carder bee. **foggy
peat** a rough, spongy PEAT¹ *20-*, now *Cai NE*
Uls. **weel-**~**it** well-off as the result of thrift
18-, *NE Ags*.
~ **house** a small garden summer-house built or
lined with mossy turf *19-*, now *Abd*.

foggie &c ['fogɪ; *Fif* 'fʌgɪ] *n* **1** a veteran soldier, an army pensioner *19-e20, local C.* **2** an **old** decrepit person *la18-.* [prob f *foggie* (FOG) moss-grown, *ie* decrepit; in Eng as *fogey &c*]

foichal [*'foixəl, *'fəixəl] *n* a girl from sixteen to twenty years of age *la18-e19.* [obscure]

foilzie &c *e19,* **fulȝe &c** *la15-e16* [*'ful(j)ɪ, *'fʌljɪ] *n* **1** a leaf of a plant or tree *la15-e16.* **2** gold leaf *la15-e16.*

gold ~ = *n* **2,** *la15-e16, e19.* [only Sc; OF *feuille; cf* Eng *foil*]

foir *see* FOWER

foir- *combs see* FOR-, FORE- *combs*

foirsate *see* FORESEAT

foisoun *see* FUSHION

foistit *see* FOOST

fold *see* FAULD²

fole &c *n* a small, soft, thick *oatcake* (AIT) *18-, chf Ork.* [see SND]

fole *see* FOAL, FUIL

folk *see* FOWK

foll *see* FOAL

follow &c, fallow &c *la14-20* [*N* 'folə; *C, S* 'folɪ; *C* 'falɪ] *vti* **1** = follow *la14-.* **2** *vt* accompany, escort *la19-, chf Sh Ork.* **3** PURSUE (a person) at law *15-e17.*

~**er &c 1** = follower *16-.* **2** a *pursuer* (PURSUE) or claimant at law *la14-e17.* **3** the young of an animal, *chf* a cow or hen, *esp* one still dependent on its mother *15-.* ~**ing 1** a *pursuing* (PURSUE) at law, the prosecution of a suit or claim *la14-e16.* **2** a body of retainers, domestic or military *18-e19.* **3** *mining* an overlying soft stratum which comes down as the coal is extracted from under it *la18-19.*

as efter ~**is** as follows *la14-e16.* ~ **furth** follow up, prosecute *la15-e17.*

follow *see* FALLOW

folly &c, foly &c *la14-e17 n* = folly *la14-.*

folyhat a hat resembling a fool's cap *e16.*

folp *see* WHALP

foly *see* FOLLY

fommle *see* WHUMMLE

fon &c *n* folly, foolishness *la15.*

vi be foolish, play the fool *la15-16.* [ME]

fond &c [fond; *Sh Cai* fʌund] *adj* **1** = fond *la15-.* **2** foolishly keen, infatuated, doting *la18-.* **3** eager, glad (to do etc)*18-, now local WC-S.*

I'd *etc* **be very** ~ **tae dae** *etc* I should never think of doing, I should certainly not do etc *la19-, now local NE-WC.*

fond *see* FOUND²

fontall &c *adj* coming from a fountain *la15.* [*cf* eModEng]

fontane *see* FUNTAIN

fonȝe *see* FUNȜE¹

foo &c, fow &c [fu] *adv* **1** = how *16-, now Sh Ork N.* **2** why, for what reason *19-, now NE.*

foo ca (ye) im &c *19,* **foustica(i)t &c** *19-, now Sh* ['fu(:)stɪ'ka(ɪ)t] *n* = what-do-you-call-him or -it. **funabe(is) &c** [*'fu:(ə)nə'bi(z)] nevertheless, however *la18-e19.* ~**'s a (wi ye)?** *greeting* how are you? *la18-, N.* **fusomever**

['fu:sʌm'ɪvər] however *la20-, Sh Ork N.* ~ **that** *conj* how, that *19-, now NE.* [var of *quhow* (HOO¹), in OSc not restricted to Sh Ork N, and even in ModSc occas found outside that area; the *f-* form has developed in N by analogy w the other *f-* interrogs, *eg fa* (WHA), *far* (WHAR); *cf* HOO¹]

foof *interj* expressing impatience or disgust *la19-, now Sh Abd Stlg.*

fool *18-,* **foul &c** *la14- n* = fowl, bird *la14-.*

fool *see* FOUL, FUIL

foolzie *see* FULYIE

foon *see* FOUND²

fooner *see* FOUNDER

fooneral *see* FUNERAL

foonge &c *vt, also* ~ **on** fawn, as a dog, flatter, show affection in a sloppy way *la18-, NE.* [see SND]

foongil &c ['fundȝəl] *n* a work-shy person; a slovenly, careless individual *la19-, chf Ags.* [see SND]

foorach &c [*'furəx, *'fir-] *n* buttermilk, whipped cream or whey with oatmeal stirred in *e20, Bnf Abd.* [Gael *fuarag* a mixture of meal and water, f *fuar* cold; *cf cauld steer* (CAULD)]

foord *see* FUIRD

foorich &c ['furəx] *n* bustle, confusion *la18-e20.* [perh extended f FOORACH]

foorth *see* FURTH

foos &c [fuz] *n pl, also (rare) in sing* **fow** [fu] the houseleek *18-, now Bnf Abd.* [uncertain]

foosh *n* a light, powdery substance, *esp* dust or soot particles *la19-, chf Ags.* [onomat]

fooshion *see* FUSHION

foost &c *19-,* **fuist &c** *17-e20;* **foosht &c** *la19-e20* [fust; *NE Ags also* fuʃt; *S also* føst] *vi* **1** become or smell mouldy *19-, now Abd Pbls SW.* **2** break wind in a suppressed way *la19-, Bnf Abd.*

n **1** a mouldy condition or smell *19-, local NE-Dmf.* **2** a suppressed breaking of wind *la19-, Bnf Abd.* **3** a dirty person, someone with disagreeable habits *la19-, Bnf Abd.*

~**it &c** *17-,* **foistit** *la16,* ~**y &c** *19-* musty, mouldy. [var of Eng *fust*]

foot *see* FIT¹

footer *see* FOUTER

footie *see* FOUTIE

for; fore &c *la14-17,* **fir** *la19-e20, Sh,* **fur** *la19-, C* [for; *C* fʌr; *unstressed* fər] *prep* **1** = for *la14-.* **2** because of, as a result of, through *la14-20.* **3** *freq with infin* = Eng infin *la14-:* '*wad ye offer for to go?*' **4 daft** *etc* with desire for, for want of *19-.* **5 be** ~ + *verbal noun or noun* inclined to have, wanting (to have), desirous of (*esp* food) *19-:* '*are ye for pudding?*' **6 frichted** *etc* ~ frightened *etc* of *19-; see* FEAR, FLEY etc. **7 ask** *or* **speir** ~ ask after (someone's health) *la19-.* **8 name** (a person etc) after *la18-; see* CA¹. **9** *elliptical in exclams, la19-, now Sh Bnf Abd:* '*see til her noo! for a braw sonsey lass*'. **10** *in negative* not to the advantage of, not good for *20-, local C-Uls.* **11**

with verbal noun, chf after a negative for fear of, to prevent *la18*-: '*my lad canna kneel..for fyling the knees o' his breeks'*.
conj = for *14*-.
a' that's ~ **somebody** *joc* what there is of someone *19*-. ~ **a' 1** for all that, all the same *la19*-, now *local*. **2** all the time, for ever *20*-, *NE*. ~ **as grand** *etc* **as..** however grand *etc.. 19*-. ~ **ordinar** *etc* ordinarily *18*-, now *local Bnf-Stlg*. ~ **that** because, since *la14-e15*. ~ **that o't** for that matter, as far as I am concerned *e20*, *local Cai-Arg*.
for *see* WHAR
for- *combs see* FORE- *combs*
forad, forader *see* FORRIT
foragainst, foraganis *see* FOREGAIN
foraneen *see* FORENUIN
foranent *see* FORENENT
foranentis *see* FORNENTIS
forarder *see* FORRIT
forbare *see* FORBEAR
forbatie &c [*?for'bɑtɪ] *adj, of taffeta* meaning unknown *la16*.
forbear *18*-, **forbere &c** *la14-e17* [for'bir] *vti, pt also* **forbare &c** *la14-e15*, **forbure &c** *15-18* [*for'ber, *for'bør] **1** = forbear *la14*-. **2** *vt* bear with, have patience with *15*, *19*-, now *midLoth*.
forby &c [for'bai, fər-] *adv* **1** = forbye, beyond, past *la14*. **2** besides, in addition, as well *la16*-. **3** near, beside; to one side *la18*-, now *Uls*. **4** *as an intensifier* unusually.., extraordinarily.. *19*-, now *Uls*: '*he was forby kind*'.
prep **1** in addition to *16*-. **2** except *19*-, *local*. **3** *followed by noun clause or infin* let alone, not to mention, far from, much less *la19*-, *Abd*. **4** compared with, relative to *la19*-, now *Sh Abd*. **5** beside, beyond *19*-, *local*.
adj extraordinary, strange; unusually good *19-e20*.
forbyes &c = *adv, prep, la19-e20*, *NE*.
be ~ **oneself** be beside oneself, out of one's wits *20*-, *Sh Ags midLoth*. ~ **that..** besides the fact that.. *20*-, *Abd*.
force &c, fors &c *la14-e17 n* **1** = force *la14*-. **2** a body, troop or company *la14*-. **3** validity (of an agreement, law etc) *la14*-. **4** the greater part, the majority *la19*-, *Bnf Uls*.
vtir = force *la14*-.
forced grun banked-up ground, ground made up in levelling *la19*-, now *local WC Kcb Uls*.
forcie &c 1 vigorous, active, forceful *la14-16*, *la19*-, now *Sh NE Ags*. **2** *of weather* warm and dry, favourable for crops *la19*-, *NE*.
force and fear *law* illegal pressure to make a person do something, duress *18*- [translating the law term *vis et metus*]. **be** ~ be necessary *la15-16*.
ford &c = for it *la15-16*.
I stand ~ I guarantee *la15-e16*. [only Sc; see 'D]
ford *see* FUIRD

fordards *see* FORDWARD[1]
fordel &c *19*-, *N*, **fordell &c** *16-e17* ['fordl] *n* **1** precedence, lead; advancement *16-e19*. **2 a** store, a reserve *20*-, *NE*.
adj in reserve, laid by; paid in advance *la16*-, *N*.
vt, chf ~ **up** store, keep in reserve, hoard *19*-, *NE*.
a fordell &c in hand; in front *la16-e17*. [only Sc; eModEng *fordele &c* advantage]
forder &c *15*-, **forthir &c** *la14-e19*, **furder &c** *la16-e19*; **further &c** ['fordər, 'fʌrðər, *'fʌrdər, *'forðər] *adv* = further *la14*-.
v **1** *vt* = further *la14*-. **2** *vi* make progress, thrive, succeed *la16*-, now *local Sh-Wgt*.
adj **1** = further *la15*-. **2** *of limbs, teeth* front, fore *la15-18*.
n furtherance, assistance; progress *16*-, now *Uls*.
~**some &c 1** rash, impetuous *la18-19*. **2** active, not slack *18*-, now *Abd*. **3** *of weather* fine, favourable for work *la19*-, now *Uls*.
guid ~ good luck! *la18*-, now *Uls*. **na** ~ no more; no longer *la16-e17*.
fordone &c [*for'døn] *adj* exhausted, worn out *19*, *S*. [eModEng (once) as *adj* f Eng *fordo*]
fordoverit &c [*for'dovərɪt] *adj* overcome with sleep *la15-e16*. [only Sc; Eng *for* + DOVER]
fordullit &c [*for'dʌlɪt] *adj* made dull or stupid *16*. [ME *fordulled*]
fordward[1] &c *16-17*, **fordwart &c** *16-e17*, **forthwart &c** *15-e16*, **furthwart** *la14-16* *adj, adv* forward.
~**is** *15-16*, **fordards** *la18-e20* forward, ahead. [ME *forthward*, OE *forðweard*; *cf* FORRIT]
fordward[2] *n* a covenant, promise *la15-e16*. [ME *foreward &c*]
fordwart *see* FORDWARD[1]
fordweblit &c [for'dweblɪt, -'dwiblɪt *&c*] *adj, literary* very weak, enfeebled *19-e20*. [Eng *for-* + DWAIBLE]
fore &c *adj* = fore *16*-.
adv **1** = fore *la16*-. **2** *golf* used as *interj* to warn anyone in the path of the ball *la19*-.
n **1** = fore, the front part *la16*-. **2** advantage, profit *19-e20*.
fore-bar *n, law* in the old *Court of Session* (SESSION), the bar at which ADVOCATES pleaded causes of first instance *18-e19*.
to &c the ~ **1** *of wealth or resources in gen* on hand, in reserve *la16*-, now *local Sh-Gall*. **2** *of persons and things* alive, still in existence *17*-. **3** in advance, ahead, *freq* **to the** ~ **wi** ahead of *17-19*.
fore *see* FOR
fore- *combs see* FOR- *combs*
forebear &c; forbear &c ['for'bir, -'ber; *'for'biər; *for'biər, *-'bir, *-'ber] *n, chf in pl* ancestors, forefathers *15*-. [orig Sc; FORE *adv* + agent noun of BE]
forebearer *la19-e20*, **forebearar &c** *la16-e17* [*for'birər] *n, chf in pl* ancestors, forebears. [only Sc; erron var of prec]

forebreist &c ['for'brist] *n* **1** the front of any-thing, forefront, van *la15, 20-, now Abd.* **2** the breast of a cloak, gown etc *16-e17.* **3** *freq* ~ **o the loft** the front (seat) of the gallery in a church *la17-, now local N-EC.* **4** the front (seat) of a cart *la19-, Ork NE.* [*fore-* + BREIST]

forebroads [**'for'brodz*] *n pl* the first milk from a cow after calving *e19, Ayr.* [*cf* Icel *brod-dur, brodd mjólk* the first milk]

forebront &c [**'for'brʌnt*] *n* the van of an army or a charge *16-e17, only Sc.*

forebuthe &c [**'for'bøθ*] *n* a front booth or shop *la15-e17, only Sc.*

fore-cadie &c *n, golf* a CADDIE[1] (*n* 4) who went on ahead of the player to watch where the ball fell *la18-19.*

forechalmer &c [**'for'tʃɑmər* &c] *n* a front room *la15-e17.* [*cf* eModEng *forechamber*]

foredask &c [**'for'dask*] *n* a desk or pew in a front position in a church *17-e18.*

foredoor &c ['for'dor, **-'dør*] *n* **1** the front door of a building *la16-, now NE Fif Ayr.* **2** the front part of a box cart, which has a seat on top for the driver *20-, Abd Arg Kcb.* [obs in Eng]

fore-elder *e19*, **fore-eldar** &c *15-e16 n, chf in pl* ancestors. [nME *foreildres; cf* ON *foreldrar*]

fore-end &c *n* the first or front part or portion (**of** something), *specif* the beginning or earlier part (**of** a period of time) *17-.* [now dial in Eng]

fore entré &c *n* a front entrance, a vestibule *16-e17, chf Sc.*

fore entres &c *n* = prec *16-17, only Sc.*

fore-face &c *n* **1** the front or forward facing part (**of** something) *la16-17.* **2** the front of a fireplace, consisting of an iron framework *la19-e20, Fif.* [eModEng (rare)]

forefit *18-, now Sh Abd Fif,* **forefute** &c *15-16* ['for'fɪt, **-'føt*] *n* **1** = forefoot *15-.* **2** the front part of the foot *la16-, now Sh Abd Fif.*

forefolk ['for'fok, *-'fʌuk*] *n* ancestors, forefa-thers *la19-, local Cai-Gall, only Sc.*

fore-front &c *n* the fore part or front (**of** some-thing) *15-.* [earlier in Sc]

forefute *see* FOREFIT

foregain &c *16-, now Ork Abd,* **forgane** &c *la14-e16,* **forganis** &c *la15-17,* **forganest** &c *16-17,* **foraganis** *la15-16,* **foragainst** &c *la16-e18;* **forgainst** &c *la16-19* [for'gen; **-'genst, *-(ə)'genz*] *prep* opposite to, over against, in front of. [chf Sc; *fore* + AGAIN, GIN[3]]

foregait &c [**'for'get*] *n* the street in front of a building *15-e17, only Sc.*

foregang &c ['for'g(j)aŋ, *-'gɛŋ*] *n* an image of a person or some other supernatural sign, *eg* a light, thought to foretell a death; any premoni-tion of misfortune *la19-, Sh Cai Bnf, only Sc.*

foregere &c ['for'gir] *n* armour for the front of the body *la15-16, only Sc.*

forego &c ['for'go] *n* = FOREGANG *la19-e20.* [anglicized var]

foregranddame &c [**'for'grandm* &c] *n* a great- or great-great-grandmother *16-17.* [only Sc; *fore-* + *grandame* (GRAND); *cf* FOREGRANTSIRE]

foregrandfather &c [**'for'grandfeðər*] *n* a great-grandfather *la16-17, only Sc.*

foregrantsire &c [**'for'grantsɪr, *-'grantʃər* &c] *n* a great- or great-great-grandfather *la15-17.* [only Sc; *fore-* + Eng *grandsire; cf* FOREGRANDDAME]

forehaimmer &c *20-,* **forehammer** &c *la16-e19* ['for'hɛmər &c] *n* a sledge-hammer.

fore-halve *n, chf in adj* **fore-halved** &c *of a sheep* having the front half of the top of the ear cut away *18-e19, local.*

forehammer &c *see* FOREHAIMMER

forehand &c ['for'han(d) &c] *adj* **1** *of payments,* now only of rents made in advance *la17-.* **2** first, foremost, leading *19-, local.* **3** *curling* (CURL) *and bowling, of the stones or bowls* approaching the TEE[1] or jack from the right, curving in anti-clockwise *20-, NE-WC.* **4** = forehand.
n **1** *curling* the first stone to be played; the player to play the first shot on either side *19.* **2** *curling and bowling* a shot coming in from the right of the TEE[1] or jack *20-, NE-WC.*
~**it** &c **1** paid in advance *la19-, local Bnf-Slk.* **2** farseeing, having thought for the future *la19-e20, local.*

foreheid &c *la15-,* **forehede** &c *la14-e16,* **foret** &c *la14-16, only Sc;* **forehead** *la19-* ['forhid; *Sh also* -hed; *St* 'forhɛd; **'forɛt*] *n* = forehead *la14-.*

forehouse &c [**'for'hus* &c] *n* a house facing the street; an outer apartment by which a house is entered *15-19, only Sc.*

foreland &c [**'for'lan(d)*] *n* **1** a piece of land next to the street; a TENEMENT facing the street *la15-18.* **2** = foreland, a headland, a cape *16.* **3** the foreshore or beach *18.*

forelap &c [**'for'lap*] *n, chf in pl* the overlap-ping front flaps of a garment *la16-e17, only Sc.*

forelins ['forlɪnz] *adv* (*adj*) forward(s), (in) front *la18-, NE.*

foremail &c *la15-e18,* **foremale** &c *la15-16* [**'for'mel*] *n* prepaid rent *la15-e18.*
vt let (property) for a prepaid rent *la15-16.* [only Sc; *fore-* + MAIL[1]]

foremaist *20-,* **formast** &c *la14-18,* **fore-most** *la18-* ['formest, *-məst*] *adj, adv* = foremost.
back side ~ back to front *la19-.*

foremale *see* FOREMAIL

foremost *see* FOREMAIST

forenail, fornale ['for'nel] *vt* let or sell (prop-erty) in advance; pledge (money) before it is earned, earmark for spending in advance *la15-, now NE.* [altered f FOREMAIL]

forenemmit &c *la14-e17,* **forenem(p)nyt** &c *la14-e15;* **for-** ['for'nɛmɪt, &c] *adj* fore-named, previously mentioned by name *la14-e17.* [*fore-* + NEM; *cf* Eng *forenamed*]

forenens, forenenst *see* FORNENTIS

forenent &c *la16-*, **fornent &c** *15-e17*, **foranent &c** *la16-19* [for'nɛnt; *-ə'nɛnt; fər-] *prep* **1** opposite to, in front of *15-*. **2** concerning, with regard to *la15-19*. **3** in return for, in exchange or payment for *la18-*, *now Ags*. [*fore* + ANENT]

forenicht &c ['for'nıxt] *n* the early part of the night, the evening; *latterly esp* the winter evening as a time of relaxation and social entertainment *16-*, *now local NE-Dmf*.

forenuin &c *la17-*, **forenoone &c** *17-*; **for(a)neen** *la19-*, *NE* ['for'nøn, -'nın; *NE* 'for(ə)'nin] *n* = forenoon, *but commoner in Sc where Eng prefers* morning *17-*.

~ **(bite, bread etc)** a mid-morning snack or drink, elevenses *19-*, *Abd Fif Rox*.

forepartie &c [*'for'pɛrtı *&c*] *n* a vanguard *la17*. [ME = the front part]

foreplace &c [*'for'ples] *n* a FORELAND (*n* 1) *16-e17*.

forerin, for-rin &c ['for'rın] *vt* outrun, outstrip in running *16*, *19*.

for(e)rinner &c = forerunner, precursor, harbinger *la14-e17*, *20-*. **for-run** [*'for'rʌn] *adj* exhausted by running *la15-e16*.

foreroom &c *la19-*, *now Sh Fif*, **for-rowme** *la16* ['for'rum] *n* the front part of a boat. [ON *fyrir-rúm*]

foresaid &c ['for'sed, *St* -'sɛd] *adj, before or after its noun, now esp law and official* aforesaid, abovementioned: **1** *in sing, la14-*; **2** *in pl*: (1) *as adj, la14-e18*; (2) *as noun* the persons, matters etc previously mentioned *16-e19*. [now rare in Eng]

foreschete &c *n* some part of a mill *la16*. [unknown]

foreschot *see* FORESHOT

foreseat &c *18-e19*; **foirsate** *la16* [*'for'sit, *-'set] *n* a front seat; *specif* a seat or bench forming the front part of an enclosed pew. [obs in Eng. DOST *fore-sete*]

foresee &c *vti* **1** = foresee *15-*. **2** *vt* consider (something) beforehand; see (someone) previously *la16-17*, *only Sc*.

foreshop [*'for'ʃop] *n* a shop fronting the street *18-e19*, *only Sc*.

foreshot &c, foreschot &c *la17* ['forʃot, *St* -ʃot] *n* **1** a projecting part of a building overhanging the street *la17-18*. **2** *distilling* the WHISKY that comes over first *la18-*.

foresicht &c; forsicht ['for'sıxt] *n* = foresight *la14-*.

~**y &c** foresighted, provident *19*.

foreside &c ['for'səid] *n* the front or front part of something *la15-*, *now local Sh-Fif*.

foresman &c ['forzmən] *n* = foreman, the head workman *la18-*, *local Sh-Dmf*, *only Sc*.

forespeak *18-*, *now Uls*, **forespeik &c** *la14-17* ['for-'spik] *vt* **1** *only in ptp* **forspoken &c** ['for'spokən] agreed, settled or mentioned beforehand *la14-16*, *la19-*, *now Uls*. **2** foretell, predict *15-16*.

forespeik *see* FORSPEAK

forest &c; forrest *la14-e18* *n* **1** = forest *la14-*, *in place-names la12-*. **2** *law* a large area of ground, not necessarily still wooded, *orig* reserved for deer-hunting and belonging to the Crown *18-*.

forestary &c [*'forɛstarı] the office of forester *la15-e17*, *only Sc* [MedL *forestaria*]. **free forester** a person who was granted or claimed the rights of *free forest*; *latterly* a person who poached on deer forests *la19-e20*. **the muckle** ~**er** the wind *20-*, *Mry Bnf*. ~**ry &c** *law* **1** the district of a forester; a hunting forest; the rights of hunting in such a forest *la16-19*. **2** = forestry.

free ~ a forest in which the hunting rights were granted to the proprietor by the Crown under charter *15-e20*. **the F**~ Ettrick Forest in Slk *18-19*. **The Flowers o the F**~ name of a tune traditionally said to be a lament for the young men of Ettrick killed at Flodden *la18-*.

foresta¹ &c *17-19*, **forestall &c** *15-*; **forstaw** *la15-e18* [for'sta; *for'stal] *vt* = forestall.

foresta² &c ['for'sta] *n* a manger, a feeding trough in a BYRE *la19-*, *NE Ags, only Sc*.

forestair &c ['for'ster] *n* an outside staircase leading to the first floor of a building *16-*, *now hist, only Sc*.

forestall *see* FORESTA¹

forestam &c [*'for'stam] *n* **1** = forestam, the prow of a boat *la15-e16*. **2** the forehead *e18*.

forestreet *18-19*, **forestreit &c** *la17* [*'for-'strit] *n* the street directly in front of a building *only Sc*.

foresupper &c ['for'sʌpər] *n* the period between the end of work and supper-time *la18-e20*, *only Sc*.

foresye &c ['for'sai] *n*, *butchering* a cut of beef from the shoulder, *varying regionally, but roughly corresponding to the Eng* forerib *and* middlerib *18-*. [only Sc; *fore-* + SEY³]

foret *see* FOREHEID

foretaiking &c;   **foretaking &c** [*'for'tekən] *n* = foretoken, an omen *la16*. [nME *fortakne*]

foretenement &c [*'for'tɛnəmənt] *n* a TENEMENT fronting a street *la16-e19*, *only Sc*.

forethaft &c ['for'θaft] *n* the seat next to the bow in a rowing boat *la19-*, *now Sh Bnf Fif*.

forethocht¹ &c [*'for'θoxt] *adj* premeditated, thought out beforehand, *chf law* ~ **felony** malice aforethought *la14-e19*.

forethocht² &c ['for'θoxt] *n* forethought *la19-*. ~**y** cautious, having foresight *19-*, *now Clcm*.

forewa *19-*, **forewall &c** *16-* ['for'wa] *n* the front wall of a building. [*cf* obs Eng *forewall* a defensive outer wall]

forewerk &c [*'for'wɛrk *&c*] *n* a front portion of a building *la15-17*, *only Sc*.

forewin &c ['for'wın] *n*, *hand-reaping* the first strip to be cut, done by the most experienced

worker; the worker who leads or sets the pace in
any farming task *la19-, now Arg.* [only Sc; *fore-*
+ WIN[1] *n* 3; cf *bandwin* (BAND[2])]
fore-writin &c [*'for'wrɪtən, *-'writən] *ptp,*
adj already set down in writing *la14-e16.*
fore-ʒett &c [*'for'jɛt] *n* a front gate *15-e17.*
[only Sc; *fore-* + YETT]
forfaictour &c; forfactour &c [*'forfaktør
&c] *n* forfeiture *15-16.* [only Sc; var of *forfature*
(FORFAULT) with *-c-* f MedL *forfactura &c*]
forfalt, forfat *see* FORFAULT
forfar bridie *see* BRIDE
forfauchlet &c [for'faxlt] *adj* worn out,
exhausted *19-e20.* [only Sc; *for-* + *fauchled*
(FAUCHLE)]
forfault &c *la15-19,* **forfalt &c** *la15-16,*
forfat *15-17;* **forfaut &c** *la14-e16* [*'forfat,
*-falt, *also* *for'fat, St *-'falt] *vti, ptp also*
forfault &c *la14-17* [*'forfat &c] **1** = forfeit
la15-e18. **2** *vt* subject (a person) to confiscation
of rights or property *la15-18.*
n = forfeit *15-17.*
~**er, ~our &c** *15-e18* [*'forfatur, *-ər] *n* **1** *also*
-ure *16-17* [*-ør] = forfeiture, deprivation of
property as a penalty *15-18.* **2** = forfeiter, a
wrongdoer *la15-16.* ~**ry &c** forfeiture; the
property forfeited *16-18.* [only Sc; by assimilation to Eng *fault*]
forfeit, forfett &c *15* *vt* **1** = forfeit *15-.* **2** *law*
subject (a person) to forfeiture, confiscate (a
person's estates and HERITABLE property) as a
penalty for treason *17-19.* [*cf* FORFAULT]
forflutten &c, forflitten *16-e17* [for'flʌtən,
*-'flɪtən] *adj* severely scolded, excessively
abused. [*for-* + ptp of FLYTE]
forfochtin &c *15-16;* **forfochten &c** *15-,*
forfoughen &c *la18-* [fər'foxən, *also*
-'foxtən, *&c; NE also* -'foxt; *S* -'fjuxən] *ptp, adj*
1 exhausted with fighting *15-e20.* **2** exhausted
with any kind of effort, *freq* **sair** ~ *17-, only Sc.*
[ME *forfoughten &c*]
forga &c [*for'ge, *&c] *vt* = forgo, do without,
give up *la14-16.* [nME]
forgadder *see* FORGAITHER
forgainst *see* FOREGAIN
forgaither &c *la19-,* **forgadder &c** *la15-e17,*
19-, now Sh; **forgather &c** *la16-* [fər'geðər,
-'gɛðər; *Sh* -'gadər] *vi* **1** assemble, gather
together, congregate *la15-.* **2** meet or fall in
with one another *la16-.* **3** meet, fall in **with,**
freq by chance: (1) *of persons, 16-;* (2) *of ships,*
la16-17, la19. **4** associate, keep company **with**
la18-, now NE midLoth. **5** come together in marriage, get married *la18-, Abd.*
~**in &c** a meeting, an assembly *19-, local NE-*
EC. [chf Sc]
forgane &c [*for'gen] *adj* exhausted with going
la14-16. [nME *forgan;* cf sME *forgon*]
forgane, forganis, forganest *see* FOREGAIN
forgather *see* FORGAITHER
forget &c *la16-,* **foryet &c** *19-, now Sh,* **forʒet**
&c *la14-e17* [fər'gɛt, *Sh* -'jɛt] *vti* = forget.

n (an instance of) forgetfulness, absent-minded-
ness *19-.*
forgettle &c *19-e20,* **forʒetil** *la14* [*for'gɛtl,
*-'jɛtl] forgetful.
forgie &c *18-,* **forgeve &c** *la15-16;* **forgif &c**
la14-e17, **forgive &c** *15-* [fər'gi; *for'giv] *vt,*
ptp also **forgevine &c** *la14-e16,* **forgien &c** *18-*
[fər'gi(:)n; *for'givən] = forgive.
forgevance &c [*for'givəns] forgiveness
la15-16, only Sc.
forhoo &c *la18-, now NE midLoth Pbls,* **forhow**
&c *16-18,* **forhooie &c** *la18-, chf NE,*
forvoo &c *la18-e20* [fər'hu; *NE also* -'huɪ; *S*
-'hʌu; *NE* 'fər'vu] *vt, chf of a bird* forsake, abandon (a nest). [ME *forhowien;* OE *forhogian*
despise; *cf* PERVOO]
forin *see* FARAN
forisfamiliate ['fɔrɪsfa'mɪlɪet] *adj, law, of a*
MINOR living independently of his or her parents
because of being married, having a separate
estate etc *la16-.*
vt provide separately for (a son or daughter)
la16-.
forisfamiliation *law* the separation of a child
from his family under such conditions *17-.* [chf
Sc; MedL *forisfamiliat-,* ptp stem of *foris-*
familiare, f *foris* outside + *familia* family]
forjeskit &c [fər'dʒɛskɪt, -'dʒaskɪt] *adj*
exhausted, worn out *la18-, local Sh-Pbls, only Sc.*
forjidget &c [*'for'dʒɪdʒɪt] *adj* extremely tired,
exhausted *la18-e19.* [appar extended f OSc
forjugeit condemned, *ie* as good as dead]
fork *n* **1** = fork *la14-.* **2** a forkful *19-, now Sh Ork*
Abd Per. **3** a thorough search *la19-, Sh NE Fif.*
vti **1** *chf* ~ **for** search, hunt for (money, work
etc) *19-, local Sh-EC.* **2** *vi* fend for oneself *la19-,*
local Sh-EC.
forker *20-, sEC, S,* **forkie &c** *20-, Ork-S,*
forkietail &c *19-, local Sh-S* the earwig. ~**in** **1**
the crotch *19-e20.* **2** the point where a river
divides into two or more streams *19-, now Abd*
Ags.
forky *adj* meaning obscure *e16.*
forl *see* WHURL
forlaithie &c *la19-e20;* **forlethie** *la18-e20*
[fər'leθɪ, -'lɪθɪ] *n* a surfeit, an excess (**of** something); a feeling of revulsion *la18-, now Bnf.*
vtr disgust through excess, sicken *la19-, Bnf Abd.*
[only Sc; *for-* + *laithie* (LAITH)]
forlane [*for'len] *adj* **1** set aside, disregarded
15-16. **2** despicable, worthless *16.* [ptp of ME
forly lie with (a woman)]
forleet &c *19-,* **forleit &c** *la15-19* [for'lit, fər-]
vt **1** forsake, neglect, leave behind *la15-, now Fif.*
2 forget *la18-e19.* [ME *forlete,* OE *forlǣtan*]
forlethie *see* FORLAITHIE
forloff &c [*?'forlof] *n* = furlough, leave of
absence *17-e18.* [chf Sc; Du *verlof*]
forloppin &c [*'for'lopən] *adj, freq of monks, fri-*
ars or priests runaway, renegade *16-17.* [only Sc;
Eng *for-* + *loppin* ptp (LEAP)]

forlore &c [*for'lor] *adj* lost, forlorn, destroyed *15-16*. [ME ptp of *forlese* lose]

forlot *see* FIRLOT

formast *see* FOREMAIST

forn *see* FARE

fornace &c *la14-e17*, **furnas &c** *15-e17* ['fʌrnəs] *n* = furnace.

fornacket &c [fər'nakət] *n* a hard slap, a wallop *19-*, *now Abd, only Sc.*

fornale *see* FORENAIL

forneen *see* FORENUIN

fornemnyt, fornempnyt *see* FORENEMMIT

fornent *see* FORENENT

fornentis *15-16*, **forenens &c** *16*, **foranentis &c** *la16-e17*; **forenenst &c** *la17-e20* [*for'nɛn(t)s, *-ə'nɛnts, -'nɛnst, fər-] *prep* = FORENENT 1. [*cf anenst* (ANENT)]

fornicatrix *n* a woman guilty of fornication *la16-e18*. [only Sc; L]

fornie &c *n, colloq* fornication *la18-e19, only Sc.* [reduced form]

fornyaw &c [*for'njɑ, *fər-] *vt, chf in ptp* ~**d** fatigued, tired, worn out *la18-e20*. [only Sc; Eng *for-* + *nyaw* for *gnaw* w extended meaning]

forout &c [*for'ut] *prep* without *la14-e17*. [ME; OE *forutan; cf* FOROUTIN]

forouth &c *la14-e15*; **forrouth &c** *la14-e16* [*for'uθ] *adv* **1** forward *la14*. **2** before, previously *la14-e15*.
prep **1** *of position* before, in front of *la14-e16*. **2** *of time* before, previous to *la14-e15*. [nME *forwith*]

foroutin &c [*for'utən] *prep* **1** without, lacking *la14-e17*. **2** besides, not taking into account *la14-16*. [OE *forūtan, forūton* without, except; *cf* FOROUT]

forow &c *la14-e16*; **forrow &c** [*'foru, *-ʌu] *adv* beforehand, previously *la14-16*.
prep **1** *of time* before, previous to *la14-e17*. **2** *of place* before, in front of *la14-15*. [only Sc; reduced f FOROUTH]

forpet &c *la18-19*, **forpett** *e17*; **forpit** *19-e20* ['forpət; *EC also* 'fʌur-] *n* = LIPPIE *n* 1, now *chf* used for the sale of root vegetables (*eg* = 3½ lb of potatoes) and oatmeal (= 1¾ lb) *17-, local Abd-Rox.* [only Sc; reduced f FOURT + PAIRT]

forquhy &c *conj* = forwhy *la14-16*.

forra *see* FORRAY

forrad *see* FORRIT

forray &c *la14-16*, **furrow &c** *la16-e17*; **forra** *15-16* [*'fore, -ə, *'fʌre, -ə] *n, vti* = foray.
~**our &c 1** = forayer *la14-e16*. **2** a person sent in advance to secure quarters or supplies *la16-e17*.
rin *or* **ride a forray** make an attack *16*.

forrest *see* FOREST

for-rin *see* FORERIN

forrit &c *18-*, **forwart &c** *16*; **furrit &c** *la19-, now C*, **forward** *16-*, **for(r)ad** *20-, Sh Cai adv, comparative* ~**er, fora(r)der** *20-, now Abd Stlg Edb* **1** = forward *16-*. **2** available for sale, on the market *19-*.

adj **1** = forward *la16-*. **2** *of a clock or watch* fast *la19-*. **3** present, at hand *la19-, now midLoth WC Rox.* **4** appearing in public for sale or a contest *20-*.
vt = forward *19-*.
~**some** forward, impudent, bold *19-, now local midLoth-S.*
back and ~ backwards and forwards, to (a place) and back *18-*. ~ **owre** bent forward, stooped *20-, Sh Rox.* **come** (*local NE-Ayr*) *or* **gang** *etc* (*now Abd*) ~ *church* come or go forward to take the SACRAMENT (*n* 2 (1)) *la19-, local NE-SW.* [*cf* FORDWARD¹]

forrouth *see* FOROUTH

forrow *see* FARROW, FOROW

for-rowme *see* FOREROOM

for-run *see* FORERIN

fors *see* FORCE

forsak &c *la14, la19-* (*Abd*), **forsake &c** *15-* [fər'sek; *Abd* fər'sak] *vt* = forsake.

forsamekle &c *la15-16* [*fors(w)e(:)'mikl, *-'mɪkl] *conj* forasmuch **as**. [chf Sc; nME *forsomykill*]

Forsday *see* FUIRSDAY

forseeth &c *la18-e19, N,* **forsuthe &c** *la14-e17* [*for'siθ, *-'søθ] *adv* = forsooth.

forsicht *see* FORESICHT

forsocht &c [*for'sox(t) &c*] *adj* premeditated, planned *15-16*. [corrupt form of FORETHOCHT¹]

forspeak &c *17-*, **forspeik &c** *17* [for'spik, fər-] *vt, chf in ptp* **forspoken &c** [fər'spokən] put under a spell, bewitched, *latterly esp* by excessive praise *17-, now Sh Ork Cai Abd.*
forespoken water water used to undo a spell *18-e20*. [ME]

forspeaker &c *la16-19*, **forspekar &c** *15-e17* [*?'for'spikər, *?for-, *?fər-] *n* a person who speaks on behalf of another, an advocate. [eME *vorspekere &c*, OE *for(e)speca &c*]

forspeik *see* FORESPEAK

forspoken *see* FORESPEAK, FORSPEAK

forsta &c [for'stɑ, fər-] *vt* understand *19-, Sh Ork Abd.* [prob f Du *verstaan*]

forstand &c [*for'stan(d) &c*] *vt* understand *18-19*. [OE *forstandan* defend, understand]

forstaw *see* FORESTA¹

forsume &c [*for'søm] *vt* neglect, misuse *la15-e16*. [only Sc; *cf* Du *verzuimen*, Ger *versäumen*, Dan *forsömme*]

forsuthe *see* FORSEETH

forswiftit [*for'swɪftɪt] *adj* swept away *e16*. [only Sc; f ON *svipta* (*v*)]

fort &c *16-*; **forth &c** *16-17, only Sc n* = fort.

fort *see* FOURT

fortak &c [fər'tak, *pt* -'tuk] *vt* hit, deal a blow at *la19-e20, NE.* [only Sc; *cf* Norw dial *fortaka* assail, assault]

fortefie *see* FORTIFEE

forteres &c *la14-16*; **fortrace &c** *la15-16, only Sc* [*'fort(ə)rɛs] *n* = fortress.

forth *see* FORT, FURTH

forthink &c [fər'θɪŋk, *pt* -'θoxt] *vti* **1** =

forthink, cause regret in *la14-16*. **2** *vt* think of with regret, regret that, repent of *la14-*, *now NE*. **3** *vi* feel repentance *la14-e17*. **4** have second thoughts, reconsider *18-*, *now NE*.

forthir *see* FORDER

forthwart *see* FORDWARD[1]

fortifee *la19-*, *NE*, **fortify &c** *la15-*; **fortefie &c** *la15-e17* ['fortɪ'fi] *vt* **1** = fortify *la15-*. **2** pet, pamper, spoil (a child etc) *la19-*, *NE*.

fortig &c *la19-*, *now Sh Abd*; **firtig** *la19* [fər'tɪg] *vt*, *n* = fatigue.

fortnicht &c ['fortnɪxt] *n* = fortnight *17-*.

fortoun &c *la14-*, **fortune** *la15-*; **forton &c** *la14-e16*, *e19* ['fortən; *'fortøn] *n* (*la14-*), *vti* (*la14-e17*) = fortune.

fortrace *see* FORTERES

fortunat *pt*, *ptp* happened, befell *la15-e16*. [only Sc; ptp stem of L *fortūnāre*; *cf* laME *fortunate* (*v*) make fortunate]

fortune *see* FORTOUN

forty &c *16-*, **fourty &c** *la14-e16* ['fortɪ; *'fʌurtɪ] *numeral*, *adj* = forty *la14-*.

the **F~-five 1** the Jacobite rising of 1745 *18-*. **2** the forty-five members representing Scotland in the British parliament (1707-1832) *18*. the **F~** (**Thieves**) a group of MINISTERS in the SYNOD of Glasgow who withdrew their support from the DISRUPTION as it became imminent and tried to find a compromise *e19*. the **F~-twa** the *Black Watch* (BLACK), *orig* the 42nd Highland Regiment of Foot *19-*, *local NE-Dmf*.

forvoo *see* FORHOO

forwandert; **forwandered** [*for'wandərt, -ərd] *adj*, *literary* weary with wandering, bewildered, lost *la19-e20*. [ME *forwander* weary oneself with wandering]

forward, forwart *see* FORRIT

forwonderit &c [*for'wʌnd(ə)rɪt &c*] *ptp* amazed, astounded *la14-15*. [nME *forwondred*]

forwrocht [*for'wroxt] *ptp* overcome with toil, exhausted *la15-e16*. [ME *forwroȝt &c*, ptp of *forwork*]

foryet *see* FORGET

forȝelde &c [*for'jild] *vt* repay, recompense, reward (a person or action), *chf* **God you &c ~** *la14-16*. [ME; OE *forȝeldan &c*]

forȝet, forȝetil *see* FORGET

fosset &c *n* a rush mat laid on a horse to prevent chafing by the CURRACH[2] *19-e20*. [uncertain]

foster &c *vt* **1** = foster *la14-*. **2** promote, encourage (something) *la14-*. **3** *chf of a mother suckling her offspring* feed, nourish *la19-*, *local Sh-Abd*.

n **1** a foster-child *16-17*. **2** an adopted child *18-*, *now Cai*.

fostership &c *16-e17*, **fostery &c** *la15* *n* forestership, the office of forester. [only Sc; f ME *foster* a forester]

fosy *see* FOZIE

fot &c *n*, *chf in pl* footless stockings serving as gaiters in bad weather *19-e20*, *S*.

fottie a baby's bootee *la19-e20*, *Rox*. [uncertain]

fotch &c *vt* shift, turn, change the position of *19-e20*. [var of FITCH[1]]

fotch *see* FESH

fother &c ['foðər] *n* = fodder, food for cattle and horses *la15-*, *local Ork-Uls*.

vt = fodder, feed (cattle and horses) with hay, straw etc *18-*, *local NE-Uls*. [eModEng]

fou &c *la17-*, **fow** *la14-e19*, **full &c**; **fu** *la18-* [fu; fʌl; *S* fʌu] *adj* **1** = full *la14-*. **2** full of food, well-fed *la15-*, *now local NE-Rox*. **3** *only* **fou &c** drunk, intoxicated *now freq with qualification*, *eg* **blin ~, roarin ~** *and in phrases*, *eg* **~ as a puggie** *16-*. **4** *only* **fou &c** comfortably well-off, well-provided for *19-e20*. **5** *only* **full** proud, pompous, conceited *la19-*, *local NE-Kcb*. **6** *only* **full** *of herrings* full of milt or roe, sexually mature *la19-*, *Sh Ork N*, *EC*.

adv fully, very, exceedingly *la14-*, *now local Ork-WC*.

n **1** a *or* one's fill, a full load *la16-e17*, *19-* (*local Sh-Uls*). **2** a FIRLOT *17-e19*. **3** *only* **full** a herring full of milt or roe *la19-*, *E*.

vt **1** = full, fulfil *la15-16*. **2** fill; load *18-*, *now NE Ags Fif*.

fuller a *filler* (FILL) *la19-*, *NE Ags*.

full bench a sitting of the *High Court of Justiciary* (JUSTICIARY) or of the *Inner House* (INNER) of the *Court of Session* (SESSION) consisting of more than the quorum required for the hearing of criminal appeals generally *la19-*. **~-hand**(**it**) **&c** having the hands full, having enough *16-*, *now Abd*. **a ~ man's leavins** a very small portion of food left by someone who can eat no more *19-*, *now local Ork-Per*. **ower ~ hauden** too well provided, too well off *la18-e20*, *S*.

fouat *e19*, **fowat** *16-e17* [*'fuət] *n* some kind of cake, *latterly* one similar to a *black bun* (BLACK). [only Sc; OF *fouac(h)e* a cake baked in the ashes]

fouchle *see* FAUCHLE

fouk *see* FOWK

foul &c *15-*; **fule &c** *la14-e20*, **fool &c** *la19-e20* [ful] *adj* **1** = foul *la14-*. **2** dirty; unwashed *la15-e20*. **3** infected with plague *la16-17*.

~ness *mining* an impurity or irregularity in a seam *la19-*, *now Fif*.

the **~ thief** *now chf in imprecations* the devil *la18-*, *now Sh*.

~ (be)fa may evil befall .. *15-e19*. **~ a ..** not a .., devil a .. *la17-19*.

foul *see* FOOL

foulsum *see* FOUSOME

foumart &c *la15-16*, *19-* (*local NE-S*), **thoumart &c** *19-e20*, **thummart &c** *la18-e19*; **fulmart &c** *15-17*, *e19*, **thulmard** *la17*, **whumart &c** *18*, *Ags Per* ['fumərt, 'θumərt, *'θʌ-, *'fulmərt, &c*] *n* **1** the polecat; *latterly chf* the ferret or weasel *15-*, *now local Abd-Dmf*. **2** term of abuse *16*, *19-*, *chf NE*. [ME *fulmart &c*, OE *fūl mearð* foul marten]

found[1] **&c** [*fund] **of** ~ made of cast metal *16-17*. [only Sc; F *fonte*, assimilated to the stem of the F verb *fondre*]

found[2] **&c, fund &c** *la14-19*; **foon &c** *la19-* [fun(d); *NE also* *f∧n(d)] *v* **1** *vt* = found *la14-*. **2** *vi* (1) *of persons* base one's opinion or conduct (**up**)**on** *la16, 19-*, now *local Sh-Fif*. (2) *of things* be based or established (**up**)**on** *19-*, now *local Sh-Fif*.

n **1** *lit and fig* a foundation, base (1) *in sing, 17-*; (2) *in pl, la19-*. **2** a ring of stones and brushwood on which a haystack is built *20-, NE*. **3** *also* **fond** *18-e20* a fund of money *la17-*, now *NE Ags*.

~**in pint** a drink given to workmen after laying the foundations of a building as an omen of good luck *la19-*, now *Ork Ags*. ~**it &c** provided for by the foundation of a college etc *la16-17*.

found[3] **&c** [*fund] *vi, only verse* go, travel, make one's way *la14-16*. [ME; OE *fundian*]

founder *la15-*; **funder &c** *16*, **fooner** *la19-*, *Abd Ayr* ['fun(d)ər; *'f∧n(d)ər] *v* **1** *vi* = founder *la15-*. **2** *fig* collapse, break down with drink, exhaustion, illness etc *la19-, Gen except Sh Ork*. **3** *vt* fell, strike down (a person, animal etc) *la18-, local NE-S*. **4** *chf in passive* be exhausted, worn out, prostrated by fatigue, shock, a cold etc *18-, local NE-S*.

n **1** a collapse, breakdown in health *19-, local NE-S*. **2** *specif* a severe chill *la20-, WC Uls*.

foundin *see* FIND

foundit &c ['fundɪt] **not a** ~ *etc* not the least little bit, not a thing *19-*, now *Gall*. [abbrev f Eng *not a confounded* ..]

four *see* FOWER

fourlet *see* FIRLOT

fourt &c *la15-e20*, **ferd &c** *la14-17*; **fort** *la16-e20*, **feird &c** *la14-e17* [fort; *Sh Ork* furt; *Bwk Rox* f∧urt; *fird, *ferd] *adj* = fourth *la14-e20*.

fourtie &c *n* a quarter of the regulation barrel, a firkin, *chf* of salt herring *20-, NE*.

the ferd &c corne used in estimates of the value of grain for sowing *la15-16*. **the ferd &c penny** one penny in every four *16*.

fourteen &c *la17-*, **fourtene &c** *la14-e17* ['fortin; *EC, S* 'f∧ur-] *numeral* **1** = fourteen *la14-*. **2** a MERK, a fourteen-shilling piece SCOTS (*ie* after its value was raised from thirteen shillings and fourpence) *la17-e18*.

fourty *see* FORTY

fous, fowse &c [*fus] *n* = fosse, a ditch *la15-e17*.

vt, only **fowse** furnish (a town, churchyard etc) with a ditch *16*. [*cf* FOUSSIE]

fousome *17-e20*, **foulsum &c** *la14-16*, **fowsum** *16*; **fusome** *19-e20* ['fu(:)səm, *'f∧ls∧m] *adj* **1** filthy, dirty, loathsome *la14-16, 19-*, now *NE Ags*. **2** *of food* filling, over-rich *17-*,

now *Sh Abd Ags*. [ME *fulsum* full, abundant; f FOU + -SOME w confusion of the first element w FOUL]

foussie &c, fowsie &c *16-e17* [*'fusɪ] *n* a ditch *16-17, 19-e20* (*hist*).

vt provide or surround (a wall, piece of land etc) with a ditch *la16-e17*. [only Sc; F *fossé*, OF *fousseis*; for vowel *cf* FOUS]

foustica(i)t *see* FOO

foustie *see* FUSTIAN

fouter &c; footer &c *la18-* ['futər] *n* **1** term of abuse, *orig* for a hateful, objectionable person, now much weaker an exasperating person *18-*, now *chf N*. **2** a slacker, a muddling, aimless person *19-*. **3** a chap, fellow *la18-*: 'a tough auld fouter'. **4** a troublesome, fiddling job *19-, local*.

v **1** *vi* potter, trifle, fiddle; work in a fiddling, unskilled way *la19-*. **2** *vt* thwart, inconvenience *20-*, now *Ork Per*.

~**ie** *of a person* fussy, inept; *of a task* trivial; fiddling, time-wasting *20-*. [OF *foutre*, L *futuere* (of a man) have sexual intercourse; *cf* Eng slang and dial]

fouth &c, fulth &c *la14-e15* *n* [fuθ; *NE also* f∧uθ; *f∧lθ] *n* abundance, plenty, an ample supply *la14-*, now *local Sh-Ags*.

~**ie &c** having abundance, prosperous *19-e20*.

at fouth *16-e17*, **afouth** *la18-e19* in abundance, fully, copiously. [ME *fulthe &c*]

foutie &c *18-*, now *Mry Abd Wgt*, **futie &c** *la17-e19*; **footie &c** *19-e20* ['futɪ] *adj* **1** mean, despicable, underhand *la17-*, now *Mry Abd Wgt*. **2** obscene, indecent *19-e20*. [see SND]

fow &c [f∧u] *n* **1** a pitchfork *la15-e17, 19-*, now *NE Gall*. **2** a kick, a restless tossing movement with the feet *la19-e20, Mry Bnf*.

vi **1** lift or toss straw, hay etc with a fork *19-, Bnf Abd Kcb Dmf*. **2** kick about restlessly, *esp* in bed *la19-, Bnf Abd*. [obscure]

fow *see* FOO, FOOS, FOU

fowat *see* FOUAT

fowd &c [f∧ud] *n* withered vegetation, long coarse grass not eaten down in summer; worn-out thatch *la18-e20, N*. [Gael *fòd* a turf]

fower &c, four &c; foir *16-17* [f∧ur] *numeral* = four *la14-*.

~**sie** ['f∧urzɪ] *game of chuckies* (CHUCK[2]) a set or group of four stones etc which have to be picked up while another is thrown in the air *la19-, local Mry-WC*. ~**some &c** **1** a group of four persons or things *la15-*. **2** *also* **foursome reel** a REEL[1] danced by four people *20-*. **3** *golf* a match consisting of four players, two on each side *la19-*.

~ **hours &c** **1** four o'clock in the afternoon *16-e17*. **2** a light meal or refreshment taken around this time *17-e20*. **four-neukit** four-cornered *la15-19*. **fower quarters** the body, the person; *transf* the personal influence (of someone) *la18-19*.

on (the) four half(is) about in the surrounding neighbourhood *15-e17.* **(up)o(n)** yer *etc*
fowers on all fours *la19-, local Cai-Kcb.*

fowk &c *18-,* **folk &c; fouk &c** *la15, la18-e20,*
fock &c *la16-19* [fok; *local Cai-Per Dmf* fʌuk;
*folk] *n, usu in sing as collective or in pl* **1** = folk
la14-. **2** people, persons, mankind *la14-.* **3** *in sing* the inhabitants of a place *la18-.* **4** the members of one's family, community etc, one's relatives *la18-.* **5** *chf in sing* servants, employees *la18-, Gen except Sh Ork.* **6** *usu with a number specified* individual persons *la18-:* 'here's twae folks come frae Glasgow'. **7** human beings as opposed to animals or supernatural beings *19-, now Abd Kcb.*
ferm ~ the workers on a farm *20-, NE Fif SW.*

fowne [*fʌun] *n* = fawn *16.* [ME, OF *foun*]

fowse *see* FOUS

fowsie *see* FOUSSIE

fowsum *see* FOUSOME

fox &c *n* = fox *la14-.*
~-fit 1 a species of crowfoot *20-, now midLoth Bwk.* **2** the fir club-moss *19-e20, S.* **fox trie &c leaves** foxglove (leaves) *e17, e19, only Sc.*

foy¹ &c *n* a farewell feast; a party to celebrate a marriage, special occasion etc *18-, local.*
drink (someone's) ~ drink farewell (to someone) *18-e19.* [eModEng; MDu *foye, voye* a celebration of a departure; OF *voie* a journey]

foy² *interj* tut tut! *19-, now Abd.* [var of Eng *fie*]

foyl3e *see* FULYIE

foze *see* WHEEZE³

fozie &c; fosy &c *18-e20,* **fozzy** *e19* ['fozɪ; S 'fuzɪ] *adj* **1** *freq of overgrown or rotten vegetables* soft, spongy *la18-.* **2** *of rope etc* ragged, frayed *18-, Abd.* **3** *of persons and animals* fat, flabby, out of condition *la18-, local NE-Gall.* **4** unintelligent, dull, stupid *18-, now midLoth.*
foziness 1 sponginess *19-, local Sh-Pbls.* **2** flabbiness *19-e20.* **3** stupidity *19-e20.* [only Sc; Du *voos* spongy, porous + *-ie*]

fozle *see* WHEEZE³

fozzy *see* FOZIE

F.P. *see* FREE

fra *see* FRAE

fra'at &c *la18-, NE,* **frithat &c** *e19* [*NE* 'frɑ'at, frɑt; *C, S* *'frɪðat &c*] *adv phr* = for all that, nevertheless.

fraca &c [frə'kɑ] *n* **1** = fracas *la18-.* **2** a fuss, a bother *19-.* **3** an intimate, demonstrative friendship, a warm affection *la19-, Abd Fif midLoth.*

fracht *see* FRAUCHT

frack *see* FRECK

fraction &c *n* **1** = fraction. **2** a proportional payment for horses used for military service; a certain number of persons required to provide and pay a leader of horse *la17, only Sc.*

frae &c *la15-, now chf literary,* **fra &c** *la14-19,* **fae &c** *la18-, orig N,* **thrae &c** *19-, Bwk S,* **fray &c** *la15-e17,* **fre** *la16* [fre; fe, fɪ; *Bwk S* frɛ, frə, θre, θrɛ] *prep* from *la14-.*

conj **1** from the time that, as soon as *la14-, now local Sh-S.* **2** since, because, seeing that *16-e17, e19.*
fra that *or* **at** from the time that *la14-e16.*
glower, look *etc* **frae one** have a fixed or vacant look, stare stupidly *19-, now S.* [nME *fra*, corresponding to midl and sME *fro; cf* THROM]

frael *see* FRAIL¹

fraer &c *la16,* **frear &c** *la16-17;* **frayar &c** *14-16* [*'freər, *frer] *n* a basket (of figs, dates or almonds). [only Sc; altered f *frael* (FRAIL¹)]

fraesta &c *interj* please *19-e20, S.* [perh 2 pers sing imperative of OSc, ME *fraist* (*v*) attempt, try; *cf seestu* (SEE)]

fraik &c *n* **1** = freak, a whim, an odd notion *la18-e19.* **2** (1) flattery; affectionate fussing *19-, Ork Cai Ags Fif.* (2) a flatterer, a wheedler *la19-, Ags Fif Dmf.* **3** a slight ailment about which too much fuss is made *20-, Ork Ags.*
v **1** *vt* flatter, make a fuss of, pet, pamper *19-, Ork Ags Fif.* **2** *vi* pretend to be ill, make a fuss about a minor ailment *20-, Ork Ags.*
~ie coaxing, wheedling *19-, now Ork.*
mak a ~ **aboot** make a fuss about (something), *esp* when showing reluctance to do something *la19-, now Ork Ags.* **mak a** ~ **wi** *or* **o** make a fuss of (someone) *la19-, now Ags.*

frail¹ *20-,* **frael** *e15* [frel, *'freɛl] *n* **1** = frail, a rush-basket *e15.* **2** a container with a circular wooden frame and a sheepskin bottom, used for winnowing corn, a WECHT² *20-, midLoth Dmf Rox.* [OF *frayel* a basket for figs; *cf* FRAER]

frail² *n* = flail, the threshing implement *19-e20.*

Frainche *see* FRENCH

fraine &c *v* **1** *vt* = frayne, ask (a person) about (something), ask **how, quhat** .. *la14-16.* **2** *vi* make enquiry *la15-16.*

frainesy &c *16-20,* **frenesy &c** *la14-19* ['frenəzɪ, 'frɛn-] *n* = frenzy.

fraise *see* PHRASE¹

frait *see* FREIT

fraith *see* FREITH

fraized *see* PHRASE²

frak *see* FRECK

frame &c *n* **1** = frame *la16-.* **2** a square or hoop of wood hung from the shoulders on which to carry pails *la19-, local Ork-Abd.* **3** an emaciated person or animal *la19-, local Sh-Kcb.*
vt = frame *la16-.*

frame *see* FREMD

France &c [*frans, *frans] *adj* French *la14-e17.* [only Sc; var of next or *attrib* use of the Eng noun]

Franche &c [*franʃ] *adj, n* French *15-e17.* [the vowel agrees with Du *Fransch,* Dan and Sw *Fransk,* Mod Icel *Franskur; cf* FRENCH]

frandie &c *n* a small rick of hay- or corn-sheaves made by a man standing on the ground *19-, Per Fif.* [only Sc; prob a dim based on *fra* (FRAE) hand, as no lifting implement is used]

frank &c adj **1** = frank la15-. **2** willing, eager, ready la18-, now Ags.
Frankis &c [*'fraŋkɪs] adj Gaulish e15. [only Sc; L Francus; cf FRANCHE]
franktenement &c [*'fraŋk'tɛnəmənt] n freehold la14-e17.
~**ar &c** a freeholder la15-16. [cf eModEng]
frase see PHRASE[1]
fratch vi quarrel, argue, disagree 19-, Dmf Rox. [ME fracchyn (v) creak]
fraucht &c; fracht la14-16 [frɑxt] n **1** the hire of a boat; the fare or freight charge for transport by water la14-, now Cai Arg. **2** a ship's cargo la15-16. **3** (1) a load, a burden 18-e20. (2) as much as can be carried or transported at one time by one person, eg two pailfuls, two cartloads etc 19-, Sh-N Fif. **4** (1) an amount, quantity, number la15-17. (2) a large amount, a generous supply la18-e20.
vt **1** transport by water 15-16. **2** also fig load with cargo 15-19. **3** hire (a boat) la16-18.
frauchtar &c 16-17, only Sc, ~**isman** 15-16, only Sc a person who loads a ship. [ME fraght, MDu, MLowGer vracht carriage by sea, transport; cf Eng freight]
frawart &c la14-e20. **fraward &c** 15-17 [*'frɑwart, *-ward] adj = froward, contrary, perverse; adverse, unfavourable la14-e20, latterly only literary.
prep, only **frawart** = froward, away from 15-e16.
fray &c n **1** = fray la14-. **2** a noise made to raise the alarm 16-17. **3** in gen a noise, a fuss, a stir la16-e20.
vti = fray la14-e17.
fray see FRAE
frayar see FRAER
Frayday see FREDDAY
fre see FRAE, FREE
frear see FRAER
freath see FREITH
freche see FRESH
freck la18-19, **frak** la14-e17; **frack** la16-e19 adj **1** bold, active, eager, forward la15-e19. **2** able-bodied, vigorous, active la18-19.
vi move swiftly e16.
~**ly &c** smartly, quickly, actively la14-e17. [ME frek, OE frec, fræc bold, greedy]
Fredday &c 16-19, chf NE, **Friday &c** 15-, **Fryday &c** la14-17; **Frayday &c** 16-e18 ['frəide, -dɪ; St also 'fraɪ-; NE 'frɛdɪ] n = Friday 15-.
Friday('s) penny etc the penny etc given to children as pocket-money la19-e20, Abd.
free 15, la17-, **fre** la14-e17; **frie &c** 16-e18, **frei &c** la14-16, e20 (S) [fri; S frəi] adj **1** = free la14-. **2** single, unmarried 18-, now local NE-midLoth. **3** ready, willing (to do etc) la18-, local Sh-Kcb. **4** of pastry etc brittle, crumbly la18-. **5** in calculating time, esp of days between a summons and a trial clear, non-inclusive la18-e20.
adv freely la14-.

vt **1** = free 15-. **2** with infin clear (someone of a suspicion), absolve or acquit (someone or something of being or intending something) 19-, Sh NE: 'I widna free 'er to try some queer pliskie on 'im'. **3** games, chf hide-and-seek etc put out of the game by reaching 'home' first 20-, local Abd-Ayr.
n **1** the **F**~ = Free or United Free Church (FREE, UNITED) la19-. **2** a member of these churches la19-.
~**dom &c 1** = freedom la14-. **2** the state of being free from subjection to an alien ruler or power la14-16. **3** the area over which the immunities of a BURGH extended la15-17. **4** full membership of a guild or trade la15-17. **5** permission 19-, local. **6** a piece of common land allotted by certain communities to their members la18-e19. ~**lins** rather, quite 20, Bnf Abd. ~**ly &c** adv **1** = freely la14-. **2** entirely, completely, fully, quite 15, 18-, now local Sh-midLoth.
F~ **Church (of Scotland)** = F~ Kirk, 19-. ~ **coal** coal which breaks or burns easily 19-, local. ~**holder**, ~**haldar &c 1** = freeholder, one who possesses a freehold estate 15-. **2** law a person who, before the 1832 Reform Act, could elect or be elected a member of Parliament by virtue of holding lands direct of the Crown assessed at or over forty shillings 18-e19. **F**~ **Kirk** name **1** adopted by the body which broke away from the Established Church at the DISRUPTION 19; **2** now applied to the minority which refused to enter the union with the United Presbyterian Church (UNITED) in 1900, 20-; cf wee free. ~**living** self-indulgent 19-, Sh NE Fif Uls. ~ **money** surplus or ready money la15-16, only Sc. ~ **port** a port open to all merchants for loading and unloading their vessels la16-. **F**~ **Presbyterian, F.P.** (esp wHighl) a member of the body which seceded from the Free Church of Scotland in 1892, la19-; cf Seceder (SECEDE). ~ **prison** prison without fetters or with the privilege of going out temporarily la15-17. ~**stane** freestone, a kind of easily worked sandstone; a block of this stone 16-, now local. ~ **trade** smuggling 19. **wee** ~ derog a member of the Free Kirk (n 2) 20-.
freen(d) see FRIEND
freenge la19-, **freinge &c** 17, **frenȝe &c** la15-e17 [frindʒ; *'frinjɪ, *'friɲɪ, *'frɪŋ(j)ɪ] n = fringe.
freest n = frost la19-e20, Abd.
freet &c 17-, now Fif, **frete &c** la14-16 v **1** vt rub, chafe, injure by friction or violence la14-, now Fif. **2** vi = fret, be vexed la16-19.
freet see FREIT, FRUIT
freeth &c 17-18, **frethe &c** la14-16; **freith &c** 15-17 [*frið] v **1** vt free or release from a claim or obligation la14-e18. **2** set free, liberate 15-e17. **3** set or make free **from** or **of** 15-17. **4** vr free or absolve oneself **of** la16-e17. [ME frethe, frithe, OE friðian free, keep in peace]
freevolous &c adj = frivolous 19-. [only Sc; cf FRIVOLE]

freff *adj* shy; cold, distant *la19-e20*. [prob by assimilation and metathesis f THARF]

frei *see* FREE

freid *see* THREID

freinge *see* FREENGE

freit &c *la16-*, **frete** *15-e16*; **freet** *la16-e20*, **frait** *la18-19* [frit; *N, EC, S also* frɛt, fret; *Sh also* *'frøt] *n* **1** *freq in pl* superstitious beliefs, observances or acts *15-*, *now local N-Rox*. **2** a superstitious saying, an adage *19-*, *now Bnf*. **3** an omen, a presage *18-*, *now Ross Ags*. **4** a whimsical notion, a fad *la18-e20*.

~**y &c** strongly believing in superstition *18-*, *now Fif*.

stand on ~**s** make a fuss about trifles, be faddy *la18-e20*. [nME (once); obscure]

freith &c *la18-*, *now Kcb Dmf*; **freath &c** *18-e20*, **fraith &c** *e19* [*S, SW* freθ; *WC Dmf* friθ] *v* **1** *vi, chf verse* foam, froth *la18-*, *now Kcb*. **2** *vt* work (a liquid) up into a froth, make a lather in *18-e20*. **3** swill (clothes) quickly through soapsuds *19-*, *Kcb Dmf*.

n **1** *chf verse* froth, foam, lather *la18-*, *now Kcb*. **2** a hasty wash given to clothes *19-*, *local Arg-Dmf*. [only Sc; OE *āfreoðan*, ON *freyða* (*v*) froth]

freith *see* FREETH

fremd &c *15-*, *now local*, **fremmit &c** *la14-e20*, **frame &c** *la16*, *e19*, **frem** *la17*, *19-e20*; **fremt** *la18-e20* [frɛm(d), frɛmt; *C also* 'frɛmɪt; *Ork Cai* frɛn(d)] *adj* **1** *of persons, places etc* strange, unfamiliar, foreign; unrelated *la14-*, *local Sh-Dmf*. **2** strange, unusual, uncommon *la15-e17*. **3** strange in manner, distant, aloof *16-e19*.

n, uninflected, now chf **the** ~ strangers, the world at large *la14-*, *now local*.

fremmitly &c strangely, in a strange or unfriendly way *la15-16*. **fremmitnes &c** strangeness, unfriendliness, unfamiliarity *la15-16*, *e20*. [ME *fremde &c*, OE *frem(e)de*]

French *18-*, **Frenche &c** *15-17*; **Frainche &c** *16-e17*, *e20* *adj*, *n* = French.

French cake a kind of small fancy sponge cake, iced and decorated *20-*. **French loaf 1** = French loaf, a long thin loaf *20-*. **2** a loaf made from dough containing a little fat and sugar and shaped so as to give a heart-shaped slice *e20*.

French and English a boys' game = *English and Scots* (ENGLISH) *la19-*, *now Fif Stlg*. [*cf* FRANCHE]

frende *see* FRIEND

frenesy *see* FRAINESY

frenʒe *see* FREENGE

frequent &c [*v* frɪ'kwɛnt, *Abd Ags* -'kwant; *adj* 'frikwənt, *frɪ'kwɛnt] *vti* **1** = frequent *la15-*. **2** *vi* associate, keep company with *e17*, *19-*, *local Sh-midLoth*.

adj = frequent *16-*.

frere *see* FRIAR

fresh &c *15-*, **fresche &c** *la14-e17*; **fres** *la14-15*, **freche** *la15-e17* [frɛʃ; *fresh la14-*. **2** *chf of a habitual drunkard* sober, recovered from a drinking bout *18-*, *now Sh-Ags*. **3** *of weather* not frosty, open, thawing *la18-*. **4** *of animals* thriving, fattening *20-*, *now midLoth SW*.

adv = fresh, freshly *15-*.

n (the setting in of) a thaw, a period of open weather *18-*, *local*.

v **1** *vi* thaw *19-*, *now NE Ags*. **2** *vt* pack (herring) in ice ungutted, for consumption as fresh *20-*, *local*.

fresher 1 a herring-buyer who packs fish as in *v* 2, *20-*, *local*. **2** = fresher.

frest *see* FRIST

frete *see* FREET, FREIT

frethe *see* FREETH

freuch &c [fr(j)ux, frʌx] *adj* dry and brittle, liable to break *la15-*, *now NE*. [ME *frough, frouh*; obscure]

freuchan ['frøxən, 'frex-, 'frʌx-] *n* the toe-cap of a boot *19-*, *now Ross Arg*. [Gael *fraochan*]

Freuchie &c ['fruxɪ, 'frʌxɪ] **gae tae F**~ (**and fry mice**) go to blazes! *19-*, *local Ags-Ayr*. [the village in Fif]

frevoll *see* FRIVOLE

freyte *see* FRUIT

frezel *see* FRIZZEL

friar &c *17-*, **frere &c** *la14-17* [*St* 'fraɪər; *'frir] *n* = friar *la14-*.

friar's chicken a soup made with veal, chicken and beaten eggs *la18-e19*.

fricht &c [frɪxt] *n* = fright *18-*.

vt frighten, terrify *18-*.

~**it for** afraid of *18-*, *now C*. ~**some** fearful, terrifying *la18-*.

nae frichts no fear *la19-*, *now Fif*.

frichten &c ['frɪx(t)ən] *vt* = frighten *la19-*.

~**ed for** frightened of *la19-*.

Friday *see* FREDDAY

friddon &c *la16-e17*, **firdoun &c** *la16* *vti* warble. [F *fredonner*; eModEng *freddon*]

frie *see* FREE

friend *18-*, **frende &c** *la14-e16*; **freend &c** *la16-e20*, **freen &c** *17-* [frin(d)] *n* **1** = friend *la14-*. **2** a relative, a kinsman *15-*.

vt = friend *15-e19*.

~**full** friendly *la14-16*. ~**lyk** *adj* (*adv*) friendly, in a friendly way *15-16*. ~**ship &c 1** = friendship *la14-*. **2** kinship; kindred, friends *la15-16*.

be ~**s to** *or* **with** be related to *la19-*, *now NE*.

frist *15-e19*, **first &c** *la14-e16*; **frest** *la14*, *18-e19* *n* **1** = frist, delay *la14-e18*. **2** *specif* the allowing of time for payment, credit *la15-16*.

v **1** *vt* sell (goods) on credit *15-e19*. **2** allow (a thing) to be delayed, suspend, postpone *17*. **3** give (a person) delay, respite or credit *la15-e17*.

frith *see* FIRTH[1]

frithat *see* FRA'AT

frivole &c *16-e17*, **frevoll &c** *la15-e17*, **fruell &c** *la15-16* [*'frɪvol, *'friv-, *-əl, *fr(j)uəl] *adj* **1** frivolous, of little account or worth *la15-e17*. **2** fickle, unreliable *la15-16*. [chf Sc; F *frivole*, L *frivolus*]

frizz *vi, of cloth etc* fray, wear out *20-, Abd Fif Slk.* [uncertain]

frizzel &c, frezel *e17 n* **1** the steel used for striking fire from a flint *17-e20.* **2** the hammer of a flintlock pistol or gun *18-19.* [perh altered f MDu *vierijser; cf* FLEERISH]

fro &c *la18-;* **froh** *la19-, NE Ags* [fro] *n* froth, foam *la18-, now local Mry-Slk.*

vi froth, foam; bubble *la18-, local Abd-Slk.*

froh milk a mixture of cream and whey beaten up and sprinkled with oatmeal *20-, NE Ags.* ~ **stick** a whisk made of wood and cows' hair *la19-, now Abd.* [reduced f Eng *froth*]

frock &c *16-,* **frog &c** *la14-17 n* **1** = frock *la14-.* **2** a sailor's or fisherman's knitted jersey *19-, Ork Abd.* **3** a short oilskin coat or cape *la20-, Sh Cai Fif.*

frock *see* THROCK

frog[1] **&c** *n* a young male horse from one to three years old *19-, Bnf Abd.* [obscure]

frog[2] **&c** *n* = frog *16-.*

~**s mouth** the monkey flower or mimulus *la19-, Fif Pbls SW.*

frog *see* FROCK

froh *see* FRO

froit *see* FRUIT

front &c; frunt *la15-e17* [frʌnt] *n* **1** = front *la14-.* **2** *elliptical* **the** front garden *la19-, local NE-Ayr.*

~ **breist** the front seat in the gallery of a church *e20.*

in ~ **of** *of time* before, prior to *20-, Sh NE Fif.*

frontale &c [*'frʌntəl] *n* **1** = frontal, a covering for the front of an altar *la15-16.* **2** a curtain for a bed *16, only Sc.*

froon *19-,* **froun &c** *vti* (*la16-*), *n* (*19-*) = frown.

frosin *see* FROZEN

frost &c *n* **1** = frost *la14-.* **2** ice *la18-, now local Sh-Fif.*

vt protect (a horse) from slipping on ice by spiking its shoes *16-.*

find ~ run into difficulties, *chf* of one's own making, suffer unpleasant consequences from one's own actions *18-, now Ork.* **it is** ~ it is freezing, there is frost *la18-.*

frostar &c *n* a forester *la14-e17, NE, only Sc.*

frothy *see* FURTH

froun *see* FROON

frow &c [frʌu] *n* a big buxom woman *la18-, chf NE.*

frowdie ['frʌudɪ] = *n, 19-e20.* **frowdie** (**mutch**) *etc* an old woman's cap, with a seam at the back *19.* [Eng = a Dutchwoman, Du *vrouw*]

frozen *19,* **frosin &c** *la15-e17 adj, also with double ptp ending* ~**ed** *19-, Ork Ags Stlg Ayr* = frozen.

fruct &c *15-e17;* **fruict** *la16-e17 n* a fruit.

~**les** *chf fig* fruitless *16, only Sc.* [ME *chf* or only a spelling var of FRUIT after L *fructus; cf* FRUIT]

fruell *see* FRIVOLE

frugal ['frugəl; *Cai* 'frʌu-] *adj* **1** = frugal. **2** frank, kindly, hospitable *la18-, Sh Cai Abd.*

fruict *see* FRUCT

fruit &c *15-,* **froit &c** *la14-16,* **freyt &c** *e15;* **freet &c** *19-, now Cai* [frøt, frɪt; *Ags Fif* fret; *Cai also* frit] *n* **1** = fruit *la14-.* **2** *only* **freet &c** milk produce; butter, cheese *19-20, Cai.* [cf FRUCT]

frull *n* = frill *19-.*

frump &c *n, chf in pl* the sulks, a bad mood *18-, now Sh.* [prob same as Eng = a sneer, jeer (obs); a dowdy woman]

frumple *vt* crease, crumple *19-, now local NE-Fif.* [laME *fromple* wrinkle; perh f MDu *verrompelen*]

frunt *see* FRONT

frunter *see* THRUNTER

frusch &c *v* **1** *vt* = frush, smash, drive back by attack *la14-16.* **2** *vi* become broken, go to pieces *la14-16.*

n **1** = frush, a charge *la14.* **2** a crashing noise, the crash of breaking weapons *la14-e15.*

frush &c *adj* **1** *of pastry etc* crisp, short, crumbly *18-, now Ork SW.* **2** *of soil* crumbly, loose *19-, now local Ork-Dmf.* **3** *of wood, vegetable fibre, cloth etc* brittle, apt to disintegrate, decayed, rotten *la18-, local Ork-Dmf.* **4** frank, bold, rash *la18-e20.* **5** tender, easily hurt or destroyed, frail *19-e20.* [appar f FRUSCH]

fruster &c *vt* frustrate, bring to nothing, make useless *16.*

adj ineffective, useless *la15-e16, only Sc.* [laME *frustre* defraud; F *frustrer,* L *frustrārī*]

fry *vti* = fry *16-.*

n **1** a small number of fish for frying, *chf* when presented as a gift *la19-, now local Sh-SW.* **2** *fig* a state of worry or distraction, a disturbance *la18-, now local Sh-Stlg.*

Fryday *see* FREDDAY

fryne &c [frəin] *vi* grumble, whine *la18-e20.* [cf Norw and Sw dial *fryna* wrinkle up one's nose, make a wry face]

frythe [*fraɪð] *vti, lit and fig* fry *la18-19.*

frything pan a frying pan *17-e18.* [Eng *fry,* perh w infl f Eng *seethe* and FREITH]

fu *see* FOU

fuaill *see* FEWALE

fud &c *n* **1** the buttocks *18-, now Dmf Rox.* **2** the tail of an animal, *chf* a hare or rabbit *18-, local NE-Rox.* **3** the female pubes *19-.*

vi frisk about; walk briskly or with a short, quick step *la18-e20.*

fuddie &c *adj, of animals* short-tailed; *of persons or things* short, thick, stumpy *la19-e20. n* a hare *19, chf Bnf Abd.*

cock its *etc* ~ *of an animal* cock its etc tail *la18-e20.* [see SND]

fud *see* WHID[1]

fudder *see* FUTHER, WHIDDER

fuddle *vti* **1** = fuddle, tipple; intoxicate. **2** *vt* get drunk on, drink the proceeds of; spend (time) drinking *19-e20.*

fude *see* FUID

fuff &c *vti* **1** emit puffs of smoke or vapour, hiss *e16, 19-, local.* **2** *vi* puff, blow gently *la16-.* **3** *of a cat etc* spit, hiss *la17-, local NE-Rox.* **4** go off in a huff, fly into a temper *la18-, local Abd-Rox.* **5** sniffle as if about to cry *19-, now midLoth.* **6** *vt* cause to emit puffs of smoke, smoke (a pipe) *la18-e20.* **7** *of a hen etc* puff (feathers) **out** *or* **up** *la20-, Sh Ork Abd.*
n **1** a puff, a gentle gust (of wind), a whiff *16-, now local Sh-Kcb.* **2** a hiss or spit of a cat etc *19-, now local NE-Kcb.* **3** a sudden outburst of temper, a huff *19-, now Bnf local EC.*
interj indicating an explosive noise, or expressing contempt, fsst!, psst!, bah! *19-, now local NE-Dmf.*
~**y** short-tempered, impatient *la19-e20.* [only Sc; onomat]

fuffle &c *v* **1** *vt* dishevel, ruffle, disarrange (clothes etc) *19-, now Cai midLoth.* **2** *vi* walk awkwardly, shuffle, fumble, be clumsy *20-, Sh Cai Ayr.*
n fuss, violent exertion *19-, S.*
fuffling rough moving about *e16.* [only Sc; onomat]

fuggle &c ['fʌgl, 'fjʌgl, 'fjugl] *n* **1** a small bundle of hay, grass, rags etc, *esp* when used to stop up a hole *la19-, NE Ags.* **2** an unburnt plug of tobacco in a pipe, the DOTTLE (*n* 2) *e20, NE.* [only Sc; *cf* Norw dial *fugge* a small bundle]

fugie &c ['f(j)udʒɪ, *also* f(j)udʒ; *N also* (*chf or only v*) *'fʌdg(ɪ)] *n* **1** a runaway, a fugitive; a coward *la18-, now Ags.* **2** *specif* a runaway cock from a cock-fight *la18-19.* **3** a light blow, accompanied by the word, given by one schoolboy to another as a challenge to fight *la19-e20.* **4** a truant from school *la19-20.*
adj cowardly *19-e20, Rox.*
vt, chf ~ **the schule** play truant *la19-, now NE.*
~ **warrant** *law* a warrant issued by a SHERIFF to a creditor to apprehend a debtor on sworn information that he intends to leave the country *19.* [see SND]

fugitate [*'fjudʒɪtet] *ptp, vt, law, chf in ptp* ~(**d**) declared a fugitive from justice, banished *la17-e19.*
fugitation *law* sentence of outlawry with confiscation of MOVEABLE property for failing to appear in court on a criminal charge *18-19.* [only Sc; ptp stem of L *fugitāre* flee; *cf* FUGITIVE]

fugitive &c [*'fødʒɪtaɪv] *n, adj* = fugitive *la14-.*
decern and adjudge *or* **declare** ~ *law* outlaw, pronounce sentence of *fugitation* (FUGITATE) on *18.*

fugitour &c [*'fødʒɪtur] *n* a fugitive *15-16.* [only Sc; L *fugitor*]

fuid &c *la15-19*, **fude** *la14-* [føid, fɪd] *n* = food.

fuil &c *la15-*, **fule** *15-*, **feel** *18-*, *N*; **fole &c** *la14-17*, **fool &c** *17-*, **feul** *20-*, *Ork* [føl, fɪl; *N* fil; *nEC* fel] *n* = fool *la14-.*
adj foolish, silly *la14-, now Sh-C.*
~-**like** foolish *19-, C.*

fuilitch &c *19-, now Abd Ags,* **fulage &c** *16-, la19-e20* ['følɪtʃ, -ɪdʒ, *&c*] *adj* foolish. [only Sc; var of Eng *foolish*, perh w infl f F *folage*]
fuillie *see* FULYIE
fuilteach &c ['fʌ(l)təx *&c*] *n, chf in pl, in contexts describing weather* a period at least partly in February, of varying date and duration *19-, now Abd.* [Gael *faoilteach* the last fortnight of winter and the first of summer, *usu* a period of stormy weather]
fuilzie *see* FULYIE
fuird &c *la15-*, **furd &c** *13-e17*, **feerd** *19-e20, Abd*; **ford &c** *12-*, **foord &c** *la16-*, *N* [førd, *C* ferd; *Cai-Abd* f(j)urd; *Abd also* fird] *n* (*la14-, in place-names 12-*), *vt* (*18-*) = ford.
fuirday &c ['for'de; *'før'de] *n, chf* ~**s 1** late in the day *e16, e19.* **2** broad daylight *18-e19.* **3** the earlier part of the day, the morning *19-, now Gall Dmf.* [*cf* ME *forth dayes*]
Fuirsday &c *la16-, now local Sh-Ayr*, **Furisday** *la14-e17*; **Forsday** *la16, 19-e20*, **Feersday &c** *20-, NE* [*Sh Ags C* 'førzdɪ, *C also* 'ferz-; *Cai* 'fjurz; *NE* 'firz-; *Gall Dmf* *'forz-] *n* = Thursday *only Sc.*
fuish, fuishen *see* FESH
fuist *see* FOOST
fuit *see* FIT[1]
fulage *see* FUILITCH
fule *see* FOUL, FUIL
full *see* FOU
fullely &c [*'fʌlɪlɪ] *adv* fully *la14-16.* [nME *fulli*, f *fully* (adj)]
fulmar ['fulmər] *n* a bird of the petrel species, *orig* breeding in St Kilda but now more widespread *la17-.* [orig Sc; Gael *fulmaire*; ON *fúll* foul + *már* gull, because of its offensive smell]
fulmart *see* FOUMART
fulth *see* FOUTH
fulyie &c *la15-e18*, **foolzie &c** *e18*, **fulʒe &c** *la15-e17*; **foylʒe &c** *la14, 17*, **fulye** *la15-e16*, **fulʒie &c** *16-17*, **fuillie &c** *la16-e17*, **fu(i)lzie** *18-e20* [*'ful(j)ɪ, *'føl(j)ɪ] *n* filth, dirt, garbage; dung, excrement *la14-e20.*
vt **1** trample underfoot, beat down, overcome *la15-e18.* **2** defile, pollute *16.* [see SND]
fulʒe *see* FOILZIE, FULYIE
fulʒie, fulzie *see* FULYIE
fum[1] *n* **1** a wet or spongy PEAT[1] or turf *la19-, now Dmf.* **2** a useless person; a big, fat, dirty woman *la19-e20, Ayr.* [obscure]
fum[2] *n* a disagreeable smell *la19-, midLoth Dmf.* [uncertain]
fummle &c, fummill &c *16* *vti* = fumble *16-.*
n a fumbling; work badly or hurriedly done *la18-.*
fummle *see* WHUMMLE
fumper *see* WHIMPER
fun *see* FIND, WHIN[1], WHIN[2]
funabe(is) *see* FOO
fund *see* FIND, FOUND[2]

fundatour &c [*'fʌndətur] *n* a founder *la15-17*.
[L *fundator*; *cf* ME *foundatoure &c*]
fundeit *see* FUNDY
funder *see* FOUNDER
fundin *see* FIND
fundit *see* FUNDY
fundlin &c *18-19*, **fundling &c** *la14-e18*;
fundline *la17-e18* ['fʌn(d)lın] *n* = foundling.
fundy &c *la14-18*; **funnie &c** *18-e19* *vi* suffer a
chill, become stiff with cold *la14-18*.
  fundyit, fund(e)it &c chilled; sensitive to cold
la16-e19. [eModEng *fundied*, ME *founded*; f OF
(en)fondre]
funeral &c; fooneral *la19-e20*, S [*St* 'fjunərəl,
S 'fun-; *'føn-, *-al] *n*, *adj* = funeral *la15-*.
  ~ **cairn** a cairn to mark resting places for the
bearers on the way to the graveyard *19-*, *Highl*.
  ~ **letter** an invitation by letter to a funeral
la19-, *local Ork-Kcb*.
fung; funk *v* **1** *only* **funk**, *vi*, *esp of a restive horse*
kick, throw up the legs *18-*, *now NE Ags Fif*. **2**
vt throw violently and abruptly, toss, fling
19-e20. **3** strike with the hands or feet *la19-*,
now NE. **4** *only* **fung**, *vi* fly up or along at high
speed and with a buzzing noise, whizz *19-e20*.
5 fly into a temper or rage, sulk *la19-*, *NE*.
  n **1** a blow from the hand or foot, a cuff, a kick
la18-, *now NE Fif Wgt*. **2** a throw, toss *19-e20*.
3 a whizzing noise, *eg* of a bird's wings *19-e20*.
4 a bad temper, huff, tantrum *19-*, *now local Sh-
Kcb*. **5** a state of excitement; a state of enthusiasm, commotion *la19-*.
  adv forcibly, violently; with a whizzing movement *la18-*, *Bnf Abd*.
  funker an animal that kicks *19-e20*. ~**ie &c**
apt to take offence, huffy *la19*.
  like fung &c violently, vehemently *la19-e20*.
  lat fung let fly *20-*, *Bnf Abd*. [onomat]
fungible ['fʌndʒıbl] *n*, *chf in pl*, *law* consumable
goods; perishable goods which may be esti-
mated by weight, number or measure *la18-*.
[only Sc; Roman Law *res fungibiles*]
funk *see* FUNG
funnie *see* FUNDY
funny &c *adj* = funny.
  n a game, *usu* of marbles, played for fun, where
no score is kept and all winnings are restored to
the loser *la19-*.
funseless &c *adj*, *of fodder*, *wood etc* dry and sap-
less *20-*, *Cai*. [uncertain]
funtain &c *la19-*, *now Abd*, **funtane** *e17*,
fontane &c *la15-e17* ['fʌntən, *-en] *n* =
fountain.
funʒe¹ &c *la14-e16*; **fonʒe &c** *la15* [*'fʌnjı] *n*,
in pl = foins, the fur of the beech-marten, *only
Sc*.
funʒe² &c [*fʌnjı] *vi* = foin, fence, make thrusts
la14-15, *only Sc*.
fup *see* WHIP
fupperty jig &c *n* a trick, dodge *19-*, *chf Abd*.
fur *see* FOR, FURR

furch &c [*fʌrtʃ] *n* = fourch, fouch, the hindquarters of a deer *16-17*, *only Sc*.
furd *see* FUIRD
furder *see* FORDER
fure &c [*før] *vt* **1** carry, convey, *chf* by sea
la14-e17. **2** bring, carry, bear *la15-16*.
  furing &c [*'førın &c] **1** transporting by sea
la15-e17. **2** the cargo of a vessel *16-e17*. **3** the
amount of cargo allowed to a mariner for his
own business use *e17*. [only Sc; LowGer *fören*,
Ger *führen*, Du *voeren*]
fure *see* FARE, FURR
furious &c, feerious *19-e20*, *NE* [*NE* 'fırıəs;
*førıəs] *adj* **1** = furious *la15-*. **2** *law*, *of persons*
mad, insane, *esp* violently *la15-19*. **3** *only* **feerious** extraordinarily good, excellent *la19-20*,
NE.
  adv, *only* **feerious** exceedingly, very *19-20*, *NE*.
  furiosity &c *16-19*, **furiosité** *la15*, *law* madness, insanity. [*cf* FURY]
Furisday *see* FUIRSDAY
furisine *see* FLEERISH
furl *n* **1** = ferrule *la20-*, *NE*. **2** the tin or wire tip
of a bootlace *la20-*, *NE*.
furl *see* WHIRL
furlet *see* FIRLOT
furlie &c *NE*, *in combs*, *eg* ~-**fa** *la19-e20* [~ 'fɑ],
~-**majigger** *20-* [~ mə'dʒıgər] **1** a whirligig
la19-e20; **2** a cheap showy ornament *la19-*; **3** a
piece of machinery or equipment, *esp* one that
revolves or has wheels *20-*. [only Sc; see SND]
furlot *see* FIRLOT
furm *18-*, *now Lnk Abd Fif*, **furme** *la14-17*,
firm &c *16-*, *now Sh Ork Per n* (*la14-*), *vt* (*e15*)
= form.
furnas *see* FORNACE
furnis &c; furnes &c, furneis &c [*'fʌrnıs,
&c] *vt* = furnish *la15-e17*, *only Sc*.
furr &c, fur, fure &c *15-e17*, *e20*, *Cai* [fʌr;
*før] *n* **1** a furrow made by the plough; the
strip of earth turned over in the process *15-*. **2**
the deep furrow or trench separating one RIG¹
from another *la18-*, *now Sh*. **3** a deep furrow or
rut cut by the plough to act as a drain for surface water *18-*, *now Sh Ork Arg*. **4** the act of
furrowing, a ploughing; a turn-over with a
spade *18-*, *now Ork NE*.
  vt **1** plough, mark or make furrows in *la18-*, *now
NE Dmf*. **2** make drills in or for, draw soil
around (plants) so as to form a ridge, earth **up**
18-, *Sh-nEC*, *SW*.
  ~-**ahin** *la18-20*, *WC*, ~-**beast** *19-*, *NE Ags WC
Dmf*, ~-**horse** *19-*, *local* the horse in a team
immediately in front of the plough on the right-
hand side.
  one ~ **ley** grassland after its first ploughing-up
18-, *now WC*. [eModEng *feure*, *fore*; OE *furh*; *cf*
FURROW]
furriour *see* FURROUR
furrit *see* FORRIT
furrour &c; furriour &c *n* a furrier *la15-16*.
[ME *furour*, *forrour*; OF *forrour*]

furrow *n* **1** = furrow. **2** the earth turned over in a furrow by the plough *la18-*. [*cf* FURR]

furrow *see* FORRAY

furth &c; foorth &c *la16-17*, **forth** *la18-*, **furt** *la19-*, *Sh* [fʌrθ; *Sh* fʌrt] *adv* **1** = forth *la14-*. **2** outside, out of doors, in(to) the open air *18-*, *now Sh NE Ags*.

prep out of, from, outside *18-*, *now local Sh-Wgt*. *n* the out-of-doors, the open air *la19-*, *now NE Ags*.

furthie &c, forthy &c, frothy *la19-*, *Bnf Abd* **1** forward in disposition, bold; go-ahead, energetic; impulsive *15-16, 19-*, *now Abd*. **2** frank, friendly, affable *18-19*. **3** generous, hospitable, liberal *18-*, *now Fif*.

furth bering &c carrying out, discharging *e16*. **~coming &c** *n* **1** = forthcoming *15-*. **2** *law*, *freq* **action** *etc* **of furth-coming** an action which the *arrester* of property must bring against the *arrestee* (ARREIST) in order to make the *arrested* property available *la17-*. **~fill &c** fulfil *la16-e17*. **~ganging &c** *n* outgoing *e16*. **furthgif** give out; pronounce (a decision) *la15-16*. **~going &c** the feast given at a bride's departure from her parents' home, a wedding entertainment *19-e20*. **furthputting &c** **1** exercising (of authority etc) *la15-e16*. **2** eviction from a place *la15-e16*. **furthrin &c** run out, elapse, expire *16*. **furthseik** seek or search out *la16*. **furthschaw &c** show forth, display, exhibit *la14-16*. **furthset** set or put forth or forward *la16*. **furthȝet** pour forth *e16*. **furth the gait &c** *adj*, *adv* candid(ly), honest(ly), straightforward(ly) *la19-*, *now NE*. **furth of 1** out of, away from, beyond the confines or limits of *la15-*, *now law, literary and NE*. **2** out of the revenues of, at the expense of *la17-e19*. **furth of Scotland** outside Scotland *19-*. **the furth** out of doors, in the open, away from home *19-*, *now Abd*.

further *see* FORDER

furthwart *see* FORDWARD[1]

fury &c [*'førɪ] *n* **1** = fury *16-*. **2** *law* violent insanity *17*. [*cf* FURIOUS]

fush *see* FISH

fushach *see* FUSSOCH

fushen *see* FESH

fushion &c *la19-*, **fusioun &c** *la15-17*, **foisoun &c** *la14-18*; **fusoun &c** *la14-15*, **fusion &c** *la14*, **fooshion &c** *e20* ['fuȝən, 'fuʃən, 'fʌʃən; *C, S also* 'føʃən &c] *n* **1** = foison, plenty etc *la14-16*. **2** the nourishing or sustaining element in food or drink *17-*, *now NE Per*. **3** physical strength, energy; bodily sensation, power of feeling *18-*, *now NE*. **4** mental or spiritual force or energy; strength of character, power *18-*, *now NE*. **~less 1** *of plants etc* without sap or pith, dried, withered *19-*, *now local Sh-Arg*. **2** *of food* lacking in nourishment, tasteless, insipid *19-*, *local Sh-C*. **3** *of actions, speech, writing etc* without substance, dull, uninspired *19-*, *now Abd C*. **4** *of persons* (1)

physically weak, without energy *18-*; (2) numb, without feeling *la18-*, *NE*. **5** *of things* without strength or durability; weak from decay *19-*. **6** *of persons etc, and their moral or mental qualities* spiritless, faint-hearted, lacking vigour or ability *19-*.

fushloch, fushnach *see* FUSSOCH

fusion, fusioun *see* FUSHION

fusker *n* a whisker, a moustache *la18-*, *NE*.

fuskie *see* WHISKY

fusome *see* FOUSOME

fusomever *see* FOO

fusoun *see* FUSHION

fussle *see* FISSLE, WHISTLE

fussoch &c *19-*, *now Bnf*; **fushloch** *19*, **fushnach** *la20-*, *Gall*, **fushach &c** *20-*, *now Abd* [*NE* 'fʌsəx, 'fʌʃəx, 'fuʃəx; *SW* 'fʌʃləx, -nəx] *n* **1** the grass that grows in stubble; waste fragments of straw, grass etc *19-*, *now Gall*. **2** a loose, untidy bundle of something *la19-*, *now Bnf Abd*. [dim of Eng *fuss*, *fuzz* loose fluffy matter]

fussy &c *adj* **1** = fussy. **2** affected in dress or manner, dressy, foppish *20-*, *Abd Ags Fif Rox*.

fustian &c; fustean &c *la15-e19*, *only Sc n* = fustian *la14-*.

~ scone &c *16-e19*, **foustie &c** *20-*, *Ags Per* ['fustɪ, 'fʌustɪ] [perh a conflation w *foosty* (FOOST)] a kind of large thick bread roll, now white and floury but *orig* containing oatmeal, so-called from its coarse texture and *perh* also its colour.

fute *see* FIT[1]

futher &c *15-19*, **fudder &c** *la15-e17*, **fidder &c** *16-17*, *only Sc* [*'fʌðər, *'fʌdər, *'fø-, *'fɪ-] *n* **1** = fother, a cart-load; a quantity of lead *15-17*. **2** a large number of people, a company *16-e17*.

peat-futherer a person who carries PEAT[1] for door-to-door sale *19*, *Mry*.

futher *see* WHIDDER

futie *see* FOUTIE

futley *see* WHITTLE[2]

futrat *see* WHITRAT

futtle *see* WHITTLE[1]

fuzzie &c *adj* effervescent, hissing, fizzing *19-*, *now Abd*. [onomat; var of Eng *fizzy*; *cf* FISS]

fy &c [faɪ] *interj* **1** = fie *15-e17*. **2** inciting a person to hurry *la17-19*. **3** *with emphatic force, esp* **~ ay** *or* **na** yes *or* no indeed!, certainly (not)! *la19-*, *NE Ags*.

fy *see* WHEY

fyachle *see* FAUCHLE

fyall &c [*'faɪəl] *n* a finial *16-e17*. [only Sc; OF *fyole &c*]

fyift *see* FIFT

fyke &c, feik &c *18-19*, **fyk &c** *16*, *e20* (*Sh*) [fəik; *Sh* fɪk, fɛk] *v* **1** *vi* (1) move about restlessly, fidget *16-*, *local Sh-SW*. (2) *fig* fret, be anxious or troubled *19-*, *now midLoth*. **2** *vt* cause pain or bother to, trouble, vex *la16-19*. **3** *vi* exert oneself, work laboriously, take trouble or pains (**with**) *18-, now local Cai-Stlg.* **4** bustle about in a trifling way, fiddle, make a fuss about nothing very much *la18-, local N-S.*

n **1** a restless movement, a twitch; *chf in pl* the itch, the fidgets, a fit of restlessness *la16-, now Cai midLoth.* **2** restlessness, a state or mood of uneasiness *la18-e20.* **3** a fuss, bustle, commotion, excitement *18-, now Ags Fif Stlg.* **4** (1) trouble, bother, worry; *in pl* petty cares *la18-e20.* (2) an intricate and (*usu*) trivial piece of work, a trifle *19-e20.* **5** a whim, a fussy fad *18-, now local EC.* **6** a fussy, fastidious person, a person who makes a fuss over trifles *20-, EC, WC, S.*

fykerie &c fuss, fastidiousness over trifles *19-, now Sh WC.* **fykie &c** **1** *of persons* (1) restless, fidgety *19-, now local NE-S*; (2) fussy, fastidious over trifles, finicky *19-.* **2** *of a task etc* tricky, troublesome, intricate and difficult to manage *19, now local.*

haud &c or **hae a fyke** flirt, have an affair *la18-e20.* **mak a fyke** make a fuss (**about**) *la18-e20.* [*chf* Sc; ON *fikjast* (*v*) be eager or restless]

fyke-fack &c *la18-e20 n, pl also* **ficks facks &c** *la16-18* **1** *chf in pl* trifling and troublesome affairs, finicky details, trifles *la16-e20.* **2** *in pl a* trivial fuss *la18-e20.* **3** a whim, a contrary or freakish mood *e19.* [only Sc; *orig* reduplicated vars of FYKE; *cf* also Du *fikfak* unnecessary fuss]

fyle &c *v* **1** *vt* = file, defame *la14-16.* **2** make dirty, soil, defile *15-, Gen except Sh.* **3** (1) soil with excrement *15-, Gen except Sh.* (2) *vi* defecate *16-, now NE Per Slk.* **4** *vt* pollute, make impure; infect *la14-e17.* **5** let (land) become overgrown with weeds *15-e16.* **6** defile morally, debauch, desecrate *la14-, now local NE-Lnk.* **7** taint through wrongdoing *16.* **8** find guilty, convict, blame *la15-18.*

~ **a bill** find the charge made in a bill justified and the accused guilty *la16.* ~ **one's fingers** *etc* **wi** have to do with, meddle with (something debasing) *la18-, now NE Ags Lnk.* ~ **the** or **one's stamach** upset the stomach, make one sick *19-, now NE-WC Rox.*

fyllies *see* WHILES
fyow *see* FEW[1]
fyrne *see* FIR

G

g' *see* GAE

ga &c *la18-*, **gall** &c *la14-*; **gaw** &c *16-* [gɑ] *n* = gall, bile etc *la14-*.

ga *see* GAE

gaady &c *16-e18*, **gaudé** &c *e16* [*'gɑdɪ] *n* one of the larger beads on a rosary; a bead. [laME *gaudy, gawdie*, MedL *gaudia*]

gaain, gaan *see* GAE

gaave *n*, *gipsy* a large village *e20, SW-S*. [Romany *gav* a village]

gab[1] &c *n* **1** speech, conversation; manner of speaking *la18-*. **2** *specif* light, entertaining talk, chat, cheek *la18-*. **3** a talkative person, chatterbox, gossip *19-*, *local Mry-Ayr*. *vi* talk, *esp* idly or volubly *18-*.
gabbie &c garrulous, chatty; fluent *18-, Gen except Sh Ork*. **gabbit** &c talkative, gossipy *18-*, *now Sh Kcb Rox*. [prob onomat]

gab[2] *n* **1** = GOB[1] 1, *18-*. **2** the palate, taste *18-19*.
-gabbit &c -mouthed; *specif* **fine-** or **nice-gabbit** fastidious, fussy about food *la19-*, *now Ags Fif*.
~-gash petulant or voluble chatter *la19-*, *now Inv*. **~-stick** a (wooden) spoon *19-e20*.
haud *or* **steek one's ~** hold one's tongue, shut up *la18-*. **set up one's ~** speak out boldly or impertinently *19-*, *local Cai-Rox*. **thraw one's ~** grimace, *eg* because of discontent or annoyance *la18-*, *now Mry Abd*.

gab[3]; **gob** *20-*, *chf Cai n* **the ~ o May** *etc* stormy weather at the beginning of May *la19-, N Kcb*. [prob f GAB[2]; *cf* SAB[1] 2]

gabar *see* GABBART

gabart &c, **gabbert** &c [*'gabərt, *'ga-] *n* = gaberdine *la15-16*.

gabbart &c *18-e20*, **gabar** *la16*, **gabert** &c *la17-19 n* a lighter, barge *chf WC*. [eModEng *gaber*, F *gabarre*]

gabber &c *vti* jabber, gibber *19-e20*. [prob onomat, but perh f GAB[1]]

gabbert *see* GABART

gabbit &c; **gabbart** &c *n* = gobbet *la18-e20*.

gaberlunzie &c *18-e20*, **gaberlungy** *17* [gabər'lʌnzı; *-'lʌnjı, *-'lønjı; *WC* *-'lunı, *-'lɪnzı] *n* a beggar, tramp, *freq* **~ man**. [obscure]

gabert *see* GABBART

gaberts &c *n pl* scaffolding *la19-*. [prob f CABER]

gable-endie &c *n* nickname for **1** an inhabitant of Montrose *la19-, Ags*; **2** *in pl*, *football* the Montrose football team *la19-*. [because small plots of land leased in the town necessitated building houses with gable-ends facing the street]

gad &c *interj* expressing disgust *la19-, Gen except S*. [altered f Eng *God*]

gad *see* GAUD[2]

gadder *see* GAITHER

gade &c *n* **1** a bar or rod of iron or steel *15-17*. **2** an iron bar with rings to which prisoners' shackles were attached, *chf* **the lang ~** *la16-17*. [only Sc; OE *gād* a goad, used in the same sense as GAUD[2]]

gade *see* GAUD

gader(ing) *see* GAITHER

gadge *vi* talk haughtily without justification *e18*.

gadge *see* GAUGE

gadger *n* a sponger *la19-*, *chf NE*. [f CADGE[1]]

gadgie &c *n* a man, fellow: **1** *in gen*, *e20*, *chf S*; **2** *now child's word*, *la20-*, *Edb*. [Romany *gadgi* a man, *chf* a non-gipsy]

gadloup,   gateloupe,   goad-loup [*'gad'lʌup, *'ged-, *'god-] *n*: **loup** *etc* **the ~** run the gauntlet *la17-e18*. [Sw *gatlopp*; *cf* eModEng *gant(e)lope*]

gae &c, **ga** *la14-16*, **go** &c *la15-* [ge] *v, pres and infin unstressed* **g'**. *pt also* **gaed** &c *la16-*, **geed** &c *18-e20*, *chf Ork N*, **gied** *19-e20*, *N-C*; **ʒeid** &c *la14-18*, **ʒude** &c *la14-e19* [f OE *ēode*] [ge(:)d; *Sh* g(j)ød; *Cai Ross Mry* gi(:)d; *NE* gɪd; *jid; *jød]. *presp also* **gaun** *18-*, **ga(a)n**, **gaain** *20-*, **gyaa(i)n, gya(u)n** *20-*, *Sh NE*, **gaein** *20-*, *local*, **dya(u)n** *e20, N* [gɑn; 'geən; *Sh Ork N also* gjɑn; *Sh NE also* 'dja(ə)n, *Abd also* 'dʒɑ-; *C also* gɪn; *SW also* 'gɑən]; combined with 'to' **gaunie** &c, **gennay** = going to *20-*, *local* ['gɑnı, 'gɪnı, &c]. *ptp also* **gane** &c *la14-*, **gein** *la16*, **geen** *20-*, *Sh N* [gen; *Sh N* gɪn] **1** *vi* = go *la14-*. **2** *vt* cover on foot *la18-*, *local Abd-Rox*. **3** *vi, of animals* graze *19-*, *now NE*. **4** *with infin expressing* movement to fulfil the purpose of the other verb *la18-19*: 'I maun gae ride.'
n, only **go 1** = go. **2** a fuss, bother; a state of anxiety, distress or excitement, *freq* **in a ~** *la19-*, *now Sh-nEC*.
gane &c **1** (1) *placed before its noun* past, ago *18-*: 'Sunday gane a week'. (2) *specif* **nae farrar gane (than)** as recently (as) *la18-*. **2** *placed before or after the number it qualifies* over, more than (a certain age) *la19-*: 'he's but eighteen gane', 'she's gane forty-twa'. **3** mad, crazy *20-*. **gaun** &c **1** brisk, active, busy *18-e19*. **2** *of a child* at the walking stage *18-*, *now Sh Ork*. **3** *also* **gaunaboot**, *of a tramp etc* vagrant, wandering, *freq* **gaun(-aboot) bodie** *la19-, local*. **gaun gear 1** the machinery of a mill *la18-*; *cf ganging graith* (GANG). **2** applied to persons in declining health, *esp* those about to die *19-e20, NE, SW*. **3** money or property that is being wasted *la19-, Abd Ags Wgt*.
~ aboot *of a disease or complaint* be prevalent *20-*, *local Sh-Ayr*. **~ about the bush** approach in a roundabout or tactful way *19-*, *local Ags-Uls*. **~ awa 1** die *19-*, *Ork NE, S*. **2** faint, swoon *la19-, Ags Fif SW*. **3** *imperative* expressing impatience, incredulity or derision *19-*: 'g'wa wi ye'. **~ back** deteriorate, run down, fall off *18-*, *Ork C-S*. **go-between** a

between-maid *la19-20*. ~ **by the** *or* **some-one's door** pass someone's house without calling in, shun *la18-*. ~ **done** be used up or worn out, come to an end *la19-*, *Gen except Sh Ork*. ~ **fae &c** stop, abstain from, lose the taste for *la19-*, *NE Renfr*. ~ **in 1** *of a church, school etc* assemble *19-*. **2** shrink, contract *19-*, *Sh Abd WC*. **3** *impersonal* = go on, approach (a point of time) *18-e19*: '*it's gaein in twa years noo*'. ~ **in twa** break in two, snap *19-*, *now NE*. ~ **in wi** agree with *la19-*, *local Sh-Dmf*. ~ **into** open and search (a bag, drawer etc) *la19-*, *local Abd-Rox*. ~ **lie** retire to bed *18-*, *SW*. ~ **on** make a fuss, talk at length in a badgering or quarrelsome way *la19-*, *local*. **go o the year** the latter part of the year *19*. ~ **ower** be beyond a person's power or control; get the better of (someone) *19-*, *local Sh-Fif*. ~ **tae** *vi* shut, close *la19-*, *Sh Abd SW*. ~ **thegither &c 1** come together, unite, close *la19-*, *local*. **2** (1) get married *la18-19*, *local*. (2) *of lovers* court *la19-*. ~ **through 1** waste, squander, *esp* ~ **through't** become bankrupt, penniless *19-*. **2** bungle, muddle (speech, a discourse) *19-*, *chf N*. ~ **through the fluir, grund** *etc* be overcome with shame, embarrassment, astonishment *19-*. ~ **through ither** make a mess of things *la19-*, *NE-Fif*. ~ **wi 1** keep company with, court (a lover) *19-*. **2** go pleasantly or smoothly for *la18-*, *now NE Per*. **upon go** *of persons, things* restlessly active; much in use *19-*, *now Sh Abd*. [*cf* GAN, GANG]

gae *see* GIE

gaebie *see* GEBBIE

gaein *see* GAE

Gael [gel] *n* a *Highlander* 1 (HIELAND), a GAELIC-speaker *la18-*. [Gael *Gaidheal*]

Gaelic &c *18-*, **Galeig** *e16*, **Gathelik &c** *16*; **Gal(l)ic** *18* [the orig GAELIC pronunciation 'ga:lɪk was current in the *Lowlands* (LAWLAND) as well as the *Highlands* (HIELAND) until *la18*, appar often w vowel-length conformed to the regular *Lowland* Scots rule, as 'galɪk; thereafter 'gelɪk has supervened in the *Lowlands*, prob w infl f spelling and f GAEL, but there is now a growing tendency to revert to 'galɪk, or, often, with the *Highland* vowel-length, 'ga:lɪk, *esp* for *n* 1 and *adj*] *n* **1** *freq* **the** ~ the Celtic language of the *Highlands and Islands* (HIELAND) *16-*. **2** = (**Irish** *or* Manx) Gaelic. *adj* of the GAELIC-speaking *Highlanders* (HIE-LAND), their language etc; *loosely*, *Highland 18-*. [Gael *gàidhlig*; also MedL *Gathelicus*; *cf* ERSE, IRISH]

gaff &c, **gawfe &c** [gɑf, gaf; *Abd* g(j)ɑv] *n* a guffaw *16-e20*. *vi* **1** guffaw *18-e20*. **2** babble, chatter *19*, *chf S*. [onomat]

gaff *see* GIE

gaffaw &c *18-e20*, **guffaw &c** *19-* [gə'fɑ] *n* a guffaw, a hearty laugh *18-*.

vi laugh loudly and heartily or coarsely, guffaw *18-*. [earlier in Sc; onomat]

gage &c *n* **1** = gage, a pledge *15-*. **2** *in pl* wages *la16-e17*, *only Sc*.

gage *see* GAUGE

gaggle *vi* laugh, giggle, cackle *la19-e20*, *Edb eLoth*. [Eng *gaggle* (of geese) cackle]

gaibie *n* a stupid person *19-*, *S*. [colloq and dial Eng *gaby*]

gaiblick &c *n* an unfledged bird *19-20*, *S*. [f **gaib* = GAB² 1]

gaif *see* GIE

gaiflock *see* GAVELOCK

gaig &c [geg, gɛg; *Cai* gjɑg; *Kcb* gɑg] *n* **1** a crack, chink *19-*, *now Cai SW*. **2** a chap in the hands *19-*, *local Bnf-Dmf*. *v* **1** *vi* split, crack, from heat or dryness *la16-e19*. **2** *of the hands* chap *20-*, *Cai Kcb*. **3** *vt* cut, wound *la19-*, *Bnf*. [ScGael *gàg*, IrGael *gág* a cleft, chink; a chap, hack]

gaikit *see* GECK

gaillie &c *20-*, **galay &c** *la14-17*, **galé &c** *15-e17*; **gellie &c** *18-* ['gelɪ, 'gɛlɪ, *Sh* 'gjɛlɪ, 'dj-] *n* **1** = galley, the ship *la14-*. **2** a garret, *esp* in a BOTHY; a BOTHY *la19-*, *NE Ags*. **3** a dirty or untidy house *e20*, *Ags*.

gaily *see* GEY

gain &c *la15-18*, **gane** *la14-e19* *vi* **1** be fitting, suitable *la14-17*. **2** suffice, serve, last *18-e19*. *adj*, *only* ~**est 1** *of a way, road* most direct *la15-18*. **2** suitable, fit *e16*. [ON *gegna*]

gain-: gain-call &c [***'gen'kal &c*] revoke, withdraw *la15*. **gain-cuming &c** [***'gen'kʌmɪŋ] *n* = again-cuming (AGAIN) *la14-16*. **gain-geving &c** [***'gen'givɪŋ] *n* restoring, giving back *la14*, *only Sc*. **gainstand &c** [gen'stand *&c*] **1** *vt* withstand, oppose *15-e20*. **2** *vi* offer resistance, be opposed to *la15-16*. **nocht gainstandand** = nocht againstandand (AGAIN) *la15*. **gain-stander &c** an opponent, enemy *la15-19*. [nME; *cf* AGAIN]

gain(d)er *see* GANNER

gaing *see* GANG

gainhekling &c *e17*, **gamhekling** *n* ? a kind of yarn; the cloth made with it *la16-e17*: '*twelf scoir of gainʒekling being sacking claith*'. [uncertain]

gainin *adj* winning, winsome *18-*, *now Uls*. [Eng *gain* persuade]

gainshot *see* GIN³

gainʒe *see* GANʒE

gain-ʒeld &c [***gen'jild, ***'genjəl] *n* a return, recompense *16*. [only Sc; *cf* Dan *gengæld*]

gair¹ &c [ger; *Ork* 'gəir(o)] *n* **1** = gore, a triangular piece of cloth in a garment *la15-e20*. **2** *ballad* a triangular opening in a garment *la18-e19*. **3** (1) a strip or patch of green grass, *usu* on a hillside *la18-*, *chf SW-S*. (2) a patch of marshy ground in heather, *freq* **green** ~ *la19-e20*, *Ork S*. **4** a dirty streak or stain on clothes *19-*, *Fif Dnbt*.

~**it &c** striped *la16-e20*. ~**y &c** name for a

striped cow *la18-e19*. **~y bee** the black and yellow striped wild bee *19-*, *now Rox.* [nME *gare*, OE *gāra*, ON *geire*]

gair² &c *adj* **1** greedy, covetous *18-19*, *C*, *S*. **2** parsimonious, niggardly; thrifty, careful *la18-19*, *C*, *S*. [see SND]

gaircule &c; **gairguill** &c [*'ger(d)køl, *-gøl &c] *n* a jupon, a short outer skirt *la16-17*. [only Sc; OF *gardecul*]

gaird &c *16-*, **gard** &c *la15-16*; **guard** *18-* *n* **1** = guard *la15-*. **2** **the ~** (1) = *town guard* (TOUN) *la17-e19*. (2) the headquarters of the GAIRD (2 (1)); the lock-up *18*. **3** curling (CURL) a stone played so as to lie in front of and guard the TEE¹ or another stone *19-*.
vt **1** = guard *la16-*. **2** curling (CURL) protect (a stone lying on or near the TEE¹) by laying another in front of it *la18-*.
~ing &c a protective, *usu* brass mat or plate placed under dishes at table *16-e18*.
~ hous &c a building for the accommodation of a guard *la16-*.
brak (**aff**) **the** *or* **a ~** curling (CURL) strike away a GAIRD (*n* 3) *19-*, *chf SW*. **flee the ~s** curling fail to strike the GAIRD (*n* 3) *19-*.

gairden &c *la16-*, **gardin** &c *la15-* *n* = garden.
gairdner &c *la16-*, **gardener** &c *14-* ['gerdnǝr; *also* 'gernǝr] = gardener. **~er's ga(i)rtens** *or* **garters** the ribbon-grass *19-*.

gairdy *see* GARDY
gair-fowl &c *n* the great auk *la17-19*. [ON *geirfugl*]
gairguill *see* GAIRCULE
gairten, gairter *see* GARTEN
gairy &c *n* a vertical outcrop of rock, a crag *la19-e20*, *SW*. [prob ultimately f Gael *garbh* rough, rugged, stony]

gais *la16*, **gaw(i)s** &c *la16-17*, **gallis** *la16-e17*, **gaze** &c *la17* [*gɑz] *n* = gauze. [earlier in Sc; F *gaze*]
gais *see* GUESS
gaishon &c *n* a thin, emaciated person, a 'skeleton' *19-e20*, *chf SW*, *S*.
ill-gaishon'd mischievous, ill-disposed *19-*, *Fif.* [see SND]

gaisling &c; **gasling** &c *la16-e19* ['gezlɪn; *Bwk* 'gøzlǝn; *'giz-] *n* a gosling *16-*, *now local*. [ON *gæslingr*]

gaist *see* GUEST
gait¹ &c *15-*, **gate** &c *16-e18*, **goat** *18-*, **gote** &c *e16* *n* = goat *15-*, *in place-names 13-*.
gait buk &c a he-goat *la15-e17*. **gait hair** *la20-*, *now Ross Kcb*, **goat('s) hair** *la19-*, *Gen except Sh Ork* cirrus cloud. **~ whey** the whey of goat's milk used as a health drink *18-e19*.
gait² &c *17-20*; **gyte** &c *la19-e20*, *NE* [get; *NE* gǝit, *also* gwǝit, gɑt] *n* a single sheaf of grain tied near the top and set up to dry *17-e20*.
vt set up (sheaves) thus *la18-20*. [see SND, DOST]
gait *see* GET

gaither *la19-*, **gader** &c *la14-16*; **gadder** &c *la14-e17*, *la19-*, *now Sh*, **gether** *la19-*, **gedder** &c *e20*, *Abd*, **gather** *18-* ['geðǝr, 'gɛðǝr; *Sh also* 'gad-; *NE Kcdn Ags also* 'gɪð-, 'gɪd-] *v* **1** *vt* = gather *la14-*. **2** *vi* accumulate wealth, save *18-*, *now local Abd-WC*. **3** *vti* make a collection (of money contributions), collect (money) in subscriptions *la19-*, *local Abd-Uls*. **4** *vi*, *harvesting* bring together enough corn to form a sheaf *la19-*, *now Abd*. **5** *vt* plough so as to throw the soil into (a central ridge) *18-*. **6** *vi* recover one's faculties, collect one's wits, pull oneself together, rally *la18-*, *local Abd-Uls*. **7** *of butter* form, collect in the churn *la19-*. **8** *vti* prepare (a fire) for the night or a long period without attention, place a *gathering-coal* on the raked embers *la18-*, *now local Cai-Fif*.
~ed, **weel-~ed** rich, well-to-do *la19-*, *local NE-S.* **~er** a person who GAITHERS (*v* 4) *la18-e20*. **~in(g)** *n* **1** = gathering *la14-*. **2** *only* **gad(d)ering** &c an assembled group, a company of followers *la14-e16*. **3** *only* **gathering** a signal on drum or bagpipe to (fighting) men to assemble; a tune used for this purpose; one of the types of PIBROCH *17-*. **4** *only* **gathering**, *esp* Highland *or* Braemar *etc* **G~ing** = Highland *etc* Games (GAME *n* 2) *19-*. **gatherin(g) coal** *or* **peat¹** a large piece of coal or PEAT¹ laid on the embers to keep a fire alive over a long period without attention *19-*, *chf C.* **gathering note** Presbyterian Church a lengthened note sung at the beginning of the first and sometimes certain subsequent lines of a hymn or psalm *20-*, *chf C.* **gathering psalm** the psalm sung at the beginning of a church service *la19-*, *local.* **~it** *esp of clerical or administrative bodies* assembled *la14-16*. **gaddery**, **geddery** an accumulation, a miscellaneous collection *19-*, *chf Sh.* **~ dam** a dam which collects water from drainage and rainfall only *18-*, *NE.* **~-up** a motley collection *20-*, *local Cai-Uls.*

gaive &c *vi* move clumsily, aimlessly or restlessly *19-e20*, *chf S.* [perh voiced var of CAVE²]
galash *18-*, *now local N*, **gallash** &c *17* [gǝ'laʃ] *n* = galosh.
Galashiels &c [galǝ'ʃilz] *n* **~ grey** a coarse grey woollen cloth manufactured at Galashiels *18-19*, *chf S.* [the town in Slk]
galat &c ['galǝt] *n* term of endearment to a girl *20-*, *NE Arg.* [Gael *galad*]
Galatian &c; **Galoshan** &c [ga'laʃǝn, -'loʃǝn, go-] *n*, *only Sc* **1** *also in pl* a play performed by boy guisers (GUISE) at HOGMANAY; a mumming play or entertainment at this time *19-e20*, *C*, *S.* **2** the name of the hero in *n* 1, a mummer, harlequin *19-*, *now Ayr Rox.* [*cf* similar Eng plays, the principal characters being identified with various historical or legendary characters]
galay *see* GAILLIE
galcoit &c *n* a coat or jacket of some sort *e16*. [obscure]

gald *see* GAUD²
gale *see* GAVEL¹, GELL³, GELL⁴
galé *see* GAILLIE
Galeig, Galic *see* GAELIC
galing *see* GELL¹
gall &c [gɑl, gal] *n* = gale, sweet-gale, bog-myrtle *18-*, *now local Bnf-Gall.*
gall *see* GA, GAW
gallant¹ &c, galland *la15-17 adj* ['galənt, *-and] **1** = gallant *16-*. **2** large, ample *19-e20*. *n* = gallant *la15-*.
vi [ga'lant] gad about, gallivant; flirt *19-*, *only Sc.*
~**ish** *of women* flirtatious, ostentatious *la18-e19*, *only Sc.*
gallant² &c [*'galənt] *n* = galloon, a kind of ornamental ribbon *la16-e17*, *only Sc.*
gallash *see* GALASH
galleytrough *see* GELLYTROCH
galliard *see* GAL3EARD
Gallic *see* GAELIC
gallis *see* GAIS
gallivaster &c [*galɪ'vastər] *n* an idle, boastful person, a gadabout *e19*, *Abd*. [Eng *gallivant* + *-ster*]
gallon *n* **1** a gallon SCOTS = (approx) 3 Imperial gallons *15-e19*. **2** = gallon.
gallop *vi* = gallop.
~**er** a five-shilling piece with a design of St George on horseback *la19-20*, *NE*. ~**in Tam** a much used sermon, *esp* one preached in several places by a candidate for a church *19-20*.
gallous *see* GALLOWS
Gallovidian &c *adj* of Galloway; *also n* a native of Galloway *17-*. [MedL *Gallovidia*, f Welsh *Gallgwyddel* foreign Gaels]
gallow- *see* GALLOWS
Galloway ['galowe] *n* **1** = Galloway, a small sturdy type of horse *18-*. **2** a breed of hornless cattle, *usu* black *la18-*.
~ **dyke** a *whinstone* (WHIN¹) wall, the lower part of *dry-stane* (DRY) construction topped by a thin course of projecting flat stones, and the upper part a tapering construction of round stones, the whole *usu* being about five feet high *la18-e19*. ~ **white(s) &c** a type of woollen cloth *17-e18*.
belted ~ a breed of GALLOWAY cattle (*n* 2) with a broad white band round a black body *20-*. [the district in south-west Scotland]
gallowis *see* GALLOWS
gallows, gallowis &c *15-e17*; **gall(o)us &c** *15-e17*, *20-* ['galəs, -əz] *n* **1** = gallows (1) *in gen*, *15-*; (2) *also* **gallow- &c** *in combs*, *esp in place-names*, *13-*. **2** a device for suspending a pot over a fire *16-17*, *e20* (*Uls*).
adj **1** villainous, rascally *la18-*, *chf WC*. **2** *chf* **gall(o)us** wild, unmanageable, bold; impish, mischievous, cheeky *20-*, *local N-S*.
galluses &c ['galəsɪz] (*double pl*) **1** (1) trouser

braces *19-*. (2) *in sing* **gallus &c** *19-20*: (a) a single brace; (b) braces; (c) *attrib*: '*gallus button*'. **2** a yoke for carrying pails *e20*.
gallow-breid &c a gallows-bird *16-e17*.
gallyie &c *n* a roar, cry *19-e20*. [prob onomat; *cf* GOLLIE]
gallytrough *see* GELLYTROCH
galore &c; gillore &c *la18-e19* [gə'lor] *adv* = galore, in abundance *la18-*.
n plenty, superabundance *la18-*, *local Cai-Kcb*.
Galoshan *see* GALATIAN
galra(i)vitch *see* GILRAVAGE
galshach &c ['galʃəx] *n*, *chf in pl*, *NE* **1** sweets, titbits *la19-*. **2** trashy (*esp* sweet) food *19-*. **3** *fig* luxuries, treats *20-*. [obscure. SND *gulsoch*]
galt *see* GAUT
galtags [?'galtagz] *n pl* inflammation of the skin between the toes *20*, *Cai*. [perh f Eng *gall* a sore + dim *-ag*]
galya [*?gə'laɪe] *n* a safe-conduct *e16*. [only Sc; LowGer, Du, Dan *geleide* a conveyance, escort]
gal3eard &c; galliard &c [*'galjard, *-jart] *adj* **1** = galliard, gallant; lively *la15-e17*. **2** *of dress etc* spruce, gay, bright, gaudy *16-e17*, *only Sc.*
gam &c *n*, *chf in pl* **1** (large) teeth *la15-*, *now Mry Abd*. **2** the jaws *la15-e20*. [see SND]
gam *see* GAME
gamaleerie &c [gamə'lɪrɪ, -'rɪrɪ] *n* a foolish clumsy person *19-*, *now Fif*. [perh altered f GOMEREL]
gamashins *see* GRAMASHES
gambade *e19*, **gambat &c** *e16*, **gamo(u)nd &c** *16-17*; **gammald &c** *e16 n* a leap; a caper. [F *gambade*; *cf* eModEng *gambold &c*]
game &c *la15-*, **gam** *15-e19*, **gemm &c** *16-*, *now local*, **gem &c** *16-e19* [gɛm, gem; *gam] *n* **1** = game *la15-*. **2** *in pl*, *freq* **Highland Games** a meeting consisting of athletics, piping and dancing, held *orig* in the *Highland* (HIE-LAND) area *19-*; *cf gathering* 4 (GAITHER).
vi = game *15-*.
gamie &c *la19-*, *Gen except Sh Ork*, **gemmie &c** *e20* familiar name for a gamekeeper.
gam(m)ing &c *n* sport, sporting *15-e17*.
~**ster 1** = gamester *la16-*. **2** a player in a game *18-e19*.
~-**watcher** a gamekeeper *la19-*, *Abd Ags*.
make ~ joke *19-*, *now Abd WC*.
gamf, gamfle *see* GUMPH
gamhekling *see* GAINHEKLING
gamie *see* GAME
gammald *see* GAMBADE
gamming *see* GAME
gammon &c *n* a person's leg or thigh *18-19*. [northern OF *gambon* ham]
gamond, gamound *see* GAMBADE
gamp &c *v* **1** *vi* gape *18-e20*, *chf Rox*. **2** *vt* eat or drink greedily, devour *19-e20*, *Rox*. [prob onomat]

gampherd &c ['gamfərt, 'gɑm-, -fərd] *adj* bespangled, adorned *19-e20*, *chf Ayr.* [uncertain]

gamphrell *see* GUMPH

gamrel &c *n* a piece of wood used to separate the legs of a carcass to facilitate butchering *19-e20, SW, S.* [eModEng, ModEng dial *gambrel*, OF *gamberel*]

gamrel *see* CAMERAL

gamster *see* GAME

gan &c *18-*, **gane** *la14-16* [gɑn, gan; *gen] *vi*, *only in infin and pres* = go *la14-, C-S.*
~ on aboot make a fuss about *20-, Fif SW.* [nME *gan(e)*, infin of *ga* (GAE); latterly w infl f GANG or presp forms of GAE]

gan *see* GAE

gandiegow &c ['gandɪgʌu, -go] *n* a squall, heavy shower *e20, Sh Ags Bwk.* [see SND]

gandy; gannie &c *vi* talk in a blustering, boastful or pert way *19-e20, NE.* [prob chf onomat]

gane *n* an ugly face *16.* [only Sc; obscure]

gane *see* GAE, GAIN, GAN, GIN[2]

ganer *see* GANNER

gang &c, **dyang** *20-, Abd*, **ging** *la16, la19-20* (*NE*); **gaing** &c *la16-e17, e20* (*Sh*), **geng** *18-e20, Sh Inv*, **gyang** &c *la19-, NE* [gaŋ; *Sh* g(j)ɛn, g(j)iŋ; *Sh Ork NE also* gjaŋ; *NE also* g(j)ɪŋ; *Abd also* djaŋ, dʒaŋ, dʒɪŋ] *vi* = go *la14-.*
n **1** (1) a journey, trip (*esp* when carrying goods) *la16-, now Stlg Lnk.* (2) a load, the quantity that can be carried at one time, *esp* of water *la16-, now local Cai-Ayr.* **2** a range or stretch of pasturage, a pasture *16-, now local Cai-Ayr.* **3** a passage, thoroughfare *20-, now local Abd-S.* **4** the course or channel of a stream *la15.* **5** a gait, way of walking *19-, now Ayr Rox.* **6** a set or usual number (of articles), a related group (of objects going or functioning together, *esp* of horseshoes) *la16-18.* **7** of *persons* a family or CLAN *la16, S.* **8** a row: (1) *in gen*, but *esp* of decoration on a garment *la16-e18*; (2) *in knitting, plaiting or weaving*, *la18-, now Sh Ork Cai.* **9** a layer, *esp* of corn-sheaves in a cart or stack *la18-, now local Sh-Ayr.*
~er &c **1** a person who goes on foot *15-, now Ayr.* **2** a person who is going away *la16-e19.*
~ing body a beggar, vagrant *la19-, now Lnk Rox*; cf *gaun* 3 (GAE). **~ing geir** the working parts of a machine or implement *la16-17*; **~ing graith** the moving parts *usu* of a mill *la15-19*; cf *gaun gear* 1 (GAE) and *standing graith* (STAND). **~ing to** the setting (of the sun) *15-e17.* **gangrel(1)** &c ['gaŋ(ə)rəl; *NE also* 'gjaŋ-] **1** a toad *la15-16.* **2** a tramp, vagrant, vagabond *16-20, Gen except Sh Ork.* **3** a child just able to walk, a toddler *la18-, N, only Sc.* **a gutts an gangyls** ['g(j)aŋəlz] nothing but stomach and legs, fit for nothing but eating and walking *la19-e20, Bnf.*
~-about a hawker *20-, Ork Ayr.* **~ water 1** the water supplied by the normal flow of a

stream to a mill etc, without a dam *20-, NE.* **2** *fig* (enough money for) the bare necessities *la19-, NE.*
~ awa = *gae awa* 2 (GAE) *la18-, NE Ags Ayr.* **~ by oneself** go mad *la19-, now Abd.* **~ done** = *gae done* (GAE) *19-, now Abd.* **~ doon the house** go to the parlour of a farmhouse, where it is down a step *la19-, SW Uls.* **~ lie** = *gae lie* (GAE) *la19-, SW.* **~ one's ways** depart, take oneself off, go away *19-, now local Sh-nEC.* **~ oot amang folk** work as a charwoman, washerwoman etc in private houses *la19-, Ork Abd Ayr.* **~ ower** overcome, beat *la19-, now Ork NE.* **~ throw** &c = *gae through* 1 (GAE) *19-, now local Sh-Kcb.* **~ together** &c = *gae thegither* 2 (1) (GAE) *la18-, Sh Abd.* [*cf* GAE, GAN]

gange &c *NE* [gan(d)ʒ] *vi* **1** chatter, gossip *19-.* **2** talk insolently *19-e20.* **3** brag; exaggerate *la19-.* [var of GANSH]

gangyls, gangrel(l) *see* GANG

gangs &c *n pl* sheep-shears *e20, Cai.* [perh f GANG *n* 6]

ganner &c *15-*, **ganer** &c *15-19*; **gainer** &c *15-e20*, **gainder** &c *19-, now Rox* ['genər, 'ganər; *C* 'gendər, 'gandər] *n* = gander *15-, now local.*
vi wander aimlessly or foolishly about *19-, Abd S.*

gannie *see* GANDY

gansel &c *n* **1** *proverb or fig* garlic sauce served with goose *la15-e18.* **2** a disagreeable comment, a scolding, an insolent remark *18-e20.*
vt scold, upbraid *la19-e20.* [ME *gaunselle*, OF *ganse aillie* garlic sauce]

gansey &c *la19-, local*; **genzie** &c *20-* ['ganzɪ; 'gɛnzɪ] *n* = guernsey, a jersey, *esp* one worn by fishermen.

gansh &c; **gaunch** &c *18-19* [ganʃ; *Rox also* genʃ] *vti* **1** *of a dog, also fig* snatch (at), snap, snarl *18-20.* **2** *vi* stammer *19-, now Ayr.*
n a stupid, clumsy or stammering person *la19-e20, Uls.* [onomat; *cf* GANGE]

gant[1]; **gaunt** *la17-e20 vi* **1** yawn *la15-, Gen except Cai.* **2** stammer, stutter *20-, Cai.*
n a yawn, gape *la15-.* [*cf* ME *gane*, OE *gāian* (*v*) yawn]

gant[2] &c *n* the gannet *la19-, now Abd Fif.* [eModEng, perh f OF *gante*]

gantree &c; **gantry** *n* **1** (1) = gantry *16-.* (2) *in pl used as sing* **gantrees** &c *16-*, **gantrice** &c *19-, now Ags.* **2** *in a bar* a bottle stand *la20-, C.*

ganʒe &c *la15-e16*; **gainʒe** &c *15-16*, **genʒie** &c *16* [*genjɪ, *'gɛnjɪ] *n* an arrow or a bolt for a crossbow. [only Sc; ScGael *gàinne*, IrGael *gáinne*]

gapus *see* GAUP

gar[1] &c *19-, local Sh-Fif*, **gare** *15 n* filth, slime. [appar var of OSc, ME *gore* &c, OE *gor* slime, excrement; *cf* ModEng *gore* blood]

gar[2] &c, **ger** &c *14-16, la19-e20*; **gare** &c *15-*,

gere *la14-e16* [gar; *Ork NE nEC also* gɛr; *Abd Loth also* gɑr; *Fif also* gër] *vt, pt chf* **gart, gert 1** cause (something to be done) *14-16*: 'we have gart our sele to be appendit'. **2** give instructions, take steps (to do or make something) *la14-e19*, *latterly literary and ballad*: 'to gar mak beil fyris'; 'the Whig Captain garr'd set up a gallows'. **3** make (a person or thing do something) *la14-*: 'to gar him come'.

garrer &c *n* a senior boy at George Heriot's Hospital who made a younger boy his fag *19*, *Edb*. **garring law** the system of fagging etc (as in prec) at George Heriot's Hospital *la18-19*, *Edb*.

~ **someone** *etc* **grue** see GRUE[1]. **gar** (**someone**) **as gude** pay (someone) back, retaliate *la17-e19*. [nME *gere, ger*, ON *gera*]

garb *n* **1** = garb. **2** poor, thin cloth *20-*, *NE*. **3** a thin coating (of frost) *20-*, *SW*.

gard see GAIRD

gardenap &c *e16*, **gardenat &c** *n* = gairding (GAIRD) *la15-16*. [OF *gardenape*]

gardevine &c [*'gardə'vəin, *-'vɪn] *n* **1** a (large) wine or spirits bottle *la18-e20*. **2** a case or chest for holding wine bottles or decanters *la19*. [only Sc; F *garder* keep + *vin* wine]

gardin see GAIRDEN

gardy &c; gairdy *la16-17, e20 n* **1** the arm; *perh specif* the forearm *16-*, *now Abd*. **2** *in pl* the hands or fists, *esp* when raised to fight *la18-e20*. ~ **chair** an armchair *la18-e19*, *NE Dmf*. [see SND, DOST]

gardyloo &c [*'gardɪ'lu] *interj* a warning call that waste, dirty water etc was about to be poured into the street from an upper storey *la17-e19, chf Edb*. [F (*prenez*) *garde à l'eau!* or *gardez* (*vous de*) *l'eau!* beware of the water!]

gare see GAR[1], GAR[2]

garfa see GEEL

gargasis *n pl* knee-breeches *la16*. [only Sc; OF *gargaisse*]

garibaldi *n* **1** = garibaldi, the biscuit. **2** a kind of bun or SCONE *la19-20*.

garitour &c [*'garɪtur, *-ər] *n* a watchman on a tower or wall *15-e17*. [only Sc; OF *garite* a watch-tower]

garment &c; garmo(u)nd &c *la15-16, only Sc n* = garment *15-*. ~ **of clais** a suit of clothes *la16-e17, only Sc*.

garnach &c [*?gar'netʃ] *n* a wine from the eastern Pyrenees *la14-e15*. [only Sc; OF *garnache*]

garnale, garnel see GIRNEL

garnis &c *vt* = garnish *la15-e17*.

garray *n* commotion, disturbance *la15*. [nME, obscure]

garrer see GAR[2]

garron[1] &c *18-*, **garrein** *e17* ['garən, 'gɛr-; *Ork* 'gjɛr-; *Cai* 'kar-; *Abd also* 'gʌr-] *n* **1** a small sturdy type of horse, used *esp* for rough hill work *17-*. **2** an old, worn-out horse *19-e20, chf*

Cai Uls. **3** *transf* a strong, thickset man or sturdy boy *19-*, *NE*. [Sc and IrGael *gearran* a gelding, hack]

garron[2] &c, garroun &c *16-e17 n* a wooden beam *16-*, *now Ork Cai*. ~ **nail** a large nail or spike, *esp* as used in fixing the body of a cart to its axle *16-*, *now local Sh-Fif*; *cf cannon nail* (CANNON) and CARRON NAIL. [perh northern OF **garron*, var of F *jarron* a branch of a tree]

garse see GIRSE

garsum see GRASSUM

gart see GAR[2]

garten &c *la16-*, **gartane &c** *16-19*, **gartare &c** *la16*; **gairten &c** *la16-*, **gairter** *la16-e17*, **gerten &c** *16-e17, e20* (*Sh Ork*), **garter** *la19- n* **1** = garter *16-*. **2** a leaf of ribbon-grass *20-*, *Per Rox*. *vt* garter *la16-*.

ga(i)rtening *of a material* used for making garters *la16-e17*.

get (**gie** *or* **wear**) **the green** ~ *lit or fig* of an older sister or brother when a younger sibling marries first *la18-*, *local Abd-Fif*. [forms in *-n* are only Sc]

garth &c *n* **1** *orig* (*la15-16*) *only verse* an enclosure, yard, garden *la15-*, *now only as place-name esp of farms*. **2** a shallow part of a river or stretch of shingle used as a ford *la18-e20*, *NE*. [nME; ON *garðr* a yard, fence]

gartling see GREAT

garvie &c *la17-, now local Inv-Edb*; **garvock** *la18-19* ['garvɪ, -ək; *Rox also* 'gɛrvɪ] *n* the sprat. [only Sc; see SND]

gascon see GASKIN

gash[1] *adj, chf literary* pale, ghastly in appearance, grim, dismal *la18-e20*. [eModEng]

gash[2] *n* a protruding chin *e19*. *vti* gnash, bare (the teeth), snap *19*, *NE*. ~**le &c 1** *vt* distort *19-*, *NE*. **2** *vi* argue bitterly *19-e20, Ayr*. ~**-beard &c** *appar* having a long, protruding chin *17-e18*. ~**-gabbit &c 1** having a protruding lower jaw *19-*, *now Ags Lnk*. **2** *also* ~**-mou'd** *la19-*, *NE Fif* having a sagging, mis-shapen mouth *19-*, *now Ags*. [see SND]

gash[3] *n* prattle, talk; pert, impudent language *la18-*. *adj* talkative, loquacious *la17-20*. *vi* talk volubly, gossip, prattle *la18-e20*. ~**-gabbit** loquacious, glib *18-, chf Fif*. [see SND]

gash[4] *adj* **1** sagacious, shrewd *18-e20*. **2** well or neatly dressed, respectable, smart *la18-e20*. [see SND]

gash-gabbit see GASH[2], GASH[3]

gashly *adj* ghastly *20-, now Ags*. [prob conflation of GASH[1] w Eng *ghastly*]

gaskin &c *la15-19*, **gascon &c** *la14-16 n* a native of Gascony *la14-16*. ~ (**wyne**) a wine of Gascony *la15-e16*.

green ~ a variety of gooseberry *la18-19*. [OF *Gascon &c*; *cf* eModEng *gaskyn*, *gascon*]

gasling *see* GAISLING

gasoliery [gasə'lɪrɪ] *n* a gas chandelier *la19-20*, *EC*. [Eng *gasolier* + *-y*]

gast &c *n* a fright, *chf* (**put**) **in a** ~ *la17-e20*. *adj* frightened *la14-e16*. [ME *gast &c* frighten, OE *gǣstan* (*v*) torment]

gast *see* GHAIST, GUEST

gastrous &c *adj* horrifying, unearthly *19*, *Abd S*. [obs Eng *gaster* frighten + *-ous*]

gat &c *n* a hole in the ground; a navigable channel *16*. [only Sc; ON, OSax, LowGer, Du]

gat *see* GET

gate¹ &c, **get &c** *la14-e20*; **geit &c** *la16-e19* [get; *Sh also* gjɛt; *Cai Arg also* gɛt] *n* **1** a way, road, path *la14-*. **2** a street *15-*, *earlier (13-) and now chf in street-names*. **3** (1) *also fig* way, course, direction *la14-*. (2) = -where, *eg* **nae &c** ~ nowhere, **some** ~ somewhere *19-*, *local Ags-Rox*. **4** *chf* **one's** ~ the way one habitually or regularly takes *la14-e17*. **5** length of a way, distance *16-*, *now local Ags-Rox*. **6** a journey, trip *la17-*, *now Fif WC*. **7** *fig* (1) way, means, method of doing something; a knack *la14-*, *now local Sh-Dmf*. (2) = -how, rate, *eg* (**at**) **ony** *or* **that** ~ at any rate, at that rate, **nae** *or* **some** ~ in no way, somehow *la14-*. (3) a way of behaving, conduct, manner; *in pl* habits, manners *18-*, *now NE Ags*.

gating a drift or passage in a mine *e17*, *only Sc*.

~lins directly, straight; towards *la18-19*, *N, S*.

~ward(s) (**to**) on the road towards, in the direction of, straight to *la16-18*. **on** *or* **in** **~wart** on the way *e16*.

~ en(d) a neighbourhood, locality *19-*. ~ **farrin &c** presentable, comely *la19-e20*, *NE*.

gatesman a person who makes drifts or passages in a coal-mine *17-19*. ~ **penny** ? a levy or tax demanded from merchants and dealers on entering a market *16-e18*.

be at the ~ **again** be recovered from an illness *la19-*, *NE Uls*. **come the** ~ (**o**) come (to), turn up (at), put in an appearance (at) *la19-20*, *Abd SW*. **ga** *or* **gang one's** ~ **1** *lit* go on one's way *la14-*. **2** *chf* **gang one's ain** ~ follow one's own opinions etc *18-*. **gang to** (**the**) ~ go to wrack and ruin, be destroyed *la17-19*, *chf WC*. **gie** (**someone**) **his** (**ain**) ~ give someone his own way, allow him free rein *19-e20*. **haud &c the** *or* **one's** ~ **1** keep to the road or one's route, stick to the proper way *la14-*. **2** hold one's own (when ill); be in a good state of health or prosperity *la19-*, *now Abd*. **in the** ~ on the way, along the road *19-*, *now Abd*. **in someone's** ~ hampering, obstructing someone *la18-19*. **a mile** *etc* **o** ~ a distance of one mile etc *16-e19*; *cf* AGAIT. **out o someone's** *or* **the** ~ out of someone's or the way *la18-*, *now local*. **out the** ~ on one's way, along the road, up the road *16-20*. **tak the** ~ **1** set off *la18-20*. **2** run

away *19*, *NE Gsw*. **weel ti the** ~ at an advanced stage, well forward *20-*, *Rox*. [ME *gate &c*, ON *gata*]

gate² &c *n* = gate *la16-*.

~ **slap** an opening, gateway *la19-20*, *NE, SW*.

gate *see* GAIT¹, GET

gateloupe *see* GADLOUP

Gathelik *see* GAELIC

gather *see* GAITHER

gathering *see* GAITHER

gattin *see* GET

gaud¹ &c, **gade &c** *17* [*gɑd] *n* a trick, deceitful practice, prank *15-e19*. [ME *gaude*]

gaud² &c *16-*, **gad &c** *15-e20*, **gald** *16-e17* [gɑd, gad] *n* **1** a rod or bar of iron or steel *15-19*. **2** a goad *la17-e20*. **3** a wooden slat *approx* nine feet long used to direct the corn to the scythe or binder *20-*, *NE*. **4** a fishing-rod *la18-*, *now Pbls*.

~(**s**)**man** *la15-19*, **goad(s)man** *la17-e20* a person who drives oxen or horses with a goad *la15-19*. ~ **wand** = *n* **2**, *la14-e16*. [ME *gadd-*, *gad*, ON *gaddr* a goad, spike; *cf* GADE¹]

gaudé *see* GAADY

gaudeamus &c ['gʌudɪ'amʌs] *n* **1** name of a student song *20-* [from its opening word]. **2** a feast, merry-making, celebration *18-19*. [see SND]

gaudy &c *adj* **1** = gaudy. **2** gay, dashing *e19*, *local*.

gauge &c *e15*, *18-*, **gage** *la16-e20*; **gadge &c** *la16-e18* [gɑdʒ, gedʒ, *gadʒ] *n* **1** = gauge, a standard measure *la16-*. **2** *net-making* a template to regulate the mesh-size *20-*, *Sh Cai Kcb*. *vti* ascertain the contents of a cask; perform the duties of an exciseman *18-e19*.

gauger &c 1 = gauger *15-e17*. **2** an exciseman *18-*. [*cf* JEDGE]

gaun &c *n* the butter-bur *19*, *WC, SW*. [var of GOWAN]

gaun *see* GAE

gaunch *see* GANSH

gaunie *see* GAE

gaunt *see* GANT¹

gaup &c, **gowp &c** [gɑp, gʌup] *vi* **1** = gawp, stare open-mouthed *19-*, *local NE-SW Uls*. **2** devour *18-e20*.

n **1** *only* **gaup &c** a simpleton, fool, a person who gapes *19-*, *chf N, SW*. **2** a large mouthful, a gulp *19*, *WC*; *cf* GOWP². **3** *only* **gowp &c** a stare *la19*, *now Ags*.

gaupie &c = *n* **1**, *19-e20*. **gaupit &c** stupid, silly *la19-*, *Abd Ags Loth Uls*. **gawpus &c**, **gapus &c** ['gɑpʌs; *Cai also* 'gepəs] *n* a fool, a clumsy, stupid lout *19-*, *now local Ork-Edb*.

gowp-the-lift &c nickname for a person who carries his head high, or has a cast in the eye *19-e20*. [obs Eng *galp* gape, yawn; yelp; MDu *galpen* yelp, bark]

gaut &c *la18-*, *now Sh Ork local N*, **galt &c** *la15-e20* [gɑt; *galt] *n* a pig, *chf* a boar or hog. [ME *galte*]

gaval &c [*gəˈval, *-ˈval] *vi* revel, carouse *19*, *Ags Ayr*. [f CABAL]

gave *see* GIE

gavel[1] &c *16-*, **gavill** &c *la14-e19*, **gayll** &c *la14-15*; **gale** &c *18-e20*, *NE* [ˈgevl; *Cai also* givl; *NE also* gel; *Gall also* gəil; *NE also* *givl] *n* **1** = gable *la14-*. **2** the part corresponding to a gable in a structure other than a building *16-17*. **3** one of the side ropes of a herring-net *20-*, *Ork NE Fif*.

~ **end** = gable-end *la18-*. **like the** ~(**end**) **of a hoose** *of persons* very big and stout *20-*, *Abd Kcb*. [nME *gavill*, ON *gafl* > OF, Eng *gable*]

gavel[2] &c [*ʔˈgevl] *vi*, *of a door* stand wide open *e20*, *NE*. [see SND]

gavelock &c *16-*, **gavillok** &c *la15-17*, **gellock** &c *17-*, *SW*; **gaiflock** *la16-e17* [ˈgevlək; *Ork* ˈgavlo, ˈgablo; *SW Rox* ˈgelək, ˈgɛlək; *Dmf also* ˈgəilək; *Rox also* ˈgjulək] *n* **1** a crowbar, lever *la15-20*. **2** an earwig or other similar insect *19-*, *now Ork Cai, SW*. [ME *gavilok* &c, OE *gafeluc* javelin]

gavill *see* GAVEL[1]

gavillok *see* GAVELOCK

gaw &c *la16-*, *now local*, **gall** *16-* [ga; *gal] *n* **1** = gall, a sore etc *16-*. **2** *only* **gaw** a defect, blemish, mark, flaw *la18-*, *now Sh*. **3** *only* **gaw** *weaving* a gap in cloth where weft threads are missing, *eg* between the end of one piece and the beginning of the next *20-*, *local Ags-S*. **4** *mining* a narrow vein of igneous rock intersecting coal strata *la18-e20*. **5** a drainage furrow or channel *la16-*, *now Fif*. **6** a boggy patch of land *17-e19*.

vt **1** = gall, make sore, *chf* **gaw(e)d** &c *la16-e19*. **2** = gall, vex, irritate *18-*.

gaw fur(row) a furrow at an *end-rig* (EN) used for drainage *19-e20*; cf *n* 5.

a gaw in someone's back 1 a bad habit, a weak spot *18-e20*. **2** a grievance *19-e20*.

gaw *see* GA

gawfe *see* GAFF

gawis *see* GAIS

gawk &c *n* an awkward, clumsy person, a fool *la18-*.

vti **1** play the fool, behave foolishly, flirt *19-*, *now Ags*. **2** fool around, wander aimlessly, idle *la19-*, *now Ags Kcb*. **3** stare idly or vacantly *la19-*, *now Ayr Kcb*.

~**ie** &c = *n* (*18-*), *v* 1 (*la19-e20*). ~**it** stupid, clumsy *19-*. **gawkus** &c a fool *la20-*, *Ork Ags*. [see SND]

gawpus *see* GAUP

gaws *see* GAIS

gawsie &c [ˈgası] *adj* **1** *of persons or their appearance* plump, fresh-complexioned, jovial-looking; handsome, imposing *18-20*. **2** *of animals* handsome, in good condition *19-e20*. **3** *of things* large, ample; handsome, imposing, showy; pleasant *la18-e20*. [see SND]

gay *see* GEY

gayll *see* GAVEL[1]

gaze *see* GAIS

gazen *see* GIZZEN

ge *see* GIE

geach &c [*ʔgix] *n*, *thieves' slang* a thief; thieving *19-e20*.

geak *see* GECK

geal *see* JEEL

gean &c, **geine** &c *17* [gin] *n* the wild cherry, its fruit *17-*. [eModEng *guyne*, F *guigne*]

gear &c *la16-*, **gere** &c *la14-19*; **ger** *la14* [gir; *nEC also* ger; *Sh Ork* gjer] *n* **1** = gear *la14-*. **2** (1) possessions, property, goods, money, *freq* **goods** &c **and** ~ *la14-*. (2) livestock, cattle *la16-*. **3** (1) stuff, material *in gen*, *la18-*, *local Abd-Rox*. (2) worthless things, rubbish *19-*, *now local N*. **4** food, drink *la18-e20*. **5** *with negative* not an iota, not a jot *19*, *chf NE*.

vt **1** *only in ptp* provided with arms and armour *la15-16*. **2** *literary* equip *19*.

~ **gatherer** a person who acquires or amasses wealth, a hoarder *19-20*, *NE-EC*. **guid** ~ (**gangs** &c) **in sma buik** &c applied to a small but capable person *la19-*, *local Abd-Rox*. **naither** ~ **nor guid** nothing at all *la19-e20*, *NE*.

gebbie &c *la18-*; **gaebie** &c *20-*, *EC n* **1** the crop of a bird *19-*, *now local nEC*. **2** a person's stomach *la18-e20*. **3** a person's mouth, a bird's beak *19-*, *now Ags Per Fif*. **4** a horn spoon *la19-e20*, *Sh Ork NE*. [prob dim of GAB[2]; *cf* Gael *geuban* a crop, gizzard]

geblet-doir *see* GIBLET

geck &c, **gek**; **geak** &c *la18-e20* [gɛk] *n* **1** a gesture of derision, a gibe, trick *16-19*. **2** a scornful or disdainful manner *19*, *chf SW*. **3** a fool *la18-e20*.

v **1** *vt* mock, deride *la16-e19*. **2** *vi* mock **at**, scoff **at** *la16-20*. **3** *vt* trick, cheat *la16-19*. **4** *vi* toss the head in scorn, raise the head proudly or disdainfully *la18-20*. **5** stare rudely *la19-*, *local N Kcb*. **6** turn the head in a coquettish or vacant, foolish way *19-*, *now Abd Ags*. **7** sport, dally, play the fool *19*.

geckin &c lively, playful *la19-*, *Bnf Dmf*. **gaikit** silly *20-*, *Sh Abd Ags*. ~-**neck**(**it**) (having) a twisted neck *19-*, *NE*. ~ (**up**) **one's head** = *v* 4, *18-e19*. [Du, LowGer *gek* a fool, *gekken* make a fool of]

ged &c *n* the pike *la14-*, *now local NE-Dmf*. [nME *gedde*, ON *gedda*]

gedder, geddery *see* GAITHER

Gedward *see* JETHART

gee &c [gi; *Rox* gəi] *n* a fit of sulkiness or temper, a mood, caprice, fancy *17-*.

tak the ~ take offence, sulk *la18-*. [obscure]

gee *see* JEE

geebald &c [*Bwk Rox* ˈdʒiːbald; *Rox also* ˈdʒibəld] *n* a type of long-handled sickle *e20*, *S*. [prob dim for *G-bill* a G-shaped hedgebill]

geed *see* GAE

geegaw [ˈgiːˈga, ˈdʒiːˈdʒa] *n* = gewgaw *la19-*, *local Sh-Dmf*.

geel &c *20, Sh Ork, only Sc*, **geill- &c** *16-e18, only Sc*, **gyle- &c** *la13-19* [*Sh Ork* gil, gɪl; **gəil*] *n* = gyle, wort in the process of fermentation *la13-20, latterly Sh Ork*.

gilfa &c, garfa &c [**'gɪlfɑ, *?'gʌr-, &c*] *fig* a fit of idleness *20, SW*. ~ **house** &c the place where the wort was set to cool *16-e18*.

geelum &c [*'gilǝm, 'gɪl-*] *n* a rabbet-plane *la19-*. [only *Sc*; F *guillaume*]

geem *see* GUM[1]

geen *see* GAE

geenie [*'ginɪ*] *n* = guinea *18-*.

geenyoch &c [**'gin(j)ǝx*] *adj* ravenous, voracious; greedy *19-e20, chf WC*. [Gael *gionach*]

geese *see* GUSE, GUSSIE

geesen *see* GIZZEN

geesie *see* GUSSIE

geeskin *see* JOSKIN

gef *see* GIE, GIF

gefe *see* GIE, GIF

geffin *see* GIE

geg[1] [*gɛg*] *n* = gig, a poacher's hook for catching fish *20-, S*.

geg[2] &c [*gɛg*] *n, vt* = gag, trick *19-e20, chf Gsw*. ~**gery** trickery *19-e20*.

geg[3] &c; **gig** *la19-e20* [*gɛg, gɪg*] *n* the article used in the game *smuggle the* ~, *eg* a penknife, a piece of wood *19-e20*. ~**gie** = *n, la19-e20*. **smuggle the** ~ a boys' game, the aim of the two teams respectively being to protect or capture the GEG[3] *la19-, now local Abd-S*.

gegger &c [**'gɛgǝr, *'gag-*] *n* an under-lip, *esp* when protruding *e19*. [*cf* Norw dial *gag, gag(a)r* bent back and eModEng *gag-tooth* a projecting tooth]

geggie &c [*'gɛgɪ*] *n* a travelling theatrical show *19-e20, chf Ags WC*. [*cf* GEG[2] and Eng *gag* a made-up story]

geiffin *see* GIE

geig *see* JEEG

geigget *see* GIGOT

geil *see* GELL[1]

geill- *see* GEEL

geill *see* JEEL

gein *see* GAE

geine *see* GEAN

geing; ging [*giŋ, gɪŋ*] *n* human excrement; filth *19-20, chf C-S*. [OE *genge* a drain, latrine]

geisen *see* GIZZEN

geist *see* JEEST[1]

geit, jeit [**dʒit*] *n* a border on a garment *e16*. *vt* put a border on (a garment etc) *16*. [only *Sc*; OF *géet, giete* a border]

geit *see* GATE[1], GET, JEET

gek *see* GECK

geld [**gɛl(d)*] *adj* barren; not giving milk *la15-19*. [ME; ON *geldr* dry of milk; *cf* YELD]

gell[1] &c *la18-e20*; **geil &c** *20-, Sh Cai* [*gɛl, gil; Rox also* gel] *vi* tingle, smart, ache with pain or cold *la18-, now Sh Cai*.

galing *e16*, ~**ing** *la18, e20* tingling, smarting. [northern eModEng *gale*]

gell[2] &c [*gɛl; Sh* gjɛl; *Rox also* gel] *vi, chf* ~**ed**, *of unseasoned wood* split or cracked in drying *19-, chf Sh Ork SW*. *n* a crack (in wood) *19-, chf SW*. [uncertain]

gell[3] &c *19-, now Cai Abd Ayr*; **gale &c** *17-* [*gɛl*] *n* **1** = gale *17-*. **2** *only* **gale** a state of spiritual uplift, an afflatus *e18, e20*. **3** a state of excitement from anger, joy etc, *chf* **in a** ~ *19-e20*. **4** *chf* **gell** a brawl, row, squabble *19-, Ayr*. **5** *only* **gell** a romp, a spree; a drinking-bout, *freq* **on the** ~ *19*. [OED *gale* (*n*[3])]

gell[4], *19*, **gale &c** *16* [*gɛl; *gel*] *vi* **1** *of the cuckoo* = gale, call *16*. **2** bawl, yell *19*.

gell[5] [**gɛl*] *adj* brisk, keen *19*. [*cf* GELL[1]]

gell[6] &c [*gɛl*] *n* a leech *18-e20*. **gellie &c** = *n, 19-e20*. [Sc and IrGael *geal*]

gelletough *see* GELLYTROCH

gellie *see* GAILLIE, GELL[6]

gellock *see* GAVELOCK

gelly *see* JELLIE

gellytroch &c *18-e19*; **gelletough** *e17*, **gall(e)ytrough &c** *la18-e19* [**'gɛlǝtrox, &c*] *n* the char, the fish *Kinr*. [see SND]

gem(m) *see* GAME

gemma &c **band**, **jammay &c band** [**'dʒɛme, *'dʒame, &c* 'band] *n* a hinge *16-e17*. [ME *gemu &c, jemew &c*, OF *gemeau* twin]

gemmie *see* GAME

gend [**gɛnd*] *adj* foolish, simple *la15-e16*. [obscure]

gene &c *la16-e17*, **jayne** *la16* [**dʒin, *dʒen*] *n* (an instrument of) torture. [only *Sc*; F *gêne*, OF *gehine, jayne &c*]

gener &c [*'dʒɛnǝr*] *n* **1** = gender *16-, now Cai Abd Uls*. **2** progeny, *chf* **puddock's** ~ frog-spawn *la19-, Fif*. *vt* = gender, beget, cause *la14-e17*.

general &c *adj* **1** = general *la14-*. **2** *Sc Univs* designating a first-year, non-specialized course *18-, now St Andrews*; see also *ordinary* (ORDINAR). *n* **1** the master of the mint *la16-17, only Sc*. **2** = general.

G~ **Assembly** *Presbyterian Churches* the highest church court as represented by delegate MINISTERS and ELDERS assembled annually, *usu and now always* in Edinburgh, and presided over by a *Moderator* (MODERATE) *la16-*. G~ **Associate Synod** that section of the *Secession Church* (SECEDE) which refused to take the *burgess oath* (BURGESS), the ANTIBURGHERS *19-e20, chf hist*. G~ **Council &c 1** = COUNSAIL 2, *15-16*. **2** the deliberative body in the four older Scottish Universities, *now* consisting of the University Court, professors, lecturers of more than one year's standing and graduates, the main functions of which are to elect the Chancellor and four Assessors of the Court and to represent the graduate body *19-*. ~ **disposition** *law* a deed meant as a conveyance but lacking the pre-requisites of *infeftment* (INFEFT), *eg* a proper description of the land *la19-*.

genetrice &c [*'dʒɛnətrəis] *n* a female parent *16*. [OF *genitrice*, L *genetrix*]

geng *see* GANG

genie &c [*'dʒini] *n* inherent ability, natural bent *19*, *chf Ayr*. [eModEng; F *genie*, L *genius* a tutelary spirit]

gennay *see* GAE

gennick *see* JONICK

gent &c [*Sh* gant; *S* gɛnt] *n* a tall, thin or lanky person *19-e20*, *Sh SW*, *S*. [Norw dial *gand* a pointed stick; a tall thin fellow]

genteelity *19-20*, **gentilité** *e16*; **gentility** &c *la16- n* **1** = gentility *16-*. **2** gentry, people of gentle birth *20-*, *now Sh WC Uls*.

gentie &c ['dʒɛnti] *adj* **1** *chf of persons* neat, dainty, graceful *18-*, *now Abd Fif*. **2** genteel; courteous, well-bred *18-*, *now Abd Fif*. **3** *of dress* tasteful *19*. [see SND]

gentilité, gentility *see* GENTEELITY

gentle, gentill &c *la14-e17 adj* **1** = gentle *la15-*. **2** well-born *la14-19*. **3** gentlemanly, genteel *19*, *NE*.
n = gentle, a person of gentle birth *15-19*.
the ~ persuasion the Episcopalian denomination, adhered to by many of the upper classes *la18-e20*, *NE*.

gentlemanny &c, **gentlemanie** &c ['dʒɛntlmani] *adj* gentlemanly *la16-*, *now Sh NE Ags*, *only Sc*.

gentré *see* GENTRY

gentrice &c ['dʒɛntrɪs; *dʒɛn'trəis] *n* **1** the character or behaviour natural to a person of gentle birth or rank *la14-16*. **2** good birth or breeding, gentility *18-e20*. **3** people of good birth or breeding, gentry *la19-20*. [ME *gentrise*, OF *genterise*, var of *gentelise*]

gentry &c, **gentré** *e16* ['dʒɛntri] *n* **1** = GENTRICE 1, *16-*, *now Abd Ags*. **2** good birth, rank of a gentleman *la18-*, *now Ags*. [ME *gentrie*]

genȝie *see* GANȝE

genzie *see* GANSEY

geordie ['dʒɔrdi] *n* a guinea coin, *chf* **yellow ~** *la18-e20*. **2** a rustic, yokel *la19-*, *local Inv-S*.
plain ~ the flat bottom crust of a loaf of bread *20-*, *Ags Per*. [pet form of *George*]

George Square informal name for George Watson's Ladies' College, from 1871-1980 situated in George Square, Edinburgh *la19-20*; cf *Queen Street* (QUEEN).

ger *see* GAR², GEAR

geraflour &c *15-e16*, **geroflé** *la16* [*?'dʒɛre'flur; *?'dʒirə'fli] *n* the gillyflower. [only Sc; OF *giroflee*, Eng *gillyflower*]

gere *see* GAR², GEAR

gernell *see* GIRNEL

geroflé *see* GERAFLOUR

gerrock &c ['gɛrək] *n* a coal-fish in its first year *19-*, *NE*. [prob f Gael *gearr* short, squat]

gers *see* GIRSE

'Gers [dʒɛrz] nickname for Rangers football team *la20-*. [cf *Light Blues* (LICHT¹), HUNS]

gersone [*?'garsun, *?'gɛrsun] *n* a fellow *e16*. [ME *garcion* &c a servant, a young man, OF a servant]

gersting *see* GIRTH²

gersum *see* GRASSUM

gert *see* GAR²

gerten *see* GARTEN

ges *see* GUESS

gesine *see* JIZZEN

gess &c [*gɛs] *n* a wooden container of standard measure for fruit; the amount thus measured *la17-e18*. [only Sc; perh altered f Eng *case* a box]

gest *see* GHAIST, GUEST, JEEST¹, JEEST²

gester &c ['dʒɛstər] *vti* **1** = gesture *20-*, *Sh Ork local EC*. **2** strut, swagger *la18-*, *now WC*.

get &c; **gete** &c *la14-e20*, **gait** &c *16-e19*, **git** &c *la19- vti* [gɛt; *Sh* also gjɪt; *Cai C*, *S* also gɪt; *sEC*, *S* also git; *Loth* also get], *pt* **gat** &c *la14-19*, **gate** &c *la14-e18*, **got** &c *18-* [gat, got]. *ptp* also **gottin** &c *la14-* ['got(ə)n], **gattin** &c *15-16*, **getten** &c *15*; **get** &c *e16* **1** = get *14-*. **2** *vt* find, get by looking *18-*: '*ye'll get it in ma pooch*'. **3** marry, get for a spouse *la18-*. **4** be called, be addressed as *la18-*: '*Mackenzie's ma name but I aye get Jock frae her*'. **5** *with verbal noun or ptp* be able, be allowed, manage (to do something), find an opportunity (for doing something) *18-*, *Gen except Sh*: '*I couldna get sleeping*'; '*I got wachled hame some wey or anither*'; '*they cannot get met on a week day*'. **6** *with infin and absol* be allowed, manage (to do something, *usu* to go somewhere) *la19-*, *Gen except Sh Ork*: '*can I get downstairs?*' **7** *vi* be struck, get a blow *19-*, *NE Arg*: '*I gat i the lug wi a steen*'.
n, also **gyte** &c *19-* [gɛt; *NE* git; *C*, *S* gəit] **1** begetting, birth *la14-16*. **2** offspring, progeny, a child *15-*, *now local N-S*. **3** *contemptuous, abusive* a brat; a bastard *16-*. **4** (1) *chf* **gyte** [gəit] name for a junior pupil at the Royal High School of Edinburgh *19-20*. (2) *chf* **geit** [gəit] name for a boy in the first year of the Upper School of the Edinburgh Academy *19-*. **5** *also* **goit** *19-*, *Gall* an unfledged nestling *19-*, *Gall Rox*. **6** a coalfish in its second stage *20-*, *now Abd Fif*.
~ling &c *also abusive* a young child, infant *18-20*.
~ awa(y) die *la19-*, *local Bnf-S*. **~ by 1** avoid, dispense with *19-*, *now Sh Abd*. **2** get past, succeed in passing *20-*. **~ forth** succeed in going onwards, progress (on a journey) *19-*, *now Wgt Rox*. **~ (one's) hands on** catch (someone) for purposes of punishment *la18-*. **~ into 1** succeed in opening (something) *la19-*. **2** become familiar with, practised in (a subject, technique etc) *la20-*, *Abd WC*. **~ on to be, ~ on for** a job as, be promoted to be *19-*. **~ on to** &c attack verbally, scold *la20-*, *local*. **~ out** give full vent to, finish off *la18-*, *now Sh Abd midLoth*.

~ out wi utter suddenly or forcibly *la19-*. **~ ower 1** last out, subsist *19-*, *now NE*. **2** get the upper hand of *la19-*. **~ (it) ower the fingers** be reprimanded *20-*. **~ roon** accomplish, master *la19-*. **~ through** escape, recover from *18-*, *now local*. **~ up in(to) years** grow old *19-*. **~ well up** rise in position, succeed *19-*.

get *see* GATE¹

gete *see* GET

gether *see* GAITHER

getten *see* GET

geud *see* GUID

geve *see* GIE, GIF

gevin *see* GIE

gey &c *19-*, **gay &c; gie** *la19-e20* [gəi; *nEC also* ge] *adj* **1** *only* **gay** = gay *15-*. **2** excellent, splendid; *latterly* (*19-*) *freq ironic or derog* disreputable, wild *la15-*. **3** *of quantity or amount* considerable, good(-sized), great *19-*.
adv **1** = gay, gaily *la15-e16*. **2** considerably, very; rather *la17-*.

gaily &c *15-*, **~lies &c** *18-* ['gəili(z)] **1** *only* **~ly &c** = gaily *15-*. **2** *with adj* pretty, rather; very *la17-20*. **3** fairly well, pretty well, pretty nearly *la18-*, *now local Abd-Dmf*. **4** *chf of health* well enough, tolerably well, middling *18-*, *now local Abd-Dmf*.
~ like = *adj* 2, *la19-*.
~ and, **~an(d) &c** rather, very *18-*. **~ kind o &c**, **~ kinna** rather badly *20-*, *local N-Rox*.

geyler *see* JILE

geyze [gəiz] *vi* become leaky, warp *la18-*, *now midLoth*. [back-formation f *geisen &c* (GIZZEN)]

ghaist &c *la15-*, **gast &c** *la14-19*, **gest &c** *la14* [gest; *Bwk Rox Kcb also* gɛst] *n* **1** = ghost *la14-*, *now local Ags-Rox*. **2** term of contempt etc, *eg* for a repulsive person or for an emaciated, sickly or undersized person *16-e20*. **3** *also* **guest** *19-e20* (a piece of) shaly coal burnt to its ashy state, a white slaty cinder *19-*, *local Fif-S*.

gheast *see* GUEST

gheeho ['gi:'ho] *n* an uncouth, blustering fellow *e20*, *Arg*. [*cf* Eng *hee haw*]

ghillie *see* GILLIE¹

Giant's Grave *n* popular name for the ruins of a neolithic chambered tomb *la19-*, *local*.

gib¹ &c [dʒɪb] *n* a kind of SWEETIE *19*, *Edb*. [*cf* Eng dial *jib*, perh f *Gibraltar rock*]

gib² &c [gɪb] *n* **1** name for a cat; a cat *la15-*. **2** *specif* a tom-cat, *esp* a castrated male *19-*, *local Ork-Dmf*.
~bie &c *la18-e20*, **~ cat** *19-e20* = *n*. [ME *gibbe*, contraction of *Gilbert*]

gib³ [gɪb] *n*, *mining* a prop *la19-20*. [prob Eng *gib* a piece of metal etc used for keeping parts of a machine tight]

gibbery¹ &c ['dʒɪb(ə)rɪ] *n* gingerbread *la18-20*, *local N*. [aphetic f GINGERBREID]

gibbery² [?'dʒɪbərɪ] *n* a variety of the game of marbles *la19-e20*, *Mry Bnf*. [perh specialized use of prec]

gibble &c ['gɪbl] *n*, *chf in pl* tools, implements; articles, wares *la18-*, *now local Bnf-nEC*.
gibblet &c *n* an implement, tool, utensil *la19-*, *now midLoth Dmf*. [uncertain]

gibble-gabble &c ['gɪbl'gabl] *n* chatter, tittle-tattle *la18-*, *now local Bnf-S*.
vi prattle, chatter *18-*, *NE, EC, S*. [reduplicated f Eng *gabble*]

gibblet *see* GIBBLE

giblet &c: giblet-check &c ['dʒɪblət'tʃɛk] *n*, *masonry* a rabbet cut in masonry to allow a door to fit flush with the wall *19-*, *now Abd Ags*.
geblet-doir a door fitting flush with the wall *e17*, *Abd*. [uncertain, but *cf* ModEng *jib-door*]

gid *see* GIE

gid gad, gid gow &c ['gɪd'gad, 'gɪd'gʌu] *interj* expressing disgust *la19-*, *Ork Ags Fif Bwk*. [altered f Eng *Good God*; *cf* GAD, GUID]

gie &c *la18-*, **ge** *la16*, **gif &c** *la14-17*, **gef &c** *la14-16*, *only Sc*, **gefe &c** *la14-e17*, **give &c** *15-*, **geve &c** *la15-e17*; **gae** *la19-e20* [gi; *Ork SW* ge; *giv; *gɪf] *vti*, *pres also in contracted forms with following pronoun, eg* **gimme &c** ['gi:mɪ *&c*, 'gɪmɪ, *&c*] give me, **gies &c** [gi:z] give us *20-*.
pt **gave &c**, **geve &c** *15-16*, **gaif &c** *la14-e17*, *la19*, **gaff &c** *la14-16*, *e19*, **gef &c** *la14-e17*, *only Sc*, **gae &c** *la18-20*, **gya** *la19-20*, *NE* [ge; *NE* gja; gev; *?giv]; **gied &c** *la18-*, *now Ork Bnf C, S*, **gid** *la18-*, *now Abd Ayr*; **gien** *20-* [gi:d, gid; *NE, SW* gɪd; gin]. *ptp* **given &c**, **giffin &c** *la14-e17*, **gevin &c** *la14-17*, **ge(i)ffin &c** *la14-16*, **gien &c** *16*, *la18-* [gi:(ə)n, gin; 'gɪvən; *'givən]; **gied** *20-*, *Sh Ork C, S* [gi:d, gid; *NE, SW* gɪd] **1** = give *la14-*. **2** *vt*, *followed by prep phrase* strike *16*, *la18-*, *now local NE-Rox*: 'give him across the head with the butt of your rod'.

given *qualifying expressions of quantity, usu implying exasperation* 'blessed' *20-*, *local*: 'A had tae sit twa given hoors'. **given name** Christian name, forename *la19-*, *now midLoth Bwk*.
~ down &c **1** admit, acknowledge *18-19*. **2** reduce, remit (an amount etc) *la16-e18*, *only Sc*.
~ ower &c give up, abandon *18-*, *now Sh NE*.
gie's-a-piece a hanger-on, a parasite *19-*, *now Ags*. **~ up** hold up (a child) for baptism *20-*, *now Abd*.

gie *see* GEY

gied *see* GAE, GIE

gien, gies *see* GIE

gif &c, gef &c *la15-16*, **gefe &c** *15-16*, *la19*, **geve &c** *la15-e17*, **give &c** *la14-e18* [gɪf, gɪv; *giv] *conj* = if *la14-*, *now chf literary*. [var of ME *ʒif*, w initial consonant assimilated to *gif* (GIE)]

gif *see* GIE

giff-gaff &c ['gɪf'gaf] *n* **1** mutual help, give and take, fair exchange *18-*. **2** interchange of talk, repartee *19-*, *now sEC Ayr*.
vti exchange, barter; bandy (words) *la18-*, *now local Inv-Bwk*. [reduplicated f *gif* (GIE)]

giffin *see* GIE

gift &c *n* = gift *la14-*.
vt give as a gift, present *17-*.

~**ie** a sense of power, an ability *la18*.

gig [gɪg, gig] *n, mining* a winding engine *19-*, now *Fif.*

~**(s)man** the man in charge of the GIG *19-*, now *Fif.* [unknown, but *cf* obs Eng *gig* something that whirls]

gig *see* GEG³, JEEG

giggie *see* GEG³

gigot &c *la18-*, **geigget &c** *la16-17* ['dʒɪgət] *n* a leg (of mutton or lamb). [F]

gilbroder *see* GUILD

gild &c *n* clamour, din *16*. [obscure]

gild *see* GUILD

gildee &c [gɪl'di] *n* a fish, the whiting pout *la18-, WC*. [uncertain]

gileynour *see* GOLEINȝEIS

gilfa *see* GEEL

gilgal &c ['gɪl'gal] *n* a commotion, uproar *la18-*, now *Sh.* [onomat]

gill¹ &c [dʒɪl] *n* one fourth of a MUTCHKIN, about three quarters of the imperial gill *la18-19*.

~ **bells** bells rung at 11.30 am, the time when many paid a visit to a tavern *e18, Edb.* [*cf* Eng]

gill² &c [gɪl; *Sh also* gjɪl] *n* a ravine, gully *la15-*, now local, *in place-names 13-*. [ME *gylle*, ON *gil*]

gillatrype(s), **jolly-tryp(s)** [*?'dʒɛlɪ'trɪp(s), *'dʒolɪ-] *n* name of a witches' dance *la16-17*. [unknown]

gillet &c [*'dʒɪlət] *n* a mare *la14-16*. [only Sc; perh f the female name *Gill*]

gillie¹ &c; ghillie *la19-* ['gɪlɪ] **1** a lad, youth *17-20*. **2** a male servant, *esp* an attendant on a *Highland* (HIELAND) chief; a *Highlander* 1, *18-19*. **3** a sportsman's attendant, *usu* in deerstalking or angling in the *Highlands 19-*.

vi act as a GILLIE¹ (*n* 3) *20-*.

~ **callum** [~ 'kaləm] the *sword-dance* (SWURD); the name of the tune to which it is danced *19-*.

~**casflue &c** *18-e19* [*~ 'kas'flu], ~**wetfoot &c** *la18-e19* [*-'wɛt'fɪt, &c*] the attendant who carried the *Highland* (HIELAND) CHIEF over wet places [Gael ~ *cas-fhliuch*]. [Gael *gille* a lad, servant]

gillie² &c [*'dʒɪlɪ] *n* a flighty girl *la17-e19*. [dim of OSc, ME *gill* a wench]

gillieperous &c [gə'lip(ə)rʌs, -əs] *n* a fool; a rough ungainly person *20-, Mry Abd*. [obscure]

gillore *see* GALORE

gillravager *see* GILRAVAGE

gilly- ['gɪlɪ] ~**gacus &c** *n* a fool *18-e19*.

~**-gawkie &c** *n* a silly young person, *esp* a girl *la18-e19, chf SW-S.* ~**-gawpus &c** *la18-*, now *Ags*, ~**-gawpy &c** *18-19 n* a stupid person, a gaping fool. [*gil-*, intensifier + derivs of GAWK, GAUP; *cf* GILRAVAGE]

gilp *see* JILP

gilpie &c ['gɪlpɪ] *n* **1** a lively, mischievous youth *18-19*. **2** a lively young girl, a tomboy *18-20*. [perh var of next]

gilpin &c ['gɪlpən, 'gʌlp-] *n* a big, stout or well-grown young person; a loutish person *19-20, chf N, SW*. [see SND]

gilravage &c *la19-e20*; **galra**(i)**vitch &c** *19-e20*, **gulravage &c** *la18-*, now *Sh*, **gulravish &c** *18-20* [gə(l)'ravɪdʒ, -ɪ(t)ʃ, -'rev-] *v* 1 *vi* eat and drink immoderately, indulge in high living *18-20*. **2** make merry, enjoy oneself noisily, create a noisy disturbance *la18-*, now *midLoth Rox.* **3** rove about, *esp* to plunder *19-e20.* **4** *vt* devour *19-e20, C.*

n **1** merry-making, horseplay, commotion, uproar *la18-20.* **2** a state of confusion, a disturbance *19-20.* **3** a noisy disorderly crowd, a mob *19-20, chf SW.*

gillravager &c a wild or lawless person *e19*. [perh *gil-*, intensifier + Eng *ravage, ravish*]

gilse *see* GRILSE

gilt¹ &c [gɪlt] *v* **1** *vt* gild *la14-*. **2** *vi* become yellow *18-*, now *Bwk.* [ME *gilte*, f *ptp* of Eng *gild*]

gilt² &c [gɪlt] *n* a young sow, *esp* before her first farrowing *la15-*. [ME; ON *gyltr*]

giltin &c [*gɪltən] *adj* gilded, gilt, golden *la15-16*. [nME *gilten*]

gilty &c [*'gɪltɪ] *adj* = GILTIN *e16*.

gim &c [dʒɪm] *adj* neat, spruce *16-*, now *Bnf Ags.* **jimmy &c** = *adj*, *19*. [perh f JIMP²]

gimme *see* GIE

gimmer &c ['gɪmər] *n* a year-old ewe; a ewe between its first and second shearing *15-*. [ME *gymbyre &c*, ON *gymbr* a ewe-lamb]

gimmer *see* CUMMER²

gimp *see* JIMP¹

gin¹ &c [dʒɪn] *n* **1** = gin, a device, a trap *la14-*. **2** a bolt, lock, latch *la15-19*.

gin² &c; gane &c *la16-e20* [gɪn; *NE also* *gin, *gen] *conj* **1** if, whether *la16-*. **2** *introducing expressions of longing* oh that, if only *la18-*, now *Ork NE midLoth.* [see SND]

gin³ &c; gain *la18-19* [gɪn; *gen] *prep* **1** by, before *la18-*, *Gen except Sh Ork.* **2** in anticipation of, in readiness for *19-*, *Abd Ags.* **3** = against *19-*, now *Uls.* **4** than *la19-*, *NE Ags.*

conj by the time that, when, before, until *la18-*.

~**shot**, *chf* **gainshot** a cover over the inlet to a millwheel *la18-e19.* [aphetic f AGAIN; *cf* GAIN-]

ging *see* GANG, GEING

ginge &c [dʒɪndʒ; *dʒɪnʃ] *n, chf attrib* ginger *18-20.* [f next]

gingebreid &c [*'dʒɪndʒ'brid, *'dʒɪnʃ-, 'dʒɪns-] *n* gingerbread *la16-20.*

adj gaudy, extravagant; unsubstantial *la18-19.* [laME = *n*; ME *gingebreed, gingebras*, OF *gingembras* ginger conserve]

gink [gɪŋk] *n* **ginkum &c** ['gɪŋkəm] **1** a trick, dodge, notion *la19-20, NE.* **2** a habit, trait *la19-20, NE.* [voiced var of Eng *kink*]

ginnle &c ['gɪnl, 'gʌnl] *n, in pl* **1** the gills (of a fish) *19-20, WC.* **2** *transf* the cheeks *19-e20.*

vt catch (a fish) by the gills *19-20, chf WC.* [only Sc; see SND]

gip [gɪp] *n* the jaw of a fish *20-*, now *Abd Fif.* [only Sc; Norw dial = gap; jaw]

gipe *see* JUPE

gird¹ &c, gir(r) &c *16-*, *C* [gɪrd; *C* gɪr; *Sh* gjɪrd] *n* **1** = girth *16-*.   **2** a band or strap used to support *esp* a bed *16*.   **3** a band or hoop for a barrel etc *la16-*.   **4** a child's hoop *la18-*.   **5** a hoop for a skirt or petticoat *la19-e20, C.*   **6** a hoop-shaped frame hung from the shoulders for carrying two pails *19-, now Bwk.*

gordie *mining* a rope and chain for pulling HUTCHES, *e19.* **gurdy** *mining* the pulley on a self-acting incline *la19-, now Fif Loth.*

~**sting** *only Sc* = girthsting (GIRTH²) *16-e17.* [perh w infl f GIRD³; *cf* GIRTH²]

gird² &c [gɪrd] *n* **1** a knock, blow *la14-20.*   **2** *chf literary* a gust, blast *19.*   **3** a moment *la18-19.* *v* **1** *vi* rush (at), perform vigorously or with force *la14-19.*   **2** *vti* pierce *15-e16.*   **3** strike, deliver a blow, *freq* **let** ~ *la15-e19.*   **4** *also fig* push, force *la19.*   [eME *girde* &c]

gird³ &c [gɪrd; *C also* *gɪr] *vt* **1** encircle, fasten with a band *la14-19.*   **2** provide (a barrel etc) with hoops *la19, now local.*

~**ing** &c **1** the act of *v* 2, *la15-.*   **2** material for girths or hoops *17.*   **3** a saddle-girth *la15-, now Sh.*   **4** a rope *la19-, now Abd.*   [ME *girde,* OE *gyrdan; cf* GIRD¹]

girdle &c, **girdill** &c *15-e18* ['gɪrdl] *n* an iron plate used for baking, *traditionally* circular with a hooped handle for hanging over a fire *15-.*

~ **scone** a SCONE baked on a GIRDLE, frying pan or hot-plate *la19-.*

like a hen on a het &c ~ restless(ly), anxious(ly), impatient(ly) *la18-.*   [metath f Eng *griddle*]

girg *see* JIRG²

girkin *see* JERKIN

girl &c [gɪrl] *vi* **1** shudder with fear or dread *19-20, S.*   **2** *of the teeth* be set on edge *19-e20, S.*   [metath f GRILL]

girls *see* GRILSE

girn¹ &c [gɪrn] *v* **1** *vi* snarl, grimace *la14-.*   **2** *vt* screw up (the face) or gnash (the teeth) in rage or disapproval *la19-.*   **3** *vi* complain peevishly, whine, grumble *18-.*   **4** grin, sneer *la18-, now Sh Ork Ags Gall.*   **5** *transf* (1) *of clothes* gape *19-, now midLoth*; (2) *of soil* crack *la19-, now midLoth Arg.* *n* **1** a snarl *18-.*   **2** a whine, whimper; whining; grumbling *la18-.*   **3** a grin, grimace *la19-, now Sh Cai.*   **4** *transf* a gaping furrow *20-, now Fif Arg.*   **5** a grousing, peevish or fault-finding person *la20-, local.*

~**ie** &c *adj* peevish, ill-tempered *19-.*   *n* a fretful, bad-tempered person *la19-, local.*   ~**ie-gib** &c = ~**ie** (*n*), *esp* a child *la19-, now Bwk Uls.*   ~**igo** &c ['gɪrnɪgo] *19-, local,* ~**igo gabbie** &c *19-e20,* ~**igo gibbie** &c *la18-, now Fif* = ~**ie** (*n*) [see SND].   [metath f Eng *grin*]

girn² &c [gɪrn] *n* a noose, snare *la14-.*   *vt, also fig* snare *la14, 19-, local Cai-Rox.*   [only Sc; metath f OE *grin*]

girnel &c *16-20,* **girnall** &c *15-,* **garnel** &c *16-20, latterly chf Ayr,* **garnale** &c *la15-e16,* **gernell** &c *la15-17,* **grinnale** &c *15-e16,*

granale &c *16,* **grenil** &c *16-e18* ['gɪrn(ə)l; *WC, SW* 'garn(ə)l; *garn-, *gren-, *gran-, *grɪn-] *n* **1** a storage chest for meal etc *la15-20.*   **2** a granary, storehouse *la15-e19.*

vt store (food etc), hold in storage *16-e18.*

~**man** &c the man in charge of a GIRNEL *16-19.* [only Sc; var of ME, OF *gerner* &c (*n*), eModEng *garner* &c (*n*)]

girner *n* = GIRNEL *la16-e17.* [only Sc; assimilated to Eng *garner*]

girnigo *see* GIRN¹

girr *see* GIRD¹

girran &c *n* a small boil or pustule *19-, now Cai Arg.* [only Sc; Gael *guirean*]

girse &c *la15-,* **garse** &c *la16-19,* **gers** &c *la14-e20,* **gress** &c *la14-, now local,* **gras** &c *la14-17,* **grass** &c *la17-,* **gris** &c *la14-17;* **greis** &c *16-17* [grɛs, gras; *Sh NE nEC, SW* gɪrs; *Fif* gɛrs; *WC* *gars; *grɪs] *n* **1** = grass *la14-.*   **2** *only* **girse** &c a stalk or blade of grass *la19-, now Abd.* *v* **1** *vti* pasture (animals) *16-e20.*   **2** *vt, transf* remove from office, 'put out to grass' *la18-e20.*   **3** = grass.

girsie &c **1** grassy *16-.*   **2** *chf* **girsie** *of cereal crops* interspersed with grass *la19-.*   **get girsie stibble** *fig* enjoy the best of fare *20-, Bnf Abd.* **girsing** &c **1** the act or fact of pasturing (animals) *16-e17.*   **2** pasturage, grazing land *la16-, now Ork Cai.*

~ **beef** &c beef from grass-fed cattle *16-.* **girse-gawed** &c *of toes* having cuts or cracks between *19-e20.* **girse heuk** the hooked metal cross-stay between shaft and blade of a scythe *20-, Ork Abd Ags.* **grass-ill 1** a disease of young lambs, a kind of BRAXY *19-e20.*   **2** a disease of horses *e20.*   ~ **maill** &c rent for pasturage *la15-18.*   ~**man** a landless tenant with only rights of pasturage *la14-19, latterly Abd.* **grass nail** = girse heuk, *19-, now local Cai-SW.* **grass sickness** = grass-ill 1 (*e20*), 2 (*20*).

girsill *see* GIRSLE, GRILSE

girsing *see* GIRSE

girsle &c, **girsill** &c ['gɪrs(ə)l] *n* **1** = gristle *la16-.*   **2** a quill pen, *esp* its shaft or stump *la18-e19.*   **3** a fragment of crisp or caked porridge etc; anything charred *19-e20.*

girst &c *n* = grist *15-, now Uls.*

girsum *see* GRASSUM

girt *see* GREAT

girth¹ &c [gɪrθ] *n* **1** = grith, security; immunity *la14-16.*   **2** *specif* sanctuary; a place of sanctuary *15-e18.*

gyrthol sanctuary *la12.*

~ **cross** a cross marking the limits of a place of sanctuary *16-, now in place-names.*

girth² &c [gɪrθ] *n* = GIRD¹ *n* 1 (*la15-, now midLoth Arg*), 3 (*la15-19*).

vt provide (a barrel etc) with hoops *16-e17.*

gurthie &c **1** corpulent *19-20.*   **2** heavy, oppressive *19-20.*   ~**ing 1** providing with hoops

16-e17. **2** material for girths *e17*. ~**sting, gersting &c** *la16* a length of wood suitable for use as a barrel-hoop *15-e17*.

girtling *see* GREAT

girzie &c ['gɪrzɪ] *n* a maid-servant *19-*, now *Ags Fif*. [only Sc; metath dim of *Grizel* the personal name]

gising *see* JIZZEN

gissie *see* GUSSIE

gist *see* JEEST[1]

git *see* GET

gitter *see* GUTTER

give *see* GIE, GIF

given *see* GIE

gizen *see* GIZZERN

gizz &c [dʒɪz] *n* **1** = JEEZY *la18*. **2** the face *19-e20* [prob f misinterpretation of Burns *Address to the Deil* xvii].

gizzen &c; geesen &c, geisen &c, gazen &c *Ork Arg Uls* ['gɪzən, 'gəiz-, 'giz-; *Ork Arg Uls* also 'gez-] *vi* **1** *of wood etc* shrink, warp, leak *18-*. **2** *also* **kizen &c** *la18-20*, *WC* ['kɪzən, *'kiz-, *'kez-] *lit and fig* dry up, wither, shrivel *la18-*, now *Sh Ork NE*. **3** *chf of the throat* be or become parched *la18-*, now *local Sh-Ags*.
adj **1** *of wooden containers* cracked, leaky *la18-*, now *local*. **2** dry, parched, shrivelled *la18-*, now *Sh Rox*. [only Sc; Icel *gisna* become leaky; *cf* Norw *gissen*]

gizzen *see* GIZZERN

gizzent &c ['gɪznt, 'giz-] *adj* sated, surfeited *20-*, *Abd Slk*. [only Sc; see SND]

gizzern *19-*, **guisserne &c** *la16-e17*; **giz(z)en** *19-*, now *Ags*, **guzzern &c** *19-e20* ['gɪzə(r)n, 'gɪzrən, 'gʌz-; *Sh* *'g(j)øz-, *'dʒ-] *n* = gizzard: **1** *of a fowl*, *20-*, *Sh Cai*; **2** *joc* the human throat *la16-*, now *Ags*. [ME = 1]

glabber *see* CLABBER

glack &c, glak *16* *n* **1** a hollow between hills, a defile, ravine *16-*, now *local N-Arg*. **2** an open area in woodland *19-*, *Abd Ags Per*. **3** a handful, morsel *la18-e20*. **4** the angle between thumb and forefinger *19-*, now *Cai*. **5** the fork of a tree *19-*, now *Abd Kcdn*.
~ **someone's mitten** put money in someone's hand, tip someone, gratify someone *18-e20*, *chf NE*. [only Sc; Sc and IrGael *glac*]

glad *see* GLED[1]

glaff *see* GLIFF

glag *n* a gurgling or choking noise *la19-*, now *Abd*. *vi* make such a noise *la19-*, now *Abd*.
glagger = *n and v*, *la19-*, *Bnf Ags*. [only Sc; onomat]

glagger *vi* be avid, long **for** *la19-*, *NE*. [only Sc; prob extension of *glagger* (GLAG)]

glaiber &c ['glebər, 'glab-] *vi* talk incessantly or idly, babble *19-*, now *Rox*. [only Sc; prob onomat, w infl f CLAVER[1]]

glaid *see* GLED[1], GLED[2], GLID

glaik &c; gleck *la17-e20* [glek] *n* **1** *in pl* tricks, deception; pranks *16-19*. **2** *derog* a silly, thoughtless person *16-*, now *local*. **3** *in pl* sensual desire, wantonness *16*. **4** *in pl* a puzzle-game or toy, *appar* involving a number of rings or interlocking pieces of wood *la16-19*. **5** a flash or gleam of reflected light *la18-20*.
vi **1** look foolishly or idly *la16-19*. **2** trifle or flirt (**with**) *la16-20*.
~**ery,** ~**rie** foolish behaviour *la16-e19*. ~**ie** thoughtless, foolish *la19-*, now *Cai Abd*. ~**it** ['glekɪt; *Per also* 'gləik-] **1** foolish, stupid, of low intelligence; thoughtless, irresponsible *la15-*. **2** playful, full of pranks; flirtatious *la18-e19*. **3** *esp of a child* over-fond, clinging *19-*, now *Fif*.
fling the ~**s in someone's een** *19*, **gie someone the** ~**s** *la18-e20* deceive someone. **get the** ~**s** be deceived *la16-18*. [only Sc; see SND]

glaiks &c *n pl* **1** a lever or shaft attached to the churn-staff to facilitate churning *19-20*, *chf Uls*. **2** an instrument for twisting ropes from straw etc *20*, *SW Uls*. [only Sc; IrGael *glac* a grip, handle; *cf* GLACK]

glaim &c *la19-*, **gleme &c** *la15-16*; **gleam** *la18-* [glim; *NE* glem] *n* **1** = gleam *la15-*. **2** a flame *la16-*, now *Ags*.

glairy *adj* ~**-flairy** gaudy, showy *19-*, now *Abd midLoth*. [Eng *glary* full of glare, dazzling]

glaise &c [glez] *n* a touch of fire, a burn; a warm at a fire *la16-e20*. [only Sc; see SND]

glaiss *see* GLASS

glaister[1] *18-e19*, **glaster** *vi* talk boastingly, brag; bawl *16-e19*.

glaister[2] **&c** *n* a thin covering of snow or ice *19-*, now *SW*. [var of GLISTER]

glaizie &c *n* **1** = glazy, glittering, shiny *18-*, now *local Kcdn-Bwk*. **2** *of sunshine* bright but watery, indicating more rain *20-*, *Arg Wgt*.

glak *see* GLACK

glam *see* GLAUM

glamer &c [*'glamər, *'glam-] *n* noise, tumult; outcry *la14-16*. [only Sc; perh f Eng *clamour*, but *cf* ME, ON *glam(m)* noise]

glammach *see* GLAUM

glamour &c ['glamər, *'glam-] *n* **1** magic, enchantment; witchcraft *18-*. **2** = glamour.
vt **1** bewitch; dazzle *18-e20*. **2** deceive, bamboozle *la19-e20*. [earlier in Sc; f Eng *grammar* in the sense of occult learning; *cf* F *grimoire* a sorcerer's book and next]

glamourie &c ['glamərɪ, *'glam-] *n* = GLAMOUR *n*, *18-e20*. [f as GRAMARIE; *cf* prec]

glamp *vi* = GLAUM *v* 1 (*19*), 3 (*18-*, now *Bnf*).
n = GLAUM *n*, *la18-*, now *Cai*. [see SND]

glamse &c [glams; *Cai* glamʃ] *vi* **1** snap (**at**) *20-*, now *Ork*. **2** make a snapping, smacking noise, eat greedily *20-*, now *Mry*. [Norw, Sw dial *glamsa*, Dan dial *glamse*]

glamshach *see* GLAUM

glance, glans *16* *vi* **1** = glance *la16-*. **2** *of things other than light* shine, gleam *16-19*. **3** *impersonal* ~ (**up**)**on** occur to *19-*, now *midLoth*.
n = glance *16-*.

glancy shiny, shining, bright *18-*, now *Abd*.

glar, glare see GLAUR

glas see GLASS

Glasgow see GLESCA

Glasgowegian see GLASWEGIAN

glaschand &c adj meaning unknown e16.

glaschewe heidit adj meaning unknown e16.

glashan &c [Arg 'glɛʃən; Gall Uls *'glasən, *'glaʃ-] n the coal-fish in its second or third year la19-, now Arg. [only Sc; Gael glaisean]

Glasite &c [*'glasəit] n a member of the religious sect founded by the Rev. John Glas (1693-1773); later known as a SANDEMANIAN la18-20.

glaslaw &c n a handcuff, manacle la16-e17. [Gael glas-làmh]

glasp &c n, vt = clasp la15-17. [northern eModEng (once)]

glass la16-, **glas** la14-17, **gless** la17-; **gles &c** la14-17, **glaiss &c** 16-, now NE [glɛs, gles] n (la14-), vt (la16-) = glass.

　glessack &c a small glass marble 20-, now Cai. **~er** = **~ie** 2, 20-, now local Bnf-Wgt. **~ie &c** 1 a home-made sweet, a kind of toffee la19-, now Bwk Kcb. 2 a glass marble 20-. **~in &c** adj = glassen, made of glass; fitted with glass 16-17. n = glazing 16-17. **~inwerk &c** glass, glazing la14-e17. **~inwricht &c** a glazier 15-e18.

　~ band one of the strips of metal or wood for securing the panes of glass in a window la16-17. **~ wrycht &c** = glassinwricht, la14-17.

　casting the glass(es) a method of fortune-telling using egg-white 19-, now Ork Cai. **talk gless haunles** speak politely, use a 'refined' accent 20-, now Fif Ayr Dmf.

glaster see GLAISTER¹

Glaswegian 19-, **Glasgowegian** 19, WC [glas'widʒən, gləs-; *'glasgo-] n, adj (of) a native or inhabitant of Glasgow. [by analogy w Norwegian; cf Eng Galwegian a native or inhabitant of Galloway]

glaum &c; glam &c vti 1 snatch, grab (at) la18-, local. 2 seize, snatch at with the jaws; devour 19-, now Bwk. 3 vi grope la18-e20. n a clutch or grab, usu ineffectual 19-, local. **glammach** v = GLAUM v 1 (la19-, NE Ags), v 3 (19-, now Abd). n = GLAUM n, 19-, NE. **glammer** = GLAUM v 3, la19-e20. **glamshach** greedy, grasping 19-e20. [only Sc; Gael glàm snatch, grab; devour]

glaums see CLAMS

glaun &c [glɑn(d)] n a clamp 19-, now Ayr Kcb. [Eng glan(d); cf glaums (CLAMS)]

glaur &c la19-, **glar &c** 16-19; **glare &c** la16-e19 [glɑr; *gler] n 1 soft, sticky mud; ooze, slime 16-. 2 fig term of contempt or abuse for a person or thing 19-, now Kinr. 3 slippery ice; slipperiness la19-e20 [perh f eModEng and US glare frost, icy conditions; ice].
vt make muddy, dirty, soil; make slimy or slippery la15-, now Bwk.
~ie &c muddy, dirty la18-, local EC-Uls.

~sel completely covered with mud la20-, S [prob glaur's sel; see SEL¹ 2]. [unknown; also in northern ModEng dial]

glaver see CLAVER¹

glaze &c vt 1 = glaze. 2 smooth (over), make smooth 20-, Sh Bnf.

gle see GLEE

gleam see GLAIM

gleb(e) see GLEIB

gleck see GLAIK

gled¹ &c la15-, **glad; glaid &c** [glɛd; *gled] adj = glad la14-.
vti, chf verse = glad, make glad la14-19.
~ar &c a person who cheers or makes glad e16.

gled² &c, glaid &c la15-e19 [glɛd] n 1 the kite, the bird 15-e20. 2 applied to other birds of prey, chf the buzzard la18-, now Inv Ags. 3 transf a rapacious or greedy person la16-.
be as (gin or if) one had fa'en frae the ~('s feet) be in disorder, dishevelled, confused 19-e20. **be in the ~'s claws** etc be in mortal danger or dire trouble with little or no hope of escape 19. **as gleg as a ~** as keen or eager as a hawk; very hungry 19-e20. [in place-names 13-; ON gleða; cf ME glede, OE glida]

gled see CLEG

glede see GLEED

gledge &c vi squint, look sidelong 19-, now Pbls. n 1 a squint 19-, now Pbls. 2 a glimpse 19-e20. [only Sc; appar var of Sc (once) glede, related to GLEY]

glee la15-, **gle** la14-16, **glew &c** la14-16; **glie** la16 [gli; *glju] n = glee, entertainment, sport, mirth la14-.

glee see GLEY

gleebrie see GLEIB

gleed &c, glede n 1 a live coal or PEAT¹, an ember la14-, now Sh-Cai S Uls. 2 a spark, glimmer of fire or light 19-, now Bwk Slk. 3 a glowing fire 18-, now Slk.
brunt &c in a ~ burnt to an ember, completely burnt la14-16. [ME; OE glēd]

gleek vi 1 jeer, gibe la18-e19. 2 look, peep 20-, now Uls. [eModEng; perh connected w GLAIK v, GLEY v]

gleem-glam see GLIM-GLAM

gleesh n, also **~ach** [-əx] a large bright fire or flame 19-e20, Bnf Abd. [var of GREESH, GREESHOCH]

gleet &c, glete 15-e16 vi, chf verse gleam, shine, glitter la14-e20, latterly Rox.
n a glistening, glitter; a shine 19-, Rox. [only Sc; ON (v), Norw dial (n) glita]

gleg &c adj 1 chf of persons (1) quick, keen in perception, freq **~ of or in sight, hearing, eye** etc, 15-; (2) quick of movement; nimble, adroit 18-, local; (3) keen, smart, alert, quick-witted, freq **~ in, of or at the uptak** la18-; (4) lively, sprightly; merry 19-, now Sh NE Per. 2 of the senses, esp the sight sharp, keen 18-, now local Ags-Rox. 3 of cutting implements sharp-pointed, keen-

edged *18-*, *now Per WC Ayr.* **4** *of mechanisms* smooth-working, quick-acting *la18-*, *now local Ags-Rox.*
adv keenly, sharply *18-e20.*
~ly 1 *of sight or hearing* sharply, keenly, quickly, attentively *la18-19.* **2** briskly, quickly *la18-*, *now Sh.* **3** smartly, skilfully, adroitly *la18-e19.*
~ness sharpness, keenness, cleverness *19-*, *now Sh Abd Rox.*
~-eared with ears cocked *20-*, *now WC.* **~-eed** = sharp-eyed *18-*, *now local.* **~-gabbit** smooth-tongued, glib, voluble *la19-*, *now WC.* **~-lug'd** sharp-eared *19-*, *now Sh.* **~-sighted** = **~-eed**, *19-*, *now Sh.* **~-tongued** = **~-gabbit**, *19-*, *now Sh midLoth Rox.* **~-witted** = *adj* 1 (3) *la19-*, *now Sh midLoth WC.* [nME (once); ON *gleggr* clear-sighted, clever, distinct; also in Mod nEng dial]

gleg *see* CLEG

gleib &c *la15-e19*, **glebe; glibe &c** *la16-*, **gleb** *la16-e19* [glib, gləib] *n* **1** *now usu* **glebe** the portion of land assigned to a parish MINISTER in addition to his *stipend* (STEEPEND) *la15-*. **2** a lump, piece, quantity of anything *16-*, *now Sh.* **3** the soil, land; cultivated land, a plot, a field *18-*, *now Sh Rox.*
vt divide (land) into lots *18.*
gleebrie a large piece of (waste) ground *20-*, *Bnf Abd.* [ME *glebe*]

gleid *see* GLEY
gleme *see* GLAIM, GLIME
glen[1] *n* **1** a valley or hollow, *chf* one traversed by a stream or river, and *freq* narrow and steep-sided; a mountain valley as opposed to a STRATH *la14-*, *in place-names la12-*. **2** the daffodil *la19-*, *Ayr* [back-formation f *G~ Saturday*].
G~garry &c [glɛn'garı, -'gerı] a kind of flat-sided cap or bonnet (shaped rather like a modern forage cap) pointed at the front and back and *freq* with two ribbons hanging behind, *appar* a development of the *cockit bonnet* (COCK[2]) *2) 19-* [f Macdonnell of Glengarry who popularized it]. **G~ Saturday** a Saturday (the first or third) in April on which the children of Kilmarnock went to Crawfurdland Castle to pick daffodils *la19-*, *Ayr*; cf *n* 2. [Sc and IrGael *gleann*, early IrGael *glenn*]
glen[2] [*glɛn, *glɛn] *vt* = glean *la16-17*, *only Sc.*
glender *n* ~ **gane** *e19*, ~ **gait** *e20*, *of a person* on the decline (in health, morals etc), in a bad way. [appar f next]
glengore &c [*'glɛn'gor, *'glɛŋgor] *n* = GRAN(D)GORE *16-18.*
glengorie &c infected with syphilis *la16-e18.* [*cf* eModEng *glangore* (once)]
glennie &c *n*, *mining* a flame safety-lamp for testing for the presence of gas *20-*, *now Fif.* [f the inventor Dr W R Clanny]
glent, glint &c *v* **1** *vi* gleam, glint, shine, sparkle *18-*. **2** move quickly, dart, flash past *la18-*,

now Sh. **3** glance, peep, squint *la17-*, *now loca Sh-Gall.* **4** *only* **glint** *vt* cause (a light) to shine flash **on** *la19-*, *now Ork Abd Ags.*
n **1** a gleam, flash of light, a faint or momentar glitter *18-*. **2** a look, glance *la18-*. **3** a glimps *19-*. **4** *only* **glint** a flash of intuition, a sligh suspicion *la19-*, *local Sh-midLoth.* **5** *only* **glent** glancing blow, a slap *19-*, *Dmf.* **6** *only* **glint** scrap, bit, vestige *la19-*, *now midLoth.*
glintin dawn, daybreak *la19-e20.*
in a ~ in a flash, in a moment *la18-*, *now Sh.* [ME *glent*, laME *glynt* (rare); *cf* ModEng *glin* and Sw dial *glänta* slip, glide]

gles *see* GLASS

Glesca &c; Glasgow &c ['glɛskə, -ı, 'glɛzgə, -ı; *St* 'glazgo] **Glasgow bailie** a salt herring of fine quality; *occas* a red herring *20-*, *Fif Gsw SW.* **Glasgow Highlanders** a battalion of part-time volunteers, *latterly* the 9th (Territorial) Battalion of the *Highland Light Infantry* (HIELAND) *la19-20.* ~ **hoosie** a variety of the game of rounders *la19-e20.* ~ **Jock** coir rope used in binding haystacks *20-*, *Mry Abd.* ~ **keelie 1** *chf contemptuous* a (rough and tough) GLASWEGIAN *20-*. **2** *in pl* nickname for the *Highland Light Infantry* (HIELAND) *20-*. **Glasgow magistrate** = ~ *bailie*, *la18-*, *now Fif Gsw.* **Glasgow punch** a punch made with rum, cold water, sugar, lemons and limes *19-e20.* ~ **screwdriver** a hammer *20-*, *now Per Fif Lnk.* [the city]

gless, glessack *see* GLASS
glet *see* GLIT
glete *see* GLEET
glevin &c [*?'glivən] *vi*, *infin* glow *e16.* [only Sc; obscure]
glew *see* GLEE
gley &c, glee *17-*; **gly &c** *la16-*, *now Sh* [Sh-nEC gləi; *sEC-Gall* gli; *nEC also* gli] *vi* **1** squint; cast a sidelong glance; look askance *la16-*, *now local.* **2** avert the eyes, look away *18-19.* **3** look with one eye, take aim *19-*, *now Abd Ags.* **4** *fig* go astray; miscarry *19-e20.*
n **1** a squint; a sidelong or sly look, a glance; a cast in the eye *19-*, *local Sh-Edb.* **2** being off the straight, irregularity; error *19-*, *Abd Ags.* **3** aim; the act of aiming *la19-20*, *NE Ags.*
adj squint-eyed *20-*, *local Ags-Rox.*
adv off the straight, awry, *esp* **gae** *or* **gang** ~ *19-*, *local Ags-Slk; cf* AGLEY.
~(e)d *la17-*, **~it** *la15-e17*, **gleid &c** *la15-* [gləid, gləit; *sEC* gli:d] **1** squint-eyed, having a squint or cast in the eye; squinting *la15-*. **2** one-eyed, blind in one eye *19-*, *now Per.* **3** off the straight, slanting; crooked, awry *la16-*, *now local.* **4** mistaken, misguided *19-*, *now midLoth.*
gleytness &c 1 the state of having a squint, being squint-eyed *17-*, *now Sh Abd.* **2** obliqueness *19-*, *now Abd.* **~d-eed** = gleyed 1, *la19-*, *local Sh-Bwk.* **~d-necked** having a twisted neck *19-*, *now Cai midLoth.* **gae** *or* **gang ~d** go astray, *esp* morally *la18-*, *now Ags midLoth.*

~**-eyed &c** = *adj, la19-, local Bnf-S.*

be aff the ~ be wide of the mark, be wrong *la19-, NE midLoth.* [now only Sc and nEng dial; ME *glee &c*; obscure]

glib &c; glibe *18-19 adj* **1** smooth, slippery, moving without friction *18-, now SW-Uls.* **2** *fig* sharp in one's dealings, smart, cunning *19-, now Sh Ags.* **3** voluble, fluent (without the implication of insincerity etc) *19-, local.* **4** = glib.

vt make smooth *18-19.*

adv smoothly, easily, readily *18-19.*

~**by &c** = *adj* 3, *la19.*

~**-gabbit** *la18-, now Abd Per midLoth,* ~**-mou(e)d** *la19-, now Abd Ags* = *adj* 3; gossipy; smooth-tongued.

glibe *see* GLEIB

glid *19;* **glaid &c** *16-e20 adj* **1** moving smoothly; free from friction *16-e20.* **2** slippery *19.*

glidder *chf in pl* small stones, SCREE *la18-e20, chf Rox.* [related to GLED[1]; MDu *glad,* OFris *gled.* DOST *glad*]

glie *see* GLEE

gliff *la14-e16, la18-,* **glaff &c** *19-,* **gloff &c** *18-,* **gluff &c** *la15, la18-;* **glouf &c** *la19-e20* [glɪf, glaf, glof, glʌf; *Renfr Ayr Dmf also* glʌuf] *vti* **1** *only* **gliff** glance (**at**), look at briefly or hurriedly *la19-, now Ags.* **2** *vt* frighten, startle *la18-, local.* **3** *vi* gasp (with surprise, cold etc) *19-, now Ork.*

n **1** a hurried or startled glance; a glimpse *16-, now local.* **2** a moment, a short while; a short snatch, 'wink' of sleep, *freq* **in a** ~ in a trice *la18-, now local Sh-Kcb.* **3** a momentary resemblance *la19-, now Abd.* **4** a flash, glint *19-20.* **5** a slight attack, touch (of an illness), *esp* **a** ~ **o** (**the**) **cauld** *la19-, local Abd-Edb.* **6** a whiff, puff, breath of air; a gust, blast of hot or cold air; a slight or suddenly perceptible smell *19-, now local Abd-S.* **7** a momentary or sudden sensation (physical or emotional) *18-, now Bwk S.* **8** a sudden fright, a scare, a shock, *freq* **get a** ~ *la18-, now local Bnf-S.*

gliffin &c *la14-e16,* **glowfin** *la16* = *v* 1. **gliffin(g)** a moment, instant *19-e20.* [ME; *cf* Norw dial *glufs* (a gust of wind)]

glim *n* **1** a gleam, glimmer *19-, now Sh Cai Uls.* **2** a glimpse, glance *17-, now Sh.* [Norw dial; *cf* Eng *gleam*]

glime &c *vi, also* **gleme &c** *e16* take a sidelong glance, squint *e16, 19-e20.*

n a sidelong look, sly glance *la18-e20.* [prob ultimately f as prec; *cf* Norw dial *glyma* look sly or roguish]

glim-glam &c; **gleem- &c** *la19-e20 n* the game of blind-man's buff *la18-e20.* [reduplicated f GLAUM]

glimmer &c *vi* **1** = glimmer *16-.* **2** *of the eyes* be dazzled; blink, wink, look unsteadily *16-, now local Ork-Kcb.*

~**in** *of the eyes* half-closed, peering *19-, now Bnf Abd.*

glimp *n* = glimpse *la19-, now Fif.* [prob a back-formation, but *cf* MDu *glimpen* burn, glow, shine, Du *glimp* a glimpse, show]

glink *vi* glance, look sidelong(**at**) *la19-20, Sh Ayr.*

n a sidelong look, peep, squint *19-e20.* [var of *glint* (GLENT)]

glint, glintin *see* GLENT

glipe *n* an uncouth, clumsy, thoughtless or stupid person *19-, now Uls.* [perh f GYPE]

glisk *vti* glance, look cursorily (at) *18-, now WC.*

n **1** a glance, cursory look, peep, glimpse *la17-, now local Sh-WC.* **2** a gleam, sparkle, flash *19-, now WC.* **3** a moment, twinkling *la18-, Pbls WC.* **4** a momentary sensation or reaction; a short spell; a whiff, trace *19-, now WC.* **5** a resemblance, a slight similarity *la19-, local Sh-Per.*

a ~ **o cauld** a touch of cold, a slight cold *19-, now Ags nEC Rox.* [*cf* Norw dial *glisa* gleam, flash, glisten]

gliss *vi, only in pt and adj* **glist** shone, glistened; shining *18-e19.* [f as prec]

glister *vi* glisten, glitter *la16-, now local.*

n glitter, brilliance *la16-, now local.* [ME *glistre &c,* eModEng *glister;* now arch or dial in Eng; *cf* GLAISTER[2]]

glit &c *la15-,* **glute** *e15-,* **glut &c** *e15, 19-;* **glet &c** *la19-* [glɪt, glet, glʌt, glit; *Ork* glut] *n* **1** filth; slimy, greasy or sticky matter *15-, now local.* **2** phlegm, mucus, the thin liquid discharging from a wound etc *16-, now local.* **3** the slimy vegetation found in ponds etc *19-, now Arg Gall Uls.* **4** *only* **glut** slime on fish or decomposing meat *19-, now Sh Bwk.*

glittie &c **1** slimy, greasy, oily, mucous *la18-, now local.* **2** smooth, slippery *19-, Kcb Rox.* **glittous &c** filthy, base, vile *16.* [eModEng *glit, glut,* ME *glet,* OF *glette*]

gliv *see* GLUIVE

gloam &c [glom] *vi* become dusk, grow dark *18-, now NE Ayr.*

n twilight, a faint light *18-, now Abd.* [back-formation f next]

gloamin &c *la18-,* **gloming &c;** **glowming** *la16-* ['gloməɪn, -ɪŋ; ***'glʌum-] *n* **1** evening twilight, dusk *15-.* **2** morning twilight, dawn *19-, now Wgt Uls.*

~ **fa** *19-e20,* ~ **grey** *19,* ~ **hour** *19-, now Ags midLoth* = *n* 1. ~ **shot** a twilight interval before the lighting of lights, a short time of relaxation in the evening *la18-e19.*

~ **tide** = *n* 1, *18-, now Abd.* [OE *glōmung*]

gloan &c *n* energy, 'go'; excitement *19-20, Abd.* [obscure]

glob *n* = blob *20-, now Ags S.* [conflation of Eng *blob* and *globe*]

glock; gluck &c [glok, glʌk; *Ross* gluk] *vi, chf of liquid* make a gurgling noise *la18, now NE Ags Rox.*

n **1** *chf of liquid* a gurgling noise, a gurgle *la19-, now Abd Ags Arg Rox.* **2** a gulp *19-e20.* [onomat; *cf* GLOG[1]]

glocken &c vi start with fright 19-e20, SW. [appar nEng dial *gloppen*, ME *glopnen*, ON *glúpna* be downcast]

glod &c adj meaning unknown e16.

gloe see GLUIVE

gloff see GLIFF

glog¹ &c vi **1** chf ∼ **ower &c** swallow, gulp down 19-, now NE. **2** gurgle 20-, NE Arg.
n **1** a gulp 19-e20, Abd. **2** a gurgling noise la19-, now NE. [onomat; cf GLOCK, GLAG and Gael *glug*]

glog² adj, chf literary black, dark 19-e20. [see SND]

gloid &c vi do something in a slovenly, messy or awkward way la19-, Ags. [prob voiced var of CLOITER]

gloit see CLOIT²

gloming see GLOAMIN

glondouris see GLUNDER

gloom 17-, **glowme &c** la15-e19 [glum; Rox also glʌum] vi **1** = gloom la15-e20. **2** of a horse show signs of ill-temper or viciousness 20-, now Arg.
n **1** a frown, scowl la16-, now Dmf Rox, only Sc. **2** = gloom. **3** in pl a state of depression 19-, now NE.

glore &c n glory la14-e20, latterly arch.
vi glory, take pride (in), boast 16-e17. [OF *glore*, *gloire*]

glorg &c vi work messily 19-, now Sh. [prob onomat w infl f GLAUR and CLAG]

glorgie &c [*?'glorgɪ] adj, of weather sultry, close 19-e20, Ayr. [see SND]

glorifee &c, glorify vt = glorify 16-.

gloriositie n self-importance, boastful bearing la16-17. [OF *gloriouseté*]

glorious &c adj **1** = glorious 15-. **2** vainglorious la15-, now Ags. **3** in a state of elation from drinking alcohol la18-.

gloss &c n **1** = gloss. **2** of a fire a bright glow la18-, now Slk. **3** a doze 20-, now Bnf Abd.
vi doze 20-, now Bnf Abd.
∼y **1** = glossy. **2** of a fire glowing, clear 20-, now Fif. [cf GLOZE]

glotten &c vi thaw partially 19-e20. [perh f next]

glottnit &c adj clotted or wet with blood; bloodshot e16. [obscure]

glouf see GLIFF

glouster &c [*'glʌustər] v ∼in blustering; loudmouthed 19-e20. [conflation of BLOUSTER and GOUSTER]

glove see GLUIVE

glowe, glow [glʌu] n, vi = glow la14-.

glower &c, glowr &c ['glʌu(ə)r] vi **1** stare, gaze intently la15-. **2** literary, of the heavenly bodies gleam, shine brightly la18-19. **3** be drunk to the point of being glassy-eyed 17-. **4** scowl la17-.
n **1** a wide-eyed stare, an intent look 17-. **2** a scowl, a fierce look 17-. [see SND]

glowfin see GLIFF

glowme see GLOOM

glowming see GLOAMIN

glowr see GLOWER

gloy n straw, esp as used for thatching etc la15-, now Sh Ork Cai.
vt thresh (corn) partially or hastily la18-e20. [ME *gloy*, MDu *gleye*, *gluye*, OF *glui*]

gloyd see GLYDE

gloze &c vi blaze, shine brightly 19-, now Ags Per.
n a blaze la19-, now Ags Per. [var of GLOSS; cf MLowGer *glosen* gleam, glitter]

gluck see GLOCK

gluf see GLUIVE

gluff see GLIFF

glugger &c ['glʌgər; Cai also 'glʌug-] vi make a gurgling noise 19-, now Cai Bnf Ags. [onomat; cf GLOG¹, glutter (GLUT¹) and Eng *glug*]

gluive &c now Ags, **gluve &c, gluf &c** la14-17, **gloe &c** la18-20; **glove &c** la16-, **gliv &c** la19-, now Sh Bnf Abd [gløv; Sh NE glɪv; *glø] n = glove la14-.
∼ **of plate** a gauntlet 15-e16.

glum vi look sullen la19-, now Ags. [laME *glom*]

glumch see GLUMSH

glump now Ags, **glumph &c** now local Sh-Dmf [glʌmp, glʌmf] vi be glum, sulk, look gloomy 19-.
n, only **glumph** a sulky or morose person 19-, now local Sh-Kcb.
∼y &c sulky, sullen, morose 19-, now Ags. [onomat, w infl f GLUM]

glumsh &c; glumch [glʌmʃ] vi be or look sulky or morose; grumble, whine 19-, now local Bnf-Fif.
n a sulky, sullen, surly mood, look or reaction la19-20.
adj **1** sulky, sour-looking la19-, now Abd Ags. **2** melancholy la19-, now Per. [onomat, f GLUM]

glunder &c [*'glʌn(d)ər] n in the ∼s &c 19 or **glondouris** e16 in the sulks. [see SND]

glundie &c [*'glʌndɪ; Gall *'glʌnɪ] n a fool la18-e20. [see SND]

Glunimie &c [*'glʌnəmɪ] n, derog a Highlander 1 (HIELAND) 18-e19. [deriv of Gael *glùn* a knee; perh here = *glùineanach* gartered, (one) wearing garters; cf GLUNTOCH]

glunsh¹ &c vi look sour, scowl; grumble, snap at; freq ∼ **and gloom** etc, 18-, now local N-Kcb.
n a sour look, scowl la18-, now WC.
adj sulky, sour, bad-tempered 19-e20.
∼y = adj, 19-, now Dmf. [cf GLUMSH]

glunsh² &c vi gobble, gulp food 20-, Cai Kcb Dmf. [see SND]

gluntie adj tall, lean, haggard 19-e20, Bwk Rox. [see SND]

gluntoch e16; **gluntow** la15 contemptuous term of address to a Highlander (HIELAND). [?Gael *glùn dubh* a black (ie hairy) knee; cf GLUNIMIE]

glush n ∼ie &c of snow soft, slushy 19-, now Fif. [onomat]

glut[1] &c *n* a gulp, draught (of liquid) *19-*, *now midLoth.*
vi swallow, gulp down *la18-*, *now midLoth.*
~ter &c ['glʌtər, 'glʌð-, 'glʌd-] *n* a gurgling noise in the throat *19-e20. v* 1 *vi* gurgle, splutter *19-e20.* 2 *vt* swallow noisily, disgustingly or voraciously *19-e20.* **gluthery** *adj* muddy; slimy *la19-*, *now Per Fif.* [eModEng]
glut[2] *n* a wooden wedge, used *eg* for adjusting a plough *18-e19.* [see SND]
glut(e) *see* GLIT
gluther &c [*?'glʌðər, *?'glʌd-] *vti* flatter *la14-16.* [nME *glother*; obscure]
gluthery *see* GLUT[1]
gluttery &c *n* gluttony *la15-e16.* [nME; OF *glotirie*]
gluve *see* GLUIVE
gly *see* GLEY
glyde &c, **gloyd** &c [*gləid, *gloid] *n* 1 an old, worn-out horse *la16-e20.* 2 *transf* an old, useless or disagreeable person *la18-19.* [obscure]
gnap &c [(g)nap; *Mry Bnf* gnɛp] *v* 1 *vi* bite, gnaw *16-*, *now NE.* 2 *vti* speak mincingly or affectedly *la18-e20.*
n a morsel, a bite of food *la18-*, *now Abd.*
gnapper = *knapper* 3 (KNAP[2]) *e16.* (**in**) **gnappin** &c **earnest** (in) dead earnest *la18-e20*, *Abd.*
~-(at)-the-win &c thin *oatcakes* (AIT), light bread, insubstantial food *la19-*, *NE.* [ME; *cf* KNAP[2] and GNIP]
gnash [(g)naʃ] *n* 1 a gnashing or snap of the teeth *19.* 2 biting, caustic talk *19-*, *now Rox.*
vt = gnash. [*cf* NASH]
gnashick &c ['gnaʃək] *n* the red bearberry *19-e20*, *Mry Bnf.* [Gael *cnàimhseag*]
gneck &c [gnɛk] *n* a notch *19-20*, *NE.* [prob f NICK]
gnib &c [gnɪb; *Sh* kn-] *adj* quick in action or speech *18-e20*, *Bnf Abd.* [onomat]
gnidge *see* KNIDGE
gnip &c [gnɪp] *vti* 1 nip, bite *15-16.* 2 *vi* talk carpingly or affectedly *la19-e20*, *Mry Bnf.*
n, *also* **~per** a morsel, a bite of food *la19*, *Bnf.*
~per for *or* **and gnapper** &c bit by bit, every bit *18-e20*, *chf NE.* [only Sc; var of KNIP[2]]
gnyauve &c [(g)n(j)ɑv] *vt* = gnaw *la18-20*, *N.*
go *interj* expressing surprise or admiration *la19-*, *local NE-Bwk.* [euphemistic f Eng *God*]
go *see* GAE
goad-loup *see* GADLOUP
goad(s)man *see* GAUD[2]
goam &c *vt*, *chf in negative* not heed or notice; not recognize or greet *la18-*, *now Pbls Bwk S.*
~less stupid *20-*, *C, S.* [f northern ModEng dial; ME *gom(e)*, ON *gaumr*]
goan &c *n* a wooden bowl or dish *18-19*, *chf SW.* [ModEng dial *gaun* &c a wooden pail or tub, Cheshire *goan* a gallon measure, shortened f *gallon*]
goat *see* GAIT[1]

gob[1] &c; **gub** *20- n* the mouth; a bird's beak *la16-.*
~-stopper a large, round, hard sweet *la20-*, *local.* [Sc and IrGael *gob* a beak; a mouth; *cf* GAB[2]]
gob[2] *n* a mass or lump, *usu* of something soft *19-*, *now local Bnf-Uls.*
vi spit *20-*, *now WC.* [ME; OF *gobe* mouthful, lump]
gob *see* GAB[3]
gobble *vt* = gobble.
n, *golf* a rapid straight PUTT[1] at the hole *la19.*
~ a putt play such a shot *la20-*, *NE Ags Fif.*
goblet &c *n* 1 = goblet *la15-.* 2 *also* **goglet** *now Abd Ags* an iron pot or pan with a straight handle and *usu* convex sides *18-*, *only Sc.*
gock &c *n*, *chf* **~ie** a deep wooden dish *la18-19*, *NE.* [perh f COG[1] or reborrowed f Gael *an cog* [ən'gok] the cog]
gock *see* GOWK[1]
god &c *n* = god *la14-.*
~ba(i)rne &c **gift** a baptismal gift to one's godchild *16-e18.* **~('s)-send** a wreck or other profitable flotsam etc *18-20*, *Sh Ork SW.*
god *see* GUID
goesomer, **goe-summer** &c [*'go'sʌmər, *-'sɪmər] *n* a spell of mild weather in late autumn, an Indian summer *17-18.* [obscure; *cf* GO-HARVEST]
gof *see* GOIF
goff *see* GOWF[1]
goffring *see* GOUFFER
gog &c *n*, *games* the TEE[1] or mark in *curling* (CURL), marbles etc *la18-20.* [obscure]
gogar &c *n* ~ **gowne** meaning unknown *la15.*
goggie &c ['gogɪ, 'gʌgɪ] *n*, *child's word* 1 an egg *20-*, *Arg Lnk.* 2 an unfledge bird, a nestling *la20-*, *Ags Kcb Dmf.* [Gael (of Arran) *gogaidh* child's word for an egg]
goggles, **gogillis** &c *la16-e17 n pl* 1 = goggles, protective spectacles *la16-.* 2 *also* **hors ~** *(e17)* blinkers *17-*, *now Abd Ags.*
goglet *see* GOBLET
go-harvest &c [*'go'herst, *-'hɛrvəst] *n* the late autumn, between harvest time and winter *18-19.* [obscure; *cf* GOESOMER]
goich [goix] *n* a haughty carriage of the head *20*, *Arg.* [Gael *goic* a tossing of the head]
goif &c, **gove** &c; **gof** &c *16* [*gov, *gof, *gʌuf] *n*, *also in pl* **govis** &c, **golffis** &c *16-17* [*govz, *gʌufs] a pillory *la15-e17.*
vt, *only* **gove** put in a pillory *la15-e17.* [obscure]
goif *see* GOVE[1]
goiff *see* GOWF[1]
goit *see* GET
goke *see* GOWK[1]
gokstule &c [*'gok'støl] *n* = cuckstool, a cucking stool *la16.*
golach &c; **golack** &c, **goulock** &c ['goləx, -ək, 'gʌl-; *nEC, WC, SW also* 'gʌul-; *Ross Inv also* 'gol(j)əxən, 'gʌl-, 'gul-] *n* 1 an insect: (1) *specif*

the carnivorous ground beetle *19-*, *NE, EC Ayr.*
(2) the earwig *19-*, *now local Cai-Uls.* **2** *derog* a
person *20-*, *now Cai Abd.*
forky ~ *la20-*, *Bnf Abd*, **hornie** *or* **horned** ~
la18-, *now local Bnf-Kcb* = n 1 (2). [Gael *gobhlag*
an earwig; a fork-shaped stick; cf *forkietail*
(FORK)]
golaich &c [go'lɛx] *n* a breed of short-legged
hen *19-*, *now Per.* [Eng *go* + LAICH]
gold, goldeine, goldie, goldilocks *see*
GOWD
goleinȝeis &c [*gə'lɛnjɪz, *-'lɪnjɪz, *-'linjɪz] *n pl*
deceitful or evasive statements or arguments
16-17.

 golenȝeour *la16*, **gileynour &c** *18-e20*
 [*gə'lɛnjər, *-'lɛŋər, *-'lɪŋər, &c] a cheat, swindler. [obscure]
golf *see* GOWF[1]
golffis *see* GOIF
golk *see* GOWK[1]
gollach &c ['goləx] *vi* yell, bawl *19-*, *now Arg.*
[onomat; *cf* GOLLER and GOLLIE]
gollan &c ['golən; *Ork* 'gʌl-] *n* name for various
wild flowers, *eg* the daisy, the corn marigold
la19-, *now Ork Cai.* [northern eModEng, ME
gollan(d) &c; prob Scand; *cf* GOWAN]
goller &c; guller &c *19-*, **gulder &c** *la19-*
['gol(d)ər, 'gʌl(d)-] *vi* **1** roar, shout, bawl *18-*,
now local. **2** make a gurgling sound *19-*, *now Sh
Rox.*
 n **1** a shout, roar, yell *19-*, *now Kcb Rox Uls.* **2** a
verbal outburst, as of oaths *20-*, *now Ork Wgt.* **3**
a loud laugh *20-*, *Ork Wgt Uls.* **4** a gurgling
noise *19-e20.* [onomat; *cf* GOLLACH and next]
gollie *vi* **1** = GOLLER *v* 1, *la18-*, *now Abd Dmf.* **2**
scold *19-*, *Ayr.* **3** weep noisily *la18-*, *now Abd.*
 n = GOLLER *n* 1, now Abd. [onomat; *cf* ON,
Norw dial *gola* and GOLLACH]
gollop &c *vi* = gulp *20-*.
 n a hasty or greedy gulp *20-*, *now Arg Ayr.*
gomach ['goməx] *n* a fool, simpleton *19-*, *now
Uls.* [*cf* IrGael *gamach*, ModIr dial *goamie*]
gomerel &c; gomral &c *n* a fool, stupid person *19-*.
 adj foolish, stupid *e19.* [GOAM + *-rel*; cf *gamphrell* (GUMPH)]
gomphion *see* GUMPHION
gomral *see* GOMEREL
gone *see* GOUN, GUN
goniel &c ['gonɪəl, 'gonjəl; *Bwk* 'gonl] *n* **1** a fool
la19-, *now Dmf Rox.* **2** BRAXY mutton; a sheep
found dead *19-e20*, *Dmf Rox.* [*cf* Eng dial
gawney, goney]
gonterns &c *interj* expressing surprise or delight
la18-e20. [prob f Eng *conscience*]
goo[1] *19-*; **gou &c** *18-e20* [gu; *S* gʌu] *n* **1** a strong,
persistent, *freq* disagreeable taste *18-*, *Gen except
Sh Ork.* **2** an offensive smell *19-*, *local Cai-Kcb.*
3 *fig* a liking, taste (**o** *or* **for**) *18-e20.*
 ~**ly** tasty, having a distinctive flavour *20-*, *now
Fif Dmf.* [F *goût*]

goo[2] &c *19-*, **goule &c** *la15-e16*; **gow** *la17-e20*
[*NE* gu, gʌu] *n* = gull *N.*
goo[3] *vi* **1** of an infant coo *la19-*, *now NE, EC Rox.* **2**
retch *la19.* [imit]
good *see* GUID
goog &c *n* something soft, moist or messy *19-*,
now Abd Ags. [see SND]
goold *see* GOWD
goom *see* GUM[1]
goon *see* GOUN
goor *la19-*, **gor(e)** *15-e20*; **gour- &c** *la16-19*
[*NE* gur; *Sh Ork Cai* gʌr, gor] *n* **1** mucus, waxy
matter, *esp* in the eye *15-*, *now Sh Ork Cai Ags.* **2**
mud, dirt; muddy, stagnant water *la19-*, *local
Sh-Kcdn.* **3** slush in running water *la19-*, *now Sh
Bnf Abd.*
 vi, of streams in thaw become choked with snow
and ice *la19-*, *now Abd.*

 gorroch &c ['gorəx] *vt* **1** mix, stir (something
 soft and messy) *19-*, *now Kcb.* **2** make a mess of,
 spoil *20-*, *now Kcb.* *n* a trampled muddy spot
 la19-, *now Kcb Dmf.*
 ~**y &c** *n, also* ~**ies** fish refuse, *freq* salmon *la16-*,
 now Abd. *adj* muddy, slimy *20-*, *now Kcdn.* [ME
 gore filth, blood, MDu *goor*, Norw dial *gor* filth,
 fish-slime]
goose *see* GUSE
goosy *see* GUSSIE
gopin *see* GOWPEN
gor &c *interj* expressing surprise or incredulity; a
mild oath *19-*, *now Sh N Ayr.*
 my *or* **by &c** ~ = *interj*, *la19-*, *now Rox Uls.*
 [euphemistic f Eng *God*]
gor *see* GOOR, GORE
gorb &c *n* **1** an unfledged bird *la18-*, *now Ags Kcb
Uls.* **2** an infant, young child *19-*, *now Dmf.* **3** a
glutton *la19-*, *Ags Per SW Uls.*
 vi eat greedily *20-*, *Gall Uls.*
 ~**el &c 1** = *n* 1, *19-*, *now NE Per Pbls.* **2** = *n* 2,
 19-, *now Lnk.* ~**ellit** *of an egg* containing a
 developing chick *20-*, *NE Per Pbls.* ~**et 1** = *n*
 1, *16-20.* **2** = *n* 2, *19-20*, *Ags.* ~**ie** = *n* 1,
 la19-e20. **God's** ~**ie** *a* clergyman *e19.* ~**lin &c**
 18-, *now NE Ags*, **gordlin** *19-e20*, *Abd* = *n* 1.
 [prob intensive of GOB[1]; but *cf* Eng dial *gor*]
gorble *vt* eat ravenously, gobble **up** *18-*, *now
Dmf.* [prob chf onomat, w infl f Eng *gobble* and
gorbel (GORB)]
gor-cock *n, chf literary* the moor-cock or male of
the red grouse *la18-20.* [*cf* GORMAW]
gordie *see* GIRD[1]
gordlin *see* GORB
Gordon Highlander *n, now freq abbreviated to*
Gordon 1 a soldier in *the Gordon Highlanders,*
la18-. **2** *the* ~**s** the regiment raised by the
fourth Duke of Gordon in 1794, *orig the 100th*
and later *the 92nd Foot* (NINETY-TWA), which
became linked in 1881 with *the 75th Highlanders,*
la18-.
gore &c, gor *la15-17 vti* = gore, stab, pierce
la15-.
 n a deep furrow *la18-20.*

gie a ploo gurr cut a furrow deeper than usual and at a slant *la20-, Bnf Abd.*

gore *see* GOOR

gorfy &c ['gorfɪ, 'gʌr-] *adj* coarse *19-, Ags.* [prob metath f GROFF]

gorge *16-e20,* **gurge** *16-,* now *Rox,* **grudge** *19-,* now *Rox v* **1** *vt* choke **up** (a channel) with mud, snow etc *16-,* now *Sh.* **2** *vi, only* **gurge** *esp of water* swell, surge *16-,* now *Rox.* [ME; OF *gorge*]

gorgeat *see* GORGET

gorge-millar *n* meaning unknown *e16.*

gorget &c *15-17;* **gorgeat** *la15-e16 n* **1** = gorget *15-e17.* **2** *in pl* an iron collar used as a form of pillory *17.*

gorlin &c *n* **1** an unfledged bird *la18-,* now *Ags Pbls SW.* **2** a very young person, an urchin *18-,* now *Kcb.* [Eng dial *gor;* cf *gorblin* (GORB)]

gormaw [*'gor'mɑ] *n* the cormorant *16-e19.* [*gor* (perh f GOOR) + MAW²]

gornal *n* a button *e20, Cai.* [f KIRNEL]

gorroch *see* GOOR

gorsk *see* GOSK

gosh *interj* = gosh! *19-.*

~**en(s)** *19-e20,* ~ **be here** *la19-, Sh Abd,* ~ **bliss me** *la19-,* now *Bnf Ags,* ~ **me,** *la19-, local Ags-Rox,* **gude** ~ *19-, Ags Rox* = *interj.*

goshens *n pl* abundance, plenty; *freq* a good catch (of fish) *la19-20.* [biblical *Goshen* the fertile land allotted to the Israelites]

gosk &c; **gorsk** *18-e20 n* coarse, rank grass produced by cattle droppings in a pasture *18-,* now *Abd Ags.*

~**ie** rank, luxuriant *19-,* now *NE Ags.* [perh f *gor* (GOOR) dirt + REESK]

gospel *n* = gospel.

~ **greedy** regularly attending church, fond of church-going *la19-,* now *Stlg Kcb Uls.*

goss, gosse *e17 n* familiar form of address; a friend, crony *17-19.* [reduced f Eng *gossip &c* a godparent; a friend]

got *see* GET

gote &c; **gott &c** *17-20;* **gut** *la18-,* now *Sh Abd Dmf Uls,* **gyte &c** *la19-,* now *NE Pbls,* **gwite** *20-, NE n* **1** a ditch, drain, watercourse *la16-20.* **2** a narrow rocky inlet of the sea, a creek; a navigable channel *18-,* now *local.*

goting &c *mining* a drainage gutter cut in the pavement of a mine or working *la18-,* now *Fif Loth.* [ME, MLowGer, MDu]

gote *see* GAIT¹

goth &c [goθ] *interj* a mild oath *19-,* now *Cai Kcb.* [altered f Eng *God*]

gotherlisch &c [*Ross NE* 'gʌðərlɪdʒ, 'godərlɪtʃ, *'goðər-, &c*] *adj* slovenly; confused *19-20, chf Abd.* [see SND]

goting *see* GOTE

gott *see* GOTE

gottin *see* GET

gou *see* GOO¹

gouch &c [*?gux, *?gox] *only literary, n* a gasp; *also as interj* ouch! *19.* [imit]

goud *see* GUID

goudie &c ['gʌudɪ] *n* = Gouda (cheese) *la19-.*

gouf &c [gʌuf] *vt, building* underpin or underbuild (a wall or building) to secure its foundations or put in a damp-course *18-, chf Gsw.* [perh f COLF]

gouff *see* GUFF¹, GUFF², GUFF³

gouffer &c [*'gʌufər] *vt* goffer; decorate (cloth), *perh* with an impressed design *la16-17.*

goffring goffering *la16-e17* [earlier in Sc]. [F *gaufrer;* cf GUFFER²]

goug *see* GUGA

goukmey &c [*?'gʌuk'məi] *n* the grey gurnard *19-e20.* [cf *gowdie* 2 (GOWD)]

gould *see* GOWD

goule *see* GOO²

goulf *see* GOWF¹

goulock *see* GOLACH

goum *see* GUM²

goun &c *la15-;* **gown, gone &c** *la15-e16,* **goon** *la19-* [gun] *n* **1** = gown *la14-.* **2** *specif, freq* ~**ie** a nightgown, nightshirt, *esp* a child's *19-.*

~ **class,** ~ **curriculum** *Glasgow Univ* a class qualifying for or the curriculum leading to the Arts degree *la18-e19.* ~ **student** *etc, Glasgow Univ* a matriculated student attending a ~ *class* and intending to take the full course for a degree, hence entitled to wear the Arts student's *red gown* (REID¹) *18.*

goun *see* GUN

gour- *see* GOOR

gourd &c [gurd] *adj* dull; heavy; stiff (to use) *15-19.*

vi, of water become pent up *18-,* now *Bnf Rox.* [F *gourd* benumbed, stiff]

Gourlay [*'gurle] *n* a superior make of golf-ball *la18-e19.* [the name of the manufacturer]

gourlins [?'gurlənz] *n pl* the edible roots or tubers of the earth-nut *19-,* now *Kcb.* [Gael *cutharlan* the earth-nut]

Gourock ['gurək] **it's all to (the) one &c side like** ~ it is lop-sided *20-, EC, WC.* [the town on the Clyde]

gouster &c ['gʌustər; *Sh also* 'gust-; *Sh Ork also* 'gʌst-] *vi* boast, bluster *la19-,* now *Sh Ork Dmf.* *n* **1** a wild, violent, blustering or swaggering person *18-,* now *chf Ork Kcb Dmf.* **2** a violent outburst *la20-, Sh Ork Dmf.*

goust(e)rous 1 hearty, vigorous *19-e20.* **2** *of weather* dark and stormy *19-,* now *Dmf.* ~**y** wet and windy, blustery *20-,* now *Sh Gall Dmf.* [prob Eng dial *gauster, goster* behave in a noisy, blustering manner]

goustly *see* GOWSTIE

goustrous *see* GOUSTER

gousty *see* GOWSTIE

govan *see* GOVE¹

govanenty &c ['govənentɪ, -endɪ] *interj* expressing surprise *la19-,* now *Cai.* [perh altered f *God defend ye, God amend it* or the like: *cf* GOVIE]

gove¹ &c; **goif &c** *la15-18* [gov] *vi* **1** stare, gaze;

stare stupidly or vacantly *la14-*, *now local Cai-S*.
2 wander aimlessly about *20-*, *now Rox*. **3** *of
animals* start (with fright), toss the head *19-e20*.
n a vacant stare *19-20*.

govan &c flighty, coquettish *e19*. **govie &c** *adj*
= *govan*, *e19*. *n* an awkward or silly person *20-*,
now Uls. [obscure]

gove² *n*, also govie nickname for a headmaster or
school governor *la19-e20*. [contracted f Eng
governor]

gove *see* GOIF

governament &c [*gʌ'vɛrnəmɛnt] *n* = government *la16-e17*.

govie &c *interj, also* ~ **dick,** ~ **ding** expressing
surprise *19-*, *now local N-S*. [euphemistic f Eng
God]

govie *see* GOVE¹, GOVE²

govis *see* GOIF

gow¹ &c [*SW* gʌu, *gjʌu] *n* a fool *19-*, *now Wgt*.
[prob Eng *gull* a fool]

gow² [gʌu] *n, chf literary* a blacksmith *la19-e20, as
a surname la16-*. [Gael *gobha*]

gow³ &c [gu; *also* *?gʌu] *n* a halo around the sun
or moon supposed to be a sign of storms *19-*,
now midLoth. [perh Eng *gull* a trick]

gow⁴ &c [gʌu, 'gu(ı)] *vt, usu* ~ **ower** wheedle,
persuade *la19-e20, NE*. [Eng *gull* cheat]

gow *see* GOO²

gowan &c ['gʌuən] *n* **1** the daisy *16-*. **2** the ox-
eye daisy or marguerite *20-*, *local*.
~**(e)d** covered with daisies, daisied *19*. ~**y &c**
1 = prec *18-*. **2** *of weather* (deceptively) bright
or fine *19-e20*.
~**-gabbit** = ~*y* 2, *19-e20*.
ewe ~ = *n* 1, *19-*, *now Ags Pbls*. **horse** ~
applied to various wild flowers, *esp:* **1** = *n* 2,
19-, *now local Inv-Rox;* **2** the dandelion *19-e20*.
lapper ~ the globe-flower *19-*, *now Rox*.
(large) white ~ = *n* 2, *19-*, *local Bnf-Per*.
lucken &c ~ = *lapper* ~, *la16-*, *now Rox*. **May**
~ = *n* 1, *19-*, *now Ags*. **not care a** ~ not care
in the least, not care a fig *19-*, *now midLoth*. **yellow** ~ any of various yellow wild flowers such
as the buttercup, marigold etc *18-*. [var of
northern eModEng *gollan(d) &c; cf* GOLLAN]

gowd &c *18-*, **goold** *19*, **gold &c; gould &c**
la15-e20 [gʌud; guld] *n* = gold *la14-*.
~**en,** ~**in &c** = golden *la14-*. **gowdanook** the
skipper or saury *la18-19*. **golden crest(ie)** the
goldcrest *la19-*, *now midLoth*. **golden knap &c,
gowdnap** an early variety of pear *e19, Stlg*.
goldin myne &c a gold mine *e16*. **golden
penny** = *gold penny, la16-e17*. **gowdie &c 1**
also **goldie** *19-*, *now EC Lnk*, **gooldie &c** *19-*,
now local Arg-S the goldfinch *19*. **2** one of various fishes, *eg* the dragonet, the gurnard, the sea
scorpion *18-*, *now Ork NE nEC*. **3** the treasurer
of a trade corporation *la19-e20*. **gowdie &c
(duck)** the golden-eye duck *la18-*, *now Sh*. **gae**

gowdie-lane *of a child* walk unaided *19*. **goldilocks** the wood crowfoot *la19-*, *now Slk*.
gowds &c pet name for a child or a married
woman *20-, Cai*.
goldeine &c [*?'gold'in, *?'gʌud-, &c] the
golden-eye duck *la16*. **gold-penny** a shipping
due *la16-17*. ~ **spink &c** the goldfinch *16-*,
now Per Pbls.

gowf¹ &c,   **golf &c; goulf** *17*,   **goiff &c**
16-e17, **goff &c** *17-18* [gʌuf; *gof] *n, formerly
freq* **the** ~ the game of golf *la15-*.
~**ing &c,** *freq* **the** ~**ing** = *n, 18-*.
~ **ba(ll) 1** a golf ball *16-*. **2** the ball used in
the game of SHINTY; the game itself *la19-e20*,
Lnk Ayr. ~ **club** a golf club *16-*. ~ **house** a
golf club-house *la18-20*. ~ **links** a golf-course
by the seashore *la18-*. ~ **stick** = ~ *club, 20-*,
now midLoth. [prob f MDu *kolf* a club used in a
game similar to golf]

gowf² &c [gʌuf] *n* a blow, slap, buffet *18-20*.
vt hit, strike, slap *18-*.
to the ~ to wrack and ruin *19, Abd*. [prob f
prec]

gowk¹ &c; golk &c *la15-16*, **goke &c** *16-e20*,
gock &c *la16-e20* [gʌuk; *Sh Ork NE, WC Uls
also* gok] *n* **1** the cuckoo *la15-*, *now local NE-Uls*.
2 *also* ~**ie** a fool, simpleton, lout *la16-*. **3** a
joke, trick, *esp* an April Fools' Day joke *20-*, *now
midLoth*.
v **1** *vt* fool, deceive, *freq* in connection with April
fooling *18-*, *now local NE-Uls*. **2** *vi* wander
about without purpose, knock about *la19-*, *now
Ags* [perh belongs w GOWK²].
~**ie** stupid, loutish *la19-*, *now midLoth*. ~**it**
foolish *la16-*, *now NE Ags midLoth*. ~**oo**
['gʌuku, 'gʌku] = *n* 1, *la19-e20*.
~ **aits** oats sown after the arrival of the cuckoo
la19-, *now Abd Rox*. ~**('s) day** April Fools' Day
la19-, *now nEC*. ~**('s) errand** a fool's errand
19-, *now local*. ~**'s hose** a bell-shaped flower,
esp the wild hyacinth or the Canterbury bell
19-. ~**'s meat** the wood sorrel *la18-e20*.
~**('s)-spit(tle(s))** cuckoo-spit *19-*, *now local
NE-S*. ~**('s) storm** a brief storm, *orig* a storm
in a teacup, later (*19-*) applied literally and
equated with a spring storm coinciding with the
arrival of the cuckoo *la16-17*, *19-*, *now local
NE-S*. ~**'s-thimles &c** the harebell (HARE)
la19-, NE.
an April ~ an April fool *19-*, *now Ags Fif
midLoth*. ~ **of Maryland &c** the cuckoo of ?
fairyland *e16*. **(the)** ~ **and (the) titlin(g)** two
inseparable and/or incongruous companions,
esp a tall and a short person seen together *19-*,
now Per Fif. **hunt (th)e gowk** *vi* go on a fool's
errand, be made a fool of, *esp* an April fool *18-*,
now EC, S. n, only **hunte**~ **&c** ['hʌntɪ'gʌuk] **1**
the game of April fool, a fool's errand, *esp* on
April Fools's Day *la19-*, *Fif sEC, WC Dmf*. **2**
April Fools' Day *la19-*, *now Fif Gall Dmf*. **3** an

April fool, a person sent on a fool's errand *la19-*, *now Ork C-S.* [ME *gowk*, ON *gaukr*, Norw dial *gauk*]

gowk[2] **&c** [gʌuk] *vi* stare *la15-*, *now Ags Per.* [uncertain; *cf* GAWK *(v)*]

gowl[1] **&c** [gʌul; *Sh also* g(j)ol] *vi* **1** howl, yell, weep noisily *la14-*. **2** scold angrily *19-*, *now Fif Ayr.* **3** scowl *19-*, *now WC Rox.* **4** *of the wind* howl, gust noisily *18-19.*
n **1** *also* **gule &c** *la15* a yell, howl, bellow, growl *la15-*. **2** a howling gust of wind *19-*, *now Sh.*
~**ie &c 1** sulky, scowling *19-*, *now Sh.* **2** *of weather* windy *20-*, *Rox.* [nME *goule*, *gowle*, ON *gaula* low, bellow; *cf* Norw dial *gaul* a gust]

gowl[2] **&c** [gʌul; *gul] *n* **1** the throat, jaws *16-19.* **2** a narrow pass or cleft between hills, *esp* **Windy G~** on Arthur's Seat in Edinburgh *la16-*. **3** the crotch, the perineal region *20-*, *now Cai Bnf Abd.* [only Sc; *n* 1 prob OF *goule*, F *gueule*; *n* 2 and 3 prob Gael *gobhal*]

gowl *see* GUIL
gowly *see* GULLIE
gown *see* GOUN

gowp[1] **&c** [gʌup] *vi* **1** *of the heart or pulse* beat strongly or wildly, palpitate *la18-20.* **2** *of sores or pains* throb, ache violently *19-*, *now local Fif-Wgt.*
n a throb of pain *19-*, *now local midLoth-Wgt.* [see SND]

gowp[2] **&c** [gʌup] *vt (17-, now Ags midLoth), n (19-, now NE midLoth)* = gulp. [*cf* GAUP *n* 2]

gowp[3] **&c** [gʌup] *vt* scoop up *(eg* water), lave with the hands, hollow out *la19-*, *now local Sh-midLoth.* [back-formation f GOWPEN]

gowp *see* GAUP

gowpen &c, gowpin *la15-20*; **gopin &c** *17-e20* ['gʌupən; *Sh* 'g(j)op-; *Ork* 'gup-, 'gʌp-; *Arg Gall Uls* 'gop-; *S* -ɪn] *n* **1** the fill of the two hands held together in the form of a bowl *la15-*. **2** the receptacle so formed by the hands *la18-*. **3** *law* one of the perquisites of the miller's servant, *only as* **lock and ~** *la18-e19; see* LOCK[2].
vt scoop up or ladle out with the hands as in *n* 1, *19-*, *now Sh Cai midLoth.*
~**fu** = *n* 1, *la18-*.
gowd in ~s *or* **gowden ~s** untold wealth *la19-*, *now Ags Rox.* [ME *goupyne* (once), ON *gaupn*]

gowst [gʌust] *vi* boast, bluster *19-20.*
n = gust *la19-20.* [perh back-formation f GOUSTER]

gowstie &c, gousty &c ['gʌustɪ; *Rox also* 'gustɪ] *adj* **1** *of places* vast, dreary, desolate; eerie *16-20.* **2** *of buildings* large, bare, cheerless *19-*, *now Bwk Rox.* **3** *of persons* (1) *also* **goustly** *16* ghastly, wasted, emaciated, pale *16-20*, *latterly Bnf Abd;* (2) breathless from being overweight, fat and flabby *20-*, *now Abd.* **4** *of wind, weather, the sea* wild, stormy; eerie *19-20.* [obscure]

gra *see* GRAY[1]

grab *n* **1** = grab. **2** a thing grabbed, plunder,

booty *la18-*, *now Abd midLoth.* **3** an advantageous bargain, an advantage of any kind, *freq* with the implication of greed or dishonesty *la19-*, *now Bnf Abd Ags.* **4** a miserly or avaricious person *19-*, *local.*
~**bie &c** greedy, avaricious *la19-*, *local N-S.*
~**ble &c** *vt* grab, grope *la19-*, *local. n* a grab, a grasping *la19-*, *Ags Per midLoth.*

grace &c *n* = grace *la14-*.
gracie &c full of spiritual grace, devout, virtuous *18-20.* **gracious &c 1** = gracious *15-*. **2** happy, prosperous; *of soil* fertile *18-19.* **3** friendly, on good terms *la18-*, *now Abd Wgt.*
~ **drink** the drink taken at the end of a meal after grace has been said *18.* **act of ~** *law* the act of 1696 providing for the maintenance of an indigent debtor in prison by the creditor responsible for his imprisonment *la17-e20.*

graddan &c *18-20*, **gradʒan &c** *la16-e18* ['gradən, 'grɛd-; *'gradʒən] *n* **1** a coarse oatmeal made from parched grain ground by hand *la16-19.* **2** home-made snuff *19-20.* **3** powdery refuse, sweepings of PEAT[1] *19-20.*
vt parch (grain) in the ear *la18-e19.*

graduand ['gradjuənd] *n* a person about to graduate *la19-*. [MedL *graduandus*]

gradʒan *see* GRADDAN

graff &c *la14-e20*, **graife &c** *la15-e20* [*Sh Abd* gref; *Sh* grof; *graf] *n (la14-e20), v (15-16)* = grave.

graft *n* a grave *19-e20, chf sEC, S.* [ON *grǫftr; cf* nEng dial *graft* a trench]

Grahame's Dike *see* GRIMES DYKE

graife *see* GRAFF

graig *vi* make a noise in the throat, *eg* in clearing it *17-20, NE.* [onomat; perh voiced var of CRAIK]

grain[1] **&c** *n* **1** = grain *la15-*. **2** *measure of weight* the smallest unit, $\frac{1}{36}$ DRAP, $\frac{1}{576}$ ounce SCOTS, .825 Troy grains *16-*. **3** *commoner with concrete than abstract nouns* a small quantity, a (little) bit *la18-*.

grain[2] **&c** *n* **1** a branch, arm, offshoot (1) of a tree *16-*, *now Per;* (2) of a family *la16;* (3) of a stream, river *16-20, in place-names la15-;* (4) of a valley *la18-*, *now only in place-names.* **2** a prong (of a fork, salmon spear etc) *16-*, *now local.*
~**it &c** pronged *16-e17.* [nME *grayne &c*, ON *grein*]

grain[3] **&c** *la15-*, **grane, groan** *18-*, **grone &c** *16-e17 vi* **1** = groan *la14-*, *now local Bnf-Rox.* **2** complain, grumble; be ailing *18-*, *now Cai Ags Rox.*
n = groan *la14-*, *now local Ags-Rox.*
groaning malt &c ale brewed to celebrate a birth *18-e19.*

grainery *n* = granary *20-*, *now local Bnf-Kcb.*

graip[1] **&c; grap** *la15-17* [grep] *n* an iron-pronged fork used in farming and gardening *la15-*.

vt fork up *20-*, *local NE-Uls*. [nME *grape*, ON *greip* the space between the thumb and fingers; *cf* Norw dial *greip* a (dung-)fork]

graip² &c *16-*, **grape** [grep] *vti* **1** *also* **growp** *20-*, *local NE-Uls* [grʌup] = grope *la14-20*. **2** *vt* search with the hands, probe; handle, touch indecently *la14-*, *now Rox*. **3** examine (the conscience, an argument) *la15-18*.

graisle &c *16-20*, **graizle** *la18*, **grasill** &c *e16* [*?'gresl, *'grezl] *vti* make a grating or creaking noise, gnash (the teeth); fizzle, crackle, crumple. [prob onomat; *cf* F *grésiller* crackle]

grait *see* GREAT

graith &c; **grath** &c *la14-19*, **greth** *16-17*, **greath** *16-18* [greθ; *Ork v* greð; *v* *greð] *v* **1** *vt* prepare, make ready (1) *in gen*, *la14-e20*; (2) (food, a meal) *la14-e17*; (3) (a horse for riding or work) *la16-*, *now local Per-Uls*; (4) equip, array, dress (a person), *esp* in armour *la15-19*. (5) *vr* make oneself ready *la15-16*. **2** *vt* deal with, treat (a person in a certain way) *la14-16*. **3** provide with appropriate or necessary additions; ornament, decorate *la15-17*. **4** *vi* make ready, prepare to do something *la15-e16*.

n **1** (1) materials or equipment (for a particular purpose, job or trade); tools, implements, machinery *la14-*, *now local NE-Gall*. (2) the penis *18-19*. **2** accessory equipment, *esp* of a mechanism, *eg* a mill, plough, loom *la15-*, *now Stlg-Dmf*. **3** *specif* the heddles for a loom *16-19*. **4** the rigging or tackle of a ship *la15-*, *now local NE-Gall*. **5** (1) the accessory apparatus of a gun or cannon; ammunition *la15-e16*. (2) the priming materials of a firearm, powder and shot *la16-17*. **6** furnishings, effects *la15-*, *now local NE-Gall*. **7** personal equipment: (1) articles of dress, clothes, attire; accessories *15-e20*; (2) armour, weapons etc, *now only* as used by the *Royal Company of Archers* (ROYAL) *la15-*. **8** the trappings, harness etc for a horse *la15-*, *now C, S*. **9** merchandise; supplies; personal luggage; cargo *la15-e20*. **10** possessions, wealth, money *16-e20*. **11** *fishing* the attachment, consisting of the SNUID and *tippin* (TIP¹), by which the hook is suspended from the line *20-*, *now NE*. **12** liquor, medicine *la18-19*. **13** (1) stale urine used in washing and dyeing *19-20*. (2) urine *20-*, *now Sh*. **14** a soapy lather; dirty, used soapsuds *18-*, *chf C, S*. **15** *contemptuous* people, riffraff *19*.

adj, *only literary* ready, prompt, clear; straight, direct *la14-15*.

~**ing** equipment, accoutrements, trappings; *specif* harness, dress *la18-e20*. ~**ly** &c *chf verse* **1** well, properly, successfully *la14-e15*. **2** carefully, attentively *la14-16*. **3** clearly, distinctly *la14-17*. **4** readily, promptly *la15*. ~ (*chf* **one's**) **gate** make a way for oneself *la15*. **horse** ~ = *n* 8, *la18-*. **iron** ~ iron equipment or accessories *la15-17*. **plough** ~ the equipment of a plough *16-*, *now local NE-Dmf*. **small** ~ small shot, *n* 5 (2), *la16-18*. [nME *graith* &c

(*v*, *n*), ME *greiðen*, ON *greiða* arrange, make ready, *greiðe* &c arrangement, order; *cf* Norw dial *greida* implements, tackle]

graitifee *vt* = gratify *la19-20*.

graititeed *see* GRATITUDE

graivel &c *n* = gravel *19-*, *now Ags*.

graizle *see* GRAISLE

gralloch &c ['graləx] *n* **1** a deer's entrails *19-*. **2** the disembowelling of a deer *la19-*. *vt* disembowel (a deer) *19-*. [Gael *greallach* entrails, intestines]

gram; grame *n* = grame, sorrow, grief; anger, malice *la15-e16*.

gramarie &c ['graməri] *n*, *literary* = GLAMOUR *n* 1, *19-e20*. [ME *gramarye*]

gramashes &c *la17-e20*, **gramashins** &c *19-e20*, *WC* [grə'maʃə(n)z] *n pl* leggings, gaiters *la17-e20*. [only Sc; altered f eModEng *gamash*]

grame *see* GRAM

Grampian (**Region**) a REGION formed from the former counties of the city of Aberdeen, Aberdeen, Kincardine, Banff and part of the former county of Moray *la20-*. [*the Grampians*, the mountain range of the Central *Highlands* (HIELAND)]

gran *see* GRIND

grana crescentia [*'granə krɛ'ʃɛnʃə, *-sɛnʃə] *n*, *law* used to describe a *thirlage* (THIRL²) which applied to all the corn grown on that particular piece of land *18-e19*. [L = growing grain]

granale *see* GIRNEL

grand &c; **graun** &c *la19-* [gran(d); grɑn(d)] *adj* **1** = grand *16-*. **2** fine, splendid *la19-*.

grandame &c *15-18*, **grannam** &c *18-e19* **1** = grandam, a grandmother *15-e19*. **2** a greatgrandmother *15-17*. ~**bairn** = grandchild *la19-*, *now Sh*. ~**childer** = grandchildren *19-*, *now Uls*. ~**da** *la19-*, *now local*, ~**daddy** *19*, ~**dey** *19-*, *now Fif* = grandfather. ~**dochter** = grand-daughter *la19-*. ~**faither**, ~**fader** = grandfather *la19-*. ~**minnie** &c *20-*, *now Sh*, ~**mither** &c *la19-*, *now local Sh-Kcb* = grandmother. ~**sher** &c *la16-e20*, ~**schir** &c *la15-e17*, **grantschir** &c *15-e16* **1** = grandsire, a grandfather *15-e16*. **2** a great-grandfather *16-e20*. ~**-wean** = grandchild *la19-*, *now Kcb Dmf*.

grand *see* GRIND

grandgore &c; **grangour** &c [*'grand'gor, *'grant-; *'graŋgor] *n* venereal disease, syphilis *la15-e17*. [only Sc; OF *grand gorre*; *cf* GLENGORE]

grane *see* GRAIN³

grangour *see* GRANDGORE

granich &c ['granjəx, 'grunix, &c] *vt* sicken, disgust *la19-e20*, *NE*. [Gael *gràinich*]

granitar &c *la15-16*, **grintar** &c *la15-17* [*'granətər, *'grentər, *?'grint-] *n* an official, *esp* of a religious house, in charge of a granary. [only Sc; F *grenetier*, MedL *granitarius*]

grank *n*, *vi* groan *16*, *e19*. [nME (once) as verb; imit or frequentative of GRAIN³]

grannam *see* GRAND

grannie &c ['granı, 'grɒnı] *n* **1** = granny *la18*-.
2 the last sheaf cut at harvest-time *la19*-, Uls. **3**
a hairy caterpillar, the larva of the tiger moth
20-, *now local SW.* **4** a chimney-cowl *20*-, *now
Abd-S.* **5** as a contemptuous riposte, with a
possessive adj, usu following the repetition of the
relevant word *la19*-, *Sh NE-S*: '*We might have
improvised ..' 'Improvised yer grannie*'.
vt, in a game defeat heavily, *freq* without the loser
scoring *la20*-, *nEC Ayr Slk.*
~('s) **bairn** a grandchild, *esp* reared by its
grandmother and spoilt *20*-, *now Abd Ags Rox.*
~('s) **mutch(es)** **1** the columbine *la19*-, *NE-
WC.* **2** the snapdragon *la20*-, *Ags Per WC.* **3** =
n 5, *20*-, *now Abd Fif Arg.* ~ **mutch(ie)** nickname for an old woman *20*-, *local.* ~ **preen** a
large pin for fastening a shawl *20*-, *now Kcb.*
~'s **sooker** a peppermint sweet, a *pan drop*
(PAN[1]) *la20*-, *NE nEC.* ~'s **tuith** *or* **teeth** *carpentry* a router plane *la20*-, *Abd Ags Per.*
~ **at** address as 'granny' *20*-.

grantschir *see* GRAND

granzie &c [*?*'granzı, *?*'grɒn-] *n, gipsy* a barn
19-e20. [appar altered f Eng *grange*]

grap *see* GRAIP[1]

grape &c *n* = gripe, a vulture *16*.

grape *see* GRAIP[2]

grapple &c *vti* **1** = grapple. **2** *vt* drag (water)
for a corpse *20*-, *now local NE-Uls.* **3** *vti* grope
la19-, *now Ags.*
grappling a method of catching salmon by
means of a special arrangement of hooks *la18*-,
now Ags Ayr Kcb.

grapus [?'grepʌs, ?'grap-] *n* the devil, a hobgoblin *19*-, *now Ags.* [perh f GRAIP[2]]

gras *see* GIRSE

grashloch &c ['graʃləx] *adj* stormy, boisterous,
blustering *19*.

grasill *see* GRAISLE

grass, grass-ill *see* GIRSE

grassum &c, gressum &c, grissum &c
16, **garsum &c** *16-17*, **gersum &c** *la15-18*,
girsum *la15-17 n, law* a sum paid by a tenant
or *feuar* (FEU) at the grant or renewal of a lease
or *feu-right*, *la15*-. [ScL *gressuma* (*la13*); ME *gersum*, OE *gærsum* a treasure, something costly; *cf*
MedL *gersuma*, ON *gorsemi*]

grat *see* GREAT, GREET[1]

grate &c *n* = grating *18-19*.

grath *see* GRAITH

gratinȝied &c [*gra'tinȝıt, *-ıd] *adj, of cloth*
pinked *la16-17.* [only Sc; f F *égratigner*]

gratis *adv* = gratis *16*-.
~ **burgess** a burgess exempted from paying
the regular entry fee for burgess-ship *18-e19.*

gratitude &c *n* **1** *also* **graititeed** *la19-20, NE*
= gratitude *la16*-. **2** a service or benefit performed, kindness or favour conferred *16-e17, chf*

Sc. **3** a free gift, contribution, *chf* to the sovereign *la15-16.* **4** a goodwill payment to a landlord in addition to the rent and GRASSUM *16.* **5**
a gratuity *la16-e20.*

graun *see* GRAND

gravat &c ['gravət, 'grɒvət, *Cai* -vəd] *n* **1** = cravat; a scarf or muffler, *now usu* woollen *la17*-. **2**
a hangman's noose, *freq* **hempen** ~ *la18-e20.*

gravatour &c [*'gravətur, *-ər] *n* a letter from
the official of an ecclesiastical court censuring a
person found guilty of an attempt to defraud or
to escape due payment *la15-16.* [only Sc;
MedL *gravatorium* aggravation of sentence]

grave[1] &c *n* = grave *15*-.
vt **1** = grave, engrave *15-e17.* **2** bury (a
corpse), inter *la14-e20.* **3** dig *la14, e20* (Sh).
~**yaird deserter** = kirkyaird deserter (KIRK)
la19-, *now NE.* ~**yaird hoast** *etc* = kirkyaird
hoast, *la19*-, *now WC.*

grave[2] *n, literary* = grove *15-16.*

gravy &c *n* **1** = gravy. **2** sauce *la18*-, *now Ags.*

grawl &c *n* = GRILSE *19*-, *SW.* [see SND]

gray[1] &c; gra *la15-e17*, **grey** *la17*- [gre] *adj* =
grey *la14*-.
n **1** grey cloth, *hodden gray* (HODDEN) *la15-e19.* **2**
dawn, twilight, *esp* **the** ~ **o the morning** *or*
evening *19*-.
vi **1** dawn *la19*-, *chf Sh Ork NE.* **2** cover with a
thin sprinkling of snow *20*-, *Kcb Dmf.*
~**back** **1** the hooded crow *20*-, *now Cai Ags Per.*
2 the flounder *20*-, *Mry Fif.* **3** a salmon or
salmon trout in the autumn run *la20*-, *SW-S.* **4**
the immature herring gull or lesser black-
backed gull *20*-, *Cai Ayr.* ~ **beard &c** a one- or
two-handled jug or pitcher for holding liquor
la18-, *now arch*; cf *beardie* (BEARD). ~ **breid &c**
bread made of rye or oats *15-e19.* ~ **cheeper**
the meadow pipit *la19*-, *now Per Pbls.* ~ **corn** a
kind of light grain *la17-19.* ~ **dark** dusk *la19*-,
now local C, S. ~ **(day)licht** dawn *19*-, *now Sh
Cai Abd.* ~ **face** a crossbred sheep, black-face
crossed with Leicester *19*-. ~ **fish** the coalfish,
esp in its second or third year *18*-, *now Sh.* ~
groat a silver fourpenny piece; something of
little value *la18-e19.* ~ **hen** the female black
grouse *15*-. ~ **horse** a louse *20*-, *now Ags Fif.*
~ **lord** the fully-grown coalfish *la17-e20.* ~
meal the refuse and sweepings of a meal-mill
17-e20. ~ **oats** an inferior kind of oats
la18-e19. ~ **paper** brown paper *19*-, *Sh Ork N.*
~ **plover** the golden plover in its summer plumage *la18*-, *now Ayr.* ~ **scool &c** an inferior
variety of salmon *19-e20, S.* ~ **sisteris** nuns of
the third order of St Francis *16.* ~ **skate** the
skate *19*-, *now Fif.* ~ **slate** laminated sandstone, *freq* used in roofing *la18*-, *now Abd Ags.*
~ **stane** a grey volcanic rock, *usu* a boulder or
monolith used as a landmark or boundary stone
la15-, *now in place-names.* ~ **willie** the herring
gull *20*-, *Inv Mry.*

(gang) a ~ gate (follow) a disastrous course, (come to) a bad end *18-, now Wgt.* **sing ~ thrums** *of a cat* purr *19-e20.*

gray² &c *n* a light wind, gentle breeze *la19-, now Fif midLoth.* [Norw dial *gråe*]

Gray *n* an arithmetic text book (by James Gray of Peebles (1781-1810)) *la19-e20.*

gre *see* GREE¹, GREE²

greance *see* GREEANCE

grease &c [griz, kriʃ] *vti* serve the ball in the game of rounders *20-, Arg.* [see SND]

great *18-,* **grete** &c *la14-20,* **gret** &c *la14-e20,* **grit** &c *la15-e20,* **gryte** &c *la14-20,* **grait** &c *la16-17,* **grat** *la15-16,* **girt** &c *la16-e20* [gret, grɪt, grɛt; *NE Ags* grəit; *Kcdn also* grit; *girt] adj* **1** = great *la14-.* **2** coarse in grain or texture *la15-, now Ags.* **3** *of things* thick, bulky, roomy *16-, now Ags.* **4** *of persons* big, stout *la19-, now Sh Abd.* **5** *of persons or animals* big with young, *now only* ~ **ewe** *la14-.* **6** *of a river etc* in flood, high *la16-, now Ork.* **7** *of the heart* full with emotion, *esp* grief *18-19.* **8** boastful, proud, elated *19-e20.* **9** intimate, friendly *17-20.* **10** *placed after its noun, of a money of account* having the same proportion to the ordinary shilling or pound as the Flemish groat or thick penny did to the ordinary penny *la15-16* [f Du *groot*].

adv = great, greatly, very *la14-16.*

n **1** = (the) great *la14-.* **2** a Flemish groat *15-e17.*

~ **avizandum** an AVISANDUM from a judge in the *Outer House* (OUTER¹) to the judges in the *Inner House* (INNER); a report by the *Lord Ordinary* (LORD) to the *Inner House* in certain actions *la19-20.* **gret dusain** &c ? a gross *la15-e16.* ~ **fish** white fish as distinct from herring *18-e20.* ~ **folk** people of rank or position *18-, now Abd Per.* ~**-hearted** having the heart filled with emotion, ready to cry, sorrowful *19-, now NE Ags Fif.* ~**lin(e)**, ~**ling, gart-, girtling** the line used in deep-water fishing *la16-, now local NE-Bwk.*

greath *see* GRAITH

greatumly *see* GRETUMLY

grece &c *n* = gris, a grey fur *la14-16.*

grede¹ *see* GREED

gree¹ &c, **gre** *15-16* [gri; *S* grəi] *v* **1** *vt* reconcile (persons); settle (matters) *la16-, now Ork Abd Ags Rox.* **2** *vi* come to terms, make an agreement, be reconciled *la16-, Gen except Sh.* **3** (1) *of persons* be or live in harmony, be friends; be of one mind *la16-.* (2) *of things etc* correspond, fit *16-.*

~**able** &c **1** = greable, agreeable *15-e16.* **2** harmonious, living in peace and goodwill *la19-, now Abd Arg Wgt.*

~**ment, griment** *la16* ['grimənt] agreement, harmony, concord *la16-, now local Ork-Arg.* [ME *gree*, aphetic f *agree* or OF *greer*; *cf* next]

gree² &c, **gre** *la14-16 n* **1** = gree, a degree, step *la14-17.* **2** a step or stage in a rising scale

(chf of virtue) *la14-16.* **3** a step in the familial line of descent; a degree of relationship *15-16.* **4** degree, rank, social position *la14-19.* **5** pre-eminence, supremacy, first place, victory in a contest; the palm, the prize, *freq* **win** *or* **bear** &c **the** ~ *15-, now literary.* **6** degree or degrees in amount, intensity, quality etc *15-16.* **7** a degree in measurement in geometry or astronomy *16.*

within ~ (**defendand**) within the forbidden degrees *16-e17.*

greeance *19-, now Abd,* **greance** *la16-e17 n* concord, agreement. [OF *greance* or aphetic f eModEng *agreeance*]

greed *18-,* **grede** &c *la16-17 n* avarice, greed. [earlier in Sc; back-formation f Eng *greedy*]

greek &c *n* = GREKING *19-e20.* [back-formation]

greek *see* GREET²

green¹ &c *17-,* **grene** &c *14-e18;* **gren** *12-e17* [grin] *adj* **1** = green *la14-.* **2** covered with grass, grassy *15-, now Sh Ork Cai,* in place-names *12-.* **3** young, youthful, full of vitality *la15-, now local Abd-Uls.* **4** *of fish, esp* herring fresh, unsalted *la16-, now Sh Dmf.* **5** *of milk* new, fresh *18-, now local Abd-S.* **6** (1) *of a woman* recently delivered *18.* (2) *of a cow* recently calved *19-, now midLoth Rox.* **7** *of manure* fresh, unrotted *la18-, now Cai Kcb Rox.* **8** *of cloth* unbleached, *esp* of unprocessed linen yarn *la18-, now Ags WC Uls.* **9** *of a fire* newly kindled and smouldering *la19-, local Bnf-WC.*

n **1** = green *15-.* **2** grassy ground; a grassy place *la14-.* **3** *specif* the grassy ground forming part of the grounds of a house or other building, *freq* **kirk, castle, back, drying** *etc* ~ *la15-.* **4** a town or village green *14-.* **5** *golf* the piece of finely-turfed grass used as the *putting* (PUTT¹) ground; *formerly also* the fairway or the whole course *18-.* **6** *in pl* green vegetables, *esp* KAIL, *freq* **beef and** ~**s** traditional fare at a *curling* (CURL) club dinner *la18-.*

~**ichtie** *19-, Bnf Abd,* ~**ichy** *la19-, Mry Ags* [-əx(t)ɪ] greenish. ~**ie** &c the greenfinch *la19-e20.*

~**-bane** &c the garfish, garpike or needlefish *18-19.* ~**-berry** the green gooseberry *20-, now Abd Dmf.* ~ **brees** &c green, stagnant water, *esp* that oozing from a dunghill or cesspool *19-, now Bnf Abd.* ~ **gaw** green slimy seaweed or green algae *20-, now Abd.* ~ **grass** a children's rhyme; the game in which it occurs *19-, now Abd Ags.* ~**-horn 1** a raw inexperienced person, a simpleton *la17-.* **2** a spoon made of a greenish horn *19-20.* ~ **kail 1** a non-curly variety of KAIL *17-, now nEC Gall Rox.* **2** a soup made from this *18-e20.* ~**-kailworm** the caterpillar of the cabbage butterfly *19-, now local Cai-S.* ~ **lady 1** a spectre, *perh* portending death, from the association in folklore of green with death *19-, now local Ross-Fif.* **2** a Health Visitor *la20, Gsw* [f the colour of her uniform]. ~ **lintie** the greenfinch *19-, Gen except Sh Ork.* ~ **ribbon** the ribbon of the *Order of the Thistle* (THRISSEL) *18-19.* **G~ Rod** the baton of the *Order of the Thistle, esp* **Usher of the G~ Rod** (see USHER). **G~ Table(s) 1** = TABLE *n 3, 17.* **2** informal name for the *Court of Session* (SESSION) *20* [*appar* because formerly furnished with green cloth]. ~ **wife** a female greengrocer *19.* ~ **wood 1** growing trees or branches, living wood *15-, now Cai Kcb.* **2** *literary* = greenwood *la15-16.*

a' ~ **thing** everything, as **that cows, dings** *etc* a' ~ **thing** that beats everything *la19-, now NE.* **keep the banes** ~ preserve good health and youthfulness *la15-e19.*

green[2] **&c** *17-,* **grene &c** *16-19;* **grien** *la18-e20* [grin] *vi* **1** long or yearn **for** *16-, now local Ork-Fif.* **2** *of a pregnant woman* have a craving (**for** particular foods) *18-, now Mry Kcb.* [nME *grene*; perh metath f ON *girna* desire]

greenichtie, greenichy *see* GREEN[1]

greep *see* GRUIP

greesh *n* a stone abutment built against the gable wall inside a cottage, forming the back of the fireplace *la18-20.* [ScGael *gris*, IrGael *grios* fire, heat]

greeshach &c ['griʃəx, 'gris-] *adj* shivery, shuddery; chilly *20-, local N.* [f ScGael *gris* horror, shuddering]

greeshoch &c ['griʃəx, -ək] *n* a glowing fire of red-hot embers; the embers themselves, *esp* of a PEAT[1] fire *19-, local NE-Uls.* [Gael *griosach*]

greet[1] **&c** *la16-,* **grete &c** *la14-19;* **gret** *la14-16* [grit] *v, pt* **grat &c, gret** *now Arg Renfr Dmf. ptp* also **grutten &c** *18-e20* **1** *vi* weep, cry, lament; complain; grumble ineffectually *la14-.* **2** *vt, also fig* weep (tears) *la14-e20.*

n **1** weeping, tears *la14-19.* **2** a sob; a fit of weeping, *freq* **hae** *or* **tak a** *or* one's ~ *19-.*

~ie &c *adj* **1** weepy, given to tears *la20-, local Sh-Dmf.* **2** inclined to rain, showery *20-, now Mry Ags. n* a child's whimper *la18-, now Bnf Abd.* **~in(g)** weeping, lamentation *la14-.* **~in ee** a watering eye *la19-, Sh Abd midLoth Kcb.* **~in face** a person who habitually looks miserable or as if he is about to weep *19-.* **~in fou** at the tearful stage of drunkenness *la19-.* **~in meetin** a farewell meeting, *specif* the last meeting of a town council before an election *la19-.* **~in Teenie** a cry-baby; a person who is always complaining *20-, Gen except Sh Ork.*

the ~ in one's craig *or* **throat** a sob in one's throat *19-, now Sh Abd.* **get one's ~ out** relieve one's feelings by weeping *la19-, now local.* [nME *grete*, OE (Anglian) *gretan*]

greet[2] *19-e20,* **grete** *e16,* **greek** *18-, now Ags Fif n* = grit: **1** gravel *e16;* **2** the grain or texture of a stone *18-.*

Gregioun &c [*'gridʒun, *-ən] *n* a Greek *15-e16.* [cf ME *Gregois* and L *graiugenus*]

greif *see* GRIEF, GRIEVE

greind- *see* GRIND

greis [*griz] *n pl* = greaves, pieces of armour for the shins *15.* [reduced f ME *grevys &c*]

greis *see* GIRSE

greittumly *see* GRETUMLY

greking &c *n* daybreak *16-e20.* [ME *greking*, MDu *griekinge*]

gremmar *n* = grammar *la19-, NE.*

gren *see* GREEN[1]

grene *see* GREEN[1], GREEN[2]

grenil *see* GIRNEL

grephoun [*grɪ'fun, &c] *n* = griffin *e16, only Sc.*

greschip *see* GRIEVE

gress *see* GIRSE

gressum *see* GRASSUM

gret *see* GREAT, GREET[1]

grete *see* GREAT, GREET[1], GREET[2]

greth *see* GRAITH

Gretna Green the village in Dmf noted for the marriages of runaway couples, which were celebrated (*la18-e20*) by the blacksmith over his anvil; see SND.

gretumly &c *la14-16;* **gritt- &c** *16-e17,* **greitt- &c** *la16-e17,* **great-** *la16-17* [*'grɪtʌmlɪ, *'grɛt-, *'grɪt-] *adv* = greatly. [only Sc; appar f OE *grēatum*, dative of *grēat* (*adj*)]

greve &c [griv] *n* = grief, an injury *la14-16.*

vti = grieve *la14-.*

grevand &c grievous, painful, hurtful *la14-15* [*cf* laME *grevinge* and GRIEF].

greve *see* GRIEVE

grew &c [gru; *Rox* also grju] *n* a greyhound, *now freq* the **~s** greyhound racing *19-, now WC-Uls.* ~ **hound &c** ['gru'hun(d), -'hʌn(d); *'gruən] = n, 15-, now Ags Wgt Uls.* ~ **whelp &c** a greyhound puppy *16-17.* [ME *grewhounde*]

grew *see* GRUE[1]

grey *see* GRAY

grib *see* GRUIP

grice &c *16-,* **gryse &c** [grəis; *Sh Cai* also grɪs] *n* a pig, *esp* a young pig, a sucking pig *la14-, local Sh-Dmf.*

bring *or* **lay the heid o the soo to the tail o the** ~ balance one's losses with one's gains *18-19.* [ME *gryse*, ON *griss*]

grief *17-,* **greif &c** *la14-17* [*n* grif; *v* griv; *adj* grif, griv] *n* = grief *la14-.*

vti = grieve *la14-16.*

adj heavy, oppressive *la15, e20.* [*cf* GREVE]

grien *see* GREEN[2]

grieve *18-,* **greve &c** *16-e19;* **greif &c** *15-17* [griv] *n* **1** the chief magistrate or PROVOST of a BURGH *e15* [= L *prepositus*]. **2** the overseer or head-workman on a farm; a farm-bailiff *la15-.* **3** the manager or overseer of a mine, works, etc; the overseer or foreman of a gang of workmen *16-19.*

vti oversee *18-20.*

~schip &c *la14-16,* **greschip &c** *la15-e17* [*'gri(v)ʃɪp] the district under the jurisdiction of the GRIEVE of the BURGHS of Cullen, Elgin and Inverness. [nME *greve*, ONorthumb *gráfa*; *cf* WSax *geréfa* > ME *reve &c* > ModEng *reeve*]

grill *20-*, *Rox*, **gril &c** *e16 vi* shiver, shudder. [ME *grille &c*, OE *grillan*]

grilse &c, **grissill &c** *la15-e17*, **girsill &c** *la15-e17*, **girls &c** *15-e17*, **gilse &c** *la16-*, *now Bwk* [grɪls; *Bwk S* gɪls; *'grɪsəl, *'gɪrsəl, *gɪrls] *n* a young salmon on its first return to fresh water *la14-*. [chf Sc; nME (once), eModEng (twice); unknown]

grime &c *19-*, **grim** [grəim] *vt* 1 = grime, begrime *la15*. 2 sprinkle, fleck, cover thinly, *esp* with snow, *freq* **a griming of snow &c** *19-*, *now SW Rox*.
adj, *only* **grim** [grɪm] grey, roan, mottled black and white; grimy *19-*, *now local Abd-Ayr*. [*cf* Norw dial *grima* make streaky, smudge, *grim* a fine shower of snow or rain]

griment *see* GREE[1]

Grimes Dyke &c; Grahame's Dike ['grəimz'dəik, 'greəmz-] *n*, *hist* the Antonine Wall *16-*. [ON *Grímr* nickname for Odin. OED *dike*]

grind &c; grun(d) *la18-e20*, **greind- &c** *la16-17* [grɪn(d), grʌn(d)]. *pt also* **grun(d)** *19-*, **gran(d)** *16-*, *now Sh Ork*. *ptp also* **grun(d) &c** *16-*, **grundin &c** *la14-16*, **grind &c** *e17* [grʌn(d); *'grʌndən; *grɪnd; *&c*] *vti* = grind *14-*.
grindable *17-e18*, **grundable** *17*, *of grain* suitable for or intended for grinding.
grunstane &c *la18-*, **grin-** *la19-*, *NE* ['grʌn(d)'sten; *NE* 'grɪn'stɪn] = grindstone.

grinnale *see* GIRNEL
grinstane *see* GRIND
grintar *see* GRANITAR

grip &c; grup &c *la18-* *v*, *ptp also* **gruppen &c** *la19-*, *S* 1 *vt* = grip *15-*. 2 seize, catch, lay hold of *la15-*, *Gen except Loth*. 3 seize, lay hands on, take possession of (lands or belongings) violently or illegally *la15-20*. 4 *vi* grasp, grab *la14-19*. 5 *vt* get the better of, outsmart *la19-*, *NE*.
n 1 = grip *15-*. 2 a hand-clasp; *specif* that used between members of a secret society, *eg* the Freemasons or *curling* (CURL) clubs *la18-*. 3 *in pl* someone's embrace or clutches *18-*, *now Sh Abd Arg*. 4 *fig* grasp, control, mastery, power *la15-*. 5 *chf in pl* sharp pains, *esp* in the bowels, gripes *la16-*, *now Sh NE nEC, SW*. 6 **the ~ building industry** = the 'lump', the system of sub-contracting work to casual labour *la20-*. 7 *piping* a *throw* (THRAW *n* 7) in which all the finger holes are closed, so sounding the lowest note G *20-*.
~per the person who catches and holds a sheep to be sheared *19-*, *now SW*. **~pie** close-fisted, avaricious, mean; inclined to sharp practice *la18-*. **gripping &c** *adj* grasping, avaricious *la16-19*. *n* 1 = gripping *la16-*. 2 *also* **grupping** a paralytic disease of sheep *la18-*. **~pit**

&c 1 seized with pain (as in *n* 5) *la16-e19*. 2 hard-up, pressed for money *la19-*, *now Abd Ags*. 3 **gruppit &c** sprained *19-*, *now local Abd-Uls*. **~ grass** goose-grass, cleavers *19*.
catch ~ o take hold of *19-*, *now Sh Ags WC Rox*. **come to ~s** close (**with**), engage in a struggle at close quarters (**with**) *17-*. **~ in** pinch, constrict *20-*, *Sh NE Ags*. **~ to** *or* **till** seize, grab, hold on to; stick close to *la15-*, *now Sh NE Ags*. **hae a guid ~ o** (**the**) **gear** 1 be well off *la19-*, *now Ags WC*. 2 be miserly *la20-*, *nEC Ayr Rox*. **hae** *or* **tak a guid grip o Scotland** have large feet *la20-*. **haud the ~** keep a firm hold; *also fig* hold to one's faith or purpose; endure, last *19-*, *now Arg Wgt*. **be, go, keep** *etc* **in ~s** wrestle, tussle with, struggle with at close quarters *16-e20*. **slip the ~** die *la18-*, *now Abd Ags*.

grip *see* GRUIP
gris *see* GIRSE
grisk *adj* greedy, avaricious *19-e20*. [Norw, Dan, Sw dial]
grissill *see* GRILSE
grissum *see* GRASSUM
grist &c *n* 1 the size or thickness of yarn *18-*, *now Abd Ayr S*. 2 size, girth *in gen*, *la18-*, *now Ork*. [prob metath f Eng *girth* + *-st*]
grit *n*, *in pl* oat kernels, grain *19-e20*. [Eng (now dial) *grit* coarse oatmeal]
grit *see* GREAT
grittumly *see* GRETUMLY
groan *see* GRAIN[3]
groat *17-*, **grote &c** *la15-17*; **grot(t)** *la15-17 n* 1 = groat, the coin *la15-*, *now hist*. 2 *with negative* nothing at all *16-17*.
~ wecht the weight of a groat ($\frac{1}{8}$ ounce) *16*.
groatie &c *n*, *also* **~ buckie &c** a species of cowrie shell *20-*, *Sh Ork Cai Abd*. [see SND]
groats *la16-*, **grotis &c** *la15-16*; **grott(i)s &c** *la15-e20 n pl* = groats, hulled grain *la15-*.
ken *or* **tell one's** (**ain**) **~ in ither folk's kail** be wily or sharp in recognizing one's own property or handiwork or one's own interests *17-e20*.
groff &c; grofe &c *16-e20* [grof; *Abd Rox* grʌuf] *adj* 1 coarse in grain or texture, inferior *la16-*, *now local Sh-N*. 2 *of language etc* vulgar, coarse; smutty, obscene *la17-e20*. 3 *of persons* coarse, rough *18-*, *now local Sh-Abd*. 4 *of the voice* harsh *20-*, *Sh Mry Abd*.
~ guess a rough guess, a pretty good idea *19-*, *now Sh*. **~ print** large type *la19-e20*, *Cai Mry*. [MDu, MLowGer *grof*; *cf* Eng *gruff*]
gromish &c *vt* crush, bruise *20-*, *Cai Abd*. [*cf* Sw dial *gramsa* grasp]
gronach ['gronəx] *vi* grumble, complain *20*, *Bnf Abd*. [var of *cronach* (CORONACH)]
grond *see* GRUND
grone *see* GRAIN[3]
gronʒe *see* GRUNYIE
groo *see* GRUE[1]
groof *18-*, **grouf &c** *la15-e19*; **grufe &c** *16-e20*, **gruff &c** *15-e16* [gruf; *Ork also* grøf, grʌf; *grøf] *n* **~lins**, **~ling(i)s** prostrate, flat

on one's face *15-*, *now Sh.* **on** ~ *la15-19*, **on one's** ~ *18-20* face downwards, prone. [ME *o grufe &c*, ON *á grúfu* face down]

grool[1] **&c; grull &c** *n* **1** gritty material, gravel, dusty refuse, coal-dust *19*, *SW*. **2** friable moss made into PEATS[1] by mixing with water to a suitable consistency and drying *19*, *WC-SW*. [appar Eng *gruel*]

grool[2] *vi* = growl *la19-20*, *Mry Abd.*

groose [grus] *n* = grouse, the bird *19-e20*.

groosie &c [*ˈgruzɪ] *adj* dirty, greasy, unsavoury *19*. [prob conflation of GRUE[1] w Eng *greasy*]

groosie *see* GRUSE

groozle &c; gruzzle &c *19-* [ˈgruzl, ˈgrʌz-, ˈgrøz-] *vi* **1** breathe heavily, make a grunting noise *la18-*, *now Kcb Dmf Rox.* **2** *of a child* gurgle *19-*, *now Rox.*
n a grunting or gurgling noise *19-*, *now Dmf.* [see SND]

gropsie &c [*ˈgropsɪ] *vi* eat gluttonously *la18-e20.* [see SND]

gros [gros] *n* a Flemish or German coin *la16-e17.* [Du, Flem]

grosar *see* GROSER

grosart *see* GROSET

grosell &c [*ˈgrozl] *n* = next *19-e20.* [F *groseille*, OF *groselle &c*]

groser *16-*, **grosar** *e16*; **grozer** *17-e20* [ˈgrozər] *n* a gooseberry *16-*, *now local NE nEC.* [eModEng *groser*, f as prec]

groset &c *la18-*; **grosart &c** *la18-*, **groz(z)-** *la18-*, **gross-** *19* [ˈgrozə(r)t] *n* = prec *la18-*.
~ **fair** an agricultural fair, *esp* the one held in Kilmarnock at the beginning of August *la19-*, *Ayr.* [GROSER + *-t*]

grot *see* GROAT

grote *see* GROAT, GROTT

grotis *see* GROATS

grotkin &c *n* a gross *la15-e17.* [only Sc; Du, Flem *grootken*]

grott *la18-*, **grote** *e15 n* a particle. [ME, OE *grot &c*, cognate w GROATS]

grott *see* GROAT

grott(i)s *see* GROATS

grouf *see* GROOF

grouff &c [grʌuf; *gruf] *vi* snore *la18-19.*
n a short, disturbed sleep; a snooze *19-e20.* [onomat]

groukar *n* meaning unknown *e16.*

ground *see* GRUND

grounge *see* GRUNCH

grow &c [grʌu] *vti*, *ptp* also **growin &c** [ˈgrʌu(ə)n] **1** = grow *la14-*. **2** *vi*, *of water or the sea* rise *16*. **3** *of land* be covered with growth (**of** vegetation) *15-e16*. **4** *of persons* increase, make progress (**in** a quality, property etc) *la14-*.
n **1** growth *la18*, *Abd.* **2** *of a river etc* a sudden rise, a flood *la18-e20*, *Mry.*
~ **th &c** [grʌuθ] **1** the action or process of growing, growth *la15-*. **2** growing plants, vegetation; yield, crop *la15-*. **3** rank vegetation,

weeds *la19-*, *now local Sh-Arg.* **4** the deposit found on the bottom of a boat *20-*, *now Sh Fif Ayr.* **5** *mining* the rate of inflow of water in a working *la20-*, *now Fif.* ~**thie &c** [ˈgrʌuθɪ] **1** *of weather* warm and moist, promoting growth *la18-*. **2** (1) *of vegetation* growing fast, luxuriant, of abundant growth; weedy *la19-*, *now local Ork-Arg.* (2) *of persons or animals* well-grown, thriving *19-*, *now local Ork-Kcb.* ~**n-up** overgrown, choked (**with** *usu* vegetation) *20-*, *local.* ~**-grey** made of natural, undyed wool *la19-*, *now Per.*

grow *see* GRUE[1]

growgrane &c [*ˈgrugren, *-grem, *-grəm, *&c*] *n* = grogram, the fabric *la16-e17.* [perh w infl f MFlem *grouvegrain*]

growin *see* GROW

growk &c [grʌuk, grok] *vi*, *esp of a child or dog* look longingly at food etc *19-*, *now Kcdn Ags Per.* [obscure]

growp *see* CROUP[1], GRAIP[2]

growze *see* GRUSE

grozart *see* GROSET

groze &c [groz; *Fif* grʌz] *vt* crush, compress *la19-e20.*
n a squeeze *la20-*, *Fif.* [only Sc; prob MDu *groezen*]

grozer *see* GROSER

grozet, grozzet *see* GROSET

gru &c [*gru] *n* a particle, atom *18-19.* [ME *grue &c*; see SND]

grub &c *vt* **1** = grub *16-*. **2** grasp at (money) *19-*, *now NE Ags Kcb.*
~**ber** an iron harrow, *usu* with cultivator tines, *esp* for weeding in drills; a scarifier *19-*.

grudge &c *la16-*, **gruch &c** *la14-16*, **grutch** *la15*, *la19* [grʌdʒ; *grʌtʃ; *grødʒ; *&c*] *v* **1** *vi* complain, be grieved, discontented or unwilling *la14-*, *now local Sh-Kcb.* **2** *vt* = grudge.
n **1** = grudge *la16-*. **2** discontent, dissatisfaction; a grievance, misgiving *16-e19.*

grudge *see* GORGE

grudget &c *n* = GROSSET *19-*, *SW.*

grue[1] **&c** *18-*, **grew &c** *la14-e20*, **grow &c** *la14-e20*, **groo &c** *la18-e20* [gru; *S* grʌu] *vi* **1** feel horror or terror, shudder, shrink in horror or fear *la14-*. **2** *of the flesh, heart, blood etc* creep, quake, run cold with horror or fear *la14-*, *now local.* **3** shiver from cold *18-*, *now C, S.* **4** make a wry face *la18-*, *now local Cai-Uls.*
n a shudder, shiver, feeling of horror or repulsion *19-*, *now local Cai-S.*
adj **1** ugly, horrible *19-e20.* **2** shuddering with fear, dread or loathing, afraid *19-*, *now Cai.* **grushion &c** [ˈgruʃən, ˈgruʒən] *freq of food* an unpleasant or glutinous mess *la19-*, *Bnf.* ~**some 1** horrible; arousing dread or loathing *la18-*. **2** *chf of appearance* ugly, repulsive, dismal *la18-19.*

it gars me, my flesh *etc* ~ it makes my etc blood run cold *19-*. **tak the** ~ (**at**) become disgusted or fed up (with) *la19-, now local Abd-Rox.* [nME *grow, gru; cf* MSw *grwa,* Norw *grua,* Dan *grue,* Du *gruwen*]

grue² &c [gru] *n* the melting snow and ice found on rivers in early spring *la18-, now NE Ags S.* [prob Gael *gruth* curds]

gruel &c ['gruəl; grul] *n* **1** = gruel *la15-.* **2** porridge *19-, now Sh Ork.* **3** food made of oatmeal; food *in gen, la19-, now Ork midLoth.*

grufe, gruff *see* GROOF

gruggle &c ['grugl, 'grʌ-] *vt* disorder, rumple, crease *19-, NE Ags.*

n a fold, crease, wrinkle *20-, NE Ags.* [only Sc; Du *kreukel(en)* crease, crumple, crimp]

grugous [*'grugəs] *adj* grim, ugly, surly *la18-e20.* [perh Gael *grùgach* surly, sulky, scowling]

gruip &c *la18-,* **grup** &c; **grip** &c *19-,* **greep** &c *19-e20* [grøp, grɪp, grʌp, grup; *N Per Arg* grip; *nEC also* grep] *n* **1** the gutter in a BYRE *la17-, Gen except Sh.* **2** a field drainage ditch *19-, now Ork Abd.*

vt, also **grib** *la18-19, carpentry* cut a groove in (a board) for fitting into a corresponding 'tongue' *17-20.* [see SND]

grull *see* GROOL¹

grulsh &c *n* a fat, squat person or animal *19-, now Uls.*

~**ie** sturdy, fat, clumsy-looking *19.* [see SND]

grumlie *see* GRUMMLE

grummel &c, **gummle** &c *19- n* rubbish, *chf* of loose earth and stones, rubble; mud, sediment *16-, now Cai Ayr Uls.*

v **1** *vt* make muddy or turbid *19-e20.* **2** *vi, only* **gummle** make an indistinct sound; gargle; mumble *la20-, midLoth.*

grumlie &c, **gumlie** &c muddy, turbid, full of dregs or gravel; confused, gloomy *18-, now local Sh-Dmf.* [*cf* eModEng *grommelles, grumbles* gritty particles, dregs; prob Scand; *cf* Sw *grummel* sediment, OFlem *grommeling* rubble]

grummle &c *vi* = grumble *la18-.*

n **1** = grumble *18-.* **2** a grudge, grievance, quarrel *la19-, local Abd-S.*

grumlie &c **1** *also fig, esp of the sea* sullen, surly, grumbling *19-, now local.* **2** *of weather* unsettled, blustery *20-, now NE.*

grumph &c *n* **1** a grunt from an animal or person *18-.* **2** name for a pig *la19-, local Abd-Wgt.* **3** a grumbler, complainer *la20-, local Bnf-Slk.*

vi grunt; grumble *19-.*

~**ie** &c *n* (name for) a pig *la18-.* *vi* grunt like a pig *20-, now Ags.* *adj* ill-natured, grumpy *20-.* [imit]

grun *see* GRIND, GRUND

grunch &c; **grounge** &c *16-, now Rox* [*Ork* grʌnʃ; *Bwk Rox* grʌnȝ] *vi* **1** grumble; object, refuse *la15-, now Rox.* **2** growl, grunt *18-, now Ork.*

n a grumble, grunt, growl *19-, now Rox.* [nasalized f Eng *grutch*]

grund &c *15-,* **ground** &c, **grond** &c

la14-16; **grun** &c *la18-* [grʌn(d); grun(d)] *n* **1** = ground *la14-.* **2** the bottom or lowest part of anything *la14-, now local Ags-Dmf.* **3** the bottom of the sea *15-, now local Sh-Bwk.* **4** *fig* the bottom, root (of a matter), basis (of a discourse), text (of a sermon) *la15-, now local Sh-Ayr.* **5** *specif* the pit of the stomach *la15-, now Ags.* **6** (1) farm-land, a farm, an estate *la15-, now local.* (2) the people belonging to a farm or estate *la15-18.* **7** (the) ground reserved for the burial of a person or family *19-, Gen except Sh Ork; cf* LAIR. **8** *piping* the theme in PIBROCH from which all the variations are derived *la18-* [translating Gael *ùrlar*]. **9** *mining, also* ~ the seam next to the floor *19-, now Edb Ayr.* **10** *in pl* (1) = grounds, lees *la19-.* (2) the refuse of flax after dressing *18-19.* (3) a kind of SOWANS *20-, Cai.*

vti = ground *15-.*

~ **annual** &c *law* a perpetual annual rent chargeable on land, the liability for it forming a real BURDEN¹ on the land, the relationship between creditor and debtor not being a feudal one *la15-20.* ~ **avy,** ~ **davy** &c = ground-ivy *19-, now Ork.* **ground bauk** &c the weighted rope at the bottom edge of a fishing net *19-, now Sh Ork.* **grund blackie** a blackbird that nests on the ground *20-, now midLoth.* ~ **ebb 1** the ebb-tide at its lowest, low water *20-, local Sh-Abd.* **2** the lowest part of the foreshore *20-, Sh Cai Abd.* **grund heid** *mining* the stratum above *n* 9, *20-, Loth Ayr.* ~ **leif** &c leave given to vessels, *esp* in port, to make use of ground on shore; the duty payable for this *la16-e17.* ~ **officer** the manager of an estate *18-, now local Ork-Kcb.* ~ **rape** = ~ **bauk,** *e16.* ~ **rich** extremely rich *la15-e17.* ~ **richt** *law* HERITABLE right; right of possession, *chf* of real property *la15-16.* **grund-shot, grunsher** *mining* one of a series of shots placed along the bottom of a seam where the coal is too hard to undercut *20-, Fif Ayr.* ~**-stane** a foundation stone *la16-, now Sh* [OE *grundstān*].

grounds and warrants *law* the reasons and documentary evidence on which a DECREE was based and which might be called for in an action of restriction *19-e20.*

grund, grundable, grundin *see* GRIND

grundiswallow &c ['grʌndɪ'swalə, -ɪ, &c] *n* = groundsel *19-, now NE Ags.* [ME *grounswili* &c, OE *grundeswylige*]

grunkle *see* CRUNKLE

grunsher *see* GRUND

grunstane *see* GRIND

gruntie &c *n, joc* a pig *la18-, local Sh-Ayr.* [Eng *grunt + -ie*]

gruntle &c, **gruntill** *16 n* **1** the snout of a pig *16-, now Rox.* **2** *contemptuous, of a person* the nose and mouth, the face or head *16-e20.* **3** a grunt or similar noise *la18-e20.*

vi grunt, make a grunting or groaning noise *la16-, now Rox.* [nME *gruntil (v)*]

grunyie &c *la16-e20*, **grunƷe** *16*; **gronƷe** &c
15-16, **grunzie** *18-e20* [*'grʌnjɪ] *n* **1** the snout
of an animal or (*contemptuous*) of a person
la14-e20. **2** a grudge *la18-19*, *Abd Bnf*. [ME
groney, *groin* &c, OF *groign*]

grup *see* GRIP, GRUIP

gruppen *see* GRIP

gruse &c; **growze** &c [gruz; *WC* grʌuz; *S also*
*grʌuz] *vi*, *n* = GRUE[1] *v* 1, 3 and *n*, *19-*, now *local*
Loth-S.

groosie &c shivery *20-*, now *midLoth Bwk Slk*.

grush &c [grʌʃ] *vt* = crush *19-20*.
n grit, fine gravel *20-*, now *Pbls Dmf*.

grushie ['grʌʃɪ] *adj* **1** *of a child* thriving
la18-e20. **2** *of vegetation* abundant, lush
la19-20. [Eng *gross* + *-ie*]

grushion *see* GRUE[1]

grutch *see* GRUDGE

grutten *see* GREET[1]

gruzzle *see* GROOZLE

gry &c [graɪ; *Rox also* groi] *n*, *gipsy* a horse *20*,
local Per-Rox. [see SND]

gryse *see* GRICE

gryte *see* GREAT

guard *see* GAIRD

gub *see* GOB[1]

gubern [*gʌ'bɛrn, *'gʌbərn] *vt* govern *la15-16*.
[only Sc; L *gubernāre*]

gubernakil &c [*gʌbər'nakl] *n* a helm, rudder
e16. [only Sc; L *gubernāculum*]

guchar *see* GUID

guckit *see* GUK

guddis *see* GUID

guddle &c *vti* **1** catch (fish) with the hands by
groping under the stones or banks of a stream
19-. **2** *vt* stab, hack (a body) *19*. **3** *vti* (1) do
dirty, messy work *19-*, now *NE*. (2) do things in
a careless, slovenly way, mess about, make a
mess *19-*, now *C, S*. (3) *specif, of children* play
messily *la19-*, now *Abd Dmf*.
n **1** (1) a crowbar *20-*, now *Per Fif*. (2) a
pointed iron bar for making holes for fence-
posts *la20-*, *Kcdn Ags Per*. **2** hard, dirty or
messy work *19-*, now *Ags midLoth Gsw*. **3** (1) a
mess, muddle, confusion *la19-*, now *C, S*. (2) a
person who does things in a messy, slovenly way
20-, *midLoth Dmf*.

guddled disordered, in a muddle *20-*, now *Ags*
S. [*cf* Eng *puddle*, *muddle*]

gude, gudein *see* GUID

gudge &c *la17-*, **guge** *e17* [gʌdƷ] *n* **1** = gouge
17-, now *Sh Ork NE*. **2** anything short and
thick, *esp* a short, strong, thickset person *la19-*,
now *Cai Bnf Abd*. **3** = gudgeon, a pivot
la17-18.
vt **1** = gouge *19-*, now *Sh Ags*. **2** raise or separate by driving in wedges *la19-*, *Bnf Ags*.

gudgie &c short and thickset, squat *19-*, now
Ags Per Lnk.

gudget &c *n* a camp-follower; a servant, a
drudge *la16-17*. [only Sc; F *goujat* a soldier's
servant]

gudling &c [*'gødlɪn, *?'gʌd-] *n* = gulden, a
coin, a guilder *la15-17*.

guess *19-*, **ges** &c *la14-17*; **gais** &c *la16-e17*
[gɛs; *ges] *n* **1** = guess *15-*. **2** *chf in pl* riddles,
conundrums *19-*, now *local Cai-Rox*.
vti, *also* **guiss** *la19-*, *N* = guess *la14-*.

guest *19-*, **gest** &c *la14-e20*, **gast** &c *la14-e17*;
gheast &c *la16-e17*, **gaist** &c *16* [gɛst; *also*
*?gest] *n* **1** = guest *la14-*. **2** an object thought
to foretell the arrival of a stranger *19-*, now *Sh*
Ork.

guest *see* GHAIST

guff[1]; **gouff** &c [gʌf; *SW, S* gʌuf; *Gall* *gof] *n* a
fool, simpleton *19-*, now *EC, S*.
~**ie** stupid *19-*, now *Rox*. [eModEng *goffe*]

guff[2] &c; **gouff** &c *la19-*, now *Fif* [gʌf; *Mry Bnf*
Fif also gʌuf] *n* **1** a (*usu* unpleasant) smell or
whiff *19-*. **2** a savour, taste, after-taste *18-*,
now *Rox*. **3** a puff, whiff, current of air, vapour
etc *19-*, now *local*.
vi give off a smell, steam, smoke etc *20-*, now
local Ork-Fif.
~**ie** &c fat, flabby or fluffy about the cheeks
19-, now *Rox*. [onomat; *cf* Norw *gufs* air, a
puff of wind etc, *guva* (*v*) smoke]

guff[3] *16-*; **gouff** &c *la18-* [gʌf; *Cai Abd* gʌuf] *n* **1**
a grunting, snuffling sound (of a pig); a low
bark (of a dog) *16-*, now *Sh*. **2** a suppressed
laugh, a snort *20-*, now *Cai*.
vi **1** snort, snuffle *18-*, now *Sh Ork*. **2** cackle
with laughter; babble, talk foolishly *la18-*, now
Rox. **3** belch *20-*, now *local*.
~**ie** name for a pig *20-*, now *Slk*. [imit; *cf*
Norw dial *goffa* grunt, *guffa* yelp]

guff[4] *n* **neither** ~ **nor sty**(**e**) nothing at all *19*,
Fif. [*cf* BUFF[4]]

guffaw *see* GAFFAW

guffer[1] *n* the eel-pout *la17-19*. [obscure]

guffer[2] *vt* = goffer *la19-*, *Abd Ags*. [*cf* GOUFFER]

guga *20-*, **goug** &c *la19-e20* ['gug(ə)] *n* the
young of the gannet *la19-*, *Hebrides*. [Gael]

guge *see* GUDGE

guid &c *15-*, **gude** &c; **god** &c *la15-e17*, **goud**
&c *16-e17*, **good** *la16-*, **gweed** &c *la18-*, *NE*,
geud *19* [gød, gɪd; *Cai* gid; *NE* gwid; *Sh also*
gjød; *nEC also* ged] *adj* **1** = good *la14-*. **2** *of*
persons distinguished in rank or social standing,
worthy, respectable *la14-*, now *local*. **3** = best:
(1) *of clothes* kept as best, formal *19-*; (2) *of a*
room the best, used on formal occasions *20-*, now
WC Kcb Rox. **4** = -in-law, *as* ~ **brither** &c,
~ **dochter** &c, ~ **father** &c, ~ **mither** &c,
~ **sister** &c, ~ **son** &c *la14-*.
n, *pl also* **guddis** &c *15-e17* **1** = good *la14-*. **2**
chf in pl livestock, cattle *la15-18*. **3** (**the**) **G**~
God *la18-*.
vt improve land by manuring *la15-e19*.
adv, *intensifier* very, pretty *19-*, *midLoth*: 'I'm very
gude sure'.
~**ing** &c manure *la15-20*. ~**less ill-less** *etc*
doing neither good nor harm, insipid, characterless *19*. ~**ly** &c **1** = goodly *la14-*. **2** =

godly, pious *19-, now NE Ags.* **~lyheid &c** *verse* goodliness, sanctity *16.* **guidness &c** God, *freq* by **~ness** *19-.* **goody-good** *adj* = goody-goody *la19-, now Ags.*

~ **breed** bread baked for weddings, baptisms or funerals; the bread used at Communion *19-, now Rox.* ~ **dame &c** a *or* (*chf*) one's grandmother *15-19.* ~ **dede &c** a benefit *la16-17.* **~een, gudein** [gø'din &c] *greeting* = good evening *la16-, now Ags Ayr.* **the ~ folks &c** the fairies, brownies etc *19-20.* ~ **gaun** going well, in good working order, active, flourishing *18.* ~ **man: A** *usu written as two words* **1** = good man *la14-16.* **2 the ~ man** *chf child's word* God *19-, now Sh NE,WC.* **B** *usu written as one word* ['~'man] **1** term of address used between equals who are not on terms of familiarity *la14-20.* **2** (1) the head of a household *la15-, now local.* (2) the head of an establishment, a manager, *esp* the keeper of a jail *17-19*: '*Goodman of the Tolbuith*'. **3** a husband *16-.* **4** the owner or tenant of a small estate or farm, ranking below a LAIRD *la16-e20.* **5** the Devil *17-e20.* **the ~man's craft** *etc* a plot of land left uncultivated to propitiate the Devil *la18-e20.* ~ **neebors** = guid folks, *la18-19.* **~sire &c** *15-e20*, **~schir &c** *16-19*, **gutcher &c** *16-20*, **gutsher &c** *16-e17*, **guchar &c** *16* ['gʌtʃər; *Cai* 'git-; *'gødsər, *-ʃər] a grandfather. ~ **toun** complimentary title, *orig of any* town, *chf* of Edinburgh *16-20.* ~ **wife &c** *usu written as one word* ['~'wəif] **1** (1) *freq as a polite term of address* the mistress of a house, a wife or woman in this capacity *la14-.* (2) the mistress **of** (a particular place, *esp* a farm) *16-, now Ags EC Ayr*: '*the guidwife of Mossat*'. (3) the landlady of an inn *la18-e20.* **2** a wife *18-, now local.* **~will** = goodwill *la14-.* **~willed** zealous *19-, now Sh.* **~willie** willing, ready; generous, hearty, cordial *16-, now local Bnf-Bwk.* **give one's ~will** = give one's consent *15-e17.* ~ **words** (*chf*) children's prayers etc *la19-, now local.*

as ~ (**as**) *of price, value, measure* as much (as), practically *16-, now local.* (**be**)**come ~ for** be surety for *19-, now local.* **dae ~** get good results, thrive, prosper *la19-, now local Sh-WC.* **get the ~ o** get what advantage or benefit is to be had from (a thing) *20-.* **a ~ bit** a long time *20-, now local.* (**the**) **G~ Book** the Bible *la19-.* **goods in communion** *law* the MOVEABLE property of a husband and wife, regarded as belonging in common *la18.* **a** *or* **some ~ mair** a good many more *la18-, now Abd Ags.* ~ **and weel** well and good, so be it *la19-, now Gen except Ork.* **hae ~ on one, hae ~ in one's mind** *chf interrog, asking for money etc* be disposed to be generous *20-, C.* **haena ~ doing something** find something difficult to do *19-, now Sh Ags.* **ken the ~ o** realize or enjoy the benefits of *20-.* **men of ~** men of

property, rank or standing *la15-16.* **tak the ~ o 1** = get the ~ o, *la20-.* **2** damage, spoil *la20-.*

guide &c, gyde &c [gəid] *v* **1** *vt* = guide *15-.* **2** (1) run (an organization etc) *16-.* (2) direct, manage, control (a matter) *18-.* (3) *specif* manage, use (money or resources well, sparingly etc) *18-.* **3** treat, use, handle, care for (persons (*esp* children) or animals) *17-.* **4** conduct oneself, behave: (1) *vr, la15-, now Sh Abd Fif*; (2) *vi, 16.*

n **1** = guide *15-.* **2** a manager, controller, *usu* of money or property *la18-, now Sh Abd Ags.* **guider &c 1** = guider *16-.* **2** a manager, administrator *16-, now Sh.* **3** *specif* a person put in charge of the guidance and upbringing of a child or young person *16-17.* **4** a home-made children's cart steered by a rope *20-, Fif Edb.* **guiding &c 1** = guiding *la15-.* **2** conduct, behaviour; management of one's own affairs *la15-e17.* **~ship &c 1** guidance, leadership *16-e19.* **2** treatment (of one person by another) *la18-, now local Sh-Ags.*

~ **us** *interj* expressing surprise or consternation *19* [short for *God guide us*].

guil &c *18-*, **guld &c** *15-e20*, **gowl &c** *la16*; **guild** *la16-e17* [gøl, gil; *Ork* gʌl; *NE* gwil; *gøld; *gul] *n* the corn marigold *15-, now NE Gall.* [ME *goolde, golde*, OE *goold &c* (GOWD), GULE]

guild *18-*, **gild &c** *15-e18* [gild] *n* **1** an association formed within a BURGH, enjoying exclusive rights of trading in it and taking a predominant part in its government, a merchant guild *15-20, latterly chf hist*; *cf* ALDERMAN, DEAN. **2** a member of a GUILD *15-17.* **~ry &c 1** membership in a GUILD *16.* **2** = GUILD 1; a municipal corporation based on this *16-.* **~schippe &c** = guildry 1, *la16-e17.* ~ **box** the treasury or funds of the GUILD *17.* ~ **brother, gilbroder &c** *16-e17* [*'gil(d)-'brøðər, &c*] a member of a GUILD *15-.* **burgess of ~** a burgess elected by virtue of his membership of the GUILD *18-.* [*cf* Eng = a trade or craft association]

guild *see* GUIL

guildry *see* GUILD

guilt &c *n* = guilt. **tak ~ til ane(sel)** feel or show guilt, be conscience-stricken *la19-, local.*

guise &c *16-*, **gyse &c** *16-19*; **guize &c** *17-e20* [gaiz] *n, also* **gy &c** *19-, now Ork* [gai] **1** = guise, fashion of dress *la15-e17.* **2** a way of doing something, a fashion in behaviour etc, a habit or custom (of a society, nation etc), *freq* **as was the ~** *16-19.* **3** a masque or masquerade; merrymaking, a piece of fun *16-e20.*

v **1** *vt* = disguise *16-, now Ork Ags Rox.* **2** *vi, chf* **guising &c** going about as a ~*er* (*n* 1) *la16-, local.*

~er &c, ~ard &c *n* **1** a mummer, masquerader, *now esp* one of a party of children who go

in disguise from door to door offering entertainment in return for gifts or money, *esp* at *Halloween* (HALLOW²) *la15-*. **2** *fig* an unprepossessing or odd-looking person, a 'geezer' *18-*, *now Abd Ags*. *vi* = *v* 2, *19-*, *now local Ags-Rox*.
hae *or* **haud a** ~ (**wi**) have (a bit of) fun (with) *19-*, *now Sh NE*. **hae the gy o** have the knack of *20-*, *Ork*. **turn the** ~ *fig* reverse roles, put the boot on the other foot *18-19*.

guiss *see* GUESS

guisserne *see* GIZZERN

guissie *see* GUSSIE

guize *see* GUISE

guk &c [*gʌk] *n* a mocking sound *la15-16*.
vi talk or behave foolishly *la16*.
~**kis** a jocular title *16-e17*. ~(**k**)**it, guckit** foolish, silly *la15-16*; *cf* gowkit (GOWK¹).

gulch &c [gʌlʃ] *vt* eat rapidly or greedily *la17-*, *now Abd*.
n a glutton *la19-*, *now Cai*. [ME]

guld *see* GUIL

gulder *see* GOLLER

gule &c [*gøl] *adj* yellow *la15-e16*.
~ **tree** the barberry *e19*. [ME *gowl* &c, ON *gulr*; *cf* GUIL]

gule *see* GOWL¹

gull *n* a thin cold mist accompanied by a chilly breeze *19-*, *NE*. [Norw dial *gul*, Icel *gol(a)* a (sea) breeze, which tends to bring mist]

guller *see* GOLLER

gullet &c *n* **1** = gullet. **2** a narrow, deep channel or rocky inlet *la18-*, *now Gall*. **3** a gully, ravine *la18-*, *now local Ags-Dmf*. **4** a narrow channel made or used for catching fish *16-e19*.

gullie &c, gully &c; gowly &c *la16-e18* ['gʌlɪ; *gulɪ] *n, also* ~ **knife** a large knife *16-*.
vt cut, knife, slash *19*.
~**gaw** *vt* wound, cut, hack, gash *19-e20*, *chf N*.
guide the ~ *fig, freq of God* manage or control events *18-e20*. **haud the** ~ **ower the dyke** (*chf* **to**) stand up for oneself (against) *la19-*, *now Ags*. [obscure; perh short for *gully* (eModEng var of *gullet-knife*)]

gullion *n* **1** a quagmire, marsh *19-e20*, *Loth Gall*. **2** a pool of mud or of semi-liquid manure and decayed vegetable matter *19-e20*, *Uls*. [IrGael *goilín* a pit, pool]

gully *see* GULLIE

gulravage, gulravish *see* GILRAVAGE

gulsa, gulset *see* GULSOCH

gulsh &c *n* a fat, thickset person *19*. [see SND]

gulsoch &c, gulset *16-e19*; **gulsa &c** *la19-*, *now Sh* [*Sh Ork* 'gʌlsə; *NE* 'gʌlʃəx; *'gʌlsəx] *n* **1** jaundice *16-*, *now Kcdn*. **2** excessive eating; nausea caused by this *19-*, *now Kcdn*. [eModEng *gulesought*, ME *gowyl sowght*, f *gule* yellow + OE *sucht* disease; *cf* Norw dial *gulsott*, ON *gulu-sótt*]

gum¹ &c, gume &c *15-16*, **geem &c** *20*, *NE*; **goom &c** *la16-e18* [*C, S* gøm, gɪm; *Sh* gum; *NE* gim, *Abd also* gwim] *n, chf in pl* = the gums (in the mouth) *15-*.

~**stick &c** a stick etc used by a teething child *18-*, *now midLoth Ayr*.

gum² &c; goum &c *16* [gʌm] *n* = gum, adhesive *16-*.
~**flour &c** an artificial flower *18-20*.

gum³ &c *n* **1** a mist, haze, condensation, *eg* on glass *16-*, *now Cai NE Ags*. **2** *also* **yella** ~ jaundice, *esp* in the newborn *la20-*, *NE Ags Ayr* [perh f obs Eng *gound* rheum]. **3** *fig* a disagreement, dispute; ill-will, rancour *18-e20*.
vi become misted over *la19-*, *NE Ags*. [only Sc; obscure]

gum⁴ &c *n* **1** a clump of ore *la16*. **2** a small parcel (of awls) *la16-e17*. [OF *gomme* a packet]

gum⁵ *n* coal-dust *la18-*, *C*. [prob related to COOM¹]

gume *see* GUM¹

gumlie, gummle *see* GRUMMEL

gump¹; gumph *vti* search, grope for; *esp* GUDDLE (fish) *19-*, *now midLoth Bwk S*. [see SND]

gump² *n* a part or portion, *esp* ~**ing** the part of a crop left standing between two reapers, *usu* **cut the** ~**ing** *19-e20*, *Gall*. [obscure]

gumph &c *n* **1** *also* **gamf &c** *19-*, *now Ags Ayr*, ~**ie &c** *19-*, *now Rox* a fool *19-*, *now local N-Uls*. **2** *in pl* the sulks, *freq* **tak the gumps** *19-*, *Fif*. **gamfle** *vi* idle, dally *19-e20*, *chf nEC*. **gumple-faced** dejected *19-e20*. **gamphrell &c** a bumptious, foolish person *la18-e20*. **gumpus** ['gʌmpəs] = *n* 1, *19-*, *now Bnf Abd Ags*. [onomat]

gumph *see* GUMP¹

gumphion &c *18-e19*, **gunfioun &c** *e15*, **gomphion** *la17* *n* a funeral banner. [ME, F *gonfanon* a banner, standard]

gumple-faced *see* GUMPH

gumption &c ['gʌm(p)ʃən] *n* **1** common sense, native wit *18-*. **2** pluck, self-confidence *la19-*, *now local*. [earlier in Sc]

gumptious ['gʌmpʃəs] *adj* = bumptious *la19-e20*.

gumpus *see* GUMPH

gumsh *vi* munch *la19-20*, *NE*. [onomat, perh w infl f GANSH]

gun &c, gone &c *la15-e18*; **goun &c** *la15-17*, **gune &c** *16-17* [gʌn; *also* *gun] *n* **1** = gun *la14-*. **2** a tobacco pipe, a briar-pipe *19-*, *now local Ags-Gall*.
vi **1** gossip, talk rapidly or animatedly *19-20*, *NE*. **2** *mining, quarrying, of a charge* go off without splitting the mineral, blow back out of the charge-hole *la19-*, *now Ags*.
~**ner** a person who shoots game for sport *la18-*, *now Ork Arg*.
~ **end** the best room, the parlour *20*, *Abd*.
be great ~**s** (**wi**) be close friends (with) *20-*, *Sh N Ags*.

gunch &c [gʌnʃ] **1** a thick piece, a hunk *la18-*, *now Cai Ayr Kcb*. **2** a short, thickset person *20-*, *chf Cai*. [prob onomat]

gundie; gunnie &c *n* the father-lasher *la19-*, *now NE Ags*. [see SND]

gundy *n* toffee *19-*. [perh (child's) var of Eng *candy*, but poss direct f Arabic or Tamil]

gune *see* GUN

gunfioun *see* GUMPHION

gunk &c *n* a bitter disappointment; *freq* **do a ~ (on someone)**, **gie (someone) the ~** cause (someone) pain or chagrin, disappoint; jilt *la18-*, *now local Pbls-Uls*.
vt disappoint, humiliate; jilt *19-*, *now Uls*. [see SND]

gunnie *see* GUNDIE

gunplucker *n* = GUNDIE[1] *la19-*, *now Abd*. [see SND]

gurdy *see* GIRD[1]

gurge *see* GORGE

gurk *n* a stout, heavily-built person *18-*, *Cai NE*. [perh var of DURK[2]]

gurl &c *vi* **1** *of the wind* roar, howl *la18-*, *now midLoth Bwk Ayr*. **2** growl *19-*, *local midLoth-S*. **3** *of water* gurgle *la19-*, *now midLoth Rox*.
adj **1** *of weather, wind etc* cold, stormy, wild *16-20*. **2** *of persons* surly *19-*, *now Dmf*.
n **1** a gale, a squall *19-20*. **2** a growl, a snarl *la18-*, *now local midLoth-Rox*. **3** a gurgling sound *la19-*, *now midLoth Rox*.
~ie 1 *of weather etc* stormy, threatening, bitter *18-*, *now local*. **2** (1) *of persons* surly *18-*, *now local Sh-SW*. (2) *of dogs* growling, snarling *la19-*, *now NE*. **3** *of trees* gnarled *19-e20*. **4** *of water* gurgling *19-*, *now midLoth*. [onomat]

gurr[1] &c *n, vi* growl, snarl *19-*, *now local*.
~y &c 1 a dogfight, a brawl *19-*, *now local SW*. **2** a hurry, a bustle, a state of confusion *la19-*, *now local C*. **~y-wurry &c 1** = *n, 19-*, *now Ags*. **2** = **~y 1**, *la19-*, *local C*. [onomat]

gurr[2] *n* a strong, thickset, ungainly person *19-e20*. [Gael *geàrr* thickset, squat; *cf* GARRON[1] 3]

gurr[3] *n* drive, spirit *20-*, *now Abd*. [perh f GORE or GURR[1]]

gurr *see* GORE

gurth *n* crushed curd for cheese-making *19-e20*, *local WC*. [voiced var of Eng *curd*; *cf* also Gael *gruth*]

gurthie *see* GIRTH[2]

gusch *see* GUSH

guschet *see* GUSHET

guse &c, geese *la19-*, *Sh-NE*; **goose &c** *la16-* [gøs, gɪs; *Sh-NE* gis] *n, pl* **geese &c 1** = goose *la14-*. **2** *only* **goose**, *piping* a bagpipe with a chanter (CHANT) but no drones *la19-*.
vt press or iron with a tailor's goose *la18-e19*.
gusing iron &c a tailor's goose *17-*, *now Per*.
~ dub &c a goose pond *la16-*, *local, freq in place-names*. **~ grass 1** = goose-grass, cleavers *19-*. **2** brome grass *la19-*, *now Ork Ayr Rox*. **~ pan &c** a large cooking-pot *la15-17*.

gus-gus *see* GUSSIE

gush, gusch *la16* *vi* **1** = gush *la16-*. **2** salivate *19-*, *now Abd*.

gushet &c *18-*, **guschet &c** *la15-e17* *n* **1** = gusset *la15-*. **2** a clock or ornamental pattern

on the side of a stocking *16-e19*. **3** the breast-pocket of a jacket or coat *la19-*, *now Cai Ayr Kcb*. **4** a triangular piece of land, *esp* between adjacent properties; an odd corner of land; a nook *la16-*, *now local Sh-WC*. **5** the triangular patch left in ploughing or reaping an irregularly-shaped field *20-*, *local Sh-WC*. **6** the corner of a building, a corner in a building *20-*, *now Ags*.
~ house a house standing at a corner or forming the angle between two roads *la19-e20*. **~ neuk** = *n 4*, *la19-*, *now Abd Ags*.

gussie &c *local Ags-S*, **gissie** *20-*, *local*; **guissie &c** *e20*, **goosy &c** *19-e20*, **gees(i)e** *20-*, *local* ['gʌs(ɪ); *local Sh-Bwk* 'gisi; *C* 'gɪs(ɪ); *Per Rox* 'gøs(ɪ)] *interj*, *also* **gus-gus &c** a call to pigs *19-*, *local Ags-S*.
n **1** a pig, *esp* a young pig or sow *19-*, *now local Ags-S*. **2** *freq as a nickname* a fat person *la19-*, *now Ags*. **3** a segment of an orange *20-*, *Ags*. [only Sc; *cf* Norw, Sw dial *gis(s)*]

gust &c [gʌst; *Rox also* gʌust] *n* taste; a taste; relish *la15-e20*.
v **1** *vt* taste (food, drink etc) *la15-*. **2** *vi* take a taste **of** (something) *la15-e16*. **3** taste good, have an agreeable taste *la15-e18*. **4** *vt, freq* **~ the gab** *etc* delight the palate, whet the appetite, fill the mouth with tasty food or drink *la15-*, *now Abd Fif*. **5** *vi* smell (strongly, bad) *16-*, *now Ags*.
~ie &c tasty, savoury *18-*, *now Ayr*. **~ily** with gusto, heartily *19-e20*. **wele** *etc* **~it &c** tasting good etc *la15-16*. **~less** in bad taste, tasteless *la16-*, *now Fif*. [ME; L *gustus*, *gustāre*]

gustard &c *n* a bustard *16-17*. [appar altered f OF *ostarde* or Eng *bustard*]

gut *n, pl* **guttis &c** *la14-17*, **guts** *18-* = gut *la14-*.
vt = gut *la16-*.
~s eat greedily or gluttonously *20-*, *local*. **~ser 1** a glutton *la20-*, *NE Ags*. **2** a belly-flop *20-*, *now Ags Fif Lnk*. **~sie 1** greedy, gluttonous *19-*. **2** *of a building* roomy, commodious *la19-*, *local Abd-Ayr*. **~ter** *specif* a woman employed in gutting fish *la19-*. **~tie** *adj* **1** thick; gross; corpulent, pot-bellied *la18-*, *now local Kcdn-Dmf*. **2** fond of good eating, gluttonous *19-*, *now Bnf Abd Kcb*. *n* **1** a corpulent, pot-bellied person *19-*, *now Dmf Rox*. **2** the minnow *19-*, *now Stlg*. **~pock** the stomach of a fish *la19-*, *now Cai*. **~pock herring** herring which feed *chf* on small crustaceans *la19-*, *now Arg*. **~-scraper** a fiddle-player *la18-e20*.
(baith) ~(s) and ga &c *adv* altogether, from top to bottom *la15*. *n* the whole contents of the stomach; the stomach *la18-19*. **~ fish afore you catch them** = count your chickens before they are hatched *19*.

gut *see* GOTE

gutcher *see* GUID

guts, gutser *see* GUT

gutsher *see* GUID

gutta *see* GUTTIE

guttag *n* a fish-gutting knife *20-*, *Cai Ayr.* [conflation of Gael *cutag* w GUT]

guttam &c *n*, *orig school usage* a drop (*orig* of ink) *e20.* [L accusative of *gutta* a drop]

gutter &c *16-*, **guttar &c** *15-16*; **gitter &c** *19-* ['gʌtər; *C, S* 'gøt-, 'gɪt-] *n* **1** = gutter *15-*. **2** *chf in pl* mud, mire, muddy puddles *18-*, now *Sh-C.* **3** the doing of something in an unskilful or dirty way *la19-*, now *Abd midLoth.* **4** a muddle, mess *la20-*, *local Cai-Dmf.* **5** a stupid, awkward, untidy or messy worker *la19-*, *local Cai-Dmf.*
v **1** *vt* = gutter *la14-*. **2** *vi* do something in a dirty, slovenly or unskilful way *19-*, *local N-S.* **3** potter, tinker, fritter away time *20-*, *local N-S.* **4** talk nonsense, gabble, gibber *20-*, now *WC.*
~**ie** muddy, miry, messy *la18-*, *local.*
~**-bluid 1** a lowly-born or ill-bred person, a guttersnipe *19-e20.* **2** a native of a particular town; a person whose ancestors have been born in the same town for generations, *esp* of Peebles *19-*, now *Bwk Pbls S.* ~ **gaw &c** a sore on the foot *la19-*, now *local Ags nEC.* ~ **hole** a drain or drainage-hole for kitchen refuse *la16-20.*

guttie &c *la19-*, **gutta** *19-20 n* anything made wholly or partly of rubber: **1** *freq also* ~ **ba** a golf-ball *19-*, now *C, S Uls*; **2** *only* **guttie** a catapult *la20-*, *Per Edb Ayr*; **3** *in pl* **gutties** gymshoes *20-*, *WC.*

gutty-perky = gutta-percha, *chf* **gutty-perky-ba** = *n* **1**, *20-*, now *local N-Uls.* [reduced f Eng *gutta-percha*]

guttis *see* GUT

gutty-perky *see* GUTTIE

guy &c *20-*, **gy &c** *la14-16* [gaɪ] *vt* = guy, guide, steer *la14-16, 20 (NE).*
n **1** a guide *15-16.* **2** *chf in pl* the handlebars of a bicycle *20-*, *NE.*

guzzern *see* GIZZERN

guzzle *n* a bout of excessive eating and drinking, a debauch *19-.*
v **1** *vi* = guzzle. **2** *vt* take by the throat, throttle *la19-*, now *local Bnf-midLoth.*

gweed *see* GUID

gweeshtens &c, **gweeshtie &c** *interj* gosh!, goodness! *la19-20*, *NE.* [f *gweed* (GUID); *cf* GOSH]

gwite *see* GOTE

gy *see* GUISE, GUY

gya *see* GIE

gyaa(i)n *see* GAE

gyang *see* GANG

gya(u)n *see* GAE

gyde *n* = gite, a cloak *la15.*

gyde *see* GUIDE

gyle- *see* GEEL

gymp *see* JIMP[2]

gyne [*?dʒɔin] *vtr* elect to an office, get oneself elected *17.* [prob reduced f ADJUNE]

gype &c [gəip] *v* **1** *vi* stare foolishly or open-mouthed *la19-*, *NE Ags Per.* **2** *vti* play the fool; make a fool of *la19-*, now *Sh Ags.*
n a foolish awkward person, a silly ass, a lout *19-*, now *Sh NE Ags.*

gyper &c *vi* talk nonsense *20*, *Abd.* *n* nonsense; fun, joking *la19-20*, *NE.* **gyperie &c** nonsense, foolishness *19-*, *Abd.* **gypit &c** silly, foolish, witless *19-*, *Sh N Per.* [cognate w ON *geip* nonsense, *geipa* talk nonsense, Norw dial *gipa* let the mouth hang open]

gyre &c [gɔir, gair; *Sh Ork also* gɔi, gai; *Sh also* g(j)ør] *n* ~ **carlin(g)** &c a supernatural being, *chf* female, an ogress, a witch *16-*, now *Sh.*
adj, *of garments or colours* odd, gaudy *la19-e20*, *Abd.* [ON *gýgr* an ogress]

gyrthol *see* GIRTH[1]

gyse *see* GUISE

gyte &c [gɔit] *adj* **1** mad, insane; mad with rage, pain etc, *freq* **gang** ~ *18-.* **2** mad or crazy with longing or desire, love-sick, eager *19-*, now *local Ork-midLoth.* **3** *of things* nonsensical, crazy, *usu* **gae** *etc* ~ go awry, go to pot *la18-*, now *local NE-EC.*
n a madman, fool *19-e20.*

gyter &c *n* **1** nonsense, foolish talk *la19-*, *NE.* **2** a stupid, talkative person, a driveller *19-*, *NE.* *vi* talk a great deal in a silly way *20-*, *Abd.* **gytit &c** half-witted, crazy *la19-*, now *Ags.* [unknown]

gyte *see* GAIT[2], GET, GOTE

H

ha &c *la15-*, **hall** &c *la14-*, in place-names, *14-* [hɑ; *hal] n **1** = hall *la14-*. **2** a farmhouse as opposed to the farm cottages *18-*, *now local*. **3** the principal room of an ordinary house *18-19*. ~-**bible** a large family bible *la18-19*. **hall binks are sliddery** &c *proverb* great men are not reliable in their support *la15-e18*. ~ **board** &c a dining-table, *latterly* in a farmhouse *17-e19*. ~ **chamer** &c a small room off a hall *15-16*. ~ **house** &c = *n* 2, *17-*, *now Sh*.
the (Divinity) Hall one of the theological colleges of the *Church of Scotland* (CHURCH) or of one of the Free Churches *la18-*.

ha *see* HAE¹, HAW²

haaf-net *see* HALF²

haar¹ &c; **haur** [har; *sEC also* hɑr] n **1** a cold easterly wind *la18-*, *chf E*. **2** a cold mist or fog, *esp* an east-coast sea fog *18-*, *Gen except Gall.*
~**y 1** *of wind* cold, piercing *19-*, *Sh midLoth*. **2** misty, foggy *19-*, *now Sh Fif Rox*. [LowGer, MDu *hare* biting cold wind]

haar² &c n a burr in one's speech *la18-e19*.
vi speak with a burr *19-*, *now Ags*. [imit]

haar³ n, *chf* **haar-frost** hoar-frost *20-*, *Cai S*. [? by confusion of HAAR¹ w HAIR *adj*]

haave *see* HALF²

haaver *see* HALF¹

hab- *see* HAPSHACKLE

habber; hubber *vi* **1** stammer, stutter *19-*, *Sh N*. **2** snarl; make a gobbling noise *19-20*, *N*.
n **1** a stammer, stutter *20-*, *Sh N*. **2** a snarl, growl; the gobble of a turkey *19-*, *NE*.
~**gaw** *vi* stumble (in speaking); make objections *19*. [imit; *cf* HABBLE]

habbie *n* an inhabitant of Kilbarchan *20-*, *Renfr*.
Standard H~ name applied by Ramsay to the stanza form aaabab, with the b's forming a bob-wheel, used in the mock elegy *The Piper of Kilbarchan*, later much used by Burns and others *18-*. [f *Habbie Simpson* piper of Kilbarchan *17*; see SND]

habbie-horse *n* = hobby-horse *la19-*, *now midLoth Arg*.

habbitrot *n* = *Whippitie-Stourie* 1 (WHIPPITIE), *specif* a fairy for the spinning *19*, *S*. [obscure]

habble &c *v l vi* = hobble *la18-*, *now Ags*. **2** *vt* perplex, confuse; hamper *19-*, *chf S*. **3** tangle (thread etc) *20-*, *now Fif Kcb*. **4** *vi* stutter; babble *e19*. **5** quarrel, wrangle *19*, *chf S*.
n **1** = HOBBLE *n* 2, *la18-*, *local nEC-S*. **2** = HOBBLE *n* 3, *la18-*, *now NE Fif Ayr*. **3** a coarse or slovenly person *19-e20*.
~ **jock** a turkey cock *la19-*, *Ags*. [only Sc; onomat; *cf* HABBER]

haben &c ['habən] *n*, *gipsy* bread *la19-*, *chf Rox*.

haberschoun, haubersione &c, **aubirchoun** &c   *15-16*;   **abirioun** &c   *16* [*(h)abər-, *'(h)abər-, *-ʃun, *-ʃon, *-sun, &c] *n* = habergeon, a coat of mail *la14-e17*.

habile, habill &c *la14-e18*; **hable** &c *la14-e17*

['hebəil, *also* 'habəil; *'hebl] *adj* **1** *of persons* having ability, power or competence *15-e19*. **2** (1) fit, competent **for** *or* **to** *15-18*. (2) able, competent (to do etc) *la14-e17*. **3** *of things or animals* fit or suitable (**to** *or* **for**) *15-e17*. **4** *law* admissible, valid; apt, competent · for some purpose *la17-*. **5** liable, likely to·do *16-e17*.
habilitie &c [*ha'bɪlɪtɪ]   *n* **1** = ability *la15-e17*. **2** *law* the legal competence of a witness *la17-e18*. [OF; L *habilis*; *cf* laME *habyll* and ABLE]

habillement *see* HABULIMENT

habilliament *see* HABILƷEMENT

habilliƷe &c [*ha'bɪljɪ] *vt* array, clothe *la15-16*. [F *habiller*, *abillier*; *cf* Eng *habille* and ABILƷEIT]

habilƷement &c;   **habilliament**   *la15*, **habulƷement** &c   *16*   [*ha'bɪljɪ(ə)mənt, *ha'bʌljɪ-] *n*, *freq in pl* apparel, equipment *la15-16*. [OF *habillement*; *cf* HABULIMENT, ABUILYIEMENT]

habit &c *n* = habit *la14-*.
be in *or* **on good** *etc* ~**s** be on good terms *la18-19*.

habit &c **and repute** ['habɪt ənd rɪ'pjut] *chf law*, *adj* held or regarded as or to be (a thief, witch, married person etc) *18-*; *cf* REPUTE.
n the state or fact of being so regarded, reputation *18-*. [MedL *habitus et reputatus* held and reputed]

habitatioun &c [*habɪ'tesɪun] *n* = habitation, *freq* **mak** ~ make one's abode *la14-e16*.

hable *see* HABILE

habuliment &c, **habillement** &c *la16-e17* [*hə'bʌlɪmənt] *n* dress, attire, (military) equipment *la16-*, *now only Sh*. [eModEng *habilliment*; laME *habillement*; *cf* HABILƷEMENT]

habulƷement *see* HABILƷEMENT

hace *see* HAIRSE

hach *see* HAUCH

hache [*(h)atʃ, *(h)etʃ] *n* a pain, pang *e16*. [ME *hache* &c]

hachel *see* HOCHLE

hack *17-*, **hak** &c *la15-e20*; **hawk** &c *17-* [hak; C *also* hɑk] n **1** a pronged tool for breaking up or raking soil etc *la18-*, *Gen except Sh Ork*. **2** a joiner's adze; a miner's pick-ended hammer *19-*, *now midLoth*. **3** a crack or chap in the skin caused by cold or frost *19-*. **4** *curling* (CURL) a cut in the ice to steady the player's foot; *now* a metal footplate *19-*. **5** a notch on a graded scale; a certain amount (of time, distance) *20-*, *NE*.
vti **1** = hack *la15-*. **2** use a HACK (*n* 1) to drag dung from a cart *19-*, *midLoth Arg*. **3** chop up (meat, firewood etc) *18-*. **4** *of the skin* crack, chap, roughen *la18-*.
~**et** *or* ~**um kail** chopped KAIL or cabbage boiled in water or milk *18-19*. ~**ing stock** &c a chopping block *16-*.
~ **muck, muck** ~ = *n* 1, *la18-*. ~ **stock** = ~**ing stock**, *17-*.

a ~ abeen the common a cut above ordinary people *la19-*, *Sh NE*. **ca, drive** *etc* **a ~ i the crook** *or* **post** celebrate an event *la19-*, *local*. **mak a** (**sad** *etc*) **~ in the post** make a large hole in or take the greater part of someone's resources *19-*, *now Ayr Kcb*. **tak, pit** *or* **haul doon a ~** *fig* 'take (someone) down a peg' *20-*, *Sh NE*. [*cf* HAG¹]

hack *see* HECK¹

hackberry *see* HAGBERRY

hackit *see* HAWKIT

hackle *see* HECKLE¹

hackum-plackum &c *adv*, *of payment or reward* equally, in equal shares *19-e20*, *S*.
adj equal in every way; hand-in-glove *19-e20*, *S*. [*see* SND]

hacky duck; hucky- &c *n* a children's game in which two teams take it in turn to leap on the lined-up backs of their opponents *20-*, *nEC*.

had *see* HAE¹, HAUD

hadden *see* HAUD

hadder *see* HEATHER

haddie &c; haddo &c ['hadɪ, 'hʌdɪ; *Ork* 'hadu; *Loth also* 'hɑdɪ] *n* **1** a haddock *la17-*. **2** nickname for an Aberdonian, *chf* **Aberdeen ~** *20-*, *Gsw*.
yellow ~ a smoked haddock *20-*, *N*. [later var of HADDOCK]

hadding *see* HAUD

haddish &c, haddisch *16-e17*, **half-disch &c** *16-e17* [*'hadɪʃ, *'hʌd-; *'haf'dɪʃ] *n* a measure of grain equal to a third or a quarter of a PECK² *16-19*, *NE*.
~ cog(ue) a container holding this amount *la18-e20*, *N*. [Eng *half + dish*]

haddo *see* HADDIE

haddock &c, haddok *la15-16*, **hathock &c** *19-e20*, *only Sc*; **hoddock** *la19-*, *NE* ['hadək; *NE* 'hað-; *NE Fif* 'hʌd-] *n* = haddock *15-*. [*cf* HADDIE]

hade &c *n* rank, estate; quality, kind *la14-e15*. [nME *hade*, midl and sME *hode*, OE *hād*]

hade *see* HEID, HIDE¹

hadin, hading *see* HAUD

hadry *see* HEATHER

hae¹ *la16-*, *only Sc*, **have &c, ha** *la16-*, **haf &c** *la14-16*, **hafe &c** *la14-e17*, **half &c** *15-e16*, **hef** *16-17*, *only Sc*, **heve &c** *16-e17*, *only Sc*; **haive** *la16*, **heif &c** *16-17*, *only Sc*, **hiv &c** *18-*, *most freq emphatic or interrog*, *esp NE* [he; hʌv; *NE, C also* hɪv; *nEC Arg Bwk Rox Uls also* hɛv; *nEC, WC also* hev; *Bwk Rox* hɛ; *hɑv; *hiv] *vti*, *infin also* (*unstressed with aux verbs*) **a** [ə]; *2 pers sing also* **hes** *la16*, *e20* (*Sh*) [hɪz, hɛz, hiz]; *3 pers sing also* **hais(e) &c** *15-e16*, **hasse &c** *15*, **hes** *la16-17*, *la19-*, *now Ags Uls*, **his** *la19-*, *now Ags Ayr* [hɪz, hʌz, hez; hez; *Sh* hiz]; *3 pers pl also* **hes** *16-e18* [hɪz, hɛz, &c]; *freq with negative suffix* **-na(e)**, *eg* **hinna** *la19-*, *now Bnf Abd Ags WC*, **henna** *la19-e20*, **hinnae &c** *20-*, *EC, SW*. *pt also* **haid &c** *la14-16*, *la19-*, *now Sh*, **hid** *la19-*, *now local Bnf-Ayr* [hɪd, hʌd, hed; *Per Rox* hɛd; *hid]. *ptp also* **haid &c** *la14-17*, *e20*; **haen &c** *la18-*, *now N* [hɪd, &c; *Sh NE* hed; hen; *Cai Ags* 'hɪdən; *Ork NE* hin; *unstressed also* hən] **1** (1) = have *la14-*. (2) *sometimes omitted after conditional aux verb before ptp*, *la15-*, *only Sc, esp in negative, eg* **suld nocht dune** *etc la15-17*, **wadna cared** *etc 18-*. (3) *imperative* [he, &c; *Rox also* hjɛ] = here!, take this! *18-*: 'hae tak that, an' be aff wi you'. (4) **had to do** *etc* = had done etc *20-*, *Ags Arg Kcb*: 'if she had tae recover she wad hae bin a help tae him'. **2** put, bring, take, send *la14-*, *now NE, WC Ags*: 'Mrs. B has her compliments to you'. **3** *vir* behave, conduct oneself *15-16*. **4** go **after** *or* **with** *la18-*, *now Ags*. **5** credit, believe, think, *freq* **what hae ye o't** *etc* would you believe it! *la19-20*.
n, *sing* **hae, hiv** [he, hɪv]; *pl* **haves** *e19* [*hevz] **1** property, possessions, *chf* **~ and heal** health and wealth *19*, *chf NE*, *only Sc*. **2** *contrasted with* **want** possession of material things or mental powers *20-*, *now Ork Uls*: 'a continual state of a hae an' a want'.
be well had be well off *la18-*, *now Ayr Uls*. **haet &c** *la18-*, **haid &c** *la16-e20* [he(:)t, he(:)d; *Rox* hjɪd] = have it *la16*. **deil** *etc* **haet** not a grain or particle, damn all *la16-*. **deil a haet, (the) fient a haet** *etc* devil a bit!, not a whit! *18-*. **no** *etc* **a haet** not the smallest amount, not an iota *19-*. **that's a haet** no matter, never mind *e20*. **haiveless, hafles** *la15*, **hawles &c** *la15*, *e20*; **haveless** *19-e20*, *N* ['hevləs] *adj* **1** destitute *la15*. **2** shiftless, incapable, careless, extravagant *19-*, *N*. **3** senseless, meaningless *19-20*, *latterly Abd*. **haver &c** *la15-*, **ha(i)far &c** *15-e17* ['havər; *'hev-] **1** an owner, possessor, occupier *la15-17*. **2** *law*, *specif* the holder of documents, *esp* those required as evidence in a court *la16-*, *only Sc*. **having &c** ['hevɪn] *n* **1** (1) bearing, behaviour, deportment *la14-16*. (2) *in pl* behaviour, manners *la15-16*, *18-20*. **2** having, possessing, keeping *la14-17*. **3** taking, removing *la15-16*. **dolorous having(is)** signs of suffering *la15-16*. **~ easy** *or* **guid** *or* **ill** *etc* **daein** *etc* be able to do easily etc *la18-*, *now Sh NE Ags*. **~ had** *or* **haen something to do** have been compelled or predetermined by fate to take a certain course of action *19-*, *Abd Ags Stlg*.

hae² *vi* **hum(ph) and ~** prevaricate, hesitate *19-*, *now local Ork-midLoth Arg*.
n a hesitation *la19-*, *now Abd midLoth*: 'wi a hum and a hae'. [*cf* HEY³]

haemmit *see* HAMIT

haen, haet, haf *see* HAE¹

haf *see* HALF¹

hafe, hafer *see* HAE¹

hafer, haff(e) *see* HALF¹

haffer *see* HALF¹

haffet &c *n* **1** *now chf literary* = HALFHEDE *la16-*. **2** *chf in pl* a side-lock of hair *18-20*. **3** the wooden side of a box-bed (BOX¹), chair etc *la18-*.

hafles *see* HAE¹

haf-net *see* HALF²
haft *see* HEFT¹, HEFT³
hag¹ &c *vti* **1** hack, cut, chop wood *la15-*, *now C S.* **2** cut down trees, prepare timber *19-e20.*
n **1** a notch, hack *16-.* **2** a portion of a wood marked for felling *17-e19.* **3** brushwood; felled wood used for fuel *19-*, *now NE.* **4** (1) a hollow of marshy ground in a moor, *eg* where channels have been made or PEATS¹ cut *16-.* (2) a hillock of firmer ground in a bog *19-.* (3) a ledge of turf overhanging a stream *19-*, *SW*, *S.*
hagger *vt* cut clumsily, hack *la19-*, *NE.* *n* a deep jagged cut *la19-*, *NE.* ~**gerty-taggerty,** ~**gerty-tag-like** *adj*, ~**gerty tag** *adv* ragged(ly) *19*, *NE.* **haggersnash** *n* offal, scraps of meat; a medley, conglomeration *19-e20.* *adj* tart; spiteful *e19*, *Ayr.* **haggle** &c, **haigle** &c *Bwk S* ['hagl; *Loth* 'hexl, &c; *Bwk S* 'hegl] *vti* **1** cut unevenly, hack *19-*, *now Sh Ork C.* **2** *vi* stumble forward, struggle on *18-*, *chf S.* **3** carry (something cumbersome) with difficulty *19-*, *now S.* *n* **1** an uneven cut, a hack; a bungle; a tangle *20-*, *now Ags Stlg Ayr.* **2** a struggle, a laborious effort *la19-*, *S.*
~**-block** *la19-*, ~**-clog** *19-*, ~**-stock** &c *16-* a chopping block *latterly SW Uls.* ~**-house** a woodshed *17-e18*, *chf Edb.* ~**man** a woodcutter or -seller *18-e19.*
strike, put *etc* **a** ~ **in the post** *or* **jamb** celebrate an event *16-*, *chf WC SW.* [ON *hǫggva* strike, fell, *hǫgg* a cutting blow; *cf* HACK]
hag² *n* **hagman** a cattleman tending stall-fed oxen *la19-*, *Fif.* [perh f HAG¹ *specif* castrate]
hag³ *vt* **haggit** *adj* weary, exhausted *19-*, *now Stlg midLoth.* [uncertain]
hagabag &c [*'hagəbag] *n* = huckaback *la17-e20.*
hagarde *see* HAGGARD
hagberry; hack-, hawk- [*N* 'hagbərɪ; *C, S* 'hak-] *n* the bird cherry *18-.* [ON *heggr*]
hagbute &c; **hagbuitt** &c, **hagbit(t)** [*'hagbøt, *-bʌt, *-bɪt] *n* = hackbut *16-17.*
~**ar** &c a soldier armed with a hackbut *16-e17.*
~ **of crok, crochat** &c a hackbut supported on a mounting by an iron hook attached to the barrel *16-e17.* [commoner in Sc; eME *hagbute*]
hage *see* HEDGE
hagg; haig &c *vi*, *of cattle* butt with the head, fight *19*, *NE.* [? f Eng dial *hag* torment, tease]
haggard &c, **hagarde** &c ['hagard] *n* a stackyard *la16-*, *chf SW Uls.* [ON *heygarðr* hay yard]
haggeis *see* HAGGIS
hagger *see* HAG¹
haggirbald &c [*'hagərbald] *n* meaning obscure *e16.*
haggis &c, **haggeis** *e16 n* **1** = haggis, the traditional Scottish dish of sheep's offal, oatmeal etc *16-*, *now chf Sc.* **2** the stomach (of a person or animal) *la18-19.*
~ **bag** the sheep's stomach in which a haggis is cooked *la18-*, *now Rox.* [ME *hagas*, *hagese* &c (*e15*), of unknown orig]

haggit *see* HAG³
haggle *see* HAG¹
haggle-bargain, hargle-bargle *19*; **haggle-baggle** &c *vi* wrangle, dispute, haggle *la19-*, *now Ags.*
n a person slow in agreeing a price; prolonged bargaining *19-e20*, *chf Rox.* [*cf argle-bargain* (ARGIE)]
hagmané *see* HOGMANAY
haiches ['hexəs] *n* a heavy fall; a thud *la18-e20*, *N.* [prob onomat f HECH *interj*]
haid *see* HAE¹, HAUD, HEID
haifelie *see* HEAVY
haifer *see* HAE¹
haiffelie *see* HEAVY
haiffer *see* HAE¹
haig *see* HAGG
haigle *see* HAG¹
haigs *see* HEGS
haik¹ &c *v* **1** *vi* go laboriously, trudge; wander aimlessly, rove; loiter *la15-*, *now local.* **2** *vt* carry or drag with difficulty *la18-*, *now Sh Abd Arg.* **3** treat roughly, drive hard *19-*, *chf Abd.*
n a person or animal given to roaming about, *freq* on the scrounge *19-*, *local Bnf-S.*
be on the ~ **for, hae a** ~ **for** be on the lookout for *20-*, *local Sh-Kcb.* [unknown]
haik² &c *n* = hack, the horse or vehicle *la18-e19*, *Edb.*
haik³ *n* a cloak or mantle, worn *chf* by women *la14-16.* [ME *heyke* (once), MDu *heyke*]
haik *see* HECK¹
haikit *see* HAWKIT
hail¹ &c, **hale** &c, **whole** &c *la16-*; **hoill** *16*, **heal** &c *la16-e19*, **quholl** *17* [hel; *Sh Ork also* hil, *Bwk Rox also* hjɪl; *St* hol] *adj*, *also* **hele** *la15-e16* **1** sound, in a healthy state; wholesome; robust, vigorous *la14-.* **2** uninjured, undamaged in body or mind *la14-.* **3** healthy or fresh in appearance *15-16.* **4** *with agent nouns* having the whole charge; complete, sole *la14-e16*: 'hale *kepare*'. **5** *of things* whole, complete, undamaged *la14-.* **6** *with pl noun*, *now esp law* **the** whole of, the full number of *la14-*: 'the whole *Heritors or their agents*'. **7** *with singular noun* all, the whole of *la14-16*: 'hail *Albion*'.
adv wholly, completely; fully *la14-.*
n the whole, the full number or amount *15-e20.*
~**ly** &c wholly, completely *la14-*, *now Sh.*
~**some** &c, **helsum** *16-e17* ['helsʌm; *'hɛl-*] *adj* **1** wholesome, health-giving *15-.* **2** mentally or morally beneficial; salutary *la14-e17.* **3** curative, medicinal *la14-16.* ~**umly** *adv* completely, undoubtedly, *chf* **think** ~**umly** feel quite sure *la18-e19.*
~**-heartit** &c undaunted, stalwart *19-.*
~**-heidit** unhurt; *of things* complete, entire *19-*, *N.* **gang** ~**-heidit for** *or* **intae** devote one's entire energy to *la19-*, *N.* **gang** ~**heid erran** go for one purpose *20-*, *Cai.* ~**scart** &c ['hel'skart] unscathed, scot-free *16-.* ~**-skinnt** having an unblemished skin *la19-*, *local.*

~-**tear** at full speed *20-*, *local Abd-Wgt.* ~ **ware &c** the whole number or amount *la16-19.* ~ **watter &c** *n* a downpour; *adv* torrentially *18-.* ~ **wheel** full tilt *la19-*, *now Ags.*

get ~ **o** recover from *la18-.* ~ **and fere** in full health and vigour; unharmed, undamaged *la14-*, *now literary.* ~ **and togidder** all in one *la15-16.* ~ **at the heart** in good spirits *20-*, *chf N.* **in** (**the**) ~ in total *15-e19.* [nME *hal*, midl and sME *hol*, OE *hāl*]

hail², **haill &c** *la14-16 n* **1** = hail *la14-.* **2** small shot, pellets *la17-e20*, *C Uls.*

hail³ &c, **haill** *16-e17 n* health *16-18.* *vt* heal *16-*, *Gen except sEC.* [var of HEAL, with vowel f HAIL¹; nME *hale* (*v*)]

hail⁴ &c, **haill** *vt*, *in a ball game* drive (the ball) through the goal etc *18-*, *now chf Rox.* *n* **1** the winning of a goal; a goal *17-*, *now Rox.* **2** the shout when a goal is scored *la18-.* **3** the goal area *la18-*, *now local.* **4** *in pl* a game like SHINTY played with CLACKANS at Edinburgh Academy *la19-.* ~ **the dool**(**s**) **&c** score a goal; be the winner; celebrate *16-e20.* [appar f Eng *hail* (*v*) greet]

haild *see* HAUD

hailist *see* HAILSE

haill *see* HAIL², HAIL³, HAIL⁴, HALE

hailly *see* HAIL¹

hailse &c, **halse &c** *la14-16*, **helse** *la16* [helz] *vti*, *pt* **hailsit** *la14-16*, **hailist &c** *la14-e15* [*'helzɪt, *'hel(ɪ)st] hail, greet, salute *la14-18.*

hailsing &c, **halsing &c** a greeting, salutation *15-e20*, *latterly Abd.* [ME *hailse*, OE *halsian*, ON *heilsa*]

hailykit *see* HALLOCK

haim &c, **hame &c**, **hem &c** *now Cai Ross Arg Kcb n*, *chf in pl* the two curved pieces of wood or metal forming or covering the collar of a draught horse *la14-.* **hae** *or* **pit the** ~**s on** (**someone**) curb, keep in order *20-*, *Ross Abd C.* [ME, MDu, MHighGer *hame*]

haim(**h**)**ald**, **haimilt** *see* HAMELT

haimmer &c, **hammer**, **halmer** *la16*, *only Sc*; **hawmer &c** *la19-*, *NE*, **hemmer &c** *16-* ['hemər, 'hɛmər; *NE* 'hamər] *n* **1** = hammer *la14-.* **2** clumsy, noisy working or walking; a clumsy noisy person *la18-19*, *Bnf Ayr.* *vti* **1** = hammer *la16-.* **2** work or walk in a clumsy, noisy way *la18-*, *chf N.* ~ (**and**) **block** (**and bible** *or* **study**) a rough game in which a boy is swung by others against another boy who crouches on hands and knees *19-e20*, *local.*

hain &c; **hen** *la17-18 vti* **1** enclose (grassland or a wood) by a hedge or fence; keep unused, preserve from grazing or cutting *15-.* **2** keep from harm, protect, spare *16-e20.* **3** *also* ~ **in, on** save (up); be thrifty, hoard *18-.* **weel-hained** *of a person* well-preserved *la20-.* ~**ing** *n* **1** the enclosing of ground by a hedge or fence; the hedge, fence or wall *16-e19.* **2** a

piece of ground so enclosed *15-*, *freq in place-names 14-.* **3** *in pl* savings *19*, *local.* [ON *hegna* hedge, protect]

hain *see* HINE

hainch &c *la16-*, **hanche &c** *la15-16*, **henche &c** *la16-*; **hinch &c** *18-e20* [henʃ, hɛnʃ, hɪnʃ; *hanʃ] *n* **1** = haunch *la15-.* **2** an underhand throw as in *v* 1, *19-*, *now local Sh-Dmf.* **3** a halt or limp in walking, lameness *la19-*, *now Rox.* **4** a 'leg-up'; a help up with a heavy object *20-*, *local.* *vti* **1** throw a stone etc by jerking the arm against the thigh *la18-*, *local.* **2** *vi* walk jerkily or with a limp *19-*, *local Abd-Uls.* ~**le &c** *n* = *n* 1, *19-*, *nEC.* *vi* = *v* 2, *19-e20*, *Rox.*

haingle &c; **hingle &c** ['heŋl, 'hɪŋl, 'haŋl, 'hanjəl] *vi* move about feebly; loiter, hang about *19-.* *n* **1** an idle good-for-nothing *la18-e20.* **2** *in pl* influenza *19-e20*, *chf Ags.* *adj* slovenly, careless; lazy, not inclined to work *la18-e20*, *NE.* **be in** *or* **hae the** ~**s** be in a lazy mood *19-e20*, *N.* [frequentative of HING]

haip *see* HEAP

hair¹ &c, **hare &c**, **heir**(**e**) *la16-17*, **here &c** *15-e17*; **har** *la14-e17* [her; *hir] *n* **1** = hair *la14-.* **2** *freq in negative* not the smallest amount, not a whit or trace *la15-.* *adj* = hair(e)*d* 2, *16.* *vt* ? edge with hair or fur *16*, *only Sc.* **hair**(**e**)**d** *17-la19*, **harit &c** *la15-16*, **hairt** *19-e20* **1** = haired, having hair, -haired *la15-.* **2** *of cattle* having a mixture of white and red or white and black hair, roan *16-e18.* **ill-haired &c** ill-tempered, surly *18-e20.* ~**en &c** *la16*, ~**n**(**e**) *la16*, *e19* made of hair. **hairy &c**, **hary** *la16-e17*, *only Sc adj* **1** = hairy *la16-.* **2** *esp of work* untidy, rough, slovenly *la20-*, *chf Kcb Dmf. n*, *orig* (*e20*, *Gsw*) a woman slumdweller; *now* a woman of loose morals, *specif* a prostitute; *also*, *more gen*, *somewhat derog* a young woman *la20-*, *chf Abd Gsw*: 'a wee hairy'. ~**y grannie** a large hairy caterpillar *20-.* ~**y hu**(**r**)**tcheon &c** a sea-urchin *19-*, *now Fif.* ~**y moggans &c** footless stockings *19-*, *now Cai Abd.* ~**y-mouldit &c** covered with mould, mouldy *20-*, *now Sh-nEC Dmf* [orig f HAIR¹ *adj*, but confused w HAIR¹ *n*]. ~**y oobit &c** the woolly-bear caterpillar *19-*, *now chf S*, *only Sc.* ~**y tatties** a dish of mashed potatoes and flaked dried salt fish *20-*, *NE.* ~**y worm** = ~ *oobit*, *la20-*, *Abd Ags Fif.* ~-**kaimer** a barber *la18.* ~ **say &c** a kind of cloth (*see* SEY²), *prob* partly made with hair *17*, *only Sc.* ~-**tether &c** *chf witchcraft* a tether made of hair *la17-*, *now Cai.* **a** ~ **in someone's** *or* **the neck** a shortcoming etc which gives another a hold over one; such a hold *la15-*, *now Ags Gsw Ayr.* **a** ~ **to make a tether** a fuss about nothing, a trifle used as an excuse *18-*, *now Sh Arg.* ~ **and hoof** every

particle *e18*, *20-*, *now Sh Ags*. ~ (**the**) **butter**
free butter from impurities, *eg* hairs, by passing
a knife through it in all directions *19-*, *now Ork*.
have a ~ **on one's head** be clever, cautious or
wise *19-*, *now Arg Ayr*. **rub again(st) the** ~
= rub up the wrong way *la18-*, *now Sh Arg*.
[see also HEERE]
hair² &c, **hare**; **har** &c *la15-e16*, *e20* [her] *adj*
1 = hoar *la15-*. **2** *of weather* frosty, cold
la15-e16, *only Sc*. **3** *of ground, rocks or stones*
grey(ish) *e16*.
vi, of ploughed ground dry up *20-*, *NE*.
~ **moul(d)** the mould on cheese, bread, jam
etc exposed to damp *19-*. ~-**mouldit** *la19-*,
now Abd Ags Stlg, ~-**moul(e)d** *18-*, *now Stlg, also
fig* covered with mould [cf *hairy-mouldit* (HAIR¹)].
~**stane** *la19-*, **harestone** *la18-* a large, grey,
moss-covered stone, *specif* a conspicuously-fixed
stone used as a boundary mark *la18-*, *now Abd,
in place-names 14-*.
hair *see* HARE, HEERE, HEIR
hairbour *see* HERBOUR
haird *see* HAIR¹, HARD
hairlt *see* HARL¹
hairm &c *la16-*, **harm** &c; **herm** &c *la16-*,
heirm &c *la16-e17* [herm, hɛrm, harm] *n* **1** =
harm *la14-*. **2** *only* **harm**, *also in pl* sorrow,
grief, distress *la15-16*, *e20* (*Sh*).
vt = harm *la15-*.
harmisay &c *interj* expressing grief or distress
la14-e17.
hairn *see* HARN¹
hairp *see* HARP
hairschip *see* HERSHIP
hairse &c *la18-*, **hers** &c *16-19*, **hace** *la15-16*;
he(a)rsh &c *la19-e20*, **hais** &c *16*, *e20* (*Cai*)
[hers, herʃ; *Rox* hjɪrs &c; *Cai* hes] *adj* = hoarse.
[see SND]
hairshach *see* HARESHARD
hairship *see* HERSHIP
hairst &c *la16-*, **harvest** &c, **hervest** &c
15-, *now Cai Arg local SW*; **hairvist** &c
la16-19, **harst** *la18-*, *now Abd*, **haist** *19-*, *Mry*
[herst, 'hɛrvɪst; *nEC* herzd; *Mry* hest] *n* **1** (1) =
harvest *la14-*. (2) *only* **hairst** *or* **harst** a harvest job, *esp* **tak a** ~ engage oneself as a harvest
labourer *19-*, *now N Kcb, only Sc*. **2** the autumn
la15-, *now Sh Abd Ags*.
v **1** *vt* = harvest. **2** *vi, also fig* work in the harvest field, gather in the crops *la19-*.
hairster a harvester *la19-e20*.
~ **fee** &c the wages paid to a harvest worker
la16, *la19-*, *now Abd*. ~ **folk** workers engaged
for the harvest *la18-*, *now local Sh-Dmf*. ~ **hog**
a lamb smeared at the end of harvest, when it is
reckoned to become a sheep *e16*, *e19*, *only Sc*. ~
plait a loop of twisted straw worn in a button-
hole, or as a decoration by the horses at harvest
time *20-*, *now Arg Kcb Uls*. ~ **play** school holidays taken during the harvest *19-*, *now Cai, only
Sc*. ~ **rig** *now chf literary* a ridge of corn ready
for harvesting; the ridge between two furrows

in a harvest field; the harvest field itself *18-*, *now
local Sh-Stlg*, *only Sc*. ~ **vacance** = ~ *play*,
17-19, *only Sc*.
hae a day in ~ **wi someone** *20-*, *now Abd Ags*,
owe someone a day *etc* **in** ~ *19-*, *now Abd Ags*
have a score to settle with someone; owe someone a favour. (**in the**) **heid o** ~ (at the)
height of the harvest *la19-*, *Abd*.
hairt *see* HAIR¹, HART, HERT
hairth *see* HARTH
hairvist *see* HAIRST
hairy *see* HAIR¹
hais *see* HAE¹, HAIRSE
haise *see* HAE¹
haissel *see* HAZEL
haist *see* HAIRST
haister &c, **haster** &c ['hestər] *vt* **1** (1) rush,
scamp (a job) *la17*. (2) *specif* cook too hastily,
scorch *19-e20*, *S*. **2** perplex, pester, harass *19-*,
now Gall.
n a confusion, a muddle, rush *19*.
~**ed** &c flustered, harassed; ill-done, scamped
e15, *la18-19*. **hasterns** early-ripening oats or
peas *la18-e19*; cf *hasting* (HEEST). [only Sc; frequentative of Eng *haste*]
haistine *see* HEEST
haith *see* OATH
haith; **heth** *la19-* [heθ, hɛθ] *interj* a mild oath or
exclam of surprise *la17-*. [only Sc; prob
euphemistic for Eng *faith*; cf *haith* (OATH) and
TETH]
haithen &c, **heathen** ['heðən] *adj* **1** = heathen. **2** *only* **haithen** outlandish, incomprehensible *la19-*, *now Sh Uls*.
n **1** = heathen. **2** *only* **haithen** an intractable
or difficult person or thing *la20-*, *now Sh*. **3** a
lump of gneiss etc, a glacial boulder *19-*, *NE*.
haive *see* HAE¹
haivel, **heave-eel** &c *la17-e19*; **have-eel** &c
[hevl] *n* the conger-eel *18-20*. [only Sc; **haive-* f
ON *haf* the open sea + Eng *eel*]
haiveless *see* HAE¹
haiven *see* HEAVEN
haiver¹ &c; **haver** ['hevər] *vti* **1** talk in a foolish or trivial way, speak nonsense *la18-*. **2** (1)
make a fuss about nothing, make a pretence of
being busy *la19-*, *now Ayr Uls*. (2) dawdle, potter about; lounge *la19-*, *now Ayr Uls*.
n **1** *chf in pl* nonsense, foolish talk, gossip, chatter *la18-*. **2** a piece of nonsense, a foolish whim
or notion *19-*, *now local*. **3** a gossip, a chat *19-*,
now local Ags-S. **4** a person who talks nonsense
20-, *Gen except Sh Ork*. **5** *chf in pl* a state of
fussy indecision; a person in this state, an idler
la19-, *now Ayr*.
haiverel &c, **haveril** &c, **hav(e)rel**
['hev(ə)rəl] *n* **1** a foolishly chattering or garrulous person, a fool, a halfwit *la18-*. **2** a
lounger, a lazy person *e18*, *la19-*, *now Sh*. *adj* **1**
garrulous, speaking foolishly *la18-*, *now Kcb*. **2**
foolish, stupid, nonsensical *la18-e20*. **havering**

19-, **havren** &c *18* ['hev(ə)rən] *adj* nonsensical, gossiping, babbling, garrulous *18-e20. n* chatter, gossip, nonsense *19-.* [see SND]

haiver[2] *n, chf* **haverel** &c ['hev(ə)rəl] a castrated he-goat *19-e20.* [OE *hæfer,* L *caper* a he-goat]

haizer &c [*C, S Uls* 'hezər(d)] *vt* dry (partially), air in the open, bleach (newly-washed clothes etc) *19-, now WC.*

hak *see* HACK, HAWK

hake &c *15-16,* **hak** *la15-e16,* **heck** *la16-17 n* a hook. [MLowGer, LowGer]

hake *see* HAWK

hala *see* HALLOW[2]

halch *see* HAUGH

halcrek &c; **halcrik** &c [*'halkrɛk, *-krɪk, &c] *n* a half-suit of light armour, worn by footmen and horsemen *16.* [only *Sc*; F *halecret*]

hald *see* HAUD

Haldan(e)ite ['haldenəit] *n* a follower of the brothers Robert and James Haldane, leaders of an early nineteenth century Scottish evangelical movement, now represented partly by the Congregational and partly by the Baptist Church in Scotland.

hale, haill &c [hel] *vti* **1** *vt, freq nautical* haul, drag, pull (up) *la15-, now Sh NE.* **2** *vi* (1) move quickly *la15-e17.* (2) *now chf of rain or perspiration* flow copiously, run down, pour *16-, now Sh midLoth.*
interj, nautical exclam used when hauling *16.*
n a haul (*esp* of fish), the hauling in of nets *la18-19.* [ME *hale,* OF *haler*]

hale *see* HAIL[1]

halé *see* HALIE

Hales *see* HALIS

half[1] &c; **halve** *la15,* **haf** &c *la14-e20,* **haff**(e) *la16-e20,* **hauf** &c *la15-, only Sc* [haf, haf; *half, *halv] *n* **1** = half *la14-.* **2** a part: (1) one of two unequal parts into which a thing has been divided *18-;* (2) one of three or more divisions or portions *20-.* **3** (1) a half-measure of a specified amount, *esp of* WHISKY = a half-gill *la19-.* (2) **a wee hauf** a quarter-gill, a small WHISKY *la20-.* **4** *of time* (1) *with the following hour, eg* **half five** = half past four *17-, almost obs esp C, only Sc;* (2) *with the preceding hour, eg* **half five** = half past five *20-.*
adj (*la15-*), *adv* (*la14-*) = half.
vt **1** divide into two equal parts, halve; go halves with *19-.* **2** divide into more than two equal shares *la20-, Abd midLoth.* **3** *only* **halve** [haf, haf; *St* hav; *hav] *golf* play (a hole, round or match) in the same number of strokes as one's opponent *19-.*

halver *19-,* **halfer** &c *la16-e20,* **haufer** &c *e16, 19-,* **haf(f)er** *19-e20,* **haaver** &c *19-e20* ['hafər, 'hafər, 'havər, 'havər] *n, chf in pl* **1** *pl freq used for sing* a half-portion, a share *16-.* **2** *in pl,* exclam used *esp* by children when claiming a half share in a find *19-, now C, S Uls. vt* halve,

divide equally; hold in partnership with someone *19-, chf N.* **go** *etc* ~**ers** share equally *19-.* **in** ~**ers** in halves; jointly, in partnership *16, e20* (*Sh Cai*). ~**ie 1** = *n.* **2** a half-holiday *19-, local, only Sc.* **halflin**(g) &c *n* **1** a half-grown boy, an adolescent youth, *freq* one engaged in farm work *la17-.* **2** a half-witted person *19-, now Cai, only Sc.* **3** a half-mature herring *la20-, Fif Loth, only Sc.* *adj* **1** *chf of a boy* = **halflang** *adj* **2,** *18-e20, only Sc.* **2** *only Sc* (1) of an intermediate or half-size *la18-.* (2) *chf* ~**lin plane** a large-size plane used by carpenters, *now* the largest used, *orig* second in size to the jointer plane *19-.* **halfling** *adv* = *halflins* **1,** *15-16.*
halflins *18-,* **halflings** *16-18,* **halfins** *19,* **hafflins** *19-e20 adv* **1** half, partly, almost *16-, now Abd.* **2** half-way, mid-way *la18-, now local ShStlg, only Sc. adj* half, partial; half-grown, young *19.*
~ **bend** a half-cocked firearm *la17.* ~**-bred** *of sheep* crossed from the Border Leicester ram and the Cheviot ewe *la19-.* ~**cock**(ie) half drunk *19-e20, only Sc.* ~**-cousin** the child of one's parent's cousin, a second cousin *19-, only Sc.* ~**-deal man** a half-share fisherman *19-, now Fif Bwk, only Sc.* ~ **dele** &c *n, adv, verse* half *la14-e16.* ~ **foot** a system of land use whereby the landlord supplied (*usu* half of) the seed, the tenant grew and harvested the crop, of which the same share was delivered to the landlord as rent *19, Highl, only Sc;* cf ~ *manor.* ~**-fou,** ~**-fu**(ll) half a FOU, *ie* approx two PECKS[2] or half a bushel *18-e19, only Sc.* ~**-gate** &c *la16,* ~ **gaits** &c *la18-* half way *now Sh Fif, only Sc.* ~ **gavill** one side of a gable which is common to two houses; the right to build on such *la17-19, local WC, only Sc.* ~ **gone** &c *adj* about the middle period of pregnancy *19-, now local, only Sc.* ~**-hag** *chf in pl* ~ **haggis** a smaller size of HAGBUTE *16-e17, only Sc.* ~**-hour** &c **1** = half hour *16-.* **2** the mechanism for striking the half hours *la16, only Sc.* ~ **house** a semi-detached house *la19-, NE.* ~**-hung-tee** pretentious, affecting gentility *20-, Abd, only Sc.* ~**-hyre** &c half of a seaman's pay for a voyage *la16-e17, only Sc.* ~ **jack**(it) *20-, now Fif,* ~ **jeck** *la20, Arg* half-witted [*jack* prob = CHACK[1] (*ie* half-cracked)]. ~**-landis** *n pl* the half-portion of a landed estate *la15-17, only Sc.* ~**lang,** ~**long** *la17 adj, only Sc* **1** *chf of swords* of half the full or usual length; short *la15-e18.* **2** *freq of a young farmworker* adolescent, half-grown *19-e20. n, only Sc* **1** = *halflin, n* **1,** *la17-e18.* **2** *tanning* a half-length hide *la16-17.* ~ **loaf** a loaf of *plain bread* (PLAIN), half the size of a standard quartern loaf, *la19-, formerly* weighing 2 pounds but successively reduced to 30 and 28 ounces *la19-.* ~ **manor** *e19,* ~ **manure** &c *la17,* ~ **maner** &c *la17* = ~ *foot, Gall, only Sc.* ~ **manurer** &c one who farms land under the terms of such a lease *la17, Gall.* ~**-marrow** &c a marriage-partner, mate *la16-, now Ags.* ~**-merk,** ~

mark *now hist* **1** a half MERK *16-*. **2** *specif* as the fee or symbol for a clandestine marriage, *freq* ~-**merk church** *la17, e19*, ~-**merk marriage** *19-e20*. ~-**mes(s)** &c a small plate *la16, e18, only Sc.* ~-**net** *la15-18*, **hanet** &c *16-19* [*'haf'nɛt, *'hanɛt] a half-share of fish caught in one net in a season, *only Abd; cf halve-net* (HALF²). ~**note** a ten-shilling note *20*. ~ **one** &c **1** a half glassful of liquor *la19-, now midLoth Uls.* **2** *golf* the allowance of a stroke at alternate holes to one's opponent *19-e20*. ~**penny, halpeny** &c *15-16* ['hap(ə)nɪ, 'hap(ə)nɪ; *'hafpɛnɪ, *'halpɛnɪ] a halfpenny, the (*orig* silver) coin of this value *15-*. ~**penny** &c **land** half a *pennyland* (PENNY) *la15-, now Arg, latterly hist.* ~-**road(s)** half-way *la19-, only Sc.* ~-**seill** the matrix of a seal *la16, only Sc.* ~-**waxed** *of rabbits etc* half-grown *20-, Dmf Rox.* ~ **ways** half-way; partly *la19-, only Sc.* ~-**year** &c, ~-**ʒeir** &c, **halʒar** *la15*, **hell(z)ier** *la18* ['haf'jir; *'haljər, *'hɛljər] a half year, six months *16-, now midLoth Arg Ayr.* **ha-year auld** &c, **hi(gh)-year auld** &c [*'ha'jir'ald, *'ha-; *'həi'jir-, *?'haɪ'jir-] *of cattle* a year and a half old *19, chf S, only Sc.*
  a .. and a ~ a .. which is large or extraordinary of its kind *19-*: '*a letter and a half*'. **a** ~ **an a** ~ a small WHISKY with a half pint of beer as chaser *20-*. ~ **an atween** *20-*, ~ **and between** *19-* neither one nor the other, not quite, *only Sc.* ~ **an(d)** ~ **1** = half and half, half of one thing and half of another *20-*. **2** half-drunk *18-, now Abd midLoth Ayr.* ~ **(of) the bait** a half-share in a boat *16, only Sc.* ~ **(of) a net** = ~ *net, la15, Abd, Montrose.*
half² &c; **haave** &c [haf, hav] *n* a bag-shaped net set or held to retain fish as the tide ebbs *17, e19, Gall Dmf.*
  halver &c a person who fishes with such a net *17-e19, Dmf.* **go haavin** fish with such a net; go salmon fishing, *esp* on the Solway *la18-, now Kcb Dmf.*
  halve-net, half-net, ha(a)f-net &c *la18-* *n* = *n, la17-, Gall Dmf.* [Scand; *cf* Norw *haav*, Sw *haf*, ON *háfr* a pock-net; *cf half-net* (HALF¹)]
half *see* HAE
half-disch *see* HADDISH
halfer *see* HALF¹
halfhede &c; **half(f)et** [*'half'hid, *-'hed, *'haf-; *'halfət] *n* the side of the head; the temple, cheek *la15-e17*. [OE *halfhēafod* forehead; *cf* HAFFET]
half-net *see* HALF²
hali *see* HALLOW²
halie &c *la14-, in place-names 13-*, **haly, holy** *la16-*; **hel(l)y** *la15-19*, **hally** &c *16-18*, **halé** &c *16-e17*, **holly** &c *la16-17* ['helɪ; St 'holɪ] *adj* = holy *la14-*.
  ~ **band** the *kirk session* (KIRK) *18, only Sc.* ~ **blude** &c **1** the blood of Christ or of a saint *la15-17*. **2** the blood of Christ, adopted as the

patron of the merchant guilds of pre-Reformation BURGHS *16, only Sc.* ~ **blud(e) mes** a mass in honour of the *haly blude* (1), *la15-e16*. ~ **dabbies** &c a kind of *shortbread* (SHORT), *esp* that used formerly in place of bread at Communion *19, chf SW.* **haliday** &c = holiday *15-e19, latterly only verse.* ~ **day** = holy day *15-e17*. ~ **day(is) claithis** Sunday or best clothes *la15-e17*. ~ **gast(e)** &c *la14-e17*, **halie ghoist** &c *la16-e17* = Holy Ghost. ~ **hoose** a church *la19-e20*. ~ **kirk** = Holy Church, the corporate church *la14-16*. **in (the) face** *etc* **of** ~ **kirk** within the Church *la15-16*. **in** ~ **kirk** in a church *15-e16*. ~ **man** *euphemistic* the devil, *chf* in names for ground left untilled as an act of propitiation, *eg* ~ **mans ley,** ~ **man('s) rig** *17-, only Sc.* ~ **spreit** *la15-16* or **sp(i)rit(e)** *la14-e17* = Holy Spirit.
Halis; Hales &c [*helz] designation of one of the PURSUIVANTS, *prob* Patrick, first Earl of Bothwell and second Lord Hailes *la15*.
halk *see* HAWK
Halkerton's &c **Cow** ['hakərtənz 'ku, 'halkər-, 'halkər-] *also* **like** ~ different or the opposite from what was expected, 'another story' *la17-e20*. [f the farm-name near Laurencekirk, Kcdn]
halkit *see* HAWKIT
hall *see* HA
halla *see* HALLOW¹, HALLOW²
hallaby &c [Sh 'haləbɪ, 'halɪpə] *n, nonsense word only in child's counting rhyme, la19-, now local.*
hallach *see* HALLOCK
hallan &c, **halland** &c ['halən; Fif also -ənt; *'haland] *n* **1** (1) an inner wall, partition, or door-screen erected between the door and the fireplace, *usu* of mud or clay mixed with stones, or moulded over a wood and straw framework *16-, now Cai.* (2) a similar partition in a BYRE or stable, or between the living-room and the BYRE *la18-20*. **2** the inside porch, passage etc formed by such a partition *19*. **3** a cottage, house *19-e20*.
  ~ **door** a door into or through the HALLAN *la19-e20*. ~-**end** the area between the wall of the house and the HALLAN 1 *la18-e20*. ~**shaker** &c a beggar, a vagabond, tramp *16-, now literary.* ~ **stane 1** the threshold, door-step *la18-19*. **2** a stone forming a dividing wall between cattle-stalls in a BYRE *20-, Cai.* ~-**wa** = *n 1, 19*. [late nME *halland* = *n 1*; uncertain]
halli *see* HALLOW²
hallicat, hallich *see* HALLOCK
hallion &c; **hullion** &c *Sh Gall* ['haljən, 'hʌl-] *n* a slovenly-looking or clumsy person, a rascal, a clown *la18-, now Sh Ags Gall Rox.* [unknown]
hallirackit, hallirakus *see* HALLOCK
hallo *see* HALLOW²
hallock &c, **halok** *e16*; **hallach** &c *la18-, now chf NE*, **hallich** *la19-, NE,* **hellock** &c

19-e20 ['halək, -əx; *SW* 'hɛlək; *Rox also* 'helək] *n* a thoughtless giddy young woman or girl or *occas* young man *e16*, *19-*, *now NE Rox.*
adj, now only **hallach 1** crazy, hare-brained *19-*, *NE.* **2** uncouth, noisy *20-*, *now NE.*
vi, only **hallach, hallich** behave in a crazy, wild or irresponsible way *la19-*, *now Ags Stlg.*
hallockit, hellicat *19-20*, **hallicat &c** *19-e20*, **hailykit &c** *la19-e20* ['haləkɪt, -ət; *also* 'hel-, 'hɛl-, 'hʌl-] *adj, esp of a girl or young woman* = *adj, la17-, Gen except NE. n* a noisy restless person, a hoyden; a fool; a good-for-nothing *19-20.*
hallirackit &c ['halɪ'rakɪt, -ət, 'halə-] *adj* = *hallockit adj, 19-, local Sh-Ags.* **hallirakus** [*'halɪ'rakəs] = *hallockit n, 19.*
hallow[1]; **halla &c** *e20* ['halə; *Loth* 'halɪ] *adj* (*la16-*), *n* (*18-*), *vt* (*19-, now Abd Ags midLoth*) = hollow. [only Sc; dissimilation of vowel]
hallow[2]; **hal(l)a-** *16-e20*, **hal(l)a-** *17-*, **hal(l)i- &c** *la17-* ['halə; *sEC, S* 'halɪ; *Per Fif also* 'halɪ; *Loth also* 'halɪ] *n, chf* **H~** *in comb* = All Saints.
~ court a meeting of a craft or trades court held on All Saints' Day, 1 Nov *17-18*, *only Sc.*
~day All Saints' Day *la16-*, *now Ags Arg.*
~een &c, ~ even ['halə'in, &c; *Ayr also* 'hal'in] 31 Oct, the eve of All Saints' Day, the last day of the year in the old Celtic calendar, associated with witches and the powers of darkness, and celebrated with bonfires, divination rites etc; *now* a children's festival when they go around as *guisers* (1) (GUISE), *freq* with turnip lanterns (see also *dooking for apples* (DOOK[1])) *la16-*; *cf Alhallow evin* (ALHALLOW). **~eve** *prec, e18, la20-* (*Uls*), *only Sc.* **~ fair** a market held on 1 Nov in various places, *esp* Edb *18-*, *only Sc.* **~ fire** *a halloween* bonfire *17-18*, *only Sc.*
~mas(s), ~mes All Saints' Day *16-*, *now Sh Ags.* **~tyd(e) &c** the first week (or day) in Nov *la17-e18*, *local W.* [short for ALHALLOW]
hally *see* HALIE
halmer *see* HAIMMER
halo- *see* HALLOW[2]
halok *see* HALLOCK
hals *see* HAUSE
halse, halsing *see* HAILSE
hals-lok *see* HAUSE
haltand, haltane *see* HAUTANE
halth *n* = health *18-*, *now Uls, only Sc.*
halve, halver *see* HALF[1]
halver *see* HALF[1], HALF[2]
haly *see* HALIE
halȝar *see* HALF[1]
ham *see* HAME, HUM
ham-a-haddie &c *n* ['hamə(n)'hadɪ, *also* 'hamɪ'hadɪ] **1** *chf exclam and in expressions of disbelief* a confused or unlikely story or situation *20-*, *C, S*: '*fine ham-a-haddie (but ye'll no fry it in my pan)!*' Compare **2** a mix-up, a fuss *20-*, *now Ags-S.* [Eng *ham* + HADDIE; see SND]
hamald *see* HAMEHALD, HAMELT
hamart *see* HAMEART

hamble *see* HAMEHALD
Hamburgh &c; hammer- &c [*'hambʌrx, *also* *'hamər] **~ barrel** a kind of large barrel, *chf* as a measure of salmon *15-e16.* **hammerstand** a kind of beer barrel *la15-e16.* [only Sc; the German seaport]
hame &c, home &c *16-*; **ham** *la14-e17*, **heem &c** *16, la19-* (*Ork*), **hem** *la16-*, *now Sh,* **heyime &c** *20, S* [hem; *Ork* him; *S* hjɪm] *n* **1** = home *la14-.* **2** *specif* the town and neighbourhood of Campbeltown *e20, Arg; cf doon hame* (DOON) of Dumfries.
adv **1** = home *la14-.* **2** at home *la15-e20, only Sc.* **3** *of birth* into the world, *freq of the mother or midwife* **bring** *etc* **~, *of the child* **come ~** *la18-*, *now local Abd-S, only Sc.* **4** *of employment* into service, *freq* **enter** *etc* **~** *17-*, *only Sc.*
~ly &c *adj, adv* **1** = homely *la14-.* **2** friendly, kind(ly), courteous *15-.* **~liness 1** familiarity, lack of ceremony, intimacy; fellow feeling; *orig also* kindness *la14-e19.* **2** bluntness in speech *la15-e17.* **3** = homeliness. **~ward, ~wart, ~wirth &c** *la19-, now Bnf,* **hameart** *la19-e20 adv* = homeward *la14-.* *adj* belonging to or made at home, native, homely *la18-e20; cf* HAMEART. **~with, ~wuth &c** *la19-e20 adv* homewards *la18-20*, *now Abd Ags.* *adj* homeward *la18-, now Bnf Ags, only Sc.*
~bider *n* a local resident, *esp* a native of Bo'ness (*wLoth*) or Anstruther (*Fif*) *20-*, *only Sc.* **~-bring** fetch from a distance or abroad, import *la16-17; cf bring ~.* **~-bringar** an importer *la16-17.* **~-bringing &c** *n* **1** the action of bringing home, of fetching from a distance or abroad, or of importing *la15-17.* **2** *specif* the action of conducting or escorting (a new queen) from abroad *la15-16, only Sc.* **~come &c** a homecoming, return, *latterly* (*19-*) arrival *la14-16, 19-*, *now Sh Abd; cf come ~.* **~coming &c 1** a coming or return home *la14-.* **2** *specif* (1) the festivities that take place on the arrival of a bride at her new home *la19-*; (2) a birth *la20-*, *only Sc.* **~-dra(u)chtit &c** *only Sc* **1** selfish, keen to further the interests of oneself or one's home *la19-, NE.* **2** homesick; fond of, or drawn to home *20-, NE.* **~-fare &c** the journey of a bride to her new home; the festivities on that occasion *19-*, *now Sh Ork, only Sc.* **~-farin** staying at home *la19-, now Sh WC, only Sc.* **~-gaun** *n* **1** a return (journey), the act of going home *la18-, now Abd Fif Dmf.* **2** death; the burial of the dead *la19-, local.* *adj* homeward bound, returning home *la19-, now local.* **~-made** *n* a home-made article *19-, local Loth-S, only Sc.* *adj* homely, rustic, unrefined *20-, local.* **~ower &c, ~over** *adv* homewards *la16-, now Sh Ags.* *adj* **1** *of speech* homely, simple, in the (Scots) vernacular *18-, now local Ork-Arg.* **2** *of habits and manners* plain, simple, natural, without reserve *19-, now local Ork-Ags.* **3** *of food* plain, homely *19-, now Ork Abd Ags.* **4** familiar, intimate *la19-, Ags, only Sc.*

~-through &c, ~trow *19-*, *Sh: only Sc* **1** all the way home *la16*. **2** straight homewards *19-*, *now Sh*.

bring *etc* ~ = ~*-bring*, *la14-e17*. **come &c** ~ **1** arrive from abroad *16*. **2** arrive at one's destination *20-*, *now Sh Ags*. **gae, gang** *etc* ~ die *19-*. **get** ~ import *18-*, *now Ork Arg, only Sc*; *cf bring* ~. **pay** ~ pay back, retaliate on, punish *18-*, *now Sh*.

hame *see* HAIM

hameart &c; ham(m)art &c *la18-19*, **hamer** *la19-*, *now Dmf* ['hemərt; *also* -ər] *adj* **1** = HAMELT *adj 1*, *la18-*, *now Ags Fif Dmf*. **2** = HAMELT *adj 2*, *la18-19*. **3** *of things* plain, without ornament; *of persons* unpolished, unsophisticated *la18-*, *now Ags*; *cf* HAMELT *adj 3*. **4** childishly attached to home *19*. **~-made** home-made *la19-*, *now Ags*. [only Sc; var of HAMELT, perh w infl f *hameart, hameward* (HAME)]

hameart *see* HAME[1]

hamehald &c; hamald &c *16-e17*, **hamble &c** *la16-e19*, **hammell &c** *la16-e17*, *e19*, **hammer** *e19* [*'heməl(d), *'haməld, *'haməl(d), *-ət, *'hamər] *n*, *only in* **borgh &c of** *or* **and** ~ (BORROW[1]). [only Sc; ON *heimold* title to or right of possession, ultimately f as HAMELT]

hamehald, hameil *see* HAMELT
hameint *see* HAMIT
hamelott *see* HAMLOTT
hamelt *18-e20*, **hamehald** *16*; **ha(i)m(h)ald** *la16-e20*, **hamel &c** *e16, 19-*, **hammel &c** *17, 19-e20*, **hameil** *la18-e20*, **ha(i)milt &c** *19* ['heməlt, -əl(d); *S* 'hjım-] *adj* **1** belonging to home, domestic, internal; of home or native growth or manufacture, homebred *16-*, *now Pbls*. **2** *also adv, of speech* vernacular; in the native (Scots) tongue *18-19*. **3** homely, familiar, plain, simple *19-*, *now Cai Bnf Ayr*.

vt, law claim (an animal) as one's own property *la16-17*. [nME (once) *hamehold*, ON *heimoll* homely, domestic, household; see HAMEHALD and *cf* HAMEART, HAMIT]

hamer *see* HAMEART

hamesucken[1] &c, hamesuk(k)in &c *la14-e17*; **hemsucken** *la17* ['hem'sʌkən] *n, law* (the crime of committing) an assault upon a person in his own house or dwelling-place *la14-*. [ME *hamsok(e)ne*, OE *hāmsōcn*, ON *heimsókn*]

hamesucken[2] *adj* greatly attached to one's home; selfish *19*. [only Sc; HAME[1] + SUCKEN[1]]

hamet *see* HAMIT
hamhald *see* HAMELT
hamill *see* HUMMEL
hamilt *see* HAMELT
hamis *see* HAIM

hamit, hamet &c *la16-e17*; **h(a)emmit &c** *la16, 19*, **hameint &c** *20-*, *eLoth Bwk* ['hemɪt; *eLoth Bwk also* 'hemɪnt] *adj* **1** home-produced, home-grown *la16-*, *now Ags Stlg*. **2** home-loving,

homely, familiar; vernacular; *sometimes derog* rough-and-ready, uncouth, untidy *20-*, *now Fif*. [only Sc; var of HAMELT or HAMEART]

hamlott &c; hamelott &c [*'ham(ə)lot] *n* a holding, ? amounting to a quarter of a forester-stead *la15-e16*, *Ettrick Forest*. [only Sc; obscure; ? *cf* HEMMEL]

hammart *see* HAMEART
hammel *see* HAMELT, HEMMEL
hammell, hammer *see* HAMEHALD
hammer *see* HAIMMER, HAMBURGH
hammle &c *vi* walk with a limp, hobble *19-e20*, *S*. [prob nasalized var of HABBLE]
hamp *vi* stutter, stammer; read with difficulty or with many mispronunciations or hesitations *la18-*, *now Rox*. [obscure]
hamper &c *vt* **1** = hamper. **2** *chf in ptp* ~(i)t confined, restrained, hindered, cramped *15-*, *now Sh Ork Arg Uls*.
hamphis &c ['hamfɪs, -fɪʃ] *vt* surround, hem in, confine; curb *la18-e20*. [only Sc; altered f obs Eng *handfast* tie the hands of, manacle]
hamrel [?'hamrəl] *n* a person who often stumbles in walking; an awkward person *19-20*, *chf Abd*. [perh nasalized deriv of HABBER; *cf* HABBLE]
hamshackle *see* HAPSHACKLE
hamshoch *see* AMSHACH
han *see* HAND
hanch &c *19-*, **hansh &c; haunsh &c** *e19*, **hum(p)sh &c** *19-*, *chf NE* [*C, S* hanʃ; *NE* hamʃ, hʌm(p)ʃ] *vti* **1** *vi, also fig* snap (**at**), show the teeth, snatch, bite voraciously *17-*, *now local NE, SW Uls*. **2** *vt, also fig* eat greedily and noisily, munch *19-*, *now Abd Gall Dmf*. **3** take for one's own use *la19-*, *Bnf*.
n a voracious snap or snatch *19-*, *now Gall*. [ME *hanch*, OF *hancher* snap at with the teeth or jaws]
hanche *see* HAINCH
hanchman &c *n* the personal attendant of a *Highland* (HIELAND) *chief*, a trusty follower or bodyguard *18-19*. [appar erron alteration of Eng *henchman*; see SND]
hand &c; haund *15-*, **han(n) &c** *la18-*, *now Ork N, SW Uls*, **haun** *19-* [han(d); *C* hand; *Edb WC also* han] *n* **1** (1) = hand: (1) *in gen*, *la1-*; (2) *with preps, after place-names, and in bowling, curling* (CURL) *etc* direction, quarter, neighbourhood *la15-*, *now Bnf Abd Ags midLoth*: 'near hand'; 'from about Auchneel hand'. **2** a handle *la15-*, *now Sh Abd midLoth*. **3** *usu in pl* a pair of bats for making butter-pats *la19-*, *Gen except Sh Ork, only Sc*. **4** a cuff *16-17*, *only Sc*; *cf* ~*band*, ~*cuff*. **5** the horse that walks on the left-hand side of a plough-team, ie on the unploughed land *la19-*, *now local Ags-Wgt, only Sc* [prob orig f misreading of Burns *To His Auld Mare*; *cf* LAND[1] *n* 4(1) and *land horse*].
vt **1** = hand. **2** advise or assist a competitor at a ploughing match, *chf* ~**er** adviser, helper *20-*, *Arg Gall Uls, only Sc*.
~ie &c ['han(d)ɪ, 'han(d)ɪ] *n* **1** = *n* 1 (1) *18-*.

2 a small wooden tub or pail for carrying liquids, *esp* a milk-pail with one of the staves projecting to form a handle *la17-, now local Stlg-Dmf.* ~**it** fitted with handles *17, only Sc.* ~**less &c 1** = handless, without hands *la16-.* **2** *of persons* awkward, clumsy, incompetent, slow *la18-.* ~**y &c** *adj* **1** ready with the hands *la15-.* **2** = handy, of, or done by, the hand; dexterous, skilful. **3** *in negative* not easy to accomplish or put up with *19-.* **4** *of an animal* quiet to handle, amenable, adaptable *la18-, NE.* ~**y labourar &c** one who works with his hands *la16-e17, only Sc.* ~**y wife** an unqualified midwife *la19-, now local Abd-Ayr, only Sc.* **nae** ~**y** (*after word qualified*) awful(ly), excessive(ly) *20-, Abd: 'at a rate nae handy'.*

~**ba(ll) 1** = hand-ball *16-.* **2** a team game played in the BORDERS in which a small ball is thrown with the hands *la19-, S, only Sc; cf* BA¹ **3.** ~**ban(d)** the wristband or cuff of a shirt *la18-, now local Sh-Loth, only Sc; cf* ~*cuff.* ~ **barrow** a wooden frame with shafts, which can be carried by two people *la18-.* ~**-breed &c** a hand's breadth *la15-.* ~**-chair** a chair easily lifted by hand, *eg* a dining chair *20-, Ags Fif, only Sc.* ~**clap** a clap of the hands; an instant *la18-.* ~**-cloot** a towel *la19-.* ~**cuff &c** a wrist-piece or cuff *17, only Sc; cf* ~*ban(d).* ~**fast** *vt* **1** betroth (two persons, *or* one **with** another) by joining of hands *la14-e20.* **2** become engaged to marry, *esp* agree to a probationary period of cohabitation with (someone) before marriage *la15-e20.* ~**fasting** betrothal; trial marriage *la15-e19.* ~**-hab(ble)** quickly, without premeditation *19, only Sc.* ~**-hav(e)and** *of a thief* with the stolen article in the hand, red-handed *16-e17.* ~**-idle** having nothing to occupy one's hands, with idle hands *19-, only Sc.* ~**lawhile** [*'han(d)lə'hwəil] a short space of time, a little while *19-e20, S.* ~**lin** *la19-, now Sh N,* ~**ling &c** *16-17* = handline. ~**-makin** the making of an article by hand *la19-, now Ags, only Sc.* ~**-plane** a carpenter's smoothing-plane *19-, only Sc.* ~**-rackle** careless, heedless *e19, S, only Sc.* ~**shaking &c** ['hand'ʃekɪŋ, &c] **1** a handshake marking the conclusion of a bargain *20-, now Sh midLoth.* **2** a grappling at close quarters; a fight to settle a grudge *19-e20, Rox, only Sc.* ~**sho &c,** ~**skuve &c** [*Ork* 'hanʃo; *Ork* *'handsku, *hand'ʃø, *-'skuv] a mitten, a fingerless glove *19-, now Ork, only Sc.* ~**spaik &c,** ~**spake 1** = handspike *16-17.* **2** a spoke or bar of wood, *esp* that used in carrying a coffin *18-e20.* ~**staff,** ~**stay** the part of a flail that is held in the hand *17-, now Ork Cai.* ~**-wale** select by hand *la20-, Abd Fif Dmf, only Sc.* ~**-waled &c** hand-picked, carefully selected, choice *la17-, only Sc.* ~**write &c** handwriting, penmanship *la15-; cf* ~ *of writ(e).* **aboot &c** ~**(s)** at hand, in the vicinity *18-, now Sh-Cai Abd Kcb, only Sc.* **aff &c one's** ~ on one's authority, on one's initiative *la17-, now*

midLoth Ayr, only Sc. **afore** *la16, la19 or* **before** *la15-e17* **the** ~ **1** in advance *la15-e17.* **2** *also* **afore &c one's** ~ beforehand, ahead (in time) *la16-e17, la19.* **amang &c** (**one's**) ~**s 1** at spare moments, at intervals *18-, now local.* **2** in one's possession *17, 20-.* (**at the**) **far** *or* **near** ~ applied to applicants for membership of the incorporated trades (INCORPORATE), *as* **far** ~ a stranger *or* **near** ~ a relative or apprentice of an existing member *la18-20, only Sc: 'John Finlay, near-hand (son)'.* **at one's own** ~ by oneself, on one's own account or initiative *la15-19.* **before the** *or* **one's** ~ see *afore the* ~. **behind the** ~ **1** after the event, *freq* **wise behind the hand** *16-, now Ags Ayr Uls.* **2** overdue *la15-e17, e19; cf ahint the hand* (AHINT). **between** ~**s** in the interval *18-.* **by** (**the**) ~ see BY. **for one's own** ~ for one's own part, for one's own interest *18-.* **fra** ~ out of hand; at once, immediately *la16-e17, only Sc.* **get, hae, pit, tak** *etc* **through** ~(**s**) deal with, dispose of, discuss or investigate (a matter) thoroughly; take (someone) to task, cross-examine *la18-, now local.* **hald** ~ (**to**) give active assistance, support *la16-e18.* ~ **for** ~ hand in hand, side by side *la14-16, only Sc.* ~ **for nieve** hand in hand, side by side; abreast; hand in glove *la18-, now Cai, only Sc.* ~ **o(f) writ(e) &c** handwriting, style of writing *18-, only Sc; cf* ~*write.* ~(**s**) **owre &c head**(**s**) indiscriminately *17-, now local; cf* OWERHEID. ~**-roun-tea** *or* **-supper** a tea or supper at which people are served individually and not seated at table *20-, only Sc.* ~ **to ni(e)ve** hand to hand *18-e19.* **in** ~ *of a sum of money* in cash *la15-.* **in** ~**s 1** in captivity, under arrest *la14-16, e19.* **2** to or at grips *la15-17.* **in** ~**s with &c** occupied with, busy with, engaged in *17-, now Abd EC SW.* **keep in** ~ keep in suspense; delay *19-, now midLoth Arg.* **off a person's** ~(**s**) from a person, on his authority *la17.* **play with** *or* **tak silver of baith the** ~**s** act dishonestly or with duplicity *la16.* **pit through** ~**s** see *get through* ~*s.* **put &c** ~**s in a person** lay hands on, attack *16-e17.* **put &c** ~ **to, in** *etc* **anesel &c** commit suicide *la16-, now Sh midLoth SW.* **put &c in** (*local*) *or* **oot one's** ~ help oneself at table *la19-.* **put &c tae one's** ~ **1** lend a hand, buckle to *la18-.* **2** = *put in one's* ~, *la19-.* **put violent** ~**s on** *la15-e17 or* **in** *16-e17* **a person** = *put* ~(*s*) *in a person.* **Scotch** ~ = *n* **3,** *la19-, now NE-Rox.* **speid** (**one's**) ~ make ready quickly, make haste *16, only Sc.* **tak through** ~**s** see *get through* ~*s.* **there's my** ~ = I assure you *la18-, now EC Kcb Rox Uls.* **tak in** ~ **wi** (**something**) *e19 or* **to do** (**something**) *la19-* undertake.

handle &c, handill &c *15-e17;* **hanle &c** *19-,* **haunle** *19-* ['han(d)l; *C* 'hanl] *n* **1** = handle. **2** the shaft of a golf-club *la19.*
vti **1** = handle *la14-.* **2** *vt* lay hands on (a person) in a hostile way, seize, capture *la15-16, only*

Sc. **3** *in passive* be afflicted (**with** a disease etc) *la16-e17, only Sc.* **4** *curling* (CURL) drag off by the handle (a stone that has failed to reach the *hog-score* (HOG¹)) *la19-, now Kcb.*

handling &c 1 = handling *16-.* **2** hostile treatment, seizure, capture *la15-e17, only Sc.* **3** (1) commercial dealing, trade, business *la16-17.* (2) a commercial transaction *la16-.* (3) a task, a job in hand *18-; specif* a difficult task, a handful *la19-.* (4) a share in some affair, a hand in something *19-.* **4** a rounding up and penning of sheep for some special purpose, *eg* dipping or shearing *la19-, now Pbls SW, S, only Sc.* **5** an entertainment, meeting, party, social gathering *19-e20, only Sc.* **6** an unpleasant experience, an ordeal *la19-, now Ork Ags, only Sc.*

handschen3ie *see* HANDSEN3E
handsel, han(d)sell &c *n* **1** a gift intended to bring good luck to something new or to a new beginning, *la14-, eg* the New Year, a new house or new clothes *la14-.* **2** *specif* (1) earnest-money, a first instalment of payment *17-19;* (2) the money received by a trader for his first sale, either the first of the day or the first of a new business, thought to bring good luck *18-, now local Ork-Loth.* **3** *fig* the first taste or experience *18-19.* **4** a piece of bread or other light snack given to farmworkers before beginning work *18-e20, chf SW Uls.*
vt **1** *also fig* give or offer a HANDSEL to (a person) at the beginning of a year or day, or to mark some special occasion; present (someone) with earnest-money at the beginning of an engagement *la15, 18-.* **2** inaugurate with some ceremony or gift etc in order to bring good luck *18-.* **3** celebrate the first use of (something) with a HANDSEL; use for the first time; be the first to try, test or taste (something) *18-.*
H∼ Monday &c the first Monday of the New Year on which the New Year's HANDSEL was given, *formerly (la18-20)* regarded as a holiday *17-, now local Ags-Ayr.* [ME *hanselle &c;* OE *handselen* giving into the hands, ON *handsal* giving of the hand]

handsen3e &c; handschen3ie &c *la16-e17* [*han(d)'sɪnʒɪ, *-'sɪŋʒɪ, *-'ʃɪnʒɪ, &c*] *n* = ANSEN3E *16-e17.* [as if f HAND + SEN3E]

hane *see* HINE
hanet *see* HALF¹
hang *see* HING
hangmanay *see* HOGMANAY
hangrell &c ['haŋrəl] *n* **1** a stick, arm etc on which something is hung *la16, 19-, specif* (1) the gallows *la16;* (2) a tree-branch used for holding bridles etc in a stable *19-e20, S.* **2** a pole notched at both ends on which a carcass is hung in a butcher's shop *19-, now Wgt.* [only Sc, ? for *hang-rail*]
hank¹ &c *n* **1** = hank, a loop, coil *15-.* **2** *specif* a skein (1) of *yarn, orig* of a certain length, varying with the material (*eg* worsted, wool, linen), and with the period, *latterly* describing

weight *la16-;* (2) of gold or silver wire or thread *16;* (3) of wire in the form of a skein *16-17.* **3** *fig* hold, influence, control *18-e20.* **4** a hesitancy in speech, natural or affected; hesitation, delay *la18-, now S.*
vti **1** *freq fig* entangle, ensnare, catch as by a loop *la14-, now EC, SW, S.* **2** *vt, freq fig* (1) fasten, secure, link, *esp* by a loop *16-;* (2) tie tightly, constrict *la18-, now NE Rox.* **3** gather into coils or hanks, loop *18-, now local Sh-Bwk.*
hankle &c *lit and fig* fasten, tie up tightly; entangle *18-, now Kcb.*
hae, hald *etc* **ane ∼** *(la16-17) or* **the ∼ in one's ain hand** *(19)* have control, be master of the situation, *only Sc.*

hank² &c *n* **1** *chf in pl or* **fore** *or* **aft ∼(s)** the places on each side of a boat where the sideboards come together at stem or stern, the quarters *la16-, now Sh.* **2** the stem or *chf* stern compartment of a boat *e20.*
∼-(oar)sman a rower seated in the stern of an open boat immediately in front of the helmsman *la19-e20, Mry Bnf.* [f as HANK¹, ON *hanki* an eye or ring on the edge of a sail or on the side of a boat, *transf in Sc* that part of a boat to which such a ring was fitted]

hanker *vi* loiter, linger expectantly; hesitate *eg* in speaking *la18-, now local.*
n hesitation, a pause *19-, now Ags.*
∼in(g) *adj* lingering, deliberate, hesitant *18-e19. n* loitering, hesitation, doubt *la19-e20.* [prob Eng *hanker,* Du *hankeren* linger expectantly, crave, but w infl f and prob taken to be frequentative of HANK¹]

hankersaidil *see* ANKERSAIDIL
hankle *see* HANK¹, HANTLE
hanlawhile *see* HAND
hanle *see* HANDLE
hann *see* HAND
hansell *see* HANDSEL
hansh *see* HANCH
hant *see* HAUNT
hantle &c, hantill *16,* **hankle &c** *18-20;* **hantla** *18-e19 n* a considerable quantity (of things), a large number (of people), a great deal *16-.*
a ∼ (sicht) a great deal, much (more etc) *19-.* [uncertain, prob reduced f OSc, ME *handfull;* see SND]

hanty &c *adj* convenient, handy *18-e20.* [only Sc; appar irreg var of *handy* (HAND)]

hap¹ &c *vt* **1** *also fig* cover, surround, so as to shelter or conceal *15-.* **2** *chf ∼* **in, up, aneath** *etc* cover over *eg* with earth, straw etc as a protection against cold or wet; pile (earth) on; thatch; bury *la18-.* **3** (1) *also fig* wrap a garment round (a person), wrap (a person) up in clothes; tuck up (in bed) *la14-.* (2) *also fig* clothe, dress *la18-.* **4** make up (a fire) so as to keep it burning for a considerable time *19-, now Ags, only Sc.*
n, also fig **1** a covering, *esp* one which protects

against the weather; protection *la16, la18-, now Loth.* **2** a wrap, shawl, or PLAID; a warm outer garment; a bed-quilt or blanket *18-.*
~**per** the last hour of a mason's working day when work is covered up against frost etc *20-, now NE Arg.* ~**in(g)** *n* **1** covering, wrapping up *la16-e17.* **2** clothing, a garment *la18-e19, only Sc.*
~ **in** cover up (dung, potatoes etc) in drills with the plough *20-, NE.* ~**warm** a warm wrap or thick outer garment *la18-20.* [nME *hap(pe)*; unknown]
hap[2] &c *la16-, only Sc,* **hop** *orig chf verse* [hop; *Ork Kcdn Ags C Uls* hap] *vi* **1** *also fig* (1) = hop, jump *la15-.* (2) walk with a limp *19-, now Ags Uls.* **2** *only* **hap** *of tears etc* trickle down *18-19.*
n = hop *16-.*
hoppin beds &c (*20-, Abd Fif*), **hap-the-beds** (*19-, chf SW*) hopscotch; *cf* BED *n* 4. **hap step** &c **and lowp** *etc n* the game of hop, step and jump *la18-. v, adj, adv* = hop, step and jump *18-.*
hap[3] &c; **haup** &c *19- interj, n* a call to an animal in harness, *esp* to horses in ploughing, to turn to the right *19.*
vti, of horses or cattle in harness, also fig turn towards the right; *sometimes the driver* command to turn to the right *19-20.*
~ **and** *or* **or wynd** *of harnessed animals* turn to the right and/or left; *of a ploughman* make the animals do so; *fig, freq in negative* not be compliant with another's wishes *18-, now Wgt.* [only Sc; imit of the call, ? *ha!* or *hau(d)* (HAUD) + *up*; *cf* HUP]
hap[4] *la18;* **haup** *19-* [hap, hɑp] *n* = hip, the fruit of the wild rose *la18-, now Kcdn Ags Per.* [only Sc; *cf* OSc, eModEng *hep*, ME *heppe*, OE *hēope*; the form poss w infl f WHAUP[2] a pod]
hap[5] *n* an implement used to scrape up ooze from the sea-bed to make salt *18-e19.* [? f HAP[1] *v*]
happen, happin &c *la14-e17;* **hap(p)n-** *la14-16,* **appin** &c *e16, only Sc v* **1** *vi* = happen (1) *in gen, la14-;* (2) *with the event etc expressed as the subject, la14-16:* 'the chance *hapnit* better nor ony man supponit'. **2** *vt* happen to, befall *la14-, now Loth Lnk Slk.*
adv perhaps *la15-e17.*
~**in(g)** *adj* casual, occasional, chance *la16-, now S, only Sc. n* chance *la14-e16.*
happer &c *n* **1** = hopper (in a mill) *la16-.* **2** a basket or container, *esp* that in which the sower carries his seed *la16-, now Ork NE Ags.*
~**-arsed** *la17-18,* ~**-hippit** *19-e20,* Rox with protuberant buttocks or hips. **happergaw** &c a gap in growing corn caused by unequal sowing *17-e19. vti* sow grain unequally (when using a HAPPER *n* 2) so that the resulting crop is patchy *19.*
happin *see* HAPPEN
happity *adj, freq of a leg* lame *19-, now Ags.* [*cf* HAP[2] and Eng dial *hoppetty* lame]
happn- *see* HAPPEN

happy &c *adj* **1** = happy *la14-.* **2** lucky, fortunate, auspicious *15-, now Cai-WC.*
hapshackle, hap-schackell *e16,* **hop-schakil** &c *e16 vt, also* **hab-, hob-** *19,* **hamshackle** &c *19* hobble (a horse etc), tie up (an animal) in such a way as to prevent it from straying *16-, now local Ags-Dmf.*
n, also fig a hobble for tethering a horse etc, a fetter, shackle *la18-e20.* [*cf* eModEng *hopschackle* (*v*), Eng *hopple* (*v*) hobble (a horse); first element doubtful, prob w infl f HAP[2] *v,* and *ham-*forms w infl f Eng *hamper; cf* OSc (once) *hamshekell* (*vt*) hamstring *la17*]
har *see* HAIR[1], HAIR[2], HARE, HARR
harber, harbour *see* HERBOUR
harboury *la16-e19,* **harbery** &c *la15-e18,* **harbory** *la16-e17,* **harbry** &c *16-17,* **harborrow** &c *la16,* **herbery** &c *la14-17,* **herbory** &c *la16-e17,* **herbry** &c *la14-17 n* **1** harbour, shelter, lodging, entertainment *la14-e19.* **2** a place of shelter, a lodging or dwelling-place; an encampment *la14-16.* **3** a harbour, shelter for ships *la16-17, only Sc.*
v **1** *vt* provide with shelter or lodging *la15-16.* **2** *vir* take shelter, lodge; encamp *la14-e16.*
herbriles &c [*'hɛrbrɪles, *'harbrɪ-] without shelter, homeless *16.* **herbriour** &c [*'hɛrbrɪur, *-ər] a harbourer *la14-16, chf specif* one who provides lodgings or shelter, a host. [nME *herbery,* eME *her(e)berʒe,* OE *herebeorg* (*n*), f *here* army + *beorg* protection, shelter, ON *herbergi;* and OE *herebeorgian* (*v*) lodge, stay, ON *herbergja* lodge, harbour; *cf* HERBOUR]
harchat(t) *see* HARESHARD
hard &c; **haird** *e17, e20,* **herd** *la14-16, 20-* (*in comb*) [hard; *C also* hɑrd; *Ags Kcb also* ? hɛrd, herd] *adj* **1** = hard *la14-.* **2** *of intoxicants* strong, undiluted, raw *19-, now Cai NE Ags Dmf.* **3** close-fisted, stingy *19-, now local.* **4** *of joints in carpentry, masonry etc* pressing closely together at one place and not at another *20-, now midLoth.* **5** *of wind* dry *la15, la20* (*NE Kcb*), *only Sc.* **6** *of* TARTAN *cloth* of a hard dense texture *19-e20, only Sc.* **7** *of hides* hardened by being allowed to dry *la15-16, only Sc.*
n **1** difficulty, hardship *chf* (1) **if** *etc* ~ **comes** *or* **goes to** ~ if the worst comes to the worst; when it comes to the crunch *18-e20;* (2) **be, come** *or* **gae through** (**the hans o**) **the** ~(**s**) experience hardship or misfortune *19-, now local Bnf-Fif.* **2** a piece of firm ground, as opposed to a bog *la19-, now midLoth Kcb.* **3** spirits *la19-, specif* **the** ~ WHISKY *19-, only Sc.*
adv **1** = hard *la14-.* **2** tightly, firmly, securely *la14-, now local.*
harden, hardin &c *la14-16 vti* **1** = harden *la14-.* **2** *vi, of weather, chf* ~**en up** clear up, become settled after rain *la19-.* ~**ie** *n* **1** a kind of white bread roll with a hard surface *20-, Ags.* **2** (1) a hard sort of butter biscuit *la20-, Abd.* (2) *specif* a variety of butter biscuit baked in

Cupar and popular as ship's biscuits *20-*, *Fif.*
~lies &c *19-*, *now midLoth,* **~lins** *20-*, *now Sh.*
harly &c *19-*, *local* hardly, scarcely.
~ birdit *of an egg* almost ready to hatch *20-*,
Ags Rox. **~ breid &c 1** a kind of thin *oatcake*
(AIT), *esp* one only baked on one side and then
toasted on the other side in front of a fire before
eating *la17-*, *now Bnf Abd Uls, only Sc.* **2** stale
bread, *esp* that hardened in the oven, suitable
for making into breadcrumbs *la20-*, *local Abd-
Loth.* **~ fish** *etc* dried or salt fish *16-*, *now local
Sh-EC.* **~-handed** = *adj* 3, *19-*, *now Sh Ayr.*
~-heads *adv, fig* butting with the head *17.* **~
heid &c 1** the sea scorpion or fatherlasher *18-*,
now Ayr. **2** name for various plants: (1) *also in
pl* sneezewort *19*; (2) black knapweed; the head
of this plant *20-*, *now Kcb*; (3) ribwort *la20-*, *Fif
Kcb Dmf.* **~ neck** *slang* 'brass neck', impudence, effrontery *la20-*. **~-neckit** lacking in
modesty, forward *20-*, *now Arg.* **~ nickle
doon** a game of marbles *20-*, *local Bnf-Per.*
~-sat &c *20*, **~-sutten** *20-*, *now local Ags-S* of
eggs almost ready to hatch after long incuba-
tion. **~-set** wilful, obstinate *19-*, *now midLoth.*
the ~ stuff *la19-*, *only Sc,* **~ tackle** *19-*, *now
Fif Rox* WHISKY. **~ up 1** *of persons* in poor
health, unwell *la19-*, *now sEC, S.* **2** *of things* in
bad condition, in a state of disrepair *20-*, *now
Kcb Rox Slk.*
hard *see* HEAR
hardement *see* HARDY
harden, hardin &c; herdin &c *16* ['hardən;
*'hɛrdən, *'herdən] *n* a very coarse cloth, *orig
also* yarn, made from HARDS *la15-*, *now Ork Abd
Rox.*
adj, of cloth or yarn made of HARDS; *of garments etc*
made of such cloth *16-e20*. [northern and midl
eModEng and ME *harden,* f *hard-,* stem of *herd-
>* HARDS; *cf* HARN²]
hardhead,   hard-hed(e)   [*'hard'hid,
*'hardit, *-ɪt] *n* a (*usu*) copper coin of Mary
and James VI, orig = 1¼d, the LION *la16*.
[appar corruption of F *hardi, hardit* name of a
coin, said to be f *hardi* surname of Philip III, the
first to issue the coin]
hardin *see* HARD, HARDEN
hards, hardis &c *la14-e17* [hardz; *'hɛrdz] *n pl*
the coarse refuse of flax or hemp separated by
heckling (HECKLE¹), oakum, tow *la14-e20*.
~ weik *16*, **hard weik &c** *la16* candle-wick
made from HARDS. [northern and nmidl ME
hardes, herdes, midl and sME *herdes,* OE *heordan;
cf* HARDEN¹]
hard weik *see* HARDS
hardy &c *adj* **1** = hardy, bold, robust *la14-*. **2**
in good health *la19-*, *now local Abd-Rox, only Sc.*
3 frosty *la19-*, *now midLoth Wgt Kcb, only Sc.*
~ment, hardement *la15-e16* *n* **1** = hardi-
ment, boldness *la14-e17*. **2** deed(s) of valour
la14-15.
keep up a ~ heart be stout-hearted *19-*, *now
Ags MidLoth Wgt.*

hare; hair &c *la15-19*, *only Sc,* **har** *15-16*,
hear(e) *la16-17*, *only Sc* [her] *n* **1** = hare *15-*.
2 the last sheaf or handful of grain cut in the
harvest-field *la19-e20*, *SW Uls.*
~bell the round-leaved bell-flower *Campanula
rotundifolia,* the *bluebell* (BLUE) of Scotland *la18-*.
~('s) lug an angling fly, the body of which is
dubbed with fur from the hare's ear *19-*, *only Sc.*
hare *see* HAIR¹, HAIR²
harel *see* HARL¹
hareshard &c *19-*, *Abd,* **harchat**(t) *la15*;
hareshaw *19-*, *now Cai NE nEC Renfr,*
hareskart &c *19-*, *now Uls,* **hairshach &c**
19-, *now Fif,* **hareshal- &c** *20-*, *Rox* ['herʃa,
NE -ʃa(r)d, *Fif* -ʃəx, *Bwk Rox* 'herʃəl, -ʃe; *Uls*
-skart; *'herʃat; *'ha(r)ʃɪ] *n* a hare-lip. [all
forms except *hareshaw* only Sc; OE *hær-sceard*]
hargle bargle *see* HAGGLE-BARGAIN
harigals &c, harigalls; harigalds *18-e20*,
chf S ['harɪgəl(d)z] *n pl, also fig* the viscera of an
animal, entrails of a fowl, the pluck; *occas* of
humans *18-*. [prob F *haricot* a ragout, stew]
haring *see* HERRIN
harit *see* HAIR¹
hark, herk *la15-e20* [hark; *EC, S* hɛrk] *vti* **1**
listen (to), hearken *la15-*. **2** whisper; mutter
la16-, *now Sh-Ags.*
n a whisper *19-*, *now Sh Cai Abd, only Sc.*
harkin *see* HEARKEN
harky &c; hirki(e) *20-*, *Sh* *n,* sea-taboo or
pet-name a pig *19-*, *now Sh.* [prob orig imit of a
pig's grunt; *cf* Norw dial *harka* make a rattling
sound in the throat]
harl¹ &c,   harle &c;   har(r)**el &c** *17-19*,
haurle &c *la18-e20* [harl; *C also* harl; *Dmf*
herl] *v* **1** *vt* drag (violently or roughly), pull,
trail behind, haul *la14-*. **2** take or bring, *esp*
by compulsion or against one's will *16-17*. **3**
draw or drain in a vehicle *la16-e18*, *only Sc.* **4** *vi*
drag oneself, trail; move over a surface in a
dragging, scraping manner; move forward
slowly, laboriously, with dragging feet *18-*, *now
Sh Ork Ags.* **5** wear trailing garments *e16*. **6**
troll for fish with a fly or minnow for bait *19-*,
now Per. **7** *vti* (1) gather by trailing or dragging, scrape, rake (together) *la17-*, *now Rox.*
(2) *fig* amass (money or goods) *la18-e20*. **8**
peel (off), rub the skin off *la18* (*Ayr*), *e20* (*Uls*).
n **1** (1) what has been gathered together as by
dragging or scraping; an accumulation, an
amount of anything, large or small *la17-*, *now
SW Uls.* (2) *specif* money or property obtained
dishonourably or with difficulty *19-e20*. **2** a
rake or scraper used for scraping up dung, soft
mud, cinders etc *16-*, *now local.* **3** the act of
dragging, a tug *19-*, *now midLoth Bwk.* **4** *fig* a
slattern, a dirty, untidy or coarse person *19-*,
now SW Rox.
ha(i)**rlt** worried- or tired-looking *20-*, *now
midLoth Bwk.*
a ~ o bones a very thin person *la20-*, *Per Fif
Slk Uls.* [nME *harle* (*v*) drag; orig unknown]

harl[2] *vt* roughcast with lime and small stones *la16-, only Sc.*
n a mixture of sand and lime used for roughcasting *la19-, only Sc.*
~ing 1 the action of roughcasting *la16-.* **2** the mixture used for roughcasting *18-.* [uncertain; connection w prec not apparent]

harl[3] **&c** *n* the reed or brittle part of the stem of flax separated from the filament *18-e19.* [eModEng, MLowGer *harle* fibre of flax or hemp]

harle &c *la17-e20;* **herald** (**duck**) *la18-, now Sh* [*Sh* 'herəld; *Ork* harl] *n, defined as* the goosander, *but more correctly* the red-breasted merganser *la17-.* [only Sc; OF, F *harle* a kind of sheldrake]

harle, harlt *see* HARL[1]

harly *see* HARD

harm, harmisay *see* HAIRM

harn[1] **&c; hairn** *la17-20,* **haurn &c** *19* [harn; *sEC, WC, S also* hern] *n, only in pl, lit and fig* brains, the brain; the intelligence *la14-.* **~less** stupid *la19-, now local Sh-Kinr.* **~pan &c** the skull *la14-, now local Sh-EC.* [northern and nmidl ME *harnes,* ON *hjarne,* MDu, MLowGer, MHighGer *herne*]

harn[2]; **harrin &c** *e17, la19 n* = HARDEN *n, la16-, now local Ork-Kcb.*
adj **1** = HARDEN *adj, 16-e20.* **2** *of rope* hempen *la16-17.* [shortened f HARDEN; also northern eModEng]

harn[3]; **haurn** *19 vt* roast on embers, toast, make crisp before the fire or on a GIRDLE, bake or fire *19-, now Sh Ork Kcb Uls.* [shortened f Eng *harden* make hard]

harnish, harnes &c *la14-17,* **hernes &c** *15-16,* **herness** *la19-, now Lnk;* **harness** *la15-,* **harnais &c** *la14-16* ['harnɪʃ, -nɛs; *Slk Lnk* 'hɛrnɛs] *n* **1** = harness *la14-.* **2** *weaving, freq attrib* (1) the mounting of a loom *la17-;* (2) *specif* an intricate form of weaving common in west Scotland, *esp* Paisley *e19.*
~ing &c the accoutrements or trappings of a riding horse; the accessories of the harness *15-e17.* **~ plaid** *la19-, sEC, WC, now hist,* **~ shawl** *19-, Ayr* a PLAID (*esp* one made in Paisley) or shawl of fine quality or intricate pattern, *only Sc.* **~ sadle** a pack-saddle *la15-e16, only Sc.* **~ tying** the process of mounting a harnessloom *19-, WC, only Sc.*

haroosh *see* HURROO

harp &c, hairp *20-, only Sc;* **herp &c** *la15-* *n* **1** = harp *la15-.* **2** *only* **harp** (1) a sieve or riddle *la17-, now Cai-Ags Kcb.* (2) *specif* the lower fine-meshed sieve in a winnowing machine, that separates weed seeds from grain *20-, Ork Mry Abd.* (3) that part of the meal mill which separates the dust from the husks *19-.* **3** *only* **harp** a sparred shovel used *eg* for *lifting* (LIFT[2]) potatoes etc *19-, now Kinr Fif.*
vti **1** = harp *16-.* **2** *vt, only* **harp** riddle, sift *18-19.*

harr, har *16-e19,* **herre &c** *la15, 20 (Sh Ork) n* the hinge of a door or gate *la15-, now Sh.* [ME *harre,* eME *herre,* OE *heorra,* ON *hjarri*]

harra *see* HARROW

harrage *see* AVERAGE

harrel *see* HARL[1]

harriage *see* AVERAGE

harrin *see* HARN[2]

harring *see* HERRIN

harro &c *interj* a cry of distress, alarm or encouragement, *latterly* (*e19*) of rejoicing *15-e16, 19-e20.* [ME *harro(w),* OF *haro; cf* HURROO]

harrow &c; harra *20-* ['harə; *EC, S* 'harɪ; *Loth* 'harɪ] *n, vt* = harrow *la14-.*
~er a young horse or *chf* mare, unbroken to the plough but used for harrowing *la18, Per, only Sc.* **~bill &c, harrowbull &c** one of the crossbars or spars of a harrow *la17-19.*
die in the ~s die while still working, die in harness *19-, now Cai Abd Per.* **have** *or* **get one's leg ower the ~s** get out of hand, become unmanageable *e19.* **rin &c aff** *or* **awa wi the ~s** let oneself go in a dogmatic, assertive way, talk unrestrainedly or exaggeratedly *19-e20.*

harrowster *n* a spawned haddock *la19, NE.* [see SND]

harry *see* HERRIE

harschip *see* HERSHIP

harsk &c *adj* **1** = harsh *la14-16.* **2** severe, offensive, rude *15-e17.* [ME *harske,* eModEng *hars, harsh(e); cf* HASK]

harst *see* HAIRST

hart &c, hert *15-16;* **hairt** *la16-e17, only Sc,* **heart** *la16-e19* [hart; *hert; *hert] *n* = hart, a stag *la14-, in place-names 14-.*
~ horn(e) the antler of a hart, hartshorn *16-17, only Sc.*

hart *see* HERT

harth &c *16-17;* **hairth &c** *16-e17,* **hearth** [herθ, herθ] *n* = hearth *16-.*

harvest *see* HAIRST

hary *see* HAIR[1], HERRIE

hary nobill &c [*herɪ 'nobl] *n* an English gold coin of Henry VI *la15-e17, only Sc.*

has *see* AS[1]

hasard &c *adj* grey, grey-haired *e16.*
n a grey-haired man *e16.* [only Sc; uncertain]

hasardour &c, **hasatour &c** *only Sc* [*hazar'dur, *-a(r)'tur, *'hazərdər, &c] *n* a player at dice, a gambler *la15-16.*

has-been *18-,* **hes-beene &c** *17* ['haz'bin, *'hɛz-] *n* something or someone no longer existing or past its etc best; a good old custom.

hasch *see* HASH

haschbald *n* meaning obscure *e16.*

haschie *see* HASHIE

haseing *see* HASSON

hash, hasch *la16 v* **1** *vt* = hash, cut (meat) into small pieces *la16-.* **2** slash, hack, mangle, as with a sharp instrument *17-.* **3** slice, cut up, chop (*eg* bread, turnips for fodder); munch, chew *19-*. **4** spoil, destroy, deface *la18-*. **5** (1) *vt* fatigue, overwork, harass *19-*. (2) *in passive* be pressed, harassed *la19-*, *now NE*. **6** *vi* talk volubly, emptily or illogically *20-*, *chf S*. **7** move or work in a muddling, flurried way *20-*, *now NE Ags SW*.

n **1** contemptuous term for a person *18-*, *now local Kcdn-Dmf*. **2** = hash, a mess, muddle; confusion, disorder *la19-*, *now NE Ags Ayr*. **3** (1) a heap, a large quantity; a crowd *19-e20*. (2) *specif* the workers on a large farm *20-*, *chf NE*. **4** a row, uproar, brawl *19-*, *now Ags*. **5** ribald talk, nonsense *19-*, *now Sh*. **6** a rush or excessive pressure of work; work done in a hasty careless way *la19-*, *now local Ork-Kcb*. **7** a strong wind, *esp* one accompanied by rain *la19-*, *now Sh Fif Kinr*. **8** grain dried in a kiln and then chopped *la20-*, *local Cai-Kcb*.

~**er 1** an implement used to slice up turnips for fodder *la19-*, *now local Sh-Fif*. **2** a careless, hustling person; a workman who does fast but rough-and-ready work *la19-*, *local NE-Kcb*. ~**ie 1** *of persons* slapdash, careless or slovenly in dress, work or habits *19-*, *now local*. **2** *of weather* wet and/or windy, stormy *19-*, *now Fif midLoth Kcb*. **hashie-holie &c** *la19*, **-bashie** *20-*, *Ags n*, *marbles* a game in which smaller marbles are knocked out of holes by striking them with a larger one. ~**ter &c** *n* work done in a slovenly way, or badly arranged; a person who works thus *19-*, *chf Uls*. *vti* work in a hurried, slovenly and wasteful way; harass *19*, *Renfr Ayr*.

hashie &c, haschie *la16* *n* = hash, a mixture of chopped meat etc *la16-*, *now Ags midLoth*. [eModEng *hachy*, OF *hachie*]

hasill *see* HAZEL

hask *adj* = harsh: **1** severe, rigorous, rough *la16-e17*, *la19*, *only Sc*. **2** *of touch and taste* hard, dry, rough *19-e20*.
vti give a short dry cough, clear the throat noisily, cough up (phlegm) *19-*, *now local Ags-Uls*. ~**y 1** husky, hoarse *la18-19*. **2** coarse to the taste, unpalatable; stale, dry *19-e20*. **3** *of persons, things or actions* rough, coarse, dirty *19-e20*. **4** *of flax or fibre* rough, coarse *19-e20*. [var of HARSK]

haslie *see* HAZEL

haslo(c)k *see* HAUSE

hasp *see* HESP[1], HESP[2]

haspal &c *n* an untidy, carelessly-dressed person *19-*, *SW*. [perh OF *haspel* a rogue, ragamuffin, but prob var of next]

haspan &c *n* a young lad, a stripling *el9*, *S*. [shortened f *half-span*]

hass *see* HAUSE

hasse *see* HAE[1]

hassel *see* HAZEL

hassock &c ['hasək; *Ork* 'haso; *NE also* 'hʌsək] *n* **1** = hassock. **2** a large round tuft of PEAT[1] used as a seat *19-*, *now Ork local NE Per*. **3** a shock of bushy hair *la18-*, *now NE*.

hasson *la19-e20*, **haseing** *la17* [*'hasin] *n*, *mining* a vertical gutter or drainpipe between water rings in a shaft. [only Sc; HAUSE + *-ing*]

hast, haste *see* HEEST

haster, hasterns *see* HAISTER

hastie *20-*, *now Abd*, **hasty &c** *e16* ['hestɪ] *vtir* hasten, hurry. [ME *hasty* (rare); Mod form perh a new formation f *haste ye* (HEEST)]

hat[1]; **hatt** *la16-e20*, **hate &c** *15-e17* [hat; *sEC also* hɑt; *het] *n* **1** = hat *la14-*. **2** a layer of froth etc forming on the surface of a liquid, *esp* of yeast in brewing *la16-*, *now Sh Ork Bnf*, *only Sc*.

like a hatter with maximum energy or vigour, with all one's might and main *la19-*, *Gen except S*, *only Sc*. **hattie &c** name of various games involving a hat or cap *19-*, *now Cai*. **hattit &c kit** a preparation of milk with a top layer of cream, variously flavoured *17-19*, *only Sc*. **hattock, huttock** ? a little hat *el6*, *chf* **horse and hattock** a call, *orig* by witches, to be covered and ride *la17*, *19-*, (*hist*), *only Sc*. ~ **pece &c** a James VI coin representing him wearing a hat *la16-el7*, *only Sc*. **gie &c someone a** *or* **one's** ~ salute someone in passing by raising one's hat *18-*, *now Ags midLoth Bwk*.

hat[2] *v* = HATE[2] *la14-e15*.
hattin *ptp* named, called *la14-e15*. [ME *hat*, OE *hātte*, pt of *hātan* > HATE[2]]

hat *see* HIT

hatch *n* a peat bank (PEAT[1]); a row of PEATS[1] spread out to dry *19-*, *now Abd*. [only Sc; appar = laME *hatch* a rack, palatalized f OE *hæc*; *cf* HECK[1]]

hate[1] **&c**; **heat &c** *la16-el7* [het] *vt* = hate *la14-*.
hate[2] *v* is *or* was named or called *15-el6*. [nME *hate*, OE *hātan*; *cf* HAT[2], HECHT[2]]

hate *see* HAT[1], HEAT, HET[1]

hat(e)red, haterent &c *la15-el7*, *only Sc*; **het(t)ret &c** *la16-el7*, **hatrent** *la15-16*, *only Sc*, **hat(e)rend &c** *la15-16*, *only Sc*, **he(i)trent &c** *la16-el7*, *only Sc* ['hetrɛd, *-'rɛt, *-'rət, *-'rɛn(d), *-'rɛnt, *'hat-, *'hɛt-] *n* = hatred *la15-*. [ME *hatered &c, hat(e)redyn &c*; for forms in *-rent cf* MANRENT]

hatesum &c *el6*, *20* (*Cai*), **hat(e)some** *la15* ['hetsʌm] *adj* hateful. [ME]

hath(e) *see* OATH

hather *see* HEATHER

hathock *see* HADDOCK

hathorne *see* HAWTHORN

hatre(n)d, hatrent *see* HAT(E)RED

hatsome *see* HATESUM

hatt *see* HAT[1], HIT

hatter &c, hettir *el7* ['hatər] *v* **1** *vt* (1) *lit and fig* batter, knock about, bruise; treat roughly, bully *la15*, *19-*, *now Sh*. (2) harass, vex, overtire *19-*, *now S*. **2** *vi* collect in crowds, swarm,

abound *19-*, *now Pbls, only Sc.* **3** move confusedly or laboriously; work in a careless, slovenly or haphazard way *19-*, *now Rox.*
n **1** (1) a heterogeneous collection of things, a confused heap *e17, 19-*, *now Kinr WC Rox.* (2) a state of disorder *19-*, *now midLoth Rox Slk.* **2** a difficulty; a struggle, flurry, fluster *20-*, *Rox.* **3** a skin eruption, a rash, *chf* **be in a ~** *la18-e20.*
~el &c 1 = *n* 1; a large number *19-*, *now Ork.* **2 be in a ~el** be covered with sores *la19-*, *now Bnf.* [*cf* Eng *batter* and HOTTER]

hattin *see* HAT²

hattyr *n* **~ gestis** *appar* maple beams *e16.* [see DOST]

haubersione *see* HABERSCHOUN

hauc(e) *see* HAUGH

hauch &c; hach &c *la18-e20* [hɑx] *vti* cough, *esp* cough up mucus etc in order to clear the throat *la18-*, *now E, Uls.*
n **1** (1) a sound expressing exertion, a grunt *16.* (2) a forcible expulsion of breath, a gasp, *specif* the act of breathing hard on a surface to moisten it before polishing *20-*, *NE.* **2** a soft loose cough; a clearing of the throat *la17-*, *now local NE-midLoth.* [onomat]

hauch *see* HAUGH

hauchames *see* HOUGHAMS

hauchle *see* HOCHLE

haud &c *16-*, *only Sc,* **hald &c** *la14-e20,* **hold &c** *la15-;* **hauld &c** *la14-e20, only Sc,* **had &c** *la16-*, *only Sc,* **hild &c** *la14-e17, only Sc,* **hud** *la19,* **hai(l)d** *16-e17, only Sc,* **howld** *la19-, Sh-Cai Ross Arg* [hɑd, had, hʌd; hɑld; *Sh-Cai Ross Arg* hʌuld] *vti, pt also* **heeld &c** *la19-e20, NE,* **hud(e)** *19, Ags,* **heed** *20-, Cai* [hɛld; *Cai* hid; *NE* hild; *Ags Per* høɡ; *Sh Ork* *høld; *hild]. *ptp also* **halden** *&c la14-e20,* **hauden &c** *la14-e20,* **hadin &c** *la14-18,* **hadden &c** *la18-e20,* **holden &c** *17,* **howlded** *20-, now Cai* ['hɑld(ə)n, 'hɑd(ə)n, 'had(ə)n, 'hʌd(ə)n; *Cai* 'hʌuldɪd]. NB *This verb is freq used where Eng has* keep: **1** = hold *la14-.* **2** keep, continue, go on, maintain oneself in a certain state *now local Ork-Ayr:* (1) *vr, la14-;* (2) *vi, la18-: 'we'll haud content', 'haud ye merry!'* **3** *vt* save (one's life) *la14-e16, only Sc.* **4** *vir* continue, keep (in health) *19-, now Ags: 'hoo are ye haudin yoursel?'* **5** *vir* **~ wi** be content with, be pleased to accept *la18-19: 'haud wi less drink neist time'.* **6** *vt* keep, cause to continue to be or to do something *la14-.* **7 ~ in** *or* **on** supply, keep applying or adding *la18-, now Ork NE Ags.* **8** (1) *vi* go on one's way, go in a certain direction, proceed *la14-, now local Sh-Bwk.* (2) *vt* continue on or along (a *or* one's way etc), keep to or walk along (a path etc) *la14-, now Ags.* **9** *specif* keep (house or shop) *15-e17.* **10** (1) *vt* keep (an appointed day or place) *la14-e16.* (2) *vi, of a market, fair etc* be observed, celebrated, held *17-, now Abd Ags Arg.* **11** (1) wager, bet *18-.* (2) **~s ye** I accept

your wager *la18-, now Bnf.* **12** *vir, chf in imperative* stop; restrain oneself, keep **away** *or* **fra** *15-, now local Sh-Ayr.* **13** *vt* restrain, keep back, govern *15-, now local NE-Slk.* **14** *chf* **~ doun** burden, oppress, afflict, *freq* **hauden &c doun** *la18-.* **15** (1) *only Sc* keep, maintain (persons *la14-e17* or animals *la15-16*). (2) keep (provisions etc) in store or in hand *la15-e16, only Sc.* (3) preserve (cattle etc) for stock *19-, now midLoth Bwk.* **16** round up, pen (*chf* sheep) *19-, now Rox.* **17** *vi, of seeds etc* strike root *18-, now Abd.* **18** *chf* **haul(d)**, *of fish* hide, lurk under stones, shelter *19-e20, chf S.*
n, also, esp in senses 3 and 4, **haul &c** *19-, only Sc* [hal] **1** (1) = hold *la14-.* (2) *specif, freq* **a ~** *or* **~s** the action of grasping, a grip *19-.* (3) the action of a sheepdog in holding up sheep at a particular spot *20-, Arg Rox, only Sc.* **2** property held, a holding; a habitation, dwelling place, *latterly freq* **house and ~** house and home *la14-e20.* **3** something to which one can hold on, a support, prop *18-, now local Sh-Arg.* **4** (1) a refuge, shelter, place of retreat *la19-, now Sh.* (2) *specif* (a) a den or lair of an animal, *eg* a rabbit-hole *19-, now Sh Ayr;* (b) the overhanging bank of a stream, or a stone, beneath which a fish lurks *19-e20.* **5** *in negative* no restraint, no check, no power of retention *19-, now Abd Kcb: 'he had no haul on his hand wi the butter'.* **6** a dispute, a tiff *la19-, now midLoth.*
~er &c a holder, in various senses of the verb *la14-.* **~er-on** *in a shipyard* a riveter's assistant *20-, Loth WC.* **~in(g), had(d)ing &c** *17-* *n* **1** the action of the verb *la14-.* **2** (1) = holding, the tenure or occupation of land *la14-.* (2) a small farm or house held on lease *la18-.* **3** possession, means of support, property *la18-, now NE Fif.* **4** furniture, equipment; the stock of a farm, *esp* sheep *la18-, now Rox.*
gang *etc* **by (the) ~(s)** *esp of a child or an infirm person* support oneself in walking by holding onto chairs etc *19-, now local.* **hae't and ~ it** hide one's feelings *20-, Abd.* **~(a)back** *call to animals* turn left or away *19-, now Abd.* **~ aff &c 1** = hold off, keep off or away *la16-.* **2** *aff* (o) **anesel** look after oneself, defend oneself or one's own interests *19-, NE Ags.* **~ aff (ye)** *call to animals* turn to the right *19-, now local N-Gsw.* **~ again** hold back, check; resist *la18-, chf NE Ags.* **~-again** *n* opposition, hindrance, obstacle *19-, now Abd.* **~ at 1** persist in, keep at (something) *la19-, now local.* **2** urge on by exhortation, criticism etc, nag *19-, now Cai NE Ayr.* **~ awa &c** *v* **1** keep away, keep out or off *17-, now Sh NE Ags midLoth.* **2** continue on one's way, go away *la18-, now local.* **~ awa frae** with the exception of *la19-, now NE.* **~ by 1** pass by, keep away from, abstain from *19-, NE.* **2** have (little etc) respect for *19-, now NE: 'ye haud light by the law'.* **~-doon** *n* a handicap, burden *20-, local Sh-Arg.* **~-fast** a staple etc used for fixing *19-, now local Per-Dmf.*

~ **one's feet** or **a fit &c** keep (on) one's feet *la15-*, *now local NE-Arg.* ~ **for** aim at, make for *la19-*, *Sh-Ags Gall.* ~ **forrit** continue to improve (in health) *20-*, *now midLoth.* ~ **haul &c** offer resistance; stand up to strain or stress; prop, support *20-*, *Cai* [ie HAUD *v* + *n* 3]. ~ **in** *n* a stinting, a lack *20-*, *NE midLoth Dmf.* *v* 1 = hold in, confine, retain; restrain *15-*. 2 *of a container* hold in the contents, not leak or spill *19-*. 3 also ~ **in about** (1) bring or come closer *19-*, *now local*; (2) save, economize, be miserly *19-*. ~ **in about** keep in order, keep a check on; repress, discipline *la18-*, *now Ags.* ~ **in wi(th)** keep in with, curry favour with *19-*. ~ **one's mooth** be silent *20-*, *now Sh Ayr.* ~ **on** *vt* carry on, keep up *16*, *la19-*, *now local Sh-midLoth.* ~ **out &c** 1 *vti* keep out *la15-*. 2 *vt* persist in maintaining *la16-*. 3 *vi* live, reside *19-*, *local Abd-WC.* ~ **sae** cease, stop doing something, *chf in imperative* stop!, enough! *la18-*, *now Bwk S.* ~ **till** keep saying *19-*, *now local NE-Ayr.* ~ **to** 1 *esp of a door* keep shut, shut *19-*, *local*. 2 keep hard at work *la18-*, *now local Sh-Ags.* ~ **your tongue!** 1 = hold your tongue! 2 say no more!, words fail me! *la19-*. ~ **up** 1 = hold up *la14-*. 2 PRESENT (a child) for baptism *la17-*, *now Abd.* 3 call to animals stand still *20-*, *local*. ~ **up to** court, make up to *la19-*, *now Abd Ayr.* ~ **up wi** keep pace with *19-*. ~ **a wee** wait a little, stop for a moment *20-*. ~ **wi** admit, acknowledge the truth of, own up to *la19-*, *now local Ork-Kcb.* **in a** ~ in difficulties, in trouble *la19-*, *now midLoth Kcb.* **(lat's) see (a) haud(s)** o, see's **a haud o** give, hand over *la19-*. **neither to** ~ **nor (to) bind** ungovernable, beyond control *19-*.

hauf, haufer *see* HALF[1]

haufer *see* HALVER

haugh &c *la16-*, **hauch &c** *13-*, **hauc(e)** *e16*, **halch &c** *la12-16*; **haw** *la18-19* [hɑx; *halx; *also* *?ha] *n* a piece of level ground, *usu* alluvial, on the banks of a river, river-meadow land *la12-*.
~**(ing) ground** *la18-19*, ~ **land** *17-* = *n*. [freq in place-names; OE *halh, healh* a corner, nook]

haugh *see* HOCH[1]

haul *vti* = haul.
n 1 = haul. 2 a very large quantity (of something) *la19-*. [cf HALE]

haul, hauld *see* HAUD

haultane *see* HAUTANE

haun, haund *see* HAND

haunle *see* HANDLE

haunsh *see* HANCH

haunt &c, hant *15-19* *vti* 1 = haunt *15-*. 2 *vt* attend (divine service etc) *la16-e17*, *only Sc.*
n 1 = haunt, frequenting; resort *la15-*. 2 a custom, habit, practice *16-*, *now Ags Kcb.*

haup *see* HAP[3], HAP[4]

haur *see* HAAR[1]

haurd *see* HEAR

haurle *see* HARL[1]

haurn *see* HARN[1], HARN[3]

hause &c *17-*, **hals &c** *la14-19*; **hass &c** *17-*, *only Sc* [has, has; *Per* haz; *hals] *n* 1 the neck *la14-*, *now local Sh-Dmf.* 2 the throat, gullet *la14-*, *now Ork Bnf Ags.* 3 a narrow place *la15-*: (1) a neck of land; a narrow stretch of water *now Ork*; (2) a defile, the head of a pass *Kcb S, in place-names* [see SND]. 4 a narrow neck-like part, *eg* of an axle *16-*, *now Abd.*
vt embrace, take in one's arms *15-e19*.
~**bane &c** the collarbone *15-20*, *only Sc.* ~**-furr** *etc* the second furrow in ploughing *20-*, *now Gall, only Sc.* ~**lock &c, haslo(c)k** the wool on a sheep's neck, *freq* regarded as the finest part of the fleece *la16-20*. ~**-pipe** the throat, windpipe *la19-*, *now Ags Ayr, only Sc.*
gae doun (into) the wrang ~ *of food etc* go down the wrong way *19-*, *now local Sh-Dmf.*
hald in the ~ have in one's power, at one's mercy *la14-e17*, *only Sc.* [ME, OE, ON *hals*]

haut &c *vi* limp, hop *19-e20*.
n the act of limping, a hop *19-e20*. [only Sc; var of Eng *halt*]

hautane &c, haltane &c *la15-16*; **haultane &c** *la15*, **haltand** *16* [*'haten, *'halt-] *adj* haughty *la14-16*. [ME, OF *hautain, haultain*]

havar *see* HAE[1]

have *see* HAE[1], HEAVE

have-eel *see* HAIVEL

haveless *see* HAE[1]

haven *see* HAVIN

haver &c ['hevər] *n, chf attrib* oats, the oat *la17-e20*.
~**-meal** oatmeal *la17-*, *now Dmf.* ~**-straw** straw from oats *19-e20*. [n and midl ME *haver*; cf ON *hafre*, MDu, MLowGer *haver*]

haver *see* HAE[1], HAIVER[1]

haverel *see* HAIVER[1], HAIVER[2]

haveril *see* HAIVER[1]

haves *see* HAE[1]

havin &c *la14-e17*; **haven &c, hevin &c** *la15-16, only Sc*, **heavin &c** *la16-e17, only Sc* ['hevən] *n* = haven *la14-*.
~**ing &c** = *n*, *la16-e17, only Sc.*
~ **silver** a harbour due *la15-17, only Sc.* [cf HINE]

havin *see* HEAVEN

havrel, havren *see* HAIVER[1]

havy *see* HEAVY

haw[1] &c, chaw &c *19-20*, *Mry* [hɑ; *Mry* hjɑ, (t)ʃɑ] *n* = haw, hawthorn(-berry) *la16-*.
~**-bush &c** the hawthorn tree *19-*, *now Per Kinr Rox.* ~**-spitter** a peashooter *20-*, *chf SW.* ~**-stone** the seed in a hawthorn berry *19-*, *now Dmf Uls.* ~**-tree** *19-*, *now local NE-Dmf.*

haw[2]; hyaave &c *20-*, *local NE* [hɑ; *NE* hjɑv] *adj* 1 of a bluish, leaden, livid or dull colour *la15-e17*. 2 of a pale, wan colouring, tinged with blue or green *18-*, *now Abd.*
ha(w) clay a kind of clay formerly used for

whitening doorsteps etc, *usu* a tough, clammy, pale-blue clay *18-, now S.* [ME *haa*, OE *hāwi, hēawi*]

haw *see* HAUGH

Hawick ['haɪk] ~ **ba 1** a game played at Shrovetide with a football in the River Teviot *19-e20, Rox.* **2** a round, brown, mint-flavoured boiled sweet made in Hawick *20-.* ~ **gill** a measure of ale or spirits equivalent to half an Imperial pint (0.28 litre) *18-e19.* [the town in Rox]

hawk, halk &c *15-17;* **hak(e)** *16-17, only Sc* [hak] *n, vti* = hawk *n* (*la15-, in place-names 14-*), *vti* (*la16-*).

hawk *see* HACK

hawkberry *see* HAGBERRY

hawkie &c *n* **1** a cow with a white face; any cow; pet name for a favourite cow *18-, now chf literary.* **2** *fig* a stupid person *la18-e19.*

hurly ~ a call to cows at milking-time *19-, Gall.* [only Sc; f stem of HAWKIT + *-ie*]

hawkit &c *16-,* **haikit &c** *17-e18, e20, only Sc;* **hackit &c** *la16-e20, only Sc,* **halkit &c** *la15-e18, la19, only Sc* ['hakɪt, 'hakɪt; *Cai* 'hekɪd] *adj* **1** *chf of cattle, also other animals* (*la18-*) spotted or streaked with white; white-faced *la15-, now Abd.* **2** *fig, of persons* foolish, stupid, harum-scarum *la18-e20.* [obscure; *cf* HAWKIE]

hawles *see* HAE[1]

hawm *vi, sometimes* ~ **ower** work in a slovenly way; lounge; loaf about *la19-, Bnf.* [*cf* Eng dial *(h)awm* idle, waste time, of unknown orig]

hawmer *see* HAIMMER

hawthorn; hathorne *15-16* ['ha'θorn] *n* = hawthorn *15-, in place-names la13-.*

hay *see* HEY[1]

ha-year *see* HALF[1]

hazel &c *la18-,* **hasill &c** *la16-19;* **ha(i)ssel** *17-e18* ['hezl] *n* = hazel *la16-.*

vt beat or thrash, as with a hazel stick *la19-, now Cai Rox.*

~**ly, haslie &c** *e19* covered with or abounding in hazels *la18-, now midLoth Kcb.*

~ **oil** *joc* a caning, a sound beating (with a hazel stick) *19-, now Ags Dmf.* ~**raw** a type of lichen *la18-e19.* [ME *hasill*, OE *hæsel; cf* HISSEL]

hazer(e)d *see* HAIZER

hazy &c *adj* **1** = hazy. **2** weak in intellect, mentally unbalanced *19-, now EC Arg Slk.*

he &c, hie *16-17, e19, e e20;* **ei** *e20, Rox;* [stressed hi, *sEC* he; *S also* həi; unstressed (h)ɪ; *sEC* (h)e] *personal pronoun* **1** (1) = he *la14-.* (2) of a boat *15.* (3) *of inanimate objects, natural phenomena etc* = it *la18-, chf Sh Ork Cai and pseudo-Highl.* **2** used by a wife of her husband or a servant of his master *19-; cf* HIMSEL. **3** *attrib* (1) = he- *la15-;* (2) *of a woman* having masculine manners or appearance *19-.*

n a man, a male person *la18-, now Abd.* [see HIMSEL, HIS]

he *see* HEICH

heac *see* HECK[1]

head, headick *see* HEID

heal[1] &c *la16-,* **hele &c** *la14-e18* *n* **1** *freq* guid ~ health, freedom from sickness, physical well-being *la14-e20.* **2** a source of health or well-being *15-16, only Sc.* **3** spiritual well-being, salvation *la14-16.*

~**ful**(1) healthy; health-giving, salutary *la14-15.* [ME *heel(e)*, *hele, hæle*, OE *hǣlu*, (*hǣl*); *cf* HAIL[3]]

heal[2] *la18-,* **hele &c,** **helde &c** *e16, only Sc;* **heild &c** *16-e17, 20, only Sc* [hil; *hild] *vti* **1** = hele, cover *la14-e16.* **2** (1) conceal, hide; keep secret *la14-, now Cai.* (2) *freq in formula of homage* ~ (**the lord's**) **counsell** *15-16.* **3** *in formulae of freemasonry* shelter, protect, *freq* ~ **and conceal** *la17-.*

heal *see* HAIL[1]

healin(g) blade, -leaf *n* the greater plaintain *19-, now Cai.*

heap &c *la17-,* **hepe &c** *la14-e17;* **haip &c** *16-,* now local, only Sc *n* **1** = heap *15-.* **2** a heaped measure of capacity *16-e19.* **3** a large number or quantity, a great deal *la16-.* **4** *as adv* **a** great deal, very much, **a** lot *la19-; cf* Eng heaps: '*a heap better'.* **5** contemptuous term for (1) a slovenly woman *19-, now local NE-Uls, only Sc;* (2) a coarse rough person *la20-, local Mry-Kinr, only Sc.*

vti **1** = heap *la14-.* **2** *vi* be untidy in one's dress, wear clothes carelessly *20-, Abd.*

be heid of the ~ be in the forefront, take first place *20-, NE midLoth.*

hear *la16-,* **here &c** *la14-17* [hir] *vti, pt, ptp also* **herd** *la14-e16,* **heer(e)d &c** *la15-e20,* **hard** *15-,* **haurd** *la20-, only Sc* [hard; *also* hɛrd, herd; *sEC* hard] **1** = hear *la14-.* **2** *vt* audit (an account) *la15-e17, only Sc.* **3** *absol* listen to a preacher, attend church *la17-e18.*

~**er &c 1** = hearer, auditor, listener *15-.* **2** *specif* one who listens to the preaching of a certain MINISTER, a churchgoer *la17-, now local.*

~**ing &c** *n* **1** = hearing, faculty or action of hearing *la14-.* **2** a scolding *19-.* **3** news; a long story; *chf* **fine** ~**ing** *ironical* unpleasant news *la19-, now Sh.*

herd &c = hear it *la15.* ~ **of** hear, listen to (something) *la15.* ~ **till,** *chf* ~ **till him!** *etc* just listen to him! *la18-.*

hear(e) *see* HARE

hearing *see* HERRIN

hearken &c *la18-,* **herkin &c** *la14-16,* **harkin &c** *16-20* ['harkən; *Loth Rox* 'hɛrkən] *vti* **1** = hearken *la14-.* **2** *also* ~ **tae** eavesdrop, play the eavesdropper *la19-, local NE-Ayr.* **3** *vt* listen to, hear with attention *16-, now local Cai-Uls.* **4** *chf* ~ **someone his lessons** *etc* hear someone repeat lessons etc *19-, now local Cai-Gall.* **5** (1) whisper (something) *19-, now local Sh-NE.* (2) ~ (**in**) **tae** whisper to (a person) *la19-, now local Sh-NE.* **6** *of the wind* blow gently *19-20.*

~**er &c** a listener, an eavesdropper *la15-e20.*

hearsh *see* HAIRSE

heart *see* HART, HERT

hearth *see* HARTH

heary &c [*'hırı] *interj* expression of endearment, *esp* used by married couples to each other *la18-e19*. [only Sc; perh f *hear ye*]

hease *see* HEEZE

heas(s)ill *see* HISSEL

heast *see* HEEST

heat *la16-*, **hete &c** *la14-e20*; **het &c** *n* (*la14-15*), *v* (*la14-*), **hate &c** *n* (*la16-e20*), *v* (*e17*) [hit; *Sh Ork nEC* het] *n* **1** = heat *la14-*. **2** the act of heating, a heating, the state of feeling hot, *latterly chf* **get** *or* **gie a** ~ make (oneself or another) warm *16-*.

vti, pt, ptp also **het &c** *15-* [hɛt], *now local* = heat *la14-*, *freq* (*la18-*) *corresponding to Mod Eng* warm. ~**er** a wedge-shaped glazed sugared bun *20-*, *NE* [f similarity in shape to a heater for a box-iron].

come a-heat become hot *la19-*, *now midLoth Bwk Slk*. ~ **the house** *etc* hold a housewarming *19-*, *now midLoth*. **house-heat(ing)** a housewarming *19-*. **run wi the** ~ *of cattle* run about in hot weather when tormented by flies *20-*, *Cai Abd Kcb*. [*cf* HET[1]]

heat *see* HATE[1]

heathen *see* HAITHEN

heather *la16-*, **hether** *la16-e18*, **hedder &c** *15-*, *now Sh Ork NE*, **hadder &c** *la14-e18*, **hather &c** *15-e20*, *in place-names* la11- *n* **1** name for plants of the genus *Erica*, *esp Calluna vulgaris*, *la14-*. **2** *specif* referring to heather-clad hills as a place of concealment *18-19*. **3** *exclam* expressing surprise, wonder, doubt, disgust *la19-*, *S*.

~**y &c** *la16-*, **hadry &c** *la15-18*, **heathry** *la17-e19* **1** heather-covered; of or like heather *la15-*. **2** rough, dishevelled; mountain-bred *la18-*. ~**y &c head** (a person with) a tousled or shaggy head of hair *19-*, *now NE Rox*.

~ **ale &c** a drink brewed from heather, hops, barm, syrup, ginger and water *19-*, *now Ork NE Ags*. ~ **ask &c** the common lizard *20-*, *Bnf Abd Kinr*. ~ **bell** the flower of the heather *18-*. ~ **berry** the black crowberry *20-*, *now Cai Abd*. ~ **besom &c** a broom made of heather *la16-*. ~**-bill** the dragonfly *la19-e20*. ~**-birn(s)** the stalks and roots of burnt heather *la18-*, *now local nEC-Dmf*. ~ **blackie** the ring ouzel *la19-*, *now local Abd-S*. ~**-bleat(er) &c** *18-*, *local Cai-Uls*. ~**-bluitter &c** *la16*, *19-e20* the common snipe. ~ **claw** a dog's dew-claw, which is apt to catch in heather and is therefore *freq* cut off *20-*, *now local Cai-Dmf*. ~**-cock** the black or the red grouse *la19-*, *now local Cai-Kinr*. ~**-cow(e) &c 1** a tuft or twig of heather *17-*, *now local Sh-Abd*. **2** a broom made of heather-twigs *19-*, *now local Sh-Abd, Kcb*. ~ **lintie 1** the twite or mountain linnet *19-*, *now local Cai-Fif*. **2** the common linnet *la19-*, *now Abd Per Slk*. ~**-lowper** a hill-dweller, countryman *20-*, *NE*. ~**-piker** term of contempt for a person living

in a poverty-stricken or miserly way *20-*, *NE*. ~**-range(r)** *18-*, *now Cai Per Kinr*, ~**-reenge** *la20-*, *Abd Kcdn Ags* a bunch of heather stems tied together and used as a pot-scourer. ~ **stak** a stack of heather *16-e17*.

bell ~ a kind of heath with bell-shaped flowerlets, *Erica cinerea*; *loosely, also* cross-leaved heath, *Erica tetralix*, *19-*. **go fae the hauch** *or* **hey tae the** ~ go from a better to a worse situation *20-*, *Abd Kinr*. ~ **an dub 1** clay mixed with cut heather used instead of mortar in house-building *la19-20*, *chf Abd*. **2** *attrib* rough, poor, unrefined *la19-*, *NE*. **set the** ~ **on fire** cause a great furore or sensation *19-*.

heather-range &c; -reenge *n* the hydrangea *la19-*, *now NE nEC*. [corrupted f botanical name, w infl f *heather-range* (HEATHER)]

heathry *see* HEATHER

heave *la16-*, **heve &c** *la14-16*, **have &c** *16*, *la19-* (*chf Ork NE*); **heif** *15-e16* [hiv; *NE* hev] *vti, pt also* **ha(i)ved** *la19-e20*; **hufe &c** *la15-16*, *only Sc*, **hove** *la18-* [hivd; *NE Ags* hevd; hov; *høv]. *ptp also* **hoven &c** *la14-* ['hovən] **1** = heave *la14-*. **2** *vt* lift (a child) from the font as sponsor; stand sponsor to; baptize *la14-17*. **3** throw, pitch, toss (*without implying effort or strain as in Eng*) *la18-*, *now Sh-EC*. **4** *vi* rise up above the surface, become prominent, come into view *la19-*, *now local Sh-midLoth*. **5** swell, distend *e19*. *n, only* **heave &c** = heave *19-*.

hoven *chf of grazing animals* blown up with having eaten too much fresh green fodder *la19-*.

get *or* **gie someone the** ~ **1** (be) push(ed), shove(d) *la19-*, *Gen except Sh Ork*. **2** (be) sack(ed) or dismiss(ed) from a job *la20-*, *Gen except Sh Ork*. [see also HOVE[1]]

heave-eel *see* HAIVEL

heaven &c *la16-*, **hevin &c** *la14-16*, **havin &c** *16*; **haiven &c** *18-19* ['hɛvən, 'hëvən; *Sh Ork C* 'hivən; *N nEC* 'hivən; *'hevən] *n* = heaven.

heavin *see* HAVIN

heavy &c *15-*, **hevy &c** *la14-e17*, **havy &c** *la15-17*, *only Sc* ['hɛvı, 'hevı; *Abd Fif Rox* 'hıvı] *adj* **1** = heavy *la14-*. **2** pregnant; in an advanced state of pregnancy *la14*, *la19-*. **3** *of a river* swollen, above its normal height *19-*, *now local Cai-S*. **4** *of a drink, chf of spirits* large, copious *la19-*. **5** *of beer, freq as noun, corresponding to Eng* bitter *20-*; *see also* EXPORT, LIGHT, PALE, *special* (SPEESHAL). *adv* = heavy, heavily *15-*.

heavily &c *la16-*, **hevily &c** *la14-16*, **havily &c** *16-e17*, *only Sc*, **haif(f)elie** *16-e17*, *only Sc* = heavily. ~**some** dull, gloomy, doleful *e18*, *la20-* (*Kcb Dmf*).

~**-footed &c** = *adj* 2, *19-*. ~ **handfu(l)** a heavy burden, an oppressive responsibility *19-*. ~**- heartit** *of the atmosphere* lowering, threatening rain *19-*, *now Kinr*.

be heavy on *la19-*, **be a heavy neighbour on**

19- be hard on (clothes), consume a great deal of (food or drink) *Gen except Sh Ork.* ~ **o** (**the**) **fit** = *adj* 2, *la19-*.

hebdomader &c [hɛb'domədər] *n, in universities and grammar schools* the member of staff whose turn it was to supervise the conduct of the students *17-19*.

~**'s room** *Univ of St Andrews* a room *orig* used by the HEBDOMADAR, *now* used for meetings of committees etc. [only Sc; Church L *hebdomadarius* a member of a college or chapter taking a weekly turn in performing church services, f Gk *hebdomás* a period of seven days; *cf* EBDOMADARE]

hech &c; **heigh** &c *18-19* [hɛx] *interj* expressing sorrow, fatigue, pain, surprise or contempt, *freq* ~ **me** *or* ~ **sirs** *la17-*.

n such an exclamation *la18-, now Ayr.*

vi **1** make such a sound *19*. **2** pant, breathe hard or uneasily *19-, now Slk.*

~ **ay** &c ['~ 'aɪ] indeed *20-, local NE-midLoth Uls.* ~ **hey** &c ['~ 'həɪ] *interj* expressing weariness or regret *la18-, now Per.* ~ **how** &c ['~ 'hʌu] *interj* = prec *18-, now Slk.* *n* a fixed routine, a fixed habit, *esp* (**the**) **auld** ~ **how** the old routine, a return to a former state (of health or circumstances) *la18-, now local Fif-S.* ~ **how hum** = ~ *hey, 19-, now local NE-midLoth.* ~ **wow** = ~ *hey, usu* expressing distress or regret *18-, now Slk.* [imit of a sigh; *cf* HOCH², ACH, Eng *heh, heigh*]

hech *see* HEICH

hech-how &c ['hɛx'(h)ʌu] *n* name for various varieties of hemlock, *esp* the hemlock water dropwort *la19-, chf Arg SW.* [appar f Gael *itheodha* &c hemlock, perh w infl f *hech how* (HECH)]

hech how *see* HECH

hechle &c; **h(e)ichle** &c [hɛxl, həɪxl] *vi* **1** pant, breathe quickly, as after considerable exertion *19-, now local Cai-S.* **2** walk or proceed with difficulty, struggle or exert oneself, as climbing a hill etc *19-, now nEC.* **3** foretell, prophesy *la18-19*.

n a struggle; a difficulty; a perplexing piece of work *20-, midLoth Rox.* [frequentative of HECH, but *cf* also HOCHLE]

hecht¹ &c *only Sc*, **hicht** &c *la14-15, la18, only Sc*; **heicht** &c *la14-e17, e19* [hɛxt; *hɪxt] *v,* *with pt, ptp forms same as pres* **1** *vt* promise, vow, pledge, undertake *la14-, now Slk.* **2** *vi* make a promise *15-e20, latterly chf verse.*

n a promise *la14-e20.*

~**ing** *n* promising, a promise *15-16.* **I** ~ *parenthetic* I undertake, I avow, I dare say *la14-16.* **if a'** ~**s haud** if all comes true *18-19.* [ME *heghte, hehte,* OE *heht* pt of *hātan; cf* next]

hecht² &c, **hicht** &c *la14-16* [*hɛxt, *hɪxt] *vi,* *with pt, ptp forms same as pres* be called, have as one's name *la14-e17.* [ME *heyghte, hehte,* f as prec; *cf* HATE²]

hecht *see* HEICHT

heck¹ &c, **hek** &c *la15-e16,* **haik** &c *la15-, latterly chf N;* **hack** &c *18-19,* **heac** &c *17-e18* [hɛk, hek; *hak] *n* **1** a rack, a slatted wooden or iron framework *17-; chf specif* (1) a rack for fodder in a stable etc (*la15-*) or on a portable frame for use in the open (*18-*); (2) *transf* the ability to eat heartily, appetite *20-, Bwk Dmf;* (3) (a) a grating placed in or across a stream etc *16-, now local;* see DOST, SND. (b) one of the bars of such a framework; *also* (*chf*) one of the open spaces or interstices between the bars *15-17;* (4) a triangular spiked frame on which fish are dried *17-, now local Sh-Fif;* (5) (a) a wooden rack (suspended from the roof) for drying cheeses etc *la17-e20.* (b) a plate- or bottle-rack *18-, now local Sh-Pbls.* **2** (1) the toothed part on a spinning-wheel for guiding the spun thread onto the bobbin *16-e19.* (2) *jacquard weaving* the corresponding part of a warping machine *19-e20.* **3** a framework of wooden bars attached to the sides of a cart to enable it to take a higher load *eg* of hay *la19-, now Abd Kcdn.* **4** a metal hook or loop on a scabbard through which the sword-belt passed *e18.*

v **1** eat greedily *e20, EC Rox.* **2** work a fringe on a small loom *la18.*

~**er** a glutton, hearty eater *20-, EC, S.*

~ **door** a hatch-door, a door divided in two horizontally *la16, e19.*

Auld Haik(e)s name for a fishing-ground off the coast of Fife *la18-e20.* **live** *etc* **at** ~ **and manger** live extravagantly, 'be in clover' *la18-, now Mry nEC, WC.* [(chf n)ME *heke* &c, OE *hec* in comb *fōdder-hec; cf* MLowGer *heck,* LowGer, Du *hek* a fence, rail, gate]

heck² *interj* a call to a horse to turn left *la19-, now Ags Clcm.*

heck *see* HAKE

heckham-peckham *see* HECKUM-PECKUM

Heckiebirnie *see* HECKLEBIRNIE

heckle¹ &c *la16-,* **hekkill** &c *la15-17* *n* **1** *also* **hackle** *18-* = hackle, heckle, a flax-comb; the long neck-feathers of a cock etc *la15-.* **2** *fig* a severe beating, sharp criticism; a person who gives this *la18-, now Dmf.* **3** *also* **hackle** *19-* a cockade of hackle-feathers dyed in various colours and worn in the bonnets of certain Scottish regiments *la18-.* **4** *angling* a hackle-fly *la19.*

v **1** *vt* dress (flax etc) with a HECKLE¹ (*n* 1) *la15-e20.* **2** *vti* speak sharply and reprovingly (to); scold severely, wrangle *16-, now Sh midLoth Uls.* **3** badger with questions, *esp* with a view to discovering the weak points of the person interrogated, *esp* a candidate at an election *19-.*

heckled, hekkillit &c *adj* **1** *of lint etc* having been combed with a HECKLE¹ (*n* 1), dressed *16-19.* **2** having a border or fringe like a cock's hackle *la15-e17, only Sc.* **heckle(d) biscuit** a type of hard biscuit made in Ags with a pinhole surface *la19-, Kcdn Ags.* **heckling house** *etc* the place where flax etc is dressed *la18-19.*

~ **biscuit** see *heckled biscuit*. ~ **house** = *heckling house*, *la18-19*, *Ags*. ~**-pin** one of the teeth of a HECKLE¹ (*n* 1), *chf* **be** (**kept**) **on** ~**-pins** be (kept) in suspense or on tenterhooks *la19-*, *now N nEC*; **come** *or* **gae oer** *or* **through the** ~**-pin**(**s**) be roughly handled; be subjected to strict examination *la18-*, *now Ags*.

heckle² *n* the network of straw ropes which covers the apex of a cornrick, or a thatched roof *la19-*, *Bnf Abd*. [only Sc; Eng *hackle* the conical roof of a beehive, straw covering of a rick; OE *hacele* a cloak, mantle]

Hecklebirnie; Heckie- ['hɛkl'bɪrnɪ, 'hɛkɪ-] *n*, *euphemistic*, *usu in imprecations* Hell *19-*, *now Bnf Abd*. [see SND]

heckum-peckum; heckham-peckham &c *n*, *angling* a type of artificial fly used for trout-fishing *la19-*, *local*. [perh reduplicated f HECKLE¹ *n* 4]

hecturi (*sheep-counting*) *e20*; **heeturi** &c (*children's rhymes*) *19* numeral six. [see ZEENDI]

hed see HAE¹, HEID, HIDE¹

hedder see HEATHER, HITHER

heddle &c, **hedill** &c; **hiddle** &c *la16-e19*, *only Sc* ['hɛdl; *'hɪdl] *n*, *chf in pl*, *weaving* = heddles.

hede see HEID

hedge &c *la16-*, **hege** *la15-16*, *in place-names la12-*, **hage** &c *la15-16*, *only Sc*; **hegg-** *la15-e16* [hɛdʒ, hedʒ] *n*, *pl also* **heggis** *la15-e16*, *vti* = hedge *la15-*.

~**ie** = ~ *spurdie*, *20-*, *now NE, SW, S, only Sc.* ~ **root** the root of a hedge *la19-*, *now Per S*, *only Sc.* ~ **spurdie**, ~ **spurgie** a hedge-sparrow *la19-*, *now NE Per*, *only Sc.*

hedger *n* a hedgehog *20-*, *now Bnf Ags*. [contracted f Eng *hedgehog*]

hedill see HEDDLE

heding see HETHING

hedy-pere see HEIDIEPEER

hee see HEICH

heech &c [hix] *interj* expressing exhilaration, uttered by dancers in a REEL¹ *la19-*. [*cf* HOOCH]

heed [hid; *local* Sh Ork Per Fif hed] *vti* = heed. **never** ~ never mind, don't bother (**about** *etc*) *18-*.

heed see HAUD

heegh see HEICH

heek see HICK²

heel, hele &c *la14-17* *n* 1 = heel *la14-*. 2 = heel, the part of a tool nearest the shaft or handle, or shaped like a heel, *specif* (1) the part of an adze into which the handle is fitted *19-*, *local*; (2) the corresponding part of a scythe *19-*, *now Gall Dmf*; (3) the fulcrum of a lever, a block of wood put under a pinch to give it purchase *la20-*, *Ags Loth WC*; (4) *golf* the part of the head of a club nearest to the shaft *la19-*. 3 (1) the rind or last portion of a cheese *la18-*. (2) each end of a loaf of bread, *esp* when cut off the loaf *19-*.

vti 1 = heel. 2 *golf* strike (the ball) with the HEEL (*n* 2 (4)) of the club, and send the ball to the side *la19-*.

~**-cap** patch, mend or reinforce the heels of (shoes or stockings) *19-*, *now Dmf*. **come to one's** ~**-hap**(**pin**) *proverb*, *of a person who persists in pursuing a wrong course* come to grief *20-*, *NE*. ~**-ring** a circular piece of metal fastened to the heel of a boot to reduce wear *la19-*, *Abd Ags Kinr*. ~**-shod** a piece of iron used to protect the heel of a heavy boot or shoe *la19-*, *now local Cai-Dmf*.

coup by the ~**s** prostrate, lay low *20-*, *now Abd Fif Edb*. **gie** ~**s to** cause to hurry, put to flight; *specif curling* (CURL) make the progress of (a stone) more rapid by sweeping the ice in front of it *19-*, *now Kcb Dmf*. ~**s ower gowdie** &c *18-e20* *or* **gowrie** &c *19*, **heelster gowdie** *or* **gowrie** *20-*, *local NE lit and fig* head-over-heels, topsy-turvy, upside-down. ~**s o**(**w**)**er heid** *la18-19*, **heelster heid**(**s**) *19-*, *now Sh Ork NE Uls* = prec; in disorder. ~**s ower hurdie**(**s**) = prec *la19-*, *now Abd Rox.* **at the** ~ **o the hunt** in the rear, behind *la19-*, *now Edb Uls*. **make one's** ~**s one's friends** run away *la19-*, *now Bnf Ags*. **take one's** (*18-*) *or* **the** (*la19-*) ~**s** take to one's heels, run away, *now local*.

heel see HEELD

heelan see HIELAND

heeld &c, **helde** &c *la14-e16*; **heel** *19* [hild; *Abd *hil] *vti* 1 lean to one side, slant, tilt, turn down; overturn, upset *la14-*, *now Sh Ork.* 2 *fig* lean (towards a party, faction etc) *la14-16*. [ME *hield*, OE *hieldan*; *cf* eMod and ModEng *heel* (*v*)]

heeld see HAUD

heelie &c *latterly* N-Fif, **hely** &c, **hiely** &c *la15*; **hehllie** *la19*, *Bnf* ['hilɪ, 'helɪ] *adj* proud, haughty, arrogant *15-16*, *la19-e20*.

vti 1 *vt* despise *la19*. 2 (1) affront, hurt, offend *la19-e20*. (2) *vi* be offended, take offence *19-20*.

n an affront, a slight; a feeling of pique *19-e20*. ~**fou** &c = *adj*, *la19-e20*. [only Sc; eME *heʒliche*, OE *hēalic* high, of high degree]

heelie see HUILIE

heeliegoleerie &c; **hilliegeleerie** &c *e19*, **hildegaleerie** &c *19* ['hiligə'liri; *'hild-, *'hɪl(d)-] *adv* topsy-turvy, in a state of confusion *19-*, *now Ags midLoth*.

n confusion, noise, a bustle *19-e20*. [appar a fanciful formation, perh orig from a children's action rhyme; *cf heelster-gowrie* (HEEL)]

heelster see HEEL

heem see HAME

heepie *n* a melancholy or foolish person *18-e19*. [reduced f Eng *hypochondriac*; see next]

heepochondreoch ['hipɪkon'driəx] *adj* listless, melancholy *20-*, *Abd Kinr*. [f Eng *hypochondriac*, w different stress accentuation; see also HYPOCHONDERIES]

heepocondry *see* HYPOCHONDERIES

heepocreet *see* HYPOCREET

heerd *see* HEAR

heere &c *18-e19*, **hair** *la16*, *e18*, **heir**(e) *17-e18*, **here** *15*, *la19* [*hir, *her] *n*, *spinning* a length of 600 yards (548 metres) of linen yarn, one sixth of a hank *15-19*.

  herrin &c band [*'hırın 'band, *'herın] a string dividing cuts or HEERES of yarn into separate bundles *19-e20*. [only Sc; appar specialized f HAIR[1]]

heered *see* HEAR

heesh *see* HISH[1]

heest &c *la19-e20*, **haste &c; hast** *la14-16*, **hest** *16-e17*, **heast** *la16-e20*, **heist &c** *la15-*, *now midLoth*, **hist** *la19-*, *now Abd*, **hisht** *e20*, *Abd* [hest, hist; *Abd EC also* hıst, hıʃt; *Per also* hiʃt; *Rox also* hjıst] *v* **1** *vi* = haste *la14-*. **2** *vr*, *la14-19*. **3** *vt*, *only Sc* (1) hasten, *esp* send in haste from one place to another, instruct (a person) to go in haste *15-17*. (2) carry out, carry on, dispatch quickly or with haste *15-16*. (3) cause to go or act quickly *16-18*.

  n = haste *la14-*.

  hasting, haistine *n*, *chf in pl* an early-flowering variety of pea *la17-e19*. **~y**, **~é** (*16-e17*) *adj* = hasty *la14-*. *n* a cattle disease, murrain *la17*, *e19*, *chf Cai*, *only Sc*. **hasty brose** a kind of quickly-made BROSE *19-*, *NE*.

  ~ ye back *etc v* 'come back again soon', an invitation to visit again *la18-*. *n* a bargain or extra given by a shopkeeper to customers to increase trade *la20-*, *Abd Kcb*.

heeturi *see* HECTURI

heeze &c *18-*, **heise &c** *16-e20*, **hese &c** *16*; **hease &c** *la16-e20*, **hyse &c** *18-*, **hize &c** *la19-*, *now chf NE* [hiz; *NE* həiz; *Abd-Fif also* haız] *v* **1** *vt* hoist, lift, raise up *16-*. **2** *fig* elevate, exalt, extol *la16-*. **3** carry, convey (a person) to a place; whisk, hurry, or hustle (a person) off *19-*, *now NE Kinr*, *only Sc*. **4** dance, perform (a dance) in a lively way *19-*, *now NE*, *only Sc*. **5** *vi* dance, romp; make merry *20-*, *now NE*, *only Sc*. **6** *chf of prices* rise *la18-19*. **7** travel fast, hasten, hurry *la19-*, *now Per Kinr*, *only Sc*. **8** swarm, abound (**with**) *la20-*, *NE Kinr*, *only Sc*.

  n, *only Sc* **1** hoisting tackle *e17*. **2** (1) a heave, a hitch up *19-*. (2) an aid, encouragement, a helping hand *18-*, *now Abd*. **3** the act of swinging; a swing *e19*. **4** a romp, a piece of clowning; a practical joke, banter, a teasing *la19-*, *NE*.

  heezie &c 1 = *n* 2 (1); *also fig*, *18-*. **2** a drubbing, rough handling *18-e19*. (**h)eezie-(h)ozie** a game in which two players stand back to back, interlink arms, and, stooping alternately, raise each other from the ground *19-*, *now Rox*.

heyser ['həizər, 'haizər] a clothes-prop *20-*, *Abd Ags*.

  ~ (**up**) **one's heart** lift up one's own or

another's heart; take or give courage to; cheer *la16-*. [LowGer *hissen*, MDu *hiesen*, Du *hijschen* raise, lift > HOISE, Eng *hoist*; *cf* HEIST]

heezel *see* HISSEL

heezie *see* HEEZE

hef *see* HAE[1]

heff *see* HEFT[3]

heffer *vi* laugh heartily, guffaw *20-*, *midLoth Bwk S.*

  n a loud laugh, guffaw *20-*, *now midLoth Bwk*.

  ~er a person who laughs loudly *20-*, *midLoth Bwk Slk*. [prob onomat]

heft[1], **haft** *la16-* *n* = haft, a handle of an implement *la14-*.

  vt = haft, fit with a handle; fix firmly **in** something *la16-*.

  ~it &c handled, fitted with a handle *18-*.

  hae (**baith**) (**the**) **~ an** (**the**) **blade** (**to haud**) **in one's hand** have complete control (of a situation), have the whip hand *la18-*, *Abd*, *only Sc*.

heft[2] *vt* **1** lift up; remove by lifting *la18-e20*. **2** lift in order to estimate the weight *20-*, *now Bnf SW*. [appar verbal extension of Eng *heft* (*n*) weight, heaviness]

heft[3]; **heff** *la17-e20*, **haft &c** *18-e19* [hɛf(t)] **1** *vtr*, *also fig* accustom (sheep or cattle) to a new pasture by constant herding to prevent them from straying, *chf* **~it** accustomed to a new pasture *18-*, *now Arg SW*, *S.* **2** *vi* (1) *of animals* become accustomed to a new pasture *la18-*, *now Dmf S.* (2) *fig* become settled or established (in a place, occupation etc) *18-*, *now SW*, *S.*

  n **1** a pasture which sheep (*la18-*) or cattle (*la17*, *Kcb*) have become familiar with and continue to frequent; the attachment of sheep to a particular pasture, *now Arg SW Rox*. **2** the number of sheep that graze on *n* 1, *20-*, *Arg SW*, *S.* **3** a dwelling, place of residence, one's situation or environment *18-e20*. [appar Scand; see SND]

heft[4] *vt* hold back (milk) in a cow's udder so that it becomes hard and distended; leave (a cow) unmilked *la19-*, *now local EC-S.*

  ~it &c 1 (1) *of an udder* hard and dry, through not being milked *20-*, *now NE Gall S.* (2) *of milk* accumulated in the udder *19-*, *now local Abd-S.* (3) *of a cow* having a large quantity of milk in the udder *18-*, *now nEC*, *WC Rox*. **2** *transf* (1) full of liquid to bursting point *19-*, *now Kinr midLoth*; (2) swollen with wind, flatulent *20-*, *now Kinr midLoth Dmf*; (3) full to repletion *20-*, *now Abd midLoth*. [chf Sc; ON *hepta* bind, impede, Norw dial *hefta* hold up, restrain, check]

hege, hegg- *see* HEDGE

hegs; haigs &c *la19-e20 interj* expressing emphatic assertion or surprise *la18-*, *now local*. [f HAITH by analogy w FEGS and Eng *faith*]

hehllie *see* HEELIE

heich &c *la14-* (*but rare before 16*), **hich** *16-17*, *la19*, **heicht &c** *la14-17*, **hicht &c** *16-e17*, **he**

&c *la14-e18*, **hey** &c *la14-e17*, **hie** &c *la14-19*; **hech** &c *la14-e17*, **hee** *la14-e19*, **high** *la16-*, **heegh** &c *17-*, **hi-** *la16-e19* [hix; *hi; *St* haɪ] *adj* **1** = high *la14-*. **2** (1) *of persons, animals, plants etc* tall *la15-*. (2) *of edging-lace or braid* broad *17*, *only Sc.* **3** *freq contrasted with* LAICH (1) occupying the higher situation, situated above another of its kind, raised *la15-*; (2) *specif* situated in the upper part or on the upper floor of a building, **the** *or* **an** upstairs (room etc) *la16-*, *now Arg Ayr.* **4** arrogant, proud, condescending *16-*. **5** (1) in high spirits, lively, excitable *19-*, *local Sh-Ayr.* (2) out of one's mind, raving in delirium *la19-*, *NE*. **6** *of wind or geographical location* north *20-*, *SW*.
adv **1** = high *la14-*. **2** (1) loudly, in a loud voice *la14-*. (2) *freq* ~ **out** aloud, audibly *la19-*, *now NE Ags Ayr, only Sc.* **3** proudly, haughtily, disdainfully *la18-*.
n [hix, hɪx] **1** = high, height, the highest point *16*. **2** a hill, height, an eminence, upland; rising ground *la16-*, *now local Abd-S*.
vt, lit and fig raise, heighten; exalt *la14-18*.
Higher *secondary education* at a more advanced or difficult level, of both a State examination and the certificate awarded to successful candidates *la19-*: 'Higher English'. *n, colloq* one of these examinations or certificates *20-* [for details see SND, and *cf Lower* (LAICH), ORDINAR *adj* 4, and see *(Higher) Leaving Certificate* (CERTIFICATE)].
high-bendit dignified in appearance, haughty, ambitious *18-*, *now midLoth.* **hie burde** &c the high table, principal table in a dining-hall *la16-e17.* **High Court** = High Court of Justiciary (JUSTICIARY); NB *in England, this refers to the supreme civil court.* **high-cutter** a type of plough used in ploughing competitions *la20-*, *local Cai-Arg.* **high door** *mining* an upper landing-place in a shaft *la19-*, *now Fif.* **high English** the stilted, affected, pedantic or distorted form of English used by Scots trying to imitate 'correct' English *la18-*, *now Per midLoth WC.* **high-flyer** &c name for a member of the Evangelical Church party, the successors of the *Covenanters* (COVENANT), as opposed to a MODERATE *18-e19.* ~ **gate** &c **1** a main road, highway *la14-18.* **2** the highway through a town, the High Street *la15-16.* **3** the best or most direct way *16-19.* ~**-heidit** = *adj* 4, *la16*, *la19-*, *now Sh N nEC.* **high heid yin(s)** see *heid yin* (HEID). **high jinks** see JINK[1]. ~ **kirk** the principal church in a town or region, *eg* St Giles in Edinburgh *15-.* ~**-nekkit** &c *of a garment* having a high neck *16-.* ~ **school** &c *now chf* **High School** name for the principal school in many Scottish BURGHS *16-*, *orig Edinburgh, then Kelso and Stirling, later (19-) in many other towns*; a grammar school; a *senior-secondary school* (SENIOR); a comprehensive school. **high tea** = TEA *n* 2.
be ~ **upon ae shouther** have one shoulder higher than the other *20-*, *Sh Abd Kcdn.* **be**

very ~ **in the bend** be very condescending *20-*, *now midLoth Dmf.* **carry a** ~ **heid** behave haughtily *la19-*, *E.* **up to high doh** in a state of extremely agitated excitement *20-*.

heichen, highen; hichten *la18-* ['hixən, 'hɪx(t)ən; *Per also* 'hɛxən] *vt* heighten, raise up, increase in intensity etc *la17-*, *Gen except S.* [*cf* HEICHT *v*]

heichland *see* HIELAND

heichle *see* HECHLE

heicht &c *only Sc*, **hecht** &c *la14-e20*, *only Sc*, **hicht** &c *la14-e20*; **height** *la16-* [hɪxt, hɛxt] **1** = height *la14-*. (2) *la18-* a high place, a hilltop etc *la14-*. (2) *only* **hicht: the** high ground, the Highlands (HIELAND) *la14-16.* **3** haughtiness, pride, insolence *la15-16.* **4** *of behaviour, emotion etc* a high pitch *18-*, *now local NE-Uls.*
vt **1** raise higher, heighten, lift *la15-*, *now Abd.* **2** (1) raise in price or value, increase (a price etc) *la16-e19.* (2) raise the rent or dues payable by (a person), *chf in passive* have one's rent increased *16-18.*
~**y** &c proud, haughty, arrogant *la15-16.* ~**ynes** = *n* 3; temerity *16.* **at** ~ at the height of greatness, dignity etc *la14-15.* **of** ~ *verse tag* of great height, high *15-16.*

heicht *see* HECHT[1], HEICH

heid &c, **hede** &c, **hade** *la15-17*, **haid** *16-e17*; **hed** &c *la14-16*, **head** *la16-*, **eid** *la19-20*, *Ork Ross Abd* [hid; *nEC* hed; *local Sh-Mry* hed] *n* **1** (1) = head *la14-*. (2) *in sing with ref to more than one*, *la15-16*: 'all the teith in thair heid'. **2** = head, the top, upper end or higher part: (1) *in gen*, *la14-*, *Gen except Sh Ork*; (2) *specif* (a) the highest part of a river, valley, parish etc *la14-*: 'the hed of Tay'; (b) *of a town, street, or passage* the end next to the main street *15-*: 'the heid of ilk clos'; (c) *of rising ground* the summit of a hill *la15-*: 'the head of the brae'; (3) the ridge of a house-roof *la19-*. **3** the piece of cloth draped from the canopy at the head of a bed *la15-17*, *only Sc.* **4** the (flat) top or upper surface (of *eg* a wall or tower *16-e17*, a piece of furniture *16-*, the floor *la19-*). **5** the part of the old *Scots* plough (SCOTS) corresponding to the modern sole *la18-*, *now Arg Kcb.* **6** *bowls and curling* (CURL) that part of the game in which all the stones or bowls on both sides are played to one end of the rink; the position of the stones or bowls thus played *19-*; *cf* EN *n* 5. **7** a measure of yarn, formerly = 4 *cuts* (CUT[1] *n* 3), but after wool was *usu* sold by weight, a bundle of one-ounce skeins (*usu* eight) *la16-*, *now local.* **8** *only* ~**s** *or dim* ~**ie** the head or top pupil in a class *20-*, *Rox*; *cf* FIT[1]. **9** (1) = head, one of the chief points of a discourse; a section of a discourse; an item *la16-*. (2) a matter under discussion, a subject *la16.* (3) the chief or essential point, purpose or intention of a matter or action *20-*, *Ork NE.* (4) *specif* a separate item of a statement of religious belief, an article (of faith) *la16-e17*, *only Sc.*

adj, chf in comb chief, principal; most important, best *15-*.
vt **1** behead, decapitate, *freq* ~ **and** *etc* **hang &c** *la14-, now hist.* **2** = head, lead, top *15-*. **3** put the finishing touches to (a rick or stack) and secure its top *17-*. **4** *lit and fig* reach the summit of *la19-, now Bnf Abd.*
headicks and pinticks &c a game played with pins *la19-, NE, now Abd.* ~**ie** *adj* **1** (1) headstrong, passionate, impetuous, violent *la16-, Gen except Sh Ork.* (2) proud, haughty *la19-, now Bnf Kcdn Per.* **2** clever, showing proof of brains *la19-.* **3** apt to make one giddy or dizzy *la19-, now midLoth Rox.* *n* **1** = *n.* **2** a headmaster *20-.* **3** *in ball-games* a header. ~**ie knite** *or* **knot(ar)** a clever fellow *la19-e20, NE.* ~**ing sheaf** **1** the last sheaf placed on the top of a STOOK[1] (in wet districts) or rick *19-, now local Abd-Uls.* **2** *fig* the last straw *la19-, now Bnf Kinr.* ~**lins,** ~**lings** *lit and fig* headlong, precipitately *la16-, now Sh Ork Bnf.* ~**maist** topmost, highest up *20-.*
~**band** **1** = headband *16-.* **2** the waistband of a garment, *chf* of trousers *17-, now local NE-Uls.* **3** a halter *la18-, now local.* ~**banger** *colloq* an idiot, very stupid person *la20-, local C.* ~**bauk** **1** the float-rope with corks attached, from which the older type of herring-net was suspended in the water *la19-20, Sh NE.* **2** the vertical edge of a fishing-net *la18-, now Sh.*
heid bummer *freq sarcastic* a manager, a prominent or important person *la19-.* ~ **burgh &c** the principal town of an area, *latterly chf law* the town where the SHERIFF held his chief court *16-18.* ~**coal** *orig* the stratum of a coal-seam next to the roof; *latterly more freq* the top portion of a coal-seam when left unworked, either permanently, or to be taken down later *19-, chf Fif.* ~ **court** *orig* one of the three principal sessions of a BURGH-, SHERIFF-, or BARON-court (which *freeholders* (FREE) were obliged to attend); *latterly*, a court without judicial function, held once a year at MICHAELMAS, when the *freeholders* (FREE) of a county met to make up the voters' rolls and, as required, to elect an MP *15-e19.* ~**dyke &c** the outer wall of a field or holding; a wall separating arable from uncultivated land, the boundary wall *15-, now Uls.* ~**gere &c** **1** what is worn on the head; a head-dress *15-.* **2** armour for the head *e16, only Sc.* ~**heich** with the head high, proudly, confidently, with dignity *20-, NE midLoth Uls.* ~**hemp(t)** ? hemp assembled in HEIDS (*n* 7) *la16-17.* ~**house** the principal house of an estate, the manor-house; the main building or great house of a manor-house group *15-16.* ~**lace** a fillet, a hair-ribbon *16-e17, only Sc.* ~ **man** **1** = head man *la16-.* **2** a stalk of rib-grass, used by children in mock duels *18-, now Uls.* ~**sman &c** a chief, commander; a leader, superior; a foreman *la15-20.*

~**mark** *orig of sheep etc, later of persons* an individual characteristic of appearance which distinguishes one from another, as opposed to any artifical means of differentiation *18-.* **know** *etc* **by** ~**mark** have a personal acquaintance with; recognize by face or appearance *19.* ~**pece &c** **1** = head-piece *la16.* **2** = *n* 3, *la16-17.* **3** an accessory for a musket *la16.* ~ **rig(g)** the ridge of land at the end of a field on which horse and plough etc are turned during ploughing, often including a strip at either side of a field ploughed along with the RIGS[1] in one continuous journey *la15-.* ~ **room &c** **1** the higher or outer part of a CROFT; that side of a CROFT lying on the boundary of the *burghlands* (BURGH) of the estate; the marginal or boundary land *15-18, but still in farm names.* **2** *fig* scope for action, authority *la19-, Gen except Sh Ork.* ~**schete &c** a sheet for the head of a bed *la15-e17.* ~**sheaf &c** **1** the last sheaf of grain placed on the top of a STOOK[1] (*now Arg*) or rick *la19-.* **2** *fig* the crowning point, finishing touch; the last straw *18-, now Mry Bnf*; see SND. **steel &c,** ~ **staill** *16-e18* = headstall, the head-piece of a bridle *la15-, now local Cai-Kcb.* ~**steke,** ~**stik** [*'hid'stik, *-'stɪk] a piece of large artillery, a kind of cannon *16.* ~**suit** a set of ribbons for trimming a head-dress *e18.* ~ **tow &c** a headrope **1** *chf* of the rigging of a ship *la15-e17*; **2** in a herring-net *la20-, Bnf Abd.* ~ **washing &c** the washing of the head as a ceremony of initiation *la16-, eg* when a new apprentice enters his trade *18-, now Ayr.* ~**werk &c** [-'wark, *&c*] a headache, pain in the head *16-e17.* ~ **yin 1** a leader, a person in authority *20-.* **2** *in pl* the authorities *20-.* **high** ~ **yin(s)** = prec 1 and 2, *20-.* ~**ʒard &c** [*'hid'jard, *-'jerd, *&c*] the (farther or outer) end of a yard or garden *la15-e16.*
aff at the ~ *19-, local,* **awa in the** ~ *la19-, local Kinr-S* off one's head. **be at** ~ **an aix wi &c** be involved, *esp* in a meddlesome or contentious way, with (a person or affair) *la19-, now Bnf.* **get** *or* **gie one's heid in one's hands** *usu in threats* receive *or* give a severe scolding or punishment *la19-.* **get one's** ~ **oot** launch out on one's own, get one's freedom of action *20-, local.* **go oot o** ~ be forgotten *la19-, now NE Ayr Slk.* **the haill** ~ the whole amount, the total *la16-17.* ~**s an heels** completely, wholly *20-, local Inv-Uls.* ~ **of kin &c** the chief of a family or CLAN *la15-e16.* ~**s an(d) thraws &c** *adv, of articles arranged in a row* (1) with alternating head and feet or top and bottom *18-, now local Cai-S;* (2) in disorder or confusion, higgledy-piggledy *19-.* *n* a game played with pins *19-e20;* cf ~*icks and pinticks.* **in** *or* **on the** ~ **o(f)** busied or occupied with, deeply involved in *19-, now Sh Abd Uls.* **i(n) the** ~ **hurry o** at the busiest time of, in the peak of *la19-20.* **ken by** ~ **and horn** know (something) intimately *la20-, local N;* cf ~ *mark.*

lay one's ~ till set about eating (something) *la19-, now Abd.* **on the ~ o(f) 1** immediately after, on top of *la19-, now Sh NE Ags.* **2** see *in the ~ o(f).* **on the ~s o** in confirmation of; on the strength or security of; over, concerning *la19-, now local Sh-Kcb.* **ower &c the ~(s) o(f)** because of, in consequence of, on account of, concerning *la19-.* **take** *or* **buy something over &c someone's ~** dispossess or deprive a person of something which he has or wants, by offering a higher price, rent etc *la15-e17.* **tak one's ~** *of alcohol, also fig* go to one's head, intoxicate *la19-.* **tak up one's ~ wi** interest oneself in *la19-, Gen except Sh Ork.* **want** *etc* **the** *or* **one's ~** be beheaded, have one's head cut off *16, only Sc.* **wi one's ~ under one's oxter** looking downcast or dejected, sorry for oneself *20-.* [in place- and personal names *13-*]

heid *see* HUID

heidiepeer &c, hedy-pere; -s *18-*['hɪdɪ-'pir(z)] *adj* of equal stature (*16-*) or age (*18-*). [only Sc; appar HEID + OF *de per* on an equality, Eng *peer* equal]

heif *see* HAE[1], HEAVE

heifer *la19-,* **hiffer** *e17* ['hifər] *n* **1** a young cow, the precise meaning varying considerably as to whether or not the animal has calved, or how often she has calved *e17, la19-.* **2** *transf, usu of a woman* a big awkward clumsy person *la20-, NE Fif midLoth.* [*cf* Eng]

heifle *see* HYPAL

heigh *see* HECH

height *see* HEICHT

heild *see* EILD[1], HEAL[2]

heing *see* HING

heir &c, hair &c *la14-e17,* **air &c** *la14-17* [er] *n, also* **ayer** *la14-16* = heir *la14-.*
vt, only **air &c** = heir, be heir to; inherit *15-17.* **arer** [*'erər] an heir *la15-.* **heirship** *la17-,* **airschip &c** *la15-e17,* **arschip &c** *la15-e16* ['erʃɪp] **1** the state or position of an heir; succession by inheritance *15-.* **2** an inheritance *la15-, now Bnf* [*cf* ARSCAP]. **airschip gudes &c, gudes of airschip** *la15-e17,* **heirship moveables** *la17-19* the best of certain MOVEABLE goods belonging to a predecessor, to which the heir in HERITAGE was entitled.
~ portioner one of several female heirs who succeed to equal portions of a HERITAGE, failing a male heir; the successor of such a joint heiress *la16-20.*
~ of conquest *law* one who succeeds to lands or HERITABLE rights acquired (not succeeded to) by his immediate predecessor *17-19.* **~-at-law** *19-20,* **~ of line** *la15-20* one who succeeds by law to the HERITABLE property of a deceased person. **~ of provision** one who succeeds in

virtue of express provisions, as in a (marriage-)settlement *17-.* **~s what-** *or* **whomsoever** heirs of whatever sort, having a right by proximity of blood to succeed as heirs, as opposed *eg* to those called by DESTINATION *18.*

heir *see* HAIR[1], HEERE

heird *see* HEAR, HERD

heire *see* HAIR[1], HEERE

heirm *see* HAIRM

heirscheip *see* HERSHIP

heiry *see* HERRIE

heise *see* HEEZE

heist &c; hyste &c *19-e20* [həist] *vti* (*la17, la19-*), *n* (*la19-, now NE Ags Fif*) = hoist. [*cf* HEEZE, HOISE]

heist *see* HEEST

heitrent *see* HAT(E)RED

hek *see* HECK[1]

hekkill *see* HECKLE[1]

heland *see* HIELAND

helde *see* HEAL[2], HEELD

hele *see* HAIL[1], HEAL[1], HEAL[2], HEEL

hell *see* HILL[1]

hellicat *see* HALLOCK

hellier *see* HALF[1]

hellock *see* HALLOCK

helly *see* HALIE

hellzier *see* HALF[1]

helm *n* **1** *chf verse* = helm, a helmet *la14-.* **2** *fig* a crowd, noisy gathering *20-, now NE.* [see SND; *cf* HEMMEL]

helmstok &c a tiller *e16.* [only Sc; MDu and Flem]

help &c *vtir* **1** = help *la14-.* **2** *vt* remedy, amend; improve, supplement *la14-e17.* **3** mend, repair *la15-e19.*
~ender &c an assistant, helper, *chf* = ~er 2, *la19-, now Abd.* **~er &c 1** = helper *la14-.* **2** a MINISTER's or teacher's assistant *la17-.* **~lie** helpful; willing to help *la15-e20.* **~like** helpful, serviceable *la14-e16, only Sc.*
~ ma bob *interj* expressing astonishment or exasperation *la19-, C* [*bob* euphemistic for *God*].

helse *see* HAILSE

helsum *see* HAIL[1]

helter[1] *n, vt* = halter *la15-.*
~-shank the rope of a halter *la19-, now local.*

helter[2] *n* the possession of an animal or article by one person which is formally challenged by another, *freq* **in ~**; the animal or article itself *15, Ayr Prestwick.* [? specialized use of HELTER[1]]

helter-skelter *see* HILTER-SKILTER

hely *see* HALIE, HEELIE

hem &c *n* **1** = hem, the border of a garment etc *la14-.* **2** the outer part of a millstone *la16-.*

hem *see* HAME, HAIM

hemis *see* HAIM

hemmel &c; hammel *n* **1** a shed and an open court communicating with it, used for housing cattle *19-, now Rox.* **2** a square rack on posts in a cattle court to hold fodder *19-, Rox.* [appar

metath f HELM in general sense of 'a covering';
cf Norw dial *hjelm* the straw covering of a rick, a
slatted roof]

hemmer *see* HAIMMER

hemmit *see* HAMIT

hemp &c; hempt *16-e17* [hɛmp] *n* = hemp
15-.

~**ie &c** *n* **1** a rogue, a person deserving to be
hanged *18-19*. **2** *joc* a mischievous or unruly
young person, *now esp* a girl *19-*, *now local*. **3**
the hedge-sparrow *la19-e20*, *chf S*. *adj* wild,
romping, roguish *18-*, *now Bwk*.

~**-rigg** a ridge of land on which hemp was
sown *la17-*, *Gall*, *now only in farm names*.

hempe *see* IMP

hempt *see* HEMP

hemsucken *see* HAMESUCKEN[1]

hen &c *n* **1** = hen *la15-*, *freq corresponding to Eng*
chicken as eg ~**-broth**, ~**-hertit**. **2** *affectionate or*
familiar term of address for a girl or woman
la18-, *C, S Uls*. **3** a dare, a challenge to some
feat *20-*, *local*.

v **1** *vi* withdraw from any undertaking or promise through cowardice, 'chicken out' *19-*, *sEC*,
SW, S. **2** *vt* challenge (someone) to perform
some special feat, dare *20-*, *local*.

henner 1 an acrobatic or gymnastic feat *20-*,
chf Edb. **2** = *n* 3, *la20-*, *midLoth*. **hennie &c**
timid, cowardly *20-*, *local Abd-Ayr*.

~ **a(i)pple, hennie(s) aipple** the fruit of the
service tree *la19-*, *now Inv*. ~**-bauk &c** a
tie-beam on the roof of a country cottage (so
called because hens roosted there) *18-*.
~**-broth** chicken BROTH *la19-*. ~**-cavie** *la16,*
19-, ~**crae** *20-*, *Ags Ayr Dmf* a hencoop.
~**('s) croft &c** part of a cornfield frequented
and damaged by fowls *20-*, *now Bnf Abd*. ~**'s**
eeran a fool's errand *20-*, *now Cai Per*. ~**('s)**
flesh goose-flesh *19-*, *now Sh S*. ~**'s gerse &c**
as much grass or land as would produce food
for a hen; *fig* something of very little value *la19-*,
now Sh. ~**-hertit &c** chicken-hearted *18-*.
~**-laft** a hen-roost; the roof-joists of a house
and the space above them *la19-*; *cf* ~**-bauk**.
~**-pen** the droppings of fowls, used as manure
19-, *now NE, C*. ~ **picks** *la20-*, *NE*,
~**-plooks** *20-*, *S* = ~**'s flesh**. ~**-ree** a hen run
20-, *NE, SW*. ~**-taed, -toed** pigeon-toed *20-*.
~ **taes** crowfoot *20-*, *local*. ~**'s taes** *of bad*
handwriting scrawls *19-*, *now local Sh-Kcb*. ~**('s)**
ware an edible seaweed *19-*, *now Kcdn*. ~**-wife**
1 a woman who has charge of, or deals in poultry *la15-*. **2** *transf* a man who concerns himself
about matters usually left to women *20-*, *now*
Per Kinr Slk. ~**-wile &c** a petty or contemptible trick or strategy *la16-e18*.

have a memory like a ~ have a bad memory, be very forgetful *20-*, *local*. **my wee** ~
familiar term of address for a little girl *20-*, *local*.

see (somebody) by the ~**s' dish** *etc* escort

(somebody) part of the way home *20-*, *NE Arg*
Kcb. **sell one's** ~**(s) on a rainy day** sell at a
disadvantage, make a bad bargain *la17-*.

hen *see* HAIN

henche *see* HAINCH

hend *see* EN

hende &c [*hind] *adj* = hend, skilful, pleasant
la15-16.

n a gentle or courteous person *la15-16*.

hendely &c [*'hindli] *adj* = *adj*, *la15-16*.

hender *see* HINDER[1], HINDER[2]

hender end *see* HINDER[2]

Henderson; Hinnerson: as hard as ~**('s**
arse *etc*) extremely hard *la20-*, *Abd Ags*.
[unknown]

heng *see* HING

henk *la19-*, *now Sh*, **hink** *la15-e18* *vi* walk or
move unsteadily, walk with a limp, hop on one
leg *la15-*, *now Sh*.

n a hesitation, faltering; a stutter *la16-19*.
[only Sc; MLowGer, MDu *hinken*, Dan *hinke*,
Icel *hinka* limp, hobble; Sh forms are prob f
Dan and Icel rather than OSc]

henmast, henmest *see* HINDMAIST

henna *see* HAE[1]

henner, hennie *see* HEN

Henry: ~ **noble** = HARY NOBILL *la15*, *only Sc*.

hensboy *n* a page of honour, a henchman *e16*.
[eModEng *hench-boy*]

henshelstane &c;   henshin-stone &c
['hɛnʃl'sten, 'henʃin-, 'hinʃin-, *Abd* -'stin] *n* the
stone shelf or slab in front of a baker's oven-
door, used to make it easier to slide trays etc
into the oven, or to square up loaves before
baking *20*. [prob deriv of HAINCH from the
approximate height of the stone + STANE]

hensure, hensour *n* ? a swaggering young fellow *16*, *e19*. [only Sc; unknown]

hent *la16-e19*, **hint &c** *vt*, *pt*, *ptp* **hint, hent**
la16-e19, **hyntit &c** ['hintit] *la15-17* **1** take
hold of (a thing or person); grasp, seize; raise
(**up** *etc*) *la14-e19*. **2** *fig* seize on, take, acquire,
get *la15-16*.

hint to lay hold of (a person or thing) *15-e16*.
[nME *hint*, midl and sME *hent(e)*, OE *hentan*]

hent *see* HINT[1]

hepe *see* HEAP

hepocreet *see* HYPOCREET

her *see* HERE[1], HERE[2], HIR, SHE

herald, herald duck *see* HARLE

herand *see* EERANT

herbere *see* HERBOUR

herbery *see* HARBOURY

herbore *see* HERBOUR

herbory *see* HARBOURY

herbour &c *la16-*, **herbore** *la16*, **herbere**
&c *la14-e17*, **harbour &c** *16-*, **harber**
16-e17; **hairbour** *la16, e19* *n* = harbour
la16-.

vti **1** = harbour, shelter *la14-*. **2** *vi* take shelter,
lodge *15-e17*, *e19*.

~**ous** hospitable *la16*. [*cf* HARBOURY]

herbri-, herbry *see* HARBOURY
herd &c, hird &c; heird &c *la16-e18*, **hurd**
20, Uls [hɪrd, hërd, hɛrd; *Uls* hʌrd] *n* **1** (1) a
person who tends or watches over sheep or cattle, *esp* in order to confine them to a particular
pasture in unfenced areas *la14-20*. (2) *specif* a
shepherd *la14-, now WC Gall S*. **2** *fig* a spiritual guide, a pastor *la14-e20*. **3** *curling* (CURL)
a stone played so as to guard the winning shot
from the stones of opponents, a GAIRD *la18-e19*,
SW.
v **1** *vt* (1) tend, watch over (sheep or cattle), *esp*
to prevent them from straying onto crops *la17-*.
(2) ~ **craws** prevent rooks from interfering
with crops *20-, Abd Ags Kinr*. **2** (1) watch
over, look after, attend to (a person or object)
la16-, now Kcb. (2) keep (someone) away
from *la19-, Abd Kinr*. **3** (1) *vi* watch over
sheep or cattle *la18-, now local Abd-Uls, only Sc*.
(2) *vt* keep (land) clear of animals *la19-, only Sc*.
~**ing &c 1** the tending and confining to their
own grazing of sheep and cattle *la16-19*. **2** a
grazing allotted to a particular herd *la17-, now
Cai S, only Sc*. **3** the post of herdsman *la19-, now
Inv Kinr Rox, only Sc*.
common ~ a HERD (*n* 1) employed by the
community *15-e18*. [ME *herd*, ME (latterly
nME), OE *hyrde*, OE *hiorde*]
herd *see* HARD, HEAR
herdin *see* HARDEN
herdwill; -wall [*ˈhɪrdwəl, *ˈhɛrd-] *adj* capable of keeping cattle in or out *la17, Rox*. [only
Sc; Eng *herd* a flock + ?]
here¹ &c; her *la14-15* [hir] *adv* **1** = here *la14-*.
2 *with omission of the verb 'to be'* *la14-16, 20-, now
nEC, WC*: '*here a sweetie shop*'.
interj expressing surprise *20-*.
~**anent** *now chf law* concerning this matter; in
regard to what has just been said *la16-*.
~**attour &c** in addition to this, furthermore,
besides *la14-15*. ~**awa**, ~ **away** *adv, also
attrib* **1** in this quarter or neighbourhood, hereabouts *la16-, now local NE-S*. **2** to this quarter,
hither *19-e20*. **3** on this earth, in this life
17-18. ~**awa(y) thereawa(y)** hither and
thither *la18-, now local Cai-S*. ~**cumming** coming here, arrival; a visit *la14-el7*. ~ **doun**
here below, here in this world *14-16, only Sc*.
~**eft** = hereafter *la15, only Sc*. ~**intill** in this
(matter, case etc) *la15-e17, only Sc*. ~**till** =
hereto, to this matter etc *la14, only Sc*.
here² &c; her [*hir] *n, chf verse* a lord, a chief; a
man of high or senior rank; a master *la14-16*.
[nME *here*, OFris *hêra*, MLowGer, MDu *hêre*]
here³ &c [*hir] *n, verse* an army, a host, a company *la15-e16*. [nME *her*, ME, OE *here*]
here *see* HAIR¹, HEAR, HEERE
hereauld *see* HERIAL
hereditare &c [*hɛˈrɛdɪtər] *adj* hereditary
la16-e17. [only Sc; F *héréditaire* or L *hērēditārius*]
herely &c [*ˈhirlɪ] *adj, adv* stately, splendid(ly)
la15. [only Sc; ? OE *hērlic* noble, or f HERE²]

hereschip *see* HERSHIP
heretrice, heretrix *see* HERITOR
herial &c, hereȝelde &c *la15-16*, **heriald**
&c *15-17*; **herȝeld &c** *la15-16*, **her(ȝ)eauld**
&c *la16-17* [*NE* ˈhɛrɪəl; *ˈhirjəl(d), *ˈhɛr-,
*ˈhar-; *ˈhɛrɪəld] *n* **1** (1) *also attrib, chf* ~ **horse**
the best living animal, *best aucht* (BEST) due by
feudal custom to the landlord on the death of a
tenant *la15-17*. (2) a money payment in lieu
16. **2** = heriot, the right to claim or take such
a payment from one's tenants *15-18*. **3** a particular animal taken or set aside to be given as
HERIAL (*n* 1) *la16-17*. **4** that which causes loss
or ruin, a great or unwarranted expense, a constant drain on one's resources *la19-, NE*. [poss
HERE² + ȝelde (YIELD), but appar related to
Eng *heriot*; see DOST, SND]
herin(g) *see* HERRIN
Herioter [ˈhɛrɪotər] a pupil or former pupil of
George Heriot's School (*formerly* Hospital) in
Edinburgh *la19-*.
herischip *see* HERSHIP
heritable &c,   heritabill &c   *la14-17*,
eritabill &c *la14-el7, only Sc* [ˈhɛrɪtəbl; *ˈɛr-]
adj **1** capable of being inherited, subject to
inheritance; *law* applied to that form of property (houses, lands, and rights pertaining to
these) which went by inheritance to the *heir-at-law* (HEIR), as opposed to MOVEABLE property
la15-20. **2** *law* pertaining to or connected with
houses, lands etc *la14-, only Sc*. **3** *of persons*
holding property, office, or privilege by hereditary right *15-*.
heritably &c *adv* **1** as a HERITABLE property, as
HERITAGE; as held by HERITABLE right, by right
of inheritance *15-19*. **2** *in the disposition of property* with HERITABLE rights to the disponee
la14-el7.
~ **bond** *law* a personal obligation for a money
loan, fortified by a conveyance of HERITAGE as
security *18-*. ~ **jurisdictions** collective term
for various ancient rights formerly enjoyed by
feudal proprietors of land or by holders of certain offices, entitling them to administer justice
in local courts; abolished by the Heritable
Jurisdictions (Scotland) Act 1747, *18*. ~
security *law* security for a loan consisting of
the right of HERITABLE property conveyed by
the debtor to the creditor *18-*.
heritage &c, eritage &c *la14-15, only Sc*
[ˈhɛrɪtedʒ; *ˈɛr-] *n* **1** = heritage, inheritance
la14-. **2** (1) property, *esp* landed property,
which descended to the *heir-at-law* (HEIR) on the
decease of the proprietor, HERITABLE estate
15-16. (2) such property inherited by a person as rightful heir, sometimes distinguished
from CONQUEST, *ie* land inherited, not acquired
by purchase; an inheritance, birthright
la14-el7. (3) *law* the technical term for property in the form of land and houses *18-; cf* CONQUEST. **3** a person's or nation's native land
15-16. **4** (1) *in reference to a* FEU the possession

of lands by HERITABLE right, *chf* **in** ~ *15-*.   (2)
HERITABLE right or title (to lands), *freq* **of** ~ by
HERITABLE right *la14-16*.

heritor &c *la16-*, **heritar** &c *la15-e16*,
heriter &c, **heritour** &c *16-17* ['hɛrɪtər,
-ər; *-ur] *n* **1** = heritor, an heir or heiress
la15-. **2** the proprietor of HERITABLE property
la15-e17, only Sc. **3** a property-owner, a landowner, a landed proprietor, *specif in parochial
law* a proprietor of land or houses formerly liable to payment of public burdens connected
with the parish, including administration of the
poor, schools, and upkeep of church property
la16-, now hist.
    heretrice *16-e17*, **heretrix** &c *la16-e18*
[*hɛrɪtrɪs, *-trɪks] a female HERITOR.

herk *see* HARK
herkin *see* HEARKEN
herle &c *e16*, *la19-e20*; **erle** &c *20-*, *nEC n* the
heron. [the *l* may be due to confusion w
HARLE]
herling &c, **hirling** &c *n* an immature sea-
trout *la17-, SW.* [uncertain; ? Eng *herle* the
barb of an angling fly]
herm *see* HAIRM
hern &c; **huron** &c *19-e20, Bwk Rox* [hɛrn; *Rox*
hørn] *n* heron *la18-*.
hernes(s) *see* HARNISH
heronious *la19-, Ayr,* **hyronius** *la16*
[hɛ'ronɪas; *hɪ'ronɪʌs] *adj, of persons* misguided
in behaviour, disregarding or defying established habits and ideas, unconventional, outrageous.   [var of Eng *erroneous*]
heronshew &c *19-e20, chf S*, **heronis-sew**
la15 ['hɛrn'ʃu; *Rox* -'sjux; &c] *n* the heron.
[ME *heronsew*, OF *heronceau* a young heron]
herp *see* HARP
herre *see* HARR
herrie, herry &c *la16-*, **hery** &c *15-17*, **hary**
&c *16-e17*; **harry** &c *17-*, **heiry** &c *la16-e17*
['hɛrɪ, 'harɪ; *'hɪrɪ] *vti* **1** = harry, rob, plunder
la14-. **2** *vt, specif* harrow (hell); *transf* lay waste
(heaven) *la15-16*. **3** despoil (a place or person) (**of** certain goods) *15-17, e19* (*literary*). **4**
also fig rob (a bird's nest) of eggs or young (*16-*)
or (a beehive) of its honey (*19-*) *Gen except Sh
Ork.* **5** take all the fish or shellfish from (a
stretch of water etc) *17, 19-e20*. **6** (1) ruin
(persons) by extortion or oppression, impoverish *la15-, now NE Dmf.*   (2) exhaust the fertility of (land), as by removing the topsoil *la19-,
Sh Ork Dmf.* **7** *mining* cut away coal from pillars left as supports; remove all coal from a
working *19-e20*.
    ~**ment 1** plundering, devastation *19*. **2** that
which causes devastation, ruination *la18-, now
Bnf.*
    ~ **hawk** a plunderer, a robber, *specif* one who
takes everything from a nest etc *20-, now wLoth.*
    ~ **out** dispossess (a person), drive out in a state
of destitution, expel (from one's home or possessions) *la18-, now Abd Ags.* ~**-watter** &c

la15-17, 20- (Cai), ~**-water-net** *17-18* **1** *also fig*
a kind of fishing net *la15-18*.   **2** a very selfish
person *20-, Cai.*

herrin &c *18-*, **herring** *la16-*, **herin(g)** &c
15-17, **haring** &c *la15-e17, only Sc;* **harring**
&c *la16-e18, only Sc*, **hearing** &c *la16-e18,
la20- (Bnf)* ['hɛrɪn, -(ə)n, 'hɛrɪn; *Bnf also* 'hɪrɪn]
n = herring.
    ~ **drave** &c the annual herring-fishing *16-e17*.
    ~ **hake** the hake *la19-, now Inv Fif WC.* ~
hog the grampus or some other species of
dolphin; the fin-whale *19-, now Uls.* ~**sile**
young herring *la19-, now local NE, Kcb.*
herrin *see* HEERE
herrischip *see* HERSHIP
hers *see* HAIRSE
hersel &c *la16-*, **hirself** &c *15-17;* **hirselvyn**
&c *la14-e16*, **herself** *18-* [(h)ər'sɛl; (h)ər'sɛlf;
*hər'sɛlvən] *pronoun* **1** = herself *la14-*. **2** *literary, supposedly of a Highlander's* (HIELAND) *speech*
myself, I *la18-19*. **3** name for the female head
of any body or institution, *eg* the mistress of the
house, a female boss *la19-, now local N-Uls; cf*
HIMSEL 2. [*cf* SHE and HE and see also *nainsell* 2
(NAIN)]
hersh *see* HAIRSE
hership *18-19*, **herschip** &c *15-19*, **hereschip** &c *la15-18;* **her(r)ischip** &c
la14-18, **heirscheip** &c *15-e17*,
hairs(c)hip &c *16-17*, **harschip** &c
la16-18 [*'hɛrʃɪp; *'hɪrʃɪp, *'her-, *'har-,
*'hɪr-; *'hɛrɪskɪp] *n* **1** *chf in pl* armed incursions,
esp to carry off cattle etc, predatory raids
la14-17. **2** the act or practice of harrying,
plundering or pillaging by an army or armed
force, *freq* **mak** ~ *15-18*. **3** harm or hardship
inflicted on a person by violence or robbery;
destitution, impoverishment caused by harrying or violent treatment *la15-19*. **4** booty,
plunder, *esp* cattle *la16-18*. [from HERE[3] or
stem of OE *hergan* > HERRIE; *cf* ON *herja* harry,
herskapr harrying]
herskit *see* HERT
hersle *see* HIRSEL[2]
hert &c, **hart** &c *la14-e17, e19*, **heart** *la16-;*
hairt &c *16-* [hɛrt; *also* hert] *n* **1** = heart
la14-. **2** the stomach *16-, now Sh-Cai Abd.* **3** the
central core of sheaves in a corn-rick *la18-.* **4** *in
pl* (**the**) **Hearts** = H~ *of Midlothian* 2, *20-.*
vt **1** *also* ~ **up** embolden, hearten *la14, 19-, now
Kcb.* **2** strike in the region of the heart so as to
wind or knock out *17-e20, only Sc.* **3** *vti* build
up the inner sheaves of a cart-load or stack of
corn *19-.*
    ~**(e)nin** &c   encouragement;   strengthening
(with food etc) *la18-, now Ork NE Ags.* ~**fully**
&c *freq verse* from the heart, with the whole
heart, heartily, sincerely *la14-e17.* ~**ie** &c *adj* **1**
= hearty, cordial *la15-.* **2** intoxicated, tipsy,
exhilarated by drink *la17-, now Sh Cai, only Sc.*
3 *chf of persons, but also of things* fond of fun and
good company, jovial, cheerful, merry *la18-,*

only Sc: 'let's be hearty wi the blythesome thrang'; 'a hearty fire'. **4** liberal, open-handed *la18-, local.* **5** *esp of guests at a meal* having a good unrestrained appetite, eager for food *19-, now NE Ags.* **6** suffering from a weak heart *20-, local.* **~ily &c** *adv* = heartily *la15-. adj* hearty *16-e17.* **~in(g)** the building up of the inner sheaves; these sheaves themselves *19-.* **~les(s)** **1** disheartened, discouraged, dejected *16-.* **2** cheerless, dismal, discouraging *la17-, now Abd WC Dmf.* **~ly** *adj* **1** from the heart, heartfelt, sincere *la14-e17.* **2** dear to the heart, beloved *16, only Sc. adv* from or with the heart, sincerely, heartily *la14-e17.* **~lynes** sincerity, heartiness *15-e17.* **~some &c** *adj* **1** encouraging, animating; cheering, attractive, pleasant *la16-.* **2** *of a meal* satisfying, substantial, hearty *la18-, now Kcb Dmf.* **3** merry, cheerful, lively *18-, now Sh NE Dmf.* **~somely** cheerfully, heartily *la17-, now Sh, only Sc.* **~someness** cheerfulness *la17-, now Sh.*

~-alane absolutely alone, lonely, desolate *la19-, now Sh Pbls.* **~-cake** *e17,* **~-kake** *20-, Sh* heart-disease. **~'s care** anxiety, deep worry *19-, now Sh Ork.* **~-dry** thoroughly dry *la19-, NE Ags.* **~-fever** a febrile condition; an illness causing a feeling of exhaustion *e17, la19 (Uls).* **~-glad** very glad, delighted *20-, Sh-Cai Ags.* **~-hale** **1** *of the body* organically sound *19-, now local Sh-Dmf.* **2** = heart-whole *la19-, now local NE-Dmf.* **~-heezin &c** encouraging, uplifting, heartwarming *19.* **~-hunger** **1** a ravenous desire for food *19-, NE Ags.* **2** a longing for affection *la19-, Sh Abd Ags.* **~-lazy** exceptionally lazy, naturally indolent *la19-.* **~-likin** affection, love *la19-, now Sh Abd.* **~-peety** deep compassion *20-, Sh Abd.* **~ pipes** translating L *praecordia* the heart, its blood vessels etc *la16-e17, only Sc.* **~-rug** a strain on the emotions *20-, now Sh Ork.* **~-sab** a sob from the heart *20-, now Per Ayr.* **~-sair &c** pain or grief of heart; a great vexation, constant grief *la14-, now local. adj* = heartsore *la17-.* **~ scad &c** *la16-,* **~ scald** *17-e20,* **~ scaud** *20-,* **he(r)skit &c** *20, Sh Ork* ['hɛrt'skɑd, &c; *Sh Ork* 'hɛ(r)skət, 'ha(r)-] *n* **1** heartburn *la16-20.* **2** *fig* a feeling of disgust or repulsion *la18-, now WC Uls.* **3** a source of bitter grief, trouble, disappointment or aversion *17-, now NE Ags Uls.* **~-scalded** vexed, sorely grieved *20-, Uls.* **~-sorry** deeply grieved *la19-.* **~-stoun(d) &c** *lit and fig* a pain at the heart *19-, Gen except Sh Ork.* **~-warm** deeply affectionate, sincerely warm, cordial *la18-, now Sh.* **gae** *or* **gang wi** *or* **tae one's ~** be appetising, palatable, or to one's liking in any respect *19-, NE Ags SW.* **gang against one's ~** be unpalatable, distasteful, disliked *19-, NE Ags SW.* **gar someone's ~ rise** make someone sick *20-, Ags Fif Rox.* **hae one's ~ an one's ee in** be extremely interested in, be eager to possess *la19-, local NE-Arg.* **the ~ o corn** one of

the best, a good fellow *la19-, Gen except Sh Ork.* **H~ of Midlothian** **1** *orig (19)* name for the old TOLBOOTH of Edinburgh (demolished 1817), *now (20-)* the site of this marked by a heart-shaped arrangement of cobbles in the roadway. **2** *only* **Heart-** name of one of the Edinburgh football teams *la19-.* **~ of the yearth** the plant self-heal *la19-20, Rox.* **taste someone's ~** be agreeable to someone's taste, be to someone's liking *20-, N.*

hert *see* HART
hervest *see* HAIRST
hery *see* HERRIE
herȝeauld *see* HERIAL
hes *see* HAE[1]
hes-beene *see* HAS-BEEN
hese *see* HEEZE
hesill *see* HISSEL
heskit *see* HERT
hesp[1]; hasp *18- n* = hasp, a catch or clasp *la15-.*
vt fasten with a hasp, fix *18-, Gen except Sh Ork.* **buckled wi ae hasp** tarred with the same brush, birds of a feather *la19-, now Sh-Cai Kcb.* **~ and staple** *chf law* symbols employed in giving SASINE, the symbols of *infeftment* (INFEFT) used in *entering* (ENTER) an heir to property held in BURGAGE tenure *la15-19.* [*cf* next]
hesp[2]; hasp *la18-19 n* a length of yarn, a HANK[1] (*n* 2) or skein of wool etc of a certain length, the precise amount varying according to district *la16-, now local Sh-WC*; see SND, *esp* Suppl.
a ravelled &c ~ a confused, obscure state of affairs, a difficult situation, a quandary *18-, now Sh-Cai, Ags.* [nME *hasp, hespe,* MDu *haspe,* ON *hespa*; poss orig f as HESP[1], the other Teutonic languages having similar developments of meaning]
hest *see* HEEST
het[1] &c, hete &c *la16-e17,* **hate &c** *la14-, now local,* **hote &c** *16-;* **hot &c** *15-* [hɛt; *Cai* heit; hot; *het; *hit] *adj* **1** = hot *la14-.* **2** warm, comfortable *19-, chf Ayr.* **3** *of peas and oats* quickly growing, early maturing *la18-19, chf Sc.* **4** *of grain or root crops* fermenting, decayed through being stored too damp or in a diseased condition *20-, local N-S.*
adv = hot *la14-.*
hot-furr &c a newly-turned strip of earth, used *esp* for sowing early peas *17-, now Abd Fif.* **~ heart** a heart suffering from bitter disappointment; the disappointment itself *19-, now NE, WC.* **~ pint** a drink made from hot spiced ale to which sugar, eggs and spirits may be added, served at christening, wedding or New Year festivities *18-, only Sc.* **~-skinned** fiery, irascible *la18-, now N nEC, only Sc.* **hot-trod &c** the tracking down and pursuit of BORDER marauders by the aggrieved party; the signal for such pursuit *la18-19, hist.* **~ waters** spirits, alcohol *17, e20.*

~ **beans and butter** children's game resembling hunt-the-thimble *19-20.* **get** *or* **gie (someone) a** ~ **skin** get *or* give (someone) a sound thrashing *19-.* **get** *or* **gie (someone) it** ~ **(an reekin)** be scolded or beaten severely, scold or beat (someone) severely *la18-, now local NE-Uls.* **keep the puddin** ~ keep the pace up, maintain the momentum *la19-, now EC Ayr Rox.* **(ower)** ~ **at** *or* **a- hame** *ironical* applied to someone who appears to have left the comforts of home for no apparent reason *19-, local N-SW.* [long vowel forms derived f OE *hāt* hot; short vowel forms f OSc, ME *het(t)*, ptp of HEAT]

het² [hɛt, hɪt] *pronoun* = it, the person who chases etc in children's games *20-, local.*

het *see* HEAT, HIT, HOOT

hete *see* HEAT, HET

heth *see* HAITH

hether *see* HEATHER

hether- *see* HITHER

hething &c *la14-16,* **heding &c** *la16-e17, only Sc* [*'hiðɪŋ, *'heð-, *'hid-] *n* scorn, derision, mockery.

~**full &c** derisive, scornful *la15-16.* [ME *hething,* ON *hæðing*]

hetrent, hetret *see* HAT(E)RED

hets *see* HOOT

hettel *see* HETTLE

hettir *see* HATTER

hettle &c, hettel *n* name given by fishermen to the rough stony sea-bottom some distance from the shore, beyond the area covered with seaweed *la17-, now Cai.* [perh var of HECKLE¹]

hettret *see* HAT(E)RED

heuch &c; huche *15-16* [hjux; *WC* hjʌx; *Abd also* hjʌx; **høx] *n, pl* ~**(s) &c** *16-,* **hews &c** *15-19* [hjuxs, &c; **hjuz] **1** a precipice, crag or cliff, a steep bank, *esp* one overhanging a river or sea *15-.* **2** a GLEN¹ or ravine with steep, overhanging sides *la15-, Gen except Sh Ork.* **3** a pit, mineshaft, quarry(-face) *15-, now Ayr.*

vt earth up (plants) in drills, trench *20-, Abd midLoth.*

~ **heid &c** the top of a cliff or precipice *16-19.* [freq as place-name *la11-;* nME *hough, hogh* hill, OE *hōh* heel (> HOCH¹) a projecting ridge of land, promontory (> Eng place-name *hoe*)]

heuch *see* HOOCH

heuicking *see* HOO³

heuk &c *la16-,* **huke &c** *la14-e18,* **hook &c** *la17-* [hjuk; *Sh Ork Per Fif WC, SW also* hjʌk; *Ork Bwk Rox also* høk] *n* **1** = hook *la14-.* **2** a reaper *16-19, only Sc.* **3** the barb of an arrow *15-16.* **4** contemptuous term for an old woman *20-, NE.* **5** the proportion of the proceeds from the sale of coal cut by a group of miners allotted to each one *19.*

hooky &c hook-shaped, crooked; *fig* crafty, grasping *19-, now midLoth Rox.*

heuk *see* YEUK

heukbane &c *19-, now local Per-Rox,* **huke-**

bane *e16;* **hook bone &c** *18-e19* ['hjuk'ben, -'bon; *Edb also* 'hjux-; **'høk'ben] *n* = huck bone, the hip-bone. [*laME hokebon,* obscure; early confused w HEUK, and perh also w HOCH¹]

heumble, heumle *see* HUMMLE

heve *see* HAE¹, HEAVE

hevily *see* HEAVY

hevin *see* HAVIN, HEAVEN

hevy *see* HEAVY

hew *see* HOW¹, HUE

hewie *see* HOOIE

hewl *see* HULE

hewmet, hewmond *see* HOOMET

hews *see* HEUCH

Hexham: to ~ *euphemistic* to Hell, to blazes *la19-, S.* [the Northumberland town]

hey¹ &c *17-,* **hay &c** [həi] *n* **1** = hay *la14-.* **2** the hay harvest *la18-, only Sc.*

~**-bog** a piece of marshy ground whose grass was formerly used for winter fodder *19-, now Cai Kcb.* ~**-bogie** a low hay-truck dragged behind a tractor *20-, local midLoth-Rox.* ~**-broo &c** a decoction or infusion of hay *19-, now Cai Abd.* ~**-fog &c** the second growth of grass in a hayfield *19-, now Ags midLoth Rox.* ~**-folk** haymakers *la19-, now midLoth Kcb.* ~**-fow** a hayfork *la19-, now Bnf Kcb Dmf.* ~**-neuk &c** a corner of a BYRE or stable in which hay is stored for immediate consumption *19-, now Sh Dmf Rox.* ~**-sned** a scythe or its shaft *20-, local midLoth-Rox.*

hey² &c [həi] *n* a halfpenny *la19-, Ags.* [diphthongized f Eng *ha'(penny)*]

hey³ *15-,* **hay &c** *la15-17* [həi] *interj* = hey, a call to attract attention etc.

vti exclaim HEY³ in order to announce one's presence or as an expression of high spirits, *eg* when dancing; summon with a shout of HEY³ *la18-.*

like ~**-ma-nanny &c** vigorously, quickly *la19-, Gen except Sh Ork.* **get (one's)** *or* **give** ~**-ma-nanny** get or give a drubbing, (be) scold(ed) or punish(ed) vigorously *20-, now NE, Per Rox.*

hey *see* HEICH

hey- *see* HI

heyime *see* HAME

heyser *see* HEEZE

hezel *see* HISSEL

hi &c [hai] *interj* a call to a horse, with various meanings in different areas, but *chf* a command to turn left, *freq* ~ **here, hey up** etc, *19-, now local.*

vt direct (a horse) to the left by using this call *la19-, now Cai Ags Rox.*

hi- *see* HEICH

Hibernian *see* IBERNIAN

Hibs, Hi-bees [hɪbz, 'hai'biz] nicknames for Hibernian football team *20-.*

hich *see* HEICH, HITCH

hichle *see* HECHLE

hicht *see* HECHT¹, HECHT², HEICH, HEICHT

hichten *see* HEICHEN

hick¹ &c *n* a hiccup, the act of hiccuping *19-*, now *Abd Ags*.
vi **1** hiccup *19-*, now *Abd Ags Fif*. **2** catch the breath and make a hiccuping sound before bursting into tears; sob noisily *19-e20*, *chf S*. [imit; *cf* Du, Da *hik*, Sw *hicka* (*v*)]

hick²; heek &c *vi* **1** delay, hesitate; waver, procrastinate; haggle in bargaining *19-*, now *Dmf Rox*. **2** hesitate in speaking *19-*, now *Abd*. [*cf* Norw dial *hika* delay; grope for a word, Sw dial *hikra* stammer; of same ultimate orig as prec]

hickertie-pickertie *adv* = higgledy-piggledy *19-*, now *midLoth*. [*cf* eModEng *hickletee-pickletee*]

hickery-pickery &c *n* a purgative of bitter aloes with other ingredients *19*. [altered f L (f Gk) *hiera picra* bitter remedy]

hid *see* HAE¹, HIDE¹, HIDE², IT

hidder *see* HITHER

hiddie-giddie &c, hiddy-giddy *adv* **1** in a giddy whirl, dizzily *la15-17*. **2** topsy-turvy, in a confused or giddy state *e19*. [rhyming jingle, prob f HEID + Eng *giddy*; *cf* also HIRDY GIRDY]

hiddie kiddie *n* wit, sense, mental stability *e20*, *Abd*. [appar humorous reduplication f HEID]

hiddil *see* HIDDLE

hiddillis &c; hidlis &c [*'hɪdlz] *n* **in** ~ in hiding, in concealment *la14-e16*. [ME *hidlis &c*, *hidels &c*, OE *hȳdels* (*sing*) f *hȳdan* > HIDE¹; *cf* HIDDLE, HIDLINS]

hiddin *see* HUID

hiddle &c, hiddil &c *n* **1** *chf in pl* hiding places, sheltered spots *15-16*, *la19-*, now *Ags*. **2** hiding, concealment; secrecy, *chf* **in** ~ *la15-e16*.
vti **1** hide, conceal *19-*, now *Sh Ags*. **2** *vi* nestle closely, take shelter *la19-*, *Kcdn Ags*.
hiddlie &c *adj* hidden, sheltered, remote *la19-*, now *Ags*. **hidlin &c** hidden, secret; secretive, furtive *19-*, now *local Ags-Bwk*. **hidlin wise &c** secretly, by stealth *la18-*, now *Dmf*. [ME *hidil*, f *hidels* (HIDDILLIS) taken to be pl; later meanings show infl of Eng *huddle*; *cf* HIDDILLIS, HIDLINS]

hiddle *see* HEDDLE

hiddlins *see* HIDLINS

hiddy-giddy *see* HIDDIE-GIDDIE

hide¹ &c *15-*; **hid &c** *la14-e18*, **hod &c** *la18-*, now *Abd Kcdn Ags*, **hoid &c** *la19-*, *Sh*, **howd &c** *19-*, *Fif* [həid; *Abd Kcdn Ags* hod; *Fif* hʌud].
pt **hid &c** *la15-*, **hade &c** *la18-19* (*S*), *la20-* (*Mry Abd Rox*), **hed** *e20*, *local*, **hod**(**e**) *20*, *Abd Kcdn Ags*; **hidit** *20*, *local N*, **hoddit &c** *20*, *local*.
ptp **hid &c, hide** *15-16*, **hod** *la19-*, *Ags*, **hidden &c** *la16-*, **hodd**(**e**)**n &c** *la19-e20*, **hu**(**i**)**d**(**en**) *16*; **hidit &c** *20*, *NE*, **hoddit &c** *20-*, now *Ags* [*ptp* hɪd, 'hɪd(ə)n, 'hod(ə)n; *Ags* hod; *Abd* also hod; *NE* 'həidɪt, *Ags* 'hodɪt] = hide, conceal *la14-*.
hidie &c *19-*, **hoddy &c** *la19-*, *Ags*, *only Sc adj* carefully concealed; very suitable for hiding anything or anyone in *20-*, *local NE-Rox*. *n* the

game of hide-and-seek; the call given by a player in this game to indicate that he is ready to be sought for *19-*, now *Per*. **hidie-hole &c** a hiding place *19-*. ~**in**(**g**) *n*, *freq in pl* ~**in**(**g**)**s** *19*, ~**ance** *la19* concealing, concealment, secrecy; hiding-places *15-e20*.

hide² &c, hid &c *la14-e17* [həid; *?*hɪd] *n* **1** (1) = hide, the skin of an animal; now *joc or contemptuous* human skin *la14-*. (2) *alliterative with* **hair** *and* **hew** *la14-20*. **2** *pejorative* a female domestic animal; a woman; *rare* a man *19*.
~ **bind** a disease of horses and cattle which causes the hide to cling to the bone *19-*, now *Ork midLoth* [cf obs Eng *hidebound*].

hidit *see* HIDE¹

hidlin *see* HIDDLE

hidlins &c, hidlingis &c *16*; **hiddlins &c** *la18-* *adv* secretly, stealthily, in secret *la15-*, now *Ags sEC Rox*.
n pl **1** hiding places, places of concealment or refuge *la16-*, now *local Ags-Arg*. **2** concealment, secrecy *19-*, now *Dmf*.
adj secret, clandestine, underhand *19-*, now *local sEC-Rox*.
in ~ in secret, clandestinely *la16-*, now *sEC Arg Kcb*. [*hid*, *ppl adj* of HIDE¹ + *adv* suffix -*lin*(*g*)*s*; see also *hidlin* (HIDDLE)]

hidlis *see* HIDDILLIS

hidowis &c *la15-e16*; **hidwis &c** *la14-e16*, *only Sc* [*'hɪd(u)wɪs, &c*] *adj* = hideous.

hie &c, hy &c [haɪ] *n*, *verse* haste, speed, *chf* **in** *etc* ~ in haste, speedily, **in, with** *etc* (**full**) **gret** *or* **all** ~ *la14-15*.
v, *chf verse* hasten, proceed quickly **1** *vr*, *la14-16*; **2** *vi*, *la15-e20*. [ME]

hie *see* HE, HEICH

hieland &c *15-*, **heland &c** *15-17*, **heichland &c** *la16-17*; **highland &c** *la17-*, **hilland &c** *la16-17*, **heelan &c** *la17-* ['hilən(d); *sEC, S* 'hilənt; *St* 'haɪlənd, 'həilənd; *** 'hixlənd] *n* **1** = highland, high ground *15-*. **2** *specif* **the** ~ *16-e17*, **the** ~**s** *16-*, *and now usu* **H**~(**s**) the mountainous district of Scotland lying north and west of the *Highland line*, the territory formerly occupied by the CLANS, where the GAELIC language was spoken; *cf* LAWLAND. **3** *elliptical* **the H**~ = *H*~ *Show*, *la19-*.
adj, *chf* **H**~ of, belonging to, or characteristic of the *Highlands* of Scotland or their people **1** *in gen*, *16-*. **2** *of clothes*, *freq as* **H**~ **dress** (*la18-*) referring to the TARTAN outfit worn by *Highlanders* and others, *ie* the KILT¹ or TREWS and PLAID, and all or any of the accessories, *eg* bonnet, belt, *dirk* (DURK¹), SPORRAN and hose *16-*. **3** *of sports, dancing etc, orig* native to the HIGHLANDS (*n 2*) *la16-*. **4** *of the language of the Highlands* (*n 2*): GAELIC, in GAELIC, GAELIC-speaking *la17-*. **5** referring to the mental or moral qualities or traits of character supposed to be typical of *Highlanders*, *freq pejorative* owing to the suspicion and dislike of them once prevalent in the *Lowlands* (LAWLAND): (1) warmly hospitable

la18-, now local; (2) having an exaggerated sense of birth and lineage, *esp* ~ **pride** *la18-*; (3) uncouth, unskilled, inelegant, rough-and-ready; *freq in negative, eg* **no sae** ~ not too bad(ly) *19-*; (4) not quite truthful or honest, shifty, evasive *19-, now NE*; (5) naive, gullible, unrealistic, impractical, 'green', *esp in negative* **no sae** ~ *la19-*. **6** of breeds of animals native to the *Highlands* (*n* 2) *eg* the long-horned, shaggy-haired cattle, and various breeds of horses and dogs *16-*.

~er, *chf* **H~er 1** a native or inhabitant of the *Highlands* (*n* 2) *17-*. **2** a soldier in one of the *Highland regiments, 18-*. **3** one of the *Highland* breed of cattle (*adj* 6) *la18-*.

Highland dance a dance, based on traditional *Highland* figures, performed as spectacle, *freq* solo (*eg Highland fling*, SHANTREWS, *sword dance* (SWURD)) *19-*; see also *Highland Reel, Reel of Tulloch* (REEL[1]), *strathspey* (STRATH). **H~ Donald** nickname for a *Highlander* 1, *la18-, now Cai Abd*. **Highland fling** a solo *Highland dance, 19-*. **Highland Games** *see* GAME *n* 2. **Highland Gathering** *see gathering* 4 (GAITHER). **H~ honours** the ceremonial drinking of a toast, involving all the company standing with one foot on their chairs and one on the table *19-e20*. **Highland Light Infantry** a Scottish regiment, raised in 1777 and so called from 1807, mainly recruited in Glasgow and its neighbourhood; *usu* referred to as **the H.L.I.**; in 1881, linked with the 74th *Highland regiment*; in 1959, merged with the *Royal Scots Fusiliers* (ROYAL) to form the *Royal Highland Fusiliers* (ROYAL) *19-20; cf Glasgow Highlanders* (GLESCA). **Highland line** name for the imaginary boundary between the *Highlands* (*n* 2) and *Lowlands* (LAWLAND) of Scotland, a line drawn approx from Dumbarton to Ballater and thence to Nairn *19-*. **H~man** = ~*er* 1, *15-*. **H~man's garters** ribbon grass *20-, now Sh Abd*. **H~ pony** one of a breed of ponies originating in the *Highlands* (*n* 2) *19-*. ~ **pyot &c** the missel thrush *la19-, NE*. **Highland reel** a REEL[1] as performed in the *Highlands*; a tune for such; *latterly specif* a *Highland dance* performed by two persons, *freq* following the *strathspey* (STRATH) *la18-*. **H~ regiment** one of the regiments in the British Army *orig* raised in and recruited from the *Highlands* (*n* 2), whose members are entitled to wear *Highland dress* (see *adj* 2), *18-*. **Highland (Region)** a REGION formed from the former counties of Caithness, Sutherland and Nairn, and parts of the former counties of Ross and Cromarty, Inverness, Moray and Argyll *la20-*. **H~ sheltie** = ~ *pony, la18-, now local*. **H~ Show, Royal H~ Show** (*20-*) a large agricultural show held annually by *The Royal Highland and Agricultural Society, orig* in different centres year by year, but since 1960 at a permanent site at Ingliston, midLoth *19-*.

the Highlands and Islands the *Highlands* (*n*

2) and the *Western Isles* (ILE) *20-*. **The Highland Society of Edinburgh** *la18*, **The Highland Society of Scotland at Edinburgh** *la18-e19*, **The Highland and Agricultural Society of Scotland** *19-20*, **The Royal Highland and Agricultural Society of Scotland** *20-* a society formed *orig* to inquire into the state of the *Highlands and Islands* of Scotland and the condition of their inhabitants, and into the means of improving the area and preserving its GAELIC culture; *latterly* (*19-*) dealing with the whole of Scotland, but almost exclusively with reference to agriculture. [HEICH + LAND[1]]

hiely *see* HEELIE
hiffer *see* HEIFER
high *see* HEICH
highen *see* HEICHEN
Higher *see* HEICH
highland *see* HIELAND
high-year *see* HALF[1]
Hi Hi ['haɪ 'haɪ] nickname for Third Lanark football team *la19-20*. [obscure; perh f a supporters' chant; *cf* WARRIORS]
hilch &c; hilsh &c *19-* [hɪl(t)ʃ] *v* **1** limp, hobble, move with a rolling, lurching gait *la18-, local Cai-SW*. **2** ~ **up** move with a jerk; hitch up (a load on one's back) *20-, Cai Kcb*.
n a limp, the act of walking with a limp; an uneven gait *19-, Cai Dmf Uls*. [palatalized var of HILT[3]]
hild *see* HAUD
hildegaleerie *see* HEELIEGOLEERIE
hill[1] &c; hell *e16*, **hull** *18-, now NE, WC* [hɪl; NE, WC also hʌl] *n* **1** (1) a hill, a (low) mountain *la14-*. (2) an (artificial) mound *16-*. **2** (1) a common moor where rough grazing rights are shared by the community *16-, now local, only Sc*. (2) any piece of rough grazing on a farm *la19-, Gen except Sh Ork, only Sc*. **3** (1) a piece of rough moorland where PEATS[1] are cut, a *peat moss* (PEAT[1]) *la17-, now local Sh-Abd, only Sc*. (2) a *peat-stack, 20-, now Cai Abd, only Sc*. **4** *mining* (see also *coal hill* (COAL)) (1) the dump of hewn coal at the pithead *16-17, only Sc*. (2) the pithead, the surface *18-, now Fif, only Sc*.
hillan a mound, heap, hillock, *esp* a molehill *la18-, now Edb, only Sc*. ~**er** a little hill, a heap, a small mound *20-, Cai, only Sc*. ~**ock &c 1** = hillock *la15-*. **2** *fig* a fat sluggish person *20-, Sh N Dmf, only Sc*. **3** a large quantity *la20-, Cai NE Ags, only Sc*.
~ **berry** the crowberry *19-, now Cai, only Sc*. ~ **cart** *mining* a small low cart *20-, now Fif*. ~-**clap** a rumbling noise in the upper air over hills, said to be caused by an air current *20-, chf Sh, only Sc*. ~ **clerk** *mining* the person who weighs the mineral dispatched *la19-, now Fif*. ~ **dyke** the wall dividing *n* 2 (1) from the lower arable land *la17-, now Sh Ork Dmf, only Sc*. ~**fit &c** *freq in pl* **1** the ground at the foot of a hill; foothills *16-19*. **2** *specif, chf in pl* the foothills of the Ochils *la18-, Stlg Fif Kinr Clcm*. ~

folk &c 1 the inhabitants of a hilly region, people who live among the hills *la19-e20*. **2** name given *orig* to the *Covenanters* (COVENANT) of *c.* 1670-1688 who worshipped secretly in the hills because of persecution, and later to their successors, the *Reformed Presbyterian Church* (REFORM) *19, hist.* ~**-head &c** the summit of a hill *la15-*, now *Sh NE Ayr, freq as farm name.* ~ **lintie** the twite *la19-*, now *Cai Ags, only Sc.* ~ **man 1** *mining* a man who worked at the pithead; a colliery official *la17-e20.* **2** one of the ~ *folk 2, la17-e20, latterly hist.* ~**-run** *adj* **1** *esp of wild moorland* hilly, upland *la19-*, *Cai Inv NE, only Sc.* **2** *fig of persons* uncultured, rough, boorish *20-*, *NE Ags Fif, only Sc.* ~ **woman** *mining* a female worker at the pithead *la19-*, now *Fif.*

gather the ~ gather together flocks pastured on a hillside *20-*, *local, only Sc.* **oot o** ~ **an heap** from whatever lies to hand, from odds and ends, by one's own resourcefulness or imagination *19.* **to the** ~ in an upward direction *19-*, now *Abd Kcb.*

hill[2] **&c** [hɪl, hʌl] *vi,* ~ **on, up** *etc* go at a fair pace, hurry *20-*, *NE.* [obscure]

hilland *see* HIELAND

hilliegeleerie *see* HEELIEGOLEERIE

hilsh *see* HILCH

hilt[1] **&c** *n* **1** = hilt, the handle of a sword etc *la14-.* **2** a plough-handle *la20-,Cai Abd Kcb-Rox, only Sc.*

hilt[2] [hɪlt, hʌlt] *n* **ilka** ~ **an(d) hair** every particle *18-*, now *Kcb Dmf.* **(neither)** ~ **(n)or hair** nothing at all, not a vestige *19-*. [perh ultimately f OE *hyldan* flay, skin; *cf* Eng *hide nor hair*]

hilt[3] *vi* walk with a limp *la18-19.* [var of Eng *halt*]

hilter-skilter *19-*, now *Ork Bnf Ags*; **helter-skelter** *18-*, **hilty-skilty &c** *la18-e20 adv* = helter-skelter, in rapid succession, confusedly *la18-.*

adj, only **hilty skilty** harum-scarum, heedless *19-e20, only Sc.*

drink helter-skelter drink heavily, while also mixing one's drinks *18-19, only Sc.*

himberry *see* HINDBERRY

hime &c [həim] *n* = hymn *20-*, *local Sh-WC, only Sc.*

himsel &c *la15-*, **himself** [hɪm'sɛl, (h)əm-, (ə)m-, -'sɛlf] *pronoun* **1** = himself *la14-.* **2** name for the head or chief male person in any body or institution, *eg* the CHIEF of a CLAN, the man in a household (*cf* HE 2), a male boss *la19-*; *cf* HERSEL 3.

hin *see* HINT[1]

hinch *see* HAINCH

hinc inde ['hɪŋk 'ɪnde, 'ɪndi] *law, chf of claims or contracts* reciprocally, on the one side and on the other *18-*. [L = on this side, on that side]

hind &c *la16-*, **hyne &c** *la15-e20* [həin(d)] *n* **1** a farm-servant, now a ploughman *la15-*, now *local*

midLoth-Rox. **2** *specif* a married skilled farm-worker who occupies a farm-cottage, and has certain perquisites in addition to wages, a *cottar* (COT) *la17-*, *chf S.* **3** *latterly only attrib and in ballads* (*la18-19*) a youth, a stripling *la14-e19.*

~**ing** *n* the work of or a situation as a HIND *n* **1** and **2** *la19-*, *midLoth Bwk Rox.* **hinds' raw** a row of cottages occupied by farm-workers *20-*, *midLoth Bwk Rox.* [eModEng *hind*, ME *hyne*; OE *hīne* (*pl*) members of a household, domestics]

hind *see* HINT[1], HYNE

hindberry &c *19-20*; **himberry &c** *la19-*, now *Lnk* ['həin(d)bɛrɪ, 'həim-] *n* the wild raspberry. [OE *hindberie*, f *hind* the female deer + *berry*; *cf* Ger *Himbeere*]

hinder[1] **&c** *la15-*, **hender &c** *la14-e17*; **hinner** *19-*, now *N, WC* ['hɪn(d)ər, *[*'hɛndər] *adj* **1** *of time* last, (recently) past *la14-*, now *Ayr, only Sc.* **2** *of place* = hinder, coming from or situated behind, in the rear etc *la15-.*

n, chf in pl the buttocks; the hindquarters of an animal *la19-*, now *Sh.*

~**lan(d)s** *19-e20* [so printed in editions of Scott's *Rob Roy*, and imitated by later writers, but MS reads *hinderlins*], ~**lets** *la18-e20*, ~**lins &c** *19* buttocks. ~**maist &c** *19-*, ~**most** *la16* ['hɪn(d)ərməst] *adj* final, last *19-.*

this *or* **the** ~**night &c** *chf verse* last night, the previous night *16-e19.*

hinder[2] **&c** *la15-*, **hender &c** *15-e20*; **hin(n)er** *19-e20* ['hɪn(d)ər; *[*'hɛndər] *vti* **1** (1) = hinder, detain, prevent, delay *15-.* (2) *freq with infin or verbal noun* = Eng 'from' *or* 'in' + *verbal noun, 18-*: '*what's to hinder us doing the same?*' **2** *vi* linger, dawdle *20-*, *Sh NE Ags.* **3** *vt* waste (time) *20-*, *Sh NE Ags.*

n a hindrance, obstruction, cause of delay, *orig* also damage *16-*, now *Sh Ork NE, EC.*

hinnerance = hindrance *la19-*, now *Cai NE.* ~**ment** hindrance, delay *la19-*, now *Sh Abd.* ~**some &c** *esp of weather* (*19-*) obstructive, troublesome, detrimental *la16-*, now *local Sh-Ayr.*

hinderend &c *la15-*, **hender end** *la15-e20*; **hinneren(d) &c** *19-* ['hɪn(d)ər'ɛn(d); *Uls* 'hɪntər-; *Abd Kcdn* -'əin; *[*'hɛndər-] *n* **1** the later or final part, the back or rear portion of anything, the extremity *la15-.* **2** the end, *esp of life or time* the concluding portion; death *16-.* **3** *of persons* the behind, the backside *19-.* **4** the remains of anything, leavings, refuse; the worst of anything *19-*, now *NE, EC Rox.* **the hinderend &c o a'** the last straw *la18-*, *chf NE.* **at** *or* **in the hinderend &c** in the long run, finally; on the Day of Judgment *la15, 18-.* **lauch one's hinderend** die laughing *19-*, *chf NE.*

you'll no ~ **me** *etc* **to do .. ** *emphatic* nothing could (have) prevent(ed) me etc from doing *19-*, *Gen except S.*

hindie(s) *see* HYNE

hindmaist &c *la15-*, **hindmest &c** *16*, **hinmest &c** *16-19*, **henmast &c** *la14-16*;

hinmaist &c *16*-, **hinmost** *16-e19*, **hind-most** *la17*-, **hint-** *la19*-, **henmest** *16-17* ['hɪnməst, 'hɪnd-, 'hɪnt-; *Sh* 'hɪd-, *Ags* 'hɛn-; *Fif* 'hɛməst; *Fif wLoth* 'hɪməst; *Bwk* 'hɪnmest] *adj* **1** last in position, furthest behind, in the rear *la14*-. **2** last, final (in order, time etc) *la15*-. *adv* finally, last, in the last place *la15*-, *now Sh NE, Kcb*. *n, chf* **hin(d)most** the last, the farthest back; *of time* the close, the end *19-e20*. [see SND]

hine &c *la18*-, **hane &c** *e16, Wgt*; **hain** *19*-, *now Ags* [hain; *Ags also* 'he(ə)n] *n* a haven, a (natural) harbour *e16, 19*-, *now Ags Fif, also in place-names*. [reduced f *haven* (HAVIN)]

hiner *see* HINDER[2]

hiney *see* HINNIE

hing &c, hang &c (*orig chf of judicial hanging*), **heng** *16-17*; **heing** *la16-e17* [hɪŋ; haŋ] *vti, pt* ~**it &c**; **hang** *16*-, *now Sh NE*, **hung** *16*-. *ptp* ~**it &c**; **hung &c** *la15*-; **hungin &c** *15-16*, **hingin** *la16* **1** *vti* = hang *la14*-. **2** *freq* ~ **to** attach, append (one's seal to a document), *chf in ptp* (**to**) ~**in** *15-16*. **3** *vti, chf in passive* have the notice of one's intention to marry displayed on a registrar's notice board, instead of having the banns read in church *20*-, *now EC, S.* **4** *vi* lean (out of a window) in order to watch events in the street below *la19*-, *Gen except Sh Ork S.* '*hingan owre the windae wi my elbaes in my hands*'. **5** delay, hover indecisively; shirk *la19*-, *now Ags Fif Arg.* **6** be in a poor state of health *la19*-, *local NE-SW.* *n* **1** (1) = hang *la19*-. (2) the act of leaning out of a window for amusement as in *v* 4, *20*-, *EC, WC Gall.* **2** *fig* a period of idleness or leisure *la19*-, *now midLoth.*

hinger &c 1 a device by which something is hung *16*-. **2** *chf in pl* hanging drapery, curtains, a tapestry *16*-, *now Abd Bwk.* **hinger-in** a person who perseveres, a conscientious, hardworking person *20*-. **hangie** *familiar* the hangman *18-19, only Sc.* ~**ing &c** *n* = hanging *16*-. *adj* **1** = hanging *la15*-. **2** *of coal* lying at a steep angle; undercut and ready to fall *la17*-. **3** *of a golf ball or its position* lying on a downward slope *la19*-. **4** *of sky etc* overcast, threatening rain *20*-, *Abd-Rox.* **hanging burn** a sheep-mark branded on the lower part of the cheek or chin *la19*-, *now Bwk Rox.* ~**ing chimney &c** = ~**ing lum**, *la18-e19.* ~**ing gate** a bar or grating hung across a stream *19*-, *now midLoth Bwk Rox.* **hingen-heedit** abashed *la19*-, *Cai NE.* ~**in-like** ill-looking *la20*-, *local Cai-Rox.* ~**ing &c lock** a padlock *la15*-. ~**ing-luggit** dejected, crestfallen, abashed *20*-. ~**ing lum &c** a wide wooden chimney, projecting from the wall, which descended from the roof above an open fire *la17-20.* **hinging mince** a non-existent thing, an absurdity for which persons are sent on fool's errands *la20*-, *NE Ags Fif.*

~**ing-mou'd &c** dejected, sulky *la19*-, *NE.* ~**ing post** one of the wooden posts supporting a roof *18*-, *now Per.* **hanging scaffold** *mining* a movable platform in a shaft *la19*-, *now Fif.* ~**ing stair** steps built into a wall at one end, and cantilevered *la18*-, *now Fif.* **hangit** judicially hanged *16*-. **hangit-faced** looking ripe for the gallows, villainous *19-e20.* **hangit-like** *or* -**looking** shamefaced, having an air of constraint or reluctance *19-e20.* **hingum-tringum &c** ['hɪŋəm-'trɪŋəm] worthless and somewhat disreputable; barely presentable *la19-e20, Bnf.* **ill-hung-tee** *or* -**thegither** *of persons etc* awkwardly knit, clumsily built; dressed without care or taste *la19*-, *local Sh-Kcb.* ~**man 1** *chf* **hangman** = hangman *la15*-. **2** *only* **hangman** a cheese made by hanging the curds up to dry in a cloth exposed to the sun instead of putting them in a press *20*-, *Abd, only Sc.* ~ **net** a vertical stake-net *19*-, *now Suth Bwk Kcb.* ~ **the cat** *or* **cleek** work slowly or to rule; lounge about, hold things up *la20*-, *Fif Ags.* ~ **by one's ain head** be independent and self-supporting, be self-reliant *18*-. ~ **in 1** carry out a task with energy, get on with a job, persevere; hurry *la19*-, *local Sh-Kcb;* cf ~**er-in.** **2** pay court assiduously, persist in courting someone; curry favour *20*-, *chf Abd.* ~ **one's** *or* **the lugs** look dejected or abashed *la17*-. ~ **on** *vi* linger expectantly, wait *18*-. *vt* delay or hinder (someone) in doing something, keep (someone) waiting *20*-, *NE, Ags.* **hing-on** *n* (a source or period of) delay, tedium or weariness; an encumbrance, hindrance *20*-, *Gen except Sh Ork.* ~ **on a** (**lang**) **face** look glum or doleful *la19*-, *now Sh Ork Ags.* ~ **the pettit lip** sulk, have an injured and offended expression *20*-. ~ **tae &c** *vi* join in, adhere, attach oneself *lit* (to something) *or fig* (to some person or cause), fall in with another's plans *19*-, *now Cai NE, midLoth.* *n* **hing-tee** a mistress, girlfriend *la20*-, *N.* ~-**the-gither** clannish *19*-, *local N-S.* ~ **up** *of weather* keep dry *20*-, *Arg Ayr.* **on the** ~ in the balance *la20*-, *Per midLoth SW.*

hingle *see* HAINGLE

hingum-tringum *see* HING

hink *see* HENK

hinkie-pinkie *see* INKIE-PINKIE

hinkum &c: ~ **sneev(l)ie** a silly stupid person; an underhand person, a tell-tale *19*-, *Abd.* [see SND]

hinmaist, hinmest, hinmost *see* HINDMAIST

hinna(e) *see* HAE[1]

hinner *see* HINDER[1], HINDER[2]

hinneren(d) *see* HINDER[2]

Hinnerson *see* HENDERSON

hinnie &c *la16*-, **huny &c** *15-e18*; **honey &c, hiney &c** *la18-19* ['hɪnɪ, 'hʌnɪ] *n* **1** = honey *la14*-. **2** term of endearment *la15*-, *Gen except N.* *adj, lit and fig* sweet as honey *la18-e20.*

~-**blob** &c **1** a drop of honey; *fig* term of endearment *e19*. **2** a big yellow variety of gooseberry *18-e20*. **hunygukkis** term of endearment *e16*. ~-**pear** a sweet pear *18-*, *now Edb SW Rox*. ~-**pig** an earthenware container for drained honey *19-*, *now Abd*. ~-**pots** a children's game *19-20* [see SND]. **hinniesickle** &c *n* = honeysuckle *la18-*, *now Ags Ayr*.

nothing but *or* a' ~ **and jo**(e) *of a person's behaviour* all affability, all smiles *la17-*, *now Ags midLoth*.

hint[1] *la18-*, **hind** &c; **hin** *19-*, *now N, WC, SW*, **hent** *20-*, *local* [hɪnt, hɪn] *adj* **1** belonging to or at the back, rear *e16, 19-*. **2** later in time *16*.

n **1** the back, rear; *now chf of time* the end; the period immediately following *19-*, *now local Abd-Dmf*. **2** *ploughing* the furrow left between two RIGS[1], the *mould furrow* (MUILD[1]) *la19-*, *WC Dmf Uls*.

adv behind, in the rear *e19*.
prep behind *la18-*, *now Ags*.

hintin(**g**) the *mould furrow* (MUILD[1]) *la18-*, *now local Stlg-Rox*.

~**backs** *adj* surreptitious, behind the back *la18, la20-* (*Sh Ork*). **hin-door** the removable backboard of a box-cart *la19-*, *Gen except Sh Ork*.

~-**end** the extremity or rear part; the latter portion (of a period of time); the hindquarters, posterior *la19-*. ~-**hairst** &c the period of the year after harvest and before winter *18-*, *now Ags*. ~-**han**(**d**) *adj* also *n*, *esp curling* (CURL), *of the last stone played in a rink, or the player(s) of such a stone* (the) last, hindmost *19-*. **2** *fig* dilatory, careless, late *la19-*. **hindhead** &c the back of the head *la16-17*. ~-**side** the rear *20-*, *local Ags-Uls*. **hint-side** foremost back to front, backwards *20-*, *Ork Kcdn Ags Dmf*.

~ **the han** stored for future use *la19-*, *now Bnf*.

hint[2] *n* a moment, instant *la18-*, *now Sh*. [Eng *hint* an opportunity; a suggestion or implication]

hint[3]: **neither** ~ **nor hair** nothing at all, not a vestige *la19-*, *NE Ags*. [altered f HILT[2] with substitution of Eng *hint* a slight indication]

hint[4] *v*, *chf* ~ **aboot**, **aifter** *or* **roun** go about in a sly or furtive way in order to further one's own interests, slink about; watch quietly *19*, *Bnf*. [see SND]

hint *see* HENT

hint- *see* HINDMAIST

hip[1] &c *n* **1** = hip, the part of the body *16-*. **2** a projecting piece of land; a curving projection on the lower slopes of a hillside *la15, 19-*, *now Kcb*.

hippin &c **1** a baby's napkin *18-*. **2** *joc* the curtain of a penny theatre *19-20*. **hippit** &c **1** = hipped *16-*. **2** *esp of workers in the harvest-field* having a feeling of stiffness or overstrain in the lower back, hips, or thighs *19-*, *only Sc*. **hipsie-dipsie** &c *n* a thorough thrashing, *chf* **gie** (**somebody**) ~ *19*.

~-**grippit** = *hippit* 2, *20-*, *Cai Abd Kcb*. ~ **locks** &c the coarse wool which grows on the hips of sheep *la17-*, *now Ork Cai SW*.

hip[2] *v* **1** *vt* miss, skip, pass over, omit to take into account *la15-*, *now Sh Fif midLoth*. **2** *vi* hop, skip *19-*, *now Rox*.

n the act of hopping, a hop *20-*, *chf Rox*.

hippertie-skippertie &c *adj* light, frivolous, frisky *19-*, *now Kcdn*. **hippity** *adv*, *chf in comb* with a limp, lamely *la19-*, *local*. *adj* lame, crippled, limping *la19-*, *now Ags Kcb*. [ME *hippen* hop; *cf* HAP[2]]

hipothecar &c; **hipoticar**(**y**) &c [*hɪˈpɒtɪkər, *-ˈpɒθ-, &c] *n* an apothecary *la16-e17*. [only Sc; var of APOTHICAR, by confusion w laL *hypothēcārius*, OF *hypothecaire* (*adj*) of a mortgage > eModEng *hypothecary*]

hippans &c *n pl* = hips, the fruit of the wild rose *19-*, *NE*. [Eng *hip* with Gael dim *-an*]

hipple &c *vi* go lame, walk with a limp, hobble *19-*, *now Bnf*. [frequentative or dim of HIP[2]; *cf* HIRPLE and see HYPAL]

hipsie-dipsie *see* HIP[1]

hir &c; **her** *18-* [*unstressed* (h)ər; *stressed* hɪr, hër, hʌr] *possessive adj* **1** = her *la14-*. **2** *pseudo-Highl* my, his, *chf* ~ **nainsel** &c *la17-*.

hirris &c *possessive pronoun* = hers *15-e17*. [*cf* SHE]

hir *see* SHE

hird &c *n* = herd, a flock *15-16*.

hird *see* HERD

hirdum-dirdum *n* uproar, noisy mirth or revelry *18-*, *now Fif*.
adv topsy-turvy *19-*, *Rox*. [reduplicated f DIRDUM]

hirdy-girdy *n* uproar, confusion, disorder *la15-*, *now Ags Fif*.
adv in disorder or confusion, topsy-turvy *la16-*, *now Ags Rox*. [intensive var of HIDDIE-GIDDIE; also *cf* prec]

hire, hyre &c *v* **1** *vt* = hire *15-*. **2** *vi* engage oneself as an employee, take service *la17-*, *Gen except NE*. **3** *vt* let out on hire *la16-*. **4** season (food), make it more palatable by the addition of rich ingredients, *chf* ~**d** &c *19-*, *now NE*.

n **1** = hire *15-*. **2** *specif* a seaman's pay for a voyage *15-e17*, *only Sc*. **3** a titbit, something tasty given as an inducement; a reward *in gen*, *19-*, *now midLoth*.

hirer 1 = hirer, one who hires (a person etc) *17-*. **2** a person who lets out something (*esp* vehicles) on hire *18-*. **3** a farm-servant; *specif* (*20-*) one engaged by the day, or for a short period *la19-*, *chf Cai*. **hiring 1** = hiring *17-*. **2** *also* **hiring fair, hiring market** *etc* a fair or market held for the purpose of engaging farm-workers *19-*, *now Bwk Rox*.

~**gang** *n* hire, lease of farm animals, utensils or land, *chf* **in** ~**gang** *16-e17*. ~ **house** a farm BOTHY; farm labour or service *la19-e20*, *chf NE*. ~-**man** a hired servant, *chf* a farmworker *la15-e19*. ~-**woman** a female servant *la16-19*.

as they were hyrit &c (run etc) willingly, eagerly, speedily *16-e19* [SND *heyrt*].

hiree *see* HURROO

hirki(e) *see* HARKY

hirling *see* HERLING

hirne &c *n, usu in pl* corners, nooks, hiding-places *15-17*. [ME, OE *hyrne*]

hirple, hirpil &c *vi* walk lamely, limp, hobble; move unevenly *la15-*.
n a limp, the act of walking unsteadily or with a limp *la18-*. [see SND; *cf* HIPPLE]

hirr &c *interj, n* a call to a dog to attack or pursue *19-*, *now Sh Cai*.

hirrie-harrie, hiry-hary &c [*'hırı'harı, &c*] *interj, n* an outcry after a thief etc, expressing rapid, tumultuous movement *e16, e19, only Sc*. [prob *orig* a cry of alarm or excitement; *cf* HARRO]

hirsally *see* HIRST

hirschle *see* HIRSEL²

hirris *see* HIR

hirsel¹ &c, hirsell ['hırsl] *n* **1** *also fig* a herd or flock, *chf and now only* a flock of sheep, the number of sheep looked after by one shepherd or on one small farm *la14-*, *now NE, S*. **2** an area of pasturage to be grazed by a flock of sheep under the care of one shepherd *19-*, *now C, S*. **3** a flock, a large number or quantity, a crowd *la18-*, *now Ags*.
vt arrange in HIRSELS (*n* 1-3); *in gen* classify, arrange in order *16-*, *now Rox*. [ME *hirsill*, ON *hirzla*, *hirðsla* safe-keeping, f *hirða* tend sheep]

hirsel² &c *la18-*, **hirsill** *e16*, **hersle** *la17, e20*; **hurs(ch)le &c** *19-e20*, **hirschle &c** *la19* ['hırsl, 'hʌrsl; *NE also* 'hırʃl, 'hʌrʃl] *v* **1** *vi* graze **against** or grate **on** (something) *16-17*. **2** move with a rustling or grating noise, *chf* **hirs(ch)lin &c** grating, rustling *19-*, *now Abd*. **3** move or slide along a surface awkwardly or without getting up, slither *18-*, *now local Sh-Ags, only Sc*. **4** *vtr* move or shift awkwardly or with difficulty; cause to slide or slip along or down; shuffle *18-e20*. **5** *vt* shrug (the shoulders) *la19-e20*, *only Sc*. **6** *vi* make haste, scramble, bustle *19-*, *now Ags Per, only Sc*. **7** wheeze, breathe noisily *20-*, *only Sc*.
n, only Sc **1** the act of moving the body sideways in a sitting position, a slithering, hitching motion *19-*. **2** the sliding, slithering or shuffling motion of something slipping or being shifted with difficulty; the noise or result of such motion, a confused fall *la19-*, *now Abd*. **3** a wheeze or catarrhal sound in the chest *la19-*. **4** an iron pin or auger used when red-hot for boring holes *19-e20*.
~ **aff** (**the stage**) *fig* die peacefully, slip away *la18-19*. ~ **yont** move further up or along (*eg* a bench) to make room for others, move over or away *19-*, *now Abd Ags Kcb*. [onomat]

hirself, hirselvyn *see* HERSEL

hirsill *see* HIRSEL²

hirst &c *n* **1** a barren, unproductive piece of

ground, *usu* a hillock, knoll, or ridge *15-e20*. **2** a bank of sand or shingle in a harbour, river etc; a ford *la16-e19*. **3** *also* **hist** a great number (**of** people), a great quantity (**of** things), a heap or accumulation (**of** objects) *la19-*, *NE*. **4** a threshold, door-sill *e16, e19* (*literary*), *only Sc*. **5** the frame of a pair of millstones, the part of the mill where the stones revolve in their framework *e20*.

hirstie &c, histie &c *la18-*, *local*, **hirs(al)ly** *la19-*, *of soil* dry and stony, barren *18-*, *now Per Fif midLoth*. [see DOST *hirst* (*n¹, n², n³*), OED *hurst*]

hirtch &c *vi* **1** move jerkily, edge forward *la19-e20*, *NE*. **2** approach in a sly ingratiating way, sidle *la19-*, *now Kcdn Ags*.
n a slight sideways push or jerky motion, a hitch; a shrug of the shoulders *la19-*, *now Ags*. [obscure; *cf* OSc *hurche* (*v*) (once) crouch (*e17*)]

hiry-hary *see* HIRRIE-HARRIE

his &c; *unstressed also* **'s** *18-* [(h)ız; *EC Arg also* hiz; *unstressed also* z] *possessive pronoun (adj)* **1** = his *la14-*. **2** = its *la15-*, *now Sh Ork*.
hissel *la17-*, **hisself** *la15-e17* himself. [see HE. DOST *he*]

his *see* BE, HAE¹, US

hish¹ &c *la19-*; **hiss &c** *19-*, **heesh** *e20* *vti* **1** make a hissing sound in order to drive (an animal) away or to scare (birds) *19-*. **2** incite (*eg* a dog) to attack *20-*.
interj a sharp hissing call to drive off animals, or to incite a dog to attack *19-*.
~ (**tae**) **cat** *also fig* a call to frighten away a cat or to incite a dog to chase it *19-e20*. [onomat; *cf* MDu *hiss(ch)en* hound on a dog, and *cf* HISK, ISK]

hish² *interj* **1** an exhortation to be quiet *la20-*, *local Cai-Kcb*. **2** a soothing sound, *esp* for rocking a child to sleep *20-*, *local NE-Per*. [onomat; *cf* HISHIE]

hish-hash *n* a muddle, confusion, untidy mess *20-*, *now Sh midLoth*. [reduplicated f HASH]

hishie; hushie *n* a very quiet sound, a whisper, *chf* **neither** *etc* ~ (**n)or w(h)ishie** not the slightest sound *19-*, *now Fif*.
vti lull to sleep, sing a lullaby *19-*, *now midLoth*. [onomat, dim of HISH² or Eng (hu)sh keep silent!]

hisht *see* HEEST

hisk *interj* a call to drive off an animal or to alert or incite a dog to pursue *la18-e20*. [onomat; *cf* HISH¹, ISK]

Hispanʒeart &c [*'hı'spanjart, *?-'spen-*] *n, adj* = Spaniard *e16*. [only Sc, after L *Hispānus*]

Hi-Spy &c ['(h)aı 'spaı] the call used in the children's game of hide-and-seek; the game itself *19-*. [appar Eng *Hi!* + *spy*]

hiss *see* HISH¹

hissel &c *17-*, *only Sc*, **hisill &c** *la16, e19, only Sc*, **hesill &c** *15-16*; **heas(s)ill &c** *la16-17*, **hizzle &c** *19-*, *NE*, **he(e)zel** *20*, *S* ['hızl; *Dmf*

Rox 'hizl; *'hɪsl] *n* **1** = hazel *15-20*. **2** *only* **hissel** &c, **hizzle** &c a hazel stick used as a cudgel; a stout stick of any wood *19-*, *now Cai*. *adj, only* **hissel** &c, **hizzle** &c = hazel *19-e20*. [nME *hesil, hesel*, ON *hesli*; *cf* HAZEL]

hissel(**f**) *see* HIS

hissill *see* HISSEL

hist *see* HEEST, HIRST

histor(**e**) [*'hɪ'stor, *'hɪstor] *n* history *la16-e18*. [only Sc; ME, F *histoire*]

hit &c *n* a blow, a stroke *15-*. *vti, pt also* **hat**(**t**) &c *16-*, *now Sh Cai NE*, **het** &c *17-e20*, **hut**(**t**) *la19-*, *now local Abd-S. ptp also* **hitten** &c *la16-*, *now Sh Abd*, **hutten** *la19-*, *now local*; **hut** *la20-*, *local Edb-Dmf* = hit *la14-*.

hit *see* IT, HOOT

hitch, hich &c *v* **1** *vi* hobble, walk with a limp; hop *16-*, *now midLoth*. **2** *vti* = hitch. *n* **1** = hitch. **2** the little hop made in playing hopscotch *la19-*, *now Abd midLoth*.

hitchie-koo *n* a ball game *20-*, *NE*. [the title of a music-hall song]

hither &c *la16-*, **hidder** &c *la14-*, *now Sh*, **hedder** &c *15-16*, **hether-** &c *la15-16* ['hɪðər, 'hɪdər] *adv* = hither *la14-*. ~-**cum**(**m**)**ing** &c coming here, arrival *16*, *only Sc*. ~**til** &c hitherto *15-*, *now Sh*. ~**tillis** &c until now, hitherto *15-17*, *only Sc*. ~ **an yon**(**t**) &c *adv* hither and thither, this way and that *18-*, *now Ork Ags. adj* untidy; careless; estranged; muddled *19-*, *now Mry midLoth*.

hits *see* HOOT

hiv *see* HAE[1], HUIF

hive *n, only in place-names* a haven, harbour, *chf* **Steenhive** &c Stonehaven *17-*, *NE*. [var of ME *hythe*, OE *hȳð* a harbour, perh by conflation w Eng *haven*]

hives, hyvis *n pl* **1** name for a skin eruption, *esp* red-gum in infants; *now* any childish ailment without distinctive symptoms *16-*. **2** inflammation of the bowels in children, causing fever and diarrhoea *20-*, *local Cai-SW*. [uncertain; *cf bowel hive* (BOWEL)]

hivie &c [*'haɪvɪ] *adj* in easy circumstances, rather wealthy *la18-e19*. [only Sc; ? as if having resources laid by, as bees store honey in a hive]

hixy-pixy ['hɪksɪ'pɪksɪ] *adv* in confusion, topsy-turvy *20-*, *now Ags Per*. [conflation of EEKSIE-PEEKSIE w *higgledy-piggledy*]

hi-year *see* HALF[1]

hiz *see* US

hize *see* HEEZE

hizzie &c, **hussy** &c ['hɪzɪ, 'hʌzɪ, 'hɪsɪ, 'hʌsɪ] *n* **1** a housewife *15-e17*. **2** the mistress of a household; the mistress of a servant, pet animal etc *16-e17*. **3** *joc or* (*slightly*) *disparaging* a woman, *esp* a frivolous woman; a servant girl *16-*. **4** a woman of bad character *16-*. **5** *only* **hussy** &c a pocket-case for holding needles, thread etc *19-*, *now Ork Cai*.

~**skep** &c housewifery, housekeeping, household management *16-e17*, *19-20*, *only Sc*. ~ **fellow** &c a man who interferes with or undertakes women's duties *e19, chf SW, only Sc*. **of** ~**mak**(**ing**) made by the housewife for family use *la15-16*, *only Sc*. [reduced f *housewife*; *cf* Eng *hussy*]

hizzle *see* HISSEL

H.L.I. *see* HIELAND

ho &c *n* nae (**ither** &c) ~ **but** no (other) choice, no hope but *19-*, *Abd*. [*hope but* > *hobbut, with later wrong division as *ho but*]

ho *see* HOSE[1]

hoam; hoom [hom, h(j)um] *vt* spoil (food) through damp or steam *e19*. ~**ed** musty, mouldy *19-*, *now Kcdn Ags*. [appar extension of OAM]

hoast &c, **host** &c, **whoast** &c *18-e20* [host; ***hwost**, *Rox* ***hwʌst**] *n* **1** (1) coughing as an ailment, a cough *la15-*. (2) (a) a single cough *16-*. (b) a cough made to attract attention or to stop someone *19-*. **2** *fig, in negative* indicating something worth little consideration or which offers no difficulty or resistance *la18-*, *now Abd Kcb*: 'that case wadna stand a hoast in the Court of Session'. *v* **1** *vi* (1) cough *la15-*. (2) cough in order to attract attention, or to cover confusion *18-*. **2** *vt, chf* ~ **out** *or* **up** *lit and fig* cough up, get something off one's chest *16-*, *now local Ork-Kcb*.

hoax *vt* **1** = hoax. **2** spoil or disorganize (a game) *la19-e20*, *Mry*, *only Sc*.

hob- *see* HAPSHACKLE

hob(**b**)**ell; hobbill** *vt* cobble, mend (shoes) roughly *16*. *n* some part of a shoe, *perh* a patch *16-e17*, *only Sc*.

hobbill *see* HOBBLE

hobbleshow *see* HUBBLESHEW

hobble &c, **hobbill** &c *16 vti* **1** = hobble *16-*. **2** rock from side to side, bob up and down *la14-*, *now local Bnf-Rox*. **3** shake with mirth *la18-*, *NE*. **4** swarm with living creatures *20-*, *NE*. **5** perplex, bother *20-*, *Cai Uls*. *n* **1** = hobble. **2** a shaking, bouncing *19*. **3** a difficulty, predicament *19-*, *now Cai*. **4** a mêlée *19-*, *now Kcdn*. **hobblie** *of the ground* quaking under the feet *la19-*, *Bnf Rox*. ~ **bog** a quagmire *la19-*, *NE*. ~ **quo** *also fig* = prec *19-e20*, *S* (*cf* QUAW). [*cf* HABBLE, HUBBLE]

hobby &c [*'hobɪ, *'hʌbɪ] *n* a person who dressed in coarse rustic clothing; a stupid slovenly fellow *18-e20*. [dim of Eng pet-name *Hob* (Robert) a rustic]

hobell *see* HOBBELL

hoburn sauch &c *n* the laburnum *19-*, *now Bnf*. [obs F *aubour* laburnum, f *alburnum metath f L *laburnum*, + SAUCH]

hobyn *n* = hobby, a small horse *la14*.

hoch[1] &c; **houch** &c, **hogch** *16-e17*, **haugh** *19-* [hox; *S* hʌux; *St* hɔx] *n, pl also* **howis** *16*

[*'hʌuz] only Sc **1** (1) = hough, hock, the hind-leg joint of an animal *la15*-. (2) *now chf* **hough** a hind-leg joint of meat, the shin *16*-. **2** *of persons* the hollow behind the knee-joint, the back of the thigh; the thigh itself, the upper part of the leg *la15*-.
vt **1** hamstring, disable by cutting or striking the tendons of *n* 1 (1) and 2, *16-20*. **2** *fig, only Sc* (1) deprive of support; put out of action, put a stop to *17*; (2) overthrow, cause to fall, defeat *18-e19*. **3** throw (a stone) from beneath one's upraised thigh *19*-, *now Abd Ags, only Sc*. **4** traverse with difficulty on foot, trudge over *la19-e20, only Sc*.
.. ~ed &c *adj* having .. thighs, ..-thighed *18-19*, *only Sc*. ~er a person who maims or hamstrings (*chf* cattle) *la16-18*.
~ **band &c** *n* a strap or cord by which the hough-sinew of an animal is constricted to curb its movement *la17*-, *only Sc*. *vt* hobble (an animal) thus *19*-, *now Sh*.
cut the ~s hamstring *16-e17*. **cruik &c** *a or* **one's** ~(s) bend one's knees; sit down, kneel, dance etc *18*-, *now Ags*. **shak one's** ~s dance *19*-, *now Ayr*. [ME *hoȝ*; OE *hōh* heel]
hoch² [hox] *interj* expressing weariness, regret or disapproval *19*-, *now Abd Uls*.
~ **aye** expression of assent, suggesting impatience or resignation *la19*-, *now Abd*. ~ **hey** *interj* expressing weariness or sadness, sometimes accompanying a yawn *la18*-, *now Abd*. [imit of a sigh; *cf* ACH, HECH, OCH]
hochems *see* HOUGHAMS
hochie &c ['hoxɪ] *n* a secret store, something saved up for a future emergency *la19*-, *Fif*. [see SND]
hochle &c; hoighel *19-e20*, **houg(h)el &c** *19*- ['hoxl; *WC Uls* 'hoixl; *Rox also* 'hʌuxl] *vi*, *also* **hauchle &c** *19*-, *now local Per-Uls*, **hachel &c** *la19-e20* ['hɑxl] walk with a slow, awkward, hobbling or tottering gait *la18*-, *Gen except Sh Ork*.
n **1** an ungainly heaving movement of the body, an awkward shifting of position *20*-, *local Abd-Uls*. **2** *also* **hachel &c** ['hɑxl] *19-e20* a person who is ungainly or slovenly in gait, dress or appearance *19*-, *now Pbls Arg*. [only Sc; frequentative of HOCH¹]
hochmagandy; hough- ['hoxmə'gandɪ, 'hʌx-; *St* 'hɔx-] *n* fornication *la17*-, *latterly in reminiscence of Burns*. [only Sc; a ludicrous formation based on HOCH¹]
hock *see* HOWK¹
hocker &c; hucker &c *vi* crouch, bend down; walk or hobble bent double; crouch over or near a fire for warmth *19-20*, *chf Cai S*. [only Sc; ON *hokra* crouch, go bent, slink away; *cf* HUNKER]
hockerty-cockerty &c *adv* seated with one's legs astride another's shoulders *19*-, *now Ags*. [see SND]

hocus &c *n* a stupid person, a simpleton *la18*-, *now Cai*. [extension of obs Eng *hocus* a conjuror, cheat]
hod *vi* **hoddin &c** *n, adj* jogging along on horseback, bumping in the saddle *la18-19*. [prob onomat; *cf* HOTCH, HOWD, HODDLE]
hod *see* HIDE¹
hodden &c, hodding &c *la16-e18*; **hodin &c** *17-18* ['hodən] *n* **1** *orig chf attrib* coarse homespun, an undyed woollen cloth of a greyish colour due to a mixture of black and white wool *la16*-. **2** *attrib and fig* rustic, homely *19*-, *now Fif*.
~ **gray 1** homespun wool (*la16-e17*) or woollen cloth (*18*-) of the natural undyed colour. **2** *attrib and fig* a person dressed in a simple rustic fashion; a homely, unaffected individual *la19*-. [only Sc; unknown]
hodden *see* HIDE¹
hoddin *see* HOD
hoddit *see* HIDE¹
hoddle &c *vi* waddle; move with an uneven hobbling gait as an old person; walk with quick short steps *18*-, *now Ags Edb Dmf*.
n a waddling gait, a quick toddling step *e20*.
hain *etc* **one's** ~ relax one's pace or effort, take things easy *19*. [only Sc; *cf* HOD]
hoddn *see* HIDE¹
hoddock *see* HADDOCK
hoddy, hode *see* HIDE¹
hode *see* HIDE¹
hodge &c *v* **1** *vi* move or walk awkwardly or jerkily, hobble along *18*-, *now Sh Ork NE, only Sc*. **2** fidget, twitch, *usu* with impatience or discomfort *19*-, *now NE, only Sc*. **3** shake, quiver, hitch the shoulders, *esp* with laughing *19*-, *now Abd Kcdn*. **4** *vt, freq* ~ **up** hitch up, tug or push in a series of jerks, heave *la18*-, *now Sh, only Sc*.
n a rough shove, a sharp push or jolt, a hitch up *la18*-, *now Sh Bnf Abd, only Sc*. [prob chf onomat; *cf* HOD, HODDLE, HOTCH]
hodgehead *see* HOGGET
hodgel &c *n* a dumpling, *usu* one made of oatmeal, fat and seasoning *19-e20*, *S*. [appar dim reduced form of next]
hodge-podge *n* **1** = hotch-potch. **2** a thick BROTH made with plenty of vegetables *18-e19*.
hodiern [*hodɪ'ɛrn] *adj* hodiernal, of the present day *e16*. [L *hodiernus*]
hodin *see* HODDEN
hoe *see* HOSE
Hoff &c *n* Julius ~ name for a round building that stood near Carron *e16*. [OE *hof* a house, hall; *cf* ARTHURIS HUFE]
hoffe *see* HOWF
hog &c, hogg [hog, hʌg] *n* **1** *now chf* **hogg** *in agric use* a young sheep from the time it is weaned until it is shorn of its first fleece, a yearling *14*-. **2** *curling* (CURL) a stone which does not pass over the ~-score, *la18*-.
vt **1** make a HOG of (a lamb), keep (a lamb) on

winter pasture during its first year *19.* **2** *curling* play (a stone) which fails to cross the *hog-score, 19-e20.*

hogged stuck, at a standstill *19-, now Dmf.*
hogget = *n* 1, *19-.* **hogging** a pasture reserved for one-year-old sheep *19-, now Per Gall Rox.*

~-**fence** a pasture saved for the HOGS' winter keep *la18-, now Rox.* ~-**score** curling (CURL), *also fig* either of the two distance lines drawn across the rink over which every scoring shot must pass *la18-20.* ~-**shouther &c** push or jostle with the shoulder, shove about *la18-e19* [appar coined by Burns].

ewe ~ a young female sheep *19-.* **tup** ~ a young ram *19-.* **wedder &c** ~ a young castrated male sheep *18-.* [also in Eng dial; *cf* St Eng = a pig]

hogch *see* HOCH[1]
hogeart [*?'hodʒərt] *n* ? a tired-out old man *e16.*

hogg *see* HOG

hogger &c, hoggar &c; hugger &c *19-* ['hogər, 'hʌg-] *n* **1** a coarse stocking without a foot, worn as a gaiter *la17-, now nEC, WC, Rox.* **2** (1) an old sock-foot worn as a slipper, or over a shoe on icy roads *19-, Ags.* (2) *specif* a kind of slipper like a stocking foot, knitted from flax rove and worn by factory-workers *20-, Ags.* **3** an old stocking-leg used as a receptacle or purse; any kind of pouch used to keep money in; a hoard *18-, now Ags WC.*
huggerfu a stocking-leg full, a hoard *19-, now Ayr.* [obscure]

hogget &c *la16-,* **hoghed &c** *la15-e17;* **hodgehead &c** *17-e18,* **hugget &c** *la16, la19* ['hogət; *'hʌgət; *'hodʒət; *'hog'hid, *'hodʒ'hid] *n* = **1** hogshead, a large cask *la15-, now Bute Ayr.* **2** a measure of liquor, fish, meal etc *la15-e20.* [omission of -s- only Sc]

Hogmanay &c *la17-,* **hagmane &c** *17-18;* **hangmanay &c** *19-e20,* **hugmanay &c** *e19* ['hogmə'ne, 'hʌg-; *Rox* 'haŋ-; *Loth also* 'hʌug-; *'hag-] *n* **1** 31 Dec, the last day of the year, New Year's Eve *la17-.* **2** (1) a New-Year's gift, *esp* (19-e20) a gift of *oatcakes* (AIT) etc given to or asked for by children on New Year's Eve *la18-.* (2) the cry uttered in asking for the New Year's gift *17-e19.* (3) *esp* **your** *etc* ~ any form of hospitality, *esp* a drink given to a guest to celebrate the New Year, or a gratuity given to tradesmen and employees on that day *20-.* **3** *specif* an *oatcake* or biscuit baked to give to the children on 31 Dec *19.*

haud *etc* ~ celebrate the passing of the old year *la18-.* [northernF dial *hoguinane,* OF *aguillanneuf* a gift given on New Year's Eve, the word shouted in asking for this; *cf* NEW-YEAR]

hograll &c *n* ? the skin of a HOG *n* 1, *15, only Sc.*

hogtoune &c, hugtoun [*'hogtun, *-tən, *'hʌg-] *n* **1** a sleeveless padded jerkin worn under the hauberk, and occasionally alone as a

fencing jacket *la15-e16.* **2** a short sleeveless jacket *16.* [OF *hocton; cf* eModEng *hocton, hacton,* ME *acton*]

hoid *see* HIDE[1]
hoighel *see* HOCHLE
hoill *see* HAIL[1]
hoillin(g) *see* HOLLAND
hoise &c [hoiz] *vt* raise, lift up, heave up, hoist (a sail); *fig* raise, exalt *17-, now nEC Arg Kcb.* *n, also fig* a lift, a heave up *la18-, now Fif Arg Kcb.* [eModEng; alternative development to HEEZE, LowGer *hissen* etc; *cf* HEIST]
hoislar *see* HOSTLAR
hoit &c *vi* move awkwardly or clumsily, *esp* of a stout person or a well-fed animal trying to move quickly, waddle *la18-19.* *n* a slow hobbling gait *19-e20.* [orig prob onomat as HOD etc; *cf* HOTTER, HYTER]
hoke *see* HOWK[1]
hokster *see* OXTER
hola *interj, nautical* haul! *16.* [OF *haler* haul; *cf* HALE]
hold, holden *see* HAUD
hole &c, holl &c *la14-e20 n* **1** = hole *la14-.* **2** *golf* the small circular cavity in the green into which the ball is to be played; the distance between each TEE[1] and its HOLE (a golf-course *usu* having 18); the point scored by the player who takes the fewest strokes to reach the HOLE *18-.* **3** *only in pl* (*la19*) or *dim* **holie** (*la19-, now N, EC Kcb*) a variety of the game of marbles in which the marbles are aimed at others in holes in the ground. **4** a small bay *la18-, now N, EC Arg, freq in place-names.* **5** a shallow pool, a puddle *la19-, local Sh-Kcb.*
vti **1** = hole *16-.* **2** dig, excavate; dig up, loosen from the ground (*now esp* potatoes (*NE Ags*) or turf (*Uls*)) *16-.* **3** *golf* play (the ball) into the HOLE (*n* 2), play (a particular HOLE) *18-;* see ~ **out.** **4** *freq* ~ **on** *or* **about** linger, *esp* linger too long in one place or at one task, loaf about; be contented with mean work *19-, now Abd.* **5** wear into holes *la19-, Gen except Sh Ork.*

holiepied &c ['holɪ'paɪd] full of holes **1** *in gen, 20-, NE Ags;* **2** *specif, of open-work embroidery or broderie anglaise, la19-, NE.*

hail ~ to the fullest or utmost extent *la19-, now Abd.* ~ **i(n) the wa 1** a small house or apartment, *freq* in a recess between two larger buildings, and entered directly from the street, *usu* used as a shop or public house *la18-, local Abd-Dmf.* **2** a box-bed (BOX[1]), a recessed bed *la20-, Abd C, S.* ~ **out** *golf* complete the playing of a HOLE (*n* 2) by striking the ball into the HOLE *la19-.* **in the** ~ on the point of childbirth *18-, now Abd Fif.* [f inflected forms of OE *hol; cf* HOWE[1], HOWE[2]]

holf *see* HOWF
holie *see* HOLE
holine, holing *see* HOLLIN
holk *see* HOWK[1], HOWK[2]

holl *see* HOLE, HOWE[1]
Holland &c; **ho(i)llin(g) &c** *16-e19* ['holən(d)] *n, freq attrib* = Holland *la15-*.
~ **hawk** the great northern diver *19-e20, only Sc.*
hollin &c, holine &c *la15-e18*; **holing &c** *16* ['holɪn, -ən; *-əin] *n* holly, a holly-tree *la15-, now Bnf.* [northern eModEng *hollyn*, ME *holyn*, OE *holen, holegn*]
hollin(g) *see* HOLLAND
holly *see* HALIE
holm *see* HOWM
holograph *adj, law, of a deed or letter* wholly in the handwriting of one person and, in the case of a will, signed by him *18-*.
n, law a document wholly in the handwriting of one person *18-*. [*cf* Eng; in Scots law such documents are valid without witnesses]
holy *see* HALIE
home *see* HAME
hommill *see* HUMMEL
homologate &c [hɔ'mɔləget] *vt, pt, ptp* also **homologat(e)** *la16-17* ratify, confirm, approve, *esp law* render valid, ratify (a deed etc which was informal or defective) *la16-*.
homologation the act of confirming by implication something not previously legally binding, ratification *la17-e20*. [MedL (f Gk) *homologare* agree]
hond *see* HUND
honder *see* HUNDER
hone *see* HUNE
honest &c, oneste *15-16 adj* **1** = honest *15-*. **2** *expressing approval* of good character and standing, worthy, estimable *15-*.
honesty &c **1** = honesty *la14-*. **2** (1) decency, decorum; a mark of respectability *18-, now Abd Per Renfr.* (2) *of clothes etc* best, *esp* **as** or **for an** ~**y** *la18-*.
~ **like** *of persons, or their dress or appearance* decent, respectable; *of things* substantial, of respectable appearance *19-20*. **the H**~ **Lad, the H**~ **Lass** the leading participants in the annual festival in Musselburgh *20-*. **the H**~ **Men** nickname for Ayr United football team *20-* [f Burns *Tam o' Shanter*]. **the H**~ **Toun** Musselburgh *la18-*.
honey *see* HINNIE
honorary *n* an honorarium, a fee for professional services, in law considered as a gift made in acknowledgment of services gratuitously rendered *18-e19*. [L *honōrārium*; *cf* ModEng = a gift, honouring distinction]
honour &c *n* **1** = honour *la14-*. **2** *in pl*, also **the H**~**s of Scotland** *la17-* the regalia of the Kingdom of Scotland, *ie* the Crown, Sceptre, and Sword of State *la16-*.
hont *see* HUNT
hoo[1] *19-, chf Sh Ork C*, **how &c, whoo** *e20*; **quhow &c** *la14-17*, **whow** *16-18* [hu; *S* hʌu; *hwu] *adv* **1** = how *la14-*. **2** why *17-, Gen except NE; cf* FOO 2.

~**anever &c** ['huən'ɪvər, *&c*] however *la18-, Cai C Uls.* ~ **gat(e)** in what way, how *la14*.
hoosever &c *19-, Gen except Sh Ork*, **howsaever &c** ['hu:'sɛvər, *&c*; *'hu:'se'ɛvər] *16* = howsoever. ~**somever** ['hu'sʌm'ɛvər, *&c*] = howsomever, notwithstanding, nevertheless, however *la18-e20*. ~ **soon &c** *17-18*, ~**sone &c** *16-17*, ~**sein &c** *la16-e17* [*'hu:'søn, *'-sin, *&c*] *adv* as soon as *only Sc.*
~ **an a' be &c** [*'hu:(ə)nɑ'bi; *S* *-'bəi; *&c*] however, nevertheless *19-e20*. ~**'s a' wi ye** ['huz 'ɑ wɪjɪ] *greeting* how are you? *la18-, now C Uls.* ~ **that** ['hu ðət, *'hu:t] in what way, how *la14-, Gen except NE.* [see also FOO]
hoo[2] **&c** [hu] *n* a cry used **1** to attract attention *la19-, now Renfr Rox*; **2** to frighten birds or cattle *la19-, NE*; **3** to encourage effort *19*.
v **1** *vt* scare (birds or straying animals) away from growing crops; *in gen* scare (people etc) away *la18-, now NE.* **2** *vi* shout in order to attract attention from a distance *19-, now Renfr Rox.* **3** (1) *of an owl* hoot; hoot like an owl *19-, now Ags.* (2) *of wind* howl *19-e20*.
hoo-hoo &c *19*, **hooie &c** ['huɪ] *la18-, now NE Per* = *n* and *v*.
hoo[3] *18-20*, **how &c** [hu] *n* **1** a cap *la14-e19, freq* (grasp etc someone) **be** ~ **and hair &c** *la14-e15*. **2** *only in combs eg* **hal(l)i(e)**~ **&c** *18-e20*, **seely**~ **&c** *18-* the caul sometimes on the head of a new-born child, regarded as a good omen. **3** a roof rafter *17-19*.
hooick &c *la19-*, **howek &c** *la19-e20* ['huɪk] a small rick of corn or hay *la19-, now NE, Ags.*
heuicking ['huɪkɪn] the preserving of corn in *hooicks* during a rainy harvest *20-, NE, Ags.*
nycht how [*'nɪxt 'hu] a nightcap *16, only Sc.* [OE *hūfe* a hood, cap; for *n* 3, *cf* cognate Norw dial *huv* ridge of a roof, ON *hūfa* a hood]
hooch &c; heuch *la19-* [hux, hjux] *interj*, also **whoogh &c** *e19* [*hwux] expressing excitement or exhilaration, *esp* when uttered by dancers during a REEL[1] *19-*.
vi **1** cry HOOCH, shout *19-*. **2** whoop with mirth *19-e20*. **3** breathe hard on an object before polishing it *19-, now Abd Ags.*
n **1** (1) a shout, a loud cry, *esp* that uttered while dancing a REEL[1] etc *la19-*. (2) a dance *la20-, local Per-S.* **2** a sudden expulsion of the breath, a puff *la19*. [imit; for *v* 3 and *n* 2 *cf* HAUCH]
hood *see* HUID
hoo-hoo *see* HOO[2]
hooick *see* HOO[3]
hooie &c; hewie *20-, Mry* [*Mry EC* 'hjuɪ; *NE* 'huɪ] *vti* exchange, barter *19-, now NE-Per Pbls.* [obscure]
hooie *see* HOO[2]
hook *see* HEUK
hook bone *see* HEUKBANE
hooker[1] *n* a glass of WHISKY, a dram *19-e20*.

hooker[2] *WC n, chf* ~**-doon** *Edb WC* a cloth cap
with a peak *20-*. [prob f the action of pulling
down the peak as if hooking it on]

hookie *n, only exclam* **by the** ~ a mild oath or
asseveration *19-, local.* [var of Eng slang *hokey*]

hool *see* HUIL.

hoolachan &c; **hullachan** &c ['hulǝxǝn] *n* a
REEL[1], *specif* the *Reel of Tulloch* (REEL[1]), *19-, now
Cai NE Arg Rox.* [Gael *(ruidhle) Thulachain*
[('rɒɪlǝ) 'hulǝxan] the *Reel of Tulloch*]

hoole *see* HUIL.

hoolet &c *19-,* **howlat** &c *la15-19* ['hulǝt] *n* **1**
= howlet, owl *la15-.* **2** *disparaging* applied to
persons showing real or imagined characteristics of the owl (*eg* stupidity *20-*) *la16-.*
v **1** *vt* henpeck *19-, Per Rox.* **2** *vi* go about with
a miserable expression; be solitary, unsociable
19-e20. [F *hulotte; howlet* &c dial in Eng; *cf*
OOL, OOLET]

hoolie *see* HUILIE.

hoom *see* HOAM.

hoomet &c *19-,* **hewmet** &c *16;* **hoomach**
20-, Mry ['humɪt; *Mry* -ǝx; *hjumǝt] *n* **1** *also*
hewmond &c [*'hjumǝnd, *-ǝnt] = helmet
16. **2** (1) a large flannel nightcap, worn by old
women *19-e20.* (2) a woman's hat of unusual
shape *20-, NE.* **3** *in pl, chf* **hoomachs** fingerless
gloves or mittens *20-, Mry.* [only Sc; *-ach* is
alternative Gael ending]

hoop *see* HOWP[1].

hoops &c *interj* encouraging someone to raise
himself or lift something heavy *20-.*
~**e up** = *interj, e20.* [emphatic alteration of
UP; *cf* OOP and colloq Eng *upsadaisy*]

hoose &c [huz] *n* a disease in cattle which produces a dry wheezy cough *la19-.* [Eng dial,
prob from an unmutated form of OE *hwēsan* (*v*)
wheeze]

hoose *see* HOUSE.

hoosht &c [huʃt] *interj* hush!, be silent! *18-e20.*
[*cf* eModEng *husht*]

hoot *la18-,* **hout** &c; **het** *la19-e20,* **hit** *la19*
[hut; *Bwk Rox also* hʌut; *Rox also* hɛt; *hɒt, *hɪt]
interj, also ~**s** *la19-* expressing dissent, incredulity, impatience, annoyance, remonstrance or
dismissal of another's opinion *16-.*
vti say HOOT to, pooh-pooh, treat or dismiss
with contempt *18-, now EC Dmf Rox.*
~ **awa 1** nonsense! *18-.* **2** *expressing pity or sympathy, esp in soothing children* oh dear! *la19-, NE.*
~ **aye** &c indeed, certainly *la18-.* ~ **fie** &c
= ~ awa 1, *la18-, now local NE-SW.* ~ **na,** ~
no a strong negative *19-.* ~**(s)-toot(s)** &c =
~ awa, *19-.* [*cf* Gael *ut!,* Eng *tut(s),* Sw *hut!*]

hoove *see* HUIF.

hoozle *see* HOSE[1].

hop *see* HAP[2], HOWP[1].

hope[1] &c *15-, freq in S place-names la12-;* **howp**
&c *17-18,* **whope** *la18, S* [hop; *S* hwʌp;
*hʌup] *n* **1** a small enclosed upland valley, a

hollow among the hills *15-, now S.* **2** a hill *18-,
now Rox.* [nME *hope,* OE *hop* a piece of
enclosed land]

hope[2] &c; **howp** &c *17-, now Abd* [hop, hʌup] *n*
a small bay or haven *15-, now only in place-names.*
[ON *hóp* a landlocked bay]

hope[3] &c [*hop, *hʌup] *n* a heap, pile, stack; a
lot (of goods for sale) *la15-e16.* [only Sc; MDu,
Flem *hoop,* MLowGer *hôp*]

hope *see* HOUP, HOWP[1].

hops *see* HOUP.

hopschakil *see* HAPSHACKLE.

hork *see* HURK.

horl &c *n* the metal tag or point of a bootlace
18-, now Gsw. [? conflation of *whorl* (WHURL) w
VIRL]

horl *see* WHURL.

horlage *see* ORLOGE.

horn &c; **whorn** &c *19-20* [horn; *Rox* hwʌrn]
n **1** = horn *la14-.* **2** anything resembling a
horn *16-, specif* (1) the constellation Ursa
Minor *16;* (2) the stem-post (or stern-post *la19-,
Sh*) of a boat, the prow *la16-, now Sh;* (3) a corn
on the foot, a piece of hard skin, a callosity
18-19; (4) a handle; a spout *la18-, now Sh Ork,
only Sc;* (5) the horn-like projection at the side
of an anvil *19-, now Ork Cai Kcb.* **3** *chf law* the
trumpet used to proclaim an outlaw, *latterly chf*
a debtor, *chf* **at the** ~, **put to the** ~ proclaimed as an outlaw or bankrupt *la14-19, only
Sc.* **4** *in pl* (*la15-17*) the metal tags or tips on
laces or thongs *la15-, now Ork, only Sc.*
vt **1** fit with horns, *chf* ~**ing** *la15-e17.* **2** *law* =
put to the ~ (*n* 3), proclaim as an outlaw or rebel
(though still competent, in practice now superseded), *chf* ~**ing** *16-, only Sc;* see *letters of horning*
(LETTER).
~**er 1** a person, *esp* a tinker, who makes articles
of horn, *esp* horn spoons or combs *la16-19.* **2** a
person who has been *put to the* ~ (*n* 3), *la16, only
Sc.* **3** an earwig *la19-, now Ags;* cf *hornie-gollach*
(GOLACH). ~**ie** *adj* = horny *16-.* *n* **1** *chf*
Auld Hornie nickname for the Devil *la18-.* **2**
a constable, a policeman *la18-20.* **3** (1) a cow
of a horned breed *19-e20.* (2) a cow *in gen,
19-, now Sh.* **4** a form of the game of tig *19-20.*
5 fair hornie fair play *19-, Gen except Sh Ork.*
hornie holes a game for four persons where
each couple tries to throw a stick into the hole
defended by their opponents *19-e20.* **hornie
(h)oolet, hornie owl** the long-eared owl *la19-,
NE.*
~ **daft** quite mad *19-, now Cai Ags.* ~**-dry** of
clothes etc thoroughly dry *19-, now Sh Cai Abd.*
~**-eel** &c the sand-eel *19, NE, EC.* ~**-en(d)**
&c the best room in a *but and ben* (BUT) *19-,
NE.* ~**-hard** *adj* as hard as horn, extremely
hard *19-, now Sh.* *adv* **sleep** ~**-hard** sleep
soundly *la18-e19.* ~**-idle** having nothing to
do, completely unemployed *la18-, now Sh Cai
Lnk Ayr.*

auld in the ~ advanced in years and experience, wise, shrewd *19-*. **bear** *etc* (**away**) **the** ~ carry off the chief prize, win a contest, excel *18-e19*. **blaw one's** (**ain**) ~ boast *20-*. **as dry as a** ~ thoroughly dry *19-*, *Sh Cai nEC, Dmf*. **get out one's** ~**s** become assertive, break free of conventions, be free to express oneself in action *la19-*. **as hard as a** *or* **the** ~ very hard, as hard as nails; *of persons* hardy *19-*. **have one's** ~ **in somebody's hip** criticize severely, be antagonistic towards *19-*, *now Ork NE Arg*. **lang in the** ~ = *auld in the* ~, *la20-, C*. **by the lug and the** ~ forcibly *19-*, *now Kcb*. **sleep as sound as a** ~ sleep very soundly *20-*, *Sh Cai Dmf*.

horneck &c *n* the earth-nut *19*, *SW*. [corruption of ARNIT]

hornis [*hornz, *'hornɪs] *adj*, *of coins* coined by the bishop of Horn *la15-16*. [only Sc; f *Hoorn*, in North Holland]

horologe *see* ORLOGE

horoyally &c ['horo'(h)jalɪ, 'hoɪrɪ-] *n* a CEILIDH, a singsong, an uproarious party *la19-*, *Highl Arg*. [Gael *ho ro eile, ho ro (gh)eallaidh &c* a meaningless refrain in songs]

horrid *adv*, *as intensifier, not necessarily disapproving* extremely, specially *la18-*, *now Sh Ork Kcb*. [appar orig Eng slang; *cf* AWFU *adv*, ODIOUS]

horse &c, hors &c *la14-17* *n* **1** = horse (1) *in sing, la14-*; (2) *without article or possessive adj, la14-16*: 'he fell off hors til erde'; (3) *uninflected in pl after numerals etc, la14-*: 'giffin for four hors to the King'. **2** a trestle, a support, *specif as used by masons to support scaffolding 19-*, *now local N-S*.

vtir **1** = horse *la14-*. **2** *vt* convey as on horseback; carry (a person) on one's back *16-e17*.

be sic mannie, sic horsie *usu contemptuous* be all of one kind, be birds of a feather *20-*, *NE*.

~**-beast** a horse *19-*, *Gen except Sh Ork*. ~**-buckie** the large whelk *la19-*, *Gen except Sh Ork, only Sc*. ~**-carriage &c** conveyance by horse *la16-e17*, *only Sc*. ~**-cock &c** the dunlin; a kind of snipe *e17, 19, only Sc*. ~**-couper** a horse-dealer *17-*, *Gen except Sh Ork*. ~**-couping** horse-dealing *la18-*, *Gen except Sh Ork*. ~ **fete &c** *n pl* the feet of horses; a horse *la14-e17*. ~**-gang 1** *land measurement* the fourth part of a plough-gate (PLEUCH), the land occupied by one of four persons sharing a plough worked by their four horses *18-19*, *only Sc*. **2** the circular track trodden by the horses in driving a threshing mill; the driving apparatus itself *19-e20*. ~**-gell(y) &c** a horse-leech *19*, *only Sc*. ~**-heid 1** = horse-head, the head of a horse *15-e16*. **2** a large unbroken lump of earth, a clod *20-*, *now Abd Ags, only Sc*. ~**-hirer** a person who hires out horses *17-*, *only Sc*. ~**-kirn** a churn worked by a horse *e20, only Sc*. ~(**'s**) **knop** *or* **knot** the black knapweed *la18-*, *now Dmf*. ~**man 1** = horseman *15-*. **2** (1) a man who tends horses, *specif* a farm servant who looks after and

works a pair of horses, on larger farms ranked according to seniority as **first, second** etc ~**man** *la17, la19-*. (2) *freq* one of a fraternity of horsemen (2 (1)) with initiation ceremonies, passwords etc, *usu* regarded as a relic of Devil-worship *la19-*, *esp in comb eg* **horseman's word** a secret word by which the initiate gains complete control over his horses *la19-*, *now local Cai-Lnk*. ~ **marschall &c** a horse-doctor *la15-16*, *only Sc*. ~**-mussel &c** a large fresh-water mussel *17-*, *now Sh Cai Kcdn, only Sc*. ~ **pa(c)k** a pack carried by a horse *la16-17*, *only Sc*. ~**-peas(e)** the common vetch *la18-*, *now Cai*. ~**-rinning** horse-racing *16*. ~**-setter** a person who has horses for hire *18-19*. ~**-tree** the swingletree of a plough or harrow *la17-*, *now midLoth Kcb*. ~ **wa(i)rd** an enclosure for horses *16-e17*.

on ~ *coupled or contrasted with* **on fute &c** on horseback *15-16*.

hort *see* HURT

hosack &c ['hozək, &c] *n* = *ho(se)-fish* (HOSE[1]) *19-, Abd*. [dim]

hose[1] **&c** *n*, *pl* **hose &c** *15-*, **hoses &c** *16-e17*. *sing also* **ho(e)** *18-*, *now NE* [back-formation f *hose* pl] **1** *chf as pl* = hose *15-*. **2** ? a case or covering of coarse cloth for a flag *16*. **3** the socket for the handle on any metal implement, *eg* a fork or rake *la16-*, *now Sh-Cai Fif*. **4** *mining* an iron clasp at the end of a rope *la19-*, *now Fif*. **5** the sheath enclosing an ear of corn *17-*, *now midLoth*.

vt remove the bark from the base of (a tree) before felling *la19-e20*.

hosing &c *n* **1** the providing or making of hose; hose themselves *16*. **2** a kind of cloth for making hose, *freq* **hosing claith, hosing gray** (**woll**) *16-e17*. **hozle &c, hoozle &c** ['hozl, 'huzl, 'hʌuzl] the socket into which the handle or shaft of a hammer, pick, fork, golf club etc is fitted *20-*, *now Edb Slk Rox*. ~**-fish** the cuttlefish *la17-e20*. ~**-grass &c** meadow soft grass *19*. ~**-net 1** a small stocking-shaped net fixed to a pole, used for fishing in small streams *18-e19*. **2** *fig* a trap, a position from which it is difficult to escape *la16-e19*. **schort** ~ knee breeches *la15-e17*, *only Sc*.

hose[2] *vt*, *of fish* swallow (the bait); *of human beings or animals* swallow voraciously *20-*, *now Bnf Abd*. [appar fig f HOSE[1] *n*, the food going down the gullet like water through a hose]

hoshen &c; hushion *la18-e20* *n* **1** a footless stocking used (*chf by outdoor workers*) to cover legs or arms in cold weather *la18-*, *now Cai SW*. **2** a stocking used as a container, *eg* a purse *la18-*, *now Cai*. [only Sc; deriv of HOSE[1]; see SND]

hoslar *see* HOSTLAR

hospitale &c *la14-e17*; **hospital** *la15-* ['hospɪtəl, *hospɪ'tel] *n* **1** = hospital *la14-*. **2** *specif* a charitable asylum for lepers, a leper-house *la15-e17*.

host¹ &c *la15-*, **ost &c** *la14-e17* (*the commoner form before 17*) *n* **1** *also* **great ~** *16* = host, an armed company *la14-*. **2** *only* **ost** a confrontation or joining in battle of two opposing armies; two such armies at the point of battle *la15-e16*, *only Sc*. **3** the assemblage or assembling of armed men summoned by the sovereign or regent for military service, *usu* on a specific occasion or for a specific campaign; the Scottish army; the campaign for which such a force is raised *15-17*, *only Sc*. **4** a multitude, a large number, an abundance (**of** something) *15-*.
vi serve in an armed force, take part in a campaign etc, raid *16-e18*.
~ing 1 campaigning, active military service *la15-16*. **2** = *n 3*, *la15-e17*, *only Sc*. **3** *only* **osting** ? an army *la15,e17*, *only Sc*. **4** *only* **hosting** *specif* military service discharged as a feudal obligation in return for the holding of land *16-e18*, *only Sc*. **5** *attrib* as used on active service, field- *la15-e17*. **in ~ing** on campaign *la15-16* [in Eng chf, and orig only, referring to Ireland].
in ost as an army *la14-16*: '*in ost thai war assemblyt thar*'.
host *see* HOAST
hostie &c *n* the host, consecrated bread *la16-e20*. [only Sc; laME *hostye*, F *hostie* a sacrifice]
hostilar *see* HOSTLAR
hostilary &c *16-e17*, **hostlary &c** *la15-e17*, *only Sc*, **ostillary &c** *15-16*, **ostlary &c** *la16-17 n* **1** = hostelry, an inn *16-17*. **2** lodging etc provided as a right to a church dignitary; a lodging belonging to a monastic community *15-e16*. **3** the business of providing lodging and entertainment for travellers etc in a public hostelry, the keeping of an inn *la16-e17*, *only Sc*.
hostlar *15-e17*, **ostlare &c** *la15-17*; **hostler** *la16-e20*, **ho(i)slar** *15-e17*, **ostler &c**, **oslar** *la16-17* [*'*(h)os(t)lər] *n* **1** a host *15-e17*, *only Sc*. **2** *also* (**h)ostilar &c** *15-e17* [*'*(h)ostɪlər] an innkeeper *la14-17*, *e19*.
~ hous, *also* (**h)ostilar &c hous** a hostelry, an inn *la15-17*, *only Sc*. **~ wife** a woman who keeps an inn etc *17-e20*, *only Sc*. [ME *hostler*, *hosteler &c*, *ostiler &c*, OF *hostelier*, *ostelier*, MedL *hostel(l)arius*]
hostlary *see* HOSTILARY
hostler *see* HOSTLAR
hot &c, **how(i)t** *la16*, **huit** *e17*; **hett** *18-19*, **hut(t)** *18-* [hot, hʌt] *n*, *now only* **hut(t) 1** a basket or pannier, *esp* one used for carrying manure or earth etc *la16*, *19-*, *Gall*. **2** a small heap *esp* of manure distributed over a field in preparation for spreading *la17-*, *now local midLoth-S*. **3** *only* **hut(t)**, **huit** a small stack of corn or hay etc built to protect the crop temporarily from the weather before its removal to the stackyard *17-*, *now Ags-Uls*. **4** *only* **hut(t)** a lazy person, a slattern *19*.

vt **1** heap up, heap together *la19-*, *now midLoth Dmf*, *only Sc*. **2** *only* **hut(t)** put up (sheaves of grain) in small stacks in the field as a protective measure against weather or birds *la18-*, *now local Ags-Uls*, *only Sc*. [nME *hott*, OF *hotte* a pannier]
hot *see* HET¹
hotch &c *v* **1** *vi* move jerkily up and down, bob; jog *la15-*, *now local Fif-S*. **2** fidget, hitch about with impatience or discomfort *la18-*, *Gen except Sh Ork*. **3** heave with laughter *la18-*, *now local Kcdn-S*, *only Sc*. **4** (1) *vt* cause to move jerkily, shrug, hitch (**up**) *19-*, *now Fif*. (2) *vr* shift along in a sitting position to make room for others *19-*, *now midLoth Slk*.
n, *only Sc* **1** a jerk, jolt, bounce, hitch, shrug; a twitch *la18-*, *now midLoth Kcb Rox*. **2** a big fat ungainly woman; a slut *la19-*, *now midLoth WC*, *S*.
~in &c *adj* **1** infested, seething, overrun **with**; abounding *la18-*, *Gen except Sh Ork*. **2** restless with impatience, extremely eager *la19-*. [nME *hotch*; *cf* Du *hotsen* (*v*) jog, jolt, MHighGer, Ger dial *hotzen* (*v*) move up and down, OF *hochier* (*v*) shake, tremble; *cf* HOD, HODGE]
hote *see* HET¹
hott *see* HOT
hotter &c *vi* **1** move in an uneven jerky way, jolt about *19-*, *now local NE-Bwk Rox*. **2** walk unsteadily, totter *19-*, *chf S*. **3** *of liquid etc or its container* seethe, bubble, boil steadily *19-*, *Gen except Sh Ork*. **4** shudder, shiver with cold or fear, shake with laughter or excitement *19-*, *now NE*. **5** crowd together, swarm *19-*, *now Abd Rox*.
n **1** a shaking or jolting, the rattling sound thus produced *19-*, *now Abd Rox*. **2** the bubbling made by boiling liquid *20-*, *now NE Fif Dmf*. **3** a shiver; a start; a quiver(ing) *19-*, *now Abd*. **4** (1) a seething mass, a crowd; a swarm (of vermin); the noise or motion of such a crowd *e19*. (2) a confused, jumbled heap of something *19-*, *now local Abd-Kcb S*.
~el &c *n* **1** = *n 5* (1) *20-*, *Bnf*. **2** a mass of festering sores or chaps; one such sore *20-*, *Abd*. **~in** *adj* **1** jolting, rumbling *19-e20*. **2** swarming, seething, crowding *19-e20*. [? frequentative of **hot-* as in HOTCH etc; *cf* Flem *hotteren* (*v*) shake and HATTER]
hottle &c [ˈhotl] *n* = hotel *19-*, *now local Cai-Edb*.
Hottopyis &c [*'*hotəˈpaɪz, &c] name for a variety of wine, and its standard measure *la16*. [see DOST Suppl]
houch *see* HOCH¹
houff *see* HOWF
hougel *see* HOCHLE
hough *see* HOCH¹, HOWE¹
houghams *e19*, **hochems &c** *17*, **hauchames &c** *17* [*'*hoxəmz] *n pl* wooden supports for panniers on a horse. [only Sc; ? f HOCH¹]

houghel *see* HOCHLE

houghmagandy *see* HOCHMAGANDY

houlk *see* OUK

houn, hound *see* HUND

hounder, houndreth *see* HUNDER

hount *see* HUNT

houp *la16-e17*, *19-*, *now Ork*, **hope** *la16* [hʌup; *hop] *n* = hops, as used in brewing: **1** *as collective sing la16-e17*, *19-* (*now Ork*), *only Sc*; **2** *as pl*, *also* **hops** *17-*.

hour *see* OOR[1]

house &c, hous &c *la14-e18*; **huse &c** *15-e17*, **hoose &c** *19-* [hus] *n* **1** = house *la14-*, *in place-names 14-*. **2** a stronghold, a castle *15-e17*, *only Sc*. **3** a separate portion of a building occupied by a single family etc and consisting of one or (*usu*) more rooms, with a separate door opening onto the common passage or stair, a flat *16-*. **4** *curling* (CURL) *and carpet-bowls* the circle round the TEE[1] within which the stones etc must lie to be counted in the score, the BROCH *la19-*.
vt **1** = house. **2** take, put, or drive (*chf* animals) into a house; shelter *15-*. **3** store (goods, crops etc) *15-*, *now Abd*.
hoosie = *n* **1**, **3**, *la19-*. **~ing &c** *n* **1** = housing *15-*. **2** a canopied niche or recess in a wall *16-17*. **3** a dwelling-place *la16*, *19-*, *now Abd*.
~ ba *game* rounders *la19-*, *now local Cai-Rox*.
~ devil a person who behaves badly at home, *freq* contrasted with *causey saint* (CAUSEY) *19-*, *NE, EC, S*. **~-en(d) 1** the end or gable of a house *la14-*. **2** *fig* a stout or heavily-built woman *20-*, *Gen except Sh Ork*. **~-fast** housebound, confined to the house *la19-*, *local Sh-Renfr*. **~-gear** household furnishings or equipment *19-*, *Gen except Sh Ork*. **~hald &c** *15-e17*, **household** *17-*, **housald &c** *la15-e17*, **~it &c** *16*, *19* ['hus'hald; *'husɑld, *'husət] *n*, *also* **housal** *19*, **housell** *la17* [*'husəl] *freq attrib* = household. **in ~hald &c** in or within the household; included in the household *la15-e17*: '*his mother being present in houshald with him*'.
~haldar *16*, **~ha(u)dder** *el7*, *19-* [*'hus'hɑldər, *-'hadər, &c] = householder. **~halding &c** *la16*, **~ haddin** *la19-* ['hus'hɑldɪn, -'hadɪn] the management of a house, housekeeping. **~-heat(ing) &c** a house-warming *19-*. **~-heid &c** the roof of a house *16*, *19-*, *now Cai Abd Rox*. **~-hicht &c** *n* the height of a house, one or more storeys *la16-*, *now midLoth Renfr*. **~-knock** = house clock *17*, *only Sc*. **~-mail &c** *16-e18*, **~-meall &c** [*'hus'mel] *la16-17* house rent, rental *only Sc*. **~ place** a situation as a domestic servant *20*, *midLoth Rox*. **~-side &c 1** the side of a house *la15-16*. **2** *fig* a big clumsy person *19-*, *now Ags midLoth Gsw*. **~-ste(a)d &c** the land on which a house is to be built, the site of a house *la15-e19*. **~-tied** = **~fast**, *la19-*, *now Cai Per Renfr*.
~ within itself a *self-contained* (SEL[1]) house or flat *la18-*, *now Abd*. **one's ~ at hame** one's

home *la18-*, *now Abd Ags Ayr*. **out o ~ an ha** *etc* (drive someone) out of every refuge *19-*, *Gen except Sh Ork*.

housour &c [*'husur, *-ər] *n* a covering, a housing *e16*. [OF *houss(e)ure*; *cf* ModEng *house*]

houster &c ['hustər, 'hʌustər; *Rox* 'høstər, 'hʌstər] *vi* gather together in a confused way *18-*, *now Fif*.
n **1** a badly-dressed, untidy person *19-e20*. **2** *chf* **houst(e)rie &c** trash, rubbish *19-e20*. [obscure]

hout *see* HOOT

houxie ['hʌuksi, 'hʌugsi] *interj* a call to a cow *20-*, *Cai*. [? dim of Eng *ox*, or perh f Norw *okse*]

houzle [*'huzl] *vt* fill the nostrils with (snuff) *19*. *n* a large pinch of snuff *19*. [perh a joc extension of *hoozle* (HOSE[1])]

hove[1], huve &c [hov] *16-*, *now Sh* [hov; *Sh* høv] *v* **1** *vt* raise, hold up *la14-e16*. **2** throw, toss, fling, cast away *18-*, *now Sh Ags Bwk*. **3** *vi* (1) *of light loose soil* rise, puff up *la18-e19*. (2) *in gen* rise above the surface *la19-*, *now local Cai-Dmf*. **4** (1) *vt* cause to swell, distend *la18-*. (2) *vi* become swollen or distended, swell, expand *19-*; see also *hoved*.
n the swelling of cattle (*cf* next) *la19-*, *now midLoth Bwk Lnk*.
hoved *adj* = *hoven* (HEAVE) *20-*, *now local*. **hovie &c** swollen, distended; *of bread etc* puffy, well-risen *la19-e20*. **hoving &c** the state of being swollen *19-*. [back-formation f *hoven*, ptp of HEAVE]

hove[2] *interj* a call to a cow to come to be milked, or housed for the night *19-*, *Bwk Rox*. [*cf* nEng dial *hoaf*]

hove, hoven *see* HEAVE

hover &c ['hovər] *vi* **1** = hover *la15-*. **2** pause, wait a little (*orig* (*16*) in deliberation, uncertainty or indecision) *16-*.
n = hover.
~ a blink wait a little *19-*. **in (a) ~** in a state of hesitation, uncertainty or indecision *16-*, *now Sh*.

hovie, hoving *see* HOVE

how[1] &c; **hew** *18-19*, **hyow &c** *20-*, *Cai NE* [hʌu; *Cai NE* hjʌu] *n* = hoe, the tool *la14-*.
vti **1** = hoe *17-e20*. **2** *specif* uproot (broom or whins) *17-19*.
come tae the hyow be ready for hoeing *20-*, *Cai NE*.

how[2] &c [hʌu] *interj* a call to attract attention, or to incite (sailors or horses etc) to action *la15-e20*; *cf* *hech how* (HECH).

how *see* HOO[1], HOO[3], HOWE[1], HOWE[2]

howd &c [hʌud] *vti* **1** sway, rock from side to side, bump up and down *la18-*, *now Abd Kcdn*. **2** *of a vessel afloat* pitch or toss about, bob up and down *19-*, *now Kcdn*.
n, *esp of the motion of a ship* a lurching rocking movement from side to side *la18-20*. **howder &c, howther &c** *19-e20* ['hʌudər, 'hʌuðər] *vi* **1** *esp of a boat or cart* move with a rocking, jolting

or bumping motion *19-*, now *NE*. **2** *of a large number of persons etc* swarm, mill around, bustle about *la18-19*. *n* **1** (1) *of a boat on a rough sea* a rocking, jolting, sideways motion *la19-*, *Bnf Abd*. (2) uncouth horseplay, a rough-and-tumble *e19*. **2** a blast of wind, a blustering wind *19-*, *NE*. **howdle &c** *vi* move with a rocking or bumping motion, limp *19-e20*. *n* a swarm or crowd (in motion), a heap *19-*, *Fif*. [var of HOD; *cf* HUDDER]

howd *see* HIDE[1]

Howdenite &c [*'hʌudənəit] *n*, *appar* a follower of John Halden, an extreme *Covenanter* (COVENANT) *la17-e18*.

howder [*'hʌudər] *vti* hide, conceal *18-e19*, *only Sc*. [frequentative of *howd* (HIDE[1])]

howder *see* HOWD

howdie &c ['hʌudɪ] *n* a midwife; *formerly* an untrained sick-nurse; *also* a woman who lays out the dead *la17-*.
~**ing** *n* **1** a confinement *19-*, now *Lnk Kcb*. **2** midwifery *19-*, now *Edb*.
~ **wife** = *n*, *la19-*, now *local Cai-Lnk*. [unknown; prob popularized by Burns]

howdle *see* HOWD

howe[1] &c, how &c, holl &c *la14-16*; **hough &c** *la17-19* [hʌu; *hol] *n* **1** = hole *la14-16*, *only Sc*. **2** a depression, a hollow or low-lying piece of ground *16-*, now *N, EC S*. **3** *chf in place-names* a stretch of country of basin formation, a wide plain bounded by hills, a vale *16-*: 'Howe o the Mearns'. **4** *in gen* a depression or hollow, a hollow space, a cavity *la17-e20*. **5** *curling* (CURL) the smooth stretch of ice down the centre of the rink along which the stones travel *la19-*, now *SW*. **6** *fig*, *in pl* a mood of depression, *freq* **be in the** ~**s** be depressed, be in the dumps *la17-*, now *midLoth*, *only Sc*.
adj **1** hollow, lying in a hollow, deep-set, sunken *la14-*. **2** hungry, famished, empty (of food) *18-*, now *Ork*. **3** deep, intense, innermost *19-*, now *Ags*. **4** *of sound, the voice etc* hollow, deep, echoing, guttural *17-*, now *Ork*.
adv hollowly, deeply *la15-19*, *only Sc*.
~ **backit 1** *of a horse* saddle-backed *la18-19*. **2** *of persons* round-shouldered; hollow-backed *20-*, now *C, S*. ~**-barrow &c** a barrow with sides *16*, *only Sc*. ~ **bonet** a bonnet with a hollow crown *la16*, *only Sc*. ~**-dumb-dead &c** the depth, the darkest point (of winter, night etc) *e19*, *e20* (*literary*), *only Sc*. ~ **ice** *curling* (CURL) = *n* 5, *la18-*, now *local Abd-Gall*.
cast *etc* **in the** ~**s** cast out, suppress, reject completely *17*. **heich(s)** *la16-* or **heicht(s)** *la16-*, now *local E* **and** ~**s** hill(s) and dale(s), ups and downs; *fig* moods, tantrums, quirks of character. ~ **enough &c** very indifferent(ly), 'so-so' *la17-19*. ~ **o the neck** the nape of the neck *la19-*, now *NE*. ~ **o the nicht** midnight or the period between 12 and 3am *19-*, now *Abd*

Kcdn Lnk. ~ **o (the) winter** *midLoth*, ~ **o the year** now *Ags* midwinter, Nov to Jan *19-*. [ME *holl*, OE *hol*; *cf* next and (HOLE)]

howe[2], how &c [hʌu] *n* **1** the hull of a ship *16-17*, *e20*. **2** a boat with neither sails nor mast up *20-*, *NE-Fif*. [appar var of *holl* (HOLE) the hold of a ship (as in Eng)]

howek *see* HOO[3]

howf &c, houff &c [hʌuf] *n* **1** (1) *also* **holf** a burial ground in the centre of Dundee, *orig* the courtyard of the Greyfriars Monastery *la16-18*. (2) *also* **hoffe** *la17* [*hof] *in gen* a burial ground, *latterly freq* a private burial ground *17* (*Abd*), *la18-*, now *Kcdn Ayr*. **3** *also* **holf** an enclosed open space, a yard, *specif* a yard for storing timber, *orig* (*17-e18*) at Leith *17-*, now *Ags Per Fif*. **4** a favourite haunt, a meeting place, *freq* a public house, sometimes implying a place of disrepute *18-*. **5** (1) a rough shelter or refuge *la18-*, now *Ags Stlg Renfr*. (2) a natural or improvised shelter used by mountaineers *20-*.
vti **1** dwell, lodge; haunt, frequent *18-*, now *EC Kcb Dmf*. **2** take shelter or refuge *la19-*, now *Ags*.
hae nae ~ **o** have no desire to associate with, have no liking for *la19-e20*. [only *Sc*; *appar* Du, Flem *hof* an enclosed place, a courtyard]

howffin &c, howffing ['hʌufən] *n* a clumsy, shy and rather stupid person *e16*, *la19-*, *NE*. [only *Sc*; uncertain]

howis *see* HOCH[1]

howit *see* HOT

howk[1] &c *la16-*, **holk** *la15-17*; **hoke &c** *la16-19*, **hock &c** *la19-*, *Sh* [hʌuk; *Sh Ork Gall Uls* hok; *holk] *v* **1** *vt* (1) dig (ground), dig into, make (a trench etc) by digging, dig out, uproot *16-*. (2) *fig* investigate, poke one's nose into *19-*. (3) *fig* unearth, bring out, extricate *19-*. **2** hollow out, scrape or scoop out the inside of (something) *17*, *la19-*. **3** hew, mine (coal), quarry (stone) *la18-*. **4** *vti*, *chf of pigs* root, burrow in the earth *18-*. **5** *freq* ~ **on** or **about** loiter, stand around idly, pass the time idly *la19-*, now *Abd Kcdn Rox*.
n the act of digging or burrowing *la18-*, now *Sh Ork*.
~**er** a person who digs *19-*; see also *tattie-howker* (TATTIE). ~**it** *adj* hollowed (out), made hollow (by digging or otherwise) *la15-16*.

howk[2] &c *19-e20*, **holk- &c** *16* [hʌuk] *n* **1** *in pl* an ailment affecting the face or eyes of a person *16*. **2** *chf in sing* **the** ~ a disease (primarily a stomach disorder) affecting the eyes of cattle *19-e20*, *chf Abd*. [see SND, DOST]

howk *see* HULK

howlat *see* HOOLET

howld &c [hʌuld; *NE* hʌul] *n* = hold (of a ship) *18-*, now *local Sh-Fif*.

howld *see* HAUD

howm &c *16-*, **holm &c** *la14-19*, *in place-names*

13- [hʌum, hom: *holm] *n* a stretch of low-lying land beside a river, a HAUGH *la14-, now C, S.*

ho(l)min(g) (**ground** *etc*) = *n, 18.* [ME *holme,* ON *holmr* a small island]

howp¹ &c *la16-, now local Cai-Rox,* **hope &c** *la14-;* **hop** *la14-e17,* **hoop** *la17, 20-* (*Sh Ork*) [hʌup; hop; *Sh Ork* hup] *n* = hope *la14-.*
vti **1** = hope *la14-.* **2** *vt* believe, suppose, think (something to be or have been the case) *la14-17.*
~fu(l) = hopeful *17-.* **be ~ful that** hope that *la18-.*
I ~ *followed by pt* blow me if he *etc* didn't *etc! 19-, now NE, Dmf: 'I hope he'd forgotten the key'.*
in ~(s) to do *etc* in the hope or expectation of doing etc *la16, 19-: 'they tend the flock in houp to get the fleece'.* **na ~ bit** no alternative but *20-, Sh Abd Kcdn.*

howp² &c [hʌup] *n* a mouthful or gulp of liquid, a draught (*esp* of liquor), a dram *la19-, NE.* [prob imit of the sound of gulping]

howp *see* HOPE¹, HOPE²

howt *see* HOT

howther *see* HOWD

howtowdie &c ['hʌu'tʌudɪ] *n* **1** a large (young) chicken for the pot, a young hen which has not begun to lay *18-20.* **2** *transf* an unmarried woman *19.* [only Sc; appar OF *hétoudeau*]

hoy¹ *v* **1** *vt* drive, urge or incite with cries of 'hoy' *16-, now Bwk Lnk.* **2** hail, summon *la18-, local Ork-Kcb.* **3** *vi* shout 'hoy' *la16-, now local Ork-Kcb.* [Eng *hoy* interj]

hoy² *vt* heave up (a heavy object), throw or toss up *20-, Sh Bwk Rox.*
n a heave, the act of heaving *20-, Sh Cai Kcb Rox.* [reduced or back-formation f HOISE]

hoy³ *vi* walk with a quick brisk step, hurry *19-, C, S.* [var of HIE *v*]

hoyes *see* OYES

hozle *see* HOSE¹

hree *see* THREE

hubber *see* HABBER

hubbilschow *see* HUBBLESHEW

hubble *n* **1** = HOBBLE *n* 4, *19-, Sh C, S.* **2** = HOBBLE *n* 3, *la19-, chf SW.*
vt = HOBBLE *v* 5, *la19-e20, C.*
be in a ~ o work be 'snowed under' with work *19-, Sh Dmf.* [*cf* also HABBLE and next 2 articles]

hubble-bubble &c *n* an uproar, tumult, hubbub *e17.* [see DOST Suppl; *cf* next]

hubbleshew &c, **hubbilschow &c** *16;* **hobble- &c, -shue &c** ['hʌbl'ʃu, 'hobl-, &c] *n* **1** an uproar, tumult, hubbub *16-, now Sh.* **2** a mob, rabble *la18-e19.* [*cf* eModEng *hubbleshowe, hubble-shubble* (*n*); eModFlem *hobbel-s(j)obbel* (*adv*) confusedly]

huche *see* HEUCH

hucker *see* HOCKER

hucky duck *see* HACKY DUCK

hud &c [hʌd] *n* **1** the back of an open fireplace,

consisting of a stone or clay block resembling a seat *la18-20, chf S.* **2** a small shelf or recess at each side of an old-fashioned fireplace, used as a hob for pots etc *19-, Kcb Dmf Rox.* **3** the seat by the fire on a blacksmith's hearth *19-20, Dmf Rox.*
~ stane the stone which forms the HUD (*n* 1) *19, SW.* [irreg var of Eng *hob*; see SND]

hud *see* HAUD, HIDE¹, HUID

hudd &c *n* = hod, a receptacle for carrying mortar *19-, now Kcb, only Sc.*

hudd *see* HUID

hudder &c; huther &c *la18-* ['hʌdər, 'hʌðər] *v* **1** *vi* act in a confused or hasty way; work or walk clumsily or hastily *19.* **2** *vt* heap together in disorder; throw **on** (clothes) hastily or untidily *la19-, now Ags.*
n **1** *now only* **huther** an untidy worker or person, a sloven *la19-, now Lnk Dmf Rox.* **2** a confused crowd or heap *19-, now Kcb.*
hudderie &c, hutherie &c *19 adj* **1** *also* **hudderie-dudderie &c** *la19-e20* slovenly, dirty or untidy in appearance or habits *19-, now local Fif-Dmf.* **2** *chf of hair* shaggy, unkempt, dishevelled *la19-, NE, C.* **hudd(e)rin &c** *adj* **1** *chf of a woman* slovenly, slatternly *18-, now Kcb Uls.* **2** awkward, clumsy *18-e20* [*cf* HUDDERON]. [var of *howder* (HOWD)]

hudderon &c, huddroun &c *e16;* **huddron &c** *n* a slovenly person *16-, now Cai Lnk.* [appar deriv of HUDDER; see SND]

hudderon *see* HUTHERON

huddoun &c *n* a species of whale *la15-16.* [nME *hodones* (*pl*); unknown]

huddron *see* HUDDERON

huddroun *see* HUDDERON, HUTHERON

hude &c [*hød] *n* a Dutch measure of dry capacity *la15-e17.* [only Sc; MDu *hoet, hoot*]

hude *see* HAUD, HUID

huden *see* HIDE¹

hudge [hʌdʒ] *n* a large quantity, a vast amount (of money etc) *19-, Ork Cai Abd.*
vt amass, heap up *la19-, now Abd.* [voiced var of Eng *hutch,* (orig) a chest for money etc]

hudge-mudge ['hʌdʒ'mʌdʒ] *n* secrecy; furtive whispering *18-, now Ags.*
hudg(e)mudgan &c *n* whispering (*esp* behind someone's back) *19-, now Abd Ags.* [parallel form to Eng *hugger-mugger* (*n*) secrecy, (*v*) conceal]

hue &c *19-,* **hew &c** *n* **1** = hue, colour, complexion *la14-.* **2** appearance, aspect *15-, now Sh Ags.* **3** a very small quantity or portion (*freq* of food or drink); **not** a whit *19-, now WC.*
neither ~ nor hair *adv* in no way, not a whit *19-, now Sh Cai.*

hufe *see* HEAVE, HUIF, HUIVE

huff *vti* **1** = huff. **2** swell, puff up *la19-, now Sh Ags.*

huff- *see* HUIVE

huge &c [*hʌdʒ] *adj* = huge *la14-.*
adv hugely *la15-e16.*

hugger *vi* **1** shudder, shiver, hug oneself (to keep warm) *19-*, *NE*. **2** crowd or huddle together as a protection against cold *la19-*, *Bnf Abd Ags*. **3** *of clothes* slip down or hang untidily, *chf* ~**ed**, ~**in** &c *20-*, *now Ags Fif*.
~**t**, ~**ing** *adj* **1** round-shouldered *20-*, *now Mry*. **2** huddled up or shrunk with cold, pinched-looking *la20-*, *NE-Per*. [only Sc; var of HOCKER; *v* 3 may be conflation of HOCKER w HUDDER]
hugger *see* HOGGER
huggery-muggery &c; **hug(ge)rie** *19-*, *now Ayr adj* furtive; disorderly, untidy *19-*, *Ags-Rox*.
adv furtively; in a confused or disorderly state *19-*, *now Dmf*. [var of Eng *hugger-mugger*]
hugget *see* HOGGET
hugly *see* UGLY
hugmahush &c ['hʌgmə'hʌʃ] *n*, *freq attrib* a slovenly person, a slattern; a lout *19-*, *now Kcdn*. [only Sc; fanciful formation w infl f *eg* HUGGERY-MUGGERY and HUSHLE[1]]
hugmanay *see* HOGMANAY
hugrie *see* HUGGERY-MUGGERY
hugtoun *see* HOGTOUN
huid &c *16-*, **hude** &c; **hood** *la18-*, **hud(d)** *la14-e20* [høð, hɪd; hʌd; *N* hid; *St* hud] *n* **1** = hood *la14-*. **2** *chf* **hood** one of a pair of sheaves of corn placed on the top of a STOOK[1] or corn stack as a protection against the weather *la18-*, *now Rox*.
vt **1** = hood *la17-*. **2** top (a STOOK[1] of corn) with two protective sheaves *19-e20*.
~**ie** ['høðɪ, &c; *Fif also* 'hʌudɪ] *n* **1** = ~ie craw 1 and 2, *la18-*. **2** a sunbonnet worn by field-workers *20-*, *now Ork Ags*. ~**ie craw** &c, **heidie** &c **craw** *la18-e20*, *Sh N* **1** the hooded crow *la18-*. **2** the carrion crow *la18-*, *Gen except Sh-Cai*. **3** the black-headed gull *la19-*, *now Sh, only Sc*. **4** *fig, contemptuous* a person with a sinister manner or aspect *la20-*, *Abd Per Rox*. **put the** ~**ie on** cap, top *20-*, *now Ork Ags*.
hoodin(g) &c = *n* 2, *20-*, *now Uls*. **huidin** &c *19-*, *now Sh Ork*, **hiddin** &c *la19-e20*, *chf NE* a point of juncture, a fastening, a hinge, *specif* **1** *of a flail* the leather hinge or wooden connection joining the two parts *19-*, *now Sh Ork*. **2** a knot used to join two parts of a fishing line *la19-e20*.
~**it** &c **1** = hooded *16-*. **2** *of birds* having head-colouring etc suggestive of a hood, *specif* ~**it craw** = ~**ie craw** 1 and 2 (*16-*), 3 (*19-*, *now Ork, only Sc*). ~**ock** = ~**ie craw** 1; *fig* an avaricious person *la18-19*.
hood sheaf = *n* 2, *la18-19*. ~**pyk** &c [*'~ 'pəik, *'~'pɪk] a miser, a mean person *16*, *only Sc*.
huid *see* HIDE[1]
huif *19-*, *now Ags Kcb*, **hufe** *la15-e16*, **hoove** &c *16-e18*, *only Sc*; **hiv** *la19-*, *now Cai NE* [høf, hɪf; *N* hɪv; *høv; *NE also* *hif; *pl* *høvz; *WC* *hevz] *n* = hoof.
huil &c (*now chf EC, S*), **huill** *la16*, **hool(e)** *17-*; **hull** *16-* [høl, hɪl; *nEC* hel] *n* **1** = hull, the

husk, pod, skin, shell of a fruit or nut etc *16-*. **2** other forms of covering: (1) the pericardium, the membrane surrounding the heart, *freq* **leap** etc (**oot o**) **the** ~ *of the heart* burst *la16-20*; (2) the skin of a person or animal *18-e20*; (3) *in pl* clothes, garments *18-e20*. **3** the body as the container of the soul; *fig* an outward or superficial aspect or appearance *la18-19*.
vt shell (peas etc), husk *la18-*.
huilie &c *20-*, **huly** &c; **hoolie** &c *18-*, **heelie** &c *19-*, *NE* ['hølɪ, 'hɪlɪ; 'hulɪ; *NE* 'hilɪ] *adj* moderate, slow, cautious, careful *orig only* ~ **pace** &c or **speid** *la15-e19*.
adv **1** moderately, slowly, gently *16-*. **2** *freq as interj* be careful!, go slow!, have patience! *la16-*.
vi pause, halt, hesitate *la19-*, *now Mry Kcdn Stlg*, *only Sc*.
ca one's hogs til a ~ **market** *fig* make a bad bargain *20-*, *NE*, *Ags*. **come** ~ **on** (*la20-*) *or* **tae** (*la19-*) have indifferent success, fare badly *now NE Stlg*. ~ **and fair(ly)** slowly and gently but steadily *18-e20*. [nME *holy, huly*, ON *hóflig-r* (*adj*), *hóflega* (*adv*)]
huill *see* HUIL
huird &c *la16-*, **hurd** &c *la14-e17* [hørd, herd; *NE* hurd] *n* = hoard *la14-*, *now Cai Abd Per*.
vt **1** = hoard *la14-*, *now Cai Abd Per*. **2** harbour, entertain (criminals or wrongdoers) *esp* secretly or clandestinely *la15-e17*, *only Sc*.
huit *see* HOT
huive &c *19-e20*, **huve** &c *15-16*, **hufe** &c *la14-e17*; **huff-** &c *15-e17* [*Rox* høv] *vi*, *chf verse*, *orig of persons on horseback* remain stationary, stay, wait, tarry. [var of Eng *hove*]
huizle &c [høzl] *vt*, *chf* **huizlin(g)** a severe drubbing *19-*, *Rox*. [uncertain]
huizle *see* WHEEZE[3]
huke &c [*høk] *vt* regard, pay attention to, take into account *la16*. [only Sc; obscure]
huke *see* HEUK
huke-bane *see* HEUKBANE
huldge: hulgie- having a hump, hunch-(backed etc) *la18-e20*, *NE*. [only Sc; var of obs or dial Eng *hulch* a hump]
hule &c; **hewl** &c [høl, hjul] *n* **1** a mischievous, perverse or objectionable person or animal *19-*, *now Kcb Dmf*. **2** = devil, deuce, *eg* **what the** ~, **a** ~ **of a** *la19-*, *now Rox*. [obscure; *cf* Ir dial *hole* = *n* 1]
hulk &c; **howk** &c *la15-e16* *n* **1** = hulk, a ship *15-*. **2** a big unwieldy mass, a hump *la18-*.
vi hang idly **about** (a place), skulk (**about**) *la19-*, *local Sh-Fif*.
hull *see* HILL[1], HUIL
hullachan *see* HOOLACHAN
hullie &c ['hʌlɪ] *adj* hollow *la19-e20*, *eLoth Bwk*.
n a receptacle for storing live crabs and lobsters, *orig* (*19*) holes in the rocks below the high-water mark, *now* (*20-*) baskets or boxes anchored in the harbour *19-*, *eLoth Bwk*. [var of HALLOW[1]]
hullion &c *n*, *appar* a heap or accumulation of articles; wealth, property *la18-e20*. [obscure]

hullion see HALLION

hullok *n* a Spanish red wine *la16-e17*. [eModEng *hollocke, hallocke,* Sp *haloque*]

hulster[1] *n* = holster *la17-e18, only Sc.*

hulster[2] **&c** *vi* **1** hoist a load onto one's back; struggle along under a heavy burden *20-, now Abd Per.* **2** walk heavily as if laden *la19-, now Abd.* **3** have on too many clothes, be cluttered up with too many clothes *20-, Abd Rox.*
n an upwards hoist, a push *la19-, Bnf Abd Per.* [uncertain]

huly see HUILIE

hum; ham &c *la19-, Ork Abd Uls v* **1** *vt* chew partially, *esp* chew (food) till soft before transferring it to an infant's mouth *19-, local.* **2** *vti, freq* ~ **amo** *or* **intae** eat greedily, take large mouthfuls of, crunch *20-, Bnf Abd.*
n a piece of food chewed as in *v* 1, and given to a child *19-, now Cai Dmf.*

hummle &c = *v* 1, *19-e20.* [uncertain]

humanity &c, humanité &c *15-16* [*St* hju'manɪtɪ; **hǝ'manɪtɪ*] *n* **1** = humanity *15-.* **2** *Sc Univs* the formal name for (1) the study of the classical languages and literature, *esp* (and *now only*) Latin *la16-*; (2) the chair or class of Latin *19-.*

humast see UMOST

humble see HUMMEL

humbug *n* **1** = humbug. **2** a nuisance, an imposition *la20-, NE.*
vti **1** = humbug. **2 be humbugged with** be pestered with, be bothered with *la19-, now NE.*

humch *vi* be sulky or bad-tempered *la19-, Bnf.* [*cf* GLUMSH]

hum-drum *adj* **1** = humdrum. **2** dejected, in low spirits; sullen *18-, now local Cai-Slk.*
n an apathetic, lazy-minded person *19-20.*

humdudgeon &c *n* a fuss; *in pl* sulks *e19.* [*cf* Eng slang *humdurgeon* the sulks]

humel- see HUMMEL

humf see HUMPH[2]

humfie, humfy see HUMPH[1]

humility, humilité &c *la14-e16* [hju'mɪlɪtɪ; **hǝ'mɪlɪtɪ*] *n* **1** = humility *la14-.* **2** a pot plant, a kind of saxifrage, Aaron's beard *la19-, Abd Ags wLoth.*

humill, humil(l)y see HUMMLE

humle-, humler, humlie see HUMMEL

humlock &c ['hʌmlǝk; *EC also* -lɪ; *S also* -lǝt, -lo] *n* **1** the common hemlock or any of the umbelliferous plants such as the cow parsnip *15-, now Ags Bwk Rox.* **2** a dried hemlock stalk used as a peashooter *19-, Fif S.* [eModEng *humlocke,* ME *hum(b)lok,* OE *hymlice*]

humly see HUMMLE

hummel &c *la17-,* **hummill &c** *la16,* **hommill &c, hamill &c** *la17-e20;* **humble &c** *la16-e20* ['hʌml; *Ork* 'haml; *Ross also* 'haml] *adj* **1** (1) *of farm animals, chf and orig only of cattle* naturally hornless; *also* polled *16-.* (2) *of deer* naturally hornless *la20-.* **2** *of corn etc* awnless,

not bearded *la15-e20.* **3** *transf* (1) without projections; with a flat, level appearance; smooth; unarmed *18-20;* (2) *specif, of a boat* without a mast or sail; lying with mast and sail lowered *20, N.*
n an animal that has no horns or has been polled *la19-, local Cai-Ags.*
vt **1** remove the awns from (barley etc) *la18-.* **2** break up (stones or large pieces of driftwood) into smaller pieces and shape for use *20-, now Sh.*
~**(e)d &c** *of cattle etc* deprived of horns *la16-, now Cai Ags WC.* **hummeller, humler** a machine for removing the awns from barley; the part of a threshing mill that does this *la18-20.* **hum(m)lie** *n* **1** = *n, 19-e20.* **2** a rustic, *specif* (1) a Highlander (HIELAND) *18-e19;* (2) a native of Buchan *la19-, Abd.* **Buchan humlie** one of the hornless *Aberdeen Angus* (ABERDEEN) type of cattle reared *chf* in Buchan *la19-, NE.*
~ **bonnet** a plain bonnet without a crest of feathers worn by *Highland regiments* (HIELAND) *19.* **hum(m)el doddie** *adj* hornless *la19-, Bnf Abd. n, in pl* woollen mitts *20-, Abd.* **hum(m)le mittens** *n* = *prec la19-, Bnf Abd.* [LowGer *hommel, hummel* a hornless animal]

hummell *n* meaning obscure *e16.*

hummer &c *vi* murmur, mumble, grumble; mutter to oneself *18-, now Cai midLoth.* [Eng *hum (v)* murmur + *-er*]

hummie[1] **&c** *19-20,* **hummock** *e17, e19* ['hʌmɪ; *NE also* 'humɪ; **'hʌmǝk*] *n* **1** the closing of the hand so that the thumb and the four fingertips are placed together (eg as a test of the suppleness of one's fingers on a cold day) *e17, e19.* **2** a pinch (of meal, salt etc), as much as can be taken up between the thumb and four fingers *19-20.* [see SND]

hummie[2] *interj, also* ~ **your side!** *etc* a cry in the game of SHINTY to warn an opponent to keep to his own side *19-e20.* [see SND]

hummill see HUMMEL

hummle &c *la16-e19,* **humill &c** *15-19;* **heum(b)le &c** *e16, la19-e20* ['hʌml; *NE also* **'h(j)uml*] *adj, vt* = humble *la15-e20.* **hum(m)il(l)y &c** *la14-17,* **humly &c** *la15-18* = humbly.

hummle see HUM

hummlie see HUMMEL

hummock see HUMMIE[1]

humour &c, eemir &c *e20, Abd* ['hjumǝr; *NE* 'imǝr; **'ømǝr*] *n* **1** = humour *15-.* **2** (1) matter or pus from a wound or sore *20-, Gen except WC, SW.* (2) a skin eruption *la20-, Abd Kcdn Rox.* **3** a feeling of resentment or ill temper *18-20.*
humoursome &c humorous, witty *19-, now N, nEC.*

humph[1] **&c** *19-, only Sc;* **hump** *la18- n* **1** =

hump, a curvature of the back or spine, a hump-back *19-, Gen except Sh Ork*. **2** the act of carrying a heavy load *la20-*.

v **1** *vt* carry about (a heavy burden), lug, hoist or lift up (something heavy) *la19-*. **2** *vi* move around laboriously under the weight of a heavy burden *20-, local NE-S*.

~**ed** hunched *20-*. ~**ie &c, humfie** *adj* **1** having a hump, hunchbacked *la18-, Gen except Sh Ork*. *n* a hunchbacked person *la18-19*.

humfy-back = ~**ie** (*n*), *la20-, Gen except Sh Ork*. ~**ie- backit** = ~**ie** (*adj*), *la19-, Gen except Sh Ork*.

~-**backed** hunchbacked *19-, Gen except Sh Ork*. **come up one's** ~ come into one's head, occur to one to do something *la19-, now C Slk*. **set up one's** ~ become angry and antagonistic *la19-, EC, WC, Slk*.

humph[2]; **humf** *la19-e20* *n* **1** an offensive smell of decaying matter, a stench *la19-, local Cai-Lnk*. **2** a 'high' flavour, a taste of a foodstuff going bad *19-e20*.

vi have or acquire a smell or taste of decay *la19-, now Abd Per midLoth*.

~**ed** stinking, putrid *la18-, now Per Fif midLoth*. ~**y** *adj* having an offensive smell or a high taste, 'off' *20-, now Per*. [perh f Eng *humph* (*interj*) expressing disgust]

humph[3] *n* name for poor quality coal *la18-e20*. [uncertain]

humple[1] *la18-, now local Stlg-Rox*, **humplock &c** *la17-, now WC* *n* a small heap or mound, a hillock *now local Stlg-Rox*. [Eng *hump* (*n*) + dim suffixes]

humple[2] *vi* walk unevenly or haltingly, as in tight shoes, hobble *19-e20, Rox*.

humplock *see* HUMPLE[1]

humpsh, humsh *see* HANCH

hun *see* HUND

hunch &c [hʌnʃ] *n* an upward thrust with the shoulders; a shrug *la20-, Abd midLoth*.

vti **1** = hunch. **2** heave or shove with the shoulder *la19-, now Ork midLoth*.

~**ie** a hunchback *19-, now Cai Abd midLoth*. ~-**cuddy-**~ a boys' team-game *20-, C*; see SND.

hund, hound &c; houn &c *la18-e20*, **hun(n)** *la18-e20*, **hond &c** *la14-e17* [hʌn(d), hun(d); *Ayr also* hʌun] *n* **1** a dog *in gen, la14-*. **2** *specif* = hound, a hunting dog *la14-*.

vti **1** = hound *16-*. **2** drive out *etc* with dogs or by violence *la16-17*. **3** *of a male dog* run about from place to place after females *20-, Abd Lnk*.

~**er** (**out**) an instigator, an inciter *la16-17*. ~**ing,** ~**ing out** *n* instigation, inciting *la16-18*.

hunder &c *now local*, **hundir &c** *la14-e19*, **hounder &c** *la16-e17*, **hunderd &c** *15-16*, **hundreth &c** *la14-e18*, **houndreth &c** *la16-e18*; **honder &c** *la14-e16*, **hundred** *18-*, **hundereth &c** *15-17*, **hun(n)er** *la14-e15*, *la18-, now local NE-Uls* ['hʌn(d)ər; 'hʌn(d)ərt;

*'hʌndrɛð, *-ið, *-əð] *n* **1** = hundred *la14-*. **2** *weaving* a unit of measurement denoting the fineness of a web *16-19*. **3** a definite number (of livestock, goods etc) which is greater than 100, *usu* 120, but varying according to time and place *la16-, now Ork*.

adj **1** = hundred *la14-*. **2** *also* **hunert &c** *la16, 20-, Sh Abd* = hundredth *15-, now NE midLoth*.

a ~ **ȝere &c** a century *15-16*.

the Auld Hunder(t), the Old Hundredth the long-metre version of the 100th Psalm in the Scottish Psalter (see PSALM); the tune to which this is sung *la19-*. **get a** ~ **pound** get a piece of good fortune, *freq* a birth in the family *20-, local Abd-midLoth*.

hune, hone &c *la14-16* [*høn] *n*, *only verse, chf but* (*la14-16, e19*), **foroutin** (*la14-16*) *or* **withoutin** (*15-16*) ~ without delay. *vi* stop; linger; delay *19*. [nME *hon(e)*; obscure]

huner, hunert *see* HUNDER

hung *see* HING

hunger &c ['hʌŋər] *n* = hunger *la14-*.

vti **1** = hunger *la14-*. **2** *vt, also fig* starve *15-*.

hungered &c *17-*, **hungert &c** *16-*, **hungrit &c** *la16* ['hʌŋərt; *'hʌŋrit], *also fig* starved(-looking), hungry *la19-*. **hungry &c** ['hʌŋ(ə)rɪ] *adj* **1** = hungry *15-*. **2** mean, miserly; greedy *la19-*.

hungrysome &c *19-, now local Cai-Kcb*, **hungersome** *19-, now Per midLoth adj* **1** hungry, having a keen appetite *19-*. **2** stimulating hunger *19-20, now midLoth*.

a ~ **and/or a burst** starvation (*or* scarcity) and/or plenty *la19-*.

hunker &c ['hʌŋkər] *vi, freq* ~ **doon 1** squat; seat oneself in a crouching position or on one's haunches, *freq derisive* in reference to kneeling and genuflexion in non-Presbyterian worship *18-*. **2** huddle, sit or settle oneself in a crouching or cramped position *la18-, local Ork-Kcb*. **3** *fig* stoop, submit, resign oneself (to circumstances) *19-, now midLoth*.

n, chf **on one's** ~**s 1** in(to) a squatting position *la18-*. **2** in a quandary; on one's last legs *19-, C*.

~-**bane** the thigh bone *20-, now Cai Per*. ~-**slide** *vi* **1** slide on ice in a crouched position *19-, Gen except Sh Ork*. **2** *fig* evade a duty or a promise, act in a shifty manner, prevaricate *20-*. ~-**slider** a slippery customer *20-*. ~-**sliding** *n* dishonourable or shifty conduct, evasive behaviour *la19-*. *adj* evasive, dishonourable *20-*. [appar a nasalized frequentative of *huk-, found in MDu *hucken*, Ger *hucken*, ON *húka* (*v*) squat > HOCKER]

hunn *see* HUND

hunner *see* HUNDER

Huns *n pl* **the** ~ abusive nickname for Rangers football team (*chf* by Celtic fans) *20-*.

hunscott &c *n* name for a type of cloth made in S Holland and Flanders *la16-e17*. [only Sc; Du *honskote(n)*]

hunt &c; ho(u)nt *la14-e17* [hʌnt] *n* **1** *in pl* ~**is** *treated as sing*: a *or* the hunt *la14-17, only Sc*. **2** = hunt *18-*.
vti = hunt *la14-*.
~**ing &c** *n* **1** = hunting *la14-*. **2** a hunting-ground *la15-17, only Sc*.
~ **hall** a hunting lodge *la15-e16, only Sc*.
Huntis up name of a song and dance and its tune, 'The Hunt is up' *la15-17*.
~ **the staigie &c** a children's game in which one player has to catch the others *la19-, NE*.
(neither) ~ **nor hare &c** nothing at all, not a vestige *la19-, local Ags-Lnk*.

huntegowk *see* GOWK[1]

huny *see* HINNIE

hup &c *interj* (*19-*), *n* (*e20*) a call to an animal in harness **1** to turn to the right or off-side *la19-, Gen except N, only Sc*; **2** to increase speed *19-, now Ork NE Uls*.
v **1** *vi, of a horse in harness* go to the right *19-, Gen except NE, only Sc*. **2** *vti, of the driver* call to a horse (1) to go to the right *19-, Gen except NE, only Sc*; (2) to go forward at a quicker pace *19-, NE*.
~ **aff &c** go to the right! *20-, now Cai Lnk SW*.
~ **back** come back, bearing right *20-, now Cai midLoth WC, Dmf*.
neither to ~ **nor wynd** (*19-, Lnk SW Rox*) *or* **gee** (*20-, Lnk*) *chf fig* move neither to the right or left on command; prove unmanageable; be obstinate. **wo** ~ slow down and bear right *la20, Cai Edb WC Rox*. [perh imit of call *ho!* + *up* or *haud up*; *cf* HAP[3]]

hupe, hup [*høp, *hup, *hʌp] *n* **1** *specif* the circular wooden frame enclosing millstones to prevent meal from being scattered *15-e19*. **2** = hoop *la15-16*.

hur *see* SHE

hurb &c *n* a puny, uncouth or good-for-nothing creature; *joc, of a child* a rascal *la19-20, NE*. [doubtful]

hurcheon &c, hurchoun &c *16*; **erchin** *19-, Abd Fif* ['hʌrtʃən; *Abd Fif* 'ɛrtʃɪn; *Rox also* 'hʌrtʃənt] *n* **1** a hedgehog *16-, now C*. **2** *fig* an unkempt, uncouth person *16-19*. [nME *hurchon*, ONF *herichon* = 1]

hurd *see* HERD, HUIRD

hurdie &c *n, chf in pl* the buttocks, hips, haunches of human beings or animals *la16-, Gen except Sh Ork*.
~**-caikle** *or* **keckle** a pain in the back and thighs caused by prolonged stooping *la19-e20*.
ower the ~**s** *fig* in difficulties, deep (in debt) *la19-, now Per Lnk*. [only Sc; unknown]

hure &c *la14-*, **whore** *17-* ['hur; *hør; *Abd* *hir] *n* = whore.

hurk &c; hork *19-20 vi* **1** (1) sit in a crouched position on one's haunches, *esp* over a fire *19-, Dmf Rox*. (2) laze idly about *la19-, now Kcb*. **2** grub (in the dirt) like a pig; *fig* poke about, rummage *19-, now Kcb Dmf*.
n the act of lounging; a person who does this, *esp*

the one who occupies the most comfortable position by the fire *20-, now Kcb*. [MDu *hurcken*, LowGer *hurken* = *v* 1]

hurkill &c *vi* come into violent collision *la15*. [only Sc; appar ME *hurtel* hurtle]

hurkle[1] &c, hurkill &c *vi* **1** *freq* ~ **doun** crouch, sit huddled in a crouched position for warmth or secrecy *16-, now Cai Pbls SW*. **2** walk with the body in a crouching position; stumble along, stagger *19-, now Bnf, only Sc*. **3** *fig, freq* ~ **doun** submit, yield *19-, now Abd Kcdn Ags, only Sc*.
~**-backit** hunchbacked, misshapen *19-, now Dmf*. ~**-bane &c** the hip-bone *18-, local*. [ME *hurkel*; see SND, OED]

hurkle[2] *n* a single horse-grubber or horse-hoe used for cleaning turnips *19-, now Pbls Lnk*. [appar f HURK *v* 2]

hurl[1] &c *vti* **1** = hurl *15-*. **2** *vi* dash, hurtle, fall from a height *la15-, now Sh nEC*. **3** *vt* convey in a wheeled vehicle, drive, push or pull along on wheels *la17-*. **4** *vi* move on wheels, bowl or trundle along, ride in a wheeled vehicle *18-*. **5** *of a ball* roll *19-, sEC*.
n **1** a violent rush forwards or downwards, *eg* of falling stones or wind *16-, now local Sh-midLoth, only Sc*. **2** a wheelbarrow *16-17, only Sc*. **3** = hurl *17-*. **4** a ride or drive in a wheeled vehicle, a life along the road *19-, only Sc*.
hurlie &c *n* **1** = ~ **barrow**, *19-*. **2** *chf mining* a HUTCH *19*. **3** = ~**ie** cart, *20-*. **4** = ~**-bed** *la19-, now C, SW*. ~**ie-barrow** = ~**-barrow**, *la18-, now Cai midLoth*. ~**ie-bed** = ~**-bed** *la19-20*. ~**ie-cart** a child's home-made cart, *eg* an orange-box on wheels *20-, local*. **hurlie-hacket** *19*, **hurly-hakcat &c** *e16 n* **1** the sport of sliding down a slope on a trough or sledge, tobogganing. **2** the trough or sledge used thus; *transf* a poor-quality carriage *e19*.
~**-barrow** a wheelbarrow; a handcart *16-*. ~**-bed** a wheeled bed, a truckle-bed *17, only Sc*. ~**-cart** a common cart *e16, only Sc*. ~**-come-gush &c** a noisy rush of water, a mountain torrent in spate *19-e20, only Sc*.

hurl[2] &c *vi* **1** make a deep rumbling hollow sound, as of rushing water *20-, Sh Cai Uls*. **2** wheeze because of phlegm in the chest *20-, Sh Ork NE Ags*.
n **1** a rumbling or grating noise as made by a heavy object in motion; thunder *la18-, now Sh Ork Ags*. **2** (1) the sound of laboured breathing resulting from phlegm in the throat or chest *20-, local Sh-Abd*. (2) the death rattle *la20-, local Ork-NE*.
hurlie congested with phlegm *la20-, Cai Abd Ags*. [prob onomat; see SND]

hurlie &c *interj* a call to a cow to come to be milked *19-, SW*. [obscure]

hurlie *see* HURL[1], HURL[2]

hurly &c *n* ~ **hinmaist &c** the last, the hindmost *la19-, NE, Ags*. [uncertain; see SND]

hurly-hakcat *see* HURL[1]

huron *see* HERN

hurr &c *vi* make a whirring sound; purr *la19-*, *chf Sh Ork Cai.*
interj a purring, murmuring sound expressing pleasure or contentment *19-*, *now Sh.* [orig onomat; *cf* ME *hurr*, Norw and Sw dial *hurra* buzz *(v)*]

hurroo; haroosh &c *19-*, *now NE, C,* **hurro &c** *la19-*, *Sh,* **hiree &c** *e20*, *NE* [hə'ru(ʃ); *Sh* hə'ro; *NE* hə'ri] *n* an excited, high-spirited, disorderly gathering, a tumult, uproar, broil *19-*, *now local.*
vt urge on with shouts *la19-*, *Sh Uls.* [orig onomat; for Sh form *cf* Norw dial *hurra* buzz, rush about noisily]

hurry *vti* = hurry.
n **1** = hurry. **2** a disturbance, riot, quarrel, commotion *18-*, *now local Inv-Uls.* **3** a scolding *19-*, *now Abd Fif.* **4** a rush of work, an exceptionally busy time *19-*.
hurried harassed, hard pressed, hard put to it (to do something) *la19-*, *local Ork-Kcb.*
~-burry *18-*, *Gen except Sh Ork,* **~ gurry** *19-*, *now midLoth Bwk Lnk* a tumult, confusion.
in a couple of hurries without delay *19-*, *Gen except Sh Ork.* **in a ~** suddenly, unexpectedly *la19-*, *Gen except Sh Ork.* **tak yer ~ (in yer han)** take your time *la19-*, *NE, WC, SW.*

hurschle, hursle *see* HIRSEL[2]

hurt &c; hort *la16-*, *now Cai n, vti* = hurt *la14-*.
~some hurtful, injurious *la16-*.

hurt-majesté &c *n* high treason *la14-e16.* [only Sc; after Med and classical legal L *laesa mājestas*, F *lèse majesté* > LESE-MAJESTY]

husband &c ['hʌzbən(d), -bənt; *'husbən(d)] *n* **1** = husband *la14-*. **2** a manorial tenant who had, in return for rent and services, a certain holding in land in addition to his homestead *15-e17.*
~ry &c 1 the land occupied by the tenant(s) of a manor or estate, as distinct from the demesne lands *la14-15*, *only Sc.* **2** the holding of land as a HUSBAND *n* 2; the letting of land to such tenants *15-e16*, *only Sc.* **3** = husbandry *16-*.
~-land in SE Scotland, *orig* the land-holding of a HUSBAND *n* 2; *later chf* a measure of arable land, varying from district to district but *usu* = two *oxgangs* (ox) *la15-17.* **~man 1** = husbandman *15-*. **2** = HUSBAND *n* 2, *15-e17*, *only Sc.* **~ town &c** a homestead occupied by a *husbandman* (*n* 2) or *usu* husbandmen, a farm-steading with its cluster of peasants' houses, a settlement of *husbandmen*, *la14-17*, *only Sc.* [as personal name *la13-*; Sc L has *husbandus* = *n* 2 (*14-e15*) and *terra* or *tofta husbandorum* (*la13-e14*)]

husche paidill *see* HUSH PADLE

huschou *see* HUSH[2]

huse *see* HOUSE

hush[1] *n* **1** a rushing, gushing sound as of swiftly moving water *la19-*, *now Sh Ork.* **2** a whisper, a slight sound; a rumour *19-*, *now Abd.* **3** *fig* an onrush of people *la18-*, *now Sh.* **4** a large

quantity or abundance (of something) *19-*, *now Sh.* **5** a fat, ungainly, dirty person *la19-*, *now Abd Kcdn.*
v **1** *vi, of water* rush forth, gush out *19-*, *now Sh Uls.* **2** *vt* fling together, bundle hurriedly or carelessly *19-*, *now Sh midLoth.* [onomat]

hush[2] &c; huschou *la19-*, *NE* [hʌʃ; *Sh Cai NE also* *hə'ʃu] *n, interj* a cry to frighten off birds etc *la19-*, *now Sh Cai NE Uls.*
vt, also fig scare or drive away (birds etc) by making this noise *18-*, *now Sh Ork midLoth.* [*cf* Eng *shoo!*]

hushie *see* HISHIE

hushie-ba &c ['hʌʃɪ'ba, -'ba, 'hʌʃə-; *Mry* 'hɪʃɪ-] *interj, n* an expression for lulling a child to sleep, a lullaby *19-*.
vt lull (a child) to sleep *la19-*. [*hush* + *a(nd)* + *ba* (as in BALLOO)]

hushion *see* HOSHEN

hushle[1] &c; hussle &c *19-e20* ['hʌʃl; *NE also* 'hʌzl; *S* 'hʌsl] *vi* **1** fidget or move about awkwardly or restlessly *la18-*, *NE.* **2** shrug the shoulders, as if to rid oneself of an irritation *19-e20*, *S.* **3** work or dress in a careless or slovenly way *la19-*, *now Sh.*
n **1** a heap, a conglomeration, an untidy bunch or mass *la19-*, *now Sh Cai.* **2** an untidy, carelessly-dressed person, a slattern *20-*, *now Sh Cai SW.* **3** a person who is unable to work as a result of ill health or incapacity *e19*, *Renfr Dmf.* **4** a rustling sound *la19-*, *Bnf Abd.* [frequentative of HUSH[1], w infl f or confused w HIRSEL[2]]

hushle[2] &c *n* a strong, drying, gusty wind *20-*, *Sh Ork Wgt.*
vti, of wind blow in gusts, blow through (sheaves etc) *20-*, *Sh-Cai Uls.* [prob chf onomat]

hushoch &c ['hʌʃəx, -ək] *n* a confused heap, a tangled mass, a loose quantity of something *19-*, *now Abd Fif.*
hushloch &c ['hʌʃləx, 'hʌs-] = *n*, *19-e20.*
hush(l)ochy *adv, adj* hurried, careless(ly), slovenly *la19-e20.* [HUSH[1] or HUSHLE[1] + dim suffixes]

hush padle &c, husche paidill *la16* ['hʌʃ'pedl, -'padl] *n* the lump-fish *la16-*, *now Kcdn.* [first element may be Du *haasje*, dim of (*zee-)haas* the lump-fish; see also PAIDLE[3]]

husk *vi* cough violently *19-*, *now Ayr Rox.* [obscure]

husling &c [*?'hʌslɪŋ] *verbal noun* ? violent shaking, clashing *e16.* [only Sc; *cf* MDu *hutselen* shake violently > Eng *hustle*]

hussle *see* HUSHLE[1]

hussy *see* HIZZIE

husta &c *interj* expressing surprise, remonstrance or alarm *la18-e20*, *NE.* [uncertain]

hut &c *n* **1** = hut. **2** a smaller second house built in the grounds of a larger mansion and occupied as a town- or suburban house by wealthy families *la18-19*, *chf Edb.*

hut *see* HIT, IT, HOT

hutch *n* **1** = hutch. **2** *mining* the box-like

container in which coal is conveyed from the face *la17-*. **3** (1) a small heap or pile, *specif* of dung *la18-e19*. (2) a small rick or temporary stack of corn *19-*, *now Lnk Kcb Dmf*. **4** an embankment built up to check erosion caused by running water *19-*, *Rox*.
vt set (sheaves of corn) in small temporary ricks to dry *la20-*, *Lnk Kcb Dmf*.

huther *see* HUDDER

hutheron &c *18-e19*, **huddroun &c** *17*; **hudderon &c** *la16-e19* [*'hʌðərən, *'hʌd(ə)rən] *n* a young heifer; the skin or meat of one *la16-e19*.
~ veal &c ? pasture-fed veal as distinct from milk fed veal *17-e19*. [only Sc; unknown]

hutit &c [*'høtɪt] *adj* reviled, execrated; detested *e16*, *only Sc*. [Eng *hoot* (*v*)]

hutt *see* HIT, HOT

hutten *see* HIT

huttock *see* HAT¹

huve *see* HOVE¹, HUIVE

huz *see* US

hy *see* HIE

hyaave *see* HAW²

hyacinth *n* = hyacinth.
wood ~ = the English bluebell, wild hyacinth, *Scilla non scripta*, *la19-*, *Gen except Sh Ork*, *only Sc*. [*cf* bluebell (BLUE)]

hyke &c *v* **1** *vi* move with a jerk *19-*, *now Uls*. **2** *vti* sway, rock, swing *la19-e20*. [obscure]

hyne &c; hyn &c *15-e20*, **hind &c** *la16-* [həin] *adv* **1** *of place* hence, away, far (off), at a distance *la14-*, *now local Ork-Loth*. **2** from this world, from this life *la14-16*. **3** *of time* (1) henceforth, thenceforth *la15-16*. (2) far on, late *20-*, *NE*.
hindie(s) ['həindɪ(z)] *chf child's word* = adv 1, 20-, *Abd*.
~ awa *adv* far away, at a great distance *19-*, *now local Ork-midLoth*. *adj* distant *la19-e20*.
fra ~ = adv, *la14-16*. **fra ~ furth**(wart *e15*) **&c** henceforth *la14-e17*. (**a**) **merry ~ to ye &c** go to the devil and good riddance to you *19-*, *Abd*. [late nME *hyne*; see DOST, SND]

hyne *see* HIND

hyntit *see* HENT

hyow *see* HOW¹

hypal &c; heifle &c *e20*, *Abd* ['həipl; *Rox*

'həipəlt; *Abd also* 'həifl] *n* an uncouth, unkempt, broken-down or good-for-nothing person or animal *18-e20*, *local*. [doubtful; *cf* HIPPLE]

hype *n* a big unattractive person *la19-*, *Cai Bnf*. [? N var of HEAP]

hypochonderies *e19* [*'həipo'kondərɪz] *n pl*, *also in sing* **heepocondry** [hipo'kondrɪ] *20-*, *Per Stlg Fif* = hypochondria. [see also HEEPOCHONDREOCH]

hypocreet &c *la19-e20*, **hypocrite &c** *la16-*; **he(e)pocreet &c** *la16-19* ['hipokrit, 'hipə-] *vi* = hypocrite.

hypothec &c [hɪ'poθɪk, ə-; *St* (*law*) 'haipoθɛk, 'hɪ-] *n*, *law* the right of a creditor to hold the effects of a debtor as security for a claim without taking possession of them *la16-*.
the hale ~, the hale apotheck &c the whole of anything, the whole business etc, everything *19-*, *only Sc*. [OF *hypotheque*, laL (f Gk) *hypothēca* a deposit, pledge]

hypothecate *vt*, *ptp also* **hypothecat** *17* [hɪ'poθəket] *law* give, take or pledge as security, mortgage *17-*, *now rare*.
hypothecation pledging *la17*, *la19-*, *now rare*. [*hypothecat-*, ptp stem of MedL *hypothecare*]

hyre *see* HIRE

hyronius *see* HERONIOUS

hyse *see* HEEZE

hyste *see* HEIST

hyte¹ &c *adj* **1** mad, highly excited, enraged *la18-e20*. **2** excessively or madly keen *la18-e20*.
gae *or* **gang ~** go mad with rage or passion, fly into a hysterical state *18-*, *now Cai Kcb*. [only Sc; see SND]

hyte² &c *interj* a call to a horse *la19-e20*. [var of Eng exclam *hait!*]

hyter &c ['həitər] *vi* walk with a lurching, unsteady movement; stumble, trip *la19-*, *NE Ags*.
n **1** a lurch, a stumble *la19-*, *NE*. **2** a stupid person *19-*, *now Kcdn*.
adv with weak or uncertain stumbling step; in a state of ruin *la19-*, *Bnf Abd Ags*. [uncertain]

hythe &c [haið, haiθ] *n* a harbour, a landing place, an inlet among rocks *18-*, *Mry Bnf*. [OE *hyð* and in Eng place-names]

hyvis *see* HIVES

I

i *see* IN[1]

I; ik &c *la15*, **A &c** *16-*, **Aw** *la19-*, *local* [*stressed* aɪ, ɑ, a', *unstressed* ɑ, a, ə; *sAgs* ɛ; **ɪk*] *personal pronoun, chf accusative and dative* **me &c, ma** *la18-* [*stressed* mi; *S* məi; *unstressed* mɪ, mə] **1** = I, me *la14-*. **2 me** as subject, in pseudo-Highl Sc *la18-*. **3 me** as indirect object *usu* preceding the direct object IT *la18-*: '*give me it*'. [see also MINE[2], MY]

Ibernian &c *e16*; **Hibernian &c** *16- adj (n)* Irish. [Eng *Hibernian, e18*]

ibone &c *n* ebony *17*. [eModEng *ebone*, L *(h)ebenus*]

ice &c *n* = ice *la15-*.
~-**lowsing &c** a thaw *20-*, *now Wgt.*
~-**schok(k)il &c** *la15-e19*, ~**shoggle &c** *18-e19*, **eeshogel** *la20-, Per Bwk Dmf* an icicle.
~-**stane** a *curling stone* (CURL) *19-*, *now Ags Per Fif.* ~-**tangle &c** an icicle *19-, NE Ags Fif.*

icker *see* AICHER

icksy-picksy *see* EEKSIE-PEEKSIE

iconomus *see* OECONOM(O)US

idaia &c [ɪ'deə, aɪ'de, aɪ'di, &c] *n* = idea *la19-*, *chf NE.*

idand *see* EIDENT

idder *see* ITHER

ident *see* EIDENT

idilsett *see* IDLESET

idilteth *see* IDLETY

idiot, idiwut *see* EEDIOT

idleset &c, idilsett *e17*; **idleseat &c** *17-, chf Abd*, **idlesee &c** *20-, Abd Sh* ['əidlsɛt; *Abd* 'əidlsi(t); *&c*] *n* **1** idleness, laziness *la16-*, *now local Sh-Kcb.* **2** lack of work, unemployment *la19-*, *now WC Rox.*
adj idle, disposed to idleness *19-e20*. [only Sc; Eng *idle (adj)* + SET[1] (*n* 9 (1)); in NE second element appar associated w *seat* a place, position]

idlety &c *19-*, *now Ork Abd*, **idilteth &c** *16* ['əidltɪ, **-tɛθ*] *n* idleness. [f Eng *idle (adj)*]

idoleeze &c [əidə'liz] *vt* = idolize *19-*.

idoneus &c [**ɪ'dɒnɪAs, *i-*] *adj* fit, competent, suitably qualified *16-e17*. [earlier in Sc; L]

ieroe *la18-20*, **eroy &c** *17-e20*; **eer(ie)oy &c** *19-, Sh-Cai* ['iroi, 'iro, 'ɪrɒi, *&c*] *n* a great-grandchild. [Gael *iar-ogha*, f *iar* after + *ogha* grandchild; *cf* OE]

if *vt* = gif (GIE) *la15*. [by analogy w GIF; *cf* also rare laME *if* (*v*)]

ift *n* = gift *la15*. [*cf* prec and rare laME *yft* (*n*)]

ignorant &c *adj* **1** = ignorant *15-*. **2** ill-mannered, presumptuous, forward *la19-*.
n, chf in pl ignorant people *la15-e17*.

ik *see* I

Ila(y) *la15-16*; **Islay** ['əile] ~ **herald &c** one of the Scottish heralds *la15-19, la20-*. [the Hebridean island]

ile &c *la14-e18*; **isle &c** *la16- n* = isle *la14-*.
the I~s the Hebrides *15-*. **the North I~s** the northern Hebrides including Skye and the Outer Hebrides *16-e17*. **the Northern Isles** the Orkney and Shetland Islands *20-*. **the South** (*16-e17*) *or* **West** (*17*) ~**s** the Hebrides south of Ardnamurchan, and also Kintyre. **the Western I~s** the Hebrides, *more specif* the Outer Hebrides *la16-*; for the administrative area, see next. **Western Isles Council** the local government body set up in 1975 to administer the area of the *Western Isles* (Lewis, Harris, North Uist, Benbecula, South Uist and Barra) *la20-*; *cf Islands Council* (ISLAND) and REGION. [*cf* ISLAND]

ile *see* ALE, AISLE, OIL

ilest *see* EE[1]

ilk[1] &c *adj* **1** this *or* that ~ *la14-e17*, **the** ~ *la15-e16* the (very) same (person, thing etc already mentioned or about to be specified). **2** *absol, chf* **that** ~ (1) to the same thing or person *la14-19*. (2) the same place, estate or name, *chf* in designations of landed proprietors, distinguishing the head of a landed family *la14-*: '*James of Dundas of that ilk*'; '*Grant of that ilk*'.
n, by extension from adj 2 (2): family, race; quality, kind *la18-*. [nME *ilke*, OE *ilca*]

ilk[2] &c *adj* each, every, of two or more *la14-*, *now chf literary and replaced by* ILKA[1].
pronoun each one, every one *la15-e20*.
~ **ane &c** ['ɪlk'en] *pronoun* each one of two or more, everybody, all and sundry *la14-*, *now local NE-Rox. adj* every *la14-16, e19.* ~ **dayis** *of clothes* everyday, not one's Sunday or holiday best *la15-17.* ~ **dele** *chf verse* altogether, entirely *la14-e16.* ~ **ither** each other, one another *la18-*, *now Ags Rox.* ~**one** [**'ɪlk'on*] *only verse, chf in rhyme* = ~ *ane* (*pronoun*) *la15-16*. [only Sc *16-*; nME *ylk*, OE (Mercian) *ylc*, OE (Wessex) *ælc* > *each*; *cf* ILKA[1]]

ilka[1] &c; ilke *15-16*, **ilkie &c** *18-e20, latterly N adj* each, every, of two (*16-*) or more (*la14-*).
~ **ane &c** each one, everyone *18-*, *now local Bnf-Ayr.* ~ **dale**, ~ **dele &c** = *ilk dele* (ILK[2]) *la14-e15, la18-e19* (*N*), *orig only verse.* ~**day** *n* a weekday *19-*, *now NE Ags. adj* ordinary, everyday as opposed to Sunday or festive *19-.* ~**day(s) claise** ordinary, everyday or working clothes *19-, local NE-Rox.* ~ **where** *19*, ~ **wye** *la19-, Abd* everywhere.
~ **body's body 1** a popular person, a general favourite, *esp* a friendly obliging person *la18-*, *local N-Kcb.* **2** *disparaging* a person who is all things to all men, a time-server *la20-, Abd Fif.* **nae ilka body** not everybody, no ordinary person *19-, N Per.* [see SND, DOST; *cf* ILK[2]]

ilka[2] *adj* that *or* this ~ the same *15*. [substituted for ILK[1] *adj*, by analogy w ILK[2] and ILKA[1]]

ilke, ilkie *see* ILKA[1]

ill &c; ull *20-, Abd adj* (*adv*), *comparative usu* WAUR, *also* ~**er** *20-. superlative* WARSE **1** = ill *la14-*. **2** (1) *of persons* evil, wicked, depraved *la14-*. (2) *of conduct, language* bad, profane, malevolent *la14-*. **3** unwholesome, harmful, noxious *la14-*, *now local Sh-Bwk*. **4** harsh, severe, cruel *15-*, *Gen except WC*. **5** difficult, troublesome *la14-*: *'it's ill carrying gudes up the stairs'*. **6** awkward, inexpert, having difficulty in *19-*, *local*: *'ill to live'*; *'ill at gyaun'*. **7** *freq in curses* unlucky; malevolent, unfriendly, hostile *la15-*, *now local*. **8** poor in quality, defective, scanty *16-*, *now Sh NE Rox*. **9** *of weather* stormy *la15-*, *now local*. **10** *of coinage* counterfeit *la17-*, *now Sh NE Ags*. **11** bad, unsatisfactory, ineffective *18-*, *now Sh Ork Abd*.

n **1** = ill *la14-*. **2** harm, injury, mischief from natural or supernatural causes *la14-*. **3** illness, disease *la14-*, *now Sh N Ags*. **4** badness, malice *20-*.

~**-aff &c 1** = ill off, poor *19-*. **2** miserable, ill used *18-*, *Gen except SW*. **3** perplexed, at a loss *19-*, *now local*. ~**-best** *adj* (*n*) the best of a bad lot *17-*, *chf Sh-N* [*cf* ON *illsbestr*]. ~ **bit** a poor, infertile piece of ground *20-*, *local sEC-S*. ~**-brew** an unfavourable opinion *la18-*, *midLoth Kcb*. ~**-chat** impudence *20-*, *NE Ags midLoth Lnk*. ~**-cleckit** misbegotten *19-*, *now Bnf Lnk*. ~**-coloured** having a bad or unhealthy colour *18-*. ~**-come 1** ill-gotten *20-*, *N nEC*. **2** illegitimate *20-*, *N* [*cf* Eng *ill-come-by*]. ~**-contrived &c**, ~**-contriv(v)en 1** tricky, mischievous, badly-behaved *la19-*, *Sh N*. **2** contradictory, intractable *la19-*, *Sh Cai Mry*. **3** awkward *la19-*, *now Sh*. ~**-daer &c 1** evildoer *18-*. **2** an animal that does not thrive *20-*. ~**-daein &c** *n* misdemeanour, bad behaviour *la15-*, *now Sh N midLoth*. *adj* badly-behaved, dissolute; not thriving *la19-*. ~**-dune &c** wrong, badly-behaved, perverse, mischievous *19-*. ~**-deedie &c** *18-*, ~**-deedit** *la18-*, *Cai Ags* *adj* mischievous, unruly, wicked; *cf evill-dedy* (EVILL). ~**-designed** evilly disposed, mischievously-minded *19-*, *Sh NE midLoth*. ~**-ee 1** the evil eye *la18-*, *now Ags Wgt*. **2** *fig* a longing, yearning *20-*, *Abd Ags*. ~**-end** a miserable death *la19-*, *now Ork*. ~**-farrant &c** ugly, unkempt, unpleasant in behaviour or appearance *19-*, *nEC Rox*. ~**-farandly** in poor condition *la15*. ~**-faured &c** ['ɪl'fard; *Abd* 'ʌl'fart] **1** *of looks, appearance etc* ill-favoured, ugly, unbecoming *la16-*. **2** *of behaviour or speech* ill-mannered, bad-tempered, coarse *19-*, *now Ork Abd Ags*. **3** *of things* hateful, obnoxious, unpleasant *19-*, *now Cai Kcb*. **4** poor in quality, unattractive, scruffy *la18-*, *Sh Ork Abd Ags*. **5** *of movement* clumsy *19*. **6** *of colour, dress etc* shabby, faded *20-*, *Ork Abd*. ~**-fittit** bringing bad luck *la19-*, *Sh Rox*. ~**-gab** *n* insolent, impudent language *la19-*, *local EC*. *vti* use abusive language, abuse (a person) *la19-*, *local C*. ~**-gaein &c** clumsy or awkward at walking due to deformity of the feet *20-*, *Ork Abd Ags*. ~**-gate &c 1** a bad habit *la19-*, *Ags Fif midLoth*. **2** *in pl* dissolute behaviour, mischievousness *la19-*, *Ags*. ~**-gated &c**, ~**-gettit &c** *of persons* badly-behaved, perverse *19-*, *local EC*.

~**-gaitedness** perverseness *19-e20*, *chf NE*. **gae** *or* **run an** *or* **the** ~ **gate &c** live an immoral life *19-*, *local Sh-Lnk*. ~**-gien &c**, ~**-gevin &c 1** addicted to evil ways; ill-disposed, malevolent *la16-*, *now Sh Lnk Dmf*. **2** mean; wayward *20-*, *Cai*. ~**-gotten** illegitimate *la18-*, *Sh Ags Kcb*. ~**-greein** *adj* quarrelsome *20-*, *N-WC*. ~**-guide** ill-use, maltreat *18-*, *local Sh-Dmf*. ~**-guided &c 1** mismanaged *18-e20*. **2** badly brought up *la19-*, *now Dmf*. ~**-guideship** maltreatment, abuse *la19-*, *now local Sh-Kcdn*. ~**-hard &c** *adj* hard up *18-19*. ~**-hauden &c** *adj* **1** oppressed, in difficulties *20-*, *Per SW*. **2** saved to no purpose, falsely economized *la19-*, *NE*. ~**-hertit** *adj* **1** malevolent *la18-*, *Gen except S*. **2** greedy, mean *20-*, *chf NE*. **3** *of a corn-rick* not packed tightly enough in the centre *la20-*, *Ork Cai NE Wgt*. ~**-inten(i)t** ill-disposed, with evil intentions *19-*, *NE*. ~**-jaw** coarse abusive language; insolence *19-*, *Sh N Kcb*. ~**-kinded** ['ɪl'kəindɪt] *adj* ill-disposed, cruel; having a wicked disposition *20-*, *EC* [ILL + *adj* f KIND disposition]. ~**-less**, **illes** ['ɪl'les, *NE* 'ʌl-] harmless, innocent, docile; free from evil intentions *la16-*, *now Sh NE*. ~**-like &c** *adj* **1** having the appearance of evil, suspect *la15-16*, *20-* (*Sh*). **2** sick-looking *17*. ~**-likeit &c** unpopular *la19-*. ~**-looked-upon** *adj* held in disfavour, unpopular *la18-20*, *Sh Ork midLoth*. ~ **man** the devil *la17-*. ~**-mou &c** vile language, a disposition to use such language, an abusive tongue *la19-*, *Bnf*. ~**-mou'd** impudent, insolent, abusive *19-*, *local Sh-EC*. ~**-muggent &c** malicious *la18-19*, *N* [extension of meaning of *ill-mogganed* having poor or shabby MOGGANS, hence mean, scurvy]. ~**-name** a bad name, a bad reputation *19-*, *local Sh-WC*. ~**-nature** bad temper, irritability *18-*. ~**-natured** bad-tempered, irritable *18-*. ~ **pa(i)rt** Hell *la18-*, *now NE*. ~**-pairtit** badly divided, shared out unequally *la19-*. ~**-peyd &c** extremely sorry *19-*, *Abd*. ~ **pit** in difficulties, baffled, hard pressed *20-*, *local Sh-WC*. ~**-pit(ten)-on** shabbily-dressed *la19-*. ~**-scrapit &c** *of the tongue* slanderous, rude, bitter *la18-*, *now Cai Mry*. ~**-set** *adj* **1** evilly disposed *la17-*, *Ork N SW*. **2** harsh, cruel *20-*, *Stlg Fif*. **3** surly, out of humour *20-*, *Ork*. **4** ungenerous, churlish *la19-e20*. *vt* be unsuitable for *la19-*, *now Abd*. ~**-setten** clumsy *la18-*, *now Ork*. ~**-shaken &c**, ~**-shaken thegither** loosely built, ungainly, shambling *20-*, *NE*. ~**-shaken-up** untidy, disordered, awkward, loutish *18-*, *Sh Ork NE*. ~**-speakin &c** given to repeating slander, slanderous talk *la19-*, *now Sh midLoth*. ~ **spoken o** slandered *la19-*, *Sh Ags*. ~**-taen &c** taken amiss, resented *la18-*, *local N-S*. ~**-thrawn &c** ill-natured, cantankerous *la20-*, *Sh Ork Cai SW*. ~**-tongue &c** *n* a malevolent or abusive tongue; bad language, abuse; slander *18-*. *vt* abuse *la19-*, *Cai Mry Abd*. ~**-tongued** slandering, abusive, vituperative *la18-*, *N midLoth SW.* ~-**trickit** &c prone to play tricks, mischievous *18-*, *Sh-Ags.* ~-**will** &c *n* dislike, enmity, malevolence *la14-. vt* wish evil to, hate *la18-20, now Abd.* ~-**willed** hostile, having a dislike *19-, now Sh.* ~-**willer** a person who wishes evil on another *16-e20.* **ha(v)e** *or* **tak (an)** ~-**will at** *19-, local Sh-Ags,* **hae** &c ~-**will to** *la16-e19* take a dislike to [nME; *cf* ON *illvili*]. ~-**willie** &c *adj* **1** malevolent, malignant *la15-e16.* **2** *freq of animals* bad-tempered *16-, now Rox.* **3** grudging, disobliging, mean *18-, now Abd.* **4** unfriendly, hostile *19-e20;* cf *evil-willy* (EVILL). ~ **wind** &c **1** scandal, slander *la19-e20, NE.* **2** abusive language *la19-, NE.*

cast ~ **on** bewitch, put the evil eye on *19.* **dee** ~ **wantin** spare with difficulty *19-, Cai.* **for na(ne)** ~ with no bad intention *la15.* ~ **aboot 1** desiring greatly, keen on, fond of *la18-, now NE.* **2** vexed, sorrowful *19-, Gen except N.* ~ **at** = ~ *aboot 2, la19, C.* ~ **for** inclined to (some bad habit etc), having a vicious propensity to *19-, N midLoth SW.* ~ **tae dae til** *(20-, local Sh-Per)* or **wi** *(la19-, N-SW)* difficult to please or humour. ~ **to see** ugly to look at *la19-, Sh Ags midLoth.* **nae** &c **that** ~ *adv* not so badly, quite well *19-. adj* not so bad, good enough *20-, Sh NE midLoth.* **pit (one's meat) in an** ~ **skin** look thin or half-starved *19-, Gen except Sh Ork.* **tak something** ~ **oot** be upset at, averse from, offended by something *la19-, local Ork-Lnk.* **tak** ~ **(wi)** take badly, find difficulty in *20-.* [freq wrongly regarded as var of *evil*; see DOST, OED]

illes *see ill-less* (ILL)

illumine &c **1** = illumine *la14-.* **2** illuminate (manuscripts etc) *16-.* **3** *fig* brighten as if with light *15-.*

illustratioun &c *la14-16;* **illustration** &c *la16- n* **1** (spiritual) enlightenment *la14-.* **2** = illustration *la16-.*

image *see* EEMAGE

imaginat *ptp, adj* imagined, devised *16.* [L *imāgināt-*, ptp stem of *imāgināre*]

imaigine [ɪˈmedʒɪn] *vti* = imagine *la19-, Ork Abd Ags.*

imang *see* AMANG

imbazel, imbesil *see* EMBEZLE

imbreve [*ɪmˈbriv] *vt* write out in the form of a BRIEF; enter in writing *la16.* [MedL *imbreviare* &c]

imbring *see* INBRING

imbuik *see* INBUKE

immatriculat *ptp* matriculated *17.* [ptp stem of MedL *immatriculare; cf* eModEng *immatriculated*]

immedantly; immidintly &c [ʔɪˈmidəntlɪ, ɪˈmɪd-] *adv* = immediately *19-20, now NE.* [intrusive -*n*- introduced by analogy, eg w *presently*]

immediat &c; **immediate** &c *adj* **1** = immediate *la15-.* **2** succeeding directly (as heir) *15-.*
adv **1** *of feudal tenure or ecclesiastical rank* directly, without intermediary *e15.* **2** preceding or following without interval, next *la15-e16.*

immen *see* BE

immer &c; **ember** &c *n, chf* ~ **goose** the great northern diver *la17-, now Sh Ork.* [Norw *imbre* &c, ON *himbrin*]

immick *see* EEMOCK

immidintly *see* IMMEDANTLY

immis &c; **eemis** &c *adj* **1** *of the weather or atmosphere* uncertain, gloomy, likely to rain etc *19-e20, chf NE.* **2** *of an object* insecurely balanced, unsteady *e19, e20 (literary).* [Norw *ymis*, ON *ýmiss* changeable]

immixtion *n* concerning oneself or meddling with property etc, *intromission* (INTROMIT) *la17.* [eModEng *immixion* mixing in, f L *immixt-*, ptp stem of *immiscēre* mingle, meddle]

immortal &c *adj* = immortal *16-.*
The I~ **Memory** name for the honorific speech in praise of Robert Burns given at *Burns Suppers* (BURNS).

immost *see* UMOST

immunitie &c *n* = immunity *la15-.*
~ **of Tayne** &c the sanctuary of St Duthac of Tain *16-e17.* [ME *ynmunite*, L *immūnitas;* also ScL *immunitas de Tayne* (e15)]

imp &c; **hempe** &c *20-, Fif n* **1** = imp *la16-.* **2** a young shoot or cutting *la15-20, now Rox.* **3** a small candle or taper *e16.* **4** a cord of twisted horsehair forming part of a fishing line, to which the hook is attached *18-, Sh-Cai, Fif Bwk. vt* **1** = imp *la16-.* **2** engraft *la15-18.*

impediment &c *n* = impediment *la14-.*
mak ~ *freq law* offer hindrance, opposition or objection *15-e17.* **without, but** *etc* ~ *chf law,* in precautionary *formulae* etc without obstruction, opposition or objection *la14-16.*

imperial &c *adj* **1** = imperial *15-.* **2** supreme, excellent *16-.*

imperiour *see* EMPERIOUR

impertinat *adj* = impertinent *la15-16.*

impesche &c *16-e17,* **empasche** &c *la16-e17* [*ɪmˈpɛʃ, *-ˈpiʃ, *-ˈpeʃ, &c] *vt* hinder, obstruct, delay, prevent. [eModEng]

impetrate &c, **impetrat** &c *ptp* **1** obtained by petition or formal application to an authority *la15-17.* **2** obtained by request, *latterly pejorative, eg* gained or contrived by fraud *la16-e18. vt* = impetrate, obtain by request *la15-.* [chf Sc in 16th century; L *impetrāt-*, ptp stem of *impetrāre*]

imphm [m(:)mmʔ] *interj* with varying intonation indicating attentiveness, decided or reluctant assent, sarcastic agreement, hesitation etc *19-.*

impident &c [ˈɪmpɪd(ə)nt, ɪmˈpɪdənt] *adj* = impudent *19-.*
impidence &c impudence *18-.*

impignorate, impignorat &c [ɪmˈpɪgnoret, *-at] *v, ptp* **impignorat,** ~**ed** pawn, pledge, mortgage *la16-, now rare*.

impignoration &c [ɪmˈpɪgnjoreʃn, *also* -ˈpɪgn-] *law* pledging; mortgage *la15-, now rare*. [chf Sc; *cf* eModEng *ptp*, ModEng *v*; MedL *impignorat-*, ptp stem of *impignorare* pledge]

impire &c *15-e17, only Sc*, **empire** &c *la14-* [*ɪmˈpaɪr, *ɛmˈ-] *n* **1** = empire *la14-*. **2 the** ~ the Roman or Holy Roman Empire *la14-17*.
vi **1** = empire, rule as emperor *16-e17*. **2** *also fig, of desires etc* rule, wield authority (*esp* tyrannically), hold sway *la16-e17*.

impit *see* IMPUT[1]

implement [*n* ˈɪmpləmɛnt, *v* ɪmpləˈmɛnt] *n, law* the fulfilment or execution of a contractual obligation *17-*.
vt complete, execute (a contract or agreement), fulfil (a condition or promise) *18-*. [L *implēmentum*, f *implēre* fulfil]

imploy *vt* **1** = employ *la16-17*. **2** apply (money) to a particular purpose; bestow, expend (money) *la16-17*.

import *vt* **1** = import *la16-*. **2** obtain for oneself, have *la16*: '*ȝe will import our special thanks*'.

importance &c *n* **1** = importance *16-*. **2** income, revenue *16, only Sc*.

importurate &c *ptp* portrayed; adorned with pictures etc *e16*. [only Sc; *cf porturat* (PORTURE)]

impreiff *see* IMPREVE

imprent &c [*ɪmˈprɛnt] *vt* = imprint *la15-16*.

impreson &c [*ɪmˈprɪsən] *vt* = imprison *la16*.

imprestable [*ɪmˈprɛstəbl] *adj* impossible to perform or discharge *la17-e18*. [only Sc; *im-* + PRESTABLE]

impreve; impreiff [*ɪmˈpriv] *vti* **1** (1) disprove (a legal document) *chf* as being forged *la15-e17*. (2) refute (an argument etc); confute (a person) *16-e17*. **2** repudiate; disapprove, condemn *la15-16*. [only Sc, replaced by IMPROVE *17-*; L *improbāre* condemn, reject; for the form *cf* PRUIVE, APPREVE, APPRUVE]

impriour *see* EMPRIOUR

impreve *see* IMPRUIVE

improbation &c, **improbatioun** *la16-e17* [ɪmproˈbeʃn] *n, law* disproof of a legal deed as invalid or (*chf*) forged; *esp* an action to annul a deed on these grounds *la16-*.

improbative [ɪmˈprobətɪv] liable to IMPROBATION; not proved to be true *la18-*. [L *improbātio*; *cf reduction* (REDUCE)]

improve [*ɪmˈprøv] *vt, chf law* disprove *la15-e18*. [F *improuver*, L *improbare* condemn, reject; see also IMPROVIN, IMPREVE]

improven *see* IMPRUIVE

improvin [*ɪmˈprovən] *ptp* **1** *chf of legal deeds etc* disproved *la16-17*. **2** *of persons* convicted of preparing or presenting disproved documents *la16-e17*. [*ptp* of IMPREVE and IMPROVE]

impruive; imprive *la18-19, N* [ɪmˈprøv,

-ˈprev; *N* -ˈpriv] *vt, ptp* **improven** &c *17-e19* [*?ɪmˈpruvən, *?-ˈprov-] ~**ed** *la18-* = improve *17-*.

impugn &c; **impung** &c *15-17* [*ɪmˈpʌŋ] *vt* = impugn *15-*.

imput[1] &c; **impute** *la16-* [*ˈɪmpøt, *?-pʌt] *vt, ptp also* **imput** *la14-16*, **impit** *16* [*ˈɪmpʌt, *-pɪt, *-pøt(ɪt)] impute, lay to the charge of, attribute (a fault, a crime, blame) **to** *la14-*. [OF *imputer*, L *imputāre*]

imput[2] &c [*ˈɪmpʌt] *vt, pt, ptp* **imput(e)** &c [*ˈɪmpʌt] **1** ~ **to, upon** impose, levy (a tax etc) on *16*. **2** *in gen* impose, bestow *15-e17*. [late alteration of ME *input*]

imput *see* INPIT

impyre &c [*ɪmˈpaɪr] *adj* **hevin** ~ the empyrean, the highest heaven *16*. [only Sc; var of eModEng *empyre*, MedL *empyreus*]

imsch *see* NIMSH

in &c; **i** *19-* [ɪ(n)] *prep* **1** = in *la14-*. **2** *chf with verb of motion* into *la14-, now local*. **3** *of place, position* on, upon, along *la14-*. **4** *of time* during, on, at *la14-*. **5** through, because of (a person's fault, failure) *la14-16*. **6** resident in, or shortlease tenant of (the place named, *latterly* only farms) *16-e19*; *cf* A[1] 1 (3) *and* OF 2 (1). **7** with *18-*: '*provided in a living*'. **8** *now chf law* to the amount or extent of *18-*: '*fined in forty shillings*'. **9** of, *freq* **good** ~ **ye** *etc* good of you etc, kind of you *la18-19*, ~ **coorse** see COORSE[2] [? *poss in* for *i*, var of o[1] *prep*]. **10** as, *freq* ~ **a compliment, gift** *etc* *18-*.
adv **1** (1) = in *la14-*; (2) *preceding the verb, 15-16*: '*the place that he is first in set*'. **2** *with omission of certain verbs* (*cf* OUT, UP *etc*): (1) *omitting verb of motion, 18-*: '*the dog wants in*'; (2) ~ **with,** *freq in imperative as in colloq Eng* put or push in *la19-*: '*he juist in wi her*'. **3** *of a gathering, meeting etc* assembled, in session *19-*. **4** *of land under* crop, ploughed and sown *la18-, now Cai Kcb*. **5** under one's breath, in a whisper, *chf* ~ **to onesel,** ~ **laich** *la19-*. **6** alert, attentive *20-, NE Ags midLoth Kcb*. **7** *of a debtor* ~ **a certain amount** (**with one's creditor**) in debt (to someone) *19-, NE Ags midLoth Gall*. **8** *golf* over the last nine holes of an 18-hole course *la19-*.
vt bring (the harvest) in from the fields *la15-*.
n **1** an entrance; an invitation or permission to enter *la19-, NE*. **2** *children's games, chf in pl* (one of) the side which is in possession of the goal or home, or whose turn it is to play *19-, now Ork nEC*.

in-below-the-bedfu &c a large assortment of things such as are *freq* stored below a bed *20-, Rox*. ~ (**i**)**t** there, present, available *19-, Highl*: '*there's nae butter in it the day*' [translating Gael *ann*]. ~ **a mistake** in error, by mistake *19-, local*. ~ **o** &c *of motion or rest* in, into, inside *la18-, local*. ~ **and out 1** inside and outside, altogether *15-*. **2** *of motion* = in and out *la16-*. ~ **the road** *etc* along the road etc, in a direction near the speaker *20-, N Fif.* **nae &c** ~ abstracted, day-dreaming *la19-, Sh NE C.* [*cf* OUT]

in *see* AND, INN

inact *see* ENACT

inadvertence *n* negligence, carelessness *16-.* [earlier in Sc; MedL *inadvertentia,* OF *inadvertence*]

inamité *see* INIMITY

inane *adj* of no account, pointless *16-.* [earlier in Sc; L *inānis*]

inanimitie &c [*ˈɪnaˈnɪmɪtɪ] *n* enmity, strife *la16.* [appar altered f INIMITY]

inarme *see* ENARM

inawing *see* ANAWIN

inband [ˈɪnˈband] *n, building* a header, a stone with its short side in a wall face, *specif* a quoin or jamb stone *la18-.* [IN *adv* + BAND¹; cf *bandstane* (BAND¹), OUTBAND]

inbearing [ˈɪnˈbirən &c] *adj* **1** impressive, persuasive *la17.* **2** officious, ingratiating, obsequious *19-, Bnf Abd Ags.* **3** meddlesome, intruding *20-, Abd nEC.* [IN + *bear*]

inbering [*ˈɪnˈbirɪn] *n* carrying in *la16-e17.* [f as prec]

inbrace *see* ENBRACE

inbreak &c [*ˈɪnˈbrɛk &c] *n* a breaking in, intrusion by force, *fig* violation *la17-19.*

inbring &c, imbring *la16-e17* [ˈɪnˈbrɪŋ, ɪnˈbrɪŋ, *ɪm-] *vt, pt ptp* **inbrocht &c** [*ˈɪnˈbroxt &c] **1** (1) bring (a thing) into or to a place, convey; import *la15-, now midLoth.* (2) fetch in (persons) as prisoners *la16-e17.* **2** *specif* (1) fetch in (taxes, fines etc) to the appropriate recipient or office, collect (such moneys etc) *la15-e17.* (2) *law, chf in ptp* seized and confiscated *la15-e18.* **3** introduce *la14-e17.* **4** cause, bring about *la14-16.*

~**ing &c 1** conveying, fetching in (**of** things) *15-e18.* **2** importation from abroad *la15-17.* **3** bringing or fetching in of persons *la15-e20.* **4** collecting (*esp* of rent, debts etc) *la15-e18.* **5** introduction *la17.* [chf Sc; ME *inbrynge,* OE *inbringan*]

inbuke &c, imbuik &c [*ˈɪnˈbøk, *ɪm- &c] *vt* enter in a book, record, enrol *la16-e17.*

inby; in by [ˈɪnˈbaɪ] *adv* **1** *with verb of motion* from outside to inside, further in, within a house or room, from the coast inland etc *18-.* **2** inside, in the inner part (of a house etc), at someone's house *19-.* **3** in that portion of farmland in the immediate vicinity of the farm-buildings *20-, Ross midLoth Bwk S; cf* INFIELD.

prep close to, beside; in the neighbourhood of *la19-, Abd midLoth.*

adj low-lying *19-, midLoth Kcb Dmf S.*

incarcer &c [*ˈɪnˈkarsər] *vt* = next *la16-17.* [only Sc; F *incarcérer,* MedL *incarcerare*]

incarcerate, incarcerat &c *16-17 vt, chf in*

ptp **incarcerat,** ~**ed** imprisoned *la16-.* [eModEng *incarcerate,* MedL *incarcerat-,* ptp stem of *incarcerare*]

incast [ˈɪnˈkast, ˈɪnkast] *n* an extra amount given by a seller to a buyer in addition to the quantity stipulated *la18-, now Fif Rox.* *v, only* ~**ing** in various senses of CAST *v, la15-e18.*

incertitude *n* uncertainty, insecurity, unpredictability *la15-.* [earlier in Sc; OF]

inch &c, insch &c *17* [ɪnʃ] *n* **1** (1) a small island *15-, in place-names la12-.* (2) a piece of rising ground in the middle of a plain *la18-.* **2** a stretch of low-lying land near a river or other water, sometimes cut off at high tide *la15-, now chf in place-names.* [Gael *innis* an island]

inchant; inshant *la16* [*ɪnˈtʃant, *ɪnˈʃant] *vt* = enchant *la16-e17.*

~**ment &c 1** = enchantment, the act of enchanting *la14-17.* **2** a method of enchanting, a spell or charm *la16-e17.*

incident diligence *n, law* a warrant issued by a law-court to enforce the production of evidence in the hands of third persons *17-e19.* [Eng *incident* (*adj*) incidental + DILIGENCE]

incline &c *vti* **1** = incline *la14-.* **2** cause to bend or curve, allow to bend down *la15-.*

inclose &c *v* **1** *vt* = enclose *la15-.* **2** (1) shut a jury in a retiring room for consideration of the verdict *18-.* (2) *vi, of a jury* retire for this purpose *la17-18.*

income *17-,* **incum** *15-17* [ˈɪnˈkʌm, ˈɪnkəm] *n* **1** an entrance, arrival *la15-, now local Bnf-Rox.* **2** a newcomer, new arrival, *esp* one who comes to settle in a place *19.* **3** (1) an illness or infirmity with no obvious external cause *19-, N Renfr.* (2) a swelling, abscess, festering sore etc *18-, now local Sh-Kcb.* (3) a sharp attack of pain, a stitch in the side *la19-, now local N-S.* *vi* enter *15-16.*

incomer, incum(m)er = incomer, stranger, immigrant, but in Sc *chf derog,* implying an intruder *16-.* ~**in(g)** *adj* **1** *of a period of time* about to begin, ensuing *19-.* **2** *of a new person* newly arrived, succeeding (in a tenancy, post etc) *la18-.* *n* **1** = incoming *15-.* **2** an invasion *la16-e17.* **3** the coming of vessels into port *la15-e17.* [*cf* ONCOME]

inconsumptive [*ɪnˈkonsʌmptaɪv] *adj* incapable of being consumed *e16.* [only Sc; *cf* eModEng *consumptive*]

incontrare &c *prep* (*adv*) **1** contrary to, in opposition to *la15-16.* **2** against, in opposition to *16.* **3** in violation **of** *la15-16.* [IN + CONTRAIR]

inconvenient &c [*ɪnkonˈvinɪənt] *n* **1** (1) a state or cause of difficulty or disturbance *15-17.* (2) trouble, difficulty, danger *16-17.* **2** personal inconvenience *la15-e17.* [ME]

incorporate, incorporat &c *16-e17 ptp, adj, also*

~**ed** *la18-* **1** = incorporate *16-*. **2** *specif* formally constituted as a corporation, *latterly freq* as **Incorporated Trades** the trade associations in a BURGH *16-*.
vt = incorporate *la16-*. [ME; L *incorporāt-*, ptp stem of *incorporāre*; *cf* next]
incorporation, incorporatioun *la15* *n* **1** = incorporation, the act of incorporation *la15-*. **2** an association of tradesmen, *orig* belonging to the same craft, with burgess rights and duties and until 1846 holding a monopoly of their craft in their BURGH *18-*; see DEACON¹; *cf* GUILD (*of merchants*).
incounsolabill &c [*'ɪnˈkunsəlebl, -abl] *adj* refusing counsel or advice *e16*.
incountrie *see* INCUNTRÉ
incre &c [*'ɪŋkər] *adj* earnest, ardent *la14*.
~**ly** *la14-e15*, **inkirly &c** *la14-e16* [*'ɪŋkərlɪ, *'ɛŋkər-] earnestly, eagerly, extremely. [only Sc; ON *einkar* specially, very]
incredule &c [*?ɪnˈkrɛdøl] *adj* unbelieving *16*. [only Sc; L *incrēdulus*]
incres &c [*'ɪnˈkrɛs] *n*, *vti* = increase *la15-e17*.
incum, incummer *see* INCOME
incuntré &c; incountrie &c [*'ɪnˈkʌntrɪ &c] *n* the inner part of a country, an inland district; *freq* the Scottish *Lowlands* (LAWLAND) as opposed to other parts of Scotland *16-17*. [only Sc; IN + *cuntre* (COUNTRA)]
Independent Companies *n pl* companies of *Highland* (HIELAND) troops first recruited during Charles II's reign, and again (1725-30) by General Wade to keep order in the *Highlands*, formed in 1739 into the *Black Watch* (BLACK) *18-*, *now hist*; see *Forty-twa* (FORTY).
indevoir *see* ENDAIVOUR
indew *see* ENDUE
indict &c [ɪnˈdɔɪt] *vt* accuse *la15-*.
~**ment, indyt(e)ment** *15-17* **1** = indictment *15-*. **2** *law* the form of process by which the accused is brought to trial at the instance of the *Lord Advocate* (LORD) *la18-*. [Eng has forms in *-ct*, *17-*; see OED]
indie &c [ˈɪnd(j)ɪ, ˈɪndʒɪ &c] *n*, *also* ~ **rubber** india-rubber *la19-*, *local N-Uls*. [Eng *India*]
indigent *n* a pauper *la16-e17*. [ME (*adj*); L *indigens* (*adj*)]
indilaitlie &c [*ɪndɪˈletlɪ] *adv* immediately *la16-e17*. [only Sc; f L *dīlātus*, ptp of *differre* postpone, delay]
inding &c [*'ɪnˈdɪŋ] *adj* = indign, unworthy *16*.
indiscreet, indiscreit *16* *adj* **1** = indiscreet *16-*. **2** rude, uncivil *la17-20*.
~**ly** impolitely *17-e20*. [*cf* DISCREET]
indisgestion &c [ɪndɪsˈdʒɛstʃ(ə)n &c] *n* = indigestion *18-*. [*cf disgeest* (DIGEEST)]
indoce &c [*'ɪnˈdos] *vt*, *ptp* **indost &c** = endoss, endorse *16*.
indors *vt* = endorse *la15-e17*.
~**atioun &c** endorsement *la15-19*.
indorsate &c [*'ɪnˈdorsat, -et] *ptp* endorsed *la15-e17*. [only Sc; MedL *indorsatus*]

indrink [*'ɪnˈdrɪŋk] *n* shrinkage, diminution *la17-19*.
induciae [ɪnˈdjuʃie] *n pl* the period of time between a citation to appear in a law court and the date fixed for the hearing *18-*. [L *indutiae* a truce, delay]
induct *v* **1** = induct *18-*. **2** *Presbyterian Churches* install (an ordained MINISTER) in a charge *19-*.
~**ion &c** **1** = induction *la15-*. **2** the act of installing an ordained MINISTER in a charge, and *in gen* the ceremonial service which takes place *19-*. [see SND]
indulge *vti* = indulge.
indulgence **1** = indulgence *15-*. **2** *specif* the licence offered to Presbyterian MINISTERS to conduct services during the reigns of Charles II and James VII under certain conditions, *eg* recognition of Episcopal authority and Royal supremacy in the church *la17-*, *now hist*.
indult *n* a special privilege, licence or permission, *esp* one granted by the Pope *la15-16*. [earlier in Sc; F; L *indultum*]
indurand, induring *see* ENDURAND
industrial *adj* **1** = industrial. **2** *law* brought about by the industry of man *la18-*.
indwell &c, indwel [*'ɪnˈdwɛl] *vti* dwell (in a place), occupy *15-18*.
~**er &c, indwaller** *la16-*, *now NE Kcb S* a resident, inhabitant *15-*. [see also DWALL]
indyte &c [*'ɪnˈdɔɪt] *n* verbal composition; something composed or committed to writing *16*. [*n* only Sc; var of ENDITE]
indyt(e)ment *see* INDICT
ine *see* EN, UNE¹
inemité *see* INIMITY
inemmell [*'ɪˈnɛml] *vt* = enamel *la16*.
inemy *see* ENEMY
ineuch *see* ENOUCH
inew *see* ENEW
infa &c, infall [ˈɪnˈfɑ, *-ˈfal] *n* **1** = infall, a raid *17*. **2** the inflow of a river, *latterly* of a tributary joining a main river *17-*, *now NE*.
infame [*'ɪnˈfem] *adj*, *n* infamous, an infamous person *16*: '*he salbe declarit infame*'. [OF *infame*, L *infāmis*; *cf* eModEng]
infamité &c [*'ɪnˈfamɪtɪ] *n* infamy *la15-16*. [only Sc; OF *infamité*]
infang [*'ɪnˈfaŋ] *n* short for next *16-e18*. [*cf* OUTFANG]
infangthief &c [*'ɪnˈfaŋ ˈθif] *n* the right of the lord of a manor to try and to punish a thief taken on his property *13-17*. [ME *infangethef*, OE *infangen þeof*; *cf* OUTFANGTHEIFF]
infare &c [*'ɪnˈfer] *n* **1** an entertainment on entering a new house *la14*. **2** *specif* the feast given by the bridegroom to celebrate the coming of his bride to her new home *la16-19*.
infar [*'ɪnˈfar] **cake** a piece of oatcake (AIT) or *shortbread* (SHORT) broken over the head of a bride as she enters her new home *la19*. [OE *infær* entrance; *cf hamefare* (HAME)]

infeck &c *la15-*, **infect** &c *la14-* [ɪn'fɛk(t)] *vt*
= infect.

infeft [ɪn'fɛft, *also* -'fift] *vt, law* **1** *chf in ptp* **infeft**
&c, **infetht** *la15, freq* ~ **in** enfeoffed, invested
with legal possession of (HERITABLE property)
15-. **2** assign (property) by *infeftment, la15-16*.

infeftment, enfeftment *15-16, law* **1** the
investing of a new owner with a real right in, or
legal possession of land or HERITAGE, *orig*
accomplished by symbolic act, *now* by registration of the deed of transfer *15-*. **2** the document
which conveys this right *15-*. **infeftment in
security** *law* temporary *infeftment* of a creditor
in HERITABLE property as security against a
loan or debt *18-e19*. [orig ptp of OSc *infeff*; ME
enfeff, OF *enfieffer* vest with a fee or fief]

infeild *see* INFIELD

infeodacione &c [*?ɪnfio'deʃɪən] *n* = *infeftment* (INFEFT) *la15-16*. [MedL *infeodatio*;
eModEng *infeodation, 17*]

infer *vt* = infer *16-*.
~ **the pain(s) of law**, ~ **a punishment** *etc*
law involve or lead to a certain penalty
la17-e19.

infetht *see* INFEFT

infield &c, **infeild** &c [*'ɪn'fild, *Abd* *-'fidl] *n*
the field or land lying nearest to the farm or
homestead; *specif* one of the two main divisions
of an arable farm before the practice of crop
rotation, consisting of the best land nearest the
farm buildings, kept continuously under crop
and well manured *la15-e19*. [*cf* OUTFIELD]

infirmité &c *la14-16;* **infirmity** &c *la15- n*
= infirmity.

infit [*'ɪn'fɪt] *n* **hae an** ~ **wi** have influence on,
be in the good graces of *la19-e20, Bnf Abd*. [IN
+ FIT¹]

inflam, inflamb *see* ENFLAMBE

inflick [ɪn'flɪk] *vt* = inflict *18-*.

information, informatioun &c *la14-17 n* **1**
= information *la14-*. **2** *law, freq in pl* a written
argument ordered by a *Lord Ordinary* (LORD) in
the *Court of Session* (SESSION), or by the *Court of
Justiciary* (JUSTICIARY) when difficult questions
of law arose *18-e19*. **3** *law, in criminal cases* a
formal written accusation or statement of the
charge *18-20*.

ingadder *see* INGAITHER

ingadge *see* ENGAGE

ingaen *see* INGAUN

ingage *see* ENGAGE

ingait *see* INGATE

ingaither *la19-*, **ingadder** &c *16-, now Sh NE;*
ingather *la16-* ['ɪn'geðər, ɪn'geðər, &c] *vt* **1**
collect (money, dues etc) *16-, now Sh-C*. **2**
gather in, harvest (crops) *17-*.

ingan &c *18-*, **ingȝoun** &c *la16-e17*, **ingon**
&c *16-19*, **inȝone** &c *e17*, **onȝeon** &c
la16-17 ['ɪŋən, *'ɪŋjun, *-jən] *n* = onion *16-*.
~ **Johnnie** an itinerant onion-seller, *usu* from
northern France *20-*. [laME *ynon*, OF
oi(n)gnon]

ingang ['ɪn'gaŋ; *Sh* -'gjɪŋ] *n* **1** a lack, deficiency,
shortage *la16-, now Abd Kcdn Rox*. **2** an
entrance, entry *20-, Sh NE Ags; cf* INGAUN.
~**in**(**g**) the act of entering, entrance, entry *15-,
now Ork Bnf Gall*. [IN + GANG]

ingate, ingait &c ['ɪn'get, *Sh* -'gjet] *n* admission, entry; a way in *la16-, now Sh*. [IN +
GATE¹]

ingather *see* INGAITHER

ingaun, ingoing &c; **ingaen** &c *20-, Ags S*
['ɪn'gɑn &c] *n* **1** the act of entering *17*. **2** an
entrance, way in *la17-, now local Cai-S*. **3** the
assembling in a building, *esp* for a church service *19-, now local Cai-S*. **4** entry to a new tenancy *20-, local Ork-Gall*. **5** *only* **ingoing, ingo**
the reveal of a door- or window-case where the
stonework turns inward at right angles to the
wall *la19-*.
adj entering, taking possession, *esp* ~ **tenant** *etc*
the person entering the tenancy of a property
on the departure of the previous occupier *19-;*
cf *incoming* (INCOME).
~ **ee** (the entrance to) a drift mine or coal
seam at the surface outcrop, *esp* where the seam
is not entered vertically *19-, now C*. [f IN +
GAE]

ingener *see* ENGENDER

ingere &c *la15-16*, **ingyre** &c *16-e17*, **engyre**
&c *16-e17* [*'ɪn'dʒir, *-'dʒaɪr] *vr* **1** take upon
oneself, presume *la15-16*. **2** push oneself in,
obtrude oneself *16-e17*. [laME (once) *ingere*, L
ingerere]

ingettin(**g**) &c [*'ɪn'gɛtɪn] *n* getting in, collecting (rents, debts etc) *16-e17*. [*cf* INGOTTIN]

ingevar, ingeving *see* INGIVE

ingie ['ɪn'gi] *vt* in weaving a pattern, hand the
requisite threads in a loom to the weaver *20-,
local Fif-S*.
ingier the person who does this *20-, local Fif-S*.
[IN + GIE; *cf* INGIVE]

Ingies &c [*?'ɪŋgɪz] *n pl* = Indies *19*.

ingill, engill, inglis &c [*'ɪŋl] *n* a goldsmith's
weight, 1/20 ounce *la15*. [MFlem *inghelsche, engels*]

ingill *see* INGLE

ingine &c *15-*, **engine** &c [*sense 1* 'ɪndʒɪn; *St*
'ɛndʒɪn, 'ɛndʒɪn; *Abd also* 'ɪndʒəin; *senses 2-4*
ɪn'dʒəin] *n* **1** = engine, a mechanical contrivance *la14-*. **2** (1) natural cleverness, wit,
genius, ingenuity *15-20*. (2) a great intellect, a
person of intellectual ability *la16-e19*. **3** (1)
mental quality, disposition, temperament
15-e17. (2) the mind or disposition of a person
or persons *16-e17*. **4** *freq* evil *or* **false** ~, **colour or** ~ deception, guile *la15-16*.

ingineer, engineer [ɪndʒɪ'nir; *St* ɛndʒɪ'nir,
ɛndʒ-] = engineer. [the *in-* form is as in the
orig L *ingenium*]

ingive [*'ɪn'gɪv, *-'gi(v)] *v* **ingiver** &c, **ingevar**
la16-e17 one who hands in or lodges a docu-
ment formally for registration etc *la16-e19*.
ingiving &c, **ingeving** *la16* giving in a document, submitting it for consideration *la16-19*.

Ingland &c ['ɪŋland] *n* = England *la14-e17*. [*cf* INGLIS]

ingle, ingill *16-e17* ['ɪŋəl] *n* **1** (1) a fire on a hearth *16-*, *now local NE-Rox.* (2) an open hearth, the fireside, a chimney corner *18-*, *now local Cai-Uls.* **2** a kiln- or furnace-fire *17-*, *now Ork Cai Kcb.* **3** fuel for a fire, burning fuel taken from the fire *17-19*.

~-**cheek** the fireside, chimney corner *la18-*, *now local Cai-Rox, only Sc.* ~-**en**(d) the side of a house or room where the fire is *la18-19*. ~ **lowe** the flame or gleam of the fire *la18-*, *now Cai Bnf.* ~-**neuk** &c = ~ *cheek, la18-.* ~-**stane** a hearthstone *la19-*, *now Per Kcb Rox.* [Gael *aingeal* fire]

ingleberry *see* ANGLEBERRY

inglis *see* INGILL

Inglis &c *la14-17*; **Inglis**(c)**h** *15-e18* ['ɪŋlɪʃ; *'ɪŋlɪs, *'ɪŋlz] *adj* **1** = ENGLISH *adj* 1, *la14-e18*. **2** designating *Inglis n* 1 (1) and (2) and writings in this language *la14-e18*.
n **1** = English *15-e18*: (1) the language of England; (2) the language of *lowland* (LAWL-AND) Scotland, thought of variously as being the same as (1) or as being different from it. **2** (1) Englishmen *15-16*. (2) the ~ = *n* 3, *la17*. **3** *in pl* ~**is** the English troops of the Commonwealth *la17*.

~**man,** ~**men** = Englishman, -men *la14-17*. ~ **schole** = *English School* (ENGLISH) *la16-17*. [*cf* ENGLISH]

ingo *see* INGAUN

ingoing *see* INGAUN

ingon *see* INGAN

ingottin [*'ɪn'gotən] *ptp* collected *la16-e17*. [IN + *ptp* of GET; *cf* INGETTIN(G)]

ingraif &c [*'ɪn'grev] *vt* = engrave *la16-e17*, *only Sc.*

ingrave[1] [*'ɪn'grev] *vt* bury *16*. [IN + Eng *grave*]

ingrave[2] &c [(*irreg*) *'ɪn'grev] *vt, fig* = engraff, engraft *la16*.

ingres &c [*'ɪn'grɛs &c] *n* inlying pasture *16*. [IN + *gress*]

ingreve *see* ENGREVE

ingy ['ɪŋɪ] *vti, of a ewe* give birth to (a lamb) *20-*, *Cai.* [Norw dial *yngja* (*v*), f *ung* young; *cf* EENIE, YEAN]

ingyre *see* INGERE

ingჳoun *see* INGAN

inhabile, inhable &c [*'ɪn'hebəil, *-'hebl] *adj, law* unfit, unqualified, inadmissible *16-e19*.

inhability &c **1** = inability *la16-17*. **2** *law* disqualification, loss of legal rights *15-18*. [OF *inhabile*, L *inhabilis* incapable; *cf* HABILE]

inhabitant &c *n* **1** = inhabitant *la15-*. **2** *in pl without of*: those inhabiting *la15-e16*: 'the tennentis and inhabitantis the saidis landis'.

inhaddin, inhald *see* INHAUD

inhance &c, **enhaunse** &c; **inhaunce** [*'ɪn'hans] *vt* appropriate (goods); monopolize (a trade) *la17*. [only Sc; eModEng *inhance* enhance]

inhaud, inhald *v* ['ɪn'hɑd, *'ɪn'hald, &c] **inhalding** *n* damming (of water) *la15-16*. ~**in, inhaddin** &c *adj* **1** frugal, stingy *la18-*, *now Abd.* **2** obsequious *19-*, *Cai-Fif.*

inherd *see* ANHERD

inhibit &c *vt, ptp* ~**ed, inhibit** &c *16-17* **1** = inhibit *16-*. **2** *law* place under *inhibition* 2 (1), *16-*.

~**ion** &c **1** = inhibition, a prohibition *la14-*. **2** *law* (1) a writ prohibiting a debtor from parting with or committing his HERITABLE property to the prejudice of a creditor *la16-*. (2) an order by which a husband may prevent credit being given to his wife *la18-20*. [see *letters of inhibition* (LETTER)]

inhonesté; inhonestie *n* disgraceful conduct; indecency *16-e17*. [laME (once); laL *inhonestas*]

inimity &c *la15-17*, **inimité** *16*, **inemité** *la15-e17*, **inamité** *16* [*'ɪ'nɪmɪtɪ, *-'nɛm-, *-'nam-] *n* = enmity. [only Sc; *cf* *inemy* &c (ENEMY)]

inimy *see* ENEMY

iniquity &c *16-*, **iniquité** &c *la14-16 n* **1** = iniquity *la14-*. **2** *law* lack of equity, partiality *17-18*.

injone *see* INJUNE

injoys *see* ENJOSE

injune &c *15-e17*, **injone** *16-e17* [*'ɪn'dʒøn] *vt* = enjoin, *only Sc.*

injure[1] &c [*'ɪn'dʒør] *n* **1** (1) injustice, wrong, mischief done to a person *la14-16*. (2) an instance of this *15-16*. **2** physical injury, maltreatment *15-e16*. **3** abuse, insult *16*. [ME (once), OF; *cf* Eng *injury*]

injure[2] &c [*'ɪn'dʒør] *vt* **1** do injustice to *la15-*. **2** hurt, harm; maltreat *la15-*. **3** abuse, insult *la16-*. [earlier in Sc; OF *injurer*]

ink &c *n* = ink *la14-*.
~**er** an ink-bottle *la19-*, *Ags.* ~-**fish** squid *la18-*. ~-**pud** an ink-bottle *19-20*.

inkie-pinkie &c; **hinkie-pinkie** &c *n* **1** weak beer *19*. **2** nonsense word in children's rhymes *19-*, *now local C.* [obscure]

inkirly *see* INCRE

inkling, inklin &c *n* **1** = inkling *la16-*. **2** a small amount *19-*, *now local.* **3** an inclination, a slight desire *19-*, *now Sh Ork N.*

in-kneed, in-kne'd *adj* knock-kneed *17-*, *now Ork N Rox.*

inks *n pl* low-lying land on the banks of a river estuary *la17-*, *SW.* [var of Eng dial *ing*, ON *eng* a riverside meadow]

inlaik &c, **inlake, enlaike** *la16-e17*; **inlack** &c *la14-19*, **inleak** *la16-* [ɪn'lek, ɪn'lik, ɪn'li:k; *'ɪn'lak] *n* **1** deficit, deficiency; a deficiency, shortage, reduction, lack *la14-*. **2** death *16-19*. *vti* **1** be deficient, lack, suffer loss (in weight, volume etc) *16-19*. **2** *of persons* (1) be or become absent, default *la16*; (2) die *16-19*. **3** fall short; become weak, decline *la16-e17*. [IN + LACK]

inlair *see* INLAY

inlairge *see* ENLAIRGE

inlake *see* INLAIK

inland &c [*'ɪn'land, *'ɪnland] *n* **1** INFIELD land on a farm or estate *la15-e17*. **2** the inlying or central area of a country *la16-e17*. **3** the inner part of a TENEMENT *16-18*, *Abd*. [ME, OE the inner part of an estate or manor]

in lang, inlangis *see* ENDLANG

inlarge *see* ENLAIRGE

inlat; inlet ['ɪnlat, 'ɪnlət] *n* **1** = inlet. **2** an entrance, avenue *19-*, *NE-Fif*. **3** *fig* an encouragement, a concession, opportunity, welcome *18-*, *now local Abd-Kcb*.

inlay [*'ɪn'le] *vt* build (the *inlair*) *la16*.

   inlair [*'ɪn'leər, *-'ler] the part of the mill dam which formed the channel of the millrace; the LADE *la16-e19*. [cf *lay in* 3 (LAY¹)]

inleak *see* INLAIK

inlet *see* INLAT

in like [*ɪn'ləik] *adv* equally; likewise *e16*.

   inlik(e)maner &c *la16*, **~wayis &c** *la16*, **inlikewise, inlikwis &c** [*'ɪn'ləikwaɪz &c] *adv* likewise, also *la15-16*. [nME = alike; *cf* ELIKE]

in litem [ɪn 'ləitəm, ɪn 'laɪtɛm] *law* **oath** ~ an oath sworn by the *pursuer* (PURSUE) in an action regarding the amount of loss suffered by him *18-*. [L = in regard to the dispute]

inlok [*ʔ'ɪn'lok] *n* ? a lock inserted in a door *15*. [only Sc]

inlow [*ʔɪn'lu] *v* = allow, accredit (to one) in an account *15-17*.

inlying [*n* 'ɪn'laɪɪn; *adj* -ən] *n* a lying-in, confinement *la18-*, *now local*.

   adj confined, in childbed *la19-*, *now local*.

inmeat; inmate &c *la19-* ['ɪnmit, -met] *n* the viscera of an animal, *esp* the edible parts *la17-*, *now Rox*. [eModEng *inmeats*]

in-myd [*'ɪn'mɪd] *adv, prep* in the middle (of) *la15-e16*.

inn &c, in &c *la14-16* *n* **1** = inn *la14-*. **2** *also in pl with sing sense* a dwelling, habitation *la14-e20*. **3** *in pl with sing sense* a lodging, tavern, hotel *16-*, *now SW Slk*.

   ~ery &c a TENEMENT to which access is gained by a common passage and stair *20-*, *Rox*.

innative &c [*'ɪ'netɪv] *adj* innate *16-e17*. [appar laL *innātus* + L *nātīvus*; *cf* Eng = native *la17*]

inner &c *adj*, *also* **enner** *la16* = inner *la14-*.

   ~lie &c **1** inlying, not exposed; in the interior of a district *19-*, *S*. **2** friendly, kindly, sympathetic, affectionate *19-*, *now S*. **3** *of a ship or of fishing grounds* near the shore *20-*, *chf Sh*.

   ~ house 1 an inner apartment of a building *la15-e17*. **2 I~ House** the first and second divisions of judges of the *Court of Session* (SESSION) *la16-*. **~mare &c** further in *la14-16*.

inner *see* INVER

innin *n* an entrance, introduction, friendly reception *la19-*, *local Abd-Dmf*. [f IN or perh INN]

innomerable &c *la15-e16*, **innowmerabill &c** *15-e16* [*ɪnʌmə'rebl, *'ɪ'nʌmərəbl, *'ɪ'numərebl, &c] *adj* = innumerable.

innouth *see* INWITH

innovat &c *adj* revised, renewed *la16-17*. [only Sc; L *innovāt-*, ptp stem of *innovāre*]

innovatioun &c *n* **1** = innovation, the alteration of an established form, practice, institution, or legal provision *la15-*. **2** the alteration or replacement of a legal obligation *la15-*, *only Sc*.

innowmerabill *see* INNOMERABLE

inopportune &c *adj* untimely, unseasonable, inconvenient *la16-*.

   inopportunitie &c an unsuitable occasion or application *16-*. [earlier in Sc; freq confused *16* with *importune* importunate]

inordourly, inorderlie &c *adv* improperly, irregularly *la15-e17*.

   adj disorderly *la16-e17*.

inorme *see* ENORM

inormité *see* ENORMITY

inouch *see* ENEUCH

in oure *see* INOWER

inower, in oure *16*, **anower &c** *la19-e20*, *Ags*; **in over &c** *la16-19* [ɪn'ʌuər; *Ags* ən-] *prep* **1** in, inside, within *16-*, *now Ork-EC*. **2** over (a fence or boundary) into the area within *16-*, *now Ork-EC, Lnk*.

   adv inside, *usu* implying that a barrier has been surmounted, close(r) in *16-*.

   ~ and out ower thoroughly *19-e20*, *S*.

inpassing *n* a passing in(wards) *16*.

inpit *la16-*, **input &c** ['ɪn'pɪt, -'put, *-'pʌt] *vt*, *also* **imput &c** *la15-17* **1** (1) grant a lease to, install (a tenant etc) *la15-18*. (2) appoint (a person) to an office or position *16-e17*. **2** (1) put (a thing) in a place, insert *la15-e18*. (2) put (a person) in prison *16*. (3) sow (crops) *la18-*, *SW*.

   n a share, contribution of money etc (for a specific purpose) *la17-20*, *only Sc*.

   input *ptp, adj* which has been put in, sown, loaded etc *18-e19*. [IN + PIT¹]

inprofitable *adj* = improfitable *la15-e17*.

input *see* INPIT

inquere *see* INQUIRE

inquest &c; inqu(e)ist &c *la15-16* [*'ɪn'kwɛst, *ɪn'kwist, &c] *n* **1** = inquest *la14-*. **2** *specif* a body of men appointed to inquire into such matters as cognition of the insane and inheritance *la15-19*. **3** a judicial and administrative body in the BURGHS of Peebles and Lanark *la15-16*.

inquire &c *15-*, **inquere &c** *la14-17*, **enquire &c** *la15-* [ɪn'kwaɪr, *'ɪn'kwir] *vti* **1** = inquire *la14-*. **2** ~ **at** inquire of, ask for information from (a person etc) *15-*. **3** ~ **for** ask about the health of (a person) *19-*.

inquiry &c ['ɪnkwɪrɪ] **1** = inquiry *la18-*. **2** an inquest, *esp* an investigation into a fatal accident *la19-*. **make inquiry at** ask or inquire from (a source of information) *18-*. [*cf* ASK², SPEIR]

inquist *see* INQUEST

inrage *see* ENRAGE

in retentis [ɪn rɪ'tɛntis] *law, of evidence* taken on oath before a case is heard *la18*-. [L = among things retained]

inrin &c [*ɪn'rɪn] *vt* commit (an offence), incur (a loss), fall into (a difficulty etc) *15-e17*. [only Sc; after L *incurrere*]

inring ['ɪn'rɪŋ] *n, curling* (CURL) **1** the innermost part of the surface of a stone, ie that nearest the TEE[1] *19-, now Kcb*. **2** a shot in which the stone being played is made to strike the inside edge of another, and glance off it so as to hit and displace the opponent's stone nearest the TEE[1], an INWICK *la18-, now Lnk Kcb Rox*.

inscales, inskells *la17 n pl* the gratings or racks placed at the lower end of a wicker salmon-trap *la17-e19*. [appar IN + *scale* a series of steps, *ie* of a salmon-ladder]

insch *see* INCH

inschew *see* ENSCHEW

inseam &c ['ɪn'sim] *n* the seam which attaches the welt to the insole and upper of a boot or shoe *la19-, local Sh-Kcb*.

inseat *see* INSET

insense [ɪn'sɛns] *vt, chf* ~ **into** convince, impress a fact on, enlighten *la19-, chf Gall Uls*. [OSc (once) *ensens*, ME *ensense*, OF *ensenser* inform]

insere [*ɪn'sir] *vt, ptp also* **insert**, *chf in ptp*: **1** included in a book etc *16*. **2** entered in an official record etc *la15-, now local Cai-Fif*. [chf Sc; L *inserere*, ptp stem *insert-*]

inserve [*ʔɪn'sɛrv] *v* serve *la16-e17*. [chf Sc; L *inservīre; cf* eModEng (rare) *la17*]

inset, insett *n* **1** *also* **inseat** (*la17*), *chf law* the INFIELD or a part of it *17-18; cf* OUTSET[2]. **2** a living room in a farm house *la17-19, chf WC*. [IN + SET[1]]

insetting [*'ɪn'sɛtɪŋ] *vbl n* setting in position, installing *16-e17*.

insew *see* ENSCHEW

inshant *see* INCHANT

insicht &c [*'ɪnsɪxt] *n, also* ~ **of houshald** *la15*, ~ (**and**) **plenissing** *16-17* furniture, household goods *la15-19*. [unknown; *cf* OUTSIGHT]

inside *n* **1** = inside. **2** *mining, chf* **gae tae the** ~ go from the pit-bottom to the coal face *20-, Fif Loth Lnk*.
adj = inside.
~ **claes** underclothing *la19-, local*. ~ **twist** *curling* (CURL) a twist causing a stone to revolve to the right *19-e20*.

insinuat &c *vti* **1** = insinuate *16-e17*. **2** *vt* announce publicly, intimate, mention *la16-17*.

insist *vi* **1** = insist *la16*-. **2** *law, freq* ~ **in** proceed with (a charge or action at law); continue with (one's case) *la16-*. **3** ~ **for** insist upon *la18-20*. **4** go on talking etc *18-e19*.

inskells *see* INSCALES

insnorl [?ɪn'snorl] *vt, lit and fig* entangle *la19-e20, N*. [IN + SNORL]

insolence &c *n* **1** = insolence *16*-. **2** wild behaviour, licentiousness *la15-16, only Sc*.

inspreth &c [*'ɪnsprɛθ, *-sprɛx(t), *-spreθ &c] *n* furniture, household furnishings *la15-17, chf WC SW*. [obscure]

instance &c [*'ɪn'stans, 'ɪnstans] *n* **1** = instance *la14*-. **2** *law* the pleading and procedure followed during the hearing of a legal action *17*-.
at *etc* **the** ~ **of** at the instigation, request or suit of *la14-17*. **to** (**someone's**) ~ to the suit or citation (of a *pursuer* (PURSUE)) *la15-e16*. **with** (**gret**) ~ *in the formula recording the procuring of a seal* (PROCURE) *15-16*.

instant &c ['ɪn'stant, *ɪn'stant] *adj* **1** = instant *16*-. **2** of the present time, contemporary, now in existence; *specif of the year or month* current *15*-.
~**ly &c** **1** = instantly *16*-. **2** now, at this moment *16-e18*.

insteid, instede &c *15-e17*; **i stead &c** *la19-, now Rox* [ɪ(n)'stid] *adv* = instead (**of**) *15-, now local*.

institor [*ʔ'ɪnstɪtor] *n, law* an agent or manager *la17-e20*. [L]

institute *n, law* the person first named in a TESTAMENT or DESTINATION of property *la17*-. [L *institutus* one instituted (as heir); *cf* SUBSTITUTE]

instruct &c; instruck &c *vt* **1** = instruct *la15*-. **2** *law* supply evidence or documentary proof of, prove clearly, vouch for (a fact) *la16*-.
~**ion &c** **1** = instruction *la15*-. **2** evidence, proof *la16-e18*.

instrument [*n* 'ɪnstrəmənt; *v* *ʔɪnstrə'mɛnt] *n* **1** = instrument *la14*-. **2** *specif law, now only church law* a formal narrative, duly authenticated, of any proceedings of which a person wishes to preserve a record, *latterly chf* with a view to protesting or appealing against them *la14*-.
vt register a protest against (a person) by means of an INSTRUMENT (*n* 2) *18*.
~**ary witness** one who witnesses the signing of an INSTRUMENT (*n* 2) *la17-19*.
ask, take *etc* ~ request, obtain etc an INSTRUMENT (*n* 2) *15-*. ~ **of sasine** the deed or document recording the transfer of property *la19*-.

insucken, insuckin *16-e17* [*ɪn'sʌkən] *n, law, also* ~ **multure** *la17-18* the MULTURE payable by persons within the SUCKEN of a mill *16-e17*.

insulane &c *n* a Hebridean *e16*. [laME *insulane* an islander, L *insulānus*]

intack *la19-*, **intact** [ɪn'tak(t)] *adj* = intact *la15*-.

intacking *see* INTAK

intae[1] &c *19-*, **into &c** ['ɪntə, 'ɪntɪ] *prep* **1** = into *la14*-. **2** in, within *la14-, now Ork Cai EC*.
be ~ **1** find fault with, scold (a person) *20-, now local*. **2** hook (a fish, *chf* a salmon) *20*-. **come, sit** *etc* ~.. come, sit *etc* forward to (the fire, table etc) *18*-. **out** ~ out of, from *19-, local Ags-Bwk*. **sing, speak** *etc* ~ **anesel** speak under one's

breath, sing *sotto voce*, *la18-*. **that's** ~ **ye** *etc of a cutting remark etc* = that's one for .. *la19-*. [freq two words; *cf* INTIL]

intae² ['ɪn'te] ~**d** *19-*, **intoed** *la18-* with turned-in toes, pigeon-toed. [IN + TAE¹]

intak &c; **intake &c** *la16-* ['ɪntak, 'ɪntek, 'ɪntək] *vt* take in *la15-*.

n **1** the place where water is diverted from a river, dam etc by a channel (*freq* to supply a mill) *la15-*, *now local Cai-Kcb, only Sc*. **2** a piece of land reclaimed and enclosed on a farm *16-*, *now Sh-Ags, Ayr*. **3** a narrowing: (1) *building* the offset on a wall, a ledge in a wall where its thickness is reduced *la17-*, *now Fif*; (2) *knitting*, *chf in pl* the number of stitches decreased in order to shape a garment, *eg* a sock *la19-*. **4** the act of taking in (*eg* food, harvest, breath) *la19-*. **5** a fraud, deception *19-*. **6** a swindler *19-*, *local Cai-Bwk*.

~**ing, intacking &c** *16-e17* **1** the act of taking in *16-*. **2** the taking of a place by assault *la16-17*. **3** the breaking in and cropping of previously fallow ground *18, Abd*. **4** the decrease of stitches in knitting socks etc *la19-*.

intelleck; intellect *n* **1** = intellect *19-*. **2** *in pl* wits, senses *la19-*, *now Rox*.

intemeit *see* INTIMATE

intend &c; inten *20-*, *NE, WC, SW* [ɪn'tɛn(d)] *v* **1** = intend *15-*. **2** *law* raise or PURSUE (legal proceedings) *la16-e18*; *cf* INTENT.

~**er** *freemasonry* a fellow of the craft chosen by a novice to instruct him in the mysteries of the craft *la16-18*.

intent *vt, chf in ptp* **intented &c**, *law, of a legal action* raised or instituted *16-e19*.

n, law the *pursuer's* (PURSUE) action in a suit *la16-e17*. [only Sc; MedL *intentare litem* institute a lawsuit; *cf* INTEND]

intent *see* ENTENT

inter *see* ENTER

interchange, intercheinge *16* [*ɪntər'tʃin(d)ʒ &c*] *vt* = interchange, exchange *la14-*.

~**ably &c, enterchangeably &c** *chf law* mutually, reciprocally *la14-e16*.

intercommune &c *la16-19*, **intercommoun &c** *la15-e17*; **intercommon &c** *la15-e18* [*ɪntər'komun, *-ən] *vi* **1** be in communication (with enemies, rebels, outlaws etc) *la15-19*, *latterly only hist, only Sc*. **2** *vt* prohibit from intercourse with others, ban, outlaw *la17-e18*. **3** *vi* take counsel together, consult *16-*. **intercommuned &c** denounced in *letters of intercommuning* (LETTER) proscribed, outlawed *la17-e18*. **intercommuning &c** the fact or practice of being in communication with rebels or denounced persons *la15-18*. [var of OSc *entercommoun*, ME *entercomen*, AF *entrecomuner* have dealings with others]

interdict *la15-*, **interdite &c** *15-e17* [*n* 'ɪntərdɪkt; *v* ɪntər'dɪkt, 'ɪntərdɪkt, *ɪntər'dəit] *n*, *also* **enterdick** *la19-e20 law* a court order prohibiting some action complained of as illegal or wrongful, until the question of right is tried in the proper court, *corresponding to Eng* injunction *la18-*.

vt **1** = interdict *15-*. **2** *vr* restrict oneself in some respect by voluntary renunciation *la16-e17*. **3** *vt, law* restrain (a spendthrift or FACILE person) by law from disposing recklessly of his estate *18-*. **4** *law* prohibit or restrain from an action by an INTERDICT (*n*) *19-*.

~**ion &c 1** = interdiction *la15-*. **2** the means whereby the actions of a FACILE person are restrained either voluntarily or by a court *la16-*.

~**or &c** a person whose consent is necessary before a FACILE person can grant any deed involving his estate *17-*.

interim ~ a provisional INTERDICT (which can be granted without the participation of the DEFENDER) *la19-*.

interes &c; intres &c, enteres, entres &c [*ɪnt(ə)rɛs, *-is, *ɛnt-] *n* **1** = interess, interest *la15-17*. **2** damage, injury, loss; compensation for these *15-17*.

v, chf in ptp ~**t 1** = interested *la16-e17*. **2** damaged, harmed *la16-17*. [*cf* INTEREST]

interes *see* ENTRESS

interest &c; intrest *17-e18 n* **1** = interest *la16-*. **2** a landed property, an estate *18*. [*cf* INTERES]

interlocutor, interlocutour &c *la15-17*; **interloquitor &c** *16-e18* [ɪntər'lɔkətər, *also* -'lɔk(j)utər] *n, law, strictly* an order or judgment given in the course of a suit by the *Court of Session* (SESSION) or a *Lord Ordinary* (LORD) before final judgment is pronounced; any court order *16-*.

~**y, interloquutoure &c** provisional, not finally decisive *la15-e17*. [MedL *interlocutorium*]

intermediate, intermediat *la16 adj* **1** = intermediate *la16-*. **2** *education* applied to the type of school providing a three year course for 12 to 14-year-old children, which ended with a state examination and the **Intermediate Certificate** *e20*. [see CERTIFICATE; *cf* HIGHER]

intermeis [*ɪntər'mis &c*] *n* something served between courses at a banquet; an entertainment taking the place of this *la16*. [ME *entremees*, OF *entremès*]

intermell [*ɪntər'mɛl*] **1** *vt* = intermell *la15-16*. **2** *vi* get into company or connection with *la15-e16*.

~**ie &c** in a confused group or crowd *la14-e15*.

intermiddill *see* ENTERMIDDILL

interpell &c [*ɪntər'pɛl*] *vt* **1** interrupt; appeal to, call upon *la16-17*. **2** *law* prohibit, prevent *18-19*, *only Sc*. [ME; L *interpellāre* interrupt]

interpone &c [*ɪntər'pon*] *vt, law* interpose *16-e19*.

~ **one's authority to** etc intervene so as to prevent something *16-19*. [eModEng; L *interpōnere*]

interpret &c; interpreit &c *16* [ɪn'tɛrprɪt &c; *ɪntər'prɪt &c] *vti* = interpret *la15-*.

interprysar &c [*ɪntər'praɪzər] *n* = enterpriser, a person who undertakes some work or action *la16*.

interrogat &c *ptp* interrogated, questioned *la16-18*. [eModEng; L *interrogāt-*, ptp stem of *interrogāre*]

interrogators &c *la16-e18*, **interrogatouris** *16* [*ɪntər'rogaturz, -ərz] *n pl, law* = interrogatories, questions to a witness etc.

interrup &c *la15-*; **interrupt** *la16-* [ɪntə'rʌp(t)] *vt* = interrupt *la15-*.

interruption &c 1 = interruption *15-*. **2** *law* the step legally required to stop the period of a *prescription* (PRESCRIBE) *15-*.

intertene, interteny *see* ENTERTEEN

intertrike &c [*ɪntər'trəik] *vt* ? disarrange, interfere with *16*. [see DOST Suppl]

intertynie *see* ENTERTEEN

interval, intervall *la16* *n* **1** = interval *la16-*. **2** the period of time between morning and afternoon church services *la19-20*.

intery *see* ENTRY

inthrow &c; introw &c *20-*, *Sh* ['ɪn'θru; *Sh* -'tru; *NE* -'θrʌu] *adv* inwards, towards an inner focal point, *eg* a fireside *la17-*, *now Sh*. *prep* **1** right through; in the heart of *16-*, *now Ork NE*. **2** by means of, through the agency of *19-*, *NE*. [IN + THRU]

intil &c; intul &c *19-*, *NE, C* ['ɪntɪl, ɪn'tɪl; *NE, C also* ɪn'tʌl] *prep* **1** into *la14-*. **2** in, inside, forming a part or ingredient of *la14-20*. *vt* enter *la20-*, *local Cai-midLoth*.

~ anesel under one's breath *19-*. **be ~ of a pointed remark** be a hit or thrust at (someone) *la19-*, *local Abd-Kcb*. [IN + TILL[1]; in early use commoner than INTAE[1]; freq written as two words; now less common than INTAE[1] in *C, S*]

intimate; intemeit &c *la16-17* *vt, pt, ptp* **intimat(e)** *16-20* = intimate, make known *16-*.

intimation &c 1 an intimation, a formal notification or announcement, *esp* (*17-*) from the pulpit *15-*. **2** *specif, law* an official notice given to persons concerned, of something required of them and the penalty in case of default *16-19*.

intimmer &c; intimber *la17-e18* ['ɪn'tɪmər] *n, only in pl* *la17-* **1** the inner timbers of a vessel *la15-e18*. **2** *of a mechanical contrivance* the internal structure, the mechanism *20-*, *Sh Ork NE Wgt*. **3** *joc, of the human body* the internal organs, *esp* stomach and bowels *19-*, *now local Sh-Stlg*. [IN + TIMMER[1]]

intimy &c [*?'ɪntɪmɪ] *vt* intimate *16-e17*. [only *Sc*; F *intimer*, L *intimāre*]

intitulat &c *ptp, chf of books or writings* entitled *16-17*. [laL *intitulāt-*, ptp stem of *intitulāre*]

intment *see* EYNTMENT

into *see* INTAE[1]

intocum [*'ɪntə'kʌm] *adv* coming next, immediately ahead *16*.

intoed *see* INTAE[2]

in-toll &c [*'ɪn'tol] *n* a payment made to the BAILLIE upon entering into possession of *burghal* (BURGH) property *la13-16*.

intoun &c ['ɪn'tun, 'ɪntun] *n* the land adjacent to the farmhouse, *orig* continuously cultivated *16-20*, *chf Abd*. [IN + TOUN; *cf* INFIELD]

intra *see* ENTRY

intrait, intreit &c; intrat [*ɪn'tret, *-'trɪt] *vt* = entreat *la16-e17*.

intrant [*?'ɪntrant] *adj* newly appointed, just beginning or entering on a profession, function etc *la16-18*.

n **1** a person who enters or becomes a member of a college, institution, association or body; a person who enters the *ministry* (MINISTER) of the church or a new charge *16-18*. **2** a person entering a place of any kind *17*. **3** *St Andrews and Glasgow Universities* the student chosen by each NATION to represent it in voting for the RECTOR *18-19*; *cf* PROCURATOR. [L *intrant-*, presp stem of *intrāre* enter]

intrat *see* INTRAIT

intré *see* ENTRY

intreit *see* INTRAIT

intres *see* ENTRESS, INTERES

intrest *see* INTERES[2], INTEREST

intrinche &c *vtr* = entrench *la16-e17*.

intrinsic &c *adj* **1** = intrinsic. **2** *law, of an explanation admitted under oath* not separable from what is sworn and thus qualifying the oath *18-*; *cf* EXTRINSIC.

intromit &c; intromet &c *la15-e18* [ɪntro'mɪt, *-'mɛt] *vt* **1** *law* handle or deal **with** (funds or property, *esp* those of another person living or dead), with or without legal authority *15-19*. **2** have to do **with**, consort, interfere **with** *la15-*, *now Abd Ags Fif*.

intromissatrix &c *la16-*, **intromissatrice &c** *la16-e17* [*ɪntro'mɪsətrɪks, *-trəis, &c] a female *intromitter*. **intromission &c 1** *law* (1) the assuming of the possession or management of another's property with or without authority *16-*; (2) *in pl also* the transactions of an agent or subordinate *18-*. **2** the conduct of any piece of business; *in pl* intermeddling *19-*, *now Ork Ags Fif*. **intromitter &c** a person who INTROMITS with another's property *la15-*. **vitious intromissatrix** a female *vitious intromitter*, *la16-*. **vitious intromission** *law* unwarrantable interference with the MOVEABLE estate of a deceased without legal title, whereby liability for all the debts of the deceased may be incurred *la17-*, *only Sc*. **vitious intromitter** *17-* a person who INTROMITS without authority. [ME; L *intrōmittere* interfere with (the property of) another]

introw *see* INTHROW

intrude *vti* **1** = intrude. **2** thrust oneself or another into any benefice or church living to which the intruder is regarded as having no claim, *esp* against the wishes of the congregation *18-*, *now hist*.

intrusion 1 = intrusion *15-*. **2** *specif, church*: the *presentation* (PRESENT) and (forcible) introduction of a MINISTER to a charge against the wishes of the congregation *18-*, *now hist*. [*cf* next]

intruse [*ɪnˈtrøz] *vtr* thrust (oneself or another) into an office etc to which one has no claim *15-17*. [L *intrūs-*, ptp stem of *intrūdere*; *cf* prec]

intrusion *see* INTRUDE

intul *see* INTIL

in-turn *n*, curling (CURL) the playing of a stone with the handle inwards, to make it swing to the right *20-*, *SW*, *S*.

inunct [*ɪnˈʌŋkt] *vt* annoint *16*. [L *inunct-*, ptp stem of *inunguere*]

inund [*ɪnˈʌnd] *vt* inundate *17*. [eModEng (once); L *inundāre*]

invade &c *vt* **1** = invade *la15-*. **2** *lit and fig* attack, assault (a person etc) *la15-*. **3** take possession of, usurp, by armed force *la15-16*.

invalesce; invales *vi*, *chf of disease etc* increase, grow worse or more grave *16*. [L *invalēscere* grow strong(er)]

invecta et illata [ɪnˈvɛkta ɛt ɪˈlata] *law* goods or effects brought onto premises, which may be held as security for rent; grain brought from outside the SUCKEN[1] to be ground at the SUPERIOR's mill *18-*. [L = things imported and brought in]

inveet &c, *18-*, *local*, **inveit &c** *17*; **invite** [ɪnˈvit, -ˈvəit] *vt* = invite *17-*.

n an invitation *la19-*.

inventar &c, **inventour &c** *16-e18*, **invitour &c** *16-17*; **inveter &c** *la17-19* [ˈɪnvɛ(n)tər, -vɪ(n)t-,-vit-] *n* **1** an inventory *la15-19*. **2** *in pl* the stock, crops etc listed in the inventory of a farm and taken over by a new tenant *20-*, *now local Bnf-midLoth*.

vt make an inventory of, catalogue *la16-e18*. [chf Sc; OF *inventaire*, *-oire*, L *inventarium*, *-orium*]

inver; inner *la15-16* *n* a confluence of streams; the mouth of a stream or river *la15-18*, *NE Arg*, *in place-names la15-*. [Gael *inbhir*]

Inverness: ~ (**cape etc**) a heavy tweed knee-length cloak with a shoulder-cape *la19-*. [the town]

invert &c *vt* = invert *la16-*.

inversion *law* the act of *inverting possession*, *19-*.

~ **possession** *law* exercise proprietary rights over the property of another, *esp* of a tenant using the SUBJECTS for a purpose not provided for in his lease *la19-*.

inveter *see* INVENTAR

invious *see* ENVY

inviroun *see* ENVERON

invite *see* INVEET

invitour *see* INVENTAR

invy *see* ENVY

inwan [ˈɪnˈwan] *adv* inwards *la19-20*, *Fif Edb*. [IN + WAN[2]]

inward; inwar &c [*ˈɪnˈward, *-ˈwer &c] *n* some feudal service, *prob* that due within the lord's demesne *la12*. [OE *inwaru*; *cf* OUTWARE]

inward *see* INWART

inwark; inwork [ˈɪnˈwark &c] *n* domestic or indoor work *la18-*, *now Ork Ags Per*. [IN + WARK]

inwart &c *la14-16*, *only Sc*, **inward &c** *adj* **1** = inward *la14-*. **2** *of persons* on intimate terms, in favour *la15-16*.

adv = inward *15-*.

inweys [ˈɪnwəiz; *Abd* ˈɪnwaɪz] *adv* inwards *20-*, *local Ork-Kcb*. [IN + WEY[1]]

inwick [ˈɪnˈwɪk] *orig curling* (CURL) *and now also carpet-bowls* (*la20-*, *SW*) *n* a shot which strikes the inside of another stone etc and glances off it towards the TEE[1]; the playing of such a shot *19-*. *vti* strike (a stone with another) in this way, reach the TEE[1] by glancing off the inner side of another force and knocking out that of an opponent *19-*. [IN + WICK[1]; *cf* INRING]

inwith &c *15-20*, **innouth &c** *15-e16*, **enouth &c** *la14-15*, **ennowe** *16* [ˈɪnˈwɪθ; *ɪˈnuθ, *əˈnu] *adv* **1** within, inside *15-19*. **2** inwards *19-20*, *chf NE*.

prep **1** within, inside *la15-e17*. **2** *only* **inwith** at less than, under (a certain price etc) *la16*. [ME; *cf* INBY]

inwork *see* INWARK

inʒet *ptp* poured in *e16*. [IN + *yet* (YAT)]

inʒone *see* INGAN

ion *see* EEAN

iorram &c *19-*; **jorram &c** *la18-19* [ˈɪrəm] *n* a GAELIC rowing-song. [Gael]

ipothecar, ipoticar *see* APOTHICAR

ipotingar &c [*ɪˈpotɪŋər &c] *n* an apothecary *la16*. [conflation of *ipoticar* (APOTHICAR) w POTTINGAR]

ir *see* BE

Irche *see* IRISH

ire *see* IRON

Ireland *see* IRLAND

iren *see* IRON

Irish &c *16-*, **Irische &c** *15-e17*, **Irsche &c** *la14-e16*, **Iris &c** *la16-e17*; **Irche &c** *la14* [ˈaɪrɪʃ, ˈəir-, *-ɪs; *ɪrʃ] *adj* **1** *of persons* of or from Ireland or (*-18*) the *Highlands* (HIELAND); GAELIC-speaking *la14-*. **2** *of language, writings etc* of the GAELIC language of Ireland or (*-18*) the *Highlands*, *16-*. **3** *of things, practices etc* Irish or (*-17*) Highland *16-*.

n **1** Irish or (*-18*) Highland (HIELAND) people *la15-*. **2** the Irish or (*-18*) Scottish GAELIC language *16-*. **3** *in pl* ~**es** (1) Irishmen *la16-e19*. (2) Highlanders (HIELAND) *la16-17*.

~**er** an Irish person *19-*. ~(**e**)**ry &c** the Irish people or nation *15-*. ~**man, Irichman** *16* **1** = Irishman *la15-*. **2** a Highlander (HIELAND) *la15-e17*. **3 Irishman's cutting** a cutting taken from a plant, with a portion of the root attached *20-*, *local Cai-WC*. [ME *Irisc*; *cf* EERISH, ERSE and GAELIC; ScGael became distinct from IrGael in its written form *c* 1750, and the senses = Highland, ScGael etc had died out by *la18*]

Irland &c *la14-e17*; **Ireland &c** ['aɪrland, 'əɪr-; *'ɪr-] *n* = Ireland *la14-*.
adj **1** Irish, characteristic of Ireland *15-17*. **2** as a designation of heraldic officers *la15-e16*.
~ **man** an Irishman *la15-e16*. [*cf* HIELAND and IRISH]

iron &c *16-*, **irne &c** *la14-e19*, **airn &c** *la16-*, **erne &c** *la15-*, **iren &c** *la15-e17* [*Sh-nEC* 'əɪr(ə)n; *WC, SW, Uls* 'ɛr(ə)n; *sEC, WC, SW* 'er(ə)n; *ɪrn] *n*, *also* **ire** *la18-, Abd* **1** = iron *la14-*. **2** *in pl* surgical instruments *la15-*, *now midLoth Bwk*. **3** *golf* one of a number of clubs with metal heads of varying shapes, used in all conditions except on the *putting green* (PUTT[1]) *19-*. **4** an iron tool for cutting PEATS[1]; the amount of PEAT[1] which can be cut with this tool in one day *la18-, Hebrides*.
adj = iron *la15-*.
~**-eer &c** ferric oxide, rust, *esp* when found as a deposit in soil or water, or as a stain on linen *la19-, N*. ~**-eerie &c** impregnated with iron; rusty *18-, NE*. ~ **fit** a shoemaker's last *19-*, *N nEC Lnk*. ~**-house** a room in a prison, *orig* the Old TOLBOOTH of Edinburgh, where prisoners were kept in irons *la16-18*. ~ **man** *fishing* a hand-winch used on boats to haul in the nets *la19-, Sh Ork E*.
fresh *or* **new aff the** ~**s** brand new; fresh from one's studies *la18-e20*.

irr *see* BE

irredeemable &c *17*, **irredimable** *17*; **irre-deemable** *la17-* *adj* not redeemable. [earlier in Sc]

irregular &c *adj* = irregular *la15-*.
n a disobedient or disqualified ecclesiastic *la15-17*.
~ **marriage** a marriage contracted without a religious ceremony or formal civil procedure *18-*.

irrelevant &c **1** *adj, law, of a legal claim or charge* not RELEVANT, not sufficient or pertinent in law to warrant the decree asked for *la16-*. **2** = irrelevant.
irrelevance, irelevancy &c **1** *law* lack of pertinence, impropriety *la16-*. **2** = irrelevance. [*cf* RELEVANT]

irresponsall &c *adj* not answerable, *esp* unable to pay, insolvent *17*. [f RESPONSAL *adj*]

irrevocabill &c [*?ɪrɛ'vokəbl] *adj* **1** *of a person* appointed as an agent etc authorized irrevocably, whose appointment may not be revoked or rescinded *15-17*. **2** = irrevocable.
~**y &c** irreversibly *la15-*.

irritant &c *adj, law* to be rendered or rendering null and void *16-*.
irritancy the nullification of a deed resulting from neglect or contravention of the law or of

an agreement *la17-*. **irritancy (of (the) feu)** *irritancy* incurred when the *feuar* fails to pay *feu-duty* (FEU) for two consecutive years *la18-*.
~ **clause** a clause in an agreement rendering it null and void if any act therein prohibited is performed *la16-*. [L *irritant-*, presp stem of *irritāre* make void; *cf* next]

irritate *vt, law* make void, nullify *la17-*. [laL *irritāt-*, ptp stem of *irritāre* make void, f *irritus* invalid; *cf* prec]

irrogat [*ɪro'gat, *-'get] *ptp, of a penalty* imposed *la16-17*.
vt impose (a penalty) *17*. [L *irrogāt-*, ptp stem of *irrogāre* propose against, impose]

Irsche *see* IRISH

is *see* AS[1], BE, SALL, THIS

ischa, ische, isché *see* ISH

ischear *see* USHER

ischew &c; ischue &c *16-18* [*'ɪʃu] *n* **1** = issue *la14-17*. **2** = ISH *n* 2, *16-e17*. **3** = ISH *n* 3, *la16-e17*. **4** **ushaw &c** [*'ʌʃə] = ISH *n* 5, *18-e19*.
vti see issue *16-e18*.

ise *see* SALL

ish &c *la16-*, **ische &c** *la14-17*, **ush &c** *la14-20*; **esche &c** *15-e16* *n, only Sc, also* **isché &c** *la15-16*, **ischa** *15-e17* [perh by anaalogy w *intré* (ENTRY)] **1** the action of going out *15-16*. **2** *law* right or means of egress, *chf* (**free**) ~ **and entry** *15-e20*. **3** *also* **oysche** *la14* the termination of a legal term, term of office or service, or any period of time; the expiry (date) of a lease etc *15-*. **4** *in pl, also* **oyscheis** proceeds or profits (in the form of fines) of a local court of justice *15-16*. **5** *only* **ush &c** *in pl* the entrails of a slaughtered animal *la16-, 20*.
vti **1** (1) go or come out, go forth *la14-e20*. (2) sally forth, make a sortie *la14-e17*. **2** flow out, pour out *16*. **3** clear (a place) of occupants *16-17*. [ME *issh &c*, OF *issir*; *cf* ISCHEW, Eng *issue*]

isill *see* AIZLE

isk; isky &c *19-*, **iskis** *19-* [ɪsk, 'ɪskɪ, 'ɪs'kɪs] *interj* coaxing call to a dog *18-*, *now Abd Fif*. [*cf* HISK]

isk *see* YESK

iskie bae *see* USQUEBAE

iskis, isky *see* ISK

island &c *17-*; **iland &c** *16-17* ['əɪland] *n* **1** = island *16-*. **2 the** ~**s** (1) the *Western Isles* (ILE) *20-, Hebrides wHighl*; (2) the *Northern Isles* (ILE) *20-, nHighl*.
~**er** a person from the *Western Isles* (ILE) *la16-* [*cf* Gael *eileanach*].
Islands Council name for the local governmment council set up in 1975 in each of Shetland, Orkney and the *Western Isles* (ILE) *la20-*; *cf* REGION.

Islay *see* ILA(Y)

isle *see* ILE

iss *see* THIS

i stead *see* INSTEID

it &c, hit &c; 't *la18-*, **hid** *la19-*, *Ork Cai*, **hut**
la19-, *local: pronoun* **1** (1) = it *la14-*. (2) as
direct object, placed after indirect object *18-*:
'*gie the bairn it*'. **2** *corresponding to Eng* there
15-e19, *latterly chf ballad*: '*sic ane ferly neuer it was*'.
3 *as a possessive* = its *16-*, *now local E.* **4** things *in*
gen, circumstances *la18-e19*. **5** *referring to a state-*
ment just made or opinion expressed, corresponding to
Eng so *20-*: '*I don't think it*'.
about it about one's usual state of health *la19-*.
awa wi't *20-*, **by wi't** *la19-* ruined in health or
fortune. **for that o't** for that matter *la20-*.
this *or* **that o't** this or that state of affairs *19-*.
throw wi't = awa wi't, *la20-*. [*cf* 'D]
it *see* AT³

Italianes &c; Italienis &c [*ɪ'talɪenz, -ɪənz] *n*
1 the Italian language *la16*. **2** *appar* lace or
braiding *e17*. [final -*is* perh by analogy w other
national designations, eg *Scottis* (SCOTS)]
itchy-coo *n* anything causing a tickling; *specif*
the prickly seeds of the dog-rose etc, put by
children down each others' backs *20-*, *Ags Fif*
WC. [conflation of Eng *itchy* w HITCHIE-KOO]
ithand *see* EIDENT
ither *la18-*, **other &c, aither &c** *la19-*, **ather**
&c *la14-15*, **oder &c** *la15-e17*; **uther &c**
la14-17, **uder &c** *la15-16*, **idder** *20-*, *Sh NE*
['ɪðər; *Sh NE* 'ɪdɪr; *EC* 'eðər; 'ʌðər; *'ʌdər] *adj*
1 = other *la14-*. **2** *chf* **the ~..** *or before a numeral*
further, additional, successive, more *la14-*. **3**
inflected, with pl noun the remaining, the rest of
the *la15-16*: '*the otheris sacramentis*'. **4** *inflected,*
with pl or collective noun remaining, additional,
further *15-17*: '*amongst others matters*'; '*utheris irne*
grayth'. **5** *with sing or collective noun, without article*
another, additional *la14-16*: '*gif scho has other*
dowar'.
pronoun **1** = other *la14-*. **2** *reciprocal* each other,
one another (1) *uninflected*, *la14-*: '*lookin' at ither*
like daft folk'; (2) *inflected*, *15-19*: '*they sall ilkane*
tak vtheris be the handis'. **3** *uninflected* others, other
people *la14-19*: '*the lasses looked what ither had*'.

adv otherwise, else *20-*, *Gen except S.*
~gates &c *15-*, **~roads** *20-*, *now Fif Lnk Uls*
otherwise. **~ some &c** some others, others
la14-19. **oderwas &c**   *16*,   **otherway &c**
la14-17, **otherwayis &c** *la14-17* **1** = otherwise
la14-. **2** in another similar way or ways, similarly *la14-e17*. **3** in all other respects, for the
rest *15-e17*. **~where(s) &c** elsewhere, in or to
another place *la14-*, *now local N-Kcb*. **~whiles**
at other times *15-*, *now Abd Ags Uls*. **~wise** =
otherwayis, *la14-*.
~ half one and a half *15-16*, *chf Ork EC*. **~**
mony many, various others in addition
la14-15.
eftir ~ in turn, in succession, one after another
la16-, *now local N-S*. **in o ~** together, in(to) one
compacted whole *20-*, *N nEC*. **~ ma** others
besides *la14-15*. **~(is)** **my** *etc* my other..
la15-e17. **nae(thing)** ~ nothing else *la18-*, *NE*.
out o ~ apart, in(to) pieces, in disorder or disintegrating *la19-*, *local N nEC*. **what ~** what
else?, naturally, of course *la18-*, *NE, WC*. [*cf*
TITHER]
ithin *see* ATHIN
ithoot *see* ATHOOT
iver &c *la18-*, **ever &c** *la16* ['ɪvər, 'ivər, 'ēvər]
adj, freq in place-names upper, higher, *esp* the
higher of two places of the same name. [only
Sc; OE *yferra*, var of *uferra* (see UVER)]
iver *see* EVER
ivery *see* EVERY
ivil &c [*'ɪvl] *n, adj, adv* = evil *la14-17*. [some-
times written, like EVILL, in place of ILL]
ivry *see* EVERY²
I wis &c [*ɪ'wɪs, *aɪ 'wɪs] *adv, only verse, usu rhyme*
certainly, indeed, truly *la14-16*. [ME *ywisse*,
OE *gewis*]
iz *see* US
izal *see* AIZLE
izzat &c [*'ɪzə(r)d, -ə(r)t] *n* the (name of the)
letter Z *la19-e20*. [Eng dial *izzard*]

J

ja *see* JAW, JAY
jab &c *vt* prick sharply *19-*.
n a prick, pricking *19-*.
~**ble** *only Sc*, **jaible &c** *20-*, *Lnk SW*, *only Sc vti*
1 *of a liquid* splash *19-*, *local*. **2** *vi*, *of the sea*
become choppy *19-*, *local*. *n* **1** a liquid and its
sediment stirred up together, *esp* a weak mixture as of tea or soup *la18-*. **2** a choppy area of
water or of the sea *19-*. **3** *fig* confusion, agitation *la19-*, *now Sh Per Slk*. [*orig Sc*; var of JOB²]
jabart¹ &c *n* ? some kind of domestic fowl *16*.
[*cf* next]
jabart² &c [*Cai* 'tʃabərt, -ərd; *'dʒab-] *n* **1** an
animal in a weak or debilitated condition *19-*,
now Cai. **2** a lean cod etc, a fish out of season
19-, *now Cai*. [*only Sc*; *cf* CABER *n* 5 (2) and
prec]
jabb *vt* tire out, exhaust, *freq* ~**it** *19-*, *NE*. [*only
Sc*; *see* SND]
jachelt &c ['dʒaxlt] *ptp* tossed, buffeted by the
wind *la19-*, *now Ayr*. [*only Sc*; var of DACKLE *v*]
jacinct &c *16-e17*; **jasink &c** *16*, *only Sc n* =
jacinth or hyacinth, the gem.
jack¹ *la17-*, **jak &c**; **jeck &c** *la19-*, **jake &c**
la17- *n* **1** J~ = JOCK *n* 1, *16-*, *now NE*. **2** =
jack *la19-*. **3** *in pl* small stones, bones or (now)
metal objects used in the game of *chuckies*
(CHUCK²) or knuckle-bones; the game itself
la19-. **4** the jackdaw *la19-*, *now EC Lnk SW*.
~**ie** the jackdaw *20-*, *EC Lnk SW*. ~**ie downie**
the fish, the bib or pout *la19-*, *chf Mry*. **jecky
forty-feet** a centipede *e20*, *Cai*.
~ **easy** indifferent, not caring one way or the
other; easy-going, offhand *la19-*. ~**fallow lyk**
of a servant presumptuous, behaving like his
master's equal *la16-e17*; *cf jock-fellow-like* (JOCK).
jeck wi the monie feet = *jecky forty-feet*, *20-*,
Arg Kcb.
jack² *n* = jakes, a privy *18*, *only Sc*.
jackman *see* JAKMAN
jackteleg *see* JOCKTELEG
Jacob *n* ~'**s ladder** belladonna *19-*, *now Lnk
Uls*. [*cf* Eng (= *Polemonium caeruleum*)]
jad *see* JAUD
jadden &c *n* the stomach of a sow; a *pudding*
(PUDDIN) made therein, a HAGGIS *19*, *Fif*. [*only
Sc*; ME *chaudoun* entrails, OF *chaudun* tripes]
jadge *see* JEDGE
jaffle *vt*, *chf* ~**d** tired, worn out *19-20*, *SW*. [*only
Sc*; *cf* JAMPH²]
jag¹ &c *vt* prick, pierce *16-*.
n **1** = jag, an ornamental tag on the edge of a
garment; *in pl* rags *15*. **2** a prick; a sharp blow,
prod; *now also transf* an injection, inoculation
la17-. **3** a prickle, a thorn; something causing a
sting, *eg* on a nettle *19-*.
jaggie &c 1 prickly, sharp-pointed, piercing
la18-. **2** *of nettles* stinging *20-*, *local C*.
the J~s nickname for a football team with *thistle* in its name, *chf* Partick Thistle *20-*. ~-**the-
flae** contemptuous name for a tailor *la18*.

jag² *n* a sharp violent shake or jolt *la19-*, *now Sh
Cai*. *vt* **1** shake violently, jolt *19-e20*, *NE Kcdn*.
2 *vi* move with a jerking motion, bump *la19-*,
now Bnf Per.
jaggie &c *of motion or a vehicle* jerky, uncomfortable *19-*, *now Per*. [var of Eng *jog*]
jag³ &c *n*, *also* ~ **purse** a bag or wallet *16-17*.
[*cf* obs and dial Eng = a load]
jaible *see* JABBLE
jaicket &c *n* = jacket *la19-*.
jail *see* JILE
jairble *see* JIRBLE
jairg *see* JIRG²
jak *see* JACK¹, JAUK
jake *see* JACK¹
jakman; jack- *n* an attendant, retainer *16-17*.
[*only Sc*; uncertain]
jallisie; jollicy &c *n* an illness *la19-20*, *Mry
Bnf*. [var of Eng *jealousy*; *see* SND]
jalling-stane *see* JAW
jalous *see* JEALOUS
jalouse &c *la19-*, **jelous** *la17-e18*; **jealouse
&c** *la17-e19* [dʒə'luz] *vt* **1** suspect, be suspicious
of (a person or thing) *la17-*. **2** *in passive* be
regarded with suspicion *la17-e18*. **3** suspect,
suppose (that..) *la17-*. [*chf* Sc; Eng *jealouse*
(*la17*), F *jalouser*; *cf* JEALOUS]
jam¹ *vt* **1** = jam, squeeze *19-*. **2** mend, patch
la18, *now Sh Ork*. **3** (1) put in a quandary,
cause to be at a loss *la19-*. (2) inconvenience
la19-, *now local Abd-Lnk*. (3) *vr* occupy one's
time to the exclusion of all else, preoccupy oneself exclusively *20-*, *Bnf Abd Ags Loth*.
~(**min**) **fu** cram full *20-*.
jam² *n* J ~ **Tarts** nickname for *Heart of Midlothian*
(HERT) football team *20-* [rhyming slang for
Hearts (HERT *n* 4)].
jamb, jam &c [dʒam] *n* **1** = jamb *16-*. **2** a
projecting wing or addition to a building *la16-*,
now NE, *only Sc*. **3** an overlarge, rambling
house *19-*, *now NE Kcb*, *only Sc*. **4** anything large
and awkward *19-e20*, *only Sc*.
~-**stane** *specif* the upright of a fireplace *19-*.
jamffe *see* JAMPH¹
jammay band *see* GEMMA BAND
jamp *see* JUMP
jamph¹ &c, **jamffe &c** [dʒamf, dʒɑmf] *v* **1** *vt*
fool, trick, mock *17-e20*. **2** *vti* trifle, slack (at)
19-e20, *NE*.
n mockery, a jeer *17-e20*. [*only Sc*; *see* SND]
jamph² &c [*dʒamf] *vti* struggle; *in passive* be
exhausted or in difficulties *la18-e19*. [nasalized
var of JAUP]
jandies ['dʒandɪz] *n* = jaundice *la17-*.
Janet Jo *n* a children's singing game *19-*, *local*.
[*cf* Eng *Jenny Jones*]
jangle, jangill &c *la15-16* ['dʒaŋl] *vti* **1** = jangle *la15*. **2** *vi* chatter, talk incessantly *la15-*,
now Uls. **3** *vt* calumniate, defame *la15-16*.
Janis &c [*dʒenz] *n*, *chf* ~ **taffatie &c** taffeta of
Genoa *16-e17*. [OF *Jannes* Genoa; *cf* Eng *jean*
&c a kind of cotton cloth]

janitor &c *n* **1** a doorkeeper; a caretaker of a public building, *esp* a school etc *la16*-. **2** an usher or junior master in a school *la16-18*.

jannie &c *colloq* a (*usu* school-) JANITOR *20*-. [L; earlier in Sc]

Janiveer *see* JANUAR

jank *vt* evade, give the slip to; fob **off** *la17*-, *now Ags*. [only Sc; prob f JINK¹]

janker &c *n* a long pole on wheels used to transport *chf* timber suspended under it *19*-. [only Sc; see SND]

janner *see* JAUNNER

Januar &c *la14-20*, **January** &c *la16*-; **Janiveer** &c *17-19*, **Janvarie** *17-e18 n* = January.

jap *see* JAUP

japple &c ['dʒapl, 'tʃ-] *vi* stamp with the feet in water, splash *20*-, *Sh Cai Ags*. [prob frequentative of JAUP; cf *jabble* (JAB)]

jar *vt* ? push *e16*, *only Sc*.

jarbe &c *n* a piece of jewellery in the form of a sheaf *la16-17*. [OF *jarbe*, F *gerbe* a sheaf; cf eModEng *garb* a sheaf, *gerbe* a firework]

jarg, jargle *see* JIRG²

jarie *see* JAURIE

jasch *n* the dash of a wave *e16*. [only Sc; appar onomat; cf JASS]

jasink *see* JACINCT

jaskit *adj* jaded, worn out *la19*-, *now Sh Ags*. [only Sc; reduced f DISJASKIT or FORJESKIT]

jass *n* a violent throw, a heavy blow *19*-, *now Abd*. [only Sc; see SND]

jauchle ['dʒaxl] *vi* ~ **through** do (something) with difficulty *19*-, *now Fif Renfr*. [only Sc; see SND]

jaud &c, **jad** &c [dʒad] *n* term of abuse for **1** a horse; a worthless, worn-out nag *17*-, *now NE Ags Rox*; **2** a woman *17*-; **3** a wilful, perverse animal *la19*-; **4** an old or useless article *19*-, *now NE Fif*. [only Sc; perh a conflation of YAUD¹ w Eng *jade*]

jaudie &c *n* **1** the stomach of a pig or sheep, used in making HAGGIS etc *19*-, *now Fif Kinr*. **2** an oatmeal *pudding* (PUDDIN) made therein; a HAGGIS *19*-, *now Fif*. [dim of JADDEN]

jauk &c *la18*-, **jak** &c *la15-18* [dʒak] *vi* **1** idle, dawdle, slack *la15*-, *now Bnf Kcb*. **2** *of footwear* be slack or loose-fitting *19*-, *NE*. [only Sc; see SND]

jaump *see* JUMP

jaunner &c; **jaunder** *e19*, **janner** *19 vi* talk idly, foolishly or jokingly *19*-, *now Per Kcb Dmf*. *n* **1** idle, foolish talk *la18*-, *SW Rox*. **2** a chatterbox *19*-, *Kcb Dmf Slk*. [voiced var of CHANNER²]

jaup &c, **jawp** &c; **jap** *19*- [dʒap] *v* **1** *vi*, *of water etc* dash, splash, spill *16*-, *now NE Uls*. **2** *vt* cause (water) to splash *18*-, *now Bnf*. **3** splash, bespatter with water, mud etc *la18*-, *now NE, C Uls*. **4** exhaust, fatigue (*chf* oneself), *freq* **jaupit** weary *la19*-, *now Bnf-Ags midLoth*.

n **1** the splashing of the sea, a breaker, the surf,

a choppy sea *16*-, *now Sh Ork SW Uls*. **2** a splash (of water, mud etc) *la18*-, *now C-Uls*. **3** a spark or flying fragment of red-hot metal etc *la19*-, *now midLoth*. **4** *chf contemptuous* a small quantity, a drop (of drink, alcohol) *19*-, *now Bnf Ags*.

adv splash!, with a splash *la18*-, *now Fif*.

~**in fu** brimming over *20*-, *now midLoth SW*.

~**y** &c splashy, muddy *la19-e20*.

ding, knock *or* **gae to** ~ be wrecked or brought to ruin *19*-, *SW*. [onomat]

jaurie &c; **jarie** &c ['dʒarɪ] *n* an earthenware marble *la19*-, *now local EC, WC Uls*. [only Sc; dim of Eng *jar* an earthenware container]

javeling &c; **jeffelling** &c *16*, *only Sc* [*'dʒavəlɪn, *'dʒɛv-] *n* = javelin *16-e17*.

javell &c, **jevill** &c [*?'dʒevl] *n* = jail *17*. [northern eModEng; cf ModF dial *javiole* a cage, MedL *gabiola, gav*-; cf JAVELOR]

javell *see* JEVEL

javelor &c *la16-e18*, **javellour** &c *16-e17*, **jevellour** &c *la15-e17*, **jeveller** &c *16-17* [*?'dʒevəlur, -ər] *n* = jailer. [chf Sc; nME (once) *jaueler*; the intrusive -*v*- perh by analogy w *gavill, gayll* (GAVEL¹) = gable etc; cf JAVELL]

jaw &c; **ja** [dʒɑ] *v* **1** *vt* pour abruptly, splash, dash, spill *16*-, *now local NE-Uls*. **2** *vi*, *of water*, waves dash, splash, surge *18-e20*.

n **1** a wave, breaker *16*-, *now NE Ags*. **2** a rush, spurt, outpouring, splash of liquid; liquid splashed or thrown *19*-, *now NE Ags Lnk*. **3** a draught, drink *la18*-, *now NE Kcb*.

~**er hole** &c = ~-*hole, la16-e17* (*Edb*), *e19* (*Ayr, hist*). **jalling-stane** = prec *e16*.

~-**box** = ~-*hole*; a sink in a kitchen or on a *common stair* (COMMON) *19*-, *C Uls*. ~-**hole** &c **1** a primitive drain; *orig* a hole in the wall of a house for pouring away slops etc *la17*-, *now Fif midLoth Dmf*. **2** the mouth of a cesspool, a sewer *19*-, *now local Abd-SW*. **3** *fig* a sink, drain, a foul place *19-e20*. ~ **stane** a stone sink in a scullery *e16*; cf ~ *box*. [see SND, and DOST Suppl]

jaw-lock *n* = lockjaw *la19*-, *local Ork-Lnk*.

jawp *see* JAUP

jawpish *la18*, **chaudpis** &c *la16* [*'dʒapɪʃ, *'tʃad'pɪs] *n* urethritis. [F *chaude pisse* hot piss]

jay *16*-, **ja** *la15-16* [dʒe] *n* = jay, the bird *la15*-. ~ **pyot** &c = *n, 19*-, *now Kcb*.

jayl *see* JILE

jayne *see* GENE

jealous &c *17*-, **jelous** *la15-16*, **jalous** &c *16-e17*, **jelius** &c *la15-16*, **jolious** &c *16* ['dʒɛləs, *'dʒaləs, *'dʒolɪʌs, &c] *adj* **1** = jealous *la15*-. **2** suspicious, apprehensive *17-19*. [cf JALOUSE]

jealouse *see* JALOUSE

jeanie &c ['dʒɪnɪ] *n* = (spinning-)jenny *la18*-, *chf Ayr*.

jebber *see* JIBBER

jeck¹ &c *vt* **1** neglect (work) *la18-20*. **2** *chf* ~ **up**

throw up, discard, abandon *20-*, *Gsw S*. **3** dislocate (a joint) *20-*, *Kcb Rox*. [sense 1 perh var of JAUK; for 2 *cf* colloq Eng *jack up* or *in* abandon (something)]

jeck² &c *vi* move smoothly; fit in (**with**) *18-*, *NE Ags*. [voiced var of CHACK¹]

jeck *see* JACK¹

Jedburgh &c ['dʒɛdbʌrə, -bʌrɪ] *n* ~ **justice** *18-*, ~ **staff** *16-17* = *Jethart justice, staff* (JETHART). [the town in Rox]

Jeddart *see* JETHART

jedge, jadge &c *la16-17 n* **1** = gauge, a standard measure, a means of verifying the standard *la16-e18*. **2** *chf and latterly only* ~ **and warrant** &c an order from a *Dean of Guild* (DEAN) specifying repairs or rebuilding (*orig also* new building) of a property *17-20*.
vt verify the capacity of (a standard measure) *la16-e17*.
jadgear &c = gauger, *esp* one who verified that the fish barrels were standard size *la16-e17*.
jadgerie &c the action or office of gauging *la16-e17*. [only Sc; F *jauge*; *cf* GAUGE]

Jedwart *see* JETHART

jee &c; **gee** [dʒi; *Ork Cai* tʃi] *interj*, command to a horse = gee *19-*.
vi **1** move, budge; move to one side or another, swerve *18-*. **2** *vt* cause to move, stir; shift to one side; raise *18-*, *now local Abd-Dmf*.
n a move, motion, a sideways turn *19-*, *now Abd Ags midLoth*.
adj see combs below.
~**d** awry, squint *la19-*, *now Abd Ags midLoth*.
~**-eed** squint-eyed *la19-*, *now Ags midLoth*.
~**-ways** squint, sideways *18-*, *now Ags midLoth*.
~ **one's ginger** *etc*, *chf in negative* not show concern, not bother one's head; not become flustered *la18-*. **on the** ~ *also fig* awry, off the straight *19-*, *now local Kcdn-Ayr*.

jeedge *see* JUDGE

jeeg &c *la18-*, **jeig** &c *la16-18*, **jig** *la18-* [dʒig] *n* **1** = jig *la16-*. **2** *in pl* carryings-on, capers *la18-*, *now NE*. **3** a jerk, sudden pull, tilt, swing *la19-*, *Cai*. **4** *only* **jig** an instrument for catching fish, a sinker or wire frame with fish hooks attached *la19-*, *local*.
vti **1** = jig *la18-*. **2** *vi, also* **geig** *e16* creak, make a creaking noise *16-20*. **3** *vti, also* **gig** *chf Bnf* move briskly *18-*. **4** *only* **jig** catch fish with a JIG (*n* 4) *la19-*, *local*.
~**er** *chf contemptuous* an odd or eccentric person *19-*, *Sh local E Lnk*. **the jiggin** dancing, a dance *19-*. ~**le** *vt* = jiggle *la19-*, *local*. ~**ly** unsteady, shaky *la19-*, *now NE nEC Ayr Uls*.

jeel &c *la18-*, **geill** &c *la15-*; **geal** *19-e20* [dʒil] *n* **1** jelly *la15-*, *now local Abd-Rox*. **2** extreme coldness, chill, frostiness *la19-*. **3** a chill, a chilling sensation *20-*, *Abd Kcdn Ags*.
vti **1** freeze, congeal, be benumbed with cold *la18-*, *N-SW*. **2** *vi, of jam, jelly, stock etc* set, congeal *18-*.

~**-cauld** &c cold as ice, stone-cold *la19-*, *NE*. [OF *gel, giel* (*n*), *geler* (*v*), L *gelāre*; *cf* next and ME *gell* (*v*) congeal]

jeelie &c; **jelly** *n* **1** = jelly, table jelly; fruit juice preserve *18-*. **2** jam *19-*, *now local*.
v **1** *vi* = jelly, set like jelly *20-*. **2** *vt* cause (the nose) to bleed *la19-20*, *EC*.
~**-can** *20-*, *Gen except NE*, ~**-jaur** *20-*, *local*, ~**-mug** *la20-*, *Ork Renfr Kcb* a jam-pot. ~ **neb** *or* **nose** a bloody nose *20-*, *local EC-Rox*. ~ **pan** a (*traditionally* brass) pan for making jam or jelly *20-*. ~ **piece, piece and** ~ C bread and jam *19-*. ~**-pig** = ~**-mug**, *20-*, *Abd Ags*.

Jeen *see* JUNE

jeep *see* JUPE

jeest¹ *la17-*, **jeist** &c *16-e19*, **jeste** &c *16-18*, **geist** &c *la15-19*, **gest** *la14-17*; **gist** *la16-e18* [dʒist, *dʒɪst, *ʔdʒɛst] *n* **1** = joist *la15-*. **2** a large timber beam *la14-17*.
vt = joist, furnish with joists *la16-18*.
~**ing** joisting, the timber work, structure or furnishing of joists *la16-*.

jeest² &c *la16-*, *now NE*, **jest** *16-*, **gest** &c *la14-16* [dʒist, dʒɛst] *n* = jest, *orig* a tale, exploit; a joke *la14-*.
vti = jest *la16-*.

jeet *la19-*, *Abd Ags*, **geit** &c *16-e18* [dʒit] *n* = jet, the mineral *16-*.
~**y** &c neat, fastidious *20-*, *Abd Ags*.

jeet, jeetle *see* JUTE

jeezy &c *n* = jasey, a wig *la18-e19*. [*cf* GIZZ]

jeffelling *see* JAVELIN

jeho &c [dʒɜ'ho, -'hu, -'hoi] *vt* give over, stop *la19-*, *chf NE*. [*cf* Eng dial *gee-ho* call to an animal to stop]

jeig *see* JEEG

jeist *see* JEEST¹

jeit *see* GEIT

jelius *see* JEALOUS

jellie, jelly &c, **gelly** &c *la16-18* [*'dʒɛlɪ] *adj* **1** = jolly *la16-e17*. **2** pleasant, attractive, agreeable *la16-e20*. **3** upright, honest, worthy, excellent *18-19*.

jelly *see* JEELIE

jelous *see* JALOUSE, JEALOUS

jenepere &c ['dʒɛnɪpər] *n* = juniper *18-*, *now Abd*. [ME; OF *genevre*]

Jenkin's hen &c: **die the death of** ~, **die like** ~ die an old maid *la18-e20*. [only Sc; appar referring to a hen which never knew the cock]

Jenny &c; **Jinny** *la19-e20 n* **1** *freq with* JOCK generic term for a woman, *esp* a country girl *17-*, *now Abd Fif*. **2** a man who occupies himself with what are regarded as female concerns; an effeminate man *20-*, *C, S Uls*; *cf* JESSIE. **3** *in pl* callipers, *specif* hermaphrodite callipers with one leg with a short bend and the other with a point *la19-*.
~ **a'thing(s)** a female owner of a small general store; her shop *la19-*; *cf* *Johnnie a'thing(s)* (JOHN). ~**'s blue een** the speedwell *20-*, *Abd*

Fif Lnk. ~ **gray** &c the black guillemot in its first or winter plumage *la19-, chf Cai.* ~ **heron** the heron *la19-, SW.* ~**-hun**(d)**er-feet** *la19-, now Cai Per Fif,* ~**-hun**(d)**er-legs** *20-, local* the centipede. ~**-lang-legs** the cranefly, daddy-long-legs *19-, now Cai Abd C, S.* ~ **Lind** a kind of fancy loaf named after the singer *20-, now local C-S.* ~ **Meggie** = ~*-lang-legs, la19-, midLoth Lnk.* ~**-mony feet** = ~*-hunder-feet, 19-, now Ags midLoth.* ~ **muck** a working woman; a female farmworker *la19-, Cai NE.* ~**-nettle**(s) **1** = ~*-lang-legs, 19-, now Ork midLoth SW.* **2** the stinging nettle *19-, Edb Lnk S.* ~ **reekie** a hollow cabbage stalk packed with tow, used to blow smoke into a house as a HALLOWEEN prank *19-, Fif Kinr.* ~ **speeder** *20-, Kcb Rox,* ~ **spinner** *19-, Cai Bnf SW, S =* ~*-lang-legs.* ~ **Wullock** a hermaphrodite, a sexually-deformed male; an effeminate man *la19-, EC, WC.* [pet form of *Jane, Jean* or *Janet*]

jeopardie &c, **jeopardy**, **juparty** &c *la14-e16;* **jeperté** &c *la14-16* [ˈdʒɛpardɪ, *-partɪ, *-pərtɪ, *ˈdʒʌ-] *n* **1** = jeopardy, peril, risk, chance *la14-.* **2** a daring exploit, a feat of arms; a battle, raid etc *la14-.* **3** martial daring, valour, prowess *e16.* **4** *chf* **juparty** &c a stratagem, trick *la14-e16.* **5** *in pl* risks, difficulties *16-e19.*

vtr = jeopardy, venture, risk *16.*

jerk *vi* ~**in** &c a jollification, *orig* on a ship's leaving port *19, only Sc.* [Eng *jerk, jerque* search a vessel, examine a ship's papers]

jerk *see* JIRG¹

jerker *n, also* **mealie** ~ a white oatmeal *pudding* (PUDDIN) *20-, Bnf Abd Ags.* [only Sc; f Eng *jerk,* f their motion when hung in strings]

jerkin &c *18-e19,* **girkin** &c *16-17* [ˈdʒɛrkɪn, ˈdʒɪrk-, *St* ˈdʒɛrk-] *n* **1** = jerkin *16-.* **2** a bodice worn by women *18-e19.*

~**et** &c = *n, la17-18.*

jerkin *see* JERK

Jerusalem *n* ~ **haddie** &c the opah or kingfish *la19-, Ross Abd Ags Fif.* ~ **traveller** a louse *20-, Ork Abd-Per.*

jesing *see* JIZZEN

jesp¹ **&c; jisp** *n* **1** a small gap or opening; a flaw, *esp* in the weave of a fabric, a broken thread *la18-, now local EC Rox.* **2** a stain, speck, blemish *19-e20.*

jesp² **&c** *n* = jasp, jasper, the precious stone *16, only Sc.*

Jessie *n, contemptuous* an effeminate man or boy *20-.*

~ **Ann** *20-, Abd,* ~ **Fisher** *la20-, Kcdn Ags Per* = *n.* [the personal name]

jest *see* JEEST²

jeste *see* JEEST¹

Jethart *la19-,* **Jedwart** &c *16-17,* **Gedward** &c *16;* **Jeddart** *19-* [ˈdʒɛðərt, ˈdʒɛd-; *ˈdʒɛdwəθ, *-wərt, &c] ~ **justice** precipitate or arbitrary justice, condemnation without a hearing *19-.* ~ **snails** a kind of toffee from

Jedburgh *20-, S.* ~ **staff** a weapon similar to a bill or halberd, *orig* from Jedburgh (represented on Jedburgh's coat-of-arms) *16-17, 19- (hist).* [only Sc; early form of Jedburgh's name, OE *Gedweard* 8th century; *cf* JEDBURGH]

jeuk *see* DEUK, JOUK

jevel &c, **jevell** &c *only Sc,* **javell** &c [*ˈdʒɛvl] *n* a ruffian, a rascal *16-e19.* [ME *javel* &c; obscure; *cf* CAVEL²]

jeveller, jevellour *see* JAVELOR

jevill *see* JAVELL

Jew &c *16-,* **Jow** &c *la14-e17* [dʒu] **1** = Jew *la14-.* **2** term of abuse for an unbeliever, infidel *e16.*

Jew's loaf *or* **roll** a small loaf rounded on top with a brownish glaze *la19-, SW.*

jewel *see* JOWEL

jeyol *see* JILE

jib &c *vt, also fig* milk (a cow) to the last drop *18-, now Lnk SW.*

jibbings &c the strippings from a cow's udder *19-, now local Lnk-S.* [uncertain]

jibber, jebber *n* silly talk, idle chatter *19-, now local N-nEC, Uls.* [onomat; *cf* Eng *gibber*]

jibble &c [ˈdʒɪbl, ˈdʒibl] *vt, also* ~ **oot, owre, up** spill (a liquid) by agitating its container *19-, now local N-Uls.*

n **1** a splash, the splashing or lapping of a liquid *20-, NE Ayr.* **2** a small quantity of a liquid or semi-liquid food or drink *19-, now NE Dmf.* [? frequentative of JIB; *cf jabble* (JAB)]

jick *vt* elude, dodge, evade *19-, now Lnk.*

~**er** move, walk, ride etc quickly *la18-, now midLoth.*

play the ~ play truant *20-, now Lnk Rox.* [var of JINK¹; *cf* JOUK]

jiff *n, also* ~**er** a person of doubtful reputation *20-, NE.* [perh voiced var of CHUFF]

jig *see* JEEG

jile &c *la19-,* **jeyol** &c *17,* **jayl** &c *17;* **jail** &c *la16-* [dʒəil] *n, vt* = jail *la16-.*

jiler &c *la19-,* **geyler** &c *la14-15,* **jylour** &c *la17, Gsw* = jailer.

get the ~ be sent to prison *la19-.*

jillet &c *n* a flighty girl, a flirt *la18-e20.* [only Sc; pet form of *Jill* or *Gillian*]

jilp &c, **jilt** *19-, now Fif;* **gilp** [dʒɪlp, dʒɪlt] *v* **1** *vt* cause (liquid) to spurt or splash, spill *19-, now NE midLoth Lnk.* **2** *vi, of a liquid* splash about or over *19-, now Sh NE Ags.*

n **1** a small quantity of liquid splashed or spilt, a splash, spurt of liquid *19-, now NE Ags midLoth.* **2** a small quantity of liquid, *esp derog* a thin or insipid drink *la19-, now Bnf Abd Kcdn Ags.* [only Sc; onomat; *cf* JAUP]

jilt¹ *n* **1** = jilt, a woman who jilts *la18-.* **2** contemptuous term for a girl or young woman *la18-e20; cf* JILLET.

jilt² *see* JILP

Jimmie *n* **1** very familiar form of address to a man, *chf* a stranger *la20-.* **2** a j~ a *white pudding*

(WHITE[1]) or oatmeal *pudding* (PUDDIN), *freq* **mealie** ~ *20-*, *local NE-Kcb*. [pet form of *James*]

jimmy *see* GIM

jimp[1], gimp [*dʒɪmp] *n* a subtle or trifling point; a quirk *la15-16*. [perh related to JIMP[2]]

jimp[2] *17-*, **gymp &c; jump &c** *la18-e20* [dʒɪmp] *adj* **1** *of persons* slender, small, graceful, neat, dainty *16-*, *now Ork N, C*. **2** *of clothes* close-fitting *19-*, *now local NE-midLoth*. **3** *of measure or quantity* scanty, scrimp, barely adequate, sparing *17-*.
adv scarcely, hardly, barely, sparingly, scantily *la18-*.
vt **1** curtail, restrict unduly, stunt *19-*, *local*. **2** scrimp, stint, keep in short supply *19-*, *now Ork-midLoth*. **3** give short or scant measure to (a person) *or* in (a measure) *la19-*, *local N-S*.
~**ie** = *adj* 1, *19-*, *now Abd Lnk*.
~ **o** lacking, short of *20-*, *Abd Edb*. [obscure]

jimp[3] *e19*, **jump** *la17-18 n* a strip or sliver, *specif* of leather as used to build up the heel of a shoe. [only Sc; perh var of JUNK]

jimp[4] &c; jump &c *18-e19 n*, *in pl or* ~**ie &c** a woman's bodice *18-e20*. [Eng *jump (la17)*]

jimp *see* JUMP
jine *see* JOIN
jing &c *n* (**by**) ~(**s**) a mild expletive *la18-*. [*cf* Eng *jingo*]

jing[2] *n*, *vti* jingle *19-*, *now Ags*.

jing-bang *n* a considerable number, *usu* **the hail** ~ the whole lot, company, concern etc *la19-*. [prob prec + BANG[2]]

jingle *see* CHINGLE

jingo-ring &c [ˈjɪŋəˈrɪŋ, ˈjɪŋgoˈrɪŋ] *n* a children's singing game *19-*.

jinipperous &c [dʒɪˈnɪp(ə)rəs] *adj* spruce, trim; finicky, over-particular, stiff *19-*, *Abd*. [perh f Eng *juniper*]

jink[1] &c [dʒɪŋk; *Fif also* dʒəɪŋk] *v* **1** *vi* turn quickly, move or dodge nimbly *la18-*. **2** progress in quick, sudden or jerky movements, dart, zigzag *la18-*, *now Sh Abd Ags Ayr*. **3** move jerkily to and fro as when spinning or playing the violin; play the violin briskly *18-19*. **4** flirt *18-*, *now Cai Kcb Rox*. **5** *vt* dodge, elude; cheat, trick *la18-*. **6** *vti* dodge (school, a class), play truant *la20-*, *N Fif*.
n **1** (1) a quick or sudden twisting movement, a jerk *la19-*, *now local NE-Kcb*. (2) a coil, twist, kink *la19-*, *now Abd*. **2** the act of dodging or eluding someone; a dodge, trick *la18-*, *now Abd*. **3** *chf in pl* playful tricks or frolics *19-*, *now Sh Abd Uls*. **4** *in pl or* ~**ie** a chasing game *19-*, *now local Abd-Loth*.
~**er** a pleasure-seeker; a libertine, a wanton *18-e19*. ~**ers** a game involving the catching or dodging of a ball thrown at a wall *20-*, *chf Per*.
high &c ~**s** *orig* a drinking game; *latterly* lively or boisterous sport, unrestrained merrymaking *18-*. [earlier in Sc]

jink[2] *n* = chink, a crack *19-*, *now midLoth Renfr*.

jinkie *adj* nonsense word in nursery rhymes *la19-*, *NE now Ork*, *only Sc*.

Jinny *see* JENNY

jinsh &c *n* a small piece of something *19-e20*, *Bnf Abd*. [only Sc; *cf* KINSH[2]]

jint *la19-*, **junt &c** *16-18*, *only Sc* [dʒəɪnt; *dʒʌnt] *n*, *vt* = joint. [*cf* JOIN]

jirble &c; jairble *19-e20*, *Rox vt* **1** splash, slop (liquid) *la18-e20*. **2** pour out unsteadily in small quantities *19-*, *now local Abd-Rox*.
n a small quantity of liquid poured out, a drop *19-*, *now Lnk S*. [only Sc; see SND]

jirg[1] &c; jerk *la19-*, *Abd Ags*, **jirje &c** *la19-e20*, *Abd* [dʒɪrg, dʒɛrg, dʒɛrk; *Abd Kcdn also* dʒɪrdʒ] *v* **1** *vi* make a squelching or splashing sound, gurgle *la18-*, *now local NE-Gall*. **2** *vt* work (something in a liquid) so as to cause a squelching sound; shake violently up and down *20-*, *now Abd*.
n a squelching sound *19-*, *NE*. [only Sc; onomat]

jirg[2] &c *19-*, **jarg &c** *16-*, **girg** *e16*; **jirk** *la18-e20*, **jairg &c** *19-e20*, *S* [dʒɪrg, dʒɛrg, dʒɪrk; *Rox* dʒɛrg; *dʒarg] *v* **1** *vi* creak, grate, jar *16-*, *now Sh Arg Gall*. **2** *only in negative* not to hesitate, waver or budge *e17*. **3** *vti* grate, grind (the teeth) *19-*, *now Cai midLoth Kcb*.
n a creaking or grating sound *la18-*, *now Arg*.
jargle &c *vi* make a sharp, shrill or harsh sound *19-*, *now Fif*. *n* clamour, noise *20-*, *Ags Fif*. [only Sc; onomat; *cf* CHIRK]

jirje *see* JIRG[1]

jirk &c *n* **1** = jerk, a sharp sudden movement *19-*. **2** a smart blow *17-*, *now Abd Ags*.
~**ie** changeable *19-*, *now midLoth*.
in a ~ in an instant *la19-*, *now Ags Per*. [*cf* YERK]

jirk *see* JIRG[2]

jirr &c *n*, *vi* quarrel *18-*, *now Abd*. [onomat; *cf* Eng *jar*]

jirt &c *n* a sudden or sharp blow, squeeze or push, a jerk *la17-*, *now Sh*.
vti jerk; move jerkily, dart *20-*, *now Sh*. [eModEng *jerte*; voiced var of CHIRT]

jise *see* JOICE
jisp *see* JESP[1]
jist *see* JUIST

jizzen &c *18-*, *now verse*, **jesing &c** *la15-16*, **gesine &c** *la15-e17*, **gising &c** *15-e17* [ˈdʒɪzn; *dʒɪˈzin, *dʒɪˈzɪn; *ˈdʒɪzɪn] *n* childbed. [ME *gesen*, OF *gesine*]

jo &c; joe [dʒo] *n*, *in OSc also occas written as* **joy**, *though still pronounced* [dʒo] **1** = joy *16*. **2** *term of endearment* sweetheart, darling, dear, *chf* **my** ~ *16-20*. **3** *now chf verse* a sweetheart, lover, *usu* male *17-*.

job[1] *vi* **1** = job. **2** *chf* ~**bing &c** illicit sexual intercourse *18-e19*.

job[2] *vti* = job, pierce, stab (*usu* more lightly than in Eng); prick *18-*, *now Sh Ork NE nEC*.
n a prick; a prickle *19-*, *now Sh NE nEC*.

jobbie &c prickly *19-, Sh NE nEC.* **~bie nettle** the stinging nettle *la20-, NE-Per.* [*cf* JAB]
job³ *vi* ? go at an easy pace, jog, amble *la16.*
~-trot &c a slow, monotonous or easy-going
pace; the settled or routine way of doing things
la17-e20 [*cf* ModEng *jog-trot*].
Jock, Jok &c *n* **1** (1) generic term for a man,
the common man: (a) *with other men's names* =
men *in gen, 16*; (b) *sometimes with* JENNY = a
rustic or countryman, a farmworker *16-, now
NE, EC Rox.* (2) (nickname for) a soldier in
one of the Scottish regiments *20-.* **2** a bull *19-,
Gall.* **3** an oatmeal *pudding* (PUDDIN), a HAGGIS
la19-, Fif. **4** *mining* (1) an iron rod attached to
the rear of a train of HUTCHES as a safety check
if a rope breaks *la19-, now Fif.* (2) a lump of
stone in the coal *20-, Fif Dmf.*
~ie &c 1 = *n* **1**, *la16-.* **2** a vagrant, gipsy
la17-e20. **3** a horse-dealer; a postillion *18-19.*
~ie blindie *or* **~ie blind-man** *game* blind-
man's buff *la18-, Ags Per.* **~ie coat** a greatcoat *la17-20.* **~ie an his owsen** notches cut
on a cowherd's stick, representing the method
of yoking of an ox-plough team *20, Abd, hist.*
~ brit *contemptuous* a miner *20-, now Stlg eLoth.*
~-fellow-like, joke- *adj* (*adv*) *of inferiors' relations with their superiors and vice-versa* intimate(ly),
familiar(ly) *18-e19*; *cf* jak-fallow *lyk* (JACK¹). **~
hack** *NE*, **~ muck** *now Cai* = *n* **1** (1) (b), a
ploughman *la19-.* **~ Scott** *angling* an artificial
fly, named after its inventor *19-e20.* **~ upaland** = *John upland* (JOHN) *la16-e17.*
afore ye could say ~amanorie
[?~əmə'norɪ] *or* **~ Hector** *or* **~ Morrison** =
before you could say Jack Robinson *la19-.* **the
deil's gane ower ~ Wabster &c** *proverb*
things have got out of hand; the fat's in the fire
18-, now Cai Kcdn. **~ the laird's brither** *proverb* a person treated with familiarity or little
respect *la17-19.* **play ~ needle ~ preen &c**
play fast and loose, act in a double-dealing or
shifty way *la19-, NE.* **~ Tamson's bairns**
the human race, common humanity; a group of
people united by a common sentiment, interest
etc, *chf* **we're a' ~ Tamson's bairns** *19-.*
[pet form of *John; cf* JACK¹]
jockteleg &c, jackteleg &c *17; -* **the leg &c**
la17-e20 ['dʒɔktələg, *'dʒak-, -ðə-] *n* a
clasp-knife *17-, now Sh Ayr.* [appar f JOCK +
Eng *leg*; see SND, DOST]
joco &c [dʒə'ko] *adj* jovial, merry, cheerful,
pleased with oneself *la19-, Gen except Sh Ork.*
[reduced f Eng *jocose*]
joctibeet &c *n* the wheatear *la19-, Cai.* [only
Sc; prob imit of its song]
joculatour *n* an entertainer, jester *la15.* [ScL
joculator (*e15*); L *joculātor* a joker, jester]
joe *see* JO
jog¹ **&c** [dʒɔg; *Per* dʒug; *Fif* dʒʌug] *vt, n* = JAG¹ *v*
(*18-, now Kcdn C Rox Uls*), *n* **2** (*20-, now Kcdn
Ags*).

jog² **&c, jok &c** *la16-e17 vt* put in the JOUGS
la16-19. [f JOUGS]
jogis *see* JOUGS
John: ~dal &c *contemptuous* a young ploughman
20-, Cai. **Johnnie a'thing(s)** an owner of a
small general store; his shop *la19-*; cf *Jennie
a'thing(s)* (JENNY).
~ Barleycorn personification of barley as the
grain from which malt liquor is made; ale or
WHISKY *la18-.* **~ o Gro(a)t's buckie &c** the
cowrie shell *18-.* **~ Gunn** a privy, latrine *20-,
Bnf Abd.* **~ Thomson's man &c** *proverb* a
hen-pecked husband *16-19.* **~ upland** *e16 or*
uponland *la16* a rustic. [the personal name]
joice; jise &c *19* [dʒois, dʒəis] *n* = juice *18-,
now local Sh-Ags.*
join &c, jone &c *la15-16,* **june &c** *la15-16;*
joune &c *16-19,* **jine** *19-* [dʒəin, dʒoin; *Fif*
*dʒʌun; *dʒøn] *vti* **1** = join *la14-.* **2** *vt* become
a communicant of (a particular religious
denomination), *esp* **a ~ed member** *la19-.* **3**
begin (work) *20-, now midLoth Arg.*
n **1** the clubbing together of several persons to
buy drink; a social gathering or outing *la19-,
now Bnf.* **2** an association of neighbours for
some communal task *19-e20, Uls.*
~er 1 a sharer, partner, confederate *la17.* **2** a
woodworker, carpenter, *not restricted as in Eng,
17-* [the usu ModSc word, replacing WRIGHT
19-]. **~ery** a joiner's workshop *20-, Abd Ags
Fif.* **joint** [*dʒəint, *dʒʌnt] *ptp* united in a
group, party, opinion etc *la15-e18.* **jointly,
juntly** = jointly *la14-15.* **jointour &c 1** =
jointure *16-17.* **2** a metal link or connecting
piece of a harness *e16.* **joint adventure** *law* a
limited partnership undertaken for a specific
purpose and restricted as regards liability etc
19-. **joint** *or* **junt feftment** *law* infeftment
made to two persons jointly *15.* [*cf* JINT]
joip *see* JUPE
jois *see* JOYSE
joiter *see* JOT
Jok *see* JOCK
jok *see* JOG²
joke &c *v* **1** *vi* = joke. **2** *vt* make a joke against,
tease *18-, now Sh Ags.*
jokie &c jocular, fond of a joke *19-.*
joke-fellow-like *see* JOCK
jokkis *see* JOUGS
jolesy &c *n* = jealousy *16.*
jolious *see* JEALOUS, JOLY
jollicy *see* JALLISIE
jolly-tryp(s) *see* GILLATRYPES
joly &c *la14-17;* **jolly &c** *la16- adj* **1** = jolly,
gay, gallant, pretty etc *la14-.* **2** *of bitches* on
heat *16-17.*
jolious jolly, merry, joyful *la16.*
jone *see* JOIN
jonet¹ *n* **~ flour** name for a flower, *orig* any of
various yellow flowers *15-17.* [chf Sc;
eModEng (once) *flour iaunette,* F *jaunet(te)*]
jonet² *n* = jennet *16, only Sc.*

jonick; gennick &c ['dʒɒnɪk, 'dʒɛn-] *adj* genuine, honest, fair, just *la19-, now NE-Per.*
n fair play, justice *e20.* [Eng dial *jannock &c*]
joogle¹, jougle &c ['dʒugl] *vi* = joggle, shake, wrestle **with** *la17-.*
n = joggle, a shaking *19-.*
joogle² *vti* = juggle *20-.* [*cf* OSc, eModEng *jouglour &c* a wizard]
jooter &c *vi* saunter, totter *20-, now midLoth.*
[prob chf onomat]
jorg &c *vi* make a squelching or grating sound *19-e20.* [voiced var of CHORK]
jornal *see* JOURNAL
jorné *see* JOURNEE
jorram *see* IORRAM
jose *see* JOYSE
joskin; geeskin &c *NE* ['dʒɒskɪn, 'dʒiskɪn] *n* a country bumpkin, yokel, farmworker *la19-, now local NE-Dmf.* [appar f next, and corresponding to Eng *bumpkin*]
joss *vt, n* jostle *e19.* [var of DOSS⁴]
jossle &c *vi* shake, totter *la19-.* [Eng *jostle*]
josyne *see* CHUSE
jot, jott; jote &c *la16-e17* *n* **1** = jot, whit, tittle *la16-.* **2** *chf in pl* small or occasional pieces of work, odd jobs *16-, now NE.*
v **1** *vt, chf* ~ **down** write down hastily or briefly, make a short note of *18-* [earlier in Sc]. **2** *vi* do light work, potter (**about** etc) *la19-, NE.*
jotter, *also* **joiter** ['dʒotər] *n* **1** a rough notebook, *now esp* a school exercise book *la19-.* **2** an odd-job-man; a ne'er-do-well, a trifler, a dawdler *la19-, now midLoth. vi* do odd jobs or light menial work; work in a dilatory fashion *la19-, now midLoth Bwk.* ~**erie** odd jobs *19-e20.*
jotting a note, memorandum, excerpt *18-.*
jottle appear busy without achieving much *19-, now midLoth.*
joug &c *la16-*, **jug &c** *16-*; **juig &c** *la16-e17* [dʒug, dʒʌg] **1** = jug *la16-.* **2** name for the various standard measures of the pint in Scotland, *esp* the principal one, the **Stirling jug &c** = about three imperial pints (1.7 litres) *la16-e19.* **3** a mug or drinking vessel *17-.*
vti **1** = jug. **2** *vi* tipple, drink *16-e19.*
jouggis *see* JOUGS
jougle *see* JOOGLE¹
jougs, jouggis &c, jogis &c, jokkis &c *la16*, **juggs &c** [*dʒʌugz, *dʒogz, *dʒoks, *dʒʌgz] *n pl, now hist or fig* an instrument of public punishment consisting of a hinged iron collar attached by a chain to a wall or post and locked round the offender's neck *la16-.* [see SND; *cf* JOG²]
jouk &c; juke &c *16-*, **jeuk &c** *la17-*, **juck &c** *18-e19* [dʒuk] *v* **1** *vi* (1) duck, dodge a blow etc *16-.* (2) *vi* duck out of sight, hide, skulk *16-.* (3) bow deferentially; humble oneself, show deference *16-, now midLoth.* (4) cower, crouch *la19-, local NE-Kcb.* **2** (1) *vti* evade, elude,

avoid (someone or something) *18-.* (2) play truant (from) *19-, local NE-Uls.* (3) *vi* shirk, flinch *18-, now local Abd-Ayr.* **3** *vi* appear and disappear quickly, dodge in and out, dart, flicker *19-, local NE-Uls.* **4** *vt* evade by trickery, cheat, deceive *la18-, local Abd-Kcb.*
n **1** a quick ducking or dodging movement *16-, now local NE-Uls.* **2** an obeisance, a bow or curtsy *la16-, now Ags.* **3** a bend, meander, twist (of a river) *la19-, now Kcb.* **4** shelter, a sheltered spot *la18-e20.* **5** a trick *la16-, now Per Ayr Slk.*
~**er** a slippery or evasive character *la20-.*
~**erie &c** trickery, deceit, roguery *la14-, now C.*
~**erie-pawk(e)ry &c** = prec *la17-* [see *pawkery* (PAWK)]. ~**ie** evasive, elusive, sly *19-, now Kcb.* ~**ing 1** the action of the *v, 16-.* **2** dodging, shiftiness, dissembling *la16-.*
~ **an let the jaw gae by** etc *proverb* give way prudently in the face of overwhelming force, submit to the force of circumstance *18-.* ~ **one's head** = *v* 1, *19-.* ~ **under** be subservient to *la19-, now Ags midLoth.* [only Sc; prob palatalized f DOOK¹; *cf jeuk* (DEUK)]
jouk *see* DEUK
joundie *see* JUNDIE
joune *see* JOIN
joup *see* JUPE
journall &c; jornal &c *15-17*, **jurnal &c** *16-17* ['dʒʌrnəl, *'dʒurnəl] *n* **1** = journal *la14-.* **2** a register of the *Court of Justiciary* (JUSTICIARY), the *Justice Aire* (JUSTICE) or another court *15-17*; *cf adjournal* (ADJOURN). **3** = JOURNEE 3, *17.*
journee &c, jorné &c, journay; jurnay &c ['dʒʌrnɪ,*'dʒurnɪ] *n* **1** = journey *la14-17.* **2** *specif* a stage or portion of a journey at the end of which new horses were provided *la16-17.* **3** one minting or portion of work in coinage, *orig* a day's work; the quantity of coins so produced *la16-17.* **4** a kind of travelling cloak worn over armour *la15-e16.*
v **1** *vi* = journey *15-.* **2** *vt* cite or summon to appear in court on an appointed day *la15-e17, only Sc.*
~ **hors** a post-horse *17.* ~ **maister** the master of a posting-station *17.*
jow &c [dʒʌu] *n* **1** a single peal or stroke of a bell; the ringing or tolling of a bell *16-, now local NE-midLoth.* **2** the surge or swell of water or waves *19-, now Kcdn Ags.* **3** a swing or act of swinging *la19-, Fif midLoth.*
v **1** (1) *vt* ring, toll (a bell) *16-, now Kcdn midLoth.* (2) *vi, of a bell* ring, toll *la16-, now Kcdn.* **2** *vti* move with a rocking motion, swing, jostle, jog *19-e20.* **3** spill (a liquid) from a container by making it move from side to side *19-, midLoth Lnk.* **4** *of a boat* rock, toss *19-, now Ags.*
~ **one's ginger** *or* **jundie** = *jee one's ginger* etc (JEE) *la19-, Bnf Ags.* [perh f as JOWL; *n* 2, *v* 3 appar w infl f JAW]
Jow *see* JEW

jowcat &c [*?'dʒukət] *n* a liquid measure less than a pint (.57 litre) *la16-e19*.

jowel &c *la14-*, *now Abd Kcdn,* **jewel** &c *16-*, **juell** &c *16-17* ['dʒuɛl, -əl] *n* = jewel *la14-*.
jewel-coal a high-grade coal with a jewel-like surface *la17-*, *C.*

jowl *chf literary* [dʒʌul] *n, vi* = jow *n* 1, *v* 1, *19-e20*. [*cf* JOW and obs and dial Eng *jowl* (*n, v*) bump etc]

jowler [*'dʒʌulər] *n* a heavy-jawed hunting dog *la18-19*. [f Eng *jowl* the jaw]

joy &c [dʒoi; *dʒaɪ] *n* 1 = joy *la14-*. 2 = jo 2 and 3, *la14-e17*.
vti = joy *la14-*.

joy *see* JO

joyse &c, **jois** &c, **jose** &c *la15-e17*; **joyis** &c *la14-16* [*dʒoiz, *dʒoz] *v* 1 *vt, law* enjoy or have the use of, be in occupation or possession of (lands, office, rights etc) *la14-e19*. 2 *in gen* have, possess, obtain *la15-16*. 3 *vi* take pleasure, rejoice **in** *la16-e17*. [OF *joiss-*, lengthened stem of *joir*; *cf* ME *joise* rejoice]

jubish &c ['dʒubiʃ, -əs] *adj, of persons* = dubious, suspicious *la19-*, *now Ork Cai C Uls*.

juck *see* CHUCK², DEUK, JOUK

judge &c, **juge** &c, **jeedge** &c *19-*, *NE* [*Sh C, S* dʒødʒ, dʒɪdʒ; *NE* dʒidʒ, *also* dʒudʒ] *n* 1 = judge *la14-*. 2 *freq with following qualifying noun or adj, eg judge ordinar(y)* (ORDINAR).
vti 1 = judge *la14-*. 2 *vi, only* **jeedge** &c swear, curse *19-*, *NE*.

jugisment = judgement, *la15-e17*, *only Sc.*
~ment &c 1 = judgment *la14-*. 2 judicial authority or the extent or territory of this; jurisdiction *la15-e17*. 3 reason, senses, wits, sanity, *esp* **lose** *or* **be out of one's ~ment** *la17-*, *only Sc.* **~ment-like** characteristic of divine displeasure, appearing to threaten divine retribution, awful *la17-20*. **in ~ment** (bring) before a court of law *15-16*. **in** (**face of**) **~ment** during the formal course of proceedings in court, before a court of law, in court *15-e17*. **furth of, out of** *or* **outwith ~ment** out of or outside the court *la15-16*. **sit in ~ment** sit as a judge or as a duly constituted court of justice *15-16*.

judicative &c *adj* judicative, judicial *la15-17*. [earlier in Sc; MedL *judicativus*]

judicatory, -ie &c [dʒu'dɪkətorɪ] *n, chf church* a court of judicature in church or state, a tribunal having judicial authority *la16-e20*. [laL *jūdicātōrium; cf* eModEng]

judicatour &c *n* = judicature *la16-17*.

judicatum solvi [dʒudɪ'ketəm 'sɔlvaɪ] *adj, law, of a security* pledged for the payment or satisfaction of a judgment *18-*. [L = that what has been awarded by the Court should be paid]

judicial &c *adj, law* = judicial, of or pertaining to judgment or the judicature, *specif* **~ declaration, ~ examination, ~ sale** *etc la16-*.
~lie &c 1 = judicially *la16-*. 2 = *in judgement* (JUDGE) *la16-17*.
~ factor a person appointed by the *Court of*

Session (SESSION) or *sheriff court* (SHERIFF) to administer *eg* the property of a person unable to administer it himself *19-*.

judicio sisti [dʒu'dɪʃɪo 'sɪstaɪ] *adj, law, of security* involving an undertaking that a debtor will appear in court to answer a claim *la18-*. [L = that one be made to appear in court]

juell *see* JOWELL

juffle &c *vi* 1 scuffle, fumble *16-17*. 2 shuffle *19-*, *now Bwk.*
~r &c an awkward or clumsy person *e16-*. [perh onomat, or var of Eng *shuffle*]

jug *see* JOUG

juge *see* JUDGE

juggins *see* DEWG

juggs *see* JOUGS

jug(g)is [dʒʌgz] *n pl* swill, dregs, foul or waste liquid *16-e17*. [obscure]

juig *see* JOUG

juist *17-e20*, **just, duist** &c *la19-e20*; **jist** &c *la19-* [dʒɪst; *Sh Ork S* dʒøst; *NE also* dʒɪst; *Kcdn Gall also* dʒust; *Bwk S also* døst] *adj* = just *la15-*.
adv 1 = just *la15-*. 2 *freq following the word or phrase it modifies* really, quite, absolutely, simply, implying no less than ..; indeed, truly *la18-*: '*I took a drammie, for I was geeled jist*'.
vt, only **just**: ascertain the accuracy of (a weight or measure), correct to the standard *la16-*, *now Sh Ork* [*cf* OF *juster*].
~ that quite so, precisely *la19-*.

juitle *see* JUTE

juke *see* JOUK

Julie &c, **July**; **Jully** &c *17-e18* ['dʒulɪ, 'dʒulaɪ] = July *15-*.

jummil *see* JUMMLE

jummle, jummil &c *vti* 1 = jumble, mix up, get mixed up with, confuse *la16-*. 2 agitate, shake, churn *la16-*. 3 *vi* make a churning or confused noise *19-*, *now Sh*.
jummlie &c turbid, muddy *19-*, *now local*.

jump, jimp *la18-*, *now Sh vi, pt also* **jamp** *19-*, *now Sh Ags Fif*, **jaump** *la19-*, *now midLoth* = jump *17-*.
~in-jack &c 1 a child's toy made from the wishbone of a fowl *la18-*, *now Abd*. 2 = jumping-jack, a dancing doll. **~in-rope** &c a skipping rope *19-*, *local Abd-S*.

jump *see* JIMP², JIMP³, JIMP⁴

jumpie *see* JIMP⁴

juncture &c *n* 1 = juncture, joining, conjunction, a joint *16-*. 2 = *jointour* 2 (JOIN) *16*.

jundie &c; **joundie** &c *la17-18*; **junny** &c *19-*, *Abd* ['dʒʌn(d)ɪ, *'dʒun-] *n* 1 a push, as with the elbow, a shove, a jolt, a blow *18-*, *now Gall Uls*. 2 a trot, an even steady pace *la19-*.
vt push, jog, jostle, elbow *la17-*, *now NE Uls*. [perh onomat]

June &c, **Jeen** &c *19*, *NE* [*Sh Ork SW* dʒøn, dʒɪn; *NE* *dʒin] *n* = June *15-*.
the lang eeleven o ~ 11 June (Old Style), the longest day of the year *la19-*, *now Uls*.

june *see* JOIN

Junii *see* JUNY

junior *adj* = junior.

~ **secondary** (**school**) a state secondary school providing less academic courses than the *senior secondary school* (SENIOR), attended by pupils who were not successful in the *qualifying examination* (QUALIFY) *20*.

junk *n* = chunk *la18-*, *local*.

junner *vt* jolt, bump against *20-*, *Kcb*.

junrells debris, ruins *19-*, *Kcb*. [f JUNDIE]

junny *see* JUNDIE

junrells *see* JUNNER

junt &c *n* **1** a large lump of something, *esp* meat or bread *18-*, *now NE*. **2** a large quantity of liquid *19-*, *Kcb*. **3** a squat, clumsy person *la18-e20*, *Abd Bnf Ags*. [fig f *junt* (JINT), perh w infl f JUNK]

junt *see* JINT, JOIN

Juny &c; Junii &c [*'dʒønɪ] *n* June *15-e17*. [ME (rare) *Juni*; L *Jūnii* genitive]

jup *see* JUPE

juparty *see* JEOPARDIE

jupe &c, jup &c *la16-19*, **joup &c** *la16-17*, **jeep** *20-*, *NE*; **joip** *e17* [dʒøp, dʒup; *Abd* dʒip; *'dʒʌp] *n* **1** a jacket, short coat or loose tunic worn by men *la16-*, *now Ork Stlg Fif*. **2** a child's smock *18-e20*. **3** *also* **gipe &c** *la19-e20* [*ʔdʒəip] a woman's bodice, jacket or kirtle *17-e20*, *only Sc*. [OF]

jupe *see* CHOOP

jurant *adj* (*n*) (a person) taking an oath of abjuration in favour of William and Mary, Anne or the House of Hanover *18*.

non-~ (a person) refusing to take such an oath *18*. [L *jūrānt-*, presp stem of *jūrāre* swear]

juratory caution ['dʒurətɔrɪ 'keʃn] *law* inadequate security allowed in some civil cases where no better security is available, *similar to Eng* entering into recognisance *19-*.

jure &c [*dʒør] *n* **1** jurisprudence *la15-16*. **2** that which substantiates a claim, a ground of right or entitlement *la15-16*. **3** a title, legal right, privilege *16*. [only Sc; L *jūr-*, stem of *jūs* law, right]

jurement [*'dʒørmɛnt] *n* an oath *la15*. [only Sc; OF]

jurmummle [dʒər'mʌml] *vt* mess or mix up; confuse *19-*, *now Rox*. [perh dial and colloq Eng *jerrymumble* shake, tumble about]

jurnal *see* JOURNAL

jurnay *see* JOURNEE

juror *n* = JURANT *18*.

jurr *n* contemptuous term for a servant-girl *la18*. [short for Eng *journeywoman* a daily help]

jus devolutum ['dʒʌs dɛvol'jutəm] *church law* the right of *presenting* (PRESENT) a MINISTER to a congregation, which falls to the PRESBYTERY if the charge has remained vacant for six months *18-*. [L = a right which has devolved]

jus mariti [dʒʌs mə'raɪtaɪ] *law* the right of property vested in the husband on marriage in all his wife's MOVEABLES except her paraphernalia (*ie* clothes, jewellery and their receptacles) *18-19*. [L = the right of the husband]

jus quaesitum tertio ['dʒʌs kwe'sitəm 'tɛrʃɪo] *law* a contractual right of one party, arising out of a contract between two others, to which the first is not a party *la17-*. [L = a right sought by a third person]

jus relictae, jus relicti ['dʒʌs rɪ'lɪkte; -taɪ, *also* -ti] *law* the share of a deceased spouse's MOVEABLE goods to which the surviving wife (*relictae*) or husband (*relicti*) is entitled: one-third if there are surviving children, one-half if there are none *18-*. [L = the right of the survivor]

just *see* JUIST

jus tertii ['dʒʌs 'tɛrʃɪaɪ] *law* the right of a third party (when it is denied that a person has the right he alleges, though it might properly be claimed by another, the third party) *19-*. [L]

justery &c; justry &c [*'dʒʌstɔrɪ] *n* **1** *appar* one of the districts into which the country was divided for administration of the law by the JUSTICES; the jurisdiction of a JUSTICE within a specified district *e15*. **2** = JUSTICIARY 1, *la15-e16*. **3** = JUSTICIARY 2, *la15-e16*. **4** a *justice aire* or other *justice court* (JUSTICE) *e15*. **5** justice, the administration of the law, equity *la15*. [only Sc; see DOST]

justice &c; justis &c *15-17* ['dʒʌstɪs; *NE* *'dʒist-*, *'dʒust-*] *n* **1** = justice *15-*. **2** *law* the *Court of Justiciary* (JUSTICIARY) *la15-e17*. **3** one of the (*orig* three, each with distinct territorial jurisdiction) officers of state who, either in person or by deputy, was charged with the holding of *justice aires* and *justice courts*, as presiding judge and in the name of the sovereign; *latterly* the supreme criminal judge but *orig* with jurisdiction also in certain civil matters *15-* [ScL *justitia* (*12*); *cf* JUSTICIAR]. **4** any judge charged with the holding of *justice courts* or *justice aires* in the name of the sovereign; the presiding judge of any particular DIET² of these courts *15-*, *now only in combs*. **5** *law* the corresponding officer of a *lord of regality* (LORD), with jurisdiction equivalent to that of the royal JUSTICES *la15-e16*. **6** *law* a person with local and separate power of JUSTICIARY over a particular area *la15-e17*. **7** *in gen*, *esp literary* a criminal judge *la15-16*.

~ **aire &c** *law* the circuit court of the sovereign's JUSTICE (*n 3-4*) or of the JUSTICE of a regality (*n 5*) *la14-17*. ~ **clerk &c** *law* **1** an officiating clerk of a DIET² of the *justice court* or *justice aire*, *15-e17*. **2** J~ **Clerk** ['~ 'klark, *joc* 'klɛrk], *chf* **Lord J~ Clerk** the principal clerk of JUSTICIARY, *orig* the *officer of state* (OFFICER) who officiated as clerk of the *justice court* or *justice aire*; *latterly* one of the principal judges and vice-president of the *Court of Justiciary* (JUSTICIARY) *la15-*. ~ **court** *or* **court of** ~ *law* **1** a court presided over by a JUSTICE (*n 3-6*) *la15-17*. **2** = *Court of Justiciary* (JUSTICIARY) *la17-e19*. ~

deput &c *law* a deputy for the *Justice General* or for a JUSTICE *n* 5, *la15-17*. **J~ General &c**, *latterly chf* **Lord J~ General** = the principal JUSTICE (*n* 3), now the president of the *Court of Justiciary* (JUSTICIARY) *15-*. **~man** *mining* a checkweighman *18-*, *now Fif Lnk*. **J~ Principal &c** *law* = *Justice General*, *16*. **Gret J~** *law* = *n* 3, *la15-e16*. **~ in that part** *law* one who has been granted particular rights of JUSTICIARY, *usu* over a particular area *la16-17*.

justiciar *n, law* = JUSTICE *3-7*, *la16-*, now the preferred *hist* term *esp* = JUSTICE 3. **~(s) aire** = *justice aire* (JUSTICE) *e17*. [laME; MedL *justitiarius*]

justiciary &c *n* **1** the office or jurisdiction of a JUSTICE or of the JUSTICES *la15-*. **2** the judicature as an official body *la15-17*.
commission of ~ a court for trying criminal causes, now absorbed into next *16-e17*. **Court of J~** *orig* a court presided over by a JUSTICIAR; *now, as* **High Court of J~**, the supreme criminal court of Scotland *16-*; cf *High Court* (HEICH). **Lord (Commissioner) of J~** *see* LORD. [chf Sc; MedL *justitiaria &c*]

justicoat &c [*'dʒʌstɪkot, *'dʒøst-, &c] *n* a jacket or sleeved waistcoat *la17-19*. [F *just au corps* a close-fitting coat, w final syllable assimilated to *coat*]

justify &c *vt* **1** = justify *15-*. **2** execute justice upon, convict, condemn; execute (a convicted criminal); put (a criminal etc) to death *15-e17*. **~ to (the) dede** put (a criminal etc) to death *la15-16*.

justis *see* JUSTICE

justry *see* JUSTERY

jute &c, jeet *19-, NE* [dʒøt, dʒɪt; dʒut; *NE* dʒit] *n* **1** weak or sour ale; bad WHISKY *18-, now Ork*. **2** any insipid drink, dregs, weak tea etc *19-, now Ork*. **3** *chf* **jeet** *contemptuous* a tippler, boozer, drunkard *la18-, now Abd*.

juitle &c, jeetle &c *e20* ['dʒøtl; *Abd* 'dʒitl; *'dʒʌtl] *v* **1** *vi only* **juitle &c** tipple *19-, now Dmf*. **2** *vti* spill, splash, overflow *19-, now Gall*. *n* a dash or small quantity of liquid *19-, now Ayr*.

jutor &c [*'dʒøtər; *'dʒʌtər] = *n* 3, *la16-17*. [OF *joute, jute*, MedL *juta* vegetables, pot-herbs, ME *joutes* (*pl*) vegetable or herb soup]

jylour *see* JILE

K

ka *see* KAE[1]

kabbelow ['kabɪlʌu] *n* cabbage and potatoes mashed together, sometimes with butter *19-e20, Ags Fif Loth.* [appar an extension of CABELEW]

kaber *see* CABER

kace *see* CASE

kach *see* CACK

kachepell, kachepule *see* CACHEPELL

kae[1] **&c, ka &c** *16-e17,* **ca(a)** *la15-16;* **kyaw &c** *20-, Mry SW* [ke; *Mry SW* kjɑ] *n* **1** the jackdaw *16-.* **2** the call of the jackdaw *la19-, now Per.* **3** contemptuous term for a person *la18-19.*
vi, of a jackdaw caw *la19-, Bnf Per.*
~-witted hare-brained, half-witted *la18-, chf Ags.* [nME *ka*; see DOST, SND]

kae[2] **&c** [ke] *interj* expressing disapproval, contempt or incredulity, pooh-pooh! *la18-20.* [*cf* MDu *ke*]

kaen [ken] *vt* split (cod) *20-, Cai.* [f the short piece of cane used to keep the split cod open when drying]

kaff *see* CAFF

kag *see* CAG

kaid *see* KED

kaif *see* KAV

kail &c, kale *17-,* **cale &c** *la14-;* **keill &c** *17-19,* **kell** *17-e19* [kel; *Ork* kil] *n* **1** = cole, brassica, *esp* the curly variety; cabbage *15-.* **2** dishes made of this *la14-:* (1) BROTH[1] or soup (a) in which cabbage etc is a principal ingredient; (b) made with vegetables with or without the addition of meat, *freq* prefixed by the name of the principal ingredient, *eg* **nettle ~, pea ~;** (2) prepared as a vegetable on its own, boiled and mashed. **3** a main meal, dinner *19-, now NE nEC Bwk.*
kail-bell the dinner-bell; a call to dinner *la17-, now Ags Per.* **~ blade** a leaf of kail *la18-, now local Sh-Dmf.* **~ broo &c, ~ bree** the juice of boiled KAIL *la19-, now local Sh-N.* **~ brose** BROSE made with the liquid from boiled kail *la18-, now N Per Ayr.* **~ gullie &c** a blade fixed at right angles to the end of an upright handle, used for cutting and chopping KAIL stems *18-, now Ork local N.* **~ kenny, ~ kennin** a dish of cabbage and potatoes mashed *19-20, N Lnk Kcb; cf* KABBELOW. **~ ladle** a tadpole *20-, Per Fif Dmf.* **~ root &c** the stump left after the head of the KAIL has been cut *20-, local N-Uls.* **~ runt 1** the stalk of the KAIL plant, a CASTOCK *17-, now local Sh-SW.* **2** contemptuous term, *esp* for an old woman *la19-, Ags Fif Gall.* **~ stock 1** = CASTOCK *18-, now local Sh-Dmf.* **2** a full-grown KAIL plant *17-20, Sh Arg Ayr.* **~ supper &c** a person who is fond of BROTH[1]; nickname for an inhabitant of Fife *la18-19.* **~ time** dinner-time *la18-, now local Ags-Lnk.* **~ wife 1** a woman who sells vegetables and herbs *la16-, now Ags.* **2** *fig* a scold, a coarse brawling woman *17-18.* **~**

worm a caterpillar *la18-, now local Ork-Ayr.* **~ yaird &c 1** a cabbage garden, a kitchen-garden *16-.* **2** name for a type of heavily sentimental fiction popular in the late 19th and early 20th centuries dealing *chf* with rural domestic life and containing dialect speech *la19-;* see SND.
earn, get *or* **mak saut to his ~** make a living *18-, now local Ork-Dmf.* **get one's** *or* **gie someone his ~ through the reek &c** *18-, now Sh-Per,* **get** *or* **hae one's kail het** *la19-, now NE Per* get *or* give someone a severe scolding. **green ~ =** *n* 1, *la17-.* **Kilmaurs ~** a strong hardy variety, *chf* used for feeding cattle *la18-, now WC.* **lang ~** great or Scotch kail, a less curly, purplish variety; a dish made with this *18-19.* **pan ~ =** *n* 2, *18-19.* **red &c ~ =** *lang ~, la16-19.* **scaud one's lips** *or* **tongue in** *or* **wi ither folk's ~** interfere, meddle *la16-, now local Cai-Fif.* **wild &c ~** the wild radish, RUNCH[1] *la18-e19, Dmf Kcb.* [nME *cale,* OE *cāl,* ON *kál*]

kailie *see* CEILIDH

kaip *see* CAIP, KEP[2]

kairn *see* CAIRN

kairy *see* CAIRIE

kaisart &c, kesart &c [***'kezər(t), **?*'kiz-] *n* a cheese-vat *la17-e19.* [only Sc; eModFlem *kaeshorde; cf* CHESSART]

kaisie *see* CASSIE

kake *see* CAKE

kale *see* KAIL

kalends &c ['kelənz, 'ka-] = calends *15-.* **the cauld ~** *Mry Abd* or **calendars** *NE Ags* the cold spell which *freq* occurs at the beginnings of the spring months, *esp* March or May *20-.*

kalk *see* CAUK[1]

kame &c, came &c *la14-e20,* **kem &c** *la14-e17;* **kamb &c** *la16-19,* **keam &c** *la16-,* **comb** *18-* [kem; *Ork also* kjem, k(j)im; ***kɛm] *n* **1** = comb *la14-.* **2** a combing *20-, NE, WC.* **3** *chf* **kame &c** a long narrow steep-sided ridge, the crest of a hill or ridge *la18-, also freq in place-names.*
vt **1** = comb *la14-.* **2** rake (loose hay or straw from a stack to trim it) *20-, local.* **3** scold *20-, NE Lnk.* **4** *vi* (1) *of a horse* rear *19-, now Ork Cai.* (2) *of a child* climb or clamber up *20-, Cai NE.*
kaming-claith &c a cloth put over the shoulders while the hair is combed *la16-e17.* **~ing stok &c** a support to which carding- or rippling-combs were fixed *16-e18.*
bring *or* **get an ill ~ for** *or* **to one's head** bring mischief upon oneself *18-, now Fif.* **claw someone's ~** give someone a drubbing *19-, Loth.* **~ against the hair** *fig* ruffle, irritate *la18-, NE Fif.* **~ someone's hair, head** *etc* **for** *or* **til him =** *v* 3, *19-, local NE-S.*

kan *see* CAN[1]

kane &c *la15-,* **cane &c; can** *12-e13,* **kean &c**

la16-19 [ken] *n* **1** a payment in kind, a portion of the produce of a tenancy payable as rent, *latterly chf* poultry; such payments collectively *12-e20*. **2** *transf* a quantity of cheese, *latterly appar* fixed at about 3 tons (3.048 tonnes) *18-20*, *WC, SW*.

canage [*'keneʤ] a custom-duty paid as *n* 1, *14-16*. **kaner &c** *16-17*, **kenner &c** *la16-e19* [*'kenər] the person appointed overseer of certain fishings and *appar* responsible for paying the KANE *Ross Mry*.

pay (the) kain pay the reckoning or *(fig)* the penalty *18-e19*. [ScGael *càin* rent, tribute, fine, IrGael *cáin* law, penalty]

kanny *see* CANNY

kape *see* CAIP

kar *see* CAR[1]

kard *see* CAIRD[1], CAIRD[2]

karle *see* CARLE[1]

karriewhitchit [kərɪ'hwɪtʃət] *n* term of endearment for a child or young animal *19-*, *Abd Ags*.

kart *see* CAIRT[1], CAIRT[2]

kartie *see* CART

kast *see* CAST

Kate: curly ~ the rounded top crust of a loaf of bread *20-*, *Ags Per*. ~ **Kennedy** a mythical personage in whose honour a historical pageant is performed annually in spring by the students of St Andrews University *la19-*, *chf Fif*.

katherane *see* CATERAN

Katie &c, Katy *n, also* **k**~ = KITTIE 1, *e16*.
~ **beardie &c 1** name for a woman with a beard or moustache *20-*, *Cai Abd Ags*. **2** the loach *20-*, *now Ags Fif midLoth* [name of a popular song *17-*]. ~ **wren** the wren *la19-*, *Abd Loth Bwk*.

katt *see* CAT[1]

katy-handed *see* KETACH

Katy *see* KATIE

kauch &c; kiaugh &c [*SW* kjɑx(t), *kɑx; *WC* *kex] *n* care, worry, bustle, anxious exertion *la18-*, *chf SW*. [perh Sc and IrGael *cath* a battle, struggle, trouble]

kav &c; kaif &c [*Sh* kɑv; *Abd* kef] *vi, of a stormy sea* foam in breaking, throw up a spray *20-*, *Sh Abd*. [Norw dial *kava*, ON *kafa* dive under water; *cf* CAVE[2]]

kavill *see* CAVEL, KEVEL[3]

keaber *see* CABER

keam *see* KAME

kean *see* KANE

keave *see* CAVE[2]

keavie, keavy, cavey *19* [*'kevɪ] *n* a species of crab *la17-19*, *chf Fif*. [obscure]

keb[1] *vi, of a ewe* **1** give birth prematurely or to a dead lamb *19-*, *SW, S*. **2** lose a lamb by early death *19-*, *chf S*.
n **1** a ewe that has given birth to a dead lamb or failed to rear a live one *16-*, *chf S*. **2** a stillborn or premature lamb *la19-*, *SW, S*.
~ **hoose 1** a small shed or shelter where a ewe

that has lost her lamb is confined while being made to adopt another *la19-e20*, *S*. **2** a shelter for young lambs in the lambing season *la19-*, *SW, S*. ~ **yowe &c** = *n* 1, *la16-*, *now Fif*. [eModEng *keb, kebbe*, of uncertain orig; *cf* Ger dial *kibbe* a ewe, MDu *kebbe* a young pig, *kabbelen* bring forth, Flem *kippe* a newly-born calf]

keb *see* COB[1], KED

kebar, kebbar *see* CABER

kebbock &c *17-*, **kebbok &c** *16*, **cabok &c** *la15-e19* [*'kɛbək, 'kebək; *Cai* 'keibəg] *n, freq* ~ **of cheese &c** a cheese, a whole cheese, *latterly esp* home-made *la15-*.
~ **heel** the hard end-piece of a cheese *la18-*, *now NE Fif Edb*. [see SND]

kebby-lebby *see* CABBY-LABBY

kechepule *see* CACHEPELL

kechin *see* KITCHEN

keck *interj* the sharp cackling sound made by **1** a jackdaw *e16*; **2** a hen *la18-*, *now Wgt*.
vi make this sound, cackle, cluck *20-*, *now NE*. [imit; *cf* KECKLE]

keckle &c, kekkill &c *16* *vi* **1** *of hens, jackdaws etc* cackle *16-*. **2** laugh noisily; giggle *la15-*. **3** laugh with joy or excitement, express unrestrained delight *18-*, *now Sh NE Ags*.
n a cackle; a chuckle *la19-*, *NE Ags Loth*. [imit; eModEng (once) *keckle*, corresponding to ME *kakelen &c*; MDu, Flem *kekelen*, MLowGer *kakelen*; *cf* CAIKLE]

ked &c *la17-*, *now local Sh-Dmf*, **kaid &c** *la16-e19*, **keb** *la17-*, *local Ork-Kcb* [kɛd, ked, kɛb] the sheep-tick. [northern eModEng *cade*; obscure]

keddie *see* CADDIE[2]

keechan *see* CAOCHAN

keech *see* KICH

keechle &c [*'kixl, 'kigl] *vi* giggle, titter *la19-*, *local Sh-Dmf*.
n a short laugh *20-*, *now Loth Dmf*. [onomat]

keeger &c *20-*, *Abd*, **quigger &c** *20-*, *Bnf Abd* [*'k(w)igər, 'k(w)ɪg-, 'kwixər] *vti* mix up messily, mess about, work in a slovenly or ineffective way *20-*, *Bnf Abd*.
n a mess, untidy mixture, muddle *20-*, *Abd*. [prob an altered frequentative of KICH]

keehoy &c; keehow *la19* [ki'hoi; *Abd* ki'hʌu] *n* the game of hide-and-seek *la19-*, *local Sh-Dmf*. [f a call uttered in the game; *cf* CAHOW and HOY[1], HOO[2]]

keek[1], keke &c [kik; *local WC, S* ki:k] *vi* peep, glance *la15-*.
n a peep, a glance *la16-*.
~**er 1** a person who watches surreptitiously, a peeping Tom *la19-*, *now Kcb*. **2** the eye *la19-*, *local nEC-S*. **3** *also* **blue** ~**er** a black eye *la19-*, *local Abd-WC*. ~**ing glass &c** a mirror *la16-*, *now Ags*.
~**-bo &c** *n* the game of peep-bo *18-*. *interj, also* **keekie-bo** *la19-*, *local Ags-WC* **1** used in the game when the player in hiding has been seen *19-*. **2** used in similar play with a young child

la19-, local Abd-Kcb [cf Du kiekeboe, LowGer kike-bu]. ~ **hole** a chink or peep-hole 19-, now local Sh-Kcb.

~ **o day** or **dawn** sunrise, peep of day 20-, NE Ags Fif. ~ **and hide** = ~-bo (n), 20-, Ork NE. [ME keke; cf MLowGer kīken, Du kijken]

keek² &c [kik, kig] n **1** a cunning, sly or malicious person 19-e20, NE. **2** contemptuous term for a young woman 20-, Abd. [uncertain]

keek³ n a linen cap for the head and neck la18-e19, Abd. [perh f KEEK¹ v]

keel¹, **kele** &c n **1** ruddle, red-ochre, esp as used for marking sheep 17-. **2** the owner's mark made with ruddle on sheep la15-. **3** weaving the mark made with ruddle by the warper at each end of his warp to ensure that the weaver returns the correct amount of woven yarn 19-, now WC Slk. **4** a coloured crayon or pencil 20-, now Ags Bwk WC.

vt mark (sheep) with ruddle la17-, now local.
~**ie** adj marked with KEEL¹ (n 1) 19-20, Gall.
~**man** a dealer in KEEL¹ (n 1) la18-e19, SW. [obscure; Gael cil ruddle may be f Sc; also in northern and n midl Eng dial]

keel² 18-, **kele** &c n **1** = keel (of a ship) la15-. **2** slang a person's bottom, the backside 18-, now Bwk.

vt to overturn, upset, throw on one's back 19-, now Sh.

~ **draucht** &c an iron or wooden covering on the outside of a boat's keel to protect it when the boat is being drawn la19-, now Cai. ~-**up** a heavy fall on one's back 20-, local Sh-Ags.

keelick &c; **keelup** &c 20-, Abd-Per ['kilək; Kcdn Per -əp] n a blow, stroke 19-, now Ags Fif.
keelakin a thud, a hard blow la19-, Abd. [see SND]

keelie¹ n, also ~ **hawk** the kestrel 19-20, local EC-S. [prob imit]

keelie² &c n a rough male city-dweller, a tough, now esp from the Glasgow area, orig with an implication of criminal tendencies 19-; cf Glesca keelie (GLESCA). [Gael gille a lad, a young man]

keelie see KEEL¹, KEELIVINE

keelin &c, **keling** &c, **killing** &c ['kilin; *'kɪl-] n a cod, esp a fully-grown or large one la14-.

~ **sound** the swimming bladder of the cod, used for glue e16. [northern and n midl ME keling; cf ON keila, Gael cilean a large cod]

keelivine &c 18-, **killavyne** &c 17-, **callivan** &c 20-, local ['kilɪvəin, 'kalɪ-, 'kɪlɪ-, 'gɪlɪ-, 'kʌlə-, &c; -vin, -vən, -fəin, -fən] n **1** black lead, graphite la17. **2** a lead pencil, a crayon or coloured pencil 19-, now local.
keelie &c = n 2, 20, Fif Bwk Rox. ~ **pen** = n 2, 17-. [see DOST, SND]

keelup see KEELICK

keen, kene &c la14-16 adj **1** = keen la14-. **2**

of persons or their actions etc brave, fierce, courageous, resolute la14-16. **3** transf (1) of combat fierce, violent la15-16; (2) of the elements, pestilence, war cruel, violent, terrible 15-e16. **4** (1) of persons lively, brisk, with renewed vigour after an illness 20-, local Sh-midLoth. (2) of animals spirited, lively, eager 20-, local N-SW. (3) curling (CURL), of ice crisp, smooth 19-, now Ayr. **5** of persons avaricious, driving a hard bargain 20-, local. **6** of prices highly competitive 20-.

be ~ **of** be eager for (something) or to (do something), be fond of, have a liking for la19-, local N-S.

keeng see KING

keep &c, **kepe** &c; la14-17; **kyp** &c la15-16 [kip] vti, pt, ptp also **kepit** &c la14-, **keiped** &c la16-18, **keipt** &c 16-18, **keip** &c 16-20 ['kipɪt, kip(t)] **1** = keep la14-. **2** vt attend to the wellbeing of; tend, take care of la14-. **3** vi give careful attention **to** 16. **4** fare (as regards health) la19-; cf HAUD v 4. **5** vt maintain, sustain, keep going (talk, noise etc) la19-, NE. **6** = KEP² v 1 and 2, 16-17.

n **1** = keep. **2** charge, custody la15-17. **3** in pl a game of marbles in which the winnings are kept 20-, local Ayr-SW.

~**er** &c **1** = keeper la14-. **2** a person who conducts or is present at a conventicle la17. **3** a store animal, one kept for fattening 20-, NE.
~**ie-in** n a pupil detained after school as a punishment la19-, now NE Per. ~**ie-up** a game of keeping a ball in the air by means of the feet, knees or head la20-, local EC, WC. ~**ing** **1** = keeping la14-. **2** keeping in food and shelter, entertainment or upkeep 15-e17. be on one's **keping** &c be a fugitive or in hiding e17. **go** or **run upon one's keping** &c save oneself by flight or concealment, abscond e17. ~**in aff** except, not counting la19-, now Ags Loth.

keep-up n = upkeep, cost of maintenance 20-, local.

~ **aff o anesel** act defensively in fighting; stand up for oneself la19-, N Fif Kcb. ~ **in aboot** restrain, keep in order, discipline la19-, local. ~ **in guid wi** keep in with, on good terms with 20-, now local Cai-Kcb. ~ **in one's hand 1** restrain oneself, refrain from striking la19-, now Bnf Fif Loth: 'Keep in your han, gudewife; the bairn meant nae ill'. **2** be stingy la19-, now NE Loth. ~ **me** or **us (a)** may God keep me or us (all) 19-, local N-S. ~ **someone's pooch** provide someone with pocket money 20-, local NE-SW. ~ **a stack** trim a hay- or corn-stack while it is being built 20-, now Kcb Dmf. ~ **steeks** or **stitch** keep pace, keep up (with) 19-, now Ags Kcb. ~ **tee** or **til (wi)** = prec, keep abreast (of) 20-, NE Ags. ~ **one's tung** keep a check or guard on one's tongue e16. ~ **up 1** stay awake la19-, local. **2** of weather stay fine 20-. **3** hoard (corn etc) la16-17. ~ **up one's rig** maintain the same rate of corn cutting as the others in the harvest field *la19-*, now *Loth Wgt.* ~ **wide** *shepherding* keep some distance from the flock so as not to disturb the sheep *la19-*, *local*. [*cf* KEP² *v* and HAUD]

keer *see* CURE

keerie &c *interj* a call to a lamb or sheep *20-*, now *Per Fif*. [Gael *ciridh* pet name for calling sheep]

keeriosity, keerious *see* CURIOUS

keeroch &c ['k(w)irəx] *n* contemptuous term for any strange or messy mixture *19-*, *NE*.
vi stir or poke about messily; work awkwardly *la19-*, now *Abd*.
   kweerichin &c awkward and unskilful *20-*, *Abd*. [see SND]

keers *n pl* a thin gruel given to feeble sheep in the spring *20-*, *S*. [uncertain]

keeslip &c ['kizlɪp, 'kɪslɪp] *n* the stomach of an animal used as a source of rennet *18-20*, *chf Slk*. [f a northern, unpalatalized form of OE *cīeslybb* rennet; *cf* MDu *kaeslibbe*]

keessar &c ['kisər] *n* a large uncomely person, *usu* female *la19-20*, *NE*. [prob var of colloq Eng *geezer*]

keest &c *n* sap, pith, substance *19*, *chf S*.
   ~**less 1** tasteless, insipid *19-e20*, *S*. **2** lacking in substance *e19*, *SW*, *S*. [MDu *keest* a kernel]

keething *see* KYTHE

keevee &c ['ki'vi] *n*, *chf* **on the** ~ = on the qui vive, on the alert; in high spirits; worked up *19-*.

keiching *see* KITCHEN

keiler ['kəilər] *n* = coiler; *specif* a person who coils ropes in the bottom of a boat; *derog* a useless or insignificant person *20-*, now *Cai*.

keill *see* KAIL

keind *see* KIND

keip, keiped, keipt *see* KEEP

keir &c [*kir] *adj*, *of horses* dun, dark brown or grey *la16-17*.
   ~ **black** dark-coloured *la16-e18*. [Gael *ciar*]

keir *see* CAIR

keist *see* KIST

keith [*? kiθ] *n* a bar across a river to prevent salmon from mounting further *la18-e19*, *Per*. [Gael *cuidh*, *cuith* an enclosure]

keke *see* KEEK¹

kekkill *see* KECKLE

keksi *see* KEX

kelchyn &c [*'kɛl(t)ʃɪn] *n* a fine paid to the kinsmen of a person killed *e15*, *e17*. [see DOST]

kelde [*kild] *adj* ? allowed to cool *e16*. [see DOST]

kele &c [*kil] *vt* = kill *16-17*. [Sc var with change of vowel appar occurring first in *pt* and *ptp*; *cf* KILL²]

kele *see* KEEL¹, KEEL²

keling *see* KEELIN

kell¹ &c *n* **1** = caul, a woman's ornamental hairnet or cap; *specif* when worn alone, the distinctive head-dress of a young unmarried woman *14-19*, *latterly ballad*. **2** an incrustation of scab, scurf or dirt on the head or face *19-*, now *Ayr*.
   ~**t**, ~**ed** covered with dirt or scurf *20-*, *Lnk Ayr*. [northern and n midl ME *kell*, F *cale &c*]

kell² &c *n* a spring, fountain, *chf* ~ **head** *la16-17*, in *place-names la13-*. [nEng dial *kell*, *keld*, ON *kelda*]

kell *see* KAIL, KILL¹

kellach &c [*'kɛləx, *'kjaləx, *'kilək] *n* a large conical wicker basket or pannier, *usu* with a lid at the lower end, *chf* for carrying dung to the fields *la18-19*, *N*. [Gael dial *ceallach*]

kelp &c *n* **1** *chf* ~**ie** a mischievous young person *19-*, *S*. **2** a big raw-boned youth *19-*, *NE Ags*. [var of GILPIE]

kelpie *n* a water demon, *usu* in the form of a horse, which is said to haunt rivers and fords, and lure the unwary to their deaths *18-*, in *place-name la17*. [prob Gael *cailpeach*, *colpach* a bullock, colt]

Kelso; Kelsae ['kɛlsɪ; *St* 'kɛlso] ~ **Laddie** the leading male participant in the Kelso *Riding of the Marches* (RIDE) *20-*. [the town in Rox]

kelt¹ *n* a salmon or sea-trout on its way back to the sea after spawning *16-*.
   ~**ed** spawned *e19*, *S*. [nME *kelt*; obscure]

kelt² &c *n* a kind of homespun black or grey cloth, used for outer garments *16-19*. [? *cf* eIr *celt* cover, dress, Mod Sc and IrGael *cealt* clothes; coarse cloth; *cf* KELTER¹]

kelter¹ &c [*Ork* 'k(j)ɛltər] *n* = KELT² *16-e20*, *latterly Ork*. [northern eModEng; ? *cf* early Ir *celtar* a covering, disguise, garment, Gael *cealtar* thick (grey) broad-cloth (but the latter may be f Sc)]

kelter² &c *v* **1** *vi* tumble headlong *19*, *S*. **2** wriggle, undulate, struggle *19-*, now only *verse*. **3** *vt* overturn, upset *la18-19*.
n a fall in which one is thrown head over heels *19-20*, *SW*, *S*. [prob frequentative of KILT²]

keltie, kelty *n*, *chf* **give someone** ~ force a large alcoholic drink on a person who has tried to avoid drinking; *fig* give someone a double dose of punishment *la17-19*. [appar eModEng (once) *turn kelty* = turn (a drinking vessel) over after emptying it; *cf* KILT² and prec]

Kelton Hill Fair a rumpus, a noisy uproar *20-*, *Gall*. [the village in Kcb]

Kelvinside ['kɛlvɪn'səid; *also, imitating the accent*, -'se(i)d] **a** ~ **accent, speak** ~ denoting a very affected, over-refined pronunciation of Scottish English *20-*. [the district of Glasgow]

kem *see* KAME

kemp [kɛmp; *Sh also* kjɛmp] *n* **1** a champion: (1) one who fights in single combat; a professional fighter *16-*, *latterly only ballad and place-names*; (2) one who fights on behalf of another or for a cause *la16-e17*. **2** *chf in pl* (1) stalks of the ribwort plantain, *esp* used in the game (*n* 2 (2)) *la16-19*, *EC*, *S*. (2) a children's game played with plantain stalks in which each contestant

tries to decapitate his opponent's stalks *19-20*, *Bwk Rox*. (3) the crested dogstail grass *20-*, *Cai Ross*. **3** a contest, *usu* to finish first in the harvest field *la18-*, *now Sh Ork Rox*.
vi **1** contend, strive *16-20*. **2** *specif* compete in a piece of work: (1) *in gen*, *la19-*, *now Sh Ork*; (2) in the harvest field *18-20*; (3) in eating *18-e20*.
~**er** a person who strives or contends, a fighter, one who strives to outdo his fellows, a keen worker *17-20*. ~**ie** *n* a bold or pugnacious person; a lively child *e16*, *19-*, *now Bnf*. *adj* energetic, vigorous *20-*, *Rox*. [ME *kemp*, OE *cempa* > ON *kempa*; *cf* also Norw dial *kjempe* the plantain, its stalks, also used in a children's game]
kempit &c *n* the pith of hemp or of a wild carrot, parsnip etc, dried and used as a candle *e19*. [uncertain]
kemple &c, kimpill &c *n* **1** a horse-load of straw or the equivalent quantity *16-e20*. **2** a bundle or load of hay or straw made up in a certain way, a truss of straw prepared for thatch *20-*, *Cai*. **3** a lump or fragment, *esp* of food *la19-20*, *NE*. [appar ON *kimbill* a little bundle; *cf* Gael *ciomboll*]
ken &c [kɛn; *Sh Ork* kın, kin; *with reduced stress* k(ı)n] *vt* **1** make known, *specif* (1) inform of, teach, tell *la14-17*; (2) show, point out (the way) *la14-16*. (3) (a) ~ **someone to a piece of land** ascertain authoritatively and point out to a person the situation and limits of his or her separate portion of land, thereby formally admitting the person to occupation of the land; recognize a person as legal successor to an inheritance, *latterly chf* ~ **a widow to her terce** *la15-20*. (b) ~ **someone (for, of** *or* **with) the land** invest with, admit to occupation of, assign the land in this way *la15-17*. **2** = know *la14-*; *cf* KNAW¹.
n knowledge, acquaintance, comprehension, insight *16-*.
~**able** obvious, easily recognizable *la19-*, *now Sh NE*. ~**ning &c** **1** (1) recognition, acquaintance *15-*, *now Sh Ork N*. (2) teaching, understanding, power of apprehension *la15-*, *now Sh N Lnk*. **2** a very little of anything, a trifle *la18-*, *local Sh-SW*. ~**t &c**, ~**d &c**, ~**nit &c** *la15-e16 ptp, adj* **1** (well-)known, familiar *15-*. **2** having a certain fame or reputation *la15-*. **be it** ~**d** *formula introducing the principal statement of a legal deed or formal declaration*, *la14-18*. **make** ~**d** make known, declare: **1** *in gen*, *15-16*; **2** *in the formula introducing a formal declaration*, *15*. **be it made** ~**d** = be it kend, *15-e16*.
~**mark &c** *n* a distinguishing mark, a mark of ownership on an animal, a brand *la19-*, *Sh N Fif* [*cf* ON *kennimark*, Du *kenmark* a mark].
~**nawhat &c** ['kɛnə'hwat; *NE* -'fat] a something-or-other *19-*, *now Sh Ork NE*. ~ **o anesel** be aware consciously or intuitively, have instinctive knowledge *la19-*, *Sh NE*. ~ **o't** *freq in threats* know by dire experience, suffer for

one's actions *20-*, *local*. ~**s faar, how, whae** *etc* (*elliptical for* **deil, guid** *etc* ~**s what** *etc*) goodness knows what etc *19-*, *now Abd Ags Loth*. [ME *ken*, OE *cennan* make known, declare, ON *kenna* know etc, teach, tell etc; KEN has superseded KNAW¹ in ModSc]
ken *see* KIN
kench *see* KINCH¹
kend *see* KEN
kendalye &c [*'kɛndəlı] *n* = Kendal cloth, a coarse green woollen cloth *la15-16*.
kendill *see* KENNLE
kene *see* KEEN
kené *see* KNEE
kenkynolle &c [*'kɛn'kınəl] *n* a CLAN CHIEF, his office *la14-e16*. [Gael *ceann-cinneil*; more freq as *hede of kin* (HEID)]
kennel *n* a channel, a street gutter *18-20*, *now Ayr*. [var of obs Eng *cannel*]
kennel *see* KINGLE
kenner *see* KANE
kennill *see* KENNLE
kennit *see* KEN
kennle &c *la16-*, **kennill** *e17*, **kendill &c** *la14-18*; **kin(n)le** *19-*, **kindle &c** *16-* ['kɛn(d)l; *Bwk Rox* 'kınl; *Bwk also* 'kır(ə)l] *vti* = kindle *la14-*.
~**in(g)** kindling material; wood, live coals or PEAT¹ used as kindling *16-*.
kenspeckle &c, kenspekill *e16*; **kenspreckle &c** *la18-e20*, *Abd* ['kɛn'spɛkl; *Abd also* -'sprɛkl] *adj* easily recognizable, conspicuous, familiar *16-*.
n a mark by which a person or thing may be known or recognized *la19-*, *now Loth Lnk*.
kenspeckled = *adj*, *la17-19*. [see DOST *kenspecke* and SND]
kensy¹ &c [*?'kɛnsı] *n* a kind of woollen cloth *la16-e17*. [only Sc; ? *cf* KENTSCHIRE]
kensy² &c *n* term of abuse for a man *16*. [obscure]
kent *n* a long staff or pole used for leaping ditches etc; a punt-pole *17-20*.
vti propel a boat by using a KENT; convey (a person) in a punt *19*, *S*. [see DOST]
kent *see* KEN
Kentschire &c: ~ **claith** a Kentish cloth *la16-e17*.
keo *see* KIOW-OW
kep¹ &c *la17-*, **caip &c** *17-*, *now local Bnf-Fif*, **cap** *la15-* *n* [kɛp, kep, kap; *Sh* kjɛp] **1** = cap *la15-*. **2** a woman's cap *la19-*, *now S*.
vt, *only* **cap** confer a degree on (a GRADUAND) by touching his or her head with a cap *la19-*.
kep² &c; kaip &c *la16-18* [kɛp; *Sh also* kjɛp] *vt* **1** (1) catch (a falling object) *la15-*. (2) *specif* catch (a liquid) in a receptacle *16-*. **2** (1) intercept; stop, head off *16-*, *now local*. (2) *specif* parry, ward off (a blow) *16-*, *now local*. **3** (1) meet, encounter *la18-*, *chf NE Ags*. (2) *specif*, *of a train, bus, etc* connect with (another) *20-*,

Kcdn Ags. **4** = KEEP, contain, restrain, guard *18-e20.* **5** hold (the hair) **up** with a band, comb etc *19-, now Cai Kcb.*

n **1** (1) the act of catching, a catch, *esp* with the hands *20-, now local N-S.* (2) the heading off or intercepting of animals *20-, NE Lnk.* **2** a contrivance for checking, stopping or holding *esp* doors or windows *18-, now Kcb.* **3** *in pl, mining* = SHUTS *la19-, now Fif.* **4** a chance, opportunity *la18-20, WC Rox.*

kepper &c 1 = keeper *la15-16.* **2** a person who is good at catching *20-, local.* **3** a thing which is easy to catch *20-, wLoth Lnk Ayr.* **4** *in pl* = catchers (CATCH) *la19-, now Lnk Kcb.* **kep-pie(s)** *n* = prec *20-, Cai Ags Kcb.* **kepping** = keeping (KEEP) *16-17.* **kepping kame &c** a large comb used to hold up a woman's hair on the back of the head *19-, now Cai.*

~ **again** check, intercept, turn back *20-, now Cai Abd SW.* ~ **a catch** *or* **slap** *or* **strait** bridge a gap, serve a turn, be useful in an emergency, do for the time being *19-, local C, S.* ~ **gushes** dam the water in a street gutter with the feet *20-, Rox.* **kep-a-gush** a splay-footed person *20-, Rox.* ~ **skaith** suffer or incur harm *16-19.* [nME *kep*, var of KEEP]

kepe *see* KEEP
kepill *see* COUPLE
kepit *see* KEEP
kepp *see* KIP[1]
kepper, keppie(s), kepping *see* KEP[2]
ker *see* CAR[1], CAR[2]
kerk *see* CARK
kerl *see* CARLE[1]
kerlyng *see* CARLINE
kern *see* KIRN[1]
kers(e) *see* CARSE[1], CARSE[2]
kerseckie *see* CARSACKIE
kesart *see* KAISART
kess *see* CASE[1]
Kessock: ~ **herring** a small variety of herring caught in the Inner Moray Firth *la18-, Ross Inv Mry.* [the village on the Beauly Firth]
kest *see* CAST
kest *see* KIST
ket[1] **&c** *n* carrion, tainted flesh, *esp* that of a sheep *19-, Bwk S.* [ME *ket* carrion, ON *kjǫt* meat, flesh]
ket[2] *n* **1** a matted fleece of wool *la18-, now Clcm Loth.* **2** (1) couch-grass *19, chf S.* (2) a spongy kind of PEAT[1] of tough matted fibres *19-e20, SW.*
adj irascible, quick-tempered *19, SW.*
ketty *of turf* matted, lumpy *19-20.* [var of Mod Eng dial, eModEng and ME *cot &c* wool matted together in the fleece]
ketach &c ['kitəx, 'kɪtəx, 'kɪtɪ] *n* the left hand *la19-, Arg Renfr Uls.*
~ *or* **katy &c handed** left-handed *19-e20, Renfr Uls.* [Gael *ciotach* the left hand, *ciotach* left-handed]
ketch *see* KEYTCH

ketharan *see* CATERAN
kethat *n* some kind of overgarment *e16.* [? corrupt; see DOST]
kethie &c *la19-, now Abd Bwk* ['kɛθɪ; Kcdn-Fif 'kiθɪ, 'kɪθɪ]; **kethock &c** *19-, now Ayr* ['kɛθək; Ayr also 'kɪθək], **kethrie &c** *la19-e20* ['kɛθrɪ] *n* the angler fish. [obscure]
ketterel *see* KITERAL
kettle &c, kettill &c *15-17 n* **1** = kettle *15-.* **2** *specif* a large cooking pot *la15-, now Sh.* **3** a riverside picnic, *esp* on the Tweed, at which newly-caught salmon are cooked on the spot *la17-, now Loth Bwk.* **4** *mining* a cylindrical or barrel-shaped vessel of wood or iron used to raise and lower materials and men during the sinking of a pit *la19-e20.* **5** *chf* **kettlie &c** the game of hopscotch *20-, Ross Inv.*
~-**bellied** = pot-bellied *la19-, now Cai Wgt.* ~ **brod** a wooden pot-lid *20-, Sh N.*
keuch &c [kjʌx; *Sh also* kjox; *Rox* kjux] *vi* cough persistently from a tickling in the throat *19-, now Bwk.*
n a troublesome, persistent, tickling cough *19-, now Bwk.* [prob var of Eng *cough*; *cf* HOAST]
kevel[1] **&c** ['kɛvl] *vi* hold oneself awkwardly, stumble *19-, now Dmf.* [perh frequentative of CAVE[2]]
kevel[2] **&c** *vi* scold, wrangle *e19, S.* [var of Eng *cavil*]
kevel[3] **&c** *17-20,* **cavell &c** *16,* **kavill &c** *16-e19* ['kɛvl; *?*'kevl] *n* a large hammer for breaking stones *16-e20.*
~ **hammer** *la16-e20,* ~ **mell** *17-e20* = *n.* [nME *kevell*; uncertain]
kevel, kevill *see* CAVEL[1], CAVEL[2]
kex &c; keksi *20-, Sh n* the cow parsnip *la18-, now Sh Ork* [appar Scand; *cf* Norw dial *-kjeks* in various plant names of the umbelliferae]
key &c; kye &c *la15-e18* [ki; *NE, S* kəi] *n* **1** = key *la14-.* **2** an accessory part of a wool-comb *la16-e17.* **3** *in pl, children's games* a state of call or call for truce *20-, now Fif WC, SW.* **4** *fig* (from *key* in music) mood, humour, *chf* **be in a** ~ *19-, local Sh-Kcb.* **5** *in pl* = BADDERLOCKS *19-e20, local Ork-N.*
vt fasten with a key, lock *la19-, Sh Uls.*
seek for a ~ **that is in the lock** waste one's time, do something futile *la19-, now Ayr.* **use** *etc* **the kingis, his hienes,** *etc* ~**is** force entry by virtue of a legal warrant *la16-e19.*
keyheid &c [*'ki'hid] *n* the westernmost or most inland part of the quay of Aberdeen *16-17.*
key-maister &c [*'ki'mestər] *n* an officer in charge of the quays in the harbour of a seaport *la16-17.* [eModDu *kayemeester, kaey-* and *meester*]
keytch &c; kytch &c, ketch &c [*kəitʃ, *kɛtʃ] *vt* pitch, toss aside or to and fro; hitch up *18-e20.*
n a toss, jerk, heave *18-19.* [*cf* CADGE[2]]
keyth *see* KYTHE
kiaugh *see* KAUCH

kibble &c ['k(j)ɪbl] *adj* sturdy, well-built, active, agile *la18-*, *NE*. [see SND]

kibbling &c *n* **1** a thick, rough stick, a cudgel *e19*, *Dmf Gall*. **2** a cudgelling, beating *la20-*, *Wgt Rox*. [laME and ModEng dial *kibble*]

kich &c; keech &c [kix, kɪx] *n* excrement, filth or dirt of any kind *la19-*.
vi defecate *la19-*.
interj an exclamation of disgust, a warning, *usu* to a child, not to touch something dirty or undesirable *19-*.
~ie filthy, nasty *20-*, *now Abd midLoth Dmf*. [child's var of *cach* (CACK)]

kiché *see* KITCHIE

kicher¹ &c ['kɪxər, 'kɛxər] *vi* have a short, persistent, tickling cough *19-*, *local Abd-SW*.
n a short sharp cough *20-*, *Abd-Fif Ayr*. [onomat]

kicher² ['kɪxər] *vi* titter, giggle *19-*, *now Sh Abd-Ags*.
n a titter *20-*, *Abd Ags*. [onomat; *cf* Ger *kichern*]

kiching *see* KITCHEN

kick &c [kɪk; *Sh Ork* kik; *Mry* kəik] *vti* **1** = kick *la16-*. **2** show off, walk haughtily *la19-20*, *N*.
n **1** = kick. **2** *esp of dress* a novelty, something new-fangled *19-*, *chf Sh Ork*. **3** a trick, caper *19-*, *NE midLoth*. **4** (1) a habit, whim *20-*, *NE Ags*. (2) *in pl* airs, manners *19-e20*, *chf NE*.
~er a tedder, a machine for spreading out new-mown hay *20-*, *Bnf Fif WC, SW*. **~y** showy, *esp* in dress, dandified *la18-*, *now Kcdn*.
~ ba &c 1 football *la19-*, *local N-S*. **2** a football *19-*, *now Cai Abd*.
~ the block (*la19-e20*) *or* **can**(**nie**) (*20-*, *local*) *etc* a game in which a player had to hunt for other hidden players while preventing any of them creeping out to kick a block of wood etc.
~ bonnety (**~**) a game played by kicking a cap or bonnet until the owner can substitute another which is in turn kicked *la19-*, *now Cai*. [for *v* 2, *n* 2 *cf* Eng slang *kick* the vogue *19*]

kicker *n* **sit the ~, stand the ~s** (**o**) resist, refuse to budge (for) or be disturbed (by) *19-*, *NE*. [see SND]

kickmaleerie [kɪkmə'liːrɪ] *n* a flimsy trifling thing *19-*, *now midLoth Rox*. [KICK + *-maleerie* a fanciful ending as in WHIGMALEERIE]

kid *vi* flirt *19*. [see SND]

kid *see* KYTHE

kidgie *see* CADGY

kiest *see* CAST

kiggle-caggle &c *vi*, *curling* (CURL) cause a *curling-stone* to make a succession of zigzag movements between other stones to reach its objective *19-*, *now Fif*. [prob reduplicated var of COGGLE]

kighle ['kɪxl] *n* a short, tickling cough *19-20*. [*cf* KICHER¹]

kilbern *see* KILL¹

kilch &c [kɪl(t)ʃ] *n* an unexpected blow, a push *19-e20*, *chf Gall*.

vt push, shove, jerk, ram *19-*, *now Dmf Rox*. [conflation of KEYTCH w KILT²]

kilchan &c *Abd*, **calchen** *Abd*, **coulichin &c** *e20*, *Mry* [*Abd* 'kɪlxən, 'kalxən; *Mry* 'kulɪxən] *n* a rack hung in the chimney for drying *fir-candles* (FIR) *19-e20*. [see SND]

Kildé *see* CULDEE

kilfuddoch &c [*kɪl'fʌd(j)ox, -əx] *n* a meeting and discussion, a debate, a dispute *19*, *Ayr*. [see SND]

kilhailie [kɪl'helɪ] *n* a somersault, a fall *20-*, *Cai*. [see SND]

kill¹ &c, kiln &c *la16-*; **kell** *la16-18* [kɪl] *n* **1** = kiln *la15-*. **2** a lime-kiln *16*. **3** the wooden tripod round which a stack of hay or corn is built for ventilation *19-*, *local NE-Dmf*. **4** *joc* a WHISKY still *20-*, *now Loth*.
vt dry (grain) in a kiln *16-17*.
~ barn &c *la17-*, *now Ork*, **kilbern** *la16* a barn attached to or containing a kiln. **~ beddin** the packed straw on the drying floor of a kiln, over which the grain was spread *la18-*, *now Sh*.
~ cast the quantity of oats taken to the mill at one time to be ground into meal for household use, *usu* enough to produce four BOLLS *19-*, *now Wgt*. **~-crack** a small crack appearing in the glazing of pottery which has cooled at an uneven temperature, *chf* **~-crackit** covered with such cracks *la19-*, *local*. **~ croft &c** the piece of ground occupied by or attached to a kiln *la15-e17*. **~ door** the steps up to the entrance to a kiln *la19-*, *chf Sh*. **~ ee** the open space in front of a kiln fireplace *e20*, *local*. **~ head** the roof of a kiln, also forming the floor of the drying chamber on which the grain is spread to dry *la18-*, *now Sh*. **~ man** the man in charge of a corn-kiln *la17-*. **~ plate** one of the perforated metal plates forming the surface of the drying floor in present-day kilns *la20-*, *local Ork-Dmf*. **~ pot** the heating chamber under a corn-kiln *18-20*, *chf SW*. **~ rib** one of the small movable wooden bars laid across the kiln joists to support the bed of straw on the drying floor *la17-*, *now Sh*. **~ stead &c** = ~ *croft*, *la15-*, *now Sh*. **~ stick**(**le**) *la17-*, *now Sh*, **~ tree &c** *16-*, *now Sh Ork* one of the beams which support the drying floor.
fire the ~ *18-*, *now Sh midLoth*, **set the ~ on fire** *or* **a-low** *la17-*, *now Sh* start trouble, raise a commotion. **the ~'s on fire** *or* **in a bleeze** *proverb* denoting a state of tumult or excitement *16-*, *now Ags Loth*.

kill² &c *vt* **1** = kill *15-*. **2** (1) thrash, beat *20-*, *local N-Uls*. (2) hurt badly *la19-*, *local*. **3** overcome from weariness *la19-*, *local Sh-SW*: 'we're kill'd wi' wark'.
~ing-time(**s**) name for the period of the greatest persecution of the *Covenanters* (COVENANT) in 1685, later extended to cover the whole period 1679-1688.
~ (**the**) **coo** *chf in negative* not a serious matter,

no bother or trouble *19-*, *now SW.* **laugh one's ~, get one's ~** (**lauchin**) 'laugh one's head off' (**at**) *20-*, *Abd Ags*. [*cf* KELE]

killavyne *see* KEELIVINE

killick &c *n* **1** the 'mouth' of a pickaxe *18-e19*. **2** *transf* a leading seaman in the Navy, the anchor badge on his sleeve being likened to a pickaxe *20-*, *WC*. [var of *gellock* (GAVELOCK)]

Killie *n* nickname for Kilmarnock football team *20-*. [f Burns *Per Contra*]

killiecoup &c [kɪlɪˈkʌup] *n* a tumble head over heels *19-20*, *chf S*. [see SND]

killieleepie &c [kɪlɪˈlipɪ] *n* the common sandpiper *19-e20*, *local*. [imit]

killiemankie &c [*kɪlɪˈmaŋkɪ] *n* = calamanco, a kind of woollen cloth *17-18*. [*cf* MANKIE]

killie-shangie *see* COLLIESHANGIE

killing *see* KEELIN

killogie &c; kiln-logie &c *18-20* [kɪˈlogɪ, kə-] *n* applied to various parts of a corn- or maltkiln: **1** the lower part, under the drying chamber; the kiln itself *16-e20*; **2** the fire or fireplace *la18-*, *now Sh*; **3** the covered space in front of the fireplace *19-20*. [KILL¹ + LOGIE; *usu* one word, latterly also two]

killyvie &c [kɪlɪˈvi] *n* a fuss, disturbance, to-do *19-20*, *WC*. [see SND]

killywimple [kɪlɪˈwɪmpl] *n* a trill or affectation in singing *19-e20*. [*killie* + WIMPLE]

Kilmarnock [kɪlˈmarnək] *n* **1** *also and orig* ~ **bonnet** a broad flat woollen bonnet of blue, black or red *19-*, *now chf hist*. **2** *also and orig* ~ **hood** *etc* a knitted woollen conical skull-cap worn as a nightcap or by indoor workers such as weavers *la18-e20*.

~ **shot** *in games, eg bowling, football* a safe shot, put deliberately wide or out of play; any kind of unsporting play *e20*, *Ags Fif Ayr*. [the Ayrshire town noted for its weaving]

Kilmaurs &c [kɪlˈmɑrz] *n* **sharp** *or* **gleg as a** ~ **whittle** quick-witted *la18-*, *Ayr*. [the Ayrshire town noted (*la17-18*) for its cutlery]

kiln *see* KILL¹

kiln-logie *see* KILLOGIE

kilt¹ &c *vt* **1** *chf of a woman* tuck (**up**) (one's clothes) *16-*. **2** lift (**up**), suspend (a thing); 'string up', hang (a person) *la17-e20*. *n* a part of modern male *Highland dress* (HIELAND): a kind of skirt, *usu* of TARTAN cloth, reaching to the knee and thickly pleated at the back *18-*; *cf* FILLEBEG. ~**ed** dressed in a KILT¹ *19-*. **high-~it** having the skirts well tucked up; *fig* immodest, indecent *la18-e20*. ~**ie** a wearer of the KILT¹; a soldier in a *Highland regiment* (HIELAND) *19-*. ~**ing &c** **1** the lap of a woman's petticoat *19-e19*. **2** a pleated frill on a petticoat *20-*, *Kcdn Ags Dmf*. [nME *kilt* (v), Norw, Dan *kilte* (v), ON *kelta*, *kjalta* (v) tuck up the clothes, ON *kilting* (n) the lap of a garment]

kilt² *vti* overturn, upset *19-*, *now midLoth S.* *n* a tilt, *esp masonry* the slope of a stone to allow water to run off, *esp* that on a staircase etc *19-20*. [obscure; perh irreg var of Eng *tilt*]

kilt³ *n* the proper way or knack of doing something *19-20*, *SW*. [prob f KILT²]

kilter &c *n* good spirits, fettle, *chf* **in** *or* **out of** ~ *18-*. [chf dial in Eng; also US]

kim *adj* **1** spirited, frolicsome, lively *19-20*, *chf Abd*. **2** spruce, nimble *19-20*, *Abd*. [unknown]

kimmer *see* CUMMER²

kimming &c *n* = cumin, the spice *16-e17*.

kimming *see* CUMMEN

kimpill *see* KEMPLE

kimpkin *see* KINKEN

kin &c; ken &c *la14-16, 20* (*Sh*) [kɪn] *n* **1** = kin, kinsfolk *la14-*. **2** a kinsman, relation *la15-*. **3** ancestral stock, familial origin, extraction, *freq* **of** (**ryal, gentle, etc**) ~ *la14-*. **4** the race or stock descended from a particular ancestor *la14-16*. *adj* related, akin *la18-*.

kindred &c, kinrede &c [*ˈkɪnrɪd, *-red, &c] *n* **1** = kindred *la16-*. **2** a *or* one's family, CLAN etc, *specif* applied to the extended family groups in the kin-based society of Celtic Scotland *16-*, *now hist*. ~**less** without noble or influential relatives *la17-19*. **kinrent &c** [*ˈkɪnrɛnt] *n* = kindred, *15-16* [only Sc; metath f ME *kinreden* > *kinrede* above; *cf* MANRENT].

kinbut(t)e &c [*ˈkɪnbøt] *n* compensation paid for manslaughter by the slayer to the *kindred* of the slain, *assythment* (ASSYTH) *15-e18*.

be of ~ be related **to** *15-17*. **redd oot** *or* **up** ~ trace one's lineage *la19-*, *local Sh-Dmf*. **store the** ~ *chf in negative* fail to keep up the stock; be unable to keep going, last or live *la19-*, *NE*.

kinallie *see* CANALLY

kinbutte *see* KIN

kinch¹ &c; kench [kɪnʃ, kɛnʃ] *n* **1** a twist or doubling in a rope, a kink; a loop, noose, running knot *19-*, *local N-S*. **2** *fig* a tight corner, predicament, a difficult problem *20-*, *Abd Fif*. **3** a sudden twist in wrestling *19-*, *now Per Fif Wgt*.
vt **1** twist a loop in (a rope) with a stick in order to tighten it *19-*, *now NE-C*. **2** tie up (a bundle etc) *19-*, *now SW*. **3** fasten a noose round the tongue, lips or muzzle of (a horse) *20-*, *local NE-Ayr*. **4** *weaving* fasten loops on to (bridles) *19-e20*. **5** throw (a stone) in a particular way, *chf* make (a flat stone) skip on the surface of water *e20*, *Fif Rox*. ~**er &c** = *n* 2, *20-*, *NE*. ~ **pin** a pin or rod used for *kinching* ropes *19-*, *now nEC*, *SW*. [parallel form to KINK¹ (as *bench* and BINK¹); *v* 5 may be a different word]

kinch² &c [*ˈkɪn(t)ʃ] *n* **1** the fall of the dice *la15*. **2** one's lot or fortune, *chf* **count one's** ~

la16-e17. [OF *keanche &c, cheance &c* the fall of the dice; also phr *conter sa keance*; *cf* MDu, MLowGer *kanse, kan(t)ze*]

kinch³ [kɪnʃ] *n* an (unexpected) advantage or opportunity *17-, chf NE Uls.*

keep ~**es** serve a turn, be useful in an emergency; fall in with the plans or ways of another *19-, chf SW.* [f KINCH¹ or KINCH²]

kind &c; keind &c *15-e20* [kəin(d)] *n* **1** = kind *14-.* **2** innate character or nature *la14-19.* **3** inherited character *15-, now S.* **4** the physical nature or constitution of a person or animal *la14-16.*

adj **1** *of a person or animal* native (**to** a place) *la14, 20- (Sh).* **2** belonging to one by birth or inheritance; lawful, rightful *la15-e18.* **3** *of a bondman or tenant* belonging by birth to the lands specified or to a particular lord *la14-e16.* **4** = kind *16-.*

vti **1** ~ **to** resemble, take after *20-, S.* **2** sort, arrange in kinds *20-, Loth Rox.*

adv, used unstressed after adjs somewhat, rather *la18-:* '*an odd kind chiel*'; *cf* LIKE¹ *adv.*

~**le** [ˈkɪn(d)l] *vi, of small animals, esp rabbits* produce young *20-, now Dmf.* ~**ly &c** [ˈkəin(d)lɪ] *adj* **1** natural; according to the natural order of things, normal; characteristic, innate; congenial *la14-, now Ork.* **2** = kindly *16-.* **3** related, of one's kindred *la16.* **4** (1) native, indigenous; true-born, rightful (ruler, subject etc) *16-19.* (2) *of a place* native to one, of one's origin *la16-e17.* **5** *of a possession, right etc* belonging to one by right of birth or heredity *16-17.* **6** *of a tenant or tacksman* (TACK²) having a right to the tenancy or TACK² in consequence of its long continued occupation by oneself or one's ancestors, rather than by *feudal* (FEU) charter etc, *chf* ~**ly tenant** *etc, now only* **King's Kindly Tenants of Lochmaben** *etc 16-.* **7** having the right of a *kindly* occupier **to** (the land etc specified) *16.* **8** *of lands, tacks* (TACK²) *etc* belonging to a person as the *kindly* occupier, *chf* ~**ly rowme, steding** *etc 16-e17.* **9** of a good or excellent nature or quality, thriving *la18-19.* ~**liness &c** the right of a ~*ly tenant (adj* 6) *17-18.* **maist** ~**ly tenant** best-entitled tenant *la16.* ~**ness &c** [ˈkəindnɛs] *n* **1** = kindness *15-.* **3** kinship, relationship by birth *15-e17.* **3** the prescriptive right of a *kindly tenant (adj* 6) to his holding or TACK² *16-e17, orig chf Lnk SW, only Sc.* **4** *appar* permission to occupy a holding with the friendly consent or goodwill of the landlord *16-17, only Sc.* **5** prescriptive or hereditary right or title *in gen, 16-e17, only Sc.*

~ **born(e)** *of a bondman* belonging by birth to a particular lord *15.* ~**lik &c** *adj* = kindly (*adj* 1) *la14-e16.*

(**a**) ~ **of** *freq in reduced form* **kinna &c** [ˈkəin(d)o, -ə, ˈkɪnə], **kin-a-wise** *C, S,* **kin-naweys** *C, S* [*C, S* ˈkɪnəˈwaɪz, -ˈwəɪz, -ˈwez] somewhat, rather *la19-.* **keind-o, no verra,**

bit gey = in a sort of way, yes and no *20-, now Bnf Fif.* **in a** ~ after a fashion *la19-, now NE Fif.* **not** *etc* **a ..** ~ not a .. of any description, not a single .. *20-, now Sh midLoth Kcb:* '*out she ran without a shawl kind on her*'. **of** ~ by birth or descent; by native constitution, naturally *15-e19.* **out of** (**the** *or* **one's**) ~ at variance with or contrary to one's inherited rank or character *16-e20.* **yon** ~ *euphemistic* not quite normal or proper; not worth or up to much, in indifferent health etc *20-, local Sh-Per WC.*

kindle *see* KENNLE

kindred *see* KIN

king &c; keeng *20, local Abd-WC* [kɪŋ, kiŋ] *n* **1** = king *la14-.* **2** *specif* = *Candlemas King* (CANLEMAS) *18-e20.* **3** *cock-fighting* the winning cock; its owner *la19, Abd Kcdn Slk.* **4** *chf* **kingis** *of silk thread, gloves, ale* of royal or excellent quality or make, of the finest sort *16.*

~**dom &c** *n* = kingdom *15-; cf* KINRICK. **the** ~**dom of Fife** Fife *la17-* [from its self-contained situation]. ~**lyke &c** = kingly, befitting a king *15* [only Sc; var of Eng *kingly*]. ~ **alison** *la19-e20, Kcdn,* ~(**'s**) **doctor ellison** *la19-e20, chf NE* the ladybird. ~ **ba &c** a children's game *20-, Ags Fif;* see SND. ~**'s chair**(**ie**) *la19-, chf NE Ags or* **cushion** *19-20, local* a seat formed by two children each of whom grasps one of his own wrists and the opposite wrist of the other child. ~**'s freemen** persons who by virtue of services rendered by themselves or their fathers or husbands in the army, navy etc had a statutory right to exercise trades as freemen without becoming members of their particular trade INCORPORATION *19.* ~**'s hood** *or* **head 1** the second of the four stomachs of a ruminant *19-, now Sh Edb Rox.* **2** *joc* the human stomach *la18.* **be a** ~ **tae** surpass, be superior to *la19-, now Sh-C Slk.* ~ (**a**)**cross the ditchie** a children's game *20-, Cai Ags;* see SND. ~ **coll-awa** the ladybird *la19-20, Kcdn.* ~ **of the herrings** the Arctic chimaera *la19-e20, Sh NE.* **K**~**'s Own Borderers** *1805-1887,* **K**~**'s Own Scottish Borderers** *1887-, now familiarly* **the KOSBs** the Scottish regiment first raised in 1689 as *Leven's* or *the Edinburgh Regiment.*

kingle &c; kennel [ˈkɪŋl, ˈkɛnl] *n* a kind of very hard sandstone *19-, now Fif.* [obscure]

kingrik *see* KINRICK

kink¹ *vti* **1** = kink, twist. **2** *vi, specif of wood* warp *la19-, now Ags Per Dmf.*

n **1** = kink, a bend, loop. **2** a crease, fold *la19-.*

kink² &c, kinke *vi* gasp or choke convulsively or spasmodically, *specif* **1** suffer an attack of coughing, *esp* whooping-cough *la18-, now local NE-Uls;* **2** choke with laughter *19-, now Abd SW, S Uls.*

n **1** a convulsive catching of the breath as in

whooping-cough; a fit of coughing *la17-*, *local Abd-Uls*. **2** a violent and irrepressible fit of laughter *la17-*, *local Abd-Uls*.

kinkers = ~ *cough, 20-, Abd Per Fif*.

~ **cough &c** *18-*, *now SW Slk*, ~ **host &c** *la16-*, *now Sh NE, EC, SW* whooping-cough. [nME *kinc*, OE *cincian*; *cf* LowGer *kinken*]

kinken, kinkin &c, kimpkin &c *la16-e17*, **quinquene &c** *la16* [*'kɪnkɪn, *'kɪŋ-, *'kɪmp-] *n* a keg, a small barrel, *appar* = a firkin or quarter barrel *la15-19*. [only Sc; MDu *kinnekijn*]

kin-kind &c [kɪn'kəin(d)] kind, sort, description, *chf* **all &c** ~ *la18-*, *now NE*. [by wrong division of *alkin kind* (A')]

kinle *see* KENNLE

kinnen, kinning *see* CUNING

kinnle *see* KENNLE

kinrede, kinrent *see* KIN

kinrick &c, kinrik, kingrik &c [*'kɪnrɪk, *'kɪŋ-] *n* = kingdom *la14-e20, latterly only literary*. [ME *kinrik, king-*, OE *cynerice, cyning-*]

kinsh¹ &c *n* a lever used in quarrying stones *19-*, *now Fif midLoth*. [see SND]

**kinsh² ** *n* a small quantity, a pinch *20-*, *Abd midLoth*. [perh parallel form to Eng *pinch*]

kintra *see* COUNTRA

Kintyre &c: ~ **pursevant &c** one of the Scottish PURSUIVANTS *la15-19*. [the district in Arg, [k(ɪ)n'taɪr]]

kinvaig *n* a small woollen plaid *19*, *chf S*. [obscure]

kiow-ow &c; keo &c *20-, SW* ['kjʌu (-'ʌu), kjo] *vi* talk or act frivolously, caper about, play the fool *la19-, N Gall Uls*.

n **1** a trick, ploy, carry-on *la19-, now Gall Uls*. **2** *chf in pl* things of no importance; silly chatter *19-, N*.

~**in** *adj* tattling, frivolous *19-, N Wgt*. ~**y** fussy, pottering *la19-, chf Ags*. [uncertain; perh imit of aimless chatter]

kip¹ &c; kepp *la16-18*, **kype** *20-* *n* **1** a jutting or projecting point on a hill; a peak *la18-*, *now midLoth, freq in place-names 17-, chf S*. **2** a turned-up nose *la19-*, *now Uls*. **3** the projecting cartilage on the lower jaw of the male salmon at spawning time *la19-, chf S*.

vi, chf **kippit &c 1** *of a hill* ? having a KIP¹ or KIPS¹ (*n* 1) *la14*; **2** *of a nose, a cow's horn etc* turned or tilted up *la16-*.

kipper pile or stack **up** carelessly *20-, now Abd*.

kippie *adj, of cattle* having upturned horns *19-*, *now Rox*. *n* a small hill *19-e20, local*.

~**-headed, -hedit** *of cattle* having upturned horns *la16-e18*. ~ **nose** a nose turned up at the tip *19-, now Rox*. [MDu, MLowGer *kippe* a point, peak]

kip² *vi* play truant from school *19-, now nEC midLoth Rox*.

play (**the**) ~ play truant *la19-, now Stlg Fif Edb*. [obscure]

kip³ *n* **1** a bundle or bunch containing a specific number (of hides, ropes or belts) *16-17*. **2** a small bundle *20-, Ork*.

vt tie up (hides, fish) in bundles *15-e16, 20* (*Sh*). [northern eModEng *kepe* a bundle of 30 or 50 hides, MDu, MLowGer *kip* a bundle, eModDu *kippen* put (fish) into kips; *cf* also ON *kippi* a bundle]

kip⁴ *n* **1** haste, hurry *19-, now Rox*. **2** a state of great excitement *20-, Abd Rox*. [prob reduced f KIPPAGE]

kipill *see* COUPLE

kippage &c *n* **1** the crew of a ship *e16-e17*. **2** disorder, confusion, fuss, predicament; a state of excitement or anger *19-e20*. **3** (good etc) spirits, fettle *20-, Cai Kcb*. [F *équipage* = *n* 1]

kipper &c *n* a large bowl; a large quantity (of food) *la19-, Bnf Kcdn*. [*cf* KYPE]

kipper *see* KIP¹

kippie &c *adj* left-handed *la19-, nEC*.

n **1** a left-handed person *la19-, now Per Fif*. **2** the left hand *20-, Per, Fif*. [obscure]

kippie, kippit *see* KIP¹

kipple *see* COUPLE

kirdandy [kɪr'dandɪ] *n* a row, uproar *la19-, Ayr Uls*. [f *Kirkdamdie* (*locally* [kɪr'dandɪ]), Barr, Ayrshire, where there was a famous and riotous fair]

kire &c [kəir] *n* = choir, a group of singers *20-*, *NE*; *cf* QUEIR.

kirk &c *n* **1** = church *la14-*, *in place-names la12-* (see DOST). **2** (1) *esp* before the Reformation, applied to the Roman Catholic Church, in Scotland and beyond *16-e17*; (2) after the Reformation, applied to the reformed church in Scotland both when episcopalian and when presbyterian in organization; since *la17* largely replaced by CHURCH in most formal contexts, but reappearing in recent years, *usu* as **the K~**, in all contexts except the official title *Church of Scotland* (CHURCH) *la16-*; see also ~ *session*, PRESBYTERY, SYNOD, *general assembly* (GENERAL), FREE, *Reformed Presbyterian Church* (REFORM), RELIEF, *seceder* (SECEDE), UNITED. **3** the ruling body or *kirk-session* of a local church *la16-e17*. **4** the *General Assembly* (GENERAL) of the *Church of Scotland* (CHURCH) *la16-e17*.

vt, chf in passive = be churched, *orig chf* of the first church attendance after a birth or marriage, *latterly* (*la19-*) also after a funeral or *eg* on the appointment of a civic or academic body *15-*.

~**ie &c** enthusiastically devoted to church affairs *20-, local*. **kirkin &c** a ceremonial attendance at church as in *v, la17-*: '*kirking of the council*'. **kirkin feast &c** a celebration held after the *kirkin, la15-e20*. **kirkin time** the time of church service *19-, Ork NE, SW*.

~**less 1** *of a* MINISTER: without a church *19-, now local Sh-Loth*. **2** *of a layman* not attending or not a member of a church *19-, now Dmf*.

~ **bedell &c** = ~ *officer*, 17. ~ **book** an official record book of a church *18-*, *now Ork Kcb*. ~ **box 1** a box in which church funds were kept; a church collection box, *latterly specif* the box containing the fund for the parish poor *17-e19*. ~ **claes** one's Sunday clothes *la19-*. ~ **door &c** = church door, *specif* the place where various public ceremonies were performed, *orig* baptisms and marriages (*la15-16*), later (*la16-17*) *esp* acts of repentance; also used for the collection of offerings, reading of proclamations etc (*la16-*). **do something at the ~ door** do something openly or in the public gaze *19-*, *now Ags Fif Loth*. ~ **folk 1** churchgoers, frequenters of the church; the congregation *la19-*. **2** church officials; ecclesiastics *19*. ~ **greedy** *chf in negative* not zealous in attendance at church *la19-*, *NE-S*. ~ **hole** the grave(yard) *la18-*, *Lnk Ayr*. ~ **house** a house belonging to or adjoining a church *16-17*. ~ **ladle** a small box on the end of a long handle for taking the collection *19-*. **~land** = church-land, a *glebe* (GLEIB) *la15-*, *now local Sh-Ayr*. ~ **man 1** an ecclesiastic *la14-*, *now Sh Ork*. **2** a regular churchgoer *la17-*, *now Sh NE*. ~ **master &c 1** the official appointed by the BURGH etc to take charge of the upkeep of the church building *la15-17*. **2** a church treasurer or DEACON[2] appointed by the ~ *session*, *la16-e17*. **3** a paid kirk *officer* appointed by the BURGH *la16-e17*, *Kcb*. **4** an elected officer of a craft or the merchant guild responsible for the upkeep of the fraternity's altar and chaplaincy in the parish church *la15-16*, *Edb Gsw*. ~ **mense** a decent appearance suitable for church, *chf* **gie claes ~ mense** wear a new garment at church for the first time *20-*, *now Bwk*. ~ **officer &c** *now usu* anglicized as *church officer* (CHURCH) a paid official with the job of keeping order in the church and parish, attending the *kirk-session* and carrying out its edicts; a *beadle* (BEDDAL) *la16-*, *now usu* anglicized as *church* ~ **reekit** bigoted *19-e20*. ~ **road** a road or path used by parishioners going to the parish church, and constituting a right of way *18-*, *chf NE*. ~ **session** *Presbyterian Church* the lowest court, consisting of the MINISTER and the ELDERS of the congregation and exercising its functions of church government within a parish *17-*; *cf* SESSION. ~ **shune** shoes kept for churchgoing *la19-*, *local Sh-Dmf*. ~ **skail(ing)** the dispersal of the congregation after worship *19-*, *local*. ~ **stile** a stile or narrow entrance to a churchyard; *latterly* common as a meeting-place, where announcements were made and the bier was received into the churchyard at funerals *15-19*. ~ **toun &c** *chf* the town or village in which the parish church is situated *15-*, *freq in place-names* *12-*. ~ **yaird &c** = churchyard *la14-*. ~ **yaird deserter** a sickly-looking person, one who looks as if he should be in his grave *19-*, *now NE*. ~ **yaird hoast** *chf joc* a churchyard

cough *20-*. ~ **werk** building work on a church *15-17*. **maister of the ~ werk** = ~ *master* 1, *15-17*, *Abd*. (**the**) **Auld K~ 1** the established Church of Scotland as opposed to other presbyterian denominations, *esp* after the DISRUPTION *19-e20*. **2** *joc* name for WHISKY *la19-*. **come into the body of the ~** *of a person sitting etc apart* come forward and join the main company *20-*. **keep the ~** (**at ..**) retain one's membership on the Communion Roll (of a particular church) though living outside its parish boundaries *19-*, *now Abd Ags*. **K~ of Scotland** title of the established reformed church in Scotland *la16-*; *cf n* 2 and *Church of Scotland* (CHURCH). ~ **and/or market** in all the public affairs of life *18-*. **mak a ~ and/or a mill o** do whatever one wishes with, make or mar, *usu* implying indifference on the part of the speaker; *orig*, make the best of *18-*. **man of ~** = ~ *man* 1, *la15-16*. **neither big ~s nor place ministers** be engaged in some questionable activity *la19-*, *NE*. **ride** (**on**) **the rigging o the ~** be an excessive partisan of one's own church *20-*, *N Fif SW*. [*n and east midl* ME, *la*OE *kirke &c*, ON *kirkja*, f OE *cirice* > *s*ME *chirche*; *cf* CHURCH]

Kirkcaldy [kɪrˈkɑdɪ, -ˈkadɪ] ~ **stripe** a distinctive stripe characteristic of certain kinds of cloth made in Kirkcaldy *la19-*, *now Ags Per Fif*. [the Fif seaport]

kirmash &c [kərˈmaʃ] *n* a crash, noise and confusion, hullabaloo *19-*, *now Ork*. [see SND]

kirn[1] &c, curn &c *20-*, *Cai Edb Arg*; **kern &c** *la17-20 n* **1** = churn; a churnful *16-*. **2** *freq in place-names* a natural feature resembling a churn in noise, motion or shape *la18-*, *chf Sh Ork*. **3** milk in the process of being churned; buttermilk *19-*, *now Abd Fif*. **4** a churning motion, a confused stirring *la19-*. **5** a sloppy mess, as of mud; a distasteful mixture of food, liquid etc *19-*, *Sh Abd Fif*. **6** a muddle, jumble, confusion *la20-*, *local Sh-Kcb*. **7** a confused stir or uproar, a throng *20-*, *NE Ags*. **8** work done in a lazy, slovenly or disgusting way *la19-*, *NE*. **9** a rummaging or pottering; an aimless trifling (**with**) *la19-*, *NE*. *vti* **1** *vt* = churn *la16-*. **2** stir, mix up or together with a churning motion *la17-*, *now Sh NE Ags*. **3** (1) cause to turn or rotate *20-*, *now Gall*. (2) bore with a drill or circular chisel *la19-*, *now Fif*. **4** *vi* (1) rummage, search, hunt or poke about *la19-*, *Sh NE-Per*. (2) work with one's hands in a sloppy, purposeless or disgusting way *19-*, *now local Sh-Fif*. **5** *of a crowd* swarm, mill about *20-*, *local Sh-Fif SW*. **6** *chf* ~ **wi** fuss over, mollycoddle; be constantly and demonstratively affectionate towards, 'pet' *la18-*, *NE*. **~ie &c** = *n* 3, *la19-*, *Ags Per Rox*. **~ing &c** *n* one complete act of churning; the quantity of milk required for this (*local*), the quantity of butter so produced (local NE-S) 20-. adj footling, inefficient 20-, NE Ags; cf v 4 (2). ~ing day the day on which churning was done la19-, now local Sh-Ags Kcb. ~ing rung the plunger of a churn 19-e20, WC Dmf.

~ milk &c buttermilk; curds made from buttermilk 16-, now local. ~ staff 17-, now Sh Ork Abd, ~ stick 20-, now Bnf (the handle of) the plunger of an upright churn.

the ~'s brok(ken) the milk is beginning to form into butter la20-, local Sh-Ayr. milk ~ a churn for milk la15-, now Sh Ork. stannin ~ an upright churn worked by a plunger 20-, Kcdn Fif Kcb.

kirn² &c n 1 a celebration marking the end of the harvest, a harvest-home 17-20, C, S. 2 the last sheaf or handful of corn of the harvest, freq plaited and ornamented etc for display 19-, now Dmf.

~ baby 19-e20, ~ dollie &c 19-, now Fif the decorated female effigy made from the last sheaf or handful of corn to be cut, a corn-dolly. ~ cut the last handful of corn to be cut 19-e20, S. ~ supper the celebration held when the corn is cut 19-, now Fif Dmf Uls.

win the ~ gain the honour of cutting the last sheaf; of a band of reapers be the first to finish la18-e20. [cf CURN¹; see SND]

kirnel &c, kirnell n 1 = kernel la15-, now Kcb. 2 a lump under the skin, esp in the neck; a swollen gland 19-, now Fif-Rox. 3 in pl animal glands used as food, lamb's fry, lamb's testicles 18-, now Gall.

wax(en) or waxing ~s = n 2, 18-, local Fif-Rox.

kirnell &c n 1 = crenel, a notch in a battlement la14-17. 2 in pl battlements 16. [northern and n midl ME kirnel, ME kernel, northern OF kernel, OF quernel, var of OF crenel]

kirnell see KIRNEL

kirr &c adj 1 cheerful, lively, brisk; self-satisfied la18-e20, SW. 2 amorous, wanton 19, SW. [see SND]

kirrie dumplin the flower cluster of the primula denticulata, 20-, Ags Per. [abbrev of the place-name Kirriemuir, where appar they are common, + dumpling f the rounded shape]

kirsp &c n = crisp, a fine fabric, gauze or crêpe la15-e16. [metath]

kirsten &c la18-, christen ['kɪrsn] vt = christen la16-.

~ing &c = christening 19-. christening bit or piece = baby's piece (PIECE) la19-, chf Edb.

kirsty ['kɪrstɪ] n a WHISKY jar 20, now Fif Loth. [f the girl's name Kirsty (short for Christine)]

kis see CAUSE

kiss &c, kis &c la14-17 n (16-), vti (la14-) = kiss.

~-my-luif &c a fawner, toady, effeminate person la19-. ~ my erse &c expression of abusive contempt 16-17.

kist &c; kest la15-e19; keist &c la16-e17 [kɪst;

Sh also kjɪst; *kɛst, *kist] n 1 (1) = chest, a trunk, large box la14-. (2) = chest, the thorax la19-. 2 a case for storing or transporting certain kinds of dry goods or merchandise; a packing case la15-e17. 3 a coffin la14-, Gen except S. 4 a kind of fish-trap, appar = CRUIVE la16-e17, Inv.

vt 1 put or enclose in a coffin 18-. 2 place or pack in a box or chest, lay up, store, save la19-, NE Ags Ayr.

~in(g) the laying of a corpse in its coffin on the night before the funeral with accompanying ceremonies and entertainment 19-e20.

~ locker a small compartment in a trunk for keeping money and valuables la18-, local. ~ neuk &c a corner of a chest reserved for money or valuables la18-, now local Sh-Ayr. flit one's ~ neuk move from one's accustomed place 20-, NE.

~ (fu) o whistles 1 derog a church organ 18-, now literary. 2 joc a wheezy chest la20-, Cai Ags Per. ~ o(f) drawers = chest of drawers la19-. [northern and n midl ME kist, ON kista; cf Norw, Sw kista, Da kiste]

kist see CAST

kit &c n 1 a small, usu wooden, tub la14-20. 2 a fair amount (of something, esp food) la19-, now Rox. 3 = kit, a soldier's equipment etc. vt place or pack in a KIT (n 1) 18-e19.

kitchen &c, kiching &c 16-17, kechin &c la14-19; keiching &c 16-e20 ['kɪtʃɪn; Sh Rox also 'kitʃɪn] n 1 = kitchen 15-. 2 an allowance of food from the kitchen (eg of meat) supplied or stored as one's provisions 14-e17. 3 anything served in addition to a plain food such as bread or potatoes la15-, Gen except N. 4 fig (1) perquisites of food, esp those given to servants la19-e20. (2) a money allowance in lieu la18-e19. 5 also and chf tea ~ a tea-urn la18-e19.

vt 1 give flavour to, season 18-. 2 make (something) go far, spin out, use sparingly 18-, now Sh S.

~less lacking anything that will give taste or savour 19-, now Sh. ~ fee tallow; dripping, formerly the perquisite of the cook la15-. ~ meit = n 2, la16-e17.

kitchie &c la16-, kiché e16 ['kɪtʃɪ] n 1 = KITCHEN n 1 (16-, chf N), 3 (la19-, now Sh N). v 1 vt = KITCHEN v 1, la19-, Sh N. 2 vi, of farm-servants take one's meals in the farm-kitchen as opposed to living in a BOTHY or cot-house (COT), live in 20-, NE.

kite [kəit] n = quoit 20-; cf QUOIT.

kiteral e20, kytrall &c la16; ketterel &c la16, e19 [*'kɛt(ə)rəl, *?'kəit-] n strong term of abuse for a person. [see DOST, SND]

kith &c [kɪθ] n 1 a person's acquaintances, neighbours and kinsfolk la14-. 2 one's native country or district; in gen a country or nation la15-e17. 3 knowledge of how to behave, courtly or refined behaviour, *only in* **cumly in, to** *or with* ~ *la15*. [northern and n midl ME *kith*, OE *cȳðð*]

kithan ['kɪθən] *n, also of women* **kithag** ['kɪθəg] a rascal, blackguard; a tricky person *20-, Cai*. [see SND]

kithing *see* KITTLIN

kittag *see* KITTOK

kittie[1] *n* **1** familiar or contemptuous term for a woman or girl, *specif* (1) a giddy, skittish young woman *16-, now NE*; (2) a woman of doubtful character, a whore *la19-, Sh NE*. **2** the jack in the game of bowls *la19-, local NE-Loth*. **3** = *kittiwake, la19-, now NE Ags Fif*.
~ **cat** the piece of wood etc hit by the sticks in the game of SHINTY *19-, S*. ~ **neddie** *or* ~ **needy** the common sandpiper *la19-, now Abd*. ~ **unsell** = *n* 1 (2), *la16*. **kittiwake &c** the kittiwake *la17-* [earlier in Sc]. ~ **wren** the wren *19-, now Loth Dmf Rox*; cf *cutty wran* (CUT[1]). [chf f pet form of *Katherine*, but see SND; cf KATIE and KITTOK]

kittie[2] *n* prison, jail, the village lock-up *la19-, S Uls*. [nEng dial and slang]

kittle[1] **&c**, **kittill &c**, **cuittle &c** *la18-, now Lnk Kcb*; **kyittle &c** *la19-, Sh Ork* ['kɪtl; *Sh Ork* 'kjɪtl; *S also* ? 'kɒtl] *vti* **1** = tickle *16-*. **2** *vt, fig, freq* ~ **up**: (1) stimulate, please; make excited *16-, now local NE-S*; (2) stir (a fire) *20-, local NE-S*; (3) provoke, annoy, tease *la19-, Gen except Sh Ork*; (4) chide, reprove *la19-, now Abd midLoth*. **3** *vi, freq* ~ **up**: (1) *of the wind* freshen, blow more strongly and gustily *19-, now NE*; (2) *of persons* become angry, moved or annoyed *la19-, now Abd*; (3) *of a horse* become restive *la19-, now NE Ags Per*; (4) *of circumstances, health etc* improve *20-, Abd Ags*. **4** set (the strings of a musical instrument) in motion, tune (**up**), strike **up** (a tune) *la18-*. **5** puzzle, perplex, nonplus *19-, now midLoth Rox*. **6** *curling* (CURL) give speed to (a stone) by sweeping the ice before it *la19-*.
n **1** = tickle *19-*. **2** an irritation (of the throat) *la19-*. **3** *fig* a pleasurable excitement, stimulus *19-*. **4** a stir, a poke (of a fire) *20-, local NE-Rox*. **5** a difficult feat *20-, Loth-Gall S*. **6** a polish, shine *20-, NE*.
adj **1** ticklish, tickly *la16-, now local*. **2** *of persons or things* (1) touchy, easily upset or offended, difficult to deal with *la16-, now local NE-Kcb*; (2) inconstant, unreliable, fickle *la16-, now local NE-S*. **3** *of a task or problem* hard to deal with, intractable, tricky, puzzling *la16-, now local*. **4** *of an angle or bend* awkward, difficult to negotiate *19-, local NE-S*. **5** *of writers, their words or thought* difficult (to understand or pronounce), obscure *18-19*. **6** cunning, adept, skilful *19-, now Ags*. **7** liable, inclined **to** .. *la18-20, SW*.
kittlie &c **1** *of things* tickly, causing a tickling sensation; *of persons* susceptible to tickling, itchy, ticklish *19-*. **2** sensitive, easily roused or

provoked *19-20*. **3** troublesome, difficult, ticklish, precarious; obscure, difficult, puzzling *19-, now NE Fif Loth*. ~**some** = *adj* 3, *20-, local NE-S*.
~ **cattle** persons (or animals) who are unmanageable, capricious, difficult *19-*. ~ **the-cowt, kittlie-cout** [*-'kʌut*] a children's game similar to 'hunt the thimble' *e19*. ~ **in the trot** quick-tempered, irritable *la19-20, NE*. [latterly (*la15-*) chf Sc, northern and n midl Eng dial; la nME *kytylle*, laME *ketil*; cf nME *kitlynge* verbal noun, laOE *kitelung*, prob f ON *kitla*]

kittle[2] **&c** *vi* **1** give birth: (1) *of cats* kitten *la18-*; (2) *of other small animals* produce young *19-, local*; (3) *contemptuous, of a woman*, *19-20*. **2** *vi and passive, of an idea etc* be engendered, spring into being *e19*.
be in kittle *of certain small animals* be (on the point of) giving birth *la20-, NE Kcb*. [prob back-formation f KITTLIN; cf Norw *kjetla*]

kittlin &c, kitling &c *n* **1** = a kitten *la16-*. **2** the young of other small animals *la18-20*. **3** *contemptuous, of persons, esp children* a whelp, brat *16-e17*. [ME *kiteling*, ON *ketlingr* dim of *kǫttr* a cat]

kittok &c *n* **1** term for a woman or girl of low rank or character *la15-16*. **2** **kittag &c** *Cai*, **kittock &c** *Ork* the kittiwake *la19*. [pet form of *Katherine*; cf KITTIE[1]. SND *kittie* (*n*[1])]

kiver *see* COVER[1]

kizen *see* GIZZEN

kizzen &c *la19-*, **cusine &c** *15-17*, **cusing &c** *la14-20*, **cusigne** *e17*, **cousigne &c** *la16-17*; **cussin(g) &c** *16-e18*, **cusa(i)n** *la17* ['kɪzn; 'kʌzn; *Fif also* 'kɪʒn, 'keʒn; *'kozɪn; *'kuzɪn] *n* = cousin.
cusines &c, cousinace &c, cousingnes &c *la15-16* [*'kozɪnɛs, *'kʌzɪn-, *'kuzɪn-] a female cousin *la14-16*.

kjunning *see* CUNING

kley *see* CLAY

klister *see* CLEESTER

klondyke *vti, freq* **klondyker, klondyking** an exporter or the exporting to the Continent of fresh fish (*orig* herring, *now chf* mackerel) *orig* by fast ship, *now* direct to factory ships for processing on board *20-*. [f *Klondyke*, Alaska = a 'gold-mine', the practice being much more profitable than salt-curing]

klurt *see* CLART[1]

knab[1] *n, chf* ~**lick &c** **1** a knot or root of fir *la19-, Bnf*. **2** a boulder *19-, NE*.
adj irregularly shaped, knotty, rough *18-20, N*. [var of Eng *knob*]

knab[2] **&c, nabb** *n* a person of importance or prestige; a person of moderate wealth, a person with social pretensions, a snob *17-, now local N-S*.
~**ery &c** gentry *19-*. **knabbie &c** having rank, means or position; genteel, pretentious *la18-19*. **nabbie** a type of herring-fishing boat *la19-, chf*

WC, SW [f its smart appearance]. **half ~bie** a
member of the middle-class *la19-20*. [see
SND]
knab &c *see* KNAP[2]
knab(b) *see* NABB
knabbie *see* KNAP[2]
knack &c, knak &c *vti* **1** make a sharp cracking noise: (1) *in gen, 19*-; (2) *vt, specif* snap (the
fingers) *18*-, *now NE Loth*; (3) break or snap
with a sharp sound *la19*-, *now local NE-Uls*. **2**
strike or slash sharply *la19*-, *local Sh-Per*. **3**
make fun of; deride *15-e16, la19-20 (Ayr)*, *only
Sc*. **4** *vi* chatter (**away**) *la19*-, *NE Uls*.
n **1** a sharp clicking, breaking or striking noise;
a sharp blow, a crack *la18*-, *now Ork NE*. **2** a
mocking retort; a gibe *la15-16, la19-20, only Sc*.
3 *in pl* a throat disease of poultry; *joc* any complaint characterized by wheezing *19-20*, *chf
Rox*.
~ aff *vt* strike or knock off, as with a sharp
implement *20*-, *Sh NE*. [imit; *cf* Eng *knack*,
MDu *knacken*, MLowGer *knaken*, Sw *knaka*]
knackie &c; nacky &c *adj* **1** adroit, deft, ingenious, skilful *18*-. **2** (1) nimble, smart *la19*-.
(2) *of persons or things* trim, neatly-built, spruce
la19-. **3** witty, pleasant in conversation, face-
tious *18*-. [f Eng *knack* a skilful way of doing
something; *cf* KNACK *v* 3, *n* 2]
knag[1] &c; nag *n* **1** a knot or spur projecting
from a tree *la18*-, *now NE Per Fif*. **2** a peg etc
for hanging things on *16*-, *now local Ags-Dmf*.
at the ~ an the widdie at variance, at loggerheads *la19-20, NE*. [laME *knag(ge)*; *cf*
MLowGer *knagge*, Norw *knag*]
knag[2] &c, knog &c *18*- *n* **1** a keg *16*-, *now Uls*.
2 a small wooden dish with one stave extended
to form the handle *la18-e20*. [see SND]
knak *see* KNACK
knap[1] &c *la16*- *n* **1** *also* **knop &c** an ornamental
knob, boss or stud *15-18*. **2** a rounded knob, a
lump or bump; a protuberance *18*-, *now Ork
NE*. **3** (1) *also* **knop &c** a tassel *la15-e18*. (2)
specif one on a bonnet or nightcap *la19*-, *now Sh
Per*. **4** (1) the point of the elbow *la16*-, *now Sh*.
(2) the kneecap *19*-, *now Kcdn Ags Fif*. **5** a shin
of beef *la17*-. **6** a hillock or knoll *19*-, *local
Ork-Fif*.
knapdarloch &c [knap'dɑrləx, -lək, -'dorlək]
1 a knot of hardened dirt and dung or matted
hair hanging from the coat or tail of an animal
la19-, *chf NE*. **2** contemptuous term for an
undersized, dirty, cheeky person *20*-, *NE*.
knappie &c 1 lumpy, bumpy *la19*-, *now Abd*.
2 friable; crisp, brittle *la18*-, *now Uls*. **knappit**
&c, knoppit ornamented with knobs or tassels
la15-e17. **knapplach &c** ['(k)naplǝx, -lǝk] a
lump, a large protuberance, a rough projection
la19-e20, NE.
~ bane *in cattle* the knee or knuckle-joint *20*-.
~ (silk) button a knob-shaped button *e17*.
[ME *knoppe &c, knappe &c*]
knap[2] &c, knab &c *19-e20*, **nab** *19 v* **1** *vt*

knock, strike sharply, rap *la15*-, *now local*. **2**
(1) break sharply, snag *19*-, *now local Sh-Kcb*.
(2) *specif* break (stones) for building, roadmaking *e17, 19*-. **3** break or snap with the teeth,
munch, eat greedily *19*-, *chf Sh*. **4** *esp of a Scot
aping 'fine' English* speak in an affected or
clipped, mincing way *la16*-, *Sh*.
n **1** a sharp knock or blow, a rap *16*-, *now local*.
2 (1) a snap, bite *la19*-, *now Sh Ork*. (2) a morsel of food, a bite *19*-, *now Sh NE Loth*.
knapper 1 *freq* **stane-knapper** a stone-
breaker *la19*-. **2** a small hammer used by
stone-breakers *la19*-, *local*. **3** one who bites or
snaps with the teeth (to drive off cats etc); a
boor *e16*. **knapper-knytlych &c** ['knapǝr(t)
'knəitlɪx, 'knɪpǝr'knatlɪx]   short-tempered;
mean *e20, Abd*.
knap at the wind *n, vi* (take) a mere bite
la19-20, Ork Abd. [imit; *cf* eModEng *knap*,
GNAP; MDu *cnappen*, MLowGer *knappen* crack,
snap etc, Norw *knapa* eat quickly and noisily]
knap[3] &c *n* a sturdy lad; a chap *19*-, *now NE*.
(k)nappy stout, sturdy, strong *19-20*. [perh f
KNAP[1]]
knap *see* NAP[1]
knapburd &c [*'knapbǝrd, &c*] *n, appar* =
clapboard *la16-17*. [*kn-* after KNAPPEL etc]
knapdarloch *see* KNAP[1]
knape &c *n* a lad, attendant *la15-e17*. [ME; OE
cnapa]
knapholt,   knappald,   knappart   *see*
KNAPPEL
knapparts,   knapper(t)s &c ['(k)napǝrts,
'gnap-] *n pl* **1** the tuberous vetch, heath pea
19-, *N*. **2** the acorn *la17-e18*. [KNAP[1] +
reduced form of *wort*; *cf* Norw *knappurt*, Dan
knapurt, MLowGer *knōpwort* as names of various
herbs]
knappel &c *16-20*, **knapholt &c** *la15-e17*,
knappet(t) &c   *16-e17*;   **knappald &c**
la15-e17,   **knappart &c**   *la16-17* [*'knapl*,
*'knap(h)ǝld, *-(h)olt, *-(h)ard, *-ǝt, &c*] *n*
clapboard, split oak smaller than wainscot, *chf*
used as barrel-staves and as panelling or boarding *la15-20*; *cf* KNAPBURD. [corresponding to
laME, eModEng *clappalde*, MLowGer, MDu
klapholt, w *kn* for *cl* as in eModDan *knapholt*
beside *klapholt*]
knappiskaw *see* KNAPSCALL
knapplach *see* KNAP[1]
knappy *see* KNAP[3]
knapscall &c; -ska(w) *la15-16*, **knappiskaw &c** *la16* [*'knapskal, *-ska, *-ske,
'knep-] *n* a metal shell or skullcap, worn
defensively, commonly under a bonnet; *latterly
sometimes also* shell and bonnet together
la15-e17.
~ bonnet a bonnet for covering a KNAPSCALL;
latterly shell and bonnet together *la16-e17*.
[obscure]
knapscap &c *n, literary or hist* = knapscall *19*.
[f prec, w substitution of *cap*]

knapska(w) *see* KNAPSCALL
knapwood &c [*'knapwɪd, &c] *n* = KNAPPEL *la17-e18.* [*cf* KNAPBURD]
knar &c *n* **1** a knot in wood *19-20.* **2** *fig* a burly, stockily-built person *20*, *NE*. [ME *knarre* a knot; a thickset fellow; *cf* Du *knar*, LowGer *knarre*]
knarholt; knerrott &c [*'knarholt, *'knarət] *n* clapboard *e16.* [MLowGer, MDu *knarholt; cf* KNAPPEL]
knave &c; **kneave** &c *la16-17* [(k)nev] *n* **1** = knave *la14-.* **2** a lad or man employed as a servant; a menial *la14-e19, latterly literary.*
~**ship, knaschip** &c *chf NE* [*'knevʃɪp, *'kne(:)ʃɪp] **1** the office of under-miller or miller's assistant; the perquisites of this *16-17.* **2** a small quantity of corn or meal in addition to the MULTURE levied on each lot of corn ground at a mill, as payment for the miller's servants *14-e19.*
~ **bairn**, ~ **child** a male child *la14-16.*
knaw[1] &c *la14-19*, **know** *la15- vti, ptp also* **knawin** &c *la14-e17*, **knawn** &c *la16-e19* **1** = know *la14-.* **2** make judicial inquiry into, take legal cognizance of *15-e17.*
knowin ['noɪn] a small amount *la19-, Wgt Uls* [*cf kenning* 2 (KEN)]. ~**lage** &c *n* **1** = knowledge *15-.* **2** judicial or authoritative knowledge; formal investigation to obtain this; legal cognizance *15-e17, freq in phrs* **gif a** ~**lage of** *or* **be** (**ane**) **assise** *la14-e15*, **tak** ~**lage** *la14-e17*, **pas, put** *or* **tak** (**something, a person**) **to the** ~**lage of ane assise** *la15-e17.* **3** knowledge, understanding or ability (to do something) *la15-16.* ~**lege** *vt* **1** = acknowledge *15-la16.* **2** = *v* 2, *e17.*
that is to ~ = that is to say, namely, to wit *e16* [*cf* L *scīlicet*]. [*cf* KEN]
knaw[2] *vti* = gnaw *16.*
kne *see* KNEE
kneave *see* KNAVE
kned [(k)nɛd] *v* **1** *vt* = knead *la16-20.* **2** tire out *20*, *Ags.* **3** *vi, of animals* breathe with effort, pant *20, Cai.*
knee &c, **kne; knie** *la16-17*, **kené** &c *16-e17* [(k)ni; *Rox* nəi; *Bwk also* ne] *n* **1** = knee *la14-.* **2** a bend in a part of a plough, as in the plough-beam (*20, Sh*) or coulter-stem (*20-, Fif Loth*). *vti* bend so as to form a knee-shaped angle: (1) *of a nail or staple, 19-, now Per Fif;* (2) *of the stalks of plants, 19-.*
kneed, kneit [(k)niːd; *'kniɪt] *adj* **1** *of a metal bar or band* having an angular bend *la16-e19.* **2** = kneed.
~ **breeks** = knee-breeches *19-.* ~ **head** &c a piece of naturally-bent timber used to secure together parts of a ship, a knee-timber in a boat *la15-, latterly (la17-) Sh Ork.* ~ **hicht** a small child, one no higher than the knee *la19-, Sh Ork Dmf.* ~ **ill**(**s**) a disease affecting *esp* the knee-joints of cattle *19-, now Ags Ayr.* ~ **lid** the

kneecap *19-, now Ags Fif Ayr.* ~ **tea** tea in which cup and plate are held on the knee *la19-, NE.*
kneef &c [knif; *Sh Ork* (k)n(j)ɪf; *Bnf also* gnɪf] *adj* **1** mentally or physically alert, agile *18-, chf Sh-N.* **2** fit, in sound health and spirits *20-, N Per.* [obscure]
kneel *see* KNELE
kneep &c [(k)nip; *Ags Per* (t)nəip] *n* a lump *la19-, NE.*
~**lach, **~**le** ['(k)nipləx, '(k)nipl] a large lump or piece *la19-, NE Ags.* [uncertain]
kneetle *see* KNUITLE
kneevle &c ['knivl] *n* a bit, lump *la18-, Mry Bnf Ayr.*
kneevlick &c ['knivlək] a big lump, as of food, *esp* cheese *la19-, chf NE.* [see SND]
kneggum &c ['knɛgəm, 'gnɛg-, '(k)nag-] *n* a pungent, disagreeable taste or flavour *la18-, local N Kcb.* [see SND]
kneit *see* KNEE
knele; kneel &c *17-* [(k)nil] *vi* = kneel: **1** *in gen, la14-;* **2** *specif* with reference to the question of kneeling to receive Communion *17.*
knell &c *vti* **1** *of a bell etc* ring *la15-17.* **2** *vt* strike with a resounding blow, knock *16-20.* *n* **1** = knell *16-.* **2** a loud echoing boom, as of a gun; a thud *la19-, NE.*
knerrott *see* KNARHOLT
knetting *see* KNIT
knevell *see* NEVEL
knewel &c, **knewill** [knil; *'kn(j)u(ə)l] *n* a cross-bar or toggle of wood or metal, *specif* **1** the wooden pin on the end of a rope or halter *17-20, NE Ags Per;* **2** the tag put through the ring on the rope or chain for tethering cattle in a stall *19-20, Abd Fif.* [MLowGer, Du *knevel*, ON *knefill*]
knibloch &c; **kniblock** &c ['knɪbləx, -lək; *'knʌb-] *n* a small rounded stone, a hard clod of earth; a lump *in gen, 19-20.* [*cf* KNAB[1]]
knicht &c, **knight** &c [knɪxt] *n* = knight *la14-.*
vt make (someone) a knight *la16-.*
~**hede** &c = knighthood *la14-e17.* **knichtit** highly gratified as by some honour, delighted with oneself *la20-, Abd.* ~**lik** &c *adj* = knightly *15-e16.* *adv* = knightly *la14-la16, only Sc.*
~ **baronet** a baronet (of Nova Scotia) *17.* ~ **preceptor** (**of Torphichen**) = the Preceptor of Torphichen *e16.*
knick; nick *19- v* **1** *vi* make a cracking, clicking or ticking sound *18-, now Ork Ags.* **2** *vt* (1) cause to make a cracking or clicking sound; *esp* of the fingers *19-, now NE Ags.* (2) break, snap *19-, now Cai.* **3** *marbles* propel smartly with thumb and forefinger, flick *19-, now Bnf Gsw Wgt.*
n a click, a cracking or sharp rapping sound *la19-, Sh Ork NE Ags.*
nicker &c *n* a marble used for striking *la19-,

now Gsw. *v* **1** *vi* make a cracking or clicking sound *20-, now Sh.* **2** *vt* propel (a marble) *la20-, Abd.* [imit; *cf* MLowGer *knicken,* Du *knikken,* Norw *knekkja* and KNACK]

knick-knack *n* **nick-nacket** = knick-knack *la18-, now NE Fif Loth.*

knickle *see* KNUCKLE

knidge &c *la18-,* **gnidge** *18-19,* N *vti* rub, squeeze, press, *esp* with the knee *la18-, now Sh N.*

n a forceful squeeze, an application of pressure, *esp* with the knees *la19-, Sh N.* [see SND]

knidge *see* KNITCH

knie *see* KNEE

knife *n* **1** = knife *la14-.* **2** a knife worn with a sword or WHINGER, *appar* in the same sheath, a *byknife* (BY) *16-17.*

knifie &c a boys' game in which each player tries to stick an open knife into the ground by sliding or tossing it from different parts of the arms and body *20-.*

pair of kniffis a pair of knives, *esp* when kept in a single sheath by a woman *la15-e17.*

knight *see* KNICHT

knip[1] *la19-,* N *n* a little, mischievous boy or girl. [see SND]

knip[2] &c *v* **1** *vi, specif of animals* bite or crop grass *e16.* **2** *vt* pull to pieces, break off, snap *20-, Sh NE Dmf.* [onomat; *cf* Norw dial *knippa* snap, Du, LowGer *knippen* clip, snip]

knipe &c *n* a lad, chap *e17, e20 (Bnf).* [uncertain; perh f KNAPE. SND *knip*[1], DOST *knape*]

knir *see* KNUR

knit &c [(k)nɪt; *Sh also* hnɪt] *v* **1** *vt, lit and fig* = knit, tie, fasten, unite *la14-.* **2** *specif* (1) join in marriage *16;* (2) (a) *vr and passive, of persons* join or combine in association or alliance *la14-e17.* (b) *chf passive* combine in military formation, form up in close order *la14-e16.*

knit *adj* **1** = knitted *la16-e18.* **2** *of joiner's or smith's work* secured by a joint, welded *e17.*

knitting &c, **knitten, -in** *la17-,* **knetting** *la16-e17 n* **1** = the action of knitting *17-.* **2** *chf in pl, appar* short pieces of string, cord or tape, *chf* used as ties or points for clothing *16-.* **3** *fig, in pl* details, particulars, items of news *20-, Abd.*

knit up *vt* **1** = knit up, fasten *la16-.* **2** *fig* make firm (friendship etc) *16.*

knitch &c; **knidge** *19- n* a bundle, truss *la16-, latterly chf Ork N.*

vt make into a bundle or truss *la19-, chf Bnf Fif.*

knidge(1) &c a (short) sturdy person *20-, Cai.*

knitshel &c, **-chell** &c *16-e17* a (small) bundle *16-, now Sh Fif.* [ME *knytche,* OE *gecnycce*]

knock[1] &c, **knok** &c *vti* **1** = knock *la14-.* **2** beat or pound (1) flax or cloth *la15-e20;* (2) grain, *chf* barley *la16-20.*

n **1** = knock, a blow *15-.* **2** a knocker on a door or gate *la16-17.* **3** a wooden mallet for beating linen etc, after bleaching *18-e19.*

~**ing mell** a mallet for pounding barley

la18-20. ~**ing-stane 1** a hollowed-out stone in which to pound barley *la16-20, latterly Sh-Cai.* **2** a flat stone on which to beat linen after bleaching *17-19.* ~**ing trough** = ~*ing-stane, la17-20.* ~**it barley,** ~**it bear** barley ground in a ~*ing-stane, la16-e19.* **six** ~**s** *law* the procedure required in the serving of a summons: six blows on the door of the principal dwelling-place *16-e18.*

knock[2] &c, **knok** &c, **nok** &c *17- n* a clock *15-.*

~ **house** the part of a building, *chf* the steeple, in which a public clock was placed *la16-19.* **keper** *la16-17,* ~ **man** *17* a person appointed to attend to a clock. ~ **laft** a clock loft or gallery in a church *18-, now Fif.* ~ **smith** a clock-maker *la17.*

knock[3] &c, **knok** *n* a hillock *19-, now only verse, in place-names 14-.* [Gael *cnoc* a hill]

knockle &c ['knokl; *NE also* 'knjokl] *n* **1** a knuckle *la16-, now NE Per.* **2** the rounded, protuberant part of a bone at a joint, the condyle *20-, Cai SW.* [ME, MLowGer *knokel*]

knog *see* KNAG[2]

knoit[1] &c; **knyte** &c *la19-,* NE [(k)noit; NE knəit] *n* **1** a large piece, a lump *la19-, NE Ags Per.* **2** a knob, a bump; a bunion *la19-, Kcdn Ayr Uls.* [altered f KNOT; *cf* next]

knoit[2] &c [(k)noit; *NE* (k)nəit] *n* a sharp blow, a knock *la18-, now local Cai-Kcb.*

v **1** *vt* knock, beat, strike sharply *18-, now Abd.* **2** *vi, of the knees* knock *18-19.* **3** hobble, walk stiffly and jerkily *19-e20.*

cry *or* **play** ~ make a sharp sound in striking or being struck *la18-, now Abd.* [see SND]

knok &c *n* a bundle (of hemp, flax etc) *la16-17.* ~ **lint** = *n, e17.* [northern eModEng; MLowGer, ModGer *knocke* &c]

knok *see* KNOCK[1], KNOCK[2], KNOCK[3]

knoll &c [nol; **knol] n, chf of food* a large piece or lump *la18-e20.* [MDu, MLowGer *knolle*]

knool &c; (**k**)**noll** &c [nul, nol] *vt* beat, strike, knock *la18-e20.*

(**k**)**noolt** crushed, dispirited *la19-e20, Gall Rox.* [see SND]

knoose *see* KNUSE

knoost &c [(k)nust; *Cai* knuʃ] *n* a large lump, a hunk, *eg* of cheese *18-e20.* [LowGer *knuust;* MDu *knoest* a knot in a tree]

knop *see* KNAP[1]

knorl- *see* KNUR

knot &c [(k)not; *Abd also* knjot] *n* **1** = knot *la15-.* **2** a closely-massed group of fighting men, a company or troop *16.* **3** (1) a lump, a broken-off chunk *la19-, now NE.* (2) a lump in porridge *20-, N Gsw Ayr.* (3) *fig* a sturdy, thickset person or animal *la19-, now Sh.* **4** a node or joint in the stem of a plant, *esp* straw *la16-, now local Cai-SW.* **5** a flowerbed, a formal garden *16-, now Cai Gall.* **6** *also* ~**berry** the cloudberry *la18-e20.*

vi **1** *of porridge,* SOWANS *etc* form or grow into

lumps; *of arthritic joints* swell, gnarl *19-*, *local Sh-SW*. **2** *specif*, *of turnips* suffer from finger-and-toe-disease *20-*, *local NE-Loth*.

~less &c futile, aimless, ineffective *la17-*, *now Loth Bwk*. **a ~less threid** a thread that has no knot and tends to slip out of the needle; *fig* an aimless, useless, futile person or thing *la18-*. **knotting** *or* **knottit sowans** SOWANS made thick and only half-boiled so as to form lumps *19-*, *NE*. **knottit ream** clotted cream *20-*, *NE*. **knotty &c** full of lumps or knobs *la19-*, *local N-S*. **knotty meal** the earth- or pig-nut *19-20*, *Inv-Mry*. **knotty tam(s), -tammies** a dish of hot milk or water and oatmeal formed into partially cooked lumps *la19-*, *chf Cai NE*. **~ grass** name for various grasses with knotty stems etc *la18-*, *chf Ork N, C*.

aff (at) the ~, affen the ~ 'off one's head', crazed, distraught *la18-*, *NE Uls*. **flower ~** = *n* 5, *19-*, *now Fif SW*. **King's K~** the grassy mound, *orig* laid out as an ornamental garden, below Stirling Castle *la18-*, *Stlg*. **a ~ in the puddin** a strangulated hernia *la19-*, *Fif Gsw Dmf*. **the ~ o one's craig** *or* **thrapple** the Adam's apple *19-*, *NE Ags*. [*cf* KNOIT¹]

knotty &c *n* **1** the game of SHINTY or a variant of it *18-*, *chf Cai*. **2** the ball used in SHINTY or football *20-*, *Sh-Cai*. [ON *knøttr*]

knoud &c [nʌud] *n* the grey gurnard *19-20*, *WC, SW Uls*. [reduced f Gael *cnòdan*]

know &c [(k)nʌu] *n* = knoll *16-*. **~ head** a hilltop *la16-*, *now local N-Kcb*.

know *see* KNAW¹

knowll- *see* KNULE

knowpert &c ['knʌupərt] *n* the crowberry *la19-*, *NE*. [see SND]

knuckle &c; (k)nickle *la19-* *n* **1** = knuckle. **2** *measure* the length of the second finger from tip to knuckle *la19-*, *Sh Ork Uls*. **3** *specif, marbles* the flick given to the striking marble; the marble so played *la19-*, *NE*.
v **1** *vt* measure in lengths of the KNUCKLE *n* 2, *la19-*, *Sh Cai Uls*. **2** strike sharply; *specif, marbles* propel (the striking marble) *e19*, *NE Kcb*. **3** *vi* submit *19-*.

knuckled cake cakes pressed out with the knuckles *la19-*, *Ork Per Bwk*. **knuckler, (k)nickler** the marble used to KNUCKLE *v* 2, *la19-*. **knucklie &c 1** a game played with marbles *20-*. **2** *in pl* the game of *chuckie-stane* (CHUCK²) *20-*, *local Abd-Kcb*.
~ deid *chf as a call* play a marble with the knuckles firmly on the ground *la19-*. **~ in** *marbles*, *chf as a call* play in a marble from wherever it lies, without the advantage of being allowed to move to first from an awkward position *20-*, *local Per-Uls*. [*cf* KNOCKLE; the form *knickle* seems due to conflation w KNICK *v*]

knuife &c [*knøv, *knøf] *vi* converse familiarly *la18-e19*. [uncertain]

knuitle &c; kneetle *20 Abd* [?'knøtl; *Abd*

'knitl] *vt* **1** strike or squeeze hard with the knuckles; keep striking *e19*. **2** press (down) *20*, *Sh Abd*. [perh f KNOIT *v*, w infl f KNUCKLE]

knule &c [(k)nul, (k)nʌl, (k)nɪl] *n* a lump, knob; *specif of cattle* a small loose horn *19-e20*, *SW Rox*. **~-kneed** having swollen or enlarged knee-joints; knock-kneed *la18-*, *chf WC-S*. **knowll-ta &c** a toe swollen at the joints *e16*. [*cf* LowGer *knolle*, *knulle* and KNOLL *n*]

knur; (k)nir *19* [(k)nʌr; *Ork* (k)noro; *WC* (k)nɪr] *n* **1** *chf in dim forms* a lump, a weal *19-*, *Abd Ork*. **2** a decrepit or dwarfish person *19-20*, *chf SW-Uls*. **knurl &c, (k)norl- &c** *la18-20* **1** a lump, bump, protuberance *la19-*. **2** *fig* a deformed person, a dwarf *18-20*, *chf WC Dmf*. **~lie** lumpy, knobbly, gnarled *la19-*, *now Cai*. **~lin** = knurl 2, *la18-19*. **~lick** = knurl 1, *la18-*. [fig extension of Eng *knurr*; *cf* ME, MDu, MHighGer *knorre*]

knuse &c; (k)noose &c [nuz; *Ork* nɪz] *vt* squeeze, press down, bruise; cuddle; pummel; drub *18-*.
noozle ['nuzl, 'nɪzl; *Rox* 'nøzl, 'nʌzl] = *v*, *19-*.

knype¹ &c; knyp [(k)nəip] *v* **1** *vt* knock, strike sharply *la19-*, *NE Uls*. **2** *vi* 'jog (on)' steadily, keep going, work away *20-*, *NE Ags*. [*cf* KNAP², KNIP²]

knype² &c [knəip; ?knɛp, ?gnɛp] *vt* tie (boats) together in harbour in order to hold them more securely than by a mooring rope alone *20*, *Fif*. **knypin &c** a short rope used for lashing boats together in this way *20-*, *Mry Fif*. [? f Norw dial *kneppa*, *knippa* tie or bind tightly together]

knyte *see* KNOIT¹

kok *see* COCK¹

koken *n* a rogue *e16*. [? OF *coquin &c* a beggar, rogue]

KOSBs *see* KING

kosch &c *adj* hollow *e16*. [*cf* Gael *còsach* cavernous, full of holes, f *còs* a hollow, cave]

kow *see* COO

Kowanday [*'kʌuənde] *n*, *prob* St Congan's Day (13 Oct), when one of Turriff's two fairs was held *16-e17*, *NE*.

kowdoch *see* CUDDOCH

koy *see* QUEY

kreill *see* CREEL

kro *see* CRUE

kuafe *see* QUEFF

kugl *see* COGGLE

kuir *see* CURE

kuke *see* CUIK

kure *see* CURE

kurn *see* CURN¹

kute *see* CUIT

kweerichin *see* KEEROCH

kwerious *see* CURIOUS

kyaard *see* CAIRD¹

kyauve &c [*Sh* kav, kev, *also* kjav; *NE* kjav] *v* **1** *vi* toil, wrestle laboriously, struggle **with** *20-*, *Sh*

NE. **2** move or toss restlessly, tumble about, wrestle in fun *la19-, Sh NE.* **3** *vt* knead *19-20, NE.*

n, also fig a struggle, exertion, a turmoil *la19-, chf N.* [var of CAVE², Norw *kava* wrestle etc, ON *kafa* plunge, dive; there may also be confusion with TYAUVE]

kyaw *see* KAE¹

kye *see* COO, KEY

kyeuk *see* CUIK

kyittle *see* KITTLE¹

kyle¹ &c *n* a narrow strait or arm of the sea or narrow part of a river *la16-, chf W Coast, freq in place-names.* [Gael *caol,* genitive *caoil, (n)* a strait, *(adj)* narrow]

kyle² &c *n* **1** a ninepin or skittle, *freq* (**the**) ~**s** the game itself *16-20.* **2** *fig* a chance, opportunity *la18-20.*

vi, of the metal ball used in a form of skittles reach the aiming point *la19-, Fif.* [corresponding to ME, eModEng *kayles,* MDu *keghel;* the Sc form may be f F *quille*]

kyle³ &c: ~ **bonnet** *or* ~ **hude** some sort of headgear *la16.* [unknown]

kyle *see* QUILE

kyloe &c; kylie &c *la18-20* ['kəilo, 'kəilɪ] *n* one of a breed of small *Highland* (HIELAND) cattle *la18-, local Cai-S.* [Gael *gaidhealach* ['ka:ələx] Gaelic, Highland]

kyp *see* KEEP

kype &c *n* **1** a small scooped-out hollow in the ground, *chf* for use in the game of marbles *19-, NE Ags.* **2** a game played with marbles aimed at a hole in the ground *17-, Cai NE.* [prob OE

cȳpe, LowGer *kipe* a basket, extended to anything of a hollow concave shape]

kype *see* KIP¹

kytch *see* KEYTCH

kyte &c *n* the stomach, belly *16-20.*
~**fu**(1) a bellyful *19.* **kytie** corpulent, *esp* as a result of good living *19-, now local N-Kcb.*
~-**clung** having the belly shrunk from hunger *19.* [see SND, DOST]

kythe &c; keyth &c *16-20, chf NE* [kaɪð; *kið] *v, ptp also* **kid &c** *la14-16, verbal noun* **keething &c** *la18-20, chf NE* **1** *vt* (1) show, display, reveal, make manifest *la14-20.* (2) exhibit (a sign or marvel), perform (a miracle) *la14-16.* **2** make known or reveal by words, declare *la15-e17.* **3** *vr* show one- or itself *16-e17.* **4** *vi with reflexive force* show or present one- or itself, appear, become manifest *la15-20.* **5** make a formal appearance in a court of law *e17.* **6** *with complements* show or reveal oneself in a specified light or character, manifest a specified quality in one's behaviour: (1) *vr, 15-e17;* (2) *vi, 17.* **7** turn out or prove (to be) *la15-e17.*

kid &c *ptp* **1** renowned *la14-e17.* **2** notorious *la14-e16.* ~**some** pleasant, of prepossessing appearance, *always* **blythsome &c** *and* ~**some** *19, Per WC.*
~ **to** *or* **wi** take after, accord with; be attracted to *la19-, now Kcdn.* **it kythes** *etc la15-e17,* **as kythed** *la16-e17 impersonal* it appears *or* as appeared evident. [ME *kythe,* OE *cȳðan* make known, *esp* in words, ptp *cȳdd*]

kytrall *see* KITERAL

L

la [*la] *article, in Latin texts preceding vernacular place-names, chf* **de la** of the *14, rare.* [AN, OF fem def art; *cf* LE, LEZ]

laar [ʔlɑr] *n* = layer *20, Sh Abd.*

lab[1] **&c** *n* **1** a lump; a portion, bit; a shred *19-, Loth S.* **2** a blow, stroke *19-, chf Bwk S.* **3** a throwing, tossing movement *19.* **4** *specif* a game of marbles *la19-, now WC.*
v **1** *vt* beat, strike *19-e20.* **2** *vi* fall flat *19.* **3** *vt* pitch, throw *19-, now Ayr.* [Eng *lob* a lump, something pendulous; *cf* LOB]

lab-[2] *adj* ~-**sided** = lop-sided *la19-, local C-Uls.*

lab *see* LAIB

laberlethin &c [*'lebər'lɛθən, *'lɛbər'lɛxən, &c] *n* a rigmarole, rambling discourse *la19-e20.* [uncertain]

labie &c, laby [*'lebɪ, *'labɪ] *n* the flap or skirt of a man's coat or shirt *la15-19.* [obscure]

labour &c; lawbour &c ['lɑbər] *n* **1** = labour *15-.* **2** *specif* agricultural work, tillage *15-, now local Sh-Loth.*
vti **1** = labour *15-.* **2** till, cultivate *15-, now local.* **3** ['lɑbər, *also* ʔ'lɑb-] beat, thrash *19-, local.*
~**er &c 1** = labourer *15-.* **2** *also* ~**er of the ground** a cultivator, a landworker *15-e18.*
~**ing &c 1** = labouring *15-.* **2** tillage *la15-, now Sh.* **3** a farm or holding, arable ground *17-19.* **laborious 1** = laborious, industrious, toilsome *16-.* **2** labouring, belonging to the peasant or artisan class *16-e17.* **laborous &c** = *laborious* 1 (*la15-16*), 2 (*la16-19*).

labrod &c; lawbroad &c *19-e20* ['la'brod, -'burd, -'børd, 'le-] *n* = lapboard, a board laid across the knees for working on *19-, now Ork Bnf.*

labster *see* LAPSTER

laby *see* LABIE

lacer ['lesər] *n* a lace, *esp* a boot-lace *la19-, local Ork-Ayr.*

lach *see* LAUCH[1], LAUCH[2]

lache *see* LAICH, LAISH, LATCH[3]

lachen *see* LAUCH[1]

lachet *see* LATCHET

lacht *see* LAUCH[1]

lachter[1] **&c; lauchter &c** *19-e20* ['lɑxtər, 'laxtər; *Rox also* 'laftər] *n* **1** the total number of eggs laid by a fowl in a season; a single clutch on which she broods *la18-, now local NE Uls.* **2** a hatch or brood of chickens *19-, local.* [ON *látr* f *lahtr* the lair of an animal]

lachter[2] **&c** *18-,* **lochtir &c** *la14-e15;* **louchter &c** *la19-, now Uls* ['lɑxtər, 'loxtər; *Gall Uls* 'lʌxtər] *n* **1** a lock of hair; a tuft of grass *la14-e15, 18-19.* **2** *reaping* the amount of corn grasped and cut in one stroke; the last sheaf cut in harvest; a handful of hay *19-, now Cai.* [ON *lagð* a tuft of wool or hair]

lachter *see* LAUCHTER

lack &c *la15-,* **lak &c** *la13-18,* **lake &c** *la14-e20* [lak, lek] *n* **1** = lack, want, deficiency

la13-. **2** blame, censure *la14-16.* **3** disgrace, shame, *freq with* **shame** *la14-e19.* **4** a fault or failing such as to bring shame or disgrace *la15-16.* **5** offence, injury; insult *15-16.*
adj, orig chf in comparative and superlative, latterly freq ballad deficient in quality, inferior *15-e19.*
vti **1** = lack *la15-.* **2** *vt* censure, blame; disparage *la15-19.*
but ~ without fault, blamelessly *la15-e16.*
think ~ think shame *la16-e19.* **to** ~ to blame; blameworthy, despicable *la14-16:* 'this Herrod wes al to lak'.

lackanee [*'lakəni] *interj* alas! *e19.* [aphetic f *alakanee* (ALAKE)]

lacrissye; lagrace, lacreische [*la'krɪs(ɪ), *-'kriʃ] *n* **sukker** ~ liquorice *la15-16.* [MDu *lacarisse; cf* ALICREESCH, LICOROUS]

lad &c; laid &c *la16-17,* **lawd &c** *16, 20-, now C* [lad; *C* lɑd; *lel] *n* **1** = lad, menial *la14-.* **2** a serving lad *la15.* **3** a youth *15-.* **4** a male child, a son *16-.* **5** a bachelor *19-, now Cai.* **6** a male sweetheart *18-; cf* LASS. **7** the young bachelor chosen as the central male participant in various annual local festivals; see *Riding of the Marches* (RIDE); *cf* LASS 6. **8** an (extreme) example of its kind, a one *20-, local:* 'ye're a lad'.
laddie; lathie &c *la18-, now Ags* ['ladɪ, 'lɑdɪ; *'laðɪ; Ags* *'laðɪ] *n* = n, *17-, Gen except Sh Ork.*
~**ry &c** base conduct or talk, ribaldry *15.*
~ **bairn** *etc* = n 4, *la18-19.* ~'**s love** southernwood *19.*
the auld (black) ~ the Devil *la19-, now Loth Uls.* ~ **o pairts** a promising boy, a talented youth *la19-.*

ladder *see* LETHER

laddle *see* LADLE

lade &c, lead &c *la16-, now local Ork-Kcb;* **leid &c** *la16-e19* [led, lid] *n* a channel bringing water to a mill; a mill-race, *freq* **mill** ~ *15-.* [only Sc; OE *gelād* a watercourse, channel; *cf* LEAD *n* 2]

lade *see* LAID

lade-gallon &c [*'led'galən] *n* a wooden bucket used for ladling and carrying liquids *la15-17; cf* LAGALLOUN, LEGLIN. [ME *lade* (*v*) ladle, load + Eng *gallon*]

ladill *see* LADLE

ladin *see* LAID

ladinar &c *e16,* **ladinster** *16-e17,* **lathenar &c** *e16* [*'ladənər, *'laðənər, *'leð-, &c] *n* a washerwoman, laundress. [metath var of ME *lander,* short for *lavender*]

ladinar *see* LAIDNER

ladle &c, ladill &c *la15-17;* **laddle &c** *16-19* ['ledl; *'ladl] *n* **1** = ladle *la15-.* **2** a ladle used to measure the duty on foodstuffs at a BURGH market; the duty itself, *orig* paid in kind but latterly (*18*) in cash *la16-18.* **3** a long-handled church collecting box *19-20.* **4** a tadpole *19-e20, chf N.*

vt **1** exact LADLE duty from (grain etc); charge with LADLE duty *la17-e18, Gsw.* **2** = ladle.

~**ar &c** a collector of LADLE duty *17, Gsw.*

~**-full** the amount levied as *n* 2, *la16-e17.* **be** *or* **hae one's caup** *or* **sit aneath somebody's** ~ become dependent on or subject to another *20-, NE.*

ladrone *see* LAIDRON

lady &c; leddy &c *16-,* **lethy &c** *20-, Ork* ['lɛdɪ, 'lɛdɪ; *Ork also* 'lɛðɪ] *n* **1** = lady *la14-.* **2** title prefixed to the name of an estate and given to a female landowner or wife of a landowner *la15-; cf* LORD 3 (1).

~**ness** the quality or character of a lady *19-, now Ork Ags Uls.*

~**'s beds** lady's bedstraw *la19-, local Ork-Per.*

~ **body** a ladylike woman *20-, Ork Abd Ags.*

~ **bracken &c** *(now Rox),* ~ **fern** *(now Dmf Uls)* the female fern *19-.* ~**'s** *or* **ladies' fingers** the cowslip *la19-, Fif Loth.* ~**'s** *or* **ladies' gairtens &c** *or* **garters 1** the striped ribbon-grass *la19-, local.* **2** the blackberry *la18-e19, S.* ~**'s gown** *law* a gift made by a buyer to the seller's wife on her renouncing her *liferent* (LIFE) in the seller's estate *18-e19.* ~ **lander(s)** *or* **launners &c** the ladybird *19-, local Ags-Rox* [for second element *cf* OSc *landar* a launderess]. ~**'s meat** the young leaves and buds of the hawthorn *19-, now Cai Kcb.* ~ **messe &c** a mass celebrated in honour of the Virgin *15-e16.* ~ **nit** the larger plantain *20-, Rox.* ~ **provost** courtesy title for the wife of a *lord provost* (LORD) *20-, now Cai Wgt Uls.* ~**'s purse** shepherd's purse *20-, now Cai Wgt Uls.* ~**'s thimbles 1** the *harebell* (HARE) *la19-, now Uls.* **2** the foxglove *la19-.*

~ **o the meadow** meadow-sweet *19-, Cai SW.*

laen *see* LEN

laest *see* LEAST[2]

lafe *see* LAIF, LAVE[1]

laft &c *17-,* **loft &c** *n* **1** = loft *la14-.* **2** *only* **loft** the deck of a ship *la15.* **3** the upper storey of a two-storey building *15-, Gen except S.* **4** *only* **loft** a joisted boarded ceiling *la15-19.* **5** a gallery in a church *16-, Gen except S.* **6** *only* **loft,** *golf* the act of striking the ball so as to make it rise; the slope on the face of the golfclub which causes this *la19-.*

v **1** *vt* provide (a building) with a loft by flooring joists etc *la15-.* **2** *only* **loft** furnish (a boat) with a deck *la17-e18.* **3** *vti* (cause to) rise off the ground *19-.* **4** *only* **loft** *golf* strike (the ball) so as to make it rise high *la19-.*

~**ing 1** = *n* 4, *16-.* **2** boarding *in gen, 16-.* **3** an upper storey *17.* **4** furnishing with a loft or joisted ceiling *17-.*

loft-house &c = *n* 3, *la15-, now Uls.*

(**up)on** ~ *chf verse* **1** in the air *la14-e16.* **2** into the air *la14-16.* **3** loudly *15.* **4** *fig, of one's spirits* raised, high *16.*

lag[1] *adj* lingering, tardy, slow *18-, now Fif Loth SW.*

n **1** = lag, a delay, an interval. **2** the last in a series or in a concerted activity, *eg* a game *la19-e20.*

lag[2] **&c** *n, also* **laggie** a call to a goose to be fed; the goose itself *19-, SW.* [see SND]

lagalloun &c *la16,* **legalloun &c** *la16-17* [***'le'galən, ***'lɛ-] *n* = LADE-GALLON; *cf also* LEGLIN.

lagamachie &c;   **legammachie &c** [lə'gamaxɪ, laŋ'gaməxɪ, &c] *n* a rigmarole, a long-winded discourse *19-, NE.* [Eng *logomachy,* Gk *logomachía* a battle of words]

lagger &c; laiger &c *19-e20 v* **1** *vt, chf* ~**it** made wet or muddy; besmeared, bespattered *16-.* **2** *vi* sink in soft ground, be encumbered by walking through snow etc *18-, Ork Abd Fif.* *n* mire, mud *la19-, chf N.*

~**y** muddy, miry *19-, chf Ags.* [see SND]

laggin &c *la16-,* **lagging &c** *16-e19;* **laigen &c** *17-19,* **leggin &c** *18-* ['lagɪn, 'leg-, 'lɛg-; *NE also* 'ljag-] *n* **1** the projection of the staves beyond the bottom of a barrel etc *16-, now local Sh-Loth.* **2** the bottom hoop of such a vessel *19.* **3** the angle inside a vessel or dish where sides and bottom meet *la18-, now Sh NE.* **4** *freq in pl* the edge, rim, *eg* of a hill or shoe *19-, now Rox.*

~**-gird,** ~**-hoop** = *n* 2, *19-, now Sh.* **cast a** ~**-gird** bear an illegitimate child *18-e19.*

claut the ~ scrape or drain a container of food or drink *la18-19.* **frae lug to** ~ from top to bottom, all over *la19-, Dmf.* [ON *lǫgg* the ledge or rim at the bottom of a cask]

laglein *see* LEGLIN

lagrace *see* LACRISSYE

laib; leb &c *la19-e20,* **lab &c** *19-, chf N* [leb, lɛb, lab] *vt* lick up, lap, gobble *18-, now Abd Ags Uls.*

n **1** a mouthful, *esp* of liquid *19-.* **2** an untidy, ill-fitting piece of clothing etc *la19-, Bnf Abd.* **3** a rigmarole, a rambling or incoherent discourse *la19-, Bnf Abd.*

~**ach &c** ['lebəx, &c] *vi* babble, chatter *la19-, NE.* *n* **1** = *n* 1, *la19-e20, NE.* **2** = *n* 3, *la19-, NE.* ~**er &c** beslobber, bespatter with food *19-e20, chf S.* [voiced var of LAIP]

laich &c *15-,* **lache &c** *la14-17,* **lauch &c** *la14-17,* **leauch &c** *la16-e17,* **law &c, low** *16-;* **leuch &c** *16-19,* **leach &c** *la16-17* [lex; *Abd also* ljɑx; *S* ljux; ***lɑ; ***lɑx] *adj* **1** = low *la14-.* **2** situated in the lower part of a building, *eg* the ground floor or basement *16-.*

adv = low *la14-.*

n **1** a stretch of low-lying ground *la14-e19; freq in place-names 16-.* **2** the low side or lowest part of anything *la14-, now Abd Fif Wgt.*

vt **1** *chf* **law** = low, abase, humble *la14-16.* **2** *chf* **law, low** lower *16-20.*

Lower *education* at a less advanced level, of both a State examination and the certificate awarded to successful candidates *la19-20.* *n, colloq* one of these examinations or certificates *la19-20;* for details see SND, and *cf Higher*

(HEICH), *ordinary* (ORDINAR) *adj* 4. **laichy &c braid** a short stocky person or animal *la19-*, *Bnf Abd*.

laich &c bigging = ~ *house* 2, *17-e18*. ~ **country, low countries** *la17* the Lowlands (LAWLAND) of Scotland *la16-*, *now Fif Ayr*. ~ **house &c 1** a room or rooms in the lower part of a building, *eg* a cellar *la16-*, *now Abd Fif Edb*. **2** a lower building, *freq* one of a group, attached to a main building of several stories; *in pl* outbuildings *la16-e18*. **3** a one-storey building, *freq* of rural cottages *18-*, *now local Ork-Gall*. **laich &c kirk** a church which is not the chief church in a town *la16-19*; *cf high kirk* (HEICH). ~ **road** *lit* the lower of two alternative roads leading to the same place; *fig* the road below the earth along which the dead were supposed to travel *19-*. **laigh room &c** = ~ *house* 1, *18-*. **laich &c-set** squat, stocky *la19-*, *now Ayr Kcb*. **laigh shop** a cellar in a shop; a basement shop *la18-*, *now Abd Fif Edb*. **flee laich &c** act prudently and cautiously; be modest and unambitious *20-*, *local Abd-Dmf*. ~ **doun, in** ~ in a low voice, under one's breath *19-*, *N Fif*. [nME *lagh &c*, eME *lāh &c* ON *lágr*; *cf* LAWLAND]

laich *see* LATCH[2]

laid &c *la15-*, **lade &c, load &c** *17-*, **lode &c** *16-*; **led** *la16-e20*, **leid &c** *la15-e19* [led; *?lid] *n* **1** = load *la14-*. **2** a measure of quantity varying according to district and commodity *la15-*, *now local C*. **3** *only* **laid &c** as much liquor as one can hold at a sitting *19-*, *chf S*. **4** *only* **load &c** a heavy attack (of cold) *la19-*, *now Sh-N Fif*.
vti, pt also **lade** *la18*, **load** *la18-*. *ptp also* **lade** *la18*, **load** *la18-*; **ladin &c** *la16-* ['ledən], **loaden** *la16-19* = load *15-*.
~**en,** ~**in** = *v*, *16-*, *now C*. ~**ening &c 1** the loading of a ship *16-18*. **2** a ship's cargo *la16-e18*. **laidin &c 1** loading a ship *la15-16*. **2** a ship's cargo *la16-e19*. **3** a load *18-*. **laidner &c** a shipper *la16-e17*.
lade hors &c a pack-horse *la15-e17*. **lade &c man, load &c man** *la17* **1** a man in charge of a pack-horse *la14-17*. **2** *specif* a miller's assistant who collected and delivered corn and meal *la17-19*. ~ **sadil &c** a pack-saddle *la14-e18*. **laid tree** the centre rail of a frame laid on a hay-cart to enable it to take a heavier load *19-e20*, *chf S*.

laid *see* LAD, LEID
laidly *see* LAITH

laidner &c *la16-e19*, **ladinar &c** *16-19*, **lardener &c** *la14-17*; **lairdner &c** *16-18* [*'le(r)d(i)nər] *n* a store-room for meat etc *la14-e18*.
~ **mart &c** *la15-17, chf SW*, ~ **mart cow &c** *17-18, Gall* a fattened ox or cow killed and salted for winter provisions. ~ **time** the season when the *laidner mart* was killed and cured *18-19, latterly hist*. [ME *lardiner &c* a larder, ME, OF = a larderer]

laidner *see* LAID
laidron, ladrone; la(i)therin &c *la18-20* ['ledrən, 'leð(ə)rən; *WC, SW also* *?'lıd-] *n, term of abuse* a rascal, loafer; a slattern, drab *16-*. [see SND, DOST]

laif &c *la15-*, *now EC, WC, S*, **lafe &c** *la14-19*; **loaf &c** *17-*, **lofe &c** *16-e20*; **leaf &c** *16-e19* [lef] *n, pl also* ~**s**, **laves &c** *la14-18*, **leaves &c** *la16-18* [lefs; *?levz] **1** = loaf *la14-*. **2** bread, *esp* wheat-flour bread *19-*.
loafie a kind of currant bun *la19-*, *Kcdn Ags*. ~ **bread &c** wheat-flour bread (as opposed to *oatcakes* (AIT)) *18-*. [*cf* BREID]

laifie *see* LUIF
Laif-So(u)nday &c *n* = Low Sunday *la15-16*. [appar altered or misread f OSc *laissonday*, var of *Law Sonday*]
laig; lyaag &c [leg; *Sh* lɑg; *NE also* ljɑg, lɑg] *vi* chatter, gossip *la19-*, *chf NE*.
n (idle) talk, gossip *19-*, *chf NE*. [*cf* Norw dial *laga* (*v*) chatter; *cf* also LIG[2] and *lay aff* (LAY[1])]
laig *see* LEG
laigen *see* LAGGIN
laiger *see* LAGGER
laigh *see* LAICH
laiglin *see* LEGLIN
laik &c *n* **1** a stake *la16*. **2** *also* **yake** *20, Mry Gsw, specif* a small marble used as a stake in a game *19-*, *chf Abd Ags*.
vi sport, amuse oneself *15-16*. [chf nME *laik* (*n, v*) sport, ON *leikr* (*n*), *leika* (*v*)]
laik *see* LEK
laikage *See* LECK[1]
laikwake *see* LYKE
lailly *see* LAITH
lain, layne &c *vt, latterly proverb and ballad* conceal or be silent about (a fact), *freq verse* **nocht to lane** *etc*, *la14-e19*.
n, verse **but** *or* **without(in)** ~ without concealment, in truth *15-16*. [chf northern and n midlME *layne &c*, ON *leyna* hide, keep secret]
lainch *see* LENCH
laing *see* LANG[1]
lainth *see* LENTH
laip &c, lape; lep &c *la16-*, *now Sh Ork* [lep; *Sh Ork* lɛp] *vti* = lap (liquid) *15-*, *now local Sh-midLoth*.
n **1** the act of lapping *19-*, *now Ags midLoth*. **2** a mouthful or small amount (of liquid) *19-*, *now Ags midLoth*. **3** a perfunctory wash, a swill *20-*, *Kcdn Ags midLoth*. [*cf* LAIB]
lair[1] &c *n, also* **layer** *la16-18* **1** a person's bed *15-*. **2** a place where animals lie down, a fold or enclosure *16-*, *now Sh, freq in place-names*. **3** the spending of a night by animals belonging to one person among the crops of another *17-*. **4** a burial place or grave, *specif* a burial space reserved by a person or family in a graveyard

or church *15-*; *cf* GRUND *n* 7. **5** (1) a place where something lies or is laid down *la16-20*. (2) *specif* a patch of ground on which cut PEATS¹ are laid to dry *17-*, *NE*.

vt **1** drive (animals) to their resting-place *17-18*. **2** bury (a person) *la18-*, *now Ags Fif*. **3** lay (*specif* a millstone) in position *20-*, *Abd Ags*.

~ **silver** the price charged for a LAIR (*n* 4) *16-e18*, *latterly NE*. ~ **stane** &c a gravestone *la16-*, *chf NE*. [ME *lair*, OE *leger*]

lair² &c *n* **1** mud, mire *17-*, *Ags midLoth Kcb*. **2** a mire *17-*, *now Abd*.

vti **1** sink in mire, become bogged (in mud, snow, etc) *la16-*, *now local N-S*. **2** cause to sink in boggy or muddy ground *la16-*, *now local NE-S*.

~**y** miry, muddy *19-*, *Abd Ags Rox*, also in *place-names 16-17*. [nME *layre*, ON *leir* mud]

lair³ &c, **lare** &c; **lear** &c *18-* [ler; *also* lir] *n* **1** = lore, act of teaching *la14-16*. **2** learning, knowledge, education, lore, doctrine *la14-*: '*book lair*'. **3** habit, custom, *usu* **ill** ~ *20-*, *Cai*.

vt learn *la14-18*.

ill-~ed *of a child* having bad habits, badly brought up, spoiled *20-*, *Cai*. (**well** *etc*)-~**ed** (well-)educated *la18-e19*.

at *or* **to** (**the**) ~ under instruction, at or to school, at study *la14-16*. [OE *lār* > Eng *lore*; *cf* LEAR with which there is some confusion, hence pronunc [lir]]

lair⁴ *n* the floor of a *peat-bank* (PEAT¹), a trench from which PEATS¹ have been cut *17*. [Gael *làr*]

lairag *see* LAIRICK

lairbair *see* LARBAR

laird &c *15-*, **lard** &c *la14-20*; **lerd** *la16-17*, **leard** &c *17-e18* [lerd; *Abd also* *ljɑrd] *n* **1** a prince or chief *la14-*, *latterly rare and literary* (*see* LORD). **2** (1) Christ *la14-16*; (2) *colloq as mild expletive*, *18-*, *now local Cai-Kcb*. **3** the landlord of landed property or an estate *15-*; *cf landislaird* (LAND¹). **4** *chf* (*15-*) *of lesser landowners* a landowner holding directly of the Crown, and so entitled to come to parliament *-e18*, but not a *lord of parliament* (LORD 2 (3) (a) and (b)) *la14-*. **5** an owner of property *in gen*, *esp* a house-owner *19-*, *NE*, *C*. **6** applied (with patronymic) to the chief of a *Highland* (HIELAND) CLAN *la16-e17*: '*the laird of M'Gregour*'. **7** *joc term of address* chum, lad *20-*, *local Abd-Loth*.

vt **1** be the owner of (an estate) *la19*. **2** lord it (**over**) *la19*.

~**ly** lordly, aristocratic; lavish, extravagant *la19-*, *chf Abd*. ~**ship** &c **1** a barony (BARON). a landed estate, *esp* that of a small freeholder *la14-*. **2** the dignity or rank of LAIRD *la15-19*. **3** *as title* = lordship *19-*, *now Loth Slk*.

auld ~ = *n* 4, the present laird, where there is a male heir *16-*. **young** ~ the male heir of *n* 4, *16-*.

~ **in the Abbey** *joc* a bankrupt *18-e19*, *Edb*; see ABBEY. [shortened f OSc *laverd*, OE *lāford* lord; *cf* LORD]

lairdner *see* LAIDNER

lairge &c *la15-*, **large** &c *la16-*, **larg** *la14-16*; **lairg** *la16-e17* [lerdʒ] *adj* **1** = large *15-*. **2** generous; lavish *la14-*, *now NE*. **3** *of speech* voluble, unrestrained *la15-e16*, *la19* (*Abd*). **4** ample in quantity, plentiful *la14-*, *now NE*. **5** *of persons* having an abundant supply **of**, rich **in** *19-*, *NE*.

adv **1** = large *la15-17*. **2** fully, quite *15-e18*.

at ~ **1** = at large *la15-*. **2** profusely *16*.

lairick &c *19*, *EC*, **larick** &c *19-*, *now Mry Ags*, **lairag** &c *20-*, *Cai* ['lerɪk, -ək; *Cai* 'lerəg] *n* = LAVEROCK. [reduced form]

laiser *see* LEISURE

laish *la17*, **lasche** &c *16-17*; **lache** *la15* [*laʃ] *adj* **1** slack, negligent *la15-17*. **2** = lash, relaxed, limp *e16*. [*cf* LATCH³ *v*]

laist *see* LAST¹, LEST¹

lait¹ &c *la15-*, **late** *la14-e16* *n* in *sing* outward appearance, bearing *la14-15*. **2** *in pl* manners, behaviour, *latterly* (*19-*) *chf* **ill** ~**s** *15-*. [n and eME *late*, pl *lates*, ON *lat* (*pl*) manners]

lait² &c *vt* seek, look for *15*. [nME *lait*, ON *leita*; *cf* northern ModEng dial]

laith &c, **lathe** &c *la14-16* [leθ; *v* leð] *adj*, *also* **leth** &c *la16-e17*, *20* (*Sh*); **leath** &c *la16-e17*, *20* (*Sh*) = loath *la14-*.

n **1** = loath, evil *la14-15*. **2** ill-will, loathing, scorn *la15-*, *now Ork*; *cf* LETH¹.

vt = loathe, detest *la14-*.

~**fu** &c **1** reluctant(ly) *18-*, *now Wgt*. **2** bashful(ly) *la18-20*. **3** disgusting(ly) *19-*, *NE Per Loth*. ~**ie** a surfeit *19-e20*. ~**ly** *adj*, *also* **laidly** *la16-e19*, **lailly** &c *19* loathsome, hideous *la14-*. *adv* foully, horribly *la14-e16*. ~**some** &c = loathsome *la16-*.

laith *see* LATH

laitherin *see* LAIDRON

Laitin &c *16-*, *now NE*, **Latine** &c *la14-17*; **Lating** &c *15-e17* ['let(ɪ)n] *n*, *adj* = Latin.

lak *see* LACK

lakay *see* LECKIE

lake¹ &c *n* **1** = lake, a body of landlocked water *17-*; *cf* LOCH. **2** a stagnant pond, a pool *la14-19*. **3** a pool left at ebb-tide, used as a fish trap *17-*, *Dmf*. **4** *palus* a pool, swamp *e16* [translating L *lacus* or *palus*]. **5** *verse* the flowing water of a river or stream *la15-16*.

lake² &c *n*, *verse* fine bleached linen *la15-e17*. [MDu, Flem *laken* (linen) cloth]

lake³ *interj* alas! *19*. [aphetic f ALAKE]

lake *see* LACK, LECK¹, LIKE²

laky *see* LECK¹

laland *see* LALLAN

laldie &c ['laldɪ] *n* a thrashing, punishment, *chf* **get** ~, **gie someone** ~ *la19-*, *C*, *S*; *also* **gie it** ~ do something vigorously or exuberantly *20-*. [perh (chf onomat) child's word or may have connection w OE *lǣl* a whip; a weal, bruise]

lallan *la18-*; **laland &c** ['lalən] *n* **1** *latterly in pl* = LAWLAND *n* 2, *la16-e19*. **2** *now chf in pl* (1) = SCOTS (*n* 1) *la18-*; (2) *specif* since about 1940, the variety of literary SCOTS (*n* 1) used by writers of the Scottish Renaissance movement.
adj **1** = LAWLAND *adj*, *18-*, *now local Kcdn-Ayr*. **2** using the speech of the *Lowlands* (LAWLAND) of Scotland, SCOTS-speaking as opposed to GAELIC- or English-speaking *la18-*.

lamb &c, lam &c; lame *la14-e16* [lam] *n* **1** = lamb *la14-*. **2** *freq* ~**ie &c, my wee lamb** affectionate term of address, *now esp* to a child *17-*.
v, see derivs below.
lambing-stick a shepherd's crook used for catching ewes by the neck at lambing-time *20-*, *WC-S*. **lambing-storm** a period of severe weather, *usu* about lambing-time in March *20-*, *N*. **lammie-meh** pet name for a lamb *20-*, *local N-S*. **lammie sourocks** sheep's sorrel *19-*, *Rox*.
~ **bed** the uterus of a ewe *19-*, *Ork Cai SW*. ~**'s ears** the hoary plantain *20-*, *Fif SW Rox*. ~**'s lugs 1** = prec *20-*, *NE Ags Loth*. **2** the plant *Stachys lanata*, *20-*. ~**'s tongue** field mint *19-*, *now Cai Wgt*.

lamber *see* LAMMER
Lambes *see* LAMMAS
lambleck *n* = lamp-black *la17*.
Lambmes *see* LAMMAS
lame¹ &c; leam &c *17-*, *now Ork* [[lem; *Sh Ork* lim; *N also* lim] *n* **1** *verse* = loam, earth *la14-e17*. **2** earthenware, china *16-*, *now Sh-N*. **3** a piece of broken crockery, *esp* one used as a plaything *la19-*, *local Sh-N, WC*.
adj made of earthenware, china *16-*, *now Sh-N*. [nME *lame*, OE *lām* clay]
lame² &c *n*, *verse* lameness, a crippling injury or infirmity *15-e16*. [nME, f the *adj*]

lame *see* LAMB
lamen &c ['lɛman; *?*'laman] *n* = leman, a lover *16-e17*.
~**ry &c, lemmanry &c** illicit or profane love *la15-16*.
lament *n* **1** a lamentation *16-*. **2** *specif* an elegy, a dirge; the air to which such a song is sung or played, *esp* on bagpipes; also in titles of such *la17-* [translating Gael *cumha*].
vti **1** = lament *16-*. **2** *vt* complain of, state as a grievance *la16*.
lameter &c ['lɛmɪtər; *Arg* *'leməntər] *n* a lame or crippled person or *occas* animal *18-*. [appar f *lamit* lamed + *-er*]
lamgabblich [lam'gablɪx] *n* a long rambling discourse, a rigmarole *20-*, *NE*. [altered f LAGAMACHIE, w infl f Eng *gabble*]
Lammas &c *15-*, **Lammes &c** *la14-17*; **Lamb(m)es &c** *16-18* ['laməs] *n* **1** Aug, a Scottish quarter day *la14-*.
~ **drave** the summer herring fishing on the Fife coast *la17-*, *now Kcdn Fif*. ~ **evin &c** LAMMAS eve *15-16*. ~ **Fair** a fair held at LAMMAS

in various places *17-*. ~ **flude(s)** a flood caused by a period of heavy rain about LAMMAS *la18-*. ~**man** a young salmon trout which begins its journey up-river from the sea for the first time about the beginning of August *la19-*.
~ **market** = ~ *Fair*, *esp* one held in Kirkwall and St Andrews *19-*. ~ **spate** = ~ *flude(s)*, *19*. ~ **stream** a high and strong tide occurring about LAMMAS *la19-*, *chf N*. [ME *lammes*, OE *hlāmmesse, hlāfmæsse* 'loaf mass' *ie* because orig a harvest festival]
lammer, lamber ['lamər, 'lɑmər; *'lambər] *n* amber *16-*.
~ **bead** an amber bead, *freq* used as a charm or amulet *16*. [ME, OF *lambre*, MedL *lambra*, Arabic *al anbar*]
Lammermuir; -moor: ~ **lion** *joc* a sheep *18-19*. [f the hilly moorland sheep country in SE Scotland]
lamp¹ &c *n* **1** = lamp *la15-*. **2** one of the heavenly bodies *16*. **3** a shining light or example, a paragon *16*.
~ **of licht** a person of extreme excellence or beauty *la15-16*. ~ **of Lothian** name *orig* for the medieval church of the Franciscan Priory in Haddington, *now* for the tower of the parish church *19-*; see SND Suppl.
lamp² *vi* **1** stride along, take long springing steps *17-*, *now local*. **2** limp, hobble *19-*, *now local*.
n a long firm stride *la19-*, *WC-S*. [see SND, DOST]
lamp³ *vt* beat, thrash; defeat *19-*, *local NE-EC*. [see SND]
lamp⁴ *vt* ~ **in the** *or* **intill ane lyme** *freq fig* trap in bird-lime *e16*. [see DOST]
lampeekoo &c *n* a variation of hide-and-seek *20*, *Abd Ags*. [obscure; *cf* PEE-COO]
lamper eel, -ele &c *16* *n* a lamprey *16-*. [ME *lampre* lamprey + Eng *eel*; *cf* RAMPER EEL]
lampet *see* LEMPIT
lan *see* LANE¹, LAND¹
Lanark, Lanerk ['lanərk] ~ **weight, stane** *etc*: referring to the *Scots Troy* (SCOTS) system of weight of which the standard was kept in the custody of the BURGH of Lanark *17-e19*.
lance &c *n* **1** = lance *15-*. **2** a surgeon's lancet, a scalpel *16-*, *now local*.
vi, *verse* bound, spring *la14-e19*.
~**-staff &c** a piked staff, a lance or pike *16-e17*.
lanche *see* LENCH
land¹ &c; lan &c [lan(d), lɑn(d)] *n* **1** = land *la14-*. **2** *in pl* the fields, the countryside *la14-e17*. **3** the country as opposed to the town *15-19*. **4** the fields as opposed to the buildings of a farm *20-*, *N-SW*. **5** (1) the soil which has still to be turned over by the ploughshare; the width of the cut made by the plough in the soil *la18-*. (2) an S-hook attaching the yoke to the muzzle of a plough, by which the LAND 5 (1) can be adjusted *la17-*, *N Fif*. **6** a holding of *burgage land* (BURGAGE), a building site; a building erected on this, a TENEMENT *15-*.

vti = land *16-*.

~er 1 = ~ *beast, la20-, local NE-Dmf.* **2** a fall on the ground, *eg* when skating *la20-, Gen except N.* **~ing &c** the journey of a plough from one side of a field to another and back again, a BOUT[2] *19-, local EC-S.*

~ beast *in a plough-team* the left-hand horse, which walks on the unturned earth *la20-, local NE-SW.* **~ birst, ~ brist, ~ burst** (*e20, Cai*) the breaking of waves on the shore *la14-e20.* **L~ Court** = *Scottish Land Court* (SCOTS) *20-.* **~('s)-end 1** the (top) end of a land or RIG[1] *16-17.* **2** the end of a furrow, where the plough turns *19-, chf SW S.* **~ feaver &c** some kind of illness *17;* cf ~ *ill.* ~ **ferme** rent for land; land valued at the rent specified *16.* **~ flesche &c-mercatt &c** = ~ *mercatt, la16-17.* **~ flescheour** a *flesher* (FLESH) from the country using the ~ *mercatt, 16.* **~ gate(s) &c** *adv* **1** by land, overland *la15-16.* **2** landwards, in the direction of the country *la18-19.* **~ horse** = ~ *beast, 19-,* now *Arg Ayr Dmf.* **~ ill** a disease, ? epilepsy *16-19*; cf ~ *feaver.* **~ labourer** a person who works on the land as a casual labourer *la17-19.* **~lady 1** the mistress of a house where one is staying, one's hostess *19-.* **2** = landlady. **~(i)s-lady &c** a landlady, the proprietrix of land or houses *la16-,* now *Ags.* **~lord 1** the head of the family where one is a guest, one's host *19-,* now *Ork SW.* **2** = landlord. **~is-lord &c** *or* **-laird &c** a landlord, the proprietor of a landed estate; the proprietor of a house let to tenants *16-17.* **~lowper &c** a person who roams about the country idly or to escape the law, a vagabond, adventurer *la16-19.* ~ **maill(is) &c** *in Lanark* the rent paid by the tenants of the BURGH's common land collectively (*pl*) or by one tenant (*sing*) for a particular holding of this land *la16-e18.* **~ marches &c** boundaries of land *17.* **~ meither** a person appointed by a corporate body to settle and inspect the boundaries of their property *la17-e18, Gsw.* **~ meithing** the fixing and inspection of boundaries *la17-e18, Gsw.* ~ **mercatt &c** *16-17,* **~ market** *la17-e18* a FLESH-market held in some BURGHS for the unfree *fleshers* (FLESH) from the country; the place where this was held, *surviving as a place-name in* **the Lawnmarket** a street in the *Old Town* (AULD) of Edinburgh. **~ mouse** the field vole *la20-, local Fif-Wgt.* **~ plate** the side-plate on the left-hand side of a plough *la20-, local Fif-Uls.* **~-rent** revenue or income from land *la16-17.* **~ rope, ~ raip** a rope passing from the end of a drag-net to the shore *17-18.* **~('s)-setting** the letting of land and farms to tenants *17-20.* **~ side** the left-hand side of the plough *la20-,* now local *N-SW.* ~ **stale &c, ~ stool &c** *la17-e19* the foundation on land of the pier of a bridge or weir *la15-19.* **~ stane** a loose stone in the soil turned up in digging or ploughing *la18-,* now *Ork SW.* **~ tack &c** a TACK[2] or tenancy of land *16-e17, Abd.* **~ wyne &c** ? wine grown up-country, not in or near the town (of Bordeaux) *e17, chf Dundee.* **get** *or* **tak** ~ strike or reach land *la14-e16.* **gie** (**a ploo**) **mair** *or* **less** ~ adjust the width of the cut to be made by the plough *la20-.* **the ~ of cakes** Scotland *la17-19* [f the importance of *oatcakes* (AIT) in the Scottish diet]. **the ~ of the leal** the land of the faithful, Heaven *la18-* [chf in reminiscence of Lady Nairne's song (1798)]. **~ and tenement** *15-16* *or* **tenement of ~** *15-18* a TENEMENT in a BURGH. **pit on** *or* **tak aff** ~ increase or decrease the width of the cut to be made by the plough *20, Fif SW.*

land[2] &c; lawnd &c *n* an open space in a wood, a clearing *e15.* [ME *launde,* MedL *landa*]

land[3] *vt* saddle (someone) **with** (a burden or obligation) *la20-.* [? var of LANT]

landart *see* LANDWARD

landier &c [*'landər, *?'landɪər] *n* an andiron *17.* [F]

landimare, landimere, landimure, landsmark *see* LANIMER

landward &c, landwart &c; landart &c *la16-* ['lan(d)ward, -wərt, -ərt] *adv* **1 to** ~ *15-17,* **in** ~ *16-18,* **fra** *or* **from** ~ *16-17* in(to) or from the country as opposed to the town. **2** *without preps* in, toward or in the direction of the country as opposed to the town *19-.*

n the country as opposed to the town, the rural area in the neighbourhood of a town, the rural part of a country district or parish *la16-18.*

adj **1** rural, in or of the country as opposed to (a particular) town, in or of a rural part of a parish or district *16-.* **2** rustic, awkward, uncouth *16-,* now *EC Ayr.*

~is = *adv* 1, *adj* 1, *15-17.*

~ bred brought up in the country, rustic *19.* [*cf* late nME *to landward,* MDu *te land(e)-waert(s)*]

lane[1], lan *la16-17* [lɑn; *len] *n* = lawn, fabric *la15-17.*

lane[2] *n* a marshy meadow; a slow-moving, winding stream or its bed *17-, SW, also in Gall place-names.* [ScGael *lèan(a),* IrGael *léana* a marshy meadow]

lane[3] &c; lean &c *la16-e18* [*len] *n* a loan, the action of lending *la14-19.*

vt lend *16-e18.* [nME *lan(e),* ON *lán* > ModEng *loan; cf* LEN, with which there may be confusion in some dials]

lane[4] &c, lone &c *17- adj* **1** = lone *19-.* **2** *with the possessive pronoun* (*16-*) (**all** (*la16-17*)), **my, his, its** *or* **thair** ~; *with the 3 pers objective pronoun* **him, it, them** ~ (*chf Sh NE*); *with pl inflexion* **our ~s, them ~s** (*17-*) (1) without a mate or companion, on one's own, solitary *la16-.* (2) *esp of a child learning to walk* unaided *18-.* (3) *as noun with preps* = -self, -selves *18-:* '*by oor lains*'; '*to his lane*'.

lanely &c lonely *la18-*. **lanerly** ['lenərlɪ] *adj* lonely, alone; reserved in manner *19-*. *adv* singly, only *19-20, Sh Cai*. **~some** lonely, lonesome *la18-*. [*cf* ALANE, ALLENARLY]

Lanerk *see* LANARK

lang¹ &c, **long &c** *15- adj, also* **laing &c** *la16-17* **1** = long *la14-*. **2** tall: (1) *of persons, la15-;* (2) *of gravestones and standing stones* (STAND¹) *16-e18*. **3** *of sums of money, prices etc* large in amount, high *la18-, now Abd.* *adv* (*la14-*), *vti* (*la15-*), *n* (*in combs*) = long. **langlins &c** *prep* along *la16-18. adv* lengthwise *la20-, Sh NE*. **langsome &c 1** lengthy, tedious *la14-*. **2** *of persons* tardy, dilatory *16-, now Sh.* **3** lonely, forlorn; bored *la19-, now Sh-Ags.* **langsumly &c** (for) long *la15-e17.* **langsomeness &c 1** tedious lengthiness *15-e17.* **2** loneliness *19, chf NE.* **~ ale** a soft drink *20-, NE.* **~ back** long ago *19-.* **~ board** a long table at which master and servants sat together *la18-19, Ags Loth.* **~ cairt &c** a two-wheeled cart with a long body and sparred sides, used *esp* for carrying grain *19-, local N-Uls.* **~ carriage &c** the feudal duty of carting goods over a relatively long distance *16-18.* **~ chair &c** = ~ *settle, 19-e20, SW, S.* **~-chafted, ~-chaffed** long- or lantern-jawed *19-, now NE-Ags.* **lang craig** a long neck; *fig* an onion which runs to stem *19, chf Ags.* **lang-craiget** *of a bird* long-necked *19-, now NE Wgt.* **the ~ day** the Day of Judgment *18-e20.* **~-drachtit &c** scheming, cunning *19.* **L~ Forties** the Forties, a North Sea fishing-ground 75 miles (120 km) off the Abd coast, and only 40 fathoms deep *la18-19.* **lang hat** a top hat *20-, Ags Ayr Slk.* **~ heid &c** shrewdness; a shrewd or sagacious person *19-.* **~-heidit &c** shrewd, sagacious *19-.* **lang helter** *or* **halter** the permitting of animals such as cattle to range at will once the crops were harvested *19.* **lang ingans** = *lang leeks, la20-, NE.* **the Long Island** the Outer Hebrides, the long chain of islands off the west coast of Scotland extending from the Butt of Lewis to Barra Head; sometimes referring only to Lewis and Harris *18-* [Gael *an t-Eilean Fada* the long island, later name for the earlier *Innse Gall* the islands of the strangers, *ie* the Norsemen]. **Long John** a brand of WHISKY *20-.* **~ kail** *see* KAIL. **~ kent** familiar *20-, local Sh-Dmf.* **lang leeks** a variety of the game of leap-frog *20-.* **lang lip** a sulky expression *la19-, Bnf Uls.* **lang lugs 1** a person with long ears; *joc* a donkey *18-, now Ags Kcb Rox.* **2** a hare *20-, Cai Ayr Rox.* **lang-luggit 1** *lit and fig* long-eared *19-, now local NE-S.* **2** shrewd *20-, local C.* **~-nebbit &c 1** *lit* having a long NEB, snout etc *19-.* **2** *fig* (1) *of things* long, tapering or pointed *19-, local;* (2) *of persons* having a gnome-like or supernatural appearance *18-, now Ork;* (3) sharp, astute, having an eye to one's own advantage *18-, now local Ags-S;* (4) inquisitive,

critical *19-, now local;* (5) *of words* polysyllabic; pedantic *19-.* **~ Sandy &c** the heron *20-, NE.* **~ settle &c** *16-,* **~ sadill &c** ['~'sadl, *'~*'sedl, *'~*'sedl] *la15-,* **~ sattill &c** *la16-17,* **~ sald &c** *e16, Abd* [*'~*'sel(d)] a long wooden bench, very common *16-17,* having a back and *freq* arms or sides, *usu* with a chest below the hinged seat, and sometimes also convertible into a bed *la15-, latterly SW.* **~ settle &c bed** a *long-settle* which opened up to form a bed *16-e17.* **~ shankit 1** long-legged *la19-, now local NE-S.* **2** having a long shank or handle *18-, now NE.* **~ sheep** a Cheviot sheep *la18-19.* **lang syne &c, long syne** *17-19 adv* long ago, long since *15-.* *adj* ancient, of long ago *la18-.* *n* old times, memories of the past, old friendship *la17-.* **auld ~ syne 1** = *lang syne* (*n*), *18-.* **2** the song or the tune of this name, *now esp* Burns' song and its tune, played and sung at the close of social gatherings and at midnight on HOGMANAY *18-.* **lang-frae-syne** *or* **lang-sin-syne** = *lang syne* (*adv*), *19-, chf Sh Abd.* **long-teethed** ? long-established, of old family; aged *20-, Abd Ags.* **lang time &c** *adv, also* **of ~ time** for, during or since a long time *la14-e17.* **the Lang Toun** nickname for various Scottish towns, *esp* Kirkcaldy, because of their layout *19-.* **~-wund** involved *19-, Sh Gall Uls.* **at (the) lang** fully; finally *la16-e17.* **at (the) lang and (the) length, at ~ and last, at (the) lang length** at long last, finally *la18-.* **at (the) ~ run** in the long run *18-, now Sh-Cai Wgt.* **(for) (this) monie (a) ~** for a long time, for many days, years etc *la18-, now NE Ags.* **i the lang length** = *at (the) ~ length, la19-, Sh Abd.* **~ drink (o water)** a tall lanky person *la19-.* **lang ere &c; langare &c** [*'laŋ'ir, *'~*'er] *adv, freq written as one word* before, formerly *la14-16.* **~ may yer lum reek** *exclam* wishing someone prosperity *20-.* **~ o(f)** slow in, dilatory about *la18-19; cf* LATE. **leave, put** *etc* **someone to the ~ sands** subject someone to a lengthy process of litigation *la17-e19.* **mak a lang airm** stretch out and help oneself *20-.* **or lang gae** before long *la18-19.* **tak lang** grow weary (for, to), long *20-, Cai.* **think ~ (for; to, till; quhill** (*la15-16*)) be or grow weary or impatient with expectation or longing (for, to, that) *la15-.*

lang² &c *vi* **~ to** *or* **till** *without prep* **1** pertain to; relate to, concern; befit; be the property or right of *la14-e16.* **2** *specif* (1) *of things* be an appurtenance or accessory of *la15-e16;* (2) *of persons* belong, as a member of a family, an adherent or dependent *15-e16.* [nME *lang*, aphetic f OE adj *gelang* (**on**) pertaining or belonging (to); *cf* BELANG]

lang³ &c *prep* along *la15-19.* [aphetic f ALANG]

langage &c; langidge &c *la18-e20, chf Abd* ['laŋɪdʒ; *'laŋedʒ*] *n* = language *la14-, now chf NE, EC.* [ME, F]

langald, langall *see* LANGLE

langer *see* LANGOUR
langett *see* LANGLE
langfad *see* LYMPHAD
langidge *see* LANGAGE
langis &c *prep* along *la15-e17*. [*cf* LANG³ *prep* and *alangis* (ALANGST)]
langle &c *la16-*, **langall** &c *la15-e20*, **langald** *la15*; **langett** &c *16-e18* ['laŋl; *'laŋə(l)t, *-ald] *n* a hobble, tether (of rope) to prevent an animal from straying *la15-*, *now N Gall Uls*.
vt **1** hobble (an animal) *la15-*, *now Ork N Gall Uls*. **2** *fig* encumber, hamper, frustrate *la17-e20*. [ME; *appar* LANG¹ + *hald* (HAUD) = long hold]
langour &c; **langer** *la16-*, **languor** &c *15-* ['laŋər; *?'laŋwur, *?-wər] *n* **1** = languor *la14-*. **2** boredom, low spirits *la15-*. **3** longing **for** *or* **of** (something or someone) *or* **to do** (something) *la16-17*.
langorius [*?laŋ'gorɪʌs] distressing, painful; distressed *e16*.
haud *or* **keep** (**someone**) **out of** *or* **frae** ~ keep someone's spirits up, amuse *la16-*, *now Sh-NE*.
langsadill [*'laŋ'sedl] *n* a pack-saddle *16-e17*. [? var of *laidsadil* (LAID)]
langsadill, langsattill *see* LANG¹
lanimer &c *la17-*, **landimere** &c *15-19*; **landimare** &c *15-e17*, **landimure** &c *la16-17* ['lanɪmər; *'land(ɪ)mɪr, *'mər, &c] *n* **1** *chf in pl* boundaries of land, *specif* of *burgh* lands (BURGH) *15-*, *chf Abd WC* (*esp Lnk*). **2** *chf in pl* used as *sing* the annual ceremony of inspecting the boundaries, *Riding the Marches* (RIDE) *15-e19*. **3** a person who inspects and adjusts boundaries within a BURGH *17-18*, *chf Bute*.
Lanimer Day *etc*, **landsmark** &c **day** *la18-e19*, the day etc of celebrations accompanying the annual *Riding of the Marches* (RIDE) in Lanark *la18-*, *Lnk*. **Lanimer Queen** the girl chosen as Queen at the *Lanimer Day* celebrations *20-*, *Lnk*. [only Sc; OE *land-gemære*; *cf* OUTLANDIMER]
lank *n* a lean creature *la19* (*Bnf*), *la20* (*Uls*). [*cf* Eng]
lant &c *n* the card game *now called* loo *18-20*.
vt **1** put in a dilemma *19-*, *now Sh*. **2** mock *19-e20*, *NE*. [reduced f Eng *lanterloo*]
lantren &c *n* ? = LANDIER *16*. [ME *laundyren*]
lap &c *vt* **1** = lap, wrap, parcel up *15-*, *now local*. **2** fold up (newly-woven linen) for storage or dispatch *18-19*. **3** patch *la19-*, *local Sh-Wgt*. **4** press round in a hostile way, hem in *la15-16*.
n **1** = lap, flap, fold *15-*. **2** a wrapping round, fold, coil *la19-*. **3** *also* ~ **cock** *la18-e20* a small truss of hay *la19-*, *Cai Uls*. **4** a lobe (of the liver, of the ear) *la17-*, *now Sh*. **5** a sheepmark made by slitting the ear so as to make a flap *18-e20*, *chf Ork*. **6** a lapful, a small amount or collection *20-*, *Sh Uls*.
lap *see* LEAP
lape *see* LAIP, LEAP

lapidar &c [*'lapɪdər] *n* a jeweller; *latterly* a connoisseur of precious stones *16-e17*. [only Sc; OF *lapidaire*]
lapper¹ &c *v* **1** *vti*, *also* **lopper** &c *16-e19*, *esp of blood or milk* clot, curdle, *freq* ~**ed** &c *16-*. **2** *of water* freeze *la18-*, *now Abd Ags*. **3** besmear with or become covered with blood etc *18-*, *now Sh Loth*. **4** *of soil* dry out in a caked or lumpy state *la19-*, *Bnf Abd*.
n **1** a clot, clotted matter, *esp* milk or blood *19-*, *now local*. **2** *specif* milk soured and thickened in preparation for butter-making *19-*, *Gen except Sh Ork Cai*. **3** *also* **lopper** &c melting, slushy snow *19-e20*, *SW, S*.
~ **milk** thick sour milk *20-*, *local NE-S*. ~**ing tub** a container used for curdling milk *20-*, *Abd Loth Dmf*. [nME *loper* &c (*v*) curdle]
lapper² &c *vi*, *of water* lap, ripple *la19-*, *local Sh-SW*.
n, *of water* a lapping sound or motion *20-*, *NE Loth*. [frequentative of Eng *lap*; *cf* LAIP, LIPPER¹]
lappie *n* a small pool of water, puddle *19-*, *Ags Per*. [dim of Eng *lap*]
lappin *see* LEAP
laproun *see* LEPRONE
lapster &c, **lapstar** *la16-e17*, **lopstar** &c *e16*; **labster** *la18-*, **lobster** *19-* *n* = lobster *la16-*.
~ **creel** a lobster trap *20-*. ~ **kist** a box floated in water in which lobsters are kept alive until sent to market *20-*, *Ork Cai Ags*.
lapt *see* LEAP
laqueat [*lakwi'at, *-'et] *ptp*, *fig*, *only verse* ensnared *16*. [only Sc; L *laqueāt-*, ptp stem of *laqueāre* ensnare]
larach &c ['larəx, 'lerəx] *n* **1** a site or foundation of a building, the remains of an old building *16-*, *chf NE Per*. **2** *also* **stack** &c ~ the foundation of a hay- or corn-stack *19-e20*. **3** *also* **lerroch** *la18* a site *in gen*, a place, situation *la18-e20*. [only Sc; ScGael *làrach*, IrGael *láithreach*]
larbar &c; **lairbair** &c *adj* exhausted, impotent *16-e17*.
n an exhausted or impotent man *16-e17*. [chf Sc; laME (once) *larbre*, obscure]
lard *see* LAIRD
lardener *see* LAIDNER
lardon *n* a gibe, a piece of sarcasm *la16*. [only Sc; F *lardon* = *n*; a piece of larding bacon]
lare *see* LAIR³
larg, large *see* LAIRGE
larges &c *la14-e17*; **lerges** *16* ['lardʒɛs; *'lerdʒɛs] *n* = largesse.
largité &c [*'lardʒɪtɪ] *n* liberality *e15*. [OF *largete*]
larick &c ['larɪk, 'lɛrɪk] *n* the larch tree (introduced into Scotland *la17-e18*) or its wood *18-*. [back-formation f L *larix*, itself in regular use in Sc *18*]
larick *see* LAIRICK

larkie *n* the game of hide-and-seek *20*, *EC*, *WC*. [dim of Eng *lark* frolic]
larrie &c *n* = lorry *la19-*.
lary &c *la17-e20*, **laury &c** *16* [*'lɑrɪ] *n* the laurel. [ME *lorry*; see SND, DOST]
lasche *see* LAISH
lase &c [*les] *n* a lease *17*. [eModEng *lese*, *lease*]
laser *see* LEISURE
lash¹ *vti* = lash, dash, beat, squander.
n **1** = lash, a blow, whip, flogging. **2** a great splash of water, a heavy fall of rain *19*. **3** a large amount, an abundance (of things or persons) *la19-*.
~angallaivie, ~gelavy &c [*Bwk S* 'laʃ(ən)-gə'lev(ɪ), -'løvɪ, -'løf, 'laʃɪ-] abundance *19-*, *chf S*.
lash² *n* a looped string fastened so as to raise groups of warp-threads in a loom together *e19*.
~er a person who fastens LASHES in a loom *19-e20*, *Renfr.* [see SND]
lasie *see* LAZY
lasour *see* LIZOUR
laskit; lesteek &c *adj* elastic *19-*. [f Eng *elastic*]
lass, las &c *la14-17* [las] *n*, *also dims* **~ie**, **~ock &c**, **~ickie &c 1** (1) a girl *la14-*. (2) *familiar or joc* a woman *16-*. **2** an unmarried woman, a maiden *18-*. **3** a daughter *la16-*. **4** a maid-servant *16-*. **5** a sweetheart *la16-*. **6** the chief female participant in various local festivals *20-*; see *Riding of the Marches* (RIDE); *cf* LAD *n* 7.
~(ie) bairn *17-*, *now local*, **~ wean** *19-e20* a daughter. **~(ie) boy** an effeminate boy *la20-*, *local*. **~like** girlish, like a girl *19-*.
lad and ~ a pair of sweethearts *la18-*. **servant ~** a servant-girl *17-20*. [ME *lasse*; see DOST, OED]
last¹ &c, laist *16-* *adj, adv, n* = last *la14-*.
(the) ~ day the previous day, yesterday, the other day *la18-19*, *local*. **the ~ heir &c** *law* = ULTIMUS HAERES *16-e19*.
last² &c *n* = last, the denomination of quantity *15-*.
~age 1 a port-duty, ? levied on the cargo of a ship *15-17*. **2** the cargo of a ship measured in LASTS *16-e17*.
last³ &c [*lest] *n*, *verse* **nocht** *or* **nevir a ~** not a trace, nothing *la14-e15*. [OE *lāst* a footstep, trace]
lat¹ &c, let &c [lat; lɛt, lot; *WC*, *SW* lɪt; *lit] *vti*, *pt also* **leit &c** *la14-20*, **lat &c** *la14-20*, **luit &c** *16-20* [lut; *Sh Ork S also* løt; *NE* lit; *C also* lɪt; *Fif also* let; *lat, *lot]. *ptp* **latten &c, letten &c, luitten &c** *19-*; **lat &c** *16-17*, *19-20*, **let &c** *16-* ['latən, 'lɛtən, 'lʌtən, 'lutən; *nEC*, *S also* løtn; *C also* 'lɪtən; *Fif also* 'lotən; let; *lat, *lit, *løt] **1** = let *la14-*. **2** *followed by an infin, eg* **~ drive**, **~ gird**, **~ skelp** let fly, strike out *15-*. **3** *chf* **~ to borch** (BORROW¹) give up (something) on security, release (a person) on bail *la14-16*. **4**

reckon, consider, believe, expect *la14-15*. **5** think (lightly, less etc) **of** (a person etc) *la14-16*. **6** declare, avow *la14-15*.
~ a-be(e) = **~ be**, *18-*. **~ aff &c** *vi* break wind *19-*. **let-aff** *n* a reduction of rent *la19-*, *local Sh-Bwk*. **~ at** *lit and fig* hit out at; make a sarcastic thrust at *18-*, *now local N-Uls*. **~ be** = **~ on** l, *la20-*, *Sh NE Slk*. **~ be** *v* leave alone or undisturbed; desist *la14-*. *adv* let alone, much less *16-*. **let be** *n*, *chf proverb* tolerance, *esp* mutual forbearance or compromise *la18-19*. **~ doun &c 1** lower the price of *19-*. **2** *of a cow* yield (milk) *17-*. **3** swallow *la20-*, *NE*, *EC*. **4** *knitting* drop (a stitch) *19-*, *now NE*. **5 ~ doun (on)** *chf in negative* not refrain from teasing (a person), not stop reproaching (a person) *20-*, *now NE*. **~ intil** strike violently, let fly at *19-*, *N.* **~ ken** make it known *18-*, *local*. **~ (it) licht** give information privately or casually *19-*, *NE.* **~ on 1** *chf in negative* not show that one knows (about something) by word or sign, not betray interest in or a connection with something *18-*: '*never let on*'. **2** pretend *18-*. **~ out 1** allow (a fire) to go out *18-*. **2** make (straw ropes) by paying out the straw through the fingers while another twists with the *thraw cruik* (THRAW) *20-*, *NE.* **~ ower** swallow *19-*, *chf NE.* **~ see &c 1** = let see, show *la14-*. **2** *specif* pass, hand over *la19-*, *NE.* **~ sit** leave things as they are *la19-*, *NE.* **~ someone wi something** concede to someone's desires or opinions in something *19-*, *N.* **~ (to) wit** *also* **~ (to) wot** *18-19* make known; let it be known *la14-*, *now Abd.* [*cf* LEET³; see SND, DOST]
lat² &c *n* a lath, *esp* one stretched across roof beams for storage *19-*, *now Kcb.* [chf nME *latt*, OE *lætt*; *cf* LATH]
lat *see* LATE, LET
latch¹ *n* **1** = latch. **2** a loop or catch of any kind *la18-*, *now Kcdn Fif Slk.* [*cf* LATCHET]
latch², leche *15-16*, **laich &c** *20-17* [latʃ; *lɛtʃ] *n* **1** a mire, patch of bog *15-e20*; **2** a small stream, *esp* one flowing through boggy ground *15-19*. [freq in place-names *13-*; nME *leche*; *cf* OE *lacu* a stream and *leccan* moisten]
latch³ &c *la19-*, *NE*, **lache &c** *16*, **leach &c** *16-e19* [latʃ; *letʃ] *vti* delay; be negligent; lag, procrastinate *16-*, *now NE.*
lacheand &c, leithand &c, lathand &c *la15-e16* [*'latʃan(d), *'letʃ-, *?'liθ-] lagging, negligent *la14-16*. **~ie** slow, dilatory *20-*, *NE.* **~in** *adj* slow, tardy, lazy *la19-*, *NE.* *n* tardiness, loitering, *chf* **without laching** *la15-16.* [see DOST and *cf* LAISH]
latchet &c, lachet *16-e17* ['latʃət] *n* **1** a small loop of string, thread, wire etc, *freq* a fastening *16-*, *now local.* **2** a window lattice; one of the pieces of wire or metal-work of which it was made *17*. [ME *lachet*, OF *lachet*, dim of *las* a lace]
late &c, lat *la14-17*, **leat &c** *la16-18* [let; *lat] *adj, adv* = late *la14-*.

~ **of** tardy in (doing something) *la18-*.
late *see* LAIT¹, LET
lated, latit &c ['letɪt, -ɪd] *adj, of iron or steel* softened or reduced in temper by heating *(16-e18)* or through rusting *(19-e20)*. [see SND, DOST]
lateron *see* LETTERN
latewake &c [*'let'wek, *-'wɑk] *n = lyke wake* (LYKE) *la17-19*. [altered form]
lath; laith *16*, **lauth(t)** *16* [laθ; *?leθ; *?lɑθ] *n, orig chf in sing as collective = lath la15-*.
~**in(g)** *n* = prec, *esp* as roof-boarding *16-17*.
lauthing &c *verbal noun* covering with laths *16*.
~ **brod,** ~ **bord** lath-boarding, laths collectively *16*. [ME *lathes* (*pl*); *cf* LAT² and see OED]
lathand *see* LATCH³
lathe *see* LAITH
lathenar *see* LADINAR
latherin *see* LAIDRON
lathie *see* LADDIE
Latine, Lating *see* LAITIN
latit *see* LATED
latrin &c; lettrin &c [*'latrən, *'lɛt-] *n, only in pl* = latrines *17*.
latter &c, letter &c *la15-e18 adj* **1** = latter *16-*. **2** belonging to the recent past or the present, recent *la14-16*.
~ **fair** the last of the annual fairs in Stirling *la16-17*. ~ **meat &c** food left over from a meal and served again, *esp* that from the master's table later served to the servants *16-e18*. ~ **meat room** a larder for storing food already cooked *17-18*. ~ **mynd** *16*, ~ **will** *16-17* a person's intention as to the disposal of his property after his death; a will.
lattit *see* LET
lattroun *see* LETTERN
latuce &c [*'latʌs] *n* = lettuce *16-e17*, only Sc.
lauch¹, lach &c *la15-* [lɑx; *Sh Ork also* lex] *vti, pt also* **leuch &c** *15-*, now *N*, **luich &c** *la16*, **lowch &c** *la15-16*; **l(e)ucht &c** *la14-e20*, **laucht &c** *17-* [l(j)ux(t); lɑxt; *Fif also* lex; *Bwk also* luft, lɑft; *EC* *løx, *lɪx]. *ptp also* **la(u)chen &c** *la16-*, now *NE*, **leuchen &c** *19-e20*; **la(u)cht &c** *17-*, **leucht &c** *la19-e20* ['lɑxən, 'l(j)uxən; lɑxt, l(j)uxt; *nEC* *'løxən] = laugh *la14-*. *n* = laugh *la19-*.
come *or* **gae** ~**in hame** *proverb, of something borrowed* be returned to the lender with a gift in recompense *18-*, now *Sh Ork Abd*. ~**in rain** an (unexpectedly long) shower of rain from a clear sky *la19-*, *Ags Uls*.
lauch² &c; lach &c *la16* [*lɑx] *n* a reckoning, a bill in a tavern *la15-16*.
fre ~ free entertainment, food and drink *16*. [see DOST; *cf* LAWIN]
lauch *see* LAW¹, LAICH
lauchen, laucht *see* LAUCH¹
lauchtane &c [*'lɑxtən] *adj* dull-coloured, grey; livid *la14-16*. [MIr, ModIrGael *lachtna*, ScGael *lachdunn*]

lauchter &c; lachter &c *16-* ['lɑxtər] *n* = laughter *15-*.
lauchter *see* LACHTER¹
laud &c *n, law* a finding in a case of arbitration *16*. [laME *laude*, MedL *laudum* a legal finding]
laurean &c; lawrane &c *n* laurel *la14-16*. [irreg var of ME *laurer* or *laurel*]
laureate &c, laureat *ptp* **1** crowned with laurel, honoured as a poet, victor, saint etc *la15-16*. **2** admitted to a university degree *la16-e18*.
vt confer a university degree on *17-e18*.
adj **1** worthy of the laurel crown symbolizing distinction, pre-eminent *16*. **2** pre-eminent in poetry, supremely eloquent; also of speech and writings *16*. **3** graduate *17*.
laureation &c university graduation, *now specif* applied to the complimentary address with which honorary graduates are promoted *17-*. [ME *lauriat*, L *laureatus* crowned with laurel]
Laurence, Lowrence &c *la15-*; **Lawrence** ['larəns, 'lʌurəns] **1** = Laurence *16-*. **2** name given to the fox *15-16*. [*cf* LOWRIE]
laury *see* LARY
lauta *see* LAWTIE
lautee, lauteth *see* LAWTIE
lauth(t) *see* LATH
lavatoure &c [*'lavatur] *n* the spiritual cleansing of baptism *e16*. [obs F *lavatoire* washing, place for washing]
lave¹ &c, lafe &c *la14-e17*; **leife &c** *16* [lev; *Abd also* ljav] *n* the rest, the remainder *la14-*.
an a' the ~ **o't** and all the rest of it, and so on *19*. **ane amang the** ~ one among many, one more of the kind *19-*, now *NE*. [nME *lave*, OE *lāf*]
lave² &c *vt* **1** bale, remove (water) with a bucket or scoop *16-*. **2** = lave *la16-*.
lashins and lavins *fig* abundance *20-*, *Cai Gall Uls*.
lave *see* LEAVE¹
lavell *see* LEVEL
lavellan &c [lə'vɛlən] *n* the water-shrew *la17-*, *Cai*. [Gael *la-bhallan*]
lave-luggit &c *adj* having drooping, pendulous ears *la17-*, now *S*. [nME *lave* drooping (of the ears) + LUG¹]
laven *see* LEAVEN
laverock &c, laverok &c; liv(e)rock &c *la19-*, *NE*, **laveroo &c** *19-*, *Ork* ['levrək; *Ork* 'levru; *NE* 'lɪvrɪk] *n* the skylark *15-*. [ME *laverok*, OE *lāferce*; *cf* LAIRICK]
laves *see* LAIF
lavie &c ['lavɪ] *n* the guillemot; the razorbill *la17-e19*, *Hebrides*. [Gael *làmhaidh*, ON *langve*]
law¹ &c [lɑ; *NE also* *ljav] *n, also* **lauch &c** [*lɑx] *only in sing la14-16, only proverb 17-e19* **1** = law *la14-*. **2** *in pl* specific points of law cited in support of a plea; the legal basis of one's case *la15-e16, only Sc*.

vti **1** = law, litigate, sue *19-*, *now Ork Abd Gall*. **2** *vt* lay down the law to; control, determine *la18-e19*.

lawer &c, lawvyer &c *la19-* ['lɑwər, 'lɑvjər] *n* **1** = lawyer *la16-*, *now local*. **2** a university professor of law *la16*. **lawful &c** *15-*, **lauchfull &c** *la14-e18* (*the commoner form la14-16*) = lawful. **~ful &c day** *etc* a day etc on which it is permissible to transact business *la14-*.

~ agent a solicitor *informally 19-*, *officially la19-e20*. **law-biding** submitting to the law *la16-17*, *only Sc*. **law-borch &c** = *lawburrows* **2**, *la15-16*. **draw oneself** *or* **one's possessions law-borgh &c** pledge oneself etc (not to injure another) *la15*. **law burrows &c, law-borowis &c** ['labʌrəs; *St* 'lɔ'bʌroz; *'la'borʌuz, *-'borəs] **1** *law* legal security required from or given by a person that he will not injure another *15-*, *now chf hist*. **2** the person standing as surety as in **1**, *freq* **becum** *etc* **lawborrowis &c for** *la15-17*. **letters of lawborrowis** the warrant charging a person to give such security *16-17* [pl of *lawborch*, treated as sing]. **~ fere &c** a lawful partner, a person in partnership with another by legal agreement *e17*. **~ lord** one of the judges of the *Court of Session* (SESSION), to whom the courtesy title of LORD is given *18-*. **~-paper** a legal document *19-*, *now Ork Ayr*. **~-plea** a lawsuit, process of litigation *la18-*, *now EC*. **~ sovertie &c** = *lawburrows*, *16-17*. **~ wark &c** theology based on Mosaic law, implying formal morality rather than evangelical religion *18-19*.

the law (*or* **laws**) **of Clan Macduff** a privilege granted to the kin of the Earls of Fife (or to Fife men) of remission of the penalty of slaughter, on payment of compensation by the slayer according to a prescribed rate *15-16* [ScL *legem de Clanmacduff*, *la14*].

law² [lɑ; *NE also* *ljɑ] *n* **1** a rounded, *usu* conical hill, *freq* isolated or conspicuous *la14-*, *in place-names*, *chf EC, S, 12-*. **2** an artificial mound, *specif* (1) a grave-mound *la16-e19*; (2) a mound of earth and shingle on a river-bank to which salmon nets are drawn to be emptied *la17-e19*, *NE*. [nME *lawe &c*, OE *hlāw &c*]

law *see* LAICH
lawage *see* LOVAGE
lawboard *see* LABROD
lawbour *see* LABOUR
lawd *see* LAD, LAWIT
lawic &c [*'laɪk] *adj* lay, not of the clergy *la15-e17*. [altered f LAWIT after Eng *laic*]
lawid *see* LAWIT
lawin &c, lawing &c *16-17* ['laɪn] *n* **1** a session of drinking or entertainment, *esp* in a tavern; a drinking party *16-17*. **2** a tavern reckoning or one's share of this *16-*, *now local*

NE-Ayr. **3** a contribution towards the refreshments at a wedding *17-19*. **4** *fig* retribution, the consequences *la18-e20*. [related to or derived f LAUCH²]

lawit &c; lawid &c, lawd &c, lewit &c *la14-e16* [*'laɪt, *-ɪd, *lad, *ljuɪt, *-ɪd] *adj* = lewd, lay; unlearned; unpolished; common *la14-17*. [*cf* LAWIC, LAYIT]

lawland &c *la15-*, *now Ags Ayr*, **lowland &c** *17-* ['lɑlən(d)] *n* **1** *in sing and pl* the low-lying area, low-lying lands *la15-17*. **2** *chf in pl* any part or all of Scotland east and south of the *Highland Line* (HIELAND) (*sometimes excluding* the BORDERS) *la15-*; cf *laich country* (LAICH). **3** = LALLAN *n* **2** (1), *la19-e20*.

adj belonging to the *Lowlands* of Scotland *16-*. **~er** a person from the *Lowlands*, *n* **2**, *20-*. [*cf* LAICH]

lawnd *see* LAND²
Lawnmarket *see* LAND¹
lawrane *see* LAUREAN
Lawrence *see* LAURENCE
lawtie &c *la14-18*, **leautee &c** *la14-15*, **lautee &c** *la14-e17*, **lauta &c** *la15-e17*, **lauteth &c** *16-e18* [*'latɪ, *-ə, *-əð, *'liatɪ, *'ljutɪ] *n* **1** loyalty, fidelity *la14-18*. **2** (1) faithful adherence to one's word; integrity *la14-16*. (2) faithful adherence to high standards of conduct, upright behaviour *la15-e17*. (3) integrity in the administration of the law, justice, equity *la14-16*. **3** the truth *la14-15*. **lautéfull &c** faithful, loyal; honourable *16*. [nME (once) *laute*, ME (once each) *lealte*, *lewted*, OF *leaute*, *lealte &c*]

lawvyer *see* LAW
lax &c *n* a salmon *la15-e19*, *chf NE*.

~fisher &c a salmon fisherman *14-18*, *chf NE*. **~ net &c** salmon-net *la15-e17*. [ME; OE *leax*, ON *lax*]

lay¹ &c [le] *vt* **1** (1) = lay *la14-*. (2) *used where Eng has* put, place, set etc *18-*. **2** flatten (crops) by wind or rain *la18-*. **3** silence, check (speech, noise) *16-e19*. **4** build *16-17*. **5** plant or make (a hedge) *la18*, *la20-*, *sEC Kcb*. **6** (1) paint *la15-16*. (2) smear (a sheep's fleece) with butter, tar etc as a protection against wet etc *la17-e20*. **7** re-steel (a plough-iron etc) *la16-*, *Gen except Sh Ork*. **8** form (a rope etc) by twisting strands together *e15*, *la18-20*. **9** lay aside, put (a plough) out of action *15-16*. **10** lay out (money), pay out *la15*. **11** supply, provide (at the place required) *la16-17*. **12** place (hope, confidence etc) **on** or **in** (a person or thing) *la14-16*. **13** *also fig* reckon up, audit (an account) *16-17*.

n **1** the re-steeling of the cutting edge of an implement *la18-*, *Gen except Sh Ork*. **2** mood, temper *la19-*, *chf Sh Ork* [perh partly f Norw *lag* mood].

laid drain a field drain formed by a row of stones laid on each side and a third course of flat stones laid above these *19-*, *now Sh Cai Gall*

Uls. **laid wark** couched work *17*. **laid wool** &c wool from sheep which have been smeared as in *v 6, 17-19*.

~ **bag** *20-*, *Ork-Per*, ~ **p(y)ock** *19-*, *chf Sh Abd* the ovary of a fowl.

be laid aff one's feet *la19-*, *now midLoth Uls*, **be laid aside** *18-* be incapacitated by illness. **I (dar)** ~ **(vow)** *etc verse* I wager, I dare say *la14-e16*. ~ **about** turn a boat round *la19-*, *Sh Ayr*. ~ **one's account for** *or* **with something** *or* **to do something** expect, reckon on *18-e19*. ~ **aff** &c *vti* recount fluently, talk volubly and confidentially (about) *19-*. *n* a harangue, rigmarole *la20-*. ~ **anker** &c drop anchor *15-e17*. ~ **aside** put out of the way, get rid of (a person) *16-17*. ~ **at** strike at, beat *la19-*, *now local Sh-Loth*. ~ **awa** *of a fowl* lay eggs away from the usual nest *19-*. ~ **by** *vti* **1** lay aside, discard *la14-*. **2** set aside, reserve *16-*. **3** (cause to) stop or rest *18-*. **4** *chf in passive* be incapacitated through illness *la18-*, *now local*. ~ **doun** &c lay in the grave, bury *19-*, *chf NE*. ~ **frae one 1** *vt* take off (one's clothes etc) *la14-17*. **2** *vi* hit out in all directions *19-*, *local Sh-Wgt*. ~ **furth 1** put out (furniture) from a house, *esp* in evicting a tenant *16*. **2** ~ **furth on** *or* **upoun breid** extend, spread out *16*. ~ **in 1** pay in (rent in kind, pledges) *16-17*. **2** = *v* 11, *la17*, *Pbls*. **3** enclose or retain (*freq* a mill-dam) by means of an embankment *la16-17*. **4** set to work energetically *la19-*. **5** ~ **oneself in** stock up, take in goods in bulk *la19-*, *now Sh Loth*. **6** (1) fold (something) down or over on itself *19-*, *now midLoth SW*. (2) *specif* turn up (a hem) *la20-*, *local Ork-Kcb*. **7** *forestry* hack a tree around the trunk before felling, eg to prevent it splitting upwards *la20-*, *local Abd-Dmf*. ~ **into** *or* **intil** eat greedily *la19-*. ~ **on** *v* **1** *of rain or snow* (*19-*) fall heavily *15-*, *now local*. **2** work hard, apply energy *19-*, *now Sh Uls*. **3** eat heartily *la19-*, *now Ags Loth Uls*. **4** ~ **on** *or* **upon someone** (**to do** *or* **for doing something**) charge, delegate *la16-e17*: '*the rest leyed upon me to be speaker*'. **lay-on** *n* a hearty meal; a surfeit *la19-*, *now Ags Loth Uls*. ~ **out** = ~ **furth** 1, *16-17*. ~ **over** &c **1** = *v* 6 (1), *16-e17*. **2** turn over (a furrow) in ploughing *la20-*, *Sh-NE Wgt*. ~ **till** *or* **tae** &c *v* **1** *vt* start to eat *la18-*, *now Sh Uls*. **2** beat *19-*, *now local*. **3** close (a door) *la19-*, *Sh-NE*. **4** *vi* set to, work vigorously *la19-*, *local*. ~ **to (the) se** to put (ships) to sea *e15*.

lay² [le] *n* **1** the framed part of a loom, which strikes home each successive weft thread, the batten *la16-*, *now local*. **2** a turning lathe *20-*. [MDu *la(ey)* = 1; ultimately cognate w Eng *lathe* of which 2 is a var]

lay³ [*lǝi] *n* **1** alloy; an alloy *la14-17*. **2** *attrib* made of alloy, debased (money etc) *la16-17*. ~**it** alloyed, *freq* ~**it money** *16-17*. [aphetic f OSc (once), eModEng *allay*, ME, northern OF *alay*]

lay⁴ [*ʔlǝi] *n* ? = delay *15-e16*.

lay *see* LEA, LIE

layer *see* LAIR¹

layit &c [*ʔ'leɪt] *adj* lay, of the laity *16*. [altered f Eng *laic*; *cf* LAWIT]

layit *see* LAY³

laylock &c ['lelǝk, 'lɛlǝk; *Bwk* 'lɪlǝk] *n* = lilac *la18-*, *now NE Fif Slk*. [*cf* LILYOAK]

layne *see* LAIN

laytil *see* LITTLE

lazarus; lazarous *n* a leper *la15-16*. [earlier in Sc]

lazy &c, **lasie** &c *la16-17* ['lezɪ] *adj* = lazy *la16-*.

n a fit of laziness *20-*, *midLoth SW, S*.

~**-bed** a method of planting (*usu* potatoes) on undug strips of soil, using manure and sods from adjacent trenches as covering *18-*, *now chf Hebrides Highl*, *now chf hist*.

le; lie &c *16-19*, **ly** *la14-16* [*li] *article* the, *in Latin texts preceding both sing and pl forms of* **1** *vernacular place-names*, *la12-e17*; **2** *other vernacular designations*, *la14-19*. [AN *le*, OF *li* masc sing def art; see DOST; *cf* LA, LEZ]

le *see* LEE²

lea¹ &c *la17-*, **ley** &c; **lay** *la16-18* [lǝi; *sEC, WC Dmf* li] *adj* **1** lea, fallow, unploughed *16-*. **2** barren, wild *18-*.

n **1** (1) = lea, ground left untilled; ground once tilled but now in pasture, *orig* part of the OUTFIELD *16-*. (2) *specif* second-year or older pasture following hay *20-*. **2** *chf verse and freq in place-names* a tract of open grassland; an open uncultivated area *16-*. **3** = ~ **corn**, *la17-*, *local*.

~ **arnut** &c *joc* a stone lying loose on the soil, and of a size easily thrown *19-*, *Abd*. ~ **break** fallow ground or old pasture due to be ploughed up in rotation *20-*, *local N-SW*. ~ **corn** *20-*, ~ **crap** *la17-* oats grown on ploughed-up grassland *local*. ~ **field** a field of established grass *20-*, *N, EC, SW*. ~ **fur**, **furrow** a ploughing of old grassland *la19-*, *local NE-SW*. ~ **girse**, ~ **grass** *e18*, *20-*, ~ **ground** *la19-* established pastureland, grassland not recently ploughed *local*. ~ **hay** hay grown on old pasture *18-*, *now SW*. ~ **land** land left unploughed *la16-18*. ~ **oats** &c = ~ **corn** *20-*, *local*. ~ **park** = ~ **field**, *la19-*, *N Gall*. ~ **rig** *now only verse* a RIG¹ or strip of grass left untilled in a ploughed field, a broad BAUK¹ *16-*.

lie ~ *lit and fig* lie fallow *16-19*. [*n* 2 orig ? OE *lēah* a clearing, which is also found (chf as second element) in Sc place-names *la12-*. The forms of this and of *n* 1, which is derived from the *adj* above, coalesce in ME, and, *esp* in combs, it is not always possible to distinguish the originals]

lea *see* LEAVE¹

leach *see* LATCH³

leache *see* LAICH

lead *16-*, **lede** &c [lid; *nEC* led] *vti*, *pt*, *ptp also*

leid &c *la14-la16* [*lid] **1** = lead *la14-*. **2** *vi*, curling (CURL) lead off for one's side, play first *19-*. **3** *vt* (1) convey in a cart *la14-*. (2) *specif* transport (PEATS¹) home from the MOSS *la16-*, now *local*. (3) carry (harvested grain or hay) home or **in** *(19-)* from the field *la14-*. **4** administer (the law(s)) *15-16*. **5** conduct (legal proceedings); hold (a court); bring (an action); deliver (a judgment) *15-17*: 'quhat-sumevir oure saidis counsalouris .. leidis to be done'. **6** *law* call, produce (evidence, witnesses etc) *15-*: 'lead proof'. **7** guide (another's hand) in writing *16*.

n, curling (CURL) **1** the first player on each side *19-*, now *Ayr Gall*. **2** the course or rink over which the stones are played *19*.

leader &c *la16-*, **ledar &c** *la14-e17* ['lidər; *'ledər] **1** = leader *la14-*. **2** a person in charge of a pack- or draught-animal; a person who carries goods in a vehicle *la15-19*. **3** a tributary of a stream *la19-*, now *Cai Uls*. **4** a tendon, sinew *la19-*, now *local*. **5** an extension in a salmon-net to lead the fish into the main trap *la20-*, *N Bwk SW*. **6** a person who administers the law(s) *la15-16*. **led farm** a smaller or outlying farm managed through an employee *17-*, *local Fif-S*.

follow one's ain ~ do as one pleases *20-*, *N local EC*.

lead *see* LADE, LEID

leaf &c *17-*; **lefe &c** *la14-17* [lif; *Sh Ork nEC* lef; *pl* lifs, lefs] *n* **1** = leaf *la14-*. **2** one of the segments of an orange *20-*, *local Cai-Uls*. [for *n* 2 *cf* LITH]

leaf *see* LAIF

league *see* LEGE

leak *see* LECK¹

leal &c *la16-*, **lele &c** [lil; *nEC* lel] *adj* **1** legally valid, just *la14-16*. **2** (1) loyal, faithful to one's allegiance or duties *la14-*, now *chf verse*. (2) faithful in religion; Christian *la14-15*. **3** faithful, constant in friendship and (*esp*) love *la14-*, now *chf verse*. **4** (1) honest, honourable, law-abiding *la14-20*. (2) *specif* applied to a person required to act (under oath) officially or legally, *esp* in testifying *la14-17*. **5** *of conduct or counsel* dutiful, trusty *la14-16*. **6** *of a report, accounts etc* true, accurate; *of doctrine* genuine, sound *la14-18*. **7** *of a measure* fair, exact, accurate *15-19*. **8** *ballad, of a woman* chaste, pure *18-19*.

adv **1** loyally, honestly, sincerely *15-e19*. **2** truly, accurately, thoroughly *15-e19*.

~**ty** loyalty *19-e20*.

~ **becumit**, ~ **come (by)** lawfully obtained, honestly earned *17*. ~**-heartit** faithful, sincere *18-*, *local Bnf-Rox*. ~ **love &c** one's true love, sweetheart *17*. ~ **won &c** = ~ *becumit*, *la15-16*.

bere ~ **(and suthefast) witnes(sing)** *chf law* give a truthful testimony *la14-17*. [nME *lele &c*, OF *leel &c* loyal, L *legalis* legal]

leam¹ *la18-*, **leme &c** [lim] *n*, *chf verse, lit and fig* light, radiance; a gleam of light *la14-*, now *chf NE*.

vi, *chf verse* shine, glitter, flash *la14-e20*. [ME *leme*, OE *lēoma*]

leam² &c [lim] *vt* take (a ripe nut) from its husk *19*, *SW, S*.

~**(m)er** a ripe nut separating easily from its husk *19-e20*, *SW, S*. [obscure]

leam *see* LAME¹, LOOM²

lean &c *la16-*, **lene &c** [lin, len] *vti* **1** = lean *la14-*. **2** *vir* recline, lie down, rest, take a seat *la14-*, now *Bnf Lnk Kcb*.

n a rest; a resting-place, seat *la18-*, *Ags Fif Loth*. [*cf* LIN]

lean *see* LANE³

leap &c *la16-*, **lepe &c**; **lape &c** *la14-19* *vti* [lip; *nEC* lep] *pt also* **lap &c** *la14-20*, **lape &c** *la14-20*, **lep &c** *19*, *Sh Ork*; **lapt** *la19-e20*. *ptp also* **loppin &c** *la14-e17*, **lappin &c** *la16-e17*, **luppen** *la18-e20* **1** = leap *la14-*. **2** ~ **out** emerge, escape *la14-17*. **3** *vi*, *of frost or snow* thaw *19-e20*. **4** (1) *of things* spring apart *16*, *19-e20*. (2) *specif, of potatoes being boiled in their skins* burst open *20-*, *wLoth S*. **5** *of the face* flush with blushing or with a skin rash *20-*, *Sh Rox*. **6** rush or spring in attack *16-e17*.

~**ing-on-stone** a mounting-block *la17-19*. **luppen sinnen &c** a ganglion *la19-*, now *Renfr SW*. ~ **abak** *or* **back** back out of an agreement *16-e17*. [*cf* LOWP¹]

lear &c *la16-*, **lere &c** [lir; *nEC* ler] *v* **1** *vt* teach, instruct *la14-e19*. **2** *vti* learn, ascertain *la14-*. **lerit &c** *adj* educated; *hence* belonging to the clergy *15-16*. [ME *leren*, OE *lǣran* teach; *cf* LAIR³]

lear *see* LARE³

leard *see* LAIRD

learn &c *la16-*, **lerne &c**; **leern** *la19-e20*, *Abd* [lɛrn; *lern; *lirn *latterly NE*] *vti* **1** = learn, ascertain *la15-*. **2** *vt* teach, instruct *la15-*.

lease¹ &c [liz] *vt* **1** separate or sort out (the yarn for the warp threads) before weaving *19-*, *chf Rox*. **2** arrange, lay in order, sort *19-e20*, *SW, S*. **3** disentangle (a complicated state of affairs), tidy up (confusion of any kind) *19-*, *SW, S*.

n **1** *weaving* the division of the threads in a warp before it is put on the loom *19-*, now *WC*. **2** *fig, of speech or thought* a continuous or coherent sequence; a clear understanding of a story or idea; one's bearings *la19-*, *midLoth SW Uls*: 'I lost the lease o't'. [ModEng *dial* lease, OE *lesan* glean, gather]

lease², **lese &c** [?lis] *vt* release *17*, *la19-e20*. [*appar* ME *lese*, OE *lēsan &c*]

leaser *see* LEISURE

leash &c *la16-*, **lesche &c** [liʃ] *n* **1** = leash *15-*. **2** (1) a long piece of string, rope, thread etc *19-*, now *NE, SW*. (2) anything long of its kind *19-e20*, *chf NE*. **3** a leash used for whipping; a stroke of a lash *16-*, now *Sh midLoth*.

v **1** = leash, tie together *la19-*. **2** lash, flog

16-, now Sh. **3** *vi, of rain* fall in torrents *20-, Sh Ags.* **4** walk or move quickly or energetically (**up, away** *etc*) *18-, chf Sh N.*
~ **at** work energetically or at great speed *la19-e20, Sh Bnf.*

leasing &c *la16-*, **lesing &c** ['lizɪŋ] *n* **1** lying, slandering *15.* **2** a lie, a slander *la14-18.*
~-**maker &c** a person who is guilty of ~-*making, 15-19.* ~-**making** *law* the spreading of calumny against the Crown likely to cause sedition or disaffection *la17-, now hist.*
but ~, **forout**(**in**) ~, **without** ~ *only verse* candidly; in truth, certainly *la14-16.* **mak** ~ lie, tell lies *la14-15.* **mak ane** ~ *or* ~**s 1** (1) = prec *la15-e17;* (2) *chf* **mak** (**a**) ~ **of** tell lies about, slander *la15-16.* **2** backbite, slander *la15-e16.* [ME *lesing*, OE *lēasung*, f *lēasian* (v); *cf* LES. SND *lease* (v¹)]

least¹, leste &c *la16-17* [list] *conj* = lest, in case *la16-, now Abd midLoth Uls; also* ~ **that** *la16-17, e19.* [eModEng ME *leste &c*, OE *þy læs þe*]

least² &c *la15-*, **leste &c** *la14-17;* **laest &c** *17-, now Sh Ork* [list; *Sh Ork NE nEC* lest] *adj* = least *la14-.*
adv **1** = least *la14-.* **2** at least *19-, now Ork.*
~**est** *double superlative adj, la19-, now Sh.*
~**ways,** ~**wise** = *adv* 2, *la19-, local.*

leasure *see* LEISURE

leat *see* LATE

leath *see* LAITH

leather &c *la16-*, **lether &c** *15-17*, **ledder &c** *15-, now Sh Ork NE* ['lɛðər; *Sh Ork NE* 'lɛdər; *'laðər; *'ladər] *n* **1** = leather *15-.* **2** the skin, hide *16-.* **3** a heavy blow *20-, N, SW.*
v **1** *vt, of a hound* wear the skin of (a quarry) *16.* **2** beat, thrash *la18-.* **3** *vti, freq* ~ **at,** ~ **up** do something fast and energetically, work hard *19-, now Ags Kcb Uls.* **4** *vi* hurry, walk briskly *19-, now Abd Loth Slk.*

leauch *see* LAICH

leautee *see* LAWTIE

leave¹ &c *la15-*, **leve &c** *la14-e20*, **lefe &c** *la14-e19*, **lea &c** *la18-;* **lave &c** *la16-, now nEC* [liv; li; *Sh Ork* lev; *nEC Gall Uls* lev, le] *vti, pt, ptp also* **levit &c** *la14-e16* [*'livit], **leeft** *la19-e20, Abd* [lift] = leave *la14-.*
leaving *see* CERTIFICATE. **left** abandoned (by God's grace), left to follow one's own foolish or sinful devices *18-.* **left to anesel** misguided, astray in one's judgment *18-.*
~ **aside** let alone, apart from, not counting *la19-, local Bnf-Wgt.* ~ **me** *etc* **alone for** I *etc* may be trusted to do or deal with *19-, now Cai SW Uls.*

leave² &c *la16-*, **leve &c** *la14-17*, **lefe &c** *la14-e17* [liv] *vt* permit, allow *la14-, now local.*
n **1** = leave, permission *la14-.* **2** *specif* (1) permission to a pupil to leave the classroom during a school lesson *20-;* (2) the playtime interval in school *20-.* **3** dismissal, notice to quit *la15-.*

~-**taking** the taking leave of a person *la14-.*
get one's ~ be given one's discharge, be dismissed *17-19.* [*cf* LEESOME², LEFUL]

leaven &c, laven &c *16* ['lɛvən; *Abd* 'livɪn] *n* **1** = leaven *16-.* **2** a mixture of oatmeal and water made up as a dough for *oatcakes* (AIT) or as food for young poultry *18-, Sh N Fif.*
~ **tub** the vessel in which dough is mixed and leavened *16, chf EC.*

leave-o &c *n* a children's game in which one side hunts out and captures the members of the other, and places them in a DEN² from which they have to be released by their own side *20-, local Ork-Ayr; cf* RELIEF, *reliever* (RELIEVE). [f a call made in the game, reduced f *relieve o*]

leaves *see* LAIF

leb, lebbach, lebber *see* LAIB

lecence *see* LEESHENCE

lecent *see* LICENT

leche *see* LATCH²

lechfull &c; leichefull &c [*?'lixfʌl] *adj* = LEFUL *la15-16.* [by analogy or blending w *lauchfull* (LAW¹)]

leck¹ *la16-, now local*, **lek** *la15-19*, **leke &c** *la16-e18;* **leak** *la18-*, **lake &c** *17-* [lɛk, lek] *n* **1** = leak *16-.* **2** a container in which bark for tanning was steeped *18-19.*
vi **1** = leak *16-.* **2** *of rain* fall in intermittent showers *17-, now Ork Stlg Uls.*
lekkage &c, laikage &c *e17* wastage of imported wine by leaking from the barrels; an allowance made for this in charging duty *16-17.*
l(**e**)**aky tide** a tide in the upper part of the Firth of Forth which seems to lose water temporarily before the full tide, and to gain it before the ebb tide *e18-, EC.* [*le*(*c*)*k* forms prob MDu, LowGer *lek* (*n*), *leken* (*v*)]

leck² &c *n* **1** a flat stone or slab; a flat rock in the sea *20-, NE Kcb, freq in Abd place-names.* **2** *also* ~ **stane, lek stain** *e17* a kind of igneous rock which breaks into flat slabs; a piece of this used as an oven-slab *e17, 19, EC.* [Sc and IrGael *leac* a slab, ledge of rock]

leckerstane &c *17-*, **likarstane &c** *15-* ['lɛkər'sten, 'lɪkər-, &c] *n* a conspicuous stone or stone-heap, *traditionally* associated with burials *15-, chf NE-nEC, now in place-names.* [see SND, DOST]

leckie &c *17-e18*, **lakay &c** *la16-17* ['lakɪ; *'lɛkɪ] *n* = lackey; *cf* ALLEKAY.

lectioun &c *n* a university lecture *la16-17.* [MedL *lectio* a lesson, lecture; *cf* eModEng *lection* reading, interpretation, L *lectio*]

lector &c, lectour &c *la15-e17* *n* **1** = lector, a reader *la15-.* **2** a pupil learning to read *16-e18.* **3** a lecturer in a university *la16-e17.* **4** a clerk, scribe *la16-e17.*
~ **schole &c** an elementary school *la16-e17.*

lectroun &c *n* = LETTERN *la15-16.* [see DOST]

lecture &c ['lɛktər] *n* **1** = lecture (in a university) *la15-*. **2** a reading in church of a passage of Scripture accompanied by a running commentary *la16-19*.
vi deliver such a reading and commentary *17-e19*.

lecturi; leetera &c *numeral* **1** *only* **lecturi** *sheep-counting* seven *e20*. **2** *only* **leetera** &c *children's rhymes* six *la19*. [see ZEENDI; *cf* SEATER]

led *see* LAID, LEAD, LID

ledar *see* LEAD

ledd *see* LEID

ledder *see* LEATHER, LETHER

leddy *see* LADY

lede[1] &c [*lid] *n*, *chf alliterative verse* **1** *in sing* a person; a man *la15-16*. **2** *in pl* people, men *la15-e16*.
  all (levand) leidis *or* **leid** [*lid(z)] all (living) people, everyone *la15-e17*. [ME *lede* &c, OE *lēod* (*masc*) a man, prince; *cf* next]

lede[2] &c [*lid] *n* a people or nation; *collectively* people, folk *la14-16*. [ME *lede*, OE *lēod* (*fem*); *cf* prec]

lede *see* LEAD, LEED, LEID

ledge[1] *vti* assert, declare, make accusations *19*. [aphetic f Eng *allege*]

ledge[2] *n* = ledge *17-*.
  ledging &c the parapet of a bridge *17-e19*.
  ~**it** the top of the lower sash of a window *la19-*, *NE*.

lee[1] *16-*, **ley** &c; **lie** &c [li; *S also* ləi] *v, pres pl also* **leyne** &c *e16*. *pt, ptp also* **leyit** *15-16*, **leyt** *la14-e17*, **leid** &c *la15-* ['lɪɪt, liːd] **1** = lie, tell lies *la14-*. **2** say something in error with no intention to deceive *la19-*, *now local*.
n **1** = lie, falsehood *la15-* [NB: OSc pl *leis* is sometimes indistinguishable f *leis*, pl of LES]. **2** a false statement not made deceitfully, *esp* by speakers correcting themselves *20-*, *local*.
  ~**some** &c incredible; shocking *19-*, *now SW, S*.
  ~**some like** like a fiction, incredible *19-*, *SW, S*.
  ~ **like** false, lying; fictional *19-*, *SW, S*.
  the father of ~**s** the Devil *la16*. ~ **on** etc tell a lie about, slander *la14-*.

lee[2] &c *la15-*, **le** *la14-e16* [li] *n* = lee, shelter *la14-*.
adj = lee *la15-*.
  ~**gaw** a sign of bad weather in the leeward part of the sky *20-*, *N*. ~**-laik** &c sheltered *17-*, *SW*. ~**side** *of a pot* the side boiling less fiercely, the cooler side *18-*, *now Ork Wgt*.

lee[3] *e19*, **ley** &c *la16-e17* [*li] *n* = lye. [late nME; OE *lēag* &c]

lee *see* LIEF, LUIF

leebel *see* LIBEL

leeberal *see* LIBERAL

leeberty *n* = liberty *19-*.

leebral *see* LIBERAL

leebrary &c *19-*, **library** &c; **liberary** &c *17-18* ['lib(ə)rəre, 'lɪb-] *n* = library *la16-*.

leecure *19-*, *now Sh*, **licoure** &c *15-16* ['likər] *n* = liquor.

leed *18-*, **lede** &c *n* **1** a language *la14-*, *now Ork*, *latterly chf verse*. **2** a manner of speaking or writing, diction, style *la15-19*. **3** a formula, refrain, the way a rhyme or song goes *la18-19*. **4** a constant or repeated theme; a long rambling story *la19-*, *NE*. [ME *lede*, *appar* reduced f *leden* &c, OE *lēoden* language]

leef *see* LUIF

leeft *see* LEAVE[1]

leefu(l) *see* LIEF

leek &c *la16-*, **leke** &c *la14-17* *n* = leek *la14-*.
  as clean as a ~ complete(ly), thorough(ly) *18-*, *now midLoth*.

leek *see* LYKE

leem *see* LUME

leemit *la19-*, **limit** &c, **lemit** &c *la15-16* ['lɪmɪt, 'lɪmɪt] *n*, *vt* = limit *15-*.
  limit &c *adj*, *of a time, place, boundary* appointed, fixed definitely or within limits *la14, 17*.
  vt circumscribe *la16-17*. [L *līmitāt-*, ptp stem of *līmitāre* limit]

leemon *n* = lemon *la19-e20*.
  ~**ade** = lemonade *20-*, *now Gall Uls*.

leen *n*, *chf in pl* pieces of grassy land in a moor or by a river, meadows, *freq* pastures of natural grass *la18-*, *Cai*. [ON *læna*, Icel *læna* a hollow or valley]

le'en *see* ELEEVEN

leenge &c *vi* slouch in walking *19-e20*. [uncertain]

leengyie *e19*, **lignie** &c *la15*, **lenȝe** &c *la14-16*; **linȝé** &c *e16* [*'lɪŋ(j)ɪ, *'linjɪ, *'lɪŋ-, *'lɪn-] *adj* fine, thin, slender **1** *in gen*, *la14-16*; **2** *specif of textiles e16*, *e19* (*Ayr*). [northern OF *ligne*, ultimately f L *līneus* of flax, linen]

leep *18-*, **lepe** &c *v* **1** *vt* heat partially, parboil *16-*, *now Sh-N Gall*. **2** *vi* sit lazily by a fire *la19-e20*.
n a warming; a parboiling; a sitting by the fire *19*, *N*.
  ~**it** &c **1** warmed up; parboiled; scalded *18-e20*. **2** fond of warmth, given to coddling oneself, pampered *18-*, *chf N*. [perh OE *hlēpan*, corresponding to ON *hleypa* cause to leap or rush; curdle (milk) as by heating it]

Lee-penny *n* a small, red, roughly heart-shaped stone set in a groat of Edward IV of England (1442-83) and possessed by the Lockharts of the Lee near Carluke, Lnk, used as a healing charm; the theme of Scott's *Talisman 19*, *Lnk*.

leepie *see* LIPPIE

leerie &c *n* **1** a lamplighter *19-20*. **2** a lamp *la19-*, *now EC Dmf*.
  ~ **pole** the pole used by lamplighters *20*, *Abd EC Gsw*. [f the children's rhyme beginning *leerie, leerie, light the lamps*, orig prob meaningless]

leerie-la &c *n* **1** the call of the cock *e19*. **2** the cock *19*.
vi crow *20-*, *Ags Fif*. [imit; *cf* COCKIELEERIE]

leern see LEARN

leerup &c *n* a sharp blow or smack, a lash *19-*, *chf N.* [Eng slang *leerip &c* (*v*) beat, thrash; *cf* Du dial *lerpen, larpen* (*v*) whip]

leeshence &c *19-*, **lecence &c** *15-e17*, **licence &c** *15-*; **leesense &c** *19-* [ˈliʃəns, ˈlis-] *n* **1** = licence *15-*. **2** *specif, Presbyterian Churches* the permission granted after examination to a divinity student by a PRESBYTERY to preach and become a *probationer* (PROBATION) available to be called to a ministerial charge, *corresponding to Eng* holy orders *18-*.
vt **1** = licence *15-*. **2** *specif, Presbyterian Churches* grant a *licence* (*n* 2) to *18-*.

leesome¹ &c *adj* **1** pleasant, lovable *la18-*, *now Ork Uls.* **2** *of weather* fine, balmy, mild and bright *la18-*, *NE.* **3** *as intensifier* one's ~ **lane** absolutely alone, on one's own *19-*, *now local N-Ayr.* [appar LIEF + -SOME, w infl f LEESOME²]

leesome² &c *17-19*, **lesum &c** *la15-18*, **lefesum &c** *la15-e17*, **levesum** *la16* [*ˈlisʌm, *ˈlivsʌm] *adj* morally or legally permissible; right, just. [ME *lefsum*, f OE *lēaf* > LEAVE²; *cf* LEFUL]

leesome see LEE¹

leet¹ *18-*, **leit &c** *la16-e19* [lit] *n* **1** a stack of PEATS¹ (*la16-*) or coal (*la18-20*) of a specific size, varying locally and from time to time, *chf NE.* **2** a section of an oblong stack of grain or beans *17-*, *now Loth WC.*
~ **peats** PEATS¹ delivered in LEETS¹ as part of a farm tenant's rent *17-e19*, *NE.* [OE *hlēte*, ON *hleyti* a lot, share, portion]

leet² &c, **leit &c** *la16-e18* [lit] *n* **1** a list of selected candidates for a post *la16-*. **2** *in pl* the persons listed as nominees or selected candidates *la16-17*. **3** the select or prize-winning animals at an agricultural show *la20-*, *SW.*
vt nominate to a list of candidates *17-*.
long ~ **1** the list of nominees for the seats of the retiring members of a BURGH council, submitted to the existing council for reduction by half *18-e19.* **2** a first list of selected candidates, to be further selected into a *short leet, 20-*. **short leet 1** the shortened list of nominees produced as described in *long leet 1, e19.* **2** the final list of candidates for a post after the preliminary rejection of the least suitable *la18-*. [only Sc; aphetic f OSc *eleit*, F *élit*; *cf* LITE]

leet³, **leit &c** [lit] *v* **1** behave as if, pretend *15-16, e19.* **2** *vti* give a sign that one knows or is taking notice; pay attention *la18-*, *now Sh-Cai.* **3** make mention, pass on information *la19-*, *local Sh-Loth.* [regular development of OE *lǣtan* let, in special uses of LAT¹. DOST *lat* (*v¹*)]

leet see LAT¹

leetany &c *n* a long rambling story, a rigmarole *19-*, *Sh NE.* [Sc var of Eng *litany*]

leetera see LECTURI

leeterary *adj* = literary *la20.*

leeteratur *e19*, **letteratoure &c** *la14-e16* [*ˈlitərətər, *ˈlɪt(ə)r-, *ˈlɛt(ə)r-, *-atør] *n* = literature.

leeve *16-*, *only Sc*, **leve &c** *la14-e20*, *only Sc*, **live &c**, **lefe &c** *la14-e17*, *only Sc*, **lif &c** *la14-16*, **luff &c** *la14-16* [lɪv, lʌv; *WC, SW, S Uls* liv] *vti* = live *la14-*.
the langar *or* **langest levand &c** *or* **levar &c** (**of thaim &c**) the survivor *la14-17.* **leevin &c 1** a person, anyone *19-*, *now local Ork-Gall.* **2** food *19-*, *now Ags SW.* **livin-like** lively, in good health *la19-*, *local Ork-Gall.*
~ **aff** = live on *20-*. ~ **under** be subject to (a government or authority) *15-16.* **weel to** ~ comfortably off *19.*

leevy, leeze see LIEF

lefe see LEAF, LEAVE¹, LEAVE², LEEVE, LIEF

lefesum see LEESOME²

left &c *adj* = left *15-*.
~-**fitter &c** *disparaging* a Roman Catholic *20-*, *C.* ~-**hand man** one of the two chief supporters of the CORNET or *standard-bearer* (STANDART) in various *Riding of the Marches* (RIDE) festivals *20-*, *sEC, S.*

left see LEAVE¹

leful &c *la14-16*, **levefull &c** *15-e16* [*ˈli(v)fʌl] *adj* legally or morally permissible; right, honest, proper. [ME *lefful &c, leveful*, f OE *lēaf* > LEAVE²; *cf* LECHFULL, LEESOME²]

leful see LIEF

leg &c; laig &c *la16-20*, **leig &c** *la16-*, *now NE*, **lig &c** *16-17, 20* (*Edb*) [lɛg; *Sh* lig; *NE Fif also* ləig; *EC also* lɪg] *n* **1** = leg *la14-*. **2** = ~-**dollor**, *la17.* **3** a measure of land, *prob* a sixteenth of a *ploughgate* (PLEUCH), a quarter of *horsegang* (HORSE) *16.*
vi walk, *usu* at a quick pace, run *la18-*, *now NE midLoth Kcb.*
tak ~ **bail** run away, decamp *la18-*, *now Bnf local C.* ~ *or* **leggit dollor &c** a Dutch silver coin equal to about fifty-six shillings SCOTS, so called from the device on its reverse *la17-e18.* ~ **sok &c** a long sock or stocking *la16-e17.*
gang fit for ~ go immediately, as quickly as possible *la19-20, Abd Uls.* **gie (a stane)** ~**s** *curling* (CURL) accelerate the pace of a stone by sweeping the ice in front of it *la19-*, *now SW.* ~ **aff** set off, depart *la19-*. ~ **on** *vi* walk or work energetically or quickly *la19-*. *n* ~-**on** speed and energy in walking and working *la19-*, *local Ork-Kcb.* **lift (a)** ~ **1** move, run, gallop *18-*, *Ags sEC Ayr.* **2** commit fornication *18-*, *now Ork Abd.* **on (the)** ~, **upon** ~ on the move, gadding about *19-*, *now local Abd-EC.* **put** ~**s and arms to &c** add to or embellish (an anecdote) *la19-*, *now local Cai-Kcb.* **tak** ~(**s**) *also fig* run off, decamp, clear out *la18-*, *local Ork-Gall.*

legacy &c *n* **1** = legacy *la15-*. **2** a delegation *la14-16.*

legal &c *adj* **1** = legal *15-*. **2** *of a preacher or his* *doctrine* stressing Old Testament law and salvation by works rather than justification by faith *18.*

n, law, also ~ **reversion &c** *17* the period, at different dates seven, five or ten years, during which a debtor may redeem HERITABLE property adjudged to his creditors *17-.*

~ **rights** the claims which the surviving spouse and/or issue have to share in a deceased's estate, whether or not there is a will *la19-*; cf *prior rights* (PRIOR), LEGITIM, JUS RELICTAE, JUS RELICTI.

legalloun *see* LAGALLOUN

legammachie *see* LAGAMACHIE

legatar, legator &c [*ˈlɛgatər, *-ur] *n* a person to whom a legacy is left *la16-e18.*
  legatrix a female legatee *17-e18.*
  universal ~ sole legatee *17-e18.* [OF *légataire*, L *lēgātārius*]

Legavrik &c [*?ˈlɛˈgavrɪk] *n* one of the eight annual fairs of Inverness, held on 1 Feb *la16-17.* [*cf* Gael *Leth-gheamhraidh* the winter half of the year]

lege &c *la15-17*, **lig &c** *15-e17*, **lieg** *la15-16*; **league** *la17-* [lig; *lɪg] *n* **1** = league, an alliance *la15-.* **2** The Solemn League and Covenant *17.*

legend &c *n* **1** = legend *la14-.* **2** a passage of Scripture or of a saint's life read as part of divine service *la15, Abd.*

lege pouste *see* LIEGE POUSTIE

leggin *see* LAGGIN

leggums [ˈlɛgəmz] *n pl* = leggings *19-, local EC, S.*

legitim &c [ˈlɛdʒɪtɪm] *n, law* that part of a person's MOVEABLE estate which goes under common law to his or (since 1881) her children (*now* (*la20-*) including illegitimate children), one third if the other parent survives, otherwise half *la17-*; LEGITIM only applies after satisfaction of any *prior rights* (PRIOR); cf *bairns part* (*of gear*) (BAIRN). [only Sc; L *legitima* (*pars*) the lawful share (Civil Law); cf *legal rights* (LEGAL)]

legitimatioun &c *n* **1** = legitimation *la15-17.* **2** legitimacy *la15-17.*

leg-laig *see* LIG²

leglin &c, laglein &c; laig- *17-18* [ˈlɛglɪn; *ˈleg-] *n* = LADE-GALLON, *latterly chf* with a projecting stave as a handle, used as a milk pail *17-20*; *cf also* LAGALLOUN.

leichefull *see* LECHFULL

leid &c, lede; laid &c *16-17*, **lead &c** *17-*, **ledd &c** *19-, Sh Ork* [lid; *Sh Ork nEC* led] *n* **1** = lead, the metal *la14-.* **2** a large vat (not necessarily of lead), as used *esp* in brewing and dyeing *15-e18.* **3** one of the lead-weights of a pendulum-clock *la19-, Sh Ork Ags Wgt.* **4** the lead sheeting covering a roof *16-17.* **5** the leaden seal of a papal bull, **under the** ~ *la15-e16.*

~**ie** a handmade lead marble or counter for the game of BUTTONS *la19-, now Wgt Rox.* **leidin myne &c** a lead mine *la16-17.*
~ **draps** small shot used in fowling *19-, now Wgt.* ~ **stane** *fishing* a lead-sinker for a handline *la16, 19-, now Sh Hebrides Ayr.* ~ **ure &c** lead-ore *la15-17.*

leid *see* LADE, LEDE¹, LEE¹, LID

leife *see* LAVE¹

leig *see* LEG

leikwake *see* LYKE

leill &c [*lil] *n, sewing* a single stitch, *eg* in a sampler *e19.* [see SND]

leink *see* LINK¹

leinth *see* LENTH

leippie *see* LIPPIE

leis *see* LIEF, LISS

leischpund *see* LISPUND

leish &c [liʃ] *adj* active, athletic, supple *19-, SW, S.* [see SND]

leisk *see* LISK

leispund *see* LISPUND

leister &c [ˈlistər] *n* a pronged spear used (*now* illegally) for salmon fishing *la16-.*
  vt spear (fish) with a LEISTER *19-.* [eModEng *lister*, ON *ljóstr* a fish-spear]

leisure &c *16-*, **leaser &c** *la16-e17*, **laiser &c** *now Sh*; **leasure** *la16-19*, **laser &c** *la14-e17* [ˈliʒər, ˈliʒər; *Sh Bnf also* ˈlezər] *n* = leisure *la14-.*
~**it &c** having the opportunity or free time, free (to do something) *16-e17.*

leit &c [*lit] *vi, verse* linger, tarry *la15-16.* [obscure]

leit *see* LEET¹, LEET², LEET³

leit *see* LAT¹

leith *see* LETH²

leithand *see* LATCH³

Leith-ax &c [*ˈliθˈeks] *n* a kind of halberd *e16.*

leit-of-camp *see* LET DE CAMP

lek &c; laik &c [*lɛk] *adj, of a ship* leaky, having leaks *16-17* [? MDu, LowGer *lek*]

lek *see* LECK¹, LECK², LIKE¹

leke *see* LECK¹, LEEK

lele *see* LEAL

lely *n* = LILY *la14-16.*

leme *see* LEAM¹

Lemistar &c; Lymmistar &c [*ˈlɛmɪstər, *ˈlɪm-] *n* ~ **blak** a type of expensive fine black cloth, *chf* used for hose *e16*; *cf* MAUCHLYNE. [ME *Leymster* Leominster in Hertfordshire, where fine (and expensive) wool was produced *15*]

lemit *see* LEEMIT

lemmanry *see* LAMEN

lempit &c *la17-*, **lempet &c** *la15-19*, **lampet &c** *la16-e17*; **lemped &c** *la19-, Ork Cai, in place-name la12*, **lempeck &c** *19-e20, Fif Bwk n* = limpet *15-.* [nME *lempet*, OE *lempedu*]

len &c, lend *16-*, **laen** *20-, Sh Ork* [lɛn] *vt* **1** lend *la14-.* **2** deal (a blow) *la16-20.*
n a loan *la16-.*

in ~ on loan *la16-e18*. ~ **an** *or* **one's ear to** listen to *la14-*. ~ **a lift to** *fig* aid, support *la16-17*. [OE *lǣnan*; see DOST; *cf* LANE³, with which there may be confusion in some dials]

lenage *see* LINIAGE

lench &c *17-*, *now Ork N*, **lanche &c** *la16*; **lainch &c** *17-19* [lɛnʃ; *lanʃ, *lenʃ] *vti* = launch.

lend¹ [*lɛnd, *lɪnd, *lind] *n*, *chf in pl* **lendis &c** the loins *la14-16*. [ME *lenden &c (pl)*, OE *lendenu (pl)*]

lend² &c; leynd &c [*lɛnd, *lind] *vti*, *ptp* **lent**, **lende** [*lɛnt, *lɛnd]: *chf verse* **1** (**be**) **lent** (1) (have) come, (be) present *la14-16*. (2) *of the affections* (have) lighted **apon**; (**be**) **lent into** (be) set on *15-e16*. **2** dwell; sojourn; remain *la14-16*. [ME *lenden*, OE *lendan*, ON *lenda*, ultimately f LAND *n*]

lend *see* LEN

lende *see* LEND²

lene *see* LEAN

lenght, length, lenht *see* LENTH

lenk *see* LINK¹

lenocinium &c [lino'sɪnjəm, lɛno'sɪnɪʌm] *n*, *law* the connivance or encouragement by one partner in a marriage of the adultery of the other (constituting a bar to divorce) *la16-*. [L = pandering, procuring]

lent *adj* slow: **1** *in gen*, *la16-17*; **2** *specif, of a fever*, *la17-e18*. [F *lent*, L *lentus*]

lent *see* LEND², LENTH

lentell *see* LINTEL

lenten- *see* LENTREN

lenth &c, length &c *la16-*, **linth &c** *la14-e17*, *chf NE-C*; **lenght** *la16-17* [lɛnθ; *Sh Ork N nEC*, *WC* *lɪnθ] *n*, *also* **leinth &c** *15-16*, *chf NE-C* [*?lɪnθ], **lainth &c** *17-18*, **lenht** *16* [*lɛnθ], **lent &c** *16-*, *Sh Ork* **1** = length *la14-*. **2** distance; extent, amount *eg* **the** ~ **of**, **my** *etc* ~, **this** ~ as far as (me, this etc) *15-*. **3** a person's stature or height *la16-*, *local*.

vt = length, lengthen, prolong *15-e17*.

lynthar &c a lengthener *la15*.

at lang ~ at long last *la19-*. **at (the)** ~ **an lang** at last, in the end *la18-*, *Sh NE*. **at mare** ~ at greater length, more fully *la15-17*. **breadth an** ~ *adv* one's full length, prone *19-*, *Fif midLoth SW*. **for a(ny)** *or* **some** ~ **o time** for a very long time *20-*. **gae** *etc* **a bonnie** *or* **all one's** ~ follow one's inclinations or feelings as far as one can or dares *la19-*, *Gen except Sh Ork*. **one's lang** ~ = breadth an ~, *19-*, *Cai NE, EC*. **on** ~ extended, spread out *la15-16*.

lentren &c, lentrin; lentron &c *16-19* [*'lɛntrən, *'lɛntərn] *n* Lent *la14-19*.

~ **kail, lenten kail** soup made with vegetables only, without meat-stock; cabbage boiled in water and then served in milk *19*. ~**ware** [*'lɛntrən'wer, &c*] *collective* a kind of lambskin *15-16*. [ONorthumb *lenctern*, corresponding to WSax *lencten*]

lenӡé *see* LEENGYIE

leo *n* = LEW² *la15-e16*. [perh assimilated to L *leo* a lion]

Leonis *see* LYONIS

lep *see* LAIP, LEAP

lepe *see* LEAP, LEEP

leper *see* LIPPER³

lepin *see* LIPPEN

leprone &c *16-18*, *la20*, **laproun &c** *16* ['lɛprən; *'lap-] *n* a young rabbit. [only Sc; OF *laperel &c*]

lerb &c *vti* lap with the tongue, slobber in drinking *19-*, *Abd*.

n a lick, a mouthful of a liquid or semi-liquid *20-*, *Abd*. [emphatic var of LAIB]

lerd *see* LAIRD

lere *see* LEAR

lerges *see* LARGES

lerioun &c *n* some animal *la15*. [see DOST]

lerne *see* LEARN

lerroch *see* LARACH

les; lese &c [*lis, *les, *lɛs] *n* falsehood, lying *la14-16*. [ME *leas*, OE *lēas*; *cf* LEASING]

les *see* LESS¹, LEZ, LISS

lesart &c [*'lɛzərt, &c] *n* **1** = lizard *la15-16*. **2** a lizard-skin *e16*.

lesche *see* LEASH

lese &c [*liz] *vti*, *ptp* **lorn &c** **1** = leese, lose *la14-e17*. **2** *vi* be lost or destroyed, perish *la15-16*.

lese *see* LEASE², LES

lesed &c [lizd] *ptp* **1** *law* injured in regard to one's interest, property, rights or reputation *la17-*. **2** *medical* impaired, injured *e18*.

the party ~ the injured party *la17-e18*. [f L *laesus*, ptp of *laedere* (v) hurt; *cf* next and LESION]

lese-majesty &c, lese-majesté &c *la15-16* ['liz'madʒɛstɪ] *n* **1** = lese-majesty, treason *la15-*. **2** *fig, in relation to God*, *la16-e18*. [F *lèse majesté*, L *laesa mājestas*; *cf* prec, LESION and HURT-MAJESTÉ]

lesing *see* LEASING

lesion &c, lesioun &c *la16-17* ['liʒn] *n* **1** = lesion *la15-*. **2** *law* detriment to a person, *esp* a minor, in respect of property or rights *la16-*; *see* ENORM. **3** *medical* a morbid change or injury to an organ *la16-*. [laME *lesion*, F *lésion*, L *laesio n*, f *laedere* (v) hurt; *cf* LESED, LESE-MAJESTY]

lesour *see* LIZOUR

lespund *see* LISPUND

less¹ &c, les *la14-17* [lɛs] *adj* **1** = less *la14-*. **2** fewer *la14-*.

adv = less *la14-*.

conj **1** unless *la15-*, *now Abd Ags*. **2** lest *16, 20-*.

~ **age &c** minority, the condition of being under legal age *16-e17*. **of** ~ **age &c** minor *16-17*.

frae ~ **to mair** from one thing to another, *esp* of something progressing in intensity *la18-*, *now N midLoth WC*. ~ **and mair &c, mair and** ~ *only following the noun or absol* **1** *of things* larger and smaller; *hence* every one, everything *15-16*. **2** *of persons* of high and low rank; everyone *la14-16*. ~ **or mair &c** *la15-17*, **mair or** ~ *la14-16* of larger or smaller amount; *of persons* of high or low station, whoever they are. ~ **or** (*or* **na**) **mair &c, mare or** (*or* **na &c**) ~ *only following the noun* of greater or lesser magnitude or consequence, of any sort, in any way, at all: '*he had na wittering mar nor les*'. ~ **than** *la14-e16*, ~ **na** *la15*, ~ **nor** *16* unless. **nothir** *etc* **mair na les &c** *absol* neither etc less nor more, the exact amount in question *15-e17*. **or** ~ = or else *20-*, *Gsw* [metath for Eng *else*].

less² *&c interj* = ALACE, ALISS *19-*, *chf Sh.* [aphetic]

less³ *n* = a lease, tenancy *20-*, *NE nEC.*

lesson &c *n* **1** = lesson *la14-*. **2** the action of reading or study *la14-e16*. **3** something from which one may learn; a rebuke etc aimed at preventing a repetition of the offence *15-*. **4** the public discourse following the examination for admission as an ADVOCATE *la17-e18*. **leir a** ~ follow advice or an example *15-16*.

lesspund *see* LISPUND

lest &c, laist *la19-* [lɛst] *vi* **1** = last, endure *la14-*, *now Sh-EC, S.* **2** extend in space, reach *e16*. *n* continuance, duration, permanence; durability, *freq* **have na** *or* **no** ~ *15-16*, *20-* (*local Sh-Loth*). ~**and,** ~**ing &c** *adj* continuing, enduring, everlasting *la14-16*. ~**ie &c** lasting *la15-*, *now Sh-EC, S*; *cf lastie* (LAST¹). ~**ing** continuance, duration, permanence, *freq* **have** ~**ing** *la14-15*. [ME *leste(n)*, OE *læstan*; *cf* LAST¹]

lest *see* LIST¹

leste *see* LEAST¹, LEAST²

lesteek *see* LASKIT

lesu *see* LIZOUR

lesum *see* LEESOME²

let &c, lat &c *la14-17*; **lete &c** *la14-15*, **late** *la14-15* [lɛt; *lat] *vt, pt, ptp also* **lettit** *la14-17*, **lattit** *15-17* **1** = let, hinder, prevent *la14-17*. **2** *with infin* neglect, refrain, desist from doing something *la14-15*. *n* **1** = let, hindrance *la14-*. **2** a slip-gate or hurdle used to stop up a gap in a hedge or wall *20-*, *SW*. **but, withoutin (mare) letting** = but *etc* ~ *la14-15*. **mak** ~**ting &c** (**to**) hinder, restrain *la14-e16*. **letles** without let or hindrance *la14*, *only Sc.* **but, withoutin** *etc* (**langar, mare** *or* **ony**) ~ *verse* without hesitation or delay, at once *la14-16*.

let *see* LAT¹

let-de-camp &c *e16*, **leit-of-camp &c** *e16*, **letacamp &c** *la15-16*, **liticant &c** *la16*, **litticamp &c** *16-e17*, **littigant &c** *la16-e17* [*'lit(d)ə'kamp, *'lɪt-, *'lɛt-, *'lɪtɪkant, *-gant, *&c] *n, also* ~ **bed** a camp-bed. [only Sc; northern OF *lit de camp*; *cf* eModDu *lit de camp &c*, *lidecant &c*]

lete *see* LET

leth¹ &c [*lɛθ] *n* ill-will, hatred; revulsion, loathing *15-16*. [ME *leþþe, laþþe*, OE *lǣðð*u; *cf* LAITH]

leth², leith [*?lið] *vti* neglect; lag, *chf* ~**and** negligent; tardy *la14-e16*. [ME *lethe(n)*, northern ModEng dial *leath*; *appar* confused w LATCH³ (*v*) (see DOST *lache* (*v*² and Suppl))]

leth *see* LAITH, LITH

lether &c *18-19*, **ledder &c** *la14-e20*, **ladder &c** *la16-* ['lɛðər; *Sh Ork NE* 'lɛdər] *n* = ladder *la14-*. *vt* set a ladder or ladders to (a wall etc), *chf* in attacking a fortified place *15-17*.

lether *see* LEATHER

lethy *see* LADY

letle *see* LITTLE

letter &c *n* **1** = letter *la14-*. **2** *now in pl, law* a WRIT or warrant in missive form, *latterly chf* one issued by the *High Court of Justiciary* (JUSTICIARY) or by the *Court of Session* (SESSION) under the SIGNET *la14-*. **3** a missive from the sovereign by which he intervened by prerogative in the processes of the courts or crown offices, or issued peremptory commands to his officers *la15-e17*. **burial** ~ an intimation of or invitation to a funeral *la17-*, *now Cai Kcb*. **criminal** ~s *law* a form of criminal charge in which the sovereign summoned the accused to answer the charge *la16-20*. ~**s of arrestment** *law* a WRIT to attach property for debt *la16-*. ~**s of caption** *law* a warrant for the arrest of a person for debt *15-18*. ~**s conform,** ~**s conformand** *15 law* a warrant issued by the supreme court to render effective the judgments of inferior courts *15-e19*. ~**s of cursing** a warrant issued by a decree of the pre-Reformation church courts excommunicating a stubborn offender *15-16*. ~**s of fire and sword** *law* a warrant from the Privy Council to enforce court DECREES of removing and ejection *17-e18*. ~**s in the first, secund, thrid, ferd form** *la15-e16*, ~**s in the four forms** *16*, ~**s of four forms** *16-17 law* the warrants (giving up to four successive charges) issued as the first step in a process of DILIGENCE against a person for debt. ~**s of horning** *law* a warrant in the name of the sovereign charging the persons named to act as ordered, *eg* to pay a debt, under the penalty of being *put to the horn* (HORN *n* 3) *16-*. ~**s of inhibition** *law* a warrant prohibiting a debtor from burdening or alienating his HERITAGE to the prejudice of his creditor *16-*. ~**s of intercommuning** a WRIT issued by the Privy Council prohibiting any communication with the persons named in it *la17-18*. ~**s of open doors** *law* a warrant authorizing the forcing open of *lockfast* (LOCK) places containing goods to be *poinded* (POIND) *18-20*. ~**(s) of panis &c** a missive containing a royal command or summons and specifying the penalties to which the recipient is liable for failure to comply *el6*. ~s **of presentation** the WRIT by which a *presentation* 3 (PRESENT¹) is intimated to the SUPERIOR *el5, la18*. ~s **of procuratory** written authorization for one person to act on behalf of another *la15-16*. ~s **of slains** *law* a WRIT subscribed by the relatives of someone killed in a private feud, acknowledging payment of compensation, abjuring all further claims or revenge, and requesting the sovereign to grant remission *15-18*. ~s **of supplement** a warrant from the *Court of Session* (SESSION) enabling an inferior judge to summon a *defender* (DEFEND) to appear when he did not live in the jurisdiction *la18-e20*. **run one's** ~s await trial; if the prosecutor failed to bring his case within the prescribed period, the prisoner was liberated *18-19*.

letter *see* LATTER

letteratoure *see* LEETERATUR

lettergae &c *n* the PRECENTOR in a church *18-*, now literary. [agent noun f *let gae* (LET) strike up a tune]

letterin(g) *see* LETTERN

lettern &c *la16-20*, **lettroun &c** *la15-19*, **lat-troun &c** *16-el8*; **letterin(g)** *16-18*, **lateron &c** *la16-e20* ['lɛtərn, -rən, 'lat-] *n* **1** a lectern *la15-e17*. **2** the desk of the reader or PRECENTOR in post-Reformation churches *17-e20*. **3** a reading or writing desk in a private house *la15-el8*. **4** a lawyer's desk, *chf* **go** *or* **be put to the** ~ pursue legal studies *la17-18*. [ME *letrune*, OF *lettrun* a reading desk]

lettit *see* LET

lettrin *see* LATRIN

lettroun *see* LETTERN

leuch *see* LAUCH¹, LAICH

leuchen, leucht *see* LAUCH¹

leuk &c *la16-*, **luke; luik &c** *16-*, **lu(c)k &c**, **look &c** *16-* [luk; *Ork Cai Fif WC Uls* lʌk; *lək; Sh Abd *ljuk] *vti* **1** = look *la14-*. **2** *vt* look at, inspect, examine *la14-*.
n **1** = look *la14-*. **2 a** ~ **o** *or* **til** *or* **to** a look or visit for the purpose of seeing or examining *la19-*.
one's ~**in een** *or* **face** one's very eyes or face *19-e20*.
~ **down &c 1** be melancholy or downcast *16*. **2** ~ **down &c on** regard with disfavour, hold in contempt *16-*. ~ **after &c** take notice of, respect *19-, Abd*. ~ **in the face** confront *la14-*. ~ **the gate o** *local*, ~ **near(han)** *now Abd* heed, see to, take an interest in; visit *19-*. ~ **on** wait for the end of (a dying person), be at the deathbed of *la18-, now Bwk*. ~ **o(w)er 1** look after, take care of, watch over *la18-, local Sh-SW*. **2** pass over, overlook, forgive *la19-*, *now Sh N*. ~ **ower the door** look outside; *hence* go outside, *esp* be in the open air after an illness *19-, Sh N, C*. ~ **ower the window** look out of the window, lean over the sill and look out *la17-, now local NE-SW*. ~ **the road someone is on** *in negative* take no interest in,

ignore *20-*. ~ **se(e)** *imperative* mark you!, look here! *la19-, NE, C*. ~ **till** *or* **to** look at, observe, behold *la14-, now Sh NE*. ~ **up** be alive *la19-*: 'had John been looking up to-day'. **lucks-tu, lu(k)sto** mark you! *19-, now Ork*.

leutenant *see* LIEUTENAND

Levand *n, attrib* from the Levant *16*.

levar *see* LIEF

leve *see* LEAVE¹, LEAVE², LEEVE, LIEF

levefull *see* LEFUL

leve-gard &c; loveguard &c [*'liv'gerd, &c] *n* = lifeguard, a bodyguard of soldiers *17*.

level &c; lavell &c *16-e17* ['lɛvl; *?'levl] *n* **1** = level, the craftsman's instrument *la16-*. **2** *mining* a water-level, a passage for drainage *16-17*. *vti* = level *la16-*.

Leveller one of a body of peasants in Galloway who had been dispossessed by the enclosure system, and who organized themselves in 1724 to knock down the walls built around fields *el8*.

lever *see* LIVER¹, LIEF

levery *see* LIVERY

levesum *see* LEESOME²

levetenand *see* LIEUTENAND

leviat &c [*?'lɛvɪat, *?'liv-] *ptp, of soldiers* enlisted, recruited *la16-el7*. [irreg f Eng *levy*]

levin *see* ELEEVEN

levit *see* LEAVE¹

lew¹ &c [lu; *Sh Ork S* lju] *adj* lukewarm, tepid *18-*.
n a warming, a slight rise in temperature, *esp* of the interior of stacks *19-, local Sh-SW*.
vi become warm *la19-, Sh Uls*.
~ **warm** = *adj*, *16-*. [ME *lewe* adj, OE *hlīewan* (*v*) warm]

lew² &c [*lju] *n* a Flemish or Dutch gold coin current in Scotland *la15-16*. [MDu, Flem *le(e)uwe* a lion, also as name of certain gold coins; *cf* LEO]

lewder &c *16-*, **louder &c** *la16-*; **louther &c** *19-* ['ludər, 'luð-; *NE* 'l(j)ʌu-] *n* **1** a wooden lever, *esp* one for lifting millstones *la16-, now NE*. **2** a stout stick *18-20*. **3** a heavy blow (from a stout stick) *19-20, Abd Per Uls*. *vt* hammer; thrash *la19-20*. [ON *luðr* a support for a millstone]

lewer ['liuər,'lʌuər] *n* = lever *19, chf SW, S*.

lewer *see* LURE

lewit *see* LAWIT

ley *see* LEA, LEE¹, LEE³, LIE

leyit *see* LEE¹

leynd *see* LEND²

leyne, leyt *see* LEE¹

lez &c; les [*?'liz] article pl, in Latin texts preceding pl nouns in the vernacular the *15-e16*, rare. [F *les*; *cf* LE, LA]

li.; lib, *pl also* **libs** *abbrevs* of L *libra* [*'laɪbra] a pound, *librae* [*'laɪbri] pounds (*of money or weight*) *15-e16*.

liable &c *adj* = liable *17-*.
~ **in** *esp law* = liable to or for *la17-*.

liart &c [*'laɪart] *n* the small French coin, a quarter of a sou *16-17*. [F *liard*]

liart *see* LYART

lib[1] **&c** *vt* **1** castrate (*esp* farm animals) *16-*. **2** *fig* mutilate, curtail, deprive *18-, chf SW*. **3** grope in the soil and remove (growing potatoes) without disturbing the tops *19-, now Per Fif Kcb*. [ME *libben*, MDu *lubben* geld]

lib[2] **&c** *n* a (healing) charm *la16-17*. *vt* heal, cure (with a charm) *la15-17*. [only Sc; OE *lyb(b)* a potion, drug]

lib *see* LI.

libber-lay &c; libber-la [*'lɪbər'le] *n* a cudgel *e16*. [obscure]

libel &c; libelt &c *e19*, S ['laɪbl; *-əlt] *n* **1** *also* **leebel &c** *19-, now Ork* ['libəl(t)] = libel *15-*; but for Scots legal usage see DEFAMATION *n* 2 and *cf* 3 below. **2** any piece of writing, formal or informal *la18-, now Kcdn midLoth Lnk*; sometimes confused with Eng *label*. **3** (1) *law* a formal statement of the grounds on which a suit or prosecution is brought *la15-*. (2) *Church law* a charge against a person in an ecclesiastical court *18-*.
vt, law **1** specify in an indictment; state as grounds for a suit or prosecution *la15-*. **2** *also Church law* make a formal charge against *la17-20*. **3** *also* **leebel** *19-, now Ork* = libel.
libellat &c [*'laɪbəlat, &c] specified in the LIBEL (*n* 3); drawn up as a LIBEL *16*. [*n* 3 f Civil Law *libelli accusatorii*; *libellat* f ptp of MedL *libellare*]

liberal &c, leeberal &c *la16, 19-,* **leebral** *19-* ['lib(ə)ral, 'lɪb-] *adj* **1** = liberal *la14-*. **2** *of offspring* legitimate *16, chf Ayr*.

liberary *see* LEEBRARY

liberate, liberat *ptp, lit and fig* set at liberty, released *17-e18*. [eModEng; L *līberātus*, ptp of *līberāre*, f *līber* free]

libertine &c *n* **1** = libertine *la15-*. **2** *in King's College Aberdeen* a student with no BURSARY or scholarship *la18*.

librar[1] **&c, librall &c** *16,* **librell &c** *e16* [*?'lɪbrar, *-əl; *?'laɪb-] *n* = library *15-e17*. [only Sc]

librar[2] **&c** [*?'lɪbrar, *?'laɪb-] *n* a bookseller *la16-e17*. [only Sc; F *libraire*]

library *see* LEEBRARY

librell *see* LIBRAR[1]

libs *see* LI.

licence *see* LEESHENCE

licent, lecent [*'laɪsɛnt, *'li-] *vt* grant permission, authorize (someone to do something) *16*. [only Sc; perh f *licence* (LEESHENCE) *n*, as verbs absent, present f corresponding nouns in *-ence*]

licentiate &c, licentiat &c *la15-17* [laɪ'sɛnsɪət] *vti* **1** = licentiate, authorize, permit *la16-17*. **2** *specif* = LEESHENCE *v* 2, *17-18*.
n **1** a person who has been licensed, *specif as in* LEESHENCE *v* 2, *19-*. **2** = licentiate, holder of the University degree of 'licence' *la15-16*. [ME; MedL *licentiatus* ptp]

lichen, lichn *see* LICHT[1]

lichour &c [*'lɪtʃur] *n* = lecher *la14-e17*.
lichory &c [*'lɪtʃərɪ] = lechery *la14-16*.

licht[1] **&c, light &c** [lɪxt; *Sh S* ləixt; *St* ləit] *adj* = light, bright *la14-*.
n **1** = light *la14-*. **2** *fig* mental or spiritual enlightenment *15-*. **3** that part of a candle which provides light, candle-wax or candle-tallow *17, Gall*. **4** *freq* ~ie the will-o'-the-wisp, jack-o'-lantern (regarded as an omen of death) *la19-, chf NE*. **5** *law, only* **light** a SERVITUDE binding one owner of property not to build or plant on it so as to obstruct the light of his neighbour *la17-*.
vt, pt, ptp also **licht** *la16-17* [*lɪxt] = light, lighten *la14-*.
adv brightly *la15-16*.
~**en &c, lich(e)n** ['lɪx(t)ən] = lighten *la15-*.
L~ies *see* *Reid Lichties* (REID[1]).
the Light Blues nickname for Rangers football team *la19-* [f the colour of their jerseys; cf 'GERS, HUNS]. ~ **coal** splint coal (used for illumination as well as heat) *la18-19*.
auld ~, new ~ *church* **1** the MODERATE or more latitudinarian element (*new* ~) as opposed to the stricter conservative and evangelical section (*auld* ~) of the *Church of Scotland* (CHURCH) *18-e19*. **2** the two corresponding groups which split both branches of the *Secession Church* (SECEDE), the *Burghers* (BURGH) in 1799 and the ANTIBURGHERS in 1806, the *New Lichts* from both combining in 1820 to form the *United Secession Church* (UNITED) and the *Auld Lichts* in 1842 to form the *Synod of Original Seceders* (ORIGINAL). **between** (**the**) ~**s** twilight *20-, NE Fif*. **canna &c see the** ~ **o day to** be blind to the faults of (a person) *19-, NE, EC, S*. **new** ~ *see auld* ~. **sit in one's own** ~ be an obstruction to oneself *16-e17*.

licht[2] **&c, light &c** [lɪxt; *S* ləi(x)t] *adj* **1** = light, not heavy *la14-*. **2** below the standard or legal weight, underweight *la15-*. **3** *of battles or fights* involving small numbers or few casualties *16-e17*. **4** (1) demented *la16-17*. (2) dizzy, light-headed *20-, Loth Renfr*. **5** ~ **on** abstemious, temperate in the use of *20-; cf* HEAVY. **6** *also used as a noun* applied to a low-gravity beer, the successor of (*e20*) mild *la20-; cf* HEAVY.
n **1** the light parts of corn seed separated out by winnowing and sifting *19-, now Ross Loth WC*. **2** *in pl, also* **lighs** *la16* [*lɪxs] the lungs (human or animal) *la15-*.
vti **1** = light, lighten *la14-*. **2** *fig* make light, lighten, ease, mitigate *la15-, now Ags Wgt*. **3** ~ **on, to, til** (1) set upon, attack *16-*. (2) *fig* upbraid *20-, now local*. **4** be brought low, *chf fig* be degraded or humiliated *15-16*. **5** *of a weapon or a blow* strike (on a particular place) *la14-16*.
adv = light(ly) *la15-*.
~**er** delivered of a child *15-e20*. ~**lie &c** *adv* **1**

= lightly *la14-*. **2** (describe or study something) briefly, superficially, not in full *15-16*. *adj* slighting, contemptuous, scornful *la15-18*. *vt* make light of, disparage, insult *la14-*, *now NE nEC Lnk*. *n* the act of disparagement, an insult *la16-19*, *only Sc.* ∼**lifie &c** [ˈlɪxtlɪfaɪ, -fi] = ∼*lie* (*v*) *19-*, *now NE Per*. ∼**liefu &c** [ˈlɪxtlɪfu] slighting, contemptuous *la16, la19- (NE)*, *only Sc.* ∼**lifullie** [*ˈlɪxtlɪfʌlɪ] slightingly, contemptuously *la16-e17*. ∼**lines** arrogance, contempt; an insult *15-16*, *only Sc.* ∼**some &c 1** carefree, cheerful *la15-*. **2** cheering, enlivening, pleasant *18-*. **3** light on one's feet, agile *la19-*.
∼**-farand &c** *la16-e17*, ∼**-farrant** *20-*, *Abd Gall* frivolous, giddy in behaviour. ∼**fit** *la19-*, *now NE Gall*, ∼**fute** *la16*, *chf verse* light-footed, nimble. ∼**-headed** frivolous; changeful *15-*. ∼ **hors(e)man** a (? mounted) raider or *reiver* (REIVE) *la16-e17*. ∼ **set** = ∼*fit*, *19-*. **lat** ∼ admit; make known *18-*, *NE*. **lat** ∼**ly of** regard with scorn, disparage *la14-e19*. ∼ **in the head** = *adj* 2 (2) *20-*. **set** ∼ think little of, despise, undervalue *la15-16*.
lichter [*ˈlɪxtər] *n* = lighter, a loading boat *la16-e17*.
lick, lik &c *n* **1** = lick *17-*. **2** (1) a small amount, the least particle (of something) *17-*. (2) *specif, esp* **a** ∼ **of goodwill** a small measure of meal given to the under-miller as a gratuity in addition to the MULTURE *la17-*. **3** a hard blow; *freq in pl* a thrashing, chastisement *18-*. **4** a smart pace, a burst of speed *19-*. *adv* with a heavy thud, *freq* **play** ∼ fall heavily *la19-*, *Kcb*. *vt* **1** = lick *la14-*. **2** take a pinch or small quantity of (something, *esp* snuff) *19-20*. **3** *vi* hasten, hurry *la19-*, *local NE-Uls*.
∼**-lip** fawning, wheedling *la19-*. ∼**-penny** a greedy, covetous or swindling person or thing *19-*, *now Ags Loth Wgt*. ∼**-spit** = lickspittle *19-*, *now Cai Fif*. ∼**-want** *chf in threats* famine, the condition of going hungry *20-*, *Abd Ags midLoth*.
∼**-ma-** or **the-dowp** an obsequious (person) *18-*, *now Ags midLoth*. ∼ **an skail** profusion, extravagance in living *20-*, *Abd Per Stlg*. ∼ (**up**) **one's winnin(s)** make the best of a bargain or of a bad job *la18*.
lickery *la19-*, **licorous &c** *la16-17*; **licorese &c** *la16-e17*, **liquorie &c** *la19-* [ˈlɪk(ə)rɪs, ˈlɪkərɪ] *n* = liquorice *la16-*.
∼ **stick** liquorice root chewed by children as a sweet *la19-*, *WC*. [*cf* LACRISSYE, ALICREESH]
licoure *see* LEECURE
lid &c; leid *la16-17*, **led** *e17, 20* [lɪd] *n* **1** = lid *la15-*. **2** one of the leaves or halves of a double door, *freq* one enclosing a *box bed* (BOX¹) *la16-*, *now Ags*. **3** one of the boards of a large book *20-*. **4** *mining* the cover or flap of a valve; a flat piece of wood on the top of a prop *la19-*, *now Fif*.

the ∼ **of the knee** the kneecap, patella *la16-17*, *only Sc.*
lidder *see* LITHER
lie &c, ly &c, ley *la14, 17* [laɪ] *vi, pt* **lay &c** *la14-*. *ptp also* **lyin &c** *15-16*, **lien &c** *17-*, *now NE* [*NE* ˈlaɪ(ə)n] **1** = lie, be in a recumbent position *la14-*. **2** be confined to bed by illness *15-*. **3** (1) lurk *la14-16*. (2) lie in wait **for** (a person) *16*. **4** *of the tongue or speech* be still, silent *19-*. **5** *of money or property* (1) ∼ **beside, by** or **with someone** or **in** (**someone's**) **hands** be in someone's possession or keeping *la14-17*. (2) be pledged, mortgaged etc *15-16*. **6** be, remain, or continue in legal dispute *15-17*.
n **1** (1) the act of lying, *esp* in bed; rest or sleep *19-*. (2) the place where one lies *19-*. **2** *golf* (1) the position of the ball, or the spot on which it lies *la18-*. (2) the inclination of the face of a golf-club as held by the player *19*. **3** a railway siding, *esp* in a coal-mine *la19-*.
lyage [*ˈlaɪedʒ] the lying of goods at a port until collected by the consignee; a charge made for this *la18*. **lyar &c** [*ˈlaɪər] **1** a carpet, rug, coverlet *la15-e16*. **2** the nether millstone *la16-17*. ∼**ing dog** a setter *17*. ∼**in money, siller** *etc* ready cash *la16-*. ∼**ing storm** a fall of snow which lies long on the ground before melting *la18-*, *now NE Lnk*. ∼**ing time** *orig mining* a period of time worked by an employee either at the beginning of a new job for which he is not immediately paid, or between the closing of the books for the week's work and the payment of wages, payment being retained until the person leaves the employment *la19-*.
∼ **day 1** one of a certain number of days allowed for the loading and unloading of a ship *16-18*. **2** a day of *lying time*, *la19-*, *local EC-WC*. ∼ **time** = *lying time*, *la19-*, *EC Lnk*.
∼ **aff** *of a sheepdog* keep at a distance from the sheep *20-*, *local Sh-SW*. ∼ **by** *vi* hold back, remain inactive or uncommitted *la16-*, *now Sh Ags midLoth*. ∼**-by** *n* **1** a person who stands aside or remains uncommitted *la16-e18, 20* (*Uls*). **2** a siding at the roadside used for storing road-metal etc *20-*, *Fif Ayr Slk*. **3** an accumulation of work postponed, arrears *20-*, *NE*. ∼ **doun** take to one's bed with illness *20-*, *Gen except S.* ∼ **furth** = ∼ *out* 2, *16-e17*. ∼ **on** *mining* work an extra shift, do overtime *20-*, *Fif Loth*. ∼ **out 1** *esp of cattle* lie in the open air all night, remain unhoused *17-*. **2** delay entering into possession of inherited property or occupation of an office *16-*. **3** withhold (**from** another) one's support, allegiance or obedience *la16*. ∼ **out of** remain unpaid in respect of (money due to one) *17*. ∼ **over 1** be postponed *la16-19*. **2** *of a debt* remain unpaid *20-*. ∼ **to** *or* **till** *vti* feel affection (for), show liking (to) *la18-*, *now Abd Ayr*. ∼ **upon** quarter oneself on, exact accommodation from

15-e17. ~ **wrang** *of a woman* lose one's chastity *la18-19.* ~ **yont** lie further over, shift over in bed etc *19-20.* **a long lie** a 'lie-in', extra time in bed *19-.* [*cf* LIG¹]

lie *see* LE, LEE¹

lief *19-,* **lefe &c; leve &c** *la14-20,* **lee** *19* [lif, liv, li], *comparative also* **levar &c** *la14-e16* **lever &c, loor &c** *18-e19,* **lourd &c** *la18-19* ['lifər, 'livər, lir; *lur(d)] adj* **1** = lief, pleased, willing *15.* **2** *chf early verse* dear, beloved, agreeable *la14-16, e19 (ballad).* **3 have ~** *in conditional expressions, chf* **I, he** *etc* **had (as) ~** *or* **had ~fer** *la14-19,* or **me, him** *etc* **had levar** *la14-e15* I would or had rather; *also with* 'had' *omitted, la15-:* '*I loor chuse to herd goats*'; hence **loor &c** taken as verb, with **lourd** as *pt, ptp,* *18-:* '*I rather lourd it had been mysel'.* **4** *chf* **I, they** *etc* **wad as ~** *or* **~er** I etc would rather *15-.* **5** *as an intensifier in combs* entire(ly), absolute(ly) (1) *with* ALANE *and* LANE⁴, *freq* **lief alane** *19-,* or **lee lane** *la19-* all by oneself, solitary. (2) *with* LANG¹, *as* **lee lang** *or* **leeve lang day** *etc, la18-,* **lee(vy) day** *etc* **lang** *19* livelong day etc, *now rather literary.* **6** *only verse,* *esp ballad* solitary, desolate, eerie *la18-19:* '*a' the lee winter nicht'.*

leful &c [*'lifʌl] **1** *only verse* willing, glad, prompt, ready (to do something, to *or* of something) *la15-16.* **2** *chf* **leefu &c** kind-hearted, considerate, compassionate *18-19.* **3** solitary *19.* **(one's) leeful(l) lane** ['lifə'len, ?'lifu-] all by oneself, solitary *18-.*

~ is me *etc, 15-e16, contracted to* **leis &c me (of)** *la16-e17,* **leeze &c me (on)** *18-* I etc am very fond of or pleased with; *latterly (18-) also* blessings on.

lieg *see* LEGE

liege poustie &c *16-,* **lege poustee &c** *la14-17* ['lidʒ 'pustɪ] *n, law, occas in non-legal contexts* the state of being in full possession of one's faculties; soundness in mind and body *la14-e20.* [nME *legge pousté,* OF *lige poesté,* MedL *potestas ligia* ? free power; *cf* POTESTATER]

lien *see* LIE

lieutenand &c, lutenand &c, luf(e)-tenand &c, levetenand &c; leutenant &c *15-16,* **lietennent &c** *e16,* **lieutenant &c** *la15-* [*'lju'tɛnand, *-ant, *'li(v)-, *'lø(v)-] *n* = lieutenant *la14-.*

~ry &c 1 the office or jurisdiction of a lieutenant, *chf* that of viceregent or deputy of the sovereign *16-17.* **2** the area over which a lieutenant is granted authority *16-e17, only Sc.* **~ general 1** = lieutenant general *15-.* **2** the senior military commander after the sovereign *la16-e18.*

liewer *see* LURE

lif *see* LEEVE

life &c; lyve &c *la14-17* [ləif; *laɪv] *n* = life *la14-.*

lifie &c full of life, vivacious, brisk *la18-, Sh-Fif S.* **lifieness** vivacity, vigour *la19-, now Sh Ork Fif.*

~lade &c [*'ləif'led, *'ləiflet, *-lət] livelihood **1** means of living, maintenance *la14-e17;* **2** property as a means of support *la15.* **living &c and ~like** hale and hearty *18-, now Sh.*

~rent ['ləif'rɛnt] *n, law* **1** a right to receive till death (or some other specified contingency) the revenue of a property, without the right to dispose of the capital, *corresponding to civil law* usufruct *la14-.* **2** the *life-rent* (*n* 1) of a VASSAL's property or of a benefice *escheated* to the SUPERIOR or the patron *16-e18 (see* ESCHEAT*).* **~rented** possessed in *~rent, la17-.* **~renter** *16-e19, fem* **~rentrix,** *fem pl* **~rentrices** *17-18* a person who has a *~rent.* **leevin and ~ thinking** = living and *~-like, 18-, now Sh.* **in ~** *la14-, now Sh midLoth,* **on ~** *la14-e19* alive. **(one's) lyvis fude** a livelihood *15-16.* **out of ~** lifeless *15-16.* **successive .. in thare ~** *of royal and papal successions* (each) in his own (successive) lifetime or reign, in succession *e15.*

liffray *see* LIVERY

lift¹ &c *n* the sky, the heavens *la14-.*

drap *or* **fa frae the ~** come or happen suddenly or unexpectedly *la19-, now local NE-EC.* **twa munes** *or* **sins in the ~** an event which never happens *19-, now Ayr Uls.* **under the ~** on earth, in this world *16.* [nME *lift,* OE *lyft*]

lift² &c *v* **1** *vt* = lift (1) *in gen, la14-;* (2) (a) take or pick up (an object from where it lies) *19-;* (b) *golf* pick up (the ball) *19-;* (c) raise (one's hat) *la19-;* (d) *knitting* pick up (stitches) *19-, now NE;* (3) serve (a dish at table) *20-, N midLoth;* (4) (a) take up or out of the ground (*eg* a crop of corn, potatoes) *19-;* (b) gather (scythed corn into a sheaf for binding) *la19-, now local;* (5) *vti* carry (a corpse) out for burial; start a funeral procession *la17-, Gen except Sh Ork;* (6) *vt, fig* raise (a sound): (a) strike up (a tune) *17-, now sEC;* (b) mention, utter (*esp* a person's name) *la19-, now local Sh-Gall;* (7) take (a lady) up to dance, lead to the floor *la19-, Cai C, S.* **2** *fig* raise (the spirits), elate *la15-.* **3** *vi* (1) get up, stand up and move off, depart *19-, now Abd;* (2) *of the chest* heave, as when there is difficulty in breathing *la19-, local C-S.* **4** *vt* (1) (a) collect and carry away (goods or persons), drive (animals) to market *la18-, NE-S.* (b) *specif of a sheep-dog* round up (sheep) and move them forward *20-, now Ork Fif Kcb.* (2) (a) collect (money, rents etc) *15-.* (b) collect or gather *in gen, 18-.* (3) take up or cash (money etc), withdraw (money from a bank) *19-.* (4) *specif* steal (cattle), take by a raid *la17-, now hist.* (5) *of the police* arrest, apprehend, take into custody *20-.* **5** hear distinctly, understand *20-, now Dmf.* **6** raise or levy (troops) *la16-e17; cf* LIST³. **7** move (one's camp or one's house) *la16-17.*

n **1** (1) the act of lifting or of assisting to lift *la16-.* (2) *specif* such an act in carrying a corpse for a funeral *la17-.* **2** *fig* help, relief, encouragement *la16-.* **3** the amount of fish, *esp* herring, that can be lifted aboard by hand in the net, about half a basketful *20-, Abd WC.* **4** the uneven rising step of a person who has one leg shorter than the other *la19-, now Fif WC.* **5** a rising swell in the sea *19-, local.* **6** the point at which a *dry-stone* (DRY) wall begins to rise above the grass at its base *19-, Gall.* **7** (1) a load, burden *16-, now local N-SW.* (2) a large amount *la18-, now NE wLoth Dmf.* **8** a collection, a whip-round *20-, Ayr.* **9** a theft, that which is stolen *19-, local N-SW.* **10** the rounding-up of sheep by a sheep-dog before penning them *20-, local Ork-SW.* **11** a trick at cards *la18-, now Dmf.* **12** *mining* the first seam of coal removed from a mine; a slice taken off a pillar of coal *la19-, now Fif.* **13** *piping* a special emphasis produced by the use of *cut notes* (CUT[1]) *20-.*

~**er** *chf in pl, in the Secession church* (SECEDE) the group which approved of the MINISTER raising the communion elements before consecrating them *la18, Ayr.* **a-~ing &c** *e17, 20-, now Sh Ork Cai,* **at the** *or* **in &c** *19-20, esp of animals* in a very debilitated state [f the practice of raising a farm animal to its feet, *eg* after winter starvation]. ~**it &c** (**up**) cheered up *19-, local.* **a dead** ~ a state in which one can exert oneself no more, a crisis *18-19.* **as fast as** *etc* **legs can** ~ as fast as one can run, at full speed *la18-, now Gall Uls.* **gie a** ~ **to** give a helping hand to; promote, encourage *la17-.* **instrumentis to** (**tak,**) (**ask,**) ~ **and raise** the legal formula in commissions of PROCURATORY *la15-17.* **lend a** ~ **to** = *gie a* ~ *to, la16-.* ~ **and lay** pick things up and lay them down again absent-mindedly or haphazardly *la19-, midLoth Gsw Uls.* ~ **one's hand** (**to**) hit, strike *19-.* ~ **one's lines** *in the Presbyterian churches* withdraw formally from the communicant membership of a certain congregation *la19-.* **tak a** ~ **wi** = *gie a* ~ *to, la18-.* **tak the** ~ **o** make a fool of *20-, NE Ags Per.*

lig[1] **&c** *vi* **1** (1) lie, recline, rest *15-, now only literary.* (2) lie in the grave, be buried *la16-e17.* (3) lie in a bed *16-.* (4) have sexual intercourse **with** *etc la15-19.* **2** lodge temporarily (in a place) *16-17.* **3** *of things* be set or have come to rest *la15-17.*

~**ger &c** a newly-spawned salmon, a foul fish *19-, chf SW.* ~ **at** (**the**) **wait** *or* **await** lie in ambush *e16.* [nME *lig,* ON *liggia; cf* LIE]

lig[2] *v, freq* **lig-lag &c, leg-laig** = LAIG *v, 19-, now Bnf.*

n chatter, idle talk; the noise of many people talking, noisy unintelligible talk *19-e20, chf NE.*

lig[3] *n* = league, the measure of distance *la15-17.*

lig *see* LEG, LEGE

liggat &c; liggett &c *n* a self-closing gate, *freq* one shutting off pasture from arable land *la17-, SW.* [OSc (? *la12*), laME *lidyate,* OE *hlidgeat* a folding door, hinged gate]

ligger &c, liggar &c *n* a military camp, *esp* of a besieging force; a siege *17-e18.* ~ **lady** a female camp-follower *la17-19.* [eModEng *legher,* Du *leger* a camp]

ligger *see* LIG[1]

lighs *see* LICHT[2]

light *see* LICHT[1], LICHT[2]

lig-lag *see* LIG[2]

lignie *see* LEENGYIE

lignott *see* LINGOTT

lik *see* LICK, LIKE[1], LIKE[2]

likarstane *see* LECKERSTANE

like[1] **&c; lik &c, lek &c** *la19-, Sh Cai* [ləik; lık] *adj, comparative* **liker** *la14-,* **mair liker** *la19-20, N Fif* **1** (1) = like *la14-.* (2) the like of, someone or something like *15-e17:* 'shee saw like ane great smoak'. **2** *freq in comparative* more apt, more befitting, more appropriate *la19-, local:* 'a worset goon's the liker you'. **3** (1) likely, probable *la15-, now local Abd-Gall.* (2) *with infin* likely to, apparently on the point of *la14-.*

adv **1** = like *la15-.* **2** added as an intensifier or modifier, *eg* ~ .. *or* .. ~ so to speak, as it were, *eg* **what a** ~**, sic a** ~**, what's** ~ **wrang** *19-, Gen except Sh Ork:* 'juist for the day like'; 'what a like thing to say'. **3** about, approximately (a certain amount or number) *la18-, now Sh.* **4** (1) likely, probably *la19-.* (2) as if about (to do something) *15-.* (3) as if, so as almost to make it appear or give the impression (that something is so) *16.*

n **1** = like *la14-.* **2 the** ~ *used to emphasize* (1) *a positive* that very thing, indeed; (2) *a negative* nothing of the sort, not at all *la19-, now local Sh-SW:* 'Ye're sleepin - I'm no the like'. **3** *golf* an equal number of strokes on both sides (at a hole in course of play); a stroke which makes the scores even, *freq* ~ **as we** *etc* **lie, play the** ~ *19-.*

vi, chf **be liken &c to** be likely or about to, look like doing or being *la16-, now local Sh-Loth:* 'I was lyken to dee'.

likely &c *17-,* **likly &c** *la14-, now NE* ['ləiklı; Sh Cai NE also* 'lık-] *adj* **1** = likely *la14-.* **2** *orig chf of men* good-looking, handsome *la15-, now Sh SW Uls.* **3** (1) capable or competent in manner *la14-, local EC-S.* (2) strong and brave-looking *la15-16.* (3) *of things* appearing to be suitable (for some purpose) *15-.* *adv* probably *la17-.* *n* likelihood, probability, chance *18-, Sh Abd Fif SW.* *vt* make (a rhyme) like its rhymeword *e16.* **the liklyest &c** the course that seems most promising or suitable in the circumstances *la14-16.* **be liklynes** to all appearances, apparently *la14-15.* **liken &c, likkin &c** *vt* **1** = liken *la14-.* **2 liken with** *or* **to** associate (a person) with (another person or thing) by repute, think of in connection with *19-, local NE-SW.* **no to leave a body** (**in**) **the** ~**ness o a dog** call someone everything that is bad, defame someone's character *19-.*

∼ as 1 = like as *15-*. **2** as if *la15-16*. **3** *introducing a principal statement referring to the previous one* likewise, similarly, furthermore *la15-19*. **∼sae** likewise, similarly *e17*, *la19-*, *now Ags midLoth*. **be ∼ to be** *etc* appear or seem to be etc *la14-17*. **be ∼ one's meat** look well-nourished *19-*, *Gen except Sh Ork*. **be ∼ onesel 1** be unchanged in appearance, *eg* after death *19-*. **2** act up to one's reputation *20-*. **∼ wha &c but him, her** *etc* quite the thing, in a grand or confident manner *19-*, *now NE*.

like² **&c; lik &c, lake** *la19-20* [ləik; *Sh Cai* lık] *v* **1** *vt* = like *la14-*. **2** *impersonal* it ∼s it pleases, suits, is agreeable to (me etc) *la14-*, *now literary*. **3** *vi, used in negative* expressing hesitation or bashfulness *19-*: 'I dinna like'. **4** *vt* love, have a strong affection for (*esp* a person of the opposite sex) *18-*.
liking 1 = liking *la14-*. **2** *chf early verse* happiness, contentment; pleasure, satisfaction *la14-e18*.
as .. as ye ∼ as .. as you can imagine, very .. *la19-*: 'as impident as ye like'. **come** *etc* **what ∼s** come what may *la18-*.

likkin *see* LIKE¹

likly *see* LIKELY

Lilias-day &c [*'lılıas'de] a July holiday and fair in Kilbarchan, Renfr *la19*. [f *St Liliosa* a Spanish saint whose day is 27 July]

lill *n* one of the holes in a wind instrument, as in the *chanter* (CHANT) of a bagpipe *18-19*. [appar Du *lul* a pipe, MDu *lul(le)pijpe* a bagpipe; *cf* LILT]

Lilles &c; Lyllis &c [*'ləilz] *chf* **∼ worset** cloth (as) made at Lille in French Flanders *16-e17*.

lill &c for lall; lill for law [*'lılfər'lal, *'lılfər'la, *lil-]: quit *or* play **∼** give tit for tat, requite *15-e16*. [*cf* OE *lǣl* a weal, stripe, *wið lǣle* = L *livorem pro livore* and eModEng *lill for loll*]

lillie &c *adj, literary, esp ballad* lovely, beautiful *la18-e20*. [reduced f obs Eng *liefly*, OE *lēoflic* lovable, lovely]

lillie *see* LILY

lillikine &c *n, in pl as collective* a kind of lace for trimming garments, ? with a floral pattern *la16-e17*. [? eModDu *leliekijn* a lily, lily of the valley, *lelie* a lily, a fleur de lis]

lillilu ['lılı'lu] *n* a lullaby *19-*, *now Sh Ork midLoth*. [onomat]

lilt &c *v* **1** raise (a loud cry) *e16*. **2** *vti, of sound* sing in a low clear voice, *usu* implying sweetness of tone and light cheerful rhythm; sing a tune on its own without the words (1) *of persons*, *la17-*; (2) *chf verse, transf of bird-song, running water, a musical instrument etc*, *18-*; (3) *vt* strike **up** (a tune or a song) *18-e19*. **3** *vi, lit and fig* move in a sprightly way, skip, dance *19-*, *now Abd midLoth Uls*. **4** move in a jerky, hopping way *e19*.

n **1** *freq in titles of tunes* a lively, sweet or rhythmical song; the tune itself *la17-*. **2** a rhythm, cadence *19-*.
∼er a singer, songster *19*. **the ∼in &c** *specif* the old setting of *The Flowers o the Forest* (FOREST) *la18-*, *Slk*.
∼ it = *v* 3, *18-e20*. [ME *lulte* (once), orig chf imit]

lily &c, lillie &c ['lılı] *n* **1** = lily *la14-*. **2** the narcissus, *esp* the common daffodil and pheasant's eye varieties, *freq* distinguished as **yellow** or **white ∼** *la19-*.

lilyoak &c ['lılı'ok] *n* the common lilac *19-*. [altered f LAYLOCK, by association with *lily* and *oak*]

limb &c *la16-*, **lim &c** [lım] *n* **1** = limb *la14-*. **2** *specif* the leg of a human or animal *15-18*.
devil's ∼ *la14-*, **∼ o the deil** *etc*, *la19-* a wicked or mischievous person or animal.

limbe &c [*lım] *n* = limbo *la15-e17*. [nME *lymbe*, L *limbus* a border, edge]

lime¹ &c *n, also* **lymb** *e17* **1** = (quick)lime *15-*. **2** mortar, cement, *freq* **stane and ∼** masonry *la14-*.
vt **1** = lime *la17-*. **2** steep (skins) in a solution of lime *17*.
∼ coal coal used for burning lime *la17-*, *now Ayr*. **∼ craig 1** a limestone quarry *17*, *WC*. **2** the working face of a limestone quarry *la18-*, *now Fif*. **∼ holl &c** *la16-17*, *SW, S*, **∼ pot(t)** *16-17* a tanner's lime-pit. **∼ quarrell** = **∼ craig** 1, *17*. **∼ shells** the unground lumps produced by burning limestone *la18-20*. **∼ stane 1** = limestone *la15-*. **2** *in pl* pieces of limestone *16-e17*. **∼ wand** a stick smeared with bird-lime for trapping birds *la15-16*. **∼ wark &c** a place where lime is worked and burned, a limekiln *19-*, *now Ayr*.

lime² &c *adj* made of earthenware, porcelain *la17-e18*. [var of LAME¹; see SND]

limfad *see* LYMPHAD

limit *see* LEEMIT

limitat &c *ptp* **1** territorially delimited, *esp* by authority *16-17*. **2** restricted (by authority) in scope, powers or action *la16-17*.
vt circumscribe *la16-17*. [L *līmitāt-*, ptp stem of *līmitāre* limit; *cf* LEEMIT]

limmer &c, limmar &c ['lımər] *n, also* **lymber &c** *17* **1** (1) *freq of* BORDER *or Highland* (HIELAND) *robbers* a rascal, villain, scoundrel *15-20*. (2) *of a mischievous child* a rascal, rogue *19-*, *now local*. **2** (1) a loose or disreputable woman; a man's mistress; a whore *16-*. (2) term of more general abuse or contempt for a woman *la18-*. **3** term of abuse for female animals or things personified *la18-e20*. [obscure]

limn [lım] *vti* = limn *16-*.
n a portrait, likeness, replica; a photograph *20-*, *Ork Ayr*.
∼er 1 a portrait-painter *la17-*. **2** *specif* the Royal portrait-painter *la16-*.

limp &c *n* = lump, the fish *la17-e18*.

lin &c [lɪn; *lin] *vi* pause, desist *17-*, *now Sh Ork.* [ME *lin*, OE *linnan* desist, ON *linna*; confused w LEAN]

lin *see* LINN¹, LINN²

lin-&c: ~**-nail &c** *la15-e20*, ~**-pin &c** *16-*, *now Ork Rox* a linch-pin.

linally *see* LINEALLIE

lincum &c: ~ **twine** twine or thread made or as made at Lincoln *la16-e17.*

linder ['lɪndər; *NE also* lɪnər] *n* **1** a woollen jacket or cardigan *la18-e19*, *chf NE.* **2** *also* **linner** *19-* a woollen or flannel undershirt *la18-*, *NE.* [perh f ON *lindi* a belt, girdle, binder]

Lindesay &c ['lɪn(d)ze] ~ **herald** title of a herald in the service of the Earl of Crawford *la15.* [the family name of the Earls of Crawford]

line¹ &c *n* **1** = line *14-.* **2** *marbles* a straight line scored on the surface of the ground *20-*, *Ags wLoth Gsw.* **3** a line of a metrical PSALM read or intoned by the PRECENTOR before being sung by the congregation, *chf* **read** (*la17-e19*) *or* **give out** (*19-20*) **the** ~. **4** (1) a line of writing; any piece of written authorization *la17-.* (2) *in pl, specif* a certificate of church-membership, *chf lift one's* ~*s* (LIFT²) *la19-.* (3) an account with a shop; a bill *20-*, *chf* **pit on a** *or* **the** ~ put (a charge) down to account *20-.* (4) a prescription *la19-.* (5) a note requesting or explaining a child's absence from school etc *la19-.* (6) a shopping list *20-.* (7) a betting slip *20-.* **5** ? a bar or sandbank in a river or harbour *16.*

vt, specif trace out (boundaries of properties in BURGHS) *15-e18.*

liner &c 1 a line-fishing boat *la19-.* **2** (1) an official appointed to measure out and fix the boundaries of properties (in BURGHS) *15-;* (2) *latterly* a member of a *Dean of Guild* (DEAN) Court which supervised the erection or alteration of buildings in certain BURGHS *16-20*, *chf Gsw;* see also *lynster* below and DEVIDER, LANIMER, OUTLANDNER. ~**y** *marbles* a game played with a LINE *n* 2, *20-*, *Ags wLoth Gsw.*

lining 1 the measuring out of holdings in the settlement of boundaries, *chf* in BURGHS *15-e17.* **2** *attrib* (a stone or post) set in position or marked as a boundary by *liners*, *la15-e16.* **breve of lining** see BRIEF. **(decree of) lining** permission to proceed with building after due inspection of the boundaries *la18-20.* **lynster &c** [*'ləinstər] = *liner* 2, *e17*, *Elgin Kirkcudbright.*

gie someone a ~ **o' one's mind** give someone a piece of one's mind *la19-*, *NE wLoth.*

line² &c *vt* **1** = line, apply a lining to *la15-.* **2** beat, thrash *19-*, *now Cai Abd.*

~ **someone's luif** grease someone's palm, bribe *la19-*, *Sh N EC Lnk.*

lineallie &c, linally &c *la15-16* ['lɪnɪalɪ; *?'lɪnəlɪ, *?'ləin-] *adv* **1** = lineally *15-.* **2** *freq in descriptions of boundaries* in a straight line, 'as the crow flies' *la15-e17*, *chf NE.*

lineatioun &c [*lɪnɪ'eʃun] *n* = lining 1 (LINE¹) *17.*

linen &c, linin &c; linning &c *16-19* ['lɪnən; *'lin-, *?'ləin-] *adj* = linen *la14-.*

n **1** = linen *la15-.* **2** *in pl, also* (*erron*) **lineis** (1) linen clothes, one's shirts or undergarments *la16-*, *now Sh;* (2) a shroud *18-*, *now Cai Ags;* (3) penitential garments *17.*

~ **clathis 1** = *n* 2 (1); articles or pieces of linen *la14-e17.* **2** = *n* 2 (3) *la15-e17.*

liney *see* LINE¹

ling¹ &c *n* a line; a rope, cord or string *la15-16;* cf *great ling* (GREAT).

vi rush forward *la14-e19.*

~**it &c** thin, lank, lean *19-20*, *EC, S.*

in(til) ane &c ~ *verse* in a straight line, straight on; immediately; quickly, impetuously *la14-e16.* [ME *li(n)gne*, OF *ligne* a line]

ling² &c *n* **1** = ling, heather *la15-.* **2** the harestail cotton-grass; the deer-grass *la17-20*, *C, S.*

pull ~ the harestail cotton-grass *la18-19*, *sEC, S.* [ultimately ON *lyng* ling, heather; the whortleberry; see SND]

lingal *see* LINGEL²

lingel¹ &c, linyel *e17;* **lingan &c** *la18-*, *chf nEC* ['lɪŋl, 'lɪŋən; *'lɪnjəl] *n* the waxed thread used by shoemakers *17-.*

~**-backit** having a long weak limp back *la19-*, *SW, S.* ~**-en(d)** the tip of the LINGEL¹ to which the BIRSE was attached for threading it through the leather; the piece of LINGEL¹ itself *19-e20*, *C S.* ~**-tailed** *fig* having a long lank tail; narrow-hipped; with long narrow trailing skirts *18-*, *now Fif Dmf.* [eModEng *lingel*, ME *lynolf*, OF *lignoel &c*, *ligneul* cobbler's thread]

lingel² &c, lingal; lynȝell &c *16* ['lɪŋl; *'lɪnjəl, *'lɪŋjəl] *n* **1** (1) a length of rope or cord *la18-*, *now Loth.* (2) *also* **linget &c** *e17*, *e19* (*Ags*) [*'lɪŋət] *specif* a rope for hobbling an animal *16-;* *cf* LANGLE. **2** any strap, thong or looped cord *16-*, *now Loth.* **3** *fig* anything long, long-drawn-out and consequently flaccid or flabby; a rigmarole; a tall lanky person *la19-*, *N.*

vt hobble (a horse etc) *la19-*, *NE.* [ME *lingell* harness, strap, appar ultimately f L *li(n)gula* strap]

linget &c ['lɪn(d)ʒət] *n* the seed of flax, linseed *la15-20*, *latterly N.*

~ **oil** linseed oil *la15-16.* ~ **seed** = *n*, *la15-e19.* **olye** ~ = ~ *oil*, *16.* [only Sc; uncertain; *cf* MF *lignette* linen cloth]

linget *see* LINGEL²

lingie ['lɪŋgɪ] *n* a long rambling story, rigmarole *20-*, *NE Fif Dmf.* [var of Eng *lingo*]

lingott &c; lignott &c, lingnot [*?'lɪŋgot, *?'lɪgnət, *?'lɪŋnət] *n* **1** a block of metal, *usu* silver or gold, which has been cast in a mould, an ingot *la15-17.* **2** an ingot mould *16-17.* [F *lingot*]

liniage &c *only Sc*, **lenage &c** ['lɪniedʒ; *'lɪnedʒ, *'lin-] *n* = lineage *15-16*.

link¹ &c; le(i)nk *16* [lɪŋk] *n* **1** (1) = link *la15-*. (2) *specif* a links in the chain from which the pot-hook hung in the fireplace *la16-*, *now Sh-N Loth.* **2** a joint of the body, *esp* one of the vertebrae *la17-20*. **3** a lock of hair, a curl *la18-*, *now Sh.* **4** *chf in pl* a string of sausages or black puddings *19-*. **5** *freq in pl, esp of the Forth* loops of a winding stream or river, the land enclosed by such *la18-*.
vti **1** (1) = link *la15-*. (2) *vt* chain, bind *la16-17*. **2** (1) *vi* go arm in arm, pass one's arm through another's *19-*. (2) *vt* take (another) on one's arm, give one's arm to; support (an infirm person) by the arms *19-*. **3** (1) ~ **on, aff, up, doun** *etc* place (a pot) on or take (it) off the pot-hook on the LINKS¹ (*n* **1** (2)); (2) ~ **up, doun** place (the pot-hook) on a higher, or lower, link *18-20*.
hae *or* **pit a** ~ **in one's tail** (? *orig of a horse*) be crafty or deceitful *19-20, SW, S.*

link² [lɪŋk; *Fif also* ləiŋk] *v* **1** (1) move fast or easily, trip along, walk briskly *18-*, *now NE Per.* (2) ~ **it** take oneself off quickly *20-*, *NE.* **2** skip, dance, caper *19-*, *NE.* **3** *vti, freq of spinning* act with speed and energy; work vigorously (**at**) *18-*, *now Cai Abd Fif.*
~**ie** a roguish person, a wag; a lightfooted girl; a deceitful, untrustworthy person *19-*, *S.* **like linkie** *20*, *Ags Lnk Ayr Rox*, **like linkum** *20-*, *now Sh* in a flash, at top speed. ~**ing &c** active, agile, brisk *la18-*, *now Fif Ayr.* [see SND]

links &c, linkis &c *la15-e17*; **linx &c** *16-17* [lɪŋks; *Fif also* ləiŋks] *n pl* **1** a stretch of undulating open sandy ground, *usu* covered with turf, bent-grass or gorse, normally near the seashore *la15-*, *chf E Coast.* **2** a golf-course, *orig* formed on seaside LINKS as at St Andrews *la16-20*. [nME *lynkys*, OE *hlincas* (*pl*), *hlinc* (*sing*) a ridge, slope, bank; *n* **1** common as place-name in many Scottish seaside BURGHS]

Linlithgow [lɪn'lɪθgo] *attrib* applied to dry measures *17-e19*. [the standard dry measures were committed to the custody of this BURGH 1617-1824; *cf* SCOTS]

linn¹, lin *n* **1** a waterfall, cataract *la15-*. **2** a deep and narrow gorge *la18-*, *SW, S.* [ONorthumb *hlynn* a torrent]

linn² &c, lin *n* the pool below a waterfall *la16-*, *Gen except Sh Ork.* [Gael *linn* a pool]

linn³ *n* a kind of fireclay formerly used in the Kilmarnock district as slate-pencil *19-e20, Ayr.* [f the Linn Bed seam of coal near Kilmarnock; prob f LINN¹]

linner *see* LINDER

linning *see* LINEN

linsey-winsey, linsie-winsie &c ['lɪnsi-'wɪnsi] *n* = linsey-woolsey *la16-*, *now Abd Stlg Rox Uls.* [*cf* WINCEY]

lint¹ &c *n* **1** the flax plant *la15-20*. **2** flax in the process of manufacture for spinning *15-*. **3** = lint, scraped linen cloth or flax-waste, *orig* used as tinder or for caulking, *now* for dressing wounds *la14-*. **4** linen thread, *esp* that used by shoemakers to make their LINGEL¹ *20-*, *Sh NE Ayr.*
~**beet** a bundle of flax cut and ready for processing *19-*, *now Renfr Uls.* ~**bell** the flower of the flax plant *19-*, *now Uls.* ~**boll** *la15-e17*, ~**bow** *la16-*, *now Uls* [~'bʌu] the seed pod of flax. ~**dresser** a flax-dresser *18-*, *now Renfr.* ~**hole** a pond in which flax is steeped *la19-*, *now Bnf Fif SW.* ~**mill** a flax-factory or its machinery *la18-*, *now local Bnf-SW*, *freq as farm-name.* ~**pot** = ~*hole, la19-, now Fif.* ~**tap** the bundle of dressed flax put on a distaff for spinning; *chf* describing very fair or grey hair *18-19*: 'hair like a lint tap'. ~**wheel &c** *17-18, 20-* (*Uls*) a spinning wheel for flax. ~**white** *chf verse, of hair* white as flax, flaxen-blond *la18-*.

lint² *vtir* rest, recline *19-20*. [f *lint*, pt of LIN¹]

lintel &c; lentell &c *la16-e18* ['lɪntl] *n* **1** = lintel *16-*. **2** a mantelpiece *la18-*. **3** the threshold of a door *la19-*, *local.*
~ **ale** a drink given to the masons at a building job when the door-lintel was put on *17-e18*.

linth *see* LENTH

lintie; lintick &c *la18-e20, Ork n* **1** *also* **brown** ~ *la19-*, *now Cai SW*, **gray** ~ *19-*, *now local*, **rose** ~ *la19-*, *now NE Fif Loth* the linnet *18-*, *Gen except Sh.* **2** a sprightly, merry girl *20-*, *now Loth Rox Uls.* [f *lint* in LINTWHITE + dim ending; the bird feeds on flax seeds; *cf* Eng *linnet*, OF *linette*, f *lin* flax]

Linton *attrib* designating a variety of black-faced hill-sheep bred in the Tweed region *la18-19*. [f *West Linton* in Pbls]

lintwhite &c, lintquhite &c *e16* ['lɪnt'hwəit] *n* the linnet *16-20*. [see SND, DOST; *cf* LINTIE]

linx *see* LINKS

linyel *see* LINGEL¹

linʒé *see* LEENGYIE

lion &c, lioun &c *15-17 n* **1** = lion *la14-*. **2** the royal emblem of Scotland (adopted by William the Lion (1165-1214) in place of the earlier dragon) *la15-*. **3** (1) a gold coin issued under Robert III and James II, *15* [ScL *leo la14*]. (2) a copper or billon coin first issued in 1555, *la16*; *cf* HARDHEAD.
~ **nobill** *la16*, ~ **pece** *la16-e17* a gold coin issued 1584-1588. **L~ Rampant** the device on the royal standard of Scotland *18-*.
half ~ a coin worth half the value of *n* **3** (1) *la15*. [see also LYON]

lion *see* LYON

lioun *see* LION, LYON

Lioun(s) *see* LYONIS

lip &c *n* **1** = lip *la14-*. **2** (1) the edge or brink of a stream, pool etc *19-*. (2) *chf in pl, sometimes* *with sing sense* the edge or brim of a hat *la16-e17, e20.* **3** a notch in the edge of a knife- or sword-blade *20-, Loth S.*

vt **1** touch with the lips, taste *la19-.* **2** break, notch or chip (a blade) *19-, now EC, S.* **3** point (a wall) *19.* **4** *vi* be full to the brim or overflowing, brim **over**, *freq* ~**pin** (**fou**) *18-.*
~**pie &c** a glass full to the brim with drink *19-e20, chf Ayr.*
~**-f(o)u** quite full, brimming over *la19-, now Sh NE Ags.* ~ **labour** *freq of prayer* empty or useless talk *17-, now Sh.*
let *or* **pit down the** ~ look dismayed, pout *20-, Sh NE-S.*

lipe &c *n, mining* a small intrusion or irregularity in the joints of a coal-seam, the joints being usually glazed *18-, Fif Ayr.*
lipey *of a coal-seam* intersected by small, irregular, glazed joints *18-, Fif Ayr.* [eModEng a fold; OF *lipe*, F *lippe* a lip]

lippen &c, lippin &c; lipne &c *la14-17,* **lepin &c** *la15-16* ['lɪpən] *vti* **1** trust, depend on: (1) *vt, la16-;* (2) *vi,* ~ **to** *etc,* **in, on** *or* **for** *15-.* **2** entrust (1) (something **to** (*la14-*) *or* **in** (*la15-16*) someone); (2) (someone **with** something) *la19-.* **3** expect confidently, count on: (1) *vt, 15-;* (2) *vi,* ~ **for** (*la16-18*), **on** (*la19-e20*), **to** (*16-17*).
no to ~ **tae &c** untrustworthy *19-, N-S.* [eME *lipnien* trust; see DOST]

lipper¹ &c, lopper *e16 vi* **1** *of water* ripple, be ruffled *e16, 19-, now Ork Cai NE.* **2** *lit and fig* be full almost to overflowing, be brimming over *19-, local Sh-Pbls.*
n a ripple; a broken or choppy sea *e16, 19- (Sh-Ags).* [prob frequentative of LIP; *cf* LAPPER²]

lipper² ['lɪpər; *Ork Cai Abd* 'ləipər; ***'lɪpər] *n* **1** leprosy *15-17.* **2** a large festering sore or mass of sores, a scab *20-, now Cai.*
~**-fat** bulging with fat, gross *19-, chf S.* [var of Eng *leper* leprosy]

lipper³ &c *15-e19,* **leper &c** [***'lɪpər, ***'lipər] *adj* **1** leprous *16-e19.* **2** *as collective noun* lepers *la16.*
n = leper *la15-17.*
~**ous &c** = leprous *15-16.* ~ **folk** lepers *15-e17.* ~**-hous** an asylum for lepers *la16-17.* ~ **man** a leper *15-17.*

lippie &c; leepie &c *la18-, NE,* **leippie &c** *la16-17* ['lɪpɪ; *N nEC also* 'lipɪ] *n* **1** *in dry measure* ¼ of a SCOTS PECK², varying in weight according to district and commodity, *now usu* = 1¾ lbs for goods sold by weight and used *esp* for oats, barley, and potatoes; a FORPET *16-, now N nEC Loth.* **2** a (wooden, box-shaped) measure of this size, *latterly esp* for measuring corn for a horse's feed *17-, now N.*
~**'s bound** the amount of ground to be covered by a LIPPIE of seed, *orig* of flax (as one of

the perquisites of a farm-servant), *later* of potatoes etc *la19-, chf Fif.* [? dim of ME *lepe*, OE *lēap* a (large) basket; see DOST]

lippie *see* LIP
lippin *see* LIPPEN
liquid *adj, law* = LIQUIDATE *adj, 16-.* [L *liquidus* clear, evident, certain]
liquidate &c *ptp, adj, of debts or other due payments* fixed in advance at a definite sum, specified exactly; *of payments in kind, material damages or services* judicially or authoritatively assessed; having a monetary equivalent ascertained and prescribed by DECREE of court and appointed to be so paid *16-.* [*cf* laL *liquidāt-,* ptp stem of *liquidāre* liquefy, f *liquidus* > LIQUID]
liquidatioun &c *n* **1** judicial valuation or ascertainment of the exact amount of a debt, rent or payment due *la16-17.* **2** the authoritative assessment of the monetary equivalent of a payment in kind or of a service *la16-17.* **3** = liquidation.
liquorie *see* LICKERY
lire¹ &c *n* **1** (1) flesh *la15-e18.* (2) **bane and** ~ *la14-e18,* ~ **and bane** *15-16* flesh and bone (a) *in gen, la15-17;* (b) *specif* in contexts of burning or utterly destroying (*chf* a person) la14-e15. **2** *specif in a carcase of beef* the slice of meat near the sternum, the upper portion of brisket *18-, now Cai Edb.* [ME *lire,* OE *līra*]
lire² *n, verse* the complexion *15-e19.* [nME *lire;* ON *hlýr* (*pl*), the cheeks; *cf* ME *lere,* OE *hlēor* cheek, complexion]
lirk¹ &c; lurk *18-e20 n* **1** a crease, rumple or fold as in cloth or paper *18-.* **2** a crease or fold of the skin, a wrinkle *la17-.* **3** a fold of the body, a joint; the angle of the elbow or knee when bent *la19-, now Slk.* **4** a fold or hollow in a hill, a recess, crevice, ravine *19-, now local Sh-Kcb.* **5** an unusual trait of character, a kink, a mental twist *18-, now Abd.*
vi rumple, crease, wrinkle *la17-, now local Sh-Kcb.* [n midlME *lerke* a wrinkle; Scand; see SND, DOST]
lirk² *la19-, NE,* **lurk &c** *vi* **1** = lurk *la14-.* **2** shrink, cower, cringe *la15-16.* **3** live quietly or out of the public eye *la14-16.*
lis *see* LISS
lishpond *see* LISPUND
lisk; leisk &c *16-e17* [lɪsk; ***lisk] *n* the groin, flank *16-, now C.* [north and east midlME *lesske;* see SND, DOST]
lispund; leispund *16-e18,* **leischpund &c** *16-17,* **les(s)pund &c** *la16,* **lishpond &c** *17* ['lɪspʌn(d); ***'lis-, ***'liʃ-] *n* a unit of weight used *orig* in the Baltic trade *16-18, chf Sh Ork.* [see SND, DOST]
liss *19-,* **lis &c** *la15-,* **les** *la14-16,* **leis &c** *16* [lɪs; ***lɛs] *v* **1** *vt* relieve (pain or suffering); relieve (a person **of** suffering) *la14-16.* **2** *vi, of pain etc* cease, abate *19-, now Uls.*

lissens, lissance ['lɪsəns; *'liʃ-] respite 19-e20. [ME *lisse*, OE *līssian*, perh also w infl f LESS[1]]

lis(si)s *n pl* lists (for jousting) *la15*. [OF *lisse* sing, MedL *liciae (pl)*]

list[1] **&c** [lɪst] *vti, also* **lest &c** *la14-16* = list, desire *la14-, now Cai*.
n **1** pleasure, enjoyment, delight *la15-16*. **2** appetite, inclination *16-, now Edb*.
at ~ *la15-16*, **at one's** (**own**) ~ *15* at one's pleasure, according to one's will.

list[2] **&c** *v* **1** *vt* = list, enter on a list *la17-*. **2** enlist into the army, recruit *la17-*. **3** *vir* enlist (oneself) as a soldier *la17-*.

list[3] **&c** *v* = LIFT[2] (*v* 6) *16-17*. [appar a misreading, but *cf* also LIST[2]]

listly &c *adv, chf verse* skilfully; cunningly, craftily *la14-e16*. [midlME *listli*, OE *listelīce*, f OE *list* skill, craft]

lit &c; litt &c *15-19 vt, also fig* dye, colour, tinge *15-, now Sh Cai*.
litster &c, litstar &c *15-16*, **littistar &c** [*'lɪ(t)stər] *15-17* a dyer *la14-19*.
n a dye, tint, dyestuff *la15-, now Sh Cai*.
~-house a dye-house *la16-17*. [ME *lit*, ON *litr* colour, *lita* (*v*) dye]

lite &c *n* **1** a bishop-elect *15*. **2** *chf in pl* = LEET[2] 2, *15-e17*. **3** = LEET[2] 1, *16-e18*.
vt = LEET[2] *v, la16-e18*.
in *or* **upon** (**the**) **~s** (presented etc) as selected nominees *la16-e17*. **in** *or* **on** (**the**) ~ standing as candidates *la16-e18*. [chf Sc; aphetic f OSc *elyte*, ME *elite* = *n* 1; OF *elit &c; cf* LEET[2]]

literatorie [*'lɪtərətoraɪi] *adv* by letter, in writing *16-e17*. [MedL *litteratorie*]

lith &c, leth &c *16-e17 n* **1** a joint in a finger or toe, a small part of the body, *freq* ~ **and limb** *la14-, now Sh N nEC*. **2** a limb *19*. **3** one of the natural divisions or segments of an orange, onion etc *19-, N, C Slk Uls; cf* LEAF. **4** *lit and fig* a joint, slice, or segment *in gen, 17-e20*.
vt disjoint, dislocate; *specif* wring the neck of (a hen) *la19-, chf NE*.
out of ~ dislocated *la16-e17*. [ME *lith*, OE *liþ*, ON *liðr*]

lithe, lythe; lyde &c *19-* [laɪð; *Ags Gall also* laɪd] *adj* **1** *of a place etc* calm, sheltered, snug *la15-, now N*. **2** *of persons etc* gentle, genial, kindly *la14, 19-, NE*.
n shelter, protection from the weather; a sheltered spot, the lee side of something *la18-, N*.
vt **1** shelter, give protection from weather to *la18-, now Abd*. **2** thicken (soup, porridge etc) with oatmeal etc *17-, now Abd Bwk Uls*.
lithin the flour, meal or milk added to soup, gravy etc *19-, now NE*. **~ly** *chf literary* readily, cheerfully *19*. **lithocks &c** ['laɪðəks, 'ləɪθ-] a kind of gruel made from fine oatmeal and *freq* buttermilk *18-, now Stlg wLoth WC*. **~some** = *adj* 2; *also of weather*, *la19-*. **lithy** *of soup etc* thick, smooth and palatable *la18-e19*. [ME, OE *līðe* gentle, OE *liðan* make mild; *cf* Eng *līthe*]

lither &c, lidder &c *la15-18* ['lɪðər; *'lɪdər] *adj* lazy, sluggish, lethargic, idle; lax, slack *15-, now Dmf*.
(**come**) **lidder speid** (come) slowly *16*. [OE *lyðre* bad, base]

lithry &c [*'lɪðrɪ, *'lɪð-] *n* a crowd, *specif* of rather disreputable characters, a rabble, mob *la18-e19*. [appar f obs Eng *livery* a collection of uniformed servants]

liticant *see* LET-DE-CAMP

litigious [lɪ'tɪdʒəs, lə'tɪdʒəs] *adj* **1** = litigious *la17-*. **2** vindictive, spiteful *19-, NE*. **3** *law, esp of property* subject to litigation, concerning which legal action is pending (and which therefore cannot be alienated) *17-*.

litill *see* LITTLE

litiscontestation &c ['ləɪtɪskɔntɛs'teʃn] *n, law* the stage at or after which an action in court begins to be contested *la15-*.
act of ~ the judicial act admitting a case to proof *17*. [L *lītis contestātio* the formal entry into a lawsuit by the calling of witnesses]

litt *see* LIT

litticamp, littigant *see* LET-DE-CAMP

littistar *see* LIT

little, litill &c *la14-17*; **letle &c** *la16-e17*, **laytil &c** *la16-e17* ['lɪtl; *also* *'ləɪtl] *adj, comparative* **littler** *la16, 19-*. *superlative* **littlest** *19-* **1** = little *la14-*. **2** *specif* (1) *as opposed to* MUCKLE the younger or less important in rank or status *la14-, common in farm-names 18-*. (2) *freq* ~ **wee** tiny *19-*. **3** used to imply modest depreciation, affection etc *la15-e17*: '*this lytle buk*'.
adv **1** = little *15-*. **2** *ironic* not at all *la14-e17*: '*he fearit him litill*'.
n = little *la14-*.

littlin, ~ ane, ~ one ['lɪtlən; *'lɪtlen] a child, an infant *la16-, now N nEC*.
~ body a child, an infant *la19-, Ags Fif Uls*. **~-boukit &c** **1** small in body or bulk, shrunken *la18-, now N nEC Dmf*. **2** of little importance, insignificant; deflated in esteem *la19-, NE*. ~ **folk(s)**, ~ **foukies** *literary* the fairies *18-*. ~ **guid 1** the devil *19*. **2** *also* ~ **gweedie** *la19-, NE* the sun-spurge *19-*. ~ **house &c** a privy, a water-closet *la16-, now local NE-Uls*. ~ **man** a junior or adolescent male farm-servant *la17-e19*. **~-thing** *chf without indef art* a small matter, a trifle *la14-, now Abd Ags*: '*the loss was little-thing to what it might have been*'. ~ **worth** of worthless character *19-*.
a ~ ago a short time ago *la19-*.

liv *see* LUIF

live *see* LEEVE

liver[1] **&c, lever &c** *15-17*, **luffer &c** *16* ['lɪvər; *'liv-] *n* = liver (of a person or animal) *la15-*.
~ **rock** a kind of sandstone *19-e20*.

liver[2] **&c** ['lɪvər] *vt* **1** discharge (a ship's cargo), deliver on shore *17-19*. **2** *of the ship* unload *17-18*. **3** unload (a ship) *la17-, now N Hebrides*. [ME; F *livrer* deliver]

liverock *see* LAVEROCK

livery &c, levery &c *la14-17,* **luveray &c** *la15-16;* **livray &c** *17,* **liffray &c** *15-17,* **luferay &c** *16,* **loveray &c** *16-e17* ['lɪv(ə)rɪ; ***'liv-, ***'løv-] *n* = livery *la14-.*
~ **meal** a certain quantity of meal given to farm-servants in lieu of board *la18-e19.*

livrock *see* LAVEROCK

lizour &c *16-e20,* **lesour &c** *la15-e19,* **lesu &c** *15-16;* **lasour &c** *la16-17* [***'lɪzər, ***'lizər, ***'lezər, ***'lizi, ***'liz(j)u] *n* a pasturage, grazing, meadow *la15-e20.*
vti pasture, graze *la15-e19.* [ME *leswe &c,* OE *lǣswe &c; -our* forms (chf Sc) prob f *pasture*]

lizure &c [***'lɪzər] *n* the selvage or edge of a web or piece of cloth *la18-e19, Renfr.* [ME *liser,* OF *lisiere*]

lo; lu &c *la14-16* [***lø] *interj* = lo! *la14-e17.*

lo *see* LUVE

load *see* LAID

loaf *see* LAIF

loan[1] &c *la16-,* **lone &c** *15-19;* **loyne &c** *la16-17* [lon] *n* **1** *also* **loune &c** *16-e18* a grassy (cattle-)track through arable land, *freq* leading to (common) grazing and also used as pasture, a milking place, a common green etc *15-,* now in place-names. **2** *specif* the part of farm ground or a roadway which leads to or adjoins the house *19-,* now NE Per. **3** a street or roadway *19, chf Ayr.*
vt drive (cattle) along a LOAN[1] (*n* 1) *17-e18.*
~**in(g) 1** = *n* 1, *15-,* now NE, C. **2** the right of passage for animals by means of a LOAN[1] (*n* 1) *la15-17.*
~ **head &c** the higher or outer end of a LOAN[1] *la16-,* *Gen except Sh Ork.*
commoun ~ public or communally owned LOAN[1] (*n* 1) *16-17.* **heid of the** ~ = ~ **head,** *la16-e17.* [OE *lone* a road, street; *cf* Eng *lane*]

loan[2], lone &c *n* provisions for a campaign *la16-e18, chf Highl NE.* [only Sc; ScGael *lòn,* Ir Gael *lón* food, provisions]

lob; lub *19, S n* a lump, a heavy unwieldy thing, a large piece or area of something *la19-,* now *Ags.* [var of LAB[1]]

lobster *see* LAPSTER

local &c *adj* **1** = local *la16-.* **2** *of stipends* (STEEPEND) assigned parish by parish out of the ecclesiastical revenues of each, *esp* out of the TEINDS of lands within each parish *la16-17.* **3** *of troops' quarterings* allocated to a specified district, not temporary or transient *17.*
vt assign (a parochial *stipend* or AUGMENTATION) out of the TEINDS or other ecclesiastical revenues of a parish; apportion the liability for payment of the same among the HERITORS *la16-.*
locality &c 1 the revenues of a certain piece of land allocated to an individual or corporate body as (part of) his or their income; the land in question *17-,* now only hist. **2** (1) the authoritative apportioning of liability for payment of

LOCAL (*adj* 2) stipend (STEEPEND) or AUGMENTATION of *stipend* among the HERITORS or other possessors of the TEINDS of lands lying within the parish *17.* (2) the liability thus apportioned for payment of (an increase in) a parish MINISTER's *stipend, 17-, now only hist.* (3) such a *stipend, 17.* (4) a schoolmaster's stipend *la17.* **3** (1) a levy or the allowance provided from it for maintaining troops in quarters, *latterly chf* a requisition of forage for their horses *17-e18, latterly chf SW.* (2) the district allocated to a particular body of troops to provide its *locality* (as in prec) *e17.* **4** = locality. **decree** (*18-*) or **decreet** (*17-e18*) **of** ~**ity** the decision of the *Commission of Teinds* (TEIND) confirming the allocation of liability as in *locality* 2 (1), now only hist. **locallie** *adv* **1** (assigned, paid) as LOCAL stipend or as appointed by a *decreet of locality, 17.* **2** *of lands* and TEINDS *from which a compulsory loan or troops' maintenance is to be levied* (distributed) district by district, separately in each district *e17.*

location, locatioun *16 n, law* the act of hiring out or renting *la16-.* [eModEng; L *locātio* letting, *locāre* let for hire]

locator [lɔ'ketər] *n, law* a person who lets for hire *la17-.* [eModEng, L *locātor,* f as prec]

loch &c; louch &c *la14-20* [lox; *S also* lʌux] *n, pl also* **lowis** *15-e16* [***lʌuz] (*cf* LOW[3]) **1** a lake, pond (applied to all natural lakes in Scotland, except the Lake of Menteith, Per); *also* a sea-loch (SEA) *la14-,* in place-names *14-.* **2** (1) a small pool or puddle *20-.* (2) a discharge of urine *la20-, Ork NE Per.*
~ **fit &c** the lower end of a LOCH *la19-.* ~ **head, locheid** *16-17* the upper end of a LOCH *16-,* *freq in place-names.* ~ **leech 1** the leech *la16-e19.* **2** *fig* a parasite, a rapacious person *la16-e18.* ~ **maw,** ~ **maa** the common gull *17-,* now *Sh Cai Wgt.* ~ **reed** the common reed-grass *18-e19.* ~**side** the side of a LOCH, the district round a LOCH *la14-.* ~ **trout** a trout which feeds in a LOCH, *usu* larger than a river-trout *19-.* [Sc and IrGael *loch,* but see DOST]

Lochaber [lox'a(:)bər] ~ **axe** *etc* a kind of long-handled battle-axe; *now only* ceremonial arms carried by the attendants of Edinburgh's *Lord Provost* (PROVOST) *16-.* [the district in Inv]

lochan ['loxən] *n* a little LOCH *la17-.* [only Sc; Gael *lochan,* dim of *loch*]

locher *see* LOGGER

Loch Fyne [lox'fəin] *attrib* applied to herring caught there *18-.* [the sea-loch (SEA) in Arg]

Lochgelly [lox'gɛle] a leather strap or *tawse* (TAW[1]) for punishing school children, manufactured in Lochgelly, Fif *20-.*

Lochiel &c [lox'il] ~**'s lantern** = *MacFarlane's bouet* (BOUET) *la19, hist.* [the name given to the chief of Clan Cameron, f the name of the *sea-loch* (SEA) in Inv]

Lochleven &c [lox'livən] ~ **trout** a variety of trout peculiar to Lochleven *la18-*. [the LOCH in Kinr]

loch-liver; loch-lubbertie, -lub(b)erton ['lox-'lɪvər, -'lʌbərtɪ, -'lʌbərtən] *n* a jelly-fish *19-, Abd*. [see SND]

locht; lucht [*loxt, *also* *lʌxt] *n* a boat-load (of a commodity) *la16-17*. [IrGael *lucht* contents, a batch, ScGael *luchd* a cargo]

lochtir *see* LACHTER²

lock¹, lok &c; louk &c *la16-e17* [lok; *also* *lʌuk] *vt* **1** (1) = lock *15-*. (2) *fig* entrap, imprison *la15-e18*. **2** *of weather, snow, mist etc* make (a place) impassable or impenetrable *la19-, now Ags*. **3** embrace *19-, Sh Ags*. *n* = lock *la14-*.
   lokkit &c 1 locked (**up**) *la14-*. **2** *fig* kept secure or hidden *16-*. **3** furnished with a lock or locks *15-*. ~**it** *book* an official register of GUILDS or crafts fitted with clasps and locks *16-*, *latterly appar only Dundee*.
   ~**fast** fastened by a lock, shut and locked, secured under lock and key against interference; breaking into a ~*fast* place constitutes an aggravation of theft *la15-*.

lock², lok &c; lowk *20-, Cai* [lok; *Cai* lʌuk] *n* **1** = lock, a tress of hair *la15-*. **2** (1) *also* **luik** *17, Ork* [*?luk] a (small) quantity, a handful, a pinch (of meal, salt etc) *la16-, now Cai Gall Uls*. (2) a bundle or handful (as of hay) *18-, Sh-Cai Gall Uls*. (3) *law* a small quantity of meal exacted as one of the SEQUELS of a mill *17-19, freq* ~ **and gowpen** *la18-e19*. **3** a (small) quantity, number or amount (of anything); a lot *la18-, now Sh-Cai Uls*.
   locker, lokker *vi, chf of hair* **lokkerand &c** *la15-e16*, **lockering** *18, 20* curling; **lokkerit &c** curled, curly *e16*.

lockanties &c *exclam* expressing surprise or disappointment *la18-e19, Ayr*. [perh altered f Eng *lack a day(s)*, but *cf* LOVANENTIE, LOKE, and Eng *lawkins*]

lockart *see* LOKKAT

Lockerbie; Lockerby ['lokərbɪ] ~ **lick** *etc* a gash or wound in the face *la18-, now hist*. [the town in Dmf]

lockerstrae &c *n* a small pointer, reed or straw used in teaching children to read, or in keeping one's place on a page when reading aloud *19-e20, NE*. [appar for *locus strae a straw for indicating the position of the word or letter, f L *locus* a place, position]

lockie *see* LOKE

lockman, lokman *n* a public executioner, *chf* of a BURGH *la15-e19, Ork C*. [uncertain; perh f LOCK² *n* 2 (3); see SND, DOST]

locumtenant &c *n* = LIEUTENAND *la15-e16*. [after MedL *locumtenens*]

locus *n, esp law* a place, site, position *18-*.
   ~ **poenitentiae** [pɪnɪ'tɛnʃie] the opportunity given to a person to withdraw from an agreement before he has confirmed it in law *18-*. [L]

Lod &c *interj* = Lord! *la19-, Cai Ags C, S*.

lode *see* LAID

lodesman *la19-, Sh*, **lodisman &c** *16* ['lodzmən] *n* a guide; a pilot; a steersman. [eModEng, ME *lodesman*]

lodge *la16-*, **loge &c** *la14-17*, **ludge &c** *15-*, **luge &c** *la14-16* [lodʒ, lʌdʒ] *n* **1** = lodge *la14-*. **2** *specif* (1) a porter's lodge *15-*; (2) any shed or cabin, *eg* for storage *la16-e17*; (3) *mining* a pithead shed or shelter *la17, la19*; (4) a fisherman's BOTHY *la14, 19-, now Sh*; (5) a shed or workshop for masons *la15-18*.
   vti **1** = lodge *la14-*. **2** *vi* be or lie **in** (a place), **on** (the ground etc) *16*. **3** *vt, law* leave (pleadings etc) in the custody of the clerk of court, *corresponding to Eng* file *19-*. **lodgeable** habitable *18-e19*. ~**ing &c 1** = lodging *la14-*. **2** a dwelling, a residential building *15-*. **3** a military camp or camping place *la14-e16*. **4** = *n* 2 (3) *la17*. **5** an animal's lair *16*. **mak ~ing** = take lodging(s) *la14-e16*. ~**ment** *mining* a reservoir or water store underground *la19-, now Fif*.

lodisman *see* LODESMAN

lodomy &c *n* = laudanum *19-, now NE Ags Loth*. [colloq alteration]

lofe *la14-e20*, **lof &c** *la14-e17*, **love &c** *la14-e19* [*n* lof; *lov; *v* *lov] *vt* **1** praise, honour; value highly *la14-16*. **2** offer (wares) at a price; *latterly* haggle over; set a price on, price *la16-e19*.
   n, chf **lof &c 1** praise; honour, glory *la14-16*. **2** an offer to sell or to buy something at a certain price *la16-e17, e20 (Dmf)*.
   lovabill &c 1 *of persons, their actions or attributes* praiseworthy, honourable, satisfactory, acceptable *15-16*. **2** *of laws etc or customs etc* laudable, acceptable; respected, established *la15-17*.
   lovage *la15-e16*, **loving &c 1** the act of praising, praise *la14-16*. **2** honour, credit; fame, glory *la14-16*. **3** an instance of praise; a writing or speech of praise *la14-16*. [see DOST]

lofe *see* LAIF

loft *see* LAFT

logan &c *n* a collection of small articles of the same kind, *eg* coins, marbles, *esp* when scattered for children to scramble for *19-e20, Abd*.
   vt scatter (coins) as at a wedding; get rid of (a collection of marbles) *19-e20, Abd*. [var of law term *lagan* jetsam, OF *lagan*]

loge *see* LODGE

loggage *n* = luggage *la19-, NE*.

loggar *e19, Dmf*, **logour &c** *la15* *n, only in pl* a kind of hose, stockings without feet. [unknown]

logger; locher &c [*'logər, *'loxər] *vt* drench, soak; slobber (food) *19-e20, Ross Fif Lnk Dmf*. [prob imit]

loggerand *adj* ? loose-jointed *la15*. [obscure]

logie &c ['logɪ] *n* **1** *also* **loggie** *la18-19* = KIL-LOGIE *la16-19*. **2** the outer opening of a venti-lation funnel in a corn-stack *la18-e20*. [appar Gael *logan, lagan*, dim of *lag* a hollow, pit]

logive *see* LOVAGE

logour *see* LOGGAR

loik hertit *see* LUKE-HERTIT

loit &c [loit, ləit; *Fif* lʌut; *Bnf also* *lit] *vti* throw down something wet and soggy in a mass on the ground; defecate; vomit *19-e20*.
n **1** a small quantity of liquid *19-e20*. **2** (1) a mass of something filthy or disgusting, liquid or semi-liquid *19-, now Kcdn*. (2) a lump of faeces *19-e20*. [orig mainly onomat, perh w some conflation w senses of LEET³; see SND]

lok *see* LOCK¹, LOCK²

lokart *see* LOKKAT

loke; loks, lockie &c *exclam, usu* expressing surprise or glee *la18-, now Rox*. [prob altered f *Lord!*; *cf* Eng *lawk(s)*, LOCKANTIES]

lokkat &c; lo(c)kart &c *only Sc n* = locket, a metal crossbar in a window *16-e17*.

lokman *see* LOCKMAN

loks *see* LOKE

loll¹ &c *n* a pampered, lazy person *18-e20, Abd*. [eModEng; *cf* Eng *v* = hang, droop]

loll² &c *vi* howl like a cat, caterwaul *19-e20, S*.

loman *see* LYOMON

Lombard *see* LUMBARD

lomfad *see* LYMPHAD

londies, London, Londoun *see* LONON

lone *see* LANE⁴, LOAN¹, LOAN²

long *see* LANG¹

longart *see* LUNKART

longavil *see* LONGUEVILLE

longsoucht *see* LUNGSOCHT

longueville *e19*, **longavil &c** *la17* [*'loŋgəvɪl] *n* a variety of pear.   [the F place-name]

lonin(g) *see* LOAN¹

lonker, lonket *see* LUNKART

lonnach &c *n* **1** couch grass, *chf in pl, esp* when indicating heaps of the weed gathered for burn-ing *la18-, now Kcdn Ags*. **2** a long piece of cord, thread or rope *la19-e20, NE*. [uncertain; perh of Gael origin]

Lonon &c, Londoun &c *16-e17*, **London &c** *16-*; **Lunnon** *18-20* ['lʌnən] = London *16-*. **Lon(d)oner &c** **1** = Londoner *17-*. **2** *in pl, also* **londies** *20-, Sh Abd Ags* [?'lʌndɪz] a skip-ping game with two ropes being simultaneously turned in opposite directions *20-, Sh Abd.XX*
~ bun a glazed bun with currants and orange peel, sprinkled with crystallized sugar *la19-*. **~ ropes** = *n* 2, *la20-, Abd Edb*.

lonsoucht *see* LUNGSOCHT

lonȝe *see* LUNYIE

loo *see* LUVE

loof *see* LUIF

loog *see* LUG¹

look *see* LEUK

loolie &c *n, child's word* a lamplighter *la19-, Inv*. [appar altered f LEERIE]

loom¹ &c *vi* = loom *19-*.
n the indistinct appearance of something seen through a haze or at a great distance; a haze or fog *19-, local*.

loom² &c; leam &c *NE* [*Sh Ork* lum; *NE* lim] *n* the red-throated diver; the great northern diver *19-, Ork Abd*. [Norw dial *lom*, ON *lómr*]

loom(b) *see* LUME

loon *see* LOUN

loonge &c *16-*, **lounge &c** *16-*, **lunge &c** *la18-, now local*; **luindge &c** *la18-*, **lunsh** *la19* [lun(d)ʒ, lʌn(d)ʒ; *Sh* lʌnʃ] *vi* = lounge, slouch, loll *16-*.
lo(u)ngeour &c an idler, layabout *16-*. [ear-lier in Sc]

loop, loup &c [lup] *n* **1** (1) = loop *16-*. (2) *knitting* a stitch *la18-*. **2** any natural bend or configuration like a loop, *eg* the winding of a river in its valley *la15, 19-*.
~ie &c deceitful, shifty, crafty *la18-, Fif SW*. **~ing** cord or braid consisting of loops, *usu* as fastening or trimming on garments *la16-e18*. **~it &c** coiled, looped, intertwined *16-*.
tak a ~ take up one's knitting, knit *la19-, now Sh N Dmf*.

loor *see* LIEF

loorach &c ['lurəx] *n* **1** *usu of clothes, rope etc* something tattered or trailing *20-, Inv NE*. **2** a much-worn coat *20-, Abd*. **3** an ungainly or untidy person, a trollop *20-, Inv NE Per*. [Gael *lùireach* a trailing, untidy garment; a lanky, clumsy person; L *lorica* a coat-of-mail]

loos- *see* LOS¹

loose [*loz] *vt, pt, ptp* **loosed &c** *only Sc* = loose, lose *17*.

loose *see* LOUSE, LOWSE

loosie *see* LOUSE

loot *n* = lout *la19*.

loozie *see* LOUSE

lope *see* LOWP¹

lopper *see* LAPPER¹, LIPPER¹

loppin *see* LEAP

lopstar *see* LAPSTER

lorane [*?'loren, *-ən] *n* = TESTAN 2, *la16*. [? f the name of the duchy or the cross of Lorraine]

lord &c *n* **1** = lord *la14-*. **2** *as in Eng* a formal title (1) of certain of those holding high office in the state *la14-*. (2) *chf in pl as collective* members of Parliament or *General Counsail* (COUNSAIL) or the sovereign's Council, or sections or commit-tees of these, *eg* **the lordis of** (**the** *etc*) **prevy** *or* **secret counsail** *la15-17*. (3) *specif* (a) a member of the peerage, with a hereditary right to individual summons to Parliament or to the *General Counsail* (COUNSAIL) *15-17*; (b) *chf in pl as* **~s of parliament** the lowest rank of the Scots parliamentary peerage, which emerged about 1445, *15-17*. (4) *specif* a judge of the *Court of Session* (SESSION) and its antecedents; *in pl* the court itself *la15-*; *cf law lord* (LAW¹). (5) with complements specifying any or all of the *Three Estates* (ESTATE) *la15-e17*. **3** *in territorial, family* *and other titles and designations*: (1) (a) the lord or proprietor **of** (a ~*ship* 2 (1), *and latterly* 2 (2)) *la14-e17*: '*the lord of Doun*'; (b) *without* **of** *la15-16*. (2) *orig* prefixed (*without* **of**) to the family name of certain important barons, and from about 1445 exclusively used as the distinctive style of a *lord of parliament*, prefixed to the family or territorial name *15-17*: '(*the*) *lord Gray, lord Halis*'. (3) as a complimentary designation of a ~ *of the session, 17-*. (4) **our** ~ *used alone or in apposition* one to whom others owe obedience, a VASSAL's feudal lord, *chf* **our** ~ **the king** *la14-15*. **4** as a mode of address: (1) *in sing* to a person entitled LORD *la14-e17*; (2) *in pl* to a group of noblemen or to Parliament or a section of it *la14-15*; (3) *in pl* to other audiences, *eg* the readers of a literary work *la14-16, only Sc*. **5** in mock titles *16-e19*: '*lord of Bonaccord*' (BONACCORD).

~**ship** &c **1** = lordship *la14-*. **2** (1) an estate or *freq* a group of estates held as a single unit by a feudal lord; an individual fief *la14-17*. (2) a fief of a *lord of parliament* as distinguished from a mere *lairdship* (LAIRD) *la16-e17*; see DOST. **3** the *superiority* (SUPERIOR) of a fief (as distinct from its lands) *e15*. **4** patronage *15-16*. **5** a royalty payable on minerals, books etc *18-*.

L~ Advocate &c the principal law officer of the Crown in Scotland *la16-*. ~**is auditoris** (**of Causis and Complaintis**) name for the judicial committees of Parliament for hearing parliamentary causes and complaints *la15*; *see also* CHEKKER. ~ **chalmerlane** &c = CHAMBERLAIN 1, *la15-16*. ~ **chancellour** = CHANCELLOR 2, *la15-17*. **L~ Chief Baron** (**of Exchequer**) the president of the *Court of Exchequer* (EXCHEQUER) set up in 1707 and abolished in 1856; *cf Barons of* (*the*) *Exchequer* (BARON). ~ (**Clerk**) **of Register** *see* REGISTER. ~**is commissionaris** (*la16-e17*), **L~** (**High** *18-*) **Commissioner** (*17-*) the representative(s) of the sovereign, *formerly* (till 1707) in the Scottish Parliament, *also* in the *General Assembly* (GENERAL). **L~ Commissioner of Justiciary** = *L~ of Justiciary, la17-*. **L~ Conservator** = CONSERVATOR 3, *17-18*. **L~ Cornet** = CORNET 2, *20-, Lnk*. **L~ High Stewart of Scotland** *see* STEWART. **L~ High Treasurer** *or* **Thesaurer** = *L~ Treasurer, 17-e18*. **L~ Justice Clerk** = *Justice Clerk* 2 (JUSTICE) *la16-*. **L~ Justice General** = *Justice General* (JUSTICE) *18-*; *cf L~ President*. **L~ Lyon** &c (**King of** *or* (*not officially approved*) **at Arms**) the chief officer of arms of Scotland and head of the *Lyon Court* (LYON) *la16-*; *cf* LYON. **the Lord's mornin** (*la19*) *or* **nicht** (*la17-19*) Sunday morning or night. **L~ Ordinary 1** one of the regular ~*s of the session, la16*; *see also extraordinar* ~. **2** *specif* one of the judges (*now* 13 in number) of the *Court of Session* (SESSION), who sit on cases of first instance in the Outer

House (OUTER) *la16-*. **L~ President** the president of the *Court of Session* (SESSION) and head of the Scottish judiciary; the same judge now also holds the position of *Lord Justice General, la16-*. **L~ Privy Seal** &c *orig* the (Lord) Keeper of the Privy Seal of Scotland, *latterly* merely a titular office *la15-e20*. **L~ Probationer** = *probationer* 2 (PROBATION) *la18-e19*. **L~ Provost** courtesy title given to the PROVOSTS (*n* 2) of Edinburgh, Glasgow, Aberdeen, Dundee, Perth *la15-*. **L~ Rector** = RECTOR *n* 2, *la16-* [the title *Lord* is erroneous and seems to have arisen from the fact that many RECTORS have been noblemen]. **the Lordis Saboth** Sunday *e17*. **Lordsake**(**s**) *exclam of surprise or protest* for the Lord's sake!, Good Heavens! *19-*. ~ **Sanct John**(**is**) see ~ (*of*) *Sanct John*(*is*). **L~ Secretary** &c the Secretary of State and assistant to the *Lord Chancellor, 16-e18*. **L~ Treasurer** *or* **Thesaurer** the chief financial officer of Scotland, *latterly chf* honorary *16-e18*.

criminall ~**s** those ~*s of the session* who became judges of the *Court of Justiciary* (JUSTICIARY) by the Act of 1672, *la17*. **extraordinar**(**y**) ~**s of session** those persons nominated by the sovereign to join the fifteen regular ~*s of the session* as additional or supernumerary members of the Court *la16-17*; *cf supernumerale* ~*is*. **L~s of** (**the**) **Articles** a committee of members of the Scottish Parliament entrusted with the preparation of acts *la15-17*. ~ **of one's awin** possessor of one's own property; a person who has full or independent ownership or control of his property *15*. ~**s of the bills** the Parliamentary *Commission for Bills, la17*. ~**s of the clergy** the Bishops as the ecclesiastical ESTATE in the post-Reformation parliament *la17*. **L~ of Justiciary** a judge of the *Court of Justiciary* (JUSTICIARY) *la17-e19*. ~ **of council and session** *chf in pl* the formal collective designation of the judges of the *Court of Session* (SESSION), the *College of Justice* (COLLEGE) *16-*; *cf* ~(*s*) *of* (*the etc*) *session*, ~*s of* (*the etc*) *sete*. **the** ~**is of** (**the, our soverane lordis** *etc*) **counsail 1** the members of the sovereign's Council in any of its various advisory, judicial, auditorial or executive capacities *la15-e17*. **2** *chf specif* = ~*s of council and session, 16-e17*. **L~ of Erection** = TITULAR *17-18*; *cf* ERECTION. **the** ~**is of** (**the, our** *or* **his**) **parliament** = *n* 2 (2) and (3) *15-16*. ~**s of plat** = PLAT² *17*. **L~ of Regality** a person to whom rights of REGALITY (2 (1)) were entrusted *15-e18*. **L~ of Register** *see* REGISTER. ~ (**of**) **Sanct John**(**is**) Preceptor of the Knights Hospitallers of St John *la15-16*. ~**s of** (**the, our** *etc*) **session** *la15-*, ~**s of** (**the** *etc*) **sete** *la15-16, less formal* = ~*s of council and session*. **the** ~**is** (**of the**) **thre estatis** the members of Parliament collectively, the *Three Estates* (ESTATE) in Parliament *la15-e16*. **ordinar** *or* ordinary ~ (of (the) session) 1 = L~ *Ordinary* 1 and 2, *la16-17.* supernumerale *or* supernumerare ~is = *extraordinar(y)* ~s *of session, la16-e17.* [a doublet of LAIRD w early (15-) differentiation in meaning; appar of nME origin, rather than f sME: see DOST]

lordane *see* LURDAN

lorie &c *interj* = LORD! *la19-, Sh-N.*

lorimer, lorimar ['lorɪmər; *'lʌur-] *n* = lorimer, a maker of the metal parts of a horse's harness, a maker of small metal-work *la15-18, as personal name la12-.*

lorn *see* LESE

Lorne &c *n, chf* ~ shoe a kind of shoe, a derby *la19-, local Sh wLoth.* [orig a proprietary trade name in honour of the Marquis of Lorne]

los¹ &c; lose *la16-17* [los] *n* = loss *la15-17.* [ME *los(se),* lose f LOSE]

los² &c; lose &c *16-e17* [*los] *vti, pt, ptp also* lost *la16-e17.* verbal noun los(s)ing *16-e17,* lowsing *la16-e17,* loosing *17* [*'losɪŋ, *?'lʌus-] 1 *of a vessel* (1) *vi* discharge cargo, be unloaded *15-e17.* (2) *vt* discharge (its cargo) *la16-e17.* 2 *vt, of persons* (1) unload (a ship) *la15-e17.* (2) unload (cargo) from a vessel *la15-e17.* [only Sc; MDu *lossen* free, redeem, unload a ship, MLowGer *lossen,* Dan *losse,* Sw *lossa* unload a ship]

los *see* LOSE, LOWSE

losane *see* LOZEN

lose &c, los, loss *la16-, now the commonest infin and pres form,* lowse &c *16-e17, la19* [loz; los] *vti, pt, ptp also* losit *la14-e17,* lossit *la14-e17,* lossed &c *la16-17* 1 = lose *la14-.* 2 *in passive* cease to exist or maintain its potency, decay, decline *la15-16.* 3 (1) *vi* suffer defeat in a contest, be unsuccessful in one's efforts *la14-.* (2) *vt* be defeated in (a battle, lawsuit etc) *la15-.* [[loz] f OE *losian* lose; [los] prob by back-formation f pt forms; *lows(e)* w infl f LOWSE (*v*); *cf* LESE and LOS¹]

lose *see* LOS¹, LOS²

losel &c [*'lozl] *n, chf literary* a scamp, scoundrel, loafer *la18-19.* [appar var of *losen,* ptp of LEESE lose]

losenge; lozange ['lozəndʒ] *n* = lozenge *la15-.*

~ armes funeral hatchments *la17.* [the usual Sc is LOZEN; eModEng, ME *losenge* a lozenge-shape, a window-pane etc]

losengeour &c [*'lozɪndʒər] *n* 1 = losenger, a deceiver *la14-e16.* 2 a sluggard, idler *16.*

losh *n, interj, also* loshins *la19,* losh me &c *19-* = Lord! *la18-.*

losing *see* LOZEN

loss *see* LOSE

lost *see* LOS²

lot &c *n* 1 = lot, share *la15-.* 2 a piece of land allotted to a particular tenant *17-e19.* 3 an allowance of corn paid to the thresher as part of his fee *la17-18.*

vt 1 = lot *la17-.* 2 *freq coupled with* SCOT: contribute a proportionate or allotted share to a common payment *la15-e18.*

~man a corn-thresher *la18-19.*

lotch *n* a fat lazy person *e19, Ayr Lnk.* [perh var of LATCH³]

Lothian *see* LOWDEN

louch [lux] *adj* in a depressed state of health or spirits *20-, wLoth WC.* [obscure; *cf* LOUGH]

louch *see* LOCH, LOUTCH

louchter *see* LACHTER²

loud &c [lud] *adj, adv* 1 = loud *la14-.* 2 *of persons* clamorous, loud-voiced *15-17.*

~ out out loud, aloud, in a loud voice *19-; cf laich in* (LAICH). ~-spoken having a loud voice, forward or overbearing in speech *la19-.* stilly or ~ clandestinely or openly, in any way, at all *la15.*

louder *see* LEWDER

lough [lux] *vi, of the wind* die down *20-, now Ags.* [perh based on LAICH and SOUCH; *cf* LOUCH]

louk &c; luk *15-16* [*luk, *lʌk] *v, ptp also* luk-kin &c *15-e16* [*'lʌkən, *'lokən] 1 *vt* close (the eyes of a dead person) *16-e17.* 2 *vi* close, draw together, form a close mass *16.* 3 *only in ptp* enclosed, surrounded, entrapped in *15-e16.*

~it *of flower-buds* closed, compact *e16.* ~it kaill cabbage *la16-e17.* [ME *louke(n),* OE *lūcan* close, lock; *cf* LUCKEN]

louk *see* LOCK¹

louman *see* LYOMON

loun &c, loon &c *17-* [lun] *n* 1 *also attrib* (1) a fellow of the lower orders, one of the riffraff, a rough; a rascally servant, a menial *la15-19;* (2) a dishonest rascal *16-17;* (3) a lawless or violent scoundrel, a robber *la16-17.* 2 *less specif* (1) a rogue, wretch, scoundrel, worthless person *16-, now local EC Uls;* (2) *milder, esp of a boy* a young scamp, a mischievous rogue *17-, now Ags mLoth.* 3 a sexually immoral person: (1) a lewd rascal *la16-17;* (2) *of a woman* a whore *la16-e19.* 4 (1) *more gen* a fellow, chap, lad *la15-, now N Fif wLoth Wgt.* (2) a young farm-worker, a *halflin(g)* (HALF¹); *among workmen* a boy who does the odd jobs *19-, N nEC.* (3) nickname for a native of Forfar *la19-, N.* (4) *in pl* nickname for Forfar Athletic football team *20-.* 5 (1) a boy or youth as opposed to a *lassie* (LASS) or QUEAN *17-, N Fif.* (2) a male child, a son, a baby boy *19-, N.*

~rie &c 1 baseness; knavery, villainy *16-e19.* 2 sexual wickedness, fornication *la16-e18.*

~-lookin knavish-looking, villainous *la19-e20.* ~-like disreputable, shabby, scruffy *17-20, latterly Ags.* ~-minister applied by the *Covenanters* (COVENANT) to a MINISTER who accepted the episcopalian and royalist régime *17.*

play the ~ 1 behave as a whoremonger or strumpet; commit fornication *la16-e20.* 2 act mischievously or wickedly, cheat *la16-e17.* [late nME *lowen* a worthless person, prob eModDu *loen* a fool; *cf* Du *loen* trick, deceit]

lounder[1] **&c; lunner &c** *la18-* ['lun(d)ər, 'lʌn(d)ər; *Abd Fif also* 'lʌundər] *vti* **1** deal heavy blows on *la18-*. **2** *vi* aim or lay on blows, hit out *la18-*. **3** *vt, also* ~ **at** *or* **on** work with energy and speed at; speak vehemently or earnestly about, hold forth or harp on about *la19-*, *now Sh Abd.*
n a heavy blow *18-*.
~**ing** *19-*, **lund'ring** *la17* a beating. [uncertain; perh f LEWDER with nasalization]

lounder[2] **&c** [*'lundər, *'lʌndər] *vi* idle, skulk *15-19*. [Du *lunderen*]

loune *see* LOAN[1]

lounge &c [*lundʒ] *vt* belabour, beat *19*. [var of Eng *lunge*]

lounge *see* LOONGE

loup *see* LOOP, LOWP[1]

lour &c [lur] *vi* **1** = lour, frown, look threatening *la16-*. **2** cower, crouch *la15-e19*. **3** (1) grovel *16*. (2) *fig, chf* ~ **(un)to** yield to, submit to (something) *la15-e17*. **4** lurk, skulk *la15-e19*.
~**y** *of the sky* dull, overcast, threatening rain *19-*, *now local.*
~**-brow** a frowning aspect *20-*, *now Ags eLoth.*
~**-shouthered &c** round-shouldered, stooping *19-20*, S.

lourd *see* LIEF

lourd &c [lurd] *adj* = lourd, sluggish, heavy, stupid *15-17*.
~**ie &c** *adj* heavy; sluggish, slow *la18-*.

louse &c, lous &c; loose [lus] *n* = louse *16-*.
loosie &c, loozie &c ['lusɪ, 'luzɪ] lousy. **lous(e)y &c arnut** ['lusɪ'arnət, 'luzɪ-] the earth-nut *19-*, *now Mry nEC Ayr.*

lout &c [lut] *v* **1** bend the body, stoop, duck: (1) *vi, la14-*; (2) *vr, la19-, chf Sh.* **2** *vi* bow respectfully, make an obeisance **to** *la14-e20*. **3** *fig* (1) submit, yield **to** *la15-e20*. (2) humble oneself *16-19*. **4** *vt, of persons and animals* bend or bow (a part of the body), lower (the head etc) *la18-e20*.
adj, of the shoulders bent, stooping, round, *chf* ~**-shouthered &c** *16-e20*.
n a bow, an inclination; *latterly* a stoop *la16-*, *now Sh.*
~**it &c** bent with age etc; round-shouldered *20-*, *N Loth.* [ME *lout(e)*, OE *lūtan*, ON *lúta*]

loutch &c *la18-*, **louch** [lutʃ] *vi* stoop, slouch *la16-*, *local Abd-Wgt.*
n a slouching gait, a stoop *la20-*, *Abd Kcdn mLoth.* [appar conflation of LOUT w Eng *slouch*]

louther *see* LEWDER, LOWDER

lovage *19-e20*, **lowage** *e16*; **lovich &c** *la18-e20*, **logive** *19, Ayr*, **lawage** *la16* ['lovɪ(t)ʃ; *'lav-; *'lodʒɪv] *adj* = lavish.

lovage *see* LOFE

lovanentie &c; lovenanty &c, lovan &c ['lovə'nɛntɪ, -'nɛndɪ, 'lovən] *exclam of surprise or*

protest dear me!, good gracious! *la19-*, *now Lnk Dmf.* [perh f eg *Lord defend thee* etc; *cf* LOCKANTIES]

love *see* LOFE, LUVE

love guard *see* LEVE-GARD

lovenanty *see* LOVANENTIE

loveray *see* LIVERY

lovey- [?'lʌvɪ-]: ~ **dick(ie)** (*now Ags mLoth Slk*), ~ **ding &c** (*now Cai Fif*) *exclams of surprise or protest*, *la19-*. [*cf* Eng *love-a-duck* and LOVANENTIE]

lovich *see* LOVAGE

lovie *see* LUVE

low[1] **&c** [lʌu] *n* **1** a flame *la14-*. **2** fire; a fire indoors or out, a blaze *la14-*. **3** a glow, a radiance as of fire etc *19-*. **4** *fig* a spiritual glow, a state of ardour or excitement, a blaze of feeling *15-*.
vi **1** burn with a bright flame, blaze *17-*. **2** gleam, glow, flare *19-*. **3** *fig, of human beings* be in a state of ardour *18-*.
get one's ~**in laid** have one's ardour quenched, one's enthusiasm dashed, be put in one's place *la18-*, *Abd Kcdn.* **in** (a) ~ **l** on fire, alight, glowing *16-*. **2** *fig* in a state of emotional tension or excitement *la16-* = *cf* ALOW[2]. **tak** ~ to catch fire, go up in flames *la17-*. [northern and midl ME *lowe* (*n, v*), ON *logi* a flame, *loga* (*v*) blaze]

low[2] [*lu, *lʌu] *vt* = allow *la15-19*.
~**ance** = allowance *la16-19*. [aphetic]

low[3] [*lʌu] *n* = LOCH *la14-e15*. [appar f an earlier inflected form of LOCH; *cf lowis* (LOCH)]

low *see* LAICH

lowage *see* LOVAGE

lowand &c-ill; lowing-ill [*'lʌuən(d)'ɪl] *n* a disease of cattle characterized by prolonged or continuous lowing or bellowing *la16*.

lowch *see* LAUCH[1]

lowden, lowdin ['lʌudən] *adj* subdued, mute *la16-e18*.
v **1** *vi, esp of sound, the wind etc* diminish in intensity *19-e20*. **2** *vt* subdue *19-e20*. [*adj* is metath f *lownd* (LOWN)]

Lowden &c *16-*, **Lothian &c** *17-*; **Lowthiane &c** *16-18* ['lʌudən, 'loðɪən; *'lʌuðɪən] = Lothian, the area in central Scotland.
Lothian (**Region**) a REGION formed from the former counties of the City of Edinburgh, East Lothian, Midlothian and West Lothian *la20-*.
The Lothians name for the (former) counties of East Lothian, Midlothian and West Lothian (with or without the City of Edinburgh) *20-*.

lowder &c; louther ['l(j)ʌudər, 'lud-, 'l(j)ʌud-, 'lʌut-] *vi* **1** loiter, idle *la19-e20*. **2** walk with a heavy rocking motion as if weary, plod; move clumsily or lazily *la18-*, *now Abd.* [prob Du *leuteren* linger, dally, MDu *loteren* sway about, hesitate > Eng *loiter*; phonology perh w infl f LEWDER]

lowen *see* LOWN

Lower *see* LAICH

lowing-ill see LOWAND ILL
lowis see LOCH
lowk see LOCK²
lowland see LAWLAND
lown &c; lowen &c *la15-e20*, **lownd** *la18-e19* [lʌun; *Bwk Rox also* lʌund] *adj* **1** (1) *of the wind* lowered, calm *la15-*, *now Loth S.* (2) *of weather* calm, still *16-*, *now local Fif-Uls.* (3) *of a place* sheltered, snug *la16-*, *now EC.* **2** *of places, circumstances etc* peaceful, undisturbed *la15-*, *now Loth Rox.* **3** (1) *of persons* subdued, restrained, undemonstrative *la15-*, *now Loth Kcb.* (2) *of sounds* quiet, hushed *la16-*. **4** humble, unassuming *19-e20.*
adv **1** *esp of wind* quietly, gently, moderately *la16-e20.* **2** calmly, peacefully *19-20.* **3** in a sheltered position, snugly, *chf* **lie** ~ lie low, skulk, keep out of trouble *18-e20.* **4** softly, in a low voice *19-*, *now Kcb.*
n **1** a peaceful sheltered spot, the lee of something *17-*, *local C.* **2** calm, unclouded weather *19-e20.* **3** tranquillity, silence, quietness *19-e20.*
v **1** *vt* give shelter from the wind, screen *la14-*. **2** *vi, also vt* (*16*), *of the wind, stormy weather etc* moderate, calm, die down *15-*, *now Fif Loth Kcb.* [ON *logn* calm weather, *lygn* calm *adj*]
lowp¹, lope &c *la16-*; **loup, lup** *la19-*, *Sh Ork* [lʌup; *Sh Ork* lup, lʌp; *Ork also* lop; *Suth* lup, lop; *Wgt* lop; *Wgt also* lup] *vti, pt, ptp also* **lowpit** *18-*; *ptp also* **lowpen** *la17-* **1** leap, spring, dash *16-*. **2** *of water* cascade, roll *19-*. **3** spring to one's feet, spring to attention *18-*. **4** start with pain, surprise, shock *la16.* **5** dance, caper, hop about *la14-*. **6** walk with a long springing step, bound *la18-*. **7** *of the heart, blood etc* throb, race *la16-*. **8** *also vt, of things* spring or fly (in some direction); pop out of (a receptacle or covering) *la15-*, *now Sh NE Kcb.* **9** *vi, of frost* thaw, break *19-*, *N.*
n **1** a leap, jump, spring *la14-*. **2** a throb, start *20-*. **3** a place where a river may be or is traditionally thought to have been crossed by leaping; a shelf in a river-bed over which water cascades, or over which fish may leap up-river *la18-*.
~in an levin *of fish* fresh, newly caught; *of persons* hale and hearty *la19-*, *chf EC.* **~in ill** a disease of sheep, symptomized by leaping *la18-*.
~in-on-stane a mounting-block *17-*, *now hist.*
~y for spang with a leap and a bound, at a gallop *la19-*, *NE.*
~ aff 1 dismount from a horse *la19-*, *Sh NE Wgt.* **2** change the subject abruptly *la19-*, *now NE.* **~ back** withdraw (from a promise), back out *18-e19.* **~-(the-)coonter** contemptuous a male shop-assistant *la19-*, *local N-Wgt; cf* COONTER-LOUPER. **~ the country** flee the country; emigrate *19-*, *NE.* **~ the cuddy** = leap-frog *la20-*, *local NE-Rox;* cf *cuddy-lowp(-the-dyke)* (CUDDY). **~-the-dyke** *attrib* undisciplined,

wayward *19-*. **~ dykes** weather troubles successfully, tackle difficulties boldly and effectively *la18-*. **~ a gutter** avoid or overcome a difficulty or loss *la19-*, *chf NE.* **~-hunt** a gadding about (esp in search of amorous adventures) *19-e20*, *N.* **~ on 1** mount (a horse) *la15-*. **2** copulate with *la16-18.* **~ ower** go beyond, transgress *18-20.* **~ a** *or* **the stank** = ~ a gutter, *la19-*, *NE.* **~ up** raise one's price suddenly when making a bargain *19-*, *NE, WC Wgt.* **~ up at** flare up angrily at, chide sharply *20-*, *Sh NE Ayr.* [ME *lope*, ON *hlaupa* (*v*), *hlaup* (*n*) leap; *n* 1 and 3 also in place-names *17-*; *cf* LEAP]
lowp²&c [*lʌup] *n* a basket for catching fish *16-17.* [ON *laupr* a basket for carrying things; *cf* LIPPIE, COUP³]
lowpen, lowpit see LOWP
Lowrence see LAURENCE
lowrie ['lʌurɪ] ~ **hook,** ~ **tow** *chf nautical* a hook or rope by which something may be dragged *20-*, *Sh Ags.* [? f Eng dial *lurry* (*v*) drag]
Lowrie &c, Lowry ['lʌurɪ] **1** the personal name, as a forename or surname *la15-*. **2** *chf literary* name for the fox *la15-19.* **3** (1) applied as a name to a crafty person *16.* (2) a crafty person, a rascal *16.* **4** name given to the great bell of a church, *freq* one dedicated to St Lawrence *la19-e20.* **5** *attrib* name of two fairs held in Rayne (Abd), and Laurencekirk (Kcdn) in mid August, dedicated to St Lawrence *18-e20.* [pet form of *Lowrence* (LAURENCE)]
lowse &c, lows &c; los &c *la14-17*; **loose &c** *la16-* [*adj* lʌus; *also* *los; *v* lʌuz; *also* *loz, *los; *St, law* lus] *adj* **1** = loose *la15-*. **2** *of persons, their way of life etc* unrestrained by moral considerations, dissolute, immoral; dishonest, lawless *la15-*. **3** unemployed; without fixed employment, vagabond *la16-18.* **4** released from an obligation, commitment or liability; absolved *la14-e17.* **5** *with pl and collective nouns* not tied or fastened together, not secured *la15-*: 'lows fedderis', 'lows hemp'. **6** *of goods* movable, transportable *16-e17*, *chf Sh Ork.* **7** *of clothes* unfastened, hanging loose; loose-fitting *la15-*. **8** *of a tie or fastening* untied, unfastened *la16-e17.* **9** *of a ship* free from its moorings *16-e17.* **10** *of the weather* unsettled *la19-*, *Sh-Cai Gall.*
adv = loose *la15-*; *see* FAST.
vti **1** = loose *la14-*. **2** (1) *vt* unbind (an animal) from a stall etc, *esp* unyoke (a horse from a plough etc or vice versa) *16-*. (2) *vi* unyoke a draught animal, stop ploughing etc *la15-*. **3** (1) *vt* release or dismiss (a workman etc) at the end of a turn of work *17.* (2) *specif* release (a MINISTER) from his charge *17.* (3) *vi* stop work or other activity *la17-*; *cf* YOKE *v* 4. **4** (1) *vt* free (lands, HERITABLE property) from encumbrance, *eg* of WADSET, by paying the debt; redeem (HERITAGE) *15-17.* (2) release (goods etc) by payment or by finding security; redeem (something confiscated or taken as a

pledge, something from pawn) *15-e19*.   (3) *law*
withdraw (*eg an arrestment* (ARREIST)) *15-*.   (4)
law revoke (a recognition of or legal interdiction on HERITABLE property) *la15-e17*.   **5** undo
the fastenings of, open up, dip into (a purse,
coffer etc) *la15-17*.   **6** *also* ~ **for** *or* **tae a mill**
(*Abd*) cut or undo the band of a sheaf of corn
before feeding it into a threshing mill *20-*.   **7**
procure, purchase *la15-17*, *chf C*.   **8** *vi* (1)
become loose or free, become unfastened *la14-*.
(2) set to with vigour (**on** a task, in conversation etc) *la19-e20*.   (3) *specif of anger or scolding*
let oneself go, explode; break **out on** (someone)
la18-, *now local Sh-midLoth*.   (4) *of frost etc* thaw
16, *19-*, *now Sh*.   (5) *of a cow* swell with milk in
the udder *19-*, *SW*.
lowsance &c [*'lʌuzəns] release *18-e19*.
lowsed ['lʌuzd] **1** freed of the day's work
la17-, *now Loth Slk*.   **2** tired, weary *20-*.
lowser ['lʌuzər] the person who opens up the
sheaves and feeds them to the mill *20-*.   **low-**
sen ['lʌusən] = loosen *19-*, *now local N-S*.
~in loft the loft onto which sheaves are
thrown for threshing *20-*, *local N-S*.   **~in time**
time to stop work, the end of the working day
la18-.   **~ness 1** = looseness *la16-*.   **2** lack of
settled government or authority, lawlessness,
disorganization *la16-17*.
~-fittit not bound to one place by one's work,
engagements etc, free to travel *18-*, *now local
Sh-Kcb*.
be castin ~ lose one's job or one's livelihood
e17.   **brek** ~ **1** break out into or turn to disorder, lawlessness, immorality etc; rise in arms
la16-17.   **2** *also* **go** *etc* ~ leave one's job; take to
vagrancy *17*.   ~ **down 1** undo and let down
(clothes) *16-e20*.   **2** open out (a parcel etc) *18-*.
lowse *see* LOSE
lowsing *see* LOS²
Lowthiane *see* LOWDEN
loyne *see* LOAN¹
lozange *see* LOSENGE
lozen &c *18-*, **losing &c** *la15-17*; **losane**
la15-16 ['lozən] *n* **1** = lozenge *la15-18*.   **2** a
pane of glass, *orig* a small diamond-shaped pane
in a latticed window *la16-*, *now local N-WC*.
vt, *chf in ptp* **1** with a diamond pattern superim-
posed, criss-crossed *la16-*, *now Mry Ags*. **2** *of a
window* glazed *20-*, *Mry Ags*.
~ **armes** funeral hatchments *17*.   [MF
loseingne, var of *lozenge* (see LOSENGE); *cf* laME
lozeyn]
lozenger &c *n* = lozenge, a flavoured sweet,
orig diamond-shaped *la19-*.
lu *see* LO
lub *see* LOB
lubbard &c; lubbert &c *n* = lubber, a lout
la16-, *now Kcb S*.
lubbertie *n* a jellyfish *20-*, *only Kcdn Ags*.   [*cf*
LOCH-LIVER]

Lubbis &c [*'lʌbɪs, *'lʌp-] *adj*, *of money of account*
of Lübeck *16*, *Abd*.   [LowGer *Lübsch*, MDu
Lub(e)sch]
luce &c [løs, lʌs] *n* **1** a skin incrustation, scurf,
dandruff, loose dead skin *19-*, *now Sh*.   **2** sebor-
rhea *19*.   [obscure]
lucerve &c [*?'lʌsərv, *?'løs-] *n* a lynx, a lynx
skin, lynx fur *16*.   [appar MF *loucerve*, OF
loucervier]
lucht *see* LAUCH¹, LOCHT
luchtach &c ['luxtəx] *n* the retinue or bodyguard of a *Highland* (HIELAND) chief *18-e20*, *chf
hist*.   [f Gael *luchd-taighe*]
Lucine &c [*lø'səin, *-'sin, *'løsəin] = Lucina,
the moon *16*.
luck &c, luk &c *n* **1** = luck *la15-*.   **2** a piece of
luck or good fortune; a useful or valuable object
come upon by chance *la19-*, *now Sh Ork*.
vi **1** fare, prosper **well** *or* **ill** *16-*, *now Sh N*.   **2**
have good fortune; succeed *la16-*, *now Abd
midLoth Bwk Kcb*.
~y, luckie &c, lukkie *adj* **1** = lucky, fortunate, bringing luck *la16-*.   **2** full, ample, more
than the standard or stipulated amount *17-*,
now local.   **3** *as a compliment or term of endearment*
attended by good fortune, good *16*. *adv*, *as
intensifier* abundantly, pretty, more than enough
la18-, *now Sh Abd*: '*I think them lucky dear*'. *n* **1**
familiar, *of an elderly woman*, *freq prefixed to a surname* old Mrs .. *17-*, *now N, EC Ayr*.   **2** *specif* (1)
a wife, married woman *la18-19*.   (2) a midwife
19-, *now Lnk*.   (3) a landlady, hostess of a tavern *18-*, *now Bnf Ags*.   (4) a witch, hag *19*.   **3**
a grandmother *18-*, *now NE; sometimes in exclams
of impatience or disdain as* **kiss your ~ie** go to
blazes!, not likely!   **~y box** a child's savings-
bank, a penny-bank *20-*, *local NE-Rox*.   **~y
dad(d)ie &c, ~y daid &c** a grandfather *17-*,
now NE Ags.   **~y minnie** a grandmother
la18-20.   **~y penny** = ~('s) *penny*, *20-*, *local Sh-
Wgt*.   **~y pock** a lucky bag, a lucky dip or lottery
la19-.
~('s) penny a sum of money given for luck, *eg*
that returned traditionally by the seller to the
buyer as a discount *18-*.   **upon ~'s head** on
the chance of success, on chance; for luck *17-*,
now Sh Ork.
luck *see* LEUK
lucken &c, lukkin &c *adj* **1** *of the hand or foot*
(1) closed tight, clenched; having the sinews
contracted *la15-18*.   (2) having webbed fingers
or toes *la15-19*.   **2** *fig* (1) *of the brows* knit, close-
set, contracted as in a frown *19*.   (2) *of flowers*
having a compact head as in a bud *18-19*; see
GOWAN.   (3) *of cabbages etc* having a firm heart
19-e20.   (4) *of a fish*, *esp a haddock or whiting* gut-
ted, but not split right down to the tail *19-*, *now
NE*.   (5) *of leather* consolidated and thickened
by tanning and hammering *18*.
n a half-split haddock for drying or smoking
19-, *NE*.

vi **1** = LOUK *v* 2, *e16*. **2** *of plants which form a bud or head* grow compact or firm *19*.

~booth &c [*'~*'buθ; *-'bøθ] a booth or covered stall which could be locked up, common in medieval Scottish towns, *specif in pl* a row of such in the High Street of Edinburgh, demolished 1817, *la15-*, *now only hist*. **luckenbooth brooch** a kind of brooch, *usu* of engraved silver in the shape of a heart or two hearts entwined, *orig* used *chf* as a love token or betrothal brooch *20-*. [ptp of LOUK; *cf* eModEng, ME *loken*, OE *(ge)locen*, ptp of *lūcan* lock]

lucrative *adj* **1** *law* gratuitous, granted as a free gift, *chf* ~ **successor,** ~ **title** where the heir accepts part of an estate as a gift before the death of the grantor, thereby involving himself in liability for any prior debts *17-e20*. **2** = lucrative *la18-*.

lucrie &c [*'lʌkrɪ, *'løk-] *n* = lucre *la16*.

lude *see* LUVE

ludge *see* LODGE

ludifie [*'lødɪfaɪ] *vt* make a fool of, ridicule *17*. [eModEng = deceive, L *lūdificāre* make a fool of, delude]

lufe[1] **&c** *16-e17*; **luff &c** [*løf] *n* **1** = luff, a contrivance for altering a ship's course *15-e17*. **2** ? the rope which carried forward the clew of a sail to windward *16*.

lufe[2] *v* ? = LOFE *or* LUVE *la15-16*. [contexts are rather ambiguous]

lufe *see* LUIF, LUVE

luferay *see* LIVERY

lufetenand *see* LIEUTENAND

luff *see* LUFE[1], LEEVE

luffage ['lʌvedʒ] *n* = lovage, the herb *la15*.

luffer *see* LIVER[1]

luftenand *see* LIEUTENAND

lug[1] **&c; loog &c** *la17, 20-* (*Cai*) [lʌg; *Cai* lug; *Mry also* lug; *Fif also* lʌug] *n* **1** *lit and fig* any projecting part of an object, *esp* one by which it may be handled, attached or lifted: (1) a flap of a cap or bonnet *la15-*; (2) the handle of a cup, bowl etc, *freq* one of a pair *la16-*; (3) a flap of a shoe *17-*; (4) a projecting flange or spike on an iron instrument, *eg* a spade *18-*, *now NE*; (5) the corner of a herring-net *19-*, *now NE Ags*; (6) one of the wings on a wing-chair *20-*; (7) one of the hand grips at the top of a full sack *20-*; (8) part of the muzzle of a plough *20-*, *local Cai-Wgt*. **2** (1) the ear as part of the body, the external ear of man and animals *la15-*. (2) *in pl* epithet for a person with prominent ears *20-*, *Abd Per midLoth*. **3** (1) the ear as the organ of hearing, the inner ear *la16-*. (2) *transf, appar hist* a hidden recess from which one might overhear the conversation in a room *19-*. **4** the pectoral fin of a fish and its attachments *19-*. **5** *chf literary* the chimney corner *19-*, *now NE nEC Uls*.

~gie &c *adj* **1** also used as a nickname with characteristic ears *la17-*, *now Mry wLoth*. **2** = ~git 1, *20-*, *now Ork*. *n* **1** a small wooden bowl etc with one or two handles formed from projecting staves, *freq* used for serving milk with porridge *18-*, *now local N-Rox*. **2** a similar but larger container used *esp* as a milking-pail *la19-*, *now local Ags-Gall*. **~git &c 1** having a LUG or LUGS (of a specified nature) *la15-*. **2** *of laces or braids* ? having ornamental loops etc projecting laterally *16-e17*.

~-bane &c the bone behind the pectoral fin of a fish *la19-*, *now Sh Ork*. **~-chair** a wing-chair *la19-*. **~-mark** *n* **1** an earmark, *esp* on a sheep *la17-*. **2** any recognizable mark *19-*. *vt* mark the ear of *17-*. **~-stane &c** one of a series of stones attached to the lower corners of a herring-net or salmon-weir to make it hang vertically in the water *18-*, *N*.

about one's ~s about one's ears, all around one *16-*. **at one's ~, at the ~ o** *18-* at one's side, close by, in close contact with *la16-*. **at the ~ o** the law at the centre of affairs, in close touch with authority *18-19*. **blaw in the ~ o** flatter, wheedle, cajole *la16-19*. **by the ~ and the horn** by main force *19-*, *now Kcb*. **get one's** *or* **gie someone his head in his hands** *or* **lap and his ~s to play wi** get or give someone a severe dressing-down *20-*, *local Ork-Gall*. **get one's ~ in one's luif** be severely taken to task *18-*, *now Ags*. **hae** *or* **tak the wrang soo by the ~** have hit on the wrong person or thing, have come to a wrong conclusion, have the wrong end of the stick *18-*, *now Sh-Per Wgt*. **lauch on the ither side o one's ~** laugh on the other side of one's face *la19-*, *now Sh Ags Wgt*. **lay one's ~** wager (that ..) *19-*, *now Sh Ags*. **lay one's ~ in(to)** eat or drink heartily of (some food or drink) *18-*, *now N wLoth Lnk*. **lay (our** *etc*) **~s thegither** lay (our etc) heads together, concert action *la19-*, *local Sh-Kcb*. **lay** *or* **lend (to) one's ~** listen attentively *e17*. **(out) ower the ~s** over head and ears, completely absorbed or immersed *18-*, *now NE Ags Per*. **a puddin ~** *interj* nonsense! *la19-*, *NE*. **tak someone be (the lap of) the ~** take someone by the ear, lay hold of someone *la16-17*. **up to the ~s** = out ower the ~s, *19-*. [earlier in Sc, gradually replacing ear *la15-*; obscure; orig Scand; *cf* Sw *lugg* forelock, *lugga* (*v*) tug at one's hair > Eng *lug* pull about]

lug[2] **&c** *n* a clumsy fellow *19-*, *now Gsw*. [uncertain]

lug[3] *adj*, *chf of crops* **luggie** growing to leaf and stem, rank and luxuriant with poorly developed fruits *la18-e19*, *chf N*. [uncertain; *cf* Eng dial *loggy*]

luge *see* LODGE

luggie *see* LUG[1], LUG[3]

luich *see* LAUCH[1]

luif &c, lufe; loof &c *17-*, **luve &c** *la18-19*, **liv &c** *la19-*, *now NE*, **leef &c** *19-*, *now Uls*, **lee** *la19-*, *chf Abd* [løf, lɪf, lɪv; *local ECoast* lɪf; *nEC* lef; *Abd also* li; *pl* løfs, lɪvz, &c] *n* **1** the palm of the hand *la15-*. **2** the paw, foot or hoof of an animal *la18-*, *now Wgt*.

~fie, laifie *20-*, *Ags* ['løfɪ, 'lɪfɪ; *Ags also* 'lefɪ] *n*
1 PALMIE *19-*, *local Ags-Slk.* **2** an early kind of
flat, handleless *curling stone* (CURL) with indentations for the thumb and fingers *19-e20.* **3** a
kind of flat bread roll *20-*, *Ags.* **~ful &c** a
handful *16-*.
aff (**ane's** *or* **the**) ~ offhand, without premeditation or preparation *18-*, *now EC.* **crack ~s**
shake hands in friendship *18-*, *now Cai.* **the
outside o the, my** *etc* ~ *in various phrs of defiance
or derision*, *19-*, *now Wgt*: '*and the outside of the loof
to them*'. [northern and n midl ME *lufe*, ON
lófe the palm of the hand; *cf* northern ModEng
dial]
luik *see* LEUK, LOCK²
luindge *see* LOONGE
luit *see* LAT¹
luk *see* LEUK, LOUK, LUCK
luke *see* LEUK
luke-hertit &c; loik-hertit [*?'lək'hɛrtɪt,
&c] *adj* ? warm-hearted *e16.* [?ME *luke* warm]
Lukismes &c; Lukismas, Luxmes *15-16*
[*'lʌks'mɛs, *'luks-, *'løks-, *-məs] *n* the festival of St Luke, 18 Oct, a customary date for
payment of debts and dues; the date of one of
the annual fairs in Rutherglen *15-17*, *chf C.*
[only Sc; *Luke* + MESS²; *cf* PATRICKMES]
lukkie *see* LUCKIE
lukkin *see* LOUK, LUCKEN
lum &c; lumb *17-18* [lʌm] *n* **1** a chimney, the
smoke-vent or flue of a fireplace, a chimney-
stack *17-*. **2** *specif* (1) a wood-lined opening in
the ridge of the roof, for light and ventilation
and the escape of smoke, less primitively having
a wooden canopy suspended over the fire to
serve as a smoke-vent *17-e20*; (2) the whole
structure of a chimney and fireplace with the
adjacent recesses, a chimney-piece, chimney-
corner *17-*, *now local Sh-Kcb.* **3** the funnel of a
steamship or locomotive *20-*. **4** a long funnel-
like passage worn by natural forces through a
cliff; a rock chimney *la18-*, *now NE.* **5** a tall
silk hat, a top-hat *la19-*.
~mie a chimney on fire *20-*, *Ags Edb.*
~-can a chimney-pot *19-*, *local Sh-Per.*
~-cheek the chimney-corner, fireside *la19-*, *Sh
Ags Per Kcb.* **~-hat** = *n* 5, *la19-*. **~-heid** the
chimney top, the part of the chimney rising
above the roof *la17-*. **~ pig(g)** = ~ *can*,
19-e20, *WC, SW.* **~-tap** the top of a chimney
or funnel *19-*, *Sh N Per Kcb.* [northern eMod-
Eng *lumbe* a roof-opening; *cf* obs Welsh *llumon*
chimney]
Lumbard &c *la15-17*, **Lombard &c** *la15-* *n*
1 = Lombard *la15-e16*, *as personal name 13-14.*
2 ? = ~ *sleve*, *16.*
adj Lombardic *la15-*.
~ paper an expensive kind of paper used for
both cartridges and books *16-17.* **lumbard
&c sleve** a style of sleeve believed to have
originated in Lombardy *16-17.*
lume &c; loom &c *17-*, **loomb &c** *17-e18*,

leem &c *17-*, *Cai NE* [løm, lɪm; *local N* lim;
nEC lem] *n* **1** (1) an instrument or tool of any
kind *la14-e20.* (2) *specif* (a) *in pl* the male genitals *el5*; (b) *in sing* the penis *16*, *18-e19* (*NE*). **2**
an open container, a tub, bowl etc *la15-*, *now
Sh.* **3** = loom, a weaving-loom *16-*.
~full *n* some dry measure, *perh* = a PECK² *el7*,
Linlithgow.
lumfad *see* LYMPHAD
luminar &c *n* a luminary *la15-16.* [laME
lumynaire, L *lūmināre*]
luminator *n*, *St Andrews Univ* a member of class
who, in return for fees paid by the other students, was responsible for providing fire and
light in the lecture-room and for keeping the
attendance-roll *la17-e19.* [laL *lūminātor*, ultimately f *lūmen* light]
luming *n* meaning unknown *el7.* [perh connected with LUM]
lummed [lʌmt] *adj* thwarted, frustrated, baffled
20-, *SW.* [obscure; perh f LUM *n*, i.e. stuck in a
chimney, gone up the chimney]
lump &c *n* **1** = lump *la14-*. **2** a lot, a large
amount or portion *20-*. **3** a lifeless or soulless
mass of material, a dead thing *15-e17.* **4** a mass
of iron in the process of manufacture *16-e17.*
a *or* **the ~ of someone's death** the chief
cause of or an important factor in someone's
death *la18-*, *now Sh Kcb.* **in til a** (*el5*) *or* **by
the** (*la17*) ~ all of a piece, as a whole,
wholesale.
lunch *n* **1** = lunch *20-*. **2** a lump, large slice of
food, chunk *la18-e19.*
lunge *see* LOONGE
lungsocht &c; lon(g)soucht &c [*'lʌŋsoxt,
*'lʌnsox(t)] *n* lung disease, *esp* in cattle *15-16.*
[Eng *lung* + Sc *-socht* disease (as in GULSOCH)]
lunk [lʌŋk] *adj*, *of weather* close, sultry *20-*, *local.*
~ie = *adj*, *19-20.* **~it &c** tepid, lukewarm *19.*
[Scand; *cf* Norw dial *lunka* warm slightly]
lunkart &c, longart *la14* ['lʌŋkər(t)] *n* **1** a
temporary shelter; a small temporary hunting-
lodge *la14*, *e17*, *la20* (*Ags*). **2** an open-air fireplace made of sods with an iron bar across the
top from which to hang a pot *la19-e20*, *N.* **3**
only **lonker &c, lonket** a hole in a wall, made
with a lintel stone, to allow sheep to pass
through, or a stream to flow under *19-*, *now Bute
SW.* **4** a large mass or nodule of one mineral
in the layers of another *19-e20.*
lunkie, lunkie-hole (*SW*) = *n* 3, *19-*,
sEC-SW. [Ir and ScGael *longphort* a harbour; a
camp; a residence, dwelling (permanent or
temporary)]
lunkie *see* LUNK, LUNKART
lunner *see* LOUNDER¹
Lunnon *see* LONON
lunsh *see* LOONGE
lunt¹ &c *n* **1** (1) a match, a fuse, a light *16-e20.*
(2) cord etc prepared for ignition *la16-17.* **2** a
column of fire and smoke, a puff of smoke or
steam etc *la18-*, *local NE-Slk.*

v **1** *vt* set fire to, kindle *la19-*, *chf S*. **2** *vi* catch fire, burn, blaze *la18-*, now *NE Ayr*. **3** *vti* smoke, emit puffs of smoke, smoke (a pipe) *la18-*, *local N-Kcb*.

~ staff, *pl* **~ staves** a staff for holding a lighted match, a linstock *17*.

set (a) **~ to** set fire to *19-e20*. **with** *or* **of ~ werk** &c *of firearms* having a matchlock *e17*. [*chf Sc*; eModDu *lonte*, MLowGer *lunte* = *n* 1; *cf* eModEng (once) and northern ModEng dial]

lunt[2] *vi* walk with a springy step, walk briskly *19-*, *SW, S*. [prob Scand; *cf* Norw dial *lunta* stroll, Sw dial *lunte* hop]

lunyie &c, **lun3e** &c *16*; **lon3e** &c *16* ['lʌn(j)ɪ; *Ork* 'lʌnjo, 'lɪnjo; ***lun(j)ɪ, ***løn-, ***løŋ-, ***lɪŋ-; *Ayr S **lun] *n* = loin *16-e19*.

~-bane the haunch-bone of an animal *la18-e20*. [OF *loigne*]

lup *see* LOWP[1]

luppen *see* LEAP

lurdan &c; **lordane** &c *e16* ['lʌrdən] *n* **1** a ruffian; an oppressor *la14-e16*. **2** *term of reproach, latterly* (*19-*) *literary*: (1) *of a man* a villain, a rogue, rascal *15-e19*; (2) *of a woman* a whore; a slut *la14-17, e20*.

adj heavy, dull; clownish, stupid, rascally *la18-19*.

~ry villainy *e16*. [ME *lurdan* a rascal, OF *lourdain* a dullard]

lure &c; **l(i)ewer** *la17* [lør; *Loth* ler; ***ljur] *n* the udder of a cow or other animal *la17-*, now *local Ork-Edb*. [*chf Sc*; uncertain]

lurk *see* LIRK[1], LIRK[2]

luschbald &c [***'lʌʃbald] *n* term of abuse for a person *e16*. [obscure]

lustart *see* LUSTER

luster &c *la16-e17*; **lustre** &c *n* = lustre *la16-*. *vt* put a glaze on (cloth), *freq* **~it, lustart** (*la16-e17*) *la16-*. [F *lustre* (*n*) gloss, sheen]

lustrale *adj, of a sacrifice* purificatory *e16*. [earlier in Sc; L *sacrificium lūstrāle* a sacrifice of purification]

lustre *see* LUSTER

lusty &c *adj* (*adv*) **1** = lusty *15-*. **2** *of ladies, their looks etc* fair, beautiful *la15-16*. **3** *of persons in gen, their looks etc* attractive *la15-e17*. **4** *of men* handsome; gallant, valiant; sturdy *la15-17*. **5** *of a ship* fair, gallant *16*.

lusum *see* LUVE

lutenand *see* LIEUTENAND

luttard *adj* ? bowed, bent *e16*. [*cf* nME *lutterde* ? bowed, crooked]

luve &c, **lufe** &c *la14-e17*, **lo** &c *e16*, *la18-e20*; **love** &c, **loo** *18-* [lʌv; *literary* lu; ***lø(v); *C **le(v); *NE **li] *vti, pt, ptp* also **lude** &c *la15-16* [***lø(:)d] *only verse* = love *la14-*; *latterly replaced in colloq use with* LIKE[2].

n = love *la14-*.

lovie a sweetheart, lover; *child's word* a hug *20-*, *local NE-Kcb*. **lovit** &c, **luvit** &c *la14-e16* &c [***'løvɪt, &c; *also **løt] beloved, dear: **1** *in gen*,

la14-16; **2** *as a term of address in formal letters or* (*chf*) *official or legal documents* (1) *in sing, la14-17*; (2) *in pl, also when referring to one person and as a noun, la15-17*: 'to our *louittis cousingis*'. **~some** &c, **lusum** &c *la15-e17* lovable, admirable; beautiful *la15-*. **luf(e)sumly** *15*, **lusumly** *la14* affectionately, cordially.

~-bairn a love-child *20-*, *Ork WC*. **~ blenk** *16*, **~-blink** *17-e20* a loving or amorous glance. **love-darg** a piece of work or a service done gratuitously out of friendliness *la18-*, *NE, EC Ayr*. **lufe-drowry** &c a love-token *15-e16*. **~-lozenger** a conversation lozenge *20-*, *NE Fif wLoth*. **luf(e)rent** &c [***'løvrɛnt, ***-rənd] **1** the state or condition of loving or of being loved, love, affection, friendship *la14-16*. **2** lust *la15-16*.

for love (**and**) **favour** (**and affection**) *law* formula in documents relating to gifts and donations *18-e19*.

luve *see* LUIF

luveray *see* LIVERY

Luxmes *see* LUKISMES

luxure [***'lʌksør] *n* lasciviousness, lechery *la15-e16*. [ME, F]

ly *see* LE, LIE

lyaag *see* LAIG

lyam &c ['laɪəm] *n* **1** = lyam, a leash for hounds *e17*. **2** (1) a leash or thong *in gen, e16*. (2) a rope, a tether *19*.

lyart &c, **liart** &c ['laɪərt; ***-ərd] *adj* **1** *of the hair* streaked with white, grizzled, silvery *15-20*. **2** *chf of a horse* dappled *la15-18*. **3** variegated, multi-coloured, streaked with two colours, *esp* red and white *la18-20*. [ME *liard*, OF *liart* = 2]

lyd *see* LYTHE

lyde *see* LITHE

lyin *see* LIE

lyke; leek *19-*, *Sh-Ross* [ləik; *Sh-Ross* lik] *n* **1** a corpse, an unburied body *la15-*, now *Sh*. **2** (1) a vigil kept over a corpse until burial, a wake; *also* the (*freq* large and riotous) gathering on such occasions *la16-20*, *chf N*. (2) *in pl* **funerall** *or* **dedelie ~is** funeral rites *e16*.

~ wake, **~ walk** *e17*, **laikwake** *17*, *chf sEC* **leikwake** &c *17-e18* [*Ork* 'lik'wɑk; ***'ləikwek, ***-wɑk, ***lɪk-] = LYKE **2** (1) *la16-20*; *cf* LATEWAKE. [northern and n midlME *like*, OE *līc*, ON *lík* a body, corpse]

Lyllis *see* LILLES

lymb *see* LIME[1]

lymber *see* LIMMER

Lymmistar *see* LEMISTAR

lymphad &c *19-*, *hist, heraldry*, **limfad** &c *17*, **lumfad** &c *la16-e17*, **langfad** *16*; **lomfad** &c *la16-e17* *n* a West *Highland* (HIELAND) (or Irish) galley. [Sc and IrGael *long-fhada* a long ship]

lynthar *see* LENTH

lyn3ell *see* LINGEL[2]

lyomon; lo(u)man &c ['l(j)omən, 'lʌumən; *'l(j)umən] *n* the leg; *in pl* the lower extremities, *latterly* the feet *la18-20, chf NE.* [obscure]

Lyon &c, Lio(u)n &c *la15-17 n* the chief officer of arms of Scotland *la16-.*
L~ Court the Court of Heralds in Scotland *18-.* **L~ Clerk** the Clerk of that Court *la17-.*
~ herald 1 *also* **~ herald King of Arms** *16-17 = n, la15-e19.* **2** a Scottish herald, i.e. a member of **the L~ Court** *17-e18.* **~ King of** (*la15-e18*) *or* **at** (*17-e18*) **Arms** = *n.* [short-ened f *Lord Lyon King of Arms* (LORD); *leo heraldus* also in ScL *la14-e15; cf* LION]

Lyonis, Leonis &c; Lioun(s) [*'laɪunz, *-ənz] **~ cammes, ~ canues** canvas from Lyons *la16-e17.* [the French town noted for its textiles]

lythe &c; lyd &c *18-* [laɪð, laɪd; *Ork also* laɪ] *n* the pollack, the PODLIE *16-, now local.* [appar ON *lýr*]

lythe *see* LITHE
lyve *see* LIFE

M

ma *see* I, MAE[1], MAK, MAY, MY

maa *see* MAE[2], MAW[1], MAW[2]

maamie *see* MAUMIE

maber &c [*'mɑbər, *'ma-] *n* marble *la16-e17*. [var of OSc, ME *marbre*, F *marbre*]

Mac &c *n* **1 mack** a person or CLAN whose surname has the prefix *Mac-*, *la17*. **2 Mac** familiar form of address to a man, *chf* a stranger *la20-*. [Gael prefix forming a patronymic, corresponding to Eng *-son*; *cf* colloq Eng = name for anyone known or thought to be a Scotsman]

macalive &c *la18*, **makhelve** *la16-17*; **mack(h)allow** *la17*, **meikalow** *la17* [*'makələ(v), *'makəlv] *n*, *freq attrib* a portion or endowment in cattle for a child put to fosterage *Highl*. [Gael *macaladh* fostering, f *mac* a son. DOST *ma(c)khelve*]

macallum [mə'kaləm] *n* a vanilla ice cream flavoured with raspberry juice *20-*, *C, S*. [only Sc; f the surname, see SND and SND Suppl]

MacClarty [mə'klartı] **Mrs** ~ &c name for a dirty slovenly housewife *19-*, *local Kcdn-SW*. [f the character in E Hamilton *Cottagers of Glenburnie*, w a pun on *clarty* (CLART[1])]

mace &c; **mass(e)** &c *la15-17*, **measse** &c *la17* [mes] *n* = mace, the weapon etc *la14-*.

macer; **ma(i)s(s)er** &c *la15-17*, *only Sc*, **meas(s)er** &c *la16-17*, *only Sc*, **mes(s)er** &c *la16-17*, *only Sc* ['mesər, *'mɛs-] *n* a macebearer *specif*: **1** an officer of the crown, under the authority of the *Lord Lyon King of Arms* (LORD) who delivered royal commands and summonses, and uttered public proclamations *15-17*, *only Sc*; **2** *chf law* an official serving as usher in a court of law etc, who keeps order, acts as messenger etc *la15-*, *only Sc*; **3** *literary* an ancient Roman official with similar duties *e16*, *only Sc*.
maserie &c *16-17*, **~ship** &c *16-19* the office of a MACER (*n* 1, 2) *only Sc*. [ME]

MacFarlane *see* BOUET

macfische &c *n* ? mackerel *e16*. [only Sc; ? short for *makrell fische*]

mach *see* MAICH, MATCH

machair &c ['maxər] *n* **1** a stretch of low-lying land adjacent to the sand of the seashore *la19-*, *chf Hebrides*. **2** *in pl, specif* **the M~s** the land bordering the Solway Firth or Luce Bay *la18-*, *Gall*. [only Sc; Gael = *n* 1; a low-lying plain]

machcolin(g) &c [*'matʃ(ə)kolın] *n* machicolations *la15-e16*. [only Sc; OF *machecoller* (*v*) machicolate > laME *ma(t)checole*]

Machiavell, Matchevell &c *only Sc* [*'matʃ(ı)əvɛl] *n* = Machiavel, an intriguer *la16*.

machine [mə'ʃin; *?'matʃın] *n* **1** = machine *16-*. **2** a horse-drawn passenger vehicle, *eg* a gig *la19-20*. **3** a motor car *la20-*, *local*.

machreach; michrach [mə'xrax] *n* a fuss, outcry, row *la20-*, *NE*. [only Sc; adapted f Gael *mo chreach* alas!]

macht *see* MAUCHT

macis &c; **meas(s)is** &c *la16-17*, *only Sc* [*'mesız] *n* = mace, the spice *14-17*. [ME *macis*]

mack, mak *adj* neat, tidy; seemly *la17*, *19-e20*. **makly** ? evenly *e16*. [laME *make, mak* apt, ON *makr* comfortable, snug]

mack *see* MAC

mackallow *see* MACALIVE

Mackay [mə'kaı] **the real** ~ the genuine article, the true original; *specif* a brand of WHISKY so-named *la19-*. [only Sc; see SND]

mackerel &c *la16-*, **makrell** &c *16-18* *n* = mackerel *16-*.
as clean as a ~ completely, effectively, entirely *la19-*, *now Ags Fif*.

mackhallow *see* MACALIVE

macky *see* MAKKY

maclarté; makrelty &c [*'maklərtı, *'makrəltı] *n* brokerage *la15*. [only Sc; MDu *makelaerdie*, f *makelaer* a broker]

Macmillanite [mək'mılənəıt] *n* a follower of Rev John MacMillan of Balmaghie, Kcb, a CAMERONIAN *n* 1, *18*. [see SND]

Macpherson's [mək'fɛrsənz] **Law** a so-called law that in any given situation the least fortunate of any possible consequences will befall the individual who least deserves it *la20-*. [orig humorously propounded by Wilfred Taylor in the *Scotsman*]

MacTavish &c [mək'tavıʃ] familiar name for a man or boy *20-*.

Macwhachle [mək'hwaxl] *n* **wee** ~ *joc* a toddling infant *20-*, *WC*.

mad; made &c *15-17* [mad] *adj* **1** = mad *la14-*. **2** upset, troubled; dismayed; dazed *la14-16*. **3** *transf* full of or expressing distress or dismay, sorrowful *15-16*, *only Sc*. **4** infuriated, beside oneself with rage; angry, annoyed *15-*. *adv, modifying adjs* extremely *la19-*: 'mad keen'. ~ **for** extremely eager for or desirous of *la19-*.

mad *see* MAUD

madam &c; **madem(e)** *la14-e16*, *only Sc* ['madəm, *ma'dem] *n* **1** = madam *la14-*. **2** a mistress (of servants), the lady (of the house), a fine lady *la18-e19*.

madder; mether &c ['madər; *Uls* 'mɛðər] *n* a square wooden container used as a measure for liquor *18-e20*, *chf SW Uls*. [Anglo-Ir, f IrGael *meadar* a measure]

madder *see* MATHER

madderam &c; **madrim** &c ['mad(ə)rəm] *n* madness, folly, frantic rage, tantrums; boisterous fun, hilarity *la19-*, *chf Sh Ork*. [only Sc; conflation of MAD w *widdrim* (WUID[2]), MAD replacing synonymous *wid* (WUID[2])]

made *see* MAD, MAK

madem(e) *see* MADAM

mader *see* MATHER

madge *n*, *contemptuous* a silly woman *19-*, *now Lnk*. [pet name for *Marjorie*]

madgie *see* MATTIE

madin *see* MAIDEN

madrim *see* MADDERAM

mae[1] &c *15-*, **ma** *la14-e19, latterly hist*; **mea** &c *la16-e17* [me] *adj* **1** *as comparative of* MONIE (1) more in number, more numerous *la14-, now Kcb Dmf Rox*; (2) additional to those already mentioned; other, extra *15-19*. **2** greater in quantity or amount *la16-*. **3** more than one, several, many *15-e16*.
n **1** a greater number of persons or objects, more *15-, now Kcb Rox*. **2** persons or things in addition to those already mentioned, others *la14-e18*.
adv more; again *la14-e20*.
be at ane ~ wi't &c be at breaking point, be at the end of one's tether; be at the point of death *19-e20, S*. **but** &c ~ (*chf early*) *verse* with no others, only *la14-16*. **the ~** the greater number *la15-e17*. [nME *ma*, OE *mā* > midl and sME *mo*]

mae[2] &c, **maa** *la19-* [me, mɛ, ma] *vi, of sheep etc* bleat *18-*.
n the sound of bleating, the cry of a sheep or lamb *18-*.
sheepie ~ *child's word* a sheep *la20-, local Abd-WC*. [only Sc; imit]

maffle *vi* **maffling** procrastination, bungling *19-, Dmf*. **maffled** half asleep, dazed *19-, Dmf*. [ModEng dial; ME mumble, stammer, MDu *maffelen* stammer]

Mag *see* MEG

Maga &c ['magə] name for *Blackwood's Magazine 19-20*.

magdum *see* MAKDOM

mager *see* MAUGRE

magg *vt, of coal-carters* pilfer (coal) to sell on their own account *la18-e19*.
n, in pl an extra payment in appreciation of services outside regular duties, a tip *la18-, now midLoth*. [only Sc; f colloq Eng *mag* a magpie]

maggie[1] *n* = magpie *20-, local Abd-S*.

maggie[2] &c *n, mining, chf attrib* an inferior quality ironstone *la18-e20*. [uncertain; perh connected w MAGG; *cf* MAG WOOD]

maggie *see* MEG

maggle &c, **mag(g)ill** &c *la15-e17*; **maigle** *la15-e17 vt* **1** cut or hack about, maim, mutilate, mangle *la15-e19*. **2** *fig* mutilate or botch (a literary work etc) *16-e18*. **3** spoil by over-handling *la20-, SW*.
mag(g)lit &c *adj* **1** maimed, mutilated or disfigured by cutting; mangled *la15-e17*. **2** *fig* botched *la16-e18*. [chf Sc; northern eModEng (once); uncertain]

maggot &c *n* **1** = maggot. **2** a whim, fancy, 'bee in one's bonnet' *18-, Gen except Sh Ork*.
~ive &c *la19-, chf NE*, **~y** *19-, now Kcdn-S* capricious, perverse.

magill *see* MAGGLE

magink [mə'gɪŋk] *n* a queer-looking object or creature *la20-*. [ma- + Eng slang *gink* a fellow]

magirkie &c, **magirky** [mə'dʒɪrkɪ] *n* a headdress of woollen material which also protects the throat *la17-e20, chf NE*. [see SND]

magister [*'madʒɪstər] *n* = MAISTER, *esp* 5 and 8, *la15-17*. [L]

magistrand &c ['madʒɪstrand] *n* an undergraduate in the fourth or final year at a Scottish university *17-, latterly St Andrews, Aberdeen, now only St Andrews*.
~ class the class in NATURAL and Moral Philosophy usually taken by students in their final year *17-19*. [MedL *magistrandus*, f *magistrari* become a Master (of Arts)]

magistrate &c *n* **1** = magistrate *la16-*. **2** *specif* title for a PROVOST or BAILIE of a BURGH as having administrative and judicial powers; also applied to stipendiary magistrates (but not to justices of the peace) *la16-20*. **3** a red herring *la19-, now Renfr* [shortened f *Glasgow magistrate* (GLESCA)].

maglit *see* MAGGLE

magne *see* MAINE[2]

magnum bonum ['magnʌm 'bonʌm] *n, also* **magnum** a bottle containing two quarts (2.27 litres) of wine or spirits *18-*. [L = a large good thing]

magowk [mə'gʌuk] *n, see phrase below*.
vt make an April fool of *20-, local; cf* BEGOWK.
~'s day April-fool's day *20-, Gsw SW*; see *gowk's day* (GOWK[1]). [ma- + GOWK[1]]

magrame *see* MEGRIM

magre *see* MAUGRE

mag wood &c *n* ? some inferior variety of coal *la17, eLoth*. [? *cf* MAGG, MAGGIE[2]]

Mahoun &c [ma'hun] **1** = Mahound, Mohammed *la15-16*. **2** name for the Devil *la15-e20, only Sc*.

maich &c *la15-e17*, **mauch** &c *la14-e17*, **mach** *la14-16*; **meuche** &c *la17* [*mex, *max, *mjux] *n* a male connection by marriage, as a son-in-law, brother-in-law, cousin, uncle or nephew by marriage *la14-17*. [northern eModEng *mawggh*, nME *magh*, midl *moʒe*, ON *mágr* a son-, brother-, father-in-law]

maid &c *n* **1** = maid *la15-*. **2** = MAIDEN 3, *specif* **the ~ of Lorn(e)** the eldest daughter of the CHIEF (*n* 2) of the CLAN MacDougall *19-*.
auld ~'s bairn *or* **wean** *chf proverb* a hypothetical well-behaved child which a spinster has in mind when criticizing the children of others *la19-*. **best ~** a bridesmaid at a wedding *la19-*. **~ in the mist** navelwort *19-, Kcb S*.

maid *see* MAITHE

maiden &c, **maidin**; **madin** &c *la14-e17 n* **1** = maiden *la14-*. **2** a daughter *la14-17*. **3** an unmarried heiress; *latterly* the eldest or only daughter of a landowner or farmer *15-, now NE*. **4** an unmarried woman, a spinster; an old maid *la15-, now NE*. **5** a female attendant, a maidservant *la14-, now Ags*. **6** designation of an 'office' held by one of the younger witches at a meeting of witches *17*. **7** *transf of a man, chf*

Malcolm IV a virgin *la15-, now hist.* **8** (1) the
last handful of corn cut in the harvest-field, *freq*
shaped into the figure of a girl *18-20.* (2) the
harvest-home feast and celebrations, the KIRN²
19. **9** name for a guillotine used in Edinburgh
for beheading criminals; any instrument of the
sort *la16-18.* **10** an upright post of a spinning-
wheel bearing the yarn-spindle *19-, now Sh Uls.*
~ barne &c a female child *la14-e17.* **~ castell** name for Edinburgh Castle *15-16* [trans-
lating L *Castellum* etc *Puellarum (12-15)*]. **~
clyack** = *n* 8 (1), *20-, NE.* **~ cummer, ~
kimmer** a young woman who acted as attendant to the mother at a christening *18-e19.* **~s
hair** the coarse sinews in certain cuts of beef
when boiled *19-, now local N.* **~ skate** a young
specimen of the thornback ray, skate, or similar
members of the ray species *la18-19.*
maidwyfe *see* MEDWYFE
maig; meg &c *n* a large ungainly hand, a paw
19-, chf Sh S.
vt spoil by over-handling *19-, S.* [Gael *màg* a
soft plump hand, a paw]
maigle *see* MAGGLE
maigne *see* MAINE²
maik &c *n* a halfpenny *19-.*
as daft (*C*) *or* **feel** (*NE*) **as a ~ watch** completely silly *20-.* [obscure; eModEng; *cf*
ModEng slang *mag*]
mail¹ &c, male; meal &c *la15-18,* **mell**
16-e18 [mel] *n* rent *la14-20.*
~er, malar &c *la14-e16* a tenant (farmer), a
cottar (COT) *la14-19.* **~ing &c 1** the action of
letting or renting *la14-17.* **2** a tenant farm *15-,
now local Bnf-Kcb.* **3** the rent paid for such
18-20.
~-fre &c rent-free *la15-17.* **~-garden(er)** a
market garden(er) *la18-19.* **~ man** = **~er,**
15-17. **~ mart** an ox paid as part of rent
15-18.
~s and duties the rents of an estate *16-19.*
[nME *male*, laOE *māl* payment, ON *mál* speech,
agreement, *máli* contract, pay]
mail² *n* a reddish spot or stain on cloth, *esp* that
caused by iron oxide *19-, now local EC-Rox.*
airn *or* **irne ~** = *n, 19-, now local EC-S.* [OE
māl (> Eng *mole*)]
mail³, male; meal &c *la17, e19* (*ballad*) [mel]
n a travelling bag, a trunk *la15-e20.* [ME, OF
male]
mail⁴ *n, weaving* a metal eye through which the
warp thread passes in a loom *19-, local.* [*cf*
MAIL3E¹, Eng *mail*]
maill &c; mal(3)ie *n, also* **~ land** a measure
of land equal to one forty-eighth of a TIRUNG
la17, Hebrides. [see DOST]
maill *see* MELL²
maill-eis *see* MALESE
maillie *n* a ewe; pet name for a favourite ewe
19-e20, Kcb. [extended use of *Mallie*, Eng
Molly, pet form of *Mary*, prob from Burns *The
Death and Dying Words of Poor Maillie*]

maillyer *see* MELDER
mail3e¹ &c; mal3(i)e &c *16-e17,* **mel3e**
la15-16, only Sc [*'mel(j)ɪ] *n* = (chain-)mail
la14-17. [*cf* MAIL⁴]
mail3e² &c, mel3ie &c *la16* [*'meljɪ] *n* a mail,
a French copper coin of low value, *chf* **nocht** *or*
nevir (worth) a ~ not (worth) a halfpenny
la15-16. [only Sc; OF *maille*]
main &c; mean &c *15-e19* [men] *n* = main
la14-.
adj **1** great of its kind *la15-, now Ork Cai.* **2** =
main *16-.* **3** unmitigated, 'out and out' *19-, Fif
Ags.*
adv exceedingly, very *la18-.*
~ly very, mightily *18-, now Wgt.*
~ coal *mining* the principal or best seam of coal
la18-, now Fif wLoth WC. **~ door** a door giving
sole access to a private house, as opposed to a
common entrance to a block of flats *19-.* **~
door flat** *or* **house** a ground-floor flat of a
block of flats, which has a door to itself direct
from the street *20-, C, S.*
man of ~ *verse, latterly only ballad* a mighty man
la14-e19.
main *see* MEAN¹
main- *see* MAINS
maine¹ &c [*men] *n* white bread of the finest
quality *15-16, usu* **~ breid &c** *15-16,* **~ flour
&c** *16* etc. [aphetic f OSc *demayn*; see DOST]
maine² &c; ma(i)gne [*men, &c] *adj* **Charlis
(the) ~** Charles the Great, Charlemagne
la15-16. [only Sc; OF; L *magnus*]
mainer *see* MANNER
mainis *see* MAINS
mainner &c *16-,* **maner &c** *la14-17;* **manner** *la15,* **menner** *la19-e20, NE* ['menər,
*ma'nir] *n* **1** = manner *la14-.* **2** the way in
which a thing is executed or made, its nature,
character, style *la14-:* 'ane ark in maner of ane
stak'.
for (the) ~(is) sake(s) in order to conform or
seem to conform with the normal practice, for
the sake of appearances *la16.* **in ~ as** as *15-16.*
mainner *see* MANNER
mains &c, mainis &c *la14-e18* [menz] *n pl* **1**
the home farm of an estate, cultivated by or for
the proprietor: (1) *treated as pl, la14-;* (2) *treated
as sing, 15-18;* (3) *attrib, 16-, earlier (la15) as*
main-. **2** as part of the farm name (1) **(the) ~
of A** *15-, now N;* (2) **(the) A ~** *15-, Gen except
N.* **3** name for the farmer of a MAINS, according
to the Sc idiom of calling a farmer by the name
of his farm *19-, Abd.* **4** the outbuildings of a
farm *18-.*
in ~ing *of land* farmed by the proprietor himself as opposed to being leased to tenants *e17.*
[aphetic f obs *domaine (lands)* demesne lands, the
lord (of the manor)'s lands]
**mainschott &c; manschet &c, menschot
&c** [*'menʃot, *'menʃət, &c] *n* = manchet, a
roll or loaf of the finest wheaten flour *la16-e17.*
[*cf* MAINE¹]

maintain *see* MANTEEN

maintenance &c *la16-*; **mant(e)inance &c** *15-e17*, **mentenance &c** *la16-17* ['mentənəns, ?&c] *n* **1** = maintenance *15-*. **2** *specif* the monthly pay due to serving troops (*appar orig* of the Army of the COVENANT); *chf* the tax first imposed on the Scottish shires and BURGHS in 1645 to provide this *17*.

maintene *see* MANTEEN

maintime *see* MEANTIME

main3ie &c; man3ie &c, men3ie &c [*'menji, *'mɛnji] *n* **1** a crippling or disabling wound or injury, a mutilation *la15-16*. **2** *fig* a defect or flaw *la15-17*.
vt, also fig maim, mutilate, disable by a wound or injury *la14-e17*. [ME *mayne*, OF *mahaing, mahaignier*, as Eng *maim*]

mair¹ &c, mare &c *la14-e17*, **more &c; meir &c** *la16-19* [mer] *adj* **1** = more *la14-*. **2** larger in physical size *la14-*. **3** greater in quantity or amount *la14-17*. **4** of greater importance, superior *la14-e16*.
n **1** = more *la14-*. **2** *adj used as noun* he who, or that which, is greater *la14-16*.
adv **1** = more *la14-*. **2** *with a comparative adj or adv*, *la14-*: 'mair aulder'.
.. and sumdele, lytill *or* **mekill ~, .. or (lytill) ~, .. with the ~, .. with sum ~** *added to expressions of quantity, number, etc to indicate that the actual amount or figure is (somewhat, much, etc) larger than that stated or expected la14-17.* **but, foroutin, withoutin** *etc* **(ony) ~** *verse* **1** *chf rhyming tag* without anything or anyone else, in all *la14-15*. **2** without more delay, at once *la14-16*. **~ at(t)oure &c** besides, over and above *la15-*. **the ~** *conj* although, in spite of the fact that *19-*, *Ags SW*. **the ~ by, be** *or* **for token &c 1** moreover, in addition *18-*, *now NE Ags SW*. **2** especially, in particular *19-*, *now NE nEC, SW*. **tae the ~ mean taikin &c** to be more explicit or precise, more particularly or especially *19-20*, *NE*. **the ~ o** any the more because of *la18-19*: 'ye'll no keep in the house the mair o't'. **~ ower &c** moreover *la15-*. **maister** *or* **mistress and ~** an autocratic, domineering master or mistress, one with the whip hand *19-*, *EC Slk*.

mair² *15-e19*; **mare** *14-17 n* **1** an executive officer of the law of the Crown or of a *lord of regality* (LORD) *14-e18*. **2** *attrib and possessive* **~('s) corn, land** etc assigned to a MAIR² as part of his perquisites *14-e17*. **3** = mayor, *chf* of an English city *15-17*.
~dome the office or jurisdiction of a MAIR² *la16-e17*. **~schip** the office of a MAIR² *la15-17*. **~ of fee 1** a MAIR² holding office, as commonly, by HERITABLE right *15-e18*. **2 ~-of-fee-schip** the office of a **~** *of fee*, *la15-e16*. **sheriff ~** *see* SHERIFF. [ME *mair(e)* a mayor, OF *maire*; ScL *marus* = *n* 1, Sc and IrGael *maor* a steward; both branches ultimately from L *mājōr*]

mair *see* MUIR

mairch, march &c; merch &c [mertʃ, mɛrtʃ] *v, n* = march *la16-*.
Mairch *la17-*, **March &c** *15-*; **Merch &c** *la15-* [mertʃ, mɛrtʃ] *n* = (the month of) March.

mairch *see* MARCH

maircheant *see* MERCHANT

mairiage *see* MAIRRIAGE

mairk *see* MERK

mairriage *la18-*, **mariage &c** *la14-e17*; **marriage &c** *la16-*, **mar(r)age &c** *16-17*, **ma(i)riage &c** *la16-17*, **meriage &c** *16*, **merr(i)age &c** *20-* ['merɪdʒ, *'merɪedʒ] *n* **1** = marriage *la14-*. **2** the feudal right of a SUPERIOR *eg* to a payment when an unmarried heir succeeded his VASSAL *15-e18*. **3** a large gathering of birds, *esp* rooks *20-*, *NE Ags wLoth*.
~ braws wedding clothes *la19-*, *NE-WC*. **~ gere** *16*, **~ gude** *la15-16* a marriage portion or dowry *N*. **~ lintel** *Fif Kcb*, **~ stone** *Bnf Fif* the lintel stone of a door bearing the initials and date of marriage (*usu* of the 17th or 18th centuries) of a couple who have set up house there *20-*.

mairry &c *16-*, **mary &c** *la14-e18*; **merry &c** *16-* ['merɪ] *vti, ptp also* **marit &c** *la14-16* = marry *la14-*.
~ on *16-*, **upon** *15-18*, **with** *14-18* marry to.

mairt *see* MART²

Mairti- *see* MARTINMAS

mairtin *n* = martin, the house martin *la19-*, *now Abd*.

mairtyr &c *18-*, **martir &c** *la14-e17*; **martyr, merter &c** *15-16, la19-e20* ['mertər; *Cai* 'mjartər] *n* **1** = martyr *la14-*. **2** *only* **martyr** *specif* one of those who suffered death in the 17th century in the cause of spiritual independence as set forth in the National Covenant or in the Solemn League and Covenant *18-*. **3** a disgusting mess, a dirty confusion *20-*, *local Cai-Ags*.
vt **1** = martyr *la14-*. **2** hurt or wound severely *la16-*, *now Sh*. **3** cover with dirt, bespatter with something nasty or sticky *19-*, *now Cai NE Ags*.
~dom &c 1 = martyrdom *la14-*. **2** slaughter, *esp* **mak (ane) (gret** *etc*) **~dom (on** *etc* the victims) *la14-15*. **martyry &c** martyrdom *e15*. **~('s) stone** etc a stone marking the grave of a martyr (*n* 2), *19-*.

mais *see* MAK, MESS¹

maise &c; maze *17-e19* [mez] *n* a measure, *chf* of fish, *esp* herring, = five hundred, *later usu* the long hundred of 120 (HUNDER *n* 3) *14-*, *chf SW*. [eModEng; *cf* MDu, MLowGer *mese, meise*, OF *meise* a measure of herrings, ON *meiss* a box, basket]

maisic *see* MUSIC

maiser *see* MACER, MASER

maisie *see* MEY

maisle &c *19-*, **mizzle &c** *18-*, *now NE, EC;*

measle &c *la17-* ['mezl; 'mɪzl] *n, in pl, also*
mesillis &c *16*, **missellis &c** *17* = measles,
the disease *16-*.

vt = measle; *specif* redden the skin of the legs by
sitting too near the fire, *chf* **measlet &c, miz-**
zled scorched, mottled, blotched *18-*, *now N*.

mizzle &c- *or* **mizlie &c-shinned** with legs
blotched, *esp* from sitting too near the fire *18-*,
local. [ME *maseles*]

maison &c [*'mezun, &c] *n* a house; a household, family *la16-e17*. [only Sc; F]

maisser *see* MACER, MASER

maissoner *see* MASONER

maist¹ &c, mast(e) *la14-17*, **most &c** *15-*
[mest] *adj* **1** = most *la14-*. **2** *of persons* chief,
most powerful, greatest *la14-*, *now Ayr Rox*. **3** *of
things* chief, principal *la14-*.

n = most *la14-*.

adv **1** = most *la14-*. **2** *with a superlative adj or adv*,
16-: *'the most hardest thing'*; *cf* MAIR. **3** for the
most part, mostly *15-*, *now Sh Bnf Ags*.

~ han in greatest measure, almost entirely
la19-, Sh NE. **~lins** almost, nearly *19-*, *now Sh
Ork Per*. **~ly 1** most of all, especially *la18-*, *now
Sh Ags SW*. **2** almost, nearly *19-*, *Gen except WC*.
the ~ penny the most money, the highest
price *e16, la19*.

maist², maste [mest] *adv* almost *16-*. [aphetic
f *amaist* (ALMOST)]

maist *see* MAST¹

maister¹ &c *la14-*, *in place-names 14-*; **master**
&c, mester *17-19*; *also abbrev* **mr &c** *16-*
['mestər] *n* **1** = master *la14-*. **2** the landlord of
a tenant; a feudal SUPERIOR *16-e20*. **3** a proprietor of lands or a business *la16-17*. **4** the manager or supervisor in a business or works *15-19*.
5 (1) a schoolmaster *la14-*; *specif latterly* (*19-*),
usu **the ~** the only or principal teacher in a
small rural community. (2) a teacher in a university *la15-17*. **6 ~ of, in(to)** a person who is
skilled or adept at (doing) something *15-16*. **7**
~ (*18- only* **master**) **of A** *15-*, **~ A** *16* title for
the heir-apparent or heir-presumptive (1) *orig*
to an earldom or *lordship* (LORD); (2) *now* for the
heir-apparent or heir presumptive to a Scottish
peerage which does not possess a subsidiary
peerage title which the heir may use as a courtesy title; *also* for a similarly untitled grandson
of an earl; *also* for the heir-apparent to a person
with a territorial designation as part of his surname; *cf younger* (YOUNG). **8** prefixed to the personal name of a man (*Gen except Sh Ork*): (1)
prefixed to the Christian name and surname,
orig, chf of a Master of Arts, *freq* a clergyman or
schoolmaster *la14-*; (2) prefixed to a surname
(a) *only* **Mr A** by a university teacher in formally designating a male student *19-*; (b) *more
gen* = *Eng* master, *later* (*17-*) *Eng* Mr., the polite
form of address *16-*.

vt = master *la14-*.

~fu(l) **&c 1** *law, of robbers, beggars or their actions*
overbearing, threatening, using force or vio-
lence *15-e19*. **2** powerful, big, strong *la15-*, *now
Sh Ork NE*. **~fully &c** forcibly, with violence
la15-18. **ma(i)strice &c** [*'mestrɪs, *-is, *-əis]
verse might, force; the display of might or skill
la14-16. **ma(i)stry &c** ['mestrɪ] **1** = mastery
la14-. **2** force, violence *la14-e16*. **maistriful**
&c = **~fu**(l) 1, *16-17*. **~ship &c 1** = master-
ship *la15-*. **2** the power or influence wielded by
a magnate, patronage *la15-17*.

~-man 1 a chief or leader, a mighty man
la14-e17. **2** a master of a craft *17-*, *now Rox*.

~-tree the main swingle-tree immediately
attached to the plough *19*, *chf Sh Ork*. **~ wood**
&c the principal beams of wood in a tenant's
house-roof *19-*, *Cai*.

~ of craft an inspector of the quality of work
produced by members of a Trade INCORPORA-
TION in a BURGH *15-e18*. **~ of the gr(o)und** a
landlord *la16-17*. **~ of household &c** *la15-16*,
only Sc, **maister &c household** *16-e18*, *only Sc*
an official having charge of the royal household. **~** (*18- only* **master**) **of wark** an official,
usu of a municipality, in charge of building
operations *15-19*.

maister² &c; master ['mestər] *n* stale urine,
used *chf* as a detergent *16-20*. [see SND,
DOST]

maister³ *n* = *maistrice* (MAISTER¹) *15-16*. [see
DOST]

maisterstick &c *n* the piece of work produced
by a craftsman to prove himself qualified for
acceptance as a 'master' *16-17*, *chf Aberdeen
Perth Dundee Dunfermline*. [eModDu *meesterstuck*
a masterpiece]

maistres &c [*'mestrɛs, &c] *n* **1** = mistress
la16-17. **2** style of the wife or widow of an heir-
apparent to an earldom or lordship *16-e17*; *cf*
MAISTER 7.

~ nurice &c title of the nurse of the child
James VI and later of the nurse of his children
la16.

maistrice, maistriful, maistry *see*
MAISTER¹

mait *see* MEAT

maithe &c, mathe; meith &c *la16-e19;*
maid *19-* [með; *Sh* ? me:d] *n* a maggot; the
egg or grub of the bluebottle etc *15-*, *now Sh-
Ags*.

vi become infested with maggots *19-*, *NE*.

mathie *la16*, **meithie** *la17*, **maidie** *e20*, *Sh*
maggoty, infested with maggots. [ME *mathe*,
OE *maþa*]

maither *see* MATHER

maitter &c *la16-*, **matere &c** *la14-e17*; **mat-**
ter &c *la15-*, **me(a)ter &c** *la15-17* ['metər;
*ma'tir] *n* = matter *la14-*.

to little ~ to little purpose, with small advantage *la18-*, *now Sh Ags*. **make (a) ~** make a fuss
la19-, local Sh-Kcb. **deil mak ~** all the same,
for all that *19*. **there is no (muckle) ~** it
doesn't (much) matter *la18-*.

majesté &c *la14-17*; **majesty** *16-* ['madʒəstɪ; *Abd Bwk* 'medʒəstɪ] *n* = majesty *la14-*.

the buke of ~, the Kingis *or* Scottis ~ the early Scottish legal compilation which opens with the words *Regiam Majestatem*; *loosely* the 'auld laws' as a whole *16-e17*.

major[1] &c [medʒər; ***'madʒər] *n* = major, the military rank *17-*.

~-mindit haughty in demeanour, high-minded *19-*, *now EC, S*.

major[2] &c *adj, n* = major, greater *15-*.

~ pars the greater part *la17, only Sc* [L].

mak &c, **ma** *la14-16, only verse*; **make** &c *la15-*, **mek** &c *la15-e20*, **meack** &c *17-e18*, **may** &c *la14-16, only verse* [mak; *sEC, S, SW* mek; *me] *vtir, pres also* **mais** &c *la14-e16, only verse* [*mez] *pt* **made** &c, **med** &c *16, la19-e20*, **meed** &c *17, la19-e20* [med]; **mak**(k)**it**. *ptp* **made** &c, **med** *la16*, **meed** &c *la16-e17* [med] **1** = make *la14-*. **2** *vt* fix (a price) *15-17*. **3** be the material or components of, go to form *15-16*. **4** make over (land or money to a person) *15-16*. **5** defray expenditure *la15-16*. **6** commit (a crime, fault or sin) *la15-16*. **7** *chf in negative or interrogative* matter, be of consequence, signify *la15-*, *now N*: 'it disna mak a fig'. **8** prepare (ground) for sowing *17-*, *now Ork NE Per*. **9** *vr* (1) prepare or exert oneself (to do something *or* for some action) *15-17*. (2) prepare to go, set out, proceed *15-17*. **10** *vr* pretend, make as if (to do something) *16-e17*. **11** *vi, of evidence or an argument* avail, 'tell' **for** *or* **against** *15-e17*. **12** *of food or drink in the process of cooking* thicken, set, infuse *la19-*. **13** *of dung* mature *20-*, *local Cai-Loth*. **14** *impersonal, of the weather* produce (*Sh Cai*) or threaten (*Kcdn Kcb*) rain etc *20-*.

n [mak, mek] **1** = make, form, shape *la14-*. **2** manner, way, style of behaviour *la14-16, only Sc*. **3** the action of manufacturing *e17*.

made &c **1** manufactured, finished, ready for use *15-*. **2** = made *16-*. **3** distressed, upset *eg* because of pain, overwork, or worry *la19-*, *NE*. **made diet** a cooked meal *20-*, *Sh NE*. **made lee** a deliberate lie *19-*, *now Sh NE Loth*. **made tie** a man's bow-tie sold with the bow ready tied *20-*, *Sh C*. **made up wi** pleased, elated with *la19-e20*. **sair made** sorely harassed, oppressed, hard put to it *19-*, *Sh-Ags*. **makar** &c, **maker** &c *16-* **1** = maker *la14-*. **2** *now chf* **makar** *and esp literary, referring to one of the 15th and early 16th century Scots poets* a poet *la15-*.

~ better improve, get better *la19-*, *now Sh*. ~ a better o *freq in negative* not improve upon, not do better with *la19-*. ~ by **1** overtake, excel *la19-*, *now Ags wLoth Kcb*. **2** make money or gain advantage by, profit by *la19-*, *Ork NE*. ~ ceremony stand on ceremony, fuss, scruple *18-*, *now Ags Uls*. ~ doon *vt* **1** dilute the strength of (spirits) *19-*, *local*. **2** prepare (a bed) by turning down the bedclothes *19-*. **3** reduce into smaller fragments, grind *la18-*, *now Abd Per*

Wgt. **makdoon** a garment altered to suit a smaller wearer *20-*, *Sh-Per*. ~ faith possess credence, be valid or trustworthy *la16-e17*. ~ for **1** *freq followed by adv with omission of verb of motion* prepare for, be on the point of *20-*. **2** *of weather* show signs of, 'look like' (snow etc) *20-*. ~ furth finish; complete the preparation or equipping of *la14-e17*. ~ (the) gait *etc* make (one's) way *la15-e17*. ~ into *or* intil make or force one's way into *la19-*. ~ in wi curry favour or ingratiate oneself with *19-*, *now Sh-Cai*. ~ or meddle (*now nEC, SW*) *or* mell (*now Sh Kcb*) interfere, meddle *la18-*. ~ nae-thing o it *of an ill person* fail to show signs of improvement *20-*. ~ o fuss over, make much of *18-*. ~ on *vt* **1** build and kindle (a fire) *la14-18*. **2** pretend, feign *la19-*, *Sh NE*. mak-on *n* a pretence, humbug; an imposter *20-*, *Sh NE*. ~ out **1** *freq* ~ it out achieve successfully, accomplish, manage *18-*. **2** *specif* make a living, keep going, succeed *19-*, *now Sh NE Uls*. **3** set out on a journey *19-*, *now Wgt*. **4** make up (weight) *20-*. ~ a prayer say or recite a prayer *la14-*. ~ rich become rich, make money *la18-*, *now Loth Wgt*. ~ (up) a sermon write a sermon *19-*, *now Cai*. ~ through wi struggle to bring to an end *19-*, *now Cai*. ~ to **1** set to work, set to *la16-17*. **2** *also* ~ till go towards *la18-*. ~ up **1** = make up *15-*. **2** make rich, establish successfully in life *16-*, *now Ork NE Uls*. **3** *law* complete, establish fully (a title) *18-19*. **4** *chf* ~ it up *with infin or that ..* (1) plan, contrive, arrange *19-*. (2) *specif* plan to get married *la19-*. **5** make (a bed) *19-*. ~ up for = ~ for 2, *la20-*, *Ork Abd Ags*. ~ up on overtake, catch up with *20-*. ~ way set about, prepare *20-*, *Sh Ork NE*. ~ weel make good, succeed *20-*, *Ork Fif*. [see SND, DOST]

mak *see* MACK, MAKE

makdom &c; **magdum** *la19-20, Sh Ork n* a person's form, shape or build *la15-e20*. [appar f MAK *n*]

make &c, **mak** [mek; *NE also* mak] *n* **1** *chf in negative* the equal or peer of a person or thing *la14-*, *now Sh-Per*. **2** the like, the same action *16, only Sc*. **3** a spouse or mate (1) *chf verse* of a person *la14-19*; (2) of an animal or bird *16-17*. **4** a close friend or companion *16-19*.

vti mate, pair; match *16-e17*.

~les matchless, peerless *15-e18*. [ME; OE *gemaca*, ON *make*]

make *see* MAK

makhelve *see* MACALIVE

makkit *see* MAK

makky &c; **macky** &c *n* name of a variety of cloth *la16*. [? the surname *Mackie, Mackay*]

makrell *see* MACKEREL

makrelty *see* MACLARTÉ

mala fama [*?'mala 'fama] *n* a report of bad behaviour, *esp* in cases of church discipline *18-e19*. [L = bad reputation, evil rumour]

malafooster &c [malə'fustər] *vt* destroy, wreck, ruin *20-, local.* [see SND]

malagrugrous &c [*malə'grug(r)əs] *adj* grim, forbidding; gloomy, melancholy *19.* [*mal-* + ALAGRUGOUS, GRUGOUS]

malagruize &c [malə'gruz, 'maləgə'ruz] *vt* **1** dishevel, disarrange, spoil *la19-, chf NE.* **2** injure, hurt, punish with physical violence *20-, NE.* [*mal-* + GROZE]

malancoly [*'malənkolɪ, &c] *vi* feel melancholy, sadness or resentment *e15.* [eModEng *melancholy (v)*, OF *melancolier*]

malar *see* MAIL[1]

malasche *see* MOLASS

malashes &c *n* = molasses *la17.* [*cf* MOLASS]

malder *see* MATHER

male *see* MAIL[1], MAIL[3], MEAL[1], MEAL[2]

malese &c; malice, maill-eis &c [*mel'iz, *-'ez] *n* **1** = malease, physical or mental unease or distress *la14-e16.* **2** *also fig* a disease or sickness *la14-e16.*

maleso(u)n *see* MALISON

maletout &c [*'mal(ə)'tʌut, &c] *n* name for some custom duty *14-15.* [AF *maletoute*, MedL *mala tolta* evil tax]

mal-grace [*'mal'gres] *n* disfavour, disgrace *chf* **in** ~ *la16-17.* [ME (once), OF *male grace* evil favour]

malice *see* MALESE

malie *see* MAILL

malign *see* MALING

malignant &c *adj* **1** = malignant *la16-.* **2** *specif* used by the *Covenanters* (COVENANT) of their adversaries *17.*
~ **kirk, kirk** ~ = church malignant (applied to the Roman Church by the early Protestants) *16.*

maling &c *la15-16* [*ma'lɪŋ] *adj* = malign *16.* *vti, also* **malign &c** *16-* **1** *vi* act wickedly or wrongfully, err *la15-16, only Sc.* **2** *vti* = malign *16-.*

malison &c, malisoun &c *15-e17*; **maleso(u)n &c** *15-19* [*Sh* 'mɛlɪʃən; *'malɪsun, *-ən] *n* a malediction, curse *la14-, now arch.* *vt* curse *la16-17, only Sc.*

malkin *see* MAUKIN

mall *see* MELL[2]

mallash *see* MOLASS

mallduck &c *n* the FULMAR *19-, chf Sh Ork.* [altered f next, w infl f Eng *duck*]

mallimoke &c *n* the FULMAR *19-, chf Sh Ork.*
mallie &c = *n, 20-, chf Sh.* [Du *mallemok; cf* prec]

malmy *see* MAUMIE

malt, malten *see* MAUT

malvader &c [*?məl'vadər] *vt* stun with a blow; punch with the fists *19-e20.* [ModIr dial *mulvather* confuse, bamboozle]

malverse &c [*?'mal'vɛrs] *vi* betray the trust attaching to an office by acting dishonestly, corruptly, or oppressively *17-e18.*

n a breach of trust, a piece of grave misconduct *18, only Sc.*

malversation &c corrupt behaviour in a position of trust *16-.* [F *malverser*, OF *malversation*]

malvesy &c *15-16*; **mavasy &c** *la15-e17, only Sc* [*'malvəzɪ, *'mavəzɪ] *n* = malvesy, malmsey.

mal3e *see* MAIL3E[1]

mal3ie *see* MAILL, MAIL3E[1]

mam *n, child's word* mother *la18-.*
~**(m)ie &c 1** = *n, la17-.* **2** a wet-nurse *17-e19, la19-e20 (Sh).* **3** a midwife *la16-19.* ~**miekeekie** ['mamɪ'kikɪ] a spoilt indulged child *20-, Lnk Dmf S.* [eModEng; *cf* PAWPIE]

mament *see* MOMENT

mamp *see* MUMP

man &c [man, *also* mɑn; *unstressed* mən, mɪn] *n* **1** = man *la14-.* **2** a husband *la14-.* **3** *vocative, used parenthetically and sometimes with the name of the man (or in ModSc occas the woman)* (1) implying surprise, remonstrance or irony: '*Maun, Will, I'm dumfounert*'; (2) *esp in the unstressed forms* **min, mon &c**, *as an emphatic expletive 15-:* '*Hey, mon!, he called to Rab*'.
~**had(e)** *15,* ~**heid &c** *la14-, now Bnf* = manhood. **mannie &c, mannikee** *la19-* **1** a little man *la17-.* **2** (1) *affectionate* of a small boy. (2) *disparaging* of an adult *la19-, now local.* **3** *only* **mannie** a skipper *20-, NE.* **4** *only* **mannie** the one who is 'it' in a game *la19-, Abd.* ~**kind 1** = mankind *la14-.* **2** the nature of man *la14-16.*
~ **bairn &c** a male child *la16-, now C.* ~**-big** grown to manhood, adult *la19-, now local Cai-S.* ~ **body** an adult man, a man as opposed to a woman *19-.* ~**-grown** = ~**-big**, *la19-, local.* ~**-keeper 1** the newt or water-lizard *la19-, chf SW Uls.* **2** the common lizard *19-20, SW, S Uls.* ~**-length** = ~**-big**, *la19-, local C.* ~ **milne &c,** *pl* **man** *or* **men mylnes &c** a handmill *16-17.* ~**-muckle,** *pl* **man** *or* **men-muckle** = ~**-big**, *19-, now Ags SW, S.* ~ *or* **men servand(i)s** = men-servants *la15-e17.*
menfolk &c men *in gen;* **the** men of a particular family or **the** male workers on a farm *19-.* **the Auld M**~ *18-, now local Ork-Ags Uls,* **the bad** ~ *la19-,* **the black** ~ *la19-, local, familiar* the devil. ~ **of business** a lawyer *la18-.* ~ **and lad, page** *etc,* ~ **and syre** every man, all of them *la14-e16.* **be** ~ **of one's meat** have a healthy appetite and digestion *la19-, now Ags Ayr.* **a** ~ **o his** *etc* **mind** one who thinks and acts for himself, a self-reliant person *20-, now Ags Ayr.* **the Men** name for a group of extremely strict spiritual leaders in a parish *19, N.* **the Men's day** the Friday preceding the half-yearly Communion service, used by the *Men* for religious exhortation *la19-.*

man *see* MAUN[1], MAUN[2]

manage *see* MANISH

manager *n* **1** = manager. **2** a member of a board of management of the temporal affairs of certain Presbyterian churches, *eg* of QUOAD

SACRA churches and of the former *United Presbyterian Church* (UNITED) *la18-*. **3** a member of the governing body of one of those small BURGHS where there was no popularly elected Town Council *la19-20*.

manance *see* MANNACE

manchon; manston &c *n* a muff *la16-17*. [only Sc; F]

mancipate &c *ptp* enslaved; made subject (**to**) *la16-17*.

manco *see* MANKIE

mand *n* a fee, fine *e17*. [aphetic f AMAND]

mand *see* MAUN³

mandate &c, mandat &c *16-17 n* **1** = mandate *16-*. **2** *specif, law* a formal warrant authorizing one person to act on behalf of another (without payment); a commission of attorneyship or proxy *16-*.

vt learn by heart, memorize *18-20, only Sc*.

mandant a person who gives a MANDATE *n* 2 *la17-*. **mandatar** [*ˈmandatər] a person to whom a MANDATE (*n* 2) is given *la17-e18*.

mandator [*ˈmandatər] = *mandant, la17-18*.

mandatory, ~ary [ˈmandətəri] = *mandatar, 18-*.

mandement *see* MANDMENT

mandill &c [*manˈdil, *ˈmandl] *n* = MANTEEL *n* 1, *la16-17*. [*cf* obs F *mandil*, Sp, Port *mandil*]

mandment &c; **mandement &c** [*ˈmand(ə)mənt, *ˈmand-] *n* **1** = mandment, command *la14-e16*. **2** = MANDATE *n* 2, *15-17, only Sc*.

mane¹ &c, mene &c, mean &c [men; *Sh-N* *also* min] *n* **1** = moan *15-*. **2** a voiced complaint, grievance, grouse *18-, now local Sh-Fif*. **3** any mournful sound *19-, now local Sh-Fif*.

vti [min, *also* men] **1** mourn, lament ((*chf* **for**) a person or thing) *la14-, now local Cai-Uls*. **2** *vr* bemoan, complain *15-la16*. **3** *vti* indicate pain or injury by flinching, or by ostentatiously nursing (the affected part) *la18-, now Abd Fif Wgt*. **4** present formally as a grievance, state as a formal complaint: (1) *vt, la15-18*; (2) *vr, 15-e18*; (3) *vi* ~ **upon** (= against) (a person) *16*, **of** *or* **on** (a grievance) *la16*. **5** *vt* pity or show sympathy towards (a person or his misfortune) *15-, now Cai Ags Rox*. **6** *vi* utter a moaning or mournful sound *19-, now Ags Fif*.

mening &c mourning, lamentation *15-16*. **mak mening** lament (**for** a person) *la14-e15*. **Deil ~ ye** *etc* = Devil take you *18-, now local Abd-SW*. **mak (a) ~ 1** lament, mourn *la14-, now local*. **2** to complain, grumble *la18-20*. **mak (nae) ~ for** *or* **about** show (no) sympathy towards *la19-, now Sh-N Uls*. **to ~ to** be pitied *16-, now local N-S*: 'they're no to mean'. [nME *man*, OE *mān* (*n*); ME *mene*, OE *mǣnan* (*v*); see SND]

mane² &c *n* **1** = mane (of *eg* a horse) *15-*. **2** *transf* applied to a person's long hair *la14-*.

maner *see* MAINNER

maner place &c [*ˈmanərˈples] *n* a manorhouse *la14-e18*.

maneswere *see* MANSWEAR

mang *vti* **1** *vt* bewilder; stupefy; misguide *la15-16*. **2** *vi* err; become perplexed; go distracted or frantic *la15-19*. **3** be extremely eager or anxious, long *la19-20, NE*.

mangit &c *16-e19*, **mangin** *e19* confused, crazed. [see SND, DOST]

mangery &c; maniory &c *15-e16, only Sc* [*ˈmendʒəri, *ˈmɑndʒ-] *n* = mangery, a banquet; feasting *la14-e16*.

mangrel &c [ˈmaŋrəl] *n* **1** = mongrel *la16-19*. **2** term of abuse for a person *la16-19*.

maniest *see* MONIE

manifest *adj* **1** = manifest, plainly evident, patent *la15-16*. **2** that is palpably or unmistakably what the noun asserts, palpable *la15-*: 'ane manifest myrakle'.

adv clearly; palpably *15-e16*.

manifestation &c *n* **1** = manifestation *la15-*. **2** an instance of this, a revelation *17-*.

maniory *see* MANGERY

manish &c *19-, local Sh-Kcb, only Sc*; **manage** [ˈmanıdʒ, -ıʃ] *v* **1** = manage *19-*. **2** *vt* succeed in reaching (a given destination) *la19-*.

manishee &c *n* a woman *20-, orig gipsy but now also Rox*. [Sanskrit *mānusī*]

mank¹ &c *n* **1** a flaw, fault; a deficiency, want *16-e19*. **2** a fuss *19-e20, Lnk Rox* [*cf* F *manque* and MANK² *adj*]

mank² &c *adj, only fig* deficient, defective; botched, ill-made *16-e18*. [eModEng *manke*, OF *manc*, L *mancus* maimed; *cf* prec and next]

mank³ &c *v* **1** *vt, also fig* mutilate; deface; spoil; botch (cloth) *15-e20*. **2** *vi* be deficient or wanting, come short *la16-e18*.

~it 1 mutilated, maimed *15-16, 20- (Abd Edb)*. **2** *fig, of a literary work* mutilated; corrupt *la16-17, 20- (Abd Edb)*. [nME *mank*; *cf* laL *mancāre* (*v*) mutilate, f *mancus*; *cf* prec]

mankie &c; manco &c *la18-e19 n* = calamanco, a kind of glossy woollen material *18-19*. [shortened f Eng]

mannace &c *la14-17*, **man(n)ance &c** *la14-e16*; **minace &c** *15-e18* [*ˈmanəs, *-əns, *ˈmınəs, &c] *v, n* = menace *la14-e18*.

manner &c *la19-, now Sh WC Kcb*, **manure &c** *la15-*; **mannour &c** *la15-17*, **main(n)er &c** *15-16, 20 (Rox)* [ˈmanər; *Rox* ˈmenər] *vt* = manure, occupy; till; spread manure on (land etc) *15-*.

n **1** = manure, dung *la17-*. **2** the utilizing or cultivation (of land) *la16-e17*.

manner *see* MAINNER

mannour *see* MANNER

Manounday *see* MONANDAY

manrent &c *n* = manredyn, manred, homage, vassalry, vassalage *la14-e18*.

~schip &c = *n, la15*.

band (*la15-17*), **bond** (*la18-, hist*) *or* **letter(is**

(la15) **of** ~ the contract between the parties concerned. [only Sc; for metathesized form in *-rent* cf *haterent* (HAT(E)RED), *kinrent* (KIN)]

manschet *see* MAINSCHOTT

manse &c *n* **1** a large or stately dwelling, a mansion; the principal residence of an estate with its attached outbuildings and land *la15-17*. **2** the dwelling-house provided for the parish MINISTER *16-*. **3** a house reserved for the occupants of particular chairs at Aberdeen University *17-e20*. **4** a measure or piece of land *la16-17*.
a son *or* **daughter of the** ~ a son *or* daughter of a Presbyterian MINISTER *la19-*. [MedL *mansus* a dwelling, a quantity of land considered sufficient to support a family]

manston *see* MANCHON

manswear &c, maneswere &c ['man'swir; 'mɛn-; *'men-] *v* **1** *vi* swear falsely, commit perjury *15-16*. **2** *vr* perjure oneself *la14-20*. **3** *vt* swear falsely or blasphemously by (a god) *la15-16*. **4** refuse or cease to acknowledge, *esp* on oath; disavow, abjure *16-e17*. **5** quit (a place) on oath not to return within the time stated *16*.
manswearing perjury, bearing false witness *la15-17*. **mansworn** *ptp, adj* **1** *of persons* forsworn, perjured *la14-*, *now only literary*. **2** *of oaths* sworn falsely, perjured *la15-e17*. [eModEng *mansweare*, OE *mān-swerian*, f *mān* wicked(ness) + *swerian* swear]

mant *vti* have a speech impediment, stammer, stutter *16-*, *Gen except Cai*.
n a speech impediment, a stammer, a stutter *19-*, *Gen except Cai*. [*cf* Sc and Ir Gael *manntach* lisping, stammering]

mantea *see* MANTIE

manteel &c,   mantele &c,   mantill &c [man'til; 'mantl] *n* **1** = mantle, a loose sleeveless cloak or wrap; a covering *la14-e19*. **2** the plaid worn as their principal garment by Highlanders (HIELAND) and Irishmen *16-e17*.
~ **wall** a curtain-, or outer wall, a rampart, a screen wall *16-e17*, *only Sc*. [eModEng, OF *mantel*; also F *mantille*, Span *mantilla*; *cf* MANDILL]

manteen &c *la15-19*, **maintene &c** *la14-19*, **maintain &c** *la16-*; **ma(y)nteme &c** *la14-16*, **mentene &c** *la15-e17, la19 (Bwk)*, **meintene &c** *la15-16, la19 (Mry Rox)*, **mentain &c** *la16-17* [*'men'tin, *men'tin, *-'tim, &c*] *vt* = maintain. [ME *maintene*, F *maintenir*; see also MAINTENANCE]

mant(e)inance *see* MAINTENANCE

mantele *see* MANTEEL

manteling *see* MANTILLING

manteme *see* MANTEEN

mantie &c, mantea ['mantɪ] *n* = mantua, manteau, a woman's loose, flowing, *usu* silk gown *la17-19*.
~**-maker &c** a dressmaker *la18-*, *now Sh NE Slk*.

mantill &c [*'mantl] *n* a set of skins of fur containing a specific number *la15-e17*.
~**ing** ? making up (furs) into MANTILLS *e16*. [OF *mantel*; ? f as MANTEEL]

mantill *see* MANTEEL

mantilling; mant(e)ling &c *n* some variety of cloth *la16-e17*. [only Sc; *cf* ME, eModEng *mantell* a kind of woollen cloth]

mantua &c *n* ~ **bonnet** a bonnet made or as made in Mantua, Italy *la16-e17, only Sc*.

manuale &c *adj, of a signature* written with the hand, autograph, *chf* **subscription** ~ *la15-17*. [*cf* Eng *manual*]

manufactor &c *n* manufacture; a manufactory *17*. [eModEng, F *manufacture*]

manumission &c *n* the conferring of a university degree upon a graduand *17*. [only Sc; ME, F *manumission*, L *manumissio* liberation from bondage]

manure *see* MANNER

many *see* MONIE

manyment &c [*'manɪmənt] *n* management *la16-e17*. [only Sc; F *maniement*]

manʒie *see* MAINʒIE

maormor *see* MORMAER

map[1] **&c** *n* = mop *18-19*.

map[2] **&c** *vti* nibble with twitching of the lips, as a rabbit or sheep *19-*, *now local Ork-Kcb*.
n, see comb below.
mappie &c 1 pet name for a rabbit *la19-*. **2** call to a rabbit *19-*. **mappie('s)-mou(s)** name for various plants *esp* of the figwort family, which have blossoms in the shape of a rabbit's mouth, as the antirrhinum, calceolaria *la19-*, *now NE-nEC*. **map-map** = mappie, *19-*. [onomat; *cf* MOUP and MUMP]

map[3] **&c** *vi* **1** = mope *20-*, *Ags*. **2** *of a bitch* be in heat *18*.

mappit stupid, thick-headed *20-*, *Abd nEC*.

mappamound &c [*'mapə'mund] *n* the globe, the world *la15-16*. [F *mappe-monde*, MedL *mappa mundi* map of the world]

mappat *see* MOPPAT

mappie *see* MAP[2]

mar[1] **&c, mer &c** [mar; *Sh S* mɛr] *vti* **1** = mar *la14-*. **2** *vt* obstruct, hinder, intercept, stop *la14-*, *now local*. **3** *fig* confuse, perplex, *chf* **marrit &c** *la14-*, *now Cai Lnk*.
n a hindrance, obstruction *17-e19, la20- (Sh Lnk)*.

mar[2] *vt* do bodily harm to, maim, injure, kill *20-*, *orig gipsy but now also Rox*. [*cf* Sanskrit *mārayate* he kills]

marage *see* MAIRRIAGE

marakle *see* MIRACLE

marble *n* = marl, a kind of soil *la17, Abd*.
marblie *of soil* marly *la17, Abd*.

march &c; merch &c, mairch *16-* [martʃ, mertʃ, mɛrtʃ] *n* **1** *usu in pl as collective* = marches, a boundary or frontier *15-*. **2** *specif, in sing* the Anglo-Scottish Border *la14-*, *now hist*. **3** (1) the boundary(-line) of a property or of lands belonging to a community *15-*. (2) the limit of a working in a coal-mine *la17-19*. **4** a boundary-marker, a landmark *la15-e18*. **5** a natural frontier or limit (of a stretch of land or water) *15-16*.

v **1** *vi* have a common boundary (**with**) *15-*, *Gen except Sh Ork*. **2** *in passive* be bounded **with** (lands, a wall etc) *15-17*. **3** *vt* border, adjoin; form the boundary of *la16-*, *now Abd*. **4** *vt* settle and mark the boundary of (land etc); fix and mark (a boundary) *la15-*, *now Loth*, *only Sc*.

~**ar** &c a march-dweller, a borderer *la14-e15*. ~ **bauk** &c a strip of land dividing two properties *la16-*, *now Bnf Fif*. ~ **blak** a type of fairly expensive (*appar* black) cloth *e16* [f the Welsh March (with England); *cf* LEMISTAR]. ~ **ditch** *19-*, ~ **dyke** &c *la15-*, ~ **fence** *19-*, ~ **stane** &c *16-*, a boundary ditch etc. ~ **roadie** a path between boundaries *20-*, *NE*. ~ **stank** = ~ *ditch*, *la19-*, *now Sh Wgt*.

day of ~ a day of truce on which a court of the wardens of the opposing MARCHES (*n* 2) heard complaints of infringements of the *laws of march*, *15-16*. **gang ower the** ~ *usu of a couple from England coming to be married according to the speedier and less formal procedure of Scots law* elope *18-*, *Rox*. **law, statutis** *etc* **of** (**the**) ~(**is**) the code of regulations governing Anglo-Scottish relations on the Border *la14-e15*. (**liand**) (**be**) **dry** ~(**is**) (dwelling on the other side of) a land frontier or boundary, *ie* one not marked by the sea or a river *15-17*. **riding of the marches** *see* RIDE.

march *see* MAIRCH
March *see* MAIRCH
marchand *see* MERCHANT
Marchmont &c; **Merchemount** &c *la15-e17* [*'martʃ(ı)mont, *'mɛrtʃ(ı)-, &c] ~ **herald** one of the Scottish heralds *15-*. [see SND Suppl, DOST]
marcie *see* MERCY
marcury *see* MERCURY
mardle[1] &c ['mardl; *Sh* 'mɛrdl] *adj*, *usu of women* heavy, clumsy, corpulent; lazy *19*, *NE Renf*. *n*, *derog* a fat, clumsy, idle woman *19-*, *Sh NE*. [prob f next]
mardle[2] &c, **merdale** &c ['mardl, 'mɛrdl; *mɛr'del, *mar-] *n* **1** *collective* camp-followers *la14-e15*. **2** a large number, a crowd, a heterogeneous collection *19-*, *NE*. [OF *merdaille* worthless rabble, f *merde* a turd]
mare *see* MAIR[1], MAIR[2], MEAR
margelene *see* MARJOLENE
margh *see* MERGH
margining &c *verbal n* annotating in the margin; marginal annotations, collectively *la16*. [appar only Sc; f *margin* to annotate]
margullie &c; **murgully** &c [*mər'gʌlı] *vt* mangle, hack about; besmirch, debase, abuse *18-e19*. [OF *margoillier* to dirty; see SND]
mariage *see* MAIRRIAGE
Marie *see* MARY

mariguld &c [*'marıgøld, &c] *n* = marigold *16*.
marikine &c [*'marıkın, *'mɛrı-, &c] *n*, *adj* = maroquin, Morocco (leather) *16-17*.
marinall &c; **marinell** &c [*'marınal, *-ɛl] *n* a sailor, seaman *la15-17*. [nME, northern eModEng *marinell*, OF *marinal*, *-el*, MedL *marinalis*]
marischal &c *now hist*, **marschall** &c ['marʃl, *'marəʃl] *n* **1** = marshal *la14-*. **2** a high *officer of state* (OFFICER) in Scotland *la14-e18*; see SND. **3** (1) *in the* BURGHS *of* Stirling, *Edinburgh and Irvine* designation of some officer or functionary *la17*. (2) *in Elgin* the BURGH hangman *la17-e18*; *cf* LOCKMAN, *staffman* (STAFF). **4** *in the army of Scotland* the title of a low-ranking regimental officer of regiments of foot *17*.

vt **1** = marshall (horses) *la15-e16*. **2** arrange (a group of persons) in order (of precedence) at a feast or ceremony *la15-*.
Marischal College a college in the University of Aberdeen, founded 1593 by the fifth Earl Marischal *la16-*. **Knight M**~ an office awarded to Sir John Keith, third son of the sixth Earl Marischal *la17*. [the early forms are usu disyllabic, trisyllabic ones becoming common only *la16*]
marit *see* MAIRRY
marjolene &c; **margelene** &c [*'mardʒəlin] *n* marjoram *16*, *chf Sc*. [OF *marjolaine*, MDu *margelleine*; *cf* ME, OF *majorane*]
mark &c; **merk** *15-*, *now S n* **1** = mark *la14-*. **2** an insensitive spot supposedly placed on the body of a witch by the Devil as a mark of his possession *la16-e18*. **3** a stone or cluster of stones of a different sort or larger size set into a string or chain of jewels *la16* [*cf* obs F *marche*]. *vti* **1** = mark *la14-*. **2** *vt* note down, make a written note of *17-*. **3** *vi* (1) take aim *la15-*, *now Kcdn EC Ayr*. (2) purpose, intend (to do something) *la15-16*, *only Sc*. **4** *vir*, *orig only verse* direct one's way, proceed *la15-16*.
~**ed** &c **1** *of a stroke in fencing etc* kept tally of, scored *16*, *only Sc*. **2** *of persons* notable, distinguished *la19-*, *local*.
~**is point** the centre of a target; *fig* the nub of the matter *la16*. ~ **stane** = *march-stane* (MARCH) *16* (*Ork*), *19-* (*Sh Ork Cai Gall*). ~ **a finger** (**up**)**on** harm in any way *la19-*, *Bnf Uls*. ~ (**a foot to**) **the ground** set foot on the ground, stand *la18-*, *now Kcb Uls*.
mark *see* MERK, MIRK
market *see* MERCAT
marl &c *n* **1** a mottle, a mottled or veined pattern *18-*. **2** *in pl chf* **mirls** &c measles *19-*, *chf NE Ags*.
~**ie**, **mirlie** &c mottled or variegated in pattern, *esp* **1** of birds and animals *la18-*, *now N-Uls*; **2** of wool or knitted garments *la18-*, *now Ork Kcb*. [see next]
marled &c, **marlit** &c, **mirled** &c *19-*, *now*

local, **merlit** &c *16-19 adj* chequered, variegated, mottled, veined, streaked *16-.* [chf Sc; ? OF *merelé* chequered, f *merelle* &c a counter; a kind of board game]

marless *see* MARROW

marlʒeoun *see* MERLʒEO(U)N

marmaid &c *n* = mermaid *la16-e19.*

~**en,** ~**yn** &c = *n, 16-e18.* ~(**en**)'**s purse** the egg-case of a ray *18-, now* Sh Ork Uls.

marmore &c *n* marble *la14-e17.* [only Sc; L *marmer*]

maroonjous &c [məˈrundʒəs] *adj* wild, obstreperous; surly, obstinate *la19-20, chf NE.* [obscure]

Maroons *n pl* **the** ~ nickname for *Heart of Midlothian* (HERT) football team *20-.* [f the colour of their strip]

marrabas &c *n* ~ **bonet** a flat cap *e16.* [only Sc; F *bonnet à la marrabaise,* f *marrabais* a pseudo-Christianized Jew or Moslem]

marrage, marriage *see* MAIRRIAGE

marrit *see* MAR¹

marrot &c *n* the common guillemot; the razorbill *18-, now* Abd Fif. [orig perh imit of its call; *cf* Eng *murre*]

marrow &c; **morrow** *la16-* [ˈmarə; *Sh Ork Uls* ˈmorə; *Loth also* ˈmarɪ] *n* **1** (1) a comrade, companion *la15-, now* Sh Ags Ayr. (2) a colleague, fellow-worker, mate; an associate or partner in business *la15-e19.* **2** a marriage-partner, spouse *la16-, only* Sc, *now chf literary.* **3** another of the same kind, a counterpart: (1) of persons *17-e20;* (2) of things *16-, latterly* (18-) *only in pl* a pair. **4** *freq in pl with sing meaning* a match, equal *16-.* **5** an opponent *16-17.*

v **1** *vtr* associate, join in partnership *15-17.* **2** *vi* enter into partnership, combine *16-20, latterly* (*la18-*) *of small farmers co-operating in certain tasks.* **3** marry: (1) *vt, 16-18;* (2) *vi,* ~ **wi** *17-e20.* **4** *vt* match, equal *la16-20.*

~**less 1** matchless, unequalled *17-, now nEC.* **2** *also* **marless** &c *of gloves etc* odd, not matching *18-.* **3** unmarried *19-, now* Ags. ~**schip** partnership; partners, associates, collectively *15-e16,* Abd. **ill-**~**ed** *of marriage partners* ill-matched *20-,* Sh NE. [laME *marwe;* ? of Scand orig]

Marrow &c [ˈmarə] short for *The Marrow of Modern Divinity* by E Fisher, whose strongly Calvinistic doctrines were condemned by the *General Assembly* (GENERAL) in 1720, a prolonged controversy ensuing *e18.*

~**-folk,** ~**-men** supporters of these doctrines *e18.*

marschall *see* MARISCHAL

Mar's year &c name given to the year 1715, when the Jacobite army was led by the Earl of Mar *la18-e19.*

mart¹ &c [mart, mert] *n* **1** = mart, a market *20-.* **2** *specif* a building used for agricultural auctions; the periodical sales themselves *la19-.*

mart² &c; **mairt** &c *16-,* **mert** &c *16-* [mart, mert] *n* **1** an ox or cow fattened for slaughter

15-20, now Sh Cai Bnf. **2** any other animal (*esp* a sheep) or bird which is to be salted or dried for winter meat *17-20.* **3** contemptuous term for a clumsy, inactive person *16-, now* NE.

~ **silver** a money payment as *feu-duty* (FEU) in lieu of a payment in kind in MARTS *16-e18.* [ScL = *n* 1, *e14;* Gael = a cow]

Marti- *see* MARTINMAS

Martin Bullion &c [? ˈbʌliən] *n* ~'**s day** the day of the Feast of the translation of St Martin, 4 July (Old Style), 15 July (New Style), St Swithin's day *19-, now* Sh. [F *Saint Martin d'été* or *le bouillant,* L *Martinus bulliens; cf* L *Martinus hiemalis* = MARTINMAS; *cf* BULLION'S DAY]

Martinmas &c *15-,* **Martinmes** &c *la14-17;* **Mertin-** &c *la16-e20,* **Marti-** &c *la14-e19,* **Merti-** &c *16-e18,* **Mairti-** &c *la15-e20 n* the feast of St Martin, 11 Nov; a Scottish quarter day, one of the *term days* (TERM) (though the date for removals and for the employment of servants was changed in 1886 to 28 Nov) *la14-.*

~ **Term** the first or autumn term in the Universities of St Andrews and Glasgow *20-.*

martir *see* MAIRTYR

martrick, martrix *see* MERTRICK

martstig &c; **martstuik** &c [*ˈmartˈstøk, *-ˈstjuk &c] *n* some kind of tax in Breadalbane and Atholl *16-e17.* [? Gael *mart-staoig,* f MART² + *staoig* a collop]

marty &c [*?ˈmarˈtaɪ] *n* = Gael *maor tighe* a major-domo *e17,* Arg.

~**schip** &c the office or function of a MARTY; the lands of a castle for the rents of which the castle's MARTY was responsible *la16-e17,* Arg.

martyr *see* MAIRTYR

mary *see* MAIRRY

Mary &c; **Marie** &c [ˈmerɪ] *n* = Mary, the female personal name *14-.*

~ **day** one of the festival days of the Virgin *la15-e18:* **1 first** ~ **day** the Annunciation (25 March) or (*chf*) the Assumption (15 Aug); **2 latter** ~ **day** *chf or only* the Nativity (8 Sep). ~**mas(s),** ~**mes** &c = *prec la15-.* ~**mas Fair** etc a Fair etc held at *Marymas,* *la19-,* Ayr. (**the Queen's**) **Maries** *orig of Mary Queen of Scots' four attendants* ladies-in-waiting, female attendants *la16-e19, latterly chf ballad.*

maryland *see* GOWK¹

mas *see* MASS

maschle, meeschle [ˈmaʃl, ˈmiʃl] *n* a mixture, muddle, mess *la19-,* Bnf Abd. [see SND]

mascorn [*?ˈmasˈkorn] *n* silverweed; its edible root *19.* [reduced f Eng *marsh* + *corn*]

masel(l) *see* MYSEL

maser &c; **mais(s)er** *16-e17, only* Sc [*ˈmezər] *n* = mazer, a drinking cup *la15-17.*

maser *see* MACER

mash¹ *n* a heavy two-faced hammer, used for stone-breaking etc *la17-, local* Cai-Dmf.

~**ie** a golf-club corresponding to the No 5 iron *la19-20.*

~ **hammer** = *n*, *la18-*. [*cf* F *masse* a sledge-hammer]

mash² *n*, *vti* = mesh (of a net) *20-*, *Ross Ags WC*; *cf* MASK².

mashlach, mashlok *see* MASLOCH

mashlum &c ['maʃləm, *also* *-lə, *-lɪ] *n* mixed grains or grains and pulses grown and ground together *18-*, *now local NE-Kcb*.

adj muddled, confused *la18-e19*. [var of Eng *maslin*; *cf* MASLOCH]

mask¹ &c *v* **1** *vt*, *brewing* mash (malt); brew (ale etc) *15-*, *now Ork*. **2** (1) make or infuse (tea) *la18-*. (2) *vi*, *of the tea* brew *la19-*. **3** *fig*, *of a storm etc* threaten, brew up *17-19*.

n **1** a single mashing of malt *16-e18*. **2** a mash of malt or draff as a feed for a horse etc *16-e18*. **3** a brew or infusion, *esp* of tea *la17-*, *now Sh Ags*. **4** a (large) quantity or amount *la19-e20*, *Abd Ags.`*

~**ing 1** the action of *v* 1; a brewing *17-e20*. **2** an infusion or pot of tea *19-e20*. ~**ing fat** *la15-e19*, ~**in tub** *la15-e16*, *SW*, *S* a mashing vat. ~**in pot** a teapot *la18-*, *Ags Ayr*.

~ **fat** = *masking fat*, *la13-e18*. ~ **rudder,** ~ **ruther** the stick used to stir the steeping malt *la16-e18*. [northern eModEng (once) *maske*, corresponding to ME *mahas-* (*v*), OE *mǽscan, ME *massh* (*n*), OE *mac-*; *cf* Sw dial *mask* draff]

mask² *n* the mesh of a net *la16-*, *now Sh-Ags*.

vti, *chf of fish* catch in a net; be trapped in a net *19-*, *now Sh-Cai*. [ME *mask* (*n*), OE *max*, *masc, ON *mǫskve*; see also MASH²; *cf* MAST²]

masloch &c; **mashlach, mashlok** &c [*'masləx, *-lək, *'maʃ-] *n* **1** mixed grain *15-e17*. **2** bread made from mixed meal *17-e19*. [altered var of ME *mastlyoun*, *cf* ModEng *maslin* and MASHLUM]

mason &c *la13-*, **masoun** &c *14-17*; **me(a)son** &c *la16-17* *n* = mason *la13-*.

masoner; maissoner &c *n* a mason *17*, *Arg Kcb*. ~**ry** &c **1** = ~ *werk* 1, *la14-e18*. **2** = masonry, stonework.

~**'s ghost** the robin redbreast *20-*, *chf S*. ~ **luge** &c a (Free)masons' lodge or meeting place *16-18*. ~ **werk 1** mason's work *la15-17*. **2** masonry, stonework *la16-17*. **the** ~**('s) word** the secret word given to a masonic initiate *17-18*.

mass &c *la16-*, **mas** *la15-e17* *n* **1** = mass, a body of matter *15-*. **2** a package or bundle (of letters or papers) *la15-e17*, *only Sc*.

~**ie** &c bumptious, full of self-importance, proud *18-*, *now nEC*, *WC*, *S*. **mawsie** &c [*'masɪ] *adj*, *of a garment* warm, thick, comfortable *la19-e20*, *chf NE*. *n* **1** an amply-proportioned, motherly-looking woman *la18-19* [perh a specialised use of *Mause* (? Mary); see SND]. **2** a warm woollen jersey etc *la19-*, *NE Ags*.

mass *see* MACE

massacker &c, **massacar** *la16-17*; **missaucre** &c *la19-* [mə'sakər, mə'ʃakər] *n* **1** = massacre *la16-17*. **2** severe injury; destruction *la19-*, *chf Sh NE*.

vt **1** = massacre *17-*. **2** maul, mutilate, bruise, beat (a person) *19-*, *now local*. **3** spoil (something) by mishandling or rough treatment *la18-*, *local*.

masse *see* MACE

Massedone &c = Macedon, Macedonia *la15*.

masser *see* MACER

massymore &c [*'masɪ'mor] *n*, *chf literary* the dungeon of a castle *la18-e20*. [popularized by Scott; Span (f Arabic) *mazmorra* a dungeon]

mast¹ &c, **maist** &c *16-e17* *n* = mast (of a ship) *la14-*.

vt equip (a ship) with masts *e16*.

to the ~**-heid** to the fullest possible extent *19-*.

mast² *n* a net *la15*.

vt net (herring) *19-*, *now Ags Uls*. [var of MASK²]

mast *see* MAIST¹

maste *see* MAIST¹, MAIST²

master *see* MAISTER¹, MAISTER²

mastis &c, **mastishe** &c *la16-e17*, *only Sc* [*'mastɪs, *-ɪʃ, &c] *n* = mastiff, the large watch-dog *15-e17*. [northern eModEng; *cf* Provençal *mastis*]

mastrice, mastry *see* MAISTER¹

mat &c *n* **1** = mat *15-*. **2** an underlay for a bed; a bedcover, *now* (*C*, *S*) one made of thick wool *16-*. **3** a sack made of matting *17-18*, *N*.

mat *see* MAUT, MOTE³

matash [mə'taʃ] *n* = moustache *la19-*, *now Ags*.

match &c *la16-*, **mach** &c *la15-e17* [matʃ] *n* **1** = match, an equal; a contest *la15-*. **2** *following a verbal noun* a bout or fit of .. *19-*: 'a greetin *match*'.

~ **play** *golf* that variety of the game in which the number of holes won by each side is reckoned, not the total number of strokes *la19-*; *cf* MEDAL 2.

Matchevell *see* MACHIAVELL

mate &c *adj* = mate, mated at chess; exhausted *la14-16*.

vti = mate, (be) checkmate(d); overcome *15-16*.

~**ed** ['metɪt; *Abd* 'mɑt-] exhausted, spent *la19-*, *Abd*.

~**out** = *adj*, *19-e20*, *S*.

matere *see* MAITTER

materes *see* MATTRASS

material &c *adj*, *n* **1** = material *la15-*. **2** *in pl* the matter from which something is made, raw materials *la15-17*. **3** *in pl* equipment, implements, tools for some operation *17*.

matermony *see* MATRIMONY

matfull &c ['mat'fʌl] *n* a sexually mature herring *la19-*, *fishing areas*. [MATTIE + *full* (FOU)]

mathe *see* MAITHE

mathelas &c *n* a mattress *la15*. [OF, var of *materas*]

mather *17-18*, **mad(d)er** &c *15-*; **maither**

&c *17-18*, **malder** &c *16* ['maðər; *'maðǝr; *'med-; *'með-; *'mad-] *n* = madder, (dye from) the root of the plant.

matin(e) &c ['matɪn; *ma'tǝin, *-'tin; *'metɪn, *-in, &c] *n, chf in pl* **1** = matins *la14-*. **2** applied to the Little Office of Our Lady *e16*.

~ **buke** a book of hours or primer *la15-16*.

matkie *see* MATTIE

matrimoniall &c *adj* = matrimonial, of or pertaining to matrimony *la16-17*.

croun ~ a regal crown claimed or obtained in Mary's reign through marriage with the sovereign *la16, only Sc*.

matrimony &c; **matermony** &c *15-16* ['matrɪmonɪ, *'matǝr-, &c] *n* = matrimony *la14-*.

matron &c [*'matrǝn] *n* **1** = matron, married woman *la14-*. **2** as the distinctive designation of a married female saint, *esp* St Anne *e16*.

~**ize** &c chaperon *e19*.

matsill &c [mǝ'tsɪl] *n* affectionate form of address to a child *20-, NE*. [*ma* my + *tsill* (CHILE) child]

matter *see* MAITTER

mattie &c; **matkie** &c *18*, **madgie** *la20, Abd* ['matɪ; *Abd also* 'madʒɪ; *'matkɪ] *n* a young maiden herring with the roe not fully developed *18-, now Sh NE Ags*. [Du *maatjes* (*haring*); *cf* MLowGer *madikes-herink*; both ultimately f LowGer *mädeken* a maiden]

mattle *vi* nibble (like a young animal) *19-e20*. [onomat]

mattrass &c *la14-, now Sh-nEC, WC*, **materes** &c *la14-17* [mǝ'tras, -'trɛs] *n* = mattress *la14-*.

mature &c *adj* = mature *16-*.

~**ly** with due deliberation, after full consideration *la15-*. **maturity** &c **1** = maturity *15-*. **2** deliberation in action or thought *la14-e16*.

matutine &c *n, chf in pl* matins *la15-16*. [MedL *matutinae* fem pl etc, f L *mātūtīnus* of the morning > laME, OSc *matutine, adj*]

mauch *see* MAICH, MAUK

mauchle &c ['maxl] *vti* botch; act or work clumsily, exert oneself to no purpose *la16, 19-, now Wgt*. [see SND]

mauchless *see* MAUCHT

Mauchlyne &c [*'maxlǝin, *-lɪn, &c] *n* = Mechelen, the Belgian town, notorious as a place of origin for counterfeit coins *16-e17*.

~ *or* **Mauchlinys** &c (**lemistar** &c) **blak** a type of expensive fine black cloth, *chf* used for hose *e16; cf* LEMISTAR.

maucht &c, **mought** &c *19-, now Ork*; **macht** &c [maxt] *n* **1** operative power, ability, capacity *la14-, latterly* (*la17-*) *freq in pl in sing sense*. **2** physical strength, mightiness *la14-*.

~**less** &c, (*chf*) **mauchless** &c feeble, powerless *la16-, now Sh-nEC*. ~**y** powerful, mighty *la18-e19, chf N*. **mak a maucht** *or* **mauchts** make a move or effort (to do something) *la19-, Ags Per*. [eME *maʒt*, appar f ON **mahtr*]

maud &c, **mad** &c [mad] *n* a checked PLAID or wrap, used as a bed-covering or worn by shepherds *la17-e20, chf S*. [see SND]

maugre &c; **magre** &c *15-16, la19-*, **mager** &c *la16, la19-*, **mauger** &c *la16-e20, latterly NE* ['magǝr; *'ma'gri, &c] *n* **1** = maugre, illwill *la14-16*. **2** odium, the state of being regarded with ill-will *15-16*.

prep in spite of, despite, notwithstanding *la14-19*.

vt act in despite of; master, worst; spite *19-, NE*.

magerful domineering, wilful *la19-, chf NE*.

in ~ **of** in spite of *15-16, la19-* (*NE*). ~ **a person's hede, neck** *etc* in spite of a person's opposition or resistance *15-19*. ~ **of** in spite of *la15-e20, latterly N*.

mauk &c *18-*, **mauch** &c *e16, 19-* [mak; *nEC* max] *n* a maggot *16-, Gen except NE*.

~**ie** &c **1** maggoty *la18-, now Fif*. **2** filthy *19-, now Inv Edb*. ~**ie fly** = ~ **flee**, *20-, S*. **maukit**, **maucht** *adj* **1** *esp of sheep* infested with maggots *19-, Cai C, S*. **2** putrid; filthy *la20-, WC*. **3** exhausted, played out *20-, S*.

~ **flee** a bluebottle *19-, C, S; cf* above.

as dead as a ~ absolutely lifeless *la18-e20*. [ME *mawke*, ON *maðkr* (*n*)]

maukin &c, **malkin** &c ['makɪn; *NE* 'mja-] *n* **1** the hare *18-, now NE nEC Kcb*. **2** an awkward, half-grown girl; a young house-servant *18-e20*. **3** a feeble person, a weakling *e20, Abd Uls*. **4** the female pudendum *e16, 18*. [ME = a female personal name, esp of the lower classes, dim of *Matilda, Maud*]

maumie &c; **malmy** &c, **maamie** &c *NE* ['mamɪ] *adj* **1** *of fruit etc* ripe, mellow *la19-*. **2** *of a liquid* thick and smooth; full-bodied *la18-*. **3** *of weather* settle, mild *20-*. **4** *fig* mellow, pleasant *18-*. [chf NE; Eng dial *malm* mellow, f ModEng, ME *malm*, OE *mealm-* soft rock, light soil]

maun[1], **man** [man; *unstressed* mǝn] *v* **1** *aux v, pres only* = must *la15-*. **2** with omission of verb of motion *15-*: 'I *maun awa in*'.

n, proverb compulsion, necessity *la18-*.

~-**be** *n* an unavoidable necessity *19-, local*. [chf Sc; nME *man*, ON *man*, var of 1 and 3 pers sing indicative of *munu; cf* MON[1]]

maun[2]; **man** &c [man] *vti* **1** manage, succeed *la18-, now SW*. **2** *vt* master, control, domineer *19-, now Sh*. [ON *magna* (*v*) strengthen, grow strong; see SND]

maun[3] &c *la18-e20*, **mand** *la15-e19* *n* **1** a basket made of wicker or wooden slats *la15-e20*. **2** a platter for *oatcakes* (AIT), *usu* made of wooden slats *la17-19, NE*. [eModEng *maund*, OF *mande*, MLowGer *mande*; OE *mand* appar did not survive]

maun[4] &c *adj* **muckle** ~ great big *18-e19*. [see SND]

maunner &c *vi, n* = maunder, babble *la18-e20, only Sc*.

maundrels nonsense, idle tales *la18-e19*.

maut &c *16-*, **mat** *16-e19*, **malt &c** *la14-*
[mɑt; *malt] *n* **1** = malt *la14-*. **2** *transf* ale,
liquor *16-19*.
~en *vi, of grain or seeds* germinate, sprout;
become malt *la18-19*. **mautent** *adj* lazy,
weary, lethargic *18-20, NE*.
~-barn a building where malt is prepared
16-19. **~man 1** a maltster *16-*, *now Cai NE
Loth*. **2** *attrib, of a kind of cloth, la16*. **~ silvir**
&c a payment to a maltster for making grain
into malt *la16-e17*. **~ whisky** WHISKY distilled
from malted barley in a pot-still, as opposed to
a blended WHISKY (made mainly from grain)
19-.
get *or* **hae in one's ~, haud the ~** be drunk
la19-e20. **the ~ gaes, is** *etc* **abune the meal**
he *etc* is drunk *17-e20*. **meal and ~** food and
drink *16-*, *now Kcdn Ags*.
mauvie &c the stomach *20-, Cai*. [Eng *maw* +
-ie; cf MYAVE]
mavasy *see* MALVESY
mavie *see* MAVIS, MUVE
mavis &c; maveis &c *15-18* ['mevɪs] *n* =
mavis, the song-thrush *15-*.
mavie = *n, la19-*.
mavité &c [*'mevɪtɪ, *'mɑv-] *n, verse* wickedness, malice, evil intent *la14-e15*. [OF *mauvitié
&c*]
maw[1] **&c** *v, pres also* **maa** *la19-, Sh Ork S*. *pt*
mawit &c *16-*; **meuw** *la19-, SW, S* [mju]. *ptp*
mawn &c *la16-* = mow, cut (hay etc) with a
scythe *15-*.
~er *la15-*, *now Gall*, **~ster** *e19, Gall* a mower.
~in girse meadow hay *la20-, Sh Ags*.
maw[2] **&c; maa** *la19-, Sh Ork n* mew, seagull,
esp the common gull *16-*.
sea ~ &c = *n, la15-, Gen except Sh Ork*. **keep**
your ain fish guts for your ain sea ~s *proverb* charity begins at home *18-*, *now NE*. [only
Sc; ON *máv-*, oblique stem of *már* mew]
maw[3] *n, child's word* = ma, mother *20-, C*.
maw[4] **&c** *n, freq in pl* the plant mallow *15-e20*,
latterly S. [late ME *mawe*, var of *malwe*]
maw[5] **&c** *vi* mew as a cat *la18-e20*.
n a miaow *19-e20, chf SW, S*. [imit; *cf* ME *maw*
(*v*), Du *mauwen*]
mawdelit &c [*'mɑdə'lɪt] *n* illness which confines one to bed, as an excuse for not appearing
in court *15*. [only Sc; OF *mal de lit*, MedL
malum lecti]
mawit *see* MAW[1]
mawmar &c *n* the discharge pipe of a ship's
pump *la15-e16*. [? *cf* Du *mamiering* a scupper-
hose]
mawn *see* MAW[1]
mawsie *see* MASS
mawster *see* MAW[1]
maxie *n* a gross error in a Latin translation,
entailing the highest deduction of marks
la19-20, chf NE. [abbrev dim of L *maximus
error*]
may &c, ma *la14-18* [me] *v, pres unstressed* **ma**

la18-e19 [*mə]; *2 pers sing* **may &c** *la14-e19*
[me; *Rox also* mɛ; *mɑi]. *pt* **micht &c** *la14-*
[mɪx(t); *Bwk Rox also* mɑi(x)t] **mith** *la16-, chf
NE* [mɪθ]; **mocht &c** *la14-e19* [*moxt] **1** =
may *14-*. **2** *with cognate object* possess, exert
(power, might) *la14-15*. **3** *in negative* not be
agreeable (to do etc); be unable to endure (to
do etc) *la15-16*.
~ fall *adv phr, verse* perhaps, perchance
la14-e15.
may *see* MAK, MY
May *see* MEY
mayan *see* MOYEN[2]
maybe &c; mibby &c *la19-* ['mebi, 'mɛbɪ; *C
'mɪbɪ] *adv, also* **maybes** ['mebɪz, *&c*] **1** perhaps, possibly *la18-*. **2** *of quantity or measurement*
approximately *la19-*: '*maybe half a mile*'. **3** *in
emphatic statements etc* = Eng then *20-, Abd WC*:
'*surely no maybe*'.
n a possibility, *chf proverb* **a ~ is not aye a
honey bee** *18-*.
~ aye and ~ hooch aye *expression of uncertainty*
perhaps he *etc* did or perhaps he didn't; *or ironic
expression of disbelief* = sure! *20-*.
maynteme *see* MANTEEN
mayock &c [*'meok] *n* ? a little maiden; ? a
mate *la16-e17*. [see DOST]
maze *vt* amaze *la19-e20, S*.
n a state of amazement, perplexity *19-, local*.
[eME]
maze *see* MAISE
me *see* I, MY
mea *see* MAE[1]
meack *see* MAK
meaddie, meadow *see* MEEDOW
meal[1] **&c** *la16-*, **mele &c, male &c** *la15-e20*
[mil; *Sh-Mry nEC Wgt Uls* mel] *n* meal; *specif*
oatmeal as distinct from other kinds, which
have defining terms *la14-*.
vi **1** *of grain* yield or turn into meal *la18-e20*. **2**
vt add meal to (soup etc) *19-, chf N*.
~ie &c 1 = mealy *17-*. **2** *of soil* friable *20-,
local*. **~ie bag, ~ie poke** a beggar's bag for
holding alms given in oatmeal *17-e19*.
~-creeshie &c, meal-a-crushie &c oatmeal
fried in fat *la19-, WC Wgt Uls*. **~ie drink** a
drink of water into which oatmeal has been
sprinkled *20-, Ork Abd Per*. **~ie dumpling** a
round *pudding* (PUDDIN) of oatmeal and fat with
seasoning, boiled or steamed *la20-*. **~ie pudding** a sausage-shaped version of prec, a *white
pudding* (WHITE[1]) *20-*.
~ ark a chest for storing oatmeal *16-*, *now C
Uls*. **~ bowie** a barrel for storing oatmeal *19-,
NE*. **~('s) corn** grain in general; food, sustenance *la16-, chf Sh-NE*. **~ kail** BROTH made
with oatmeal and KAIL *18-19*. **~ kist** = **~ ark**,
la16-. **~maker** a person who prepares and
deals in meal *la15-18*. **~man** a dealer in meal
15-17. **~ mob** a riotous crowd protesting
about shortage and high price of oatmeal

la18-e19, chf N. **M~ Monday** a Monday holiday in the Universities of St Andrews, Edinburgh and Glasgow (see SND) *la19-20.* **~-monger** a dealer in meal *la17-19.* **~ pock &c** a bag for holding oatmeal *la16-,* now *Sh-Ags Gall.* **~ seed &c** the husk of a grain of oats, used for making sowANS *19-, Sh-Fif.* **~ an ale &c** the traditional dish (also containing WHISKY) at harvest-home celebrations; the celebration itself *la19-, NE-Per.* **~ an bree** = BROSE *la18-,* now *Uls.* **~ an kail** = **~** *kail, la17-19, NE.* **~ and maut** *see* MAUT. **~ an thrammel** meal stirred up with water or ale, taken as a snack *la18-e19, NE.*

meal² **&c** *la17-,* **male &c** *16-e20* [mil; *Bnf nEC, WC-S* mel] *n* **1** = meal, a repast *la15-.* **2** a single milking of a cow or cows *la17-e20.* **~ o' meat** = *n* 1, *la17-, chf SW, S.* [see DOST, SND]

meal *see* MAIL¹, MAIL³

meall, mealock *see* MUILD¹

mealtit *see* MELTITH

mean¹ **&c** *la16-,* **mene &c** *la14-e19;* **main &c** *17 adj* **1** = mean, common; inferior *16-.* **2** *esp of farm-land and facilities shared by several tenants* possessed jointly or in common, joint- *la16-e20.* **3** *of an animal* in poor condition, thin *la19-,* now *Ags Uls.* **in ~(is)** in common, as a joint possession or undertaking *la16-17.*

mean² **&c** *la15-,* **mene &c** *14-18 n* **1** = mean *14-.* **2** *in sing* (1) a means; an instrument; an opportunity *la14-19;* (2) resources, possessions, means of support *la16-19.* **mak a ~** make an attempt *la16-,* now *Sh.* [*cf* MOYEN¹]

mean³ **&c** *la16-,* **mene &c** *la14-e20 vt, pt, ptp* **~it &c** *15-e17,* **~ed &c** *la16-e19,* **ment &c** *15-16* **1** = mean *la14-.* **2** convey in words, declare, say *la14-18.*

mean *see* MAIN, MANE¹

meantime &c *la16-,* **mene time &c** *la14-e17;* **maintime &c** *16-la19,* **myntime &c** *16 n* = meantime *la14-.* *adv* **1** = meanwhile *la16-.* **2** for the time being, at present *la20-.* **in the ~** = *adv, la14-.* **in the ~ of** during *la14-e17.* **(in) the ~ that** while *15-16.* **in the mids &c of the ~** *local NE-Dmf,* **the ~** *la19-, Sh Cai Per* = *adv* 2. **the ~, all this** *or* **that ~** = *adv* 1, *la14-e15.*

mear &c *la16-,* **mere &c** *15-e20,* **mare &c** *la15-* [mir; *nEC* mer] *n* **1** = mare, a female horse *15-, freq proverb.* **2** a wooden frame (1) on which wrongdoers were made to 'ride' as a public punishment *17;* (2) used as a trestle to support scaffolding *la17-,* now *NE.* **3** a bricklayer's hod *la16-19, C.* **~ie &c** = *n* 1, *la17-e20.* **Tamson's ~** Shanks' pony, on foot *la19-, Abd EC, WC.*

mearing &c, mering &c ['mirɪŋ] *n* a strip of uncultivated land, *usu* marking a boundary, a BAUK¹ *la16-e20, N.* [eModEng *mearing,* ME *mere,* OE *gemǣre* boundary; *cf* LANIMER]

mease &c *la16-e19,* **mese &c** [*miz, *mez] *vt* **1** pacify, assuage (1) (a person) *la15-e18;* (2) (some emotion, passion or sorrow) *la15-e19.* **2** pacify, make calm (1) (strife, tumult etc) *la15-e17;* (2) (the elements, weather etc) *16.* **3** quench (a fire), cool down (something hot) *la14-16.* **4** mitigate, allay (pain) *e16.* **mesing** pacifying, setting at rest *15-e16.* [northern and n midl ME *mere,* aphetic f AMEISE]

measer *see* MACER

measinger *see* MESSENGER

measis *see* MACIS

measle *see* MAISLE

meason *see* MASON

measse *see* MACE

measser *see* MACER

meassis *see* MACIS

measure &c, mesure &c *la14-e17,* **missour &c** *16-17, only Sc;* **mussour &c** *16, only Sc,* **mizzer &c** *20-, Sh Abd, only Sc* ['mɪzər, 'mɪʒər; *mɛ'zør, *-'zur, &c] *n, vti* = measure *la14-.* **be &c ~** by measuring (out), as determined by measurement *15-17.* **tak** *or* **do missour &c** ? make necessary arrangements, take necessary steps *la16.*

meat &c *la16-,* **mete &c;** **mait &c** *la16-* [mit; *Sh-nEC Uls* met] *n* **1** food *in gen,* for men or animals *la14-.* **2** = meat, flesh as food *la15-.* **3** produce, animal or cereal, while still alive or growing *16-17.* **4** livelihood, living *la14-17.* *v* **1** *vt* provide food for, feed *la16-,* now *Sh-nEC.* **2** *vi* eat a meal, receive one's meals *la16-,* now *Sh Abd.* **~rife &c** having a plentiful food supply *19-e20, chf S.* **~ almery &c** a food cupboard *la15-e17.* **~ burde &c** a dining-table *15-e17.* **~-butter** better quality butter, used for food *la16-18, Ork Ags.* **~-fisch &c** freshly-caught fish, as opposed to barrelled or salted fish *16-17, chf N.* **~-hail &c** having a healthy appetite *la18-,* now *Sh NE Fif.* **a good** *etc* **~ house** a house where there is always plenty of good food *18-, Gen except Sh Ork.* **~-like and claith-like** well-fed and -dressed *la17-,* now *Sh Ags.* **~ scheip** *etc* a sheep etc intended to be slaughtered for food, not grown for wool *16-17.* **~ tea** *high tea* (HEICH), tea with a cooked dish *20-, WC.* **ae coo's ~** enough land to grow food for one cow *20-, Sh-Fif.* **hae one's ~ and one's mense baith &c** said when one's hospitality has been refused, so that one has the credit of hospitality without any expenditure of food *17-19.* **like one's ~** plump, well-nourished in appearance *la17-.*

meater *see* MAITTER

meath *see* MEITH

meble see MOBILL

mec(h)anic(k) &c *adj, n* **1** = mechanic *16-*. **2** *of a person* that performs manual labour or belongs to the class of artisans *e16*.

med see MAK

medal &c *la17-*, **medalʒie** &c *la16* [ˈmɛdl, *məˈdeljɪ] *n* **1** = medal *la16-*. **2** *golf* a medallion given as a prize in a competition, the scoring being by the total number of strokes, not the number of holes won in a round, *chf* ~ **competition**, ~ **play** *la19-*; cf *match play* (MATCH).

medcinare see MEDICINER

meddill see MIDDLE¹, MIDDLE²

meddle see MIDDLE¹

med(d)um &c *n* some white substance, ? starch *la16-e17*. [perh connected w SMEDDUM]

mede see MEID

medecinare see MEDICINER

medhop &c; **medop(e)** *n* meaning obscure *la16-e17*. [see DOST]

mediat¹ &c *adj, n* **1** = mediate *la16-17*. **2** *of a person* intermediary, intervening; that acts for another *16-17*. **3** *of an heir* not lineal, collateral *la15-16*.

mediat² &c *adv* = IMMEDIAT *15-16*. [aphetic]

medicinary &c [*mɛˈdɪsɪnərɪ, *ˈmɛdsɪn-] *n* the art or practice of medicine *16*. [only Sc; *cf* eModEng *medicinary* (*adj*) curative]

medicine [*ˈmɛdɪsəɪn, *-sɪn] *n* **1** = medicine, healing, medicament *la14-*. **2** *transf and fig* (1) a spiritual remedy *la15-16*; (2) a remedy or cure for anything *15-e17*.

mediciner &c *la15-e19*, **medicinare** &c *la14-17*; **med(e)cinare** &c *la14-e17* [*mɛˈdɪsɪnər, *-ɪr; *ˈmɛdsɪn-, *ˈmɛtsən-] *n* **1** a physician, practitioner of medicine *la14-17*. **2** title of the Professor of Medicine at King's College, Aberdeen *la16-e19*. [eModEng (once); *cf* OF *medecineur*]

medick; methick [ˈmidɪk, ˈmið-] *n* the dandelion *20-*, *Bnf*. [transf of Eng *medick* a plant of the genus *Medicago*, esp lucerne]

medie [*ˈmidɪ] *n* an error in Latin translation less serious than a MAXIE, with a lesser penalty *la19-e20*, *Abd*. [abbrev dim of L *medius error*]

Mediterrane &c [*mɛdɪtɛˈren, *mɛdɪˈtɛrən] *adj* Mediterranean *15-e17*. [L *mediterrāneus*; *cf* eModEng]

medling see MIDDLIN

medop(e) see MEDHOP

medow see MEEDOW

medum see MEDDUM

medwyfe; meidwif &c *la15-e17*, **maidwyfe** &c *16* [*ˈmidˈwəif, *ˈmed-] *n* = midwife *la14-17*.

meechie &c [ˈmixɪ] *adj* mean, stingy *20-*, *local N-WC*. [see SND]

meed see MAK

meedow &c *la19-*, **medow** &c *la14-17*; **meadow** &c *la17-*, **meaddie** &c *la19-*, *chf EC*, **mödow** &c *20-*, *Sh* [ˈmidə, *C* -ɪ; *Sh* ˈmɪdu;

C also ˈmɛdɪ] *n* **1** = (a) meadow *la14-*, *in place-names la12-*. **2** marshy grassland where the natural coarse grasses are often cut for hay ?*16-*.

meef see MUITH

meelackie see MUILD¹

meelie see MUILD²

meen see MUNE

meenie; minnie *n* a fine awl *20-*, *Cai Ross*. [Gael *minidh* an awl]

meenit see MINUTE

meer see MUIR

meer-swine *18-e19*, **mereswyne** &c; **mer-** *15-16* [*ˈmirˈswəin, *ˈmer-, *ˈmɛr-] *n* a dolphin; a porpoise *15-e19*. [ME *mersuine*, OE *mereswīn* (*lit*) sea-swine]

meeschle see MASCHLE

meese *vi* = muse *e20*, *NE*.

meeser see MISERT

meeserable &c *17-*, *now local*, **miserable, miserabill** &c *la15-17* [ˈmizərəbl] *adj* **1** = miserable *la15-*. **2** wretchedly poor, poverty-stricken *la15-17*. **3** mean, stingy, miserly *la19-*.

meesery *la19-*, *now Sh Ork Per*, **miserie** &c *la15-e17*; **meserie** &c *16-17* [ˈmizərɪ] *n* = misery.

meesick see MUSIC

meet¹ &c *la16-*, **mete** &c *la14-e17* *adj, adv* **1** well-fitting, of the right dimensions *la14-e19*. **2** = meet *15-*.

meet² &c *17-*, **mete** &c *la14-17* *vti, pt, ptp* **met** &c; **meit** &c *la14-e17* [mɛt] **1** = meet *la14-*. **2** *vt, transf* (1) respond to, offer a rejoinder to *15-e17*; (2) combat, counter (something nonmaterial) *16*; (3) *law* provide an adequate answer to (contrary allegations etc) *la16-e17*. **3** *vi, of a group meeting by arrangement* assemble, convene *la14-*. **4** *of non-material things or events* unite; occur or exist simultaneously *16-*.

~**ing 1** = meeting *la14-*. **2** the action of meeting (a person) *la15-16*. **3** the action of engaging (an enemy) in battle; a fight *la14-16*.

~ **in** *wi* meet (a person) *19-*.

meeth see MUITH

meeve see MUVE

meffin &c *n* the act of warming oneself at the fire by sitting in front of it with the legs apart *20-*, *Ags Per*. [obscure]

meg see MAIG

Meg &c; **Mag** &c *la17-19*, *chf N n* **1** a rather unsophisticated girl, *esp* a rough country girl *16-e20*. **2** applied to a large cannon, *appar* = *Mons Meg* (MONS) *la16-e17*.

maggie &c *17-*, **meggie** *19-* = *n* 1.
~**gie(-lickie)-spinnie** a spider *19-*, *N*. ~(**gie**) (**o** *or* **wi the**) **mony feet** the centipede *la18-*. ~(**gie**) **Mulloch** &c a familiar spirit traditionally associated with the Grants of Tullochgorum in Strathspey *la17-*, *chf Mry Bnf*. **Maggie Robb** &c **1** a counterfeit halfpenny *e18*, *N*. **2** a scolding shrewish woman *19-e20*.

M~'s hole a rift in the sky to the south-west, foretelling clearer weather *20-, now Lnk Ayr.* [pet forms of the name *Margaret*]

megir [*'migər] *adj* = meagre, thin *e16, only Sc.*

megrim &c *la17-,* **magrame &c** *16* ['migrəm, *'meg-, *'mɪg-] *n* **1** = megrim, migraine, severe headache *16-19.* **2** a whim, preposterous notion *19-, local Per-Uls.*

megstie &c; mexty &c *interj* expressing surprise, distress or disapproval, *chf* ~ **me** *19-, Gen except Sh Ork.* [altered f MIGHTY]

meichie *see* MUITH

meid &c, mede [*mid] *n* **1** = meed, reward for merit *la14-16.* **2** the quality of deserving well, merit, worth *la14-18.* **3** assistance, support *15-e17.*

meid *see* MEITH, MID, MUID

meidwif *see* MEDWYFE

meikalow *see* MACALIVE

meikle *see* MUCKLE

meild *see* MUILD[1]

meill *see* MELL[2]

meintene *see* MANTEEN

meinȝe *see* MENYIE

meir *see* MAIR[1]

meis *see* MESS[1]

meit *see* MEET[2]

meith &c, **methe; meath &c** *la16-19,* **mithe &c** *la16-17, NE-Fif,* **meid &c** *Sh* [mið; *Sh* mi:d; *n pl* miz; *Cai sing also* miz; *chf v* *maɪð] *freq coupled with synonyms, esp* MARCH *n* **1** a boundary marker *la15-, now Sh Rox.* **2** *chf in pl with sing sense* a boundary *15-, now Sh Rox.* **3** (1) a point of reference, indication, guide *16-e19.* (2) a distinguishing feature, a distinctive mark *la18-e20.* **4** a sea-mark: (1) a marker in the water *la16-17*; (2) a landmark used by sailors to steer by *18-.* **5** a turning-post; a terminus; a course *e16* [translating L *mēta*]. *vt* settle and/or mark the boundaries of (a piece of land) *la15-18.* [only Sc; ON *mið* a fishing-bank marked by landmarks, *miða* mark the position of something; *cf* MYTH]

meith *see* MAITHE

mek *see* MAK

mekill *see* MUCKLE

melder &c; meller &c *e19,* **maillyer** *20-, NE* ['mɛl(d)ər; *NE also* 'mɛljər] *n* **1** the quantity of one person's corn taken to the mill to be ground at one time *la17-, now NE.* **2** the occasion of such a grinding *la18-, now Bnf.* **3** the meal ground from the corn which formed part of a farm-servant's wages *19.*

~ing &c the meal produced in a MELDER *la18-e20.*

(salt) ~ meal mixed with salt, sprinkled over sacrifices *e16* [translating L *mola (salsa)*]. [laME (once) *meltyre*, ON *meldr* flour or corn in the mill]

meldrop &c *n* (a drop of) mucus from the nose *la15-e20, latterly Rox.* [ME (once) *maldrope*; OE *mǣldropa* phlegm, ON *mél-dropi* foam from a horse's mouth, f *mél* snaffle-bit + *dropi* drop]

mele[1] **&c** *n* a measure of dry goods *la12-17.* [ON *mælir* a measure]

mele[2] **&c** *vti* speak, tell *la14-15.* [OE *mǣlan*, ON *mæla; cf* MELL[3]]

mele *see* MEAL[1]

melg *n* the milt of a male fish *la16, Inv, 19-, NE.* [Gael *mealg*; Scand]

melgs *n* the plant the white goosefoot *19-e20, Nai Mry.* [see SND]

meliorate *18-e19,* **meliorat** *la16-17 vt, law, chf of a tenant* make improvements on (the buildings, land etc occupied), *chf* **meliorat(ed)** *la16-e19.*

melioration &c 1 an improvement made by a tenant on the property rented *la16-e19.* **2** *chf in pl* the allowance made for such improvements on the termination of the lease *17-19.* [eModEng *meliorate*, laL *meliōrāt-*, ultimately f *melior* better]

mell[1] **&c** *vti* **1** mix, mingle, blend *la14-, now local.* **2** *vi* mingle, come together (1) in combat *la14-e19*; (2) *transf* in a *flyting* (FLYTE) *la16.* **3** associate, have dealings **with** *16-, now Sh Ags.* **4** concern or busy oneself improperly or intrusively (*chf* **with** an affair, action; goods, property; a person) *la14-, now Sh Kcb Slk.* **5** have sexual intercourse (**with**) *la14-e17.*

milled &c [*mɪld, mɪlt] *of a ewe* mated to a ram of a different breed *la19-, now Cai Slk.* [ME *mell*, OF *meller*, var of *mesler*]

mell[2] **&c;** **maill &c** *la16-20,* **meill &c** *la16-e19,* **mall &c** *19-e20* [mɛl; *Sh* mal] *n* **1** = maul, a heavy hammer; a club *15-.* **2** the mallet awarded to the last in a race etc *la17-e19.* **3** a heavy blow, as given by a large hammer *la17-e20.* **4** a clenched fist *la19.* *vt* **1** strike with a heavy hammer *18-, now local Per-Kcb.* **2** strike as with a heavy hammer, thrash; trounce *la18-, now local Abd S.*

~-heid 1 a blunt-shaped head; a stupid person, blockhead *20-, Rox.* **2** **~-heidit** hammer-headed; stupid *16-, now Rox.*

cast the ~ assign the stations in *halve-net* (HALF[2]) fishing *la20-, SW.* **keep (the)** ~ **in (the) shaft** keep in a good state of order, health or prosperity *19.*

mell[3] *vi* speak, converse *15-16.* [n, midlME *mell(e)*, OE *meðlan; cf* MELE[2]]

mell *see* MAIL[1]

mellay[1] **&c; mella** [*'mɛlɪ] *n, adj* (a cloth) of a mixed weave or mixture of colours *16-17.* [ME *melle, melly*, f as MELLÉ]

mellay[2] [*'mɛlɪ] *vi* mingle in combat, fight *e15.* [only Sc; f MELLÉ]

mellé; mellie &c [*'mɛ·li, *'mɛlɪ] *n* **1** fighting, *esp* close combat *la14-16.* **2** a battle or engagement, *esp* one involving *n* 1, *la14-e16.* **3** a close combat between individuals *la14-16*. **4** a closely-packed mass of men fighting *la15-e16*. [n midlME (twice), OF *mellée*]

meller *see* MELDER

mellie *see* MELLÉ

mellifluat &c [*mɛ'lɪfluat, *-et] *adj, verse, chf fig* flowing with honey, mellifluous *la15-e16*. [only Sc; L *mellifluus*]

melmot &c *19*, **melmet** *e17 n* juniper *Nai Mry*. [obscure]

melody &c *n* **1** = (a) melody *la14-*. **2** rejoicing, joy *15-e16*.

melt *n* **1** = milt, the spleen (*la15-*, *now local*); the milt of a male fish (*16-*). **2** the tongue *la19-20*. *vt* fell (a person or animal) with a blow near the spleen; thrash *la16-*, *now Fif WC*.

meltith &c,   **melteth &c**;   **meltat &c** *la16-e19*, **mealtit &c** *17-e19* [*'mɛltɪð, *-tɪθ, *-tɪt, &c] *n* **1** a meal, repast *16-20*. **2** a single milking; the quantity of milk from such *la16-e19*. [only Sc; eModEng *meal tyde*, ME *mel tid*, f OE *mǣl* mealtime + *tīd* time; *cf* laON *máltíð* and MEAL²]

melvie &c *vt* coat (clothes) with a film of meal or flour *la18-e19*. [ultimately f OE *melu* meal]

mel3e *see* MAIL3E¹

mel3ie *see* MAIL3E²

mem *n, vt* = ma'am, madame *19-20*.

member *n* **1** = a member *15-*. **2** an agent or 'limb' of Satan *la14-16*.

memorance &c [*'mɛmorans] *n* memory, remembrance *la15-17*. [ME (once), as if f L *memorantia*, f *memorāre* bring to remembrance, *memorāri* remember]

memorandum &c *n* **1** = memorandum *la15-*. **2** a memento, souvenir *la19-20*.

memorative &c *adj* mindful *e16*. [only Sc; *cf* late ME = commemorative]

memore &c [*mɛ'mor, *also* *mɛ'mur; *'mɛmor] *n* **1** = memory *la14-16*. **2** the mental faculty, (one's) mind or wits *15-e16*. **3** the fact or state of being remembered (*esp* after one's death), *chf* in ~ *la14-16*. **of gude** ~ of happy or blessed memory *la14-16*. **past** ~ **of man** from time immemorial *la15-16*. [ME *memore*, OF *memoire*, L *memoria*; *cf* MEMORY]

memorial &c *n* **1** = memorial *15-*. **2** posthumous reputation, fame *la15-17*. **3** (1) a record, chronicle, report *15-16*. (2) a memorandum of instructions or proposals *16-17*. (3) a register, inventory *la16-17*. **4** *law* (1) a statement of facts submitted to the *Lord Ordinary* (LORD) as a preliminary to a hearing *18-19*; (2) a document prepared by a solicitor for counsel, giving certain facts and circumstances and indicating the question on which counsel's opinion is sought *la18-*.

memory &c ['mɛmorɪ, *mɛ'morɪ] *n* = memory *la14-*.

past ~ **of man** from time immemorial *la16-17*. **put in** ~ to record in writing *la15-16*. [*cf* MEMORE]

men *see* MAN

menage &c; **menodge &c** [mə'nadʒ, -'nadʒ] *n* a kind of savings club to which each member contributes a fixed sum weekly for a stated period *19-*, *C, S*; see SND. [F *ménage* housekeeping; thrift, economy]

mence *see* MENSE¹

mend &c *vti* **1** = mend *la14-*. **2** *vtr* reform, improve (a person, his character or habits, either oneself or another) *la14-*, *now local*. **3** *vi* reform oneself *la15-*. **4** *vt* emend, correct (a writing; verse etc) *15-17*. **5** (1) restore to health, heal *la14-e20*. (2) *vi*, ~ **of** recover from (an illness) *la15-*. (3) *of a wound, disease etc* get better *16-*. **6** *vti, in negative and interrog, freq impersonal* avail; profit, advantage (a person) *la15-16*, *only Sc*. **7** improve in quality, ameliorate *la14-e16*. **8** *vti* fatten, (cause to) grow plump *19-*, *now Kcb Uls*.

mending &c **1** = mending *la14-*. **2** amends, redress *15-16*, *only Sc*. **there's no ane o them to** ~ **anither** they're all equally bad *19-*, *C, S*.

mendiment *see* MENIMENT

mendis *see* MENDS

mendment *see* MENIMENT

mends &c *la16-*, **mendis &c** *15-17*; **mens(e) &c** *la16-* [mɛnz; *also* mɛndz] *n* **1** compensation, reparation; atonement *15-*. **2** a *or* ane ~ [by analysis of *amendis* (AMENDS)] = prec *15-*. **3** *also fig* healing, a remedy *la15-e17*, *only Sc*. **4** improvement, betterment (in morals or fortune) *la15-e17*. **get** *or* **hae** (a *or* the) ~ **of** get satisfaction from *16-e20*. **get a seing** ~ **of** see oneself revenged on *17*. **mak** (a) ~ **of** make recompense for *15-e16*. **to the** ~ to boot, as an extra *17-e19*, *only Sc*. [ME *mendes*; aphetic f AMENDS]

mene &c [*min] *n* = mien, bearing *e16*. [aphetic f laME *demene*; *cf* eModEng *meane &c*]

mene *see* MANE¹, MEAN¹, MEAN², MEAN³

mene time *see* MEANTIME

meng *see* MING¹

mengyie *see* MENYIE

meniment &c *19-e20*, **mendment** *15*; **mendiment** [*'mɛn(d)ɪmənt] *n* = mendment, amendment *15-e20*. [for trisyllabic pronunciation *cf* ME, OF *mendement*]

mening &c [*'minɪŋ] *n* = minning, a peal of bells rung to commemorate a departed soul *e16*. [see DOST]

mennent *see* MINNON

menner *see* MAINNER

menodge *see* MENAGE

menorité *see* MINOR

menoun *see* MINNON

mens *see* MENDS

mensal &c *adj* applied to a church or benefice the revenues of which were appropriated to the bishopric, ? *orig* for the maintenance of the bishop's table *la17-18, hist.* [only Sc and Ir; *cf* laME *mensal* table-, laL *mensālis*, f *mensa* table]

menschot *see* MAIN(S)CHOTT

mense[1] **&c; mence** *n* **1** honour, credit *15-*, now *SW, S.* **2** dignity; moderation; courtesy, hospitality *18-*, now *sEC, SW, S.* **3** something which brings credit or honour to one *19-*, *chf SW, S.* **4** a reward, prize *e19.* **5** common sense, intelligence *18-*, *Gen except Sh Ork.*

vt do honour to; grace, adorn; honour with one's presence *16-*, now *SW.*

~ful &c 1 *of persons* good-mannered, polite; sensible *la16-*, now *N, SW, S.* **2** *of things* seemly, proper *19-e20.* **~less 1** unmannerly, objectionable in behaviour *la15-.* **2** greedy, grasping *18-*, now *Kcb.* **3** stupid, foolish *19-*, now *Bnf EC, S.* **4** *of prices etc* inordinate, extortionate *la18-e20.*

gie a garment kirk *or* **Sunday ~** wear something for the first time at church on Sunday *20-*, *Bwk SW, S.* [later var of MENSK]

mense[2] **&c** *n* a great amount, large quantity *la19-*, now *Sh Uls.* [aphetic f Eng *immense*]

mense *see* MENDS

mensk *n, vt* honour, credit, reverence *la14-16.* [ME *mensk, mensca,* ON *mennska; cf* MENSE[1]]

menstral &c *la14-19*, **minstral &c** *14-16*; **minstrel** *la15- n* = minstrel, an entertainer *14-16*; *specif* a musician *15-*.

~(l)er = prec *la16-e17, only Sc.* **~(l)ing** *la16-e17, only Sc,* **~(l)y &c** *la14-e17, only Sc* minstrelsy, musical entertainment.

the commoun ~ the public musician (of a BURGH) *16-e17.*

ment *see* MEAN[3]

mentain *see* MANTEEN

mentenance *see* MAINTENANCE

mentenant &c *n* a person who is under the protection of another as his vassal or dependant *16-17.* [back-formation f MAINTENANCE]

mentene *see* MANTEEN

mention &c, mentioun &c *la14-16 n* **1** = mention *la14-.* **2** a trifle, trace, particle *20-*, *Sh Ork Uls.*

vt = mention *16-.*

mentionat &c *ptp, adj* mentioned, designated, *freq* **abuve ~, before ~, after ~** *etc, 16-e18.*

vt specify, designate *la16-17.* [eModEng *mentionate,* MedL *mentionat-,* ptp stem of *mentionare* > MENTION *v*]

mento &c *n* **in** *or* **out of someone's ~** under or free from obligation to someone *19-e20, NE.* [see SND]

menwt *see* MINUTE

menyie &c, menȝe &c *la14-16*; **mengyie &c, meinȝe &c** *15-16* ['menȝ(j)ɪ, 'mɪŋ(j)ɪ, 'menjɪ, *'menzɪ] *n* **1** a family, household *la14-19.* **2** a tribe, race, nation *la15-e16, only Sc.* **3** (1) a retinue, suite of followers *la14-19.* (2) a body of troops *la14-e18.* **4** a crowd, multitude;

disparaging a rabble *la14-*, now *NE Edb.* **5** a large or heterogeneous collection of things *la18-e20, chf N.*

(a) few ~ a small party, few companions *la14-e16.* [ME (chf n) *menȝe,* (midl and s) *maine,* OF *meyné, mesnie,* ultimately f L *mansio* a dwelling]

menȝell *see* MINȜELL

menȝie *see* MAINȜIE

mer *see* MAR[1]

mercat &c, market &c [*C, S* 'merkət] *n* **1** = market *la14-.* **2** the Forum of Rome *15-e16.* **3** the action or business of buying and selling; a commercial transaction *la15-*, now *Kcb.* **4** *transf* the marriage market, *chf* **make (one's) ~** find a husband or wife, become engaged to be married *16-.* **5** a *fairing* (FAIR[1]) *la19-, N.*

~-cross &c, ~-cors &c *15-e16* a market cross *15-.* **~-gate 1** a market-street in a town *14-*, *chf in place-names.* **2** a high-road leading to a market-place *15-e17.* **~-like** fit for the market, marketable *la15-e16.* **~-met** measured (as) by the standard measures used in a public market *16.* **~ mixtures** an assortment of small hard sweets, commonly sold at markets *20-, Ags Fif.* **~-stance** the site where a market or fair is held *19-, Sh-Ags.* **~-steid &c** a market-place *16-17.* **in** *or* **to kirk and ~** in or to public places, in public, abroad *la15-17.* **mak ~** buy and sell, do business *la15-17.* **mak ~ of** offer for sale, sell *la15-17.*

merch *see* MAIRCH, MARCH, MERGH

Merch *see* MAIRCH

merchant &c, marchand &c *la14-19*; **maircheant &c** *la16-17* [*Sh NE* 'mertʃən; *C, S* 'mertʃ(ə)nt; 'mεr-] *n* **1** = merchant *la14-.* **2** a retail shopkeeper, *esp* of a grocery and general store *15-.* **3** an itinerant salesman, packman *la16-18.* **4** *freq attrib* a member of the GUILD of merchants of a BURGH *15-.* **5** a customer, buyer *19-*, now *NE.*

adj **1** = merchant, trading- *la16-.* **2** *of a commodity* that is bought or sold; that is fit for selling *16-e17.*

~rise = merchandise *la14-e17, only Sc.*

~-buthe &c a shop or stall kept by a MERCHANT (*n* 2), *16-17, only Sc.* **~-geir &c** merchandise *16-e17.* **~ gude &c** *or* **~ ware &c** *only Sc* **1** *also in pl* merchandise, marketable goods *15-17.* **2** satisfactory, good quality merchandise *la15-16.* **general ~** = *n* 2, *20-.* **his** *etc* **eye is his ~** *proverb,* approximating to L caveat emptor *la17-.* **meet wi one's ~** meet one's match *19-, C.*

Merchemount *see* MARCHMONT

merciment &c *n* **1** = mercement, a fine imposed by a court *15-17.* **2** the condition of being liable to a fine at the 'mercy' or discretion of a court or judge *15-17.* **3** the discretion, disposal, mercy (of a person *in gen*), *chf* **in someone's ~** at his mercy *la16-20.*

mercury, mercure *la16* [*mɛr'kør] *n* **1** = mercury *la16-*. **2** *also* **marcury &c** ['mark(ə)rɪ] a barometer *la19-*, *now NE*.

mercy &c; marcie &c *16-e17, only S n* **1** = mercy *la14-*. **2** *chf* **the mercies** liquor, *esp* WHISKY *19-, NE, WC*.

merdale *see* MARDLE²

mere *see* MEAR

mereit *see* MERITE

mere-swyne *see* MEER-SWINE

mergh *18-*, *now Sh*, **merch &c** *la14-e17*; **margh &c** *la16-18* [mɛrx, marx] *n* = marrow (of bones) *la14-*, *now Sh*.

merchie &c ['mɛrgɪ, -kɪ] *fig* full of substance, effective *la17*. **mergie, merky &c** = *n*, *la19-*, *Sh Ork*.

meriage *see* MAIRRIAGE

meridian &c *adj* (*n*) **1** = meridian *16-*. **2** a social mid-day drink, *esp* among business and professional men *la18-19*.

mering *see* MEARING

merite &c *la14-17*; **merit &c, mereit &c** *la15-e17* [*n* 'mɛrɪt; *mɛ'rəit, *-'rit; *'mɪrɪt, &c; *v* 'mɛrɪt, *-it] *n* **1** = merit *la14-*. **2** *in pl* the condition or fact of deserving well, of being entitled to reward or gratitude *la15-17*. **3** *pl and sing* the intrinsic rights and wrongs (of a matter) *16-e17*. *vt* = merit *16-*.

meritabill &c worthy of reward or praise *15-e16*. **~o(u)r &c** = meritory, *esp* serving to earn reward from God *la15-e16, only Sc*.

merk &c *la16-*, **mark &c; mairk** *la16-e17 n* **1** = mark, the unit of weight = ⅔ lb *15-e17*. **2** *sing, pl and collective* a money of account = ⅔ of the pound of currency concerned, *ie* when SCOTS, depreciating along with the rest of the currency, finally (*la17*) reaching 13⅓ pence of English currency, and continuing at that valuation as a money of account even after the official abolition of the SCOTS currency in 1707, *la14-*, *now only arch in legal use*. **3** the name of a coin of the value of *n* 2, *chf as* ~ **pece** *la16-17*. **4** *chf* **~land** a measure of land, *orig* valued at one MERK *la15-*, *now hist and in place-names*.

~is worth of land *etc* land etc assessed as yielding the specified number of MERKS in rent per annum *la14-e17, NE-nEC, SW, S*.

Ten M~ Court a municipal court dealing with small debts (up to ten MERKS), and with the recovery of servants' wages *18, Edb*. [ScL *marca* = *n* 2 (*la12*), *n* 4 (*e14*)]

merk *see* MARK, MIRK

merky *see* MERGH

merl, merle *n*, *chf verse* the blackbird, *freq* ~ **and mavis** *15-*. [eModEng, F *merle*]

merlin &c *n*, *erron* the blackbird *19*. [by confusion w MERL]

merlit *see* MARLED

merlʒeo(u)n &c; marlʒeoun &c [*'mɛrljun, *'marl-, &c] *n* = merlin, the falcon *la15-17*. [ME *merlioun*]

merour &c [*'mirur] *n* = mirror *la14-15*.

merrage *see* MAIRRIAGE

merrans &c *n* obstruction, impediment *la15-16*. [OF *marance* an affliction, fault, f *marer* (*v*), cognate w *mer* (MAR¹)]

merriage *see* MAIRRIAGE

merry &c *la16-*, **mery &c** *la14-18*; **mirrie &c** *15-17* ['mɛrɪ; *'mirɪ; *'mɪrɪ] *adj* = merry *la14-*.

~nes &c 1 = merriness, joyfulness *16*. **2** merrymaking; fun *la15-e17*.

~-begotten conceived out of wedlock, illegitimate *la18-*, *local*. **~-courant &c** a riotous revel; a sudden unceremonious dismissal *la19-*, *chf SW*. **~ dancers** the aurora borealis, northern lights *la17-*, *Sh-Ags*. **~-ma-tanzie &c** corrupted phrase found in the refrain of a children's ring game etc *19-*, *Gen except Sh Ork*. **~-meat** a meal to celebrate the birth of a child *19*; *cf blithemeat* (BLITHE).

merry *see* MAIRRY

mers &c *n*, *nautical* a round-top, top-castle *la15-e16*. [MDu *merse* the 'top' of a mast, *lit* a basket]

merse, mers &c *n* **1** *usu* **the M~** the district of Berwickshire lying between the Lammermuirs and the Tweed; *also* the whole of the county *la14-*. **2** flat alluvial land by a river or estuary, *specif* that bordering the Solway *16-*, *SW*. [only Sc; var of MERSK]

mersk &c *n* **1** *chf in pl* = MERSE 1, *13-14*. **2** = MERSE 2, *e16*. **3** marshland, a marsh *15-17, NE*. [only Sc; corresponding to ME *mersch*, OE *mersc* marsh; *cf* prec]

mer-swyne *see* MEER-SWINE

mert *see* MART²

merter *see* MAIRTYR

Merti-, Mertin- *see* MARTINMAS

mertrick *la15-e19*, **martrik &c** *15-17 n*, *pl and as collective* **~s**, **martrix** *15-e17* the pine-marten; its fur. [only Sc; MedL *martrix*, fem form coined from *martor*, but in Sc taken as a *pl*]

mervel &c, mervaill &c *la14-16 vti*, *n* = marvel *la14-19*.

~lous &c 1 = marvellous *15-19*. **2** *specif* marvellous on account of great size etc; very great, huge, tremendous *la15-e17*.

mery *see* MERRY

mes *see* MESS¹, MESS²

Mes; Mess [*unstressed* məs, mɪs] *n* = MAISTER¹ *n* 8 (1), *specif* of a clergyman *17-19*.

~ John *freq joc* name for a (*chf* Presbyterian) MINISTER, or for MINISTERS as a class *la17-19*. [shortened f MAISTER¹; *cf* eModEng *mas*]

meschant &c, mischant &c ['mɪʃən(t), mə'ʃant] *adj*, *of persons, their character and conduct* **1** wicked, bad *16-17*. **2** spiritless, feeble, worthless *16-17*.

~ly &c 1 wickedly; wrongfully *la16-e19*. **2** miserably; feebly, cowardly *la16-e17*. **~ness &c** (a) heinous villainy, wickedness *la16, e20*. [laME *myschaunt*, OF *mescheant*]

mese *see* MEASE
mesell *see* MISELL
meser *see* MACER
meserie *see* MEESERY
mesill *see* MAISLE
mesillis *see* MAISLE
mesingere *see* MESSENGER
mesmerise &c *vt* **1** = mesmerize. **2** surprise, astound, dumbfound *20-.*
meson *see* MASON
mess¹ &c *17-*, **mes** *15-e16*; **meis &c** *15-*, *now NE*, **mais &c** *la15-17* [mɛs; *mis; *mes] *n* **1** = mess, a serving of food *15-e17*. **2** *transf* a plate, platter, dish *16-17, only Sc*. **3** provision or supply of food for a person's or household's meals *la15-e17, only Sc*.
vt [mɛs; *NE* mis] measure out (a portion for a meal, an ingredient in cooking) *19-, chf NE*.
at (**the** *or* **one's**) ~ at a meal, at (one's) table *la15-16*. ~ **and mell** to interfere; mix *or* have dealings (**with**) *19*.
mess² &c *la14-e19*, **mes** *la14-e17* *n* = (the) mass, Eucharist.
Mess *see* MES
message &c *n* **1** = message *la14-*. **2** a person or party of persons conveying a communication; an envoy, embassage *la14-16*. **3** *in pl* purchases, one's shopping *20-*.
~ **boy** an errand-boy *la19-*.
go *etc* **a** ~ go an errand *la18-*. **go the** ~**s** do one's shopping *20-*. **mak** *or* **ma** (**a**) ~ carry out an errand, deliver a message *15*.
messan &c; messen *17-e18*, **messin** *la17-19* ['mɛsən] *n* **1** *also* ~ **dog** *or* ~ **tyke** *16-e20* (1) a small pet dog, a lapdog *la15-e18*. (2) *contemptuous* a cur, mongrel *la18-, chf C*. **2** contemptuous term for a person *18-, now local sEC-SW*. [only Sc; Sc and IrGael *measan* = 1 (1)]
messenger &c, **mes(s)ingere &c** *la14-17*; **measinger &c** *la15-16* *n* **1** = messenger *la14-*. **2** a messenger of the Scottish Crown; from before 1510 under the authority of the *Lord Lyon* (LORD), with the main function of executing summonses and letters of DILIGENCE *15-*.
~**y &c** the office of a MESSENGER 2, *16-18*.
~ **of** (*la16-e18*) *or* **at** (*la16-*) **arms** = *n* 2.
messer *see* MACER
messin *see* MESSAN
messingere *see* MESSENGER
mester *see* MAISTER¹
mesure *see* MEASURE
met &c *ptp, adj* measured *la14-e18*. [f Eng *mete* (*v*) or METT²; *cf* laME *mett*, ptp of *mete*]
met *see* MEET², METT¹, METT²
metal &c, **mettall &c** *n* **1** = metal *15-*. **2** *heraldry* either of the tinctures *or or* argent *la15*. **3** *in sing and pl* metallic ore, in the mine or before refinement *la15-17*. **4** *mining, chf in pl* the geological strata in which minerals occur *18-, now Fif*. **5** rock broken up and used in road-making *la18-*.

mete &c [*mit] *n* = METT¹ *15-18*. [rare in Eng; lengthened vowel f Eng *mete* (*v*)]
mete *see* MEAT, MEET¹, MEET²
meter *see* MAITTER
methe *see* MEITH
mether *see* MADDER
methery *see* MUNDHERI
methick *see* MEDICK
mett¹ &c, **met** *n* **1** measure, measurement; a standard or system of measurement (only of quantity or dimension, not weight; *cf* MEASURE) *la15-20*. **2** a unit of measurement of capacity; a specific quantity measured out in accordance with this *la15-*, *specif* (1) of herring *18*; (2) of coal *17-, Abd Ags*. **3** a standard instrument for measuring capacity *la15-e18*.
~**lume &c** = *n* 3, *16-e17*. ~**-stick** a stick cut to the exact length of the foot and sent to the shoemaker as a measure for fitting shoes *19*.
Sanct Nicholas ~ a duty on salt brought into Aberdeen, used for the upkeep of St Nicholas' Church *16, Abd*. [ME *met*, OE *gemet*; *cf* MET and next]
mett² &c, **met** *vt* = mete, measure as to quantity or dimension *15-e19*.
mettage &c 1 (1) the measuring of goods, *chf* by a *metter*, *16-e17*. (2) the duty payable for this *16-e17*. **2** the measuring of land, *chf* for the settling of boundaries *la16-17*. ~**er &c** *la15-18*, ~**ster &c** *la16-e19, only Sc* a person who measures, *chf* an official legally authorized to measure saleable goods or land. [short vowel ? f pt, ptp of *mete* (see MET (*ptp*)), or f METT¹]
mettall *see* METAL
mettick &c *n* a soft crab *19-e20, Abd*.
mettle &c *adj* spirited, mettlesome *la18-, now Abd C, S*. [eModEng, f Eng *mettle* (*n*) spirit]
meubles *see* MOBILL
meuche *see* MAICH
meuggle &c ['mjugl, 'mjʌgl] *vt* bespatter with dirt *20-, Cai*. [frequentative f Dan *møg*, Norw *myk*, ON *myki* muck, dung]
meuis *see* MOY¹
meuw *see* MAW¹
mewt &c *vi, of a cat* mew *17-e18*. [ME; imit]
mexty *see* MEGSTIE
Mey &c *la16-*, **May &c** [məi] *n* = May, the month *la14-*.
~**sie, maisie** ['məizɪ] the common wild primrose *la19-, Ags*.
~ **bird** the whimbrel *la18-, now Uls*. ~ **flood** a high tide occurring in May *la19-, chf Ork*. ~ **kow, ~ wedder** an animal paid for in May *la17, Gall*. ~ **play** *chf in pl* the entertainments etc of May Day or early May *la16-e17*. ~ **skin &c** the skin of a lamb which has ? died or ? been slaughtered in May *la15-17*. ~**-spink** = *Meysie*, *la19-, now Ags Per*.
as mim as a ~ **puddock** very demure and staid *la18-* [the frog is popularly supposed to remain silent from May till the end of summer].
mi *see* MY

miauve &c [mjɑ(v)] *v, n* = miaow *19-*, NE. [*cf*
MEWT]
mibby *see* MAYBE
mich &c *la15-e16, 20- (Highl)*, **much &c** *adj, n,*
adv = much.
　much aboot it much the same *la18-*. **not**
　make much of it show little improvement in
　an illness *20-*. [*cf* MUCKLE]
mice *see* MOUSE
Michael, Michell &c ['mɪxl] *n* **1** *only in comb*
= Michaelmas, 29 Sep *17-*. **2** a person of lowly
rank, a rustic *16-e20*. **3** *also* **mickey &c** *joc* (1)
a chamber-pot *la19-*, *Gen except Sh Ork Cai*. (2)
a privy *la19-*, *now C* [prob short for micturating
(pot)].
　~day Michaelmas day *17-e18*, *Abd*. ~ **Fair** a
　fair held in Oct at Aboyne *20-*, *Abd Ags*.
Michaelmas &c, **-mes &c** ['mɪxlməs;
*'mixl-] *n* = Michaelmas, 29 Sep *15-*.
　~ **(heid) court** = *heid court* (HEID) *la15-e19*.
　~ **moon** the harvest moon; the booty from
　Highland (HIELAND) and BORDER raids at this
　time of year *18-e19*.
michane *n* meaning unknown *e16*.
Michell *see* MICHAEL
michrach *see* MACHREACH
micht &c [mɪxt] *n* **1** = might *la14-*. **2** *in pl*
divine powers or influence *la14-e18*. [*cf*
MAUCHT]
micht *see* MAY
michty &c ['mɪxtɪ] *adj* **1** = mighty *la14-*. **2** disgraceful, scandalous *la19-*, *chf NE Ags*.
adv greatly, thoroughly, drastically *la19-*, *Ags*.
n **the Almighty** *la19-*, *now Sh Kcb*.
interj *also* ~ **be here,** ~ **me,** ~ **on's** *etc*, expressing surprise or exasperation, *la19-* [reduced f *God*
Almighty].
micken *n* the common spignel, meu *la18-*, N
nEC. [Gael *muilceann*]
mickey *see* MICHAEL
mickle *see* MUCKLE
mid &c; meid *16* [mɪd] *adj* **1** = mid *la14-*. **2**
situated midway up a building *16-17*. **3** of
medium size, quality or age *16-e17*. **4** equal in
amount *la14-16*.
n **1** the middle, midst *la19-*. **2** a lamb of middle
quality or growth *19-*.
　~-age(d) middle age(d) *la15-19*. **~-couple**
&c 1 a loop of cowhide or eelskin connecting
the hand-staff of a flail to the beater *17-*, *now*
Uls. **2** *law* a piece of evidence linking a claimant with the right claimed *la17-*. **~field &c 1**
= midfield *la15-*. **2** the centre division of an
army *16*. **~-finger** the middle finger *15-*, *now*
Sh Gall Uls. **~gate(s) &c** halfway *16-19*. ~
house 1 the central storey(s) of a building
16-e17. **2** the small middle room of a *but-and-
ben* (BUT) *la19-*, *Bnf Abd*. **~-impediment** *law*
any event happening between two others which
prevents the latter event from becoming effective *la18-*. **~-lentroun &c** the middle of Lent
15-e17. **~man** a mediator *la15-17*. **~nicht**

midnight *la14-*, *rare in Sh Ork S*. ~ **persoun &c**
a mediator; an intermediary *16-e17*. **~-place**
= ~ *house* 2, *la19-*, *now Abd*. **~-rig &c** = MIDS
5, *18-*, *local NE-Uls*. **~schip** the middle part of
a vessel *la15-16*. **~-superior** *law* a person who
holds an intermediate position of *superiority*
(SUPERIOR) in the occupancy of land between
an over-SUPERIOR and a VASSAL or series of VAS-
SALS *19-*. **~-superiority** such a holding *19-*.
in the ~ time in the meantime *15-17*.
midden &c, midding &c ['mɪdən; *'mid-] *n*
1 (1) a dunghill, compost heap, refuse heap
la14-. (2) a domestic ash-pit *e20*. (3) a dustbin
la20-, C. **2** a muddle, shambles, mess *20-*, *local*.
3 a dirty, slovenly person *19-*. **4** a gluttonous
person or animal *19-*, *NE Ags*.
vt heap into a dunghill *la16-e19*.
　~ **bree** the effluent from a midden *la20-*, NE.
　~ **cock** a barnyard cock *19-*, *now Kcb Uls*. ~
dub the pool of seepage from a dunghill
la18-e19, *chf SW*. ~ **dyke** a wall round a dunghill *la19-*. ~ **feals &c** turfs laid on a dunghill
to aid the maturing process *la17-*, *now Ork*. ~
flee a dung-fly *18-*, *now Per Rox*. ~ **fool &c** a
barnyard fowl *la17-e20*. ~ **heap** a domestic
ash-pit or refuse heap *la19-*, *Cai C*. ~ **heid** the
top of a MIDDEN; *fig* a person's home territory
la17-. ~ **hole** the hollowed-out foundation of
a dunghill *la18-*, *local Cai-SW*. ~ **mavis** *joc* a
female searcher of refuse heaps *la19-*. **~-raker**
a searcher of refuse heaps *la19-*, *now WC*.
~-stead &c the site of a MIDDEN; *fig* a stamping
ground *la16-*, *now local Sh-SW*. ~ **tap** = ~
heid, *la18-*, *now Ags*. ~ **weed** a kind of goosefoot, fat hen; knotgrass *19-*, *now Loth Rox*.
either (in) the moon &c or the ~ (in) one of
two extremes of mood or behaviour *20-*, C, S.
be (on her back) in the ~ *of the moon* be surrounded by a lunar bow, foretelling a storm
20-, NE. **craw on one's ain ~** be boastful in
one's own environment *19-*. **knacker's ~** a
mess, a shambles; a glutton *la20-*, C, S. **look** *or*
glower at the moon till one falls in the ~
be so lost in one's dreams that one loses touch
with reality and comes to grief *18-*. [ME *myd-
dyng*, ON *mykidyngja a muck heap; *cf* ODan
møgdynge]
midder *see* MITHER
middest *see* MIDS
middill *see* MIDDLE[1], MIDDLE[2]
midding *see* MIDDEN
middis *see* MIDS
middle[1] &c, middill &c *16-e17*, **meddill &c**
16-17; **meddle &c** *vti* **1** = meddle *16-*. **2** *vt*
interfere with, bother, harm *18-*, *local*. **3** *vti*
have to do or associate **with** *la16-*, *now local*
Bnf-Kcb. [ME *medle*; vowel ? f next]
middle[2] &c, middill &c *12-e17;* **meddill &c**
15-16 adj = middle *la14-*, *in place-names 12-*.
　~-erd &c the world, viewed as half-way
　between heaven and hell *16-19*.
middlin &c, midling &c; medling &c

16-e17 ['mɪdlɪn] *adj* **1** of medium size, stature or quality *15-*. **2** intermediate in position or rank *la15-16*. **3** fair, tolerable *19-*.
adv fairly, tolerably *19-*.
n pl goods of an intermediate sort *16-e18*: '*any coloured cloaths except midlings and fyne cinamons*'.
~ **way** the middle course, mean *la15*. [orig Sc; eModEng]

middrit &c *la16-e19*, **midred &c** *la15-e17*; **mitherit &c** *la18-19* [*'mɪdrɪt &c*; *'mɪð-*] *n* **1** the diaphragm, midriff *la15-e19*. **2** *in pl* the heart and skirt of a bullock *17-19*. [ME *miderede*, OE *midhriðre*]

midge &c, mige &c *la15-e18*; **mudge** *20-*, *Highl* ['mɪdʒ, *Sh Ork Arg also* 'mʌdʒ] *n* **1** = midge *la15-*. **2** a small insignificant person or animal *la18-*.
    midgeck &c *Abd*, **mudgeick &c** *Sh Ork*, **midgie** = *n* 1, *la19-*.

midge *see* MUDGE

midgie *n*, *in comb* (domestic) rubbish *la20-*, *local*: '*midgie men*'; '*midgie bin*'. [altered f MIDDEN *n* 1]

midling *see* MIDDLIN

midmest &c *adj* **1** = midmost *15-e17*. **2** second-best *la16-e17*.

midred *see* MIDDRIT

mids &c, middis &c *la14-17 n* **1** the middle, centre, midst, *freq* **in** (**the**) ~ *la14-*. **2** *also* **middest &c** *17* a middle course, compromise *la15-*, *now NE*. **3** a means to an end, an expedient *la16-e18*. **4** *logic* the grounds from which a conclusion follows *17*. **5** *ploughing* the dividing furrow between two ridges *18-*, *NE*; cf *mid-rig* (MID).
    a good ~ a compromise *18-e19*. **in the** ~ **of the meantime** meanwhile; at present *la19-*, *Abd*. [ME *middes*, OE *in, on middan* in sense 1; other senses only Sc]

mige *see* MIDGE

mignard *see* MINꝫARD

mik &c *n* a wedge for sighting a cannon *la15-16*. [ME (once) *mike* a crutch supporting a boom, MDu *micke, mic* a forked prop; *cf* MITCH]

mikill *see* MUCKLE

mildis *see* MYLES

mile; myll &c *15-17*, **mylne &c** *la16-17* [məil] *n, freq uninflected in pl after numerals etc* **1** = mile; *also* = a *Scots mile* (SCOTS) *la14-*. **2** *fig* a great distance *15-*.
    gae &c one's ~(**s**) go as far as one dares (in wild conduct) *20-*.

miles *see* MYLES

milk &c [mɪlk, mʌlk] *n* **1** = milk *la14-*. **2** an annual entertainment in a school, when the pupils presented a small gift or sum of money to the teacher and were given a treat of curds and cream etc *la17-e19*.
    v **1** *vt* = milk *la15-*. **2** add milk to (tea) *la20-*. **3** *vi, of a cow or ewe* yield milk (well, badly etc) *19-*, *local*.
    ~**ness &c 1** an animal's yield of milk *la16-18*.

2 the quantity of milk obtained; its products *la15-e20*. ~**y thrissle &c** the milk-thistle *20-*, *local Abd-S*.
    ~**-beal**(**in**) a whitlow *20-*, *SW Uls*. ~**-bowie** a wooden milk bucket *18-*, *now NE Ags Per*. ~**-boyne &c** a broad, shallow wooden vessel for holding milk *19-*, *C*. ~ **brose** oatmeal mixed with boiling milk *la19-*, *local Sh-Dmf*. ~ **broth** a dish made with barley and milk *19-*, *N*. ~ **cellar** a small room used as a dairy *la18-*, *Ork Abd*. ~ **cow &c** a milch cow *la15-*. ~ **ewe &c** a ewe in milk *16-17*. ~ **house** a dairy *18-*. ~ **meat** a dish of milk and meal or bread; BROTH made with skimmed milk *17-*, *now NE*. ~ **porridge &c** porridge boiled in milk *la16-*. ~ **soup** soup made with milk, *freq* including eggs or fish *la18-*, *chf N*. ~**-sye &c** *19-*, ~**-syth &c** *la16-e19*, **milsie &c** *la17-* ['mɪlk'sɑɪ, *&c*; 'mɪlsɪ, 'mʌlsɪ] a milk-strainer. ~ **wife** a wet nurse *16*.
    ~ **and breid** oatcakes (AIT) crumbled in milk *la18-*. ~ **and watter &c** bluish-white; a cloth of this colour *16*.

mill &c, miln &c *14-18*, *in place-names 13-*, **milve &c** *16-17*, *chf SW*; **mull &c** *19-* [mɪl; *Abd-Fif WC* mʌl; **'mɪl*(ə)n, **mɪlv*] *n* **1** = mill *14-*. **2** a threshing-mill *la18-e20*. **3** a snuff-box, *orig* incorporating a grinder *18-*. **4** a tin box or canister with a lid *19-*, *chf NE*.
    millart &c *16-*, **milnward &c** *la16-17*, **milware &c** *17* ['mɪlərt; *NE also* 'mʌl-; **'mɪlwart, *-wər, &c*; **'mɪlnward*] *n* = millward, a miller *16-*, *NE*. **millart('s) word** a secret password, supposedly current among millers, conferring supernatural powers *19*, *Bnf Abd*. **miller &c** *la15-*, **milnar &c** *14-e18 n* = miller *14-*. **miller's lift** an upward thrust with the handle of a crowbar, as in setting a millstone *la19-*, *now Cai Fif Ayr*. **droon** *etc* **the miller** add too much water to tea or WHISKY *la20-*.
    ~ **bannock** a large round oatmeal cake baked at a mill and given to mill-servants or poor people *17-e20*. ~ **bitch** a bag into which the miller secretly diverted some of a customer's meal *19*. ~ **caul**, ~ **call &c** a mill-dam *17-*. ~ **clap** the clapper of a mill *la16-e20*. ~ **close &c** the sluice of a mill *la16-e19*. ~ **coorse** the circular path trodden by the horses driving a threshing-mill *la20-*, *Ork Bnf Abd*. ~ **damheid &c** the embankment forming a mill-dam *la16-e18*. ~ **dozen** every thirteenth peck of grain milled, payable to the mill-owner *e17*. ~ **ee &c 1** = mill-eye, the opening through which meal comes from the millstones *la18-19*. **2** the profits of the mill *17*, *NE*. ~ **gang** the five- or six-sided building which formerly housed the driving apparatus of a horse-driven threshing-mill *la20-*, *Cai EC, S*. ~ **gault &c** a young pig or castrated boar paid to the miller by estate tenants *17-18*; cf ~ **swine**. ~ **graith &c** the equipment of a mill *16-18*. ~ **knave &c**

an undermiller *la14-e18.* ~ **lade &c**, ~**-lead**
&c a channel bringing water to a mill; a mill-
race *15-.* ~ **lavers** the beams to which the
horses driving a threshing-mill were harnessed
la19-, Ork NE. ~ **pick &c** a small tool for
roughening the surface of a millwheel *16-, now*
Ork. ~ **reek** a disease contracted by lead-
workers from poisonous fumes *la18-e19, C.*
~**-rind &c** [~-'rəin(d); *Abd also* 'mʌlrɪn] **1** =
mill-rind *la15-.* **2** a coin bearing an impression
apparently resembling a mill-rind *17.* ~**-ring**
the space between the millstones and the surrounding kerb; the meal remaining there *19.*
~**-rink** = ~ **gang**, *la20-, local Bnf-Dmf.* ~
seeds husks of corn with meal adhering to
them *19-, now Ork Kcb.* ~ **services** tasks connected with a mill performed by estate tenants
as part of their rent *17-18.* ~ **stead &c** the
ground and buildings comprising a mill *16-e19.*
~ **swine &c** a pig given as a due to the miller
la16-e19; cf ~ **gault.** ~ **toon &c** the buildings
comprising a mill; *freq* the adjacent farm or
hamlet *la15-, in place-names 13-.* ~ **trow &c** [~
'trʌu] the wooden conduit carrying water to a
mill-wheel *18.* ~ **wand** a spar pushed through
the central hole of a millstone to trundle it
along *18-e19.* ~ **yins** ['mɪl'jɪnz] factory workers *20-, Edb S.*
gang on like a tume ~ chatter on without
pause *20-, now Ags Per.* **throo the** ~ *n* an
ordeal, a searching examination *la19-, NE, SW*
Uls.

milled *see* MELL¹
millen *see* MUILD¹
miln, milnar, milnward, milve,
milware *see* MILL
milygant &c [*'mɪlɪgənt] *n, derog* ? a rascal,
scrounger *la15-16.*
mim &c *adj* prim, restrained in manner or behaviour, *esp* in a prudish or affected way *16-.*
adv in a mincing, prudish way *la18-.*
vi move or act in a prim, affected way *la19-e20.*
~**-moued &c** [~-'mu:d, -'mu:t, -'muθt] affectedly prim or demure in speaking or eating *18-.*
~**-spoken** prim or shy in speech, quiet-spoken
la19-. [imit of pursing the mouth; *cf* MIMP]
mimmerkin &c [*'mɪmərkɪn, *?'mɛm-] *n* a
dwarf, a dwarfish creature *e16.* [obscure]
mimp *vi* **1** speak or act affectedly *la19-, NE Kcb*
Rox. **2** eat with the mouth nearly closed *20-,*
Ork Kcb S. [*cf* MUMP and MIM]
min &c *adj* less, lesser, *only* **mare and (na)** ~
&c *la14-16.* [ME *minne*]
min *see* MAN, MUNE
minace *see* MANNACE
minch &c *la16-20;* **minsch &c** *16,* **mince**
la18- [mɪnʃ] *vti* **1** = mince *la16-.* **2** cut short,
diminish, remove a part (from) *16-e19.*
n minced meat *18-.*
~**e(d) collops** minced steak cooked with
oatmeal, onion, carrot etc *18-.* ~**ed &c pie 1** a

pie of finely-chopped meat *la17-19.* **2** a (fruit
etc) mincemeat pie *18-e19.* **minschie &c** a
crumb, morsel *la19-, Bnf Abd Ags.*
mince-pie = -ed *pie, 20-.*
mind &c; mine &c *la16-* [məin(d)] *n* **1** =
mind *la14-.* **2** a memory, recollection *19-, now*
Abd. **3** one's opinion, judgment *15-19.*
v **1** remember, recollect, call to mind: (1) *vt,*
la17-; (2) *vir* ~ **o, (up)on** *18-.* **2** *vt* remember
(a person) in a will, give (someone) a small gift
18-. **3** mention in one's prayers, pray for *la17-,*
now Sh Abd Ags. **4** remind (a person) (*chf*) **of..**
16-. **5** recall (one person) **to** (another) by conveying greetings *la17-.* **6** have in mind, intend,
desire *16-19.*
~**ing &c 1** a small gift made by way of remembrance, a token of goodwill *19-.* **2** a memory,
recollection *20-.* **that's weel** ~**it** what a good
thing that you etc remembered *18-.*
be *etc* **a mind tae** intend to *la18-, chf SW Uls.*
hae ~ (**o**) recall, have recollection (of) *15-.*
keep ~ (**o**) bear in mind, take heed (of) *la18-,*
local. **lose** ~ forget *20-, Sh-Ags Ayr.*
mine¹ &c; mind &c *la15-19* [məin; *məind] *n*
1 = mine *15-.* **2** *mining* a passageway or tunnel
running from the surface to a mine-working or
connecting one underground working with
another; a drift, level *17-.*
vti = mine *15-.*
mine² &c *possessive pronoun* = mine *la14-.*
mines [məinz] mine, my one(s) *17-* [*by analogy*
with yours, theirs].
~ **ain, own &c** my own *la15-17, 20-* (*Sh, NE).*
[*cf* MY].
mine *see* MIND
mineer &c [mɪ'nir] *vti* make a din; stupefy with
noise *la19-e20, NE.*
n an uproar, a noisy gathering, a tumult, a fuss
la19-, Bnf Abd Kcdn. [aphetic f DOMINEER]
minent *see* MINUTE
mines *see* MINE²
ming¹ &c, meng &c *vt* **1** mix, blend; mix up,
confuse *la14-19.* **2** *specif* mix (tar etc) for sheep-
shearing *19-e20, S.*
~**-mang** *v, n* muddle *la19-e20, C.*
ming² *n* a smell *20-, C, S.*
~**in** *adj* having a bad smell, stinking; very
drunk *la20-, local EC-Ayr.* [obscure]
minister &c ['mɪnɪstər] *n* **1** = minister *la14-.*
2 a clergyman, *esp* of the *Church of Scotland*
(CHURCH) *la16-.*
ministry &c 1 the profession of MINISTER, *esp* of
the *Church of Scotland,* *la16-.* **2** *collective* the MINIS-
TERS of the Church, the clergy *la16-.* **3** the MIN-
ISTER and ELDERS of a congregation as a court of
the Church; the *kirk session* (KIRK) *la16-e17.*
~**'s man** the manservant of a MINISTER, *freq*
also in country parishes performing the duties
of *church officer* (CHURCH) *19-20.*
ministrat &c *vti* = minister *16-e17.* [only Sc;
L *ministrāt,* ptp stem of *ministrāre*]
mink; munk *19-, Kcdn Fif n* **1** a noose, loop

19-, Cai NE. **2** *fig* an entanglement, snare; matrimony *la19-, Abd Ags.* **3** a cow's tether; a horse's halter *19-, local Bnf-Fif.*

~er a ragamuffin, vagrant; a gallows-bird *la20-, Abd Edb.* [Sc and IrGael *muince* a collar; *cf* Gael *muinghiall* a halter]

minnie &c *n* **1** *of persons* affectionate name for a mother *16-.* **2** *of animals* a mother, dam *la18-19, C, S.*

vtr, of a young animal run back to its mother; *of a shepherd* put (a lamb) to its mother *la18-e19.*

~'s bairn a mother's pet *18-, now Ags.* [northern eModEng; ? f baby language]

minnie *see* MEENIE

minnon &c, menoun &c; mennen(t) &c *19-e20, chf S* ['mɪnən, 'mɛnən(t)] *n* a minnow; any small freshwater fish *la14-, Gen except Sh Ork.* [only Sc; ? AF form of OE *myne* a small fish]

minnonette &c ['mɪnənɛt, 'min-] *n* = mignonette *la19-, Abd, Ags Wgt.*

minor, minour &c *16-17 n (adj) law* = minor, (a person) under 21 or (*now*) 18 years of age; *Sc law* a male over 14 or a female over 12 and under 18 or 21, *16-; cf* PUPIL.

~ity &c, menorité &c *16* the state of being a MINOR, *latterly freq* **~ity and lesion** (see LESION) *la15-.*

minsch *see* MINCH

minstral *see* MENSTRAL

mint &c *vti* **1** intend, attempt (to do), aim, aspire **at, to** *etc, la14-.* **2** *vt* plan, scheme, attempt (something) *19-, now Abd.* **3** *vi* (1) make a threatening movement, feint *15-, now NE;* (2) **~ to** make as if to draw (a weapon etc) *16-e19.* **4** *vt* brandish (a weapon), aim (a blow), threaten (a person) *la16-, now NE.* **5** insinuate, hint, suggest (1) *vt, 19-e20;* (2) *vi,* **~ at** *19-, now NE.* **6** mention, speak of, utter *la18-, now local Sh-Kcb.*

n **1** an attempt, effort, intention *la16-e20.* **2** a pretended blow, a feint *16-, now NE.* **3** a physical movement towards doing something *16-e17.* **ill-~ed** evil-intentioned *la19-, now Sh Ork.* [chf Sc (16-); ME]

minute &c, minut &c *la15-17,* **menwt &c** *la16-e17;* **meenit &c** *la19-,* **minent &c** *19-, local* ['minət, -ənt] *n* **1** = minute *la15-.* **2** *in a school* an interval or recreation time; *in a factory* a tea-break *la19-, NE Ags.* **3** *law* (1) a note of the judgments, acts, decrees etc of a court or judge or of the intentions of a party in a suit regarding matters of procedure *la16-.* (2) *in the Register of Sasines* (SASINE) *etc* a summary of the contents of a deed presented for registration, to be recorded in the *minute book, la18-.* (3) a memorandum setting out the heads of an agreement *la16-.*

vt = minute *la16-.*

~ book a systematically kept register of transactions, *esp* those of a notary or court *la16-.* **at**

the ~(heid &c) instantly, without hesitation *la19-.* **on the ~heid** punctually, 'on the dot' *20-.*

in a ~ readily, without a second thought *20-.* **a wee ~** a moment, a short space of time *20-.*

minuwae &c [*'mɪnəwe] *n* a minuet *la18-19.* [f pronunciation of F *menuet*]

minȝard &c; mignard [*'mɪnjard] *adj* dainty, mincing, effeminate *la16-17.* [F *mignard; cf* eModEng *migniard*]

minȝell &c, monȝeall &c *e16,* **menȝell &c** [*'mɪnjəl, *'mʌn-, *'min-, *'mʌnjl] *n* = monial, a mullion in a window *16-e17.* [ME *moynell &c,* OF *moinel, meigneaul*]

minȝeoun &c [*'mɪnjən] *n* = minion *la15-16.*

miracle &c; marakle &c *la14-16, la19- (Sh)* ['mɪrakl; *Sh* mə'rakl; *Ork* *'mirəkl] *n* = miracle *la14-.*

miraculous &c [mɪ'rak(j)ələs, mə'rakləs] *adj* **1** = miraculous *la16-.* **2** very drunk *la19-.* **3** clumsy, loutish *20-, Cai Abd.*

mird *vti* **1** meddle, have dealings or association **with**; sport, dally **with** *17-, chf NE.* **2** venture, dare (*chf* to do etc) *18-19, chf NE.* [*cf* MARDLE[1], MARDLE[2], MIDDLE[1]]

mire &c, myre &c *n* **1** = mire *la14-.* **2** a PEAT[1]-bog *16, la19- (Sh).*

~ drum the bittern *la19-e20.* **~ duck** the wild duck, the mallard *19-, local Abd Gall.* **~ snipe** the common snipe *15-, now Ork Cai Wgt.* **meet with a ~ snipe** meet with a misfortune *la17-e19* [*cf* ON *mýrisnýpa*].

mire *see* REEK

mirk &c; murk *17-,* **merk &c** *la14-e20,* **mark** *la16-e20 adj* **1** dark, black, gloomy, obscure *la14-.* **2** *of air, weather etc* dull, murky, lowering *la14-19.* **3** *fig* unenlightened, deluded *la15-e19.* **4** *fig* obscure, difficult to comprehend *la14-16.*

n darkness, night, twilight *la15-.*

vti darken, make or grow dark *la15-.*

mirken &c, mirkn- &c *vti* **1** darken, obscure *15-e16.* **2** grow dark *16-, now Sh.* **~enin &c** late twilight *la18-, now Sh.* **~ing &c** dusk, nightfall *la18-e20.* **~ness &c 1** darkness, gloom *la14-.* **2** blindness *la14-19.* **3** spiritual darkness, unenlightenment *la14-16.* **4** obscurity, secrecy *15-16.* **~some &c** dark, gloomy *la19-, now Sh.* **~y** dark, sombre; dirty *la18-, Gen except NE.*

(a) ~ mirrour something difficult to comprehend *la15-e17.* **~ Mon(an)day** 29 March 1652 (Old Style), on which occurred a total eclipse of the sun, the day being later regarded as one of supernatural darkness *la18-19.* **~ nicht &c** the dead of night *la14-, now Ags Ayr.* [ME *mirke,* OE *mirce,* ON *myrkr*]

mirkie &c *adj* merry, cheerful, mischievous *la18-, now NE.*

adv cheerfully, pleasantly, merrily *19-e20, NE.* [? Gael *mireagach* merry, playful]

mirl *see* MARL, MURL

mirled *see* MARLED

mirligoes &c ['mɪrlɪgoz; *'mɛrlɪ-; *Bwk, Rox* -gogz] *n pl* vertigo, dizziness, light-headedness *la18-e20*.
in *or* **on the** ~ light-headed, confused *19-e20*. [based on *mirled* (MARLED) + *-igo* f *vertigo*]
mirrie *see* MERRY
mis &c [*mɪs] *adv* (*adj*) = mis, amiss *la15-16*.
ga *or* **go** ~ go astray, err *e16*.
mis *see* MISS
misanswer [mɪs'ansər] *vti* disobey; give a rude answer *la20-, Bnf Abd Uls*.
misbeet &c [*mɪs'bit] *vti, weaving, of thread or yarn* become crossed or tangled *19*. [*mis* + BEET¹]
misbehaden &c *19-, now Sh Ork NE,* **misbehalding** *el7* [mɪsbɪ'had(ə)n, -'had-] *adj* out-of-place, improper, impolite. [eModEng *misbeholden*]
misbelieve *19-,* **misbeleve &c** *la15-e16 vt* disbelieve, doubt.
misca &c *18-,* **miscall &c** [mɪs'ka] *vt* **1** call (a person) bad names, abuse verbally, denounce *la16-*. **2** speak ill of, slander, disparage *la16-*. **3** mispronounce (a word) in reading *19-, local*. [ME]
miscairry *la19-,* **miscary &c** *16-17;* **miscarry &c** *17-* [mɪs'kɛrɪ] *vti* **1** = miscarry *16-*. **2** *vt* fail to obtain (one's desire) *18-19, chf Abd*. **3** *vi* be pregnant when unmarried *18-, now Sh*.
~**ing** *adj* erring, blundering *17*.
miscall *see* MISCA
miscarry, miscary *see* MISCAIRRY
mischancit &c [*mɪs'tʃansɪt] *adj* unlucky, unfortunate, ill-fated *la15-16*.
mischancy &c [mɪs'tʃansɪ] *adj* **1** = MISCHANCIT *16-, now local NE-S*. **2** risky, dangerous *19-*.
mischant *see* MESCHANT
mischefe *see* MISCHIEF
mischeiff, mischeve *see* MISCHIEVE
mischevous *see* MISCHIEVOUS
mischief &c, mischefe &c [mɪs'tʃif; *Sh Ork* mis'ʃif; *St* 'mɪstʃif] *n* **1** = mischief *la14-*. **2** strife, discord *la16-e17*. **3** misfortune, trouble *la14-, now Sh Ork Ags Uls*. **4** a physical injury; bodily harm *la18-*.
mischieve, mischeve &c; mischeiff &c *16-e17* [mɪs'tʃiv; *Sh* mɪ'ʃiv] *vir* **1** = mischieve *la15-17*. **2** *vt* injure, give a beating to (a person), treat cruelly *16-, now Sh NE Ags*.
mischievous, mischevous &c; mischievious &c *18-e20* [mɪs'tʃivəs; mɪs'tʃiviəs] *adj* = mischievous *16-*.
miscomfit [mɪskʌm'fɪt] *vt* displease, offend *20-, Bnf Abd*.
misconstruct &c *vt* misconstrue, put a wrong interpretation on *17-e19*. [only Sc; f L *construct-*, ptp stem of L *construere* > Eng *construe*]
miscontent *n* discontent, dissatisfaction *17, only Sc*.
~**it &c** *adj* discontented, dissatisfied *16-, now Bnf*.

~**ment &c** *n* **1** = miscontentment, discontent *la16-17*. **2** mutual bad feeling, discord *17*.
miscook *17-19,* **miscuke &c** *16* [*mɪs'kuk, *-'køk, &c] *vt* **1** spoil (food) in cooking *16-19*. **2** *fig* bungle, mismanage *16-19*.
misdoubt &c [mɪs'dut] *vt* **1** distrust, doubt, disbelieve *19-*. **2** presuppose, suspect, be afraid (that) *17-, now Sh SW*.
n a doubt, suspicion, fear *19-, now Ags Ayr*. [eModEng *misdoubt* (*v*)]
misell &c, mesell &c *15-e16* [*mɪzl, *'mizl] *adj* **1** = mesel, leprous *la14-e17*. **2** *of fish and swine* infected, tainted *16, only Sc*.
miserabill, miserable *see* MEESERABLE
misericorde &c [*mɪ'zɛrɪkord] *adj* compassionate, merciful *la15-16*. [only Sc; OF *misericord*, L *misericors*]
miserie *see* MEESERY
miseritie &c [*mɪ'zɛrɪtɪ] *n* misery *e16, only Sc*.
misert &c ['maɪzərt] *n, also* **meeser &c** *19* ['mizər] = miser *19-*.
adj = mean, miserly *19-, now Sh Ags*.
~ **pig** a child's (earthenware) moneybox *la19-, now Sh*.
misfare &c [mɪs'fer; *pt* -før; *ptp* -'for(ə)n, *-'fer(ə)n] *vti* **1** misfare, come to grief *la14-, now Sh*. **2** *of an enterprise* go amiss, miscarry, fail *la14-e16, only Sc*. **3** *vt* impair, bring to ruin; mismanage *la15-16, only Sc*.
n misfortune *15-19*. [ME; OE *misfaran*, ON *misfara*]
misfit [mɪs'fɪt] *vt* offend, displease *la19-, Bnf Abd, only Sc*.
misfortune &c [mɪs'fortən, *-'fortøn] *n* **1** misfortune *la15-*. **2** a breach of chastity resulting in the birth of an illegitimate child; the child itself *la18-*.
~**at &c,** ~**it** unfortunate, unlucky *la15-, now NE Gsw Uls*. **misfortunately** unfortunately *la17-19, only Sc*.
misga *see* MISGIE
misgae *18-,* **misga, misgo** *16-e19* [mɪs'ge, *-'go] *vi* **1** = misgo, go astray *15-e19*. **2** go wrong, fail, miscarry *18-, now Bnf Ags*.
misgide *see* MISGUIDE
misgie *19-,* **misgif** *la16;* **misgive &c** *la16-* [mɪs'gi, -'gɪv] *vti, pt also* **misga** *la16* [mɪs'ge(v)] **1** = misgive *la15-*. **2** fail, go wrong; *of crops* give a poor yield, fail to grow *la16-e19*. **3** *vi, of a gun* fail to go off, misfire *la16-18*. **4** *vt* (cause to) fail, let (a person) down *19-, now Sh Ayr*.
vt play false, let down *19-, now Sh Ayr*.
misgo *see* MISGAE
misgoveraunce &c [*mɪs'gʌvərans] *n* = misgovernance *la15-16, only Sc*.
misgrown [mɪs'grʌun] *adj* stunted, deformed *la18-, now Sh*. [eModEng]
misguggle &c [mɪs'gʌgl, -'gugl, *-'grʌgl] *vt* handle roughly or clumsily; rumple; bungle; hack *la18-, now Bnf Fif, only Sc*. [see SND]
misguide &c, misgide &c *vt* **1** = misguide

16-. **2** treat badly, neglect; bring up badly or cruelly *la16-*, *now local Sh-nEC Uls*. **3** waste, squander, mismanage *la18-*, *now Sh NE Ags*.

misguiding &c 1 = misguiding *16-*. **2** misrule, mismanagement, ill-treatment *16-e17*. **3** steering (of a boat) incompetently *16-e17*.

mishandle &c,   mishandil   *la16* [mɪsˈhan(d)l] *vt* **1** = mishandle *la16-*. **2** mangle, maim, knock about *la19-*, *now Sh Uls*.

mishanter &c [mɪˈʃantər; *Sh Ork* mɪsˈantər] *n* **1** a mishap, disaster; misfortune *la18-*, *now Sh-Ags*. **2** a physical hurt or injury *la19-*, *now local Sh-Ags*.

vt hurt, injure *la19-e20*, *Bnf Abd*.

the ~, Auld ~ *in imprecations* the Devil *la18-19*. [reduced f OSc, ME *mysaventure &c*, OF *mesaventure*]

mish-mash *n* = mishmash. *vti* mix up, throw together confusedly *la18-19*, *Bnf Abd Edb*.

misk *n* a damp, boggy, low-lying stretch of grassland *18-e20*, *WC*. [obscure]

misken &c [mɪsˈkɛn] *vt* **1** be ignorant or unaware of, not know *la14-e18*. **2** misunderstand, mistake *la14-e17*. **3** fail to recognize or identify *16-*, *now Sh NE*. **4** refuse to recognize, spurn, ignore *15-e19*. **5** leave off (doing something), desist *e19*, *Ayr Rox*. **6** *vr* have mistaken ideas of one's own importance, get above oneself *la14-*, *now NE*.

~nand, -ning &c *adj* **1** ignorant, uncomprehending *la16-e17*. **2** disdainful (of others), neglectful *17*. [chf Sc; ON *miskenna*]

misknaw &c, misknow &c *la16-17* [*mɪs-ˈ(k)nɑ, *-ˈknɔ] *vt* **1** be ignorant or unaware of *15-e20*. **2** be unfamiliar with, be unversed in *la14-16*. **3** misunderstand, misjudge *la14-16*. **4** fail to recognize or identify *la14-e19*. **5** repudiate, ignore, disavow *la15-e17*. **6** *vr* have an exaggerated opinion of oneself *16*.

~lage &c *n* = misknowledge, lack of knowledge *15-e17*. *vt* refuse to acknowledge, disown, repudiate, neglect *la16-e17*, *only Sc*. [chf Sc; nME (once); *cf* MISKEN]

mislabour *vt* impoverish (land) by overcropping and bad husbandry *la17-18*, *Abd Ags*.

mislear, mislere &c [mɪsˈlir, -ˈler] *vt* **1** misinform, misguide, lead astray *17-19*. **2** hurt, abuse, maltreat *17-e19*. **3** *vt, also* ~ **oneself to** (**someone**) abuse, vilify *e17*, *only Linlithgow*.

~(e)d, -it *adj* **1** misinformed, mistaken, erroneous *19-*, *now Cai Per*. **2** ill-bred, unmannerly, rude *la16-*, *now Ork Ags Per*. **3** excessively selfish, greedy *19-*, *now Abd*. [ME *mislere(n)*, OE *mislǣran*]

mislernit &c [*mɪsˈlirn(ɪ)t, *&c*] *adj, of persons* ill-bred, misconducted; *of speech* unmannerly, abusive *e17*. [*cf* prec]

mislikely &c *vt* make unlikely; depreciate; smirch *19*, *only Sc*.

misliken *vt* speak ill of, disparage; undervalue *e19*, *only Sc*.

mislippen &c, mislippin &c [mɪsˈlɪpən] *vt* **1**

defraud, disappoint *la16-17*. **2** distrust, doubt, suspect *19-*, *local NE-S*. **3** neglect, overlook *la16-*, *Gen except Sh Ork*. **4** deceive, lead astray *19-20*. [chf Sc; *cf* northern eModEng *mislicken*]

misluck, misluk &c [mɪsˈlʌk] *n* bad luck, misfortune *la16-*, *now Sh Bnf Uls*.

vi meet with bad luck; miscarry *17-19*.

~it &c dogged with bad luck, unfortunate *la19-*, *NE*. [chf Sc]

mislushious &c [mɪsˈlʌʃəs] *adj* malicious, ill-intentioned *18-20*. [altered f *malicious*, w infl f *mis-*]

mismade *see* MISMAK

mismaggle &c [*mɪsˈmagl] *vt* disarrange, interfere with; spoil *la18-e19*, *N Fif*.

mismak &c [mɪsˈmak; *sEC, S* -ˈmek] *vt* **1** make badly, misshape *16-e19*. **2** unmake, destroy *la16-e17*. **3** prepare or cook (food) badly *19-*, *now Ags*. **4** *chf vr* disturb (oneself), put (oneself) about, trouble (oneself) *19-*, *now WC, S*.

mismade misshapen, deformed *la14-16*. [chf Sc; ME *mysmake*, *mysmaad*]

mismarrow &c [mɪsˈmarə, -o, *&c*] *vt* mismatch, join together although incompatible *la18-e20*.

~ed mismatched, ill-assorted *19-20*, *Sh Bnf Lnk*. [only Sc]

mismay &c [mɪsˈme] *vtr* trouble, bother, upset *15-20*. [chf Sc]

mismuive &c [*mɪsˈmøv] *vtr* trouble, disturb; alarm *19*. [only Sc]

misnurtourit &c [*mɪsˈnʌrtərɪt, *&c*] *adj* ill-bred, unmannerly, boorish *la16-e17*, *only Sc*.

misordinate &c *adj* disorderly, immoderate *la15*, *only Sc*. [ME *ordinate*]

mispersoun &c *vt* treat (a person) with indignity; abuse verbally *16-e17*. [only Sc]

misred &c [mɪsˈrɛd, -ˈrɪd] *adj* tangled, involved, confused *la18-*, *now Sh Cai Kcb*. [only Sc; *mis-* + REDD[1]]

misregard &c [*mɪsrɪˈgard, *-ˈgerd] *vt* disregard, treat with disrespect, despise, ignore *la16-e18*, *only Sc*.

n = misregard, disregard, neglect *17*.

~ful &c heedless, neglectful *17*.

misremember *vt* forget; remember incorrectly *19-*, *now Ayr Uls*.

misrestit [mɪsˈrɛstɪt] *adj* suffering from loss of sleep *20-*, *Sh Abd SW*, *only Sc*.

miss &c, mis &c *la14-16* *vtir, pt, ptp also* **mist 1** = miss *la14-*. **2** *chf with infin, occas with* **but** fail *la16-*, *now local*: 'they never miss to find out'; 'how can he miss but thrive?'. **3** fail to happen *la18-*, *local NE-Uls*. **4** *of crops* fail to germinate or grow; *of a breeding animal* fail to conceive *la19-*, *now local Sh-Per*. **5** *vt* avoid, escape *16-*, *now local Sh-Per*. **6** escape the notice of *la19-*. **7** pass over, skip, *eg* in reading *la19-*, *local Ork-Per*. **8** *vr* miss something good or entertaining by being absent *la20-*: 'you really missed yourself at the party last night'.

n **1** = miss *la14-*. **2** a loss, want, cause for regret or mourning *la19-*. **3** harm, injury; offence, fault *la14-e19*.

in ~ing absent, lost, lacking *la16-e17*. **~ a fit** trip, stumble *la18-*.

missaucre *see* MASSACKER

missell *see* MUZZLE

missellis *see* MAISLE

misset, missit [mɪs'sɛt; *mɪs'sɪt, pt *-'sat] *vti* displease, annoy, disconcert; be displeasing **to** *la14-19, only Sc*.

missie *n* the eldest unmarried daughter of a farmer *20-, NE, EC Uls, only Sc*.

missionar &c ['mɪʃənər] *n* an itinerant evangelical preacher; a member of an Independent church *19-, now NE Ags Uls, only Sc*.

missionary *n* **1** = missionary. **2** a lay preacher, *esp* in the *Free* and *F.P. Churches* (FREE) *20-, now Hebrides Highl*.

missit *see* MISSET

missive &c *n* **1** (1) = missive, a formal letter. (2) *specif law* a letter in which a transaction is agreed upon, which may then be succeeded by a more formal legal document, and which may or may not be binding according as whether the contract in view does not or does demand formal writing *16-*. **2** the official letter sent to each of the members of the *Convention of Burghs* (CONVENTION) announcing a meeting of the CONVENTION and listing the agenda *la16-e17*.

~ dues the proportion of administrative expenses allocated to each member of the *Convention of (Royal) Burghs la17-*.

~ of lease (*19-*) *or* **tack** (*e19*) a lease drawn up in the form of a MISSIVE (*n* 1 (2)).

misslie &c; mistlie &c ['mɪslɪ] *adj* **1** alone, lonely through absence of a usual companion *19-20*. **2** missed, regretted owing to being absent *19-e20, SW Uls*. [? *mist* ptp of MISS + *-lie*]

missour *see* MEASURE

misswear [*mɪs'swɪr] *vtr* swear falsely, perjure, *chf adj* **missworn** *la16-19, chf Abd* [*mɪs'sworn]. [eModEng (once) *myssworone*]

mist *see* MISS

mistak &c [mɪs'tak; *sEC, S* -'tek] *vti* **1** = mistake *la14-*. **2** *vi* do wrong, transgress *la14-, now Ork Ags*. **3** *vr* make a mistake, go wrong *la17-*. *n* **1** = mistake *17-*. **2** a breach of chastity by a woman *20-, local*.

mistaen &c 1 ~ with overcome by, under the influence of (drink) *18*. **2** *of a remark* taken amiss, misunderstood *20-, Sh-EC Kcb*.

in a ~ *adj* mistaken, labouring under a misapprehension. *adv* in error, by mistake *18-*. **nae ~ but** without doubt, certainly *la19-*.

mistell [mɪs'tɛl] *vt* misinform *20-, Fif Slk*.

mistemper [mɪs'tɛmpər] *vt* disturb, upset *la15-e17*.

~ance &c over-indulgence, excess *la15-e16*.

mister &c *n* **1** = mister, craft *la14-15*. **2** need, necessity; pressure of circumstances *la14-e20*. **3** an emergency, crisis, plight *la14-e19*. **4** needy circumstances, destitution, poverty *la14-17*. **5** want, lack, *freq* **of** (something) *la14-16*. **6** *in pl* requirements, needs *la15-e17*.

vti **1** require, need; have need (of *or* to do something) *15-e18*. **2** be in needy circumstances *la15-16*. **3** be necessary, needful *la14-16*. **4** *of things* be lacking in some respect, be faulty *la16-e17*.

~ful &c 1 needy, necessitous *la14-17*. **2** needful, necessary *15*.

at ~(s) in case of necessity *la15-17*. **beet a ~** fulfil a need, make good a deficiency *la14-19*. **gif** *or* **as** *or* **when** (**it**) **~s** if etc (it is) necessary *15-16*. **gif ~ be** *la14-e17*, **quhen ~ is** *15-16* if need be. **have ~ 1** be in need *14-16*. **2** need, require (to do ..); have need (of) *la14-e17*. **3** be in distress, be in straits *la14-15*. **4** be impoverished, destitute *la14-16*. **in one's (maist** *etc*) **~** *etc* when one is in (most etc) difficulty or need *la14-17*. **what &c ~s (me** *etc*) **..** what need is there (for me) ..? *15-e18*.

misthrive &c *vi* fail to prosper, do badly *la16-, now Sh Ags Abd*.

~n not prosperous, in straits; undernourished *la18-, Sh Ags Abd*. [only Sc]

mistime *vi* keep irregular hours, depart from routine in sleeping and eating *19-, now NE Ags*.

~ous irregular, unpunctual, slovenly *20-, Cai NE*.

mistlie *see* MISSLIE

mistoneit &c [*mɪs'tɒnɪt] *adj* discordant, out of tune *16*. [eModE *mystonyd* (once)]

mistress, mistres &c *la16-17* ['mɪstrɛs] *n* **1** = mistress *la16-*. **2** prefixed in full to the name of a married woman, = Mrs *la16-*. **3 the** wife of a person of standing in the community, such as a farmer, MINISTER *or* shopkeeper *la17-*. **4** designation of one's own or another person's wife *17-*. **5** *mining* a protective covering for a miner working in a wet shaft or for a miner's lamp *la19-, now Fif*.

mistrow &c [*mɪs'tru] *vt* **1** = mistrow *la14-15*. **2** disbelieve, doubt (something) *la14-e15*.

~and *adj* unbelieving, infidel *15*. *n* an unbeliever, infidel *15*. **~ar** = prec (*n*) *la15*.

mistryst [mɪs'trəist] *vti* **1** fail to meet, let down, break faith (**with**); seduce *la17-, now Kcdn Slk*. **2** delude, perplex, dismay *e19*. [chf Sc]

mitch *n* the crutch or rest in which the top of a mast lies when lowered *20, Cai Fif*. [eModEng *miche* or ModEng *mitch-board; cf* MIK]

mite, myte &c *n* **1** = mite, a small insect *17-*. **2** a small clay marble *la19-e20, Mry Ags*. **3** the smaller size of button used in the game of *buttony* (BUTTON); *in pl* the game itself *20-, Ags Stlg*.

mith *see* MAY

mithe *see* MEITH

mither, mother &c *la15-*, **moder &c** *la14-16, 20* (*Sh*); **midder** *la19-, Sh NE* ['mɪdər; *Sh NE* 'mɪdər; *mødər, *mʌdər, *møðər, &c] *n* = mother *la14-*.

motherie a small delicately-coloured shell used for making necklaces *la20-, Suth Bnf Ags*.
~**'s bairn** a spoilt, indulged child *la19-*. ~ **brother** *la15-17*, ~ **sister** *16-e17* a maternal uncle or aunt. ~**'s pet** the youngest child of a family *19-*. ~ **side** the maternal line of descent *la16-*.
gud ~ **tochter** the daughter of a good mother *la15-e17*.

mitherit *see* MIDDRIT
mitilatioun *see* MUTILATION
mitre *see* MYTER
mitten¹, mittane &c *n* **1** any kind of glove, with or without separate fingers etc *la15-*. **2** a small squat person or child *19-e20, Bnf Abd Ags*. *vt* grab hold of, seize *la19-, Sh Abd Ags*.
claw (*19-, chf Fif Rox*) or **lay** (*la18-e19, Abd*) **up** (*someone's*) ~**s** kill, polish off, 'do for'; trounce.
mitten², mittane &c *n* a bird of prey; the male hen-harrier *16-19*. [obscure]
mittle &c *vt* do bodily harm to, mutilate *19-*, now *Ags Per*. [only *Sc*; eModEng *mutile* (once), F *mutiler*]
mix &c *vti* **1** = mix *16-*. **2** *of greying hair* become mixed in colour *20-, local Ork-Kcb*.
~**ed &c** mentally confused, muddled with drink *19-, local Sh-Per*. **mixt cloth** cloth woven with more than one colour of yarn, marled *17-18*.
mixter &c *n* = mixture *19-*.
mixtie-maxtie &c;   mixter-maxter &c, mixie-maxie &c *n* a jumble of objects, a mixture, confusion *19-*.
adj heterogeneous; jumbled; in a state of confusion *la18-*. [reduplicated f *mixed*, MIXTER]
mizle *see* MUZZLE
mizzer *see* MEASURE
mizzle &c *vi* vanish, melt away *la19-, now Ags*.
mizzle *see* MAISLE, MUZZLE
moabill *see* MOVEABLE
mob *n, vti* = mob.
~**bing and rioting** *law* the joining together of a number of people to act in a way which is against peace and good order *la19-*.
mobill &c, meble &c *la14* [*'mobl, *'møbl, *'mibl] *n, pl also* **meubles &c** *in collective sing and pl* MOVEABLE property, chattels; possessions, wealth *la14-16*.
adj, of goods MOVEABLE *la14-15*. [ME *moble, mobylles*, L *mobilis*]
moch¹ &c [mox] *n* a moth *17-, now Sh-nEC*.
vi be infested with moths *20-, Abd*.
~**ie &c** full of moths, moth-eaten *19-, Sh-N*.
~-**eaten** moth-eaten; infested with woodworm *la19-, chf NE*. [nME *moghe*, ONorthumb *mohðe*; *cf* MOUD]
moch² &c [mox; *Ayr also* *mɔix; *Bwk* *moix] *n* a warm moist atmosphere, close misty weather *la19-, Abd Gall Uls*.
adj = ~**ie** *1, 16-e20, local*.

vi, of corn, meat, meal etc become tainted, fusty or rotten *17-, NE*.
~**ie &c** **1** *also* **muchtie** *20-, Abd* ['mʌxtɪ] *of weather* humid; misty and oppressive, muggy *la18-, local NE-SW*. **2** *of stored articles* impaired by damp, mouldy *19-, NE*. [see SND]
Mochrum elder ['moxrəm-] *n* the cormorant *la19-, Gall*. [see SND]
mocht *see* MAY
mock &c, mok &c *la15-17 vti* = mock *la15-*. *n* **1** = mock *la15-*. **2** the very small egg sometimes laid by a hen and regarded as an omen of misfortune *la19-, now wLoth Rox*.
~**rife &c** scornful, mocking *19-e20*.
mod *n* **1** *in Celtic areas* a council or parliament *19-, now hist*. **2** **the M**~ the annual GAELIC festival of music and literature first held at Oban in 1892. [Gael *mòd* a meeting, assembly]
modderit *see* MOIDER
model &c *n* **1** = model *17-*. **2** an exact likeness, the 'image' of *19-, now Sh*.
moder *see* MITHER
moderate &c, moderat &c *vti* **1** = moderate *la16-*. **2** preside over, act as chairman of (any of the courts of the Presbyterian Churches) *17-*. *adj* **1** = moderate *16-*. **2** applied to the less rigorously Calvinist party in the *Church of Scotland* (CHURCH) *18-e19*.
n a member of the MODERATE party in the *Church of Scotland* (CHURCH) *19-, now hist*.
~**ion &c** **1** = moderation *16-*. **2** the office of a *moderator, la16-e17*. **3** the principles of the *moderate* party of the Church *18-e19*. ~**or** **1** the MINISTER who presides over a Presbyterian church court *la16-*. **2** *specif* **the M**~ the MINISTER chosen to preside (*now specif* for one year) over the *General Assembly* (GENERAL) of the *Church of Scotland* (CHURCH) and to perform certain ceremonial duties *la16-*. **3** the chairman of the *High Constables* 2 (CONSTABILL) *17-*.
~ (**in**) **a call** *of a* PRESBYTERY preside over the election and *induction* (INDUCT) of a MINISTER to a vacant charge *la17-e20*. [F *modérateur* the president of a French Protestant assembly *17-18*, following Calvin's freq use of *modérer* etc]
moderne &c *adj, of persons* now living; currently holding a position or title *la15-e17*. [F; laL *modernus; cf* eModEng]
modewarp *see* MOWDIEWORT
modify &c ['modɪfaɪ, -fi] *vt* **1** *law* specify the exact amount of (a payment, fine etc), assess at (a precise sum) *15-19*. **2** (1) award (a payment) **to** *la16-e17*. (2) *specif* determine the amount of (a parish MINISTER's *stipend* (STEEPEND)) *la16-19*. **3** determine and decree the nature and extent of (a penalty or punishment) *la15-e18*. **4** = modify *la17-*.
modifiar &c a person who prescribed the amount of a MINISTER's *stipend la16-e17*. **modification &c** **1** = modification *la15-*. **2** the assessment of a MINISTER's *stipend* (STEEPEND) *la16-*. [ME *modify* limit; appease]

mödow *see* MEEDOW

mofabil *see* MOVEABLE

Moffat: ~ **measure** a liberal measure *la20-, Kcb Dmf Slk.* [the town in Dmf (once noted for the amount of ale brewed)]

moger &c ['mogər; *N also* 'mugər, 'mjogər, 'mjɑgər] *vti* work in a slovenly or messy way, botch (a piece of work) *20-, N, WC.*
n a muddle, mess, bungle *19-, Cai WC.* [see SND]

moggan &c; moggin &c *Abd* ['mogən; *Cai* 'mu-] *n* **1** the leg of a stocking; a coarse footless stocking; a protective covering for the legs, of sacking or straw ropes, worn for farm work *la18-, N.* **2** a woollen stocking; a stocking foot worn indoors over the stocking or out of doors over the shoe in wet or frosty weather *la18-, Ork N Ags.* **3** an old stocking leg used as a purse; a hoard of money *19-, NE.* **4** a glove with one compartment for the thumb and another for the fingers, a mitt *20-, Ork N Per.*
mix (one's) ~**s** have sexual intercourse (**with**); marry *18-e19, Abd Fif.* **wet (the sma end o')** **one's** ~**s** be over the ankles in water *18-e20, Mry Abd.* [see SND]

moider &c *v, chf* **moidert, modderit** confused, dazed, *esp* as a result of blows, drink, mental strain etc *19-, WC, S Uls.* [also in Eng and Ir dial]

moietie &c [*'mɔiɛtɪ] *n, of a fine, levy etc* a half payment; an instalment of a total payment *la17-e18.* [ME *moitie*, OF *moitié*]

moif *see* MUVE

mois *see* MOSS

moist *see* MUIST

moister *n* = moisture *19-.*

moistify *vt, joc, of topers drinking* moisten, wet *la18-19.* [appar coined by Burns f *moist* adj]

mok *see* MOCK

molass &c *la18-19,* **malasche** *la16;* **mallash &c** *la18-e19* [*mə'las, *mə'laʃ] *n* a spirit distilled from molasses; WHISKY adulterated with this.
~**ed** *adj* drunk, *esp* with this spirit *la18-e19, local.* [Eng *molasses; cf* MALASHES]

mold *see* MUILD¹, MUILD²

mole *n* = mole.
vi, also **mollach &c** ['moləx] loiter about, wander idly *20-, NE, only Sc.*
molie &c *n (chf* name for) a mole-catcher *la19-, N, EC Lnk.* **moleskin** *adj* true, reliable *20-, NE nEC, WC, SW.*

mole *see* MULL¹

molendinar; molendinary [molən-'dəinər(ɪ)] *adj* pertaining to a mill or miller *19, in place-name* la12-, Gsw. [only Sc; MedL *molendinarius*]

molestation &c, molestatioune &c *15-17*
n **1** = molestation *la15-.* **2** *law* (1) the troubling or disturbing of a holder or occupier of lands in his legal possession *15-19;* (2) *also*

action of ~ an action taken by a proprietor of land against those who disturb his possession *la16-19.*

Moll: molly-dolly an Aunt Sally at a fair *20-, Dnbt Ayr, only Sc.*

moll *see* MOW²

mollach *see* MOLE

mollett¹ &c *n* the rowel of a spur; *heraldry* a mullet *la15-e16.* [ME, AF *molet* a mullet in heraldry, OF *molette* a rowel, mullet]

mollett² &c *n* a severe spiked or studded bit for a horse *16.*
~ **bit,** ~ **bridil**(1) *16.* [? OF *molette* a spurrowel; *cf* prec]

molligrant &c; mulligrumph &c ['molɪ-'grant, -'grʌmf, -'grʌnt; &c] *n* a complaint, lamentation; *freq in pl* a state of dissatisfaction, a fit of sulks *19-, now Ork EC.*
vi complain, grumble *la19-, now Abd EC Lnk.* [*cf* next]

molligrups &c ['molɪ'grʌps, 'mulɪ'grʌbz, &c] *n* = mulligrubs, a fit of melancholy or sulks; stomach-ache, colic *18-e20.*

mollop &c *vi* toss the head disdainfully; give oneself airs *19-e20, S.*
n pl airs, antics, capers *19-e20, Rox.* [? f MOLLET²]

moltin *see* MOUTEN

moment ['mom(ə)nt] *n, also* **mament &c** *16-20* ['mam(ə)nt] = moment *15-.*
~ **hand** the second hand of a timepiece *19-, now nEC.*

mon¹ &c *la14-e17;* **mun** *la16-e18* [mʌn; *?mon]
v = must. [ME, ON *mun, mon*, ON 1 and 3 pers sing indicative of *munu* shall, will; *cf* MAUN¹]

mon² *prep* among *20-, Abd Ags* [aphetic f *amon* (AMANG)]

mon *see* MAN

Monanday &c *17-, now local Sh-Ayr,* **Monounday &c** *la14-17,* **Manounday &c** *la16-17,* **Mounday &c** *la15-17;* **Munonday &c** *la15-e18,* **Monday &c** *la16-* ['manənde; 'mʌnde; *also* *'mon-, *'man-] *n* = Monday.
~**'s haddie** a fish that has lost its freshness *la19-, now Bnf Per Slk.*

monarchy &c *n* **1** = monarchy *15-.* **2** a group of nations or states under the dominion of a single nation or its ruler, an empire *la16, only Sc.*

Monday *see* MONANDAY

mone *see* MUNE

mones &c *vt* monish, admonish *la14-17.* [orig back-formation f MONEST]

monest &c *vti, also (chf) pt, ptp* admonish(ed), charge(d), exhort(ed) *la14-16.* [nME; OF *monester*, popular L *monestāre* ultimately f L *monēre* warn]

monet(e) &c [*?'mʌnɛt] *n* money *15-16.* [*cf* L *monēta* and next]

moneth &c [*?'mʌnɛð] *n* money *la15-e17.* [*cf* OF *moneide* and prec]

moneth *see* MONTH

money &c *n* **1** = money *la14-*. **2 the** Scottish coinage; the Scottish mint *15*.

monie &c, **mony** &c, **many** &c *la15-* ['monɪ, 'mʌnɪ] *adj* **1** = many *la14-*. **2** *with sing noun* = many a *la14-19*: 'money time'. **3** *with pl or collective noun* big, great, considerable *la18-*, *now Sh Ags*: 'mony pricis', 'many company'.

moniest &c, **maniest** *adj* most *16-e18*. *n*, *only* **moniest** &c the greatest number, the majority *16-e19*. ~**way**, ~**wise** &c in many ways, many times over *la14-16*.

~ **a** ~ very many *19*, *Mry Ags Gall*. ~ **ane** *adj*, *following noun* many *la14-e19*. *pronoun* many a person *la14-e20*, *now Sh NE*. ~'s **the** .. many a *la18-*.

moniefauld &c ['monɪ'fɑld] *n* the third stomach of a ruminant; *in pl* the intestines *la18-*, *now Ags*. [Eng dial *manifold*; *cf* MONIPLIES]

moniest *see* MONIE

moniment &c, **monument** &c ['monɪmənt] *n* **1** = monument *la14-*. **2** an object of ridicule or distaste, a 'sight', a laughing-stock; a rascal; a silly person *la18-*, *Sh-Per*.

moniplies ['monɪ'plaɪz] *n pl* **1** the third stomach of a ruminant *19-20*. **2** *fig* a tortuous argument or statement *18-e20*, *only Sc*. [Eng (chf dial) *manyplies* = 1; *cf* MONIEFAULD]

monitioun &c *la14-e17*; **monition** &c *n* **1** = monition *la14-*. **2** a formal charge or warning by an ecclesiastical authority to a backslider to amend *15-16*. **3** a formal charge or injunction by an ecclesiastical judge that a certain action be carried out or refrained from, or that the terms of a contract be adhered to *16-e17*.

monitour &c *n* a monitory, a missive setting out a formal charge or injunction of an ecclesiastical judge; the charge or injunction itself *e16*. [MedL *monitoria*; F *monitoire*]

monkey &c, **monké** *la16 n* **1** = monkey *la16-*. **2** a tool with a ratchet for tensing fencing wire *20-*, *C, S*.

~-**chip** &c a variety of the game of marbles *20-*, *Mry Abd Ayr*.

monopole [*'monopol] *n* a seditious faction; a conspiracy *16-e17*. [OF *monopole*, MedL *monopolium*]

Monounday *see* MONANDAY

Mons &c, **Mounts** *17-18* [monz; *mons; *mʌns] *n* a large 15th century cannon cast probably at Mons in Flanders and now at Edinburgh Castle *15-17*.

~ **Meg** the name later (*c* 1650) given to this cannon *17-*. [see SND *Meg*]

mont *see* MONTH², MUNT¹, MUNT²

montane *see* MOUNTAIN

monter &c; **munter** &c, **mounter** &c [*'mʌntər] *n* a watch *la16-17*. [only Sc; F *montre*]

month¹ &c, **moneth** &c *la14-e18* [mʌnθ, *'mʌnəθ] *n* **1** *freq uninflected in pl after numerals etc* = month *la14-*: 'twa month'. **2 X** etc ~ = (the month of) X etc *15-*, *now Ags Per*: 'about August month'.

month² &c, **mont** &c; **mounth** &c, **mount** &c [mʌnθ; *St* mʌunθ, mʌunt; *mʌnt] *n* **1** *chf* **the M**~ name for the mountains at the eastern end of the Grampians, *chf* in Ags and Kcdn *la12-*. **2** a stretch of hilly or high ground; a mountain, hill, moor *15-*, *latterly only in place-names*.

~ **grass** the sheathed cotton-grass *la19*, *Ags*.

the Cairn o' Mount(h) [*St* 'kern o 'mʌunt] a road over the Grampians in Kcdn, now the B974, *la18-*. **the cawsay** *etc* **of the** ~ a main road over the Grampians south of Aberdeen *la14-e17*. [Gael *monadh* a hill, moor, range of hills; the *St* forms have been influenced by Eng *mount* and the forms in *-t* by MUNT²; *cf* MUNT²]

monument *see* MONIMENT

mony *see* MONIE

monȝeall *see* MINȝELL

monzie *see* MUNSIE

mood *see* MUID

moog *see* MUG¹

mool *see* MUILD¹

mooler *see* MUILDER

moolet &c *vi* whimper, whine *19-*, *Ayr, Lnk*. [? perh imit]

moon *see* MUNE

moor *see* MUIR

moose *see* MOUSE

moosh &c *adj* (*n*) crumbly (material) *20-*, *Cai*. *vi* crumble away *la20-*, *Cai*. [perh conflation of Gael *musg* grow mouldy or musty w Eng *mush*]

moost &c *n*, *vi* = must, mould(er) *la19-*, *now Bnf*. [see SND; *cf* FOOST]

moot *la16-*, **mute** &c *vti* [mut; *møt] *vti* **1** ~ **of, in** speak, discuss *la14-e17*. **2** *vt* say, utter, divulge; hint, insinuate *la14-*, *now Sh Abd Ags Kcb*. **3** *vi* argue, plead; protest, object *la14-17*. **4** *vi and impersonal* take (a matter or person) to court, litigate *15-e17*. **5** = moot, raise for discussion.

n a whisper, hint *19-*, *now Sh Abd*. [ME *mote*]

moot *see* MOUT

mooth *see* MOUTH

mop-mop *see* MOUP

moppat &c; **mappat** &c *n* a mop, *esp* for cleaning gun barrels, applying liquids etc *16-e17*. [only Sc; *cf* ME *mappel*]

moppie *see* MOUP

mora ['mora] *n*, *law* delay in pressing a claim or obligation which may infer that the action has been abandoned by the *pursuer* (PURSUE) *18-*. [L = delay]

Morave *n* an inhabitant of Moray *16*. [ScL *Moravus*, Gael *Moireabh*]

Moray &c ['mʌrɪ; *NE* 'mʌrə] ~ **coast** &c a hard subsoil such as is found along the coast of the Moray Firth *la18-e19*, *Ross Mry*.

more *see* MAIR¹, MUIR

More &c *n* **1** = Moor; a blackamoor or negro

16-e17. **2** a person disguised as a Moor when taking part in a Morris dance, pageant, *guising* (GUISE) etc *la16.*
adj Moorish; negro *e16.*

morgeoun *see* MURGEON

Morisonian &c *n* a follower of the Rev James Morison of Kilmarnock, who was suspended from his charge in 1841 for opposition to certain Calvinist doctrines and later founded the Evangelical Union *19.*

morkin *see* MORT

mormaer &c; maormor [*St* 'mɔr'mer] *n* a high steward of one of the ancient Celtic provinces of Scotland *19-, hist.* [ScGael *12*, prob f Gael *mór* great + *maer* a steward; translated in ScL documents as *comes* earl; *cf* TOISEACH]

morn &c, morne &c *n* **1** = morn *la14-.* **2 the ~** (1) tomorrow, the following morning or day *la14-;* (2) *adv* tomorrow, on the following morning or day *la14-.* (3) **the ~'s ~, -morning, -nicht** *etc* tomorrow morning etc *19-.*
here the day and awa the ~ said of someone unreliable or changeable *la20-.* **the ~-come-never** the morrow that never comes, the end of time *19-, Edb Bwk Dmb.* **the ~ day** the following day *la14-16.* **(the)** ~ **i'e morning &c** daybreak, first light *19-, Gall.* **the ~ (nixt) eftir** (..) the day following (..) *la14-e17.* **uther ~ the** day after tomorrow *la16.*

morn *see* MURN

mornin &c *la15-,* **morning &c** *n* **1** = morning *la14-.* **2** a glass of spirits or a snack taken before breakfast; a mid-morning drink or snack *18-.*
~ blink the first glimmer of daylight *la17-, now Sh.* **~ drink** *la16-e18,* **~ piece** *la19-, now Sh Ork Uls* a drink or snack taken during the mid-morning break from work. **~ gift** = MORWYNGIFT *16.* **~ roll** a soft bread roll *20-.*
in the ~s in the morning *la19-, now Sh Ork Abd.*

morow *see* MORROW

morowing &c *n, verse* morn, morning *16.* [ME *morowyng(e)*]

morrow &c *16-,* **morow &c** *15-17 n* = morrow *15-.*
the ~(s) morn(ing) the following morning, tomorrow morning *la17-20, chf Kcb Uls.*

morrow *see* MARROW

mors(e) *vt* prime (a gun) *16-e17.*
moshin &c hole, motion &c hole the touchhole of a gun *la18-e19.* **morsing &c powder** priming powder *la16-19.* [aphetic f F *amorcer* prime (a gun)]

mort &c *n* **1** a dead body *la15-e19.* **2** = ~ **lambskin,** *19-, S.*
morkin &c a sheep that has died a natural death *la18-e20, Ayr Dmf Slk.* **mortuall &c** some kind of skin, *perh* that of a young sheep *16.* **~ bell** the bell rung at funerals *la16-17, WC, SW.* **~ cauld &c** a severe cold, one's 'death' of cold *18-, now Sh.* **~charge &c** 'dead weight' goods, which had a high weight-to-bulk ratio

and which therefore paid lower freightage *16-e17.* **~ chest** *la17-18,* **~ chist** *la17,* a coffin. **~-cloth &c, ~-clathe &c 1** a pall covering a coffin on its way to the grave, *latterly chf* hired out by the *kirk session* (KIRK) *la15-, now local Sh-Kcb.* **2** *in pl, also* **mortcloth money** the fees received from the hire of a *mortcloth, 17-18.* **~ hede &c 1** a human skull, a death's head *17.* **2** *chf heraldry* a representation of a skull *la16-e20.* **3** a turnip lantern representing a skull *19-20, NE.* **~ kist** = ~ **chest,** *la16-, now Sh.* **~ lambskin** the skin of a sheep or lamb that has died a natural death *la17-, S.* **~ safe** an iron grid placed over a grave or over the coffin to deter body-snatchers *19, local.* **~ stand** a set of ecclesiastical vestments or altar-cloths for funeral services *16.*
(one's) morth o' cauld = ~ *cauld, 19-, now Uls.* [ME *mort(e)* death, F *mort*]

mortal &c *adj* **1** = mortal *15-.* **2** extremely intoxicated, dead drunk *19-.*
adv very, *chf* ~ **drunk,** ~ **fou** *19-.*
~ly &c very, exceedingly *la18-.*
~ end the end of everything *la20-, local.*

mortancestor, mortancestry *see* BRIEF

mortar stane &c *n* a hollowed stone in which barley was pounded to remove the husks *16-19.* [see SND]

mortercheyn &c, mortichein &c [*'mɔrtə(r)'ʃin] *n* a disease of horses, glanders *17-19.* [only Sc; ? F *mort d'eschine* death of the spine]

mortfundyit &c *adj* deadly cold *e16.* [only Sc; var of Eng *morfound &c* be benumbed with cold]

morth *see* MORT

morthour *see* MURTHER[1]

mortichein *see* MORTERCHEYN

mortify ['mɔrtɪfaɪ, *-fi] *vt* **1** = mortify *la15-.* **2** *law* assign or bequeath in perpetuity (lands, property or money) to an ecclesiastical or other body or institution *la15-e19.*
mortification 1 = mortification *la15-.* **2** *law* lands, property or money *mortified;* the deed of making such an allocation *la15-, only Sc.* **master of mortifications** a member of the Town Council of Aberdeen appointed to administer the city's *mortified* property *17-e19, only Sc; cf* MAISTER[1]. **mortifier** the donor of a *mortification, 2, 17-e19.*

mortis causa ['mɔrtɪs 'kɔzə] *law, of a deed, bequest* etc taking effect on the death of the grantor *la19-.*

mortoun &c [*'mɔrtən, *'mart-] *n* a (? sea-)bird, *perh* the guillemot or razorbill *la15-16.*

mortuall *see* MORT

morwyngift &c [*'mɔrwɪn'gɪft, *'mɔrʌuɪn-] *n* a settlement or endowment of money or property made by the husband to the wife on the morning after the marriage *15-16.* [ME *morwen* morn + *gift*]

mos *see* MOSS

mosh *n, marbles* a hollow scooped in the ground in which the target marble is placed *20-, Fif midLoth WC.*

~ie &c a game involving three such hollows *20-, Gsw Lnk.*

moshin hole *see* MORS(E)

moss &c, mos &c *la14-17;* **mois &c** *la16-17* [mos] *n* **1** boggy ground, moorland *la14-.* **2** a PEAT¹ bog; a stretch of moorland allocated to tenants for cutting fuel *la15-.* **3** = PEAT¹ *n* 1 (1), *16-19.* **4** = moss, the plant *17-.* **5** = *moss-crop, la18-, now Cai wLoth.*

vi work at cutting PEATS¹ etc in a PEAT¹ bog *19-, now NE wLoth Uls.*

~er 1 = *moss trooper, la17.* **2** a person who cuts and dries PEATS¹ *la19-, NE Rox.* **~ing** a crop of cotton grass *la19-, N.* **~y** boggy, *peaty* (PEAT¹) *16-e20.*

~ aik, ~ oak bog oak *la18-, SW.* **~ bank** = *peat-bank* (PEAT¹) *la18-, N, Per.* **~ bluiter &c** the common snipe *19-, Kcb S.* **~ cheeper &c** the meadow pipit *la17-, C, S Uls.* **~crop &c** cotton grass, *esp* the harestail *la17-, now Ork N, C.* **~ duck** the mallard *19-e20, NE Renfr.* **~ fir** the wood of ancient fir trees sunk into *peaty* (PEAT¹) soil, bog fir *18-, now Per.* **~ flow** a wet PEAT¹ bog, a swamp *19-e20, C.* **~ grieve &c** the estate official in charge of the rights of PEAT¹-cutting in a MOSS *la17-, NE.* **~ ground &c** soil, turf or PEAT¹ from a bog *17.* **~ hag &c** *18-, now C,* **~ hole** *la17-, Gen except Sh Ork* = *peat hag* (PEAT¹); *in pl* dangerous boggy moorland. **~ laird** *joc* a tenant given an area of rough moorland rent-free or at reduced rent in return for making it arable *la18-19, Per Stlg.* **~ leave &c, ~ lefe &c** the right or permission to cut PEATS¹ etc in a MOSS *la16-e18.* **~ mail &c** rent paid for the right of cutting PEAT¹ etc in a MOSS *16-19.* **~ mingin &c** the cranberry *19, Renfr Lnk.* **~ pot** a water-filled pit in a PEAT¹ bog *18-, NE.* **~ road** a track to a *peat moss* (PEAT¹) *la19-, now Abd.* **~ room &c** the portion of a *peat moss* assigned to a tenant for his own use *16-e18, WC, SW.* **~ trooper** a BORDER cattle-*reiver* (REIVE) *17-e19.*

~ o' Byth [bɔiθ] the ace of spades *20-, Bnf Abd* [see SND]. [in place-names *13-;* nME, OE *mos* bog]

most¹ *n* a mast *19-, now Bnf Abd.*

most² &c *v* = must *la15-e18, 20- (Sh).*

most *see* MAIST¹

mot *n, also* **motie &c** *derog* the old woman, the *wifie* (WIFE) *20-, Bnf Abd.* [cf Eng slang *mot* a girl, wench and eModEng *mort* a girl, woman]

mot *see* MOTE³

mote¹ &c *n* **1** a mound or hillock; an embankment *15-, now Sh Uls.* **2** the tidal moat which encircled Kirkcudbright town *la16-17.*

v, mining reinforce the stonework of a mining shaft with a mixture of clay and water, making it watertight *19.* [ME, OF]

mote² &c *n* **1** = mote, a particle of dust *la14-.* **2**

a minute speck, a small fragment *16-, now Sh Ork.* **3** a flaw, blemish; a drawback *la16-, now Abd.*

vt **1** pick specks of fluff etc from (something) *la17-, now Abd Kcdn.* **2** find fault with *16, 19, only Sc.*

motie &c, motty &c flecked with specks of dust etc, smutty *la16-, now Sh NE.*

mote³ &c *15-19,* **mot &c** *la14-e19,* **mat &c** *la16-e20* *v* = mot, may, might, must *la14-e20, latterly arch.*

mote *see* MUTE

moth *adj, chf* **mothy** unaired, fusty *18-, now Bwk.*

mother *see* MITHER

motif *see* MOTIVE

motion hole *see* MORS(E)

motive &c; motif &c *16* **1** = motive *15-.* **2** *chf* **of one's awin (fre, proper) ~** of one's own free will *la15-e18, chf Sc.*

adj, freq law **of one's owin (fre, proper) ~ will** = prec *16-17, only Sc.*

motoun *see* MUTTON

mott *n, chf quoits or marbles* a mark or target *19-, local.* [appar F *motte* a hillock, butt; *cf* MOTE¹]

motty *see* MOTE²

mou &c, mow &c [mu; *S* mʌu] *n* **1** a large heap of grain, hay etc; a pile of unthreshed grain stored in a barn *la14-, Gen except Sh Ork.* **2** the division in a barn where unthreshed grain is heaped *la19-, now Per.* **3** a large vertical section of a house-shaped hay- or corn-stack *la20-, Bnf Ags Kcb.* **4** a pile or stack of PEATS¹ *la18-19, WC, S.*

vt pile up (unthreshed grain or hay) in a barn *19.* [ME *mowe*, OE *mūʒa*, ON *múge* a swath]

mou *see* MOUTH, MOWS

moud &c [mʌud] *n* the clothes moth *19-e20, Bwk, S.* [var of nEng dial *mowt*, ME *moughte*, OE *mohðe; cf* MOCH¹]

moud *see* MUILD¹

mou'd *see* MOUTH

mouden *see* MOUTEN

moudie *see* MOWDIEWORT

mouf *see* MUFF

mought *see* MAUCHT

mougre ['mugər] *vi, lit and fig* hang gloomily, cast a shadow *19-, Arg.* [Gael *mùig* suppress; become gloomy]

moul¹ &c [mul] *vi* grow mouldy *la16-e19.*

moul, ~d, ~it mouldy *15-, now Abd Fif.* **~ie &c 1** mouldy; *fig* little used *la16-, now NE Fif WC.* **2** mean, stingy *la19-, C, S.* [eME *muwlen*, ON **mugla* grow mouldy]

moul² &c [mul] *n* a chilblain, *esp* a broken one on the heel *16-, now Ayr.*

moulie &c affected with chilblains *la18-, now Cai.* [laME *mowlle*, ME *mule*, MedL *mula* a chilblain]

mould *see* MUILD¹, MUILD²

moulder *see* MUILDER

Mounday *see* MONANDAY

mount *see* MONTH[2], MUNT[1], MUNT[2]

mountain &c *la15-*, **montane &c** *la14-17*; **muntain &c** *18-e20*, *C* ['mʌntən, *-en; *'munt-] *n* = mountain *la14-*.
~ **dew** WHISKY, *esp* if illicitly distilled *19.* ~ **men**, ~ **folk** *etc* the persecuted *Covenanters* (COVENANT) (1670-88) who took refuge in the mountains, *esp* of Galloway; the MACMILLANITES *18-e19*.

mounté *n* a mountain, hill-top *la14.* [OF *mountee*]

mounter *see* MONTER

mounth *see* MONTH[2]

Mounts *see* MONS

moup &c, mowp [mʌup, mup] *vti* **1** *also* ~ **on** *or* **at** repeatedly twitch the lips; nibble, munch; mumble *16-*, *now Edb Ayr Kcb.* **2** consort or live **with** *la18-*, *SW.*
n, also **moppie, mup-mup &c** (*Ayr S*) **1** *familiar or child's word* a rabbit *20-*, *local N-S.* **2** *also* **mop-mop** the antirrhinum *20-*, *Ayr S; cf mappie mou* (MAP[2]). [onomat; eModEng *moppe* move the lips, grimace; *cf* MAP[2] *and* MUMP]

mourn *see* MURN

mouse &c, mous &c; moose &c *19-* [mus] *n* **1** = mouse *15-.* **2** *also* ~ **end &c** the lump of flesh or tissue at the end of a leg of mutton *la18-e19.* **3** a small lead weight tied to a cord, used by joiners to guide cords into a sash window and by electricians to drop wires *la20-.*
~ **cheep** the squeak of a mouse *la19-.* ~ **fa**, ~ **fall** a mousetrap *la17-*, *now Fif.* ~ **moulding** a narrow moulding filling the angle between floor and skirting board or wall *la20-.* ~ **pea**, ~ **pease** various species of vetch *la16-*, *now Sh-Cai SW.* ~ **wab**, ~ **web**, ~ **wob** a spider's web, cobweb *la16-.* ~ **weasel** a small female weasel *la20-*, *N Kcb.*
mak mice feet o', mak like mice feet reduce to fragments; confound *18-*, *Sh NE.*

mout &c; moot *19-* [mut] *vti* **1** = moult *la15-*, *now C, S.* **2** *vt* fritter **away**, consume gradually *19-*, *now Sh.* **3** *vti* crumble away, decay slowly *19-e20*, *Sh EC, S.*
n, freq **the** ~ *of birds* the process or period of moulting *19-*, *C, S Uls.*
~**it &c** *adj* moulted; worn away, bare, shabby *16-19.*

moutache &c [mu'taʃ] *n* a moustache *la19-*, *NE, nEC.* [? w infl f *mou* (MOUTH)]

mouten &c *la16-e20*, **moltin &c** *la14-17*; **mouden** *e20*, *Mry Bnf* ['mʌutən; *Mry Bnf* 'mʌud-; *'molt-] *adj* **1** *of metal etc* molten, melted; moulded, cast *la14-17.* **2** *of fat* clarified *e20*, *Mry Bnf.*
vti melt, dissolve; clarify (fat) *la19-e20*, *chf Mry Bnf.* [ME *molten*]

mouter *see* MULTURE

mouth &c, mow &c *la15-*; **mou** *la17-*, **mooth** *la19-* [muθ; *NE, C* mu; *S* mʌu] *n* **1** = mouth *la14-.* **2** a threshold or entrance to an

enclosed place or tract of country *la17-*, *now local C.* **3** *of a peat stack* (PEAT[1]) the end from which one begins to draw away the PEATS[1] for fuel *la19-*, *Abd.* **4** the beginning (of a season, day, event etc) *19-*, *local NE-Kcb.* **5** the open top of a shoe *20-*, *Ork NE Kcb.* **6** the blade (of a shovel or spade) *19-*, *Sh-nEC, SW.* **7** a speech, utterance *la18-*, *now Kcb.* **8** a garrulous, boastful person *la19-*, *Gen except Sh Ork.*
vt tell, utter, mention *19-*, *now Sh C.*
-mou'd &c [-'mu:d] -mouthed. **tak a ~fu o** enunciate deliberately or emphatically *la20-*, *Sh C.* ~**ie** a mouth-organ *20-.*
~**-bag** a horse's nosebag *la19-.* ~**-ban(d)** utter, express, mention *la17-*, *chf N, C.* ~**-bund** tongue-tied; unable to master a pronunciation *20-*, *local.* ~**-cloth** a cloth for wiping the mouth, a face-cloth *17-e18.* ~ **cord** the rope linking the inner bit rings of a pair of horses to keep them together *20-*, *WC.* ~ **poke** = ~ *bag*, *19-*, *Gen except Sh Ork NE.*
ask *etc* **if someone has a** ~ invite someone to eat or drink *la19-.* **doon o** ~ in low spirits, down in the mouth *la19-*, *local.* **fin one's** ~ convey food to one's mouth *20-*, *Sh Ork NE, SW.* **get roun the mou wi an English dishclout** become affectedly anglicized in speech *la20-*, *NE nEC.* **in the** ~ **o the pock** at the outset, barely started *19-*, *NE nEC Ayr.* **mak a puir** ~ complain of one's poverty, exaggerate one's need *19-.* **wi** ~ **and een** (**baith**) in a gaping, staring manner *la19-*, *now Abd.*

moutoun *see* MUTTON

movabill *see* MOVEABLE

move *see* MUVE

moveable &c, movabill &c *15-17*, **moabill &c** *e16*, **mufabill &c** *15-e16*, *only Sc*; **mofabil &c** *15* ['muvəbl; *'mø(v)-] *adj, law* **1** applied to that form of property which is not HERITABLE (personal belongings etc), and which formerly passed to the next of kin instead of to the *heir-at-law* (HEIR) *15-.* **2** *of a tenant* removable, as opposed to RENTALLED tenants, who could not be removed *la17.*
n, law, chf in pl MOVEABLE property *la16-.* [ME = able to be moved; L *mobilia bona* movable goods]

movir &c [*'mʌvər] *adj* quiet, gentle, mild *e15.* [late nME *moyre*, OF *meür*; for *-v-* cf SOVER and *sure* (SHUIR)]

mow[1] &c [mʌu] *vti, of males* copulate, have sexual intercourse (with) *16-e20.* [perh f MOWS jest, make fun of]

mow[2] &c *la15-18*, **moll &c** *la14-e16* [mʌu; *mol] *n* dust, mould, crumbled fragments *la14-18.*
mulloch &c [*'mʌlox, *'mol-] crumbled refuse of PEAT[1], *eg* as found at the bottom of a *peat-stack* (PEAT[1]) *19.* [ME *mol &c, mul &c*]

mow *see* MOU, MOUTH, MOWS

mowar *see* MOWS

mowdiewort &c, modewarp &c ['mʌudɪ-

wʌrt, -wart, -warp, -wʌrk, &c; *NE Loth* also
'mudɪ-; *'mo(l)d(ɪ)-] *n* **1** the mole, the small
burrowing animal *la15-, Gen except Sh Ork.* **2** a
sneaking, underhand person *19-, now wLoth Ayr.*
3 a recluse; a slow-witted or slovenly person
la19-e20, Abd Fif Loth. **4** a small dark child
with a lot of hair *la16-19.* **5** *joc* a mole on the
skin, a wart *20-, now Renfr Ayr.*
vi **mowdy** loiter or prowl furtively about *20-,
Lnk Ayr.*
    moudie &c **1** = *n* 1, *la18-, C.* **2** a mole-catcher
la19-, now C, S. **moudieman** = *prec* 2, *19-,
now wLoth SW, S.* **moudieskin** the skin of a
mole *19-, now Kcb.* ~(**wort**) **brod** the
mouldboard of a plough *17-e19.* ~(**wort**)
hill(**ock**) a molehill *16-, now Dmf.* [ME
mold(e)warp(e) &c, OE *molde* mould + *weorpan*
throw]
mowdy *see* MOWDIEWORT
mowence [*?'mjuəns] *n* change, mutation *la14.*
[OF *muance; cf* eModEng *muance*]
mowlin *see* MOYLIE
mowp *see* MOUP
mowrie &c ['mʌurɪ] *n* **1** gravel mingled with
sand, shingle *la17-e20, Mry.* **2** a gravelly
sea-beach *la19-, Bnf.* [of Gael orig; see SND]
mows &c *(pl)*, **mow** &c *(sing)*; **mou** [mʌu] *n*
1 a grimace, *esp* derisive *la15-e17.* **2** a piece of
foolery, a jest, a laughing matter *16-e17, only Sc.*
3 *in pl* banter, jesting; a joke, a laughing matter
16-, latterly chf NE, Ags.
vi, only **mow** jest, joke (**with**); speak without
seriousness *16.*
adj, only **mows** &c safe, harmless, circumspect
la19-, NE.
    mowar a person who mocks or jests *la15-e16.*
in ~**s** (**or ernist**) as a joke (or seriously)
16-e18. **mak a mow** *or* **mows 1** pull a face,
esp in derision *la15-e17.* **2** make a grimace of
disapproval, reluctance etc *la18-, chf Abd.* **mak**
(**mony**) ~**is** sport, jest, have fun *la15-e17.* **nae**
~**s** no laughing matter; serious, dangerous,
uncanny *16-, now NE Ags.* [ME *mouwe, mowe,*
MDu *mouwe* a thick lip; a pout; *cf* F *moue* a
pout]
moy[1] &c *(sing)*, **meuis** &c [*'mjuz] *(pl) n* a dry
measure, used *esp* of salt *15-16.* [ME *mauys* &c
(pl), OF *moi* &c]
moy[2] *adj* demure, prim, meek *la15-e18.*
    mak (**sa** *etc*) ~ behave demurely, affect gentil-
ity *la15-16.* [appar MDu *mooy* elegant,
handsome]
moyar &c *n* ? some small domestic article; ? a
fitting or fastening for a garment *16-e17.*
moyen[1] &c, **myane** &c *15-20* ['moiən, moin,
'maiən] *n* **1** power to exert influence; influence
exerted, mediation, steps taken *15-, now Abd.* **2**
a means, agency *la15-17.* **3** an agent, intermediary *la16-e17.* **4** power, credit, standing (in a
community, at court etc) *16-e18.* **5** means,
resources, funds *16-17.* **6** forewarning, news in
advance, *chf* **get** (**a**) ~(**s**) **o** *la19-, NE.*

vt **1** bring about, contrive; arrange, negotiate
la16-e17. **2** direct, guide (something); persuade, induce (someone) *la19-, Abd Ags.* **3** recommend, back (a person) *la19-, now NE.*
    ~**ar** an agent, intermediary; a backer *la16-e17,
only Sc.*
lay *or* **mak** ~(**s**) take steps (towards some
objective), use influence *16-, now NE.* [laME
moyen, MF *moien; cf* MEAN[1]]
moyen[2] &c,   **myane** &c,   **mayan** &c
[*'moiən, *'maiən] *adj, of a culverin* of the middle size *16.*
    n a medium-sized culverin *16-e17.* [only Sc;
MF *(coulevrine) moyenne; cf* CULVERING]
moylie &c; **mowlin** ['moilɪ, 'mʌulən] *n* a
hornless or polled cow or bullock; a hornless
wild goat *19-, Gall.* [ModIr dial *moiley* a hornless cow, IrGael *maolán,* f *maol* bald; *cf mulloch*
(MULL[1])]
moze &c [moz; *Sh Cai* also muz] *n,* see deriv
below.
    vi decay, become musty or mouldy *20-, Sh Ork
Cai.*
    mozie &c decayed, fusty, mouldy *la19-, Sh Ork
Renfr Ayr.*
mozey &c ['mozɪ] **coal mozey** a coal seam of
variable thickness *la18-, Clcm.* [? f *prec*]
mr. *see* MAISTER[1]
much *see* MICH, MUTCH
muchin, muchkin, muchskin *see* MUTCHKIN
muchtie *see* MOCH[2]
muck &c *la16-, **muk** &c *la14-17 n* **1** dung,
farmyard manure *la15-.* **2** dirt, filth; refuse,
rubbish *la15-.*
    vti **1** (1) clear of dirt, clean out *la14-, now Abd
Kcb.* (2) *specif* clean dung out of (a BYRE or stable) *16-.* **2** spread with dung, fertilize *16-.* **3**
clutter up, mar the appearance of *20-, Sh NE.*
    ~ **bell** a silver bell given annually in Dumfries
to the winner of the *muckmen's* horse-races
la17-e18. ~ **creel** &c a pannier or hamper
used for taking dung to the fields *la15-e19.* ~
fail &c turf mixed with dung to form a manure
or compost *17-e19, chf Abd.* ~ **flee** a bluebottle; a dung-fly *la20-, local.* ~**man** a day-
labourer whose chief duty was to act as a street
cleaner *la16-e18.* ~ **midden** &c a dunghill
la16-.
    as drunk as ~ very drunk *la19-, now Sh Ags
Per.* **Lord** *or* **Lady M**~ name for a person who
puts on airs *20-.* ~**-a** *or* **the-byre** *contemptuous* a
farmer *la18-, now Bnf Per.* **wet as** ~ soaking
wet *19-, now Sh Kcb.* [eME *muk* &c; *cf* ON *myki*
dung]
muckie &c; **muckack** *n* the fruit of the dog-
rose, a rose-hip *20-, Cai Ross Inv.* [Gael *mucag*]
muckle &c *la17-, **mekill** &c *la14-e18, **mikill**
&c, **mukill** &c *la16-e17;* **meikle** &c *la16-,
mickle &c *16-* ['mʌkl; 'mikl; 'mɪkl] *adj* **1**
large in size or bulk, big, great *la14-.* **2** *specif*
applied to the larger of two farms, estates etc of
the same name *14-.* **3** much in quantity or

degree, a great deal of *la14-*. **4** full-grown, adult *17-*, *now Sh Ork NE Kcb*. **5** of high rank or social standing; self-important *la18-*, *now local Sh-Edb*. **6** *of letters of the alphabet* capital *la19-*, *Sh NE*.

adv to a large extent, much, greatly, very *la14-*.

n a large quantity, a great deal *la14-*.

~dom &c size, bulk *la16-17*, *only Sc*. **Mucklie &c** the fair held on **M~** *Friday*, *la19-*, *Kcdn Ags Fif*.

~-boukit &c 1 physically big and broad, burly *19-e20*. **2** pregnant *19-*, *now local Sh-wLoth*. **~ chair** a large armchair *18-*, *local Sh-Kcb*. **~ coat &c** an overcoat *18-*, *now Sh NE Edb*. **~ deil &c** the Devil, Satan *17-*, *now Sh Loth Gall*. **~ feck** the greater part, the lion's share *la19-*, *NE Edb*. **M~ Friday** the Friday on which the half-yearly *hiring market* (HIRE) was held; the hiring market itself *la19-e20*, *Abd Ags*. **~ furth** the open air, the outdoors *la19-*, *Abd Kcdn*. **~ hell** the depths of hell *la19-*, *now Sh*. **~ kirk** the parish church; the *Church of Scotland* (CHURCH) *19-*, *now Sh Ork NE*. **~-kited** pot-bellied *e17*, *20-*, *NE, Fif*. **~-moued &c** having an unusually large mouth *18-*, *now Sh Ork nEC*. **~ pot** the largest cooking pot, a cauldron *la18-*, *now Sh Ork Bnf*. **~ tae** the big toe *la16-*, *now local Sh-Kcb*. **mekill thing &c** a great deal, much *la14-16*. **~ tohoi, ~ tae hae** ['~ tə'hoi, '~ tɪ'he] a gawky empty-headed fellow *20-*, *now Ags Rox*. **~ wame** the stomach of a cow or bullock (as contrasted with the smaller one of a sheep) *16-19*. **~ wheel** a spinning wheel consisting of a large hand-turned wheel connected by a band to the spindle *18-20*. **~ wort** deadly nightshade *16-e17*, *only Sc*.

..an as ~ *used as an intensifying exclam*, *la19-*, *now NE, Ags*. **I've seen as ~ as** *la19-*, **I wadna ~ say but** *19-*, *now Sh Abd* I would not be surprised if. **man** *or* **woman ~** grown-up *la19-*, *now Clcm Kcb Rox*. **mony a mickle maks a muckle** *roughly corresponding to Eng* every little helps *20-* [? altered f *mony a little..*]. **~ aboot it** much the same, without change *la19-*, *now Abd*. **~ an nae little** no small amount of *19-*, *now Abd*. **not to mak ~ o't** show little improvement in an illness *la19-*, *now Sh NE Ags*. [nME *mikel*, OE *micel*, ON *mikill* great, large; *cf* MICH]

mud¹ *la15-*, **mude &c** *15-e17* [mʌd; **məd] n =* mud *15-*.

~ fish *etc* codfish preserved by being salted wet in bulk in the hold of a fishing vessel *la15-20*, *Sh-N, only Sc*.

mud² *n* a small-headed stud for the heels of boots or shoes *19-20*. [obscure; ? *cf* Norw dial *mod*, ON *moð* small objects, refuse of hay etc]

muddle *vti* **1** = muddle. **2** grub about in soil etc with the fingers, *esp* work (potatoes) away from the root by hand leaving the stem undisturbed *la19-*, *now Sh Ayr*.

mude *see* MUD¹, MUID

mudge &c, midge *19-*, *local Ork-WC* [mʌdʒ, mɪdʒ; *Ayr *mudʒ] vti* (cause to) move, stir, shift *la18-*.

n **1** a movement *19-*, *now local Ork-SW*. **2** a sound, a whisper; a rumour *19-*, *now NE nEC Dnbt*.

mudgins &c, mudgeoune &c *la16* movements, *esp* movements of the features, grimaces *la16-e20*. [see SND, and DOST *mudgeoune*; *cf* also MURGEON]

mudge *see* MIDGE
mufabill *see* MOVEABLE
mufe *see* MUVE
muff &c, mouf &c *16-17*, *only Sc* [mʌf] *n* = muff, *now freq in bird-name combs 16-*: '*muff cock*'; '*muffie wheybeard*'.

muffed &c *of a domestic fowl* having a crest or tuft of feathers at the head, or round the neck or legs *18-e19*.

muffell &c *n* a muffler or chin-cloth *16-e17*. [*cf* northern eModEng (once) *muffle* (*n*), eModEng *mofeler*, *muffler* (*n*), f laME *muffle* (*v*) and *cf* MUZZLE *n* 3]

muffle &c, muffil *la16 n* a mitten *la16-e20*. [F *moufle*, MedL *muffula*, MDu *moffel*; *cf* obs Eng = a boxing-glove]

mug¹ &c *n* **1** an earthenware container or jar *16-19*. **2** *also* **moog** *la19-e20*, *Cai Mry* = mug, a drinking vessel.

mugger an itinerant tinker *19-*, *Bnf sEC, S* [*orig* one who sold earthenware mugs *etc*].

mug² *n, marbles* **1** the hole in the ground used as a target *19-*, *now Ayr*. **2** *chf* **muggie** the name of the game itself *la19-*, *now WC*. [perh extension of prec]

mug³ *v* **muggin** a beating *la19-*, *now wLoth Lnk*. [Eng boxing slang *mug* strike on the *mug* (face)]

mug⁴ &c *n* drizzling rain, *freq* with mist or fog *19-*, *now Abd Ags*.

vi drizzle, *esp* in misty weather *19-*, *now Ags*.

muggle = *v*, *19-*, *now Abd*. **muggy &c 1** drizzling, wet and misty *19-*, *now Sh-NE Uls*. **2** = muggy. [ME (once) *v*; *cf* Norw dial *mugga* (*v*), *mugg* (*n*) drizzle, ON *mugga* soft drizzling mist]

mug⁵ &c *n, freq attrib* a breed of very woolly sheep with wool even covering the face, imported from England to improve the quality of wool in the Scottish breeds *la18-19*. [eModEng, obscure; perh *orig* = hornless; *cf* ModEng *mugged cow* a hornless cow]

muggart &c ['mʌgərt; *Cai* 'mugərd; *Arg Dmf* 'mugər] *n =* mugwort *19-20*.

~ kail = *n* *19-*, *now Cai*.

muggie *see* MUG²
muggin *see* MUG³
muggins &c ['mʌgənz; *Arg* 'mug-] *n* mugwort *la19-*, *now Abd Uls*. [shortened f MUGGART + *-ins*]

muggle *see* MUG⁴
muid &c *16-*, *now Sh Ags Kcb*, **mude** *la14-e17*, **meid &c** *la16-20*, *NE*; **mood** *la15-* [məd; *mɪd; NE* mid] *n, in OSc only verse* = mood *la14-*.

mudie &c *adj, chf early verse* brave, bold *la14-18* [there are poss early forms in vars of the surname *Moodie, la13-*].

muif *see* MUITH

muild[1] &c *16-e17*, **muld &c** *15-e17*, **mule &c** *la15-17*, **mold &c** *la15-e17*, **mould &c** *la17-*, **meild &c** *la16-18, NE*, **meall &c** *la17-20, NE*; **mool &c** *17-*, **moud &c** *19-* [møl(d), mïl(d); mul(d); mold, mʌud; *NE* mil(d)] *n* **1** = mould, earth etc *la15-*. **2** soil broken up in the process of cultivation, loose soil, lumps of earth (1) *in sing, 16-e17*; (2) *in pl, la16-*. **3** (1) *chf in pl* the earth of the grave *15-*. (2) *in sing* the grave *15-*. (3) *chf in pl, freq with ref to witchcraft* earth as the remains of a buried corpse *16-17*.

v, only **mule, meall &c, mool 1** *vt* crumble (one substance **in** with another) *la16-, now NE*. **2** *lit and fig* crumble down, reduce to fragments *18-, now NE Ags*. **3** *vi, of persons, chf* ~ **in** (1) mix well together, fraternize or associate (**with**) *la16-, now Ork NE Edb*; (2) curry favour **with** *20-, now Abd*.

mealock &c, moolock &c a crumb, a small fragment *la19-*. **meelackie** = *prec 19-, now Abd Ags*. ~**ie &c** *n* a child's marble of burnt clay *la19-, now Ayr*. *adj* **1** liable to crumble, crumbling *la19-, now Fif Ayr*. **2** *of earth* crumbled, finely broken up *19-, now Ork Sh*. **3** earthy, deep in the soil *19-, local Sh-SW*.

moolin(g) &c *la18-*, **millen &c** *la19-, lit and fig* a crumb, a fragment *18-*. **moolock** *see* mealock. ~ **bred &c** = mouldboard *la14-*. ~ **fur(row)** the last furrow of a RIG[1], ploughed on soil from which the sod has already been turned over *la19-, local Ork-Per*. **mulde-meyt** [*-mit] *appar* food sacrificed over a grave *e16*.

abune the ~ alive, in this world *20-, Sh Ork NE*.

muild[2] &c *16-e18, only Sc*, **muld &c** *la15-e17, only Sc*, **mule &c** *17-e20*, **mold** *la16*; **mould** *16-* [møl(d); *NE* mil] *n* **1** = mould, a pattern etc *la15-*. **2** a button-mould of bone or metal; a button made of such a mould covered with cloth; *latterly* a flat linen-covered button *18-e20*.

muldry &c [*'møldrɪ] moulded work, moulding; ornamental masonry on the cornices etc of a building, similar ornamentation in joinery *16-17, only Sc*. **meelie** = *n* 2, *e20, NE*.

muilder &c *la17-*, **moulder** *17-*; **mooler &c** *18-* ['møldər; *Rox* 'mølər; *SW, S* 'mulər] *vti* = moulder.

n crumbled fragments of oatcake (AIT) *la19-, now Sh Uls*.

muir &c *la15-, only Sc*, **mure &c** *la14-e19*; **more &c** *15-17*, **moor** *17-*, **meer &c** *18-, NE, only Sc*, **mair** *la19-, C, only Sc* [mør, mer; *NE* mir; *NE also* mjur; *St* mjur, mur] *n* **1** = moor *la14-*. **2** rough, uncultivated heathery land considered as part of an estate *la15-*. **3** (1) a tract of unenclosed uncultivated ground held by a proprietor or *chf* a community, the common; *latterly freq* the market green *la15-, Gen*

except *Sh Ork, freq in place-names*. (2) *in pl, 15-17*. **4** PEAT[1], peaty soil; a layer of PEAT[1] *la18-, now Sh Ork*.

~**y &c** *18-19*, ~**ish** *17-e19* consisting of or abounding in moorland.

~**band &c** a hard subsoil of sand and clay with embedded stone, impervious to water *19-, now Fif Rox*. ~**burn** the controlled burning of moorland to clear the way for new growth, *freq* **make** ~**burn** *15-, only Sc*. ~**cheeper** the meadow pipit *20-, now Per WC*. ~**cock &c** the male red grouse *15-*. ~ **duck** the wild duck, the mallard *la19-, now Bnf Kcb*. ~ **fowl &c** the red grouse *16-, only Sc*. ~**hen** (female of the) red grouse *16-*. ~**ill &c** red-water, a disease of cattle *la16-e19*. ~**land** = moorland; *freq attrib* moorland-bred or -grown, rustic, uncouth *16-*. ~ **pout &c** a young red grouse *16-e20*. ~ **road** a road leading through moorland *20-, now NE Ayr*. ~**stone** the stone from outcrop rock on moorland, *freq* granite *la18-, now Bnf*.

throu the ~ a dressing-down, a severe scolding *la20-, Abd Ags Per*. [in place-names *la12-*]

muirment &c, murement [*'mørmənt, &c] *n* stones and rubbish which blocked up the workings in Sheriffhall Colliery *la17-18, midLoth*. [only Sc; ? OSc *mure* (once, *la14*), laME *mure(n)*, F *murer*, L *mūrāre* block up by building a wall]

muist &c *la16-e19*, **muste &c** *la15-17*; **moist** *la15-e16* [*mʌst, *møst, *must] *n* **1** = musk, *freq attrib, eg* ~ **ball** a pomander *la15-e19*. **2** hair powder *la18-e19*.

vt apply hair powder to, powder (a wig) *la18-e19*.

~**it &c** perfumed with musk; ? containing musk *la16-e17, only Sc*. [only Sc; OF *must*, var of *musc* musk]

muith &c *19-e20*; **meeth &c** *la18-e19, chf Abd*, **meef** *la20-, Sh-Cai*, **muif &c** *20-, Sh Ork Rox*, **meich- &c** *20, local* [møθ; *NE* miθ; *Sh Ork* møf; *Cai* mif; *Ayr Rox also* mix] *adj* **1** (1) *of the atmosphere* oppressively close and humid *la18-e20*. (2) *of persons* oppressed or exhausted by heat *la18-, now Cai*. **2** cheerful *la18-e19*. ~**lie &c** in a soft, smooth way *19-e20*. ~**y** = *adj* **1** (1) *20-, now Ork Edb Ayr*. ~**ness** an oppressively hot and moist atmosphere *la18-e20*. [ON *móða* condensed vapour, mist]

muk *see* MUCK

mukill *see* MUCKLE

mulberry *n* **1** = mulberry. **2** the white beam *la19-, Abd Kcdn nEC, only Sc*.

mulctur *see* MULTURE

muld *see* MUILD[1], MUILD[2]

muldoan *n* the basking shark *20-, Abd Ayr*. [only Sc; obscure; perh Gael]

mule &c [*møl, *mʌl] *n* a kind of soft shoe or slipper *la16-17*. [F; *cf* eModEng (twice) *moyle* and ModEng re-introduction of F form = a backless slipper]

mule *see* MUILD[1], MUILD[2]

mull[1] *la16-*, **mule** &c *la15-18*; **mole** &c *14-e15* [mʌl; *SW* mul, moil, &c; *møl] *n, chf in place-names* a promontory, headland *14-*.
adj in deriv etc.
~**och** &c a cow without horns *19-e20, WC, SW; cf* MOYLIE. [Gael *maol* (*adj*) bald, bare; hornless; (*n*) a headland; *maolag* a hornless cow]

mull[2] *n* **1** *in pl* the labia of the vulva *e16*. **2** *in sing* the mouth or muzzle of an animal; the lip of (*chf*) a cow; *also transf of a person, 16-, chf Sh Ork, now Fif*. [Norw dial *mule* the lips of an animal, ON *múli* the muzzle]

mull *see* MILL

mullach ['mʌləx] *n, affectionate term of address* my dear *20-, Cai*. [only Sc; Gael *muileach* dear]

muller &c, **mullo(u)r** *16 n* a frame or moulding, *chf of wood 16-19*.
~**it** furnished with a moulding or ornamental framing, framed *la16-17*. [F *moulure* (*n*), *mouler* (*v*) mould; *cf* eModEng (once) *muller* (*n*)]

mulligrumph *see* MOLLIGRANT

mullor, mullour *see* MULLER

multiplepoinding ['mʌltɪpl'pɪndɪŋ] *n, law* an action which may be brought by or in the name of the holder of a fund or property, to determine which of several claimants has preferential right thereto or in what proportions the fund or property is to be divided *17-*. [only Sc; Eng *multiple* + verbal noun of POIND]

multiplie &c [*'mʌltɪpli, *-plaɪ] *n* multitude, (a) (large) number or quantity *la15-16*. [only Sc; OF *multepli*, f *multiplier* (*v*)]

multure &c; **mouter** &c *la15-e20*, **mutter** *la15-17*, **mulctur** &c *16* ['mutər; *Bnf* 'mju-; *'multər; *'mʌltər, *'mʌtər] *n* a duty consisting of a proportion of the grain or meal payable to the proprietor or tenant of a mill on corn ground there; the right to this duty *15-19*.
vt pay MULTURE on (grain); charge MULTURE against (a person); levy MULTURE on (grain) (at a particular rate) *15-e20*.
~**er** &c *14-18*, **multrar** &c *la14-16* an official with the duty or right of collecting MULTURE.
~ **aith** &c an oath as to the amount and kind of grain which one has had ground other than at the mill to which one is *astricted* (ASTRICT) *la16-e17, only Sc*. ~ **free** &c exempted from payment of MULTURE; without having to pay MULTURE; without exacting payment of MULTURE *15-19*. ~ **malt, meal** *etc* malt, meal etc paid or payable as MULTURE *16-18*. ~ **schaiff** &c *appar* some proportion (? a tithe) of the corn growing within a SUCKEN[1] appropriated as a due to the mill *la15-17, only Sc*. [ScL *multura* ?*13-e14*; nME *multir*, eModEng *multer*, *mulcture*, *mooter*, OF *molture*, MedL *multura*, earlier *mol(i)tura*, f *molere* (*v*) grind]

mum *n, chf in negative* not a word, not a murmur *la16-20*.
vi utter the least sound; mutter, mumble *la16-e20*. [ME]

mumble *see* MUMMLE

mumchance *see* MUMSCHANCE

mummle &c, **mummill** &c; **mumble** &c *17- vti* = mumble *la16-*.
mumbler an implement for breaking clods, a kind of heavy harrow *20-, now Fif wLoth Rox*.

mump &c; **mamp** *e19 vti* **1** *vt, or vi* (~ **at**) nibble by twitching the lips in a succession of rapid movements like a rabbit *18-, now WC-S Uls, only Sc*. **2** *vt, or vi* (~ **at**) mumble, mutter *19-, Gen except Sh Ork*. **3** *only Sc* (1) grumble, complain peevishly *19-, Gen except Sh Ork*; (2) sulk, mope around; loaf around *19-20*. **4** communicate by gesture and grimace without overt speech *18-, now Bnf Abd, only Sc*.
n a word, a whisper, the merest suggestion (of something) *19-, now Bnf, only Sc*.
adj depressed, sullen *la19-, local NE-S, only Sc*. [Eng; *adj* perh another word; *cf* MOUP and MAP[2]]

mum(s)chance &c *n* (a) masquerade, mumming *la16*. [MLowGer *mummen-schanze* a game of dice, a masquerade, MDu *momme-canse*, f *mummen* act in dumb show + *schanz* f F *chance*; *cf* eModEng *mumchance*]

mun &c *n, cant or gipsy, chf in pl* the mouth, the 'chops' *19-e20, local*. [prob f LowGer *mund* mouth]

mun *see* MON[1]

mundan(e) *adj* **1** = mundane *la15-*. **2** of the world, of the earth *16-e17, only Sc*.

mundheri (*sheep-counting*), **methery** (*children's rhymes*) numeral four *e20*. [see ZEENDI]

mundiall &c *adj* worldly *la15-16*. [Eccl L *mundiālis*, OF *mundial* &c, f L *mundus* world; *cf* eModEng (once)]

mundy *n* a kind of heavy hammer weighing about 20-28 lbs (9-13 kilos) used *esp* by shipwrights *20-, Edb WC*. [prob f name of the firm of shipsmiths, J Mundy, Partick *la19-e20*]

mune &c *15-*, **mone** &c *la14-e17*; **moon** &c *15-*, **meen** *la19-, NE*, **min** *la19-e20* [møn, mɪn; *N* min; *nEC* men] *n* **1** = moon *la14-*. **2** a (lunar) month *la15-, now Rox*. **3** a very long period of time, an 'eternity', an 'age' *la18-e20*. **4** that part of a clock which exhibited the phases of the moon *16-e17*. **5** the goldcrest *la19-, Rox*.
~ **bow** *la19-, now local*, ~ **broch** *la19-* a halo round the moon, believed to be a sign of an approaching storm. ~**licht flitting**, **meen-lichtie flitting** *20-, NE* a secret removal during the night *la18-*.
the auld ~ in the airm(s) o the new *etc* the disc of the full moon faintly illuminated within the crescent moon, believed to be a sign of an approaching storm *la18-*. **at the back of the ~** at a very great distance *la19-, now Sh nEC Uls*. **a month o ~s** a month of Sundays, an impossibly long time, an eternity *la19-, now Sh Ags Uls*.

munge[1] *n* a heap, mixture *e16*. [see DOST]

munge² &c [mun(d)ʒ] *vi* grumble; sulk *la18-e20*.
[orig chf imit, perh w infl f Eng *moon* (*v*) mope
and WHINGE]

munk *see* MINK

munn &c *n* a short-handled horn spoon *18-e20*.
[prob same word as MUN, perh orig in cant of
tinkers, who made horn spoons]

Munonday *see* MONANDAY

Munro [mʌn'ro] *mountaineering* name for any
Scottish peak of 3000 feet (914.4 metres) or
more *la19-*.
~**-bagger,** ~**-bagging** a person who aims or
the act or process of aiming to climb every
MUNRO *la20-*. [f Sir Hugh T Munro, who published a list in 1891; *cf* CORBETT and DONALD]

munsie &c *19-,* **monzie** &c *la17-e19* ['mʌnsi]
n **1** *disparaging* a Frenchman *la17*. **2** a person
deserving contempt and ridicule; an odd-looking or ridiculously-dressed person *19-,* now *Abd*.
3 a person who is in a sorry state, who has been
knocked about etc *la19-e20,* *NE*. **4** the jack or
knave in a set of playing cards *la19-20,* *NE*.
mak a ~ **o** reduce to a ridiculous or sorry
state, spoil, bungle *la19-,* *NE*. [reduced f F *mon-
sieur* a gentleman]

munt¹ *la16-,* **mont** &c *16-17;* **mount** *15-*
[mʌnt; *munt] *vti* **1** = mount *la15-*. **2** *vt* provide (a person) with clothing or equipment
17-18, *only Sc*. **3** adorn, trim (a garment etc)
17-, *Gen except Sh Ork,* *only Sc*. **4** *vi* prepare to set
off; depart *la18-e20*.
n, *in pl* fittings, decoration, *esp* of metalwork on
wood *la19-,* *local C*.
munting &c equipment, dress, *esp* a bride's
trousseau *la19-,* now *wLoth Kcb Slk*.

munt² &c *la16-,* **mont** *la14-17;* **mount** &c
15- [mʌnt] *n* **1** = mount, a hill *la14-*. **2** hilly
land, high land, moorland *la16-e17,* *only Sc*. **3** a
low tree-covered hill *la19-,* *Fif Ayr*. [*cf* MONTH²]

muntain *see* MOUNTAIN

munter *see* MONTER

mup-mup *see* MOUP

murder *see* MURTHER¹

murdris &c *la15-17;* **murthrys** &c *la14-e16*
[*'mʌrdrɪs, *'mʌrðrɪs, *'mʌrdərs] *vt, pt, ptp* ~**t**
la14-17, **murderist** &c *16,* **murdre(i)ssit**
16-e17 murder; *without implication of blame* slay
(a person) *la14-17*.
murderisar &c *16,* **murdre(i)s(s)ar** *16* a
murderer.
murdreis hoill a loop or loop-hole in a fortification for the defenders to shoot through
la16-e17. [OF *murdriss-,* lengthened stem of
murdrir; cf eModEng (once) *murtrish* and
MURTHER¹]

mure *see* MUIR

murement *see* MUIRMENT

murgeon &c, **murgeoun** &c *16;*
morgeoun &c *16,* **murgon** &c *la16-e20*
['mʌrdʒən] *n* a grotesque movement of the
body or face; a contortion, a grimace *16-e20*.

vti mock with exaggerated posturing or
grimaces; grimace, posture *la16-e20*. [appar
var with intrusive *-r-* of *mudgeoune* (MUDGE)]

murgully *see* MARGULLIE

murk *see* MIRK

murl, murle; mirl &c *la19-e20* [mʌrl, mɪrl] *v,*
freq ~ **doon 1** *vt, also fig* crumble, reduce to
fragments, ruin *la15, 19-*. **2** *vi* crumble away as
from decay, moulder *19-,* now *Ork NE, EC*.
n a crumb, fragment, *esp* of oatcakes (AIT) *la19-,*
NE nEC.
murlack &c = *n,* *la19-e20*. **murlie** &c crumbly, friable *19-,* *NE, EC*. **murlin** *n* a crumb,
fragment *la19-,* *N, EC*. *adj* crumbling, mould-
ering *20-,* *NE Fif wLoth*. [see SND]

murle &c *vi* murmur, burble, babble *19*. [fre-
quentative of MURR]

murlin &c *n* a round narrow-mouthed basket
used *chf* by fishermen *la18-,* now *Abd*. [ScGael
mùrluinn, mùrlag a basket for holding wool,
IrGael *murlóg, murlán* a basket as in *n*]

murmell &c, **murmill** *vt* grumble at; mutter,
mumble *16-e20*.
n the expression of discontent *e16*. [only *Sc; cf*
OF *mormeler, murmeler,* Ger *murmeln* murmur]

murmichan ['mʌrmɪxən] *n* a BOGLE or wicked
fairy used to frighten children *20-,* now *Ags*.
[obscure]

murmill *see* MURMELL

murmur &c *vti* **1** = murmur *15-*. **2** *in impersonal and passive as* it is *etc* (**heavily** *etc*) ~**it**
that .. (great) discontentment is expressed that
.. 15-17, *only Sc*. **3** *vt* complain against; calumniate; *latterly specif law* cast reflection on the
character or integrity of (a judge) *15-,* *only Sc*.
~**ashen** *20-,* *Sh,* ~**atio(u)n** &c *la15-17* a murmur or clamour of rumour (*la15-17*) or discontent (*la15-*); the expression of discontent,
grumbling.

murn, murne &c; **mourn** &c *la16-,* **morn**
&c *la16* [mʌrn] *vti* **1** = mourn *la14-*. **2** *vi* complain, show resentment, grumble *la19-,* *only Sc*.
n, see phrase below.
~**ing** &c *n* **1** = mourning *la14-*. **2** *in pl* the
black garments worn to show grief *la17-*. ~**ing**
hem *joc* the inner rim of a tea-cup visible
between the tea and the lip of the cup, *usu*
implying that not enough tea has been served
la20-, *local Per-Lnk,* *only Sc*. ~**ing letter** a
black-edged letter of invitation to a funeral *20-,*
local Sh-Kcb, *only Sc*. ~**ing string** a black sash
or a black streamer for a hat etc, worn as a sign
of mourning *la17-e18,* *only Sc*.
mak (a) ~ **for** *or* **ower** lament, bewail *la19-,*
now *Abd*.

murr &c [mʌr] *vi* make a continuous vibrating,
murmuring or purring sound; *of a cat* purr;
growl *19-,* now *Abd*.
n a purring, whirring or murmuring sound as
made by a cat, a baby, the sea etc *19-e20*.
[onomat]

Murra(**y**) the province or district of Moray *16-17*.

murther[1] **&c** *13-e20*; **murder &c** *la15-*, **morthour &c** *16* *n* = murder *13-*.
vt **1** = murder *15-*. **2** harass, torment, distress *19-*, now *Sh Per Uls*.
~**er &c, murdrer** *la15-16* **1** = murderer *la14-*. **2** *only* **murderer** a device for catching deep-sea fish *la19-*, *local Sh-Kcb*.
mak ~ (**up**)**on** = *v* **1**, *la15-16*, *only Sc*. [*cf* MURDRIS]

murther[2] *vi, of a child* murmur, whimper, sob quietly *19-e20*. [*chf* onomat; *cf* MURR and Eng *murmur, mutter* etc]

murther[3] **&c** *n* a murderer *la14-e17*. [only Sc; OE *myrðra*]

murthrys *see* MURDRIS

musche taffetie &c *n* ? = *muschit taffetie* (MUSCHIT) *la16*. [only Sc; *cf* F *mouche* a spot as part of a design, but perh altered f next]

muschit &c *adj, chf of taffeta* spotted *la16*. [only Sc; OF *mouchete*; *cf* prec]

muschkin *see* MUTCHKIN

Muscovia Muscovy; Russia *e17*. [only Sc; ModL; *cf* eModEng *Muskovie*]

Muscovy *adj* **m~ cat** a tortoiseshell cat *la20-*, *SW*.

muse *n* a room to be used for meditation or study *la17*. [only Sc; *cf* Eng *muse* (*v*) and obs Eng *musæum* a place dedicated to the pursuit of learning etc]

mush[1] *n* **1** = mush. **2** the mixture of oak saw-dust and chips burned when smoking herring to make kippers, *chf* ~ **house** a store for the mixture *20-*, *Sh NE*.
~**och &c** [*ˈmʌʃox, &c*] a heap of grain, *chf* threshed seed-corn *18-e19, SW*.

mush[2] *n, in negative* not a whisper, not a sound *19*. [only Sc; onomat]

mush[3] *vt, needlework* gather, flounce, puff (**out**); scallop, cut into a pattern with a stamp *17-*, now *Abd Edb*. [? OF *moucher* trim]

music *la15-*, **musike &c** *15-20*; **maisic &c** *la19-e20, only Sc*, **meesick &c** *la18-20, NE, only Sc* [ˈmøzɪk, ˈmezɪk; *NE* ˈmɪzɪk; *Ork Kcb* also ˈmuzɪk] *n* = music *15-*.
~**er &c** a musician *19-e20*.

musicianer &c [məˈzɪʃ(ə)nər] *n* a musician *16-*, now *SW Uls*. [obs in Eng]

musie &c *n, verse* = muse *la18-19, only Sc*.

musike *see* MUSIC

muskan &c *n* a razor-fish *19-*, *Wgt*. [Gael *mùsgan*]

muskane &c *adj, of a tree* rotten, decayed *16*. [only Sc; see DOST]

musken *see* MUTCHKIN

muslin &c *17-*, **musseline &c** *17-18* *n* **1** = muslin *17-*. **2** a fine linen fabric *18*.
~ **kail** a thin soup made from barley and vegetables without any meat-stock *la18-e20, only Sc*.

mussel &c, mussill &c *16* *n* = mussel *16-*.
~ **brose** BROSE made from mussel-BREE[1] mixed with oatmeal *la18-19*. ~ **midden** *lit and fig* a refuse heap where mussel-shells are thrown *la19-*, now *Fif*. ~**-picker &c** the oyster-catcher *la19-20*. ~ **scaup &c** a mussel-bed *la15-*, now *Sh NE Fif*.

musseline *see* MUSLIN

mussell *see* MUZZLE

mussill *see* MUSSEL

mussour *see* MEASURE

mustard &c; mustart &c *la15-*, **mustar &c** *16-e17, chf Sc* *n* = mustard *15-*.
~ **stane &c** a stone on or with which mustard is pounded *16-e17*.

must-cat *n, appar* a musk-deer or a civet cat *e16*. [only Sc; *cf* eModEng *musk-cat*]

muste *see* MUIST

mutch &c *la16-*, **much &c** *la15-e17* [mʌtʃ] *n* **1** a kind of hood or coif, *chf* of linen etc (1) worn by men, *chf or only* as a nightcap etc *la15-e17, only Sc*; (2) worn by women by night or day, *specif* a close-fitting cap worn by married women *la16-e20*. **2** an old woman *20-, Fif SW*.
~ **string** the string for tying a MUTCH under the chin *la19-*, now *Ork Per*.
auld wife's ~**es** a plant with a bonnet-like flower, *eg* the columbine *la19-*, *local Abd-Ayr*.
night ~ a nightcap *la18-*, now *Ork*. [MDu *mutse &c*, MLowGer *mutze &c*, EFris *mütse &c*; *cf* eModEng (once) and ModGer *Mütze* a cap]

mutchkin &c *la16-*, **muchkin &c** *15-18*, **muchin &c** *17-e18*; **muschkin &c** *la16-17*, **musken &c** *la16-*, now *Dmf Kcb*, **mutchin &c** *16-e19*, **mu**(**t**)**chskin &c** *16-17*, **mut-skin &c** *la16-18* [ˈmʌtʃkɪn; *Dmf, Kcb* ˈmʌskən; *ˈmʌtʃɪn; *ˈmʌtskɪn] *n* a measure of capacity for (*chf*) liquids or for powdered or granulated solids = ¼ pint SCOTS, *ie* ¾ pint imperial (.43 litre); a container of this capacity *15-*; *latterly* (*18-*) sometimes = an imperial pint *esp* of spirits *la17-e20*. [only Sc; eModDu *mudseken* a measure of capacity, dim of *mutse* a measure of wine]

mute &c; mote [*møt] *n* **1** a formal meeting to discuss and transact official or legal business *15-e16*. **2** (1) an action at law, a plea *15-e17*. (2) *in sing without article* litigation *15-e17*. [ME *mote, moot*(*e*), *imot*, OE (*ge*)*mōt*, ON *mót*]

mute *see* MOOT

mute-hill *n, appar* a hill on which assemblies were held, but sometimes *perh* simply a mound *15-e16*. [appar MUTE + Eng *hill* but perh orig *mot hill* a mound or hillock, f MOTE[1]]

mutilation, mutilatioun &c *16-e17*; **mutulatioun** *16-e17, only Sc*, **mitilatioun &c** *la16-e17, only Sc* [*mətəˈleʃun, &c*] *n* **1** = mutilation *16-*. **2** *law* the (crime of) wounding or disabling of a person in a limb, whether or not it is severed *16-e19, only Sc*.

mutilit &c [*møtəlɪt] *ptp, adj* mutilated, maimed *la16-e17*. [*cf* eModEng (once) *mutil'd*]

mutskin *see* MUTCHKIN

mutter *see* MULTURE

muttie &c *n* a measure for grain, *orig* equal to a third or a quarter of a peck, *latterly prob* a smaller measure; the vessel containing this amount *la17-e20, N*; *cf* HADDISH. [obscure]

mutton &c, muttoun &c *15-17*; **motoun &c** *la14-16*, **moutoun &c** *15-16* ['mʌtən; *'mut-] *n* **1** = mutton *la14-*. **2** *collectively* the carcasses of sheep *15-e17, only Sc*. **3** *of gloves* sheepskin *la16, only Sc*.

~ **bouk &c** the carcass of a sheep *16-e18, only Sc*. ~ **ham** a leg of mutton cured in the same way as a ham *19*.

Mutual Instruction Association; Mutual Improvement Society &c a local society for the dissemination of knowledge on learned topics by means of papers given and discussions held by its members *19-20*.

mutulatioun *see* MUTILATION

mutuum ['mjutjuʌm] *n, law* a contract by which the borrower of goods for consumption, *eg* food, agrees to repay a like quantity of the same goods instead of the actual goods borrowed *la17-*. [L = a loan]

muve &c *16-e20*, **move &c** *la14-*, **mufe &c** *15-16, only Sc*, **meeve** *la19-20, NE*; **moif &c** *15-16, only Sc* [møv; *NE* miv] *vti, n* = move. **meevie nor mavie** *in negative* not a movement or sound *19, NE*.

muzzle &c *la16-*, **mussell &c** *la15-18*, **missell &c** *16-17, only Sc*; **miz(z)le** *18-e20, only Sc* ['mʌzl, 'mɪzl] *n* **1** = muzzle *la15-*. **2** the bridle of a plough *16-, now C Uls*. **3** a muffler or chincloth as worn by women for protection or disguise *16-e17, chf Sc*; *cf* MUFFELL.
vti = muzzle *la16-*.
~**it** having the face covered with a muffler etc, masked, *chf* for concealment or disguise *la15-e17, only Sc*.

my &c, me &c *la15-17, la19-e20*; **may &c** *16-17*, **ma** *19-*, **mi** *e16, e20 (Sh)* [maɪ; ma, *unstressed* mə; *Sh Ork* mi, mɪ] *possessive adj* **1** = my, *orig commoner than* MINE[2] *before consonants except* h-, *but also occurring before vowels (15-) and* h- *(la14-) la14-*. **2** used with certain nouns where Eng omits *eg* bed, dinner etc *la18-, only Sc*: '*I am going to my bed*'; *cf* THE.

myane *see* MOYEN[1], MOYEN[2]

myave [mjɑv] *n* = maw, stomach *la19-20, NE*; *cf* MAUVIE.

myles *la17-*, **miles** *19-*, **mildis &c** *e16* [məilz, *məildz] *n pl* name for several varieties of the *Chenopodeae* and for several of the orache plant family *16-, now SW Uls*. [ME *mielde*, OE *melde*]

myll, mylne *see* MILE

myntime *see* MEANTIME

myowt &c [mjʌut] *n, chf in negative* not a sound, not a whisper *esp* of complaint or protest *la19-, NE*. [var of MOOT *n*]

myre *see* MIRE

myrthus *n* the myrtle *e16*. [ME, L *myrtus*]

mysel &c *16-*, **myself &c** *15-*; **my selfin &c** *la14-16*, **masel(l) &c** *la19-* [mə'sɛl, *Sh Ork* mi'sɛl; maɪ'sɛlf, *-'sɛl(vən)] *pronoun* = myself.

myslin &c ['məislɪn, ?'mɛs-] *n* a poor quality coal *la18-e20*. [var of MASHLUM]

myte *see* MITE

myter &c *la15-17*; **mitre &c** *la16-* ['məitər, *St* 'maɪtər] *n* **1** = mitre, the head-dress *la15-*. **2** a paper hat worn as a punishment, *usu* inscribed with the nature of the offence *la16-17, only Sc*.

myth &c [*maɪð] *vt* **1** indicate, reveal, show *la15-16*. **2** observe, notice *la15*. [ME *(once) miþe*, ON *miða*; *cf* MEITH]

myting &c [*'məitɪŋ] *n, abusive, chf flyting* (FLYTE) ? a dwarf, a runt *16*. [late nME *mytyng*, eModEng *myting*; ? f Eng *mite* the insect]

na[1] **&c** [na, nɑ] *adv* **1** *chf immediately before a verb* not, in no way, by no means *la14-16*: '*that he na louit him never a deill*'. **2** = no, the negative response *la14-*.
conj that .. not, but (that), other than *la14-16*.
~ **had** (**nocht bene**) had it not been (**that**), but for *la14-e15*. ~ **war** (**it**) were it not (**that**) *la14-e15*. [nME *na*, OE *nā*, ? f *ne* + *ā* ever; *cf* NAE[2]; see DOST]

na[2], **nae** *18-*, **ne** *16-* [nə; *EC* nɪ] *adv*, *unstressed*, *chf used with aux verbs as* **canna**, **dinna** = not *16-*. [unstressed var of NO[1]; see DOST, SND]

na[3], **nae**, **no** *NE* [nə, nɪ; *NE also* no] *adv*, *freq toning down a question or request* now, then *19-*. [unstressed form of NOO]

na[4], **nay** *15-16*, **ne** *15-16* [nə; *nɪ] *conj* **1** nor, and not *la14-16*. **2** than *la14-*. [n, eME *na*, OE *nā*, special use of NA[1]; *cf* NO[2], NO[3]]

na[5] [na] *interj* really, indeed *18-*, *now Sh NE*. [see SND]

na *see* NAE[1]

naar *see* NAR

nab **&c** *n* a peg or nail on which to hang things *18-*, *now Abd Ayr Uls*. [see SND]

nab *see* KNAP[2]

nabal **&c**; **nabald** **&c** *e20*, *Sh Ork* ['nɑbəl(d), 'nabl] *n* a miser *la18-20*.
adj grasping, churlish *la19-*, *now Abd Kcdn*. [f the biblical Nabal, I Samuel xxv]

nabb **&c**; **knab**(**b**) *Sh Ork* [(k)nab] *n* a hillock, summit *19-e20*, *chf Sh*. [also in nEng dial; Norw dial *(k)nabb*, ON *nabbi*; *cf also* NAB]

nabb, **nabbery** *see* KNAB[2]

nabble *vti* **1** = nibble *20-*, *now Sh*. **2** *vi*, *chf clothmaking* work with speed and deftness *20-*, *Ags Per*.

nabery *see* KNAB[2]

nace; **ness** [*nes] *adj* pitiable, destitute *la18-19*, *Abd*. [ME *nais*, ON *neiss*]

nacked *see* NAKIT

nacket[1] **&c**, **nakket** **&c**; **nocket** **&c** *19-e20* *n* **1** a type of small fine loaf *la16-e20*. **2** a packed lunch, a snack *19-e20*, *chf SW*, *S*. [see SND, DOST]

nacket[2] **&c** *n* **1** a boy, youngster; *specif* a cook's or miller's lad *16-e18*. **2** (1) a small, neat person *la18-*. (2) a pert or precocious child, an imp *la19-*, *now Sh Ork NE*. **3** a little ball *19-*, *now Lnk*.
~**y** **&c** neat *la18-*, *now NE Per*. [OF *nacquet* the ball boy in tennis]

nacky *see* KNACKIE

nadir *see* NEDDER

nae[1] **&c** *la16-*, **na** *la14-18*; **nay** *la15-16*, **ne** *la14-16* [ne] *adj*, *adv* = no, not any *la14-*.
~ **ane** no one *19-*. ~ **kin** *adj* no kind of, not any, no *la14-16*.
be *or* **on** ~ **kin way** *or* **wys** by no means, in no way *la14-16*. ~ **ma** *adj* no greater in number, no further *15-16*. *n* no more *la14-e17*.
~ **mar**(**e**) **&c** *n* nothing more, nothing else *15-*.
adj no further, no other *la14-16*. *adv* **1** no longer, not again; never again *la14-*. **2** in no greater degree, to no greater extent *15*. [nME *na*, reduced f *nān* > NANE, orig only before consonants]

nae[2] **&c** *adv* not *18-*, *chf NE*.
~ **bit &c** no more than, just *20-*, *NE*; *cf* nae a bit (BIT). [perh a re-stressed form of NA[2]]

nae[3] **&c** *adv* = nay, no *19-*. [eModEng *nay*, ON *nei*; *cf* the more usual NA[1] 2]

nae *see* NA[2], NA[3]

nael; **nile** **&c**, **nyvle** **&c** ['nɔi(v)l; *nel] *n* = navel *la18-e20*, *chf SW*. [*cf* gale &c (GAVEL[1])]

naesay *see* NA-SAY

naether *see* NAITHER

naffle *see* NEVEL

nag[1] *n*, *in pl*, *marbles* a game in which the loser is struck on the knuckles by the other players' marbles; the blows so struck *19*. [see SND]

nag[2]; **niag** *20-*, *Uls* [n(j)ag] *n* a hard ball used in SHINTY *la19-*. [var of KNAG[1] *n* 1]

nag *see* KNAG[1], NAIG

nage *see* NAIG

nagus *n* term of abuse for a stingy person *e16*. [*cf* Mod Lancashire dial *nagas*]

naider *see* NAITHER

naig **&c** *16-*, **nag** **&c** *la15-*; **nage** *16-18* [neg; *Cai NE also* njɑg] *n* **1** = nag, a small horse or pony *la15-17*. **2** a horse *in gen*, *18-*.
~**ie** = *n* 1, *18-19*.

nail **&c** *n* = nail *15-*.
vt **1** = nail *la14-*. **2** *fig* clinch (an argument or bargain) *la18-*, *now Sh NE Uls*. **3** hit, strike down, kill *la18-*, *now local*. **4** beat; scold *la19-*, *chf Rox*.
~ **string** the iron rod from which nails are cut *18-19*. **aff at the** ~ deranged *18-*.

nain **&c**, **nane** *adj*, *also* **naun** *la15*, **nawn** **&c** *19-20* (one's) own *la14-e16*, *la18-*, *now local*. *n* what is one's own, one's due *19-e20*.
~**sell 1** = ainsel (AIN) *la19-*, *chf NE*. **2** *chf* **her** ~**sell** (1) *pronoun* a Highlander's (HIELAND) supposed way of speaking of himself, as if = I *la17*: '*her nainsell lives by thift*'. (2) *n*, *joc* a Highlander, *18-*.
by one's ~ alone *19-*, *chf NE*. [wrong division of *myn ain*, *mine awn* (AIN)]

naiphouse **&c**, **napehous**; **nep**(**ho**)**us** [*'nep'hus, *'nɛp-; *'nɛpəs] *n* a dormer *17-e19*. [see SND, DOST]

naipkin **&c**, **napkin** **&c**; **nepkin**, **neepyin** **&c** *la19-*, *local C* ['nepkin, 'n(j)ɛp-, 'nip-, 'nɪp-, 'nɪb-; 'nep(j)ɪn, 'nip-; 'nɛptɪn, 'nip-; *Ross* 'nimkɪn; *Bnf* 'nɛmpən] *n* **1** a pocket-handkerchief; a neckerchief *15-*. **2** *rare* = napkin *la17-*; for Sc word see SERVIT.

nairra **&c** *la16-*, **naro**(**w**) **&c** *la14-16*; **narrow** **&c** ['nɛrə, 'nɛrɑ, *Ork Cai* -o, -u; 'narə; *EC*, *WC*, *S also* 'nɛrɪ, 'nɛrɪ, 'narɪ] *adj* = narrow *la14-*, *in place-names 13-*.
~**ly** **&c** scarcely, barely *la14-e16*.

~-begaun = *near-begaun* (NEAR) *19-*, *local*.
~-boukit thin, lean *la20-*, *Abd Ags Per*.
~-nebbit &c sharp-nosed; *fig* bigoted, *esp* in
religious matters, strict *19-*, *now Uls*. **~ seis**
straits, narrows *16-17*.
nait &c *n* use; profit; purpose *la15-e16*.
adj quick and effective, deft *16*.
~ly &c *adv* skilfully, cleverly *e16*. [nME *nait*,
ON *neyte*]
naither &c;   **nather &c**,   **naether &c**
la16-e20, **naider &c** *la16-e20* ['neðər; *Sh Ork
NE also* 'nedər] *adv* (*conj*), *adj* (*pronoun*) =
neither *la15-*.
~ins *adv, pronoun, following another negative* either
19-, *now NE*: '*A dinna like naitherins o' them*'. **~s**
adv = *prec, 19-e20*: '*the bairns wasna nae great
shake neithers*'. [see DOST, SND and *cf*
AITHER, NOWTHER]
naitional ['neʃənəl] *adj* = national *20-*, *Ork
Abd*.
naitral *see* NATURAL
naitur *see* NATURE
nakit &c;   **nacked &c**   *la16-e18*,   **naked &c**
['nekɪt; *NE also* 'njɑkɪt, 'njakɪt; ***'nakɪt] *adj* **1**
= naked *la14-*.   **2** wearing only an undergarment *16-17*.   **3** unarmed *la14-17*.   **4** exposed
to attack *15-17*.   **5** *of land* bare, barren *16-17*.
6 thin, lean, emaciated *la20-*, *Ags Per Loth*.   **7**
of alcoholic drink neat *19-*, *now Fif Wgt*.
nakket *see* NACKET[1]
nam &c [nam; *Sh Abd* njam] *vt* **1** seize, grab *19-*,
Sh Rox.   **2** eat up greedily *19-*, *chf S*. [see
SND]
name &c; **neam &c** *16-17*, **neem** *la19-*, *Sh-
Cai n, also* **nem** *16-* **1** = name *la14-*.   **2** a title
of rank or dignity; the authority or state which
a title conveys *15-17*.   **3** those bearing a particular name, *esp* a family or CLAN *16-17*.
vt = name *15-*.
namely noted, famed, of good repute *e17, 19-*
[translating Gael *ainmeil* famous f *ainm* a name].
namer, *also* **namie** one of the two chief players
in a children's guessing game (see SND)
la19-e20, *Sh-Abd*.
~ dochter *19-*, **~ son** *la18-* a girl or boy who
has been called after someone *now Sh Ork*.   **~
faither &c** *la17-*, **~ mother &c** *la18-* the man
or woman after whom someone is named.
be ~ed to 1 be assigned or allotted to *la15*.   **2**
specif be named as the sweetheart of *la19-*, *Abd
Uls*. **cannot** *etc* **~** be unable to call by the right
name *la17-*, *now NE Per SW Uls*. **ca (someone) out of his ~ 1** miscall, speak to the detriment of *19-*.   **2** give a nickname to *la19-*, *chf
Uls*. **get the ~** have a child named after one
la19-. **gie (a bairn) its** *or* **a ~** christen (a
child) *20-*. **gie in** *or* **up the ~s** supply the
names for the *proclamation* (PROCLAIM) of marriage banns *19-*. **in ~ of (male, ferme** *etc*)
as payment of (a due) *la14-e17*. **i(n) the ~ (o
a')** *exclam* in heaven's name *la19-*, *NE, WC*.
[*cf* NEM]

nammit *see* NEM
nane &c, **none &c** [nen; *Sh N also* nin; ***non]
pronoun **1** = none *la14-*.   **2** neither (of two) *19-*.
adj = none *la14-*.
adv **1** *with comparative adjs and advs* not any, no
15-e16.   **2** *as an emphatic negative* not at all, in no
way *15-16, 18-*: '*she slept none*'.
~ o the twa neither *19-*. **~ other** *adj, pronoun* = no other *la14-16*.
nane *see* NAIN
nanes &c, **nanis &c** *la14-16* [nens; ***nenz] **for
the ~ 1** for that very purpose, on purpose,
expressly *16*.   **2** *verse, only as rhyme* (1) suitably
for the purpose, accordingly *la14-16*; (2) *as a tag*
certainly, assuredly *la14-16, 19-*.   **3** for a joke
20-, *Cai*. [nME (*for*) *the nanes*, *for þan anes*,
midl and sME *nones*]
nap[1]; knap *18-e20*, *WC-S n, also* **nappie &c** a
bowl, a drinking vessel *18-*. [eME *nap*, OE
hnæpp, ON *hnappr*, MDu *nap*]
nap[2] *n* **tak one's** *or* **the ~ aff (a person)** make
fun of, mock *la19-*. [see SND]
nap *see* NOP
nape *n* an ape *la15-17*. [wrong division]
napehous *see* NAIPHOUSE
naperie &c, **napery &c** ['nep(ə)rɪ] *n* =
napery, *esp* table linen *la15-*.
~ press a linen cupboard *17-*.
Napillis &c; **Naplis &c** ['neplz; ***'nap-] **~
taffetie &c** Naples taffeta *la16-e17*.
napkin *see* NAIPKIN
nappie &c *adj* **1** *of ale etc* foaming, strong *18-*, *chf
literary*.   **2** *of persons* slightly intoxicated,
'merry' *la18-19*.
n (strong) ale *la18-e20*. [eModEng *nappy* =
adj 1]
nappie *see* NAP[1]
nappy *see* KNAP[3]
nar &c, **ner &c**; **naur** *18-*, **naar** *19-*, *Sh NE*,
nerr *19-*, *S* [nar, nɑr; *S* nɛr] *adj* **1** near, close
17, *19-*, *now Kcb Uls*.   **2** near or left-hand
(side) *17*, *la19-*, *now local Abd-Kcb*.   **3** nearer,
closer to the speaker *20-*, *local Sh-Kcb*.
adv **1** *with comparative force* nearer, closer *la14-*.
2 near, close by, nearby *15-e17, 19-*, *now NE*.
3 nearly, almost *19-e20*.
prep close to, beside *la14-*.
narrer *comparative adv* (*la14-*), *prep* (*la16-17*),
narrest *superlative adj* (*15-*), *adv* (*16-17*), *prep*
(*16-17*), nearer, nearest. **~lans**, **~lins** *19-*, *chf
Sh Ork* = *nearlins* (NEAR).
~by ['nar'baɪ, *&c*] *adv, prep* (*la16-19*), **~ hand**
16- = nearby, near hand (NEAR). [nME *narre*,
ME *nerre*, OE *nēarra* comparative of *nēah* nigh,
ON *nære*, northern ModEng dial *nar*; *cf* NEAR]
nar *see* NARR, NOR[1]
narg &c [n(j)arg; *Sh also* n(j)ɪrg] *vi* keep grumbling, nag *19-*, *now Sh-Cai*.
n nagging *19-*, *now Sh*. [see SND]
naro(w) *see* NAIRRA
narr, nar; nyarr &c [n(j)ar] *vi* **1** *of a dog* snarl

e16, la18-, now Bnf Abd. **2** *fig of persons* be discontented or complaining, fret *19-.* [chf NE; imit; eModEng *narr, gnar* = 1; *cf* NURR]

narrate; narret(e) *la17-e18* [naˈret; *ˈnaret, *-ət] *vt* **1** *law* set forth (the relevant facts) in a document *la17-18.* **2** = narrate, relate *la17-.*

narration &c 1 = narration *16-.* **2** the act of reporting, *esp* by way of accusation, complaint or slander; a report or accusation, *freq* **fals** *or* **wrang narratioun** false report, misrepresentation *16-e17.* **3** *law* = narrative 2, *16.* **narrative** *n* **1** = narrative *la16-.* **2** *law* a statement of alleged facts as the basis of a legal action, *freq* **wrang** *etc* **narrative** *la16-17.* **3** *law* that part of a legal document which contains the statement of the alleged facts on which the plea is based *16-e17.* **4** *law* that part of a legal deed which states the relevant essential facts *17-.*

narration &c [noˈreʃən, nə-] *n* an uproar, fuss, clamour *la19-, chf SW, S.* [f wrong division of Eng dial *an oration*]

narret(e) *see* NARRATE

narrow *see* NAIRRA

na-say *18-,* **naysay** *la16-e20;* **naesay** *19-* [ˈnɑˈse, ˈne-] *n* a refusal, denial *la16-.*
vt refuse, deny *18-.* [chf Sc; NA¹ and NAE² *adv* + *say*]

nasche *see* NESH

nash *n* impudent or caustic talk *18-, chf Rox.*
~-gab garrulous or impudent talk *19-, chf Rox;* cf *snash-gab* (SNASH). [*cf* GNASH, SNASH]

nasty *see* NESTIE

nat &c *n* a small-sized, sharp-tempered person *la19-, now Sh Abd.* [see SND]

natch &c *n* **1** a notch or indentation *18-.* **2** *specif, curling* (CURL) a cut made in the ice to hold a player's foot when delivering the stone, a HACK *n* 4, *19-.* **3** ? small scissors used by tailors *18-e19.*
vt make a notch or incision in *18-, chf Sh Abd.* [eModEng; var of Eng *notch*]

nate *see* NEAT

nather *see* NAITHER, NETHER²

natie *see* NEAT

nation &c, natioun &c *la14-e17* [ˈneʃən, *ˈnaʃən] *n* **1** = nation *la14-.* **2** one of the privileged bodies of foreign nationals trading in continental towns, *chf* **the ~ of Scotland, the Scottis ~** *16-e17.* **3** one of the regional divisions of the student body in the Universities of Glasgow and Aberdeen, and until 1858 St Andrews *la15-.* **4** birth; breed, race *la14-16.*
be *or* **of** (**Scottis** *etc*) **~** belonging to the (Scottish etc) nation, (Scottish etc) by nationality *la14-16.*

native &c *adj* **1** = native *15-.* **2** by kinship *16:* 'native moder'. **3** *of lands* belonging to one by right *16.*
n **1** = native *la14-.* **2** a bond tenant or bondman *la14-17.* **3** the district of one's birth *19-, now NE Ags Dmf.*

~ bond, bond ~ a bondman or bond tenant *15.* **~ born &c** born in a country or place; having a certain status by virture of birth *la15-e17.* **~ man 1** = **~** *bond,* 15. **2** a KINDLY tenant *16.* **3** a person's servant, dependant or tenant of long standing or from birth; one born to his service *la14-e17.* **~ servant** = **~** *man* 3, *la16-e17.* **~ tenant** = **~** *man* 2, *la16-e17.*

natter &c; nyatter &c *chf NE,* **nitter- &c** *chf Sh Ork* [ˈn(j)atər; *Sh Ork also* ˈnɪtər] *vi* chatter, *esp* peevishly, nag, grouse *19-.*
n **1** grousing, nagging talk; aimless chatter *la19-.* **2** a bad-tempered, nagging person; a chatterer *20-, Sh NE SW S.*
~ie &c peevish, bad-tempered *la19-, now local.*
nitteret &c ill-natured *la19-, chf Sh Ork.* [see SND]

nattle &c [ˈn(j)atl; *Sh also* n(j)ɪtl] *vt* nibble, chew awkwardly, mumble toothlessly *19-, Sh Rox.* [var of prec]

natural &c [ˈnet(ə)rəl; *St* ˈnatjurəl] *adj* **1** = natural *15-.* **2** native-born, true-born *15-17.* **3** ? sagacious, ? *orig and chf* knowing a country as or as if a native *16-17.* **4** *as adv* = naturally *la19-.*
naturality &c *n* **1** a native endowment, *esp* mental; ability, intelligence *16-e17, e19.* **2** the rights or position of a native-born subject *16-e17.* **3** natural human sympathy *16-17, 19.*
naitral-hertit &c kindly, affectionate *la19-, now Uls.* **~ philosophy** = natural philosophy, the study of natural phenomena, physics: **1** *in gen,* 15-; **2** *Sc Univs* the formal name of the subject and its chair *18-;* see also *philosophour natural* (PHILOSOPHOUR) and PHILOSOPHY. **~ possession** *law* owner-occupancy of a property *17-.*

nature &c; naitur *19-* [ˈnetər] *n* **1** = nature *la14-.* **2** the tenor or purport (of a statute, written agreement etc) *15-17.*
~ grass grass which grows wild and luxuriantly *18-, now NE.*

naturell &c [ˈnetərəl; *ˈnetørɛl] *adj* = NATURAL *15-16.* [ME; F *naturel*]

nauchtie *see* NOCHT

naun *see* NAIN

naur *see* NAR

naval *adj* naval *la15-.*

nave¹ &c; neve &c *la16-e17, only Sc* [nev; *?niv] *n* = nave, the hub of a wheel *16-.*

**nave² [*nev] *n* = NIEVE *la14-e17.* [perh partly corresponding to Norw dial *nava*]

navis-bore &c [*ˈnɑvəsˈbor] *n* a knot-hole in wood *19-20, Bnf Abd.* [orig *navarsbor,* Norw dial *navar,* ON *nafarr* an auger + Norw dial *bor* or Eng *bore* a hole]

navyne &c [*ˈnɑˈvəin, *ˈnevɪn] *n* = navy, a fleet *la14-e16.* [only Sc; see DOST]

nawn *see* NAIN

nay *see* NA⁴, NAE¹

naysay *see* NA-SAY

ne *see* NA², NA⁴, NAE¹

neam *see* NAME

near, nere &c [nir; *nEC, SW also* ner] *adv* **1** = near *la14-*. **2** nearly, almost, all but *la14-*. **3** *specif* with terms of number, quantity or extent *la14-*. **4** narrowly, only just *19-*, *now Sh Ags SW.*
prep **1** = near *la14-*. **2** closely related to or associated with *la14-16*.
adj **1** closely related by blood or kinship *la14-*. **2** = near *15-*.
vti draw near (to), approach *16-*.
at the ~est by the shortest or quickest way *18-*. **~lins** almost *la18-*, *now Sh Abd.* **~nes** closeness of kinship *15-e17*.
~ about(s) *prep (adv)* close by, in the vicinity (of) *15*, *17*, *la19-*. *adv* almost, by and large *la19-*. **~-begaun &c** miserly *19-*, *local.* **~ beside** *adv, prep* near *la14-17*. **~by** ['nir'baɪ] *adv* **1** close at hand *la14-*. **2** nearly *la15-*, *chf Sc. prep* near, beside *la14-*. **~ cut** a short cut *la18-*. **~ gaun** = **~ begaun**, *la18-*, *chf Sh-N, S.* **~ hand** *adv* **1** near at hand, close by *la14-*. **2** almost, all but *la14-*. *adj* close, near, neighbouring *la18-*. *prep* near, close to *la14-*. **~ hand beside** *adv (15-16)*, **~ hand by** *adv (la14-18)*, *prep (la14-e16)* = **~ hand**. **~-hand cut** = **~ cut**, *la18-*.
as ~ nearly (as good), near enough *la18*, *la20-*, *local Sh-Kcb.* **~ the bane &c** miserly *la19-*. **~ the bit 1** = **~ the bane**, *20-*, *WC Kcb.* **2** pretty well correct, near the mark *20-*, *Sh NE, S.* **~ thereby** ['~ 'ðer'baɪ] **1** near at hand, close by *la14-e15*. **2** approximately *15-e16*. [*cf* NAR]

neat &c *la16-*, **nete &c** *la15-17*; **nate &c** *la17-* [net; *nɛt] *adj* **1** = neat *la15-*. **2** *of persons* trim, smart *18-*. **3** *also as adv* exact, precise; nett *la17-*.
nettie &c, **natie &c** sheer, unmitigated *la18-e19, NE.*

neath, nethe &c; neth *19-* [niθ, nɛθ] *prep, chf verse* beneath *e15, la17-*.
nethmast &c *15-e20*, **~most** *16, 18-*, *now NE, EC*, **nedmast &c** *16-17*, **nyowmost &c** *la18-e20, chf Abd* ['nɛθməst; *NE also* 'njʌuməst; *'nɛd-, *'n(j)u-] *adj* lowest, undermost. [aphetic f ANEATH]

neb &c *n* **1** the beak of a bird *la14-*. **2** *transf* (1) a person's nose *17-*. (2) the whole face *la19-*. **3** any projecting tip or point: (1) on a person's body, as (a) of fingers or toes *la16-*; (b) of the tongue *la16-19*; (2) *in gen* (a) of a piece of land or rock *19-*, *local*; (b) the toe of a shoe *la19-*; (c) the point or nib of a pen or pencil *la18-*, *now local Abd-Lnk*; (d) the point of a pin, knife etc *19-*, *now Sh*. **4** *transf* sharpness, pungency, *esp* of liquor *19*.
vti **1** *of birds* bill *19-20*. **2** *vt* put a point on (a quill-pen or pencil) *la19-20*.
nebbie &c *adj* **1** biting, nippy, sharp; *fig* smart *20-*, *now Fif WC Kcb*. **2** brusque *la19-*, *now*

local sEC-S. **3** cheeky *20-*, *local wLoth-Gall.* **4** inquisitive *20-*, *local sEC-Uls.* **nebbit &c** *adj, usu in comb* having a beak, nose or point of a specified kind *la16-*: *'red-nebbit'*. **~sie &c** *adj* impudent, pert *20-*, *now eLoth.*
~-end the tip of the nose *20*, *local Edb-S.* **~fu** a beakful; a small quantity *esp* of liquor, a drop *19-*, *local Sh-Edb.*
cock (up) one's ~ look haughtily *la19-*. **lead by the ~** *fig* lead by the nose *20-*. **see far afore one's ~** have foresight *19-*, *now Sh Ork Ags*. [ME *neb*, OE *nebb*; *cf* NIB]

nebour *see* NEIBOUR

nece &c [nis] *n* **1** = niece *15-e18*. **2** a nephew *15-e17*.

necessar &c, necessare &c ['nɛsɛsər] *adj* **1** necessary *la14-*, *now Sh NE, EC Ayr*. **2** profitable, useful; appropriate *16-17*. **3** *of persons* giving necessary or useful service *16-17*. **4** inevitably determined *la14-16*. **5** determined by circumstance *16-17*.
n, in pl **1** necessaries *la14-*, *now Sh*. **2** *in non-material uses*: (1) necessary rights of access or use (in property) *16*; (2) necessary business; necessary or useful work *16-e17*. [L *necessārius*; *cf* F *nécessaire*, Eng *necessary*]
necessitat &c *vt* = necessitate, oblige, compel (a person to do something) *17-*.
necessitate, necessitat *ptp* compelled, *chf* by circumstance (to do something) *la16-e18, la20-* (*NE*).
adj compelled by necessity, unavoidable *17*. [MedL *necessitat-*, ptp stem of *necessitare*]

nechbour *see* NEIBOUR

neche &c *la14-e15*, **nich &c** *la14-16* [*nix, *nɪx] *vi* approach. [ME *neghen*, f *negh (adv)* ? OE *nēah* nigh]

neck &c, nek *n* **1** = neck *la14-*. **2** the collar of a coat or shirt *16-*, *now local NE-Uls*. **3** the throat, gullet *20-*. **4** *mining* the upper part of a shaft, above the coal *18-*, *Fif*.
vt **1** break the neck of (a person, bottle etc) *19-*, *now Kcb*. **2** embrace *19-*.
(double, single *or* **side) nekkit bonnet &c** a bonnet having a flap or flaps covering the neck as described by the adj *la15-e16*.
~ break *fig, chf religious* one's downfall, a cause of this; a stumbling block *la17*. **~hering &c** ? a variety of herring, ? the shad *la15*; *see* DOST.
(in) spite o one's ~ in defiance of one's efforts, wishes etc *19-*. **mak a lang ~** stretch the neck to reach or see anything *la18-*, *now Ags*. **strike in the ~** *of disaster etc* overtake (a person) *e16*.

neck *see* NICK

nedder &c; nadir *19* ['nɛdər] *n* an extension placed below a beehive to give extra room for breeding *19*.
vi place a NEDDER below a hive *la19-*. [f NETHER² *adj*; *cf* Eng *super-hive*]
nedder *see* NETHER²

neddyr *see* NETHER[1]
nede *see* NEED
nedecessitie *see* NEEDCESSITY
nede-fyre *see* NEEDFIRE
nedenaill *see* NEED-NAIL
nedill, nedling *see* NEEDLE
nedmast *see* NEATH

need &c *la16-*, **nede &c** *la14-e18 vti* **1** = need *la14-*. **2** *absol* have to be; be of necessity *la19-*: 'are you a good driver? — I would need'. **3** *with ptp* (where Eng has *verbal noun*) *20-*: 'this lock needs sortit'. **4** *impersonal, chf* **what needs?** (1) + *active infin* what need is there (to do something) *la15-18*: 'but what needs this or that to name?'; (2) + *indirect object and active infin la14-*, *now NE*: 'what needs ye speak so loud?'; (3) + *noun or pronoun object* what is the need or use of?; there is no need for *la15-17*: 'quat nedis wordis mor?'. *n* = need *la14-*.

~fu &c *adj* having need or want of, needy; in straitened circumstances *18-*, *now local*. *n, in pl* necessaries *la18-19*. **~lingis &c** necessarily *la14-e16*. **~way** *la14, only Sc*, **~wayis** *la14-e16* necessarily. **~y &c** *adj* **1** = needy *16-*. **2** that acts as if in need, parsimonious *la15-16*, *only Sc*.

needfire &c ['nid'faɪr] fire produced by the friction of dry wood, having reputed magical or prophylactic properties *17-e20*. **tak ~ fyre** take fire spontaneously *16-17*. **of** *or* **on ~force** of necessity, perforce *la15-e17*.

hae mair ~ to do *censorious* ought rather to do, would be better employed doing *20-*. **not out of (the) ~ o** still in need of *la19-*. **he, it** *etc* **will** *or* **winna ~ to** = he, it etc had better (not) *la19-*.

needcessity &c, **nedecessitie &c** [nid'sɛsɪtɪ] *n* **1** necessity, need *la16-*. **2** *in pl* the necessities *la19-*, *now Uls*. [conflation of *necessity* w NEED]

needle &c, **nedill &c** *la15-e17*; **nidle &c** *la16-17* ['nidl] *n* **1** = needle *la15-*. **2** a type of brooch or ornamental pin *la16-17*. **3** a spar used as a support, *eg* in scaffolding *16-17*. *vti* move like a needle rapidly through, or in and out *19-*.

needlach &c ['nidləx, -lək] a young eel *la19-*, *Inv*. **nedling** [*'nidlɪŋ] the setting up of transverse supports *la16-17*. **the ~ ee** a children's game *19-*; see SND. **~-naked** stark-naked *la20-*, *Sh Cai Kcdn*.

need-nail &c, nedenaill &c *vt* fasten securely, nail up *la16-e19*. [LowGer *nednagel* a clinched nail]

neef &c *n* difficulty, bother *18-e20*, *Abd*. [only Sc; obscure]

neeger &c ['nigər] *n* **1** *contemptuous* a nigger *20-*. **2** a hard or reckless person; a savage, barbarous person *la18-20*. *vi* head a ball *la20*, *Edb*. [F *nègre*]

neem *see* NAME
neen *see* NUNE

neep *18-*, **nepe &c; nip &c** *la17-e19* [nip] *n* **1** a turnip; *in Scotland, chf* the swede *la14-*; *cf* TURNEEP. **2** *in pl* the time of the year when turnips are hoed *la19-*, *Sh NE Per*. **3** *joc, implying stupidity* the head *la19-*, *local Sh-EC*. **4** a turnip watch *la19-*, *local Ork-Kcb*.

vt **1** feed (cattle) with turnips *la19-*, *Sh-EC*. **2** sow (land) with turnips *la20-*, *Bnf Abd Loth*.

~y candle = ~ lantern, *20-*, *NE*.

~ brose BROSE made with the liquid in which turnips have been boiled *20-*, *chf NE Uls*. **~ cleek** a hooked implement for pulling up turnips *20-*, *NE-Loth Kcb*. **~-cutter** a turnip slicer *la19-*, *Ork nEC, WC*. **~ grund &c** ground prepared for turnips *20-*, *Sh Ork NE*. **~ hack** a two-pronged iron implement for pulling turnips out of frozen ground *19-*, *now WC*. **~ heid** a stupid person *19-*, *local Sh-EC*. **~ land** ground from which a crop of turnips has been taken *la19-*, *now Sh Ork*. **~ lantern** a turnip-lantern, *esp* as at *Halloween* (HALLOW[2]) *la19-*, *Sh-nEC*. **~ machine** a horse-drawn machine for sowing turnips *la19-*, *NE Per*. **~ muck** manure for putting on turnip ground *20-*, *Sh NE*. **~ re(e)t** land from which a turnip crop has been taken, and still so called under the subsequent corn-crop *la19-*, *NE*. **~ seed 1** turnip seed *la19-*. **2** the time for sowing turnips *la19-*, *NE*. **~ shawin** turnip sowing *20-*, *NE*. [ME; OE *nǣp*]

neepyin *see* NAIPKIN
neer *see* NEIR[2]
Neer- *see* NEW-YEAR
neerice *see* NOURICE
neese &c, nese &c [niz] *vi* (*16-*), *n* (*18-*) sneeze *now Sh Ork NE*. [ME *nese(n)*; see DOST]
neet *see* NIT[2]
nef *see* NIEVE
nefare *see* NIFFER
nefe *see* NIEVE
neffie *see* NEVOY
negart *see* NIGGAR
negative[1] **&c** ['nɛgətɪv; *'nɛgataɪv] *adj* = negative *16-*.

N~ Confession *religion* the King's Confession, or Second Confession of Faith (1580-1) *la16-17*, *now hist*.

negative[2] **&c** [nɛga'taɪvɪ] *adv, law* in the negative *16-*. [laL *negātīvē*]

negleck &c *only Sc*, **neglect &c** [nɪ'glɛk] *n, vt* = neglect *16-*.

neibour &c *la16-*, **nebour &c** *16-*, **nichbour &c** *la14-17, only Sc*, **nechbour &c** *la14-e17*; **neighbour &c** *la16-*; **nybour &c** *la16-e18*, **neiper &c** *la16-*, *NE* ['nibər; *NE* 'nipər; **'nixbur, *-bər, *'nix-] *n* **1** = neighbour *la14-*. **2** (1) *specif* a fellow-inhabitant of a BURGH; a fellow-member of a community *15-17*. (2) a person admitted to full citizenship of a BURGH or membership of a community, a burgess *la15-17*. (3) *in pl* the citizenry, the community as a whole *15-17*. **3** a workman's mate *la17*.

4 a husband or wife, a bedfellow, partner *la19-*.
5 *of persons or things* a match, one of a set or pair *la18-*.
adj **1** of one's neighbour, between neighbours *la14-16*. **2** that is a neighbour, neighbouring *la15-17*. **3** *of enmity or war* internal, domestic *la15-e17*.
vi **1** ~ **wi** (1) *of persons or things* be situated near, consort with *19-20*. (2) co-operate with (one's neighbours), *esp* in agricultural jobs *la18-*, *local NE-Uls*. **2** *vt* (1) associate with, consort with *la19-*. (2) match, form a set with *20-*.
~**heid &c**, ~**hood &c** *18-*, **nechbourret &c** *la15-e17* (but see DOST) ['nibərhid, &c; *'nixburhid, &c; *'nixburət, *'nibərət] **1** friendly relations between neighbours, *freq* **gude &c** ~**heid**, **evill** *etc* ~**heid &c** *16-*. **2** neighbourly relations or conduct within a BURGH, estate or other community; mutual obligations of the members of a community *la15-*. **3** (1) a dispute between neighbours over property rights, boundaries etc *la15-17*: '*all questions of nichbourheid*'. (2) ? the site of such a dispute *la16-e17*. **4** = neighbourhood, the vicinity etc *17-*. **Act of** ~**bourheid &c** an act for the regulation of disputes (as in ~**heid** 3 above) *la16-17*. **give** *etc* **aith of (lawfull)** ~**heid &c** swear to comply with the obligations of a burgess *la16-e17*. **hald** *etc* **gude** ~**heid &c** observe the rules as in ~**heid** 2, *la15-18*. ~**less** *of one of a pair* lacking the other *la19-*. ~**like 1** neighbourly *15-*. **2** emulating or aping one's neighbours *18-*. ~**schip &c (till)** the fact of being neighbour (**to**); neighbourly relations, amicable behaviour (**to**) *la15-e16*. **hald** ~**schip to** act as a neighbour towards *la16*. ~**t(r)ie &c** [*NE* 'nipərt(r)ı; *Abd* *'nıxburtı] neighbourliness *17-*, *NE*.
be ~**s &c to 1** be next to, be adjacent to *15-16*. **2** *also* **be** ~**s wi** have (a person) as neighbour *la19-*, *NE*. **Guid Nychburris festival** the Dumfries festival of the *Riding of the Marches* (RIDE) *20-*, *Dmf* [revival of OSc spelling]. **our** *or* **the guid &c** ~**s** the fairies *la16-17*. **ane lawful** *or* **sufficiand** ~ a good citizen or neighbour *15-17*.
neicht *see* NICHT
neighbour, neiper *see* NEIBOUR
neir¹ **&c**, **nere** [nir] *n* a kidney, *latterly esp* of an animal *la14-*, *now Sh-N*.
~ **leather** the back or belly-band of a horse's harness *20-*, *now Renfr*; *cf* EAR-LEATHER. ~ **strap** a strap in a horse's harness *la19-20*. [nME and eModEng, ? OE]
neir² **&c** *16-e18*; **neer &c** *la16-*, **noor** *la19-*, *Cai* [nir, ner; *Cai* nur] *adv* = NEVER *16-*, *now chf literary*.
~**-do-gude &c** *e19*, ~**-do-weel &c** *18-* ['~'də'wil, &c] a good-for-nothing, a rake, debauchee. [SND *never*]
neist &c, **neste &c** [nist; *NE also* niʃt] *adj* = next, nearest etc *la14-*, *now Gen except SW*.

adv = next *la14-*, *now Sh Ork NE*.
prep = next *la19-*, *now Sh NE*.
~**en** *adj*, ballad, *with extra syllable for the metre* = *adj*, *e19*; *cf firsten* (FIRST). ~**most** the next again *la19-*, *Sh NE*. [nME *neste*, OE *nēahst*, superlative of *nēah* near, ON *næst*; *cf* NEXT]
neit &c [nit] *adv* nor yet *la18-*, *NE*. [*ne* (NA⁴) + *yet*]
neither *see* NETHER²
nek *see* NECK, NICK
nem; neme [*nɛm] *vt*, *ptp also* **nammit &c** [*'nɛmıt] **1** = name *la14-16*. **2** specify as to amount or value *15-16*. **3** nominate to an office *la15-16*.
above nemmit above mentioned *la15-16*. **als wele nocht nemmyt** *or* **unnemmyt as nemmyt** *etc* legal formulae used in the specification of possessions, lands etc *la14-16*. [ME *nemme*; OE *nemde*, pt of *nemnan*; *cf* NEMMIN]
nem *see* NAME
nemmin &c *vt* = NEM *la14-15*. [OE *nemnan*, ON *nemna*]
nepe &c [*nip] *vi*, *of a ship* be stranded at neap tide *16*. [*cf* ModEng *neipe*]
nepe *see* NEEP
nephew, nepho *see* NEVOY
nephous *see* NAIPHOUSE
nepkin *see* NAIPKIN
nepote; nepott [*?'nɛpot] *n* **1** a grandson *16-e17*. **2** a nephew *16-e17*. [L *nepōt-*, stem of *nepos*]
nepus *see* NAIPHOUSE
nepvo *see* NEVOY
ner *see* NAR
nere *see* NEAR, NEIR
nerr *see* NAR
nerve &c *n* **1** = nerve *16-*. **2** a band of material used to decorate a garment *e16*, *only Sc*.
vt apply such a band to (a garment) *e16*, *only Sc*.
nervish &c *adj* nervous, easily agitated *19-*, *N-S*.
nese *see* NEESE, NIZ
nesh &c, nesch [nɛʃ, neʃ] *adj* soft *la14*, *la19-*. *n*, *also* **nasche &c** soft ground, a bog *la15-e17*, *NE*. [ME *nesche*, OE *(h)nesc(e)*, *næsc*]
ness &c, nes &c *n* a headland *la15-*, *chf Sh Ork*, *in place-names la12-*. [ME *-nesse*, OE *næs*, *nes*, ON *nes*]
ness *see* NACE
nest *n* = nest *15-*.
look ower the ~ *of a young person* begin to act independently *la19-*, *SW*, *S*.
neste *see* NEIST
nestie &c, nesty; nasty *adj* = nasty *la17-*. *vt*, *chf* **nasty** dirty, befoul *18-*.
nestreis [*'nɛstrız] *n pl* privies, *or perh* a privy *la16*.
net *see* NIT¹
nete *see* NEAT
neth, nethe *see* NEATH

nether[1] *19-, now Cai*, **neddyr &c** *la15-e20* ['nɛðər, 'nɛd-] *n* an adder. [ME *neddre, nadre*, OE *nædre. cf* ETHER[1]]

nether[2] **&c**, **nedder &c** *la15-, now Sh Ork*, **nather &c** *la16-17*, **neither &c** *17-18* ['nɛðər, 'nɛd-; *'nɪð-, *'nɪd-] *adj* **1** lower, under *la14-*. **2** *in place-names* the lower-situated of two places, roads etc of the same name *la14-*. **3** *describing localized features, buildings etc* lower *15-*: 'at the nether cairn'. **4** the downstairs or basement (part of a building) *la15-17*: 'over kitching .. nedder kitching'; 'the nether tolbuith'.
~ **end** the posterior *17-*.

nether *see* NITHER

nettercap &c *n* = ATTERCAP 1 (*la19-, Kcdn nEC*), 2 (*la19-, now Kcdn*).
netterie = *n, la19-, chf Kcdn Ags Per*.
nettie &c *n* a woman who goes about the country collecting wool *la19-20, chf Slk*. [see SND]
nettie *see* NEAT

nettle &c, nettill &c *la15-e17 n* = nettle *la15-*. ~ **brose** BROSE made with the juice of boiled young nettle-tops *la19-, NE.* ~ **broth** BROTH made from nettle-tops *19-, now Kcb Uls.* ~ **claith &c** a type of cloth *la16-e17.* **nettl(i)e-creeper** the whitethroat *la19-, now Clcm.* ~ **kail &c** = ~ *broth, la16-19*.
on ~**s** on tenterhooks, impatient, ill-humoured *la19-*.

nettle-earnest &c ['nɛtl'ɛrnəst; *Rox* -'jɪrnəst] *n* dead earnest *19-, S Uls*. [wrong division of *in ettle earnest* (ETTLE)]

neuk &c *la15-*, **nuke &c** *la14-17*; **nook &c** *17-*, **nok &c** *15-16* [nøk; *N sEC* njuk; *nEC, WC* njʌk; *Fif also* nʌk] *n* **1** = nook *la14-*. **2** a projecting point of land, *esp* into the sea *la14-*. **3** an external angle of a building; the corner of a street *15-*. **4** a corner made in a fold of a garment or napkin *la16-e17*. **5** an outlying or remote place *16-*. **6** *also fig* an obscure corner, a lurking-place *la14-*.
~**it &c 1** having corners; crooked *16-*. **2** *fig* cantankerous *20-, NE*. **four** *or* **three** ~**it** having four *or* three corners *la16-*. (**four**) ~**it bonet** *or* **cap** a square cap, *esp* as worn by Roman Catholic or Episcopal clergy *la16-17*. **the East N**~ the eastern corner of Fife *la17-*. **hold, keep** *or* **put** (one) **in his ain** ~ keep under strict control *19-, Sh NE*. **in a** *or* **the** ~, **in** ~**is** clandestinely *16*.

neuth &c [*njuθ] *prep, adv* beneath *la14-e15*. [only Sc; see DOST]

neutral &c *adj* **1** = neutral *la15-*. **2** *grammar* = neuter *16*.

neve *see* NAVE[1], NIEVE

nevel &c, nevell &c; knevell &c *19*, **naffle** *la19-e20, Fif Clcm* ['nɛvl, 'nɪvl, 'nivl, 'kn-; *Fif* 'nɛfl; *'nɪfl, &c] *n* a sharp blow with the fist, a punch *16-*.
vt **1** punch, pummel, batter *la16-*. **2** squeeze, pinch *19-20*. [f NIEVE *n*]

never &c; niver &c *17-* ['nɪvər, 'nɛvər, 'nēvər] *adv* = never *la14-*.
~**mass &c** never, a time that never comes *18-e20*. ~ **nane** no one, none at all *15-e16*. ~ **a** not a single, absolutely no *la15-*. ~ **a bit** *interj* really? *20-, NE Per*. **the** ~ (**a**) = ~ *a, la18-19*. ~ (ʒit) **quhare** never anywhere (as yet) *la14-e15*. [*cf* NEIR[2]]

nevew *see* NEVOY

nevin &c [*'nivən] *vt, verse, chf rhyme* name, mention, declare *la14-16*. [northern and n midlME *neven*, ON *nefna; cf* NEMMIN, NEM, NAME]

nevoy &c *16-*, **nevo &c** *la14-e19*, **nepvo &c** *la16-e17*; **nepho &c** *16*, **nephew &c** *17-*, **nevow &c** *15*, **nevew &c** *15-e17*, **nevy &c** *16-e20*, **neffie &c** *la19-, local* ['nɛfi, 'nɛvi, 'nɛfji; *'nɛvo, *-(j)u] *n* **1** = nephew *la14-*. **2** a grandson; a great-grandson *15-*. **3** *literary* a descendant *e16*. **4** a grand-daughter; a niece *16-e17*.

nevval &c ['nevl] *n, only* **a nevval** upside down, on the back, tumbled over *20, Cai*. [wrong division of *on aival* (AVALD[1])]

nevy *see* NEVOY

new[1] **&c**, **now &c** *15-17*; **nue &c** *la16* [nju; *Ork also* nʌu, nø-; *NE also* njʌu; *nEC* nu] *adj* **1** = new *la14-, in place-names 12-*. **2** *with verbs of fashioning, repairing etc* = so as to restore or make new again, *eg* **make** *or* **mend** (**something**) ~ *la15-16*.
adv **1** newly, recently, just *la14-*. **2** (1) anew, afresh *15-16*. (2) *in prefixed position* = *Eng* re- *la15-19*: 'they'll help ye to new sklate'.
n, see phrases below.
vt = new *la14-15*.
~**in(g) 1** the working of yeast in the making of ale *la16-*. **2** *in pl* novelties, wonders *la16-e17, la19-* (*chf Gall Uls*). ~**lins &c**, ~**lingis &c 1** = newly, recently *la14-, latterly chf NE*. **2** anew *15-16*. ~**ly &c** for the first time, without precedent *la15-16*.
~ **calf(f)it**, ~ **cal(d)** *of cows* newly calved *la15-*. ~ **cheese** a dish made from the cream of a newly-calved cow's milk *19-, NE*. ~ **corn &c** harvest-time *la16-17, S*. ~ **fangle**, ~ **fangill** *adj* (excessively) fond of novelty *16-19*. *n* novelty, innovation *la18-*. ~ **farrant** novel, new-fangled *20-, NE*. ~**start-up** *adj* (*n*) (an) upstart *la16*. **N**~ **Town** name for the part of Edinburgh to the north of the Castle ridge which was developed as a planned residential area in the late 18th and early 19th centuries; *cf Old Town* (AULD).
in the ~ = *of* (*the*) ~ 2 and 3, *18-20*. **jist** ~ = *adv* 1, *la19-*. **of** (**the**) ~ **1** newly, freshly *15-16*. **2** *also* **of** ~ **agane** *la16-17* afresh, anew *la14-*. **3** of late, recently *la14-*. **on** ~ = *of* (*the*) ~ 2, *la14-e15*.

new[2], **nyow-** [*njʌu] *vt* master, oppress, curb *la18-19, NE*. [reduced f NEATH]

New(e)r *see* NEW-YEAR

news &c *la17-*, **newis** &c *la15-17* [njuz; *nEC* nuz] *n pl* **1** = news *la15-*. **2** *treated as a sing* talk, conversation; a gossip *la19-*, *chf Sh N*. *vi* talk, chat, gossip *19-*, *chf Sh Cai NE*. **newser** a person who is fond of chat; *of a child* a good talker *20-*, *Sh N*. **newsie** gossipy, talkative *19-*, *chf NE*.

New-year &c, **New-ȝere** &c *la15-17*; **New(e)r-** &c *16-*, **Neer-** &c *la19-* ['nju'(j)ir, 'nju(ə)r; *Cai* 'nivər; *nEC* 'nu'ir; *C,S* ner; *SW* nir; *nur] *n* **1** the New Year *la15-*. **2** a gift, or a drink or food given in hospitality at the New Year *la19-*.
~ **day** *la15-*, ~**'s day** *16-* **1** New Year's Day *la15-*. **2** = *n 2*, *la19-*. ~ **even** *16-*, ~**'s even** *17-* New Year's Eve, HOGMANAY. ~(**is**) **gift** a New Year gift *16-17*. ~(**'s**) **mas** = New Year's day or tide *la15-*, *now Sh*. [the contracted forms are only *Sc*; uncapitalized forms are also common in all senses, *esp* in the early period]

next &c, **nixt** &c [nıkst, nëkst, nɛkst] *adj* **1** = next *15-*. **2** *with names of days or months, usu contrasted with* FIRST *or 'this'*: the next but one *18-*: *'Friday first .. Friday next'; 'this October .. next October'.*
~**an**, ~**in** *adj, ballad, with extra syllable for the metre* = *adj, la18-e19*.
~ **adjacent** next in order (**to**) *la16-17*. ~ **cumis** = ~*-to-cum, 16*. ~ **hand** *prep* nearest to, immediately following; second only to *15-e16*. ~**-to-cum** *of a date, time etc* immediately following, next *15-e18*: *'on Monunday nixtocum'.* [*cf* NEIST]

niag *see* NAG[2]

nib, nibb *n* **1** = NEB 1 *la18-*, 2 (1) *la18-*, 3 *la17-*. **2** a nip; a prod *la19-20*.
~**ie** &c a walking stick with a hooked handle; a shepherd's crook *19-*, *chf SW, S*. ~**ie staff** a walking stick *la19-*, *SW, S*. ~**lick** &c the golf club corresponding to the No 8 or 9 IRON *la19-e20*.

nibbit *n* an *oatcake* (AIT) sandwich *la18-19*. [see SND]

nibble, nibbill &c *la15-e16* *vt* **1** = nibble *16-*. **2** fiddle with *19-20*.
n **1** = nibble *la15-*. **2** a stroke of luck *20-*, *S*.

nice &c *adj* **1** = nice *la15-*. **2** disdainful, haughty *la15*. **3** involving precision, intricate *la15-16*.
~**nes** hauteur; reserve, caution *la16-e17*. ~**-gabbit** fussy, fastidious about food *19-e20*.

nich *see* NECHE

nichbour *see* NEIBOUR

nicher &c *18-*, **nikkir** &c *la16-e20* ['nıxər, 'nık-; *Sh also* nj-] *vi* **1** *of a horse* snicker, neigh *la16-*. **2** snigger *19-*.
n **1** a whinny, neigh *la18-*. **2** a snigger *19-*.
nickerers *pl* new shoes *19-e20*. [onomat]

nichil &c [*'nıtʃəl, *?'nıxəl] *n* nothing *la15-16*. [MedL *nichil*, L *nihil*; *cf* eModEng *nihil, nichel*]

nicht &c; **night** &c *16-* [nıxt; *Cai Rox also* nəixt] *n*, *also* **neicht** &c *16-19*, **nyt(e)** *la16-17*, *only Sc* = night *la14-*.
v **1** *in passive* be benighted, be overtaken by night *la16-*, *now Abd*. **2** *vi* pass the night *17*, *20-*, *now NE*.
~ **clock** a night-flying beetle *19-*, *now Sh Kcb Uls*. ~ **glas(s)** *appar* a sand-glass used on a ship to time the night watches *16-e17*. ~ **waker** &c, ~ **walkar** &c [*'~'wekər, *'~'wɑkər] a person who stays up late engaged in revelry; a person who goes about at night, *esp* for nefarious purposes *16-17*. ~ **waking** &c keeping awake at night, *esp* for revelry or riotousness *la15-e17*. ~ **walk** [*'~'wɑk] a wake held at night *17*. ~ **walking** [*'~'wɑkıŋ] = ~ *waking*; going about at night *la15-e18*.
be *or* **on** ~**ertale** &c by night *la14-17*. **the nicht afore the morn** the eve of an important occasion, *eg* the *Common Ridings* (COMMON) in the BORDERS or the *Lammas Fair* (LAMMAS) in Kirkwall *la19-*, *Ork S*. **under** ~ under cover of night *16-17*.

nichtingale *see* NIGHTINGALE

nick &c *la15-*, **nik** &c *17-*, *now Sh Ork*; **ne(c)k** *la16-e19* [nık] *n* **1** = nick *17-*. **2** *specif* one of the notches or growth-rings on an animal's horns *la18-*. **3** a notch in a stick as a means of reckoning *la17, e19*. **4** *chf in place-names* a narrow gap in a range of hills *17-*, *chf SW S*. **5** a broken-off fragment, a scrap *la17-*, *chf Sh Uls*. **6** prison, the police-station *19-*.
vt **1** = nick, notch *la15-*. **2** cut off, sever; *fig* make away with *18-*. **3** *lit and fig* catch, seize *la18-*. **4** imprison *20-*. **5** cheat, trick *19-*.
~**ie** an *oatcake* (AIT) or bun with an indented edge *la19-*, *chf Fif*. **as auld farrant as a** ~**it bake** (*wLoth Kcb*) or **bap** (*Bnf*) *of a child* old-fashioned, quaint *20-*.
~ **stick** a tally, reckoning stick *la17-*.
a ~ **in** *or* **on one's horn** *fig* **1** a year of one's life *19-*. **2** *in pl* age or experience *19-*. ~ **the thread** *fig* kill *la18-19*. [*cf* NITCH]

nick *see* KNICK

Nick *n* the devil *18-e19*, *more freq* **Auld** ~ (AULD).
~**ie** *19*, ~**ie-ben** *la18-e20* = *n*. **nickum** &c a scamp, a rogue, a mischievous boy *19-*, *NE nEC, SW*. [see SND]

nicker *see* KNICK

nickerers *see* NICHER

nickie-tam &c *n*, *chf in pl* a pair of straps or pieces of string, used by farmworkers to secure the trousers immediately below the knees, to keep the legs above the knee clean or to relieve the weight of mud at the ankles *20-*. [see SND]

nickle &c *n* ~ **naething** the term represented by the letter N on a TOTUM[1], which indicated 'nothing' for the player to whom it fell *la19-*, *NE Per*. [*cf* NICHIL and see SND]

nickle *see* KNUCKLE

nickum *see* NICK

nidder *see* NITHER

niddle &c *vi* **1** *of the fingers* carry out intricate or laborious work quickly or perseveringly *19-, now Abd Fif.* **2** fiddle, toy, potter *19-, now Abd.* [imit of short jerky movements]

nidge *vt* dress (a building stone) roughly, by picking with a sharp-pointed hammer *19-.* [voiced var of NITCH]

nidle *see* NEEDLE

nieve &c *16-,* **neve &c** *la14-16,* **nefe &c** *la14-19;* **nef &c** *15-e17,* **nive &c** *la16-* [niv, nɛv, nɪv; *Sh Ork* nev; **nif, *nɪf, *nev*] *n* **1** a fist *la14-.* **2** one's grasp or possession *16.* **3** *in pl* fisticuffs *18-, now Sh Ork.* **4** *measures* a hand's breadth *la17-e18.*

vt GUDDLE (fish) *e19, SW.*

~**ful**(**l**) ['nivfu, -fɪ, 'nɛv-, 'nɪv-, 'nifɪ, 'nɛfɪ, 'nɪfɪ; **'*nifu, *&c, *'*nivl, **'*nɪvl] a fistful, handful *la14-.* **nevie-nevie-nak &c** *e17,* **nievie-nievie-nicknack &c** *18-* first line of a rhyme in a children's guessing game. [ME *neve,* ON *(h)nefe;* see DOST, SND; *cf* NAVE², NEVEL]

niffer &c, **nefare &c** ['nɪfər; *nEC* 'nifər; **'*ni(v)'fer] *v* **1** *vt* barter, trade *16-, now Sh NE-WC.* **2** *vi* haggle, bargain *la16-, now local Sh-WC.*

n the process of exchange or barter; an exchange *16-, now Sh NE-WC.* [chf Sc; see DOST]

niffler &c *n, weaving* a comb-like appliance between whose teeth the web is spread on the loom, an EVENER *la18-, chf Fif.* [f NEVEL *v*]

niffnaff &c ['n(j)ɪf'n(j)af] *vi* trifle, dilly-dally *18-20.*

n a small, insignificant or trifling person or thing *19-, now Sh Bnf Lnk.* [see SND]

nigg-naye *see* NIG NAY

niggar &c, **negart &c** ['nɪgər, 'ni-, **-*ərt] *n* = niggard, a miser *la16-, now Ags Kcb Uls.*

nigh &c [naɪ; *Uls also* nəɪ] *adv* = nigh *la16-.* ~ **hand &c** nearly, almost *19-, now Bnf Abd.*

night *see* NICHT

nightingale &c, **nichtingale &c** ['nəɪtɪŋgel; **'*nɪxtɪŋgel, **-*gal] *n* = nightingale *la14-.* **Scotch** ~ the woodlark; the sedgewarbler *19-, now local C.*

nig nay &c, **nigg-naye &c** *n* a nicknack, trifle *la17-e20.*

vi trifle, fuss *la19-e20.* [see SND]

nik *see* NICK

nikkie-now &c [**'*nɪkɪ'nʌu] *only proverb* a NIT²-infested head *la16-e17.*

nikkir *see* NICHER

nile *see* NAEL

nimious ['nɪmɪʌs] *adj, law* excessive, vexatiously burdensome *la17-, now chf* ~ **and oppressive.** [L *nimius*]

nimm &c [n(j)ɪm] *interj* expression of pleasure (by or to a child) at something good to eat = yum-yum *20-, chf Sh.*

nimmle &c, nimmill &c *15-16 adj* = nimble *15-.*

nimp &c; nyim &c [n(j)ɪm(p)] *n* a morsel *19-.* [see SND]

nimsh; imsh *n* a tiny piece *20-, Cai Bnf-Ags.* [see SND]

nine &c, **nyne &c** *n* **1** = nine *la14-.* **2** ninth *la14-e17.*

~**sie** the ninth movement in the game of *chuckies* (CHUCK²) *20-.* **nint** [nəint] = ninth *la14-, now NE.* ~**teen** *adj* **1** = nineteen *la14-.* **2** = nineteenth *16-.* *n* a lease of a farm for nineteen years *19-, now local Ork-Loth.* **Ninety Twa** the 92nd Regiment of Foot, the GORDON HIGHLANDERS *19-.*

~-**eyed-eel** the lamprey *19.* ~ **holes** the cut of beef below the breast *19-, now local Ags-S.* (**up**) **to the nine**(**s**) to perfection *18-.*

nip &c, **nipp** *n* **1** = nip, a pinch *la16-.* **2** pungency, sharpness of flavour *19-, only Sc.* **3** *mining* an interruption in a seam of coal *19.* **4** *fig* an advantage, *esp* in bargaining *la19-20, NE.* **5** a fragment, piece, a pinch *17-.* **6** a sheepmark, a notch cut in the ear *la18-, local NE-S.*

vti **1** = nip *la15-.* **2** *baking* pinch dough at its edges, make indentations round pastry etc *20-.* **3** *esp of animals* nibble; graze *18-, now Abd Per.* **4** *of clothes* (cause to) fit tightly, grip, constrict, *chf in ptp* ~**it** tight-fitting *19-.* **5** *vt, lit and fig* cause to tingle or smart (1) *in gen,* *16-;* (2) *specif of cold, la18-;* (3) *of food or its taste, 19-;* (4) *fig, of a sarcastic speaker or his words, la19-.* **6** *vi* ache, tingle with cold *18-.* **7** *vt* get the better of (in bargaining), cheat *la19-, now Gall.* **8** seize, catch; snatch, make off with *la18-.*

nippit &c **1** curt, bad-tempered *la19-.* **2** pinched with hunger *la19-.* **3** niggardly *19-.* **4** narrow in outlook *la19-.* **nippity** quick and jerky, with short sharp movements *20-.* **nippy &c** = nippit 1 (*la19-*), 3 (*19-*).

~**caik** a miser *e16.* ~-**lug** backbiting, squabbling *19-.* ~-**nebs** Jack Frost *la19-.* ~**scart** a niggardly person *19-e20.* ~ **of hunger** the pinch of hunger, the effect of hunger on farm stock *20-, Bwk Rox.*

nip *see* NEEP

nipschot &c *n, of a bowman, of cannon, and fig* **schute** *or* **play** ~ *appar* shoot amiss in some way *16-e17.* [obscure]

nir *see* KNUR, NOR¹

nirl &c; nurl *18-* [nɪrl; *Sh also* njɪrl] *n* **1** a fragment, crumb, a small object *19-, now Uls.* **2** **the** ~**s** a disease characterized by inflamed pustules, a rash *17-, now Ork Per Loth.*

v **1** *vt* shrink, shrivel, stunt in growth, pinch with cold *19-, local Sh-Lnk.* **2** *vi* shrivel up in oneself, cringe with cold *19-, now Sh.*

~**ie &c** **1** *of animals or plants* dwarfish, stunted *19-, now Sh Ork.* **2** *of cold* pinching, nipping *la19-, now Sh Fif.* [var of *knurl* (KNUR)]

nise *see* NIZ

nit¹ &c *17-,* **nut &c** *15-;* **net &c** *e17, la19-20* (*Kcdn Ags*) [nɪt] *n* **1** = nut *15-.* **2** some accessory part of a gun *16.*

~**gall** &c an oak-gall, *chf* used as a dye-stuff *la16*. ~**mug** &c a nutmeg *17-19*.

nit² &c; **neet** &c *la17*- *n* = nit, the egg of the louse, *now chf* the head louse *la16*-.

neetie &c *n* a mean or disobliging person *19*-. *adj* stingy *19*-.

nitch &c *n* a notch, small incision *18*-, *now Sh Ork Ags*. [var of NICK; see SND]

nither &c *17*-, **nether** &c *la14-el7*; **nidder** &c *16*- ['nɪðər, 'nɪd-; *'nɛð-, *'nɛd-] *v* **1** *vt* (1) make low, abase *la15-el7*. (2) constrict, confine *16-el8*. (3) oppress, vex *la15, 18-e20*. **2** pinch or stunt with cold or hunger *18*-, *now Rox*. **3** *vi* shrink or huddle as with cold, shiver *la19*-, *now Loth Lnk S*. [eME *niþeren*, OE *niðerian*, ON *niðra* bring low]

Nithsdale ['nɪθsdel] ~ **measure**, ~ **peck**, ~ **pint** *etc* measures of capacity about one-tenth larger than the standard SCOTS equivalents *18-el9, Dmf eKcb*. [the valley in Dmf]

nitteret *see* NATTER

nitty- *see* NOW

nive *see* NIEVE

niver *see* NEVER

nixt *see* NEXT

niz &c *la18*-, *chf NE*, **nese** &c *la13-e20*; **nise** &c *la16-18* [nɪz; *Abd also* niz] *n* **1** *now joc* the nose *la14*-. **2** *appar* a promontory, a NESS *la13-el6*.

~**zin** &c **1** a buffeting by the weather *la19, NE*. **2** *fig* a sharp reproof *la19-20*.

nesethrill &c a nostril *la14-el7*. ~**wise** *fig* far-seeing, perceptive *17*-, *now Abd Kcdn*.

stink *in or* **into someone's nese** be offensive to someone *la15-16*. [early and nME *nese*; *cf* NOSE]

njirr *see* NURR

no¹ &c *adv* **1** = not *la15*-. **2** *with adjs, advs etc*, *giving an impression of understatement or qualified admission or approval, as* ~ **bad** pretty good; ~ **canny** risky, unlucky; ~ **weel** ill *19*-. **3** *placed before a main verb, with omission of aux, 19*-: 'ye that no kens', 'a no want to'.

~ **utherwayis** &c *adv* = no otherwise, in no other way *15-17*. [reduced f NOCHT; see DOST; *cf* NAE²]

no² *conj* nor *la14-16*. [eME *no*; *cf* NA⁴ 1]

no³ *conj* than *e16*. [quasi-anglicized var of NA⁴ 2]

no *see* NA³

nob¹ *n* **1** the nose *la18-20*. **2** the toe of a shoe *19*-, *Edb*. [Eng *knob*]

nob² *n* a blackleg in a strike; an interloper or unqualified person in a trade *19*. [reduced f Eng *knobstick*]

nobile officium ['nobɪle ɔ'fɪʃɪʌm] *law*: the Court of Session's (SESSION) power of equitable jurisdiction in cases where the law itself does not provide a clear remedy *la18*-. [L = function pertaining to the supreme authority]

nobilitate, **nobilitat** *adj* distinguished, renowned *la16-18, only Sc*.

vt, pt, ptp also **nobilitat(e)** raise to the rank of titled nobility *la16-el8*. [L *nōbilitāt-*, ptp stem of *nōbilitāre; cf* eModEng *nobilitate* (*v*)]

nobill &c *la14-17*; **noble** *adj* **1** *of attributes, actions or reputations of persons* of or like a noble person *15*-. **2** distinguished for ability or learning *la15-16*.

n **1** = noble, a nobleman, one of the nobility *la14*-. **2** a person of great distinction or renown *la15-el6, only Sc*.

~ **part** a vital bodily organ *la16-el7*.

the nine ~**s** = the nine worthies (of ancient and medieval history and legend) *la15-el6*.

nocht &c; **noucht** &c, **noth** &c *15-e20, latterly NE* [nɔxt; *NE* noθ; *S* nʌuxt] *n* = nought, nothing *la14*-, *Gen except Sh Ork*.

adv **1** *now chf literary and arch* = not *la14*-. **2** *placed before nouns* = non- *16-el7*.

~**ie** &c, **nauchtie** &c *la16-el9* [*'naxtɪ] **1** *of persons* good-for-nothing, insignificant *19-e20*. **2** *of things* small, worthless, unfit for use *la18*-, *now local Sh-Fif*. **nochtifie** &c disparage *la19*-, *Sh Ags Per*. ~**less** worthless, of no account *19*-, *now Sh S*.

~ **gaynstandand** *la15*, ~**gaynstanding** *la14-el6*, ~ **obstant** *la15-16* = ~*withstanding*. ~ **than** nevertheless, for all that, even so *la14-15*, *only Sc*. ~**-the-les** nevertheless *la14-el7, only Sc*. ~**withstanding 1** = notwithstanding *15-16*. **2** *specif* in spite **of** *16-el7*. [*cf* NO¹, NOT, NOWT²]

nocket *see* NACKET¹

nocturne &c [*'noktʌrn] *adj, verse* nocturnal *16*.

nod *vti* = nod *la15*-.

(**nid**) **nid nodding** nodding repeatedly, as when dozing *la18-20*.

noddy *n* a kind of light two-wheeled cab *19-e20, local C, S*. [see SND]

nodge *vt* nudge, push *la18*-, *now Sh*.

n a nudge, a jog *e19* (*Ayr*), *20-* (*Sh*). [*cf* KNIDGE]

noisome *adj* noisy, rowdy *19, Abd Edb*. [see SND]

nok¹ *n* the tip or extremity of a yard-arm *16*. [laME (once); MDu *nocke*, EFris or LowGer *nok(ke)*]

nok² *n* a small hook; a hook holding the thread in a distaff *la15-16*. [eModEng *nock*; see DOST]

nok *see* KNOCK², NEUK

nolder *see* NOWTHER

noll *see* KNOOL

nolt *see* NOWT¹

no-mare &c *n, adv* = no more *la14-17*. [partly anglicized var of *nae mar(e)* (NAE¹)]

nominal *adj* = nominal.

~ **raiser** see *raiser* (RAISE).

nominate *adj, law* **executor** *or* **tutor** ~ an executor or TUTOR named and appointed in the will of the testator or parent *la18*-; *cf* DATIVE.

non-conform, -covenanter, -subscriver *etc* see the second elements.

Non [non] *n, Church* a person who disagrees with the policy of *intrusion* (INTRUDE) *la19-20, chf Abd Ags.*

non-conform *see* CONFORM

non-covenanter *see* COVENANTER

none *see* NANE, NUNE

non-entry &c; non-entré &c *la15-16 n, law* **1** the failure of an heir to a deceased VASSAL to obtain ENTRY (*n* (5)); the CASUALTY (*n* (2)) payable to the SUPERIOR in the case of such failure *la15-19.* **2** failure to present oneself or another at some appointed place, *chf* in a court of law for trial *la15-16.*

non-so-prettie [*'non'so'prɛtɪ] a kind of cloth *e17.* [Eng *none-so-pretty* an article of haberdashery]

nonsunt &c [*'non'sʌnt] *n* the twelve-penny groat coined under Francis and Mary 1558-9. [f the L words *non sunt* in the inscription on the reverse of the coin]

noo *19-, Gen except S*, **now &c; nu** *Sh Abd* [nu; *S* nʌu] *adv* **1** = now *la14-.* **2** under the present circumstances, in view of these facts *15-.*

~ **an than**, ~**s an thans** now and then, from time to time *18-, now NE.* ~ **as then, than as** ~ *law* at or for all or any present or future time, for all time *15-e17.* ~**na** *expressing sympathy or mild remonstrance* well then!, now then!, really! *19-, now C, S.* **now-on-dayes** = now-a-days *la15-e16.* **than as** ~: see ~ *as then.* **the** ~ **1** just now, at present; just a moment ago *18-.* **2** in a moment, soon *la19-.*

noof *see* NUIF

nook *see* NEUK

noop *n* the cloudberry *la19-, N S.* [see SND]

noor *see* NEIR

noose *see* KNUSE

noozle *n* one of a row of cords attaching the mesh-work to the headrope of a fishing-net *20-, Cai Fif Bwk.* [ME *nostylle* a short cord fastened to a net, OE *nos(t)le* a band or fillet; *cf* OSEL]

noozle *see* KNUSE

nop¹ &c *la14-16*, **nap &c** *16-17*; **nope-** *n, only in pl* wool flock *la14-17.*

~ **bed**, ~ **sek** a flock mattress *15-16.* [laME, eModEng *noppe*, eModEng *nap &c* nap of cloth, MDu *noppe* wool flock, nap of cloth]

nop² *vi* = nap, take a short sleep, *only* ~ **and nod** *la15-16.*

nor¹ &c, nar *16, 18-20 (Abd S)*; **nir** *la18-20, chf NE* [nor; *unstressed also* nər] *conj* **1** = nor *la15-.* **2** than *16-; cf* NA¹ *conj.* **3** that .. not, (but) that *la15-16, la18- (chf NE)*: 'nae wonder nor you're thin'; *cf* NA¹ *adv.* **4** *in imprecations* (God) ~ *la15-,* Deil ~ *la18-,* **fient** ~ *18-,* **shame** ~ *18-,* **sorrow** ~ *19-* would that, (God) (grant) that, would to the devil that etc: 'God nor that I hang'; 'sorrow nor the drink wad chock ye'. [see SND, DOST]

nor² *conj* = nor: **1** used for emphasis in negative replies or contradictions, before the main word

repeated from the preceding question or statement *20-*: 'is it sore?—no, nor sore'; **2** followed by another negative *19-20*: 'ye nor me havena been there'.

nor-, norat *see* NORTH

norie¹; norrie &c *n* a whim, a fancy *la18-, chf S.* [see SND]

norie² **&c** *n* the puffin *la18-, Sh Ork Kcdn, now Sh.* [perh imit of its cry; *cf tammie-norie* (TAMMIE)]

noris *see* NOURICE

Norish *see* NORSE

norl- *see* KNURL

norland *see* NORTH

Norn &c *n, adj, of language* Norse, Norwegian, *esp* that spoken in Sh and Ork, now surviving mainly in items of vocabulary *la15-.* [ON *norréna*]

norrie *see* NORIE¹

Norroway &c ['norəwe, -wə] = Norway *16-, now Sh Ork NE.*

~**is** [*'norowez, *-wɪz] *n pl* Norwegians, Norsemen *la15-e16.*

Norse &c *adj, also* **Norish &c** *la17* **1** *of language* = Norse; Norwegian *la17-.* **2** *of nationality* Norwegian *19-.*

n **1** the Norwegian language *la17-.* **2** (1) a Norwegian *e17.* (2) the Norwegian people *e18.* (3) *as pl* **the** ~ the Norwegians *20-.*

norter &c, nurture &c ['nortər; *'nʌrtər] *n* **1** = nurture *la14-.* **2** rigorous discipline, chastisement, rough treatment *20-, Abd.*

vt **1** = nurture *la15-.* **2** discipline, chastise *16-, now Abd.*

north &c; nor- *adv see combs below.*

n **1** the north *15-.* **2** *specif* **the** north and north-east of Scotland *la16-.*

northart &c, norat &c, *20- adv* northward, to the north *16-, now Sh Ork NE.* *n* (the direction of) the north *17-, now Sh Ork NE.* ~**er &c** *of two places of the same name* the more northerly *16-e17.* ~**erlie &c** *16-,* ~**lins** *la18-, now Sh Ork* towards the north, in a northerly direction *16-.* **the Northern Isles** *see* ILE. **Northern Meeting** a social gathering held at Inverness, *orig* with *Highland Games* (HIELAND) etc, *now* a formal ball held in late summer and at Christmas-time *la18-.*

~ **cuntré &c** = *n* 2, *la14-17; cf* ~ *land.* ~**land &c** *la15-e18,* **norland &c** *la16-,* **norlan &c** *17-* **1** = *n* 2, *freq attrib, eg* ~**land men,** ~**land plaidis** *la15-.* **2** a person from the north or north-east of Scotland *la17-, now Fif.* **3** a *Highland* (HIELAND) bull, cow or steer *e19.* ~**man** a Norman *16.* ~**mest** *16-e17,* ~**most** *la16-* most northerly. ~ **ower,** ~**our** northwards *e16 (Bnf),* *20- (Sh).* ~ **part &c** the northern part (**of** a place) *la15-16.* ~ **partis &c** *n pl* = *n* 2, *15-16.*

(**on**) ~ **half(f) &c** (on) the north side (of), (to) the north (of) *la14-15.* **on** *or* **upon the** ~ **part** on the north side *15-16.*

Northway Norway *16-e17*. [*cf* ME *Norþways* Norwegians, MedL *Northwegia* Norway]

nose &c *n* **1** = nose *la15-*. **2** *mining, also* ∼ **o coal** coal left protruding where it has been inadequately stripped *la19-, now Fif.*

nosie a throw in the game of *knife* (KNIFE) *20-*.

∼**thirl** = *nesethrill* (NIZ) *16-e17, 18-* (*Sh N*). [*cf* NIZ]

not *adv* ∼ **obstant** *e17,* ∼ **the les** *16-e17,* ∼**withstanding of** *la16-e19* = NOCHT-.

not *see* NOTE[1], NOTE[2]

notablie &c *adv* ∼ **knawin** = *notourly knawin* (NOTOUR) *e16*.

notar &c *n* **1** = notary, a notary public, *freq* ∼ **public, public** ∼ *la14-18*. **2** a clerk of court *la15-e17*. **3** a clerk or scribe *in gen, 16-e17*.

∼**ial** = notarial. ∼**ial instrument** *law* a formal document made out by a notary, declaring that certain things have been done, *formerly esp* in connection with conveyance of land *la18-*.

notarial protest a *notarial instrument* in which the notary PROTESTS that a debtor shall be liable on non-payment to the consequences set forth in the INSTRUMENT *la18-*.

notarie &c *n* **office of** ∼ the profession of notaryship *la15-e17*. [only Sc; MedL *notaria* office of a notary]

note[1] &c; not(t) &c *la16-e19 n* **1** = note *la14-*. **2** *law* a formal record, *esp* in a court register (1) *in gen, la15-; specif* (2) an appendix to a DECREE (*n* 2) in which a judge gives the reasons for his decision *20-*. (3) a step in *Inner House* (INNER) proceedings used for making an incidental application *19-*. **3** a one-pound banknote *la18-*. *vt* **1** = note *la14-*. **2** mark out from others, specify *15-e17*.

note[2] &c *vt* **1** make use of, need *la15-19, latterly N*. **2** *also* **not(t)**, *ptp* **nott(en), note** used as *pt, ptp* of NEED *la18-, NE*. [ME *note(n)*, OE *notian*]

noth *see* NOCHT

notice &c *vt* heed, watch; tend, see to *la17-, now Sh Ork NE*.

n **1** = notice, information; heed *la15-;* see DOST. **2** care, attentive help *19-, Sh Abd.*

notion &c *n* **1** = notion. **2** ∼ **o, tae** *etc* a liking or affection for (a person) *la18-*.

∼**ate** full of whims or caprices *la19-, now Kcb.*

notorieté &c; notorité &c [*?'noto'raɪ(ə)tɪ, *?'no'turətɪ] *n* = notoriety *la16-e17*.

notorious &c *adj* **1** = notorious. **2** *also adv, semi-joc* great(ly), exceeding(ly) *la19-, now Uls.*

notorité *see* NOTORIETÉ

notory &c *adv* ∼ **knawin** = *notourly knawin* (NOTOUR) *la15-e16*. [MedL *notorie*]

notour &c [no'tur, 'notur, -ər] *adj* **1** *of wrongdoers:* (1) known by common knowledge, notorious *15-20*. (2) openly admitted, *eg* ∼ **bankrupt** *la17-, now only law*. **2** *of facts:* commonly known or manifest: (1) *chf law* of crimes or other discreditable circumstances, *now* ∼ **adultery,** ∼ **bankruptcy** *15-;* (2) of facts or circumstances involving no discredit *la15-18*.

∼**ly,** *chf* ∼**ly knawin** notoriously, openly, publicly known *15-19*.

make (**it**) ∼ make (it) known *17*. [chf Sc; MedL *notorius*, F *notoire; cf* laME, eModEng (rare) *notoire*]

nott *see* NOTE[1], NOTE[2]

notten *see* NOTE[2]

noucht *see* NOCHT

noumer *see* NUMMER

noun *see* NUNE

noup &c [nup] *n, esp of the elbow* a knob or protuberance *19-, chf Ags S.* [see SND]

nourice &c, nuris &c *la14-e17,* **nurisch(e)** *la15-e18;* **noris** *16,* **neerice &c** *la18-20, NE* [*n* nʌrɪs; *NE* 'nirɪs, norɪs; *v* 'nʌrɪʃ, 'norɪʃ; *'nʌrɪs, *'nør-, *'nor-] *n* a child's nurse, *esp* a wet-nurse or foster-mother *la14-20, latterly chf literary and ballad*.

vt = nourish *15-20*.

∼ **father** a foster-father *la16-e17.* ∼ **fee** the wages given to a wet-nurse *la18-e19, chf NE*. ∼**s(c)hip** the occupation or post of NOURICE *la16-e19*. [ME *nuris, norice*, OF *nurice; cf* Eng *nurse*]

novatioun &c *16-17;* **novation &c** *n* **1** change (*chf* undesirable) in established practice; an innovation *16-17*. **2** *specif* (1) (a) the alteration of a legal obligation or status *16-17;* (b) the substitution of a new debt or debtor for a former *la17-;* (2) a (*chf* wrongful or undesirable) change or innovation in religious doctrine or polity *la16-17;* (3) a newly-introduced and oppressive tax *la16;* (4) the wrongful appropriation to one's own use of land (*esp* common or public) adjacent to one's own; land of this sort *la16-17, Inv Abd.* [eModEng, F *novation,* L *novātio* an innovation]

novator &c [*?'novatər] *n* an innovator, one who makes wrongful or undesirable changes in religious matters *17; cf* NOVATIOUN 2 (2). [F *novateur,* L *novātor* an innovator]

novelle &c [no'vɛl] *n* = novel, a work of fiction *la18-e20*.

novodamus [nɔvə'demʌs, novo'damʌs] *n, law* the formal renewal of a grant by a feudal SUPERIOR in order to alter or correct a former grant *17-*. [L (*de*) *novo damus* we grant anew]

now &c [*nʌu] *n* = noll, the head, *only proverb* **nitty** ∼, *la16, e18*.

now *see* NEW[1], NOO

nowder *see* NOWTHER

nowt[1] &c; nolt &c *15-* [nʌut; *Sh* nut, nød; *not] *n* **1** (1) *collective* cattle *la14-, Gen except Sh Ork SW*. (2) *sing* an ox, steer *15-, now NE*. **2** a big unwieldy person, an oaf, a blockhead *la18-, now local Sh-nEC Rox.*

∼ **beast** a bovine animal *la17-, now NE*. **nowt('s) feet** *chf in pl* calves' feet, cow-heels as a dish *16-20.* **nolt(is) price** payment due for cattle *la16-17, SW*. [ME *nowt,* ON *naut* cattle;

the *-l-* forms are scribal, by analogy w words where an original *-l-* is vocalized in Sc, *eg* COWT]

nowt[2]; **nowts &c** [nʌut] *n* **1** = nought, nothing *19-*, *S*. **2** *in pl, marbles* a shout by one's opponent preventing the player from firing from any spot he chooses *20-*, *Dmf Rox*. [reduced f NOCHT; orig only in sSc and nEng]

nowther &c; **nowder &c** *la15-16*, **nolder &c** *16* ['nʌuðər; *'nʌudər] *adj* (*la14-e16*), *pronoun* (*15-16*) neither.
conj **1** ~ **nor** *etc* neither *la14-20*. **2** = and not, nor, nor yet *16*. [ME *nowther &c*, OE *nowðer*, contracted f *nōhwæðer*; *cf* NAITHER and OWTHER]

nowther-quhare &c [*'nʌuðər'hwer] *adv* nowhere, in no respect *e15*. [see DOST]

noy &c *vt* **1** annoy, vex, irritate *la14-e19*. **2** *in passive* be troubled, *chf* be incensed, angry *la14-e19*.
n **1** vexation, harm *la14-19*. **2** *in pl* wrongs, injuries *la14-17*. [aphetic f Eng *annoy*]

noyne *see* NUNE

nu *see* NOO

nub &c *n*, *also* ~**bie &c** nickname for a club-footed person *18-e19*, *Rox*.
~ **berrie** = NOOP *la18-*, *S*. [var of eModEng *knub* a small lump, MLowGer *knubbe, knobbe* a knot, knob, lump]

nue *see* NEW[1]

nuif &c; **noof** [nøf] *adj* neat, spruce *la18-20*, *Gall*. [obscure]

nuke *see* NEUK

null &c *adj* **1** without legal force, void, invalid *16-17*. **2** *law, prefixed to a noun of action* (*orig only* ~ **defence**) expressing failure to perform what the noun denotes, = non-, not- *la15-17*.
~**ing** *n* rendering null, cancellation *16-e17*.

nullité &c ['nʌliti] *n* = nullity.

numerat &c [*'nʌmərat] *adj* (*16-17*), *pt, ptp* (*la15-16*) counted out, paid in cash. [only Sc; L *numerāt-*, ptp stem of *numerāre*; *cf* laME, eModEng *numerate* (*v*) reckon and NUMMER]

numeration &c [*nʌmər'esiun, -'eʃ(i)ən] *n* **1** = numeration, counting *16-*. **2** a counting out in cash; payment in cash *16-17*.

nummer &c *15-*, **noumer &c** *la14-16* ['nʌmər; *'numər] *n* = number *la14-*.
vt **1** = number *15-*. **2** count out (a sum of money) in payment; pay over in cash *la15-16*.
~**able 1** = numerable, capable of being numbered *la15-*. **2** numerous *la16-17*, *only Sc*.
~**it** *of money or payment* counted out in cash; given in cash *la15-e17*.

nuncupative [nʌnkju'petɪv] *adj, law, usu of a will* oral as opposed to written *la17-*. [MedL *nuncupativus*]

nune &c *16-*, **none &c** *la14-17*; **noun &c** *la15-17*, **noyne &c** *la14-e17*, *latterly N*, **neen** *20*, *N* [nøn, nɪn; *N* nin] *n* = noon *15-*.
noneschankis &c *n pl* an afternoon snack, = four hours (FOWER); a workmen's afternoon break *la14-16*.

nunlaw &c *n* = UNLAW *15*. [by wrong division]

nuris, nurisch(e) *see* NOURICE

nurl *see* NIRL

nurr; njirr *la19-*, *Sh-Cai* [n(j)ʌr; *Sh Ork* njɪr] *vi* **1** growl like an angry dog, snarl like a cat *19-*, *now Sh Cai*. **2** *of a cat* purr *19-*, *chf Sh*.
n the growl or snarl of an angry dog *19-*, *now Sh Rox*.
~**ing &c** growling, snarling; fault-finding *19-*, *now Sh Cai*. [imit; *cf* NARR and Norw *knurre*, Du *knorren* (*v*) growl, OE *gnyrran* creak)]

nurture *see* NORTER

nut *see* NIT[1]

nyaff &c [njaf; *local C also* naf] *vi* **1** *of a small dog* yelp, yap *19-*. **2** *fig* talk senselessly or irritatingly, yap *19-*, *now Sh*.
n **1** a puny, insignificant person; a small conceited impudent person *19-*. **2** a worthless person, good-for-nothing *20-*. [prob imit; see SND]

nyarb &c [njarb] *vi* be discontented or complaining *19-*, *NE*. [see SND]

nyarr *see* NARR

nyatter *see* NATTER

nybour, Nychburris *see* NEIBOUR

nyim *see* NIMP

nyne *see* NINE

nyod [njod] *interj* = God! *la19-*, *NE Fif*. [euphemistic alteration; *cf* DOD[2]]

nyow *see* NEW[2]

nyowl &c [njʌul] *vi* howl like a cat *20-*, *Sh NE*. [imit]

nyowmost *see* NEATH

nyte &c *vt* **1** deny; refuse to admit (something) *la14-e16*. **2** disown, abjure (a person) *la14-16*. **3** refuse to another (a request etc) *la14-16*. [nME *nite*, ON *níta*]

nyt(e) *see* NICHT

nyvle *see* NAEL

O

o¹, a *la15-17* [o, ə, ɪ] *prep* **1** = OF (1) *in gen, la14-*; (2) *with pronouns* (a) ~ **me** *etc* my *etc, 18-, now local Sh-Kcb*: 'I wad hae thrawn the neck o'm'; (b) *as reflexive pronoun* **the sell o'm, the sell o ye** *etc* himself, yourself *etc 19-, now NE Per*; (c) *elliptical* some of, a number or quantity of, a few of *19-, now local*: 'o them faucht, o them fled'; (3) *in designations of tenant farmers, with the farm-name la18-, now Sh Ork*: 'Tam o Shanter'; *cf* OF 2 (1) and IN *prep* 6; (4) omitted in expressions of quantity *16-*: 'a pint milk; a wee drap parritch'. **2** = on *15-*. **3** *where Eng has a different prep etc* (1) as regards, about, as far as concerns *la18-, now Sh*: 'he is ill to please o worldly bliss'; (2) *after an adj, freq comparative, esp* BETTER, WAUR: for; on account of; in return for *18-, Gen except Sh Ork*; (3) from *19-, now Sh Abd Ags*: 'he takes dat o his midder'; (4) in, in respect of, in the matter of *18-*: 'it's a queer thing o me, gentlemen'; (5) with, in consequence of, as a result of *19-*: 'the lassie's greetin o hunger'; (6) *used with verb of remembering* about, concerning *18-*: 'do ye mind o her?'; (7) *with adj implying proficiency* at, in respect of *19-, now Abd*: 'claer o the Laitin'; (8) during, in the course of *19-, now NE Loth*. [reduced f OF and ON; assimilation in form leads to confusion and transference of usage between OF and ON; *cf* IN]

o² *interj* **1** = o, oh! *15-*. **2** *ballad* added after the rhyme-word at the end of a line or half-line *18-, chf Sc*: 'green grow the rashes, o' [*cf* eModEng -a].

o³ *indef art* = A¹ *la14-16*. [irreg anglicized var]

o *see* OE

O &c; oy &c *la16-e17* [o] *n* **1** = O, anything shaped like an O *16-*. **2** a circular window *la16-e18*. **3** the looped brass fitting for raising a window sash *la19-, Per WC*.

round ~ **1** = *n* 2, *16-19*. **2** *fig, of a person* a cipher, a nonentity *la19-*.

O *see* ORDINAR

oam &c, ome; yoam &c *la19-* [(j)om; *Sh Ork* øm] *n* **1** *translating L 'vapor', la16*. **2** steam, vapour; condensation *19-, now Sh Ork NE*. **3** a warm aroma, *eg* from cooking *la19-, Sh Ork NE*. **4** a warm stuffy atmosphere; a gust of hot air; a heat haze *la19-, Sh NE*. **5** a jet of thick billowing smoke *la19-, Sh NE*.

vi **1** *of smoke* pour out thickly *20-, Sh NE*. **2** *of a smoker* puff *la19-, Abd*. [Norw dial *oma* be hot and hazy, smell; *ome* smoke; the smell of burning; a warm breeze]

oanshach ['o(n)ʃəx] *n* a foolish person, an idiot *la20-, Mry Abd Arg*. [Gael *oinnseach* an idiot]

oat *see* AIT

oath &c *17-*, **othe &c** *15-*, **aith &c** *la14-19*, **athe &c** *la14-16*, **haith** *la15*, **hathe &c** *la14-15*; **eath &c** *16-e17* [eθ, oθ] *n* = oath *la14-*.

oath of calumny an oath taken at the outset of an action by which both parties swear that the facts pleaded are true *la16-20*. **oath in supplement** an oath by which a litigant could give evidence in his own favour when impartial legal evidence was incomplete or defective *la17-19*. **oath of verity** an oath as to the truth of the averment of debt required to be made by a creditor petitioning for or claiming in *sequestration* (SEQUESTRATE) *la17-*.

obbit *see* OBIT

obedience &c *n* **1** = obedience *la14-*. **2** ~ **of** *or* **to** the compliance with or performance of (a command etc) *la15-17*.

do, gif *etc* ~ render obedience or dutiful service; submit *la15-17*. **mak (one's)** ~ do ceremonial reverence, show one's respect by a curtsy or bow; do homage *la14-20*.

obedient &c *adj* = obedient *15-*.

n an obedient or dutiful person; a person who is subject to authority *16-17, chf Sc*.

~**al** *law, of an obligation* imposed by law as distinct from contract *la17-*.

obefore *see* OF-BEFORE

obeit *see* OBIT

oberin &c; obran ['ob(ə)rɪn] *n* a trifle; *in pl* odds and ends; trivial work; scraps *la19-, now Kcdn*. [var of *overins* (OWER)]

obeyand &c [*o'biand &c*] *adj* submitting, obedient or subject (**to**) *la15-e16*. [Eng *obey*]

obit &c; obite &c *15-e17*, **obeit &c** *la15-e17*, **obbit** *la15-e16* *n* **1** = obit *la14-*. **2** *after the Reformation* an endowment, or the revenue from it, *orig* intended for the provision of an annual memorial service as in *n* 1, *la16-17*.

~ **silver** = *n* 2; payment for such a service *16-17*.

object &c; objeck &c *la15-* [*n* 'obdʒɛk(t); *v* əb'dʒɛk(t)] *n* **1** = object *la16-*. **2** a deformed or diseased person; an imbecile; someone deserving of pity *18-*.

vti, pt also **object** *la15-16* **1** = object *la15-*. **2** *vt* mention in reproach, disparagement or mockery *16*.

objection &c, objectioun &c *la16-17* *n* = objection *16-*.

have no objections have no objection *la18-*.

objure [*əb'dʒør*] *vt* = abjure *16-17, only Sc*.

obleege &c *la16-*, **oblige &c, oblis &c** *la14-17*; **oble(i)s &c** *la15-e18*, **oblych &c** *la14-e15*, **oblish &c** *la16-e18* [o'blidʒ; *-'blɪs, *-'blis, *-'blɪʃ] *vtir* **1** = oblige *la14-*. **2** *vi* bind or pledge oneself; promise *15-19, only Sc*. **3** *in passive* (1) be legally or morally bound or pledged; be bound by oath, promise or contract (to someone, to do something *or* that something be done *etc*) *la14-17*; (2) be bound or contracted **to** *etc* another: (a) in support, homage, service *etc 15-16*: 'as he is oblist till his lord'; (b) **in** = for (a sum of money) *15*: 'oblist tyll Thomas Purvais in a somme of siluer'; (3) be pledged or sworn *la16-17*: 'Jhone Hagy is oblist cautioun for hir'; (4) be under necessity of, need (to do something) *la14-e17*. **4** *in passive* be under obligation to pay, be owing *16-e17*. **5** *vt* compel, constrain;

consign, commit *15-16*. **6** *vr* commit, engage oneself (**to** another) **in** = for (a sum of money) *15, only Sc*: '*I oblist me, my ayris .. in fourty pvnd.*' **oblissing &c 1** a binding contract, undertaking, oath; the document expressing this *15-16*. **2** the fact of having pledged or committed one's goods as security *la15-16*. **~ment 1** a formal contract or agreement *freq* to pay a sum of money; an obligation *la15*-. **2** an act of kindness, a favour *18*-.

obligacoun *see* OBLIGATIOUN

obligant ['oblɪgənt] *n, law* a person who binds himself or is legally bound by a contract, bond or some other obligation *la16*-. [only Sc; L *obligant-*, presp stem of *obligāre* bind]

obligatioun &c *la14-17*; **obligacoun** *15 n* = obligation.

obligatour &c [*o'blɪgətur, *-or, *oblɪ'getər] *adj* = obligatory *17*. *n* = *lettre* ~, *la16-17*.
lettre, lettris *etc* ~(**is**) a written contract or bond embodying a legally-binding undertaking *la14-e17*.

oblige, oblis, oblish, oblych *see* OBLEEGE
obolus *n* a halfpenny *16*. [see DOST]

obran *see* OBERIN

obreption *n, law* the obtaining of a gift, dispensation etc by false statement *la17-20*. [F *obreption*, L *obreptio* a creeping up on unawares]

obscure &c *adj* **1** = obscure *la15*-. **2** *of persons or things* hidden, concealed *la16-17, only Sc*.

observar &c; observer *n* = observer *17*-.
party ~ **&c** *law, in penalty clause of contract* the party who keeps the terms of a contract, as against the party who fails to do so *17, only Sc*.

observe &c *vti* = observe. *n* an observation, scientific or otherwise; a remark, comment *la17*-, *now Sh Fif wLoth*.

obsolve &c [*əb'solv] *vt* = absolve *la16-17*.

obstant [*ob'stant, *also* *'obstant] *adj* opposing, resistant, adverse *la15-16*. [earlier in Sc; L *obstans*, presp of *obstāre* stand against]

obstene *see* ABSTEEN

obteen &c *17*-, *now local Sh-EC,* **obtene &c** *15-17*, **optene &c** *15-16*; **obtine &c** *16-17*, **obtain &c** *16-*, **ouptene &c** *la15-16* [əb'tin; ob-, *op-, *əp-] *vt* **1** = obtain *15*-. **2** take (a person) into custody or into one's hands *la16, only Sc*. **3** *law* be successful in, win (an action at law) *15-16*. **4** gain possession of by conquest *la15-16*. **5** *chf* **optene upon** succeed in getting (costs etc) against (someone) *la15-e16*.

obtemper &c [ob'tempər] *vti, law* comply with, submit **to**, obey (*esp* a court order etc) *16*-.
~ance (**of**) complying (with); obedience *la16-e17*. [chf Sc; eModEng *obtempre*, F *obtempérer*, L *obtemperāre* obey]

obtemperat [*ob'tempərat] *ptp* complied with, obeyed *16*. [L *obtemperāt-*, ptp stem of *obtemperāre*; *cf* prec]

obtemperate *18-19*, **obtemperat &c** *la16-17* [*ob'tempərat, -et] *vt* = OBTEMPER *la17-19*. [laME *obtemperate*]

obtend [*ob'tend] *vt* put forward as an argument or pretension; pretend, allege, maintain *la16-e17*. [earlier in Sc; L *obtendere* spread in front of]

obtene, obtine *see* OBTEEN

ocation *see* OCCASION

occanȝe **gluffis &c; okkenȝie- &c** [*o'kenjɪ-] *n pl* goose-skin gloves *la16*. [only Sc; MF *gands occaignez*]

occasion &c, **occasioun &c** *la14-17*; **oc(c)ation &c** *la16-17 n* **1** = occasion *la14*-. **2** *specif, Presbyterian Church* the celebration of the Lord's Supper; the periodical Communion Service *17-20, only Sc*.
vti = occasion.

occasioun *n* the setting (of the sun) *e16*. [only Sc; L *occāsio* taken as *n* of action from *occidere* go down (the actual L word was *occāsus*)]

occation *see* OCCASION

occident *adj* situated in the western part of the sky or of the earth, western *16*. [only Sc as *adj*]

occisioun &c [*o'kɪzun] *n* **1** = occision, slaughter, mass killing *la14-16*. **2** the killing of one person, murder *la15-e16, only Sc*.

occour *see* OCKER

occupatioun &c *15-e17*; **occupation** *n* **1** = occupation *la15*-. **2** the body of those following a particular trade or occupation, a craft INCORPORATION (*n* 2) *16, only Sc*.

occupe &c [*'okəp, *also* *o'køp] *vt* = OCCUPY *la14-16*. [only Sc; perh var of OCCUPY but *cf* OF *occuper*, L *occupāre*]

occupy &c; occupee &c *la19-e20* ['ok(j)əpɪ; *'okøpaɪ, -pi] *vti* **1** = occupy *la14*-. **2** *vt* (1) take or hold possession of (territory etc) by conquest or settlement *la14*-. (2) gain or have (authority or rule) by conquest or usurpation *la14-15*. (3) usurp the possession of; appropriate to one's use *la15-16*. (4) *of a disease* take possession of, grip (the victim) *16*. **3** employ, make use of; be busy with, enjoy the use or possession of *15-e19*. [*cf* OCCUPE]

occur &c; accur &c *16-e17 vti* **1** = occur *la15*-. **2** come **to** (someone's mind) *la15*.

och &c [ox] *interj, orig* expressing sorrow, pain, regret; *now chf* expressing exasperation, weariness etc *16*-.
~ane &c; o(c)hone &c *18-* ['o'xon, *'o'xen] *interj* expressing sorrow *la15*- [used orig and *freq* in Gaelic contexts]. **~anee** ['oxəni] = OCH *la19*-. [Sc and IrGael *och, ocha(i)n &c*; *cf* nME *oghane*; *cf* ACH, HECH, HOCH², OUCH, ANEE]

ochiern *see* OGTHIERN

ochone *see* OCH

ocht¹; oucht &c *la14-e20*, **owt** *20-*, *now Ork S* [oxt; *Ork S also* ʌut] *n* (*pronoun*) **1** *also* **aucht &c** *la15-e20* [*'ɑxt] = aught, anything *la14*-. **2** *with negatives* nothing *la20*-: '*nae end o nabbery that were fit for ocht else*'.

adj any *19*.
adv **1** *verse* = aught, to any extent *la14-16*. **2**
somewhat, rather, in some way *la14-e20*.
~**lins** *adv* in any way, at all, in the least degree
18-20. *n* aught, anything *18-e20*.
ocht²; ought [oxt] *vti* = ought, be bound or
under obligation (to do etc) *la16-*. [*cf* AUCHT³]
ocht *see* AWE²
ocker &c, ok(k)er &c; occour &c *la16 n* **1**
usury, the lending of money at (more or less
excessive) interest (*usu* regarded as a crime or
sin) *la15-e18*. **2** an instance of this; interest; a
rate of interest *la14-e17, only Sc*.
~**ar &c** a usurer *15-17*. [ME *oker*, ON *okr*]
Octavian &c *n, chf* (**the**) ~**s** a committee of
eight members appointed by James VI in
1595-6 to control Crown revenues and the
exchequer *la16-, latterly hist*. [only Sc; f L *octāvus*
eighth]
octo *n* a measure of arable land; a
half-*farthingland* (FARDEN), the eighth part of a
pennyland (PENNY) *18-19, Cai Suth*. [only Sc;
Gael *ochdamh* an eighth; *orig* an eighth of a
DAVACH or *ounceland* (OUNCE)]
od &c; odd(s) *19- interj, as a mild oath* = God
la18-, Sh NE, EC.
~ **sake(s)** *la19-, now NE, WC*, ~ **saffs &c** (*lit*
God save us) *19-, now Sh*, a mild oath. [aphetic;
eModEng]
odd &c, od &c *la14-17*; **ode** *la14-17 adj* = odd
la14-.
adv in an unusual manner; in a unique state
la19-, now Ags.
n, golf the handicap given to a weak opponent
by deducting one stroke from his total at every
hole *la19-; cf* ODDS 4.
~**land** land additional to, or not forming part
of some main body of land *15-16, only Sc*.
play the ~ play one more stroke than one's
adversary *la19-*.
for ~ **or evin** on any account *la14-15*.
oddis *see* ODDS
oddisman *see* ODDSMAN
odds, od(d)is &c *16-17 n pl* **1** = odds *17-*. **2**
freq (*17-*) *as sing, chf* ~ **of, on** difference in,
disparity between, inequality *la16-*: '*forty years
makes a great odds of a girl*'. **3** a small surplus
sum or number in addition to that specified;
something over; an indefinite additional
amount *16-*. **4** *golf* one stroke more than one's
opponent has played or conceded in a handicap
match *19-; cf* ODD *n*.
make (**a person's**) ~ **even** equalize or level
inequalities, adjust; *orig* (*16*) *also* atone for or
remit his shortcomings or transgressions *16-*. ~
and *or* **or evens** (*children's*) game = odd and
even *la19-*. (**the**) ~ **of** over, more than *19-, Sh
NE Uls*.
odds *see* OD
oddsman *la17-18*, **oddisman** *la16-e17 n* =
ODMAN. [w infl f ODDS]
ode *see* ODD

odeman *see* ODMAN
oder *see* ITHER
odger *see* OGEOUR
odious &c *adj* **1** = odious *15-*. **2** full of hate or
enmity; hostile *15-16, only Sc*. **3** *as intensive* very
big, excessive, intense etc *19-, now Sh*.
adv very, exceedingly *la19-, now Sh Uls*.
odis *see* ODDS
odman &c; odeman &c *n* **1** *in a body of arbitrators* the third, fifth *etc* person, who was accepted
as neutral and might give the casting vote
15-e17. **2** *in pl* arbitrators *16-17*. [ON
oddamaðr; eModEng *odd man; cf* ODDSMAN,
ODPERSOUN]
odorative *adj* aromatic, fragrant *la16*. [only Sc;
L *odōrātīvus*]
odpersoun &c *n* = ODMAN *16, only Sc*.
odwood *n, mining* (*Fawside colliery*) ? coal supplied in addition to the amount regularly contracted for *la17*. [only Sc]
oe &c *16-*, **o** *la15-19*, **oy(e) &c** *la15-20*; **oo**
la15-e17 [o; oi; (*disyllabic*) 'oɪ] *n* **1** a grandchild
la15-, now N Arg. **2** a nephew; *orig also* a niece
la16-e20. [ScGael *ogha*, IrGael *ó* a grandson,
descendant; see also IEROE]
oeconomus &c [*?ɔi'konomʌs, *?i-] *n* **1** *also*
iconomus &c *la16-17* the steward or manager
of property and finances, *esp* of a religious house
or a college *la16-e18*. **2** *also* **economus &c**
la16-17, Abd St Andrews, **economist &c** *la18,
Abd, specif* the keeper of student lodgings at a
university [L (f Gk) *oeconomus* steward]
oecumenick &c *adj* ecumenical *la15-17*. [F
oecuménique, L *oecumenicus*]
oen *see* UNE¹
o'er *see* OWER
o'ercome *see* OVERCOME
o'erpit, o'erput *see* OWERPIT
of; off *la14-17 prep* **1** = of *la14-*. **2** (1) (*cf* IN *prep*
6 and o¹ 1 (3)) *in designations* indicating that the
person named is the CLAN CHIEFTAIN, proprietor
or principal tenant of the place; the designation
remains, even if the lands are alienated *la14-*;
(2) *specif* **Viscount** ~ = Viscount *18-*. **3** in
describing taxation etc, indicating the unit on
which payment is levied *15-e17*: '*of ilk otyr skyn a
halfpeny*'; '*of friemen iiij d*'. **4** *used with certain verbs
concerning, in regard to *18-19*: '*we forbid you of
it*'. **5** *after verbal noun, la18-e19*: '*he said he was
shooting of game*'. **6** for; with, through, in respect
of, in consequence of: (1) *after certain adjs, la14-*:
'*a field rich of clover*'; '*a boy big of his age*'; (2) *after
a comparative adj, esp* BETTER, WAUR *18-; cf* o¹ 3
(2); (3) = o¹ 3 (4) *la18-*: '*she had been so long of
sending for assistance*'. **7** *in telling the time* to,
before (an hour) *20-, Sh NE Uls*: '*a quarter of
twelve*'. **8** with *18-*: '*it was pouring of rain*'. **9**
resulting from ambiguity of o¹ = on, upon *18-e19*.
five *etc* **of a family** a family of five *la18-*. [*see*
AFF, o¹]
of *see* AFF

of-before &c *la14-18*, **obefore &c** *15-e17*, **abefore &c** *la15-17* [*ovbɪ'for, *obɪ-, *əbɪ-] *adv* earlier, previously, formerly.
~ **time** in the past, formerly *e15*. [only Sc; OF + BEFORE]

ofcom *see* OFFCOME

off *see* AFF, OF

offcome, ofcom *la17 n* **1** the conclusion of an argument *17*, *only Sc*. **2** the way in which one comes out of an affair, or is seen to conduct oneself in it *la17*, *only Sc*. **3** an excuse, pretext, evasion *18-e19*, *only Sc*. **4** a (good or bad) result *20-*, *S*, *only Sc*. [eModEng *offcome* the product of multiplication; see *affcome* (AFF)]

offeecial [o'fiʃ(ɪə)l] *n*, *adj* = official *la19-*.

offeecious [o'fiʃ(ɪ)əs] *adj* = officious *la19-*.

offen *la19-*, **offend &c** [o'fɛn(d)] *vti* **1** = offend *15-*. **2** *vi* be offended *la16-17*, *only Sc*: 'the Queen offendeth that I vse the title and arms of England'.

offer &c *vti* **1** = offer *la14-*. **2** *vtr* (1) offer (another or oneself) to the service of a superior authority *la14-16*. (2) offer (oneself) in battle *la15-16*. (3) put forward (a person) to fulfil some function *16*. **3** *with infin* threaten; make as if (to..); attempt, try *la17-*. **4** *of persons and weather* look like being.., appear to be turning out.. *la17-e20*: 'Sabbath being calm and offring fair'.
n **1** = offer *la15-*. **2** an attempt, feeble effort, gesture *19-*, *now NE Ags Edb*.
~**ing &c 1** = offering *la15-*. **2** a small quantity; a feeble attempt *20-*, *Sh NE Lnk*.
in one's ~ at one's choice; at one's disposal; for the taking *la18-19*.

offerand &c; offrand &c *la15-16 n* **1** = off-rand, a religious offering *la14-16*. **2** *sing and pl*, *specif* Church offerings, *esp* as viewed as part of the regular income of a church or benefice *la15-16*. **3** ? the offertory, the point in the Mass when offerings were made *e15*. **4** the Presentation of Christ in the Temple, as celebrated at Candlemas *15*, *Abd*, *only Sc*.

office &c *n* **1** = office *la14-*. **2** a workshop, factory, shop *la18-19*.
~**-hous &c** a workshop, an outbuilding *la15-e18*. ~**-man** an officer, official *la15-17*, *only Sc*.
~ **of arms** the business of heralds, the science of heraldry; the corporate body of Scottish heralds; the LYON office *la15-16*.

officer &c, officere &c *la14-17*, **officher &c** *16-e17*, *only Sc*, **officiar &c** *15-e18*, *only Sc*; **offisher &c** *16-*, *only Sc* ['ofɪsər, 'ofɪʃər] *n* **1** = officer *la14-*. **2** an official of any legal, municipal or ecclesiastical court, or similar body whose duty is to keep order at meetings, deliver messages, summonses etc *15-*.
~**ship &c** the position and functions of an officer *la16-*.

officiary, officiarie &c *la16-17* **1** the position and functions of an officer of a BURGH, barony (BARON), craft etc, or of a *ground officer* (GRUND) of *n* 2, *la16-17*. **2** a division in a large Highland

(HIELAND) estate, each *orig* under the care of one *ground officer* (*esp* of the Breadalbane estates, Per) *la16-*, *only Sc*.
~ **corn** grain paid by tenants towards the emoluments of the officer of a *baron-court* (BARON) *17-18*. ~ **of armes** any officer, *esp* a herald or PURSUIVANT, under the authority of the *Lord Lyon King of Arms* (LORD) *la15-16*.
officer of state one of the important officials of state in Scotland, *eg* the *Lord Lyon*, *Lord Advocate* (LORD) *17-*. [*officiar* f MedL *officiarius*]

offie &c *n* a privy, dry closet *19-*, *local Ags-S*. [f obs Eng (*house of*) *office*]

offisher *see* OFFICER

offrand *see* OFFERAND

offreis, offrez *see* ORPHUS

oftsyse &c [*'oft'saɪz] *adv*, *chf verse* often, repeatedly; *as* is often the case, commonly *la14-16*. [nME (once) *of sise*, reduced f ME *oftsithes*]

ogart &c; ogert &c *la15-e19* [*'ogərt] *n* pride, arrogance, presumption *la14-e17*.
ogertfu dainty, affected, fastidious *18-e19*. [northern and midl ME *ougard* arrogant; *cf* ON *ágjart* ambition]

ogeour; odger &c [*'odʒər] *n* ? an ogee arch, or a moulding which when doubled constituted such an arch; a stone cut for such an arch *16-e17*. [see DOST]

ogert *see* OGART

ogie &c ['ogɪ] *n* = KILLOGIE 2 and 3, *19*. [aphetic f LOGIE, by wrong division of KILLOGIE]

ogthiern &c; ochiern *la17* [*?'og'tiərn &c] *n*, *law* one who ranked with the son or grandson of a THANE[1] *13-17*, *latterly hist*. [only Sc; Gael *òg-thighearna* a young lord, chief's son]

ohone *see* OCH

oik *see* OUK

oil &c, ile *19-*, *Gen except S*, **uilie &c** *la14-*, *now Sh*, **olȝe &c** *la14-e17*, **eelie &c** *19-e20*; **ole &c** *la15-e17*, **oyell &c** *la16-17*, **oilie &c** *15-19*, **ule &c** *la15-e17*, **ollie &c** *16-19*, **ulyie &c** *19-e20* [əil, *øl, *(j)ul; 'øl(j)ɪ, 'ulɪ, *'oilɪ, *'olɪ, *'ʌlɪ; *NE also* 'ilɪ] *n* (*la14-*), *v* (*la16-*) = oil.
~ **colour &c** *orig only in pl* oil-paint *la15-*. ~**ie cruisie** an oil lamp *19-e20*. ~ **dolive &c** *16*, ~ **de olive** *16*, ~ **doly &c** *la15-17*, ~ **olive** *16-e17* olive oil. **eelie dolly 1** oil of any kind *19*, *Abd*. **2** an oil lamp *la19-*, *NE*. **ulie &c peter** rock oil, petroleum *la16*. **uilie pig** an oil barrel etc *la18-*, *now Sh*.

oise *see* USE

oismont *see* OSMOND

oix *see* OX

ok *see* OUK

oker *see* OCKER

okkenȝie- *see* OCCANȝE GLUFFIS

okker *see* OCKER

okstare *see* OXTER

old *see* AULD

older *see* OWTHER

ole *see* OIL

oleit *see* OLITE

olif *see* OLIVE

olite &c *17-e20*, **oleit** &c *la16-e19* [*'olit, *-ləit, *-lət, &c] *adj* **1** eager, ready, willing; cheerful *la16-e20*. **2** active, energetic, nimble *la16-19*. [only Sc; appar reduced f ON *offléttr* prompt, ready]

olive &c; **olif** *16* *n* = olive *15-*.

olk *see* OUK

ollie, olȝe *see* OIL

oman *see* WOMAN

ome *see* OAM

omnigaddrum &c *16-17*; **omnigatherum** &c *n* **1** = omnium gatherum, a miscellaneous collection etc *16-e19*. **2** *in pl* things or persons forming such *la17*. **3** a miscellaneous group of crafts, not *incorporated* (INCORPORATE) separately, and treated for certain purposes as a single unit *17*, *Stirling*.

on *prep* **1** = on *la14-*. **2** *esp with* CONDESCEND, MIND, TELL *etc* about, concerning *la14-*. **3** at, near, beside, by *la14-*. **4** supported by, by means of, with *la14-*: 'go on a stick'. **5** in *la14-*. **6** to: (1) *chf* **cry** *etc* ~ summon or attract the attention of (someone) by calling out *15-*; (2) *see* MAIRRY *16-*. **7** for, in anticipation of; per *16-*; *see eg* WAIT[1]. **8** of *la16-19*.
adv **1** = on *la14-*. **2** *idiomatic with eg* LAT[1], MAK, PIT[1].
~ **a(n)**, ~ **o(n)**, ~ **upon** (on)to, upon *la18-*, *now N, EC*. ~ **about** occupied in talking about, harping on *20-*. ~ **fit** afoot *20-*, *Ork Ags Kcb*. ~ **for** keen on, in favour of, eager for, taken up with *la19-*, *NE, C*. ~ **oneself** on one's own account, independent(ly) *la19-*. ~ **tae**, ~ **til 1** *with verbs of placing, fixing etc* on(to) *19-*. **2** approaching, getting on for *19-*, *Sh-N Kcb Uls*. ~ **wi** = on for, *la19-*, *NE-S*. [*cf* o[1], IN]

on- *see* UN-

onabill *see* UNABLE

onamovit [*onə'møvɪt] *adj* unmoved *e16*. [only Sc. OED *unamoved*]

on-ane &c, **onone** &c; **one-ane** *la14-e15* [*on'en,*-'on] *adv, verse, chf or only in rhyme* **1** forthwith, straight away *la14-e16*. **2** continuously *la15-e16*.
sone ~ immediately, quickly *la14-15*. [northern and n midl ME *on an*, eME *anan*, *onon*, OE *on ān* into one, *on āne* in one; *cf* Eng *anon*]

onbaykyn [*'on'bekən] *adj, of brick etc* not baked in a kiln, not exposed to heat *e16*, *only Sc*. [OED *unbaken*]

onbeast *la18-e20*, **unbeast** &c *la14-e19* [*'on'bist, *'ʌn-] *n* a monster, a wild beast; a frightening bird or animal. [nME *unbest*]

onbekend *see* UNBEKENT

oncairry &c; **oncarry** ['on'kerɪ] *n* a fuss, an instance of rowdy behaviour, a 'carry-on' *19-*, *Sh-nEC*.

oncanny *see* UNCANNIE

oncarry *see* ONCAIRRY

oncassin *see* UNCASSEN

oncast &c *n*, *knitting* the first row of stitches; the casting on of this *la19-*, *local Sh-Arg, only Sc*.

once *see* AINCE

oncle &c *n* = uncle *16-17*.

oncome ['onkʌm,'oŋ-] *n* **1** the approach or beginning of something; the setting about an action; development, progress in something *19-*, *now Sh NE*. **2** a heavy fall of rain or snow *19-*, *now local Ags-Uls*. **3** an attack of a disease of unknown origin; a sharp attack of illness *19-*, *S*; *cf* INCOME.
oncomin ready to make advances, friendly *20-*, *local*.

oncorn *see* UNCORN

oncost &c *n* **1** *also* **uncost** *la15-16*, *freq mining*: *chf in pl 15-16*, *only in sing 17-* additional expenses; overheads *15-*, *now Fif*. **2** *mining, also* **oncoster**, ~ **man** a timeworker *la18-*, *now Fif*. [MDu *onkosten* expenses]

ondag *n* a shower, a heavy fall of rain *20-*, *NE*. [ON + DAG[1]]

ondantit *see* UNDANTIT

onder *see* UNDER

onderstand *see* UNDERSTAND

ondertaking *see* UNDER

onding *n* **1** a heavy continuous fall of rain or snow, a downpour *la18-*. **2** an attack, onset, outburst (*esp* of noise) *la19-e20*.
vi, also fig rain or snow heavily *19-e20*. [only Sc; ON + DING]

ondocht *see* UNDOCHT

ondreyd [*'on'drid] *adj* not dreaded *e16*, *Abd*. [OED *undreaded*]

one &c *indef art* = ANE[2] *15-17*. [wrong anglicization by analogy w ANE[1]]

one *see* ANE[1]

one- *see* UN-

one-ane *see* ON-ANE

oneratioun &c *n* a financial burden or charge; a written statement or account of this *16*. [only Sc; MedL *oneratio*; *cf* Eng *oneration* the action of loading *la17*]

onerous &c *adj* **1** = onerous. **2** *law* involving payment; granted or created in return for money, services etc received *la17-*; *cf* GRATUITOUS.
onerosity *law* the fact or condition of being ONEROUS.

onerstan(d) *see* UNDERSTAND

one servit *see* UNSERVED

oneste *see* HONEST

one to *see* ONTO

onfa &c *19-*, **onfall** &c ['onfɑ, -fə, *-fal] *n* **1** a military attack *la17*. **2** a heavy fall of rain or snow *19-*, *local*. **3** an attack of a disease, *freq* one of unknown origin *19-*, *chf S*. **4** the fall of evening *19-*, *S*. [nME *on-fall*, OE *onfeall* an attack of disease or other calamity]

onfarrand *see* UNFARRANT

onfowllit [*'on'fulɪt] *adj* unexhausted *e16*, *only Sc*. [OED *unfouled*]

ongae *19-;* **ongo** ['on'ge, -'go] *n* **1** *also* **ongoing** movement, progress *17-e20.* **2** stir, fuss, uproar *la19-, Sh NE, S.*

ongaein &c, ongoing &c, ongaun &c *chf in pl* goings-on, behaviour, *esp* of a specified kind, *eg* wild or rowdy behaviour *la17-.* [ON + GAE; *cf* ModEng *ongoing* and ONGANG]

ongang &c ['on'gaŋ] *n* **1** the starting up or setting in motion of machinery, *esp* a mill *la19-, NE.* **2** rowdy unrestrained behaviour; antics *la19-, now Abd.* [only Sc; ON + GANG; *cf* ONGAE]

ongaun, ongo *see* ONGAE

ongris &c [*'ʌngrɪs] *adj, only in coin names* Hungarian *la15, only Sc.* [see DOST]

ongrit [*'on'grɪt] *adj* small *e16.* [only Sc. OED *ungreat*]

onhabill *see* UNABLE

onhanger ['on'haŋər] *n* a hanger-on *19-, now Uls, only Sc.*

onhing ['on'hɪŋ] *n* the act of waiting around lazily; tedious delay *la20-, NE-Per.*

onie &c, ony &c ['onɪ] *adj, pronoun* = any *la14-. adv* in any way, at all *la18-, only Sc: 'can ye fish ony?'*

~ **ane** anyone *16-.* ~**gate** anywhere *19-, EC, SW, S.* ~ **ither wey** anywhere else *la19-, now NE.* ~**kin,** ~ **kyne** = anykyn, of any kind or sort *la14-15.* ~**way(s) &c** *la14-,* ~**wise &c** *la14-16* anyhow, in any way, anywhere.

onis *see* ONCE

onkent *see* UNKEN

onlay *vt, chf* ~**ing** laying on *la16-.*

on-leping *see* ONLOWPING

onless *see* UNLESS

onlowping &c *la16-e17,* **on-leping &c** *la15-e17* [*'on'lʌupɪŋ, *-'lip-] *n* the act of mounting a horse to depart *only Sc.*

on na way *la16,* **on-na-wayis &c** *la15-e17,* **on-na-wise &c** *15-e17,* **on-no-wise &c** *la15-e17* [*on'ne'wez, *-'waɪz, *-'no-] *adv* in no way or manner, by no means, not at all, on no account.

onone *see* ON-ANE

onpit *17-,* **onput &c** *16-19* ['on'pɪt, *-'pʌt] *vt* put into position; install *16-17. n* that which is put on, dress *la19-, now Rox.*

onputting &c 1 the action of putting on or installing *16-17, chf C, S.* **2** = *n, la19-, now Rox.*

onprisit; unprisit [*'on'praɪzɪt, *ʌn-] *adj* untested as to quality or value; unpriced *e15.* [only Sc; *cf* Eng *unprized.* OED *unprized*]

onput *see* ONPIT

onrestles [*'on'rɛstləs] *adj, appar* restless *e16.* [only Sc. OED *unrestless*]

ons *see* OUNCE

onset¹ &c *n* **1** = onset *16-.* **2** a scolding *la18-e20.*

onsetter &c 1 an assailant *la16-e17.* **2** *mining* the person who loads the hoist at the pit bottom *la20-, now Fif.*

onset² &c *n* a dwelling-site, a *steading* (STEID¹)

with the dwelling-house and outhouses built on it, a small cluster of houses *15-20, orig chf Ork S, latterly chf SW Uls.* [OE *set* a seat, residence, stall etc; OE *gesete* a seat, habitation; *cf* ONSTEAD]

onsetting &c [*'on'sɛtɪŋ] *n* **1** the action of fixing (things) on *16-e17.* **2** attacking, assailing *la16.*

onspulʒeit &c [*'on'spuljɪt, &c] *adj* = unspoiled *16-17.* [only Sc. OED *unspulyied*]

onstead &c, onsted ['onstɛd; *Rox* 'onstid] *n* = *steading* (STEID¹) *la16-, chf S.* [*cf* ONSET²]

ontak &c ['on'tak] *n* (the taking on of) a task or responsibility; a big job *20-, Sh NE.*

~**ing &c 1** (the start of) an undertaking *18-, now Sc.* **2** engaging oneself for a post, enlisting as a soldier *la17-e18.*

on-takis-man &c [*'on'taksmən] *n* a person who does not hold a TACK² of part of the common *e17, Inverurie.*

ontil *see* UNTIL

onto *la14-16,* **unto; one to** *la14-e16* [*'on'tø, *ʌn-] *prep, in OSc chf before consonants* (*cf* UNTIL) = unto *la14-.*

conj = until *la15-16.*

ontynt [*'on'tɪnt] *adj* not lost *e16.* [only Sc. OED *untint*]

onwait &c ['on'wet, *NE* -'wəit] *vi, chf* ~**er** a person who waits or is made to wait long or expectantly; a person who attends to another; an attendant, assistant, servant *17, only Sc;* ~**ing** (long, *freq* enforced) waiting (**for** something); patient expectation; attendance, service *la16-.*

n the act of waiting, a long wait; a person, *eg* an invalid, requiring constant attention; a person who causes a long wait *la19-, NE.*

onwal &c ['anwal] *adj* = annual *la19-e20, chf N.*

onwart &c *adv* = onward *15-e16.*

n **in** ~ *of payment* in advance *la15-e16, only Sc.*

ony *see* ONIE

onʒeon *see* INGAN

oo¹ &c *16-,* **oull &c** *15-e20,* **wool &c** *17-;* **woll &c** *la14-16,* **wow &c** *la15-e19,* **woo** *18-* [u, ul, wu] *n* **1** = wool *la15-.* **2** *in pl* **oos &c, ooze &c** [uz, us] woollen fluff; fluff from cotton etc *19-, Gen except Sh Ork; cf* CADDIS.

~**en &c** *la15-,* **woon &c** *la16-18* woollen. **oosie &c** ['uzɪ, 'usɪ] fluffy; furry; having a good nap or pile *18-, now C.* ~**ster** a wool-stapler *la16.* **oother &c, ouder &c** ['uðər, '(w)udər] *n* **1** fluff from wool, cotton etc when it begins to fray *19-, S.* **2** a light morning mist or haze; a heat haze *e19, Slk.* ~**y &c** woolly, covered with wool *la18-, Sh-EC, Kcb.*

wollbutter butter used to salve sheep's wool *e17, only Sc.* ~**-card** the spiked board used for teasing wool *17-, now Sh Ork.* ~**-mill &c** a tweed mill *la19-, NE Ayr.* ~ **wheel** a spinning wheel *17-19, only Sc.*

a(**w**) **ae** ∼ all one wool; all one, all the same; of one stock; on an equal footing *19-, now Sh-N, Fif.*

oo² *19-e20,* **ow** &c *17* [u] *vt* = woo.

oo³; ou *n* [*ʌu, *(disyllabic)* *'ʌuu] *n, only in street cry* **caller** ∼ fresh oysters *19-e20, Edb.* [reduced f *owster,* EC var of Eng *oyster*]

oo *see* OE, WE

oobit &c *la18-,* **woubit** &c *16-e19;* **wobat** *16-* ['ubət, *'wu-] *n, freq* **hairy** ∼ *19-, Fif Bwk S* a hairy caterpillar, *esp* the larva of the tiger moth *16-.* [ME *wolbode;* first element appar f Eng *wool*]

oof *la18-20,* **wolf** &c; **wowf** &c *16-, now Abd* [(w)uf; *Abd also* wʌuf] *n* **1** = wolf *la14-.* **2** the angler-fish *la19-, NE.*

v **1** *vi, of a grain crop* grow leaves profusely without producing seed-heads *la18-20.* **2** *vt* = wolf, consume ravenously *20-.*

oogly *see* UGLY

ool *19-, now Sh NE Ags,* **oule** &c *16-e17;* **owl** &c [ul] *n* = owl *la14-.*

v **1** *vt* treat harshly, ill-use, bully; wreck the health or spirits of *19-.* **2** *vi* be dejected, subdued, as from illness *20-, Sh Uls.*

∼d, ∼t downcast, cowed, nervous, bewildered *20-, now NE.* [*cf* OOLET, HOOLET]

ool *see* WE

oolet &c *n* **1** = OOL *n, 20-, NE, WC.* **2** *fig* a disgruntled, peevish, dismal person *20-, Sh NE Ags.* [conflation of HOOLET w Eng *owlet*]

oon *see* UNE¹

oon- *see* UN-

ooncanny *see* UNCANNIE

oonder *see* UNDER

oonderstan(**d**) *see* UNDERSTAND

oon-egg *see* WIND¹

ooner *see* UNDER

oonerstan(**d**) *see* UNDERSTAND

oonken- *see* UNKEN

oopie, oopsie *see* UP

oor¹ &c *la19-,* **our** &c, **hour** &c [ur] *n* **1** = hour *la14-.* **2** *in pl* o'clock *15-19:* '*twa oors*'. [see also *fower-hours* (FOWER)]

oor² &c [ur] *vi* crouch, shiver with cold; huddle *la19.*

∼it &c **1** cold, shivery, hunched up with cold or discomfort *la19-, now local Sh-Dmf.* **2** tired or ailing-looking, dejected *la19-e20.* [appar var of OOL *v; cf* next]

oor *see* EVER, OUR

oorie &c, **oorich**(**ie**) *la19-e20, local* ['urɪ(xɪ)] *adj* **1** (1) *of persons or things* dismal, gloomy, miserable-looking from cold, illness, etc *18-, now local Sh-Arg.* (2) *of weather* dull and chilly, raw *19-e20.* **2** uncannie, strange and disquieting *la19-, now Sh.*

oorlich &c ['urləx] *adj* **1** *of persons* miserable looking from cold, hunger or illness *la18-e20.* **2** *of weather* damp, raw, bleak *19-, N.* **3** *of things* sad and depressing, EERIE *20-, NE.* [appar f OOL *n, v,* and OOR²; *adj* 2 w infl f EERIE]

oos *see* OO¹

oosie, ooster *see* OO¹

oot, ooten *see* OUT

oother *see* OO¹

ootleuk &c ['ut'l(j)uk &c] *n* = outlook *la19-, Sh Ork Abd.*

ooze *see* OO¹

oozlie &c *adj* slovenly, untidy, unkempt, dirty *19-e20, SW.* [*cf* ME *usell* wretched, miserable; ON *úsæll* unhappiness, *úsælligr* poor-looking]

opeenion *la19-,* **opinioun** &c *15-e17;* **opinion** &c, **opunyone** &c *la14-e16,* **opingan** &c *la19, Abd* [ə'pinjən, ə'pɪŋən] *n* **1** = opinion *la14-.* **2** one's estimation of the worth of a person or thing; esteem *la14-.*

open *la16-,* **opin** &c *la14-e17,* **apen** &c *la16-e20,* **apin** &c *la15-16,* **wuppen** &c *la19-e20, S;* **oppin** &c *la14-19,* **appin** &c *16-e17* ['op(ə)n, 'ap-; *S* 'wʌp-] *adj* **1** = open *la14-.* **2** *of female animals* ready to bear young; bearing young; not sterilized *la18-19.* **3** free (to do ..), available, not prevented by previous engagement or duty *20-, EC, S.*

n an opening, gap, space *la15-, now NE.*

vti **1** = open *la14-.* **2** *vt* initiate (a proceeding or business); raise (a matter) *la15-.* **3** make available **to**, grant *la15-16.* **4** *vi* ∼ **on, to** *etc, of a door etc* face onto or towards (a place or direction) *la15-.*

open account *law* a debt entered in a book, not constituted by voucher or DECREE, *eg* for goods supplied by shops *18-.* **∼-cast** *mining* a method of working coal from the surface *17-.* **∼ gate** the public street; a free or open access-road *la15-16, only Sc.* **opin** &c **renȝeis** freedom, licence *e16, only Sc.* **∼steek** *needlework* a kind of openwork stitch *19-, now Ork.*

by, with *etc* ∼ **voce 1** audibly and publicly *16.* **2** by public fame or rumour *16-e17.* **go** *etc* **to the apen furth** go *etc* out of doors *19-e20.* **the ∼ o the heid** the front suture of the skull, the fontanelle *la18-, now Sh.*

operatioun &c *n* **1** = operation *la15-16.* **2** practical work of some kind *esp* as a trade or occupation; craftsman's work; a job of work *la15-17.*

opin *see* OPEN

opingan, opinion, opinioun *see* OPEENION

oppin *see* OPEN

oppone &c *la15-18,* **appone** &c *la15-17* [*o'pon, *ə-] *vtir* **1** = oppone, oppose *la16-17.* **2** *vt, chf law* oppose by argument, say or bring evidence to the contrary of, advance as an objection *la15-18.*

oppose &c *la15-,* **appose** &c *16-17* *vtr* **1** = oppose *16-.* **2** *vt* resist by force; obstruct, restrain *la15-.*

oppugn &c; **oppung** &c *la16-e17, only Sc* [*o'pʌŋ] *vti* = oppugn *la16-.*

optene *see* OBTEEN

opunyone *see* OPEENION

or &c *prep* **1** before *la14-*. **2** until *19-*, *Sh*, *NE*, *EC*, *S*.

conj, *also* **ir** *la19-*, *Sh NE* **1** before; until *la14-*, *now Sh-Ags*. **2** sooner than, rather than *la14-*, *now local NE-Uls*. **3** than *16-*, *now Sh Ork*.

or ever *conj* before ever, even before *la14-*, *now NE*. **or a' be dune &c** before it's all over *la19-*, *Ork NE Ags*. [ME, corresponding to regular nME *ar(e)*, f ON *ár* early; *cf* AIR⁵, ERE; see DOST]

or *see* OWER

ora *see* ORRA

oraisoun *see* ORISOUN

orange &c; orenge &c *16-e17*, **oringe &c** *la16-e17* *n* **1** = orange *16-*. **2** the colour orange *la16-*. [*cf* ORENƷE]

oranger; orenger &c *la16-17*, **oringer &c** *17-19* *n* an orange *la16-*. [only *Sc*; appar erron f F *oranger* an orange tree]

oratioun &c *n* **1** the act of praying, prayer; a prayer *la14-16*. **2** = oration *la16-e17*.

orator *see* ORATOUR²

oratory &c [*'orətorı, &c*] *n* **1** = oratory *la15-*. **2** a study *15-16, only Sc*. **3** an inner shrine of a temple, as the seat of an oracle *e16*. [*cf* ORATOUR¹]

oratour¹ &c; oritore &c *la15-16* *n* = ORATORY 1 (*la14-e17*), 2 (*la15-16*), 3 (*e16*). [nME (once) *oritore*, OF *oratur*]

oratour² &c *la15-e17*; **orator** *16-* *n* **1** = orator *la15-*. **2** a person who offers up prayers for another: (1) applied by the sovereign to members of the clergy *la15-16*; (2) applied by petitioners to themselves as praying for the person addressed (*freq* the sovereign) *16-e17*; (3) a person whose duty or employment it is to pray on another's behalf, *chf* a chaplain, a bedesman *la15-16*. **3** an oracle *e16*.

oratrye &c *n* = oratory, the art of the orator etc *16, only Sc*.

orchard *15-*, **orchat &c** *e16, only Sc*; **orchart &c** *la15-e17*, **orchaird &c** *la16-e17*, **orcheard &c** *la16-17*, **orchyard &c** *16-e18*, **orscheat &c** *la15-e16, only Sc* *n* = orchard.

orchard-litt &c; orcheart- &c *n* name of some dye *la16-17*. [perh altered f eModEng *orchell*, OF *orchel*, the red or violet dye, orchil, obtained from certain lichens]

ordeen &c, ordain &c; ordine &c *la14-e17* [or'din, or'den, *or'dan(d), *'ordən] *vtir, pt, ptp also* **ordand** *la14-16*, **ordoned &c** *la16-e17* **1** = ordain *la14-*. **2** *now only* **ordain**, *Presbyterian Church* admit (an ELDER or DEACON²) to office *la16-*. **3** *with infin* sentence (someone) to suffer a certain penalty or punishment *16-e17*.

ordinar [*?or'dinər, *?'ordənər] a person who appoints, settles or decrees something; a person who invests or ordains (an ecclesiastic) *la16-17*.

order &c; ordour &c *15-17* *n* **1** = order *la14-*. **2** the badge or insignia of a society of knights *16-*. **3** the action of putting or keeping in order; regulation, control, discipline *15-e17*.

4 decorous personal behaviour, decency, propriety *la15-17, only Sc*. **5** a scheme of the actual or proposed arrangement for a person's or persons' maintenance; regular provision or allowance of board and lodging; one's living standard as determined by this *la16, only Sc*. **6** *Reformed Church* a scheme for territorial reorganization or for the regular and settled provision of MINISTERS' *stipends* (STEEPEND) *la16, only Sc*; see PLAT². **7** *in pl* one's requirements or gear; all that one needs for some purpose *la18-, only Sc*.

as the ~ of law will, is usit *etc* according to the law, in regular legal form *la14-e15, only Sc*. **~ of table** the sequence set out in a list of the succession in which causes etc were to be called *16, only Sc*. **per ~** in order, in proper sequence *la14-e16, only Sc*. **put ~ to, in** *etc* impose order on, exercise authority over, regulate, set to rights, take disciplinary action against *16, only Sc*. **tak (ane) ~ 1** give directions, make arrangements, take measures (1) *absol, la16-17*; (2) **that, how** *etc* (something should be done) *la16-e17*; (3) **for** (doing something) *or* **for** (some concern) *la16-e17*. **2** impose order, exercise authority; make arrangements, take measures **in, anent** *etc* (some concern). **take (an) ~ with** *or* **o** impose order on, exercise authority or discipline over; take measures concerning, make arrangements for, see to *la16-, now Abd*.

ordinance &c; ordnance &c *15-*, **ordonnance &c** *15-e17*, **ordines &c** *16* *n* **1** = ordinance *la14-*. **2** = ordnance *16-*.

ordinar &c, ordinary &c *la16-*; **ordnar &c** *la16-e20* ['or(d)nər, 'ord(ı)nərı] *adj* **1** = ordinary *la15-*. **2** *law, now only* **ordinary** (1) *freq* **judge ~, sheriff ~** *etc* a judge etc with a fixed and regular jurisdiction in all actions of the same general nature *15-*. (2) (a) applied to the regular *lords of session* (LORD) and to the office of such *la16-e17*. (b) applied to the *lord of session* taking his turn of sitting separately on cases of first instance etc *la16-e17*. (3) *specif* **judge ~** a *Sheriff-substitute* (SHERIFF); a *Lord Ordinary* (LORD) *18-e20*. **3** *only* **ordinary**, *Sc Univs* (1) applied in the Faculties of Arts and Science to the general courses in any particular subject, passes in a certain number of which lead either to an *Ordinary Degree* or to the higher classes of an Honours course *la19-* (*Abd Gsw*), *la19-20* (*Edb*), *la19-e20* (*St Andrews*); see also GENERAL 2. (2) *also* **Ordinary Degree** an academic degree gained by a number of passes in *ordinary* courses, according to varying regulations *la19-*, (*Abd Gsw*), *la19-20* (*Edb*), *20-* (*Dundee, St Andrews*). **4** *only* **Ordinary** *or* (*chf*) **O**, *secondary education* (1) at a less advanced level, of a state examination, the course leading to it or the certificate awarded to successful candidates *la20-*. (2) *as a noun, chf* **O** (**Grade**) one of these examinations, courses or certificates *la20-* [the *O*

Grade Certificate replaced the Lower Leaving Certificate 1962; see Lower (LAICH), (Higher) Leaving Certificate (CERTIFICATE), and cf Higher (HEICH) and Standard Grade (STANDART)]. **5** regular, frequent in attendance; common, habitual la16-17.

adv ordinarily, usually, in the usual way; somewhat, but not excessively la16-e20.

n **1** = ordinary 15-. **2** *chf* **a person's ordinar &c** the usual state of things; what is customary or habitual to a person etc 17-, *now local Sh-Per.* **3** one's regular allowance of (*chf*) food and drink, or pay; a fixed portion or permitted serving; a usual share or amount of anything 16-19. **4** (1) (one of) a series of sermons given by a MINISTER on one text la17-20, *only Sc.* (2) **ordinary** (**reading**) a regular reading from the Bible as a religious observance within a household la17, *only Sc.* **5** = Lord Ordinary (LORD) la16-19, *only Sc.* **6** = judge ordinary (see adj 2) 15-17, *only Sc.* **7** (1) an officer or other person who had a regular or permanent appointment or engagement la16-17. (2) *specif* a (permanently engaged) gunner la16-e17, *only Sc.*

~is lettres letters from an ecclesiastical ordinary, *eg* a bishop la15-e16. **ordinar letters, letters ~** a decree from an ordinary court, including an ecclesiastical court la15-16; cf *letters conform* (LETTER). **~ pure** those officially registered as parish poor, who received aid from parish funds la16-17, *only Sc.* **aff** (**o**) *or* **past** (**the**) **~** unusual(ly), out of the ordinary, extraordinar(il)y 19-; cf *by-ordinar* (BY). **collatioun ~** regular induction to a benefice la15-16. **for ~** normally, usually, as a rule 17-. **nae ~** *following the word governed* unusual(ly), extraordinar(il)y, in no ordinary manner la19-, *local Sh-Ags.* **nor ~** 20-, **than ~** la18- than usual.

ordinar *see* ORDEEN
ordinary *see* ORDINAR
ordine *see* ORDEEN
ordines, ordnance *see* ORDINANCE
ordnar *see* ORDINAR
ordoned *see* ORDEEN
ordonnance *see* ORDINANCE
ordour *see* ORDER
oreeginal *see* ORIGINAL
orenge *see* ORANGE
orenger *see* ORANGER
orenʒe &c [*o'rinʒɪ] *n, adj* = orange 16, *only Sc.* [Du *oranje*]
organ &c; orgain &c 16 *n* = organ la15-.
~ loft an organ-gallery, *esp* in a church 16-.
orgement &c, orge-moundé la16 [*?'ordʒmənt, 'ordʒ'mundɪ] *n* barley with its outer husk removed; boiled barley; barley soup or porridge la16-e18. [only Sc; F *orge mondé*]
original &c; oreeginal &c la19-, *now Abd adj* **1** = original 15-. **2** *of histories etc* describing beginnings or early times e15, *only Sc.*

n **1** = original 15-. **2** origin, birth, descent 15-, *now Abd.* **3** birthplace 17-, *now Abd.*

~ justice innate sense of justice la15, *only Sc.* **O~ Seceder** a member of the church formed in 1842 by the reuniting of the *Burgher* (BURGH) and ANTIBURGHER elements in the *Auld Licht* (LICHT¹) church, now merged with the *Church of Scotland* (CHURCH) 19-20.

orilyeit [*?'orɪljɪt] *n* an ear-covering attached to a lady's head-dress la16. [eModEng *orlett*, F *oreillette* a little ear, a covering for the ear]

oringe *see* ORANGE
oringer *see* ORANGER
orishon &c [?'orɪʃən] *n, contemptuous* a wild person; an odd-looking or insignificant person 19-, *SW.* [obscure]

orisioun &c *n* a prayer la15-16. [only Sc; appar conflation of ORISOUN w ORATIOUN]

orisoun &c, oraisoun &c la15-16; **urison &c** la16 [*'orɪzun, *-ezun, *'ʌr-] *n* **1** = orison la14-16. **2** a formal or set speech; an oration, harangue, oral address; a formal written discourse or address 16-e17. **3** *grammar, only Sc:* (1) a sentence 16-17; (2) **part of ~** part of speech 16.

oritore *see* ORATOUR¹
orkie, orquie &c *n* a Dutch or Flemish coin worth two DOITS 17-e18. [Du *oortken*, dim of *oort* > ORT²]
Orkney la16-, **Orknay** 16; **Orkynnay** la15-e16 the Orkney islands la15-.
~ chair a wooden armchair with a high (often curved) back made of woven straw or bent grass la19-. **~ cheese** cheese made in Orkney after the DUNLOP method (which was introduced into Orkney la18) 20-.

orloge &c 16-e19, **orlage &c** la15-17, **horologe &c** la16-19; **orlege &c** 16-e17, **horlage &c** 16-e17, **horlage &c** 16-17 [*'orlodʒ, *-lədʒ, *'(h)oro-, *'(h)orə-] *n* = horologe, a clock; the dial of a clock or sundial.

Ormond &c one of the Scottish PURSUIVANTS la15-. [only Sc; f the title, *Marquis of Ormonde*, of the second son of James III]

ornament, ournement &c la15-e17 *n* **1** = ornament 15-. **2** *in pl, specif* insignia, regalia la15-17.

orp, orpe; wurp la19-e20, *S vi* fret, grumble, complain in a peevish, nagging way la16-, *now Ags.*
~it fretful, discontented, peevish la15-e20. [see SND]

orphant &c 17-, **orphan &c** *n* = orphan la15-. [eModEng]

orphus &c, offreis; orph(e)is &c, offrez *n* = orphrey, an ornamental band or border on an ecclesiastical vestment etc 16.
orpheist &c, orpheoust &c adorned with an orphrey; bordered **with** (some rich material) la16. [only Sc]

orpie, orpy; wurpie 19-e20, *S n* = orpine, the herbaceous plant la15-e20.

orquie *see* ORKIE

orra *17-;* **ora** *18-e20,* **orray &c** *la16-e19,*
orrow *la18-19* ['orə; *C also* *'orɪ] *adj* **1** (1) *of
persons or things* spare, unoccupied; unemployed
la16-, now *Sh-Per.* (2) *specif of women* unattached
(either in marriage or as a servant) *la16-17, C.*
(3) *specif of one of a pair* without a partner;
unmatched, odd *19-, Sh-Ags.* **2** spare, extra,
odd, superfluous *18-,* now *NE nEC, WC.* **3** (1)
occasional, coming at irregular or infrequent
intervals, appearing here and there *la18-, local
NE-S.* (2) *specif* (a) *of a job* casual, odd,
unskilled *19-;* (b) *of a person or animal* doing casual or unskilled work *la19-.* **4** miscellaneous,
nondescript *19-,* now *NE Ags Per.* **5** strange,
uncommon, abnormal *la19-,* now *EC.* **6** *of persons or things* worthless, shabby, disreputable
19-, NE Ags Per.
n what is left over; an article not in immediate
use; *in pl* odds and ends *la18-,* now local *NE-Arg.*
orral &c a scrap, fragment, remnant; *chf in pl*
bits and pieces, odds and ends; leftovers *19-,
NE Ags Per.* **orraster** an extra hand, casual
labourer; a disreputable person *20-, Bnf Abd.*
~ **beast** *19-, NE,* ~ **horse** *19-* a horse kept for
odd jobs. ~ **billie** *20-, NE,* ~ **laddie,** ~ **lassie** *la19-,* ~ **loon &c** *19-, NE,* ~**man** *19-* **1** a
person who does odd jobs, *esp* on a farm. **2** *only*
~**man** any mechanical contrivance used by a
man working single-handed *20-, NE.* [perh
reduced f OWER + A': see also DOST; *cf* Eng
odd]

orral, orraster, orray, orrow *see* ORRA

orscheat *see* ORCHARD

ort[1] **&c** *n, chf in pl* **1** what is useless and has been
cast aside; leavings, leftovers *la16-,* now *Sh Fif
Uls.* **2** food for horses etc *19.*
vt **1** reject, throw away; refuse *19-e20.* **2** use
(food) wastefully *19-e20.* [ME *ortus* (*pl*) leavings etc. DOST *ortis*]

ort[2] *n* ? a quarter of a dollar which had been cut
in four; a coin valued at a quarter-dollar *16-17.*
[only Sc; see DOST; *cf* ORKIE]

osare &c *n* = osier, a species of willow *la15-16,
only Sc.*

osel &c; oz(z)el &c *la19-* ['ozl; *Sh* 'osl] *n* one of
the short cords by which a herring-net is
attached to the head-rope *la18-, local Sh-Arg.*
[wrong division of *a nossel,* ME *nostylle,* OE
nos(t)le a band > NOOZLE]

osill &c [*'ozl] *n* = ouzel, blackbird, merle; *perh
also* the ring-ouzel *la15-16, only Sc.*

oslar *see* HOSTLAR

oslin &c *n* a variety of early apple *19, Kcdn Ags.*
[? F place-name]

osmond &c; oismont &c *la16-e17* [*'oz-
mund, *-mənd, *-mənt, &c] *n* = osmund, a
superior quality of imported iron *15-e17.*

Osnaburg &c, ozenbrigs [*'oznəbʌrg,
*'ozən-, *-bʌrʌ, &c] *n, orig* a kind of coarse

linen; *latterly* a strong coarse cotton *la16-,* now
hist. [*Osnabrück* the town in NW Germany,
where it was orig made]

ospital *19-,* **ospittall &c** *la15-16 n* =
hospital.

ost *see* HOST[1], HOST[2]

ostad *n* a kind of cloth *e16, Abd.* [only Sc; OF
ostade serge, worsted; MedL *ostadum* kind of
cloth]

ostage-fedder &c *n* = ostrich-feather *16,* only
Sc.

ostend *vt* **1** = ostend, show, exhibit *la15-16.* **2**
law exhibit or present (a document) for scrutiny
la15-16, only Sc.

ostensioun &c *n* **1** = ostension, manifestation
la15-16. **2** *specif, law* presentation (of a document etc) for scrutiny *la15-e16, only Sc.* **3** the
action of presenting (? by holding up) one's
hand in taking of an oath etc *16, only Sc.*

ostentive [*o'stɛntɪv] *adj* ostentatious *17-e18.*
[eModEng (once); L *ostent-,* ptp stem of *ostendere*
+ suffix -*ive*]

oster *see* OYSTER
ostillar *see* HOSTLAR
ostillary *see* HOSTILARY
osting *see* HOSTING
ostlare *see* HOSTLAR
ostlary *see* HOSTILARY
ostler *see* HOSTLAR
ote *see* AIT
othe *see* OATH
other *see* ITHER
otherane *see* OWTHER
otow *see* OUTWITH

otter &c *n* **1** = otter *la15-,* in place-names *la13-.* **2**
the barb of a fishing-hook or LEISTER *la19-,* now
S, only Sc. **3** a piece of fishing-tackle used by
poachers of salmon or trout *la19-.*
~ **skin** *15-.*

ou; ow [u, ʌu] *interj* expressing surprise or vexation = oh! *la18-.*
~ **ay &c** oh yes, yes, indeed, that's so; *sometimes*
expressing impatience or dissatisfaction *19-.* ~
yea really?, is that so? *19-, NE.* [ME *owe &c*]

ou *see* OO[3]

ouch [ux] *interj* a sound like a gasp or grunt used
exclam of exertion, pain, or disgust *la19-.* [*cf*
OCH, ACH]

oucht *see* OCHT[1]
ouder *see* OO[1]
ouer *see* OUR, OWER

ouf &c [uf; *S* juf] *n* **1** a puny insignificant creature *19-e20.* **2** an imbecile, a stupid fool *19-,*
now *Bnf.* [obs Eng *ouph* an elf, var of *oaf, auf* an
elf's child, an idiot]

oug *see* UG

ought *see* AUCHT[3], OCHT[2]

ouk &c *la14-20,* latterly *Sh NE,* **week &c** *16-,*
wick *18-,* now *NE;* **houlk &c** *16-e17,* **oik**
16-19, **ok** *la15-16,* **olk &c** *15-e17,* **owik &c**

16-e17, **wouk** &c *la14-18,* **wok** *la15-e16,* **wo(u)lk** *15-e16* [uk; *NE* wɪk; **wuk] n =* week.

~ly *adj (16-),* adv *(la15-).*

~-day 1 = weekday *la16-.* **2** a day of the week other than market-day *la15-17.* **~(i)s penny** *la15-16,* **~ly penny** the weekly contribution to the funds of a craft made by its freemen *la15-e17.* [forms with loss of initial *w-* only Sc; in Sh, Ork perh direct f Norw *uke*]

oule *see* OOL

oull *see* OO¹

oun *see* WOUND

ounce *la15-,* **unce** &c; **ons** &c *16-17* [ʌns] *n, uninflected in pl after numerals etc* = ounce, the unit of weight *15-.*

~land, *also* ~ **of land** = urisland (URE⁵) *17-19, Hebrides Highl SW; cf pennyland* (PENNY), TIRUNG. [translation of ON *eyrisland*]

oup *see* UP

ouptene *see* OBTEEN

our &c, *unstressed* wir *la19-;* **ouer** *la15-16,* **oor** *la19-, unstressed* wer *la19-, now Uls,* **wur** *la19-, stressed* weer *20-, NE Per* [ur; *unstressed* wər, wɪr; *stressed* wir] *possessive pronoun* **1** = our: (1) *in gen, la14-;* (2) *with pl inflexion, la15-16:* 'the said landis of ovrez predecessovris'. **2** used as in royal usage by others, *chf* members of the nobility *la14-e17:* 'We Archibald Erile of Angus..in oure naymn'. **3** with the first name of a member of one's family *20-:* 'it's oor Ann at the door'.

~ **ane** &c my wife; my husband *la19-, now C Uls.* ~ **anes** &c my family *20-, now Uls.* **~-self** &c = ourself *la14-,* **~-selfis** &c *16-e17,* **~-sel(1)(s)** &c *la16-* = ourselves; *now (20-) usu* **~sel** is collective, **~sel(1)s** is individual *eg 'we do everything oursel',* but *'we'll settle it atween oursels'.*

our *see* OOR¹, OWER

our- *see* OVER-, OWER-

ourcum *see* OWERCOME

ourdrive &c, **overdrive** &c *la15-16* [*ʌur-'draɪv] *vti, pt also* **-drafe** &c [*-'drev]. *ptp also* **-drevin** &c [*-'drivən] **1** *vt* come through (hardship etc) more or less successfully; live through, pass through *la14-16, only Sc.* **2** (1) *vt* pass through (any period of time); cause (time) to pass; pass, spend, occupy (time); live out (one's life) *la14-e17.* (2) *vi* allow time to pass or elapse *la14-e16.* (3) *in passive* be brought to an end, be spent; have passed away *la14-e16.* **3** *vt* drive, or move over so as to cover, blow over *la15-e16, only Sc.* [late nME *our-drave (pt)* allowed time to pass; laME *ore-drafe* drove, moved over]

oureyhude, ourga, ourgo *see* OWERGAE

ourhelde, ourhele *see* OVERHELE

ourisman *see* OWERSMAN

ourlard *see* OURLORD

ourloft &c *la15-e16,* **overloft** &c *16-e17* [*ʌurloft] *n* = OURLOP. [only Sc; conflation w *loft* (LAFT)]

ourlop &c *la15-17,* **overlope** &c *la16-17* [*ʌurlop] *n, orig* the platform or raised gangway(s) joining the raised half-decks at the ends of ships; the deck of a ship; one of the decks, where a ship has more than one *la15-e17.* [eMDu *overloop,* f MLowGer, MDu *overlopen* run over; *cf* Eng *orlop*]

ourlord &c *la14-16,* **ourlard** &c *la14-e16,* **overlord** &c *15-* [*ʌurlord, *-lerd] *n* the feudal SUPERIOR of a VASSAL or a fief *la14-.*

ourluke *see* OWERLEUK

ourman *see* OWERSMAN

ournement *see* ORNAMENT

our-se *see* OWERSEA

oursé, oursie *see* OWERSEE

ourstrenkle &c [*ʌur'strɛŋkl &c] *vt* sprinkle, besprinkle *la15.* [only Sc; OWER + *strenkell* (STRINKLE)]

oursyll *see* OVERSILE

ourta &c *la14-16,* **overta** &c *la15-16* [*ʌur'te] *vt, ptp* **-tane** &c **1** = overtake *la14-16.* **2** come at or get at with hostility *la14-16, only Sc.* **3** seize, arrest, catch *la15.* **4** *in passive* be found guilty or be convicted in a court of law (**of** *or* **with** the offence, **for** (= as) an offender) *la14-16.* **5** tackle, deal with; get through, cover *la14-e16.* [*cf* eModEng *oretane,* nME *over-tane* ptp and OWERTAK]

ourthourt *see* OURTHWORT

ourthrow *see* OWERTHRAW

ourthwort *la14-e16,* **overthort** &c *15-16;* **ourthourt** &c *15-e16,* **overthuart** *16-17* [*ʌur'θ(w)ort] *adv* = overthwart, across, from side to side *la14-16.*

prep **1** = overthwart, from side to side of, so as to cross, across *la15-16.* **2** *only* **over-** all over, throughout *15-16, only Sc.* **3** *only* **our-** to and fro in, through *e16.*

owerter &c [*?'ʌurtər] crossways *e19, SW.*

ourtirve &c *la14-16,* **overtirve** &c *16;* **ourtirf** &c *e15* [*ʌur'tɪrv] *vt* overturn; overthrow. [ME *over-terve, over + tirve* &c turn over or upside down]

ourtre *see* OWERTREE

ourtummyll &c; **overtumble** *16-17* [*ʌur'tʌml] *vti* **1** *vi* tumble over, capsize, fall down *la14-e17, only Sc.* **2** *vt* cause to tumble over, upset *16-17.*

ourwelt [*ʌur'wɛlt] *vt* turn over, throw over or down *e16.* [OWER + *welt* (WALT²); *cf* ME *overwalt* and Mod Yorkshire dial *owerwelt* &c]

ourȝeid *see* OWERGAE

our-ȝeir *see* OWERYEAR

ous *see* US

oussen *see* OX

out &c; **oot** *19-* [ut] *adv* **1** = out *la14-.* **2** *of a cup etc, or its contents* emptied, drained, consumed *la15-:* 'is your cup out?'; *cf cap out* (CAP¹). **3** *of a gathering of people, church congregation, school etc* dismissed and out of the building, dispersed; *of the meeting itself* over, concluded *la16-:* 'the school was out'. **4** *following an adj or adv* very *la14-e15:* 'fer *out'*. **5** (1) *following a noun phr stating a period of time* to the end, fully *15-16*: '*ane moneth out'*. (2) *with numeral, esp of one's age* fully, quite *la16-*, now NE: '*I'm fifty oot.'* **6** *referring to* (1) *the Jacobite Risings of 1715 or 1745*: in arms against the Hanoverian Government *la18-*, now *hist*; (2) *the* DISRUPTION *of 1843*: having left the established Church for the *Free Church* (FREE) *la19-*, now *hist*. **7** *omitting verb of motion, eg* **need** ~ need etc to go out *la19-*; *see also* WANT *v* 6. **8** *golf* over the first nine holes of an 18-hole course *la19-*.

prep **1** out of, from *la14-*, now *C, S*. **2** beyond, outside, not in *la15-19*. **3** *also adv* along, up (a road) in an outward direction away from the speaker *16-*: '*out the way homeward'*.

vti **1** = out. **2** *vt, chf in ptp* (*esp of a clergyman from his parish, 17*) ejected, turned out *15-20*. **3** exhibit; utter, express, reveal *la16-e19*. **4** put up for sale; release for sale; sell *la16-e17*. **5** issue, circulate (counterfeit money) *la16-17, only Sc*.

n, see phrases below.

adj **1** = out, outlying etc *la15-*. **2** belonging to, coming from or happening in some other place *la15-16*. **3** (working) out of doors or in the fields, *specif and chf of farmworkers* (*chf female*), *eg* ~-**servant** *la16-18*, ~**work(er)** *la18-*, ~-**girl** *la19-*. **4** *attrib, of a fire* extinguished, burned out *19-*: '*I came home til an oot fire and a caul hoose'*.

interj, chf in combs attracting attention and urgency, expressing indignation etc, *eg* ~ **harrow** *la15-16*, ~ ~ *15-*.

ooten out of *la19-*. ~**ing &c 1** an expedition, excursion, trip *la14-*. **2** = outing, expulsion *17*. **in** ~**ing(is)** in going, *or* being abroad or away from home; while abroad etc *la16-e17*.

~ **about** *only Sc, adv* out of doors, out in the garden or fields, at some distance from one's home, in an isolated spot *la18-*. *adj* outdoor *19-*, *NE*. *n* a piece of business transacted away from home; an outing *19-*, *NE*. ~ **amang**, ~ **amo(n)** out of, away from, out from, among *19-*, *now local Sh-Ork, only Sc*. ~ **at** out of, from (a door, window etc) *la14-*, *now local Sh-Fif, only Sc*. ~ **on, ooten** out of, outside *20-*, *now Abd Kcb, only Sc*. ~ **o** *prep* out of, from out of, outside, beyond *19-*. **be** ~ **o't 1** be in an exalted state of mind *20-*, *NE*. **2** be mistaken, in error *20-*. ~ **o anesel** beside oneself (with grief, anxiety etc) *18-*, *now Ork SW Slk*. ~ **o ither** *lit and fig* disjointed, disintegrated, in(to) pieces, apart *la19-*. ~ **o one's head** off one's head, out of one's mind *la19-*, *now local*. ~ **of** *prep* **1** = out of *la14-*. **2** indicating privation or separation *la14-*: '*to put the King out of his estait'*. **3** indicating the source from which payment is provided, from *la16-*: '*the minister has payit him out off the bishopric three hundred merks off money'*. ~ **ower**, ~ **our**, ~ **over** [~ 'ʌur] *prep* **1** *of motion* outwards and over; over the top of; over to the other side of; across; out of *la14-*. **2** *of position* (1) above, over, on top of *16-*; (2) bent over (a

drink, task etc) *18-*; (3) on the other side of, on either side of *la18-*, *now local*. **3** over, more than, in excess of, beyond *la14-e19*. *adv* **1** across in an outwards direction *la14-16*. **2** at a distance; aside; apart *la18-*, *now Sh-Ags*. **3** out of bed, up *la19-*, *now Sh-Ags*. **4** throughout, all over; completely, to the full *18-e20*. **by and outover** see BY. ~ **ower the door** out of doors *18-*. ~ **ower the head** *or* **lugs** *measurement of depth* over the head or ears *la18-*, *now NE* [*cf* ATOUR *and* INOWER]. ~ **thro(ugh) &c**, ~ **throw &c** *prep, only Sc, also* ~ **t(h)rouch &c** *16* **1** throughout, through, (all) over, right across *la14-*. **2** across (a thing, region etc) to(wards) its opposite side or end *16*: '*owt throu the feld com rynnand'*. **3** right through (something) *la15-17*. *adv* right through, through and through, throughout *la14-e20*.

~ **and in** *adv* **1** = out and in *15-*. **2** *also* **in and** ~ all over, throughout, entirely *la15-16*, *only Sc*. *adj, of neighbours* paying frequent short calls, used to dropping in *la19-*, *nEC, WC*. ~**s and ins** = ins and outs, details (of something) *la18-*. [*cf* IN]

outainsell *e18*, **utensel &c** *la14-e16* [*'øtɛnsɪl, *-sɛl, *-'ut-] *n, in sing as collective* domestic equipment. [OED *utensil*]

outakin, outane *see* OUT-TAK

outawing &c [*'ut'ɑən] *presp, of a debt* that one owes (**to** another) *17, SW*.

outband &c; outbo(u)nd ['ut'band] *n, building* a stretcher, a stone with its long side along a wall face, *specif* a quoin or jamb stone *la18-*. **out and in bond &c** alternate headers and stretchers in the angles of walls, and of window and door jambs *la19-*. [*only Sc;* OUT + BAND[1] *or Eng bond; cf* INBAND]

outbirst *see* OUTBURST

outbo(u)nd *see* OUTBAND

out-braid &c [*'ut'bred] *vti* break into speech, blurt out *16*. [*cf* eModEng = upbraid]

outbreak, outbreke &c [*'ut'brɛk, *-'brak] *vi* ~**ing** an outburst; a breaking out into sin or rebellion; a bout of disorderly conduct *17-e19*.

outbrist *see* OUTBURST

out-burges &c [*'ut'bʌrdʒɛs] *n* a burgess resident outside the BURGH *la15-16, only Sc*.

outburst *la19*, **outbirst** *la16*, **outbrist** *15-16* ['ut'bʌrst, &c] *vti* = outburst, burst out.

outby [*adv* ut'baɪ; *Sh Ork also* 'u(d)bɪ, *'ubdɪ; *adj* 'ut'baɪ; *Sh Ork* 'u(d)bɪ; *prep* 'ut'baɪ, 'utbɪ]] *adv* **1** outwards; out and a little way off, beyond, to or at some distance from a point; away from the shore, out at sea etc *17-*. **2** out of doors, outside, out in the fields *17-*. **3** away from home, not at hand *19-e20*. **4** away from the populous part of a district, in an outlying, *usu* upland part *19-*, *Kcb S*. **5** in or towards the outer part of a room, away from the fire, nearer the door *la18-*, *now Sh Ork*.

adj **1** (1) outlying, out of the way, distant, away from the main or central part *19-*, *now Sh NE*

Uls. (2) *specif of a farm or farmland* (a) away from the steading *19-*, *now Uls*; (b) in the outlying fields, in an upland or more pastoral area *19-*, *SW*, *S*. **2** out of doors, outside, in the fields, rural, *freq* ~ **worker** field labourer *la19-*, *now Loth*.

prep on the outskirts *or* in the neighbourhood of *20-*, *NE Uls*. [late nME (once); *cf* INBY]

outca &c *n* a small enclosed pasturage for cattle *19-e20*, *SW*. [OUT + CA¹ *v*]

outcast &c ['ut'kast] *n* a quarrel *17-*, *now Sh-Ags SW*. [only Sc]

outcome &c, outcum ['ut'kʌm] *n* **1** a coming out, appearance; escape *la14-*. **2** *specif* the drawing out of the year, the time when the days begin to lengthen *la17-e20*, *only Sc*. **3** the result, effect, end-product *la18-*. **4** produce, product; the difference in cost between raw material and manufactured article; profit *19-*, *now Sh Kcb*, *only Sc*.

outcum &c *la16*, **outcummit** *la16-17* [*'ut'kʌm(ɪt)] *adj*, *of a sheep* ? that is in lamb [only Sc; see DOST]. **~ing &c 1** = outcoming, coming forth *la15-17*. **2** profit, gain; worthwhile result *19*.

out-dichtings &c ['ut'dɪxtɪnz] *n pl* refuse of threshed grain, the sweepings from the mill *16-e20*, *only Sc*.

outding [ut'dɪŋ] *vt* beat, exceed, surpass *19-*, *now NE*.

outdraucht &c [*'ut'drɑxt] *n* an extract, abstract or partial copy (of a record or account) *16*. [laME (once) *outdrauʒt*; appar after L *extractum*]

outdwelland &c [*'ut'dwɛlan(d)] *adj* living outside the BURGH *15-16*, *only Sc*.

outdwellar [*'ut'dwɛlər] *n* one who lives outside the BURGH; a stranger, outsider *15-16*.

outen ['utən] *prep*, *freq literary* without, lacking *20-*. [reduced f *withouten* (WITHOUT), perh conflated w *out on* (OUT)]

outer¹ &c ['utər] *adj* **1** = outer *16-*. **2** = utter *16-19*.

~lin(g) the weakling of a brood; *fig* the black sheep of a family, a reprobate *la19-e20*, *only Sc*. **~ly** *of wind* blowing offshore *la19-*, *now Sh*.

O~ House *law* that part of the *Court of Session* (SESSION) in which cases of first instance are heard *la17-*. **O~ Isles** the Outer Hebrides *20-*; *cf* OUT ILE 1. [*cf* UTTER]

outer² &c; utter &c [*'utər, *'ʌtər] *vi*, *of a horse or its rider, in combat* ? swerve aside, refuse the encounter *16*. [only Sc; unknown; perh *cf* OF *ou(l)trer* go or pass beyond a place]

outeral *see* OUTREL

outfa &c, outfall ['ut'fa] *n* a quarrel *17-*, *now Sh*. [only Sc; *cf* Eng *fall out* (*v*)]

outfall &c [*'ut'fal, *-'fɑ] *n* a sally, sortie *17*. [only Sc; Du *uitval*, Ger *ausfall*]

outfall *see* OUTFA

outfang [*'ut'faŋ] *n*, *also attrib*, *chf coupled with*

INFANG ? theft committed outside the jurisdiction, *but perh merely formulaic, la16-*, *now hist*. [short for next]

outfangtheiff &c *16-17*, **outfangand-thefe &c** *la14-15* [*'ut'faŋ(ən)'θif] *n*, *law* a franchise granted to the lord of a private jurisdiction, *presum orig* the right to pursue a thief outside one's own jurisdiction and to bring him back for trial; *also* the right to try a thief coming from outside one's jurisdiction. [eME *utefangthef*, *utfangene þeof*; *cf* INFANGTHIEF]

out-farm &c ['ut'fɛrm, &c] *n* an outlying farm, *chf* one worked by a manager or subtenant *la18-*, *now local NE-Lnk*, *only Sc*.

outfield &c, outfeild ['ut'fil(d), &c] *n* **1** *in the early agric system before enclosures and crop-rotation* the more outlying and less fertile parts of a farm *16-*, *now hist*. **2** a poorer outlying patch of ground (previously uncultivated) *20-*, *only Sh*. **3** *attrib* outlying, remote; out of doors *la17-19*. [see also INFIELD]

outgae &c ['ut'ge] *vi* **outgane &c** ['ut'gen] *of a period of time, or (chf) a person's or animal's age* past, fully *la14-*, *now Sh*: '*a youth, no twenty-twae outgaen*'. **outga(u)n &c** *19-*, **outgoing &c** *la16-* ['ut'gan, &c] *n* = outgoing *la16-*. *adj* **1** *of a tenant* = outgoing, removing, leaving *20-*. **2** *specif of the tide* ebbing *20-*, *Sh Ags SW*.

outgang &c ['ut'gaŋ; 'utgɪŋ] *n* **1** the exportation of goods; the duty on this *la15-16*. **2** a way out, a means of getting out *16-*, *now local Sh-EC*. **3** an outgoing, departure, *eg* the end of a season etc, one's removal (from a tenancy) *la19-e20*. **4** an open pasture for cattle *19-*, *chf SW*. **5** expense, outlay *la19-*, *local Sh-EC*.

vi = outgo, go out, outstrip *la17-*. **~ing** = outgoing, going out *16-*.

outgate &c; outget *la16-17* ['utget] *n* **1** a way out, exit; *lit and fig* an outlet *16-*, *now Sh*. **2** *fig* (*freq theol e18*) a way out of *esp* a moral or spiritual problem; a solution *la15-19*. **3** an outcome of a situation or events *la16-17*, *only Sc*. **4** a market, sale, means of disposal of merchandise *la19-*, *now Sh*.

outgaun *see* OUTGAE

outget *see* OUTGATE

outgif &c [*'ut'gɪv] *vt* give out, issue, pay out *la15-17*, *only Sc*.

outgiving &c *n* **1** *esp law* giving out, delivering, issuing *la16-e18*. **2** *in pl* disbursements *la17-e19*, *only Sc*. [SND *outgie*]

outgoing *see* OUTGAE

outh &c [*?uθ] *prep* above in position or authority, over; above the top of; on top of *la14-e15*. *adv* above; *also* **at** ~ above in authority *la14-15*. [only Sc; obscure, perh OE *uf-* above + *-with*]

outhald &c [*'ut'hald, &c] *vt* = outhold, hold out, retain *la15-e17*.

~ing holding or keeping out or back; keeping out (by force) *la15-e17*.

outhand ['ut'han(d)] *adv, curling* (CURL) with the stone directed outwards from the hand, so as to give it a bias from right to left *20-*.

outhave [*'ut'hev] *v, only in derivs* carry or convey out or away; export *la15-16, only Sc.*

outheidie [*ut'hidɪ] *adj* headstrong, rash *la19-20, Kcdn Ags.* [cf *heidie* (HEID)]

outhorn &c [*'ut'horn] *n* a horn blown by officers of the crown to give the alarm, *eg* to summon the lieges in pursuit of a fugitive *15-16.* [ME]

outhound; outhund [*'ut'hund, *-'hʌnd] *vt* **1** incite (to mischief or crime) *la17-18.* **2** set a dog to attack or chase (animals or persons); raid (cattle) with a dog *18.*
~er instigator *la16-18.* [only Sc]

out ile &c [*'ut 'əil] *n, chf in pl* islands lying away from the mainland, *specif* **1** the Hebrides *la14-e17;* **2** Shetland and Orkney, *latterly esp* applied by the islanders themselves to the more distant of the islands *la16-e20.* [cf *Outer Isles* (OUTER)]

outins &c ['utɪnz] *adv (adj)* outside, out of doors *19-e20, Lnk Rox.*

outintoun &c [*'utən'tun] *adj* coming from outside the boundaries of a town; *freq of dues* payable by those from outside the SUCKEN[1] of a mill *la16-18.*
~is &c [*'utən'tunz] *adj* coming from outside the town, *also orig* the barony or estate; pertaining to persons or things from outside the town *la16-18.*
~isman a man from outside the town *la16-17, Rothesay Gsw.* **~is multure** *etc* = *outsucken multure* (OUTSUCKEN) *17-18.* [only Sc; *cf* OUT-TOUN]

outjet *n* a projection, jutting-out part of a building *la17-e19.*
~ting jutting out *la17-e18.* [OUT + eModEng (once) *jet* a projection; *cf* eModEng (once) *outjetty*]

outland &c; outlin &c *18-e20,* **outlan** *19-,* **utland &c** *la16-17* ['utlan(d), -lən] *n* **1** land held in addition to but lying outside the principal holding or estate *16-e17.* **2** outlying land, rough ground on the edge of arable marginal land *18-e20; cf* OUTFIELD. **3** an outsider, stranger, outcast *18-, now local Sh-Fif.*
adj foreign; outlying, remote, distant; from or living outside the bounds of a town or district; coming from a remote place; alien, strange; outcast *la15-e20.*
~er = *n* 2, *17-20.* **~is &c** [*'utlan(d)z, *-lənz] coming from outside, not belonging to or residing in the BURGH *la15-e17, only Sc.* **~isch &c 1** = outlandish, foreign *la16-17.* **2** from or of a place outside or distant from the BURGH *17.* [*cf* Eng]

outlandimer &c [*?'ut'lan(d)ɪmər] *n* a person appointed to perambulate and survey land boundaries, ? round or outside the BURGH limits *la16, Gsw.* [only Sc; *cf* LANIMER]

outlat &c ['utlət] *n* = outlet *20-.*

~ting, outletting 1 letting out *la16-.* **2** *specif, only* **-latting:** *knitting* the increase in the stitches in the heel of a stocking *la19-, Sh Abd.*

outlaw; utlaw &c *la14-17* ['ut'lɑ; *also* *'ʌt-] *n* (*la14-*), *v* (*15-*) = outlaw.

outlay ['ut'le] *n* expenditure, the laying out of money *la18-.*
v **1** *only in verbal noun* (*la17*) *and ptp, adj* (*e19*) expend, lay out money. **2** *of a hen* lay away from the regular nest *19-, only Sc.*

outleeve &c *e20,* **outleve &c** *la16-e17* ['ut'liv] *vi* = outlive.

outler &c ['utlər] *n* = OUTLIER 1, *la18-, now verse.* [perh reduced f *outlayer,* f *lay* = lie]

outletting *see* OUTLAT

outleve *see* OUTLEEVE

outlie &c ['ut'lai] *n* **1** an outlying piece of ground *la20-, NE.* **2** money put out on loan or on mortgage *19-e20.*
outlying &c *n* staying away, absence (from church services etc) *e17.* *adj, of animals* not housed in winter *la19-, chf SW.* [*cf* OUTLER, OUTLIER]

outlie *see* OUTLY

outlier &c, outlyer ['ut'laiər] *n* **1** a farm animal which remains outside during the winter *18-, now local.* **2** a person from a different or remote district, or from outside the BURGH *18-, now Sh, only Sc.* **3** *in pl* stones found loose above ground, not quarried *la18-19, only Sc.* **4** an absentee from church *e17, only Sc.*

outlin *see* OUTLAND

outliveray [*'ut'lɪvərɪ] *n, chf in pl* **-liverais &c** bounty given to servants *la16, only Sc.*

outlordschip [*'ut'lordʃɪp] *n* patronage or support from a lord or magnate from outside the BURGH *la15-16, only Sc.*

outly, outlie ['utlɪ] *adv* fully, completely *17-19.* [ME *outliche*]

outlyer *see* OUTLIER

outlying *see* OUTLIE

outmaist *see* OUTMOST

outman &c [*'ut'man] *n* a man coming from outside the community or BURGH; an outsider *la15-16, local C.* [northern eModEng (once) *la16*]

outmarchis &c [*'ut'martʃɪz] *n pl* the outer borders of a country *la15-e16, only Sc.*

outmest *see* OUTMOST

outmiln &c; outmyll &c [*'ut'mɪl(n)] *n* a mill outside the town; a mill other than those to which the townspeople were *astricted* (ASTRICT) *16-17, Edb.*

outmost &c, outmest &c *la16-e17,* **utmaist &c** *la14-e19,* **outmaist** *16-e20* ['utməst, *'ʌt-] *adj* **1** = outmost, outermost, most remote *16-e20.* **2** utmost, most extreme, maximum, last *la16-18.*
n (do one's) utmost *16-19.* [OED *utmost*]

outmyll *see* OUTMILN

outouth, outow *see* OUTWITH

outpait *see* OUTPAY

out-parochine; outparish [*'ut'parotʃən, &c] n that part of a BURGH parish lying outside the BURGH itself; the rural part of a BURGH parish la16-e17. [cf Eng outparish]

outpassage [*'ut'pasɪdʒ] n a means of exit or escape e16. [ME (once)]

outpassing &c [*'ut'pasɪŋ] n 1 (1) going out, departure 16-e17. (2) specif of exported goods departure; exportation la15-16. 2 passing out of, or retirement from office 16, Dundee Perth. 3 expiry la15-e17. [ME]

outpat see OUTPUT

outpay vt, only pt, ptp -pa(y)it paid in full, settled 16, Slk Rox.

outpenny &c [*'ut'pɛnɪ] n a penny paid to the BAILIE by an outgoing property-owner in the BURGH in token of resignation of the property la15-e16. [cf OUT-TOLL and INTOLL]

outpit see OUTPUT

outpour &c [*'ut'pur] n a heavy fall of rain etc, a downpour la19-20, NE Ork.

output &c; outpit 20 ['ut'pɪt, 'utpɪt, -put, &c] vt, pt also -pat &c la16-e17 1 put or send out; emit, eject; discharge 16-e20. 2 specif issue (false coinage) la16-e18.

~**tar &c** 1 a person who puts out others' property (as in ~ting 2 (2)) 16-e17. 2 a person who issues or circulates eg coinage unlawfully la16-e17, only Sc. 3 a person responsible for finding and equipping men for military service 17, only Sc. ~**ting &c** 1 expulsion, ejection; banishment la16-e17. 2 (1) ? moving or lifting out (something) 16-e17. (2) orig and chf the conveying of stolen goods out of the district etc; also perh the exposure of another's property to thieves with whom one is in league la15-e17, only Sc. 3 issuing (of false coin) la16-e17, only Sc. 4 the finding and equipping of men for military service 17-e18.

outquit &c, outquite &c [*'ut'kwɪt, *-'kwəit] vt, ptp also **outqueit &c** la16-e17 [*'ut'kwɪt, &c] law redeem, free (land, HERITAGE or annual rent from property) from encumbrance by payment of a debt 15-17.

outquitting &c redemption from attachment or pawn: 1 of HERITAGE etc la15-e18; 2 of MOVEABLES 16-e18. [only Sc]

outrad see OUTRED

outrage &c [*'ut'redʒ, *'utredʒ] n 1 = outrage la14-. 2 excessive boldness; foolhardiness, rashness; presumption la14-15. 3 a sense of injury; anger, rage la15-16, only Sc.

outraik &c ['utrek] n 1 an extensive grazing area 19-e20, Rox. 2 fig scope, outlet, opportunity; behaviour 19, S. [OUT + RAIK]

outraik see OUTREIK

outreche n, vt = OUTREIK 17, only Sc.

outred &c; outrad la15-e17, **outreid &c** la15-17, **outrid** la16-17, **outterd** la16 [*'ut'red, *-'rid, *-'rɪd, *'ut'rɛd, &c] vt, pt chf **outred** 1 (1) settle by payment; pay (a sum

due), meet or discharge (a debt), pay for (goods or services); redeem (lands etc from pledge etc) by due payment la15-17. (2) pay (what is due) **to** (another) la15-e18. 2 settle one's obligations to (another) by payment of the sum due; pay (another) what he is due la15-16. 3 discharge, carry through (a piece of business) by payment etc 16-17. 4 finish off, complete (a piece of work or an artefact) 16-e18. 5 fit out, equip (1) (a ship) la16-17; (a person or troops) for an expedition etc la16-e17; cf OUTREIK.

n 1 the settlement of a debt or liability; final payment of a creditor; clearing up, settling an affair by payment la15-17. 2 completion (of a piece of work) la16-17. 3 (1) fitting out (a ship) with equipment and provisions for a voyage la15-e17. (2) fitting out (a person) for an expedition la16. (3) the equipment or outfit itself la16-e17. [only Sc; OUT + REDD[1]]

outreik &c, outreke; outraik 17, **outrike &c** la16-17, **utrique &c** la17 [*'ut'rik, *-'rɪk, *'ut'rik, &c] vti 1 vt fit out, equip; supply with necessaries la16-17. 2 specif make (a ship etc) ready for a voyage or service 17-e18. 3 provide and equip etc (esp men for military or naval service) 17.

n 1 (1) equipping a ship for a voyage 17-e18. (2) the act of outfitting a ship; an outfit (of tackle and stores) la16-17. 2 also attrib (1) finding and equipping troops or their mounts; fitting out troops etc for military service 17-e18. (2) a levy of troops; a tax or contribution raised for the finding or equipping of troops 17. 3 fitting out a private person for an expedition or other special occasion 17-19.

~**er &c** a person who finds and equips a man for military service 17; cf outputtar (OUTPUT). [only Sc; OUT + REIK; cf OUTRECHE, OUTRIG]

outrel &c; outeral &c ['ut(ə)rəl] n a person from a different country, district or family; an alien, stranger, incomer la19-, now local, Sh-Lnk. [only Sc]

out-relation &c ['ut rə'leʃn] n a distant relative la19-, now Abd, only Sc.

outricht &c ['utrɪxt] adv, adj = outright la19-.

outrid see OUTRED

outrig &c [ut'rɪg, 'ut'rɪg] n 1 = OUTREIK n 1 and 2, 17. 2 rig-out, dress; outward appearance, get-up la19-, now Sh Ags.

vt fit out, equip; get ready, prepare 18-e20.

~**(g)ing** supplying, fitting out la16-e18. [only Sc; cf Eng rig out]

outrike see OUTREIK

outrin see OUTRUN

outring ['ut'rɪŋ] n, curling (CURL) the side of the curling stone away from the TEE[1]; a method of striking one curling stone with another on its outer edge so as to drive it towards the TEE[1], an OUTWICK 19-; cf INRING.

outriving &c [*'ut'raɪvɪŋ] *n* unauthorized cultivating (of land not one's own) and so adding to one's own land; breaking into another's land thus *la15-17, only Sc.*

outroom &c ['ut'rum] *n* an outer room, *latterly specif* of a room attached to a cottage and under the same roof, but entered from the outside by a separate door *la17-20, N.*

outrun &c, out-rin [*n* 'ut'rʌn, 'utrʌn; *v* ut'rʌn, ut'rɪn] *n* **1** an area of outlying grazing land on an arable farm *la19-, Sh-N, WC, SW.* **2** the way in which a dog runs out and round sheep in order to gather them for penning *20-, Ork SW, S.*
vti, ptp also **outrunnin &c** *la15-16* **1** run out (of), flow (from) *16.* **2** *vi, of time, a due date, contract etc* expire, run out *la15-17, only Sc.*
~ning &c 1 the expiry of a set period of time etc *la15-17, only Sc.* **2** *specif* the running out of an hour-glass *16-e19, only Sc.*

outschot &c [*'ut'ʃot] *adj, chf of animal skins* reject, of inferior quality *la16-e17.* [*cf* MDu *uteschot* (*n*) cullings, refuse, and see also *shot* (*n*) (SHUIT)]

outschot *see* OUTSHOT

outschute &c [*'ut'ʃøt] *vtr, pt* **-shot &c 1** = outshoot *la16-17.* **2** *vr* over-reach oneself, go too far *la16-17, only Sc.*

outseam &c ['ut'sim] *n* ~**ed** *of gloves* sewn on the outside *la17.*
~ awl an awl for sewing shoes from the outside *la19-20, Sh-Per.* [only Sc]

outseit *see* OUTSET²

outset¹ &c [*n, v* 'utsɛt; *v* also 'ut'sɛt] *n* **1** a setting or sending out, *eg* the issue of a book *17-e19.* **2** a setting out to advantage, display, arrangement; ornament, embellishment *17-, now local, only Sc.*
vt set forth, display, maintain with proper splendour *16, only Sc.* [*cf* OUTSETTING]

outset² &c; outseit &c *16-, latterly only place-names* ['utsɛt; *-sit, *-set] *n* **1** a smaller piece of land outlying or detached from, but dependent on, a main estate or holding *16-17.* **2** a patch of reclaimed and newly-cultivated (or *orig* newly-inhabited) land, *freq* taken in from moorland etc *16-, now Sh.* **3** = ONSET² *16-e17.* [only Sc; uncertain]

outsetter *n* some implement used in gunnery *e17, only Sc.*

outsetting &c ['ut'sɛtɪn] *n* **1** making publicly known, publication, proclamation *la16-e17, only Sc.* **2** the putting on or producing (of a show etc), *chf* impressively or with splendour *la16, only Sc.* **3** support, maintenance with money, provisions, equipment or troops; equipping *la16, only Sc.* **4** the letting out (of land) on lease or FEU *17, only Sc.* **5** departure *la17-, now Sh Abd.*

outshot &c *la17-,* **outschot &c** *la16-e17*

['utʃot] *n* a projecting part of a wall or building; an extension built onto the side of a building *la16-, now local C-Uls.*
adj projecting, protruding, bulging *19-, now EC, S; cf* SHUIT *v* 10.

outshot *see* OUTSCHUTE

outsight *17-e19,* **outsicht &c** *la16-e17* [*'utsɪxt] *n, chf coupled with* INSIGHT, *and usu* ~ **plenishing** goods kept or used out of doors, *eg* animals, implements. [form after INSIGHT]

out-stair ['ut'ster] *n* an outer stair on a house, giving separate access to an upper flat, a FORESTAIR *la18-20.*

outstander *n* a person who opposed the National Covenant or its adherents *la17, only Sc.*

outstanding *adj, of debts etc* that remain to be collected or paid; unpaid *17-.* [appar earlier in Sc]

outsted; outsteid &c [*'ut'stid, &c] *n* a settlement or farm at or near the edge of an estate *la16-e18, chf SE.* [OUT + STEID¹]

outsteik &c ['utstik] *n, in pl, or* ~ **shune** shoes with the soles stitched from the outside *18-20, S.* [OUT + STEEK²]

outstrapalous &c [*ut'strapələʌs] *adj, joc* = obstreperous *19-.*

outstreek ['utstrik] *v* ~**it &c** outstretched *19-, now Sh Abd Kcb.* [see STREEK¹]

outstrik, outstrike [*'ut'stroik, -'strɪk] *vt* ~**ing &c** (**of**) striking out, making an opening (for a door etc) *la14-e18.* **outstriking** *n* an eruption of the skin, a rash *la17-, now Ags.*

outsucken &c, outsuckin &c *la16-e17* [*'ut'sʌkən] *n, law, freq* ~ **multure** MULTURE payable on corn brought in from outside the SUCKEN¹ of a mill *la16-19.*
outsuckiner &c *a* person from outside a SUCKEN¹ *la17-18.* [*cf* INSUCKEN]

out-tak &c ['ut'tak] *vt* exclude, except, reserve; extract, remove *15-16.*
~ing &c *n* a taking out, removal *15-, now Ork.*
prep, also **out-takand &c** *15* [*'ut'tak(and), *u'tak(and)] excepting; except, leaving aside *15-16.* **out-takin &c, outakin** [*u'takən] *la14 prep* = *out-tane* (*prep*) *la14-e16, e19.* **out-tane &c, outane &c** *la14-15* [*'u'takən, *'ut'ten, *u'ten] *ptp, used absol and at the end of its clause* **1** *chf in bonds of* MANRENT excluded, excepted *15-e16, only Sc:* 'saiffand the Kingis grace allegiance alanerlye owttane'. **2** disclaimed, repudiated *la14-e16:* 'all maner of fraude, gyle, exceptioun and cauillatioun owtane'. *prep* except, except for, with the exception of *la14-e16. conj* except (**that**) *la14-15.*

outterd *see* OUTRED

out-thraw &c [*'ut'θra] *vi, pt* **-threw** come out with a twisting or spinning motion; press out in a confused mass; billow out *la15-e16, only Sc.*

out-toll &c [*'ut'tol] *n* = OUTPENNY *la13-e18, chf Abd.* [*cf* INTOLL]

out-toun &c ['ut'tun] *n* **1** an outlying field on a

farm, the OUTFIELD *17-e19*, *chf* NE. **2** ? an outlying estate, detached from the main property
la17, SW.
adj = OUTINTOUN *la16-e19.*
out-tounis &c [*'ut'tunz] *adj* = *outintounis*
(OUTINTOUN) *la15-e18, Lanark Prestwick.*
~**isman** = *outintounis man* (OUTINTOUN) *16,
SW.* [only Sc; *cf* OUTINTOUN]
out-turn &c ['ut'tʌrn] *n, curling* (CURL) the
playing of the stone with the handle outwards
so that it travels in an inward arc *la19-, now
local C.*
outwach *la15-e16;* **outwatch &c** *la16-e17*
[*'ut'watʃ] *n, chf in pl* an outlying watch or
watchmen; guards etc placed outside the body
of an army, a town etc *la15-e17.*
outwale &c; outwyle &c *la16-, now N nEC*
['ut'wel; *N nEC* -'wəil; *Ork Uls* -'wɑl] *n* **1** an
outcast, an unworthy person *15-16.* **2** *chf in pl*
the remainder, rejects, refuse, leavings *la16-,
now Sh Uls.*
vt select, pick out, choose; reject *la16-19.*
outwilin &c *chf in pl* = *n* 2, *la19-, now Sh-NE.*
[OUT + WALE; *cf* also Norw dial *utval* choice,
selection]
outwan &c ['utwən] *adv* outwards *la19-, now
Fif.*
outward &c *la16-,* **outwart &c** *la14-e17;* **outwert &c** *la15-16* ['utwərd, -wərt] *adj* **1** = outward *la14-.* **2** cold in manner, aloof, reserved
19-, Rox.
adv = outward *la14-.*
outware; utware &c, utwarde *la12*
[*'ut'wer, *-'ward] *n, appar* services due by
tenants on land other than the lord's demesne
lands *la12-e13.* [OE *ūtwaru; cf* INWARD]
outwart *see* OUTWARD
outwatch *see* OUTWACH
outwert *see* OUTWARD
outwick &c ['ut'wɪk] *curling* (CURL) *n* a shot
which strikes an already-played stone on the
outside at such an angle as to drive it towards
the TEE[1] *19-.*
vti, also carpet bowls play such a shot, strike (a
stone) in this way *19-.* [OUT + WICK[1]; *cf*
INWICK, OUTRING]
outwile *see* OUTWALE
outwinter ['ut'wɪntər] *vt* keep (cattle) out of
doors throughout the winter *la18-.*
outwith &c *15-,* **outouth &c** *la14-16,* **outow
&c** *la16;* **utwith** *la15-e19,* **utouth &c**
la14-16, **otow &c** *la15* ['ut'wɪθ, *'ʌt-, *u'tuθ,
*u'tu, &c] *prep* outside, out of, beyond; out of
the control of; away from *la14-.*
adv outside; out of doors; outwards *la14-, now
NE.*
adj outer; outermost, outlying *la16-, now Abd.*
[*cf* INWITH]
outwitten [*'ut'wɪtən] *adv* ~(**s**) **o**(**f**) unknown
to, without the knowledge of *la18-e19.* [see
SND]
outwyle *see* OUTWALE

ouverture *see* OVERTURE
oven *see* UNE[1]
over *n, children's rhymes* a numeral, *prob* eight
la19-, local. [see ZEENDI]
over *see* OWER, UVER
over- *see* OWER-
overcum *see* OWERCOME
overdrive *see* OURDRIVE
overeengie *see* AIPPLERINGIE
overflete &c *16,* **ourflete &c** *15-16* [*ʌur'flit]
vti, pt, ptp -**flet** [*-'flɛt] flow over, overflow.
[chf Sc; *cf* ME *pt ouerflet*]
over-fret,   ourfret &c;   ower   fret &c
[*ʌur'frɛt] *ptp* ~ **with** or **of** decorated,
adorned all over with *la15-16.* [laME]
overgilt &c, ourgilt &c [*ʌur'gɪlt] *vt, pt, ptp*
-**gilt, -giltit** gild over; overlay **with** (gold)
la15-e17.
overgive &c *16-e19,* **ourgive &c** *la15-17*
[*ʌur'giv, &c] *vt* give up, renounce, resign, surrender (property etc) *la15-e19.* [chf Sc; ME
ouerʒouun (*ptp*) (once) given over, expended,
eModEng *overgive* give up *16.* SND *owergie*]
overgo *see* OWERGAE
overharle &c, ourharle &c [*ʌur'harl] *vt* **1**
oppress, tyrannize over; despoil *la16-e17.* **2**
overthrow, overwhelm *la15-e17.* [only Sc]
overhele &c *la15-16,* **ourhele &c** *la15-16,*
ourhelde &c *e16, only Sc* [*ʌur'hil] *vt, ptp also*
-**he**(**i**)**d** *lit and fig* cover over. [ME *overhelen*, OE
oferhelian]
overhye *see* OWERHIE
overisman *see* OWERSMAN
overla(**i**)**r** *see* OWERLAY
overlap *see* OWERLEAP
overlar *see* OWERLAY
overledder &c [*ʔ'ʌur'lɛdər, *ʔ'ʌvər-] *n* the
upper of a shoe *16-e17.* [ME *overlether*]
overloft *see* OURLOFT
overlope *see* OURLOP
overlord *see* OURLORD
overluke *see* OWERLEUK
overman *see* OWERSMAN
overmare &c *la14,* **ourmare &c** *la15*
[*'ʌur'mer] *adv* farther over, farther away. [*as
uppermair* (UPPER); *cf* ME *overmore* moreover,
further in time]
overput *see* OWERPIT
overquhelme &c *la15-16,* **ourquhelme &c**
16, -**quhemle** *e16* [*ʌur'hwɛlm, *-'hwɛml,
&c] *vt* = overwhelm.
oversailyie [*ʌur'seljɪ] *vt* bridge over (a CLOSE[2]
or alley) *la17.* [only Sc; MF *sursaillir*]
over-se *see* OWERSEA
oversé, oversie *see* OWERSEE
oversile &c *16-e17,* **oursile &c** *la15-16;* -**syll**
16-e17 [ʌur'sɔil] *vt* **1** *lit and fig* cover, obscure,
conceal *la15-16.* **2** dim, dull, impair (mental or
physical sight) *16-e17, only Sc.* **3** *only* **over-**
deceive, delude (a person) *16-e17, only Sc.*
overslide &c *16-e17,* **ourslide &c** *la15-16*
[*ʌur'slɔid, *also* 'ʌur-] *vi* **1** *of time* pass, elapse

16. **2** *of an event or action* (**let** a matter) pass unnoticed *la15-e17.* **3** *vt* glide over (water) *e16.* [ME]

oversyll *see* OVERSILE

overta *see* OURTA

overthort *see* OURTHWORT

overthrall &c *vt, prob* var of *overthraw* (OWER-THRAW) *e16.*

overthuart *see* OURTHWORT

overtirve *see* OURTIRVE

overtumble *see* OURTUMMYLL

overture &c; ouverture &c *la16-17* [*'ovər-tər, *'uvər-, *-tər] *n* **1** = overture *la16-.* **2** a proposal or recommendation drawn up for the consideration of a legislative body; a bill etc *la16-e18, only Sc.* **3** *Presbyterian Churches* a proposal or call for legislation brought before a higher church court by a lower body, *usu* made by a PRESBYTERY to the *General Assembly* (GENERAL) *la16-, only Sc.*
vti submit as a more or less formal proposal to (a legislative or deliberative assembly); propose (a motion) formally; petition *la17-.*

overturn *see* OWERTURN

overwent *see* OWERGAE

ovin *see* UNE[1]

ow *see* AWE[2], OO[2], OU

owder *see* OWTHER

owdience &c ['ʌudɪəns] *n* = audience, hearers, hearing *18-e20, Sh NE.*

owe *see* AWE[2]

owen *see* OWN

ower &c *15-*, **over &c**, **our &c** *la14-e19;* **ouer** *la15-e20,* **o('e)r** *17-e19* [ʌur] *prep* **1** = over *la14-.* **2** (down) from, out of, out at (a door, window, bed etc) *la16-.* **3** beyond the control or capabilities of, too much for *la19-, Sh NE Ags.*
adv **1** = over *la14-.* **2** *with adjs, advs* too, overmuch, excessively *la14-.* **3** *with preps* indicating position or direction, *eg* ~ **abune** over there above *15-, now Sh NE Uls.* **4** *as second part of a compound adv of motion* = and over, and across, -wards *la15-e17, only Sc: 'north-over'.* **5** *of time* well on, late, far advanced *la18-, Sh NE.* **6** off to sleep *la18-, only Sc.*
adj, of ropes etc going across or over *la20-, Bnf Stlg Wgt.*
vr (be able to) do what is necessary for oneself without help; cope with a situation, bestir oneself *19-e20, only Sc;* cf *may* ~.
n, only in *pl, chf proverb* excesses, extremes; leftovers, remnants; odds and ends *16-e18.*
~ance &c ['ʌurəns] control, mastery *la16-, now Rox.* **owrins, overins** [*'ʌurɪnz] odds and ends, remnants; trivial activities *19-e20.* **~ly** (*chf* **over-**) *adv* **1** carelessly, superficially, in a casual manner, by chance *17-, now Bnf.* **2** excessively, too, too much, in the extreme *19-.* *adj* **1** superficial, casual, careless *la17-, now Abd.* **2** excessive, exaggerated; unrestrained, unconventional, unusual *19-, now Sh.* **~um,**

~(h)im, ~(th)em *adv* turning over and over or inwards one side after another *19-, now Rox.*
n (*adj*) (in) a state of muddle or confusion *20-, Rox.*
~ **all &c 1** all over, everywhere *la14-, now Ags.* **2** above all else, most of all *la15-17.* ~ **allquhare** everywhere, in all directions *la14-16, only Sc.* **our-ane** [*?ʌur'en] in one, together *e16* [usu written as one word]. ~ **weel** in very good health *20-, Sh-Cai Uls.*
may ~ have power over, have mastery or control of *la15-16: 'gif ony of thame may our his falow be strenth'.* ~ **and abune &c** over and above, as well *la17-19.* ~ **somebody's heid** at the expense of someone, in spite of someone, without consulting the wishes or rights of someone *la18-, now local Ork-SW.* **take** *etc* **something** *or* **someone ~ another's heid** dispossess someone of land, customers etc unfairly (*eg* by offering better prices) *la16-17.*

owerblaw &c, overblaw &c, ourblaw &c *16-e17* [*'ʌur'bla] *vt* = overblow, *esp* cover (with snow or sand) *16-e19.*

owerbuird *la19,* **over-burde &c** *la16-e17,* **our-burd &c** *15-16* [*'ʌur'børd] *adv* = overboard.

owerby &c, over-by &c ['ʌur'baɪ] *adv* over, across at or to a place understood from the context (*usu* at a distance from the speaker), over there *la17-.*

owercap &c [ʌur'kap] *vt* overlap; be superior to, beat *19-, now Sh.*

owercast &c, overcast &c *la16-,* **ourcast** *la15-16* [ʌur'kast] *vti, ptp also* **-cassin &c** *la15-e20* **1** = overcast *la15-.* **2** *vt* recover from; throw off (an illness etc); get over *la18-e20, only Sc.* **3** look over; read through, inspect *la16, only Sc.*

owerclad &c, overcled &c, ourcled &c [ʌur'klɛd, *also* *-'klad] *adj, chf verse* clothed over, overclad; *chf fig* covered over (with), overspread *la15-, now Sh.* [only Sc; ptp of OSc *ovir-clethe;* cf ME *overclothe*]

owercome &c, overcum *16-e17,* **ourcum &c; o'er-** *18-e20* [*v* ʌur'kʌm; *n* 'ʌurkʌm] *vti, ptp also* **~(m)in &c** *la14-16* **1** = overcome *la14-.* **2** *vi* revive, recover **from** (shock, sickness etc) *la14-19.*
n **1** a surplus, extra, excess *15-19, only Sc.* **2** a sudden attack of illness *19-, only Sc;* cf INCOME *n* 3. **3** (1) a refrain, burden of a song, a chorus *19-, local wLoth-Wgt.* (2) a frequently-repeated phrase or theme, a saying *19-, now verse* [only Sc; cf OWERWORD]
~ing the act of coming across; crossing *la15-19, only Sc.*

owercoup &c [ʌur'kʌup] *vti, lit and fig* overturn, upset *18-e20.*

owercroun &c ['ʌurkrun] *n, chf* ~ **mutch** a peaked MUTCH worn by married women *19-20, NE, only Sc.*

owerday [ˈʌurde] *n* ~'s **breid** *etc* bread which has been kept for more than one day *la18-, now Sh NE Bwk.*

owerend &c, over-end [ʌurˈɛnd] *vti* turn up, set on end, tip up; turn topsy-turvy *17-.*
adv (adj) upright, standing up *17-, now Sh.* [only Sc]

owerfa &c *vi* **at the** ~**in** [ˈʌurˈfaən] on the point of falling down, very dilapidated *20-, Abd Ags.*

owerfret *see* OVER-FRET

owergae, overga, ourga &c *la14-16,* **ourgo** *15-16,* **overgo** *la16-19* [ʌurˈge, &c] *vti, pt also* **ourʒeid &c** *la15-18* [*ʌurˈjid], **oureyhude &c** *16* [*ʌurˈjød], **overwent** *la16-19. ptp* -**gane &c** *15-,* -**geen &c** *20-, Sh N* [-ˈgin] *chf in pt, ptp and derivs* **1** go over, pass through or over, cross *la14-19.* **2** *vt* overflow; *fig* overrun, infest, cover over (**with** weeds, dirt etc) *15-, now Sh Ork Wgt.* **3** (1) overpower, overwhelm, oppress *la15-, now Sh.* (2) surpass, excel *la14-, now Sh.* **4** *vi, of time* pass, elapse *la14-e20: 'the time's lang owregane'.*
~**ing &c** [-ˈgeɪn, -ˈgan, &c] *n* **1** a crossing, a way across *la16-, now NE.* **2** the act of working over an area etc, *eg* in cleaning, painting *la19-, chf NE.* **3** *fig* a severe reproof *20-, Sh NE Ags.*
in the owergaun &c in crossing, on the way across *la19-, now NE.* **owrgaun rapes** ropes which go vertically over the thatch on a cornstack *19-20, latterly Loth Kcb.*
lat overgo, lat ourgo let pass; omit *la15-17.* [ME *overga(n),* OE *ofergān;* eModEng *overgo; cf* OWERGANG]

owergaff &c [*ʌurˈgaf] *vi, of the sky* become overcast after a clear morning *19-e20, S.* [uncertain]

owergane *see* OWERGAE

owergang &c *la16-,* **overgang &c** *la15-e17,* **ourgang &c** [*v* ʌurˈgaŋ, &c; *n* ˈʌurgaŋ] *vt, only in pres and infin* **1** overcome, oppress, dominate *la15-, now Sh.* **2** spread over, overrun, infest *la16-e19.* **3** exceed, surpass *18-, now Sh wLoth Rox, only Sc.* **4** oversee, superintend *la19.*
n, only Sc **1** a going over, an application of something to a surface, *eg* a rake, coat of paint *20-, Sh NE Kcb.* **2** a drubbing, dressing-down *20-, Sh NE Kcb.* [ME *overgange(n),* OE *ofergangan; cf* OWERGAE]

owergaun, owergeen *see* OWERGAE

owerget *la19,* **overget** *la16,* **ourget** *la15* [*ʌurˈgɛt] *vt* overtake, catch up with. [ME *overget*]

owerhail &c, overhale &c, ourhale &c [*ʌurˈhel] *vt* **1** overtake *16-e18.* **2** *only* **our**- consider, survey *e15, only Sc.* **3** pass over, disregard, overlook *la15-16, only Sc.* **4** = overhale, oppress; overthrow *16-e17.*

owerhan &c *18-, now local,* **overhand &c** *la14-e18,* **ourhand &c** *la15-e16* [ˈʌurˈhan(d) &c, ˈʌurhan(d), *ˈʌvər-] *n* the upper hand; mastery, victory. [ME *overhand &c*]

owerhaul &c [?ˈʌurˈhɑl] *vt* drive (a screw or bolt) too tightly, so that the thread is damaged *19-, latterly N.* [*cf* ModEng *overhaul*]

owerheid &c *16-,* **overhede &c** *16-17,* **ourhede &c** *la15-17;* **overhead &c** *18-* [*adv* ʌurˈhid; *adj* ?ˈʌurhid] *adv* **1** (1) at an average rate per item *la15-, now Sh NE Wgt.* (2) in gross, overall *16-e20.* **2** precipitately; in a commotion, in confusion; untidily *16-, now Sh Ork NE, only Sc.*
adj untidy, slovenly, rough and ready, careless *la19-, now Sh Ork, only Sc.* [nME *ower-heued,* OE *ofer heafod* > ModEng *overhead*]

owerhie *la16-19,* **overhye &c** *la16-e19,* **ourhye** *la14-16* [*ʌurˈhaɪ] *vt* overtake, catch.

owerhing &c, overhing *vti* (*17-*), *n* (*20-*) [?ˈʌurˈhɪŋ] = overhang.

owerhip &c [*ʌurˈhɪp] *adv, of a smith* striking the metal by raising the hammer over the shoulder; *fig* forcibly *la18-19, only Sc.*

owerlap *see* OWERLEAP

owerlay &c, overlay, ourlay &c [*n* ˈʌurle, *v* ʌurˈle] *n* **1** a turn-down collar, a falling band *la16-e17, only Sc.* **2** a necktie, cravat; *latterly also* a scarf *18-e20, only Sc.* **3** the kind of hem in which one part of the cloth is folded or laid over the other *19-, only Sc.*
vt **1** = overlay *la16-17.* **2** *specif* paint (timber or metal) *16-e17.* **3** sew (a hem) as in *n* 3, *19-, now Sh Ork Ags, only Sc.*
~**er &c, -la(i)r** = *n* 1, *16-e17, only Sc.*

owerleap, overlepe, ourlepe [*ʌurˈlip] *vti, pt* -**lap** = overleap *la15-19.*

owerleuk &c *la19-, now local,* **overluke &c** *16-e17,* **ourluke** *la15-e17* [ʌurˈljuk, &c] *vt* = overlook *16-.*

owerloup &c, overloup, ourloupe [*?ˈʌurlʌup] *n* **1** the right of (? occasional) grazing of one's animals in land next to one's own *la17-18, Kcb.* **2** the spring tide at the change of the moon *18.*

owermaist &c, overmaste &c [ˈʌurmest, -məst] *adj* **1** uppermost *16-e20.* **2** farthest off or over *19-, Sh NE, only Sc.* [nME *ouermast,* eModEng *overmost*]

owermaister &c [ʌurˈmestər] *vt* = overmaster *19-e20.*

owerpit &c, overput &c *la16;* **o'er-** *18-e19* [*ʌurˈpɪt, &c] *vti* come through (a trial, danger), get over, recover from, get the better of *la16-e19.* [nME *ouerput*]

owerplus &c *la19-,* **overplus** *la17-18,* -**plush** *19-e20* [ˈʌurplʌs, -plʌʃ] *n, also fig* a surplus, excess, what is left over *la17-, now Bwk Kcb Uls.* [ME]

ower-pooer &c [ʌurˈpuər] *vt* = overpower *la19-, now Sh Cai.*

ower-rax &c [ʌurˈraks] *vt* stretch or reach over, over-reach *la19-, local N-S.*

owerreach *la19*, **ourreche &c** *la16*, **ourreke &c** *la15-16* [*ʌur'ritʃ, *-'rik] *v* **1** = overreach *la15-16*. **2** come upon, overtake, catch up with *16-19*.

ower-rin &c *la19-*, **overrin &c** *16-e17*, **ourrin &c** *la14-16*; **overrun** *16-* [ʌur'rɪn, &c] *vti* **1** = overrun *la15-*. **2** *vi, of time* come to an end, run out *la14-e15*. **3** *vt* flow over (a surface) *la15-*. **4** run down, run over (a person) *la16-*, *now Ork*.

owersea &c, **over-se &c**, **our-se &c** [*adj* 'ʌursi; *adv* *ʌur'si] *adj* **1** foreign, from over the sea *la16-*, *now Sh Ayr*. **2** *fig* far-fetched *17*. *adv* = overseas; from overseas *la14-17*.

owersee *16-*, **oversé &c** *16-17*, **oursé** *la15-e17*; **-sie** *16-17*, **oversee** *18-* [ʌur'si] *vt* **1** = oversee *16-*. **2** *specif* tend, look after (animals) *la15-*, *now Sh Ork Bnf*. **3** fail to take action against; allow to go uncensured or unpunished; overlook, tolerate (1) (a crime, fault) *la16-17*; (2) (a person) *16-17*; (3) *with infin* (a person doing something) *la16-17*. **4** neglect to insist upon, forego *la16-17*.

owerset &c *la15-*, *now Sh*, **overset &c** *la16-*, **ourset &c** *la14-16* [ʌur'sɛt] *vt* **1** = overset, overturn *la14-*. **2** overcome, get the better of (a trouble, difficulty etc) *la15-16*. **3** *chf in ptp* overwhelmed, beaten down (by hostile natural forces, *eg* a storm) *la15-*. *n, only* **our-** [*ʔ'ʌursɛt] the threat of defeat; the condition of being hard pressed or violently attacked; overthrow, subjugation by force *la15-e16*.

owersicht, **oversicht**, **oursicht &c** *la16-e17* ['ʌursɪxt] *n* **1** = oversight *la16-e20*. **2** *only Sc* (1) failure to take preventive or punitive action; licence, indulgence, toleration, connivance *la16-e17*; (2) allowance, special permission (to do something) *la16-e17*.

owersman &c *la16-*, **oversman &c** *la15-*, **ourisman &c** *la15-19*, **overman &c** *la15-e17*, **ourman &c** *la14-e17* ['ʌurzmən, *'ʌurman] *n* **1** = overman, a person with authority over others, one's superior, a head *la14-18*. **2** *specif* a craftsman appointed to supervise his fellows and their work *la15-e18*. **3** *specif* (1) the PROVOST of Prestwick and Wigtown *la15-16*, *only Sc*; (2) one of the leading officials of a BURGH, a magistrate *16*, *only Sc*. **4** *only* **~sman** *mining* (1) ? the manager (*appar* one superior to the overseer) of a coalmine *la17*; (2) an overseer or inspector in a coalmine *18-*, *now C*. **5** a chief ARBITER, appointed to have the final decision in the event of deadlock *15-*. **6** (1) a chief and arbitrating executor *16*. (2) *specif* a person appointed by a testament to see that its terms are carried out, and/or to look after the interests of the widow and/or PUPIL or MINOR heirs *16-e17*, *only Sc*.

owersoum &c, **oversoum &c**, **oursoum &c** [*ʌur'sum] *n* an animal or number of animals in excess of what constitutes a SOUM[1]; the keeping of such animals in excess of the allotted SOUM[1]; a fine or payment for this *la15-e19*.

owerstap, **overstap** [ʌur'stap] *vt* = overstep, step over or across *17-*, *now Bnf Ags*.

owerstent, **overstentit &c** [*ʌur'stɛnt(ɪt)] *ptp, orig only of tax* assessed at too high a rate, excessive *la17-19*, *only Sc*.

owertak &c *15-*, **overtak &c** *la16-18*, **ourtak &c** *la14-e17*; **overtake** *17-* [ʌur'tak, &c] *vt, ptp* **-taken &c** *15-*, **owertaen &c** *la18-* [-'takən, -'ten, &c] **1** = overtake *la14-*. **2** catch up with and punish *17*. **3** (1) deal with, get through (work etc) *la15-e17*. (2) catch up on (a piece of work or business) *la18-e20*. **4** *of a body of persons* occupy, fill (a space) *la14-15*, *only Sc*. **owertaen &c**, **overtaken** (**with** *or* **in** *la17-19*) deranged, made helpless, overcome (*specif* by liquor) *17-*, *now Per*. [*cf* OURTA]

owerter *see* OURTHWORT

owerthraw &c *la15-19*, **overthraw &c** *la15-17*, **ourthraw &c** *la15-17*, **ourthrow &c** *la16-e17* [*ʌur'θra] *vt, n* = overthrow.

owertree &c, **ourtre** *16*; **overtree** *18-* ['ʌur'tri] *n* a crossbeam, lintel *16-*, *now Ayr, only Sc*.

owerturn &c *19-*, **ourturn** *la15-e16*; **overturn** [*v* ʌur'tʌrn; *n* 'ʌurtʌrn] *vt* = overturn *la15-*. *n* **1** the burden or chorus of a song; a repetition of a story *19*, *only Sc*. **2** *commerce* turnover *la19-*.

owerword &c, **ourword &c** *16* ['ʌurwʌrd] *n* the burden or refrain of a poem or song; *latterly* also a repeated saying *16-*, *now C*.

oweryear, **our-ȝeir** *e16* [*'ʌur'jir] *adj, latterly of animals* left or kept over from the previous year *16-19*.

owik *see* OUK

owl *see* OOL

owld *see* AULD

own &c, **awn**; **owen &c** *la17* [ʌun; ɑn] *v* **1** = own *la17-*. **2** acknowledge as a relation or acquaintance, give recognition to; deign to be associated with; have to do with; attend to; come into contact with; lay claim to *la17-*. **awner 1** = owner *la15-e20*. **2** *specif* a shipowner *17*. [see OED and *cf* AWE[2]]

owne *see* AWE[2]

owrins *see* OWER

owse *see* OX

owt *see* OCHT[1]

owther &c; **owder &c** *la15-16* ['ʌuðər; *'ʌudər] *adj* either *la14-*, *now S*. *pronoun* either *la14-e16*. *adv, also* **older** *16*, **authir &c** *la14, e17* [*'aðər] either *la14-e20*. *conj or e16*. **~ance &c** *la15-19*, **o(w)therane** *la15 adv* either. [ME, eModEng *owther*, OE *ōwðer*, ultimately f *ō* ever; *cf* AITHER and NOWTHER]

owthor *see* AUTHOR

ox &c *15-*, *in place-names la12-*; **oix** *16 n, pl also* **oussen &c** *15-* ['ʌusən] *and back-formation as sing* **owse** *chf in combs, la18-20* [ʌus] *n* **1** = ox *15-*. **2** *pl used as sing, la15-16: 'ane tuithles oxine'.*

~in bow, oussen bow a curved wooden collar for a draught ox *la15-e20*. **~ ee &c 1** the great tit *16-*, *now Fif midLoth*. **2** the blue tit *la18-*, *now nEC Rox*. **~gang** *14-*, **~gate** *la16-*, **oxingang &c** *la15-*, **oxingate &c** *la16-* a measure of land, a division (*usu* one eighth) of a *ploughgate* (PLEUCH) or *occas* (*Suth Ross*) of a DAVACH, *now only hist and in place-names*. **~ gers &c** the extent of pasturage suitable for one ox *16*. **oxin tilth &c** a measure of land, *appar = oxgang e16, only Sc*.

oxter &c; oxster &c *16-e17*, **okstare &c** *la16-e18*, **hokster &c** *16-e17 n* **1** the armpit; the under part of the (upper) arm *15-*. **2** the corresponding part of an animal, the underside of its shoulder *la16-*. **3** the corresponding part of a garment; the armhole *la19-*.

vti **1** take, lead, support by the arm *la18-*, *NE-S*. **2** hold, carry under the arm *la18-*, *local Sh-Kcb*. **3** *also* **~ with** *19-* take (someone) on one's arm *la18-*, *local*. **4** *also* **~ at** embrace, cuddle *la19-*, *NE-WC*, *only Sc*. **5** elbow, shove, jostle *la19-*, *local, only Sc*.

~-cog help a person to walk by supporting him under the arm *la19-*, *Uls*. **~f(o)u** *also fig* an armful; as much as one can hold in the crook of an arm *18-*. **~ lift** as much as can be carried

under the arm or in the arms *la19-*, *now Sh*. **~ pickle &c** the small grain *freq* attached to the full one within the husk in oats *19-*, *NE*. **~ pouch &c** a breast-pocket *la18-*. **~ staff** a crutch *19-*, *NE*.

gie an ~ lend an arm **to** (someone) in walking *la19-*, *now NE*. **in one's ~** in one's armpit, in one's arms *la16-*. **in** (**utheris**) **~is** arm in arm; in one another's arms *16*. **lead** *etc* **by the ~** lead by the arm *16*. **under one's ~** under one's arm, in one's armpit *la15-*. **wi one's airms in one's ~s** with one's arms folded (sometimes implying idleness) *20-*. **wi one's heid under one's ~** with a downcast, drooping look *20-*, *now Ork Uls*. [northern eModEng *oxtere*, appar altered f OE *ōhsta*, *ōxta*]

oy *see* O, OE

oye *see* OE

oyell *see* OIL

oyes &c *la15-17*, **hoyes &c** *16-19*, *only Sc* [*'oˈjɛs, *'oiˈjɛs, *'ho-, *'hoi-, *-'je] *v, in imperative as interj* = oyez *la15-19*.

n, pl also **~(s)es** = oyez *la16-17*.

oyne *see* UNE[1]

oysche *see* ISH

oyster &c; oster &c *16-17* ['oistər; *'ostər] *n* = oyster *15-*.

~ plant seaside smooth gromwell *la19*.

ozel *see* OSEL

ozenbrigs *see* OSNABURG

ozzel *see* OSEL

P

pa *17-e19*, **pall** &c *la14-* [*pɑ, *pal] *n* = pall, rich cloth.

pa *see* PEY

paal *see* PALL

pace *see* PAISE, PEACE, PIECE¹, PASS¹

Pace, Pasche &c *la14-e20*, **Pask** &c *la14-20*, **Pax** &c *15-e17*; **Pas** &c *la14-15, la19*, **Pasce** *15*, **Paisch** &c *16-e17*, **Peasche** *16-17*, **Pes** &c *16-20*, **Pesche** &c *la16-17, e20*, **Peace** *la16-e20*, **Peax** &c *16-e17* [pes; *peʃ; *pask; *peks] *n* **1** = Pasch, Easter *la14-*. **2** = Pasch, the Passover *15-16*.

Pasch Court the Easter session of the *head court* 1 (HEID) of each BURGH *18*. **~ Day** Easter Day *la14-17, e20*. **p~ egg** an Easter egg *19-*, now *Sh-N Rox*. **pace egg day** Easter Monday *20-, Bwk Rox*. **~ evin** &c Easter eve; the day before Easter or the Passover *la14-16*. **Pasch &c Fair** a fair held in various districts at Eastertime *18*. **Pasch(e)-finis** &c collective term for a certain payment made at Easter in local churches *16*. **~ market** a market held at Eastertime *la15-19*. **~ Saturday, Sunday** *etc* Easter Saturday, Easter Sunday etc *la16-*, now *Sh Cai*. **Pace-yaud** &c a person who fails to observe the custom of wearing something new for Easter *19-*, now *Ags*. [see SND]

pacient *la14-16*; **patient** *la15-* ['peʃənt] *adj* **1** = patient *la14-*. **2** passive, inactive, inert *16*. *n* = patient *16-*.

~fu long-suffering, very patient, submissive *la18-e20*.

pack¹ &c *la15-*, **pak** &c now *Sh n* **1** = pack *15-*. **2** an initial stock of merchandise; a means of setting up in business; a means of living *16-17*. **3** one's worldly goods, property, fortune *16-*, now *Abd-Ags*. **4** a measure of wool (*usu* 12 stones SCOTS in weight) or of cloth (of varying length) *16-19*. **5** a number of sheep owned by a shepherd which are allowed to pasture along with his master's sheep as one of his perquisites *19-*, now *Cai Ags Lnk S*. **6** the state of being packed or crowded together, a crush, a squeeze *20-, Sh NE Ags*.

v **1** *vtr* = pack *la15-*. **2** *vt, transf* stuff (oneself or one's stomach with food) *la16-17*. **3** *fig* **~ up** bring (a dispute) to an amicable agreement *la16-e17*. **4** *ploughing* lay (the furrows) close together *la19-, local Sh-Wgt*.

~ie &c = **~man** 1, *19-*, now *Cai Fif Kcb*.

~-house a warehouse, a shed for storing merchandise *la16-e19*. **~man 1** a pedlar, a travelling merchant, *esp* in soft goods *la16-*, now *Sh-N Ayr*, *chf Sc*. **2** a type of cloud formation *la19-, local* [so called because of its shape resembling a man with a pack on his back]. **~ merchant 1** = **~man** 1, *19, Abd*. **2** = **~man** 2, *la19-20*.

bring *or* **ca one's ~ to the pins** *or* **till a preen** squander one's fortune, be at the end of one's resources *18-*, now *Abd Kcdn Ags*. **~**

and *or* **or peel** &c **1** pack and unpack bulk merchandise; act as a wholesale merchant in export and import trade *la15-e18*. **2** have dealings **with** (unfreemen) in trade, associate **with** (unprivileged merchants) by allowing them the rights of trade belonging to the guilds *la16-e19*.

pack² *n* an agreement, plot, conspiracy *usu* secret, *chf* **in ~** in collusion, in league *la19-*, now *Ayr Kcb Uls*. [perh f obs Eng = a secret agreement or plot, or may be Sc form of Eng *pact*]

pack³ *adj* on intimate and friendly terms, linked by mutual feeling or understanding, in league *18-*, now *EC, WC, S*. [see SND]

packed *see* PAKKET

packet &c *n* a pannier, a load-saddle *18-e20, NE*. [perh f *pakkald* (PAUCHLE¹)]

packet *see* PAKKET

pacok &c *14-16*, **paco** &c *16*, *only Sc* [*'peko(k)] *n* = peacock. [nME *pacok* &c]

paction &c *16-e20*, **pactioun** &c *16-17 n* an agreement, bargain, understanding, *freq* of an informal, underhand or conspiratorial nature; the act of making an agreement; *law* an unofficial agreement as distinct from a legally binding contract *16-e20*.

vi make an agreement or bargain, enter into a compact *la17-e19, only Sc*. [ME *paccion*]

pactorial *adj, law* of the nature of or pertaining to a pact or agreement *la19*. [only Sc; Eng *pact* + *-orial*]

pad *n* **1** a footpath, a narrow, unsurfaced track or way *18-*, now *WC, S, Uls*. **2** *chf in place-names* a route over a natural obstacle, a pass through hills etc *19-e20, C*.

vi **1** travel on foot, trot along steadily and purposefully *la18-*. **2** depart, take oneself off, *eg* after being dismissed, *usu* with the implication of haste *la19-e20*.

~ded &c *20-*, now *Sh Abd*, **~dered** &c *la18-*, now *Sh Abd* trampled, well-trodden.

~ the road *etc* trudge around, *usu* looking for work *19-e20*. [*n* orig cant f LowGer or Du = a path; for *v cf* LowGer *padden* tread a path]

paddill *see* PAIDLE³

paddle *see* PAIDLE¹, PAIDLE², PAIDLE³

paddo(k) *see* PUDDOCK

paddok-lok &c *n* a portable lock; a padlock *16-17*. [only Sc; appar altered f Eng *padlock* perh because of some fancied resemblance to a *paddok* (PUDDOCK)]

paddy *see* PUDDOCK

Paddy *n* = Paddy, nickname for an Irishman.

~ barrow a barrow without sides, *freq* used for carrying large stones *20-, local Ork-Ayr* [so called from its frequent use by Irish labourers].

~'s Market 1 a street market in Glasgow frequented by Irish members of the population *la19-, Gsw*. **2** any confused scene, an untidy room etc *20-, Ags WC*. **~'s Milestone** *joc* name for Ailsa Craig in the Firth of Clyde, a conspicuous landmark for Irish immigrants sailing to Scotland *la19-*.

come (**the**) ~ **ower** get the upper hand of by a trick, bamboozle *19*.

padill *see* PAIDLE², PAIDLE⁴

padȝeane *see* PAGEANT

paek *see* PECK

paewae &c *18-*; **pauw-wauw** &c *e20, Rox* [*NE* 'pe'we; *nEC* 'pju'wju; *Slk* 'pi'wi; *Rox* 'pʌu'wʌu, 'piu'wjʌu] *adj, of a person* pallid, sickly; drooping, spiritless *now Sh NE Fif.* [prob chf imit of a whining sound w infl f WAE¹, wow²; cf *peelie-wally* (PEELIE)]

paffle &c *la17-20*, **poffill** &c *la15-17, in placenames la13-*; **poffle** &c *la18-e20 n* a small piece of land, a CROFT, an allotment *la15-20, in placenames la13-*.

paffler &c a person who farms a PAFFLE, a small tenant-farmer *la18-19.* [perh f OE **pofel* a piece of low-lying sandy ground]

page &c *la14-*; **pege** *16-e17, only Sc,* **peage** &c *la16-e17* [pedȝ] *n* = page, a boy servant.

pageant &c *16-*; **pegane** &c *16,* **padȝeane** &c *16* ['pedȝənt; *-ən(d)*; *'bedȝ-*] *n* = pageant.

paich *see* PECH

paidle¹ &c; **paddle** &c ['pedl] *vti* **1** (1) = paddle *la18-*. (2) *vi* move with short quick steps, toddle, walk slowly or aimlessly *la18-, now local Sh-WC*. **2** *vt* press or beat with the feet, trample, tread down *la18-, now Ork Fif Kcb Uls*. *n* the act of wading or paddling in water etc *la19-, now Cai Bnf Ayr*.

paidling &c toddling, waddling; aimless, feckless *la18-e20*.

paidle² &c, **padill** *la16-17*; **paddle** &c *18-e20* [*local Per sEC Rox* 'pedl] *n* a long-handled tool for weeding, scraping earth etc from a hard surface or clearing the coulter of a plough in the furrow; a hoe *la16-, local*.

vti scrape (floors etc) clean; use a hoe, clean or clear by means of a hoe *la16-, now eLoth*. [ME *padell* a small, long-handled, spade-like implement, ModEng *paddle* an oar; *cf* PATTLE]

paidle³ &c *la16, 19-*, **paddill** &c *16-e17*; **paddle** &c *18-19* ['pedl; **'padl*] *n* the lump-fish or lump-sucker *16-, now Sh Cai Kcdn Fif*.

~ **cock** the male lump-fish *la19-, now Kcdn Ags*. [only Sc; see SND]

paidle⁴ &c *19-*, **padill** *la16* ['pedl] *n* **1** a small leather bag or wallet; a flat leather pouch *la16, 19*. **2** the pocket or trap in a fishing-net, *esp* in the small stake-net used for catching flounders etc *19-20, SW*.

~-**net** a fishing-net containing a PAIDLE⁴ (*n* 2), *la19-, now Kcb*. [only Sc; perh dim of eModEng *pad* a pannier, basket]

paik &c *v* **1** vt beat, strike, thrash, punish *16-, now Kcdn Ags Ayr Uls*. **2** *vi* trudge, tramp along, stump *19-e20*.

n **1** *in pl, chf* **get one's** *or* **gie someone his** ~**s**

get one's or give someone his deserts *16-*. **2** a blow, stroke, thump *la18-, now Bnf Ayr*. **3** a worthless creature, *specif* of women or female animals *19-e20*.

~**in** &c a thrashing, punishment, 'beating-up' *la19-, local*. [only Sc; see SND]

pail &c *16-e20*, **paill** &c *16-17*; **peal** &c *17-e18* [**pel*] *n* **1** a canopy for a bed etc; a covering of state for a royal personage etc *16-17*. **2** a cloth for draping a coffin or a corpse, a pall *16-e19*. **3** a hearse *19-e20*. [only Sc; OF *paile* &c, L *pallium*]

pailace &c *la19*, **palice** &c *la15-e17*; **paleis** &c *la15-e17* ['paləs; **'pel-*] *n* **1** = palace *la15-19*. **2** an official residence of the Scottish sovereign; the precinct of such a residence *la15-e17*.

pailin(**g**) *see* PALE²

pailister *n* the game of quoits *18-20*. [only Sc; Gael *peilistear* a quoit, flat stone]

paill *see* PAIL

pailȝoun(**e**) *see* PALLION²

paiment *see* PAMENT

pain &c; **pan** *la14-16, only Sc* [pen] *n* **1** = pain *la14-*. **2** (**the**) ~**s** chronic rheumatism, rheumatic twinges *la18-*.

vtr = pain *la14-*.

~**ful 1** = painful *la15-*. **2** causing or involving hardship or difficulty; troublesome, laborious *la14-17*. **3** *of persons* painstaking, laborious, assiduous, diligent *la16-17*.

dey in(**to**) **the** ~ die in the attempt *la14-e16*.

set one's ~ *la14-e16*, **tak** ~(**s**) **upon oneself** *la16-17* expend much effort, exert oneself, take the trouble (to do something).

painch &c *16-*, **panche** &c *16-17*; **penche** &c *la15-e20*, **paunch** [penʃ, penʃ, panʃ; **panʃ*] *n* **1** = paunch *la14-*. **2** *in pl* the bowels or intestines of a person or animal *la17-, now Ayr Uls*. **3** *in pl* the entrails of an animal, *esp* as food; tripe *16-e20*.

vt **1** = paunch, disembowel, stab. **2** *specif* puncture the large stomach of (an animal, *esp* a ruminant) to allow accumulated gases to escape, probe *19*.

paunchings &c the intestines of an animal, *esp* as used for food, tripe served in potato soup *la19-, now Sh*.

paint &c; **pent** *la17-*, **pint** &c *la17-e20* [pent, pent; *Abd also* pɪnt] *vtr* = paint *la14-*.

n **1** = paint. **2** the painted woodwork of a room or building, the paintwork *20-*.

~**it** &c **1** = painted *15-*. **2** *of glass* coloured, 'stained' *e16*. **3** *fig, of words, speeches etc* highly 'coloured' for show or to deceive; feigned, deceitful, insincere *16*. ~**it werk** stained glass *e16*.

paintrie &c *15-e17*; **paintre** *16* [**'*pentrɪ] *n* **1** *collective* painters' work, painted pictures or designs *15-e17*. **2** painters' material; paint or pigment *16-e17*. [MF *peintrie*]

paintrie *see* PANTRÉ

paip[1] &c *n* **1** the stone or kernel of a fruit, a pip *20-, now Dmf Slk.* **2** *specif* a dried cherrystone used as a counter and as currency in children's games *19-, now midLoth S.* **3** the ~**s** a game, varying between districts, played with cherrystones as counters and stakes *19-, now midLoth S.* [var of Eng *pip*]

paip[2], **pape** *n* **1** = pope *la14-e20.* **2** *derog* a member of the Roman Catholic Church *20-, chf WC* [shortened f Eng *papist*].

papery &c popery *la16-, now Ayr Kcb.* **papish** *la16-, now local Ags-Uls,* **papisher** &c *e19 n, chf derog* a Roman Catholic, a papist. **papist** &c *n* = papist *la16-.* *adj* papistical, popish *la16-17.*

paiper *see* PAPER

pair &c; **peare** *17,* **perr** *20-, local* [per; *Rox* pɛr; *Gsw also* pɛr] *n* **1** = pair *15-.* **2** (1) a set, not limited to two, of related objects, *esp* ~ **of arrows** a set of three arrows *18-e20, latterly hist;* ~ **of bagpipes** a set of bagpipes *la17-, now Sh Ags;* ~ **of beads** a string of beads *la15-, now local Ross C-Uls;* ~ **of cards** a pack of cards *la16-, now NE, WC Slk.* (2) a single object viewed as a collection of its component parts, *esp* ~ **of blankets** *etc* one large blanket etc used folded in two *la15-;* ~ **o questions** the *Shorter Catechism* (SHORT) *la20-, local NE-WC;* ~ **o taws(e)** (TAW[1]) a schoolmaster's strap with several thongs *19-, now Sh Ags Kcb.* **3** *specif* (1) a team of two horses for ploughing and other farm jobs *la19-;* (2) *attrib* **an ae** *etc* ~ (**horse**) **place** *etc* a farm with one etc team of horses *la19-, now NE.*

ane *etc* ~ (**buttis**) *measure of distance* one pair of butts (BUTT[2]) *17.*

paircel &c *20-,* **parcel** &c; **parcial** &c *la15-16,* **perciall** &c *la15-e17,* **partial** &c *la16-e17,* **persell** &c *17-e20* ['pɛrsəl, 'parsəl; ***'pɛrsəl, ***'parʃəl, ***'pɛrʃəl] *n* **1** = parcel *la15-.* **2** a small company or collection (of people or animals); a group, herd, flock *la17-, now Sh Ayr Uls.*

vt = parcel *la16-.*

in parcel(s) &c in parts, part by part, piecemeal, by instalments *16-17.*

pairin *see* PARE

Pairis *see* PARIS

pairish &c *la17-e20,* **parische** &c *la15-16,* **parioch** &c *la16-e18,* **paroche** &c *la14-e18;* **parise** &c *la14-17,* **perish** &c *la15-e20,* **perroche** &c *16,* **pareis** &c *la16-19,* **parish** *17-* ['pɛrɪʃ, *NE also* -ɪs; ***'paro(t)ʃ, ***-ɪo(t)ʃ] *n* **1** *chf in combs until la16* = parish *la14-, latterly only church; see* QUOAD OMNIA, QUOAD SACRA. **2** the inhabitants of a parish *la16-17.* **3** *curling* (CURL) the ring surrounding the TEE[1], the HOUSE *la19-, now Renfr Ayr.*

parischin &c *15-17,* **parochin** &c *15-20, latterly chf literary,* **pariochine** *la16-e17, chf NE,* **prochin** &c *16* ['pɛrɪʃən; ***'p(a)ro(t)ʃən, ***'parɪo(t)ʃ-, ***'parɪʃ-, &c] **1** a parish *15-20.* **2**

the inhabitants or members of a parish *la15-17.*

parischinar &c *15-17,* **parochinar** &c *la15-e18,* **pariochiner** *la17,* **pareeshioner** *20-* [pə'rɪʃənər; ***pa'r(ɪ)o(t)ʃ-] a parishioner, a member or inhabitant of a parish. **parochial** [pa'roxɪəl] **board** &c an elected body, set up in each parish by the Poor Law Amendment (Scotland) Act of 1845, responsible for the Poor Law provisions and much of the parish administration *19.* **parochial school** = *parish school, la18-19.* **parochial visitation** a periodical inspection, by the PRESBYTERY, of the religious affairs of a parish *18-19.*

parish school one of the schools set up by the *Church of Scotland* (CHURCH) to provide instruction in the rudiments of education and in Latin, and to equip promising pupils for University entrance *la17-19.*

pairk *see* PARK

pairlament *see* PARLIAMENT[1]

pairling *see* PEARL[2]

pairls &c *19-,* **parleis** &c *la16-e17,* **perrillis** &c *e17;* **perils** &c *19-e20* [perlz, pɛrlz; ***'parlɪs] *n, chf* the ~ paralysis; a paralytic tremor or weakness *la16-, now Slk.*

adj **pairlt** &c [perlt, pɛrlt, parlt] affected with paralysis or a paralytic tremor *19-, now Slk.* [only Sc; reduced f PARLESY; *cf* Gael *pairilis*]

pairple &c *18-20,* **parpall** &c *la15-e20;* **perpell** &c *la15-e19 n, also* ~ **wall** *la15-e18* a partition, *freq* of wood or a similar light material. [only Sc; var of PARPEN]

pairse *see* PIERCE

pairt &c *15-,* **part** &c; **pert** *15-19* [pert, pɛrt] *n* **1** = part *la14-.* **2** a portion of land, part of an estate held by a smaller landowner, one of a number of pieces of land into which an estate might be divided for separate disposition *la14-17.* **3** (1) *in sing where Eng uses pl* a place, area, neighbourhood *15-, now Sh Ork NE.* (2) a site, a clearly defined spot *19-, now Sh Ags Kcb Uls.* **4** one's way of life *15-16.*

vti **1** = part *la14-.* **2** *vt* divide into parts or portions, share (1) *in gen, 15-;* (2) *specif* (food at table) *20-, now NE.* **3** leave, depart from, separate from, part with *17-, now Uls.* **4** (1) *vi* leave one's spouse after being authorized to do so *e16.* (2) *vt, in passive* be separated formally from one's spouse *la16.* **5** *vi, of property, food etc* be divided or divisible *19-, now Sh NE Ags.*

~**isman** a person who shares or takes part with (another) **in** or **of** (an undertaking); a partaker **of** (a benefit); a partner *la15-16, only Sc.* ~**lik** proportionally, *chf* ~ (**and**) ~**lik** in fair or equal shares *16-e17, only Sc.* ~**lingis** in part; partly *la16, only Sc.*

~**-tak** &c **1** = partake *17-.* **2** support, side with, defend *16-19.* ~**-taker 1** = partaker *16-.* **2** a supporter, an ally; an accomplice *16-18.*

for that ~ **o** for the matter of .., in regard to .., as far as concerns .. *la19-, now local Ork-Kcb.*

be guid, ill *etc* one's ~ *of an action, thought etc* be (in)consistent etc with one's duty, (un)becoming etc in one, (un)worthy etc of one *18-, now Bnf.* **in that part 1** on or concerning that point; in that respect *la15-e17.* **2** *of an official or office* by special appointment and with jurisdiction limited either to particular matters or with respect to time or place *la15-*; see *eg* JUSTICE, SHERIFF. **keep one's ain pairt** look after one's own interests, 'keep one's end up' *19-, now Ork Ags.* **kepe (a) gude** *etc* **part to** behave towards (a person) in a good etc way *la15-16.* **(all) part(s) (pendicles) and pertinents** *16-*, **parts and pendicles** *16-19, law* everything connected with or forming part of lands conveyed (except the REGALIA) that is not specially reserved from the grant. ~ **wi bairn** *or* **child** give birth to a premature or stillborn baby; suffer a miscarriage *la15-, now Sh NE Uls.*

pairt *see* PERT

pairtclaith *see* PARTCLAITH

pairtiner *see* PAIRTNER

pairtisay &c ['pertısı] *n* a thing done by or belonging to more than one person, a joint venture or possession *19-e20.* [only Sc; F *partisé* joint, mutual, shared]

pairtissing *see* PARTISING

pairtner *17-*, **partinere &c** *la14-e17*; **pairtiner &c** *la16-e17* ['pertnər, 'pɛrt-; *pairtiner &c] n = partner *la14-*.
~y **&c** partnership *15-e20.*

pairtrick *see* PAITRICK

pairty &c *la15-*, **partie &c**; **perty &c** *15-e18* ['pertı, 'pɛrtı] *n* **1** = party *la14-*. **2** a match, equal *16*. **3** a person proposed or intended as a marriage partner; a lover; a spouse *la15-e17*. **4** *as adj* (1) concerned, personally involved; active in *la15-17*; (2) antagonistic, hostile to *la16-e17*.
vti **1** take sides, make common cause with *la16-18*. **2** *vt* support, take the part of *la16-e17*.

pais *see* PAISE, PASS[1], PEACE

Paisch *see* PACE

paise &c *15-19*, **pais &c** *15-17*; **pas** *la15-e17*, **pace** *la15-19*, **pease** *la16-e18* [*n* pes; *v* pez; *Rox also* pəiz; *v also* *pes] *vt* **1** = peise, measure the weight of, in or as in a balance *la15-17*. **2** assess the weight of something by holding it, estimate *16-19*. **3** *fig* weigh in the mind; deliberate upon, consider *16-e17*.
n **1** = peise, standard weight *15-16*. **2** the weights and prices of different kinds of bread, periodically laid down by the magistrates of BURGHS etc; the official list or table of this *15-17*. **3** (1) a stone or metal weight, *esp* one used in a pulley mechanism *16-18*. (2) *specif* (a) one of the weights of a pendulum clock *la16-e19*; (b) *weaving* one of the weights in the pulley which controls the tension of the warp threads *19-20*. **of pais** conforming to the prescribed or standard weight *la15-e16*.

Paisley &c ['pezlı] *attrib* with reference to the thread and textile industries of PAISLEY, *esp* the manufacture of shawls of the *Paisley pattern*; the pattern itself or any fabric bearing it *19-*.
~ **bodie &c** a native of Paisley *la17-, now WC*.
~ **pattern** an elaborate colourful design based on Hindu and Arabic motifs, used in the *Paisley shawl* (1805-1870) and subsequently copied throughout the world *20-*. ~ **screw** a screw driven home with a hammer instead of a screwdriver, suggesting laziness *20, WC*. ~ **screwdriver** a hammer *20, WC*; cf *Glesca screwdriver* (GLESCA). ~ **shawl** a shawl of the *Paisley pattern* made of cashmere and wool or silk, or cotton and wool, and *freq* acquired by a woman on her marriage *19-*. [the town in Renfr]

pais-penny &c [*?'pez-] *n, appar* one of a number of coins found as treasure *la15-e16*. [only Sc; perh f POSE[1] but the vowel change is unexplained]

paiter &c *la19*, **patter &c** ['petər, patər] *vti* **1** = patter, repeat prayers *16-*. **2** *vi* talk in a persistent, monotonous way, chatter on endlessly *19-e20*.

paith(e) *see* PETH

paitrick &c *la15-, Gen except Sh Ork*, **partridge &c** *la16-*, **partrik &c** *la14-20*, **patrick &c** *16-e20*; **pertrik &c** *15-16, la19*, **pairtrick &c** *16-e20*, **peirtrick &c** *la16, e20*, **pertridge &c** *17* ['petrɪk, 'pertrɪk; *Sh C, S also* 'pertrɪdʒ; *Mry C, S also* 'patrɪk; *NE also* 'partrɪk; *WC Uls also* 'patrɪdʒ; *&c*] *n* = partridge. [*cf* PERDRIX]

paittern *la19*, **patron &c** *la14-19*, **patroune &c** *la14-16*; **pattern** ['petər(ə)n, 'patrən; *pa'trun] *n* = pattern.

paiument [*?'pevmənt] *n, vt* pavement, pave *la16*. [? var of Eng *pavement* but ? *cf* ME *pauiment* f L *pavīmentum*; *cf* PAMENT]

paix *see* PEACE

pak *see* PACK[1], PAWK

pakk *see* PAWK

pakkald *see* PAUCHLE[1]

pakket &c *16-17*; **packet, packed** *la16-e17* ['pakət, *-əd] *n* **1** = packet *la16-*. **2** a larger bundle or package of goods or merchandise, tied together for transportation or storage *16-e17*.

palaver; palaiver *now local Ork-Per* [pə'lavər; *N* pə'levər; *Loth* pə'lavər] *n* **1** = palaver. **2** a fussy way of behaving, an ostentatious procedure, a great fuss about nothing *la19-*. **3** a foolishly ostentatious person, an extremely fussy person *la19-, now Cai NE Per*.
vi **1** behave in a silly or ostentatious way, fiddle about *la19-e20*. **2** waste time, trifle, make a great deal of a small task, *freq* of a child, delaying bed-time *19-, now Sh Per WC*.
~**in** *n* an ostentatious fuss, an 'act' *la19-, now local Ork-Per*. *adj* capering, ostentatious *la19-, now local Ork-Per*.

paldie *see* PALLALL

pale[1] **&c** *n* a small shovel or scoop, used for taking samples of food, *esp* cheese *19-, now Lnk Gall.* *vt* pierce (cheese etc) with a PALE[1], remove a sample with a PALE[1] *18-, now Kcb.* [F *pelle* a shovel, paddle-blade, shutter of a sluice, OF *pele* > ModEng *peel* a baker's shovel]

pale[2] **&c; peal &c** *17-e19* [pel] *n* **1** = pale, a pointed stake used in fencing; a fence *la15-.* **2** a peg used as a stopper *16-e19, only Sc;* cf *cock and pail* (COCK[1]).

paling, pailin &c, pealin(g) &c *n* = paling *16-.* *vt, freq* **pailin aff, up** enclose with a fence or paling *20-.* **pailing-stab &c** a paling post *la20-, local Sh-Kcb.*

pale[3] **&c** *n* = peal, the ringing of bells *17.*

pale[4] **&c** *adj* = pale, lacking colour*15-.*
~ **ale,** *formally* **India P~ Ale** a kind of low-gravity beer *20-;* *cf* HEAVY.

paleis *see* PAILACE

palfurner &c [*pal'fʌrnər] *n* a man in charge of horses, a groom *16.* [only Sc; F *palefournier* (*16*), rare var of *pal(e)frenier* > eModEng *pal-freynyer &c*]

palice *see* PAILACE

palie[1] *19-;* **paulie &c** *la18-e19,* **pallie &c** *19-20* ['palɪ; *'pelɪ] *adj* **1** thin, having a pallid, sickly appearance, listless *19-, now local Fif-S.* **2** (1) stunted in growth, underdeveloped, delicate *19-, now Ayr S.* (2) *specif, of young animals, esp lambs* undersized, not thriving *19-e20.* **3** (1) defective, deformed, lame *la18-, now C, S.* (2) *of the limbs etc* incapacitated, affected by injury or disease, paralysed *19-, now Per Rox.* *n* **1** a lethargic, sluggish person; a feeble weakling *19-e20.* **2** an undersized, ailing lamb *19-, now Kcb.*

pally-handit *or* **-fittit 1** having a damaged or useless hand or foot *20-, C, S.* **2** (1) left-handed *la20-, EC.* (2) splay-footed, flat-footed *la18-e19.* [f PALE[4], with vowel variation as in *pape, paup* (PAP[1]), *wake* (WAUK) etc]

palie[2] [*?'palɪ] *adj, Heriot's Hospital slang* sweet-tasting, delicious *19-e20.* [reduced f Eng *palatable*]

palinode *18-e20, latterly hist,* **palinod** *e17* ['palɪnod] *n, law* a formal retraction of a defamatory statement which a *pursuer* (PURSUE) could demand of the *defender* (DEFEND) as part of the damages in a libel action; an apology. [*cf* eModEng = an ode etc in which an author retracts something]

pall; paal *19-20,* **pawl &c** *19-e20* [pɑl] *n* **1** a pole, a stout post, a beam, *esp* a mooring post for ships *18-, now N Ayr Kcb.* **2** a prop or stay, a support, a fulcrum *19-, now Ork.* *vt* **1** puzzle, perplex, thwart *19-, now Sh-Cai Mry.* **2** surprise, astonish *20-, Sh Ork Bnf.* **3** exceed, surpass, *chf* ~ **aa** beat everything *la19-, Sh Ork NE.* [var of nautical Eng *pawl* (*n*) a bar used to lock a capstan etc, (*v*) check, stop]

pall *see* PA

pallack *see* PELLOCK

pallall &c ['pa'lal, -'lal, pə'lal; p(ə)'ral; &c] *n* **1** *freq in pl* the game of PEEVER[1], hopscotch *la18-, now Ags Fif Loth.* **2** the counter with which the game is played *la19-, Ags Fif.* **3** the name of one of the squares, *usu* the seventh, on which the game is played *la19-, Ags Fif.*
pallie *la19-e20,* **paldie** *20-, Ags Fif* ['pal(d)ɪ] = *n.* [only Sc; altered f F *palet* a stone etc used to throw at a target in various games]

pallat *see* PALLET

pallawa ['paləwə] *n, also* **pallie** *la20* ['palɪ] a small edible crab, *freq* used for bait *19-20, Fif.* [obscure]

palle &c [*pal] *n, heraldry* a pale *la15-16.* [only Sc; F *pal* a stake, a pale in heraldry]

palleis *see* PALLIASSE

pallet &c *la17-,* **pallat &c** *16-e18* ['palət; *Cai* 'peləd] *n* **1** *chf verse, contemptuous* the head, pate *16-19.* **2** a tadpole *20, Cai.* **3** a ball of any kind, *specif* the glass or metal float on a fishing net *19-, NE Fif Bwk.* [see SND]

palliasse &c *17-,* **palʒas &c** *16-e17,* **palleis &c** *la16-17;* **palʒeis &c** *16-e17* ['palɪəs, 'paljas; *(-j)es, *(-j)is, &c; *'pel-] *n* a straw mattress. [OF *paillasse &c,* f *paille* straw; adopted into Eng *18*]

pallie *see* PALIE[1], PALLALL, PALLAWA

pallion[1] **&c** ['paljən, 'pʌl-] *n* **1** = pallion, a cloak, mantle *la15.* **2** *chf in pl* rags, tatters, useless or worn-out clothing *19-e20.* **3** *fig* a big, gangling, raw-boned person, a rough, ungainly or worthless person, a scold *e20, NE.*

pallion[2] **&c** *16-e19,* **palʒoun &c** *la15-e17;* **pailʒoune &c** *la14-16,* **paulʒon &c** *e16* [*'paljun, *'pel-, *'pal-] *n* **1** (1) *in sing* a large and stately tent, a pavilion *la15-e19.* (2) *in pl* a tented camp; an army's lines *la14-e16.* **2** a flag or banner *la16.* [ME *palyon* f as PAVILION]

pallo *see* PELLOCK

palm[1] **&c** [pam, pɑm] *n* **1** = palm (of the hand) *15-.* **2** *transf* (1) the blade of an oar *e16.* (2) the hand of a clock *17-19, only Sc.* (3) the grippers or claws of a pair of tongs *19-, now Ork Uls.*

palm[2] **&c** [pɑm] *n* **1** = palm, the tree *15-.* **2** one of the various native trees or shrubs, *esp* the willow, used by Roman Catholics or Episcopalians to represent the palm on Palm Sunday; a sprig or branch of one of these trees *la14-, now local NE-Uls.*
~ **fair** an annual two-day fair formerly beginning on the fifth Monday in Lent *la16-18, SW.*
~ **tree** = *n* 1 and 2, *la14-16, e20.*

palmer &c, palmere &c; paumer &c *19-e20* ['pɑmər] *n* = palmer, a pilgrim *13-.* *vi* **1** walk about aimlessly, saunter *19-e20.* **2** move or walk clumsily and noisily, stamp around *la19-, now NE.*

palmie &c; pawmie &c *19-e20* ['pɑmɪ, 'pamɪ] *n* a stroke with a strap or cane on the palm of the hand as a punishment *la18-.* *vt* administer PALMIES to *19-e20.* [see SND]

palp *see* PAP[1]

palsify [*?'palsɪfaɪ] *vt, also fig* afflict with palsy, paralyse *la19*.

palt *see* PELT[1]

palȝardrie &c *la16*, **palȝardy** *16* [*'paljard(r)ɪ, *'pel-] *n* knavery; deception; treachery. [only *Sc*; F *paillardie*]

palȝas, palȝeis *see* PALLIASSE

palȝoun *see* PALLION[2]

pam &c [pam] *n* **1** = pam, the knave of clubs *e19*. **2** the knave of any other suit *19-, now Sh*.
pawmie ['pamɪ] = *n, 19-, now Sh*.

pament &c; paiment [*'pemənt] *n* paving; a pavement *16-17*.
vt pave *la16-e17*. [nME and northern eModEng; var of midl and s *pavement*; *cf* PAIUMENT]

pamphelet [*'pamf(ə)lɛt] *n* a woman of easy virtue *e16*. [only *Sc*; see DOST]

pan[1] *la15-*; **pane** *la14-17* [pan; *Loth also* pɑn] *n* **1** = pan, a cooking vessel *la14-*. **2** a similar container used to heat substances in nondomestic uses *la14-*. **3** *pl, freq in place-names* a group of salt pans or the site occupied by them; a salt works of this kind *la15-17*. **4** ? the bowl containing the fuel and wick of a lamp; ? a lamp *16*. **5** the skull, the cranium *19-, now Sh Bnf*. **6** a hard stratum lying below the soil which is impervious to moisture *la18-19*. **7** a conveyor in a coal or shale-mine *la20-, Fif wLoth*.
v **1** *vt* tie a pan or kettle to (*eg* a dog's tail), *esp* to make it go home *la19-, now Ork Ags*. **2** *vi, of soil* form into a PAN (*n* 6), become impervious to rain *la19-*.
pannie &c kindling, firewood *20-, now Kcdn EC* [shortened f *pan-wood*].
~ **bread** bread baked in a pan or tin *20*; *cf* ~ *loaf*. ~**cake 1** = *dropped scone* (SCONE) *20-*. **2** = pancake. ~ **coal** = *pan-wood, la18-19*. ~ **cratch &c** a precipitate of lime forming on the sides of salt pans, formerly used for rendering or *harling* (HARL[2]) walls *17-18*. ~**door &c** ['pan'dor] the entrance to or environs of a salt pan *la18*. ~**door &c oyster** *18, also* ~**door &c** *la18-19* a large succulent type of oyster found in the Forth, *esp* around Prestonpans. ~ **drop &c** a round peppermint sweet, a mint imperial *la19-*. ~ **haggis** oatmeal, sometimes mixed with scraps of meat etc, and fried in fat, *skirlie* (SKIRL[1]) *la20-, Ayr Kcb Rox*. ~**-jotral(s) &c 1** a dish made from the offal of slaughtered animals; odds and ends of food; left-overs *19-, now Mry Bnf Slk*. **2** a type of cake made from scraps of other cakes or the scrapings of the baker's board with the addition of fruit *20, Abd*. ~ **loaf 1** a loaf with a hard smooth crust, baked in a pan or tin *la19-*. **2** *fig* an affected, ultra-refined way of speaking adopted to impress others *20-, Gen except Sh Ork* [so called because the *pan loaf* was more expensive than the *plain loaf* (PLAIN)]. ~ **scone** = ~*cake* 1,

la20-, chf Dmf. ~**-wood &c** *only Sc* **1** small coal or DROSS, *chf* used as the fuel of salt pans *16-e20, latterly hist*. **2** a measure of coal or DROSS used as such *la17*.

clerk of the pannis [panz] *appar* a person who kept a record of some part of the royal household expenditure *la15-e16*. **knock one's ~ out** *or* **in** work very hard, exert oneself to the point of exhaustion *20-, C*.

pan[2] **&c** *n* one of a number of horizontal timbers fixed to the COUPLES of a roof and running at right angles to them, a purlin *16-, now Dmf*.
vi, chf in phrs, eg ~ **and ruif** build a roof *la15-17*.
~ **tree &c** = *n, la16-18*. [ME *panne* a wall plate, F *panne*, MedL *panna &c*]

pan *see* PAIN

panche *see* PAINCH

pand *la16-*; **pawn &c** *la17-e20* [pan(d); *EC, WC* pɑn(d)] *n* a flounce draping the legs of a bed, *orig* also the canopy above it, a valance. [only *Sc*; *appar* f OF *pandre*, L *pendēre* hang, perh w *infl* f OF *pan*, Eng *pane* a piece of cloth, counterpane]

pand *see* PAWN

pander &c ['pandər; *WC* 'pɑn(d)ər] *vi* wander about aimlessly, drift around in an idle purposeless way *19-, now Dmf Rox*. [perh conflation of PALMER w Eng *wander*]

pandie &c *n* a stroke with a cane etc on the palm of the hand, a beating, *esp* from a schoolmaster *19-*.
vti beat on the palm of the hand with a cane etc; punish *la19-, local NE-Uls*.
get a ~ *or* ~**s** be beaten with a cane etc *19-e20*. [*chf Sc*; L *pande* (*palmam, manum*) stretch out (your hand)]

pane *see* PAN[1]

panel &c, pannell &c *la16-, now rare, only law*; **pannall &c** *16-e18 n, law* **1** the place of arraignment in a court, the dock, the bar *18-19*. **2** a prisoner or (*formerly also*) a group of prisoners at the bar of the court, the accused *la16-*.
vt, chf in passive be brought to trial, be indicted *la16-e19*.
enter in *or* **on** ~ present for trial *la16-e17*. **put** *or* **set** (**up**)**on** (**the** *or* **ane**) ~ arraign, try *16-e17*. [only *Sc*; obscure; see DOST]

panetar &c [*'panɪtər] *n* the officer of a household in charge of the pantry *la14-16*. [ME *paneter*, OF *panetier*; *cf* PANTRÉ]

pang *vt* **1** pack (a receptacle) tight, cram full, stuff *17-, Gen except Sh Ork*. **2** cram (the stomach) with food, gorge *17-, now NE*. **3** *chf in adj* ~**ed &c** pressed together, packed closely side by side *19-e20*.
adj completely filled, full to overflowing; crammed with food *la16-20*.
~ **f(o)u** *19-, now NE wLoth Uls*, ~**'d-fu &c** *19-e20* stuffed, full to overflowing. [uncertain]

pani &c ['panɪ] *n* water; rain *20-*, *Rox*. [gipsy *pani*, Hindi *pani, panee*, Sanskrit *pānīya* water, liquid]

panitrie *see* PANTRÉ

pannall *see* PANEL

pannell &c *n* **1** = panel *la15-e17*. **2** a rectangular pane of glass in a mullioned window *16-e17*. **3** a prefabricated section of wooden walling making up part of the external wall, *eg* of a house *la16-e17*.

~**ing** (wooden) panels or panel-work *17*.

pannell *see* PANEL

pannoun &c *n* a pennon *la15*. [only *Sc*; OF]

pans &c [*pans] *n* = paunce, a piece of armour to protect the belly or abdomen *15-e17*.

panse &c, **pans** [*pans] *v* **1** *vt* think about, *usu* deeply or seriously, reflect on, consider *16-17*. **2** *vi* (1) think, ponder, meditate *la15-e17*. (2) *chf in negative or implied negative* pay no heed, not care *la16-e17*. **3** *vt* care for (a person) medically or surgically *la16-17*. **4** dress (a wound) *la16-e18*. [only *Sc*; OF *panser* take thought for, take care of, treat (the sick, wounds); *cf* PENSE¹]

panshit &c; **panshine** &c ['panʃɪt, -ʃait, -ʃəin; *Sh also* 'panʃəd] *n* a state of excitement, panic, muddle *19-*, *now NE*. [see SND]

pansive &c *adj* = pensive *16-e17*.

pant¹ *n, also* ~**-well** *19-20* (the mouth of) a public well, fountain etc *18-20*, *Bwk S*. [appar f nEng dial = a well, pool]

pant² *n* a prank, a 'lark', a piece of fun *la19-*, *now C, S*. [reduced f Eng *pantomime*]

pant *see* POINT

pantin &c *la19-e20*, *Sh*, **pantoun** &c *la15-17 n* a kind of soft shoe, a slipper. [perh related to obs Eng *pantofle*]

pantré *la14-e16*; **panitrie** &c *16-e17*, **pantry** &c *15-* [pantrɪ; *pan̩ɪtrɪ] *n* = pantry *la14-*.

~**man** a man in charge of or employed in a pantry *16-e17*, only *Sc*. [*panitrie* &c is sometimes misread as *paintrie* &c]

pan-velvot &c *n* a fabric similar to velvet but with a longer nap, plush *la16-e17*. [F *panne* (*de velours*)]

panȝell &c [*'panjəl] *n* = pannier, a large basket *15*.

paon *see* POWN

pap¹; **pape** &c *la14-17*, **palp** *la15-e17*, **paup** &c *la15-16* [pap, pɑp; *pep] *n* **1** = pap, a teat or nipple *la14-*. **2** one of the teats of an animal *la15-17*. **3** *also* ~ **glas** *or* glas ~ ? some kind of artificial teat made of glass *la16-e17*. **4** the uvula *17-*, *chf* ~ **o the** *or* **one's hause** *18-*, *now C, S*, ~ **o the throat** *la20-*, *Cai NE*. **5** *chf in place-names* a conical hill *la15-*. **6** one of the segments of an orange *20-*, *NE*. **7** the sea anemone *18-*, *now Kcdn Fif*.

~**-bairn** a child at the breast, a suckling *la18-19*. ~**-milk** breast-milk *la19-*, *now Sh*.

pap² &c *n* **1** = pap, a soft semi-liquid substance. **2** *weaving* a paste or dressing, *eg* of flour and water, used to give body to a web *19-e20*.

pappin &c = *n* 2, *19-e20, S*.

pap³ &c *la18-*; **pop** *vti* **1** = pop. **2** *vt and vi* ~ **on** touch or strike lightly and smartly, tap, rap *18-*, *now NE Ags Loth*. **3** *vt* beat, thrash *19-e20*. **4** (1) aim (an object), throw, shoot (a missile) *18-*, *now NE, C*. (2) strike with a missile, pelt *la19-*, *now Ags*. **5** *vi* fall or drop with a quick, light sound, 'plop' *la18-19*.

n a tap, rap; a swift blow *19-20*.

pappin a whipping, drubbing *la19*.

~**-in** a drink made of light ale and oatmeal with a small quantity of WHISKY or brandy added *18-19*.

pap⁴ &c *vt* sound (the horn of a car, *esp* of the rubber-balled sort), toot *20*, *NE Ags*. [imit]

paparap &c [*?'papərəp] *n* a device consisting of three hooks lashed together and fastened to a weighted string, used in poaching to draw a line out of a river *19-e20*, *Mry*. [perh f PAP³, *ie* 'a popper up']

pape *see* PAIP², PAP¹

papejay &c [*'pep'dʒe, &c] *n* the parrot *la15-17*. [eME *papeiai*, thereafter appar only northern; *cf* PAPINGA(Y) and PAPINGO]

paper &c; **peper** &c *16-19*, **peyper** &c *16-e20*, **paiper** &c *la16-17*, **peaper** *17-e18* ['pepər, 'pɛpər, 'pɪpər; *'pɑp-] *n* **1** = paper *la14-*. **2** *freq* **the** ~ the manuscript of a sermon *18-*; see ~ *minister*. **3** a printed proclamation or notice *la19-*, *now Sh*.

vt set down on paper for publication, issue a bill or insert a notice in a newspaper concerning (a person or thing, *eg* repudiation of a spouse's debts) *la19-*, *now local NE-Kcb*.

~ **minister** *or* **priest** *derog* a MINISTER or priest who read his sermon; this was looked on as a sign of a lack of inspiration or real conviction *la18-19*. ~ **note** a (one-pound) banknote *la19-*, *now Sh Ork Cai Bnf*. ~ **pound** a one-pound note *la19-*, *now Ork Cai*.

papingo &c; **pepingo** &c *17-e19* ['papɪŋgo; *'pep-; &c] *n* **1** *also* **papingay** &c *16* a parrot *16-*, *latterly arch, hist, literary or as a heraldic device*. **2** a representation of a parrot used as a target in archery *la16-*, *now Ayr*. [Sc vars of ME *papengay* a popinjay; *cf* PAPEJAY]

pappin *see* PAP², PAP³

papple¹ &c *18-*; **popule** *15-16, only Sc*, **popill** *16-17 vi* **1** *also fig* = popple, flow, bubble up *15-*, *now Abd Loth*. **2** *of fat in cooking* sizzle, sputter *19-*, *local Mry-Wgt*. **3** *of persons* stream with perspiration, be too hot; be extremely excited *19-*.

n **1** ? a swelling or bulge like, or caused by, a bubble *e17*. **2** a bubble, as in a cooking pot *e19*. [OED *popple*]

papple² &c *n* = popple, the corn-cockle or corn-campion *18-19*.

parade *see* PARAWD

paraffin *n* **1** = paraffin. **2** *slang* a smart, flashy appearance, *esp* in dress, a 'get-up' *20*.

paraffle &c [*?pə'rafl] *n* a flourish, an ostentatious display *e19*. [only Sc; f F *parafe* &c a flourish added to a signature]

parage &c [*pa'redʒ] *n* **1** = parage, (noble) lineage *la15-e16*. **2** equality in rank *16*.

parale &c [*'parəl] *vt*, *fig* equip or array **with** *la15*.

paraling &c, **per(r)aling** &c [*'parəlıŋ] **1** equipping, fitting out; equipment, furniture *la15-e17*. **2** an ornamental trimming for a vestment or for clothing generally *la16-e17*. **3** ? a wall decoration; a wall-hanging *la15-e16*. [ME *parail* &c, aphetic f *apparel*]

paraphernal &c [*parəfər'nal, *-'nal] *n*, *usu in pl* the personal effects of a married woman, which remained her own property after her marriage *19*. [noun usage of Eng *paraphernal* pertaining to a married woman's personal property]

paraphrase &c *n* **1** = paraphrase. **2** *Presbyterian Church* one of a collection of metrical versions of scriptural passages, collected and prepared by a Committee of the *General Assembly* (GENERAL) for congregational singing, adopted in 1781 and now printed with the metrical PSALMS at the end of the Scottish Bible *18-*.

parawd &c *la19-*, **parade** &c [pə'rad] *n* **1** = parade. **2** a procession, march, *esp* one in support of a political object, cause etc *la17-*, *now Ayr* [also US and now entering St Eng].

parbruilyeid &c, **perbrouilʒeit** &c [*par'brøljıd, *?-'bru(ı)ljıt] *adj* besmeared; confused, disordered *la16*. [only Sc; var of ptp of *barbulʒe* (BARBULYIE)]

parcage &c *n*, *only in documents concerning* BORDER *disputes* the act of enclosing stray cattle or sheep; the fine payable to obtain their release *la15-16*. [OF *parcage*, f *parc* a pound or enclosure]

parcel *see* PAIRCEL

parch &c *la17-e19*, **perch** &c [pɛrtʃ; *partʃ] *n* **1** = perch, a pole set up in a sea-way to guide navigation *17*. **2** piles of stones used for this purpose in the Firth of Clyde *18-e20*.

parchment &c; **perchment** *la16-17* ['partʃmənt; *'per(t)ʃ-, *'pɛrtʃ-, &c] *n* **1** = parchment *la15-*. **2** *orig* a parchment certificate issued to a qualified teacher in a state school on which comments on his proficiency were annually recorded by the School Inspectorate and which served as an authorization to teach; *latterly* a certificate given to a qualified teacher on satisfactory completion of a two-year probation period *19-20*.

parcial *see* PAIRCEL

parcionar &c [*'parsıonər, *'parʃ(ı)onər] *n* a joint-owner, joint-heir *la15-e16*. [only Sc; MedL *partionarius*; *cf* Eng *parcener*]

pardoos &c [pər'dus] *n* a thump; a resounding blow, whack; a violent fall *la19-*, *now Sh*. [*per-* + DOOSE]

pare &c *vt* = pare *la14-*.

pairin-meal, -flour a coarse meal or flour made from the husks of the grain *19*.

~ **and burn** burn the top layer of turf cut from a field before ploughing, for use as manure *18-e19*.

pareeshioner, pareis *see* PAIRISH

Pareis *see* PARIS

paremptour *see* PEREMPTOR

pargen [*'pardʒən] *vt* ? cover or daub with plaster, plaster *16*.

~**ar** a plasterer *16*. [ME *parget*; *cf* SPARGEN]

parify &c [*'parıfaı] *vt* represent as equal, equate, compare *e15*. [OF *parifier*, MedL *parificare*; *cf* eModEng]

parioch *see* PAIRISH

Paris &c; **Pareis** *16-e17*, **Pairis** *la19-* ['parıs, 'pɛrıs] = Paris *la15-*.
Pairiser = *Pa(i)ris bun*, *la19-*. **Parisian barm** flour, malt and water stocked or stored with mature or old barm and used as a medium for the growth of yeast *e20*.

~ **black** &c a kind of cloth *16-e17*. **Pa(i)ris bun** a sweet, sugar-topped, sponge-like bun *20-*.

parische, parise, parish *see* PAIRISH

park &c; **pairk** *16-e20*, **perk** &c *16-e20* [park, perk; *Bwk Rox* pɛrk] *n* **1** = park, an enclosed piece of land *12-*. **2** an area of enclosed farmground, a field *la16-*.
vt **1** = park, enclose (forest etc) (**with** a wall or ditch), form (land) into fields etc *16-*, *now Sh*. **2** lodge (troops) in a camp or fortification *e16*. **3** rear (animals) in a field or enclosure instead of on free range *la18-*, *now Sh*.

~**ie** *child's word* a park-keeper or attendant *20-*, *EC, WC*.

~**-dyke** a field wall *16-e19*. ~**-lamb**, ~**-sheep** a lamb or sheep reared in a field as opposed to moorland pasture *19-*, *now Cai*.

parkes &c [*parks] *n pl* the Fates *la16*. [only Sc; L *Parcae*]

parkin; perkin *n* a hard, round, ginger-flavoured biscuit made of oatmeal, flour and treacle, with an almond in the centre *la19-*. [unknown]

parleis *see* PAIRLS

parlesy &c [*'parləsı] *n* palsy *la14-16*. [nME; reduced f ME *paralisie*]

parlet *see* PATLET

parley, parlie &c *n* **1** = parley *17-*. **2** *games* a state of neutrality, a period of truce, respite; *interj* the call for such a truce etc *18-*, *now Bnf Ags*. [*cf barley* (BIRLIE)]

parliament[1]; **perlament** &c *la15-16*, **pairlament** &c *la16-17* ['parləmənt; *'parlı(ə)mɛnt, *'perl-] *n* = parliament *la14-*. *vi* attend Parliament *la18*.

~**ary** = parliamentary. ~**ary church** *or* **parish** one of a number of QUOAD SACRA churches or their parishes, *esp* in the *Highlands and Islands* (HIELAND), created by Acts of Parliament in 1810 and 1824, *19-20*, *latterly hist*.

~ary road a road built and maintained jointly by the government and local landowners under the *Highland* Roads and Bridges Act of 1803, *19.* **P~ary school** a school in one of the *parliamentary parishes* in the *Highlands,* supported by State aid *19-e20.* ~**er &c** a member of Parliament *la17-,* now *Sh.* ~**in(g)** a discussion, conversation, parley *la16-e19.*

P~ Hall the hall of *Parliament House* which was the meeting place of the Scottish Parliament from 1639 to 1707 and which later became the ante-room to the *Court of Session* (SESSION); *also* applied to apartments in Edinburgh and Stirling Castles where the medieval Scottish Parliament met. **P~ House** the building in the High Street of Edinburgh where the Scottish Parliament met; *now* the *Court of Session, la16-.* ~ **man** a member of Parliament *17-e19.*

parliament² [*?'parl(ə)mɛnt] *n* some part of a cloak or gown, *perh* a facing *e16.* [? f rare Eng *apparelment*]

parlie &c *n* a crisp, rectangular, ginger biscuit *19-20.* [only Sc; shortened f Eng *parliament-cake*]

parlie *see* PARLEY

paroche, parochial *see* PAIRISH

parochy &c [*'parotʃɪ] *n* a parish *15-16.* [only Sc; MF *parochie,* laL *parochia*]

parokett &c *n* a parrot *16-17.* [OF *paroquet*]

parpall *see* PAIRPLE

parpen &c *la16-,* **parpan &c** *la15-19 n* **1** *building* a stone which passes through the entire thickness of a wall *la15-20.* **2** (1) = ~ *wall, la16-e17.* (2) the parapet of a bridge *19-e20. adj, of a door, window-frame etc* in exact alignment, true, exactly parallel or perpendicular *la19-,* now *NE.*

~ **wall** a thin wall (? *orig* of PARPEN stones) used as a partition; a partition wall of any material *16-17.* [ME *perpoynt, perpend,* OF *parpaigne*]

parplait *see* PATLET

parquere *see* PERQUEER

parr &c *n* a young salmon with dark stripes on its side, at the stage before it becomes a *smolt* (SMOWT¹) *la18-.* [earlier in Sc; unknown]

parrat *see* PARROT

parreck *see* PARROCK

parritch &c; parridge *la18-e20,* **porritch** *la18,* **porridge** *n, formerly freq treated as a pl* = porridge, the dish of oatmeal (or rolled oats) boiled in salted water; *freq* food *in gen,* one's sustenance, daily bread *la18-.*

parritch cap a wooden porridge-bowl *la18-e19.* ~ **spurtle** *la18-,* ~ **stick** *19-e20* a stick used for stirring porridge.

as plain as ~ self-evident, as clear as crystal *la18-e20.* **auld claes an** ~ one's usual daily routine, the daily grind *la19-.* **keep** or **save one's breath to cool one's** ~ save one's breath; hold one's tongue, *usu in imperative* mind your own business!, shut up! *19-.*

parrock &c; parreck &c *19-e20,* **parroch &c** *19-e20* ['parək, -əx] *n* **1** (1) *also* **parrok** *la13* a small enclosure or pen *la13, 19-e20.* (2) *specif* a pen in which a sheep is familiarized with a strange or neglected lamb *19-,* now *SW, S.* **2** a group of people, animals or things closely packed or huddled together *19-20, NE Ags.* *vt* confine (animals etc) in a PARROCK, enclose, herd together (*specif* a ewe with a lamb it is intended she should foster) *la18-e20.* [OE *pearroc* a fence or enclosure]

parrot &c, parrat &c *e17 n* = *parrot coal, 17-20.*

~ **coal** *18-, Kcdn C Rox,* **parrat coll &c** *la16-e17* a highly volatile bituminous coal which ignites easily and burns with a clear bright flame and a crackling sound. [uncertain]

parry &c *vti* **1** = parry. **2** *vi* trifle, waste time, dawdle or delay in order to avoid action *la19-,* now *Lnk.* **3** meddle or tamper **with,** have dealings or occupy oneself **with** *19-,* now *Fif wLoth.*

parrymauk &c ['parɪ'm(j)ɑk, 'pɪrɪ-] *n* an exact replica, the very same, the 'living image' *e20, Abd.* [? f Eng *par, peer* equal + MAKE]

parsell *see* PERSEL

parsment *see* PARTIMENT

parson &c *n* **1** = parson *la15-.* **2** a person *16-e17.*

~ **gray** a dark shade of grey, 'clerical grey' *19-.* [*cf* PERSON]

parsonage &c *n* **1** *also* **personage** *15-e18* = parsonage *la15-.* **2** = *parsonage teinds* (TEIND) *la15-,* now *hist.*

parson hoop *see* PASS²

part *see* PAIRT, PERT

partan &c *n* **1** the common edible crab *15-.* **2** *term of abuse* an ugly, bad-tempered or stupid person, *freq* ~**-face(d)** *la19-,* now *Bnf Ags Fif.*

~**('s) cairt(ie)** a toy cart made from a crab's shell and pulled along on a string *la19-,* now *Ork Bnf.* ~ **pie** a dish of seasoned crab meat cooked and served in the shell *18-e19.* ~**('s) ta(e)** the claw of a crab *16-e20.* ~**-taed** having a pigeon-toed gait like a crab *la20-, Sh-Ags.* **as fu as a** ~ brimful, full to the top *la19-, Ork Bnf Abd.* [Gael *partan* a small crab]

partclaith &c; pairtclaith [*'pert'kleθ, &c*] *n* = PATLET *la16-e17.* [only Sc; var of Eng *partlet* w the final syllable altered to CLAITH; *cf* PATECLATHE]

parteeklar *see* PARTICULAR

partial &c *adj* = partial *la15-.*

~ **counsel &c** *n, law* advice, information etc given improperly to a witness in a case by a judge, juror, witness or other member of the court and constituting a ground for excluding his evidence as biased *la15-19; cf* PURGE.

partial *see* PAIRCEL

partibus ['partɪbʌs] *n, law* a note written in the margin of a *Court of Session* (SESSION) summons listing the contestants in a case and their counsel and solicitors *18-*. [only Sc; L = the parties being]

particate, particat &c *n* a square measure of land consisting of ¼ of a *Scots acre* (SCOTS) *la15-18*.

~ **man** the owner or tenant of a PARTICATE of land *18-19*, *Rox, latterly hist*. [only Sc; MedL *perticata, particata* an *orig* linear measure of land common in charters, L *pertica* a measuring rod, a perch, the area of land so measured]

particular &c; **perticular** &c *15-19*, **parteeklar** &c *la19-*, *now Sh* [pər'tɪklər, -'tɪk(ɪ)lər, &c; *Sh also* -'tɪkwɪlər; *per-; *-'tɪkølər, &c] *adj* **1** = particular *15-*. **2** private, confidential *15-*, *now Sh-N Loth*. **3** remarkable, worthy of note, exceptional; odd, peculiar *16-*, *now Ork Ags*. **4** clean, hygenic, *esp* in cooking *20-*, *local*.
adv particularly, markedly, especially *la19-*.
n = particular *la15-*.
~**ie** &c = particularly, individually *la15-e17*, *only Sc*. ~**ity** &c [*par'tɪkølarɪtɪ, *-'tɪkwɪlarɪtɪ, &c] **1** = particularity *la16-*. **2** (an instance of) self-interest, private advantage; a private grievance or feud *16-e17*, *only Sc*. **3** a personal or private trait or characteristic, an idiosyncrasy; a detail, particular *la18-*, *now Sh Ags*.

particule ['partɪkøl] *n* a small part of anything, a detail, particle *16-e18*. [eModEng (once), F *particule*, L *particula*]

partie *see* PAIRTY

partiment &c, **parsment** &c *n* a division; a company *e16*. [MedL *partimentum* a division; *cf* eModEng = a constituent part]

partinence *see* PERTINENCE

partinere *see* PAIRTNER

partisan &c ['partɪzan, *-ən, &c] *n* = partisan, a long-handled spear *17*.
~ **staff** &c = *n*, *17*, *only Sc*.

partising &c *la14-e17*; **pairtissing** &c *la16* [*'partɪsɪŋ, *'pert-, &c] *n* **1** a formal division (of land, goods etc) into shares or portions *la14-e17*. **2** *law* a legal separation or divorce *la15-e17*. [only Sc; OF *partison* &c partition, separation, w verbal noun ending]

partle *vti* waste (time), work in a half-hearted way, trifle *la18-20*. [prob a var of nEng *pawtle, po(w)tle*, frequentative of PAWT]

partnery *see* PAIRTNER

partridge, partrik *see* PAITRICK

pas *see* PAISE, PASS²

Pas *see* PACE

pasalm *see* PSALM

Pasce, Pasche *see* PACE

pascioune *see* PASSION

pase &c [*pes] *n* pasteboard *la16*. [only Sc; shortened f next]

paseburde &c [*'pes'børd, *-'brod, &c] *n* = pasteboard *17*.

pash *n*, *joc* the head, 'nut' *la7-19*. [unknown]

pasiment *see* PASSMENT

Pask *see* PACE

pasment, pasmont *see* PASSMENT

pasneip &c *n* = parsnip *la16-e18*.

pasper &c *la17-e19*, *Gall*, **paspier** &c *17*, *SW* [*'paspər, *-pir] *n* the plant samphire. [F *passe-pierre*, var of *perce-pierre* literally 'pierce-stone', samphire, saxifrage etc; *cf* obs Eng *percepier*]

paspie *n* = prec *la16-17*. [reduced form]

paspier *see* PASPER

paspyll &c [*'pas'pøil] *n* a kind of ornamental trimming or facing on a garment *e17*. [only Sc; F *passpoil*]

pass¹, pace &c; **pais** &c *15-17* [pas, pes] *n* **1** = pace, a step *la14-*. **2** a predicament; a critical position, a certain point (in an affair) *15-16*. **3** an indoor passage or corridor *la18-*, *now Uls*; *specif* (1) the passage between the pews in a church, an aisle *la19-*, *now NE*; (2) a passage between looms in a weaving shop or machines in a factory; a team of weavers etc *la18-*, *now Renfr Ayr*. **4** the ~ (of Calies &c) the Straits of Dover *16*, *only Sc* [F *pas de Calais*].
vti = pace *15-*.

pass² &c, **pas** &c *la14-e18* [pas] *vti* **1** = pass *la14-*. **2** *vi, of a route, boundary etc* lead, run (from one place to another) *15-e17*. **3** *vt, chf of persons* surpass, excel *la14-17*. **4** *vi, of an action, activity etc* take place, happen *la14-e17*. **5** *of an inquiry or decision* take place; be put into effect *la15-17*. **6** *of a legal grant, award etc* be issued *la15-e17*. **7** *chf* ~ (**up**)**on** serve or sit on a jury, inquest etc *15-e20*. **8** *vt* issue, give effect to, execute (a grant, warrant etc) *la14-17*. **9** *vi, of a criminal or a crime* go unpunished *15-17*. **10** *vt, freq of a judicial body* let (someone) off all or part of a penalty, obligation etc; remit (a punishment) *la17-19*. **11** overlook, disregard *la16-e19*. **12** give up, abandon *18-e20*.
n = pass *la15-*.
~**er** *20-*, *NE Gsw*, **parson hoop** *20-*, *NE* [f *passin(g) hoop*] a large iron hoop for holding the staves of a barrel in position during construction. ~**ing** &c *adj* **1** = passing *la15-*. **2** *of money* legally current *la17*, *only Sc*. **burn-** etc ~**ing** the act of crossing a burn etc; a crossing-place; the right to cross *15-17*. ~**it by** gone by, at an end, finished *15-16*.
~**-gilt** &c money acceptable as currency *la17*, *only Sc*. ~**-key** a key for opening a particular lock *17-*. ~**-lock** one of a set of locks which can be opened by the same key(s) *17-e18*, *only Sc*.
it ~**es me** etc it is beyond my etc comprehension, 'it beats me' *la19-*, *local*. ~ (**ap**)**on** **1** *of an adjudicator etc* = pass upon, proceed to give judgment on *la15-e17*. **2** *of a grant, award or decree* be issued or given effect concerning *la15-17*. **3** make an attack on *16*. ~ **to assise** *or* **probation** *of an accused person or a legal issue* go for trial or adjudication *la16-17*. ~ **doun** *or* **to** *of the sun or moon* set, go down *la16*.

~ **fra &c** give up, renounce, abandon (a right, obligation etc) *15-17, chf Sc.* ~ **the irnis &c** *of an issue of coins* be struck and put into circulation *la16-17.* ~ **our &c** *vi* **1** = pass over, cross a stretch of water *15-16.* **2** *of time or an occasion* run its course *la15.* ~**-ower &c** *n* an intentional omission, something quickly passed over or ignored, *esp* because it is not understood *19-, now Abd Ags Uls.* ~ **(under) the great, privy** *etc* **seal** undergo the process of authentication required for royal grants, deeds etc *la16-17.* ~ **water** *mining, of a bucket* leak *la19-, now Fif.*

passage &c *n* **1** = passage *la14-.* **2** a military or naval expedition *la15-e16.* **3** an unimpeded flow (of water etc) *16.* **4** a water-course, gutter, conduit *16-17.* **5** an enclosed passage in a building or underground; a corridor or a tunnel *la15-.* **6** *of money* the fact of passing current or being generally acceptable; currency *la15-17.*
lang &c ~ prolonged time, long distance *la15-e16.*

passager *see* PASSENGER
passement *see* PASSMENT
passenger *17-,* **passinger &c** *16-17,* **passager &c** *17* ['pasɪndʒər; *'pasedʒər] *n* **1** = passenger *16-.* **2** a (passing) traveller, a passer-by *16-19.*

passion *la15-,* **passioun &c** *la14-17;* **pascioune &c** *la15-e16,* **patients** *19-e20,* **patience** *la19-, local* ['paʃən, 'peʃənt, -ən(t)s; *'paʃən] *n* = passion *la14-.*
ma patience! *exclam* expressing wonder, disbelief, exasperation etc *la19-, local.* **passioun(is) of dede** *15-16,* **patient(s) o deed** *or* **death** *19-e20* the death throes, the last agonies.

passit *see* PAST
passive &c *adj* **1** = passive *15-.* **2** *law, of an heir etc* liable for the debts of an estate *la16-e17, only Sc.*
~ **debt** *law* a debt owed to another *e18, only Sc.*
~ **title** the title or right of possession to an inherited estate which carries with it liability for the debts of the granter *la17-, only Sc.*

passment *18-e19,* **pasment** *la16-e20,* **pasiment &c** *la16;* **pasmont &c** *e16,* **pesment &c** *la16-e19,* **pessiment &c** *la16-19,* **passement** *la16-19* [*'pas(ə)mənt, *'pes(ɪ)-, *'pɛs(ə)-, &c] *n, usu in pl, also fig* passement, decorative edging, *esp* of gold, silver or silk *16-e20, latterly literary.*
pasmentar &c a passement-weaver or -worker *la16, only Sc.* ~**ed &c** trimmed or edged with passements *16-19.* [eModEng, F *passement*]

past *la15-,* **passit** *15* *prep* = past, beyond *15-.* *adv* **1** = past. **2** on one side, out of the way; over, done with *19-.* *adj* **1** = past. **2** *after a date, month etc* last, preceding *20-:* '*I haena seen him this year past*'. **3** having reached a specified age on one's last birthday *20-:* '*Wee Bob's nine past*'.
lay, put, set *etc* ~ put away, set aside for later use; put aside for a rainy day *19-.* **not to (be able to) see** ~ **someone** be obsessed with someone's virtues or merits, favour someone to the exclusion of all others *la20-.* ~ **a'** unspeakable, beyond belief, intolerable *la19-, now Sh Cai.* ~ **ordinar** outstanding, remarkable, exceptional *19-, now Uls.* **pit** ~ *vt* put (a person) off something *la19-.* *n* **pit-**~ **&c** a hasty or makeshift meal, a quick snack *la20-, Gen except Sh Ork.*

paster[1] **&c** *19-,* **pasture &c** *16-18* ['pastər, 'pɛstər, 'pɛstər; *Loth* 'pɛstjər] *n* the pastern. [ME *pastour,* F *pâture,* OF *pasture* grassland, pasture, *later* the clog by which a grazing horse is tethered by the pastern]

paster[2] *18-20,* **pasture &c** *n, vti* = pasture *la14-.*

pasturage &c **1** = pasturage *16-.* **2** *law* the SERVITUDE right of pasturing animals on another's land *la16-.* **pasturall &c** pasture land; grazing *la16, only Sc.*

pasvelour &c [*'pasvə'lur] *adj* ? velvety in texture, ? purple *la16-e17.* [eModEng *passeuelours,* F *passe-velours* the plant amaranth]

pasvoland &c [*'pasvo'land, *-'volən(d), *-'volənt] *n* = passe-volant, a type of small cannon *16.*

pat &c *la17-19,* **pate** *la17- n* = pate, the head.
pat *see* PIT[1], POT
pate *see* PAT, PEAT[1]

pateclathe &c [*'petkleθ] *n* = PATLET *la16-e17.* [only Sc; var of *patelet* (PATLET) w the final syllable altered to *clathe* (CLAITH); *cf* PARTCLAITH]
patelet *see* PATLET

patent &c ['petənt; *Loth also* *'pɑ-] *adj* **1** = patent, evident *la15-.* **2** *of a doorway etc* wide, unobstructed, open *la15-e19.* **3** *of premises, a route, document etc* open to all, generally accessible, public *16-e19, chf Sc.* **4** open, accessible, exposed *la15-17.* **5** exposed or liable (to harm) *16.*
make ~ **doors** *law, of a messenger-at-arms in a poinding* (POIND) *action* force a *lockfast* (LOCK[1]) place with the authority of a warrant *la16-e18.*
the most ~ **door** *of a church etc* the main door, that at which public proclamations were made *la16-19.*

patentar &c [*'petəntər] *n* a patentee, a person to whom a patent has been granted *17.* [only Sc; f Eng *patent* a document conferring a privilege, right etc]

patesar *see* PATISAR
path *see* PETH
pathe &c [*peð] *vt, chf in ptp, also fig* paved *16-e19.*
~**ment &c** pavement *la14-, now Ags, only Sc.* [SND *peth*]

patie &c ['petɪ] *n* the puffin *19-, Ayr.* [dim of *Peter* or *Patrick*]

patience *see* PASSION
patient *see* PACIENT

patients see PASSION

patill see PATTLE

patisar &c *la16-e17*, **potissar &c** *la16*; **patesar &c** *16* [*'patɪsər, &c; *?'pot-, *-ɪʃər] *n* a pastry-cook *la16-e17*.

patisserie &c, potissarie &c pastries *la16*. [only Sc; F *pâtissier*]

patlet *16-e18*, **patelet &c** *16-17*, **parlet &c** *e16*, **parplait &c** *e16* [*'patlət, *pet-, *'par(t)-, *'per(t)-, *'parplet] *n* a partlet, a covering for the neck worn by women. [northern eModEng *patlett*; MF *patelette* a band of stuff]

Patrickmes &c [*'patrɪk'mɛs] *n* **1** the feast of St Patrick, 17 Mar *la15-e18*, *chf WC, SW*. **2** the date of one of the annual fairs in Dumbarton *17*. [only Sc; *Patrick* + MESS²; *cf* LUKISMES]

patrik see PAITRICK

patrimonial &c *adj* **1** constituting part of the patrimony of a bishopric *17*. **2** *law* referring to property or money, pecuniary *la18-*. [*cf* Eng, referring to inherited wealth]

patrocine &c *n* patronage *la16-e17*. [only Sc; F]

patron &c, patroune &c; pawtron *19* ['petrən, 'patrən] *n* = patron *15-*.

patron see PAITTERN, PATROUNE

patrontash &c, patrontasche &c [*'patrən'taʃ, &c] *n* a pouch or case for holding cartridges and other ammunition *la17-e18*. [only Sc; Du *patroontasch*, Ger *patronentasche*]

patroune &c; patron [*pa'trun, *'patrən] *n* a paper container for the charge of a cannon or pistol; a (paper) cartridge *16-17*. [only Sc; MLowGer *patrone* a paper cartridge-case; *cf* prec]

patroune see PAITTERN, PATRON

patruell &c *n* a paternal first cousin *e16*. [eModEng *patruel*; L *patruēlis*]

patt see POT

patter *vt* trample (ground etc), beat down by constant treading *la19-*, now *Bnf*. [only Sc; perh a frequentative of PAWT w infl f Eng *pat* beat gently]

patter see PAITER

pattern see PAITTERN

pattle &c *17-*, **patill &c** *la14-16*; **pettle &c** *la18-20* ['patl, 'petl; *'petl] *n* a small spade-like tool, used *esp* for clearing the mould-board of a plough *la14-20*.

vi poke or dabble idly in some substance *la19-*, now *Sh Ork*.

~ing &c scraping clean with, or as with, a PATTLE *la16*. [nME *pattyl*; appar irreg var of Eng *paddle*; *cf* PAIDLE²]

pauchle¹ &c *19-*, **pakkald &c** *16-17*; **pechle &c** *e19*, **pochle &c** *20-* [*C, S* 'paxl, 'pakl, *'pexl; *'pakəld, *'pakl] *n* **1** a bundle, a small load (of goods or merchandise); the personal belongings of someone in service and living away from home, *usu* as kept in a trunk etc *16-*, now *Per Fif eLoth*. **2** a small bundle or parcel of something, a quantity of something; *now specif* a

small quantity of something taken by an employee from his employer, either furtively or as a perquisite *la16-*, now *local Per-Slk*. **3** a packet (of letters) *16-e17*. **4** a swindle, a piece of trickery, a 'fiddle' *la20-*, *Per WC*.

vti **1** be guilty of a minor dishonesty, cheat; *specif* 'rig' (an election etc) *20-*, *local C*. **2** *vt* steal, embezzle, pocket *la20-*, *C, S*. **3** shuffle (playing cards) *20-*, *Lnk Ayr*.

pechler &c a pedlar dealing in earthenware, a travelling handyman or tinker *e19*. [nME *pakald*; appar f PACK¹]

pauchle² &c ['p(j)axl] *vti* **1** *chf* ~ **alang, awa, on** *etc* move feebly but persistently, shuffle, hobble, struggle along *la19-*, now *Uls Slk*. **2** *vi* struggle, strive, expend effort and energy *20*. **3** work ineffectually, bungle, potter *20-*, *Fif Loth Gsw*.

be in a ~ be in a chaotic, disorganized state, be behind with one's work *la20-*, *Mry Fif Uls*. [only Sc; prob onomat; *v* 1 perh related to prec, *ie* walk as if with a burden; *cf peuchle* (PEUCH)]

pauchtie &c ['paxtɪ] *adj* **1** supercilious, conceited, haughty, arrogant; insolent, cheeky; self-important *la16-*, now *Kcb*. **2** stout-hearted, spirited, gallant *la18-e19*.

pauchtily &c haughtily, arrogantly, superciliously *la17-e19*. [nEng dial *pauchtie &c*, *pafty*; obscure]

pauk see PAWK

paulie see PALIE¹

paulʒon see PALLION²

paumer see PALMER

paunch see PAINCH

paup see PAP¹

pauper &c *n* **1** = pauper. **2** a school pupil who received free education in return for various cleaning and supervisory duties *19-e20*, *N, only Sc*.

paut see PAWT

pautener &c [*'patənɪr, *-ər] *adj, of persons* cruel, deadly *la14-e15*. [nME; ME *pautener(e)* a vagabond, AF *pautener*, OF *pautonier*]

pauw-wauw see PAEWAE

pavee see PAVIE

pavey-waveys ['pevɪ'wevɪz] *n* a girls' skipping game in which the rope is made to wave either horizontally or vertically on the ground, the object being to jump over it without touching it *la20-*, *WC*. [f Eng *pave(ment)* + *wave*]

pavie &c; pavise &c *19-e20*, **pavee** *19-e20* ['pevɪ, 'pavɪ, -vi, pə'vi; *'pevɪs, *'pe'vi] *n* **1** a caper, a fantastic movement of the body; a flamboyant or affected gesture; a stately or strutting carriage *la16-e19*. **2** a trick, practical joke *17-e19*. **3** a fuss about nothing, a commotion; a great state of excitement *19-*, now *Ags Fif Bwk*.

vi **1** caper, frisk, move in a quick light way, cavort *19*. **2** adopt an exaggeratedly courtly bearing, strut, parade oneself *19-e20*. [unknown; *cf* PAW¹]

pavilion &c *15-*, **pavilloune** &c *15-e17*; **pavilʒeoun** &c *16* [*paˈvɪljun, *ˈpavɪl(j)un, *pɑ-] *n* = pavilion, a tent.

pavise *see* PAVIE

paw[1] &c [pɑ; *Sh* pjɑ] *n* a slight movement, a feeble gesture or motion *18-*, *now Sh.*

no play ~ not make the slightest movement, show no signs of life *la18-e20.* **play a** ~ play a trick *la16-17.* [only Sc; perh connected w PAVIE; *cf* BRAW and PYAUVE]

paw[2] *n* = pa, dad *20-*, *C.* [*cf* PAWPIE]

pawk &c, **pauk** &c *la16-e20*; **pak(k)** &c *la16-e18* [pɑk] *n* a trick, stratagem; a wile *16-e19.*

pawkery &c trickery, slyness *e19.* ~**ie 1** wily, crafty; shrewd, astute; stubborn *17-20.* **2** having a matter-of-fact, humorously critical outlook on life, characterized by a sly, quiet wit *19-.* **3** roguish, coquettish; lively, merry *18-e20.* **4** quaint, fantastic, amusing *19-*, *now Cai.* **pawkie-witted** = *pawkie* 1, *18-20.* [obscure; *cf* northern ModEng dial = impudence, cheek]

pawkie &c [ˈpɑkɪ; *Bwk* ˈpokɪ] *n* a mitten *19-*, *Bnf C Slk.* [perh double dim of Eng *paw* + *-ock* + *-ie*, orig in children's usage; *cf hummel doddie* (HUMMEL), *doddie-mitten* (DODDIE)]

pawl &c *vi* **1** make clutching or groping movements with the hands, fumble *e19*, *S.* **2** ~ **at** play with one's food *e20*, *S.* [perh dim or frequentative of Eng *paw*]

pawl *see* PALL

pawmie *see* PALMIE, PAM

pawn &c *la16-*, **pand** *16-e18*, *chf Sc*; **pawnd** &c *15-e20* [pɑn(d); *pand] *n* **1** = pawn, a pledge *15-.* **2** *usu in pl* a sum of money deposited with the *kirk session* (KIRK) by a couple as a guarantee of their intention to marry within forty days and of their chaste conduct in the interval *la16-e19.* **3** a pawnshop *19-.*

vt **1** = pawn, pledge, stake *la16-.* **2** foist **on to**, palm off **on** *19-20.*

lay a ~, **lay doon the** ~**s** make official notification of one's intention to marry, arrange for the proclamation of banns *18-e20.* **(lay) in** ~ (put) in pawn, (lay down) as a pledge or security *15-17.*

pawn *see* PAND

pawnd *see* PAWN

pawne *see* POWN

pawpie *n*, *child's word* grandfather *19-*, *Fif Bwk Kcb.* [Eng *pappa*; *cf* PAW[2], BOBBIE, *mammie* (MAM)]

pawrent &c [ˈpɑrənt] *n* = parent *19-e20.*

pawt, paut [pɑt; *Cai also* pjɑt] *vti* **1** strike the ground with the foot, stamp (the foot) in rage; *of a horse etc* paw (the ground) *la17-*, *now Sh Abd Ayr.* **2** *vi* walk in a heavy uncoordinated way, stamp around angrily *la19-*, *now Cai.* **3** *vt* ~ **at** touch or feel with the hand, finger, 'paw' *la18-20.*

n a movement with the foot, a stamping, heavy step, a kick *18-*, *now Sh Abd.* [var of (now dial) Eng *pote*, ME *pote(n)*, OE *potian*; *cf* POWT]

pawtron *see* PATRON

Pax *see* PACE

pay *see* PEY

paysie [ˈpeːsɪ] *n* a peahen *la20-*, *NE.* [var of *pea-* (f *peahen*) + *-sie*]

pbroo *see* PROO

pea; pey &c *la19-20* [pi; *NE, S* pəi] *n* **1** = pea. **2** a small marble *la19-*, *now Loth; cf peaser, peasie* (PEASE[1]), PEEDGIE. **3** *in pl* a grade of very small coal *la19-*, *Loth.*

~**-bree** &c the liquid in which peas have been boiled, pea-soup *20-*, *Ags Loth WC.* ~ **cod** *18-*, *now Ags,* ~**-huil** &c *18-*, *Fif Loth S,* ~**-shaup** *19-*, *now Fif WC* a pea-pod. ~**-splittin** *of persons* petty, fussy, cheese-paring *la19-*, *now Uls.* ~**-tree** the laburnum *19-*, *now S.* [*cf* PEASE[1]]

peace &c *la15-*, **pais** &c *16-e17*, *la19*, **pese** &c *la14-20*; **pace** &c *la15-e20*, **paix** *16-e17* [pis; *Sh-Mry nEC, SW Uls* pes] *n* **1** = peace *la14-.* **2** an outlaw's pardon; his re-admission to allegiance *16-17.* **3** *as a substitute for* God *etc in phrs, eg* **I wish to** ~, **surely to** ~ *la18-.*

interj a call for a truce in a game, 'pax!' *la19-*, *nEC Slk Uls.*

v **1** *vt* reconcile; end (a war); moderate (one's anger etc) *la14-15.* **2** *vti* = peace, be or become silent, reduce to silence *16.*

~**-warning** a notice to a tenant to quit *la19.*

be, sit *etc* **at** *or* **in** ~ *freq imperative to a child* sit still, don't fidget *la19-.* **give me** *etc* ~ *usu imperative* leave me etc alone, don't disturb me etc *20-.* **hald** *or* **kepe in** ~ maintain in a state of peace *15-e17.* **in (the)** ~ = *in tyme of* ~, *la14-16.* **in(to)** ~ in freedom from war or strife, in tranquillity *la14-e17.* **in tyme of** ~ *used in documents, referring to land valuation, perh* = by *auld extent* (EXTENT) *15-17*; see DOST. **pas, come** *etc* **to** *or* **till (someone's)** ~ come etc to the allegiance of a particular sovereign etc *la14-15.* ~ **of the fair** &c the special protection granted to merchants and traders travelling to or from, or attending, a fair *15-16.* **set** *or* **put in** ~ pacify, make peaceful *la14-e16.* **wi** ~ in peace, peacefully, without disturbance *la19-*, *now Sh Ork.*

Peace *see* PACE

peage *see* PAGE

peak &c *n* **1** = peak. **2** a type of lace with a pointed, scalloped edge *19-*, *now Ork.*

vti = peak.

~**it** &c *of lace* having a scalloped or frilled edge *20-*, *now Ork Kcb.*

peal *see* PAIL, PALE[2]

peaper *see* PAPER

pear *see* PEER[2]

pearl[1] &c *16-*, **perle** &c *15-17*; **per(r)ill** &c *la16-e17* [pɛrl; *Bwk* perl; *pirl] *n* **1** = pearl *15-.*

2 a cataract (on the eye) *la16-, now Uls.* **3** a small piece of coal of the next size to DROSS *20-, now WC.*

pearlin &c 1 = pearling. **2** *in pl* a string of pearls *19-e20.* **perlit &c** = pearled, set etc (as) with pearls *la16-e17.*

pearl² 17-, perle &c *16-e17 n* **1** = purl, embroidery or edging, *esp* of gold or silver wire *16.* **2** = purl, a stitch in knitting *19-.*
vt, chf in ptp = purled, edged with lace, ornamented with a knitted border *la16-20.*
perling &c *la16-e20,* **pairling &c** *17,* **pearling &c** *17-e20, latterly literary* = *n* 1; *in pl* lace-trimming. [orig chf Sc]

peare *see* PAIR

Peasche *see* PACE

pease¹ &c *la16-,* **pese &c** *15-19,* **pise** *la15-e18;* **pes** *la15-16,* **peyes &c** *la16-17,* **pies &c** *la17-18,* **pis &c** *la15-19,* **piz(z)** *19-e20* [piz; *Inv-Buchan* pez; *Abd nEC* pɪz; *Mry Abd Bwk Rox also* pəiz] *n* = pease *15-.*
peaser &c 1 *also* **peesil** *20-, Fif* a small marble *20-, Ags Fif.* **2** *in pl, joc* pease-pudding *la19-, N, WC, S.* **peasie &c** *adj* made of or like ~*-meal, e20.* *n* a small marble *20-, Gen except Sh Ork.* **peasy-bannock &c** a BANNOCK made of ~*-meal, 20-, now Loth.* **peasie whin &c** a type of stone, *usu* granite, with a marled granular surface *la18-20, chf Bnf Abd Kcdn.*
~ **bannock** = *peasy-bannock, la17-e20.* ~**-bogle** a scarecrow *19; cf tattie-bogle* (TATTIE). ~**-brose** a dish made of ~*-meal* and boiling water stirred to a paste *19-.* ~**-clod** a roll or loaf made of ~*-meal, la18.* ~**cod tree** the laburnum *la17-e19.* ~**-kill 1** a quantity of peas roasted as in *(orig* in) a kiln *17-18.* **2** *fig* a source of enjoyment or gain; a state of confusion *e19.* ~**-meal &c** a flour made of ground pease *17-.* ~**-pistils** = *pease-brose, e20.* ~**-scone** a SCONE made of ~*-meal, 18-19.* ~ **strae &c** the stalks and foliage of the pea plant used as cheap fodder or bedding for animals *la16-, now Kcb.* **(Clean) Pease Strae** name of a Scottish country dance and its tune *18-.* ~ **wisp &c** *fig* an inextricable tangle, a small bundle of anything tossed roughly together like a wisp of pea straw *la19-, local.* [*cf* PEA]

pease² &c *interj* a call to food to a tame pigeon *19-, Ross Inv C, S.*
peasie = *interj, 20-, Per Kcb.* [uncertain]

pease *see* PAISE

peaser &c [*'pizər] *n* a draught of liquor, *esp* WHISKY *la19.* [aphetic f Eng *appeaser*]

peat¹ &c *la16-,* **pete &c** *la14-e20;* **pet(t)** *15-19,* **pate &c** *16-20,* **pit &c** *la16-e18,* [pit; *Sh Ork Bnf nEC* pet; **pɛt] *n* **1** (1) **a** ~, *pl* ~**s** a piece of the semi-carbonized decayed vegetable matter found under the surface of boggy moorland, *usu* cut into brick-shaped pieces, dried and burned as fuel *la14-.* (2) **the** ~**s** the work of digging

and preparing PEAT¹ for fuel *20-.* **2** the substance itself *15-.* **3** applied to objects resembling a PEAT¹ in shape or colour, *specif* (1) a bar of soap *19-e20;* (2) a gable stone supporting a coping-stone; a coping-stone; the keystone of an arch, *chf* ~ **stane** *16-20.*
vt fuel with PEATS¹, stoke (a fire etc) with PEATS¹ *la17-18.*

~**ery &c** *hist* a ~ *moss* belonging to a landed estate; the right to cut PEATS¹ from this *19-e20.*
peting &c the action of getting PEAT¹; the right to cut, or the service of cutting PEAT¹ *la15-17.*
~**y** of or like PEAT¹; *freq of water* PEAT¹-stained *la18-.*

~**-bank** the bank or vertical face from which PEATS¹ are cut *la19-.* ~**-barra &c** a flat barrow with a high end and no sides used for carrying PEATS¹ *20-.* ~ **bing** a heap of PEATS¹, *usu* the winter's supply, stacked against the gable of the house *20-, Sh Bnf WC.* ~ **bree &c** the water which drains from PEAT¹ soil, ~*y* water *19-, now NE.* ~**-cassie &c** = ~*-creel, la19-, now Sh Ork Uls.* ~**-caster** a person who cuts PEATS¹ and lays them out to dry *17-.* ~**-castin** the act of doing this *la17-.* ~**-clod** a single PEAT¹, *esp* one which is still earthy and friable *19-, Sh N Wgt Uls.* ~**-coom** PEAT¹ dust, the crumbly remains of PEAT¹ *la19-, Cai SW, S.* ~**-creel &c** a large straw or rush basket for carrying PEATS¹ on the back *la17-, NE, C Highl Uls.* ~**-gate &c** the track, road or right-of-way leading to a ~ *moss, 17-e19, chf Abd.* ~**-greeshoch &c** a red-hot smouldering PEAT¹ or PEAT¹-fire, PEAT¹ embers *la19-, NE, SW.* ~ **hag &c** a hole or pit left in an old PEAT¹-working *19-.* ~**-hill** a ~ *moss, la19-, now Sh Ork.* ~**-hole &c** an old PEAT¹-working on a moor, *freq* one filled with rainwater *la17-, now Uls.* ~**-house** an outhouse used for storing the winter's supply of PEAT¹ *16-, now Sh Bnf.* ~ **lair, ~-larach &c** the area of moor on which newly cut PEATS¹ are laid out to dry *20-, Sh N, SW.* ~**-leading** the carting of cut and dried PEATS¹ from the ~ *moss, la16-18.* ~**-low(e)** a PEAT¹ fire, the glow from such a fire *19-e20.* ~**man** an estate servant in charge of the PEAT¹ supply; an itinerant PEAT¹-merchant *18-19.* ~ **moss &c** a PEAT¹-bog or -moor, the place where PEATS¹ are dug *16-.* ~ **muild &c** = ~*-coom, la19-.* ~**-neuk &c** a corner or alcove, *usu* in the kitchen, used for storing PEATS¹ for immediate use *18-, now Sh-N, Wgt.* ~**-pot &c** a hole from which PEATS¹ have been dug *15-e19.* ~**-ree** an enclosed recess, either inside or outside, for storing PEATS¹ *la20-, local NE-Kcb.* ~**-reek &c 1** the pungent smoke from a PEAT¹ fire *la18-.* **2** *transf: Highland* (HIE-LAND) WHISKY, whose characteristic flavour is allegedly from the smoke of the PEAT¹ fire used in the drying of the malt *la18-.* ~ **rickle** a small heap of three or four PEATS¹ set up on end

to dry *19-*, *now Abd*.   ~ **spad(e)** &c a spe-
cially-shaped spade used for PEAT¹-cutting
la15-.   ~**-stack** &c a large pile of dried PEATS¹
erected out-of-doors as a fuel-store *la16-*.   ~
ʒaird &c a place where PEATS¹ are dug
la16-e17.

fit the ~**s** set PEATS¹ on end to dry *la20-*, *Uls*.
[ScL *peta*, *la12*, perh f the Celtic base *pett-* a
portion; cf MedL *petia*, F *pièce* a piece]

peat² &c, **pete** *la17-e19* [pit; *also* *pet] *n* **1** term
of endearment, *esp* for a child *la19-*, *now Abd*.
2 term of reproach or scorn for a woman, *freq*
proud ~ *19-e20*.   **3** an ADVOCATE reputed to
be the protégé of a particular judge *la17-19*,
only Sc. [eModEng *peat(e)*; cf MDu *pete* godmother, in ModFlem also used as a familiar
greeting; appar not connected w PET¹]

peatch &c *la17-e18*, **piatch** *la17* [*'piatʃ] *n* =
piazza, an arcade. [eModEng *piazza*; Ital
piazza a public square]

peath *see* PETH

Peax *see* PACE

pebble *see* PEEBLE

pece *see* PIECE¹

pech &c; **peich** &c *16*, **paich** &c *20* [pɛx] *vi* **1**
breathe hard as from exertion, puff, pant, gasp
for breath *16-*.   **2** move or work so as to pant
or gasp with the exertion *la18-*, *NE*, *WC Kcb*.
3 cough in a subdued asthmatic way *la20-*, *now
Ayr*.   **4** expel the breath slowly and audibly,
sigh, groan *la18-e20*.

n **1** a laboured breath, a pant, gasp; one's
breath *16-*.   **2** an asthmatic wheeze, a breathless cough *la19-*, *NE*, *C*.   **3** a sigh of weariness,
relief, satisfaction etc *19-*.

~**ie** short-winded, asthmatic, wheezy *20-*, *Gen
except Sh Ork*.   ~**in** &c shortness of breath; the
act of panting *18-*.   ~(l)**t**, ~(l)**ed** out of
breath, exhausted *19-*, *Abd nEC*, *S* [perh a var
of PAUCHLE²].

get over something with a ~ get something
done by dint of great effort *20-*, *NE Ags Wgt*.
a sair ~ a prolonged and weary effort, an
exhausting struggle *20-*. [late nME; onomat; cf
northern ModEng dial *peff*, *peck* and PEUCH]

pech *see* PECHT

pechan &c ['pɛxən] *n* the stomach as a receptacle for food, the belly *la18-19*. [only Sc;
obscure]

pecher *see* PITCH

pechle *see* PAUCHLE¹

pecht &c *la14-e20*, **picht** &c *la14-e20*, *only Sc*,
pict &c *la15-*; **peicht** &c *15-17*, **pech** &c
17-e20, **pick** &c *la18-e20* [pɛxt; pɪk; pɪkt;
*pɪxt] *n* **1** P~ = Pict, one of an ancient people
who inhabited Scotland north of the Forth
la14-; see SND.   **2** contemptuous term for a
small undersized person or *occas* animal or thing
17-, *now Sh Bnf Abd*.

Pictish &c of or like the Picts *la16-*. ~**s'**
house an underground dwelling, a WEEM or

earth house, *chf* dating from the first two centuries AD *18-*, *Sh Ork N*.   **P~land** the territory
of the Picts *16-*, *now hist*. [nME *Peght* &c, OE
Pechtas, *Pihtas* (*pl*); laL *Pictī*, appar = *pictī* pl
ptp adj of *pingere* (*v*) paint, *ie* the painted or
tattooed people, or poss merely assimilated to
this f a native name]

pecifee &c *e20*, **pecify** &c *16-e20* [*Cai* 'pisɪfi;
NE 'pes-; *'pisɪfai, &c] *vt* = pacify.

peck¹ &c; **paek** &c *20*, *Sh* [pɛk] *vti* = peck,
strike with the beak *19-*.

n a small quantity of something edible, what
can be pecked, a scrap of food *la19-*, *local*.

peck² &c, **pek** &c *15-17*; **pect** *16-17*, **peick**
&c *la16-17* [pɛk] *n* **1** = peck, a dry measure, in
Scotland *chf* equivalent to a quarter of a FIRLOT
but varying according to district and commodity; a vessel used as a PECK² measure *15-e19*.   **2**
a plot of land, *prob* one requiring a PECK² of oat
seed to sow it *19*, *Per*.

~ **of land** a land-measure *17-18*, *Ross*.

pedagoge &c [*'pɛdagog] *n* = next *la15-e17*.
[only Sc; MF]

pedagogy &c ['pɛdəgogɪ] *n* **1** *appar* the *orig*
name of the teaching institution of the Faculty
of Arts (1) in St Andrews Univ, with the building housing it, (2) in Glasgow Univ, with its
body of teachers; (3) alternative term for the
University or College (of St Andrews or Glasgow) viewed as a teaching institution *15-16*.   **2**
= pedagogy.

peddell *see* BEDDAL

pedder &c *la15-e20*, **peddar** *e16*, **pethar** &c
la17-e19 ['pɛdər; *'pɛð-] *n* a pedlar, packman.
[ME *peoddare*, *ped(d)er* &c pedlar, maker of panniers, appar f ME *ped* a pannier]

pedell *see* BEDDAL

pee¹ &c *vti* urinate, wet with urine *la18-*.

n urine; the act of urinating *19-*.

~**ins** urine *la20-*, *NE Ags*.

~**-the-bed** the dandelion *20-*, *N Ags Edb* [f its
diuretic properties].   [earlier in Sc; prob f the
name of the letter *p* as the first letter of *piss*]

pee² &c *la15-e17*; **pey** &c *la15-16*, **pye** &c
16-17 [*pi, *paɪ] *n* a kind of (? loose-fitting, ?
short) coat or jacket. [eModEng *P*, *pee*,
laMDu *pie* a coat of coarse woollen material; cf
ModEng *pea-jacket*]

peeack *see* PEEK¹

pee-ay *see* PREE²

peeble &c *18-*, *now NE Slk*; **pebble** *la18-* *n* **1** =
pebble *18-*, *now NE Slk*.   **2** a semi-precious
stone, *usu* agate or rock-crystal, found in large
numbers in streams and rocks, *freq* set in silver,
making a distinctively Scottish type of jewellery
18-19; cf *Scots pebble* (SCOTS).

pee-coo &c [*'pi'ku, *-'kʌu] *n* a game resembling hide-and-seek or prisoners' base *19*, *chf
Ags*.   [cf LAMPEEKOO]

peedie *see* PEERIE

peedgie &c ['pidʒɪ, 'pitʃɪ] *n* a small glass marble
20, *Ross-Mry*.   [prob f PEA]

peefer &c *19-e20*; **pif(f)er** &c *e19 vi* complain querulously, 'moan', fret *19-e20*.

~**in** trifling, feckless, ineffectual *19*. [only Sc; orig prob imit; *cf* Eng *piffle*]

peek[1] &c *19-*; **peeack** &c *la19* ['pi(ə)k] *interj, freq* ~-~ a sound representing the cry of a small animal or bird, or the shrill voice of a child *la19-, NE Ags Uls*.

n **1** the cry of a small animal or bird, a shrill, piping noise, a cheep, an insignificant sound *la19-, NE Ags Uls*. **2** a person with a weak piping voice; an unimpressive, insignificant individual *la19, Bnf Abd*.

vi **1** cheep, chirp, cry feebly like a small animal or bird *19-, Sh NE Uls*. **2** complain, grumble, whine, whimper *19-, NE Ags*. [onomat]

peek[2] &c *n* a tiny bead or point of light, a little tongue or jet of flame, *freq* **a** ~ **o light** *etc*, *19-*. [only Sc; prob a noun usage of Eng *peek* peep, on the analogy of PEEP[1]]

peek- *see* PICK[3]

peel[1] &c *17-*, **pele** &c *15-17 vti* **1** = peel *15-*. **2** *vt* plunder, rob, pillage, cheat *la15-19*. **3** unpack or unwrap (bulk goods); separate into smaller packages for retailing *16-e17*; *cf pack and* ~ (PACK[1]). **4** skin (one's leg, arm etc), rub or scrape skin off, *usu* by accident *19-*.

n = peel.

adj, of fish untreated (as by drying) and bulk packed *la16-e17*.

peeled &c **1** = peeled, stripped of possessions, an outer layer etc *la15-*. **2** = *adj, la16-e17*.

~**ed egg** a stroke of good fortune one has not had to strive for, a windfall *18-e20*. ~**er** &c a small crab which has just cast or is about to cast its shell and is therefore suitable for bait *la19-, now NE Ags*. ~**ock** (**potato**) a potato cooked and served in its skin *19-, SW*.

in ~ *of fish* not packed *16-e18*. ~**-an-eat** *n* = ~*ock*; a meal made up of these *la18-, now local NE-S*. *adj, of a person* unhealthy-looking, delicate, sickly *19-e20*. ~ **one's wands** *fig* begin something (new), *specif* married life, or an apprenticeship etc *20-, S* [prob a metaphor f basket-making].

peel[2] &c *vti* equal, match; *in curling* (CURL), *bowls etc* tie, have equal scores *18-, WC, S*.

n an equal, a match (for another person or thing) *18-e19*.

be, lie, stand etc ~**s** *of the contestants in a game etc or the game itself* have equal scores on both sides *la19-, C, S*. [only Sc; obscure]

peel[3] &c *17-*, **pele** &c *la14-20 n* a defensive palisade or stockade; the ground enclosed by such; a fortified house or small defensive tower, *? orig* one built within a palisade (*chf* in the BORDER counties of both England and Scotland) *la14-, latterly hist, also in place-names as* **the P**~ **of X**.

vti stake up, support or protect by means of stakes *la16-18*.

~**-house** a fortified dwelling or refuge *la16-19, latterly hist*. **pil(1)muir** &c *appar* a piece of

common land enclosed by a fence and cultivated as arable ground *18-e20, also freq in place-names*. [ScL *pela* a fortified house *e14*; ME *pel(e)* a stake, a palisade, a castle, OF *pel, piel*, MedL *pela, -um* a stake, palisade]

peel[4] *18-*, **peill** &c *la17-e18* [pil] *n* = pill, a tablet.

peel *see* PUIL

peelick &c *n* a blow, buffet *la19-20, Ags Per*. [dim f Eng (now dial) *peal* (*v*) strike, pelt, batter]

peelie &c *adj, chf* ~-**wally** ['~-'walɪ] sickly, feeble, pallid, thin and ill-looking *19-, now C*.

~-**wersh** &c sickly, delicate; insipid, nondescript *19-, now Rox*. [orig prob imit of a whining feeble sound, w formal infl f PALIE[1]]

peen[1] *n* = pane, a sheet of glass *18-, now NE*.

peen[2] &c *la18-, local N-SW*, **pene** &c *e16*; **piend** &c *19-, now N Loth* [pin(d)] *n* **1** a peak or apex, a point; a coping *18-, now Sh Mry Ags*. **2** *building* one of the sloping ridges at the corner of a hipped roof, where two adjacent sloping surfaces meet *la18-, now Abd C*.

vt **1** hammer metal (**out**) flat and thin *e16*. **2** bring to a point, taper *la19-, Cai Abd Ayr*.

~**er** a mason's peen-hammer *la20-, N Fif Loth*. ~-**roof** a hipped, regular or pavilion roof *la19-, now N Loth*. [eModEng *pen*, ModEng *peen* &c the pointed end of a hammerhead; *cf* Norw dial *pen, pænn* the pointed end of a hammer, Sw dial *pena* beat with a hammer]

peen *see* PIN

peenge &c *la18-*; **pinge** *now Kcdn Ags* [pin(d)ʒ, pɪn(d)ʒ] *vi* **1** whine, complain, whimper *la18-*. **2** droop, pine, mope, look cold and miserable *18-, now Kcdn Ags*.

n a feeble, sickly-looking person; a fretful child *20-, Fif S*.

peengie &c **1** *freq of a child* peevish, fractious *20-, NE, C, S*. **2** sickly-looking, puny, not in good health *19-, now NE Ags Fif*. **peeng(e)in** &c **1** = *peengie* 1; mean, grudging *19-e20*. **2** ailing, pinched and cold-looking *18-e20*. [onomat, w infl f WHINGE, PEEK[1] etc]

peenie &c *n* **1** = pinafore, *esp* one worn by children; an apron *la19-*. **2** *child's word* the 'tummy' *20-, C*.

peeoy &c ['pi'oi] *n* a schoolboy's home-made firework made of a small cone of moistened gunpowder set off by a light applied to the top *19-e20*. [only Sc; imit of the noise it makes]

peep[1] &c, **pepe** &c *e16 n* **1** = peep, a quick glance. **2** a PEEK[2], *freq* of a gas-jet *la19-e20*. **3** a small opening, a little aperture or crack *19-, now Sh Ags Uls*.

vi, also **pype** *la15* = peep *la15-*.

put &c **the** (*lit*) **or someone's** (*fig*) **gas at** *or* **in a** ~ (*lit*) reduce the pressure of a gas jet to the lowest point at which it will remain alight; *fig* put someone in his place *20-, Gen except Sh Ork*.

peep[2] *la16-*, **pepe** &c *la15-e17, e19 n, v* = peep, a squeak *la15-*.

heather ~er 1 the meadow pipit *la19-*, *Bnf*. **2** the sandpiper *la19-*, *now Per*.

peep³ *n* a small marble *la19-*, *eLoth*. [perh a var of Eng *pip*; *cf* PAIP¹]

peer¹ *vi* = peer, look narrowly.

~ie-wearie &c strained or short-sighted-looking *19-*, *now Slk*.

peer² *17-*, *Gen except nEC*, **pere &c** *15-17*; **pear &c** *la16-* [pir; *local Sh-Clcm Wgt Uls* per; *Gsw also* pɛr] *n* **1** = pear *15-*. **2** *fig* something of little value *15-16*.

~ie &c ['piri; *EC*, *WC Rox also* 'pɛri, 'pɪri] **1** *also* **pirie &c** *e19* a child's spinning-top *la17-*, *Gen except Sh Ork*. **2** a fir cone *la20-*, *S*. **3** *mining* a surveyor's large brass plumb-bob *la20-*, *Fif*. **4** a small stone marble *20-*, *NE*. **~ie cord** *etc* the string with which the *peerie* (*n* 1) is set in motion *19-20*. **~ie heel** a high, sharply-pointed heel of a shoe, a stiletto heel *la20-*, *C*, *S*. **~ie-heidit** in a state of mental confusion *20-*, *now C*, *S*. **~ie ring** a game played with *peeries* (*n* 1) *la19-*, *now Loth*. **French ~ie** a humming top *19-*, *now Loth Dnbt*. **sleep like** *or* **as sound as a ~ie** sleep like a top *19-*, *C*, *S*. **treacle &c ~ie** *see* TRAICLE.

peer³, **pere &c** *16-e18 vt*, *also* **peerie &c** *la18-e19* pour in trickles or small drops, trickle. [uncertain; *cf* Norw dial *pira* (*v*) trickle]

peer *see* PERE, PUIR

peerie &c, peedie *20-*, *Sh Ork Cai Fif adj* small, little, tiny *la19-*, *now Sh Ork Cai*.

~-weerie *adj* = *adj*, *19-e20*; *n* a tiny creature *19-*, *now Sh Per*. **~-winkie** *nursery rhymes* the little finger or toe *la19-*, *Sh Ork Renfr*. [see SND]

peeryorie &c [pir'jari] *n*, *street-cry* a potato *19-e20*, *Edb*. [only Sc; altered f PAWTIE]

peesie ['pizi] *adj*, *slang and child's word* excellent, splendid *la20-*, *Loth WC*. [altered f BEEZER]

peesie(-weesie) *see* PEESWEEP

peesil *see* PEASE¹

peesweep &c; peewee *la19-*, **peeweet &c** *19-*, **peesie &c** *la20-*, *now Ags Per* ['pi(z)'wip, 'pizi'wip, 'piwi(t), 'pizi] *n* **1** the lapwing *la18-*. **2 peeweet** a miner's singlet, *usu* blue-grey (the colour of a lapwing's wings) *la20-*, *Fif*.

adj, *chf* **peesie-weesie** *of persons* sharp-featured, gaunt; shrill-voiced, whining, complaining; ailing *19-*, *now Wgt*. [imit of the bird's cry]

peety *la19-*, **peté &c** *la14-16*, **pité &c** *la14-16*; **peite &c** *15-17*, **pity &c** ['piti] *n* (*la14-*), *vt* (*la16-*) = pity.

~fu(l) &c 1 = pitiful *la16-*. **2** *of persons* arousing pity and compassion, pitiable *la16-*. **pet(e)ous &c** *la15-16*, *chf Sc*, **petuous &c** *la14-16*, *chf Sc* = piteous. **pietuous** deserving pity; compassionate; pious *16*, *only Sc*.

it's a *or* **the ~ o 1** it's a pity about *19-*, *Ork C*, *S Uls*. **2** *as a threat* it's a bad lookout for; *ironic* it serves (you etc) right *20-*, *Sh Cai Ags Per*. **~ me!** *exclam* expressing surprise, disapproval, disgust etc *19-*. [*cf* PIETÉ]

peever¹ &c *n* **1** the flat stone used in the game of hopscotch *19-*, *C Uls*. **2** *freq in pl* the game itself *la19-*, *C*, *S*.

~(ie) beds = beds (BED *n* 4) *20-*, *C*. [only Sc; unknown; *cf* next]

peever² *n* a very small marble *la19-*, *NE Fif*. [only Sc; uncertain; *cf* prec]

peewee, peeweet *see* PEESWEEP

peg &c *n* **1** = peg. **2** *slang* a policeman *la19-20*, *local NE-WC*.

vti **1** = peg. **2** *vt* whack, beat *la19*.

peggin a beating, drubbing *20-*, *wLoth S*.

Peg: peggie a household implement for stirring and pounding clothes in the wash-tub *la20-*, *now Kcdn*. [the girl's name]

pegane *see* PAGEANT

pege *see* PAGE

peges-nos &c [*?'pɛgz'noz] *n* ? the projecting part of the prow, ? the figurehead of a ship *la16*. [uncertain]

pegral &c *la19-e20*, **pegrall &c** *16* ['pɛgrəl, 'pi-] *adj* **1** petty, paltry, trifling *16*. **2** mean, greedy, miserly *la19-e20*. [only Sc; perh altered f OSc *pedral*, metath var of Eng *pedlar*, *ie* one who deals in a petty way]

pegy-mast &c; piggé *e16* [*?'pɛgi-, *?'pɪgi] *n* ? a small mast of some kind; ? a top-mast or ? a small mast or yard for a pennant on a ship *la15-e16*. [only Sc; obscure]

peich *see* PECH

peicht *see* PECHT

peick *see* PECK²

peiffer *see* PIFER

peik *see* PICK⁵

peill *see* PEEL⁴

peint *see* PINT

peirell *see* PERILL

peirse *see* PIERCE

peirtrick *see* PAITRICK

peist [*chf NE* pəist] *vi*, *chf* **~er 1** work in a lethargic half-hearted way *la19-e20*. **2** make one's way with difficulty, struggle along *20-*, *Mry Bnf*. [only Sc; obscure]

peite *see* PEETY

peittiecott *see* PETTICOAT

pek *see* PECK²

pekar *see* PIKE

pekery *see* PICK¹

pelat [*?'pɛlət] *n* = pallet, a straw mattress or bed *e16*.

pelcher ['pɛltʃər] *n* the grey mullet *la19-*, *Cai*. [appar f Eng *pilchard* w transf meaning]

pele *see* PEEL¹, PEEL³

pell¹ *n*, *contemptuous* a dirty, worthless person, reprobate, tramp *19-*, *now Sh Ork*. [see SND]

pell² *n* buttermilk, *chf* **as soor** *etc* **as ~** *19-e20*, *S*. [obscure]

pellack *see* PELLOCK

pellar *see* PILLAR

pellet¹ &c *n* a pelt, a raw skin of a sheep etc

before dressing or tanning *15-*, *now Slk.*
[laME; OF *pelete &c* dim of *pel* a skin, L *pellis* a
skin; ScL *pellete* (*pl*) *e14*]

pellet² &c *n* **1** = pellet, a ball used as a missile
la15-. **2** = *pellok-bow* (PELLOK) *la16-e17*.

pellile &c [pə'lil] *n* the redshank *la19-e20, NE.*
[? imit of its call]

pellock &c *la16-*, **pellok** *16-e17*; **pellack**
17-e20, **pallack** &c *la17-e20*, **pallo** *la19-e20*,
Ork *n* **1** the porpoise; ? *orig also* the dolphin *16-*.
2 the flesh of the porpoise *16-e17*. **3** *fig* anything bulky and clumsy; a short fat person
la18-, *now Ork Bnf.* [only Sc; ScL *peloca* (*e14*);
unknown]

pellok *n* a more or less spherical missile shot
from a *pellok-bow*, gun etc; a ball, bullet or
canon-ball *15-e16*.
~ **bow** a type of hand-bow or crossbow which
shot pellets *16-e17*. [altered f Eng *pellet*]

pelsh &c *n* a drenching shower of rain, a downpour *20, NE.* [obscure]

pelt¹ &c *v* **1** *vt* = pelt *19-*. **2** *vi* keep hammering
or striking (**at** etc) *e16, 19*. **3** *vti, fig* work energetically, exert oneself (**at**) *la19-*, *now Sh Bnf.*
n, *also* **palt** *e16* a hard blow, a buffet *la15-*, *now
Ork Ags.*
~**er** a state of great excitement *la19-*, *Sh Abd.*
~**ie** a shipyard hammer *20-*, *WC.*

pelt² &c *n* **1** a person or thing of little value;
trash, rubbish *la16-19*. **2** *specif* a low-grade
type of coal containing a large proportion of
stone, shale and slate *19-*, *now wLoth.*
~**in-pyock** ['~ɪn'pjok] a shabby garment, a
worthless rag, *esp* one worn as protective clothing for rough work *la19-e20, NE.* ~**ry** &c *n*,
also fig worthless objects, trash, rubbish *la16-19*.
adj worthless, rubbishy, unpleasant *la16-*, *now
Bnf.* [see SND]

pen¹ &c *n* **1** a plume, feather; the quill or barrel
of a feather *la15-*, *now local.* **2** = pen, a writing
implement *la14-*. **3** *transf* a man's penis *16*. **4**
a small spoon or similar object for taking snuff,
orig one made from a quill *la18-*, *Ork Bnf.* **5**
the stalk of a plant or vegetable, a stalk of straw
la18-e20.
vt = pen, write down *16-*.
~**fu** &c *n* **1** amount (of food or drink)
18-19. ~**ner** &c **1** a case or sheath for holding
pens *la15-20*. **2** *joc* a top-hat *la19-e20, Bnf Abd.*
~**ner-inkhorn** &c a pen-case and inkhorn
combined   *la16-17*,   *only*   *Sc.* ~**ne(r)th**
[*?'pɛnə(r)θ] a case or sheath for pens or needles *17*, *chf Edb.*
~**ball** a (*prob* golf-)ball stuffed with feathers
la16-e17, *only Sc.*   ~**gun** a kind of pop-gun or
pea-shooter made from a bird's quill *18-e20.*
crack, talk *etc* **like a** ~**gun** keep up a continuous flow of talk, chatter *19-*, *now NE Loth.*
~**point** a pen-nib *la19-*, *N Ayr.*

pen² *n* a pointed conical hill *la18-*, *chf S*, *chf in
place-names as* **X** ~: '*Ettrick Pen*'. [OWelsh *pen* a
head, top]

pen *see* PEND¹, PIN

penalité &c [*pɪ'nalɪtɪ] *n* a troubled state of
mind due to an awareness of the weakness of
human nature and sin *la15*. [eModEng *penal-
ite* &c pain, suffering, punishment, F *pénalité*,
MedL *penalitas* punishment]

penche *see* PAINCH

pend¹ &c, **pen(n)** *16-* [pɛn(d)] *n* **1** an arch,
vault, the arch of a bridge, gateway etc; *fig* the
sky *la15-20*. **2** *as collective* = ~ *stones*; the
stonework of an arch or vault *16-e17*. **3** a
vaulted or arched passageway or ENTRY, *esp* one
leading from the street into the back-court of a
block of houses, *orig* running through the building, *later* between houses whether built over or
not *16-*. **4** a covered drain or sewer, the
entrance to or grating over a drain or sewer
19-, *Ayr Kcb S.*
vt **1** form into an archway, vault *15-e19*. **2** furnish with arching or vaulting, arch or vault
over *la15-17*.
~**close** = *n* **3**, *19-e20*. **P~ Folk** a small
religious sect, of Baptist principles, taking its
name from its meeting-house in a ~*close* in the
High Street of Paisley *la19*.   ~ **gate** &c **1** an
arched gate *e17*.   **2** a gate closing the entrance
to a PEND¹ (*n* **3**) *la19-*, *Ags Per.*   ~**mouth** the
entrance to a PEND¹ (*n* **3**) *la19-*, *NE Ags Per WC.*
~ **stone** &c a stone shaped for building into an
archway *la16-e19*. [ultimately f OF *pendre*, L
pendēre hang]

pend² &c [*pɛn(d)] *n* a valance for an altar or
bed *16-e17*. [only Sc; MF *pente*, F *pendre*; *cf*
PAND]

pendakill *see* PENDICLE

pendale &c [*'pɛndel, *-əl] *n* a valance or
hanging for an altar *e16*. [only Sc; MedL
pendale &c a hanging, curtain; *cf* PENDICLE (*n* **3**
(1)), PENDLE]

pendas *see* PENDICE

pendecle *see* PENDICLE

penden &c *n* = PEND² *la15-16*. [? var of
PENDALE]

pendice &c *16-e18*, **pendas** &c *la15-16*;
pendes *la15-16* [*'pɛndes, *-ɪs] *n* something
ornamental which hangs down, *eg* on the end of
a strap or belt; an ornamental strip hanging
from a bishop's mitre. [only Sc; OF *pendace* a
hanging breast or pap, f as PEND¹]

pendicle &c; **pendakill** &c   *la15-e16*,
pendecle &c *la15-e17*, **pendicule** *16*
['pɛndɪkl] *n* **1** something dependent on or
subordinate to something else: (1) a piece of
land etc regarded as subsidiary to a main estate
15-19; (2) a small piece of ground forming part
of a larger holding or farm and *freq* let to a subtenant *la18-*, *now C, S*; (3) a place, district etc
regarded as a detached portion of a larger territory, a place etc administratively dependent on
another area *16-e18*; (4) an ecclesiastical depen-
dency *16-18*; (5) applied to non-material
things, *eg* a story *la15-e19*; (6) a specialized craft

regarded as a subdivision of a general craft *17*.
2 *in the organization of the Trades* INCORPORATIONS
a trade or tradesman not fully incorporated
and having limited rights or occupying an
ancillary or subordinate position *18-e20*. **3** (1)
a hanging cloth such as a valance, *eg* on an
altar, a bed *la15-e17*. (2) a hanging ornament
or attachment, a pendant *la16-17*.

pendicler &c the tenant of a PENDICLE, a
smallholder *la18-20*.

parts and ~s *see* PAIRT. [only Sc; MedL
pendiculum f L *pendēre* (*v*) hang]

pendle &c *n* **1** a pendant or drop earring *e19*.
2 the pendulum of a clock *18-20*. [*cf* F *pendule* a
pendulum, *pendille* a hanging or dangling object
and PENDALE]

pendula &c [*'pɛndələ, *-ɪ] *n* a pendulum, *chf*
~ **knock** a pendulum clock *la17-e18*. [only
Sc; prob f Ital *pendolo* a pendulum; *cf* Eng *pendulum clock* and Eng dial *pendilo*]

pene *see* PEEN²

penetrive &c [*'pɛnɪtraɪv] *adj* penetrating,
piercing, keen, sharp *la15-e16*. [only Sc; ?
shortened f Eng *penetrative* w infl f F *pénétrer*]

penitent &c *adj*, *n* = penitent *la14-*.
~ **stuil &c** = *stool of repentance* (REPENT) *la16*,
Fif.

penn *see* PEND¹

penné *see* PENNY

penne(r)th *see* PEN¹

penneyis *see* PENNY

pennok &c *la15-e17*; **pinnok &c** *15-16*
[*'pɪnok; *?'pɛn-] *n* a measure or quantity of
skins. [only Sc; ? f or f as obs Eng *pane* fur, *esp*
used for lining a garment]

penny &c; penné *15-17* ['pɛnɪ] *n*, *pl also* **penneyis &c** *16-e17* **1** = penny, *chf* the SCOTS (*adj*
4) coin: (1) *in gen, la14-*; (2) *freq* as a symbolical
payment, *chf* in property transactions *15-17*: '*be
deliverance of earth and staine and of ane penny as use
is*'. **2** money in general; a sum of money *la15-*.
~ **book(ie)** a child's first school primer, *orig*
costing a penny; *hence* the first class in a primary
school *la19-e20* [other classes were referred to as
the tippeny (see TIPPENY), *sixpenny* etc according
to the price of the reading book used]. ~ **bridal &c** = ~ *wedding, la16-19*. **~-buff** a
child's first school reading book *20* [f its buff
cover]. ~ **chap** a game at dominoes in which
a penny forfeit is paid when a player CHAPS³
20-, *local Kcdn-S*. ~ **dog** a dog that follows
constantly at his master's heels; *fig, of persons* a
sycophant, toady *18-19*. **~-fee &c** *chf verse*
cash, wages, earnings *la18-e20*. **~-full** *of the
moon* round like a penny, full *la15*. ~ **geggie**
= GEGGIE *la19-e20* [f the admission fee].
~land 1 a measure of land, varying in size, *orig*
reckoned *eg* as $\frac{1}{18}$ of an *urisland* (URE⁵) (*Ork Cai*),
$\frac{1}{20}$ of an *ounceland* (OUNCE) (*Hebrides Highl SW*),
later $\frac{1}{6}$ of a DAVACH (*Suth*) *16-*, *now hist and in
place-names*. **2** a measure of land of one penny
rental in the EXTENT *la12, 16-*, *C, now hist and in*

place-names; cf *merkland* (MERK *n* 4), *pundland*
(PUND¹). **~-mail &c** the part of a rent paid in
money, rent in cash *la15-e18*. ~ **pig** an earthenware money-box *17-*, *Ork, local NE-S*. ~
purs ? a purse for small coins *e16*. **~-rattler**
a shop selling small cheap goods costing only a
few pence *la20-*, *Bnf Abd*. ~ **reel** a dance at
which a dancer paid a penny each time he took
the floor *19*. ~ **siller** money, fortune *la18-19*.
~stane a round flat stone used as a quoit; the
game of quoits *la16-e19*. **~-stane-cast** the
distance to which a *pennystane* can be thrown, a
stone's throw *la14-19*. ~ **thing** a fancy cake
or biscuit, *orig* costing a penny *20-*, *Ags Loth
WC*. **~-wabble** a thin weak ale formerly sold
at a penny a bottle *la19-*, *Bnf Abd*. ~ **wedding &c** a wedding at which a guest contributed a small sum of money, or *occas* food and
drink, towards the cost of the entertainment,
the surplus of which was given to the couple as
a gift *la17-*, *now Cai Kcb*. **~-whaup &c** =
~-wabble, *la18-19*. **~worth &c 1** = penny-
worth *15-20*. **2** = **~-land** 2, *la15-e16*. **3** *chf in
pl* the equivalent of a certain sum or amount in
money or, *chf*, in goods; equivalent payment
15-17. **4** *in pl* an amount of merchandise for
retail sale *15-e17*. **5** a bargain, value for
money *19*. **get one's (flesh) ~(s)worths
(out) o** get one's own back on, revenge oneself
on, get the better of *20-*, *local*. **hang in
~(s)worths** *of the hair* droop in lank wisps
la18-, *now Kcb*.

a bonnie, braw *or* **gey ~** a considerable sum
of money, 'a pretty penny' *19-*. **hae een like
~ bowls** have a startled wide-eyed expression,
be 'saucer-eyed' *la19-*, *Ork Ags Gall*. **mak ~
of** realize as negotiable funds, turn into money;
sell *la15-17*. **~ and** *or* **or ~worth(is)** cash
and *or* or its equivalent *16-17*.

pensall *see* PENSIL

pense¹ &c *la16-*, **pens** *la15-16* [pɛns] *v* **1** *vi*
think, ponder *la15-16*. **2** *vt* take thought of,
consider; call to mind *la15-16*.
~fu thoughtful, meditative, pensive *la19-*, *now
Ags*. **pensie &c 1** *of persons* responsible, sensible, respectable, self-respecting, fastidious about
one's appearance *18-20*, *latterly NE*. **2** self-
important, affected, pompous, priggish, prim
18-e20. **pensit &c** proud, conceited, arrogant; puffed with pride *16*. [only Sc; F *penser*
think, be thoughtful, L *pensāre* weigh, ponder,
consider; *cf* PANSE]

pense² *n* a (spell of) study, a school exercise
17-e18. [only Sc; L *pensum* a piece of work
assigned]

pensil &c *16-e19*, **pensell &c** *16-e19*, **pinsell
&c** *la16-17*; **-sall &c** *la14-e17* *n* **1** a (small)
pennon or streamer, a standard, a set of colours
la15-19. **2** *specif* the standard carried at the
celebration of the *Common Riding* (COMMON) in
Hawick *e18*. [ME *pensile &c*, AF *pencel*]

pensionar &c *n* **1** = pensioner *16-*. **2** the recipient of a pension from an ecclesiastical benefice; a beneficed person *16-e17*.

pensionary &c *n* an ecclesiastical benefice which pays out a pension *16*. [only Sc; *cf* MedL *ecclesia* etc *pensionaria* a church etc burdened with having to pay a regular fixed payment]

pent *see* PAINT, PINT

penult &c [*pɛˈnʌlt] *adj* last but one, penultimate (*orig* day of the month) *la15-e19*.
n the last day but one (of a month) *la16-17*, *only Sc*. [earlier in Sc; ? *orig* a written abbreviation of L *paenultima*; *cf* eModEng]

penure &c; pin(n)er &c [ˈpɛnər; *ˈpɪnər] *n* **~-pig** a slotted earthenware money-box for small savings, used *esp* by children *la18-20*. [appar reduced f Eng *penury*]

penurious; perneurious &c *la20-*, NE [pə(r)ˈnjurɪʌs] *adj* **1** = penurious. **2** *freq of a child* bad-tempered, whining *20-*, NE. **3** attentive to detail, scrupulous, fastidious, *esp* about food *20-*, NE.

penurité &c [pɛˈnørɪtɪ] *n* **1** destitution, want, poverty *la15-16*. **2** deficiency, dearth, scarcity (of food etc) *16*. [only Sc; L *pēnūria* penury, w altered suffix]

peonar *see* PIONER

pepane &c [*ˈpipən, *ˈpɪp-] *n* a doll; a puppet *15-16*. [appar altered f ME, eModEng *popyn &c*]

pepe *see* PEEP¹, PEEP²

peper *see* PAPER, PEPPER

pepher *see* PIFER

pepill &c *la14-17*; **pipell &c** *la16-e17* [ˈpipl] *n* = people.

pepingo *see* PAPINGO

pepper &c *la15-*, **peper &c** *15-17* [ˈpɛpər] *n* = pepper *15-*; *cf* SPICE.
~ curn &c a pepper-mill *16-e19*. **~ dilse &c** a pungent edible seaweed, jagged fucus *la18-e19*.
~ and mustard (**breed, terrier** *etc*) applied to a dog of the BORDER breed now called Dandie Dinmont *19-20* [f its brindled grey or yellow colour].

peppin &c [ˈpɛpɪn] *vt, chf in adj* **peppint &c** petted, spoilt, pampered *19-*, *Mry Bnf*. [deriv of *paip* pap, soft baby- or invalid food]

peraling *see* PARALE

perance &c [*ˈpirəns] *n* appearance, in sight, before a court etc *la14-15*. [aphetic f *apperance* (APPEARANCE)]

peratt *see* PIRATE

perbrouilʒeit *see* PARBRUILYEID

perceptioune &c *la15*; **perception** *16- n* **1** the (? *chf* wrongful) collection or levy of rents etc *la15-e16*. **2** = perception *la16-*.

perch *see* PARCH

perchment *see* PARCHMENT

perciall *see* PAIRCEL

percill *see* PERSEL

perconnon &c *la18-*, *Abd Kcdn*, **percunnand** *e15* [pɛrˈkʌnən, pri-; *pɛrˈkʌnənd] *conj* (*n*) **~ that, on** *etc* **that** *etc* **~ that** on the understanding that, on condition that, with the proviso that. [only Sc; *per-* + *cunnand* (CONAND), representing OF *par* (*tel*) *covent*]

perdrix &c *n* a partridge *la15*. [only Sc; OF *perdriz*, F *perdrix*; *cf* PAITRICK]

perduellion, perduellioun *e16* [*pɛrdjuˈɛliən] *n*, *law* hostility against the state or government, treason *16-e19*. [only Sc; L *perduellio*, f *perduellis* a public or private enemy]

pere &c *la14-17*; **peer &c** *la15-* [pir; *per] *n*, *vt* = peer, equal *la14-*.
~ and ~ as equal(s) or associate(s) *la14-e15*.

pere *see* PEER², PEER³

pereis(che) *see* PERISH

peremptor &c, peremptour &c *la14-e19*; **paremptour &c** *17*, **peremptory** *18-* [pəˈrɛm(p)tər(ɪ)] *adj* **1** = peremptory *la14-*. **2** *of things* urgent, pressing, unavoidable *e18*. **3** *of persons* positive, absolutely certain *e18*. **4** *of persons* excessively careful, fussy *19-*, *now Sh*.
adv, also **~ly &c** *15-18* = peremptorily *15-e19*.
~ (*la16-17*) *or* **~y** (*la17-*) **defence** *law* a defence put forward by a litigant which, if proved, annuls further proceedings forever; *cf* *dilatory defence* (DILATOR).
be *etc* (**up**)**on** *or* **be put to one's ~s** be precise and formal in one's attitude, stand firm on one's ground *e19*.

perfeck, perfect *see* PERFIT

perfervid [pərˈfɛrvɪd] *adj* ardent; enthusiastically patriotic *19-*. [see SND]

perfit &c *15-e20*, **perfite** *15-e19*, **perfect** *16-*; **perfeck &c** *la19* [*adj* ˈpɛrfɪt, -ˈfəit, -ˈfɛk; *pərˈfəit, *-ˈfɛk; *ˈpar-, *par-; *v* pərˈfɛk, -ˈfəit] *adj* = perfect *15-*.
adv perfectly, faultlessly; completely, absolutely *la15-e20*.
vt **1** = perfect *la15-*. **2** complete (a task etc), finish a job *la16-19*. **3** *specif* train or instruct (a person) completely in a trade, skill etc *la18-e19*.
~ age *etc, chf in legal contexts* the age at which a person attained legal competence, *usu* the age of majority, 21 years *la15-18*.

perfornis *see* PERFURNIS

perfunctorious &c *adj* perfunctory *la16-17*. [only Sc; L *perfunctōrius*]

perfurnis &c *15-16*; **perfornis &c** *la14-e16*, **perfurneis** *16* [*pərˈfʌrnɪs] *vt* **1** bring to completion, finish, carry out (a task, request etc) *la14-16*. **2** complete (a payment), make up (a required total) *15-16*. **3** provide (for), supply *16*. **4** ? provide or construct (an artefact or structure) *e16*. **5** complete or supply with necessary accessories *16*. [nME *perfurnysche &c*, F *parfourniss-*, extended stem of *parfournir*, in OF achieve, complete, furnish completely]

pergaddus &c [pər'gadəs] *n* a heavy blow or fall, thump; a noisy burst of energy *19-e20, Abd Ags Fif.* [prob onomat]

peril &c; peirell &c *17* ['pɛrɪl; *'parəl, *pə'rɔil] *n* **1** = peril *la14-.* **2** the hazard of loss of goods bought or borrowed (as falling on the person in possession at the time) *15-, now rare* [legal L *periculum*].
vt = peril *la16-e17.*

perill *see* PEARL¹

perils *see* PAIRLS

perish &c *16-*, **peris &c** *la14-e17*; **per(r)eis &c** *la15-e17*, **pereische &c** *la16-e17* ['pɛrɪʃ, *-ɪs] *v* **1** *vi* = perish *la14-.* **2** *vt* destroy, kill, bring about the destruction of (a person), *latterly freq* ~**ed with cold &c** *la15-.* **3** squander (money), dissipate, wreck (a ship etc); *joc* 'polish off', finish (food or drink) *la18-, local Sh-SW.*
~ **the pack** squander one's money and possessions, spend all one has *19.*

perish *see* PAIRISH

perjink &c [pər'dʒɪŋk] *adj* **1** trim, neat, smart in appearance *la18-.* **2** prim, strait-laced *la18-.* **3** exact, precise, scrupulously careful, fussy *la18-.*
adv primly, fastidiously, in a precise and careful way *20-.*
n, in pl fussy details, niceties *e19.* [only *Sc; per-* intensifier + prob onomat second element w infl f DINK, JINK¹ etc]

perjure &c [*'pɛrdʒər, *pər'dʒør] *n* perjury *la15-16.*
adj perjured, perjurious *la16-e17.*
vr perjure oneself, commit perjury *16-.* [ME; OF *parjure,* L *perjŭrium*]

perk &c *n* **1** = perk, a pole, perch *la14-e19.* **2** *specif* a wooden pole or rod projecting from a wall or window on which clothes were hung to dry; *latterly* an indoor drying rail or rope *17-20.* **3** a linear measure varying according to district *19-e20, Ayr* [not in normal Scottish linear measure, prob an adaptation of imperial standard].
vir = perk, perch (oneself) *16-e17.*
~-**tree &c** = *n* 1; a clothes-post *la14-19.*

perk *see* PARK

perkin *see* PARKIN

perlaig &c *la20-*; **perlyaag &c** *e20* [pər'l(j)ɑg, -'leg] *n* trash, rubbish; a worthless object; a disgusting mixture of scraps, *esp* rubbishy food *20-, Bnf Abd.* [only *Sc; Eng per-* + *lag* fall behind, w infl f LAGGER]

perlament *see* PARLIAMENT¹

perle *see* PEARL¹, PEARL²

perlicket &c [pər'lɪkɪt] *n* a trace, scrap, an iota *20-, Cai NE.* [only *Sc;* alteration of *(deil) be-licket* (BE-LICKET)]

perling *see* PEARL²

perlit *see* PEARL¹

perlyaag *see* PERLAIG

perma *see* PIRR¹

permanence &c *n* **1** = permanence *la16-.* **2** steadfastness *la16, only Sc.*

permutation *n* **1** = permutation. **2** *law* an exchange of MOVEABLE goods under a contract of consent *la18-19.*

perneurious *see* PENURIOUS

pernicketie &c; pirnickitie &c *19* [pər-'nɪkɪtɪ, &c] *adj* **1** *of persons and their actions* (1) very precise, obsessed by detail, fussy *19-*; (2) cantankerous, touchy, bad-tempered *19-e20.* **2** *of things* requiring close attention or great care, fiddling, troublesome *19-.* [uncertain]

peroffer &c [*pər'ofər] *vt, n* = proffer *la14-16, only Sc.*

peronall [*'pɛronəl] *n* a wanton woman, harlot; *more gen* a young woman *e16.* [appar ME *pernel, parnel*]

perpell *see* PAIRPLE

perpetual &c; perpetuale *15-e16 adj* (15-), *adv* (15-16) = perpetual.
in ~ in perpetuity *la15-16, only Sc.*

perqueer &c *la14-e19*, **parquere &c** *la14-e17*; **perquire &c** *16-e18*, **prequeer &c** *la18-20* [pər'kwir, prə-; *par'kwir, *par'kør] *adv* **1** by heart, from memory; perfectly, accurately *la14-e19.* **2** exactly, without hesitation, distinctly *la18-e19.*
adj **1** *of a person* thoroughly-versed, word-perfect, expert, knowledgeable *16-18.* **2** *of things* clear, distinct, accurate, skilfully made, elaborate *la18.* **3** clearly seen, distinctly visible *20, Ork.*
~**ly** = *adv* 2, *la18-e19.*
leif ~ be short of money, live without financial resources *la16-17.* [only *Sc;* OF *par queur &c*]

perr *see* PAIR

perraling *see* PARALE

perreis *see* PERISH

perrill *see* PEARL¹

perrillis *see* PAIRLS

perroche *see* PAIRISH

pers *see* PIERCE

persave &c *la14-e17*; **perseif &c** *la16-e17* [pər'siv; *-'sev] *vt* = perceive.

persecute &c *vt* = persecute *la15-.*
persecuting time(s) the worst period of the persecution of the Covenanters (COVENANT) *e19, hist; cf killing time(s)* (KILL²). **persecutioun &c of** (legal) prosecution **1** of a person or an action at law; **2** of a legal claim to (a property etc) *la15-e16.*

perseif *see* PERSAVE

persel &c *la16-e19*, **percill &c** *la15-16*; **parsell &c** *la16-18 n* = parsley.

persell *see* PAIRCEL

persevand *see* PURSUIVANT

persew(t) *see* PURSUE

perskeet &c [pər'skit] *adj* fastidious, precise, over-particular; hard-to-please *19-, now Sh.* [obscure]

persoit *see* PURSUE

personage *see* PARSONAGE

person &c ['pɛrsən; *pər'sun] *n* **1** = person *la14-*. **2** a parson *la14-17*.

personal &c = personal *15-*. **personal bar** *law* an impediment to a legal right or action due to a person's own previous statements or behaviour, *corresponding to Eng* estoppel *20-*. **personal diligence** *18-19*, **personal execution** *e19*, *law* the procedure of imprisonment for debt; *cf* DILIGENCE. **personal exception** *20-*, **personal objection** *e19*, *law* = *personal bar*. [ScL *persona* = *n 2*, *la11-e13*; *cf* PARSON]

persow *see* PURSUE

persuade *see* PERSWAD

persuit, persutt *see* PURSUE

perswad &c *16-e20*, **persuade &c** *la15-* [pər'swed, pər'swɑd] *vt* = persuade.

pert &c *la14-*; **pa(i)rt** *la15-e17* [pɛrt; *part, *pirt] *adj* = pert, open; clever etc.

pert *see* PAIRT

perteen &c *17-*, **pertene &c** *la14-17*; **pertine &c** *16-e17* [pər'tin] *v* **1** *vi* = pertain *la14-*. **2** ~ (**un**)**to** *of a legal issue etc* come under the jurisdiction of *15-e17*. **3** *vt* belong to, be connected with (a person or thing) *15-17, la19*. **4** befit (a person) (to do); be suitable or appropriate for *la15-16*: 'Quhat pertenis ane knycht to do'.

Perthshire: ~ **Light Infantry** a Scottish regiment, raised in 1794 as The 90th Perthshire Volunteers; 1815 became 90th Perthshire Light Infantry *19-20*; *cf* CAMERONIAN 2. [the county]

particular *see* PARTICULAR

pertine *see* PERTEEN

pertinence &c; partinence &c *16*, **pertinench &c** *e16* ['pɛrtɪnəns; *'par-, *-ənʃ] *n* **1** = pertinence, an adjunct; the fact of being pertinent *la14-*. **2** *specif* accompaniments to a main dish *16*.

pertinene &c [*?'pɛrtɪnən] *n* an adjunct, accompaniment *15-e16*. [? shortened f next or ? anomalous sing f PERTINENCE taken as a pl]

pertinent &c *n* **1** *law, freq in pl* anything connected with or forming part of a piece of land or HERITABLE property (except the REGALIA) that is not specially reserved from the grant, *eg* buildings on a piece of land, a right of pasturage *15-e20*; see *all part(s) (pendicles) and pertinents* (PAIRT). **2** an accessory, adjunct, appendage *16-, now* Ork.
adj = pertinent *15-*.

pertridge, pertrik *see* PAITRICK

pertrubbil &c [*pɛr'trʌbl] *vt* disturb greatly, cause disorder among *e16*. [chf Sc; OF *pertroubler &c*]

perty *see* PAIRTY

pervene [*pər'vin] *vt* reach *la18*. [L *prevenīre*]

perverst &c *la15-16*; **perversit &c** *la15-e17* [*'pɛrvɛrst; *pər'vɛrs(ɪ)t] *adj* perverted. [chf Sc; Sc ptp form based on L *perversus*]

pervise &c [*?pər'vaɪz] *vt* look over, examine *la16-e17*. [see DOST]

pervoo &c [pər'vu] *vt, of a bird* abandon (its

nest); *of persons* stop keeping regular company with (someone), drop (a friend) *20-, Abd.* [var of FORHOO]

pes *see* PEASE[1]

Pes(che) *see* PACE

pese *see* PEACE, PEASE[1]

pes(si)ment *see* PASSMENT

pest &c *n* **1** (an outbreak of) any virulent or deadly epidemic disease, *specif* bubonic plague *la15-19*. **2** a troublesome, annoying person or thing *16-*.
vt trouble, annoy, plague, pester *18-, local Sh-SW*. [F *peste*, L *pestis* plague, contagious disease]

pestell &c *15-e17*; **pistoll &c** *la16-17* *n* = pestle.

pester &c *vt* **1** = pester *la17-*. **2** encumber, obstruct, impede *17-, now Ags Ayr*.

pestilentious &c *adj* **1** tending to produce pestilence, noxious to life or health *16-e17*. **2** *fig* = pestilentious, morally pernicious *16*. [earlier in Sc]

pestinence &c *n* plague, pestilence; a moral mischief, source of corruption *e16*. [only Sc; altered f Eng *pestilence*]

pestolat *see* PISTOLET[1]

pestole *see* PISTOLL[2]

pestolet *see* PISTOLET[2]

pestoll *see* PISTOLL[1]

pet[1], pett *n* **1** an animal which has been domesticated and treated with affection, *freq* a hand-reared lamb or sheep *16-*. **2** *also fig, orig* (*16*) **carlingis** ~ a favourite person, a petted or spoiled child *16-*. **3** a day of sunshine in the middle of a spell of bad weather, *freq* ~ **day** *19-, local C-S*.
vt make a PET[1] of, treat with special favour, fondle, cuddle *17-*.
interj a call to a sheep or lamb *20-, now Cai Ags Kcb*.

pettle &c = *v, la18-, now S*.

~**-willed &c** headstrong, self-willed, obstinate *20-, NE*. [orig chf Sc; northern eModEng *pette*, OIr *peat(t)a*, ScGael *peata* a domesticated animal; a fine day; appar not connected w PEAT[2]]

pet[2] &c, pett *n* = pet, ill-humour *la16-*.
vti (cause to) take offence, anger, upset *18-*.

pet *see* PEAT[1], PEAT[2], PIT[1]

pete &c [*pit, *pet] *n* = *peat-stane* (PEAT[1]) *16-e17*. [? shortened forms; *cf* PUTT[2]]

pete *see* PEAT[1], PEAT[2]

peté *see* PEETY

pete *see* PETTY

peteous *see* PEETY

peter *n* come the ~ **ower** act in a domineering way over, dictate to *20-*. **pit the** ~ **on** put a firm and sudden stop to, bring up short *la19-*. [uncertain; *cf* Eng slang *peter* stop, leave off]

Peter: petrie-ball *prob* = ~ *bowie*, *la19-e20, NE Fif*. ~(**ie**) *or* (**-a**)**-dick** a rhythmic pattern of two or three short beats followed by one long, *freq* beaten out by the feet as a dance step or with the knuckles on a board; a child's toy which can be used to reproduce this rhythm *19-, Sh-N Renfr Uls*.

~ &c **bowie** a wedge or stick used by shoemakers for rubbing the seams of shoes before sewing *19*. ~ **evin** &c the eve of *Petermes, la16-e17, only Sc*. ~ **fyir** a bonfire made for *Petermes, la16, only Sc*. ~**mes** &c the feast of St Peter and St Paul (29 June); the feast of St Peter ad Vincula, LAMMAS (1 Aug) *15-e16*. ~**'s plough** the constellation *Ursa Major*, the Plough *19-e20*. ~**'s thoom** &c *la20-, Sh-N, WC, (St)* ~**'s mark** *19-, Cai NE, WC* one of the black marks behind the gills of a haddock [popularly thought to be the fingerprint of St Peter when he caught the fish for the tribute money (Matthew xvii 27)]. [the personal name]

peth &c *now NE Loth Ayr S*, **path** &c, **paith**(e) *16-19*; **peath** &c *16-e18* [pɛθ, paθ; *peθ] *n* **1** a cleft etc running up and down the slope of a steep hill; a steep track or road leading down into a ravine and up the other side *la14-, in place-names 12-*. **2 the peths** &c name for several ravines crossing the coastal route from Scotland to England near Cockburnspath *16-e17*. **3** = path *16-*.

pethar *see* PEDDER

petition, petitioune &c *15-17 n* **1** = petition *15-*. **2** *law* one of the methods by which proceedings can be brought before the *Court of Session* (SESSION) or the *High Court of Justiciary* (JUSTICIARY) *19-; cf* SUMMONS.

~ **and complaint** an application to the *Court of Session* (SESSION) for redress of *eg* complaints of professional misconduct brought against MAGISTRATES etc; *formerly also* the form for bringing under review by the *Court of Session* the actions of *freeholders* (FREE) and MAGISTRATES of *royal burghs* (ROYAL) at their *head courts* (HEID) *19-*.

petitor, petitour &c *15-17 n* **1** = petition *15-*.

petitor, petitour &c *15-17 adj* = ~*y, la15-e17*.

~**y** ['pɛtɪtərɪ] *chf of an action, freq contrasted with* **possessory** in which the court is asked to order the *defender* (DEFEND) to do something, *eg* to pay money, to deliver goods *15-*.

petous *see* PEETY

petrie-ball *see* PETER

Petronella [pɛtrəˈnɛlə] *n* name of a Scottish country dance, said to have been introduced by the fiddler Nathaniel Gow *19-*.

pett *see* PEAT[1], PET[1], PET[2]

pette *see* PETTY

petticoat &c *la17-*, **petticote** &c *la15-e17*; **pit**(t)**iecoat** &c *la16-e18*, **peittiecott** &c *e17* ['pɛtɪkot; *'pɪtɪ-] *n* = petticoat *la15-*.

~ **tails** triangular *shortbread* (SHORT) biscuits cut from a round, with the outer edge scalloped *19-*.

pettle *see* PATTLE, PET[1]

petty &c; **pet**(t)**é** *la15-e16*, **pittie** &c *la15-e18*

adj **1** = petty *15-*. **2** *with a proper name, forming a nickname* small in size or stature *la15-17*: 'Pette Johnne'.

~**-commo**(**u**)**nis** an allowance of food, or sometimes money, assigned to a member of a society *la16-e17*. ~**pan** a small metal pan or mould used for pastry *18-e19*. ~**-point** petit point *17-e19*.

petuous *see* PEETY

peuch &c; **pugh** &c *e19*, **pyoch** &c *la19-* [pjux, pjox; *pux] *interj* **1** imitating the sound of the wind etc, puff! *la19-e20*. **2** expressing impatience, disgust, disbelief etc, pooh! *19-, now Sh Ags Per*.

n a light blast of air, a puff of wind or breath *19-, now Sh Abd*.

vi, freq **pyocher, peughle** puff, blow, give a gusty sigh *la19-, now Sh Ags*.

peuchle &c *19-e20*, **pyocher** &c *20-, Sh NE Ags vi* **1** fuss about or work ineffectually, make a poor attempt at something *19-, now Sh*. **2** cough in a choking, asthmatic way, repeatedly clear one's throat and chest of catarrh *20-, now Sh NE Ags*. *n, also* **peucher** *la20-, NE* a persistent choking cough *20-, now NE*. [onomat; *cf* PECH]

peuch *see* PLEUCH

peuchtie &c; **pituchtie** &c [p(ɪt)ˈjuxtɪ] *n* a young saithe or coalfish *20, Arg Ayr*. [perh altered f Gael *piocach* ['pɪxkəx]]

peudenite &c [*?ˈpjudənis] *n* a kind of fur *e16*. [perh misreading for *peudenice*, ? *peau de Nice*]

peug &c [*pjug] *n* = puke, a high quality woollen cloth *la16*.

peughle *see* PEUCH

peumonie &c *n, joc* = pneumonia *20-*.

peur *see* PUIR

peuther[1] *17-e18*, **pewther** *17-19*, **pewder** &c *la15-17*; **pouder** &c *la15-e18*, **podir** &c *16*, **puder** &c *16-e18*, **pulder** *16*, **puther** *17-18* ['pjutər; *'putər, *'p(j)uθər, *'p(j)udər] *n* = pewter *la15-*.

~**er** &c *16-17*, **pewder-makkar** &c *la16, only Sc* a worker in pewter and also in lead and tin; a pewterer.

peuther[2] &c; **pewter** &c *19* ['pjuθər, 'pjutər] *v* **1** *vi* fuss about doing nothing, fumble, make a great show of working *19-, Ork Ags Uls*. **2** *vti* importune in a fussy and ingratiating way, bustle about trying to win favour; *specif* canvass for votes using flattery *18-e20*. [see SND]

pevagely *see* PEVYCH

pevych &c [*?ˈpivɪʃ, *?-ɪtʃ] *adj* = peevish *e16*.

pevagely [*?ˈpivɪdʒlɪ] = peevishly *e16*.

pew &c; **pue** *19-e20, SW n* **1** the cry of a bird, *esp* the kite *la15-16*. **2** a stream of air, a breath, the sound made by exhaling *la19-, now Sh*. **3** a puff or breath of smoke, wind etc *19-, SW*. **4** a small quantity of a substance, a trace *19-, now Sh*.

vi **1** *of birds* cry, peep *e16*. **2** *of smoke, vapour etc* puff out, rise through the air *19-, now Kcb*.

play ~ *chf in negative* stop breathing; have no effect; make no impression; be unable to compete *18-e19*. [only Sc; imit]

pewder &c *n* = *pewderer* (PEUTHER¹) *17*. [? altered or erron form]

pewder *see* PEUTHER¹

pewl &c; pule *19-e20*, **pyowl &c** *la19-e20* [pjul; *Sh* pjurl; *NE also* pjʌul] *vi* **1** = pule, whine, complain; cry in a shrill piercing tone *19-*, *now local Sh-Per*. **2** (1) *chf of animals* be in a weak state, pine *19-e20*. (2) *fig, of people* be only half-alive, scrape a bare living, live from hand to mouth *19-*, *Ags Per*. **3** *of snow or rain* fall thinly, intermittently or in small amounts *19-e20*, *Rox*.

n **1** a wailing cry, shriek; a moan, complaint *20-*, *Abd Per*. **2** (1) a seagull, *specif* the herringgull, from its wailing cry *19-*, *NE*. (2) *in pl* nickname for the inhabitants of some of the remote Buchan fishing villages perched on or overhung by cliffs *20*, *Bnf Abd*. **3** a thin curl or wisp (of smoke or vapour) *19-e20*. **4** a small morsel (of food), a bite, nibble (*esp* of grass for an animal) *19*.

~**ie** (**Willie**) = *n* 2 (1), *e20*.

~ **amang, at** *or* **ower one's food** eat listlessly and without appetite, pick at one's food *18-20*.

pewter *see* PEUTHER²

pewther *see* PEUTHER¹

pey &c *la15-*, **pay &c; pa &c** *la15-e16*, **py** *17-20* [pəi] *vti* **1** = pay *la14-*. **2** beat, chastise *15-*. **3** *vt, of a source of income* yield or provide (a certain payment) *15-*. **4** pay for *19-*: '*it'll help tae pey the coal*'.

n **1** = pay *15-*. **2** a blow, punishment, chastisement: (1) *in sing, la14-15*; (2) *in pl, 19-, now Ork Ags*.

~**ment &c** **1** = payment *la14-*. **2** punishment, chastisement, a beating, thrashing *la14-*, *now Bnf Abd*. **3** means of payment, currency, *usu* **Scots** ~**ment** *etc*, *15-16*, *only Sc*. ~**ment making** = payment, the action of paying *la16-e17*.

~**master &c** **1** = paymaster. **2** a person made responsible for discharging a debt or refunding a loss to another *17*, *only Sc*.

~**-wedding &c** = *penny wedding* (PENNY) *19-*, *now Loth Kcb*.

~ **aff** pay for others' drink or entertainment *20-*, *Ags WC*. ~ (**someone**) **when a' man** ~**s ither** pay (one's creditor) when everyone else does, *ie* never *20-*, *NE*. ~ (**someone**) **hame** give (someone) his deserts, repay in full *la16-e19*. ~ **on, alang** *etc* go quickly, hurry *19-*, *now Bnf*. ~ **someone's skin** *etc* give someone a good beating, thrash someone *18-*, *now Sh*. ~ **up** do (something) with energy and application *la19-*, *now Abd*.

pey *see* PEA, PEE²

peyes *see* PEASE¹

peyet *see* PYOT

peyper *see* PAPER

peyzart &c ['pəizərt, -ərd] *n* a miser, skinflint *19-e20*. [obscure]

phalme *see* PSALM

phan &c [*fen] *n* = vane, a weathercock *16-17*.

phanatik &c [*ʔfə'natɪk] *adj, n* = fanatic *la16-17*.

pharmacian [*fər'masɪən] *n* a pharmacist, apothecary *la17-e18*. [F *pharmacien*]

pheare, pheere *see* FERE²

pheise *see* PHISE

phesand &c ['fezənd; 'fezənt, 'feʒən; *-ənd] *n* = pheasant *la15-17*.

philabeg *see* FILLEBEG

philagram *n* = filigree *la17*.

philamort *see* FEILAMORT

philosell &c [*'fɪlosɛl] *n* = filoselle, rough silk thread *la16*.

philosophour &c *n* = philosopher *la15-16*.

~ **naturall** a student of natural phenomena *la15-e16*; *cf natural philosophy* (NATURAL).

philosophy &c *n* **1** = philosophy *la14-*. **2** *specif, Sc Univs* applied to the courses in Ethics, Physics and Metaphysics which constituted the later and greater part of the MA degree; the term was extended to cover the preliminary studies in Latin and Greek and so came to designate the Arts course as a whole *e18* [on the abolition of the REGENT system the Arts subjects were departmentalized and the name PHILOSOPHY reverted to its proper categories while *Arts* was used for the faculty and its combined disciplines; *cf* PEDAGOGY and see also *natural philosophy* (NATURAL)].

phiscall *see* FISCALE

phise &c *la16*; **pheise &c** [fiz] *n* **1** ? a device operated by screws, for mounting a cannon or attaching a cannon to its stock; ? a type of vice or clamp operated by turning a screw *la16*. **2** ? a mechanical device used in warehouses; ? a type of screw-operated hoist *e17*, *Abd*. [only Sc; var of *fize* (FEEZE)]

phisik &c ['fɪzɪk; *'fiz-] *n* = physic *la15-17*.

under (**the cure of**) ~ under medical care, receiving medical treatment *17*.

phrais *see* FARCE

phrase¹ &c; fra(i)se &c *18-20 n* **1** = phrase *16-*. **2** an elaborate flowery speech, gushing and effusive talk, flattery *18-*, *now NE*. **3** a great or ostentatious talk about something, a palaver *la18-*, *now Abd Ags*. **4** something false and misleading, a pretence, delusion *la19-*, *now NE Ags*.

v **1** *vt* = phrase. **2** (1) flatter, praise in an ingratiating and often insincere way, fawn on *la18-*, *NE*. (2) *vi* ~ (**wi**) make fine speeches, use flowery, gushing language (to) *20-*, *NE*.

faizle = *v* 2, *19*. **phraser &c** a wheedler, sycophant *19-*, *Bnf Abd*. **phrasie &c 1** gushing, fulsome *19-*, *now Abd*. **2** fussy, fastidious *20-*, *Bnf Abd*. **phrasing &c** *adj* fulsome, ingratiating, insincere in speech *19-20*. *n* flattery, 'gush' *19-e20*.

haud a ~ wi = mak a ~ wi, *la18-, now Abd.*
mak a ~ l make a 'song and dance', make an outcry *17-e20.* **2** boast, brag, exaggerate, gush *18-e19.* **mak a ~ wi** *etc* flatter, 'butter up' *la18-e20.*
phrase[2] *vt, chf in ptp* **fraized** greatly surprised, having a wild, staring look *19-e20.* [conflation of FAIZE[2] and RAISE]
piatch *see* PEATCH
pibroch &c ['pibrox] *n* the music of the Scottish bagpipe, *now* limited to traditional *gatherings* (GAITHER), marches, salutes, laments etc (in Gaelic called *ceòl mor* literally = great music); a piece of this, consisting of a theme (the URLAR) and a series of variations *18-.* [Gael *pìobaireachd* piping]
piccatarrie *see* PICTARNIE
pice *see* PIECE[1]
pichar &c *la15-e16;* **pitcher** *la16-* ['pɪtʃər; *'pitʃ-] *n* **1** = pitcher *la15-.* **2** the quantity, *esp* of ale held by a pitcher, *appar* accepted as a standard measure *la15-17.*
picher &c ['pɪxər] *n* **1** a state of confusion or muddle, an excited or overwrought state of mind *la19-, NE Ags.* **2** a useless, ineffective person, a person who is habitually in a 'flap' *la19-, Bnf Abd.*
vi work in an unplanned and disorganized way, muddle along *la19-, now NE.*
~in fumbling, ineffectual, unmethodical *la19-, now NE.* **~t** at a loss, perplexed, unable to cope *20-, Bnf Abd.* [perh altered f colloq obs Eng *pucker* fluster, agitation, w infl f Eng *pickle* a predicament]
picht *see* PECHT, PITCH
pick[1] **&c** *la16-,* **pik &c** *la14-e16 vti* **1** = pick *la14-.* **2** *vi* be a petty thief, pilfer *18-e19.* **3** *vt* question or pump (someone), 'pick someone's brains' *20-, Ork NE Ags Slk.*
n **1** = pick, one's unrestricted choice, a choice article. **2** a pecking, (a quantity of) food, one's keep *18-19.* **3** a small quantity, trace, scrap *la19-.*
~er 1 *weaving* the person who cuts off any loose or protruding threads from the web *19-, now Ayr.* **2** *in a sawmill* the man who arranges the sawn timber according to size *la20-, NE Ags.* **3** *mining* a sharp piece of metal used to trim the wick of a miner's lamp *19-20.* **~ery &c** *la15-e19,* **pekery &c** *17, WC, SW* ['pɪk(ə)rɪ; *WC, SW also* *'pik-] **1** *law* theft, *esp* petty theft, pilfering *la15-e20, latterly hist.* **2** articles pilfered *16-e17.* **3** an act of *pickery,* a petty theft *la16-e19.* **~et &c** meagre, scraggy, shrunken; mean *la18-e20.* **~ie** a person who picks at his food, a poor eater *la19-, now local C-S.* **hae a ~ie (o) say** have a certain amount of authority or responsibility, be in a position of influence, *specif* of a farm servant etc who has had promotion *e20.* **~ie-say &c (hat)** the narrow-brimmed tweed hat, worn as a badge of authority by a foreman or gaffer on a farm *20-,*

NE. **~in(g) &c** a mouthful of food, a frugal meal *19-.* **~le &c** peck (up) repeatedly and delicately; *of persons* eat in a sparing way, nibble *16-e19.* **~le in one's ain pock-neuk** rely on one's own resources, be self-supporting *17-e19.* **~le oot o ae pock** *of a number of persons* share a common means of livelihood, live together *la18-19.*
~-thank *n* a person who curries favour by discreditable means, a sycophant, sneak, gossip *16-19.* *adj* ungrateful, unappreciative *la19-, NE.*
~ an dab a light meal, snack, *specif* of potatoes dipped in salt *19-20.* **~ one's lane** be self-supporting, able to fend for oneself *19.* **~ someone up** understand someone, get someone's meaning *la19-, Sh-Per, WC.* **~ and wale** = **1** *n* 1, *la18-, now Sh Bnf Abd.* [*cf* PIKE]
pick[2] *17-,* **pik &c** *la14-e20 n* **1** = pick, the tool *la14-.* **2** a chap on the skin *20-, Ork Bnf Abd.* **3** a light stroke or tap, *usu* with a pointed instrument *16-20.*
vt **1** = pick, pierce with a pick or sharp instrument *17-.* **2** *vi,* **~ on** *lit and fig* make an impression on, affect *19-, Kcb.*
~it &c roughened, pitted, uneven *la19-, now NE Loth.*
~(ie)man &c *la16-, now Sh* ['pɪk(ɪ)'man], **pikeman** *la16,* **pikkeman &c** *la16-17* **1** a man who dresses millstones with a *mill pick* (MILL) *la16-, now Sh.* **2** *only* **~man** a miner, coal hewer *17-, now Fif.* **~-staff** a pike-staff *la15-e19.*
~ and mell with utmost vigour, 'hammer and tongs' *la19-, now Wgt.*
pick[3] **&c;** **peek-** *la19-20 vti* **1** throw, pitch, hurl; thrust, drive *19-e20.* **2** *weaving* throw the shuttle across the loom *la20-, local Ags-Uls.* **3** *vt* **~ (up)on** pitch on, fix on, choose *19-.* **4** *of a female (farm-)animal* abort (her young), give birth to prematurely, *freq* **pick calf** *la18-, NE-S.*
n **1** a marble, *usu* of earthenware, which was thrown or pitched at the other marbles instead of being rolled *20-, Bnf-Ags.* **2** an aborted or stillborn animal *20-, now WC, S Uls.*
~er *19-20,* **~er stick** *etc, 20-, now Ayr, weaving* a mechanism for shooting the shuttle across the loom. **tak a ~(ie)** *marbles* throw or aim a marble (**at** another) instead of rolling it, pitch from a height *20-, Ags.* [nME *pykke, pikke* (v) pitch]
pick[4] **&c,** **pik** *la16-e17 n* = pique *la16-e18.*
~ant &c ['pɪkən(t)] = piquant, sharp, keen, biting, tart *la16-, now NE.*
hae *or* **tak a ~ at** have or form a dislike for, bear (someone) a grudge *18-, now N Ags Kcb.*
pick[5] *16-,* **pik &c** *la14-e20;* **peik &c** *la16-e17* [pɪk] *n* = pitch, the black, resinous substance *la14-.*
vt = pitch, daub or smear with pitch *la14-e19.*

~y &c of or like pitch *e16*. **~y-fingered** 'sticky-' or 'tarry-fingered' *19-, now Per*.

~ **black** *etc* pitch-dark, as black as night *la18-20*. ~ **tar** = *n*, 20-.

pick[6] **&c** a spade in playing cards *19-, Bnf Abd*. [only Sc; F *pique*]

pick *see* PECHT

pickerel &c, pikkerel *n* the dunlin; any small wading bird *la17-e20*. [f PICK[1] or Eng *picker* + *-rel*]

pickery, picket *see* PICK[1]

picket-a *see* PICTARNIE

pickie &c *n* the young of the SAITHE, any small fry of fish *la19-, now Ayr*. [Gael *piocach*; *cf* PEUCHTIE]

pickindail &c, pikkindaill &c *n* = piccadill, a decorative collar *17-e18*.

pickle[1] **&c, pikkill &c** *la16-e17* *n* **1** (1) = pickle, a liquid for preserving food *la16-*. (2) = pickle, a predicament *19-*. **2** an elaborate and demanding piece of work, a fiddling awkward job *la20-, now WC* [perh var of PICHER]. **~ty &c** = *n* 1 (2), *19-, local NE-SW*.

pickle[2] **&c, pikkill &c** *la16-17*; **puckle** *la19-* ['pɪkl; *sEC-S also* 'pʌkl] *n* **1** a grain of oats, barley or wheat *la16-20*. **2** a small particle or grain of salt, meal etc, a granule, speck *17-, now Sh*. **3** a small or indefinite amount of something, a number of persons or things, a little, a few *17-*.

adv, only **puckles** occasionally, now and then *la20-, NE*. [unknown]

pickle *see* PICK[1]

pickmaw &c *19-, now local*, **pikmaw** *la15* *n* the black-headed gull.

pickie-maw &c = *n*, 20-, *Rox*. [only Sc; perh PICK[2] or PICK[5] + MAW[2]]

pict *see* PECHT

pictarnie &c; picktarntie &c *19-20*, **piccatarrie &c** *la19-e20*, **picket-a** *19* ['pɪ(k)'tar(n)ɪ, -'tɑr(n)ɪ, -'tɛrnɪ, 'pɪkɪ-, &c] *n* **1** the common or arctic tern *la18-, now Sh Ork Fif*. **2** the black-headed gull *18-, local*. **3** *fig* a thin wretched-looking person, a 'scarecrow'; a bad-tempered person *19-e20*. [only Sc; *pick* as in PICKMAW + Eng *tern*]

picter &c *la16-*, **picture &c** *16-* *n* = picture.

pie[1] **&c** *la16-*, **py** *16-18* *n* **1** = pie *16-*. **2** an affair, matter, PLOY[1], escapade *la19-20*.

pie[2] **&c** *vi* peer closely, squint *19-20*.

~-eyed cross-eyed, having a squint; drunk *la20-, Kcdn WC*. [perh f Eng *spy* by wrong division of *he's spying* etc]

pie *see* PIE-HOLE

piece[1] **&c** *la16-*, **pece &c** *la14-e18*; **pace** *16-17*, **pice** *16-e18* [pis] *n* **1** = piece (1) *in gen, la14-*; (2) *uninflected in pl after numerals etc, la15-*; (3) *with omission of* OF *etc, 16-*. **2** an area of land, stretch of water; a district, territory *la15-17*. **3** an indefinite distance, *esp* a short distance *15-, now Sh-Per* [short for ~ *of ground* etc]. **4** a portion or space of time *19-, Abd*. **5** a head (of

cattle etc) *la15-e18*. **6** (1) a goblet, *usu* of silver *la15-17*. (2) one of the containers used for collecting church offerings *la16, Dundee Edb*. **7** *law* a writ establishing a right or title *la16-e17*. **8** a piece of food, a snack, *now usu* a piece of bread, SCONE etc with butter, jam etc *17-*. **9** *derog* a (bad etc) untrustworthy etc person, 'type' *18-19*. **10** the ~ each, apiece *18-*.

a piecie a little, somewhat, rather *20-, local Sh-EC*.

~ **box** the box in which a workman or schoolchild carries a lunchtime snack *20-, local*. ~ **denner &c** a lunchtime snack of sandwiches etc *la20-, NE, EC, S*. ~ **poke** the paper bag etc in which a snack is carried *20-, local NE-Kcb*. ~ **time** a break for a meal or snack during working or school hours *la19-*.

a piece = *a piecie, 20-, local Sh-EC*. **baby's** ~ a slice of cake, cheese and a coin offered to the first person to see a baby after its christening *20-, local EC*. **noon(ing)-piece** = ~ *denner, la19-*. ~ **and** ~ piece by piece, little by little, gradually *16-18*. **play** ~ a mid-morning snack at school *20-*. **schule &c** ~ a child's mid-morning or lunchtime snack at school *20-*. **tea** ~ a mid-afternoon snack *la19-, Abd Fif*.

piece[2] *conj* although *la18-e19*. [reduced f *apiece* (ALBUIST)]

pie-hole &c *18-* *n*, also **py** *la16-17*, **pie** *la19* a hole made in fabric or leather to allow a lace or cord to pass through, an eyelet *la16-*. [uncertain]

piend *see* PEEN[2]

pierce &c *la16-*, **pers &c** *la14-17*; **peirse &c** *la15-e17*, **pairse &c** *16, la19* [pirs; *C also* pers] *vti* = pierce *la14-*.

piercing-shot *mining* a blast of explosive in the roof or *brushing* (BRUSH[2]), designed to bring down an increasing thickness of stone *la19-, now Fif*.

pies *see* PEASE[1]

piet *see* PYOT

pieté &c ['pitɪ, 'paɪətɪ] *n* **1** = piety *la15-e17*. **2** godliness, devoutness, reverence *la15-17*. [*cf* PEETY]

pietuous *see* PEETY

pifer &c; pepher &c, peiffer &c [*'pɪfər, *'pifər] *n* **1** a player on the fife *la16*. **2** a fife or other wind instrument *la16-17*.

~er &c = *n* 1, *la16-e17*. [only Sc; F *pif(f)re*, Ital *piffero*, MedL *piffarus &c* a fife]

pif(f)er *see* PEEFER

pig[1] **&c** *n* **1** = pig *la15-*. **2** a small, stunted lamb fattened for the market instead of being kept for breeding *e19, S*.

~-crue &c *la19-, now Ags Per*, **~-hoose** *20-* a pigsty.

pig[2] **&c** *n* **1** a container, *usu* of earthenware; a pot, jar, pitcher; *in pl* crockery *la15-*. **2** *specif* (1) a cinerary urn *e16*; (2) an earthenware chimney-pot *la17-, now Ayr*; (3) a flower vase *18-, Abd Ags Loth*; (4) a chamber-pot *19-, now*

Ags Loth; (5) an earthenware money-box, *now* sometimes shaped like the animal *19-*; (6) an earthenware hot-water bottle *la19-*. **3** earthenware as a material; a fragment or sherd of earthenware, *esp* as used in children's games *la16-20*.

~(**g**)**er 1** a dealer in earthenware, a maker or seller of crockery *17-*, *now NE Ags*. **2** an earthenware or clay marble *la19-*, *now Ags*. ~**gery &c** crockery, dishes *19-*, *Abd Kcdn*. ~**fu &c** a quantity filling a PIG² (*n* 1), a dishful *la16-e19*. ~**gie &c bank** = *n* 2 (5), *20-*. ~**gy bool** a clay marble *la20-*, *NE Ags*. ~**gie money** broken bits of earthenware used by children as money when playing at 'shops' *la20-*, *EC Rox*. ~-**cart** the cart carrying the crockery-merchant's stock *la19-20*, *WC*. ~ **maker &c** a potter, a maker of coarse pottery *16-e18*. ~**man** a pottery merchant, *freq* an itinerant one, a *pig-an'-ragger*, *la17-*, *NE-S*. ~ **shop &c** a stall or shop selling cheap crockery, a china-shop *la19-*, *EC*. ~-**wife** a female crockery-seller, *usu* one going from door to door giving pottery in exchange for rags *19-*, *now nEC*. ~-**an'-ragger** a travelling hawker giving crockery in exchange for rags *la19-*, *NE*. ~**s an**(**d**) **whistles** odds and ends, bits and pieces, trivialities *la17-e19*. **to** ~**s an' whistles** to pieces, to ruin *la18-*. [ME *pygg*]

piggé *see* PEGY-MAST

piggin &c ['pɪgɪn] *n* a container, *usu* of wood, tub-shaped and with one stave extended to form a handle, used as a milk-pail, feeding dish etc *la18-*, *now Uls*. [uncertain]

pik &c *n* **1** a weapon consisting of a long wooden shaft or pike-staff, with a pointed head of iron or steel; a pike-staff *16-17*. **2** *literary* applied to earlier staff weapons *la16*. [chf Sc; eModEng *pick*(*e*) collateral form of *pike*, F *pique*]

pik *see* PICK¹, PICK², PICK⁴, PICK⁵

pikant &c [*'pɪkən(d), *-ənt] *n* a prickle, thorn *la15*. [F *piquant* (*adj*) used as noun, f *piquer* prick, sting]

pike &c [pəik] *n* **1** a pick, pickaxe *la16-e19*. **2** a pointed tip or end (of a horn etc); a spike (of a railing etc) *la15-*, *now Ork NE, EC, S*. **3** (1) a thorn or prickle on a plant; a spine or quill of an animal *la15-*, *now Ork*. (2) a long, pointed piece of lead for ruling paper; a slate pencil *19*, *NE*. (3) the pin on the sternpost of a boat *20-*, *Kcdn*. **4** that which has been picked, a picking, *specif* a bite of food, a light meal *la19-*, *Per*. **5** a round, conical-topped hay-rick for drying hay before stacking *19-*, *now SW, S Uls*. **6** = PICK⁴ *20-*, *Bnf Abd*.

vti **1** = pick, probe with a pointed instrument; peck; choose *la14-*, *now Ork NE nEC Rox*. **2** (1) steal, pilfer; indulge in petty theft *la15-*, *now Abd*. (2) *vt, of illness, hunger etc* make (a person or animal) thin and emaciated, reduce to skin and bone *la19-*, *now Ork*. (3) *vti, freq of pasturing animals* eat in a delicate leisurely way, nibble, pick (at food) *la18-*, *now NE, S*. **3** *vt* provide with a pike or pikes or with a spike or spikes, *specif* shoe (a horse) with *sharps* (SHAIRP) to give a grip on icy roads *19-*, *now Abd*. **4** scold, beat, chastise *19-e20*. **5** build (hay) into a PIKE (*n* 5) *19-*, *chf S*.

piker &c 1 *also* **pekar** *la17*, *Arg* [*'pɪkər] a thief, robber, pilferer *la14-e18*. **2** a person who builds hay into PIKES (*n* 5) *20-*, *S*. **pikery &c** ['pəik(ə)rɪ] petty theft *16-e19*. **pikie &c** spiked, jagged, barbed *19-*, *NE Ags Fif*. **pikin**(**g**) *n* the action of stealing, petty theft *la15-17*. *adj* engaged in petty theft, dishonest *16-19*. **pikit &c 1** = piked, spiky *16-e17*. **2** *also* **piket-like** *la19-*, *now EC, of a person or animal* having a gaunt emaciated appearance, thin and unhealthy-looking *la19-*, *now EC*. **pikit weir** barbed wire *20-*, *NE Ags*.

~-**purse** a person who steals purses or their contents *la16-17*. ~-**staff** a long walking-stick with a spike on the lower end *la15-e19*. **ding on, rain** *etc* **auld wives** *or* **puir men an** ~ **staves** teem with rain, rain cats and dogs *19-*, *now NE Ags*. ~-**thank** *n* (*18-*, *now Cai*), *adj* (*19-*, *Bnf Abd*) = *pick-thank* (PICK¹). **a** ~-**at-one's-meat** a poor or fussy eater *20-*, *local NE-S*. ~ **up** sail along, sail close to (the coast) *e16*. [*cf* PICK¹]

Pikkardie &c *adj*, *of hemp* of or from Picardy *la16-e17*. [the French province]

pikkerel *see* PICKEREL

pikkill *see* PICKLE¹, PICKLE²

pikkillar &c [*'pɪk(ə)lər] *n* a petty thief or pilferer *la16*, *Fif*. [? altered f Eng *picker* a thief or *piker* (PIKE) or ? f *pickle &c* (PICK¹)]

pikkindaill *see* PICKINDAIL

pikmaw *see* PICKMAW

pik-moyane &c *n* a kind of culverin, a large cannon *e16*. [only Sc; *pik* of uncertain origin + MOYEN²]

pikoneir &c [*'pɪkə'nir, *?'pɪkənər] *n* a soldier armed with a pike *16-17*. [only Sc; MDu *pikenier*, OF *piquenaire*]

pilch *see* PILSH

pildagerst &c [*'pɪl(d)ə'gɛrst, &c] *n* the groats from the naked oat or barley *17*. [? *pilled* ptp of eModEng *pill* peel, strip the rind etc from + GIRST]

pile¹ &c *n* **1** = pile, a pointed stake *15-*. **2** a blade (of grass etc) *16-e20*. **3** a grain (of corn etc); a leaf (of tea etc); a husk; a pellet (of shot) *la18-*, *now Dnbt Kcb*. **4** a snowflake *20-*, *WC*. *vt, chf in verbal noun* **piling &c** driving in stakes, *chf* to indicate the limits of mineral workings *la16-18*.

piling a paling, fence *19-*, *SW, S*. **pilin lett** a slat of wood in a fence *la20-*, *SW, S*.

pile² &c *n* = pile, a heap *la16-*.

v **1** *vt* = pile, make into a heap. **2** *vtir* increase the motion or speed of a swing, scooter etc by moving the body or feet *la20-, now Kcdn Per Fif*.
piler a boy's home-made cart, propelled as in *v* 2, *la20-, EC, WC*.

pilgat(e) *see* PILGET²

pilget¹ &c ['pɪlgɪt] *n* **1** a quarrel, disagreement, wrangle; *also fig* a fight, struggle, battle against odds *la18-, NE*.   **2** a state of distress or excitement, a fluster, panic *la19-, now NE*.
vi, freq of children quarrel, wrangle, bicker *19*. [unknown]

pilget² *17-e18*, **pilȝet** *e16*, **pilgate** &c *16-e17* [*'pɪl(d)jət] *n* a soft saddle used by women. [only Sc; altered f *pilȝane* (PILLION)]

pilgrim &c; **pilgrame** &c *la14-16 n* = pilgrim *la14-*.
~**er** &c *also fig* a pilgrim *16-e20*.

pilk &c [pɪlk; *Sh also* pəilk] *v* **1** *vt* pick out, shell, peel; top and tail (gooseberries) *18-, now Sh*.   **2** *vti* pilfer, pocket, indulge in petty theft *la18-, now Sh*.   **3** *vt* milk (a cow etc) down to the last drops, STRIP³ of milk *19-, now Wgt*.
n a husk, an empty shell; a morsel, scrap *20-, now Sh*. [ME *pilk* pluck, LowGer *pülken*, Du *pulken; cf* Norw, Faeroese *pilka* pick, scrape]

pill *n, chf* ~**ie** the penis *la16-, now local*. [*cf* Norw dial *pill*]

pillage &c *n* **1** = pillage *la15-*.   **2** *specif* the share of the contents of a prize-ship due by law to the ordinary members of the ship's company which made the capture *la16-e17*.

pillan *see* PILLER

pillar &c; **pellar** &c *la16* ['pɪlər] *n* **1** = pillar *la14-*.   **2** a pillar in a church or street regarded as a place of public repentance, punishment etc; a raised platform on which wrongdoers were ordered to appear publicly at specified times *la15-18*.

pillé; pillie, pilȝe &c [*'pɪl(j)ɪ] *vt* rob, plunder (a ship or those sailing in it) *16-e17*.   **2** steal (goods or possessions), *esp* from a ship *la16-e17*. [only Sc; F *piller*, representing laL *piliāre* for L *pilāre* deprive of hair]

pillé *see* PULLEY

piller &c *la19-*; **pillan** *18- n* a small crab which has just cast or is about to cast its shell and is useful for bait *Ork-EC*. [*cf* Eng dial *pill*, var of *peel* strip or shed skin]

pilleurichie &c [?pɪ'lurəxɪ, ?-'larəxɪ] *n* a fuss, hullaballoo, uproar *la19-, Abd*. [onomat]

pillie *see* PILLÉ, PULLEY

pilliedacus &c [pɪlɪ'dɑkəs, bɪlɪ-] *n, chf* **the heid** ~ *usu with critical and sarcastic implication* the person in command, 'the big cheese' *la19-, now NE nEC*. [perh BILLY + a mock Latin element]

pillie-wantoun *n* an amorous, lecherous or randy person *e16*. [prob *pillie* (PILL) + Eng *wanton*]

pilliewinkis &c *n* an instrument of torture for squeezing the fingers *la16-17*. [altered f laME *pyrewinkes*]

pillion &c *17-*, **pilȝane** &c *16-17* ['pɪljən] *n* **1** a sack stuffed with rags, a cushion, used as a saddle, *esp* for a woman or for carrying luggage etc *16-e19*.   **2** *only* **pillion** = pillion. [earlier in Sc; Gael *pillin, pillean*, f L *pellis* a skin, pelt]

pillmuir *see* PEEL³

pillow &c ['pɪlə, -ɪ] *n* = pillow *16-*.
~**-ber(e)** &c ['~'bir; *'~bər] *n* a pillowcase *16-, now Slk*.

pilmuir *see* PEEL³

pilpert *n* a badly-fed, cold-looking child *e20, NE*. [uncertain]

pilsh &c *la19-*, **pilch** *e16, 19-, e20* [pɪlʃ] *n, also* **pilshach** &c *19-e20, NE* ['pɪlʃəx, -ək] **1** = pilch, a garment of skin dressed with the hair still on; a triangular piece of material bound over a baby's nappy to keep it in place *16-*.   **2** an ill-fitting garment, an ugly, thick article of dress *la19-, Mry Bnf*.   **3** a piece of dirty thick cloth *la19-e20, Bnf Abd*.   **4** a gross thickset man; a boorish, low character *19-, NE*.

piltock &c, **piltok; piltick** &c *la19-e20 n* the coalfish in its early stages, *usu* in the second year *la17-, now Sh Ork*. [dim of ON *pilt* a boy w extended meaning]

pilty-cock *n* an early form of *curling stone* (CURL), with indentations for the fingers and thumb instead of a handle *19-e20, hist*.

pily &c *adj* having a (? coarse) hairy surface, having a (? hairy) pile or nap, *freq* ~ **gray** *16*. [Eng *pile* + -*y*]

pilȝane *see* PILLION

pilȝe *see* PILLÉ

pilȝet *see* PILGET²

pin &c; **pen** *la15-e17*, **peen** *20-, now EC, S* [pɪn, pin] *n* **1** = pin *15-*.   **2** part of a gallows, *perh* the peg over which the rope was slung *16-e17*.   **3** a kind of door-knocker consisting of a vertical, serrated, metal rod fixed to the door and a ring which was drawn up and down it to produce a rattling noise *16-e20, latterly hist*.   **4** *literary* the latch of a door *e19*.   **5** *mining* a miner's distinctive tally used to label the HUTCHES of coal he has filled *la19-, now Fif*.   **6** *golf* the flagpole marking each hole *20-*.   **7** *in pl* small stones wedged into the crevices between larger stones in a wall to consolidate it *la19-*.   **8** a small, neat person or animal, a small child *la19-e20, Bnf Abd*.   **9** as much washing as will go through a mangle at one time *20, EC, S*.   **10** a mood, frame of mind, *freq* **in a merry** etc ~ *18-, now Sh Ork*.
v **1** *vt* = pin *la15-*.   **2** *building* consolidate (masonry) with PINS (*n* 7) *la16-*.   **3** strike as with a small sharp-pointed missile, hit a sharp quick blow, pelt with stones etc *19-, local Sh-C*.   **4** beat, thrash *la19-, now Cai S*.   **5** *also fig* grab, grasp at, seize *la19-, now Abd*.   **6** *vi* move with

speed and vigour *19-, now Ork N.* **7** put a PIN (*n* 5) on a HUTCH of coal, *esp* substitute one's own PIN for that of the rightful owner *20-, C.*

~**ned &c 1** = pinned. **2** *fig, of persons* tied down (to work), not having a moment's leisure *20-, now Mry Bnf.* ~**ner &c 1** a piece or rafter of wood used to fasten or stabilize a structure *la16-e17.* **2** a game played along a road or gutter in which the aim is to strike an opponent's missile with one's own; the piece of iron used as the missile *la20, Ags.* **3** an unscrupulous person, one with an eye on the main chance *la19-, Bnf S.* **4** something large or good of its kind; a heavy drinking bout *19-e20.* ~**fu &c** = *n* 9, *20-, Fif Loth S.* ~**nin(g) &c 1** the action of PIN (*v* 2), *la16-.* **2** *chf in pl* small stones used in *pinning* masonry *la16-, now Sh NE.* **3** a beating, scolding *la19-, now Wgt Slk.*

peen-heid the young fry of the minnow or stickleback *20-, EC, S.* ~**-leg** a wooden leg *20-.* ~ **reel** a round dance in which one unpartnered person dances alone in the centre of a ring of dancers *20-, Sh Ork NE.* ~ **stones** = *n* 7, *la19-.*

full ~ at full speed *la19-, Sh-EC.* ~ **in** hurry (over a task etc), get a move on *20-, Bnf Abd.* ~**-the-widdie &c** a small haddock, unsplit, which is hung in the smoke of the chimney to cure *19-20.* **pit in the** ~ give up drinking *19-e20.* [*cf* PREEN]

pin *see* POIND

pinch &c, pinsche &c *la16-17 vti* **1** = pinch *la16-.* **2** spend or give meanly, stint, be excessively economical *la16-.* **3** *vt* puzzle, put into difficulty, bring (an argument etc) to a standstill *la18-19.* **4** move (a heavy object) by levering it *la18-.*
n **1** = pinch *la16-.* **2** a pointed iron rod or bar for levering or making post holes, a crowbar *la17-.*
~**er 1** = pincher. **2** *in pl* a tool for pinching, *eg* tweezers, pliers *la18-.* **3** a crowbar *la18-, local.* **4** a blunt chisel used for chipping the edge of a squared-off stone *la19-20.* ~**ing bar** = *pincher* 3, *la18-, local.*

pind *see* POIND

pinding &c ['pɪn(d)ɪn] *n* a bowel disorder affecting lambs fed on over-rich milk *19-, latterly S.* [f obs Eng *pind* enclose, stop up; *cf* POIND]

pine &c *n* **1** = pine, hardship, effort *la14-16.* **2** suffering, distress, pain, either physical or mental *la14-, now Sh Ork NE.* **3** suffering inflicted as punishment or torture, the pains of Hell *la14-e19, latterly ballad.* **4** a disease of sheep or cows due to mineral deficiency *19-e20.*
v **1** *vt* cause pain and suffering, torment, torture *la14-19.* **2** *vi, la15-:* (1) = pine, languish from grief etc; (2) waste away from disease, become exhausted or emaciated, *now Ork-Per Kcb.* **3** *vti, of fish, hay etc* shrink by drying in the open air *la16-, now Sh.*

pined &c, pinit &c 1 in pain, tortured, tormented *16-19.* **2** emaciated, reduced to skin and bone *16-19.* **piner 1** an animal suffering from PINE (*n* 4); an animal or person that is not thriving *20-.* **2** *also* **piner wind, sea piner** *20-, NE* a strong north or north-east wind that dies away by degrees *la19-, NE.* **pining** a disease of sheep, VANQUISH *19.*

piner &c *la16-e20,* **pinor &c** *15-19;* **pynor &c** *la15-e17* ['pəɪnər] *n* **1** a labourer or porter; *specif, in Aberdeen* applied to a member of a society of porters instituted in 1498 and still existing as the *Society of Shore Porters* (SHORE¹) *15-19, latterly hist.* **2** = piner, a pioneer *16.*
~**ie &c** *16-e18, Per,* ~**schip** *16, chf Per* the office or duties of a PINER (*n* 1) *only Sc.* [*cf* PIONER]

piner *see* PENURE

pinge *see* PEENGE

pingle¹ &c *la16-,* **pingill &c** *16-e17* ['pɪŋl] *v* **1** *vi* contend, compete; quarrel, disagree *16-e19.* **2** *vt* press or force (a boat etc) forward as in a contest; compete with (a person); oppose *16-e17.* **3** *vi* struggle at a difficult task, exert oneself at something; work hard with little result, drudge *16-20.* **4** trifle, dabble or meddle **with**, work in a lazy, ineffectual way *19-, now S.*
n **1** a contest, competition; disagreement, quarrel *la16-e19.* **2** an effort, struggle, fight against odds; a labour with little result *18-, now Fif.*
pingled hard put to it, harassed with difficulties, overcome with exhaustion *18-e20.*
pingling *n* contention, exertion; labour with little success *la16-19.* *adj* **1** *of persons* painstaking, meticulous *19-, local.* **2** *of work* fiddling, tedious, demanding *la19-, Sh WC, S.* **3** *of persons* ineffectual, feeble, lacking character or energy *19-e20.* [*cf* eModEng *pyngle* (*n*) contest, (*v*) meddle, trifle]

pingle² &c ['pɪŋl] *n, also* ~**-pan** a small, shallow, metal cooking-pan, *usu* with a long handle, a saucepan *la18-, local EC-S.* [only Sc; uncertain]

pinit *see* PINE

pink¹ &c *n* **1** *chf* ~**ie** the primrose *la18-, now NE Ags Ayr.* **2** = pink, the garden flower; *fig* the finest example of excellence.
speak ~ speak in a very affected over-refined way, in an unsuccessful attempt at Received Pronunciation *la20-, Kcdn Ags Fif.*

pink² &c *n, now chf* ~**ie** anything very small, a small thing or creature; a speck, tiny hole, speck of light *la16-e20.*
vi, also fig, of the eyes become small and narrow, be half-shut; *of persons* narrow the eyes, blink, peer *19.*
~**ie** *n* **1** see *n* 1. **2** the little finger *19-.* *adj* **1** tiny, minute *19-, now Loth Lnk.* **2** *of the eyes* narrowed, peering, winking *18-e19.* [*cf* Du *pink* the little finger, *pinken* (*v*) blink and *cf* eModEng]

pink³ &c [pɪŋk, piŋk] v **1** vi, of small drops of moisture drip, fall with a sharp, tinkling sound, plop la18-, now Ork Abd. **2** vt strike with a small object so as to make a tiny sharp sound; impel or catapult a small object through the air 19-, now local NE-S.

~in a beating, thrashing la20-, S. **~le** of hunger pangs prick, produce a prickling or tingling sensation 19-, now Rox. [only Sc; v 1 onomat, v 2 perh confused w or extended f ME pynk pierce, prick]

pink⁴ vt **1** = pink, ornament (cloth) by slashing or scalloping it 16-. **2** adorn, dress **up** la19-, now Sh Ork Uls.

n = pink, a hole or eyelet in a garment e16.

pinkie n weak beer e19. [reduced f INKIE-PINKIE]

pinnage &c n = pinnace, a small light ship la16-e17, only Sc.

pinner see PENURE

pinnet n a small flag or standard, an ensign, streamer 18-19. [only Sc; alteration of Eng pennant]

pinnok see PENNOK

pinor see PINER

pinsall see PENSIL

pinsche see PINCH

pinsell see PENSIL

pint &c, point &c la15-17; **pe(i)nt &c** la15-e17 [pəint] n = pint; formerly (and officially until e19) the SCOTS measure, the JOUG (surviving later in the bakery trade as four imperial pints) la14-.

~-pig = PIG² n 2 (5) 19, Abd. **~ stowp &c** a tankard or drinking vessel containing a SCOTS PINT (see n) 16-e20.

pint see PAINT, POINT

pintle la16-, **pintill &c** 15-e17 ['pɪntl] n the penis 15-, now local.

~ fish the sand-eel la16-e18. [ME; OE pintel]

pinto &c [*'pɪnto] n, weaving a pin or bolt used as a handgrip for turning the beam in a loom e19. [var of prec; cf Eng use of pintle a pin, bolt]

pinule &c [*?'pəinəl] n a young pine tree la15. [only Sc; F pinel]

pioner &c 16-17, **peonar &c** 16 [*'paɪənər, *'piənər] n **1** = pioneer 16-17. **2** = PINER n 1, 16. [eModEng; OF pionnier &c, peonnier &c]

pipe &c n **1** (1) = pipe 15-. (2) also in pl, freq **the ~s** the Scottish bagpipe(s) 16-. **2** a large ripe acorn with its stalk 20-, Bwk S.

vti **1** = pipe; specif play (a tune) on the bagpipes 15-. **2** vi, of the wind make a low moaning sound; blow gently and softly 18-19. **3** vt flute (cloth), goffer, frill with a special iron la19-.

piper &c 1 (1) = piper, specif one who plays the bagpipes 15-. (2) military title given to certain members of a regimental **~ band**, la19-. **2** an unsplit, half-dried haddock 19-, NE.

piper's bidding a belated, last-minute invitation 19-, local Ork-SW. **piper's news** stale or out-of-date news, usu already known to the listener 19-. **as fou as a piper** extremely drunk 19-. **pipie** informal name for a ~ major, 20-.

~y-dottle the plug of tobacco and ash in a half-smoked pipe la20-.

~ band a band made up of pipers and drummers with a drum-major 20-. **~(-an(d))-dottle** a PIPE (n 2) 'smoked' by children as a tobacco-pipe 20-, now Bwk S. **~ major** the leader of a ~ band; specif as a military title, the equivalent of the regimental bandmaster in an English regiment la19-. **~-maker** a maker of PIPES, chf a specialist in the making of bagpipes la17-. **~-riper** a pipe-cleaner la19-, Sh-C. **~-shank** the stem of a tobacco-pipe la19-. **~-shankit** of persons or animals having long, thin legs la20-, C, S. **~-stapple &c 1** = **~-shank**, la18-. **2** = pipe-(an(d))dottle, 20-, S.

(the) great ~ the Highland (HIELAND) bagpipe la16-19 [translation of Gael piob mhor]. **~s and drums** the formal collective name for the pipers and drummers who make up a pipe band, 20-. **pit oot someone's ~** put someone in his place, thwart someone 18-e20. **tune one's ~s** start to cry, wail like the sound of bagpipes being tuned la17-19.

pipell see PEPILL

pippane &c n a reel onto which a definite length of thread was wound la15-16. [only Sc; see DOST]

pipsyllis &c n a disease, possibly epilepsy; malingering, feigned illness 20, Abd. [altered f Eng epilepsy]

pirameitt &c [*'pɪrəmit, &c] n = pyramid e17.

pirate &c 16-; **peratt &c** la16 [*'pɪrət, *'pir-] n = pirate.

pirhe see PIRR²

pirie see PEER²

piriwik la17-e18; **piriwig &c** la17 [*'pɪrɪwɪk, *-wɪg, *'pirɪ-, &c] n = periwig, a wig.

pirk &c n a sharp point, thorn, prickle la19-, now Cai.

~le usu in pl the spiked nose-band used to prevent a calf sucking la20-, Cai Bnf Bute. [perh partly f Eng perk make spruce, stick up and partly f Norw pirk(e) poke, prod]

pirkas &c ['pɪrkəs] n **1** a thing worth having, a lucky acquisition; ironic a small matter 20-, Cai. **2** a finicky, troublesome matter, a bother, predicament 20-, Cai. [reduced and altered f Eng perquisite]

pirl &c; purl &c la18- v **1** vi thrust, poke **at** la15. **2** vt (1) twist, twirl, coil, curl 19-, local NE-S. (2) (a) roll, cause to rotate, whirl 19-, local Bnf-S. (b) manoeuvre (a small object) by poking it with the finger, a stick etc la18-, now NE. (c) specif, in football, hockey etc drive (the ball) with quick light strokes or kicks, dribble 20-, Bnf Abd. (3) stir, agitate, mix, poke (a fire) *19-, Sh NE.* **3** *vi* (1) spin, whirl round, rotate *19-, NE.* (2) *of snow, wind, water etc* swirl, eddy, ripple *la18-, now NE, S Uls.* (3) fumble with the hands or feet, grope, poke about; move or work idly or half-heartedly *la19-, now Mry Bnf.*

n **1** (1) a curl, twist, coil *la19-, Loth WC, S.* (2) a twist or knot of hair at the back of a woman's head, a bun *la20-, Ags Fif Wgt.* **2** an eddy or swirl in air or water, a ripple, gentle breeze *19-, now NE Rox.* **3** a snowflake *20-, local C, S.*

~**er** an odd-job man on a farm; a cattleman *la19-, now Ags.* ~**ie &c** *adj* curly, curled, twisted *19-, now S.* *n* **1** anything very small *19-, now Ork Per.* **2** the little finger *19-, now Ags.* **3** *also* ~**ie &c pig** *la18-, local Sh-SW,* **pirrell pig** *la17* a *usu* circular, earthenware money-box with a coin-slot, *specif* one used by the Town Council of Dundee for collecting fines from absentee members *19-e20.* ~**ie-winkie &c** = *pirlie (n 2) 19-, now local NE-Wgt.* [see SND]

pirlag *see* PURL

pirlicue &c ['pɪrlɪkju] *n* **1** a flourish or ornament at the end of a handwritten word *19-20, Bnf Abd Dmf.* **2** a follow-on, sequel, *specif* (1) *Presbyterian Church* the summary formerly delivered by the parish MINISTER at the end of the four-day Communion season, of the sermons preached during that time by visiting MINISTERS *19*; (2) a resumé, conclusion *19-e20.*

vi, Presbyterian Church deliver the PIRLICUE *(n 2* (1)) *19.* [*orig* a school expression referring to handwriting, *appar* f *pirlie* (PIRL) + ? Eng *cue,* F *queue* a tail]

pirn &c; pirm &c *18-e20, Sh Ork,* **purn** *20* *n* **1** a small spool of sewing thread, *orig* of gold, silk etc; a reel of or for thread *la15-.* **2** *weaving* a spool for holding the weft yarn in the shuttle, a bobbin *17-.* **3** the amount of yarn that can be wound on a PIRN *la15-, now Mry Slk.* **4** the reel of a fishing rod *la18-, now local NE-Kcb.* **5** *mining* a disc on which flat ropes are wound *la18-, now Dmf.* **6** a twitch for quietening a horse *20-, Bwk S.* **7** a stripe or band in a piece of cloth, of a different colour or texture from the rest; an irregularity, flaw *la17-e18.* **8** something trivial or of little value, an iota *la19-, now Sh Ags.*

vi ~ **in** *or* **out** *fishing* reel a fishing line in or out *la19-e20.*

~**ed** *17-e19,* ~**it &c** *la15-e17* woven of threads of different colours or textures, striped, variegated. ~**ie &c** *adj* variegated, striped, uneven or irregular in weave *la16-e19.* *n, also* ~**ie cap** *19-e20* a type of woollen nightcap, *esp* one made in Kilmarnock, Ayr, *orig* striped in a variety of colours *19-, now S.* ~**ie plaid** a PLAID *or* mantle with a stripe instead of the usual chequered pattern *18-19.* ~**ie &c-taed** pigeon-toed *20-, NE nEC.*

~**-mill** a mill where weavers' bobbins are

made *20-, Ags Per.* ~ **satin** *etc* satin etc variegated with a contrasting thread, *eg* gold *16-e17.* ~**-taed &c** = ~*ie-taed, 20-, Sh NE nEC.* ~ **wheel &c** a wheel for winding yarn onto bobbins *16-20.* ~**-winder** a person who loads a weaver's bobbins with yarn *la18-19.*

fill a ~ wind yarn on to a weaver's bobbin *la18-, now Ags.* **a ravelled** ~ a confused or complicated matter *la19-, now Bnf.* **wind (oneself** *or* **another) a** ~ *or* **into a bonnie** *etc* ~ create difficulties for oneself or another *18-e20.* [see SND]

pirnickitie *see* PERNICKETIE

pirr[1] **&c** *n* the common tern *19-e20.* ~**-maw &c** *19-,* **perma** *20-* the black-headed gull *now Ayr Wgt.* [imit f the bird's cry]

pirr[2] **&c** *la17-,* **pirhe &c** *17-19* *n* **1** a sudden sharp breeze; a gentle breath of wind *17-, now Sh NE.* **2** a sudden burst of activity: (1) a harassed, over-excited state of mind, a panic, rage *la19-, now Sh Ork NE*; (2) a fit of temper, sudden rage *la19-, Sh Ork NE Bwk S.*

vi **1** *of liquid* ripple; flow, stream *19-, now Sh Uls.* **2** tremble with anger, fizz with rage *20-, now Sh.*

pirrie &c 1 *of persons* given to sudden bursts of activity, unpredictable, unreliable *la19-, now Sh.* **2** quick-tempered, touchy, easily annoyed *19-, Bwk Rox.* [onomat; *cf* BIRR[1]]

pirrell pig *see* PIRL

pirrie &c *adj* **stane** ~ hare-brained, scatty *la20-, S.* [prob orig f PIRR[2] *n 2,* w a play on the name of *Pirrie* the manufacturer of stone ginger in Hawick]

pis *see* PEASE[1]

piscence *see* PISSANCE

pische *see* PISH

pise *see* PEASE[1]

pish *17-,* **pische &c** *16-17* *vti* **1** = piss *16-.* **2** *vi, of water* gush, rush, splash out *la18-, now NE Kcb.*

n = piss, urine *la17-.*

~**-minnie** *19-, SW, S,* **pismire** *la18-* [*local WC, SW, S* 'pɪsmaɪr; *Rox* 'pɪsmər, 'pɪʃ-; *Uls* 'pɪsməɪr, 'pɪʃ-], ~**-mither &c** *19-, now Gall,* ~**mool** *la19-e20,* **pismuill** *e17* [*Ayr Uls* 'pɪʃmul, 'pɪs-; **-møl*] the ant [f the smell of an ant-heap]. ~**-oot** a heavy downpour of rain, a *thunder-plump* (THUNNER) *20-, NE Kcb.* ~**-pot** a chamber-pot *19-.* ~**-the-bed** the dandelion *la19-, local* [f its diuretic properties].

piskie[1] **&c** *n, colloq* a member of the Scottish Episcopal Church *la19-.* [reduced f Eng *Episcopalian*]

piskie[2] **&c** *adj, of grass, hair etc* dry, withered, shrivelled *19-e20, SW.* [obscure]

pismire, pismuill *see* PISH

piss &c *interj* a call to a cat or kitten *19-, local.* *vt* incite (a dog) to attack *20-, Cai Abd Dnbt.* **pistack it!** ['pɪs'takɪt] a cry to chase off a cat or dog *19-, now Cai.* [prob Scand]

pissance &c, puissance &c; piscence &c *e16,* **pusiance** *16* ['pwɪsəns; ***'pɪsəns,

*?'pəsəns] *n* **1** = puissance, power, influence *la15-16*. **2** supernatural power *16*. **3** financial resources *16*.

pissane &c [*'pɪzən, *'pizən] *n* a pisane, a piece of armour to protect the upper chest and neck *la15-e16*. [see DOST]

pissant &c *la15-e17*, **puissant** *la15-*; **pussant &c** *16-e17* ['pwɪsənt; *'pɪsənt, *?'pøsənt] *adj* = puissant.

pistack *see* PISS

pistill *see* PYSTLE

pistolet¹ &c; pistolat &c, pestolat &c [*'pɪstolət] *n* = pistolet, the fire-arm *la16-e17*.

pistolet² &c; pistolat, pestolet &c [*'pɪstolət] *n* = pistolet, a name for certain foreign gold coins *la16-e17*. [*cf* PISTOLL²]

pistoll¹ &c *la16-*; **pestoll &c** *la16-17* ['pɪstol] *n* = pistol.

pistoll² &c *17*; **pestole** *la16* [*'pɪstol] *n* = pistole, a name for certain foreign gold goins. [*cf* PISTOLET²]

pistoll *see* PESTELL

pit¹, pitt, put &c; pet *17-e20*, **powt** *16* [pɪt, pʌt; *local EC* pɛt; *'pøt] *v*, *pt also* **put, pat &c** *16-*, *now local*, **pit** *la19-*, *local Cai-WC* [pat, pʌt, pɪt; *Fif also* pot; *'pøt]. *ptp* **put, pit** *16-*, *now Cai NE, WC*; **putten &c** *la18-*, *local NE-S*, **pitten &c** *la18-*, *local Sh-WC*, **potten** *la19-e20* [pʌt, pɪt, 'pʌtən, 'pɪtən; *EC also* 'pøtən, 'putən; *Fif also* 'potən; *'pøt] *vti* **1** = put *la14-*. **2** *vt, used where Eng has* send, make, take etc *18-*: '*It was him who pat me mad*'; '*A wis juist pittin aff ma claes, gaen tae ma bed*'.

n = put, an act of putting *16-e17*.

~ **about 1** inconvenience, cause trouble to; distress, upset (oneself or another) *19-*. **2** clothe, wrap (*usu* oneself) up well; wrap up (a parcel) *la19-*, *Sh Uls*. ~ **at** make demands on, press; proceed against, attack, prosecute *16-20*. ~ **awa &c** *v* **1** *vt* = put away *la16-*. **2** dismiss from employment, sack *20-*, *now Sh-Per*. **3** bury *la19-*, *local N-Uls*. **4** *vr* commit suicide *la19-*. ~ **by** *v* **1** *vt* = put by, set aside *16-*. **2** dispose of, do away with; *specif* inter, bury *la19-*, *SW Uls*. **3** *vti* achieve, pass, complete, put behind one; spend time, stay *la19-*, *local N-Uls*. **4** make do **with**, tide (oneself or another) over **with** *19-*. **5** *vt* last out, survive (a period of time) *la19-*, *now Abd Lnk*. *n* ~**-by** **1** a hoard, stand-by *la19-*. **2** a snack, light meal *20-*. **I** *etc* **wadna** ~ **it by him** *etc* I wouldn't put it past him etc (to do something discreditable) *20-*. ~ **someone by the door** turn someone away, reject, spurn *20-*, *Sh Abd Uls*. ~ **down &c 1** kill, put to death (human beings) *la16-19*. **2** suffocate (bees) with sulphur in order to get at the honey *19-e20*. **3** defeat, beat, overcome *la19-*, *now Sh Uls*. **4** set (plants, *esp* potatoes) in the ground *20-*, *Cai Uls*. **5** inter, bury *la19-*, *now Cai Abd Uls*. ~ **frae &c 1** prevent, hinder, stop *18-*. **2** put (a person) off (a thing or person), give (a person) a

distaste for (a thing) *la19-*, *Abd Uls*. ~ **into** insinuate or suggest to, impose (an idea etc) on *la19-*, *NE Ags*. ~ **off &c 1** = put off *la14-*. **2** do away with, kill *la15*. **3** ~ **off &c** (**time**) waste time, delay *17-*. ~ **on** *v* **1** *vi* put on one's clothes, dress *la18-19*. **2** *vt* impress, impose on, fool *20-*, *now Cai Per*. *n* ~**-on** insincerity, pretence, falseness *20-*, *now Sh Abd*. **pitten on** *of persons* affected, conceited, insincere *20-*, *now N-C*. **sair pit on** ill *20-*, *Cai Per*. **ill, weel** *etc* **pit(ten)-on** shabbily, finely etc dressed *19-*. ~ **oot** fit (a person) out with clothes and accessories *20-*, *now Abd*. **put out the line** *of a* PRECENTOR: sing the line of a PSALM for the congregation to repeat *20-*, *Hebrides Highl*. ~ **owre &c** *v* **1** *vt* swallow, consume; wash down, make palatable *la19-*. **2** get (a thing) behind one, accomplish, have done with *la18-*, *now Sh NE*. **3** make (a period of time, hardship etc) pass more quickly or easily, get through *18-*, *now Sh NE*. **4** *vti* last out, survive, make do; tide (a person) over *19-*, *now Cai NE*. **5** *vt* defer, postpone *19-*, *Lnk S*. *n* ~**-ower** a snack, makeshift meal *la19-*, *now NE*. ~ **past** *see* PAST. ~ **someone through a thing** make something clear to someone, explain something in detail to someone *19-*, *Sh-Per*. ~ **to 1** close (a door), sometimes with the implication of not engaging the catch *18-*. **2** kindle (a fire), set (a fire) alight *20-*, *NE Ags Dnbt*. **3** apprentice (someone) to (a trade) *19-*. **hard, ill, sair** *etc* **pit(ten) to &c** hard-pressed, in difficulties *la18-*. ~ **up 1** = put up *la15-*. **2** vomit, bring up *la19-*. [see also PUTT¹]

pit² &c, pitt &c *n* **1** = pit *la14-*. **2** one of a series of holes dug to mark a land-boundary *la16-18*.
vti **1** = pit *la14-*. **2** *vt* define (a land-boundary) by means of a series of holes *la18-e19*.
~**-bottomer** *mining* = onsetter (ONSET¹) *la19-*, *now Fif Dnbt*. ~**-mirk &c** *adj*, *n* pitch-dark(ness), dark as a pit *18-*. ~**-stone** a boundary stone *la17-e19*.
~ **and gallows** a right of jurisdiction over criminals found within baronial lands *15-e18* [translating ScL *furca et fossa*; see DOST].

pit *see* PEAT¹

pitawtie &c *la19*, **pitato** *la17*; **potato &c** *la18-* [*pə'tɑtɪ, *-ə, *-o, *-tat-] *n* = potato *la17-*.
~ **bogle** *lit and fig* a scarecrow *19*. **potato scone** = tattie scone (TATTIE) *20-*. [*cf* TATTIE]

Pitcaithly [pɪt'keθlɪ] **&c Bannock** *n* a round flat cake of thick *shortbread* (SHORT) containing chopped almonds and citron peel *19-20*. [the place in Per, formerly a spa]

pitch &c *17-*, **picht &c** *la15-e17* [pɪtʃ; *pɪxt; *pt, ptp* *pɪxt] *vti* (*la15-*), *n* (*17-*) = pitch, fix; throw.
~**er, pecher 1** the flat stone etc used in the game of hopscotch *la19-e20*. **2** the game itself *la19-*, *now Bnf*. **3** a marble which is thrown

rather than rolled in games with marbles *la19*-, now *Bnf Abd Ags*. **~ie** = *pitcher* 1, *la20*-, *Mry Bnf Abd*.

pitcher *see* PICHAR

pité *see* PEETY

pith &c *n* **1** = pith *la14*-. **2** the strength-giving quality of food or drink *la15-17*.

~y &c **1** = pithy *la16*-. **2** strong, solid, robust, powerful; prosperous, well-to-do *la16-20*.

a' one's ~ with all one's energy *la19*-, now *Ork N*. **the ~ o maut** WHISKY *e19*.

piti(e)coat *see* PETTICOAT

pitt *see* PIT[1], PIT[2]

pittance-silver &c *16-e17*; **pittane-silver &c** *16 n* the revenue from a bequest or endowment, *orig* given to a religious house to make additional provision of food, wine etc for the religious on special occasions. [only *Sc*; Eng *pittance + silver*]

pitten *see* PIT[1]

pitter-patter *vt* repeat (words, prayers etc) rapidly and mechanically *17-e19*. [*cf* Eng noun]

pittie *see* PETTY

pittiecoat *see* PETTICOAT

pittie-pattie &c *adv* = pit-a-pat *18-e19*.

pituchtie *see* PEUCHTIE

pity *see* PEETY

piz(z) *see* PEASE[1]

pla *see* PLAY

placad &c *la16-e20*, **placard &c** *la16*- [*St* 'plakard; *'*'plakə(r)t, *plə*'kad] *n* = placard *la16*-.

vt **1** = placard, publish using a placard *la17*-. **2** publish or utter derogatory statements about (a person), tell tales about *18-e20*.

place &c; plece &c *16-17*, *e20* [ples; *Loth also* plɪs] *n* **1** = place *la14*-. **2** an area or building customarily used for a certain (*freq* specified) purpose, *eg* **buriall ~** *la14*-. **3** a suitable place, *freq* **time and ~** *15*-. **4** *also* **placie** *la19*-, *now Ork-Ags* a holding of land, an estate, farm or CROFT *la14-e20*. **5** *mining* the length of coal-face assigned to each miner *la19*-, *now Fif Ayr*.

vt, *ptp also* **plaist** *16* **1** = place *16*-. **2** *Presbyterian Church*: settle (SATTLE) (a probationer (PROBATION)) in his first charge; *occas* induct (an ordained MINISTER) to a new charge *la16-e20*.

~d minister *etc* an ordained or practising clergyman in charge of a parish or congregation *18-e20*.

~ haldand *la15*, **~ haldar &c** *la16-e17* a deputy, a person acting in the place of another. **have ~ 1** = have etc place *la15*-. **2** *also* **give ~** have or give entitlement or a right (to) *la15-16*. **3** *only* **have ~** *of a procedure, argument etc* have credence or validity *la15-e17*. **nae, ony, some** *etc* **~** no-, any-, some- etc where *la18*-. **the bad ~** Hell *la19*-, *NE*. **the guid**

&c ~ Heaven *19*-, *now Sh*. **the ill ~** = *the bad* **~**, *19*-, *now Sh*. **the ~ of** the mansion-house (of a particular estate) *15-19*. **the secret, quiet** *etc* **~** ? euphemisms for the lavatory, the privy *16-17*.

plack &c *la16*-, **plak &c** *la15-e18 n* **1** (1) a small billon or (*later*) copper coin, *usu* valued at four pennies SCOTS *la15-e17*; see SND. (2) as a money of account *17-18*. **2** *in negative*, *common in proverbs* nothing of any value, nothing at all *16*-, *now NE Ags Per*. **3** money *in gen*, a sum of money, cash; one's worldly wealth *19-e20*.

~less penniless, hard-up *la18-e20*.

~ bill *law* informal term for a bill of *Signet letters* (see SIGNET, LETTER), the summons or warrant presented to a debtor etc in small civil actions *la18-e19*. **~ pie &c** a pie costing a PLACK *18-e19*. **~sworth** *lit and fig* as much as can be bought for a PLACK, a very small amount *17-18*. **catch the ~** make money, increase one's wealth *la18-e19*. **mak one's ~ a bawbee** make money; profit from something *18-19*. **~ an bawbee, farthing** *etc* to the last penny, every farthing etc, in full *19*. **twa an a ~** *freq ironic* a considerable sum of money *la17-19*.

plad *see* PLAID

pladge *see* PLEDGE

plage *see* PLAGUE, PLEDGE

plagium ['pledʒɪʌm] *n*, *law* the offence of childstealing or kidnapping *19*-. [laL = the stealing of children or slaves, *plagiāre* kidnap, abduct]

plague &c *16*-, **plage &c** *la15-e17*; **pleague &c** *la16-e17* [pleg; *Ork Abd also* plɑg; *Abd also* pjɑg] *n* (*la15*-), *vt* (*la16*-) = plague.

~d &c 1 = plagued *la16*-. **2** confounded, blasted, damned *18-e19*.

plaid &c; plad &c *16-e18*, **plyde &c** *la16-19*, **pled** *la16-17*, **pleyde** *la16-e17*, **plead** *17* [pled, plɔid, plad; *sEC also* plɛd] *n* **1** a rectangular length of twilled woollen cloth, *usu* in TARTAN, *formerly* worn as an outer garment *esp* in rural areas, *later* also as a shawl by women in towns, and *now* surviving as part of the ceremonial dress of members of the *pipe bands* (PIPE) of Scottish regiments *16*-. **2** the woollen cloth of which PLAIDS are made *16-e19*. **3** a PLAID or TARTAN cloth used as a blanket or bed-covering *18-e20*.

vti dress (oneself or another) in (a) PLAID *19-e20*.

~ie &c = *n* 1, *18*-. **~ing &c** = *n* 2, *16*-.

~ing market *joc* bed *la20*-, *Abd Kcb* [f the common use of *plaiding* as material for blankets].

~-neuk &c a fold or flap in a PLAID used as a pocket, *esp* by shepherds for carrying young lambs *la16*-, *now eLoth WC*, *S*.

belted ~(y) &c a long PLAID wound round the middle of the body and held in place with a

belt, *prob* an early form of KILT *18*; *cf* FILLEBEG.
[*appar orig* Sc (> Gael *plaide*), perh a *ptp* of
PLY¹]

plaid *see* PLEAD

plaig *see* PLAY

plaik *see* PLAY

plain &c; plenn *la15-20*, **plean &c** *17* [plen;
nEC Ayr plɛn] *adj* **1** = plain *la14-*. **2** *of ground
etc* free from hills, water etc; unwooded, open; *of
any surface* flat, smooth, level *la14-*, *now Sh*. **3** *of
a court or market* held in the public view and
hearing, open *la14-16*.

adv **1** = plain *la14-*. **2** clearly, audibly *15-e16*.

n **1** = plain *la14-*. **2** a small or limited stretch
of level ground *la15-e16*.

~**ie 1** *games* any movement or manoeuvre in its
simplest form, before complications and variations are introduced *20-*, *Mry C, S*. **2** *in pl* a
pavement *la19-20*, *Ags*.

~ **bread** bread baked as a ~ *loaf*, *20-*. ~
loaf a flat-sided white loaf with a hard black
crust on top and a floury brown crust at the
bottom, a batch loaf, *formerly* commoner than
the *pan loaf* (PAN¹) *20-*. ~**-soled** flat-footed
19-e20. ~ **stane &c** *chf in pl* **1** flat stones used
for paving *17-18*, *only Sc*. **2** a pavement (at the
side of a street); a paved area surrounding a
town's *mercat cross* (MERCAT) or *Town House*
(TOUN) *17-*, *now local*.

plainen *n* coarse linen *la18-20*. [*appar f Eng
plain*]

plainschour *see* PLENSHER

plaint &c; plent *la16-e17*, *la19 n* **1** = plaint
la14-. **2** a complaint, protest, grievance; an
expression of distress or grief *la15-20*. **3** =
court plaint (COURT) *15-17*.

v **1** *vi, freq* ~ **of** or (**up**)**on** complain about, find
fault with *16-e19*. **2** *vt* express as a grievance,
complain of *la16*.

plaint *see* PLANT

plaintie *see* PLENTY

plaintis &c *la15-e16*; **plenteis** *la16* [*'plɛntɪs,
*'plɛnt-] *adj* = PLAINTUOUS. [only Sc; OF
plaintis, var of *plaintif* plaintive]

plaintuous &c *15-e17*; **plantuous &c**
la15-16, **plentuous &c** *16-e17*, **plenteous
&c** *16-e17*, **playntous &c** *15-e17*
[*'plɛntju(w)us, *-wəs, *'plɛnt(ɪ)us, *'plɛnt-]
adj be ~ (**of** or **on**) have a grievance (about);
express a complaint, *esp* a formal one (about).
[only Sc; MedL *planctuosus*]

plainʒe *see* PLEEN

plaip &c *vi* = plap, flap, make a slapping noise
la19-, *chf Ags*.

plais *see* PLEASE

plaist *see* PLACE

plaister &c, plaster &c *15-*; **plester &c** *17-*
[*'plɛstər] *n* **1** = plaster *la14-*. **2** a chastisement, beating; a dressing-down, swearing *la18-*,
now Sh Cai. **3** (1) a person who thrusts himself
on the attention or company of others, a fawning or ingratiating person or animal *20-*, *now*

WC. (2) an excessive flatterer *la20-*, *nEC Dmf
Uls*. **4** a botched or mismanaged job, a mess,
shambles *20-*, *local Ags-Uls*. **5** a piece of showy
adornment, excessive jewellery, frills etc in
one's dress *la19-*, *now WC*.

v **1** *vt* = plaster *16-*. **2** *vi* work or go about in a
slovenly slapdash way, mess around *la19-*, *local
N-Dmf*. **3** make a fuss or useless bother, be
over-attentive, fawn, intrude obsequiously or
inopportunely *20-*, *Kcdn nEC Rox*.

~**y** a showy, overdressed person *la20-*, *WC*.

~**man** a plasterer *e16*.

plait *see* PLAY, PLET

plak *see* PLACK

plan &c *n* **1** = plan. **2** a plot of ground, an
allotted RIG¹ on the *runrig¹* (RIN) system; a
CROFT *18-e19*.

vt = plan.

~**ner 1** = planner. **2** a landscape gardener
la18-19.

plancheoun-naill *see* PLENCHEOUN-NAILL

plane¹ &c *n*, *also* ~ **tree** *la16-e20* = plane, the
tree; the sycamore *la16-*.

plane² &c *vt* **1** = plane, make smooth *la15-*. **2**
make plain, demonstrate, declare *la15-16*.

n **1** = plane, a level surface. **2** *mining* a working room driven at right angles to or facing the
plane joints *la19-*, *now Fif*.

planeis *see* PLENISH

planet &c; plenit &c *la15*, *19-e20* [*'planət;
Bwk also* 'plɛn-] *n* **1** = planet *la14-*. **2** an area
of ground *19*. **3** a heavy localized shower of
rain *e20*.

planisch *see* PLENISH

plank &c *n* **1** = plank *15-*. **2** something which
has been *planked* (*v* 3), a hidden hoard; the
place where something has been deposited for
later use, a hidey-hole *la20-*.

vt **1** = plank *17-*. **2** set down, place, *usu* with
a thump or in a decisive way *la19-*. **3** put in a
secret place, hide, stow away for later use *la19-*,
N, C.

planchoir, planschour *see* PLENSHER

plant; plaint &c *la14-e17* [plant] *n* = plant
15-.

vti **1** = plant *la14-*. **2** *vt* provide (a church
etc) **with** (a MINISTER); appoint (a MINISTER) to
a charge *la16-19*. **3** *carpentry* attach or lay in a
piece of moulding *la19-*.

~**ation &c 1** = plantation *la15-*. **2** the action
of appointing a MINISTER or schoolmaster; the
action of supplying a church or school with an
incumbent *la16-e18*. ~**in(g) &c 1** = planting
16-. **2** *usu in sing as collective* young trees, seedlings *16-18*. **3** a small wood or grove of trees, a
plantation *la16-*.

plantuous *see* PLAINTUOUS

planys *see* PLENISH

plapper &c *vi* **1** *of a liquid* bubble and plop
when boiling *20-*, *NE*. **2** splash about in water
la19-, *now Mry*. [onomat]

plash¹ &c *18-*, **plasch &c** *16-17 n* **1** a splash, the noise made by something falling into water *16-, now Sh NE Ags.* **2** a sudden sharp downpour of rain, a heavy shower *19-*. **3** an insipid, tasteless liquid or drink; a large quantity of something liquid *19-e20*. **4** a shallow pool; a sticky, miry place *19*.

v **1** *vi* splash, squelch; *specif, of rain etc* fall in torrents, lash, pelt down *la17-, now local Sh-Lnk.* **2** *vt* splash (a person, thing etc) with a liquid, wet, drench *la18-, now Sh*. **3** *vi* walk on waterlogged ground, squelch along through mud *18-, local Sh-Kcb*. **4** *freq* ~ **at** work in a messy, slovenly way, mess about in liquids *la19-, now Sh.*
adv, occas as interj splash!, with a splash *19-, now Sh NE Ags.*
~**in** squelching or splashing with moisture, soaking wet *19-e20*. ~**y &c 1** causing splashes; water-logged, soaking wet *19*. **2** rainy, showery *la18-e20*.
~**-mill** a fulling mill driven by a water-wheel *la18-19*. ~**-miller** the operator of a fulling mill *19*. [eModEng; *cf* MLowGer, LowGer *plasken, plaschen*, MDu, Du, LowGer *plassen* etc]
plash² *n, chf* ~**ack**, ~**ach** *e20* ['~ək, -əx], ~**-fluke** *19-e20* the plaice *chf N*. [uncertain]
plaster &c [*'plestər, *'plastər] *n* a plasterer *17*. [short for OSc *plasterar &c*]
plaster *see* PLAISTER
plat¹ &c; plet &c *19-* adj **1** flat, level, even; low-lying *la15-, now Sh*. **2** direct, clear, downright, *freq* ~ **and plain** *la14, 19-, now Sh*.
adv **1** flat; flat on the ground, (seated) with the legs stretched out horizontally *15-16, 20-* (Sh). **2** *freq of direction* exactly, due, straight *16-, now Sh*. **3** in a plain, direct way, straightforwardly, flatly, outright, *freq* ~ **and plain** *16-, now Sh*.
n **1** = plat, a sheet of metal *la16-e17*. **2** *freq* ~ **copper, leid** *etc* sheet metal *16-e17*. **3** a household plate; a shallow dish *16-17*. **4** *in sing as collective* silver or gold vessels *la16-17*. **5** a landing (on a stair) *17-, now Ags Per Kcb*.
v **1** *vt* place or set (an object) down flat, clap into place *15-, now Sh*. **2** *vi, of a person* fall down flat (on one's face, knees etc), prostrate oneself *16*. **3** *vt* flatten down (the point of the nails attaching the shoe to a horse's hoof), clinch (a nail) *19-, now Sh*.
~**ten &c** = *v* 3, *19-, now Sh*. **plettie &c** = *n* 5, *20-, Dundee*. **pletty-stanes** a pavement *la20-, Ags Per Clcm*.
~ **fute &c** flat-foot, the name of a dance and its tune *16, only Sc*.
cow-~ a cow-pat *19-, now Rox*.
plat² &c *n* **1** = plat, a plan *16-17*. **2** a plan for a villainous action, a plot, conspiracy *la16-e17*. **3** a scheme of the actual or proposed distribution of churches and arrangements for their supply, within a particular area or over a limited period *la16-17*. **4** (1) the scheme for the reorganization on the Presbyterian system of the post-Reformation church, *esp* in regard to

parishes and *stipends* (STEEPEND) *la16-e20, latterly hist;* (2) the body which implemented and administered this scheme, *later (1617)* replaced by the *Commission of Teinds* (TEIND) *la16-e20, latterly hist.*
vt plot, plan (*usu* something evil) *e17*.
~**ter &c** a plotter, conspirator *la16-e17, only Sc*. **Commission of P**~ = *n* 4 (2) *17-18*. **decreet &c of** ~ an official ruling or authorized scheme of the PLAT² (*n* 4 (2)) *17-18*. [*cf* PLOT²]
plat *see* PLATT
platch¹; plotch *19-20, chf S n* **1** a splashing, a step or stamping movement in water or mud; a splash of mud etc *la19-, Sh midLoth Lnk S*. **2** a large spot; a patch of cloth *la19-, now Sh Rox*.
adv with a splash *20-, Sh S*.
v **1** *vt* splash, cover with mud *19-, now Sh Bnf*. **2** *vi* walk through mud or mire *19-20, Sh Fif S*. **3** go about or work in a sloppy way, potter *19-, Sh Per S*.
~**ie** wet, muddy *19-, now Rox*. ~**in** soaking, sopping *19-, S*. [partly onomat and partly var of PLASH¹ w infl f next and f Eng *patch; cf* CLATCH¹]
platch² *vi* plant down one's feet in an awkward flat-footed way, walk in a heavy ungainly way *19-, Sh Rox*. [var of PLAT¹]
plate &c; pleit &c *la16-e17*, **pleat &c** *la16-17*, **plet &c** *la16-19* [plet; *plɛt] *n, vt* = plate *la14-*.
~**ful &c** the amount contained on a plate *la16-*. ~ **glufe** or **slefe &c** a glove or sleeve consisting of or reinforced by plate-armour *la16-17*.
platform &c; pletforme &c *16-17, e20*, **platfurme &c** *la16-17 n* **1** = platform *16-*. **2** a flat roof; *orig also* a partially flat roof serving as a walk on top of a building *16-17, la20*. **3** *mining* a junction of two or more lines in a HUTCH railway, *orig* laid on a raised board *la19-20*.
vt provide (a building) with a flat roof or roof-walk *la16-e17*.
~ **ruf &c** = *n* 2, *16-17*.
platt, plat &c *n* a blow, stroke *e16, e19*. [only Sc; OE *plætt*]
platter; plotter *la19-e20 vi* **1** dabble with the hands in a liquid, work in a messy, slovenly way *la19*. **2** splash noisily and clumsily through mud or water *la19-, now Sh*. [prob chf onomat; *cf* Eng *splatter*]
plausibill &c; plausable &c *only Sc adj* **1** = plausible *la16-17*. **2** only apparently deserving approval, having only the appearance of being acceptable or trustworthy *la16-17*.
play &c; pley &c *la15-e17, la19*, **pla** *16-e18* [ple; *also* *ploi] *vti, pt, ptp, also* **plait** *la15-e16* **1** = play *la14-*. **2** *vr* amuse oneself, sport *la14-*. **3** *vi, of a liquid or the vessel containing it* boil, seethe *15-20*. **4** *vt, before a noun used adverbially, where Eng uses* go *la18-20*: 'the door played clink'.
n **1** = play *la14-*. **2** a game, sport, pastime

15-, *now Sh.* **3** *usu* **the** ~ time off school for recreation; a holiday from work, school or college *17-20*. **4** a country fair or festival *la15-19, only Sc.* **5** an act of playing on a musical instrument, a performance *la19-*.

~**ock &c** *15-*, **plaig &c** *16-e20*, **plaik &c** *19* **1** a plaything, a toy *15-*, *now NE Dmf.* **2** a game, pastime *19*. ~**rife** [*~rəif, *~rɪf] playful, light-hearted, fond of fun *19*.

~ **club** *golf* a wooden-headed club for driving the ball long distances, a driver *la17-19*. ~ **cote &c** a coat or garment worn by a player in a performance, masque etc *16*. ~ **day 1** a day of festivity or one on which a play or pageant was performed; a day of recreation or freedom from task-work *la16-17*. **2** a holiday or half-holiday, *esp* from school *la16-17*. ~**fare &c** a plaything, toy *la18-20*. ~ **feild &c** an open space for public festivities, performances etc *la16-17*. ~ **fere &c** a playmate; a jester *16-e19*. ~ **fuil &c** a jester *16-e18*. ~**gin &c** ['plegən] a plaything, toy, *freq* applied to potsherds used as toys *19-20*, *Bwk Rox* [prob reduced f nEng dial *play-laking*]. ~**-Saturday, -Tuesday** *etc* the Saturday, Tuesday etc of a PLAY (*n* 3 or 4) *la18-19*.

(**away, go** *etc* **and**) ~ **yersel** go to blazes!, go away! *20-*. **gar** *or* **mak the** *or* **one's pat** ~ (**broon**) provide someone with food, support someone *19*. **the** ~ **be done** *or* **ended** the matter is concluded *la15-17*. ~ **the wort** *brewing* ? stir or ? boil the wort before adding the yeast *la16-17, only Sc.* ~ **up wi** play the devil with, do harm to, spoil, destroy *la19-, Sh-Per.*

play *see* PLEA

playntous *see* PLAINTUOUS

playock, playrife *see* PLAY

plea *17-*, **pley &c** *15-20*; **plie** *la15-17, e20*, **play &c** *16-e17* [pli; *pləi] *n* **1** *law* an action at law, a lawsuit *la15-19*. **2** *law* = plea *15-*. **3** a quarrel, disagreement, argument; strife, discord, enmity *16-, now Mry Ags.*

v **1** *vi, law* litigate, go to law *la15-e18*. **2** *law* state or maintain the claim of a party to a lawsuit, plead as an advocate **for** (a person) *or* **in** (a matter) *la15-e17*. **3** quarrel, disagree, argue *la15-, now Ags.* **4** *law* put forward a plea; make a formal allegation *16*. **5** *vt, law* sue (a person); take to court *16-e17*. **6** *law* maintain (a plea or cause) by argument *la16-e17*. **7** *law* contest (a matter), make the subject of litigation *la15-19*.

~**abill &c** *law* **1** *of a thing in dispute* that is (to be) a subject of litigation *la15-16*. **2** *of a dispute* that is being, or may be, argued and decided by a legal process *16*. **pleyar &c** *law* a litigant; a disturber of the peace *la16-e17*.

be in ~ *law, of a thing in dispute* be the subject of litigation *la15-e17*. **but** *or* **without** (**ony**) ~ *law* without litigation or objection; not liable to plea or counter-plea *la15-e17*. **enter** *etc* **in** ~

law, of a person engage or be engaged in litigation *15-e17*. **move** ~ *law* institute legal proceedings *la15-e17*. ~ **in bar of trial** *etc law* a statement or objection by the counsel for the accused, giving reasons why judgment should not be passed or why criminal proceedings should be dropped *20-*. ~ **in law** *law* a short legal proposition at the end of a pleading showing exactly the relief sought and why *19-*. **the** (**four**) ~**s of the Crown** *law* criminal cases on murder, robbery, rape and arson, which could only be heard in the *Court of Justiciary* (JUSTICIARY); robbery and arson can now be tried in a *Sheriff Court* (SHERIFF) *17-*.

plead &c *la16-*, **plede &c** *la14-17*; **pled** *15-e16*, **plaid** *la16-17* [plid; *pled] *n* **1** an action at law, litigation *la14-15*. **2** a plea by or on behalf of a litigant; an allegation, a claim *la15-e17*. **3** a verbal dispute; contention, opposition *la15-16*.

vti, pt also **pled** *la17-* **1** = plead *15-*. **2** contend, argue, debate in a court of law; *transf* entreat for *15-*.

pledar &c 1 = pleader *la16-17*. **2** a litigant *17*.

plead *see* PLAID

pleague *see* PLAGUE

plean *see* PLAIN

pleasance &c *la16-*, **plesance &c** *la14-16*; **pleasants** *18-19* ['plizəns; *St* 'plɛzəns; *'plezəns] *n* **1** = pleasance, the action of pleasing *la14-16*. **2** the feeling of pleasure, joy, happiness, satisfaction *la15-19*. **3** *in sing and pl* a source of pleasure; a pleasure or delight *la14-15*. **4** a pleasure-ground or park, either attached to a castle etc or on its own, *now only* as a street- or district-name as in Edinburgh and Falkirk *16-*.

pleasant &c *16-*, **plesand &c** *la14-e17* ['plizənt; *nEC* 'plez-; *-ən(d)] *adj* **1** = pleasant *la14-*. **2** *of a person's appearance* agreeable, pleasing *15-17*. **3** *of persons* having a pleasing manner or personality *15-*. **4** *of persons* humorous, witty, jocular, merry *la19-, now NE, WC, SW.*

n = pleasant, a jester, fool, clown *la16-17*.

~**ly &c 1** = pleasantly *la15-*. **2** *referring to the making of a payment* satisfactorily; adequately; ? in full *16-17*.

pleasants *see* PLEASANCE

please &c *16-*, **plese &c** *la14-17*; **plais &c** *16-17, e20* [pliz; *nEC* plez] *vti* **1** = please *la14-*. **2** *vt* satisfy (a person): (1) by payment of compensation **for** (harm done to another) *la15-e16*; (2) by payment **of** *or* **for** (an amount due etc) *la15-e16, only Sc.* **3** like, approve of, be pleased or satisfied with *la15-e18, only Sc.* **4** *vi, usu in negative* not be pleased, not show contentment *la19-, now NE*: 'He frettit aye an wadna please'.

plesit &c may it please *la15-e16* [contraction of *plese it*].

~ madame &c a type of dyestuff; the colour obtained by its use, or a stuff of this colour *la16-e17*.

nae hae a ~ be incapable of being pleased, be perpetually dissatisfied *19-, NE Ags*.

pleasure &c *16-*, **plesour &c** *la15-e17*, **pleseir &c** *la15-16*; **pleassour &c** *la16-17*, *19* ['plizər, 'pliʒər; *Sh NE also* 'plezər; *'pli'zir, *'pli'zur, *'plizur, &c] *n* **1** = pleasure *la15-*. **2** a service, good turn, favour; a payment (? made in good-will); a benefaction *16-e17*. **3** the wish or inclination to please; courtesy *16-e17*.
vt please, content, give pleasure to, satisfy *la16-, now local NE-SW*.

pleat [plit] *n* **1** = pleat. **2** a pigtail, plait *20-*. [*cf* PLET]

pleat *see* PLATE

pleban &c *n* a rural dean *la15, Pbls*. [only Sc; MedL *plebanus*, f *plebs, plebes* a diocese, parish, parish church]

plece *see* PLACE

pled *see* PLAID, PLEAD

plede *see* PLEAD

pledge &c *16-*, **plege &c** *15-e17*; **plage &c** *16*, **pladge &c** *la16-e17* [*plidʒ, *pledʒ] *n, vti* = pledge *15-*.
~ chalmer &c *la16-e17*, **~ house &c** *17-e18* a room or house for confining hostages, sureties or *later* debtors *Dumfries*.
(up)on plegis in return for, or after receipt of, pledges *16-e17*.

plee &c *n* a seagull; the young of the gull before it changes its first plumage *la19-, now Sh Fif*. [imit of its call; *cf* PLEENGIE]

pleen &c *la17-19*, **plene &c** *la15-e17*, **plenʒe &c** *la14-17*, **plainʒe &c** *15-16*; **plenye &c** *la15-16*, **pleinʒe &c** *la15-16*, **pleinye &c** *la15-16* [*plin, *'pliŋɪ, *'plinʒɪ, *'pliŋʒɪ, *'plen(ʒ)ɪ, &c] *vti* **1** = plain, make a formal complaint; lament *la14-e17*. **2** *vi, freq* **~ of** complain, grumble, mourn, whine *la14-19*.
n a complaint, an objection, an expression of dissatisfaction *19-e20*.
plenʒeand &c making formal complaint *e15*.
(party) pleinʒeand &c *la14-e17*, **plenʒeour &c** *15-16* the complainant or *pursuer* (PURSUE).

pleengie &c ['pliŋ(ɪ), 'pliŋ(ɪ)] *n* a sea-gull, *specif* the young herring gull *19-, now Kcdn*. [prob chf imit of its call, w infl f prec; *cf* PLEE]

pleep &c *n* a sea-bird with a thin, high-pitched cry, *specif* **1** the oyster-catcher *la19-, now Mry Slk*; **2** the redshank *la19-, now Mry Per*.
vi, usu of birds utter a shrill, high-pitched cry, peep *la19-, chf Sh Cai Per*. [imit]

plege, plegis *see* PLEDGE

pleinye, pleinʒe *see* PLEEN

pleit *see* PLATE

pleiter *see* PLOWTER

plencheoun-naill &c, plancheoun-naill &c [*'plɛnʃən'nel, *'planʃ-] *n* a flooring nail *la16-17*. [var of *planschour &c(-naill)* (PLEN-SHER); *cf* PLENSHIN]

plene *see* PLEEN

plenish &c *16-*, **plenis &c** *15-17*; **pleneis &c** *la15-17*, **planeis** *la15-16*, **planys &c** *16*, **plenesch &c** *la16-17*, **planisch &c** *17*, **plinis(h)** *la16-e20* ['plɛnɪʃ, *-ɪs] *v* **1** *vt* furnish, provide (**with**), fill *la15-19*. **2** *vti, specif* stock (land) with trees etc or livestock *la15-18*. **3** *vt* furnish (a house etc) *16-*.
n = *plenishing*, *18-19*.
weel *etc* **plenished** well etc provided, well etc stocked, rich *16-, now Sh-Per, Uls*. **~ing &c 1** goods, necessary accessories, equipment, provisions *16-17*. **2** *also* **~ment** *la17-, now Sh* furniture, household equipment, *freq* that brought by a bride to her new home *la16-*. [OF *pleniss-*, stem of *plenir* (*v*) fill, L *plēnus* full]

plenit *see* PLANET

plenn *see* PLAIN

plenschell &c-naill *n* = PLENCHEOUN-NAILL *16-e17*.

plensher &c *la16-18*, **planschour &c** *la15-17*, **plenshour &c** *la16-17*; **plan-schoir** *e16*, **plainschour &c** *16-e17* [*'plɛnʃər, *'planʃər, &c] *n* = **~ nail**, *16-e18*.
~ nail a flooring nail *la15-18*. [ME *plaunchoure*, OF *plancher &c* planking; *cf* next]

plenshin &c, plenshion &c ['plɛnʃɪn, 'planʃ-] *n* = **~ naill**, *17-e18*.
~(g) naill a flooring nail *17-20*. [short for PLENCHEOUN-NAILL; *cf* prec]

plenshour *see* PLENSHER

plent *see* PLAINT

plenté *see* PLENTY

plenteis *see* PLAINTIS

plenteous, plentuous *see* PLAINTUOUS

plenty &c *15-*, **plenté &c** *la14-e16*; **plaintie &c** *16-e17* ['plɛntɪ; *'plentɪ] *n* **1** = plenty *la14-*. **2** *not implying sufficiency as in Eng* a great number of, many, a large proportion of *19-*: '*plenty of them play football*'.

plenye, plenʒe *see* PLEEN

plert &c *n* a heavy fall into soft earth, mud etc, a splat *la19-, now Ork Wgt*. [prob partly ono-mat, partly var of *plart*, rare intensive var of PLAT¹]

plesance *see* PLEASANCE

plesand *see* PLEASANT

plesandis &c ['plizəns] *n* = PLEASANCE *n 2*, *la14-16*.

plese *see* PLEASE

pleseir *see* PLEASURE

plesit *see* PLEASE

plesour *see* PLEASURE

plester *see* PLAISTER

plet &c; plait *la18-* *v* **1** *vt* = plait *la15-*. **2** cross or fold (one's legs or arms) *la15-, now local NE-Rox*. **3** **~ in (one's) arms** embrace (someone or each other) *15-16*. **4** *chf in ptp* **plet** *of a thing* clasped, fixed closely, tied **to** or **on** (another thing) *16*. **5** fold (cloth etc) *18-, now Sh Ags Kcb*. **6** *vi* twist, cross; *of the limbs* intertwine as a result of weariness, nervousness

CSD-R

etc, fold under one *la18*-, *now NE nEC*. **7** (1) walk in an unsteady, pigeon-toed way *20*-, *Per Fif Kinr*. (2) stagger as with drink *la20*-, *nEC, S*.

n **1** = plait *la16*. **2** a pleat in a garment, a fold, crease *16*-, *now local Sh-Per*. **3** a predicament, quandary *20*-, *S*.

adj **1** intertwined, interwoven, braided *16-17*. **2** *of metal bars in gratings, window openings etc* set criss-cross, interwoven *16-e17*.

    yplet [*ɪ'plɛt] *ptp*, *of hair* plaited *e16*. [*cf* PLEAT]

plet *see* PLAT¹, PLATE

pletforme *see* PLATFORM

plettie *see* PLAT¹

pleuch &c, plew &c; pluch &c *la14-17*, **pluich &c** *15-e17*, **plouch &c** *16-e17*, **plewh** *17*, **plooch** *la19-20*, **plough &c** *17*-, **plu &c** *15-17*, *e20*, **ploo** *la19*-, **peuch &c** *la19-e20*, **pue &c** *la19*-, *now local C* [*n* plu; *Sh* pljʌx; *NE Ags also* plux; *nEC Ayr Gall also* plʌx; *nEC also* pjʌx; *Ayr also* pju; *SW, S also* plju(x); **pløx; v* plu; *nEC Ayr also* pju; *S also* plju] *n* **1** = plough *la14*-. **2** = ~*gate*, *15-e19*, *latterly hist*. **3** the constellation *Ursa Major*, the Plough *16*-. **4** a team of plough-horses or oxen *la17-e20*. **5** the persons working a plough; the tenants of a ~*gate*, *la15-17*.

    vti = plough *16*-.

    pleuchie &c a ploughman; a rustic, yokel *la19*-, *now Ags Per Fif*.

    ~ **feast &c** a ritual entertainment given at the first ploughing of the new season *la16*, *19*.   ~ **gang &c** a measure of arable land, sometimes equated with the ~*gate*, *16-e20*, *latterly hist, only Sc*; see SND.   ~**gate &c** *latterly chf* **plough-gate** an area of land which could be tilled by an eight-oxen plough in a year, *usu* taken to be 104 *Scots acres* (SCOTS); used *eg* for tax assessment *17*-, *now hist*; *cf* DAVACH.   ~ **graith &c** the movable fittings and attachments of a plough *16-e19*.   ~ **guids &c** the oxen used for ploughing, a plough-team *la16-17*.   ~ **irons &c** the metal parts of a plough, *esp* the coulter and share *15*-.   ~ **land &c 1** an area of land, *freq* equated with the ~*gate*, *la14*-, *now in place-names*; see SND. **2** land suitable for ploughing, arable land *la19*-, *now Bnf*. ~**man's love** southernwood, the plant *la20*-, *Kcdn nEC*. ~ **rynes** the reins used for a plough-team *la19*-, *now Kcb*.   ~ **slings** the hooks connecting the swingle-trees to the plough *19*-, *now NE-Per*.   ~ **soam &c** the rope or chain by which horses or oxen are yoked to the plough, the traces; the ~ *slings*, *la17*-, *now Kcb*.   ~ **sock** a plough-share *la17*-.   ~ **stilt &c 1** *usu in pl* the shafts or handles of a plough *la16-20*. **2** a unit of land measurement equal to half a ~*gate*, *la16-e18*, *Gall*.   ~ **theats** the plough-traces *la18*-, *now NE*.

    haud one's *or* **the** ~ drive a plough, be a working farmer *18*-. **pick something up at**

the ~ *freq suggesting bad manners etc* learn something from observation of life rather than by formal instruction *la20*-, *WC*.

pleuder &c [*'pljudər, &c*] *n* pewter *la16-17*. [only *Sc*; irreg var of *pewder* (PEUTHER¹) and *Eng pewter*]

pleuter *see* PLOWTER

pleven &c [*'plivən, *'plevən*] *n* = plevin, a pledge, an assurance *la15*.

    adj of guaranteed (good) quality *e16*.

plever *see* PLIVER

plew, plewh *see* PLEUCH

pley *see* PLAY, PLEA

pleyde *see* PLAID

plicht¹ &c [plɪxt] *n* = plight, state, condition *15-e20*.

plicht² &c [*plɪxt] *vt* = plight, pledge *15-19*, *latterly literary*.

    n **1** = plight *15-16*. **2** wrongdoing, sin, crime *la14-e16*.

plie *see* PLEA

plight-anchor *la17-18*, **plicht-ankir &c** *16-e17* [*plɪxt'aŋkər] *n*, *fig* a support or refuge in a crisis or emergency, a sheet anchor. [only *Sc*; *LowGer plicht-anker*, *Du plechtanker* the main anchor of a ship]

plinis(h) *see* PLENISH

plink &c *n* a short sharp sound like that made by the sudden release of a taut string, *hence* the sound of the violin or fiddle *la19*-.

    vi make a sudden sharp sound *la19*-.

    ~**in** *of water etc* tinkling, pattering *la19*-. [onomat]

plinth *la19*-, **plint** *la17* *n* **1** = plinth. **2** *building* the uppermost projecting part of a cornice; the eaves course or wall-head course *la17-20*.

plish-plash &c *n* a splashing noise or motion, a splash *17-19*.

    vi, *of a liquid* splash, dash, cascade *19*.

    adv with a splashing noise *la19*-, *Sh NE Ags*. [onomat; *cf* PLASH¹]

pliskie &c *n* **1** *also* **plisk** *e18* a practical joke, a trick, escapade, *chf* **play someone a** ~ play a (dirty) trick on someone *18*-. **2** a plight, predicament, a sorry state *19*-, *now local Sh-Fif*. **3** a wild idea, a 'bee in one's bonnet' *la19*-, *now Abd Kcdn*.

    adj mischievous, full of tricks, wily *la19-e20*. [obscure]

pliver &c *la16*-, **pluvar &c** *15-17*, **plever &c** *16-e17*; **plover &c** *16*- ['plɪvər; *'plivər] *n* = plover *15*-.

    ~**'s page** the dunlin *la19*-, *now Cai* [f its habit of flying with plovers].

plleuter *see* PLOWTER

plod *see* PLOUD

plodge &c [plodʒ, plotʃ] *vi* walk on muddy or waterlogged ground, squelch along in a heavy slow way *19*-, *now midLoth S*. [intensive var of *Eng plod*]

ploiter *see* PLOWTER

ploo(ch) *see* PLEUCH

plook *see* PLOUK

ploom &c *17-*, **ploume** &c, **plum** &c *la16-* [plum] *n* **1** = plum *la15-*.   **2** the fruit of the potato-plant *la18-*, *Gen except Sh Ork*.

~ **damas** &c a damson plum, damson; a dried plum or prune *16-*, *now Slk, only Sc.*

plot[1] **&c, plote; plout** &c *la19-20* [plot; *also* ?plʌut] *v* **1** *vt* (1) scald (an object) with boiling water in order to clean or sterilize it *18-*.   (2) *specif* (a) immerse (the carcass of a fowl, pig etc) in boiling water to ease plucking or scraping; remove hair, feathers etc from (skins) by scalding *la17-*, *local Sh-SW*; (b) foment (a sore) in very hot water *19-*.   (3) *freq fig* expose to great heat, overheat, burn, roast, scorch, boil, stew *17-*, *now NE-Per*.   (4) *also fig* pluck wool from (a sheep) or feathers from (a bird) *19-e20*.   **2** *vi* become very hot, 'boil'; *also fig, of persons and animals* 'stew', swelter *19-*.

n **1** a scalding, an immersion in boiling water *la19-*, *local Sh-WC*.   **2** an overheated state, a 'sweat', swelter *la19-*, *Sh-Fif*.

plottie &c a hot drink, *specif* mulled wine *18-e20*.   **plot(tin) het** &c scalding hot *19-*, *now Abd Fif Dmf*.   **plottit** bare, despoiled, having a miserable or sickly appearance *19-e20*, *S*. [MDu *ploten* remove wool from a fleece, *esp* by immersion in a hot alkaline solution]

plot[2] **&c** *n* **1** = plot *la16-*.   **2** = PLAT[2] *n* 3 and 4, *e17*.

plotch *see* PLATCH[1]

Plotcock &c *18-e19*, *chf hist*, **Plotcok** *la16* name for the, or a, devil. [only *Sc*; appar a popular var of *Pluto* + ? suffix *-ock*]

plote *see* PLOT[1]

plotter &c *n*, *weaving* a person who trimmed the nap on woollen cloth *17*.   [only *Sc*; Du *ploter*; *cf* PLOT[1]]

plotter *see* PLATTER

plouch *see* PLEUCH

ploud &c *la18-e19*, **plod** *16-17* [*?plʌud; *plod] *n* a green sod, a thick piece of turf.   [unknown]

plough *see* PLEUCH

plouk *la16-*, **pluk(e) &c** *15-e20*; **plook** *la18-* [pluk, *also* plʌk; *NE also* pjuk] *n* **1** pluk *15*, **pluck** *20-*, *NE* sheep-rot.   **2** a growth, a swelling; a boil; a pimple *la16-*.   **3** a knob, protuberance, *specif* a small knob etc marking a measure on the inside of a container *la16-e20*, *latterly hist*.

plookit covered with pimples, spotty *la19-*.   **plouky &c** covered with growths, pustules or pimples, spotty *16-*. [eModEng, laME *plowke* &c]

ploume *see* PLOOM

plounge *see* PLUNGE

plout *see* PLOT[1]

plover *see* PLIVER

plowd &c [plʌud, plud] *vi* **1** *chf* ~**er** *la19-*, *now Bnf* walk in a heavy-footed way (**through**

water, mud etc), waddle or plod along, paddle around in water *19-20*.   **2** *fig* work perseveringly towards a goal, strive, plod *20-*, *now NE*.

n **1** a heavy ungainly carriage or walk, a waddle *la19-*, *Mry Bnf*.   **2** a heavy fall, a thud, bump *la19-*, *Mry Bnf*.

pludisome dogged, persevering, painstaking *20-*, *now NE*. [intensive var of PLOWT[1], PLOWTER]

plowp &c [plʌup] *vi*, *n*, *adv* = plop *19-*, *Abd Kcdn Ayr S*.

plowster &c; pluister *19-20* ['plʌustər, 'plustər] *vi* work messily in mud etc, flounder about *19-*, *now Rox*.

n **1** a mess; a muddle, 'shambles' *19-*, *now Rox*.   **2** an incompetent, messy worker, a bungler *19-*, *now Rox*. [chf onomat, w infl f next, PLOWTER, PLAISTER etc]

plowt[1] **&c** [plʌut; *also* plut, plʌt, &c] *v* **1** *vt* plunge or thrust (something) **into** (a liquid), submerge quickly **in** *19-*, *now WC*.   **2** set down suddenly and heavily, plump or slap down *la19-*, *now Abd*.   **3** *vi* fall heavily, *freq* into a liquid *la19-*, *now NE Per Wgt*.   **4** walk through water or over wet ground, squelch along; dabble in water or mud *19-*, *now Sh Abd Ags*.   **5** *of liquids*, *esp rain* fall with a splash, pelt down *la19-*, *now Sh Abd Ags*.

n **1** a noisy fall or plunge, *esp* into water etc; a splash, plop *19-*, *now Sh-Ags, Wgt*.   **2** a heavy shower or cascade, a downpour of rain, a *thunder-plump* (THUNNER) *18-*, *now Sh NE nEC*.   **3** a clumsy, blundering person or animal, a clod-hopper *20-*, *now Mry Fif*.   **4** a dull blow, punch, thump *20-*, *Sh Abd*.

~ **kirn &c** a churn operated by a plunger *18-*, *now Ork*. [onomat]

plowt[2] [plʌut] *n*, *joc* a dish made of meat boiled and jellied in a mould, *esp potted heid* (POT) *la20*, *Fif*. [cf PLOT[1] *v* 1 (3) and next]

plowt[3] [plʌut] *n* popular name for the Fleshmarket Close in Edinburgh, *orig* the meat-market and slaughter-house *e20*. [unknown]

plowter &c; plutter &c *19-e20*, **pl(l)euter** *19-20*, **ploiter** *la19-e20*, **pleiter &c** *20* ['plʌutər, 'ploitər; *NE also* 'pjʌut-, 'pleit-; *C also* 'plut-, 'plɒt-, 'plɪt-] *v* **1** *vi* dabble with the hands or feet, *usu* in a liquid, splash aimlessly in mud or water, wade messily through wet ground *19-*.   **2** work or act idly or aimlessly, potter or fiddle **about** *19-*.   **3** fumble about, rummage or grope in the dark *20-*, *local Per-Slk*.   **4** *vt* make a mess of, spoil (*esp* a piece of land by bad cultivation) *19-*, *now Sh Abd*.

n **1** the act of working or walking in wetness or mud, a splashing about; a (disagreeable) messy task; a botched job, an exhibition of slovenliness or inefficiency *19-*.   **2** a splash, dashing of liquid *19-*, *now Sh Ags*.   **3** a wet, muddy spot, a bog, mire *19-20*.   **4** a sloppy or sticky mess of food etc *la19-*, *local Sh-SW*.   **5** a messy inefficient worker, a muddler *20-*, *now C*.

~**y &c** *of the weather etc* wet, showery, rainy, puddly *la19-20*. [chf Sc; frequentative of PLOWT[1]; *cf* also Du *ploeteren* dabble in water, drudge]

ploy[1] **&c** *n* **1** a venture, undertaking; a piece of business, a scheme *la17-*. **2** a light-hearted plan or enterprise for one's own amusement, a piece of fun, a trick, practical joke *18-*. **3** a social gathering, party *la18-*, *now Sh*. [perh aphetic f obs Eng *employ* an occupation, activity]

ploy[2] *n* a legal action; a quarrel, disagreement, breach of the peace *la16-e20*. [only Sc; F *ploit* a plea]

plu(ch) *see* PLEUCH

pluck &c, pluk &c *vti* **1** = pluck *15-*. **2** *vt* steal (livestock) **from** (a person) *16-17*. **3** take (turnips) out of the ground with a PLUCK (*n* 5) *la20-*, *NE*.

n **1** = pluck. **2** *also fig* a mouthful of grass etc taken by an animal as food *la17-*, *now Sh NE Wgt*. **3** *fig* an attempt to snatch at a prize, *specif* an eager demand for or 'rush' on something *la19-*, *now Bnf*. **4** a moulting state in fowls or animals *20-*, *Ork Cai Mry Kcb*. **5** a two-pronged, mattock-type implement used for taking turnips from hard ground, forking dung etc *19-*, *now NE*.

~**er** a kind of spokeshave, a tool for planing a curved surface, *eg* the outside of a barrel *la19-*, *now Bnf Abd*.

play ~ at the craw play a game in which one player is pulled about by the others; *fig* take what one can get by any means to hand *16*.

~**-up fair &c** a 'grab and buy' sale; a scramble in which everyone tries to get as much as he can for himself *la16-17*, *only Sc*.

pluck *see* PLOUK

pludisome *see* PLOWD

pluff &c *adv* with a puff, whoof! *la19-*, *now Sh Abd Ags*.

n **1** a mild explosion, a whiff or puff or air, smoke, gunpowder etc *16-*, *now Sh NE Kcb*. **2** a firework, squib *la19*. **3** *also* ~ **gun** a tube used as a pea-shooter or as a simple form of bellows *la17-*, *now Sh*. **4** the instrument used for throwing out hair-powder *18-e19*. **5** a piece of padding, *esp* used in a garment, a pad *18-*, *now Kcb*. **6** a small quantity, a pinch of powder, dust etc *19-*, *now Sh*.

v **1** *vt* discharge (smoke, breath etc) with a small explosion, puff (something) out in a cloud; blow (something) **out** by puffing air on it *17-*, *now local*. **2** puff out, give a puffy appearance to *19-*, *now Sh Abd*. **3** *vi* become inflated, swell up, puff out *20-*, *local*. **4** explode, go up in a puff of smoke *20-*, *now Sh NE*.

~**er** a pea-shooter *la19-*, *now Sh NE Uls*.

~**ing &c 1** firing, shooting *17-e19*. **2** *in pl* the refuse of corn, husks, chaff *19-*, *S*. ~**y &c** *adj*,

freq of living things having a 'well-padded' appearance, plump, 'puffy', fleshy *19-*. *n* a kind of toffee made fluffy and brittle by the addition of bicarbonate of soda, puff candy *20-*, *Ags Slk*.

~ **grass, pyuff** [pjʌf] **girse** the creeping or meadow soft grass *19-e20*, *NE* [f the lightness and fluffiness of its seeds]. [only Sc; *cf* LowGer *pluf*, Du *plof* (*interj*), LowGer *ploffen*, Du *pluffen* (*v*) puff, explode]

plug[1] *n* = plug.
vti, *mining* blast rock by means of *plug shots*, *la19-*, *now Fif*.
~ **shot** *mining* a charge in a small hole to break up a stone *la19-*, *now Fif*.

plug[2] *vti* dodge (school), play truant, absent oneself without leave *20-*, *C, S*. [perh var of PLUNK[2]]

pluich *see* PLEUCH

pluister *see* PLOWSTER

pluk *see* PLOUK, PLUCK

pluke &c [*?pløk] *n* a club, bludgeon; a stout stick *la14-e15*. [only Sc; Gael *ploc* (genitive *pluic*) a sod; a club, MIr *pluc* a round mass, knob; *hence* a mace or club]

pluke *see* PLOUK

pluking &c [*'plʌkɪŋ] *n* the action of stopping up a barrel with a plug or wedge *16*. [*cf* MLowGer, LowGer *pluck*, *plock* and Eng *plug* a wooden plug or pin]

plum *see* PLOOM

plumb &c [plʌm; *plʌmb] *n* **1** = plumb *la15-*. **2** a deep hole used as a privy *e16*. **3** a deep pool in a river or on the seabed, a drop *la18-*, *now Ayr Rox*.
vt = plumb *la16-*.
~ **lede** unworked or untreated lead; the colour of this *la15-16*, *only Sc*.

plummet &c *15-*; **plumbat &c** *16-e17* *n* **1** = plummet *16-*. **2** the pommel on the hilt of a sword, *freq* weighted with lead *15-18*, *only Sc*.

plump[1] **&c** *n* an assemblage or collection: **1** *of persons or animals* a group, body, band, flock; **2** *of things* a clump, *eg* of trees, a cluster, patch *la16-19*. [unknown]

plump[2] **&c** *vti* **1** = plump, fall. **2** *vi, of rain* fall heavily, pour, fall in sheets *19-*. **3** *of a* (*semi-*)*liquid* make a loud bubbling or plopping noise, *eg* when boiling *la18-*, *now Uls*.
n **1** = plump, a heavy fall *la16-*. **2** a heavy downpour of rain, a deluge, *freq* following thunder *19-*; *cf thunder-plump* (THUNNER).
~**er** the plunger of a *plunge churn* (PLUNGE) *la19-*, *NE*.
~**-hasher** a heavy implement for slicing turnips etc *20-*, *Bnf Abd*. ~ **kirn &c** a *plunge churn* (PLUNGE) *20-*, *NE*. ~ **shower** = *n* 2, *la17-e18*.
play ~ plunge, dive *20-*, *now Sh Per*.

plumrose &c *n* = primrose *la18-19*, *only Sc*.

plunge &c; plounge &c *la15*,   *la18-19*

[plʌn(d)ʒ] *vti* **1** = plunge *la14-*. **2** *vt* penetrate by diving or plunging, plunge into *la15-e18*, *only Sc*.

n **1** = plunge *16-*. **2** a heavy fall of water, a downpour of rain *la18-19*.

~ **churn** &c a churn worked by moving a plunger up and down *19*.

plunk[1] **&c** *adv, interj* with a dull, heavy sound, plump!; in a sudden way, quickly *la19-*.

n **1** a heavy fall, plump or plunge; the sound of this *19-*, *local Sh-SW*. **2** the sound of a cork being drawn from a bottle, a popping sound *19-*. **3** a sharp forward jerk or thrust, a flick; *specif* the act of propelling a marble by the thumb and forefinger; the game of marbles played thus *la19-*, *now NE-S*.

v **1** *vi* fall with a dull heavy sound, *usu* into water etc, plop *19-*. **2** *vti* make a plopping or gurgling noise as when drawing a cork, swallowing etc *19-*, *now Ags Kcb*. **3** *vt* drop (an object) into water, plop, put (something) down with a thump *19-*. **4** *specif, marbles* propel (a marble) with a thrust or jerk, pitch, throw *19-*, *Gen except Sh Ork*. **5** strike with a dull thud, hit with a thump *20-*, *local Sh-SW*. **6** pluck (the strings of a musical instrument) to make a popping or twanging noise *19-*, *Lnk Kcb S*.

~**er** a heavy clay, glass or metal marble designed to be played as in *v* 4, *la19-*, *Gen except Sh Ork*. ~**ie &c 1** the game of marbles played as in *n* 3, *e20*. **2** a kind of homemade sweet made of treacle or syrup and flour *la19-*, *NE* [so called because it is thrown into cold water to harden after boiling]. [onomat]

plunk[2] *vti* dodge (school), absent oneself from school without leave *19-*, *C, S*.

~**er** a truant *19-*, *C, S*. [only Sc; uncertain]

plurality &c *16-*, **pluralite(e)** *la15-17* *n* **1** = plurality *la15-*. **2** the greater proportion of a number (of things, persons etc), the majority *la16-*.

plusquamperfect &c [*plʌskwam'pɛrfɛkt] *adj* pluperfect *16-17*. [only Sc; L *plus quam perfectum* more than perfect]

plutter *see* PLOWTER

pluvar *see* PLIVER

ply[1] **&c** *n* **1** a fold, a layer or thickness of any material, a strand or twist of rope, wool etc *15-*. **2** *applied to fishing rivers* condition, state, fettle, *chf* **in** (**good** etc) or **oot o'** ~ *15-*. **3** *mining* a thin layer of hard rock separated by a softer one from another hard layer, a rib *la18-*, *now Fif*.

v **1** *vi* = ply, bend; be pliable *la15-*. **2** *vt* fold or double over (cloth, paper etc) *la14-15*. **3** ? provide a lining for (a garment etc); ? reinforce with extra material *17*.

~**ing &c** providing a garment with lining; pleating, pleats; ? a type of pleated material *la17-e19*. ~**ing hammer** a heavy double-faced hammer, used *esp* in shipyards *la19-*, *now WC*.

two etc ~ *la18-*, or -**plyed** *e18*, *of wool etc* made of two etc strands twisted together.

ply[2] *v* **1** *vi* = ply, tack, work to windward *la15-*. **2** *vtir* apply (oneself) to (a task), work hard and perseveringly *17-19*.

plyde *see* PLAID

plype &c *n* (the noise of) a sudden dash of water; a sudden heavy shower of rain; (the noise of) a fall into water *la19-*, *now NE Ags*.

vi **1** drop suddenly into a liquid, plunge or splash in(to) mud or water *la19-*, *NE Ags*. **2** *also* **plyper &c** *la19-e20* dabble or work messily and carelessly in a liquid or some wet material *19-*, *NE Ags*. **3** walk on wet or muddy ground, squelch along *la19-*, *NE Ags*.

adv suddenly, with a splash, plop! *la19*, *Bnf Abd*. [onomat]

plyven &c [*'plevən &c*] *n* the flower of the white or red clover *19-e20*.

pneumatic &c, pnewmatick *la17-e18* *n*, *chf in pl* **1** *Sc Univs* pneumatology, a branch of metaphysics *la17-e20*, *latterly hist*; *see* SND. **2** = pneumatic.

'po *see* UPON

poach[1] **&c; potch** *19-e20*, *Abd* [potʃ] *vti* **1** = poach, catch game illegally *19-*. **2** *vt* (1) stir or poke with a stick etc, push, prod, thrust *19-*, *now NE Rox*. (2) reduce (something, *eg* food in a dish) to mush by over-handling, mess about with *19-*, *Bnf Abd*. (3) pound or stamp on (clothes) in washing *20-*, *Mry Bnf Per*. **3** *vi* work in an aimless or messy way **at**, mess **about** *la19-*, *now S*.

n a wet, muddy area of ground, a puddle; *fig* a disordered state of affairs, a shambles, mess *la19-*, *now Abd*.

poach[2] *20-*, *now Ags*, **poch &c** *la16-e18* [potʃ] *n* the armed bullhead or pogge, the fish. [only Sc; obscure]

pob &c *n*, *also* ~ **tow** *18-e19* the refuse of flax (*later* also of jute) after scutching, any fibrous or dusty waste material; rope or twine teased into fibres *18-*, *now Bnf*. [perh Gael *pab* shag, rough hair; oakum]

poch [pox] *adj*, *of persons* slightly unwell, out of sorts *20*, *Mry Abd*. [perh onomat, suggesting exhaustion; *cf* PECH]

poch *see* POACH[2]

pochle *see* PAUCHLE[1]

pock[1] **&c, pok &c** *16-e17*; **polk** *16-e17* [pok; *pʌuk] *n* **1** = pock, an eruption or pustule on the skin *16-*. **2** the disease causing this, *eg* chicken-pox *19-*, *now local Sh-SW*.

~(**y**)**arred &c** pock-marked, having a scarred or pitted skin *19-*, *now Ayr*.

pock[2] *la16-*, **poke &c; pok &c** *15-17*, *la19-20* (*Sh*), **polk** *la15-17*, **pook &c** *la16-e18* [pok; *NE also* pjok; *pʌuk] *n* **1** (1) a bag or pouch, a small sack, *appar* sometimes as a measure of a commodity *15-*. (2) a shopkeeper's paper bag *la19-*. (3) a beggar's bag used for collecting meal etc given in charity *la17-e20*. **2** a kind of fishing net varying between localities *la16-*, *now Sh Ork Cai SW*. **3** (1) ? a loosely-hanging appendage to a hat *17*. (2) ? a similarly-shaped hood or hat *17*. **4** a pouch-like swelling under the jaw of a sheep caused by sheep-rot; the disease itself *la18-*, *now local Sh-Pbls*. **5** the udder of a milch animal *la19-*, *now Kcb*. **6** the stomach of a fish; *joc* the human stomach *20*, *Cai Wgt*.

v **1** *vt* put into a *poke* (*n* 1), *freq* ~ **up** store away (in ·a bag), save *la16-19*. **2** *vti* fish or catch (fish) with a ~-*net*, *la16-*, *now Sh Ork SW*.

pocked &c *of sheep* having a swelling under the jaw, infected with sheep-rot *la17-19*.   **pockle** a bagful *19-20*, *Ags* [reduced f *pockful*].

~**man** a porter *la16-17*.   ~-**net &c** = *n* 2, *la17-20*.   ~ **neuk &c** the bottom or corner of a bag etc, *esp* one used to hold money *la16-19*. **be on one's own** *or* **another's** ~ **neuk** be relying on one's own or another's resources *e19*.

~ **puddin(g) &c 1** a DUMPLING or steamed pudding cooked in *eg* a muslin bag *la17-*, *now WC*. **2** *joc* or *pejorative* nickname for an Englishman *18-20* [f the supposed fondness of the English for steamed puddings, w an implication of stolidity].   ~ **shakings &c 1** the last child of a large family *19-*, *local*. **2** the smallest pig in a litter *19-*.

be on one's ain ~ be relying on one's own resources *19-*, *WC Dmf*; cf *pock neuk*. **gang wi the** ~ go about begging *la18-*, *now Per Kcb*. **let the cat oot o the** ~ 'let the cat out of the bag' *19-*, *local Cai-Kcb*. **lowse** *etc* **one's** ~ tell one's news, give a full account of something *18-19*. [ME *poke*; ScL ablative pl or poss Sc pl *pokis* (*e14*)]

pockmantie &c *la16-19*, **pokemantie &c** *la16-19*, **pokemantle &c** *17-e19* [*'pok-'mantɪ, *-'mantl] *n* a travelling-bag, a portmanteau. [altered f Eng *portmanteau*, w infl f prec]

pod *see* PUD[1]

poddock *see* PUDDOCK

podir *see* PEUTHER[1]

podlie &c *la17-*, **podlok &c** *16-17*; **podlo** *16-17*, **pudlo** *la17* *n* **1** *also* **podler** *la17-e19* the young of the coalfish at the second stage of its development; the pollack, the LYTHE *16-*, *now NE Ags Fif*. **2** a tadpole *19-*, *now Ags Fif*. **3** a red-breasted minnow *20-*, *now Loth Rox*. **4** term of affection for a child *la19*, *Abd Ags*. [perh an early form of Eng *pollack*; *cf* POLLACK, PULLACH]

poffill, poffle *see* PAFFLE

poind &c, pind &c *15-19*; **puind &c** *15-18*, **poyn &c** *la15-17*, **pin** *la17-19* [pɪn(d); *NE* pin] *vti* **1** *law* seize and sell the goods of a debtor; impound (goods); distrain upon (a person) *15-*. **2** *vt* impound (stray animals etc) as surety for compensation for damage committed by them *16-*, *now Cai Loth S*.

n **1** an article or animal which has been *poinded*, the goods impounded *15-e20*. **2** an animal or cattle seized as plunder *15-16*. **3** an act of *poinding*, a distraint, seizure of goods for debt *19*.

~**able &c** *of persons, goods etc and property* liable or in a position to be distrained *16-*, *only Sc*. ~**age** the right of impounding trespassing cattle; the fine payable for their release *la16*.   ~**er &c**, ~**ler &c** *la16-e19* **1** an estate officer authorized to impound straying or trespassing animals *16-e19*. **2** a creditor who distrains his debtor's goods *la16-19*.

~**fold &c** an enclosure or building in which forfeit animals etc were kept, a pound *la15-19*. ~ **money** the money realized on distrained goods *la18-19*. ~ **the ground** take the goods on land (*eg* furniture, farm equipment) in enforcement of a real BURDEN possessed over the land *la18-*. [*cf* nME; *cf* eModEng *pynd(e)*, OE *pyndan* enclose; the spelling *poind* is an arch legal survival of an OSc spelling var -*oi*-, in ModSc usu found as -*ui*-, pronounced [ɪ] when short; *cf* PUND[2] and MULTIPLEPOINDING]

point &c; pint &c *la14-20*, **pwint &c** *15-16*, **poinet &c** *15-e17*, **pount &c** *16-19* [pəint; *Fif* also *pʌunt] *n*, *also* **pant** *16* **1** = point *la14-*. **2** a tagged length of cord, twisted yarn etc, used as a fastening, *latterly specif* a shoe- or boot-lace *la15-*, *now Sh-nEC*. **3** the leading member of a team of reapers, the man at the front left-hand-side of the team *19*. **4** the tapering part of a field which is not completely rectangular, the furrows or drills shortened because of this *la20-*, *NE wLoth Kcb*.

vti **1** = point *15-*. **2** *building* indent a stone face with a pointed tool *la20-*, *NE Per*.

~**ed &c 1** = pointed *16-*. **2** *of persons* precise, (over-)attentive to detail, demanding; punctual, exact *18-*, *Ork, local N, S*.   ~**edly** accurately, punctiliously, punctually, immediately *19-*, *now Ags*.   **pointie** a throw in the game of *knifie* (KNIFE) *20-*, *Bnf Ags Ayr*.

~ **game** *curling* (CURL) a game played by a *curler* as an individual as opposed to one played in a team *la19-*, *now Kcb*. ~ **lace &c, poinet(t) lace &c** ? lacing for making POINTS (*n* 2) *e17*.

at ~ **1** properly, fitly, aptly *la14-16*. **2** in full readiness, ready *la15-16*.

point *see* PINT

pointal &c [*'pəintəl] *n* **1** = pointel, a pointed weapon *15-e16*. **2** a plectrum *e16*, *only Sc*.

poinȝé &c *la14-e15*; **pugny** *la15*; **punȝe &c** *la14* [*'pʌnjɪ, *'pəinjɪ] *la14* *n* = poygné, a battle, skirmish. [OED *poygné*]

poiss- *see* POSE[2]

pok *see* POCK[1], POCK[2]

poke *see* POCK[2]

pokemantie, pokemantle *see* POCKMANTIE

pokey-hat *n* an ice-cream cone *20-*, *C*. [colloq Eng *hokey-pokey* ice-cream + *hat* f its shape]

polacie *see* POLICY
polder *see* POUTHER
pole *see* POW¹, POWL
polece *see* POLICE
poleist *see* POLISH
policat *see* PULLICATE
police &c; polece &c *16-19*, polis &c *20-*
[po'lis, pə-; *C, S* 'polɪs] *n* 1 (1) the civil administration and organization of a community, the
public services, *eg* lighting, cleansing (*later* controlled by Town Councils) and the preservation
of law and order *la15-e19*. (2) = police, the
official body enforcing law and order *la18-*. 2
= POLICY *n* 2, *la15-16*. 3 *also joc* polly &c *la19*
a policeman, police-officer *la19-*.
vt 1 improve or develop (land) by cultivation
and planting *16*, *only Sc*. 2 = police.
~ burgh a BURGH set up under various public
Acts, in which MAGISTRATES and *police commissioners* were elected with powers similar to those
of the councils of the older BURGHS *la19-20*, *latterly hist*. ~ commissioner = *Commissioner of
P~*, *e20*. ~ dung dung and waste material
collected in the streets of a city *e19*. ~man 1
= policeman. 2 *fig, mining* a movable guard
over or round a pitmouth or at mid-workings,
safety gates *la19-*, *now Fif*.
Commissioner of P~ a member of a popularly elected body in a BURGH which supervised
the watching, lighting and cleansing of the
town *19*.
policy &c, policie &c *la16-17*; police &c
la16, polacie &c *16-17* ['polɪsɪ] *n* 1 = policy
la15-. 2 the improvement or development of a
town, estate etc by the erection of buildings,
plantation or enclosure etc, (provision of)
amenity; the buildings etc involved in this
15-e18, *only Sc*. 3 polish of manners, refinement, cultivation, civilization *16-e17*, *only Sc*.
4 *now chf in pl* the enclosed grounds of a large
house, the park of an estate *18-*.
polis *see* POLICE, POLISH
polish *19-*, polis &c *15-e17* ['polɪʃ, *-ɪs*] *vt* =
polish *15-*.
polished &c *19-*, polist &c *now Sh Uls*, poleist
15-e16 1 = polished *la14-*. 2 *transf and fig, of
persons or their appearance* bright, beautiful;
? adorned, embellished *la14-e16*. 3 complete,
utter, out and out *19-*, *now Sh Uls*.
politik &c; pollutick &c *la16-17* ['polɪtɪk] *adj*
1 = politic *la15-17*. 2 refined, cultured, polished *la16* [erron for L *polītus*].
polk *see* POCK¹, POCK²
polk breik *n* ? a TARTAN or chequered bag; ? a
PLAID *e16*. [Gael *poca* a bag + *breac* speckled,
chequered]
poll *see* POW¹, POW², POWL
pollack &c *n* the POWAN *18-e19*. [ScGael *pollag*,
IrGael *pollog*, dim of IrGael *poll* a lake; *cf* POD-
LIE, PULLACH and Eng *pollack* the LYTHE]
pollutick *see* POLITIK
polly *see* POLICE

pollywag ['polɪ'wag] *n* a tadpole *la19-*, *Per Fif
Ayr*. [ME *polwygle*]
polonie &c ['pol(ə)nɪ, pə'lonɪ] *n* 1 a kind of
loose-fitting gown worn *occas* by women but *more
freq* by young boys; a greatcoat for older boys or
men *18-19*. 2 a loose ill-fitting garment, a
clumsy, outlandish article of dress *20-*, *now Sh
Bnf Abd*. [obs Eng *Polony*, F *Pologne*, MedL
Polonia Poland; *cf* obs Eng *polony* Polish]
pomate &c [*n* *'pomət; *v* *?po'met*] *n, vt* (dress
the hair with) a pomade *la18-e19*. [Eng
pomatum]
pome *n* 1 a pomander *e16*. 2 = pome *la16*.
poney *see* POWN
pong-pong *n, also* pong a kind of artificial
flower, rosette etc for a woman's dress or hat
la18. [var of Eng *pom-pom*]
pontioune *see* PUNCHEON²
pony *see* POWN
poo &c *n* the common edible crab *19-20*, *Loth
Bwk*. [perh f POU]
pooch *see* POUCH
poochle &c *20-*; puchal &c *19* ['puxl; *'pʌxl*]
adj proud, self-assured, self-confident; cocky
NE. [perh deriv of *pooch*, onomat of a puff of
wind, *ie* inflated, w infl f PAUCHTIE]
pooer &c *la19-*, power &c; puer *16-17*, poor
&c *18-e20* ['pu(ə)r; *'pu'ir*] *n* 1 = power *la14-*.
2 power of control, jurisdiction, command
la18-19. 3 *used in the subscription of a letter, chf* at
(all) *or* (one's) ~, to (one's) ~ to the best of
one's ability *16-17*.
abuif &c one's ~ beyond one's ability, capacity or resources *la15-16*. stand, ly *etc* in one's
~(s) be within one's capacity to do *la15-e16*.
with (all) ~ by force, forcibly *15*. with (lefe
and) (ful) ~ with full authority *15-17*.
pooer *see* POUR
pook *see* POCK², POUK, POWK¹
pool *see* PUIL
poolicks &c *n pl* old clothes, rags, tatters; finery
19-, *now Fif*.
poon *see* PUND²
poopit *see* PUPIT
poor *see* POOER, POUR, PUIR
poortith *see* PUIRTITH
poose *see* POSE¹
pooshin *see* PUSHION
poosie *see* POUSS
pooster *see* POUSTIE
pop *n* 1 = pop. 2 a small round sheep-mark
made by dabbing on the marking substance
with a stick *la19-*, *Dmf Slk Rox*.
pop *see* PAP³
popill *see* PAPPLE¹
poplexy &c *la17-e19*, poplesie &c *16-17*
[*'popleksɪ, *'popləsɪ*] *n* = apoplexy, a stroke
of apoplexy. [aphetic]
poppy *see* PUPPIE¹
popular &c *adj* = popular *16-*.
n 1 = popular, a commoner; the common people *la16*. 2 a pawn in chess *la15*.

~ sermon the sermon preached to the people of the parish by a *probationer* (PROBATION) as part of his TRIALS for entry to the *ministry* (MINISTER) *la17-e18*.

popule *see* PAPPLE[1]

porciunkle &c [*'pɔrsɪʌŋkl] *n* a small portion (of land) *la15-e16*. [only Sc; F *portioncule, portiuncule*, L *portiuncula*, dim of *portiō*]

pore *see* PORR

pork *vt* prod, poke, push; *of a bird* peck, damage by pecking; *of a cow etc* prod with the horns, gore *la19-, now SW Rox*.
n a thrust, prod, poke *20-, SW Rox*. [prob intensive f Eng *poke*, perh w infl f next]

porr; pore &c *la16-e18*, **purr &c** *vti* **1** prod, poke, thrust at; *of a cow etc* prod with the horns, gore *la16-, now SW*. **2** *vt* prick, stab *19-20*.
n **1** (the noise made by) a thrust, stab, poke, prod *la16-, now SW*. **2** a poker *17-e18*. **3** a thorn, prickle, barb; a thistle *20, Cai*.
porring &c iron = *n* 2, *la16-e19*. [ME *porre*, Du, LowGer *porren* (*v*) poke, thrust]

porridge, porritch *see* PARRITCH

port[1] **&c** *n* **1** *also in pl used as sing, e16* a gateway or entrance, *esp* of a walled town or a castle *15-, now only in place-names*. **2** *chf in pl* the limits or boundaries (of a town, property etc) *16*. **3** the road passing through or leading to a PORT (*n* 1); the area adjacent *17*. **4** a piece of open ground near a town gate used as the site of a *hiring market* (HIRE), *esp* for farm-workers; the market itself *la18-e20*. **5** = port, an opening in the side of a ship *15-*. **6** an opening in a beehive for the passage of the bees *la20-, Bnf Uls*. **7** *curling* (CURL), *bowls* a narrow passage between two stones or bowls through which a third can be aimed, *freq* **block** *or* **enter a ~** *la18-*.
vi, curling (CURL), *bowls, also fig* send a *curling stone* or bowl between two stationary stones or bowls lying close together *19*.
~ boulls &c the game of bowls *la16-e17, Mry*.

port[2] **&c** [port; *Gael* porʃt] *n* a tune, catch, theme, *esp* played on the bagpipes *18-20, latterly hist*.
~-a-beul [*Gael* 'pɔrʃtə'bial, &c] a fast tune, *usu* a REEL[1] etc of GAELIC or *Lowland* (LOWLAND) origin to which GAELIC words of a repetitive nature have been added to make it easier to sing, sometimes used as an accompaniment to dancing in the absence of instrumental music *20-* [Gael 'music from mouth']. **~-youl &c** [*'pɔr'tjul] a sad outcry, a doleful moan, howl, *freq* **sing ~-youl** cry, lament *la17-19*. [Sc and IrGael *port* a tune played on a musical instrument]

port[3] **&c** *n, v* = port, bear(ing) etc *la15-*.
~able &c 1 that is or has to be borne, *only in* **~able charges** etc *la15-17, only Sc*. **2** = portable *17-*. **~er &c 1** = porter *la15-*. **2** *weaving* a section of the reed in a loom containing 20 interstices through which the warp threads are passed *18-e20*.

portary &c *n* citizenship or burghership in a Flemish or Dutch city, and its rights and privileges *la16*. [only Sc; MFlem *porterie &c*]

portative &c *adj* **1** = portative, portable *16*. **2** navigable *la16-17, only Sc*.
n = portative, a portable organ *15-16*.

portculis &c *15-16*, **portcul3eis &c** *16-e17*; **portcules** *la15-e17*, **portculeis** *16* [*'pɔrt'kʌl(j)ɪs, *-ɪs] *n* = portcullis.

porteous *la15-19*, **port(u)ous &c** *la15-e19*; **portuis &c** *15-16*, **porteus &c** *la15-e18* [*'pɔrtjəs, *-ju(ə)s, *-(ɪ)us, *-(ɪ)əs] *n* **1** = portas, a portable breviary *la15-e16*. **2** an official list of persons to be indicted or otherwise proceeded against *15-e17, only Sc*. **3** *only in* on an official list of names drawn up for some other purpose *e16*.
P~ clerk *law* one of a number of legal officers who investigated the circumstances of crimes to be prosecuted in the circuit courts *e18*. **~ roll** a list of persons drawn up by the *Justice Clerk* (JUSTICE) for indictment before the Circuit *Court of Justiciary* (JUSTICIARY) *la17-e19*.

porter biscuit *n* a large round flattish bun resembling a roll in texture *20-, C*. [appar because commonly eaten with porter beer]

porteus *see* PORTEOUS

portion &c, portioun &c *la14-17 n* **1** = portion *la14-*. **2** *specif* a passage chosen from the Bible for reading, *esp* at family worship *la18-, now Abd*.
portionat *ptp* (*v*) provide(d) with a portion of an inheritance *la16*. **portioner &c 1** *law* the proprietor of a small estate or piece of land once part of a larger estate, *orig also* a joint heir, *esp* female, or her successor; a joint tenant; a joint proprietor *la15-*; cf *heir portioner* (HEIR). **2** a joint owner, joint proprietor (1) of land *15-16*; (2) in gen *17*. **3** a person who shares with another in a joint venture or jointly-owned commercial property *16-e17*.
~ natural *law* = LEGITIM *la16-19*.

portous *see* PORTEOUS

portrature &c *15-17*; **portratoure &c** *la14-e17 n* **1** = portraiture *la14-17*. **2** the external appearance of a person or animal *la14-e17*.

portuis, portuous *see* PORTEOUS

porture &c *vt, ptp also* **porturat &c 1** = porture, portray, depict *15-e16*. **2** *chf in ptp* shaped, formed, fashioned *la14-e16*.

pory *adj* spongy, porous in texture *19-, now Sh*. [obs in Eng]

pose[1] **&c; poose** *e20, Rox* [poz; *Rox also* puz] *vt* place (an object) in a specified position, *freq* with the aim of hiding it; hide, cache; save **up** (money), lay **by** *la19-, Inv NE Ags*.
n **1** *chf* **posie &c** *19-, now NE Ags*, **posel(ie) &c** *19-20* that which has been deposited or laid down, a heap, pile, collection of objects, a quantity of some substance *e19*. **2** *freq* **posie &c** *la19-20* a collection of money or valuables

hidden away for safe-keeping, a person's private hoard, savings *16-20*. **3** a fund or stock of money *la16-e17*.

in ~ *of money or treasure* set by in safe-keeping; in hand, on deposit *la15-17*. [laME (once) *pos*, appar F *poser* lay down]

pose² &c; **poiss-** [*poz] *vt* **1** *freq church* put a question or questions to, interrogate, question *la16-e18*. **2** charge (someone) **to declare** (something) *la16-17*. [aphetic f Eng *appose* or *oppose*]

posel(ie) *see* POSE¹

posh &c *n*, *freq* ~**ie** *la19-*, *local Ork-WC*, *child's word* porridge *la19-*. [perh onomat or a child's form of *porridge*; perh w infl f Eng dial *posh* a soft pulpy mass]

positive¹ &c *adj* **1** = positive *la15-*. **2** *of persons* determined, adamant, pig-headed, obstinate *18-*, *N, C*.

positive² &c [*?pozɪˈtaɪvɪ] *adv* explicitly, without reservation; by explicit statement; affirmatively *17*. [only Sc; L *positīvē*, f as prec]

poss *vt* **1** strike or hit with the knees or feet, knee, kick, trample *16-e17*. **2** press, squeeze down, pound *19-e20*, *S Uls*. **3** knead or press down (clothes etc) in washing, trample (a washing) in order to extract the dirt *19-*, *local Per-S*.

~**er** a stick, *freq* with a flat disc at one end, used to pound clothes in the wash-tub *la18-*, *now SW, S*. ~**ing tub** a deep barrel-shaped wash-tub *19-*, *now Dmf S*. ~ **stick** = ~**er**, *20-*, *now Mry S*. [perh a var of POUSS; *cf* POST³]

possede &c [*poˈsid] *vt* **1** = possede, possess *la14-e17*. **2** take or obtain possession of, gain, win *16-e17*.

possess &c *v* **1** *vt* = possess *15-*. **2** *vt* ~ **with** cause (land) to be occupied by (cattle) *16*, *Slk*. **3** be in possession or occupancy of (property etc) as owner or (*freq*) tenant *16-18*.

~**ion** &c **1** = possession *la14-*. **2** (a) giving of possession to another; a property given by one to another to possess *15-16*. **3** a property enjoyed or occupied though not necessarily owned; a tenancy, a piece of ground, small farm etc held under lease *la14-19*.

~**ory** &c = possessory *16-*. ~**ory judgment** *law* the legal rule by which an occupant of at least seven years standing cannot be dispossessed by a rival claimant except by a court action of *reduction* (REDUCE) *17-e20*, *only Sc*. ~**our**(e) *adj* = possessory *la15-e17*.

posset &c *n* **1** = posset *16-17*. **2** a poisonous drink *la16-17*, *only Sc*.

possibill &c *la15-e17*; **possible** ['pɒsɪbl] *adj* **1** = possible *la14-*. **2** (the) greatest possible *la15-17*, *only Sc*.

adv = possible, possibly *la16-17*.

possodie &c [*poˈsodɪ] *n* **1** term of endearment *e16*. **2** a poisonous drink *la16*. [*cf* POSSET and POWSOWDIE]

post¹ &c *n* **1** = post, an upright of timber *15-*.

2 *mining etc* a thick layer or seam of (particularly hard) stone, *usu* sandstone or limestone; the working face between main joints in a granite quarry *la18-*, *now Fif*.

~-**stone** a very hard, fine-grained sandstone *20-*, *Fif*.

post² &c *n* **1** = post, *orig* a letter-carrier on a post-road, *latterly* a postal delivery *16-*. **2** a letter-carrier, *orig* a courier carrying mails, *now* a Post Office postman *16-*. **3** one of a series of stations where post-horses were kept for relays, a stage *17*. **4** ? a message-bearer (on a single occasion) *la16-e17*.

vti **1** = post *16-*. **2** *vi* act as a postman *la20-*, *NE*.

adv = post, at great speed *la16-17*.

~**ie** &c = *n* 2, *17-*.

at (**the**) ~ **1** *of a message or messenger* as or by express courier; at express speed *16-e17*. **2** *of a person* by relays of horses at post-stages; at great speed *16*. **rin, ride** *or* **pas the** ~ go as an express messenger or despatch rider, ? using relays of horses; *transf* travel at express speed *16*.

post³ *vt* = POSS *v* 3, *19-*, *now Mry Bnf*. [Gael *post*, borrowed f POSS]

postillat *see* POSTULAT²

postpone &c *vti* **1** defer, delay, put off till later *la15-*. **2** *vt* keep (a person) waiting for something promised or due *16-17*. **3** set aside; disregard, neglect; quit, leave off *la15-16*, *only Sc*. **4** subordinate (one thing **to** etc another); treat as of lesser importance; esteem less *16-e17*. **5** *law* relegate the claims of (a creditor) by giving others priority of repayment, demote in the *ranking* (RANK¹ *v* 2) of creditors *18-e20*. [rare in Eng before *la17*]

postrum &c; **postrome** &c [*ˈpostrəm] *n* a back or side door; a private door; a door or gate other than the main entrance *15-16*. [var of Eng *postern*]

postulat¹ &c [*ˈpostølat, &c] *n* a person nominated *eg* to a bishopric, although canonically disqualified, while awaiting a papal dispensation of the impediment *la15-e17*.

adj nominated and awaiting papal sanction as in *n*, *e16*. [only Sc; L *postulāt-*, ptp stem of *postulāre*]

postulat² &c; **postillat** &c [*ˈpostølat, *ˈpost(ə)lat] *n* one of various similar base-gold coins from the Low Countries *la15*. [see DOST]

posy &c *n* **1** = posy *la15*. **2** term of endearment for a child or woman, sweetheart *19-*, *now WC Kcb*.

pot, pott, pat(t) *la16-e20*; **pote** &c *la14-17* [pot; *EC, WC also* pat] *n* **1** = pot *la14-*. **2** a kind of WHISKY still in which heat is applied directly to the pot; *orig* one made by adding an attachment to a cauldron-type cooking pot *la18-19*. **3** = PEEVER¹ *n* 2, *la19-*, *now Mry Bnf*. **4** *chf* **pottie** &c a marble made of fine clay or earthenware *la19-*, *now Abd*. **5** a pit or hole in the ground whether natural or man-made *la14-18, in place-names 13-*. **6** *specif* (1) a tanner's pit for bark or lime *15-17*; (2) a pit from which PEATS[1] have been dug *la15-, now Wgt Slk*; (3) a mine or pit for minerals; a mine shaft *16-17*; (4) *also in place-names* a (deep) hole in a river, a pool *la15-*. **7** a deep chasm or abyss: (1) of hell *la15-17*; (2) *fig* of a (reprehensible) quality *la16*: 'the pot of ignorance'.

vti **1** = pot. **2** *vt* dig pits in, fill with pits *la14-16*. **3** *specif* dig holes (in the ground) (1) to indicate a land boundary *16-e18*; (2) to extract PEAT[1] *18-19*. **4** place (a boundary-stone) in a pit or hole *la16-e18*. **5** mark off the limits of (a piece of land) by pits as in *v* 3 (1) and *v* 4, *la7*.

potted &c heid &c *or* **hoch** *now local* a dish made of meat from the head *or* shin of a cow or pig, boiled, shredded and served cold in a jelly made from the stock *la19-*. **pottie &c** = *n* 6 (4), *19-*. **pottie &c bod** = *n* 4, *20-, NE*. **pottie &c heid** = *potted heid, la19-, now WC Kcb*. **gin I be pottie ye're pannie** you are as bad as I am, you are in no position to criticize *la19-, Bnf Abd*. **pottle &c** a potful *la18-, now Kcdn*.

~ **barley** barley from which the outer husk has been removed in milling, used for making BROTH[1] etc *la18-20*. ~ **black** very black or dirty *20-, WC Uls*. ~ **bool &c** a device for lifting or hanging a pot *la16-, now Ork Cai*. ~ **brod** a (wooden) pot-lid *17-, now Sh*. ~ **brose** a kind of quickly-boiled porridge *la19-, NE*. ~ **clip &c** = ~ *bool, la16-e18*. **pot fit** one of the legs or feet of a cauldron pot *20-, NE*. **out like a pot fit** *of persons* in a state of discord, not on speaking terms *la20-, NE*. **stick out like a pot fit** be very noticeable, 'stick out like a sore thumb' *20-, NE*. **pot hole 1** a pool in the rocks on the seashore *20-*. **2** a small depression in a field which is difficult to drain *20-*. **3** a puddle-hole *18-*. ~ **lid** *curling* (CURL) a shot which exactly covers the TEE[1]; the TEE[1] itself *19-20*. **pot lug** the ear or loop by which a pot is suspended *18-, now Sh Ork*. ~ **pece &c** a gun with a large bore, a mortar *la16-17, only Sc*. ~ **stick** a stick for stirring porridge etc in cooking, a SPURTLE *19-, now SW Uls*. ~**-still** = *n* 2, *la18-*. ~**-tastit &c** tasting of the pot; *fig* stale, unpalatable *la19-, now Ork NE*.

as black as the ~ very black or dirty *la19-*. **pot and gallows** = *pit and gallows* (PIT[2]) *19-e20, latterly hist*.

potage *see* POTTAGE
potato *see* PITAWTIE
potch *see* POACH[1]
potch potch *interj, also* ~**ie** ~**ie** a call to a pig *la20-, Ross Inv Nai*. [Gael *poitidh poitidh* ['pɔtʃi 'pɔtʃi], perh f *poit* a pot]
pote *see* POT

potegar &c [*'pɔtɪgar] *n* an apothecary *la16-17*.
~**y &c** *in pl* an apothecary's drugs, medicines *la15*. [only Sc; altered f *pothecar* (POTICARY); *cf* POTTINGAR]
potent &c *adj* powerful, having great power *15-*. [earlier in Sc]
potestater &c [pɔtə'statər] *n, only* **in one's** ~ at the height of one's career, influence etc, in a state of full well-being and prosperity, in one's prime *la19-, Sh NE*. [f the Sc legal phr *in (ligia) potestate* [pɔtə'statɪ] sound in body and mind; *cf* LIEGE POUSTIE]
poticary *la19-, Kcb*, **pothecar &c** *la15-e17* ['pɔtɪkər(ɪ); *'poθɪkər] *n* = apothecary, a druggist. [aphetic]
potingair *see* POTTINGAR
potissar *see* PATISAR
pott *see* POT
pottage &c *la16-*, **potage &c** *15-17* ['pɔtɪdʒ, -ɪtʃ] *n* **1** = pottage *15-*. **2** *formerly freq treated as a pl* oatmeal porridge; one's breakfast, food in gen, *la17-, now NE*.
milk ~ porridge made with milk instead of water *la16-, now NE*. [*cf* PARRITCH]
potten *see* PIT[1]
potterlow &c [pɔtər'lʌu] *n, freq of food spoilt in cooking* a broken or ruined condition, smithereens, pulp *20, Bnf Abd*.
(gane) tae ~ reduced to pulp or fragments, completely spoilt; *of persons or circumstances* 'gone to the devil', to wreck and ruin *la19-, NE*. [prob orig nonce based on the phr *go to pot*, perh w a pun on *Waterloo*; *cf* next]
potterneeshin &c [pɔtər'niʃən] *n* a state of ruin or chaos, a mess, shambles, *chf* **gae to** ~ get into a state of ruination, 'go to the dogs' *20-, Abd*. [conflation of prec w *crockanition* (CROCK[2]), infl by a play on *pot* and *crock*]
pottie &c *n, vt* = putty *18-*.
it winna ~ *of a story, plan etc* it won't do, 'it won't hold water' *la19-, now WC*.
pottingar &c, potingar &c; potingair &c *la15-17* [*'pɔtɪŋgər] *n* an apothecary *la15-e19*.
~**y &c 1** the art or practice of an apothecary, pharmacy *la15-e17*. **2** the drugs or medicines of an apothecary *la15-e16*. [only Sc; var of *pothecar* (POTICARY); *cf* POTEGAR]
pottinger &c [*'pɔtɪndʒər] *n* a bowl for soup, porridge etc, a porringer *18-e19*. [obs in Eng *la17*]
pottle *see* POT
pou &c, pow &c *la15-e20*, **pull; pu** *la18-* [pu, pʌl; *S also* pʌu] *vti* **1** = pull *la15-*. **2** *vt* pluck (fruit, flowers etc) from the plants or trees on which they grow, gather or collect produce of any kind *la15-*. **3** strip (a bird) of feathers, pluck (a fowl) *16-, now NE Fif SW*. **4** draw or extract (a tooth) *19-*. **5** *vi, of a vent, chimney etc* have a strong draught, draw *20-, local NE-SW*.

like pulling teeth extremely difficult (to get money, a response etc from an unresponsive person) *20-*.

pull-ling, purlaing [*'pʌl'lɪŋ, *'pʌrlɪŋ] the harestail cotton-grass *la18-19, Pbls Bwk*.

~ **stalks &c** pluck stalks of corn or cabbage plants for use in divination, *eg* at *Halloween* (HALLOW²) *la18*.

pouch &c, pouche &c; putch *la16-e18*, **pooch &c** *la19-* [putʃ] *n* **1** = pouch *la16-*. **2** a pocket in a garment *16-*. **3** the pocket as containing one's money or cash, one's purse or finances *la17-*. **4** a deep hole in the bed of a river *la20-, Fif WC*.

vt **1** put (something) into one's pocket, take (something) either legitimately or dishonestly; *fig* steal, pocket *18-*. **2** eat (something) greedily and with relish, gulp down *la19-, Bnf Ags*.

poud [pʌud] *vt* bump, swing, jostle from side to side *20, Bnf Abd*. [see SND]

pouder *see* PEUTHER¹, POUTHER

pouder &c ['pudər] **violet &c** *n* a powder made from violets, ? as a perfume *16*. [only Sc; F *poudre de violette*, OF *pourre volete*]

pouk &c *la18-*, **pook &c** *la18-*; **puke &c** *17-19* [puk] *v* **1** *vt* (1) pluck, twitch, tug, pull sharply *17-, now C, S*. (2) pull out the loose hay at the foot of (a stack) to let air in *19-, local Per-SW*. **2** *specif* remove the feathers from (a bird), pluck (a fowl) *19-, C, S*. **3** *vi* ~ **at** pluck or tug at, pull at sharply; *fig* annoy, harass; criticize *19-, now Kcb*. **4** *in card games* take an extra card or cards from the pack, *esp* when unable to play from one's hand *la20-, Stlg Lnk Ayr*.

n **1** a plucking motion, a twitch, tug, a sharp pull *la18-, local Per-Slk*. **2** (1) what has been or is to be plucked (off), a picking, *freq* tufts of wool from a sheep, fluff, a tuft of hair; a mouthful or bite *19-, now Per*. (2) a small quantity, a little *la19-, now WC Uls*. **3** a moulting condition in birds *19-, now Per Stlg WC*. **4** the short unfledged feathers of a fowl, when they begin to grow after moulting *19-, now Kcb*.

~**ie &c** *of persons* dejected-looking, thin and unhealthy-looking *la19-, WC Kcb Uls*. ~**in** the moult *la19-, C*. ~**it &c** plucked; *of persons or things* having a miserable, emaciated appearance, scraggy and thin-looking; shabby, threadbare *19-, now C, S*.

in the ~ **1** *of birds* moulting *la19-, C*. **2** not very well, below par *19-e20*. **play** ~ **at** clutch at, try to grasp or tug *19-, SW*. [obscure]

pouldar *see* POUTHER

poulie &c ['pulɪ] *n* a louse *19-, C*. [doubtful]

poullie &c ['pulɪ] *n* a young hen, *esp* one for the table, a chicken, pullet *19-, now Uls*. [only Sc; appar a late borrowing of F *poulet* a chicken]

poultry *see* POUTRIE

poun *see* PUND¹

pounce *see* PUNCE

pouncioun *see* PUNCHEON¹

pound &c [pʌund] *n* an enclosed stretch of

water, a pond, pool, reservoir *19-, now local C, S*. [appar of recent Eng dial origin; ultimately of the same origin as PUND²]

pound *see* PUND¹, PUND²

pount *see* POINT

pour &c, poure &c; pooer &c *la16-17, 19*, **poor** *19-* [pur; *Uls also* pʌur] *vt* **1** = pour *16-*. **2** (1) empty (a container) by pouring out its contents *la19-*. (2) pour the liquid from (boiled food, *esp* potatoes), drain *la19-*. **3** smear (sheep) with an oily compound as a protection against insects and wet *la19*.

n **1** a small quantity of a liquid, a drop *19-, now Uls*. **2** a heavy shower of rain, a downpour *la18-*.

pourie &c 1 a vessel with a spout for pouring, a jug, *esp* a cream jug *la18-, now C, S*. **2** a small oil can with a spout *la19-, now C, S*. **3** = *n* 1, *la19-, now Ags Per*. **pourin &c 1** = pouring *la16-*. **2** = *n* 1, *19-, now Sh Ags Uls*. **3** *usu in pl* (1) the liquid strained off as in *v* 2 (2) *20-, now WC*; (2) *specif* the liquid strained off sowans after their fermentation *19-20*; (3) the last drops of liquid left in a container, the dregs *19-, now WC Uls*.

~ **out!** *exclam* the shout raised at a wedding by children, for coins to be scattered in the street for them to scramble for *19-, now Loth*. ~-**out &c** *n* the scattering of coins as in *exclam*, *19-, now C, S; cf* SCATTER. ~ (**the**) **tea** pour out tea *20-*.

pouse *see* POUSS

pouskered ['puskərd] *adj, of persons* exhausted, worn out *la20-, Ags WC*. [perh altered f *poustit* (POUST)]

pouss &c *la16-e20*, **pouse &c** *la16-19*; **pusche** *la16*, **push &c** *17-* [pʌʃ; *pus] *vt* **1** = push *la16-*. **2** incite, urge, egg on *la16-*. **3** poke or thrust (a stick etc); prod, strike with a sharp thrusting blow, punch *18-e19*.

n **1** = push. **2** a thrust, prod, blow, stroke, knock, push *la17-e19*.

poosie ['pusɪ] **knickle &c** *marbles* a faulty shot in which the marble is lobbed rather than flicked *20-, now Ayr*. [the Sc form remained unpalatalized, but *push* was adopted later f Eng]

poussie *see* PUSS

poust &c [pust, pʌust] *n* strength, vigour, power, force *19-, now S*.

~**it &c** drained of strength or virtue, powerless; not in one's normal state of health or mind, suffering sickness or pain *19-e20, chf Ork*. [shortened f POUSTIE]

pousté *see* POUSTIE

pouster &c [*Sh Ork* 'pustər; *NE* 'pʌu-] *n* **1** = posture *e18*. **2** a position in space, situation, location *la19-e20*.

poustie &c *16, 19-e20*, **pousté** *la14-16*; **poweste** *la14*, **pooster &c** *la17, 19-20* (*Sh Ork*) ['pustɪ; *Sh Ork* 'puster; *po-, *pʌu-] *n* **1** power, strength, force, authority, control *la14-20*. **2** ability to do or effect something, capacity, might *la14-e15*. **3** (1) sound physical health *la14-e15*. (2) the physical capacity or use of a part of the body *16-e20*. [ME *pouste &c*; OF *poesté*, L *potestās* power]

pout &c [put; *Kcdn Ags Arg* pʌut] *n* **1** *also* **putt** *e17* = poult, a young game-bird *16-*, *now Cai Mry Bnf Kcb*. **2** *freq* ~**ie &c** (1) a small haddock *19-20*; (2) term of affection for a child or young person, *freq* a young girl or sweetheart *18-20*.

~**in(g)** the sport of hunting game-birds; a shoot *la17-e20*.

pouther &c *17-*, **pouder &c**; **powder &c**, **polder &c** *16*, **pouldar &c** *la16-e17*, **pudder** *17*, **puther** *la17* ['puðər, 'pudər] *n* **1** = powder *la14-*. **2** *curling* (CURL) the force or strength behind the delivery of a stone, the impetus with which a stone is played *19-*, *now Kcb*.

vt **1** = powder *16-*. **2** sprinkle (food) with salt or spices in order to preserve it, salt, cure (meat, butter etc) *la15-*.

pouthery &c like powder, charged with powder *la18-e20*.

~ **lumbard &c** *appar* the name of some kind of spice *la14*. **pouder &c myll &c** a mill for making gunpowder; ? the place where this was done; ? a mill for pulverizing stone *16-17*.

lat oot the ~ reveal a secret, 'let the cat out of the bag' *la19-*, *NE*.

poutrie &c, **poultry** *18-*; **pultrie** *la15-16* ['putrɪ; *'pʌltrɪ] *n* **1** = poultry *la15-*. **2** *also treated as pl after numerals etc*, *la15-e18*: 'six poutrie'.

povereese &c [povə'riz, 'povəriz] *vt* reduce to a condition of poverty, exhaust (land etc) by overworking, impoverish, over-exploit *la19-*, *now Ork N, SW*. [var of obs or dial Eng *poverish*]

pow¹ &c *16-*, **poll &c**; **pole &c** *la16-e20* [pʌu, pol] *n* **1** the head of a human being or an animal, the crown of the head, the scalp, the skull *la15-*. **2** = poll, a person as a unit; voting etc *15-*. **3** *only* **pow** [pʌu], *fig* the end part of a variety of inanimate objects, *specif* the blunt or rounded part of an axe-head *la19-*, *Sh NE Kcb*. **4** *only* **poll &c** [pol] a haircut *20-*, *now Cai*. *vti*, *only* **poll &c** [pol] **1** = poll *16-*. **2** cut the hair of (a person, animal, head) *la16-17*, *e20*.

powie ['pʌuɪ] a smith's hand-hammer with both striking faces bevelled or rounded off *la20-*, *nEC midLoth*.

~ **penny** a charitable offering made at a funeral etc, as it were on behalf of the deceased *la15-e16*.

pow² &c *16-*, *in place-names la15-*, **poll** *la14-17*, *in place-names 14-* [pʌu; *pol] *n* **1** a slow-moving, ditch-like stream flowing through CARSE¹ land, *esp* bordering the Tay, Forth and Solway *la14-*, *now Per*. **2** a creek or inlet (? at the mouth of *n* 1) serving as a wharf for small vessels *16-*, *now SW*. **3** (1) a pool of water, *chf* a shallow or

marshy one, a watery or marshy place; a sea-pool in the rocks *18-*, *now Sh Cai Abd*. (2) a puddle, a *pot hole* (POT) in the street *20-*, *Sh Ross*. [Sc and IrGael *poll* a pit, mire, pool, gulf; cognate w PUIL]

pow³ [pʌu] *n* ~ **net** the first net *shot* (see SHUIT) after the buoy from a herring-boat *20-*, *now Fif*. [appar a var of BOW⁴, perh w infl f POW¹ *n* 3]

pow *see* POU

powan &c ['pʌuən] *n* a species of freshwater fish, found in Scotland only in Loch Lomond and Loch Eck *17-*, *WC*. [Gael *pollan*; *cf* POLLACK]

powa(r)t *see* POWHEID

powder *see* POUTHER

power *see* POOER

poweste *see* POUSTIE

powheid &c *la18-*, **powart** *17-e19*; **powat &c** *18-19*, **powrit** *19-e20*, *Fif* ['pʌuhid, 'pʌuət; *Fif* 'pʌurət; *'pʌuərt] *n*, *also* **powowit** *la18-e20* ['pʌuʌuət], **powie** *19-*, *now Per Fif* ['pʌuɪ] a tadpole *17-*, *now local nEC-S*. [perh f *poll* (POW¹) + HEID; *cf* eModEng *pole-head &c*, ME *polheved*]

powin *see* POWN, PUND¹

powk¹ &c; **pook** *la19-20* [pʌuk; *chf Sh Ork* puk] *vti* **1** = poke. **2** dig or excavate in a careless, clumsy way *18-*, *Bnf Ags*.

n a hole or hollow in the ground, *usu* waterlogged or marshy *19-*, *now Mry Per*.

powk² [pʌuk] *vi*, *n* walk making a dull, thudding sound; such a sound *la19-*, *Bnf*. [prob onomat, but perh w infl f prec and POWT]

powl &c *la16-*, **pole &c**; **poll** *la15-e17*, *la19* [pʌul, pol] *n* **1** = pole, a long, thin, round shaft of wood *la15-*. **2** a walking stick, stilt, crutch *la19-20*.

v **1** *vt* = pole, furnish with poles. **2** (1) *vr* propel oneself with the aid of a crutch *19-*, *now Kcb*. (2) *vi* walk at a good steady pace, bowl along *la19-*, *now Ayr Gall*.

pown &c *15-e17*, **pawne &c** *la16*; **powin &c** *la15-16*, **paon** *la15-16* [*pʌun, *pɑn] *n* a peacock *15-e17*.

pownie &c *18-e19*, **pon(e)y** *e19* [*'pʌunɪ] the turkey, *esp* the female turkey. **pownie &c cock** the male turkey, a turkey cock *18-e19* (the turkey was freq confused w the peacock). [chf Sc; OF *poun &c*, F *paon* peacock]

pownie &c, **powny &c** ['pʌunɪ] *n* **1** = pony, *specif* a riding horse *la17-*. **2** a carpenter's trestle for supporting planks of wood for sawing etc *20-*, *N Fif Uls*. [earlier in Sc]

powowit, **powrit** *see* POWHEID

powsowdie &c *la18-20*, **powsodie &c** *la17*, *e20* [pʌu'sʌudɪ, '-sodɪ] *n* **1** BROTH¹ or thick soup made from a sheep's head *la17-e20*. **2** a mixture of various ingredients, a messy hotchpotch, a mush *19-20*. [perh POW¹ + SOWDIE; *cf* POSSODIE]

powt &c [pʌut] *vti* **1** poke, prod, *esp* with a long stick etc *e16*, *19-*, *now Slk*. **2** *vi* walk with a heavy exhausted step *19*, *Bnf*.

n a poking or prodding movement, a thrust *19-e20*.

~ **net** a stocking-shaped net fastened to poles, used to force out or catch fish resting under projecting river-banks *la17-*, *now Slk*. [var of eModEng, ME *pote &c*, OE *potian*; *cf* PAWT]

powt *see* PIT[1]

powter &c ['pʌutər] *vti* **1** *also fig* poke or prod repeatedly, keep up a continual poking action *e16*, *19-*, *now Renfr Lnk Wgt*. **2** = potter *19-*, *local*. **3** *vi* paddle or poke about in a liquid, make a noise in a liquid *la19-*, *now Ags Wgt*.
n (the noise made by) a poking or prodding movement, stirring, prod or thrust *19*, *Ayr*.

pox *vt* botch (a job), ruin (a piece of work), *specif* in stone-dressing spoil (a stone) by bad cutting *20-*, *now Abd*. [obs Eng *pox* infect with the pox]

poyn *see* POIND

poysonit *see* PUSHION

pozie *n* a narrow alleyway or passage between buildings, a CLOSE[2] *20-*, *now Bnf*. [obscure]

pra *see* PRAY

pract *vti* practise *la15*. [only Sc; f stem of Eng *practic*, *practice*]

practeeze &c *18-*; **practisse** *16*, **practiz &c** *16*, *e19*, **pratize** *la16* [prak'tiz] *vti* = practise *16-*, *now Cai NE Ags*.
practeezing a dancing-class *18-*, *now Ork*. [OED *practise*]

practicate &c [*'pra(k)tɪkat, *-et] *adj* **1** practised, experienced, skilled *la15-16*. **2** *as ptp* legally decided *la16*. [only Sc; MedL *practicāt-*, ptp stem of *practicāre*]

practice &c ['praktɪs, *-iz] *n* = practice *la16-*.
~ **chanter** = chanter 2 (2) (CHANT) *20-*.

practician &c *16-19*; **preticiane** *la15* [prak'tɪʃən; *prə'tɪsɪən] *n* a person who practises any art, profession etc; a practical man as opposed to a theorist, a doer. [obs F *practicien &c*]

practick *see* PRATTICK

practisse, practiz *see* PRACTEEZE

praecipuum [pri'sɪpjuʌm] *n*, *law* an indivisible right, *eg* to a peerage, which went to the eldest and not jointly to all *heirs portioners* (HEIR) *18-20*. [L = that which is taken from an inheritance before the general distribution begins]

praedial *see* PREDIAL

praefer *see* PREFER

praepositura [pripɔzɪ'tjurə] *n*, *law* the right of a wife to incur debts on behalf of her husband for food and household requirements *la18-*. [L = the position of (a wife) *praeposita negotiis*, *ie* set over the management (of a household)]

praevene *see* PREVEEN

prais *see* PRESS

praisant *see* PRESENT[1]

praise &c *n* **1** = praise *la16-*. **2** *euphemistic* God, Lord etc, *eg* ~ **be blessed** *18-*.
vt = praise *16-*.

pram &c *vt* **1** press down, squeeze; exert pressure or force on *19-*, *Sh Kcdn*. **2** stuff (a receptacle) with something, press (an object) into a small area *19-*, *now Sh Kcdn*. [only Sc; MLowGer, MDu *pram(m)en* (*v*) press, squeeze]

pran &c *vt* **1** crush, squeeze, compress, reduce to pulp, pound, trample *19-*, *NE*. **2** bruise, buffet, beat, punish *18-*, *NE*. [only Sc; Gael *pronn*, *prann* pound, mash, grind; *cf* PRON]

prang *n* = prong *19-*, *now Mry Abd Per*.

prank *n* = prank.
vi **1** play pranks, meddle, interfere, act in a lighthearted, careless way *19-*, *now Bnf Ags*. **2** sport, gambol, amuse oneself *la19*.

prap *la18-*, **prop** *n* **1** = prop. **2** an object or objects set up as a marker, *eg* a heap of stones, a pole etc, *specif* (1) as a boundary-mark *la15-e20*; (2) as a memorial, to mark a grave *19-e20*; (3) as a target for shooting or throwing at *la15-*, *now Abd*; (4) *ploughing* as a guide to mark the course and end of the first furrow of the RIG[1] *la19-*, *Ork NE*.
vti **1** = prop. **2** *vt* mark (a boundary etc) by means of PRAPS *la15-*, *now Bnf*. **3** set up (any object) on end; set up as a target for throwing or shooting at *19-*, *now Sh*. **4** *vti* aim or throw (stones, marbles etc) at a target *19*.

prat &c *16-19*; **prot** *18-*, *now Cai*, **pret &c** *17-20* *n* **1** a trick, prank, practical joke, piece of mischief *16-*, *now Cai*. **2** an act of disobedience or a bad habit in a horse, *freq* **tak the** ~ be disobedient, refuse *18-e19*.
vi **1** play tricks, lark around; *of a horse* be disobedient, jib *la16-e20*. **2** meddle or interfere **with**, tamper or fiddle **with** *la19-20*.
~**ty &c** mischievous, naughty, restive *la17-e19*.
ill-~**ty &c** mischievous, naughty *18-19*. [ME, OE *præt &c* a trick, guile]

prat *see* PRATT

pratize *see* PRACTEEZE

prat(t) *vti* = prate *16*. [OED *prate*]

prattick &c *la15-*, *now NE*, **practick &c** *15-20*, **prettik &c** *16*, **prottick &c** *18-*, *NE* *n* **1** = practic, the action of practising, practice as opposed to theory *la15-16*. **2** an act, practice, way of doing things; a custom, habit, usage *la15-e19*. **3** *law* (1) a customary usage, a precedent, the usual practice *16-18*; (2) *specif*, *in pl* the recorded decisions of the *Court of Session* (SESSION), forming a system of case-law *18-20*, *latterly hist*. **4** *also* **prettikin &c** *19-*, *Sh Ork* ['prɛtɪkɪn] (1) an exploit, feat of daring or physical skill, a caper *18-19*; (2) an escapade, *esp* a discreditable one, a piece of mischief *18-*, *now NE*. **5** a venture, undertaking, experiment; an artful scheme, trick, dodge *la15-*, *now NE*.
vt, *only Sc* **1** put into action or operation *15-16*. **2** influence or activate craftily *la16*. **3** *in ptp* practised, versed *16*.

prieve &c *a* ~ *or* **one's** ~**s** practise schemes, use wiles **on** (a person) *16-19*. [OED *practic*]

pratty *see* PRETTY

prauein *see* PREVEEN

pray; pra *16* [pre] *vti* = pray *la14-*.

preach &c *la16-*; **prech** *la14*, *la19* [pritʃ; *nEC also* pretʃ; *NE also* *prɔitʃ] *vti* = preach *la14-*.
~**ing &c 1** = preaching *la16-*. **2** a sermon, a religious service, *specif* one leading up to and following the communion service *16-20*.
~ **in** conduct a service to welcome (a MINISTER) to a new charge after his *induction* (INDUCT) *20-*.

prebendar [*'prɛbəndər] *n* a prebendary *16*, *only Sc*.

precable *adj* that may be asked or demanded as feudal service, impost or tax *la16*. [only Sc; L *precābilis* entreating, praying, f *precārī* ask, beg]

precarious &c [prə'keriʌs, -'kariʌs] *adj* = precarious.
~ **loan** *law* = PRECARIUM *la18* [adopted f next].

precarium [prə'keriʌm, -'kariʌm] *n*, *law* a loan given gratuitously and recallable at will *la17-*. [L = something lent at the pleasure of the owner]

precary &c [*?prɛ'keri] *n* a grant on request, at the will and during the pleasure of the grantor *la16*, *only Sc*. [f as prec]

precede *vti* **1** go before or beyond (another) in quality or degree; surpass; exceed *la14*. **2** = precede.

preceese &c [prə'siz] *adj* = precise *19-*.
adv exactly, precisely *19-*.

preceid *see* PRESIDE

precent &c [pri'sɛnt] *v* **1** *vi* lead the singing in a church, act as PRECENTOR *la17-*, *now chf Hebrides Highl*. **2** *vt* sing (a line of a PSALM etc) as a lead to a church congregation *18-*, *Hebrides Highl*. [back-formation f next]

precentor &c [pri'sɛntor, prɪ'zɛntər] *n* **1** = precentor, a person who leads or directs the singing of a choir etc *la16-*. **2** *Presbyterian churches* an official appointed by the *Kirk Session* (KIRK) to lead the singing by singing the line for the congregation to repeat, *now chf* in the smaller denominations where instrumental music is disapproved *17-*, *now chf Hebrides Highl*.

precept &c ['prisɛpt, *-sɛp] *n* **1** = precept *16-*. **2** *law* a document instructing or authorizing a certain action, a warrant granted by a judge to give possession of something or to confer a privilege *16-e19*. **3** a written authorization issued by an individual or corporate body to make a payment from funds, *freq* in reference to payments made by the *kirk sessions* (KIRK) to the poor *18*.
~**ive 1** = preceptive. **2** conveying a command, mandatory *la15-*.
~ **of clare constat** ['klari'kɔnstat] *law* a precept of sasine by which an heir is recognized by the SUPERIOR *la16-* [L = it is clearly established, the opening words of the document].
~ **of sasine &c** *law* the mandate by which the SUPERIOR authorized his agent to give possession

16-, *latterly hist*. ~ **of warning** *law* a written instruction given by a landlord to his agent to notify a tenant to remove from his property within 40 days *18-*.

prech *see* PREACH

preclare &c [*pri'kler] *adj* **1** very clear *e16*. **2** distinguished, illustrious *la15-16*. [chf Sc; L *praeclarus* very bright]

precogitate &c *ptp*, *adj* precogitated, premeditated *la16-17*. [only Sc; L *paecōgitāt-*, ptp stem of *praecōgitāre*]

precognition [prɛkɔg'nɪʃn, pri-] *n* **1** = precognition. **2** *law* the process of *precognoscing* (PRECOGNOSCE); a statement made by a witness during this investigation *la17-*.

precognosce [prɛkɔg'noz, -'nos, pri-] *vti*, *law* carry out an initial investigation of the facts of a case by interrogating the witnesses to find out if there is a case to answer and to make it possible to prepare a relevant charge and defence; examine a witness in preparation for a trial; in criminal cases *orig* carried out by the SHERIFF or *judge ordinary* (ORDINAR (*adj* 2)), *now* done by the *procurator fiscal* (PROCURATOR) *la17-*. [only Sc; *pre-* + COGNOSCE]

precordial [*pri'kordɪal] *adj* **1** = precordial, very cordial *e16*. **2** *fig* very comforting or cheering *la16*, *only Sc*.

predetermination *n* **1** a decision made beforehand *17-*. **2** a previous determining or fixing of the limits or extent **of** (something) *e17*. **3** = predetermination, a previous settling or determination.

predial; praedial ['pridɪal] *adj* = predial, pertaining to land.
~ **servitude** *etc*, *law* a SERVITUDE etc connected with land *la17-*.

pree[1]; **prie** *18* [pri] *vt* **1** have experience of, try out, sample *19-*, *now Cai*. **2** try by tasting *18-*, *now chf literary*.
n an experiencing or trying of something, a tasting or testing; a small quantity of the substance tested or tried, a sample, pinch *19*.
preein(g) 1 a small quantity of something, a sample *19-*, *now Bnf Ags*. **2** a taste, tasting *19-*, *now Ags Per midLoth*.
~ **(someone's) lips** *or* **mou** kiss *18-e20*. [short for *prieve* (PRUIVE); *cf* GIE, HAE[1] etc]

pree[2] *la20-*, *local Ross-Uls interj*, *freq repeated, also in extended forms* ~**ay** *20-*, *NE*, ~**a** *20-*, *now Ayr*, **pee-ay** *20-*, *now Ross Wgt*, ~ **leddy &c** *e20*, ~**-may** *e20* call-name for a cow or calf, *chf used* to call cows in for milking. [perh var of PROO]

preek *see* PRICK

preen &c; pren(n) *la16-18*, **prin** *la15-20* [prin; *v also* *prɪn] *n* **1** a metal pin (1) *in gen*, *la14-*; (2) as a symbol of something of very little value *la15-*. **2** *in pl* a game played with pins or in which pins were the stakes *19*. **3** a fishing-hook *la15*, *la19-* (*Sh*).
vt **1** sew, stitch up *e16*. **2** fasten with a pin, pin *la16-*.

~**ack** a pine-needle *20-*, *NE*.

~**-cod** &c a pin-cushion *16-*, *now Ork Cai EC*.

~**-heid** **1** a pin-head; *hence* something of very little value or consequence *la18-*, *now Sh NE*. **2** the fry of the minnow *la19-*, *C, S*. ~**-heidit** *of persons* stupid, of low intelligence *la19-*, *NE nEC*. ~**-tail day** the day following All Fools' Day when paper tails were attached to the backs of unsuspecting persons as a joke *20-*, *Bwk Rox*.

~ **one's lugs back** *fig* listen carefully, pay great attention *la20-*. ~ **something to one's sleeve** make a special effort to remember something, take a mental note of something *20-*, *Mry Abd*. ~**-tae** &c **1** a person or thing attached to another *la20-*, *Fif Edb*. **2** *specif* an illicit sexual partner, a mistress *20-*, *now WC*. **be sittin on** ~**s** be in a very nervous, apprehensive state, be on tenterhooks *la19-*. [nME; OE *prēon* a pin, brooch; *cf* PIN]

preese *see* PRESS

preevely *see* PRIVY[1]

pre-excellence *n* pre-eminent excellence *la15*. [F; *cf* eModEng *pre-excellency, pre-excellent*]

preface ['prifes] *vti* **1** = preface. **2** *vt and* ~ **on**, *Presbyterian church, of a* MINISTER deliver a paraphrase of or commentary (on a PSALM to be sung by the congregation) *18-19*.

prefalie *see* PRIVY[1]

prefec *see* PREFETE

prefer &c; **praefer** *16* [pri'fɛr; *-'far] *vt* **1** = prefer *la16-*. **2** be preferable to; surpass, excel *e16*.

prefete &c; **prefec** *n* = prefect *la14*. [OED *prefect*]

preif *see* PRUIVE

preis *see* PRESS

preiss *see* PRIZE

preivin *see* PRUIVE

prejudge &c *vt* **1** = prejudge *la16-*. **2** affect unfavourably, work to the prejudice of, harm, hinder, interfere with *16-e18*, *only Sc*.

prelation &c *n* **1** utterance, pronunciation *la14*. **2** = prelation *la16*.

prele(i)ttis *see* PRELOT

preliminary *adj* = preliminary. ~ **defences** *law* = dilatory defences (DILATOR) *19-*. ~ **examination**, *colloq* **prelim** ['prilɪm] **1** an examination for entry to a Scottish University set annually by each of the Universities for their own prospective students *la19-20*. **2** applied unofficially to the class examinations taken before the *Highers* (HEICH) etc to provide an estimate of the candidate's ability *20-*, *local*.

prelimit [pri'lɪmɪt] *vt* limit beforehand; confine within limits previously fixed *17*. [earlier in Sc]

prelocutor *la16*; **preloquutour** *e17* [*pri'lokøtur, *-ər, *-'lokwɪt-] *n* a prolocutor, advocate, pleader. [only Sc; MedL *praelocūtor*; L *praeloquī* speak beforehand or before another]

prelot ['prɛlət; *prɪ'lat, *-'let] *n*, *pl* **preleittis**, **prelettis** ['prɛləts, &c] = prelate *16*. [OED *prelate*]

prelucent; **preluciand** [*pri'løsənt, *-ənd] *adj* shining, resplendent *16*. [only Sc; L *praelūcent-*, presp stem of *praelūcēre* shine forth]

premention &c *n* a mention beforehand, previous notice *la17*.

premonition &c [primə'nɪʃən; *-mə'nɪʃ(ɪ)ən] *n* **1** = premonition *la16-*. **2** *law* an official notification or warning, an obligatory period of notice, *freq* **instrument of** ~ a formal notification made by the debtor to the creditor in a WADSET to appear at an agreed place and receive payment of the debt *16-18*.

pren *see* PREEN

prence *see* PRINCE

principal *see* PRINCIPAL

prenn *see* PREEN

prent &c, **print** &c *16-* *n* **1** = print *15-*. **2** form, appearance *la15-e16*, *only Sc*. **3** a pat of butter (*usu* a quarter- or half-pound) imprinted with a decorative motif using a mould *19-*, *NE, C Uls*.

vti, ptp also **prent** *16* = print *16-*.

~**er** &c **1** = printer *16-*. **2** a coiner *la16*.

~ **buik** a printed book, *freq* **speak like a** ~ **buik** speak with an air of knowledge; speak in an affected way *18-20*. **printfield** a cotton-printing works *18-*, *now in place-names* [because orig established on a bleaching field].

prentice &c *la14, 18-20*; **prenteis** &c *la14-16*, **printeis** *la14-17* ['prɛntɪs; *'prɪnt-] *n* = apprentice, a learner *la14-20*.

vt apprentice (a youth) to a trade or craft, indenture or bind as an apprentice *la18-*, *now Abd*.

entered ~ *freemasonry* one who has passed his first degree *18-e20*, *latterly hist* [f the Scottish practice of entering a mason's new apprentice in the records]. [aphetic]

preordine [*pri'ordən] *vt* = preordain *e16*. [only Sc. OED *preordain*]

prepare &c *vti* = prepare *la16-*.

n act of preparing, preparation *16-e19*.

preparation = preparation *la16-*. **preparation-day, -Sabbath, -Saturday** *etc* the day(s) preceding the communion service when special services of preparation were conducted *17-e19*. **preparative** &c **1** = preparative. **2** a precedent, excuse, an example *16-e18*, *only Sc*. **preparatory** = preparatory. **preparatory service** a service held on a weekday, *usu* the preceding Friday, in preparation for the communion service *20-*.

prepositor *n*, *law* a person who employs an agent etc to manage an enterprise, the principal in a business negotiation or undertaking *la17-e19*. [Roman Law term]

prequeer *see* PERQUEER

prerogative *adj* held or enjoyed by privilege *15-*. [earlier in Sc]

presbyterial *see* PRESBYTERY
Presbyterian *adj* (*n*), *church* = presbyterian, applied to a system in which the church is governed by ELDERS *18-*; see SND and KIRK.
presbytery &c *n* **1** = presbytery. **2** an ecclesiastical court above the *kirk session* (KIRK) and below the SYNOD, consisting of the MINISTER and one *ruling elder* (RULE) from each parish or congregation within a designated area *la16-*. **3** the area represented by and under the jurisdiction of a PRESBYTERY 2, one of the units of organization in the *Church of Scotland* (CHURCH) *la16-*.
presbyterial of or belonging to a PRESBYTERY or its functions *17-*.
prescribe &c *vti* **1** = prescribe. **2** *vi, law, of an action, a right etc* become invalid through the passage of time, lapse; *of a debt, crime etc* be immune from prosecution through lapse of time *17-*. **3** *vt, law* make or declare invalid through lapse of time *18-e19*.
prescriptibility liability to PRESCRIBE, the state of being subject to *prescription, e18*. **prescription &c 1** = prescription. **2** the lapse of time after which a right is either established *or* rendered invalid or a debt etc annulled, if previously unchallenged or unclaimed *la15-*.
prescriptive arising from *prescription, freq* **prescriptive title** *etc, 19-*.
prescrive &c [*pri'skraiv] *v* **1** *vt* lay down as a rule or direction to be followed; prescribe *la16-19*. **2** *vi* become valid by *prescription* (PRESCRIBE) *la15*. **3** *of a right or claim* cease to be valid; *of the prescribed period* elapse, run out *la15-17*. **4** *vt* condemn, prohibit *la16*.
~r a prescriber, one who appoints or ordains *17*. [only Sc; OF *prescriv-*, f *prescrire*, L *praescrĭbere* prescribe]
presence &c ['prɛzəns, 'pre-; *'pri-] *n* = presence *la14-*.
(hearing) in ~ the hearing before an enlarged Court of a case in which the Judges of the *Inner House* (INNER) have been equally divided *18-e20*.
present¹; praisant &c *16, la19-e20* [*v* prɪ'zɛnt; *'prizɛnt; *n* 'prɛzənt, 'pre-; *'pri-; *-and] *v* **1** *vt* = present *la14-*. **2** *vr* come into the presence and sight of another or others, or into a particular place, *esp* in a formal manner *la14-*. **3** *vt, Presbyterian Church* (1) put forward the name of (a *licensed* (LEESHENCE) *probationer* (PROBATION) or MINISTER) to the PRESBYTERY so that he may be approved for admission to a parish *la18-19*, see SND; (2) offer (a child) for baptism *18-*.
n **1** = present *la14-*. **2** a white speck on the fingernail, commonly believed to presage the arrival of a gift *la19-, Ork NE, C*. **3** a form of cash payment of rent for land *18*.
~ation [prɛzɛn'teʃən, pri-] **1** = presentation. **2** the action of PRESENTING (*v* 3 (1)) *la18-e20*. **3** *law* the granting by the Sovereign to a

DONATORY of HERITAGE acquired by the Crown by ESCHEAT *la18*. **bond of ~ation** *law* a written obligation binding the obliger to produce a person freed from custody for debt at a particular time and place, a bail-bond *18-e20*.
give, bring *etc* **in a ~** give, bring etc as a present, make a present of *18-*.
present² &c ['prɛzənt, 'pre-; *'pri-] *adj* (*16-*), *n* (*la14-*) = present.
~ly 1 = presently *la14-*. **2** now, at this moment, at present *la16-*.
preserve &c [prɪ'zɛr(v), pri-] *vti* = preserve *la14-*.
n **1** = preserve. **2** *in pl* weak spectacles intended to preserve the sight *19-, local Sh-SW*. **(Guid** *etc*) **~ us** (**a**) *interj* expressing surprise or dismay *la18-*.
preses &c ['prisez, -ɪz; *-ɛs] *n* the person who presides at a meeting etc, the chairman, president; the spokesman or leader of a group *17-*. [chf Sc; L *praeses* a president, chief, guardian]
preside; preceid &c *la17* [*pri'sid] *vti* = preside *la17-*.
president &c [*'prɛsɪdənt, *-sid-] *n* **1** = president *la14-*. **2** *specif* the head of the *Court of Session* (SESSION) *16-17*; cf *Lord P~* (LORD).
presome *see* PRESUME
preson *see* PRISON
press &c, preese &c *19-e20*; **preis &c** *15-17*, **prais** *16* [prɛs, pris; *pres] *vti* **1** = press *la14-*. **2** *vir* endeavour, strive, contend *la14*. **3** *vr* move or push (forward) with force or against obstacles *la14-e15*. **4** *vi* make a charge or an assault (**on**) *la14*. **5** *vr* presume, take upon oneself *e16*.
n **1** = press *la14-*. **2** the act of pressing, pressure *e16*. **3** a strong but ineffectual urge to defecate *19-, local Ork-Fif*. **4** *only* **press &c** a large cupboard, *usu* one built into a recess in the wall *la15-*.
press bed a bed built into a recess in the wall and shut off from the room by wooden doors *18-20*; cf *box bed* (BOX¹).
prestable *17-*; **prestible** *la17 adj* able to be carried out, practicable, enforceable; *of money etc* able to be paid out, usable, negotiable, transferable, exigible. [only Sc; OF = able to be lent, ready to provide]
prestation *n, law* = prestation, the performance of an obligation or duty *la17-*. [now commoner in Sc]
presume &c; presome *16 vti* = presume *la14-*.
n anticipation, expectation *la15*.
presumptive 1 giving reasonable grounds for presumption *la16-*. **2** = presumptive, presumed.
presuppone [*prisʌ'pon] *vt* presuppose, assume beforehand *la16-e17*. [chf Sc; ME (once); MedL *praesuppōnere*, or perh f *pre-* + SUPPONE]
pret *adj* ready *e16*. [only Sc; F *prêt*]

pret *see* PRAT

pretence &c *n* = pretence *la16-*.
vt **1** = pretence, pretend *la16*. **2** intend, purpose, design *la16*.

pretend *vtir* **1** = pretend *la14-*. **2** *vi* form designs, plot **against** *la16*.

pretext *adj* ~ **goune** the purple-bordered *toga praetexta* worn by Roman magistrates etc *e16*. [L *praetexta*]

preticiane *see* PRACTICIAN

prettik(in) *see* PRATTICK

pretty &c; pratty &c *la16*, *la19-e20*, **protty &c** *17-e20*, *chf NE* ['prɛtɪ; *NE* 'protɪ; *'pratɪ] *adj* **1** = pretty *la15-*. **2** mean, petty, insignificant *e16*. **3** (1) (a) *of persons* fine, good-looking, having an impressive and dignified bearing *18-e20*. (b) *specif* (i) *of men* courageous, gallant, manly *la18-*, *Sh NE Ags Slk*; (ii) *of women* well-built, buxom *la18-*, *NE*. (2) *of animals* well-grown, sturdy, well-bred, in good condition *20-*, *Sh NE*. (3) *of things* well-made, of good quality or finish, attractive *la18-*, *Sh Ork N*.

preuine *see* PREVEEN

prevail &c *la16-*; **prevele** *la15* [prɪ'vel] *vti* **1** = prevail *la15-*. **2** *vt* prevail over, have superiority over, outstrip *e16*, *only Sc*.

prevat *see* PRIVATE

preveen *la17-18*, **prevene &c** *15-17*; **praevene** *la16*, **prowein &c** *la16*, **prauein** *e17*, **preuine** *e17* [*prɪ'vin, *pri-] *vt* **1** anticipate, prevent (danger) etc, forestall *15-18*. **2** *theol, of God's grace* prevent, go before with spiritual guidance *la16-17*. **3** *law, of a court or judge* take from (another) the preferable right of jurisdiction, by exercising the first judicial act *la17*. **4** take in advance: (1) preoccupy *e16*; (2) *of death etc* overtake prematurely *la16*; (3) anticipate (a time) by earlier action; provide beforehand for (a coming event) *la16*. **5** come or go before, precede *la16*. [chf Sc; L *praevenīre* come before, anticipate, hinder]

prevele *see* PREVAIL

prevely *see* PRIVY[1]

prevene *see* PREVEEN

prevention &c *n* **1** = prevention *la16-*. **2** *law* a privilege exercised by a superior judge or civil magistrate *la17*.

prevert [*pri'vɛrt] *vt* go beyond, outstrip *e16*. [only Sc; L *praevertere* outstrip]

price &c *n* (*la14-*), *vt* (*16-*) = price.
be the ~ o someone *of an event or happening* serve someone right, be just what someone deserves *20-*. **twa, three** *etc* **~s** two, three etc times the market or former price *19-*.

prick &c; preek &c *la14-19* *vti* **1** = prick *la14-*. **2** *vt, mining* (1) pierce (rock etc) with the point of a pick *la19-*, *now Fif*; (2) cut into a layer of soft fireclay at the bottom of a seam by

hand *20-*, *now Fif*. **3** *vi, of grazing cattle* stampede in an attempt to escape from the stings of insects *18-*, *NE*. **4** *vt* fasten or secure with a pin etc *18-e19*.
n **1** = prick *16-*. **2** a pointed implement, *specif* (1) a skewer; a pin etc for fastening one's clothes *18*; (2) a knitting-needle *17-l18*.
~er &c a light horseman, skirmisher, *esp* a *reiver* 1 (REIVE); the light pony on which he rode *la16-19*. **~ing** *mining* a thin stratum suitable for holing in *la19-*, *now Fif*. **~y** having sharp points or spines, prickly *la19-*, *now NE, SW*.
~ measure, ~ mett an iron rod used as a measure for grain *e17*, *only Sc*.
~ (ap)on (someone) attack (someone) *la14*. **~-the-louse** *la18-19*, **~louse** *16* *contemptuous* a tailor. **~-me-dainty &c** *n* an affected, self-conscious person *19-*, *now Mry*. *adj* over-refined, mincing *19-*, *now Bnf Renfr S*. **~ and prin oneself** dress oneself up, take excessive pains with one's appearance *la18*.

pricket &c *n* **1** = pricket, a candle *la16-e17*. **2** a pinnacle or small spire on a building, a pointed finial *17-e20*.

prickle &c *n* **1** = prickle *16-*. **2** a prickling or stinging sensation *la19-*, *Sh Cai WC Uls*.
vt **1** = prickle *16-*. **2** *fig* cause (a person) to feel pain or guilt *e16*, *only Sc*. **3** stand on end, stick up, rise erect *19-*, *now Ork Bnf*.

pride &c *n* = pride *la14-*.
v **1** *vi* take pride **in**, feel proud **of**, be or become proud *la15-e19*. **2** *vtr* = pride (oneself etc) *la18-*.
~fu &c ['~fu, '~fɪ] full of pride (1) *in a bad sense* haughty, arrogant, snobbish, vain *16-20*; (2) (*less freq*) *in a good sense* self-respecting, fastidious; pleased *19-20*. **prydy** characterized by pride, proud *la15*.

prie *see* PREE[1]

prief *see* PRUIF, PRUIVE

priest &c *n* = priest *la14-*.
vt = priest, ordain to the priesthood *e16*.
be someone's ~ cause someone's death, 'be the death of' *la18-e19*, *N*. **~ and devil** a shoemaker's last *la20-*, *Per Uls*.

prieve *see* PRUIVE

prig &c *v* **1** *vi, also fig* haggle over the price of something; drive a hard bargain *17-*, *now NE Ags WC*. **2** *vt* beat **down** the price of (an article) by bargaining; beat (someone) **down** to a lower price *18-*, *now local NE-Rox*. **3** *vi* plead **with** (someone) **for** (something) *18-*, *now Sh-nEC Kcb*. **4** *vt* beseech, entreat, importune *19-*.
~-penny a person who haggles over pennies, a hard bargainer *e16*, *la19*, *only Sc*. [see SND]

primacy &c *n* **1** = primacy *la16-*. **2** the ecclesiastical province or see of a primate *la16*.

primar &c ['praimər] *n* **1** the PRINCIPAL of a college or university *17-e18*. **2** *St Andrews Univ* a student of the first grade in social rank, the son of a nobleman, who paid higher University fees than the *secondars* (SECOND) and TERNARS and wore a better-quality gown *la17-e19*.

~**iat** [*?prəi'mariat] the office of PRINCIPAL 2, *17*. [only Sc; MedL *primarius* a principal, f *primus* first]

prime[1] *n* **1** *in Scots Troy* (SCOTS) *measure* a unit of weight for gold and silver consisting of $\frac{1}{24}$ of a grain *17*. **2** = prime, a prime number.

prime[2] **&c** *vti* **1** = prime. **2** *vt, also fig* fill, stuff, charge, load *16-*.

~ **gilt** a sum of money paid to the master and crew of a ship for the loading and care of the cargo *16-e19*.

primineary &c [*primə'neri, *-'niri] *n, joc* = praemunire, a fix, predicament, scrape *e19*.

primp *v* **1** *vt* make prim and over-neat, arrange or do up in a stiff, affected way *la16, 19-*. **2** *vi* behave or talk in a mincing or affected style *19-, NE-S*.
adj fastidious, straight-laced, prim; haughty, conceited *19-, now Sh*.
n a straight-laced and self-conciously correct person, a prig, a show-off *20-, S*.
~**ed &c** *of things or speech* stiff, formal, over-elaborate, correct; *of persons* affected, elaborately and formally dressed *19-e20*. [f Eng *prim*]

primsie &c ['primzi, ?'primsi] *adj* self-consciously correct, demure, straight-laced, old-maidish *la18-, now Sh Ork*. [Eng *prim* + *-sie*]

Primus &c ['prəimʌs] *n, Scottish Episcopal Church* the bishop chosen by his colleagues to be the president of their episcopal meetings, but without metropolitan or special authority *18-*. [L, = first]

prin *see* PREEN

prince &c; prence *la16, la19* *n* = prince *la14-*.
P~ Charlie('s) rose the *white rose* (WHITE[1]) *la19-, now Abd Per Rox*. **P~ of Scotland** title of the eldest son of the Sovereign before the Union of the Crowns in 1603, *now* used only in connection with the lands of the *Principality of Scotland* (PRINCIPALITY) *la18-*.

principal &c, prencipal &c *la15-19* *adj* **1** = principal *la14-*. **2** excellent, first-rate, outstandingly good *19-, now Sh*. **3** *of a document* original, not in the form of a copy *la18-*.
n **1** = principal, chief *la14-*. **2** *now chf* **P~** the academic head of a (university) college; *latterly also* the head of a university (who also acts as Vice-Chancellor) *la16-*. **3** a person for whom another is surety, the person primarily liable for a debt *la16-17*. **4** the original of a document *la15-*.

principality &c *n* = principality.
P~ of Scotland the *lordship* (LORD) of certain lands in Scotland, *esp* in Ayr, Renfr and Ross, held as of right by the eldest son of the Sovereign as *Prince and Steward of Scotland* (PRINCE, STEWARD) and failing him by the Crown itself *la15-*.

prink &c; prunk *20-, Sh Ork* *v* **1** *vt* make smart or pretty, titivate *18-*. **2** *vi* strut, move with a swagger, walk in a jaunty, self-conscious way *la19-, Ork Ags*.

~**ie &c** over-meticulous in dress or appearance, fussy over details, ostentatious, conceited *19-, now Ork Bnf*. [eModEng, appar a var of Eng *prank* deck out, adorn, f Du *pronk* show, finery, Ger *prunk*]

prinkle[1] **&c** *v* **1** *vi* have the sensation of pins and needles, tingle, thrill, prickle *18-, now Bnf Abd S*. **2** *vt* cause to tingle, set pricking; jab with a pin *la19-, now Per*. **3** *vi* twinkle, glitter, sparkle; *of a boiling pot* bubble, simmer *18-e20*.

prinkly prickly, tingling *e20, S*. [only Sc; appar var form of PRICKLE; *v* 3 may be a separate word]

prinkle[2] *n* a young coalfish *19-, NE*. [obscure]

print *see* PRENT

printeis *see* PRENTICE

prior *adj* = prior *18-*.
~ **rights** the statutory rights of the spouse of a person dying intestate to the deceased's dwelling-house with furnishings and *plenishings* (PLENISH) and a financial provision out of the remaining estate *la20-*; *cf legal rights* (LEGAL).

prioressy &c *n* a nunnery or convent presided over by a prioress *la16-e17*. [only Sc; Eng *prioress* + *-y*]

pris *see* PRIZE

prise &c [praiz] *n* an instrument used for levering, a lever *e16, 19-, now Ags Per Slk*. [ME; = a grasp, grip; *cf* Eng *v*. OED *prize* (*n*[4])]

prisk *adj* ancient, primitive *e16*. [only Sc; L *priscus* old, primitive, old-fashioned]

prison &c;   preson &c *la14-e18* ['prizən; *'prizun, &c] *n* = prison *la14-*.
vt take or keep prisoner, imprison *15-, now Sh Ork*.

private &c *la16-*; **prevat &c** *16, 19* ['praivət; *'privat] *adj* = private *16-*.
private school 1 *Edb Univ* a small classroom *e17*. **2** *in pl, St Andrews Univ* a seminar or tutorial as opposed to a public lecture *e18*.

privative *adj* **1** = privative. **2** *law, of the jurisdiction of a court* exclusive, not shared or exercised by others *la18-*.

prive *see* PRUIVE

privilege &c ['privilidʒ; *'priv-] *n* (*la14-*), *v* (*16-*) = privilege.
privileged debt *law* a debt owed by the estate of a deceased person, *eg* for funeral expenses, which takes precedence over the debts of ordinary creditors *la18-*. **privileged deed** *law* a deed which does not require the signatures of witnesses to validate it, *eg* on the grounds of necessity or expediency *e19*. **privileged summons** *law* a summons in which the normal period of 27 days between the citation of a person and his appearance in court is shortened *la18-*. **privileged writing** *law* = *privileged deed, e20*.

privitate &c *n* a secret matter, design etc, a secret *e16*. [only Sc; appar as if f L **prīvitās*, abstract noun f *prīvus* private]

privy¹ &c ['prɪvɪ; ***'privɪ] *adj, n* (*la14-*), *adv* (*e16*) = privy.

prevely &c *la14-16*, **preevely &c** *16*, **prefalie** *16* ['prɪvɪlɪ; ***'priv-] = privily, privately.

~ **censures** *Presbyterian Church* a meeting of a *kirk session* (KIRK) or PRESBYTERY at which each member was examined separately and questions were put to his fellow-members about his church duties and his behaviour in his private life *18-e19*.   **P~ Council** the official body consisting of high *officers of state* (OFFICER) and other magnates presided over by the CHANCELLOR, which, nominally subject to Parliament, exercised judicial, legislative and executive power *16-e18*.   ~ **seal** the seal used to authenticate a royal grant of personal or assignable rights; it was not abolished by the Act of Union but continued subject to regulations made by ensuing Parliaments and is still in existence although no longer a requirement *15-*.

privy² &c *n* = privet, *chf* ~ **hedge** etc *la18-*, now *NE, C.*

prize &c; pris &c *la14-e16*, **preiss &c** *15-16* [*v, n* praɪz; ***prəis] *vt* **1** = prize, value, appraise *15*. **2** estimate the quality and money value of (some commodity), valuate *la14-e19*. **3** value or esteem highly, think much of *la14-*. **4** praise, commend *la14-16*.
n = prize.

proadge &c [prodʒ] *vti* make poking or prodding movements with a long instrument *19-*, *Sh SW*. [var of Eng *prod*]

prob *n* **1** = probe. **2** *specif* a sharp-pointed instrument for piercing the stomach of swollen cattle to release the accumulated gas *20-*, *Ork NE*. **3** a prod, poke, jab *19-*, *NE nEC.*
vti **1** = probe. **2** *vt, specif* release gas from the stomach of (cattle) by piercing *20-*, *Bnf Abd*. **3** *also fig* prod, poke, jab, stab *19-*, *Sh NE nEC.*

probation &c *n* **1** = probation *la16-*. **2** the act of proving, demonstration *16-19*. **3** *law* the hearing of evidence in court before a judge; evidence, proof and the procedure for demonstrating it *la15-*.
~**ary** relating to a *probationer* 1, *18-e20*.   ~**er &c 1** *Presbyterian Churches* a student MINISTER during the period between his *licensing* (LEESHENCE) and his ordination *18-*. **2** *law* a newly-appointed judge of the *Court of Session* (SESSION) after he has presented his letter of appointment and before he takes the oath *la18-e20*; cf *Lord Probationer* (LORD).
conjunct ~ *law* the process of disproving by evidence an opponent's allegations, carried on as part of the process of proving a party's own case *20-*.

probative *adj* **1** = probative. **2** *law, chf of a*

document having the quality or function of proving or demonstrating, carrying evidence of its own validity and authenticity *la17-*.

process &c *n* **1** = process *la14-*. **2** *law* the legal papers in an action LODGED in court by both parties *la15-*.
vt **1** proceed against in law, sue, bring to trial *la15-19*. **2** = process.
~ **caption** *law* a warrant to imprison a person who has borrowed a PROCESS (*n* 2) and has failed to return it *19-*.
no ~ *law* a preliminary defence based or sustained on the grounds of a technical error in the procedure which bars trial *la17-e19*.

prochin *see* PAIRISH

proclaim &c *vt* **1** = proclaim *16-*. **2** *in regard to banns of marriage* read, publish; read the banns of, announce the impending marriage of *la16-*.
n the action of proclaiming, proclamation *e16*.
proclamation &c 1 = proclamation *16-*. **2** the publication of banns *la16-*.

procurator &c;   **procurature** *16*, **procutor &c** *17-e19* ['prɔkjuretər; ***pro'kørətur, ***'prokəratur *&c*, ***'prokøtur, ***'prokətər] *n* **1** = procurator *la14-*. **2** a solicitor or lawyer practising before the lower courts *15-*, *now only in formal contexts*. **3** *church* an ADVOCATE appointed as official advisor in legal matters to the *General Assembly* (GENERAL) *la16-*. **4** *Abd Univ* (*la17-20*), *Gsw and St Andrews Univs* (*18-19*) a student representative appointed by each NATION to preside over it (and in Aberdeen to vote on its behalf) in *Rectorial* (RECTOR) elections.
~ **fiscal &c,** ~ **phiscall** *la16* the public prosecutor in a *Sheriff Court* (SHERIFF), appointed *formerly* by the SHERIFF or magistrates, *now* by the *Lord Advocate* (LORD), who initiates the prosecution of crimes, and carries out to some extent the duties of an English coroner *16-*. [OED *proctor, procurator*]

pro-curator ['pro'kjurətər] *n, law* a guardian or CURATOR who has not been legally appointed *la17-*. [only Sc; L *pro-* + CURATOR]

procuratory &c [prɔkju'retɔrɪ, 'prɔkjurətərɪ] *n, law* the authorization of one person to act for another *16-*.
~ **of resignation** *la18-19*, ~ **to resign** .. *e16*, *law* a disposition executed by a VASSAL in which he resigns his lands to his SUPERIOR, requesting that they be retained by the SUPERIOR or transferred to another VASSAL. [MedL *procuratorium* proxy]

procurature *see* PROCURATOR

procure &c *n* procurement *la16*.
vti **1** = procure *la14-*. **2** *vt* obtain by formal application, *freq* ~ **a person's seal** *la14-17*. **3** care for, take care of, attend to *e15*. **4** *vi* plead, make supplication *la16-e17*, *only Sc*. **5** *vt, law* prevail upon, induce, persuade (a person to do something criminal) *19-e20*.
procuration &c 1 = procuration *15-*. **2**

management for another, stewardship *la16-17*.

procurur *la14*, **prokerrour** *la16* [*pro'kørur, *prokə'rur] = procurer.

procutor *see* PROCURATOR

prod[1] **&c** *n* **1** = prod. **2** a wooden pin or skewer, *esp* one used as a thatching-pin *18-*, *now Per*. **3** a thorn, prickle *19-*, *SW*. **4** a prick, stab; the sting of an insect *19-*, *now SW*.
vti = prod.
proddled poked, stirred up, jabbed at; pricked as by a thorn *la19-*, *Gall Uls*.

prod[2] **&c** *n*, *contemptuous, of a person or animal* a waster, lazy creature, fool *la19-e20*. [short for Eng *prodigal*]

Prod *n*, *also* **Proddie** contemptuous term for a Protestant *20-*, *local C Uls*. [reduced f *prodistan* (PROTEST)].

proddled *see* PROD[1]

prodie *n* a trinket, plaything *19*, *Edb*. [shortened f Eng *prodigy*]

prodigue *n* a prodigal *la16*. [F. OED *prodig*]

prodistan &c *see* PROTEST

production &c *n* **1** = production; *specif, law* the exhibiting of a document in court *la15-*. **2** *law* an article or document produced as evidence, an exhibit *19-*. **3** extending or lengthening of time or space *e16*.
satisfy ~ *law* produce a document when challenged to do so in a court of law *19-e20*.

profession &c *n* **1** = profession *la14-*. **2** a religious system or sect *18-e20*.
~al examination one of a series of examinations, called the **First, Second** *etc* **Professional Examination**, taken by students of medicine and veterinary medicine *la19-*.

professor &c *n* **1** = professor *la16-*. **2** a person who makes open profession of religious faith, an acknowledged adherent of some religious doctrine *17-e20*.

profit &c *n* **1** = profit *la14-*. **2** natural produce, *eg* milk, grain, the yield (*esp* of a cow) *18-*, *now Sh Kcb*.
vti **1** = profit. **2** *vt* render profitable *la16*.
put to ~ put to a remunerative employment *la16*. **upon &c** ~ at interest *la16-e17*, *only Sc*.

profite [pro'fəit] *adj* proficient, skilful, expert *19-*, *now Bnf*. [altered f PERFIT, perh w infl f Eng *profit*]

prog &c; progue *la18-e20* [prog; *Cai also* prʌug] *n* **1** (1) a piercing weapon or instrument, a barb, dart, arrow *la18-*, *now Sh Ork Cai*. (2) a thorn, spine, prickle *la19-*, *now Per Ayr*. **2** a stab, thrust, poke etc, the act of pricking or stabbing *19-*, *local*.
v **1** *vt* stab, pierce, prick; poke, prod, jab *18-*, *local*. **2** *vi* make poking, prodding movements, poke **about** *la19-*, *now Sh*.
progger 1 a pricker, marking point *la20-*, *WC*. **2** a long spike or rod *la20-*, *local EC, WC*. [eModEng = a piercing instrument, perh a conflation of BROG w PROD[1]]

progenytrys [*pro'dʒɛnɪtrɪs] *n* an ancestress *la15*. [earlier in Sc; *cf* eModEng *progenitrice*]

prognostic &c *n* = PROGNOSTICATION 2, *19-*, *Abd*.

prognostication *n* **1** = prognostication. **2** an almanac *17-18* [appar f the prognostications about weather it contained].

program &c *n* a public notice, official notification or advertisement *17-e19*. [L (f Gk) *programma*; *cf* Eng *programme* f F (*19*)]

progress &c *n* **1** = progress *16-*. **2** *law* a series or progression, *esp* (1) **charter by** ~ a *feu charter* (FEU) which repeated or confirmed a grant of land as distinct from that conveying the original grant *18-19*; (2) ~ (**of title**(**s**) *or* **title-deeds** *etc*) the series of title-deeds, extending over at least ten years, which constitute a person's title to land *la16-*; (3) **right by** ~ a right established under *charter by* ~, *18-e19*.
vi = progress *17-*.
be ~ione in succession, gradually *e16*. **~ive 1** = progressive *la17-*. **2** *law, of writs or deeds* constituting a series or PROGRESS *e19*.

progue *see* PROG

prohemiate [*pro'himɪet] *vi* write or compose a proem *la16*. [L *prooemiāt-*, ptp stem of L *prooemiāri* make a proem. OED *proemiate*]

project; projeck &c *la19-* [*n* 'prodʒɛk(t); *v* pro'dʒɛk(t)] *n*, *vti* = project.

proke *vi* poke about, make a poking movement *19-*, *now Kcb*.
~r a poker *19-*, *now Uls*. [ME *prokien* prod, poke; prob f Eng dial, perh via Ireland]

prokerrour *see* PROCURE

prolixt; prolixit &c [*pro'lɪks(ɪ)t] *adj* = prolix, lengthy *la15-e16*.
prolixitnes = prolixity *e16*. [only Sc; *cf* *taxt* (TAX)]

prolocutor [*?pro'lokøtur, *-or] *n* **1** *law* a spokesman in court, an ADVOCATE *la15-e18*. **2** = prolocutor.

prolong [*pro'loŋ] *n* delay, procrastination *la15*. [only Sc; obs F, f *prolonger* prolong]

promene; promine [*pro'min] *vi, also* **purmein** *e17* [*pʌr'min] walk about, take a walk *la16-e17*.
n a royal progress *la16*. [only Sc; OF *promener*, *pourmener &c*]

promise &c *15-*; **promeis** *la16-17* ['promɪs] *n, vti* = promise.

promitt &c [*v* *pro'mɪt; *n* *'promɪt] *vti* promise *la15-e18*.
n a promise *16*, *only Sc*. [eModEng; L *prōmittere*]

promote &c *vt* **1** = promote. **2** *curling* (CURL) cause a stone to move forward by striking it with another stone *20-*, *Abd nEC SW*.
~r &c 1 = promoter *la14-*. **2** *now only* **promotor** *Sc Univs* the official, *usu* a senior member of the academic staff, who presents students for their degrees at graduation ceremonies *la17-*.

promove &c [*pro'møv] v 1 vt support, foster, promote 15-e18. 2 vi = promove, advance la16.

promoval &c promotion, furtherance, advancement la17, only Sc.

pron &c n the residue of oat husks and oatmeal remaining from the milling process, bran, SEEDS 18-, local N.

~**ack** &c ['pronək, -əx] a crumb, fragment, splinter; a state of mush, a mess, hotchpotch 19-, now Cai Per. [Gael pronn, prann (v) pound; mash, grind, pronnag a crumb; cf PRAN]

pronepot [*?'pro'nɛpot] n = next e16. [only Sc; L pronepōt-, stem of pronepos]

pronevoy 16; **pronewowe** &c 15, **pronepuoy** la16-e17 [*'pro'nɛvo, *-(j)u] n a great-grandson. [only Sc; pro- + Eng nephew after F pronepveu; cf PRONEPOT. OED pronephew]

pronounce &c; **pronunce** 16-e17 [prə'nuns; *'pro'nʌns] vti 1 = pronounce la16-. 2 vi make a pronouncement, assert 15-.

pronȝe see PRUNȜE

pronȝeand [*?'prʌnjənd] adj poignant, pricking e16.

prunȝeandlie poignantly, piercingly la16. [only Sc; altered f Eng poignant perh after PREEN, Eng prick etc]

proo &c 19-; **pbroo** e19 [pru] interj 1 a command to a horse to stop 19-, now S. 2 also **pruitchie** &c(-leddy) 19-e20, ~-**leddy** 20-, now Lnk Ayr, **proochie** la20 ['prutʃɪ] a call to a cow or calf 19-20. [see SND]

prood see PROUD

proof see PRUIF

prop n a stopper, bung, wedge e16, la19- (Sh). vt cram, stuff, load la16, only Sc. [Du prop, MDu proppe a broach, skewer, plug]

prop see PRAP

propale &c [*pro'pel] vt make public, divulge, publicize, announce 16-e19. [eModEng; MedL propalare, f pro before + palam openly]

propel vt 1 = propel. 2 law, of an heir of entail anticipate (the succession of his heir-apparent) by giving him enjoyment of the entailed property before his succession 19-.

propulsion 1 = propulsion. 2 the act of propelling (v 2) la19-.

propense [*pro'pɛns] adj liable or subject (**to** physical influence) la16. [obs Eng = inclined, disposed etc]

proper &c adj = proper la14-. adv excellently, handsomely; genuinely; thoroughly la15. n = proper, one's own property la15. ~ **improbation** law the setting aside or discrediting of a document on the grounds of its falsity or the fact that it has been forged la18; cf reduction-improbation (REDUCE). ~ **jurisdiction** law the authority of a judge when acting in his own person as distinct from the authority delegated by him to a deputy la18-e19.

propiciant [*pro'pɪsɪant] adj propitious, well-disposed e16. [only Sc; L propitiänt-, presp stem of propitiāre propitiate]

propine &c [*pro'pəin] n 1 drink-money la16-18. 2 a gift, tribute, reward, benefit 15-19. vt 1 also fig offer or give to drink, present with drink la16-e18. 2 offer as a present; put before someone, propose 16-19. 3 endow, present (a person) with 16-19. [chf Sc; ME = give to drink, F = drink-money, L propīnāre drink to someone's health, pledge, Gk propínein drink to another, give one to drink, give or present]

propone [pro'pon] v 1 vt put forward (a matter) for discussion or action, suggest la14-e20. 2 law advance or state in a court of law 15-. 3 vr offer oneself, offer e16. 4 vt = propone, offer as a reward or example la16-17. 5 vti have the intention of doing something, purpose, propose la16-e18. ~ **defences** state or move a defence la18. [L prōpōnere set forth, intend; cf eModEng]

proport &c [*pro'port] vt convey meaning, signify, purport la14-e18, chf Sc. n = purport, bearing la16, only Sc. [OF proporter, var of porporter purport]

proportion &c n 1 = proportion 16-. 2 Presbyterian Church the district assigned to an ELDER for visiting etc, a QUARTER 18-e19. vt = proportion.

proposely &c [*?pro'pozlɪ] adv on purpose, purposely la16. [only Sc; obs Eng propose purpose + -ly]

propulsion see PROPEL

pro-rector n, St Andrews Univ the vice-RECTOR 19. [pro- + RECTOR]

pro re nata ['pro 're 'netə] as the occasion requires; for an unforeseen contingency la16-. [earlier in Sc; L = for the matter which has arisen]

prorogate &c ['proroget, *-at] vt, ptp also **prorogate** la17-e18 1 defer, postpone 16-e19. 2 defer the termination of (a period of time), extend, prolong (esp a lease) la16-. 3 extend (the jurisdiction of a judge or court), usu by waiving objection to an incompetent jurisdiction la17-. [chf Sc; L prōrogāt-, ptp stem of prōrogāre]

prosecute ptp = prosecuted e17, only Sc.

prospect n 1 = prospect. 2 a spy-glass, telescope 18-e19.

prosper [*'prospər] adj prosperous, successful e16. [ME prospere, F prospère or L prosper(us) favourable, fortunate, prosperous]

pross &c vi put on airs, show off; gossip 19-e20. [perh var of Eng prowess used as a v]

prot see PRAT

proteck 19-, **protect** la14- [pro'tɛk(t)] vt = protect.

protectrix n a protectress 16-e17. [MedL]

protest *vti* **1** = protest *la16-*. **2** make a formal request, demand as a right, stipulate *la15-*, *only Sc*.
n = protest.
~**ant &c** *la16-*, ~**ane** *la16*, **prodistan** *20-*, *Gsw Uls* = protestant. ~**ation &c 1** = protestation *la16-*. **2** *law* the procedure by which a *defender* (DEFEND) in the *Court of Session* (SESSION) compels the *pursuer* (PURSUE) either to proceed with his action or to end it *la16-*. **P~ers &c** the name given to those Presbyterians who opposed union with the Royalist party in 1650, *la17*.
protocol &c; **prothogall &c** *16-e18 n* **1** = protocol *la15-*. **2** the book or register in which a notary etc recorded the details of transactions *la16-e19*.
~ **book &c** *or* **record** *etc* = *n* 2, *la15-*.
prottick *see* PRATTICK
protty *see* PRETTY
pro-tutor *n* a guardian of a PUPIL who has not been legally appointed *18-*.
pro-tutrix a female PRO-TUTOR *18-*. [L *pro-* + TUTOR; *cf* PRO-CURATOR]
proud &c; **prude &c** *la16*, *la19-e20*, **prood** *la19-* [prud] *adj* **1** = proud *la14-*. **2** highly pleasing *la14*. **3** *of persons* pleased, gratified, glad *la19-*. **4** *of fish* slow to take the bait, difficult to catch *la19-*, *now SW*. **5** over-grown, full-bodied, of luxuriant growth etc, *specif*: (1) *of growing crops* (over-)luxuriant *la18-*, *now Sh Mry*; (2) *of the sea or a river* running high, swollen *la18-*, *now Mry*; (3) *of an object or surface, eg a high-pitched roof, a high relief pattern* set higher than or not flush with its immediate surroundings *19-*.
n a proud person; a person of high degree *16*.
~**fu &c** haughty, prideful *la16-*, *now Bnf Ags Kcb*.
prounȝe *see* PRUNȝE
provay &c [*pro've] *vt* = purvey, provide *16*. [OED *purvey*]
prove *see* PRUIVE
proveist *see* PROVOST
proven *see* PRUIVE
provenient [*pro'viniənt] *adj* forthcoming *la16*. [only Sc; L *prōvenient-*, presp stem of *prōvenīre* come forward]
proves, provest *see* PROVOST
proviance &c *la16*; **pruwiance** *la14* [*?'provians] *n* provision; providence. [only Sc; OF *proveance*]
proviant &c [*'proviant] *n* provision, food supply, *esp* for an army *e17*. [Ger *proviant*, Du *proviand*; imported by soldiers serving in the Thirty Years' War]
provide &c *vti* **1** = provide *la15-*. **2** ~ **in** = provide or supply with *la16-18*.
provided 1 = provided. **2** prearranged *la16*.
providing 1 = providing. **2** the household articles, linen etc laid aside by a young woman for her bottom drawer *la18-*.

provincial &c *adj* = provincial *la16-*.
n **1** = provincial *15-*. **2** a provincial synod *17*.
provisor [pro'vaɪzər, -ər] *n* **1** a person in charge of getting provisions, *usu* for an institution *la15-18*. **2** *Abd Univ* the title of the steward of the Students' Union *20*. [ME = a manager]
provoke &c [*v, n* pro'vok] *vt* = provoke *16-*.
n **1** a provocation, challenge, invitation, summons *la18-e19*. **2** a person or thing which causes annoyance, a nuisance, pest *la19-*.
provokshin &c [pro'vokʃən] provocation, temptation *la19-*, *now Sh*.
provost &c *la15-*; **provest &c** *la14-e18*, **proveist** *e17*, **proves &c** *la18-e19*, *Ayr* ['provəst, -ost; *-əs] *n* **1** = provost *la14-*. **2** the head of a Scottish municipal corporation or BURGH, who was the civic head and chairman of the town or BURGH council and the chief magistrate, *corresponding to Eng* mayor; since 1975 used only in the title *Lord P~* (LORD) and as a courtesy title in some authorities *la14-*. **3** *Scottish Episcopal Church* the MINISTER of a cathedral church *la19-*.
~**ry &c 1** = provostry *la16-e17*. **2** the status or term of office of a PROVOST (*n* 2) *16-e19*.
~**schipe** the office or position of a PROVOST (*n* 2) *la16*.
prowdence *see* PRUDENCE
prowein *see* PREVEEN
prude *see* PROUD
prudence &c; **prowdence &c** *16* ['prudəns; *?'prodɛns] *n* **1** = prudence *la14-*. **2** a woollen wrap for the head worn by women, *esp* in winter *20-*, *now Bnf Abd Lnk*.
pruff *see* PRUIF
prufe *see* PRUIVE
pruif &c *15-19*, **proof** *18-*; **pruff &c** *la14-15*, **prief &c** *la14-16*, *19-* [prøf, prɪf, prif; *St* pruf; *pl* *prøvz, *privz] *n* **1** = proof *15-*. **2** a person who gives evidence, a witness *la15-16*. **3** (1) *agriculture* the act of estimating the quality and yield of a grain-crop by examining a random sample; the sample itself *16-*, *now Uls*. (2) *chf in pl, Presbyterian Church* scriptural texts used as proof or illustration of the doctrines in the catechisms, *esp* those of the *Shorter Catechism* (SHORT), printed as a schoolbook *18-19*. (3) *law* the method by which the disputed facts in a case are judicially determined, including the taking of evidence by a judge or (until *e19*) by a commissioner appointed by the Court, to determine the issues on which trial will take place; *also* (since the introduction of jury trial in 1815) trial before a judge only *18-*.
vt assess the quality and content of (a given quantity of grain) by examining a random sample *19-*, *now Ork NE Wgt*.
~ **barley, corn** *etc agriculture* the barley, corn etc selected as a sample for PRUIF (*n* 3 (1)) *18-*, *now Abd Per*. ~ **man** *agriculture* the person appointed to PRUIF grain *18-e19*.

~ **of lead** *or* **shot** a supposed magic protection from bullets *la17-e19*. [*cf* PRUIVE]

pruitchuie *see* PROO

pruive &c, prove &c; prufe &c *la14-16*, **preif &c** *la14-16*, **prief** *16-e17*, **prive** *18*, **prieve &c** *16-e20* [priv; *prøv] *vti, ptp also* **proven &c** *la16-* ['provən; *also* 'pruvən; *NE also* 'privən] **1** = prove *la14-*. **2** *vt* give proof of, *esp* by action *la14-15*. **3** (1) try out, put to the test, sample *la14-e20*. (2) try by tasting, taste *la16-*, *now Sh Ork NE*. **4** = PRUIF *19-*, *now NE*.

proven ['provən, 'pruvən] *adj* = proved *16-*. **proven rental** *law* a scheme of a MINISTER'S rental proved in a process of AUGMENTATION *la18-e20*. **not proven** *law* a verdict by the jury in a criminal trial when a majority find that although there is a suspicion of guilt, the case against the accused has not been proved beyond reasonable doubt; he is then unconditionally discharged *18-*. **previn** ['privɪn] a taste, a very small quantity; a kiss *la18-e19*. [*cf* PREE[1], PRUIF]

prunk *see* PRINK

prunʒe &c *15-16*; **prounʒe** *la16*, **pronʒe** *e16* [*'prʌnʒɪ] *vti* = prune, trim; dress up. [only Sc; OED *prune* (v[1])]

prunʒeandlie *see* PRONʒEAND

prute *interj* expressing scorn or defiance, *freq* ~ no!, prutish!, pruts! *la18-e19*.

pruwiance *see* PROVIANCE

pry[1] *vt* = prise, move by leverage *20-*, *Gen except Sh Ork*. [back-formation]

pry[2] &c *n* one of various species of sedge common in southern Scotland and used for sheep-feeding *la18-19*. [eModEng *prie*]

prydy *see* PRIDE

prynsace ['prɪnsɛs] *n* = princess *la15*. [only Sc; OED *princess*]

psalm &c, pasalm &c *la16-e17*, **phalme &c** *la16-17*, **pschalme** *17*, *only Sc*, **saum &c** *19* [sam; *St* sam] *n* = psalm, in Scotland *esp* referring to the metrical version of the Psalms adopted from French Protestant usage in the 16th century, the 1650 version being regularly used in congregational praise in the Presbyterian Churches *la16-*.

vt recount (a story etc) at great length and in monotonous detail, reel **off** endlessly in a monotonous whining voice *20-*, *NE*.

psalmistry psalms *e16*.

ptarmigan *see* TARMAGAN

pu *see* POU

puber *n* a youth, a person between the age of puberty and maturity *e16*. [ME; L *pūbes &c* (*adj*) having attained puberty, (*n*) a youth]

public &c *la15-*; **publict &c** *16-e18* *adj, n* = public *la16-*.

vt = public, make public *la15-e16*.

~ **burdens** taxes etc as they affect land, rates and taxes *18-*. ~ **right** *law* a HERITABLE right acquired when the purchaser of a property

completes his feudal title with the seller's SUPE-RIOR, *orig* a distinct procedure but *latterly* merely formal in conveyancing practice *la18-e19*. ~ **room** a room in a house in which visitors are received and entertained, *eg* a sitting room, dining room *19-*. ~ **school** a state-controlled school run by the local education authority, *usu* non-fee-paying and supported by contributions from local and national taxation *la17-20*, *officially la19-e20*.

publican &c *n* **1** = publican. **2** an excommunicated person *la14-17*.

publict *see* PUBLIC

puchal *see* POOCHLE

puckle *see* PICKLE[2]

pud[1] &c *19-*; **pod** *18-e20* [pʌd, pod; *S also* pud] *n* **1** a small, neat, *esp* plump person or animal *18-*, *now Uls*. **2** term of endearment for a child or small squat animal *la19-*, *Fif wLoth Lnk*. **3** name for a pigeon *20-*, *now Ags Per*.

puddie &c = *n* 3, *20-*, *now Rox*.

pud(die)-doo &c = *n* 3; a tame pigeon *19-*, *now Per Fif*. [perh f colloq Eng *pud* a pudding, but *cf* Eng *podgy, pudsy* plump, tubby]

pud[2] &c *n* an ink-holder, ink-pot *19-e20*, *chf S*. [perh var of Eng *pot*, w some association w prec]

pudder *see* POUTHER

puddin &c *18-*, **pudding &c** ['pʌd(ɪ)n] *n* **1** = pudding. **2** a kind of sausage made from the stomach or entrails of a sheep, pig etc stuffed with various mixtures of oatmeal, onions, suet, seasoning, blood etc, and boiled and stored for future use *la15-*; *see also* BLACK, *mealie* (MEAL), WHITE[1]. **3** *in pl* entrails, viscera, guts (of persons or animals) *16-*. **4** a stupid or clumsy person *20-*.

~ **bree &c** the water in which a PUDDIN has been boiled *18-*, *Ork Abd Per Kcb*. ~ **fillar** a person who lives to eat, a glutton *e16*. ~ **lug** *exclam* expressing impatience *la19-*, *now Abd*. *n* an ear which has swollen as the result of a blow, a 'thick ear' *la20-*, *WC* [one of the projecting ends of a PUDDIN (*n* 2)]. ~ **market** *child's word* the stomach *la20-*, *Ork Kcdn Ags*. ~ **supper** *see* SUPPER.

haud *or* **keep the** ~ **boilin, het** *etc* keep the pot boiling *19-*, *C*. ~**s an' wort!** *exclam* expressing contempt or disbelief *20-*, *now Kcb*.

puddle &c *n* **1** = puddle *16-*. **2** a street gutter *20-*, *NE*. **3** a state of disorder, a muddle, mess, confusion *la18-19*. **4** an untidy or disorganized worker, a muddler, bungler *19-*, *now Ags*.

v **1** *vi* work in a muddling, inefficient way, muddle along, mess about *la16-*, *NE Ags Gall Uls*. **2** *vt* wet with mud or dirty water *e16*. **3** *vi* walk with short steps, plod; *of the feet* work up and down *19-e20*, *chf S*.

puddock *la16-*, **paddok &c** *la14-e20*, **poddock &c** *17-20*, **paddo &c** *la14-e16*, *19*; **paddy &c** *19-e20* ['pʌdək, 'padək; *Ork also* 'pado; *Mry also* 'paðək; *NE also* 'podək; *sEC, S also* 'padı; *Loth also* 'pɑdı; *Dmf also* 'padə] *n* **1** the frog; *also* the toad *la14-, in place-names 14-*. **2** term of abuse or contempt for (1) a spiteful or arrogant person *19-e20*; (2) a clumsy, ungainly or ugly person *19-, now Bnf Abd*. **3** *agriculture* a flat, wooden, *usu* triangular platform etc, shaped rather like a frog, used for transporting heavy loads of hay etc *18-20*. **4** *in pl* a game with local variations, a kind of makeshift cricket *la19-, now Cai Edb*.

vt move (stones etc) by means of a PUDDOCK (*n* 3) *la19-, NE*.

~ **barrow** = *n* 3, *19-, now Ross Abd*. ~('s) **crud(d)les &c** frogspawn *la19-, local NE-Kcb*. ~ **hair** the down or fluff growing on very young creatures, *esp* birds *19-e20*. **be in the** ~ **hair** *freq of persons* be very young, be an infant *e19*. **paddy &c ladle** a tadpole *la19-, now S*. ~ **pipes** a kind of grass, the marsh horse-tail *17-, now local NE-Kcb*. ~('s) **pony &c** = *paddy ladle, 20-, Per*. ~ **redd &c** = ~('s) **crud(dles)**, *18-, now Wgt S*. **paddy's rhubarb** the butter-bur *la20-, Loth S*. ~ **rude &c** = *puddock('s) crud(dles)*, *e16, 19-, now Cai*. ~'s **spindle** the spotted orchid *la19-, now Ags Ayr*. ~('s) **spit(tle) &c** cuckoo-spit *la19-*. ~-**stane &c** a toadstone *la15-e18*. ~ **stool &c** a toadstool or mushroom; any fungus, *usu* stalked *la16-*. [ME *paddoke*, f obs Eng *pad &c*, *pode &c + -ock*]

puddy *n* a kind of cloth *e18*. [perh reduced f Eng *paduasoy*, a common 18th century grosgrain silk]

puder *see* PEUTHER[1]

pudge &c *n* = pudge, a small, plump, thickset person or animal *la19-, local*.

pudget *la19-e20*, **pudgie &c** *la18-, now Sh Abd*, **pudgle &c** *19-, now Bnf Abd Slk* = *n*; a heavy eater.

pudlo *see* PODLIE

pue *see* PEW, PLEUCH

puer *see* POOER

puff &c *vti* **1** = puff *la16-*. **2** *vi* boast, brag *19-, local Abd-Kcb*.

n = puff *16-*.

~**er** a small steamboat used to carry cargo around the west coast of Scotland and the Hebrides *20-*. ~**ie** *20-, Abd Ags Fif*, ~**y dunter** *la19-, now NE* the porpoise.

pug[1] &c *n* **1** = pug, a courtesan; a pug-dog *la17-*. **2** *now chf* ~**gie &c** a monkey *la17-, now C*. **3** *chf* ~**gie** term of disrespect or abuse for a person *la19-, now Per*.

~**gy bun** a bun consisting of a treacle sponge mixture in a pastry case *la20-, Per Fif* [f its resemblance to a monkey's face]. ~**gie pipe** the cup and stalk of the acorn, which children put in their mouths and 'smoke' *la20-, now Loth*. **as fou as a** ~**gie** extremely drunk *20-, Cai C, S*. **get one's** ~**gy up** *la19-, now Fif*, **lose one's** ~**gy** *la20-, C, S* lose one's temper.

pug[2] *vt* pull, tug *19-, chf Per Fif*. [eModEng; obscure]

puggie *n* **1** *marbles* a hole into which the marbles are rolled *la20-, Ags Fif Bwk Ayr*. **2** the bank, kitty, jackpot or pool in a game of cards etc *la20-, Ags WC*.

puggle &c *vt, chf in adj* **puggled &c** at a standstill due to exhaustion or frustration, done for, at the end of one's resources *20-*. [perh extended f Eng slang *puggled* very drunk, or euphemistic alteration of Eng slang *buggered*]

pugh *see* PEUCH

pugny *see* POINȝÉ

pugs *n pl, mining* a stratum of hard coal in a *free coal* (FREE) seam *la19-, now Lnk*. [prob extended f Eng *pug* loam or hard pounded clay used to make bricks etc]

puidge &c [pødʒ] *n* **1** (1) a small enclosure, pen or sty, a hut, hovel *19-e20*. (2) *specif* a small enclosure used for fattening cattle *la20-, S*. **2** *fig* a mess, muddle, a pigsty *20-, S*. [obscure]

puil &c *now Sh C, S*, **pool, peel** *19-e20, NE* [pøl, pıl; *Cai NE* pil; *nEC also* pel] *n* = pool, a body of water *la14-*.

vt, only **puil &c** = pool, make a hole in *18-e20*. **peel rushich &c** a heavy shower, downpour; a torrent *e20*. [cf POW[2]]

puind *see* POIND

puir &c, poor &c *la16-*; **pur** *la14-16, la19* (*Sh*), **peur &c** *la16, la19* (*Ork*), **peer &c** *19-20, NE* [pør, per; *NE* pir] *adj* = poor *la14-*.

n **1** = poor, the poor people *la14-*. **2** (1) a poor person, someone receiving charity *16-e19*. (2) *law, followed by a person's name* indicating that he had been given free legal aid because his name was on the *poor's roll*, *la18-e20*.

vt = poor, make poor *la15*.

puiranis &c poor ones, poor people *la16*. ~ **bodie** a beggar *la18-, now Sh Abd Per*. ~'s **box** a collecting box for poor relief kept by the *kirk session* (KIRK); the poor fund itself *18*. ~**shouse &c** a poorhouse, workhouse *la18-, now hist*. ~('s) **inspector**, *formally* **the Inspector of Poor** an official in each parish who investigated cases of poverty and paid out relief; his duties are now carried out by a Social Security official *la19-20, latterly NE*. ~ **man 1** = poor man. **2** a kind of candlestick used for holding up a *candle fir* (CANNLE) etc *la19-, NE, hist* [because this was thought to have formerly been done by paupers in return for alms etc]. **3** a dish made from the remains of a shoulderbone of mutton *18-19*. ~ **man's clover** selfheal *la20-, Bnf Ags Per*. **ding on** *or* **rain** ~ **men and pike staves** (**and the pike ends neathmost**) rain heavily, pour with rain *19-, NE*. **peer page** = ~ *man 2, 19-e20, NE*. ~'s **rates** = poor-rate *la18-e20*. ~'s **roll 1** a list of paupers in a parish who received poor relief *18-*. **2** a roll of persons officially recognized as qualifying because of poverty for free legal aid under the Act of 1424, *la18-20*.

mak a ~ mou(th) plead poverty as an excuse for meanness, claim to be poor when in fact one is quite well off *19-*.

puirtith &c *la19-, now literary,* **poortith &c** *18-e20;* **purteth** *e16,* **puirteith** *la16* ['pørtəð, -təθ] *n* = poverty. [for *-ith* cf DAINTITH]

puissance *see* PISSANCE

puissant *see* PISSANT

puist[1] [pøst] *vt* cram, stuff full; *specif* cram (the stomach or oneself) with food *19-e20, chf Rox.* *adj, of persons* in easy circumstances, comfortably off *19-, now Kcb Dmf.* [only Sc; perh connected w POSS, POUSS]

puist[2] **&c** [pøst] *vt* urge forward, push, impel; *fig* criticize *19-e20.* [perh f as prec]

puke *see* POUK

pulder *see* PEUTHER[1]

pule *see* PEWL

pull *see* POU

pullach &c ['puləx] *n* a species of cod *la19-, now Bnf.* [var of Eng *pollack; cf* PODLIE, POLLACK]

pullan &c *n* a kind of sail-cloth *e16.* [var of eModEng *polaine*]

pullane &c *n* = polayn, a piece of defensive armour covering the knee *la15.* [OED *polayn*]

pulley &c, **pillé &c** *16;* **pillie &c** *16-e19* ['pʌlɪ; *'pɪlɪ] *n* = pulley *la15-.* **~shee** *18-, ~* **scheif** *16-17* **1** the sheave or grooved roller over which a rope runs in a pulley-block *16-17.* **2** a pulley, *esp* a rope on a pole, used to hang clothes out of a window to dry *18-, now local Ags-Ayr.*

pullicate &c *la18-e19;* **policat &c** *e19* [*'pʌlɪkət] *n* a coloured, *freq* checked gingham-type cotton produced in Scotland; a PULLICATE handkerchief. [f the town of Pulicat, Madras, where handkerchiefs of this material were first made]

pullie &c *n* a turkey *la19-, now Bnf Uls.* [uncertain; Gael *pulaidh* is f Sc]

pulloch &c ['pʌləx, 'pol-] *n* a small edible crab *18-, now Bnf Kcdn.*

pulpit *see* PUPIT

pult &c [pʌlt] *n* a short stout person *19-, now Ork Per Uls.* [uncertain]

pultice ['pʌltɪs] *n* = poultice *la19-.*

pultrie *see* POUTRIE

pump[1] **&c** *n, vti* = pump *16-.* **~ed &c** *of a tree* affected by *pumping* or heartrot, having a hollow stem or trunk *la19-, NE-Kcb.* **~ing** a disease affecting trees, a form of heart-rot which leaves the stem hollow like a pump-shaft *la19.* **~staff** a pump-rod *la16.*

pump[2] **&c** [pʌmp; *Abd* pɪmp] *n, slang or colloq* a breaking of wind *19-.* *vi* break wind *19-.* [onomat]

pumphal &c *19-;* **pumphel &c** *17-20* ['pʌmfl] *n* **1** a *usu* square enclosure for livestock *la19-, now NE.* **2** a kind of square church pew,

with a seat or bench round the inside, entered by a door or gate and with a small table in the centre *17-, now NE.* *vt* shut up in a PUMPHAL (*n* 1) *la19-e20, NE.* [only Sc; altered f PUND[2] or POIND + FAULD[2]]

pun *see* PUND[1]

punce &c *16-e20,* **pounce** *19-* [pʌns] *n* **1** = pounce *16-.* **2** a dagger *e16, only Sc.* **3** a light blow with the elbow, foot etc, a nudge, poke, thrust *19-e20.* *v* **1** *vi* = pounce. **2** *vt* (1) buffet *e17.* (2) poke or jog, *usu* with the foot, elbow etc, *esp* when lying in bed *19-e20.*

Punch *n* = Punch, the puppet. **punchie &c** *n, also* **punchik(ie)** a short, stout person or animal *la19-, now NE. adj, of persons or animals* thickset and short *19-, now NE.*

punch-bowl *n* = punch-bowl. **bottom of the ~** name of a Scottish dance tune and country-dance *20-.* **round about the ~** a children's game *la19-, now Uls.*

puncheon[1] **&c;** **pouncioun** *15* ['pʌnʃən; *'pʌns(ɪ)un, *'pʌnʃ(ɪ)un] *n* = puncheon, a dagger *la14-.* **~ irn** an instrument for punching *eg* letters on plate, coinage dies etc *e16.*

puncheon[2] **&c** *16;* **punsioun &c** *la15-16,* **puntion** *16,* **pontioune** *16* ['pʌnʃən; *'pʌns(ɪ)un, *'pʌnʃ(ɪ)un] *n* = puncheon, a large cask.

punct; punt *la16* [*pʌŋkt, *pʌnt] *n* **1** a point, dot, speck *e16.* **2** a point, full stop *e17.* **3** = punct, point, a moment *e16.* **4** an item, detail *la14-16, only Sc.* *vt* appoint *la15, only Sc.*

pund[1] **&c,** **pound &c;** **poun &c** *19-20,* **pun** *la19-,* **powin &c** *la19-20* [pʌn(d); *pun(d); *n* **2** *NE also* 'pʌu(ə)n] *n, uninflected in pl after numerals etc* **1** = pound, a measure of weight; *specif* (until *e19*) a measure varying in value according to whether the standard was the *Scots Troy* (SCOTS) or TRON *la14-.* **2** *freq ~* **Scots** *18* a money of account *la14-;* see SCOTS. **~land** a measure of land, *orig* assessed at the annual value of one pound in the EXTENT, fixed (*la16*) at half a *ploughgate* (PLEUCH) *16-, now hist and in SW place-names.*

pund[2] **&c,** **pound &c** *15-;* **poon** *la18-e19* [pʌn(d); *pun(d)] *n* **1** a seizure of animals in a raid etc; cattle so taken *la14-15, only Sc.* **2** an animal or article taken by distraint *16-e17.* **3** = pound, an enclosure for animals *18-.* **4** *only* **pound** a pond, *esp* a fish-pond *la16-e17* [*cf* POUND]. *vt* **1** = pound, impound straying animals *la19-.* **2** = POIND *v* 1; fine, levy *15, e18.* **~ler &c** a person whose main duty was *orig* the impounding of livestock, *later* looking after tree plantations *16-, now Mry Bnf.* **~law** a fine for something impounded *la15-16, only Sc.*

pundar *see* PUNDLER

pundie &c *n* **1** a strong type of beer; liquor *in gen, 19-, now Loth Slk.* **2** a measure of beer given free to brewery workers *la20-, Loth Slk.* [obscure]

pundlane &c, pundlene [*'pʌndlen, &c] *n, also fig* the due payable for the release of animals impounded for trespass *la13-e16.* [first element appar PUND²; for second element *?cf* LANE³. OED *pound-lien*]

pundler &c *17-20;* **pundar &c** *la18-e20* ['pʌn(d)lər; *'pʌndər] *n* a weighing instrument of the steelyard type *chf Sh Ork.* [altered, w infl f *pundler* (PUND²), f ON *pundari* steelyard. OED *pundlar*]

Punic &c *adj* **1** = Punic, Carthaginian *16-.* **2** **p~** purple *e16.*

punish &c *15-;* **punis &c** *la14-16,* **puneish &c** *la16* ['pʌnɪʃ; *latterly chf Sh Ork* 'pønɪʃ; *Cai* 'pinɪʃ; *'pʌnɪs, *'pøn-] *vti* **1** = punish *la14-.* **2** *vt* stint, limit; *specif* reduce (a stone) in size by cutting and dressing *19-, now Cai.*

punkie *n, usu in pl* a variety of the game of marbles played in three holes in the ground; the holes themselves *la19-e20, Ross Inv.* [appar var of *plunkie* (PLUNK¹)]

punse &c *n* = pulse, the beat of a person's blood *la16.* [only Sc; perh w infl f PUNCE]

punsioun *see* PUNCHEON²

punt *see* PUNCT

puntion *see* PUNCHEON²

punʒe¹ [*'pʌnʒi] *n* a handful of men, *usu* soldiers *e16.* [F *poignée,* OF also *pugnie &c* a handful. OED *punye (n)*]

punʒe² [*'pʌnʒi] *vt* prick, pierce; spur *15.* [only Sc; F *poign-,* f *poindre* pierce. OED *punye (v)*]

punʒe *see* POINʒÉ

pup *n* **1** = pup, a young dog. **2** a small size of brick *la20-, Stlg Fif WC Rox.*

pupil &c *n* **1** = pupil, a schoolchild etc. **2** *law* a child under the age of *minority* (MINOR), 12 for girls and 14 for boys *la15-.*

~larity &c *law* the state of being a PUPIL (*n* 2) *la16-.*

pupit &c *la19-,* **pulpit &c;** **poopit &c** *la18-e20* ['pupɪt] *n* **1** = pulpit *16-.* **2** the poop of a ship, from which directions were given *e16.* **wag one's pow** *etc* **in a** ~ be a MINISTER *18-.*

puppie¹ &c; **poppy &c** *la18-e20* *n* ~ **show** *etc* a puppet show, a Punch-and-Judy show etc *18-e20.* **mak a ~-show o anesel** make a fool of oneself, make an exhibition of oneself *la18-, now nEC, WC.* [F *poupée* a doll; *cf* Eng *puppy, puppet*]

puppie² &c *n* = poppy *18-, now WC-S.*

pur *see* PUIR

purchase &c; purchass &c *la14, e18* *vt* **1** = purchase *la14-.* **2** procure, obtain, gain possession of, acquire *la14-19.*

n **1** = purchase *la14-.* **2** concubinage *e16.*

pure &c [*pør] *adj* = pure *la14-.*

n **1** = pure. **2** 'pured' fur, fur trimmed so as to show only one colour *e16.*

pureale [*?pʌ'ralɪ] *n, law* = puralé, a perambulation to determine boundaries *15.* [OED *puralé*]

purfle *v, only* **purfled &c, purfe(i)t** ['pʌrfɪt] *of persons* fat and asthmatic, corpulent, plump and wheezing *18-e20.* [perh intensive of *puffle,* Eng dial deriv of Eng *puff*]

purge *vt* **1** = purge *la15-.* **2** *law* (1) clear off an irritancy (IRRITANT) by remedying the failure which produced it *17-;* (2) *freq* **~d of partial counsel** *of a witness etc* having taken an oath as to the disinterestedness and impartiality of the evidence he is about to give *la16-19.* **3** *church* check or verify (the roll of communicants in a congregation) by removing the names of lapsed members *la19-e20.*

purify &c [(*St*) 'pjurɪfaɪ; *'pørɪfaɪ; *NE* *'pirɪ-] *vt* **1** = purify *16-.* **2** *law* fulfil or carry out (a condition), bring an agreement etc into operation by complying with a proviso in it *18-.*

purk *n* = pork *la19-, Sh NE Ags.*

purl &c [pʌrl; *Sh-Fif Lnk also* pɪrl] *n, chf in pl* the small balls of dung excreted by sheep, rabbits etc *18-.*

vi, of animals defecate *19-, now Sh.*

pirlag *20-, Ork Cai,* **~ack** *la20-, Per* = *n.* [perh orig a var of Eng *pearl*]

purl *see* PIRL

purlack *see* PURL

purlaing *see* POU

purmein *see* PROMENE

purn *see* PIRN

purpest *see* PURPOSE

purpie¹ &c *n* the colour purple *la18-, now Mry.* *adj* of a purple colour, gaudy *la17-19.*

~ **fever &c** some kind of fever causing purplish discolouration of the skin, *prob chf* typhus *la17-e19.* [reduced f obs Eng *purpur*]

purpie² &c *n* the name of some plant, *perh* purslane (but see SND) *la15-e18, only Sc.*

purpoir *see* PURPUR

purpose &c *16-;* **purposs &c** *la14-15* ['pʌrpos; *n, v* *'pʌr'poz] *n* **1** = purpose *la14-.* **2** efficiency, neatness, tidiness *la19-, now Ork Uls.*

vt, pt also **purpest** *e16* = purpose *la14-.* *adj* well-ordered, tidy, methodical; tidy-looking *19-, Sh-nEC Uls.*

~-like &c *of persons* neat, tidy, methodical, efficient *la15-, Gen except Sh Ork.*

tak ~ resolve, determine *la14-16.*

purpress [*?pʌr'prɛs] *vi, law* commit purpresture, encroach on another's land etc *la16.* [only Sc; var of next, appar w infl f Eng *purpresture*]

purprise [*?pʌr'praɪz] *vti, law* make a purpresture or illegal encroachment; enclose or encroach upon *la15-e17.* [only Sc; F *porprendre, pur-; cf* next]

purprision &c *la15-e19;* **purprusioun** *16* [*pʌr'prɪʒən] *n, law* encroachment on another's lands, *esp* on royal or common land, purpresture. [only Sc; OF *porprison*, MedL *porprensio* occupation, usurpation; *cf prec*]

purpur &c *la14-e17*; **purpoir** *e16* [*'pʌrpər, *-ør] *n, adj* = purpur, purple (cloth).

purpurare [*'pʌrpərər] *n* a purpuress, a female seller of purple *e16*. [only Sc; f laL *purpurāria* a female dyer of purple]

purr *see* PORR

purry *n* a savoury dish consisting of oatmeal BROSE with chopped KAIL stirred into it *la18-19*. [F *purée* sieved pulp of vegetables etc; *cf* obs Eng *porray*]

purse &c *n, vt* = purse *la16-*.
~ **maister &c** a purse-bearer, treasurer, bursar *la16-17, chf Sc*. ~ **mou** the opening of a purse; *fig* a boat-shaped cloud said to presage high wind *la19-, now Ags Per*. ~ **penny** a coin, *usu* of high value, kept in the purse for luck *17-e18*. **purspyk** [*'pʌrspɪk] a thief who picks purses, a pickpocket *e16*.

pursevant, pursifant *see* PURSUIVANT

purspyk *see* PURSE

pursue &c *la15-*, **persew &c** *15-17*; **persow &c** *16* [pər'ʃu, -'su] *vti* **1** = pursue *15-*. **2** *vt* attack, assail, besiege *la15-17, only Sc*. **3** harass, worry, persecute (a person or group), beg (a person) persistently to do something *la15-, now Kcb*. **4** follow (a person) persistently with one's attentions *16*. **5** beg (someone) for favours; pay suit to as a lover *16*. **6** *law* (1) *vt* prosecute in a court of law, sue: (a) *with a person as object, la15-19*; (b) *with the offence as object, la15-17*: 'the master may *persew* ejection committed against his tenant'; (2) carry on (an action at law), prosecute (a case), claim (damages) in litigation *la15-*; (3) *vi* raise an action in a law court, take part in litigation *15-*. **7** institute a claim **for** by legal action *16-17*.

pursuer &c, persewer &c *16* **1** = pursuer *16-*. **2** an assailant, a besieger *la16-e17, only Sc*. **3** *law* the active party in a civil action, the plaintiff, prosecutor *la16-*. **pursuit &c** *16-*, **persuit &c** *la14-17*, **persutt &c** *la15-e17*, **persewt &c** *la15-e17*, **persoit &c** *la15-16* [pər'ʃut, &c; *pər'søt] *n* **1** = pursuit *la15-*. **2** *law* (1) the action of prosecuting or bringing a suit; an action, suit, prosecution *la14-18, latterly chf Sc*; (2) the prosecution or suing **of** (a person) by another *16-e17*; (3) the prosecution **of** (a legal action or suit) **aganis** *or* **upoun** (another) *la15-e17*; (4) the action of seeking to obtain or recover something by legal means *la15-17*. **3** *only Sc* (1) an attack, assault *16-17*; (2) a siege *la16-e17*. *vt, only Sc* **1** persecute *la16*. **2** submit (a proposal) for consideration *la17*.

pursuivant *la18-*; **pursifant &c** *15-16*, **persevand** *15-16*, **pursevant &c** *15-e18* ['pʌrs(w)ɪvant, *-and] *n* **1** = pursuivant; a member of the *Lyon Court* (LYON); there were *formerly* six, *later* (1867-) three, *ie* CARRICK, UNICORN and KINTYRE *15-*. **2** (1) a follower, an

attendant *e16*. (2) *specif* an attendant on the CORNET at the *Riding of the Marches* (RIDE) ceremony at Dumfries *la20-*.

purteth *see* PUIRTITH

pusche, push *see* POUSS

pushion *19-*; **pusoun &c** *la14-16*, **pooshin &c** *la19-e20*, **pushin &c** *la19-e20*, **pusion &c** *la19-e20*, **puzhen &c** *19-e20* ['puʒən, 'puʃən, 'pəizən; *Bnf also* 'paiʒ-; *local C* 'pøʒ-, 'pɪʒ-; *Fif also* 'peʒ-; *sEC* 'pʌʒ-, 'pʌʃ-; *Ayr also* 'pʌʒ-; *Bwk S* 'pʌz-] *n* **1** = poison *la14-*. **2** an unpleasant person or thing, a 'horror' *la19-, Sh N*.
adj, of persons or things unpleasant, detestable, foul *19-, now Sh Ork Fif*.
vt **1** = poison *la14-*. **2** make unpleasant, spoil; *specif* make (food) unpalatable or nauseating; cause discomfort to *19-*.
~ **able** poisonous; unpleasant *la16-, now Per Dnbt*. **pooshinous &c 1** = poisonous *19-*. **2** unpleasant, detestable, horrible *20-, Sh N*. ~**t 1** *also* **poysonit** *16* = poisoned *16-*. **2** *of persons* unpleasant, spiteful, malicious; *of things* unhealthy- or unwholesome-looking, dingy, discoloured *19-, now Rox*.
~ **berry** the woody nightshade or bittersweet *la19-, now Lnk*. [OED *poison*]

pusiance *see* PISSANCE

pusion *see* PUSHION

puslick &c ['pʌʃlək] *n, chf in pl* the (dried) droppings of a cow or sheep *19-, now Abd*. [uncertain]

pusoun *see* PUSHION

puss [pus] *n, also* **pussy &c** *la18-*, **poussie &c** *la18-19* ['pusɪ] **1** = puss. **2** a hare *la18-, now Uls*.
pussy-baudrons &c affectionate name for a cat *la19-, now Abd*. **as quiet, calm** *etc* **as** ~**ie** in a quiet, tranquil way *19-, now local*.

pussant *see* PISSANT

put *see* PIT[1], PUTT[1]

putch *see* POUCH

puther *see* PEUTHER[1], POUTHER

putt[1] &c, put [pʌt] *vti* (1) push, shove; nudge gently, prod; *of an animal* push or prod with the head or horns, butt *15-, now Sh-NE*. (2) *vt, esp athletics* hurl (a stone or heavy metal ball) by means of a strong thrust from the shoulder *la16-*. (3) *vti, golf* strike (the ball) with a (series of) gentle tap(s) so as to move it towards the hole *la17-*. **2** *vi* (1) make a nudging, poking or thrusting movement, nudge or knock **at** or (**up**)**on** *la16-, now Ork Cai*. (2) pulsate, throb *la19-, now S*.
n **1** a gentle touch or push; a butt from an animal; the recoil from a gun *16-, now Sh-N, Kcb*. **2** (1) *golf* the gentle tapping stroke used to impel the ball across the GREEN[1] and into the hole *18-*. (2) *athletics* the thrusting movement by which a *putting stane* or weight is propelled *19-*.
~**er 1** *mining* a person whose job it is to push a

loaded HUTCH from the coal-face to the pit-bottom *la18-20*. **2** *golf* a person who PUTTS; the flat-faced club used for putting *18-*. **driving** ~**er** *golf* the flat-faced club used for pitching shots onto the GREEN¹ *19*. ~**ing green** *golf* the area of close-cut turf surrounding the hole; a GREEN¹ containing a series of short holes used for *putting* practice or for recreational *putting* competitions *19-*. ~**in(g) stane** the stone thrown as in PUTT¹ *v* 1 (2), *la18-19*. **mak** *or* **keep one's** ~ **guid** succeed in a venture, gain one's object *la17-*, *now WC, SW*. ~ **an row** *fig* trying as hard as one can, using every means at one's disposal *la18-*, *now Bnf*. [early var of PIT¹, differentiated by pronunciation and in ModSc by the regular use of the weak conjugation]

putt², **put** [pʌt] *n* **1** a piece of masonry projecting from a wall, a buttress *16-e19*. **2** a buttress of a bridge *e17*. **3** a jetty or stone buttress projecting from a river bank, used to alter the current, protect the bank etc *la17-e20, S*. ~ **stone** = *peat stane* (PEAT¹) *la19-*, *now Cai.* [only Sc; uncertain]

putt *see* POUT
putten *see* PIT¹
puttock &c *n* the buzzard *la19-e20, Dmf.* [uncertain]
puzhen *see* PUSHION
pwint *see* POINT
py *see* PEY, PIE¹, PIE-HOLE
pyat *see* PYOT

pyauve &c [pjɑv] *vi, chf* **pyauvin &c** sickly, ailing; suffering from the heat *20-*, *now Cai Abd.*
n, only **pyauvie &c** an attack of sickness or faintness, a fit of nausea *20-*, *now Cai.* [N form of PAW¹, w extension of meaning]
pye &c *n* a counting-out rhyme, *freq* **count** *or* **say a** ~ *la20-*, *Abd Kcdn.* [uncertain]
pye *see* PEE²
pynor *see* PINER
pyoch *see* PEUCH
pyock *see* POCK²
pyot &c *la15-*, **piet &c** *15-20*; **pyat &c** *16-e20*, **peyet &c** *la18-19* ['paɪət] *n* **1** the magpie *15-20*. **2** applied to other birds with pied plumage *eg* (**water**) ~ the dipper, **sea** ~ the oyster-catcher *19-*, *now Abd Ags Gall.* **3** nickname for a person *la16-e20*. **4** contemptuous term for a chattering, irresponsible person *la18-e20*. **5** a piebald horse *la18-*, *Mry Abd midLoth.* **6** a farm-hand who stands on a corn stack and passes the sheaves from the forker to the builder *la19-*, *NE.*
adj **1** resembling a magpie in colouring, piebald, multi-coloured, variegated *16-e20*. **2** *of speech* loud, empty, voluble *la16*, *19-e20*. [ME *piot*; *cf* F *piette* the dipper, dim of *pie* magpie]
pyowl *see* PEWL
pype *see* PEEP¹
pystle &c, **pistill &c** *la14-16* [*'pɪstəl] *n* **1** = *pistle*, a New Testament epistle *la14-16*. **2** a letter *la15-18*.
pyuff-girse *see* PLUFF

Q

qhiche *see* WHILK²

qua *see* QUAW, TWA, WHA

quaa *see* QUAW

quachet &c *n* the name of a kind of loaf of white bread *e15*. [obscure]

quackie *n* a duck *19-*, *now Abd Stlg Slk.*

quad *see* QUED

quader &c ['kwadər] *v* 1 *vt* make square, quadrate *19-e20*.   2 *vi* agree, 'get along' *19-20*, *Abd.* [ME *quadre*]

quadrant &c ['kwadrənt] *n* 1 = quadrant *16-*.   2 a farthing *15-e17*.

quadrate &c [*'kwadrat, *-et] *adj, ptp, of a thing* square, squared *la16*.   [L *quadrāt-*, ptp stem of *quadrāre* (*v*) square]

quadriennium *n* ~ utile [kwɔdrɪ'ɛnɪʌm 'jutɪlɪ] *law* the four years following on the attainment of majority during which a person may by legal action seek to withdraw from any deed done to his prejudice during his minority *la18-* [only Sc; L = the useful period of four years].

quadrulapse &c [*'kwadrəlaps, *'kwɔdrə-] *n* a fourth offence against church discipline *la16-19*. [only Sc; L *quadru-* four- + Eng *lapse*; *cf* DULAPSE]

quadruplait [*'kwadrəplet] *adj* quadruple *la15*. [OED *quadruplate*]

quadruple &c [*'kwadrʌpl] *vt* increase fourfold *la14-*.

quadruply [*'kwadrəplaɪ, *'kwɔd-] *n*, *law* a fourth answer, made by the *defender* (DEFEND) in reply to the TRIPLY of the *pursuer* (PURSUE) *17-e19*.
vi answer in a QUADRUPLY *16-e18*. [OF *quadruplique* (*n*), MedL *quadruplicare* (*v*) rebut, multiply by four; *cf* DUPLY, TRIPLY, QUINTUPLY, SEXTUPLY, SEPTUPLY]

quaestor ['kwistər] *n*, *St Andrews University* the chief financial officer of the University, the University Treasurer *la18-*.   [L = one of the financial officers of the Roman State]

quaich &c *18-*; quhaich *e16*, quech &c *la17-e19*, queff *la17-e18* [kwex, *kwɛx, *kwix, *kwɛf] *n* a shallow bowl-shaped drinking cup, *orig* made of wooden staves hooped with metal, and with two ears or handles, sometimes with silver mountings or made entirely of silver, *now chf* ornamental *16-*.   [only Sc; Sc and IrGael *cuach* a cup, bowl]

quaick &c [kwek] *vi* quack, as a duck *16-*, *now Bnf Abd.* [imit. OED *quake*]

quaid *see* QUED

quaiet *see* QUATE

quaiff *see* QUEFF

quaik *see* QUAK

quailʒe &c [*'kweljɪ] *n* 1 = quail *16-17*.   2 ? the corncrake *la15*. [OED *quail*]

quair &c *n* 1 = quire *18-e19*.   2 a literary work of any length, *orig* one that might occupy a quire of paper *la15, 20-, latterly literary.*

quaird &c *n* a division of the INFIELD land on a farm, used for crop rotation *18*. [perh a var of eModEng *quart* a quarter, as sometimes the INFIELD was divided into four parts for manuring]

quaisteen *see* QUESTION

quak &c *now local*; quaik *15-16* [kwak] *v*, *pt also* quouk *la14-15*, qu(h)oik *16*, quuik *e16* [*kwøk] *vi* = quake *la14-*, *now local Sh-Wgt.*
~in-bog a quagmire *la19-*, *now Bnf-Wgt.*   ~in a(i)sh &c *la18-*, *now Abd Kcb*, ~in asp &c *18-19* the aspen. ~(k)in moss *la19-*, *now Cai*, ~(k)in qua *19-*, *Kcb* = quakin-bog, ~in trei = quakin a(i)sh, *20-*, *S.*

qual *see* TWAL

qualify &c ['kwalɪfi; *St* 'kwɔlɪfaɪ] *vti* 1 = qualify *la16-*.   2 *vt*, *law* establish by evidence, authenticate, testify *la16-*.   3 *vti* acquire or give legal sanction to by the taking or administration of an oath, *specif* in regard to the Scottish Episcopalians who until 1792 were not permitted to practise their faith until they renounced allegiance to the Jacobite monarchy; swear allegiance to *18*.   4 pass the *qualifying examination* for admission to secondary education *20*.
qualified = qualified *la16-*.   qualified chapel *etc* an Episcopalian Chapel etc whose members had renounced allegiance to the Jacobite monarchy *18*.   qualified oath *law* an oath upon *reference* (REFER) qualified by special limitations restricting it, which must be INTRINSIC to be valid *la18-e19*.   qualifying examination, *colloq* the quallie ['kwɔlɪ] an examination at the end of primary education which decided which type of secondary education pupils should have *20*; see SND. quallie ['kwɔlɪ] dance a party for pupils in their last year at primary school *20-*, *Edb.*

quality &c *16-*, qualitee *la15* ['kwalɪtɪ] *n* 1 = quality *la15-*.   2 *chf law* a proviso, qualification, reservation *17-18*.

quall *see* QUELL

quallie *see* QUALIFY

quantity &c; quantité *la14* ['kwantətɪ] *n* 1 = quantity *la14-*.   2 number, numbers *la14-16*.

quarnell &c [*'kwarnəl] *adj* square *e16*.
quernallit *e16*, quarnelt *e19* [*'kwɛrnəl(ɪ)t, *'kwarn-] squared; having corners. [only Sc; uncertain]

quarrel¹ &c; querell &c *16* ['kwarəl; *?'kwɛr-] *n* 1 a stone-quarry *16-*, *now Per SW*, *also in place-names.*   2 the stone etc taken from a quarry *16-*, *now N, only Sc.* [ME *quarer*, OF *quarriere* a quarry]

quarrel² &c; querel &c *15-17* ['kwarəl; *'kwɛr-] *v* 1 *vi* = quarrel.   2 *vt* dispute (a fact or claim), challenge the truth or validity of, take objection to *la16-19*.   3 find fault with (a person), reprove, rebuke *la16-*.
n = quarrel *15-*.

quarrente *see* WARRAND

quart [kwart] *n* **1** = quart *16-*. **2** a gallon, *chf* of wine, ale or oil *17-18* [because one *Scots pint* (SCOTS) was commonly said to be four English pints (see SND *pint*)]. **3** ? the fourth part of the great tithes *e17*.

quarten &c ['kwartən] *n* = quartern, a quarter (pint) *la18*.
~ **loaf** a quartern loaf, a four-pound loaf *la18-20*.

quarter &c ['kwartər; *St* 'kwɔrtər] *n* **1** = quarter *la14-*. **2** one of the areas, *orig* a fourth part, into which BURGHS and parishes were divided for administrative purposes, *esp* for poor relief and the distribution of ELDERS' duties; *latterly* a locality, district *16-*, *now Ork*. **3** *also* **corter** the fourth part of a round of *oatcakes* (AIT) *la18-*, *now NE*; cf FARL. **4** a quarter-pound *la19-*. **5** the fourth part of a year, *specif* referring to a school term or similar period of instruction *18-20*.
vt = quarter *16-*.
~**er** a poor person who is given temporary lodgings by way of charity *19-e20*. **quarterly** *adv, adj, n* = quarterly *la15-*. *n* an examination held at the end of a school term *18-20*.
~**land** a piece of land, *orig* assessed at a quarter of the DAVACH in the *Highlands* (HIELAND) and a quarter of a *husband-land* (HUSBAND) or of a *ploughgate* (PLEUCH) in the BORDERS *18-e19*.
~**man** a farm-worker who does miscellaneous jobs and errands *la19-*, *Loth.* ~ **master** an official in an *incorporated* (INCORPORATE) trade who looked after the affairs and probably collected the dues of a quarter or sub-division of the members *e18.* ~ **moon** the crescent moon *19-*, *local.* ~**-pennies** the sum of money contributed per quarter by each member of an *incorporated* trade etc *18-19.* ~ **seal** one of the seals of the Chancery of Scotland, still available for use but in practice no longer used, *orig* a quarter of the great seal *18-*. **Q~-sessions** *law* a court of review and appeal held quarterly by the Justices of the Peace on days appointed by statute *la17-19.* ~**-sponge** the first stage of bread-making in which a quarter of the water required has been used *20*.

quasi-delict ['kwezaɪ 'dilɪkt] *n*, *law* an act of negligence not motivated by criminal intent but making a person liable to an action for damages *19-*. [only Sc; L *quasi* almost + *delictum* an offence, a petty crime; *cf* DELICT]

quastion *see* QUESTION

quat &c; quate &c *la16-19*, **quett &c** *la17-20* [kwat, ʔkwɛt; *kwet] *v* **1** *vt* leave, forsake; give up *la16-*, *now local EC-Uls.* **2** require *la17.* **3** *vti* cease, desist, stop *la18-*, *now local.*
quattin time time to stop work, 'knocking-off time' *19-*, *now SW.* [only Sc; pt of QUIT]

quat *see* QUIT, WHAT¹

quate &c *18-*, **quiet &c; queat** *la16*, **quyit &c** *la16*, **quaiet &c** *la19-e20* ['kwe(ə)t; *EC*

kwəit] *adj* **1** = quiet. **2** secret, private *la16-*. **3** remote, peaceful *16.* **4** sheltered from the wind *la16.* **5** acting or living quietly; remaining secret; fast asleep *16-17.* **6** *of weather* windless, still, calm *la19-*.
adv quietly; stealthily *la19-*.
n = quiet *la14-*.
quietlike *adj, adv* quiet(ly) *la15-*, *only Sc.*
quate wi ye! *interj* be quiet! *la19-*.

quate *see* QUAT, QUIT

quatern [*ʔ'kwatərn] *n* a quire of paper *la16.* [F *quaterne*]

quatorziem &c [*ʔ'kwatorzɪəm] *n* = quatorzain, a fourteen-line piece of verse *e17.*

quatridual [*ʔkwa'trɪdjuəl] *adj* lasting for four days *e17.* [only Sc; stem of L *quatriduum* a period of four days + *-al*]

quatt *see* QUIT

quavyr &c [*'kwevər] *n*, *also* ~ **case** = quiver, a case for arrows *16.* [OED *quiver*]

quaw &c *15-*; **quaa** *la18-e19*, **qua &c** *19-20* [kwɑ; *Gall also* hwɑ] *n* a bog, quagmire, marsh *chf Gall.* [only Sc; see SND]

quay *see* COME

queak &c *vi* make a weak, squeaking noise, cheep *la19-*, *now Bnf Slk.* [only Sc; onomat]

quean *18-e20*, **coin** *la19-e20*, *Ags*; **qwen** *e15*, **queyn &c** *la15-e20*, **quine &c** *18-*, *now NE Ags* [*NE* kwəin, *Ags* kəin; *kwin; *nEC* *kwen] *n* **1** a young (*chf* unmarried) woman, a girl *15-*, *now NE Ags.* **2** a female child, a girl up to the end of her schooldays *19-*, *now NE Ags.* **3** a daughter *20-*, *NE Ags.* **4** a maidservant *19-*, *now NE.* **5** a female sweetheart, a lass *19-*, *now NE.* **6** *term of abuse* (1) a bold, impudent woman, hussy, slut *18-*, *now NE*; (2) a mistress, concubine *19-*.

quenry [*ʔ'kwɛn(ə)rɪ] associating with prostitutes *la16.* [ME *quene* a woman, a prostitute, OE *cwene*; *cf* QUEEN]

queat *see* QUATE

quech *see* QUAICH

qued *la19*, *only slang*; **quaid &c** *16*, **quad** *la16* *adj* vile, bad. [ME; *cf* MDu *quaed*]

queel *see* CUIL

queem *19-e20*, **queme &c** *la14-e20*; **quim** *18-e19 adj* **1** = queme, pleasing, agreeable *la14-e15.* **2** quiet, still *la14.* **3** close- or well-fitting, snug, neat; *fig* friendly, intimate *18-19.*
adv pleasingly, smoothly, calmly, neatly *la14-e16, 19.*
vi, also fig join or fit closely *e16, 19.*

quemfully [*ʔ'kwimfʌlɪ] pleasantly, agreeably; graciously *la14.*

queen *la18-*; **quene &c** *la14-16*, **quen** *la16* [kwin; *Sh Ork* hwin] *n* = queen *la14-*.
~**ist** a partisan of Mary, Queen of Scots *la16.*
Q~ Ann(e) a long-barrelled, large-bore flintlock musket *19-e20.* ~**'s chair** a method of carrying a girl seated on the crossed and joined arms of two bearers *20-*, *now Ork Abd Slk.* **Q~ Mary** a girls' ring dance accompanied by a

song beginning with these words *la19-*. **Q~ Street** informal name for The Mary Erskine School for Girls (*earlier* The Edinburgh Ladies' College), from 1871-1967 situated in Queen Street, Edinburgh *la19-20*; *cf* GEORGE SQUARE. **Queen's and Lord Treasurer's Remembrancer** the general administrator of Crown revenues in Scotland *19-*. **~ of (the) meadow** meadowsweet *19-*, *Gen except Sh Ork*. **The Queen's Own Cameron Highlanders** the name from 1881 of the regiment raised in 1793 as the *79th* or *Cameronian Volunteers* by Major Alan Cameron of Erracht, *later* (1806) known as the *79th* or *Cameron Highlanders* and in 1873 granted the title *79th Queen's Own Cameron Highlanders* by Queen Victoria *la19-20*. **Queen's Own Highlander** a soldier in the *Queen's Own Highlanders (Seaforth and Camerons) la20-*. **Queen's Own Highlanders (Seaforth and Camerons)** the regiment formed in 1961 by the amalgamation of the *Seaforth Highlanders* (SEAFORTH) and *The Queen's Own Cameron Highlanders, la20-*. **Q~ of the South** nickname for the town of Dumfries; official name for the Dumfries football team; *latterly* also the Dumfries schoolgirl chosen as the festival queen at the annual local *Riding of the Marches* (RIDE) *la19-*. [ultimately f the same Indo-European root as QUEAN]

queeple &c *vi* peep, quack in a squeaking high-pitched tone like a duckling *la19-*, *now Bnf Per*. [onomat; *cf wheeple* (WHEEP)]

queer &c *adj* **1** = queer *16-*. **2** amusing, funny, entertaining *la18-e19*. **3** considerable, very great *20-*.
~ways ['~wəiz, &c] *adv* in not quite a normal state, slightly unwell *19-*, *now Ork Kcb*. **~y** *adj* rather strange, oddish *la19-*, *Ags Per*. *n* an oddity, a queer thing or person *19-*, *now Ags Edb*.

queeriosity *see* QUERIOUS
queern *see* QUERN¹
queesitive *adj* = inquisitive *la19-20*, *local Sh-Per*.
queet *see* COOT, CUIT
queeth *see* CUITHE
queff *la20-*, *Abd*; **quaiff &c** *15-e17*, **kuafe** *e16* [kwef] *n* = coif, a close-fitting cap. [OED *coif*]
queff *see* QUAICH
queir &c *la14-20*; **quer** *la14* [kwir] *n* = choir, *chf* a chancel; *latterly* a pre-Reformation cruciform church or its ruin; *cf* KIRE.
queith [*kwið] *n* speech *e16*. [ME *quethe* a sound, cry. OED *quethe*]
quel *see* TWAL
quell &c *v* **1** *vt* = quell *la16-*. **2** knock **down**, strike *e16*. **3** *vi*, *only* **quall &c** [kwal], *of wind etc*, *also fig* abate, calm down *19-*, *now Abd*.
quelpe *see* WHALP
queme, quemfully *see* QUEEM
quen(e) *see* QUEEN

quenry *see* QUEAN
quent¹ *adj* acquainted *e16*, *only Sc*. [aphetic f *acquent* (ACQUANT¹); *cf* QUENTANCE]
quent² &c *adj* = quaint *16*.
adv skilfully, cunningly *la16*. [OED *quaint*]
quentance *15-17*; **quyntans** *la14* [*'kwɛntəns, *'kwɒint-] *n* = quaintance, acquaintance. [OED *quaintance*]
quer *see* QUEIR
queral *adj* = coral *e16*.
querche *see* CURCH
querel *see* QUARREL²
querell *see* QUARREL¹
quereour [*'kwɛrɪur] *n* = quarrier, a person who quarries stone *la14-15*. [only Sc. OED *quarrier* (*n*¹)]
querious [*'kwɪrɪəs] *adj* curious *e19*.
queeriosity [kwɪrɪ'ozɪtɪ] a curiosity, something strange *20-*, *NE Per*. [only Sc; conflation of Eng *queer* w *curious*]
quern¹ *now Sh Ork*; **queern &c** *now NE*, **quirn** *19-*, *now Cai* [kwɛrn; *NE* kwirn; *sense 2 NE also* kjurn] *n* **1** = quern *16-*. **2** *transf* the stomach of a fowl, the gizzard *19-*, *now NE*.
quern² &c *n*, *also fig* a granule, small seed etc *19-*, *now Mry Abd*.
~y &c *of honey, coarse sugar etc* granular, composed of small grains or particles, coarse to the tongue *la18-*, *now Bnf*. [perh a var of CURN¹]
quernallit *see* QUARNELL
querty &c *adj* vivacious, active, in good spirits; full of fun or mischief *la18-19*. [ME *quert* healthy, sound; *in quert* in good spirits]
question &c; quastion &c *la19-e20*, **quaisteen &c** *la19-e20*, **queystion** *la19-20* ['kwɛst(ɪ)ən; *Sh* 'hwɛst-, 'hwɪst-; *NE* 'kwəist-; *C* 'kwast-; *Bwk also* 'kwɛsən; *S also* 'kwɛstɪn] *n* **1** = question *la14-*. **2** a legal dispute, a litigation *la14*. **3** *Presbyterian Church, chf in pl* (the questions in) the *Shorter Catechism* (SHORT) of 1648, so called because it takes the form of a series of questions and answers on Calvinist doctrines *18-*, *only Sc*. **4** *elliptical, expressing doubt or wonder* I wonder, goodness knows .. *20-*, *Lnk Dmf Rox*: 'quaisteen if hei can finnd the road'.
question book a copy of the Catechism *18-19*.
questorie *n* = quaestorship *e16*, *only Sc*. [OED *quaestorship*]
quet *see* QUIT
quett *see* QUAT
quey &c *15-20*, **koy** *16-17*, **coy** *16-17*; **quoy** *16-18* [kwəi; *Ork also* kwoi; *Mry-Per also* k(w)oi; *sEC, WC, S also* kwaɪ] *n* a heifer *15-20*.
queyock &c [*Sh* hweg, hwek; *Ork Cai* 'kwəiək; *Ork also* kweg, 'kwoio; *Cai also* 'kwoiəg; *NE* 'kwe(ə)k] = prec *la15-20*. [ME *quy*; ON *kvíga*]
queyn *see* QUEAN
queystion *see* QUESTION
quha *see* WHA
quhaich *see* QUAICH
quhaik *see* WHEEK

quhaill *see* WHAAL
quhaip *see* WHAUP[1]
quhais *see* WHA
quhaitt *see* WHAT[1]
quhalm [*kwalm] *n* = qualm, loss, damage *e16*. [OED *qualm* (*n*[1])]
quhalp *see* WHALP
quham *see* WHA
quhane *see* WHAN
quhang *see* WHANG
quhap *see* WHAUP[1]
quhare *see* WHAR
quhasill *see* WEASEL
quhat *see* WHAT[1]
quhattin *see* WHATTEN
quhawm *see* WHAM[1]
quhay *see* WHA
quhaye *see* WHEY
quhedir *see* WHETHER, WHIDDER
quheil *see* WHEEL
quheiss [*hwis] *n* a blow with something pliant, a lash *la16*. [onomat. OED *whiss*]
quheit *see* WHEET[2]
quhel *see* WHEEL, WHILE
quhelk *see* WHILK[2]
quhell *see* WHAAL
quhelm [hwɛlm] *vt* = whelm, overturn; *of fortune* turn (its wheel) downwards *15-16*. [OED *whelm*]
quhelpe *see* WHALP
quhem *see* WHA
quhemle *see* WHUMMLE
quhen *see* WHAN, WHEEN
quhence &c *adv, conj* = whence *16*. [OED *whence*]
quhene *see* WHAN, WHEEN
quhere *see* WHAR
quherle *see* WHIRL
quhete *see* WHAT[2], WHITE[3]
quhether *see* WHITHER
quhethir *see* WHETHER, WHIDDER
quhew(e) [*hwju] *n* = whew, a whistling sound *16*.
interj whew! *15*. [OED *whew*]
quheyn(e) *see* WHEEN
quheythir *see* WHETHER
quhich *see* WHILK[2]
quhidder *see* WHETHER, WHIDDER, WHITHER
quhile *see* WHILE, WILE[1]
quhilis *see* WHILES
quhilk *see* WHILK[2]
quhill *see* WHILE
quhillylillie [*'hwɪlɪ'lɪlɪ] *n, familiar* the penis *e16*. [unknown]
quhilom *see* WHILOM
quhingar *see* WHINGER
quhinge *see* WHINGE
quhinne *see* WHIN[2]
quhinȝear *see* WHINGER
quhip *see* WHIP
quhirll *see* WHIRL
quhirre *see* WHIRR

quhisch *see* WHUSH
quhisk *see* WHISK
quhisper *see* WHUSPER
quhissel *see* WISSEL
quhistle *see* WHISTLE
quhit *see* WHEET[2]
quhit- *see* WHAT[2]
quhit(e) *see* WHITE[1]
quhite *see* WHITE[2], WHITE[3]
quhither *see* WHETHER
quhiting *see* WHITIN
quhitrat, quhitred, quhitret *see* WHITRAT
quhittil *see* WHITTLE[1]
quhittine *see* WHITIN
quhittour *see* WHITTER[4]
quho *see* WHA
quhoik *see* QUAK
quholl *see* HAIL[1]
quholpe *see* WHALP
quhome *see* WHA
quhomle *see* WHUMMLE
quhon &c *la14*; **quhoyne &c** *la14-e16* [*hwøn] *n, adj* (a) few. [nME *whon*, OE *hwōn; cf* WHEEN. OED *whon*]
quhone *see* WHAN
quhorle *see* WHURL
quhose, quhoum *see* WHA
quhow *see* HOO[1]
quhoyne *see* QUHON
quhryne *see* WHRYNE
quhuir- *see* WHIRR
quhy *see* WHY
quhyd *see* WHID[1]
quhymper *see* WHIMPER
quhyn *vi* = whine *16*.
quhyn *see* WHIN[1]
quhyne &c [*hwəin] *adv* whence *la14-e16*. [nME *quein &c*; contraction of ME *whethen*. OED *whyne*]
quhyt *see* QUITE, WYTE
quich *see* WHILK[2]
quick &c *adj* **1** = quick *la14-*. **2** (1) living, alive *15-19*. (2) swarming, infested *20-*, *Sh Ork Uls*.
~**enin &c** yeast, any fermenting agent *18-e19*. ~ **moss** moss which trembles or in which a person can sink *la18-e19*. ~ **water** the current (of a river), running water *20-*, *Gall Slk*.
quicken &c ['kwɪkən; *Bwk Rox also* 'hwɪkən] *n, chf in pl* couch grass *la17-, now EC, SW*. [nME *cuik*, OE *cwice*, f *cwic* quick, full of vitality]
quickenin *see* QUICK
quid *see* CAN[2], COOD[1], COOD[2]
quidder *adv* **quick and** ~ alive and full of vigour *e17*.
quiet *see* QUATE
quietie &c, quieté [*'kwaɪətɪ] *n* quietness *la15-e16*. [only Sc; OF *quieté*. OED *quiety*]
quigger *see* KEEGER
quigrich &c *la18-e20*; **coygerach** *la19-e20* ['kwɪgrɪx, 'koigrəx] *n* the name given to the pastoral staff of St Fillan. [Gael *coigreach* a

stranger, foreigner; so called because it was carried to distant places for the recovery of stolen property]

quile &c *19-*; **quoil &c** *la17-20*, **kyle** *19-20*, **coil &c** *la17-e20* [koil; *C, S also* kəil; *local Ags-Kcb also* kwəil; *WC Dmf also* kwoil] *n* the small heap into which hay is gathered after being cut *la18-, now WC Gall.*

vt rake (hay) into such heaps *17-, now WC Gall.* [appar vars of Eng *coil (n)* a spiral mass, *(v)* gather into such a heap; OF *coillir* gather; *cf* COLE]

quile *see* COAL

quilpe *see* WHALP

quim *see* QUEEM

quin *vt* study, learn *la16.* [var of Eng *con*]

quine *see* QUEAN

quinie *see* CUNYIE

quink &c *n, now chf* ~ **goose** the brent goose or the greylag goose *la16-, now Ork.* [only Sc; perh imit; *cf* Norw dial *kvinka*, ON *kveinka* whine, wail]

quinkill &c *v, of a light* go out *e16.* [only Sc; appar OE *cwincan*; *cf* Eng *quench.* OED *quinkle*]

quinkins &c *n pl* **1** dregs or leavings of any kind, scum of a liquid, charred traces of food stuck to the saucepan *19-, now Ags.* **2** a worthless trifle *19-, now Abd Kcdn.* [only Sc; uncertain]

quinquene *see* KINKEN

quinter *see* TWINTER

quintis [*?'kwəintɪs] *n* = quaintise, a badge, heraldic device *la14.*

quintra *see* COUNTRA

quintuply [*'kwɪntəplaɪ, *'kwɪntju-] *law, n* a fifth answer, made by the *pursuer* (PURSUE) in reply to the *defender's* (DEFEND) QUADRUPLY *la17-e19.*

vi answer in a QUINTUPLY *17-18.* [formed on L *quintus* etc by analogy w QUADRUPLY etc]

quinȝie, quinzie *see* CUNYIE

quirk *n* **1** = quirk. **2** a riddle, catch question, an arithmetical problem *20-, Sh Abd Ags.*

vt trick, fox, get the better of, cheat *la18-, now NE Ags.*

~**y &c 1** intricate, twisted, complicated *la19-, now Bnf Abd Ags Kcb.* **2** cunning, resourceful, tricky *19-, now Bnf Abd Ags Kcb.*

quirn *see* QUERN[1]

quirre *see* WHIRR

quisquous &c [*'kwɪsk(w)əs] *adj* perplexing, doubtful, debatable, dubious *la17-19.* [only Sc; perh f L *quisquis* whoever, whatever, *ie* uncertain, undefined]

quit &c; **quite &c** *la15-, now Ork* [kwɪt; *Sh* hwɛt; *Ork* kwəit] *v, pt* **quat** *la16-e20*, **quate** *la18-, now Abd Per* [kwat, kwet]. *ptp* **quet** *15*, **quyite** *16*, **quat(t)** *la19-* [kwat; *kwɛt, *kwəit] **1** *vtir* = quit *la14-.* **2** *vi or vt, with verbal noun* cease, give up, stop *19-, now local:* 'he quat drinkin'. **3** *vt* free, exonerate, acquit *19.*

adj **1** *also* **quat** *18-* [kwat] = quit, free *la14-.* **2** destitute, deprived **of** *la16.*

quittance 1 = quittance, release, acquittal *la14-e17.* **2** the discharge of a debt etc, a receipt, payment; *also fig* an account, a valid explanation *la18-, now Sh WC.*

make quit (of) do away with, dispose of; make a clearance *la15-e16, only Sc.* [see also QUAT]

quite &c; **quhyt** *la14-15* [kwəit] *adv* **1** = quite *la14-.* **2** *followed by adj or adv* completely, totally, absolutely *la14-.*

quite *see* COAT, QUIT

quither *see* WHETHER

quittance *see* QUIT

quitter, quittour *see* WHITTER[4]

quo &c *18-e20*, **co &c** *la18-e20, chf N*; **quod** *la15-18* [k(w)o; *kwod] *v, pt* **1** = quoth. **2** *only* **quod** used at the end of a piece of writing to introduce the name of the author *16-18, chf Sc.*

quoad omnia ['kwoad, 'kwɔd 'ɔmnɪə] **1** applied to a parish which combined secular as well as ecclesiastical functions *19-.* **2** *of a church constitution* in which the *kirk session* (KIRK) is responsible for all matters and which does not allocate secular functions to a congregational board *19-.* [L = as regards all matters]

quoad sacra ['kwoad, 'kwɔd 'sakrə] applied to a parish which functions for religious purposes only, created by statute because the existing parish became too large for a single MINISTER; the original parish remained the unit for civil administration until such matters were transferred to other local government bodies *18-.* [L = as regards sacred matters]

quoad ultra ['kwoad 'ʌltrə] *law* used in the written pleadings of an action to indicate the point beyond which the *defender* (DEFEND) makes no further admission of the *pursuer's* (PURSUE) allegations *la19-.* [L = as regards the rest]

quod *see* QUO

quoik *see* QUAK

quoil *see* QUILE

quoit &c *19-e20, chf SW*, **coit** *19-e20, Ags*; **cute** *19-e20, WC* [k(w)oit, k(w)oit; ?kjut] *vi* play at the game of *curling* (CURL), play a *curling stone, 19-e20.*

n, also ~**in(g) stane** a *curling stone* (CURL) *19, chf SW.* [*cf* Eng]

quoniam attachiamenta ['kwonɪəm ə'ta(t)ʃɪəmɛntə] *n, law* name given, from its opening words, to an ancient (now thought to be late 14th century) work of Scots Law *18-, hist.* [only Sc; MedL = since arrestments ..]

quorum &c *17-*, **coarum** *20-, NE n* **1** = quorum *17-.* **2** a gathering, *esp* of friends for social purposes, a company *la18-, NE.* [*cf* CORAM]

quoss *see* COSE

quot &c *la16-e18*, **cote &c** *16-e17*, **cot &c**

16-e17 *n* the share (one twentieth) of the MOVE-
ABLE estate of a deceased person due to the
bishop of his diocese. [OF *cote, quote,* L *quota*
(*pars*) how great a part.   OED *quote* (*n¹*)]

quotation &c *n* **1** = quotation.   **2** a numbering, number *la15.*

quote &c *vt* = quote *la16-.*

~ **a paper** *law* endorse the title of a paper *la18.*

quouk *see* QUAK

quow *see* COO

quoy *see* QUEY

quuik *see* QUAK

quyin *see* WHIN²

quyit *see* QUATE

quyite *see* QUIT

quyntans *see* QUENTANCE

quyschile *see* WHISTLE

quysson *see* WHITSUN

qware *see* WHAR

qwen *see* QUEAN, WHAN

qwet *see* WHITE³

qwhayne *see* WHEEN

qwhyssonday *see* WHITSUNDAY

qwilke *see* WHILK²

qwistle *see* WHISTLE

qwyl *see* WHILE

qwylum *see* WHILOM

qwyssonday *see* WHITSUNDAY

R

ra *see* RAE[1], RAE[2], RAW[2]

raan [rɑn] *n* a disease of turnips *la20-*, NE Kcb. **~ed** affected with RAAN *la20-*, NE Kcb. [perh fig f RAWN, f a supposed similarity in appearance]

raan *see* RAWN

raaz *see* RAZE

Rab *see* ROB

rabat &c *la16*, **rebat &c** *17* [*'rabat] *n* a kind of collar. [only Sc; F = a turned-down collar; cf Eng *rebato* a kind of stiff collar]

rabbet *see* RYBAT

rabbit *n* = rabbit. **~'s sugar** *child's word* the seeds of the common sorrel *20-*, Mry Bnf. **~ thissle** the common annual sow-thistle *20-*, midLoth S.

rabblach, rabble *see* RAIBLE

rabel *see* REBEL

rabiator &c *18-e20*; **rubeatour &c** *16* [rubɪ'atər; *ra-; *rʌbɪ'etur] *n* a scoundrel, villain; a violent, ruthless person; a lout, boor. [only Sc; see SND. OED *rubiator*]

rabut *see* REBUT

raccunys *see* RECOGNIZE

race[1] **&c** *n* **1** = race *la14-*. **2** a run, journey at speed; a flying visit; the act of running; a short run before jumping *la14-*. **3** a shock, blow *e16*. **4** a passage along a wall where sheep are graded or separated *la20-*, local Bnf-midLoth. *vti* = race, run. **~r** nickname for a loose woman *la18*. **rew a** *etc* **~** repent of the course one has taken *la15-16*.

race[2] *n* **1** = race (of people) *16-*. **2** a set (of articles used together) *19-*, NE.

rachan *see* RAUCHAN

rachle *see* RAUCHLE, RAUCLE

rach-ma-reeshil &c ['raxmə'riʃl, 'rak-] *adj* confused, mixed-up, higgledy-piggledy *19-*, now Per Fif. [first element uncertain; for second element ? cf *reeshle* (REESLE)]

racht *see* RECK

rack[1] *n* **1** = rack, a frame. **2** *specif* a framework of spars on a wall for holding crockery and cutlery *19-*. **3** *in pl, also* **rax**, *sometimes understood as sing with double pl* **raxes** a set of bars to support a roasting spit *16-e19*.

rack[2] **&c** *v* **1** *vt* = rack, stretch *17-*. **2** *vti* stretch, pull, increase in length *16-*, now local nEC-S, chf Sc. **3** *vi* reach, extend *la19-*, Lnk SW, S. **4** *vti* stretch (the neck); hang, be hanged *19*. **5** *vt* wrench, dislocate, twist *16-*, local. **6** *vi, fig* worry needlessly, be over-anxious *20-*, Kcb Rox. **7** *vt* tie the latch of (a door) so that it will not open *la19-*, now Per.
n **1** = rack, an instrument of torture *17-*. **2** a sprain, wrench, dislocation *la18-*, Gen except Sh Ork. **3** a frame for stretching wet cloth in the process of fulling *19-*, now Ags Slk. **4** a stretch or reach of a river *17-*, now Ags, only Sc; cf RAIK *n* 5. **5** a ford in a river, a ridge of gravel or a shallow place *la17-*, now Kcb Dmf, only Sc. **6** a path, track *la20-*, chf Ags [perh var of RAIK]. **7** *curling* (CURL) = RINK *n* 5, 6, *la18-e20*, WC.
~ ban &c *or* **chain** the chain connecting the bridle of a plough with the swingletree *la19-*, NE Kcb. **~ pin** a stick used to tighten a rope or chain, *eg* on a loaded cart *19-*, now local Per-Lnk. **~ sauch** a gallowsbird *e16*, only Sc. **~ stick** = **~ pin**, *19-e20*. **tak owre (the) ~ stock** take severely to task *la19-e20*, Bnf Abd. **~ strap** = *fit fang* (FIT[1]) *20-*, Bnf Abd.

rack[3] **&c** *n* **1** a heavy blow, a crash, shock *15-19*. **2** a rush (of wind) *e16*. **3** driving mist or fog *16-*, now local Mry midLoth. *vi* **1** *of a gun* go off, fire *e16*. **2** *of clouds* fly before the wind, clear away *e19*. **~abimus** [*?rakə'bɪməs] a sudden jolt or fall *e19*, Ags. **~ing** *of clouds* flying before the wind; *of wind* driving *19-*, now Per Slk. **~ up** *of weather* clear *19-*, now local Per-Rox. [ME; cf Norw dial *rak* wreckage, refuse, cognate w WRACK[1] *n* 1]

rack[4] *n* a stay, strut *la20-*, local Mry-midLoth. [perh extended f RACK[1] or RACK[2]]

rack *see* WRACK[1]

rackabimus *see* RACK[3]

racket[1] **&c** *n* **1** = racket, a bat; *in pl* the game *16-*. **2** a violent stunning blow, a thump, stroke *18-*, now Sh.

racket[2] *n* = rocket, a firework; a missile *19-e20*. [cf F *raquette*, Du *raket*]

rackle &c *n* **1** *also* **reckle** *e17* a chain *17-e20*. **2** *specif* a small chain on a pipe stem, attaching the lid and a pin for clearing out the pipe *la19-*, now Abd. **3** the rattling, jingling noise made by a chain *la19-*, now Mry Ags. *vi* rattle, clank *e16*, *la19*. [see SND. OED *reckle*]

rackle *see* RAUCLE

rackless *see* RECK

rackon &c *now NE Fif*, **reckon &c** *v* **1** *vt* = reckon *la14-*. **2** enumerate, mention one after another *la15-e16*. **3** repeat, recite *16-e17*. **4** *vi* name things in order *la15-e16*. **~ing &c 1** = reckoning *la14-*. **2** mode of numbering *la14*.

racord *see* RECORD

rad &c; **red &c** *la14-18*, **rede &c** *la18-e19* *adj* frightened, afraid, alarmed *la14-e20*. **~our &c** fear, terror *la14-e16*, only Sc. [ME *rad*, ON *hræddr*]

rad *see* REDD[3]

radde *see* RAID

rade *see* REDD[1], RIDE

rademe &c [rə'dim] *v* **1** *vt* = redeem *la15*. **2** rescue, deliver *la15-16*. **3** *vi* return **to** (a state) *la15*. *n* the act of redeeming *la15*, only Sc. [OED *redeem*]

radge *adj* **1** *also* **radgie** mad, violently excited, furious, wild *la19-*. **2** sexually excited *20-*, *Gen except Sh Ork*. **3** silly, weak-minded *20*.
n a loose-living woman *20-*, *local Abd S*. [see SND]

radical &c *n* **1** = radical. **2** a wild, unruly person, a rogue, rascal *19-*, *now Sh Bnf Abd*.
~ **right** *law* the ultimate proprietary right of a *truster* (TRUST) which survives if the fulfilment of the trust purposes does not exhaust the whole estate *19-*.

radical *see* RETICULE

radicate *ptp* rooted *la15*. [L *rādīcāt-*, ptp stem of *rādīcāre* take root]

radote [*ra'dot] *vi* mutter disconnectedly *la16*. [only Sc; F *radoter*]

radoun *see* REDOUND

radres *see* REDRESS

rady *see* READY

rae¹ &c *16-*; **ra &c** *la14-16* [re] *n* = roe, the deer *la14-*, *now Ayr Slk*.
roebuck berry the fruit of the stone bramble *la18-19*. [OED *roe¹*]

rae² &c *la16-*, **ra** *la15-16* [re] *n* a sailyard *la15-*, *now Sh*.
~**band** the rope attaching the sail to the yard *16-*, *now Sh Cai*. [only Sc; MDu *ra(e)*, ON *rá*]

raeffle *see* RAIVEL

rael &c *19-*, **real** [rel; *St* 'ri(ə)l] *adj* **1** = real *la17-*. **2** *of character* honest, forthright, genuine *19-*, *now Sh Ags Wgt*.
adv, as intensifier very, extremely *19-*.

rael *see* RAIVEL

raem, raemikle *see* REAM

raep [rep] *vti* = reap *la16-*, *now Sh Ork Bnf nEC*. [OED *reap*]

raff¹; **raft** *la19-*, *SW n* **1** plenty, abundance; a large number *la18-*, *now Bnf Abd Kcb*. **2** rank growth *19-*, *now Bnf*.
raffie &c 1 abundant, generous, well-supplied *la19-*, *NE*. **2** *of crops, animals etc* thriving, flourishing *20-*, *now Abd*. [appar f Eng *riff and raff* one and all]

raff² *n* a short sharp shower, accompanied by gusts of wind *la18-*, *now Abd*. [perh onomat]

raff³ *vi, chf* **raffin &c** roistering, merry, boisterously hearty *18-*, *now Per*. [perh extended f RAFF¹]

raffell &c ['rafl] *n* ? some kind of animal skin *la15-e16*. [obscure]

raffle *see* RAIVEL

rafreyn *see* REFRAIN

raft *n* a rafter *la16-20*. [ME; ON *raptr*]

raft *see* RAFF¹

rag¹ &c *n* **1** = rag *la14-*. **2** a rough projection on a surface, *eg* after sawing, filing *la20-*. **3** a lean, scraggy animal or fish *la19-*, *local Sh-Dmf*. **4** the poorest pig in a litter *la20-*, *SW, S*. **5** a partial winnowing of corn *la18-19*.
v **1** *vt* winnow partially *19*. **2** *vi, of oats* reach the stage of growth where the grain begins to appear *e19*, *SW*.

~**ger** a person who collects rags *20-*, *N*. ~**gety &c** = ~**git**, *la19-*, *only Sc*. ~**gie &c** *adj* ragged *19-*, *local*. *n* a (diseased) salmon *la19-*, *Bwk S*.
~**gie biscuit** a locally-made biscuit with an uneven edge *la20-*, *Per Fif*. ~**git &c 1** = ragged *la15-*. **2** *of persons* wearing ragged clothes *la14-*. ~**gle &c** make an uneven or ragged cut in, cut jaggedly *la17-*, *now Sh Ayr*.
~**glish &c** erratic; *of weather* uncertain, gusty with rain; *of persons* wild, unreliable *19-*, *NE*.
~ **fauch &c** *or* **fallow** a system of fallowing land by ploughing in the old crop of hay or grass in summer and ploughing once or twice again with manure, before preparing for autumn sowing of wheat *la18-19*. ~**-footed** *fig* ill thought out *e17*. ~**nail** a loose piece of skin or broken nail at the side of a fingernail, a hangnail *la19-*, *local*. ~ **pock** a bag for holding rags *la19-*, *local*. ~**weed** the ragwort *la18-*, *now local NE-Uls*.
lose one's *or* **the** ~ lose one's temper *20-*.

rag² *vt* scold, reproach severely *19-*, *now local Bnf-Uls*.
hae a ~ **oot o** enjoy a joke at the expense of, get a laugh out of *la19-*, *local*. **tak the** ~ **o** make fun of, make a fool of *20-*, *local Sh-SW*. [Eng dial; obscure; *cf* Eng *rag* a piece of horseplay]

rag³ &c; **raggle &c** *la20-*, *Abd n* a wet mist, drizzle *20-*, *Sh Ork Abd*. [Scand; *cf* Sw dial *ragg(a)* (*v, n*), Icel *hragla* (*v*) drizzle]

rag⁴ *n* a whetstone *la19-*, *now Fif Edb Rox*. [Eng = a kind of hard stone]

rag⁵ *vi, of a wall* develop cracks and bulges, come out of alignment *18-e19*, *Renfr*. [perh var of RACK² *n* 2, or extended f Eng *rag*]

ragabash &c; **ragabrash** *la19-e20*, *SW* ['ragəb(r)aʃ, &c] *n* **1** a good-for-nothing, a ragamuffin *18-19*. **2** *collective* a ragged, motley crew, riff-raff *19-*, *now Ayr*.
adj rough, uncouth; good-for-nothing *e19*, *chf S*. [eModEng; perh f Eng *rag*]

rage &c *n* = rage *la14-*.
vti **1** = rage *16-*. **2** ~ (**at** *or* **on**) scold, berate *19-*, *Gen except Sh Ork*.
raging a scolding *la20-*, *Gen except Sh Ork*.

raggety *see* RAG¹

raggle¹ &c *vti* **1** *masonry* (*latterly also carpentry*) cut a groove in stone (or wood) to receive another stone etc, *eg* in the steps of a stair, the edge of a roof *16-*. **2** *mining* cut into the coal-face *la19-*, *now Fif midLoth*.
n the groove cut in stone or wood as in *v* 1, *19-*.
raglet &c ['raglət] *masonry* = *n*, *19-20*.
rag(g)lin &c = *n*; *specif, freq in pl* the space for the edges of the slates under the coping-stones of a gable *16-*. [*cf* laME and eModEng *regyll*, *regall* a groove, slot, OF *rigole* a narrow channel, MDu *regel* a straight line, L *rēgula* a straight piece of wood; the Sc vowel is difficult to account for]

raggle² *n* straggling order *la16*, *only Sc*.

raggle³ *vi*, *n* wrangle, dispute *19-*, *now Abd.*
[perh conflation of ModEng *wrangle* w *haggle*; *cf* also RAG²]
raggle *see* RAG¹, RAG³
ragglin *see* RAGGLE¹
ragglish *see* RAG¹
raghter &c *n* = rafter *15-20.*
raglet, raglin *see* RAGGLE¹
ragman &c *n* 1 = ragman, a document; *specif* that by which the Scottish nobles acknowledged Edward I as their overlord in 1291, returned by Edward III in 1328, *la14-e15.* 2 *only* **ragment** a legal agreement *la15-e16.* 3 *only* **ragment** a long rambling discourse *16*, *only Sc.*
rahatour *see* REHATOR
rahers *see* REHEARSE
raible &c *la18-e20*, **rabble &c**, **reeble &c** *la19* *n* 1 = rabble *16-.* 2 a disorderly outpouring of words or noises, a rigmarole; nonsensical talk *17-*, *now local.* 3 a carelessly erected building etc, something ruinous or dilapidated *la19-*, *now Sh Bnf.*
v 1 *vt* mob, assault with overwhelming numbers (*specif* an Episcopalian clergyman by a hostile Presbyterian congregation, after the Revolution settlement of 1688-89) *la17-*, *now hist.* 2 *vti* utter (a torrent of words), speak or read hastily and indistinctly *la18-*, *now Sh Ayr.*
rabblach = *n*, *la19-20.*
raiche *see* RASH¹
raid &c; radde *e17*, **reid &c** *la15-17* [red; **rid*] *n* 1 (1) a foray or predatory expedition on horseback *15-.* (2) *more gen* a sudden or surprise attack *19-* [introduced into Eng via Scott]. (3) *ironic* an outing, jaunt *e19.* 2 a roadstead for ships *15-e20* [perh partly f Du *reede* or F *rade*; *cf* REID²]. [Sc form of OE *rād* a riding, a mounted foray > Eng *road*]
raid *see* REDD²
raif *see* RAVE¹
raiffell *vi* meaning unknown *e16.* [? nEng dial *raffle* lounge about]
raik &c; reck &c *18-e20* [rek] *v* 1 *vi* move, go forward, *esp* with speed *la14-*, *now Ayr.* 2 journey, go, *later usu* implying unnecessary effort; walk, stroll; gad about, rove *la16-.* 3 *of grazing animals* spread out in a line, straggle *la15-e20.* 4 *vt* pursue (one's way) *e15.* 5 range over, wander through *18-*, *local Sh-Kcb.* 6 *vi* work energetically and speedily *la19-*, *Bnf.*
n 1 the act of going; a journey; a long or tiring walk; a stroll *15-*, *now local.* 2 (1) a journey, *esp* one to or fro for a specified purpose, *eg* to fetch a load, a trip, run *17-*, *Cai Bnf C, S.* (2) (a) as much as can be carried in one load *la18-*, *now local Cai-S.* (b) *specif mining* a train of loaded HUTCHES *la19-*, *local Stlg-Lnk.* (3) *of food* a spoonful; a helping *20.* 3 speed, pace, rate *la18-*, *now Slk.* 4 a cattle- or sheep-walk, a pasture *15-*, *now nEC.* 5 a stretch of river used for

salmon-fishing *la14-e19*; *cf* RACK² *n* 4. 6 a roving person or animal, *esp* a person who wanders about in search of gossip or entertainment *19-*, *local.*
~er a vagabond *la16.* [ON *reik(a)* (*n*, *v*) walk, stroll, *rák* a streak, path, OE *racian* run, rush]
raik *see* REAK, RECK
rail¹ **&c** *n* 1 = rail. 2 a row of protective studs in the sole of a boot or shoe *la18-19.*
vt 1 *only* **ralye** [*reljɪ] = rail, set in order, adorn *e16.* 2 (1) = rail, provide with rails. (2) *specif* fit (a stair) with a handrail *la19-*, *now Abd.*
~ing &c 1 = railing *19-.* 2 a handrail *la19-.*
~ stair a stair with a *railing* 2, *la16-*, *now Abd Lnk.*
rail² *n*, *also* **raillie &c** a woman's short-sleeved front- or over-bodice, worn on dress occasions *18-19.* [ME *raile* a kind of neck-cloth, OE *hrægel* a garment, mantle]
railya [*reljɪ] *adj* striped, decorated to give a striped effect *e16.* [only Sc; OF *reillié*]
railyet *n* ? a band, ribbon *la16.* [only Sc; *cf* prec]
raing *la18-e19*, **rang** *la15-16* [*raŋ, *reŋ] *n* a range, rank, row. [only Sc; F *rang*]
raing *see* RING¹
raip &c, rope *17-* *n* 1 = rope *la14-.* 2 *specif agric* a straw or hay rope *19-.* 3 a clothes-line *19-.* 4 the ropes securing thatch on a roof or, most *freq*, on a corn-rick *la18-*, *Gen except Sh Ork*; see also *thack and raip* (THACK¹). 5 a straw band for a sheaf of corn *19-*, *now NE Loth Rox.*
vt 1 = rope. 2 *specif* secure the thatch of (a corn-rick) with a network of (straw) ropes *la19-*, *local.*
raperee [?*repərɪ*] a ropery, ropeworks *19-20.*
~fu &c 1 what a rope can hold *19-*, *now Sh.* 2 *fig* a gallowsbird *la16*, *la19.*
a thraw *or* **a whaup in the ~** a snag, drawback, unforeseen difficulty *17-e20.* **trail the ~** bring bad luck by twisting a straw rope and pulling it round anticlockwise *la19*, *NE.*
raip *see* RIP¹
rair &c, roar &c *la16-* *vti* 1 = roar *la14-.* 2 *vi*, *of animals or birds* not thought of as roaring call loudly *16-e20.* 3 CRY (*v* 3 and *cry in*), summon with a loud shout; pay a flying visit *la19-*, *now Sh EC.* 4 *of cracking ice etc* make a resounding, cracking noise *la18-e19.* 5 *curling* (CURL), *of a stone* make a roaring noise as it moves rapidly on the ice *19-*, *local Per-Gall.* 6 weep, cry, *usu*, but not necessarily, loudly, *freq* **roar and greet** *18-.*
n 1 = roar *15-.* 2 a call, as to a neighbour in passing, a doorstep visit *20-*, *local nEC-Lnk.* 3 a loud report; a belch *19-*, *now Ags Abd.*
roarie &c 1 loud, noisy, roaring *20-*, *now Sh Ork Ags Kcb.* 2 drunk *la19-*, *now Sh Per Gsw.* 3 *of colours* bright, showy; *now chf* glaring, garish, loud *la19-*, *Gen except NE.* **~ing buckie** a kind of whelk shell which when held to the ear

makes a roaring sound thought to sound like the sea *19-*, *now Ags Fif*. **~ing game** the game of *curling* (CURL) *la19-*.

raird *see* REIRD

raise &c; rease &c *la16-18* [rez] *vt* **1** = raise *la14-*. **2** *law* draw up (a summons, LETTER etc), bring, institute (an action) *15-*. **3** *curling* (CURL) strike and move forward (another stone of one's own side) towards the TEE[1] *19-e20*. **4** arouse, rouse from sleep *15-*, *now local Sh-Kcb*. **5** infuriate, enrage, drive into a frenzy *la18-*, *now Sh-N, SW, S*.

n a state of extreme bad temper, a frenzy *la19-*, *Ags-Stlg*.

~d &c infuriated, wild, over-excited *la16-*.
raiser *law* the holder of the disputed property in a MULTIPLEPOINDING, called the **nominal raiser** when a claimant initiates proceedings or the **real raiser** when the holder himself initiates *19-*.

~ net a fixed fishing net which rises and falls with the level of the tide *la16-e19*, *Dmf*.

~ on turn on in anger, attack *19-*, *local NE-Ayr*.

raise *see* RISE

raisin &c *n* = raisin *15-*.

~ kail: BROTH[1] with raisins added, a traditional dish at weddings *19*. **~ Monday** *St Andrews Univ* a Monday in the winter term when senior students formerly demanded of first-year students a pound of raisins in return for their protection *la19-*.

raison *see* RIZZON

raith &c; rath *la14*, **reath &c** *la18-19* [reθ] *n* **1** a quarter of a year; a period of three months *la14*, *la18-20*. **2** *specif* a term at school, three months of full-time education *19-e20*. [chf Sc; ScGael *ràithe*, OIr *rá(i)the*]

raither &c *la19-*, **rather &c; rether** *16*, *la19-*, *now Cai*, **redder** *20-*, *Sh NE* ['reðər; *Sh NE* rɛðər; *Cai NE Fif* rɛðər] *adv* = rather *15-*.

~ly rather *19-*, *now Cai*.

raivel &c *19-*, **ravel; reavel &c** *la18-e20*, **raffle &c** *20-*, *Ork*, **raeffle** *la19*, *Sh*, **rael &c** *19-e20*, **rile &c** *19-*, *SW*, **reul &c** *19-e20*, **rowl** *20-*, *Per* ['revl; *Sh also* 'refl; *Ork also* 'rafl; *Per* rʌul; *SW, S* rəil, rjul; **rel*] *vti* **1** *in gen and specif of thread, yarn etc, also fig* get into a tangle or confusion; muddle, disorder *la16-20*. **2** *vi, of thread or yarn* unwind itself from a reel *la18-20*. **3** speak incoherently, ramble, be delirious *la19-*, *now NE nEC Lnk*. **4** *vt* confuse, perplex, make incapable of coherent thought *la19-*, *Gen except Sh Ork*. **5** bamboozle, outwit *20-*, *Sh Ork Mry*.

n **1** a muddle, tangle, confusion *la19-*. **2** a broken or frayed thread, a loose end *19-*, *now Ags Uls*.

~ed &c 1 tangled, confused, in difficulties *19-*. **2** *of hair* dishevelled, unkempt *20-*, *NE, EC, SW*. **3** confused in mind; rambling, delirious *la19-*,

Gen except Sh Ork. **~ed hesp, pirn** *etc* a knotty problem, a state of confusion *18-*, *now local Ork-Lnk*. **ravelment** a confusion, tangle *e19*.

reavel-ravel *la17*, **revill-raill** *la15* [**'rivl-'revl, *-'rel*] a rigmarole; cf *reel-rall* (REEL[1]). [Du *ravelen, rafelen* tangle, fray out; *cf* Eng *ravel* unravel, disentangle]

rajose &c *vti* = rejoice *la15-e16*.

rak *see* RECK

rake &c *vti* **1** = rake; *specif* rake together stalks of corn left behind on a harvested field *19-*. **2** *vt* turn over and smooth out (seaweed) in the last stages of kelp-burning *la19-*, *now Sh Ork*. **3** bank up, cover (a fire) with small coal, ashes etc so that it will smoulder all night *16-*, *now Ork C*. **4** search (a person) *la20-*, *Bnf C Slk*. **5** *also* **rauk &c** rub (the eyes); scratch *18-*, *now Sh Abd, only Sc*.

n **1** = rake *la15-*. **2** an accumulation, hoard, what has been gathered together *la19-*, *NE nEC*. **3** a grasping, hoarding person *20-*. **4** a very thin person *19-*. **5** *only* **rauk &c** a scratch, groove, rut; the sound of a sharp point scratched on a hard surface *la19-e20*.

~r 1 a person who follows the reapers with a rake to glean *19-e20*. **2** *also* **rakin coal** *19-*, *WC-S* a large lump of coal put on a fire to keep it burning through the night *20-*, *local Fif-Ayr*.

raklie *see* RAUCLE

ralef *see* RELIEVE

raleyff *see* RELIEF

ralliach *see* ROIL

rally[1] **&c; ralyie &c** *18-e20* ['ralɪ; **'raljɪ*] *vti* **1** = rally. **2** *vi* crowd, bunch together; romp around together *la19-*, *now Sh*.

n **1** = rally. **2** a disorderly crowd; a piece of boisterous fun *19-*, *now Sh*.

rally[2] **&c** *vti, freq* **~ on** scold, speak angrily to *la19-*, *local*. [F *railler* mock, banter; *cf* Eng *rail*]

ralye *see* RAIL[1]

ralyie *see* RALLY[1]

ram[1] **&c** *n* = ram *la15-*.

~horn &c (spoon) a spoon made from the horn of a ram *18-*, *now Kcb*. **~ race &c 1** *lit and fig* a headlong rush *16-*, *now Sh Lnk Slk*. **2** a short burst of speed *la17-*, *now Sh Lnk Slk*. **~ reel** *now chf freemasonry* a REEL[1] danced by men only *19-*, *now Kcdn Per*.

ram[2] *v* **1** *vt* = ram, drive down; stuff with food etc *18-*. **2** *vti* push, shove, clear one's way by pushing and shoving *la19-*, *local*. **3** *vt* punish by bumping the buttocks against a wall or by caning the soles of the feet *la19-e20*.

~-full crammed full (of food or drink) *la20-*, *Gen except Sh Ork*.

ram- &c *prefix, intensifier*. [see SND]

ramagiechan [ramə'gixən] *n* a big, rawboned, awkward, impetuous person *19-20*. [obscure]

ramail *see* RAMMEL

ramasse *n* a summary *e17*. [only Sc; F *ramas* a heap, collection. OED *ramass*]

ramayn see REMAIN

rambarre [*?ram'bar] vt beat or force back e17. [only Sc; F rembarrer]

ramble see RAMMEL, RAMMLE

ramburse [*ram'bʌrs] vt reimburse la16. [only Sc; F rembourser]

rambust &c [?ram'bʌst, -'bʌsk] adj = robust 19-20, Bnf S.

rame &c; **rem** &c 18-19, **rhame** &c 19-e20 [rem; Sh rɛm; Ork røm] v **1** vi cry aloud, shout, roar 16-e19. **2** vti repeat, recite something; drone on monotonously 18-, now Uls. **3** vi, also ~ **on** or **about** dwell on something, harp on **about** (one's troubles) la19-e20. **4** talk nonsense, rave 19-e20.
n a phrase, remark etc repeated over and over 19-e20. [only Sc; ON remja roar; rh- forms prob w infl f RHYME]

ramember see REMEMBER

ramemmor see REMEMOR

ramfeezle &c; **ramfoozle** &c 19-e20 [ram-'fizl, -'fuzl] vt muddle, confuse; exhaust la18-, now local Abd-Fif. [only Sc; appar coined by Burns; see SND]

ramforce see RANFORCE

ramgunshoch &c [ram'gʌnʃəx] adj bad-tempered, rude and boorish 18-, now Wgt. [RAM- + ? cf GLUNSH[1], GANSH]

ramiegeister &c [ramɪ'dʒistər] n, lit and fig a sharp stroke or blow 19-e20, NE. [unknown; cf REBEGEASTOR]

rammage &c adj **1** also **rammasche** e16, of animals or birds, esp hawks = ramage, wild, untamed la15-e17. **2** of persons violent, wild, unruly; frenzied la15-e19. [cf RAMMISH]

rammel &c; **ramble** 18, **ramail** &c la13 ['raml; *ra'mel] n **1** chf in sing as collective small or crooked branches; the rough timber of such la13-19. **2** brushwood, undergrowth 16. [chf nME; OF ramaille branches]

rammish 17-, **rammis** &c la15-16, **rammist** &c 15-e16; **ramsh** la18-e20, **ramse** 18-, Ork adj, of persons or animals mad, crazy; impetuous, uncontrolled la15-, now Ork.
vi, chf **rammis** &c rush about frantically la15-e20. [prob altered f RAMMAGE]

rammle &c; **ramble** vi **1** = ramble 19-. **2** wander about aimlessly, esp under the influence of drink 18-, now local Bnf-Uls.
n a piece of noisy or riotous behaviour, specif a noisy drinking bout 18-, local NE-S.
on the rammle drinking heavily la19-e20.

rammock[1] &c n **1** a big rough piece of wood, a stick; a worthless object la19-, now Bnf. **2** a big, coarse person; a large, worthless animal 19-, now Bnf. [altered f RAMMEL]

rammock[2] &c; **reemick** &c 19-, Abd Kcdn n couch-grass; its roots 19-e20, chf Abd. [doubtful; cf RONNACH]

rammy n a free-for-all, violent disturbance, scuffle 20-. [perh reduced dim of RAMMLE]

ramove see REMUVE

ramp[1] &c v **1** vi = ramp la15-. **2** of plants climb, ramble la20-, Bnf Uls. **3** romp boisterously 19-, now local NE-Uls. **4** vti stamp, beat the floor with the feet la18-, local nEC-Lnk.
n **1** an outburst of temper, a violent mood la19-, NE Ags. **2** a romp, scuffle 19-, now Abd. ~**le** &c vi romp, sport 19-20.

ramp[2] adj **1** wild, bold, unrestrained la17-e19. **2** having a strong, coarse flavour or smell 19-e20, chf SW Uls. [only Sc; prob altered f Eng rank, perh w infl f prec, RAMMISH, RAMSH[2]]

ramp[3] vi, of milk etc become glutinous 19. [perh f prec]

rampage &c [ram'pedʒ, -'padʒ; 'rampedʒ; Gall *'rʌmpɪʃ] vi rage or rush about furiously; play roughly or boisterously la17-.
n an outburst of rage, violent, disorderly behaviour; riotous living 19-. [earlier in Sc; conflation of RAMP[1] w Eng rage]

ramper eel la18-e20 n, also **ramper** 19-e20 the sea or river lamprey; any large eel. [altered f LAMPER EEL]

ramps &c n the wild garlic 17-20. [OE hramsa &c; cf Eng ramson]

ramscallion &c [ram'skaliən, -'skʌliən] n = rapscallion la19-20.

ramscooter &c [ram'skutər; Abd -'skwiter] vt trounce, drub, drive off in terror la19-, local N-Kcb. [see SND]

ramse see RAMMISH

ramsh[1] &c [ramʃ; also ranʃ] vti munch, crunch, chew vigorously 19-, local Bnf-Loth. [onomat]

ramsh[2] &c [ramʃ; Sh Ork rams] adj **1** of food rank, unpleasant, coarse 19-, local Sh-Fif. **2** of persons brusque, testy la19-, Abd. **3** of yarn etc rough and coarse-textured 20-, now Kcdn Per. [appar f Eng rammish rank etc; cf Dan ramsk]

ramsh see RAMMISH

ramshackle &c adj **1** = ramshackle. **2** of persons unkempt, untidy, rough la19-, now Ork Bnf Ags.
vt throw into confusion or disorder 19.

ram-stam &c; **ram tam** 18-e19 adj headstrong, rash, heedless, unrestrained 18-.
adv in a headlong, precipitate way, rudely, in confusion 18-.
n **1** a headstrong, impetuous person or action la18-e20. **2** freq **ram tam** brewing the strongest kind of ale, that drawn from the first mash la18-e19.
vi rush or blunder about in a headlong, impetuous way 19-, Gen except Sh Ork.
~**phish** [*ram'stamfɪʃ] rough-and-ready, unceremonious 19-e20. [prob RAM- or Eng ram the animal + STAM[2], STAMMER]

ramstoorie [ram'sturɪ] adj, of a worker vigorous but slapdash, rough-and-ready 20-, Kcdn-Stlg. [RAM- + STOUR]

ramstougar [ram'stugər] adj, also **ramstougerous** &c rough in manner, boisterous, disorderly 19-, now Lnk. [RAM- + second element perh f STUG[2]]

ram tam *see* RAM-STAM
ramuff *see* REMUVE
ramverse *vt* reverse, withdraw *17*. [F *renverser*; *cf* eModEng = overthrow]
ramvert *vt* overthrow *e17*. [only Sc; altered f prec after *convert* etc]
ran *see* RAND[1]
rance &c *n* **1** a prop, wooden post used as a stay or strut, *specif* the stretcher of a table or chair *19-*, *now Mry Ags Kcb*. **2** a bar for securing a door *19-*, *now Loth*. **3** *mining* a prop to strengthen a wall of coal or the roof of a working; a pillar of coal left for this purpose *19-*, *now Fif*. **4** the crossbar of a fence *la18-e20*.
vt **1** prop up, brace, stay (a building etc) *la17-*, *now Fif midLoth Lnk*. **2** make fast, close up, *esp* by wedging a bar across an opening, fasten firmly to prevent motion *19-*, *now Per Loth Stlg*. ~ **wall** *mining* a wall of coal supporting the roof of a working *18*. [chf Sc; appar OF *ranche* a crossbar or stay, F a pole, bar, rung]
Rance *see* RENS
rancie &c *adj* ruddy-complexioned *e19*, *Fif*. [unknown]
rancounter *see* RENCOUNTER
rand[1] &c; ran &c *19-e20* *n* **1** = rand, a border, rim *18-*, *now Sh*. **2** a strip, a narrow section *19-*, *now Per*. **3** a stripe or section of a different colour or texture *la18-*, *now Kcb*.
~**it &c** striped or streaked with different colours *19-*, *now Rox*.
rand[2] *vt* = rend, melt (tallow) *la16*. [*cf* RIND[2]]
rander &c *16-*, **render** *vti* **1** = render *16-*. **2** *vt* hand over, commit **to** (another) *la14-17*. **3** *vi* talk idly or nonsensically, ramble, maunder *19-*, *now Sh Cai Uls*. **4** *of a wound* discharge pus *la19-*, *local*.
n **1** a great talker *19-*, *Rox*. **2** *freq in pl* senseless, incoherent talk *19-e20*, *chf S*. **3** order, restraint, decorousness, conformity *la18-*, *now Kcdn*. **4** *only* **ranter** order, tidiness *e20*, *Abd*. **5** clarified fat, dripping *la19-*, *now Ork Ags*.
randie &c *adj* **1** rough, belligerent, riotous, aggressive, *freq* ~ **beggar** *la17-*, *now Sh C*. **2** *of a woman* loud-voiced, coarse and aggressive *19-*, *now Bnf Ags midLoth*. **3** *of persons* (1) boisterous, wild, dissipated *18-*, *now Sh C*; (2) = randy, lustful; sexually excited *la20-*. **4** *of language* coarse, uncouth; obscene *la19-*, *now local Ags-S*.
n **1** a (*usu* rude or hectoring) beggar, a ruffian *18-*, *now Cai EC Wgt*. **2** (1) a beggar-woman; any foul-mouthed, brawling, bad-tempered woman *la18-*. (2) a loose or dissolute woman *19-*. **3** a boisterous, mischievous person *20-*, *now Abd Kcb*. **4** a romp, frolic *la19-20*.
vi behave belligerently, scold *19*. [*cf* obs Eng *rand* rave, rant, obs Flem *randen*]
randle *see* RANTLE
randon; randoun &c *n* = random, speed, force *la14-e17*.
vti ? flow swiftly; ? set in line *la15*.

at ~ **1** = at random *e17*. **2** ? at full speed *e17*.
in ~ in a straight course or line *la14-e16*, *only Sc*. [OED *random, randon*]
randyvoo *see* RENDEVOUSE
rane &c, rone *la19-*, *chf Ags Per n* a constant refrain, a prolonged or repeated utterance, *freq* a complaint or demand *15-*, *now Ags*.
vti **1** keep on repeating; complain; demand, ask persistently *16-*, *now Ags Fif*. **2** recite (a song, ballad etc) monotonously *19-e20*, *local C*.
rennie &c, ronnie &c = *n* and *v* 1, *la19-e20*, *Abd Ags*.
in a ~ continuously, without stopping *la14-16*. [only Sc; perh var of RAME]
ranegill &c ['ranɪgɪl, *'rɛnɪgəl] *n* a rough character, *esp* a tinker *19-*, *Abd Kcdn Rox*. [see SND]
ranew *see* RENEW
ranforce &c, ramforce &c *chf Sc vt* **1** = ranforce, strengthen, fortify *16*. **2** *only* **ramforce** (1) *also fig* block up, barricade (a door etc) *la16-e17*; (2) ? jam up (cannon) *e17*. **3** *only* **ranforce** force, break open (a door) *e17*.
rang *see* RAING, RING[3]
rangald, rangale, rangat *see* RANGLE
range &c *vti* **1** = range *la14-*. **2** = REENGE *v* 2, *18-*. **3** *vt* agitate (water) to drive fish from a hiding place *19-*, *S*. **4** = REENGE *v* 3, *la19-*, *Ags Fif S*.
n **1** = range *la14-*. **2** a stroll, walk *la19-*, *local NE-midLoth*. **3** = REENGE *n* 2, *la20-*, *NE*.
range *see* RINSE
rangiebus *see* REGIBUS
rangle &c *18-e20*, **rangale &c** *la14-e15*, **rangat &c** *16-e17*, *e20*; **rangald** *la14-e16* ['raŋl, 'raŋət; *raŋ'(g)el, *'raŋald] *n* **1** camp followers *la14-e15*. **2** a rabble (*esp* of soldiers); a crowd, group *la14-e20*. **3** disorder, commotion *la15-16*.
ringat-rangat [*'rɪŋət'raŋət] a rabble *e16*, *only Sc*. [chf Sc; OF *ringaille* the riff-raff, *esp* of an army]
rank[1] &c *v* **1** *vt* = rank *la16-*. **2** *vti, law* place (a creditor) in his due place on the list of accredited claimants to the realized estate of a bankrupt; *of a creditor* be placed thus *la17-*. **3** *also* **runk &c** *e20*, *Abd* (1) *vtr* get ready, prepare, *esp* dress before going out *la19-*, *NE*; (2) *vt* prepare for use, lay **out** in readiness *19-*, *NE*.
n **1** = rank *16-*. **2** *St Andrews Univ* a division in the order of merit awarded to students at the end of the class work of the academic year (before the degree examinations) *la19-*.
~**ing**, *also* **renkning** *la16*, *only Sc* [*?'rɛŋkɪŋ] = ranking.
~**ing and sale** *law* the process whereby a bankrupt estate is sold and the price divided among the creditors *18-20*.
rank[2] &c *adj* **1** = rank *16-*. **2** proud; noble, grand *la16*. **3** stout, strong *la15-e17*, *e19*. **4** swift, impetuous, turbulent, given to violence or excess *16-e17*, *e19*. **5** abundant, copious; thick, dense *la15-e19*.

rankel *n* a festering sore *la16*. [ME, OF *rancle*. OED *rankle*]

rannle *see* RANTLE

rannoch ['ranəx] *n* fern; bracken *20-, now Per.* [only Sc; Gael *raineach*]

ranowne *see* RENOWNE

ranshackle &c [ran'ʃakl, -'ʃekl, ram-] *vt* search minutely, ransack *19-, now Rox Uls.* [eModEng *ransackle*, f *ransack* + *-le*]

ransom &c *n* **1** = ransom *la14-.* **2** an exorbitant price or rent *19-, only Sc.*
vt = ransom *la14-.*

rant *v* **1** *vi* = rant, talk foolishly *la17.* **2** romp, make merry, indulge in boisterous fun *18-, now local Sh-Ayr.* **3** *vti* play or sing a lively tune, *esp* for a dance *la18-19.* **4** *vi* make a great noisy fuss, complain at length *la19-, Cai Kcb Uls.*
n **1** a romp, boisterous or riotous merry-making *la18-, now Bnf Abd.* **2** a festive gathering with music and dancing *la18-20.* **3** a lively tune or song, *esp* one suitable for an energetic dance; *freq* in titles of dance tunes *18-, now local Sh-Lnk.*
~**er 1** = ranter *la19-.* **2** *specif* a person who played for dancers, *esp* a strolling minstrel *la18-e19, literary.* ~**ie &c** frolicsome, full of boisterous fun *la18-19.* ~**in 1** roistering, merry, uproarious *18-, local.* **2** *of a fire* burning strongly, blazing *18-19.* ~**inlie &c** merrily, uproariously *18-19.*

ranter &c *vt* **1** *also fig* sew together, darn, mend *17-, now Cai.* **2** mend or stitch hastily or roughly *19-e20.*
n a rough, hasty stitching or sewing *20.* [F *rentraire* darn, mend]

ranter *see* RANDER

rantie-tantie &c *n* a reddish-leaved plant found in cornfields, formerly eaten as a vegetable, *prob* the common sorrel *18-19.* [obscure]

rantle &c; rannle &c *19-e20,* **randle &c** *e19 n* a wooden or iron bar across a chimney from which the chain and pot-hook were suspended *la17.*
~ **tree 1** *also* **rannle bauk &c** *19-e20* = *n, la18-, local NE-Slk.* **2** a roof-beam, rafter *la18-e19.* **3** a thin, stick-like person or thing *19-20.* [*cf* Norw dial *randa-tre, rand-aas* = *n*]

rantree &c *n* a RANTLE *19-20.* [reduced f Norw dial *randa-tre*]

rap¹ &c *v* **1** *vti* dash, thump, knock, strike or fall with a sharp thud *16-, now local Sh-Kcb.* **2** *vt* send **forth** with a clap *e16.* **3** = rap (at a door) *16-.* **4** *vt* cause to strike sharply, make a rapping action or noise with *19-, now local Sh-Kcb.* **5** *vi* fall rapidly in a shower or in drops *16-, now Sh Ork, only Sc.* **6** make a rapping or banging noise *la19-, Sh NE Ags.*
n **1** = rap (at a door) *17-.* **2** an instant, moment, *freq* **in a** ~ *18-, Gen except Sh Ork, only Sc.*
hap weel, ~ **weel** come what may *19.* ~ **to** slam (a door) *17-, now Sh.* ~ **up** rouse by knocking *la19-, now Cai Kcb.*

rap² *n* a good-for-nothing, a cheat, a rake *19-, now Fif.* [*cf* Eng = a counterfeit coin; something of no value]

rap³ *n, chf in pl* = rape, the plant *18-, now SW.* [perh Du *raap*]

raparal &c [*rə'parəl] *vt* = reparel, repair; array *la15-16.* [OED *reparel*]

rapayr *see* REPAIR¹

rape *adv* hastily *la16.* [ME = quick, hasty, ? f ME *rapely*]

raperee *see* RAIP

raploch &c; roploch *e16* ['raplox] *n, also* ~ **grey** coarse, homespun, undyed, woollen cloth; a garment made of this *16-20.*
adj **1** made of RAPLOCH, coarse, homespun, undyed *18-e19.* **2** (1) home-made, crude, rough-and-ready *la18-19.* (2) *of persons* ordinary, undistinguished; crude, uncouth *la19-, now Ags.* [only Sc; obscure]

raport *see* REPORT

rapple &c ['rapl; *Rox also* 'ropl] *v* **1** *vi* grow rapidly, shoot up *19-e20.* **2** *vt* make or mend hurriedly and roughly *19-e20.* [perh f ME *rap* hasten]

rapreiff *see* REPREE

rapt *n* **1** rape *16-17.* **2** an abducted woman *e17.* **3** = rapt, a forcible movement, a carrying away *e17.* **4** robbery, plunder *e17.*

rapture &c ['raptər] *n* **1** = rapture. **2** a paroxysm, fit, *esp* of rage *19-, now local Per-Dmf.*

raquest *see* REQUEESHT

rascal *n* = rascal.
R~ Fair a *hiring market* (HIRE) for the engagement of men who had failed to get employment at the regular market *la19-e20, Abd.* ~ **knot** a kind of knot tied on the straw bands of corn sheaves *20-, now Abd Rox.*

raser &c [*'rezər] *n* the redcurrant *la16-17.* [var of RUSSER-BERRÉ; *cf* RIZZAR]

rash¹ &c *16-, Gen except Sh,* **thrash** *19-, now WC;* **raiche** *la16,* **resh &c** *la15-20,* **thresh** *19-, now EC, S* [raʃ, rɛʃ; *EC, WC also* θraʃ; *EC, S also* θrɛʃ] *n* **1** = rush, the plant *la15-.* **2** a peeled rush used for a lamp wick *19-e20, N.*
rashen &c = rushen, made of rushes *la18-e20.*
rasher = *n, la19-e20, Bwk Rox.* ~**ie &c** *n* = *n, 19-e20. adj* made of rushes; overgrown with rushes *18-.* **Rashiecoat** name of the heroine of a Scottish version of *Cinderella,* who wore a coat of rushes *20-.*
~ **bush &c, thrush bush** *la17* a clump of rushes, *formerly freq* **the** ~ **bush keeps the cow** *etc, proverb* referring to a time of peace and security from marauders *16-, now NE, SW.* **rush corn** inferior oats fed unthreshed to livestock *18.*

rash²&c *v* **1** *vi* rush violently or hastily *16, e19.* **2** *vt* cast or pour out hurriedly *e16, e18.* **3** *vi, of rain* pour, come down in torrents *19-, now Ork Cai.* **4** *vt* dash **together, against** *etc, 16-17.* **5** smash, break with violence *e16.* **6** *vi* produce a stabbing or searing pain, throb *la19-e20.*

n **1** a crash or clashing noise *la15-e16.* **2** a sudden downpour of rain or hail *19-e20.* [chf *Sc*; prob onomat]

rash³ &c *adj* **1** = rash. **2** active, agile, vigorous *19-, now Rox.*

rasp *n* **1** the fruit or plant of the raspberry *18-.* **2** a mole; a birthmark, naevus *20-, Per Fif.* [ME; also in Eng dial]

rassaif *see* RECEIVE

rasyst *see* RESIST

rat¹ *n* = rat.

~('s) **tail** the greater plantain; its seed-head *la19-, Gen except Sh Ork.* [*cf* RATTON]

rat² &c *n* a rut, groove, deep scratch *16-, now S. vti* scratch, make a rut or groove (in) *16-20.* [obscure]

ratch¹ &c *17-e18*; **roch &c** *la16* [*ratʃ, *rotʃ] *n* the barrel of a gun. [shortened f Eng *ratchet*, F *rochet* a lancehead; a spool]

ratch² &c *n, also fig* a gundog or hound which hunts by scent *la15-19.*
vi range about ravenously; prowl *19-, now Rox.* [ME *rache &c*, OE *ræcc*]

ratch³ *vt* damage by rough usage, tear, scratch *19-, now S.*
n a scratch, line *la19-, now SW.* [prob onomat or conflation of RAT² w Eng *scratch*]

ratchell &c *n* a hard stony crust under the soil, a gravelly TILL² (*n* 1) *la18-19.*
~ **salt &c** coarse-grained salt *la16, la19.* [perh f F *rochaille* an agglomeration of small stones; *ratchell salt* perh f *La Rochelle* the town in France]

rate &c *n* = rate *la15-.*
at nae &c ~ not under any circumstances, by no means *la18-, now Ags.*

rate *see* RATT

rath &c [raθ] *n* a circular earthwork, a defensive homestead or settlement *19-, freq in place-names.* [ScGael *ràth*, IrGael *ráth* [ra:]; commoner in Ireland]

rath *see* RAITH

rather *see* RAITHER

ratificatory *adj, law* confirmatory *e17.* [only *Sc*; MedL *ratificare* ratify]

ratihabit *vt* express approval of, sanction *la17-e18, only Sc.*
~**ion &c** *law* approval, approbation, sanction *16-e18.* [MedL *ratihabere*, laL *ratihabitio*; *cf* obs Eng law *ratihabition*]

rationable &c *adj* reasonable, just, right *15-16.* [chf *Sc*; L *ratiōnābilis*]

ratorn *see* RETURN

rat rane *see* RAT-RHYME

ratret *see* RETREAT

rat-rhyme &c *18-e20*, **rat-rime &c** *la16-19*, **rat rane** *e16 n* a piece of doggerel verse; a nonsensical rigmarole, a tedious repetition. [orig and chf *Sc*; perh var of Eng *rote* + *rhyme*]

ratt &c, rot; rate [*rat, *rot] *n* a file (of soldiers) *17.*

the Town R~s the *town guard* (TOUN) *e19.* [Du, OF *rot*; *cf* Eng *rout.* OED *rat* (*n⁵*)]

rattle &c *vti* **1** = rattle *la15-.* **2** strike or beat repeatedly, (cause to) hit, crash noisily *19-, now local Sh-Per.* **3** *vi* pronounce a strong uvular *r*, speak with a burr *la18-, now local Sh-Dmf.* **4** *vt* do with great haste, make speedily and not too carefully, *freq* ~ **up** *19-.*
n **1** = rattle. **2** a rattling sound *16-.* **3** a sharp blow, a thump, crash *17-.* **4** a strong uvular *r*, burr *18-, now Abd.*

~**bag** a stone-filled bag on the end of a stick, used to make a rattling noise *la18-e19.* ~**head** *mining* a suction pipe *la19-, now Fif.* ~**scull** a giddy, thoughtless, empty-headed person *18-19.* ~**stane &c** *children's rhyme* a hailstone *la19-, local NE-Kcb.*

rattle gold &c *n* goldleaf or tinsel *e16.* [only *Sc*; MDu *raetelgoud*]

ratton &c; rottan &c *la17-20 n* **1** a rat *15-, Gen except Sh Ork.* **2** contemptuous term or term of endearment for a person *la16-e20.*
~ **fa &c** a rat-trap *la17-e19.* ~**'s nest** a state of perpetual unrest and bustle *19-e20.* [ME; OF *raton*, MedL *rato*]

raturn *see* RETURN

rauchan &c; rachan &c *la17-e20* ['raxən] *n* a PLAID or wrap, a MAUD; a clumsy garment *la17-, now Per.* [only *Sc*; Gael *rachda* a TARTAN PLAID worn as a cloak]

rauchle &c; rachle ['raxl, 'raxl] *n* a loose, untidy heap of objects; something ramshackle or dilapidated *la19-.* [perh var of *ruckle* (RICKLE¹) w infl f RAUCLE]

rauchle *see* RAUCLE

raucht *see* REAK

raucle &c *19-*, **rackle &c** *16-e20*; **rauchle &c** *la19-20*, **rachle** *19-* ['rakl, 'rakl; 'raxl, 'raxl] *adj* **1** bold, impulsive, rash *16-, now Fif.* **2** *of persons or things* (1) strong, sturdy, robust *19-e20*; (2) hard, stern, grim, unbending *19-20.* **3** *of persons, rarely of things* rough, crude, tough, uncouth *la18-e20.* **4** *of speech* rough, unpolished, blunt to the point of rudeness *la18-e20.*
rachlie dirty and disorderly *19-20.* **raklie** rapidly, impetuously *la15.*
rackle-handed 1 = *adj* 1 and 2 (2), *18-e20.* **2** having powerful hands *la19-e20.* [ME *rakel &c*]

rauk &c *adj* hoarse, raucous *la15-e16, e19.*
vi clear the chest or throat of phlegm, hawk *la19-, Ags Fif.* [only *Sc*; OF *rauque*, L *raucus*]

rauk *see* RAKE, ROUK¹

raun- *see* ROWAN¹

raux *see* RAX

rave¹ &c; raif &c *la15-16, only Sc* [rev] *vi* = rave *la15-.*
n **1** a person who talks volubly and nonsensically, a windbag *20-, local Stlg-SW.* **2** a vague rumour, an unlikely story *19.*

rave² *vi* wander, stray, roam *la16, 19.* [ME; *cf* Icel *rafa*, or perh altered f Eng *rove*]

rave *see* REIVE, RIVE

ravel &c; revel &c, reavil &c *18* ['revl; *Rox* rəil] *n* **1** a rail, railing; a balustrade; a bridge parapet *17-e20*. **2** the horizontal beam in a BYRE fixed to the tops of the stakes for the tethers *18-e19*.
vt supply or enclose with a railing *17-19*.
~**ing &c** railing; railings *17-19*.
~**tree &c, realtree &c** *19, SW-S* ['revl'tri; *SW-S* *'rel-] = *n* **2**, *la17-e20*. [perh Scand; *cf* Faeroese *revil* a fillet of wood etc, ON *refill* a strip of cloth; not connected with RAIL¹]

ravel *see* RAIVEL

raverie &c, reverie &c ['revərɪ] *n* **1** *only* **reverie &c** (1) wantonness, wildness *e16*; (2) noise, din *e16, only Sc*. **2** raving, furious or deranged speech; nonsense, foolish talk *la16-, now Abd*. **3** a rumour, a piece of gossip *la18-, now Bnf Kcdn*. [OF; *cf* ModEng *reverie* a daydream etc]

ravest &c [rə'vɛst] *vt, pt, ptp also* **ravest &c** = revest, clothe *15-e16*. [OED *revest* (v¹)]

ravis &c *la14-16*; **revis &c** *16* [*'ravɪs, *?'rev-] *vt* = ravish. [OED *ravish*]

ravissant *adj, esp of wolves* ravening *la15-e16*. [F presp of *ravir* seize, take away; *cf* prec]

raw¹ &c, row &c *la18-* [rɑ; *Mry* *rjɑv] *n* **1** = row, a line *la14-*. **2** a ring of people, *esp* children *19-, now Kcb*. **3** a row of houses, *usu* of a uniform construction with common gables, *freq* applied to miners' or farm-workers' cottages; a street of such houses *15-, in street-names 14-*.
v **1** *vt* set up in a row, arrange in a line *19-, now Ork Kcb*. **2** *vti, of root crops* plant, come up in rows *19-, now Kcb*. **3** *vt* bring (late-lambing ewes) in single file to a field beside the shepherd's house to keep them under observation *la19-20*.
on ~ 1 in a line *la14-e16*. **2** in order *16-e18*. **on ~s &c** in lines *la15-e16*. **twa &c in a ~** two abreast *20-, local*.

raw²; ra &c *20, Sh Ork NE* [rɑ] *adj* **1** = raw. **2** *of corn-sheaves* damp, not fully dried out *la19-, now Sh*.
n neat WHISKY *19-, now Sh Cai*.
~**-gabbed** *la19-e20, Sh*, ~**-mowit** *e16* voluble in an ignorant, ill-informed way. ~ **sowens &c** *19-, now Sh Ork NE*, ~**sins** *20-, now NE* uncooked SOWANS.

rawn &c; raan &c *la18-20, N*, **rown &c, rowan &c** *la18-e20*, **roan &c** *la18-19* [rɑn; *EC, S* 'rʌu(ə)n; *EC also* *'ro(ə)n] *n* **1** the roe of a fish *16-, now E Kcb*. **2** the turbot, *freq* ~ **fleuk** *la18-, now Abd*.
~**er** an unspawned salmon *19-, now Per Slk*. [ME *rowne, rawne* roe; *cf* Dan *ravn, raun* and ON *hrogn*]

rawsins *see* RAW²

rax &c; raux *19*, **wrax** *19*, **rex** *la19-20, Sh Ork* [raks; *Sh Ork also* rɛks] *v* **1** (1) *vir* stretch oneself after sleep etc *la14-*. (2) *vt* stretch (a cramped limb etc) *19-*. **2** (1) put (oneself) to great effort, overexert, strain ((a part of) oneself) *16-*.

(2) sprain (a limb) *la19-*. **3** (1) *also fig* stretch in order to lengthen etc, pull out *18-*. (2) stretch (a person's neck), hang (a person) *la18-*. (3) stretch or extend (something) to its full reach or capacity *la18-, now Sh-EC*. **4** (1) *also* ~ **up** extend, raise (the head or eyes) in order to look or listen *la19-, now Sh Abd*. (2) *freq* ~ **out**, ~ **ower** *etc* extend, reach out (the hand or arm) *18-*. (3) stretch out, crane (the neck) *19-, now E Lnk*. **5** *vi* extend one's power; rule; prevail *la15-e16, only Sc*. **6** *vt, also* ~ **doon &c**, *and vi, chf* ~ **for**, ~ **till** *etc, also fig* reach, stretch out to take or grasp (something); *specif* at table, help oneself to (food) *20-*. **7** *vt* (1) *freq* ~ **doon**, ~ **ower** *etc* hand (a person an object) *19-*; (2) give (a person one's hand) *la18-*; (3) deal (a person a blow) *18-, now local*. **8** *vi* (1) *also fig* stretch, expand, elongate *18-, now Sh Abd*. (2) grow, develop *la18-19*. (3) *of the day, time* ~ **oot** stretch out *la19-, now Sh Abd Per*. **9** extend in distance from one point to another, reach *20-, now local*.
n **1** the act of stretching *la18-, now Sh NE, EC*. **2** a strain, sprain *la19-*. **3** the act of reaching; reach *19-, now local Sh-Lnk*. [nME *rax*, OE *raxan* stretch; *rex* perh by conflation w Norw dial *rekkja* strain, stretch out]

rax *see* RACK¹, REX
raxes *see* RACK¹
ray [*re] *n* = ray, a king, used as a respectful or ironical term for a man *e16*.
raze; raaz &c [rɑz] *vt* gash, cut, tear *la18-, now Sh*. [eModEng]
razzor &c ['razər] *n* = razor *20*.
reable &c, rehabile &c *16* [*'ri:'ebl] *vt* restore to a former state or position; legitimize *16-17*. *adj* legitimate *la16*. [only Sc; Eng *re-* + *able*, prob after F *ra-, rhabiller*]
reach &c [ritʃ; *Sh* retʃ] *vi* retch, try to vomit *la19-*. [eModEng]
read &c; rede &c *la14-16 vti* **1** = read *la14-*. **2** *vi, of a preacher* read a sermon, rather than preach extempore *la18-20*. **3** speak or tell **of** *la14-16*. **4** *vt* interpret (a dream, riddle etc), foretell the future, *freq* ~ **(the) cups, cards** *etc, la18-* [orig REDE¹ *v* 3].
n **1** = read. **2** a loan (of a book etc) for the purpose of reading it, a perusal *19-*.
~**er &c 1** = reader *la16-*. **2** a person appointed to read Scriptures etc in the absence of an ordained MINISTER, *officially la16, unofficially 17-*. **reediemadeasy &c** ['ridimə'dizɪ, -'dezɪ] a first school reading book *19-20*. ~**ing &c 1** = reading. **2** = *n* 2, *19-, now Ork Ayr*. **3** a reading from the Bible, *esp* in family worship *19-20*. ~**in sweetie** a conversation lozenge *20-*.
~ **richt** have or take a correct view *16*. ~ **up** read aloud *19-, now Fif Wgt*.
ready &c *17-*; **redy &c** *la14-18*, **reddy &c** *la14-e18, only Sc*, **rady &c** *la16, only Sc* ['rɛdɪ;

*?'rad-] adj 1 = ready la14-. 2 with infin or verbal noun apt, liable, likely to la16-, now local: 'ready makin mistakes'.

v 1 make ready, prepare: (1) vr, la14-e16; (2) vt, 19-e20. 2 cook (food), prepare (a meal) 18-, now Stlg WC, SW.

readily &c 1 = readily la14-. 2 probably; naturally, in the normal course of events 17-19.

reak &c la19-; reik &c, raik &c la19-e20, rike &c la18-19, reck &c 19-e20, Sh [rek; Sh also rɛk; *rik, *rəik] vti, ptp also raucht &c la14-e20, roucht &c la14 [raxt] 1 = reach la14-. 2 vt reach for 19-, now Sh Ork Kcb: 'I raekid a floo'r bannick an cleev'd him in twa'. 3 deliver (a blow) la14-, now Sh Kcb. 4 vi stretch or extend between two points 19-, now Sh.

n = reach 16-, now Sh. [OED reach]

real see RAEL

realtree see RAVEL

realty &c [*'rialtı, *'rɪɑtɪ] n 1 (1) = realty, royalty la14-15. (2) used as a title, la14. 2 a kingdom, realm la14-e15. 3 a part, or the parts, of a kingdom directly under the king's jurisdiction 15-16; cf REGALITY.

ream &c 18-; reme &c e16, raem &c 19-, chf Sh [rim; Sh nEC rem] n 1 cream (as a food and a cosmetic) 16-, now Sh NE, C. 2 the froth on top of ale etc la18-, now Bnf.

v 1 vi, of milk form cream la19-e20. 2 vt skim the cream off (milk) 18-, NE-S. 3 vi form a froth or foam (1) of liquor, suds etc, 18-e20; (2) of a turbulent stream, 19-e20; (3) fig, of liquor rouse confusion (in the mind) la18-e20. 4 (1) be full of a frothy liquid, bubble to the brim 16-, now Mry Bnf Lnk. (2) of emotion etc bubble over, effervesce la19-e20.

~er 19-e20, ~ing dish 18-e19 a shallow dish for skimming cream off milk. ~in fou &c full of frothy liquid la18-, now Sh. ~y &c 1 of a creamy consistency; consisting of or made with cream 19-e20. 2 frothing 19-, now Bnf.

~ breid oatcakes (AIT) made with cream e20, Abd. ~ cheese cheese made from cream la18-, now Bnf. raemikle &c ['remık(ə)l, -ol, 'røm-] a round wooden tub for holding milk etc; a pail la19-, now Sh [REAM + Norw kolla a vessel, bucket; cf Norw rjomekolla]. ~ pig, stoupie etc a jug for holding cream la18-, now NE nEC Kcb. ~ ower &c overflow, run over la18-, Sh N, C Slk. [ME reme &c, OE réam]

rease see RAISE

reason see RIZZON

reat [*'riat] n offence, wrongdoing e16. [only Sc; L reātus accused]

reath see RAITH

reave see REEVE², REIVE

reavel(-ravel) see RAIVEL

reavil see RAVEL

rebaghle [*?rə'baxl] n disparagement, reproach 19-e20. [only Sc; appar var of REBALK]

rebaik see REBALK

rebald see REEBALD

rebalk &c la15-e16; rebaik &c la16 [*rə'balk, *-'bɑk] vt abuse, reproach. [only Sc; obscure]

rebat [rə'bat] vi give a curt, brusque or discouraging reply la19-, NE. [appar irreg f obs Eng rebate repress, blunt]

rebat see RABAT

rebegeaster [*?rɛbɪ'dʒistər] n a stroke with a stick e16. [unknown; cf RAMIEGEISTER]

rebel &c; rabel &c la15-16 [n 'rɛbl, *'rabl; v rə'bɛl] n 1 = rebel la16-. 2 law a person who disregards or flouts authority; a lawbreaker, disobeyer of summons; a person, latterly (la18-e19) specif a debtor, declared outside the law by being put to the horn (HORN) 14-. 3 opposition la15.

adj = rebel la14-.

v 1 = rebel: (1) vi, la14-; (2) vr, la15. 2 vt oppose rebelliously la15.

~lion &c 1 = rebellion la16-. 2 law disobedience to a legal summons; the consequences of this; latterly specif of a debtor as in n 2, freq civil ~lion 15-e19.

rebet [*rə'bɛt] vi renew one's attack on la15. [only Sc; appar F (se) rebattre turn]

rebet see RYBAT

rebig [?ri'bɪg] vt rebuild la17-, Sh Ork N. [re- + BIG¹]

rebook &c v, n = rebuke 18-e20.

rebound &c; reboun &c la19, NE [rə'bun(d)] n 1 = rebound. 2 a loud explosive noise as of gunshot, a reverberation la19-, now Abd Kcdn Fif. 3 a reprimand, severe rebuke 20-, Abd-Stlg.

vti 1 = rebound 16-. 2 vi leap up e16.

rebourse [*rə'burs] n at ~ &c on the wrong side; in the wrong way; in the opposite direction la14-e15. [chf Sc; F rebours rough, perverse. OED rebours]

rebous [*rə'bus] n ? din, disturbance e16. [only Sc; perh connected w prec]

reboyt see REBUT

reburse [*?rə'bʌrs] vt = reimburse la16.

rebut &c, rebute 16-19; reboyt &c la14-16, rabut &c la15-16 [rə'bʌt; *rə'bøt] v 1 vt revile, rebuke, reproach la14-15. 2 = rebut, repel, repulse la14-. 3 deprive of (something) by driving the person off e16. 4 repel, reject (something offered) la16. 5 vi, curling (CURL) play a very forceful shot in the late stages of a game 19.

n rebuke, reproach la15-16.

reca [rə'kɑ] vt = recall 19-e20.

recamby [*rə'kambı] n = RECHENG la15. [only Sc; MedL *recambium]

receed &c [*rə'sid] vi = reside 17-e19.

receipt &c la17-; recept &c la14-e18, ressait &c 15-19 [rə'sit, rə'set; *rə'sɛpt] n 1 = receipt 15-. 2 a (medical) prescription or preparation la16-, now Ags Ayr Uls. 3 a recipe 19-, local Cai-Kcb.

vt 1 = RESET v 1, la14-e18. 2 = RESET v 2, 16-e18.

tekat of ~ = n 1, la16.

receive &c   *la16-*;   **ressave** &c   *la14-16*,
resaive *la14-19*, **resaif** &c *la14-16*, **rassaif**
16, only Sc, **reschave** *la14, only Sc* [rəˈsiv;
*rəˈsev] *vti* **1** = receive *la14-*. **2** *vt, in imprecations* seize, carry off *la19-20*: 'God receive me'.

recept *see* RECEIPT

receptation &c *n* being received (into a place)
la16-e17. [only Sc; MedL *receptātio*, L *receptāre*
receive]

recheng &c [*ˀriˈtʃindʒ] *n* = rechange, the
re-exchange of a bill *la15*. [OED *rechange*; *cf*
RECAMBY]

reciprocous [*ˀrəˈsɪprokəs] *adj* reciprocal *la16*.
[L *reciprocus*]

reck &c *16-*; **rak** &c *la14-e17*, **raik** *19* [rɛk;
*rak] *vti, pt also* **racht** *la14-15*, **roucht** *16*
[*raxt, *roxt] **1** = reck, (take) heed *la14-e16*.
2 reckon, consider *la18-19*.
n = reck, heed *la15*.
rackless &c *la14-, now Sh Ork Wgt*, **reckless**
&c *16- adj* **1** = reckless *la14-*. **2** accidental,
unintentional *e19, only Sc*. *vt* neglect; be negligent or heedless of *la16*. **~lessly** &c **1** = recklessly *la15-*. **2** through carelessness; accidentally *la14-17, only Sc*.
what &c **~(s)** what does it matter? *16-e20*.

reck *see* RAIK, REAK
reckle *see* RACKLE
reckless *see* RECK
reckon *see* RACKON

reclaim &c *v* **1** *vt* = reclaim *la16-*. **2** *vi* protest,
object, be in opposition *la16-e19*. **3** *vt* make a
claim against, sue at law *la15, only Sc*. **4** *vi, law*
appeal, *now* from the *Outer House* (OUTER¹) to
the *Inner House* (INNER) of the *Court of Session*
(SESSION) *la16-, only Sc*.
reclamation &c **1** = reclamation *16-*. **2** an
appeal at law *la16, only Sc*. **~ing note** *etc*
18-19, **~ing motion** *20-* the procedure by
which an appeal is made as in *v* 4.

reclead &c [rəˈklid] *vt* reclothe *la19-, now Sh
Ags*. [*re-* + CLEED]

recognition &c *n* **1** = recognition *17-*. **2** *law*
the resumption of land by a SUPERIOR, *latterly
specif* when a VASSAL had alienated half or more
of it without the SUPERIOR's consent *la15-e18*.

recognize &c [*ˀrəˈkʌnɪs, *-ˈkognɪs] *vt* **1** = recognize. **2** *also* **raccunys** &c *la15* =
RECOGNOSCE 1 (1), *la14-e17*. **3** = RECOGNOSCE
5, *e17, e19*.

recognosce &c [*ˀrikogˈnos] *v* **1** *law* (1) *vt, of a
feudal* SUPERIOR: resume possession of (lands)
la15-e18; *see* RECOGNITION; (2) *vi, of lands* return
to a SUPERIOR by RECOGNITION *la18, hist*. **2** *vt*
recognize, identify *e16*. **3** recognize, acknowledge *la16-e17*. **4** revise, amend *la16-18*. **5** reconnoitre *e17*. [chf Sc; L *recognoscere* recognize;
review]

recolleck &c *19-*, **recollect** *vt* = recollect *16-*.
n, in pl memoirs, collections *e16, only Sc*.

recommend *vt* = recommend *la16-*.

~ A to B as a servant recommend A to have
B as a servant *19, now Abd Ags*: 'I wadna
recommend you to him as a servant'.

recompense &c *vt, also* **recompanse** *16* **1** =
recompense *la16-*. **2** *law* put forward a counterclaim in a debt action *e18*.
n **1** = recompense *16-*. **2** = *recompensation* 2, *19*.
3 a non-contractual obligation by which a person is obliged to restore a benefit derived from
another's loss *la17-*.
recompensation &c **1** = recompensation *16*.
2 *law* a counter-claim in a debt action *la17-19*.

reconter, recontre [*rəˈkontər] *vt, n* encounter *16*. [only Sc; vars of Eng *recounter*]

reconvention [rikənˈvenʃn] *n, law* the right
to sue a person who has brought an action
against one, even if that person lives in another
country and is thus in another jurisdiction *16-*.
[F; *cf* MedL *reconventio*]¹

recoorse *see* RECOURSE¹

record; racord *15, only Sc* [*n sense 1* ˈrɛkord,
-ərd; *senses 2, 3* *rəˈkord; *sense 4* rɪˈkord; *v*
rəˈkord; *also* *ˈrɛkord] *n* **1** = record *la15-*. **2**
repute, account *15, 19*. **3** a reply; a statement
la15, only Sc. **4** *law* the statements and answers
of both parties to an action; when adjusted, the
RECORD is closed and the action proceeds to
proof or debate *la15-*.
v **1** *vt* = record *la14-*. **2** *vi* pertain or belong (to
someone) *la15*.
Keeper of the R~s 1 *also* **Deputy Keeper of
the R~s** *la18-e20* an official responsible to the
Lord Clerk Register (REGISTER) for custody of the
public records of Scotland *la17-e18*. **2** the official responsible for the preservation of the public registers, records and rolls of Scotland *20-*; *cf*
Keeper of the Registers (REGISTER).

recounsel &c; **recounsale** &c [*rəˈkunsel,
*-ˈkunsl] *vt* **1** = recounsel, reconcile *la14-16*. **2**
bring (a person) back **to** (peace or favour) *16*.

recounter &c [*rəˈkuntər] *vt* **1** = recounter,
encounter in battle etc *15-16*. **2** *law* oppose
(the giving of a pledge) *e15*.
n, law a counter-pledge or security *15*.

recourse¹; recoorse *la19-* [rəˈkurs; *St* rɪˈkors,
ri-] *n* **1** *law* the right of the assignee to claim
compensation from the assignor, *esp* in the case
of failure to honour a bill of exchange or in the
case of eviction *18-*. **2** a visit *e17*. **3** =
recourse.
vi = recourse, return *la15-e17*.

recourse² [*rəˈkurs] *n* (*16-e17*), *vt* (*16*) =
RESCOURS, rescue. [only Sc]

recreu &c [*ˀrəˈkrju] *n* = recrew, a body of
soldiers as reinforcements *e17*.
vt reinforce (an army) *e17*. [OED *recrew*]

recrimination *n* **1** = recrimination *la17-*. **2**
specif law, in a divorce action a counter-charge on
grounds of adultery *la18-*.

recry [*ˀrəˈkrai] *vt* retract *la15-e16*.
n recall, revocation *e16*. [only Sc]

recryand [*?'rɛkraɪand] *adj* = recreant *la14-e16*. [only Sc. OED *recreant*]

recryat [*?rə'kraɪat] *vi* ? surrender *e16*. [only Sc; perh OF *recreant*, presp of *recroire* give up, yield or erron form of RECRY]

rector *n* **1** *Sc Univs* a high-ranking official, the office varying in the four older Scottish Universities and throughout the centuries; the RECTOR is now a public figure elected for three years by the students; he or she represents them on the University Court and gives a *rectorial* address at his or her inauguration *16-*; see also *Lord Rector* (LORD) and DOST. **2** a headteacher of a secondary school *18-*. **3** = REGENT *n* 2, *e16*. **4** = rector, a ruler; the incumbent of a parish *la16-e17*. **5** a clergyman in charge of a full congregation of the Scottish Episcopal Church *la19-*.
R~ate the office of RECTOR *n* 1, *la19*. **~ial** *adj* of a RECTOR *n* 1, *18-*. *n* the canvassing and ceremonial connected with the election and inauguration of a RECTOR *n* 1, *la19-*. **R~ship** the office of RECTOR *n* 1 and 2, *la18-*. [ScL = *n* 1, *15*; L = ruler, one who governs]

red *see* RAD, REDD¹, REID¹, RIDE

redargue [*rɛ'dargju] *vt* **1** = redargue, blame, reprove *la16*. **2** confute (a person) by argument *la17-e18*. **3** *law* refute, disprove (an argument, statement etc) *18-19*.

redcoll &c *n* the horse-radish *la17-e20*. [eModEng; ME *radcolle*]

redd¹ &c; red, rade &c *19* [rɛd] *vt, pt, ptp* **~it &c** *15-16*, **red(d)** *la16-* **1** save, rescue *la16-e18*. **2** save from burning; put out (a fire) (1) *in gen*, *la14-18*; (2) *freq fig* in expressions implying great haste *la19-*, *NE*: '*fleein like tae redd fire*'. **3** free, rid, relieve (another or oneself) **of** *la15-*. **4** (1) clear (a space, the way or a passage), make room, remove obstructions from *15-*. (2) clear (land) by reaping, ploughing etc *18-e20*. (3) clear out (a ditch, channel etc), remove rubbish or silt from *15-*, *now NE-C*. (4) clear (the throat, nose, stomach etc) *19-*, *N*. (5) clear (a fireplace, tobacco pipe) of ashes, poke up or out *la19-*, *Sh NE-C*. **5** clean (the intestines of a slaughtered animal) of fat *la20-*, *Sh Ork Rox*. **6** *law* vacate (a property), leave (a house etc) ready for the next occupant, *freq* **void and redd** cleared and ready for a new occupant *la15-*. **7** clear away, remove (a thing or person) *16-*, *now NE-S*. **8** *also specif mining* clear away waste or debris from *16-*. **9** disentangle, unravel, sort out *lit and fig*, *esp* (1) (thread, yarn etc) *17-*; (2) (fishing lines or nets) *16-*, *now NE, WC*; (3) comb (the hair) *18-*. **10** *also* **~ up** arrange; settle (affairs etc); clear up, sort out (problems, difficulties etc) *la17-*. **11** fix exactly, verify or determine (the boundaries of a piece of land) *15-*; *cf* RID, RIDE, **~ the marches**. **12** bring (animals or people) under control *16*. **13** separate (combatants); put an end to (fighting) *16-*, *now Abd*. **14** *also* **~ up** (1) put (things) in order, tidy up (a room, building etc) *16-*; (2) tidy (one's clothes or oneself) *la16-*; (3) clean out and renew the bedding of (a housed animal) *19-*, *now NE*.

n **1** the act of clearing away or tidying **up**; a putting in order; a cleaning, tidying *la15-*. **2** the curvature of a ploughshare which helps keep it clear of obstructions *la18-19*. **3** the power to clear or sweep aside obstacles; energy, drive *la19-*, *now Sh Ork*. **4** (1) rubbish, rubble etc which has been or is to be cleared away *16-e20*. (2) *specif* waste material from a coalpit or quarry *18-*, *now local EC, S*. **5** a combing and arranging of the hair *la19-*, *now local Sh-Stlg*.

~er &c a person who intervenes to stop a fight or quarrel *la15-e19*. **~er's lick** *etc* a blow received by a person trying to stop a fight *19-*, *now Bnf*. **~in &c 1** the action of *redding*, *la15-*. **2** *in pl* (1) clearance, riddance *19* [w infl f Eng]; (2) fat removed from an animal's intestines, *esp* used for making PUDDINS *la19-*, *now Sh Dmf*. **~in kame &c** a comb for the hair *19-*, *local*. **~in straik** *etc* = **~er's lick**; *fig* a severe blow (of fate) *17-*, *now local Sh-EC*. **~ing-up** a scolding, rebuke *19-*, *local Sh-Kcb*. **redment 1** *also* **reddiment** a settlement of affairs etc *19-e20*. **2** a tidying-up *20-*, *Rox*.

~ bing a mound of waste at the surface of a mine or quarry *la19-*, *now Fif Loth*. **~ box** *mining* a truck for carrying rubbish to the pit-head *la19-*, *now Fif*. **~ han** a freeing, a clearance, a free hand *la19-*, *local Sh-Kcb*. **redland** *etc* land cleared of its crop, bare after cropping or ploughing *la16-*, *now Abd C*. **redland oats** a crop of oats sown after a cleaning crop, *eg* turnips *la20-*, *WC, SW*. **~sman** *mining* the person who keeps the passages in a pit clear of debris *18-*, *now Fif*.

mak ~ make progress or headway in business etc *la19-*, *now Ork*. **~ one's crap** *fig* get something off one's chest *la19-*, *now Abd*. **~ one's fit** *etc* clear the way for action or progress, extricate oneself from some difficulty *19-*, *now Sh-Per Kcb*. **~ the hoose** *or* **the ice** *curling* (CURL) clear the TEE¹ of stones with a fast, forceful shot *19-*. **the marches** *also fig* go round the boundaries of a BURGH, parish etc *la15-19*; *cf* RID, RIDE. **roads** *or* **the bout** scythe corn round the edges of a field to allow space for a reaping machine *la20-*, *NE*. **~ up** *vt, also* **~ out** scold, give a dressing-down to; speak critically of *la18-*, *local Sh-SW*. *n* **~-up** a scolding, rebuke *la19-*, *now local NE-SW*. **~ up** *or* **out kin(dred)** *etc* trace lineage *19-*, *local Sh-SW*. [*v* senses 1-3 f OE *hreddan* rescue; senses 4-14 prob f the cognate MLowGer, MDu *reden* put in order etc; *cf* REDE², RID]

redd² &c; **raid** *e17*, **rid &c** *18-e19* *n* **1** fish- or frog-spawn, *freq* **fish-~**, **paddock ~** *17-*, *now Per Wgt Rox*. **2** the rut in a riverbed made by salmon for spawning in *19-*.

vi, of fish spawn *18-, now Per Wgt.* [obscure; *cf* RODD]

redd[3] &c, **rad** &c *la15-19 adj* **1** = rad, quick, hasty *la15.* **2** prepared, willing *16-19.* **3** *also* ~-**handit** &c quick and skilful (with one's hands) *la18-19.*

adv readily, **as** ~ **.. as** as soon .. as *20, NE: 'as redd be sleepin 's harkenin'.*

redd *see* REDE[1]

reddendo &c [rɛˈdɛndo, rɪ-] *law* the duty or service to be paid by a VASSAL to a SUPERIOR as set out in a *feu charter* (FEU); the clause in which this is set out *17-.* [L = by giving in return (the first word of the clause)]

redder *see* RAITHER

reddicle *see* RETICULE

reddie *see* REID[1]

reddiment *see* REDD[1]

reddy *see* READY

rede[1] &c; **redd** &c *16-19* [rid; *rɛd] *v, ptp* **rede** &c *la19,* **redd** &c *la18-19* **1** *vt* = rede, guard, protect *la14-15.* **2** *vti* advise, counsel; warn *la14-e20.* **3** *vt* interpret, explain *18-20; cf* READ *v* 4. **4** *vti* think, consider, reckon *la18-19.*

n **1** advice, counsel; plan, determination *la14-19.* **2** a tale, narrative *la14, e19.*

my *etc* **dream is** ~ my etc wish has come true; my etc fate is sealed *la18-, now Abd.*

rede[2] &c [rid] *vt* = REDD[1] *v* 4 (*16, 19*), 6 (*la15*), 13 (*17-19*), 14 (*e19*).

n = REDD[1] *n* 4, *18-19.* [OE *rǣdan* arrange, dispose, put in order etc; *cf* MDu, MLowGer *reden*]

rede[3] *n* a sound *la15, only Sc.*

rede *see* RAD, READ, REID[1]

redimite &c; **redomyt** [*ˈrɛdɪməit] *adj* wreathed, crowned; adorned, beautiful *e16.* [only Sc; L *redimītus*]

redment *see* REDD[1]

redomyt *see* REDIMITE

redound &c; **radoun** *la15* [*rəˈdun(d)] *vti* **1** = redound *la15-.* **2** *vi* penetrate **to** *16, only Sc.* **3** *vt* return, refund (money, costs) *la16, only Sc.*

redress &c; **radres** &c *la14-15* [rəˈdrɛs] *n* redress *la14-.*

vt **1** = redress *la15-.* **2** (1) restore, give back *e16.* (2) make good (a bill) *la16.*

redschip *n* tackle, equipment *la16.* [only Sc; obs Du *reedschap, reeden* set in order, fit out; *cf* REDE[2]. OED *redship*]

reduce &c *vt* **1** = reduce *la14-.* **2** *law* annul, set aside by legal process *la15-.*

reducible &c *of a deed etc* capable of being set aside by legal process *16-.* **reduction** &c **1** = reduction *16-.* **2** the bringing back (of money) to the mint again *la16, only Sc.* **3** *law* the process of *reducing* a deed etc as in *v* 2, *16-.* **reduction-improbation** a *reduction* (*n* 3) sought on grounds of forgery *la18-.* **reduction-reductive** the annulment of an improperly-obtained *reduction* (*n* 3), *19-.*

redvore &c *n* ? some piece of equipment used in weaving *e15.* [ME *radevore* &c]

redy *see* READY

ree[1] &c, **reeve** &c *la18-, now NE Per;* **reed** &c [ri; *NE* riv, rɪv; *C* rid] *n* **1** a yard or enclosure for storing coal and from which it may be sold retail *18-, C.* **2** an enclosure or pen for animals, *specif* (1) *freq* **reed** a stone-built yard, wholly or partly covered, in which cattle are wintered *la18-, now EC, WC;* (2) a permanent stone sheepfold, used during stormy weather, shearing etc *la17-, now SW;* (3) a pigsty, *usu* a building and an outdoor run *la19-, local NE-SW;* (4) a chicken run *20-, NE, SW.* **3** *chf* **reeve** *by extension* a prehistoric hill-fort *la18-19.* [only Sc; see SND]

ree[2] &c *adj* **1** tipsy, befuddled with drink *la18-, now Ork; cf* REEZIE. **2** over-excited, delirious, crazy *la18-, now Ork Fif.*

n a state of great excitement or frenzy *18-e20.* *vi* become extremely excited, fly into a rage *la19-, now Ork.* [*cf* eME *rei, reȝ-,* OE *hrēoh* disturbed in mind]

ree[3] &c *n* a medium-sized sieve or riddle for cleaning grain, peas, beans etc *18-, now Stlg midLoth.*

vt clean (grain, grass-seed, peas, beans etc) by sieving in a REE[3] *la18-, now midLoth.* [also in Eng dial; ME *ree, rye* &c (*v*) sieve; obscure]

reebald &c *la19-,* **ribald** &c; **rebald** *la14-16,* **reebal** *la19-* [ˈribəl(d); *ˈribal(d), &c] *n* a good-for-nothing, a scoundrel *la15-, now Sh Ork.* *adj* = ribald *16-.*

~**aill** &c [*ˈribaldel, *ˈrɪ-] rabble; low company *la14-e16.* [OF *ribaldaille*]

reeble *see* RAIBLE

reechnie &c [ˈrixnɪ, ˈrɛx-] *n* a rough, uncouth person, *esp* a woman or girl *la19-e20, Bnf Abd.* [obscure]

reed[1] *n* **1** (the direction of) the grain in wood, stone or metal *la18-, now local C.* **2** *mining* the line in a coal seam along which the strata split off *la18-, now midLoth.* **3** a longitudinal defect in a lead pipe *la20-, WC.*

vi, of a lead pipe split longitudinally *la20-, WC.* ~**ie** *of a lead pipe* liable to split (as in *v*) *la20-, local EC, WC.* [obscure]

reed[2] &c *n* **1** = read, the stomach of an animal *la15.* **2** *specif* the fourth stomach of a ruminant *la19-20.* [OED *read* (*n*[1])]

reed *see* REE[1], RUID

reediemadeasy *see* READ

reef &c *n* a skin disease producing scabs *la16-19.* [OE *hrēofa* leprosy, *hrēof* scabby, leprous]

reef *see* REEVE[1], RUIF

reefort *see* RIFART

reeg *see* RIG[1]

reeho *n* a state of excited impatience, a stir *20, Bnf Abd.* [perh onomat]

reek[1] &c; **rick** *la20-, NE n* **1** smoke, vapour *la14-.* **2** a cloud or column of smoke *la18-, now Sh Ork Cai.* **3** a house with a fire burning on the hearth, an inhabited house *la16-*, *now Sh Ork*. **4** mist, *esp* a morning mist rising from the ground *la18-*, *now Sh Abd*. **5** the act of smoking a pipe etc, a smoke, a whiff, puff *la19-*.

v **1** *vi*, *of something burning* emit smoke *16-e19*. **2** *of a house etc* have smoke coming out of the chimney as a sign of habitation *la16-20*. **3** *of a chimney* (1) emit smoke, *esp* as a sign of human habitation *19-*; (2) fail to emit smoke properly, sending it back into the room *la19-*. **4** *vti* smoke (a pipe etc) *20-*, *now Stlg*. **5** *vi* = reek *16-*. **6** *of hot liquid, damp hay, corn etc* emit vapour or steam *18-*, *now local Sh-Kcb*. **7** show anger or fury, fume *la19-*, *now Ayr*.

~ie &c **1** smoky, smoke-filled; blackened or begrimed by smoke *16-*. **2** of or like smoke; misty, damp *16-e19*. **~ie-mire &c** a hollowed cabbage-stalk packed with oily waste, used to blow smoke into a house as a prank *la19-*, *Mry Bnf*. **~ie Peter** a CRUISIE *la19*, *NE*. **~ing &c** inhabited *la18-*, *now Sh Ork*. **~in hot** *of a bowl or quoit* delivered at great speed *la19-*, *Per Fif*. **a ~in lum** **1** an inhabited house *la20-*. **2** a chimney which smokes (as in *v* 3 (2)); *hence* a source of annoyance which drives one from the house, *esp* a nagging wife *20-*, *now local Sh-Fif*. **get** (*or* **gie someone**) **it het and ~in** be scolded or beaten severely, scold or beat someone severely *la20-*, *Sh Per*. **~it &c** **1** begrimed, blackened with smoke or soot, sooty *la18-*, *now local Sh-Kcb*. **2** *of food* smoke-cured; smoke-tainted, acrid *16-*.

~ fowl, **~ hen** a hen paid as part of rental for every house with a hearth *16-19*.

borrowed ~ smoke from a neighbouring chimney blown down another by the wind *la20-*, *NE*. **raise a ~** make a great fuss, cause a stir *la18-*, *now local Sh-Lnk*. **a** (**sour**) **~ in the house** *fig* something unpleasant at home, *esp* a nagging wife *18-e20*. [chf nME *reke &c*; OE *rēc* smoke, ON *reykr* smoke, steam]

reek² &c *n* a wild, irresponsible trick, a subterfuge *19-*, *now Rox*. [eModEng *reakes*]

reek *see* REIK

reel¹ &c *n* **1** = reel, a rotatory device; a whirl or whirling movement *la16-*. **2** (1) a lively dance with setting steps and travelling figures, danced by a minimum of three dancers, but now *usu* by a set of two, three or four couples *la16-*; see also *foursome reel* (FOWER), *eightsome reel* (AUCHT¹). (2) the music to which a REEL¹ is danced *la16-*. **3** a rapid careless delivery (of a speech etc) *la16*, *only Sc*. **4** a commotion, clamour, stir, *freq* **make a ~** *16-e18*. **5** a noise, crash, peal *la16-*, *now Sh Stlg*.

v **1** *vt* wind (yarn etc) on a reel; fill (a spool) with thread *la16-20*. **2** *vi* turn with a circular motion, whirl or spin around *16-19*. **3** *of the eyes* roll or revolve with excitement, greed etc *16-*, *now NE Ags*. **4** *of the head or senses* be in a whirl, become confused *la18-*. **5** rush about in a furious or violent way; behave riotously *la14-19*. **6**

of an army etc waver, give way *la14-16*. **7** *vti* = reel; (cause to) stagger *16-*. **8** *vti* dance a REEL¹; *specif* execute a figure-of-eight travelling movement *la15-*. **9** *vi* make a great noise, clamour or clatter *18-19*.

~-foot a club-foot *la19-e20*. **~-fitted &c** having a **~-foot**, *la19-*, *local Sh-Wgt*. **~-rall &c** [cf *reavel-ravel* (RAIVEL)] *n* a state of confusion, a muddle of objects, sounds etc *la18-*, *NE local C*. *adj* confused, disorganized, higgledy-piggledy *19-*, *N-C*. *adv* in a confused way, higgledy-piggledy *19-*, *N-C*.

dance the ~ o Bogie etc, *euphemistic* have sexual intercourse *18-e20*. **in gweed ~** in step, in good order, tidy *la20-*, *NE*. **out o** (**the**) **~** out of step or tune, astray, disarranged *la19-*, *NE*. **R~ of Tulloch &c** **1** *also* **Tullich R~** *e18* a tune of uncertain origin used for dancing a REEL¹ *18-*. **2** a *Highland dance* (HIELAND) performed by four persons, *prob* originating in the Central *Highlands* (HIELAND); *freq* danced after the two-couple *strathspey* (STRATH) *19-*; *cf* HOOLACHAN.

reel² *n* a mason's medium-weight hammer with two oblong faces *la19-*. [perh f prec (*v* 9) f the noise it makes]

reemage *see* RUMMAGE

reemick *see* RAMMOCK²

reemis &c; reemish ['rimɪs, -ɪʃ] *n* **1** a resounding crash or rumble, as of falling masonry etc *la18-*, *Bnf Abd*. **2** *of a lighter sound* a scuffle, din, clatter *19-*, *now Abd*. **3** a heavy stroke, blow or beating *la18-*, *Bnf Abd*.

vi move about with a crashing or clattering sound, jolt, jar *20-*, *NE*. [var of RUMMISS]

reemish *see* RUMMAGE

reemle &c *vi* make a sharp, tremulous noise; make a lot of noise *la19-*, *Bnf*. [altered f RUMMLE w infl f prec]

reen *see* REIN, RIND¹

reenge &c; ringe &c *19-e20*, *C* [rin(d)ʒ, rɪn(d)ʒ] *v* **1** *vt* traverse, wander over, travel through *la19-*, *Sh NE*, *C*. **2** *vti* search (a place) widely and thoroughly *19-*, *now Sh NE*, *C*. **3** *vt* poke ashes from (a fire), *esp* through the bars of a grate to let air circulate *19-*, *now Ags Fif WC*. **4** *vi* bustle about noisily, pace hither and thither *19-*, *now local Sh-WC*. **5** make a clattering or rumbling noise *19-*.

n **1** range, distance, bounds *la19-*, *now NE*. **2** the seat(s) in a church just below the pulpit, used by the ELDERS etc *19*, *Fif*. **3** a thorough search, a tour of inspection *la19-*, *now Kcdn EC*, *WC*. **4** a clattering, ringing noise *19-e20*.

~ the ribs = *v* 3, *la18-e20*. [ME *renge*, OF *renge(r)* (set in) line or rank; var of RANGE; cf *cheenge* (CHANGE)]

reenge *see* RINSE

re-enter *vti* **1** = re-enter *16-*. **2** put (a person) **in** (a place of custody) again *la16*, *only Sc*.

re-entry **1** = re-entry. **2** the act of *re-entering* (*v* 2) *la16*, *only Sc*.

reep &c n familiar, slightly derog term for a person 19, Bnf Abd. [obscure]

reerie &c n a noisy quarrel or disturbance, a row, uproar 19-, NE. [uncertain]

ree-ruck &c n a small rick of corn set up to aid drying 19-e20, S. [first element uncertain + RUCK]

reese see RUISE

reeshle see REESLE

reesk &c n **1** also **risk &c** la15, 18 a piece of moor or marshy ground covered with natural grass la15-, now Abd Kcdn, freq in place-names Cai, local WC-Kcb. **2** a growth of natural coarse grasses or rushes on rough, waste or marshy ground 18-, now Bnf Abd.

~ie &c of ground having a REESK n 2, 18-e20, Abd. [only Sc; ScGael riasg sedge-grass, land covered with this, OIr riasc a fen]

reesle &c la18-; **reestle &c** 19-e20, **reeshle &c** 19-, **rissle &c** 18-20 ['risl, 'riʃl, 'rɪsl] v **1** vi = rustle 18-, now local. **2** of wind etc whistle la19-, now local. **3** (1) of doors, crockery etc clatter, rattle 19-, local Sh-WC. (2) rap **at** (a door) la19-, now Rox. **4** of persons or animals move about noisily or with a clatter, crash about 19-, now Sh NE. **5** go **through** with a scuffling noise, rummage **through** 20-, now Ags Per. **6** vt move or shake (an object) so as to make it rustle or rattle la19-, now Sh-Per wLoth. **7** beat, whack, thrash 18-, now Ags wLoth. **8** (1) shake, stir, agitate 20-, now local Sh-Per. (2) riddle (ashes) la20-, WC. **9** vi shiver, shudder la19-, now Sh [cf Norw rysja shudder].

n **1** a rustling sound la19-, now N. **2** a loud clattering, knocking or banging noise la18-, Sh-EC. **3** something which clatters or rattles by being loose or unstable, something rickety or likely to collapse la19-, chf Ags. **4** a shake producing a rattling or jingling sound, a jolt, jerk 19-, local Sh-Stlg. **5** a heavy blow or stroke 19-, now Sh EC. **6** a spell of bad weather, esp windy weather at harvest-time 20-, Cai. **7** an involuntary shiver or shudder la19-e20. **8** a large crowd or amount 20-, now Sh.

adv with a rustling noise; with a clash or clatter la19-, now Sh Ags. [onomat; cf MDu rysselen, Eng rustle]

reest¹ &c v **1** vt cure (fish, ham etc) by drying or smoking 16-, now local Sh-Wgt. **2** vi, of fish, ham etc be cured (as in v 1) 18-, now Sh.

n a wood or rope framework on which fish, meat etc is smoked 19-, now Sh. [only Sc; appar Scand; cf Norw, Dan riste broil, grill, Icel, Norw rist a gridiron]

reest² &c 18-; **reist &c** la15-19, **rest** la16-e20, **rist** la19-20 [chf rist; also rɛst, rɪst, riʃt] v **1** vt arrest, seize (goods), chf for debt, POIND la16-, now Rox. **2** bring to a halt, arrest the motion or action of la17-, now NE. **3** freq **rest** cover or damp down (a fire) for the night la18-, local Sh-Fif [perh formally confused w Eng rest]. **4** vi, of horses, also of other animals, persons, vehicles stop

and refuse to move, jib, balk la18-, now NE sEC-S. **5** of a person or his limbs come to a (sudden) halt, become rooted to the spot 19-, now Kcb.

n **1** = rest, a piece of armour which held the butt end of a lance la15-16. **2** esp of horses the act of stopping and refusing to move, freq **tak the ~** jib 19-, now Stlg.

~er a jibbing horse; a stubborn person la19-e20. **~ie &c** of a horse, also fig inclined to jib 18-, local EC-S. **~in clod** or **peat** a turf or PEAT¹ laid over a fire to keep it burning slowly all night la19-, Sh NE. [aphetic f ARREIST]

reest³ &c n the mould-board of a plough 18-, now Abd C.

vi tilt a plough to the right (ie to the mould-board side) 20-, local EC-WC. [ModEng dial, eModEng; cf WREST²]

reest see ROOST¹

reestle see REESLE

reet see RUIT¹, RUIT²

reeve¹; reef vi chatter, babble 19. [perh F rêver dream > Eng rave talk incoherently]

reeve² &c, reave vti, pt, ptp **reft** tear, rend, grab, snatch forcibly (**at**) la14-, now Ork.

reevin of wind high, gusty; fig, of persons rash, excitable 19-e20; cf REEZE. [ME; appar conflation of REIVE w RIVE; Sh Ork prob direct f Norw rive]

reeve³ vi, chf **reevin** blazing 20-, NE. [perh extended f prec]

reeve see REE¹

reevick &c [S 'rivək; Rox also 'rið-] n a very thin, flimsy piece of cloth, specif of muslin cheesecloth 19-e20, S. [perh dim of obs or dial Eng reeve a long narrow strip of cloth]

re-examinat ptp re-examined la16, only Sc.

reeze &c vi, of the wind blow strongly 19.

reezie &c windy, blowy; gusty 19-e20, EC. [perh chf onomat; cf REEVE²]

reezie &c adj light-headed, esp from drink, tipsy 19-, now Slk. [uncertain; cf prec and REE²]

ref see REIF

refar see REFER

refase, refeese see REFUISE

refer; refar &c 18-20, chf Abd-Ags [rə'fɛr, rə'far] vti **1** = refer la15-. **2** vt, law, in a civil action, chf **~ a matter to an oath** submit a fact at issue to proof by the oath of a defender (DEFEND), esp in a debt case la16-. **3** vi defer, delay, put off making a decision 18-20.

n, only Sc **1** a matter referred for consideration 17. **2** a reference (in a book) la17.

~ence ['rɛfərəns] **1** = reference. **2** law the act of referring (v 2) la18-. **~rance** ['rɛfərəns] = reference la16, only Sc. **~rer** law a person who REFERS (v 2) la17-.

refete &c [*rə'fit] v **1** vt = refete, refect, refresh la14-e15. **2** vi recover, recuperate la15.

refleck vt = reflect 19-.

refloir [*rə'flor] vt cause to flourish again la16. [only Sc. OED reflore]

refond see REFOUND[2]

reform &c vti **1** = reform la14-. **2** vt repair, make good (damage, a loss etc) la15-e17.

Reformed Presbyterian Church the church (or any of its courts) descending from those *Covenanters* (COVENANT) who continued to oppose the Revolution Settlement after 1688 and who consider themselves to be the surviving remnant of the true *Covenanted* KIRK; most of them joined with the *Free Church* (FREE) in 1876 and only a few congregations remain *18-*; see also SOCIETY and CAMERONIAN [so called because their leaders re-formed a PRESBYTERY out of the SOCIETIES in 1743]. ~**er 1** = reformer la16-. **2** also ~**ier** = reformado, an officer left without a command but retaining his rank and receiving full or half pay *e17*. **3 R~er** a member of the *R~ed Presbyterian Church, 18-*.

refound[1] [*rəˈfund] vt found again, re-establish *e16*. [OF *refonder*]

refound[2] la15-e18; **refond** e15 [rəˈfʌnd, *rəˈfund] vt **1** refund *15-e18*. **2** make good, repair (an injury etc) la16. **3** cast the blame of (something) **on** (a person or thing) la17. [only Sc; var of Eng *refund*]

refoys see REFUSE

refraiche see REFRESH

refrain &c *16-*; **refrenȝe** la14-e16, **rafreyn** la15 [reˈfren; *reˈfrin, *rəˈfrenʃi] vti **1** = refrain la14-. **2** vt hold, contain e16, only Sc. **3** avoid, shun (danger) la16, only Sc.
n restraint la16, only Sc.

refresh &c; **refres** la14, **refraiche** la16 [rəˈfrɛʃ; *rəˈfrɛs, *?-ˈfrɛʃ] vt **1** = refresh la14-. **2** restore, renovate (a building) la14. **3** cool (desire) la16.

reft n robbery la15-16. [only Sc; altered f REIF, after ptp of REIVE]

reft see REEVE[2], REIVE

refuise &c *16-*, **refuse &c**; **refoys &c** *15-16*, **refase &c** la19-e20, **refeese &c** *19-20, NE* [rəˈføz; *NE* rəˈfiz; *C* rəˈfez; *Loth* also rəˈfjez] vti **1** = refuse la14-. **2** vt deny *18*.
n a refusal e17, 20-, now local NE-Wgt.
adj refused, rejected e16.

refurm [*rəˈfʌrm] vt = re-form, form again e15. [only Sc. OED *re-form* (v^2)]

refuse see REFUISE

refutation &c n **1** military repulse **of** (a person) la16, only Sc. **2** = refutation.

regaird, regard &c [rəˈgerd] n (*15-*), v (*16-*) = regard.
~**less &c 1** attrib (1) heedless, uncaring la17-; (2) specif heedless of religious practices, irreligious la19-, now Sh Cai. **2** = regardless.
without ~ of = without regard to la16-e17.

regal see REGALL

regalia n **1** = regalia; cf HONOUR n 2. **2** law rights held by the Crown, comprising ~ **majora**, which are inalienable, and ~ **minora**, which may be conveyed to subjects by royal grant la17-.

regality &c; rigalitie *16, only Sc* [rɪˈgalɪti] **1** = regality. **2** (1) a jurisdiction almost co-extensive with that of the Crown, granted by the sovereign to a powerful subject *15-e18*; see *lord of* ~ (LORD). (2) land or territory subject to such jurisdiction *16-e18*. (3) a particular area under such jurisdiction *15-e18*.
~ **court, court of** ~ a court held by a *lord of* ~ (LORD) and presided over by a BAILIE or STEWART as the LORD's deputy la17-e18.

regall e18, **regal &c** n = REGALITY 2, la14-e18. adj = regal *16-*.

regard see REGAIRD

regent &c n **1** = regent la15-. **2** *Sc Univs* a teacher who took a class of students through the full four-year Arts course in language, physics and philosophy *16-18*. **3** *St Andrews and Aberdeen Univs* a lecturer etc who acts as adviser and consultant to students assigned to him la20- [a revival of the title of n 2 but with different duties].
vi act as a REGENT (n 2) *17-18*.
~**rie** the office or function of a REGENT (n 1 and n 2) la16, only Sc.

regibus &c; rangiebus &c [*?ˈrɛdʒɪbʌs, *?ˈrendʒɪbʌs, *?ˈrenɪbʌs] n a boys' game, usu involving one side trying to capture the other side's caps la19-e20, NE. [appar schoolboy usage of L *regibus*, dative pl of *rex* a king; cf REX]

regimen &c n **1** government, rule la15-e16. **2** = regimen.

regimental n, in pl **1** formal dress or livery, one's best clothes la19-. **2** = regimentals.

reginal adj queenly la16. [obs F]

region &c n **1** = region la14-. **2** one of the nine larger units into which Scotland (*except* Orkney, Shetland and *the Western Isles* (ILE)) was divided for local government purposes in 1975, la20-; cf *district* (DESTRICK), *Islands Council* (ISLAND) and BORDERS, CENTRAL, DUMFRIES AND GALLOWAY, FIFE, GRAMPIAN, *Highland* (*Region*) (HIELAND), *Lothian* (LOWDEN), *Strathclyde* (STRATH), TAYSIDE.
~**al 1** = regional. **2** of a REGION (n 2) la20-; '*Regional Council*'. ~**alization &c** the reorganization of Scotland into REGIONS (n 2) la20-.

register &c n **1** the record of royal charters etc under the Great Seal *15-e16*. **2** the collection of State and official papers, including parliamentary and judicial records and private deeds, *latterly esp* those concerned with the transfer of HERITABLE property, preserved in *R~ House*, la15-e19. **3** = register la15-. **4** (1) = clerk ~, *16-17*. (2) = *Lord Clerk R~, e18*.
R~ House &c *16-*, **R~ Office** la18, **General R~ House** la17- the various building(s) in Edinburgh in which the REGISTER has been kept.
Clerk of (the or **his)** ~ la15-e17, **clerk** ~ *17-e18*, **Lord (Clerk) of R~** la16-17, **Lord R~** *17-18*, **Lord Clerk R~** *18-* the official, later *officer of state* (OFFICER), responsible for the framing and custody of the main state registers

and records; *latterly* (*la19-*) a titular office only, giving the holder precedence after the *Lord Justice General* (LORD); he is also *Keeper of the Signet* (SIGNET); *cf* next. **Deputy (Clerk) R~** *19-e20*, **Keeper of the R~s and Records** *e20* the official appointed to carry out the duties of the (titular) *Lord Clerk R~*; *cf* prec. **Keeper of the R~s 1** = *Keeper of the Records* 1 (RECORD) *la17-e18*. **2** the official responsible for framing the registers of SASINES, deeds etc *20-*; *cf Keeper of the Records* (RECORD). **Lord (Clerk) (of) R~** see *Clerk of (the or his) R~*.

registrate &c *ptp*, *adj* registered, recorded *15-18.*

vt register *la16-19.* [chf Sc; MedL *registrat-*, ptp stem of *registrare*, f *registrum* a register]

registration &c *n* the act of registering or recording; an instance of this *la16-*.

reglar &c *la19-e20*, **regular** ['reglər] *adj* = regular *16-*.

n **1** *only* **reguleir** [*rɛgøˈlir] a regulator *e16*, *only Sc.* **2** = regular.

regne see RING³

regour &c [*ˈrigər] *n* = rigour *la16.*

regrate &c [*rəˈgret] *v* **1** *vt* lament, feel or express sorrow at *la14-e18.* **2** lament or mourn the death or loss of (a person or thing) *la14-e18.* **3** *vi* lament, mourn *e17.*

n (an expression of) grief, sorrow or disappointment *la14-e18.* [only Sc; OF *regrater*, var of *regreter &c* > Eng *regret*]

regress *n* **1** = regress *la14-*. **2** *law* an obligation by a SUPERIOR to re-admit a VASSAL to land which he had conveyed in WADSET, once he was able to redeem it, *freq* **letters of~** *15-18.*

regular see REGLAR

regulation *n* = regulation.

R~ roll a roll of the *Court of Session* (SESSION) listing jury cases or those where no appearance had been made for the *defender* (DEFEND) *e19.*

reguleir see REGLAR

regyne &c [*rəˈdʒəin] *n* a queen *e16.* [only Sc; L *rēgīna.* OED *regine*]

regyre &c [*rəˈdʒəir] *vt* return, retort *e17.* [only Sc; L *regȳrare* turn about]

rehabile see REABLE

rehabilitate &c *vt* **1** restore by decree (an attainted or degraded person) to former privileges, rank and possession *16-*. **2** = rehabilitate *la17-*.

rehator &c; rahatour [*rəˈhetər] *n* term of abuse for a person *e16.* [only Sc; obscure]

rehearse &c; rahers &c *la15*, **reheirs** *la16* [rəˈhɛrs; *-ˈhirs] *vti* = rehearse *la14-*.

n = rehearsal, a recital, repetition, recitation *la14-16.*

reid¹ &c *16-*, **red &c**; **rede** *la14-e16*, **rid** *16-*, **rud &c** *18-e20* [rid; *Sh C* rɪd; *Rox also* rɪd] *adj* **1** = red *la14-*. **2** bloody, resulting in bloodshed *19.* **3** mad, furious *19.*

vti redden, make or become red *19-20.*

~ie &c, reddie [ˈrɪdɪ, ˈrɛdɪ] a red clay marble *la19-*, WC.

~-arsie &c a bee with red markings behind *19-*, *now NE Ags.* **red biddy** *slang* a mixture of cheap red wine and methylated spirit or other alcohol *20-* [perh thought of as drunk by the Irish in Gsw, f *Biddy*, pet form of *Bridget*, a common female name in Ireland]. **~ brae** the gullet *20-*, *local Ags-SW.* **Redcap** a fairy or goblin said to haunt old buildings *19-e20.* **~coat &c 1** R~coat = Redcoat, a soldier in the British army. **2** a ladybird *19-*, *chf Rox.* **~ etin &c** *also fig* a giant, a savage monster *16-e19.* **~ face** a blushing face, as a sign of embarrassment or shame, *freq* **give &c** someone *or* **get a ~ face** *19-*. **~ fish 1** a male salmon at spawning time when it turns reddish *15-*, *now WC, SW.* **2** *used where the name 'salmon' is taboo* salmon *in gen*, *la19-20.* **gae roon a bodie's hert like a ~ yaird o ~ flannan** warm the heart, be very palatable or flattering *la20-*, *Sh-N.* **~ friar &c** a Templar *16-18*, *latterly hist.* **~ gibbie &c** the stickleback *20-*, *Ags.* **red gown** the scarlet gown worn **1** by a judge of the *Court of Session* (SESSION) in his capacity as a *Lord of Justiciary* (LORD) dealing with criminal cases *18*; **2** by an arts undergraduate of one of the four older universities, *now* not worn regularly *la18-*; *cf* TOGA. **~ hand**, *also* **with ~ hand** *la16-e17* (captured) in the act of a crime *15-* [Eng *red-handed* is a coinage of Scott's based on this]. **~ hawk &c 1** the merlin *e16.* **2** the kestrel *la19.* **Red-head tax** a freight tax on coal carried by sea further north than Red-Head, a promontory in Ags *la18*, *Sh N.* **~-heidit &c** having red hair and thus popularly believed to be excitable and impetuous *la19-*, *Gen except Sh Ork.* **Red Hose Race** an annual foot-race at Carnwath, Lnk with a pair of red hose as the prize *19-*. **~ lane** = **~ brae**, *la20-*, *local.* **red-legged crow** the chough *la18-e20.* **~ lichtie** nickname for a native or inhabitant of Arbroath *la19-*, *Ags* [see SND]. **R~ Lichties** nickname for the Arbroath football team *la20-*. **~ mad** furiously angry, demented *19-*, *now Sh Cai.* **~ nakit** stark naked *la19-*, *local Abd-Per.* **~ neb &c 1** a red nose *19-*. **2** the oyster-catcher *la20-*, *Bnf Abd.* **3** a variety of potato with red markings at one end *la18-e19.* **~-nebbit pussy** the puffin *la20-*, *Mry Bnf.* **~ Rab** the robin redbreast *20-*, *now wLoth Slk.* **~ road** = **~ brae**, *la20-*, *local.* **~-shank &c 1** nickname for a *Highlander* (HIELAND) *esp* a *kilted* (KILT¹) soldier, from his bare legs *16-19*, *latterly hist.* **2** = redshank, the bird *16-*. **3** name for various weeds with red stems or seed spikes, *esp* the common sorrel, the broad-leaved dock *19-*, *now C-S.* **~ ware &c** the seaweed *Laminaria digitata*, from its red colour *la18-*, *now Sh-N Fif.* **redware cod(ling)** a young inshore cod *19-*, *now Sh-EC.* **~-wat literary** blood-stained *19.* **~-wat shod** *literary* up to the ankles in blood *la18-e19.* **~ wood &c** the wood at the heart of trees *e19*. ~ **wud &c** stark staring mad, beside oneself with rage, mentally unbalanced *16-*, *now local N-SW*.

reid² **&c** [*ˀrid] *n* = RAID 2, *la16-17*. [perh directly f Du *reede* or LowGer *rêde*]

reid *see* RAID

reif &c; ref &c *la14-16* [*rif] *n* **1** plunder, booty, spoil *la14-e19*. **2** the act or practice of robbery; plundering *la14-19*.

fowl &c of ~ a bird of prey *la15*. [OE *rēaf*; *cf* REIVE]

reif *see* REIVE

rei interventus [ˈreaɪ, ˈrɪaɪ ɪntərˈvɛntʌs] *n, law* conduct by one party to an uncompleted and informal contract with the knowledge and permission of the other party, which makes the contract binding *la18-*. [L = the intervention of a circumstance]

reik &c; reek [rik] *vt* fit or rig **out**, equip *la16-*, *now Kcdn Ags Lnk*. [only Sc; obscure]

reik *see* REAK

rein &c *la15-*; **renȝe &c** *la14-16*, **renyie &c** *18-e19*, **rine &c** *la18-20*, **reen &c** *19* [*NE, WC, SW* rəin; *sEC, S* rin; *ˀrɛn(j)ɪ, *ˀrɛɲɪ, ?&c] *n, vt* = rein.

reing *see* RING¹

reinge *see* RING³

reingres [*ˀriˈɪnˈgrɛs] *n* renewed ingress *e16*. [OED *reingress*]

reir &c [*rir] *vi* go backwards, retreat *la14-15*. *n* **on** ~ ? back; ? in the background *la15*. [appar aphetic f *arere* (AREAR)]

reird &c *la15-*, **rerde &c** *15-16*; **raird** *16-e20* [rerd, rird] *n* **1** a roar; a loud uproar or clamour *15-e20*. **2** (a) din, loud noise *la15-e19*. **3** a loud outburst, *eg* of laughter or scolding *18-*, *now Rox*. **4** a noisy breaking of wind *18-*, *now Abd*.

vi **1** shout, roar, make a noise *15-e19*. **2** make a loud crashing or cracking noise *la15-*, *now Kcb*. **3** scold loudly *19*.

rerdour clamour, tumult *e16*. [ME *rerde &c*, OE *reord* voice, cry]

reis *see* RICE

reist *see* REEST²

reithe &c, rethe &c *15* [*rið] *adj* **1** fierce, cruel; terrible, furious *15*. **2** zealous, keen *e19*, *only Sc*. [nME *reth*, OE *rēþe* harsh, severe]

reive &c, reave *la18-*, **rave** *16*; **reve &c** *la14-15*, **reif &c** *la14-e19* [riv; *rev] *v, pt, ptp* *also* **reft** **1** *vi* rob, plunder, pillage, *later esp* in the course of a RAID *la14-*, *now local NE-S*. **2** *vt* despoil, rob; deprive (a person) **of** (something) *la14-19*. **3** take away; steal, remove by theft or pillage *la14-*, *now Bnf Ags*. **4** rescue (a person) by carrying off *la16-e17*.

reiver &c, reiffar &c *la14-19*, *latterly literary* **1** a plunderer, robber, *esp* one riding on a RAID *la14-*, *now hist*. **2** a pirate, sea-robber *la14-15*. **3** the chief male participant in the annual festival at Duns, Bwk *la20-*, *Bwk*. **Reiver's Lass** the female partner of *reiver* 3, *la20-*, *Bwk*.

~ **up** snatch or lift up *la16-e18*. [OE *rēafian* plunder; *cf* REIF]

rejeck &c, reject &c [rɪˈdʒɛk(t)] *vt* **1** = reject *16-*. **2** dismiss from one's mind *la16*.

relapse *n* **1** = relapse *16-*. **2** *also adj* (a person) having twice offended against church discipline *e18*; *cf* DULAPSE.

relax *vti* **1** *chf law* release from a legal process or penalty, *esp* from outlawry *16-18*: 'relax from the horn'. **2** = relax.

~**ation &c** **1** *law* release from a judicial penalty, *esp* outlawry *16-18*. **2** = relaxation.

release &c [rəˈlis; *S also* rəˈliʃ] *vt* = release *la14-*.

n **1** = release *15-*. **2** a variety of the game of tig in which players who have been touched by the catcher may be released by the touch of an uncaught player *20-*, *NE nEC, WC*; *cf* RELIEF, *reliever* (RELIEVE).

relect [*rəlɛkt] *ptp* read again *la16*. [only Sc; L *relect-*, ptp stem of *relegere*]

releegion &c *la16-*, **religion &c** [rəˈlidʒən] *n* **1** = religion *la15-*. **2** *as collective* members of a religious order *la14-15*.

releegious &c [rəˈlidʒəs] = religious *la16-*.

releif *see* RELIEVE

releit *see* RELY

relevant &c *adj* **1** pertinent to the matter in hand *la16-*. **2** *law, esp of a charge or claim* pertinent, sufficient to justify the appropriate penalty or remedy, if the alleged facts are proved *16-*.

relevancy &c *esp law* the state of being RELEVANT *la16-*. [*cf* IRRELEVANT]

relict &c [ˈrɛlɪk(t)] *n* **1** = relict, a relic *16-*. **2** a widow *la15-*, *now arch*. **3** *in pl* the remains of a dead person *17-e19*.

relief &c; raleyff *e15* [rəˈlif] *n* **1** *law* (1) a payment made by an heir of a deceased VASSAL to the SUPERIOR for his recognition as lawful successor *la14-e20*; (2) the right of a person standing security for a debt to reclaim payment from his principal or from his fellow *cautioners* (CAUTION) if he has paid more than his share *la17-*. **2** = relief *la15-*. **3** freedom from ecclesiastical oppression, *esp* with reference to the 18th century controversy in the *Church of Scotland* (CHURCH) led by Thomas Gillespie, concerning the right of a congregation to elect its own MINISTER; this led to the formation of the **Relief Church** *la18-e19*. **4** *in a variety of the game of tig* a call by which an uncaught player may release one who has been touched by the catcher and made to stand still *20-*, *local NE-Ayr*; *cf* RELEASE, LEAVE-O.

relieve &c; releif &c *la14-16*, **ralef** *e16* [rəˈliv] *vt* **1** = relieve *la14-*. **2** *law* release from a legal obligation; *specif* refund the payment of (a *cautioner* (CAUTION) or guarantor) *la15-e19*. **3** provide **with** (something); assist **with** (munitions of war) *la14*. **4** release from captivity, set free *la16-e20.* **5** recover, regain *la16, only Sc.* **6** bring (something) into prominence, make clear or evident *la16, only Sc.*

reliever 1 a member of the *Relief Church* (RELIEF) *la19, hist.* **2** = RELEASE *n* 2, *20-, local Inv-WC.*

religion *see* RELEEGION

relocation [rilə'keʃn, rɛ-] *n* **1** tacit ~ *law* the assumed continuation of a lease or contract of employment on unchanged terms if no action is taken at the date of expiry *la17-.* **2** = relocation.

relusand [*rə'løsand] *adj* relucent, shining *la15.* [ME *relusaunt,* OF *reluisant,* presp of *reluire.* OED *relusant*]

rely &c *vti, pt also* **releit &c** *la14* [*rə'liːt] **1** = rely *la14-.* **2** *vi, freq* ~ **tae** *or* **til** make one's home with *20-, Bnf Abd.*

rem *see* RAME

remain &c; ramayn &c *15* [rə'men] *vi* **1** = remain *la14-.* **2** continue to belong **to** *e15.* **3** live, dwell, reside *la15-e16.* **4** be left **with** (a responsibility) *la15, only Sc.*

n **1** (1) *also in pl* = remain(s), the remainder, the rest; what is left; a dead body *la15-.* (2) *in pl* the surviving members of a group *la15.* **2** a stay, sojourn *la15.*

~and, ~ant, reman- [*rə'menand, *-ant] *n* the rest, the remainder *la14-17.* **~der &c 1** = remainder *la16-.* **2** [*Ork NE* 'rɛməndər] a remnant of cloth at the end of a bale *20-.* **~der sale** a sale of such remnants at reduced prices *la20-.*

~ **on** wait for *16, only Sc.*

remanent &c ['rɛmənɛnt, -ənt] *n* = remanent, the remainder, the rest *la15-e17.*

adj **1** remaining *la15-e17.* **2** *specif* remaining over and above, other, additional *16-e20.*

remark *n, vti* = remark.

~**in** observation, notice; a spectacle *la18-19.*

reme *see* REAM

remede *see* REMEID

remeeve *see* REMUVE

remeid *16-,* **remede &c** *la14-e20* [rə'mid] *n* **1** remedy, redress *la14-, now local NE-SW.* **2** the remedy or small margin by which coins may deviate from standard weight etc *la16.*

vt remedy, redress *la14-19.*

remeidar a person who remedies *e16.*

~ **of** *or* **in law** redress for one's grievances through the appropriate legal channels, *esp* by appeal to a higher court against the decision of a lower one *15-19.* [ME, OF *remede &c*]

remel *see* RYMMYLL

remember &c; ramember &c *16* [rə'mɛmbər] *vti* **1** = remember *la14-.* **2** *vi,* ~ **of** *or* **on** have memory of, recollect *la15-, now Sh Inv C.* **3** *vt* remind (a person) **of** or **about** *16-, now Fif.* **4** ~ **something to someone** remember to repay someone for something *la19-, now local NE-SW:* '*I'll remember it to you on term day*'.

~**ing prayer** the intercessory prayer *e19.*

rememmorat *see* REMEMORATE

rememor &c; ramemmor [*rə'mɛmor] *vt* = remember *e16.* [only Sc; *cf* next]

rememorant [*rə'mɛmorant] *adj* mindful *e16.* [only Sc; prob L *rememorant-,* presp stem of *rememorāri* remember]

rememorate [*rə'mɛmoret, *-at] *vt, ptp* **rememmorat** remind *la15.* [ptp stem of laL *rememorāri, -āre*]

remission &c *n* **1** = remission *16-.* **2** a formal pardon; a document conveying this *la15-e17, only Sc.*

remit &c [rɪ'mɪt; *n* 3 'rɪmɪt] *vti* = remit *la14-.* *n* **1** remission, pardon *15-16.* **2** a cross-reference in a book *la17.* **3** *law or formal* the referring of a matter to another authority for opinion, information, execution etc, *specif* the transfer of a case from one court to another; the terms and limits of such a reference *la17-.*

remnant *n* **1** *hist* name (used by themselves) for the extreme *Covenanters* (COVENANT) who refused to accept the Revolution Settlement of 1688, *esp* members of the *Societies* (SOCIETY), the MACMILLANITES, the *Reformed Presbyterian Church* (REFORM) *18-e19.* **2** = remnant.

remofe *see* REMUVE

remord &c *pt, ptp also* **remord &c** [*rə'mord] *v* **1** *vt* afflict with remorse or painful feelings *16-e17.* **2** examine (one's conscience etc) in a penitent spirit *la15-16.* **3** recall to mind with remorse or regret *la15-16.* **4** ponder *e16.* **5** *vi* feel remorse *la15-e17.* **6** awaken remorse *la16.* **7** *vt* = remord, blame, rebuke *e17.*

n a taint *la15.*

remorse *vti* express regret or remorse (about), repent, lament *la19-e20, chf Abd.* [eModEng]

remuve &c *la18-e20,* **remove &c; remufe &c** *15-16,* **remofe &c** *la14-16,* **ramove &c** *e15,* **ramuff** *la15,* **remeeve &c** *e16, 20, NE* [rə'møv; *NE* rə'miv] *vti* **1** = remove *la14-.* **2** *vt, of a landlord* compel (a tenant) to quit his holding *16-.* **3** *vi, of a tenant* quit a property *15-.*

removing &c 1 = removing *17-.* **2** *law* the *removing* (as in *v* 2) of a tenant by a landlord *la16-.*

renaig &c; renegue &c [rə'neg, rə'nig] *vi* refuse to do work; shirk; shy away from a responsibility, engagement or challenge *20-.* [*cf* Eng *renegue* deny, renounce]

rence *n* = raines, a fine linen *la16.* [only Sc. OED *raines*]

renchel &c ['rɛnʃəl, 'rɛn-] *n* a thin, spindly thing or person *19-, now Slk.* [perh f RANCE]

rencounter; rancounter [*rɛn'kuntər, *ran-] *n, vti* = rencounter, encounter *16-e17.*

~ **with** meet *17, only Sc.*

rendal *see* RIN

render *see* RANDER

rendevouse &c *18-e19;* **randyvoo &c** *e17, e19-20* ['randɪvu; *rɛndɪvuz] *n, v* = rendezvous.

renegue *see* RENAIG

renew; ranew *la15* [rə'nju] *vti* **1** = renew *la15*-. **2** *vi* begin a fresh attack **upon** *la15*.

renk *see* RINK

renkning *see* RANK[1]

rennie *see* RANE

rennish *n* a sudden crashing or clanging noise *19-e20, SW.* [obscure]

renounce *see* RENUNCE

renove [*rə'nov] *vt* renew *la16.* [ME; OF *renover &c* or L *renovāre*]

renown &c; ranowne &c *la14-15* [rə'nun] *n*, *vt* = renown *la14-*.
of ~ in respect of fame or distinction *15-e16.*
with great ~ with much distinction or display *la16.*

renownee &c [*rənu'ni] *n* renown *la14-e16.* [conflation of prec w obs Eng *renomee*]

Rens *e16*; **Rynche** *la15*, **Rance** *16* [*rɛns, *rɪnʃ, *rəinʃ, &c] *adj, of wine* = Rhenish. [OED *Rhenish*]

rent[1] *vti* rend, tear, crack, split *la14-, now local Abd-S.*
n **1** = rent, tear. **2** a breach between persons *18-e19.*

rent[2] *n* **1** = rent *la14-.* **2** profit, value *e16.*
on ~ at interest *e17, only Sc.*

rental &c *n* **1** a rent-roll, register of tenants *14-, now hist.* **2** the amount paid or received as rent *15-.* **3** (1) a kind of lease granted on favourable terms by a landlord to a tenant *16-19*; cf *kindly* 6 (KIND). (2) an extract from a *rental book* etc confirming such a lease *16-e17.*
vt **1** enter (a person) in a RENTAL (*n* 1), or grant (a person) a lease as in *n* 3 (1), *la15-16.* **2** record details of (a piece of land, a lease, rent etc) in a RENTAL (*n* 1); lease (land) on rent *la15-18.*
~**ler &c** a person who held land by being entered in a RENTAL (*n* 1), *latterly* as in *n* 3 (1), a *kindly tenant* (KIND) *la16-18.*
~ **book** = *n* 1, *16-18.*

renunce *now Abd*, **renounce** *17-* [rə'nʌns; *St* -'nʌuns] *vti* **1** = renounce *la14-.* **2** *law, specif* surrender (a lease, inheritance etc) *17-.*
renunciation &c **1** = renunciation. **2** *law, specif* the act of renouncing as in *n* 2, *la16-.*

renyie, renȝe *see* REIN

renȝe [*'rɛnjɪ] *vt* = raign, arraign *la15, only Sc.*

repair[1] **&c; rapayr &c** *15* [rə'per] *n* **1** = repair, (a) resort *la14-, now arch.* **2** a resort, stay, sojourn **in** or **at** *la14-19, only Sc.* **3** intercourse, association (**with** others) *16-17.* **4** a gathering of people; a frequent coming or going *17-19.*
vi = repair, resort *la14-.*
out of, but *etc* ~ away from people *16.*

repair[2] **&c** *vt* **1** = repair, mend, remedy *16-.* **2** make good, make amends for *la16-.*

reparation &c *n* **1** = reparation *15-.* **2** furniture, furnishings *la16, only Sc.* **3** *law* the redress of a civil wrong, *usu* by award of damages *la17-.*

repater [*rə'petər] *vt* feed *e16.* [only Sc; F *repaître*]

repeat &c *v* **1** *vt* say over again; reiterate *la14-.* **2** *vti* = repeat, recite etc *la16-.* **3** *vt* trace back *16, only Sc* [translating L *repetere*]. **4** *law* (1) ask back (money or goods); claim *la16-e17*; (2) repay, refund, make restitution of *18-.*
repetition &c **1** = repetition *la16-.* **2** *law* (1) the claiming of restitution or repayment *16-18*; (2) restitution, repayment *la18-.*

repel &c *vt* **1** = repel *16-.* **2** *law, of a court* reject (a plea or submission); overrule (an objection) *16-.*

repent *vtir* = repent *la14-.*
~**ance &c** = repentance *la14-.* **place of** ~**ance** the area of a church where penitents stood to be rebuked *18-, now hist.* ~**ance stool &c, stool of** ~**ance, ~ing stool** a seat in a prominent place in a church, *usu* in front of the pulpit, on which offenders, *esp* against chastity, sat to be rebuked *la16-, now hist.*

repet *see* RIPPET

repetition *see* REPEAT

repey *vt* = repay *20-.*

replait; resplate [*rə'plet, *rə'splet] *vt* adjourn (a cause); remand (a person) *16.* [only Sc; OF *replait &c* the re-hearing of a plea]

replede &c [*rə'plid] *vi* plead again, raise a further plea *la14-e16.* [OED *replead*]

repledge &c [rə'plɛdʒ] *vt, law* **1** *also transf* withdraw (a person or cause) from the jurisdiction of another court to that of one's own, under the pledge that justice would continue to be done *la15-e18.* **2** take back or take over (something forfeited or impounded) on proper security *la16-e17.*
~**r** *law, also fig* a person who REPLEDGES a criminal *17-e18.* **repledgiation &c** the act of *repledging, 16-e18.*

replenish *vt* **1** = replenish. **2** repair; rehabilitate *la19-20.*

reply &c *n* **1** *law* a counter-answer by the *pursuer* (PURSUE) to the answer of the *defender* (DEFEND); *sometimes* this was called the answer and the REPLY was the second rejoinder by the *defender*, *la15-e19.* **2** = reply *17-.*
vi **1** = reply. **2** *specif law* answer the plea of a *defender* (DEFEND) *la15-e17.*

repone &c [rɪ'pon] *v* **1** *vt* restore to office or to rights previously held, reinstate *la15-19.* **2** *specif, church* restore (a deposed MINISTER) to his charge *la16-19.* **3** *law* restore (a *defender* (DEFEND)) to his right to defend his case, *esp* after judgment has been given against him in his absence *la16-.* **4** put (a person or thing) back **in** (a place) *la16-e17.* **5** *vi* give as a reply; answer *17-e19.* [only Sc; L *reponere* replace, restore]

report; raport &c *16-e17* [rə'port] *vti* **1** = report *16-.* **2** *vt* bring in return, bring in; *of persons* obtain, get *16-e17.* **3** *law, of a judge of first* *instance* remit (a case or part of it) to a body of one's colleagues, *chf* the *Inner House* (INNER), for decision *18-*.

n **1** = report *la15-*. **2** *law* the act of *reporting* (*v* 3) *17-*.

~er 1 = reporter. **2** *law* the officer responsible for bringing cases before children's hearings *la20-*.

repose &c *vti* **1** = repose *16-*. **2** = REPONE (*v* 1, 2) *la16-e17*, *only Sc.*

reposition [*?ripo'zɪʃn] **1** the restoration of a person to an office or to rights from which he has been deposed; *esp* the reinstatement of a clergyman *16-19*, *only Sc*; *cf* REPONE. **2** = reposition, a laying aside *la17*.

repossess &c *vt* **1** = repossess. **2** restore (a person) **to**, reinstate **in** *la16-e17*, *e19*, *only Sc.*

~ion &c 1 = repossession *la16-*. **2** restoration (as in *v* 2) *la16-e17*, *only Sc.*

repouss &c [*rə'pus] *vt* = repulse *la16*, *e19*.

repree *19*, *Abd*; **repreif &c** *la14-16*, **rapreiff** *15*, **reprove, reprow** *la14-15* [*n* *rə'prif, *-'prɒf, *-'prɒv; *v* *Abd* rə'pri; *Bwk* rə'prev; *rə'priv, *rə'prɒv] *vt* **1** *also* **reprow** *la14-15* = reprove *16-*. **2** set aside as invalid *la15*.

n = reproof *la14-16*. [only Sc. OED *reproof, reprove*]

reprehend *vt* **1** = reprehend. **2** take (a person) in the act of doing wrong *e16*, *only Sc.*

repreif *see* REPREE

represe [*rə'prim] *vt* repress *16*. [only Sc; L *reprimere*]

represent *vt* **1** = represent *la14-*. **2** render (service); present (a thing **to** a person) *15-16*.

~ation 1 = representation. **2** *law* an appeal against the decision of a judge of the *Court of Session* (SESSION) presented in the form of written pleadings *e19*, *hist.* **3** *law* the right to succeed to HERITABLE property because one represents a deceased direct heir (*eg* of a grandson succeeding his grandfather) *la17-*. **4** *law* the right to inherit an estate which carries with it liability for the debts of one's predecessor *18-e20*.

~ing days the 20 days from the pronouncement of a *Court of Session* (SESSION) judgment during which an appeal against it might be lodged *la18-e19*.

reprise *n* **1** *building* an indentation of stone *e16*. **2** = reprise *la17-*.

reproach &c; reproche *16* [rə'protʃ] *vt* **1** = reproach *16-*. **2** recall (*eg* a promise) with reproaches *e16*.

n = reproach *16-*.

reprobate *vt* **1** = reprobate *la17-*. **2** *law*, *see* APPROBATE.

reprobator &c [*?rə'probətər, *?-ətər] *n*, *law*, *also* **action of ~** an action to challenge the impartiality or honesty of a witness *la17-e19*. [MedL (*actio*) *reprobatoria*; *cf* prec]

reproche *see* REPROACH

repromit [*ripro'mɪt] *vt* promise in return *e17*. [only Sc; L *reprōmittere*]

reprove, reprow *see* REPREE

repute &c [*rɪ'pøt, *'rɛpøt; *NE* *rɪ'pit] *ptp*, *also* **~ and halden &c** *16-e18* reputed, considered, reckoned *la14-e19*; *cf* HABIT AND REPUTE. [reduced form of ptp, as DEPUTE etc]

require *see* REQUERE

requeesht *19*, **request; requeist &c** *16-e19*, **raquest** *15* [*rə'kwist, *-'kwiʃt] *n*, *vt* = request *la14-*.

Master of R~s title give to a member of the *Privy Council* (PRIVY[1]) whose duty it was to deal with petitions etc submitted to the *Privy Council* *la16-17*. **~ of** ask, beg of (a person) *la18-*.

requere &c *la14-16*, *la19* (*Abd*); **requare &c** *la19-e20*, *Abd* [rə'kwaɪr; *Abd* -'kwer; *-'kwir] *vt* = require. [OED *require*]

request *see* REQUEESHT

requisition &c *n* **1** = requisition *la16-*. **2** *law* a demand by a creditor for repayment of a debt *17-*.

requit [*rə'kwɪt] *n* requital, compensation *la18*. [*cf* verb in eModEng]

rerde, rerdour *see* REIRD

rere [*rir] *vi* resound; cry, roar *la15-e16*. [only Sc; obscure]

resaive, resaif, reschave *see* RECEIVE

rescissory &c *adj*, *law* **1** *of a legal action* purporting to declare a deed or illegal act void *la17-*. **2** *specif* of the Act of the Scottish Parliament of 1661 which rescinded all acts since 1633, *la17*. [chf Sc; laL *rescissōri-*, f ptp stem of *rescindere* rescind]

rescours &c [*rɛ'skurs] *n* = rescours, rescue *la14-e16*.

vt rescue *e16*, *only Sc.*

reset &c [*v* rɪ'sɛt, *also* 'risɛt; *n* 'risɛt; *rɪ'sɛt] *vt*, *ptp also* **reset &c** *16-* [rɪ'sɛt, *also* 'risɛt] **1** receive, harbour, give shelter or protection to (*esp* a criminal, enemy, fugitive etc) *la14-*. **2** receive (stolen goods), *usu* with the intention of reselling *la14-*.

n **1** refuge, shelter *16-17*. **2** a place of refuge, *later esp* for criminals etc; an abode, residence, haunt *la14-e18*. **3** a person who receives or shelters (*esp* a criminal) *la15-e18*. **4** *law* the receiving or harbouring of criminals *la15-e19*. **5** the act of receiving *16*. **6** *law* the receiving of stolen goods, *freq* **~ of theft &c** *16-*.

~ter a person who RESETS *18-*. [OF *recet*(*er*) &c, L *receptāre* (*v*), *receptum* (*n*); *cf* RECEIPT]

resh *see* RASH[1]

residence &c *n* = residence *16-*.

mak ~ stay at or in a place for a certain time *la14-16*.

resident &c *n* = resident *la15-*.

~er &c [rɛsɪ'dɛntər] a resident, inhabitant, *esp* one of long standing *17-*. **~ing** [*rɛsɪ'dɛntɪŋ] residing, dwelling *18-e19*.

residuary &c *adj* **1** = residuary *19-*. **2** *chf derog after the* DISRUPTION: pertaining to the Established Church of Scotland *19*.

resign &c; **resing** &c *la14-16* [rɪ'zəin; *rɪ'sɪŋ] *vti* **1** = resign *16-*. **2** *law, of a* VASSAL: surrender his FEU to his SUPERIOR *la14-*.

resignation &c **1** = resignation *la16-*. **2** *law* the way in which a VASSAL *resigned* his FEU *la14-19*.

resile &c [rɪ'səil, -'zəil] *vi* **1** draw back, withdraw (**from** an agreement, undertaking etc) *la16-*. **2** recoil (**from** something), shrink away in distaste or disgust *la17-e20*. [chf Sc; OF *resilir* &c, L *resilīre* jump back, recoil]

resing *see* RESING

resist *la14-*; **rasyst** [rə'zɪst] *15-16, only Sc vt* = resist.

resolution &c *n* **1** = resolution *la16-*. **2** a state of dissolution or decay *e16*.

R~er one of the church party which in opposition to the *Protesters* (PROTEST), supported the *engagement* (ENGAGE) *la17*.

resolutive [rɪ'zɔljutɪv] *adj* ~ **clause** *law* a clause in an agreement whereby it becomes void if some specified event intervenes *18-*. [*cf* next *v* 2]

resolve &c [rɪ'zɔlv; *rɪ'zɔl] *vti* **1** = resolve *16-*. **2** *law* make or render void, (cause to) lapse *la18-e19*.

respeck &c, **respect** &c *la16-* [rɪ'spɛk(t), rə-] *n* **1** = respect *la15-*. **2** affectionate esteem, *freq* **show** ~ attend the funeral of a friend *la19-*. *vt* **1** = respect. **2** regard affectionately, esteem *la19-*.

respective *adj* = respective *17-*. *adv* [*rɪspɛk'taɪvɪ] respectively *16-e18, only Sc.*

resplate *see* REPLAIT

responde; respondie *e17* [*rɪ'spondi, *-ɪ] *n, law* **1** *chf* ~ **book**, *also* **buik** &c **of** ~ *16* a book in which records or receipts were kept, *specif* (1) one in which NON-ENTRY and RELIEF duties due by heirs were entered in CHANCERY *16-e19*; (2) one in which decrees and acts were entered by the Clerk of *the Session* (SESSION), providing a record for the charging of fees *18-e19*. **2** a single entry in *n* 1 (1) *la16-17*. [only Sc; L *responde* reply, the first word of each article in the book]

responsal &c [*rə'sponsəl; *n* *rɛspon'sel] *n* = responsal, reply *la15*. *adj* answerable, responsible, trustworthy *la15-e18*.

ressait *see* RECEIPT

ressave *see* RECEIVE

rest[1] &c; **rist** &c *la14, la19-* (*chf NE*) *n* **1** = rest, repose etc *la14-*. **2** some part of the ironwork of a gate *e16, only Sc.* *vti* **1** = rest *la14-*. **2** *vi, of arable land* lie fallow or in grass *la18-, Sh-EC.* ~**ing chair** &c a settle *17-, now Sh.* ~**ing stane** &c a stone used as a resting place; *specif* one on the road to a churchyard where the coffin was laid while the bearers rested *la19-20*. **ristit** *of land* having lain fallow *20-, Sh-EC.*

rest[2] &c; **rist** *16 n* **1** = rest, remainder etc *16-*. **2** *freq in pl* sums of money due, arrears *16-e18.*

v **1** *vi, also* ~ **unpayt**, *of a sum* remain due or unpaid, be overdue *la15-, now Sh Ork.* **2** *vt, of a person* owe (someone something) *la16-, now Sh.* **3** = rest, remain, be left *la16-*.

~**ing owing** &c *adj* **1** *of a person* owing, in debt *la15-e19*. **2** *of a debt* unpaid *16-*. *n* the state of a debt being unpaid *19-*.

the auld &c ~ **1** = *n* 2, *la15-e16*. **2** name of a disease *la16.*

rest *see* REEST[2]

restagn [*rə'stagn] *vt* dam up (water), cause (water) to cease to flow *17-e18*. [only Sc; OF *restagner*]

restauration &c *n* **1** the reinstatement of man in divine favour *la14*. **2** restoration of stolen goods *la17*. [ME, F = restoration]

restling *n* wriggling or twisting about *la15*. [only Sc; var of Eng *wrestling*]

restore &c *v* **1** *vt* = restore *la14-*. **2** *vi* recover, revive *16.*

restreen *e20, Kcb*; **restrene** *e15*, **restrenȝe** *la14-16* [rə'strin; *rə'strɛnjɪ, *-'strinjɪ, &c] *vt* = restrain. [OED *restrain*]

restrict; restrick &c *now Abd vt* confine, limit *16-*. [earlier in Sc; L *restrict-*, ptp stem of *restringere* confine]

resume *vti* **1** = resume. **2** *vt, law, of a landlord* repossess (part of a piece of land which has been let) in accordance with the terms of the lease *la18-*. **resumptions** *n* **1** = resumption. **2** *law* the act of *resuming* (*v* 2) *la18-*.

resurse [*rə'sʌrs] *vi* rise again *e16*. [only Sc; OF *resurs-*, pt stem of *resourdre*]

reteener *see* RETENE

reteir *see* RETIRE

retene &c [*rə'tin] *vti* = retain *16-17*. **retener** &c *16*, **reteener** *e19* = retainer, a servant.

retention &c *n* **1** = retention *la16-*. **2** *law* the right not to fulfil one's own part of a contract until the other party has fulfilled his, *eg* not to deliver goods until the buyer has paid for them *17-*.

rethe *see* REITHE

rether *see* RAITHER

rethorie *see* RHETORY

reticule &c; **radical** &c *la19-e20*, **reddicle** *20* ['rɛtɪkl, 'rɛd-, 'rad-] *n* = reticule. ~ **basket** a woven bag for carrying on the arm *la19-, Cai nEC, SW.*

retire &c *la16-*; **reteir** &c *16-e18* [rə'taɪr; *rə'tir] *vti* **1** = retire *16-*. **2** *vt* rally, bring back *la16*. **3** withdraw from currency, pay up (a bill of exchange etc) when due *la17-e19*. **4** *of a debtor* seek sanctuary, *specif* in the Abbey of Holyroodhouse in Edinburgh *18-e19*. **retiral** retirement from office etc *20-, now chf Sc.* **retiring collection** *church* an extra collection for some special purpose taken as the congregation leaves *20-*.

retour &c [rə'tur] *n* **1** (1) a return, a return

journey *la14-19*. (2) *specif* a return journey at reduced rates in a carriage or on a horse hired by another for the outward journey *18-e19*. **2 a** round, a turn, a bout; a second helping of food, round of drinks etc *la19-*, *chf Abd*. **3** *law* the return or extract of a decision sent to CHANCERY by a jury or INQUEST, *esp* one declaring a successor heir to his ancestor; the record of such a return, *esp* one specifying the annual taxable value of the land *la15-*.

v **1** *vi* return or revert *la15-e16*. **2** *vt*, *law* make a return to CHANCERY, *esp* one declaring a person heir; declare formally as heir; declare the annual taxable value of (the land concerned) on such a return, *freq* ~ed &c *16-*.

~**able** *of a document, esp a brieve* (BRIEF): returnable to the authority issuing it *la18-*, *now hist*.

~**ed duty** the amount of tax payable based on the value recorded in the RETOUR (*n* 3), *la17-*.

~ **duty** *etc* = ~ed *duty*, *la17-e19*. [*chf Sc; OF retour return*]

retractation &c *n* **1** = retraction, withdrawal, revocation *16*. **2** ? disinclination, reluctance *la16*.

retrahibition &c [*?'rɛtrəhɪ'bɪʃən, *?'rɪtrə-] *n* a withdrawal of a previous prohibition *la16*. [only Sc; conflation of *retro-* w *-hibition* as in *prohibition*]

retreat &c; ratret *la14-e16* [rə'trit] *n* = retreat *la14-*.

vti **1** = retreat *la16-*. **2** *vt* retract, revoke *la15-17*, *only Sc*.

retrocess &c [*rɛtro'sɛs] *vt*, *chf law* restore (a right temporarily assigned to another), reinstate (a person) in a post or office *la17-18*. [prob back-formation f next]

retrocession [rɛtro'sɛʃn] *n*, *law* a returning of a right to the person who granted it *la16-*. [F *rétrocession* the ceding or giving back; *cf* Eng = ceding back of territory]

retrospiciant &c [*rɛtro'spɪʃ(ɪ)an(t)] *n* a person who turns back; a renegade *e17*. [only Sc; altered f L *retrōspicient-*, presp stem of *retrōspicere*]

retrotraction [*rɛtro'trakʃ(ɪ)ən] *n* retraction, withdrawal *la17*, *only Sc*.

retroversion &c *n* ? = REVERSION 2, *la16*. [only Sc; *cf* ModEng = turning or looking back]

return &c *vti*, *also* **ratorn** *15*, **raturn** *la15* [rə'tʌrn] **1** = return *la14-*. **2** *vi* change or turn **into** (something else) *e16*, *only Sc*.

n = return *16-*.

clause of ~ *law* a provision whereby the granter of a right provides that in certain circumstances it may return to himself and his heirs *18-*.

reuall; riwell [*?'r(j)uəl] *n* ? a circular or wheel-shaped ornament *la15*. [? OF *rouelle* a little wheel]

reuch *see* RUCH

reul *see* RAIVEL

reule *see* RULE

revay [*rɪ've, *-'vəi] *n* hunting or hawking on the banks of rivers *la15*. [ME (*v*) = hunt, hawk on banks of rivers, northern OF *rivieer*]

reve *see* REIVE

revel &c *n* a severe blow *e17, e19*. [only Sc; perh extended f Eng *revel* riotous merrymaking]

revel *see* RAVEL

revelyng *see* RIVLIN

revenge &c *v* **1** *vr* avenge oneself *la14-*. **2** *vt* = revenge *15-*.

n = revenge.

~**ance &c** revenge, vengeance *la14-15*.

rever [*?'revər, *?'rivər] *n*, *archery* = rover, a mark selected at random *la16*.

reverence &c *n* = reverence *la15-*.

in *etc or* **out of the** ~ **of** under or not under an obligation to; in or out of the power or mercy of *la16-*, *latterly esp Highl*, *now Arg*.

reverie *see* RAVERIE

reverse &c *vti* = reverse *la14-*.

reverser 1 = reverser. **2** *law* a person who borrows money on security of land, a mortgager *18-*. **reversion &c 1** = reversion. **2** *law* (the right of) redeeming *esp* mortgaged lands *la15-*.

revert &c [rə'vɛrt; *-'vart, *-'vert] *vti* **1** = revert *15-*. **2** recover, bring back or return to one's normal state of mind or spirits; recover consciousness *la15-e19*, *latterly N*.

revill-raill *see* RAIVEL

revin *see* RIVE

revince [*rə'vɪns] *vt* restore (a person) **to** (a possession) *la16*. [only Sc; *cf* eModEng = refute, disprove]

revis *see* RAVIS

revolve &c *vti* **1** = revolve *la15-*. **2** *vt* destine, purpose *e16*, *only Sc*.

rew &c *n* a street; a village *la14-16*. [only Sc; F *rue*]

rew *see* RUE

rewaird &c *15-e20*, **reward &c** *la14-* [rə'werd] *vti*, *n* = reward.

rewburd *see* RHUBARB

rewvine, rewyne *see* RUIN

rex; rax *n* a children's chasing game *la19-e20*. [L *rex* a king; *cf* REGIBUS]

rex *see* RAX

reylock [*'ri:lək] *n* robbery *la15*, *only Sc*. [OSc, ME *revelaik*, f REIVE]

rhame *see* RAME

rhetory &c; rethorie &c [*'rɛtorɪ, *?'rɛθ-] *n* rhetoric; eloquence *la15-e16*. [only Sc; laL (f Gk) *rhetoria &c*,]

rheum &c [rum; *rjum] *n* **1** = rheum *16-*, *now arch*. **2** *chf in pl* rheumatic pains *la18-*, *now Bnf Ags Per*.

rheumatise &c ['rumatiz, -ɪz] *n* = rheumatism *19-e20*.

Rhinns &c; Rynnis &c *16* [rɪnz] *n pl*, *chf* **the** ~ **of Galloway** the western peninsula of Wigtownshire *16-*. [Sc and IrGael *rinn* a promontory, headland]

rhone *see* RONE[1]

rhubarb &c; rewburd *20-, local N-S,* **roob-rub** &c *la19-, now Cai Arg* ['rubərb, 'rubərd, -ərt, 'rub(ə)rʌb; *Fif* *'rʌbərb] *n* = rhubarb *la19-*.

gie someone ~ give someone a sound thrashing *20-, Abd Gsw, Wgt*.

rhyme &c *la18-,* **rime &c** *vti* **1** = rhyme *16-*. **2** repeat, drone **on** monotonously; talk nonsense *la19-, local Bnf-Uls*.

n = rhyme *la14-*.

~less without reason, meaningless; *of persons* irresponsible, reckless, ineffective *19-, now Bnf*.

riach &c [*Ork* 'rio, 'reo; *'riəx] *adj, freq of black and white wool mixed in cloth* greyish-white, drab, brindled *la17-e20, Sh Ork N*. [Gael *riabhach*]

rial &c [*'raiəl] *adj* **1** = rial, royal *la14-e18*. **2** notable, remarkable *la14-16, only Sc*.

n **1** = rial, real, a prince; a Spanish coin *15-e16*. **2** (1) a French gold coin current in Scotland *la15-e16*. (2) one of several Scottish silver coins *la16*.

~ty &c 1 = rialty, royalty *la14-15*. **2** a district directly under the sovereign *15-e17, only Sc*; *cf* REGALITY *n* 2.

rib &c *n* **1** = rib *la14-*. **2** a horizontal roof-timber joining rafters *16-, now Bnf midLoth*. **3** *in pl* the bars of a grate *la17-*. **4** *ploughing* the ridge left unploughed as in *v* 2, *18-e19*. **5** *mining* a wall of solid coal or other mineral *la19-, now Fif*.

vti **1** = rib. **2** *ploughing* plough every alternate furrow, turning the soil over onto the adjacent unploughed strip *la18-, local N-S*.

deep ~bit *of a cow or a woman* large-chested *la19-, now Sh Kcb*.

~-side *mining* a face of solid mineral left projecting beyond the next face *la19-, now Fif*.

ribald *see* REEBALD

ribble-rabble &c *adv* in a state of great confusion *la19-, now wLoth Slk*.

n = ribble-rabble, a rabble *la17-, now Ags*.

ribe &c *n* **1** a tall thin (cabbage) plant *e19*. **2** a long-legged, thin person; an emaciated animal *19-, now Gall*. [doubtful]

rice &c; rys &c *la15-e20,* **reis &c** *19-e20* [rais] *n* **1** *collectively* twigs or small branches, brushwood *la15-, now Per Ayr*. **2** a branch, a twig; a stick *16-e20*.

stake and ~ *n* (*18-*)*, also* **stab and ~** (*la17-e20*) a method of construction by which twigs are horizontally woven between vertical stakes; a fence constructed thus. *adj, fig* sketchy, in outline only *19-e20, only Sc*. [eME; OE *-hris*, ON *hris*; *cf* MDu *rijs* and Ger *Reis*]

rich &c; ryke &c *la15-16* [rɪtʃ; *'rəik,* *rɪk] *adj* **1** *of persons* powerful, mighty; *of things* powerful, strong *la15-e16*. **2** = rich *la18-*.

vt = rich, make rich *la14*.

richt &c, right &c [rɪxt; *Sh Ork S* rəi(x)t] *adj* **1** = right *la14-*. **2** *chf in negative* not in one's right mind, mentally unbalanced; simple-minded;

abnormal, UNCANNY *17-*. **3** sober, not drunk, living in a sober, well-behaved way *la19-, local Sh-Kcb*.

adv **1** = right *la14-*. **2** *as intensifier* very, exceedingly *la14-*. **3** rightly, by right *e16, only Sc*. **4** thoroughly, very much, very well *la19-, Abd Ags*. **5** adequately, properly, satisfactorily *la18-, local Sh-Kcb*.

n **1** = right *la14-*. **2** *mining* a document substantiating a claim or title *16-e17*.

vt = right *la14-*.

~(e)ous &c [*'rɪxtwɪs, *-wəs, *-(i)əs] **1** = righteous *la14-*. **2** rightful, lawful, legitimate *la14-18*. **richtify** put to rights *20-, NE-C*.

~lins &c rightly *la19-, Sh NE*.

~-like just, fair, equitable *la19-, NE Ags*.

at all ~ = at all rights, at every point *la14-15*.

at ~ properly, aright *la14-e16, only Sc*. **ken the ~ side o a shillin** *etc* be knowing with money, be good at getting the best value for money *la19-, local Sh-WC*. **~ an** *as intensifier* very, completely *la18-, now Slk Uls*. **~ eneuch** comfortably off, well provided for *la19-, Ork-C*. **the ~ gate** in no uncertain manner, thoroughly, properly *la19-, NE*. **~ now** immediately *la19-*. **~ oot &c** outright, unequivocally *20-*. **the ~ way o't** the true account or story, the genuine version *la19-*.

rick *see* REEK[1]

ricket *n* a noisy disturbance, racket, row *19-, now Ags*.

~ie &c 1 a wooden rattle consisting of a small frame whirled round on wooden ratchets, used *formerly* by policemen to raise an alarm, *now chf* by children and football supporters *la18-, now local EC, WC*. **2** a ratchet brace or drill *la19-, now Fif WC*. [onomat f Eng *racket*]

rickietickie *n* a button etc on a thread, used by boys to rattle on a window *20-, Mry EC Ayr*. [imit, based on Eng *tick*]

rickle[1] &c; ruckle *19- n* **1** a heap, pile, collection (of objects), *esp* one loosely or carelessly thrown together *la16-*. **2** a broken-down person or thing: (1) a ramshackle or disintegrating object *la19-, Gen except SW*; (3) an emaciated, broken-down person or animal, *freq* **a ~ o banes** *la18-*. **3** an untidy collection or huddle of buildings *19-, now Sh Ork Abd*. **4** a dry-stone (DRY) wall; a layer of small stones placed on top of larger stones as a coping to such a wall *la19-, local Ork-C*. **5** a small temporary stack of grain or seed-hay *la18-, WC, SW*. **6** a small heap of PEATS[1] or turfs, stacked loosely for drying *18-, now local N-Ayr*.

vt **1** pile together loosely; construct loosely or insecurely *la16-, local*. **2** build without mortar; *freq* **~ up** build (a dry-stone (DRY) wall) *18-, now Fif*. **3** build (grain) into small temporary ricks *la18-, WC, SW*. **4** stack (PEATS[1]) loosely for drying *la18-, now local N-SW*.

ricklie &c badly-constructed, ramshackle, rickety *18-*. [prob Scand; *cf* Norw *rygla* a small, loose heap, ON *hraukr* a small pile (of PEATS[1])]

rickle[2] &c *vi* rattle, move with a rattling or clattering sound, rattle **down** *la17, 20-, NE Fif*. *n* a clatter *e16, la20-, NE Fif*. [nME *rekil* (*v*) rattle; onomat]

rickling; wreckling &c *n* the smallest, weakest animal in a litter *20-, Per SW*. [prob Scand; *cf* Icel *rekling* an outcast and RIGLEN]

rickmatick &c ['rɪkmə'tɪk] *n* a group of people or things, *freq* **the hale** ~ the whole lot *la19-*. [altered f Eng *arithmetic*]

rid &c *vt* **1** = rid *la16-*. **2** = REDD[1] *v* 4 (2) (*17*), 9 (*la18-e20*), 10 (*15-16*), 11 (*la15-19*), 13 (*e18*). ~**der** = *redder* (REDD[1]) *17-e18, only Sc*. [ON *ryðja*; there has been confusion w REDD[1] f an early date]

rid *see* REDD[2], REID[1], RIDE

riddle &c *n* **1** = riddle, a coarse sieve *16-*. **2** a measure of claret, thirteen bottles arranged round a *magnum* (MAGNUM BONUM) *19-* [f the practice of carrying it in at ceremonial dinners in a riddle].
vt = riddle.
riddling heids the refuse of corn left after riddling *20-, Cai SW*.
turning (of) the ~ **(and the shears &c)** a method of divination, used *esp* for the discovery of theft *la16-e19*.

ride &c *v, pt also* **rade &c** *la14-20,* **red &c** *la16-e20,* **rid** *18-19. ptp also* **rode** *la18-e19* **1** *vti* = ride *la14-*. **2** *vi* ride out on a foray, *esp* in the BORDERS *15-, now hist*. **3** *vt* fix during perambulation (the boundaries of land or the TEINDS payable on growing crops) *la15-; cf* REDD[1] 11 [prob f REDD[1] or RID, confused w RIDE as the inspection was *usu* carried out on horseback]. **4** *vi* ride in a ceremonial procession *17*. **5** (1) *vt* cross (a stretch of water) on horseback, ford (a river) *16-e20*. (2) *vi, chf in negative, of a river etc* not be fordable by a rider, not allow a rider to cross *17-19*. **6** *vti*, curling (CURL), *also in bowls, freq* ~ **out** play a stone with such force that it moves (an opponent's stone which was blocking its path to the TEE[1]) *la18-; cf redd the hoose* (REDD[1]). **7** *mining* travel up and down the shaft in a cage *la19-, now Fif Lnk*. **8** *of a harrow* override another being drawn alongside it and become interlocked with it *la18-, now Kcb*.
n = ride.
~**r &c** **1** = rider *la15-*. **2** a person who rode as in *v* 2, a *reiver* (REIVE) *16-, now hist*. **3** a Scottish gold coin with the figure of the king on horseback on the obverse *la15-e18* [*cf* Du *rijder* a 15th century gold coin]. **4** *law* a *riding claimant*; a *riding claim, 19-*. **5** curling (CURL), *also in bowls* a shot played as in *v* 6, *la19-*. **6** *gardening* a standard fruit tree used to fill space on a high wall until smaller permanent trees grew high enough *19*. ~**ing &c 1** = riding. **2** a raid on horseback *la14-, now hist*. **riding claim** *law* a

LIQUID claim on a claimant in a MULTIPLEPOINDING which may be lodged in the MULTIPLE-POINDING itself *20-*. **riding claimant** a person who makes such a claim *20-*. **riding commission** *or* **committee** *church* a committee appointed to examine the causes of rejection of a candidate by a PRESBYTERY or congregation, and to override these if they are found to be insufficient *18*. **riding interest** = *riding claim, 19-*. **Riding of the Marches** the traditional ceremony of riding round the boundaries of common land to inspect landmarks, boundary stones etc, *latterly* the focus of an annual local festival in certain, *esp* BORDER towns *18-*. **riding season** *or* **time** the breeding season of animals *la17-, now Ork*.

no tae ~ **the ford** *or* **water on** *or* **wi** not to be depended on, unreliable, untrustworthy *la18-, local NE-S.* ~ **(in) the fair** *or* **market** open a fair or market with a ceremonial procession of MAGISTRATES and council *la16-18*. ~ **the marches** perform the ceremony of *Riding of the Marches, 18-; cf* REDD[1] *v* 11. ~**-out** one of a series of rehearsal rides of a section of the boundaries in the weeks before the *Riding of the Marches, la20-, Dmf Rox*. R~ **the Parliament** open Parliament with a ceremonial procession *la16-e18*. ~ **at the ring** take part in a competition in which a rider tried to spear and carry off a small ring suspended from an overhead crossbar *18*. ~ **the shaft** *or* **tow** *mining* go down the pit by sliding down the shaft rope *la19-, now Fif*.

rideeculas &c [rɪ'dik(ju)ləs] *adj* = ridiculous *la19-e20*.

ridlaik *n* a species of wild goose *la16, only Sc*.

rif *see* RIVE

rifart &c *la17-e19;* **reefort &c** *la18-e20* ['rifərt; *ʔ'rɪf-] *n* a radish. [OF *reffort, riffort; cf* F, *raifort;* eModEng *raifort &c*]

rife &c *adj* **1** = rife *la15-*. **2** *with collective or sing noun* plentiful, abundant *17-*. **3** ~ **o** *or* **wi** having plenty of, well supplied with, rich in *18-, now local Sh-Kcb*. **4** quick, ready, eager **for** *la19-, now Sh Ork*.
adv plentifully, abundantly *la18-*.
-rife &c [-rəif, -rɪf] *suffix* **1** *with nouns* having an abundance of, notable for, liable to, *eg* **cauldrife, salerife**. **2** *with verbs* liable to, likely to, having a tendency to, *eg* **mockrife, waukrife**. **3** *with adjs* sometimes with intensive force, *eg* **auldrife, wildrife**.

riff *see* RUIF

riffle[1] &c *vt* = rifle, plunder *e15*.
n a depredation, sacking *e15, only Sc*. [OED *rifle* (*n*[1], *v*[1])]

riffle[2] &c *n, vti* = ruffle *17-18*.

rift[1] &c *vi* **1** belch *la15-*. **2** exaggerate, brag *18-, now Abd*.
n **1** a belch *15-*. **2** an exaggerated account; a boast *19-, now Abd*. **3** a lively chat *19*.
~**in fou &c** full to bursting point *19-*.

hae the ∼ o have (food) repeating *la19-*, *Ags Per*. ∼ **up** *also fig* rise on the stomach *e17*. [ME *rift &c*, ON *rypta &c*]

rift² &c *n* **1** a cleft, fissure in a rock etc *15-*, now local *Sh-Per*. **2** = rift, a break, split, crack *16-*. *vti* = rift.

rig¹ &c; **reeg** &c *la19-e20, Sh Cai n* **1** the back or backbone of a person or animal *15-*, now *Sh Cai*. **2** a (*freq* white) strip running along the back of an animal *la19-*, now *Sh*. **3** a ridge of high ground, a long narrow hill, a hill-crest *la14-*, now local, in place-names *la12-*. **4** (1) an extent of land, longer rather than broad *la15-*. (2) *early farming* (see eg *runrig* (RIN)) each separate strip of ploughed land, raised in the middle and sloping gradually to a furrow on either side, and *usu* bounded by patches of uncultivated grazing; now one of the divisions of a field ploughed in a single operation *16-*. (3) *also* **corn** ∼ such a piece of land when planted with a crop or being harvested *18-*, now *Ork NE Ags*. (4) the team of reapers, *usu* three, assigned to each RIG¹ *la18-19*. (5) a measure of land, *usu* fifteen feet wide and varying in length *16-*, now *Arg*. **5** (1) *in pl, chf literary* the arable land belonging to one farm or proprietor *18-e20*. (2) a strip of ground leased for building in a BURGH *18*. **6** that part of a town left free for cultivation *16-17*. **7** *weaving* the centre line of a web of cloth along which it is folded, the folded edge *la15*.

vt plough (land) in RIGS¹ (4 (2)) *la18-*, now local *C-S*.

∼**ged and furred** ribbed *la18-e20*; cf ∼ *and fur*. ∼**gin** &c *n* = *n* 1, *16-*, now local *Ork-Stlg*. **2** the ridge of a roof; the roof itself; the materials of which it is made *16-*. **3** (1) the top, the highest part of a wall, a cornstack, a ridge of corn etc *16-*, now local. (2) the top of a stretch of high ground; a high ridge of land, *esp* running along the side of a plain *la16-*, now in place-names. **4** the central point of a period of time, *chf* **the** ∼**gin o the nicht** *la19-*, *NE*. *vt* roof (a building) *la18-e20*. ∼**gin-bane** = ∼*-bane*, *la18-*, now *Ork*. ∼**gin divot** &c a turf used as a ridge-coping for a thatched roof *la17-*, *chf NE*. ∼**gin-heid** the ridge of a roof *20-*, *NE nEC, WC, SW*. ∼**gin stane** &c a stone used as a ridge stone of a roof *16-*, now *NE-C*. ∼**gin tree** &c the ridge-beam of a roof *17-*, now *Sh Per*. **ride on the** ∼**gin** &c o *fig* be completely preoccupied (with); be very officious (about) *18-*, now local *Ork-SW*. ∼**git** &c *esp of cows* having a stripe as in *n* 2, *la16*, now *Sh*. ∼**lin** &c a male animal or *occas* a man with one testicle undescended *la16-*, now *Ork EC, SW-S* [the undescended testicle was thought to remain in the back; *cf* RIGLEN]. ∼**gy** &c name for a cow with markings as in *n* 2, *la18-*, now *Sh*.

∼**-back** *la16-*, now *Sh*, ∼**-bane** *la15-*, now *Sh midLoth* the backbone, spine. ∼**body** &c = ∼*widdie*, *la19-*, *EC Arg*. ∼**-end** = *endrig* (EN)

19. ∼**-fit** the foot or lower end of a RIG¹ (*n* 4) *la20-*. ∼**-heid** &c the crown or high part of the RIG¹ (*n* 4 (2)) *la19-*, now *Sh*. ∼**-len(g)th** the length of a RIG¹ (*n* 4) as a measurement of distance *17-*, now *Sh*. ∼**widdie** &c *n* a band (*orig* one made of WIDDIES) passing over the back of a carthorse and supporting the cart-shafts *16-*, now *NE-C*. *adj*, *of a person* **1** *esp of an old woman* wizened, gnarled, tough and rugged-looking, mis-shapen *la17-19*. **2** stubborn, obstinate; perverse *19-e20*.

∼**-about** the *runrig* (RIN) system of land tenure *19-*, *latterly hist*. ∼ **and baulk** &c arable strips of land separated by uncultivated strips onto which stones and rubbish from the cultivated strips were cleared *19-*. ∼ **and fur, ∼ and furrow** *of the pattern on a ploughed field, also fig, of knitting* ribbed; corrugated *la18-*. ∼ **and rendal** &c = *rundale* (RIN) *16-20*, *latterly Sh Ork Cai*. [nME, perh f ON *hryggr* a back, ridge, corresponding to OE *hrycg* > ModEng *ridge*]

rig² &c *n* **on the** ∼ out for fun or mischief *19-e20*. **play the** ∼ **wi** *etc* hoax, play a trick on, make fun of *la19-20*. **run** (**the** *etc* ∼(**s**)) run riot, have a wild time, have fun *la18-e20*; cf *rin the hills* (RIN). **run the** ∼ **on** = *play the* ∼ *wi*, *la18-19*. [perh f prec]

rig³ &c *n* the smallest animal or weakling of a litter *la19-*, now local *Sh-SW*. [unknown; appar related in some way to RIGLEN]

rigalitie see REGALITY

rigger *n* = rigger (of a ship).
∼ **worm** a kind of marine worm used as bait *20-*, local *EC*.

right see RICHT

riglen, wregling *la17 n* **1** an undersized or weak animal or person *18-*, now *Fif SW*. **2** the smallest animal in a litter *la19-*, now *Ags Per SW*. [appar altered f RICKLING, perh w infl f *riglin* (RIG¹), but *cf* also RIG³]

riglin see RIG¹

rigmarie &c ['rɪgmə'ri] *n* **1** something of little or no value *la17-19*. **2** a frivolous gathering, a frolic *19-e20*. [supposed to be name for low-value coins of Queen Mary, bearing the inscription *Reg[ina] Maria*; sense 2 perh conflation of RIG² w Eng *rigmarole*]

rike see REAK

rile see RAIVEL

rilling see RIVLIN

rim¹ *n* = rim *16-*.
∼**mer** a hoop or band, *specif* one used to protect the runner-stone of a mill or to shape a cheese *18-e20*.

rim² &c *n* **1** = rim, a membrane, skin *e16*. **2** the peritoneum *la16-e19*.
∼**burs(t)in** *15-e20*, ∼**burst** &c *la16-*, now *Ags Per ptp* ruptured; *n* a rupture, a hernia. ∼**burstenness** = prec *n*, *la16-17*. ∼**fu** *20-*, now *Wgt*, ∼**rax(in)** *e20*, *Abd* a large meal. ∼ **side** the flesh-side of a skin *la15*, only *Sc*.

rime &c *n* **1** hoar-frost *16-*. **2** a frosty haze or mist *16-*, *now Sh Ork Ags*.
　rimie &c frosty *20-*. [rare in ME; dial or literary in ModEng]
rime *see* RHYME
rimle *vt, mining* probe or stir *la19-*, *now Fif*.
rimpin *n* a miserable or annoying person or animal, *eg* a mean old woman *19-20*, *SW, S*. [obscure]
rimple *n, vti* wrinkle; ripple *19-*, *now Ork Ags*. [ME, ModEng dial]
rim-ram *adj* confused, higgledy-piggledy, disordered *19-*, *now Mry Bnf*. [chf onomat, w infl f *reel-rall* (REEL[1]) etc]
rimwale &c ['rımwǝl; *EC* 'rʌml] *n* a board round the gunwale of a boat *20-*, *Sh Fif*. [*cf* Faeroese *rim* the uppermost strake, ON *rim* a rail, ultimately f as Eng *rim* + *wale* a gunwale]
rin &c, **run** &c *v, pt also* **run** *18*. *ptp also* **runnyn** &c *la14-e16* [*'rʌnǝn], **roun** &c *la14-e16* [rʌn] **1** = run (1) *vti, la14-*; (2) *vi, verse,* contrasted with **ride** go quickly on foot *la14-e19*: 'the Scotts they rade, the Scotts they ran'. **2** *of a dog* move sheep at a brisk pace, range out in herding sheep *la20-*, *SW, S*. **3** be covered with water, mud etc, be awash; leak, stop being watertight *19-*, *local Sh-Per*. **4** *of milk* coagulate, curdle *19-*, *chf Sh Ork*. **5** *vt* draw (liquor); distil (WHISKY) *18-19*. **6** hold (the hands etc) under running water, swill *20-*. **7** *bowls* drive (another bowl or the jack) away with a strong shot *18-20*. **8** put (a batch of loaves etc) in the oven for baking *20-*, *now Fif*.
　n **1** a stream, rivulet, water channel *la16-19*. **2** a flow of water *19-*. **3** the course of a river or stream, *freq* with the lands bordering it, a river valley *la18-*, *now NE Slk*. **4** = run.
　~ner &c **1** = runner *la14-*. **2** a tapster *e17, only Sc*. **3** a small water-channel, a ditch, runnel *la18-*, *now Ork Fif SW*. **4** a thin cut of meat from the forepart of the flank *18-e20*. **~ning** &c *adj* = running *la14-*. *n* **1** = running *la15-*. **2** a raid or foray *la14-16*. **3** *in pl* the main points of a story, sermon etc, the outline, gist *la19-*, *chf NE*. **running stock** *agric* a system of stock-management whereby all stock is sold at regular intervals, and breeding stock is bought in when required *la18-e20*, *WC, SW*. **~dale** &c *15-18*, **rendal** &c *la18-e20* a landholding system similar to *runrig* but involving larger portions of (*chf* OUTFIELD) land. **run deil** an out-and-out rogue *la18-19*. **run-joist** &c a beam running along the side of a roof across the rafters to support the thatch, a purlin *la18-e19*.
run-knot a slip-knot which has been pulled tight *la19-*, *Sh NE-SW*. **~ lime** mortar poured liquid into the crevices of stonework and left to set *19-*, *chf NE*. **run-line** the singing of a PSALM by a congregation in two or more continuous lines, instead of the earlier practice of one line at a time after the PRECENTOR had read or intoned it *19*. **~rig** &c, *latterly only* **runrig** *n* a

system of joint landholding by which each tenant had several detached RIGS[1] allocated in rotation by lot each year, so that each would have a share in turn of the more fertile land; such a portion of land *15-20*, *latterly only Hebrides*. *adj, adv* held under this system of tenure, divided by this system *la17-e20*. **~-roof** &c the roof over the main part of a building *16-e19*.
runtree a continuous horizontal beam or bar, *chf* one which holds vertical posts firm, *eg* in a fence, BYRE-stall etc *la18-e19*. **~-wall** &c a light partition wall from one side of a house to the other *la18-e19*. **rin-water** &c a natural flow of water, *esp* one which will drive a millwheel without a dam *20-*, *Abd*.
rinabout &c ['rınǝbut] *adj* runabout, roving *la19-*. *n* a vagabond, rover; a restless person, a gadabout *19-*. **~ ahin** ['rınǝ'hın] **1** run close behind or at the heels of *la19-*. **2** be in arrears, fall into debt *la19-*, *now Abd EC, WC*. **rin the cutter** evade the revenue cutter when smuggling; *joc* bring home liquor unobserved *la19-*. **run errands** go on errands *16-*. **~ the hills** roam about in a wild, unrestrained way, rush or gad about *19-*, *NE-Per*. **~ in by** *or* **in to** pay a short call on (a person) *la19-*. **~-a-mile** *game* a variation on hide-and-seek *20-*, *now Lnk*. **~ neeps** *or* **neep dreels** hoe between drills of turnips with a horse-hoe *la20-*, *NE midLoth*. **~ out** *of a vessel* leak *18-*. **~ o the rig** the direction or angle at which a field has been ploughed *la20-*, *local Per-S*. **~ stockings** strengthen stocking heels by darning them with a running stitch *19-*, *NE-S*. **~thereout** &c ['rınðerut, -ðǝrut] a vagrant, roving person *19-*, *now NE Ags*.
rinagate &c ['rınǝget] *n* = runagate, a fugitive, rascal *19-*, *local Sh-SW*.
rind[1] &c [rǝin(d), rın(d)] *n* **1** = rind *16-*. **2** *also* **reen** &c *la19-*, *chf N* a strip or slat of wood, a thin piece cut off the edge of a board, a piece of beading *18-*, *now Sh-nEC*. **3** the edge, *eg* of a strip of cultivated land or a *peat-bank* (PEAT[1]) *18-20*. [*cf* RUIND]
rind[2] &c [rǝin(d)] *vt* melt down, render (fat, tallow), clarify (butter etc) *16-*, *now local Sh-Dmf*. *n* melted tallow *la18-*, *now Ags Stlg*. [nME, eModEng *rend*, F *rendre*; *cf* RAND[2]]
rind[3] &c [rǝin(d)] *n* hoar-frost *e16, 19-*, *now Bwk Dmf*. [eModEng; prob altered f RIME]
rind *see* RUIND
rine *see* REIN
ring[1] &c, **raing** &c *la19-e20*, *Mry Bnf*; **reing** &c *la15-e18* [rıŋ; *'rıŋ] *n* **1** = ring *la14-*. **2** popular name for a circular ditch and rampart of a prehistoric hill-fort, *esp* of the early Iron Age *la18-e19*. **3** a traditional dance of circular formation *18-e19*. **4** *marbles, freq* **the ~** a circle on the ground used as a target; the game itself *19-*. **5** the meal which falls into the space between a millstone and its casing, regarded as the miller's perquisite *16-e19*.

vt **1** = ring *la17-*. **2** put a metal tyre round the rim of (a wheel) *la19-*, *now Ork NE Ags*; *cf* ~*ing bed*.

~**er** *curling* (CURL) a stone which lies within the ring surrounding the TEE[1] *19-*. ~**ie &c** = *n* 4, *la19-*. ~**ing bed** *etc* a bed of stone or a metal plate on which a red-hot metal rim is placed on a wheel and shrunk to fit it *20-*, *N-Fif*; *cf v* 2. ~**it &c 1** *of the eye* having a white circle round the iris; *of persons* wall-eyed *19-*, *now Sh Per Kcb*. **2** *of animals* having a ring of white hair round the eye *e16*, *la20-* (*Sh*). ~**gle &c ee &c** ['rɪŋl-] a wall eye; *of an animal* an eye with a ring of white hair round it *18-*. ~**gle-eed &c**, ~**lit-eed &c** ['rɪŋl'iːd, 'rɪŋlɪt-, 'rɪŋlt-] having a ~*le eye*, *la16-*.

~**-bear &c**, ~**-corn** = *n* 5, *la15-e19*. ~**-cutter** *curling* (CURL) an instrument for marking the circles round the TEES[1] *la18-*. ~ **fowl(ie)** ['~'ful(ɪ)] the reed-bunting *19-*, *now Abd*. ~**-gang** the topmost circle of sheaves in the vertical wall of a stack, made to project as eaves *la18-19*. ~**-malt** = ~**-bear**, *la15-e19*. ~**-net** a herring net suspended between two boats which gradually sail closer to one another with a circular sweep until the net closes and traps the fish *16-*. ~**-netter** a boat used in ~*-netting*, *20-*. ~**-netting** fishing with ~ *nets*, *20-*. ~ **sang** a choral dancing song *e16*.

~ **the mill** provide the first grain for a mill to grind after the millstones have been picked; *fig* keep someone going *19-e20*.

ring[2] **&c** *vti* **1** = ring *la14-*. **2** *vt* give a resounding blow to (*esp* the ear, the head) *20-*, *now Sh N-C*. **3** *vi*, *of ice or frosty ground* make a ringing sound under impact or friction *19-*, *local NE-S*. *n* **1** = ring. **2** the striking of a clock, the stroke *la19-*, *Sh NE-C*. **3** a resounding blow or cuff, *esp* on the ear or head *la19-*, *Sh NE-C*.

~**er** = *n* 3, *20-*, *local*. **ringin(g) frost** a hard, prolonged frost *19-*, *local*. ~**le** ['rɪŋl] a ringing, jingling sound *20-*, *local Abd-WC*.

~ **in 1** *of church bells* increase in tempo before stopping or reducing to a single bell as a sign that a service is about to begin *19-*, *now NE Ags Fif*. **2** give way, abandon an effort or struggle; be near the end of one's powers of endurance; be at death's door *19-*, *now NE Ags Per*.

ring[3] **&c; reinge &c** *la14*, **regne &c** *la14-e18* [rɪŋ] *v*, *pt* ~**it &c** *la14-19*, **rang** *la15-e20*. *ptp* also **rongyn** *15*, **rung** *16* [*'rʌŋ(ən)] **1** *vi* = reign *la14-e20*. **2** *vti* rant, storm, behave in a domineering way (towards) *19*.
n = reign *16-e19*.

~**in &c** *adj* **1** domineering *19-e20*. **2** *as intensifier* out-and-out, downright *19-*, *now Cai Bnf midLoth*. *adv* forcefully, with ease *la19-*, *Bnf*. [OED *reign*]

ringat-rangat *see* RANGLE

ringe *see* REENGE, RINSE

rink &c *la15-*; **renk** *la14-19 n* **1** the piece of ground marked out for a contest, combat, race etc *la14-*, *now arch or hist*. **2** the course or way on which one is going *la15-e16*. **3** a spell of running; a run, course; the act of running *la15-16*. **4** a course in a joust or tournament *la15-16*. **5** (1) *curling* (CURL), *quoits* the marked-out area of play *la18-*. (2) = rink, a stretch of ice etc for skating *la19-*. **6** the team forming a side in a game (now four in *curling* or (carpet-)bowling, two in quoits) *la18-*. **7** *curling* a game, one of a series of games constituting a match *19-*. **8** a straight line; a line of demarcation or division, *esp* the boundary between Scotland and England *la18-19*, *chf S*. **9** (1) a ranging up and down, a restless, *esp* noisy, prowling or hunting *la19-*, *NE*. (2) a rattling noise *la19-*, *Mry Bnf*. *v* **1** *vi* range or prowl **about** restlessly and *esp* noisily *19-*, *now Abd*. **2** *vti* search thoroughly, rummage (in) *la19-*, *NE*. **3** *vi* climb, clamber *la19-*, *now Abd*.

~**er** a round woollen cap of the type worn by *curlers* (CURL) *20-*, *local Sh-WC*.

~ **roume** a tournament ground *e16*. [*appar* OF *renc &c* a row, line, rank; *cf* F *rang*, Eng *rank*, *range*]

rinse &c *18-*, **reenge &c** *la19-*, *now local Sh-Lnk*; **ringe &c** *la16-19*, **range &c** *18-e20* [rɪns; *local Sh-Uls* rin(d)ʒ, rɪn(d)ʒ, ren(d)ʒ, rɛnʃ, rɛns; *Bwk Ayr Uls also* rɪnz] *vt* **1** = rinse *la16-*. **2** *not* **rinse** clean (a pan etc) by scraping or scrubbing, scour *la19-*, *now Rox*. **3** *only* **rinse:** wash **down** (a meal) with liquor *19-*, *now Bnf Ags*.
n **1** = rinse *la19-*. **2** a scourer made of heather twigs, *esp* for cleaning out pans etc *19-*, *now NE-WC*.

ranger, reenger = *n* 2, *18-*, *now WC*. [the Sc [-n(d)ʒ], [-nʃ] forms are appar f northern F *rincher*]

riot &c *n* **1** = riot *la14-*. **2** unlawful bodily harm or violence to another person, assault and battery *17-e18*.
adj wanton, licentious *e16*.
v **1** *vt* ravage, harry (a country) *la14-e15*. **2** *vti* = riot *la16-*.

ryatous &c ['raɪətʌs] = riotous *16*.

rip[1] **&c** *vti* *also* **raip** *la19-*, *NE* = rip. **2** strip off turf before digging *la18-*, *now Sh*. **3** *vt*, ~ **out** *or* **down** undo (a piece of knitting) *la19-*. **4** *vi* fish with a *ripper*, *20-*, *Sh-nEC*.
n **1** = rip. **2** the act of sawing wood etc along the grain *20-*, *now Sh-Per WC*.

~**per** a heavy metal bar fitted with hooks and attached to a fishing line *20-*, *Sh-nEC*.

rip[2] **&c** *n* **1** a handful of stalks of unthreshed grain or hay *17-*, *now local Ork-Bwk*. **2** *law* a sample of a crop carried to the market cross as a symbol of the right to POIND it, and as a sample of its quality *18-*. [perh f prec]

rip[3] *n* a round wicker (or straw) basket used for carrying fish, eggs or fishing lines *19-*, *Kcdn Ags Fif*.

~ie a kind of circular net used in crab-fishing or salmon-poaching *la19-20, Bnf Abd.* [ME *rippe*, ON *hrip* a fish-basket]

ripe¹ &c *adj* **1** = ripe *la14-*. **2** *of persons* (1) fully developed mentally or physically *la14, e18*; (2) advanced in years *la14-*.
vti = ripe, ripen *la15-e16*.

ripe² &c *vti* **1** search thoroughly, examine (*esp* for stolen property); hunt through, grope, rummage *15-*. **2** *vt, specif* rummage through, turn out the contents of (a pocket, wallet etc); pick (a pocket) *18-*. **3** rifle, plunder *la18-20*. **4** (1) clear (the bars of a fireplace etc) of ash, *freq* **~ the ribs** *19-, NE-C.* (2) clear (ash etc) out of a pipe; clear (a pipe) of ash *la19-, Sh-C.* **5** strip (*eg* berries from a bush) *la19-, Sh Abd.*
n a poke, stir to clear an obstruction *la19-, Sh-C.* [OE *rȳpan* engage in robbery]

rippet &c; repet &c *e16* ['rɪpət] *n* **1** a noisy disturbance, uproar; the sound of boisterous merrymaking *16-, now NE Pbls WC.* **2** a row, noisy quarrel *19-, now NE, WC.*
vi create a row or disturbance, quarrel loudly *19.* [perh onomat]

ripple¹ &c *n* **1** *chf in pl* a disease affecting the back and loins, *perh* a venereal disease *16-e20.* **2** *appar* a dance or dancing step performed *orig* to the song in the *Merry Muses* beginning 'I rede you beware o' the ripples' *la17-e20.* [only Sc; obscure]

ripple² *n* **~-grass &c** the ribwort plantain; the greater plantain *19-e20.* [appar nEng dial = a cut, scratch (for which the leaves were used); *cf* Norw *ripla* (*v*) scratch]

ripture ['rɪptər] *n* = rupture *19-.*

rise &c [raɪz; *C, S also* rəiz; *n al so* ***rəis] *vti, pt also* **raise &c** [rez], **ris &c** *la19-, now Stlg Lnk Kcb* [rɪz] **1** = rise *la14-.* **2** *vi* get out of bed in the morning *la14-.* **3** *vt* cause to rise up, lift up; bring about, produce *18-e20.* **4** *vi* ascend, mount, climb up *la19-, chf SW.*
n **1** = rise *la17-.* **2** the act of getting out of bed in the morning *20-.* **3** the layer of new wool next to the skin of a sheep at shearing time which represents the growth of the new coat *19-, C, S.* **4** a piece of fun at someone's expense, a joke, hoax *18-e20.*
~r 1 = riser. **2** *rubble-walling* a stone which reaches to the full height of the course *la20-.*
rising &c 1 = rising *la14-.* **2** *of a period of time* approaching *la19-, local Sh-Kcb: 'it's rising fower (o'clock)'.*
~band ['rɪzban(d), &c; *'rəis-] *masonry* a vertical joint rising through several courses without bonding *la18-, Per Dnbt.*

risk &c *vi* make a ripping, tearing sound, as of roots being torn up *la16-, now Kcb.* [perh partly onomat and partly altered f RISP¹, w infl f REESK]

risk *see* REESK

risp¹ &c *v* **1** *vt* file, smooth off with a file; cut or saw roughly *16-.* **2** grind (two surfaces)

together; grind (the teeth) *la17-, now Abd.* **3** *vi* make a harsh, grating sound *la17-, now Sh-NE Rox.* **4** *vti* make a grating noise with a RISP¹ 2; use (a RISP¹ 2) *19-e20.*
n **1** a coarse file or rasp *16-.* **2** = PIN *n* 3, *19-e20.* **3** a harsh grating sound, as from the friction of two surfaces *la19-, now Sh NE Ags.* [ME *rispe* grate, ON *rispa* scratch, score]

risp² &c *n, also* **~ grass &c** a species of sedge or reed *16-e20.* [only Sc; obscure]

rissert *see* RIZZAR

rissle *see* REESLE

rissom &c ['rɪsəm, 'rɛs-] *n* **1** a single head or ear of oats *19-e20.* **2** *chf in negative* not an atom or particle *19-, now Ork-NE, SW.* [ME; Scand; *cf* Sw dial *ressma* an ear of grain, *esp* oats]

rist *n* ? a stringed instrument played with a plectrum *la15.* [*cf* ME and eModEng *wreste* a tuning key, a plectrum]

rist *see* REEST², REST¹, REST²

ristle &c ['rɪstl] *n* a kind of small plough with a sickle-shaped coulter for cutting a narrow deep rut through strong roots *18-, chf Hebrides Highl, now hist.* [Gael *risteal*; ON *ristill* a ploughshare; *cf* REEST³]

rit &c; rut *19-* *vt* **1** scratch, score, groove *19-, now Sh Cai Edb.* **2** mark with a shallow trench or furrow as a guide in ploughing, draining etc *la17-, now Sh-Cai Gall.* **3** slit (a sheep) in the ear as an earmark *19-, now Sh Slk.* **4** thrust (a sword etc) through; stab *la17-, now Sh.*
n **1** a scratch, score, groove *18-, now local Sh-Kcb.* **2** the shallow preliminary cut or furrow made in ploughing, draining etc *19-, now Cai.* **3** a sheepmark in the form of a slit in the ear (or nostril) *20-, Sh Ork SW.*
rutter a marker on a drill plough, which cuts the line of the next drill *20-, now Arg Kcb.*
~tin(g)-spade a double-handled spade for making the first cuts in draining *19-, now Cai WC-S.*
~ irne a turf-cutter *la16.* [ME *ritte &c*, cognate w OHighGer *rizzan*, Ger *ritzen*; *rut* prob due to confusion w Eng *rut*]

rit *see* RUIT¹

rither *see* RUTHER¹

rittocks *n pl* the refuse of melted lard or tallow *19-, chf SW.* [? *cf* Eng dial *ritt &c* animal entrails]

rive &c; rif &c *la14-16* [raiv; *Bwk S* rəiv] *vti, pt also* **rave &c** [rev; *NE* riv]; **rived &c**; *ptp* **riven &c**, **revin &c** *la14-16* ['rɪvən, 'rɪən; *Rox also* 'ri:ən; *'rivən] **riven'd** *19-e20* **1** *vti* tear, rip, lacerate *la14-.* **2** *vt, specif* tear up (a document etc) in order to destroy or cancel it *la15-e18.* **3** wrench, pull apart, break up (into pieces) *la15-, now local.* **4** wrench or force **out**, dig **up** *la15-, now local Sh-Kcb.* **5** *also* **~ out** break up (untilled) ground) with the plough; cultivate (moorland) *16-, now Cai Abd Ags.* **6** *vti* pull or tug roughly or vigorously *la15-, now local Sh-Kcb.* **7** *vt, specif* tear (the hair), *esp* in grief or anguish *la14-*, *now Sh NE nEC*. **8** *vi* tear at or maul an opponent in a fight *la18-20*. **9** *vti, of wind* blow violently, *chf* **riving wind, a riving storm** *la19-*, *now Sh N*. **10** *vi* work (1) with a tugging or tearing motion *la18-*, *now Sh NE*; (2) hard or in a laborious way; toil *19-*, *local Sh-Wgt*. **11** *vti, freq* ~ **at** eat voraciously, tear into (food) *19-*, *local Sh-Wgt*. **12** *vtir* force one's way forward, plough **through** *19-*, *now EC*. **13** *vti* burst, crack, split *16-*, *now local*. **14** *vi, of cloud* break up, disperse *la19-*, *now Sh Fif Wgt*. **15** *fig* (1) *of the stomach* burst from eating and drinking too much *la17-*, *now N Per Lnk*; (2) *vti* burst with laughing *18-*, *now Sh N Lnk*; (3) burst with pain or anguish *la18-*, *local Sh-SW*. **16** = REIVE *v* 1 and 2, *la15-16*.

n **1** a tear, rip, scratch (in cloth, the skin etc) *la18-*, *now local Sh-Lnk*. **2** an uprooting, severance, break *19-*, *now Sh Abd Ags*. **3** a pull, jerk, wrench, grab; a hug *19-*, *now N nEC Lnk*. **4** a bite, a large mouthful; a good feed *la18-*, *now local NE-Kcb*. **5** energy in working, vigorous activity *la19-*, *now Sh*. **6** a split, crack, fissure *19-*, *now Sh*. **7** a large quantity or company *19-*, *now Abd*.

~ **someone's bonnet &c** excel or go one better than someone, *esp* said of a son excelling his father *19-e20*. [ME; ON *rífa*]

riveling *see* RIVLIN

riven('d) *see* RIVE

rivlin &c *19-*, *Sh Ork*, **riveling &c** *la19*, **rilling &c** *16-*, *now Cai, only Sc*, **rullion &c** *17-e20*; **revelyng &c** *15* ['rʌljən; *Sh Ork* 'rɪvlɪn; *Cai* 'rɪlɪn; *'rɪvəlɪŋ, *'rɪv-] *n* **1** a shoe of undressed hide *15-*, *now Cai*. **2** *in pl* rags, tatters, cheap cloth *19-*, *now Cai*. **3** *chf* **rullion** a coarse, ungainly, rough-looking person or animal *19-e20*. [OE *rifeling*, ON *hriflingr*]

riwell *see* REUALL

rizzar &c; **russle &c** *17-e20*, **rissert &c** *la17-e19* ['rɪzər; *SW* 'rɪsl, 'rʌsl; *'rɪzərt, &c] *n* the redcurrant *17-*, *now local EC Ayr*.

black ~ the blackcurrant *e18*. **white** ~ the white currant *18-*, *now Fif*. [appar var of RASER]

rizzer &c *vt, freq* ~**ed &c 1** dried, parched; *specif of haddock* sun-dried *18-*, *now local EC*. **2** *of clothes* sun-dried, thoroughly aired *19-*, *now EC*. [only Sc; obs F *ressoré* dried up, shrivelled]

rizzon &c *la19-*, *now NE*, **reason &c**; **raison &c** *16-*, *now Ork nEC* ['rezən; *NE* 'rɪzən] *n* (*la14-*), *vti* (*la16-*) = reason.

out o (**a'**) ~ unreasonable, exorbitant *19-*, *Sh N*. **out o one's** ~ out of one's mind *la19-*, *now local Sh-Per*. ~ **or nane** with or without reason on one's side; obstinately *la19-*, *now NE*.

ro &c *la14*, *e20* (*Sh*); **ruf &c** *la15-16*, **roif &c** *la16* [*Sh* ro, *also* rø; **rø(v)*] *n* = ro, rest, peace *la14-16*.

vi take a rest, rest (in one place) *la16*, *e20* (*Sh*), *only Sc*.

road &c; **rod &c** *19-*, *now Sh n* **1** = road *la16-*.

2 *freq* ~**ie** an unmetalled road, a track *18-*, *Gen except WC*. **3** a hand-cut path round a grain field to clear the way for a reaping machine *la19-*. **4** a way, direction, course, route *la19-*: *'what road are you going?'* **5** a way, method, manner *20-*, *local*: *'that's nae the road to dee it'*. **6** a condition, state *20-*, *now Abd*.

v **1** *vi* travel on a road, set out on a journey *la19-*, *NE Ags*. **2** *vt* send (a person) off (on an errand or in a particular direction) *20-*, *Abd Ags*.

~**it** on the road, off on a journey; *of a child* able to walk *la19-*, *NE Ags*.

~ **board &c** a local government committee which supervised the making and repair of roads in a county *la19-e20*. ~ **coal** coal cut from the face at road-level *19-*, *Fif Loth*. ~**-en(d)** the junction where a side road meets a main road *la19-*, *freq in place-names*. ~**-harl** a scraper for removing mud from a road *20-*, *now Stlg*. ~**head** *mining* the end of an underground passage at the working face *la19-*, *now Fif Loth Lnk*. ~**(s)man** a mine official responsible for the making and maintenance of haulage roads *la19-*, *now Fif Loth Lnk*. ~**-money** a tax levied on the inhabitants of a district for the upkeep of roads *la18-19*.

a' ~**s** everywhere *la19-*, *Gen except Sh Ork*. **a' the** ~ all the way, during the whole extent of a journey *la19-*. **get the** ~ be dismissed, get the sack *20-*, *Per WC Kcb*. **hae one's ain** ~ follow one's own inclination, go one's own way *20-*. **in one's** *or* **the** ~ in one's way, causing one inconvenience *19-*. **nae** ~ by no means, in no possible way *la20-*, *local NE-Ayr*. **on the** ~ *of a woman* pregnant *la20-*, *NE-S*. **ony** ~ anyway, anyhow *20-*. **out of one's** *or* **the** ~ out of one's or the way *la17-*. **never out of one's** ~ always able to turn things to one's own advantage; not easily upset *19-*, *now Abd*. **out of the** ~ *of* unaccustomed to, out of the way of *18-*, *local N-S*. **tae the** ~ recovered after an illness, able to be about again *la19-*, *NE Ags*. **tak in the** ~ travel along the road, cover the distance, *esp* at speed *20-*, *NE Ags*. **tak the** ~ set off (on a journey) *la18-*. [borrowed f Eng *16*; *cf* RAID and ROD]

roan &c *adj* = roan.

~**t &c** of a roan or variegated colour *20-*, *Abd SW*.

roan *see* RAWN, RONE[1]

roar *see* RAIR

roast *18-*; **rost &c** *vti, ptp also* ~**in &c** *16-e20*, **rossin &c** *la16-e20* = roast *la14-*.

n **1** = roast *la15-*. **2** a part of an animal, prepared or intended for roasting *18-*.

~**it &c 1** uncomfortably hot *la19-*, *local Sh-Kcb*. **2** *of cheese* toasted *la18-*.

rob; rub *16-e20* *vt* = rob *16-*.

~**bers and rangers** a kind of hide-and-seek *la19-*, *now Ags*.

Rob; Rab *n* **1** familiar form of Robert. **2 the Rabs** the players in the Kirkintilloch Rob Roy football team *20-, WC.*

Rabbie Burns the *usu* current affectionate form of the name of Robert Burns among Scots. **Robbie Burns** an old-fashioned kind of plough with wooden stilts and beam and an iron body, without a coulter *la20-, NE-C* [perh because associated w Burns f portraits]. **Robbie Dye** a rabid enthusiast for the town of Hawick, *esp* for its Rugby team *la20-, Rox* [f the nickname of one such]. **Robbie-rin-the-hedge &c** the goose-grass *la19-, local NE-S.*

Rob Gib(b)'s contract *freq as a motto or toast* disinterested love and loyalty *18-, now hist* [f a Master of Horse to King James V who, on being asked by the king why he served him, replied 'for stark love and kindness']. **Rab Ha** a glutton, voracious eater *la19-, WC, SW* [f a vagrant, Robert Hall, noted for his gastronomic feats]. **Rob Roy,** *also* **Rob Roy tartan** name given by TARTAN-makers to a red-and-black checked pattern in cloth *19-* [f the nickname of the famous *Highland* (HIELAND) freebooter Robert MacGregor of Glengyle (1671-1734)]. **Rob Sorby,** *also* **Sorbie** *joc* name for various sharp-edged tools, *eg* a scythe, a sickle, a saw *la19-, NE Kcdn Per* [f Robert Sorby, a Sheffield edge-tool manufacturer].

robe; rob &c *now Sh n* = robe *15-.*
~-coat a loose outer garment formerly worn by women; an overdress *18-, now Sh Ork.*

Robin &c; Robene &c *la15-17 n* **1** = Robin; robin *la15-.* **2** *child's word* the penis *la20-, NE-S.* **~ Hood &c 1** = Robin Hood *15-.* **2** a mummer's play with Robin Hood as the leading character *la16.*
~-a-ree(rie) name for a burning stick used in a children's game *19-, now Per Ayr.* **~-rin-the-hedge &c** *19-, now Kcb,* **~-roond-the-hedge** *la19-, now Wgt Rox* = Robbie-rin-the-hedge (ROB).

roch *see* RATCH[1], RUCH

rochel [?'rotʃəl] *n* a porch, vestibule *19-e20, Bnf.* [obscure]

rochian ['rɔxɪən] *n* a ruffian *la20-, NE Per.* [conflation of *roch* (RUCH) w Eng *ruffian*]

rock[1]; **roke &c** *n* **1** = rock *16-.* **2** *curler's* (CURL) name for a *curling-stone, la20-.* **3** *also* ~ **partan** the common edible crab *la19-, now NE, WC.*
~lie pebbly *19-, local EC, SW.* **~y-on** a pile of stones built by boys to try to stem the incoming tide *la19-, Abd Kdn.*
~ bool a round, hard, candied-sugar sweet *20-, local sEC-Rox.* **~ cod (fish)** *or* **codling** a kind of cod which lives amongs rocks *19-.* **~-halibut** the coal-fish *20-, NE Ags.* **~-herring** the allis or twaite shad *19-, now Bnf.* **~ lintie** the twite; the rock pipit *la19-, now Cai.* **~ sole** the Dover sole *la19-, now NE.* **~ turbot** the flesh of the catfish or wolf-fish *20-, NE Ags Bwk.*

rock[2] **&c** *vti* **1** = rock *15-.* **2** *vi* stagger or reel in walking *18-, now Sh NE Kcb.*
~er &c 1 = rocker. **2** a nurse or attendant whose duty it was to rock a child in its cradle *16-e17, only Sc.* **~ie** *or* **~etie-row &c** with a rocking or rolling motion *19-, now Fif Kcb.*

rock[3] **&c** *n* **1** = rock, a distaff *15-, now arch.* **2** a distaff with the wool or flax attached; the quantity of wool or flax placed on a distaff for spinning *16-19.*
~in(g) a gathering of women neighbours to spin and chat together; any convivial gathering of neighbours *la18-19.*

rocket &c *n* = rochet, a bishop's surplice *la15-e19, latterly hist.*

rocketie-row *see* ROCK[2]

rod &c; rode &c *13-17 n* a path, way; a track *la14-17.*
~ding &c a narrow track or path, *specif* one trodden out by sheep *la18-20.* [only Sc; perh by wrong analysis of OE *fūt-trod* a track, foot-path; cf ROAD, w which there is some confusion]

rod *see* ROAD

rodd &c; rod *e16* [rod; *Cai* rʌd] *n* fish- or frog-spawn *e16, 19-, now Cai.*
~en &c, *freq* **~en fluke &c** the turbot *la18-e20;* cf *rawn fleuk* (RAWN). **~ing** spawning *la15, la18.* [obscure; cf REDD[2]. OED *rud* (*n*[3])]

rodden &c *n* the berry of the ROWAN[1]; *occas* the tree itself *la16-, now N.*
~ tree the *rowan-tree* (ROWAN[1]) *16-, now N, local C.*
nae to care a ~ not to care a fig *20-, NE Ags.* **have had ~s tae one's supper** be in a sour or surly humour *20-, NE.* **as sour as ~s** very sour or bitter *la19-, chf NE Ags Ayr.* [prob Scand; cf ON *roð* redness, *roði* reddening and Eng *red*]

roddikin &c *n* the fourth stomach of a ruminant; tripe *la16-, now local sEC, S.* [obs Du *roodeken,* dim of *roode;* cognate w REED[2]]

roddle *vti* rock, shake, totter *la19-, Lnk.* [perh altered f Eng dial *roggle*]

rode *see* RIDE, ROD

roebuck berry *see* RAE[1]

rogue &c *n* = rogue.
~-money a local tax levied for the expenses of arrest and detention of criminals *18-19.*

roid &c *adj* **1** roughly or hurriedly made, not well finished *la14-15.* **2** unlearned; unrefined; inelegant *la14-16.* **3** violent, rough, uncivil *la14-16.* [ME, eModEng *royde,* OF *roide &c,* L *rigidum* rigid or perh var of Eng *rude*]

roif *see* RO

roil *n* a storm, a heavy sea *la19-, Arg.*
ralliach &c ['raljəx, 'roiləx] choppy, stormy *la19-e20, Arg.* [cf Gael *roithleach* rolling, tossing and obs Eng *roil* agitation (of water)]

roising *see* ROSE

roiter *see* ROYET

roke *see* ROCK[1], ROUK[1]

rokelay &c [*'rokli] *n, also fig* a kind of short cloak *18-e19.* [altered f F *roquelaure,* f the Duc de Roquelaure]

roll, rolment *see* ROW[1]

rolp *see* ROUP[2]

romanis &c [*'romans] *n* = romance *la14-e16.*

romany [*'romǝni] *n* ~ **buge** &c some kind of small fur used for lining garments *la15-e16.* [only Sc; OF *romine* &c]

rone[1] &c; **roan** *la17-,* **rhone** *la18- n* **1** the horizontal gutter for rainwater, running along the eaves of a roof; *also occas* = ~ *pipe, 18-.* **2** the pipe of a boat's pump *17.* **3** *mining* a wooden water-channel *la17-, now Fif.*

~ **pipe** the more or less vertical pipe for draining water from the RONE[1] (*n* 1); *also occas* = *n* 1, *20-.* [perh f or f as RIN; *cf* Norw *run, ron* a watercourse and obs Eng *run* = *n* 1]

rone[2] &c *n* a thicket of brushwood, thorns etc; a patch of a dense stunted woodland *la15-20.* [ME; *cf* Norw dial *rune* &c, ON *runnr*]

rone[3] &c *n* a strip or patch of ice on the ground; *specif* a children's slide *16-20, latterly NE.* [perh f Eng *run*]

rone *see* RANE, ROWAN[1]

ronge *see* RUNDGE

rongyn *see* RING[3]

ronnach ['ronǝx] *n, in pl* couch-grass *19-, now Kcdn.* [appar altered f LONNACH; *cf* RAMMOCK[2]]

ronnie *see* RANE

roobrub *see* RHUBARB

rood *see* RUID

rood-goose &c [*'rød'gøs, *'red-, *'rid-] *n, also* **rutt** *la16* the brent goose *la18-19, Sh Ork Ross.* [ON *hrotgás; cf* Dan *radgaas*]

roof *see* RUIF

rook[1] &c; **ruke** &c *15-18* [ruk; *Kcb* rʌk; *røk, *rjuk, *rjʌk] *n* **1** = rook, the bird (*more usu* CRAW[1]) *15-.* **2** term of abuse *16-19.* **3** *esp marbles* a complete loss of what one has *la19-, C, S. vt* **1** plunder, clean **out** *18-.* **2** = rook, cheat, overcharge deceitfully *19-.* **3** rob (a bird's nest) of eggs *19-, Gen except Sh Ork.* **4** *marbles* win (all an opponent's marbles); win all the marbles of (one's opponent) *la19-.*

~**ie** *marbles* a game in which the winner takes all *la20-, local.*

the hindmost ~ one's last farthing *la18-, now WC Wgt.*

rook[2] *n* **1** a quarrel, uproar, fuss *19-, now Ags.* **2** a noisy group of people *la19-, now Ags.* [obscure]

rook *see* ROUK[1]

rooketty &c; **ruckity** &c *interj* imitating the first notes in the call of a pigeon.

~**-coo** *n* the call of a pigeon *20-, Gen except Sh Ork. vi* coo; *of lovers* bill and coo *19-20.* ~ **doo** a tame pigeon *la19-, local C.* [imit; *cf* LowGer *rukke* (*v*) coo]

roolyie *20-, Cai;* **rul3e** &c *e15* [*Cai* 'rulji; *'rʌlji &c] *vt* rumble or stir noisily. [ME *roylen* roll, f OF *roillier* &c related to *roelle* a wheel]

room &c *17-;* **roum** &c *la12-e20* [rum] *n* **1** = room *la14-.* **2** a place in a series, logical sequence, queue etc *la16-18, only Sc: 'in the first room'.* **3** *in pl* domains, territories *la15-16, only Sc.* **4** an estate; a piece of land rented from a landowner, a farm, a TACK[2], arable holding *16-, only Sc, now chf hist and in place-names.* **5** seating space for one in a church pew *e18.* **6** the compartment or space between the thwarts of a boat *la18-, chf Sh.* **7** *orig* the apartment of a *but and ben* (BUT) not used as the kitchen; *hence more gen* a sitting-room, best room *la18-.* **8** *mining* the working space left between supporting pillars of coal *18-, now wLoth Ayr.*

adj **1** = roomy, spacious, wide *la15-19.* **2** empty, unobstructed, clear *17-e19, only Sc.*

vt **1** = room, clear; leave; extend *15-e16.* **2** install *la16-17, only Sc.*

~**-end** the end of a *but and ben* (BUT) away from the kitchen *19-, now local C.* ~ **free** &c not incurring the payment levied on corn for occupying space in a mill while awaiting grinding *la12-e17.* ~ **se** the open sea *la14.*

in ~ **of** in place of *la20-, NE, C.* ~ **and kitchen** a dwelling, *usu* a FLAT[1], consisting of a kitchen(/living-room) and another room *20-.* ~ **and rance** *mining* a kind of *stoup-and-room* (STOUP) working *19-20.*

Room &c = Rome *la16-, now Bnf.*

roon *see* ROUND, RUIND

roond *see* ROUND

roop *see* ROUP[1], ROUP[2], ROUP[3], ROUP[6]

roose *see* ROUSE[1], ROUSE[2], RUISE

rooshel *vt* hustle *la20-, NE Ags.* [conflation of *reeshle* (REESLE) w Eng *rustle*]

Rooshian *n, adj* = Russian *la19-, Sh-C.*

rooshie-doo *see* RUSH

rooshter *see* ROOSTER

roost[1]; **reest** &c *19-, chf NE n* **1** = roost. **2** the open cross-joists of a cottage living room *la18-, now Sh.*

vi = roost.

roost[2] *19-,* **rust** *la18-;* **roust** &c [rust] *n* **1** = rust *16-.* **2** rancour *e16, only Sc.* **3** *only* **roost** *chf in negative* not a penny, not a brass farthing *20-, local Cai-SW.*

vti = rust *16-.*

~**ie** &c **1** = rusty *16-.* **2** *of verse* rough, unpolished *16, only Sc.* **3** *of the throat or voice* rough, dry; hoarse, raucous *18-, local Sh-Kcb.* ~**ie nail** a dram of WHISKY *20-, now EC-Wgt.* ~**it** &c **1** = rusted *16-.* **2** *of the throat* = ~*ie* 3, *la18-, local Sh-WC.*

rooster &c; **rooshter** *n* useless rubbish *19-, NE.* [appar var of prec, w infl f TROOSHTER]

root *see* ROWT, RUIT[1], RUIT[2]

roove *see* RUIVE

roow *n* a wheel *la16.* [only Sc; F *roue.* OED *row* (*n*[6])]

ropach ['ropǝx] *adj* untidy, dirty, slatternly *20-, Highl Per.* [Gael *ròpach* squalid, slovenly]

rope *see* RAIP, ROUP[1]

roploch *see* RAPLOCH

rorie &c *n* something large of its kind, *specif* a large turnip *la19-20, Bnf Abd*. [uncertain]

rose &c *n* **1** = rose *la14-*. **2** *also* ~ **end** the crown end of a potato tuber *19*.

rosie &c *adj* = rosy *16-*. *n* **1** a reddish marble *la19-, now Bnf*. **2** an effect of light indicating a change in the weather or bad weather *e20, Mry*.

rosy-posy term of endearment *la19-, now Abd Ags*. **roising** ['rozən] rosy *la15*.

~ **lintie &c 1** the male of the linnet (which has bright red plumage during the breeding season) *19-, now Ork Cai*. **2** the lesser redpoll *la19-e20*.

roseegar &c, roseager [*roz'igər] *n* darnel *la17-e18, chf SW*. [only Sc; f Eng *rosaker, rosager* realgar, disulphide of arsenic, darnel being supposed to have similar narcotic properties]

roset &c ['rozət] *n* = resin, rosin *la15-*.
vt rub with resin; *specif* rub (a fiddle-bow) with rosin *16-*.
adj resinous *la19-, local Sh-Per*.

~**(t)y** of, full of or covered with ROSET *19-*.
~**ty-en(d)** a shoemaker's thread *la19-, now Kcb*. ~**ty ruits &c** fir-roots used as fuel *la19-, now Ags Per*.

~**-en(d)** a resined thread, used for sewing leather *19-, NE-C*.

rosidandrum &c [rozɪ'dandrəm] *n* rhododendron *20-, local Bnf-Uls*. [f the supposed similarity to the flower of the rose]

rosine [*ro'zəin] *n* a rose *e16*. [L *rosa*, w infl f REGYNE]

Ross: ~ **Herald** one of the former Scottish heralds *la15-19*. ~**-shire Buffs** see *Seaforth Highlanders* (SEAFORTH) *la18-20*. [the former county, now *district* (DESTRICK), of *Ross and Cromarty*]

rosignell [*?'rosɪnjəl] *n* the nightingale *la16*. [F *rossignol*. OED *rossignol*]

rossin, rost *see* ROAST

rot &c *n* (*la16-*), *vti* (*la14-*) = rot.
~**tack &c** an old, discarded, decayed object, a piece of rubbish *19-e20, NE*. ~**ten &c 1** = rotten *la14-*. **2** *also* ~**ten drunk** drunk *20-, Sh-SW*. **3** *of rock* crumbling *la18-*.

~ **grass** one of several grasses supposed to be poisonous to sheep *la18-19*.

rot *see* RATT

Rothesay &c [St 'rɔθse; 'rosɪ]: ~ **Herald** one of the Scottish heralds *15-*.
Duke of ~ a title of the monarch's eldest son *la14-*. [the town in Bute, site of a (now ruined) royal castle)]

rothick &c ['roðək, 'rodək; *Cai* 'rʌθəg] *n* a young edible crab *19-, local N*. [Gael *rudhag* a crab (*lit* little red one)]

rothos &c; rothie ['roθəs, 'roθɪ] *n* **1** a tumult, uproar; a tangle, muddle *19-, now Mry*. **2** a rude, coarse person *20-, Abd*. [perh connected w RUCH or RUDDIE]

rottack *see* ROT
rottan *see* RATTON
rouch(le) *see* RUCH

roucht *see* REAK, RECK
roudes *see* RUDAS
roug *see* RUG
rough *see* RUCH
roughie *see* RUFFIE[1]

rouk[1] &c, roke &c *16-19*, **rauk** *18-e20*; **rook** *18-* [ruk; *Rox also* rʌuk; *rok, *rɑk] *n* mist, fog *16-, now local*.
~**ie &c** misty, damp, drizzly; muggy *18-, now local Cai-S*. [ON *raukr, Sw dial *rauk* vapour, smoke; *cf* Du dial *rock*, Du *rook* smoke; also in nEng dial]

rouk[2] &c [*?ruk] *vi* ~ **and roun(d)** talk privately *15-16*. [perh ME, eModEng *rouke, ruck &c* crouch, huddle together; *cf* nME *runk*, OFlem *ronken* mutter]

rouk *see* RUCK
roul *see* ROW[1]
roule *see* RULE
roum *see* ROOM

roun &c; round *16-19* [*run(d)] *vti* **1** whisper, tell or talk quietly or privately *la14-e20*. **2** *vt* discuss, talk **over** *16-e17*.
~**ar** = rouner, a talebearer *16-e17*. [obs or dial Eng *roun(d)*. OED *rouner*]

roun *see* RIN, ROUND
rounall *see* ROUNDEL

round &c; roun *la18-*, **roond** *la19-*, **roon** *20-* [run(d)] *adj* **1** = round *la14-*. **2** *of cloth* made of thick thread *la15-16, only Sc*. **3** *of speech* honest, plain *15-16*. **4** sizable, big *18-e20*.
adv = round *16-*.
n **1** = round *16-*. **2** *specif* (1) = ROUNDEL 3, *18-20*; (2) a circular sheep-fold *19-, local SW, S*; *cf* ROUNDEL 4. **3** the ~ the surrounding country, neighbourhood *19-, Sh Ork local EC*. **4** *golf* a complete circuit of the course in which all the holes are played *la18-*. **5** *of time, chf* **a** *or* **the ~ o the clock** a complete circuit of the hour-hand of a clock, twelve hours *la19-, local Sh-Kcb*: '*he slept the round of the clock*'. **6** the correct sequence; one's turn in a sequence *la18-19*. **7** *also* ~**-steak** a cut of meat, *esp* beef, taken from the hindquarter *19-; cf* Eng *rump*.
vti = round *16-*.

~ **about** *adv, prep* = round about *16-*. *n*
~**about 1** = roundabout. **2** a circular prehistoric fort *19-, now Ayr Rox*. **3** a circular roll made of coarse flour; a circular *oatcake* (AIT) *19-, now Bnf*. ~ **meal** coarsely-ground oatmeal *19-, now Bnf Abd*. **roun soun** ['run 'sun] *used emphatically* complete, whole *19-, SW*: '*a roun soun dizzen*'.

round *see* ROUN

roundel &c; rounall &c *la18-e20* ['run(d)əl] *n* **1** = roundel *15-*. **2** a small round table *e16, only Sc*. **3** a round turret *18-, now nEC, SW; cf* ROUN *n* 2 (1). **4** a circular sheepfold *20-, local Cai-Lnk; cf* ROUN *n* 2 (2). **5** a circular patch of grass worn smooth by cattle *19-, now wLoth Lnk*. **6** a round heap *20-, now Per wLoth*.

rounge *see* RUNDGE

rountre *see* ROWAN[1]

roup[1] **&c;** **roop** *la17-e20*, **rope &c** *17-e18* [rʌup; *Sh Suth* rup; *Ork Bute Ayr SW* rop] *vt* **1** sell or let by public auction *la16-*. **2** sell up, *esp* turn out (a bankrupt) and sell his effects, *freq* ~ **out** *etc*, *19-*.

n a sale or let by public auction *la16-*.

~**er** a person who puts up goods for sale by auction; *occas* an auctioneer *18-e19*. ~**ing** a selling or letting by public auction, an auction *la16-e20*. ~**ing clerk** = *clerk of the* ~, *la19-*, *now Cai Lnk*. ~**ing roll** a record of transactions at an auction sale *18-*, *local N-S*. ~**ing wife** *etc* a woman who buys and resells second-hand furniture; a female auctioneer *la18-e20*.

~**-bill** a list of items for sale at an auction *la19-*, *now Sh Cai Ags*. ~**-day** the day on which an auction sale is to be held *la19-*, *Sh-nEC*. ~**-price** the price fetched at an auction *la20-*, *Sh NE*. ~**-roll** = ~*ing roll*, *la18-*, *now Cai WC Kcb*.

articles of ~ a formal statement of the conditions of sale at an auction *18-*. **bring to the** ~ bring to bankruptcy, ruin *20-*, *local EC-WC*. **clerk of the** ~ an auctioneer's clerk *la19-*, *now N*. **cry** *etc* **a** ~ proclaim publicly that an auction sale is to take place *19-20*. **judge of the** ~ a person appointed as ARBITER[1] in any dispute arising from buying or selling at an auction *18-*, *now N*. **put to the** ~ offer for sale or let to the highest bidder *la18-*, *Sh-Per*. [f next; *cf* Norw *rope op* sell by auction]

roup[2] **&c;** **roop** [rup; *local also* rʌup] *v* **1** *vi*, also **rolp** *la15* cry, shout, roar; croak *la15-*, *now NE wLoth Ayr*. **2** *vt*, *only Sc* (1) proclaim loudly *16*; (2) invoke loudly *e16*.

n **1** *freq* **the** ~ hoarseness, huskiness, any inflamed condition of the throat *la16-*, *now local Cai-Fif*. **2** a catarrhal disease of the mouth or throat in poultry *19-*.

~**er** a person who cries or shouts *la16*. ~**ie &c** hoarse, rough husky *la18-*, *local N-SW*. ~**it &c** hoarse, rough, raucous *la18-*, *now local C*. [ON *raupa* boast, brag; *cf* prec]

roup[3] **&c;** **roop** [rup] *vt* **1** plunder, rob, deprive of everything *19-*, *local NE-S*. **2** prune (a hedge etc) very severely *la20-*, *Per Fif*. **3** take (the marbles of a defeated opponent) in a game of *roopie*, *20-*, *now Per Fif*.

roopie a variety of the game of marbles in which the winner claimed all the loser's marbles *e20*, *Sh Ork*. [appar altered f ROOK[1], perh w infl f RIPE[2] and STOUP AND ROUP]

roup[4] [rʌup] *vi* vomit *la19-20*, *NE*. [onomat]

roup[5] **&c** [rʌup] *n*, *chf in pl* the stems of seaweed, *specif* of the oar-weed *la19-20*, *Bnf Abd*. [perh var of Eng *rope*]

roup[6]**; roop** [rup] *n* a dense mist *la19-e20*, *SW*, *S*. [prob altered f ROUK[1]]

rous *n* a heavy fall or crash *e16*. [only Sc; obscure]

rouschit *see* RUSH

rouse[1] **&c;** **roose &c** *la19-e20* [ruz] *v* **1** *vt* = rouse. **2** *vi* move with violence or speed, rush *la19-*, *Sh Ork Bnf*. **3** become agitated, excited or enraged *la19-*, *NE-S*.

rousie &c *of an animal* restless, easily excited *la20-*, *S*. **rousing bell** a bell rung to let distant worshippers know it is time to get up for church *la19-*, *local EC*.

~ **on** become enraged at *20-*, *NE nEC wLoth*.

rouse[2] **&c;** **roose &c** *la19-* [ruz] *vt* **1** sprinkle (fish) with salt to cure them *18-*, *now Sh-N Fif*. **2** sprinkle with water; water with a watering can *la19-*, *NE Ags*.

rouser &c a watering-can *la18-*, *local NE-WC*. [aphetic f ME *arrouse*, OF *arrouser* bedew; sprinkle]

roust *see* ROOST[2], ROWST[1]

rout[1] **&c** [rut] *vi*, *of the sea, winds, thunder etc* roar, rumble, make a loud noise *la14-*.

~**ing &c** roaring, rumbling *16-*, *freq in place-names*. [ME *rute &c*; prob Scand; *cf* Norw *ruta*]

rout[2] **&c** [*rut] *vi* snore *la14*, *e19* (*prob arch*). [ME]

rout[3] **&c** [*rut] *n* a violent movement, a heavy blow, stroke *la14-19*. [nME; OE *hrūtan* rush, move with violence]

rout[4] **&c** [*rut] *n* **bane and** ~, **stout and** ~ completely *la14*; *cf stoup and roup* (STOUP). [only Sc; obscure]

rout[5] **&c** [*?rut] *n* a species of wild goose *la16-e17*. [only Sc; obscure; *cf* ROOD-GOOSE]

rout *see* ROWT

routh &c [rʌuθ] *n* plenty, abundance, profusion *la17-*.

adj plentiful, abundant, profuse, well-endowed *la18-e20*.

~**ie** = *adj*, *la18-*, *now N Per Rox*. [obscure]

rove[1] **&c** *vi* **1** = rove *17-*. **2** wander in thought or speech, be delirious, rave *18-*, *now Sh-Cai Ags*.

n a ramble or wandering, *freq* **on the** ~ *19-*, *now Sh Per*.

rove[2] *vi*, *of a fire* burn well, blaze, *freq* **rovin** *la19-*, *NE*.

rover a large blazing fire *la20-*, *Sh N*. [perh extended f prec; *cf* REEVE[3]]

rovin *adj* ~ **fu** full to the brim *la19-*, *Per Fif*. [obscure]

row[1] **&c** *la15-*, **roll &c**; **roul &c** *la18-20* [rʌu; *also* rʌul] *vti* **1** = roll *la14-*. **2** *vi* ride in a carriage *e16*. **3** *vt* convey in a wheeled vehicle, wheel *18-*. **4** trundle (*specif* a GIRD[1] *n* 4) forward *19-*. **5** *also freq fig*, *of life*: (1) play (a bowl or curling-stone (CURL)) *la18-*, *now Bnf Ags Ayr*; (2) *vi*, *of bowls* roll towards the jack *18-*, *now Bnf Ags Kcb*: 'see how the bowls roll.' **6** *vt* form (cotton or newly-carded wool) into a roll before it is spun *18-19* [*cf* Eng *rove*]. **7** wind, twist, twine *19-*, *Sh-C*. **8** wrap **up** *or* **in**, envelop **in**; wrap around *19-*. **9** wind **up** (a clock etc) *18-*, *now Sh C*, *S*. **10** *chf in passive* **be** ~**ed intae** be involved or embroiled in *la18-*, *C*, *S*. **11** *vi* move about with a rolling or staggering gait, waddle, lurch or stumble along *19-, now local Sh-Kcb*. **12** move about, fidget, toss and turn restlessly *la19-, now Sh N, C*. **13** *of sheep* roll over on the back *20-, EC, WC*.

n **1** = roll *la15-*. **2** *law, only* **roll** a list of cases, applications, motions etc set down for hearing in court *la17-*. **3** a roll of wool etc drawn out and slightly twisted *la17, e20* [cf *v* 6]. **4** a roll of tobacco *19-, local Sh-Kcb*; *cf* BOGIE¹. **5** the high-water mark on a beach; a roll of seaweed along this line *20-, Ross Mry*. **6** a rounded stick or roller for levelling grain in a measure *18-19*. **7** a plump person, a fat, untidy, lazy woman *20-, SW*.

~**er &c 1** a rolling pin, *freq* a ribbed or grooved one used in making *oatcakes* (AIT) *19-, now NE Kcb*. **2** = *n* 6, *18-, now Cai*. **rowie &c** a flaky bread roll made with a lot of butter *la20-, NE Ags*. **rollie-pin &c** [ˈrolɪˈpɪn] *games* a rolling action of the hands between the bouncing and catching of a ball *la20-, now Stlg Kcb*. ~**ing &c 1** = rolling *la16-*. **2** a roll of cotton or wool rolled as in *v* 6, *18-20*. **rolment &c** [*ˈrolmənt, *ˈrʌu-] enrolment *la15-17*.

~ **bowls** the game of bowls *e16*. **row-chow** [ˈrʌuˈtʃʌu] *vi, esp of children at play* roll, tumble *20-, local Per-Kcb. adj* rolling, revolving; mixed-up, tangled *la19-, now WC Kcb*. **row-chow tobacco &c** a game in which a chain of boys coil round a large boy and all sway to and fro shouting the name of the game until they fall in a noisy heap *19-, now local Per-Kcb*. **row-shoudert** round-shouldered *la20-, NE Ags*.

as ready to row as rin said of a very fat person *20-, Ork Bnf Abd*.

row² &c [rʌu] *vti* **1** = row (a boat) *la14-*. **2** *vi, of a boat* move along in the water easily or smoothly *la18-, now Sh Abd Ags*.

~**age** rowing dues or charges *la17*. ~**th** [*~θ] *only Sc* **1** rowing *15-e16*. **2** a stroke of the oar(s) *e16*.

row *see* RAW¹

rowan¹ &c; rone &c *la16-18*, **raun- &c** *la17-e20* [ˈrʌuən; *NE* ran; *ˈro(ə)n; *rʌun] *n* **1** *also* ~-**tree, rountre** *la16* the mountain ash *la16-*. **2** the fruit of the mountain ash *19-*.

~ **berry** = *n* 2, *18-*. ~ **buss &c** = *n* 1, *19-20*. ~ **jelly** a tart-flavoured preserve made of ~ *berries*, served with game or meat *la19-*. [eModEng; Scand; *cf* Norw dial *raun*, ON *reynir*; also in nEng dial]

rowan² &c [*ʔˈruən, *ʔˈrʌuən] *n, attrib* a kind of cloth *la15-e16*. [appar *Rouen* the French town]

rowan *see* RAWN

rowl *see* RAIVEL

rowlie-powlie &c [ˈrʌuliˈpʌuli] *n* **1** = roly-poly, a game; a kind of pudding. **2** *specif* a form of KYLES² or ninepins played at fairs *19-e20*. **3** a fairground stallholder in charge of *n* 2, *19*.

rown *see* RAWN

rowst¹ &c, roust &c [rʌust] *vi* shout, roar, bellow *16-, now Ags*.

n a shout, roar, bellow; the act of roaring or bellowing *la14-, now Ags*.

~**y &c** *of weather* windy, blustery *la20-, Ags Fif*.

rowst² &c [rʌust] *vt* arouse, stir to action, rout out *la19-, now Ags Kcb*. [altered f Eng *rouse*, perh by conflation w Eng *rout*]

rowt &c, rout; root &c *la19, Sh Ork Bnf* [rʌut; *Sh Ork* rut; *Bnf also* rut] *vi* **1** *of cattle* bellow, roar *15-, now local Sh-SW*. **2** *of other animals* roar, cry *la16-, now Ags Per Ayr*. **3** *of persons* (1) shout, bawl, make a great noise *15-, now Ags Kcb*; (2) play **on** (a horn); *of a horn* toot *19*; (3) *transf* break wind *la19-, now Fif wLoth*. **4** *of wind, water etc* roar loudly *18-19*.

n **1** the bellowing or lowing of cattle; the act of bellowing *15-, now local Sh-Gall*. **2** a shout, outcry, clamour, fuss *18-19*. **3** a loud crashing noise *16-19*. [ME *rowt &c*, ON *rauta* bellow]

rowth *see* ROW²

roy¹ *n, freq verse* = roy, a prince, sovereign *la15-16*.

roy² *vi* talk nonsense *e16*. [obscure]

roy³ *n* a variety of trunk rot in conifers, *esp* the larch *la18-, now Mry Bnf*.

vt, only ~**ed** affected with ROY³ *la18-, now Mry Bnf*. [Gael *ruaidhe* redness; a defect in fir timber]

royal &c *adj* = royal *16-*.

n **1** = royal. **2** R~ *informal* a soldier in the *Royal Scots*.

~**ty &c 1** an area of land or a district held by or directly of the Crown *la16-*; *cf* REGALITY, *barony* (BARON). **2** = royalty.

~ **bounty** an annual payment made by the Crown to the *Church of Scotland* (CHURCH) for the promotion of religion in *the Highlands and Islands* (HIELAND) *18-19*. ~ **burgh &c, burgh** ~ *la17-e18* a BURGH deriving its charter and its lands and privileges directly from the Crown *17-20*; the *Royal Burghs* formed a separate estate in the Scottish Parliament; see *Convention of R~ Burghs* (CONVENTION). **R~ Company of Archers** the Sovereign's bodyguard in Scotland *18-*. **R~ Highland Fusiliers** a regiment formed in 1959 by the amalgamation of the *Royal Scots Fusiliers* and the *Highland Light Infantry* (HIELAND). **R~ Highland Show** see *Highland Show* (HIELAND). **R~ Mile** the street in Edinburgh extending from the Castle to the Palace of Holyroodhouse, consisting of the *Lawnmarket* (LAND¹), the High Street and the Canongate *20-*. **R~ Scots** a regiment, *orig* raised 1633 as a regiment in the French service; so called since 1812; from 1920, **The Royal Scots (The Royal Regiment)**. **Royal Scots Dragoon Guards (Carabiniers and Greys)** a regiment formed in 1971 by the amalgamation of the *Royal Scots Greys* and the 3rd Carabiniers (Prince of Wales Dragoon Guards). **R~ Scots Fusiliers** a regiment, *orig* raised

1678; so called 1881-1959; cf *R~ Highland Fusiliers*. **R~ Scots Greys** name given officially to the *Scots Greys* (SCOTS) in 1877, *la19-20*; cf *Royal Scots Dragoon Guards*.

royet &c; royt &c, royd &c *19 adj* **1** extravagant, nonsensical *la16*. **2** *esp of children* wild, unruly, mischievous *la16-, now local Sh-Fif*. **3** *of weather* wild, stormy, variable *la19-, NE*. **4** irregular, turbulent *19-20*.
n **1** an unruly, troublesome person, *esp* a bad-tempered woman *19-e20, C*. **2** a troublesome animal, *esp* a roaming or noisy cow *18-e19*.
roiter &c talk nonsense, babble, rave *19-e20, Renfr Ayr*. [perh irreg var of Eng *riot*; cf ROY², ROID]

royn [*?ron] *adj* ? red, vermilion *e16*. [only Sc; ? OF *roun*]

royne [*ron] *n* some kind of leather *e15*. [obscure. OED *roan* (*n²*)]

royt *see* ROYET

rub &c *vti* **1** = rub *16-*. **2** *vt, bowls, curling* (CURL) move (a stone or bowl) aside by knocking gently against it with another *19-*. **3** fix (a charge etc) **on** (a person) *17*.
n **1** = rub. **2** *golf* factors affecting the resting place of the ball in play which must be accepted by the players *19-*. **3** a slight jibe, reproof or teasing *la19-, local Ork-Kcb*.
~(**b**)**er** a hard brush for rubbing or scrubbing, a scrubbing-brush *18-, now Lnk*. ~**bing bottle** a bottle of liniment or embrocation *20-, now local Cai-Wgt*. ~**bin stane** a piece of pipeclay used to whiten doorsteps *20-, Ork C, S*. ~**bing stick** a stick used by shoemakers to rub leather smooth *20-, now Ork*. ~**bing stock** a post in a field for cattle to rub themselves against *18-, now Ork Per*.

rub *see* ROB

ruban &c [*'rʌbən] *n* a ribbon *la15-e16*. [F; cf eModEng]

rubbage &c *n* = rubbish *18-, now local Sh-Kcb*.

rubber &c *la16-e18*, **rubbour &c** *la15-16 n* a cask, barrel. [nME; obscure]

rubeatour *see* RABIATOR

rubigo *n* the penis *la16*. [only Sc; presum L *rūbīgo* redness; modesty; shame]

ruch &c *16-*, **rough** *17-*; **rouch &c** *la15-*, **reuch &c** *la14-e20*, **roch &c** *16-e20* [*Ork S* rʌux; *N Fif* rox; *C* rʌx; **rux] *adj* **1** = rough *la14-*. **2** (1) *of hides* undressed, untanned (with the hair still on) *la14-e18*. (2) *of sheep* unshorn, unclipped *19-, Bwk SW, S*. **3** *of the growth of grass or crops* strong, luxuriant, dense *19-, local Sh-Kcb*. **4** abundant; plentifully supplied, *esp* with good plain fare *18-, now C*: '*a guid rouch house*'. **5** *of a bone* having meat on it *la18-, now Per Stlg Ayr*. **6** lewd, foul-mouthed, indecent *19-, local NE-Kcb*.
adv **1** = rough *la16-*. **2** in a comfortable or well-supplied state *la19-, Ags Per Kcb*.

n **1** = rough. **2** rough ground *la15-*. **3** *specif* the rough ground along the edges of a golf-course *20-*. **4** *agric* land in an unimproved, virgin condition *20-, Sh N Ayr*. **5** the major part of something *19-, local NE-Gall*.
vt = rough *19-*.
~**ie &c 1** a wild rough boy *la20-, N*. **2** a rough, coarse woman *20-, Abd*. **3** = ~-*back*, *19-e20, NE*. **rouchle &c** toss about, shake roughly, tousle *19-, chf Arg* [perh w infl f Eng *ruffle*]. ~**some** somewhat rough or uneven; rough, crude, uncouth *la17-, now Dnbt Kcb*.
~**-back** (**fluke**) the long rough dab *la18-, now Bnf*. ~ **bear** = BEAR¹ *la17-e20*. ~ **blade** the mature leaf of a plant as opposed to the seed leaf *la20-, local Ork-Wgt*. **the rough bounds** name for the mountainous region in the *West Highlands* (WAST) from Loch Sunart (Arg) to Loch Horn (Inv) *19-* [translating Gael *Na Garbhchriochan*]. ~ **coal** a kind of inferior coal *la18-, now Fif Lnk*. ~ **dram** enough liquor to cause drunkenness *la19-, N*. ~**-head &c** a turf or PEAT¹, *esp* one with the surface grass still attached *19-20*. ~**-living** *of a man* living in a dissolute, debauched or immoral way *19-, now Sh NE Per*. ~**-spun** coarsely-made; *of manners* rough, crude, unpolished *la18-, now nEC*. ~ **stane** a natural boulder *20-, local Per-Gall*. ~**-stane dyke** a *dry-stone* (DRY) wall *20-, now Ayr Gall*.
~ **and right 1** entirely, taking everything into consideration *la18-, now Ags*. **2** rough and ready, having somewhat rough manners, blunt *la19-, now Sh*. ~ **and round** simple, homely; *of food* plain but substantial *e19*.

ruck &c; rouk &c [rʌk; *Ross Inv Arg* ruk] *n* **1** a hay- or corn-stack of a standard shape and size *16-, now NE-S*. **2** a stack or heap, *orig* of fuel, *later also specif* of PEATS¹ *16-, now Bnf Abd*. **3** a small temporary haystack in the field to allow the hay to dry *19-, local Cai-S*.
vt pile up, stack up, build (hay, corn etc) into a stack *18-, now local*.
~ **foun**(**d**) **&c** a circular foundation of stones etc on which a stack is built *20-, NE nEC, SW*. ~ **heid** the tapering top of a stack *20-, NE nEC, SW*. ~ **tow** the rope used to bind the thatch on a stack *20-, NE Per*. [ME; prob Scand; cf Norw *ruka* a heap, stack, cognate w OE *hrēac*, ON *hraukr* a rick]

ruckie *n* a stone; a marble *20-, S*. [perh conflation of *yuckie* (dim of YUCK) w Eng *rock*]

ruckity *see* ROOKETTY

ruckle¹ &c *vi* make a rattling, gurgling or roaring sound, *specif* of the breathing of a dying person *16-e20*.
n a rattling or gurgling sound, *specif* the death-rattle *19-, now Rox*. [Scand; cf Norw dial *rukla* (*v*), *rukl* (*n*)]

ruckle² &c *vt* wrinkle, crease, work into folds *la19-, local Sh-SW*.

n a wrinkle, fold, crease *la19-, local Sh-SW*. [*cf* Norw dial *rukla* a wrinkle, ridge, ON *hrukka* a wrinkle > Eng *ruck* a crease, fold]

ruckle *see* RICKLE[1]

rud *see* REID[1]

rudas &c *19-*; **roudes &c** *18-e19* ['rudəs] *n*, *chf* **auld** ~ a coarse or masculine-looking woman; an ill-natured hag, an old witch *18-, now Bnf.* *adj* **1** *of a woman* ugly, cantankerous, witch-like *19-e20*. **2** *of a man* cantankerous, stubborn, rough-mannered *e19*. **3** wild, undisciplined, irresponsible *la19-, now Mry*. [only Sc; obscure]

ruddie *n* a loud, reverberating, *freq* repeated, noise *19-, now Kcdn Ags*.
vi make a loud, repeated noise, beat noisily **on** *19-, now Kcdn*. [obscure; *cf* ROTHOS]

ruddoch &c [*'rʌdəx, &c*] *n* term of contempt for a (bad-tempered) old person *la18-19*. [appar altered f RUDAS]

rude [*røð] *n* = rud, red; complexion *la15-e19*. [OED *rud* (*n*[1])]

rude *see* RUID

rue; rew *15-e20* [ru; *Rox* riu] *n* = rue *15-*.
vti **1** = rue *la14-*. **2** *vi* repent **of** *e17*. **3** ~ **on** have pity on, feel compassion for *17-, now Ags Fif*. **4** regret a promise, bargain etc, withdraw from a bargain or contract *18-, now N Per Kcb*.
~**fu &c 1** = rueful. **2** terrible, dreadful *19*.
~**-bargain** money given as compensation for breaking a bargain or withdrawing from an agreement *19-, now Gall*.
mak a ~ *now local EC Wgt*, **tak the** ~ **1** repent, regret; change one's mind about a course of action *la18-, NE-S*. **2** take offence or a dislike *la20-, Ayr Dmf Slk*.

ruf *see* RO, RUIF

rufe *see* RUIVE

ruff &c *vti* **1** beat (a drum); beat a RUFF (*n* 1) on (a drum); *of a drum* sound a roll *18-, now Bnf Fif*. **2** (1) applaud or show approval by stamping the feet *la16-, now NE Fif*. (2) *freq* ~ **down** show disapproval, silence (a speaker) by stamping or shuffling with the feet *la18-, now Bnf Fif*.
n **1** the beating of a drum, a drum-roll preceding a proclamation *la18-e19*. **2** a drumming on the floor with the feet to indicate approval or applause *19-, now Mry Kcdn*. [obs in Eng; perh onomat]

ruffie[1] &c; roughie *e19* ['rʌfɪ] *n* a torch or light, a fir-brand, a wick of rag smeared with tallow; *specif* a torch used when fishing for salmon at night *la18-e20*. [*cf* obs Eng *ruff* a candle(-wick)]

ruffie[2] &c, ruffy *n* **1** R~ (name for) a devil or fiend *la15-16*. **2** a person impersonating a fiend *e16*. **3** R~ cant or slang name for the Devil *19-, now Ayr*. **4** a ruffian *16*. [reduced f obs Eng *ruffin*]

ruffle &c *n* **1** a check, defeat; an impairment *la16-e18, only Sc*. **2** = ruffle.
vti = ruffle, disorder, disarrange; struggle etc *la14-*.

ruffy *see* RUFFIE[2]

rug &c; ruk *la14*, **roug &c** *la19-e20, chf Cai* [rʌg; *Cai* rug] *v* **1** *vt, freq* ~ **down, out, up** *etc* pull vigorously or forcibly, tug, drag, draw *la14-*. **2** *vi* pull, tug, draw (**at**) *15-*. **3** *of pain, hunger, an empty stomach* gnaw, ache, nag *18-, now NE Ags*.
n **1** a pull, a rough, hasty tug *15-*. **2** *specif* a tug on a fishing line when a fish has been hooked, a bite *la19-, Sh-C*. **3** *of grazing animals* a bite of grass, a feed *la18-, now Bnf Kcb*. **4** a strong undercurrent in the sea, a strong tide *la19-, now Sh-Per*. **5** a twinge or pang of nerves or emotions *la19-, local NE-Ayr*. **6** a knot or tangle of hair *la19-, now Ork Bnf Abd*. **7** (1) a bargain, *esp* one which takes unfair advantage of the seller; a high profit, a cut, a rake-off *18-, now NE-Ags*. (2) a good match, a catch, *freq* **no great** ~ no great shakes *18-, now Ork*. **8** a share, portion, *esp* of a quality *19-, now Cai*.
~**gie &c** *of hair* difficult to comb, tangled; *fig* rough, hard *la19-, local NE-Lnk*.
~ **saw** a two-handed or cross-cut saw *la16-18*. ~ **and reive** practise robbery *16*. ~ **and rive** pull or tug vigorously; struggle, tussle *la16-*. [nME; Scand; *cf* Norw, Icel, Faeroese *rugga* sway, rock]

ruge [*'rʌdʒ] *n* roaring *e16*. [only Sc; L *rugīre* roar]

ruid &c, rood *18-*; **rude, reed &c** *la18-, NE Dmf* [røð, rɪd; *Cai NE Dmf* rid] *n* **1** = rood, the cross of Christ; the measure *la14-*. **2** *specif* (1) *freq also* **short** ~ a square measure, *corresponding to Eng* square rod, $\frac{1}{160}$ of a Scots acre (SCOTS) or 36 square ELLS; a small plot of ground of this size *15-, now Bnf Ags*; (2) *masonry or slaterwork* an area of 36 square ELLS or *later* yards *16-19*. **3** a piece of ground belonging to a BURGH rented or feued (FEU) for building and cultivating *15-, now in place-names; cf burgh rudis* (BURGH).
~ **altar &c** an altar of the Holy Cross *la15-17, only Sc*. R~ **day 1** *also* R~ **Day in barlan** the day of the Invention of the Cross, 3 May *18-e20*. **2** *also* R~ **day in hairst** the day of the Exaltation of the Cross, 14 September *16-e20*. R~ **even &c** the eve of R~ *day, la14, 19-e20, latterly N*. R~ **fair** a fair or market held on R~ *day, la17-, now SW, only Sc*. ~**mass &c** = R~ *day, 19-, now Cai*.

ruif &c, roof *17-*; **ruf &c** *la14-16, la19- (Sh)*, **reef** *18-, NE*, **riff** *la19-, now Fif* [røf, rɪf; *N* rif; *nEC also* ref; *Bwk also* rif] *n* **1** = roof *la14-*. **2** a canopy, tester *e16, only Sc*. **3** the ceiling of a room *la18-*.
~**-tree 1** the main beam or ridge of a roof *la16-*. **2** *fig* a house, home *18-*.

ruin &c; rewyne &c *16*, **rewvine &c** *la16* ['rʊɪn; *'rju'əɪn] *n* (*la14-*), *vtir* (*la16-*) = ruin.
~**age** destruction, spoiling, ruination *20-, now Sh Abd*.

ruind &c *la18-*; **rund** *la17-19*, **rind &c** *la18-20*, **roon &c** *la18-19* [røn(d), rɪn(d);

*?run(d), *?rʌnd] *n* **1** the border or selvage of a web of cloth; a strip of cloth *in gen, la17-, now Ork Slk.* **2** any thin strip of material, a shred, fragment *la18-e19.*

~ **shune** &c shoes made of strips of selvages of cloth *19-e20.* [obscure; there is much confusion w RIND[1]]

ruise &c, **roose** &c *17-;* **reese** &c *la18-, NE* [*v* røz, rez; *n* røs, res; (*n, v*) *N* riz] *v* **1** boast (**of**): (1) *vi, 15;* (2) *vr, 16-17.* **2** *vt* praise, extol, *esp* exaggeratedly, flatter *15-, now Sh-N Kcb.*
n praise, commendation, flattery; boasting; a boast *la14-.*
mak &c (**a**) (**toom**) ~ give (empty) praise or flattery; boast (unjustifiably) *16-19.* [eME *ros* &c (*n*), *rosen* &c (*v*); ON *hrós* (*n*), *hrósa* (*v*) praise]

ruit[1] &c *la15-,* **root** &c *la16-;* **rut** &c *la14-16, e20* (*Sh*), **rit** &c *19-e20,* **reet** &c *19-, N* [røt, rɪt; *N* rit; *nEC* ret] *n* **1** = root *la14-.* **2** a dried tree root used as firewood, *esp* one dug up from a bog *19-, now NE Ags WC.* **3** the bottom of a hedge *19-, now Ags Per Kcb.*
vti = root *la15-.*
at the ~ **o one's tongue** on the tip of one's tongue *la19-, local Sh-Kcb.* (**the**) **reet and** (**the**) **rise** the source and every aspect of something *la19-, NE.*

ruit[2], **root; reet** *chf Cai* [røt, rɪt; *N* rit] *vti* **1** = root, dig up with the snout. **2** *vi* poke about, rummage, search, leave things in confusion as a result of searching *la19-, Sh-N, SW.* **3** work in a clumsy, ineffective way, *freq* **reet and fyke** *20-, Cai.*

ruive &c *16-;* **rufe** &c *la15-17,* **roove** *17-e20* [røv, rev; *N* riv] *n, esp boat-building* a burr, a metal washer on which the point of a nail or bolt can be clinched; a rivet *la15-, now local Sh-Kcb; cf* SEAM[2] .
vt, also fig rivet, clinch (a nail or bolt) *la16-, now local Sh-Kcb.* [ON *ró,* > nautical Eng *rove* a burr]

ruk *see* RUG
ruke *see* ROOK[1]
rule &c; **reule** &c *la14-16,* **rull** &c *la16,* **roule** &c *la19-, NE* [rul; *NE also* rʌul; *rjul] n* = rule *la14-.*
vti **1** = rule *16-.* **2** *vt* have charge of; make (good) use of; regulate (a clock) *16, only Sc.* **3** *vi, of prices* be at a certain rate, be current *17.* **4** *vt* arrange or set in order *la16, only Sc.*
ruling elder *Presbyterian church* a person who has been ordained as an ELDER, *strictly* any ELDER, *but in practice* one who is not a MINISTER *17-.*
~-**right** as straight or exact as a rule; exactly *la16, only Sc.*

rullion *see* RIVLIN
rulȝe *see* ROOLYIE
rum[1] *adj* **1** = rum, queer, odd. **2** boorish, coarse in manner or speech *la20-, NE Lnk SW.*

rum[2] &c *n, freq in pl, mining* an inferior bituminous shale; a bend or dislocation in a stratum *19.* [perh var of Eng *rim*]
rumballiach &c [*ram'balɪəx, *rəm-] *adj, of weather or temperament* tempestuous, stormy *19-e20, S.* [obscure]
rumbisch *see* RUMMISS
rumble *see* RUMMLE
rumford &c [rʌm'førd, -'ferd, &c] *vt* improve the draught of (a chimney) by narrowing the vent *e19.*
~-**in** &c a sheet of metal used as a lining or casing for the back of a fireplace *20-, now Ags Per Slk.* [f Count von Rumford (1753-1814) who suggested this method of improving smoky chimneys; *cf* Eng *rumfordize*]
rumgumption [rʌm'gʌm(p)ʃən] *n* commonsense, understanding, shrewdness *la17-, local Sh-Wgt.* [RAM- + GUMPTION; *cf* RUMMLE-GUMPTION]
rummage &c *v* **1** *vi* = rummage. **2** *also* **reemage, reemish** &c ['rimɪdʒ, -ɪʃ] search noisily, poke around *19-, NE Ags.*
n, only **reemage, -ish** a careful, thorough search *la19-, now Abd Ags.*
rummiss &c, **rummish** &c *la18;* **rumbisch** *la16* [*'rʌmɪs, *-ɪʃ] *v* **1** *vi* roar, bellow, make a rumbling noise *la15-e18.* **2** protest loudly, make an uproar *e16.* **3** *vti* knock over with a crash *la18-e19.* [perh OF *rumir, romir* (> ME *romy* roar); *cf* REEMIS]
rummle &c; **rumble** &c *17-* *vti* **1** = rumble *16-.* **2** *vi* make a noise or disturbance; move about noisily or riotously *la16-19.* **3** knock over or throw stones (at a door) as a prank *20-, local NE-Ayr.* **4** strike or beat severely; jolt, handle roughly *la19-, C, S.* **5** *vi* toss about restlessly in bed *20-, local Abd-S.* **6** *vt* stir or shake vigorously; mash (potatoes); scramble (eggs) *18-, now Kcb.* **7** clear (a narrow passage, *esp* a tobacco pipe) with a rod or wire *la19-, now local Bnf-Lnk.* **8** *vi* feel (in one's pocket) for something *20-, C, S.* **9** *vt* pick (someone's pocket), rob *e19.*
n **1** = rumble *16-.* **2** a movement causing a rumbling sound; a vigorous stir, a rough jolting; a resounding blow or whack *la19-, now local Sh-Ayr.* **3** a rough knocking or beating *19-, now NE, WC.* **4** a badly-built piece of masonry, a ruin *la19-, Sh NE.* **5** something ugly or dilapidated, *eg* a room, a piece of furniture *la19-, now Sh Abd.* **6** derog term for a large clumsy person, a 'lump'; a rough reckless boy *20-, WC, SW.* **7** a sudden impetus, a rush *la19-, local Sh-Ayr.* **8** a mixture, concoction; something confused or disordered *19-, now Sh.*
adj, of a drain filled with loose stones *20-, Cai Ayr.*
rummlie &c **1** *of soil* rough and stony; *hence* loose and crumbly *la20-, NE Ayr Wgt.* **2** *of the mind* disordered, jumbled *20-, now Mry.* **rummlieguts** ['rʌmlɪ'gʌts] *contemptuous* a 'windbag'

la20-, Loth Dmf. **rummlin &c 1** *of a person* boisterous, full of mischief; slapdash *19-e20.* **2** *of a drain etc* filled with loose stones *la18-19.*
rummlin kirn a deep narrow gully on the shore where the tide makes a loud rumbling noise *19-, Kcb.*
∼**(de)thump &c 1** mashed potatoes with milk, butter and seasoning *19-, now Ayr.* **2** mashed potatoes with cabbage (or turnip) *19-, now Ags Stlg Fif.* **3** = *skirlie* (SKIRL¹), *20-, now Ags.*
∼**garie &c** ['rʌml'gerɪ] *adj* wild, unruly, devil-may-care *18-e19.* *n* a wild, reckless, or thoughtless person *la18-e20.* ∼**-skeerie** a wild reckless person *la19-, local Per-Ayr.* **rumble-tumble &c** (full of) noisy confusion *la19-, now Ags.*
∼ **up** *football* jostle, charge (one's opponent); play a rough attacking game against *la20-.*
rummle-gumption &c *n* **1** understanding, common-sense, level-headedness *la18-, now N, C.* **2** *joc, freq in pl* wind in the stomach, flatulence *la19-, now WC Kcb.* [var of RUMGUMPTION, w infl f prec]
rump *n* **1** = rump; in Scotland, a cut of beef corresponding to Eng *topside + silverside, now usu* called *round-steak* (ROUND). **2** contemptuous term for a person or animal *16-19.*
vt **1** cut, clip or crop very short *la18-, local Bnf-S.* **2** eat down to the roots *la19-, now Kcb.* **3** (1) = ROOK¹ *v* 1, *19-, local Bnf-Slk.* (2) = ROOK¹ *v* 4, *la20-, nEC, WC.*
∼**ie &c** a small crusty loaf or roll *19-, now Per WC.* ∼**le &c** the rump, tail, haunches (of an animal); the buttocks, seat (of a person) *16-, now Sh.* ∼**ple-bane** the rump-bone, the coccyx *la19-, now local.*
∼ **and stump** completely, to the very last piece or fragment *19-, local*; *cf stump and rump* (STUMP).
rumption &c ['rʌmʃən] *n* a state of noisy, bustling disorder, an uproar *19-20* [altered f Eng *ruction* and *eruption*; *cf* RUMMLE]
run *see* RIN
runch¹ &c [rʌnʃ] *n* the wild radish, found as a weed in cornfields *la16-, now local*; *cf* SKELLOCH² (with which it is sometimes confused because of the similarity in their flowers).
∼**ick &c,** ∼**ech &c,** ∼**ie &c** *19-e20, chf Sh* ['∼ək, '∼əx, '∼ɪ, 'rʌnsɪ] = *n, la16-, now Ork.* [obscure]
runch² [rʌnʃ] *vti* crunch, grind, crush *la19-, now Dnbt.*
n a crunching, grinding *19.* [perh var of RUNDGE w infl f Eng *crunch*]
runch *see* WRANCH
runchie &c ['rʌnʃɪ] *n, adj* (a) coarsely-built, raw-boned (person) *19-e20.* [uncertain; *cf* RAMSH²]
rund *see* RUIND
rundge &c, rounge &c [*rʌndʒ] *vti* **1** = rounge, gnaw, champ; devour greedily *16-e18.* **2** *vt, also* **ronge** *e16* clip (coin) *16-e17, only Sc.*
rung &c *n* **1** = rung. **2** a stout stick; a cudgel

16-, now N Kcb. **3** a blow with a stick; a thump, whack *la19-, local Sh-Stlg.* **4** contemptuous term for a bad-tempered person, a large, ugly person or animal or a thin, scraggy animal *19-, now Mry Abd Bwk.*
vt **1** make or fit with spans or rungs *16-e20.* **2** beat with a stick, cudgel *19-, now local Sh-N.*
∼**-backed** *of a chair* having a back of wooden spokes or spars *20-, Sh-Cai Kcb.* ∼ **cart** an early type of cart made of spars and having solid wooden wheels *la18-19.*
rung *see* RING³
runk¹ &c [rʌŋk; *Cai* rʌuŋk] *n* **1** a cabbage-stalk, *esp* when hard and withered *e20, Cai Mry.* **2** an emaciated, worn-out person, animal or thing *19-20, chf Sh-N.* **3** contemptuous term, *esp* for a bad-tempered woman *20-, Mry Abd.* [altered f RUNT¹, perh by association w RUNKLE]
runk² *vt* deprive (a person) of all his money, possessions etc, 'clean out', bankrupt *19-, now local NE-Fif.* [prob conflation of ROOK¹ w RUMP; *cf* RUNT¹ *v* 2]
runk *see* RANK¹
runker &c *n* **1** the lumpfish *la19-, now Cai.* **2** one of several species of wrasse *e20, NE.* [see SND]
runkle &c *vt* **1** wrinkle *la15-.* **2** crease, rumple, crush *18-, now Sh-nEC, WC, SW.* **3** gnarl, twist, distort, curl *18-, now local C.*
n a wrinkle, crease, ridged indentation *16-.*
runkly &c wrinkled *la18-, now NE nEC, WC, S.* [prob OScand *runkla* wrinkle; *cf* Dan *runken* wrinkled, Sw *rynka* wrinkle, Norw dial *rukka* a wrinkle; *cf* WRUNKLE]
runnyn *see* RIN
runsy &c *n* = rouncy, a horse *la15-e16.*
runt¹ *n* **1** an old or decayed tree-stump *16-, now local.* **2** the hardened, withered stem of a cabbage or KAIL plant, a CASTOCK *18-.* **3** (1) a short, thickset person; an undersized or dwarfish person or animal *20-, local.* (2) = runt, the smallest pig in a litter *la20-, now Ork C-S.* **4** the tail of an animal; the rump, the upper part of the tail *la18-, SW.* **5** contemptuous term, *esp* for a coarse, gnarled, ill-natured person, an old woman *18-, now local Sh-Fif.*
v, only ∼**it &c 1** stunted in growth *la18-, Ayr Kcb.* **2** completely deprived of one's possessions, made bankrupt; *marbles* having lost all one's marbles to one's opponent *la19-, now NE*; *cf* RUNK². [uncertain]
runt² *n* an ox or cow for fattening and slaughter, a store animal, *freq* a Highland (HIELAND) cow or ox; an old cow (past breeding and fattened for slaughter) *17-, now local Cai-SW.* [prob MDu *runt,* Du *rund,* perh w later infl f prec]
rural *adj* **1** = rural. **2** *law, of a lease etc* relating to land as opposed to buildings (whether in the country or in town) *la17-*; *cf* URBAN.
ruryk *adj* rustic *la15.* [only Sc; *cf* MedL *ruricus.* OED *ruric*]
rush &c *vti, pt also* **rouschit &c** *la14-15* [rʌʃ; *also*

ruʃ] **1** = rush *la14*-. **2** *vi, esp of sheep or cattle* suffer from dysentry *20*-, *now Cai Rox.* **3** *vt* flirt with, court (a girl) *la20*-, *local Cai-SW.*

n **1** = rush *15*-. **2** dysentry, *esp* in sheep or cattle *la18-e19*. **3** a skin eruption, rash, *specif* of scarlet fever *18*-, *now local.* **4** a luxuriant growth of vegetation or hair *20*-, *Sh Ork Ags.* ∼**ie,** *freq* **rooshie-doo &c** a noisy squabble or scramble *la19*-, *now Abd Fif.* ∼**-fever** scarlet fever *la18*-, *now wLoth Ayr.*

rush corn *see* RASH[1]

rushyroo &c ['rʌʃɪru] *n* the shrew *20*-, *now Per.* [altered f ME *erdshrew* earthshrew]

rusk *n* a blow *e15.* [only Sc; perh related to ME *rusk* (*v*) disturb, shake]

ruskie[1] &c *n* **1** (1) a straw basket etc *la17*-, *now local Abd-Ayr.* (2) *specif* a basket for holding meal or seed-corn *18-e20.* **2** a straw beehive *la19*-, *NE, EC, S.* **3** a coarse-straw sunbonnet *19, S.* [Gael *rùsgan* a kind of basket; a kind of dish used to measure meal etc]

ruskie[2] &c *n* (*adj*) (a) strong, vigorous, *usu* rough-mannered (person) *19.* [obscure]

russer berré *n* the redcurrant *la16.* [prob var of *russle* (RIZZAR) + Eng *berry*; *cf* F *rousseur* redness and RASER]

russle *see* RIZZAR

rust *see* ROOST[2]

rusticate *adj* countrified, boorish *la15, only Sc.* [L *rusticāt*-, ptp stem of *rusticārī* live in the country]

rut *see* RIT, RUIT[1]

ruther[1] &c *15-e19*, **rither &c** *18*-, *now Fif Kcb* ['rɪðər, 'rɪdər; *'rʌðər] *n* = rudder. [OED *rudder*]

ruther[2] &c ['rʌðər, 'rʌdər] *n* **1** an outcry, uproar *la18-19.* **2** turmoil, chaos, ruin *e20, Abd.* [obscure]

rutt *see* ROOD-GOOSE

ryatous *see* RIOT

rybat &c *17*-; **rabbet &c** *15*-, **rebet &c** *la16-18* ['raɪbət, 'rɪbət; *'rɛbət] *n* = rabbet.

ryke *see* RICH

rymmyll *la14*, **remel** *la15* [*'rɪməl; *?'rɪməl] *n* a blow. [obscure. OED *rimmel*]

Rynche *see* RENS

rynd &c [*raɪnd] *vi, chf* ∼ **to** belong or pertain to; tend to *16.* [ME *rine &c*, OE *hrīnan* touch. OED *rine*]

Rynnis *see* RHINNS

rys *see* RICE

S

s [ɛs] *n* the draught-hook of a plough etc *19-*, *now local Ork-Loth.* [from the shape; *cf* ESS²]

s *see* SALL, US

's *see* HIS

sa *see* SAE², SAY, SEE

sab¹ &c *la18-20, only Sc*, **sob &c** *vi* = sob *la15-.* *n* **1** = sob *la15-.* **2** the noise made by a gust of wind or by the rise and fall of the sea; a full sea, as on the east coast in May *19-e20.*

sab² &c *vti* (cause to) subside or sink, sag; droop *18-e19.* [uncertain]

Sabbath &c; Sawbath &c *19-e20* ['sabəθ, 'sɑbəθ] *n* **1** = Sabbath, Sunday *16-.* **2** *esp among older speakers* Sunday as a day of the week without specific connotation of its religious significance *la19-.*
~**ly** (recurring) Sunday by Sunday, every Sunday *17-e19, only Sc.*

sable &c *n* **1** = sable, black *16-.* **2** blackness, darkness *e16.*

sace *vi* = cease *la16, only Sc.*

sacerdott *n* a priest *la17.* [only Sc; L *sacerdōt-*]

sack *n* **1** = sack *17-.* **2** a dry measure of oatmeal = 1 or 2 BOLLS *20-, local Abd-Ayr.*
vt = sack, put in a sack etc.
~**en** *chf of the penitential garment* made of sackcloth *18-19.* **give someone a ~fu o sair banes** give someone a beating *la19-, now local* [altered f *sarkfu* (SARK)].
~ **brab** *e18*, ~ **goun** *la17-e19* a sackcloth garment worn while doing public penance *only Sc.* [*cf* SECK¹]

sacket &c *n* **1** a small sack or bag *16-, now Wgt.* **2** *term of abuse* a scamp, rascal, a pert impudent person *la19-, Ags.* [ME *sakett*, OF *saquet* dim of *sac* (*n*) sack; for *n* 2 *cf* Ger *sack*]

sackless *see* SAKELESS

sacrament &c *n* **1** = sacrament *16-.* **2** *specif* (1) **the** Eucharist *16-.* (2) **the** periodical Communion service of the Presbyterian Churches *la18-.* (3) *in pl* the period Thursday to the following Monday including the Communion and other services *20-, now Hebrides Highl.* ~ **house** a tabernacle *la16, only Sc.* ~ **Sunday** *etc* the Sunday of the Communion service *la18-19.*

sacrist ['sakrɪst] *n* **1** the chief porter and macebearer of King's College and of Marischal College *la17-, Abd, only Sc; cf* BEDELLUS. **2** = sacrist.

sad &c; said &c *la16*, **sod** *la19-, chf N, now Abd* *adj* **1** = sad *la14-.* **2** *of persons* grave, sedate *la14-19.* **3** causing sorrow, distressing, lamentable *la14-.* **4** remarkable, outstandingly good *la18-e20, chf NE.* **5** (1) solid, dense, hard and compact *19-.* (2) *specif, of bread or pastry* not risen, heavy *19-, now Ork NE-S.*
adv severely, heavily *e16, e17, la19.*
v **1** *vt* make SAD (*adj* 5(1)), cause to sink or settle down *18-e19.* **2** *vi, of soil, a haystack etc* become SAD (*adj* 5(1)), shrink in bulk, subside *19-, now Ags Fif.*
n a thud, a thump *19-e20, only Sc.*

sadden *vt* = *v* 1, *la18-, now Lnk Kcb.* **saddit** *adj* **1** = sadded, made sad *e17.* **2** *also* **sadden** (1) *of earth etc* beaten hard, hard-packed *18-, now local Kcdn-Lnk.* (2) *of bread* heavy, not fully baked *20-, local sEC-S.*

sad *see* SAY

saddle *see* SAIDLE

sade &c *n* (a) turf, (a) sod *e19.* [only Sc; *appar* orig LowGer]

sadle *see* SATTLE

sae¹ &c *18-*, **say &c** *e15, e18*; **s(e)y &c** *18-19* [se] *n* **1** a bucket *e15.* **2** a wooden tub, carried by two persons on a pole or rope, used for transporting water *18-, now Sh Ork Cai.* [ON *sár* a cask]

sae² ** *la16-*, **so; **sa** *la14-19*, **say** *la14-e16, e20*, **swa &c** *la14-e18*, **swae &c** *16-e18* [se, *swe] *adv* **1** = so *la14-.* **2** (1) **so it** etc is indeed it is etc *19-, now WC Kcb*: 'you're a wee dodger, so you *are!*'; (2) *also with negative*: neither it is etc: '*she never lifted her hand, so she didna*'.
sagat, swagat(is) = sogate(s), thus *la14-e15.*
~ **like** such like, much the same (**as**), similar *16-20.*
ilka ~ lang every so often, now and again *la18-, NE nEC.* ~ **.. as l** as .. as *la18-, now C.* **2** *with exclam force* so!, how! *la18-e20*: '*sae weel's I see it yet!*'. ~ **as** in order that *la19-.* **(gif) ~ beis (that)** *la15-e16*, ~ **be('t)** *la18-, now Sh* it being the case (that), provided (that).
~ **bein('s) &c** provided that, if only; seeing that, since *16-, now local Sh-SW.*

sae *see* SEE

safe *see* SAUF

safer *see* SAUFEY

saff *see* SAUF

saffron &c *16-*; **saipheron** *la15* *n* = saffron *la15-.*

safity *see* SAUF

saft &c *la16-*, **soft** *adj* **1** = soft *la14-.* **2** *of weather* mild, not frosty; in a state of thaw *la15, 19-.* **3** wet, rainy, damp *19-.* **4** *of cloth* of a loose, soft, and pliable texture *16, e19.*
n a thaw; rain, moisture *la19-, local Ags-Ayr.*
v **1** *vt* = soft, make soft; abate *la14-e16.* **2** *vr* calm or restrain oneself *la15, only Sc.*
~**en** **1** = soften *15-.* **2** thaw *19-, now NE.*
~**ie** **1** = softie, a weak(-minded) person *la19-.* **2** = ~ *biscuit, la20-, local Sh-Fif.* **3** *also* **saftick** *NE* an edible crab which has lost its shell, *freq* used for bait *la19-, NE Ags Fif.* **4** a soft (carpet-)slipper *la20-, NE Ags Ayr.*
~ **biscuit** a kind of plain floury bun or roll with a dent in the middle *la19-, local Ork-Per.*
on *or* **up someone's ~ side** into someone's

good graces or favour *20-*. **have a ~ side to** have a special liking for, be well-disposed towards *20-*.

saga *n* a witch *la16*. [only Sc; L = a female soothsayer]

sagan &c ['sagən, 'segən] *n, contemptuous* a surly, uncouth or clumsy person *20, Abd.* [perh euphemistic alteration of SAWTAN]

sagat *see* SAE²

saich *see* SICH

saicret *see* SECRET

said *see* SAD

saidle &c *la16-*, **saddle &c; seddle** *la19- n* **1** = saddle *la14-*. **2** *nautical* a block of wood fastened to a spar to take the bearing of another spar attached to it *e16*. **3** the part of a stall on which an animal stands *la19, Fif.*
vti = saddle *la16-*.
~ band ? the band of a pedlar's pack *e17, only Sc.* **~ crub** the steel groove in the saddle of a cart-horse in which the back-chain works *20-*, *now NE.* **~ curall** the curule chair *e16, only Sc* [translating L *sella curulis*]. **~ lap** the side-flaps of a saddle *e19*.

saige *see* SIEGE

sail &c; saule *e16 n* **1** = sail *la14-*. **2** a ride in a cart or other vehicle or on horseback *19-*, *now Cai SW Uls.*
vti **1** = sail *la14-*. **2** *vi* be covered over with liquid, be swimming or awash *18-*, *now Kcdn Ags Fif.* **3** ride or drive in a vehicle *20-*, *now Cai Arg SW Uls.*
~age ? the speed of a ship under sail *e17, only Sc.* **~rif** abounding in sails *e16*.

sailȝe [*seljɪ] *v* **1** *vt* make an assault on *la15*. **2** *vi* make an attempt *e16*. [only Sc; aphetic f Eng *assail*. OED *sailyie*]

sain &c *v* **1** *vt also* **sene** *la17* protect from harm by a ritual sign, *esp* by making the sign of the cross, consecrate, bless: (1) *with the hand etc or with an object*, *la14-e20*; (2) *vr* cross oneself, protect oneself from harm by prayer, incantation etc *la14-20*; (3) *vi for vr*, *la16*; (4) *vi* **~ aboot, o(n)** *etc*, *19-20*; (5) *vt* inaugurate with some act or ceremony *la18-*, *now Bnf.* **2** bless, call down blessings on (*esp* as a sign of gratitude) *16-e20*. **3** heal, cure *e20* [also in literary Eng *19*, by confusion w ME *sane* (*v*) heal].
n a blessing, a gesture or invocation of goodwill and good fortune *19-e20*.
(God) ~ .. (God) bless ..! *18-e20*. [ME *sayne &c*, OE *segnian*]

sain *see* SAY

saint &c, saunt &c *18-*, *only Sc*; **sant, sanct** *la14-19, chf Sc* [sent, sant, *?saŋkt] *n* **1** = saint *la14-*. **2 the S~s** nickname for St Johnstone and St Mirren (cf *buddies* (BODY)) football teams *20-*.
vti **1** = saint, canonize; play the saint *la14-*. **2** *vi* disappear, vanish, *esp* in a sudden or mysterious manner *18-*, *now S.* **3** *vt* cause to vanish quickly or inexplicably, spirit away *19-*, *now Sh.*

St Andrew's House informal name for the Scottish Office in Edinburgh, from 1939 in St Andrew's House, Regent Road; most departments are now in New St Andrew's House, St James Centre *20-*. **St Faith's cattle** *or* **drove** cattle collected, *chf* from Galloway, into one large herd and driven to St Faith's Market, near Norwich *la18-e19*. **St John's nut** a double hazelnut, supposed to be a charm against witchcraft *19-e20*. **St Johnsto(u)n 1** name for the town of Perth, of which St John the Baptist is patron *la18-e19*. **2 St Johnstone** official name for the Perth football team; cf *the Saints.* **St Johnston('s) ribbon** *etc* the hangman's noose or rope *18-e20*. **St Michael's cake** *etc* a kind of cake baked in the Hebrides, *esp* in the Roman Catholic areas, on Michaelmas Eve, the STRUAN *18-e20*. **St Mungo** name for the city of Glasgow, of which St Kentigern or Mungo is patron *la18-19*.

saip &c *15-20*, **soap &c** *17- n* = soap *15-*.
soapery &c a soap factory *la17-18*. **~y suds** soapsuds, soapy lather *la18-e19*.
~ bells soap bubbles *18-e19*. **~(y) graith** = **~y** suds, *la19-*, *now local Ags-Rox.* **~man** a soapmaker, soap-boiler *17-e19*. **~(ie) sapples** = **~y** suds, *19-*, *now C.* **~work(s)** = **~ery**, *17-18*.

saipheron *see* SAFFRON

sair &c, sore &c *16-*; **sar** *la14-e16* [ser; sor] *adj* **1** = sore *la14-*. **2** causing or involving physical pain or distress: (1) *of an illness, pain* severe *la14-*; (2) *of a task, activity etc* causing physical strain *la15-*. **3** (1) causing or involving mental distress or grief *la15-e20*. (2) pressing hard upon one, hard to bear, oppressive *16-e20*. (3) *specif of trials or temptations*, *la16-*. **4** (1) involving hardship, difficulty, danger etc *la15-20*. (2) *of a battle, struggle etc* hard, severe, fierce, *now freq (of life in gen)* **it's a sair fecht** *16-*. **5** *of the weather, the elements* severe, stormy *19-e20*. **6** *freq as intensifier of something unpleasant etc* serious, considerable, thoroughgoing, 'sorry' *la18-20*. **7** (1) *of the head* aching, painful, throbbing *la18-*, *only Sc*; cf **~ heid.** (2) *of the heart* aching, grief-stricken, sorrowful *la16-*; cf **~ heart.** **8** *of persons (also* **~ on** *etc)* harsh in discipline, treatment or judgment (towards) *la18-*. **9 ~ on** destructive, harmful, giving hard wear or usage to *20-*: '*she's sair on her claes*'.
n **1** = sore *la15-*. **2** a wound, injury *16-e19*. **3** a grief, a sorrow *18-e20*.
adv **1** sorely, severely, harshly, so as to cause pain or suffering *la14-*. **2** *chf of weeping* in a distressed manner *la14-*. **3** hard, with great exertion, laboriously *la16-*, *now NE.* **4** with vehemence or intensity, with all one's strength or feeling *la18-*. **5** *as intensifier* (1) *with verbs* very much, greatly *la14-e20*; (2) *with adjs, advs* very, extremely *la16-*.
~ aff badly off, very hard up *19-20*. **~ done** *of meat* well done, overcooked *19-*, *now NE.* **~**

face a pathetic expression assumed to elicit sympathy *la20-, local Sh-Per*. ~ **fit &c** a time of need or difficulty, an emergency, *chf* **lay something aside** *etc* **for a** ~ **fit** *18-e20*. ~ **hand &c 1** a mess, a piece of unskilled workmanship *20-, now Ayr*. **2** a large thick slice of bread with butter or jam (which looks like a bandaged hand) *20-, C*. ~ **heid &c 1** a headache *16-, only Sc*. **2** *chf* ~ **heidie** a small plain sponge cake with a paper band round the lower part of it *20-, NE-Fif*. ~ **hert &c** a sad or sorrowful state of mind; a cause for grief, a great disappointment *18-*. ~ **herted &c** sad at heart *la16-19*. ~ **leg** = ~ *fit, 18-, now Ags Per*. ~ **teeth** toothache *20-, Sh-nEC*. **a** ~ **wame &c** colic, stomach-ache *19-, now N-nEC*. ~ **awa wi't** *of persons or things* far gone, worn out by illness, hard usage etc *20-, NE-nEC*. ~ **not** badly needed *la19-, NE*. ~ **pit on** suffering from an illness *20-, Cai Per*. **sit** *or* **set someone** ~ distress someone *la15-16*.

sair *see* SAUR, SER, SERVE[1]

sairgint *see* SERGEANT

sairie &c *la14-20*, **sorry &c** *16-* *adj* **1** = sorry *la14-*. **2** distressed, sad, sorrowful *la14-e20*. **3** serious, solemn *19*. **4** in a poor or sorry state; puny; incompetent *la15-19*. **5** expressing compassion or affection: 'poor old ..' *18-e19*.

sairious &c *adj* = serious *la19-e20*.

saison &c *17-, now Sh Ork*, **season &c** *16-*, **sizzon** *la19-, now NE*, **cessone** *16*; **ses(s)oun &c** *la14-e16* ['sezn; 'sızn] *n* **1** = season *la14-*. **2** a time of ripeness and maturity *e16*.
vt = season *la14-*.
by ~ at the right time, in time *la16, only Sc*.
out of ~ not in season *16-*.

Saiterday *see* SETURDAY

saithe &c *la18-*, **sey &c** *la17-e19*; **seeth &c** *17-e19* [seð; *se, *səið, *səi] *n* the full-grown coalfish in its third or (*local*) fourth year. [only Sc; ON *seiðr*, Norw, Dan *seid, sei*]

saitin *la19-20*; **saiting &c** *la16, only Sc*, **salting** *la16, only Sc* [*'setın, *'satın] *n* = satin. [OED *satin*]

saitisfee &c ['setısfi] *vti* = satisfy *18-*. [*cf* SATIFY]

saiven *see* SEEVEN

sake &c *n* = sake *la14-*.
for any &c ~ for Heaven's sake *19-*. **~s me!** dear me! *la19-, now Cai Ayr*.

sakeless &c *16-*, **sackless &c** *la14-19* *adj* **1** = sackless, secure; without just cause *la15-16*. **2** innocent (**of**) *la14-e20*. **3** (1) guileless, simple; inoffensive, harmless *la16-e20*. (2) without sense, silly; lacking drive or energy *19-20*, *S*.
~ly &c innocently, without cause *16-e17*.

sal *see* SAUL

salair *see* SELLARIE

salamonicall *see* SOLOMONICAL

sald *see* SELL[1]

sale *see* SEAL

salerife *see* SELL[1]

salfer *see* SAUFEY

sall &c, shall &c, *reduced form* (*only after personal pronouns*) **s(e)** *la16-* [sal, səl; *reduced* s, z] *aux v, pt* **suld &c** *la14-20*, **sould &c** *16-19*, **sud &c** *18-, now Sh*, **should &c** *la16-*, **sid** *19-, now NE*, **shid** *20-, now NE* [sud, səd, søð, sıd, ʃıd]. *pres negative also* **sanna &c** *la18-20*, **shanna** *la18-20* ['sanə, 'sənə, 'salnə, 'ʃanə] **1** = shall *la14-*. **2** *cf* WILL[1]: (1) *in 1 pers*, used to express will or intention, rather than mere futurity *la14-*. (2) *in 2, 3 pers* used to express futurity *la15-*. **3** *1 pers, freq* **I's(e)**: (1) *with verbs of asseveration* as a kind of emphatic present *18-, now local Sh-Wgt*: 'I'se warrant'; (2) *wrongly used for* am (*due to misunderstanding of 3* (1)), *la18-19*.

should &c *pt* **1** = should *la14-*. **2** in indirect statements to express past time (*freq* implying that the speaker does not guarantee the truth of the reported fact) (1) *la16-e20*: 'it was alledgit that my lord of Arrane .. sould oppin this conspiracie.' (2) *with omission of* have *la15-*: 'it appeared that they should matched'. **suld bene** would have had to be *e16*.

salmon, salmond, salmont *see* SAUMON

salrar *n* = cellarer *la15, only Sc*.

sals *see* SAUCE

salsar [*'sasər] *n* = saucer *la15-e16*. [only Sc. OED *saucer*]

salt *see* SAUT

salting *see* SAITIN

Saltoun &c ['saltən] ~ **barley** fanner-dressed pot barley *18-, now hist*. [the process was introduced by Andrew Fletcher of Saltoun, East Lothian]

salus &c [*'saløs] *vti* salute *la14-16*. [nME; ME *n* a salutation]

salutaire [*'saløtər] *adj* salutary *la16*. [ME (once) *saluter*; F]

salutiffere [*sa'løtıfər] *adj* salutiferous, conducive to health *e16*. [only Sc; OF. OED *salutifere*]

salve *see* SAUF

salvendo *see* SOLVENDIE

sam *see* SAME[2]

same[1] &c *15-, now local*, **seam &c** *18-19* [sem; Cai sam] *n* fat, *esp* of pigs, grease, lard. [ME *saym(e)*, OF *saim(e)* lard]

same[2] &c; sam &c *now Sh Ork Cai* [sem; *Sh Ork Cai* sam] *adj, n* = same *la14-*.
same-like = *adj, 19*. **samen** [*'semən, *'sam-] = *adj, la14-20, only Sc*.
the ~ **as** in the same way as, just as (if) *19-*.
the ~ **day** today *la15*.

samen *see* SAME[2]

sanal *see* SAND

sanct *see* SAINT

sanctitude &c [*'saŋktıtød] *n* holiness, sanctity *la15-*. [earlier in Sc]

Sanct Nicholas bischop *n* a boy bishop elected for a festival of choirboys or schoolboys on or following St Nicholas Day *la15-16, only Sc.*

sanctuar &c [*'saŋktjuər] *n* a sanctuary *la14.* [nME *santuare*, laL *sanctuārium*. OED *saintuaire*]

sand [san(d), sɑn(d)] *n* = sand *la14-.*

vt **1** = sand. **2** run (a ship) ashore on sand *e19.* **3** mix with sand, adulterate (a coin) with sand in the smelting *18.*

san(d)al &c, san(d)le &c *la18-, local Cai-Fif,* **~lin** *19-, now Bnf* the sand-eel. **~y, sannie &c** *adj* = sandy. *n, chf* **sannie, ~y** = *sandshoe, 20-, Ags WC, EC.* **~y laverock, ~y lairick &c** the ringed plover *18-, now Cai Abd.* **~y lowper** a sand-flea *la19-, Fif midLoth.* **big** *etc* **~y mills** (wi) be intimate (with), be a friend or playmate (of) *la18-19.* **~y swallow** the sand-martin *la19-e20.*

~ bed a very heavy drinker, a 'soak' *19-, now Rox.* **~ blin(d)** = sand-blind, half-blind; *specif* having the poor sight associated with albinism *la16-, now Sh.* **~ bunker** a (golf-course) BUNKER *19-.* **~ dab** the dab *20-, local Bnf-Kcb.* **~ dorbie** the sandpiper *20-, Mry Abd.* **~ fleuk** the smear-dab *19-, now Bnf Fif.* **~ jumper** = **~y lowper**, *19-, now Mry Ayr.* **~ laverock &c, ~ lairick &c** = **~y laverock**; *more loosely* the sandpiper *la18-, now Abd.* **~ lowper** = **~y lowper**, *18-, now Ags Per Fif.* **~shoe** a gym shoe, plimsoll *20-.*

Sandemanian ['sandɪmanɪən, sandə'menjən] *n* a member of a religious body organized from the GLASITES *19-e20, hist.* [f Robert Sandeman, Glas's son-in-law, who became minister of this church in London and later in the USA]

Sandie &c, Sandy; Sawnie &c, Saunders &c, Sannock *la18-19* ['san(d)ɪ, 'sɑn(d)ɪ, 'san(d)ərz, 'sɑn(d)ərz, 'sanok] *n* **1** a young man, *esp* a countryman, yokel; *chf Eng slang* a Scotsman *la18-19.* **2** *freq* **auld ~** the devil, Satan *la18-e19.*

~ (Campbell &c) *joc, freq taboo* a pig; pork or bacon *la19-, now local Cai-Lnk* [in allusion to the boar's head crest on the Campbell coat-of-arms]. **~ oat** a variety of oat *19-20, NE.* [as a personal name *la15-*, short for *Alexander*]

sandle *see* SAND

sandre *n* a kind of striped silk *e16.* [only Sc; short for Eng *Alexander* in the same sense]

Sandy *see* SANDIE

sang¹, song *la16- n* **1** = song *la14-.* **2** the noise of the sea breaking on the shore *la19-, local Sh-Kcdn.* **3** a fuss, clamour, outcry, *freq* **mak a ~ aboot** *etc 18-.*

sang buik &c a book of songs *la15-.* **sang-schaw** a song festival *e20* [a new coining based on WAPPENSHAW]. **sang scule &c** a school attached to a church, for the teaching of (chf ecclesiastical) singing and music *16-e17, 20-, local.*

an auld sang an old story or saying, a proverb

la19-, local Sh-Kcb. **the end o an auld sang** the last of an old custom, institution etc, the end of an era *18-* [f the remark by the Earl of Seafield after signing the Act of Union in 1707, 'Now there's ane end of ane old song'].

sang²&c *interj* expressing surprise etc, *freq* **by my ~** *la19-, local Sh-Sw.* [appar F (*par le*) *sang* (*de Dieu*); *cf* Eng *'odsblood*]

sang *see* SING²

sanle *see* SAND

sanna *see* SALL

sannie *see* SAND

Sannock *see* SANDIE

Sanquhar ['sanxər, 'sanxwər] **~ gloves** *la18-,* **~ hose** *la18-e19* gloves, hose etc knitted in various ornamental patterns with a double thread *SW.* [the town in Dmf, formerly noted for its knitting industry, where they were made]

sanshach &c ['sanʃəx] *adj* **1** wily, shrewd, pawkie (PAWK) *19-, now Bnf.* **2** disdainful, surly *19-, NE.* **3** (over-)precise, irritable *19-, now NE.* **4** pleasant, genial *la20-, NE.* [only Sc; see SND]

sant *see* SAINT

sap¹&c *n* **1** = sap. **2** a quantity of liquid, *usu* to be consumed with food *la18-, now Sh Ork Cai Abd.*

~ money money given to workers in lieu of a milk or ale allowance *la18-e20.* **~ spail &c** the sap-wood of a tree *19-, now local Bnf-Per.*

sap² *la17-,* **sop** *n* **1** = sop *la14-.* **2 sop of ..** a person in respect of some pervading specified quality *la15-16*: '*sop of sorrow*'. **3 saps** pieces of bread etc soaked or boiled in milk etc, *freq* as food for children *la17-.*

vt = sop, soak, steep, saturate *19-.*

sapsy ['sapsɪ] *adj, lit and fig* like SAPS (n 3), soft, sloppy; effeminate *20-, Per Stlg WC.* *n* a soft, weak-willed, characterless person *la20-, Fif WC.*

sappie &c *adj* **1** = sappy. **2** *of meat etc* juicy, succulent *16-.* **3** *fig* full of goodness; *of persons* unctuous, over-full of fervour *19.* **4** *chf of persons* plump, sleek, fleshy *19-, now Abd Gall.* **5** wet, soppy, sodden *la15, 19-, now NE, C.* **6** given to drinking too much *19-e20.* **7** *of food* soft, soggy, like SAPS (n 3) *la19-, now local Sh-Per.* **8** *of a bed etc* soft, yielding, comfortable *la18-19.* **9** *of a kiss* soft, long-drawn out *la18-, now Ork Abd.*

~-headed simple-minded, silly, foolish *la19-, Ags Per.* [orig *chf* SAP¹ but some meanings f SAP²]

sapple *vt* soak, saturate with water, rain etc; *specif* steep (clothes) in soapy water *19-, now local Stlg-Kcb.*

n, chf in pl soapsuds, lather for washing *19-, now local C.* [f SAP²]

sapsy *see* SAP²

sar *see* SAIR, SAUR, SERVE¹

sardiane *n* = sardine, a precious stone *la14, only Sc.*

sardonice *n* = sardonyx *e16, only Sc.*

sark &c; serk *16-* [sark; *C, S* sɛrk] *n* **1** a man's shirt *15-*. **2** a woman's shift or chemise *17-20*. **3** a surplice *18-19*.

vt **1** clothe in or provide with a shirt *18-, now local Sh-Ayr.* **2** cover the rafters of (a roof) with wooden boards, line (a roof) with wood for the slates to be nailed on *16-*.

~**et &c** an undershirt, a woollen vest *la18-, now Abd.* **a** ~**fu o sair banes &c** a person stiff or sore from hard labour or from a beating *17-, now local; cf* SACK. ~**ing 1** shirting(-material) *la16-, now local Sh-Ayr.* **2** roof boarding *16-.* ~**less** without a shirt or shift *la18-20.* ~ **alane** in one's SARK only *16-e20.* ~ **neck** a shirt-collar-band *la18-.* [nME *serc*, OE *serce*, ON *serkr* a shirt]

sarray *adv* sarraly, in close order or array *la14.* [only Sc; F *serré*]

sasiabilitie [*ˈsɛsɪəˈbɪlɪtɪ] *n* capability of being satisfied *e16, only Sc.* [OED *satiability*]

sasine &c *16-*, **seisin &c** *la14-e19;* **sessing &c** *la14-16* [*ˈsezɪn] *n* **1** = seisin, possession *la14.* **2** *law* the act or procedure of giving possession of feudal property, *orig* by symbolic delivery of earth and stones, *now* by registry at the General Register of SASINES in Edinburgh, *freq* **give, take** *etc* ~ *la14-, only Sc.* **3** *law* the document which attested SASINE 2, the INSTRU-MENT *18-19, only Sc.*

vt take **root** *la16, only Sc.*

sessonar a lawful possessor (of lands) *la15, only Sc.*

~ **ox** an ox due as a perquisite to a sheriff when he gave *infeftment* (INFEFT) to crown lands *la16.* [laL *saysina*, F *saisine* = 2; *cf* Eng *seize*]

Sassenach &c [ˈsasənəx] *adj* English (-speaking); *formerly* also applied by Highlanders (HIELAND) to the *Lowlanders* (LAWLAND) of Scotland *18-.*

n an Englishman or -woman *18-.* [Gael *sasunnach* Saxon, English; a non-GAELIC-speaking Lowlander, the Scots and English languages not being differentiated in Gael]

sassenger &c *n, now rather joc* = sausage *19-, now Ork Cai WC.*

sasser &c [ˈsasər] *n* a sausage *la18-20.* [corruption of F *saucisse*, prob w infl f next]

saster &c [ˈsastər] *n* a kind of sausage with a HAGGIS stuffing *la16, 19-20.* [reduced f ME *saucister*]

sate *see* SEAT

Sathan *see* SAWTAN

satify &c *16;* **settifee** *e20* [*ˈsetɪfi, *ˈsɛtɪfi] *vt* = satisfy. [chf Sc; OF *satifier &c*, var of *satisfier; cf* SAITISFEE]

sattle &c *16-*, **settle &c** *la16-* *vti* **1** = settle *la16-.* **2** (cause (troops) to) fall back, yield ground *16.* **3** *vi* become composed, settle oneself *la16-.* **4** *vt, Presbyterian Church* install (a MINISTER) formally in a charge; provide (a vacant parish) with a MINISTER *18-.*

n **1** *also* **sadle &c** *la15-18* [ˈsadl, ˈsedl] = settle, a bench *la15-.* **2** a ledge or raised platform, *specif* in a BYRE where the cattle stand *19-, now Ags.*

settleder more settled *19-, now NE.* ~**ment** **1** *law* the disposition of one's property by will, a testament *18-.* **2** the placing of a MINISTER in a charge *18-.* ~ **bed** a wooden bed which can be folded up to form a seat during the day; a divan bed *19-, now local Stlg-SW.*

Saturday, Saturnday, Saturnsday *see* SETURDAY

sauce &c; sals &c *la14-e16* [sɑs] *n* = sauce *la14-.*

saucy &c 1 = saucy *16-.* **2** vain, conceited *la18-, local.* **3** fastidious about food or dress *la18-, now WC-S.*

sauch, saugh *18-* [sɑx] *n* **1** = sallow, the willow; a willow rod, willow wood *la15-.* **2** a rope of twisted willow withes *16.*

~**en 1** of or pertaining to willow *18-, now local Bnf-wLoth.* **2** tough as willow; *of persons* DOUR, stubborn and sullen *17-, now Bnf Abd.* **3** soft, yielding as willow, lacking in energy or spirit *18-, now Abd.* ~**ie** made of willow; abounding in willows *19-.*

~ **buss &c** a willow tree, *prob specif* a low-growing variety *la18-, now NE Kcb.* ~ **tree** a willow tree *16-, now Ags.* ~ **wan(d)** a twig or branch of willow *la18-.* ~ **willie** the willow *20-, local.* [nME *salfe*, OE *salh*, corresponding to WSaxon *sealh* > Eng *sallow*]

sauch *see* SEE

saucht *la14-e20*, **saught** *la18-19* [sɑxt] *n* peace, quiet *17-e20.*

adj in agreement, at peace, reconciled *la14-16.* *vi* become reconciled *la14-e15.*

~**en &c** reconcile *la14-e16.* [nME *saght*, eME, laOE *seht &c*, ON *saht &c*]

sauf &c, safe &c, save &c *la14-* (v), *16-17* (adj) [saf, sef, sev] *adj* = safe *la14-.*

vt, also **saiff &c** *la14-e19*, **salve** *la15-16* [*saf, *sav] **1** = save *la14-.* **2** give protection from *la16, only Sc.* **3** draw (a boat) up on the shore for the winter *la19-, now Cai* [appar translating Gael *gleidh* (v) preserve].

saving &c *prep* **1** = saving, except; having regard to *16-.* **2** but for *e16, only Sc.* **3** with the reservation of *la15-e17, only Sc.* **saving stone** a stone built over a lintel to distribute the load of the wall above onto the jambs *la20-, now Per Ayr.* ~**ty &c, savité** *la14,* **safity** *la19, Abd* **1** = safety *la14-.* **2** protection *la15-16, only Sc.*

safe lintel &c a wooden lintel placed for additional support behind the stone lintel of a door or window *18-, Gen except Sh Ork.*

(Lord *etc)* **sauf** *or* **safe us** *etc* exclam of surprise, apprehension, protest *19-, now Ork Bnf Ags.* **to** ~ *only Sc* **1** saving, having regard to *la14-15.* **2** saving, except *e15.*

saufey &c *la16-19*; **safer &c** *la16-17*, **saufer &c** *la16-e18*, *only Sc*, **salf- &c** *la16* [*'safe, *'safər, *'sefər] *n* a sum paid for recovering lost property *la16-19*.
vt redeem by payment of SAUFEY *la16*. [nME; prob connected w SAUF]

saugh *see* SAUCH

saughrin *see* SOCHER

saught *see* SAUCHT

saul &c *la14-*, *now local Sh-SW*, **sowl** *la19-*, **soul &c** *17-* [sɑl, sʌul] *n* **1** = soul *la14-*.   **2** *chf* **saul** spirit, mettle, courage *la18-e20*.
interj, *also* **sal &c** *la18-e20*, emphatic or asseverative upon my word *la18-20*.
~**ful &c** *n* enough to fill the soul *17-e20*.
~ **hird &c** a shepherd of souls *la14*.   ~ **mass** a mass for the soul of a dead person *la15-e19*.
for sowl and body with great vigour, as if one's life depended on it *20-*, *now Ork*.   **say one's ~ is one's own** *in negative* not be independent of others *16-*.   **the (wee) ~, my (wee) ~** term of familiarity, pity or mild disparagement *la19-*.

sauld *see* SELL¹

saule *see* SAIL

saulie &c *n* a hired mourner at a funeral who preceded the cortège with a black staff etc, a mute *17-18*.   [doubtful, but prob f SAUL]

saum *see* PSALM

saumon &c *la18-*, **salmon &c**; **salmond** *la14-18*, **-mont** *la16* ['saman, *'samənd, *'samənt] *n* = salmon *la14-*.
~ **coble &c** a flat-bottomed boat used in salmon-fishing *la18-*, *now local*.   ~ **cruive** a trap in a river to catch salmon *la18-*, *local*.   ~ **lowp 1** a salmon leap.   **2** *also* ~'**s lowp** a kind of leapfrog *20-*, *now Per*.   ~ **rawn** salmon roe *18-*, *now Kcb*.

Saunders *see* SANDIE

saunt *see* SAINT

saur &c *16-20*, **savour &c**; **sair &c** *16-19*, **sar &c** *18-e20* [sar, *ser] *vti* **1** = savour *la14-*.   **2** *vi* have a certain taste or odour *18-e20*.   **3** smell **of** *16-e18*.
n **1** = savour *16-*.   **2** a smell, *specif* an evil or sickening one *e19*.   **3** a slight wind, gentle breeze *19-20*, *Arg Ayr*.
savoring something that gives a faint notion *e16*, *only Sc*.   ~**less 1** tasteless, insipid *la16-*.   **2** lacking in wit, spirit, energy *19-20*, *NE*.
savorous &c of good savour *la15-e16*.

saut &c *18-*, **salt** [sɑt] *n* = salt *la14-*.
adj **1** = salt *la14-*.   **2** *of experience etc* painful, severe, bitter *16-*, *now Kcb*.   **3** *of prices etc* dear, stinging *18-*, *now N-S*.   **4** *of speech, manner* harsh, unkind *la19-*, *now Kcb*.
vt **1** = salt *la14-*.   **2** punish, take revenge on; snub, treat severely; over-charge, 'sting' *la18-*.
~**er 1** = salter, a saltmaker; a salt-worker *la16-*.   **2** a shrew, termagant; harsh or severe punishment *la19-*, *local Abd-Per*.   ~**ie** *adj* =

salty *la19-*.   *n* the dab *19-*, *now Bnf*.   ~**ie bannock** an oatmeal BANNOCK with a fair amount of salt, baked on Shrove Tuesday *19-*, *now hist*.
~ **backet &c** a salt-box, now *usu* one with a flat back and a curved front made to hang on the wall *18-*, *now NE nEC*, *only Sc*.   ~ **bree** salt water, water in which salt has been mixed or boiled *la18-*, *Sh NE*.   **the ~ burgh** nickname for Dysart, Fife, once a centre of the salt trade *20*, *hist*.
~ **dish** a salt cellar *19-*.   ~ **fail &c** seaside turf *18*.   ~ **fat &c** *la15-*, *now local Sh-Fif*, ~ **foot** *la17-19* = ~ **dish**.   ~**man** an itinerant seller of salt *19-20*.   ~**-master** a collector of salt-duty *la17*.   ~ **stack** a mound of earth from which salt was manufactured *17*.   ~ **water** the seaside, *esp* as a place for holidaying or recuperation *19*.   ~ **willie** a salt jar *20-*, *now Fif*.
lay (something) in ~ *freq in threats of something unpleasant* lay aside, keep in reserve *la18-19*.   **small ~** table salt *la16*.   **nae sma ~** 'no small beer' *la20-*, *Ags Per Fif*.   **as ~ as lick** very salty *19-*, *local C*.

savage &c [*'savidʒ, *sə'vedʒ] *adj* **1** = savage *la16-*.   **2** intrepid, valiant *la15*.

savagiously [*sə'vedʒəslɪ] *adv* savagely *e17*.

save, savité *see* SAUF

saving *n* = savin, the shrub which produces an abortifacient drug, *freq* ~ **tree** *la18-e19*.

savor-, savour *see* SAUR

saw¹ &c, **sow** *la15-*; **shaw &c** *15-*, *chf NE*, **shaave &c** *la19-*, *NE* [sɑ; *NE also* ʃɑ(v)] *v*, *pt also* **sew** *16-*, *now NE* [su], **schew(e) &c** *18-*, *now Sh NE*, *only Sc* [ʃu]; ~**ed &c** *19-*, *now NE*. *ptp* ~**n &c**; **saw** *e16*; ~**ed &c** *la18-e20* *vti* **1** = sow *la14-*.   **2** *vt* shed (blood) *e16*, *only Sc*.   **3** throw out (a fishing-line) from a boat, shoot (a line) *e20*, *NE*.
~**in happer** *e20*, *Ork Abd Ayr*, ~**in sheet** *19-20*, *local* a canvas sheet from which seed was broadcast.   ~**in time** seed-time *20-*, *NE*.
~ **doun, out** *etc specif* sow (land) for a grass-crop, sow grass as a rotation crop with corn *la18-*.

saw² &c *n* salve, a healing ointment *la14-20*.   [only Sc. OED *salve* (*n*¹)]

saw³ *n*, *vti* = saw ((for) wood) *15-*.
~**ing 1** = sawing *16-*.   **2** ~**in(g)s** sawdust *19-*, *now Abd Lnk*.
~ **neb** the goosander; the red-breasted merganser *la19-e20*.

Sawbath *see* SABBATH

sawn *see* SAW¹

Sawnie *see* SANDIE

Sawtan &c *la19-20*; **Sathan** *la16-e20* ['satən, 'saθən] *n* **1** = Satan, the devil *la16-e20*.   **2** *only* **sawtan, sawtie** a small light shooting marble *20-*, *Stlg*.   [OED *Satan*]

sax *now chf Sh Ork N*, **six** *la17-*; **sex** *la14-19* *numeral* = six *la14-*.

sick(ie) &c sixpence *la19-*, *Kcdn Ags Fif*. **six-sie** a move in the game of *chuckies* (CHUCK²) *la20-*, *local NE-Dmf*. ~**some** &c a group of six (people), *latterly esp* in a dance *la14-*. ~**some reel** a REEL¹ danced in sets of three couples *19-*, *now Ork*. ~**t** = sixth *la14-*. ~**teen** &c 1 = sixteen *la14-*. 2 **the** ~**teen** the sixteen representatives of the pre-Union peerage of Scotland elected from their own number after each general election (until 1963) to sit in the House of Lords *la18-20*. **sixteensome** a REEL¹ danced in sets of eight couples *20-*.
sax-month a period of six months *20-*, *local Sh-Ags*.
six(es) and sax(es) very much alike, six and half a dozen *20-*, *now NE, WC, SW*.

saxeane *adj* made of stone *la16*, *only Sc*. [only Sc; L *saxeus*]

say; sa *la14-e16*, *only Sc* [se; *pres* sez, se] *vti*, *pres 3 pers pl also* **sigge** [*sɪdʒ] *la14*, *only Sc*. *pt also* **sad** *la14*, *only Sc*. *ptp also* **sad** *la14-16*, **sain** &c *la19-*, *now local Sh-Ags* [*pt, ptp* sed, sen] = say *la14-*.
n 1 what is said; a remark, piece of gossip *la16-*, *now local Sh-Ayr*. 2 a saying, proverb *la18-*, *Sh Ork N*. 3 talk, speech *la18-e20*.
~**er** &c 1 = sayer *la16-*. 2 a poet, story-teller *e16*. **be easy said til** be yielding or amenable *la19-*, *Abd Kcdn Ags*.
~ **ae wey** (**wi**) agree, be in harmony (with) *20-*, *local NE-Ayr*. ~ **awa(y)** *vi* 1 say on, hold forth, speak one's mind *19-*, *now local Sh-Per*. 2 say grace before a meal *19-*, *now Ork Bnf Abd*. *n* 1 a long rambling discourse, a rigmarole *19-*, *local NE-S*. 2 a loquacious person *20-*, *S*. ~ **for** vouch for *17-*, *now local*. ~ **ower** recite, repeat from memory *la19-*. ~ **thegither** agree, be of one mind; be on good terms *la20-*, *NE nEC*. ~ **wi** agree with, concur with *20-*. ~ (**a body**) **wrang** speak ill of (someone) *la19-*, *local Sh-Ags*. **I winna** *etc* **say** (**but** (**what**)) I dare say, I won't deny (that) *la19-*, *local Ork-Kcb*.
say *see* SAE¹, SAE², SEY¹, SEY², SEY³

saynd &c [*send] *n* = sand, the act of sending, a message, gift, God's ordinance; a messenger *la14-15*. [only Sc. OED *sand* (*n*¹)]

scab *n* 1 = scab. 2 one of the umbelliferae, *eg* hemlock *20-*, *S*.
v 1 *vt* form scabs on *e17*, *only Sc*. 2 *vi* = scab. **scabbert** &c *n* 1 a person suffering from scab; *fig* contemptuous term for a person *19*. 2 a bare, stony piece of land *19*, *NE*. *adj* scabbed, bare *19-e20*. **scabbie-heid** applied to a person with head lice *20-*, *local C*. **scabbit** &c 1 = scabbed *16-*. 2 *of land* bare, infertile *la19-*, *now local Sh-Per*. 3 *of a person* mean, worthless *18-*. ~ **pikar** ? a person who treats sheep for scab *la15*, *only Sc*.

scad *see* SCAUD

scaddin &c *n* 1 a thin flaky turf, the top paring of PEAT¹ from a bog; a PEAT¹ turf used for thatching *18-e20*. 2 a lean, emaciated person or animal *la19-*, *now Abd*. 3 contemptuous term for a person or thing; *occas* the lowest playing card in a game *la19-*, *NE*. [only Sc; *cf* Du *schadde* turf, grass]

scaddow *see* SHEDDA

scadlips *see* SCAUD

scaff¹ &c *n* a light boat, skiff *la14-e20*. [chf Sc; OF *scaphe* &c, L (f Gk) *scapha*]

scaff² &c *vti* 1 scrounge (*esp* food), go about looking for what may be picked up *16-*, *now local Cai-Per*. 2 wander about *la19-*, *NE Kcdn*. 3 eat or drink greedily *19-*, *now Sh*.
n 1 food, provisions *la18-*, *now Sh*. 2 *also* ~ **and raff** (worthless) rubbish; riff-raff *19*. 3 going about idly, roaming in search of amusement or on the scrounge *la19-*, *local Cai-Ags*. ~**er** a parasite, sponger; an extortioner *16*. ~**ery** &c extortion *la16-17*. [only Sc; see SND]

scaffat *la14-16*, **skaffell** *la16* *n* = scaffold. [OED *scaffold*]

scaffie &c *n* a street-sweeper, refuse collector *la19-*. ~ **cairt** a refuse-collector's cart or lorry *la19-*, *local*. [only Sc; reduced dim of Eng *scavenger*]

scag *vi* 1 *of fish* become rotten by exposure to sun or air *e19*. 2 *of the human face etc* become wrinkled, lose the bloom *la20-*, *Cai*.
n a putrid fish *la19-20*. [only Sc; ? Gael *sgag* crack, split, become weather-beaten]

scailie &c *18-20*; **scailȝe** &c *la15-e16*, **scailyie** &c *la16-18*, **scallie** &c *18-*, *local*, **skylie** &c *la18-*, *local*, **skeely** &c *la19-e20* [*skeli*; *EC, S* *skilr*; *NE Ags also* 'skəili, 'skali, 'skali; *'skeljɪ] *n* 1 (a) slate *la15-20*. 2 a slate pencil *19-20*.
~ **brod** &c a slate for writing on *18-e19*. [only Sc; MDu *schaelie*, f OF *escaille* a shell; a (fish-)scale, lamina]

scaith [*skeθ] *n* a kind of light fishing boat *la19-e20*, *Bnf*. [only Sc; prob altered f SCAFF¹]

scal *see* SCAULD

scalade; scallet *n* 1 = (e)scalade *17-19*. 2 *only* **scallet** a scaling ladder *e17*.

scalbert *see* SCAWBART

scald *see* SCAUD, SCAULD

scaldrick *see* SKELDOCK

scaldrie *see* SCAULD

scale¹ &c *n* 1 = scale, the pan of a balance *la14-*. 2 a shallow drinking bowl; a shallow dish for skimming milk *18-*, *now Lnk Rox*.

scale² &c *n* = scale, a ladder *la16*. ~ **stair** a straight (as opposed to a spiral) stair *17-e20*, *only Sc*.

scaledrake *see* SKELLDRAKE

scalie *see* SKELLIE¹

scall *see* SCAW

scallag &c ['skalək] *n* a farm labourer; *latterly* form of address to a boy *la17-e20*, *Highl*. [only Sc; Gael *sgalag*; *cf* SCOLOC]

scallet *see* SCALADE

scallie *see* SCAILIE

scallion *n* **1** = scallion *19-*. **2** a spring onion *la20-*, *C Uls*; *cf* SYBOW.

scalp *see* SCAUP

scam, scaum &c *19-20* [skɑm] *vt* **1** burn slightly, scorch, singe *17-*, *now local*. **2** *of frost* scorch, blight (plants) *la19-*, *now N Per*. **3** scold severely *20-*, *now Bnf Per*. **4** cover with a film of moisture, a haze etc *19-e20*.

n **1** a burn, singe, or its mark *19-*, *now local*. **2** a withering or scorching of plants by frost etc *la20-*, *N Per*. **3** a hurt to one's feelings, a wound, cause of suffering *la19-*, *Bnf Abd*. **4** a spot, crack, injury *19-*, *now local Sh-Fif*. **5** a film of vapour, a haze etc *19-e20*. [chf Sc; see SND]

scamble *see* SKEMMEL

scambler *18*; **scamler &c** *e16*, **skemler** *e20* *n* a sponger, parasite. [only Sc; see SND]

scamp *vi* go, wander **about** etc, *freq* with an idea of mischief *la19-*, *now Bnf*. [*cf* Eng (*orig* cant) *v* = wander about; *n* a footpad; Du *schampen* decamp, run away]

scance &c *v* **1** *vt* scan, analyse the metre of; scrutinize, look critically at *la16-20*. **2** give the appearance of *la15*. **3** *vi* reflect, comment **on** *or* **about** *17-e19*. **4** *vt, also vi* ~ **at** criticize, reproach *19-*, *now Cai*. **5** *vi* gleam, glitter, shine *la18-e20*. **6** talk pompously, exaggerate *e19*.

n **1** a quick (appraising) look, a cursory survey *la18-*, *now local Sh-WC*. **2** a gleam, a brief, quick appearance, a tinge *19-*, *now local Ags-Ayr*. [chf Sc; see SND]

scandal *n*, *law* an actionable report defaming a person's character, defamation *18-19*.

~**eese &c** = scandalize *la19-20*.

scant¹ &c *n* a scanty supply, lack, scarcity *la15-*, *now Ork N, WC*.

adj = scant *16-*.

adv **1** scarcely, hardly *la16*, *la19*. **2** scantily *e17*.

~**lins** scarcely, hardly *la18-e20*, *only Sc*.

~**ness 1** = scantness *17-*. **2** scarcity *e16*, *only Sc*.

~**-o-grace** a scapegrace, reprobate *18-19*, *only Sc*.

scant² *n* a type or size of slate *la20-*, *Abd Per*. [reduced f Eng dial *scantle*]

scantack &c *n*, *fishing* a hooked and baited line fixed along a shore or in a stream, *freq* used by night poachers *19*, *Mry*. [only Sc; see SND]

scantlins *see* SCANT¹

scap *see* SCAUP

scar &c *la15-*; **scaur** *la18-e20*, **sker &c** *15-e20* [skar, skɑr, skɛr] *adj*, *also* **skair &c** *la19-e20* [sker] *esp of animals* timid, shy, wild, apt to run away *16-*, *now Ork*.

n a fright, scare *19-*, *now Ork Kcb*, *only Sc*.

v, *also* **scare** *19-* **1** *vt* = scare, frighten (away) *16-*. **2** *vi* take fright, run away in fear *la15-*.

~**-craw** a scarecrow *18-e20*. [*cf* SKEER]

scar *see* SCAUR¹

scarce *la17-*; **scars &c** *la14-e16*, **skairs &c** *la16-17* [skers] *adj* = scarce *la16-*.

~**lins** scarcely *la20-*, *Sh Fif SW*. ~**ment**, **scarsement 1** *building* a horizontal ledge *e16*, *la18-*, *chf Sc*. **2** the edge of a ditch cut to form a ledge on which bushes etc may be planted *la18-e20*, *only Sc*.

scare *see* SCAR

scarf &c *la17-*, *now Sh-Uls*, **scart &c** *18-*, *now local Ags-SW*, **scrath &c** *la17-*, *chf NE*; **scarth** *la15-e16* [skarf, skart, skert; *skraθ, *skarθ] *n* the cormorant; the shag. [only Sc; ON *skarfr*; *cf* Norw *skarv*]

scargivenet &c [*?skər'gɪfnət] *n* a skinny adolescent *19-e20*. [only Sc; obscure]

scarnach &c ['skarnəx] *n* **1** heaps of loose stones on hillsides, SCREE¹, detritus *la18-e19*. **2** a great number or crowd of things or people *19-e20*. [Gael *sgàirneach* = *n* 1; the noise (as) of their falling]

scarp &c *n* a bare barren piece of ground *20-*, *now Sh*. [only Sc; *cf* Norw *skarp*, ON *skarpr* barren; or *perh* altered f SCAUP]

scarrow &c ['skarə] *n* **1** a faint light or reflection of light *la18-*, *SW*. **2** a shadow, shade *19-e20*, *chf SW*. [only Sc; irreg var of Eng *shadow*]

scars, scarsement *see* SCARCE

scart¹ &c *vti* **1** scratch, scrape with the nails, claws etc *la14-*. **2** *vt* scrape or scratch (the ground) in search of food *19-*. **3** scrape with a spoon, take the last of food from (a dish) *18-*. **4** scrape or gather together in a niggardly, acquisitive way *17-*, *now C, S*. **5** strike (a match) *la19-*, *now Ork NE-S*. **6** mark (a surface) with a scratch *19-*. **7** mark (a paper) with a pen, write, *esp* carelessly, scribble (a note etc) *19-*. **8** *vi* make a scraping, grating, or rasping noise *20-*.

n **1** a scratch with the nails etc *la16-*. **2** a mark or scrape of a pen, a scribble *la18-*. **3** a furrow or mark on the ground *20-*, *local Sh-Kcb*. **4** the smallest quantity of something, a grain, trace *19-*, *now C, S*.

~**le** *vti* scrape together in little bits; make little scratching movements *19-e20*. *n* a scraper, hoe or rake *19-20*.

~ **free** *18-e20*, ~ **hale** *la19-*, *nEC* unscathed, scot free.

~ **someone's buttons** run one's fingers down another's jacket buttons, as a challenge to fight *19-*, *now Rox*. [only Sc; metath f the rarer SCRAT¹]

scart² *n* **1** *also* **scarth &c** *16* a hermaphrodite; a monster *16*, *20-*, *now Rox*. **2** a puny, shrunken person; *also in gen* term of abuse *19-*, *now Per Dmf*. [only Sc; metath f SCRAT²; OED *scarth*]

scart *see* SCARF

scarth *see* SCARF, SCART²

scash &c *vi* **1** quarrel, squabble *19-20*, *Abd*. **2**

esp of feet or gait twist, turn to one side; shuffle along with the toes turned out *la19-*, *NE*. **3** dress in a slovenly way *19*.

adj, esp of the feet or mouth twisted, turned to one side *la19-*, *now Abd Kcdn*.

n **1** a quarrel, dispute, brawl *la18-e19*. **2** an untidy or slovenly person or garment *la19-e20*.
~**le &c** = *v* 2 and 3 and *n*, *19-*. [only Sc; see SND]

scat¹ **&c** *n* a tax or tribute: **1** *in gen*, *e16*; **2** *specif* one of various local taxes *la16*. [also = a land tax *la15-*, *Sh Ork* (see SND *skatt*); ON *skattr*; *cf* SCOT]

scat² *n*, *chf in combs* term of abuse *la18-e20*. [only Sc; obscure]

scat *see* SCOT

scatch *see* SKETCH¹

scath, scathe *see* SKAITH

scattan; scatyin &c ['skatən, 'skatjən] *n* a herring *19-*, *now NE Bute Ayr*. [only Sc; Gael *sgadan*]

scatter &c *vti* **1** = scatter *la16-*. **2** *specif, at a wedding* throw handfuls of coins or sweets in the street for children to scramble for *20-*, *C, S*; *cf pour-out* (POUR).
n **1** = scatter. **2** the scattering of money etc, *eg* as in *v* 2, *20-*, *now C, S*.
~**ment &c** a scattering, dispersal, rout *la19-*, *now Abd*.
~**-wit &c** a scatterbrain *la19-*, *now local Abd-Slk*.

scatyin *see* SCATTAN

scaud &c *16-*, **scald &c**; **schald &c** *la14-e16*, **scad** *16-* [skad] *vti* **1** (1) = scald *16-*. (2) make (tea) *la20-*, *Kcb S*. **2** (cause to) burn with desire *la14-e16*. **3** *vt, of words, language* burn, scald *e16*. **4** *vti, chf scad of cloth* (cause to) become faded or shabby *la19-*, *now local Kcdn-S*. **5** *vt, chf scaud* cause grief or pain to, punish *19-*, *now Ags Wc*.
n **1** = scald. **2** a quantity of scalding liquid *e16*. **3** a sore caused by chafing of the skin *18-*, *now C, S*. **4** *joc* tea *19-*, *nEC, WC, SW*. **5** a hurt to the feelings; vexation *18-e20*. **6** *chf scad* a faint appearance of colour or light; a reflection *la17-*, *now Per Lnk*, *only Sc*.
scalder &c a jellyfish, medusa *la19-*, *Cai NE, SW*. ~**ing &c** *adj* **1** = scalding *16-*. **2** *of the sea* boiling, seething *e16*. **3** *of desire* burning, fervent *la14*. *n* a sheepskin of small value *15-17*, *chf Sc*. **scaddit scone** a scone of barley- or wheat-meal mixed with hot milk or water *la20-*, *Bnf Lnk SW*. •
scadlips &c BROTH with a small amount of barley (and thus more likely to burn the mouth) *la17-19*, *only Sc*.

scauld *18-*; **scald &c** *16-e20*, **scaul &c** *18-e20*, **scal &c** *la18-20* [skal(d); *Sh Ork Cai* skʌuld] *n* **1** = scold, a scolding, abusive woman *16-20*. **2** scolding, railing, abuse *la18-*.
vti = scold *18-*.

scaldrie abusive speech *e16*, *only Sc*. **scaulin pyock** a loose fold of skin under the jaws of a fat person *20-*, *Bnf Abd*. [OED *scold*]

scaum *see* SCAM

scaup &c, **scalp &c** *la16-*; **scap &c** *la15-19* [skap] *n* **1** = scalp *la15-*. **2** the skull, cranium *18-19*. **3** thin shallow soil; a piece of infertile, stony ground; a small bare hill or piece of rock *16-*, *now Sh NE*. **4** a bank for shellfish in the sea *la15-*. **5** the shellfish found on rocks between high and low tide *19-*, *now Cai*.
vt pare off the top soil etc from (a piece of ground); denude (soil) *19-e20*, *chf Sh*.
scappy &c bare and exposed; *of soil* thin and shallow *18*.

scaur¹ **&c** *19-*, **scar &c** *16-e20*; **sker &c** *19-*, *S* [skar; *S* skɛr] *n, freq in place-names* a sheer rock, precipice; a steep, eroded hill *16-*, *now NE-S*. [ME *skerre &c*, ON *sker*; *cf* SCORE²]

scaur² [skar] *n, vti* = scar *la19-e20*.

scaur *see* SCAR

scaw &c, **scall &c** *e17* [ska] *n* **1** a scaly skin disease *la14-*, *now Ork Ayr*. **2** a barnacle, a mass of barnacles *19-*, *now Cai*.
scawt &c, **skaid** *16-17 adj* **1** affected with scab, itch, ringworm etc; scabby, scruffy *16-*, *now NE Ayr*. **2** spoiled in appearance, shabby, faded *la18-*, *now NE, WC Dmf*. **3** scruffy, mean; scanty *17-e20*. **4** *of rocks* covered with barnacles etc *la19-*, *now Cai*. [ME *scall* = *n* 1; ON *skalle* a bald head]

scawbart &c *e16*; **scalbert &c** *la15-e16*, **scawburne** *la15* [*'skabərt*, *-barn*] *n* = scabbard. [only Sc. OED *scabbard*]

scawt *see* SCAW

SCE *see* CERTIFICATE

sceldrick *see* SKELDOCK

scent &c [sɛnt, sɛnt, sınt] *n* **1** = scent *la14-*. **2** a small quantity, drop, pinch *19-*, *local Stlg-Kcb*.

schadow *see* SHEDDA

schaffroun *see* CHAFFERON

schald *see* SCAUD, SHAULD

schalk [*ʃalk*] *n* a servant; a man *la15-e16*. [ME; OE *scealc*. OED *shalk*]

schallow &c [*ʃalə*] *n* a drove, flock *la16*, *only Sc*. [Gael *sealbh*; OED *shallow* (*n*¹)]

schame *see* SCHEME

schamlich *see* SHAMMLE

schammo *see* SHAMBO

schand [*ʃɛnd*] *adj* ? beautiful, handsome *la15*. [only Sc. OED *shand*]

schane *see* SHEEN

schapen *see* SHAPE

schare *see* SHEAR¹

schargant *see* SERGEANT

scharpentyn *n* = serpentine, a kind of (ship's) cannon *e16*, *only Sc*.

schaw *see* SEE

schawd *see* SHAULD

schawis *see* SHEAVE

schearstane *see* SHIRE¹

schefe *see* SHEAVE

scheid *see* SHED
scheip *see* SHIP
scheir *see* CHEER[1]
scheirly *see* SHEER[1]
scheld *see* SHIEL[2]
scheme, schame *18-e20* [skim, * skem] *n* **1** = scheme. **2** *also* **housing** ~ a local-authority housing estate *20-*. *vti* = scheme.
scherald *see* SHIRREL
Scherand [*?'ʃirand] name for a kind of wine *16*. [only Sc; perh f F *Gironde* (the river)]
scherard, scheratt *see* SHIRREL
schervice *see* SERVICE
schervitour *see* SERVITOR
schervitude *see* SERVITUDE
scherviture [*'sɛrvɪtør, *'ʃɛr-] *n* service, servitude *e16, only Sc.* [*cf* Eng. OED *serviture*]
schevin *see* SHAVE
schew *see* SAW[1], SHUVE
schewd *see* SHOWD
schewe *see* SAW[1]
scheyff [*ʃiv] *vi*, ~ **fra** avoid *la15*. [only Sc; aphetic f Eng *eschew*]
schief *see* SHAIF
schinder *see* CINNER
schip *see* SHEEP
schiphird *see* SHEPHERD
schir *see* SIR
schirly *see* SHIRE[2]
schirpe *see* SHAIRP
schirryve *see* SHRIVE
schlorach *see* SLORACH
scho *see* SHAE, SHE
schocht *see* SEEK[1]
schoir &c [*ʃor] *adj* steep; rugged *la14-16.* [chf Sc. OED *shore (adj)*]
schoir *see* SHORE[1]
scholar &c *18-*; **scoller &c** *la16-e17 n* **1** = scholar *la16-.* **2** a school pupil *18-.*
schomd *ptp, of a horse* adorned with some kind of ornament *e16.* [appar f ME *shome* (once) ? a horse-ornament. OED *shome*]
schon *see* SIN[1]
schonk *v* **1** *vt* shatter *la15.* **2** *vi* burst forth *la15.* [only Sc; obscure. OED *shonk*]
school, schooladge *see* SCHULE
schorling *see* SHORELING
schoun, schoyne, schoys *see* SHAE
schrif *see* SHRIVE
schuif *see* SHAVE
schulder *see* SHOUDER
schuldir: in ~ ? into fragments *e16.* [altered f *in schundir* (SINDER)]
schule &c *16-*, **school** *17-*; **scule &c, squeel &c** *19-*, NE, **skeel &c** *la20-*, Cai-Ross [skøl, skɪl; *Cai-Ross* skil; *NE* skwil; *nEC* skel] *n* **1** = school *16-.* **2** the place where an ancient Greek or Roman philosopher taught *la14-.*
~**adge &c** school fees *la15-e18, only Sc.*
school board &c an elected body set up in

each parish or BURGH by the Education Act of 1872 to provide universal elementary education there *la19-e20.*
~ **wages** school fees *18-19.* ~ **wean** a schoolchild *19-, WC, SW.*
learn the ~ be a pupil at school *19-, now NE, EC.*
schunder *see* SINDER
schune *see* SHAE
schup *see* SHAPE
schyffis *see* SHEAVE
schyll [*ʃɪl] *n* = sill *16, only Sc.* [OED *sill* (*n*[1])]
scientive *adj* well-versed, learned *la16.* [only Sc; OF *scientif*]
scillop &c ['skɪləp, 'skʌləp] *n, esp cooperage* an auger with a rounded tapering blade *la18-, now local.* [only Sc; see SND]
scintill *vi* sparkle *la17.* [only Sc; F *scintiller* or L *scintillāre*]
scisma &c *n* = schism *la15-e16, only Sc.*
scission *n* **1** schism *15-19.* **2** = scission, cutting.
sclaff &c [sklaf; *Inv* slaf, ʃlaf] *v* **1** *vt* strike with the open hand or with something flat, slap *la19-, now Abd C.* **2** *golf* graze (the ground) with the club when striking the ball; hit (the ball) thus *la19-.* **3** *vi* walk in a flat-footed or shuffling way *la19-, now NE, C.*
n **1** a blow with the palm of the hand or with something flat, a falling flat, a thud; the noise of this *la19-, NE, C.* **2** *golf* a muffed shot when the club grazes the ground before hitting the ball *la19-.* **3** a light loose-fitting shoe or slipper; an old worn-down shoe *la19-, NE Ags Per Fif.* **4** a thin flat piece of something *la19-, now Abd.*
~**er** *v* = *v* 3, *la19-, now NE.* *n* **1** = *n* 3, *la19-, now NE.* **2** a big clumsy flat-footed person; a flat foot *la19-, now NE Ags Per.* ~**ert &c 1** a blow with the palm of the hand or with something flat *la18-, N.* **2** a clumsy flat-footed person *20-, Bnf Abd.* ~**y** = *sklaff-fittit, la19-e20.*
sklaff-fittit flat-footed *la20-, local N-SW.* [chf Sc; onomat; *cf* SKLEFF]
sclaik *see* SLAKE[2]
sclair *see* SLAIR
sclam *see* SCLIM
sclammer[1] **&c** *vi* = clamber *19-, local Abd-Slk, only Sc.*
sclammer[2] **&c** *vi, n* = clamour *20, NE, only Sc.*
sclander &c *la14-e18*, **slander &c** *vti* **1** = slander *la14-.* **2** *vt* charge **with**, accuse **of** (a crime or offence) *16-e17, only Sc.*
n = slander *la14-;* but for Sc legal usage see DEFAMATION *n* 2.
sclap &c *vi* walk in a flat-footed or shuffling way *la20-, NE.*
n a heavy blow, hard smack, *esp* with something flat *la19-, now NE.* [only Sc; var of SLAP[1]; *cf* SCLAFF]
sclatch &c *v* **1** *vt* smear or cover over with some wet or messy substance *la19-, now local Sh-Wgt.*

2 *vti* work messily; make or use clumsily, untidily or carelessly *19-*, *now local Abd-Fif.* **3** *vi* walk or move in an ungainly, slovenly way, shuffle *19-*, *now Ags Per.*

n **1** a large smudge, smear; a daub of something wet or dirty *19-*, *now local Sh-Clcm.* **2** a mess, bungle *19-*, *local Abd-S.* **3** a heavy fall, *esp* into water or mud; a slap, smack; the noise of this *19-*, *now NE.* [only *Sc*; see *SND*]

sclate *see* SLATE[1]

sclave[1] &c *16-20*, **slave &c** *la16- n* = slave *16-.*

sclave[2] &c *vt* spread (a story) by gossip, *specif* as a malicious rumour; slander (a person) *19-*, *NE.*

    n a gossip, scandalmonger *la20-*, *NE.*

    sclaver = *v*, *la19-*, *NE.* [only *Sc*; prob back-formation f *sclaver*, var of CLAVER[1] w prothetic *s-*]

sclender &c *la15-19*; **sclinder** *la16*, **-nner** *19-*, *NE* ['sklɛn(d)ǝr, 'sklɪnǝr] *adj* = slender.

sclenter &c *n*, *in pl* loose stones, SCREE[1], a stony hillside *la18-e20.* [appar nasalized var of SLIDDER, perh w infl f CLINT]

sclew *see* SLAY

sclice &c *n*, *vti* = slice *15-.*

sclidder *see* SLIDDER

sclim &c *vti*, *pt* **sclimmed &c** *la19-*, **sclam &c** *e20* = climb *la18-.* [only *Sc*; Eng *climb* + intensifying prothetic *s-*]

sclinder, sclinner *see* SCLENDER

sclit *n*, *mining* slaty or fissile coal, coaly BLAES; a clayey stratum *la18-*, *now Fif Lnk.* [only *Sc*; var, w altered vowel, of *sclate* (SLATE[1])]

sclither *see* SLIDDER

sclore &c [sklor, *Rox* ʃlor] *vi* chat, gossip, BLETHER[1] (at length) *la19-e20.*

    n rubbishy talk, a long rambling story *la19-e20.* [only *Sc*; see *SND*]

scloy *see* SCLY

sclunsh *vi* walk with a slow heavy tread, stump along *la18-*, *local Abd-Fif.* [prob onomat, perh w infl f SLOUNGE]

sclushach ['sklʌʃǝx] *n* a crab during the shell-less stage after it has cast its old shell *20-*, *Bnf Abd.* [only *Sc*; ? var of CLOSHACH]

sclutter *see* SLUTTER

scly &c *19-*, **sly &c** *la19-*; **scloy** *19-e20 vi* slide, skate (as) on ice *19-*, *now local Pbls-S.*

    n **1** a strip of ice etc used as a slide *19-*, *local EC-S.* **2** the act of sliding on ice etc *la19-*, *local Lnk-S.*

    sklire &c = *v*, *e19*, *Loth Dmf.* [perh reduced f nME *slithe*, var of *slide*]

sclẏddyn *see* SLIDE

sclype *see* SLYPE

sclyster *see* SLAISTER

scob[1] &c *18-*, **scobe** *17-e20* [*S* skʌub] *n* **1** a twig or cane of willow or hazel, *esp* one bent over to fasten down thatch, make baskets etc *16-*, *now SW.* **2** a rod of wood, or *occas* metal, used for various purposes *la18-e19.* **3** a slat of wood

used as a splint for broken bones, for repairing a wooden shaft etc *la19-*, *now NE Ags.* **4** *weaving* a defect in which the shuttle passes on the wrong side of the warp threads *19-*, *local Ags-Slk.*

    vt **1** close or obstruct (the mouth) *17-e18.* **2** put (a broken bone) in splints *19-*, *now NE Ags.* **3** *weaving* miss (threads), allow the weft to miss (the warp) *la19-*, *now nEC Slk.* [ScGael *sgolb*, IrGael *scolb* a splinter; a thatching rod; a thin stick]

scob[2] &c [skob] *vt* **1** scoop out, hollow, gnaw out with the teeth *19-e20.* **2** remove pieces or quantities from the inside of a heap etc, leaving the outside undisturbed *la19-e20.* [appar Gael *sgob* snatch; scoop out; nibble, peck]

scobe *see* SCOB[1]

scodge &c; **scudge &c** [skodʒ, skʌdʒ] *n* **1** a servant who does light, rough or dirty work, *esp* a kitchen-boy or -girl *la18-*, *now local Cai-WC.* **2** = *scodgie brat*, *20-*, *wLoth S.*

    vi **1** do rough menial work *19-*, *now EC, WC.* **2** act slyly, sneak idly about *19-*, *now Cai.*

    scodgie &c ['skodʒɪ, 'skʌdʒɪ; *Per* 'skwodʒɪ] = *n* **1** (*la18-*, *now local Cai-WC*), n **2**, (*20-*, *wLoth S*), *v* **1** (*la19-*, *now EC, WC.*) **scodgie brat** a rough apron worn for dirty work *20-*, *wLoth S.* **scodgie claes** one's second-best or working clothes *la20-*, *Kcdn Ags Per.* [only *Sc*; see *SND*]

scodgebell *see* COACHBELL

scoff[1] *la17-*; **scouf &c** *19-e20* [skof, skʌuf] *vt* **1** steal, plunder; sponge, scrounge *la17-20.* **2** swallow (food or drink) quickly *19-.* [appar var of SCAFF[2]]

scoff[2] *vt* dodge, avoid doing *la20-*, *NE Kcdn.* [perh var of SCUFF[1]]

scog *see* SCUG

scoll *see* SKOLE

scoller *see* SCHOLAR

scoloc &c *n*, *Celtic church*, *orig* the first-born son of a monastic tenant, given to the church to receive an ecclesiastical education; *later* any monastic tenant *19-*, *hist.* [ScL *scoloci* (*pl*) *e13*; OIr *scolóc*, f *scol* school; *cf* IrGael *scológ &c* a farmer, rustic; *cf* SCALLAG]

scomfish &c *la18-*; **scunfis &c** *la14-20* ['skʌmfɪʃ, *'skʌmfɪs*] *vt* **1** discomfit *la14.* **2** suffocate, stifle, choke, overpower with heat etc *la18-*, *now local.* **3** disgust, sicken *la19-*, *now Sh NE Ags.*

    n a suffocating atmosphere; a state of suffocation *19-*, *now Ork.*

    get *or* **tak a ~ at** take a strong dislike to, be disgusted at *la19-*, *now Sh NE Ags.* [aphetic f DISCOMFISH]

scon *see* SCONE

sconce[1] &c *n* a screen or shelter (of stone, wood etc) against the weather, fire, or for concealment, defence etc *16-.* [*cf* eModEng = an earthwork]

sconce[2] *vi* cheat, get something by false pretences *la18-e20.* [see *SND*]

sconce[3] &c *vr* settle oneself, take up one's position *la19-*, *NE*. [prob aphetic f Eng *ensconce*]

scondies *see* SCONE

scone &c; **scon(n)** *n* **1** a large, *usu* round semi-sweet cake made of wheat flour, baked on a GIRDLE etc, or in an oven, and cut into four three-sided pieces; one of these pieces; a similar small round individual-sized cake *16-*. **2** an *oatcake* (AIT) *18-*, *now Sh*. **3** *chf* ~ **bonnet** or **cap** = *Kilmarnock bonnet* (KILMARNOCK) *19-*, *now local Kcdn-Ayr*. **4** a slap (with the flat of the hand), smack *19-*, *local NE-Lnk*.

vt **1** strike the surface of (something) with a flat object, crush flat with a slap *19-*, *now local Ork-Ags*. **2** slap with the open hand, smack (*esp* a child's bottom) *18-*, *NE*.

scondies *child's word* smacks, a spanking *la20-*, *NE*.

~face nickname for a person or thing with a round flat face *20-*, *now local Ags-WC*.

a ~ o the day's *etc* **baking** one of the same kind as others, an average or typical person *la19-*. **drop(ped)** ~ a small, round, flat cake, made by allowing thick batter to drop onto a GIRDLE, frying pan etc, smaller and thicker than an English pancake and *usu* eaten cold with butter, jam etc, a *pancake* (PAN[1]) *20-*. **my wee** ~ term of endearment, *esp* to a child *20-*, *local C*. **who stole your ~?** why are you so glum? *20-*, *C*. [orig Sc; perh MDu *schoonbrot* fine bread, a kind of flat loaf]

sconner *see* SCUNNER

scoo *see* SCULL[1]

scoonrel &c; **scoondrel** &c ['skun(d)rəl] *n* = scoundrel *18-*.

scoop *see* SCUIP

scoor *see* SCOUR[1], SCOUR[2], SCOUR[3]

scoot *see* SCOUT[1], SCOUT[2]

scorchet *see* SCROCHAT

score[1] &c *n* **1** = score, a set of twenty *la14-*. **2** a line, stroke, mark, scratch *16-*. **3** *games etc* a mark or line on the ground, *eg* the starting line *16-*, *now Loth*. **4** a line, wrinkle on the skin, *esp* of the hand as used in palmistry; a scar left by a wound, a weal *la18-*, *now Sh N, WC*. **5** a parting in the hair *20-*, *local C*.

vt = score *16-*.

scorie &c scratched, notched *19-20*.

~ **abune the breath** make a scratch (*freq* the sign of the cross) on the forehead of a suspected witch, *usu* with an iron instrument, as a means of thwarting her power *18-19*, *only Sc*. **over the ~** beyond the bounds of reason, moderation etc *18-*.

score[2] *n* a crevice, cleft, gully in a cliff face *19-*, *now chf in place-names*. [only Sc; see SND]

scorie *see* SCORE[1]

scorn &c *n* **1** = scorn *la14-*. **2** a snub, brusque rejection, *esp* of a would-be lover *la18-19*.

v **1** *vt* = scorn *la14-*. **2** *vi* jeer, scoff **at** *16-*, *now Sh*. **3** *vt* ~ (**someone**) **wi** tease (*esp* a girl) about (a lover) *la18-19*.

scorp *vi* mock, scoff *16*. [only Sc; *cf* SKIRP]

scoskie &c *n* the starfish *la19-20*, *N*. [by assimilation, f Gael *crosgag, crosgan*]

scot &c *16-e19*, **scat** &c *16-e17* *n* = scot, a tax.

~ **and lot** pay equal contributions towards a charge or cost in a BURGH; pay a local tax as a free burgess *la16-e18* [only Sc as a *v*]. [the form *scat* is by association w SCAT[1]]

Scot &c *n*, *pl also* **Scottis** &c *la14-16* = Scot; a native of Scotland; *orig and hist* a member of the people which crossed from Ireland to Argyll in the 5th century *la14-*.

scot *see* SQUAT

Scots &c *17-*; **Scottis** &c *la14-17*, **Scottish** &c, **Scotch** *la17-*

A *Forms*: **Scots** (the descendant of the historical Sc form) survived till *19* only in certain locutions, but has gradually re-established itself as preferable to *Scotch* in general contexts among Scottish speakers when speaking Eng. **Scottish** (the full Eng form) was used in general contexts by anglicizing Scots (*17-18*); then retained in formal contexts stressing national or historical aspects (*la18-*): 'Scottish burgh', 'Scottish Crown'. **Scotch** (the contracted Eng form and the prevailing form in England *17-*) was adopted into Sc and was the prevailing Sc form (*la18-19*), is still the regular vernacular form but is now acceptable in Scottish Standard English only in certain compounds: 'Scotch broth', 'Scotch whisky'.

B *adj* **1** (1) = Scottish *la14-*. (2) of the mainland of Scotland *la20-*, *Sh Ork*. (3) *specif* of military bodies consisting of Scotsmen, both as mercenaries in foreign service and in the British Army *17-*. **2** *chf* **Scots** applied to the distinctive Scottish legal system developed from the Civil Law in the 17th century *18-*. **3** *chf* **Scots**, applied to measures (1) of length or area, based on the SCOTS yard or ELL *18-19*; (2) of weight, based on the *Lanark stone* (LANARK) *18-e19*; (3) of dry capacity, based on the LINLITHGOW FIRLOT; of liquids, based on the *Stirling jug* (JOUG) *18-e19*. **4** **Scots** &c *chf following its noun* of the Scottish value (of the pound etc), by 1700 worth one twelfth of the corresponding Eng sum (separate currencies were abolished by the Act of Union, 1707, but calculations were still made on the basis of the Scottish system till *la18*, and still survive in some archaic legal usages) *16-*. **5** speaking or expressed in SCOTS (*n* 1), *la16-*.

n **1** the Scots language, the speech of Lowland Scotland; that treated in this dictionary *la15-*. **2** the (Scottish) Gaelic language *la16-*, *latterly hist*, translating L 'lingua Scotica'.

Scots acre an area of 5760 square ELLS, approx 1.3 imperial acres (0.5 hectares) *la18-e19*. **Scots blanket** a blanket of hard unbrushed texture *la18-*. **Scotch bun** = *black bun* (BLACK) *la19-*. **Scottish Certificate of Education** *see* CERTIFICATE. **Scots collops**

thin slices of meat stewed with stock and flavouring *18-*. **Scots Confession** the 1560 Confession of Faith of the reformed Scottish Church, the first published document of the Scottish Reformation; cf *Negative Confession* (NEGATIVE). **Scotch convoy** the accompanying of a guest a part or all of the way back to his home *19-*, *Gen except Sh Ork*. **Scotch cousin** a distant relative *la19-, now NE, C*. **Scotch cuddy** a pedlar, travelling packman or draper *20-*, *WC, SW*. **Scots dyke** an earthwork (built *la16*) along part of the Scottish-English border *18-e19*. **Scots &c ell** the Scottish yard of 37 inches (940 mm) *la18-e19*. **~ Episcopal 1** *now only* **Scottish Episcopal** a member of the Scottish Episcopal Church *18-*. **2** *specif* **old Scots Episcopal** an adherent of that branch of the church which had been proscribed for its Jacobitism and whose clergy were not *qualified* (QUALIFY) *18-e19*. **Scotch &c flummery** a kind of steamed custard *la18-*. **Scotch gravat** a hug, cuddle *la20-, NE, C Slk*. **The Scots Greys** a Scottish (cavalry) regiment (2nd Dragoons formed from Independent Troops of Dragoons in 1681) *18-19, informally la19-20*; cf *Royal Scots Greys* (ROYAL). **Scotch hand** = HAND *n 3, la19-, now NE, C, Rox*. **Scotch horses** a formation of children running etc with arms linked behind their backs *20-*. **Scottish Land Court** a court set up by statute with a legally-qualified chairman and members with agricultural expertise; its jurisdiction covers the various forms of agricultural tenancy *20-*. **Scotch mahogany** the wood of the alder, which turns red when exposed to light and weather *la19-, now WC, Kcb*. **~man** (*orig written as separate words*) a male native of Scotland *la14-*. **Scots mile** the mile of around 1980 imperial yards (approx 1810 metres) *17-19*. **Scotch muffler** a drink of liquor, *esp* (regarded as keeping one warm) *la20-, Abd nEC Lnk*. **Scotch &c nightingale** *see* NIGHTINGALE. **Scots pebble** a semi-precious stone (*eg* an agate) found on hills, in streams etc in Scotland *18-*. **Scots &c pint** = *Stirling jug* (JOUG) *la17-19*. **Scots &c plough** a kind of swing- or wheel-less plough *la18-19*. **~ thistle** one of the thistle family (the exact species being disputed) adopted as the national badge of Scotland *la18-*. **Scots Troy** a standard measure of weight for meal, meat, iron etc, based on the *Lanark stone* (LANARK) *la18-e19*; cf *adj 3* (2). **Scotswoman** a female native of Scotland *19-*. **Scotch and English** *etc* name for various boys' games, in which two opposing sides try to capture one another, or some object, across a dividing line *19-20*.

Scottis *see* SCOT, SCOTS
Scottish *see* SCOTS
scoudrum *see* SCOWDER
scouf *see* SCOFF[1]
scoug *see* SCUG

scouk &c *la15-*, **skulk** *17-*; **scowk** *la14, la19* [skuk] *v* **1** *vi* = skulk *la14-*. **2** *vt* shun, avoid (in a skulking manner) *17-e19*. **3** (1) *vi* scowl, look balefully or furtively from under the eyebrows *18-, now local Cai-Fif*. (2) *vt* draw (the brows) together in a frown *19-, Bnf Abd*. *n* **1** a furtive look (from under the brows); a frown *18-, now Bnf Abd Ags*. **2** a skulking, cowardly person, a sneak *la19-, now Cai Inv*. **scoul &c** [skul] *vi* = scowl *18-, now Abd*. **~ horned** *of a cow* having downward-pointing horns *la17, 20-, now Ayr*.
scoup *see* SCOWP[1], SCUIP
scour[1] &c; **scoor &c** *la19-* [skur] *n* a shower of rain, *esp* intermittent with gusts of wind *la18-, now local Cai-Ayr*. **~y** blustery with rain, wet and squally *la18-, now local NE-Dmf*. [ON *skúr* a shower, cognate w Eng *scour* rush about, and *shower*]
scour[2] &c; **scoor &c** *la19-* [skur] *vti* = scour, rush about etc *la14-*. *n* **1** a run, rush, quick pace *la18-, now N*. **2** a blow, stroke, box (on the ear) *la19-, NE*. [uncertain; *cf* Norw *skura* (*v*) rush, perh cognate w SCOUR[3]]
scour[3] &c; **scoor &c** *la19-* [skur] *vt* **1** = scour, cleanse *la14-*. **2** purge or clear out (the bowels, stomach) *la18-*. **3** flush out with liquid; *joc* drink **off**; wet (one's throat etc) *18-19*. **4** drive (an enemy) **out of** *la15*. **5** reprimand severely *19-, now Sh Lnk*. *n* **1** the act of scouring *19-*. **2** an apparatus for washing gold-bearing soil *17-e19*. **3** a large hearty drink (*esp* of liquor) *18-e19, only Sc*. **4** a purging of the bowels *19-, now Ork Abd Per*. **~in clout** a rough cloth for washing floors etc *20-*. **~-oot** the scattering of coins at a wedding for children to scramble for *la20-, Ags Fif*.
scourge &c [skʌrdʒ] *n* **1** = scourge *la14-*. **2** the whip of a spinning top *la19-, now Lnk*. **3** a brawling domineering woman *la19-, now SW*. *vt* **1** = scourge *16-*. **2** exhaust the fertility of (land) *la18-19, only Sc*.
scourie &c ['skurɪ, 'skʌurɪ] *adj* **1** *of persons* scruffy, disreputable, broken down (in appearance) *16-, now Stlg Ayr*. **2** *of clothes* shabby, worn *la18-19*. *n* a scruffy, disreputable-looking person, a rascal *18-e19*. [only Sc; perh f SCOUR[3]]
scoury *see* SCURRY
scout[1] &c; **scoot** [skut; *Fif Uls* skʌut] *v* **1** *vt* cause (water etc) to spout or spurt out, squirt *19-*. **2** *vi*, *of liquid* spurt or squirt out *19-*. *n* **1** a sudden gush or flow of water from a spout etc; the pipe from which it comes *19-, now NE, C*. **2** (1) a squirt, syringe, *esp* one used as a water gun *19-, now Per Loth*. (2) a peashooter, *esp* one made from a plant stem *la19-, now Fif wLoth Ayr*. **3** diarrhoea, *esp* of birds or animals *la19-, now local Cai-Slk*. **4** contemptuous term for a person *19-, now local Abd-Kcb*.

scooter 1 a squirt, syringe *la19-, now NE, C Rox.* **2** = *n* 2 (2), *20-, N-S.* ~**ie** worthless in character, scruffy; small, insignificant *la19-, now Per WC.*

~ **gun** = *n* 2 (1), *19-, now Per Loth.* [only Sc; see SND]

scout² &c; scoot *la19* [skut] *n* one of various seabirds, *eg* the razorbill, the guillemot *la16-e20.* [perh f scout¹]

scouth *see* scowth

scouther *see* scowder

scove &c [*skov, *?skuv] *vi, of a bird* fly smoothly, glide *la18-19.* [perh altered f skiff¹ or scuff¹]

scow¹ &c [skʌu] *n* a flat-bottomed boat, *eg* a lighter, barge *19-, now local Cai-Kcb.* [also US; Du *schouw*]

scow² &c [skʌu] *n, chf in pl* **1** barrel staves, thin planks *la15-, now Sh.* **2** splinters, slivers of wood; fragments, shattered pieces *19-, now Ork Cai.*

ding tae ~**s** smash to atoms *19-e20.* [only Sc; Du *schooven, pl* of *schoof* a sheaf of corn, a bundle of staves]

scow³ *la19-e20,* **scrow** *19-, now NE Ags Per* [sk(r)ʌu] *n* a sudden, heavy, squally shower of rain. [unknown]

scowder &c; scouther &c *la17-,* **skolder** *e16* ['skʌudər, -ðər; *Sh Ork* 'skuðər, 'skʌ-] *v* **1** *vt* burn, scorch, singe; over-toast (bread etc) *16-.* **2** *of frost or rain* wither, blight (foliage etc) *la19-, now local Per-Slk.* **3** *vi* become scorched, burn *19-, local Sh-Gall.* **4** rain or snow slightly *la19-, now Ork.*

n **1** a scorch, singe, burn; the mark made by such *la18-.* **2** a jellyfish (because of its burning sting) *19-, now Arg.* **3** a slight shower (of rain) *19-, now local Ork-Ayr.*

scoutherin *adj* reproving (severely), blistering (with rebuke) *19.* **scoudrum** chastisement *19-, Bnf Abd.* ~**y** beginning or threatening to rain or snow *19-, now Lnk.* [only Sc; see SND]

scowf *see* scowth

scowk *see* scouk

scowner *see* scunner

scowp¹ &c, scoup &c [*skʌup; *Sh Gsw* *skup] *vi* bound, dart, skip, run hither and thither *la16-19.*

~**er** a dancer *la16, only Sc.* [chf Sc; ME *scoupe, scope,* perh f ON *skopa skeið* take a run]

scowp² &c [skʌup; *Sh* skup] *n* = scope *la18-, now chf N.*

scowth &c *18-,* **scouth &c; scowf &c** *20-, local* [skʌuθ; *local* skʌuf; *Cai* skʌu; *local* skuθ, skuf] *n* **1** *lit and fig* freedom of movement, (elbow) room, scope *la16-, now local Ork-Wgt.* **2** scope, chance to improve or prosper *20-, now local Cai-Wgt.* **3** abundance, plenty *e19.*

~**ie** capacious, bulky, big *la19-, NE.*

~ **and rowth &c** freedom, room to range; plenty, abundance *19-e20.* [only Sc; see SND]

scraap *see* scrape

scrab¹ &c *16-,* **scribe &c** *19-, local WC n* **1** the crab-apple *16-, now Fif Loth Dnbt Ayr.* **2** *only* **scrab** a shrivelled or stunted person or thing, *esp* a tree or plant *la18-, now Bnf.* [nME; *cf* Sw dial *skrabba* a shrivelled apple, Norw dial *skrabb* a shrunken or feeble little creature]

scrab² [skrab, skrɑb] *vt* scratch, scrape *la19-20.* [Gael *sgrab,* Eng dial *scrab,* Du *schrabben,* cognate w Eng *scrape*]

scrae &c *n* **1** a stunted, shrivelled, or under-developed person or animal *19-, now NE.* **2** a shrivelled dried-up object, *esp* one overexposed to heat *18-, now Cai.* **3** an ill-natured person; a miser *la19-, now Cai.* [only Sc; ON *skrá* a piece of dried skin or parchment]

scraffle &c ['skrafl, 'skravl] *vi* scramble, claw about with the hands *19-, now Sh Ork Cai.* [only Sc; see SND]

scrag *see* scrog

scraible *n* something to one's own advantage got by roundabout means, a 'wangle' *la20-, local C.* [var with extended meaning of Eng *scrabble*]

scraich *see* skreek

scrammle &c *vti, n* = scramble *19-.*

scran &c *n* **1** food *19-, now local Ork-SW.* **2** scraps or leavings of food, *freq* those acquired by begging *19-, now NE.* **3** any refuse or rubbish which may be picked up by a beggar or scrounger *20-, now Abd Stlg Ayr.* **4** odd fish, *eg* mackerel among herring, claimed by the crew of a boat *la20-, NE.* **5** the picking up of discarded odds and ends, **the** scrounge *20-, local.*

v **1** *vt* scrounge about for (food etc); scrape together frugally *19-.* **2** *vi* poke about in or scrounge from dustbins *e20, Abd.* **3** *vt* take (the odd fish found in a catch) as a perquisite *la19-, Bnf Fif.*

~ **bag** etc a bag in which a beggar collected scraps of food etc *19-, now Sh Abd WC, latterly hist.* [obscure]

scranch &c [skran(t)ʃ] *vt* crush with a grating noise, crunch *la18-20.* [appar Du, Flem *schran(t)sen* (grind with the teeth, crush; perh conflated w Eng *crunch*]

scrape *vti, also* **scrap &c** *la18-,* **scraup &c** *la19,* **scraap &c** *la20-, Abd* = scrape *16-.*

n **1** = scrape. **2** *chf* **a** ~ **of the pen** a mark made by a pen; a hasty scribble or letter *la17-, only Sc.* **3** the shallow first furrow made in commencing a rig¹ *20-, WC Kcb.*

scrapie a sheep disease causing constant itch *20.*

scrat¹ &c *vti* **1** scratch, claw; make a scratching noise *la14, 19-, now NE-WC.* **2** ~ **aff** mark out with shallow furrows the rigs¹ to be ploughed in (a field) *la20-, Ork NE Ags.*

n **1** a scratch, slight wound; the noise made by scratching *19-, now Ork nNE.* **2** the shallow first furrow made in commencing a rig¹ *la20-, Ork NE.* [ME; obscure; *cf* scart¹]

scrat² &c *n* **1** = scrat, a hermaphrodite *la16*. **2** a puny or stunted person or animal *19-*, now *NE Ags*. [*cf* SCART²]

scratch *n* (*la16-*), *vti* = scratch.

~**er** ['skratʃər] **1** *slang* a bed *20-* [appar *orig* a public lodging-house term]. **2** a trawler which fishes as close as possible to the three-mile limit *la20-*, *NE*.

scrath *see* SCARF

scrauchle &c ['skrɑxl, ?'skraxl] *vi* scramble with hands and feet, clamber hastily and clumsily *la19-*, *local Stlg-Slk*. [only Sc; var of SCRAFFLE, perh w infl f SPRAUCHLE]

scraup *see* SCRAPE

scraw &c *n* a thin turf or sod, *esp* as used for roofing *la18-20*. [ScGael *sgrath*, IrGael *scraith*]

scree¹ &c *n* a mass of loose stones on a steep hillside *19-*. [ultimately f ON *skríða* a landslide]

scree² &c *n* **1** a riddle or sieve, *esp* box-shaped, for sifting grain, sand, coal etc *19-*, *local Per-Ayr*. **2** an arrangement of parallel bars for riddling coal at a pit-head *la19-e20*.

vt riddle, sift (coal etc) *20-*, now *Fif Loth Lnk*. [appar reduced f Eng *screen*]

screebie *see* SCRUBIE

screechan *see* SCREICH

screed &c [skrid; *S* *skridʒ] *n* **1** a long narrow strip: (1) of cloth, twine, paper etc; a torn piece, shred *16*, *19-*, now *local Inv-Ayr*; (2) of land *la19-*, *chf NE SW*; (3) *fig* a piece, a detached portion (of time etc) *19-20*. **2** *freq disparaging* a long discourse or piece of writing (*freq* one which can be recited) *la18-*. **3** a tear, gash, slash; a scratch *18-*, now *Fif*, only *Sc*. **4** the sound of tearing etc; a grating, scraping noise; *joc* a tune on the fiddle *la18-*, now *Ayr Uls*, only *Sc*. **5** a bout of drinking, a few days *on the bash* (BASH) *19-e20*.

v **1** *vt* tear, rip *la18-*, now *local Per-Wgt*. **2** *vi* tear, come apart *19-e20*. **3** *vti* make a shrill or screeching noise; play (a tune) on a fiddle or bagpipe *18-19*, only *Sc*. **4** (1) *freq* ~ **aff** read volubly, recite fluently, reel off *la18-*, now *Sh EC Wgt*. (2) *freq* ~ **away, doun** *etc* compose (a piece of writing) rapidly and lengthily; write rapidly *19-20*. [var of Eng *shred*, OE *scrēade* a strip, *scrēadian* cut]

screef *see* SCRUIF

screel *vi* scream, screech *la19-*. [*cf* SKIRL¹]

screen *n* **1** = screen. **2** a shawl, headscarf *18-19*.

vt = screen.

~**er** *linen trade* a person who examines cloth for flaws and faults *20-*, *Per Fif*.

screenge¹ &c; **scringe** &c *19-e20* [skrin(d)ʒ, skrindʒ] *v* **1** *vt* rub or scour energetically *19-e20*. **2** whip, flog *la18-*, now *Bnf Abd*. **3** *vti* search eagerly or inquisitively; *specif* fish the sea bottom inshore with a small net *19-*, now *nEC local WC*. **4** *vi* prowl about, wander about aimlessly *la19-*, *NE*.

n **1** a rubbing, scrubbing, scouring *la19*, *Bnf Ags*. **2** a lash of a whip etc, a beating *19-20*.

screenger 1 a person who hunts about to pick up or find things *la19-20*. **2** a person who fishes with a *screenge* net, *la19-*, now *Fif*.

~ **net** a small seine net used as in *v* 3, *la19-*, now *Arg Ayr*. [reduced f *scrimmage* (SCRIM¹)]

screenge² &c *vti* shrink, contract *20*, *Gall Rox*. [Eng *cringe* w prothetic *s-*]

screeve &c *v* **1** *vt* graze (the skin), peel or tear off (a surface etc), scratch, scrape *19-*, now *nEC Lnk S*. **2** *vti* make a scraping motion or sound; draw an object over another with a screeching noise, *esp* a bow over fiddle strings *19-*, now *Ags*.

n **1** a large scratch *19-*, now *local Kcdn-Rox*. **2** a scraping or grating sound *20-*, now *Ags Ayr*.

screever a *dropped scone* (SCONE) cooked on a GIRDLE *la20-*, *Pbls Lnk Ayr*. **screevie** a slate pencil *la20-*, *local Fif-Dmf*. [see SND]

screich &c [skrix] *n*, *slang* WHISKY *19*.

screechan &c ['skrixən] = *n*, *20-*, *Sh*. [perh joc extension of SKREICH]

screw¹ &c [skru] *n* = shrew, the animal *19-*, now *local Ags-SW*. [northern form; OE *scrēawe*]

screw² *19-e20*; **scrow** *la17-e19* [skru] *n* a freshwater shrimp etc. [perh extension of Eng *screw*]

screw *see* SCROO

scrib *see* SCRIBE

scribble &c ['skrɪbl, *'skrʌbl] *vt* card or tease (wool) mechanically *la17-*.

scribbler a person who cards wool *la17-18*. [LowGer *schrubbeln* &c]

scribe &c *n*, also **scrib** *la16-e18* a mark made with a pen; a piece of writing, letter *la16-*, now *Sh*.

vti [*skrɪb] write *19-e20*. [see SND]

scribe *see* SCRAB¹

scriddan &c *n* a mountain stream, torrent; rocks and gravel brought down by such *la19-e20*. [Gael *sgriodan*]

scrieve¹ &c *v* **1** *vi* move, glide along, speed on smoothly *la18-*, now *local NE-SW*. **2** work vigorously *19-*, now *Ork*. **3** *vti* talk fluently and at some length; reel **off** (a long story) *19-*, now *Sh*.

n a long animated story or chat; a harangue *19-*, now *Sh*. [only Sc; perh ON *skrefa* (*v*) stride, w infl f SCREEVE]

scrieve² &c *la18-*; **scrive** *16-19* *vti* **1** write, *esp* easily and copiously *16-*, now *local Sh-Edb*. **2** scratch or incise a mark on (wood), *eg* to show the shape in which something is to be made *la19-*, now *Ayr*.

n **1** a piece of writing, a letter or its contents *19-*, now *local Sh-Lnk*. **2** *thieves' slang* a banknote, *esp* a pound note; a pound (*la18-e19*.

scriever &c *esp derog* a writer, scribbler *19-e20*. [see SND]

scriff, scriffin *see* SCRUIF

scrift &c *n* a long account, a long passage of prose or verse recited or read *la18-*, now *Kcdn Ags*.

vti recite, declaim, reel **off** *la18-e20*. [see SND]

scrim[1] **&c, skrim &c** *v* **1** *vi* = skirmish *la14-e16*. **2** dart, rush *la15-e16*. **3** *vt* beat, strike vigorously *la18-19*.

scrimmage &c *vi* = *v* 3, *la19*. *n* = skirmish *la15*. [only Sc; see SND]

scrim[2] *n* a kind of thin coarse linen or canvas, made in narrow widths *la18-*.

vt, plastering fill (a crevice, joint etc) with SCRIM[2] *la20-*. [perh reduced f *scrimp-claith*, from its narrow width and loose texture]

scrimmage *see* SCRIM[1]

scrimp &c *adj* **1** scant, in short supply *la17-*. **2** *of clothes* short, constricted *18-*, now local *Sh-nEC*. **3** *of numbers* limited, bare *18*. **4** *of persons* having a scanty supply, in want *la18-*, now *Sh NE Ags*. **5** parsimonious, ungenerous, sparing *18-*.

adv scarcely, almost but not quite; parsimoniously *la18-*.

v **1** *vt* restrict in supplies, stint *18-*. **2** restrict or cut down in amount; use or consume frugally or meanly *la18-*. **3** *vi* economize, be parsimonious *20-*.

~**it &c** scanty; restricted; undersized; mean *18-*. ~**ness** scantiness, deficiency, *esp* in wits *la20-*. ~**y** *adj* scanty, inadequate *20-*. *n* a scanty measure *la19-*. [see SND]

scrimple &c *vt* shrivel with heat; crumple, crinkle *16*. [only Sc; *cf* SCRUMPLE, Ger *schrumpeln* &c and Eng *crumple*]

scringe *see* SCREENGE[1]

scrip &c *vti* mock, jeer, scoff (at) *la15-18*.

n a scornful grimace *la15*. [only Sc; see SND]

scripter &c, scripture ['skrɪptər] *n* = scripture, *esp* Holy Writ *la16-*.

scriptured warranted by Holy Scripture *e17*, only *Sc*.

scriptor &c *n* a writer, scribe *e16, e19*. [only Sc; L]

scripture *see* SCRIPTER

scrive *see* SCRIEVE[2]

scroban *n* the crop of a fowl; the human gullet or chest *la19-*, *Cai-Inv Per Arg Bute*. [only Sc; Gael *sgròban*]

scroch &c [skrɔtʃ] *vt, esp of sun or wind* = scorch *18-e20*. [metath]

scrochat &c; scorchet &c [*'skrɔtʃət, *'skɔrtʃət] *n* a kind of sweetmeat *15-e17*. [only Sc; obscure]

scrocken &c, skurken ['skrokən, 'skroxən; 'skrʌkən; *Sh* 'skʌrkən] *vti* dry out (*esp* PEATS[1]), shrink or shrivel up with heat or drought *la17, la19-*, *chf Sh NE*.

scrockle &c ['skrokl] = *v*, *20*. [only Sc; *cf* Norw dial *skrokken* (*ptp*) shrivelled, cognate w Eng *shrunken*; *cf* SKRINK]

scrog &c, scrag *la19-*; **scrug &c** *la18-20*, **skroug &c** *la20*, *Cai* [skrog, skrag; *Cai* skrʌug] *n* **1** a stunted or crooked bush or tree; *in pl* brushwood or undergrowth *16-*, now local *N-Uls*. **2** a gnarled or crooked stump etc of a

tree *19-*, now *Ork NE Ags*. **3** the crab-apple (tree) *la19-*, now *sEC, S*. **4** a dried-up or shrivelled thing; a lean scraggy animal or person *20-*, now *Cai*.

scroggie &c **1** full of SCROGS, covered with undergrowth *16-*, now *N, EC, SW*. **2** *of a tree* stunted or crooked *18-*, now *N, EC, SW*. [see SND]

scrog *see* SCRUG

scroll *n* **1** = scroll. **2** a rough draft or copy; a writing-pad etc for rough drafts or notes *la17-*, now *Ork NE Ags*, only *Sc*.

vt **1** = scroll, write in a scroll *e17*. **2** make a copy of (a document) *18-19*, only *Sc*.

~-**book &c** **1** a book in which drafts or copies of documents are written *la17-19*, only *Sc*. **2** a school rough notebook *la20-*, *Edb*. [*cf* SCROW]

scronach &c ['skronəx] *n* a shrill cry, outcry, loud lamentation *la18-*, now *NE*.

vi **1** shriek, yell, cry out *19-*, now *Bnf Abd Kcdn*. **2** make a great outcry or fuss, grouse *la19-*, now *Bnf*. [only Sc; emphat var of *cronach* (CORONACH)]

scroo &c *la19-*; **screw** *18-*, **scrow** *17-18* [skru] *n* a stack of corn, hay etc, or of corn sheaves *17-*, *Sh Ork N*.

vt build (corn etc) into stacks *17-*, now *Sh Ork*. [only Sc; Norw dial *skruv*, ON *skrúf* a stack of corn etc]

scroosh &c [*skruʃ] *n, freq disparaging* a large number of people, *esp* children, a worthless lot *e20*. [only Sc; see SND]

scrow &c [skrʌu] *n* **1** = scroll *la16*. **2** *in pl* writings *la15-e17*. **3** *in pl* long strips or thin scraps of hides or skins, used for making glue *la18-19*. **4** a long list of people; a crowd, mob *19*.

~ **buik** = *scroll-book* 1 (SCROLL) *la16*.

clerk of the scrow = *Clerk Register* (REGISTER) *la16*, only *Sc*. [var of SCROLL]

scrow *see* SCOW[3], SCREW[2], SCROO

scrub &c *vt* **1** = scrub. **2** beat down in bargaining, treat meanly *19*.

n **1** a pot-scrubber *19-*, now *Mry Fif Lnk*. **2** a mean avaricious person, a hard bargainer *la18-e20*.

scrubber a pot-scrubber, *esp* one made of a bunch of heather twigs *19-e20*. **scrubby** sordid, mean, niggardly *la19-*, now *Bnf Abd Loth*.

scrubie &c *17-e19*, **screebie &c** *la19-20*, *NE* [*'skrøbi, *NE* *'skribɪ] *n* = scurvy.

scruff *see* SCRUIF

scrug &c *19-*; **scrog &c** *18-* [skrʌg, ?skrog] *vt* tug (one's cap) forward over one's brow so as to give one a jaunty or bold air *18-*, now *Ags*. [only Sc; see SND]

scrug *see* SCROG

scruif &c, scruff &c *la17-*; **scriff &c** *19-e20*, **screef &c** *19-*, *NE* [skrøf, skrɪf; *NE* skrif] *n* **1** = scruff, scurf *la16-*, now *Sh C, S*. **2** a hardened scab, piece of encrusted skin, hair, dirt etc *la18-*, now *Ork C*. **3** the skin, epidermis *18-19*.

4 a thin surface layer, a film, crust etc *la16-*, now *Sh Ork N*.   **5** the layer of vegetation on the surface of the ground *la17-*, now *Sh Cai Abd*.   **6** the surface of water or the sea *19-*, now *NE*.   **7** *chf* **scruff** a worthless person or persons, riffraff *20-*, *C*.

vt **1** *chf* ~ **over** cover with a thin crust or layer; *fig* gloss over, treat superficially *17-*, now *Sh*.   **2** (1) scrape (off) the surface of, graze, skin *la16*, *19-20*.   (2) loosen topsoil or skim off weeds etc from *19-*, now *Sh Bnf Abd*.

scruiffin &c 1 a thin paring or scraping, *eg* of butter or cheese *la20-*, *Stlg Fif Lnk*.   **2** *chf* **scriffin &c** a thin crust or covering; the face of the earth *19-e20*.   **scruiffy** filthy, caked with dirt *19-*, now *Ayr*.

scrump¹ &c *n* something crisp and hard; a crust, hard surface layer *la19-*, now *Bnf*.
~**ie &c** baked hard and crisp *19-*, now *Bnf Abd*. [see SND]

scrump² &c *vt* crunch, munch, chew (something hard and crisp) *la19-*, *Bnf Abd Kcdn*. [var of CRUMP, w infl f SCRUMP¹]

scrumple &c *n* a wrinkle, crease *e16*, *only Sc*.   *vt* crush, wrinkle *la16*.   [var of Eng *crumple*]

scrunt¹ &c *n* **1** something shrunken or worn down by use, age etc, *eg* a stump of a tree, pen etc *e16*, *19-*, now *NE*, *C*.   **2** a person shrunken or withered by age, illness etc, a thin scraggy person; a poorly-developed unthriving animal or plant *19-*, now *NE*, *C*.   **3** a mean miserly person *19-*, *local Bnf-S*.
~**it &c** shrivelled, shrunken, stunted in growth *19-*, now *local Bnf-SW*.   ~**y 1** stunted, shrivelled, stumpy, wizened *19-*, now *SW*, *S Uls*.   **2** mean, niggardly *19-*, *local Bnf-S*. [only Sc; see SND]

scrunt² &c *v* **1** *vt* scrape, scrub, scratch, grind *19-*, now *Ags*.   **2** plane (a board) roughly to remove a thick shaving; rough down (pointing) with a handpick *la20-*, *local Abd-Lnk*.   **3** *vti* produce a harsh sound by scraping *la18-19*.
n **1** the act of planing roughly; a thick or rough shaving of wood *la19-*, now *Abd Lnk*.   **2** a harsh grating sound made by scraping on wood etc *19-e20*. [only Sc; prob onomat, w infl f SCRUNT¹]

scry &c *n* **1** = scry, a cry, yell, clamour *15-e16*.   **2** a public proclamation, *esp* one made by a crier after church *la18-20*, *NE*.
vt proclaim, make known by public proclamation *18-19*, *N*.

scud &c *v* **1** *vi* = scud.   **2** *vt* pass, sail quickly over *e17*.   **3** *vti* throw (a flat stone) so as to make it skip over the water, play ducks and drakes *la19-*, now *local Ork-Ayr*.   **4** *vt* beat with the open hand or a strap, smack, spank *19-*.
n **1** = scud.   **2** a blow, smack with the open hand, a stroke with the *tawse* (TAW) or cane *19-*.   **3** a turn at doing something, a SHOT¹ *20-*, now *Inv*.   **4** *in pl* brisk or foaming ale; beer with a head *18-e20*.

scudder *n* a driving shower of rain or snow *20-*, *Bnf Abd*.   *vi*, *of wind etc* sweep along in rainy gusts *la19-*, now *Bnf Abd*.   **scuddie** a game like SHINTY or hockey; the club or the ball used in it *la19-e20*.   **scuddrie** *adj* with cold driving showers *la19-*, now *Bnf Abd*. [see SND]

scud *see* SCUDDIE

scuddie &c *adj* **1** naked, without clothes, or with one garment only *19-*, now *C*, *S*.   **2** mean, scruffy, shabby-looking, in want or straitened circumstances *la19-e20*.   **3** stingy, penurious; insufficient, too small *la19-*, *Bnf Abd*.
n **1** the bare skin, a state of nudity *la19-*, now *Abd Kcdn Per WC*.   **2** *also* **scud** *la20-*, *local WC* a nestling, a young unfledged bird *la19-*, now *Lnk*.
bare scud = *n* 1, *la20-*, *C*. [only Sc; see SND]

scuddie *see* SCUD

scuddle¹ &c *v* **1** *vt* wash (dishes) *la16*.   **2** *vi* work in a slatternly way, mess about at domestic work *la19-*, now *NE Per*.   **3** *vt* soil (one's clothes), make shabby or shapeless by rough usage *19-*, now *Abd Ags*.
scuddlin claes one's second-best clothes *20-*, *local Ork-Per*. [only Sc; back-formation f SCUDDLER]

scuddle² *vi*, *of persons or animals*, *esp dogs* scurry, roam about aimlessly, often with the intention of keeping out of sight; dodge, shirk work *la19-*, now *Cai*. [perh Eng dial *scuddle* run away]

scuddler &c *la16*, *e20*, **scudler** *la15-e18* *n* a scullion, kitchen-boy; *latterly* a maid-of-all-work. [only Sc; prob OF *escudeler*, escuelier, f L *scutella* a dish, pan]

scuddrie *see* SCUD

scudge *see* SCODGE

scudler *see* SCUDDLER

scuff¹ &c *v* **1** *vt*, *only* **skoof** slur over *la16*.   **2** ? evade, shirk (duty) *la16*, *only Sc*.   **3** touch lightly in passing, draw one's hand etc quickly over; brush off or away *18-*.   **4** hit, strike with a glancing blow *19-20*.   **5** *vti* shuffle with the feet, draw the feet over (the ground etc) lightly but noisily, scuffle *la18-*.   **6** *vt* wear away (clothes) with hard usage, make worn and shabby; tarnish *19-*.
n **1** a jibe *la16*.   **2** a glancing or brushing stroke of the hand, a slight touch in passing, a hasty wipe *19-*.   **3** a slight passing shower of rain *19-*, now *NE Loth SW*.   **4** riff-raff, the scum of the population *19-*, now *local Per-WC*.   *adv* with a whizzing or scuffling noise; grazing as it passes *la19-*, now *Abd Ags*.
~**in** *of clothes* second-best *la19-*, *local Fif-Dmf*.   ~**le** graze, rub slightly; wear away; tarnish *la19-*, now *Abd Ags*.   ~**y &c 1** *lit and fig* shabby, worn, tarnished, mean-looking *la19-*, now *NE-S*.   **2** niggardly *20-*, *NE*. [see SND]

scuff² &c *n* = scoff, mockery *16-e17*. [only Sc. OED *scoff* (*n²*)]

scuffin *see* SCUFF¹

scuffle *n* a bakers' swab for cleaning out ovens *la19-, now Kcdn Rox.* [var of obs Eng *scovel*]

scuffle *see* SCUFF[1]

scug &c *16-;* **scoug** &c, **scog** &c *16-20* [skʌg; skug; skog; *Cai* skʌug] *vt* **1** conceal, screen, hide *e16, la18-, now nEC.* **2** shelter, shield, protect *19-e20.* **3** *vir* (1) take shelter or refuge *la18-, now local Sh-Fif.* (2) hide, skulk *19-, now NE.* **4** *vt* take shelter from, avoid, evade (bad weather etc) *19-, now Sh Cai Per Fif.*
n **1** shadow *e16.* **2** *also fig* the shade, shelter, protection (of a rock etc) *la16-, now local Sh-Fif.* **3** a pretence, pretext, hypocritical excuse *la15-, now local Sh-Kcdn.*
~**ry** concealment, secrecy *la16.* ~**y** shady; sheltering *16-18, only Sc.* [ON *skugge* shadow]

scuif &c [skøf, skɪf] *n* a scoop, small hand-shovel, as used by grocers, seedmen etc *20-, Loth Rox.* [altered f SCUIP, perh w infl f SCUFF[1] and SKIFF[1]]

scuill *see* SCULE

scuip *19-,* **scoup** &c *e16, 19,* **scoop** *19-;* **scupe** &c *e16, 19,* **skip** &c *19-* [skøp, skɪp; *local nEC* skep; **skup, *skʌup; NE *skip] n* **1** = scoop *16-.* **2** a kind of (flat) hat or bonnet with a protruding brim *19-e20.* **3** *chf* **skip** the front brim of a hat, the peak of a cap *20-, now local Fif-Gall.*
skippit &c **bonnet** &c a cloth cap with a peak *19-, now local Fif-Gall.*
scoup &c **aff** *or* **up** drink or toss off (liquor) *19.*

scuit &c [skøt] *n* a shallow, wooden, scoop-shaped drinking cup, *freq* ~**ifu** the full contents of this *19-, now Slk.* [var of SCUIP]

sculduddery &c [skʌl'dʌdərɪ] *n* **1** *literary or joc* fornication, unchastity *18-.* **2** obscenity, indecency, *esp* in language *19-e20.* [orig Sc; obscure; in US *la19* as *skulduggery* misappropriation of funds]

scule &c *19-e20;* **scuill** *la16* [*skøl] *n* = school (of fish). [OED *school* (*n*[2])]

scule *see* SCHULE

scull[1] &c *17-,* **skull** &c; **skill** *e16,* **scoo** &c *19-, local Ork-Bnf* [skʌl; *N also* sku, skʌu] *n* **1** a shallow container *e16* [translating L *cymbium* and *cratera*]. **2** (1) a shallow, scoop-shaped basket for carrying PEATS[1], potatoes, grain etc *16-, now local NE-Kcb.* (2) *fishing* a similar-shaped basket for holding fish or baited lines *16-, now NE.*
scullgab a cloud-formation thought to resemble a SCULL, indicating wind direction *la19-e20, Bnf Abd.* [northern eModEng; see SND]

scull[2] *n, vti* = scull, oar, row.
~**row** a notch in the stern of a boat used as a kind of rowlock when the boat is propelled by a single oar *19-, now WC.*

scult &c *vt* **1** strike with the palm of the hand, slap, smack *18-, now Ags.* **2** strike on (the palm), cane, *tawse* (TAW[1]) *19-e20.*

n a blow with the flat of the hand, a slap, stroke of the cane or *tawse* (TAW[1]) on the hand *18-.* [only Sc; onomat; *cf* SCUD and SKELP[1]]

scum &c *n* **1** = scum *17-.* **2** a thin coating of ice *20-, Cai Kcb.* **3** a worthless disreputable person *18-, now local Sh-Ayr* [*cf* Eng collective usage].
v **1** *only Sc* (1) *vt* pass lightly over *e16.* (2) *vi* ? skim the air *16.* **2** *vti* skim, remove scum (from) *19-, Gen except Sh Ork.* **3** *vt* catch with a small round net on a long pole (any herring fallen back into the sea as the nets are hauled aboard) *la19-, N.* **4** strike with the hand across (the cheek), slap (someone's face) *18-e19.*
adj skimmed, *esp* ~ **milk** *19-, Gen except Sh Ork.*
scummer &c **1** = scummer (of the sea), a pirate *la14.* **2** a ladle or shallow dish for skimming *18-, now N, EC.* **3** a young crew member who SCUMS (*v* 3) *la19-, N.* **scum(ming) net** a scoop-net for catching salmon in rivers or herring dropped from nets *la18-20.*

scuncheon &c *n, masonry* the inner edge of a window or door jamb; the open finished end of a wall *17-.* [laME *sconcheon* &c]

scunder *see* SCUNNER

scunfis *see* SCOMFISH

scunge &c; **squeenge** &c *20-, NE* [skʌndʒ; *NE* skwindʒ; *Per also *skundʒ] vi* **1** *of dogs or persons* prowl or slink about (in search of something), sponge, scrounge *19-, local Sh-SW.* **2** rummage about, as in a drawer or cupboard *e20, NE.*
n a person who SCUNGES *20-, now local Loth-SW.*
scunger &c a prowler, moocher *la20-, NE.* [perh altered f Eng *scrounge* w infl f SCONCE[2]]

scunner &c; **sconner** &c *15-19,* **scowner** &c *la14-e15.* **scunder** &c *la20-, Ross Uls* ['skʌnər; *Ross Uls* 'skʌndər] *v* **1** *vi* shrink back, flinch; hesitate *la14, 19-e20.* **2** get a feeling of aversion, disgust or loathing, feel nauseated or surfeited *15-.* **3** *freq* ~ **at** feel disgust for, be sickened by, be bored or repelled by *18-20.* **4** *vt* (1) cause a feeling of repulsion, aversion or loathing in (a person), nauseate, surfeit *19-.* (2) *fig* make bored, uninterested or antipathetic, *freq* ~**ed, scunnert** disgusted, bored,'fed up' *19-.*
n **1** (1) a feeling of disgust, loathing, nausea or surfeit; *fig* repugnance, distaste, dislike, loss of interest or enthusiasm, *freq* **tak a** ~ (**at** *or* **against**) *16-.* (2) a shudder indicating physical or moral repugnance; a sudden shock *la19-e20.* **2** (1) a thing or action which causes loathing, aversion or disgust, a nuisance *19-.* (2) a person who causes disgust or dislike, a troublesome or objectionable person *la18-.*
~**ation** &c an object of dislike or disgust, an offensive sight *la19-, local Sh-Kcb.* ~**fu** *la19-, NE-S,* ~**some** *la19-, Gen except Sh Ork* disgusting, nauseating, objectionable. [uncertain; see SND]

scupe *see* SCUIP

scur[1] &c *n* **1** a scab or cicatrix which forms over a healing sore or wound *19-, now Abd*. **2** a rudimentary, loosely-attached horn in polled or hornless cattle *19-, now SW*. **3** a despicable person, rascal, 'scab' *19*. **4** a *sheriff officer* (SHERIFF) or his assistant *19*.
vi, of a wound or sore form a scab, crust over in healing *la19-, Bnf Abd*. [perh var of Eng *scurf*]

scur[2] *n* the mayfly immediately after its larva stage, *freq* used as angler's bait *la19-20, chf Ayr*. [see SND]

scurdie &c *n* a kind of *whinstone* (WHIN[1]) or basalt, *specif* that intrusive into old red sandstone *la18-, now Ags*. [only Sc; prob from *Scurdy Ness* near Montrose, Ags, which is formed of such rock]

scurl *n* = SCUR[1] *n* 1, *19-, now NE Ags Per Rox*. [dim]

scurr[1] &c *vi* slither, slide, skate, skid *20-, now Bnf Abd*. [var of SKIRR, perh w infl f SCOUR[3]]

scurr[2] &c *n* a buffoon, jester *la16*. [only Sc; L *scurra* a buffoon]

scurry &c ['skʌrɪ, 'skurɪ; *NE also* 'skwɪrɪ] *vi* **1** = scurry. **2** *also* **scoury** &c *20-, NE,* **squeerie** &c *la19-, Bnf Abd* roam about, wander idly, prowl about a district like a dog on the hunt *19-, now NE*.

scurryvaig &c [skʌrɪ'veg] *n* a vagabond; an idle, unkempt, or slatternly person; a lout; a scullion *e16, 19-e20*.
vti range or roam about or aimlessly (over); live in idleness and dissipation *19-e20*. [only Sc; see SND]

scush &c [skʌʃ; *Cai* skuʃ] *vi* shuffle, walk with a shambling gait *20-, now NE*.
n a shuffling, scuffling with the feet; the noise of this *19-, now NE*.
~le &c ['skʌʃl; *Cai* 'skuʃl] *v* = *vi, 19-, now NE*.
n an old worn-down shoe *19-, now Bnf*. [onomat, perh w infl f SCASH]

scutarde *n, contemptuous* ? a person who defecates *e16*. [only Sc; perh f SCOUT[1], or var of SKITTER[1]]

scutch[1] &c *vt* **1** dress (*esp* flax) by beating *la16-e20*. **2** strike off (the ears of corn) from the stalk with a stick *la18-e19*.
n the stick used for *scutching* flax, a swingle; the corresponding part in a machine *la18-19*.
~er = *n, la18-e20*. [see SND]

scutch[2] &c *v* **1** *vt* skim or graze the surface of one object with another, flick, SCUFF[1], sweep, hoe etc, *esp* rather perfunctorily *la19-, Cai Bnf*. **2** *vi* (1) walk quickly with a light scuffling step *la19-, now Cai*. (2) slide on ice, skate, sledge *20-, now Bnf*.
n the act of *scutching* (*v* 1), a grazing or scuffling movement or sound, a swift light motion over a surface, *eg* in sweeping *la19-, now Cai*.

scutch[3] &c *vt* **1** cut or shear with a hook or knife, slash, trim (a hedge) *la19-, now Loth WC,*

SW. **2** (1) *masonry* dress (a stone) roughly with a pick *19-e20*. (2) *mining* make a vertical cut in a coal face with a pick *la19-, now Fif*.
n a slash, a cutting of twigs, thistles etc, the trimming of a hedge *la19-, now SW*. [only Sc; appar var of Eng *scotch* cut, gash]

scutch[4] &c *n* = scotch, a wedge put under a wheel to prevent it slipping *la20-, now EC, WC*.

scutter &c *vti* **1** do something in a slovenly or bungling way, make a mess (of), spill or splash about *19-, now Sh-Per*. **2** *vi* be engaged in time-wasting, pointless work, fiddle about aimlessly or confusedly, dawdle *la19-, now N Per*. **3** *vt* hinder with something unimportant, detain through some needless or annoying cause *la19-, NE Ags Per*.
n **1** the doing of work awkwardly or dirtily, a botch, bungle; a footling, time-consuming, and irritating occupation *la19-, Sh Ork N nEC*. **2** a person who works in an ineffective, muddled, or dirty way *la19-, N Per*.
scutterie troublesome; *of a job* time-wasting, muddling, footling *la19-, NE*. [see SND]

scuttle &c *vt* serve on a plate, dish up (food); pour (liquid) from one container to another, spill in so doing *e19*.
n refuse water, dishwater, *chf* ~ *or* **scutter hole** a hole in the ground into which this is poured, a sewage pit, drain *16-e20*. [ME *scutel* a dish etc]

scythe &c *n* [səið, səið; *St* saıθ] **1** = scythe *17-*. **2** a scytheman *20-, NE*.
vt [səiθ; *St* saıð] cut with a scythe, mow *19-*.
~-sned the curved wooden handle or shaft of a scythe *19-, now NE Per*. **~-straik** a scythe sharpener *19-, now NE Kcb*.

se *see* SALL, SEA, SEE

sea *la16-*; **se** &c *la14-e16*, **sie** *la16*, **sey** &c *15-e20* [si; *Mry Firth S also* səi] *n* = sea *la14-*.
~ **box** a mariner's friendly society, so called from the box in which the funds were kept *17-19*. ~ **breve** a document allowing reprisals at sea *e16*. **be ~ burd** &c by sea *e16, only Sc*. ~ **car** &c an embankment against the sea, a sea-wall *18-e19*. ~ **cat** the wolf-fish *16-e20*. ~ **coulter** the puffin *la17, only Sc*. ~ **cowbell** a sea-going COBLE[2] *e16*. ~ **craig** a rock by or in the sea *la16, only Sc*. ~ **daisy** the thrift or sea-pink *19-, now Ork*. ~ **dog** the dogfish *la18-e20*. ~ **doo** &c the black guillemot *la19-, now Arg*. ~ **fire** sea phosphorescence *19*. ~ **flech** a sand-flea *20-, Sh Kcdn Ags*. ~ **fyke** a powder made from the crushed dried egg-capsules of the whelk *Buccinum undatum*, which causes skin irritation *la18-e19*. ~ **goo** a seagull *la19-, Abd*. ~ **green** land partially reclaimed from the sea, but still overflowed by spring tides *18-19*. ~ **gust** salt spume driven by wind onto the land *e17, la19- (Sh Ork)*. ~ **haar** a sea fog *19-, E*. ~ **hen** the common guillemot *la19-, now Cai*. ~ **lark** the dunlin *la19-, now Per*. ~ **lintie** the rock

pipit *la19-, now Ayr*.   ~ **loch** an arm of the sea,
esp fiord-shaped *17-*.   ~ **pa(a)p** *chf in pl* sea
anemones *la19-, Mry Fif Bwk*.   ~ **plover** the
Squatarola helvetica, la17, only Sc.   ~ **pyot** &c
the oyster-catcher *18-, local NE-Gall*.   ~ **revar**
&c a pirate *16*; cf *reiver* (REIVE).   ~ **skar** a sea-
cliff *e16, only Sc*.   ~ **sleech** &c mud formed by
a tidal river or estuary *18-19*.   ~ **soo,** *pl sometimes* ~ **swine** the small-mouthed wrasse *19-*,
now Kcdn.   ~ **toun** &c a seaport town or village *18-, freq in place-names*.   ~ **ware** seaweed,
esp the coarse kind washed up by the tide and
used as manure *16-, now Sh Ork NE*.   ~
wrack 1 = ~ *ware, 18-e19*.   **2** property cast
up by the sea *e16, only Sc*.

Seaforth ['si'forθ] **1 a** ~ a soldier in the regiment raised in 1778 by the Earl of Seaforth; a
Seaforth Highlander, la18-20.   **2 The** ~(**s**) the
Seaforth Highlanders, la19-20.
~ **Highlander** a soldier in the *Seaforth Highlanders, la19-20*.   ~ **Highlanders** name given
to the regiment formed in 1881 by amalgamation of the *72nd Duke of Albany's Own Highlanders*
(raised by the Earl of Seaforth in 1778) and the
78th Highlanders, Ross-shire Buffs (raised in 1793
by Colonel Francis Humberston MacKenzie),
now (since 1961) amalgamated with *The Queen's
Own Cameron Highlanders* (QUEEN) to form the
Queen's Own Highlanders (Seaforth and Camerons)
(QUEEN) *la19-20*.
seal &c; **sell** *la14-15*, **seill** &c *la15-e17*, **sale**
&c *16-17* [sil; *'siəl, *'seəl, *sɛl] *n* **1** = seal
la14-.   **2** *specif*, as a mark or sign of *office, la15-*.
vt **1** = seal *la14-*.   **2** impress (a mark) **on** *la16*.
~**ing ordinance**(**s**) the Sacrament of the
Lord's Supper and/or baptism *17-, now formal*.
burning ~ an iron for branding casks *la17, only
Sc*.   **pass (by, through** *or* **under) the
(Great, Privy** *etc*) ~(**s**) *of a document making a
gift, granting a warrant etc* be approved and
authenticated by being sealed with the appropriate seal with the authority of the Chancery
of Scotland or of the *Court of Session* (SESSION)
la16-.   ~ **of cause** a charter granted by a
town council to a body of craftsmen, forming
them into an INCORPORATION *la15-19*.
seal *see* SELL²
seam¹ &c [sim; *Sh nEC* sem] *n* **1** = seam *la16-*.
2 a row of natural or, *more usu*, artificial teeth,
freq **a** ~ **o teeth** *la19-, now NE-Per*.   **3** the parting of the hair *20-, local Sh-wLoth*.   **4** a woman's
sewing or needlework *18-*.   **5** any task, piece of
work *la19-, local Per-S*.
vt fit one edge of (a plank) to another *19-, now
Sh Cai*.
~ **biter** *joc* a tailor *e16, only Sc*.
seam² &c; **sem** *la19-20, Sh* [sim; *Sh* sem,
?sɛm] *n* a nail used to fix together the planks of
a clinker-built boat, riveted by a RUIVE, *freq*
seam and ruive *la15-, now Sh*. [correspond-
ing to ON *saumr*, prob cognate w SEAM¹]

seam *see* SAME¹
seann triubhas *see* SHANTREWS
search¹ &c, **cerse** &c *16-e17*; **sers** &c *16*
[sɛrtʃ; *sɛrs] *vti* = search *16-*.
n **1** = search.   **2** *specif* an investigation into the
Register of SASINES, in order to discover the
nature of the title, details of the BURDENS etc,
which affect a property offered for sale *la18-*.
~**er**; **seircear** &c *la16, only Sc* **1** = searcher
la16-.   **2** a church ELDER or other official
appointed to look out for and report to the *kirk
session* (KIRK) any absences from divine service,
disorderly behaviour etc *17-e19*.   ~**ery** *law* the
office of a *searcher, esp* a customs-officer *la16-e18,
only Sc*.
search² [sɛrtʃ] *n* a sieve, strainer, riddle *18-, now
NE Ags*.
vt put through a sieve, sift, strain *18-, now NE
Ags*. [*cf* Eng *searce*. OED *searce*]
season *see* SAISON
seat &c *la16-*; **sate** &c *16-*, **seit** &c *la15-e20*
[sit; *Sh Ork Cai nEC, WC* set] *n* **1** = seat *16-*.   **2**
also ~ **of Session** the *Court of Session* (SESSION)
16, only Sc.   **3** name for the *kirk session* (KIRK)
la16, only Sc.
~ **rent** the rent paid for the use of a seat in
church *18-20*.   ~ **tree** the weaver's seat in a
handloom *la18-19*.
seater &c [*'sitər, *'sitəri, *'zitəri] *numeral, children's rhymes* seven *e20*. [see ZEENDI; *cf*
LECTURI]
sebowe *see* SYBOW
secede [sə'sid, 'si'sid] *vi* **1** = secede.   **2** in reference to the *secession* (*n* 2) *18*.
Seceder &c **1** a member of any of the branches
of the *Secession Church, 18-e20*.   **2** a member of
the *Free Presbyterian* (FREE) Church *20-, Highl*.
secession 1 = secession *16-*.   **2** the departure
from the *Church of Scotland* (CHURCH) in 1732 by
a group of MINISTERS led by Ebenezer and
Ralph Erskine; *chf* **Secession Church** the
church formed after this event; the term was
first used officially in 1820 in the title *United
Secession Church* (UNITED) *18-20*.
sech *see* SICH
seck¹ &c *n* = sack *la14-*.
vt put in a bag, bag, stuff *18-*.   [ON *sekkr* cognate of OE *sacc* > SACK. OED *sack* (*n*¹)]
seck² &c *n* = sack, the wine *la16-e18*.
seck³; **sect** *n* = sex *19*. [*cf* Eng *sect*]
seckie *n* a kind of linen overall worn by foremen
in a weaving factory *la20-, Ross Lnk Ayr*.
[aphetic f *carseckie* (CARSACKIE)]
second &c; **secont** &c *19-e20* ['sekənt; *Per Fif
also* 'sikənt] *adj, n* **1** = second *la14-*.   **2**
(an)other, additional to the first *la14-*.   **3**
applied to the storey immediately above the
ground floor of a building *la18-20*.
~**ar** *adj* = secondary, of second quality; of the
second size *la15-16, only Sc*. *n, also* ~**er**, *St
Andrews and* (*la17*) *Glasgow Univs* a student of

social rank just below a nobleman, who had special privileges and paid higher fees *la17-e19*; *cf* PRIMAR, TERNAR.

~-handed second-hand *la19-*, *Gen except Sh Ork*.

~ pair the pair of horses worked by the second or assistant horseman on a farm *la19-*, *N, SW*.

~ sight a supposed faculty or power of seeing future or distant things as if they were actually present; the image thus seen; *more gen*, the ability to foretell future events, telepathic powers *la16-*.   **~ sighted** having this faculty *18-*.   **~ stature** ? medium height *e17*, *only Sc*.

~ in blood *etc, law* a person related in the second degree of consanguinity *la16-18*, *only Sc*.

secré [*sə'kri] *adj* **1** intimate, privy *e16*, *only Sc*. **2** *of a place* secluded *e16*.

n = secre, (a) secret *la14-15*.

secret &c, saicret &c *la19-*, *now Sh Ork Bnf Ags*, **secreit** *16-e17* ['sekrət; 'sikrɪt; *sə'krit] *adj* = secret *la14-*.

n **1** = secret *la15-*.   **2** a coat-of-mail concealed under one's ordinary clothes *la16-e17*, *only Sc*.

S~ Council the Scottish *Privy Council* (PRIVY) *16-17*.

secretar &c ['sɛkrətər, 'sekrətər] *n* = secretary *15-*, *now NE Ags*, *only Sc*.

sect *see* SECK[3]

secting *verbal noun* cutting *e16*. [L *sect-*, ptp stem of *secāre* cut; *cf* ModEng *sect* cut]

secularity *n* **1** secular jurisdiction or power *e16*. **2** = secularity.

sedarin *see* SEDERUNT

seddle *see* SAIDLE

sederunt &c [sə'dɛrunt, -ənt] *n* **1** in minutes of deliberative bodies, used to introduce the list of those present at a meeting; the list itself; the persons who attended *la17-*.   **2** a meeting of a deliberative or judicial body: (1) of the *Court of Session* (SESSION) *17-e19*; (2) of the *General Assembly* (GENERAL) or other court of the Presbyterian Churches *la17-19*; (3) of Parliament, Town Councils etc *17-e20*.   **3** a meeting or sitting of an informal or social nature *18-*, *now local NE-Wgt*.   **4** *also* **sedarin &c** [sə'dɛrɪn, -əns] an unpleasant interview, a scolding, a dressing-down *19-*, *now Abd Ags Per*.   **5** ? an individual's record of attendance at a sitting *e17*.

~ book a minute book *17-18*.   **~ day** a day appointed for a sitting of the *Court of Session* (SESSION) *la17-e19*.

Act of S~ an ordinance drawn up by the judges of the *Court of Session* (SESSION) to regulate its procedure *16-*.   **Books of S~** the records of the *Court of Session* (SESSION), including the *Acts of Sederunt*, *17-*. [only Sc; L *sēdērunt* there sat down]

seduce *16-*; **sedouse &c** *16* [*sə'døs] *v* **1** *vt* = seduce *16-*.   **2** *vi* **~ with** seduce *la16*, *only Sc*.

see *16-*; **se** *la14-17*, **sie** *16-e17*, *only Sc*, **sei &c** *la19-e20*, *chf S* [si; *ECoast S also* səi] *vti, pres 2 pers sing also* **seis** [siz] *la14-16*, *with the 2 pers sing*

pronoun **seestu &c** *19-*, *now Sh Ork Dmf* ['siztu, 'sistu, 'sɪstdu, 'sɪstə]; *3 pers sing also* **sies** *e17*, *only Sc* [siz], *pl also* **sie** *16* [si], **seis** *la14-16* [siz]. *pt also* **sa &c** *la14-16*, *only Sc*, **schaw** *la14*, *only Sc*, **sauch** *e16*, **seed &c** *18-e20* [sɑ, si:d]. *ptp also* **sein &c** *la14-17*, **sen** *15-16* [sin] **1** = see *la14-*.   **2** *vt, freq imperative* look at, examine, inspect *17-*, *now local Ork-Kcb*.   **3** *vi* take measures or steps **to** .., contrive **to** .. *la18-20*.   **4** *in imperative* (1) hand or pass, give into a person's hand, let (a person) have *19-*: '*see me the teapot*' [*orig* **let me** *etc* **~** (**a haud o**); *cf* HAUD)]; (2) *also* **sae** *la19-*, *Ags, parenthetic, pointing something out or for emphasis*, *la19-*, *Abd Ags*: '*come awa, noo sey, Marget*'; (3) *vt, introducing a person or thing about to be discussed*, *la20-*, *C*: '*see him, he canny drive*'.

~in(g) glass a mirror *20-*, *now local Abd-Ayr*. **I've seen myself** *or* **me** (**do(ing) something**) I can remember .., I have often .., I have seen the day when .. etc *20-*.   **I think I see** .. *ironic* there is no chance, fear etc .. *la19-*.   **~ about** look after, enquire about (a person) *la18-*, *now local NE-Ayr*.   **~ after 1** look after (a person), attend to the wants of *la19-*.   **2** take steps to obtain, make enquiries for *la20-*, *local Inv-Ayr*.   **~ her ain** *of a woman* menstruate *20-*, *Fif*.   **~ at 1** *usu imperative* look at, observe *la19-*, *NE*.   **2** consult, inquire of *la19-*, *NE-WC*.   **~ day aboot wi** be even with, get one's own back on *19-*, *now Cai*.   **~ someone far enough** *expression of annoyance* wish that someone were out of the way, had not appeared etc *la19-*.   **~ for** look for, try to find *e16*.   **~ on** look on, look at *e16*.   **~ thegither** see eye to eye, agree *20-*, *NE, EC*.   **~ till, seetle** *19-*, *now Sh Ork NE nEC*, **~ to** *la18-e19* = *see at* 1.

seestu &c 1 you understand, let me tell you *19-*, *now Sh Ork Dmf*.   **2** nickname for the town of Paisley (because once considered to be characteristic of Paisley speech) *19-20*, *WC*.

seeck &c, sick *la18-* [sik] *adj* = sick *la14-*.

~ rife ['sikrɪf] **1** sickly, slightly ill *19-*, *now literary*.   **2** sickening, nauseating; tiresome *la19-*, *Fif Ags*.   **sick-laith** extremely unwilling, very reluctant *la18-e20*.   **sick-sair(t) &c** thoroughly sated or bored, sick to death *19-*, *Ork NE*.   **sick sorry 1** = *sick sair(t)*, *19-e20*. **2** very sorry *la19-*, *now Ork Cai*.   **seek-stawed &c** = *sick sair(t)*, *20-*, *local wLoth-Dmf*.   **sick-tired** = sick and tired *19-*.

seed &c *n* **1** = seed *la14-*.   **2** seed-time, *freq* **bear** *etc* **~** *la16-19*.   **3** *also* **sid**, *la17-*, *Sh-N Per*, *chf in pl* particles of (oat-)bran, *freq* used to make SOWANS *la17-*, *now local Sh-Gall*.   **4** a small particle or grain (**of** something) *la19-*, *now Ags*.

vti **1** = seed.   **2** *vt* weave a pattern of spots, resembling seeds, in (a piece of muslin or linen) *19*.

~ie full of oat husks *18-e19*.

~ bird the wagtail *la18-*, *now Slk*.   **~ fur** the

furrow into which grain is to be sown and har-
rowed *18-*, now *N*.   ~ **lady** the pied wagtail
la19-, now *Ayr*.   ~**-like** *of soil* ready for sowing
la19-, *Cai Bnf*.

never lat *or* **say sid(s)** never say a word,
never make the least remark (**about**) *la20-*,
NE.   **a** ~ **in one's teeth** *etc* something which
irritates or annoys one *la18-e20*.

seed *see* SEE
seefer *see* CEEPHER

seek[1] **&c; sek** *la14*, **sik &c** *18-20* [sik, sɪk] *vti*,
pt also **schocht** *la14*, *only Sc*.   *pt, ptp also* **socht**
&c *only Sc*, **soucht &c** *la14-e20*, *only Sc* [soxt] **1**
= seek *la14-*.   **2** *vt* search for, look for *la14-*.
3 ask for, request: (1) by begging *la15, 18-*, *now*
local Sh-Kcb; (2) with intention to purchase,
hire etc *la18-*, *now Sh-C*; (3) as a price, as
wages etc *la19-*, *Sh-C*; (4) require, demand,
expect as one's due *18-*, *now Cai Ags Per*.   **4** (1)
search (a place), look through *la14-*, *now local*
Sh-SW.   (2) examine, consult (a register) *la17*.
5 (1) invite, bid (a person) (to come, do etc)
la19-, *now local Sh-Wgt*.   (2) *specif, of a farmer*
invite (a servant) to remain for the next half-
year *18-20*.   **6** *vi* make an attempt or request
to go, come etc **to, in(to), away** *etc*, *la15-*, *now*
local Sh-Wgt.   **7** *vt* seek in marriage, ask for the
hand of (a woman), propose to *la18-*.   **8** *with*
infin wish, desire *la19-*, *now local Sh-Kcb*.   **9**
bring, fetch *20-*, *S*.

socht exhausted *19-*, *now NE Ags*.
~**-an-hod** hide-and-seek *19-*, *Ags*.   ~ **in** invite
(a person) *la17*, *only Sc*.   ~ **to** resort or apply
to, strive for *la18-*, *now Sh-nEC*.   ~ **up for** *nau-*
tical bear up for, sail towards *e17*, *only Sc*.

seek[2] *vi* percolate, soak, ooze *la19-*, *local Kcdn-*
SW.   [only Sc; perh extended f SEEK[1]; *cf also*
Eng dial *seak*]

seelence *la18-e20*, **silence &c** *n*, *vt* = silence
la14-.

putting to silence *law* the court action to
INTERDICT another from putting about an
unfounded claim to be married to the *pursuer*
(PURSUE) *19-e20*.

seelent &c *adj* = silent *la19-e20*, *Sh Ork Abd*.
seelyhoo *see* HOO[3]

seem &c *vt* **1** (1) = seem *la14-*.   (2) *with confused*
construction, as if impersonal, *la14*: 'And tournys sa
mony tyme his stede, That semys off ws he had na
dred.' (3) *with omission of* **to** *e16*.   **2** look
becoming in (a piece of clothing) *e20*, *S*.
n outward appearance or semblance, image
18-e19.

~**ly, sembly** *15-e16*, **symly** *la15*, *only Sc* **1** =
seemly *15-*.   **2** of pleasing appearance, handsome *la15-e16*, *la19-*, *now Sh Cai*.

seen *see* SEEVEN, SUNE, SYNE

seendil &c, sendle &c *16-e19*;   **sindle &c**
la15-19,   **sinnle &c** *17-e20* *adv*   =   seldom
la15-, *now literary*.

~ **times** rarely, seldom *17-e18*.   [only Sc;
metath form of ME *selden &c*, OE *seldan*, the
orig form of Eng *seldom*; *cf* SELDOM]

seep &c *vi*, *also* **sip** drip, ooze, trickle, leak *la18-*.
n leakage, dripping, oozing *19-*.
~**age** = *n*, *20-*.   ~**in** *of rain* soaking *la19-*, *now*
NE.   ~**it** soaked, wet through *19-*.   [earlier in
Sc; perh OE *sipian* soak, be soaked; *cf* SYPE]

seer &c *n* **1** = seer.   **2** an overseer; an inspector
la15-e17, *only Sc*.

seerup *la19-*;   **serop** *la15-e16* *n*   =   syrup.
[OED *syrup*]

seestu *see* SEE
seet *see* SUIT[2]
seeth *see* SAITHE
seetiation *see* SITUATE
seetle *see* SEE

seeven &c *17-*,   **seven &c;**   **saiven &c**
la19-e20, *chf Abd*, **siven &c** *la19-e20*, *N*, **seen**
&c *la18-e20* ['siv(ə)n; *Bnf nEC Uls* 'sev(ə)n;
Abd 'səiv(ə)n; *St* 'sɛvn; ***'sɪv(ə)n, ***sin] *n* **1** =
seven *la14-*.   **2** *rugby football* a team of seven
players only; *in pl* a rugby competition among
such teams, *orig* from various BORDER towns
20-.

sevensie the seventh game in the series at
chuckies (CHUCK[2]) *la20-*, *local Bnf-Dmf*.   ~**some**
seven in all, a group of seven *18-*, *only Sc*.   ~**t**
= seventh *la14-*.   **2** seventeenth *la14-e20*.   ~**teen &c** **1** = seventeen
la14-.   **2** seventeenth *la14-e20*.   ~**ty** *la14-*,
sinty *la18-*, *now WC* = seventy.

~ **night &c** *la14-e20*, **sennicht &c** *18-19* a
week, a period of seven nights.   ~ **pence**
sevenpence; a late 17th century half-MERK (=
seven shillings SCOTS) *la17-*.   ~ **the** ~ **Sisters 1**
the Pleiades *20-*, *now local Cai-Dmf*.   **2** seven
similar cannon used at the Battle of Flodden *16*,
only Sc.

seven-a-sides *also attrib in sing* = *n* **2** *pl*, *20-*.

seg[1] **&c** *n* **1** = sedge *15-e20*.   **2** *specif* the yellow
flag-iris *18-*.   **3** a kind of float made of bundles
of SEGS used by children learning to swim *19*.
seggan &c the wild iris *19-*, *now Arg Bute Ayr*
[prob Gael dim suffix *-an*].   **seg(g)ing** a disease of oat-plants *19-*, *now Kcdn Loth*.   **seggy**
abounding in SEGS[1], sedgy *19-e20*, *in place-names*
14-.

seg[2] **&c** *vi* = sag *la17-*, *now NE-WC*.
seg[3] **&c** *vt*, *of sour fruit etc* set (the teeth) on edge
la18-20.   [extended f northern ModEng dial
sage &c (*n, v*) saw]

segg &c *n* an animal, *esp* a bull, which has been
castrated when fully grown *la18-e19*.   [prob
Scand; *cf* Dan dial *seg*, *sæg* a castrated boar]

segnett *see* SIGNET

segstar [***'sɛgstər] *n* a sexton *e16*.   [only Sc;
MedL *sacristārius*, prob through OF]

segyrstane &c [***'sɛgərstən] *n* the sacristan in
a religious house *la14-e15*.   [(chf n)ME *seger-*
stane &c, AF *segerstaine*, OF *segrestein*, semi-pop-
ular f MedL *sacristānus* > Eng *sacristan*; *cf* ME
var *sekesteyn &c* > Eng *sexton* (see OED *sexton*)]

sei *see* SEE
seich *see* SICH
seil &c, **sele** &c [sil] *n* happiness, bliss, prosperity, good fortune *la14-e20*.
~**fu** happy, lucky; pleasant *la18-e20*. ~**y 1** blessed, lucky, happy *la14*, *la18-e20*. **2** = seely, holy, innocent, helpless *la15*. ~**yhoo** &c *18-, now NE Fif*, **ceeliehoo** &c *20-, Abd Fif* a caul on the head of a newborn child, thought to be very lucky.
seil *see* SILE²
seill *see* SEAL
sein *see* SEE
seinye *see* SENƷE
seircear *see* SEARCH¹
seis *see* SEE
seisin *see* SASINE
seit *see* SEAT, SET¹
seize &c; **sess** *la14* [siz; *sez] *vt* = seize *la14-*.
seizer = *searcher* 2 (SEARCH¹) *18-e19*.
sek *see* SEEK¹
sekir *see* SICKER
sel¹ &c *la15-*, **self** &c (*the usu form for combs*) *pronoun, adj, n* **1** = self *la14-*. **2** *following noun in possessive, eg* **saut's sel** salt itself, very salty *20-, Kcb Rox*. **3** *with personal pronoun, eg* **himsel** alone, by himself etc *la19-*.
sellie &c selfish(ness) *18-e20*.
self-contained *orig only of houses, but latterly also of flats* having their accommodation and entrance restricted to the use of one household *la18-*.
self and same selfsame, identical *19-, now Ork*. **the self** itself *15-e17, chf Sc*. **the sel o't** *etc used for the emphatic or reflexive pronoun* itself etc *19-e20*.
sel² *n* = cell *la14*.
selch &c *12-, now NE*; **selk** *e16* [sɛlx] *n* **1** = seal, the animal *12-*. **2** a fat clumsy person *la19-, now Bnf*.
selchy *e19*, **selkie** &c *19-, Sh Ork Cai NE* ['sɛlxɪ, 'sɛlkɪ; *Sh Ork N also* 'sɪlkɪ] = *n* 1. [OED *seal*]
seldom &c *adv* = seldom. *adj* **1** = seldom *e16*. **2** scanty, poor in quantity *20-, now Mry*. [*cf* SEENDIL]
sele *see* SEIL
self *see* SEL¹
selk *see* SELCH
selkhorn *see* SHILCORN
Selkirk: ~ **bannock** *or* **bannie** a kind of rich fruit loaf, made as a speciality by Selkirk bakers *19-*. ~ **grace** a rhymed grace before meals (wrongly ascribed to Burns) *19-*. [the BORDER town]
sell¹ &c *vti, pt also* **sald** &c *18-, now Sh*, **sauld** &c *la16-e20*, **sel(l)t** &c *la18-, ptp also* **sald** *la14-, now Sh*, **sauld** *la14-e20*, **sel(l)t** &c *la16-* [sɑl(d); sɛld, sɛlt] = sell *la14-*.
~**able 1** = sellable *la16-*. **2** venal *e17, only Sc*.
~**rife** &c *e16, e19*, **salerife** *la18* [*'sɛlrɪf, *'sel-] *of goods* saleable, easy to sell.

to ~ for sale, to be sold *19-*.
sell² &c *19-, now NE*; **seal** &c *la16-e20* [sel] *n* the rope, iron loop or chain by which cattle are bound by the neck to their stalls, *specif* the part of the chain round the animal's neck. [ON *seil* a rope (*cf* OE *sāl*); *cf* ModEng dial *seal* tie up cattle]
sell *see* SEAL
sellarie &c *18-e20*, **cellarie** &c *la17*; **salair** &c *la15-17* ['sɛlərɪ, *sə'ler] *n* = salary. [OED *salary*]
sellet &c *n* = sallet, a light helmet, some kind of iron container *e16*. [OED *sallet*]
sellie *see* SEL¹
sellt, selt *see* SELL¹
sem *see* SEAM²
semat *see* SEMMIT
sembland *n* = semblant, appearance *la14*.
by ~ in appearance *e16*.
semblé &c [*'sɛmblɪ] *n* **1** = sembly, an assembly *la14-15*. **2** a hostile meeting, conflict *la15-e16*. [OED *sembly*]
semble *see* SEMMLE
sembly *see* SEEM
semi &c ['sɛmɪ] *n* a second-year university student, *usu* in the Arts faculty *17-, latterly Abd, St Andrews, now only St Andrews*.
~ **bajan** &c = *n, la16-20*. ~ **class** the second-year class as in *n, la17-18*. [only Sc; *appar* reduced f *semi-bajan*; see also BEJAN]
seminate *adj* disseminated *la16*. [only Sc; L *sēmināt-*, ptp stem of *sēmināre* sow]
semlit *see* SEMMLE
semmit &c *la19-*; **semat** *la15 n* **1** applied to a Roman tunic *la15*. **2** a (*usu*) man's undershirt or vest, *usu* of wool or flannel *la19-*. [see SND]
semmle &c *20-*, **semble** *la15-e16 vti, pt also* **semlit** *la14-16* **1** *vi* = semble, assemble *la14-e16, la20-, now Ork*. **2** meet in conflict *la15-e16*. **3** *vt* gather (things) together in order to make a selection, choose *20-, now Fif*.
semple &c *15-*, **simple** &c *adj* **1** = simple *la14-*. **2** *law* without any strengthening circumstances *16-18*.
gentle and semple gentry and commoners alike *16-*.
semys [*'sɪmɪs] *adj* ~ **leddir** some kind of leather *e16*. [only Sc; *appar* Ger *sämisch* a kind of soft leather]
sen *see* SEE, SEND, SYNE
senator *n* = senator *16-*.
S~ **of the College of Justice** official title of a judge of the *Court of Session* (SESSION) *16-*.
senatus [sə'netəs] *n, in full* **S**~ **Academicus**, *latterly also* (*usu less formally*) **Senate** *in the older Sc Univs* the body, consisting of the Principal, Professors and, more recently, a number of Readers and Lecturers, which superintends and regulates the teaching and discipline of the University *17-*. [L = a senate]

send; sen [sɛnd; *N, WC* sɛn] *vti* **1** = send *la14-*. **2** *vt* export *la16*.

n **1** the action of sending *la15-16, only Sc*. **2** a message, summons or intimation sent *18-19, only Sc*. **3** a messenger sent ahead of a bridegroom at a wedding to summon the bride *la18-e20*.

sendle *see* SEENDIL

sene *see* SAIN, SYNE

senior *adj* = senior.

~ **secondary** (**school**) a state secondary school providing more academic courses than the *junior secondary school* (JUNIOR), attended by pupils who were successful in the *qualifying examination* (QUALIFY) *20*.

sennachie *see* SHENACHIE

sennicht *see* SEVEN

senown *see* SINNON

sensament *see* SENSEMENT

sense *n* essence, pith, juice *la19-, NE Ags*. [aphetic f Eng *essence* w orig F stress on second syllable]

sensement &c, censement &c; sensament &c *n* a decision, judgment *la15-16*. [only Sc; OF]

sensyne *see* SYNE

sentence &c *n* = sentence *la14-*.

~ **money** *or* **silver** *law* a percentage of the sum decreed, payable as a fee to the *sheriff depute* (SHERIFF) by the litigants in a case *17-e18*.

sentiner *see* CENTINER

sentrell *see* CENTRELL

sentrice *see* CENTREIS

senʒe &c; seinye &c, seyne *e15* [*'sin(j)ɪ] *n* **1** = senye, a distinguishing mark *15*. **2** a battle-cry, rallying cry *e16, only Sc*. **3** a signboard *la16, only Sc*. [OED *senye*]

senʒeour &c [*'sinjər] *n* **1** = seignior, a lord *la16*. **2** used to represent Ital *Signor* and F *Seigneur* in designations of Italians and Frenchmen *la16*.

~**abill** of a lord, lordly *la15, only Sc*. [OED *seignior*]

senzie &c *16-e19, latterly hist*; **senʒe &c** *15-e16* [*'sinjɪ] *n* a synod, deliberative meeting of clergy. [only Sc; appar altered f ME, OF *sene &c*. OED *senyie*]

separate *vti* **1** = separate. **2** *vt* divide into parts *la16*.

sepone [*sə'pon] *vt* set apart *e17*. [only Sc; L *sēpōnere*]

septuply [*'sɛptjuplaɪ] *vi, law, of the pursuer* (PURSUE) make a seventh answer, in reply to the SEXTUPLY of the *defender* (DEFEND) *la18*. [formed on L *sept(imus* etc) by analogy w QUADRUPLY etc]

sequel &c *n* **1** = sequel. **2** *in pl, law* the small quantities of meal, or money in lieu, given by the tenants *thirled* (THIRL[2]) to the mill to the miller's assistants for their services *17-, only Sc*.

adj following, subsequent *e17, only Sc*.

sequestrate [sikwə'stret] *v* **1** *vt* = sequestrate,

remove *16-19*. **2** confiscate *17-*. **3** *vti, law* (1) divert (the income of an estate etc) into other hands *e17*; (2) place (lands or other HERITABLE property) under a FACTOR or trustee appointed by the *Court of Session* (SESSION) to administer the property and rents from it, *usu* while the ownership is the subject of a legal action *18-19*; (3) *specif* put (the property of a bankrupt) into the hands of a trustee, by appointment of a court, for equitable division among his creditors; make a person bankrupt *18-*.

adj **1** = sequestrate, cut off *la16-e17*. **2** politically separate, independent *e17, only Sc*. **3** sequestered, secluded *17-e19, only Sc*.

sequestration the act or process of the *v*, *la16-*.

ser; sair *vt* ~'s, **sirs, surce &c** *exclam* (God etc) preserve us! *18-, now local N-SW*. [*cf* eModEng, ME *serve*]

ser *see* SERVE[1]

sere *see* SHUIR

serefe *see* SHERIFF

serenity &c *n* **1** = serenity. **2** honorific title given to reigning princes etc *la15-16*.

sergeant &c; sergeand &c *la14-e18*, **seriand** *la14-e16*, **sairgint** *la19-20* ['sɛrdʒənt, 'serdʒənt] *n* **1** = sergeant *la14-*. **2** *only Sc* **schargant** an officer of a guild *la16, only Sc*.

serjeandrie &c the office of sergeant in a *sheriffdom* (SHERIFF) whose duty it was to arrest and incarcerate those accused or suspected of crime under a SHERIFF's warrant *la16-e18*.

serk *see* SARK

sermon &c *n* **1** = sermon *16-*. **2** *without the article* divine service, an act of church worship *la16-19*.

~**ing** talk, discourse, conversation *la14-e16*.

sero [*'siro] *adv* (*adj*) late *17-e18*. [only Sc; L]

serop *see* SEERUP

serpens *see* SERPENT

serpent *la15-* ['sɛrpənt] *n, pl also* **serpens** *la14-e16, only Sc* [*'sɛrpnz] *n* = serpent *la14-*.

~ **toung** a jeweller's ornament shaped like a snake's tongue *la15, only Sc*.

serplaith &c [*'sɛrpləð, *'sarpləð] *n* = sarplier, a large wool-sack *15-e17*. [OED *sarplier*]

sers *see* SEARCH[1]

serten *see* CERTAIN

servable *see* SERVIABLE

servan *see* SERVANT

servant &c; servan *19-, now NE n* **1** = servant *la14-*. **2** a workman's assistant *la16, only Sc*.

~ **chiel** a young male servant *la19-, now Abd*. ~ **lass** a maidservant *la17-*. [-*an* forms reduced f -*and* (found in OSc and ME), due to infl f presp forms]

serve[1] &c, ser *la15, la18-*; **sar** *la16*, **sair** *18-* [sɛr(v), ser] *vti* **1** = serve *la14-*. **2** *vt* attack (**with** weapons) *la14*. **3** *law* declare (a person) heir to an estate *e16*; see also *serve heir*. **4** *of clothes* fit, suit *18-, now Bnf Ags Per*. **5** give alms, *esp* food or drink, to (a beggar) *19*. **6** (1) satisfy or content, *esp* with food or drink *la18-*. (2) satiate, sate, glut *la18-*, now *N*. **7** *only* **ser &c** treat (in a certain way), behave (in a certain way) towards *19-*, *local Sh-Kcb*: '*to sair a bairn like that!*'

n, *only* **ser &c** one's fill, enough, satiety *19-*, now *NE Ags Rox*.

saired &c having one's appetite satisfied, full up *la18-*, now *local*. **ill-saired** not having had enough food at a meal *19-*, now *NE*. **weel-saired &c** well satisfied with food or drink *la18-*, now *NE*. **server 1** a person who hands round refreshments at a funeral *la19-*, now *SW*. **2** a salver, tray *18-*, now *local NE-Renfr*. **sairin &c 1** one's fill (*esp* of food) *la18-*, now *local Sh-Lnk*. **2** enough of something unpleasant; a thorough beating or trouncing *19-*, now *NE*. **servin(g) lass** a maidservant *la19-e20*.

serve a person heir *law* declare a person heir to an estate through legal process, formerly by an INQUEST and RETOUR, *latterly* (*19-20*) by petition to the SHERIFF *la16-20*.

serve² *vt* = deserve *la14-18*.

serviable &c *16-e17 adj* **1** *also* **servable &c** *la15-e17*, *only Sc* willing to serve, obedient *la15-e17*. **2** belonging to the servant class *e17*, *only Sc*. [OF *serv(i)able*]

service &c; schervice *e16*, *only Sc n* **1** = service *la14-*. **2** compulsory or forced labour as a penalty for crime, penal servitude *la18*. **3** labouring or unskilled work, *specif* in building a house *18*. **4** (1) *Presbyterian church* the serving of the elements at Communion *la16-*. (2) the serving of refreshments, *specif* at a funeral or wedding *la18-*, now *nEC Lnk*. **5** *law* the procedure by which HERITABLE property was transmitted to an heir, a **special ~** referring to particular lands, a **general ~** having no such restriction *la16-20*; *cf serve heir* (SERVE¹).

servient *adj*, *law*, *of persons or property* subjected to a SERVITUDE, *freq* **~ tenement** *la16-*; *cf* DOMINANT TENEMENT. [*cf* Eng]

servit &c *la16-*, now *Cai Fif Lnk*, **serviette &c** *16-*; **serviot &c** *la15-e17 n* **1** a table-napkin, serviette *la15-*. **2** a small tray *19*.

servitting &c material for table napkins *e17*, *only Sc*. [F; orig only Sc; in *19* borrowed into Eng f F; *n* 2 is prob by confusion w *server* 2 (SERVE¹)]

servitor &c; schervitour *16 n* **1** (1) = servitor, a (male) servant *la15-e20*. (2) *Edinburgh Univ* a janitor or attendant *la19-*. **2** an apprentice, *esp* to a lawyer, a lawyer's clerk *la15-18*, *only Sc*. **3** *deferential*: **your** humble servant *la16-18*. **4** a table-napkin *16-*, now *Lnk* [by confusion w SERVIT].

servitrix &c *la16-18*, **servitrice &c** *la15-e17* a female servant.

servitude &c; schervitude *la16 n* **1** = servitude *la16-*. **2** *law* an obligation attached to a

piece of property limiting the owner's use of it or permitting others to exercise specified rights over it *la16-*.

sesnit &c, cesnat &c *n* = sarsenet, a fine soft material *e17*.

sesoun *see* SAISON

sess *see* SEIZE

sessing *see* SASINE

session &c, cessioun(e) &c *la15-16 n* **1** = session *la15-*. **2** *law* (1) a court of justice consisting of the CHANCELLOR and other persons chosen by the king, which determined causes previously brought before the king and his council *15-16*. (2) **the S~**, now **the Court of S~** the supreme civil judicature in Scotland *16-*. **3** = kirk session (KIRK) *la16-*. **4** *Sc Univs* the portion of the year during which teaching is carried on *18-*.

vt **1** *chf in passive*, *of a betrothed couple* be called before the *kirk session* (KIRK) to record their intention to marry and to lay down their PAWNS *18-19*. **2** summon or take before the *kirk session* for offences against church discipline *la19-e20*.

~al relating to or administered by the *kirk session* (KIRK) *18-e20*. **~er &c 1** a member of the *Court of Session*, *la16-17*. **2** a member of a *kirk session*, *17*. **~ book** the minute-book and register of a *kirk session* (KIRK) *18-*. **~ box** the box or chest containing the church funds, *esp* those to be distributed as charity *18-*. **~ clerk** the clerk or secretary of a *kirk session*, *18-*. **~ house 1** the building where the *Court of Session* was held *17-e18*. **2** the room in or attached to a church, in which the *kirk session* meets *la18-*. **Court of S~** *see n* 2. **on the ~** in receipt of poor relief *19*.

sessonar *see* SASINE

sessoun *see* SAISON

set¹; sett, seit *la14-16* [sɛt; *also* *sit] *vti*, *ptp also* **setten &c** *la16-*, now *NE* **1** = set *la14-*. **2** (1) *vtr* cause or make to sit, seat, place on a seat *la14*, *la18-*. (2) *vt* cause (an assembly etc) to sit *la14-16*. **3** *vi* sit, be seated *la14*, *18-*. **4** stack (PEATS¹) in RICKLES¹ to dry *20-*, *NE*. **5** dislocate (one's neck) *20-*, *local Sh-SW*. **6** bring (a mill) to a stop by turning off the water from the wheel *18-*, now *Bnf Ags Slk*. **7** *vi and in passive*, *of plants and animals* stop growing, have the growth checked *19-*, now *local Ork-WC*. **8** *vt* disgust, nauseate *19-*, now *NE Ags*. **9** *vi*, *of a horse* jib, become restive, refuse to obey the rider or driver *la19-*, *NE Kcb*. **10** (1) start off, set out, make one's way *17-*, now *Sh Ork*. (2) *vt* direct or guide in a certain course *19-*, now *NE Ags*. (3) cause to go, send (a person or thing) *la18-*, now *Ags Bwk*. (4) accompany, escort, convey (a person *home* etc) *18-*, now *Bwk Kcb S*. **11** leave (milk) standing for the cream to rise *20-*. **12** (1) let by contract, lease *15-*, now *local*. (2) *vi* be leased, hired out, fetch a rent *18-*, now

Sh SW Rox. **13** apply oneself (to do something) *la15.* **14** *vt* sight or make (land) *e17, only Sc.* **15** *law* reject, set aside *la17.* **16** (1) *freq impersonal, with infin, of a thing or action, now sometimes ironic* be seemly or suitable for, become, suit *la15-*: '*It sets us to be dumb a while*'. (2) *of a person* look becoming in *19-, now local; cf* SUIT[1].

n **1** (1) = set, a young plant etc used for planting *16-*. (2) a potato, or (*orig*) a portion of it, used for planting *la18-*. **2** a berth (in a harbour) *15-e16.* **3** a letting or leasing of a farm, house etc, a lease (*esp* thought of from the lessor's point of view) *15-, now Bnf Abd Wgt, only Sc.* **4** *law, chf* **action of** ~ (**and sale**) an action in which a part-owner of a ship can request to buy out or be bought out by his partners or to have the ship sold *la17-.* **5** a check or stoppage, as in growth; a setback, a disappointment *la17-, now NE Ags.* **6** a feeling of disgust or repulsion *la18-, NE Ags.* **7** a carry-on, wrangle, fuss *la19-, local Abd-Gall* **8** a joke, piece of fun, frolic *la19-, now WC, SW.* **9** (1) the manner or position in which a thing is set, fixed or arranged; the way in which a thing goes or works; a condition, state (of affairs) *19-, now local Sh-WC.* (2) a twist or warp in a piece of wood *la19-, now WC Kcb.* (3) *of a person* build, physique, kind *19-, now local Sh-SW.* (4) a person's attitude, customary manner *la20-, local NE-Gall.* (5) the way in which a tune is arranged, the setting of a piece of music *la17-.* (6) the way in which something is set down in writing *e16, only Sc.* (7) *now freq* **sett** a checked pattern in cloth, *esp* (the arrangement of) the squares and stripes in a TARTAN, the pattern of TARTAN associated with a particular CLAN *18-.* (8) *chf* **sett** the constitution or form of organization of a BURGH *la17-e20.* **10** an arrangement or contract for regular supply from a producer, *esp* of milk, a standing order, the amount supplied *18-19.* **11** a whetstone *19-, Fif Loth Rox.*
conj although *la14-e16, only Sc.*

set *ptp, adj* **1** = set *la14-.* **2** *of a battle* pitched *la14-15.* **3** disposed, inclined, determined, obstinate, *freq* **well-set, ill-set** *16-, now Sh-C.* **4** *of cloth, esp* TARTAN having a certain pattern *la17-e18.* **5** *esp of a horse's tail* stiffened or cocked up *la18.* **6** pleased *20-, now Bnf Abd.* NB *For combs with ptp, see below.*
set(t)en on burnt, frizzled, shrivelled (in cooking) *19-, now Lnk Wgt Rox.* **setter 1** = setter *la17·.* **2** a person who lets or gives out on lease, a lessor *la15-e19, only Sc.* **3** a jibbing horse *20-, Bnf Abd Per.* **4** baking a strip of wood supporting the row of end- or side-loaves in a batch in an oven *19-e20.* **5** a large lump of coal put on to keep a fire going *la20-, Fif Loth Lnk.* **setting &c** *n* **1** = setting *la14-.* **2** the action of letting or leasing (land etc); the right to do this; a lease *la14-e17.* **3** a young plant;

the quantity of potatoes planted as seed *la19-. adj* fit, suitable, becoming; *of a person* attractive in looks or manner *la18-, now NE-Per.* **setting down &c** an equipping or providing for marriage *la19-, now Ags.*
~ **burd** *only Sc* **1** ? a washboard in a ship *e16.* **2** some kind of table *e16.* ~ **stane** a whetstone for razors, chisels etc *19-.*
Deil *or* **sorra** ~ **you** etc *as imprecation, 19-e20, Abd.* ~ **aff &c 1** = set off. **2** send off or away, dismiss from one's home or job *19-e20.* **3** plant out *19-, local Sh-Per.* **4** dawdle, be dilatory *19-, NE Kcb.* **5** cause to explode, let off an explosive charge, shot etc *la19-, now Abd Kcb.* ~ **after** set off in pursuit of, follow after *la19-, now Sh N, C.* ~ **awa &c** *vi* set off, start on a journey etc *19-, now local Sh-Wgt.* *n* a fuss; a row, scolding; a send-off *20-, local NE-S.* ~ **by 1** lay aside, clear away, set aside for future use *la18-, now local Sh-Kcb.* **2** provide with a makeshift meal *la18-19.* ~ **caution** put down a pledge *17.* ~ **down &c** *v* **1** = set down *15-.* **2** put down, quell *la16.* **3** cause to sit down, *esp* at a table for a meal *19-, now local Sh-C, freq in ptp* **set down** *of a meal* formally served at table *20-, local NE-WC.* **4** go bankrupt *20-, NE Kcb.* *n* a formal meal, a 'spread' *20-.* ~ **ensample** give an example *la14.* ~ **for** send for, summon *la20-, Ags Fif.* ~ **in** bring in (a meal), lay (a table for a meal) *19-, now Sh Abd Ags.* ~ **-in** inserted, inset *16-.* ~ **on 1** put (an unweaned animal) to suck, *esp* a strange lamb to a ewe that has lost her own *la19-, Bwk Lnk S.* **2** set in motion, start off (a mill etc) *18-e20.* **3** make and kindle (a fire) *19-, local Sh-Kcb.* **4** set to work, begin in earnest *la19-, now Sh.* ~ **-on** equipped, dressed, fed *19-, local Sh-Lnk.* ~ **out** *v* **1** = set out *16-.* **2** send out, eject forcibly *la19-, now Ags.* *n* a display, show, turn-out *la19-, now local N-Kcb.* ~ **ower &c** ferry across (a river etc) *la14, la20-, now Sh.* ~ **a scull** arrange baited fish-lines in a SCULL[1] or basket *20-, Bnf Abd Kcdn.* ~ **to &c 1** = set to *17-.* **2** set upon, attack *19-, NE-S.* ~ **up 1** = set up *la14-.* **2** drive up *la15, only Sc.* **3** earth up (a plant) *la18-.* **4** arouse, stir up; incite *19-, now Sh Ork.* **5** join together (the parts of a fishing line) *la19-, local Sh-Ayr.* **6** set (a chimney) on fire *la20-, local Sh-Kcb.* **7** *chf imperative* ~ **him** *etc* **up**, *ironic or contemptuous, of a person who gives himself airs* what a cheek!, the impudence etc! *18-.* ~ **&c-up** conceited, affected, 'stuck up' *la19-, local Inv-Slk.* ~ **up one's gab** *etc* utter impudent remarks etc *19-, local Sh-Kcb.* **tak a** ~ **o land** take one's bearings *e20, Mry Ags Loth.*
set[2] *n* **1** = set, a group *16-.* **2** a team to build corn-stacks; the number of RIGS[1] reaped at one time by a band of reapers *19-, local sEC-Uls.*
seteesh [sə'tiʃ] *n* = schottische *20-, Ork NE.* [corrupt form]

setis [*sits] *n pl* groups of men posted to intercept and shoot game *la14-e16*. [only Sc; obscure. OED *sete*]

sett *see* SET[1]

setterel &c [*ˈsɛtrəl] *adj* **1** small and thickset *la18-20*. **2** short-tempered, sarcastic *la19-20*, *NE*. [appar Eng *set* (*adj*) + -*rel*]

settifee *see* SATIFY

settle *see* SATTLE

Saturday &c, **Saturday &c** *la17-*; **Saturn(s)day** *17-e18, only Sc,* **Saiterday &c** *la19* [ˈsɛtərde, -dɪ] *n* = Saturday *la14-*.
blin Saturday the Saturday of the week in which no pay is given to the fortnightly-paid *la20-, local nEC-Slk.* ~'s **penny** *etc* a penny etc given to a child as pocket money *la19-*.

seuch *see* SHEUCH, SOUCH

seur *see* SHUIR

seven *see* SEEVEN

sevendable *see* SEVENDLE

sevendle &c [*səˈvɛndl] *adj* **1** strong, firm, securely made, built or fixed *19-20*. **2** *also* **sevendable &c** [*səˈvɛndəbl] thorough, out-and-out, extreme *19-20*. [only Sc; altered f SOLVENDIE]

several &c *n, in pl* ~s several persons or things *la17-, now Inv NE Stlg Bwk.*
adj = several.

sew *see* SAW[1], SHEW

sewane *n* ? a spice *e16*.

sex *see* SAX

sextern *n* = sestern, a container for liquid *15, only Sc.*

sextuply [*ˈsɛkstəplaɪ] *vi, law, of the defender* (DEFEND) make a sixth reply in answer to the QUINTUPLY of the *pursuer* (PURSUE) *la17-18.* [formed on L *sextus* etc by analogy w QUADRUPLY etc; *cf* eModEng *sextiply* multiply by six]

sey[1], **say** [*səɪ] *vti, latterly literary* **1** test, try *16-e19.* **2** attempt (something difficult) *la16-19.*
n **1** = say, tasting of food or drink *la15.* **2** a trying out, test, putting to the proof *la15-e19.* **3** a trial, trouble *la16, only Sc.* **4** a test-piece, sample, *specif* one submitted as proof of competence for entry to a trade INCORPORATION *la17-e19.*
~ **box** the chest in which coins were deposited at the Mint for future examination *16-e17.* ~ **drink** a round of drinks paid for by an entrant to a trade when submitting his SEY[1] (*n* 4) *17-e18.* ~ **piece** = *n* 4, *16-e19.* ~ **shot** *in games* an opportunity to regain what one has lost *la17-e19.*

sey[2] *18-19;* **say** *16-17* [*səɪ] *n* a kind of serge-like woollen cloth. [ME *say*]

sey[3] **&c;** **say** [saɪ] *n* **1** *butchering* a cut of beef from the shoulder to the loin, *corresponding to Eng* shoulder steak and sirloin *18-e19;* see also *back-sey* (BACK[1]) and FORESYE. **2** *tailoring* the armhole of a sleeve *la17-.* [see SND]

sey *see* SAE[1], SAITHE, SEA, SYE[1]

seynd *see* SYND

seyne *see* SENƷE

sgian *see* SKEAN

sha &c [ʃɑ] *interj* a call to a dog to chase prey *19-, now Bwk Arg SW.* [Sc and IrGael *seo* here!]

shaave *see* SAW[1]

shabble, shable &c *n* **1** a curved sword, a sabre, cutlass *17-e19.* **2** a little, insignificant person or thing *e19.* [see SND]

shabby *adj* **1** = shabby. **2** unwell, in poor health *20-, Loth Bwk Rox.*

shable *see* SHABBLE

shachle *see* SHAUCHLE

shackle &c; **sheckle &c** *la16-e20* *n* **1** = shackle *16-.* **2** the wrist *20-, now Fif Ayr.* **3** the link-fitting which connects the plough-beam with the swingletree *19-, now Cai Kcb.* **4** the clamp which holds the shaft of a plough coulter to the beam *20-, local Cai-Kcb.*
~ **bane &c** = *n* 2, *la16-, now Sh-Per.*

shaddie *see* SHEDDA

shade &c *n* **1** = shade. **2** a shed, a roofed structure used as a shelter or store *18.* [*cf* Eng *shed*, f a short-vowel variant]

shade *see* SHED

shadow *see* SHEDDA

shae &c *la19-,* **shoe &c** *la17-;* **scho** *la14-e16,* **shee &c** *la18-, chf NE* [ʃø, ʃe; *NE* ʃi] *n, pl also* **schoyne** *la14,* **schoys** *la15,* **schoun &c** *15-16,* **shone &c** *16-18,* **shune** *la18-,* **shoon &c** *17-,* **sheen** *18-, now NE Dmf* [ʃøn, ʃɪn; *NE* ʃin; *local nEC* ʃen] *n* **1** = shoe *la14-.* **2** applied to a lover or spouse, *chf* **auld shune** an old sweetheart, discarded lover *la18-, now local Sh-SW.* **3** the plate or iron strip on the underside of an old wooden plough etc *18.* **4** the shute carrying grain from the hopper to the millstone *la19-, now local Sh-Ayr.*
vt **1** = shoe. **2** fit with metal rims, studs, tips etc; hobnail (shoes) *la15-, now local Ags-Kcb.*
~**in box** the box in which a blacksmith keeps his smaller tools *la19-, Abd Kcb.* ~**in shed** a shed as part of a smithy in which horses are tied up to be shod *20-, Ork Abd Kcb.* ~**less &c** without shoes *la14-.* **schone &c horne 1** a shoehorn *la16-e17.* **2** something which facilitates a transaction *e17.*
~ **head** the top or upper edges of a shoe *la19-, local.* ~ **latch** a shoelace or thong for fastening shoes *la19-, now NE.* ~ **pint** a shoelace *20-, now NE.*
cast a ~ have an illegitimate child *20-, now Ayr.* **gie a story hose and sheen** magnify a story in the telling *la20-, Abd Kcb.* [see also SHOD]

shaft *see* CHAFT[1]

shag[1] **&c** *n* the refuse of oats, barley etc *18-, now Kcdn Ags Per.* [*n* use of obs Eng *shag* (*v*) shake]

shag² *n* an ox castrated incompletely or when fully grown *18-, now Cai.* [prob irreg var of SEGG]

shaif &c, sheaf *18-;* **shave &c** *la15-, now Ags,* **schief &c** *16,* **sheave** *e19 n* = sheaf *15-.*

~ **laft** a barn loft where sheaves are stacked before being put through the threshing mill *la20-, Ork N Kcb.*

shair *see* SHUIR

shaird &c *17-,* **shard &c** *la18-;* **sherd** *17-* *n* **1** (1) = shard, sherd, a fragment *17-.* (2) the remains of something broken or decayed *la18-19, only Sc.* **2** a puny or deformed person or animal; a bad-tempered or malicious person *la18-, now Bnf.*

shairn &c *18-,* **sharn** *17-;* **shearn &c** *la16-18* [ʃern; *Sh Ork N* ʃarn] *n* dung, excrement, *esp* of cattle *la16-.*

vt smear or soil with cow-dung *la19-, local Sh-Wgt.*

~**y** of cow-dung; smeared with dung *17-.* ~**y flee &c** a dung-fly *20-, local Sh-Kcb.*

~ **bree** the ooze from farmyard manure *la19-, Abd.* ~ **midden** a dung hill *19-, Abd.*

shairp *la16-,* **sharp &c;** **schirpe** *la16,* **sherp** *16-19 adj* **1** = sharp *la14-.* **2** *of soil* containing sand and grit, gravelly, open and loose *19-.*

n **1** the act of sharpening (an implement etc) *19-, now NE Kcb.* **2** a frost-nail on a horse's shoe *20-, now N, C.*

vt **1** sharpen *la14-.* **2** make (the sea) rough *e16, only Sc.* **3** provide (a horseshoe) with frost-nails, rough (a horse) *19-, N, C.*

~**ing stone &c** a whetstone *la17-, only Sc.*

~**-nibbit** having a pointed nose *20-, Sh Abd.*

~ **set** keen, eager, *specif* for food, sex etc *la18-, now Ayr.*

be ~ **upon** be hard or severe on *la16-.*

shak &c, shake &c [ʃek; *Sh Ork NE Ags Per* ʃak] *16-* *v, pt also* **shuk &c** *la14-e20,* **shuke &c** *16-e20;* **shakit** *la19-e20* [*ʃøk, ʃʌk, 'ʃekɪt] *ptp also* **shakken &c** *16-,* **sheuken &c** *la19-, now local,* **shucken &c** *19-, now EC Lnk,* **shooken** *19-, now S;* **shook** *la18-, now Ayr* ['ʃakən, 'ʃukən, &c; also 'ʃøkn] **1** *vti* = shake *la14-.* **2** *vi, of a group of people* reel, give way *la14.* **3** *vt* shake the faith of (a person) *la14-.*

n **1** = shake *la18-.* **2** the shaking of grain from an ear of corn, *esp* in wind etc; the loss of grain so caused *la18-, now Sh Ork N.* **3** *wrestling* a twist or throw, a bout *19.*

shaker &c **1** *in pl* a dress trimming of thin metal plates which vibrated as the wearer moved; *also transf* applied to dewdrops *16, only Sc.* **2** *chf in pl* (1) the moving racks in a threshing mill *19-, now local Ork-Kcb.* (2) the quaking-grass *la19-, now Loth Kcb Rox.* (3) a fit of shaking, from disease or fear; a state of terror or intimidation *la19-, Sh-C.* **shakie tremlie &c** *adj* wobbly, insecure; giddy *la19-, Kcdn Ags Per.*

n, chf in pl = shaker *2(2), la19-, now NE Ags.*

shakins &c herring which have to be shaken out of the net and are thus damaged, inferior herring *la20-, Sh N.* **the shakins o the poke &c** the last remnants; the last-born of a family *20-.*

shakefork a pitchfork; *heraldry* a Y-shaped charge on the shield *la17-19.* **shake-wind** a strong blustery wind which shakes off ripe ears of corn *la18-19.*

~**-down &c** a makeshift or temporary bed *18-.* ~ **a fa** try a fall, have a wrestling bout or tussle *18-20, chf Bnf Abd.* ~ **a** *or* **one's fit, shanks** *etc* dance *la18-, local.* ~ **out 1** cast out the contents of *e17.* **2** unfurl and let out (a sail etc) with a shake *e16.* ~ **a trot** name of a dance *e16, only Sc.* **shak-and-trumble** = shaker *2(2), la19-, NE Ags.*

shakbotter *n* a player on the sackbut *e16.* [OED *sackbut*]

shake *see* SHAK

shall *see* SALL, SHELL

shalla &c *adj, n* = shallow *la19-.*

shalter &c *n* = shelter *18-, now Sh Ross.*

shaltie *see* SHELTIE

sham¹ &c *n* the leg *19-e20.* [only Sc; F *jambe*]

sham² *la19-,* **shan &c** *vi* make a wry face, grimace *19-, now Sh.*

shammie-leggit bandy-legged *la20-, Per Stlg Gsw.*

~**-gabbit** *etc* having the lower jaw protruding beyond the upper, with a projecting lower lip *19-, now C, SW.* [appar back-formation f SHAMMLE]

sham *see* SHAME

shamble *see* SHAMMLE

shambo &c *17-e19;* **schammo** *la16* *n* = chamois, goatskin leather *only Sc.*

shame &c; **sham &c** *la15-e19 n, vti* = shame *la14-.*

~**ful 1** = shameful *la14-.* **2** shaming, affording shame to *la16, only Sc.* ~**fully 1** = shamefully *16-.* **2** shamefacedly, modestly *la14.* **shamit &c reel** = shame reel, *19-e20, N.* ~ **reel** *etc* the first dance at a wedding (danced by the bride and best man, the bridegroom and bridesmaid) *19.* ~ **spring** the tune played for this *19, NE.* ~ **a ..!** *interj* not a blessed ..! *18-e20.* **think (black burnin** *la18-)* ~ be (very) ashamed *la15-.*

shamell *see* SHAMMLE

shamloch *e19;* **shamloh &c** *16-17* [*'ʃamlox &c] *n* a FARROW cow. [*cf* Gael *seamlach* a cow that gives milk without having a calf beside her]

shamloh *see* SHAMLOCH

shammade *vt* ornament with lace *la17.* [only Sc; appar F *chamarrer*]

shammle &c *19-, now NE,* **shamble** *19-;* **shamell** *18-19* ['ʃaml] *v* **1** *vi* = shamble, walk awkwardly etc. **2** *vt* (1) twist, strain, dislocate *19-e20*. (2) *specif* twist (the face), make (a wry mouth) *18-e19*.

shambling, shammelt now *esp of teeth* twisted, out of alignment *20-*, *NE*. **schamlich** *vi* walk with a shambling gait *la19-e20*, *NE*. *n* a weak, puny, or slovenly person or animal *la19-*, *NE*. **~-shanks** *etc* a bandy-legged person *la18-19*.

shan &c *adj* **1** of poor quality, bad, shabby *18-*, now *Rox*. **2** bashful, timid, frightened *19-*, now *Cai*. [see SND]

shan *see* SHAM[2]

shanacle *see* SHANNACK

shandeller *see* CHANDLER

shane *see* SHINE[1]

shangie[1] **&c** *la18-*, **shangan &c** *la18-e19* ['ʃaŋɪ, 'ʃaŋən] *n* **1** *also* **shanie** *la17* a cleft stick, tin can etc put on a dog's tail *la17-19*. **2** *mining etc* a (straw or hemp) washer put round a drill or bolt to prevent leakage *la19-*, now *Abd WC*. **3** *in pl* manacles, handcuffs *19-*, now *Abd Ags Per*. **4** a forked stick used to make a catapult *la20-*, *local Bnf-SW*.

vt, *also fig* put a SHANGIE on (a dog's tail) *la18-e20*. [see SND]

shangie[2] **&c** ['ʃaŋɪ] *n* a row, disturbance, fight *20-*, now *local Bnf-Lnk*. [reduced f COLLIESHANGIE]

shangie[3] **&c** [*'ʃaŋɪ] *adj* thin, scraggy, gaunt *19*.

~-moud with gaunt cheeks, lantern-jawed *18*. [Gael *seang* thin, slender]

shanie *see* SHANGIE[1]

shank &c *n* **1** = shank *16-*. **2** a leg of meat *19-*. **3** the leg of a stocking; a stocking, or *later* any garment, in the process of being knitted *16-*, now *local Bnf-WC*, only *Sc*. **4** the stem or shaft of an implement, *eg* a spoon, brush, glass *la18-*. **5** the stem or stalk of a tree, plant, or fruit *16-*. **6** (1) the lower part or sides of a cornstack *la19-*, *N*, *local C*. (2) a chimney-stack *la20-*, *WC*. **7** the vertical shaft of a mine *17-*, now *Fif*, only *Sc*. **8** a downward spur or slope of a hill *17-*, now *Ags S*.

vti **1** walk, go, or cover on foot, *freq* ~ **it** *18-*, now *local Mry-S*, only *Sc*. **2** *vt* send off on foot, dismiss *18-*, now *Lnk*, only *Sc*. **3** *vi* knit stockings etc *19-*, now *Abd-Ags*, only *Sc*. **4** *vt* fit (a tool etc) with a SHANK (*n* 4) or handle *la19-*, *local Ags-SW*. **5** *vti* sink (a shaft) *18-*, now *Fif*, only *Sc*.

~er 1 a knitter of stockings *17-*, *chf Abd*, only *Sc*. **2** a gadabout; a (young) active person *19-*, *Mry Abd*. **~er's naigie** = ~*s'*(*s*) naig(ie), *20-*, *local Ags-Ayr*. **~ie** a small cooking pan with a long handle *19-*, now *Dmf*, only *Sc*. **..-~it** having legs of a specified kind *la18-e20*: '*sturdy-shankit*'.

~s'(**s**) **naig(ie) &c** shanks' pony *18-*, now *C, S*.

shankie &c *n* a lavatory *la20-*, *C*. [f *Shanks*, Barrhead, Renfr, the well-known manufacturers of lavatory equipment]

shanna *see* SALL

shannack &c *n* a *Halloween* (HALLOW[2]) bonfire; now more *gen* any outdoor fire *19-*, *Per Fif*. **shanacle &c** = *n*, *19-*, *Per Fif*. [only *Sc*; Gael *samhnag* a Halloween bonfire, f *Samhuinn* Hallowtide; *cf* SOWNACK]

shantieglan *n* an itinerant knife-grinder *la20-*, *WC*. [obscure]

shantrews &c; seann triubhas &c ['ʃan-'truz] *n* a solo *Highland dance* (HIELAND); the tune played for it *la18-*, only *Sc*. [Gael *sean triubhas* old trousers]

shap *see* CHAP[3], SHAPE, SHAUP, SHOP

shape &c; shap &c *la14-19 v*, *pt also* **schup &c** *la14-18* [*ʃøp*]. *ptp also* **shapen &c** *la14-18* **1** *vti* = shape *la14-*. **2** attempt, endeavour, contrive (to do etc) *la14-*, now *Cai*. **3** *vr* set about, prepare (to do etc or for) *la14-16*. **4** *vi*, *chf* ~ **to** turn out, show promise of being etc; adapt oneself to *la18-20*. **5** ~ **to** direct one's course to, set out for *la19-*, now *Cai Ayr*. **6** *vi* cut (cloth) in a certain pattern or shape, *freq* ~ **and sew** *18-*, now *Sh-N*.

n **1** = shape *la15-*. **2** a dressmaking pattern, a pattern piece *20-*. **3** an attitude, posture; conduct, manner *la19-*. **4** an odd or droll figure *20-*, *Wgt Rox*.

schapen naturally fitted **for** *la14*. **shapin(g)s** *dress-making* leftover cuttings or shreds of cloth *19-*, now *Abd*.

mak a ~ make an effort (**at**) *la19-*.

shapen *see* SHAPE

shapio(u) &c *n* a type of hat *e16*, only *Sc*. [? F *chapeau*]

shard *see* SHAIRD

share &c *adj* = sheer, bright *la16*. *vt* pour off (top liquid), separate (a liquid) from its dregs *19-*, now *SW*. [*cf* SHEER[1]]

share *see* SHEAR[1]

sharg &c *n* a stunted starved-looking person; a short bow-legged man; an impudent man *17-e20*. **~ar &c 1** a puny, weakly person *18-*, now *NE Ags*. **2** the weakest of a brood or litter *la19-*, *NE*. **~art** stunted *la19-*, now *Abd*. [Gael *searg* a puny creature]

sharn *see* SHAIRN

sharp *see* SHAIRP

sharrie &c *n*, *vi* quarrel, fight *la19-20*, *NE*. [only *Sc*; see SND]

sharrow &c *adj* bitter to the taste *19-*, now *Cai*. [Gael *searbh* bitter, tart, sarcastic]

shathmont *n* the distance from the knuckle of the little finger in the clenched fist to the tip of the extended thumb, *approx* six inches (150 mm) *la18-e19*, only *Sc*. [var of Eng *shaftment*]

shatter &c *vi* = chatter, chirp, rattle *la16-e20*. **shatters** *see* CHATTERS

shauch &c [ʃax] *adj* awry, askew, twisted *19-e20*. [perh back-formation f next]

shauchle &c *19-*; **shachle &c, shochle &c** ['ʃaxl] *v* **1** *vi* walk without lifting the feet, shuffle, walk clumsily *18-*, *Gen except Sh Ork*. **2** *vt* wear (a garment, shoes etc) out of shape *19-*, now *WC Kcb*. **3** ~ **off** shuffle or shake off, get rid of *20-*, now *Abd Kcdn*.

n **1** a shuffling, shambling gait *20-*, now *Abd Kcdn*. **2** an old worn-out shoe, slipper etc *19-e20*. **3** a weakly, stunted, or deformed person or animal *20-*, now *Ags Per*.

shachled &c now *C*, **shauchlie** now *NE*, *C* = *shauchlin* 1, *19-*. **shauchlin &c 1** unsteady or weak on one's feet, shuffling; knock-kneed; wearing worn-out shoes *19-*, now *N-S*. **2** of shoes out of shape, down at heel and worn, badly-fitting *19-*, *local N-S*. [only Sc; see SND]

shauld &c *15-*; **schald &c** *lal4-el7*, **schawd** *lal4*, **shaul &c** *lal6-20* [ʃɑl(d); *ʃɑd] adj **1** shallow, not deep *lal4-*, now *local Sh-Kcb*. **2** shallow in character, empty-headed *18-*, now *Sh*.

n a shallow part in the sea or a river, a shoal *lal4-*, now *local Sh-Ayr*. [OE *sceald*. OED *shoal*]

shaup &c; shap &c *18-e19 n* **1** the seed husk of a leguminous plant; a pea-pod *18-*, now *C*. **2** an empty-headed, frivolous person, a useless creature *18-e19*. **3** usu in pl bits, smithereens *lal9-*, *Bnf Abd Kcdn*.

vt shell (pea-pods), take (peas) from the husks *lal9-*, now *Stlg WC*.

~**ie** lank, not plump *19-*, now *Lnk Ayr*. [see SND]

shave &c *vti, pt also* **schuif** *lal4-el6* [*ʃøf]. pt also **schevin** *el6* [*'ʃevən] = shave *lal4*.

shavelin *19-e20*, **chaveling** *el6* a tool for smoothing hollow or circular wood *NE*.

shavie a trick, prank, swindle, *freq* **play a shavie** *18-19*, *only Sc*. **to a shavin** exactly, to a nicety *19-*, now *Cai Ayr*.

shave *see* SHAIF, SHEAVE

shavel *see* SHEVEL

shaviter *n* a slovenly disreputable-looking character *19-e20*. [prob altered f Eng *shaver* a rogue]

shaw¹ &c, show &c *15- v, pt also* **shawit &c** now *Sh*; **shew** now *Sh* [ʃ(j)u]. ptp also **shawn &c** *lal6-*, now *Sh* **1** *vti* = show *lal4-*. **2** *vt* display, unfurl (a banner etc) *lal5-16*. **3** inflict (shame etc) *el6*. **4** *law* decree, award *el6*. **5** prove, make out (a person or thing) **to be** (something) *lal6-*. **6** *vi* ~ **well** etc have a good etc appearance, make a good etc show *lal4-*. **7** *vt, chf* **shaw** cut off the SHAWS of *(turnips* (TURNEEP)) *lal9-*, *Gen except Sh*.

n **1** = show *16-*. **2** *in pl, chf* **shaws** the stalks and leaves of potatoes, *turnips* (TURNEEP) etc *18-*.

shewer ['ʃoər] *law* a person appointed by a court to show a jury premises etc on which litigation is based *19-*.

show-buik ['ʃo'buk] a child's picture-book *20-*, now *Stlg wLoth Lnk*.

shaw furth come forth into view *lal4*. **the shows** [ʃoz] a fair with roundabouts, sideshows etc *20-*, *C*.

shaw² *n* a small, *esp* natural wood, a thicket *lal4-*, now *chf literary and in place-names*. [ME]

shaw *see* SAW¹

shawis *see* SHEAVE

shawl &c *n* = shawl.

~**ie** *n* **1** = *n*, *lal9-*. **2** an urban working-class woman or girl *e20*, *Gsw Uls*. adj *(of a* ~**ie** n 2) wearing a shawl over the head and shoulders as an outdoor garment *e20*, *Abd C Uls*.

shawn *see* SHAW¹

shayth *n* reason, what is reasonable; (a person's) rights *el6*, *Mry*. [only Sc; ? Gael *seadh*]

she &c *lal6-*, **scho &c** *lal4-18*; **sheu &c** *lal6-el8, 20-* (Sh Ork) [ʃi; Sh Ork ʃo; Ork also ʃe; *sEC, SW, S* ʃe; *unstressed* ʃə] personal pronoun, accusative and dative **her** *18-*, **hir &c, hur &c** *19-* [hɪr, hër, hʌr] **1** = she, her *lal4-*. **2** used by a husband of his wife or by a servant of his or her mistress *lal9-*. **3** referring to an inanimate object, *eg* a mill, bell, church, clock *lal4-e20*. **4** *pseudo-Highl, also with* **her** *as subject* I, me *lal5-19*.

he or ~, ~ **and he** this one or that, everyone *16*.

sheaf *see* SHAIF

shear¹ &c; share &c *19-e20* [ʃir; *Sh Ork nEC* ʃer] *vti, pt also* **schare &c** *lal4-el6*, **shure &c** *16*, now *Sh* [ʃør, ʃer; *NE* ʃur] **1** = shear *lal4*. **2** *vt* cut (a person) for the extraction of a stone, *chf* **shorne of the stane** *lal6*, *only Sc*. **3** reap (corn), cut (crops) with a sickle *16-*, now *local Sh-Per*.

n **1** the act of cutting *(esp* corn) *18-*, now *Sh*. **2** a shorn animal *lal7*, *only Sc*. **3** a cut edge, *esp* the cut end of a sheaf of corn *la20-*, *Mry Abd*.

~**ed** *of a coin* clipped *el7*. ~**er 1** a corn-reaper, sickleman *16-*, now *Sh*. **2** a person who removes the nap of cloth by shearing *lal5*. ~**er's bannock, scone** etc a large bread roll etc eaten on the harvest field *lal9-*, *local Ags-Bwk*. ~**ing &c 1** = shearing *lal5-*. **2** a cleavage, parting *el5*, *only Sc*. **3** reaping; harvest *19-20*. **4** *mining* a preliminary vertical cut *lal8-19*. ~**ing darg** = ~ *darg*, *lal6*, *only Sc*. **shorn 1** = shorn *15-*. **2** *of meat or vegetables* chopped up *lal6-el9*. **3** carved *16-el8*.

~ **darg &c** a day's work at reaping or shearing (as a feudal service to a landlord) *17-18*, *only Sc*. ~ **mouse** the shrew *lal9-*, *local Cai-Ayr*. ~ **shope** a place where cloth is manufactured *lal7*, *only Sc*.

where wind and water *or* **weather** ~**s** on a watershed or high ridge *lal6-el9*, *only Sc*. [cognate w SHEAR²]

shear² &c [ʃir; *Sh Ork nEC* ʃer] *n* **1** *in pl, also* **cheris &c** *el7* = shears *17-*. **2** *in pl* (a pair of) scissors; (sheep-)clippers *17-*. **3** *in sing* a pair of shears *lal6-19*. **4** *chf in pl* (1) a piece of metal in which the axle-ends of a wheel or roller turn; the beam of a farm cart between which the shafts are placed *18-*, *now Per Kcb.* (2) *mining* a contrivance for attaching coal HUTCHES to the haulage rope *19-*, *now Fif.*

~ grinder a person who grinds SHEARS *la17-19.*

calke is no ~s *proverb* chalking the cloth is not cutting it *e17*, *only Sc.* [cognate w SHEAR¹]

shearn *see* SHAIRN

sheath &c [ʃiθ, ʃeθ; *Sh* ʃed] *n* **1** = sheath *la15-*. **2** a pad on a belt used to hold knitting needles when not in use *la18-*, *now Sh N-WC.*

sheave &c *la18-*; **schefe** *la14*, **shave &c** *18-e20*, *only Sc* [ʃiv, ʃev, ʃef] *n*, *pl also* **schyffis &c** *la15-16*, **s(c)hawis** *la16* **1** = sheave, a pulley(-wheel) *15-*. **2** a slice of bread, cheese etc *la14*, *18-*.

vt cut into slices *la19-*, *now Sh Abd.* [*cf* SHIVE]

sheave *see* SHAIF

sheckle *see* SHACKLE, SHOCKLE

shed &c, **shade &c** *16-20*; **shede &c** *now Sh Ork NE* [ʃɛd; *Sh Ork N* ʃid; *nEC* ʃed] *vti*, *pt also* **scheid &c** *15-16*. **1** = shed *la14-*. **2** *vt* separate, divide (*now esp* lambs from ewes) *la15-*, *Gen except Sh Ork.* **3** separate, part company (1) *vi*, *la15-e19*; (2) *vr*, *la16.* **4** *vi* be dispersed, scatter *la14-16*. **5** *vt* (1) cleave (with a weapon) *la15-e16*, *only Sc.* **6** (1) part or comb (the hair, a sheep's fleece etc) to one side or the other *la18-*. (2) *vi*, *of the hair* part, be combed one way or the other *18-*, *now Abd.*

n **1** the act of sorting out sheep, *freq* as a test in sheepdog trials *20-*, *Gen except Sh Ork.* **2** the parting of the hair on the head or the wool on a sheep's back *16-*. **3** *chf* **sheed** a slice, piece divided off *18-e20*, *chf Ags.* **4** a clot (of blood) *e16.* **5** a strip of land, a distinct or separate piece of ground *la15-*, *only Sc*, *now chf in place-names.* **6** an opening, gap, *esp* between the two sets of threads in a loom *la19-*, *now C.*

shedder an instrument for parting, a pen for sorting sheep *20-*, *Gen except Sh Ork.* **shedding 1** the act of separating sheep *19-20.* **2** a place where roads branch, a parting of ways *18-*, *now C.*

shame is past the ~ of his *etc* **hair** he etc has lost all sense of shame *la16-e18.* **~ someone's shanks** set someone's legs apart *la16*, *only Sc.*

shedda &c *la18-*, *now Sh*, **shadow** *17-*, **scaddow** *19-e20*, *S*; **schadow &c** *la14-16*, **shaddie &c** *la19-e20*, *Loth Bwk n* (*la14-*), *v* (*16-*) = shadow.

~ half the portion of a piece of land facing north *16-19*, *only Sc.*

shede *see* SHED

shee *see* SHAE

sheed *see* SHED

sheel &c; **shill &c** [ʃil; *C also* ʃɪl] *vt* **1** shell (peas, grain, flax seeds etc), take out of the husk or pod *la15-*, *now local Sh-Lnk.* **2** cut (a mussel) from its shell *19-*, *now local Sh-Bwk.* **3** 'rook' (a

person), win staked money, marbles etc from *la19-*, *now NE Dmf.* **4** 'shell **out**' (money) *19-*, *now N.* **5** throw **out** or scatter right and left *la20-*, *NE.*

n the act of husking corn; the act of turning something out of its container, a throwing about *la20-*, *NE.*

~ing 1 the action of SHEEL *v*, *la16-*. **2** *freq in pl* the grain removed from the husk by milling; *occas* the husks thus removed, the bran *16-*, *now local Sh-Wgt.* **~ing hill** a piece of rising ground where grain was winnowed by the wind *la16-*, *now in place-names.* **~ing seeds** the husks removed from the grain in the first process of milling *18-e20*; *see* SEED. **~ing stane** a millstone, *specif* one to remove the husks in the first process *la18-*, *now Loth.* **~ock &c** *chf in pl* the small or light grains of corn blown away during winnowing; the chaff and broken straw riddled off in threshing *17-*, *now NE.*

~blade a knife for scooping out mussels for bait *20-*, *NE Fif.*

like a mill ~ing at a quick, steady pace; volubly *19-e20.* [ME *schylle*; related to Eng *shale* and SHELL]

sheemach &c [ˈʃiməx] *n* **1** a tangled or matted mass of hair etc *la19-20*, *NE.* **2** a pad or woven covering, used as a saddle; a kind of pack-saddle *19-20*, *chf Abd.* **3** *contemptuous* a worthless or worn-out thing, a puny person or animal *19-20*, *N.* [only Sc; *perh* connected w Gael *sìoman* a rope of twisted straw or hay]

sheen &c *adj*, *also* **schane** *e16* = sheen, beautiful, bright *la14-e19.*

n **1** = sheen *la18-*. **2** the pupil (of the eye) *e16*, *e19.*

vt shine, gleam, glisten *la14-*, *now Sh NE-WC.*

sheen *see* SHAE, SUNE

sheep &c *la14-*; **schip** *la16* *n* = sheep *la14-*.

~ie 1 = *n*, *la19-*. **2** the cone of the Scots pine *la20-*, *Bnf Abd.* **~ie mae &c 1** a sheep, so-called from its bleat *20-*, *local.* **2** a flower of the wild white clover *20-*, *local Cai-Arg.* **~ie's silver** = *sheep siller*, *la20-*, *N.*

~ bucht &c a sheep pen, *esp* at a market or for milking-ewes *18-*, *Gen except Sh Ork.* **~ drain** an open or surface drain in pasture land *la19-*, *Gen except Sh Ork.* **~ eik** the natural grease in a sheep's wool *19-*, *Bwk Wgt S.* **~ fank** a (*dry-stone*) (DRY) enclosure where sheep are gathered for shelter, dipping, shearing etc *19-*. **~ fauld &c** = sheepfold *la16-*, *now Cai.* **~ gang** a sheep pasture, *esp* of hill-grazing *la18-*, *now Loth S.* **~ head &c** a sheep's head, *esp* one used to make BROTH¹ *16-19*, *only Sc.* **~ hewit** of the colour of a sheep's fleece *la16*, *only Sc.* **~man** ? a sheepstealer, rogue *e17*, *only Sc.* **~ money** a yearly payment to a farm-servant in lieu of permission to pasture a few of his own sheep on the farm *la18-e20*, *Bwk.* **~ net** a net on stakes to confine sheep on a *turnip* (TURNEEP) field *19-*. **~'s purls** sheep-dung *20-*. **~**

raik a path or strip of ground trodden by grazing sheep *19-e20.* ~ **ree** = ~ *fank, 19-,* now *Wgt.* ~ **rodding** a sheep-track *19-20.*
sheep shank the leg of a sheep, *freq fig* **nae** ~ **shank** a person of some importance *la18-,* now *Stlg SW, only Sc.* ~ **siller** white mica, *esp* in small scales *19-,* now *WC.* ~ **steid &c** a sheep farm *la16-e17, only Sc.* ~ **stell** = ~ *fank, 19-,* now *Cai Bwk S.* ~ **taid &c** a sheep tick *19-,* *WC-Rox.* ~ **troddles** = ~'*s purls, 20-,* *Lnk Kcb S.*
sheer¹ &c *adj* = sheer.
vti pour off (top liquid), separate a liquid from its dregs *20-,* now *Lnk.*
scheirly brightly, clearly *la15, only Sc.* [ME var of SHIRE²]
sheer² *adj* ~ **dog** *etc* the tope or Portugal shark *19-e20.* [see SND]
sheer *see* SHUIR
sheet &c *n* **1** = sheet *la14-.* **2** a sheet of canvas folded into a pouch to hold corn-seed when sowing *la18-,* now *Cai.* **3** a large canvas sheet made into a pocket for holding wool; the amount it contains, 240 lb (108 kg) *la19-,* now *Cai.*
~ **shaking &c** remains of meal etc shaken from a SHEET *16, Abd, only Sc.*
sheet *see* SHUIT
shelband *see* SHELVIN
shell &c; shall &c *la19-, Sh Ork N* *n* **1** = shell *la14-.* **2** (1) a scale of a balance *16-e20, only Sc.* (2) the bowl or pan which holds the oil in a CRUISIE *la19, NE.* (3) a saucer *la19-, Bnf Abd.* **3** *in pl* fragments, sherds *la16-,* now *Sh, only Sc.* **4** *in pl* the lumps of burnt limestone before it is slaked, underground quicklime *18-,* now local *Bnf-Ayr.*
v **1** *vt* = shell *18-.* **2** *vi and passive, of sheep or their wool* become caked with driven snow *la18-19.*
~**ing** husked oats etc; chaff *17-19.* ~**ing seeds &c** bran *18-20.* ~**y coat &c** **1** a water-sprite wearing a shell-covered coat *18-19, only Sc.* **2** a *sheriff officer* (SHERIFF), bailiff *la18.*
~ **paddock** a tortoise *la16-17, only Sc.*
shute at *etc* **the shell 1** shoot at a target *la15.* **2** *of a man* have sexual intercourse *e16.* [*cf* SHEEL]
shellwing, shelmont *see* SHELVIN
shelt *see* SHELTIE
shelter *n* = shelter *la17-.*
~**age** a place of shelter *17-e19, only Sc.*
sheltie &c; shaltie &c *la17-19,* **shelt &c** *19-,* *Ork Abd* ['ʃelt(ɪ); *Abd* 'ʃalt(ɪ), 'ʃʌlt(ɪ); *Ork* 'ʃolt(ɪ)] **1** a Shetland pony, one of a breed of very small horses, *orig* native to Shetland; also applied to any pony, *usu* a GARRON¹ *17-.* **2** *chf joc* a Shetlander *la18-, Sh N.* [see SND]
shelvin &c *la19-,* now *NE;* **shilvin &c** *19,* **shellwing &c** *17-,* now *Sh-Cai,* **shelmont &c** *18-,* now local *Per-S,* **shelband &c** *19-,* now *Ayr* *n, usu in pl* part of the sides of a cart, *now usu*

movable boards to allow the carrying of higher or bulkier loads. [eModEng *shelvinge,* verbal noun of Eng *shelve;* later alterations are by association of the second element with Eng *band* etc]
shenachie &c *la15-;* **sennachie &c** *la18-* ['ʃɛnəxɪ] *n, orig* a professional recorder and reciter of family history, genealogy etc; *now* a teller of traditional GAELIC heroic tales *la15-.* [Sc and IrGael *seanachaidh*]
shent &c *ptp, adj* **1** put to shame, disgraced, ruined *la14-e20.* **2** defeated (in a fight) *la14-15.*
vt destroy, ruin *la16.*
n disgrace *la14-15, only Sc.* [ptp of obs Eng *shend.* OED *shend*]
shepherd &c; schiphird &c *16* ['ʃɛpərd; *St* 'ʃepərd] *n* = shepherd *16-.*
~('**s**) **check** = ~'*s tartan, la19-.* ~'**s club** the common mullein *18.* ~'**s plaid** a PLAID worn by shepherds, *esp* one in ~'*s tartan,* a MAUD *19-.* ~'**s stirk** a calf reared by a shepherd as one of his perquisites *la20-, WC Dmf.* ~('**s**) **tartan** (a cloth of) black-and-white check *la19-.*
sherd *see* SHAIRD
sheriff &c *15-;* **shir(r)eff &c** *la14-18,* **serefe &c** *la14-15,* **shirra &c,** **sherra &c** *15-* *n* **1** = sheriff *la14-.* **2** the (hereditary) chief officer of a shire or county, responsible to the sovereign for peace and order, and having civil and criminal jurisdiction *la14-e18;* see ~ *depute* 1 and ~ *principal* 1. **3** the chief judge of a *sheriffdom, 18-;* see ~ *depute* 2 and ~ *principal* 2. **4** a legal officer who performs judicial duties and certain administrative duties, some of the latter delegated by the *sheriff principal, popularly 18-20, officially la20-;* see also ~ *substitute.*
~**dom 1** the area under the jurisdiction of a sheriff, now a group of REGIONS or a division of a REGION *la14-, only Sc.* **2** = sheriffdom, the office of a sheriff *la16.* ~**ship** the office of a sheriff *la15-.*
~ **clerk** the clerk of the *sheriff court, la14-.* **S~ Court &c** the court presided over by the SHERIFF *15-.* ~ **depute 1** the lawyer appointed to perform the judicial duties of the SHERIFF *n* 2, *15-e18.* **2** = *n* 3, *18-e19.* ~ **fee** a fee payable to the SHERIFF *17-18, only Sc.* ~('**s**) **fiars** = FIARS *la17-18, only Sc.* ~('**s**) **gloves** a perquisite of the SHERIFF levied at a fair *16-e17, only Sc.* ~ **mair** *18-e19,* ~ **officer** *la17-* an official or messenger who carries out the warrants of a SHERIFF, enforces DILIGENCE (*n* 2), serves WRITS, etc. ~ **principal 1** = *n* 2, *la15-e18.* **2** = *n* 3, *18-.* ~ **roll** the roll on which *sheriff-court* proceedings were recorded *e16, only Sc.* ~ **substitute** = *n* 4; *orig* appointed by the SHERIFF (*n* 3), *latterly* (*la19-20*) appointed by the Crown *18-20.*
~ **in that part** a person appointed to substitute for the SHERIFF in certain duties *la15-;* see *in that part* (PAIRT).
sherp *see* SHAIRP

sherra *see* SHERIFF

sherrack &c; shirrak &c *n* a noisy squabble, rumpus *19-*, *now Gsw.*

vt raise a riot about (a person), incite a mob against (a person) by publicly reviling and denouncing him *20-*, *now WC*. [uncertain]

sherville *n* = chervil *la17*.

shet *see* SHIT

sheth &c [ʃɛθ] *n* **1** a crossbar, *esp* a spar in the frame or sides of a cart etc *la15-*, *now Per Bwk*. **2** a division of land *e15*. **3** a connecting bar or strut in a plough *18-e20*. [*see* SND]

Shetland ['ʃɛtlən(d); *NE also* 'ʃitlən] ~ **hose** stockings made of *Shetland wool*, *19*. ~ **shawl** a kind of very fine lacework shawl made of *Shetland wool*, *la19-*. ~ **sheep** a breed of small sheep native to Shetland, now much interbred *la18-*. ~ **wool** *orig* wool from the Shetland sheep; *now, unless qualified by* **real, pure,** *or* **genuine,** used as a general term for pure wool of a similar quality *la18-*. [the place-name; *see also* ZETLAND]

sheu *see* SHE

sheuch &c *18-*, **sheugh &c** *18-*, **sough &c** *la16-*; **seuch &c** *16-e19*, **shough &c** *la17-e20* [*N sEC* ʃux; *nEC, WC* ʃ(j)ʌx; *S* ʃjux; *Sh* ʃox; *Ork* søx] *n* **1** a trench in the ground, *esp* for drainage, a ditch, open drain *16-*. **2** a temporary trench or furrow for plants *19-*. **3** a furrow made by a plough *19-e20*. **4** a street gutter *la19-*, *nEC Loth WC*.

vti **1** dig, trench, make a ditch or furrow (in) *16-*, *now local Per-Wgt*. **2** *vt* lay (a plant etc) in the ground; *specif* put (seedlings etc) in a temporary trench for later transplantation or storage *18-*. **3** bury, cover with earth *18-19*.

in a *or* **the** ~ in a state of squalor or misery, ruined *la19-*, *now wLoth SW*. **up a** *or* **the** ~ in error, mistaken *la20-*, *WC Dmf*. [northern eME *sogh* a swamp]

sheuken *see* SHAK

sheul *see* SHUIL

shevel &c *16-*, **showl &c** *la18-*, *now N Per*; **shavel &c** *la18-20*, **shile &c** *19-*, *SW* ['ʃevl; *local* ʃʌul; *SW* ʃəil] *adj*, *of the mouth* distorted, twisted *16-19*.

v **1** *vt* twist out of shape; distort (the mouth), screw up (the face) *la16-*, *now N Per*. **2** *vi* become distorted; make a wry mouth, grimace from vexation, pain, a bitter taste etc *19-*, *now N Per SW*.

n a wry smile, grimace *la19-*, *now SW*.

~(**ing**) **gabbit** *etc* having a wry or twisted mouth *18-19*. [also northern ModEng dial; *appar* cognate w Eng dial *shail*, ME *schayle* walk crookedly]

shew &c, sew; sue &c *la16-19*, **she &c** *la16-19*, **show &c** *18-e19* [ʃu] *vti*, *ptp also* **shewed** *19-e20* = sew *16-*.

n the act of sewing; a spell of needlework *20-*.

~**ing gold** gold thread *16*. ~**ing silver** silver thread *e16*. ~**ster** a seamstress, needlewoman *17-*, *now NE*.

~-**up** the closure or shutting-down of a business, bankruptcy *20-*, *local Ags-S*.

shew *see* SAW[1], SHAW[1]

shewe *see* SAW[1]

shiak &c ['ʃaɪək] *n*, *chf in pl* a kind of grey-striped black oats *18-e20*. [only Sc; obscure]

shid *see* SALL

shidder *n*, *vti* = shudder *19-20*, *chf Ags*, *only Sc*.

shide *vt* cleave, split *e16*. [ME ptp *ischyt*]

shiel[1] **&c** *la15-*, *in place-names la12-*; **shield &c** *la15-18* [ʃil] *n* **1** a temporary or roughly-made hut or shed, *freq* one used by (salmon) fishermen or shepherds (and their animals), a *shieling* (*n* 2) *la15-20*. **2** a small house, hovel *la16-e19*. **3** a summer pasture with a shepherd's hut or huts *17-e19*.

vti live in a summer-pasture hut, herd (sheep and cattle) at a SHIEL *la18-e19*.

~**ing &c** *only Sc* **1** a high or remote summer pasture, *usu* with a shepherd's hut or huts *la16-*, *now hist*. **2** a roughly-made hut, *esp* one for shepherds and dairymaids on a *shieling* (*n* 1) *17-*, *now hist* [ScL *scalinga*, *la12*]. ~ **house** a shepherd's or fisherman's hut *la16-e20*. ~ **toun** = *n* 3, *e17*. [nME]

shiel[2] *19-*, *now NE*, **shield &c** *16-*; **scheld** *la14-e16* [ʃil(d)] *n* **1** = shield *la14-*. **2** (the seat of) a privy *16*, *only Sc*. **3** a keyhole plate *e17*, *only Sc*.

with spear and ~ in battle array; by force of arms *16*.

shiel *see* SHUIL

shield *see* SHIEL[1], SHIEL[2]

shiffle *see* SHUFFLE, SHUIL

shift &c *vti* **1** = shift *la16-*. **2** *vi* change places with *la18-*, *now Abd Ags*. **3** (1) *vt* change (one's clothes, shoes etc) *la18-*. (2) change the clothes of (another person), provide (someone) with (fresh clothes) *18-*, *now local Sh-Per*. (3) *vir* change one's clothes, put on clean clothes *19-*. **4** *vti*, *jute and linen spinning* change the bobbins on a spinning frame *la20-*, *EC Renfr*. **5** *vi* make a move in the game of draughts *la19-*. **6** (1) *vti*, *with infinitive or gerund* put off, defer *18*. (2) *vt* evade, dodge *e18*.

n **1** = shift *17-*. **2** a way of earning one's living, *chf* **honest** ~ *la16-18*, *only Sc*. **3** a change of situation, abode or employment *la19-*, *local*. **4** each successive crop in a system of crop-rotation; the land or field on which this is grown *18-*, *Gen except Sh Ork*. **5** a change of clothing *19-*. **6** a move in the game of draughts *la19-*.

~**in claes** one's second-best clothes, those worn when changing from one's working clothes *la19-*, *EC, WC*.

~ **one's feet** change one's shoes and stockings *20-*.

shig *n* a small temporary hay- or cornstack *20-*, *now Wgt*. [ModIr dial; IrGael *síog* a rick of corn, a swath]

shilagie &c [ʃə'lagɪ] *n* the coltsfoot, *esp* its leaves used by juvenile smokers as a substitute for tobacco *la19-*, *now local Ags-Lnk*. [short for TUSHILAGO]

shilcorn &c *19-20*, **selkhorn** *la17*, *only Sc n* a pimple, a blackhead. [obscure]

shile *see* SHEVEL

shilfa &c *19-*, *now Cai C, S*; **shoulfall** *la17*, **shilly &c** *la19-*, *now Fif n* the chaffinch. [only Sc; see SND]

shill¹ &c *adj, adv* shrill(y) *la15-19*. [ME]

shill² *adj* = chill *la16, e20*. [also northern ModEng dial]

shill *see* SHEEL

shilling &c *n* **1** = shilling *15-*. **2** the weight of twelve silver pennies *e15*, *only Sc*. **3** used until the 1950s in the classification of the strength of beer, from the price per barrel, *eg* **forty-~ ale** (*usu written* **40/-**) a very light beer; *later* re-introduced (without reference to the price) in the 'real-ale' boom of the 1970s, *la19-*.

~ **land** land of which the annual product was valued at a SHILLING under the *auld extent* (EXTENT), fixed (*la16*) at $\frac{1}{40}$ of a *ploughgate* (PLEUCH) or 2.6 *Scots acres* (SCOTS) *la16-*, *now hist and in place-names*.

want tippence *etc* **o the** ~ be mentally defective, be 'not all there' *19-*, *local Sh-Kcb*.

shilly *see* SHILFA

shilp *adj*, *also fig* sour, sharp, acid *20-*, *Cai*. [only Sc; back-formation f SHILPIT]

shilpie &c *adj* thin, puny, pinched-looking *19-e20*. [only Sc; var of next]

shilpit &c *adj* **1** *chf of persons* thin, puny, shrunken, starved- or drawn-looking *17-*, *Gen except Sh Ork*. **2** *of liquor* insipid, thin *19-*, *now Sh Ork*. **3** sour, bitter; no longer fresh *19-*, *now Sh Ork Cai*. [perh var of *shirpit* (SHIRP)]

shilvin *see* SHELVIN

shim *n* a horse-hoe, a kind of small plough for weeding, earthing up etc *19-*, *NE*.

vi use a horse-hoe, weed etc with a SHIM *la19-*, *NE*. [also in Eng dial; perh 'anglicized' f Eng *skim* (*cf* SKAIR² and Eng *share*)]

shimee &c ['ʃɪmɪ] *n* a straw rope *la20-*, *Suth-Inv*. [Gael *sìoman*]

shimley *see* CHIMLEY

shimmer *see* SKIMMER

shimmie *see* SHINTY

shin &c *n* **1** = shin *la15-*. **2** a ridge or steep hill-face, a projecting part of a piece of high ground *19-*, *now NE wLoth, only Sc*.

shin *see* SUNE

shine¹ &c *vti, pt also* **shane** *la14-e19*; **shined &c** *la15-e19* = shine *la14-*.

n **1** = shine. **2** a social gathering, mild jollification, party, *freq* **tea ~, cookie ~** *19-*, *now local Abd-Lnk*. **3** a stir, turmoil, row *la19-*, *now Sh Ork Cai Ags*.

shine² *vt* throw with force or violence, pitch, fling *la19-*, *chf S*. [uncertain]

shinner *see* CINNER

shinnon *see* SINNON

shinty &c *18-*, **shinny &c** *la17-e20*, **shimmie &c** *la19-e20 n* **1** a game like hockey played towards HAILS⁴ *n* 3, *now chf* in the *Highlands* (HIELAND) *la17-*. **2** a CAMAN, the club or stick used in the game *la18-*. **3** the ball or knot of wood etc used in the game *19*. [perh the cry *shin (to) ye*]

ship &c; scheip &c *la14-16*, **chep- &c** *15 n, v* = ship *la14-*.

~ **broken** shipwrecked; ruined by shipwreck *la14-e17*, *chf Sc*. ~ **fontane** a device for making salt water fresh *e17*, *only Sc*. ~ **rae** a sailyard *la16*, *only Sc*. ~ **rede** a roadstead *la16*, *only Sc*. ~ **wrack** = shipwreck *la16-*, *now Sh*.

shire¹ &c *n* **1** = shire *15-*. **2** a district or area, much smaller than the modern county, *prob* at one time under some separate (*eg* baronial or ecclesiastical) jurisdiction and with its own administrative centre *la18-*, *hist*. **3** **the S~** the county of Wigtown *la19-*, *SW*. **4** nickname for East Stirling football team *20-* [full name is *East Stirlingshire*].

schearstane &c a stone boundary mark of a SHIRE *e16*.

shire² &c *adj* **1** = shire, bright *la15-e18*. **2** *of liquid etc* clear, unclouded *15-e18*. **3** complete, sheer, utter *16-e19*. **4** thin; watery; sparse *16-e20*.

adv **1** brightly, clearly *la14-e16*. **2** sheer or straight down *e16*.

vti **1** pour off top liquid, separate a liquid from its dregs *19-20*. **2** *of the mind* (allow to) become clear *la19-*, *now Uls*.

shirins &c liquid which rises to the top and is poured off *19-e20*. **schirly** brightly *la15*. [*cf* SHEER¹]

shire *see* CHEER¹

shireff *see* SHERIFF

shirins *see* SHIRE²

shirp *vi* wither, shrivel *17*.

~it &c thin, shrunken, with sharp, drawn features *19-*, *EC, WC*. [only Sc; perh var of *sherp* (SHAIRP)]

shirra *see* SHERIFF

shirrak *see* SHERRACK

shirramuir &c; shirramere &c *NE* [ʃɪrə'mør, -'mer; *NE* -'mir] *n* **1** **the S~** the Jacobite rising of 1715 which ended in the battle of Sheriffmuir, near Stirling *la18-19*. **2** a noisy row, rumpus; a dressing-down *19-*, *now NE*.

shirreff *see* SHERIFF

shirrel &c *18-20*; **scherald** *e16*, **scherard** *la16*, **scheratt** *la16-19* ['ʃɪrl, *'ʃɪrət; *'ʃɪr-; &c] *n* a (piece of) turf, *esp* from the surface of a PEAT¹ bog. [only Sc; appar deriv of SHEAR¹]

shirrow &c *la16-e20*, **shrew &c** [ʃə'ru] *n, vt* = shrew *la14-*.

adj wicked, bad *e17*.

shissors &c *n pl* = scissors *18-e19*.
shit &c *n* **1** shit, excrement *la16-*. **2** contemptuous term for a person *16-*.
vti, pt also **schate** *e16*, **shet** *e17, lit and fig* = shit *16-*.
shither[1] &c ['ʃɪðər] *vi, n* shiver, shudder *19-, now Rox.* [see SND]
shither[2] &c ['ʃɪðər] *n pl* people; natives of a particular district; kinsfolk *20-, Cai.* [only Sc; var of *childer* &c obs pl of CHIELD]
shittle *see* SHUTTLE[1]
shiv *see* SHUVE
shive &c *n* a slice (of bread) *18-, now Pbls Bwk S.* [eME *schive; cf* SHEAVE]
shiver[1] &c ['ʃɪvər] *vti* = shiver *la15-*.
~**ing** &c *or* ~**y bite** a mouthful of food taken after bathing to allay shivering *la19-, now local C* [cf *chitterin bit* (CHITTER)].
shiver[2] ['ʃɪvər, 'ʃaɪvər] *n* **1** = shiver. **2** *chf in pl* splinters of stone, *esp* as broken off in stone-dressing *la18-, now EC Lnk.*
shivereens [ʃɪvəˈrinz] *n pl* fragments, small bits *la19-, local, N-SW.* [conflation of Eng *shivers* w *smithereens*]
shiverine &c *n* ? a goat-skin; *in pl* goat-skin gloves or ? breeches *16-17.* [only Sc; prob var of CHEVERON]
shoad *see* SHOD
shochle *see* SHAUCHLE
shock[1] *n* **1** = shock. **2** a (paralytic) stroke, cerebral haemorrhage or thrombosis *la19-*.
shock[2] *n* a roll of cloth containing 28 ELLS *e17, only Sc.* [Eng *shock* a lot of 60 pieces]
shockle &c *la16-e20*; **sheckle** *e17*, **shuchle** &c *e19* ['ʃokl, 'ʃogl; *'ʃʌxl; &c] *n* an icicle. [also northern ModEng dial; shortened f *ice-schok(k)il* (ICE)]
shod; shoad &c *pt, ptp* = shod.
vt, pt, ptp **shod(d)it 1** furnish with shoes, put shoes on; shoe (a horse) *19-*. **2** fit (a bootlace, arrow, spade etc) with a metal tip etc *18-*. **3** put iron toe- and heel-pieces on (a shoe), cover (shoe soles) with studs etc *la19-, now Sh Abd Ayr.* *n* **1** a shoe, *esp* a child's shoe *18-19.* **2** an iron tip etc on a (*usu* wooden) object to prevent wear; the metal tyre of a cartwheel *19-, local.* **3** a metal plate on the toe or heel of a shoe; a hobnail *19-, now Mry.*
shodding &c **1** boots and shoes, footwear *18-19.* **2** metal tips or edging *19-e20.*
shod shovel a wooden shovel with a metal rim *17-e18.* [pt, ptp of SHAE]
shoddie *n* a natural building stone, used roughly dressed *la20-, local Inv-Ayr.* [perh a noun form f OE *scādan*, Eng *shed* (*v*) divide; *cf* local Eng *shoad* loose fragments of ore]
shoe *see* SHAE
shog &c; **shogue** &c *18-*, **shug** *la18-*, **shoog** &c *19-* [ʃog, ʃʌg; *Fif also* ʃʌug; *Inv Mry sEC, S also* ʃug] *v* **1** *vt* shake, jog, cause to swing or rock *16-*. **2** *vi* sway, swing, rock from side to side,

wobble *18-, now NE, C.* **3** proceed at a leisurely but steady pace, jog along, keep going *18-, now Sh.*
n **1** a shaking state *la16.* **2** a jog, shake, nudge *18-, now Sh NE, C.* **3** the act or motion of swinging or rocking; a swinging-rope; a child's swing *la19-, now local Mry-Per.*
shoggie &c *v* = *v* 2, *19-20.* *n* = *n* 3, *20-, now C, S.* *adj* shaky, unsteady, wobbly *la19-, NE-Per Ayr.* **sho(o)gie boat** a swing-boat at a fair *la19-, local.* **shoggie bog** = ~ *bog, 20-, now Lnk Dmf.* ~**y-shoo** &c **1** a seesaw, the game of seesaw; *also interj, la17-e20.* **2** a swing *19-, now local EC-S.* *vi* seesaw *19-.* **shoggin boat** = *sho(o)gie boat, la19-, local.* **shoggle** &c *19-*, **shoogle** &c *19-*, **shuggle** *19-20* ['ʃugl, 'ʃʌgl; *NE, S* 'ʃogl; *Fif also* 'ʃʌugl] *v* **1** *vi* sway, move unsteadily, rock, wobble, swing *18-, now local.* **2** *vt* shake, joggle, cause to totter or rock *19-, now local Sh-C.* **3** *vi* jog along, move with little unsteady jerks; shuffle *19-, now Sh Cai.* *n* **1** a jog, jolt, shake *19-, now Sh-Ags.* **2** the act of swinging on a rope, tree-branch etc *la20-, local Ags-Ayr.* **shooglie** &c shaky, unsteady, tottery, insecure *19-.* **shooglie jock** brawn in jelly *20-, now Stlg wLoth Lnk.*
shoog boat = *sho(o)gie boat, 20-, local.* ~ **bog** a soft watery bog, a quagmire *19-20.* [ME]
shogue *see* SHOG
shone *see* SHAE
shoo &c *interj* **1** = shoo. **2** *rejecting another's statement etc* pooh!, nonsense! *19.*
shoog, shoogle *see* SHOG
shook, shooken *see* SHAK
shoom *n, vi* (make) a low buzzing or humming sound *e20, Kcdn.* [onomat]
shoon *see* SHAE
shoot *see* SHUIT, SUIT[1]
shop &c, **shap** &c *la15-e20*, **chop** &c *16-*, **tchop** *20-, NE n* = shop *la15-*.
~ **door** the front flap or fly of trousers *la19-.* ~ **lassie** a female shop-assistant *la19-, now NE.*
shore[1] &c; **schoir** *la16 n* **1** = shore *la15-.* **2** *with a place-name or* **the** ~ a quay, landing-place, harbour *la15-, now N Fif, only Sc.* ~ **due** a harbour-due *la17-19, only Sc.* ~ **head** the ground on the upper or land side of a quay or harbour *19-, Fif, only Sc.* ~ **levy** a duty on ships entering a harbour *la16, only Sc.* ~ **mail** = ~ *due, e17, only Sc.* ~ **master** &c a harbour-master *17-19, only Sc.* ~ **porter** *specif, in Aberdeen* a member of an incorporated society of porters, **the Society of S**~ **Porters** (*orig* called PINERS), no longer only working at the harbour, but also carrying out house removals etc *19-, only Sc.* ~ **silver** = ~ *due, la16, only Sc.*
shore[2] *n, chf* **shorie** a variety of the game of marbles *la19-, now Per wLoth.* [obscure]
shore[3] &c *vti* **1** threaten, use menaces (to) *la14-e20.* **2** *specif of weather* threaten (rain or

snow) *18-19*. **3** *vt* scold, upbraid *la18-*, *now* Sh. **4** urge, incite; hound (a dog) *19*, *S*. **5** offer as a mark of favour *la18-19*.

n menace, threatening *la14-18*.

shoring &c = *n*, *la16-e18*. [also nEng dial; perh cognate w SCHOIR]

shoreling &c *18-e19*, **schorling &c** *14-e17*, *only Sc n* the skin of a recently-shorn sheep; such a sheep. [f ptp *shorn* (SHEAR¹) + Eng *-ling*. OED *shorling*]

shorie *see* SHORE²

shorn(e) *see* SHEAR¹

short &c *adj* **1** = short *la14-*. **2** *of a hill* low *la16*, *only Sc*. **3** *of black-face sheep* relatively short in the body (compared with the CHEVIOT etc) *la18-19*.

adv **1** = short *17-*. **2** (1) for a brief while *17-19*. (2) in a brief space of time *la16-e17*.

n **1** = short. **2** a short time, an instant *la18-*, *Abd*. **3** *in pl* the refuse of flax tow after carding *la18-e19*, *Abd Ags*.

vti **1** = short *16-*. **2** *vt* make time seem short for, amuse *e16*, *la19*, *only Sc*.

~en &c 1 = shorten. **2** = *v* 2, *la16-e19*. **Shorter Catechism**: *Presbyterian Churches* the shorter of two catechisms approved by the *General Assembly* (GENERAL) in 1648, *17-*. **~ie &c** = *shortbread*, *la19-*, *local*. **~lins** = *shortly* 1 and 3, *la18-*, *local*. **~ly &c 1** = shortly *la14-*. **2** in a small compass *la16*. **3** recently *la18-*. **~some** *of persons, things, situations* lively and entertaining, cheerful, making time pass quickly *18-*, *now N Per*. **~bread** a kind of biscuit made of a short dough of flour, butter and sugar *la16-*. **~ butter** butter which is soft and crumbly from being churned too hot *la20-*, *NE Wgt*. **~ coal** coal with wide joints in the seam *20-*, *Fif*. **~come** a deficiency, shortage; a fault in character or conduct *la18-*, *local Sh-SW*. **~coming** = *shortcome*, *la17-* [earlier in Sc]. **~ days** a short time; *also adv* in a short time *16*, *only Sc*. **~ ended** short-winded *la16*, *only Sc*. **~ game** *golf* the playing of short strokes when approaching the hole and putting *la19-*. **~ gown &c** ['ʃort'gun, 'ʃorgən] a kind of long loose blouse of strong cloth, worn by women while doing housework etc *la15-*, *now nEC Pbls WC*. **~ hose** knee-breeches *la15-e17*. **~ hour** an early hour (of the morning) *la18-e19*. **~-set** small and stockily-built *la19-*, *local Sh-WC*. **~ sword** short-bladed sword *la15-*, *now hist*. **at ~ 1** in short *16*, *only Sc*. **2** in a short time, quickly *16*, *only Sc*. **~ ago** a short time ago *la20-*, *Sh-Per*. **~ and lang** in brief, summarily *19-*, *now WC Wgt*. **the ~ and lang** (**o it**) the long and the short of it *la19-*, *now NE Ags*. **~ (sin) syne &c** a short time ago *18-*, *now local Sh-WC*. **~ in the trot** (*NE*), **~ in the pile** (*SW*), **on** *etc* **~ trot** in a bad temper, curt and uncivil *la19-*. **~ while** (during) a short time *17-e19*.

shot¹ &c *n* **1** = shot *la14-*. **2** a discharge, flow (of blood etc) from the body *16-*, *now Kcb*. **3** a sheet (of ice) *e17*, *only Sc*. **4** *curling* (CURL) the playing of a stone towards the TEE¹; the score awarded to any stone nearer the TEE¹ than its opponents; a stone so played *la17-*. **5** *weaving* a single movement of the shuttle carrying the weft across the web *la18-*, *now local Ags-Ayr*. **6** the *shooting* (SHUIT *v* 3(2)) of a fishing-net etc *la15-19*, *only Sc*. **7** a piece of ground, *esp* one cropped rotationally *la16-*, *now only in place-names*. **8** a brief loan; a temporary use (of something); a 'turn' *20-*.

vti, only in pres and infin (for pt and ptp see SHUIT) **1** *also* **shut** *20-*, *Sh Ork* shoot *la16-*, *now Sh-nEC*. **2** *vt* cast (lines or nets) *la19-*, *NE*.

interj a warning among children of the approach of a policeman, teacher etc *20-*, *Fif Loth*.

shotter a missile, weapon *la16*, *only Sc*. **~ whaip** a kind of curlew *e17*, *only Sc*. **great ~** (a person's) chief aim *e17*, *only Sc*.

shot² &c *n*, *also* **~ window** a small opening in the wall of a house, closed by hinged shutters, sometimes with a few panes of glass at the top *16-*, *now hist*. **~ hole** the opening for this *19-e20*, *hist*. [obscure]

shot *see* SHUIT

shott &c *n* a young pig after weaning *la16-*, *now C, S*. [ME *shote*; *cf* Du dial *schote*]

shotten *see* SHUIT

shottle &c *la16-*, **shuttle** *17-e20 n* **1** a small compartment at the top of a trunk, chest etc, *usu* with a lid or drawer *la16-*, *now local*. **2** a small compartment in a set of shelves or a drawer etc *17-e19*. [see SND]

shouder &c *16-*, **shoulder &c** *la16-*; **schulder** *la14-16*, **shouther &c** *la18-*, **shud(d)er &c** *16-19* ['ʃudər, 'ʃuðər] *n* **1** = shoulder *la14-*. **2** the part of a garment covering the shoulder *la15-*. **3** *in pl* a coat-hanger *la20-*, *local C*. **4** the swelling part of a wave rising to the crest *20-*, *local Bnf-Gall*. **5** the dome-shaped upper part of the pot of a WHISKY-still *la18-*, *now NE*.

vti **1** = shoulder. **2** *vi* walk heavily, plod *la19-*, *now Bnf*. **3** *vt, plastering* point (the inside joints of slating) with mortar *20-*.

~ar a person who shoulders *e16*, *only Sc*. **~ie** a shoulder shawl *la20-*, *Cai Dnbt SW*. **~ cleek** the hook on a cart-shaft to which the shoulder-chain is attached *20-*, *now Loth Dnbt*. **~ heid** the socket of the shoulder-bone; the shoulder joint *la19-*, *NE, EC, S*. **~ lire &c** a cut of beef from the upper foreleg *18-20*, *only Sc*. **~ pick** a pick-axe which is wielded over the shoulder *la20-*, *NE*.

never look ower one's ~ 'never look back', go steadily forward, not fail or relapse *20-*,

NE-S. ~-**the-win** *n* (*adj*) (having) a deformity in which one shoulder is higher than the other *la20-*, *local N-Gall.*

shough *see* SHEUCH

should *see* SALL

shoulder *see* SHOUDER

shoulfall *see* SHILFA

shour &c, shower &c [ʃur] *n* **1** = shower (of rain etc) *la14-*. **2** a pang or paroxysm of pain etc, *specif* of childbirth *la16-20*.
vti = shower *17-*.
a ~ **in the** (**dam-**)**heids** a fit of weeping *19-20*.

shout &c [ʃut] *n* **1** = shout *la14-*. **2** a loud noise made *eg* by a bird or musical instrument *16*.
v **1** *vi* (1) = shout *la14-*. (2) *of birds* give a loud cry *16*. (3) *of a place* resound with shouts *e16*, *la19*. **2** *vt* shout at, greet with shouts (of insult or welcome) *la14-19*. **3** utter with a loud voice *la14-*. **4** *vi*, *of a woman* be in labour, give birth *19-*, *now Kcb*.
~**ing** childbirth; a merrymaking to celebrate it *19-e20*.
~ **and cry** *or* **hoyes** hue and cry *e17*, *only Sc.*

shouther *see* SHOUDER

shove *see* SHUVE

shovel *see* SHUIL

show &c [ʃu, ʃo] *n* the refuse of flax stems broken off in scutching *la18-*, *now Renfr.* [var of Eng *shove*, itself perh var of SHIVE (now also in Eng dial); *cf* SHIVER[2]]

show *see* SHAW[1], SHEW

showd &c *19-*; **schewd** *la16* [ʃʌud] *v* **1** *vi* swing to and fro, rock; have a rocking, waddling gait *la16-*, *now Inv NE.* **2** *vt* cause to sway or rock; dandle (a child) in one's arms *19-*, *now Abd.*
n **1** a rocking, swaying motion; the act of swinging *19-*, *now NE.* **2** a ride in a cart or barrow *20-*, *Ross Inv.*
~**ie** = *n* 1, *la19-e20.* [perh cognate w MLowGer *schudden* shake, wag]

shower *see* SHOUR

showl *see* SHEVEL

shraich [*ʃrex] *n* = shriek *la16*, *only Sc.* [*cf* SKRAICH. OED *shriek*]

shreed *n* = shred *la19-*, *now NE.* [ME *shrēde*, OE *scrēad*, the vowel being shortened later in Eng (*cf* BREID)]

shrew *see* SHIRROW

shrive &c; schrif &c *la14-16*, **schirryve** *e16*, *only Sc* [ʃraɪv] *vt* = shrive *la14-*.
~ **oneself of** renounce *16*, *only Sc.*

shrood &c *20-*, **shroud &c** *la15-* [ʃrud] *n* = shroud *la15-*.
vt **1** = shroud *la15-*. **2** deck, adorn *e16*.

shroud *see* SHROOD

shrunkled *adj* shrunken, shrivelled *la19-*, *NE*, *EC Rox.* [conflation of *skrunkle* (SKRUNK) w Eng *shrink*]

shuchle *see* SHOCKLE

shucken *see* SHAK

shud *n* **1** a large piece of loose ice etc in a river *19-e20*, *chf S.* **2** a large segment or lump of something *19-20*, *S.* [perh connected w SHED]

shud(d)er *see* SHOUDER

shue &c [ʃu] *vti* **1** swing, rock or sway backwards and forwards; swing or rock on a rope, gate, or seesaw *19-*, *now S.* **2** *rowing* back water, row (a boat) backwards *19-*, *now Sh Ork Cai.*
n **1** a rocking; a swing, seesaw *19-e20.* **2** a push, shove, a pushing backwards and forwards *la19-e20.*
~ **shuggie** *exclam* said when dandling a child *e20.* [var of Eng *shove*; *cf* SHUVE]

shuet &c *n* = suet *18-*, *now NE local C.*

shuffle &c *17-*; **shiffle &c** *vti* **1** = shuffle *la16-*. **2** *vt* treat (a matter) equivocally *17-e18*, *only Sc.*
shuffle-the-brogue the game of hunt-the-slipper *19-e20*, *Kcb Uls.*

shuffle *see* SHUIL

shug *see* SHOG

shuggar *see* SUCCAR

shuggle *see* SHOG

shuil &c, shuffle &c *17-*, **shovel &c; shiffle &c** *18-*, *Sh N*, **shiel &c** *la18-*, *chf N*, **shull &c** *15*, *la19-20*, **sheul** *la19-e20*, *Ork* [ʃøl, ʃɪl; 'ʃʌfl; *N* ʃil; *NE also* 'ʃɪfl] *n* **1** = shovel *la14-*. **2** *chf* **shiel &c** a kind of long-bladed PEAT[1]-cutter *20-*, *Cai.* **3** an act of shovelling *la18-*, *now NE*, *C.*
vti **1** shovel, work or clean out with a shovel *18-*. **2** *vt* dig (a hole etc) with a shovel *la15-*. **3** cut the top turf of a *peat-bank* (PEAT[1]) with a *shiel* (*n* 2), *20-*, *Cai Ross Inv.* **4** *fig* 'clean (someone) out', take away (someone's) store of something *la19-*, *local.* **5** *vti* (cause a flat object to) move along the ground as a shovel moves, slide; shuffle (the feet) *19-*, *now Ags Rox.*
shuily &c *specif of the feet* like a shovel, flat and splayed out *20-*, *now Ayr.*
shuil-fit a person with flat shuffling feet *20-*, *now Stlg Ayr.*
shuil-the-board &c a kind of draughts game where the winner is the first to get all his men off the board *la16-*, *now local Sh-Per.* **shuil down** destroy by shovelling away *la16*, *only Sc.*

shuir &c *la18-e20*, **sure; suir &c** *16-20*, **seur &c** *la15-e20*, **shair &c** *la19-*, **sere &c** *la18-e19*, *Abd*, **sheer &c** *la18-e20*, *NE* [ʃør, ʃer; *NE* *sir, *ʃir] *adj* = sure *la15-*.
adv **1** = sure *16-*. **2** surely, indeed, for certain *la16-*.
~**ly** = surely *la14-*.

shuit &c *la16-*, **shoot &c** *la16-*; **shute &c** *la14-19*, **sheet** *18-*, *N* [ʃøt, ʃɪt; *N* ʃit] *v*, *pt also* **shuit &c** *la19-*; **sheetit** *la20-*, *NE.* *ptp also* **shotten** *la19-*, *now NE*, **shuten &c** *la19*; **sheetit** *la20-*, *NE* **1** *vti* = shoot *la14-*. **2** *vi*, *of blood, tears etc* stream out *la15*, *only Sc.* **3** *vt* (1) launch (a ship) *la14.* (2) position (a fishing-net) in water *la16-*. **4** throw or pull **down** *la14-e16*, *only Sc.* **5** emit (flames, rays etc) swiftly and forcibly *la14-*. **6** ~ **out** *of animals* produce (horns etc) *la16*. **7** avoid, escape *16-17, only Sc*; cf *shot (ptp 3)*. **8** push, jerk forward, thrust roughly *18-*, now *Sh Ork*. **9** *vti, esp in buying and selling cattle and sheep* separate the good from the bad; reject (the poorer) after selection *la18-*, now *Dmf*; see also *shot (n)* below. **10** *vi, of walls etc* protrude, bulge; collapse, avalanche *18-*, now *Ork*. **11** *of plants* go to seed; *of grain* come into ear *la18-*.

n **1** = shoot *16-*. **2** a push, shove *19*.

shot *ptp* **1** *of plants* having run to seed *18-*. **2** *also* **shotten**, *of fish* spawned *20-*, now *EC*. **3** ~ **of** rid of, free from *18-*. *n* an inferior animal, *esp* a sheep, left over *eg* after a buyer's selection *18-*. **shot blade** the leaf enclosing the corn-stalk and ear *17-*, now *local*. **shot-cock** a young cockerel, to be preserved for breeding *20-*, *NE*. **shot heuch &c** a landslip *la16, e19*. **shot joint** a joint deformed by rheumatism *20-*, *local*. **shot star &c 1** a shooting star, meteor *18-19*. **2** *chf in pl* jelly-like algae found in pastures after rain (thought to be *eg* the remains of a shooting star) *la18-e19*.

~**-aboot** a makeshift meal *la19-*, *Kcdn Ags*. ~ **by** manage somehow, make a shift *la18-*, now *Ags-Stlg*. ~ **a** *or* **the craw** order drinks without paying; abscond without paying one's debts *la20-*, *Edb WC*. ~ **to** *or* **a deid &c** kill or harm (*esp* cattle) by magic (*eg* by fairy arrows) *la18-19*. ~ **forth** *etc* drive out or away, expel *16*. ~ **out one's fit** *etc* give a convulsive kick, as in a fit or death-agony *la18-19*. ~ **ower** last over (a period); tide (someone) over *18-e20*.

shuit *see* SUIT[1]

shuk, shuke *see* SHAK

shull *see* SHUIL

shunder, shunner *see* CINNER

shune *see* SUNE

shure *see* SHEAR[1]

shurf &c *n, contemptuous* an insignificant person *19-*, *S*. [*cf* Eng *scurf*]

shusy &c ['ʃuzi] *n* **1** a corpse (*prob orig* female) used for anatomical dissection and demonstration, *esp* one stolen from a grave *19*. **2** a woman, *esp* a silly, empty-headed one *20-*, now *Bnf*. [f the personal name *Susie*]

shut &c *vti, ptp also* **shuttit** *la19-*, *NE* = shut *16-*.

n **1** *chf in pl* window shutters *la18-20*. **2** *in pl, mining* sliding or hinged boards on which the cage rests at the pithead *la19-*, now *Fif*.

~ **day** a holiday on which shops are shut for the whole or part of the day, an early-closing day *20-*, *C*. ~ **to** close (*esp* a door) properly *la19-*.

shut *see* SHOT[1]

shute *see* SHUIT, SUIT[2]

shuttle[1]; shittle *n* = shuttle *17-*.

v **1** *vi* weave, drive the shuttle in a loom, be a weaver *la19-*, now *Ags Stlg Ayr*. **2** *vti* move to and fro like a shuttle *19-*.

shuttler, shittler a weaver; a boy who fills carriages and bobbins in a lace factory *la19-*, now *Ags Stlg Ayr*.

~ **gab &c** a misshapen mouth, with one jaw protruding beyond the other, *esp* of an animal *20*.

shuttle[2] *adj* quick, active, making sudden hasty movements *la19-20*. [var of eModEng *shittle* inconstant, unstable]

shuttle *see* SHOTTLE

shuve &c *19-e20*, **shove &c**; **shiv &c** *la19-20* [ʃøv, ʃiv] *vti, pt also* **schew** [*ʃiv] *la16* = shove *la15-*.

shover &c a person who shoves *16-*.

shove-by, shove-ower a hastily-prepared or makeshift meal *la19-*, *local*. ~ **forward** *fig* urge on (in a course of action) *la16-*. [*cf* SHUE]

shyve *vt* throw (*specif* a rope, *eg* from boat to pier) *la20-*, *NE*. [var of Eng *shy* throw, perh w infl f SHUVE]

sib &c *adj, comparative* **sibber**, *superlative* **sibbest**, *chf* ~ **to 1** related by blood to, of the same kindred (KIN) or lineage as *la14-*. **2** *transf* closely akin to, allied with, of the same sort as *16-*, now *local Ork-Dmf*. **3** likely to inherit or acquire, having a claim to, *esp* by right of kinship *18-19*. **4** bound by ties of affection, familiarity etc, well-disposed (to) *19-*, now *local NE-Slk*.

n **1** = sib, a relative *la14*. **2** *as pl*: kindred (KIN), relatives, *freq* ~ **and fremd** *la18-*, now *Sh*.

~**like**, ~**ly** friendly, like members of the same family *19-e20*. ~**nes(s)** *lit and fig* kinship, relationship, affinity *16-e20*. ~**rent &c** = sibred, kinship *e15, only Sc*; *cf* MANRENT.

sic &c, **sich** *15-*, **such &c** *la16-*, **swilk &c** *la14-e16*; **swik** *e16*, **silk &c** *la14* [sɪk, sɪtʃ; *swɪ(l)k, *sɪlk] *adj, pronoun* = such *la14-*.

adv, as exclam with adjs how ..!, so ..! *20-*, *Abd Kcdn*: 'sic bonnie she is!'

siccan &c, **si(t)chan** *la19-e20* ['sɪkən, 'sɪtʃən]; *when followed by the indef art* **sicna** *20-* ['sɪknə] **1** such, of such a kind, of a sort already mentioned *16-*. **2** *as exclam with nouns* what (a) ..!; *with adjs* how ..! *19-* [SIC + *-kin* kind]. **siccan like &c** = siclike, *19-*, now local NE-SW. **siccan-a-like yin** so-and-so *20-*, *sEC, SW, S*.

~**like &c** ['sɪkləik, sɪ'kləik, 'sɪklɪk] *adj* **1** = suchlike *15-*. **2** *of health, quality etc* much about the same; so-so, indifferent *la20-*, *local Sh-Dmf*. *pronoun* = suchlike *la15-*. *adv* **1** similarly, in like manner *la15-*, now local Sh-Kcb. **2** *introducing a subsequent detail in a list etc* likewise, item *18*. (**be**) **sic ten** *etc* **better** *etc* ten etc times better etc *la15-16, only Sc*. **sic a** *with pl noun* what a lot of ..! *e20*. **sic a bodie** so-and-so, such a person *20-*, *NE-S*. **sic a like** *exclam, indicating surprise and usu disparagement* what a ..! *19-*, *Gen except Sh*. **sic-an-sae &c** alike, similar, much of a muchness *la19-*, now *Dnbt Lnk S*. **sic-an-sic** such-and-such, so-and-so *18-*. **sic-an-sic-like** = sic-an-sae, *19-*, now local *Sh-Ags*.

siccar *see* SICKER

sich *la14-20*; **sicht** *la14-15*, **seich &c** *la19-e20*, **saich &c** *la19-e20*, **sech** *la19-e20* [SIX, SEX; *Sh Ork S* sǝix] *vti, n* = sigh.

sich *see* SIC, SICHT

sichan *see* SIC

sicht &c, sight *la16-*; **sich** *la16* [SIXT] *n* **1** = sight *la14-*. **2** a close look, examination; supervision *la14-*. **3** a place on a riverbank from which salmon can be watched *la18*. **4** the pupil (of the eye) *19-*, *local Sh-Lnk*.
vt **1** = sight *17-*. **2** examine, scrutinize *only Sc*: (1) *in gen, la16-*, *now local Sh-C*; (2) *specif* inspect (a newborn animal) for its sex *la20-*, *local Sh-Edb*; (3) scrutinize (a person) indecently *la20-*, *local Sh-Edb*.
~**less 1** = sightless *la16-*. **2** deprived of the sight **of** *e17*, *only Sc*. **3** out of sight *17-e19*.
~**y 1** = sighty, visible *e16*. **2** sightly, handsome *e16*.
at one ~ in a single look *la15-e17*. **at the** ~ **of** under the supervision or scrutiny of *18-e19*.
a ~ **for sair een** a welcome or pleasing sight *19-*.

sick *interj* a call to a lamb or calf to come to be fed from its bottle *20-*, *NE Ags*.
n, also ~ **lamb** a pet lamb brought up on the bottle *20-*, *Bnf Abd*.
~**ie &c** = *interj and n, 20-*, *NE*. [prob altered f SOUK]

sick *see* SAX, SEECK

sicker &c; **sekir &c** *14-e16*, **siccar &c** *19-* ['sɪkər, *'sikər] *adj* **1** (1) safe, secure, free from danger etc *la14-*, *now local NE-Wgt*. (2) *specif, of places, paths, e16*. **2** (1) firm, stable, fixed *la14-*, *now local*. (2) securely under control, held firm *la16-*, *now Ags*. **3** confident, having a sense of security *la14*. **4** dependable, reliable: (1) *of things* not liable to sudden change, failure etc *la14-*, *Gen except Sh Ork S*; (2) *of persons* reliable, loyal; steady, sure *16-*, *now NE Bwk Wgt*; (3) *of armour*, *la16*. **5** prudent, cautious, *esp* with money, wary *la17-*, *now local Ork-Rox*. **6** *of a blow* hard and effective, telling *la15-*, *now Sh Ork*. **7** (1) having assurance or certainty (**of**) *la16-*, *now Sh Abd*. (2) having sure mastery (**of** an art) *la15*. **8** *of laws, weather etc* harsh, rigorous *19-*, *now Ork*.
adv **1** *with verbs of saying* as a fact *e16*. **2** securely, firmly, stably *17-*, *now Abd Ags*. **3** accurately, precisely *18-19*.
vt **1** = sicker, assure *la14*. **2** make firm and secure, fix firmly *18-*, *now local NE-Wgt*.
~**ly 1** = sickerly, with full certainty *la14-16*. **2** safely, without danger *la14-19*. **3** (1) firmly, fast *la14, e19*. (2) in a stable or steady manner *la16-19*. **4** undoubtedly; certainly, assuredly *la14-e19*. **5** sharply, severely *la16-19*. **6** prudently, cautiously *18-*, *now NE*. ~**ness 1** = sickerness, certainty *14-e16*. **2** safe custody *la17*.
~ **set** firmly set or seated, established *la16, 19*.

mak ~ make sure or certain *19-* [freq in reminiscence of the phrase traditionally said to have been used by Sir John Kirkpatrick to Robert the Bruce at the murder of the Red Comyn]. [ME *siker &c*, OE *sicor*]

sickie *see* SAX

sid *see* SALL, SEED

sidderwud *see* SITHERWOOD

siddle *vi* = sidle *la19-*, *Per*.

side¹ &c *n* **1** = side *la14-*. **2** *usu following a place-name* direction, district *la18-*, *now local Sh-SW*: 'I'm newcome frae Dumbartonside.'
~**lin(s) &c** *la17-*, **sidlings &c** ['sǝidlɪn(z), 'sɪd-] *adv* **1** *chf* ~**s** sideways, side on, to one side *la15-*, *now local Ork-Kcb*. **2** side by side *la16*. **3** *of speech or look* indirectly, obliquely *la18-*, *now local Sh-Kcb*. *adj* **1** sidelong, oblique, moving or glancing sideways *la18-*, *now Sh Abd Kcb*. **2** sloping, on an incline *19-*, *now Ork Abd Kcb*. *n* a sloping piece of ground, a hillside *la17-*, *now C Rox*. **sidieweys &c** sideways *20-*, *Gen except Sh Ork*. **sid(i)e for sidie** side by side, step for step *19*.
~ **bar** a secondary bar in the *Outer House* (OUTER) of the *Court of Session* (SESSION) *e18*. ~ **casting** the act of ploughing along the side of a slope *la20-*, *Per Arg Gall*. ~ **ill &c** a kind of paralytic disease of sheep *18-e19*, *only Sc*. ~ **legs** sidesaddle *19-*, *local*. ~ **school** a subsidiary school, *esp* in an outlying part of a parish *19-e20*, *only Sc*.

side² &c *adj* **1** *esp of clothes, hair etc* long, hanging low *la14-e19*. **2** hard or severe **on** *19-e20*, *Abd*.
adv **1** *esp of clothing* trailing(ly), low down, towards the ground *16-e20*. **2** proudly, boastfully *e16*, *only Sc*.
~ **coat** a long coat with a long frock or tails, a greatcoat *18-19*. ~ **tailed** *of a horse*, a coat etc having a long tail *18-e19*.
~ **and wide** extending in every way, long and large *19-e20*. [OE *sīd*, ON *sīðr* long, hanging low]

sidlings *see* SIDE¹

sie *see* SEA, SEE, SYE¹

siege &c; **saige** *16 n* **1** = siege *la14-*. **2** a place on which a ship lies *15-e16*. **3** (1) a bench or form; a class *la16-e17*, *only Sc*. (2) a wooden or stone bench on which a mason dresses his stones *la18-*.
v **1** *vt* = siege, besiege *la14-e19*. **2** place *e15*. **3** *vti* scold severely, storm **at** *20-*, *NE*.

sies *see* SEE

sieth *see* SUITH

siff &c *n* = sieve *16-e17*. [OED *sieve*]

sigge *see* SAY

sight *see* SICHT

signacle *see* SINACLE

signat *see* SIGNET

signator *n* = SIGNATURE 2, *la15-17*. [only Sc; L *signātōrius*]

signature *n* **1** = signature. **2** *law* a document presented to the *Baron of Exchequer* (BARON) by a *writer to the signet* (WRITE), as the ground of a royal grant to the person in whose name it was presented *16-19, only Sc.*

signe *see* SING[2]

signery *see* SIGNORY

signet &c; segnett &c *la14-e15, only Sc,* **singnet** *la15, only Sc n* **1** = signet *la14-.* **2** one of the Crown seals of Scotland, *orig* used for private and some official documents of the Sovereign, *latterly (17-)* used as the seal of the *Court of Session* (SESSION) *la15-*; see also *writer* (WRITE), CLARK.

vt, also **signat** *la16, ptp* **signet(t)ed** *law* stamp (a document) with a SIGNET, *latterly (17-)* as the symbol of the authority of the *Court of Session* (SESSION) *la15-, only Sc.*

Keeper of the S~ the custodian of the SIGNET, now a titular office, the holder also being *Lord Clerk Register* (REGISTER); the actual custodian is now the **Deputy Keeper of the S~** *la16-.*

signory *e16;* **signery &c** *la14, only Sc* [*'sɪnjərɪ, *'sɪŋ-] *n* = signory, lordship.

sik *see* SEEK[1]

sike *see* SYKE

silder *see* SILLER

sile[1] &c *vt* **1** cover (the eyes or sight) *16-e17.* **2** deceive (the sight) *e17.* **3** deceive, beguile, mislead (a person) *16.* **4** cover, hide, conceal *la15-16.* [chf Sc; OF *cillier* blink; sew up a hawk's eyes, f *cil* an eyelash]

sile[2] &c *19-;* **seil &c** *18-e20* [səil] *vt* pass (a liquid, *esp* milk) through a sieve, strain, filter *18-, now Bwk WC-S.*
n a sieve, strainer, filter, *esp* for milk *la19-, Bwk WC-S.* [nME; Scand; *cf* SYE[1]]

sile[3] &c; sill &c *19-, local* [səil; *chf Sh Fif* sɪl] *n* the newly-hatched young of fish, *esp* of herring *18-, local Sh-WC.* [ON *síld* herring]

sile[4] &c *n* a roof rafter or couple, *usu* one of a pair *16-e20.* [nME; obscure]

sile[5] *vt* = ceil, cover (an interior roof or walls) *la15-16.* [also northern eModEng]

sile[6] *n* = soil *19-e20, only Sc.*

silence *see* SEELENCE

silk *see* SIC

sill *see* SILE[3]

siller, silver &c; silder *18-e20* ['sɪlər; *nEC also* 'sɪldər] *n* **1** = silver *la14-.* **2** *now only* **siller** silver coin; money *in gen, la14-.*
adj **1** = silver *15-.* **2** *of payments etc* made or levied in (silver) money *la16, only Sc.*
vti = silver *19-.*
sillered &c monied, wealthy *19-, now NE-WC.* **siller bridal** a *penny wedding* (PENNY) *17-e19.* **siller-fish** the bib or pout *la19-, now Abd.* **siller fluke** the brill; the megrim *la18-e19, NE Kcdn.* **siller gun** a small silver replica of a gun used as a shooting trophy, *esp* that presented to the *Incorporated Trades* (INCORPORATE) of Dumfries by James VI, *17-, Dmf Kcb.* **~ rent** rent paid in cash *la17-e19.* **silver-seck** avaricious

la15. **siller shakers &c** the quaking grass *19-, now Loth Rox.* **~ willie** the pyramid shell *19-, now local Ork-eLoth.*

silly &c *adj* **1** = silly *16-.* **2** (1) deserving of pity or sympathy *16-19.* (2) *esp of women* helpless, unable to fend for oneself *19-, now C Rox.* **3** (1) weak(ly), sickly, delicate *la16-20.* (2) *of things* weak, shaky, unsubstantial *18-, now NE-C.* **4** mentally deficient *16-, now local Sh-Kcb.*
~ cuddies the game of leap-frog *20-, WC.*

silver *see* SILLER

Sim &c, *chf in dim* **Sim(m)ie &c** *joc* name for the Devil *la18-e20.* [f the proper name *Simon, Simeon*]

siming *see* SIMMEN

simmen &c, simmon; siming *e17,* **simmond &c** *la18-20* ['sɪmən &c; *Sh* 'sɪmə(n)t] *n,* *usu in pl* ropes made of straw, heather, rushes etc, used with stone weights to hold down thatch on houses and stacks *17-, now Sh Ork Cai Ross.* [see SND]

simmer[1] &c *16-,* **summer &c** *la16-;* **somir &c** *la14-e17 n* **1** = summer *la14-.* **2** *attrib, also (more freq than in Eng)* **~'s** *16-.*
vi spend the summer *la19-, now local Sh-SW.*
~ blink a momentary gleam or spell of sunshine *17-, now Sh Per.* **~ cowt &c** *freq in pl* a heat haze, the shimmering of the air on a hot day *la18-e20.* **~ meill** meal for use until harvest *e16, only Sc.* **simmer tre** a flower-bedecked pole erected during summer games *la16, only Sc.* **summer weed** bovine mastitis *la20-, local Abd-SW.*
~ and winter go into (something) at length and in great detail, discuss (something) in all its aspects; be long-winded in telling a story *17-, now local Abd-Rox.*

simmer[2] &c *16-e19,* **summer &c** *n* **1** = summer, a packhorse *la14.* **2** (1) = summer, a beam *la14-.* (2) *specif* a beam or joist in the floor of a corn-kiln *la17-e19.*

simmerset *n* = somersault *la19-, now Bnf Kcb.*

Simmie *see* SIM

simmon, simmond *see* SIMMEN

simple *see* SEMPLE

simpliciter [sɪm'plɪsɪtər] *adv, chf law* simply, unconditionally, without further condition or reservation *16-.* [chf Sc; L = simply]

simulate &c *adj* simulated, feigned, based on false pretences *la16-e20.*
~ly by or with pretence *la16-e18.* [L *simulāt-,* ptp stem of *simulāre* pretend]

sin[1] &c *la18-, now N,* **son &c; soun &c** *16,* **schon** *la16* [sɪn; sʌn] *n* = son *la14-.*
son-afore-the-father name of various plants whose flowers appear before their leaves *19-, now Kcdn* [*cf* Eng *son-before-the-father*]. **Son of the Rock 1** a native of Dumbarton or Stirling *19-, Per Stlg wLoth Dnbt* [f Dumbarton Rock

and Stirling Castle Rock]. **2 the Sons (of the Rock)** nickname for Dumbarton football team *20-* [*cf* WARRIORS].

sin² &c *n* **1** = sin *la14-*. **2** pity, a sense of sympathy or shame *la14-*, *now Sh*. **3** a fear of doing wrong *la15*.

~ **guilt** an act of sinning *e17*.

hae nae ~ **o** bear no blame or reproach for *la19-*, *now Sh*. ~ **one's soul** incur the guilt of sin (*esp* by telling lies) *la19-*, *local Sh-Kcb*.

sin *see* SUN, SUNE, SYNE

sinacle &c, **signacle** &c [*sɪˈgnakl, *ˈsɪnəkl] *n* **1** *only* **signacle** = signacle, a sign *e16*. **2** *only* **sinacle** vestige, trace *la18, NE, only Sc*.

sinder &c, **sunder** &c; **schunder** &c *la15-e16*, **sinner** &c *19-* [ˈsɪndər &c; *N, WC, SW* ˈsɪnər] *vti* **1** (1) = sunder *15-*. (2) *vt, specif* single, hoe out (overcrowded seedlings) *la20-, NE*. **2** *vi* part company (**from**); part (**with**) *16-, now Ayr*.

adj = sunder, separate *la14-e16*.

~**ing** **1** = sundering *la16-*. **2** *freq in pl* **sindrins** a fork in the road *19-, local NE-SW*.

sindry &c *la14-*, **sundry** *18-*, **sinnery** &c *la19-20 adj* **1** = sundry *la14-*. **2** separate, apart and by itself, distinct *la14-*, *now local Sh-SW*. *n, in sing and pl* several people, a number of persons or things indiscriminately *la14-20, chf Sc*. *adv* asunder, apart, separately; in or to pieces *la14-*, *now Sh Ork Cai C*. **syndrely** &c **1** = sundrily, separately *la14-e15*. **2** diversely, variously *e15*. **syndrynes** diversity, variety *la14-e15*. **all and sundry** &c one and all, all collectively and severally *la14-* [*orig law, translating* L *omnes universi et singuli*].

sindle *see* SEENDIL

sindrins, sindry *see* SINDER

sine quo non [*ˈsaɪnɪ ˈkwo ˈnon] *law* an indispensable person *la17-19*. [L = without whom not]

sing¹ *vti* = sing *la14-*.

n a whizzing blow, wallop *20-, now NE Dmf Rox*.

~**in cake** a sweet biscuit given to children on HOGMANAY in return for a song etc *la19-e20, Fif*.

~**in e'en** HOGMANAY, when children went from house to house singing songs for cakes etc *19-e20, Ags Fif*.

lat ~ let fly, hit out *la20-, NE Ags Dmf*. ~ **dool** lament, bewail one's luck *la18-19*. ~ **dumb** keep silent *18-*. ~ **sma** adopt a deferential or submissive tone or attitude *19-*.

it *etc* **will** ~ it is fit for singeing *19-, now NE*. [chf Sc; the conjugation has been infl by SING¹]

sing³ &c *n, v* = sign *16-e17*. [OED *sign*]

single &c [ˈsɪŋl] *adj* **1** = single *la14-*. **2** *of members of the armed forces* of the lowest rank *18-19*. **3** *in fish-and-chip-shop usage* not served with chips, by itself *la20-, local*: 'single fish', 'single pudding'.

n **1** = single. **2** a handful or small bundle of gleaned corn *16-, now local Bwk-Rox*. **3** one half of a doubled amount *la16, only Sc*. **4** the one-stone-thick upper part of a dry-stone wall *la20-, SW*.

vti **1** = single *la17-*. **2** *vt* thin out (seedlings, *esp* turnips) *19-*.

singlin [ˈsɪŋlɪn] **1** = singling. **2** = *n* 2, *la19-, local Fif-Rox*. **3** **singling** *piping* the form in which a *ground* (GRUND) or variation is first played *20-*. **singly** &c **1** = singly. **2** sincerely, honestly *e17*.

~ **catechism(s)** &c *la16-19*, ~ **carritch(er(s))** *la18-19* the *Shorter Catechism* (SHORT) without the scripture-proofs appended to each question. ~ **end** a one-roomed house *la19-, Gen except Sh Ork*. ~**-horse-tree** a swingletree of a plough to which the traces of a single horse are attached *la18-, now Per Kcb*. ~ **note** a one-pound banknote *19-*. ~ **soled** *of boots and shoes* with a single thickness of material in the sole *16-e19*.

singnet *see* SIGNET

singular [*ˈsɪŋ(j)ələr] *adj* = singular *16-*.

~ **combat** single combat *la16-18*. ~ **successor** *law* a person who acquires HERITABLE property by a single title, normally by purchase, as opposed to an heir, whose title is general or UNIVERSAL *17-*.

sinistrous, sinistruous *only Sc* [*ˈsɪnɪstrəs, *sɪnɪˈstruəs] *adj* **1** = sinistrous, inauspicious *e17*. **2** erroneous, perverse, heretical *la16-e17*. **3** malicious, unfair, prejudiced *la16-17*.

sink *vti, ptp also* **sonkin** &c *15-16* [ˈsʌŋkən], **sucken** *16-19* **1** = sink *15-*. **2** *vt, in imprecations* blast, ruin *la19-, now Sh*.

n **1** = sink *16-*. **2** *founding* ? a hole dug in the ground for a gun-mould *e16, only Sc*. **3** *mining* a pit-shaft, a coal-pit *la16-*. **4** a hollow, low-lying area where water collects to form a boggy place *la16-, now Sh and in place-names*.

~**er** **1** a person who engraves designs on dies *16-17, chf Sc*. **2** a (stone or lead) weight attached to the lower corners of a herring-net to make it sink *19-e20, local N*. **3** a weight attached to the rope of a horse's stall-collar to keep it forward in its stall *19-, now N, C*.

~**(s)man** a person who sinks pit-shafts *la17-, now Fif*.

sinner *see* SINDER

sinnie &c *n* = senna *la16-, now Sh Ork Bnf*.

sinnie *see* SINNON

sinnle *see* SEENDIL

sinnon &c *19-, now Sh NE, C*, **sinnie** &c *18-e19*; **senown** *la15-16*, **shinnon** &c *19-e20* [ˈsɪnən, ˈsɛnən; *WC Gall* ˈʃɪnən, ˈʃɛnən; *Rox also* ˈsɛnə(n)t] *n* = sinew. [OED *sinew*]

sinse *n* = sense *20-, NE*.

---

sing²; signe *la16 v, pt* ~**it** &c *19-, now Ags Per*, **sang** *e19*, **sung** *la20-, Abd. ptp* ~**it** &c *la16-e20*, **sung** *18-, now local NE-Dmf vt* = singe *16-, now local NE-Dmf*.

n the act of singeing, a scorch, a burn(ing) *19-, now Abd Ags Lnk*.

~**it** stunted, shrivelled, puny *la18-, now Per*.

sinsyne *see* SYNE
sinty *see* SEEVEN
sip *vt* eat in spoonfuls or in good mouthfuls *la18-*, now *Bnf Ags*. [perh Eng *sip*, but may be altered f Eng *sup*]
sip *see* SEEP
sipe *see* SYPE
sipling &c *e16, e19*; **suppline** *e16* *n* a sapling, young tree. [see SND]
sipper *see* SUPPER
sipple &c *17-19*, **sirple** *18-*, now *S vti* sip continuously, go on drinking in small quantities, tipple *17-*, now *S*.
n, only **sirple** a sip, mouthful, *esp* of liquor *19*. [frequentative of Eng *sip*]
sir; schir &c *la14-16, la19* [sɪr, sër, sʌr] *n* 1 = sir *la14-*. 2 as a form of address between men of equal rank, *freq* among miners *la20-, local Stlg-Ayr*.
sirken; sirkent *adj* fond of one's comforts, coddling oneself *19*. [see SND]
sirple *see* SIPPLE
sirs *see* SER
sis *see* SITH
sist &c *v* 1 *vt, law* stop, stay or halt (a legal process or procedure) by judicial decree, both in civil and ecclesiastical courts *17-*. 2 *in gen* stop, end *19*. 3 *vi* cease, stop, come to a standstill *17-e18*. 4 *vt, law* summon or cite to appear in a court case *17-*. 5 *vr, law* present oneself before a court, appear for trial or as a litigant *17-*.
n a stay or suspension of a proceeding; *specif, law* an order by a judge to stay judgment or execution *la17-*. [only Sc; L *sistere* make to stand or stop]
sister &c *n* = sister *la14-*.
~ **bairn** the child of a parent's sister, a cousin *la16-*, now *Sh Cai*. ~ **douchtar** a niece, the daughter of one's sister *15-16*. ~('s) **son** a nephew, the son of one's sister *la14-*, now *Sh Ork*.
sistre *n* = sistrum, an oriental musical instrument *la16, only Sc*.
sit; site &c *16 vti, pt also* **sut** *20-, WC, SW Uls*. *ptp also* **sitten &c** now *Sh-EC*, **sutten &c** *la18-*, now *NE, WC-S* 1 = sit *la14-*. 2 *vi, of plants* stop growing or developing, be stunted *18-*, now *NE-Per Gall*. 3 *vt, orig vi with dative* suit, fit *la14, 19-e20*. 4 ignore, pay no attention to (a command, request etc) *la15-19*.
n 1 a sinking or settling down of the surface of the ground or of anything built on it *la18-*, now *NE*. 2 *specif mining* a subsidence due to excavation below *la18-*, now *Fif Loth Ayr*.
sitten *ptp, conjugated with verb 'to be', la16-*, now *Sh-Per*. *adj* 1 *of tea* stewed, strong and bitter *la20-, N*. 2 *of an egg on which a bird has been sitting* with a developed chick inside, near to hatching *20-, local*. **sitten-doun &c** *adj, of a cold etc* persistent, chronic *19-*, now *Rox*. **sitten &c on** 1 singed in the pan *19-, local Per-Rox*. 2 **sutten on** stunted, dwarfed *19-*, now *Kcb Rox*. **sitten-up** set in one's ways *la17, only Sc*. **weill**

sitten having a good seat (on horseback) *16*.
sitter a person who regularly occupies a seat in a church *19, only Sc*. **sitting** 1 = sitting. 2 *also* **sitting up**, *specif* the act of watching over a corpse before burial *19-*, now *Kcb*. **sitting doun &c** *n* 1 *of a ship* a going aground *la16*. 2 a settlement in marriage *20-, Cai C. adj* = sitten-doun *(adj) la19-*, now *Fif*.
~ **house** a residence, a dwelling-house, *esp* on a farm *17-e19*.
~ **below** attend the church of, listen to the preaching of (a certain MINISTER) *19-*, now *Per Kcb*. ~ **down &c** *v* 1 = sit down *la15-*. 2 settle oneself in a place or situation, make one's home *16-*. 3 *of a court, school, meeting etc* begin its sitting or business, sit *18-e19*. 4 *of the wind* become calm, moderate *la16, 19*. *n* 1 a chance or spell of being seated, a seat *20-*. 2 a home, settlement, *esp* one gained by marriage, a situation *la19-*, now *Ags Per*. ~ (**doun**) **on one's knees** sink to one's knees, kneel, remain kneeling *la14-*, now *local NE-SW*. ~**fast** *n* 1 a stone deeply and firmly embedded in the earth *la18-*, now *Cai Wgt*. 2 a plant, *eg* the creeping crowfoot, with roots clinging tenaciously to the soil *la18-e20. adj, of a stone* earthfast *la18-e19*. ~ **in** draw one's chair in (**to** a fire, a table), take one's seat at a meal *19-*. ~ **in about** *absol* = prec *19-, now NE-Per*. ~ **on** *esp of a tenant at the end of a lease* remain in a place or house; stay on *la19-*, now *Sh NE Per*. ~ **on a person's coat-tail(s)** depend on or make use of someone else for one's own convenience or advantage *la18-*, now *Bnf-Per*. ~**-ooterie** *joc* an alcove, recess etc where one may sit out a dance etc *20-*, now *NE*. ~**-sicker &c** *n* name for various species of crowfoot *19-*, now *NE*; cf ~*fast* (*n* 2). ~ (**someone**) **sore &c** grieve (someone) greatly *la15-e16*. ~ **to** = ~ *in* (to), *18-*. ~ **with** put up with, tolerate *la15-e18, only Sc*.
sit *see* SUIT²
sitable *see* SUIT¹
sitchan *see* SIC
site *see* SIT, SYTE
sitevate *see* SITUATE
sith &c *la14-16*; **syith** *e16, only Sc* [*saɪð] *n, pl also* **sis &c** *la14-16, only Sc*, **cyse** *la14* [*saɪz] sithe, time *la14-16*.
in ane ~ at one and the same time *la15*. [OED *sithe*]
sithe [saɪð] *n* a chive *20-, local Loth-Rox*. [eModEng; var of ME *syve*]
sithean ['ʃiən] *n* a natural or artifical mound, *freq* a prehistoric burial place; a fairy hill or mound &c *la19-, freq in place-names*. [ScGael *sithean*, pl or dim of *sith* a fairy (hill), IrGael *siodh* a tumulus where fairies were thought to live]
sitherwood; sidderwud &c *n* = southernwood *la19-e20*. [*cf* eModEng *souther* southern, perh w infl f Eng *cedarwood*]
sitivation *see* SITUATE
sittel- *see* SUTELL

sitten *see* SIT

situate &c *18-*, *now NE and law*, **cituate &c**
la16-e17; **sitwat** *la15*, **sitevate** *e18* ['sɪtjuet,
*-at, *'sɪtɪvet, *'sɪtɪwat, &c] *ptp, adj* = situated
la15, 18-.

　sitivation &c *18-19*, **seetiation &c** *la19-*
　[sɪtɪ'eʃn; *sɪtɪ've ʃn, *sɪtɪ-] = situation. [laL
　situat-, ptp stem of *situāre* (in MedL), f L *situs* a
　site]

siven &c ['sɪvən] *n* **1** the wild raspberry *19-20*.
2 *chf in pl* a venereal disease characterized by
raspberry-like sores *la18-19*. [only Sc; Gael
suibhean, var of *suibheag* a raspberry; a venereal
sore]

siven *see* SEEVEN

six *see* SAX

size &c *n* **1** = size *la16-*. **2** a jury *la15-16, only
Sc*. **3** the established order of things *e15, only
Sc*. **4** a duty, in money or kind, levied on
imported goods by the Crown, BURGHS etc, an
impost *la16-e18*.

　~ **boll** an amount payable, as import duty
　16-18.

sizzie *see* SUSSIE

sizzon *see* SAISON

skaed *see* SKAITH

skaffell *see* SCAFFAT

skaich *see* SKECH

skaid *see* SCAW, SKAITH

skaik &c, **skawk** *e20, Mry* [skek; *NE also*
skɑk, skjɑx] *vti* smear, plaster with a soft wet
substance, streak, blotch *19-*, *NE Ags*.
n a smear, daub; a surface coating of paint *20-*,
Abd Ags. [only Sc; see SND]

skaiken *see* SKEICH

skail¹ &c; **skell &c** *la18-19*, **skale &c**, **skyle**
&c *la18-e20* [skel; *WC also* skǝil] *v* **1** *vt* (1) scatter, disperse, throw or spread about (a cluster
or collection of things) *la14-*. (2) spread (a
rumour etc) *la14-e16*. (3) spread (manure,
PEAT¹ etc) over the surface of the ground *19-*,
now Cai Per WC, SW. (4) plough **out** (a ridge)
so that the furrows fall outward on either side of
the *hintin* (HINT¹) *la18-*, *now N, C*. **2** (1) shed,
cast, throw (from a container) *19-e20*. (2)
pour out; shed, spill (accidentally) *16-*. **3**
burst (a garment) at a seam *la18-*, *now Cai Ross*.
4 (1) disperse, scatter (a group of people);
rout, put to flight *la14-*, *Gen except Sh Ork*. (2)
dismiss (a meeting, congregation, school) *la16-*.
(3) break up (one's home) *la16-e17*. (4) *in
passive* be in a scattered or dispersed state
la14-16. **5** annul (a proclamation) *la16*. **6**
raise (a siege) *15-16*. **7** *vi* (1) *of a group of persons, eg in a school, church etc* break up, disperse,
separate *la14-*. (2) *of persons or things* become
detached or separated *19-e20*. **8** (1) *of a smell,
rain etc* spread, pour down *la15-16*. (2) *of a
container or its contents* spill out or over, overflow
or leak out *18-*.
n **1** a dispersed company *la14*. **2** the dismissal

or dispersal of a group of people *17-*, *Gen except
Sh Ork*. **3** a strong, scattering or driving
storm-wind *la18-e20*.
　~**(a)ment &c** a scattering, dispersal *la18-19*.
　~**wind** a scattering wind, hurricane *la17-e20*.
　[nME; see SND]

skail² **&c** *n* **1** = scale (on fish etc) *16*. **2** *only in
uninflected pl after numerals etc* kinds or varieties
(of fish) *la16, only Sc*: 'dyuers skaile of fysh'. [OED
scale (*n*²)]

skainie &c *la18-19*; **skanʒe &c** *16*, **sken-**
16-19, **skeen-** *la18-*, **-y(i)e &c** *la16-19*, **-zie**
19, **-gie &c** *la19-*, *local* ['skenɪ, 'skeŋɪ, 'skɪnɪ,
'skɪŋɪ; *'skenjɪ, *'skeŋjɪ, &c] *n* **1** = skein *e16*.
2 a certain length (of girth web) *la16*. **3**
string, twine, pack-thread *18-20*. [only Sc; OF
escaigne. OED *skein*]

skair¹ &c *n* **1** = share, a portion, allotted part
la16-19. **2** a plot of land, *esp* one of the many
parcelled out of common lands *18, Dmf*.
vt = share *la15-e20*. [see SND]

skair² &c; **skaird &c**, **skjaard &c** *la19-*, *Sh*
[sker; *Sh* skerd, skjɑrd] *n* **1** a slanting cut or
notch in a piece of wood by which it can be
joined to another of similar shape *la18-*, *now
local Sh-Fif*. **2** a piece of wood so fashioned,
specif one of the segments of a fishing rod *19-*,
now Sh Cai Per. **3** the joint at the end of a golf-
club shaft where the head is fixed *la19-e20*. **4**
a thumb-knot join in a fishing line between the
tippin (TIP¹) and the SNUID *20-*, *Mry Abd*.
vt **1** splice (two pieces of wood etc) *la18-*, *now Sh
Ork Cai Fif*. **2** join (the *tippin* (TIP¹)) to the
SNUID of a fishing line) with a thumb-knot *20-*,
Mry Abd. [only Sc; ON *skor-, skar-* an edge,
joint in a ship's planking]

skair³ *n* ~ **scone &c** a kind of oatmeal-
and-flour SCONE made with beaten egg and
milk *19-20*. [shortened f CARECAKE, with *s-*
from SCONE]

skair *see* SCAR

skaird *see* SKAIR²

skairs *see* SCARCE

skairsburn &c [*?'skerzbʌrn] *n* ~ **warning**
no warning at all (of a sudden disaster)
la17-e20, Gall. [from the Skyre Burn ['skaɪr
'bʌrn] in Kcb (said to flood very quickly);
adapted from Eng *Scarborough warning*]

skaitbird *n* meaning unknown *e16, only Sc*.

skaith &c *15-*, **scathe**, **scath &c** *la14-e15*,
skeath *18*, **skaid** *la18-e20* [*n* skeθ, *v* skeð; *n
and v also local* *sked] *n* **1** (1) damage, hurt,
injury, harm, *sometimes in phrs with* **scorn** *la14-*.
(2) damage done by trespass of animals; the
act or offence of trespass, *freq* **in his, that** *etc* ~
trespassing on him, that place etc *18-19*. (3)
harm or injury attributed to witchcraft or the
evil eye *la18-19*. **2** damage etc involving compensation; damages: (1) *in sing, la14-e20*; (2) *in
pl, la15-e16*. **3** (a liability for) a compensation
paid for one's trouble or services *18*. **4** something which harms *la18-19*.

vti, ptp also **skaed** la19 **1** harm, injure, damage la14-, local. **2** vt penalize, fine la15-e19. **~ful &c** harmful, injurious la14-19. **~less** unharmed; free of financial loss or penalty la14-e19. **do ~** do harm or injury la14-19. **get, tak** etc **~** be hurt, damaged etc la14-, now local Kcdn-Lnk. [cf arch and dial Eng]

skaivie see SKAVE

skaken see SKEICH

skaldock see SKELDOCK

skale see SKAIL¹

skamyll see SKEMMEL

skane see SKEAN, SKIN

skanʒe see SKAINIE

skape see SKEP

skarrach ['skarəx] n a flying shower of rain; a light fall of snow 19-, now Ags Fif. [only Sc; obscure]

skate¹ &c n **1** = skate, the fish la16-. **2** contemptuous term for a stupid or objectionable person 18-, local. **~ bread** a kind of very small fish la17. **~ bree** the water in which skate has been boiled, skate soup, said to have aphrodisiac and other properties la19-, now Wgt. **~ bubble** a jellyfish e20. **~ purse** the ovarium of a skate 19-, local. **~ rumple** the part of the backbone of a skate above the root of the tail 18-19.

skate² &c 19-, **skeet &c** 18- n = (ice-)skate 19-. vti **1** = skate (on ice) 18-. **2** vt, only **skeet** make (a stone) skim over water la20-, Sh Cai Arg Lnk. **skater** C, **skeeter** Cai a water beetle 20-.

skathie [*?'skaðɪ, *?'skeðɪ] n a rough shelter, esp a fence or wall used as a windbreak in front of a door 19-20, chf NE. [only Sc; dim based on ScGael sgàth a wattle fence or door; shelter; IrGael scáth a shadow, shelter]

skave [skev] adj **skived &c** [skaɪvd] over to one side, off the straight, tilted 20-, now NE Loth Kcb. **sk(a)ivie, skeevie &c** ['skevɪ, 'skivɪ] harebrained, daft, mentally deranged 19. **skavle &c** ['skevl; Ork 'skjevl] walk with a crooked twisting gait, totter, reel la19-, now Ork. [Norw dial skeiv, ON skeifr oblique, askew; perh w infl f SKEICH]

skavie &c, skeevie &c ['skevɪ, 'skivɪ] n **1** a trick, piece of mischief 19-, Bnf Abd. **2** a mishap, accident; a disappointment la19-20, Bnf Abd. vi rush about in an idle, silly or ostentatious way la19-, now Bnf. [only Sc; uncertain]

skavle see SKAVE

skawk see SKAIK

skean &c; skane e17, **sgian &c** la19- ['skiən, skin] n a (Highlander's (HIELAND)) short-bladed black-hilted sheath-knife or dagger 18-e20. **~ dhu, sgian dubh** ['skiən 'du, 'skin 'du] = n, now commonly worn in the stocking as part of Highland dress (HIELAND) 19-. **skeen occle**

&c a SKEAN concealed in the upper part of the sleeve under the armpit 18-e19. [Sc and IrGael sgian a knife, sgian dubh a black knife, sgian-achlais an armpit knife]

skeath see SKAITH

skech &c; skaich &c, skeich &c [skex, skix; *skɛx] vti **1** obtain (something) in an underhand way by wiles, wheedling or filching; scrounge; freq wander about in search of (food), scrounge (a meal) 19-. **2** vi go about in a silly, vain, idle way la19-, Bnf Abd. n **1** the act of skeching, freq **on the ~**; what has been thus obtained, loot la19-, now Abd WC Kcb. **2** a scrounger, sponger la19-, local Abd-WC. **skaicher &c** = n 2, 19-, now Mry. [only Sc; perh ME skeck &c (n, v) raid]

skechan see SKEICH

skeechan &c ['skixən] n an intoxicating malt liquor produced in the later stages of brewing and formerly used by bakers instead of yeast; sometimes mixed with treacle etc and sold as a kind of beer 19-20. [only Sc; var of keechan (CAOCHAN)]

skeeg¹ &c n the smallest amount (esp of liquid), the least drop la18-20. **~le &c** a little drop la20-, Ags Per Ayr. [only Sc; obscure]

skeeg², skeg, skig v **1** vt whip, strike, slap, spank la18-, chf NE. **2** move nimbly, hurry, walk with long inelegant steps 19. n a blow, smack, esp on the bottom 19-, NE. [only Sc; perh onomat, w infl f SKELP¹ and FLEG²]

skeel¹ &c la18-, **skill** la14- n **1** = skill la14-. **2** skill in the art of healing (people or animals), freq of a non-professional kind 19-, now NE Ags. vt **1** order, dispose e17, only Sc. **2** scan expertly, investigate, determine, specif when looking for weather signs 20-, Bnf Abd. **~y 1** skilled, experienced, practised la18-, now NE, C. **2** having real or supposed skill in the art of healing 19-, now NE Fif. **~y wife** etc a woman credited with great or supernatural healing powers, esp one called to emergencies or confinements la18-20. **hae ~ o** be experienced in, have practice in; have a liking for or favourable opinion of la18-e20. **man** or **woman of skill** an expert in a subject, esp one called in by a court 18-.

skeel² &c n a kind of wooden tub for milk or water, freq with handles formed by elongated staves 16-, now Ags. [nME skele, ON skjóla]

skeel see SCHULE

skeeling &c n = sheldrake la16. **~ goose &c** = n, la16-17, 19-e20 (Sh Ork). [cf SKELLDRAKE]

skeely see SCAILIE

skeen occle see SKEAN

skeenie, skeenyie, skeenzie see SKAINIE

skeer &c 19-; **skyre &c** 19, **skir &c** la14, 19- vt = scare la14, 19-.

adj, of persons or animals, esp horses nervous, fearful, restive, agitated; *of a girl* flighty, skittish; behaving irrationally, mentally unstable *19-e20*.

∼ie &c = *adj, 19-, now local. [cf* SCAR. OED *scare*]

skeet *n* the pollack *e20, N.* [see SND]

skeet *see* SKATE², SKITE¹

skeetch *see* SKETCH¹

skeevie *see* SKAVE, SKAVIE

skeg *see* SKEEG²

skeich &c, skey *e16, la19-, now Ags* [skɪx, *ski *adj* **1** *of horses* inclined to shy, restive, frisky, spirited *16-, now Stlg WC Wgt.* **2** *of persons* (1) in high spirits, animated, daft, skittish *16-*; (2) *esp of women* shy, coy, disdainful, saucy, haughty *18-, now Lnk Ayr Wgt.*
adv shyly, coyly, disdainfully, saucily, spiritedly *la18-19*.
v **1** *vi* shy, startle *16-, now Ayr.* **2** *vt, only* **skey** ? startle, come upon suddenly *e16*.

∼en &c *la19-,* **ska(i)ken** *20,* **skechan &c** *20-* ['skɪxən, 'skɛx-, 'skɪx-, &c] *adj* **1** timid, easily scared, nervous *la19-20, Abd.* **2** *also* **skiten** fastidious about food, easily upset or nauseated *20-, NE.* *n* fastidiousness or fussiness about food; a feeling of disgust for something edible *19-, now Bnf Abd.* *vti* (feel) disgust, (be) repel(led), (be) nauseate(d) *la19-, now Bnf Abd.* [only Sc; see SND. OED *skeigh, skey* (*v*)]

skeich *see* SKECK

skeir *see* SKIRE

skel *see* SKELF²

skelb *n* **1** a thin flake, slice, or splinter of wood, stone, or metal, now *esp* one lodged in the skin *la16-, now NE nEC.* **2** any thin slice *la19-, NE.* *vti* cut or form into flakes or splinters *19-, now Ags Fif.* [only Sc; ScGael *sgealb,* IrGael *scealb* a splinter, flake; *cf* SKELF² and SKELP²]

skeldock &c; sceldrick, skaldock, scaldrick [*'skɛldək, *'skaldək, *'skaldrɪk, &c] *n* the wild mustard *la17-e19.* [only Sc; perh ME *kedlock; cf* SKELLOCH²]

skelet &c [*'skɛlət] *n* a skeleton *18-e19.* [eModEng *skellette,* F *squellette*]

skelf¹ &c *n* **1** = shelf *la15-, now Ork Cai NE Ags.* **2** a shelf above a *box bed* (BOX¹), *freq* used as a bunk for young children *18-, now Ork EC.*
skelvy *of a river bank etc* shelving *la18-, now Sh.* [nME; see SND]

skelf² &c; skelve, skel *n* **1** a thin flat fragment or slice, a flake, lamina; a splinter or small chip of wood, *esp* one lodged in the skin *17-, now Sh Ork Cai C.* **2** a wedge of wood driven into the cut in a tree being felled (to ease the motion of the saw) *la20-, WC.* **3** a small thin insignificant person *20-, WC Rox.*
v **1** *vt* take off (as) in flakes, slice *20-, local Sh-WC.* **2** *vi* flake, break into flat slices *19-, now Ork.* [see SND; *cf* SKELB]

skell *see* SKAIL¹

skellach &c ['skɛləx] *n* = SKELLET¹ *la17-19.* [altered var]

skellat *see* SKELLET¹

skelldrake &c *17-e19,* **scaledrake &c** *la18-e19* [*'skɛl'drek] *n* = sheldrake. [see SND *skell-*]

skellet¹ &c *la16-, now Lnk,* **skellat** *16-18,* **skillet &c** *18-e19 n, also* ∼ **bell** a handbell, a small bell, *eg* one used by a public crier *16-*.
∼ bellman &c a bellman, public crier *18-e19.* [nME; northern OF *escalete &c*]

skellet² &c *n* **1** = skillet, a saucepan *e18.* **2** a tin water-scoop *la19-, now Cai Inv Mry.*

skellie¹ &c; scalie &c *la18-19* ['skɛlɪ] *adj* **1** *also* ∼-**eyed** squinting, squint-eyed *la18-, now C (except Ags) S.* **2** lop-sided; awry *20-, local C, S.*
n **1** a cast in the eye, a squint; a squint or sidelong glance *la18-, now Per-S.* **2** an error, a going astray *20-, chf SW.*
vi **1** squint, be cross-eyed *la18-, now local Abd-S.* **2** make a mistake in a statement, exaggerate *la18-, chf SW.* [also in northern ModEng dial; *cf* ON *skelgjask* (*vr*) squint, *skjalgr* squint, awry, cognate w SHAUCH]

skellie² &c *n* a ridge of rock running out to sea, *usu* covered at high tide, a SKERRIE, reef *e16, 19-, now Abd Ags Fif, freq in place-names.* [only Sc; see SND]

skellie *see* SKELLOCH²

skelloch¹ &c ['skɛləx] *vi* shriek, scream, cry shrilly *19-, now NE Ags.*
n a scream, screech, shrill cry *19-, now local NE-Ayr.* [only Sc; see SND]

skelloch² &c, skellie ['skɛləx, 'skɛlɪ] *n, freq in pl* the charlock or wild mustard *la17-, now local Cai-Lnk.* [only Sc; see SND; *cf* SKELDOCK]

skellum &c *n, contemptuous term for a man, now sometimes playfully to a boy* a scamp, rogue, scoundrel *la18-20.* [obs Eng slang, Du *schelm*]

skelly &c *n* the chub *la17-e20, S.* [see SND]

skelp¹; skilp *19-20 vti* **1** (1) strike, hit, *esp* with something flat, *eg* the palm of the hand, slap, smack (*specif* someone's bottom) *la16-.* (2) hit, strike, drive with blows, kicks etc; beat, hammer *la18-.* (3) *of the blows of misfortune* hit *19-.* **2** *vi* throb, pulsate; *of a clock* tick *18-e20.* **3** work with energy or gusto (**at**), be vigorously busy *la18-, now local.* **4** *vt* do (a piece of work) vigorously, reel or rattle off *19-, now Kcb.* **5** *vi* strike the ground with the feet or hooves, scamper along, gallop, move quickly *18-.* **6** *vti, of liquids* (cause to) splash or dash, spatter, pelt *la18-, local Sh-Kcb.*
n **1** a stroke, blow, *esp* with a flat object, a smack with the open hand, a sword, whip etc *16-.* **2** the sound of such a blow, a crack *19-.* **3** a blast of wind, squall, downpour of rain; a splash of liquid *19-e20.* **4** a blow of misfortune *la18-.* **5** an indirect satirical reference, a hit (**at** someone) *20-, NE wLoth Ayr.* **6** an attempt, try, SHOT *20-, local Sh-Kcb.*
adv with a smack or crack, vigorously *la18-.*

~**ie** *n, also* ~**ie limmer** *la18* a naughty, mischievous girl *la18-19. adj* naughty *la9.* ~**ing** big of its kind, 'thumping' *la18-, now local.* ~**it leathering** a thrashing, spanking *20-, Per WC.*

skelp[2] *n* **1** = SKELF[2] *n* 1, *18-, now local Inv-Lnk.* **2** a large slice or chunk, a slab, *eg* of cheese or butter *19-, now local Ork-Arg.* **3** a long strip or expanse, *esp* of ground, an indefinite area *la19-, local.* [prob var of SKELB]

skelter &c *vi* scurry, scamper, rush headlong *la19-, Mry Bnf C, S.* [appar Eng *-skelter* in *helter-skelter*]

skelve *see* SKELF[2]

skelvy *see* SKELF[1]

skemler *see* SCAMBLER

skemmel &c *la16-,* **scamble &c** *la16-e18;* **skamyll &c** *la15-16* ['skɛml; *'skaml] *n* **1** a bench *la15.* **2** *in pl with sing meaning* a shambles, slaughter-house; a meat or fish market *la16-, now NE Ags.* **3** a *peat bank* (PEAT[1]), the HAG[1] (*n* 4(1)) left in a MOSS from which PEATS[1] have been cut *20-, only Sc.* [var of Eng *shamble; cf* ON *skemill,* Dan *skammel* a footstool]

skemp &c *n* = scamp *19-, local N-S.*

sken3e *see* SKAINIE

skep &c; skape &c *18-19* [skɛp] *n* **1** a wickerwork or straw basket, *esp* one for carrying grain, meal, or potatoes *la14, 18-.* **2** a beehive *la16-. vt* put (a swarm of bees) into a hive *19-.*
skeppie, ~ **bee** the hive- or honey-bee *la20-, Abd Kcdn nEC.* **skeppit &c** put to bed, tucked up for the night *la18-, now Bwk Lnk.*
~ **in wi** share accommodation with, live or hobnob with *la18-19.* [ME *sceppe;* ON *skeppa* a basket]

sker *adj* **skerry-handit** *19-, now S,* ~**-handed** *19* left-handed. [var of *ker* (CAR[2])]

sker *see* SCAR, SCAUR[1]

skerrie &c, skerry *n* an isolated rock or islet in the sea, *freq* one covered at high tide *16-, chf Sh Ork.* [dim of ON *sker*]

sketch[1], **scatch &c** *la17-19;* **skeetch &c, skytch &c** [sketʃ, skɪtʃ; *Sh N* skitʃ; *WC* skəitʃ; *'skatʃ] *n* **1** *only* **scatch** = scatch, a stilt *la17.* **2** an ice-skate *19-, now Ags.* **3** the act of skating, a turn or spell of skating *la19-, Sh Ags. v* **1** *vi* skate *la18-, now Sh Ags Per.* **2** *vti, of a stone* skim along the surface of water; cause (stones) to do this, play at ducks and drakes *20-, now Ross Inv Fif.*
skeetcher &c 1 *also* **skeetchie &c** the flat stone etc kicked in the game of PEEVER[1]; *chf in pl* the game itself *la20-, local Ross-Fif.* **2** a skimming stone *la20-, local Ross-Fif.* **3** *also* **skytcher &c** (1) a skater *20-, now Sh Ags.* (2) an ice-skate *19-, now Ags.*

sketch[2] **&c** *n* **1** = sketch. **2** a brief period of time *20-, Rox.*

skeuch *see* SKEW[2]

skew[1] **&c** [skju] *n* a stone forming part of the coping of the sloping part of the gable; the coping itself *16-.*

vt build a SKEW[1] on *18-e20.*
~ **corbel** *la19-,* ~ **putt** *la19-,* ~ **stone** *19-, now Kcb* the lowest stone in a gable coping. [ME *scu(w)e*]

skew[2] **&c; skyow &c** *la19-, chf NE,* **skeuch &c** *19-, NE* [skju; *NE* skjʌu, skjux] *v* **1** *vi* go obliquely or off the straight, move sideways; sway affectedly *la15, 19-, now Bnf Abd.* **2** *vti* twist, turn sideways, screw round *19-, now local NE-SW.* **3** *of the feet, legs, or gait* splay, turn outwards *la19-, Bnf Abd.* **4** *of the eyes or glance* squint naturally or on purpose *la19-e20.* **5** fall out, disagree *20-, NE.*
adj = skew *20-.*
adv at a slant, askew, this way and that *la19-e20.*
n **1** *mining* a piece of rock slanting upwards and overhanging a working place *la18-e20.* **2** a twist, turn, sideways movement *la19-, local.* **3** a squint, sidelong glance *20-, now Mry Abd.* **4** a quarrel, row *20-, Mry Abd.*
~**-fittit** splay-footed *la19-, local NE-Lnk.* ~**-whiff &c** awry, at a rakish angle *la18-.* [*cf* Eng]

skew[3] *n* meaning unknown *la15, only Sc.*

skewl; skyowl [skjul, skjʌul] *vt* **1** turn aside, deflect from its normal course or position *19-, now Rox.* **2** screw up, twist (the mouth) *19.* **3** wear (shoes) to one side *19-e20.*
n a turning aside, a twist *la19-, now Rox.* [see SND]

skey [*ski, &c] *vi* get clear, sheer **off** *la15.* [only Sc; obscure]

skey *see* SKEICH

skibby *adj* left-handed *20-, Lnk Ayr.* [perh var of KIPPIE]

skibo &c ['skibə, 'skibɪ] *n* a *Highland* (HIELAND) bovine animal *19-, chf Ags.* [orig of a breed of small cattle bred on the Skibo estate in Suth]

skice &c *vi* make off quickly and unobtrusively, clear out *la19-, NE.* [eModEng]

skiddle[1] *19-;* **skittle &c** *19-e20 vti* splash (a liquid), squirt (water) about, spill, dabble, potter or splash **about** *19-, Mry C.*
n **1** a thin watery liquid, *esp contemptuous* weak tea *la19-, WC.* **2** a mess, muddle, confusion, *esp* with spilling of liquid *20-, nEC Loth WC.* **3** contemptuous term for a small thing, matter, person, or animal *19-20.* [var of SCUDDLE[1]]

skiddle[2] *vi* move rapidly and lightly *20-, local Stlg-Rox.* [var of SCUDDLE[2]; *cf* Eng *skid* scud, run]

skier *see* SKIRE

skiff[1] **&c** *v* **1** *vi* move lightly, airily, barely touching the ground, skim, glide, skip *18-.* **2** rain or snow very slightly *la19-.* **3** ~ **by** *or* **ower** do work carelessly or superficially *la19-, Sh N Per.* **4** *vt* touch lightly in passing, brush, graze; brush off, flick *19-.* **5** throw (an object) along the surface of something, make (a flat stone) skip over water, or over the ground as in PEEVER[1] *19-.*

n **1** a slight touch or graze in passing, an abrasion *la19-*. **2** a slight gust of wind *19-*, *now local*. **3** a slight touch (of an illness) *la19-*, *now Cai Ags WC*. **4** a slight or flying shower of rain or snow, a light drizzle, a fleeting patch of wet mist *19-*.

~**er** a flat stone used in playing ducks and drakes *la20-*, *C, S*. ~**in 1** a slight fall of snow *la19-*. **2** a thin partition or screen *la20-*, *now NE Fif*. ~**le** *n* a slight shower of rain *20-*, *local NE-Rox*. *vi*, *eg of a stone on water* skip or skim across a flat surface *la20-*, *Cai Bwk Kcb S*.
skiffler = *skiffer*, *la20-*, *Cai Bwk Kcb Slk*.
skifflers the game of ducks and drakes *20-*, *Cai Bwk Kcb S*. [only Sc; onomat; var of SCUFF[1], but confused w SKIFT]

skiff[2] *20-*, *NE*, *C (coast)*, **skift** *la19-e20* *n*, *specif* a type of small fishing boat with oars and a lugsail. [*cf* Eng]

skiffle &c *vt* raise or produce (sparks etc) by scuffling the feet *la20-*, *Lnk Ayr Rox*. [var of Eng *scuffle*]

skiffle *see* SKIFF[1]

skift &c *vi* **1** move lightly, skim, skip *la16-e19*. **2** *specif*, *of rain or snow* fall lightly *19*.
n **1** = skift, a shift, change *e15*. **2** a light shower of rain or snow *la19-e20*. **3** a hurried or cursory dusting *20-*, *local Ags-Rox*.
~**er 1** = *n* 2, *20-*, *local Sh-Loth*. **2** *in pl* the game of ducks and drakes *20-*, *now Cai Loth*. ~**in** a light fall or sprinkling of snow *20-*, *local*, *NE-Lnk*, *Rox*. [see SND]

skift *see* SKIFF[2]

skifting &c *n* a narrow piece of boarding, *esp* (*also* ~ **board**) skirting-board *la18-*, *EC, WC, S*. [only Sc; see SND]

skig *see* SKEEG[2]
skill *see* SCULL[1], SKEEL[1]
skillet *see* SKELLET[1]
skilp *see* SKELP[1]

skilt *vi* move **about** quickly and lightly, dart, skip, gad **about** *la17-*, *S*.
n a flighty, giddy young person, a gadabout *la17-19*. [see SND]

skim *vti* = skim.
~**-the-milk** a figure in the game of *chucks* (CHUCK[2]) *20-*, *Inv WC*.

skime &c *vi* glance, shine with reflected light, gleam *19-e20*.
n **1** a glance of the eye, a quick (often sideways) or angry look *19-*, *now Kcb*. **2** a gleam of light, flash; a brief glimpse or appearance *19-*, *now Sh*. [*cf* ON *skima* peer, look about, *skimi* a gleam of light]

skimmer &c *vi* **1** (1) *of light or a bright object* twinkle, gleam *19-e20*. (2) *of clothes* be bright, resplendent *la18-20*. **2** glide along easily and quickly *la18-e20*.
n, *also* **shimmer** *la20-*, *local Per-Lnk* a light sprinkling, *esp* of snow or rain *la19-*, *Sh NE*.
~**ing** a light sprinkling (of snow) *la19-*, *Sh NE Per*. [see SND]

skin &c; skane &c *19-e20*, *Sh n* **1** = skin *15-*.
2 *slang* a robbery, what has been stolen; a petty swindle; a small private gain on the side *la19-*, *C*.
vt **1** = skin. **2** pare the surface layer of soil etc off (land) *20-*, *N, EC, Ayr*.
skinnin a small amount; a piece of petty economy or profit *la19-*, *NE nEC Kcb Rox*.
at the ~ (soaked through) to the skin *la19-*, *Sh Abd*. ~**-the-cuddy** a kind of leapfrog *20-*, *NE Loth WC*. ~**-for-**~ *mining*, *of props etc* set so close as to be touching *la19-*, *now Fif*.
weel-skinnt having a healthy clear skin or smooth appearance *19-*, *now Sh*.

skink[1] **&c** *n* **1** a shin, knuckle, *hough* (HOCH[1]) of beef *17-*, *now Sh N Per*. **2** a soup, *esp* one made from this (but *cf* CULLEN SKINK) *la16-*, *now Sh NE Ags*. [only Sc; MDu *schenke* shin, hough, ham]

skink[2] *v* **1** *vt* pour out (liquor for drinking) *16-19*. **2** pour (a small amount of liquid) from one container to another; mix (liquids) thus *18-e20*. **3** *vti* make (someone) a present of *e16*. **4** dispose of or spend recklessly *e17*, *la19-*, *now Ags*.
n **1** drink, liquor, *esp* of a weak, wishy-washy kind *19-e20*. **2** a kind of thin, oatmeal-and-water gruel *la19-20*.
~**in** easily poured, thinly diluted *la18-19*, *only Sc*. ~**le** *vt* sprinkle, scatter, spray, or spill in small quantities *19*. *n* a very small quantity, *esp* of something liquid or powdery *19*. [ME *skynk* pour (wine)]

skink[3] *vt* crush (something soft or brittle), squash by weight or pressure *19-e20*. [see SND]

skinkle *vi*, *now chf verse* glitter, gleam, sparkle *la18-*, *now Per Stlg WC*. [perh a var of SCINTILL]

skinkle *see* SKINK[2]

skinny[1] *n* a bread roll, *esp* a breakfast roll *20-*, *Dmf Rox*.

skinny[2] *adj* = skinny.
~**malink(ie) &c** ['~mə'lɪŋkɪ] a thin, skinny person or animal *la19-*. ~ **tatie** a potato boiled in its skin *la20-*, *WC-S*.

skintie *adj* small, scrimp, meagre, scanty *la20-*, *wLoth Lnk S*. [conflation of Eng *skimpy* w *scanty*]

skip[1] *v*, *n* = skip *16-*.
skippie *of roads etc* slippery, icy *20-*, *Abd Per*.
~ **rape** a skipping rope *la19-*, *now Per Stlg Wgt*.

skip[2] *n*, *curling* (CURL) *and bowls* the captain and director of play of a RINK or side *19-*.
vt, *freq* ~ **a rink** act as SKIP to a team *20-*. [reduced f Eng *skipper*]

skip *see* SCUIP

skipe *see* SKYBE

skippie &c; skippack &c ['skɪpɪ, 'skɪbɪ, 'skɪpək, 'skɪpək] *n*, *also* ~**lickie** *la20-* the game of tig *la19-*, *Cai-Inv*. [only Sc; Gael *sgiabag*, f *sgiab* touch or snatch at quickly]

skir *see* SKEER

skire &c, **skyre** *16-*; **skeir** &c *18-e20*, **skier** &c *17-19* [skaɪr, skir; *NE* skəir] *adj, of flames, light etc* clear; bright *la16, la19-e20*.
adv absolutely, utterly, altogether, *esp* ~ **mad** *etc, la16-19*.
vi **1** ? be mad *la16*; *cf* prec. **2** shine brightly, glitter; be gaudy; wear gaudy, garish clothes *la17-, now Ork NE*.
n meaning unknown *e16*.
skyrin, skyrie bright; gaudy in colour, garish *18-, now Ork NE*.
S~(s) Thursday Maundy Thursday; a fair or market held on that day *15-e20*. [see SND]

skirfen *see* SKIRVEN

skirl¹ &c *v* **1** *vi* scream, cry out with fear, pain or grief *16-*. **2** *vti* utter with a high-pitched discordant sound, cry or sing shrilly, raise a clamour *la18-*. **3** *vi* shriek with excitement or laughter *la18-*. **4** *of birds* scream, screech *19-e20*. **5** *of the wind* blow with a shrill noise, whistle *la19-e20*. **6** creak, make a crackling, screeching, or whistling sound *19-20*. **7** (1) *of bagpipes etc* make a shrill sound *la17-*. (2) *vti, of a (chf bagpipe-)player* make a shrill sound (on (the bagpipes)) *19-*. **8** *vi, of something very hot, esp in frying* sizzle, crackle, sputter *19-, now Per*.
n **1** a scream or shriek of pain, anguish, fear etc *16-*. **2** a shriek of laughter etc *18-*. **3** the loud cry, wail, or whistle of a bird *19-*. **4** *piping* the shrill sound of bagpipes; a wrong note accidentally played *la19-*. **5** (1) the high-pitched sound of a strong wind; the wind itself, gusty weather *19-*. (2) a flurry (of snow or hail) *19-, now NE Ags Per*. **6** a screeching, whirring or whistling noise made by something mechanical *la19-e20*.
~ie *n* **1** a dish of oatmeal and onions fried in a pan *20-*. **2** = *n* 5(2), *la19-20*. **~y wheeter** the oystercatcher *20-, Bnf Abd* [perh connected w OSc *scurliquitor* (once) term of abuse *la16*].
~-in-the-pan = ~ie 1, *20-, now Cai Ags Per*. [nME; Scand]

skirl² *adv, chf* ~ **naked** completely or stark-naked *19-, now local Ags-S*. [var of SKIRE, confused in form w SKIRL¹]

skirp *vti* **1** *also* ~ **at** mock, treat with contempt *la15-e18*. **2** *vt* sprinkle (water etc), splash in small drops or squirts *19-, chf NE*. **3** *vi, of water, mud etc* splash, fly up in small drops; rain slightly, spit *la19-, chf NE*.
n **1** a small drop, splash, or spurt of liquid, *specif* a slight shower or spot of rain *la19-, chf NE*. **2** a drop of liquor, a dram *19-, NE*. **3** a small flying fragment of metal, stone etc, a pellet, splinter *20-, NE*. [eME = behave with contempt, ON *skirpa* spit]

skirr &c *vi* scurry about, travel rapidly, rush, whizz *19-, now Ork*. [eModEng *skyr* run away, rush about]

skirt &c *n* **1** = skirt *16-*. **2** a woman *la16-*. **3** the border, outlying part (**of** a territory etc) *la15*.

v **1** *vi* run away, decamp; elope *19-, local NE-Kcb*. **2** *vti* elude, evade; lurk, skulk, play truant from (school) *la19-, now eLoth WC Kcb*.

skirvin &c; **skirfen** *n* **1** **skirfen** crust *e17*. **2** **skirvin** a thin covering of soil, snow etc *20-, S*. [metath f *scriffin* (SCRUIF)]

skit¹ &c *n* **1** a frivolous, vain woman *la16, e19*. **2** a trick, hoax *19-, now local Sh-Kcb*. **3** a squirt of water, a jet; a sharp short shower *la19-e20*. [perh *skyt-*, a short-vowel form f ON *skjóta*; *cf* SKITE¹]

skit² *n* **1** diarrhoea *20-, local Sh-Gall*. **2** *fig, esp of a woman* an arrogant or disagreeable person *19-, now Sh* [*cf* SKIT¹ *n* 1].
vi defecate *e16, 19-, now Sh*. [see SND]

skite¹ &c; **skeet** *la19-, Sh Ork v* **1** *vi* dart through the air suddenly, forcibly and *freq* obliquely *18-*. **2** rebound, ricochet *19-*. **3** (1) slip, slither or slide on a slippery surface *la19-*. (2) skate (on ice) *la19-e20*. **4** *vt* throw suddenly and forcibly, send flying, make (something) shoot off at an angle; cause (a stone) to skip over the surface of water *19-*. **5** *vti* cause a spray or splash of liquid, squirt, splash *19-, now Sh-Ags SW*. **6** *vi* act wildly or boisterously; carouse *20-, now Bwk*. **7** *vt* strike, hit (a person) *la20-, Cai. C*.
adv with a sharp rap or blow, forcibly and with a rebound *19-, now NE Ags Per*.
adj off one's head, daft *20-, now Bnf Abd*.
n **1** a sudden sharp glancing blow *la18-, Gen except Sh Ork*. **2** (1) the act of shooting out or squirting liquid; a squirt, a syringe *19-, now N*. (2) a small amount of water; a short sharp shower of rain *19-, now local Bnf-Wgt*. (3) a small amount of liquor, a dram *la19-, NE Ags*. **3** a jollification, spree, blow-out, *freq* **on the** ~ *la19-*. **4** a slip, slither, skid *19-, now Sh, N, C*. **5** the yellowhammer *19-e20, chf NE*.
skiter &c a squirt, syringe, instrument for spraying etc; a pea- or water-shooter, *esp* one made from a plant stem *la19-, Sh NE Ags*.
skitie &c slippery *20-*.
gie *or* **play someone a** ~ deal unfairly or deceitfully with someone *la18-e20*. [chf Sc; ON *skýt-*, stem of *skjóta* shoot, propel, dart]

skite² *vti* have diarrhoea; soil with excrement *16-e20*.
n a nasty or objectionable person *19-, now local Inv-Lnk*.
skiter term of abuse *la19-, Bnf Mry*. [ON *skíta*, corresp to OE *scítan* > Eng *shite*]

skiten *see* SKEICH
skitie *see* SKITE¹

skitter¹ &c *n* **1** diarrhoea, liquid excrement *16-*. **2** anything dirty or disgusting, a mess, rubbish *19-, now local Sh-Per*.
vi **1** have diarrhoea, void liquid excrement *16-*. **2** waste time doing footling jobs, potter **about** aimlessly *20-, local*.

~**ie 1** trifling, contemptibly small or inadequate *la20-, local*. **2** *of a task* fiddly, time-consuming *la20-, C*. ~**y feltie** the fieldfare *la20-, local Stlg-SW*. **skitterie winter** the last person to arrive for or leave work on HOGMANAY *la20-, WC*. [frequentative of SKITE²]

skitter² &c *vi* slither, slip in a jerky awkward way *la19-, now Abd Ags*. [appar frequentative of SKITE¹]

skittle *see* SKIDDLE¹

skive¹ *vi* roam or prowl about (like a dog in search of food) *la19-, now local NE-SW*.
skiver a prowler, prying person *la19-, now Lnk Ayr Dmf*. [see SND]

skive² *vt* **1** = skive, pare (leather). **2** shave, pare, slice off a thin layer from *la20-, local NE-Lnk*. [*cf* SHIVE]

skived *see* SKAVE

skiver &c ['skɪvər] *n* **1** = skewer *la18*. **2** a splinter of wood in the skin *la20-, local Ork-WC*. *vt* pierce or stab as with a skewer *19-, now Dnbt*.

skivet¹ &c ['skɪvət] *n* a sharp hard blow *19-, S*. [only Sc; uncertain; *cf* SKIFF¹ and SCUFF¹]

skivet² &c [*'skɪvət, *'skɪfət] *n* a smith's firetool *17-e19*. [only Sc; see SND]

skivie *see* SKAVE

skjaard *see* SKAIR²

sklaik *see* SLAIK

sklatter *n* an untidy splash, daub *la20-, Abd Kcdn Ags*. [altered f Eng dial *slat(ter)* (*v*) splash, smudge, perh w infl f SCLATCH]

skleat *see* SLATE

skleet *see* SKLUTE

skleff &c *adj* **1** *of a dish* shallow, flat *19-, now Loth*. **2** thin and flat; *of persons* thin; flat-chested *19-, chf S*. **3** equal, even (in a competition etc) *20-, Rox*.
on *etc* **the** ~ on the flat, along level ground *20-, Rox*. [onomat; *cf* SCLAFF]

skleg *see* SLIG

sklent¹ &c; **sklint** *19-e20* *v* **1** *vi* also **slent** *17-, local* move obliquely, turn sideways, zigzag *16-, now Sh wLoth Kcb*. **2** slope, slant, lie to one side *la18-, now local*. **3** (1) *vt* aim (something) obliquely or sideways, send across *la16-, now Sh*. (2) *vi* reflect sarcastically **on**, hint **at** by insinuation *19*. **4** deviate from the truth etc *la16-19*. **5** (1) *vt* cast (the eyes) sideways *e19*. (2) *vi* glance sideways, look askance, squint *19-, now local*. (3) *of light etc* shine in a slanting direction *la18-, now Sh*.
n **1** a slanting cut; a slope, incline *la16-, now local Cai-Dmf*. **2** (1) a sideways movement, change of direction *la18-, now Sh*. (2) *specif of wind or rain* a slanting motion *la19-e20*. **3** a sidelong glance *19-, now local Sh-Dmf*.
adj **1** slanting, to one side, oblique *19-, now local Sh-Ayr*. **2** *of a look or glance* sidelong, cast askance *19-, now Sh*.
adv at a slant, off the straight, obliquely *20-, now Sh Abd Fif*.

prep across, athwart *19*. [also northern ModEng dial; var of ME *slent*, of Scand orig]

sklent² &c *vt* split, tear (*esp* clothes) *19-, now Sh. n* a rip, tear *la19-, Sh Abd*. [see SND]

sklent³ &c [sklɛnt; *Sh* sklant] *n* a chance, opportunity *20-, now Sh*. [var of slang (*orig* nautical) Eng *slant*]

skleush &c [skl(j)uʃ] *vi* walk in a clumsy, shuffling, or leg-weary manner *la19-, now Cai Bnf Abd*.
n a trailing, shuffling, heavy-footed gait *la19-, now Cai Abd*. [emphatic var of SLUSH]

skleuter *see* SLUTTER

skliff &c; **skluif** &c *19-e20*, **skloof** &c *19-e20* [sklɪf; *NE* sklʌuf; *Ags* skluf; *Bwk Rox* sklɵf] *v* **1** *vi* walk with a heavy, shuffling step, drag the feet, scuffle *19-, now NE, C*. **2** *vt* strike with a glancing blow, scuff, rub against *la19-, local Stlg-Rox*. **3** cut away the upper surface or covering of, pare, slice *20-, local*.
n **1** a shuffling, trailing way of walking; the noise of this *la19-, now local EC-Gall*. **2** a clumsy, worn-out shoe *la19-, now Loth Per Kcb*. **3** a blow with a flat surface, a swipe in passing; the noise of this *19-, now Loth WC Rox*. **4** a segment, *eg* of the moon, of an orange *20-, Per wLoth WC, SW*.
adv with a heavy sound, plump! *la19-20*.
~**er** a flake, thin sheet or layer *19-e20*. [onomat]

sklint *see* SKLENT¹

sklinter &c *vi* splinter, break off in fragments or flakes *19-e20*. [altered f SPLINDER and Eng *splinter*]

sklire *see* SCLY

skloit *see* SKLYTE

sklone *n* a large amount of any soft plastic substance, a pancake-like mass *la19-, Bnf Abd*. [perh altered f SCONE w extended meaning]

skloof, skluif *see* SKLIFF

sklute &c *19-, now Rox*, **skleet** *20-, Cai* [*Cai* sklit, sklet; *Rox* sklɵt; *sklj)ut] *vi* set the feet down clumsily in walking, walk in a flat-footed, shuffling, or splay-footed way. [onomat; see SND]

sklyte &c; **skloit** &c *la19-e20* [sklɔit] *n* **1** a heavy fall; the sound of this, a thud *la19-, NE, nEC*. **2** a soft, wet, half-liquid mass *la19-, NE Ags*. **3** a broken-down object, *esp* a worn-out shoe *19*. **4** a big, clumsy, slovenly person or animal *20-, Abd*.
vi **1** fall with a thud or thump; slip, slither, go with a clatter *20-, NE Ags Per*. **2** pour or throw liquid in a careless noisy way, slop, splash *la19-, NE Ags*. **3** work messily or clumsily *20, EC*.
adv with a thud or plump, *esp* into something soft or wet *la19-, NE Ags Per*.
sklyter &c = *n, v, adv, la19-, chf NE*. [only Sc; onomat; see SND]

skoal *see* SKOLE

skoil *see* SQUEAL

skolder *see* SCOWDER

skole &c *17-e18*, **skoal &c** *e17*; **scoll &c** *la16*
vi drink toasts; drink out *la16-e18, only Sc.*
n a toast, a health in drinking *17*. [Norw, Dan
skaal, ON *skál* a bowl; *cf* Norw, Dan *skaal!* your
health!, now adopted in Eng as *skol*]

skoof *see* SCUFF[1]

skoosh &c *vti* (cause to) gush in spurts or
splashes, squirt; *of solid objects* dart, glide, or
move rapidly with a swishing sound *la19-*.
n **1** a splash, spurt, jet (of liquid) *la20-, N, C.*
2 lemonade or other aerated water *la20-, C.*
adv with a splash or swish *la20-, NE, C.*
~**er** a device for sprinkling or spraying, a sprinkler *la20-, local Inv-C.*
~ **car** a tramcar *la20, WC.* [only Sc;
onomat]

skoot *vi* look about one attentively or cautiously
20-, now Inv Bnf. [perh altered f SCOUK w infl f
Eng *scout*]

skourick &c [*'skurək, *'skʌrək] *n* a minute
amount; *chf in negative* not a scrap, not a bit
19-e20. [obscure]

skraich &c *18-*; **skraik &c** *19-20* [skrex;
skrek] *vi, of birds* screech, utter a high-pitched
cry; *of persons* shriek, scream *17-, Gen except Sh
Ork.*
n **1** a shriek, screech, shrill strident sound *la18-.*
2 a puny, shrill-voiced person *la19-, now Abd.*
[onomat; *cf* SKREICH]

skrank &c *adj* thin, slender, skinny *19-e20.*
[appar back-formation f next]

skrankie *adj, lit and fig* thin, scraggy, meagre,
shrivelled *18-, now local Sh-Lnk.* [Scand]

skrauch [skrɑx] *vi* utter a shrill cry, scream,
shriek, shout *19-, now N, S.*
n a shriek, screech, a shrill or harsh discordant
sound *19-, local.* [onomat; *cf* SKREICH]

skreek &c *19-*; **skreich &c** *la18-, scraich*
&c *la19-e20* [skrik, skrix, skrex] *n* ~ **o day**
first light, the crack of dawn *la18-, local Ork-S.*
[only Sc; var of CREEK[2], w infl f forms of
SKREICH and SKRAICH]

skreich &c, **skreigh &c** *17-*; **skreek &c**
18-e20 [skrix, skrik] *v* **1** *vi* shriek, screech, utter
a high shrill cry *16-.* **2** *vt* shriek out, utter in a
shrill tone *la18-, now Sh N Per.*
n a scream, screech, shriek; a shrill cry or call
16-. [onomat; altered f Eng *screak; cf* SKRAICH
and SKRAUCH]

skreich *see* SKREEK

skreigh *see* SKREICH

skrim *see* SCRIM[1]

skrink &c *vi* shrink, shrivel up *19-, now Loth
Rox.*
n a shrivelled, unpleasant, or contemptible person, *esp* a woman *19-, now Rox.*
~**ie** thin, wrinkled, shrivelled *19-, now Rox.*
~**ie-faced** with a wrinkled face (and an
unpleasant manner) *19-e20.* [Scand, corresponding to Eng *shrink*]

skroug *see* SCROG

skrunk &c *vti, chf* ~**it** shrunk, shrivelled
la19-e20.
~**le** = *v, la16-e20.* [see SND]

skule &c [*Sh Ork* skøl; *N* skil; *NE* skwil; *Sh* also
*skjøl] *n, freq in pl* an inflammatory disease of
the gums and palate of a horse *la17-, now N.*
[only Sc; Norw dial *skjo, skjøl*, Icel *skjal*]

skulk *v* **1** *vi* = skulk. **2** *vt* shun, avoid; *now
specif* play truant from (school) *17-, now Ork NE
Ags.*

skulk *see* SCOUK

skull &c *n* = skull *17-.*
~**-cap** *or* -**hat** a tight-fitting cap, *specif* one
worn out of doors or by children (*cf* Eng)
la18-19.

skull *see* SCULL[1]

skunk &c *n* the sole or messenger rope of a herring drift net *la18-e20, WC.* [obscure]

skurel &c *n* = squirrel *15.* [OED *squirrel*]

skurken *see* SCROCKEN

sky &c *n* **1** = sky *la15-.* **2** daylight, the light of
the sun, *esp* at dawn or sunset *17-e20.* **3** the
outline of a hill as seen against the sky, the skyline *la18-19, Abd.*
v **1** (1) *vi* look towards the horizon, shading
one's eyes with one's hand *la19-, NE.* (2) *vti*
shade (a patch of water) so as to see the bottom
la19-, now NE Ags. **2** *vi* look about one *la20-,
NE Ags.*
~ **break(ing) &c** daybreak *17-19.* ~
set(ting) nightfall *la17-e20.*

skybald &c; skybal &c ['skaɪbəl(d), -bəlt;
'skɪbəl(t), &c] *n* **1** a rascal, rogue, worthless
person; a poor wretch *la16-20.* **2** a ragged,
unkempt person, ragamuffin *18-e20.*
adj **1** rascally, disreputable, worthless; tattered,
ragged *la16-e20.* **2** not having enough, needy;
not providing enough, scrimp *la19-20, Bnf Abd.*
[also northern ModEng dial; obscure]

skybe &c; skipe &c *n* a mean rogue, a
bad-mannered or worthless person *18-, now
Rox.* [only Sc; reduced f SKYBALD]

skyle *see* SKAIL[1]

skylie *see* SCAILIE

skyow *see* SKEW[2]

skyowl *see* SKEWL

skyre *see* SKEER

skyre, skyrie, skyrin *see* SKIRE

skytch *see* SKETCH[1]

sla *see* SLAY

slab[1] *n* **1** = slab. **2** the first slice cut off a loaf,
with one side crusty *la20-, local EC Lnk.* **3** a
thin person with a broad frame *la19-, NE Ags.*

slab[2] *v* **1** *vi* slaver, *esp* while eating, eat or drink
noisily, slobber *la17-e19.* **2** *vt* eat **up** noisily,
eat **up** greedily *la18-, now Kcdn Ags.*
~**ber &c** *v* **1** *vt* wet with saliva, beslobber; stain
(one's clothes etc) with saliva or with food
when eating *18-, now Cai C, SW.* **2** wet with a
messy semi-liquid substance *19-, now C, S.* **3** *vi*
slaver, dribble; eat or drink noisily, sloppily
la18-, now local N-Dmf. **4** make a snorting,

bubbling sound as in weeping or sleeping *19-*, *now Dnbt SW.* **5** work carelessly, messily or with something wet or messy *19-*, *now Kcb.* **6** talk drivel, babble *la20-*, *Fif WC.* *n* **1** a greedy or noisy mouthful, a slobber *la19-*, *now Ags.* **2** *freq in pl* senseless or foolish talk, idle chatter *la20-*, *Fif WC, SW.* **3** mud; muddy, trampled soil *la19-*, *now Abd Kcdn.* **4** something liquid or messy, *esp* food *la20-*, *Abd Per.* **5** a slovenly slack-lipped person, a slobberer *19-*, *now EC Lnk Gall.* **~bery** *of roads* waterlogged, muddy *la19-*, *WC.* [*cf* obs and dial Eng]

slack¹ &c *adj* **1** = slack *la16-*. **2** *of money* scarce; *of persons* short of money *la18-*, *now local Ags-Lnk.* **3** *of a ewe* past breeding age, about to be sold for meat *la18-e20.* **4** *of a building etc* untenanted, thinly occupied, not busy *e19.*
n a slackening, loosening *la19-*.
vti **1** = slack *la16-*. **2** *vi* slacken off, become less tense or active, grow flaccid *la18-*, *local Sh-Kcb.*

slack² &c *n* **1** *freq in place-names* a hollow, *esp* between hills, a saddle in a hill-ridge, a pass *la14-*, *now local.* **2** a pit, hole *e15*, *only Sc.* **3** a low-lying, boggy depression in the ground *19-*, *S.* [ON *slakki* = *n* 1, with some of the place-names perh f Gael *sloc(hd)* (*cf* SLOCK²)]

slacky *n* a kind of sling or catapult *la17-e19.* [obscure]

slad *see* SLIDE

slade *see* SLED, SLIDE

slae¹ *n, freq attrib* = sloe *la16-*, *Gen except Sh Ork.*

slae² &c *n* the slow- or blindworm *19-*, *Arg Gall Rox.* [*cf* nEng dial *slea-worm*; ME *slaworme*, OE *slawyrm*, later > *slow-worm* by association w *slow*]

slae *see* SLAY

slag¹ &c [slag, slɑg] *n* a large blob of something wet, soft, or messy *la18-*, *now Ags.*
vti mess about with food, gobble up in large spoonfuls *e19.*
slaiger &c, **~ger &c** ['slegər; *also* 'slagər] *v* **1** *vt* (1) besmear with something soft and wet, bedaub with mud etc *la19-*, *local Cai-S.* (2) smear or daub (a soft wet substance) (**on**) *20-*, *now Cai.* **2** *vi* (1) eat or drink messily *19-*, *local NE-S.* (2) walk messily in mud etc, plod wearily or carelessly *19-*, *now Pbls WC.* *n* **1** a wet, soggy, or slimy mess, a daub, smear of sloppy food etc *19-*, *EC, WC, S.* **2** the act of bedaubing; slovenly work *la19-*, *now local Stlg-S.* **slaigerin** dirty, slovenly, slatternly *la19-*, *local.* [perh onomat, w infl f SLAG², SLOCK¹]

slag² &c [slag] *n* a marshy place, morass *19-*, *now Rox.* [ME = wet, muddy, ON = dampness]

slaich *see* SLAIK

slaiger *see* SLAG¹

slaik, slake &c *18-*; **slaich &c** *la19-*, **sklaik &c** *20*, *NE* [slek; *NE also* sklek, s(k)lex, sklɑk, sl(j)ɑx, sklax] *vti* **1** (1) lick, smear with the tongue, beslobber *16-*, *now local Ags-Wgt.* (2) *esp of a pet animal* lick (dishes) or

consume (food) on the sly *19-e20.* (3) kiss, caress, fondle over-sloppily *19-*, *now Ags.* **2** besmear, bedaub, streak *la18-*, *now local.*
n **1** a lick with the tongue, a slobbering lick or kiss *18-*, *now local EC-S.* **2** the act of daubing or smearing; something soft, wet, or messy which has been smeared on *19-*, *now Ags Per WC.* **3** a careless or slatternly wash, a hasty clean or wipe; a dirty, messy way of working *la19-*, *local Ags-SW.* **4** a person who eats or drinks excessively *20-*, *local Per-Rox.* [ON *sleikja* lick]

slaip &c *adj* slippery, smooth, sleek *19-*, *now Rox.* [nEng dial, ME *slape*; ON *sleipr* slippery]

slair &c; sclair- &c *20* *vt* smear, cover (with something soft, wet, messy) *19-*, *now local Ags-Dmf.*
slairie &c *vt* = *v*, *la18-20.* *n* a smear, daub, a lick of paint *la19-*, *local Kcdn-Dmf.* *adj* slovenly in one's eating habits *la20-*, *Clcm Renfr Lnk.* [only Sc; see SND]

slairg &c; slairk &c *v* **1** *vt* (1) smear, bespatter (with something wet and dirty) *19-*, *now SW Rox.* (2) smear **on** *or* **in** *18-e20.* **2** *vi* sup liquid noisily, slobber at one's food *19-*, *now Rox.*
n a quantity of something messy or semi-liquid, a dollop, smear *19-*, *now Fif Rox.* [see SND]

slaister; slester *la18-20*, **slyster &c** *19-e20*, **sclyster &c** *la19-*, *nEC* ['slestər; *Cai* 'sləi-; *nEC also* 'skləi-] *v* **1** *vi* (1) work messily or splash the hands about in a liquid; work awkwardly, clumsily, or ineffectively *18-*, *Gen except NE.* (2) wade in mud or water *19-*, *now Sh Cai.* (3) eat or drink messily or greedily *19-e20.* **2** *vt* (1) make messy, smear *la18-*, *now local.* (2) smear (a substance) on a surface, spread or scatter messily *20-*, *C, S.*
n **1** a state of wetness and dirt, a splashy mess, dirty water, slops *19-*, *Gen except NE.* **2** an unpalatable or nauseating mixture of foods etc *la18-*, *EC, WC, S.* **3** a state of confusion *la19-*, *local.* **4** a slovenly, dirty worker, a slut; a messy person, *esp* a messy eater *19-*, *C, S.*
~in untidy, slovenly *la19-e20.* **~y** wet and dirty, muddy, slimy *19-e20.*
~ kyte a messy eater, glutton *la18-e20.* [perh Scand, w infl f PLAISTER; *cf* Dan *sleske*, Dan dial *sleste* cajole, fawn, *slesk* unctuous]

slait &c *n* a dirty, slovenly or nasty person *18-e19.* [only Sc; obscure]

slake¹ &c *la16-*, **slawk &c** *18-*, *now Ork*; **slak &c** *la15-e20*, **sloke &c** *la18-e20* [slek, slɑk; *Abd also* sljɑx] *n* one of various species of edible fresh- and salt-water algae *la15-*, *now Sh Ork Cai.*
slawkie &c covered with such weed, slimy; smooth, soft and flabby *19.* [chf Sc; IrGael *sleabhac, slabhac,* ScGael *slòcan, slabhagan; cf* Icel, Faeroese *slavak,* of the same Celtic origin]

slake² &c; sclaik *v* **1** *vt* = slake, diminish,

decrease *la15-*. **2** *vi* (1) weaken or decrease one's efforts *la16*. (2) ∼ **of** weaken in *la15-e17*. **3** *vt* relieve **of** (sorrow etc) *la14-16*.

slaken *vt* assuage, mitigate *e17, only Sc.*

slake *see* SLAIK

slam &c *n* slime, something slimy or oozy *20, Abd.*

slammach *chf in pl* gossamer, spiders' webs *19-, Bnf Abd.* [only Sc; MLowGer *slam(m)* mud; *cf* LowGer *schlammatje*]

slammach *see* SLAM

slamp *adj* slim, lithe, supple *19-, local Ross-Per.* [see SND]

slan *see* SLAY

slander *see* SCLANDER

slane *see* SLAY

slap¹, slop *la19-, N n* **1** = slap, a smack. **2** a large quantity, a dollop *la19-, now Sh Ags.* *vt* **1** = slap, smack. **2** exceed, beat, go beyond *la19-, now local Fif-Kcb.*

full ∼ at full speed *20-, local Sh-Ayr.*

slap² &c *la16-*; **slop &c** *la14-e20 n* **1** a gap or opening in a wall, hedge etc *la14-*. **2** a gash or wound *la14*. **3** ? a break in the clouds *e16*. **4** a gap to let water into or out of a dam, drain, ditch etc *18-e19*. **5** an opening left temporarily in a salmon weir to allow the fish to swim up-river to spawn *15-e20*. **6** a narrow passage or lane between houses *la19-, Mry Bnf.* **7** a pass or shallow valley between hills *18-, now EC, WC, freq in place-names.* **8** a gap or breach in the ranks (of an army etc) *la15-19*. **9** *in gen* a hole, missing part, break in continuity; a lack, want *19-, now Sh Ags Kcb.*

vt **1** *building* make a gap or break in (a wall etc) or for (a door, window etc) *16-*. **2** make breaks or breaches in (a body of troops) *e16*. **3** thin out (seedlings etc) *la20-, NE.*

slapped &c notched, roughened at the edge *18-, now Sh.*

∼ **riddle** a wide-meshed riddle for separating grain from broken straw *18-e19*.

Saturday('s) ∼ the period from Saturday night till Monday morning, fixed by law for the free passage of fish up-river *15-e20*. [only Sc; MDu, MLowGer *slop* a gap, narrow entrance, Flem *slop* an opening in a dam]

slap³ &c, slop *n* **1** *chf in pl* = slops, sloppy food etc. **2** a careless or dirty person *la19-, WC Gall.*

∼ **bowl** a slop basin *la18-*.

slash &c *n* a violent dash or clash, *esp* of something wet, a splash *19-, now Sh Bnf Ags.*

v **1** *vt* throw (liquid) with a splash; strike with something wet *la19-, now Sh Ork Ags SW.* **2** *vi* rush with violence, dash forward *19-, now Sh Ags.*

adv with a clash or splash, with violence *20-, now Sh Ags.* [obscure, w some infl f Eng]

slasy *adj* ludicrous term of endearment *e16*. [unknown. OED *slawsy*]

slatch &c *vi* **1** work in something messy, potter

or dabble in mud etc *19-, now Rox.* **2** walk or splash through mud, wade about messily *19-, now Rox.*

n **1** a messy dirty worker; a dirty coarse woman *19-, now Rox.* **2** a wet and muddy place *20-, S.* **3** a resounding blow, a heavy thud *la19-, now Sh Slk.* [onomat; *cf* CLATCH¹ and SLASH]

slate¹ &c *18-*, **sclate; skleat &c** *17-18* [s(k)let] *n* (*la15-*), *v* (*17-*) = slate.

slater &c 1 = slater *la14-*. **2** the woodlouse *la17-*.

∼ **band** a kind of schist *19-, now Fif Lnk.* ∼ **diamond** popular name for iron-pyrite crystals *19-, now Bwk WC.* ∼ **house** a house with a slate roof *la16-, now Sh Ags, only Sc.* **sclate stane** *freq in proverbs and similes concerning money* a piece of slate or slate-like stone *18-*.

want a ∼ be feeble-minded, 'have a slate loose' *20-*.

slate² &c *vt* incite or set (a dog) on *la14-16*. [ON **sleita*, corresponding to OE *slǣtan*]

slate *see* SLITE

slather &c ['slaðər, 'sleðər] *n* a smear, slobber, a quantity of any messy substance *20-, now Bute Rox.* [*cf* Eng dial *v* = slobber]

slattyvarrie &c *n* the edible seaweed *Laminaria digitata*, *la19-e20, chf Arg.* [Gael *slatmhara*, pl *slatanmara*]

slauch *see* SLOCH²

slauchter &c, slaughter &c ['slɑxtər] *vt, n* = slaughter *la14-*.

slaurie &c *vt* daub or splash with mud etc; dirty (one's clothes) *19-, now Stlg WC Kcb.*

n a smear, smudge, daub of something soft and sticky *la19-, now Stlg SW.* [ME *slory*; *cf* ModEng dial *slurry*]

slave *see* SCLAVE¹

slaver &c; slever *la19-*, **sliver &c** *19-, NE* ['slevər; *NE* 'slɪvər] *vi* **1** = slaver *la15-*. **2** talk nonsense, chatter in a silly way, BLETHER¹ *la19-, local Cai-S.* **3** *vi* canoodle *20-, local Stlg-Dmf.*

n **1** = slaver, saliva *18-*. **2** *in pl* = prec *la18-, only Sc.*

slaw &c *adj* = slow *16-*.

adv, verse slowly, in a leisurely way *16-e20*. [OED *slow*]

slaw *see* SLAY

slawk *see* SLAKE¹

slay; sla *la14-e17*, **slae &c** *16-e17*, **sley &c** *16-e17* [sle] *vti, pt also* **slaw &c** *la14-16*, **sleuch** *la14*, **sclew** *la14-15* [*sla, *sl(j)ux, *s(k)l(j)u]; *ptp also* **slane** *la14-16* [slen] **1** = slay *la14-*. **2** *vt* strike (fire from flint) *la14-e16*. **3** destroy (vegetation) *16-e19*.

∼ **doune** kill completely *la14-16*.

sle, slea *see* SLEE

sled, slade &c *la15-e19 n* **1** a sledge *la14-*. **2** a child's cart, *usu* made of short planks on the chassis of a disused pram *la20-, Ags Edb Ayr.*

sledder &c a man who drives or uses a SLED *16-18*. [ME; MDu, MLowGer *sledde*]

sled *see* SLIDE

slee *16-, now chf verse except S,* **sly** *la18-;* **sle**
la14-16, **slie &c** *16-18,* **slea** *la14-16* [sli] *adj* **1**
= sly *la14-.* **2** *of persons* (1) skilled, clever,
expert; wise *la14-e20.* (2) ~ **in** *or* **of** skilled at
la14-e16. **3** *of things* well-made; showing the
skill of their creator or user *la15-e20.*
adv slyly, cunningly, stealthily *19-e20.*
vi go or come silently or slyly *la18-19.*

slee *see* SLEIVE

slee-band *n* an iron ring round the beam of an
old plough to strengthen it where the coulter
was attached *16-e19.* [only Sc; the first element is perh reduced f Eng *sleeve* a metal ring]

sleech *see* SLEEK²

sleek¹ &c [slik; *NE also* slɪk] *adj* **1** = sleek. **2**
smooth, oily, fawning and deceitful; cunning,
self-seeking, sly *la18-.* *now local Abd-S.*
v **1** *vt* = smooth. **2** *specif in measuring* level off
(*esp* grain or fruit) at the top of the container;
of the commodity fill (its container) *19-, now local
Abd-S, only Sc.* **3** *vi* walk or move smoothly or
furtively, slink, sneak *19-, local Sh-Dmf.* **4** *vt*
flatter, wheedle, ingratiate oneself with *la18-,
local EC-S.*
n a measure of capacity, *esp* of grain or fruit
la17-, now Lnk, only Sc.
~**ie** **1** sleek, smooth, slippery *16-20.* **2** = *adj*
2, *la18-, now local Abd-S.* ~**it &c 1** smooth,
having an even surface or glossy skin *16-, now
local Cai-SW.* **2** smooth in manner, plausible;
sly, cunning, not to be trusted *15-, only Sc.*

sleek² &c *18-e19;* **slike &c** *now Fif,* **sleech**
&c *la18-* [slik; slitʃ; *Fif* sləik] *n* an alluvial
deposit of mud or sludge left behind by the sea
or a river, silt *la14-, now Ags Fif Kcb.* [only Sc;
see SND]

sleep &c; **slep** *la14-16* [slip] *vti, pt also* ~**it,**
slept *18-19* **1** = sleep *la14-.* **2** *vi, of a top*
spin so fast and so smoothly as to appear
motionless *la19-, now Inv Bnf C; cf* DOZE. **3** *law,
of an action* lapse through passage of time and
failure of prosecution *18-; cf* ASLEEP, WAUKEN *v*
4.
n = sleep *la14-.*
~**ery &c 1** sleep-inducing *e16.* **2** sleepy, som-
nolent *la16-, now Rox.* ~**ie men, things** *etc*
the little specks of matter which form in the
eyes during sleep *20-, local.* ~**ies** the smooth
rye brome-grass *e19.* ~**ryfe** bringing sleep *e16,
only Sc.*
be ~**it oot** have slept one's fill *20-.* ~ **in**
oversleep *19-.*

sleesh &c [sliʃ; *NE also* sklɪʃ, sкləiʃ] *n* **1** a slice
la19-, now Abd. **2** a swipe, cutting stroke; a
lash, as with a whip *20, Ork Bwk Rox.*
~**ack &c** ['sliʃək, -əx] *freq in pl* a dish of potatoes fried in slices *la20-, Ross Inv.* ~**er** something outstanding of its kind *20-, Bwk Rox.*

sleeth &c [sliθ] *n* a slow, lazy person; a worthless person *18-e19, NE.* [var of SLOUTH]

sleive &c *16-19;* **slee** *19* [sliv, sli] *v* **1** *vt* slip

(something) **out of, over** *etc* (something)
la15-19. **2** *vi* ~ **ower** slip past *e16.* [ME
slefe, OE *slēfan.* OED *sleve*]

slemmer *see* SLIM
slent *see* SKLENT¹
slep *see* SLEEP

slerp &c *v* **1** *vi* salivate or slobber, splutter messily, spit *20-, Ork Fif Rox.* **2** *vt* smear or *slabber*
(SLAB²) with something wet or messy *e20, Ork
Rox.* **3** consume noisily or messily *20-, now Edb
Kcb Dmf.*
n **1** a spoonful of liquid taken with a slobbering
sound *20-, now Wgt Rox.* **2** a slovenly woman,
slut *19-, Per Fif.* [onomat var of SLORP]

slester *see* SLAISTER
sleuch *see* SLAY

sleug &c [*sljug] *n* an ugly or ungainly person;
an unpleasant person *19-e20.* [only Sc;
obscure]

sleugh [*sljux] *n* = slough, a marsh, quagmire
la18-e19, SW.

sleugh-hound *see* SLEUTH
sleum *see* SLOOM²

sleuth &c; **sloth &c** *la15,* **slow &c** *18-19*
[sljuθ; *sløθ, *sløx, *sl(j)ux] *n* **1** a track or trail
(of a person or animal) *la14-15.* **2** = sleuth.
~**hound &c** *la14-,* **sleugh-** &c *la18-19,*
slughan &c *18-,* **slow-hound** *18-19,* **slowan**
&c *19-e20* ['sluan; *Rox* 'slʌuxən; *'sljuθ'hund,
*'sl(j)ux'hund, *'slu'hund, *'sljuθən,
*'sl(j)uxən, *slun] **1** a breed of bloodhound formerly used, *esp* in the BORDERS, for hunting or
tracking game or fugitives *la14-e20.* **2** *esp*
slughan, slowan &c (1) a slow-moving, lazy,
soft person *18-, now Ork Cai Rox.* (2) a covetous or greedy person *19-, now Rox.* [ME *sloth,*
ON *slóð* a path, trail]

sleuth *see* SLOUTH
slever *see* SLAVER

slewie [*'slur] *vi* walk with a heavy swinging or
swaying gait *la14-e20, NE.* [only Sc; deriv of
Eng *slew* swing round]

sley *see* SLAY
slib *adj* slippery *e19.*
slibb(er)ie = *adj,* *19-, now Ags.* [perh
back-formation, w infl f SLID, f eModEng, ME
slibberie, MDu *slibber* slime, MLowGer *slib-
ber(ig)* slippery]

slicht¹ &c [slɪxt; *Ork* sləixt] *n* **1** = sleight, craft,
cunning, skill *la14-.* **2** the trick, method, or
knack (of doing something) *la19-, now Stlg.*
~**fully** cunningly *la14, only Sc.* [OED *sleight*]

slicht², slight &c [slɪxt; *Ork* sləit] *adj* **1** =
slight *la14-.* **2** of loose moral character
la17-18.
vt raze to the ground, demolish *17-19.*

slid; slide &c *e16 adj* **1** *of surfaces* slippery,
smooth *16-, now Lnk Kcb S.* **2** changeable,
uncertain *e16.* **3** *of persons or their actions*
smooth, cunning; oily, cajoling *18-, now Lnk Slk.*
[only Sc; perh back-formation f SLIDDER]

slidden *see* SLIDE

slidder &c *la15-*; **sclidder &c** *19-*, **sclither &c** *19-e20 v* **1** *vi* slip, slide, slither *19-*, now *NE-S.* **2** walk or move in a casual or lazy way *la19-*, now *Ags WC.* **3** *vt* cause to slip or slide *19-*, now *Sh Ags.*

adj, also fig slippery *la15-17.*

n **1** a sliding, slithering movement, a slip, skid *19-*, *local Per-Kcb.* **2** ice, an icy surface *20-*, *NE Ags.* **3** a narrow steep hollow or track down a hillside, *esp* when stony, a scree¹ *19-*, now *S.* **4** a slow-moving or dilatory person, a sluggard *la19-*, now *WC.*

~ie 1 slippery: (1) causing slipping or sliding *16-*, now *local*; (2) having a slippery surface, not easy to hold on to *la16*, *la19-*, now *NE Ags.* **2** *of food* soft, sloppy *19-*, now *Sh Ags.* **3** insecure, unstable to stand on etc, shaky; changeable, uncertain *la16-*, now *local.* **4** *of persons or actions* sly, deceitful, unreliable, untrustworthy *la18-*, now *local.* [see SND]

slide &c *v*, *pt also* **slade &c** now *local Sh-WC*, **slad** *la14-15*, **sled** *la18-20.* *ptp also* **slidden &c** now *local*, **sclyddyn** *la14* **1** *vti* = slide *la14-.* **2** deviate from the strict truth, tell a mild lie, exaggerate *19-*, now *Bnf Abd.*

n = slide *la16-.*

slider 1 the movable metal loop sliding on a rod on a cart-shaft, to which the back-chain is hooked *20-*, *Ork-EC.* **2** an ice-cream wafer or sandwich *20-.* **slid(e)y** *of surfaces* slippery, very smooth *17-*, now *local NE-Dmf.*

~ on slummir *or* **upon a sleip** fall asleep *la15-e16.*

slide *see* SLID

slidy *see* SLIDE

slie *see* SLEE

slig; skleg *vi* lie, practise deceit *19*, *SW, S.* [obscure]

slight *see* SLICHT²

slike *see* SLEEK²

slim &c *adj* **1** = slim. **2** *of clothes, shoes etc* flimsy, thin *19-*, now *Sh Bnf Ags.* **3** wily, sly, crafty *la18-*, now *Abd Kcb.*

vt, freq **~ ower** treat (work) with insufficient care, scamp (a job) *19-*, *local Cai-Rox.*

slemmer &c a person who scamps his work; a lazy, idle person *la19-*, now *Ags.*

~ jim a kind of sweet consisting of long strips of coconut or liquorice *la19-*, *WC.*

sling *v* **1** *vt* = sling *la16-.* **2** *vi* walk with a long vigorous stride, swing along *19-*, now *Rox.*

n **1** the swivels, hooks and chains of the draught-harness of a cart *la19-*, now *local Abd-Wgt.* **2** a swinging vigorous gait, a long striding step *19-*, now *Rox.*

~er 1 *usu in pl* sausages *la20-*, *Inv-WC.* **2** a dish consisting of bread sops boiled in milk *la20-*, *Bnf Abd.* [*n* 1 and ~er may have different origins]

sling *see* SLUNG¹

slinger &c *vi* swing, sway, roll, reel *la18-*, now *Sh.* [Du *slingeren*]

slink *v*, *pt also* **slunkit &c** *18-* **1** *vi* = slink. **2** *vti* cheat, deceive, act dishonestly *19.*

n **1** a smooth crafty person; a low despicable character *19-*, now *C Rox.* **2** an aborted, premature, or newly-born unfed calf or other animal *18-*, now *C.* **3** an emaciated or spent fish, *esp* a cod or salmon, a KELT¹ *19-*, now *Ayr.* *adj* thin, scraggy, lank *19-e20.*

slunken &c *adj* lank- or emaciated-looking, sunken *19-*, *Sh Lnk Dmf Rox.*

slip¹ &c *vti* **1** = slip, slide etc *16-.* **2** *vt* allow (a chance etc) to slip, fail or omit (to do something) *la16-*, now *Ork Per.* **3** *in passive, of a cow* have the pelvic ligaments relaxed before calving *20-*, *local Bnf-SW.*

n **1** = slip, sliding; error etc. **2** a metal ring attaching the swingle-trees of a plough to the trace-chains from the harness *19-*, now *Cai.* **3** a device for drawing ships out of the water for repair *19.* **4** a loose (protective) garment for slipping over one's clothes, a pinafore *19-.* **5** an abortion, miscarriage *20-*, *local Cai-Dnbt.*

~per *adj* slippery, smooth *la16-18.* *n* a slippery state or condition; that which causes slipperiness, ice etc *la19-*, now *Bnf Abd.* **~py** slippery *la18-.*

~ body an under-bodice, camisole *la19-20.* **~ bolt** a door- or sash-bolt made to slip into a cylindrical socket, a barrel-bolt *la20-.* **~ raip** a straw binding for a sheaf which, because of a defective knot, slips open *la20-*, *NE Per Lnk.* **~shod 1** = slipshod *la17-.* **2** wearing shoes but no stockings *19-*, *local nEC-S.* **3** having one's shoelaces hanging loose *20-*, *WC-S.*

~ away die quietly *la18-.* **~-by** a carelessly-performed task, shoddy work *la19-*, *local Sh-WC.* **~-ma-labor &c** ['~ma'labər] a lazy untrustworthy person *20-*, now *Sh.* **~ the timmers** die *20-*, *Bnf Abd.*

slip² &c *n* **1** = slip, a plant etc. **2** a measure of yarn, *usu* in the form of a two-pound hank, consisting of 12 CUTs¹ *la16-*, now *Rox.*

slipe¹ &c *18-*; **slyp &c** *la15-e19* [sləip] *n* **1** (1) a wooden wheelless platform for moving heavy loads, a kind of sledge *la15-*, now *C, S.* (2) *mining* a curved wooden box on iron runners for taking coal away from the cutting-face *19.* **2** a rail or wooden runner by which barrels etc are unloaded from a lorry *la20-*, *WC Rox.*

vt transport by means of a drag or sledge, haul (a load) on a SLIPE *18-*, now *midLoth Dmf Uls.* [LowGer *slipe* a sledge, MDu *slijp* a kind of drag or harrow]

slipe² *vi* move in a slanting direction, fall (**over**) sideways *la18-e20.* [*cf* MLowGer *slipen* slip, slide]

slit *n* **1** = slit. **2** *specif* name for a kind of sheep-mark consisting of a cut in the ear *la18-*, now *Kcb.*

slite *vt*, *pt* **slate &c.** *ptp* **slitten 1** slit, rip up, split *e16*, *19-*, now *local C, S.* **2** make sharp, whet *la18-e19.*

slitter; sluiter &c ['slɪtər; *Bwk S* 'sløtər] *v* **1** *vi* work or walk messily in water etc, splash about untidily; eat or drink messily *la19-, now C.* **2** *vt* besmear with something wet or messy, make messy or stained *la19-, now C Rox.*
n **1** (messy) semi-liquid matter, an unpalatable mixture of food; a state of untidiness or dirt *20-, now C.* **2** a slovenly, untidy, or messy person *20-, C, S.*
~**y &c** wet and messy, sloppy *19-, C, S.* [var of SLUTTER]

slive *vt* slice off, separate by slicing *19-, now Rox.*
n a thin slice, a sliver *20-, S.* [OE *-slīfan* cleave, slice]

sliver *see* SLAVER

sloam *see* SLOOM[1]

sloan *n* a sharp retort, a snub, reproof *19-e20, Rox.* [obscure]

sloch[1] *18-*, **slough** *la17-*; **slowch &c** *16-e18*, **sluch &c** *la16-e20* [slox, slʌx; *NE also* sljʌx] *n* **1** = slough, an outer skin *16-.* **2** a skin or membrane enclosing the body or some part of it *la16, 20-, now Ork.* **3** a suit (of clothes) *la16, e19.* **4** the outer skin or husk of certain fruits or vegetables *la17-, now local Cai-Ayr.* **5** the pelt or coat (taken skin and wool together) from a dead sheep *18-, Per Arg SW.* **6** a lumpish or soft person *19.*
vti **1** = slough. **2** remove the wool from a dead sheep by skinning rather than clipping or shearing *19-, SW.*

sloch[2]; **slauch &c** [slox, slɑx] *vt* swallow (food or drink) in a noisy slobbering way *19-, local Inv-WC.*
n a noisy intake of food or drink; a hearty drink, a good swig *la19-, now Per.*
~**y** slimy, dirty and disgusting *la19-, now Ags Per Kcb.* [only Sc; see SND]

sloch *see* SLOCK[2]
slochen *see* SLOCKEN

slock[1] **&c; sloke &c** *e16, la19-e20* [slok; *NE also* sljok] *v* **1** *vt* (1) quench (thirst etc), *freq* ~ **one's drouth** *etc, la18-.* (2) appease the thirst of (a person, animal); appease the wishes or desires of *16-.* **2** slake (lime) *la17-.* **3** moisten, soak, drench *la19-, Bnf Abd Ags.* **4** extinguish, quench (a fire etc) *la14-, now Sh Ork Cai Wgt.* **5** suppress, bring to an end *la15.* **6** *vi*, *of fire* go out *la15, la19-, now Sh Ork Cai.*
n a draught of liquid, a drink *19-, now local Sh-Ayr.*
~**in** *n* enough (drink) to slake one's thirst, a drink *19-, Sh Ork NE.* ~**it** drunk *20-, Ork Abd.* [chf Sc; see SND]

slock[2]; **sloch** [slok, slox] *n* **1** *also* **slug** *la18-e20, Abd-Ags* [slʌg] a hollow between hills, a pass *19-, now Cai Inv Mry, freq in place-names.* **2** a creek or gully in the sea, a long deep inlet between rocks, often revealed at low tide *19-, Abd-Ags Gall.*
the S~ nickname for the village of Portessie,

which is built on a SLOCK *n* 2, Sloch Hythe *la19-, Bnf.* **the Slug (Road)** the road through the pass between Banchory and Stonehaven *19-, Kcdn.* [chf Sc; Gael *sloc(hd)* a hollow, dell, pool]

slocken &c; slochen &c *la19-e20, EC* ['slokən; *EC also* *'sloxən] *v* **1** *vt* quench, extinguish (fire, flame) *la14-, now Cai Wgt Rox.* **2** (1) quench (thirst), satisfy (the desire to drink) *la16-.* (2) quench the thirst of (a person or animal) *18-.* (3) inaugurate or celebrate with a drink *19-e20.* (4) sate, satisfy (desire) *16.* **3** abate, subdue, do away with, suppress *16-19.* **4** (1) moisten, drench, soak *18-, now Per.* (2) slake (lime) *la19-, now N, C.* (3) make a paste of (meal) *19-, now local.* **5** *vi*, *of fire* go out, be extinguished *e16.* **6** *of thirst* become slaked; have one's thirst slaked *19-e20.*
~**er** a thirst-quencher, a drink *19-, NE-S.* [nME *slokken* extinguish (a fire), ON *slokna* (of a fire) go out]

slogan &c *la16-*; **slog(h)orn &c** *16-e18*, **slug(h)orn &c** *la16-e19* *n* **1** a war- or rally-ing-cry, *usu* the name of a CLAN chief or CLAN rendezvous, used by *Highlanders* (HIELAND) and *Borderers* (BORDER), *orig* as a signal to arms or as a password *16-.* **2** a catchword or motto adopted by a person or group of persons and used to distinguish them from others *18-.* [Gael *sluaghghairm* the cry of an army; into StEng via Scott]

slogg *n* a marsh, bog *19-, now Rox.* [perh var of SLAG[2] w infl f SLOCK[2]]

slogger *n* a slovenly, dirty, or untidy person *19-, local Pbls-Rox.*
~**in** slovenly in appearance, dirtily or untidily dressed *19-, local Pbls-Rox.* [uncertain]

sloghorn *see* SLOGAN

slogie-riddle *n* a wide-meshed riddle for sepa-rating vegetables *19-e20, S.* [only Sc; unknown]

slogorn *see* SLOGAN

sloit &c *19*; **slowt &c** *20-, Fif* [sloit; *Fif* slʌut] *vi* walk in a slow, slouching way, stroll idly or carelessly about *20-, now Fif.*
n a lazy, slovenly person *19.*
~**er** = *v, la19-20.* [only Sc; see SND]

sloke *see* SLAKE[1], SLOCK[1]

slong *see* SLUNG[1]

slonk *see* SLUNK[1]

slooch &c, slouch [slutʃ] *vti* **1** = slouch *la17-.* **2** *vi* crouch, cower, skulk furtively *18-, now local Sh-C.*
n **1** = slouch. **2** an idle, work-shy person *la19-, now Sh Ags Per.*

sloom[1] **&c; sloam &c** *18-20, chf Gall Uls* [slum; *Gall Uls* slom] *n* a dreamy or sleepy state, a daydream, a light or unsettled sleep *19-, now Kcdn Ags.*
v **1** *vi* sleep lightly or fitfully, doze *la18-19.* **2** *lit and fig* slip along easily and quietly *la19-20.*

3 *vti, chf of plants* (cause to) become soft or flaccid; (cause to) wilt and decay *la18-19*. **4** *of plants* (cause to) grow or sprout unnaturally *la19-20, Uls.*

~**y** *of corn etc* not well filled out, stunted *18-e19*. [see SND]

sloom² &c; sleum [sl(j)um] *n* a rumour, piece of hearsay or gossip *la19-20, Bnf Abd.*

~**in** a secret or stealthy report, a rumour *la19, Bnf Abd.* [only Sc; obscure]

sloosh &c; slus &c [sluʃ] *n* **1** = sluice. **2** a dash of water, a splashing *la19-.*
vti splash with water, throw water about in large splashes, flush *la20-.*

sloosht &c [sluʃt] *n* a disreputable character, a reprobate *20, Abd.* [see SND]

slop *e16, la20-, now NE nEC;* **slope** *la19-20 n* a kind of loose-fitting jacket or tunic, formerly worn by field workers or fishermen. [ME]

slop *see* SLAP¹, SLAP², SLAP³

slope &c *v* **1** *vt* avoid paying, defraud *la19-, now Fif.* **2** *vi* shirk one's work, dodge duty, idle *la20-, NE Lnk Gall.*

sloper a shirker *20-, now Abd Loth.* [appar US Eng = run away, decamp]

slope *see* SLOP

slorach &c; schlorach &c *e20, Abd Kcdn* ['slorəx; *Abd Kcdn* 'sklor-] *vti* **1** eat or drink messily and noisily, slobber, slaver *la19-, local NE-Per.* **2** *vi* clear the throat loudly and inelegantly, breathe or speak through catarrh *la19-, Bnf Abd Per.*
n **1** a noisy gulping down of food *la19-e20, Bnf Kcdn.* **2** a wet, disgusting mess (**of** something) *la19-, now NE.* [only Sc; see SND]

slork &c *vti* **1** make a slobbering noise, *eg* when eating or drinking; suck up (food or drink) noisily *19-, Lnk SW, S.* **2** *vi* reinhale nasal mucus, sniff or snort *20-, Lnk SW.* **3** *of shoes or persons* make a squelching noise in walking *19-, Dmf Rox.*
n a noisy sucking up of food or drink *20-, Lnk SW, S.* [only Sc; orig onomat; *cf* Norw *slurk(e)*, Sw dial *slurk(a)*]

slorp &c *vti* **1** eat or drink noisily and slobberingly *19-, local Kcdn-S.* **2** *vi, of shoes etc* make a wet squelching sound *19-e20, Rox.*
n a noisy mouthful, a slobber, swig *19-, now Loth Kcb Rox.*

~ **an greet** weep noisily and with gulps of indrawn breath, sob convulsively *19-, now Rox.* [MDu *slorpen* sup in long gulps; *cf* SLERP, SLORK and informal Eng *slurp*]

slot¹ &c, slote *16-e19 n* **1** a bar or bolt for a door, window etc *la15-, now local.* **2** (1) a metal rod *la15-e16.* (2) a cross-piece or bar, *esp* in a harrow or cart *la18-, now Cai Kcb.*
vt bolt, lock (a door, window), secure with a bolt or bar *la16-, now local Cai-SW.*
~ **staff** some kind of staff used as a weapon *la16, only Sc.* [ME *slotte*, MDu, MLowGer *slot* a door-bolt]

slot² &c *n* **1** the hollow depression running down the middle of the breast, *freq* ~ **of his** *etc* **breast** *18-e20.* **2** = slot, slit. **3** a pit, hole in the ground, *specif* that on the shores of Carlingwark Loch at Castle Douglas *19-, Kcb.* **4** the hem of a garment etc in which a draw-string runs *19-, now Cai Per.*
vi **1** make one or more slits or scores on (the carcass of a slaughtered animal) *17-e18.* **2** = slot, slit.

slotch &c *vi* move or walk in a slouching, hang-dog way, drag the feet in walking *19-, now Fif Loth Rox.*
n a lazy, slouching person, a layabout, ne'er-do-well *19-, now Loth Rox.* [onomat; var of SLATCH, perh connected w Eng *slouch*]

slote *see* SLOT¹

sloth *see* SLEUTH

slotter *vi* act in a slovenly way, work messily in a liquid; act slothfully *16-e19.*
~**y** sluggish, slothful *e16, e19.* [see SND]

slouch *see* SLOOCH

slough *see* SLOCH¹

slounge &c *la18-;* **slunge** [slun(d)ʒ, slʌn(d)ʒ] *vi* **1** idle or loaf about, walk in a slouching, lethargic way *la17-, now local.* **2** (1) behave furtively and stealthily *19-e20.* (2) hang about in the hope of getting food *20-, Sh Wgt Rox.*
n **1** a lazy, lounging, hangdog person *19-, local.* **2** a person or animal always on the look-out for food, a scrounger, glutton *19-, Loth Wgt Rox.* **3** a skulking, sneaking, sly, trouble-making person *19-, chf SW.*

slounger &c an idler, loafer *19-, now Cai.* [also in nEng dial; appar f LOONGE + prothetic *s*-]

slounge *see* SLUNGE

slour &c [slur] *n* a noisy gulp (of food or drink), a mouthful of soft sloppy food *19-e20, Abd Kcdn.* [onomat]

slouster &c; sluister *19-e20* ['slustər] *vi* **1** dabble in water or mud, work untidily or messily *19-, now Ags Fif Uls.* **2** swallow noisily and ungracefully, gulp, slobber *20-, now Fif Lnk.* **3** kiss in a sloppy way *19-e20, Uls.*
n something wet or messy *19.* [only Sc; orig perh chf onomat, w infl f SLAISTER, SLOOSH, SLUSH]

slouter &c ['slutər] *n* a coarse, slovenly, idle person *la19-, now local Cai-Ags.* [var of SLOTTER, SLUTTER]

slouth &c *la16-,* **sleuth &c** *la15-19* [*NE Ags* slʌuθ; **sl(j)uθ*] *n* = sleuth, sloth; laziness *16-e17.*
adj slothful, slow, lethargic *16, only Sc.*
vt **1** carry out (a task) in a lazy, idle, careless way, treat with indifference or neglect *la15-16, la19-, now Abd Kcdn Ags.* **2** waste (time) in sloth *la16, only Sc.*
~**ful &c** slothful *la15-e17, la19.*

slow, slowan *see* SLEUTH

slowch *see* SLOCH¹

slow-hound *see* SLEUTH

slowt *see* SLOIT

slubber *vi* slobber, swallow sloppy food, eat or drink in a noisy, gulping way *20-, Sh, N, EC, SW.*
n **1** a noisy, slobbering way of eating *19-, now Ork N.* **2** any sloppy, jelly-like matter *19-, now local Cai-Ags.* [var of Eng *slobber*; cf *slabber* (SLAB²)]

sluch &c [slʌx, slux] *n* = slough, a mire *la19-, now Sh NE.*

sluch *see* SLOCH¹

sludder &c ['slʌdər, 'slʌðər] *n* something wet and slimy, mud, filth *19-e20.* [see SND]

sludge; slutch *n* = sludge.
vi walk or move heavy-footedly and messily through mud etc *e19.*

slug¹ *n* **1** = slug, sluggard, snail etc. **2** a sleep, nap, a state of inactivity *20-, WC, SW.*

slug² *n* a loose upper garment worn to protect the clothing *la18-, now Dmf.* [prob Scand; cf Sw *sloka* hang down loosely]

slug *see* SLOCK²

sluggard &c; sluggart *15-17, only Sc* *n* = sluggard *15-.*
sluggardry *n* = sluggardy, slothfulness *e16, only Sc.*

slughan *see* SLEUTH
slughorn, slugorn *see* SLOGAN
sluister *see* SLOUSTER
sluiter *see* SLITTER

slumber; slummer &c *la15-16, only Sc* *n* **1** = slumber *16-.* **2** a period or occasion for sleep or rest *la15-16.*

slump¹ *n* **1** a large quantity, great number *e19.* **2** *building* a rough estimate *la19-.*
vt treat (several things) as one, lump together, deal with as a whole *18-, now local Sh-WC.*
~ number, reckoning, sum *etc* a number etc reckoned in round figures *la17-.*
at, in *etc* (**a** *or* **the**) **~** taken as a whole, in total, not sequentially; by a rough-and-ready computation *la17-, now local Sh-Gall.* [chf Sc; LowGer *slump* a heap, mass]

slump² *n* a marsh, boggy place, morass *19-, now Rox.*
~y marshy, muddy; *of ice* soft, unsafe *19-e20.* [perh conflation of Eng *sump* w SLUNK¹, w infl f SLUMP³]

slump³ *vi* sink (gradually and slowly) into mud, slush etc *19-, now Kcb.* [onomat; cf Norw dial *slump(a)*]

slung¹ &c, sling *17-; **slong &c** 15* *n* **1** = sling (for hurling stones) *15-.* **2** *only* **slung** a tall lanky stupid person; a disreputable person, a rascal *19-, NE.*
like a slung-stane like a bolt from the blue *la18-, Abd.*

slung² *n* = sling, a serpentine or culverin *la16, only Sc.* [OED *sling (n⁴)*]

slunge; slounge &c [slʌn(d)ʒ; *Bwk S also* slun(d)ʒ] *v* **1** *vi* (1) make a plunging movement

or noise *19-, local Cai-S.* (2) wade through water or mud in a clumsy, splashing way *la18-20.* **2** *vt* souse with water *20-, Inv C, S.*
n a plunging motion, a headlong fall, a splash made by a heavy object *la19-, now nEC Dnbt.* [onomat, perh based on Eng *plunge* and *lunge*]

slunge *see* SLOUNGE

slunk¹ *la17-,* **slonk** *la15-19* *n* a wet and muddy hollow, a soft, deep, wet rut in a road, a ditch *la15-, now Wgt.*
~y *of roads* muddy, rutted, full of wet holes *la19-e20, Uls.* [appar Scand; cf Dan dial *slank*, *slunk* a hollow in the ground; prob cognate w SLACK²]

slunk² [slʌŋk; *Cai* slʌuŋk] *n, contemptuous* a lazy, sneaking person, a shirker *20-, now Cai.* [see SND]

slunken, slunkit *see* SLINK
slus *see* SLOOSH

slush &c *n* **1** = slush. **2** a wet marshy place, a puddle, quagmire *18-19.* **3** a slovenly, untidy person, a slut; a menial worker, drudge *19.* **4** a speech peculiarity in which *sh* [ʃ] or some similar sound is used in place of the normal *s* [s] *la20-, Stlg midLoth Lnk.*
vi wade messily through wet mud etc, walk with shuffling or dragging steps *la19-e20.*
~y *of drink etc* weak, insipid *19-, now Sh Ork Cai.*

slutch *see* SLUDGE

slute &c [*Ork Cai* slut; *SW* sløt] *n* a slovenly, sluggish person *la17-, now Ork Cai SW.*
adj, also **slutt** *la16* sluttish, untidy *16.* [prob Eng *slut.* OED *slut (adj)*]

slutt *see* SLUTE

slutter &c; sclutter *la19-e20,* **skleuter &c** *la19-e20* ['slʌtər, 'sl(j)utər, 'slʌtər; *nEC Bwk* 'sløtər; 'skl-; -ðər] *vi* **1** work in a slovenly, dirty way, or in something messy *la19-, now Cai, C, S.* **2** walk in a slouching, slovenly way *la19-, local Ork-Per.* **3** make a splashing sound; plunge, flounder in mud *la19-, Bnf Ags.*
n **1** a mess, a mass of dirty (semi-)liquid *la19-, now Sh Ork EC, WC.* **2** a state of confusion, a muddle *20-, Per Stlg Dnbt.* **3** a splash, slop *19-e20.*
~y &c **1** slovenly, sluttish *19-, now EC, WC.* **2** messy, soft and wet, sloppy and sticky *la19-, now EC, WC.* [see SND; cf SLITTER]

sly *see* SCLY, SLEE
slyp *see* SLIPE¹

slype &c; sclype &c *la19-, NE* [s(k)ləip] *n* **1** a hard slap or smack, a thud caused by falling heavily, the noise of such *la19-, NE.* **2** *highly contemptuous* a lazy, coarse, dissolute, worthless person, *usu* a man *18-, now NE.*
vti **1** throw or fall down forcibly with a hard smack *la19-, Bnf Abd.* **2** *vi* walk with a heavy, flat-footed step *la19-, Bnf Abd.* [see SND]

slyre &c *n* a kind of fine linen or lawn *17.* [only Sc; LowGer *sleier, slijer,* Ger *Schleier* fine linen, a veil]

slyster *see* SLAISTER

sma &c *18-*, **small; smaill** &c *15-16*, **smaw**
la15-16 [smɑ; *smal; *smel] *adj* **1** = small
la14-. **2** *of persons, animals* slim, slender,
slightly-built; *of things* narrow, thin, of small
width or diameter *19-, now Sh NE Per.* **3** fine,
composed of small particles or droplets *la16-*.
4 *of cloth, mesh* fine in texture *la14-, now local Sh-
Kcb.* **5** *only Sc* (1) *of the sea, a lake etc* smooth,
calm, undisturbed *la18-, Cai NE, C;* (2) *of a river
etc* low, not in SPATE *la18-, NE-S.*

n **1** a small quantity or amount, a little, not
much *17-, now local Sh-Loth.* **2** *only Sc* a small
thing: (1) *chf in pl* units of small change *20-, NE
Ags;* (2) *in pl* small wares, small (drapery) goods
la19-, now Ork Per. **3** a period of calm at sea, a
lull *la19-e20.*

adv in a small voice, quietly *la19-, now Ags Per
WC.*

smally &c ['smalɪ] *of persons* undersized, small
and slight, weakly; *of things* small, slight, meagre *la18-, now C, S.*

∼-bouk(it) little bulk, small, compact
la19-, only Sc. **∼ breid** &c *tea bread* (TEA) *19-,
only Sc.* **small corn** = *small oats, la18-19, only
Sc.* **small debt court** a court set up under a
JP in 1801 for dealing with debts under £5,
and under a SHERIFF in 1837 for debts up to
£20, *19-, only Sc.* **∼ faimily** &c a family of
young children *18-, now local.* **small fish** fish
such as haddock, herring etc, caught inshore
with *small lines, la18-, now Sh Ags Kcb, only Sc.*
∼ hours, *freq* **wee ∼ hours** the very early
hours of the morning, just after midnight *18-.*
∼ *etc* **laird** a small landowner *la19-, now Ork; cf
bonnet laird* (BONNET). **∼ lines** ['smɑ'lɔinz,
'smalɪnz] the lines used by inshore fishermen to
catch *small fish, la14-, now Sh N, EC, only Sc.*
small music *piping* light music such as REELS[1],
STRATHSPEYS etc *la20-; cf* PIBROCH. **small oats**
a kind of oat sown on the poorest soil *18-20, only
Sc.* **small pennyis** &c money in small denominations or small sums *16-17.* **∼ shot** a strong
strengthening thread inserted in *Paisley shawls*
(PAISLEY) at intervals *la19-e20, Renfr.* **∼ shot
(Satur)day** a Paisley holiday on the first Saturday of July (*orig* a weavers' union holiday)
la19-, Renfr. **∼ thing** a small sum of money
20-, now N nEC Wgt. **sma write** small text,
ordinary cursive handwriting *19-, now NE.*

be, think anesel *etc* **nae ∼ drink** be, think
oneself to be a person of some importance *la18-.*
by *or* **in ∼s** in small amounts, piecemeal, little
by little *16-, now local Sh-Loth, only Sc.* **∼
stanes and slew** *etc* the dust kicked up by sudden flight or hurry *20-, Bnf Abd.*

smacher &c ['smaxər, *'smexər] *vi* eat in a
secretive way, nibble (**at**), munch unobtrusively *19-, now Kcdn.*

∼ie &c, **smachrie** &c, **smaggrie** ['smax(ə)rɪ,
'smagrɪ] **1** a large number of small objects or

people (*esp* children), *esp* in disorder or confusion *19-, now Abd.* **2** a hotchpotch or mixture
of food, *esp* sweets etc *la18-, now NE Ags.* [only
Sc; appar altered f SMATTER]

smack &c *vti* **1** = smack (the lips etc), strike.
2 *vt* kiss, *esp* in a loud hearty way *la19-.* **3** *vi*
move along with speed *19-, now Ags Per, only Sc.*
n = smack.

∼ smooth *adj, adv* completely smooth(ly) and
even(ly), level, flush with the surface *la18-e19.*

smad; smud &c *19- n* a small stain, smut,
dirty mark; a very small quantity of anything
19-, now Sh NE Ags.

v **1** *vt* stain, soil, blemish with dirt *la15-, now Sh
NE Ags.* **2** *vi, of a fire* smoulder and emit
clouds of sooty smoke, cause smuts *19-20, Gall
Uls.* [see SND]

smag &c *n* a sweet, a tasty titbit *la19-, Bnf Abd.*
[prob back-formation f *smaggrie* (SMACHER)]

smaggrie *see* SMACHER

smaik &c *n* contemptuous term for a person; a
rogue, rascal *la15-e20.*

∼ry mean or contemptible behaviour; roguery,
trickery *la16.* [only Sc; see SND]

smaill *see* SMA

smairg &c *vt* besmear with something oily or
messy; *specif* = SMEAR *v, 19-, now WC Wgt Rox.*
[only Sc; conflation of SMEAR w SLAIRG]

smairt, smart; smert *adj* = smart *la16-.*

∼er *20-, Cai C,* **smartie** *20-* a lively and efficient person, one who is quick to understand
and act.

∼ly 1 = smartly *la14-.* **2** sharply, keenly
la17-.

small *see* SMA

smarrach &c ['smarəx] *n* a confused crowd or
collection, *esp* of children *la19-, Bnf Abd.*
[appar metath f SMACHER but also confused w
SWARRACH]

smart *see* SMAIRT

smash *vti* = smash *19-.*

n **1** = smash *19-.* **2** a shattered, smashed or
pulpy state, *freq* **a-, in** *or* **to ∼** *la18-.*

∼(e)rie destruction, utter ruin, annihilation
e19, only Sc. **∼ie** a variety of the game of marbles (see SND), the game of DAIGIE; the heavy
marble used in this game *20-, EC, WC Kcb, only
Sc.* **∼ing** &c *of persons* well-built, strapping,
vigorous *19, only Sc.*

smat *see* SMITE[1]

smatchet &c *19-,* **smatchert** &c *la16-e20*
['smatʃət; *Sh Ork Cai* 'smatʃərd, -ər(t)] *n* a small
insignificant person (or animal), *esp* a pert or
mischievous child, a little rogue; *of an adult* an
impudent, worthless person, a rascal *la16, 19-,
now Sh Ork N.* [only Sc; obscure]

smatter &c; **smather** &c ['smatər; *Mry Bnf*
*-ðər; *S also* 'smʌt-] *v* **1** *vt* smash, shatter *la19-,
now Wgt S.* **2** *vi* work untidily or unmethodi-
cally, (appear to) be busy with trivial jobs
19-e20.

n **1** *in pl* bits and pieces, smithereens; odds and

ends, small amounts *la18-*, *now Ags.* **2** a small jumbled collection of people or things, *specif* of children *la18-*, *local NE-Dmf.*

~**ie** = *n* 2, *19-*, *now wLoth.* ~**ing &c** a small amount (in Sc not restricted to knowledge) *20-*, *Sh Ork N.*

~ **awa** consume or dissipate bit by bit, fritter away (money); nibble at (food) *19-*, *now Ags.* [see SND]

smaw *see* SMA

smear *la18-*; **smeir &c** *la16-e19*, **smeer &c** *20-*, *Mry Abd* [smir; *nEC* smer] *vt* **1** = smear *la16-*. **2** treat (a sheep's fleece) with a tar-and-grease compound to protect it from damp and parasites *la16-e20*.

smeerich ['smɪrɪx] *n* a thin layer or spread (of butter etc) *20-*, *Inv NE*, *only Sc.* *vt* besmear; make a mess of *19-*, *now Abd.* ~**ing house** *etc* the shed etc in which sheep were treated as in *v* 2, *19-e20*, *only Sc.*

~ **dock(en)** Good King Henry, a kind of goosefoot used in folk-medicine in ointment for itch *la18-19*, *only Sc.*

smeddum &c *n* **1** a fine powder, *specif* a finely ground meal or malt; a medicinal powder *la17-e20*. **2** the pith, strength or essence of a substance *la18-e19*, *only Sc.* **3** spirit, energy, drive, vigorous commonsense and resourcefulness *la18-*, *only Sc.* [OE *smed(e)ma*, *smeo-* fine flour; *cf* eModEng *smitham* = *n* 1]

smeech *see* SMIACH

smeek &c *18-*; **smeke** *la14*, **smeik** *15-16* [smik] *n* **1** *also fig* the fumes from something burning, smoke, REEK[1] *15-*, *now C-Uls.* **2** an unpleasant smell, a stuffy fetid atmosphere *18-*, *now Fif wLoth SW*, *only Sc.* **3** a contrivance for smoking out bees *20-*, *Bwk-S*, *only Sc.* **4** a whiff, stifling puff of fumes; the act of smelling, a sniff *20-*, *Cai WC Wgt*, *only Sc.*

v **1** *vt*, *also fig* affect or suffocate with smoke or soot, make smoky *la14-*, *now C, S.* **2** *vi*, *also fig* emit smoke or fumes, REEK[1], smoke *la18-*, *Gen except Sh Ork NE.* **3** *vt* smoke (fish, meat etc), *eg* in order to preserve *19-e20*. **4** fumigate with smoke *la19-*, *now C, S.* **5** *freq* ~ **out** drive out (bees etc) with smoke fumes; smoke out (persons) as a joke *19-*, *now C, S.*

~**er** a contrivance for smoking out bees (or playing practical jokes) *la19-*, *now Per Fif Kcb*, *only Sc.* ~**it 1** smoke-stained; stifled or blinded by smoke *19-e20*. **2** drunk *la19-*, *chf WC, SW*, *only Sc.* ~**y** smoky *la16-20*. [ME *smek(e)*, OE *smēc(n)*, *smēocan* (*v*) smoke; *cf* SMOKE and SMUIK]

smeer, smeerich *see* SMEAR

smeerless *see* SMERGH

smeeth *see* SMUITH

smeik *see* SMEEK

smeir *see* SMEAR

smeke *see* SMEEK

smell *n* **1** = smell *16-*. **2** a small quantity, a taste, 'a sensation' (*esp* of drink) *la15*, *la19-*, *now local Sh-Kcb.*

~**ed** *in comb* -scented, -smelling *e17.*

smelt[1] *n* = SMOWT[1] *la18-*. [*cf* Eng = a small salmon-like fish]

smelt[2] **&c,** **smilt &c** [smɛlt(ʃ), smɪlt(ʃ), smʌltʃ] *n* a calm patch on the sea *e20.* [only Sc; *appar* OE *smylte* calm, peaceful, serene; *cf* SMOLT]

smergh &c *la18-*; **smeuch &c** *20-*, *Cai* [smɛrx; *Cai* smjux, *smjʌx] *n* **1** bone-marrow, pith *la18-e19*. **2** *fig* pith, energy, vitality *la18-*, *now Cai.*

~**less, smeerless &c** *of persons* lacking in spirit or energy, sluggish, feckless, stupid; *of things* insipid, uninteresting *18-*, *N.* **smervie &c** *adj*, *of food*, *also fig* full of substance or flavour *la18-19*, *NE.* [only Sc; see SND]

smert *see* SMAIRT

smervie, smeuch *see* SMERGH

smeuk *see* SMUIK

smiach; smeech [smix; *N also* 'smiəx, smjax] *n*, *in negative* not a sound, whisper, murmur; not a trace, not a sign of life *20-*, *now Cai.*

vi, *in negative* not utter a sound, keep quiet *20-*, *now Cai.* [only Sc; Gael = a syllable, sound]

smick *n* a spot, trace; a small unimportant trifle *19*, *N.* [only Sc; *prob var* of Eng *smack* a taste, small quantity]

smicker &c *vi* smile or laugh in a sniggering or leering way; smile seductively; smile affectedly *19-e20.* [see SND]

smiddy &c *15-*, **smithy &c** *n* = smithy *la14-.* ~ **coal** *18-*, ~ **coom** *la19-*, *now Kcb* a small smokeless type of coal suitable for smiths' work. ~ **craft** smithcraft *e16.* ~ **sparks** the sparks of iron which fly off a smith's anvil *19-*, *now NE Ags Per.*

smile &c; smyl(l) &c *15-17 vi* (*la14-*), *n* (*17-*) = smile.

smiler *joc* a kind of wide-toothed wooden rake for stubble *la20-*, *N*, *only Sc.*

smilt *see* SMELT[2]

smird *n* a smut, smudge, a spot of dirt, rain etc *20-*, *Sh Bnf Abd.* [only Sc; *perh var* of SMIT]

smirk[1] *vi* **1** smile in a pleasant friendly way, have a smiling amiable expression; have a roguish or flirtatious smile *15-e20*. **2** = smirk, smile affectedly *la19-.*

n **1** a pleasant smile, a friendly expression *16-.* **2** = smirk, an affected smile. ~**ie** having a good-natured, amiable, friendly expression *18-e20.* ~**le** *n*, *v* = *n* 1, *v* 1, *18-19.*

smirk[2] *n* a kiss *la19-*, *NE.* [only Sc; see SND]

smirk[3] *vt*, *chf literary* smirch *la19-*, *now Mry Abd Fif.* [only Sc; by analogy w BIRK[1], Eng *birch* etc]

smirkle *see* SMIRK[1]

smirl &c *n* a sneer, mocking smile; a snigger, sneering laugh *la19.* [only Sc; *perh reduced f* SMIRTLE]

smirr &c *only Sc*, **smurr &c** *n* a fine rain, drizzle, *freq* ~ **o rain**; *occas* sleet or snow *19-*, *Gen except Sh Ork.*

vi, of rain or snow fall gently and softly in fine clouds, drizzle *19-*. [poss onomat, w infl f SMORE and SMUIR]

smirtle *la17-e20*; **smurtle &c** *18-e19 vi* smile in an arch or knowing way, smirk; laugh coyly, giggle, snigger *la17-e19*.
n a sarcastic smile, a smirk of satisfaction *la18-e19*. [only Sc; var of *smirkle* (SMIRK[1])]

smit &c *v, pt* smit *la19-*, **smittit &c** *la14-e20. ptp* smit *19-*, **smittit &c** *15-*, **smitten** *20-* 1 *vt* = smit, stain *la14-15*. **2** contaminate or affect (**with**) *15-*. **3** *of an infectious or contagious disease or patient, also fig* affect by contagion, infect, taint *la14-*.
n **1** *also fig* a smut, smudge; a taint, blemish *la14-e20*. **2** infection, contagion, *chf* **gie** *or* **get the smit** infect or be infected by a disease; *also fig, esp* fall in love *la19-*.
~**tal &c** *la16-*, ~**tle** *18-*, ~**tin** *19-e20*, ~**some** *la19-*, now Ork also fig infectious, contagious.

smitch &c *n* **1** *also fig* a stain, blemish, taint, smudge *19-, now Dnbt Ayr*. **2** a very small amount, speck, trace *19-e20*. [see SND]

smite[1] *v, pt, ptp also* **smat** *19, literary* = smite *la14-*.

smite[2] &c *n* a small insignificant person, a weak or puny creature *la19-, NE Ags*. [only Sc; see SND]

smith &c *n* = smith *la16-*.
the auld ~ the devil *la19-20, NE, only Sc*.

smithy *see* SMIDDY

smittal, smittle *see* SMIT

smizzle *vi* rain lightly and thinly, drizzle *20-, SW Rox*. [only Sc; conflation of SMIRR w Eng *drizzle*]

smoar *see* SMORE

smoath *see* SMUITH

smoch[1] &c [smox; *Rox also* smʌux] *n* thick choking smoke; thick fog *20-, Ags Fif Rox*.
~**y &c** smoky; *of the air* close, sultry, stifling *19-, now Fif*. [only Sc; appar var of Eng *smoke*, perh w infl f MOCH[2]]

smoch[2] *e16*, **smush** *e17 adj* meaning uncertain. [only Sc]

smochle &c ['smoxl] *vi* grope about with the hands, as in the dark, fumble awkwardly *la19-, chf Per*. [only Sc; see SND]

smoke &c *la17-*; **smoik** *16* [smok] *n* **1** = smoke *16-*. **2** an inhabited house *la18-20, esp Highl* [poss translating Gael *deatach* smoke; (a sign of) an inhabited house].
(**Arbroath**) **smokie** an unsplit smoked haddock *la19-, only Sc*.
~ **board &c** a wooden flap etc over a fireplace to regulate the draught and prevent the chimney from smoking *la19-20, Gen except Sh Ork, only Sc*.
~ **o tobacco** as much tobacco as will fill a pipe *19-, local Sh-Kcb, only Sc*. [*cf* SMUIK and SMEEK]

smolt; smowt *only Sc* [*smolt, *smʌut] *adj, of weather* fine, fair, calm *e16*. [ME, OE]

smolt *see* SMOWT[1]

smook; smuk &c [smuk; *Sh also* sm(j)ug] *vi* slink or sneak (**about**), go about furtively looking for something to pilfer *19-, now local Sh-Ayr*. [only Sc; see SND]

smook *see* SMUIK

smool[1] &c; smu(i)l [smul] *v* **1** *vi* slink, sneak, go about furtively *19-, now NE*. **2** curry favour, fawn, wheedle *19-, now Ags Per Fif*. **3** *vt, literary* remove stealthily, filch *19-e20*.
n, freq of a child a wheedler; a diminutive or insignificant person *20-, NE*.
~ **in wi** cajole, 'suck up to' *20-, now Ags*. [only Sc; see SND]

smool[2] *vi* look petulant or discontented, scowl, frown; look scornful and unfriendly *la19-, SW*.
n a scowl; a snarl by a horse when threatening to bite *20-, SW*. [only Sc; see SND]

smoor *see* SMUIR

smoost *see* SMUIST

smooth *see* SMUITH

smore; smoar *la16-18 v* **1** *vt* smother, suffocate, stifle (*eg* with smoke) *15-, now Sh NE Ags*. **2** *vi* be smothered or stifled, choke *la15-, only Sc*. **3** *vt* suppress, conceal (*eg* feelings); hush **up** (a rumour etc) *la14-*. **4** *also fig* extinguish (a fire, light etc), put out, obliterate *la18-, now NE Ags, only Sc*. **5** confine or cover thickly with snow etc *la18-, only Sc*. **6** *vi, of snow, smoke etc* fall or come out in a dense stifling cloud; *of atmosphere* be thick with snow, smoke etc *19-, only Sc*.
n a thick, close, stifling atmosphere full of smoke, snow, fine rain, dust etc *la19-*.
smorin *of a head-cold* thick, choking, heavy *la20-, only Sc*. **be smorin wi the caul** have a very bad cold *la20-, only Sc*. [now *chf* NE; ME; OE *smorian*, cognate w Eng *smother*; *cf* SMUIR]

smot &c *vt* mark (sheep) with tar or other colouring as a sign of ownership *16-, now Bwk*.
n a mark of ownership on a sheep; sheep or a sheep thus marked *16-, now Bwk*.
~**ter** *vt* bespatter; soil or stain *e16, 19, only Sc*. [*cf* Eng *smut*]

smother *see* SMUDDER

smouder &c ['smudər; *nEC* 'smuðər] *vi, n* = smoulder *la19-*.

smout *see* SMOWT[1]

smowt[1] &c *20-*, **smolt &c**; **smout** *18-* [smʌut; *St* smolt] *n* **1** a young salmon (or sea trout) between the PARR and GRILSE stages *la15-*. **2** *chf* **smout** a small insignificant person, a small child, animal or thing *la18-, Gen except Sh Ork*. [see SND]

smowt[2] &c [smʌut] *n* a term in marbles *20-, WC, SW, only Sc; see SND*. [? reduced f *that's me out*]

smowt *see* SMOLT

smucht &c [smʌxt] *n* = SMUCHTER *n* 1, *la20-, Bnf Abd*.
~**y** smoky, fuggy; misty, close *20-, Bnf Abd*. [only Sc; back-formation f next]

smuchter &c ['smʌxtər, 'smuxtər] *vi* **1** smoulder, emit thick black smoke, burn slowly *la19-*, *NE*. **2** *of rain, snow etc* fall in a fine mist, drizzle down persistently *la19-*, *Bnf Abd*. **3** *of persons* be short of breath, breathe with difficulty; *of the voice* be muffled or thick *19-e20*, *Abd*.
n **1** thick smoke, *freq* from damp fuel or a faulty chimney; slight smoke from a fire not properly lit; a thick stuffy atmosphere *la19-*, *NE*. **2** a thin light mist or rain *la19-*, *Mry-Kcdn*. **3** a thick choking cold, a heavy catarrh *la20-*, *Bnf Abd*.

smud *see* SMAD

smudder *la16-*, **smother** *17-* *vti* = smother.

smudge &c [smʌdʒ, smudʒ] *vi* laugh in a suppressed way, laugh quietly to oneself, smirk *18-*, *local*.
n a quiet half-suppressed laugh, a smirk, simper *19-*, *local*. [see SND]

smue &c [sm(j)u] *vi* smile placidly, blandly or ingratiatingly, smirk; laugh in a suppressed or furtive way *19-*, *now Ork*. [see SND]

smuggle &c *vti* **1** = smuggle. **2** *in handball* (HAND) (*Ork Rox*) *and rugby football* (*now also Eng*) get (the ball) unobtrusively out of a scrimmage; *in the game of smuggle-the-geg* (GEG³) (*Ork Rox*), dispose of (the hidden object) unobserved by the opposing side *20-*.
n, *in handball* (HAND) a struggle for the ball in which one side tries to pass the ball out of sight of their opponents towards the goal *20-*, *Ork Rox, only Sc*.

smuik &c, **smook** *la19-*; **smeuk &c** *16-19* [smøk; *Ork Cai, local Ags-S also* smuk; **smjuk; N nEC also **sm(j)ux] *n* **1** smoke, fumes *16-*, *now local Ags-S*. **2** fine thick snow or rain *19-*, *Ork Cai Bnf, only Sc*.
v **1** *vi* smoke, REEK¹, smoulder with thick smoke *16-*, *now Ags Rox*. **2** *vt* (expose to) smoke, fumigate; cure (meat) by smoking; smoke out (bees); discolour by smoke *19-*, *now SW, S*. [MDu *smuyck(en)* &c smoke; *cf* SMOKE, SMEEK]

smuil *see* SMOOL¹

smuir &c *16-*, **smoor** *17-*; **smure &c** *15-19* [*C, S* smør, smer; *Ork N* smur; *Mry* smjur; *C also* smur] *v* **1** *vt* (1) *also fig* be choked, suffocated, die from lack of air, *esp* by being buried in a snowdrift *15-*, *only Sc*. (2) drown in a river or bog *19-e20*, *only Sc*. **2** *vt* (1) cause (persons or animals) to suffocate, smother, crush the breath out of *la17-*. (2) bury, cover over thickly, envelop in a dense covering of smoke, snow, vegetation etc *19-e20*, *only Sc*. **3** damp down (a fire) so that it smoulders quietly *18-*, *now local, only Sc*. **4** cover with a thin coating, smear (*eg* a sheep with tar) *la19-*, *now Cai*. **5** *fig* conceal; suppress; deaden; quench *16-20*, *only Sc*.
n a thick atmosphere, a dense enveloping cloud of smoke, snow, rain, mist *la19-*, *now local Ork-Kcb, only Sc*.
smooring (**the fire**) a ritual damping down of

the domestic fire at night, once common in Highland (HIELAND) Catholic districts *20-*, *only Sc*. [Gen except NE; *cf* SMORE; see SND]

smuirich &c ['smørəx, 'smurəx; *Mry* 'smjur-; *Abd* 'smir-] *vti* exchange kisses, canoodle, cuddle *19-*, *now NE Ags Per*.
n a kiss, caress, hug, cuddle *la19-*, *now Sh NE Ags Per*. [only Sc; intensive of SMUIR and SMORE]

smuist; smoost &c [smøst, smɪst, smust; *Abd* smuʃt] *vi* emit smoke without much fire, smoulder, burn slowly *19-*, *now Stlg Rox*.
n a thick, choking, sulphurous smoke or its smell *19-*, *now Dmf*.
~er &c = *v*; be smoky *19*. [only Sc; perh altered f Eng *smutch* begrime]

smuith &c *19-e20*, **smooth; smeeth** *19-e20*, *N*, **smoath** *el7* [*C* smøð, smeð; *Ross Mry* smjuð; *NE **smið] *adj* = smooth *17-*.
n a smooth or level place, *specif* the sandy sea-bottom *e20*, *Ross Mry Kcdn*.

smuk *see* SMOOK

smul *see* SMOOL¹

smurach &c ['smurəx; *Mry* 'smjur-] *n* fine dust or powder, *specif* crumbled PEAT¹ *19-*, *now Cai Ross Inv*. [only Sc; Gael *smùrach* dust, ashes; prob orig f SMUIR]

smure *see* SMUIR

smurl *vi*, *of people or animals*, *esp if ill* eat little and slowly (without appetite), nibble half-heartedly or furtively *la19-20*. [only Sc; var of MURL]

smurr *see* SMIRR

smurtle *see* SMIRTLE

smush¹ &c *vt* break into very small fragments, crush, smash *19-*, *local Sh-Rox*.
n **1** a mass of tiny crushed fragments, something reduced to pulp or powder, *eg* over-boiled potatoes *19-*. **2** a collection of small objects; fragments, scraps of food etc *19-e20*.
~lach &c = *n*, *la19-e20*. [only Sc; var of MUSH¹]

smush² *n* a thick cloud of smoke or soot particles, grime, a sulphurous smell *19-*, *now Ork Bnf*. [only Sc; altered f SMUIST, Eng *smudge*, *smutch*, perh infl in form by SMUSH¹]

smush *see* SMOCH²

smushlach *see* SMUSH¹

smy *n* a knave, rascal *16*. [only Sc; obscure]

smyagger &c ['smjagər] *vt* smear, daub, bespatter *20-*, *Cai*.
n a smear; a mess, bespattered state *20-*, *Cai*. [see SND]

smyl(l) *see* SMILE

smyte¹ *n*, *chf* **smytrie &c** *contemptuous* a collection of people (*esp* children) or small objects *la18-*, *now Bnf Abd*. [only Sc; see SND]

smyte² *n* a rope attached to one of the lower corners of a sail *la15-e16*. [only Sc; MDu *smiete* or MLowGer *smite*. OED *smite*]

smytrie *see* SMYTE¹

snab[1] *only Sc*; **snob** *n* a cobbler; a cobbler's boy or apprentice *19-, now nEC Gsw Rox.*
~**bin** shoemaking, cobbling *la19-, now Fif Edb.* [Eng (now dial) *snob*; *cf* developed meaning in StEng]

snab[2] **&c** *n* a steep short slope, a projection of rock *la18-, now midLoth WC Rox.* [see SND]

snack[1] **&c** *n* **1** a bite, snap, *esp* of a dog *16-.* **2** a short time *e16.* **3** = snack.
vti snap with the teeth, bite *17-, now EC-S.*

snack[2] *adj* **1** *of persons* nimble, active, quick *18-20.* **2** quick in mind, acute, clever, sharp-witted *18-, now Cai Abd.* **3** sharp or severe in one's dealings or manner, exacting *la19.*
adv quickly, sharply *18-19.*
~**ie** = *adj* 1 and 2, *20-, Abd Dmf.*

snaffle &c *la16-* *vi, also* **snavil** *la14* snuffle, speak through the nose *la14, la16.*
n term of contempt for a wicked or ineffective person *19-, now Lnk Dmf.*
snaffler = *n, e17.* [see SND. OED *snaffle* (*v*[3]), *snavel*]

snag &c *vti* snarl (at); nag, grumble, taunt *19-, now Kcdn.*
n a titbit, dainty, *esp* a sweet *la19-, now NE Ags.*
snagger *vi* snarl, growl; snore harshly *la19-20, Bnf Abd, only Sc.* **snaggy** sarcastic, snappish *19.* [var of SNACK[1]]

snaik &c *vi* sneak, skulk about, do something in a mean, furtive or underhand way *la17-, now Ags.* [only Sc; ON *snaka* go snuffing or searching about]

snail *n* **1** = snail. **2** a slug *20-.*

snake &c *n* a slug, *esp* the large grey or black garden slug *20-, now Cai.* [only Sc; see SND]

snaker &c *n* = sneaker, a small bowl of punch *18-e19, only Sc.*

snap[1] **&c** *vti* **1** = snap. **2** *vt* snatch, catch or seize quickly or suddenly *19-, now Bnf Abd.* **3** gobble (**up**), eat hastily or with relish *19-.*
n **1** = snap. **2** a small piece, scrap, *specif* of food *la18-, now local Sh-Per.* **3** a ginger snap *la18-.* **4** a sharp blow *la19-, Sh N, only Sc.*
adj, only Sc **1** quick, eager, smart *18-19.* **2** short-tempered, giving a short or evasive reply, ready to find fault *20-, now Sh.*
~**per** *adj, also* ~**pert** snappish, tart, curt *la17-e19, only Sc.* *n* something large, heavy or excellent of its kind *19-, now Ags Per.* ~**pit** *only Sc, adj, adv* snappish(ly) *la19-, now Ork Ags.*
~**pous &c** hasty in temper, testy *19-, now Abd, only Sc.* ~**py &c** *adj* hard-bargaining *19-, Ags, only Sc.* *n* a small cod or haddock *20-, local Ork-Crom.*
~ **gun** *e17,* ~ **work &c** *la16-17, only Sc* a firelock.
~ **and rattle &c** toasted *oatcakes* (AIT) crumbled in milk *la20-, NE, only Sc.* **in a** *or* **upon** ~ like a shot, with no delay *la18-, now Sh Cai.*

snap[2] *n* the top layer or coping of stones on a *Galloway dyke* (GALLOWAY), set on their edges so as to taper upwards *la18-19.*

~(-**topped**)-**dyke** a wall built thus *18-, now Kcb.* [only Sc; see SND]

snapper &c *vi* **1** stumble, trip, fall suddenly *la15-, now Sh Bnf Abd.* **2** make a slip in conduct, get into trouble *la15-e18.*
n, only Sc **1** a stumble, false step, jolting motion *la16-, now Abd.* **2** a slip in conduct, blunder; an unfortunate accident *la16-19.* [ME *snapir* &c]

snapper, snappous *see* SNAP[1]

snar &c *adj* **1** severe, strict, tart *19-e20.* **2** astute, sharp (in one's dealings); *of a housewife* shrewd, efficient *e19.* [ON *snarr* hard-twisted, keen, sharp; *cf* ME *snart* sharply, severely]

snarl *n, vt* **1** = snarl, tangle. **2** snare *la20-, local.*

snarp *adj* sharp, keen *la14.* [nME; ON *snarpr*]

snash &c *v* **1** *vi* snap, bite *la19-, now Ork.* **2** *vt* insult, speak impertinently to, sneer at *19-e20.*
n abuse, hard words, impudence *la18-, Gen except Sh Ork.*
~**gab** petulant, insolent talk *19-, now Loth Rox.* [only Sc; prob onomat; *cf* Fris *snasje,* Sw *snaska* snatch at food, munch; *cf* next]

snashter &c *n, in pl,* contemptuous sweets, cakes, pastries etc; trashy food *19-, now local Per-WC.* [only Sc; *cf* SNASH and MLowGer *snascherie* eating of dainties, Sw *snask* sweets]

snatchack &c *n* a small quantity of intoxicating liquor, a dram *20-, now Ross Inv Mry.* [only Sc; prob Eng *snatch* + Gael dim ending]

snauchle &c ['snɑxl] *n* an insignificant, puny or feeble person, a dwarf *19-e20, chf SW.* [only Sc; see SND]

snavil *see* SNAFFLE

snaw &c, snow *17-;* **snyauve &c** *19-20, local Bnf Abd n* = snow *la14-.*
vti, pt also **snew** *la19-, now Sh* = snow *15-.*
throw *or* **cast** ~ **baws** jeer, make insulting remarks *18-e20, only Sc.* ~ **bree** *la19-, now NE Dmf, only Sc,* ~ **broo &c** *la18-, now Kcdn-S, only Sc* melted snow or ice, *freq* that carried down in rivers, slush. ~ **flake &c** the snow bunting *la17-e20.* ~ **mail** a payment made to owners of lowland pasture for grazing hill sheep *e19.* ~ **wreath &c** a snowdrift *19-, Gen except Sh Ork.*
like ~ **aff a dyke** (disappear) very quickly *19-, only Sc.*

snead *see* SNED[1]

sneck[1] **&c**; **snick &c** *la18-* *n* **1** a latch, catch of a door etc *la15-.* **2** *masonry* (1) *in pl* small stones packed in between the larger ones in a rubble wall *la18-, NE.* (2) a portion of a dry-stone wall built of large stones extending through the whole width of the wall *19-, now Rox.* **3** *mining* points on a HUTCH railway *la18-.*
v **1** *vt* latch, fasten (**up**) with a latch etc; make (a catch) fast *la16-.* **2** *fig* shut (one's mouth), shut **up** *20-, now Ags Ayr, only Sc.* **3** lock **up** *or* **in**, catch (something) **in** (a door), jam or squeeze between two objects *19-, now WC-Slk,*

only Sc.   **4** switch or turn **off** (an electrical appliance) *20-*, now *Sh NE nEC, only Sc.*   **5** *vi, of a door* close on a latch, shut *la19-*.   **6** *vt, masonry* close or fill **up** (a crevice in a rubble wall) by packing smaller stones tightly between the large ones, or by filling the interstices with lime *la18-*, now *NE, only Sc.*

~-**draw(er)** a crafty, deceitful person *19-e20*.
~-**drawing** *n, adj* guile(ful), artful(ness) *la18-e20*.   ~-**shifter** *mining* a pointsman *20-*, now *Fif*; cf *n* 3.

draw *or* **lift a** ~ open a latch; *fig* insinuate oneself into something surreptitiously, act craftily or stealthily *16-, only Sc.*   **aff the** ~ *of a door etc* unlatched, with the catch left off *la19-*.   **on the** ~ latched but not locked *19-*.   [nME; see SND]

sneck² &c *n* **1** a notch, a slight cut or incision; an indentation in an animal's horn as a sign of age *la18-*, now local *Sh-Per*.   **2** the power or act of cutting; *fig* a cutting remark, snub *19-*, now *Cai Ags Per, only Sc.*   **3** a dip in the ground, a saddle between hills *la19-*, local *Sh-Ags, only Sc.*
vt **1** cut sharply, cut into or **off**, prune, notch *la16-*, now local *Sh-Ayr*.   **2** surpass, beat *la19-*, *Abd Kcdn Ags, only Sc.*   [see SND]

sneck³ &c; **snick** *vt* snatch, seize, steal *19-*, now local *Abd-Rox.*
n a greedy grasping person; nickname for an Aberdonian *19-*, local *Ork-Fif.*   [see SND]

sneckler *n* a short circle of rope attached to the stern of a COBLE², for taking a rolling hitch on standing gear etc *la20, Cai NE.*   [cf Eng *snickle* (catch with) a noose]

sned¹ &c; **snead** &c [snɛd; *NE also* snɛð] *n* the shaft of a scythe, to which the blade is attached *la17-*.   [OE *snǣd*]

sned² &c *vt* **1** chop, lop off (a branch); *specif* prune (a tree) *16-*.   **2** cut **off** the tops (and roots) of (turnips, thistles etc) *la18-*, *Gen except Sh Ork.*   **3** *also fig* cut **off**, trim *la18-*, now *NE, C.*
n a cut, cutting; a slash, slight wound; a lopping or pruning *19-*.
snedder a pruner *la16-20*.   **snedding** pruning; *in pl* prunings, branches etc removed *la18-e19*.   **snedding knife** *etc* a pruning knife etc *18-19*.   [OE *snǣdan* prune, trim]

sneed *see* SNUID
sneel *see* SNEEVIL, SNUIL

sneer &c *v* **1** *vi* snort, twitch the nose, snuffle, inhale or exhale heavily or noisily *16-*, now *Ork.*   **2** *vti* = sneer.
n **1** *esp of a horse* a snort, noisy breathing (in or out) through the nose *la15-e19, only Sc.*   **2** = sneer.

sneesh &c; **snish** &c *18-e19 n* (a pinch of) snuff *la18-*.
vti, only Sc **1** take snuff, sniff it up the nostrils *19-20, local Abd-S.*   **2** *vi* sneeze *20-*, *sEC, WC, Rox.*   [back-formation f SNEESHIN; cf SNUFF²]

sneeshin &c; **snishin(g)** &c *n, chf literary, esp in Highl contexts* (a pinch of) snuff; *fig* something of little value *la17-*.
~ **box** a snuff box *18-19*.   ~ &c **draps** drops of snuff-laden nasal mucus *19-e20, Bnf Ags.*   ~ **horn** a snuffbox shaped from a horn *la18-*, now *Per.*   ~ **mull** &c a snuffbox, *orig* one which ground the snuff *18-*.   ~ **pen** a small quill or spoon for taking snuff *19-e20*.   [appar f Highl pronunciation of Eng *sneezing* &c snuff; cf Gael *snaoisean* and SNEISING]

sneet *see* SNITE¹, SNUIT

sneeter &c *vi* **1** giggle, snigger *20-*, local *Ork-Ayr.*   **2** weep, blubber *20-*, now *Cai.*   [only Sc; see SND; cf SNITTER]

sneevil &c, **snivel** &c *la17-*; **snevil** *16*, **sneel** &c *19, Gall* ['snivl, 'snevl; *SW* snil] *vti* **1** = snivel *16-*.   **2** speak through the nose, speak with a nasal snuffling tone, whine *18-*, now local *NE-SW.*   **3** *vi* cringe, act sycophantically or insincerely *la18-*.
n **1** *in pl* a severe cold in the nose, causing difficulty in breathing *19-*, now *Ork N, C.*   **2** a nasal intonation, twang; a snuffle in one's speech *19-*.

sneg &c *18-e20*, **snig** *vt, also fig* cut (**off**) with a sharp instrument, snip, chop *18-*.
~ **off at the web('s) end** cut off someone's hopes *18*.   [only Sc; voiced var of SNECK²]

sneir [*snir] *vi* sail *la16*.   [only Sc; perh OE *snyrian, snyrgan* hasten]

sneising &c, **snising** &c *n* = sneezing, snuff *17*.   [cf SNEESHIN.   OED *sneezing*]

sneist &c; **snist** *19-20* [snist, snɪst, snəist] *vi* behave in a contemptuous arrogant way, be scornful or supercilious *18-e20*.
n a taunt, jibe, air of disdain, impertinence *19-e20*.
~**er** laugh in a suppressed way, snigger *19-*, now *Sh.*   ~**y** cheeky, sneering, uncivil, tart *19-*, now *Rox.*   [only Sc; see SND]

sneith [*sniθ] *adj, also fig* smooth, polished *16-e19*.   [only Sc; obscure]

snell &c *adj* **1** quick, nimble, active, clever, sharp, smart *la16-e19*.   **2** severe in manner or speech, tart, sarcastic *la16-*, now *Sh NE Ags.*   **3** *of weather* biting, bitter, severe *la14-*.   **4** *of a blow, fortune etc* hard, severe, harsh *18-*, now *Abd WC.*   **5** sharp to the taste or smell, pungent, acrid *la18-*, now *Bnf.*   **6** sharp to the ear, clear-sounding, shrill *19-e20*.
adv **1** quickly, keenly, eagerly *18-e20*.   **2** harshly, unfeelingly, vigorously *15-e20*.   **3** *of winds* keenly, piercingly, with a nip *18-*.   [nME, OE]

sneuter ['snjutər] *n* a slow, unskilful, stupid person *la20-, NE.*   [see SND]

snevil *see* SNEEVIL
snew *see* SNAW

sneyster &c ['snəistər] *vt* burn, scorch, roast; cauterize *19-e20*.
n a piece of grilled meat, a roasted joint; a pork sausage for grilling *19*.   [only Sc; obscure]

snib &c *vt* **1** check, restrain, reprove, punish *15-19*. **2** shut **in**; catch in a trap *la18-19, only Sc*. **3** fasten (a door etc) with a catch *19-, only Sc*. **4** cut (short or off), slice, cut into *la18-, now local Sh-Ayr, only Sc*.
n **1** a check, rebuke, rebuff, calamity, reverse *la18-e19*. **2** a catch, small bolt for a door etc *19-*. **3** a short steep hill or ascent *la20-, Per Stlg Ayr, only Sc*. **4** *slang* a sixpence *e20, N, only Sc*.
~**bit &c** cut short, curtailed, trimmed; *of hair* cropped very close *la19-, now Mry, only Sc*.
~**ble** *mining* a bar of wood or iron used as a brake or drag on a waggon etc *la18-, now local Fif-Ayr*. [see SND]
snicher &c; snichter ['snɪxər, 'snɪxtər] *vi* snigger, laugh in a suppressed way *19-*.
n a snigger, titter *la19-*. [only Sc; onomat; *cf* NICHER]
snick *see* SNECK[1], SNECK[3]
sniffle &c *vi* **1** = sniffle. **2** be slow in motion or action, loiter *19-, now Bnf Abd, only Sc*.
n = sniffle.
~**r** a strong gusty wind; *fig* a difficult business *la18-19, only Sc*. **snifflin &c** slow, sluggish, lazy, procrastinating, frivolous *la16-, Bnf Abd, only Sc*.
snift *vi* puff, snort, blow *la19-e20*.
~**y** *only Sc, n* an insignificant person *la17*. *adj* haughty, disdainful *20-, sEC Wgt Rox*. [prob reduced f next]
snifter &c *vi* **1** sniff; snivel, snuffle (*eg* with a cold); snort, snore *18-*. **2** *of wind* blow in strong gusts; *of vapour etc* escape in clouds *20-, now Sh, only Sc*.
n **1** a (noisy) sniff, from a cold, grief, disdain etc, a snivel, whimper, snigger *19-, only Sc*. **2** *chf* **the ~s** a (severe) head cold, catarrh, stuffed nose *19-, only Sc*. **3** a strong blast, gust, flurry (of wind, sleet etc) *18-, now local Sh-Loth*. **4** a shock, reverse, rebuff, quarrel *19-, now Rox*. [see SND]
snig &c *n* a sharp jerk, sudden pull *20-, Cai*.
vt pull sharply, jerk *20-, now Cai*. [only Sc; onomat; *cf* Eng *nick, snick*]
snig *see* SNEG
snigger *vti* catch (salmon) illegally by dragging a cluster of weighted hooks along the river bed; fish (a pool) by this method *la19-, Gen except Sh Ork*.
n the grappling implement used in *sniggering, 20-, Cai NE*. [var of Eng *sniggle*]
snip &c *vt* = snip.
~**pin &c** nipping, biting cold *16-19, only Sc*.
~**pit 1** quick in speech, tart *la19-, local Ork-Loth, only Sc*. **2** niggardly, giving short measure *la19-, now Sh N Slk, only Sc*. **3** *of a horse* with a white patch on the face *17-, now Abd*. ~**py** = snippit 1, *la19-, now Fif Loth*.
~ **white** bright, dazzling *e19, only Sc*.
go *or* **rin ~s** go shares, divide profits equally *la17-e20*.

snipe[1] *n* **1** = snipe, the bird. **2** contemptuous term for a person *la19-*.
snipie *only Sc* **1** *also* **snippy** a kettle or teapot *la19-e20*. **2** a variety of the game of marbles *20-, Stlg Fif*. [see SND]
snipe[2] **&c** *n* **1** a smart blow *18-, now Rox*. **2** a setback, a loss by being cheated, a let-down, fraud, cheat *la19-, Bnf Abd*.
vt **1** strike smartly *19-, now Rox*. **2** cheat, defraud, bring loss on *la19-, Bnf Abd*. [appar emphatic alteration of SNIP, perh w infl f SNIPE[1]]
snippy *see* SNIPE[1]
snirk &c *vi* snort, wrinkle the nose, snigger *20-, now Dmf*.
n a snort, snigger *20-, Sh Dmf Rox*.
~**et** *of a face* pinched, wizened, puckered *20-, Sh Rox*. [only Sc; Norw dial *snerka* shrivel, shrink in, become puckered, Faeroese, ON *snerkja* wrinkle, screw up one's face]
snirl *vi* snigger, laugh in a suppressed way *19-, Rox*.
~**y** a gusty biting wind *la20-, Sh SW*. [only Sc; altered f Eng *snarl*]
snirl *see* SNORL
snirt *vi* **1** snigger, make a noise through the nose when trying to stifle laughter, sneer *18-*. **2** snort, breathe sharply and jerkily through the nose *19-e20*.
n **1** a snigger, suppressed laugh *19-, now local Stlg-Rox*. **2** a snort *la18-e20, only Sc*. **3** a small insignificant person *19-, now Loth Rox, only Sc*. **snirtle** = *v* (*la18-e20*), *n* 1 and 2 (*e19*). [see SND]
snish *see* SNEESH
snishin(g) *see* SNEESHIN
snising *see* SNEISING
snist *see* SNEIST
snitcher *n, in pl* handcuffs *la19-, now local Mry-SW*. [only Sc; Eng *snitch* catch with a noose or loop]
snite[1] **&c; sneet &c** *la19-20* [snəit; *Sh Ork NE* snit] *vt* **1** blow (one's nose), *esp* with the finger and thumb, wipe (mucus) from the nose *la16-, now Sh Ork NE*. **2** *freq* ~ **someone's niz &c** tweak someone's nose; *fig* take someone down a peg; taunt someone *19-, now SW, only Sc*. **3** strike off (the burnt tip of a candle), snuff *19-, now Bnf*. **4** strike, hit, deliver a blow at *19-, now Rox*.
n, only Sc **1** a blowing or wiping of the nose *19-, now Sh NE*. **2** a sharp blow, *esp* on the nose *19-e20*. [ME *snyten* = *v* 1 and 3, OE *snȳten*, ON *snȳta*]
snite[2] *n, esp contemptuous or abusive* a worthless person, a small insignificant person or thing *17-, now Sh Bnf Abd*. [only Sc; perh f Eng *snite* the snipe or f SNITE[1]]
snite *see* SNUIT
snitter &c *vi* laugh in a suppressed way, giggle, snigger *19-, now Ayr S*. [prob onomat, w infl f SNIRT; *cf* SNEETER]
snivel *see* SNEEVIL

snivie *see* SNUVE

snob *see* SNAB[1]

snocher *la18*-; **snocker &c** *18-19* ['snoxər, 'snokər] *vi* snort, breathe heavily and noisily through the nose, snuffle *18*-, *now NE nEC*.
n **1** a snort, snore, the act of breathing heavily through the nose *19*-, *now NE nEC*. **2 the ~s** a severe nose cold, causing blockage of the nostrils *19*-, *now NE nEC*. [only Sc; onomat; cf *clocher* (CLOCH)]

snochter &c ['snoxtər; *Wgt* 'snoixtər] *n* nasal mucus, phlegm blown from the nose *la20*-, *Abd WC, SW*.
~-dichter a handkerchief *la20*-, *WC, SW*. [only Sc; onomat; prob conflation of SNOCHER w *snotter* (SNOT)]

snock *see* SNOKE

snocker *see* SNOCHER

snod *adj* **1** smooth, level, evenly cut *la15*-, *now local Ork-Kcb*. **2** *esp of persons* neat, trim, spruce, smart *18*-. **3** *of things* neat, tidy, compact, well laid out, in good order *18*-, *now Ork N Per*. **4** comfortable, snug, at ease *la18*-, *now N-SW*.
vt **1** make trim or neat, tidy, put in order *la19*-, *now NE-SW*. **2** prune, cut, trim, smooth, make level *la18*-, *now local NE-SW*. **3** put to rights morally, put (someone) in his place, punish, defeat *la19*, *only Sc*.
~(die)-up a tidying, smartening *la19*-, *now NE, SW, only Sc*. [see SND]

snoddie *n* a stupid person *19*-, *Rox*. [only Sc; var of Eng *noddy*]

snodge *vi* walk deliberately or steadily *19*-, *Pbls Rox*. [only Sc; perh onomat]

snog *see* SNUG

snoif *see* SNUVE

snoit *vi*, *chf* **~er** breathe loudly through the nose, snore; snooze *19*-, *now Ags*. [only Sc; see SND]

snoke &c *18*-; **snock &c** *16-19*, **snook &c** *18*-, **snowk** *la18*- [snok, snuk, snʌuk] *vti* **1** sniff, smell, scent out (as a dog), snuff, poke with the nose *16*-, *now nEC, WC, SW*. **2** *vi* snort, snigger *la19-20*. **3** hunt, nose one's way, prowl, go about furtively *la18*-, *now local Sh-SW*.
n a smell(ing), sniff *la18*-, *now Stlg WC, SW, only Sc*. [see SND]

snoke *see* SNUKE

snood *see* SNUID

snook *see* SNOKE

snool *see* SNUIL

snoot *see* SNOUT

snoove *see* SNUVE

snoozle *vi* **1** snooze, doze *la19*-, *now Abd Ags*. **2** nuzzle, poke with the nose; snuggle *la19*-, *now Lnk Ayr*. [frequentative of Eng *snooze*; in 2, conflated w Eng *nuzzle*]

snore &c *vi* **1** = snore. **2** *of animals* snort *la18*-, *now Kcb*. **3** *esp of wind, fire etc* make a rushing,

whirring, droning sound *19*-, *now local Sh-Kcb*. **4** move at speed with a rushing, roaring sound *19*-, *now local Sh-Kcb*.
n **1** a snort, roar, loud roaring or droning noise *e16*, *19*-, *now Sh Cai*. **2** *in pl* an animal disease causing snuffling, the snivels *la16*, *19*.

snork &c *vi* **1** snort, snore, snuffle *19*-, *WC-S*. **2** *of things* make a roaring or explosive sound *19-e20*, *S*.

snorl &c *19*-; **snurl &c** *18-e20*, **snirl** *20* [snorl, snʌrl; *Sh Ork Uls also* snɪrl] *n* **1** a knot, tangle, kink or twist in a thread, rope etc, a mix-up *19*-, *now Sh N, SW*. **2** a predicament, scrape, muddle, confusion *19*-, *now Sh Cai NE*.
vti, *lit and fig* ruffle, wrinkle, twist, tangle *18*-, *now local Sh-Kcb*.
~y &c twisted, tangled, knotted *19-20*. [var of SNARL]

snort *n* a tangle *19*-, *now Kcdn*. [only Sc; perh conflation of SNORL w Eng *knot*; cf Northumb dial *snot-snarl* a ravelled skein]

snosh &c *adj* chubby and contented *19*. [? conflation of SNOD or Eng *snug* and COSH]

snot *n* **1** = snot. **2** the snuff or burnt wick of a candle *19*-, *now Bnf*. **3** a contemptible, worthless, or stupid person *19*-, *now local Ags-Rox*.
v **1** *vr* blow or clear the nose *la17*. **2** *vt* snub, reprove *la19*-, *now local Inv-Rox*.
~ter *n* **1** *chf in pl* nasal mucus, *esp* when hanging from the nose *la17*-, *Gen except Sh Ork*. **2** = SNOT *n* 2, *18*-, *now NE Kcb*. **3** the red membraneous part of a turkey-cock's beak *19*-, *now Cai Per Fif*. **4** = SNOT *n* 3, *la18*-, *now Cai*. **5** a snub, rebuke *la19*-, *now nEC, SW, S, only Sc*. *vi* **1** snuffle, snort, breathe heavily through the nose *18*-, *now Ags*. **2** snivel, weep noisily, blubber *19*-, *now WC Kcb*. **3** snooze, doze *18-20*, *only Sc*. **~ter box** *only Sc* **1** the nose *la18-20*. **2** a soft, stupid, untidy person *la19-e20*. **~ter-dichter** a handkerchief *la20*-, *Gen except Sh Ork, only Sc*. **~tery &c** **1** slimy, running at the nose *19*-, *only Sc*. **2** tearful, lugubrious *20*-, *WC Kcb*. **3** surly, brusque, snooty *la20*-, *nEC, WC, SW*. **~ty** short-tempered, curt, huffy *la19*-, *Gen except Sh Ork*.

snout *la16*-; **snowt** *la15-e18*, **snoot** *la18-20* [snut] *n* **1** = snout *la15*-. **2** *contemptuous* the nose *16*-. **3** *contemptuous* the face, head *18-20*. **4** the peak (of a cap) *la18*-. **5** a projecting point of land etc *la16-19*. **6** *slang* a detective, policeman *20*-, *local Abd-Wgt, only Sc*.
~it *of a cap* peaked *la18-20*, *only Sc*.

snow *see* SNAW

Snowdon [*'snɑdən] **~ (herald)** one of the Scottish heralds *15-19*. [appar the name of part of the hill on which Stirling Castle is built]

snowk *see* SNOKE

snowt *see* SNOUT

snubbert &c *n* **1** *joc or contemptuous* the nose *19-20*, *NE*. **2** the red membraneous part of a turkey-cock's beak *la20*, *NE*. [only Sc; deriv of Eng *snub*]

snuff[1] **&c** *vti* = snuff, sniff, clear (the nose) *la17-*.

n **1** a persistent snuffling; a disease in sheep *la16*. **2** = snuff, a sniff.

snuff[2] **&c** *n* **1** = snuff, the powdered tobacco *la17-*. **2** a pinch of snuff *18-*, *Gen except Sh Ork*, *only Sc*. **3** a very small amount (**of** something), something of little significance or value *19-*.

vi take snuff *18-*.

interj = stuff!, nonsense! *18-19*, *only Sc*.

snuffing the taking of snuff, *specif* as part of the *Common Riding* (COMMON) ceremony in Hawick *20-*, *Rox*. ~**y hanky** a handkerchief for use after taking snuff *20-*, *now Per Kcb*, *only Sc*.

~ **horn** a snuffbox, *specif* one made from a horn tip *19-*, *now Sh Ags Per*, *only Sc*. ~**mill** *la17-*, ~**mull** *19-* a snuffbox, *only Sc*. ~ **pen** a small quill or spoon for taking snuff *19*, *only Sc*. [*cf* SNEESH and SNEESHIN]

snuff[3] *n* a rage, huff *19*.

~**y** sulky, touchy, huffily displeased *19-*, *now local*. [Eng *snuff* the ash of a burnt candlewick]

snug[1] **&c** *18-*, **snog &c** *e16*, *20 adj* **1** smooth, sleek, close-cropped *16-*, *now Sh Ork*. **2** neat, trim, tidy *18-*, *now Ork Cai*. **3** = snug.

snug[2] **&c** *vt*, *of cattle* strike, push, try to prod with the horns *19-*, *now Sh*. [only Sc; *cf* Norw dial *snugga*, *snoga* push, shove]

snuid &c; snood *17-*; **sneed &c** *19-*, *NE* [snød; snɪd; snud; *NE* snid] *n* **1** = snood, *specif* a ribbon etc bound round the brow and tied at the back under the hair, worn *esp* by young unmarried women; *fig* a symbol of virginity *16-*. **2** *fishing* the hemp part of a sea-line to which the hook is attached; the twisted loop of horsehair by which the hook is sometimes attached to this, the *tippin* (TIP[1]) *la16-*, *now N-WC*.

vt **1** bind (one's hair) with a band *18-*, *latterly hist*. **2** *fishing* tie (the short hair line) to the hook *la19-*, *now EC*.

snuil &c *19-*; **snool &c** *18-e20*, **sneel** *19*, *NE* [snøl; snɪl; snul; *NE* snil] *n* a spiritless, cringing, abject or cowardly person; a lazy, inactive person *18-*, *now Sh Ags*.

v **1** *vt* subdue, keep in subjection, humiliate, reprove, snub *18-*, *now Ork*, *only Sc*. **2** *vi* submit tamely, cringe, act meanly, deceitfully or spiritlessly *la18-e20*. **3** show lack of energy, loaf about shiftlessly, move slowly and lethargically *19-e20*, *only Sc*. [see SND]

snuit; snite &c *la19-*, *NE* [snøt; *NE* snit, snəit] *vi* move about or work in a lazy, careless or stupefied way, laze about, be listless, be at a loose end *19-*, *now Abd*. [only Sc; see SND]

snuivie *see* SNUVE

snuke &c *la14-15*; **snoke** *la13* [*snøk, *snjuk] *n* a promontory. [obscure; *cf* Eng *nook*. OED *snook* (*n*[1])]

snurkle *vi*, *of hard-twisted thread* tangle, run into knots *19-*, *S*. [only Sc; see SND]

snurl *see* SNORL

snuve &c *19-*, **snoove** *18-e20*; **snoif** *e16* [snuv; *Bwk Rox* snøv] *vti* **1** twist, twirl, spin, make yarn *16-e20*. **2** *vi* move smoothly or easily, at a steady, even pace, glide *18-e20*. **3** move carelessly, lazily or abjectly, slink, sneak, idle *la18-*, *now Rox*.

sn(u)ivie a layabout; an abject or cringing person; a dull-witted person *19-*, *chf Rox*. [only Sc; see SND]

snyauve *see* SNAW

snyster ['snəistər] *n*, *esp in pl* sweets, cakes, dainties *19-*, *now WC*. [only Sc; altered f SNASHTER, perh by conflation w Eng *spice* or confusion w SNEYSTER]

so *see* SAE[2]

soach *see* SOUCH

soad *see* SOD

soam &c *16-*; **soyme** *la14*, **soum &c** *16-e18* [som; *saum] *n*, *pl also* **sommys** *la15* a chain or rope attaching a draught-ox or -horse to a plough etc *la14-*, *now local Kcdn-Kcb*.

soap *see* SAIP

sob *see* SAB[1]

sober &c *adj* **1** = sober *la14-*. **2** poor, mean, paltry, miserable *la16-*, *now NE*. **3** moderate or few in number *16*. **4** of low degree; humble *16*, *only Sc*. **5** small, slightly-built *la19-*, *NE*. **6** in poor or only moderate health, sickly, weak *19-*, *now NE Ags Per*.

socher &c [*'saxər, *'soxər] *vi* pamper oneself, be fussy about one's health *19-20*.

saughrin &c lacking in energy, sluggish, soft and flaccid in character or action *la18-19*. [by conflation of Gael *socair* (*n*, *adj*) calm, ease, quiet, with *sochar* softness, compliance, indulgence]

socht *see* SEEK[1]

social &c *adj* **1** capable of being associated or united **to** *la16*, *only Sc*. **2** = social.

~**ly &c** **1** in company *e16*, *only Sc*. **2** = socially.

society &c *n* **1** = society *la16-*. **2** *in pl and as* **S~-Men** *etc* name for certain groups of Presbyterians who refused to recognize the 1679 Indulgence and 1688 Revolution Settlement, and who later united to form what is now the *Reformed Presbyterian Church* (REFORM), CAMERONIANS 1, *18-*, *now hist*.

sock[1] **&c** *n* a ploughshare *16-*.

~ **spade** a spade for removing stones which might obstruct the SOCK[1] *la20-*, *Fif Loth WC*. ~ **and scythe** ploughing and mowing *la16-e19*. [nME *sokk*, OF *soc*]

sock[2] *vti* = soak *la18-19*.

socket *vi*, *golf* hit the ball in the angle between the head and the shaft of the club *20-*.

sod &c; soad *19-* *n* **1** = sod. **2** *specif* a piece of surface turf used as fuel *19-*, *local Ork-Rox*. **3** *chf in pl*, *orig* pieces of turf used as a saddle; *hence* a rough cloth saddle stuffed with straw *la16-e19*. **4** a kind of bread, a roll made of coarse flour *la18-e20*.

soadie &c a big stout woman, a slut *20-*, *now Stlg*.

sod *see* SAD

sodand, soddane *see* SUDDENT

sodden &c *adj* **1** = sodden. **2** boiled, cooked by boiling *la15-19*.

sodger &c *la16-*, **soldier &c** *n* **1** = soldier *la14-*. **2** (1) *chf in pl* the stems and flower-heads of the plantain, *esp* the ribwort plantain *la19-*, *now local*. (2) *in pl* a game played with these *la19-20*. **3** name for various small reddish-coloured creatures: (1) a ladybird *19-*, *now local Inv-Dmf*; (2) the red-breasted minnow *20-*, *now Abd Lnk Ayr*. **4** *in pl* small sparks, *eg* on the edge of burning paper; smuts of burning soot *la19-*, *now local Inv-Dmf*. **5** a native of Ceres, Fife *20-*, *Fif*. **6** a wounded or injured child or animal *la20-*, *local Abd-Dmf*. **7** *tech* a packing piece or plug, used *eg* to fill a bolt-hole *la20-*, *now Loth Ayr*.
vi **1** = soldier *19-*. **2** march in a stolid, dogged way, trudge *la20-*, *local NE-Wgt*.
red ~ = *n* **3** (1), *la20-*, *Abd Fif Kcb*. **~-clad but major-minded** *usu complimentary* having a strong sense of pride and self-respect in spite of a humble position *20-*, *now Abd Ags Stlg*. **sunny** ~ the red wild bee *la20-*, *Stlg Fif WC*.

sodie &c *n* = soda *19-*, *now Ork Per*.
~ **heid** a featherbrain, flibbertigibbet *la20-*, *local*.

soft *see* SAFT

sog *v*, *chf in ptp* ~**git** soaked *la20-*, *NE*. [prob same as eModEng, ModEng dial *sog* a wet place, *soggy* wet; prob Scand]

soilie *see* SOILZIE

soilȝe [*'sɔɪljɪ, *'søljɪ] *vt* = soil, answer (a question) *e16*. [only Sc. OED *soil* (*v*²)]

soilzie *e17*, **sulȝe &c** *15-16*, **soilie** *e15* [*'sɔɪl(j)ɪ, *'søljɪ, *'sʌljɪ] *n* = soil, land. [only Sc. OED *sulye*]

soir &c [*sɔr] *adj* **1** *falconry* = sore, applied to a young bird of prey still with red plumage *e16*. **2** *also* **sorre** *la17*, *of a horse* of a sorrel colour *la15-17*.
sorit = *adj* 2, *la16*, *e19*. [OED *sore* (*adj*²)]

soirée *see* SUREE

soit *see* SUIT¹

sojourn &c; sudiorne &c *la14-16*, *only Sc* [*'sʌdʒərn] *n* **1** = sojourn *la14-*. **2** a digression *e16*.
vt = sojourn *la14-*.

solan &c *la15-*; **soland &c** *la16-18* ['solən] *n*, *also* ~ **goose** the gannet. [orig Sc; ON *súla*; second element poss ON *ǫnd, and-* a duck]

solar *adj* of the sun *la15-*. [earlier in Sc]

solatium [sɔ'leʃɪʌm] *n*, *law* damages for injury to feelings or for pain and suffering *19-*.

sold *see* SOWD¹

solder *see* SOWTHER

soldier *see* SODGER

sole &c *n* **1** = sole *la16-*. **2** the lower part, bottom or base of something, *specif*: (1) the flat bottom of a golf club *la19-*; (2) the smooth under-surface of a *curling-stone* (CURL) *19-*; (3) the lower crust of a loaf of bread *18-*, *now local Cai-Ayr*; (4) the bottom rope of a fishing net *la19-*, *now Sh Wgt*; (5) a flat plate under a gravy boat, cheese-dish etc *18-*, *NE*; (6) the bell-end of a bagpipe *chanter* (CHANT) *la20-*; (7) the sub-soil; the under-surface of land *la17-e20*; (8) the sward or surface vegetation of a pasture *20-*, *local N-Gall*. **3** a sill, a supporting or strengthening beam, *esp* in a window or door-case *16-*.
vt **1** = sole *la17-*. **2** throw (a *curling-stone* (CURL)) so that it lands smoothly on the ice *20-*.
~ **clout** the iron shoe covering the sole of a plough *19-*, *now Kcb*. ~ **raip** = *n* **2** (4), *la19-*, *now local Sh-Ayr*. ~ **shaif** the end slice of a loaf, the HEEL *la20-*, *local Cai-Ayr*. ~ **tree** a horizontal beam of wood, *usu* on the ground, which supports posts, *specif* that forming the manger on the floor of a BYRE *18-*, *now Sh Per*.

solemn &c *adj* **1** = solemn *la16-*. **2** famous, renowned *la16*.
solem(p)niouslie &c solemnly *la16*, *e20*, *only Sc*. **solem(p)nit &c** *la14-16*, **solempt** *15-e16*, **solennit** *la16* solemn *only Sc*.

solicit¹ &c; solist &c *adj* **1** characterized by solicitude or care *16-e17*. **2** solicitous; anxious; careful *16-e17*. [chf Sc; L *sollicitus*]

solicit²; solist *la15-17* *vti* = solicit *la15-*.
solistation &c = solicitation *la15-e17*, *only Sc*.
solistar &c = soliciter, a person who manages affairs for another *16*. **solicitor** *n*, *law* = solicitor *formally 20-*, *informally 18-*; *cf* AGENT, *writer* (WRITE). **Solicitor General (for Scotland)** a senior ADVOCATE who as a member of the government is the deputy and chief assistant of the *Lord Advocate* (LORD) *19-*. **The King's** *or* **His Majesty's Solicitor** = *Solicitor General*, *e18*. **Solicitor in** *etc* **the Supreme Court(s) (of Scotland), S.S.C.** a member of an incorporated society of solicitors practising in Edinburgh *la18-*.

solid; solit &c *la19-*, *now Bwk Ayr* *adj* **1** = solid *la16-*. **2** sane; in full possession of one's mental faculties *17-*, *now Ags*. **3** *of persons* having a large supply, well-stocked **with**; *of things* in large supply, plentiful *la20-*, *Sh Bnf Ags*.

solist *see* SOLICIT¹, SOLICIT²

solit *see* SOLID

solitare &c [*'solɪtər] *adj* = solitaire, solitary *la15-e17*.

soll *vt* make foul, defile *la14*. [prob OE *solian* become foul; *cf* MDu, MLowGer *solen*]

solomonical *la16*; **salamonicall** *e16* *adj* characteristic of Solomon *only Sc*.

solp *see* SOWP³

solum *n*, *orig law* soil or ground, *specif* the ground on which a building stands *18-*. [L]

solvendie &c [səl'vɛndɪ, *&c*] *adj* **1** *also*

solvendo solvent *17-e19*. **2** *also* **salvendo &c** *e20* (1) *of things* firm, safe, adequate, sure *19-*, *now Kcdn*. (2) *of persons* strong, in good health, fit *20*. [L *solvendo esse* be solvent]

some &c; sum &c *pronoun* = some *la14-*. *adj* **1** = some *la14-*. **2** *qualifying a sing noun* (1) a certain *la16*: '*sum godlie man*'; (2) large, considerable *20-*, *Ags*: '*a some hack on my thoomb*'. *adv* **1** *modifying adjs* somewhat, a little; very, a great deal *la16-*. **2** *modifying verbs* to some extent, rather, a little *la18-*, *now local Sh-Per*. **all and summyn(g)** = all and some *e16*, *only Sc*.

somebit somewhere *20-*, *WC-S*. **~deal &c** *adv, n* a good deal *la14-19*. **~gate &c 1** somewhere *19-*, *now local Kcdn-Slk*. **2** somehow, in some way *19-*, *now local Mry-WC*. **~ part &c** *only Sc* **1** somewhat *la14-e17*. **2** somewhere *20-*, *now C*. **someplace** somewhere *la18-*. **~thing** *n* = something *la15-*. *adv* somewhat, a little *la16-*, *now Ayr*. **someway &c 1** somehow *19-*. **2** somewhere *19-*, *now Sh NE*. **and some** and more so *la18-*, *now Bnf Ags*. **~ .., othir ~ ..:** some .., others .. *la14-16*. **some idder een** someone else *20-*, *Sh Ork NE*. **some ither wey** somewhere else *la19-*, *now NE*.

-some &c *suffix* **1** = -some, forming adjs, more productive in Sc, *eg* **eeriesome** (EERIE), **waesome** (WAE¹). **2** after cardinal numbers to denote a group, team etc of that number, *now freq* used in country-dancing and golf *la15-*; for examples see the numbers.

somir *see* SIMMER¹

somler; summeleir [*'sʌmlər] *n* a butler *la16*. [chf Sc; OF *sommelier*]

sommair *see* SUMMAR

sommys *see* SOAM

somond *see* SUMMON

son *see* SIN¹

sonce *see* SONSE

Sonda *see* SUNDAY

sone *see* SUN, SUNE

song *see* SANG¹

sonk *see* SUNK

sonkin *see* SINK

sonnet &c *n* **1** = sonnet *la16-*. **2** a song, ditty *la18-*, *now Bnf Ags Per*. **3** a tale, yarn, a (tall) story, nonsense *la19-*, *now Abd Ags*. **4** a fuss, to-do *la19-*, *Ags*.

sonse &c; sonce &c *16-20* [sons] *n* abundance, plenty; prosperity, good fortune *14-20*. **sonsie &c 1** bringing good fortune; lucky *16-20*. **2** friendly, hearty, jolly; good, honest: (1) *freq as a general term of approbation*, *18-*, *now local Sh-Gall*; (2) *of the appearance*, looks, face, *la18-*, *now local Sh-Kcb*. **3** *esp of women* comely, attractive; *freq of the figure* buxom, plump; *of young children* chubby, sturdy *18-*. **4** *of things or personifications* (1) fine, handsome, impressive;

pleasant, cheery *la18-e19*; (2) big, roomy, substantial *18-20*. **5** sensible, shrewd *la17-e18*. **6** *of animals* tractable, manageable *la18-19*. **~ fa ye** *or* **on ye** *etc* may you etc have good fortune, bless you etc *18-20*. [only Sc; Gael *sonas* good luck, prosperity]

sonyie &c; sonȝe &c, sunȝie [*'sʌnjɪ] *n* **1** an excuse; a plea *15-17*. **2** hesitation; delay *la15-e16*. *vir* hesitate, delay, refuse *la15-16*. [only Sc; var of chf nME *soign*, OF *soigne*]

soo¹ &c *la19-*, **sow** [su] *n* **1** = sow *la14-*. **2** *in gen* a pig *la18-e20*. **3** a ridge-shaped mass, *eg* a large oblong stack of hay (*la17-*) or straw (*la20-*), *Gen except Sh Ork*. **4** the small ball or puck used in SHINTY *19*. **5** the ballan wrasse *20-*, *now Bnf Kcdn*. **sooie** a lump of dough trimmed off the edges of an *oatcake* (AIT) before baking *e20*, *NE*. **~('s) back &c 1** (1) a ridge or natural hump *19-e20*. (2) *specif mining* a ridge in the roof or pavement of a coalworking *la19-*, *now Fif Lnk Ayr*. **2** *also* **~-back(it) mutch** a woman's cap with a ridge from back to front *19-e20*. **~('s) cruive &c, ~('s) crave &c** a pigsty *la19-*, *now Ork C, S*. **~ kiln &c** an old type of mound-shaped limekiln *la18-19*. **sow-libber** a sow-gelder *la17*, *only Sc*. **~'s lug 1** one of the mould-boards of a drill- or double-breasted plough *20-*, *NE Ags Fif*. **2** *in soldering* an overlap of lead to strengthen a joint at a corner *la20-*, *now Inv*. **3** a similarly overlapped corner of paper, as in grocers' packages *la20-*, *now Inv*. **~-luggit &c** *of animals* having long, loose-hanging ears *18-*, *now Per*. **~-mouthed &c** *of animals* having a projecting upper jaw *la20-*, *NE*, *C*. **~ stack** = *n* 3, *20-*, *now Fif Kcb*. **~'s tail** a wrongly-tied knot *la19-*, *Ork Per*. **~'s tail tae ye** *etc* expression of defiance or derision *18-e20*. **~'s troch** a pig's trough *20-*, *local Sh-Per*.

soo² &c *19-*, **sow** *la14-e19* [su] *v* **1** *vt* inflict pain on *la14*. **2** *vi* ache; throb, tingle with pain, etc *la14-*, *now Lnk Ayr Dmf*. [nME *sow*]

soo³ &c *vi, of wind* breathe, murmur, sigh *la19-*, *now Sh*. [reduced f SOUCH]

sooans *see* SOWANS

sook *see* SOUK

sookan &c *n* a one-ply rope of straw etc, used *chf* for binding straw, thatching ricks etc *la19-*, *Ork Dnbt Bute*. [only Sc; Gael *sùgan* a hay- or straw-rope]

sool *see* SWEEL³

soom¹ &c *la16-*, *Gen except Sh Ork*, **swim &c**, **sweem &c** *la14-*, *now Ork NE Per*; **swome** *la14-19*, **swoom &c** *la16-19* vti, pt *also* ~ed &c *la16-*, *now NE*. ptp *also* ~ed &c *16-*, *now Sh Ags* = swim *la14-*. *n* an extremely wet state, a flood, *freq* **in a ~** *la19-*, *local Sh-Ags*. **be swimming full of** abound with (fish) *la16*.

soom[2] **&c** *n* the swimming- or air-bladder of a fish *la18-20*. [altered f SOUND[4] w infl f SOOM[1]]

soomans *see* SUMMON

soon *see* SUNE

soop *see* SWEEP

soople &c *17-20*; **supple &c** *18-e20 n* 1 = swipple, the part of a flail which beats the grain *17-20*. 2 a cudgel, a stout stick *e19*.

soorldab &c [surl'dab] *n, freq* **gie someone** *or* **something his** *or* **its** ~ put paid to, finish off, spoil *la20-, local C*. [see SND]

soosh &c *v* 1 *vt* beat, punish severely; deal rigorously with *19-e20*. 2 taunt, upbraid *e19, Ayr*. 3 *vti* swill, splash, wash over *la19-, NE*. [only Sc; onomat, perh w infl f Eng *swish* and *souse*]

soosler &c ['suslər, 'suʃ-] *n* a thin fish, *esp* a cod, in poor condition *20-, Cai*. [obscure]

soot *see* SUIT[2]

sooth *see* SUITH

soother ['suðər] *vt* 1 soothe, calm *la19-20*. 2 coax, cajole, flatter *la19-20, chf Arg Uls*. [frequentative of Eng *soothe*; appar Anglo-Ir]

sooze &c *vi* smoulder with a hissing sound *20-, now Bnf*. [onomat]

sop[1] *n* 1 = sop, a troop (of soldiers) *la14-e16*. 2 a cloud **of** (mist or smoke) *e16, only Sc*.

sop[2] *n* sap *16*. [*cf* MDu, WFris *sop*]

sop *see* SAP[2]

sophistic *adj* 1 sophistical, given to sophistry *e16*. 2 engaged in speculation *e16, only Sc*. [*cf* Eng = of sophistry or sophists]

sopit &c [*'sopɪt] *adj* rendered dull or sluggish; sunk **in** (sleep, sorrow etc) *e16*. [only Sc; appar L *sōpīt-, ptp* stem of *sōpīre* (*cf* next]

sopite; sopit [so'pəɪt; *'sopɪt] *vt, ptp* **sopit(e)** *chf law* settle, adjust, put an end to (a dispute etc) *la15-19*. [L *sōpīt-, ptp* stem of *sōpīre* put to sleep]

Sorbie *see* ROB

sore *see* SAIR

sorit *see* SOIR

sorn &c *v* 1 *vi* exact free board and lodging by force or threats, beg importunately, *freq* **thig and** ~ *la15-, now hist*. 2 (1) *vt* trouble or harass by exacting free board and lodging *la16*. (2) *vti, also* ~ **on** scrounge or sponge (on), abuse someone's hospitality, act as a parasite *la16-, now N Per*. (3) *vi* scrounge food, forage *19-, now Cai Ags*. 3 idle, loaf *e19*.

~**er &c**, *also* **soroner** *la17* a person who SORNS *15-, now N Per*. [only Sc; altered f *sorryn &c*, found in ScL texts *la13-14*, f obs IrGael *sorthan* free quarters]

sornie *n* the flue from the fireplace to the underside of the drying platform of a kiln; the fireplace itself *19-, Cai*. [only Sc; dim f Gael *sòrn* the flue of a kiln or oven]

soroner *see* SORN

sorp *vi* be soaked or drenched *19-, S*. [emphatic var of *sop* (SAP[1])]

sorple *vi* make a sucking noise when drinking *20, Dmf Rox*. [poss a conflation of *sirple* (SIPPLE) and SLORP]

sorra *19-*, **sorrow &c**; **sorry &c** *19-e20* ['sorə; *Sh Cai* -o; *sEC, S* -ɪ] *n* 1 = sorrow *la14-*. 2 (1) (**the**) Devil *18-, now local Sh-Wgt*. (2) a rascal, a troublesome child, a pest of a person *19-, now Sh N Per*. (3) *in phrs of malediction, exasperation etc, eg* ~ **fa ye** *etc*, (**a**) ~ **on ye** *etc, la18-, now Sh N*. (4) *as emphatic negative, freq* ~ **a** not a *la16-, now Sh N*. (5) *in impatient questions, eg* **what &c** (**the**) ~ (**way**), **where in** (**the**) ~ *17-, now Sh N*.

adj sad, sorry *19-, now Cai* [prob by confusion w Eng *sorry*].

~**fu &c** 1 = sorrowful *la14-*. 2 causing vexation, troublesome *19-, now Sh Cai Per*.

not have one's ~(**s**) **to seek** have plenty of trouble on one's hands *la19-, Sh N, C*. ~ **care** too bad!, bad luck! *la18-e20*.

sorre *see* SOIR

sorrow *see* SORRA

sorry *see* SAIRIE, SORRA

sort[1] *v* 1 *vt* = sort *16-*. 2 put in order, arrange, tidy **up**; tidy (oneself) *19-*. 3 (1) restore to proper or working order, repair, mend, fix **up**; heal *19-*. (2) *euphemistic* castrate *la20-, Sh NE*. 4 provide for, furnish or supply (**with** etc) *la18-20*. 5 (1) feed and litter (*esp* a horse) *19-, now N, C*. (2) attend to the wants of (a child or sick person) *la19-, now NE*. 6 deal with by rebuke or punishment, put (a person) in his place, scold *la18-*. 7 (1) bring together, pair, match *e19*. (2) *vi* come together, keep company, live in harmony (*with*) *la18-19*. (3) come to an agreement *la17-e19, only Sc*.

n 1 = sort, a kind (**of**) etc *16-*. 2 a considerable number, a fair amount (**of**) *19-20, S*. 3 a setting to rights, a repair, a tidying up *19-*.

of this ~ in this way *e16, only Sc*.

sort[2] *vi* sally out; make a sortie *la16*. [only Sc; F *sortir*]

sortition *n* 1 = sortition, the casting of lots. 2 an allotted share or portion *la17, only Sc*.

sosh[1] *adj* sociable, frank, open *la18-19*. [reduced f Eng *sociable*]

sosh[2] *n* a Co-operative Society shop *la19-, now Ags Fif*. [back-formation f Eng *society*]

soss[1] **&c** *n* 1 a mixture of food or drink, a wet, soggy mess of food *18-, now Sh N Per*. 2 a wet state, a sopping condition, a dirty wet mess *19-, now local Sh-Fif*. 3 a state of dirt and disorder, a muddle, confusion *la19-, Sh N nEC*. 4 a slattern, slut *20-, now Ags Per*.

v 1 *vi* eat incongruous, sloppy or messy food; eat in an uncouth, slovenly way *la18-e20*. 2 *vt* mix (*esp* liquids) in a messy, incongruous way *19-, now Sh Ags*. 3 make wet and dirty, make a mess of *20-, now Sh NE Ags*. 4 *vi* make a mess, work dirtily or in dirty conditions *la19-, N nEC*. 5 *vt* nurse over-tenderly, fuss over; pester *la19-, now Bnf.* **6** *vti, also* ~ **up,** ~ **about** cuddle *20-, now Abd.* **7** *vi* take one's ease, lie or remain idle *la19-, now Abd.* [see SND]

soss² **&c** *n* a thud, a heavy awkward fall, a heavy blow *18-20.*
vi fall or set **down** with a thud *la18-20.* [perh onomat; *cf* SOUSE¹]

sot¹ *n* **1** = sot. **2** a fool, simpleton, stupid person *la18-20.*

sot²; sut **&c** *adv, esp child's word, used to contradict a negative* on the contrary, far from it *la19-:* '*It is not. — It is sot.*' [alteration of *so* (SAE²) after Eng *not; cf* YO]

sotter **&c** *v* **1** *vi* boil, cook slowly, bubble or sputter in cooking *la18-, now local Ork-SW.* **2** sputter, crackle; come bubbling **out** *la19-e20.* **3** *vti* saturate, soak, wallow *19-, Bwk SW.* **4** work in a dirty unskilful way; handle in a disgusting way *la19-, local Sh-Per.* **5** *vi* idle, loaf, potter **about** *la19-e20, Bnf Ags Per.* **6** abound, swarm *20-, Rox.*
n **1** the noise made by something boiling, frying or bubbling up *19-, now Ags Kcb.* **2** a state of wetness *la19-, NE.* **3** a mess, muddle, confused mass, chaos *la19-, now local Sh-Per.* **4** a considerable number, *esp* of small creatures, a swarm *19-, Rox.*
in a ~**el** affected by a skin disease *e20, Abd.* [see SND]

sottle **&c** *vi* = SOTTER 1, *19-e20.*

souch **&c** *16-,* **sough** **&c** *18-;* **swo(u)ch** **&c** *la15-19,* **sugh** **&c** *la18-e20,* **seuch** **&c** *la19-e20,* **soach** **&c** *19-20* [sux, sʌx; *Sh Cai* sox; *S* sʌux, sjux, ʃux; *swux, *swʌx, *swox] *n* **1** the sound of the wind, *esp* when long-drawn-out *16-.* **2** the rushing, roaring or murmuring of water *la18-, now local Sh-Kcb.* **3** a rustling or whizzing sound, as of an object moving rapidly through the air; a whizzing blow *la18-, now local Sh-wLoth.* **4** (1) a deep sigh or gasp, heavy breathing, panting *la18-, local Sh-Gall.* (2) heavy breathing in sleep; a snooze *19-, now Kcb.* **5** a song, tune, melody *19-, now NE Ags.* **6** (1) the sound or timbre of a voice, an accent, way of speaking *la18-, now Abd Kcdn Lnk.* (2) *specif* a high-pitched, nasal way of speaking, a whine, *esp* in preaching *18-e20.* **7** general feeling or opinion, attitude, style *18-, now Ayr.* **8** gossip, rumour, scandal *19-, now NE-S.* **9** an uproar, fuss *la19-, local NE-Uls.*
v **1** *vi, of objects moving through the air* whizz, buzz, drone, flap, whirr *la15-, now local Sh-Kcb.* **2** *of leaves etc* rustle, whisper; *of water* ripple, gurgle, make a slapping sound *16-, now local Sh-Per.* **3** *of wind* make a rushing, moaning, murmuring sound *la18-.* **4** breathe heavily, sigh, wheeze, splutter, gurgle *18-, now Sh N Gall.* **5** ~ **awa** breathe one's last *la18-, now local Sh-Ayr.* **6** *vti* sing softly, hum, whistle *18-, now NE-Per.* **7** *vi, of music* sound, waft *19-, now Abd Ags.*
keep *etc* **a calm** *etc* ~ keep quiet, hold one's

tongue; *fig* keep calm or still *19-.* [ME *swow* &c (*n*), *swoʒen* (*v*), OE *swogan* (*v*) make a rushing sound]

soucht *see* SEEK¹

soucye [*'susɪ] *n* the marigold *e16.* [only Sc; OF *soucie,* L *solsequium; cf* ME, OF *solsecle.* OED *soucy*]

soud *see* SOUTH¹

souder *see* SOWTHER

souflet **&c** ['sʌflət, *'?suf-] *n* a stroke, a blow with the hand, a smack *19-e20, local Sh-Kcdn.* [only Sc; appar F *soufflet* a blow]

sough *see* SHEUCH, SOUCH

souk **&c, suck** **&c; sook** **&c** *19-* [suk] *vti* **1** = suck *la14-.* **2** *vi* flow in a certain direction, as if drawn by suction *la19-, now Ork Ags Per.* **3** *vt* suckle, give suck to *20-.*
n **1** = suck *16-.* **2** a stupid person *19-, now Rox.* **3** a cheat, deception, swindle *la20-, NE.* **4** a sycophant, toady *20-, C, S.*
interj, chf ~ ~ a call to an animal, *esp* to a calf *la19-, now local Ork-SW.*
~**er** = sucker *16-.* **auld wifie's** *etc* ~**ers** mint imperials, *pan drops* (PAN¹) *20-, NE, EC, S.* ~**ie** **&c** *n* **1** (1) a suckling *la20-, Per Ags Rox.* (2) *contemptuous* a petted or over-indulged child *20-, now local Cai-SW.* **2** *as a plant name* (1) clover *in gen, 18-, now Kcdn Ags Fif;* (2) the common red clover *19-, now Sh. adj, only* **sucky** *of a wound or blow* painful, stinging *20-, now Fif Edb. interj* = interj, *e20.* ~**ie leather** a sucker as a child's toy *20-, local Per-Rox.* ~**ie mae,** ~**y mammy** a clover flowerhead *20-, now Stlg Fif.* ~**ie soo** the flower of the clover *19-, now midLoth.* ~**ie sourocks** **&c** wood-sorrel *la20-, N nEC Ayr.* ~**ing** **&c** *adj* = sucking *la14-.* ~**in bairn** *etc, also fig* a child at the breast, a suckling *19.* **soukand** **&c sand** a quicksand *e16.* ~**in teuchit** **&c** *20-, NE,* ~ **turkey** *etc 19-, now Sh-N, SW* a feeble or foolish person. ~**it** *of animals* fatigued, exhausted *19-, now Cai.* ~**it gimmer** a ewe that has lambed *la20-, SW.*
~**-the-bluid** a kind of red beetle *20-, now Stlg Rox.* ~ **in** curry favour, ingratiate oneself (**with**) *la19-.* ~**-the-pappie** *contemptuous* a fairly old but babyish child, a 'big baby'; an effeminate person *la20-, local Cai-Kcb.*

soul *see* SAUL

sould *see* SALL

souldart *see* SUDDART

soum¹ **&c, sum** *lal7-* [sum; *only in v* 1, *n* 1 *St* sʌm] *n* **1** = sum *la14-, now Per.* **2** *chf* **soum** **&c** *only Sc* (1) the unit of pasturage which will support a certain fixed number of livestock *16-20.* (2) the number of livestock (*usu* a cow or a proportionate number of sheep) which can be supported by a SOUM¹ 2 (1), *16-, now Sh Highl Per.* *v* **1** (1) *vti* = sum *15-.* (2) *in passive* amount to *e15.* **2** *vt only* **soum** **&c** determine the number of soums[1] which can be supported by (a common pasture) in order to allocate a share among the tenants *la17-*, *now Sh Highl, only Sc.*

souming and rouming a legal action to determine each tenant's soum[1] 2(1), *la17-19, only Sc.*

soum's grass = *n* 2(1), *la16-18, only Sc.*

in a sum briefly *la17.*

soum[2] **&c** [*sum] *n* a horse-load; a pack *15-16.*

~**er** a sumpter horse *la15.* [only Sc; OF *soume*, var of *some*; *cf* eModEng *some*]

soum[3] [sum] *vt* surmise *19-*, *now Abd Kcdn.* [reduced f Eng *assume*]

soum *see* SOAM

soun *see* SIN[1], SOUND[1], SOUND[2], SOUND[3], SOUND[4], SUN, SUNE

sound[1] **&c** *16-*; **soun &c** [sun(d)] *n* 1 = sound, noise *la14-*. 2 a rumour; report; widespread talk or gossip *la19-*, *local Ork-Kcb.*

vti 1 = sound *16-*. 2 *vt* test (a building) for its acoustics *la19.*

~**ing &c** = sounding *16-*. **soundin box** a canopy etc over a pulpit to bounce the speaker's voice out into the congregation *la19-*, *now Sh Ags Per.*

sounstick the sound-post of a violin *19-*, *now Sh WC Kcb.*

sound[2] **&c**; **soun &c** *19* [sun(d)] *adj* 1 = sound, in good condition *la14-*. 2 smooth, even, level *19-*, *now Cai.*

sound[3] **&c**; **soun &c** [sun(d)] *vi* swoon or faint **away** *16-*, *now Sh Ork Dnbt.*

n a swoon, faint; faintness, *freq* **in** (**a**) ~ *16-*, *now Sh Ork.*

a ~ in a faint *18-*, *now Sh Ork.* [ME *sowne* (*n*), *soun(ye)* (*v*) faint, var of *swo(ʒe)ne* swoon]

sound[4]; **soun** [sun(d)] *n* 1 = sound, a narrow channel *16-*. 2 the swimming-bladder of a fish *16-*, *now local Sh-Fif.*

sound[5] [*sund] *n* a sounding-line or -lead *e17.* [*cf* Eng = a sounding; a surgical probe]

Sounday *see* SUNDAY

soup[1] **&c** [sup] *n* = SUP 1; *also ironic* a considerable amount, *esp* of spirits *17-*, *now local Fif-Rox.* [OE *sūpa(n)* sup (*n, v*); *cf* sowp[1] and SUP. OED *sup* (*n*)]

soup[2] **&c** [sup] *n* = soup *la17-*.

~ **tatties** potato soup *20-*, *now NE.*

soup[3] **&c** *16, 19*; **supe** *la16* [*sup] *vi* = sup, have supper. [OED *sup*]

souple &c *15-*, **supple** *la16-* ['supl] *adj* 1 = supple *15-*. 2 ingenious, cunning, astute, devious *18-*, *now local Sh-Kcb.* 3 *of speech* fluent, tripping, prattling *la18-e19.* 4 limp, helpless (with laughter, drink etc) *la19-*, *local.*

adv nimbly, agilely *18-*, *now Ork NE Per.*

vt 1 = supple *16-*. 2 soften by soaking, soak; wash *la18-19.*

~ **scones** thin, pliable scones, *usu* of barley-meal *la18-19.* ~ **Tam** a jointed wooden toy figure *19.* ~-**tongued** ready of speech *la19-*, *now Sh Per.*

sour &c [sur] *adj* 1 = sour *16-*. 2 *of wood* green *la15.* 3 *of weather* cold and wet, inclement *la18-*, *now local NE-Lnk.*

vti 1 = sour. 2 *esp of water on lime* macerate, soften, slake *18-*, *now local.*

~**ock &c**, ~**och &c** *la16-18* ['surək] 1 name for various kinds of sorrel *la15-*. 2 a sulky, perverse, sour-tempered person *18-*, *now local NE-WC* [*cf* MDu *zuric, suerik*, MLowGer *sureke* sorrel].

~ **cake &c** a kind of oatcake (AIT) baked with sour leaven for festivals, *eg* in Rutherglen for St Luke's Fair *la16-19.* ~ **cloot** a person of harsh, gloomy or fault-finding disposition *20-*, *now local Abd-Kcb.* ~ **cogue** a sour-cream dish the same as or similar to *hattit kit* (HAT[1]) *la17-e19.* ~ **dock(en)** the common sorrel *la19-*, *Bwk Kcb S.* ~ **dook &c** 1 buttermilk; *latterly also* yoghurt *19-*. 2 *fig* a sour, mean person *19-*, *local N-SW.* 3 *also* ~-**dook sodger** nickname for a member of the Lothian militia *19-e20.* ~ **drap** *also fig* an acid drop *la19-*, *now Sh.* ~ **face** = ~*cloot*, *20-*, *C.* ~ **kit** = ~ **cogue**, *e16, only Sc.* ~ **leek &c** = ~ *dock(en)*, *la19-*, *now Kcb Rox.* ~ **milk** 1 = sour milk. 2 buttermilk *18-*, *now Sh Ayr.* ~-**moued &c** sulky-looking *la18-*, *now NE Ags Per.* ~-**like-mood**, ~-**mood-like** = *prec, la19-*, *NE.* ~ **ploom** 1 *in pl* = 'sour grapes' *19-*, *now C.* 2 a native of Galashiels *18-*, *now Lnk S.* 3 a tart-flavoured round green boiled sweet (*orig* associated with Galashiels) *20-*, *EC, WC.* 4 = ~ *cloot*, *20-*, *EC, WC.* ~ **poos &c** *la18-e20*, ~ **scone &c** *19-e20* a coarse, sour-flavoured kind of oat bread or SCONE baked at Christmas-time.

sourd *see* SWURD

souse[1] **&c** [sus, ?sʌus] *v* 1 *vt* strike, cuff, thump *la16-*, *now Cai WC Wgt.* 2 *vir* fall or sit (DOWN) heavily *19-20.*

n 1 a heavy blow, *esp* on the head, a thump *la17-*, *now Cai SW.* 2 (the sound of) a heavy fall *la18-20.*

adv violently, heavily, with a thud *19-*, *now SW.*

sous(t)er &c something very large, a large amount *20-*, *Cai EC.* [*perh* onomat; *cf* MHighGer *sus* noise, din; *cf* soss[2]]

souse[2] **&c** [sus] *vt* reprove, put (a person) in his place, silence *la18-*, *now Ags Per.* [*perh* f prec or Eng *souse* drench, steep]

sout &c [sʌut] *n* a sudden leap, bounce, jolt or bump (as when a plough strikes against a stone) *19-*, *SW.*

vi shake or heave convulsively with sobs *19*, *N.* [ME, F *saut* a leap]

souster *see* SOUSE[1]

souter &c *15-*; **suter &c** ['sutər] *n* 1 a shoemaker, cobbler *14-*. 2 (1) a native of Selkirk (once noted for its shoe-manufacture) *la18-*, *Lnk S.* (2) *similarly* a native of Forfar *la19-*, *Ags.* 3 **the Souters &c** the two hills at the entrance to the Cromarty Firth *19-*.

vti 1 cobble, make or mend shoes *19-*, *now NE,*

SW. **2** *vt* get the better of, worst, trounce; *occas in games* defeat without one's opponent scoring *la19-, now Dmf*.
~**'s clod** a small coarse loaf *la18-e19*. ~('**s**) **ends** *19-, now Bnf Abd Per*, **sutter's lingles** *la18-, now Abd Per* the waxed thread used by cobblers, *lingel-ends* (LINGEL¹). [ME; OE *sūtere*, L *sūtor*]
south¹ **&c; soud &c** *la18-, now Sh* [suθ; *Sh also* sud] *adv* **1** = south *la14-*. **2** *as prep* southwards along *la16*.
adj **1** = south *la14-*. **2** characteristic of or belonging to the south *la15-20*.
~**en &c** *esp ballad* south(ern) *16-19*. ~**ert** ['suðərt; *Sh* 'sʌdərt] = southward *18-, now Sh Ork*. ~**ie** left-handed *20-, Ayr*. ~**ron &c** ['sʌð(ə)rən, 'sʌd(ə)rən] *chf Sc adj* **1** *of persons* belonging to or living in England, English *la15-, now literary*. **2** *of things* of or characteristic of England or the English *la18-19*. *n* **1** (1) an Englishman *la15-e19*; (2) *in sing as collective* the English *la15-e19*. **2** the English language as opposed to SCOTS *16-e19*. **suddren wud &c** southernwood *20-, now N, SW*.
on ~ **half &c** on or to the south (of) *la14-e16*.
~**land &c** southern, from the south *la15-e20*.
~ **awa** *la20-*, ~ **by**(**e**) *la18-* in the south *now local Sh-Wgt*.
south² **&c** [sʌuθ, suθ] *n: sotto voce* singing or whistling, a low murmur (of music) *18-e20*.
vt hum, sing or whistle softly *la18-, now Abd-Ags*. [only Sc; altered f SOWFF]
sover &c; suffer *la15* [*'sʌvər] *adj* sure, secure, safe *la14-16*.
adv surely, securely *e16*.
v **1** *vi* trust **in** (something) *la15*. **2** *vt* make safe, *esp* by a formal pledge *la15-16*.
~**ance &c** assurance; safe-conduct; truce *la15-16*. ~**ty &c 1** surety *15-18*. **2** a person who becomes surety *16*. [only Sc; OF *soür*, var of *seür*; cf *sure* (SHUIR); for *-v-* cf MOVIR]
soverane &c *n, adj* = sovereign *la14-17, chf Sc*. [OED *sovereign*]
sow &c [*sʌu] *n* **1** a bride's outfit of clothes, a trousseau *la17-19*. **2** a shroud, winding-sheet *la18-19*. [only Sc; obscure]
sow *see* SAW¹, SOO¹, SOO²
sowans &c, sowens &c; sooans &c *18-*, **swins &c** *la18-19* ['suənz, -ɪnz, 'sʌu-, 'so-; *Lnk* swinz] *n pl* **1** a dish made from oat husks and fine meal steeped in water for about a week; after straining, the liquor was again left to ferment and separate, the solid matter at the bottom being the SOWANS, the liquor SWATS; *usu* eaten like porridge, boiled with water and salt *la16-20*. **2** *usu in sing, weaving* a flour-and-water size applied to warp threads *18-, now Ags*. **sowan boat** *la18-e19*, **sowan bowie** *la18-e20*, **sowan kit** *18-e19* a wooden barrel or tub used for fermenting SOWANS. ~ **nicht** Christmas Eve (Old Style) *20-, NE*.

sowan(**s**) **pot** the pot in which SOWANS was cooked *la18-19*. **sowan seeds &c** the rough husks of oats used in making SOWANS *la17-, now Cai NE*. ~ **sieve &c** a strainer for SOWANS (after the initial steeping) *18-e20*. **sowanswats** the liquid poured off SOWANS *la19-, now Sh Ork Cai*.
drinking ~ *19-, now NE*, **knotting** ~ *19-, NE* the liquor left after straining SOWANS but before fermenting, *usu* thickened a little by heating. [ScGael *sùghan* = *n* 1, IrGael *súgán &c* sap, juice]
sowce &c [sʌus] *n* a (messy) mixture of food, *specif* some oatmeal dish such as porridge *la18-, now Cai*. [var of SOSS¹]
sowd¹ **&c** *18-*, **sold** *15-e16* [sʌud] *n* **1** = sold, (soldiers') pay *15*. **2** a (large) quantity or amount of money or possessions *16-20*. **3** *in gen* a large amount or number *19-e20*. **4** a large ungainly person *20-, Bnf Abd Ags*.
~**ie** *esp of a woman* = *n* 4, *19-, now Abd Ags*.
sowd² **&c** [*sʌud] *vt* **1** = sowd, sold, solder *la15-e16*. **2** agree (to), sympathize with (so as to curry favour) *la19-e20*.
sowdie &c [*'sʌudɪ] *n* a hotchpotch, a heterogeneous mixture *18-19*. [doubtful; *cf* POWSOWDIE]
sowens *see* SOWANS
sowf &c [sʌuf] *n* a fool, simpleton, stupid, silly person *19-, now Abd*. [*cf* SUMPH]
sowff &c [sʌuf] *vti* **1** sing, hum or whistle softly or under one's breath *18-, now NE*. **2** *vi* pant, sob, snore, doze *19*. **3** *of wind, water etc* murmur softly; *of a breeze or smoke* puff gently *la19-20*.
n **1** a low whistling, singing or humming *la18-e20, Abd Ags*. **2** wheezing, heavy breathing; a snooze, sleep *19-e20*. **3** a stroke, blow, smack *18-, Abd-Ags*. **4** a person's (normal) line of thought or action *19-, now Kcdn*. **5** a copious drink, a draught *la18-19*. [only Sc; prob eModEng *solf* sing in sol-fa, w infl f SOUCH; *cf* SOUTH²]
sowl *see* SAUL
sownack &c ['sʌunək] *n* a (*Halloween* (HALLOW²)) bonfire; a heavy bog-fir torch used in *Halloween* fires *la19-, now Per*. [only Sc; Gael *samhnag* a Halloween bonfire, f *Samhuinn* Hallowtide, 1 Nov; *cf* SHANNACK]
sowp¹ **&c** [sʌup] *n* **1** = SUP *n* 1; *also ironic* a larger amount, *esp* of spirits *16-, now local Stlg-WC*. **2** a drink; something to drink *18-20*. [ON *saup* semi-liquid food, *supa* (*v*) sup; *cf* OE *sūpan; cf* SOUP¹ and SUP]
sowp² **&c** [sʌup] *vti* soak, drench, saturate, steep *16-, now local Bnf-Dmf*.
n **1** rain, wet weather *18-e20*. **2** a state of wetness; a bog *la19-e20*. **3** water for washing, lather *19-, now Lnk SW*. [Eng *sop*]
sowp³ *16-e19*; **solp** *la15-16* [*sʌup] *vi* weary, tire; become worn out *la15-16*.

~it exhausted, worn out; sunk **in** (sorrow etc) *la15-e19*. [only Sc; back-formation f SOPIT with variant pronunc; *cf* HOWP[1] and Eng *hope*]

sowther &c *la18-*, **solder &c; souder &c** *la17-e20* ['sʌuðər, 'sʌudər; *also* 'suðər] *v* **1** *vt* = solder *17-*. **2** unite in matrimony; make (a marriage) *19-*, *now Bnf Ags*. **3** settle, patch **up** (a quarrel, disagreement) *la18-*, *now Ork-C*. **4** mitigate, alleviate (sorrow, pain, anger etc) *19-*, *now Ags*. **5** confirm, strengthen (a friendship); seal, cement (a bargain etc) *19-*, *now NE*. **6** *vi* agree, get on well together *18-*, *now Ags wLoth*.

soy &c [*soi] *n* silk *la18-*, *now arch*. [only Sc; F *soie*, obs F *soy*]

soyme *see* SOAM

space[1] **&c** *n* **1** = space *la14-*. **2** an extent, distance **of** *la14-e17*: '*the space of sex myle*'. **3** a pace, stride, used as a unit of measurement, *approx* 3 feet (1 metre) *18-*, *now Sh Cai*, *only Sc*. *vti* **1** = space *la16-*. **2** *vt* measure by pacing *19-*, *now Sh-WC*, *only Sc*.

space[2] *n* a species, kind (**of** money etc) *la16*. [only Sc; F *espèce*]

spaceir &c [*spa'sir] *vi* walk, stroll; pace up and down *e16*. [only Sc; MDu *spacieren*, OF *espacier*]

spad &c *vi*, *freq* **~ on** walk energetically *20-*, *NE*. [only Sc; see SND]

spade &c; spead *18-*, *now NE*, **spadd &c** *18-20*, *chf NE*, **spaud** *la19-e20*, *NE* [sped; *NE* spɑd] *n* = spade *15-*.

  spadin(g) a spade's depth (or breadth) of earth; a trench of one spade-depth *la18-*, *now local*. **~'s casting** one of various measurements in PEAT[1]-cutting *la18-e20*, *only Sc*. **spadar(r)ack &c** the number of PEATS[1] that can be cut with a spade by one man in one day *18*, *only Sc* [reduced f *spade darg*]. **~ silver** payment for work with a spade *e17*, *only Sc*.

spae &c *la15-*; **spay** *15-19*, **spe(e)** *la16-e20*, **spey** *18-* [spe] *v* **1** *vt* prophesy, foretell, predict, tell (fortunes) *la15-*, *now literary*. **2** read (someone's) hand *la19-*, *now Bnf Abd*. **3** *vi* utter prophecy, tell the future **about** *18-20*. *n* a prediction; an omen *la16*.

  ~ craft the art of predicting the future *18-19*, *only Sc*. **~man** a fortuneteller; a diviner, prophet *la15-19*, *only Sc*. **~wife** a female fortuneteller *18-*, *only Sc*. [ME *spa*, ON *spá*]

spag &c; spaig &c *20-*, *Cai* [sp(j)ɑg; *Cai also* speg] *n* a paw, hand, foot, *esp* a big clumsy hand or foot *20-*, *now Cai*.

  ~ach ['~ɔx] flat-footed, with clumsy or misshapen feet *la19-*, *now Cai Inv*. [only Sc; Gael *spàg* a claw, paw, (animal's) foot; *cf* SPYOG]

spaik *16-*, *now local Inv-S*, **spoke &c** *17-*; **spake** *la14-e20* [spek; *Abd* spjɑk] *n* **1** = spoke (of a wheel etc) *la14-*. **2** a wooden bar, rod or batten; *specif* a stake or pale in a wooden fence etc *la15-*, *now Inv Lnk*. **3** the perch of a bird's

cage, a roosting bar *19-*, *now Inv Lnk S*, *only Sc*. **4** one of the rungs of a ladder *la19-*, *now local Per-Rox*. **5** one of the bars of wood on which a coffin is carried to the graveside *17-*, *now Per Kcb Rox*, *only Sc*. **6** *fig*, *chf in negative* an unsupportive person *19-e20*.

  ~it made of spokes or bars of wood *17-*, *now Lnk Rox*.

drap *or* **fa aff the ~** collapse with weariness, sleep or astonishment *20-*, *S*, *only Sc*.

spail &c, spale; speal *18-e20*, **spell** *18-*, *now Abd* [spel; *local* spil] *n* **1** a splinter, chip or sliver of wood (broken off by an axe or plane); a wood-shaving; a thin strip or lath of wood *la15-*. **2** a splinter in the skin *20-*, *Gen except Sh Ork*, *only Sc*. **3** a wooden spill or taper used for lighting etc *18-*, *now local Ork-Lnk*, *only Sc*. **4** a small piece of something, a fragment; something of little or no value *la18-e20*, *only Sc*. **5** a shroud-like shape of candlegrease on a guttered candle, thought to foretell the death of the person in whose direction it forms *la18-*, *now Mry Ags Per*, *only Sc*.

  ~ing a wood-shaving *la19-*, *now Per*, *only Sc*. **~ basket** a two-handled (potato-)basket made of thin strips of wood *20-*. **~ box** a (*usu* small) box made of thin strips of wood, used for money, pills etc *18-*, *now Ork Abd WC*. [see SND]

spail *see* SPEEL[1]

spaingie *la19-*, *Bnf Abd*; **Spane** *14-15*, **Spanʒe &c** *la14-16*, **Spenʒe** *la15-16*, **Spangyie** *la16*, **spainyie &c** *19-e20*, **spengie &c** *la19-20*, *NE* ['spen(j)ɪ, *spenjɪ] *n* **1** (1) Spain *la14-16*. (2) *attrib* Spanish, of a Spanish breed *la14-20*. **2** Spanish cane, or any cane, as used for punishment; for stiffening a cap; as a fishing rod; as a substitute for tobacco etc *19-20*.

  ~ wan = *n* 2, *la19-*, *Bnf Abd*. [only Sc; aphetic f OF *Espaigne*. OED *Spain*]

spairge &c, sparge; sperge *la19-e20* *vt* **1** plaster; roughcast *16-17*. **2** bespatter, besprinkle *la16-e20*, *only Sc*. **3** scatter, sprinkle, dash (water, mud etc) (**about**) *18-*, *now Abd*, *only Sc*. *n* **1** a splash, sprinkling, splodge of water, mud etc *19*, *only Sc*. **2** a drink, a mouthful, a drop of spirits, as much liquid as will moisten one's lips *19-e20*, *only Sc*. [OF *espargier*; *cf* SPARGEN]

spaiver &c *n* the opening in the front of trousers *19-*, *now local*. [only Sc; var of SPARE[1]]

spak *see* SPEAK

spake *see* SPAIK

spald &c [spal(d); *Cai* spʌul] *v* **1** *vir* sprawl, lie stretched out *e16*. **2** *vt* split, lay open or flat (*esp* a fish) *19*.

  ~er = *v*, *19-e20*. [laME = *v* 2; *cf* SPELD]

spald *see* SPAUL

spale *see* SPAIL

spale-bone *see* SPAUL

spalter &c ['spaltər] *vi* walk awkwardly, stumble; splash through water, flounder *20-*, *now Wgt*. [Eng dial = split, splinter; cf *spalder* (SPALD)]

span *see* SPANG¹

spane *see* SPEAN

Spane *see* SPAINGIE

spang¹ *19-*, **span** *16-*; **spayn** *la14* *n* = span *la19-*.
vt = span *la14-*.
~**ie** &c a game played with marbles etc *19-*, *now Fif wLoth WC*.
a ~ **nievefu** as much of something as can be grasped in the hand *20-*, *Loth Rox*. ~ **the nose** thumb one's nose *la20-*, *Stlg Fif EC, SW*. [the form *spang* may be due to conflation w SPANG²]

spang² *n* **1** a jerk, sudden violent movement *16-17*. **2** a smart rap, a sharp blow *la16-e18*, *only Sc*. **3** a pace, a long vigorous step or bound *18-*, *now local Sh-Per*.
v **1** *vi* stride out vigorously, walk with long steps, leap, bound *16-*, *now local Sh-Per*. **2** *vt* cross with a stride or bound; make (**one's way**) by leaping or in haste; measure by pacing *20-*, *now local Sh-Per*. **3** throw, jerk, flick (**up**) *16-20*.
~**hew** &c *vt* jerk or catapult violently into the air (*esp* a frog etc, as a game) *19-*, *now Bwk Rox*. [also Mod nEng dial; prob onomat]

spang-new; **spankie-new** &c *adj* = split-new (SPLIT) *19-*, *now Cai WC Wgt*. [only Sc; vars of Eng (now dial) *span-new*, ON *spán-nyr*, f *spánn* a chip of wood]

Spangyie *see* SPAINGIE

spanis &c *la14-e15* [*'spanɪs] *vi*, *chf in ptp* **spanist**, **spynist** *e16*, *of a flower* expanded, open. [chf Sc; OF *espaniss-*, f *espanir* (ModF *épanouir*) expand, spread out. OED *spanish* (*v*¹)]

spank *vi*, ~ **awa**, **aff** *etc* move nimbly and briskly on foot, horseback or in a vehicle *19-*.
~**er** **1** a spirited fast horse *19-*, *now N Per Kcb*. **2** a person who walks quickly with a brisk regular stride *19-*, *now N, WC*. ~**ie** &c *of animals* frisky, nimble, spirited *la18-e20*. [see SND]

spankie-new *see* SPANG-NEW

Spanʒe *see* SPAINGIE

Spanʒell [*'spanjəl, *'spen-] *n* = Spaniel, a Spaniard *e15*. [only Sc. OED *Spaniel*]

spar¹ &c; **spare** *la14, 19-e20* (*Rox*), **sperr** *e16, e20* (*Sh*) *n* **1** = spar *16-*. **2** a wooden bolt for securing a door, a linchpin *19-*, *now WC Wgt Rox*. **3** a bar or rail of a wooden fence or gate *la19-*, *now NE*. **4** a rung of a chair or ladder *la19-*, *NE, C, S*. **5** a crossbar or wooden slat in a kitchen dresser *la19-*, *now local NE-Lnk*.
vt **1** fasten (a door or gate) with a bolt *la14, e19*. **2** brace (the limbs) in order to resist a strain *la19-*, *now Bnf Abd*.
sparred slatted *la20-*. **sparret** a small spar or bar *e17*, *only Sc*.

spar² *n* ~(**ry**) **coal** a kind of coal 'the backs or joints of which are filled with carbonate of lime' *19-e20*, *Fif*. [Eng *spar* the mineral]

spare¹ &c *n* **1** the opening or slit in a woman's skirt, petticoat etc *la16-*, *now Sh Ork C, S*. **2** the opening in the front of trousers *la18-*, *now local Cai-Dmf*. [see SND]

spare² &c *adj* = spare.
adv sparely, in a spare frugal manner *19*.

spare *see* SPAR¹

sparfle *see* SPARPLE

sparge *see* SPAIRGE

spargen &c [*'spardʒən, &c] *vt* parget, plaster *16-e17*. [only Sc; cf laME *sparget* and *pargen*; cf SPAIRGE]

spark &c; **sperk** *16-*, *now S*, **spirk** *la19-*, *chf Abd* *n* **1** = spark *la15-*. **2** a very small amount (**of** something liquid or semi-liquid), a drop *la16-*, *now local Sh-Fif*; *specif* (1) a nip of spirits *19*; (2) a drop of water, a raindrop *19-*, *now NE Ags*; (3) a splash or spot of mud etc *19-*, *now NE*. **3** a small diamond, ruby etc *16-e19*.
vti **1** = spark. **2** *vt* set alight; light (a match, fire etc) *19-*, *now nEC, WC, SW*. **3** spatter with liquid or mud; spot with mud etc *17-*, *now Sh Ork NE*. **4** ~ **in** sprinkle, scatter (seed, dung etc) *19-*, *now Ork*. **5** *vi* throw out a fine spray; sputter, spit forth; come out etc as or like sparks *16-*, *now local Sh-SW*. **6** rain slightly; spit with rain *19-*, *now Sh Ork NE*.
~**ie** emitting sparks; *fig* bright, sharp, quick-witted; lively *19-*, *now Abd Kcdn Per*.

sparling *see* SPIRLING

sparple &c *16-e19*, **sparfle** *la16*, **sperfle** *19-e20*; **sperple** &c *la15-e16* *vti* **1** scatter, spread about, disperse; squander *la15-e20*. **2** distribute, divide (among persons) *16-e17*, *chf Sc*. [ME; OF *esparpeillier*]

sparra *see* SPARROW

sparret *see* SPAR¹

sparrow &c, **sporrow** *la19-*, *now Sh Ork*; **sparra** *la19-*, **sparry** &c *la19-e20* *n* = sparrow *la15-*.
sparrabaldy having thin legs *la20-*, *Bnf Abd*.
~ **drift** *or* **hail** *or* **shot** shot for shooting small birds *la19-*, *now local NE-Rox*.

sparry *see* SPARROW

sparse *adj* **1** = sparse. **2** *of writing* spread out, widely spaced *18-e20*, *only Sc*.

spart *vti* scatter (dung); bespatter *20-*, *now Sh Cai*. [perh altered f SPARK *v* 4; *cf* Gael *spairt* plaster, spatter]

sparth *n* meaning unknown *la15*.

spartickles *see* SPENTACLES

spartle *18-e19*; **spurtle** *19-e20* *vi* move the body or limbs in a sprawling or struggling way; kick about, wriggle. [only Sc; Du, LowGer *spartelen*]

sparwort [*'sparvər(t)] *n* = sparver, a canopy for a bed *la15*. [only Sc. OED *sparver*]

spashious *see* SPAWCIOUS

spat *la18-*, **spot** &c *n* = spot *la15-*.

spatril &c a musical note, *esp* as written on a score *19-e20*. **spottie** the will o' the wisp, *esp* **like spottie** at once, with great speed *19-*, *now Abd*.

~ **o prins &c** a round pincushion with pins in it *19-20*. **spot pin &c** a pin, as used in playing with a teetotum *18-e20*.

spatch *n* a patch, as on a garment *19-*, *now Rox*. *vt* patch, mend (clothes etc) *19-*, *S*. [only *Sc*; var of Eng *patch*]

spatchell &c *adj* well-dressed, neat *20-*, *now Inv Mry*. [only *Sc*; Gael *spaideil*]

spate &c; speat &c *la16-19* [spet; *Sh* spit] *n* **1** a flood, a sudden rise of water *15-*. **2** flooding, swollen condition (of water etc); heavy downpouring (of rain) *16-19*. **3** a torrential fall or heavy downpour (of rain) *18-*. **4** a flood of tears *la18-*. **5** a bout (of drinking) *19*. **6** a torrent (of words etc); an outburst of emotion or activity *17-*. **7** an overwhelming rush of incidents or events; one thing after another in quick succession *la19-*. **8** a powerful public outcry *e18*.

v, only Sc **1** *vt* flood, swell *19*. **2** *vi* rain heavily *la19-*, *now local*.

in ~ in flood *16-*. [earlier in *Sc*; obscure]

spatril *see* SPAT

spaud *see* SPADE

spaul &c *18-*, **spauld &c; spald** *16-19*, **spule &c** *la18-19* [spal(d); *?sp(j)ul, *?spøl] *n* **1** the shoulder (in man or animals); the shoulder-bone *14-e20*. **2** a limb: (1) one of the four quarters of an animal, an animal's leg *18-e19*; (2) *chf in pl* human legs *19*, *only Sc*. **3** a joint, a shoulder or leg (of mutton, beef etc); the wing or leg of a fowl; a shoulder cut of beef, shoulder steak *18-*, *now Bnf Abd*.

~ **bane 1** a shoulderblade *la18-19*. **2 spalebone** a cut of beef from the shoulder, blade-bone steak *20-*, *local*.

black spauld a cattle disease which affects the quarters, a form of anthrax *la18-20*. [see SND]

spave &c *vt* spay, neuter (a female animal) *la18-*, *now Kcb*. [altered f Eng *spay*]

spavie &c ['spevɪ] *n* = spavin; *also joc* a human rheumatic disease *la17-*, *now local Ork-Kcb*.

~**d &c** *adj*, *lit and fig* affected with spavin *18-20*. [only *Sc*]

spawcious &c; spashious &c ['spaʃəs] *adj* = spacious *la19-*, *now Bnf Abd Per*.

spay *see* SPAE

spayn *see* SPANG[1]

spe *see* SPAE

spead *see* SPADE

speak *la16-*; **speik &c** *15-e20*, *only Sc*, **spek** *la14-e20*, **speke &c** *la14-e17*, **spike &c** *la19-e20*, *NE*, *only Sc*, **spick &c** *e20*, *Abd*, *only Sc* [spik; *Sh Ork Cai* spɛk; *NE* spɪk, spəik] *vti*, *pt also* **spak &c** *now Sh-WC* **1** = speak *la14-*. **2**

freq in imperative listen **to**, attend **to** *la18-20*, *only Sc*. **3** order (goods), bespeak *20-*, *now local Sh-Dnbt*, *only Sc*.

n **1** (power of) speech *la14*. **2** the action of speaking; manner of speaking *la14-e15*. **3** a chat, conversation *la19-*, *now Sh*. **4** a speech, statement, comment; a popular saying *la18-*, *now Abd Kcdn Ags*, *only Sc*. **5** a 'story' without substance; a piece of make-believe *20-*, *Sh NE*, *only Sc*. **6** gossip, scandalmongering *la19-*, *now local*, *only Sc*. **7** a subject of conversation, *esp* current gossip or rumour, the talk (of a place) *la18-*, *now local Sh-Kcb*, *only Sc*.

~**ing &c 1** = speaking *la14-*. **2** the faculty or power of speech *la14*. ~**ing drink** a payment by the master of an applicant for entry to a trade INCORPORATION *la18-e19*, *only Sc*. ~**ing time** the time of year at which employers, *esp* farmers, renew or terminate workers' contracts *la19-20*, *only Sc*. **spoken** *after names of places or areas* having the speech of *la20-*: 'South-spoken'.

~ **back** reply (in argument); *latterly* reply impertinently and defiantly, talk back *la18-*, *only Sc*. ~ **in** pay a fleeting visit, drop in *19-*, *now Ork Per Kcb*, *only Sc*. ~ **to 1** ask in marriage *20*, *only Sc*. **2** *of a farmer etc* engage (a worker) for a further term *19-20*, *only Sc*.

speal *see* SPAIL

spean &c *la16-*; **spane &c** *16-e20*, **spen &c** *la18-e20* [spen, spin] *v* **1** *vt* wean (an infant or suckling animal) *16-*. **2** put (a person or animal) off food through disgust, fear etc *la18-*, *now NE Per Kcb*. **3** *fig* draw (a person) away **from** (a habit, idea etc); separate, part **from** *la18-*, *now NE nEC Lnk*. **4** *vi* be (in the process of being) weaned *la18-*, *now Ags Per*.

new ~**ed** newly weaned, just weaned *19-*, *now Sh Ork N Kcb*. ~**ing brash** an illness affecting children or young animals on being weaned *19-*, *now Kcb*. ~**ing time** weaning time *18-*, *now Cai*. [ME *spane*, MDu, MLowGer *spanen*, *spenen*]

spear *19-*; **sper &c** *la14-e16*, **speir** *la14-16* [spir] *n* = spear *la14-*.

~**iment &c** *n* = spearmint *la19-*, *Ags Fif WC*, *S*.

~ **running** jousting with spears *16*. ~ **silver** a form of military tax or levy *la15*, *only Sc*.

speat *see* SPATE

specht &c [*spɛxt] *n* the green woodpecker *la15-e16*. [see OED *speight*]

special *see* SPEESHAL

specify &c *vt* **1** = specify *la14-*. **2** make special mention of (a person), celebrate *la15*, *only Sc*.

speciose *adj* beautiful, lovely *la15*. [only *Sc*; *cf* Eng *specious*]

spectaculous *adj* spectacular *e17*, *only Sc*.

speculation &c *n* **1** = speculation *16-*. **2** a spectacle, subject for remark or gossip, an object of contempt *la19*.

spede *see* SPEED

spee *see* SPAE

speeach &c ['spiək] *n* an oak stake; an oak branch without the bark; a small stick *20-, now Per.* [only Sc; ScGael *spéic, speuc* a spike, bar, Gael dial = a branch, prob orig f SPAIK]

speech &c *n* = speech *la14-*.

tak ~ in hand make a speech, hold forth *19-e20.*

speed *17-*; **spede** *la14-e19*, **speid** *la14-e19* [spid] *n* **1** = speed *la14-*. **2** success, prosperity, good fortune *la18-20.*

vti, ptp also **spede** *la14* = speed *la14-*.

~**full &c** profitable, advantageous, expedient *la14-e19.* ~**y** swift *la14-*.

come (good, bad *etc*) ~ be (very, not at all *etc*) successful *la16-, now Ork NE, EC, only Sc.* ~ **of foot** fleetness of movement *la18-*. **speed the ploo &c 1** a well-wishing phrase at a *pleuch feast* (PLEUCH) *la19.* **2 Speed the Plough** a popular country dance; its tune *19-.*

speeder &c; spider *17-*, **speedart &c** *19-e20, SW n* **1** = spider *la16-*. **2** *in pl* **the Spiders** nickname for Queen's Park football team *la20-* [from their black-and-white-hooped jerseys]. **3** a pennyfarthing bicycle *20, Ork Bnf Abd, only Sc.* **4** a trout-fly dressed without wings *20-*.

speeder jenny *20-, now SW, S*, **speederlegs** *la20-, Sh Ork Rox* the cranefly, daddy-long-legs *only Sc.* **spider webster** a spider *20-, now Per Ayr, only Sc.*

speel[1] **&c** *19-*; **spail &c** *la18-20*, **spell** *n* **1** = spell (of time) *19-*. **2** a time of rest or relaxation, a break in work *la18-, now local Sh-Wgt.*

v **1** *vt* take a turn at work for (someone), relieve (someone) at work, substitute for (someone) *20-, now local Sh-Gall.* **2** *vi, freq* ~ **on** work or walk with great energy *la19-, now Wgt.*

speel[2] *18-*; **speil &c** [spil; *Mry* spel] *v* **1** *vi, also fig* climb, clamber **up, down** *etc 16-*. **2** *vt, also fig* climb, clamber up *la16-, Gen except Sh Ork.*

n the act of climbing; a climb *19-, now NE-S, only Sc.*

~**er 1** a spiked iron attached to the foot for climbing trees *18-e20, only Sc.* **2** a climber *20.*

~**-the-wa** (a nip of) a cheap inferior WHISKY (from its supposed effects on the drinker) *la19-, now Lnk SW Rox, only Sc.* [perh a back-formation f SPELAR; *cf* MDu *spelen* (*v*) play]

speel *see* SPIEL

speen *see* SPUNE

speendrift *see* SPINDRIFT

speengie rose [*'spiŋɪ 'roz] *n* the peony *la19-e20.* [only Sc; corruption of Eng *peony*, perh w infl f form of SPAINGIE]

speer *see* SPEIR

speerack *adj* a lively alert person *la20-, Cai Ross Inv.* [only Sc; perh Gael *speireag, spiorag* a sparrow-hawk; a tall thin girl]

speerit *19-*, **spirit, spreit &c** *la15-20;*

sperit &c *la14-19*, **sprit &c** *la14-e18*, **spret &c** *la14-20* ['spirɪt; *sprit, *sprɪt] *n* **1** = spirit *la14-*. **2** *in pl* the mind as the source of emotion, *esp* as affected by circumstances *la14-*.

vt, only **sprete** inspire **with** (courage) *e16, only Sc.*

spiritual &c *adj* = spiritual *la15-*. *n* an ecclesiastic or cleric *la15.* **spirituality &c 1** ecclesiastical property etc received for spiritual services *la15.* **2** = spirituality *la15-*. ~**y** spirited, vivacious, full of energy *16-*. [OED *spirit, sprite*]

speeshal *la19-e20*, **special &c** *adj* **1** = special *la14-*. **2** *only* **special**, of courses in Sc Univs, latterly of a second or sometimes third year class at St Andrews advanced *18-20.* **3** *also as n, only* **special**, of beer applied to a later, carbonated version of HEAVY *la20-, only Sc.*

in special(i)té &c in detail, in particular *la14-15.* **but specialitie** without partiality or favour *la15.*

speet *la17-*, **spit &c** *la16-*; **spite** *la16*, **speit** *16-17* [spit] *n* **1** = (roasting-)spit *16-*. **2** a pointed stick or skewer on which fish are hung up to dry *19-, local Sh-Bwk.* **3** a rod for suspending the wicks in the making of tallow candles *e20.*

vt **1** = spit *16-*. **2** hang (fish) **up** by the heads or gills on a *spit* (*n* 2) to dry *la19-, local Sh-Bwk.*

spit rack a rack for supporting a spit or spits *la17.*

speid *see* SPEED

speik *see* SPEAK

speil *see* SPEEL[2]

speild *see* SPELD

speir &c, speer *17-*; **spyr** *la14* [spir] *v* **1** *vi* ask a question, inquire, make inquiries (**at, o** a person) *la14-, Gen except Sh.* **2** ask **after** (*la14-16*), **for** (*la16-*), Gen except Sh. **3** inquire one's way; make one's way **to** *e16.* **4** *vt* ask for (a piece of information, an opinion etc) *la14-*. **5** request (a thing, help, permission etc); ask (a person) **for** *18-e20.* **6** (1) ask, put a question to (a person) *19-, now Ork Cai WC Kcb.* (2) *also vi* ~ **for** (*la18-, now local NE-Wgt*) ask in marriage, make a proposal of marriage to, ask for the hand of *la19-, Gen except Sh Ork.* **7** invite *19-, now local N-Kcb, only Sc.* **8** *chf* ~ **out** search, track down, trace (by inquiry) *la14-, now Ork N, C Slk.*

n, only Sc **1** a question(ing), inquiry, investigation *la18-, now NE Ags Kcb.* **2** a person who is continually asking questions; a prying inquisitive person *la19-, now local Bnf-Slk.*

~**ing** *n* **1** *freq in pl* questioning, inquiry; prying interrogation or investigation *la14-*. **2** *freq in pl* information (obtained by inquiry), news *la14-, now wLoth SW Slk.* **3** a proposal of marriage *la19-e20. adj* inquisitive, searching *la19-*.

~ **guesses** ask riddles *la19-, now Fif Dmf.* ~

someone's price *joc* make a proposal of marriage to someone *la18-, now local NE-WC*. ~ **questions** catechize *la19-20*. [nME *spire, spere &c*, OE *spyrian*, ON *spyrja*]

speir *see* SPEAR

speit *see* SPEET

spek, speke *see* SPEAK

spel *see* SPELD

spelar &c [*'spilər] *n* an acrobat, performer *la15-e16*. [only Sc; prob MDu *speler* a player, actor.　OED *speeler*[1]]

spelch [*spɛlx] *n* a chip or splinter *la16*.　[*cf* SPELK]

speld &c; speild *16-17,* **spel** *la19-e20* [spɛl(d)] *vt, only Sc* **1** lay flat or extended; spread out; split, cut, slice open (*esp* fish to dry) *la15-, now Sh Cai*.　**2** split, crack *e17*.　*n, only* **speild** a piece, part or strip *la17*.
　spelder &c 1 *vt* spread or pull open or apart *18-, now local*.　**2** *vr* wrench oneself or pull one's muscles by falling with the legs apart *19-, now Ork Rox*.　**3** *vi* stretch out, sprawl; thrash about awkwardly *18-e20*.　~**ing &c** *19-, now Sh N*, **speldrin &c** *19-, now Fif Bwk* a split and dried (or smoked) fish, *esp* a haddock or whiting *only Sc*.　[*see* SND; *cf* SPALD]

spelk &c; spyolk &c *la19-, Sh* [spɛlk; *Sh* spjolk] *n* **1** a sharp splinter (of wood, glass, iron etc); a small strip of wood *19-, local*.　**2** a surgical splint *19-, now Sh Ork Bwk Rox*.
　vti **1** splinter; fly about like splinters *la19-e20*.　**2** *vt* bind (a broken limb) with splints, repair (something broken) with splints etc *19-, now Sh Ork Cai Bwk*.　[ME *spelke* a splinter; a thatching rod, OE *spelc* a splint; for Sh form *cf* Norw dial *spjelk &c*, ON *spjalk* a splinter]

spell[1] **&c** *vt* = spell.
　n **1** spelling, a spelling lesson *la19-, now Bwk*.　**2** a spelling book *19*.
　~ **book** *n* **2,** *19*.
　big *etc* ~(**-book**) a spelling book in capital letters *19*.　**wee** ~(**-book**) a spelling book in lower-case letters *19*.

spell[2] **&c** *vi* **1** = spell, talk *e15*.　**2** state falsely; exaggerate *la18-, now Kcb*.　**3** swear, blaspheme *la19-, Kcdn C Rox*.
　n = spell, discourse; a magical incantation *la14-*.

spell *see* SPAIL, SPEEL[1]

spen *see* SPEAN

spence; spense &c *n* an inner apartment of a house, used as a sitting room, small bedroom etc, or for storage *15-, now NE, SW*.　[ME = a pantry, aphetic f *dispense*]

spend[1] *vti, pt, ptp also* ~**it** *15-16* = spend *15-*.
　~**ing 1** = spending *16-*.　**2** goods, money, cash; means of support *16-e17*.　**spent** *adj, of a fish, esp a herring* spawned, in poor condition after spawning *la18-*.　*n* a **spent** fish *la19-*.
　spyntie ['spəɪntɪ] = prec *la19-, NE*.　~**rife** *adj* (*n*) (a) spendthrift *19-, NE Ags*.

spend[2] *vi* spring, leap, dash *16-e19*.

n a spring, bound, leap *19-e20*.　[only Sc; perh altered f STEND[1] w infl f SPANG[2]]

spengie *see* SPAINGIE

spense *see* SPENCE

spent *see* SPEND[1]

spentacles &c *la18-,* **spartickles &c** *la19 n pl* = spectacles.

Spenȝe *see* SPAINGIE

sper *see* SPEAR

sperfle *see* SPARPLE

sperge *see* SPAIRGE

sperit *see* SPEERIT

sperk *see* SPARK

sperling *see* SPIRLING

sperple *see* SPARPLE

sperr *see* SPAR[1]

sperthe *n, arch* a battle-axe *19*.　[ME *sparthe*, ON *sparða* a kind of axe]

speshie &c ['spiʃɪ] *n* = species *19-, now local N-Lnk*.　[only Sc; back-formation f Eng *species*, thought of as a *pl*]

speuchan *see* SPLEUCHAN

speug *see* SPUG

spew *see* SPUE

spey *see* SPAE

spice &c *n* **1** = spice.　**2** pepper *la18-, now Sh Ork N, only Sc*.
　spicy 1 = spicy.　**2** peppered, peppery; *fig* proud, testy *la18-e20*.
　~ **house** a store for keeping spices *la16*.

spick *see* SPEAK

spicket &c; spigot ['spɪkət, 'spɪɡət; *Per Kcb also* 'spikət; *Fif Stlg also* 'spig-] *n* **1** = spigot *la17-*.　**2** *also* **spriggit &c** *only Sc* an outdoor tap, *freq* one supplying water for a locality *20-, local*.

spider *see* SPEEDER

spiel &c *19-;* **speel &c** *la18-19* [spil] *n* **1** any kind of game or play *19*.　**2** a curling match *la18-; cf* BONSPIEL. [only Sc; *see* SND]

spigot *see* SPICKET

spike *see* SPEAK

spile[1] **&c** *n* **1** a splinter, chip, narrow strip of wood *e16*.　**2** a wooden plug for stopping the vent of a cask, a spigot *20-, Sh-Kcb*.
　vt hang **up** (fishing lines) on a pole to be cleaned *la20-, NE*.
　spilin tree *e20,* ~ **tree** *la19-* a pole on which fishing lines are hung to be cleaned or baited, *chf NE*.

spile[2] **&c** *vti see* SPILE[1]

spilin tree *see* SPILE[1]

spilk *vt* shell (peas) *19-e20, NE*.
　~**in(g)s** split peas *la19-e20*.　[only Sc; *cf* ME *spelk* bruise or crush beans; perh conflation of PILK w Eng dial *spelt*]

spill &c *v* **1** *vt* = spill, destroy *la14-16*.　**2** spoil, mar, make imperfect *la14-e19*.　**3** ravish, violate (a woman) *la14-15*.　**4** *vi* go to ruin *16*.　**5** *of food etc* degenerate, deteriorate, spoil, *freq in adj* **spilt** *la16-19*.

spin *vti* **1** = spin *16-*.　**2** *vt* roll (tobacco leaf) into a continuous rope or coil, twist (tobacco) 18-19. **3** *vi* progress favourably, go well *20-, Bnf Abd Ags.*

n **1** = spin. **2** a (made-up) story, gossip, rumour *la19-, Bnf Abd.*

spinner 1 the cranefly, daddy-long-legs *19-,* now *local.* **2** a garden spider *19-,* now *Abd.*

spinnin jenny 1 = *spinner* 1, *20-, local N-S.* **2** a home-made spinning toy *20-, Lnk Rox.*

spin(nin) maggie &c = *spinner* 1, *la19-, local NE-S.*

on the ~ on a drinking spree *la19-,* now *Ags Dmf.* ~ **the knife** a party game *20-, nEC, WC, SW.*

spindle *see* SPINLE

spindrift *19-;* **speen- &c** *17-, NE,* **spune- &c** *la19-e20, Sh NE* ['spɪn'drɪft, 'spɪndrɪft; *Sh* 'spøn-; *NE* 'spin-] *n* **1** spray whipped up by gusts of wind and driven across the tops of waves *17-.* **2** snow blown up from the ground in swirls by gusts of wind, driving snow *19-20, chf NE.* [see SND]

spink[1] *n* **1** one of several species of flower, *eg* the lady's smock, common primrose or maiden pink *la18-, local NE-EC.* **2** an attractive young person *19.* [appar var of PINK[1]]

spink[2] *n* **1** the chaffinch *la17-,* now *Rox.* **2** term of abuse for a person *e16, only Sc.*
vi, of a bird utter the note 'spink' *la19-,* now *Bnf.* [imit; see also *gowdspink* (GOWD)]

spinle &c *15-,* **spindle &c** *18-,* **spinnel &c** *la16-20* ['spɪnl] *n* **1** = spindle *15-.* **2** [*also* *'spəɪnl] a (varying) measure of yarn *18-19.*

spinnelled &c *chf of diseased teats of animals* spindle-shaped *18-19.*

spire[1] *n* **1** = spire, a stem, pointed tower etc. **2** *also* ~-**wall** a wall or screen between the fire and the door, *freq* fitted with a seat, a HALLAN *18-e19.*

spirie tall, slender, spindly *19.*

spire[2] **&c** *v* **1** *vi* dry out; become parched *la18-e19.* **2** *vt* wither, cause to fade, dry up *19-, sEC Rox.*

spirie *see* SPIRE[1]

spirit *see* SPEERIT

spirk *see* SPARK

spirl[1] *n* **1** a small slender shoot *20-, Fif Loth Slk.* **2** a tall thin person *20-, Bnf Abd Slk.*
~**ie &c** *adj* slender, thin, spindly *la18-,* now *Loth S. n* a slender person *19-,* now *Fif Loth S.* [only Sc; see SND]

spirl[2] *vi* run about in a lively way; whirl around *19.* [only Sc; appar var of PIRL w prothetic *s*-]

spirling &c; sparling &c *la18-20,* **sperling** *16-e19 n* **1** the smelt *16-,* now *Per Ayr.* **2** a sprat *18-e19.*

spirtle *see* SPURTLE

spit &c *vti, pt also* **spitted &c** *16-e19. ptp also* **spitten &c** *20-,* **spitted** *16-e18* = spit *16-.*
spitten image the exact likeness **of** *20-.*
spitter *n* **1** a slight shower of rain or snow *19-,*

now *N, C.* **2** *in pl* small drops of wind-driven rain or snow *la18-,* now *NE Ags Dmf.* *vi, of rain or snow* fall in small drops or flakes, drizzle *la19-,* now *local N-C.* **spittery** a spittoon *la17, only Sc.* **spittin &c 1** *freq in pl* spittle *la19-, Gen except Sh Ork.* **2** a small hot-tempered person or animal *19-, Bnf Abd.* **spittle &c** *n* 1 = spittle. **2** a quantity of saliva ejected at one time *18-,* now *local Ork-WC, only Sc.* **spitty** nickname for someone who spits frequently *la20-, local Sh-Fif.*

~ **and gie (it) ower** *or* **up** give in, admit defeat *19-,* now *Abd Kcdn Ags.*

spit *see* SPEET

spital &c [*'spɪtl] *n* = spital, a charity hospital *15-.* [in place-names = a hospice or shelter for travellers, *esp* in mountainous country *13-.* OED *spittle* (*n*[1])]

spite *n* **1** = spite *la16-.* **2** a disappointment, a cause for annoyance or grief *la19-,* now *Abd Ayr.*

spite *see* SPEET

spitten, spitty *see* SPIT

splae &c [sple; *Ross nEC WC also* spləɪ; *C also* 'splevɪ; *Ork SW also* splɑ] *adj* = splay(-foot(ed)) *19-,* now *Dnbt.*

splairge &c [splerdʒ; *Bwk S* splerg] *v* **1** *vt* (1) slander, besmirch *la18-20.* (2) bespatter, splash (a person etc) *19-,* now *C, S.* **2** sprinkle, splash (a liquid etc) *20-,* now *nEC, WC, SW.* **3** *vi* fly or splash in all directions, scatter itself *19-,* now *Wgt Rox.* **4** move clumsily through water, mud etc *la19-,* now *Ags Per.* **5** run wild, squander one's resources or talents heedlessly *la19-,* now *Kcdn Per.*
n a splash, sprinkling, splodge of water, mud etc *19-,* now *Loth WC-S.* [only Sc; altered f SPAIRGE]

splash[1] **&c** *n* the plaice *20-,* now *Abd.*
~**ack** = *n, la20-, local N.* [var of PLASH[2]]

splash[2] *vti* **1** = splash *19-.* **2** *vi* fish with a *splash net, la19-,* now *WC Kcb, only Sc.*
~ **net** a net suspended in the water, into which fish are driven by a splashing in the water *19-,* now *Arg Kcb.* ~ **netting** a method of fishing using a *splash net, la19-,* now *Arg Kcb.*

splash[3] *adj* ~ **foot** splay foot *19-,* now *Abd.* [only Sc; perh f SPLASH[1]]

splatch *n* a splodge, blot, *esp* of something semi-liquid or sticky, a patch of colour, dirt etc *19-, local.* [onomat]
vt bedaub, splash *19-, local.*

splatter *v* **1** *vt* scatter, splash, sprinkle about, spatter *la19-.* **2** *fig* blurt out, babble, spout *la18-,* now *WC.* **3** bespatter, bedaub, splash with liquid, mud etc *19-.* **4** *vi* splash noisily; walk or run with a clattering or rattling noise *19-, local.*
n **1** a splashing, clattering or rattling sound; a commotion *19-,* now *N nEC Gall.* **2** a splash of liquid, mud etc *19-,* now *Sh Cai.* **3** a thin sprinkling *20-,* now *Sh Ags.* [conflation of Eng *spatter* w *splash*]

splay &c *vti* **1** = splay. ˙**2** *sewing* finish a seam by hemming the upper projecting edge down over the lower one *19-*, *local Sh-SW*.
n **1** = splay. **2** a hem sewn as in *v*, *19-*, *now Abd Ayr*. **3** a stroke, slap *19-20*, *Rox*.
~ **on** work vigorously *20-*, *Loth Rox*. [only Sc]
spleen *n* = spleen.
from (*la15-16*) *or* **to** (*la16*) **the** ~ from *or* to the heart *only Sc*.
spleet &c *vti*, *pt*, *ptp* **spleet** = split *la17-*, *now Sh Ork N*, *EC Rox*.
spleeter a person who splits fish and removes the backbone *la19-*, *Sh Cai Kcdn*.
~ **new** = *split new* (SPLIT) *la18-*, *now Sh Ork N*. [see SND; *cf* SPLIT]
spleiter &c ['spləitər, 'splitər] *n* **1** a splash, patch of spilt liquid, blot *20-*, *now NE Ags*. **2** a wind-driven shower of rain, snow etc *20-*, *now Bnf Abd*.
vti spill, spatter messily over an area *20-*, *NE Ags*. [only Sc; onomat; *cf* SPLATTER and Eng *splutter*]
splenner *vi* stride or stand with the feet apart *19-*, *chf Kcb*. [only Sc; see SND]
splent see SPLINT
splerrie ['splɛrɪ] *vt* bespatter, splash with liquid, dirt etc *20-*, *now wLoth*. [only Sc; altered f *slairie* (SLAIR), with *-p-* f SPLATTER, Eng *splash* etc]
splet see SPLIT
spleuchan &c; **speuchan** &c ['spl(j)uxən, 'spjuxən] *n* **1** a tobacco pouch, *usu* of leather *la18-*, *local Ork-Gall*. **2** a pouch for holding money, *usu* of skin or leather *la18-*, *now Ork Per*. [ScGael *spliùchan*, IrGael *spliuchán*]
spleut &c [splʌut] *n* the noise caused by a sudden spluttering gush; the liquid shed or spilled in this way *la19-*, *now Abd*.
~**er** &c burst or gush out with a spluttering noise *la19-*, *Bnf*. ~**erie** &c [*NE also* 'spjutərɪ] *n* weak watery food; a dirty mess *la19-*, *now Bnf Abd*. *adj* **1** weak and watery *la19-*, *now Bnf Abd*. **2** *of weather* wet, rainy *la20-*, *NE Per Fif*. [only Sc; onomat, w infl f SPLOIT, SPLEITER etc]
splew &c *vti* spit out, spew, vomit *19*. [only Sc; altered f Eng *spew*, with *-l-* by analogy w SPLATTER, Eng *splash* etc]
splice *n* **1** = splice. **2** a sliver of wood, splinter *20-*, *now sEC*, *S*, *only Sc*.
splicer an instrument for twisting straw ropes, a *thrawcruik* (THRAW) *la20-*, *Fif WC Rox*.
splinder &c *n* a splinter, fragment *la15-*, *now Sh Ork*.
~ **new** = *split new* (SPLIT) *19-*, *now Sh Ork*. [chf Sc; ME *splyndre*; cf ODan *splinder*; Norw dial *splindra* a chip or sliver of wood]
splint *18-*; **splent** *la15-19* *n* **1** = splint *la15-*. **2** *also* ~ **coal** a hard coarse splintering coal which burns with great heat *18-*, *C*, *chf Sc*.
~**y** *of coal* like ~ *coal*, *20-*, *now Fif*.
~ **new** = *split new* (SPLIT) *la19-*, *local Ags-SW*.

split &c *vti*, *pt*, *ptp* *also* **splet** **1** = split *la17-*. **2** *vt*, *curling* (CURL) separate (two stones lying together) by striking them with a third *la19-*. **3** part (the hair) *20-*, *now local Stlg-SW*.
n **1** = split *la17-*. **2** *weaving* a small piece of split reed etc, *later* thin metal, forming one of the divisions through which a warp thread passes in a loom *la18-*, *now nEC*, *WC*, *S*. **3** a quarrel, rift *18-*.
~ **new** brand new, absolutely new, as new as *split wood la17-*, *C*. [*cf* SPLEET]
splitter &c *n* (the noise of) a splashing or splattering of liquid; a hubbub *la19-*, *now Ork C*.
vi splutter, make a spluttering noise; make a mess by splashing liquid about *la19-*, *now Ork C*. [only Sc; onomat; *cf* SPLEUT, Eng *splutter* etc]
sploit &c [splɔit] *vi* spout, squirt; splash *la18-*, *now Sh*. [var of *ploit* (see PLOWT¹); *cf* also SPLEITER]
splore &c *n* **1** a party, spree, jollification, *freq* with drinking *la18-*. **2** a controversy, quarrel; a state of excitement or commotion, a fuss *la18-20*. **3** an exploit, escapade *19-*, *Ork N*, *C*.
vi **1** frolic, make merry *la18-*, *now local Ags-Rox*. **2** show off, boast, brag (**about**) *19-*, *now Lnk*. [only Sc; see SND]
sploy *n* a frolic; a merry tale *la18-19*. [only Sc; var of PLOY¹, perh w infl f Eng *exploit*]
splunt *SW*, *S*, **sprunt** *chf Rox vi* go wooing or courting *19-e20*. [only Sc; see SND]
splurt &c *vti* squirt, eject liquid from the mouth in a splash *la18-*, *now local Sh-Per*.
n, *also fig* a spurt, splutter *19-*, *now Ags Per*. [onomat]
splush *n* = plush *20-*, *now Rox*, *only Sc*.
spoach &c [spotʃ] *vi* **1** = poach *19-*, *Rox*. **2** sponge, scrounge around for favours *19-*, *now Bwk*. **3** pry, rummage, poke about **in** *20*, *Bwk Rox*.
n a person who pokes about, a prying, inquisitive person *19-*, *now Rox*.
~**er 1** a poacher *19-*, *chf Rox*. **2** a sponger, scrounger *19-*, *now Bwk*. [only Sc]
spoilȝe see SPULYIE
spoke see SPAIK, SPEAK
spoliate *adj* destitute, devoid *la15*. [only Sc; L *spoliāt-*, ptp stem of *spoliāre* despoil]
spolȝe see SPULYIE
spon see SPUNE
spone [*spon] *vt* spend *la15*. [only Sc; aphetic f Eng *dispone*]
sponge see SPOONGE
sponk see SPUNK
sponsible *adj* **1** safe, dependable *e16*. **2** responsible, reliable, respectable *18-19*. [aphetic f Eng *responsible*]
spool see SPULE
spoon see SPUNE
spoonge *la18-20*, **sponge** &c *la18-*; **spounge** &c *la15-e19* [spundʒ] *n*, *vti* = sponge.
sporran &c *n* a purse or pouch, *specif* the (*usu*

ornamented) leather pouch worn in front of a man's KILT[1], used to hold money etc *la18-*. [only Sc; Gael *sporan*]

sporrow *see* SPARROW

sport *n* = sport *16-*.
vtir = sport.
~**our** a person who amuses others, a jester *16*, *only Sc*. ~**sum** amusing, diverting, sportive *e16*, *only Sc*.
~**staff** a quarter-staff *e17*, *only Sc*.

spot *see* SPAT

spoucher &c ['sputʃər] *n* a (*usu* long-handled) wooden ladle or scoop, *esp* for baling a boat or lifting fish from a net *16-20*. [ME *spojour*, northern OF *espuchoir*, f northern OF *espuchier*, OF *espuisier* (*v*) drain, empty of water; *cf* F *épuiser*]

spounge *see* SPOONGE

spouse &c [spus] *n* = spouse *la14-*.
vt [*spuz] = spouse, espouse, betroth *la14-e16*.
spousing *freq in combs* marriage-; betrothal- *la15-18*.
~ **one's fortune** try one's luck, seek one's fortune *e19*.

spout &c [sput] *n* **1** = spout, a pipe *16-*. **2** a forceful discharge of liquid from the mouth of a pipe etc *16-*. **3** a natural spring of water streaming from the ground or from a cleft in a rock; *latterly also* an outside tap or standpipe *18-*, *now local Abd-Rox*. **4** a waterfall, cataract *19-*, *freq in place-names, now local*. **5** a narrow enclosed pathway; a gully in a cliff-face *19-, freq in place-names*. **6** a horizontal roof gutter, a RONE[1] *18-*, *now local Sh-S*. **7** the razor-fish or -clam *16-*, *now Sh Ork Cai Wgt, only Sc*. **8** a squirt, a toy (water-)gun, *usu* made from a plant stem *la19-*, *now local Sh-Wgt*. **9** a small quantity of liquid *20-*, *local EC-SW*. **10** a rush, dart, sudden movement *la18-*, *now Sh Cai*.
vti **1** = spout *16-*. **2** *vi* dart, spring, bound **out** etc suddenly *19-*, *now local Sh-Wgt*.
~**ie &c** *of soil* full of springs, marshy, undrained *18-*, *now NE nEC*. ~**iness** a soggy condition (of soil) *la18-e19*. ~**rach &c** [*'~rəx] weak, thin drink *19*, *Abd Gall, only Sc*.
~ **fish** = *n* 7, *18-*. ~ **gun** a popgun *la19-*, *now Fif Loth Wgt*. ~ **well** = *n* 3, *18-19*.
~**-ma-gruel &c** any unappetizing food *20-*, *now Bnf*.

sprachle *see* SPRAUCHLE

sprack[1] *adj*, *chf literary* lively, animated, alert *19-*, *now Cai*. [ME *sprakliche* smartly, appar f OE **spræc*, corresponding to ON *sprækr* active, lively]

sprack[2] *n* a chip of wood, splinter; *freq in sing as collective* waste scraps of wood, tree branches etc, wood or straw litter *e20*, *Ork Arg*. [see SND]

sprackle *see* SPRAUCHLE, SPRECKLE.

sprag *n* a bradnail *20-*, *now NE nEC, WC*. [see SND]

spraich[1] **&c**; **sprauch &c** *16-e20*, **sprech** *la19-20* [sprex; *NE also* *spr(j)ɑx] *vi* cry shrilly, scream, shriek *19-*, *now Abd*.
n a scream, cry, shriek; the sound of weeping or wailing *16-20*. [only Sc; onomat]

spraich[2] **&c** [sprex; *C also* sprɑx] *n* ~ **of day** break of day *la19-*, *now Fif Lnk Ayr*. [only Sc; forming a homonymous pair w SPRAICH[1] similar to SKRAICH and *scraich* (SKREEK)]

spraikle *see* SPRECKLE

spraing &c; **sprang** *16-18* [spreŋ] *n* a (*usu* glittering or brightly-coloured) stripe, streak or ray of colour *16-e20*.
vt variegate, diversify with stripes or streaks *16-e20*.
spraingled &c ['spreŋlt] striped, streaked *18-e19*. [only Sc; see SND]

spraint *see* SPRENT[1]

sprang *see* SPRAING

sprat &c *now Stlg Bwk*, **spret &c** *18-*, *now WC, SW, S*, **spreat &c** *la16-e19*; **sprit &c** *la18-20* [sprat, sprɛt, sprɪt] *n* a coarse reedy rush or grass growing on marshy ground and sometimes used in rope-making and stack-thatching *la16-*.
~**ty 1** rush-like, rushy *la18-19*. **2** producing or abounding in rushes *18-*, *now Ayr Dmf*. [chf Sc; see SND; *cf* SPROT[1]]

sprattle &c *vi* scramble, struggle, sprawl *la18-e20*.
n a scramble, sprawl, strenuous effort; contest; struggle *19-20*. [only Sc; prob metath f SPARTLE]

sprauch *see* SPRAICH[1]

sprauchle &c *19-*; **sprachle &c** *la19-*, **sprackle &c** *la18-20* ['sprɑxl; *'sprakl, *'sprexl, &c] *vi* move laboriously or in a hasty, clumsy way (*esp* upwards), clamber; struggle (*esp* to get out of or through something), flounder about, sprawl *la18-*.
n **1** *lit and fig* a scramble, struggle *la19-*. **2** a stunted feeble creature, a weakling *20-*, *SW*. [only Sc; see SND]

sprawl *19-*; **sprewl &c** *15-e19*, **spravle** *20*, *Cai* [sprɑl, *Cai also* *'sprɑvl; *Rox also* 'sprawəl, *sprjul] *vi* = sprawl *15-*.
n **1** a sprawl. **2** a rush, struggle, scramble *la18-*, *now Abd, only Sc*.
~**ach &c** *only Sc*, *vi* sprawl, flail about with the limbs, flounder *19-*, *NE*. *n* a sprawling, flailing movement of the limbs *19-*, *Bnf*.

spreach *see* SPREATH

spread *la17-*; **spreid &c** *16-e20*, **spred** *la14-16* [sprid; *nEC* spred; *pt* sprɛd, sprid; *ptp* sprɛd] *vti* **1** = spread *la14-*. **2** *vt* extend, make larger or wider *la16*. **3** spread butter, jam etc on (a slice of bread etc) *19-*. **4** turn the top covers of (a bed) **down** *or* **up** *la19-*.
~**-field** the ground where cut PEAT[1] is spread for drying *la18-20*.

spreat *see* SPRAT

spreath &c *la17-*; **spreith &c** *15-e20*,

spreach &c *16-19* [spreθ, sprex; *NE* spriθ] *n*
1 cattle, *specif* a herd (of cattle) stolen and
driven off in a RAID, *esp* by *Highlanders* (HIE-
LAND) to the *Lowlands* (LAWLAND) *16-19*. **2**
also fig booty, plunder *15-19*. **3** a foray to steal
cattle, a cattle RAID *18*. **4** driftwood, wreckage
from ships *20-*, *now Abd Ags*. **5** a great many, a
crowd, collection *18-e20*.
vt, only **spreth** pillage, plunder *e15*.

spreacherie &c 1 household odds and ends
la16-e19. **2** booty, plunder, loot; things
acquired furtively or on the sly *la18-e20*. [only
Sc; ScGael *spreidh*, IrGael *spreid* (a dowry consisting of) cattle, ultimately f L *praeda* booty]

sprech *see* SPRAICH[1]

spreckle &c *la18-*; **spraikle &c** *16-19*,
sprackle &c *20 n* a speckle, spot, freckle *16-*.
vt, chf **spreckled &c** speckled, mottled, flecked,
variegated *la18-*. [*cf* Norw dial *sprekla* a fleck,
MHighGer *spreckel* a speckle]

spred *see* SPREAD

spree[1] &c *n* **1** = spree *19-*. **2** a boisterous
quarrel, a spirited argument; a disturbance,
fuss *19*.

spree[2] &c *only Sc*, **spry** *adj* **1** = spry *la18-*. **2**
spruce, neat, smartly dressed *19-*, *now Ags Per
Lnk*.
vti, also fig spruce **up**, smarten **up** *la19-*, *now Ags
Fif Lnk*. [see SND]

spreid *see* SPREAD

spreit *see* SPEERIT

spreith *see* SPREATH

sprent[1] &c; spraint *19 vi* **1** spring (forward),
bound; move with agility *la14-19*. **2** split,
burst apart (**in(to)** splinters) *la15*.
n **1** a spring, leap, bound *e16*. **2** *also fig* the
spring of a lock etc *17-19*, *only Sc*. **3** the clasp,
hasp of a chest, trunk etc *16-19*. [see SND]

sprent[2] *n, baking* a hollow made in a heap of
flour to contain liquid before mixing *19-e20*.

spret *see* SPEERIT, SPRAT

sprete *see* SPEERIT

spreth *see* SPREATH

sprewl *see* SPRAWL

sprig *n* a tune, a snatch of song, a dance tune
la19-, *now local N-SW*. [only Sc; altered f
SPRING]

spriggit *see* SPICKET

spriklybag &c *n* the stickleback *19-20*, *Ayr Uls*.
[var of Eng *prickly* + *bag*]

spring *vti* **1** = spring *la14-*. **2** gush (**with**
blood) *e16*. **3** rise up in the sky *e16*, *only Sc*.
n **1** = spring *17-*. **2** the growth of vegetation,
specif in spring *la18-e19*. **3** the rise, slope,
height (of an arch) *la17-*, *now WC Kcb*, *only Sc*.
4 *also fig* a lively dance(-tune) *la15-*, *chf Sc*.
~ing grazing from the first grass of the year,
spring pasture *la20-*, *SW*.
~ bauk &c the main top-rope of a herring-net
la19-, *now Mry*.

play oneself a ~, tak a ~ o one's ain fiddle
etc go one's own way, do what one pleases *la18-*,
now Sh.

sprinkle &c *vi* wriggle; dart quickly *e16*. [only
Sc; perh f Eng *sprinkle* sparkle]

sprit *see* SPEERIT, SPRAT

sprit-new *adj* = split-new (SPLIT) *19-*, *now Stlg
Fif WC*.

sprittle &c *la18-e19*, **spruttle &c** *16-e18*;
spurtle *n, only* **spruttle &c** a small spot,
speckle *e16*.
~d &c speckled, spotted *16-*, *now Rox*. [only
Sc; *cf* MLowGer *sprut(e)le*, *sprottel* a freckle]

sprool &c [sprul; *Sh* also sprøl; *Ork* sprol] *n, fishing* a short length of wire etc pushed through
the sinker of a hand-line, with a hook attached
at either end *la19-*, *local E*.
vi fish offshore with a SPROOL *la20-*, *Bnf Ags Fif*.
[only Sc; perh the same word as *sprewl*
(SPRAWL); *cf* Norw *sprellemann* a jumping-jack]

sproosh *see* SPRUSH

sproot *see* SPROUT

sprose &c; sprowse &c [sproz; *WC* also
sprʌuz] *v* **1** *vi* boast, make a great show, swagger *la18-20*, *chf WC*. **2** *vtr* brag about (oneself
or another) *19*. **3** *vi* exaggerate, tell a tall
story in order to impress *19-*, *now Ayr*.
n a bragging or boasting, swagger, bravado
la18-e19. [see SND]

sprot[1] &c [sprot; *WC* sprʌt] *n* a rush, the reedy
plant *both in gen and specif of particular species*,
la16-, *now NE Ags Per*.
~ty of or like rushes; abounding in rushes *18-*,
now Abd. [chf Sc; see SND; *cf* SPRAT]

sprot[2] *n* a small stick or twig, *esp* as used for fuel
e19. [nME *sprote* a twig, chip of wood, OE
sprota a shoot, sprout]

sproug *see* SPRUG

sprout; spruit &c *la16-e20*, **sproot** *19-*
[sprut] *vti* **1** = sprout *la16-*. **2** *vt* rub or break
off the sprouts of (potatoes) *20-*, *Sh Ork N*.
n **1** = sprout. **2** a child *19-*, *now local Bnf-S*.

sprowse *see* SPROSE

spruce, spruch *see* SPRUSH

sprud &c *n* a knife for prising limpets from a
rock *la19-*, *Abd Kcdn*. [only Sc; altered f Eng
spud applied to various (chisel-shaped) tools]

sprug &c; sproug &c *la19-e20* [sprʌg; *Cai Fif*
sprʌug; *Per Fif* also sprog] *n* **1** *joc or child's word*
the house-sparrow *19-*, *now Cai Fif sEC*. **2** a
bright but undersized boy *la20-*, *Cai Fif Lnk*.
[metath f SPURG]

spruit *see* SPROUT

sprunt[1] *vi* = sprint *la19-e20*.

sprunt[2] *n* the yarn a weaver contrived to keep
for himself *e20*, *Fif*. [unknown]

sprunt *see* SPLUNT

sprush &c *18-*, **spruce &c; spruch** *17-18*
[spruʃ, sprʌʃ] *n* **1** *only* **Spruce** the Prussian
people *e17*. **2** = spruce, the fir *la18-*. **3** *only*

sprush &c a sprucing or smartening up, a tidying or setting in order *la19-, now Sh Ags Per.* **4** *only* **sproosh** lemonade *la20-, NE.*
adj **1** = spruce *la17-.* **2** brisk, smart in one's movements, spry *la18-.*
vt = spruce *la19-.*
~ **stane** &c *16-e17,* ~ **wecht** *e16* a weight formerly used in Prussia = 28 lb troy (25 lb avoirdupois, 11 kg) *only Sc.*

spruttle *see* SPRITTLE

spry *see* SPREE

spue &c *19-,* **spew** &c [spju] *vti* **1** = spew *16-.* **2** *vi, of a pudding* (PUDDIN) burst, split open *la19-, Sh Abd.* **3** *of liquid, smoke etc* flow, pour (**out** *etc*) in a copious stream, billow out *la18-.*
n **1** = spew. **2** (a puff of) smoke *la19-, now Sh Ags* [perh partly altered f PEW]. **3** a retch, a vomiting motion *19-.*
spuin fou replete, *esp* with drink, to the point of vomiting *18-, now NE Ags Kcb.*

spug; speug &c *la19-* [sp(j)ʌg; *local C* spjʌx] *n* **1** *joc or child's word* the house-sparrow *19-, Gen except Sh.* **2** *transf* a child, a small person etc *20-, now Per.* [var of SPURG; *cf* SPRUG]

spuilzie *see* SPULYIE

spule &c; **spool** *la19-* [spøl; *Per* *spil] *n* **1** = spool, a bobbin *16-.* **2** the shuttle in which the bobbin is placed *19-, now Sh Ags.*

spule *see* SPAUL

spulie *see* SPULYIE

spult *n* a spout *la14-15.* [late nME; *cf* WFlem *spulten* (*v*) spout]

spulyie &c *la16-;* **-ʒe** &c *la14-16,* **-zie** *la16-,* **spo(i)lʒe** &c *la14-16,* **spulie** &c *la16-* ['spul(j)ɪ, *'spøl(j)ɪ, &c] *v* **1** *vt* rob, despoil, plunder (a person or place) *la14-20.* **2** deprive (someone) **of** (something) by stealing *16-e20.* **3** take as spoil or plunder, steal; *law* carry off (another's MOVEABLE possessions) without legal warrant or against his will *la15-, now Abd.* **4** *vi* plunder, maraud *18-, now Per.* **5** *vt* spoil, mar, harm *la18-.*
n **1** (an instance of) depredation, spoliation, plundering, devastation *la15-e20.* **2** *chf* **spuilzie** (1) *civil law* the taking away or meddling with the MOVEABLE goods of another without the owner's consent; an action for the restitution of such *la17-.* (2) *criminal law* an illegal seizure of another's goods, differing from theft in being done openly with the intention of claiming them as one's own or of returning them after use *la17-19.* **3** booty, spoil, plunder *16-e20.* **4** jetsam, anything cast ashore *la19-, now Ork.*
~**r** a robber, plunderer *la16-e19.*
action *etc* **of spuilzie** *law* an action for restitution as in *n* 2 (1) *18-e20.* [chf Sc; OF *espoillier* (*v*), *espoille, espuille* (*n*) spoil]

spune &c, **spoon** *18-;* **spon** *15,* **speen** *18-, NE* [spøn; *NE* spin; *nEC* spen; *C* spɪn] *n* **1** = spoon *15-.* **2** a spoon-shaped implement, *eg* (1) for heating, assaying *la15;* (2) *golf* a wooden

club with a slightly hollowed head and backward-sloping face, corresponding to the number 3 wood *19-e20.*
~**ful** *la15-,* **speenifu** *20-, NE* = spoonful.
spoon creel a small basket hung on a kitchen wall for holding spoons *19-, now local Ags-Ayr.*
~**-gabbit** having a thick, protruding lower lip *la20-, local Fif-SW.* ~ **meat** soft or liquid food eaten with a spoon *la19-, now local Ork-Dmf.*
have mair than *or* **nothing but what the** ~ **pits in** (**the heid** *etc*) be more than usually clever *or* stupid *la19-, now local NE-Kcb.* **mak a** ~ **or spoil a horn** either succeed or fail in a big way *19-20.* **pit in one's** ~ interfere in another's affairs *la20-, NE Fif WC.*

spunedrift *see* SPINDRIFT

spung &c *n* **1** a purse, pouch for money, *freq* with a spring clasp *18-20.* **2** a fob, watch-pocket in trousers *la18-20.*
vt rob (someone **of** something); pick someone's pocket *18-e19.* [only Sc; f OE *pung* a purse]

spunk &c *la16-;* **sponk** *16-18* [spʌŋk; *Cai* spʌuŋk] *n* **1** a spark (of fire), quick flicker of light, glimmer *16-, now N nEC, SW.* **2** a tiny, poor, miserable fire *la18-19.* **3** *fig* the least particle or vestige (*esp* of some moral quality) *18-e20.* **4** the spark (of life); life *la18-19.* **5** (1) tinder, touchwood; a sliver of wood tipped with sulphur etc for producing fire *18-e19.* (2) a match *la19-.* (3) a thin sliver of wood for making SPUNKS 5 (1); any splinter, chip *19-e20.* **6** a hot-tempered, irascible person *19.*
vt emit sparks (in all directions) *la19-, now Sh Per.*
~**ie** &c **1** = SPUNK *n* 1 (*19-20*), 2 (*19-20*), 6 (*19*). **2** the will-o'-the-wisp *18-20.* **3** a spirited, lively young person *19-, now NE, C.* **4** WHISKY, spirits *la18.*
a ~ **o fire** = *n* 2, *19-, now Abd.* ~ **out** *of news, scandal etc* leak out, become known *19-, now Mry.* ~ **up 1** become heated, flare up in anger or passion *la19-, now Fif Wgt, only Sc.* **2** revive in spirits, cheer up *19-, now Ags Per.* [see SND]

spur¹ &c *n* = spur *la14-.*
vti **1** = spur *la16-.* **2** *vi* hasten, hurry *e16, 20-, now Sh.* **3** scrape or scratch around, as a fowl in search of food *19-, Rox.*
~ **band** a strut or diagonal stay in a roof *14-e18.* ~ **haste** great haste *e17, only Sc.* ~**(-leather)-whang** the leather strap or thong attaching a spur to the heel; *fig* something of little value *19.* ~ **silver** money paid to choristers in certain privileged chapels by anyone entering with spurs on *e16, only Sc.*

spur² &c *n, chf in combs* a sparrow *19-e20.*
~**die 1** = *n, la19-, now NE Ags Loth.* **2** the hedge-sparrow *20-, Loth Bwk.* **3** a small lively person *la19-, NE.* [prob Scand; *cf* Norw dial *spoor, spør,* ON *spörr; cf* next and SPRUG, SPUG]

spurg *n* the house-sparrow *19-e20.*

~**ie** = *n*, *19-*, *NE*. [only Sc; prob reduced f SPUR[2] + dim suffix *-ock*; *cf* SPRUG, SPUG]

spurge *vi* spout or gush **out** in a stream *la15*. [ultimately f L *exporgere*; *cf* Eng *purge*]

spurkle *see* SPURTLE

spurl &c *vi* struggle, sprawl, kick or throw the legs about *19-e20*. [frequentative of Eng *spur*]

spurn *vi* **1** = spurn *la15-*. **2** *contrasted with* **speed** trip or stumble *15-e16*, *chf Sc*.

spurtle &c; **spirtle** *20*, **spurkle** &c *la18-e20* ['spʌrtl; 'spɪrtl; *local N, C also* 'spʌrkl, 'spɪrkl] *n* **1** *baking* a long-handled, flat-bladed implement for turning oatcakes (AIT), SCONES etc *16-*, now *Ags Per*. **2** a short round stick for stirring porridge, soup etc *16-*, *Gen but rare in Ags* (*see* THEEVIL). **3** *literary, disparaging, or joc* a sword *la17-e20*.

~ **grup** a sudden gripping pain, a stitch *la19-e20*, *Ayr*. ~ **leg** a thin leg like a porridge stick *la19-e20*. ~**-leggit** having ~ legs, *la19-*, now *NE, C*. ~ **shank** = ~ *leg*, *19-*, now *Ayr*. [see SND]

spurtle *see* SPARTLE, SPRITTLE

spy *n* = spy *la14-*.
vti **1** = spy *la14-*. **2** *vi* make stealthy observations, pry *la15-*.

spyale [*'spaɪəl] spying; observation, watch *la14*.

spycarie [*'spikərɪ, *'spəik-] *n* spikenard *e16*. [only Sc; MedL *spicarius*, L *spīca* a spike. OED *specary*]

spynist *see* SPANIS

spyntie *see* SPEND[1]

spyog &c [spjog; *Cai Gall* spog] *n* **1** a paw, hand, foot, or leg *la18-*, now *Cai*. **2** a bare stumpy branch *20-*, *Inv Mry Bnf*.
vi walk in a stilted, stiff-legged, or sedate way *la19-*, now *Ork*. [Gael *spòg* a paw, claw; *cf* SPAG]

spyolk *see* SPELK

spyr *see* SPEIR

squabash [*skwa'baʃ] *vt* silence (a person) by demolishing his arguments, pretensions etc, squash *e19*. [only Sc; conflation of Eng *squash* and *bash*]

squabblement [*'skwablmənt] *n* a wrangle, disturbance of the peace, associated *esp* with the Langholm *Common Riding* (COMMON) *18-19*.

squach *see* SQUAIK

squadrat *adj, rare* square-shaped; rectangular *e17*. [Ital *squadrato* squared. OED *squadrate*]

Squadrone &c [skwa'dronɪ] *n, in full* ~ **Volante** [vo'lantɪ] the New Party, a group of politicians in the last Scottish parliament, which vacillated between the opposition and government parties, and finally decided the Union issue in 1707; the group continued till 1725 in the British Parliament *e18*. [only Sc; Ital = a flying squadron (of ships), applied (*17*) to a group of cardinals who vacillated between parties in the Church]

squaik &c; **squeck** &c *19-e20*, **squak** &c *19-e20*, **squa(i)ch** &c *19-20* [skwek, skwex, skwak, skwɑx, skwɛk; *skwɛx] *vi, esp of birds or trapped animals* squeal, squeak, screech, squawk *19-*, now local.
n, esp of a trapped bird or animal a loud scream or screech *19-*, now local. [only Sc; onomat]

squaint *see* SQUINT

squak *see* SQUAIK

squall &c [*skwal] *n* **1** = squall, a sudden gust of wind *la18-*. **2** a row, disturbance, quarrel *la18-e19*.

~**och** &c ['skwaləx] *only Sc, vi* scream, cry out shrilly, make a noise and commotion *19-*, *NE*.
n the noise of children playing *20-*, *NE*.

square &c *16-*; **squar** &c *la14-20* [skwer; *Sh also* skwar; *NE* skwɑr] *adj, vti* = square *la14-*.
n **1** = square *16*. **2 the** ~ farm buildings, a farm steading, *esp* when forming the four sides of a square *20-*, local, *only Sc*.

~**man** a workman who regularly uses a square, *esp* a carpenter or mason *17-*, now *only freemasonry*, *only Sc*. ~**men** the *Incorporated Trade* (INCORPORATE) which comprised these in a BURGH *18-19*, *only Sc*. ~**wright** a carpenter, *specif* one who makes furniture *la17-e20*, *only Sc*.

squat; scot *19-*, *Kcdn* [skwat] *n* **1** a heavy fall, a blow, a jolt *16-19*. **2** = squat, the act of squatting.
vti **1** = squat. **2** *vt* strike with the open hand, smack, slap *19-*, now *Kcdn*.

~**tle** squat, lie low, nestle *la18*.

squatter &c ['skwatər] *v* **1** *vi* flutter in water like a duck, flap about in mud or water, splash along *la18-*, now *WC Kcb*. **2** *vt, lit and fig* scatter about; squander *la17-*, now *Ayr Dmf*.
n a large number of small creatures or objects, a disorderly, confused crowd *la19-*, local *Abd-S*, *only Sc*. [onomat]

squeak &c *n* **1** = squeak. **2** *joc* a local newspaper *20-*, *only Sc*.

squeal &c *la18-*; **squele** &c *la14-16*, **squile** &c *la19-*, *NE*, **skoil** *la17-19*, *chf Ags vti* = squeal *la14-*.
n **1** = squeal *la18-*. **2** an outcry, uproar; a spree *la18-19*, *only Sc*.

squeck *see* SQUAIK

squeeb *n* **1** = squib *la19-*. **2** a mean, scrounging, insignificant person *20-*, *NE*.

squeef &c *n* term of abuse for a mean, disreputable, shabby, or worthless person *19-*, now *WC-S*. [only Sc; perh conflation of COOF and SQUEEB]

squeegee &c ['skwi'dʒi] *adj* askew, twisted, at the wrong angle, out of shape *20-*. [only Sc; conflation of SKEW[2] and AJEE]

squeel *see* SCHULE

squeenge *see* SCUNGE

squeerie *see* SCURRY

squeeter *vti* spatter, (cause to) fly in all directions *la19-*, *NE*.

n a state of confusion, a mix-up, a botched job *la19-*, *NE*. [only Sc; emphatic var of SKITTER[1] w semantic development as SCUTTER]

squele *see* SQUEAL

squere &c *la15-19*, **squire &c** [*skwir, *skwer] *n*, *vt* = squire *la15-*.

squyary = squiry, squires collectively *la14-15*.

squile *see* SQUEAL

squink-eyed *adj* = squint-eyed *e17, only Sc*.

squint &c *la17-*; **squaint &c** *18-e20 vi*, *n* = squint.

adj off the straight, set at a slant, oblique *18-*.

~**ie**, **squin(n)y**, ~**ie &c mutch** a kind of woman's plain bonnet tied under the chin *19, only Sc*.

squire *see* SQUERE

squirk *vti* squirt out suddenly *20-, now Stlg Fif Lnk*. [only Sc; prob var of Eng *squirt*]

squirl *n*, *in writing* an ornamental flourish at the end of a letter; *in clothes etc* a piece of trimming, a flounce *19-, now Cai Bnf Per*. [only Sc; prob var of SWIRL w infl f Eng *curl*, *twirl* etc]

squische *vt* crush, squash *e16*.

squyary *see* SQUERE

S.R.C. *see* STUDENT

S.S.C. *see* SOLICIT[2]

St *see* SAINT

sta &c *la16-*, **stall**; **staw** *16-* [stɑ; *stal] *n* **1** = stall *la15-*. **2** quarters, accommodation (in an almshouse) *la16, only Sc*. **3** *chf* **staw**, *also fig* a surfeit, a feeling of nausea, disgust or aversion caused by satiety, *freq* **gie**, **get** *etc* **a** ~ *la18-, now C, S*. **4** *chf* **staw** an annoyance, nuisance; a pest, a bore *19-e20, local Bwk-S*.

vtir **1** = stall *15-*. **2** *vi* become cloyed or sated with or nauseated by food etc; become bored or fed up *18-, local Ags-S*. **3** (1) *vt, also fig* satiate, sicken or disgust with too much food *la18-, C, S*. (2) *vtr* tire, weary, bore with monotony or repetition *la19-, now chf SE, S*.

stawsome &c 1 *of food* nauseous, repugnant to the taste or appetite *19-, C, S*. **2** *fig* tiresome, boring *19-e20*.

sta *see* STEAL

stab *v* **1** *vi* use a pointed weapon to kill or wound *la14-*. **2** make thrusts with a staff or club *e16, only Sc*. **3** *vt* = stab.

n **1** = stab, the act of stabbing etc. **2** a prickle, thorn, a piece of wood in the skin *la19-*. [*cf* STOB]

stab *see* STOB

stable[1], **stabill &c** *n*, *vti* = stable *16-*.

stabler &c a public stable-keeper *16-e19*.

stable[2] **&c** *v* **1** *vt* = stable, make stable, establish *la14-e16*. **2** establish or install (a person) in an office *la15-e16*. **3** *vi* secure **to** (oneself etc) *e16, only Sc*.

stablish *17-*; **stablis** *la14-e15 vt* **1** = stablish, establish *la14-, now arch*. **2** place (a person) permanently in an office etc *la14-e15*.

stacher *la18-*; **stakker &c** *16, 19*, **staucher &c** *la19-* [ˈstaxər, ˈstɑxər; *ˈstakər] *vi* stagger, totter *16-, Gen except Sh*.

n, *lit and fig* a stumble, stagger, a false step *la19-, NE nEC, SW*.

staucherie unsteady in gait *20-, NE nEC, SW*. [ME *stacker*, ON *stakra* (*v*). OED *stacker*]

stack &c *n* **1** = stack *la17-*. **2** a PEAT[1]-stack *la20-, Sh Cai NE*. **3** a tall column of rock rising out of the sea, separated from the cliffs by weathering *la18-, Sh-Bnf*.

~ **hill** the ground or mound on which a STACK (*n* 2) is built *19-e20*. ~ **mou** that end of a STACK (*n* 2) from which the PEATS[1] are drawn for use *la19-, Bnf Abd*. ~ **yaird** a rick-yard *la16*. [for *n* 3 *cf* Faeroese *stakkur*]

stack *see* STICK[1]

stacket *n* a palisade *e17, only Sc*. [LowGer]

stack rope *see* STALK

stad *see* STEID[1]

stad(d)le *see* STATHEL

staelt *see* STEAL

staff; **stafe** *15-16, e18*, **stalf** *e16, only Sc n, pl* **staves &c** *16-*, **sta(i)f(f)is** *15-16* [staf; *stef, *staf; *Gall also *stɑv; *pl* stevz; *Abd* stɑvz; *stefs] *n* **1** = staff *15-*. **2** a walking-stick *18-e20*. **3** a stave, a section of a cask etc, *freq* **a** ~ **out o one's bicker** *etc* a reduction in one's income, a drain on one's resources *19*.

staffing the action of striking with staves *la14*.

~**man 1** an official carrying a staff of office, *eg* a constable *17-e18, C*. **2** the BURGH hangman *la17-e18, Stlg*. ~ **sling &c** a sling (*ie* the weapon), the cords of which are attached to the end of a staff *la14-16*.

ding in *or* **fa in(to)** ~**s** *lit and fig* smash *or* fall to pieces *18-, now Sh Ork Ags Per*. **keep someone at (the) staff('s) end** keep someone at a distance, keep aloof from someone *la18-19*. ~ **and stik** (*la14*) *or* **bastoun** (*la14-e18*) *or* **baton** (*18-19*) the symbols by which a VASSAL resigned his FEU into the hands of his SUPERIOR *la15-e19*.

staffage *adj* = staffish, stubborn, unmanageable *16, only Sc*. [OED *staffish*]

stafis *see* STAFF

stag *vt* support with piles *e17, Abd*. [only Sc; uncertain]

stag *see* STAIG

stage &c *n* **1** = stage *16-*. **2** = stadium, an ancient Greek and Roman measure of length *la14-16, only Sc*.

v **1** *vt* bring (a person) to trial before a court, *esp* a church court *la17-e18, only Sc*. **2** *vi* strut about in a stately way (as if on a stage) *e19*.

bring to (*la17*) *or* **keep on** (*e18*) **the** ~ bring to *or* prolong a trial before a church court *only Sc*.

staif(f)is *see* STAFF

staig &c, **stag &c** *la15-18* [steg; *NE also* st(j)ag; *stag] *n* **1** a young horse of either sex, of one to three years old, not broken to work

la15-, *now* Sh-Cai EC, WC Wgt. **2** a stallion *la15-*, *now* Ork-nEC Arg SW. **3** a young castrated horse, a gelding *19-*, *local*.

staiger a groom who accompanies a stud-horse *20-*, *NE Per Fif*. **~ie &c** = *n*, *la18-e19*. [var of Eng *stag*, poss infl by cognate ON *steggi* a male bird]

stail *vi*, *chess* undergo stalemate *la16*. [only Sc; laME *vt* = stalemate. OED *stale* (*v³*)]

staill *see* STELL¹

stainch *see* STENCH¹, STENCH²

stainchel &c *la19-*, **stanchel &c** *la16-19*; **stenchel &c** *la16-19* ['stenʃəl; *'stɛnʃ-] *n* **1** an iron bar, *usu* as part of a grating for a window etc *la16-*, *now* SW, S. **2** a bar for securing a door or gate *19-*, *now* WC, SW.
vt fit (a window) with iron bars *18-19*, *only Sc*. [var of next]

staincheon &c *la16-*, *now* Ork Cai Bnf; **stenchion &c** *17-e19* ['stenʃən; *'stɛnʃ-] *n* = stanchion. [*cf* prec and next. OED *stanchion*]

staincher *18-*, **stancher &c** *la16-18*; **stansour** *la15*, **stencher** *la17-18* ['stenʃər; *'stɛnʃ-, *'stanʃ-] *n* an iron bar forming part of a window-grating *la15-*, *now local*. [only Sc; var of prec]

staint *see* STENT²

stainyie *see* STENȜIE

stair¹ *n* **1** a flight of steps or stairs leading from one floor of a building to the next, a staircase *la15-*. **2** *specif* = *common stair* (COMMON) *19-*. **3** = stair.
~fit &c the foot of the staircase, and the adjacent space or flat *18-*. **~heid &c** *n* **1** the landing at the top of a flight of stairs or at the top of a STAIR *n* 2, *18-*. **2** used to describe something, *eg* a quarrel, which takes place on a *~heid*, *ie* among neighbours *20-*: '*stairheid rammy*'.
down *or* **up the ~** down- *or* upstairs *19-*.

stair² *vt* thrust (a weapon) *e16*. [nME; ? ON *støyra* (*v*), *staurr* a stake]

stairch &c *la19-e20*; **sterch &c** *18-e20* [stertʃ, stertʃ] *n* = starch.

stairge *vi* stalk, strut *19-*, *Rox*. [emphatic or intensive var of STAGE *v* 2]

stairt *see* START¹

stak *see* STEIK²

stake¹ &c *n* **1** = stake *la16-*. **2** ? a stick (of a fan) *e17*, *only Sc*. **3** a young ling *la18-*, *Abd*.
stakie = *n* 3, *20-*, *Abd*.
~ net a salmon-fishing net fixed on stakes in tidal waters *19-*.

stake² &c *v* **1** *vt* be sufficient for, supply the needs or wants of, provide with enough of something, satisfy *16-e18*. **2** *vi* suffice *la16*. [only Sc; obscure; *cf* Eng *stock*]

stake³ *vt* place *e16*. [only Sc; uncertain; *cf* MDu *staken* fix, place]

stakey *n*, *marbles* a game in which stakes are laid *la19-20*, *Fif Lnk Ayr*.

stakker *see* STACHER

stal, stald *see* STEAL

stale¹ &c *n* **1** = stale, a fixed position *la14*. **2** a body of armed men (posted in a particular place for ambush etc); the main body of an army *la14-16*. **3** a band of hunters *15-e16*, *only Sc*.
in ~ 1 in ambush *15-e16*. **2** in battle array *e16*, *only Sc*.

stale² &c *n* **1** the foundation, made of a layer of stones, brushwood etc, on which a corn- or haystack is built *la16-*, *now local Per-Rox*. **2** the original hive in a colony of bees, from which swarms have come off; a stock of bees *e16*, *e19*. [only Sc; see SND; *cf* STATHEL]

stale³ &c *n* urine, *esp* that collected for making bleach or manuring *19-*, *now Per*. [ME]

stale *see* STEAL

stalf *see* STAFF

stalk &c [stɑk] *n* **1** an appendage to a halter *la15-e16*, *only Sc*. **2** a chimney-stack *19-*, *NE-S*. **3** = stalk.
~ raip, stack rope a rope passed through a ring on a stable manger, weighted at one end and tied to the horse's stall halter at the other *20-*, *now Fif Lnk Dmf*.
be ca'ed *or* **loup** *etc* **off the ~** *of the heart* be stopped by a sudden fright etc *19-*, *now Fif*.

stalker &c ['stɑkər] *n* **1** a person who prowls about for purposes of theft *e16*, *only Sc*. **2** a person who stalks game illegally, a poacher *15-16*. **3** = stalker.

stall *see* STA, STEAL

stallar [*'stalər] *n*, *church* a vicar who served in a cathedral *la16*.
stallary [*'staləri] *n* the office of a STALLAR *e17*. [only Sc; MedL *stallarius*, f *stallum*, *stalla* a stall]

stallenge &c [*'staləndȝ] *n* the fee paid by a STALLENGER *16-e17*. [only Sc; var of Eng *stallage* by analogy w STALLENGER]

stallenger &c [*'staləndȝər] *n* a small trader or craftsman who was neither a member of a merchant guild or trade INCORPORATION nor a freeman of the BURGH, who paid a fee for the privilege of trading at fairs or in the BURGH market(s) *15-e18*. [chf Sc; altered f *stallager*, OF *estalagier* one who pays *stallage*, a stall tax at a fair; *cf* ScL *stallangiarius*]

stalp *n* ? some kind of trap *e16*. [only Sc; *cf* WFrisian *stap* and STAMP²]

stalwart &c, stalworth *e19* ['stalwart, -ward, -wʌrθ] *adj* **1** strongly built, sturdy (1) *of persons*, *la14-*; (2) *of their limbs*, *la14*, *e19*. **2** *of animals*, *chf horses* strong, sturdy *la14-15*, *only Sc*. **3** *of things* firmly made, strong *la14-18*. **4** *of persons or their attributes* resolute, determined *la14*, *19-*. **5** valiant, courageous *la14-16*, *19-*. **6** *of actions or a fight* severe, hard, violent *la14-e16*, *only Sc*. **7** *of a storm* violent *e16*.
n **1** a strong valiant man *la15*. **2** = stalwart, a dependable supporter.
~ly strongly, bravely *la14-15*. [*stalwart &c*

orig only Sc, var of Eng *stalworth*, introduced into Eng by Scott *e19*; *stalworth* obs in Eng f *17*, reintroduced by Scott *e19*]

stam¹ *n* the stem or prow of a ship *e16*. [laME *stam*, ME *stampne*, ON *stamn*]

stam² *vi* walk with a quick heavy tread, stamp along; stumble or blunder onwards, stagger *19-*, *now Bwk Rox.* [prob back-formation f STAMMER]

stamack &c *la18-*, **stomach &c**; **stammach &c** *19-e20* ['stamək, -əx; *Ork* -o; *Bwk also* 'stom-] *n* **1** = stomach *la14-*. **2** *only Sc* (1) a stomacher *la15-16*; (2) a chest-covering for a horse *e16*.
find the bottom *or* **grund(s) o one's** ~ feel ravenously hungry *la19-*, *NE Ags Per.* **hae a good** *or* **bad** ~ have a hearty *or* poor appetite *la18-*.

stamagast &c; **stammygaster &c** *20-*, *now the commoner form* [stamə'gast(ər), stamɪ-] *n* a great and sudden disappointment, an unpleasant surprise, a shock *la18-*, *NE Ags.*
vt **1** give a sudden surprise or disappointment to, flabbergast, bewilder *la19-*, *now NE Ags Dmf.* **2** sicken with a surfeit of food, nauseate *20-*, *Abd Fif WC.* [perh conflation of eModEng, Eng dial *stam* astonish w Eng *aghast*, w infl f *flabbergast*, and also (in *v* 2) f prec]

stame *see* STEAM

staminger &c [*'stamənᴣər] *n* = stomacher *17-e18, only Sc.*

stammach *see* STAMACK

stammer &c *vti* **1** = stammer. **2** *vi, of persons or animals, esp horses* stumble, stagger, falter, blunder about *18-*.
n **1** = stammer. **2** *freq of horses* a stumble, stagger; a missed footing; a staggering shambling gait *la19-*, *local NE-SW.*
~**al**, **stam(m)rel** *n*, *adj* (an) awkward, clumsy, stupid (person) *la18-e20.* ~**and** *la15*, ~**ing** *la18-19 adj, of horses* stumbling, not surefooted *la15*, *la18.* ~**y** stumbling, uncertain of one's footing *la20-*, *NE-Fif, SW.* [*cf* STAMMER]

stammle &c *vi* stagger, stumble, blunder, hobble *19-*, *now Rox.* [var of prec; *cf* Du, LowGer *stamelen (v)* stammer]

stammrel *see* STAMMER

stammygaster *see* STAMAGAST

stamp¹ **&c** *vti* = stamp (with the foot etc) *la14-*.
n = stamp *16-*.
~ **cole** *19, Dmf*, **stankle** *20-*, *Ork Cai Inv SW* a small temporary hay-rick.

stamp² *n* a (rat-*etc*)trap, *esp* one which grips the victim by the foot, a gin-trap *la17-*, *now Per Fif.* [see SND and *cf* STALP]

stamrel *see* STAMMER

stan *see* STAND¹

stance &c *n* **1** *lit and fig* = stance, a standing place, position *la16-*. **2** *specif* (1) a site or foundation on which something is laid or set up *17-*, *now local Sh-nEC Bwk, only Sc*; (2) a building-site for a house etc *17-*, *only Sc*; (3) a site for an

open-air market, fair etc *la17-*; (4) a space for a single stand, side-show etc, a street-trader's pitch *19-*; (5) an overnight stopping-place for a drove of cattle *19-*, *now hist*; (6) a station or terminus for buses etc, a place where public vehicles etc stand waiting for passengers, *eg* at the beginning of a run *20-*: 'taxi stance'; (7) *occas* a halt or stop on a bus route *20-*, *local*; (8) a stall etc for an animal in a stable *20-*, *Cai.* **3** (1) a room, cell *e17, only Sc.* (2) a compartment in a shield *e17, only Sc.* **4** *golf* the position of a player's feet when about to strike the ball *la18-*.
vt, *chf in ptp* placed on a certain spot, assigned a position; *of an animal* exhibited for sale at a market *18-*, *NE Ags.*
at a ~ at a standstill *la17, only Sc.* **building** ~ = *n* 2(2), *19-*. **take (up) a** *or* **one's** ~ take (up) one's stand or position *20-*.

stanch *see* STENCH¹

stanchel &c; **stenchil &c** *la16-18* [*'stanʃl, *'sten-] *n* the kestrel *la15-e19.* [irreg var of OE *stängella*; *cf* ModEng dial *staniel*]

stanchel *see* STAINCHEL

stancher *see* STAINCHER

stand¹ **&c**; **staun &c** *la18-*, **stan** *la14, 19-* [stand; *NE* stan, *WC* stan(d)] *v, pt, ptp also* **stude &c**, **steed** *19-*, *now NE* [stød, stɪd; *Cai NE,* stid] **stan't** *la18-*, *now NE.* *ptp also* **standyn** *la14*, **stand &c** *la16-e18*, **stuiden &c** *16-*, *now C, S* ['stødn, 'stɪdn] *vti* **1** = stand *la14-*. **2** *vi, in imperative, now only in calls to a horse* stop!, stand quiet! *16-*, *N, nEC, WC, S.* **3** ~ **on** be charged to, be the responsibility of (a person) *15-e16, only Sc.* **4** *in negative* not hesitate, not be reluctant (to do etc *or* about) *la16-e19.* **5** *esp of a wedding* take place, be celebrated *la16-19, only Sc.* **6** *vt* abide by, obey (a decree) *la16.* **7** cost (someone something) *18-e20.*
n **1** = stand *16-*. **2** a stall or booth at a market etc, *freq* (*19-*) including the goods exposed for sale *16-*. **3** a complete set or outfit: (1) (a) of various kinds of equipment *eg* ropes, knitting needles *la15-*, *now Sh-EC, SW Rox.* (b) *uninflected in pl after numerals etc*, *18*: 'fourtein stand of ropes'; (2) ~ **of pipes** a complete set of Scottish bagpipes, *ie* bag, drones and *chanter* (CHANT) *19-*, *only Sc*; (3) a set or suit (of clothes) *la15-*, *now NE Ags Fif.*
~**ing &c** *n* = standing *17-*. *adj* **1** = standing *12-*. **2** constant, permanent *la14-*. ~**ing drink** a drink taken standing; a DEOCHANDORUS *e17, 19.* ~**ing graith** the fixed or stationary parts of a mill *la16-19*; *cf ganging graith* (GANG). ~**ing kirn** a churn worked by pushing a plunger up and down *20-*, *Cai Stlg.* ~**ing &c room** space in which to stand *17-*. ~**ing &c stone &c**, **-stane &c** a monolith, a menhir *la12-*. **be standing** *of a clock etc* have stopped, not be going *la18-*, *Sh-EC S.*
~ **bed** a freestanding bed as opposed to a

box-bed (BOX[1]) or a folding one *la15, 18.* ~
burd a freestanding as opposed to a folding
table *la16, only Sc.* ~**fray** aloof, rebellious
la15. ~ **maill** the rent paid for a pitch at a
market *17-e18, only Sc.* ~ **mesoure** standard
measure *la16, only Sc.*

I ~ **for it &c** *parenthetic* I warrant *la15-16, only
Sc.* ~ **about** stand farther off, keep one's distance, get out of the way *la18-19, only Sc.* ~
at = *v* 6, *la15-16.* ~ **aw of someone** be
afraid of someone, stand in awe of someone
la15-16. ~ **by 1** stand near at hand, be present *la14-.* 2 be excluded from *e17.* ~ **for** =
stand for *la14-.* ~ **good for** *la18-, Sh-WC,* ~
in for *la19-, now Sh Abd Ags* stand surety for,
guarantee. ~ **out** remain solvent *20-, Bnf
Abd.* ~ **ower** *command to a horse* move to the
other side of the stall *20-, Abd Per.* **stan-tae &c**
a set-to, a tussle *la20-, Sh N Fif Wgt.* ~ **to the
wa** *of a door* be wide open *19-, Sh Ork NE-Per.*
~ **yon(t)** = ~ *about, 19-, now NE nEC Rox.*

stand[2] **&c** *n* a tub, barrel or cask set upright to
contain water, meal, salted beef etc *la15-, now
Per.* [eME *stonde; cf* LowGer *stande;* ultimately
f as prec]

standart &c; standard *18-;* **stannert &c**
19-e20 *n* 1 = standard *la14-.* 2 a rule or principle *la16-.* 3 an upright timber, pole, post
etc, a support *17-.*

standard-bearer the chief male participant in
the Selkirk *Common Riding* (COMMON), who carries the BURGH flag round the town's boundaries *la19-, Slk.* **Standard Grade** applied to a
certificate, examination or course (replacing
the *O Grade* (ORDINAR) in stages from 1984 on)
awarded to all pupils in secondary schools at
the end of the fourth year *la20-.* **standard
security** the form of HERITABLE security which
is now the only way of creating a security over
land *la20-.*

stander &c *n* a candlestick *17-19.* [*cf* Eng, or
perh reduced f prec]

stane &c, stone &c *la16-;* **steen &c** *la16-, now
Ork N* [sten; *Ork N* stin] *n* 1 = stone *la14-.* 2
(1) a measure of weight, varying according to
time, district, and the commodity *la15-.* (2) a
piece of metal used as a standard stone-weight
la16, Pbls, only Sc. 3 curling = curling stone
(CURL) *18-.* 4 a testicle *20-.*

vti 1 = stone *la16-.* 2 *vt, freq proverb* press (a
cheese) by putting a large box of stones on top
of the cheese vat *19-, now Abd Ayr.*

stonack &c = *ston(e)der, la19-e20, Inv.*
stoned &c 1 = stoned *16-.* 2 *of fruit* having a
stone or stones *16-.* 3 *of a horse* not castrated,
entire *16-, now Sh Ork Rox.* **ston(e)der** *la20,
NE,* **stondie &c** *20-, Abd,* **stoner** *la19-, NE Stlg*
a large brown glazed earthenware marble.
stonie *adj* = stony *16-.* *n* a small coloured
marble *la19-, NE Fif WC, SW.* **stonie (tig)**
name for varieties of the game of tig *19-, now
Kcb Dmf.*

~ **bing** a heap or pile of stones *la19-, Fif WC
Kcb.* ~ **blind** *lit and fig* completely blind *la14-.*
~ **cast** a stone's throw *la14, 18-, now local Sh-
Fif.* ~ **chack &c,** ~ **chacker &c,** ~ **chackart 1** the stonechat *18-, now local Ags-S.* 2 the
wheatear *19-, now Sh NE.* ~ **chipper** the
wheatear *20-, Lnk SW.* ~ **crase &c,** ~ **graze**
? a boil or abscess in the foot *e19, SW.* ~
dumb completely silent *19-, now Sh.* ~ **dyke**
a (*usu*) dry-stane (DRY) wall *la15-.* ~ **dyker** a
person who builds (*dry-stane*) walls *20-.* ~
fish the gunnel *16-e19.* ~ **horse** *etc* an uncas-
trated horse *18-e20.* ~ **(k)napper** a person
who breaks stones *la19-, NE-S.* ~ **knot** a very
tight knot *la18-19.* ~ **mine** *mining* a road
from underground workings which cuts across
the strata *20-, Fif Lnk Ayr.* ~ **raw** the lichen
Parmelia saxatilis, used for dyeing *la18-, now SW.*
~ **tired** very tired; lazy, bone idle *20-, S.*
~**-wring** ? colic attributed to the presence of a
stone in the kidneys *e16, only Sc.*

~ **and lime** masonry, masoned stone *18-.*

stanelock *see* STENLOCK
stanery *see* STANNERS
stang[1] **&c** *v* 1 *vt* = sting *la14-, Gen except Sh Ork.*
2 *vi, lit and fig* shoot with pain, throb, ache *19-.*
n 1 (1) a sting (of an insect etc) *15-.* (2) *fig*
the capacity to injure in word or deed, a harsh
or cutting remark *la18-, now Sh Abd.* 2 *lit and
fig* a sharp pain, such as that caused by a sting,
a pang *16-.* 3 the wound caused by a sting or
sharp object *19-.* 4 *transf* the sting of death
18-19. [ME *stang,* ON *stanga* prick, goad,
gore, ultimately f as STING[1]]

stang[2] *n* 1 a pole, wooden bar or rod *16-, now
NE Per Fif.* 2 *specif* a rough pole or tree-trunk
on which an offender against the laws or local
conventions (*eg* a wife-beater, nagger, adul-
terer) was mounted astride and carried about
in public; the punishment itself *18-e19.* 3 a
shaft or draught-pole of a cart *la19-e20.* 4 a
spike, prong etc of metal *17-, chf Abd.* 5 the
tongue or metal reed in a jew's harp, *chf* **the ~
o the trump** the indispensable or most effective person in a group or activity, the best of the
bunch *19-, NE Ags.*

vt cause to ride the ~, humiliate (a person) thus
la17-e19.

ride the ~ suffer the punishment as in *n* 2,
18-e19. **ride the** ~ **on** deal out this punishment to an effigy of, or someone impersonating
(the offender); hold up to public ridicule
18-e19. [ME *stong, stang,* ON *stong, stang-* a
pole, stake; *cf* STING[2]]

stang *see* STING[1]
stank &c; stunk *e17, only Sc n* 1 a pond, a
pool; a small semi-stagnant sheet of water, *esp*
one overgrown with vegetation, a swampy
place *la14-, Gen except Sh, freq in place-names.* 2
(1) a moat *e16.* (2) a ditch, an open water-
course, *freq* a natural stream which has been
straightened to serve as a boundary or as part

of a drainage system *18-*, *local*. (3) *fig* an obstacle, difficulty, *chf* **lowp a** ~ circumvent obstacles, achieve an object or a stage towards it *20-*, *Abd*. **3** (1) a street gutter *20-*, *EC*, *WC*. (2) a grating in a gutter *20-*, *WC*. *vt* **1** make a ditch in *la15*, *only Sc*. **2** surround with a moat *16-17*, *only Sc*. **3** *chf* ~**it**: (1) dammed up, blocked; choked *la19-*, *now Kcdn Ags*; (2) *fig* sated with food, satisfied *19-*, *Abd Ags*.

stankie (**hen**) the water-hen *19-*, *now Per-S*.
~ **brae &c** the edge of a STANK *la16-17*, *only Sc*.
~ **hen** = ~*ie* (*hen*), *la18-*, *now Ags*.
doun the ~ *lit and fig* irretrievably lost; *of money* squandered *20-*, *C*. [ME *stank*, OF *estanc*, L *stagnum* a pool]

stankle *see* STAMP[1]

stanlock *see* STENLOCK

stanners &c ['stanərz, 'sten-] *n pl* shingle *16-*, *also in place-names*, *only Sc*.
stan(n)ery &c stony, gravelly *16-18*. [ONorthumb *stǣner* a stony place, f OE *stān* stone]

stannert *see* STANDART

stansour *see* STAINCHER

stan't, stan-tae *see* STAND[1]

stap[1], **staup &c** *19-*, *S vti*, *n* = step *17-*, *now NE Ags Fif Rox*.
stand on stappin stanes be excessively fussy; dither *17-19*.
hae *or* **tak a** ~ take a short walk, make a short journey *19-*, *now Abd Ags*. **like** *etc* ~**s and stairs** *of a family of children* born in quick succession *19-*, *Sh Ags*. [*prob* f Du *stappen* (*v*) step, stride, *stap* (*n*) step, pace; *cf* STEP. OED *step*]

stap[2] *la17-*, **stop &c**; *step la16-17 vti* **1** = stop, block up, halt *la14-*. **2** *vt* push, thrust, cram, poke (something or someone **in**(**to**) something) *la14-*. **3** stuff, pack (a receptacle **with** something) *la14, 18-*. **4** *vi* gorge oneself with food *20-*, *local Sh-Per*. **5** *vt* tuck or pack bedclothes around (someone) *la19-*, *NE Ags*, *only Sc*. **6** exclude (someone) **from** *la16*, *only Sc*.
n **1** = stop *16-*. **2** the act of cramming or stuffing, of blocking up a hole; a surfeit *la19-*, *Sh Ork NE Kcb*.
stappin *cookery* stuffing, *specif* that used for filling fishes' heads *19-*, *Abd Ags*. **stappit 1** stuffed; replete, gorged *la18-*, *now Sh NE Ags Per*. **2** *only* **stoppit** hoarse *la15*, *only Sc*.
stappit haddie a stuffed haddock *la19-*, *Cai Bnf Abd*. **stappit heidies &c** stuffed fish heads *19-*, *now Cai Bnf Abd*.
~ **someone's breath** *of death* stifle someone, end someone's life *18-e19*.

stap[3] **&c** *17-*; **step** *la16, la19, only Sc*, **staup &c** *e19*, *only Sc n* a stave of a wooden cask or pail etc *la15-*, *now Rox*.
fa aa ~**s, gae** (**aa**) **to** ~**s** *lit and fig* fall to pieces, go to ruin *la18-e20*. **tak a** ~ **oot o someone's bicker** *or* **cog** *fig* humble someone

la18-e20. [*prob orig* f LowGer; *cf* MLowGer *stappe* a splint, a wooden vessel with one stave extended as a handle, LowGer *stap*, Ger *stab* a stave]

stap- *la16-*, *now Kcdn Fif*, *only Sc*, **step-** *prefix* = step- *16-*.
stappy &c = step-father *19-e20*.
step-bairn *only Sc n* a step-child *16-*. *vt* treat as a step-child *el7*. **mak a step-bairn o** treat unkindly, neglect, spurn *19-e20*.

staple &c *n* = staple, a town etc with the exclusive right of purchase of certain goods intended for export etc; Scotland only ever had one, varying from time to time, in the Low Countries *15-e18*.
~ **gud**(**is**) = staple-ware, such goods as were the monopoly of the STAPLE *la15-16*. ~ **hand** ? = staple-ware *la14*, *only Sc*.

staple *see* STAPPLE[3]

stapple[1] **&c** *19-e20*, *only Sc*, **stopple &c** *la15-16 n* = stopple, a stopper, plug, bung etc.

stapple[2] **&c** *n* a bundle of straw or rushes tied like a sheaf and used for thatching houses or corn-stacks *19-*, *now Stlg-SW*. [*only Sc*; *appar* Du *stoppel* stubble, corn straw, with *-a-* for *-o-* by analogy w STAP[2] etc]

stapple[3] **&c** *19-*, *only Sc*, **stopple &c** *la17-18*, *20-* (*Rox*), **staple &c** *n* **1** = staple, a metal loop used as a fastening *16-*. **2** the stem of a (clay) tobacco-pipe *la17-*, *now local*. **3** *only* **stap**(**p**)**le** *coal-mining* a short shaft connecting one coal-seam vertically with another *19-*, *now Fif*. [OE *stapol*, MDu *stapel* a stem, stalk; *-o-* forms *perh* by analogy w STAPPLE[1]]

stappy *see* STAP-

star[1] **&c** *la18-*; **ster**(**r**) **&c** *now Rox* [star; *S* stɛr] *n* = star *la14-*.
starrie a kind of sweet *20-*, *Ags* [*dim* of *star rock* a sweet made in Kirriemuir, *Ags*, the cross-section showing a star-like shape].
the ~ **o the ee** the pupil of the eye *20-*, *local*, *only Sc*. [*cf* STARN[1]]

star[2] **&c** *n* name for various kinds of grass or sedge, *usu* growing in moorish or boggy ground, *freq* ~ **grass** etc, *la18-*, *also in* (*esp NE*) *place-names*. [ME *star* rushes, ON *storr* bent-grass]

stare &c *n* **1** = stare. **2** a state of staring amazement, horror, admiration etc *la15-e16*.

stark &c *adj* **1** = stark *la14-*. **2** strong, *specif* (1) *of persons or animals* physically strong, sturdy, vigorous *la14-*, *now Ork Cai*; (2) *of things* strongly made, durable, hard *la14-*, *now Uls*; (3) *of a reason*, *la15-16*, *only Sc*; (4) *of action* vigorous *la16*, *only Sc*; (5) *of liquor* potent *la16-19*. **3** *qualifying a pejorative* arrant, unmitigated *la14*: 'sterk thefis'. **4** *of a question etc* hard, difficult *la15*, *only Sc*. **5** *of an instrument of torture etc* inflicting severe pain *16*. **6** *of natural forces*, eg a river or wind violent, rough *la16-*, *now Ork*.
adv vigorously, energetically; rigidly; fully, completely *la16-*, *now Lnk*.

starlin(**g**) *see* STERLIN

starn[1] **&c, stern &c** *la14-e20* [starn; *S* stɛrn] *n*
1 a star *la14-*, *now Sh-N, Lnk Dmf.* **2** *transf* a
medal or decoration in the form of a star
la18-e19. **3** *usu with omission of* OF *etc* a grain, a
particle; a small amount (of anything, *orig and
specif* of some granulated substance, *rarely* of
liquids) *18-*, *now NE, only Sc.*
starnie &c *la18-*, **sternie &c** *adj* starry, covered with stars *la16-*, *now Ork.* *n, only Sc* = *n* 1
(*la18-19*), 3 (*la19-*, *now NE*). **sternit** starred,
starry *e16.*
~licht starlight *la19-*, *now Abd, only Sc.* **~
schot** a shooting star *e16, only Sc.*
the ~ o the eye the pupil of the eye *19-*, *S, only
Sc.* [ME *sterne, steorrne*, ON *stjarna; cf* STAR[1]]
starn[2] *n* = stern (of a boat etc) *19-*.
~ stuil &c the short seat furthest aft in a small
boat, on which the steersman sits *20-*, *Bnf Kcdn
Fif.*
starrach ['starəx] *adj, of weather etc* cold, bleak,
disagreeable *20-*, *Cai.* [prob var of STARK *adj* 6;
pronunc poss infl by Gael]
start[1]; **stert** *la15-*, *now local*, **stairt** *16,
la19-e20, only Sc* [start; *local* stɛrt] *v, pt, ptp also*
stert *la15-e20*, **start** *la16, e20* **1** *vti* = start
la14-. **2** *vt* startle, disturb suddenly *la15-*. **3**
ride (a horse) at full speed *la15, only Sc.* **4** *vi, of
the hair* stick up in an unkempt fashion, bristle
20-, *Lnk Slk.*
n, chf **start 1** a short time, a moment *la14-*, *now
Sh.* **2** = start, a leap, sudden movement *17-*.
~y *adj, of a horse* nervous, restive *19-*, *now Sh-
Cai.*
~ and owerlowp &c the trespassing of farm-
animals on a neighbour's land, in which a certain limited latitude was permissible *18-e19*,
only Sc.
start[2] *n* **1** = start, part of a bucket on a water-
wheel *e16.* **2** one of the uprights of a box-cart
onto which the side-boards are nailed *19-*, *now
Abd Per Gall.*
startle *17-*; **stertle** *la14-e20* ['startl; *S* 'stɛrtl] *v*
1 *vi* rush about wildly, stampede, *esp* of cattle
when stung by flies *la14-*, *now SW, S.* **2** *vti* =
startle. **3** *vi, of the eyes* start from their sockets
e17, only Sc.
starve *see* STERVE
stashie &c; stushie &c, stishie &c *n* an
uproar, commotion, quarrel, row; a (*usu* unnecessary) fuss, bother *19-*. [poss aphetic f Eng
ecstasy]
state &c *n* **1** = state (1) *in gen, la14-*; (2) *attrib,
la15-.* **2** right or title to property *e15.* **3** (1)
an estate of the realm *la15-e18.* (2) *in pl, chf*
the S~s of Scotland = *the Estates* (ESTATE)
e15, e19 (hist). **4** a person's proper form, shape
or nature *e16.* **5** a statement (1) of facts or
figures, *eg* in the pleas of a law-suit or in financial transactions etc *18-*; (2) *freq* **~ of a vote**
the formulation of a motion as it is to be put to
a vote *18-e19.*

vt **1** *only* **steat** constitute, give (a person) the
status of *la17, only Sc.* **2** = state.
~like in a stately manner *la15.*
give *or* **receive** *etc* **~ and sasine** *etc, law* give
over or get HERITABLE property by a formal act
15-19, chf Sc. **in ~** in possession or seised **of**
(land) *la15-e16, only Sc.*
stathel &c; stad(d)le &c *19-* ['steθl, 'staθl,
'stedl, 'stadl] *n* **1** the foundation of a stack of
grain, built of stone, wood etc, to protect from
vermin and damp *la18-*, *now local Cai-SW.* **2**
the main part of a corn-stack; a stack in the
process of building or dismantling *17-*, *now local
N.*
stethlin &c the foundations of a stack, the
materials used for this *la19-*, *now Per.*
[eModEng *staddle* the lower part of a corn-
stack, OE *staðol* a foundation, base; *cf* STALE[2]]
station *n* = station *17-*.
~ie &c = station-master *20-*, *NE-Per, only Sc.*
~ agent a station-master, whose duties were
orig chf to bring traffic to the railway *20-*, *Gen
except Sh Ork.*
stationeir [*steʃə'nir] *adj* = stationary *la15.*
[only Sc. OED *stationary*]
statute &c *n* = statute *15-*.
vt, ptp freq also **statute &c** *15-e17* **1** ordain,
decree *la15-19.* **2** appoint (a term, a time of
payment etc) *la16, only Sc.* **3** set (a kingdom
etc) in order *la15, only Sc.*
staucher *see* STACHER
stauk *vti* = stalk, stride *la18-e19.*
staul [stal] *vi, n* squint *la19-*, *now Mry.*
[uncertain]
staun *see* STAND[1]
staunch *see* STENCH[2]
staup *see* STAP[1], STAP[3]
stave &c [stev] *n* **1** = stave, a stick of wood etc
18-. **2** a forceful blow, a jab *19.* **3** a sprain
or wrench of a joint *19-*, *only Sc.*
v **1** *vt* = stave *la17-*. **2** jab, thrust *16-17.* **3**
(1) thicken (iron) by heating and hammering
la18-, *now Inv WC Kcb.* (2) hammer (two
pieces of metal) together, make a joint by striking (*esp* lead) when heated *la19-*. **4** sprain or
bruise (a joint) *19-*, *local Sh-Ayr.* **5** *vti* aim
blows **at**, hit, belabour *19.* **6** *vi* stagger, totter;
barge **on** *19-*, *local Abd-S.*
stavie walk in a leisurely way, saunter, stroll
la19-, *Bnf Abd.* **stavin &c** staggering with
drunkenness, *stottin* (STOT[2]) *20-*, *now Inv.* [*v* 6
may be partly a back-formation f STAVER]
stavel &c; stevel *19* ['stevl] *vi* walk in a halting
uncertain way, stumble, blunder on *19-*, *now
Fif.*
n a stumble *19-*, *Rox.* [var of STAVER]
staver ['stevər] *vi* stagger, stumble about, walk
unsteadily *e15, 18-*, *now Fif.* [prob *orig* Scand;
cf Norw *stavre* stagger, totter, *staver* a stake,
post]
staves *see* STAFF
staw *see* STA

staw, stawn see STEAL

stay see STEY¹, STEY²

stead see STEID¹

steady &c *18-*; **studdie &c** *17, la19-, now Sh Gall* ['stɛdɪ, 'stɪ-, 'stʌ-, 'sti-] *adj* = steady *18-*.
adv **1** = steady *17-*. **2** continuously, all the time *la19-, only Sc*.
vt = steady.

steal *19-*; **steil &c** *la14-16, only Sc,* **stel(l)** *la14-e16, only Sc* [stil; *Bnf nEC Wgt* stel] *v, pt also* **stale &c** *la14-19, only Sc,* **stal(l)** *la14-e19* [*stal], **stald** *e15* [*stald], **staw** *la14-e20, only Sc,* **sta &c** *15, la18-e20, only Sc* [stɑ], **stule &c** *la19-, Sh, only Sc* [støl]; **steal(e)d** *la16, la18-19,* **stealt** *la18-, now NE,* **staelt** *20-, Ork NE.* *ptp also* **stow(e)n &c** *now Sh NE* ['stʌu(ə)n], **stone** *15, only Sc,* **stawn** *la18-19, only Sc*; **stealed** *la18-19,* **stealt** *la18-, now NE,* **staelt** *20-, nEC vti* = steal *la14-*.
n, golf a long PUTT which reaches the hole contrary to expectation *19-*.

stow(n)lins [*'stʌu(ə)nlɪnz, *'stʌulɪnz] in a hidden or secretive way, furtively *la18-e20*.

∼ **someone doun** ruin by secret means *la16, only Sc*.

steam; stame &c *la19-, NE* [stim; *NE nEC* stem] *n, vti* = steam.
∼**ie** a public wash-house *20-, local C, S.* ∼**in** (**wi drink**) very drunk *20-, Ork-C.*
∼ **mill** a (travelling) threshing-mill driven by a steam-engine *la19-20*.

steat see STATE

stech &c; steigh &c *19-,* **stoich &c** *19-, local WC* [stɛx, stix; *WC* stoix] *v* **1** *vti* stuff or cram (oneself, one's stomach etc) with food *18-, now nEC Loth.* **2** create a strong unpleasant stifling atmosphere (in), fill with bad air or fumes, stink *19-, now Bnf Abd.* **3** *vi* gasp, pant, puff etc (1) from repletion *19-, now Ayr*; (2) from exertion or effort *19-,local Per-S.*
n **1** a gasp, a grunt *19-, now Loth Wgt Rox.* **2** (1) the stuffy fetid atmosphere produced by a dense crowd in a small place, a fug *19-, local N.* (2) any disorder or lack of cleanliness, smelly or dirty rubbish *19-, now Ags.* [perh chf onomat]

stechie &c ['stɛxɪ] *adj, of persons* stiff-jointed, slow-moving due to stiffness, corpulence or indolence, stodgy *19-, local C.* [prob f STECH perh *orig* meaning 'fat, short-winded']

steck see STEEK¹

sted see STEID¹, STEID²

stedding see STEID¹

stedy see STUDDIE

steed see STAND¹

steek¹ &c; steck &c *la19-, now Sh v, pt* ∼**it &c,** **stickit &c** *la18-19. ptp* **stek** *15, only Sc*; **stekine** *la14, only Sc* [*'stikən]; **stokyt** *la14, only Sc,* ∼**it** *18-,* **stickit &c** *la18-19* **1** *vt* = steek, shut out (a person etc), shut up (a place) *la14-16.* **2** (1) ∼ **someone** *etc* **out** *la16-* or **in** *20-* close a door on someone etc so as to keep

him etc out *or* in *now local NE-SW.* (2) shut up, lock away (a person or thing) *la18-e20.* **3** close, shut, fasten (something), close the entry to: (1) *in gen, la16-, now local Sh-SW*; (2) *specif* shut (a book) *19-, now Ags*; (3) close (the eyes) *15-*; (4) ∼ **one's mouth** *etc, lit and fig* shut one's mouth, keep silent *18-, now local NE-SW*; (5) ∼ **one's lugs** *or* **hert** *fig* refuse to listen, harden (one's heart) *e20.* **4** shut, make fast (a door etc) *18-.* **5** stop up, block (an opening etc) *la14, la18.* **6** *vi, of a door etc* shut, come to *15-.*
n a clasp, a fastening *20-, now Abd Kcdn.*
∼**er 1** a boot-lace *la19-, eLoth Bwk SW.* **2** the back-board of a farm cart *20-, Per Fif.*
stekin(g) &c [*'stikɪŋ, *-ɪn] a lock *la14-e15, only Sc.* ∼**it nieve &c** the clenched fist *18-.*
∼ **and hide &c** the game of hide-and-seek *la18-e20.* ∼ **one's nieve on** keep quiet about; settle for (a price in bargaining) *la19-, NE.*

steek² &c; stick &c [*Sh Abd also* *stɪk] *vt* stitch, sew *16-, Gen except Ork.*
n **1** *sewing or knitting* a stitch *18-.* **2** (1) the least article of clothing, 'a stitch' *19-.* (2) a fragment of cloth etc *19-20.* **3** a sharp pain, a stitch in the side *la19-.* **4** a quick rate or pace, *chf in phrs eg* **at sic a** ∼ *la19-, Ags.*
keep *etc* ∼(**s**) **wi** keep pace with; compete with *la18-, now Kcb Dmf Slk.* **let doun a** ∼ make a mistake, commit a fault *19-, now Sh.* **tak up a** ∼ (**in one's stocking**) amend a fault, retrieve a mistake *19-, now Sh.* [prob f northern OE *stice* a stitch, but *cf* STEIK² and STICK¹ *v*]

steel¹ &c; steil &c *la15-16* [stil] *n* **1** = steel *la14-.* **2** a steelyard, a weighing bar *20-, Per Kcb.*
steelie a marble made of steel, *usu* a ball-bearing *20-.*
steelbow [*'stilbu, *also* *?-bʌu] *freq attrib* a form of land-tenancy whereby a landlord provided the tenant with stock, grain, implements etc under contract that the equivalent should be returned at the end of the lease; the stock belonging to the landlord under this arrangement *15-19* (the comb in *-bow* (BOW¹) suggests that the practice came to Scotland from Scandinavia. **the Steelmen** nickname for Motherwell football team *20-.* ∼ **sadill &c** ? a saddle with a steel frame *16, only Sc.*

steel² &c *n, chf place-name, freq in comb* a steep bank, *esp* a spur on a hill ridge *19-, S.* [only Sc; OE *stīgel*, the inflected forms of which > Eng *stile*]

steel see STUIL

steen see STANE

steenge [stindʒ] *n* a sharp pain *20-, local Ags-Rox.*
vt attack with a sharp pain *20-, Bwk Kcb Rox.* [var of Eng *sting; cf* SING² and Eng *singe*]

steep &c *vt* = steep, soak, saturate *17-.*
n **1** = steep, the act or process of steeping *18-.*

2 a place or container in which things are put to soak *17-20*. **3** rennet or some substitute for curdling milk *la19-*, *now Wgt*.

~**ies** bread sops as food for children, pets etc *la19-*, *NE-Fif*. **steepit** wet through, sodden *19-*.

~ **stone &c** a hollowed stone trough in which something may be steeped *la16-18*.

in ~ in the process of being soaked or macerated *la18-*, *now Abd*. **lat something steep** allow something to mature *20-*, *Abd Kcb*. **set** *etc* **one's brains** *etc* **in** ~ *la19-e20*, **set one's brains or harns to** ~, ~ **one's brains** *la19-*, *C, S* think hard about a problem, use one's wits.

~ **your heid** don't be silly! *la20-*, *N, C*.

steepend &c, stipend &c ['stipən(d)] *n* **1** *specif and chf in Sc* the salary of a Presbyterian MINISTER *la16-*. **2** = stipend.

preach according tae one's ~**(s)** act as one's circumstances will allow, use discretion *la19-20*.

upon one's ain ~ at one's own expense *la16*.

steepid *see* STUPIT

steeple &c; stiple &c *18*, *only Sc* ['stipl] *n* = staple (for securing a bolt etc) *18-*. [see SND]

steer¹ *18-*; **steir &c** *la14-17* [stir] *vti* **1** = stir *la14-*. **2** *vt* disturb, molest, pester *la15-*, *now local Abd-Kcb*. **3** plough, *specif* replough in spring (land already ploughed in the autumn) *la18-20*, *local*. **4** *vi* start off on a journey, set out on one's way *la18-*, *local Abd-Kcb*, *only Sc*. **5** *of persons etc* be in a bustle; be hard-pressed with work etc; work or go about in a confused, harassed way *la19-*.

n = stir, movement, bustle *la15-*.

~**age** movement, commotion *16-18*. **sterand steid** a swift horse *la14-15*. **steerie** *n* a bustle, commotion, muddle *la18-e20*. *adj* lively, bustling *19-*, *N nEC Rox*. **steeriefyke** confused bustle, agitation, excitement *19-e20*. ~**ing &c** *n* **1** = stirring *la14-*. **2** *freq attrib* ploughing *18-19*. *adj* **1** *of persons*, *esp children* active, restless, lively *la19-*. **2** *of places etc* full of activity, in a tumult *la19-*.

cauld ~**(ie)** oatmeal stirred in cold water, cold BROSE *19-*, *now N-Per*. **on** ~ astir, in motion *la14-20*, *only Sc*; *cf* ASTEER. ~ **one's fit** *19-* or **tail** *la16-e17*, *only Sc* bestir oneself. ~ **one's time** make vigorous use of one's opportunity *la16*, *only Sc*.

steer² *17-*; **stere &c** *la14-15 vti* **1** = steer, guide (a ship etc) *la14-*. **2** *vt* guide (a plough) *la15-*.

n **1** *lit and fig* = steer, a rudder *la14-16*. **2** the action of directing or governing; guidance, control, rule, government *15-16*.

~**age 1** management (of goods) *la15*, *only Sc*. **2** = steerage *19-*. ~**er** a rudder *e17, 19-* (*Sh, fishermen's taboo*).

steesh &c *n* the home or base in games *20-*, *Ags*. [prob child's deformation of Eng *station*]

steet *see* STUIT

steeth *see* STEID¹

steeve *see* STIEVE, STIVE

steevil *see* STIEVE

stefe [?stif] *n*, *chf* **stiffie &c** a broad vertical bar of light across the moon or sun, a sign of bad weather *20-*, *local N*. [see SND]

steg¹ *vt* cause a hold-up of work in (a factory, mine etc) *la19-*, *Lnk Ayr*.

n a hold-up of work in a factory etc *la20-*, *Lnk Ayr*. [Scand; *cf* Norw and Sw dial *stagga* bring to a stop]

steg² *n* a gander *19-*, *now Rox*. [eModEng *stegge*; ON *steggr* a male bird]

steg³ &c *vi* walk with long heavy steps, stride, stalk, prowl *19-*, *now local midLoth-SW*. [see SND]

steich *see* STEY¹

steid¹ &c, stead *17-*; **sted &c** *la14-e20*, **steeth &c** *18-*, *Sh-Cai* [stid, stɛd; *Sh-Cai* stið; ***sted] *n* **1** = stead *la14-*. **2** a site, foundation, base: (1) of a building or wall *17-*, *now Sh-Cai*; (2) of a corn-, hay-, or *peat-stack* (PEAT¹) *18-*, *Sh-Cai*. **3** a *steading* (*n* 1) *18-*, *now SW*. **4** a mark, imprint, impression, a track *16-*, *now SW*, *only Sc*. **5** avail, profit, service *16-*, *now Ork*.

vt, *pt*, *ptp also* ~**it** *la14*, *and in senses 1-3* **stad** *la14-e16*, **sted** *la14-19* **1** place *la14-*, *now Slk*. **2** put into a certain condition, settle *la15*, *only Sc*. **3** *in passive* be placed in a difficult or bad condition or position *la14-19*. **4** suffice for, serve the needs of *la15-16*, *only Sc*. **5** = stead, serve, be useful *la16*. **6** lay a foundation for, make the base of (*eg* a *peat-stack* (PEAT¹) or building) *la18-*, *Sh Ork*.

~**able &c** *la15-17*, *only Sc*, ~**ful** *la16* serviceable, helpful. **steadin(g)** *la17-*, **sted(d)ing** *la15-19* [*N nEC, WC, SW* 'stɛdın, *Ork sEC, S* 'stidın] *n* **1** the buildings on a farm, sometimes but not always including the farmhouse *la15-*. **2** a building site; a piece of ground on which a house or row of houses is built; the site of the buildings on a farm *la17-20*.

~ **haldand** *la14*, *only Sc*, ~ **haldar** *la15* substitute, deputy [*cf* Eng *stadholder*].

in the ~ instead of something, as a substitute *la15-16*. ~ **of** instead of *18-*, *C, S*.

steid² *la14-17*, **sted** *la14-15* [***stid] *n* = steed, a horse.

~ **horse** *e15* or **meir** *la16* a stud-horse *or* -mare *only Sc*. [OED *steed*]

steif *see* STIEVE

steigh *see* STECH

steik¹ [***stik] *n* **1** a cask of wine *la15*. **2** a coin of specified value *la16*. **3** a piece (of work) *la16*. [only Sc; Flem or LowGer *stuk*, *stik* a piece. OED *steek* (*n¹*)]

steik² *15-16*, *only Sc*; **stek-** *la14-e16* [***stik] *v*, *pt* **stekit** *la14-e15*, **stak &c** *15-16*. *ptp* **stekit** *la14-16*, **stokit** *16*, *only Sc*, **stokin** *16* **1** *vt* pierce, stab; transfix *la14-16*. **2** *vti* = steek, fix; pierce and remain fixed; be hindered *16*. **3** *vr* set oneself in position *e15*. [*cf* STEEK², STICK¹. OED *steek* (*v²*)]

steil *see* STEAL, STEEL[1]
steillit *see* STELL[1]
stein3ie *see* STEN3IE
steir *see* STEER[1]
stek *see* STEEK[1]
stek- *see* STEIK[2]
stekill [*'stɛkl] *n* the bar of a door *la15.* [ME *steckle.* OED *steckle*]
stekin, stekine, steking *see* STEEK[1]
stel *see* STEAL
stell[1]; **stile &c** *la16-19* [stɛl] *v, ptp also* **steillit &c** *la15-16* **1** *vt* place in position, set up, prop *la15-, now Lnk SW.* **2** *vtr* brace or stay (oneself or one's feet) by planting the feet against some immovable object *la18-, now WC-Rox.* **3** *vt* keep (the eyes) rigid, set (them) in a fixed stare *19-, now WC-S.* **4** halt, bring to a standstill, make immobile *la19-, now WC, SW.* **5** load (a ship) evenly, trim the cargo in (a ship) *18.* **6** put (sheep) in a STELL[1] (*n* 2); *chf fig* corner, shut in *19-e20.* **7** *vi* (come to a) stop *la19-, now Kcb.* **8** *of the eyes* become fixed in a stare of astonishment, horror etc, stand out *19-, now local Lnk-Rox.*

n, also **staill &c** *la16-e17* **1** a place in a river over which nets are drawn to catch salmon *la15-e19.* **2** an open, *usu* circular, enclosure of *dry-stane* (DRY) walling, used as a shelter for sheep on a hillside *18-, now WC-S.* **3** a clump or plantation of trees used as a shelter for sheep *la18-e20.* **4** *chf mining* a prop, wooden stay etc used for underpinning a roof *19-, now local Fif-Ayr.* **5** *curling* (CURL) the notches in the ice to prevent the players' feet from slipping when delivering the stone; *later* (*la20-*) the CRAMPET (*n* 5 (2)) which replaced these *19-, now Kcb*
~**ing place** a place of shelter *e16.*
~ **fishing** *etc* a fishery with a STELL[1] (*n* 1) *18.*
~ **net** a net stretched out into or across a river *la16-19.* [*chf Sc*; OE *stellan* lay down, establish]
stell[2] *18-, now local Suth-Gall*; **still** *la18-* *n* = still, for whisky etc *18-.*
vt distil; discharge (liquid) in small drops *18-19.*
sma ~ *usu attrib, freq implying illicit distillation* a type of small still, supposed to produce mellower whisky *19.*
stell[3] *vi* go with a firm, purposeful step, stride *19-, now Lnk.* [only *Sc*; uncertain]
stell *see* STEAL
stellage *n* a local tax on a brewery within a district, *specif* as due to the BURGH of Wigtown from the county *18-e19.* [only *Sc*; extended use of Eng *stillage* a stand for brewers' casks, MDu *stellagje* a platform, stand, stage]
stellate &c *adj* **1** verse, *of the sky* studded with stars *e16.* **2** = stellate. [only *Sc*]
stellionate &c *n, law* a crime for which there is no specific name, applied to **1** a kind of fraud in which the same right is granted to two or more different people *la17-*; **2** a real injury against

the person *la18-19.* [Civil Law L *stellionatus*, f *stellio* a kind of lizard with starlike spots; a fraudulent person]
stem[1] *vt* **1** = stem, dam up. **2** stop, staunch (bleeding etc) *la15-, only Sc.*
n a dam of stones in a stream, used as a fishtrap or to form a watering-place for cattle *e18, 20-, local Cai-Lnk.*
stem[2] *n* the peak of a cap *20-, SW.*
~(**med**) **bonnet** *or* **cap** a bonnet etc with a peak *la19-, now SW.* [extended use of Eng *stem* the prow of a boat]
stem[3] *v* **1** *vi, nautical* keep a certain course *la14.* **2** *vt* = stem (the tide).
steming &c [*'stɛmɪn] *n* = stamin, a kind of woollen or worsted cloth *16-17.* [only *Sc.* OED *stamin*]
sten *see* STEND[1]
stench[1] **&c** *la16-*, **stanch &c**; **stainch** *la16-e20* [stenʃ, stɛnʃ] *v* **1** *vt* = stanch, check the flow of *la14-.* **2** *vi* cease flowing *la16.* **3** *vt* restrain (**from** violence etc) *16, only Sc.* **4** *vi, of storm, war, dissension* come to an end; *of persons* cease from violence *16.* **5** *vt* allay (hunger or thirst); satisfy (a person) with food, satiate *la15-, now NE Ags.*
n a satisfying, *esp* of hunger *la16-, now NE.*
stench[2] *now NE, EC*; **staunch** *la18-*, **stainch** *la19-20*, **stinch &c** *19-, Abd Ags* [stenʃ, stɛnʃ] *adj* **1** = staunch *18-.* **2** serious, severe-looking, reserved; inflexible, uncompromising; austere, rigid *la18-, now NE.* **3** *of persons, animals, things* strong, dependable, firm; in good health *la19-, now NE.*
adv strictly, closely, exactly *la19-, NE.*
stenchel *see* STAINCHEL
stencher *see* STAINCHER
stenchil *see* STANCHEL
stenchion *see* STAINCHEON
stend[1]; **sten(n)** *18-e20* *vi* **1** leap, bound, spring up *la16-e20.* **2** *of animals* rear, start, be restive *la16-e20.* **3** stride, walk or march purposefully *18-, now Sh.*
n **1** a leap, spring, bound *15-, now Sh Ayr.* **2** a long firm bouncing step, a stride *18-, now Sh.* **3** *fig* a sudden start, a thrill of excitement, fear etc *la18-19.*
~**le** leap or bound frequently *e16.* [only *Sc*; perh aphetic f Eng *extend*]
stend[2] *vt* erect (a tent) *la16.* [only *Sc*; aphetic f Eng *extend*; *cf* STENT[1] *v* 1]
stendie *n* a stroke of the *tawse* (TAW[1]) *19-20, chf Fif.* [only *Sc*; L *extende* (*manum*) hold out (your hand)]
steng *see* STING[2]
stenlock &c;   **stan(e)lock &c** ['stenlək, 'stɛn-] *n* the coalfish, *esp* in its fully-grown or SAITHE stage *19-, now Arg Ayr.* [only *Sc*; see SND]
stenn *see* STEND[1]
stennis &c *vt, n* sprain *19.* [only *Sc*; uncertain]

stent[1]; **stint** *la14-20 v* **1** *vt* extend, stretch out (a sail, net etc) in its proper position; pitch (a tent); make taut *la14-*. **2** *transf* erect (a tomb) *e16*. **3** hang (a window) with curtains *e16*. **4** extend (a person) **on** *etc* (an instrument of torture) *la14-e18*. **5** keep in place, stiffen (a garment) *la15-16*. **6** distend (the stomach with food) *19-e20*. **7** *vi* strive, exert oneself (1) *in gen*, *la18-e20*; (2) ~ **at** *la20-, Sh*.

~**er 1** a person who sets up tents *e16*. **2** *cloth-milling* a tenter *18*. **3** a clothes prop *la20-, local Stlg-SW*. ~**ing &c 1** extending etc *16-*. **2** material used for stiffening a garment *la15-18*. ~**ing post** a strainer in a wire fence *la19-, now local C, S*. ~**(it)** extended, stretched, taut; stiff *16-e20*. ~**our** stiffening for a doublet *e16*. ~ **net** a fishing net stretched on stakes across a river *18-19*. ~ **tree** = stenter 2, *e18*. [only Sc; perh var of STEND[2]; also infl by STENT[2], STENT[3]]

stent[2] *16-e20*; **stint** *18-e20 n, also* **staint** *la17* **1** an (annual) assessment of the value of property, *esp* land for taxation purposes; the amount so fixed, (money paid in) tax, *specif* (1) the valuation and taxes on land held direct of the king by barons and BURGHS, *esp* that paid by the BURGHS (and burgesses) *16-19*; (2) an assessment for ecclesiastical or parochial purposes *18-19*. **2** a tax *in gen, 18-e20*.

vt, ptp, adj **stent** *16-17, only Sc* **1** assess for taxation purposes, tax *16-18*. **2** levy (a sum) as an assessment; impose (a tax etc) on *17-19*.

~**er** an assessor (as in *n* 1) *16-e19, only Sc*. ~**-master** *only Sc* **1** a person appointed to assess the taxes of a town or parish *17-19*. **2** *in pl* a committee of final-year students at Glasgow University appointed to assess the graduation fee for their fellow-GRADUANDS *18-19*. ~ **oylie &c** ? the quantity of oil claimed as duty on the year's produce *e17, only Sc*. **trade('s)** ~ an assessment on the trade done by each burgess of a town *la18-e19, only Sc*. [ME; OF *estente*, laL *extenta* valuation; *cf* EXTENT]

stent[3] *n* **1** = stint, cessation of action etc *e15*. **2** limits, bounds, restraint; the limit to which one is prepared to go *18-, now local Fif-Dmf*. **3** the proportion of pasture in a common allocated to each tenant; the number of animals allowed on each pasturage *e15, 18-e20*. **4** an allotted task, a portion of work to be covered in a given time *18-, now NE-S*.

v **1** *vi* = STINT *v* 1, *la15-e19*. **2** *vt* confine, limit, check; stint *la17-, now Rox*. **3** apportion (work); allocate an amount of work to (a person); make (a person) work hard *la15, la18-e20* [ME, var of STINT]

stent[4] *n* ? a staple or hole for the end of a bar *la15*. [only Sc; obscure]

stenʒie &c *16-e17*, **steinʒie &c** *16*, **stainyie &c** *16*, **stinʒe** *la16* [*'stɛnjɪ, *'stin-, *'stiŋ-, *'sten-, &c] *vti* = stain.

step *n* **1** = step *la14-*. **2** a short portion (of a highway), a patch (of road) *18-, now NE Ags Kcb*. **3** a stepping-stone in a river *18-, now Per Kcb, also in place-names, only Sc*. **4** *mining* a fault or slip in the strata of a mine *la18-, Ayr*. *vti* = step *la14-*. ~ **aside** commit a fault, go astray *la17-20*. **tak a** ~ walk, stroll, make a short journey *la19-*. [*cf* STAP[1]]

step *see* STAP[3]
step- *see* STAP-
ster *see* STAR[1]
sterand steid *see* STEER[1]
sterch *see* STAIRCH
stere *adj* harsh, austere, stern, rigorous *la19-e20*. [also in nEng dial; ME *stere* strong, stout; prob cognate w STURE[1]]
stere *see* STEER[2]
sterlin &c *e19*, **sterling &c**; **starlin(g)** *la16-e19*, **stirling &c** *16-e17 n* **1** = sterling, the English silver penny, English money etc *15-*. **2** the Scottish silver penny *la14-e17, only Sc*.
adj, also **striviling &c** *la15-e17, only Sc*, **stirviling &c** *la16, only Sc* [by confusion with the place-name *Striviling &c* = Stirling] sterling *la15-*.
stern *vt* cast down *la16*. [only Sc; appar f L *sternere*]
stern *see* STARN[1]
sterop *see* STIRRUP
sterr *see* STAR[1]
stert *see* START[1]
stertle *see* STARTLE
sterve &c, starve *la18- vti* **1** = starve *la14-*. **2** (1) *vi, chf* ~ **o** *or* **wi cauld** be much affected by cold, feel chilled *la18-*. (2) *vt* affect with extreme cold, freeze *19-*.
stervation bitter cold *20-*.
stethlin *see* STATHEL
steuch *see* STEW
steug *see* STUG[1]
stevel *see* STAVEL
steven[1] **&c** [*'stivən] *n, chf verse* **1** a voice *la14-19*. **2** a loud outcry, din *16-e19*. [ME; OE *stefn*]
steven[2] [*'stivən] *n* the prow *or* stern of a boat *16-19*. [only Sc; Du (*achter-)steven*, cognate w Eng *stem* f OE *stefn* prow or stern]
stew; stue &c *la19-20*, **steuch &c** *la19-* [stju(x)] *n* **1** (1) (a cloud of) dust *la14-, now Sh N*. (2) *fig* a hubbub, uproar; trouble *la19-, now Sh, only Sc*. (3) *fig in phrases implying rapid energetic movement or sudden disappearance 20-, NE, only Sc*. **2** a stench; a suffocating vapour *la16-, now Sh WC Kcb*. **3** a coating or sprinkling of dust or powder *20-, now Abd, only Sc; cf* STOUR.
vi stink, cause a stench *la16, la19-, now Sh Stlg WC, SW, only Sc*.

stewat a stinker *e16*, *only Sc*. **stewie &c** dusty, dust-stained *20-*, *NE*, *only Sc*. [see SND]

stewart &c, **steward** *la15-*; **stuart &c** *la15-e18* **1** = steward *15-*. **2** (1) an official appointed by the Crown having jurisdiction over a *stewartry*, *15-e18*. (2) the SHERIFF of Orkney and Shetland or of Kirkcudbright *18-19*.

~**ry** *only Sc* **1** (1) the territory under the jurisdiction of a STEWART (*n* 2) *la15-e18*. (2) applied to areas formerly = prec and continuing to be so called after the abolition of the *stewartry* as an administrative unit: Kirkcudbright *la15-*; Orkney and Shetland *la18-e20*. **2** the office of STEWART (*n* 2) *la15-e18*.

~ **compt** the statement of the accounts of a *stewartry*, *la16*, *only Sc*. ~ **court** the court having jurisdiction within a *stewartry*, *la15-18*, *only Sc*. ~ **deput(e)** the judge delegated by the STEWART (*n* 2) to administer justice etc in the *stewartry*, *17-18*, *only Sc*.

(**Lord High**) **S~ of Scotland** title of the chief officer of the Royal Household (*only hist*), transferred, as (**Great**) **S~ of Scotland** to be a title of the monarch's eldest son *16-* [see SND, OED].

stewat *see* STEW

stey¹ *18-*; **stay** *la14-e20*, **steich &c** *la19-20* [stəi; ?stix; *?sti] *adj* **1** *of a hill, road etc* (very) steep; difficult to climb *la14-20*. **2** *transf* upright, unbending; *of persons* reserved, haughty *la16-e17*, *only Sc*.

~ **coal** a coal seam set at a very steep angle *la20-*, *Fif midLoth*.

set *etc* **a stout heart to a ~ brae** face difficulties with resolution *18-*, *only Sc*. [prob OE *stǣge; cf OE stǣgel steep, ON stegi, stigi a steep ascent]

stey² &c *19-*, *now C, S*, **stay** [stəi] *vti* **1** = stay, stop *la16-*. **2** *vi* dwell, reside; make one's home *18-*.

n = stay *la16-*.

stey³ [stəi] *vti*, *n* = stay, support.

~**band** a crossbar of a door; a bar to fasten the two leaves of a double door from the inside *19-*, *now local Abd-Lnk*, *only Sc*.

stibblart &c *n* a young lad, a (half-grown) youth *18-e19*, *Abd*. [only Sc; see SND]

stibble &c, **stubble** *19-* *n* = stubble *la16-*.

stibbler 1 a harvest-worker who gathers up odd straws, a gleaner *la18-e19*. **2** a *probationer* (PROBATION) in the Presbyterian church not yet in a *settled* (SATTLE) charge, who preaches here and there as required *la18-e20*, *only Sc*.

~ **butter** high-quality butter made from the milk of cows grazed on stubbles *19-*, *now local N-SW*, *only Sc*.

~ **land** the stubble of the first crop of corn after grass *19-e20*. ~ **rig** *only Sc* **1** a ridge of stubble left after harvest *la18-e20*. **2** the leader in a team of reapers *la18-e19*.

stichle &c ['stɪxl] *vi* rustle, stir, bustle *16-*, *now Kcdn*.

n a rustle, bustling noise *19-*, *now Kcdn*. [only Sc; prob var of ME *stightle* bestir oneself]

sticht &c [*stɪxt] *n* battle array *la14*, *only Sc*. [ME *stight* set in order. OED *stight*]

stick¹ &c *v*, *pt also* **stack** *17-*, *now NE*; **stickit &c** *la16-*. *ptp also* **stucken &c** *la16-*, *now Sh NE, C*, **sticken** *e17, e19*; **stickit &c** *la15-* **1** *vti* = stick *la16-*. **2** *vt*, *pt*, *ptp chf* ~**it &c** stab, thrust a knife into, finish off *la16-*. **3** *of a horned animal* gore, stab or butt with its horns *la18-*, *now local*. **4** *in sorting fishing-lines* turn each hook back into the horse-hair of the SNUID to prevent its entangling the line *20-*, *Ags*. **5** come to a premature halt in, break down in the middle of (a job etc), botch *18-*, *now Sh-Per, Kcb*.

n a stoppage, breakdown, standstill; an obstacle *17-*, *now Sh*.

~**er** a stabber, a slaughterer *la16-e20*. ~**ers** goose-grass *20-*, *now Fif Wgt Rox*, *only Sc*. ~**in** stiff and unsocial in manner, unwilling to join in; obstinate *19-*, *now C*. ~**it &c 1** *of a task etc* left spoilt or incomplete *la18-*, *now Per*. **2** *of persons* halted in their trade or profession, failed, insufficiently qualified *la18-20*: 'stickit minister'. **3** *chf of plants* stunted, checked in growth *19-*, *now Cai Per*. ~**y-fingered** having a tendency to steal *19-*, *only Sc*. ~**y-Willie** = ~**ers**, *20-*, *Gen except Sh Ork*, *only Sc*. **stuck** = ~**it**, *la19-*. ~**dirt** *flyting* (FLYTE): term of abuse *la16*, *only Sc*.

~ **by 1** be constant to (a principle etc) *e17*. **2** = stick by. ~ **one's eyne in** subject (someone) to a piercing gaze *la15*. ~ **in** *sometimes with* **tae** *or* **wi** persist doggedly, work hard, persevere, go energetically (at) *19-*. ~ **tee** adhere, keep close (**to**) *20-*, *Sh Abd*. ~ **up to 1** *usu of a lover* pay court to, ingratiate oneself with *la18-*, *Abd*. **2** stand up to, oppose defiantly *19-*.

stick² &c *n* = stick, a staff etc *la14-*.

adj wooden, made of timber *18-*, *local NE-Rox*, *only Sc*.

~**le** a small stick, *esp specif* one laid across the joists of a mill kiln to support the straw etc on which the grain was dried *19*, *only Sc*.

all to ~s (**and staves &c**) all to pieces, to ruin; completely and utterly *19-*. **nae great ~s** at not adept at, not very good at *19-*, *now Sh NE Ags*. **tak up the ~s** exert oneself, 'enter the fray' *la19-*, *Sh NE*.

stick *see* STEEK²

stickit *see* STEEK¹

stickle *vi* have scruples, raise objections; hesitate, scruple (to do etc) *17-20*. [prob back-formation f Eng *stickler*]

stickly &c *adj* prickly, bristly, stubbly; *of* PEAT¹ rough, fibrous, full of little roots etc *19-e20*. [only Sc; see SND]

stiddie *see* STUDDIE

stiel &c [stil] *n* the handle of a barrow, plough etc *16-, now Rox.* [ME *stele* a handle, shaft, OE *stela* a stalk, stem]

stieve &c, steeve *la18-e20;* **stive** *la18-19,* **steif** *la16* [stiv] *adj* **1** firmly fixed, stable, rigid, compact, stiff *la16-20.* **2** *of persons, animals, their limbs* firm, strong, sturdy *la18-, now local Per-Dmf.* **3** *fig* steady, resolute, staunch; loyal, dependable *la18-, now Per Stlg.* **4** hard-hearted, relentless, obstinate *19-, now Per.* **5** shrewd in business, prudent, slightly mean *la18-e20.* **6** *of a struggle* hard, grim; *of haste* pressing *19-e20.* **7** *of a road* difficult, steep and rough *la19-, now Sh.* **8** *of food or drink* strong, thick, full of body *la18-e20.*
adv firmly, stoutly, stiffly, securely, staunchly *la16-20.*
vt make firm, stiff, taut *la16-e20.*
steevil &c ['stivl; *Ork also* 'stɪvl] = *adj* 8, *19-, now Ork.* [chf *Sc;* ME *stef,* perh f OE **stif* var of *stíf* stiff]

stife &c *n* a suffocating atmosphere, smoke, or vapour *19-, now S.*
vt, chf **stifin** stifling *20-, now Lnk Ayr, only Sc.* [appar back-formation f Eng *stifle*]

stiff *adj* = stiff *la15-.*
~en starch (clothes) *19-, local.* **~ing &c** *la16-, now N Rox, only Sc,* **~ening &c** *19-, now Stlg WC* starch.

stiffie *see* STEFE

stifin *see* STIFE

stifle &c ['stəifl] *vti* = stifle.
n, mining foul air from an underground fire; miners' asthma (from this or from coaldust), pneumoconiosis *19-, now Fif.*

stilch [stɪltʃ] *n* a young fat clumsy man *19-, now Kcb.* [only *Sc;* var of STILT, f the way of walking]

stile *see* STELL[1]

still &c *adj* **1** = still *la14-.* **2** reserved, taciturn, unforthcoming *19-, now NE Ags Rox.*
adv = still *la14-.*
vti **1** = still, (become) quiet *17-.* **2** *vi* remain quiet and silent, be at peace *la18-, now Sh.*
n **1** = still. **2** *of the tide* the pause between ebb and flow *19-, Sh Wgt, only Sc.*
interj a call to stop, *eg* in games or to a horse *la19-, now Abd Ags, only Sc.*
~stand an armistice *e17, only Sc.*
~ and on 1 yet, nevertheless, for all that *la18-.* **2** always, continuously, without intermission *la18-e20.*

still *see* STELL[2]

stillicide [stɪlɪ'səid] *n, law* = EAVESDROP *la17-.* [L *stillicidium* a drip(ping) from the eaves]

stilp &c *vi* walk with long stiff steps, stump about, stalk *la18-, now Bnf-Ags.*
~ert &c *n* **1** a stilt *la19-, NE.* **2** a tall lanky person or animal with long legs *la19-, now NE.*
vi walk with long stiff strides, lifting the feet high *la19-, local NE.* [only *Sc;* altered f STILT, w infl f STAP[1] and Eng *stump, stamp*]

stilt; stult *la19 n* **1** one of the handles of a plough *18-.* **2** a crutch *la17-, now local Stlg-Wgt.* **3** a prop, support *e17, only Sc.* **4** = stilt.
v, only Sc **1** *vi* go on stilts or crutches *19-, now local Stlg-Rox.* **2** walk stiffly, haltingly, lift the legs high in walking *la18-e19.* **3** *vt* cross (a river) on stilts *la18-, now Lnk Wgt.*

stime *la18-,* **styme &c** *la15-20 n* **1** *chf in negative* (be unable to see) the least thing or trace of *la15-, now local Sh-Kcb.* **2** a tiny amount, particle, jot *la18-, now local Sh-Ags.* **3** *now chf literary* a glimmer or glimpse of light *la18-, now Sh N Stlg.*
vi blink, look through half-shut eyes, peer *e17, 19-20.*
stymel &c a person who does not see or understand quickly *19-20, chf Rox.* **stymie &c** a person who does not see well *17-e19.* [chf *Sc;* obscure]

stimie &c; stymie ['stəimɪ] *n, golf* a shot in which one's ball lands on the green not less than six inches from one's opponent's ball, in a direct line between it and the hole, so as to obstruct his putt (abolished from the rules in 1952) *19-20.*
vti **1** *of a ball or player* lie *or* play as a STIMIE *la19-20.* **2** *fig* obstruct, thwart *la19-.* [obscure]

stimpart &c *n* **1** *in dry measure* the fourth part of a* PECK[2] *la18-, now local Stlg-Dmf.* **2** a measure of land, the fourth part of a RIG[1] *la19-e20.* [only *Sc;* aphetic f *sixteen(t) part* = one sixteenth of a FIRLOT[2]

stinch *see* STENCH

sting[1] *vti, pt also* **stang** *la18-, now NE* = sting.
~ing ether [-'ɛðər] the dragonfly *la20-, local Stlg-Lnk.* [*cf* STANG[1]]

sting[2] **&c** *15-e20;* **steng &c** *la14-e19 n* **1** a pole, staff, *freq specif* one carried on the shoulders of two men, with a load suspended from it *la14-19.* **2** a staff etc used as a weapon, the shaft of a pike etc, *freq* **staff and ~** *la15-16.* **3** a pole used to push off a boat or in punting *la18-e20.* **4** a stick with a forked iron tip used by thatchers to push straw into the roof *e19.*
vti **1** punt *19.* **2** use a STING[2] (*n* 4) in thatching; thatch with a STING[2] *18-e20.*
stingis-dint a fine for an assault with a stick *15.* **~man** one who carries loads with a STING[2] *la16.*
~ and ling 1 by means of a STING[2] resting on the shoulders of two bearers *la16-19.* **2** *fig* lock, stock and barrel, without ceremony, forcibly *e19.* [chf *Sc;* OE *steng* a stick; *cf* STANG[2]]

stingy ['stɪndʒɪ] *adj* **1** = stingy. **2** haughty, supercilious; peevish, petulant *la18-e19.*

stink &c *vti* **1** = stink *la16.* **2** *vt* fill (a place) or affect (a person) with an offensive smell, foul atmosphere etc *18-, now Sh Ork NE nEC.*
n = stink *16-.*
~ing &c *adj* **1** = stinking *la16-.* **2** offensively

haughty, snobbish, supercilious *la18-*, *now Sh NE Ags*. ~**ing Billy** sweet william *20-*, *local*. ~**ing coal** an impure kind of coal which burns with a strong sulphurous smell *la19-*, *now Fif Lnk*. ~**ing Elshender** [-ˈɛlʃən(d)ər] = ~*in Willie*, *19-*, *now Per Stlg Fif*, *only Sc*. ~**in Tam(my)** name for various strong-smelling plants, *esp* the rayless mayweed *la19-*, *now Bwk S*, *only Sc*. ~**in Willie** the ragwort *19-*, *now local NE-SW*.

stint *v* **1** *vi* stop, desist, halt *la14-*, *now Bnf Ags*. **2** *vt* (1) = stint, discontinue, cause to stop *la14-e15*. (2) *specif* stop (a blow) *la15*. **3** = stint, limit, restrict, keep short *16-*. **4** *vi*, *of plants* shrivel, droop *la18-*, *now Ork*, *only Sc*. *n* = stint *la14-*. [*cf* STENT³]

stint *see* STENT¹, STENT²

stinȝe *see* STENȜIE

stipend *see* STEEPEND

stiple *see* STEEPLE

stippit *see* STUPIT

stir *n*, *polite form of address* sir *la18-e19*. [only Sc; prob altered f Eng *sir* by conflation w MAISTER¹; *cf* STIRRAH]

stirk &c *n* **1** a young bullock or (*less freq*) heifer after weaning, kept for slaughter at the age of two or three *14-*, *freq in comb denoting sex, eg* **bull(ock)** ~ *19-*, **heifer** ~ *20-*. **2** a stupid oafish fellow *la16-*, *now N nEC, S*. **3** a sturdy young man *18-*, *now N Stlg Ayr*. ~**ie** = *n*, *la18-*, *only Sc*.

there's aye some water whaur the ~(ie) drouns there's no smoke without a fire, there must be some truth in the story *18-*. **be (putten) in the stirk(ie)'s sta** *etc*, *of a child* be supplanted in its parents' attention by the birth of a new baby *19-*, *local N-S*. [*cf* Eng]

stirk *see* STRIK

stirlin &c *16-*; **stirling &c** *15-e19* *n* = starling. [only Sc. OED *starling*]

stirling *see* STERLIN

Stirling *see* JOUG

stirrah &c *la18-*; **stirrow** *la17* *n* **1** a (sturdy) young lad *la17-e20*. **2** contemptuous term for a man, *esp* a rough unmannerly youth *19-*, *now Rox*. [only Sc; var of Eng *sirrah*; *cf* STIR]

stirrup &c *la17-*; **sterop &c** *la14*, *e16* [*ˈstirəp] *n* = stirrup *la14-*.

steropmanschip the office of a groom of the stirrup (in the royal household) *e16*.

stirviling *see* STERLIN

stishie *see* STASHIE

stitch¹ *n* = stitch.

~**y** a kind of sunbonnet *la19-*, *now Rox*.

stitch² *n* a furrow or drill *eg* of turnips *19-*, *SW*. [dial in Eng; prob f as prec]

stith &c [*staiθ, *staið] *adj* **1** = stith, unyielding, strong *la14-e16*. **2** *of a stream* strong-flowing *la14-e16*, *only Sc*. **3** *of the weather* hard, severe *e15*, *e19*. **4** stiff, rigid as in death *la18-19*, *only Sc*.

vt set firmly, cause to remain immovable *la14*, *only Sc*.

stithy *see* STUDDIE

stive *la18-*; **steeve &c** *la17-e20* *vt* stuff, pack, cram, *esp* gorge with food *la17-*, *now Per*. [ME *stive*, OF *estiver*]

stive *see* STIEVE

stoat weasel &c *n* the common stoat or ermine *la18-*, *now local NE-S*, *only Sc*.

stob &c *n* **1** *also* **stab** *la17-* a stake, a post *la15-*. **2** (1) a short thick nail *la15*, *18-e20*. (2) *only* **stab** a stout thickset man *la19-*, *now Sh Uls*, *only Sc*. **3** (1) a prickle, a thorn or spike; a splinter of wood, *esp* one driven into the skin *17-*, *now NE-Fif*. (2) the wound made thus *20-*, *NE-Fif*. **4** a stab-wound; a poke, a prod *17-19*, *only Sc*. **5** a bradawl *la19-*, *now Sh NE Ags*. **6** a Y-shaped stick used like a staple in thatching; a two-pronged stick used to push thatching straw into position *la16*, *19-20* (*NE*). **7** an incomplete rainbow showing only the lower ends of the bow, believed to forewarn of a storm at sea *19-*, *local E*, *only Sc*.

vt **1** stab *16-18*. **2** prick or jab with a pointed object *19-*, *now NE Ags*. **3** (1) *also* **stab** *la18-*, *now Sh* fence with stakes, mark or bound with posts *16-*, *now local WC-S*. (2) prop up (*eg* plants) with stakes *la18-*, *now local WC-S*. **4** thatch with STOBS (*n* 6) *16-*, *now Bnf*, *only Sc*. **5** dress or trim (a stack of grain) with a hay-fork *la19-*, *now Ork Bnf Abd*, *only Sc*.

stober a thatcher *la17*, *only Sc*. **stobby &c** rough and spiky, prickly, bristly *19-*, *now NE Ags*, *only Sc*.

~**-feathert** *of a young bird* having stumpy, not fully developed feathers; *of persons* beginning to be equipped for life *19-e20*, *chf NE*. ~ **fence** a wire fence fixed on wooden posts *la20-*. ~ **nail** = *n* 2 (1), *18-*, *now Bnf Rox*, *only Sc*. ~ **thack &c** thatch with STOBS (*n* 6), *freq* ~**-thackit &c** *la18-*, *now NE*.

hald *etc* ~ **and stake &c** hold property (in a place) *la15-16*, *only Sc*. [ME *stob* a twig, a stump, var of Eng *stub*; *cf* ON, Du *stobbe* a stump; also infl by Eng *stab* (*cf* STAB)]

stock¹ &c; **stouk** *17* [stok; *?stʌuk] *n* **1** = stock *la14-*. **2** a block of wood, log; a tree-stump *la15-*, *now Bnf Abd*. **3** the hard stalk or stem of a plant, *esp* of a cabbage etc; the whole plant *17-*, *now Sh*, *chf Sc*. **4** a stem on which a graft is inserted *la15*. **5** a butcher's or fishmonger's cutting block or table *la15-16*, *only Sc*. **6** a saddle-tree *la15-e18*, *only Sc*. **7** the rail of a bed, *orig* a box bed (BOX¹), the side of a bed away from the wall *17-20*. **8** the socket of a bagpipe drone, to which the bag is tied *20-*, *only Sc*. **9** a pack of playing cards *18-e20*. **10** that proportion of a crop etc left over after the amount (or its value) apportioned to TEINDS had been taken away *18-e20*, *only Sc*. **11** *usu sympathetic, sometimes disparaging, chf of men* a chap, 'bloke', creature *19-*, *now NE Ags*.

vti **1** = stock _16-_. **2** _vi, of the body, limbs_ become stiff, unwieldy or cramped with cold _19-20, only Sc._ **3** _of plants_ send out shoots, sprout _la18-, now N._ **4** _vt, also_ ~ **out** fund, invest (money) _18-19._

~**er** a workman who makes or fits gunstocks _e17._ ~**ing 1** the parts forming the stock of a gun _e16_. **2** the livestock and gear needed to run a farm _18-, only Sc._ ~**it &c** obstinate, stubborn _la19-, Bnf Abd._

~ **annet &c** the sheldrake _18-, now Ags Fif SW._ ~ **boat** _fishing_ a boat used to transport cured herring and equipment between outlying fishing stations and the depots _20-, now Sh Bnf Abd._ ~**isdynt** = _stingis-dint_ (STING²) _15, only Sc._ **stokmaker** a maker of gun-carriages _la16._ ~**purse** a fund kept for the common purposes of a group _la17._ **stok sadill** ? a saddle with a wooden tree _e16, only Sc._ **stoke quhele** ? a wheel for a gun-carriage _e16, only Sc._ ~ **still** quite still, _chf_ **stand** ~ **still** _la15-._ ~ **and teind** _law_ the gross produce of a farm etc, without deduction of the TEIND _la16-e17, only Sc._

stock² _n_ ~ **horn** _la16_, ~ **and horn &c** _18-19_ a kind of (clarinet-type) wind instrument. [only Sc; Sc and IrGael _stoc_, ONorthumb _stocc_ a horn, trumpet; prob same as prec]

stock³ &c _n_ ~ **swerd &c** a thrusting sword _16_. [only Sc; F _estoc_, Ital _stocco_; prob orig Germanic; _cf_ STOCK¹]

stockin; stocking _n_ **1** = stocking _18-._ **2** a stocking used as a receptacle for savings; savings, a hoard _la19-, Gen except Sh Ork._ ~ **fit** = _n_ 2, _la19-e20, only Sc._ ~ **needle** a darning needle _la18-, Gen except Sh, only Sc._

throw the ~ throw the stocking of the bride or bridegroom among the guests at a wedding as a way of predicting who will marry next _la18-e20, only Sc._

stockisdynt _see_ STOCK¹
stod _see_ STUD
stoddert &c an area of green grass on a hill or heath surrounding a spring of water _e20, NE._ [only Sc; prob altered f STROTHER]
stodge; studge _vi_ walk with a long slow step, stump; step uncertainly or unsteadily _20-, now Sh NE Wgt S._

stodgel &c, stodger a slow, lumbering, rather stupid person _la19-, now NE._ [see SND]
stog _see_ STUG¹, STUG²
stoich _see_ STECH
stoit &c; styte &c _19-_ [stoit, stəit; _Fif_ stʌut] _vti, only Sc_ **1** (cause to) bounce, rebound _19-._ **2** _vi_ stagger, stumble from drink etc, walk in a dazed uncertain way _18-, local NE-Uls;_ **3** walk in a casual easy way, saunter _la19-, NE Ags._

_n_ **1** a buffet, blow _20-, now Dmf Rox, only Sc._ **2** a lurch, stagger, tottering step _19-, now NE Ags, only Sc._ **3** a stupid, ungainly, blundering person _19-, now Abd._ **4** foolish talk, stupid rubbish, nonsense _19-, now Ork Cai NE._

adv with a bump or bounce _la19-, now NE Ags Dmf, only Sc._

~**er** ['stoitər, 'stəit-; _Cai Fif_ 'stʌut-; _Uls_ 'stʌuθ-] _vi_ **1** walk unsteadily, reel, totter _18-, now local._ **2** stumble or falter in speech, stammer, stutter _19-, now Kcb, only Sc._ _n_ a staggering motion, stumble, reeling about _19-, now local Sh-Wgt._ [Du _stuit_ a bounce of a ball etc, _stuiten_ brake, bounce, bump; prob cognate w STOT²]

stoke _vt_ **1** = stoke, pierce, make a thrust at _la14._ **2** thrust, drive home (a sword) _e16._

stokin, stokit _see_ STEIK²
stokyt _see_ STEEK¹
stole _see_ STUIL
stolum &c _n_ **1** a pen-nibful of ink _la18-, now Cai Mry._ **2** a large piece broken or cut off something _19._ [see SND]
stomach _see_ STAMACK
stomachat &c, stomakat [*'stoməxat, *-et, *'stomək-] _adj_ indignant, angry _la16._ [only Sc; L _stomachāt-_, ptp stem of _stomachārī_ be resentful. OED _stomachate_]
stonack, stonder, stondie _see_ STANE
stone &c _la18-e19_; **stoun** _la17_ [*ston, *stʌun] _n_ a tree stump or trunk left after felling; a cluster of new shoots etc growing on a (cut) tree root _la17-e19._

vi, of plants, trees throw out new growth after pruning etc _la18-e19._ [only Sc; var of Eng dial, ME _stoven_, OE _stofn_ a tree stump; prob cognate w STOO; _cf_ also _stole_ (STUIL)]

stone _see_ STANE, STEAL
stoneder _see_ STANE
stoo _la18-_; **stow &c** _16-e20_ [stu] _vt_ **1** cut (off) (_specif_ an animal's tail or part of its ear as a mark of ownership) _16-, now Sh._ **2** cut off (the stem or shoots of a plant or tree) _la18-, now Sh Abd._

_n_ **1** a slice, chunk, piece cut _18-e19._ **2** a cut on the ear (_eg_ of a sheep) as a mark of ownership _18-, now Sh._

stowans &c ['stuənz] _n_ lopped leaves etc, _esp_ the young leaves of the colewort, used as food. [reduced f Eng dial _stove_, f ON _stúfr_ a stump; _cf_ ON _stýfa_ cut off]

stook¹ _18-_; **stouk &c** _la15-18_ [stuk] _n_ **1** a shock of cut sheaves, _usu_ ten or twelve set up to dry in a field _la15-._ **2** a bundle (of straw) _la16-._

_v_ **1** _vt_ set up (sheaves etc) in STOOKS¹ _la16-._ **2** _vi, of corn_ go into STOOKS¹ _19-, now Sh Bnf Ags._

~**er** the worker who sets up the cut sheaves in STOOKS¹ _19-._ ~**ie Sunday** the Sunday at the height of harvest when all the corn has been cut and stands in STOOKS¹ _la19-, now Ork-EC Wgt._ ~ **o duds** _etc_ a person dressed in rags _19-, now Abd._ [nME _stouk_; MLowGer _stuke_ a bundle of flax or grain]

stook² _vt, in adj_ ~**it** having short upright horns; _in gen_ peaked, crested _19-20._ [perh f STUG², w infl f prec]

stookie &c ['stuki; _NE_ 'stukə, 'stugə] _n_ **1** = stucco, plaster of Paris; _specif_ a plaster-cast encasing a broken limb *la18-*. **2** pipeclay *20-*, *Lnk Gall*. **3** a stucco figure *la19-*. **4** a slow-witted, dull, or shy person *la19-*, *now N, C Rox*. **5** *in pl* a children's game in which the players try to remain motionless as long as possible *la20-*, *EC-Dmf*.

~ **eemage** *etc* a plaster statue(tte) *la19-e20*.

stand *etc* **like a** ~ stand in a helpless bemused way as if unable to move *la19-*. [only *Sc*]

stool *see* STUIL

stoop &c *vti* **1** = stoop *la14-*. **2** *vt* plunge (a knife) **in** (a person's body) *la17, only Sc*.

stoor *see* STOUR, STURE[1]

stoorack, stoorin *see* STOUR

stoot *see* STOUT, STUIT, STUT

stooter *see* STOT[2]

stoothe &c [stuð] *vt* make or cover (a wall etc) with lath and plaster *la18-*, *SW, S*. [nME *stothe* a wooden post (*esp* in a lath and plaster wall), OE *studu* var of *studu* stud]

stop *see* STAP[2], STOWP

stope *see* STAP[2]

stopple *see* STAPPLE[1], STAPPLE[3]

store *n* **1** = store *la15-*. **2 the** Co-op, popular name for an area's Co-operative Society or its local retail branch *20-, local*.

vt = store.

storour a person who keeps something in store *e16*.

~ **farm** a farm, *usu* in the hills, on which sheep are reared and grazed *la18-*, *now SW, S, only Sc*. ~ **farmer** *19, only Sc*, ~ **master** *la16-18* one who runs such a farm. ~ **room** a sheepfarm *17-18, only Sc*.

~ **the kin** *etc, chf in negative* fail to keep the human race in existence; not survive, not last out, not keep going *la19-, NE Ags, only Sc*.

store *see* STOWER

storken *see* STURKEN

storm *n* **1** = storm *16-*. **2** fallen snow, *esp* when lying on the ground in some quantity for a long time; a period of wintry weather with alternating frost and snow *18-*, *now N Per, only Sc*.

vti **1** = storm *la16-*. **2** *vt* block, cover (up) with snow or frost *la18-19, only Sc*.

~**y 1** = stormy. **2** associated with or indicating storms *la16*.

~ **cock** the missel-thrush *20-, local N-S, only Sc*.

~**head** *or* ~**ont window** a projecting window with a small roof and sides, a dormer window *la17-, now Cai Kcb*. ~**-stayed** *or* **-stead** held up on a journey by bad weather *la15-, chf Sc*. ~ **window &c** = ~**head window**, *16-*.

storour *see* STORE

stortkyn &c *n* some measure of quantity *e16*. [only *Sc*; uncertain]

story *see* TORIE

stot[1] **&c** *n* **1** a young castrated ox, a bullock, *usu* in its second year or more *la14-*. **2** *fig* a stupid clumsy person *la19-*.

~ **stirk** a bullock in its second year *19-, now*

Cai, only Sc. [ME *stotte* a steer; a horse, OE *stott* a poor horse; prob cognate w Norw, Sw *stut*, ON *stútr* an ox, bull]

stot[2] *v* **1** *vi*, *of a ball etc* bounce, rebound; *fig* jump up, get up with a spring *16-*. **2** *vt* cause to bounce etc *la19-, Gen except Sh Ork*. **3** *vi* bounce, raise the body in walking, walk with a precise, springy or stately step *la18-, now local*. **4** *of an animal* bound, go by leaps *la19-, now Bnf Ags*. **5** stagger, walk unsteadily, *eg* from drink, weakness *18-*. **6** stutter, stammer *la18-, now Ork*.

n **1** a bounce, rebound, the act of rebounding; a spring, hop in a dance *16-, Gen except Sh Ork*. **2** a sharp (recoiling) blow *19-, Ags Dmf*. **3** (1) a sudden erratic movement, a fitful motion; a stumble, stagger *la19-, now Sh*. (2) *in pl* a fit of the sulks, a whim *la19-, now Sh*. **4** the beat of a tune, rhythm (of speech or dance); the go or swing of any activity *18-, now NE Per*. **5** the sequence of events in a story, the details, the thread of a speech etc *la19-e20*. **6** a stroll, saunter *20-, now Bnf*. **7** a stammer, stutter, speech impediment *la19-, now Ork*.

adv with a rebound, with a bouncing thump *19-*.

stotter, stooter &c *vi* stagger, totter, stumble *19-, local N-SW*. *n* **1** the act of *stottering*, a stumble, stagger, unsteady gait *la18-, local N-S*. **2** *term of admiration for* (*chf*) women a smasher *la20-*. **stottin bits** scraps of meat used by butchers as make-weights etc *20-, now Ags*. **stottin (fou)** reeling drunk *la19-, local N-SW*. **aff the** *or* **one's** ~ out of the rhythm of a tune etc; losing the regular pace etc of something; off one's stride; off the mark *la19-, local NE-S*. [chf *Sc*; see SND]

stote *la15*; **stot** *la14 v* **1** *vi* = stote, halt, stop *la15*. **2** *vt* cause to halt *la14, only Sc*.

stouk *see* STOCK[1], STOOK[1]

stoun *see* STONE, STOUND[1], STOUND[2]

stound[1] **&c**; **stoun &c** *18-* [stun(d); *Sh also* stoind, stjund] *n* **1** a period of time, a while *la14-, now Sh*. **2** a sharp throb of pain; an intermittent ache *la14-*. **3** a pang of mental pain or emotion: a throb of grief, a thrill of pleasure or excitement *la16-, now Ork-C*. **4** a mood, whim, a fit of depression, sullenness etc *20-, Ork N, only Sc*.

vti (cause to) throb, ache, smart, thrill with pain or emotion *16-*.

in a ~ in a short time, in a moment *16-e19*. [ME *stounde*, OE *stund* a period of time, a time of trial or pain; *cf* Ger *Stunde* an hour]

stound[2] **&c**; **stoun &c** [stun(d)] *v* **1** *vt* stun, stupefy, make insensible with a blow *19-, local EC, S*. **2** stupefy with noise or astonishment, bewilder *19-e20*. **3** *vi* resound, reverberate, ring with noise *18-, now Ags, only Sc*.

n **1** *also fig* a stunning blow *la18-, now Ags, only Sc*. **2** a stupefying din, a resounding noise (*esp* of water) *19-, now Ags, only Sc*. **3** a stunned condition, state of insensibility *19-*, *now local Bnf-Dmf*. [ME *stund* stun, stupefy, eModEng *stound* stupefaction, prob reduced f *astound*, OF *estoner* astonish, cognate w *stun*]

stoup &c [stup; *Abd also* stʌup; *Fif also* støp, step, stɪp] *n* **1** a wooden post, pillar, prop, *eg* a table-leg, gatepost *la15-*, *now local Sh-Kcb*. **2** the butt-end of the under-rail of a farm cart, on which it rests when tilted; the STILT or handle of a plough *la19-*, *now NE*. **3** a post etc marking out a circular racetrack, *esp* the turning- and winning-posts *18-e19*. **4** the pillar of a gateway *20-*, *now Sh Abd*. **5** *mining* a pillar of coal left to support the roof of the working *18-*. **6** *fig* a loyal enthusiastic supporter, a 'pillar' (*esp* of a church) *la16-*, *now local Sh-WC*.

~**ed** *of a bed* having posts *18-e20*.
~ **bed** a poster-bed *19-*, *now wLoth*.
the four ~**s o misery** *weaving* the (four-posted) hand-loom, from the poor living it provided in competition with industrial looms *19*.
~**-and-room** pillar-and-stall, a method of working coal by leaving pillars of coal to support the roof *19-*.

stoup *see* STOWP

stoup and roup &c *18-*, *now local*; **stout and rout** *la14* ['stup ən(d) 'rup; *Dmf* 'stʌup ən(d) ?'rʌup; ***'stut ən(d) 'rut] completely, absolutely, lock, stock and barrel; *cf* ROUT[4]; *see* SND. OED *stoop and roop*]

stour &c; stoor *la18-19*, **stower** *la18-19* [stur] *n* **1** *chf literary* strife, conflict, battle *la14-*, *now local Bnf-Wgt*. **2** a death struggle *e16*. **3** the strain and stress of a struggle, *esp* with adverse conditions or hardship, *chf* **bide** *etc* **the** ~ *la18-19*. **4** commotion, fuss, disturbance, *freq* **raise** *etc* **a** ~ *la18-*. **5** a storm, wild weather; a blizzard *19-*, *now Sh Ork*. **6** dust in motion, flying, swirling dust; (a layer of) dust; any fine powdery substance, *esp* produced by grinding etc *la15-*; *see also* STEW, which is more freq in NE. **7** a (cloud of) fine spray *16-*, *now Sh, only Sc*. **8** a pouring out of liquid, a steady outflow, a gush *19-*, *now NE, only Sc*.

v, only Sc **1** *vi* run swiftly, rush (on), bustle (about) *16-*, *now Sh-C*. **2** *of dust, spray etc* swirl, rise in a cloud *19-*, *now Sh Ork Rox*. **3** *vt* spray with dust etc, cover with some powdery substance, blow dust into *19-*, *now Cai Abd, only Sc*. **4** *vti* (cause to) gush out in a strong stream *19-*, *now Sh NE*.

~**ie** *n*, *18-*, *now Ork*, *also* **stoorack &c** *20-*, *N*, **stoorin &c** *19-*, *NE Ags*, ~**ie drink &c** *20-*, *now Ags Per* a kind of liquid fine-oatmeal gruel *only Sc*. *adj*, *only Sc* **1** dusty, full of choking whirling dust, covered with dust *la18-*. **2** *esp of a young child* active, restless *19-*, *now Ags Fif WC*.
~**ie fit &c** in Falkland and Peebles, a resident who is not a native of the town, an incomer *la20-*, *Fif Pbls*, *only Sc* [*orig* a traveller, a stranger who has arrived on foot]. ~**y lungs** pneumoconiosis; silicosis *la20-*, *Fif Edb wLoth*, *only Sc*.

knock (**the**) ~ **out of** beat, thrash (someone) *20-*, *now local*. **like** ~ like a whirl of dust, with a rush *20-*, *Gen except Sh Ork, only Sc*. [ME *st(o)ur*, OF *estour* tumult, conflict, cognate w Eng *storm*]

stour *see* STOWER, STURE[1]

stoussie &c ['stusɪ, 'stuʃɪ] *adj* stout and stocky, sturdy, chubby *la18-19*.
n a plump sturdy little child *19-e20*. [only Sc; *perh* Eng *stout* + suffix *-sie*]

stout &c; stult *16*, **stoot** *19-* [stut] *adj* **1** = stout *la14-*. **2** in good health, robust, *freq* with reference to recovery after an illness *la18-*, *now Sh-N Kcb*.
n a brave, valiant person *la15*, *only Sc*.
adv with power, strenuously, strongly *la15*, *la18-19*.
~**fullie** stoutly *la16*, *only Sc*. ~**rife** strongly built, powerful *20*, *Wgt Dmf Rox*, *only Sc*.

stout and rout *see* ROUT[4], STOUP AND ROUP

stouth &c [stuθ] *n* **1** theft, robbery *15-e19*. **2** stealth, clandestine transactions *e16*, *only Sc*.
~**erie &c** theft; stolen goods; gear, goods and chattels *19-*. ~**reif &c** theft with violence, forcible theft *la15-e20*, *only Sc*. [nME *stulth*, ON *stulþr* stealing]

stoutrife *see* STOUT

stove *n* **1** a hot-air bath; a sweating room *la15*. **2** a mist or vapour rising from the ground *16-e19*. **3** = stove. **4** *cooking* a stew *18-e20*, *only Sc*.
v, only Sc **1** *vr* have a hot-air bath *la15*. **2** *vt, cooking* stew *17-*, *now local Sh-Bwk*. **3** *vi* steam, emit vapour; *of smoke* billow out in clouds; *of persons* reek with alcoholic fumes *la18-*, *now Stlg WC*.
stovies &c, stoved tatties &c a dish of *stoved* (*v* 2) potatoes, onions etc, sometimes with small pieces of meat etc *la19-*, *only Sc*.

stow[1] &c [stʌu] *vt* **1** = stow *15-*. **2** fill (the stomach) with food, feed (oneself or another) *18-*, *now local Sh-Kcb, only Sc*.
n, coopering a stack or stockpile of barrels stored away ready for use *la20-*, *local NE-SW, only Sc*.

stow[2] &c [stʌu] *n* only as second element in phrases such as **stick and** ~ *la18-e20*, **stab and** ~ *18-19* completely, entirely. [*cf* Du *stik of stol*]

stow, stowans *see* STOO
stowen *see* STEAL
stower *la19*; **stour &c** *16*, **store** *la14* [stʌur] *n* a stake, post (in a fence, for a fishing net etc) *la14-*, *now Dmf*. [ME *st(o)ure*, Norw, ON *staur(r)* a stake]

stower *see* STOUR
stowf &c [*stʌuf] *literary*, *n* dust, fine powder *e19*.
vti send up *or* rise in clouds as a vapour *e19*. [only Sc; *poss* Du *stof* dust]

stowff &c [stʌuf] *vi* walk with a slow dull heavy step, stump *or* plod along *la19-*, *NE*.

n (the sound of) a dull heavy-footed gait *la19-*, *NE*. [only Sc; see SND]

stowfie ['stʌufɪ] *adj* sturdily built, stocky, stout, stolid *19-*, *now Bnf Abd*. [var of *stuffie* (STUFF¹)]

stowlins *see* STEAL

stowmpe *see* STUMP

stown, stownlins *see* STEAL

stowp &c *16-*, **stop &c** *la15-20*; **stoup &c** *17-* [stʌup; *Sh Ork* stup; *WC Uls* stop] *n* **1** a wooden pail or bucket, *esp* a narrow-mouthed one for carrying water from a well *la16-*, *now local NE-Rox*. **2** a flagon, tankard, decanter, mug etc, *freq with its capacity prefixed, eg* **pint** ~; the measure itself *la15-*, *now nEC Lnk Wgt, only Sc*. **3** a jug, *esp* for milk or cream *la18-*, *now NE Ags, only Sc*. [see SND]

stoy¹ &c ['stuɪ, stoi] *n* a cork float used to mark the position of sunken fishing-lines or crab-traps *la18-*, *now Mry Bnf Abd*. [only Sc; Gael *stuthaidh* a marker buoy]

stoy² [stoi] *vi* walk in a leisurely careless manner, saunter, stroll *la19-*, *now Bnf Abd*. [only Sc; perh reduced f STOIT]

stra *see* STRAE

strab &c *n* a stalk of corn that has been missed or merely broken by the scythe or reaper; any odd or loose straw *19-*, *Bnf Abd*. [only Sc; var of STRAP]

strabush *see* STRAMASH

strachle; strauchle ['straxl, 'strɑxl] *vi* **1** move or walk laboriously or with difficulty, struggle; labour ineffectually *19-*, *now Wgt Dmf*. **2** straggle, grow in a loose untidy way *20-*, *now local Loth-Dmf*. [only Sc; conflation of Eng *struggle* or *straggle* w TRAUCHLE]

stracht *see* STRAUCHT

strade *see* STRIDE

strae &c *16-*, **straw &c** *17-*; **stray &c** *16-e19*, **stra** *la14-e16*, **stro** *15-16* [stre] *n* = straw *la14-*.

vt supply with straw, *eg* for animal fodder or bedding *la20-*, *only Sc*.

stray breid *e16*, **strae bread** *19-*, *now Sh* the breadth of a straw. **straw crook** a rope-twister, *thrawcruik* (THRAW) *20-*, *now Cai Per Loth, only Sc*. ~ **death** natural death (in one's bed), *freq* **a fair** ~ **death** *17-*, *now Sh Stlg SW, only Sc*. **strae en &c** the end of a barn where the straw is built up *la19-*, *now Ork N Loth, only Sc*. **strae heuk** = *straw crook*, *la20-*, *local Sh-Bute*. **strae house** a straw-shed or -barn *la16-*, *now Ork Abd Kcb, only Sc*. ~ **mouse** the shrew *19-*, *now Mry Abd Fif Kcb, only Sc*. **strae raip** a rope of twisted straw *la19-*. ~ **sonk** a straw cushion used as a saddle *18-19*, *only Sc*. **strae-thackit &c** thatched with straw *19-*, *now Ork NE Ags, only Sc*. ~ **wald &c** dyer's rocket or yellow-weed *la16-e19*, *only Sc*.

be able *etc* **to bind** *or* **tie someone wi a** ~ used to describe someone who is helpless with laughter *la18-*, *now Kcb*: '*ye might hae bund me wi' a strae*'. **in the strae** in childbed *19-e20*.

strag &c *n* **1** a thin, straggly crop, as of corn; *also transf* thin wispy hair *19-*, *now Lnk, only Sc*. **2** a vagabond, roaming person; a loose woman *20-*, *now Dnbt Lnk Dmf, only Sc*. **3** a stray pigeon *20-*, *C, S*. [reduced f Eng *straggle*]

straggle &c *vi*, *also* **straiggle &c** *la19-e20*, *only Sc* = straggle.

n = straggle *19-*.

at *or* **to (the)** ~ in straggling order *la15-e16*, *only Sc*.

straif *see* STRIVE

straiggle *see* STRAGGLE

straight *see* STRAUCHT

straik &c *15-*, **strake** *16-e20*; **strak** *la14-e20*, **strek** *la16*, **streek &c** *18-19* [strek; *Abd also* str(j)ak] *n* **1** = stroke, a blow etc *la14-*. **2** coinage, imprint of coin *15-16*, *only Sc*. **3** (the sound of) the striking of a clock *e15*. **4** a whetting or paring motion *20-*, *now Sh Cai*. **5** a stroke, mark of a pen etc *20-*, *Sh Ags*. **6** the motion or marks of a harrow; the ground covered by one journey of a harrow *19-*, *now local Sh-Gall*. **7** a stroking, caressing movement of the hand; a sleeking, smoothing action *19-*, *local Sh-Kcb, only Sc*. **8** a stripe of colour, ray of light etc *18-*, *now local NE-Dmf, only Sc*. **9** a small amount *la18-*, *now Sh, only Sc*. **10** a rounded stick with one straight edge for levelling something, *usu* corn, in a measure; the container itself *15-*, *now local Sh-SW*. **11** *specif* a level measure (of malt); (the measure of the strength of) the liquor brewed or distilled from this *e19*, *only Sc*: '*ale o twice the straik of malt*'. **12** a measure of timber *e16*, *only Sc*. **13** a tool for sharpening scythes etc *18-*, *now NE Fif SW*. **14** a (*usu* long, narrow) tract of land or water; a sheep-walk *la16-*, *now Mry*. **15** a journey, long walk *19-*, *now Fif*.

vti **1** = stroke *16-*. **2** strike, beat, aim a blow **at** *16-19*. **3** *vt* harrow (a piece of ground) *20-*, *now N Ags Per, only Sc*. **4** smear, sprinkle, spread with something oily or greasy, streak *16-*, *now local Sh-SW*. **5** streak, mark with streaks of a different colour *la19-*, *now Ork Abd Ags Ayr*. **6** level off (grain etc) in a measure *la14-*, *now local Sh-SW*. **7** fill (a road etc) with snow up to its fences etc *la19-*, *now Cai, only Sc*. **8** sharpen (a scythe etc) with a STRAIK (*n* 13) *20-*, *now local NE-SW*. **9** *vti* stretch, extend *la15-*, *now Ork Ags*. **10** *vt* lay out (a corpse) *la16-*, *now Ork Ags*.

on the *or* **upon** ~ in motion, in a state of activity, on the move *19-*. ~ **hands** *etc* shake hands, in friendship or to confirm a bargain *16-19*. ~ **tails** exchange or barter (**with**) *19-*, *chf Cai, only Sc*. ~ **wi** *or* **against the hair** soothe, humour or annoy, ruffle someone's feelings *la16-19*. [see SND. OED *straik, strake, stroke*]

straik *see* STRIK

straiken &c *n* a kind of coarse linen, a little

finer than HARDEN *la16-e19*. [northern eModEng *straykyng*; perh ptp of STRAIK, w ref to the preparation of the flax by beating]

strain *see* STREEN

strait &c; strat *la14*, **stret &c** *la19-*, now *NE* [stret] *adj* **1** = strait, narrow; strict *la14-*. **2** *of bindings, clothing etc* tight, close-fitting *la16-*, now *local Sh-Rox*. **3** tense, taut, rigid; full to bursting *20-*, now *Sh NE Lnk*. **4** *of mountains etc, also fig, of a bargain* steep *16-*, now *local Sh-Per, chf Sc*. **5** *of a legal* INSTRUMENT: stringently worded, peremptory *16-e17*, *only Sc*.

n = strait *la14-*.

vt **1** = strait, bring into straits, restrict, stint *la16-17*. **2** tighten, tauten, put tension on *la18-*, now *Bnf Abd*.

~**en** *vt* **1** = straiten. **2** tighten (a knot etc) *la18-*, now *Sh NE Ags*. **3** press hard, put in difficulty; *vr* exert oneself to the utmost *18-*. ~**ing** straitening *la16*. ~**ly** **1** = straitly *la14-16*. **2** in close confinement *la14*. [OED *strait, straight*]

strak *see* STRAIK, STREKE, STRIK

strake *see* STRAIK

strakin *see* STRIK

stram *n* a big clumsy blundering man *la18-e20*, *Bnf Abd*. [only Sc; see SND]

stramash &c *19-*, **strabush &c** *19-*, *chf Fif* [stra'maʃ; stra'bʌʃ; strə-] *n* **1** an uproar, commotion, row *19-*. **2** a state of great excitement or rage *20-*, now *Sh Cai*. **3** a smash, crash, accident, disaster *la19-*, now *Sh Ork Ags*. **4** a state of ruin, wreckage, a smashed or shattered state *19-*, now *Sh Ags*.

vi create a disturbance, be rowdy *la19-*, *local Sh-SW*. [see SND]

stramlach &c ['stramləx] *n* **1** anything long and trailing, *eg* a rope or a torn piece of dress *19-e20*. **2** a tall, lanky, gangling person *20-*, *Bnf Abd*. [only Sc; see SND]

stramp *v* **1** *vi* bring the foot down heavily, stamp, tread, trample *15-*, now *local*. **2** *vt* tread on, trample upon, crush with the foot *16-*, now *local*. **3** *vi* go about with a firm or heavy step; stump about, march energetically or purposefully *la19-*, now *local*.

n a tread or stamp of the foot; a trampling on something *la16-*, now *Sh Ork Cai Rox*. **strample** = *v* 2, *17-e20*. [only Sc; conflation of Eng *stamp* w *tramp*]

strand¹ **&c** *n* a beach or shore of the sea; a sandbank etc exposed at low water *la18-*, now *Ork Cai*. [prob ON *strond* rather than OE *strand*]

strand², **straun &c** *19-* [stran(d), strɑn(d)] *n* **1** a little stream, rivulet *la15-*, now *Lnk SW*. **2** the sea *e16*. **3** an artificial water-channel, a (street-)gutter *la16-*, now *local N-Renfr, only Sc*. [see SND]

strang, strong *la16-* *adj, adv* = strong *la14-*. *n, only* **strang** = ~ *wesche, la18-*, now *Sh Ork N, only Sc*.

~ **hole** a seepage pit in a MIDDEN *la20-*, *Sh Abd,*

only Sc. ~ **pig** a large jar etc for holding STRANG *19-*, now *Ork Abd, only Sc*. ~ **wesche** urine which has been allowed to stand for some time, used as a bleach or in making manure *la15-e16*, *only Sc*.

strang *see* STRING

strange; strenge *16-17*, **strynge &c** *la19-* [strendʒ, strəindʒ] *adj* **1** = strange *la14-*. **2** aloof; *esp of children* shy, self-conscious *20-*.

vt marvel or wonder (**at**) *la18-*, now *Sh*.

stranger &c **1** = stranger *la14-*. **2** anything thought to foretell the arrival of an unexpected visitor, *eg* a tea-leaf etc floating on the surface of a cup of tea *la18-*. **stringie** ['strəindʒɪ] *adj* aloof, shy, stiff, affected *19-*, now *Ags Per*.

strap &c *la16-*, **strop &c** *n* **1** = strap, a strip of leather etc *la14-*. **2** a string or bunch of objects tied or linked together (with string etc); a cluster of berries, *esp* currants *19-*, now *S*. **3** *only* **strap** the band of corn-stalks used to tie up a sheaf at harvest *la18-*, *SW, only Sc*. **4** *only* **strap** ? a piece of timber fastening two things together *la16*. **5** *only* **strap**, *building* a strip of wood serving as a base to which something else may be nailed *19-*. **6** black treacle, molasses *20-*, *local NE-Per*.

v **1** *vt* string (beads etc) together, tie together in a bunch *20-*, now *local Stlg-Wgt, only Sc*. **2** *only* **strap** (1) bind and hang (a person); (2) *vi* be hanged *e19*, *only Sc*. **3** *vt, only* **strap**, *building* fix strips of wood on (a wall) as a base for lath, skirting etc *19-*, *only Sc*. **4** *only* **strap** groom (a horse), *chf* ~**per** a groom *19-*, *Gen except Sh Ork*. [see SND]

strat *see* STRAIT

strath [straθ] *n* a river valley, *esp* when broad and flat *16-*, *in place-names 9-*.

S~clyde [straθ'klɔid] **1** *hist* name for the ancient kingdom of the Britons in the area of south-west Scotland south of the kingdom of the *Scots* (SCOT) in Dalriada. **2** *also* ~ **Region** a REGION formed from the former counties of the City of Glasgow, Bute, Dunbarton, Lanark, Renfrew and Ayr and parts of the former counties of Argyll and Stirling *la20-*. ~**spey &c** [straθ'spe, -'spəi] **1** a kind of dance, slower than a REEL¹; a tune for such *la18-*. **2** *specif* one of the *Highland dances* (HIELAND), performed by four persons *20-*. ~**spey minuet** *appar* a slow strathspey, *la18*. ~ **spey reel** = ~*spey*, *18* [the Mry place-name]. [Sc and IrGael *srath*]

strauchle *see* STRACHLE

straucht &c, **straight &c** *18-*; **stracht** *la14-*, **strecht** *16-e20*, **streight** *la16-e18* [strɑxt, strext; *Bwk S* strəi(x)t] *adj* (*n*) = straight *14-*.

adv **1** = straight *la14-*. **2** immediately, without delay *la14-*.

vti **1** stretch *la14-e20*. **2** *vt, lit and fig* make straight, straighten; smooth, set to rights *18-*, now *Sh N, EC*. **3** lay out (a corpse) by straightening the limbs *18-*, now *NE*.

~en straighten the limbs of, lay out (a corpse) *19-, now local NE-SW, only Sc.* **~in brod &c** = *streekin buird* (STREEK[1]) *19-, now NE Kcb.*

~-forrit *adj, adv* straightforward, straight ahead *19-.* **~-oot(-the-gate)** frank, candid *la19-, now Ork.* **~way** *la16-19,* **~wise** *la16* = straightway.

straucht *see* STREEK[1]

straun *see* STRAND[2]

stravaig; stravague &c [stra'veg; *-'vɑg] *v* **1** *vi* roam, wander about in an aimless casual way *la18-.* **2** *vt* traverse, go up and down (a place) *la19-, now Sh NE Per, only Sc.*

n a roaming about, an aimless casual ramble, a stroll *19-, only Sc.* [aphetic f EXTRAVAGE; *cf* VAIG]

strave *see* STRIVE

straw &c *vt* = strew, scatter, sprinkle *15-, now local Sh-Loth.* [ME *strawen,* dial var of *strewen,* OE *streawian, stre(o)wian; cf* STROW[1]]

straw, stray *see* STRAE

streaker; strekour &c *la14-e16* [*'strikər] *n* **1** a kind of hunting dog *la14, e19.* **2** term of abuse for a person *e16.* [AF **stracour; cf* OF *estrac* track]

stream *la16-;* **streme &c** *la14-16 n, vti* = stream *la14-.*

~er *n* **1** = streamer. **2** *mining* a person who washes deposits to obtain ore *e17.* **3** *in pl* the Aurora Borealis *la18-, now Per Kcb.* **4** the male minnow near spawning time *19-, now Lnk Ayr, only Sc.*

vt deck with streamers *e19.*

(up)on the ~ *of a ship* lying off the shore of a river *la14-16.*

strecht *see* STRAUCHT

streck *see* STRIK

streek[1] *la17-;* **streik** *la15-e20,* **streke &c** *la14-19,* **strek &c** *la14-e19,* **strick &c** *16-19* [strik] *v, pt also* **straucht &c** *la14-e18* **1** *vt* stretch (oneself or one's limbs); stretch or spread out (a thing) *la14-, now Sh NE, S.* **2** lay out (a corpse) *la18-, now local Sh-Wgt.* **3** stretch (a person) on a rack etc *la14, only Sc.* **4** *of a heavenly body* emit (light) *la14, only Sc.* **5** hold out, launch (a weapon etc) *la14-16, only Sc.* **6** *vti* put (a plough etc) into action; start work, get going *la15-, now Bnf Abd.* **7** *vt* question closely, cross-examine *e20, Bwk Rox, only Sc.* **8** *vi* extend, reach out (in a certain direction), be stretched out (in a line etc) *la14-e20.* **9** extend oneself full length, stretch out *18-19.* **10** hurry, hasten; go at full speed *16-, now local Sh-Kcb, only Sc.*

n **1** a stretch, drawing out; the full extent, maximum length to which a thing can be stretched *19-, now local Ags-Slk, only Sc.* **2** a continuous extent of time or space, a spell *la19-e20, only Sc.* **3** *mining* the horizontal course or direction of a seam of coal, a coal level *la17-19.*

~er a very tall thin person *la19-, now NE, only Sc.* **~in &c** tall and agile *19-, Rox, only Sc.*

~in buird &c the board on which a corpse is laid out for burial *la19-, now NE, only Sc.* **~ing (time)** ploughing time *la15-17, only Sc.*

~ one's hoch(s), shanks *etc* stretch one's legs, take a walk; hurry *la18-, now Ayr.* [see SND; *cf* STREETCH]

streek[2] &c *n* = strick, a bundle of broken flax for scutching *18-19.*

streek[3] *n* ~ **o day** *etc* daybreak, the first light of day *20-, local Sh-Per.* [altered f SKREEK, prob w infl f STRAIK (*n* 8)]

streek *see* STRAIK

streel *see* STRULE

streen &c *19-, now Bwk Dmf,* **strain** *17-;* **stre(i)nʒe &c** *la14-16,* **stre(i)nze &c** *17-18* [strin; *Bwk S also* strind; ***'strɛnʒɪ, ***'strɪnʒɪ, ***'strɪnʒɪ, *&c*] *vti* **1** = strain, squeeze etc *la14-.* **2** *vt* extort (money, confessions etc) *la17.*

n **1** = strain *16-.* **2** constraint, bondage *e16, only Sc.*

street &c *n* = street *la15-.*

on the ~(s) 1 in the street, out-of-doors *la18-.* **2** roaming the streets; homeless, down-and-out *la19-.*

streetch &c, stretch *vti* **1** = stretch *la16-.* **2** *vi* stretch the legs, walk, take exercise by walking or dancing; strut about haughtily *la18-, now Kcb.* **3** *vt* lay out (a corpse) *19.*

n **1** = stretch, extent, spell *la18-.* **2** a straining or relaxation of the strict import of a law, statement etc; a forced argument or claim; an unwarranted exercise of power *la17-e18, chf Sc.*

~er a clothes-prop *la19-, only Sc.* **~ing board &c** = *streekin buird* (STREEK[1]) *19.* [see SND; *cf* STREEK[1]]

streeve *see* STRIVE

streiche [*'stritʃ] *adj* stiff, affected *e16.* [only Sc; ? representing OE *stræc* rigid]

streight *see* STRAUCHT

streik *see* STREEK[1]

streinth *see* STRENTH

streinʒe, streinze *see* STREEN

strek *see* STRAIK, STREEK[1]

streke &c [**strɛk] *adj* straight *la14.*

adv, also **strak** *la14* in a straight course *la14-e16.* [root **strak-* of Eng *stretch; cf* OE *stræc, strec* rigorous, severe. OED *streck*]

streke *see* STREEK[1]

strekour *see* STREAKER

streme *see* STREAM

strenge *see* STRANGE

strength *see* STRENTH

strenkell *see* STRINKLE

strenth, strength *16-;* **strynth &c** *la14-16,* **streinth** *15* [strɛnθ; ***strɪnθ, ***strɪnθ] *n, vt* = strength *la14-.*

~ily *la15-16,* **~ly** *la14-16, only Sc* strongly. **~y 1** *of persons* strong, powerful *la14-16.* **2** *of a position etc* strong against assault *16, only Sc.* **3** *of action etc* difficult to contend with *16, only Sc.* **4** *of a person's body etc* physically strong *la15-e19.*

strenth silver *appar* money received by a tenant of a *steelbow* (STEEL[1]) farm from his landlord on entering *e17, only Sc.*

strenȝe &c *law* [*'strɪŋjɪ, *'strɪŋjɪ] *vt* = strain, distrain *la15-e17.*

~**able &c** subject to distraint, liable to be distrained *16-e17, only Sc.* [OED *strain* (v^2)]

strenȝe, strenze *see* STREEN

stress &c *n* **1** = stress *15-.* **2** bodily suffering or injury *e16, only Sc.* **3** the overpowering pressure of some adverse force *e16.*

vt **1** = stress *16-.* **2** overwork, fatigue *18-, now local Per-Rox.*

stret *see* STRAIT

stretch *see* STREETCH

strib *see* STRIP[3]

stribbly *adj, of hair* straggly, loose and trailing *20, NE.* [conflation of Eng *straggly* w *dribbly* or perh *stibbly* (STIBBLE)]

strick[1] *la15-*, **strict** *17-* *adj* = strict.

strick[2] &c *18-20*; **strict** *17-e19 adj, of running water* rapid, swift-flowing *17-e20.*

n the most rapid part (of a river), the centre of the current *18-20.* [only Sc; see SND]

strick *see* STREEK[1]

stricken *see* STRIK

strict *see* STRICK[1], STRICK[2]

striddle; stridle *16-e20* ['strɪdl] *vti* **1** straddle *la16-, now local Fif-S.* **2** *vi* walk with long straddling steps, stride, step out *la18-e20, only Sc.*

n a standing or sitting with legs apart; the spreading apart of the legs in walking, dancing etc; a wide stride or pace *18-e20, only Sc.*

striddler a farmhand who stands on a cornstack and passes sheaves from the cart to the stack-builder *e20, Bwk Rox, only Sc.*

~ **legs &c** straddle-wise, with the legs set apart *e20, S.* [eModEng]

stride *vi, pt also* **strade &c** *la15-, now local* = stride *la15-.*

n **1** = stride *17-.* **2** *in pl* trousers *la19-20.*

~**leg(s) &c** astride *la18-.*

stridle *see* STRIDDLE

stridlins &c ['strɪdlɪnz, 'strəɪd-] *adv* astride, with the legs apart *16-, now local Sh-Kcb.* [laME *stridlyngis*]

striffin &c ['strɪfən; *Cai* 'strɛfən] *n* a thin skin, membrane or film; a long thin strip *18-, now Sh Ork Cai.* [eModEng *striffen*; perh OIr *srebann* a film, membrane, Gael *s(t)reabhann* a membrane, amnion]

strik &c, strike; stirk *la14*, **streck** *17-19 v, pt also* **strak &c** *now NE*, **straik &c** *la15-e20*, **strook &c** *19-e20.* *ptp also* **stricken &c**, **strucken &c** *la15-*, **strakin &c** *16* **1** *vti* = strike *la14-.* **2** *vi, of a boundary, path etc* take a specified direction, *esp* with reference to compass points *la15-16.* **3** *vt* mark (a surface) with a line or lines *e16.* **4** fight (a battle) *la14-e19, chf Sc.* **5** *of a snake etc* wound with its fangs *la14.* **6** *vi, of a bird of prey* dart **at** and seize *e16.*

7 *vt* inflict suffering, sickness or death on *la14-16.* **8** *vt, curling* (CURL) hit away (an opponent's stone) with one's own *la18-e20.* **9** beat (flax) before heckling; tie (it) in bundles; beat (threshed barley) to remove the awns *la18-19.* **10** *ptp also* **striked** level (a measure) *la18-, now SW.* **11** *vi, of fish* become enmeshed in a net *la19-, now Sh E Kcb.* **12** *vt, of maggots* infest (a sheep's wool) *la20-, SW.*

n **1** a stroke, blow; a striking; a quarrel, dispute *la16-19.* **2** the infestation of sheep by maggots *la20-, Gen except Sh Ork.*

strucken &c hour a whole hour by the clock (with implication of tediousness) *19-.* **striker &c 1** = striker *la16-.* **2** a person who coins money *15-17, only Sc.*

~ **by** consign to oblivion *la15, only Sc.* ~ **off** cut off with a stroke of a sword, axe etc *la14-.* ~ **out 1** *vi and in passive, of the head or face* break out in sores or a rash *18.* **2** *vt* make (a door or window) by knocking a hole through a wall *la18-, now Abd, only Sc.* ~ **up** break or burst open *la14-16, only Sc.*

strike *see* STRIK

strin *see* STRIND[2]

strind[1] &c [strəɪn(d)] *n* descent, lineage; the inherited qualities which come from this *15-, now Sh.* [ME *strende, strunde*, OE *strynd* generation, stock]

strind[2] &c; strin &c *18-e20* [strɪn; *Mry also* strɪn; *strɪnd] *n* **1** a very small stream; a trickle of water; the run from spilt liquid *15-e20.* **2** the jet of milk from a cow's teat *la19-, Bnf Abd, only Sc.*

vti spray, trickle *la19-e20, NE.* [eME *strunde*]

string *n* **1** = string *la15-.* **2** a section or proportional length of a fishing-line *la19-, now E.* **3** a road crossing a watershed or hill ridge *la20-, Ayr, freq in place-names la17-, WC, only Sc.* *vt, pt also* **strang** *la18-, now Sh NE* **1** draw **up** in a line or row *la17.* **2** = string. **3** *of seedlings, esp turnips* sprout in a line along the drills *20, Bnf Abd, only Sc.*

~**ing** ornamental lace or tape *16-, now Ags Dnbt, only Sc.* ~**le** a thread, string or row of objects tied together, a long trailing piece or strip *la19-, now Abd Ags, only Sc.*

~ **girse** couch-grass *la20-, local Bnf-Stlg, only Sc.*

stringie *see* STRANGE

strinkle &c; strenkell &c *16 vt* **1** besprinkle (**with**) *la15-18.* **2** scatter, strew, sprinkle (something) **in, over, on** *16-, now Sh N Rox.*

n, also **strinkling &c** *18-, now Abd* a sprinkling; a small amount, *esp* of something liquid or granular *18-, now Abd Stlg Wgt.* [ME *strenkil*; eME *strenncle* a sprinkler, prob altered f Eng *sprinkle*]

strintle *vti* sprinkle, scatter, strew; squirt, spurt; trickle, straggle *20-, now Cai.*

n a small stream or trickle of liquid; a spurt, squirt *20-, Cai.* [only Sc; altered f *prec*]

strip[1] *n* **1** a stripe, a long thin line of colour, light etc; the 'stripe' of a non-commissioned officer *la18-, now Abd.* **2** a long narrow belt of trees *19-, NE-S.* **3** *chf* ~ **of a laddie** *etc* a young fellow, a youth *19-, now Ork Lnk.* **4** a single journey or turn of harrows over a ploughed field *la20-, N Loth Kcb.*
vt **1** *chf in ptp* ~**pit** marked or ornamented with stripes etc, variegated, ribbed *18-.* **2** pull up (a turnip crop) in strips, pull up every alternate drill or set of drills *19.*
~**pit ba** a round peppermint *boiling* (BILE[1]) *usu* with black and white stripes *20-.* [only *Sc*; see SND]
strip[2] *n* **1** = strip, a narrow piece etc. **2** ? some piece of armour *e16, only Sc.*
strip[3] *vt* **1** *also* **strib** *now local* squeeze the last drops of milk from (a cow) with the fingers, *now esp* after a mechanical milker *19-.* **2** draw an edged tool across a rough surface in order to trim or sharpen it *la20-, Bnf-Ags Kcb.*
~**pin**(**g**)**s** the last milk drawn off at a milking; *fig* the profitable residue, pickings, gleanings *la19-.* ~**pin**(**g**) **block** a block or frame with a flat file, over which a saw is drawn to reduce the teeth to a uniform height before sharpening *la20-, Bnf-Ags Kcb.* [*cf* Flem *strippen* squeeze out between the fingers, LowGer *strippen*, Dan, Sw *strippe, strippa* milk out]
strip[4] **&c** *n* = stirrup *la18-e20.* [only *Sc*; reduced form]
stripe[1] *n* **1** = stripe. **2** a narrow tract or strip of country *18-e19.* **3** a long narrow belt of trees *la18-e19, only Sc.*
vti **1** = stripe *17-.* **2** *vi* ? form a stripe *e17.*
stripey *n* a red-and-yellow striped worm used as angling bait, a bramble-worm *20-, now Dnbt Kcb, only Sc.*
stripe[2] **&c** *n* **1** a small stream, a rivulet *15-, now Sh Ork NE.* **2** a street gutter *la19-e20.* [only *Sc*; see SND]
stripe[3] *n* **1** = stripe, a blow. **2** *of a person* a scourge *la16, only Sc.*
stripe[4] *vt* thrust, pull, or draw (an object) **off, over, through** (another, between the fingers etc), *eg* in order to wipe or sharpen it *la18-, now Sh.* [var of STRIP[3]]
stristle *see* STRUISSLE
strive &c *vi, pt also* **straif &c** *la14-16,* **strave &c** *la16-, now Sh Rox,* **streeve** *19-, now NE* **1** = strive *la14-.* **2** *also* ~ **wi** quarrel, dispute (with); take a dislike (to) or distaste (for) *18-, now Sh NE.* **3** scatter coins or sweets at a wedding for children to scramble for *20-, Dmf Rox, only Sc.*
n a scattering of coins etc, *esp* at a wedding, for children to scramble for *20-, now Inv S, only Sc.*
striven ['strɪvən] *adj* having quarrelled, at loggerheads, out of friendship *19-, NE, only Sc.*
striviling *see* STERLIN
stro *see* STRAE

strod &c; strodge [strod; *S also* strodʒ] *vi* stride or strut along *19-e20, Rox Slk.* [only *Sc*; see SND]
strone &c *vti* **1** *freq of dogs* urinate *18-, now Ags Edb Rox.* **2** *of water etc* spout, spurt, gush *18-20.*
n **1** the discharge of urine *19-, now Edb Rox.* **2** a gush or spurt of liquid; the stream of milk from a cow's teat *la19-, now Stlg Bute Kcb.* [only *Sc*; obscure]
strong *see* STRANG
strontian &c [*St* 'strɒntɪən, 'strɒnʃɪən] *n* a carbonate containing the element strontium *la18-19.* [f Strontian [str(o)n'tiən], Arg, where it was first found, in the waste from lead mines]
strook *see* STRIK
stroop *see* STROUP
stroosh *see* STRUSH
strop *see* STRAP
strother &c [*'strʌðər, *'strʌd-] *n* a marsh *la15-16.* [nME; appar OE *strōd*]
strounge &c; strunge &c *la18-e20* [strun(d)ʒ, strʌnʒ] *adj* **1** harsh to the taste, rank, astringent, bitter *la19-e20.* **2** *of persons* gruff, surly, sullen, morose *la18-, now N.* [only *Sc*; prob a var of Eng *strange*]
strouble &c [*'strubl, *strʌbl, *'strobl] *vt* **1** disturb, trouble *la14-e16.* **2** make turbid or cloudy *la14-15, only Sc.*
adj full of troubles *la15, only Sc.*
stroublance disturbance, molestation *15-16, only Sc.* [aphetic f DISTROUBLE]
strouse-man *n* ? a keeper or stalker *la17, only Sc.*
stroup &c; stroop [strup] *n* **1** the spout or mouth of a kettle, jug, pump etc *16-, now Sh-C.* **2** the throat, gullet *la17.* **3** the faucet, spout or outlet of a spring or well, a water-tap *la19-, now N Per, chf Sc.* **4** ? a hood *la16, only Sc.*
~**ach** [-əx], ~**an** *Gaelicized* a drink of tea *20-, Cai-Inv, only Sc.* ~**ie** *usu joc* a teapot *la19-, now Sh, only Sc.* [nME *stroupe* the throat, gullet, ON *strúpi* the sputing of blood from a cut throat, Norw dial *strupe* a throat, narrow opening]
strouth *n* force, violence, might *19-20.* [obscure]
strow[1] [strʌu] *vt* = strew *la14-e20.*
n a contention, struggle, quarrel; a commotion, bustle, to-do *la18-20.* [*cf* STRAW]
strow[2] **&c** [strʌu] *n* the shrew *la18-, Kcb.* [only *Sc*; possibly altered f SCREW[1]]
strowd &c [strʌud] *n* **1** a popular, *usu* anonymous, light or nonsensical song, a street ballad; *disparaging* any piece of verse *19-, now Abd.* **2** a piece of nonsense; rubbishy talk or writing *la19-, Abd.* [only *Sc*; obscure]
struan ['struən] *n* a cake made from the various cereals grown on a farm, *usu* oats, barley, and rye, and baked with a special ritual on Michaelmas Eve (29 Sep) *20, Hebrides.* [only *Sc*; Gael *strùthan*]

strucken *see* STRIK

structure *n* = structure.

vt build or form into a structure *la17-*.

struie [*'struɪ] *vi* sweep threshed straw to the side with one movement of the flail *e20, Cai*. [only Sc; *cf* Norw dial *strøya* sweep aside, Dan *strø* strew]

struissle; strussel &c, stristle &c ['strøsl, 'strøʃl, 'strɪsl; *NE* struʃl] *n* a struggle; contention; toil; a hard or exacting task *19-*, *now local Bnf-SW*.

vi, lit and fig struggle, wrestle with something bulky and unmanageable *19-e20*. [only Sc; uncertain]

strule &c; streel *19-e20, chf Fif* [*NE Fif* stril; *strøl] *n* a stream or steady trickle of liquid *la19-e20*. [only Sc; MDu *struylen*, Du dial *struilen*, *streylen* urinate]

strum¹ &c *n* a fit of pique or bad humour, a perverse mood, the huff, *freq* **tak the ~(s)** *la18-*, *now Mry Abd Per*.

vi sulk, go into a huff, look surly *19-*, *Abd Ags Fif*. [only Sc; see SND]

strum² *n, mining* the fuse of a shot or explosive charge, a narrow tube of paper etc filled with gunpowder and placed in a blasting borehole *la19-*, *now local Fif-Kcb*. [only Sc; obscure]

strummel¹ &c *n* the half-smoked tobacco left at the bottom of a pipe, a DOTTLE *19-e20*. [only Sc; see SND]

strummel² &c *adj* disparaging term for a horse or STIRK *e16*.

n term of contempt for a person *e16*. [only Sc; obscure]

strunge *see* STROUNGE

strunt¹ *n* **1** a huff, the sulks, *freq* **tak the ~(s)** *18-*, *now C, S*. **2** strife, enmity, hostility *la18-19, only Sc*.

v **1** *vt* offend, pique, affront *19-e20, only Sc*. **2** *vi* sulk, go about in a huff *la19-*, *now local Inv-Rox, only Sc*.

~it offended, in a huff *19-e20*. [see SND]

strunt² *vi* = strut, walk about in a stately or affected way *la18-*, *now local Ork-Gall, only Sc*.

strunt³ *n* spirits, *esp* WHISKY, toddy *la18-19*. [only Sc; obscure]

struntin &c *n* a kind of coarse narrow worsted tape or braid *17-e19*. [only Sc; uncertain]

strunty *adj* short, stumpy, stunted, shrunken, of poor growth *la18-*, *now Lnk*. [see SND]

strush; stroosh *20-* [strʌʃ, struʃ] *n* **1** a disturbance, tumult, squabble; a commotion, throng or press of an excited crowd; a romp *19-*, *now local EC-S*. **2** a bustling, swaggering gait *la20-*, *Cai*.

vi bustle, strut, swagger *20-*, *Cai*.

~ie = *n* 1, *la19-e20*. **~in &c** a disturbance, uproar, fuss *19-*, *Rox*. **~ie &c, ~lach &c** [-ləx] *adj* untidy, slovenly, disorderly *la19-*, *NE*.

n an untidy, slovenly person, a slut, slattern *20-*, *now NE*. [only Sc; see SND]

strussel *see* STRUISSLE

strute &c [*strut] *adj* crammed full and bulging, stretched to capacity *18-e19*.

strutly ? proudly *la14, only Sc*. [eModEng *strut*; ME *strout* (*v*) swell, OE *strūtian* stand out stiffly]

strynge *see* STRANGE

strynth *see* STRENTH

strypal ['strəɪpl] *n* anything long and slender; a tall, slender, rather handsome person *la19-20, Cai Bnf*. [only Sc; dim or frequentative of Eng *stripe* a strip of cloth etc]

stryth [*?strəɪθ] *n* the work-animals on a farm, plough-horses and -oxen *19-e20, Cai*. [only Sc; Gael *spréidh* cattle (see SPREATH)]

stuart *see* STEWART

stubble *see* STIBBLE

stuck, stucken *see* STICK¹

stuckie, stushie *n* the starling *20-*, *EC, WC*. [only Sc; prob imit of its song]

stuckin &c *n* a stake *19-*, *now nEC, S*. [only Sc; prob f STOCK¹, perh w infl f STUG²]

stud &c *la15-*; **stod** *la16* [*stɔd] *n* **1** = stud (of horses) *16-*. **2** a brood-mare *la15-16, only Sc*.

stodfald an enclosure for brood-mares *la16*.

studdie &c *15-*, **stithy &c** *la14-e15*, **stiddie &c** *16-19* ['stɪðɪ; 'stʌdɪ; *'stɛðɪ, *'stɛdɪ, *'stɪdɪ] *n* = stithy, an anvil *15-*, *now local*.

studdie *see* STEADY

stude *see* STAND¹

student *16-*; **studyand &c** *la15*, **studient** *e17* [*'stɔdənt, *-ɪand, *-ɪənt] **1** = student *la15-*. **2** an undergraduate; a pupil of a particular university teacher *16-*.

S~s' Representative Council, S.R.C. a statutory body elected by the matriculated students of each of the Scottish universities to discuss student affairs etc, and represented on the University Court *20-*.

studge *see* STODGE

studient, studyand *see* STUDENT

stue *see* STEW

stuff¹ &c *n* **1** = stuff *la14-*. **2** the quilted material worn under armour; defensive armour itself *la15-e16*. **3** provisions, a store of food *16-*, *now Ork Ags*. **4** corn, grain, a crop *la15-*, *now local Ork-SW*.

vti **1** = stuff *la14-*. **2** *vt* furnish (troops) with support; support, aid (a war) *la15-16*.

~ie *only Sc, n* **the ~ie** WHISKY *la19-*, *now NE Ags*. *adj* **1** in good health, sturdy, full of vigour *19-*, *now nEC-S*. **2** spirited, plucky, game *19-*, *local Ags-Wgt*.

stuff² *vi* become out of breath *la15, only Sc*. [ME *vt* = stifle, OF *estofer*]

stuffat &c *n* ? a groom, lackey; ? a vague term of abuse *e16*. [only Sc; ? F *estafette*, Ital *staffetta*, dim of *staffa* a stirrup]

stug¹ &c *18-*, **stog &c** *la16-e20*, **steug &c** *la18-19* [stʌg, stog; *stjʌg] *vt* **1** stab, prick, jab *la16-e20*. **2** dress (stone) roughly with a pointed chisel *20-*, *now EC Rox*.

n a prick, stab with some pointed object; such an object, a dart *la16-e20*. [only *Sc*; prob var of STOCK³; F *estoc* (*n*), *estoquer* (*v*) (stab with) a pointed weapon]

stug² &c; **stog** &c *19-e20* [stʌg; stog; *NE also* stjʌg, stjog] *n* **1** a jagged or uneven cut, anything left rough by careless cutting; *specif, in pl* unevenly-cut stubble *18-e20*. **2** a stump of a tree or bush *19-e20*. **3** a stocky coarsely-built person (or animal), one whose movements are stiff and awkward *la18-20*.
v **1** *vt* cut with a rough edge, *esp* in harvesting grain with a sickle; cut (the stubble) unevenly *la17-e19*. **2** *vi*, *of a clumsy, old or infirm person* walk in a heavy-footed way, plod, stump *19-e20*.
~-tailed &c *of a horse* with a docked tail *la16-18*. [only *Sc*; see SND]

stuiden *see* STAND¹

stuil &c *16-*, **stool** &c *la16-*; **stule** &c, **stole**, **steel** *18-*, *now NE* [støl, stɪl; *NE* stil] *n* **1** = stool *la14-*. **2** = ~ *of repentance* (REPENT) *la16-e19*. **3** a bench, counter, trestle *16-*, *now NE nEC Ayr*. **4** a matted bed *chf* of vegetation, *esp* thick dense grass roots *19-*, *now Sh Ork*. **5** *chf* **stole** *forestry* a tree-stump; a new shoot rising from a group of such stumps after cutting *la18-*, *now Kcb*. **6** = stall (as in finger-stall, head-stall) *18-*, *now local* [see SND].
vi, *chf* **stole**, *of a tree-stump* throw up new shoots *la18-e19*.
~ing the framework supporting a mill *la16-e17*, *only Sc*.
~ bent the heath-rush *la18-e20*, *only Sc*.

stuir &c, **sture** &c [stør] *n* a Dutch stiver; *latterly* a penny *la15-*, *now Sh*. [reduced f Du *stuiver*]

stuir *see* STURE¹

stuit *19-*, **stut** *la16-e19*; **stoot** &c *17-*, **steet** *19-*, *N* [støt; stut, stʌt; *N* stit] *vt* prop, support, shore up *17-*, *now Kcdn Ags*.
n a prop, support (*eg* for a beached boat) *la16*, *19-*, *now Kcdn Ags*. [only *Sc*; see SND]

stulage &c *n* ? ballast *e16*. [only *Sc*; unknown]

stule *see* STEAL, STUIL

stult *see* STILT, STOUT

stumble *see* STUMMLE

stummer *vi* stumble, stagger *la15-*, *now Ork*. [ON *stumra*; *cf* STAMMER]

stummle &c *la16*, *19-*, **stumble** *17-* *vi*, *n* = stumble.

stump *16-*; **stowmpe** *15*, *only Sc* [stʌmp] *n* **1** = stump *15-*. **2** ? the body of a coat *e16*, *only Sc*. **3** the core of an apple, what is left after the flesh has been eaten *20-*, *now local EC-Rox*, *only Sc*. **4** a short stocky person or animal; a stiff, slow-moving or sluggish person *la18-*, *now Sh Cai Inv*, *only Sc*. **5** a stupid person *19-*, *now Rox*, *only Sc*.
~art *only Sc*, *n*, *in pl*: (*usu* sturdy) legs *20-*, *NE*.
vi walk heavily, in a stumping clumsy way

la19-, *Bnf Abd*. **~er** walk with a clumsy, heavy or hobbling step, stump *la19-*, *Bnf Abd*, *only Sc*. **~ie** *only Sc* **1** the stump of a quill pen, *esp* a much-sharpened one *la18-19*. **2** a short, stocky or dumpy person; a plump sturdy young child *19-*, *now Cai Ags*. **~it** short, stunted; *of a person* stocky, dumpy *la18-*, *now local Sh-Dmf*. **~le** walk with a stiff hobbling gait, stump *e19*, *only Sc*.
~ and rump completely, absolutely, entirely *la19-*, *now local NE-WC*, *only Sc*; *cf rump and stump* (RUMP).

stunk¹ *vi* sulk, go into a huff *la19-*, *now Abd Kcdn*. **the ~les** &c the sulks *19-*, *Abd Kcdn*. [only *Sc*; prob back-formation f STUNKARD]

stunk² *n*, *now chf in pl* the stake in a game of marbles; the game itself *19-*, *now local Fif-Rox*. [*cf* Eng dial *stonks*; perh altered f Eng *stock(s)* a fund, store]

stunk *see* STANK

stunkard &c *adj* sulky, surly, perversely or sullenly obstinate *la17-*, *now Lnk Wgt Dmf*. [only *Sc*; see SND]

stunt *vi* bound, bounce, walk with a springy step *19-*, *now WC, SW Rox*. [only *Sc*; prob onomat; *cf* STOT²]

stupe &c [støp, stjup] *n* a fool, stupid person *19-*, *now local Inv-wLoth*. [back-formation f Eng *stupid*]

stupefact [*'støpəfak(t)] *ptp* stupefied *16*. [chf *Sc*; L *stupefact-*, ptp stem of *stupefacere* stupefy]

stupit &c *19-*, *now Sh*, **stippit** &c *la19-*, *now C, S*; **steepid** &c *e20*, *Abd* ['st(j)upɪt, *C, S* 'stɪpɪt, -ɪd; *'støpɪt; *NE* *'stɪpɪd] *adj* = stupid.

stupration *n* violation (of a woman) *e16*. [OF, or L *stuprātio*]

sturdy &c *adj* **1** = sturdy *la14-*. **2** giddy-headed *18-*, *now Sh Cai*.
n **1** a brain disease in sheep, causing giddiness, staggering and ultimately collapse *18-e20*. **2** a sheep affected with STURDY (*n* 1) *19-*, *now Kcb*, *only Sc*. **3** a fit of sulks, a perverse mood, *freq* **tak the ~** or **sturdies** *la18-*, *now local Ags-SW*, *only Sc*.
sturdied 1 *of a sheep* affected with STURDY (*n* 1) *la18-20*. **2** *of a person* giddy-headed *18-*, *now Sh Cai*.

sture¹, **stour** *la15-*; **stoor** *18-e20*, **stuir** *la16-19* [stur; stør, ster; *NE* *stir] *adj* **1** = stour, violent, severe *la14-16*. **2** big, stout, burly, substantial *la14-*, *now Sh*. **3** strong, sturdy, valiant *la14-*, *now Sh*. **4** rough in manner or appearance; grim, gruff, stern; hard, determined, unyielding *16-*, *now Slk*. **5** *of a sound, esp the voice* deep and hoarse, harsh, rough *la18-*, *now Lnk Rox*.

sture² [*stør] *n* a sturgeon *la15-16*. [perh AF *estuir; popular L has *sturio*]

sture *see* STUIR

sturken &c *19-e20*, **storken** &c *15-e16* *v* **1** *vi* become strong; thrive *15-e16*. **2** *vti* restore to robustness; recover one's strength *19-e20*, *S*. [ON, Norw dial *storkna* congeal, coagulate]

sturt &c *n* strife, trouble, disquiet, annoyance; contentious or violent behaviour, *freq* ~ **and strife** *la14-e20*.

v **1** *vi* = sturt, contend, make trouble *la14*. **2** *vt* trouble, disturb, annoy *16-*, *now Sh, only Sc*.

~**ful** contentious *la15, only Sc*. ~**some** disturbing, troublesome, annoying *la16*. [ME; metath f Eng *strut*]

sturtin *n* ~ **stringin &c** a coarse worsted thread, with blue and red strands, like carpet-binding *19-20*. [only Sc; altered f STRUNTIN]

stushie *see* STASHIE, STUCKIE

stut &c *la18-*; **stoot** *la17-e19* [stʌt; støt, stɪt] *vi* stutter, stammer. [ME; some forms perh f cognate ME *stote*]

stut *see* STUIT

stuthe [*støð] *n* a stud or knob *e16*. [nME *stothe*, either f OE *studu* or ON *stoð* a stud]

styan &c; styal *e20, Cai* ['staɪən; *Cai* 'staɪəl] *n* a sty on the eyelid *18-*, *now Ork Mry Abd*. [also ModEng dial; OE *stīgend*]

stye *see* BUFF[3]

style &c *n* **1** = style *la15-*. **2** *law* the approved form or model for drawing up a legal document *la15-*. **3** one's condition as revealed to others *la15, only Sc*: 'Robene, I stand in sic a styll; I sicht, and þat full sair'.

vt **1** = style *la16-*. **2** name or address with honorific titles; honour with a title *16, only Sc*.

~ **book** *law* a book containing a collection of STYLES (*n* 2), *la16-e20*.

styme, stymel *see* STIME

stymie *see* STIME, STIMIE

styte *see* STOIT

suave &c [*swev] *adj* **1** = suave, pleasing; smooth-mannered *la16-*. **2** gracious, kindly *16, only Sc*.

sub *vt*, school slang kick *la20-*, *WC*. [obscure]

subaltern *adj* **1** = subaltern *la16-*. **2** *law, of a land-holder or the land* holding or held of a SUPE-RIOR who is himself a VASSAL, subinfeudated *17-*.

~**ly** *law* by subinfeudation *la17*.

subbasmont [*sʌb'basmənt] *n* a valance (of a bed) *e16*. [only Sc; OF *soub-, subbassement*]

subcharge [*'sʌbtʃardʒ, *sʌb'tʃardʒ] *n* a second dish or course *la15-e16, only Sc*.

subchet *n* ? = prec *e16*. [? erron]

subcommit &c *vt* refer (a matter) to a subcommittee *la17-e18, only Sc*.

subdane *see* SUDDENT

subdelegat *n* a deputy for a delegate *16*. [OED *subdelegate*]

subdit &c [*'sʌbdɪt] *adj* subject **to** *la15-e16*.
n a (monarch's) subject *la14-16*. [chf Sc; L *subditus* (in MedL as *n* = a subject), ptp of *subdere* bring under]

subduce *vt* **1** seduce, withdraw from allegiance *la16, only Sc*. **2** = subduce, subtract *la16*.

suberbillis [*'sʌbərblz] *n pl* = suburbs *e16*. [ME (once) *subarblis*. OED *suburbles*]

subfeu &c ['sʌb'fju] *law*, *n* a FEU granted by a VASSAL to a SUB-VASSAL *la17-*.
vt make a grant of (lands) in SUBFEU, subinfeudate *18-*.
~**dation** subinfeudation *la17*.

subject &c; subjeck &c *la16-* *n* **1** = subject *15-*. **2** (1) a piece of property; *in pl* one's estate or effects *18-19*. (2) *specif, law* a piece of HERITABLE property, *eg* a piece of land, a house *18-*.
~ **superior** = SUPERIOR (*n* 2), *freq* when he holds a *superiority* 2(2) (SUPERIOR) *18-e19*.

submission *n* **1** = submission. **2** *law* a contract, or the document embodying it, by which parties in a dispute agree to submit the matter to arbitration *la16-*.

submitter *n*, *law* a person who makes a SUBMIS-SION *17-e19*.

subordinate &c *adj* = subordinate: **1** *in gen*, *la17-*; **2** *of power, command etc*, *la15-*; **3** *of things in a series*, *la15-*.

sub-principal *n* the deputy of the PRINCIPAL of King's College, Aberdeen *la16-19*.

subreption *n* **1** = subreption. **2** *law* the act of obtaining gifts of ESCHEAT etc from the Crown by concealing certain facts *la17-e19*.

subscribent [*sʌb'skrəibənt] *n* a subscriber, a person who subscribes (to an object or scheme) *17-e18*. [only Sc; L presp stem of *subscrībere* underwrite, subscribe]

subscription *n* = subscription *la15-*.
sign *etc* **and** ~ **manual** signature, signed name *la15-e17, only Sc*.

subscrive &c [*sʌb'skraɪv] *v* **1** *vt* = subscribe, put one's name to (as a supporter) *la15-e19*. **2** *vi* = subscribe, become a subscriber (**to**) *la15-e19*. **3** *in passive* be engaged in a plot (**against**) *la16*.
subscriver &c = subscriber *la16-e18*. [ME (once); OF *soubscriv-*, pres stem of *soubscrire*]

subservient *adj* **1** = subservient *la17-*. **2** *law* subject to a SERVITUDE *la17*.

subset &c [*'sʌb'sɛt] *vt* sublet *la17-19*.
n a sub-lease *18-e19*. [only Sc]

subsidiarie [*sʌb'sɪdɪ'erɪi] *adv, law* in a secondary or subsidiary manner, as a second resort *la18-e19*. [only Sc; L]

subsist *vi* **1** = subsist *la17-*. **2** keep on, persevere *e17, only Sc*. **3** cease, stop at a certain point *17, only Sc*.

substantious &c *adj* **1** weighty, important; solid, firm; effective *la15-19*. **2** *of structures* substantial, solid *e16*. **3** wealthy, well-to-do *16-e17*. **4** *of provision* ample *16-e17*.
~**ly** with substantial means, support or effect *16-e17*. ~**ness** wealth *la16*. [chf Sc; OF *substantieux*, MedL *substantiōsus* full of substance]

substenance *n* = sustenance *e17, only Sc*.

substitute &c *n* **1** = substitute *la14-*. **2** a

beneficiary who will take a gift of property after the death of the first beneficiary *la17-*; *cf* INSTITUTE.

adj **1** = substitute *la17-*. **2** *in combs, usu following noun*: (1) nominated to act in place of another, as a deputy *la17-20*; *cf* SHERIFF; (2) nominated to replace a predeceasing person in an inheritance *la17-20*.

substitution 1 = substitution *la17-*. **2** a writ or deed appointing a substitute or deputy *18*, *only Sc*.

heir ~, ~ heir *law* an heir of entail *la17-e20*.

substract &c *v* **1** *vt* = subtract *la16-20*. **2** *vr* withdraw oneself, retire **from** *la16, only Sc*.

~ion = subtraction *17-20*. [L *substract-*, ptp stem of *substrahere*, var of *subtrahere*; *cf* SUBTRACK]

subsume [*'sʌb'søm] *vti* **1** = subsume *la16-*. **2** *vt* add, subjoin *e16*. **3** *law* state (in detail) *e18*.

subsumption = subsumption *la17-*. **subsumption (of the libel)** a detailed description of an alleged crime *17-19*.

subsynod [*'sʌb'sɪnod] *n* a division of a SYNOD *la16, only Sc*.

subtack [*'sʌb'tak] *n* a sub-lease or sub-let; a house or land so held *17-e20*.

~sman a person who holds a subordinate TACK² *17-e18*.

subtenant ['sʌb'tɛnənt] *n* an undertenant *la14-, chf Sc*.

subtrack *vt* = subtract *la19-, local*. [*cf* SUBSTRACT]

subumbrage [*sʌb'ʌmbredʒ] *vt* overshadow *la16, only Sc*. [*sub-* + Eng *umbrage* (*v*) shadow]

subvassal &c ['sʌb'vasl] *n* an under-VASSAL, a VASSAL of a VASSAL *la15-e19, chf Sc*.

subvassour [*'sʌb'vasur, *-'vɑvəsur] *e17*, **subvavassour** *e15 n* a SUBVASSAL. [only Sc; MedL *subvassor* for *subvavassour*]

succar &c *now Sh Ork EC, WC*, **sugar &c** *16-*; **sucker** *la16-*, **shuggar &c** *17-* ['sʌkər, 'sʌgər, 'ʃʌgər] *n* = sugar *la15*.

sugary &c *adj* = sugary. *n* a sugar factory *la17-e18*.

sucker &c alacreische liquorice *la16*.
sugarallie &c [ʃugər'alɪ; *WC* -'alɪ; *N, EC* also -'ɛlɪ] = prec, *esp* when made up as a sweet; a stick etc of liquorice *19-, Gen except Sh Ork*. **sugarallie hat** a tall black silk hat, *specif* as *orig* worn by policemen *la19-20, C*. **sugarallie water** a children's drink made by dissolving a piece of liquorice in water *la19-*. **sugar biscuit &c** a kind of thin crisp sponge biscuit, baked with sugar on top *la18-e19*. **sugar bool** *la19-*, **sugardoddle &c** *20-, local nEC Lnk* a round boiled sweet, *freq* striped. **sugar piece** a slice of bread buttered and sprinkled with sugar *la19-, now N Per Kcb*. **sugar &c work** a sugar factory *la17-e18*.

succeed &c, succed *la14-e16* [sʌk'sid] *vi* **1** = succeed *la14-*. **2** turn out (to one's advantage, disadvantage) *e16, only Sc*.

success ['sʌksɛs] *n* = success *la16-*.

succession &c *n* **1** = succession *la14-*. **2** lapse (of time) *la15*.

succine [*'sʌkɪn] *n* amber *la16*. [only Sc; L *succinum, sūcinum*. OED *succin*]

succudrus &c [*'sʌkwɪdrəs, *'sʌkədrəs] *adj* = surquidrous, presumptuous, arrogant *la14-e16*. [only Sc. OED *succudrous*]

succudry &c [*'sʌkwɪdrɪ, *'sʌkədrɪ] = surquidry, presumption, arrogance *la14-16*. [only Sc. OED *succudry*]

succumb *v* **1** *vt* bring low, overwhelm *e16*. **2** *vi, law* fail (in a suit), *usu* for lack of proof *16-e18, only Sc*. **3** = succumb *17-, orig chf Sc*.

such see SIC

suck see SOUK

sucken¹ &c ['sʌkən; *Ork* 'sukən] *n, only Sc* **1** an obligation on tenants on an estate to use a certain mill; the payment due in kind, service or money for the use of the mill *15-e19*. **2** the lands of an estate on which there was a SUCKEN¹ **1**; all the tenants of such land *18-19*. **3** the area of a bailiff's jurisdiction *la17*.

adj bound to a certain mill *18-19* [reduced f BUNSUCKEN].

~er a tenant of a SUCKEN¹ *la16-e19, only Sc*. [ME *soken*; OE *sōcn* a seeking; an attendance at a place, ON *sókn* an assembling of people]

sucken² &c *n* a small drag or grapnel, *esp* one used by fishermen in searching for lost lines *la19-, now Abd*. [*cf* Norw dial *sokn*, ON *sókn*]

sucken see SINK

sucker see SUCCAR

suckler &c *n* **1** *also attrib, of farm animals* a suckling; a cow giving suck *la15-, now C, S*. **2** term of endearment *e16, only Sc*. **3** *chf in pl* the flowerheads of clover *18-, now Stlg midLoth*. [deriv of Eng *suckle*]

sud see SALL

suddand see SUDDENT

suddart &c *16*; **souldart &c** *la16-e17* [*'sʌdərt, *-ərd, *sud-, &c] *n* = soldier. [only Sc; OF *so(u)ldart, -art,* f *soude, so(u)lde* pay]

suddent &c *la16-*; **suddand** *la14-16*, **sodand** *la14-15*, **soddane &c** *la14-16*, **subdane** *la16* ['sʌdən; *'sʌdənd, *-ənt, *'sud-] *adj* = sudden. [OED *sudden*]

suddenty &c *n* **1** = suddenness, *freq* **on** etc **a ~** all of a sudden *la15-, now N*. **2** *esp law* a sudden outburst of rage, an act done in hot blood, *freq* **of** *or* **on (a) ~** without premeditation *la15-19*. [chf Sc; ME *sudeynte*, OF *sodeinete*]

suddle &c *vt* soil, dirty *16-, now local*.
adj filthy *e16, only Sc*.

suddly &c soiled, dirty *la15-16, only Sc*. [*cf* MHighGer *sudelen*]

suddren wud see SOUTH¹

sudiorne see SOJOURN

sue see SHEW

Suethin see SWADEN

suffer see SOVER

sufficiand see SUFFICIENT

sufficience &c [*'sʌfɪʃəns] *n* = sufficience *16-*.
at ~ in sufficient quantity *la15-e16, only Sc.* **in**
~ in comfort *e16, only Sc.*
sufficient &c; sufficiand &c *la14-16 adj* **1** =
sufficient *la14-*. **2** satisfactory, good enough
la14, only Sc. **3** *of things* substantial, solid, of
adequate strength or quality *la14-20, only Sc.*
suffissand &c *adj* = suffisant, sufficient
la14-15. [OED *suffisant*]
sugar, sugarallie *see* SUCCAR
sugg &c *n* a fat, easy-going person *19-, now Ork*
NE. [prob Scand; *cf* Norw dial *sugg* a slovenly, lazy person, a big stout man]
suggeroun *la16-el7;* **suggeorne** *la16*
[*'sʌdʒər(ə)n] *n* a kind of oats. [only Sc; *cf*
north-eastern F dial *soco(u)ran &c* and OF
secourjon. OED *suggeron*]
sugh *see* SOUCH
sugurat &c *adj, of sound, words* sweet, honeyed
e16. [only Sc; MedL *suguratus* sugared]
suin *see* SUNE
suir *see* SHUIR
suirve *see* SWARVE
suit¹ &c, shoot &c *19-;* **soit &c** *la15-el7,*
shuit &c *19-* [søt, sɪt; ʃut; *ʃøt, *ʃɪt; *NE* *sit]
n = suit *la14-*.
vti **1** = suit *la16-*. **2** *vt, law* make an application or appeal for; sue for in a court of law
la16-e18, only Sc. **3** pursue, follow *la16, only Sc.*
4 pursue, aim at; seek to obtain *la16-17, only Sc.*
5 seek **in marriage**, woo *17, chf Sc.* **6** (1) be
agreeable or convenient to *la17-.* (2) please,
give pleasure to, *chf in ptp* pleased, satisfied *20-,*
Gen except Sh Ork. **7** *with personal subject* look
becoming in (a colour, dress etc) *20-: 'she suits*
blue'.
~**able** *16-*, **sitable** ['sɪtəbl] *20-, C* = suitable.
~ **roll** a list of tenants bound to attend at a
particular court *16-e18, only Sc.* ~ **stock** *etc,*
carpentry, masonry a bevel, adjustable square
la18-, now N.
call the ~**s** call the names or designations of
those bound to attend at a particular court
la15-e18, only Sc.
suit² &c, soot *18-;* **seet &c** *19-, chf Abd,* **sit**
20-, Abd, **shute &c** *la19-* [søt, ʃøt, sɪt, ʃɪt; *NE*
sit; *Cai* *ʃit] *n* = soot *la16-*.
~(**t**)**y** = sooty. ~**yman** a chimney-sweep
la18-e19, only Sc. **Auld Suitie** nickname for
the devil *la18-, local Bnf-Rox.*
~ **drap** a flake of soot, *esp* when hanging from
a ceiling *18-, now Sh N Fif.*
suit *see* SWEET²
suith &c *la15-*, **sooth** *17-;* **suthe** *la14-18* [søθ,
sɪθ; *NE* *sɪθ] *n, adj* = sooth *la14-*.
adv, chf **sieth &c** *chf NE, as interj* = sooth,
really *la18-19.*
~**fast** = soothfast, truthful, reliable: **1** *in gen,*
la14-e20; **2** *law, of an oath or evidence,* *16-, now*
arch, chf Sc.

(by) my ~ upon my word, to tell the truth
la18-, now Bnf Ags Kcb. [obs in Eng *17-e19,*
when it was revived by Scott and others]
suld *see* SALL
sulliart &c *la18;* **sulȝart** *16* [*'sʌljərt] *adj, of a*
horse bright, clear-coloured. [only Sc; appar
Gael *soilleir* bright]
sulȝe *see* SOILZIE
sum *see* SOME, SOUM¹
summa *n* a sum-total *la16-18.* [L; *cf* Eng = an
amount; a summary]
summar &c; sommair *la16 adj, chf law* summary, *esp* of proceedings in minor cases in
which written pleadings are dispensed with and
formalities reduced *16-e18.*
~**ly** *chf law* in a summary manner, without the
formalities of the common law *la16-18.*
~ **roll** a roll of cases which require speedy disposal, going before the *Inner House* (INNER) of
the *Court of Session* (SESSION) *19-e20.* [only Sc;
F *sommaire*]
summary *adj* **1** = summary. **2** *in combs, law*
applied to procedures which dispense with the
full formalities of the law *la18-.* [*cf* SUMMAR]
summeleir *see* SOMLER
summer *see* SIMMER¹, SIMMER²
summité &c [*'sʌmɪtɪ] *n* **1** = summity, the
topmost part *la14.* **2** the summit, top of a
mountain *la14-e15.* [OED *summity*]
summock &c *n* a cloth or pad placed under a
pack-saddle to prevent chafing of the horse's
back *16-e19.* [only Sc; Gael *sumag*]
summon, summond &c *15-18,* **summons**
&c *17-;* **somond &c** *15-16* ['sʌmən(z), *-ənd;
Ork 'sumən(z)] *vt* **1** = summon *15-.* **2** *of a*
monarch call (barons) to an assembly *la14.* **3**
only **summons** take out a SUMMONS against, *esp*
in actions of removal from a tenancy *la19-.*
n, chf **summons**; *also* **summonds &c** *15-17,*
soomans &c *19-e20* **1** = summons *15-.* **2** *law*
an official document, *corresponding to the Eng*
writ, from the *Court of Session* (SESSION) or (*formerly* in small-debt actions, *now* in SUMMARY
causes) from a SHERIFF, informing a person that
civil proceedings are being taken against him,
detailing the circumstances of the action and
the redress sought, and granting warrant to cite
him to appear in court *17-.* **3** (1) an order
similar to *n* 2 served on an accused person in
criminal cases *18-19.* (2) *informal* a citation to
appear in a criminal court *20-.*
summyn(g) *see* SOME
sump *n* **1** = sump *la18-.* **2** a sudden heavy fall
of rain, a deluge *e19, Gall S.*
sumph &c [sʌmf] *n* **1** a slow-witted person, *usu*
a man, an oaf, simpleton *18-, now N-S.* **2** a
surly, sullen, sulky person *19-, now NE-S.*
vt act like a SUMPH; loaf or lie about in a dull,
stupid way; sulk, be sullen *la17-, now NE, C.*
~**ish** *18-, now NE, C,* ~**y** *la19-, now NE* stupid,
doltish. [obscure]
sumphion *see* SYMPHION

sun &c *15-*; **sone** &c *la14-17, chf Sc,* **soun** &c *la14-e16, only Sc,* **sin** &c *la16-20, only Sc* [sʌn; *sun; *sɪn] *n* = sun *la14-.*
vt **1** = sun. **2** spear (a salmon) while dazzling it with reflected sunlight in the water *e19.*
~**ny half** *etc* = sun half, *la16-e18, only Sc.*
~ **blink** a gleam of sunshine *17-, only Sc.* ~ **broch** a halo round the sun *la19-, now E.*
~**down** &c sunset *19-.* ~ **gates** &c = *sunways, 16-, now Sh, only Sc.* ~ **half,** *la16-e17, only Sc,* ~ **side** *18-, now local N-Lnk* the side or aspect of a place facing the sun, the south side.
~**ways** following the sun, *ie* from east to west *la17-e20, only Sc.*
between *etc* **the** ~ **and the sky** between dawn and sunrise *19.*
Sunday &c; **Sounday** &c *la14-16, only Sc,* **Sonda** &c *15, only Sc* ['sʌnde; *'sun-] *n* = Sunday *la14-.*
NB: *in combs freq* ~'**s,** *now almost obs.* ~ **blacks** the black suit formerly universally worn by men for attending church on Sunday *20-.* ~('**s)** **claes** one's church-going clothes, one's best clothes *la18-.* ~('**s) face** a solemn, somewhat sanctimonious look *la18-.* ~ **Monday** name of a ball game *20-, NE Ags.* ~ **name** one's formal baptismal name, as opposed to a familiar form of it *la19-, C.* ~ **salt** salt made at the weekend, large-grained from having been left longer to crystallize *la18-e20.* ~('**s) sark** one's best shirt; a clean shirt *la18-.* ~ **strae** an extra amount of straw threshed to tide the animals over the weekend and so avoid threshing on Sunday *19-, Sh-N.*
sunder, sundry *see* SINDER
sune &c *15-,* **soon** *17-;* **suin** &c *la16-e20,* **sone** &c *la14-16,* **soun** &c *la14-16, only Sc,* **seen** &c *18-, NE,* **sin** *la19-e20,* **shune** &c *la16-e20,* **shin** *20-, EC, WC,* **sheen** *la19-, Cai* [søn, sɪn; *NE* sin; *Cai* ʃin; *Sh Ork EC, WC also* ʃøn, ʃɪn] *adv* **1** = soon *la14-.* **2** early, before it is late *la18-, now Sh Dmf.*
adj, freq in superlative quickest, most direct *19-, now local Sh-Per.*
late and ~ early and late, at all times *la18-19.*
~ **as syne** sooner rather than later, soon for preference *19-, now midLoth Lnk.* ~ **or syne** sooner or later *la16-, now Sh.*
sung *see* SING[2]
sunk *18-;* **sonk** *16-e19* [sʌŋk; *soŋk] *n* **1** a turf seat, a kind of sofa made of layers of sods, *freq* at a fireside or against a sunny gable *16-e20.* **2** a bank or wall, *esp* of earth or turf *19, Bnf Abd.* **3** (1) a straw pad or cushion, *esp* used as a substitute for a saddle, *freq* in a pair slung on either side of the horse *16-19.* (2) a hefty corpulent person, with a sack-like figure *19-, now Kcdn Ags.*
~**ie** a little bench or stool, *eg* a milking-stool *19-e20, S.* [also northern ModEng dial = 3(1); obscure]

sunket &c *n* **1** *also in pl* something *18-19.* **2** *chf in pl* eatables, provisions, *esp* titbits or delicacies *18-e20.*
adv somewhat, rather *la17-18.* [prob f OSc *sumquhat* somewhat]
sunȝie *see* SONYIE
sup *vti* **1** = sup *16-.* **2** *vt* take (liquid or soft food) into the mouth, *esp* with a spoon *16-.*
n **1** *freq with omission of* OF *etc* a mouthful, an amount sufficient to satisfy one for the time being; a drink (of liquor) *la17-:* 'a sup tea'. **2** a quantity, amount (of other liquids, *esp* rain) *la19-, now local NE-Ayr.*
~**pable** fit to be *supped,* palatable *19-, now NE, EC, SW, S.* ~**pie** = *n* 1, *la19-20.* ~**pins** soft, semi-liquid food *la18.* ~**pin sowans** sowans thick enough to eat with a spoon *la20-, Ork NE.* [*cf* SOUP[1] and SOWP[1]]
supe *see* SOUP[3]
superannuate &c [sʌpər'an(u)wət, -əwət] *adj* mentally deranged, senile; stupefied, dazed *18-, now Fif.* [*cf* Eng (now rare) = superannuated]
superb *adj* **1** *of buildings etc* of noble proportions etc *16-.* **2** = superb.
supercloth *n* a cloth placed over a corpse *e17.*
superexcrescence [*sʌpər-] *n* increase in excess *la15-e16, only Sc.*
superexpend, superspend [*sʌpər-] *vt* **1** *chf in ptp* ~**it** &c, *of persons or funds* overspent, in arrears *la15-e18.* **2** *only* **superexpend** spend (time) wastefully *e16.* [only Sc]
superexpense [*sʌpər-] *n, in pl* expenditure above receipts or income; out-of-pocket expenses *la15-e17.* [only Sc]
superexpone *vt* = SUPEREXPEND *la15, only Sc.*
superflue; superflew [*sʌpər'fl(j)u] *only Sc, adj* **1** superfluous *16.* **2** excessive, immoderate *la16.*
adv in excess, excessively *16.*
superinduce [*sʌpərɪn'døs] *vt, chf in deriv* **superinduction,** *law* the substitution or insertion of a word or letter in a document in place of another *la17-e18.*
superintendence *n* **1** a body of SUPERINTENDENTS (*n* 2) *la16, only Sc.* **2** = superintendence.
superintendent &c *n* **1** = superintendent. **2** *church* a MINISTER appointed to supervise the administration of the newly-reformed Church in a particular district *la16.*
superintromission [*sʌpər-] *n, law:* intromission (INTROMIT) beyond one's legal rights *la17-18.*
superior [sʌ'pirɪor] *n* **1** = superior *la16-.* **2** *law* a person who has made a grant of land in FEU to a VASSAL in return for a *feu duty* (FEU) or (*orig*) for the performance of certain services *la15-.*
adj = superior *17-.*
~**ate** = ~*ity* 2(1), *la16, only Sc.* ~**ity** &c **1** = superiority. **2** (1) the position or right of a SUPERIOR (*n* 2) *la14-.* (2) *specif* a FEU-title held

of the Crown, *orig* of forty-shilling land of old EXTENT, *later* of land of £400 SCOTS of valued rent, which conferred the county franchise on its holder before the 1832 Reform Act *la17-e19*, *only Sc*.

superplus [*?'sʌpər-] *n* a surplus, excess *la16-19*. [chf Sc; MedL]

superscription &c [*'sʌpər-] *n* **1** = superscription *la15-*. **2** *joc or illiterate* = subscription, *esp* a collection of money *19-20*.

superscrive [*'sʌpər-] *vt* = superscribe *e17*, *la19*, *only Sc*. [*cf* SCRIEVE², SUBSCRIVE]

supersede &c [supər-; *sʌpər-] *v* **1** *vt*, *chf law* postpone, defer, put off *la15-*, *only Sc*. **2** defer taking action with respect to; put (a thing) aside; put (a person) off *16*, *only Sc*. **3** *vi* defer action, hesitate *la16-e17*, *only Sc*. **4** *vi* (*for passive*) be postponed *la16*, *only Sc*. **5** *vti* = supersede *la16-*.

~**ment** postponement, adjournment *la15-16*, *only Sc*.

supersedere &c [supersə'derɪ; *sʌpərsə'diɪɪ] *n*, *law* a halt or cessation of the process of law, *specif* an agreement among creditors or a DECREE of a court to postpone action against a common debtor *16-e20*. [L = forbear, refrain from]

superspend *see* SUPEREXPEND

superstition &c *n* **1** = superstition *la16-*. **2** religious observance *e16*, *only Sc* [translating L *superstitio*].

superterranean [*sʌpər-] *adj*, *usu contrasted with 'subterranean'* above-ground *la17*.

supervenient [supər-; *sʌpər-] *adj* **1** = supervenient, supervening *la16-*. **2** *law*, *of a right* acquired by the *disponer* (DISPONE) subsequently to the act of transmission *17*.

superveniency *law* the fact or condition of being SUPERVENIENT *la17-e18*.

supire [sʌ'paɪr] *vi* sigh *la16*. [only Sc; OF *supirer; *cf* SUSPIRE]

supper &c; sipper *la18-19 n* **1** = supper *la14-*. **2** the last meal of the day given to an animal *19-*.

vt **1** *occas* ~ **up** give (an animal) its last meal of the day *la18-*. **2** serve or suffice for the supper of *la18-*, *now Cai Abd*.

fish-~, pudding-~ etc fish-, (*black or white*) pudding (BLACK, WHITE¹)- etc-and-chips, *esp* as bought from a fish-and-chip shop *20-*.

supple *see* SOOPLE, SOUPLE

supplé, supplee *see* SUPPLY

supplement *see* LETTER, OATH

supplementary *adj* applied to a course between the end of the Primary course and the school-leaving age, for children who were not intending to continue with academic education; *as noun* the course itself *e20*.

supplicant *n* **1** = supplicant *17-*. **2** an indigent person who has become an object of charity *la17-19*.

suppline *see* SIPLING

supply &c; supplé &c *la14-16*, **supplee** *e18* [sʌ'plaɪ; *-'pli] *vt* **1** = supply *la14-*. **2** help, aid *la14-16*. **3** make up (a whole) by adding something *la14*. **4** add to (something), supplement *la14*. **5** fill (another's place) *la14*.

n **1** (1) assistance, support, relief *15-20*. (2) charity, the giving of food, money etc to one in need *18-e19*. (3) a collection of money for charity *la17-e18*. **2** = supply *16-*. **3** an additional body of troops *la15*. **4** the CESS (*n* 1) *la17-e19*.

supplier 1 = supplier. **2** a person who takes the place of another *la15*, *only Sc*. **3** a helper, supporter *16*.

suppone [*sʌ'pon] *vt* = suppose *16-e17*. [chf Sc; MedL *supponere*]

support &c *vt* **1** = support *la15-*. **2** supply *16-e17*, *only Sc*. **3** make good (a deficiency) *16*. *n* **1** = support *16-*. **2** spiritual help *e16*. **3** bearing or defraying (**of** charges) *la16*. **4** *law* the SERVITUDE whereby a building etc rests on the *servient tenement* (SERVIENT); *also* the right of an owner of land to have it *upheld* (UPHAUD 2) in its natural state, and hence to object to anything prejudicial to this being done by a neighbour *la17-*.

suppose &c *vt* **1** = suppose *la14-*. **2** *in passive* (1) be expected, required **to** .. *20-*: '*ye're supposed tae be here at nine o'clock*'; (2) *in negative* not be permitted **to** .. *20-*: '*ye're no supposed to dae that*'. **3** *in imperative*, used as *conj* if, even if, although *la14-*, *only Sc*: '*I wadna tell you suppose I kent*'.

suppost *n* **1** = suppost, a supporter *la16-e17*. **2** *also* **supposit** *e16* a member of St Andrews or Glasgow Universities *16-*, *latterly hist*, *only Sc*. [OF *suppost*, L *suppositus* a subordinate, supporter, ptp of *supponere*]

supprise &c [*sʌ'praɪz; *n also* *sʌ'prəis] *vt* **1** = supprise, injure, attack unexpectedly *la14-e17*. **2** ensnare, betray *la16*.

n **1** injury, outrage, oppression *15-e16*. **2** surprise, unexpected attack *la15*. **3** conquest, defeat *e15*. [chf Sc; ME; AF, OF *suprise*]

surage &c [*'sʌrɪʃ, *-ɪdʒ] *n* ~ **gray** some kind of textile fabric *e16*. [only Sc; perh north-eastern OF **souriche &c*, central OF *sourise* a female mouse]

surce *see* SER

surcharge &c [*'sʌrtʃardʒ, *sʌr'tʃardʒ] *n* an additional or second dish or course *la14-e16*. [only Sc; prob var of SUBCHARGE]

surcoat &c ['sʌrkət] *n* a kind of undershirt or waistcoat; a fisherman's jersey *la18-*, *now Kcdn*, *only Sc*. [Eng *surcoat* an outer coat, appar w infl f *sarket* (SARK)]

sure &c [*sør, *'sju(ə)r] *vt* **1** = sure, make safe, secure, bind *16*. **2** *chf in 1 pers* assure, tell (a person) for certain *la16-*, *now NE* [perh merely aphetic f Eng *assure* rather than a survival of ME *sure*].

sure *see* SHUIR

suree &c; **soirée, swaree** &c [s(w)ə'ri] *n* =
soirée, a social gathering, *esp* one organized by
a church, Sunday school etc *19-*.

surety &c [*'sɔrtɪ] *n* **1** = surety *la16-*. **2** a
bond or obligation between parties that they
will keep the peace and not assault or molest
each other *18-e19, only Sc.*

surfeit &c; **surfat** &c   *16 adj*   excessive,
immoderate, intemperate *16-e20, chf Sc.*
n, vti = surfeit *16-*.

surfle &c *vti* gather, ruck a hem; overcast an
edge of cloth; trim with lace bordering
la19-e20. [ME *surful* &c, Norman F **surfiler*,
MedL *superfilare* embroider]

surigeoner *see* SURRIGINE

surioure [*sʌr'dʒur] *n* = sojour, sojourn *la14*.
[only Sc.   OED *sojour*]

surmatch [*sʌr'matʃ] *vt* excel, surpass *la16,
only Sc.*

surname &c *n* **1** = surname *la14-*. **2** a family,
CLAN *la15-e17, only Sc.*

surprise; surpreese *la19-, now SW, only Sc vt,
n* = surprise.

surrender *n* **1** = surrender *la17-*. **2** *law* the
submission of tithes to the Crown *17*.
vti **1** = surrender *17-*. **2** *vt* submit (tithes) to
the Crown *e17*.

~**er** a person who surrenders tithes to the
Crown *e17*.

at an awfu ~ at a great rate, at breakneck
speed *la19-20, Mry Bnf* [see SND].

surregerie *n* = surgery *e16*.   [only Sc.   OED
surgery]

surrigine &c *n* = surgeon *16, only Sc.*
surigeoner &c = surgeon *16, only Sc.* [*cf*
CHIRURGIAN.   OED *surgeon*]

surrogate &c *vt* **1** = surrogate, appoint as a
substitute *16-e17*. **2** substitute in respect of a
right or claim *16-e18*.

surrogatum [sʌro'getəm] *n, law* something
which stands in the place of another, *eg* the
price of a thing instead of the thing itself *la18-*.
[only Sc; L = something which is substituted]

suscitate &c *ptp, law, of an action* promoted *la16,
only Sc.* [*cf* Eng *v*]

suspeck[1] &c [*'sʌspɛk(t)] *n* = suspect, suspicion *la14-16*.   [only Sc.   OED *suspect* (*n*[1])]

suspeck[2] &c, **suspect** *vt* [sə'spɛk(t)], *adj* (*n*)
['sʌspɛk(t)] = suspect *16-*. [OED *suspect* (*adj,
n*[2], *v*)]

suspeecion *20-, only Sc,* **suspicion** &c *la14-;*
suspetion &c *16, only Sc* [sə'spiʃ(ɪ)ən] *n* =
suspicion.

suspend *vt* **1** = suspend *16-*. **2** *law* (1) *of a
court* defer or stay (execution of a sentence etc)
until the case has been reviewed *la15-*; (2) *vi, of
a litigant or convicted person* ask for SUSPENSION as a
form of appeal *la17-*.

~**er 1** a person who puts a stop to something
e16. **2** *law* a person who SUSPENDS (*v* 2 (2))
la17-. **3** = suspender.

suspension *n* **1** = suspension *la16-*. **2** *law* (a

warrant for) stay of execution of a DECREE or
sentence until the matter can be reviewed, used
when ordinary appeal is incompetent, *freq* **bill
etc of** ~ *la16-*.

suspensive *adj* **1** liable to be suspended *e16*. **2**
kept undetermined, subject to doubt *e16*. **3** =
suspensive.

~ **condition** *law* a condition which suspends
the coming into force of a contract until the
condition is fulfilled *19-*.

suspetion, suspicion *see* SUSPEECION

suspire *v* **1** *vi* = suspire, sigh *e16*. **2** *vt* utter
with a sigh *e16*.
n = suspire, sigh *e16*.

sussie &c, **sussy; sizzie** &c *19-* ['sʌsi, *SW*
'sɪzi] *n* care, trouble, bother, *latterly freq* in dealing with a fractious drunk person *16-, now Sh
Fif Kcb.*
v, always in negative **1** *vi* not care, not be anxious
or concerned *la16-, now Sh*; **2** not refuse (to do
something) *la16*; **3** *vt* not care for or regard
la16; **4** *vi* not shrink or hesitate *19-, now Sh.*
[only Sc; OF *soussy* (*n*), *soussier* (*v*); *cf* F *souci*]

sustain &c *la17-;* **susteen** &c *15-20 vt* **1** =
sustain *15-*. **2** *law, of a court* support the validity of (a claim), uphold authoritatively,
approve *la18-19*. **3** *of a church court, specif a*
PRESBYTERY: give formal approval to (a call
from a congregation to a new MINISTER) *18-*.

sustentation &c *n* = sustentation *la14-*.
~ **fund** *Free Church of Scotland* (FREE) a fund for
the support of the ministry *19-e20*.

sut *see* SIT, SOT[2]

sutell &c *la14-15*, **suttaille** &c *la15, only Sc,*
sittel- *la16* [*'sʌtl] *adj* = subtle. [OED *subtle*]

suter *see* SOUTER

suth(e) *see* SUITH

Sutherland *n, also* ~ **Highlander** etc a soldier
in the ~ *Highlanders, 18-19.*
~ **Clearances** *hist* the *clearances* (CLEAR) in the
county of Sutherland *la19-*. ~ **Highlanders** a
regiment raised *orig* in 1799 as the 93rd Highland regiment; in 1861 it became the 93rd *Sutherland Highlanders*; *cf Argyll and Sutherland
Highlanders* (ARGYLL).   [the county]

suttaille *see* SUTELL

sutten *see* SIT

sutter *see* SOUTER

svinglent *see* SWINGLE[1]

swa *see* SAE[2]

swab [swab] *n* a pea- or bean-pod *19-, Dmf Rox.*
[eModEng; *cf* SWAP[3]]

swabble &c ['swabl] *vt* beat, thrash with a belt,
cane etc *19-, now Rox.*
n **1** a thrashing *e20, Bwk.*   **2** a long pliant stick;
fig a tall thin person *19-, now Rox.*   [only Sc; see
SND]

swack[1] &c *n* **1** a sudden heavy blow, the sound
made by a heavy blow or fall; a sudden or powerful movement *la14-, now Loth Rox.* **2** a big
mouthful, a deep draught of liquor *la18-, now
Edb Rox.*

vt throw forcibly, dash down; brandish (a sword) *la14-19*. [chf Sc; onomat; *cf* MDu *swacken* shake, wave]

swack[2] **&c** *n* **1** soft, moist and easily moulded; *of cheese* not crumbly *18-*, *now N*. **2** pliant, easily bent or stretched *18-*, *now N*. **3** *of persons, animals, or their limbs* active, lithe, supple *la18-*, *now local Sh-Fif*.

~en *vti* make or become soft and pliant, loosen *19-*, *Sh Ork N*. [only Sc; Flem *zwak* lithe, MDu *swac* lithe, pliant, weak; *cf* Ger *schwach* weak]

Swade &c, Swad &c [swed, swɛd; *NE* swad] *n* **1** = Swede *18-20*, *NE*. **2** **s~** = swede, the variety of turnip *17-*; *cf* NEEP, TURNEEP.

Swaden &c; **Suethin &c** [*'swedən, *'swɛðən, *'swadən] = Sweden *16-e17*, *only Sc*. [*cf* SWANE. OED *Sweden*]

swae *see* SAE[2]

swag[1] **&c** *vi* sway from side to side, wag to and fro; hang down heavily and lopsidedly *18-e20*. *n* **1** (the act of) swinging or swaying *19-*, *now Kcb*. **2** a bag or wallet, *esp* one carried by a beggar or thief *18-e19*. **3** a quantity of liquid or liquor, a long draught *19-*, *now Sh Ork* [poss a different word; see SND]. [prob Scand; *cf* Norw dial *swagga* sway]

swag[2] *vi* **I'll ~** I'll bet *la19-*, *Ags Per*. [altered by wrong division f *I'se wad* (see WAD[1])]

swagat(is) *see* SAE[2]

swage &c [swadʒ, *swedʒ] *v* **1** *vt* assuage, relieve, reduce *15-18*. **2** *vi, of floods, the stomach after a meal, etc* subside, settle down, shrink from a swollen state *la18-*, *now Sh Ork N*. **3** *vt* take in and digest (food) *20-*, *now Sh Cai*. **4** *vi* relax after a good meal, sit back and let it digest *20-*, *Ork N*. [ME; aphetic f Eng *assuage*]

swagger &c *vi* **1** = swagger. **2** stagger, sway *18-e19*.

swaible &c *vt* mop up, wash, scour energetically *e20*, *Rox*. [see SND]

swail[1] **&c;** **swell** *la18*, **swyle** *la19-20*, *NE n* a wet hollow, a boggy place *16-*, *now Bnf*. [obscure. OED *swale*]

swail[2] **&c** *adj* meaning and orig unknown *e16*.

swaip &c *n* a slanting direction, a slope *20-*, *Rox*. *adj* slanting or sloping, oblique *19-e20*, *Bwk S*. *vi, of a road etc* rise or descend obliquely *20-*, *now Rox*. [ON *sveipa* sweep, wrap, be twisted, *sveipr* a fold in a garment, *sveipóttr* eddying, OE *swāpan* sweep, swoop]

swaird *16-e20*, *only Sc*, **sward &c** [swerd] *n* = sward *la14-*.
~-cut chop up the turf of (old pasture), *chf* as **~-cutter** a machine which does this *la18*. **swear dyke** ['swer'dəik] a wall of turf *la20-*, *Mry Bnf*. **sward-erd &c** grassland *16-e17*, *only Sc*.

swairm *vti, n* = swarm *la19-e20*.

swait *see* SWEET[1]

swaits *see* SWATS

swall &c *la16-*, *only Sc*; **swoll** *16*, *only Sc* [swal] *vti, ptp* also **swallen** *19-e20* ['swalən; *swʌun] = swell *16-*. [OED *swell*]

swalla &c; **swallow** [*N, WC* 'swalə; *EC, S* 'swalɪ] *n* **1** = swallow, the bird *la18-*. **2** the martin *la19-*, *N-WC, S*.

swallie[1] **&c** *la16-*, **swallow** *16-*; **swellie &c** *la14-16*, **swolly** *la16* ['swalɪ; *Abd Fif* 'swalə; *'swɛlɪ; *'swolɪ] *vti, pt* also **swellit &c** *la14-16*. *ptp* also **swolit** *e16*, *only Sc* = swallow (food etc) *la14-*.

swallie[2] **&c;** **swellie** ['swalɪ; *Abd* 'swalə; *'swɛlɪ] *n* = swallow, an abyss; the throat, gullet; an act of swallowing etc *la14-*.

swallow *see* SWALLA, SWALLIE[1]

swalm &c; **swame** *only Sc* [*swalm, *swam] *n* swelling *16*.
vi faint, swoon *la16*. [ME]

swamp &c [swamp] *adj, esp of a formerly plump person* thin, lean *la14-20*. [also northern ModEng dial; see SND]

swander &c ['swandər] *vi* become giddy or faint; reel about, stagger; hesitate, dither *19-20*, *Sh Ork Fif*. [perh conflation of SWAGGER w Eng *wander*]

Swane &c [swen] = Sweden *16*. [only Sc; contracted f SWADEN; *cf* AF *suane* (*12-13*). OED *Sweden*]

swang *see* SWING[1]

swank &c *adj, of persons or animals* lithe, agile, strong; *esp of a young man* smart, well set-up *la18-*, *now nEC Lnk Slk*.
~ie &c *adj, of persons* = adj, *19-*, *now local Cai-wLoth*. *n* a smart, active, strapping young man *16-*, *now local nEC-Wgt*. **~in &c** *adj* active, agile, athletic *19-e20*, *only Sc*. *n* = swankie (*n*) *e16*, *only Sc*. [MDu *swanc* supple, pliant, slender]

Swankie: ~'s doo *etc, joc* a seagull *la20-*, *Ags*. [surname common in Arbroath]

swap[1] **&c** [swap] *v* **1** *vt* strike, hit *la14-*, *now Sh*. **2** throw or move briskly or forcibly, fling *la18-*, *now Sh*. **3** brandish (a weapon), make a swipe with (a sword etc), wave about *la18-*, *now Sh*. **4** (1) fold or wind (a rope, strip of cloth etc) over on itself, criss-cross *la19-*, *Sh NE*. (2) *specif* throw (a straw-rope) up and over a hay- or cornstack to hold down the thatch; rope (a stack) thus, EDDER *la19-*, *NE*. **5** *vi* swirl, swing, move with haste or violence *la14-*, *now Sh*. **6** *vt* drink in long quick gulps, toss off *16-19*. **7** exchange, barter *19-*.
n **1** a blow, stroke, slap *19-*, *now Sh*. **2** an exchange, a give-and-take *la18-*.
adv with a sudden violent movement, forcibly *19-*, *now Sh*.
~pit ? very big *e16*, *only Sc*.
~ thak wooden slats used in thatching *la15*, *only Sc*. [see SND]

swap[2] **&c** [swap] *n*, also **swype** *la19-*, *NE Per* [swəip] the cast of someone's features, *esp* as it resembles his relatives, a facial trait or characteristic in a family *19-*, *now Sh NE Per.*

vt resemble in (*esp* facial) appearance, show a family likeness to *19-*, *now Ork Wgt.* [see SND]

swap³ [swap] *n* the shell or pod of peas or beans before they begin to swell; the peas or beans themselves *19-*, *now Loth.* [var of SWAB]

swar *n* a snare *la15*. [only Sc; unknown, poss a misreading]

swarbit &c: Deil ~ on the Devil's curse on *la16-e18*. [eModEng *swarbout*, a corruption of (*God*)*s forbote* God's forbidding]

sward *see* SWAIRD

sware *see* SWEER, SWIRE

swaree *see* SUREE

swarf &c *now Sh*; **swerf &c** *16-19* [swarf, *swarθ, *swerf, *swɛrv; *v also* *swarv] *v* **1** *vi* faint, swoon *16-*, *now Sh.* **2** *vt* cause to faint; stupefy *19-e20*.

n a swoon, faint; a stupor *la15-*, *now Sh.* [only Sc; var of Eng *swerve* turn to one side; *cf* cognate ON *svarfa* upset, overturn]

swarra &c [*Sh* 'swarə; *Mry Bnf* sə'warə] *n* **1** a kind of thick, heavy, woollen yarn used for knitting jerseys, scarves and underclothing *19-*, *now Sh.* **2** a garment knitted with this wool *la19-*, *now Sh.* [only Sc; unknown]

swarrach &c ['swarəx] *n* a crowd, swarm (*esp* of young children in a family) *19-*, *NE.*

vi, of a place swarm with living creatures *20-*, *Bnf Abd.* [only Sc; see SND]

swarth [swarθ] *n* = swath, the cut made by one sweep of a scythe *la18-19*.

swarve &c *la16-19*; **suirve** *16*, *only Sc* [*swarv] *vti, ptp also* **swarven** *16* = swerve. [OED *swerve*]

swasch &c *16*; **swesch &c** *16-e17*, **swische &c** [*swaʃ, *swɛʃ, *swɪʃ] *n* **1** a kind of drum *16-17*. **2** *prob erron* a trumpet *16-e17*.

~er a drummer *16*. [only Sc; unknown. OED *swash* (*n²*)]

swash [swaʃ] *v* **1** *vt* (1) dash down, cast against the ground; slash; beat *18-*, *now Kcb.* (2) dash or splash (liquid) about or over *19-*, *now Sh Ork.* **2** *vi* (1) rush to and fro, move about excitedly and energetically *17-19*. (2) bluster with or as with weapons; swagger, cut a dash *17-*, *now Abd Ags.*

n **1** (the noise of) a severe blow, a clashing against or on *18-19*. **2** a splash or plunge in water; a dash of water, the wash of waves against something *la18-*, *now Sh Ork.* **3** (1) a large amount of drink or food *19-*, *now Sh Ork.* (2) *in gen* a large amount *19-e20*. **4** (1) affected ostentatious behaviour; a swagger; a strutting, haughty gait *19-20*. (2) a swaggerer, a vain, ostentatious person *19*.

adj **1** fuddled with drink *18-19*. **2** ? squat *18-e19*.

~y ostentatious, dashing; strapping *la19-*, *now Abd.* [eModEng; onomat]

swat *see* SWEET¹

swatch &c [swatʃ] *n* **1** a pattern or sample of a piece of cloth *17-*. **2** *transf* a typical piece, example, selection etc *18-20*. **3** a point or amount of similarity, a feature in common *18-*, *now Sh Per.* **4** a glimpse, a partial view, a half-look *la19-*, *local Per-Ayr.* **5** a short spell, turn, SHOT¹ *la20-*, *Stlg Gsw.*

vt **1** match, select; make, copy, or supply according to a pattern *la19*. **2** look appraisingly at, size up *la19-*, *now Per Fif.*

tak (**a**) **~ o** *etc* take an appraising, critical look at, scrutinize *la19-*, *now Per.* **tak** *etc* **the ~ o** take the measure of, be a match for *la19-*, *now Bnf.* [northern eModEng *swache* the counterstock of a tally *e16*]

swats &c *la17-*; **swaits &c** *16* [swats; *swets] *n pl* **1** newly-brewed weak beer; a substitute for this, made of molasses, water and yeast *16-*, *now Sh Lnk.* **2** the liquor resulting from the steeping of oatmeal husks in the making of SOWANS *la19-20*, *Sh Ork N.* [only Sc; OE *swatan* (*n pl*) beer]

swatter &c ['swatər] *vi, also* **swetter** *e16*, *also fig* flutter and splash in water (like ducks or geese), dabble, flounder about *16-*, *now Kcb.*

n **1** a splashing or floundering about in water etc *19*. **2** a large collection or crowd, *esp* of small creatures, a swarm *19-*, *now Bnf Abd.* [onomat; *cf* Du dial *zwaddern*, LowGer *schwadern*]

swattit *see* SWEET¹

swattle &c ['swatl] *vi* **1** splash about in something wet, wallow *19-e20*. **2** drink greedily or noisily *19*. [onomat; var of SWATTER; *cf* Ger dial *schwatteln*]

swaver ['swevər] *vi* totter, sway, move unsteadily or wearily *la18-*, *now Sh Ork NE.*

n an inclination to one side, a lurch, stagger *la19-*, *NE.* [nME *swafre*; *cf* Norw dial *sveiva* (*v*) swing, Icel *sveifa* hover, glide]

swaw &c *n* a wave, a ripple *19-e20*.

vi form waves, ripple; undulate *e19*. [prob Scand; *cf* Norw dial *svaga* (*v*) sway, swing; cognate w SWAG¹]

sway &c [swe; *nEC also* swaɪ, swəi] *n* = swathe, the row of cuts of grass made by a scythe *19-*, *nEC, WC, S.*

sway *see* SWEY

sweamish *adj* = squeamish *20-*, *now Sh Ork Fif.*

swear *see* SWEER

swear dyke *see* SWAIRD

sweat *see* SWEET¹

swecht &c, sweight [*swɛxt] *n* a rush, impetus, force *16-e19*. [ME]

swedge &c [swɛdʒ; *swedʒ] *n* a tool for making the grooves and nail-holes in a horseshoe *la17-*.

vt make a groove or hole in (metal), *eg* on a horseshoe *19-*, *now Bnf.* [var of Eng *swage* a groove]

swee *see* SWEY

sweech [swix] *n* a sweeping blow, a swipe *la19-*, *Ags*. [onomat; *cf* WHEECH¹]

sweek *see* SWICK

sweel¹ &c, swill *la17- vti* **1** = swill *la16-*. **2** *vt* wash (the throat) down with liquor *18-*. **3** wash away; wash (food) down with a drink *19-*, *local Sh-Kcb*. **4** dash or throw (water) about, cause (a liquid) to swirl round, swallow in copious draughts *la18-*, *local Sh-Kcb*. **5** *vi, of water, waves* roll, flow with a swirling motion *la19-*, *local Sh-Kcb*. **6** (1) swirl, spin or revolve (quickly), roll *19-*, *now Sh-C*. (2) *of dancers* whirl, spin round *19-*, *local Ags-Kcb*.
n **1** = swill. **2** a hearty drinking *la19-*, *now NE*. **3** a rinsing, washing or swilling *la18-*. **4** a circular motion, a swirl, spin, twist *19-*, *now NE, EC Dmf*.

sweel² &c *la16-*; **swele** *e15*, **swyle &c** *17-* [swil; *NE* swəil] *vt* **1** wrap (a person) in cloth or clothing, swathe, swaddle *15-*, *now Kcb*. **2** *in gen* wrap, wind, tie or bind round *19-*, *now Uls*.
n the act of swathing or swaddling *la19-e20*.
~**er** a cloth body-belt, a binder, *esp* for an infant *19-*, *local Bnf-Kcb*. [only *Sc*; reduced f ME *swedle &c, swethel* (*v*), *swaddle* (*n*) swaddling clothes, OE *swepel* swaddling clothes]

sweel³ &c, swivel &c, sweevil &c *19-*, *now NE Ayr*, **sool &c** *now Cai Per*; **swoul** *e16*, **swill &c** *18-e20* [swil, 'swivl, sul; *Sh Ork* swɪl; *Sh also* 'swevl] *n* **1** = swivel *16-*. **2** *only* **sweevil &c** a gust of wind, a short, sharp gale *la19-*, *now Sh Ork*.
vt tether (animals) together with a swivel on the rope to allow them limited freedom of movement *la19-*, *now Sh*.
swiveltree the swingletree of a plough *20-*, *now Ork Per*.

sweel *see* SWILL

sweem *see* SOOM¹

sweeng *see* SWING¹

sweep &c, soop &c *now Cai C, S*; **swoop** *19-e20*, **swype &c** *17-*, *NE vti, pt also* ~**it &c** *18-* **1** = sweep *la15-*. **2** *chf* **soop**, curling sweep (the ice) in the path of a *curling-stone* (CURL) in order to assist its progress *19-*.
n **1** = sweep. **2** *only* **sweep** a cord or piece of rope by which the stone-sinkers of a herring-net were attached *la19, Mry Bnf*.
s(w)ooper a brush *19-e20*. **sweepit** *n, chf in negative* not a particle, not the least little bit *20-*, *now Ork* [shortened f *deil sweep it &c* (*cf* DEIL)].
sweep-the-fluir a move in the game of CHUCKS *20-, Ags Fif WC*. **soop up** speed (a *curling-stone* (CURL)) by *sooping* (*v* 2) *19-*.

sweer &c, swear [swir; *nEC* swer] *la17- vti, pt also* **swour &c** *la14-15, only Sc*, **swoor** *la18-19*, **swure &c** *19-, now Sh Ork WC-S*, **sware &c** *la14, 19-* [swɔr, swer]; ~**ed** *la19-, now Ayr Wgt Rox* [swird, swerd] = swear *la14-*.
n **1** a bout of swearing *la19-*. **2** a swear-word *20-*.

sweer *see* SWEIR

sweerie &c ['swirɪ, -o, *-ək] *n* a box or basket for holding bobbins of yarn, constructed so as to make easier the spinning of two- or three-ply thread *18-*, *now Sh Ork*. [prob deriv of SWEIR, from the idea of saving work]

sweesh &c *n, v, adv* = swish *la19-*, *local Sh-Kcb*.

sweet¹ &c *18-*, **sweat &c**; **sweit &c** *15-e20, only Sc*, **swat &c** *la14-e15, la19-e20*, **swait &c** *e16, la19*, **swite &c** *19-, now NE Ags* [swit; *Sh Ork nEC Uls* swet; *NE Ags Per* swəit; *Ags Uls* *swat] *vti, pt also* **swat** *18-, now local*, **swattit &c** *20-, local* **sweitit &c** *20-, N* [swat, 'swatɪt, 'switt]. *ptp also* **swat** *19*, **swutten** *la19-, now Abd Dmf*, **sweeten** *e20, Rox*; **sweitit &c** *20-, now NE* ['swʌtən, swatən, swat; 'switɪt; *Rox also* 'switən] = sweat *la16-*.
n **1** = sweat *la14-*. **2** stress, exertion; a state of anxiety or excitement *18-*.
~**ing 1** = sweating *la19-*. **2** sweating sickness *la16, only Sc*. [OED *sweat, swote*]

sweet² &c; sweit &c *la14-18, only Sc*, **suit** *18-e19, only Sc* [swit] *adj, n* **1** = sweet *la14-*. **2** *of milk* fresh, untreated, not skimmed or sour *18-*.
~**en** *vt* **1** = sweeten. **2** bribe *la18-*. ~**nin** a sweet(meat), a titbit *20-, Ork Bnf Abd*.
~-**bread** fancy cakes, pastries *la18-*, *now Sh Ork*. ~ **butter** fresh, unsalted butter *la18-*, *now Ork NE nEC*. ~-**milk cheese** cheese made from unskimmed milk, *specif* DUNLOP cheese *la18-*, *now N*.

sweetie &c *n* **1** a sweet(meat) *18-*. **2** *term of endearment* darling *la19-*. **3** a considerable sum of money, a stiff price *20-, NE*.
~ **bool(ie)** a round boiled sweet *la20-, Abd*. ~ **bottle** a glass jar for holding sweets *la19-, Abd*. ~ **bun** *19-, now Sh*, ~ **loaf &c** *la18-e20* a bun baked with sweetmeats or with raisins. ~-**man** a confectioner, sweet-seller *20-*. ~ **poke &c** a bag of sweets *la18-, Sh Ork Cai C*. ~ **scone &c** = ~ bun, *19-e20*. ~ **shop** a sweet-shop *la19-*. ~ **stan(d)** a sweet-stall at a fair etc *la19-*, *now Abd Per*. ~-**wife 1** a female sweet-seller *la18-*. **2** *freq of a(n effeminate) man* a garrulous, gossipy person *20-, local Cai-S*.
Aberdeen ~ a sharp tap on the head with a flick of the thumb *la19-, now Mry Bnf*. **work for** ~**s** work for a pittance *la20-, Ags Gsw*.

sweevil *see* SWEEL³

sweight *see* SWECHT

sweir &c *16-*, **sweer &c** [swir] *adj* **1** oppressed in mind, sad *la14*. **2** lazy, slothful, unwilling to work *la14-, now N, EC, SW*. **3** unwilling, reluctant, loath *la14-*.
~**ie** rather lazy; somewhat reluctant (to do something) *19-, now Sh Ork*. ~**ie well** a well which is dependable only after rain *19-, now Cai*. ~**t &c** [swirt; swird] = *adj* 2 and 3, *19-, now Sh NE, C*. ~**tie &c** laziness *19-, Sh NE*.
~-**arse &c,** ~-**draw** a game in which two persons sitting on the ground, holding a stick between them, each try to pull the other up

la19-e20. **~-drawn** reluctant, hesitating *19-e20,* S. **~-tree** = *~arse, 19-20.* [ONorthumb *swǣr* oppressive; lazy, OE *swǣrnes* sloth; cognate w Ger *schwer* heavy, difficult]

sweit *see* SWEET[1], SWEET[2]

swelch, swelth &c [*swɛlx, *swɛlθ, *swɛlf] *n* a whirlpool *la14-e17.*

    swelchie &c ['swɛlkɪ, 'swɪlkɪ; *'swɛlxɪ] a whirlpool in the sea *la17, Ork Cai.* [chf Sc; ME (once); ON *svelgr*; *cf* OE *geswelg*]

swele *see* SWEEL[2]

swell *see* SWAIL[1]

swellie *see* SWALLIE[1], SWALLIE[2]

swelt &c *vi* **1** = swelt, die *la14-e16.* **2** become faint with weakness or emotion, be physically overcome, swoon *la15-e20.*

    ~in a cod in poor condition *19-e20, Sh Kcdn.*

swelter *vi* **1** = swelter *17-.* **2** welter, wallow, flounder or flop about *16-e19.*

    sweltry oppressively hot, sweltering, sultry *19-, Sh Ork NE, C.*

swelth *see* SWELCH

sweltry *see* SWELTER

swentʒour *see* SWINGER

swepyr *see* SWIPPER

swerd *see* SWURD

swerf *see* SWARF

swesch *see* SWASCH

swetter *see* SWATTER

sweving &c [*'swiv(ə)n] *n* = sweven, a dream *e16, only Sc.*

    sweyning [*?'swinɪŋ, -ɪn] = swevening, dreaming *la16, only Sc.* [OED *sweven, swevening*]

swey &c, sway &c *18-*; **swee &c** *la16-,* **swy(e)** *la18-, Sh NE* [swi; *Sh Cai nEC, S* swəi; *NE* swəi] *vti* **1** = sway *16-.* **2** *vi* vacillate *la16, 19-e20.* **3** *vt* (1) make to sway or swing, move (an object) to one side *la18-, now Sh N.* (2) press down, bend to one side *19.*

    n **1** = sway *16-.* **2** (1) a swinging semi-circular motion; a sudden move to one side, a swerve, lurch; a swinging blow; a veering of wind *16-.* (2) an inclination or bias, a trend, tendency *18-e19.* **3** (1) a swing for children *19-, now Sh Cai C.* (2) *chf* ~ **boat** a swing-boat at a fair *20-, Kcdn nEC midLoth.* **4** a lever, crowbar, *esp* one used in a quarry to raise stones *16-, now Sh.* **5** ? the pole of a cart *e16, only Sc.* **6** a derrick or crane for lifting heavy objects; a steelyard *18-e19.* **7** *chf* **swey, swee** a movable iron bar over a fire, on which pots, kettles etc can be hung *la18-.* **8** a (street-)lamp bracket *la17-18.*

    swee chain the chain hanging from the SWEY (*n* 7) *20-, now Cai Ags.* [ME *sweʒe* go, move, OE *swegan;* StEng *sway* is f LowGer *swajen,* Du *zwaaien* swing, wave, go on a slant]

sweyning *see* SWEVING

swick &c; sweek &c *16-e20 n* **1** (a piece of) deceit, a trick, swindle *15-, now local Sh-SW.* **2** a cheating rogue, swindler, deceiver *la19-, Sh-WC.*

    vt cheat, swindle, deceive *16-.*

    ~ery cheating, swindling *la19-, now NE.* **~ful** deceitful, treacherous *e15.*

    the ~ o 1 the responsibility for (something bad or unfortunate) *19-e20, NE.* **2** the knack or ability to do (something) *19-e20.* [OE *swic(a)* (*n*) deceit, f *swican* (*v*) cheat, which led to ME and northern ModEng dial *swike* (*n*) deceit etc. OED *swike*]

swidder *see* SWITHER[1]

swiff &c; swuff *n* the motion itself or the hissing or whizzing sound of an object flying through the air, a rush of air, a whirr *19-, now Sh Abd.*

    vi rush through the air with a hissing noise, whizz *19.* [imit, perh w infl f SOUCH &c]

swift; swoft &c *la16, only Sc,* **swuft** *e16, only Sc adj, adv* = swift *la14-.*

    swift horse rinning horse-racing *e16, only Sc.*

swig[1] *vi* go with a swinging motion, rock, jog *19-20.* [prob Scand; *cf* Norw dial *sviga* swing, work quickly, beat, *sveiga* walk with a swing; *cf* SWAG[2]]

swig[2] *n* = swig.

    play at ~ indulge in drinking *la17.*

swik, swilk *see* SIC

swill; swull, sweel [swɪl, swʌl, swil, sol, sul] *n* a large shallow basket for carrying potatoes, clothes etc *19-, Bwk Rox.* [see SND]

swill *see* SWEEL[1], SWEEL[3]

swim *see* SOOM[1]

swine &c *n sing and pl* a pig, pigs *la14-.*

    ~('s) arnit &c the tall oat-grass, *esp* its tuberous roots *18-, now Abd.* ~ **crue &c** *la19-,* ~ **cruive &c** *16-, only Sc* a pigsty now *nEC.* ~ **meat** pigswill *20-, Ork NE, C.* ~ **pork** a pig *la15.* ~ **pot** a pot in which pigs' food is boiled *20-, now Ork Abd Kcb.* ~('s) **same &c** lard, pig's fat *la16-, now local N-S.* ~ **th(r)issle &c** the sow-thistle *19-, now Rox.*

    the ~ has run *etc* **through it** the plan, affair etc has come to nothing, been completely ruined *18-, now Ork Mry Dmf.*

swing[1] **&c; sweeng** *19-20, Abd Ags vti, pt* also **swang** *la15-, now Sh Abd* = swing *la15-.*

    n **1** = swing *la14-.* **2** *also* ~ **rope** a hawser for making fast a boat; *herring-fishing* the line of nets to the stern of the boat etc *19-, now N Ags Fif.* ~ **tree** a swingletree of a plough etc *19-, now Ork Bnf.*

    into a ~ suddenly *la14, only Sc.*

swing[2] *vi* labour, toil *la15.* [ME; OE *swingan; cf* SWINK]

swinge &c [swɪn(d)ʒ, swin(d)ʒ] *vt* beat, flog, drive with blows *la18-, now Sh.*

    n a heavy blow, a dash or clash, a forcible impetus *la18-, now local wLoth-Dmf.* [eModEng var of ME *swenge; cf* ModEng *swingeing* (*adj*)]

swinger &c *16-18;* **swentʒour** *e16, e17,*

swounger *e17* [*'swɛntʒər, *'swɛndʒər, *'swɪndʒ-, *'swundʒ-] *n* a rogue, scoundrel. [only Sc; prob cant; perh MDu or Flem; *cf* MDu, MLowGer *swentzen*, Ger *schwänzen* roam about idly]

swingle[1] **&c** ['swɪŋl] *vt* = swingle (flax) *la15-*. ~ **&c hand** *e19*, **svinglent** *la17, only Sc*, **swinglind** *e19, only Sc* a swingle. ~ **tree 1** = swingletree (of a plough) *19-*. **2** the free arm or beater of a flail *la18-, now Sh Ork*. **3** = *sweir tree* (SWEIR) *la19-, NE Fif Lnk, only Sc*.

swingle[2] ['swɪŋl] *vi* **1** swing from side to side, be hung or suspended, oscillate *19-, now Dmf*. **2** *specif of sheep* walk with a swinging jerky motion due to disease of the spine *la19-, Cai*. [ME, frequentative of Eng *swing*]

swinglind *see* SWINGLE[1]

swink *vi* work hard, toil; struggle hard or intensely *la18-20*. [ME; OE *swinc(an)* (*v, n*)]

swins *see* SOWANS

swipe[1] **&c** *n* **1** a blow with a full swing of the arm, a sweeping stroke *18-*. **2** such a stroke made with a golf-club or cricket bat *19*. *vi* deliver a long swinging blow or stroke *19-*. [prob var of SWEEP]

swipe[2] **&c** *n*, *mining* a crossing-switch or curved plate in a mine railway *la19-, now Fif Ayr*. [see SND]

swipper &c *16-*; **swepyr &c** *la14-16, only Sc*, **swippert &c** *la18-20, NE Ags, only Sc* ['swɪpər(t); *'swɪpər] *adj* quick, nimble, active *la14-, now NE*. *n* a lithe, agile person *20-, NE*. *adv* agilely, nimbly, quickly, abruptly *la19-, NE*. [ME *swiper &c*; OE *swipor* crafty, cunning]

swird *see* SWURD

swire &c; sware &c *la15-e19* *n* **1** = swire, the neck *la15-e16*. **2** a hollow or declivity between hills, *freq* one with a road; a hollow or level place near the top of a hill *16-, now Pbls Lnk S, freq* in place-names *la14-, chf Pbls S*. [ONorthumb *swira* a neck, ON *svíri* a neck, a ridge of land]

swirk *vt* spring **forth** *e16*. [only Sc; perh f root of SWIRL + -*k*]

swirl &c; sworl &c *16-e20, only Sc*, **swurl** *19-e20* *n* **1** a whirling movement of water, smoke etc, an eddy, whirlpool *15-*. **2** (1) a twist, twirl, coil; a twisted or tangled state *la18-, now Sh Ork Cai nEC*. (2) a twist or knot in the grain of wood *19-, now Kcb*. **3** a tuft or curl of hair, a forelock *19-, now Sh*. *vti* **1** (cause to) move round and round, whirl, eddy; wave, brandish *16-*. **2** have a twist, give a twist or curl to *e19*. ~**ie 1** *esp of the hair* having a marked curl or coil, curly, frizzy *19-, now Sh SW*. **2** *of wood* with twists in the grain, knotty, gnarly; *of rock* knobby, with an uneven grain *la18-, now Sh Cai*

Abd. **3** *also fig* tangled, twisted *19-, now Sh Kcb*. [orig Sc; prob onomat; *cf* Norw, Dan *svirra*, Norw dial *svirla*, Du *swirreln* (*v*) whirl]

swische *see* SWASCH

switch *vt* **1** = switch. **2** thresh (grain); beat, scutch (flax) *19*. **3** trim (a tree, hedge etc) *19-e20*.

switchbell *see* COACHBELL

swite *see* SWEET[1]

swith &c *la14-e20*; **swythe &c** *15-19* [swɪθ, swaɪð] *adv* **1** quickly, rapidly; at once *la14-e20*. **2** *as exclam, 19-e20*. *interj, chf* ~ **&c** *freq as an order to a dog* quick!, away! *18-19*. *adj* quick, speedy *19-e20*. *vir* be gone, speed away *la18-19, NE*. [ME *swith(e)*; OE *swīðe* very much]

swither[1] *18-*; **swidder &c** *now chf NE*, **swuther** *19-e20* ['swɪðər; *NE* 'swɪdər] *vi* **1** be uncertain, be perplexed about what to do or choose, doubt, hesitate, dither *16-*. **2** *chf literary, of things* be indeterminate or uncertain, have a doubtful appearance, fluctuate, move fitfully *19-, now local Sh-Per*. **3** feel faint or sick *e19*. *n* **1** a state of indecision or doubt, hesitation, uncertainty *18-*. **2** a state of nervousness or agitation, a panic, fluster *la18-, now local Sh-Ayr*. **3** a state of confusion, a tangled or muddled condition *la19-, local Sh-Gall*. **4** a dithering, undecided person *20-, local*. [perh extended f SWITHER[2]]

swither[2] **&c** ['swɪðər; *Sh* swɪdər] *vi* rush, swirl, move with haste and flurry *19-, now Sh*. *n* a rushing movement, swirl, flurry *20-, now Sh*. [prob related to Norw dial *svidra, svid(d)a* (*v*) rush to and fro; Icel *sviðra* (*v*) swirl]

swither[3] [*'swɪðər] *vti* beat (hard), batter (a person) *la18-e19, Ayr Rox*. [uncertain]

swither[4] **&c** ['swɪðər] *vi, of weather* be very hot, swelter *la19-, now Sh Kcdn*. *n* a swelter, a great heat *20-, now Sh*. ~**el &c** a jellyfish, medusa (from its stinging properties) *20-, now Fif*. [Norw dial *svidra* feel a smarting pain, ON *sviðra* burn, singe]

switter *vi* struggle like a drowning person, splash or flounder about; *of water* plash, ripple *la17-e20*. [only Sc; see SND]

swivel *see* SWEEL[3]

swoch *see* SOUCH

swoft *see* SWIFT

swolit *see* SWALLIE[1]

swoll *see* SWALL

swolly *see* SWALLIE[1]

swome *see* SOOM[1]

swoof *vi* make a rustling, swishing sound, as the wind etc *la16-, now Sh*. [prob onomat var of SOUCH w infl f SOWFF]

swoom *see* SOOM[1]

swoop *see* SWEEP

swoor *see* SWEER

sword *see* SWURD

sworl see SWIRL
swouch see SOUCH
swoul see SWEEL[3]
swounger see SWINGER
swour see SWEER
swourd see SWURD
swuff see SWIFF
swuft see SWIFT
swull see SWILL
swurd &c 19-, now Ork, **sword &c** la16-;
swerd &c la14-19, **swourd &c** 16-20,
swird la19-e20, **sourd &c** 18-e20 [Ork
swΛrd; Sh Ork swird; *swɛrd, *swurd, *surd] n
1 = sword la14-. **2** (1) the crossbar in a
barred gate or between chair- or table-legs 19-,
now Cai. (2) a slat of wood or tang of metal on
the end of a ladder, used to prevent it from
slipping la20-, Per Fif.
~ **belt** a belt from which a sword in its scabbard is suspended 16-. ~ **dance** the Highland
dance (HIELAND), usu solo, consisting of a series of
steps between swords laid cross-wise on the
ground 19-. **sword dollar** a silver coin of
James VI (of 30 shillings SCOTS) with a sword
on the reverse 19. ~ **slipper** a sword-sharp-
ener 16-19.
swure see SWEER
swurl see SWIRL
swuther see SWITHER[1]
swutten see SWEET[1]
swy(e) see SWEY
swyle see SWAIL[1], SWEEL[2]
swype see SWAP[2], SWEEP
swythare see SYCHARE
swythe see SWITH
sy see SAE[1]
sybow &c; sebowe &c la16-e19, **syboe** 19-,
sybae &c 18-19, **sybie &c** la16 ['səibə,
'səibɪ; C also 'saɪbɪ; Bwk S also 'səivɪ; *'sɪbɪ, &c]
n the spring onion; orig a different kind of onion
la16-, Gen except Sh Ork.
~ **tail** the green shoots of the young onion
la18-19. [only Sc; centralF ciboule, northernF
chiboule, L cepula a little onion; cf obs and dial
Eng chibol &c a kind of onion and ModF ciboule
chives]
sychare &c,   swythare;   sythware
[*?sɪ'x(w)er, *?saɪ'x(w)er] n a period or point of
time la14. [nME siquare. OED sychare,
siquare, swythare]
sycht [*sɪxt] n, in pl the front parts of a gown,
coat etc e16, only Sc. [obscure]
sye[1] &c; sey &c la18-, **sie &c** 19- [saɪ] vt pass
(liquid) through a sieve, drain, filter 18-, now
local.
n a strainer or sieve for liquids, esp for milk
la19-, now NE, WC.
syer &c = n, la19-, now Sh-Per.
sey clout a piece of gauze etc, usu stretched
across a round wooden frame, used for straining
liquid 20-, now Sh-N. ~ **dish** 18-, now NE,
nEC, ~ **milk** 18-, now NE a milk-strainer.

~-**sowans &c** a strainer for SOWANS la19-20.
[OE síon, ON sía strain, filter; cf also ON sía,
MDu sye a strainer; cf SYTHE]
sye[2] [saɪ] n, chf in pl chives 19-, now NE Ags.
[reduced f obs Eng cive; for loss of -v- cf GIE,
HAE[1]]
syith see SITH
syke &c,   sike n **1** a small stream or
water-course, esp one in a hollow or on flat,
boggy ground, and often dry in summer la14-,
now Bwk Lnk S. **2** a marshy hollow, esp one
with a stream, a cleft in the ground 18-, now
Dmf Rox.
sykie &c of ground full of sluggish rivulets, soft,
boggy, though dry in summer la18-e19. [ScL
sicum (e13); nME; cf s and midlEng sitch; OE síc,
ON sík]
syle &c vt put up a ceiling over, roof la16-e18,
e20 (Abd). [cf CIEL. OED syllit]
syllab &c ['sɪləb, -əp] n = syllable 16-e20.
vi divide words into syllables, esp in teaching a
child to read 18-e19.
sylour &c [*'səilør, *-ur, *-ər] n a silour, ceiling
la15-e16. [OED silour]
sylvan n **1** = sylvan, a wood spirit e17. **2** ? a
forest tree, shrub etc e17.
symbolic, symbolical adj = symbolic(al).
~ **delivery, possession** etc, law the transference of HERITABLE property by the delivery of
symbols, eg earth and stone la17-e19.
symly see SEEM
symphioun, sumphion n = symphan, sym-
phony, name for various musical instruments
la16, only Sc.
synd &c, seynd la16; **syne &c** la18- [səin(d)]
vt **1** now freq ~ **out** rinse (a container etc), swill,
wash out 18-, now Cai C-S. **2** wash (the face,
clothes etc), give a quick swill to (an object) by
drawing it through water la15-, now Cai C-S. **3**
wash (food) down with drink, swill (something)
away or out with water etc la18-, now C-S.
n a washing or rinsing out, a swill, a hasty wash
la18-, now Cai C-S.
~**ins** rinsings, slops, swill 19. [nME sind; prob
Scand]
syndrely, syndrnes see SINDER
syne &c; sin &c, sen la14-e18, **sene &c**
la14-e18; **seen** la19-e20, NE [adv, n səin; NE also
sin; adv 3 also sɪn; conj, prep sɪn, sən] adv **1** thereupon, directly after, next, afterwards la14-, Gen
except Sh Ork. **2** inferential in that case, so, then
la19-, now NE-nEC: 'and syne, ye're no gaun'. **3**
retrospective ago, since, before now 16-, Gen except
Sh Ork. **4** prospective from then, since, thereafter
la19-, now NE, nEC, SW.
n, governed by preps that time, then la19-, now Sh:
'fae syne'.
conj **1** since, from the time that la14-, now NE-S.
2 only sin, sen since, because, seeing that la14-,
now Sh NE Fif.
prep, now chf **sin** since (the time of) la14-.
sinsyne &c, sensyne &c la16-17 since then,

from or after that time *la14-, now local.* [ME, reduced f ME *sithen,* OE *siþþan;* see also *lang syne* (LANG)]

syne *see* SYND

synod &c *n* **1** = synod. **2** *Presbyterian Churches* a court intermediate between the PRESBYTERY and the *General Assembly* (GENERAL); in the smaller churches with no *General Assembly,* the SYNOD is the supreme court *18-.*
~**al** *n* a synodal assembly, a synod *la16, only Sc.*

syon &c *n* a kind of coat *e16, only Sc.*

sype &c, sipe *v* **1** *vi* = SEEP *18-, now local.* **2** *vti, of a container* drip, leak *18-, now Sh Ork NE, S.* **3** *vt* cause to drip or ooze; draw liquid from, drain; drip-dry (clothes) *la19-, now Sh Ork Cai Dmf.*
n **1** an oozing, leakage *la15-, now local Sh-Fif.* **2** (1) a small trickle of water, a small spring *19.* (2) a drip *la20-, local Sh-Ags.* **3** a small quantity of liquid, that which drips from an emptied bottle *19-, now Sh Ork.*

sypin, sypit soaked *19-, now Sh Abd.* **sypins** oozings, leakage; the last drops from a container *19-, now Ork NE Fif.* [chf Sc; prob development of OE *sipian* soak, be soaked; *cf* SEEP]

syre *see* SYVER

SYS *see* CERTIFICATE

Systeus *see* CISTEUS

syte, site, sytt *la16* [*sǝit] *n* sorrow, grief, suffering *la15-18.* [ME]

syth &c *15-17;* **cythe** *la16* [*v* *?saɪð; *n* *?sǝiθ] *v* **1** *vt* satisfy, give satisfaction to *15-16.* **2** *vi* be satisfied *e17.*
n satisfaction, compensation *la16.*
~**ment** [*?'sǝiθmǝnt] satisfaction, compensation, indemnification *16-18.*
get one's heart's syth *or* **syte of** *or* **on** be revenged on *la17-e18.* [only Sc; aphetic f ASSYTH]

sythe &c *la18-;* **syth &c** *la16-18* [saɪð; *nEC also* ?saɪd] *vt* strain (*esp* milk) through a sieve, filter *la16-, now Per.*
n a (milk-)strainer, filter *la16-, now Per.* [ME *cyth; cf* SYE[1]. OED *sithe*]

sythware *see* SYCHARE

sytt *see* SYTE

syver &c *16-,* **syre &c** *16-e20* ['saɪvǝr, saɪr; *NE, S* sǝir] *n* **1** a ditch, drain, water-channel, *specif* a (covered-in) stone-lined field-drain *16-, now Ork N Wgt.* **2** a street gutter *18-, C-S.* **3** the opening of the drain-trap in a street gutter, *freq* including the grating which covers it *19-, Gen except Sh Ork.* [chf Sc; prob F dial form f OF *essavier, essevour* a drainage channel; *cf* Eng *sewer*]

T

't *see* IT[1]

ta *see* TAE[1], TAE[3], TAE[4], TAK, THE

tab *n* **1** = tab. **2** *chf* **tabbie** a cigarette stub *20-*, *now NE nEC.*

tabacha *see* TOBACCO

table &c *n* **1** = table *la16-*. **2** *church, freq* **the ~(s)** the Communion table; Communion; a series of dispensings of the SACRAMENT by relays *la16-20*. **3** *usu in pl* the four boards or committees, consisting of representatives of nobles, MINISTERS, LAIRDS and burgesses which framed the National Covenant (COVENANT) *17-*, *latterly hist*. **4** *mining* a platform or plate on which coals are screened and picked *la19-*, *now Fif wLoth WC*. *v* **1** *vt* appoint to a certain duty by entering someone's name on a list *16*. **2** lay (something) for consideration before a meeting etc *18-*. **3** *vi, law* LODGE a SUMMONS before a court as a preliminary to its being called *16-*.
tabling *masonry* the stone coping of a wall or gable *18-*.
~ cloot = tablecloth *la19-*. **~ heid** the surface of a table, a table-top *la19-*, *local Cai-Lnk*. **~ stone &c 1** a flat stone *la16*. **2** *also* **~ tombstone** a horizontal gravestone *la18-*.
serve (the) ~s *of a clergyman* administer the SACRAMENT; *of the* ELDERS distribute the elements to the TABLES (*n* 2) *18-e19*.

tablet &c ['tablət, 'teblət] *n* **1** = tablet *16-*. **2** a kind of SWEETIE, made of butter, sugar etc, *now usu* of the consistency of a stiff, friable fudge *18-*.

tabour &c, toober; tober ['tabər, 'tubər, 'tobər] *vt* beat, thrash *19-*, C, S. [Eng *tabour* (beat on) a drum]

tabron &c, talburn &c *la15-16* [*'taburn, *'tabrən] *n* = taborn, tabour, a drum *16*. [OED *taborn*]

tabulet [*?'tabølet] *adj* panelled *la16*. [only Sc. OED *tabulate* (adj)]

tac &c *n* = tact *la19-*, *now Sh NE*.

tach *see* TASH[1], TYACH

tache *see* TASH[2]

tacht &c [taxt] *adj* = taut *19-*, *now N*. [appar ME *taught, toʒt*]

tacit relocation *see* RELOCATION

taciturnity &c *n* **1** = taciturnity. **2** *law* the silence of a creditor in regard to a debt or obligation, which can be pleaded in extinction of it, as implying that the claim has been satisfied or abandoned *la16-*.

tack[1] &c *n* **1** = tack, a nail etc *16-*. **2** a 'stitch' of clothing *20*, *Uls*.
vt = tack, stitch temporarily.
tongue-~it &c *lit and fig* tongue-tied, having a speech impediment, dumb, mute *la17-*, *Gen except Sh Ork*. **~le &c** join, unite, *esp* loosely or slackly *la19-e20*.
hing by a ~ hang by a thread *19-*. **keep ~ till** keep pace with, keep up with *la20-*, *Kcdn Ags Fif*.

tack[2] &c *n* **1** a lease, tenancy, *esp* the leasehold tenure of a farm, mill, mining or fishing rights, tax- or toll-collecting etc; the period of tenure *la14-*, *now rare*. **2** the farm or piece of land held on a lease *15-*, *now local Sh-Wgt, only Sc*. **3** a customary payment levied by a feudal SUPERIOR etc *la16*. **4** an agreement, bargain *la18-e20*, *only Sc*. **5** a specific period of time, *eg* a lease (of life), a spell (of weather) *18-*, *now local Ork-Loth*.
~ie = *n* 2, *la19-*, *N*.
takkar a person who grants a TACK (*n* 1) *la16*.
~-duty duty payable on land held in leasehold; rent paid by a *tacksman* 2, *17-*, *now Ork*.
~sman 1 a person who holds a TACK[2], a tenant or lessee *la15-*, *now Mry Bnf Kcdn*. **2** a chief tenant, *freq* a relative of the landowner, who leased land directly from him and sublet it to lesser tenants *la16-19*, *chf Highl*. **~swoman** a female tenant or lessee *la16-18*.
in ~ (**and assedation**) on lease, on leasehold terms *18*. [chf Sc and nEng extension of TAK; *cf* ON *taka* a taking; revenue; tenure of land]

tack, tacken *see* TAK

tacket &c *n* a small nail, *latterly esp* a hobnail, used to stud the soles of shoes etc *16-*.
~ed, ~y studded with TACKETS, hobnailed *la19-*: '*tackety boots*'. **~y jock** a shoemaker's last *la19-*, *local Stlg-Ayr*.
~ boot &c a hobnailed boot *la19-*.

tackle &c; taickle &c *16-20 n, vti* = tackle *la14-*.
~ to &c set to work vigorously on *la19-e20*.

taddy *n* a kind of snuff *la19-e20*. [f Taddy and Co., the London makers]

tadge *see* TARGE

tae[1] &c *16-*, **toe; ta** *16* [te] *n* **1** = toe *16-*. **2** a prong of a fork, rake, salmon spear etc *la18-*. **3** one of the thongs at the end of a *tawse* (TAW[1]) *19-*, *now Sh Ork N*. **4** *only* **toe,** *golf* the point or fore-part of a club *la19-*.
tae-bit the iron toe-plate on the front of the sole of boots *la19-*, *local Sh-Lnk*. **tae('s) length** the length of one's toe; *fig* a very short distance *19-*, *now local Sh-Wgt*.
fecht with one's ain taes be very quarrelsome *la20-*, *Sh Cai Abd*.

tae[2] *n, fishing* a section of deep-sea line, with a specified number of hooks attached (*usu* 100 or 120) *19-*, *now Fif*. [var of Eng *tie*]

tae[3] &c *18-*; **ta** *la14-16* [te] *adj, freq contrasted with* TITHER, **his** etc (*e16*) *or* **the** (*la14-*) one (of two). [nME *ta*; *cf* TANE and AE. OED *to* (adj)]

tae[4] &c *19-*, **to; ta** *16-*, **too** *la14-e19*, **te** *18-20*, **ti** *19-e20*, **tee** *19-*, *now NE*, **tu** *19-20* [*unstressed* (*prep, conj*) tɪ, tə; *Cai* ti; *stressed* (*adv, comb*) tø, te; *N* ti] *prep* **1** = to *la14-*. **2** (1) *as sign of infin* (*where* Eng *would use gerund or an abstract noun with a different prep*) *18-*, *now Sh NE, WC*: '*incapable to walk*'; '*I know him to see him*'. (2) *omitted as sign of infin where* Eng *retains it, 18-*: '*he knows better* *than say that'.* **3** as an accusation against, to the detriment of *18-19*: '*she never heard anything to him*'. **4** *of food* with, for, to the accompaniment of *19-*: '*an egg to his tea*'. **5** *in various idioms where Eng uses a different prep etc*: (1) *with verbs of looking at 19-*, *now Sh N*: '*look to that picture*'; (2) by: (a) **to surname** *e16*; (b) **to trade** *etc, 18-*; (c) *referring to paternity* with (a specified person) as the father *18-*: '*she had a child to her cousin*'; (3) compared with *la19-*: '*I'm but a puir man to you*'; (4) for: (a) on behalf of, for the use of, in the service of *18-*: '*he worked to Mr G.*'; (b) as (being), in the capacity or relationship of *19-e20*: '*having had an outlaw to his father*'; (c) **easy** ~ *la19-*, *Sh Abd Ags*: '*it's easy to you to do it*'; (5) of: (a) concerning, about, with reference to *la18-e20*: '*have you any word to your brother?*'; (b) *expressing family relationship, 18-*: '*son to the Sheriff*'. (6) (hatred, wrath etc) towards, against *la19-e20*: '*he had a triple wrath to his son.*'

adv **1** = to *la14-*. **2** expressing assent or favour *la15*: '*sum said to and sum fra*'. **3** *implying direction towards, closeness or contact* (1) *of a door* so as to shut or close, closed *18-*: '*close the door to*'; (2) close, on, together, in contact *la19-e20*, *chf NE*. **4** too, also, as well *la14-*.

conj **1** = to, while *la14*. **2** till, until *la19-*, *now C, S*.

tobackie [təˈbaki] one of the actions in a children's ball-game *20-*, *Edb Renfr.* ~**-bread** an extra loaf etc given free as a discount after the purchase of a certain amount *la19-*, *now Stlg Ayr Rox.* ~**-come** *n* **1** (1) arrival, approach *e16*. (2) means of access *e16*, *only Sc.* **2** a profit on resale; (an extra loaf etc as) a discount *20-*, *Fif*; cf ~*-bread.* *vt* come to *la16*, *only Sc.* ~**-coming &c** coming, advent *16.* ~**-fall &c** **1** a lean-to porch or outhouse *15-*, *now local Sh-SW.* **2** an addition, accretion; an extra charge, burden etc *19-e20.* **3** *freq* ~**-fall &c o the day** *or* **nicht** evening, dusk *18-e19.* **to-gang** go away *la16.* **to-hang** append *la15.* ~**-look &c** an outlook, prospect, something to look forward to *la16-e19*, *only Sc.* ~**-name** an additional name, a nickname or additional surname, *esp* one used in a community where many have the same surname *la16-*, *now NE.* ~**-put** affix, add *la14-e15.* ~**-set** *vt* affix *la14-15.* *n, only* **teeset &c** *fishing* the first of a fleet of lines to be *shot* (SHUIT) from a boat; the man whose turn it is to *shoot* the first line and to whom its catch is assigned *20-*, *NE.* **to-stack** *pt* stuck, adhered *la16.*

be ~ have gone to *19-*: '*arena ye tae yir bed?*' **be tee** be up to schedule *20-*, *NE.* **weel tee &c** up to time, well in hand *20-*, *NE.* [*cf* TILL[1]]

tae *see* DEY[2], TEA

ta'en *see* TAK

taffel &c *n* a (small) table *la16-e20.* [only Sc; prob Du *tafel*]

taffie &c *19-*, *now S*; **toffee** *n* = toffee *19-*.

~ **apple &c** an apple dipped in slightly candied sugar and held on a stick to be eaten *20-*.

taffie join a social gathering of young people who club together to buy treacle to make toffee *la19-e20.*

taffle &c *la19-*, *now Per*, **tuffle** *19-*, *now Ayr* [*chf nEC* 'tafl, 'tefl; *SW*, *S* 'tʌfl] *vt* handle roughly, ruffle, rumple, disarrange. [prob onomat]

taft &c *17-*, *only Sc*, **toft &c** *la14-* *n* **1** = toft, a homestead and its land etc *la14-*, *now Ags Stlg Fif*, *freq in Sh Ork place-names.* **2** *freq* **plant** ~ a small patch of enclosed ground for rearing cabbages etc *la18-20*, *Cai.*

~**ing &c** = TAFT (*n* 1); the tenancy of a TAFT *la18-e19.*

taft dyke a (turf) wall round a TAFT; a turf wall *in gen*, *la18-e19*, *SW.*

taft *see* THAFT

tag &c *n* **1** = tag *16-*. **2** *specif* a perforated leather buckle-strap *16-18.* **3** a long thin strip or slice of flesh or tissue *18-*, *now Sh.* **4** the strap used for punishment in schools, the *tawse* (TAW[1]) *19-*, *NE Ags.* **5** a skinny, worn-out horse *20-*, *Bnf Abd.* **6** *also* ~ **hole** a weaving fault in cloth, producing a hole where there should be pattern *la20-*, *Stlg Fif Ayr.*

vt **1** = tag *16-*. **2** beat with a TAG (*n* 4) *la19-*, *NE.*

~**gie &c** *of a cow* having a white-tipped tail *la16-19.* ~**ing iron &c** a tailor's tool for tagging cloth *e15*, *only Sc.*

tagrag(g)ery a hotch-potch, a mass of bits and pieces *19.*

be in the ~ be oppressed with hard work *20-*, *NE.*

taghairm *n* a form of (magical) divination said to have been practised in *the Highlands* (HIELAND) *la18-*, *hist.* [ScGael; IrGael *toghairm* a summons, invocation]

taibet &c; **tebbit &c,** **tibit &c,** **tapet &c** ['tebɪt, 'tep–, 'tɛb–, 'tɛp–] *n, freq in pl* physical sensation, feeling; energy, strength *19.*

~**less 1** without feeling, numb; dull, lethargic, spiritless *la18-*, *now local Abd-Bwk.* **2** heedless, foolish, silly *la18-e20.* [obscure]

taickle *see* TACKLE

taid &c, **toad &c** *la17-*; **ted &c** *20* [ted] *n* **1** = toad *la15-*, *Gen except Sh Ork.* **2** term of endearment, *esp* for a child or a young woman *la18-*, *now NE Ags.* **3** a sheep-tick *19-*, *WC, SW Rox.* ~**ie** a little toad *la17-*.

taigle &c; **teagle &c** *17-e19* ['tegl] *v* **1** *vt* (en)tangle, confuse, muddle *la16-*, *now Cai C, S.* **2** hinder, get in the way of, harass *17-*, *now C.* **3** confound (in an argument), bamboozle; perplex *la19-*, *now Loth Dmf.* **4** *vi* delay, linger, dawdle, hang about *la18-*, *now Stlg WC Kcb.* **5** *vti* drag (the feet) slowly and heavily, walk along slowly or haltingly *la19-e20.*

n a tangle, muddle *20-*, *now nEC Wgt Rox.*

taigled &c tired, weary, harassed *19-*, *now local sEC-Rox.* ~**ment** (a cause of) delay *e19.*

~**some** &c **1** time-consuming, causing delay
19-, now local Stlg-Wgt. **2** tiring, tedious *20-,
local sEC-Rox.*
~ **the cleek 1** *mining* hinder the working of a
pit *la19-, now Fif.* **2** *fig* hinder progress *la20-,
local Fif-Ayr.* ~ **wi** *etc* hang around, follow
about (*esp* a woman) *19.* [nME *tagle* entangle,
prob of Scand origin]
taik &c *n* **1** *nautical* = tack *18-, now N Fif.* **2** a
stroll, saunter, *freq* **tak a** ~ *20-, Sh N.* **3** a
mood, humour, disposition *20-, Sh Abd.*
vi **1** *nautical* = tack *18-, now N Fif.* **2** stroll,
saunter; move unobtrusively *20-, N.*
taiken &c *la16-20,* **token** &c *17-;* **takin** &c
la14-e19 ['tekən; *Abd also* 'tjɑkən] *n* **1** = token
la15-. **2** *usu* **token,** *church* (1) a metal badge
worn by beggars to indicate a right to beg
within a parish *la14-e18;* (2) a small piece of
stamped metal used as a pass to the Communion service in a Presbyterian (and sometimes
in an Episcopal) church (now replaced by a
printed card) *la16-e20.*
takinar &c *a* portent *e16.*
tail &c *n* **1** = tail *la14-.* **2** a long narrow piece
of land jutting out from a larger piece, *esp* from
a CROFT etc *la15-e20.* **3** *mining* the end or edge
of water in a mine *la19-, now Fif Ayr.* **4** *damask
weaving* the horizontal section of the cords in the
harness of a loom *e19.* **5** *in pl* onion leaves
la19-, now Loth S. **6** the end (of a period of
time or of an activity) *la18-, now NE, C.* **7** the
retinue or entourage of a *Highland* (HIELAND)
CHIEF *19-, now hist.* **8** a prostitute *20-, C.*
~**er(t)** &c a hand turnip-cutter *20-, Ork N.*
~**ie** (**day**) **2** April, when children fix paper
tails with various messages to the backs of
unsuspecting victims *20-, local Ork-Rox.*
~**-dam** the tail-race of a mill *la17-, now sEC.*
~**-ill** a supposed disease of the tail in cattle *19.*
~**-lead** = ~**-dam,** *la18-, now Bnf.* ~**sman** a
sawmill worker who takes and sorts the timber
from the saw *la20-, Gen except Sh Ork.* ~**-net** the
herring-net first to be *shot* (SHUIT) and therefore
the farthest from the boat *la19-, now Sh Cai.*
~**-toddle** sexual intercourse *la18.*
~ **of level** *mining* the lower or discharging end
of a drainage shaft etc *la19-, now Fif Ayr.*
taillie *see* TAILYIE
tailor &c; **tailyour** &c *15-e20, only Sc,* **teylor**
&c *20-, NE-S,* **tylor** &c *18-e20* ['tɔilər, 'tɔiljər;
Sh 'tiljər; *Rox* 'teljər] *n* = tailor *15-.*
~**'s gartens** &c ribbon-grass *la19-, local
Abd-Rox.*
tailyie &c *la15-,* **tailye** &c *la14-19;* **talȝe** &c
la14-15, **tailz(i)e** &c *16-20,* **taillie** ['tel(j)ɪ,
'tɔil(j)ɪ] *n* **1** a cut or slice of meat for boiling or
roasting, *now esp* of pork *la15-, now Bwk Rox.* **2**
arrangement, fixture *e15.* **3** an account, reckoning *la15-e16.* **4** *law* an entail, the settlement
of HERITABLE property on a specified line of
heirs *la14-18.*

vt **1** cut (to shape) *la16.* **2** determine, appoint,
arrange *la14-15.* **3** keep account or tally of
la15-e16. **4** *law* determine or prescribe the succession to (an estate), entail *la14-e19.* [only
Sc; OF *tailler* (*v*), *tailliee* (*n*) cut]
tailyour *see* TAILOR
tailȝevey &c [*'teljɪvi] *vi, n* rock, reel from side
to side *16.* [only *Sc*; obscure. OED *tailyevey*]
tailz(i)e *see* TAILYIE
taim *see* TUME
tainchel *see* TINCHEL
tainghle &c [*?'teŋxl] *vt* harass, weary with
hard work *e19.* [see SND]
taings *see* TANGS
taint *see* TINT
tair *see* TEAR²
taird *see* TUIRD
tairge *n* = targe, a shield *16, only Sc.*
tairge *see* TARGE
tairm *see* TERM
tairrie *see* TARRY
tairt &c [tert, tɛrt] *n* **1** = tart *la17-.* **2** a girlfriend *la19-20.*
taisch &c [*taɪʃ] *n* a vision seen in *second sight*
(SECOND), *esp* an apparition of a person about to
die *la18-e19.* [Gael *taibhse* ['taɪʃ(ə)] an apparition, ghost]
taise *see* TEASE
taisel *see* TOSSEL
taisle &c *19-;* **teazle** &c *la18-19,* **tassel** &c
18-e19 ['tezl; *'tesl] *vti* **1** entangle, mix up, put
or get into disorder *la19-, now local Loth-SW.* **2**
vt toss, throw about; stir up, turn over (hay)
19-, now Ags Kcb. **3** tease, irritate, vex *19-, now
Kcb.*
n **1** a buffeting or knocking about; a severe
brush or tussle *18-, now Kcb.* **2** a vexing or
teasing; a bamboozling with questions *19-, now
Kcb.* [frequentative of *taise* (TEASE), perh w
infl f Eng *teasel*]
taistrel &c *n* a gawky, slovenly, unmethodical
person *19-20, Gall Rox.* [obscure]
tait¹ &c *17-,* **tate;** **tet** &c *19-e20,* **teat** &c
la18-e20, **tit** *20, NE* [tet] *n* **1** a small tuft or
bundle of hair, wool etc *16-, now local Sh-Kcb.*
2 a tuft of grass, a small bundle or wisp of hay
or corn *la18-, now local Sh-SW.* **3** a small
amount (of something); *also* **a** (**wee**) ~ somewhat *18-.*
vt pull or pluck out (fibres etc), tease out *la19-,
now Sh.* [prob Scand; *cf* Icel *tæta* a shred, cognate w TAUT]
tait² *adj* lively, active, nimble *la15-e16.* [ME
teyte, ON *teitr* glad, cheerful; *cf* TATE]
taiver¹ &c *19-,* **taver** ['tevər] *v* **1** *vi* wander
about aimlessly or idly; dally, waste time *la16-,
now Stlg Lnk.* **2** wander in mind or speech,
rave *19-, now Per.* **3** *vt* annoy, irritate; bewilder with talk or questioning *la19-20.*
n, in pl idle, foolish talk *la19-, now Stlg Ayr.*

~t **1** exhausted with wandering *e16*. **2** bewildered, mentally confused, *esp* through exhaustion or harassment *16-*, *now Per-Fif*. [only Sc; see SND]

taiver² **&c** ['tevər; *Ork also* 'tɑvər; **'tafər*] *n*, *in pl* rags, tatters, shreds, *freq of meat* **boiled to ~s** *la18-*, *now Sh Ork*. [only Sc; prob Scand]

tak **&c**, **take &c**; **tack** *la16-18*, **ta** *la14-16*, **tay** *la14* [tak; *sEC*, *S* tek; **te*] *v*, *pt also* **tuk &c** *la14-e20*, **teuk** *la18-e20*, **tyeuk** *18-19*, *chf Abd* [tøk, tuk; *WC Uls* t(j)ʌk; *NE *tjuk*]. *ptp also* **tane &c**, **ta'en** *18-e20*, **teine &c** *la16-e20*, **teen &c** *18-*, *now Sh N*, **tone** *la15-e16*; **tacken &c** *18-*, **tooken &c** *la19-*, *now Abd Bwk Dnbt* [ten; *Sh N* tin; 'takən, 'tukən; **'tʌkən*; *Fif *'tøkən*; *only in verse *ton*] **1** *vti* = take *la14-*. **2** *vt* catch (one's foot) on; *of the foot etc* be caught on or tripped by *18-*, *now local NE-WC*. **3 ~ someone (up) to** *or* **over**, *of water* come up as far on a person as, reach **up to** (a certain height) on a person *la18-*. **4** *vr* check oneself, stop oneself from doing or saying something which one might later regret *la18-*, *now NE*. **5** *vt*, *freq of a woman* marry, take in marriage *18-*. **6** (1) lease, take on lease *19-*. (2) take over (a crop) for the grazing of livestock *la19-*, *NE Per*. **7** require or accept a promise etc in a formal matter from, *freq* **~ someone bound** *etc 18-e19*. **8** require the utmost strength and effort from *19-*, *now Fif*. **9** make for, resort to *19-e20*. **10** *vi* (1) catch fire *la20-*, *local Sh-Dmf*. (2) burn brightly; gleam, glow like fire *20-*, *Cai*.

n **1** an act of seizing, a capture, catch *20-*. **2** what has been taken or captured, *specif* a catch or haul of fish *la16-*, *now local N-WC*. **3** a state of excitement, agitation, rage *etc 19-*, *now S*. **4** a state of growth, the sprouting of a crop *la20-*, *local N-Rox*.

taen(-**like**) surprised, embarrassed, disconcerted; bewitched *19-*, *now Stlg WC*. **taker-up 1** a PRECENTOR *la16*, *only Sc*. **2** a person who receives rents etc *e17*. **takkie &c** the game of tig; the pursuer in the game *la19-*, *NE Ags*. **be on the ~** *of fish* rise readily to the bait *20-*. **tak-a'** a school attendance officer *20*, *Bnf Abd*. **~ about &c 1** take care of, look after; handle, manage *la18-*, *Sh Ork NE*. **2** prepare (a corpse) for burial *20-*, *Ork Ross NE*. **3** secure (a crop), harvest successfully *la18-*, *now Sh NE*. **~ aff &c 1** take measurements for (new clothes) *18-e19*. **2** take after, resemble *la19-*, *now Sh Ags*. **~ again** take back, withdraw (a promise etc) *18*. **~ the air** *or* **lift** *of frost* rise, disperse *19-*, *now Sh Ork Cai*. **~ awa 1** eat or drink up, eat heartily, toss off (liquor) *19-*, *now Sh Ork*. **2** *of the fairies* take away (a human child) and substitute one of their own, *chf* **ta'en-awa** a fairy changeling *19-20*. **~ back** return *19-*, *now Sh*. **~ someone's breath** *or* **wind** choke someone *la19-*, *local Sh-Kcb*. **~ one's death** get one's death, die *20-*, *Sh Abd Ags*. **~ the door after, to** *or* **wi oneself, ~**

the door tae leave a room, closing a door behind one *la18-*, *local Sh-Dmf*. **~ doun &c 1** impair in health or strength, weaken, cause to lose weight *19-*, *now local Sh-SW*. **2** reduce the potency of (spirits), dilute *la20-*, *Sh Per Kcb*. **3** make (one garment) from another *la18-*, *now Sh Kcb*. **4** reduce in circumstances, impoverish, bankrupt *la19-*, *Ork N*. **~ one's hand aff** (**someone's face** *etc*) slap, smack someone *20-*, *now Abd*. **~ on** (*la14-*) *or* **in** (*16-*) **hand 1** undertake (**to**) *la14-*. **2** *chf* **~ upon hand** *in prohibitions* dare, presume **to** *la14-e17*. **I ~ on hand** I dare say *la14-16*. **~ someone's head** go to someone's head, make someone giddy *la19-*, *now Per*. **~ ill** *or* **naeweel** become ill *19-*, *now local*. **~ in 1** house (farm stock), bring under cover *la19-*, *Sh N Per*. **2** dismantle (a cornstack) and carry the sheaves to be threshed *la19-*. **3** arrest, take into custody *20-*, *local Ork-Kcb*. **4** *of a boat* let in (water), leak *la16-*, *now Sh N Per*. **5** bring in, welcome (a new day, year etc) *20-*, *Hebrides Highl NE*. **6** catch up with, overtake *19-20*, *Bnf Abd*. **7** get over (a road), cover (a distance) *la18-*, *NE*. **~ in about** take (a person) in hand, curb, discipline *19-*, *now Sh NE*. **tak o** take after, resemble *19-*, *now Ork Cai*. **~ o it** resign oneself to something, take the consequences, 'lump it' *la19-*, *NE*. **~ on 1** = take on, put on (clothing) *la16*. **2** = take on (board) *la16-*. **3** take up (arms) *la16*, *only Sc*. **4** buy on credit or account *la18-*. **5** affect physically *la19-*, *local NE-wLoth*. **6** have (a person) on, chaff *la19-*, *local NE-Slk*. **7** *with infin* start, begin *19-*, *now Cai*. **8** get excited or emotional, be worked up; mope *19-*. **9** take the consequences, make the best of it *la19-*, *now Sh*. **~ on with** *chf in passive* take a liking to, be attracted by *20-*, *Gen except Sh Ork*. **~ out 1** enrol in (a class) or for (a subject) at a university *la20-*. **2** drink up, drain (a glass) *la18-*, *now Sh*. **~ tae &c oneself** acknowledge the truth of (an accusation), feel guilt or remorse, be sensitive about *19-*, *now local*. **~ up 1** (1) = take up. (2) *specif* take (a collection) at a meeting *20-*. **2** take (land) into occupation *la15*. **3** lead (the praise) in church, act as PRECENTOR *la16-e20*, *only Sc*. **4** raise or lift (one's foot) to kick *la18-*, *Abd Ags*. **5** *chf vi*, *of a school or college* reopen after a holiday *18-*. **6** *vt* understand, get the meaning of *19-*, *now local Sh-wLoth*. **7** *vr* improve in conduct or character, pull oneself together *la19-*, *now Per Rox*. **8** *vi* run into debt, live on credit *la19-*, *now local Ork-wLoth*. **9** *of wind* rise, begin to blow *20-*, *Sh SW*. **~ up about** *or* **wi** *in passive* be charmed by, find agreeable *la19-*, *local Sh-Kcb*. **~ up house** set up house; become a householder *17-*, *only Sc*. **~ wi 1** *freq of paternity* acknowledge, admit one's connection with; own, acquiesce in *18-*, *now NE Ags*. **2** find agreeable, take kindly to *la18-*, *now local Sh-Dmf*.

tak *see* TAUK

take *see* TAK

takin *see* TAIKEN

takkie *see* TAK

talbart &c, tawbart ['tɑbərt] *n* = tabard *e16*. [only Sc. OED *tabard*]

talburn *see* TABRON

talch *see* TAUCH

tald *see* TELL

tale &c [tel; *Sh Ork* til] *n* **1** = tale *la14-*. **2** a reckoning, calculation; a number *la14, 19*.

~**sman** a storyteller; the source for a story or statement *la15, la17-, now Sh*. ~**-pyot &c** a telltale *19-, now local Per-S*.

by *or* **with my** *etc* ~ according to my etc story, as I etc would have others believe *19-, now local Sh-Wgt*.

talian iron *see* TALLIE

talieduce &c [*'talɪ'dus] *n* = taille-douce, a kind of metal engraving *la17-e18*. [OED *tali-douce*]

Tallie &c ['talɪ] *n, now joc or disparaging, esp of a seller of ice cream, fish and chips etc* an Italian *19-*.

t~ iron, talian &c ['talɪ(ə)n] **iron** an Italian or goffering iron *20-, now Fif Lnk Rox*. [reduced f Eng *Italian*]

tallon, tallow, tally *see* TAUCH

talȝe *see* TAILYIE

Tam *n* **1** = Tom. **2 t~** a bite, a morsel of food *e20*.

t~ trot a kind of toffee *19-e20, Rox*.

~ **o' Shanter** a man's round, flat-crowned woollen cap, *freq* with a *tourie* (TOUR[1]), once regularly worn by the Scottish peasantry; *later* (*e20*) a kind of beret worn by women and girls *19-* [f the hero of Burns' poem, described as wearing such a cap; *cf* TAMMIE]. ~ **o' tae end** a kind of large HAGGIS; *now* the skin in which a HAGGIS is stuffed *19-, SW*. **trimmlin ~ 1** potted head *la19-, now Ags Per Lnk*. **2** a fruit jelly *20-, now EC, WC*.

tam *see* NICKIE-TAM, WALTAM

tame *n, freq* **tamet &c** the line on a fishing rod; a handline with one or two hooks *20, Bnf Abd Ags*. [see SND]

Tammie &c *n* **1** = Tommy. **2 t~** = *Tam o' Shanter* (TAM) *20-*. **3 t~** a loaf of coarse brown bread; food, provisions *19-e20*.

~**-a'thing** = *Johnnie a'thing* (JOHN) *la19-, Fif Loth S*. **t~ book** a shop account-book recording goods supplied on credit *la19-20*. ~ **cheekie &c** = ~ *norrie, 19-20, Abd Kcdn Ags*. ~**-nid-nod** the chrysalis of the butterfly *20-, Lnk Rox* [from the jerking motion of its head]. ~ **norrie &c** the puffin *18-*. **t~ reekie &c** a kind of smoke gun made from a cabbage stem, used to blow smoke through keyholes to annoy those inside *la19-, local Ork-Rox*.

trimmling ~ a fruit jelly *20-, EC, WC Dmf*.

tammock *see* TUMMOCK

tandle *see* TANNEL

tane &c; teen &c *la19-, now NE pronoun, freq contrasted with* TITHER: **the** one (of two). [nME *tan(e); cf* TAE[3]. OED *tone*]

tane *see* TAK

tang[1] &c *n* general name for large, coarse seaweed growing above low-water mark, *esp* the genus *Fucus, 18-, chf Sh Ork*.

~**le &c** ['taŋl; *Per also* 'taŋkl; *Rox also* 'teŋl] *n* **1** (1) *also* **sea ~le** = *n, 16-*. (2) the long stalk and fronds of this *18-*. **2** a tall, lanky person *la18-, now Sh N*. **3** an icicle *la17-, now local NE-Fif*. *adj* long and limp, lank and loose-jointed *e19*.

yellow ~ the knotted TANG[1], a kind of bladderwrack *la18-19*. [*tangle n* 3 and *adj* may possibly not belong here]

tang[2] &c [taŋ, teŋ; *Sh Ork also* tiŋ; *Abd also* tjaŋ] *n* **1** (1) = tang, a projecting piece of metal etc. (2) *specif* the prong of a digging- or pitchfork *18-, now Sh Cai C*. **2** the tongue of a Jew's harp *la19-, now Sh Ork Cai Lnk*.

Tangerines: the ~ nickname for Dundee United football team *la20-*. [f the team's colours]

tangs &c; taings *now Abd*, **tings** *19-e20*, **teengs &c** *20-, now Sh Ork*, **tyangs** *20-, Abd* [teŋz, tɪŋz; *Ork* tiŋz; *WC, SW Uls* taŋz; *Abd also* tjaŋz] *n pl, freq treated as sing* = tongs *la15-*: 'a *tangs and shovel*'.

find something where the Hielandman fand the ~ take something from its rightful place and appropriate it, steal something *19-e20*. [OED *tongs*]

tanist &c ['tanɪst] *n, Celtic law* the successor to a Celtic king or chief (of Ireland or Scotland), elected during his predecessor's lifetime from within certain degrees of kinship *la18-, hist*.

~**ic** of a TANIST, *19-, hist*. ~**ry** the system of succession through a TANIST; the office of a TANIST *la17-, hist*. [ScGael *tànaiste*, IrGael *tánaiste* something second to another; the next heir]

tanker &c *17-, now EC, S*; **tankert** *e16, only Sc n* = tankard *16-*.

~**-backit &c** round-shouldered and hollowbacked *20-, EC, WC, S*.

tannage *n* a tannery, leatherworks *18-19, only Sc*.

tannel &c *la18-e20*; **tandle &c** *la18, in placename la15-* ['tanl, 'tɑnl] *n* a beacon; a bonfire, *esp* one kindled at certain festivals, *eg* at Midsummer Eve or *Halloween* (HALLOW[2]). [MIr *teannáil, tendál* a (bon)fire, beacon; see SND]

tanner &c *n, chf in pl* the fibres, small or fibrous roots of a tree or other plant *19-e20*. [perh reduced f obs Eng *tendron* a young shoot]

tanner *see* TENOR[2]

tannie &c *adj* = tawny *la15-19*. [F *tanné* tancoloured. OED *tawny*]

tansy &c *n* **1** = tansy, the plant *16-*. **2** *more freq* ragwort *19-, now local N-S*.

tant *n, vti* = taunt *la16-18*.

Tantallon [tən'talon, -ən, tan-] **ding doun** ~ perform the impossible, go beyond all bounds in feats or conduct *18-e20*. [the eLoth castle, once a (proverbially impregnable) stronghold of the Douglas family]

tantersome *adj* exasperating, annoying *20-*, *NE*. [perh based on Eng *tantalize*]

tanterwallop ['tantər'waləp] *n*, *chf in pl* hanging tatters or rags; *in sing* a tall thin man *la19-*, *Ags Per*. [var of *tatterwallop* (TATTER¹)]

Tantonie: ~ **bell** a small church bell; a hand-bell *la16*. [shortened f *St Anthony*. OED *Tantony*]

tantrum *n* **1** = tantrum. **2** affected airs, whims *19-*, *now Sh Ork Ags*.

tap¹ *16-*, **top &c** *n* **1** = top *la14-*. **2** a tuft of hair, wool, feathers etc; a forelock; a bird's crest *la15-e20*. **3** *spinning* the tuft of flax or tow put on a distaff at one time *la17-19*. **4** the head *19-*, *now local Sh-Per*. **5** (1) the tip, end *19-*, *now local Sh-Per*. (2) a fir cone *la19-*, *now Mry Stlg Rox*. **6** the surface of water *18-*. **7** *chf in pl* a framework fitted round a cart to facilitate the transport of large loads of hay etc *19-*, *now Per Fif*. **8** *in pl*, *also* ~ **coal** *mining* the uppermost division of a seam of coal or mineral *la19-*, *now Fif*. **9** *chf* **tops** the best sheep or lambs in a flock *19-*, *Gen except Sh Ork*.

vt **1** = top *15-*. **2** oppose *e17*. **3** *freq* **top** cut the tip of the ear of (an animal) as an ownership mark *18-*, *now Sh Kcb*. **4** *chf* **top** *golf* hit (the ball) on its upper part, making it spin rather than fly forward *la19-*.

adv first-rate, excellent; *specif of sheep* of the best grade *19-*.

~**pie**, ~**pack** pet name for a hen with a tufted crest *la19-*, *now Sh Ork*. ~**pin &c** **1** the top *la19*. **2** a tuft or crest of feathers on a bird's head *19-*, *now Wgt*. **3** a crest or topknot of hair, *esp* of an early 19th century men's hairstyle *19-e20*. **4** the woollen *tourie* (TOUR¹) on the crown of a bonnet *e19*. **5** the peaked top of a hill; a CAIRN on a hilltop *20-*, *now Ayr*. ~**pin lift** a halyard to set the peak of a mainsail *19-*, *now Sh*. **tappint &c** *of a fowl* = next *19-e20*. ~**pit** *esp of a bird* crested, tufted *19-*. ~**pit hen 1** a tufted hen *18-20*. **2** a kind of (*usu* pewter) decanter, containing a standard measure, its lid knob resembling a fowl's tuft *18-*, *now hist*.

top annual *law*, *perh* an annual BURDEN payable on a building or buildings as distinct from land *la16*. (**in**) ~ **flood** *of water* in full flood, at its highest point *18-*, *now Sh*. ~**sman** the chief man in charge of a drove of cattle, the head drover *la18-e20*. ~ **pickle &c** the highest ear on a stalk of oats, *usu* considered to be of the best quality *la18-*, *now Sh*. ~ **royal** a topgallant royal (sail) *e16*. ~ **swarm** the first swarm of bees from a hive *la17-19*. **taptaes** tiptoes *19-*, *now Sh EC Lnk*. ~**-thrawn** headstrong, perverse, obstinate *19-e20*.

never off someone's ~ always chiding or criticizing, continually quarrelling with someone *19-*. **on someone's** ~ attacking, severely reproving someone *la17-*. **take one's tap in one's lap** pack up and go, leave in a hurry *19-e20* [f the practice of taking flax to spin in a neighbour's house and wrapping it in one's apron on departure]. ~ **o lint** *or* **tow 1** = *n* 3, *la17-e19*. **2** a head of flaxen hair *la18-*, *now Kinr wLoth WC*. **3** a fiery-tempered, irritable person *19-e20*. **the** ~ **o the road** the middle of the road, *esp* in referring to setting out on one's way *20-*, *Sh N*. ~ **ower tail &c** upside down, head-over-heels, topsy-turvy *la14-e19*. ~, **tail (n)or main** etc head (n)or tail *18-*, *now local NE-Kcb*. **the** ~ **o the water** high water, full tide *20-*, *Sh N*, *EC*.

tap² *n* **1** = top, the toy, *esp* the whipping top *17-*; cf *peerie* (PEER²). **2** *rope-making* a conical, grooved piece of wood used to keep the strands apart and tensed *la20-*, *now Sh Cai*.

tap³ *n* = tap, a spigot.
v **1** *vt* = tap, provide with a tap; draw off (liquid). **2** *also* **top &c** *17-e18* = tap, draw and sell (liquor) in small quantities *17-*. **3** *also* **top &c** retail (any commodity) *15-e18*, *only Sc*. **4** *vi* beg, solicit alms *19-*, *local Fif-Dmf*.
tapper *e17*, **topper &c** *la15-e18* a retailer *only Sc*.
~**-tree** *esp brewing* a bung inserted in the outlet hole of a (mash-)tub *la17-e18*.

tape &c *n* = tape.
vt **1** = tape. **2** measure exactly (with a tape-measure); *hence* deal **out** or use sparingly *18-*, *now Kcdn nEC*.

taper *vt* use (food) sparingly, eke **out** *la19-*, *now Sh Ags*. [Eng *taper*, by confusion w TAPE *v* 2]

tapescher [*'tapɪʃər] *n* = tapisser, a tapestry-maker *e16*. [only Sc. OED *tapisser*]

tapet *see* TAIBET

tapie *see* TAUPIE

tapner, tapon *see* TAUPIN

tappietourie &c ['tapɪ'turɪ] *n* **1** something which rises to a peak; an ornament on top of something *19-*, *now local Ork-WC*. **2** *specif* (1) a pile or heap; a CAIRN on a hilltop *19-e20*. (2) a turret, towered structure *19-e20*. (3) a topknot of hair, a bun *la19*. (4) a knot of ribbons, wool etc on the top of a cap, a tassel, pompom; a bonnet with this *la19-*, *local Mry-Rox*. (5) a knob of pastry over the centre hole in a pie *19-*, *Ayr*. [dim of TAP¹ and TOUR¹]

tappint *see* TAP¹

tapsalteerie &c *la18-*; **topsoltiria &c** *17*, **tapsie-teerie &c** *19-20*, **tapsie-turvie** *la18-19* ['tapsəl'tɪrɪ; *Ross* 'topsɪ'tɪrɪ; *sEC, S Uls also* 'tapsɪ'tɪrɪ; *wLoth also* 'topsəl'tɪrɪ; **'topsʌur'tɪrɪə] *adv* upside down, topsy-turvy, in(to) utter confusion or disorder *17-*.
adj chaotic, muddled, disorderly *19-e20*.
n a state of disorder or of being topsy-turvy *19-e20*. [OED *topsy-turvy*]

tar[1] *16-;* **ter** *&c la14-e20* [tɑr; *Sh S* tɛr] *n* = tar *la14-.*

~**ry** *&c la16-,* **taurie** *&c 19-* **1** = tarry *la16-.* **2** = ~*ry-fingered, 19-, now local Sh-Kcb.* ~**ry breeks** *etc* nickname for a sailor *18-e20.* ~**ry-fingered** *&c* light-fingered, having a tendency to pilfer *19-.* ~**ry oo** *etc* wool from a sheep which has been smeared with tar *18-19.*

~ **buist** a box containing tar for smearing and marking sheep *19-, local Cai-S.*

tar[2] *vi* ~ **and tig** *etc* sport or toy (*esp* with one's victim or prey) *la15-16.* [ME *tarre &c, terre &c* provoke, OE **terw(i)an*]

tarbet; **tarbert** *&c n* an isthmus or neck of land between two navigable stretches of water, *specif* one over which a boat could be drawn *19-, freq in place-names.* [only Sc; Gael *tairbeart,* f *t(h)ar* across + *beir* carry]

tards *&c 16-20;* **tawrds** *&c 19-e20,* **targe** *20, Ross Inv Mry n* a school punishment strap, a *tawse* (TAW[1]).

tare *see* TEAR[2]

targe; **tairge** *19-e20,* **terge** *&c la19,* **tadge** *20-, now Stlg Fif v* **1** *vt* treat strictly or severely, *specif* (1) question closely, cross-examine rigorously *la18-19;* (2) scold severely *19-, now local Stlg-SW.* **2** *vi* bustle about, hustle, do something actively or vigorously *19-, now Wgt.*

n a violent, scolding woman, a shrew, virago *la19-, local Ork-Uls.*

targer *&c* **1** a violent, quarrelsome, domineering person, *esp* a woman *la19-, local Cai-Kcb;* cf *n.* **2** nickname for a big, active, hustling person *19-, now Dmf.* **targin** *&c* a scolding *19-, now Stlg, SW.* [only Sc; obscure]

targe *see* TARDS

target[1] *&c;* **terget** *&c 16-e18* ['tɑrgət; ***'tɛrgət] *n* **1** = target, a shield; something to aim at *16-.* **2** a shield-shaped, *freq* jewelled, metal ornament, worn *esp* on a head-dress *16.*

~**ting** target-like trimmings (on women's dresses) *la16-17, only Sc.*

target[2] *&c* ['tɑrgət; *S also* 'tɛrgət] *n* **1** a long narrow shred of cloth, a tatter; an oddly- or untidily-dressed person *la18-, now Mry Abd.* **2** a thin strip of flesh, *esp* from a lacerated wound; a long thin strip of dried skate *la18-, now Sh.* [only Sc; uncertain]

targin *see* TARGE

tariment, tarisum *see* TARRY

tarleather *&c la16-e19;* **tarledder** *&c la16-, now Sh,* **tarladder** *la16* [*Sh* 'tar'lɛdər; ***'tar'lɛðər, *&c*] *n* a strong strip of hide, taken from the belly of the animal, dressed and used as a thong, strap etc *la16-, now Sh.*

~**ed** *of a hide* having had a TARLEATHER cut off *la16-18.* [only Sc; appar Gael *tàrr-leathar* hide from the lower part of the belly]

tarloch *&c* ['tarlɔx] *n* a small, weak or worthless person, animal, or *occas* thing *17-, now Bnf Abd.* [see SND]

tarmagan *&c la18,* **ptarmigan** *la17-;* **tarmachan** *18,* **termigant** *&c la16-18,* **tormican** *&c la17-e18* ['tarmɔgən; ***'tɛrmigən(t), ***'tormɔxən] *n* the ptarmigan. [Gael *tàrmachan;* the (pseudo-Gk) Eng form was adopted (*la18*) by Thomas Pennant from Robert Sibbald's *Scotia Illustrata* (1684)]

tarmanick; **tarmaluk** *n* = turmeric *la17.* [OED *turmeric*]

tarmegant *n* = termagant, a violent, blustering, quarrelsome person *e16.*

Tarnty *&c* = Trinity *17-e20.*

tarragat *vt* question closely and persistently; pester *19-, now Sh Per Fif.* [only Sc, aphetic f Eng *interrogate*]

tarraneese *see* TIRRAN

tarrie *&c;* **terrie** *&c n, also* ~ **dog** a terrier *la18-, now Stlg Ayr.* [reduced f obs Eng var *tarrier*]

tarrock *&c,* **tirrick** *&c 19-, Sh n* **1** the common tern *la18-, now Sh.* **2** the (*esp* young) kittiwake *20-, now Fif.* [see SND]

tarrow *&c* ['tarɔ; *Ork* 'taro] *vi* **1** delay, tarry, linger, hesitate *la14-, now Sh Ork.* **2** ~ **at** *or* **on** feel or show reluctance for, show disdain or hesitation at, spurn, refuse *17-19.* **3** complain; be perverse *19-, now Sh.* [only Sc; appar var of Eng *tarry*]

tarry *&c;* **tairrie** *&c la16 vti* = tarry *la14-.*

n **1** = tarry, tarrying *la14-16.* **2** a temporary residence, stay *la14-16.*

taryage *la15,* **tariment** *la16* tarrying, delay *only Sc.* **tarisum** *&c* slow, lingering; wearisome *e16, only Sc.*

~ **upon** wait for (someone) *e17, only Sc.*

tartan *&c;* **tertane** *&c 16, la19,* **teartane** *e16* ['tartən, 'tertən; ***'tɛrtən] *n* **1** a woollen cloth with a pattern of stripes of different colours crossing at right angles; such a pattern, *esp* one associated with a particular CLAN (although the ascribing of particular TARTANS to CLANS is largely unhistorical; see SND) *la15-.* **2** a TARTAN garment, *esp* a *Highland* (HIELAND) PLAID *18-e19.* **3** *transf* the GAELIC language *19-e20.* *adj* made of TARTAN (*n* 1); having a pattern like TARTAN *16-.*

~**ed** dressed in TARTAN (*n* 1) *19.*

tartan purry *&c* a dish of boiled oatmeal mixed with chopped red cabbage or boiled with cabbage water *18-e20.*

fireside ~ *20-, local Mry-Ayr,* **Grannie's** ~ *la20-, local EC-Dmf,* **tink(1)er's** ~ *20-, now local N-EC* mottled skin on the legs caused by sitting too close to a fire. **tear the** ~ speak GAELIC *20-, local Ork-Gall.* [perh OF *tiretaine, tertaine* a kind of cloth of wool and linen or cotton mixed]

tartar *&c vi* move about restlessly and noisily *20-, Cai.*

n a disturbance, noise, row *20-, Cai.* [extended f Eng *Tartar*]

tartle[1] &c *v* **1** *vi* hesitate, be uncertain, *eg* in recognizing a person or thing *18-19*. **2** *vt* recognize, *esp* after some uncertainty *la17-e20*. [perh metath f OE *tealtrian* waver, be uncertain; *cf* TOLTER]

tartle[2] &c *n* **1** a tuft of hair or wool at an animal's tail which has become matted with excrement or mud *20-*, *now Stlg WC Gall*. **2** *in pl* tatters, torn or trailing edges of (dirty) cloth *la19-*, *now WC*. [ME *tridil, tyrdyl*, OE *tyrdel*, dim of *turd; cf* TROTTLE]

tary &c ['terɪ, *NE* -ə; *'tarɪ] *n* **1** vexation, trouble, harm *16, e19, only Sc*. **2** *freq in imprecations* the Devil *18-e20, NE*.
vt provoke, harass *la16*. [ME *tarie* &c, OE *tergan* (*v*)]

taryage *see* TARRY

tascal &c *n* ∼ **money** a reward offered in *the Highlands* (HIELAND) for information about stolen cattle and their thieves *17-e18*.
vt restore (stolen property, *esp* cattle) after payment of a reward *17*. [only Sc; Gael *taisgeal* the finding of something lost]

tash[1] &c *18-e20*; **tach** *la15-e16*, **tatch** *17-19* [taʃ; *tatʃ] *n* **1** a clasp, buckle, fastening *18-19*. **2** a rope or strap, *esp* one for tying bundles of flax *la17-e20*.
vt = tache, attach; seize, arrest *la15-e17*. [OED *tache* (*n*[2], *v*[2])]

tash[2] &c, **tache** &c *17-19* [taʃ; *S also* tatʃ] *n* **1** a stain, smudge, blemish; a spoiling, damage *la16-*, *now NE nEC Dnbt*. **2** *fig* a blot on one's character, slur, stigma *17-*, *now Sh*.
vt **1** *also fig* stain, tarnish, deface; spoil (*esp* flowers or clothes) by handling roughly or carelessly *17-*, *now local Sh-Dmf*. **2** fatigue, weary (with hard work) *la19-*, *now local Sh-Kcb*.
∼**y** &c having a tattered, slovenly appearance, unkempt *19-*, *local NE-S*. [ME *taiche, tatche* &c, F *tache(r)* &c (*v, n*) stain]

task *n* **1** = task. **2** a set lesson to be prepared, a piece of school homework *la18-*, *now local Sh-Per*.
vt = task.
∼**er** &c a worker paid for specified tasks; a pieceworker; *esp* a thresher of corn *la14-e20*.
∼**it** &c fatigued by hard work, exhausted; stressed, harassed *19-*, *now local Ork-Wgt*.

tass &c *n* a cup, goblet etc, *esp* for spirits *16-*, *now literary*.
∼**ie** = *n, la18-*, *latterly literary, only Sc*. [OF *tasse*]

tassel *see* TAISLE

taste &c; **test** *la16 vti* **1** = taste *la14-*. **2** *vt, fig* savour of *la16, only Sc*. **3** *vi* drink liquor in small amounts, have a tipple *la18-*.
n **1** = taste *16-*. **2** (1) a small quantity of alcoholic drink, a DRAM *la19-*. (2) *in gen* a small quantity *la19-*, *now Sh-Kcb*.
tastin &c the drinking of DRAMS, a DRAM *19-*.
lose ∼ **o** lose interest in or liking for *la20-*, *local*

Ork-Per. ∼ **one's gab, hert** *etc* cause a pleasant taste in one's mouth, stimulate the appetite *la18-*, *now local Ork-Rox*.

tat *see* TAUT, THAT

tatch *see* TASH[1]

tate *adj* untamed *la14*. [only Sc; prob var of TAIT[2]]

tate *see* TAIT[1]

tathe &c *18-*, **tath** *la15-e19*; **toth** &c *18-e20* [taθ; *n* teθ, *v* teð; *NE* toθ, toð; *nEC* *ted] *n* **1** the dung of cattle or sheep left for manure on their grazing land *la15-e19*. **2** coarse rank grass which grows on ground thus manured *la18-*, *now Lnk*.
vti **1** *also* **ted** &c *la18-e19*, *of animals* drop dung on land so as to manure it *18-e19*. **2** *vt* manure (land) by turning cattle or sheep onto it *18-19*.
∼**fold** &c a piece of enclosed ground on which cattle and sheep are confined to manure it with their dung *la16-e19*. [ME; ON *tað* dung, *teðja* (*v*) manure]

tatie *see* TATTIE

tatter[1] &c *n* = tatter.
∼**y** &c **1** ragged, hanging loose *19*. **2** very windy *la20-*, *Lnk S*.
∼**wallop** &c ['tatər'waləp] **1** *chf in pl* rags, tatters *19-*, *now local Sh-Per*. **2** a ragged person, ragamuffin *la20-*, *Ork NE*.

tatter[2] *vi* talk idly; scold *la19-*, *now S*. [ME *tater*]

tattie &c; **tatie** &c, **tawtie** &c ['tatɪ, 'tɑtɪ; *Uls also* 'tetɪ] *n* **1** = potato *18-*. **2** *contemptuous* (1) the head *la19-*, *now Sh*; (2) a stupid person, a simpleton *la19-*, *local Ork-WC*.
∼**ait** a kind of oat, the potato-oat *20-*. ∼**bannock** &c = ∼ *scone, 20-*, *now Sh Ork Cai*. ∼**beetle** &c a wooden pestle for mashing potatoes *18-*, *Ork C, S*. ∼**bing** a clamp of potatoes *19-*, *now Sh Ayr*. ∼**bloom** &c the flower or complete foliage of the potato *20-*, *now Cai*. ∼**bogie** *20-*, *now NE*, ∼**bogle** &c *19-*, *Gen except Sh Ork NE*, ∼**boodie** &c *19-*, *NE* **1** a scarecrow, *esp* one in a potato field *19-*. **2** *transf* a ragged, unkempt or grotesquely-dressed person *la19-*. **3** a large raw potato with matchsticks stuck in it as a toy *la20-*, *Fif Edb Rox*. **4** a turnip-lantern used at *Halloween* (HALLOW[2]) *la20-*, *nEC*. ∼**bree, -broo** &c water in which potatoes have been boiled *la19-*, *now Ork NE*. ∼**broth** potato soup *20-*, *now Ork Ags*. ∼**champer** &c, ∼**chapper** a potato-masher or pestle *19-*, *now local*. ∼**claw** potato soup *20-*, *now Bwk Rox*. ∼**creel** a basket for gathering potatoes *19-e20*. ∼ **deevil** &c a machine for digging potatoes *20-*, *NE Ags Fif*. ∼ **doolie** &c a scarecrow; *transf* a ragamuffin *19-*, *now Kcdn-Per*. ∼ **grubber** a kind of harrow for digging up potatoes *la19-*, *now NE Per*. ∼ **grund** &c potato ground *la19-*. ∼ **holidays** an autumn school holiday to allow children to help with the potato harvest *20-*. ∼ **holin** = ∼ *howkin, 20-*, *Bnf Abd Ags*. ∼

howker a person who works at the potato harvest, *esp* a temporary worker from Ireland *la19-, Gen except Sh Ork.* ~ **howkin** the potato-harvest *19-, Gen except Sh Ork.* ~**-liftin** = ~ *howkin, 19-.* ~**-man** an itinerant potato-seller or greengrocer *la19-, now NE.* ~**-parer** a potato-peeler *la19-.* ~ **park** a field of potatoes *20-, N-Per.* ~**-peel** potato peeling *la19-, now local Sh-Ayr.* ~**-peelin 1** = potato peeling. **2** *attrib, fig, of speech* affected, prim *la20-, local Stlg-Pbls.* ~ **pie** shepherd's pie *la19-, Gen except Sh.* ~ **pit** = ~ *bing, 19-, Gen except Sh.* ~**-ploom** the seed-box of the potato plant *20-, now local NE-Kcb.* ~**-poke &c** a sack for holding potatoes *20-, now NE-Per.* ~ **pourins** = ~ *bree, la19-, local NE-S.* ~**-scone** a (flat) SCONE made of flour, milk and mashed potato *la18-.* ~**-shaw &c** *chf in pl* the stalk and leaves of the potato plant *la19-.* ~**-soup** = potato soup. **that's the ticket for** ~ **soup** that's the very thing, that's just what was wanted *la19-, now Bnf Per.* ~**-swinger** a foreman, overseer, *esp* of farm-workers at the potato harvest *20-, now Lnk.* ~**-trap** *disparaging* the mouth *la19-, now Per WC.* ~ **weather** weather favourable for the potato harvest *20-, local Sh-Per.*

the (**clean**) ~ the right person, one who can be trusted or relied on *la19-, Gen except Sh Ork.* ~**s and dab** *or* **dip** potatoes boiled in their skins and dipped in melted fat, gravy etc *la19-, now local Ork-WC.* ~**s and point** a frugal meal of potatoes only (the non-existent meat etc being symbolically pointed at) *la19-, now local Sh-WC.* **the vera** ~ the very thing *20-, Gen except Sh Ork.* [*cf* PITAWTIE]

tauch &c *16-20,* **tallow** *18-;* **talch &c** *15-19,* **tallon &c** *la15-20,* **tally &c** *18-* [tax; ˈtalə; *Sh* ˈtalən; *C, S* ˈtalɪ; *talx] *n* = tallow, **tauch** being sometimes used for the substance in its natural state and **tallow** when it has been melted down *15-.* ~**ie** smeared with tallow or fat, greasy *la18-, now Stlg.*

tally lamp a miner's lamp *20-, Fif Ayr* [*orig* tallow was used as fuel].

taucht *see* TEACH

tauk &c *la15-e19;* **tak** *16* [tɑk] *vti, n* = talk. [only Sc. OED *talk*]

taul(d) *see* TELL

taum &c *n* a fit of rage, bad temper, a sullen, sulky mood *19-e20.* [ME *talme* (*v*) faint, (*n*) faintness; ON *talma* hinder, obstruct]

taunt *vt* hoist (a sail) *la16, only Sc.* [appar f obs Eng *taunt* (*adj*), *of masts* very tall]

taupie &c; tapie &c *18-19* [ˈtɑpɪ] *n* a giddy, scatterbrained, untidy, awkward or careless person, *esp* a young woman *18-, Gen except Sh Ork.* *adj* foolish, awkward, slovenly, foolishly thoughtless *18-19.*

taupit &c foolish *19.* [only Sc; Scand; *cf* Norw *tåp* a half-wit, *esp* a woman, Dan *taabe* a fool, Sw *tåpig* foolish, weak-minded]

taupin &c, tapon &c [ˈtɑpən, ˈtap-] *n* **1** a peg in a drinking vessel *16.* **2** a peg acting as a tappet *e17.* **3** a main branch of a root; a subsidiary root; a tap-root, *esp* of a turnip *17-, now NE Per.*

taupiner, tapner &c a curved knife with a hooked tip for *lifting* (LIFT[2]) and topping and tailing turnips *20-, NE Ags.* ~ **staff** ? the stave containing the vent-peg in a barrel *la17.* [only Sc; OF *tapon* a plug]

taupit *see* TAUPIE

taurie *see* TAR[1]

taut &c *la18-;* **tat** [tɑt; *Uls* tat] *n* a tangled, matted tuft or lock of wool, hair etc *16-, now local Sh-SW.* *vti* mat, tangle; make matted or tangled *la19-20.* ~**ie &c** *16-, now C, S,* ~**it &c** *18-, now local Sh-SW, of hair, wool etc* matted, entangled, shaggy, unkempt; *of persons or animals* having a rough, shaggy head or coat. [only Sc; perh OE *tættec* a rag, tatter, ON *tǫtrar* rags, tatters; *cf* TAIT[1]. OED *tatty* (*adj*)]

tauve *see* TYAUVE

taver *see* TAIVER[1]

tavern &c *n* = tavern *15-.* ~**it** sold in taverns *15.* ~**rie** tavern expenses *la17, only Sc.*

taw[1] &c *v* **1** *vt* (1) = taw, prepare (leather, flax) *15-.* (2) knead, draw out, twist (something adhesive, plastic, stringy or fibrous) *19-, now Ags Pbls.* (3) pull and tug at *19-e20.* **2** *vi* work laboriously, struggle *la18-, now Kcdn.* **3** *vt, also* **tawse &c** beat, whip with a *tawse* (*n* 1) *la18-.* *n* **1** *chf in pl* **taws(e) &c,** *sometimes treated as sing and occas with double pl* **tawses** a whip with tails; the lash for a whipping top; *specif* a leather punishment strap with thongs, used in schools (since 1983 only rarely and only in certain REGIONS) *16-.* **2** *child's word* the penis *la20-, Stlg Fif WC.* [*cf* TEW[1], TYAUVE]

taw[2] &c; tyave &c *NE* [tɑ; *NE* tjɑv] *n* a fibre or filament of a plant or tree, a fibrous root, *specif* a conifer preserved in PEAT[1] *19-, now Sh.* [see SND]

tawbart *see* TALBART

tawne *vt* tame, subdue, soften *e17.* [prob misreading of *taume,* var of Eng *tame*]

tawrds *see* TARDS

taws(e) *see* TAW[1]

tawtie *see* TATTIE

tax; taxt *15-e18, only Sc n, vt* = tax *15-.*

taxator *15-16,* **taxter** *la15-e18* a tax assessor. **taxed** *or* **taxt ward** a form of feudal land tenure in which a fixed annual sum was paid to the SUPERIOR in lieu of the full income from the lands, abolished 1747, *17-e18.* ~ **roll** a list of its members drawn up by the

Convention of *Royal Burghs* (CONVENTION), with the proportionate liability of each in the total tax payable by the BURGHS *16-e18*.

tay *see* TAK

Tayside ['te:səid] *also* ~ **Region** a REGION formed from the former counties of the City of Dundee, Angus and Kinross and part of the former county of Perth *la20-*.

Taysiders *sporting journalism* nickname for Dundee football team *20-* [*cf* DEE and *Dark Blues* (DARK)].

tazie *see* TEASE

tchick &c *interj, n, vi 19-, now local Ork-Kcb* **1** expressing annoyance = tut-tut. **2** sound made to urge on a horse.

tchop *see* SHOP

te *see* TAE[4]

tea; tae &c *la19-20, chf Sh NE* [ti; *Sh N Uls* te; *Sh Ross Bwk S also* təi; *Fif also* te] *n* **1** = tea *la17-*. **2** *also* **high tea** a meal eaten in the early evening, *usu* consisting of one cooked course followed by bread, cakes etc and tea *20-*.

~**-blade &c** a tea leaf *la19-, nEC*. ~**-bread** buns, SCONES etc, eaten with tea *19-*. ~**-drinker** a light or dress shoe (such as might be worn at a tea-party) *la20, N*. ~**-hand** *la19-*, ~**-jenny** (*applied to men as well as women*) *20-, N-C* a person who drinks a lot of tea. ~**-skiddle**, ~**-skittle** *derog* a tea-party *20-, now Stlg WC*.

~ **and till't** tea served with a cooked meal, TEA (*n* 2), *20-, C*.

teach &c *la16-*; **tech &c** *la14-16*, **teiche &c** *la16* [titʃ; *nEC* tetʃ] *vt, pt, ptp also* **taucht &c** *la14-e20*; ~**it &c** *la15-16*, ~**ed &c** *la16-, now local Sh-Per* [tɑxt; titʃt] = teach *la14-*.

~**ment** teaching, instruction *la16, only Sc*.

teagle *see* TAIGLE

teal &c [til] *vt* entice, coax, wheedle by flattery *la19-20*. [ME *tele* deceive, entrap, ON *tæla* betray, entice]

tear[1] &c [tir; *Sh Ork nEC* ter] *n, also* **techyr &c** *e16, only Sc* [*'tixər, *'tɪxər] = tear (in the eye) *la14-*.

v **1** *vi* weep *18-e19*. **2** *vt* fill with tears *e17*. **3** *vi* **teicher, ticher &c** ['tixər, 'tɪxər] *esp of a slight wound or sore* exude moisture, ooze *19-e20, Bwk SW, S*.

wi the ~ in one's ee in an emotional or tearful state, in mourning or grief *la18-, now Per WC Kcb*.

tear[2] *17-*; **teir &c** *now NE*, **tair &c** *la19-, now Uls*, **terr &c** *20-, C* [tir; *Sh nEC* ter; *Gsw also* tɛr] *vti, pt also* **tor** *e16*, **tare** *18-, now Stlg*, **tuir &c** *19-e20* [tor, ter; *Sh* tør]. *ptp also* **tore** *19-* **1** = tear, rend, rip *16-*. **2** *vi, of wind* blow hard, sweep along in violent gusts, rage *la19-, now local Sh-Lnk*. **3** *freq* ~ **awa, on** *etc* work strenuously, energetically and with speed (**at**) *19-*. **4** *vti* rage (at) *19*.

n **1** = tear, a rent etc *19-*. **2** *of a plough* the

angle of adjustment between the coulter and the point of the ploughshare, which regulates the cut in the furrow *la20-, local Cai-Rox*. **3** a piece of fun, a spree, a lark, joke *20-, local*. **4** a lively entertaining person, a comic *20-, local Cai-S*. **5** a (great etc) quantity, a (large etc) amount **of** *20-, Sh NE Ags Uls*.

~**er** a passionate, irascible person; *of a woman* a shrew, vixen *la19-, now Sh Cai Lnk*. ~**in** *n* **1** an angry reproof, a thorough dressing-down *20-, Kcdn nEC Lnk*. **2** rowdy behaviour *la19*. *adj* rowdy, boisterous *la19-, now N, C*. **torn bellie** a herring which has been split or broken by careless handling *la19-, now Sh N Fif*. **torndoun** disreputable, dissipated, broken-down *19-, now Sh*. **torn face** (a person with) a bad-tempered, sulky, glum face *la20-, now Cai C*. **torn-hattie** *derog* name for a native of Brechin (used by the people of Montrose) *20-, Ags*. **be torn out** be asked out a lot, be popular *la20-, NE*.

~ **at, up** *etc* go at, set about, tackle with great vigour *la19-*. ~ **in** reclaim (waste or rough ground) *19-, now N*.

teartane *see* TARTAN

tease &c; taise &c [tiz; *Sh nEC* tez] *vt* = tease *19-*.

tazie &c, teesie &c a struggle, tussle, strenuous effort *19-, now Ags Per*.

teasicke *see* TEESICKE

teat *see* TAIT[1]

teaz *see* TEE[1]

teazle *see* TAISLE

tebbit *see* TAIBET

tech *see* TEACH

techyr *see* TEAR[1]

tect-demolished *adj* having the roof removed *e17*. [only Sc; L *tectum* a roof]

ted &c *vt* **1** = ted, spread out (grass) to dry. **2** *fig* scatter, strew, dissipate *la16-19*. **3** spread out in an orderly way, make (*esp* hair) tidy *la19*.

ted *see* TAID, TATHE

tedder *see* TETHER

tedisome &c; teedisome &c *adj* ['tidɪsəm] **1** tedious, tiresome, boring *19-, now local*. **2** peevish and slow in one's actions *la19-, Per Fif*. [Eng *tedious* + -SOME]

tee[1] *18-* [ti] *n, pl also* **teaz** *la17* **1** *golf* the small heap of sand, peg etc from which the ball is driven at the start of each hole; *now also* the patch of ground from which this is done *la17-*. **2** *curling* (CURL) the target, a mark on the ice in the centre of several concentric circles *la18-*. **3** *quoits, carpet bowls* the target or goal *19-, now SW*.

v **1** *vt, also* **teaz** *la17* place (a golf ball) on a TEE[1] *la17-*. **2** *vi* ~ **off** *golf* = tee off, begin to play. ~'**d ball &c** a golf ball which has been placed on a TEE[1]; *fig* a person or state of affairs bound to succeed *18-19*. ~('))**d shot** *golf* the first

stroke for every hole, played from a TEE[1] *la19-*.
~**ing ground** the small level patch from which
a ball is TEED *la19*. [earlier in Sc; unknown]

tee[2] *n, appar* some part of a horse's bridle, ? a
curb- or snaffle-rein *la15-18; cf* CURPLE. [only
Sc; prob OE *tǽg* a tie or fastening]

tee *see* TAE[4], TIE

teedisome *see* TEDISOME

teedle *vi* sing or hum a tune without the words;
sing softly so that the words are scarcely heard
19-, now WC. [only Sc; onomat; *cf* DIDDLE[2]]

teedy &c; teethy ['tidɪ, 'tiðɪ] *adj, esp of children*
cross, fractious; bad-tempered *19-, now Wgt*.
[nME *tethee*, nEng dial *teathy &c*]

teef *see* THIEF

teeger &c *19-*; **tegir &c** *16* ['tigər] **1** = tiger.
2 *fig* a person with a fierce quarrelsome nature
16-e20.
vi look fierce; clench the teeth and fists *la19-*,
eLoth Bwk.
tigirnes ferocity *e16, only Sc*.

teel &c *vti* = till (land) *15-, now Sh*.
~ **land** *e15*, ~ **ryge** *e16* [*'~ 'rɪg] tilled land.

teel *see* TUIL

teem &c *v* **1** *vt* empty (a container etc), *now esp*
of liquid *la14-, now C, S*. **2** pour, empty out
(the contents) from a container *la15-, now nEC,
S*. **3** drain water from (potatoes) *20-, now Per
Stlg*. **4** *vi, of rain* pour, come down in torrents
19-, Gen except Sh Ork. **5** *of water* flow or gush
copiously *la19-, Gen except Sh Ork*.
n a very heavy, long-lasting downpour of rain
19-, now C, S.
~**ie** *child's word* urinating *la20-, C*. [ME *teme*,
ON *tœma* (*v*); *cf* TUME]

teem *see* TUME

teemse &c [*?timz, *?temz] *n* a fine sieve, *esp*
for sifting flour *18-e19*. [OE *temes*]

teen[1] **&c** *la18-*; **tene &c** *la14-19* [tin; *v* tin(d)] *n*
1 = teen, harm, hurt; sorrow, grief *la14-e20*.
2 wrath, anger, rage *la14-19*.
adj **1** = teen, angry *la14-16*. **2** vexatious;
troublesome, distressing *la15, only Sc*.
vt, pt also ~**ded &c** **1** trouble, annoy, provoke
16-20. **2** = teen, hurt *la16*.
~**full &c** angry; malicious; sorrowful *la16-18*.

teen[2] = at een (EVEN[1]) *la18-e19*. [abbreviated
form]

teen *see* TAK, TANE, TUNE

teended *see* TEEN[1]

teenge &c [tindʒ] *n* **1** = tinge. **2** colic, *usu* in
horses *19-, now Ags Per*.

teengs *see* TANGS

teenie &c *n, derog* a junior domestic servant; an
effeminate man *20-, Gen except Sh Ork*.
~**-bash** familiar, *freq derog* form of address or
reference for a woman or girl *20-, EC*.
greeting T~ a weepy, complaining person
(male or female) *20-*. **T**~ **f(r)ae Troon** *20-*,
local WC-S or **f(r)ae the neeps** *la20-, Ags Fif* a
woman, *esp* an odd-looking, oddly-dressed or
over-dressed one. [Sc familiar form of *Christina*]

teenty &c *numeral, children's rhymes* two *la19-*.
[see ZEENDI]

teep *19-, now C*, **type** *n* = type, a representation; stamp; letters etc in printing *la15-*.
vt stamp (a letter, figure etc) on wood or metal
with a die *la20-, C*.

teep *see* TUIP

teepical *adj* = typical *20-, now Sh NE*.

teer[1] **&c** *vt* **1** = teer, coat with plaster etc *e17*.
2 *calico printing* coat with colour the pad etc on
which the printer presses his block *e19*.
~**er**, ~ **boy** the person who TEERS (*v* 2) *19*.

teer[2] **&c** *n* = tare, the wild vetch *la19-, NE Ags,
sEC*.

teer[3] **&c** *adv* **a' by** ~, **a' the** ~ barely, by the
skin of one's teeth, touch and go *19-e20*.
[reduced f *all that ever* (*one could etc ..*)]

teerie-orrie *n, game* throwing a ball against a
wall, catching and bouncing it in various ways
20-, Stlg Fif. [appar f the nonsense words
eerie-orrie, used in the game]

tee-set *see* TAE[4]

teesick &c ['tizɪk] *n* **1** = *also* **teasicke** =
phthisic, consumption *la16-e17*. **2** a spell of illness, *freq* of an indefinite nature *e20*.

teesie *see* TEASE

teet[1] **&c; tete** *16 vi* peep, peer, glance slyly, surreptitiously etc *16-, now Sh-nEC*.
n a shy peep, a sly, secretive glance *19-, Sh-nEC*.
titbore tatbore *e17*, ~(**ie**) **bo** *n, interj* the
game of peep-bo; the exclamation in the game
la18-, now local. [perh onomat or f ME *toote*,
OE *totian* peep. OED *titbore*]

teet[2] *n* the smallest sound or word, a squeak
la19-, Sh N. [imit]

teeter *vi* **1** = teeter. **2** totter or walk with
short, tripping or uncertain steps *20-*. **3** hesitate, hover indecisively *20-, local Sh-Bnf*.

teeth *see* TUITH

teethe *v* **1** *vi* = teethe, cut teeth. **2** *vt* set teeth
in, furnish with teeth or spikes *la18-, now Sh Cai*.
3 point (a wall etc) with mortar *la18-e19*. **4**
face, stand up to, set one's teeth against *la19-20,
Bnf Abd*.

teethy *see* TEEDY

teetle &c *19-e20*; **title &c** ['titl, 'tɪtl] *n* **1** = title
la15-. **2** *chf in pl* the title-deeds of land or
property *19-*.

teet-meet *see* TOOT-MOOT

teetotum &c *n* **1** = teetotum. **2** *fig* a very
small, insignificant person *19-, local N-Dmf*.

teewheet, teewhip *see* TEUCHIT

tegir *see* TEEGER

teh *interj* expressing impatience or derision *la19-,
EC Lnk Rox*.

te-hent [?ti'hɪnt, ?tɪ'hɪnt] *prep* behind *la19-, Kcdn
Ags Fif*. [reduced f *tae the hent* (see HINT[1]), used
as a prep on the analogy of AHINT]

teiche *see* TEACH

teicher *see* TEAR[1]

teicht *see* TICHT

teind &c; tend &c *la14-e15*, **tein &c** *la15-19*

[tind; *tin] *n* **1** a tenth part *la14-19, latterly literary*. **2** *church law, chf in pl* an allocation of a tenth of the produce of a parish for the support of religion, after the Reformation expropriated by the Crown and granted to landowners; *now* an amount, in 1925 standardized (on the average *fiar's prices* (FIAR) from 1875-1925), payable by the owner to the *Church of Scotland* (CHURCH) and used as part of the parish MINISTER's *stipend* (STEEPEND) *la14-*.
vt tithe, take the TEIND of (crops etc); assess for TEIND *16-e20*.

~er and thirder a tenant holding a lease under the *third and teind* system *la18-19, latterly hist*.

~ barn a tithe barn *18-19*. **T~ Clerk** = *Clerk of T~s, 19-*. **~ corn** *15*, **~ fish** *etc 16-18* corn, fish etc paid as TEIND or sometimes cash paid in lieu. **T~ Court** = *Commission of T~s, 19-*. **~ free** exempt from payment of TEIND *17-e18*. **~ sheaf &c** every tenth sheaf, paid as TEIND *15-, now hist*. **~ silver &c** money paid as TEIND in lieu of goods *16-18*.
Clerk of T~s the principal clerk to the *Court of Teinds, 19-*. **Commission(ers) of T~s, Court of T~s** the names (at various dates) of the body administering the TEINDS, since 1707 as part of the *Court of Session* (SESSION) *17-*. **drawn ~** = **~ sheaf**, *18-, now hist*. **exhausted ~s** the *valued* ~ already used in its entirety for payment of the MINISTER's *stipend* (STEEPEND), and thus with no surplus left to provide an increase *19-*. **free ~** that part of the TEIND not yet allocated to the MINISTER's *stipend, 18-*. **great ~s** *18-*, **parsonage ~s** *la16-*, **personage ~s** *la16-17* that part of the TEIND of a parish formerly due to the parson; cf *vicarage ~s*. **small ~s** = *vicarage ~s, la18-e19*. **~ to hell** a tribute or price required of his minions by the Devil *la18-e20*. **third &c and ~** a method of renting land whereby in return for the crop on some stock and equipment, the landlord took a tenth of the crop as TEIND and a third of the remainder as rent *18, chf S*. **unexhausted ~** = *free ~, la19-e20*. **valued ~** the TEIND assessed by a less variable method than crop-size, *eg* the value of the land, etc *18-*. **vicarage ~s** TEINDS taken from produce other than grain, *orig* paid to the vicar of a parish *18-19*; cf *parsonage ~*. [nME *tend &c* = *n*, also tenth; cf TEN and ON *tiunde* a tenth]

teine *see* TAK
teir *see* TEAR²
Teisday *see* TYSDAY
teistie &c *19-, now Sh Ork Cai*; **toist &c** *18-e19* ['təist(ɪ)] *n* the black guillemot. [Norw *dial teiste*, ON *þeist(i)*]
tell &c; tol(**l**) *la18-e20 v, pt, ptp also* **tald &c** *la14-e20*, **tauld &c** *only Sc*, **taul** *19-e20, NE*, **telled &c** *la16-20*, **telt &c** *19-* [tɛlt, tɛld, *also* tɑl(d); *Sh also* tʌuld] *vti* = tell *la14-*.
~ie-speirie a tell-tale *20-, Ags Per*. **~ing** a

warning, admonition, lesson, *freq* **let that be a ~ing tae ye, take a ~ing** *19-*. **it would be** *etc* **~ing** it would be to the interest or advantage of (a person) *17-*.
~ pie(**t**) **&c** ['~'paɪ(ət)] a tell-tale *20-, now Ork Cai*.
d'ye ~ me (so)? indeed, you don't say *20-, local*. **~ down** count out (money) in payment *18-, now Sh*. **~ on** *19-*, **~ upon** *la18-e19* inform against, tell tales about.
temerare &c [*'tɛmərər, *-er] *adj* = temerarious, reckless, rash *16*. [only Sc; F *téméraire*, L *temerārius*]
temerarité [*tɛmə'rerɪtɪ] *n, law* reprehensible or culpable heedlessness or negligence *la15*. [only Sc; L *temerārius* rash + *-ity*. OED *temerarity*]
temerat [*'tɛmərət] *adj* adventurous, head-strong *la16*. [only Sc; L *temerāt-*, ptp stem of *temerāre*, f *temere* (*adv*) rashly]
temming &c; timmen &c [*'tɛmɪn] *n* = (s)tamen, a kind of thin woollen cloth *la16-e19*.
temp &c *la15-*, **tent** *18-19 vti* = tempt.
temper *n* = temper.
vt **1** = temper. **2** regulate (a clock) *16, only Sc*. **~-pin 1** the wooden screw which controls the tension of the band of a spinning-wheel *18-20*. **2** a tuning peg on a violin *la18*.
tempil *see* TEMPLE¹
templary *n* an estate or benefice belonging to the Knights Templar *la16*. [ME = a Templar, the Templars]
temple¹ &c; tempil &c *n* = temple *la14-*.
~-land land belonging to the Knights Templar and as such not subject to TEINDS *la14-, now only in place-names*.
temple² &c *n* a (hazel) rod used to hold down thatch *la17-18*. [Eng = a flat rod used to keep cloth in a loom at its proper width]
temptise *vt* incite to evil *e16*.
ten &c *numeral* = ten *la14-*.
~aby &c *children's rhymes* ten *la19-, now Sh Ork Cai*.
~fauld = tenfold *19*. **~some &c** (a group of) ten *la16-19, only Sc*. **~t &c** *la16-20*, **teynt** *15-16* [tɛnt; *?tint] = tenth [cf TEIND].
~-hours ten o'clock; a small feed given in the middle of the morning to a horse at work *18-e20*. **~-hour bell** a bell rung at 10 pm, *esp* in Edinburgh, to warn citizens to go home *18-e19*.
tenant &c *la16-*; **tenand &c** *la14-18*, **tenan** *la19-, NE* ['tɛnən(t); *-ənd] *n* = tenant *la14-*.
tenandry &c 1 = tenantry, being a tenant; tenants collectively; tenancy *la14-e18*. **2** land held of or rented from a SUPERIOR by a tenant; rent etc paid by a tenant *la14-e18*.
~-stead &c occupied by a tenant, let *la17-18*.
Tenants-Day &c a fair day and holiday held on 18 Aug (Old Style) in the town of Beith in Ayrshire *19-, now Ayr*. [altered f *Saint Inan's Day*, f the 9th-century Celtic saint]

tench *n* ? a taunt, reproach *e16*. [only Sc; north-eastern OF *tenche*, OF *tence* a dispute]

tend &c [tɛn(d)] *vti* **1** = tend, intend *16-e17*. **2** *vt* understand *la15*. **3** *vti* attend (**to**), look after, see (**to**) *la19-*, *Gen except Sh Ork*.

~**our** a person who tends or waits on another *la15*.

tend *see* TEIND

tender[1] **&c; tener &c** *la19-e20*, *Abd* ['tɛndər; *NE*, *WC* 'tɛnər] *adj* **1** = tender *la14-*. **2** in delicate health, ailing, weakly *17-*, *now local Sh-Ags*. **3** *of colour or light* delicate; soft *e16*. **4** dear, beloved *la15*. **5** nearly related, akin, *freq* ~ **of blood** *16-e17*, *only Sc*. **6** *of coal etc* soft, easily broken or split off *la18-e19*, *WC*.

tender[2] *n* **1** = tender. **2** *law* an offer of a sum in settlement made during an action by the *defender* (DEFEND) to the *pursuer* (PURSUE) *la19-* [the English *tender* is an offer before an action].

tene *see* TEEN[1]

tenement *n* **1** = tenement, a holding; *specif* land held in tenure and built on *15-*. **2** a large building, *usu* of three or more storeys divided into FLATS for separate householders; the section of such a building served by one stair *la16-* [f *tenement of land* or *houses*].

~**er** the holder of a TENEMENT, a person who has a FEU of land in a village *la16-*, *chf Ayr*.

tenendas [tə'nɛndas, -əz] *n*, *law* the clause in a feudal charter which expresses the manner in which lands are to be held of a SUPERIOR *la17-*. [L = to be held; f the first words in the clause *tenendas praedictas terras*]

tener *see* TENDER

tenon ['tɛnən] *n* = tendon *19-*, *now NE*.

tenor[1] **&c** *n*, *orig law* = tenor, the substance of a document *la14-*.

~**all** of the tenor or ordinary course or procedure *e17*, *only Sc*.

proving the ~ *law* an action in which the *pursuer* (PURSUE) seeks to set up a lost or destroyed document by proof of its contents *la17-*.

tenor[2] **&c; tanner** ['tɛnər, 'tanər] *n* (*16-*), *vt* (*19-*) = tenon.

~ **saw** = tenon saw *17-*.

tensal *see* TINSEL

tent[1] *n* **1** = tent, a portable shelter *la14-*. **2** *church* a movable pulpit (with steps and canopy) erected in the open air, *esp* at half-yearly Communion services when the congregation was too large for the church *la17-19*.

tent[2] **&c** *n* attention, heed, care *la14-*.

vt **1** pay attention to, listen to, heed *la15-*, *now WC*, *SW*. **2** (1) watch over, take good care of *la18-*, *now Ags*. (2) *specif* tend, take charge of, look after (animals or children) *la17-*, *now Wgt*. **3** observe, take notice of *18-e19*. **4** beware, be careful of *18-e19*.

adj watchful, attentive, intent *la18-19*.

~**er** a weaver's assistant, *now specif* a loom-tuner *19-*, *now nEC*, *WC*. ~**ie &c** **1**

watchful; attentive; heedful *la16-e20*. **2** cautious, careful, prudent *18-*, *now Abd*. ~**ily** attentively, with care, gently *18-19*. ~**ive** attentive *la16-18*. ~**less** inattentive, heedless, careless *la16-*, *now NE*, *WC*, *SW*.

tak ~ **1** be careful, beware *16-*. **2** notice, observe, take note *19-*, *Gen except Sh Ork*. **tak** ~ **o 1** take (good) care of, heed *19-e20*. **2** pay attention to, keep watch on *la19-*, *now NE*. **3** beware of, be on one's guard against *la18-e20*. **tak** ~ **to &c** listen to, give heed to *la14-*, *now C*. [ME; aphetic f obs Eng *attent* heed or *intent* give heed; *cf* TEND]

tent[3] *vt* ? embroider in a frame *e16*, *only Sc*. [reduced f TENTER]

tent *see* TEMP, TEN

tenter *n* **1** = tenter, a frame for stretching cloth. **2** a bar of wood fitted with hooks on which fish are hung to dry *la20-*, *NE Ags Fif*.

tepat *see* TIP[1]

ter *see* TAR[1]

teran *see* TIRRAN

terbuck *see* TREBUCK

terce &c *n* **1** = tierce, a third part, the third canonical hour *la14-15*. **2** *law* the right of a widow to the *liferent* (LIFE) of one third of her husband's HERITABLE estate, if no other provision has been made for her, **greater** ~ being applicable when the husband's entire HERITAGE was available, **lesser** ~ when the widow of a predecessor still enjoyed TERCE in the lands *la15-20*.

tersaill a tierce (of wine) *16*, *Abd*. **tercer &c** a widow who has TERCE *la16-e19*.

~ **land** the land of which the rent is assigned to a widow's TERCE *la16*. [OED *terce*, *tierce*]

tere &c *adj* difficult, tedious *la15-e16*.

~**full, tyrefull** = *adj*, *la15*. [nME; obscure]

terebynthine [*terəbɪn'θəin] *n* the terebinth *e16*. [OED *terebinthine*]

tere pyle *see* TERPOILE

terge *see* TARGE

terget *see* TARGET[1]

teri &c ['tɪrɪ] *n* a native or inhabitant of Hawick, Rox *la19-*, *S*. [shortened f next]

teribus &c; tiribus &c ['tɪrɪbas] *n*, *also* ~ **and teriodin** ['~ ən(d) 'tɪrɪ'odɪn] **&c** the SLOGAN (*n* 1) of the town of Hawick, Rox; a local popular song with these words in its chorus, sung *esp* at the Hawick *Common Riding* (COMMON) *19-*, *Rox*. [see SND]

terlys *see* TIRLESS

term &c; tairm *la19-e20* *n* **1** = term *la14-*. **2** *law* one of the four days of the year on which certain payments, *eg* rent or interest, become due, leases begin and end, and (*formerly*) contracts of employment, *esp* on farms, began and ended, *Candlemas* (CANLEMAS), WHITSUNDAY, LAMMAS, MARTINMAS; *latterly* (*la19-*) removal TERMS only were fixed as 28 May and 28 Nov *la14-*.

~**ly 1** occurring or falling due every TERM (*n* 2) or at the end of a TERM, *la17-*. **2** in each TERM (*n* 2), once every TERM *la15-e19*.
~ **day,** *also* ~ **time** = *n* 2, *la18-*. **but** ~ **day** without end, forever *la14*.
~ **an(d) life** for all time, for ever and a day *19-, now Sh*.
termigant *see* TARMAGAN
terminable *adj* = terminable.
in terminablis [*ɪn 'tɛrmɪnablz] ? in definite terms, definitely *la16, only Sc*.
ternar &c *n, St Andrews Univ* a student of the third or lowest social rank *la17-e19; cf* PRIMAR, *secondar* (SECOND). [laL *ternarius* in third place]
terne &c *adj* gloomy, fierce *16-e17*.
n gloom *e16*. [only Sc; F = dull, tarnished]
ternion *n* a quire of three sheets, each folded in two *e17*. [L *ternio* a group of three, a triad; *cf* eModEng = a set of three]
terpoile; tere pyle [*'tɛr'pəil] *adj, of patterned velvet etc* three-pile; pile upon pile *la15-e16*. [only Sc; OF *a treis poils* three-pile]
terr *see* TEAR²
terreall *adj* earthly, terrestial, mundane *la16*. [only Sc; L *terreus* + *-al*. OED *terreal*]
terrible &c; terrel &c *la19-, now Stlg SW* ['tɛrɪbl; *Abd SW also* 'tɛr(ə)l] *adj* = terrible *la15-*.
adv, as intensifier very much, extremely, awfully *19-*.
terrie *see* TARRIE
terrifee *vt* = terrify *la19-, now NE*.
terrification &c the action of terrifying; a state or condition of terror, alarm or fright *17-, now Sh NE, chf Sc*.
territoire *la15*; **territour &c** [*'tɛrɪtor, *-ur] *n* territory, land *la15-e16*. [F]
territory *n* **1** = territory. **2** *law* the area over which a judge holds jurisdiction *18-*.
territorial 1 = territorial. **2** *law, of a jurisdiction, esp that of a* SHERIFF: limited to a defined area or district *la18-*. **3** *church* of a church (*esp* in a large town) serving an area not coterminous with the parish *19-*.
terror &c *n* the state of being terrified *la14-*.
tersaill *see* TERCE
tersie versie &c *adj, adv* topsy-turvy, in a random, disorderly way *19-e20, S*. [altered euphemistic form f obs Eng *arsy-versy*, perh w infl f Eng *topsy-turvy*]
tertane *see* TARTAN
tertian *Sc Univs n* a third-year Arts student *la17-, latterly St Andrews and Aberdeen, now only St Andrews*.
adj in the third year of the Arts course, third-year *18-19*. [L *tertianus* of or belonging to the third]
terty *see* THIRTY
tesment *see* TESTAMENT
test¹ *n* **1** = test. **2** *specif* the oath or declaration prescribed by the Test Act of 1681, aimed at

imposing on the extreme *Covenanters* (COVENANT) compliance with Episcopacy in the *Church of Scotland* (CHURCH) *la17-, now hist*.
test² *n* evidence, witness borne *la15*.
v **1** *vt* leave by will or testament *la15-e18*. **2** *vi* make a will, execute a testament *la17-*.
~**ing clause** *law* the attestation clause which authenticates a deed by naming the witnesses and date and place of execution *la18-*.
test *see* TASTE
testament; tesment &c *e16, 19* (*NE*) *n* **1** = testament *la14-*. **2** *specif* that part of a will in which an executor is appointed, ~ ~**ar(y)** when the testator appoints an *executor nominate* (NOMINATE), or ~ **dative** when the SHERIFF appoints an *executor dative* (DATIVE) *16-*. **3** the executor specified in a will *17-*. **4** the New Testament as distinct from the Old *16-* [earlier in Sc].
vt leave by will, bequeath *la19, Bnf Abd*.
~**ar &c** = testamentary *la15-; cf n* 2. **tutor** *or* **tutrix** ~**ar** *see* TUTOR.
testan &c *n* **1** = teston, an Italian or English silver coin *16*. **2** a Scottish silver coin of the reign of Mary (*orig* with her portrait), of the value of four shillings SCOTS *la16-e17*.
make a mark of one's ~ make a profit, invest one's capital or efforts to advantage *e18*. [OED *teston*]
testifee *vti* = testify *la19-*.
n pl **testefeis** [*'tɛstɪfiz] certificates *la16, only Sc*. [OED *testify*]
testificate *n* **1** a solemn declaration of fact or belief put in writing, a certificate, testimonial, *esp* a character reference, issued by a MINISTER or *kirk session* (KIRK) to a person applying for membership of another church *17-e19*. **2** evidence, indication *17-e19*. [chf Sc; L *testificatum* (that which is) testified]
tet *see* TAIT¹
tete *see* TEET¹
teth *interj* a mild oath *19*. [perh euphemistic for Eng *faith; cf* HAITH]
tether *la16-*; **tedder &c** *now Sh Ork N n* **1** = tether *la17-*. **2** *fig* scope, the limits (of conduct, resources, endurance etc), 'rope' *19-, now Sh Ork N*. **3** a halter, hangman's noose *16-e19, only Sc*.
vt **1** = tether *la16-*. **2** confine, bind, restrict the freedom of *la15-, now Ork NE*. **3** tie up, moor (a vessel) *18-e19*. **4** *chf sarcastic* marry, unite in marriage *19-, now N*.
go the length of one's ~ use up one's resources, exhaust one's means *20-, now Sh*.
put a ~ **to someone's tongue** silence a person, restrain someone from speaking *19-, now Sh Cai*. **win to the end o one's** ~ reach the limit of one's resources *la19-, Sh Ork N*.
tethery &c *numeral, children's rhymes* three *19-, now Per*. [see ZEENDI]
tetht *see* TUITH
teuch &c *15-, only Sc*, **tough; tuch &c**

la14-e19, **tyeuch &c** 20, **tyoch** la20-, Sh Ork
Cai Ross, **teugh &c** la15-, **cheuch &c**
la19-e20 [tjux, tʃux; nEC, WC Uls tjʌx, tʃʌx; Sh-
Ross tjox; *tøx] adj **1** = tough la14-. **2** persistent, durable, protracted la16-19. **3** (1) of persons rough, coarse la19-, local Sh-Wgt. (2) of
weather rough, wet and windy 20-, now Sh Cai.
adv vigorously, stoutly; persistently, pertina-
ciously la15-19.
teuchen &c toughen 19-. **teuchie** toughish
20-, Kcdn.
~ **Jean** a kind of sticky, chewy boiled sweet
20-, local Ags-SW.
teuchit &c 19-, now NE nEC, **teewheet &c**
17-, now Pbls SW; **teewhip &c** 20-, Ork,
tuchit &c la15-e20 ['tjuxət, 'tʃux-; 'tjʌxət,
'tʃʌx-; Ork ti'hwʌp &c; Cai 'ʃoxad; Pbls SW
'ti:'(h)wit, *t(ə)'wɪt, &c] n the lapwing, peewit,
or green plover la15-.
~('s) **storm** a period of bleak wintry weather
in March (when the TEUCHITS arrive and begin
to nest), the date varying in different districts
and seasons 19-, NE, nEC. [imit of the bird's
cry; cf PEESWEEP]
teuchter ['tjuxtər, 'tʃuxtər] n, freq disparaging
or contemptuous term for a Highlander (HIE-
LAND), esp a GAELIC-speaker, or for anyone from
the North; an uncouth, countrified person 20-,
now Cai EC, WC. [see SND]
teuk see TAK
teud [tød] n a tooth 19-e20, Fif. [appar var of
TUITH, perh w infl f Gael deud]
teug see TUG
teugh see TEUCH
teuk see TAK
teulie see TULYIE
tevell [*?'tɛvl] n lace, the fabric e17. [only Sc;
appar obs F tavelle a kind of lace]
teven [?'tɛvən] numeral, children's rhymes seven
la19-, now Cai. [prob altered f Eng seven]
tew[1] **&c** vi = TAW[1] v 2, 19-e20.
n a piece of hard work or exertion 19.
~**ed 1** of food tough, shrivelled 19-, now S. **2**
exhausted 19-, now Wgt. [cf TAW[1]]
tew[2] **&c** [tju(x)] interj expressing disgust, contempt, impatience la19-, Ayr.
tew see TYAUVE
tewk see TUCK
tewl see TUIL
teylor see TAILOR
teynt see TEN
tha see THAE, THAI
thack[1] **&c**, **thatch** la17-; **theck &c** 20-, now
Bnf Cai, **thaik &c** 17-, now Cai [θak; Ork also
tek; N also θek] n **1** = thatch la14-. **2** transf
the skin la14, only Sc.
vt = thatch 17-.
thack-divot &c = ~-turf, e16. ~ **gate &c**
the sloping top of a gable-wall which has no
coping and is overlaid by the thatch la17-, now
Sh, only Sc. ~ **house** a thatched house 16-20.

thack-pin a wooden peg used to fasten down
thatch la19-, now Ags Per. **thack-raip** a
straw-rope used to secure thatch on a house or
stack la19-. **thack-turf** a roofing turf la16.
thack and raip the thatch of a house, stack etc
and the ropes tying it down; also fig describing
something tidy, comfortable, well-secured
la18-20. [ME thakk, OE þæc (n); Eng thatch is f
the OE v þecc(e)an; cf THEEK]
thack[2] **&c** vt, chf ~**in** a beating; a severe scolding la19-e20. [ME]
thae &c la16-; **tha &c** la14-16, **thai &c**
la14-e19, **they** la16-, **thea &c** la16-e20 [ðe]
pronoun, pl of THAT = those la14-, now C, S.
adj **1** = those la14-; see also THAT adj 2. **2** occas
= these la19-; cf THIS adj 3. [nME, OE þā, tha,
corresponding to sME tho, which was later
altered to those]
thaft &c 19-, now Ork-EC, only Sc, **thoft** e16;
taft &c 19-, Sh [θaft; *θoft] n a rower's bench,
thwart. [ME thoft, OE þofte, ON þopta]
thai &c, tha &c [ðe] personal pronoun = they
la14-16. [OED they]
thai see THAE
thaik see THACK[1]
thaim see THEM
thair &c e15, 19-20, **tharf** la15; **thar &c**
la14-15, la20 (Cai) [θer, θar; *θarf, *θarθ], vi, pt
2 pers also **thur(s)t** la14, e19 [*θʌr(s)t], freq in
negative need not, not be obliged to. [ME 1
pers sing and pl thar, 3 pers sing tharf, OE 1 pers
sing þearf, f þurfan (v) need]
thair see THEIR, THERE
thairm &c la19-; **tharm** 16-e18, **therm &c**
18-20 [θerm; Sh tɛrm] n **1** a human or animal
bowel, gut, intestine; a gut used as the skin of a
sausage etc 16-, now local Sh-WC. **2** gut dried
and twisted into a string or cord for various
purposes, catgut: (1) in gen, 19-, now Sh Per; (2)
freq **therm** as a cord for the mechanism of a
pendulum clock or watch 18-, now Abd Ags
Renfr; (3) for the driving-belt of a spinning-
wheel la19-, now Sh; (4) as a fiddle-string la18-,
now Sh Lnk. [ME tharm, OE þearm]
thame see THEME
than &c, then &c (adv la14-, conj (in compari-
sons) la14-e19), **an** 19- [ðan; NE also an; conj
(unstressed) (ə)n] adv, also **dan &c** la19-, Sh Ork
= then la14-.
conj **1** = than la14-. **2** except, but la14.
noos an thans ['nuz ən '(ð)ans] now and then
20-, local Sh-Dmf. **or than, or thance &c** la18-
or, if not, then; or else; or even la14-, only Sc.
than-a- or **-o-days** in those days, at that time
la18-, now NE. **weel than** in that case; yes
indeed, very much so la18-, Gen except Sh Ork.
thanage see THANE[1]
thance see THAN
thane[1] n **1** hist a minor noble who acted as an
official of the Crown with certain fiscal, and
later judicial, authority over a tract of land; a

baron under the feudal system *15*-; *cf* TOISEACH.
2 *usu joc* any nobleman; *specif* an earl *18-e19*,
arch.

thanage &c ['θenedʒ], **~dom** *hist* the domain
or jurisdiction of a THANE 1, *15*-. [ScL *tha-
norum* of thanes *e13*; OE *þegn* &c a servant; a
follower; one who held lands of the Crown]

thane² &c *n* **1** a pennon, banner *la15-e18*. **2** a
vane, weathercock *la16-18*. [var of obs Eng
fane]

thane³ &c *adj* moist, damp, *specif* of meal from
oats which have not been properly kiln-dried
19-20. [Eng dial *thone*, OE *þān*]

thang *see* WHANG

thank &c; **thang** &c *la14*, **thenk** *la19*-, *freq
associated with affected pseudo-Eng speech*: *n*, in sing
la14-, in pl *la16*- = thank(s).
vt = thank *la14*-.
~ful &c **1** = thankful *la14*-. **2** *of a payment*
satisfactory, giving satisfaction *la15-17*.
~fully &c **1** = thankfully. **2** graciously; with
satisfaction *la14-16*. **3** so as to please, accepta-
bly, satisfactorily *la14-16*. **~fulness 1** =
thankfulness. **2** gratification, satisfaction *la15*.
thankrife full of thanks, grateful *la20*-, *Fif Ayr
SW.*
thanksgiving 1 = thanksgiving *la16*-. **2**
thanksgiving (**service**) *Presbyterian Church* the
service after Communion, in which special
thanks are given to God *18*-.
(**aa**) **one's** or **the ~** *used in reproach or displeasure*
the thanks for or recognition of a service, which
the speaker feels is inadequate *19*-, *now local
Ork-Kcb.* **be ~it** (= **God be ~it**) *exclam*
expressing thanks or relief *la18-19*. **give ~s**
say grace after (*and later* also before) a meal
19-20. **not .. for ~ ye** not .. for nothing *20*-,
local Bnf-Dmf. **~s be** *exclam* expressing relief
20-, *now Sh Cai Ags.*

thar *see* THAIR, THEIR, THERE

tharf &c *la19*; **thraf** &c *la15, e18* *adj* cold, stiff
in manner, unsocial, reluctant *18-19*.
thraf caik = tharf cake, a cake of unleavened
bread *la15*. [common in nEng dial; ME *tharf*,
OE *þeorf* unleavened]

tharf *see* THAIR

tharm *see* THAIRM

that &c, **dat** *la19*-, *Sh Ork*; **tat** *19, WC and
pseudo-Highl*: demonstrative pronoun, also **at** *20*-, *N*
1 = that *la14*-. **2** this *19*-; *cf* THIS *adj* 3. **3** *also*
aa that *20*-, *Cai C* used to emphasize a previous
phrase *19*-: '*It's very cold. It is that.*'
demonstrative *adj* **1** *also* **at** *20*-, *N* = that *la14*-.
2 *used as a pl* = those *la15*-, *now Sh-Per*: '*that
men*'. **3** parenthetic, without its following
noun (which is understood from the previous
clause) *19*-: '*she's the clever one that*'. **4** *also* **thattan** *e20* (*cf siccan* (SIC)), **that a ..** such, so much
la18-e20: '*she had that a cauld*'.
demonstrative *adv* so, to such a degree; to that
extent; very *la16*-.
relative pronoun (*cf* AT³) **1** = that, who(m),

which *la14*-. **2** *freq omitted in Sc*, *la14*-: '*wha was
the leddy gaed doon the road afore ye?*' **3** *possessive
expressed by various circumlocutions*: (1) **that** + *possessive adj*, *la14*-, *now NE*: '*the crew that their boat
wis vrackit*'; **that's** (= that his) was later construed as having a possessive ending (*as Eng* its)
and is now used of all antecedents (masc, fem,
neuter, sing, pl): '*the woman that's sister mairriet
the postie*'; (2) *not used of persons* **that .. o't, ~ o
them** *la19*-: '*the hoose 'at the end o't fell*'.
conj = that *la14*-.
and ~ and so on, et cetera *20*-. **like aa ~** like
anything, at full speed etc *la20*-. **or ~** or the
like, or something similar *20*-, *now local.* [*cf*
AT³]

thatch *see* THACK¹

thattan *see* THAT

thaveless *see* THOWLESS

thaw *see* THOW

the &c, **de** *la18*-, *now Kcdn*, **da** *la19*-, *Sh*, **ee** &c
19-, *chf N*; **ta** *la18-e19*, *pseudo-Highl* [ðə; *Sh
ECoast* də; *N also* i] *def art* **1** = the *la14*-. **2**
used before a relative pronoun *la14*-, *now only
law*: '*the which day, the Judge said ..*'. **3** used
instead of possessive pronoun: (1) with names of
relatives, *esp* **~ wife** *19*-; (2) with the names of
parts of the body *16*-, *Gen except Sh Ork*: '*keep the
heid!*'; see FIT¹, HAND, HEID. **4** used before nouns
denoting (1) public institutions *la18*-: '*he's at the
school now*'; '*they go to the church*'; '*he's in the jail*';
(2) aspects of domestic life etc *18*-: '*up the stair*';
'*sit at the table*'; '*say the grace*'; '*fish for the tea*'; (3)
commodities *la18*-: '*the price of the milk*'; (4) a fit
of annoyance or sulks *18*-: '*take the huff*'; *cf*
BUNG¹, STRUNT¹. **5** with names of diseases etc
18-: '*he's got the measles*'; '*he was a terrible man for
the drink*'; '*the dry rot*'. **6** with the names of various pursuits and activities (1) with verbal noun
(a) in gen *19*-: '*you've been at the smoking*'; (b)
denoting trades or crafts *la18*-: '*they're at the fishing*'. (2) of branches of learning, languages etc
18-, *almost obs except* **~ Gaelic**, **~ English**
[*after Gael*]: '*a minister's no muckle worth withoot
the Greek*'. (3) of sports, games etc *18*-: '*they
were playing at the chess*'. **7** with proper nouns
(1) before a surname (a) to indicate the chief or
leading member of a family *la14*-, *now hist*: '*Robert the Bruce*'; '*the Chisholm*' [translating F *le* or
altered f *de*]; (b) to denote the chief of a *Highland* (HIELAND) CLAN *19*-: '*the Mackintosh*' [prob
due to a misinterpretation of '*you, that dare to
claim kindred with the MacGregor*' in Scott *Rob
Roy*]. (2) before certain place-names *la14*-: '*the
Langholm*'; '*the Crail*'. (3) before the names of
schools or colleges *19*-: '*at the Waid Academy*'.
(4) before the names of feast days or times associated (at some period) with religious observance *18-19*: '*about the Martinmas*'. (5) omitted
before river names *18*-, *almost obs except place-
names*: '*drowned in Dee*'; '*Bridge of Don*' [prob represents orig Gael usage]. **8** with the numerals

expressing a certain year *17-*, *obs except* '*the Fif-teen*', '*the Forty-five*' (see FEIFTEEN, FORTY): '*in the 1664*'; '*since the ninety-nine*'. **9** used, where Eng omits in (1) ~ **baith &c** *la19-*, *now local*: '*the baith of them*'; (2) ~ **maist** *18-*, *now local*: '*the maist fouks*'; (3) ~ **ne(v)er** *e19*: '*the ne'er a thing*'. **10** (1) in various idioms *la18-*: '*for the matter of a fortnight*'; '*all one wants is the health*'; '*he wears the kilt*'; (2) in expressions of admiration etc *20-*: '*they tell me you're to be the great surgeon*' [prob after Gael]. **11** as a corrupt form of other prefixes and particles (1) ~ **noo &c** = EENOO *18-*; (2) = there *18-e20*: '*the ben*'; *cf* BEN[1], BUT, FURTH, THERE; (3) ~ **morn, ~ nicht** today, tomorrow, tonight *15-*; *cf* YESTREEN. **12** ~ **year** this year *la15-* [by analogy w 11 (3)]. **13** *only* **ee &c** *19-*, *now Abd Ags*: (1) in the; (2) on the; (3) of the. [cf *Dean of the Guild* (DEAN); THEGITHER]

the *see* THE

thea *see* THAE

theat &c [θit; *nEC* θet] *n* **1** *chf in pl*, *also fig* the traces (attaching a horse to a vehicle, plough etc) *la15-*, *now N nEC*. **2** a tow, pull by a trace-horse *20-*, *Ags Per*.

~**er** a trace-horse of a cart or plough *20-*, *nEC Lnk*.

hae (**nae**) ~ **o** (not) like, (not) have an incli-nation for *la19*. **kick** *etc* **ower the** ~**s** kick over the traces *la19-*, *now NE Ags*. **out of** (**the**) ~(**s**) **1** disordered; out of control; going beyond normal bounds *18-*, *now NE Ags*. **2 out of** ~ in addition to what is expected or needed *la20-*, *Mry Abd*. [only Sc; see SND]

theck *see* THACK[1]

thee[1] **&c** [θi] *vi*, *chf ballad* thrive, prosper *la18-19*. [ME]

thee[2] **&c** *now Sh C*, **thigh &c** *la16-*; **thei** *la14-e20* [θi; *S* θəi] *n* **1** = thigh *la14-*. **2** the part of a garment covering the thigh *e16*.

~ **pess** a piece of armour for the thigh *la15*.

thee *see* THOU, THY

theedle *see* THEEVIL

theek &c; thick &c *16-20* [θik, θɪk] *vt* **1** roof (a building) **with** (stone, slate, lead etc) *la14-18*. **2** *specif* roof, cover (a building, hay-, corn-, or peat-stack (PEAT[1])) **with** (thatch) *16-*. **3** cover (as with thatch), protect with a thick covering of hair, clothes etc *la17-*, *now local*.

n **1** thatch *la19-*, *now WC, SW*. **2** any thick covering of foliage, hair etc *la19-*, *now Ags Per*.

~**er** a thatcher; a roofer of houses *14-20*.

~**ing spurtle** a flat-bladed implement, some-times forked, for pushing thatching straw into position on a roof *19-20*. [nME *theke*, OE *þeccan* (*v*); *cf* THACK[1]]

theel *see* THEEVIL

theer *see* THERE

theevil &c *18-*, *now local N-Dmf*; **thivel &c** *la18-e19*, **theedle &c** *19-*, *now local Cai-Fif*, **theel &c** *19-*, *Fif Kinr* [*local NE-C* 'θivl; *Fif*

Kinr 'θidl, θil] *n* a short tapering stick used to stir food as it cooks, a SPURTLE (*n* 2). [ME *thyvelle*]

theft &c *la17-*; **thift &c** *15-e17*, **thieft-** *la16-17* [θɪft] *n* = theft *15-* [a legal term in Sc; in Eng the legal term was *larceny* until the Theft Act of 1968].

~**dom** theft; thievery *la16-e19*, *only Sc*. ~**fully** *e15*, *only Sc*, ~**ly** *15* by stealth. ~**uous &c** [***~WIS, ***~WƏS] thievish, pilfer-ing; furtive, stealthy *15-19*.

~**bute** [***~bøt] = theft-boot, the taking of money from a thief in compensation or as a bribe to prevent prosecution *la15-17* [*theft-* form earlier in Sc; ME *thefbote &c*].

by ~ stealthily, furtively *la15*, *only Sc*.

thegither &c *la18-*, *only Sc*, **together &c** *la16-*; **thegidder &c** *15-e20*, *only Sc*, **togider &c** *la14-e18*, **thegether** *19-e20*, *only Sc* [ðɪ'gɪðər, tɪ'gɪðər; *Sh* tɪ'gɪdər; *Abd* ðɪ'gɪdər; *St* tɪ'gëðər] *adv* = together *la14-*.

a' .. **thegither** altogether, nothing but .. *la18-*. ~ **with** along with, in addition to *la15-*.

thei *see* THEE[2]

their &c; thair &c *la14-16*, **thar &c** *la14-e16*, **thir** *la18-* [ðer; *unstressed also* ðər] *pronoun, also* **der &c** *la19-*, *Sh* = their *la14-*.

~**sel &c** *la18-* (*chf collective*), ~**sels &c** *la16-* themselves; cf *themsel* (THEM).

them &c, dem *la19-*, *Sh*; **thaim &c** *la14-* [ðem; *unstressed also* ðəm] *pronoun* **1** = them *la14-*. **2** *as the antecedent of a relative pronoun* those *19-*: '*them 'at sent it kens best*'.

~**sel &c** (*chf collective*), ~**sels &c** = themselves *18-*; cf *theirsel* (THEIR). ~**selves two &c** just the two of them *18-*. ~**selvin &c** = them-selves *la14-e15*.

theme &c *15-17*, **thame** *17*, *only Sc* [***tim; (*erron*) ***θim, ***θem] *n* = team, the right of juris-diction in a suit for the recovery of goods alleged to have been stolen; the process having become obs in *12*, *chf* found in fossilized lists of rights etc in charters as **toll and** ~, whence it was misunderstood to mean some kind of duty or impost. [OED *team*]

then *see* THAN

thenk *see* THANK

theologue &c *n* **1** a theologian *15-e16*. **2** a theological student *la17*. [earlier in Sc; L (f Gk) *theologus* a person who gives an account of the gods or of God]

ther *see* THIS

there &c; thar &c *la14-16*, **thair &c** *la14-e19*, **theer** *20*, *S* [ðer; *unstressed also* ðər] *adv, also* **der(e) &c** *19-*, *Sh Ork* **1** *also reduced forms* **the, they** *la18-*, **de(y)** *19-*, *Sh* [ðe, ðɪ, ð(ə)] = there *la14-*: '*they'll be nae peace*'; '*dey wir no a flooer ta be seen*'. **2** *also* **dir, dere &c** *19-*, *Sh Ork*, *elliptical for* there is, there are *17-*, *now local*: '*there naebody in*'.

~**anent** *16-19*, ~**anents** *la16* about or relating to what has been said above. ~**atour &c** over and beyond that; relating to what has been said above *la14-e16, only Sc.* ~ **awa**(**y**) away to or in that place; in that general direction *la14-, now C.* ~**ben** &c [*'ðɛr'bɛn] = BEN¹ *adv,* *16-19, only Sc.* ~**by** ['ðɛr'baɪ] = thereby *la14-.* **come** ~**by** 'come by' or get possession of that *la16.* **or thereby** *of a number or amount* or thereabouts, or round about the figure mentioned *15-.* ~**down** [*'ðɛr'dun] down there, down below *la14-18.* ~**fra**(**e**) [*'ðɛr'fre] from there, thence *la14-19.* ~**furth** [*'ðɛr'fʌrθ] outside; in the open *e16.* ~**in** ['ðɛr'ɪn] **1** = therein *la14-.* **2** at home, in(doors) *19-e20.* ~**intil**(**l**) [*'ðɛr'ɪntl] therein(to) *la15-e19, only Sc.* ~ **out** &c ['ðɛr'ut] **1** outside that place *la14-19.* **2** out of doors, in the open *la16-e20.* **3** abroad, in existence *la16-e18.* **4** out of that; out of that place *la14-.* **thairquhyne** [*'ðɛr'hwəin] from whence *la15, only Sc.* ~**till** &c ['ðɛr'tɪl] thereto *la14-e20.* ~**upon** &c ['ðɛrʌpon] **1** = thereupon *la14-.* **2** thereabouts, approximately *e17, only Sc.*

thereckly &c [ðɪ'rɛklɪ] *adv* = directly *la19-, Kcb S.*

therm *see* THAIRM

therteen *see* THIRTEEN

therty *see* THIRTY

thesaure &c [*'θɛ'zɑr, *?'θɛzɑr, *?'θizɑr] *n* treasure *la15-16.*

thesaurary &c [*?'θɛzɑrərɪ, *?'θi-] **1** the office of treasurer *la15-16.* **2** *also* **thesaurary hous, thesaurer houss** a treasury *la15-16.* **thesaurer** &c [*?'θɛzɑrər, *?'θi-] a treasurer *la15-18.* **thesaury** &c a treasury, the office of treasurer *16-e18.*

thesaurhous a treasury *la15-16.* **Lord** (**High**) **Thesaurer** *see* LORD. [chf Sc; L (f Gk) *thēsaurus, thēsaurārius,* MedL *thesaur*(*ar*)*ia*]

these [*'θiz] *n* = thesis, a proposition *e17.* [only Sc; F *thèse* or MedL *thesis*]

these *see* THIS

the streen *see* YESTREEN

thevis nek *see* THIEF

thewless *see* THOWLESS

thewtill *see* WHITTLE¹

they *see* THAE, THERE

theyn furth *see* THYNE

theyng *see* THING

thibet ['θɪbət] *n* (cloth made from) a kind of fine wool, *freq* used for women's dress aprons *19-20.* [var of *Tibet* [*'tɪbət], the country in Central Asia, from which it orig came]

thicht *see* THIGHT

thick &c *adj* **1** = thick *la14-.* **2** thickset, muscular, burly *18-, local Ork-Wgt.* *vi* flock, crowd *16.*

~**enin**(**g**) an agent which curdles milk, rennet *20-, WC.* ~**est** *n* the thickest part (of a crowd) *la14-15.* ~**fald** thickly together; in

crowds *e16.* ~**ness 1** = thickness. **2** a dense fog or sea-mist *la19-, local.* ~ **black** a brand of strong tobacco *20-.* ~ **and three-fauld** &c **1** in large numbers, in a crowd *19-, now Cai.* **2** very friendly, intimate *la19-, now Sh Per Uls.*

thick *see* THEEK

thief &c; **teef** &c *la19-, Sh Ork n* **1** = thief *la14-.* **2** general term of contempt for a person; a rascal, scoundrel *la14-.* **3** *freq* **the auld, black** *etc* ~ the Devil, Satan *la17-, now Sh Ork.* *vi* steal *20-, local Cai-SW.*

~**like** thievish; disreputable; stealthy, furtive *la18-, now Sh.* ~**ly** by stealth *la16.* ~(**t**)**ie** &c ['θifɪ; *also* 'θiftɪ; *Bwk* 'θivɪ] = thieflike, *la19-, local.*

~'**s** [θifs, θivz] **hole** &c a cell or dungeon, *esp* in a TOLBOOTH, in which thieves and other malefactors were imprisoned *16-18.* **thevis nek** [*'θivz 'nɛk] the call of the lapwing *la15-16* [OED *thevis nek*]. ~-**taker** a person who detects and captures a thief *e16.*

thieft- *see* THEFT

thieveless *see* THOWLESS

thift *see* THEFT

thig &c *vti* **1** beg, ask for charity, cadge; *latterly esp* solicit gifts from friends, *eg* when setting up house or a business *la14-, now Sh Ork Bnf Wgt; cf* SORN. **2** *vt* take for one's own use with or without permission *18-e20.* **3** *vti* crave, beseech, invoke (a favour, a curse) *la14-e19.*

thigger &c a person who THIGS, *esp* (*15-19*) a beggar who lives by begging food and lodging from particular houses *15-.* **thigging** &c **1** the practice of *thigging* (*v* 1) *16-, now hist.* **2** a gift or contribution so obtained *18-e20.*

go a thigging &c go begging *18-19, NE.* [chf Sc; ME *thigge* beg, ON *þiggja* receive, cognate w OE *þicgan*]

thigh *see* THEE²

thight *19-, now Ork;* **thicht** &c *la14-e16* [θəit; *'θɪxt] *adj* **1** tight, close in texture, watertight *la14-e16, 19-* (*Sh Ork*). **2** *of rain* heavy *la14.* [ON *þéttr*]

thimble, thimmle *see* THUMMLE

thin &c; **tin** *la19-, Sh adj* **1** = thin *la14-.* **2** *bowls, curling* (CURL), *of a shot* narrow, not having enough bias *20-.* **3** *of wind, weather* cold, bitter, piercing *la20-, Gen except Sh Ork.* **4** piqued, annoyed; unfriendly *la19-, Abd Ayr.* **the** ~ diarrhoea *la20-, NE Ags.*

thin *see* THYNE

thing &c; **theyng** *la15,* **ting** *la19-, Sh Ork* [θɪŋ] *n, pl also* **thing** *in eg* **a'thing** (A'), **ither thing** *20,* **monie thing** *20* **1** = thing *la14-.* **2** *unstressed, referring back to a previous noun* kind, sort, stuff *19-, now Per WC Kcb:* 'some black ink, or some blue thing'. **3** *freq with adjs of quantity* amount, number, extent, cost *la18-:* 'an awfu thing o port'.

aa ither ~ everything else *la20-*, *NE*. **an**(**d**) ~ and so on, et cetera *20-*, *S*. **a wee** *etc* ~(**ie**) *adv* somewhat, rather, a little *19-*.

think[1] **&c; tink** *la20-*, *Sh Ork vti, pres negative* **thinkna** *la18-e20*.   *pt, ptp* **thocht &c** *la14-*, *Gen except Sh Ork*, **thoucht &c** *la14-e20*, **toucht &c** *20-*, *Sh Ork* [θoxt; *Sh Ork* tʌu(x)t; *Bwk Rox* θʌu(x)t] = think *la14-*.
n = think.

I'm ~**ing; I** unk *e20*, *S, freq parenthetic* I presume, it's my opinion *la18-*.   **my** *etc* **ain** ~ my *etc* own private thoughts or opinion *19-*, *now Abd*.   ~ **ill to do** *etc* be unwilling to do, have scruples about doing *la19-*, *now Sh Cai*.   ~ **lang &c** long (**for**) *la15-*, *now Sh-Per*.   ~ **on 1** think of or about *la18-*.   **2** devise, hit upon *la20-*, *NE*.

think[2] *vi, pt* **thocht, thoucht &c** [*θoxt, *θʌuxt] = think, seem; *freq* **him** *etc* **thinks** it seems to him *la14-e16*.

thir *see* THEIR, THIS

third *17-;* **thrid &c** *la14-e19*, **threid** *la16*, **trid** *la19-*, *Sh* [θɪrd, θërd; *Sh* trɪd; *θrɪd] *adj* = third *la14-*.
n **1** = third *la14-*. **2** *in pl, church* a third of the ecclesiastical revenues, collected by the Crown and used in particular to ensure adequate pay for the reformed clergy *la16, only Sc*. **3** *in pl* the residue of grain left after milling or brewing, third quality flour *la19-*, *now NE-S*.
vt divide into thirds *la15-*.
~**ie** a loaf of coarse or inferior flour, with a large admixture of bran *la19, Kcdn Ags*.
thirdsman a third person, *esp* one acting as ARBITER[1] between two disputants *la18-*, *local NE-S*.
~**s of benefices** *etc* = *n* 2, *la16, only Sc*.   ~(**s**) **of kin** related in the third degree of consanguinity *16-*, *now Sh*.

thirl[1] **&c; tirl** *la20-*, *Sh Ork v* **1** *vt, also* **thrill** pierce, bore through, perforate *la14-*, *now Ags*. **2** *mining* cut through (a wall of coal) *la18-*, *now Fif*. **3** pierce or affect with emotion; thrill *la15-*, *now literary*. **4** *vi* vibrate, quiver, pass through with a tingling sensation *18-e20*.
n **1** (1) a hole, aperture *16-e20*. (2) *specif* a nostril *e16*.   **2** = ~**ing** (*n*) *la19-*, *now Fif*. **3** a thrill *la19*.
~**ing &c** *n, mining* a hole connecting one working with another *la18-19*.   *adj, of weather* piercing cold, bitter *19*, *N*. [ME; OE *þyrel* a hole, *þyrlian* (*v*) bore; ModStEng has adopted the metath form *thrill* (in fig senses)]

thirl[2] **&c, thrill &c** *la14-16*, **threll &c** *la14 vt* **1** reduce to or hold in bondage or servitude *la15-16*. **2** subject **to** (some condition) *16*. **3** *law* bind (lands or tenants) to have grain ground at a particular mill *15-e19*. **4** mortgage (land etc) *la16*. **5** (1) bind or oblige (a person) to give his services or custom to a particular person *19*. (2) engage as a servant *20-*, *now Bwk*. **6** bind with ties of affection, sense of duty or loyalty, force of habit etc *la16-*.
n **1** *only* **thrill &c, threll** a person bound in servitude *la14-15*. **2** *law* (1) the obligation of being bound in *thirlage* to a certain mill etc *la15-e19*; (2) the lands subject to *thirlage*, the SUCKEN[1] of a mill *la16-e19*; (3) the body of tenants *thirled* to a particular mill *18*.
adj bound in *thirlage* **to** *la16*.

thirlage &c 1 *also* **thrillage &c** thraldom, bondage *la14-e17*. **2** a mortgage *la16*. **3** *law* (1) the obligation on the tenants of an estate to grind their corn at a particular mill and to pay a MULTURE or duty, *usu* in kind *la16-e19*; (2) the MULTURE or payment thus made *18-e19*; (3) the land or body of tenants *thirled* to a certain mill *18*.   ~**dom** = thraldom, bondage *la14-e17*.
~**ed &c** bound in *thirlage* or by ties of affection, duty etc; *latterly freq* hidebound by an idea, belief etc *la16-*.   ~**er** a person under *thirlage*, *la17*.

~ **multure &c** *law* the MULTURE paid by tenants bound by *thirlage*; the right to exact this MULTURE *la14-e18*.   [chf Sc; OE *þræl*, ON *þræll* thrall]

thirl[3] *vt* = furl *16-e17, only Sc*.
thirstle *see* THRISSEL
thirteen &c *18-;* **thretten &c** *la14-e20*, **thrattene &c** *la14*, **thertene &c** *la14-e20*, **tretten &c** *20-*, *Sh* ['θɪrtin, 'θër-; *Sh* 'trɛtən; *C, S* 'θɛrtin, -ən; *'θrɛtin, *-ən] *numeral* **1** = thirteen *la14-*. **2** *as ordinal* thirteenth *la14-20*.
~**t** = thirteenth *la16-*, *now NE*.

thirty &c *17-;* **thretty &c** *la14-e20*, **therty** *e15, 19-*, *now Sh Ork C, S*, **terty** *e20*, *Ork*, **tretty &c** *la19-e20*, *Sh Ork* ['θɪrtɪ, 'θëtɪ, 'θrɛtɪ; *C, S* 'θɛrtɪ; *Ork also* 'tɛrtɪ; *'θrɪtɪ] *numeral* = thirty *la14-*.
~**twosome** a REEL[1] danced in sets of thirty-two dancers *20-*.

this &c, dis *la19-*, *now Sh*; **is**(**s**) *la19-*, *now N. pl also* **thir &c** *now C-S*, **ther** *la14-17* [ðɪr, ðër] *pronoun* **1** = this *la14-*. **2** *elliptical for* this time, this place, now, here *16-*: 'he gaed fae this tae Ayr'. **3** *in sing with sing verb* 'to be' *and pl predicate* these *la18-*, *Sh NE*: 'this is them'.
adj **1** = this *la14-*. **2** *in sing, used as pl* these *18-*, *now Sh-N, Kcb*. **3** *in pl, chf* **these** those *19-*, *now NE Ags*; *cf* THAT *pronoun* 2, THAE *adj* 2. **4** *in combs* ~ **day**, ~ **nicht** today, tonight *19-*, *now Sh-WC*; *cf* THE 11 (3).
adv **1** = this, thus *la14-16*. **2** *qualifying an adj* so, to such a degree or extent *la16-*, *now Sh NE*.   ~ **gait** in this way, thus *e16*.
this o't this state of affairs, this point or pitch *19-e20*.

thissell-cok *see* THROSTLE
thistle *see* THRISSEL
thivel *see* THEEVIL
tho *la18-;* **thouch &c** *la14-19, only Sc*, **thoch**

&c *16-18*, **thoucht** &c *la14-16*, **thocht** &c *la14-16*, **to** &c *la19-*, *Sh Ork* [θo; *θɔx, *θʌux] *conj*, *adv* = though. [see SND. OED *though*]

thocht, thought *la18-*; **thoucht** &c *la14-e20*, **thoft** *la16*, **thot** *e17*, **tought** &c *la19-e20*, *Sh Ork* [θoxt; *Sh Ork also* tʌu(x)t; *Bwk S* θʌu(x)t] *n* **1** = thought *la14-*. **2** anxiety, care, trouble; a cause for anxiety, a burden, worry *la19-*. **3 a** (**wee** *etc*) ~ a very small amount (of), a little; somewhat, rather *la18-*.

thochtful on careful of *la14*. ~**ie** &c *adj* heedful, attentive; serious-minded; anxious *la14-e20*. *n* = *n* 3, *la18-*. ~**iness** anxiety; melancholy *la17-e18*. **thouchtish** serious, pensive *20-*, *Rox*. ~**it** worried, anxious, troubled *la19-*, *now Loth*. **ill-~ed** having nasty or suspicious thoughts, nasty-minded *19-*, *local Sh-EC*.

~**-bane** &c a wishbone *19-*, *NE*.

it's my *etc* ~ it's my belief *la19-*, *now Sh*.

thocht *see* THINK[1], THINK[2], THO

thock *vi* pant, breathe heavily with exertion *19-20*, *S*. [obscure]

thoft *see* THAFT, THOCHT

thole &c; **tholl** *la16-18 v* **1** *vt* suffer, have to bear (pain, grief etc); be subjected to; be afflicted with *la14-*. **2** endure with patience or fortitude, put up with, tolerate *la14-*. **3** allow, permit, suffer *la14-19*. **4** be able to endure; have capacity for *la18-*, *now local N-WC*. **5** *vi* be patient, wait patiently *la14, 18-*, *now N Per*. *n* patience, endurance *20-*, *Gall Uls*.

~**able** bearable, tolerable *19-*, *Gen except Sh Ork*. **tholance** &c sufferance, toleration *la15-e16*, *only Sc*. **tholing** &c sufferance, permission, leave *la14-15*, *only Sc*. ~**mode** &c, ~**mude** &c [*~mød] patient, submissive, meek *la14-e16*. ~**moody** &c ['~mødɪ] patient; pensive *18-e20*.

~ **amends** &c *freq of health* be capable of improvement *la18-*, *now Dmf*. ~ **an assize** *etc law* stand trial *15-*. ~ **fire and water** *of grain* be dried and ground at a mill *18-e19*. [translating charter phrase (*grana quae*) *aquam et ignem patiuntur*]. ~ **through** pull through an illness *la19-*, *Ags wLoth*. ~ **wi** put up with, tolerate *19-*. [ME; OE *þolian*, ON *þola* endure]

tholl *see* TOLL

tholmont *see* TOWMOND

tholoney *e16*; **tholnie** *e17* [*'tol(o)nɪ, *'θol-] *n* a toll. [eModEng (once) *toloney*; Med and laL *t(h)olonēum*. OED *toloney*]

thon &c [ðon] *pronoun, indicating a thing or person more remote from the speaker than another or others* that *19-*, *Gen except Sh Ork*. *adj* that; those *19-*, *Gen except Sh Ork*. [conflation of YON w THAT; *cf* next]

thonder; thonner *now NE, WC* ['ðon(d)ər] *adv* over there, at some distance, yonder *la19-*, *Gen except Sh Ork*. [conflation of YONDER w THAT, THERE etc; *cf* prec]

thoo *see* THOU

thoomack *see* THOUM

thorl *see* WHURL

thorn &c; **torn** &c *la19-*, *Sh n* = thorn *la14-*. ~**ie** &c (**back**) the thornback ray *la18-*, *now Sh*. ~ **rone** an undergrowth of thorns *la14*.

thorow &c; **thorough** ['θorə, -ɪ] *prep* = through *18*. *adj* **1** = thorough. **2** mentally alert, sane *19-*, *now Bwk SW, S*. *vt* clean thoroughly *20-*, *now N-WC, S*. *n* a thorough cleaning or tidying *la20-*, *Gen except Sh Ork*.

thorough-band a stone which goes through the whole thickness of a wall *19-*. [*cf* THROU]

thorow other *see* THROUITHER

thort; twart *Sh Ork prep, with motion implied* across, from side to side *19-e20*. [chf Sc; Eng *thwart*; for form see SND]

thorter &c; **thourtour** *la15*, **thwortour** &c *la15* ['θortər; *Sh Ork* 'twartər; *'θ(w)ortʌur, *'θwartər] *prep* on or to the other side of, across, over *16-*, *now Sh*. *adv* across *la15*, *19-e20*. *adj* **1** crossing, lying across *la15-e18*, *now in place-names*. **2** obstructing, opposing *e16*. *n* opposition, obstruction *la16*. *v* **1** *vt* cross the path of; thwart, oppose *la16-e20*. **2** *vti* do something in a direction at right angles to what one has done before, *specif* (1) in ploughing or harrowing *19-*, *now Abd*; (2) in spreading butter on bread *la19-*, *now Abd*.

thortron [*'θortrən] transverse *la16*. ~**some** obstructive *e17*.

~ **ill** a kind of paralysis in sheep causing distortion of the neck etc *la18-e20*. ~ **knot** a knot in wood where a branch has grown out of the tree *e19*. [only Sc; ME *þwertouer* athwart over]

thot *see* THOCHT

thou &c, **du** &c *19-*, *Sh Ork*; **tou** &c *la18-e20*, **thoo** *la19-*, *now Ork Ross* [ðu; *S* ðʌu; *also* *tu] *pronoun, nominative also* **thee** &c *la14-15*, *la18-19*; *unstressed, after aux verb* **-ta** &c *la18-e20*, **-ter** &c *la18-e19* [*-tə]: 'ista'; 'wilter'. *accusative* **thee** &c, **dee** &c *la19-*, *Sh Ork* = thou, thee *la14-*: **1** *in gen*; **2** as used between equals and intimates, by adults to children, by masters to servants, etc (*cf* F *tu*), used *Gen* until *e19* (*latterly esp WC*), now only *Sh Ork local Ross and (almost obs) local Dmf*; *cf* THY 2. [see also E and *cf* YE]

thouch *see* THO

thoucht *see* THINK[1], THINK[2], THO, THOCHT

thought *see* THOCHT

thoum &c, **thumb** &c *la17-*; **toom** &c *20-*, *Sh Ork* [θum] *n* = thumb **1** *in gen*, *la14-*; **2** in reference to the practice of confirming a bargain etc by licking and joining thumbs, *freq* **there's my** ~, **lick**, **wet** *etc* ~**s** *17-*. *vt* **1** = thumb, touch with the thumb *18-*. **2** rub or massage (*esp* a sprain) with the thumb *20-*, *Sh NE Ags*. **3** dab or press (butter on bread etc) with a moistened thumb *la19-20*.

thoomack &c a violin peg *la19-20*, *Abd Ags*.

thoumie &c the wren *20-, Mry Abd.*

thumbikins &c a thumbscrew used to torture *Covenanters* (COVENANT) during the 1680s *la17-, now hist.*

thoum-hand &c the nearest free available hand, *specif* the right hand *la19-, NE Ags.*

thumb note *piping* high A, the top note of the bagpipe scale *20-.* **~-piece** a slice of bread with butter spread on with the thumb *20-, Ork NE-S.* **~-raip &c** a hay- or straw-rope made by twisting the strands under the tip of the thumb *19-, local Bnf-Gall.* **thumb variation** *piping*: a *doubling* (DOOBLE) of the *ground* (GRUND) in which the *thumb* note is usually substituted for the highest note in each phrase *20-.*

aboon &c one's **~** beyond one's reach, power or ability *la18-19.* **aside** one's **~** in an ineffectual, inept, or uncertain way *20-, now Bnf.* **clap** *etc* one's **~ on** keep secret, keep silent about *19-, now N Ags Per.* **come to** someone's **~** dawn on someone, reach someone's consciousness *20-, Mry Abd.* **crack one's ~s** snap one's fingers in pleasure or derision *19-, now Sh NE.* **the crack o a ~** a snap of the fingers *19-, now local Bnf-WC.* **no care the crack o a ~** be completely indifferent *19-, now Bnf.* **fash** one's **~** *in negative* pay no heed, never worry or concern oneself *la18-, now NE-Per.* **no be able to see one's ~** be unable to see ahead of one (in the dark etc) *la19-, now Sh Cai Per.* **turn one's ~** make an effort, bestir oneself *20-, Abd Ags SW.* **under ~** secretly, confidentially *la16-17.*

thoumart *see* FOUMART

thourch *see* THROU

thourtour *see* THORTER

thousand &c ['θuzən(d)] *numeral* = thousand *la14-.*

~-fold &c 1 = thousandfold. **2** a thousand times (in succession) *e16, only Sc.*

thout *see* ATHOOT

thow &c, thaw &c *17-;* **tow &c** *la19-, Sh Ork* [θʌu] *vti, pt, ptp* also **thowt &c** *19-, now NE* = thaw *la16-.*
n = thaw *17-.*

thow wind a wind bringing a thaw *20-, now Cai Per WC, SW.*

dirty ~ a thaw brought on by rain *20-, Sh NE Per Ayr.* **dry ~** a thaw after a high wind *la20-, local Sh-Wgt.* **weet ~** a thaw unaccompanied by wind or rain *la20-, NE, C.*

thowl &c *la19-, Gen except Sh Ork;* **thow &c** *18-, now N-EC* [θʌul; *N-EC* θʌu] *n,* also **~ pin** *la19-, now N-EC* = thole, the pin which holds the oar. [see SND]

thowless &c *Gen except Sh Ork, only Sc,* **thewless &c** *16-, now Loth WC Rox,* **thieveless &c** *la17-, now Abd WC, only Sc;* **thaveless &c** *e20, Per Uls* ['θʌuləs; 'θju-; *Abd WC* 'θiv-; *nEC Uls* 'θev-] *adj* **1** immoral, dissolute *la14-e16.* **2**

lacking energy or spirit, listless, inactive; lacking initiative, ineffectual *18-.* **3** *only* **thieveless** *of an action* ineffective; unconvincing *18-19.* **4** *only* **thieveless &c** cold, frigid, forbidding (in manner) *la18-e19.* [ME *theweles* = 1; OE *þeaw* a characteristic, an attribute]

thowt *see* THOW

thra *see* THRAE

thrab *vi, n* = throb *19-, now Ayr.*

thrae *19;* **thra** *la14-e17, chf Sc;* **tray &c** *19-e20, Sh Ork Gall* [θre; *Sh Ork Gall* tre] *n* eagerness, haste *la15-e16, only Sc.*
adj **1** obstinate, persistent; perverse; reluctant, unwilling *la14-e20.* **2** stubborn in fight, sturdy, bold *la15-e16.* **3** = thro, angry, violent *la14.* **4** keen, zealous, earnest *la14-e15.*
adv obstinately; boldly *la15.*
thrafullie violently *e16, only Sc.* [OED *thro, thrafully*]

thrae *see* FRAE

thraf *see* THARF, THREAVE

thraif *see* THREAVE, THRIVE

thraill &c *n* = thrall, servitude *la16.* [only Sc; *cf* THIRL[2]. OED *thrall*]

thrain; thren &c [θren] *n* a (sad) refrain, dirge, lamentation *la19, EC.*
vi harp constantly on a theme, beg persistently *la19-, Fif.* [only Sc; var of obs Eng *threne* a dirge (*in pl* = the Book of Lamentations), Gk *thrênos*]

thraip *see* THREAP

thram *vi* thrive *la18-e20, Mry Abd Kcdn.*
ill ~ *..* woe betide *..,* curse *.. 20-, Cai.* [only Sc; obscure]

thrammel &c *n* the rope or chain by which cattle are tied in their stalls, *specif* the part linking the post etc to the SELL[2] *19-, chf NE.* [var of Eng *trammel; cf* TRAMALT]

thrammel *see* THRUMMLE

thrang, throng *16-;* **trang** *la19-, Sh Ork n* **1** = throng *la14-.* **2** a large quantity or number *la19-, now Bnf Abd.* **3** pressure (of work or business), (a time of) great activity *la17-, now Sh C, S.* **4** close friendship, intimacy *la18-e19.*
adj, now chf **thrang 1** crowded (closely together); full, well-packed *16-, now NE-S.* **2** numerous, in crowds *18-, now C.* **3** *of places* thronged, crowded with people *la16-, now Sh NE-S.* **4** *of times, seasons, activities etc* busy, busily occupied *18-.* **5** *of persons or animals* busy, fully occupied *18-.* **6** intimately associated, on very friendly terms (**with**) *la18-, now local Sh-S.*
adv **1** closely, in large numbers *18-19.* **2** busily, assiduously *la18-20.*
vti = throng.
thronged 1 = thronged, crowded. **2** busily occupied, stressed with work *18.* **thrangity &c 1** a bustling crowd, a press of people *20-, now Per Stlg.* **2** busyness, pressure of work; bustle, stir *19-, now Per Stlg.*
~ o(f) full of, crowded with *18-e19.*

thrapple[1] &c *17-,* **thropple &c** *la14-e20;*

trapple &c *la19-, Sh Ork n* the windpipe; *more loosely* the throat, the gullet (of a person or animal) *la14-*.

vt grip by the throat, throttle *la18-*.

~-bow the Adam's apple *20-, chf Mry*.

weet &c **one's** ~ have something to drink, quench one's thirst *la18-*. [see SND]

thrapple²; thropple *v* **1** *vi, of wool etc* tangle *e20, Rox.* **2** *vt* draw (a hole in cloth) roughly together, instead of darning *20-, Bwk S.* [var of RAPPLE, perh by confusion w form of prec]

thrapple³ &c *n* ~ **plough** a kind of single-stilted wooden plough used *esp* in Cai *la18-, hist.* [see SND]

thrash &c *la18-;* **thresh** &c, **tresh** *la19-, Sh Ork* [θraʃ, θrɛʃ] *v, pt also* **thru**(**i**)**sh** &c *la18-e20,* **throosh** *19-e20,* **treush** &c *la19-, Sh Ork,* **threesh** *20-, NE* [θrøʃ, θrıʃ; *NE* θrıʃ; *Ork NE also* θruʃ; *WC* *θrʌs]. *ptp also* **threaschin** *e17,* **thrashen** *la18-, now NE, WC,* **thrushen** &c *19-e20,* **treshen** &c *la19-, Sh Ork* [ˈθraʃən; ˈθrøʃən; *Sh Ork* ˈtrɛʃən; *ˈθrʌʃən, *ˈθruʃən] *vt* = thresh, thrash *la14-* [since *17,* Eng has distinguished between *thresh* beat (corn) and *thrash* beat, chastise; in Sc the distinction is not made and the form is now *chf* THRASH].

~ing machine, ~ing mill a power-driven machine for threshing *la18-*.

thrash *see* RASH¹

thrashel &c *la16-, now Mry Abd Dnbt;* **threshwart** &c *19-e20* [ˈθraʃl; *Sh* ˈtrɛʃl; *ˈθraʃəld; *ʔˈθrɛʃ(w)ərt] *n* = threshold.

thratch &c *vi* twist the body about, writhe, *specif* in the death agony *18-20*.

n a jerk, twist of the body, *specif* in the death agony *17-20.* [only Sc; prob *chf* onomat, w infl f THRAW and perh FRATCH]

thrattene *see* THIRTEEN

thrave *see* THREAVE, THRIVE

thraveless *see* THRIEVELESS

thraw &c, **throw** &c *17-;* **traa** &c *la19-, Sh Ork* [θra; *NE also* θrav; *St* θro] *v, pt also* **thrawed** *la18-e20. ptp also* **thrawn** *15-* (see also THRAWN *adj*), **traan** *20-, Sh Ork* [θran; *Bwk also* θrun; *S* *θriun] **1** *only* **thraw** &c *vt* (1) twist, turn; wring; distort *la14-*. (2) *specif* turn (a key) in a lock, (a knob) on a door etc *la18-, now local N-Kcb, only Sc.* (3) twist (straw, withies etc) together, make (a rope) thus *19-, now Sh N-Per, only Sc.* (4) twist (a part of the body), wrench, sprain (a joint etc) *la18-, now Sh NE nEC, only Sc.* (5) *fig* distort, *esp* pervert the meaning or interpretation of *la16-e20, only Sc.* (6) *also fig* obtain by twisting or wrenching; extort *16, only Sc.* (7) force by torture or violence *la16, only Sc.* **2** *vi, only* **thraw** &c turn, twist, writhe; curl, become warped or twisted *la15-, now Sh Bnf Abd, chf Sc.* **3** *vt, only* **thraw** &c (1) thwart, oppose, cross *la18-, now NE, nEC, WC, chf Sc.* (2) *vi* act perversely, quarrel, grumble *19-, now NE local C, S.* (3) quarrel, contend **with** *19-, now NE, local C, Rox, only Sc.*

4 *vti, as* **thraw** now *chf Loth S* = throw *la14-*. **5** *vt* ? deliver a blow at, strike *la15, only Sc.* **6** *used without an adv, in contrast to Eng:* (1) throw away, aside, off *19-e20;* (2) *only* **throw** throw up, vomit *la19-, now N, WC, SW.* **7** *vti* discolour, (cause to) fade *19-, now Lnk.*

n, only **thraw** *in all senses except* 1 *and* 7: **1** throw. **2** a turn, twist, act of twisting *17-, now Sh N.* **3** a turn, distortion, tilt, warp *la16-, now Sh-nEC, WC.* **4** a wrench of a muscle etc, a sprain *la18-, now Sh NE, nEC.* **5** a twisting of the face, a wry expression *la19-, now Sh Ork Bnf Abd.* **6** a twisting of the body in pain, a convulsion, spasm *17-, now Dmf;* see also **deid** ~ (DEID). **7** *only* **throw** *piping* a series of gracenotes preceding a melody note of higher pitch *20-.* **8** *mining* a fault or dislocation in a vein or stratum *la19-, now Fif Lnk.* **9** a fit of obstinacy or ill-humour, the sulks *la18-, now NE nEC, WC.* **10** an argument, dispute, quarrel *19-, now NE nEC, WC Rox.* **11** a check, reverse, setback *19-, now Bnf Abd.*

adj, only **thraw** twisted, awry *e16, la19.*

~er 1 = thrower. **2** *only* **thrawer** a perverter of a meaning *la16, only Sc.* **be** *or* **get thrown back** suffer a relapse in an illness *20-, now local Per-Rox.*

~ **clet** &c *la20-, Renfr Ayr Dmf,* **~cruik** &c *la16-, now Sh-WC, Rox,* **~huik** &c *20-, now NE Arg* [ˈθraˈkruk, -ˈh(j)uk; *Ork Ags Per also* ˈkraˈkruk; *nEC also* ˈθraˈkrʌk; *Loth also* ˈθraˈθrap; *WC also* ˈθraklət, -krət; &c] **1** an implement for twisting straw etc into rope *la16-.* **2** a twisted straw rope *la20-, local Per-Kcb.* **thraw-mou** &c *appar* name for a cannon *la16.* **thraw-mouse** the common shrew *20-, NE.* **~-rape** &c = **~cruik**, *20-, local Bnf-SW.* **heads and** *or* **or thraws** lying in opposite directions; higgledy-piggledy *la18-.* **out o thraw** masonry, *of a stone* into alignment, straightened, squared *19-, now Abd Wgt.* **thraw one's face, gab** *etc* screw up, twist the face, mouth etc as a sign of pain, exertion, displeasure or disdain *18-.* ~ **the neck** *etc* wring the neck (of a fowl or, in threats, of a person) *la16-.* [OED *thraw, throe, throw*]

thrawart &c,   **thraward** &c *16-19;* **traaward** &c *20-, Sh Ork* [ˈθrawərt; *Sh Ork* ˈtrawərd] *adj* **1** perverse, contrary; adverse *la15-, now Sh Ork.* **2** twisted, crooked *19.* **head**(**s**) **and ~**(**s**) lying or facing in opposite directions; higgledy-piggledy *19.* [only Sc; var of FRAWART, w infl f THRAW]

thrawn &c;   **throwin** &c *la16,* **trawn** &c *la20-, Sh Ork Uls* [θran; *Abd also* ˈθr(j)avən] *adj* **1** twisted, crooked, distorted, misshapen *16-.* **2** *of the mouth, face* wry, twisted with pain, rage etc, surly *16-.* **3** *of persons, animals, events* perverse, obstinate; intractable; cross, in a DOUR, sullen mood *la15-.* **4** *of the weather* disagreeable, inclement *la19-, now NE.*

~-faced, ~-gabbit &c having a wry, twisted

face or mouth *18-e20*. **~-headed** perverse, contrary *la18-*, now *Ags Per Rox*. **~-mou'd &c** = ~ *gabbit*; *also of a gun*, *16-18*; cf *thraw-mou* (THRAW). [only Sc; ptp of THRAW]

thrawn *see* THRAW

thread *see* THREID

threap &c; thraip &c *la19-20*, **traep &c** *la19-*, *Sh Ork* [θrip; *Sh Ork* trep; *Mry Bnf nEC* θrep; *Cai-Inv also* θrep] *v* **1** *vi* argue, contend, be disputatious; quarrel *la15-*, now *Sh-Per SW*. **2** *vt* assert (something) positively, vehemently or persistently, *esp* against contradiction *la15-*. **3** *vi* **~ at, wi** *etc* nag at, be insistent with *19-*, now *SW*.

n **1** a controversial discussion, argument; a dispute, quarrel *15-*, now *Sh Abd Ags Rox*. **2** a vehemently held opinion etc, an aggressive assertion of one's beliefs etc *la17-*, now *N nEC*. **3** an old superstition, idea or saying *19-e20*, *C*, *S*. **4** *ploughing* (1) the angle between the points of the coulter and of the share *20*, *Ags Per*; (2) a swingletree *19-*, *SW*.

keep (**up** *etc*) *or* **stand** *etc* **to one's ~** keep to one's opinions despite all opposition or contradiction, stick to one's guns *la18-e20*. **~ down someone's throat** *etc 19-*, **~(up)on** *etc* **someone** *19-20* force one's opinion(s) on someone, try to make someone believe .. **~ kindness on** *etc* beg kindness, mercy etc from (God etc) *la16-e18*. [*threapland* etc land of which the ownership is in dispute, *specif* the *debatable land* (DEBATE) of the Scottish-English border, in place-names *la13-*; ME *threpe*, OE *þrēapian*]

threaschin *see* THRASH

threat; thret &c *la14-e17*, **threit &c** *la16-e20* [θret; *Abd* θrit] *n* = threat *la16-*.

vt **1** press, urge, *esp* by threatening *e17*. **2** threaten *la14-e20*.

threat *adj* forced, obtained by threats *la14*.

threave &c *18-20*, **thrave &c** *18-20*; **thre(i)f &c** *16-17*, **thra(i)f** *15-e16*, **trave** *la19-*, *Sh Ork* [θriv, θrev] *n* **1** a measure of cut grain, straw, reeds or other thatching material, consisting of two STOOKS[1], *usu* with twelve sheaves each but varying locally *16-20*. **2** a large number or quantity, a crowd *16-*, now *Sh*.

vi act as a *threaver*, *19*.

threaver &c a reaper paid by the THREAVE *19-20*. [ME *threve*, *thrave*, of Scand origin; see SND]

three &c, chree *20-*, now *Fif*; **threy &c** *19-e20*, *S*, **tree** *la19-*, *Sh Ork*, **hree &c** *20-*, now *WC* [θri; *S* θrəi] *numeral* = three *la14-*.

~sie 1 a move in the game of CHUCKS[2] *la20-*, *EC*, *WC*. **2** *also* **threeie** the third square or box in the game of PEEVER[1] *la20-*, *C*. **~some &c** (of) a group or company of three *la14-*.

~-bawbee costing three halfpence; *hence* cheap, worthless *19-e20*. **~fold** the marsh trefoil, the bog-bean *19-*, now *Sh*. **~ four** three or four, **a** few *la19-*, now *NE Per Ayr*.

threeple &c *adj* triple, threefold, three times over *19-*, now *NE Ags*.

vt increase threefold, treble *20-*, *NE Ags*.

threeplet one of three born together, a triplet *la20-*, *N-S*. [altered f Eng *triple* by conflation w *three*]

threesh *see* THRASH

thref *see* THREAVE

threid &c, thread; treed &c *la19-*, *Sh Ork*, **freid** *la15-16* [θrid; *frid] *n* = thread, *freq* linen thread *15-*.

~ dry completely dry *la19-*, now *Sh Ayr*.

get the richt ~ o have a correct understanding of, get the hang of *la20-*, *NE nEC*, *SW*.

threid *see* THIRD

threif *see* THREAVE

threit *see* THREAT

threll *see* THIRL[2]

thren *see* THRAIN

thresh *see* RASH[1], THRASH

threshwart *see* THRASHEL

thret *see* THREAT

threte &c [*θrit] *n* meaning obscure; *perh* a crowd, throng *e16*. [see OED]

thretten *see* THIRTEEN

thretty *see* THIRTY

threy *see* THREE

thrid *see* THIRD

thrieveless; thraveless *adj* thriftless, careless, negligent *19-e20*, *Gsw Uls*. [var, prob orig Ir, of *thieveless* (THOWLESS), w infl f Eng *thrift*, *thrive*]

thrife *see* THRIVE

thrift &c; trift *la19-*, *Sh Ork n* **1** = thrift *16-*. **2** prosperity, success, good luck *18-19*. **3** work, industry, profitable occupation *18-*, now *Sh Per Fif*. **4** willingness to work, energy, enthusiasm *19-*, now *Ork*.

~ie a child's moneybox *20-*, *Fif Edb S*. **~less 1** = thriftless, unfortunate; not thrifty *la16-*. **2** unprofitable, useless *19*.

thrill *see* THIRL[1], THIRL[2]

thrimble, thrimlar, thrimmle *see* THRUMMLE

thrimp *see* THRUMP

thrinfald &c *adv* threefold; triple *la14-16*. [nME; assimilation of nME *thrifald* to nME *thrin &c* threefold, thrice]

thring &c *v* **1** *vi* press, crowd, throng *la14-e16*. **2** press or push one's way forward *la15-e19*. **3** *vt* = thring, thrust *la15-16*.

~ down &c throw down, overthrow *la15*; cf *down thring* (DOON[1]).

thripplin kame &c *n* = rippling comb, a ripple (for removing the seeds from flax) *18-19*.

thrissel &c *Gen except Sh Ork*, **thistle &c** *la17-*; **thirstle &c** *la16-*, now *Cai*, **thrustle &c** *la19-*, *C*, **thustle** *19-*, *C*, **tistle** *20-*, *Sh Ork* ['θrɪsl; *Cai* 'θɪrsl; *C also* 'θ(r)ʌsl] *n* **1** = thistle *15-*. **2** a thistle or a representation of such: (1) as the emblem of Scotland *la15-*; (2) *only* **this-tle** as the badge of the **Order of the Thistle**, a Scottish order of knighthood, comprising the sovereign and sixteen members, with a Dean and Secretary *la17-*.

~ **noble** a Scottish gold half MERK of James VI, with a thistle on the reverse *la16*.

thrist[1] *la14-*, now *Sh Ork NE*; **trist** *20-*, *Sh Ork vi, n* = thirst.

thrist[2] *la14-e19*, **thurst** *18-19*; **trist** *19-*, *Sh Ork vti, ptp* also **thrustine &c** *la14* **1** = thrust *la14-e19*. **2** *vi* strike **together**, collide *e16*. **3** *vt* squeeze, press (down), wring *16-*, now *Sh Ork*. *n* = thrust *16, e19*. [OED *thrust*]

thrist *see* TRIST[1]

thristle *see* THROSTLE

thritty *see* THIRTY

thrive &c; thrife &c *la14-e16*, **trive &c** *la19-*, *Sh Ork* [θraɪv] *vi, pt* also **thrave** *la14-*, now *Cai C*, **thraif** *la16*, **thrueff** *la16* [θrev]. *ptp* also **triven &c** *19-*, *Sh Ork* = thrive *la14-*. *n* prosperity, a thriving state, boom *17-*, now *SW*.

ill-thriven &c badly-nourished, lean, scraggy *19-*. **well-thriven &c** well-grown, plump *20-*, now *Sh*.

throat &c *la16-*; **throt &c** *la14-18*, **trot** *la19-e20*, *Sh Ork n* = throat *la14-*.

~**cutter** a cut-throat, an assassin *16, chf Sc*.

throch *see* THROU, THROUCH, THRUCH

throcht *see* TROCH

throck, frock *n* the third, fourth, or fifth pair of oxen in a twelve-oxen plough team *19*, *NE*. [*cf* ModEng dial *throck* the sharebeam of a plough, OE *þroc*]

throm *prep* = from *la20-*, *Ross Abd Bwk*. [cf *thrae* (FRAE)]

throng *see* THRANG

throomb *see* THRUM[1]

throosh *vt* play truant from (school) *la19-e20*, *Kcb*. [obscure]

throosh *see* THRASH

thropple *see* THRAPPLE[1], THRAPPLE[2]

throstle &c *la18-e20*; **thristle &c** *la14, 19 n* the song-thrush *la14-*, now *literary*; *cf* MAVIS.

~**-cock** *19*, **thissell-cock** *la16* the male song-thrush or missel-thrush. [ME, OE]

throt *see* THROAT

throttle *n* **1** the throat, gullet, windpipe *19-*, *Gen except Sh Ork*. **2** = thróttle.

weet &c one's ~ slake one's thirst *19*; *cf* THRAPPLE[1].

throu &c, through &c; throw &c, thru &c *la14-15*, **throuch &c** *only Sc*, **throch &c** *la15-20*, **troch** *la16, only Sc*, **trou &c** *la19-*, *Sh Ork*, **thourch** *15, only Sc* [θru; *Sh Ork N, S also* θrʌu; *Abd Uls also* θrox; *v Dmf* θrʌx; *θrʌx, θrux*] *prep* **1** = through *la14-*. **2** (1) further into, in the interior of, in another part or end of *18-*, now *Sh, N-S*. (2) across, over the surface of *la18-*, now *Sh NE nEC*. (3) on the other side of (a wall), in an adjacent room etc to *la19-*, *Sh, N-S*. **3** during, in (the course of) *18-*: '*through the day*'; see also ~ *the week*.

adv **1** = through *la14-*. **2** *referring to the extent or direction of a journey* across country, from start to destination; having completed one's journey, arrived *18-*: '*they came through from Ayr*'. **3** at or near one's end, done for *20-*, *Sh-C*.

v **1** *vt* carry through, put into effect, complete *17-e18, only Sc*. **2** *vi, only* **throuch &c** succeed, win through *la18-, chf SW*.

thrower &c, througher &c ['θruər, 'θrʌuər] *n, mining* a passage made by the removal of coal from a seam worked *stoup and room* (STOUP); a ROOM driven between two levels etc for ventilation *17-*, now *Fif*. **throwly &c** thoroughly, completely *18-19*.

throu &c-band a stone etc which goes through the whole thickness of a wall *18-, local*.

through bearing &c support, livelihood, maintenance; a way out of difficulty or hardship *la17-*, now *Sh, only Sc*. **through-ca &c** energy, drive *20-*, now *NE Ags*. **throucome &c** what one has to come through, an ordeal, hardship *20-, Sh NE*. **through flat** a TENEMENT flat with rooms facing both the front and the back *la20-, local*. **througang &c 1** a way through *16-*, now *Sh Ork*. **2** a passage(way), thoroughfare, lane, corridor *la15-*, now *Ork wLoth WC*. **througate &c** a passage(way), alley, lane *la15-*, now *wLoth WC, SW* [OED *thoroughgate*]. **through-gaun &c**, ~ **gaen &c** *adj* **1** passing through *20-*, now *Ags*. **2** providing access from one street, house etc to another *la19-*, now *C*. **3** energetic, active *19-*, now *Fif Lnk Slk*. *n* **1** a passageway, alley *la19-*, *Stlg WC Wgt*. **2** a strict and censorious examination of a person's conduct *19-*, now *local NE-Rox*. **through-hochie** *marbles* a throw in which the marble is thrown through the legs from behind *la20, Bnf Abd*. **through house** a house whose rooms lead off one another, with no lobby *la20-, Fif Ayr Dmf*. **throughlet** a narrow passage or channel, *esp* at sea *la18-e19, Renfr Ayr*. **through-pit &c 1** production, output *20-*. **2** energy, activity, capacity for or progress at work *19-*, now *Sh Abd Per Dmf*. **through-pittin** a rough handling, a severe rating or cross-examination *19-*, now *Stlg WC SW*.

gang throu it dissipate one's resources, come a cropper, go bankrupt *la19-*, *NE Ags*. **gie someone** ~ **the wud, laddie** give someone a severe scolding *19-e20, SW, S*. **throu the boil &c** up to boiling point and allowed to boil for a short time *20-*, *Gen except Sh Ork*. **through the cold &c** *of speaking* thickly, in a choked manner *la19-*, now *NE Per*. **through the floor** *etc* from one side of the room to another *18-*, now *NE nEC Lnk*. **throu-the-muir &c** *n* a severe dressing down, a violent row *la19-*, now *local NE-Stlg*. *adj* untidy, heedless, devil-may-care *la20-*, *NE*. **throch-an(d)-throw &c** through and through, completely *19-e20*. **through time** in time, eventually *18-*, now *Sh Ork NE, C*. **through the week** during the week: on a weekday; on weekdays *20*-: '*if I dinnae see ye through the week, I'll see ye through the windae*'. [*cf* THOROW]

throuch &c *16-e17*; **thrugh** *e16*, **throch** *la16* [*θrux, *θrʌx, *θrox] *n* a sheet (of paper). [only Sc; unknown]

througal [*'θrugəl] *adj* = frugal *19-e20*, *Ayr*.

through *see* THROU, THRUCH

throuither &c *18-*, **through other &c**; **thorow other** *la17-e18*, **throuther &c** *la18-20* ['θru(ı)ðər, 'θrʌu-; *Abd also* 'θrʌudər; *θrux'ʌðər, *θorə'ʌðər, *-'ıðər] *adv* **1** *orig two words* (mingled) indiscriminately one with another *la16-20*. **2** *predic* mingled or mixed up; into a state of muddle or confusion, in(to) disorder, higgledy-piggledy *17-*.

adj **1** *of persons* untidy, disorganized, slovenly, unruly *19-*. **2** *of things* confused, untidy or badly arranged *18-*.

n **1** a confusion, row; a muddle, mess *la18-*, *now Abd*. **2** an unmethodical person who is always in a muddle *20-*, *Ags Lnk Rox*.

~**ness** muddle-headedness, lack of method *la19-*, *now NE*. [*cf* Ger *durcheinander* in confusion]

throw *see* THRAW, THROU

throwand [*'θrʌuand] *presp*, *adj* suffering the throes of death *la14-e16*. [only Sc; see OED]

throwin *see* THRAWN

throwth *see* TROWTH

thru *see* THROU

thruch *16-*, **through &c** *la15-e20*; **throch &c** *19-e20*, **trouch &c** *la19-e20* [θrʌx, θrux; *S* θrʌux; θrʌf] *n* a flat gravestone, *strictly* one resting on the ground, but also applied to one resting on four feet *16-e20*.

~ **stane &c** = *n*, *la15-*, *now SW Rox*. [ME *thrugh, throgh stone*]

thrueff *see* THRIVE

thrugh *see* THROUCH

thruish *see* THRASH

thrum¹ &c; throomb *la16*, *only Sc* [θrʌm] *n* **1** *chf in pl* = thrums, the ends of (warp-)threads, scraps of waste thread etc *15-*. **2** *fig* a (perverse) streak in a person's character; a whim, fit of ill-humour *la19-*, *now Ags*. **3** *fig, with negative* not a scrap, not a bit *19*.

vt twist, coil or tie loosely, carelessly, or in a makeshift way *19*.

~**mie &c** covered with or made of THRUMS, like THRUMS, frayed *la19-e20*, *Kcdn Ags*. ~**my** (**caip**) the Devil *la19-e20*, *NE*.

~ **hat** a hat made of thrums *e16*. ~ **keel** *also fig* the ruddle mark at the end of a web of cloth *19*.

sing *etc* (**gray**) ~**s** *of a cat* purr *19-*, *Abd-Ags*, *WC*. **three** *etc* **threeds and** *or* **in a thrum** description of a cat's purr *19-*, *now Ork*. [*cf* next]

thrum² &c *vi* **1** = thrum, strum. **2** *of a cat* purr *19-*, *now Abd Kcdn*. [*cf* prec]

thrummle &c *19-*, **thrumble** *la16-e17*;

thrimmle &c *16-e20*, **thrimble &c** *16-e19* *v* **1** *vt* press, squeeze *16-e20*. **2** *vi* push, jostle, squeeze one's way (through a crowd etc) *la16-e19*. **3** (1) *vt* press, rub or twist between the fingers; grasp (something) by fumbling or groping *18-*, *now Kcb Dmf*. (2) *vi*, *also* **thrammel** *la18-e19* fumble or grope with the fingers; work (with) the fingers in a cramped or awkward way *la18-e20*, *chf Abd*.

thrimlar a pusher, jostler, hustler *e16*. [see SND]

thrump *e19*, **thrimp &c** *e16* *vti* press, push, squeeze (as in a crowd). [var of ME, eModEng *thrum* with -*p*- from -*b*- of *thrimble* (THRUMMLE)]

thrumple *vt* crumple up, crush *19-20*.

n the state or condition of being creased, crumpled, or knocked about *la20-*, *NE Ags*. [var of FRUMPLE w infl f THRUMMLE and prec]

thrunter &c, **trunter &c** *n* a three-year-old sheep, *esp* a ewe *19*, *S*. [nME *trynter, thrwenter*; OE *þri-winter* of three winters; *cf* TWINTER]

thrusche &c *vt* **1** *only* **thrus**, **thursch** ? cut, cleave *la15*. **2** thrust, push *la16*. [only Sc; obscure; perh two separate words]

thrush *see* THRASH

thrush bush *see* RASH¹

thrustine *see* THRIST²

thrustle *see* THRISSEL

thud &c; tud *la19-*, *Sh Ork* *v* **1** *vi*, *of wind* come in noisy blasts, bluster *16-*, *now Sh*, *only Sc*. **2** make a dull sound on impact *la18-*. **3** *vt* beat, strike, thump *19*, *only Sc*.

n **1** a (noisy) blast of wind, a sudden squall, gust *15-*, *now Sh Ork*, *only Sc*. **2** a loud sound (*eg* of thunder, of a cannon) *16-18*, *only Sc*. **3** the dull sound of a heavy impact *19-*. **4** *also fig* a buffet, thump, blow with the fist *18-*, *now Ork Cai*.

thudder = *v*, *la19*. **thuddert** a tempest *la16*. **thuddin** a beating; a severe scolding *la19-*, *now local Stlg-Rox*. [earlier in Sc; see SND]

thulmard *see* FOUMART

thumb(ikins) *see* THOUM

thumble *see* THUMMLE

thummart *see* FOUMART

thummle &c *la19-*, **thimble** *la18-*; **thimmle &c** *la16-*, **thumble** *18-19*, **timmele** *la15* *n* **1** = thimble *la15-*. **2** *in pl* name for various plants, *eg* (1) the foxglove *20-*, *now Ags Bwk*; (2) raspberries *la20-*, *Mry Abd*. **3** *mining* an iron ring etc round a heart-joint in a pumping apparatus *la19-*, *now Fif*.

wha's got the thimble a variety of hunt-the-thimble *la19-*, *now Per Ayr*.

thump; tump *Sh vti* **1** = thump. **2** *vi* beat the ground with the feet; dance *la18-19*.

n **1** = thump. **2** a large piece or portion *19-*, *now Dnbt*. **3** a sturdy child *la19-*, *now Per*.

thunner &c, **thunder &c**; **tunnir &c** *la19-*, *Sh n*, *vti* = thunder *16-*.

~**ed** *of liquids*, *esp milk* tainted, soured, affected by thundery weather *la19-*, *NE nEC Dmf Rox*.

thunder-plump a sudden heavy thunder-shower *19-*. ~ **spale &c** a thin piece of wood whirled round on a string to make a thunder-like noise *19-e20*.

thunner-an-lichtenin the lungwort or other plant with white-spotted leaves *la19-, local Bnf-Ayr*.

thursch *see* THRUSCHE

thurst *see* THAIR, THRIST²

thurt *see* THAIR

thus &c *adv* = thus *la14-*.

~**ga(i)t**, ~**gatis** in this way, thus *la14-e16*.

thustle *see* THRISSEL

thwa *see* TWA

thwa(y)ng *see* WHANG

thwortour *see* THORTER

thy &c, dy *19-, Sh*, **dee** *19-, Sh Ork*; **thee &c** *19-20 possessive pronoun* = thy *la14-*: **1** *in gen*; **2** used between intimates etc *now only Sh Ork Cai Ross and (almost obs) Dmf*; *cf* THOU 2.

thyne &c; **thin &c** *la16* [*ˈðəin] *adv* thence *la14-e17*.

~ **furth**, **theyn furth &c** *la14-e15* [*ˈðəinˈfʌrθ] thenceforth *la14-16*. [(chf n)ME; appar reduced f eME *thethen &c*, ON *þeðan*]

ti *see* TAE⁴

tial &c [ˈtaiəl] *n* a tie, fastenening, something used for tying, *eg* a cord, ribbon *19-, now Sh Ork*. [eModEng *tyall* a rope, ME *tiel* a rein, OE *tigel* a tow-rope]

tibit *see* TAIBET

Tibbie Thiefie &c the sandpiper *20-, now Ags*. [imit of the bird's cry, assimilated to the personal name *Tibbie*]

tice &c *la19-*; **tyse &c** *la14, la19-20, latterly Sh Ork*, **tyss &c** *la15-16, only Sc*, **tyst &c** *16-e18, only Sc* [təis, taiz; *ˈtəist] *vt* entice, coax, wheedle. [ME *tyce*, aphetic f OF *atisier* stir up; *cf* eModEng *attice &c*, and Eng *entice*]

ticher *see* TEAR¹

tichit *see* TIE

tichle &c [*ˈtɪxl] *n, usu contemptuous* a troop, string (of people or animals) *e19, Slk*. [only Sc; uncertain; see TUCKLE]

ticht &c, tight &c [tɪxt; *Rox* təi(x)t] *adj* **1** close in texture *e16*. **2** = tight *la16-*. **3** firmly fixed *e16*. **4** competent, capable, alert, vigorous *la17-e20*. **5** (1) *of persons* parsimonious, close-fisted; *of things* scrimp, in short supply *la19-*. (2) short of money *la19-*. **6** neat in build, well-made, shapely *la18-e20*. **7** (1) *of persons* neat, smart, tidily or carefully dressed *18-e20*. (2) *of things* neatly kept or arranged, snug *la18-, local Sh-Wgt*. **8** *of ale* strong, brisk *la18-*. **9** strict, severely critical *la18-, now Cai*.

adv tightly, closely, neatly *19-*.

vt, also **teicht** [txt] *16* tighten, make close, secure or watertight *16-, now Sh-C*.

n a tightening *20-, local Sh-Kcb*.

~**en** *vt* = tighten *la19-*. *n* a tightening *la20-, local*.

ticht-hauden &c hard-pressed, harassed *20-, SW Rox*.

tick¹ &c *n* **1** = tick, a light tap or click. **2** a small quantity, a grain, drop *la19-, N-WC Kcb Rox*. **3** the game of tig *la19-, now Sh*.

vti tap lightly, *esp* in the game of tig *19-, local Sh-Ayr*.

~**ie** = *n* 2, *la19-, local*. ~**ie-tak &c** = *n* 3, *20-, now NE Ags Per*.

tic-tac-toe &c a game played with a slate and slate pencil *la19*; see SND.

tick² *n* play the ~ play truant *la20-, Fif*. [perh TICK¹ *n* 3, or altered f KIP²]

tick³ *interj, freq* ~**ie**, ~ ~ **&c** a call to chickens to come for food *19-, Ork-Per*.

~**ie** *child's word* a hen or chicken *la20-, NE Ags*. ~**ie-taed** pigeon-toed *20-, Per Fif Loth*; *cf* hentoed (HEN). [imit; *cf* TUCK]

tickerie &c *numeral, children's rhymes, prob* four *19-e20*. [alternative for *methery* (MUNDHERI), alliterating w TETHERY; *cf* ZEENDI]

ticket &c *n* **1** a notice posted in a public place *16*. **2** a certificate; a warrant, licence *16*. **3** a bill, a signed obligation *la18*. **4** = ticket. **5** *church* a Communion *token* (TAIKEN) *la16-e20, Ags Ayr*. **6** a severe beating or punishment *19*. **7** a person dressed in a slovenly, dishevelled or odd way, a 'sight' *20-*.

vt **1** = ticket. **2** *specif, of Glasgow Town Council* put an official notice on the door of (a house) to certify its cubic capacity and the number of people allowed to spend the night in it *20, hist*.

in ~ in writing *la16, only Sc*.

tickle¹ &c *vt* **1** = tickle *la16-*. **2** puzzle, perplex *19-, local Sh-SW*.

~**r** a problem, puzzle *19-*. **tickly &c 1** = tickly, ticklish. **2** puzzling, difficult *19-, now Abd*.

tickle² *vi* catch, tangle, become entangled **in** *la19-, nEC*. [see SND]

tic-tac-toe *see* TICK¹

tid &c *n* **1** a favourable time or season, an occasion or opportunity *18-, now local Ags-WC*. **2** *specif agric* (1) the proper or favourable season for ploughing, harrowing etc *19-, now C*; (2) a suitable condition of the soil for cultivation *la18-, now C*. **3** a mood, humour *la18-, now C, S Uls*.

vt cultivate at the right season *la18-19*.

in (the) ~ *of a river* in the proper condition for angling; *of a fish* ready to take the bait *la19-e20*. [only Sc; var of TIDE, perh orig unstressed, like [tɪm] (TIME)]

tidder *see* TITHER

tiddie *see* TIDY

tide &c *n* **1** = tide *16-*. **2** (a) time *la14-20*. **3** the sea, ocean *19-e20*. **4** the foreshore, the land between high and low water marks *la19-, now Ags Fif*.

v **1** *vi* befall, happen *la14-19*. **2** *vti* leave (fishing lines) for sufficient time to let fish take the bait *19-, now Sh Ayr*.

722

tidin &c ['təidɪn; *NE also* 'taɪðɪn; *Ayr* 'tɪdɪn] the period during which the lines are left down (as in *v* 2) *20*, *NE Ayr*. **∼ment** time, season *la16*, *only Sc*.

∼-line the last section of a fishing line to be *shot* (SHUIT (*v* 3 (2))) *la20-*, *Abd Kcdn Ags*.

tideus &c [*'tɪdɪəs] *adj* = tedious *e16*. [only Sc. OED *tedious*]

tidin &c *e16*, *19*; **tithand &c** *la14-16* [*'təidɪn, *'taɪðan(d)] *n, pl also* **tydance** *la16*, **tythance** *la16*: *chf in pl* = tidings. [OED *tiding*]

tidin *see* TIDE

tidy &c; tiddie &c *17-e19*, **tithy** *la15*, *e19* ['təidɪ; *'tɪdɪ, *'təiðɪ] *adj* **1** *of human beings and animals* in good condition, shapely, plump *16-*, *now Ork*. **2** *of a cow* giving milk; in calf, pregnant *la15-20*, *only Sc*. **3** = tidy, orderly *19-*.

tie &c *n* **1** *also* **tee &c** *la15-e16* = tie, something for tying *la15-*. **2** an obligation, a restricting force, constraint *18-*.

vt, ptp also **tichit &c** *la15* [*'tɪx(ɪ)t] **1** = tie *la15-*. **2** fasten or fix (with nails) *e16*. **3** *usu in passive* be married *la18-*.

tied *of persons or circumstances* obliged, certain (to be etc), inevitable *la19-e20*.

∼-back a short rope etc tied between two horses of a plough team to prevent their heads moving to the side *la20-*.

tift¹ &c; tiff *18-19* *n* order, state, condition; humour, fettle, frame of mind *18-*, *now Ayr Wgt Rox*.

vt adjust, put in good order or spirits *la18-e19*, *N*.

adj prepared *la14*.

in ∼, a-tift in(to) good or proper condition *18-19*. [var of obs Eng *tiff* attire, adorn, put in order, OF *tif(f)er*, F *attifer*]

tift²; tiff *19-* *n* **1** = tiff, a quarrel, dispute; the act of quarrelling *la17-*, *now local*. **2** a fit of ill-humour, the sulks *la18-*, *now Loth WC*. **3** *also fig* a sudden breeze, gust of wind *la18-19*.

∼er = *n* 1 and 2, *19-e20*. **∼y** quarrelsome, touchy *20-*, *Bwk WC Rox*.

tift³ *vt* drink, toss off (liquor) *18-e19*. [perh onomat]

tig &c *v* **1** *vi* (1) dally, have playful or amorous dealings **with** *la15-*, *now Sh NE*. (2) meddle, have to do **with** *la15-19*. **2** *vti* touch, twitch, pull playfully, teasingly or amorously *18-*, *now Sh*. **3** *vt* tap or touch lightly with the hand, *esp* in the game of tig *19-*, *Gen except NE*. **4** *vi, of cattle* run up and down, dash about when tormented by flies *19-*, *now Per Kinr*. **5** take a sudden whim, go off in a huff *la19-*, *now Ags*.

n **1** a light (playful) touch, tap, slap, *specif* the tap given in the game of tig, *usu* accompanied by the *interj* TIG *18-*. **2** = tig, the children's game *19-*. **3** a sudden whim, mood or humour; a fit of sullenness *la18-*, *now NE Ags Per*.

interj used in the game of tig when the pursuer touches someone *19-*, *Gen except NE*.

∼gie &c fractious, cross *19-*, *now Ags Per*.

∼-tag &c dally; haggle *17-*, *now Sh*. **∼-tire &c** a state of suspense *19-*, *local Ork-Kcdn*.

∼-tow &c [?'∼'tʌu] *n* the game of tig *19-e20*. *vi* play at tig; romp, flirt *19-*, *now Gall*.

chain(y) ∼, high ∼, lame ∼ variants of the game of tig *20-*, *now Gsw Kcb*. **tak a** *or* **the ∼** take a sudden whim or notion; get a fit of the sulks *19-*, *local NE nEC*.

tight [*tɪxt] *vt* **1** = tight, appoint *la15*. **2** set **with** (jewels) *la15*. [see OED]

tight *see* TICHT

tigirnes *see* TEEGER

tike¹ &c *18-*, **tyke &c** *la15-* [təik; *Sh Ork Cai* tɪk, tɛk] *n* **1** *usu contemptuous* a dog, a cur *la15-*. **2** *contemptuous* a rough person, a clumsy, ill-mannered boor *la16-*. **3** *more playfully, 19-*, *now N* (1) a mischievous child; (2) a fellow, chap.

∼-auld &c very old *19-*, *now NE*. **∼-tired** dog-tired, worn out *la18-20*. [ME; ON *tík* a bitch, female dog]

tike² &c *n* = tick, a mattress cover; ticking *la15-*. **tyking &c 1** = *n*, *la16-e20*. **2** the mattress itself *19-*, *now Edb*.

∼-o-bed &c a mattress *19-*, *now Lnk Dmf Rox*. [OED *tick* (*n²*)]

tile &c *n* **1** *also* **tild &c** *15-16* [*təild] = tile *15-*. **2** *also* **∼ hat** a top hat *20-*.

tilfoir *see* TILL¹

til-giddere *see* TILL¹

till¹ &c; tull &c *la19-* *prep* **1** = till *la16-*. **2** to (a person, thing, or place) *la14-*, *now esp Sh Ork N*, *in C, S usu before vowels or h-*. **3** *as prep governing the infin*, *la14-*, *now Cai*: 'If ye're keen till ken'. **4** *elliptical, with a verb of motion understood*, *freq implying setting about something 18-*: '*Till her, John*'. **5** *in various idioms where Eng uses a different prep etc*: (1) *freq with verbs of looking* at *18-19*; (2) by: (a) *referring to paternity* with (a specified person) as the father *la18-*, *now Sh N*; (b) **∼ name, trade** *19*; (3) for, on behalf of, for the benefit of *la18-*, *now local Sh-Per*; (4) with, for, as an accompaniment of (food) *la19-*: '*take some saut till't*'.

conj **1** = till, until *la14-*. **2** while *la14*, *e20*. **3** *after a negative clause* before, when *17-*, *now local Sh-Ayr*. **4** in order that *la19-*, *local Sh-WC*.

adv, with verbs implying setting to work etc = to *la19-*, *now Sh*.

tilfoir [*tɪl'fʊr] = tofore, before *16*, *only Sc*. **til-giddere** [*tɪl'gɪdər] together *la14*, *only Sc*. [Norse; *cf* TAE⁴]

till² &c *n* **1** a stiff, *usu* impervious, clay, found in glacial deposits and forming a poor sub-soil *la18-* [now adopted in Eng as a geological term]. **2** *mining* a hard laminated shale formed from TILL² (*n* 1), a kind of fireclay or *blaes* (BLAE) *la17-19*.

∼ie &c composed of TILL² *la18-19*. **∼ie clay** cold, stiff, unproductive soil *la18-e19*.

~ **airn** a crowbar *la19-, now Ayr Wgt*. [perh *cf* nME *thill* fireclay etc, poss f OE *þille*, ON *þilja* planking, a floor]

tiller *vi, of corn etc* produce side-shoots from the root or base of the stem *18-, now local Ags-Wgt*. [chf dial in Eng]

till-hew [*'tɪl'hju] *vt* hew or cut to pieces *la14*. [TILL¹ for *to-* + Eng *hew*]

tillie *n* a tiller (of a boat) *20-, now Fif*. [reduced f Eng *tiller*]

tillieloot &c [tɒlɪ'lət] *n* a cry of reproach, a taunt of Galashiels boys to those of the neighbouring parish of Bowden *19-e20, S*. [obscure]

tillie-pan &c *n* a flat iron cooking pan; a saucepan *18-, NE*. [perh one with a long handle like a tiller (*cf* TILLIE)]

tilliesoul &c [*tɪlɪ'sʌu(l)] *n* a small private inn erected by a landowner for the servants and horses of his guests and any others whom he did not want to entertain himself *18-19, now in place-names*. [obscure]

tim *see* TUME

timber *see* TIMMER¹

time &c [təim; *unstressed* tɪm] *n* **1** = time *la14-*. **2** a fuss, great excitement *la19-e20*.

~**ous &c** *17-*, **timous &c** *la15-* ['təiməs; *occas* 'tɪmɪəs] *adj* **1** (sufficiently) early, in good time *la15-, now law*. **2** at the proper time or season, well-timed, timely *17-*. *adv* early, betimes *la16-19, chf Sc*.

~**-taker** a time-server *17*.

at aa &c ~ at any time, at all times *la20-*. **at a** ~ at times, now and again *la19-, local*. **haud a** ~ (**wi**) make a fuss (of) *la20-, Sh N*. **in** (**all**) ~ **coming &c** for all time to come, for the indefinite future *la16-*. **this side of** ~ in this world, while life lasts *la19-, now Sh NE Ayr*. ~ **about** alternately, in turn(s) *16-, chf Sc*. ~ **o day 1** a clock *la20-, Sh N sEC*. **2** the appropriate time *18-*. **3** *ironic* a severe manhandling or reproof *la19-, now Lnk Ayr*. **a fine** ~ **of day** a pretty pass *20-*. **the** ~ **that** while, during the time that *18-*. **a** ~ **or twa** once or twice *20-, now Sh N Per*.

timid *adj* lacking in boldness *16-*. [earlier in Sc]

timmele *see* THUMMLE

timmen *see* TEMMING

timmer¹ &c, timber &c *la16-* *n* **1** = timber *la14-*. **2** wood as a material, *esp* as used for making small articles *la19-*. **3** a wooden dish, cup or utensil *18-19*.
adj **1** wooden, made of wood *18-*. **2** wooden, dull, stupid, unresponsive *19-e20*. **3** unmelodious, unmusical, tuneless *19-, now Sh Ags Per, only Sc*.
v **1** *vt* beat, thrash *19-, now NE Ayr Uls*. **2** *vti, freq* ~ **up** *etc* act or move briskly or vigorously, go at (something) with verve and energy *19-, NE*.

~**man** a carpenter *la15-e17, only Sc*. ~ **market &c 1** a timber market *la15*. **2** a fair held in Aberdeen at the end of Aug (*orig chf* for the sale of wood or wooden objects) *la18-*. ~ **meir** a kind of wooden horse used as an instrument of punishment *la17*. ~**-tongue** the disease actinomycosis which causes swelling and hardening of the tongue in cattle *20-, N Per WC*. ~**-tuned** having a harsh unmusical voice, tone-deaf, unable to sing in tune *19-, now NE, C*.

timmer² &c *n* a quantity of skins *la15-16*. [ScL *tymbria e12*; OF *timbre*]

timmer³ &c *adj* bashful, afraid *e20, Bwk Renfr Rox*. [appar back-formation f next or Eng *timorous*]

timorsome &c ['tɪmərsəm] *adj* nervous, timid, fearful *19-, now nEC, WC, S*. [eModEng *timersome &c, timbersome &c*]

timothy [*'tɪməθɪ] *n* a drink, dram, a glass (of toddy etc) *la19*. [perh the proper name; *cf* I Timothy v 23]

timous *see* TIME

timpan *see* TYMPANY

tin; tun &c *16, Abd* [tɪn; *Abd* *?tin] *n* = tin *16-*. ~**nie &c 1** a small tin mug etc, *esp* one used by children *19-*. **2** name for a tinsmith *la18-, now local NE-Rox*.

tin *see* THIN, TUNE

tinchel &c *la16-18*, **tainchel &c** *16-18* [*'tɪŋxəl, *'tɪŋkl] *n, deer-hunting* a ring of hunters who surrounded an area and closed in to entrap a deer *16-18*. [only Sc; ScGael *timchioll*, OIr *timchell* a surrounding, a circuit, round]

tincklarian *see* TINKLER

tindle &c ['tɪndl, 'tʌndl] *n* = tinder *la18-e20, Pbls Lnk S*. [var of Eng *tinder*, perh w infl f TANNEL; *cf* TUNDER]

tindling *n* a kind of cloth, *appar* linen *la16*. [only Sc; uncertain]

tine *see* TYNE

ting &c *vt, also vr* (*of cattle*) stuff (oneself etc) to the point of acute discomfort *la19-e20, Renfr Ayr*.

~**ed** swollen, ready to burst through eating fresh green fodder, *esp* clover *20-, now Ayr*. [*cf* obs Eng dial = split, crack]

ting *see* THING

tingle¹ ['tɪŋl] *vti* **1** = tingle. **2** (cause to) tinkle, ring or chime lightly *19-, local NE-S*.
n **1** = tingle. **2** a ringing, jingling noise *la20-, Abd-Per*.

tingle² ['tɪŋl] *vi* patch a leak in the clinkers of a boat *20-, local Mry-midLoth*. [appar extended f Eng *tingle* a small nail, a metal clip]

tings *see* TANGS

tink *see* THINK¹

tinker &c *n* **1** an itinerant pedlar or trader, *freq* living in a tent, caravan etc, and dealing in small metal wares, brushes, baskets etc, some being descendants of dispossessed *Highland* (HIELAND) peasantry, some of mixed gipsy descent etc *18-*. **2** *now usu* **tink** contemptuous term for a person, *specif* a foul-mouthed, vituperative, quarrelsome, vulgar person *19-*.

tink = *n*, *la19-*. **tinkie** = *n* 1, *20-*, *NE Ags Per*. **tinking &c** an abusive scolding, a slanging *la20-*, *Bnf Abd*.

~'s **tea &c** tea brewed in a pan rather than in a teapot *la20-*. [see SND; *cf* TINKLER]

tinkle *vti* **1** = tinkle *la16-*. **2** *vi* ~ **on** *etc* sing the praises of *17-19*.

tinkler &c *n* **1** a tinker, worker in metal; an itinerant tinsmith and pedlar *16-*, *in personal names la12-*. **2** a coarse, foul-mouthed, abusive person; a tough malicious person *la18-*.

tincklarian &c of the tinker sort *18-e19* [devised to describe himself by the *e18* Edinburgh pamphleteer, William Mitchell, a tinsmith by trade].

not to care *or* **be worth a** ~'s **curse** *etc* not to care etc at all *19-*. [appar altered f TINKER, though recorded earlier; perh by analogy w Eng *pedlar*, PEDDER]

tinneis ['tɛnɪs] *n* = tennis *e17*. [OED *tennis*]

tinsel &c; tinsal &c *n* **1** loss, damage by loss or harm *la14-18*. **2** perdition, damnation *la14*. **3** *law* forfeiture of a thing or right by failure to perform some stipulated condition *la14-e19*.

vt, also **tensal** *la15* subject to loss; punish by a fine *la15-e17*.

~ **of the feu** forfeiture of a FEU by failure to pay the *feu duty*, *19-*. [ME; ON **týnsla* f *týna* destroy, lose, perish; *cf* TYNE]

tint *la18-19*, **taint &c** *15-e17*, *e20* *n* **1** a conviction; *specif* a verdict by a jury *la15-e17*. **2** proof, indication *la18-e20*.

vt **1** = taint, convict *la14-15*. **2** prove (a charge) *e15*.

tint *see* TYNE

tinwall &c [***'tɪnwəl] *n* a funnel for transferring liquid *18*. [var of Eng *tunnel* now dial in this sense]

tip¹ *n* = tip, an end, apex.

v **1** *vt* = tip, put a tip on *la15-*. **2** remove the tip of *la19-*, *now Per*. **3** *vti* walk or dance on tiptoe, trip with a light delicate step *19-*, *now local Sh-Ayr*.

~**per &c** walk on tiptoe, trip, teeter *la18-e19*. ~**pertin &c** a piece of cardboard pierced by a pointed stick on which it is spun like a teetotum *19-*, *now Bnf Abd*. ~**pet &c** **1** *also* **tepat &c** *la15-e16*, **tuppat** *la15*, *only Sc* [?'tɪpət] = tippet *la15-*. **2** *fishing* a length of twisted horsehair to which the hook is attached on a line *19-*, *now Kcdn Ags*; cf *tippin*. **3** a handful of stalks of straw, used *eg* in thatching; a plait, tuft or handful of hair, wool, straw etc *19-*, *now Bnf Abd*. ~**pin &c** *fishing* the horsehair or (*now more freq*) nylon cord used to attach the hook to the SNUID *la19-*, *now N Ags Fif*; cf *tippet*. ~**pit &c** **1** = tipped *la15-*. **2** *of a pipe, sink etc* choked to

overflowing *la20-*, *Bnf Abd*. ~**pit wand** a tipstaff, a metal-tipped staff *la16*. ~**ple** *n* a bundle of hay tied near the top so that it tapers to a point *e19*. *vi* tie hay thus *e19*. ~**py &c** fashionable, stylish *19-*, *local Cai-S*.

~ **up** dress up, smarten oneself, titivate *la19-*, *NE Ags*.

tip² *n* = tip, a piece of special information.

have a guid ~ **o onesel** have a good opinion of oneself *la20-*, *local Loth-Rox*.

tip³ &c *vt* **1** = tip, tap or touch lightly. **2** *football* kick lightly with the point of the toe *19-*, *now Sh NE*.

tip *see* TUIP

tippence &c *n* = twopence *17-*.

tippeny &c *18-*, **two-penny &c** *18-*; **twa-penny &c** *16*, **tuppeny &c** *18-* ['tɪp(ə)nɪ; ***'twɑ'pɛnɪ] *n* **1** = tuppeny, twopenny *16-*. **2** *also* ~ **book** a child's elementary reading book, succeeding the *penny book* (PENNY) *la19-20*. **3** weak ale or beer sold at twopence a Scots *pint* (SCOTS) *18*.

The Twa-penny Faith popular name for Archbishop Hamilton's tract *Ane Godlie Exhortatioun* published in 1559, *la16*. **tuppeny tightener** *joc* a twopenny portion of fish and chips *e20*.

tippeny-nippeny &c *n* a kind of leapfrog *20-*, *local EC-S*. [perh reduplicated f Eng *tip* touch lightly, assimilated to prec]

tippertin, tippet, tippin, tippit *see* TIP¹

tire¹ &c [taɪr, təir] *vti* **1** = tire, exhaust etc *la15-*. **2** *vi* become or be weary or sick **of** *16-*. **3** grow weary of waiting **for**, long **for** or **to** *la18-e19*.

n a state of being or becoming tired, fatigue, weariness *19-*, *now local Sh-Stlg*.

tire² &c [***taɪr, ***təir] *n* = tier, a row, *specif* of stones or turf on a wall *17-18*. [OED *tier*]

tiribus *see* TERIBUS

tirl¹ &c *vt* **1** pull or strip off (a covering, *eg* clothes, bedclothes, thatch) *la15-*, *now local*. **2** take the covering off (a person or thing) *18-*, *now Bwk Rox*. **3** take the surface off (a piece of ground), *esp* for quarrying or PEAT¹-cutting *19-e20*. [see SND]

tirl² &c; turl &c *la19-e20* *v* **1** *vt* (1) cause to rotate or spin, turn, twirl *17-*, *now local Sh-WC*. (2) *specif* turn, twiddle, move (some movable fitting on a door etc) to and fro to produce a rattling, tapping noise; tap, knock, rattle on (a door etc) *17-*, *now Bnf Per*. **2** turn or bowl over, upset, trip *20-*, *now Sh Ork Cai*. **3** *vi* turn over, rotate in moving or falling, swirl, whirl *la18-*, *now local Sh-Per*.

n **1** an act of rotating, a turn, twirl *17-*, *now Sh Ork Cai Lnk*. **2** a short spell of some activity: (1) a bout, round or turn of doing something enjoyable, *eg* dancing, drinking *la17-18*; (2) a breeze; a flurry of snow etc *18-*, *now NE*. **3** ? a whirled pattern *la16*. **4** some disease (*perh* St

Vitus dance) *la16*. **5** a knock, rattle, tap (on a door etc) *19-*, *now NE nEC*. **6** a slight pat; a pecking kiss *19*.

~ie &c something which curls, twirls, or spins round *la19-*, *now Ork*. **~y mirlie** = *~ie-whirlie* **4**, *e16*. **~ie-tod** the greater plantain *20-*, *Abd Kcdn*. **~ie-whirlie &c** **1** an ornament, nick-nack *la18-*, *now local Sh-WC*. **2** *singing* a trill, grace-note *la19-*, *now Sh*. **3** an intricate device or mechanism, a gadget *la18-e19*. **4** the female pudendum *la18-e19*.

~in pin = PIN *n* 3, *la19-e20*.

~ at *etc* **1** = *v* 1 (1), *19-*, *local Sh-C*. **2** = *v* 1 (2), *freq* **~ at the pin** *16-20*. [metath f ME *trill* revolve, spin; *cf* Norw, Sw *trilla* roll, wheel, EFrisian *trüllen*, *tir(re)len* turn or wheel round]

tirl³ &c *v* **1** (1) *vi* pluck **at** (a beard) or **on** (the strings of a musical instrument) *la15*, *e20*. (2) *vt* cause to vibrate or tremble; sound (a musical instrument) by plucking the strings etc *la19-20*. **2** *vi* quiver, vibrate, thrill *19*. [see SND]

tirl *see* THIRL¹

tirless &c; tirlies &c *16-19*, **tirlas &c** *la17-19*, **treilȝeis** *e16*, **traleis** *la16* ['tɪrlɪs; *'tɛrlɪs, *'trelɪs, &c] *n* **1** = trellis, a lattice, grill, grating, *esp* for a door or window *la15-*. **2** such a framework on which climbing plants are trained *16-*. **3** *also* **tirlie**, *also attrib* a barred wicket etc; a turnstile *17-*, *now local*. **4** a grid or rack for drying articles indoors *e20*, *Bnf Abd*. *vt* **1** *only* **terlys** enclose in a trellis or grating *la15*. **2** = trellis, fit (a window etc) with a trellis, lattice, grate *16-18*. [OED *trellis*]

tirn *see* TURN

tirr¹ &c, tirve *now Ork Cai* *v* **1** *vt* take the top layer off (a piece of ground), remove surface turf or soil from (ground), so as to allow digging for PEAT¹, quarrying for stone etc *la16-*, *now N Bwk Rox*. **2** *also* **turr** *la18-19* strip or tear off (a covering, *esp* thatch, roofing etc) *16-*, *now N Fif*. **3** (1) *vtr* strip, undress (a person, oneself) *16-*, *now NE Ags*. (2) *vi* take off one's clothes, strip, undress *la18-*, *NE Ags*. **4** *vt* strip (a room, bed etc); dismantle *20-*, *local Abd-nEC*. **5** rob (a fruit-tree) *la20-*, *NE*.
n the layer of turf, soil etc removed from the rock of a quarry *la18-*, *local N-Rox*.

~in &c **1** the act of *tirring*, *18-*, *now Ork N*. **2** the layer removed before digging or quarrying *18-*, *now Ork N*. **~in pick, spade** *etc* one used for *tirring* (*v* 1), *la18-20*.

~ the kirk to theek the quire *etc*, *proverb* rob Peter to pay Paul *la16-e19*. [ME *tirve*, perh related to TURR]

tirr² *vi*, *of one's heart etc* beat, thump *20-*, *Ags*. *n* a thumping, shaking *19*, *Ags*. [perh extended f prec]

tirr³ *n* a passion, a fit of bad temper or rage *20-*, *now Sh Ork Dmf*. *adj* bad-tempered, quarrelsome *19-e20*. [see SND]

tirran &c *la16-20*; **tyran &c** *now Sh*, **teran &c** *la14-16*, *only Sc*, **tyrand &c** *la14-e16*, **tirrant &c** *16*, *only Sc* ['tɪran, 'tɔɪrən; *'tɪrand, *-ant, *'tir-, *'tɔɪr-] *n* **1** = tyrant *la14-*. **2** a cantankerous, awkward, or exasperating person *19-*, *now Cai*.

~eese &c, tarraneese &c **1** harass with overwork; tease, irritate *20-*, *NE Ags*. **2** treat roughly, bash or batter about *la19-e20*, *Bnf Abd*.
tyranfull tyrannical, tyrannous *e16*, *only Sc*.
tirranitie tyranny *e16*, *only Sc*. [OED *tyrant*]

tirrick *see* TARROCK

tirrivee &c [tɪr'vi, 'tɪrɪvi; *Loth also* 'tɛrɪ-, *WC also* 'tʌrɪ-] *n* **1** a fit of rage or bad temper, a tantrum; a wild extravagant mood, *freq* **take a ~** *19-*, *C*, *S*. **2** a state of excitement or bustle; a disturbance, fight *19-*, *N*, *C*, *S*. [perh based on TIRR³ or TAILȝEVEY]

tirr-wirr &c ['tɪr'wɪr, 'tʌr'wʌr] *n* a commotion, disturbance; a noisy quarrel, scolding match *la19-*, *now NE nEC*. *vi* quarrel, fight noisily; speak snappishly *la19-*, *Ags Per Stlg*. [TIRR³ + WIRR]

tirung &c [*tir'uŋ] *n* = *ounceland* (OUNCE) *16-17*, *Hebrides*. [Gael *tir-unga* ounceland]

tirve *see* TIRR¹

tirvis *see* TURR

tische *see* TISHIE

Tiseday *see* TYSDAY

tishie *la19-*, *local NE-Rox*; **tische &c** *e16*, *only Sc*, **tusche &c** *la15*, *only Sc* ['tɪʃɪ; *'tʌʃɪ] *n* = tissue *la15-*. [OED *tissue*]

tissle &c *vi*, *n* = tussle, struggle *19-*, *now Ork*.

tissu *ptp* woven *e16*. [only Sc; F]

tistle *see* THRISSEL

tit¹ &c *v*, *pt*, *ptp* **tit &c** *la14-e16*, *~tit &c* *19-* **1** (1) *vt* pull, tug, jerk, twitch *la14-*, *now Sh NE Ags*. (2) *vi* pull or tug **at** *la15-19*. **2** *vt* pull **up**, *esp* in a halter; hang *la14-e16*. **3** catch forcibly, clutch, seize *15*. *n* a short, sharp pull, a tug, jerk, twitch *15-*, *now Sh NE Ags*.

titup the trigger of a crossbow *e16*. [chf Sc; obscure]

tit² *vti* strike lightly, tap *e20*, *C*. [onomat]

tit³ *n* a nipple or teat, applied to women, animals and artificial teats *la19-*. [*cf* Eng dial and slang]

tit⁴ *n* a fit of bad temper or rage *la19-*, *now Bnf Ags Fif*.
~tie &c short-tempered, irritable *19-*, *now Fif*. [var of TID]

tit *see* TAIT¹

titbore tatbore *see* TEET¹

titch *see* TOUCH

tite &c *adv* quickly, without delay, directly, in rapid succession *la14-20*.

titter &c sooner, rather *la14-e19*.

titersome *see* TOIT

tithand *see* TIDIN

tither &c *18-*, **tother &c**; **tidder &c** *la19-*, *Sh*

Abd ['tɪðər, 'tʌðər; *Sh NE* 'tɪdər] *pronoun, freq contrasted with* TANE: **the** other or second (of two) *la14-*.

adj, also **tuther** *15-19, freq* **the** ~ **1** (the) other, alternative, second of two (or more), another; previous, recent *la14-*. **2** additional, yet another, next *18-*. [ME *tothir &c*; by wrong division of OE *þæt ōðer*]

tithy *see* TIDY

title *see* TEETLE

titlin &c, titling ['tɪtlɪn; *Cai* 'tɪtlɪn, -lag] *n* **1** the meadow pipit *16-*, now *Ork Cai* [*freq* seen with the cuckoo, hence *the gowk and the titlin* (GOWK¹)]. **2** the smallest and weakest in a brood, *esp* in a litter of pigs *la20-, Kcdn Ags Uls.* [Scand]

tits *see* TOOT²

tit-tat &c ['tɪt'tat, 'tɪt-] *n* an argument, altercation *20-, Cai.* [extended f Eng *tit (for) tat*]

titter *see* TITE

tittie &c *n* familiar term for a sister *17-20.* [orig child's word]

tittit *see* TIT¹

tittle &c ['tɪtl, 'tɪtl] *vi* gossip, tell someone something, *esp* by whispering in their ear; whisper, chatter *la15-, now local Sh-WC.* [laME *title*; appar onomat]

titular *n, also* ~ **of the teinds** *etc law* a layman to whom, after the Reformation, the Crown transferred the title to church lands, *more specif* to the tithes of church benefices, a *Lord of Erection* (LORD) *16-, now hist.*

to- [*only unstressed* *to-, *tə-] *prefix*, used as *intensifier, eg* **tobasyt** *adj* abashed *e16.* **tobet** *ptp* beaten *e16.* **tochange** *vt* change completely *e16.* **to holkyt** [*to 'hʌukɪt] *ptp* dug up *e16.* **to-perse** pierce entirely *la15, only Sc.* **to smyte** *ptp* struck very hard *e16.* **to-waver &c** waver uncertainly, wander *la14.* [freq in Douglas as an archaism; see OED *to- (prefix* ²)]

to *see* TAE⁴, THO

toad *see* TAID

toal *see* TOUL

toast &c *n, vti* = toast *16-*.

~**er 1** a metal rack or (*formerly*) a stone for drying and toasting *oatcakes* (AIT) in front of an open fire after baking *la19-, now Abd Ags.* **2** = toaster.

tobacco &c; tabacha &c *la19-, now Sh* [tə'bakə, -'bakə; *Sh* -'baxə] *n* = tobacco *17-*.

tobacco fleuk the lemon sole *20-, NE.*

tobacco lord a tobacco-importer, *specif* one who made a large fortune in Glasgow in the mid 18th century *19-, hist.*

tobackie *see* TAE⁴

tobasyt *see* TO-

tobeeth *see* TOLBOOTH

tober *see* TABOUR

tobet *see* TO-

tobooth *see* TOLBOOTH

toby &c *n* **1** a stopcock or valve in a water- or gas-main, *usu* in a roadway, at which the supply may be cut off *la19-*. **2** *joc* the penis *la20-, Abd Ags.* [perh Eng thieves' slang *toby*, Ir tinker's slang *tobar* a road]

toch &c [tox] *interj* call to a calf to come to food *20-, Cai Suth.*

tochachderety *see* TOISEACH

tochange *see* TO-

tocher &c; toucher &c *16-19*, **toquhir &c** *la15-16* ['toxər; *S* *'tʌuxər] *n* a marriage portion, *esp* a bride's dowry *la15-, now chf literary.* *vt* endow with a TOCHER, dower *la16-19.*

weel *etc* ~**ed &c** well etc provided with a TOCHER; well etc endowed, settled *18-*. ~**less** having no TOCHER *la18-e20*.

~ **band** a marriage settlement *la18-e19*. ~ **gude &c** property given as a TOCHER *16-e19*. [OIr, OScGael *tochar* an apportionment; *cf* ModScGael *tochradh* = *n*, and *tochar* a (small) present]

tod¹ &c *n* **1** a fox *15-20, in place-names la13-*. **2** a sly, cunning, untrustworthy person *16-, now local Per-SW.* **3** *in pl* fox-skin *15-16.*

~**die's grund &c** *children's games* a place of sanctuary *la19-, now Lnk Ayr.* ~**ly** foxy, crafty *la16.*

~'s **birds** an evil brood *la16-e18.* ~('s) **hole** *also fig* a fox's hole or den *la18-19.* ~**-hunt** a fox-hunt *19-e20.* ~**-hunter** a person employed to exterminate foxes *la19.* ~**-lowrie &c** the fox *la15-, now literary.* ~ **pult &c** meaning uncertain *e16.* ~ **stripe** a strip of woodland in which foxes have their holes *e15.* ~('s) **tail(s) 1** the stagshorn clubmoss *19-, now N.* **2** the foxglove *20-, Rox.*

hunt the ~ the game of hide-and-seek *la19-, now Bnf Abd.* (**the**) ~ **and** (**the**) **lambs** a draughts-like board game, fox and geese *19-, now Abd Per.* ~**-i-the-faul(d)** name of various games *19-20.* [northern eME; unknown]

tod² &c [tod; *Bwk* todʒ] *n, freq* ~**die &c** a round cake, SCONE etc *la18-, now S.* [prob var of DAD *n* 2]

tod³ *interj* a minced oath *la19, Ags Fif.* [euphemistic alteration of Eng *God*]

toddle &c *la18-*; **todle &c** *16-e20 vi* **1** play or toy **with** *e16.* **2** *of a young child or animal, of an old, infirm or drunk person* walk with short, rocking, uncertain or unsteady steps *17-.* **3** *more gen, freq in reference to setting off (usu home)* walk in an unhurried but rather ungainly way *19-.* **4** *of running water* glide, purl, ripple *la18-19.*

n **1** a leisurely walk or stroll *la19-*. **2** a toddler, toddling child; a small neat person *19.* [orig Sc; obscure]

toe *n, freq* **toesee &c** [to'zi] the mark at which a *curler* (CURL) aims his stones, the TEE¹ *la18-19.* [perh connected w Eng *taw* the line from which one shoots a marble]

toe *see* TAE¹

toffee *see* TAFFIE

toft *see* TAFT

toga *n* **1** = toga. **2** *Sc Univs* the scarlet gown worn by undergraduates, *esp* at Aberdeen *la19-*; cf *red gown* (REID¹).

together, togider *see* THEGITHER

to holkyt *see* TO-

toil &c *v* **1** *vi* = toil. **2** *vr* exhaust oneself with hard work *la19-*, *now Sh*. [*cf* TULYIE]

toilʒe *see* TULYIE

toiseach &c ['toʃəx; *Gael* 'tɔːʃəx] *n* the head of a *kindred* (KIN) in Gaelic-speaking parts of Scotland in the early medieval period *la18-*, *hist*.

toschachdor &c [*'toʃə(x)dər] an official in Gaelic-speaking areas whose duties evolved into those of the *mair of fee* (MAIR²) *16-*, *now hist*.

tossachiorschip *la14* ['toʃəxərʃɪp], **tochachderety** *e15* [*?'toʃəxdəraxɪ], **toshachdorach &c** *19-* ['toʃə(x)d(ə)rəx] the office of *toschachdor*. [Gael *toiseach* (translated in ScL documents as *thenus* (see THANE¹)), *toiseadrach, toiseadaireachd*; *cf* MORMAER]

toist *see* TEISTIE

toit &c [toit, tɔit] *vi* **1** walk with short unsteady steps, totter, *esp* from weakness or old age *la18-*, *now Bnf Abd*. **2** move about doing odd jobs, work steadily but not very strenuously *19-*, *now Abd*.
n **1** an attack of illness, a dizzy turn *19-*, *now Ork SW*. **2** a fit of bad temper *e19*.
~er &c = *v* 1, *19-*, *now Abd Ags*. **titersome** ['tɔitərsʌm] *of a job* fiddling, tediously difficult *20-*, *NE*. **~le &c** *vi* totter; toddle; idle about aimlessly *la19-*, *now NE*. *n* a short, quick or uncertain step, a toddle *la19-*, *NE*. [var of TOT³]

token *see* TAIKEN

tol *see* TELL

tolbooth &c; towbooth &c *la15-19*, **towbeeth &c** *18-e20*, *N*, **tobooth &c** *18-e20* ['tolbuθ; *Abd also* 'tʌubiθ; *Ayr also* tə'beθ; *'tolbøð, *-bøθ, *'tʌu-; *tə'bøθ; *Cai* *-'bið, *-'biθ] *n* **1** a booth or office at which tolls, market dues etc were collected *la14*. **2** a town hall, *freq* incorporating *n* 1 and *n* 3, *15-*, *now hist*, or applied to a building (or part of it) *orig* used as such in certain towns and still standing. **3** a town prison, jail (*formerly freq* consisting of cells under the town hall) *la15-*, *now hist*. [chf Sc; ME *tol-boþe*]

toldie *see* DOLL

tolerance &c *n* **1** a licence or permission given, *freq* by tacit consent, to someone to do or enjoy something to which he cannot establish a formal right *la16-e20*. **2** = tolerance.

toll &c; tholl &c *16-17*, **towl-** *19-e20* [tol; *tʌul] *n* **1** = toll *la14-*. **2** *fig* something paid as a duty *la14*. **3** a checkpoint on a turnpike road where tolls were collected, a toll-bar *la18-*, *now in place-names*.
~ie &c nickname for a toll-collector *19-e20*.
~-bar 1 = toll-bar. **2** the toll gatekeeper's house; the turnpike road itself *19-e20*. **~ road** a road on which tolls were charged, a turnpike road *la18-*, *now hist*.

toll *see* TELL, TOWL

tollet &c [*'tolət; *?'tølət] *n* = toilet: **1** *also* **tulat** a piece of cloth for wrapping clothes *e16*; **2** *also misreading* **tollar** a long, narrow, *freq* embroidered cloth for laying over a table etc *e18*. [OED *toilet*]

tollie *see* DOLL

tolmowth *see* TOWMOND

tolter &c; towter *la16* [Ork 'tultər; *'toltər, *'tʌutər] *adj* unsteady, unstable; insecure, precarious *15-16*, *la19-* (Ork). [laME; *appar* MDu *touteren* waver, totter]

toman &c [*'tomən] *n* a little hill, mound, *freq* one formed by the moraine of a glacier, in folklore associated with a fairy dwelling *19*. [Gael *toman*, dim of *tom* a hillock]

toman *see* TOWMOND

tomb *see* TOME

tombe [tom] *n* = tome *la17*. [only Sc. OED *tome*]

tome &c *18-*; **toum &c** *la17-*, *now Cai*, **tomb** *18-e20*, *Sh* [tom; *Cai* tʌum; *Rox also* *tum] *n* a cord of twisted horsehair used as a fishing-line; the cord to which the hook is attached in floating lines; the SNUID joining the hook to the hemp in a handline *la17-*, *now Sh Ork Cai Ags*. [ON *taumr* a rein, string, cord; *cf* Norw dial *taum* also a fishing-line]

tome *see* TUME

to-morrow *adv* **1** = tomorrow. **2** on the next day *la17-e18*, *only Sc*.

tone¹ *n* = tone.
toner a person who talks endlessly on the same subject *20-*, *now Lnk Kcb*.

tone² *n* the buttocks; the anus *e16*. [only Sc; Gael *tòn*]

tone *see* TUNE, TAK

tongue &c; toung &c *la14-18* [tʌŋ; *tuŋ] *n* **1** = tongue *la14-*. **2** impudence, abuse, violent language *la19-*, *NE Ags WC, SW*.
vt scold, revile *la19-*.
tonguie &c glib, loquacious, fluent *la18-*, *now Sh Cai*.
~-betrusht blunt, outspoken *e20*, *chf Abd*. **~-deaving** tiresomely talkative *la19-*, *now Sh Bnf*. **~-raik &c** volubility, flow of language *19-e20*. **~-tack(it)** tongue-tie(d) *17-*, *now local Sh-Per*.
be ~ by word of mouth *16*, *only Sc*.

tonie *n* the jellyfish, medusa *20-*, *Mry*. [reduced f Ork, Cai *clunkertonie*, of Scand origin (*cf* Dan *klynger-torn* a bramble)]

tontine *n* = tontine, a kind of annuity.
T~ face a grimace, distortion of the face from laughing, glumness etc *19-e20*, *Gsw*; see SND.

too *see* TAE⁴

toober *see* TABOUR

tooch [tux] *n* the sound of a shot, a bang, puff *20-*, *Bwk S*.

interj implying an immediate or instantaneous result *la19-, Kcdn Ags Dmf*. [onomat]

too-hoo ['tu'hu; *S* 'tø'hø] *n* **1** a fuss; hullabaloo *la19-, now Sh Ags Dmf*. **2** a spiritless, useless person *19-, local Kcdn-S*. [onomat, 1 of an outcry, 2 ? of an owl]

tooken *see* TAK

tool(y)ie *see* TULYIE

toom *see* THOUM, TUME

toon *see* TUNE

toontie *see* TWENTY

toop *see* TUIP

toorie *see* TOUR[1]

toosh &c nonsense word used in children's games *20*.

toosht &c *n* **1** a loose untidy bundle (of rags, straw etc); a bunch, tuft *la19-, NE*. **2** a slattern; *more gen* a nasty unpleasant person *la19-, now Bnf Abd*.

v **1** *vt* rumple, bundle up carelessly *la19-, now Ags*. **2** *vi* toss or be strewn about; dash hither and thither *la19-, now Abd*.

　　tooshlich &c ['tuʃləx] = *n* 1, *la19-, now Bnf*. [see SND]

toot[1]; **tut** [tut; *tøt] *v* ~**-mou'd &c** having protruding lips *16-17*. ~**-net** a salmon-net hung between the shore and a boat (in the Tay estuary), and hauled as soon as a watcher in the boat saw a fish strike the net *la18-e20, Ags-Fif*. [ME *tote* protrude, *tute* peep]

toot[2]; **toots, tits &c** [tut(s); tøts, trts] *interj, freq* reduplicated, expressing disapproval or expostulation nonsense! *18-*.

vi utter the exclam TOOT[2], *19-, now local Ork-Per*. [see SND]

toot *see* TOUT[1], TOUT[2]

tooter &c *vi* **1** work ineffectually, potter ineptly *la19-, N*. **2** toddle, walk with short mincing steps *la19-, now Mry Abd*.

n, la19-, NE: **1** ineffectual working; a botch, bungle. **2** a feckless worker, a botcher. **3** a tottery gait, toddle.

　　~**er** a person who TOOTERS (*v* 1) *la19-, N*. ~**ie** *of persons* fussy, pottering; *of things* fiddling, irritatingly trivial or intricate; *of weather* changeable, and so preventing steady outdoor work *la19-, NE*. [see SND]

tooth *see* TUITH

toot-moot &c; teet-meet *NE* ['tut'mut; *NE* also 'tit-'mit] *n* a low muttered conversation, a whispering together *19-20*.

vi converse in a low mutter, whisper *la19, Bnf Abd Ags*. [see SND]

toots *see* TOOT[2]

toove *see* TOVE[1]

top *see* TAP[1], TAP[3]

to-perse *see* TO-

topsoltiria *see* TAPSALTEERIE

toquhir *see* TOCHER

tor *see* TEAR[2]

tore *see* TEAR[2], TORR

torfle *19-e20, S v* **1** *vi* decline in health, pine away; perish, be lost. **2** *vti* toss or tumble about. [see SND]

torie &c *NE n, also* **story &c** *la18-, Sh Ork Cai* the grub of the cranefly or daddy-long-legs, which attacks the roots of grain crops *18-, chf NE*.

　　toriet infested with crane-fly grubs *la19-, NE*. ~**-eaten** *of land* infested with these grubs *18-, chf NE*.

tormican *see* TARMAGAN

torn *see* TEAR[2], THORN

torne *n* a tower *e17*. [only Sc; see OED]

torquess *adj* twisted, bent *la16*. [only Sc; see OED. OED *torques*]

torr, tore &c *n* **1** any ornamental projection *la15-16, 19-20, local*. **2** the bow or pommel of a saddle *la17-19*.

　　~**-bane** the prominence on the pelvic bone of a horse, cow or sheep *la19-, now SW*. [Gael *torr* a conical hill, heap, *torran* a knob]

torter &c *n, vt* = torture *17-, now Sh N*.

tortie &c *n* = tortoise *18-*. [*cf* ME, F *tortu*]

toschachdor *see* TOISEACH

tosh &c *adj* **1** neat, tidy, smart *18-*. **2** intimate, friendly *19-e20*.

adv neatly; in a comfortable, friendly way *la18-e20*.

vt make neat or tidy, smarten **up** *19-*.

　　~**-up &c** *n* a tidy-up *la19-*. [only Sc; prob related to TOSIE]

toshachdorach *see* TOISEACH

tosie ['tozɪ] *adj* **1** comfortable, cosy, snug *18-e20*. **2** slightly intoxicated, tipsy and merry *18-e20*. **3** *of the cheeks* flushed *19-e20*. [only Sc; obscure]

to smyte *see* TO-

toss[1] *vt* **1** *also* **tost** *e17* = toss *17-*. **2** toss a coin with (a person) *20-, NE-Per*.

toss[2] *n* = toast, a drink to someone's health; the subject of a toast *18-e20*. [prob w infl f TASS]

tossachiorschip *see* TOISEACH

tossel; taisel &c *18* ['tosl; *tɛsl] *n* **1** = tassel *la17-*. **2** a tuft or fringe of hair *20-, Sh NE-Per*. **3** the penis *la20-, local Abd-SW*.

tosslin *weaving* the forming of the thread-ends of a web into tassels *la20-, nEC Ayr*.

tost *see* TOSS[1]

tot[1] *n* **1** a small child, toddler *18-*. **2** *child's word* the penis *la20-, N*.

　　~**(t)ie** *n* = *n* 1, *19-*. *adj* small, tiny *20-, Cai C, S*. [orig Sc; obscure]

tot[2] **&c** *n* = tote, the sum total, the whole lot, *freq* **the hail &c** ~ *19-, chf WC*.

tot[3] *vi* toddle; totter *19-, now Lnk Ayr*. [only Sc; back-formation f Eng *totter* or TOTTLE]

total *adj* teetotal *19-, now NE Rox*. [reduced form]

toth *see* TATHE

tother *see* TITHER

totie *see* TOT[1]

totter *vi* = TOTTLE *v* 1 and 3, *19-, now Ags*.

tottie *see* TOT[1]

tottle &c *v* **1** *vi* simmer, boil gently *19-*, *now Ags.* **2** *vt* cause to simmer *18*. **3** *vi*, *of running water* ripple, purl *19*. **4** walk unsteadily, toddle, totter *19-*, *now Ags*. **5** totter and fall, topple over *19-*, *now Ork Ags*. [prob onomat; *cf* TOTTER and Eng *totter*]

tottum *see* TOTUM[2]

totum[1] **&c** *n* a teetotum, the four-sided top spun in games of chance; the game itself *16-*, *now local Sh-SW*. [L = the whole lot]

totum[2]; **tottum &c** *n* **1** a small child, a little tot *la19-*, *now local N-Lnk*. **2** any diminutive neat person, animal or thing *la18-*, *now local N-Dmf*. [deriv of TOT[1] w infl f prec]

tou *see* THOU

touch; twech &c *la14-16*, *chf Sc*, **twich &c** *la14-18*, *chf Sc*, **titch &c** *la18-e20* [tɪtʃ; *twɪtʃ, *twitʃ] *vti* **1** = touch *15-*. **2** *vt* ratify (an Act of the Scottish Parliament) by touching it with the sceptre *la17*, *only Sc*. **3** grieve, vex *16*, *only Sc*.

n **1** = touch *16-*. **2** a short space of time, a moment *la18-e19*.

toucher *see* TOCHER

toucht *see* THINK[1]

tough *see* TEUCH

tought *see* THOCHT

touk[1] **&c** *16-20*, **tuck** *la18-19*; **tuik &c** *la15-e18* [tuk; *tʌk] *v* **1** (1) *vi*, *of a drum* sound, beat *la15-17*. (2) *vt* beat (a drum) *17-19*. **2** *vi*, *of the wind* blow in gusts *19-20*.

n the beat or tap of a drum *16-19*.

by ~ of drum *of a proclamation* (made) by a public crier with his drum *17-18*. [chf Sc; ME *tukke* (*v*) touch, beat the drum, *tuk* the blast of a trumpet]

touk[2] **&c** *17-*, *now local*, **tuck &c** *16-* [tuk] *vt* = tuck, gather in folds etc *16-*.

n **1** = tuck, a fold in cloth etc *19-*. **2** an embankment or jetty built to prevent soil erosion *18-*, *now Wgt*. **3** a hasty tug or pull *18-e20*.

touk[3] [tuk; *tjuk] *n* a disagreeable flavour or aftertaste *19-*, *now local midLoth-Dmf*. [obscure]

toul &c; toal *20-*, *Gall* ['tu(ə)l; *Gall* 'toəl] *n* = towel *16-*.

toum *see* TOME

toun &c, town [tun] *n* **1** (1) an area of arable land on an estate, occupied by a number of farmers as co-tenants *la14-*, *now local*. (2) a farm with its buildings and the immediately surrounding area *la17-*, *Gen except Sh Ork*. (3) *freq in combs and place-names* a cluster of houses belonging to the tenants of TOUN *n* 1 (1), a village *16-*. **2** = town *la14-*.

~die the person left in charge of a farm when the rest of the household are away *20-*, *NE*.

~ie an inhabitant of a town *20-*, *Sh Abd Ags*.

~ser *usu disparaging* a town-dweller as opposed

to a countryman etc *20-*, *NE-Per*. **~ship 1** = township *la16-*. **2** = *n* **1** (1), *esp Highl* of a community of *crofters* (CROFT) *19-*.

~'s bairn a native of a particular town *17-19*. **~'s bodie** a town-dweller *la18-*, *now Sh Ork NE*. **~ champion** the chief male participant in the festival of the *Riding the Marches* (RIDE) at Musselburgh, with the duty of protecting the *Turf Cutter* (TURR) *20-*. **~('s) drummer** a drummer employed to make BURGH proclamations to the beating of his drum *18-19*. **~ end 1** the end of or way out from a town *la15-e20*. **2** a row of cottages, *usu* on a farm *20-*, *NE Uls.* **~ fit** *freq in place-names* the lower end of a town *19-*. **~'s folk** townspeople *20-*. **~ gate** the main street of a town or village *la18-e20*, *S*. **~ guard &c** an armed corps, *chf* of ex-soldiers, enrolled for police duties *la17-e19*, *Edb.* **~ heid &c** *freq in place-names* the higher or upper end of a town *la16-*. **~ herd** the public herdsman who looked after the cows on the common pasture *la18-19*. **~('s) house** a town hall, the headquarters of a municipality *18-*. **~-keeper &c 1** an official acting as a kind of constable *la18-e19*. **2** = *~die*, *20-*, *NE*. **~land** the land of a TOUN 1 (1) or (2) *17-*, *now Sh*. **~-loan** an open space round a farmstead or hamlet *18-*, *now NE*. **~ major** the major of the *~ guard*, *la17*, *Edb*. **~ officer** an official attending on the PROVOST, councillors etc in the Council Chamber and in public *la16-20*. **~('s) piper** the official bagpiper of a town council *17-18*. **~ sergeant** = *~ officer* in Aberdeen and (*formerly*) Dundee *18-*. **~'s speak** the talk of the town, the local scandal *20-*, *local NE-S*. **a clean ~** a farm from which all the hired servants have left at one term *la19-20*. **keep (the) ~** act as *~die*, *la19-*, *NE*.

toundir *see* TUNDER

toung *see* TONGUE

toupie *la19-*, *Sh* [*Sh* 'tupɪ] *n*, *chf* **toupican, -ichen** *la19-*, *NE* [*NE* 'tupɪkən, -ɪxən] any high pointed object, a knob on the top of something. [extended f Eng *toupee* top-knot]

tour[1], **tower; tuire** *16* [tur] *n* = tower **1** *in gen*, *la14-*; **2** *specif* used in names of *tower houses*: '*Smailholm Tower*'.

~ie &c, *freq* **toorie 1** a little tower; something rising to a point; a heap (of sand, stones etc) *19-*, *now Sh Abd*. **2** the pompom on a *Tam-o'-Shanter* (TAM) *la19-*. **3** a top-knot or bun of hair *la19-*, *now Sh Cai*. **~ock 1** = *~ie* 1, *19-*. **2** an ornamental top, tuft etc *la19-*, *now Sh*.

~ house (*now only* **tower-**) a high tower *orig* used both as a residence and for defence (mostly built *14-16*), a PEEL[3] *18-*.

tour[2] **&c; tower** *20-* *n* **1** [tur] one's turn or spell in a regular sequence *16-*. **2** ['tʌuər] = tour, a circular route *la18-*.

tour about, tour and turn [tur-] turn about, alternately *18-*, *now local Loth-Rox*.

toure *see* TURR

touse &c [tuz] *vt* **1** pull or knock about, handle (*esp* a woman) roughly *18-*, *now local Sh-WC*. **2** disorder, dishevel (hair, clothes etc) *19-*, *now local Sh WC*. **3** tease out *20-*, *now WC*.

tousie &c ['tuzɪ; *St* 'tʌuzɪ] **1** *chf of the hair* dishevelled; tangled *16-*. **2** untidy, in a disorderly state *19-*, *local Sh-SW*. **3** rough, boisterous, rowdy, violent *la19-*, *now Ayr Rox*. **tousie &c tea**: high tea (TEA) *19-*, *local nEC-Rox*. **tousle &c, tussle &c** *la15-19*; **tuzle &c** *19* ['tuzl; *'tʌzl] *v* **1** *vt* = tousle, pull about (roughly); rumple *la15-*. **2** *vi*, *of lovers* pull one another about playfully, fondle one another *19-e20*. **3** *vt* rummage about in, turn **out** the contents of; unravel, disentangle *19-*, *now Cai Bnf*. *n* **1** a struggle, tussle, contest *19-*. **2** a rough romp with a person of the opposite sex *la18-*, *now Sh NE*. **touslie &c** ['tuzlɪ] **1** *of the hair* dishevelled, ruffled *20-*, *C*. **2** *of wind* blustery, boisterous *20-*, *now Stlg Ayr*. [ME *to-tused &c* knocked about; *cf* Ger *zausen* pull to pieces]

toush [tuʃ] *n* a woman's jacket or short-skirted working-dress *19*. [shortened f CARTOUSH]

toust &c [*ʔtust, *ʔtʌust] *n*, *law* a rate levied, tax *la16-e17*. *vt* tax *la16*. [only Sc; see OED]

toustie ['tustɪ] *adj* testy, irascible *19-e20*. [perh conflation of TOWT w Eng *testy*]

tout¹ &c, toot [tut] *vti* **1** = toot *17-*. **2** trumpet, make a noise like a horn; speak loudly, shout *19-e20*. **3** *vi*, *esp of a child* cry, sob *19-e20*. **4** *vt* spread (a report), blab, broadcast *la18-19*. *n* = toot *17-*. **~er** *n* **1** *also* **~eroo** *NE* a horn, trumpet, *freq* a toy trumpet *la19-*, *N nEC*. **2** trivial gossip, tittle-tattle *la19-*, *Bnf Abd*. *vti* = *v* 3 and 4, *la19-e20*. **~ing horn** a cow's horn sounded by a cowherd driving his animals *18-e20*. **a new ~ in** *etc* **an auld &c horn** an old idea or piece of news dressed up as new *17-e19*. **~ (on) one's ain horn** *or* **trumpet** blow one's own trumpet *la19-*, *N-WC, S*.

tout² &c; toot [tut] *v* **1** *vi* drink copiously, tipple *la18-*, *now local NE-Ayr*. **2** *vt* drink down, empty (a glass etc) to the last drop *la18-e20*. *n* **1** a draught, swig, *orig* a large single drink, but now rather a small but repeated drink, a tipple *la18-*, *now local Sh-Loth*. **2** a drinker, tippler *20-*, *now WC*. **~ie 1** = *n* 2, *la18-e19*. **2** *also* **~lie** = *n* 1, *19-*, *now NE*. [see SND]

tout *see* TOWT

touteroo *see* TOUT¹

touther &c; towder &c *19-20*, **tudder** *20-* ['tuðər, 'tudər, 'tʌdər, 'tʌuðər, 'tʌudər] *vt* handle roughly, throw into disorder *19-*, *now Sh Fif*. *n* a rough handling; a throwing into confusion; a state of disorder, a mess *19-*, *now Sh Fif Loth*. **~ie &c** dishevelled, untidy, slovenly *19-*, *now local Sh-Dmf*. [see SND]

toutlie *see* TOUT²

toutour *see* TUTOR

tove¹ &c; toove &c *la19-e20* *v* **1** (1) *vt*, *of a fire etc* emit (smoke or flames) *19-*, *now Rox*. (2) *vi*, *of smoke* billow out, rise in the air *19-e20*, *Rox*. **2** rise into the air, soar; hurry along *19-*, *now Bwk*. **3** swarm or stream out *la19-20*, *Bwk Rox*. **4** *vt* puff up with praise, flatter *19*. **tovie & 1** steaming; *fig* giving warmth and comfort *e19*. **2** boastful, *esp* in drink *19*. **~ at** smoke, puff (a pipe etc) *la19-*, *now Rox*. [appar aphetic f STOVE, perh by wrong division of *it's* etc *stovin*]

tove² *vi* talk in a friendly, animated way, gossip, chat *19-e20*. *n* a chat, talk, gossip *la19-e20*. [perh connected w TOVE¹]

tow¹ &c [tʌu] *n* = tow, flax or hemp fibre *19-*. **~ band &c** a strap or band of woven tow; a skirt- or trouser-waistband *19-*, *now Bnf Abd*. **~-card** a toothed instrument for carding flax *18-e19*. **~-gun** a popgun with tow wadding *19-*, *local Ags-Ayr*. **~-rock** a distaff used in spinning hemp *la18*. **hae ither ~ on one's rock** *18-e20*, **hae ither ~ to tease** *19-20* have other concerns or intentions.

tow² &c [tʌu] *n* **1** a rope, cord, length of strong twine, string etc *la15-*. **2** *specif* (1) a skipping-rope *20-*, *local Sh-Ayr*; (2) a coffin cord *la20-*, *NE*; (3) a whip, whiplash *20-*, *now Bnf wLoth*. **2** a gallows rope, hangman's noose *la16-e20*. **3** *mining* (1) the winding-rope which hoists or lowers a cage *la19-*, *now Fif Loth WC*; (2) the cage itself *la19-*, *now Fif Loth WC*; (3) the journey up or down in the cage *la20-*, *Fif*. *vt* raise or lower by means of a rope *la16-18*. **lat the ~ gang wi the bucket** *proverb* give up, get rid of something impatiently, cut one's losses *20-*, *NE nEC*. **ower the ~** over the traces, out of control, beyond bounds *la18-19*. [chf Sc; see OED]

tow *see* THOW

towbooth *see* TOLBOOTH

towart &c [*'tøwart, *tə'wart] *adv*, *prep* = toward *la14-16*. **~is** [*ʔtə'warts] = towards *16*. [only Sc. OED *toward*]

to-waver *see* TO-

towbeeth, towbooth *see* TOLBOOTH

towdent &c ['t(j)ʌudənt] *adj* ill-**~** poorly-clad, neglected-looking; unkempt *20*, *Bnf Abd*. [obscure]

towder *see* TOUTHER

towdy &c [*'tʌudɪ] *n* the buttocks, the posterior *16-e19*. **~ mowdy** term of endearment *e16* [cf *tirly-mirlie* (TIRL²) and *crowdie mowdy* (CROWDIE¹)]. [obscure]

tower *see* TOUR¹, TOUR²

towin &c; town &c ['tʌu(ɪ)n] *v* **1** *vt* beat; tame by beating *18-e19*. **2** toss, rumple, disorder (clothes, straw etc) *19-e20, SW.* **3** *vi* toss and turn, bustle (about), rummage *la19-20, SW.* [see SND]

towk [*?tʌuk] *n* a large tippet *e16.* [only Sc; F *toque* a kind of hat. OED *toque*]

towl; toll [tʌul] *vti* **1** = toll (a bell etc) *18-.* **2** *vi, of a (queen) bee* emit an intermittent series of single clear notes as a swarming signal *18-e19.*

towl- *see* TOLL

towler ['tʌulər] *n* a large marble *20-, Bwk Rox.* [cf *doller* (DOLL)]

towmond &c *la16-;* **tholmont** *e15,* **tolmowth** *la16,* **toman &c** *la18-e19* ['tʌumən(d), -mənθ, -mənt; *'to-; *'tolmənt, *-məθ] *n* **1** (the period of) a year *15-.* **2** a sheep or wether in its second year *19-, Rox* [perh partly confused w *dilmont* (DINMONT)].

towmondall &c [*'tʌumənd'ɑld, *'tʌumən(d)əl, *-əl, &c] a yearling cow, steer or colt *la18-e19* [eModEng *towlmonyth &c,* appar ON *tólfmánuðr;* cf *twalmonth* (TWAL)]

town *see* TOUN, TOWIN

townty *see* TWENTY

towrow ['tʌu'rʌu] *n* a noisy uproar, rumpus, disturbance *la19-, now Sh Bnf Ags.* [reduplicated f Eng *row* a commotion]

towt &c, tout &c *la18-* [tʌut] *n* **1** a slight or temporary ailment, an indisposition *19-, now Cai Abd C, S.* **2** a sudden (*usu* bad) mood, huff *la18-, now local Ork-Wgt.* **3** a teasing remark, taunt *20-, Bwk S.*
vt **1** *also fig* toss about, upset, put in disorder *la16-19.* **2** tease, annoy, taunt *la18-, now Bwk Rox.*
~**ie &c 1** subject to frequent attacks of slight illness *19-, now nEC, WC Wgt.* **2** touchy, irritable *20-, now local Abd-SW.* **3** *of things* uncertain, changeable *e19.* [only Sc; see SND]

towter *see* TOLTER

toy[1] *n* a linen or wool cap with a flat crown and a back-flap reaching to the shoulders, worn by married and elderly women, a style of MUTCH *17-, now hist.* [only Sc; prob Du *tooi* attire, finery]

toy[2] *n* = toy.
v **1** *vi* = toy. **2** *vt* treat (a person) in an offhand, frivolous or dismissive way *la19-, now Rox.*

traa(n) *see* THRAW

traaward *see* THRAWART

trabuschet *see* TREBUSCHET

trace[1]**; tress** *19-e20 n* = trace, a draught rope etc *19-.*
tracer 1 a trace-horse *19-.* **2** the man in charge of a trace-horse *la19-e20.*

trace[2] **&c** *n* = trace *la14-.*
traschor [*?'treʃər] ? a tracer, a tool for marking out designs *e16.* [OED *trace* (*n*[1]), *tracer*[1]]

trace[3] **&c, tres &c** [*tres, *trɛs] *n* a flat braid of *eg* gold or silver thread for trimming a garment etc *16, only Sc.*

tracing &c braiding, embroidery *16-17, only Sc.*

trast &c [*trest] braided *la15-e19.* [perh altered f Eng *tress*]

tracent [*?'tresənt] *n* a French coin *e16.* [only Sc; F *treizain*]

trachle *see* TRAUCHLE

track[1] *n* **1** = track. **2** a trench *la20-, N sEC, WC, SW.*
vt **1** = track. **2** train or break in (a young animal or *transf* a human being) *la19-, NE.*

track[2] **&c; tract-** *18-20 vt* = track, tow (a boat) *18-.*
trackie &c = ~-*pot, la19-20, NE.*
~**-boat** a boat which is towed *17-e19* [Du *trek-schuit*]. ~-**pot** a teapot *18-20.*

track[3] **&c** *n* = tract, a (religious) pamphlet *la18-, now N.*

track[4] **&c, tract** *17- n* **1** = tract (of land, time etc). **2** a continuing state, a settled and protracted condition (**of** something) *17-, now Sh.* **3** a period of time; a spell of weather, *freq* **track o time** *19-, local Sh-WC.* **4** a feature, trait *16-, now Sh.*

track *see* TRAG

tracteit [*'traktet] *n* = tractate, a treatise *e16.* [OED *tractate*]

tractive *n* a tractate, treatise *la16.* [only Sc; L *tractāre* (*v*) treat + *-ive*]

trackle *see* TRAUCHLE

tract *see* TRACK[4]

tract- *see* TRACK[2]

trad *see* TRADE

traddle *see* TREADLE

trade &c *15-;* **trad &c** *la14-18,* **tred &c** *16-e20,* **tread &c** *la16-e20* [trɛd, tred; *also* trəid; *trad] *n* **1** a course, way *la14-15.* **2** a track or trail of foot- or hoofprints *la15-e19.* **3** = trade *la15-.* **4** a corporation of master craftsmen in any one trade in a BURGH, which formerly elected members to the town council *18-.* **5** coming and going between people; *latterly* a fuss *la16-, now Ags Per.* **6** a continued practice, a habit, *freq* **mak a ~ o** *la16-, now NE Ags.* **7 the T~s** = *trades holidays, 20-.*
~**s bailie** or **councillor** *etc* a BAILIE or member of a town council elected by the TRADES of a BURGH. ~**s hall &c** a meeting house of the TRADES in a BURGH *la18-19.* ~**s holiday(s)** the annual summer holiday, *orig* of the craftsmen of a town, *esp* Edb, *later* extended more generally (*orig* one day, *now* two to three weeks) *la19-; cf* FAIR. ~**s hospital** a home for pensioners of the TRADES of a BURGH, *specif* Gsw *18-19.* ~**s house** a deliberative body or council consisting of representatives of the fourteen *Incorporated Trades* (INCORPORATE) of Glasgow, presided over by the *Deacon Convener* (DEACON[1]) *18-.* ~**sman** a person who practices a trade, an artisan, craftsman *18-.*
to ~ by profession or occupation *19-: 'a* tailor *to* trade'; *cf* TAE[4] *prep* 5 (2) (b). [OED *trade, tread*]

trade *see* TREAD

tradewiddie *see* TREADWIDDIE

tradition *n* **1** = tradition *la16-*. **2** *law* delivery, handing over *la17-*.

traditor &c *n* a betrayer, traitor *la14-17*. [L]

traduct [*tra'dʌkt] *n* a passage, channel *e16*. [only Sc; L *trāductus, trādūcere* lead across]

traep *see* THREAP

traffeck &c, trafficque &c *la16-e20*; **treffik** *la16, only Sc,* **traffect** *16-18,* **trafike &c** *la19-e20,* N, **traffic** [tra'fɛk; N *also* trə'fəik; Ags trə'fik] *n* **1** = traffic *la16-*. **2** dealings, familiar communication, transactions *19-*, *now local Sh-Ags*. **3** work, progress with a job, activity *la19-, Sh Bnf Ags*. **4** *in pl* odds and ends; spare parts; trash *20-, now Sh*.
vti **1** = traffic. **2** *vi* (1) deal, have to do, or have relations (**with**) *19-, now Sh NE Ags*. (2) have illicit or secret dealings, intrigue, conspire **with** *la16-17*. **3** *vt* negotiate *e17*.

trafficker &c **1** = trafficker *la16-*. **2** a go-between, negotiator; an intriguer *la16-19*.

trag &c *n* **1** something of poor quality or little value, trash *19-, Sh Abd*. **2** *only* **track &c** a poorly- or untidily-dressed person, a 'sight' *20-*, NE. **3** riff-raff *19-, Bnf Abd*. [perh altered f *trog* (TROKE)]

traicle &c *19-*; **treacle** *19-*, **tryacle &c** *la15-e20,* **trykle &c** *la18-20,* **trekkle &c** *la19-e20* ['trɛkl; NE Bwk also 'trəikl; EC also 'trɛkl; S 'traɪ(ə)kl] *n* = treacle; in Scotland, *freq* used of any of molasses, treacle or syrup *la15-*. **~ ale &c** *19-, now local NE-SW,* **~ bendy** *la19-, now Lnk Slk* light ale brewed from treacle, water and yeast. **~ gundy** candy or toffee made from treacle *20-, N, C.* **~ peerie** = **~** *ale, la19-, nEC, S.* **~ piece** a slice of bread etc spread with treacle *la19-, now local Sh-Per.* **~ pig** a treacle jar *la20-, N.* **~ scone** a SCONE made with treacle *la19-*. **~ wheech &c** = **~** *ale, la19-, now Bwk.*
black ~ molasses *la20-, N, WC, Gall.*

traik &c *v* **1** *vi* be ailing or ill, decline in health; become weak; pine and die *16-e20*. **2** *freq of young poultry* wander, stray, become lost *19-20*. **3** roam, wander about idly or aimlessly, prowl *19-*. **4** tramp, trudge, walk wearily or with difficulty *la19-*. **5** *vt* **~ after** *or* **upon** follow, pursue in courtship *19-*.
n **1** (1) a plague, pestilence *e16*. (2) an illness, *esp* of an epidemic type *la18-20*. **2** (1) misfortune, loss, *specif* that caused by disease in farm animals *18-e20*. (2) the flesh of sheep which have died of exhaustion or disease *19-e20*. **3** (1) the act of *traiking* (*v* 3, 4) *la19-, now Sh Ags Kcb*. (2) a person or animal who is always roving about; a gadabout *la19-, now WC, S.* (3) a long tiring walk, a trudge *la19-*.
~ie &c sickly, ailing, declining *la18-19*. **~it 1** wasted, worn out; fatigued *16-, now WC Wgt*. **2** *of animals* having died of exhaustion or disease *19.* [only Sc; see SND, OED]

trail &c *vti* **1** = trail *la14-*. **2** tramp, trudge (laboriously or dispiritedly); wander about idly *19-*.
n **1** = trail. **2** a trailing piece of material etc, a rag *la19-e20*. **3** a large accumulation of articles, a haul *la19-, NE Ags Per*. **4** a long wearisome walk, a tramp, trudge *la19-*. **5** a careless, dirty, slovenly person, *esp* a woman *19-, now NE Ags*.
~ach &c [*'trɛləx] = *n* 5, *19, Bnf SW.*
~-en(d) the first of a fleet of herring nets to be shot (SHUIT) and hence the furthest from the boat *20-, Sh NE.* **~-fly** the last fly on a trout-fishing line *e19*. **~ syde** *of a garment* so long that it trails *e16, only Sc.*

trailye &c; trelȝe [*'trɛljɪ, *'trɪl(j)ɪ] *n* a kind of cloth *la15-16*. [only Sc; appar OF *treillis* netting, network]

traipse &c ['trep(ə)s] *vi* tramp, trudge wearily; shuffle through mud and dirt; go about, gad about *20-, Gen except Sh Ork.*
n a long weary trudge, a tiring walk *la20-, Ags Per WC.*
traipsing, trapezing &c *la19-e20* [trə'pizən, -ɪn] = trudging, gadding about. [see SND]

traise &c *vt, ptp* **trasit** *e16, only Sc* [*'trezɪt] = traised, betrayed.

traison &c *la15-16, e20,* **treason &c** ['trizən; *'trezun] *n* = treason *la14-*.
~able &c of or characteristic of treason; treacherous *la14-*.

traissle &c *vt* tread or trample down (growing crops or grass) *19-, now Rox*. [altered f TAISLE, with *tr-* prob f *eg* Eng *tread, trample*]

traist &c, trest *la15-e17*; **trast &c** *la14-16* [*'trest] *vti* **1** trust, have confidence **in** *la14-16*. **2** *vt* commit in trust *la15*. **3** expect *e16*.
n confidence, trust; assurance *la15-17*.
adj **1** firm, strong *la15*. **2** assured, confident *la14-15*. **3** trusty, trustworthy *15-e17*.
adv firmly; confidently *la15*.
~ful &c sure, secure; trustworthy *15-e16*. **~ly &c** securely; confidently; faithfully *la14-16*. **~nes** trustiness *la15*. **~y** trusty *e16*. [chf Sc and nEng; ON *treysta, trøysta* make firm, strong, or safe; cognate w TRUST]

traist *see* TRESS
trait *see* TREAT

traith &c [*ʔtreð] *n* a herring-fishing ground *17-19*. [perh var of TRADE (*n* 1)]

traivel *see* TRAVEL

traleel [tra'lil] *n* something long and trailing; something of poor quality *la19-e20, Abd*. [obscure; *cf* TRAIL]

traleis *see* TIRLESS
trallop *see* TROLLOP

tram¹ &c [tram; EC *also* trɑm] *n* **1** a shaft of a barrow, cart etc *16-*. **2** *in pl* the two upright posts of a gallows *la17*. **3** *in pl, esp joc or contemptuous* the legs *19-, now local Sh-SW.* **4** a very tall, thin, ungainly person (with long legs) *la19-*, *NE*. **5** = tram, a passenger car on rails; a car in a coalmine.

~ **girth** a loose girth attached to the shafts of a cart to prevent a load from tipping back *19-*, *now Ork*. ~ **horse** a horse harnessed between the shafts of a cart (as opposed to a trace horse) *la18-*, *now Ork*. ~**sach &c** ['tramsəx, -ʃəx] **1** a big, ungainly person or animal *la19-e20*, *Bnf*. **2** a rough, untidy person *20*, *N*.

tram²&c *n* **1** = tram, a machine, engine *la14*. **2** a scheme, plot *e17*.

tramalt [*'traməlt] *n* = trammel, a fishing net *la16*. [only *Sc*; *cf* THRAMMEL. OED *trammel-net*]

tramort [*tra'mort] *n* a putrefying carcass; a corpse *e16*. [only *Sc*; appar *L trā-, trans* beyond + *mors, mort-* death]

tramp¹&c *vti* **1** = tramp. **2** *vi* stamp or tread heavily **on**, trample **on** *la15-*. **3** *vt* tread, press down, crush by treading or stamping *16-*, *now local Sh-Per*. **4** *specif* wash (clothes or bedclothes) by treading them in soapsuds *18-20*. **5** press down compactly by hand, compress or pack firmly *19-*, *now Ags*.
n **1** = tramp. **2** a stamp of the foot; an injury to the foot by having it trodden on *19-e20*. **3** an iron plate on the sole of a boot or shoe in digging *19-*, *N*, *WC Rox*. **4** a horizontal strip of iron on the top of a spade blade for the foot to press on *19-*, *now local Ork-Ayr*. **5** *curling* (CURL) a piece of spiked iron on a boot sole to prevent slipping on the ice *19-*, *now WC, SW*.
~**ers 1** the feet *19-*, *now N nEC Ayr*. **2** heavy walking boots *la18-19*. ~**ie** a tramp, vagrant *20-*, *now NE Ags*. ~-**cock** *la18-20*, ~-**cole &c** *18-*, *now local Sh-WC* ['tramp'kol; *also* 'traŋkl] a cock of hay compressed by *tramping*. ~-**pick** a pick or crowbar with an iron bracket for the foot to press on *19-*, *now N Ayr*. ~-**rick &c** = ~-*cock*, *la16-19*. ~-**wife** a female tramp *la19-*, *NE Ags*. ~ **on a person's taes** encroach on a person's interests or preserves, take advantage of, offend a person *19-*, *now Sh N Per*.

tramp²&c *vt* steep, soak (**in**) *la16-*. [only *Sc*; F *tremper*]

trance &c *n* **1** *also fig* a narrow passage between buildings, an alley, lane *16-*, *now local Sh-Kcb*. **2** a passage within a building, *esp* that connecting the two main rooms of a cottage, a lobby, corridor *17-*, *now N Ags Lnk*. **3** an aisle in a church *16-20*.
~ **door** the door of a passage, *esp* an inner door leading from the outside door to the kitchen of a cottage *19-*, *now NE Ags WC*. [only *Sc*; prob OF *transe* the passage from life to death, f L *transitus* a passage, way through]

trang *see* THRANG

trannet &c *n* some piece of horse harness *e16*, *only Sc*.

tranont &c [*tra'nunt, *-'nəint, *'tra-] *vi* shift

one's position, *esp* rapidly and stealthily; make a forced march **upon** *la14-e16*. [only *Sc*; unknown]

transack &c *la19-*, **transact** [tran'zak] *n* a transaction, matter of business *la19-*, *local Bnf-Rox*.
vt = transact *la16-*.

transference &c *la17-*, **transfering** *la16 n*, *law* the procedure by which an action is transferred to his representative from a person who dies during the process.

translate &c *vt* **1** = translate *16-*. **2** *church* transfer (a MINISTER) from one charge to another *la16-*.
translation 1 = translation *la15-*. **2** the act or procedure of *translating* (*v* 2) *18-*.

transmeridiane *n* the region beyond the meridian in the Atlantic which separates the New from the Old World *e16*. [only *Sc*; *trans-* + L *meridiānus*. OED *transmeridian*]

transport *vt* **1** = transport *la16-*. **2** *church* = TRANSLATE *v* 2, *17-e20*, *only Sc*. **3** remove (a congregation) to a different part of a parish or to a different parish *18-*, *only Sc*.
act of ~**ability** a formal permission granted by a PRESBYTERY to one of its MINISTERS to accept a call from another congregation if *presented* (PRESENT¹) *la17-e18*. ~**able** enabled by prec to be *transported* (*v* 2) *la16-e20*. ~**ation** the act of *transporting* (*v* 2) *la16-18*.

transume *la16-18*; **transsump** *la15 vt*, *law* make an official copy of (a legal document) *la15-18*.
transsump *la15*, **transumpt** *la17-e19*, *law* a transcript or copy of a document. [laL *transumere* transcribe, copy, ptp stem *trans(s)umpt-*]

trantle &c *la17-e20*, **trental** *16 n*, *chf in pl* **1** = trental, a set of thirty *16*. **2** trifles; odds and ends; miscellaneous bits of equipment etc *la16-e20*.
~**ment** *20*, *Abd Kcdn*, **trantlum &c** *la18-e20* = *n* 2. [only *Sc*; prob w infl f Eng *trinket* and LUME]

trantle *see* TRINNLE

trantlum *see* TRANTLE

trap¹&c *vti* **1** = trap. **2** *vi* correct another pupil's mistake and thus take his place in order of merit in a school class *19-20*.

trap²&c *n* a ladder, a (movable) flight of steps (leading up to a loft etc) *16-*, *now local*.
~ **ladder** *la19-*, *now Ork*, ~ **stair(s)** *19-*, *now local N-S* = *n*. [only *Sc*; Du *trap*]

trap³&c *n* an idle, slovenly person, *esp* a woman *e20*, *Cai*.
~**ach** ['trapəx] slovenly, slatternly *20-*, *Cai*. [Gael *dràb(ach)* slattern(ly), Eng *drab*]

trapezing *see* TRAIPSE

trappin &c *n* **1** *chf in pl* = trappings. **2** material used to trim or tie garments, lace, tape, ribbon *la18-*, *now Ork NE Ags*. **3** small wares, a hawker's stock-in-trade *la19-*, *now Rox*.

trapple *see* THRAPPLE¹

traschor *see* TRACE²

trash *vt* wear out, exhaust, abuse with overwork and exertion *19-*, *now Dmf Rox.*

~**y** &c **1** fatiguing *la20-*, *S.* **2** *of weather* wet, dirty *19-e20.* [eModEng *trash* flounder through mire]

trashtrie &c *n* trash, useless or worthless rubbish *la18-e20.* [Eng *trash*]

trasit *see* TRAISE

trast *see* TRACE³, TRAIST

trate &c *n* a piece of cloth dipped in a mixture of beeswax, lard etc, used as a dressing for sores or boils *la18-20, Cai Kcdn Fif.* [ME *treet* a salve or plaster, aphetic f OF *entrait* an adhesive plaster]

tratel *see* TRATTLE

trath *see* TROWTH

tratour &c ['tretər] *n* = traitor *la14-16.* [OED *traitor*]

trattle &c *16-e20;* **tratel** &c *15-16* ['tratl] *vti* talk idly; chatter, prattle, gossip *15-e20.*

n, in pl idle talk or tales; gossip; chatter *16.* [chf Sc; see OED]

trauchle, trachle &c; **trackle** &c *la18-e20* ['trɑxl, 'traxl; 'trakl] *v* **1** *vt* bedraggle, injure, spoil (by dragging, trampling, knocking about etc), *freq in ptp, 16-, now local NE-SW.* **2** *vti* trail, draggle through mud etc *la19-e20.* **3** *vi* walk slowly and wearily, drag oneself along *19-.* **4** *vt* exhaust with overwork, travelling etc, overburden, harass, *freq in ptp, la16-.* **5** hamper, trouble, worry *19-e20.* **6** *vi* drudge, labour on in a harassed way, toil and moil *19-.*

n **1** a struggle, a hard time *la17.* **2** a long, tiring trudge or walk *19-, now NE, C.* **3** tiring labour, drudgery, fatiguing or dispiriting work *la19-.* **4** a state of chronic muddle caused by having too much to do *20-, local NE-Wgt.* **5** a source of trouble or anxiety, a burden, encumbrance *la19-, now NE.* **6** a careless incompetent person, an inefficient slovenly worker *la19-, now local Stlg-Dmf.*

~**some** exhausting, laborious *la20-, NE Ags.* [only Sc; appar Du; *cf* Flem *tragelen, trakelen* walk with difficulty; drudge]

travaill *see* TRAVEL

travally *see* TREVALLIE

trave *see* THREAVE

travel &c; **traivel** &c *la19-* ['trevl, 'trɛvl] *v* **1** *vi, also* **travaill** &c *la14-16* [*tra'vel]* = travel *la14-.* **2** *vti* = travail *la14-16.* **3** *vt* labour at, perform *la16.* **4** (1) *vi* walk; go about or make a journey on foot *16-, now local Sh-SW.* (2) *vt* walk back and forth, pace up and down *19-, NE.* (3) do (a journey) on foot *la19-20.* **5** *vi* go about on foot begging or hawking small wares, *freq* ~ **the roads** *etc, la17-, now local NE-Lnk.* **6** *vt* drive (cattle etc) from place to place along a road *la19-, now NE Loth Dmf.*

n **1** *also* **travaill** &c [*tra'vel]* = travel *la14-.* **2** = travail *la14-e16.* **3** a walk, journey on foot *18-, now Sh N Ags.*

~**led** *of soil, stones etc* deposited (by natural or human agency) at some distance from the original site *19-* [now also Eng geol term]. ~**ler** &c **1** = traveller *la14-.* **2** a hawker, tinker, gipsy *19-.* **3** *joc* a head-louse *la20-, Ork NE Dmf.* [OED *travail, travel*]

travise &c *e15, 18-;* **trevis(s)** &c *la15-e20* ['trevis, 'trevis, 'trivis; *Cai* 'trɛfis; *Bwk S* 'trevidʒ, 'trividʒ] *n* **1** *only* **trevis** &c = traverse, a screen, partition *la15-e16.* **2** the wooden partition between two stalls in a stable or cowshed *18-, now local.* **3** *also* **triffice** &c a stall or loose-box in a stable *18-19.*

vti, also **traverse** &c [tra'vɛrs] **1** = traverse *16-.* **2** *vi* move (to and fro) across *la14-16.* **3** *vt* mount, bestride (a horse) *e15.* [OED *traverse*]

trawl *n* = trawl (-net); *also* a seine-net *la19-.* *vi* fish with a seine-net, by encircling shoals of herring *la19-.*

trawn *see* THRAWN

tray *see* THRAE

treacle *see* TRAICLE

tread &c; **tred** &c *la16,* **trade** &c *17-e19* [tred; *local also* trid] *vti, pt also* **tred** *la16,* **tread** *19-, Abd Ags Ayr. ptp also* **tred** *16-17,* **treddin** &c *e16, la19-, now Ayr* = tread *16-.*

n **1** = tread *16-.* **2** a felloe of a wooden wheel *la19-, local Stlg-Lnk.*

~ **the feet of** trace the footprints of *la16, only Sc.*

tread *see* TRADE

treadle &c; **traddle** &c *19 n* = treadle. *vi* **1** = treadle. **2** tramp, trudge, go frequently and with difficulty *la18-e19.*

treadle-hole an open space under the loom for the treadle shafts *19-, now Lnk Ayr.*

treadwiddie &c; **trade-** &c, **trod-** &c *18-19* ['trɛdwɪdɪ; *'trod-, *'tɔrwɪdɪ, &c] *n* the draught-chain (*orig* a twisted withy), with hook and swivel connecting a plough or harrow to the swingle-trees *la17-e20.* [? *tread* (TRADE) + WIDDIE]

treason *see* TRAISON

treat &c *la16-;* **trete** &c *la14-e19,* **trait** &c *la15-, now Sh nEC* [trit, tret] *vti, pt, ptp also* **treat** *16-19,* **tret** &c *16-, now local* [trɛt] **1** = treat *la14-.* **2** *vt* deal with, carry on, manage *la14-16.* **3** consider or regard (something in a particular way) *la15-.* **4** *vti* feast, regale (someone (**with** something)) *16-.* **5** beseech, beg, request *la14-19.*

n = treat *la14-.*

~**er** &c a negotiator *la14-16.*

trebling *n* **1** = trebling. **2** *piping, in* PIBROCH the form in which the *doubling* (DOOBLE) of a variation is sometimes repeated with further development *20-.* [*cf* TRIPLING]

trebuck &c; **terbuck** &c [*Ayr* tər'bʌtʃɪ, -'bʌtsmɪ; *trə'bʌk, *tər-] used as a call, *eg* when a player has made a false move in a game and wants to make a second attempt *la19-20*. [only Sc; northern F dial *trebuquer*, OF *trebucher* stumble]

trebuschet *e17*; **trabuschet** *la16* [*?trə'bʌʃət] *n* an assay balance or pair of scales. [F; *cf* Eng *trebuchet* a siege-engine]

tred *see* TRADE, TREAD

tree &c [tri; *S* trəi] *n* **1** = tree *la14-*. **2** *freq ballad* wood, timber *la14-e19*. **3** a rod, stick *la14-19*. **4** a cudgel, club *la15-e19*. **5** a staff, walking stick *la17-19*. **6** a long, wooden bar, post or pole *la14-e18*. **7** a wooden rafter, beam, strut etc *17-19*. **8** *mining* a pit-prop *la20-*, *now Fif Loth WC*. **9** a wooden, barrel, keg, *esp* for ale *16-19*.
vt **1** = tree. **2** provide (*eg* the roof of a coal working) with supporting timbers or props *la19*.
~**n &c** [*tri:n] wooden, made of wood *la14-19*.
~**n mare** a kind of wooden horse used as an instrument of punishment *18-19*.
~ **buits** wooden boots *la16*. ~ **crop** a treetop *la16*. ~**-leg** a wooden leg *la18-19*. ~**-speeler &c** the tree-creeper *la19-*, *now local Loth-Dmf*.

tree *see* THREE

treed *see* THREID

treelip *see* TROLLOP

treeple &c *la17-*, *now NE*; **tribill &c** *la14-e19* ['tripl; *'trɪbl] *n* = treble, triple *16-19*.
adj = treble *la14-15*.
vti **1** = treble, triple *20-*, *NE*. **2** play (a tune) in triple time or dance to it, waltz; beat time with the foot to a dance tune *la17-*, *now Mry Abd* [perh conflated w Eng *tripple*, frequentative of *trip*]. [OED *treble*]

treesh &c [triʃ(t), tris(t)] *v* **1** *vi*, *freq* ~ **wi** entreat, cajole, entice in a kind and flattering way *19-*, *now Abd*. **2** run *after*, court *19-*, *now Bnf Abd*. **3** *vti* call an animal *la19-20*, *Bnf Abd*.
interj a call to cattle, *esp* calves, to come *la19-*, *NE Ags Per*. [see SND]

treetle; trytle &c *20-*, *now Abd* ['tritl; *Abd also* 'trɔitl; *Gall* *'trɪtl] *vi* **1** trickle, fall in drops or in a thin stream *la19-*, *Sh Ork NE*. **2** walk with short steps, trot *20-*, *now NE*. [prob altered f Eng *trickle*, partly conflated w DRIDDLE]

treffik *see* TRAFFECK

tregallion *see* TREVALLIE

treilʒeis [*'trilʒɪz] *n pl* ? curry-combs *e16*. [see OED *treilʒe*]

treilʒeis *see* TIRLESS

trekkle *see* TRAICLE

trelapse *see* TRILAPSE

trelʒe *see* TRAILYE

tremble *see* TREMMLE

tremebund [*'trɛmɪbʌnd] *adj* inclined to tremble; timorous, timid *la16*. [only Sc; L *tremebundus* trembling]

tremendous &c; tremendious *20-* *adj* = tremendous *17-*.
adv very much, extremely *la19-*.

tremmle &c, tremble &c *17-*; **trimmle &c, trimble &c** *la14-17* ['trɛml, 'trɪml, 'trʌml] *vi* = tremble *la14-*.

tremmlin &c a virus disease of sheep, causing paralysis, tremor and spasms *19-*, *now Per WC, SW*. **tremmlin aixies &c** *la17-19*, **tremmlin fever(s) &c** *17-e19* ague. **tremmlin &c tree** the aspen *20-*, *local Mry-Wgt*. **trimmlin &c strae(s)** unthreshed straw *20-*, *Bnf Abd*.

trensand [*'trɛnsand] *adj* = trenchant, cutting *la15*. [only Sc. OED *trenchant*]

trental *see* TRANTLE

tres *see* TRACE³

tres-ace [*'trɛs'es] *n* a game somewhat like musical chairs *la18-e19*. [var of Eng *trey* the three at dice etc + *ace*]

tresgressor [*'trɛs'grɛsər] *n* = transgressor *e16*, *only Sc*.

tresh *see* THRASH

trespass &c ['trɛspas; *trɛs'pas] *vti* **1** = trespass, commit (an offence) *la14-*. **2** *vi*, *law* enter another's land without his permission *15-*. *n* = trespass *la14-*.

tress *16-*, **trest** *16-e18*; **traist &c** *la15-16* *n* **1** a trestle for holding up a board, table etc, *freq* including the bench it supports *la15-*, *now local*. **2** a rest for a fire-arm *e16*. **3** a tripod *e16*. [OF *trest*, *trast*]

tress *see* TRACE¹

trest *see* TRAIST, TRESS

tret &c *adj* = tretis, well-proportioned *la15*, *only Sc*.

tret(e) *see* TREAT

tretten *see* THIRTEEN

tretty *see* THIRTY

treukour *see* TRUKER

treush *see* THRASH

treuth *see* TROWTH

trevallie &c; travally &c *e18*, *e20*, *Ork Uls* [trə'val(j)ɪ, -'vɛl(j)ɪ] *n* **1** a startling noise, a crash, a prolonged clatter *e20*. **2** a disturbance, brawl *19-20*. **3** *also* **tregallion &c** *usu contemptuous* a miscellaneous collection; a retinue of followers, a swarm, rabble *19-20*. [eModEng *trevally*]

trevis(s) *see* TRAVISE

trew¹ *la14-*, **trow &c** *la14-20*; **true &c** *la14-*, *now Sh* [tru] *vti* = trow, believe. [see SND]

trew² *la14-16* *n*, *also in pl* (*freq treated as sing*) **trewis &c** *la14-e17*, **trowis** *la14* [*tr(j)uz] **1** = truce *la14-16*. **2** a document recording the terms of a truce *e16*, *only Sc*. **3** *law* a suspension of judicial proceedings *e17*.
vt grant a truce to *la14-e15*, *only Sc*.
day of ~ (a day appointed for) a court held by the Wardens of the MARCHES of England and Scotland (on which a truce was held) *la16*. [OED *trew*, *truce*]

trew *see* TRUE

trewbute [*?'trjubøt] *n* = tribute *la15*, *only Sc*.

trewis *see* TREW²

trews &c; **trowse** &c *18* [truz] *n* **1** close-fitting trousers made of fine, *usu* TARTAN cloth, with the legs extended to cover the feet (somewhat like modern tights), formerly worn by *Highlanders* (HIELAND); *later* TARTAN trousers worn by certain Scottish regiments *or* short TARTAN trunks worn under a KILT¹ *la16-*. **2** trousers *in gen, 19-20*. [Gael *triubhas*]

trewthelie *see* TROWTH

trial &c; **tryell** &c *la16-17 n* **1** = trial *la16-*; NB *law* in civil cases in Scotland, used only of a trial before a jury. **2** *usu in pl* (1) *Presbyterian Church* the examinations of a *probationer* (PROBATION) by a PRESBYTERY before he is *licenced* (LEESHENCE) as a preacher *17-*; (2) *law* the testing of a *probationer* (PROBATION) before he is admitted to the bench *18-e20*.
take *etc* ~ (**of**) make enquiry (about), investigate, examine *la16-e18, only Sc*.

triangle *vi* ? lie or extend in the form of a triangle *la16*. [only Sc; extension of Eng (*n*)]

tribble *see* TROUBLE

tribill *see* TREEPLE

tribul &c [*'trɪbl] *vt* bring tribulation upon; distress, harass, afflict *la14-16, chf Sc*.
n, also **trible** &c tribulation, distress, affliction *16, only Sc*.
~**ance** tribulation *la16, only Sc*. *n, also* **trible** &c tribulation, distress, affliction *16, only Sc*.
~**nes** = *n, la14, only Sc*. ~**us** full of tribulation *la16, only Sc*. [OF *tribuler*]

tribulat [*'trɪbəlat] *ptp* afflicted *la16*. [only Sc; L *trībulātus*; *cf* prec]

tricker¹ &c *n* the catch or trigger (of a gun) *18-, now N Lnk*. [Du *trekker*; *trekken* (*v*) pull]

tricker² *n, curling* (CURL) the iron plate on which a player places his foot to prevent it from slipping on the ice *19*. [perh f Eng *trig* make firm]

trid *see* THIRD

triffice *see* TRAVISE

triffle¹ &c *n* = trifle, a small amount *la16-, now NE Edb Ayr*.

triffle² &c *n* = trefoil, the name of various plants *19*.

trift *see* THRIFT

trig &c *adj* **1** active, nimble, brisk, alert *la15-e20, only Sc*. **2** trim, neat in figure, dress or manner, well turned out; *of places, things* neat, tidy *16-, chf Sc*.
vti, freq ~ **up, out** make TRIG, smarten up *la17-, now NE*.
~**ly** neatly, smartly *la18-e20*. [eME (once), nEng dial *trigg* trusty, ON *tryggr* faithful; secure]

trigidy &c *n* = tragedy *e16*.

trigit &c [*'trə'dʒɛt, *?-'dʒɪt] *n* = treget, trickery, deceit *la14-e16*. [only Sc; *cf* TRINKET. OED *treget*]

trigle &c [*'trɪgl] *vi* = trickle *la14-e16*. [only Sc. OED *trickle*]

trigram *n* an inscription of three letters *e17*. [Gk *tri-* three- + *grámma* a letter]

trilapse &c; **trelapse** &c [*'trilaps] *adj, of a person* guilty of a TRILAPSE; *of the offence* occurring for the third time *la16-e18*.
n a third offence against church discipline, *esp* fornication *la17-19*.
trelapse a person who is guilty of a TRILAPSE *17-19*. [only Sc; L *tri-* three- + Eng *lapse*; *cf* DULAPSE]

trim &c; **trum** &c *la16, e20 vti, n, adj* = trim *16-*.
trimmie a pert, impudent girl, a hussy *19-e20*.

trimble, trimmle *see* TREMMLE

trindle *see* TRINNLE

trink &c *n* **1** a trench, channel, ditch, gutter *la16-, now NE Ags Fif*. **2** a narrow coastal inlet *la18-, now Sh-Ags Fif*. **3** a rut in a road *la19-, NE Ags*.
~**it** rutted, filled with ruts *la19-, Bnf Abd*. [northern F dial *trenque*; *cf* OF *trenche* &c and TRINSCH]

trinket *vi* have secret or underhand dealings (**with**) *17-e19*. [chf Sc; perh connected w Eng *trinket* or *trick*; *cf* TRIGIT]

trinkle¹ &c *v* **1** *vi* = trickle *16-, now local NE-WC*. **2** *vt* shed (tears) *e17*. **3** besprinkle, scatter over *la19-, NE*.
n = trickle *la19-, local Ork-WC*.

trinkle² &c *vi* = tingle *e17, only Sc*.

trinkum &c *n, chf in pl* trinkets, knick-knacks, odds and ends *la18-19*. [appar joc alteration of Eng *trinket*]

trinnle &c *16-*, **trindle** *la16-e19*; **trundill** *la15*, **trunnel** &c *19-e20 n* **1** = trindle, a wheel or similar circular object *la15-*. **2** *specif* (1) a wheelbarrow wheel *18-, now Stlg Ayr*; (2) a lantern- or cogwheel, *esp* in the gearing machinery of a mill *16-19*. **3** *only* **trintle** a rolling or flowing motion *19, WC*.
v, also **trintle** *19-*, **truntle** *la18-19*, **trantle** *19* **1** *vi, of an object, vehicle etc, also fig* roll, trundle, bowl along *17-, now local Stlg-Rox*. **2** *of persons etc* move along; waddle; straggle *19-, now Abd*. **3** *of water etc* flow, trickle *la18-, now Abd*. **4** *vt* cause to roll, flow, trickle *la18-, now Stlg Fif Ayr*.
trinnly &c roundish, suitable for rolling *20-, Bwk Rox*. **trintlet** &c a small ball or pellet, *specif* of sheep's dung *20-, now Per Stlg WC*.
trinnle-bed &c = trundle-bed, a truckle-bed *17-19*. ~**-board** &c one of the two parallel plates on a TRINNLE (*n* 2 (2)) *la16-e18*. [*cf* Eng *trundle*]

trinsch &c *n, vti* = trench *16, only Sc*.

trintle(**t**) *see* TRINNLE

trip¹ *n* **1** = trip. **2** a turn at dancing *18-e19*.

trip² &c *n* **1** = trip, a small flock *la15-e16*. **2** a troop, company (of men) *la16*.

tripe &c *n* = tripe, entrails *la15-*.
trypal &c [*'trəipl] *n* a tall, thin, ungainly person *18-, now Abd* [F *tripaille* = *n*]. **triping** coal from which the larger lumps have been separated; *later* unscreened coal from the workings; a kind of *drossy* (DROSS) coal *la19-, now Fif WC*.

triplar &c [*'trɪplər] *adj* = triple *la15*. [only
Sc; laL *triplāris*, L *triplus*]

tripling *n, esp in* PIBROCH *or strathspey* (STRATH) a
melody note divided into three by the insertion
of two short *cutting* (CUT¹) grace-notes *la19-*.

triply [*'trɪplaɪ] *n, law* a third answer, made by
the *pursuer* (PURSUE) in reply to the DUPLY of the
defender (DEFEND); *occas also* a second rejoinder
by the *defender*, *16-18*.
vi make a TRIPLY *16-e18*. [only Sc; OF
triplique; *cf* DUPLY]

trist¹ *adj* = TRAIST *adj 3, e16*.
vti, only **thrist** give credit to (a person) for
goods, supply (goods *to* a person) on credit
la16-e17, only Sc. [ME; *appar* related to
TRAIST, TRUST]

trist² *adj* = trist, sad; doleful *e16*.
n sadness, sorrow, affliction *e16, only Sc*.
~**sum** sad, woeful *la16, only Sc*.

trist *see* THRIST¹, THRIST²

trith *see* TROWTH

trittle-trattle &c *interj* expressing contempt
e16.
n, in pl **1** foolish or idle talk *la16*. **2** cheap tawdry articles *la19*. [only Sc; reduplicated f
TRATTLE, in *n* 2 perh by confusion w TRINKUM
and TRANTLE]

trive(n) *see* THRIVE

troce *see* TROYES

troch &c *only Sc*, **trough** *18-*; **trouch** &c *now
Ags, only Sc*, **throcht** *la16, only Sc* [trox, trʌu; *S
also* trʌux] *n, pl also* **trows** &c *la16-* [trʌuz] **1** =
trough *la15-*. **2** *usu in pl, latterly* **trows** a channel or wooden conduit for water, *esp* that leading to a millwheel *la16-, now local Ork-Wgt*. **3**
(1) the channel or bed of a river, *esp* a rough
part; a similar channel among sea rocks *16-e20*.
(2) the valley or basin of certain rivers in south-
west Scotland *18-e19*: '*the trow of Clyde*'. **4** *freq*
trochie &c a narrow passage between houses, a
CLOSE², VENNEL *19-, now Abd*. **5** *in pl* a kind of
flat-bottomed river barge in two sections with a
space through which salmon could be speared
19-e20, Dmf Rox. **6** *contemptuous* a person who
eats or drinks to excess *19-, local Cai-Dmf*.
trowmill a watermill *now in place-names in S*.
~**stane** a stone trough *19-, local Stlg-WC*.

troch *see* THROU, TROKE

trock *see* TROKE

trod &c *vt* trace, track down *17-e19*. [eME]

troddle &c *vi* toddle, trot, walk with short,
quick steps *19-e20*. [conflation of TODDLE w
Eng *trot*]

troddle *see* TROTTLE

trodge *vi* = trudge *19-, now Sh Ork Ags*.

trodwiddie *see* TREADWIDDIE

trog *see* TROKE

trogs &c; **trugs** &c *n pl, used as a mild oath or
expletive* faith, troth, *freq* **by my** ~ *la18-e20*.
[altered f Eng *troth, truth*]

trois *see* TROYES, TURSE

troke &c; **truck** &c, **trock** &c *la18-, now Sh*

Cai, **troch** *20*, **trouk** &c *18-, now Sh Ork*,
trog &c *la18-, now SW Uls* [trok; WC, SW Uls
trog; *Sh Ork also* truk, tʌk; *Mry Ags also* trox] *v*
1 *vt* = truck, bargain, barter *la16-*. **2** *vi* trade,
deal in a small way **with** *18-, now NE, EC, SW,
S*. **3** *vt* spread, carry about (news, gossip etc)
la19-, now Mry Bnf. **4** *vi* associate, have to do
with, have nefarious or illicit dealings **with**, be
on friendly or intimate terms **with** *18-*. **5** potter or bustle (**about**) fussily, occupy oneself
with trivial matters *la18-, now Bnf Ags Per, only
Sc*.
n **1** = truck, barter, exchange; a bargain or
business deal *la16-*. **2** *chf in pl* small articles of
merchandise, odds and ends, trinkets *18-, now N
nEC*. **3** any worthless or rubbishy goods;
insubstantial trash *19-, local Sh-Dmf*. **4** *of persons or animals* worthless specimens, riff-raff *19-,
N Bwk Lnk*. **5** = truck, dealings, association
(sometimes implying improper familiarity)
la18-. **6** a small piece of work or business, a
task, errand *19-, Sh NE nEC*. **7** nonsensical
talk, rubbish *20-, Sh N*.

troker &c, **trocker** &c, **trucker** &c, **trogger**
&c a bargainer, dealer, petty trader, pedlar
la18-, now local Bnf-SW. **trockerie** &c *la19-,
now Sh Bnf*, **troggin** &c *la18-e20* = *n* 2. [*cf*
TRUKER]

troll &c *n* an untidy, slovenly person, a slattern
la19-e20, Mry Bnf Rox. [obs Eng *trull* a
prostitute]

trollie-bags &c *n* **1** the intestines or entrails of
persons or animals *19-e20*. **2** a fat, unshapely
person *la20-, local N-Lnk*. [altered f Eng
trillibubs]

trollop; trallop &c *la19-*, **treelip** *la19-, NE*
n **1** = trollop. **2** a long, gangling, ungainly
person or animal *la19-, local Ork-WC*. **3** a
long, trailing piece of cloth, a tatter; a large,
ugly, straggling mass of something *19-, now Sh
N, only Sc*.
vi hang or trail loosely or untidily *la19-, local
Bnf-Stlg*.

trolollay &c [*'trolə'le] *interj* **1** used in a HOG-
MANAY rhyme *la18-e19*. **2** *only* **trolylow**
[*'trolɪ'lʌu] expression of contempt *e16*. [only
Sc; vars of ME *trolly-lolly* used as a refrain.
OED *trolly-lolly*]

tron *18-*; **trone** &c *14-19 n* **1** a steelyard,
weighing machine, *esp* a public one in a BURGH,
set up in or near a market-place for weighing
merchandise, *esp* locally-produced butter,
cheese, wool etc *14-, now hist*. **2** the place or
building where the TRON stood and the area
round it; the market-place; the town centre *16-,
now in place-names in Edb Gsw*. **3** a pillory, the
post of the TRON being used as such, or as a
place of public exposure and punishment
15-e19. **4** the standard weight for home-produced commodities, varying in different locali-
ties *la16-e17* (*officially*), *la16-e19* (*in practice*). [*cf*
TROYES]

vt weigh on a TRON (*n* 1) *17-e19*.

tronar &c an official who had charge of weighing at the TRON *la14-e17*.

T~ Church *or* **Kirk** name of a church standing near the site of the TRON *18-*, *Edb Gsw*. **~ lord** *appar* one of a group of porters, odd-job men etc (who *prob* stood for hire around the TRON) *17*, *Edb*. **~-man 1** = prec *17-18*, *Edb*. **2** a city chimney-sweep (*orig* with headquarters near the TRON) *18-e19*, *Edb*. **~ pound** *or* **stane** &c a pound or stone of *tron* weight, *la16-19*. **~ weight** = *n* 4, *la16-e19*. [chf Sc; ScL *trona*, OF *trone*, L *trutina* a weighbeam, scales]

trone *see* TROON, TRUAN

tronie &c *n* a long story, rambling chat *19-*, *Ags*. [perh altered f *ronnie* (RANE)]

troo &c *interj* a call to cows or calves *la19-e20*. [prob var of PROO]

troon *la19-*; **trone** *19-*, **truan** &c *19-*, **troo** &c *19-*, *N*, **trowane** *16*. ['tru(ə)n; *Cai* trʌu; *NE* tru; *WC*, *SW* tro(:)n; *Rox also* 'trʌuənt] *n* 1 = truant, a vagabond *e16*. **2** = truant (from school), *freq* **play the ~** *19-20*.

vti play truant (from), *freq* **~ the schule** &c *19-*, *local Cai-Dmf*.

adj trivial, trite *la16*. [OED *truant*]

troosers *n pl* = trousers *20-*.

troosh *interj* a command to an animal, *esp* a dog, to get out of the way *la19-e20*, *Arg*. [Gael *truis*, Eng *truss*]

trooshlach &c ['truʃləx] *n* trash, worthless things or people *la19-20*, *Abd Arg Wgt*. *adj*, *of persons* dirty, slovenly *20*, *NE*. [appar altered f Gael *trusdaireachd* trash, dirt, perh w infl f DRUSH; *cf* next and TRUSDAR]]

trooshter &c *n* 1 useless rubbish *la19-e20*, *NE*. **2** *contemptuous* troublesome children *20-*, *now Ross*. [Gael *trusdaireachd*; *cf* prec and TRUSDAR]

troot *see* TROUT

trosk *n* a silly, talkative person; a slow-witted, slovenly person, *esp* a woman *20-*, *Cai*. [Gael *trosg* a cod; a silly person, ON *þorskr* a cod]

trot &c *n*, *vti* = trot *16-*.

~tin *of a stream etc* babbling *18-19*. **~tle** &c ['trotl; *SW* *'trøtl] **1** = TODDLE *v* 2, *19-e20*. **2** dawdle, idle *20-*, *SW* [perh var of DRIDDLE].

back-door ~ *euphemistic* diarrhoea *la20-*, *local Ork-Ayr*. **short in the ~**, **on short ~** short-tempered *la19-*, *NE*.

trot *see* THROAT

trotcosy &c [*'trot'kozɪ] *n* a hood, *perh usu* as part of a cloak or other warm outer garment *la18-19*. [only Sc; perh Eng *throat* or *trot* + *cosy*]

troth *see* TROWTH

trottle &c; **troddle** *n*, *usu in pl* small round pellets of excrement, *esp* of sheep *la19-*, *local NE-S*. **trottlick** &c = *n*, *la19-e20*. [metath f TARTLE²]

trou *see* THROU

trouble &c; **trubill** &c *16-e17*, **tribble** &c *19-*, *now NE nEC Slk* ['trʌbl, 'trɪbl] *n* **1** = trouble *la16-*. **2** sickness, disease; an ailment *18-*: '*he'll diagnose yer tribble*'. **3** *mining* a break or intrusion in strata; a fault *la17-*, *now C*.

vt **1** = trouble *la15-*. **2** harm; injure; oppress *la14-e18*.

trublance &c troubling; trouble; disturbance *16-e17*. **~some** &c **1** = troublesome *17-*. **2** troubled in mind *la16*, *only Sc*.

trouch *see* THRUCH, TROCH

trough *see* TROCH

trouk *see* TROKE

trouker *see* TRUKER

trounce¹ &c *vt* **1** = trounce *18-*. **2** beat down, smash *la19-*, *SW*.

trounce² [*?trʌuns] *vti* rush off or along briskly *e19*. [perh var of ME *traunce* move briskly]

troune &c *la14-16*, **trune** *e16* [*trøn] *n* = throne. [only Sc. OED *throne*]

troush &c [truʃ; *Ags* *trøʃ, *trøs] *interj* a call to cattle *19-*, *now Bnf Kcdn*. [altered f *pruch*, var of PROO; *cf* TREESH]

trouss *see* TURSE

trout &c; **troot** *la19-* [trut] *n* **1** = trout *la14-*. **2** *freq* **~ie** term of endearment to a child *la19-*, *local Bnf-Dmf*.

vi catch trout *17-e19*.

there's a ~(ie) in the well &c said of a woman expecting a child, *esp* if illegitimate *la19-*, *now Abd*.

trow &c; **trowl** &c [trʌu(l)] *v* **1** *vi* = troll, roll, descend by rolling, spin round *la18-e20*. **2** *vtr* cause to roll, spin, turn round *19-e20*. **3** *vi* walk with a rolling or waddling gait *19-e20*, *Rox*.

trow *see* TREW¹, TROCH, TRUE

trowane *see* TROON

trowen *see* TRUAN

trowis *see* TREW²

trowl *see* TROW

trows *see* TROCH

trowse *see* TREWS

trowth &c *now Cai*, **truth** &c *16-*, **troth** *16-*; **treuth** &c *la14-19*, **truith** *la16-e20*, **trith** *la19-*, *now Loth*, **throwth** &c *la19-20*, **trath** &c *la19*, *Sh Ork* [trʌuθ; trøθ, trɪθ; troθ; *Sh Ork* traθ; *nEC* treθ; *trjuθ] *n* **1** = truth, troth *la14-*. **2** *chf* **trowth, troth** [trʌuθ, troθ] *as interj*, *freq* **in ~** indeed!, upon my word! *18-e20*. **3** *only* **troth, truth** (*la18-20*) = troth, one's pledged word.

trewthelie [*'trjuθlɪ] honestly *la15*, *only Sc*.

(**the**) **God's truth 1** the absolute truth *la19-*. **2** *used as interj* (*as in n* 2).

troyes &c *la16-e19*; **trois** &c *la15-e18*, **troce** *la16* [*troiz, *tros] *n* = troy, a standard system of weight. [*cf* TRON]

truaghan ['truəxən] *n* a poor, destitute person, a down-and-out; *also joc* a small child *20-*, *now Cai*. [Gael *truaghan*, f *truagh* wretched, pitiful]

truan &c; **trowen** &c *la18-19*, **trone** *19-*, *now*

Per ['truən, 'trʌuən, tron] *n* **1** a trowel *19-*, *now local.* **2** a tool for smoothing cement or plaster *la19-*, *now Fif Dnbt.* [altered f TRUEL]

truan *see* TROON

trubill, trublance *see* TROUBLE

truck *see* TROKE

trucker *see* TRUKER

trudder *n* rubbish, trash *19-e20*, *Abd.* [var of *tudder* (TOUTHER), perh w infl f Eng *trash* etc]

true *17-*; **trew** &c *la14-e17*, **trow** *la16-18* [tru; *Rox* triu] *adj* = true *la14-*.
~**lins** &c truly, indeed *la18-20*.

true blue *adj, n* (of) a 17th century *Covenanter* (COVENANT) (from their chosen colour, the blue of the St Andrew flag); *hence* (of) any staunch or devoted Presbyterian; (of) a supporter of the WHIGS[3] of the 17th and 18th centuries *18-*, *now hist.*

true *see* TREW[1]

truel &c ['truəl] *n* = trowel *19-*, *Ork N Per.* [*cf* TRUAN]

truff *vt* steal, pilfer *18*, *only Sc.*
trufinge [*'trʌfɪŋ] deceit *la14*, *only Sc.* [ME = trifle (with), OF *truf(f)er* mock; *cf* TRUPHANE]

truff *see* TURR

trufinge *see* TRUFF

trugs *see* TROGS

truiffis *see* TURR

truith *see* TROWTH

truker &c *la15-16*, **treukour** &c *16-17*, **trouker** &c *16-20*, **trucker** *la18-e20* [*Sh Ork* 'trukər, 'trʌkər; *'trøkər, *'trjukur] *n* a deceiver, cheat; a rascal, rogue. [ME *troke* &c fail, deceive, OE *trucian* fail, later perh w infl f *troker* (TROKE). OED *troker*]

trule [*trøl] *n* a game, *appar* played with balls or bowls *e16*. [only Sc; *cf* Eng *troll* roll, bundle]

trum *see* TRIM

trump[1] &c; **trum** &c *e16*, **trumb** *e16* [trʌmp; *trʌm] *n* **1** = trump, a trumpet *la14-*. **2** a Jew's harp *16-*, *now local Sh-Ayr.*
vi **1** = trump, trumpet *la14-e16*. **2** march or go (as at the sound of a trumpet) *e16*, *only Sc.*
the tongue of the ~ the main or most active person in a group; the spokesman *la18-19*.

trump[2] &c *vt* deceive, cheat *la14-e16*.
~**er** a deceiver, cheat *la15-e17*. ~**ery** &c **1** deceit, trickery *la15-16*. **2** *of beliefs, practices etc* nonsense, rubbish *la15*. **3** **trumphery** ['trʌmfərɪ] trash, rubbish *la18-*, *now local Sh-Ags.* [F *tromper*; *cf* eModEng]

trump[3] *n* a thing of small value, a trifle *e16*. [only Sc; perh back-formation f *trumpery* (TRUMP[2])]

trumph &c [trʌmf] *n* = trump, the chief suit in a card game; a splendid person etc *19-*.
what's (**to be**) ~(**s**)? what's doing?, how are things?; what's to be done next? *la20-*, *Sh NE Per.*

trumphery *see* TRUMP[2]

truncher &c,   **trunscheour** &c   *16*;

trunʒour *e16* ['trʌnʃər] *n* **1** = trencher *16-*, *now Sh Lnk.* **2** a knife *la16*. [OED *trencher*, *truncheour*]

trundill *see* TRINNLE

trune *see* TROUNE

trunnel *see* TRINNLE

trunscheour *see* TRUNCHER

truntle *see* TRINNLE

trunʒour *see* TRUNCHER

truphane [*?'trʌfən] *n* a deceiver, impostor *la15*. [only Sc; *appar* OF *truffant* or MedL *truffanus* f *truffa* fraud; *cf* TRUFF]

trusdar &c ['trusdər, 'truʃtər] *n* an untrustworthy person, a rascal *19-e20*, *N Highl Arg.* [Gael = a nasty person; *cf* TROOSHTER, TROOSHLACH]

trushel &c *n* a muddle, confusion; a slovenly or ungainly person *20*, *Cai.* [see SND]

trust &c *n* **1** = trust *17-*. **2** credit *la17-e19*. *vti, ptp also* **trust** *la16* = trust *la16-*.
~**er** *law* a person who sets up a trust for the administration of property or funds *la17-*. [*cf* TRAIST]

truth *see* TROWTH

trwoo &c *interj* a call to cows or calves *19-20*, *Abd Fif.* [altered f *ptrue* var of PROO; *cf* PREE[2]]

tryacle *see* TRAICLE

tryell *see* TRIAL

trykle *see* TRAICLE

tryne *n* = train, a retinue; a set of consequences *16*, *only Sc.*

trypal *see* TRIPE

tryst &c [trəist] *n* **1** an agreement, covenant, a mutual pledge *la14-e20*. **2** an appointment to meet at a specified time and place; an assignation, *freq* **set, make, keep** etc ~ *la14-*. **3** an appointed meeting or assembly, a rendezvous *15-*. **4** an appointed meeting-place *la14-*, *now Bnf Ags Per.* **5** a conspicuous object chosen as a rendezvous, *eg* for huntsmen etc *19-e20*, *freq in place-names.* **6** an appointed time *la15*. **7** a market, *esp* for the sale of livestock, a fair (though not one fixed by charter or statute) *la16-*, *now Bnf Ags Per.*
v **1** *vi* (1) make an appointment or assignation, fix a time and place of meeting *la14-*, *Gen except Sh Ork.* (2) meet **with** by pre-arrangement *la17-*, *now Bnf Ags.* **2** *vt* arrange with (a person) to be in a certain place at a certain time or to perform some service etc *18-*, *now local Kcdn-SW.* **3** betroth, engage to be married *19-*, *now C.* **4** order (something) in advance; cause (some thing or service) to be done; arrange for the making or delivery of *18-*, *now local Ags-SW.* **5** fix, arrange (a time or occasion) *la16-*, *now Ags.* **6** *of God, fate etc* (1) appoint, ordain (a person's lot), arrange for *18-19*; (2) bless **with** *e18*; (3) visit **with** (misfortune) *17-19*. **7** *vi* coincide (in time) **with** *la17*. **8** negotiate **with** *la16-17*. **9** (1) *vt* invite, encourage, entice *19-20*. (2) *vi* ~ **wi** make a fuss of, coax, wheedle *la19-*, *N.*

~**ed** *of persons* hired or engaged in advance; *of things* made to order *19-*, *now Dmf.* ~**er** a person who arranges a meeting *la17.* ~**ing &c** in combs, specifying the place or time for a TRYST (*n 3*) *17-e20*: '*trysting place*'; '*trysting tree*'.
bide (**one's**) ~ wait for someone at a prearranged meeting-place *19-20.* **haud &c** (**one's**) ~ fulfil one's commitment, keep one's word *19-e20.* [only Sc until *19*; appar f ME *trist*, OF *triste*, MedL *trista* an appointed place of ambush in hunting; perh related to TRAIST]

trytle *see* TREETLE

tsill *see* CHILD

tu *see* TAE⁴

tub &c *n* **1** = tub. **2** *mining* a HUTCH for carrying cut coal; a measure of coal (varying in weight) *19-*, *now Fif.*

tuch *see* TEUCH

tuchin &c ['t(j)uxən] *n* a husky cough, hoarseness *20-*, *Inv Mry.* [Gael *tùchan* hoarseness]

tuchit *see* TEUCHIT

tuck &c; tewk &c [t(j)ʌk, tjuk] *interj* a call to hens to come for food *19-*, *now N Per Ayr.* ~**ie**, *freq* ~**ie hen** *child's word* a hen or chicken *19-*, *now local NE-midLoth.* [imit; *cf* CHUCK¹, TICK³]

tuck *see* TOUK¹, TOUK²

tuckie &c *adj* awkward, clumsy; *of a limb etc* disabled, deformed *20-*, *NE.* [prob Eng *tuck* truss up; hamper]

tuckle &c *n* a row or file of people sledging or skating *20*, *Slk.* [var of TICHLE]

tud *see* THUD

tudder *see* TOUTHER

Tuesday ['tjuzdɪ; *Ags also* 'tuz-] *n* = Tuesday. [*cf* TYSDAY]

tuffing *n* caulking material; oakum *e16.* [f Eng *tuff*, *tuft*]

tuffle *see* TAFFLE

tug &c; chug *la19-*, *now local C;* **teug** *19-*, *now Cai Kcb* [tʌg, tjug; *C also* tjʌg, tʃʌg; **tug*] *n* **1** = tug *16-*. **2** a strip of hide or skin *16-e19* [f being freq used for the traces of horse harness]. *vti* = tug *la16-*.
teugie a moment, instant *20-*, *now Cai.* **tuggle &c** *la15-20*, **chuggle &c** *20-*, *chf Dmf vt* pull (about) roughly and jerkily. *n* a pulling about; *fig* a struggle *20*, *Sh Cai Abd.* **tuggled &c** pulled about; fatigued, harassed *la15-e19.*
~**-net** a salmon net pulled behind a boat at the mouth of a river, *esp* the Spey *15-e19*, *only Sc.* ~ **quhiting** a whiting caught by a handline *la17*, *only Sc.*

tugs *n pl* = togs, clothes *19.*

tuik *see* TOUK¹

tuil &c; teel &c *la19-*, *now NE*, **tewl &c** *19-e20*, *chf Sh Ork* [tøl, til; *Sh Ork* 'tju(ə)l; *NE* til; *nEC* tel; *Bwk also* til; *Gall also* tjul] *n* **1** = tool; *freq also* applied somewhat *joc* to any implement, piece of equipment etc *la18-*. **2** term of contempt for a person *19-*, *now Ork.*

tuill, tuilyie, tuilʒ(i)e, tuilz(i)e *see* TULYIE

tuin *see* TUNE

tuip *la16-*; **tup &c, toop &c** *18-e19*, **tip** *17-*, **teep** *la18-*, *NE* [*local Sh-Abd* tup; *NE also* tip; *C, S Uls* tøp, tɪp; *nEC* tep; *Bwk also* tip; *St* tʌp] *n* **1** a ram *15-*. **2** familiar or disparaging term for a man *19-*, *now Cai.*
vti, *of a ram* copulate; sire *18-*.
tup-yeld &c *of a ewe* barren, infertile *19-*, *now C, S.* **tup-hog** a male sheep till its first shearing *la18-e19.* ~**-horn** (a) ram's horn, *esp* one made into a spoon etc or used as a musical instrument *18-e19.* ~**-lamb** a male lamb *la18-*. [chf Sc and nEng; unknown]

tuir *see* TEAR²

tuird &c *la16-*, *now Ork*; **taird &c** *19-*, *now C* [tørd; *Abd* tird, tjurd; *C* terd] *n* = turd.

tuire *see* TOUR¹

tuith &c *16-*, **tooth &c, teeth** (*as sing*) *19-*, *now Sh N Dmf* [tiθ; *nEC* teθ; *C, S also* tøθ, tɪθ] *n*, *pl also* **tetht** *la14* [tiθ] *n* **1** = tooth *la14-*. **2** a fragment of rainbow seen near the horizon, regarded as a sign of bad weather *20-*, *NE.*
~**fu**(**l**) a mouthful, *esp* of liquor *la18-*. ~**y &c** **1** *lit and fig* sharp-toothed; ravenous *19.* **2** sharp in manner; critical, acrimonious *la18-*, *now local Fif-Wgt.*
teethache &c = toothache *19-*. **tuith tuil** *masonry* a serrated chisel or punch used for the second dressing of stones *la20-*, *Fif Bwk Rox.* ~ **wark** toothache *la14.*
in spite of someone's teeth despite someone's wishes or efforts, in defiance of someone *18-*.

tuix *see* TWIXT

tuk *see* TAK

tulat *see* TOLLET

tulchan &c ['tʌlxən] *n* **1** a calfskin, *usu* that of her own dead calf, stuffed with straw or wrapped round another calf and put beside a cow to induce her to give milk freely *la16-19.* **2** *fig* a substitute, a person appointed nominally to some office, the power and emoluments being diverted to another; *specif* one of the bishops created by Regent Morton in 1572 to enable him and his supporters to appropriate Church revenues *la16-*, *now hist.* **3** a large or fat person *19-e20*, *Bnf Abd Ags.* [Gael *tulchan* = *n* 1, *tulachan* a little mound (the calfskin sometimes being merely laid over a heap of earth beside the cow)]

tull *see* TILL¹

tulloch ['tʌləx] *n* a mound, hillock; *freq* a fairy mound *19-e20*, *Cai Per*, *in place-names 13-*. [Gael *tulach* a small hill]

tully *see* TULYIE

tulshoch ['tʌlʃəx] *n* a small bundle or heap; *also* contemptuous term for a person *19-e20*, *Abd Kcdn.* [altered f *dulshoch* (DULSHET)]

tulyie &c *16-*, **tuilyie &c** *15-19*, **tu**(**i**)**lʒ**(**i**)**e** *la14-16*, **tu**(**i**)**lz**(**i**)**e** *16-e20*, **toilʒe &c** *la14-16*, **teulie &c** *la16-*, *now Ork*, **tool**(**y**)**ie &c** *18-e20*, **tweelie &c** *la18-e19*, *SW*, **tully &c**

la18-20, **tuill &c** *15-16* ['tulɪ; *Sh Ork* 'tøl(j)ɪ; *SW* 'twil(j)ɪ; *Rox also* 'tøljɪ; **'tuljɪ] n* **1** a quarrel, brawl, fight; a noisy contest, dispute; a struggle, turmoil *la14-*, *now local Sh-Bwk*. **2** a verbal quarrel, wrangle *18-*, *now Sh Ork Mry Abd*. **3** quarrelling, contention *la16-18*. **4** trouble, turmoil; toil, exertion *la16-*, *now Sh, chf literary*.

v **1** *vt* harass; quarrel with; assault *la14-16*. **2** *vi* quarrel, contend, fight *15-*, *now Sh Ork Mry*. **3** quarrel verbally, argue, squabble *18-*, *now Sh Ork Mry*.

~r &c a quarrelsome person, a brawler *15-e17*.
~some &c quarrelsome, contentious *la16, e19*.
~-mulie a quarrel, broil, turmoil *19*. [only Sc; OF *to(u)illier* stir up, strive, dispute; *cf* Eng *toil*]

tumble *see* TUMMLE

tume &c *15-*, **toom &c** *la16-*; **tome &c** *la14-16*, **teem** *18-*, *N*, **taim &c** *e20*, *Ags Fif*, **tim &c** *20-*, *C*, *S* [tøm, tim; *N Uls* tim; *nEC* tem; *local EC, S* tim] *adj* **1** *also fig* empty; unoccupied, vacant *15-*. **2** *of a person or his limbs etc* thin, lean, lank *19-*, *now local Sh-Stlg*. **3** empty of food, fasting, hungry *la18-*, *now local Sh-Per*. **4** hollow-sounding, echoing *la20-*, *NE, C*. **5** empty-headed, foolish, witless *la18-*, *now Sh*. **6** *of words etc* vain, hollow, insubstantial *la16-*, *now Sh*. **7** *of machinery* idling, not actually processing material *20-*, *now Per Stlg Loth*.

v **1** *vt* = TEEM *v* 1, *16-*. **2** empty (a glass etc) by drinking *la16-*. **3** = TEEM *v* 2, *16-*. **4** discharge (a gun) *la18-*, *now Abd Ags Stlg*. **5** *vi* empty, be or become empty *la18-*, *now Sh N*. **6** = TEEM *v* 4, *la19-*, *local*.

n **1** sufficient time, leisure (to do something) *la14-e16*. **2** a place where rubbish is emptied, a dump *19-*, *now local Stlg-Rox*.

~-handit empty-handed, bearing no gifts *18-*, *now Sh NE-WC*. **~-heidit &c** silly, foolish *17-*. [ME *tome &c*, OE *tōm*, ON *tómr* (*adj*); *cf* TEEM]

tumfie &c; **tumphie &c** *n* a dull, stupid, soft person *la18-*. [only Sc; uncertain; *cf* SUMPH]

tumill *see* TUN

tummle &c; **tumble** *16-* *vti* = tumble *la14-*. *n* = tumble.

tumbler &c 1 a kind of light box-cart with fixed (solid) wheels *16-e19*. **2** *mining* an apparatus for tipping coal HUTCHES etc *la19-*, *now Fif*. **tumbling cart &c** = *tumbler 1*, *la16-19*. **tummlin shakker** a revolving straw-shaker in a threshing mill *la20-*, *NE*. **tummlin Tam &c 1** a kind of scales for weighing heavy copper George III coins *la18-e19*. **2** a horse-drawn hay-gatherer which turns right over when depositing its load *20-*, *Ork-S*. **tumbling verse** a kind of irregular anapaestic verse *la16*. **tummle the cat** *etc* do a somersault, go head over heels *20-*, *Sh NE*; *cf tummle one's wilkies &c* (WILD).

tummock &c *19-*, *now Wgt*; **tammock**

la18-19 *n* a small hillock; a tuft or tussock of grass; a molehill [Gael *tom* a knoll; a bush, thicket; a tuft, + *-ock*]

tump *see* THUMP

tumphie *see* TUMFIE

tumphy *n*, *mining* coaly fireclay *la19-*, *now Fif*. [unknown; *cf* HUMPH³]

tumshie &c *n*, *joc or colloq* a turnip *20-*, *C, S*. [appar f *turmit* (TURNEEP) + *-sie*; Eng dial *tummit*]

tun &c *n* = tun, ton, a cask, measure etc *la14-*. **~ster** ? an officer who superintended the tunning of liquor *e17*, *only Sc*.

tumill &c [**'tʌml] a funnel used for pouring the wort of ale into casks *la16-e18* [f *tunmill*]. **~ silver** a duty on casks of merchandise *e17*, *only Sc*.

tun *see* TIN

tunag &c [**'tonək, *?'tʌn-] *n* a short woollen mantle or cloak worn by women in some parts of the *Highlands* (HIELAND) *la18-e19*. [only Sc; Gael *tonnag*, OIr *tonach* a woollen shawl, L *tunica* a tunic]

tunder &c *la19-*, *now Ags*; **toundir &c** *la15*, *only Sc* ['tʌndər; **'tʌnər] *n* = tinder. [OED *tinder*]

tune &c; **toon &c** *16-e20*, **tuin** *la16*, **tone** *16*, **tin &c** *la19-e20*, *C*, **teen** *la18-20*, *NE* [tøn, tin; *NE* tin; *nEC also* ten; *Per also* tjøn] *n* **1** = tune *la15-*. **2** intonation (of speech), *freq* that associated with a particular dialect *la18-*, *now local*. **3** mood, humour, temper, *freq* (**in**) **guid &c** or **ill ~** *la18-*, *local Sh-Wgt*.

vt **1** = tune *17-*. **2** put (an implement) in proper working order, adjust *19-*, *now Cai*.

tunie moody, changeable in temperament *19-*, *S*.

hae *or* **tak a ~ to oneself** play a tune by oneself *19-*, *now Ork NE-Per*.

tunk *vt* **~it** *marbles and transf* 'cleaned out', bankrupt *e20*. [aphetic f STUNK²]

tunnir *see* THUNNER

tup *see* TUIP

tuppat *see* TIP¹

tuppeny *see* TIPPENY

turbot &c *n* **1** = turbot *la16-*. **2** the halibut *la18-e20*.

Turcas *see* TURK

turf *see* TURR

Turk &c *n* **1** = Turk *la14-*. **2** **t~** a kind of cloth *la17*.

adj **t~** fierce, truculent, sullen *la19-*, *now NE Ags*.

Turcas [**tʌr'kes, *'tʌrkəs] Turkish *e16* [OED *Turkeys*].

~ upon ~ some kind of upholstery fabric, *perh* of wool and canvas *18-19*.

turkas &c *la15-*, *now NE*, **turkis &c** *17-e20* ['tʌrkəs] *n* a pair of pincers or pliers, *esp* as used by a blacksmith etc. [chf Sc; ME *thourkeys*, OF *turcaise &c*]

turl *see* TIRL²

turmit see TURNEEP

turn &c; **tirn** *la19-e20 vti* **1** = turn *la14-*. **2** *vt* twist or spin (a rope) from straw *20*. **3** turn (cut hay, PEATS¹ etc) to dry; dismantle and rebuild (a small stack etc of such) for drying *19-*. **4** *vi, of property* return **to** (the former owner) *15-16, only Sc*. **5** have a tendency **to** *la16*. **6** become, grow: (1) *with complement preceding, 19-, N-S*: '*it's richt caul turnin*'; (2) *of physical or mental development, la18-, now local Sh-WC*: '*ye're turnin a big boy*'.

n **1** = turn *16-*. **2** a stroke or spell of work; a piece of work, a chore, duty *la14-, now Ags, only Sc*. **3** a trick, prank *la18-19*. **4** a rebuff, setback, a heading-off *19-, now Cai*. **5** *music* a section or passage of a tune *19-20*.

~ing &c **1** = turning *la14-*. **2** *esp ballad* = *n* 6, *e19*. **~ing loom** a turning lathe *19-, now Sh*. **~ing tree** a wooden stick for stirring *19-, now Sh*.

~-fittin &c building piles of PEATS¹ (as *v* 3) *19-, now Wgt S*. **~grese** &c [*'~gris] *la15-e17*, **~gree** *e16* a spiral staircase. **~pike** &c *15-*, **~pek** &c *16-17* **1** = turnpike, a spiked barrier *e15*. **2** *also* **~pike stair** *18-19* a spiral stair, a stair revolving round a central axis *16-, now Cai Stlg WC, only Sc*. **~pike foot** &c the foot of a *~pike stair*, *la16-e18*. **~pike heid** the head of a *~pike stair*, *e17, only Sc*. **~pike yett** a gate or door at the foot of a *~pike stair*, *e16, only Sc*.

aff &c **the ~** *chf in negative, of a door* at rest, still *la19-, local Abd-Ayr*: '*the door's never off the turn wi' them.*' **the day** *or* **year is on the ~** the days are changing in length of daylight, temperature etc *19-*. **do the** *etc* **~** serve a (useful) purpose, suffice for a particular occasion *la16-*. **tak the ~ out o** trick, fool *20-, now Sh Per*. **~ agane** retreat, flee *la14*. **~ one's bridill** turn one's horse *la14*. **~ someone's hand** provide someone with the money for something, relieve someone from financial straits *la19-, now N Kcb*. **~ someone's head** &c make someone feel giddy, intoxicate someone *la19-, local Sh-Per*. **the ~ of the nicht** midnight, the dead of night *la19-, local*. **~ ower in** *or* **tae** &c **years** grow old, age *la19-, NE Ags Fif*. **~ to the door** put out of one's house, eject, expel *20-, now Sh Cai Abd*. **~ up the wee finger** tipple, indulge in drinking *19-, Gen except Sh*. **~ the** (**wull**) **cat** do a somersault, go head over heels *la20-, Sh N-Per*; *cf* tummle one's wilkies &c (WILD). **the ~ o the year** the time of year when the days begin to lengthen *la19-*.

turneep &c *la17-, now Ork*, **turnip**, **turmit** &c *la19-, local Stlg-S n* = turnip, *in Scotland chf* a swede; *cf* NEEP.

turner &c *18-, now hist*, **turnover** (*erron*) *17*; **turnour** *la16-17 n* a small copper coin current in the 17th century, *also* called a twopenny piece or BODLE, *usu* valued at one sixth of an English penny *la16-e18*. [F *tournois* a similar coin]

turr &c *la15-, only Sc*, **truff** &c *la16-, now Ross Bnf*, **turf; toure** &c *la18-e20* [tʌr, trʌf; *tur] *n, pl also* **turreffis** *16-17, only Sc*, **truiffis** *16-17, only Sc*, **tirvis** *la16, only Sc* [*trʌvz, *tɪrvz] **1** = turf *la15-*. **2** a surface PEAT¹ or turf cut as fuel *15-, now local N-Rox*. **3** *only* **truff** &c the turf over a grave; the grave itself *la17-19*.

vt, not **truff** remove surface turf from *la19-, now Cai Mry Bnf*.

turvin &c the cutting of turf; sods, surface PEATS¹ *19-e20, chf Sh*.

Turf Cutter one of the participants in the *Riding of the Marches* (RIDE) ceremony at Musselburgh, with the duty of marking the MARCHES by digging a turf at each *20-*. **~ stack** &c a *peat-stack* (PEAT¹) *la16-e19*. [*cf* TIRR¹]

turr see TIRR¹

Turra &c *n* = Turriff, the town in Abd *19-*. **~ coo** a cow which was distrained for debt in 1913 because of the refusal of her owner, a farmer near Turriff, to pay his employees' National Health insurance contributions *20-, chf NE*. **~ neep** *or* **~ tattie** nickname for a native or inhabitant of Turriff *la20-, Bnf Abd*.

turreffis see TURR

tursal &c *n* = trussell, a bundle *15-16*. [OED *trussell*]

turse &c, **trouss** &c *la17-e20*; **trois** &c *15-e20* [tʌrs, trus] *v* **1** *vt* = truss, pack up, make into a bale etc *la14-, now Cai Bnf*. **2** pack up and carry away, carry in a pack *16*. **3** send packing, drive off *la16*. **4** *vtir* adjust or tuck up (a garment etc); get dressed *la17-, now Cai*. **5** *vi* start off, set to work; take oneself off *la18-19*.

n **1** = truss, a bundle, bale, *specif* of straw, thatch, sticks etc *la15-, now Ork Cai Arg*. **2** *only* **trouss** &c a tuck, fold, or hem in a garment *19-e20*.

tursabill capable of being packed up and carried off *la17*. [OED *truss*]

turvin see TURR

tusche see TISHIE

tushery *n* a conventional style of historical fiction, using many archaisms (such as 'tush') *la19-*. [coined by R L Stevenson, f Eng *tush*]

tushilago &c [tʌʃɪ'legə, -ɪ] *n* **1** *also* **dishilago** &c *19-* [dɪʃɪ'lago, -'lagɪ, -'legɪ &c] = tussilago, coltsfoot *la18-20*. **2** the butter bur *la20-, local*.

tusk¹ &c [tʌsk; *Sh also* to(r)sk] *n, also* **~ fish** a ling-like fish of the cod family, found *chf* in northern Scottish waters; *usu* dried, it was one of the chief exports of Shetland *18-, now Sh Ork Cai*. [Norw *to(r)sk*, ON *þo(r)skr*]

tusk² *n* **1** = tusk *la15-*. **2** *chf in pl, also* **~ stones** *building* projecting end-stones for bonding with an adjoining wall, toothing *la18-, now local Abd-Loth* [*cf* nEng *tuss*]. **3** the projecting wing on the blade of a *peat spade* (PEAT¹) *20-, now Bnf*.

vt cut (PEAT¹) from above the bank *la19-, N*. **~in**(**g**) (**stones**) = *n* 2, *la18-, local NE-Edb*.

tusk[3] *vt* empty (out) the contents of (a bag etc); empty one container into another *20-*, *local EC-Rox.* [only Sc; Gael *taosg* pour out, empty]

tussle *see* TOUSE

tut *see* TOOT[1]

tuther *see* TITHER

tutivillar [*'tøtɪvɪlər] *n* = titiviller, a rascal *e16*. [OED *titiviller*]

tutlyng [*?'tøt(ə)lɪŋ] *n* a blowing (of a horn) *la14*. [OF *tuteler; cf* TOUT[1]]

tutor &c; toutour *la16*, **tuttar** *la16* ['tjutər; *'tøtur, *?'tʌtər] *n* **1** = tutor. **2** (1) *law* the guardian and administrator of the estate of a PUPIL *la14-*. (2) used as a title, with the name of the estate over which the TUTOR had charge *16-*, *now hist: 'the T~ of Weem'.*

~**ial** of a TUTOR or his office *18-*. **tutrix** *16-e18*, **tutrice** *la15-e16* [*'tøtrɪks, *'tøtrɪs] a female TUTOR. ~**y &c** guardianship, protection; the office of a TUTOR *la14-*.

~ **dative** a TUTOR appointed by a court, *orig* by the Crown *la15-*. ~ **legitim** = tutor at law, *la18-e19*. ~ **nominate** *la17-*, ~ **testamentar &c** *16-*, **testamentary** ~ *16-* a TUTOR appointed *orig* by the father, *now* by either parent of a PUPIL to act in the event of his or her death.

~ **at** (*la19-*) *or* **of** (*16-*) *law* the nearest male relative on the father's side, who becomes TUTOR of a PUPIL in default of one appointed by the parents. [*cf* CURATOR w which it is sometimes confused]

tutti-taiti(e) &c [*'tʌtɪ'tetɪ, *-'tatɪ] *exclam* **1** representing the sound of a trumpet *la18-e19*. **2** expressing impatience, disbelief, derision *la18-e19*. [imit]

tuzle *see* TOUSE

twa &c, two &c, qua &c *18-20;* **tway &c** *la14-e19*, **twae &c** *la16-*, *only Sc*, **thwa** *e16*, *only Sc*, **tweae &c** *19*, *S* [twɑ; *sEC Lnk S* twe; *EC also* kwɑ; *kwe] *numeral* = two *la14-*.

~**erie** *children's rhymes* two *19*. **twaeock, tweck** in the game of *buttony* (BUTTON), a larger button counting as two in scoring *20-*, *Ags Stlg.* **twosie** ['tuzɪ] the second move etc in various games, *eg* CHUCKS[2] *la20-*, *EC, WC Rox.* ~**some &c** *chf Sc* **1** (of or for) a group or company of two *la14-*. **2** (a Scottish country dance, *specif* a *strathspey* (STRATH)) performed by two people *la18-*, *now NE Fif WC.*

~**-bedded** twin-bedded *20-*, *now local Sh-N.* **twa-eyed (beef)steak** *joc* a herring or kipper *la19-*, *now Cai Bnf Per.* **twa-fanglet** indecisive *la20-*, *NE.* ~**-faul(d) &c** **1** = twofold. **2** *freq of persons bent with age etc* bent double *15-*, *now local Sh-Ayr.* **3** deceitful, two-faced *la18-*, *now NE.* ~**-han(d) &c crack** *19-e20*, ~**-han(d)it &c crack** *19-*, *now nEC Dnbt Ayr* a conversation between two people. **twa-han(d)it work &c** work so badly about one that it has to be done again *19-*, *now local Sh-Fif.* **twa-horse ferm &c** *or* **place** a farm needing only two horses to work it

la19-, *now local Ork-Per.* ~**-horse tree** the swingle-tree of a two-horse plough *la18-*, *now Ork.* **twa-pair** *of a farm* worked by two pairs of horses *20-*, *Ork Cai NE.* **(the) twa part &c** two thirds *la14-*, *now local Sh-Wgt.* **twa-skippet** *la19-*, *local Per-WC*, **twa-snooted** *la19-*, *local NE-Bwk*, *of a cap* with a peak back and front. **two or three &c** *16-*, ~ **three &c** *la16-*, ~**ree &c** *19-e20*, **twartree &c** *19-e20*, *chf Sh Ork* ['twɑ'θri, 'twɑ'ri; *sEC, S* 'twe-; *S also* -'(θ)rəi; 'twɑr'θri] *adj, also used as noun, 19-*, *now NE* two or three, a few, several. **twa words** a discussion, argument, dispute *19-*, *now Ags Per.*

twa year'l *la19-*, *Sh Ork* ['twɑ'jirəl(d)], **twa year al(d)** *la20-*, *Ayr* ['twajɪr'al(d)] = two-year-old.

nane o the ~ neither *20-*. **ony o the** ~ either *19-*.

twad *see* WILL[1]

twae *see* TWA

twal &c *la16-*, **twelve** *la18-*, **qual &c** *18-20;* **twelf &c** *la14-16*, **twel &c** *16-*, **twol &c** *la16-20*, **twull &c** *la19-20*, **quel** *e20* [twal; *local* kwal; *nEC also* twɛl, kwɛl; *SW, S also* twʌl; *S also* twol; *twɛlf] *numeral* = twelve *la14-*.

n **1** a set or group of twelve persons or things *la16-*. **2** the ~ twelve o'clock, *esp* midnight, *freq* ~ **o nicht** etc, *la18-*, *local NE-Lnk.*

twelf &c *la14-e17*, *chf Sc*, **twelft** *la14-16*, **twelt &c** *16-e20*, *now Sh NE, WC* [twalt; *nEC* twɛlt; *Abd also* twʌlt; *twɛlf(t)] = twelfth *la14-*. **twelvesie** the last move in the game of CHUCKS[2], in which uncaught stones must be laid in a row *la20-*, *nEC Dnbt Lnk.*

~ **hours &c, twaloors &c 1** twelve noon (or *occas* midnight) *16-20*. **2** a midday snack or drink; a midday meal *19-*, *now Sh Ork.* **twal hundred &c** (of) medium-fine linen woven on a reed of twelve hundred splits *la18-*, *now Ork.* ~**month &c** ['twalmʌnθ, -mənθ, -mənt, 'twʌl-; *EC* twɛl-;*'twɛlfmʌn(ə)θ] (the period of) a year *la15-* [*cf* TOWMOND]. ~**penny &c** (costing) twelve pennies *la18-20*. ~**pennies &c** a shilling SCOTS; *later* a shilling in British money *la16-19*. ~**some &c** (of) a group of twelve *la19*.

twan *see* TWINE

twang *n* **1** = twang. **2** *lit and fig* a sudden sharp pain, an acute pang *18-*, *now local Ags-Rox.*

twantie *see* TWENTY

twa-penny *see* TIPPENY

twar *see* BE

twart *see* THORT

tway, tweae *see* TWA

twech *see* TOUCH

tweck *see* TWA

twee *interj* a call to calves at feeding time *20-*, *now Mry.* [*cf* PREE[2], PROO, TROO]

tweed *n* a strong, *usu* rough-textured, twilled woollen cloth, *usu* of yarn of two or more colours, manufactured *chf* in the BORDERS and in the Outer Hebrides (**Harris tweed**) *19-*. [supposed to have been a misreading of TWEEL[1] in a letter to a London merchant, but more prob f *tweeled* (TWEEL[1]) or TWEEDLE[1], w confusion w the name of the River Tweed]

tweedle[1] &c *vt* (*17-e19*), *n* (*la18-20*) = TWEEL[1].

tweedling &c *16-18*, **twidling** &c *la16-e18* twilled cloth, *esp* linen. [only Sc; perh metath f *tweel(e)d* (TWEEL[1])]

tweedle[2] *vt* **1** = twiddle (the fingers etc) *e19*. **2** cheat, deceive *19-*, *now Mry Abd*.

tweel[1] &c *18-*, *now local*, **twill** &c; **tweyll** &c *14-e19* [twil] *n* **1** twill, a diagonally-ribbed cloth produced by passing the weft threads over one and under two or more warp threads *14-*. **2** *ploughing* the angle at which the coulter is set in the beam, which determines the lie of the furrow *la20-*, *now Stlg Fif*.
vt weave as in *n* 1, *19-e20*.
~**ing** &c cloth, *usu* linen, woven thus *la16-19*. [orig Sc and nME; *cf* Eng *twilly*]

tweel[2] *interj* truly!, indeed! *la18-*, *now local Stlg-Ayr*. [contraction of (*I*) *wat weel* (see WAT, WEEL[1]); *cf* ATWEEL]

tweelie *see* **tulyie**

tween *prep* between *la18-20*.
~ **hands** between times, meantime *20-*, *local Ork-Wgt*. ~ **heid** *ploughing* the part of the reins joining the heads of two horses in a team *20-*, *local Stlg-Wgt*. [aphetic f ATWEEN]

tweesh(t) *see* ATWEESH

tweest *see* ATWEESH, TWIST

tweeter *vti* = twitter *20-*, *now Sh Ags*.

tweetle &c *vi* whistle, warble, sing *20-*.
n a dance, a 'hop' *19*, *Mry*. [altered f Eng *tweedle*]

tweezlick *see* TWIST

twel(f), **twel(f)t**, **twelve(sie)** *see* TWAL

twene *see* TWIN

twenty &c; **twinty** &c *18-e20*, **twantie** &c *16-e18*, **twonty** &c *15-20*, **townty** *e16*, **twunty** *la18-*, *now Ross EC Uls*, **toontie** &c *la19-*, *now S* ['twɪntɪ, 'twʌntɪ, 'twɛntɪ; *NE, S also* 'tuntɪ; *Per also* 'kwʌntɪ; *Rox also* 't(w)ontɪ; *'twantɪ, *'kwantɪ] *numeral* **1** = twenty *la14-*. **2** *used as an ordinal* twentieth *la14-18*. **3** in large number, plentiful, numerous *la15-e16*, *la19, latterly Sh*.
~ **days** three weeks *e18*.

tweyll *see* TWEEL[1]

twice; **twise** &c *now Sh Ork*, **tweys** &c *16, 20*, **twic(e)t** *la19-*, *now Per WC* [twəis; *Sh Ork also* twaɪz; *Abd WC also* twəiz; *Per WC also* twəist] *adv* = twice *la14-*.

twiser &c *in the game of* BUTTONS a button valued at two shots *la19-e20, Ags*.
at ~ twice *la15, la19-e20*. **be** ~ doubly *la16, only Sc*. **the twice(t)** for a second time *20-*, *local Abd-Dmf*.

twich *see* TOUCH

twict *see* TWICE

twidling *see* TWEEDLE[1]

twig[1] *vt, n* jerk, tug, twitch *la18-*, *now Sh Ork*. [chf onomat, prob w infl f Eng *tweak*, *twitch*]

twig[2] *n* a quick or sidelong glance; a glimpse *19-*, *NE*. [extended f colloq Eng *twig* (*v*) watch]

twill *see* TWEEL[1]

twilt &c [twɪlt, twʌlt; *S also* t(w)olt] *n, vti* = quilt *la17-*, *now local*.

twin &c; **twene** *la14* [twɪn, twʌn] *adj, n* = twin *la14-*.
v, also **twine** &c [twəin] **1** *vt* divide, separate, part *la15-*, *now Sh*. **2** *vi* part company, go one's separate way *la14-*, *now Sh*. **3** depart *la14-e17*. **4** part **with**, relinquish *la16-*, *now Sh Ork Cai*. **5** *vt* take (something) from (a person), deprive (a person) **of** (something) *18-e20*. **6** *vti* take a lamb from a weak ewe and give it to a strong one to suckle with her own *20-*, *C, S*.

twine &c *n* **1** (1) = twine *16-*. (2) string *20-*. **2** a short attack of (some ailment) *19, Bnf Ags*.
vti, pt also **twan** &c *16-19* **1** = twine *la15-*. **2** join, unite in marriage *19*. **3** twist (*esp* part of the body); twist the body, wriggle, writhe *19-*, *now N Wgt*.

twiner the person or machine employed to twist spun yarn into a thicker thread *la19-*, *S*.

twine *see* TWIN

twinter &c *16-*, *now Phls Ayr Slk*, **quinter** *la18-*, *SW, S, only Sc* *n* a two-year old farm animal, *esp* a thrice-shorn ewe. [chf nEng, OE *twi-wintre* of two winters; *cf* THRUNTER]

twinty *see* TWENTY

twise *see* TWICE

twist &c, **tweest** *19-*, *now Ork NE n* **1** = twist, a twig; (a) thread; an act of twisting *la14-*. **2** *only* **tweest** &c [twist, twiʃt] a small amount (of food or drink); a small, undersized person *20-*, *now Abd*.
vti, pt also **twust** *17* = twist *17-*.

tweezlick &c an instrument used to twist straw or rush ropes, a simplified *thrawcruik* (THRAW) *20, NE* [see SND]. **twistle 1** the action of twisting etc *la18-19*. **2** rough treatment, a shaking, pulling about *la18-19*.

twit *vi* chirp, twitter *la19-*, *now Ork Ags*. [imit; *cf* Eng *tweet*]

twit *see* WHITE[2]

twitter[1] *vti* **1** = twitter. **2** (cause to) quiver or tremble *19-*, *local Sh-Wgt*.
n = twitter.

twitter[2] *n* **1** a thin part of unevenly spun yarn *18-20*. **2** a very slender, small or feeble person or thing *19-e20*. [nEng dial; obscure]

twixt; **tuix** *la16-e17* [twɪks(t)] *prep* = twixt *la16-*.
~ **and ..** between now and .., before .. *la17-e18*: '*twixt and the fifteenth of November*'.

two *see* TWA

twol *see* TWAL

twonty *see* TWENTY

two-penny *see* TIPPENY

twosie *see* TWA

twull *see* TWAL

twunty *see* TWENTY

twust *see* TWIST

twynrys *n* form and meaning doubtful *e16*, *only Sc.*

tyach &c; tach &c [t(j)ax, tjʌx] *interj* expressing impatience, contempt or petulance *la19-*.

tyangs *see* TANGS

tyarr [tjar, tʃar] *vi* fight, be prone to quarrel *20-*, *now Cai*. [voiceless var, due to Gael infl, of Eng *jar*]

tyauve &c; tauve &c *19* [tjɒv, tʃɒv; *tɑv] *v*, *pt*, *ptp* ~**d &c** *20-*; *pt* **tew &c** *19-e20*, **tyeuve &c** *19* [tju; *tjuv] **1** *vt* knead, work (dough) *19-*, *now Cai*. **2** pull or knock about, treat roughly *la19-20*, *NE*. **3** fatigue, wear out *20-*, *now Abd*. **4** *vi* struggle physically, tumble or toss about *19-*, *NE*. **5** *also* **chauve &c** strive, struggle (*freq* with little result), live or work hard, exert oneself *la19-*, *NE*. **6** walk heavily or with difficulty through snow, mud etc *19-e20*, *NE*.

n, *also* **chauve &c** an act of labouring, exertion, a hard struggle; a laborious walk *la19-*, *NE*. [NE form of TAW¹; see SND]

tyave *see* TAW²

tyce &c [təis] *vi* move about slowly and easily, walk cautiously *la18-20*, *Abd*. [unknown]

tydance *see* TIDIN

tye &c [taɪ] *adv*, *interj* yes, indeed, certainly *la19-20*, *Abd*. [contracted f *hoot aye* (HOOT)]

tyeuch *see* TEUCH

tyeuk *see* TAK

tyeuve *see* TYAUVE

tyke *see* TIKE¹

tyking *see* TIKE²

tyld &c [təild] *vt* cover (*eg* a window) with a curtain, blind etc *e16*, *19-e20*. [ME *tild &c*, OE *teldian* spread, pitch a tent. OED *teld*]

tylor *see* TAILOR

tymber, tymbrall *see* TYMMER²

tymmer¹ [*'tɪmər] *n* = timbre, a percussion instrument *la16*.

~ **wecht** a tambourine *la16*. [OED *timbre*]

tymmer², tymber [*'tɪm(b)ər] *n* the crest of a helmet *la14-e16*.

tymeral *la15*, **tymbrall** *e16* [*'tɪmbral, *'tɪmərəl] = *n*, *only Sc*. [f as prec]

tympany &c; timpan &c ['tɪmpan(ɪ)] *n* the gable-shaped raised middle part of the front of a house *18-*, *now Abd*. [Eng *tympan(um)*, L *tympanum* a pediment, f Gk *týmpanon* a kettledrum]

tympathy [*'tɪmpaθɪ] *n* a morbid swelling or tumour *e19*. [joc conflation of obs Eng *tympany* a swelling w *sympathy*]

tynd &c [*?tɪnd, *?təind] *n* = tine, a prong, spike *la14-e19*.

tynd nale a large sharp-pointed nail, a spike *la16*.

tyne &c, tine [təin] *v*, *pt*, *ptp* **tint &c** now local, **tyned &c** *19* **1** *vt* lose, suffer the loss, destruction or disappearance of, cease to have or enjoy; mislay *la14-*, *Gen except Sh Ork*. **2** lose, cause the loss of *la15-16*, *19-e20*. **3** ruin, destroy *15-16*. **4** (1) fail to obtain, miss, come short of, forfeit, be deprived of *la14-*, *now NE Ags*. (2) (a) incur (a penalty) *15*. (b) lose (a cause) at law *16-e19*. (3) *vtr* lose one or miss (one's) way, stray from (the right road), get lost *la18-*, *now local Sh-Per*. (4) *vt* lose (one's footing), miss (a step) *18-*, *Bnf Abd*. (5) lose by letting fall; *knitting* drop (a stitch) *la19-*, *Abd*. **5** get rid of, free oneself from, abandon *la18-e20*. **6** fail to hold in the memory, forget, be oblivious of *16-*, *now NE Ags*. **7** spend unprofitably or in vain, waste (time, labour etc) *15-e20*. **8** draw away from, leave behind *la19-e20*, *Abd*. **9** *vi*, *of things* decline, lose value or prestige, fade away; *of persons or animals* perish, die *la15-*, *now Sh Bnf Ags*. **10** suffer loss **of** *la15*. **11** *also fig* lose one's way, stray, wander; go astray *18-20*.

between &c (the) tyning and (the) winning in a critical or doubtful state, hovering between success and failure *la18-e19*. **tint** lost; forlorn, bewildered *18-e20*.

able to ~ and win etc, *law* have the means to risk loss while aiming at profit *la15-17*. [nME; ON *týna* destroy, lose, perish; *cf* TINSEL]

tyoch *see* TEUCH

type¹ *vti* **typin** toilsome *20-*, *Abd*. **typit &c** worn out by hard work *la19-*, *Bnf Abd*. [see SND]

type² *n* a low conical hill *20-*, *Dmf*, *freq in placenames*. [obs Eng *tipe* a dome; obscure]

type *see* TEEP

tyran(d) *see* TIRRAN

tyre &c [*taɪr] *vt* inter *e15*.

~**ment** interment *e16*. [only Sc; aphetic f *entyre &c*, var of *inter*]

tyrefull *see* TERE

Tysday &c *la14-*, *now local Sh-Fif*; **Teisday &c** *la18-19*, **Tiseday &c** *la14-20* ['taɪzdɪ] *n* = Tuesday. [nME *tisdaei*, ON *Týsdagr* the day of the god Tyr (Eng *Tuesday* is f *Tiw*, the OE form of the name)]

tyse, tyss, tyst *see* TICE

tyster &c [*?'tɪstər] *n* = tester, a canopy *e15*. [OED *tester*]

tythance *see* TIDIN

U

ubiquiter [*ø'bɪkwɪtər] *n, theol* a ubiquitarian *la16, only Sc*. [*cf* obs Eng *ubiquitary*]

ucha *see* UHUH

uche &c [*ʌtʃ] *n* = ouch, clasp, buckle, brooch etc *la14-e16*.

udder &c, **ether** &c *18-, now local Ork-nEC*; **uther** *18-, now Fif*, **edder** *19-, NE* [*Ork* 'ɪðər; *Cai NE nEC* 'ɛðər; *C, S* 'ʌðər; *Cai also* 'ɪðər; *NE also* 'ɛdər] *n* = udder *16-*.

udderlock *n, chf in pl* locks of wool growing beside a ewe's udder *la18-, now Cai C, S. vi* pluck the wool from a ewe's udder to facilitate suckling *la18-, now WC*.

uder *see* ITHER

U.F. *see* UNITED

ug &c; **oug** &c *la19-* [ʌg, ug] *v* **1** *vt* find offensive or repellent; dislike, feel disgust or horror at *la16-, now literary*. **2** *vi* (1) feel dread or apprehension *15-16*. (2) be sickened, nauseated; feel repulsion *la16-, now Sh*. **3** *vt* disgust, nauseate; annoy, upset, exasperate *19-, now Sh NE*.

n, only Sc **1** a dislike; a sensation of nausea, *freq* **take an** ~ **at** take a dislike to *la19-, NE Ags*. **2** an object of disgust; a person with disgusting manners *la19-, NE*.

~**gin** &c *n* dread, loathing *la17. adj* disgusting, loathsome; objectionable; annoying, vexatious *19-, now NE, only Sc*. ~**git** upset, annoyed; disgusted; fed up *20-, now Sh NE*. ~**(g)some** &c disgusting, repulsive, horrible *15-*. ~**rines** horror *la14, only Sc*. [eME *uggi*, ON *ugga* fear, dread]

ugly, oogly &c *la16-, now local N-Uls*; **hugly** *la14* ['ʌglɪ; *N nEC Uls* 'uglɪ] *adj* = ugly *la14-*. *n* a protective shade attached to the front of a woman's bonnet; *specif* a protective bonnet on a high cane frame, worn by women field-workers *20-, local EC, S*.

uhuh &c; **ucha** *20-* ['ʌ'hʌ] *interj* indicating attentiveness or agreement *19-*. [*cf* IMPHM]

uilie, ule, ulie *see* OIL

ulipy [*ølɪ'paɪ] *n* ? an oilskin coat or jacket *16, only Sc*. [prob Du or Flem *oliepij(e)* f *olie* oil + *pij(e)* coat]

ull *see* ILL

ultimus haeres ['ʌltɪmʌs 'hirez, -'herəz] *n, law* last or ultimate heir, a title applied to the Crown when succeeding to the property of someone who has died intestate without any known heir *18-*. [only Sc; L]

ultroneous &c [ʌl'tronɪʌs] *adj* **1** = ultroneous, voluntary *17-*. **2** *specif, law, of a witness* one who gives evidence spontaneously without being formally cited; *of evidence* given voluntarily *18-, only Sc*. ~**ness** voluntary action *17-18*.

ulyie *see* OIL

ulȝeat *n* a stud for armour *e16*. [only Sc; var of ME *olyet*, ModEng *oillet* &c an eyelet]

umbecast &c [*ʌmbɪ'kast] *vti, pt* **umbekest** [*-'kɛst] **1** make the circuit of, go round *la15*. **2** consider, meditate (that) .. *la14-e15, only Sc*. [ME]

umberauch *v*, *pt*, *ptp* **umberaucht** [*ʌmbɪ'rɑx(t)] surrounded *e16, only Sc*. [OED *umbereach* (*umbe-*)]

umberella *see* UMBRELL

umbersorrow &c *adj* fit, robust; resisting disease or the effects of severe weather *19-e20, S*. [only Sc; obscure]

umbeschew &c; **umchew** &c *e16* [*ʌmbɪ'ʃu, *ʌm'ʃu] *vt* avoid, shun *la15-e16*. [only Sc; obs Eng *umb-* + *eschew*]

umbeset &c; **unbesett** *la16-e17* [*ʌmbɪ'sɛt] *vt* surround, beset *la14-e17*. [ME]

umbeweround [*ʌmbɪ'virund] *adj* surrounded *la14, only Sc*. [OED *umbeviron* (*umbe-*)]

umbrakle &c [*ʌm'brakl] *n* shade, shadow *e16*. [L *umbrāculum* a shady place. OED *umbracle*]

umbrate *adj* shady *e16*. [only Sc; L *umbrāt-*, ptp stem of *umbrāre* (*v*) shade]

umbrell *e19*; **umberella** *20-* [ʌmbə'rɛlə; *ʌm'brɛl] *n* = umbrella.

umchew *see* UMBESCHEW

umest *see* UMOST

umff *interj* = umph *la16*. [earlier in Sc. OED *umph*]

umgang [*?'ʌm'gaŋ] *n* **1** circumference *la15-e16*. **2** *only* **ungang** a turn or spell of work *e16, Abd*. [ME]

umman *see* WOMAN

umost *18-19*, **umest** &c *15-20*, **eemost** &c *19-, chf NE*, **humast** &c *la15*; **immost** &c *la18-e19, chf NE* ['øməst; *NE* 'iməst, *'ɪməst] *adj* **1** uppermost, highest *15-*. **2** *specif, of (freq bed-)clothes etc* uppermost, outer *15-16*. **3** most important or prominent *16*. [ME *ovemest*, OE *ufemest; cf* UPMAIST]

umquhile &c; **umquhill** *16-e18* [*'ʌmhwəil, *-hwɪl] *adv* **1** = umwhile, at times, sometimes *la14-16*. **2** formerly *la14-19*. **3** at some time later, by-and-by *la14-e16, only Sc*.
adj, chf of persons former, late; *esp law, freq without article* deceased *15-, now literary or arch*.

umrage &c *n* = umbrage *la19-, NE Ags*.

un-, on- *la15-20*; **one-** *16*, **oon-** *19-20, Sh Abd* [ʌn-, on-; *Sh Abd also* un-] *prefix* (NOTE: self-evident combinations with *un-* have on the whole been omitted from the Dictionary) **1** = un-, expressing both negation and deprivation or reversal; as in Eng, chf with adjs or advs, but also with participles, nouns, verbs, *la14-*: '*unsonsie, unawaurs, onbekent, unattempting, oonhonesty, unfankle*'. (NOTE: in colloq Sc the negative is freq expressed by NO, (*NE*) NAE + *adj*). **2** *with participles functioning as verbs* not (having been done etc), or without (something being done etc), not *or* without (doing etc) (1) with passive ptps or ptp phrases *la15-19*: '*gif thar be ony of thar gudis in place ondisponit apoun*'; '*that the said Issobell* *did it on imployit be hir'*; (2) with active ptps or presps *la15-20*: *'he mist sum of the Strathbogie men oncum thair'*; *'onspeckand ane word to the barne'*; *'for keping of his guides and cattell unentering in the said forest'*. (3) as 2 (1) or 2 (2), used with first item only of a series of negated items *16-e17*, *la19*: *'onhurt or slaine'*.

unabasit &c [*ʌnaˈbesɪt] *adj* undaunted *la15-16*.

~**ly** boldly *la14-16*, *only Sc.* [var of Eng *unabashed*; *cf* ABAIS. OED *unabased*]

unable &c, onabill &c *16-e17*; **onhabill &c** *16 adj* **1** = unable *la15-*. **2** physically weak, incapacitated *17-19*. **3** awkward; unlucky *la16*, *only Sc.*

~ **for** unfit for, incapable of; *specif* having no appetite for (food) *19-*. [*cf* ABLE]

unaffectionat *adj* unbiased, impartial *la16*, *only Sc.* [OED *unaffectionate*]

unagaist &c [*ʌnaˈgast] *adj* not aghast; unafraid *16*. [only Sc. OED *unaghast*]

unalike *adj* different, dissimilar, unlike *20-*, *now Sh Per.* [*cf* eModEng *unalike* differently (once)]

unanalyt [*ʌnəˈnelɪt] *adj*, *law* unalienated *e16*. [only Sc. OED *unanalied*]

unarmed; unermit &c *15 adj* = unarmed *la14-*.

unawarnist [*ʌnəˈwarnɪst] *adj* unannounced *e16*.

~**lie** without warning *e16*. [only Sc]

unawaurs &c [ʌnəˈwɑrz, *un-] *adv* = unawares *19-e20*.

unbawndonit [*ʌnˈbɑndʊnɪt] *adj*, *of animals* loose, not fastened or under control *la14*. [only Sc. OED *unbandoned*]

unbeast *see* ONBEAST

unbedraw &c [*ʌmbɪˈdrɑ] *vir* withdraw *la15-e16*. [only Sc. OED *umbedraw* (*umbe-*)]

unbekent *19-*; **onbekend** *e16* [ʌnbɪˈkɛnt, -ˈkɛnd; *on-] *adj* **1** unknown, strange, unfamiliar (**to**) *e16-*. **2** unobserved, unnoticed *20-*, *chf Per.* [UN- + ptp of BEKEN; *cf* UNKEN. OED *unbekend*]

unbeknowins [ʌnbɪˈno(ə)ns] *adj*, *adv* unperceived, unnoticed, secretly, unobtrusively *la19-*, *now Abd Ags Per.*

unbend *v* **1** = unbend *la14-*. **2** uncock (a firearm) *e17*, *only Sc.*

unbesett *see* UMBESET

unblomit [*ʌnˈblømɪt] *adj*, *verse* without blossom *e16*. [OED *unbloomed*]

unbonnie [ʌnˈbonɪ] *adj*, *chf in negative* not ugly, not unsightly *19-*: *'that's no unbonny'*.

unbowsome [ʌnˈbʌusəm] *adj* stiff; unable to bend or stoop *19-e20*, *S.* [ME *unbowsom*, *onbouȝsum* intractable, disobedient]

unbrachte [*ʌnˈbraʃt] *adj* unattacked, unassailed *la16*. [only Sc. OED *unbrashed*]

unbranslable *adj* unshakable *e17*. [only Sc; *cf* Eng *branle*]

unbraw [ʌnˈbrɑ] *adj* plain, unattractive *20-*, *local WC, SW.*

unca *see* UNCO

unca'd; uncald [ʌnˈkɑd, &c] *adj* = uncalled, not invited *la15-e19*. [OED *uncalled*]

uncan *see* UNCO

uncannie &c, uncanny; o(o)ncanny *la19-e20*, *local N* [ʌnˈkanɪ; *N* un-] *adj* **1** *of persons* unskilful, clumsy, careless *17-e19*. **2** *of things* awkward, not easy to manage *la19-*, *local Sh-Fif.* **3** *esp of a blow or fall* hard, violent, severe *la18-*, *now NE Ags Per.* **4** (1) dangerous, unreliable, insecure, treacherous, threatening *17-*. (2) *of things* unlucky, inauspicious, tempting Providence *19-*, *now Sh Cai Abd.* **5** *of persons* mischievous, malicious, malignant; not safe to meddle with, as being in league with supernatural forces etc *la16-*, *now local Sh-Lnk.* **6** *esp of things* mysterious, ominous, EERIE 2, *19-*.

uncassen *20-*, *Sh-Ags*; **uncastin** *la14-e16*, **oncasin** *la16* [ʌnˈkasən, &c] *adj* **1** not cast or thrown *la14-16*. **2** *of clothes* not faded or worn *20-*, *NE Ags, only Sc.* **3** *of* PEATS[1] not cut *20-*, *Sh NE, only Sc.* [Eng *uncast*; see CAST. OED *uncast*]

unce *see* OUNCE

uncert [*ʌnˈsert] *adj* uncertain *e16*, *only Sc, rare.* [f L *incertus*]

uncertifieit *adj* not made certain, not assured *e16*. [OED *uncertified*]

unchance &c [ʌnˈtʃans] *n* misfortune, calamity *16-e19*.

unchancy &c *chf Sc* **1** inauspicious, unlucky; ill-omened, ill-fated *16-*. **2** dangerous, threatening, treacherous, not to be meddled with *la18-*. [nME; *cf chancy* (CHANCE)]

unchargit [*ʌnˈtʃardʒɪt, &c] *adj* **1** not called upon, not summoned *la15-e16*, *only Sc.* **2** not burdened *la15*. [*cf* Eng *uncharged*. OED *uncharged*]

unchestiable [*ʌnˈtʃestɪəbl, &c] *adj* unchastizable, impossible to chastize *la16*. [only Sc. OED *unchastisable*]

unco &c *18-*; **uncow &c** *16-e18*, **unca** *19-*, *now Abd*, **uncan &c** *19-*, *Sh*, **unkin &c** *la19-e20*, *Sh Ork* [ˈʌŋkə; *Bwk Rox* ˈʌŋkɪ; *Edb also* ˈʌŋkɪ; *ˈʌŋku] *adj* **1** (1) *of people, animals, things, places* (a) unknown, unfamiliar, strange *16-*, *now NE, C*; (b) so much altered as to be scarcely recognizable *19-*, *now Abd.* (2) *of countries or lands* foreign *19-*, *now Sh, only Sc*; *cf* UNCOUTH 2. **2** *also comparative* ~**er** *la19-*, *superlative* ~**est** *18-* unusual; odd, strange, peculiar *18-*. **3** remarkable, extraordinary, great, awful etc *18-*, *now NE Ags WC, only Sc*: *'ye mak an unco sang about your taxes'*. **4** rude, uncouth, unseemly *18-e19*, *only Sc.* **5** reserved, shy, bashful *19-*, *now Sh, only Sc.*
adv very, exceedingly, extremely *18-*.
n **1** *chf in pl* (1) strange or unusual things, rarities, novelties *19-*, *now Sh NE*; (2) news, items of news or gossip *la18-*, *now Sh NE, WC.* **2** *in pl* strangers, foreigners; *in sing as collective* the world outside one's own circle, strangers *la18-19*.

~**ly &c** very much, to a great or remarkable

degree *19-*, *now literary, only Sc.* ∼**ness** strangeness, peculiarity, eccentricity *17-*, *now Sh, only Sc.*

∼ **body** a stranger, outsider, newcomer *19.* ∼ **folk** (*also used as pl of prec*) strangers *la18-*, *now NE nEC, SW.* **the unco guid** *chf literary* (*after Burns*) the self-righteously moral or pious *la18-*. ∼ **like** *adj* **1** = *adj*, *19-*. **2** *also* ∼ **leukin** having a strange or wild appearance; looking out of sorts, woebegone *la19-*, *now local NE-Ayr.* *adv* in a strange manner *e17.* ∼ **men** strangers, outsiders, newcomers *la18-e20.* [laME *unkow*; shortened f UNCOUTH]

uncoakit [ʌnkoˈakɪt] *adj* = uncoacted, not compelled or constrained *e16.* [OED *uncoacted*]

unconform *adj* non-conforming *la17.*

∼**ist** nonconformist *17.* [only Sc; see *non-conform* (CONFORM)]

unconsultit *adj* uncounselled, unadvised *la16.* [only Sc. OED *unconsulted*]

uncorduall *adj* uncongenial *la15.* [only Sc; OED *uncordial*]

uncorn *18-e19*; **oncorn** *e16* [*ʌnˈkorn*, *on-*] *n* poor quality oats; *fig* wild oats. [*un-* as pejorative as in OE and occas in ME]

uncost *see* ONCOST

uncouth &c [*ˈʌnkuθ*] *adj* **1** = uncouth *15-*. **2** foreign *15-e16*, *only Sc.* **3** unknowing, ignorant *e17.* [*cf* UNCO]

uncouthie &c [ʌnˈkuθɪ] *adj* unfriendly, fear-inspiring *la18-e19.*

uncow *see* UNCO

uncredible &c *adj* incredulous *e16*, *only Sc.*

uncshin *see* UNCTION[2]

unction[1] *n* **1** = unction *la16-*. **2** *ironic* punishment; an unpleasant or dangerous experience *e20*, *NE.*

unction[2]; **uncshin &c** [ˈʌŋ(k)ʃən] *n*, *vt* = auction *19-*. [confused in form with UNCTION[1] *n* 1, perh with ironic reference to the smooth talk of an auctioneer]

uncustom *n* an improper or illegal tax *la16*, *only Sc.*

uncustumate &c *adj*, *of goods* not having paid duty *16.* [only Sc. OED *uncustomate*]

undantit &c; **ondantit** [ʌnˈdantɪt, on-] *adj* **1** = undaunted *16-*. **2** *of horses* not broken in *la16.* **3** *fig* unbridled, unrestrained *16.* **4** undisciplined, disorderly *e16*, *only Sc.* [OED *undaunted*]

undecent &c *adj* = indecent *la16-*.

undeemous &c; **undemus &c** *la14-19* [ʌnˈdiməs; *Sh* -ˈdøm(ɪ)əs; on-, *ʌun-] *adj* extraordinary; *esp of size or amount* immense, incalculable *la14-20*, *chf Sh N.* [nME *undemes*; f ON *údǽmi* a monstrous, inconceivable thing or deed]

undegraid *adj* not degraded *la16.* [only Sc. OED *undegrade*]

undelivered &c *adj* **1** = undelivered *la16-*. **2** not dispatched or disposed of *e16*, *only Sc.*

undemus *see* UNDEEMOUS

under &c, onder &c *15-e20*; **unner** *19-*, *local*, **oon(d)er** *la19-e20*, *Sh N prep* **1** = under *la14-*. **2** *of land* planted, sown or stocked with; used for growing or rearing *la16-*. **3** subject to the instruction, direction or guidance of *16-*. *adv* = under *la14-*.

∼**board &c** *of a corpse* laid out awaiting burial *18-20*, *now Uls, only Sc.* ∼**cast** consider, reflect *la15*, *only Sc.* ∼**cause** a subordinate or secondary cause *e17.* ∼**coatie &c** a petticoat *la18-e19.* ∼**cot &c** *chf fig* suppurate or fester inwardly *la16-e18*, *only Sc.* ∼ **followand** the following (*eg* in a document) *15*, *only Sc.* ∼**foot &c** down below; underneath; underground *la17-19.* ∼**lay** provide with a lining or backing *e16*, *only Sc.* **underlie &c, onderly &c** *la15-e17 vt* **1** = underlie *la14-*. **2** (1) be subject(ed) to, submit to, undergo *15-19.* (2) ∼**ly &c the law** be liable to legal procedures and penalties *15-19*, *only Sc.* **undermind &c** *16-18*, **oon(d)ermin(d)** *19 vt* = undermine. ∼ **night &c** during the night, by night *15-e20*, *only Sc.* ∼**ply** *mining* a band or division of the upper portion of a thick seam of coal *19-.* ∼**set** *n* = undersettle, a subtenant *e16.* *vt* beset *la15.* ∼**specified &c** specified below *16-17*, *only Sc.* ∼**stane** the nether or lower millstone; the bedstone *20-.* **undersubscrive &c, undersubscribe** *vi*, *chf in presp* subscribing to, signing a document *la16-e18.* ∼**subscriber &c** a subscriber to a document, the undersigned *la17-18.* **undertak(e), unnertak** *la19-e20*, **underta** *la14-15 v* **1** = undertake *la14-*. **2** give a pledge or promise; enter into a compact or contract *la14-.* ∼**taking &c, ondertaking &c** *16-17*, *only Sc* **1** = undertaking *la14-*. **2** an action or work undertaken or attempted; an enterprise *la14-.* ∼ **thoum** secretly, in an underhand manner *19-e20.* ∼**water** water below the surface of the ground; water that has accumulated in the foundations of a house *17-*, *now Sh Ork NE.*

at ∼ in an inferior place or position; in subjection *la14-17*, *only Sc.* ∼ **ane time** at the same time *e16*, *only Sc.*

understand &c, understand &c *16-e17*; **un(d)erstan &c** *la19-*, **oon(d)erstan(d)** *la19-e20*, **onerstan(d)** *la19-*, **winnerstan** *20*, *NE* [*N, WC* ʌnərˈstan; *WC, SW* ʌnərˈstɔn; *NE also* unər-, wɪnər-] *vti*, *pt also* **unersteed &c** *la18-e20*, *NE* = understand *la14-*.

n **1** understanding, knowledge *e15.* **2** support, basis *la16*, *only Sc.*

undo [ʌnˈdø, &c] *vt* **1** = undo *la14-*. **2** unbind, release from a covering etc *e16.* **3** remove, take away; cut off *e16.*

undocht &c, undought, ondocht &c [*Cai* ˈʌndoxt; *Sh Ork Cai* ˈondoxt] *n* a feeble, weak or ineffective person *16-*, *now Cai.* [only Sc; *cf* WANDOCHT]

undoutand [*ʌnˈdutand] *adj* (*adv*) undoubted(ly) *15-16*, *only Sc.*

~**ly 1** unhesitatingly, with confidence *e15*. **2** undoubtedly, without doubt *la16*, *only Sc.* [OED *undoubting, -ly*]

undrawn &c *adj, of straw* not arranged in uniform length for thatching *la19-, Sh Ork Bnf.*

unduchtie [*ʌn'dʌxtɪ, &c] *adj* lacking in good qualities; worthless, vile *la16*. [laME *undughty.* OED *undoughty*]

une¹ &c, oven &c *la16-*, **ovin &c** *16-e17*; **oyne** *la14-16*, **oon** *18-19*, **oen** *la18-19*, **ine** *e20* [øn, ɪn; 'ovən; *'øvən; *NE* *in] *n* = oven *16-*.

oon &c cake a thick bun made from oatmeal and yeast, baked in the oven *19*, *chf Fif.* ~ **pot** *etc* a large shallow pan used as an oven by being set among the glowing embers of a fire *la19-, local NE-S.*

Arthur's Oon see ARTHURIS HUFE.

une² [*øn] ~**ing** uniting *e16, only Sc.* [f L *ūnīre; cf* UNIT]

uneis &c [*ʌn'ɪz] *adv* not easily, (only) with difficulty, scarcely *la14-e16*. [nME *unnes* var of *unnethes,* ME *unneþe(s) &c,* OE *uneaþe.* OED *uneaths*]

unermit *see* UNARMED

unerstan, unersteed *see* UNDERSTAND

unfaithful &c *adj* **1** = unfaithful *la15-*. **2** not in accordance with faith, irreligious *e16, only Sc.*

unfarrant &c *19-20*; **onfarrand &c** *e16, la19* [ʌn'farənt, on-, &c] *adj* unattractive, unpleasant; unrefined, unsophisticated, rude. [*cf* eModEng *unfaryng &c* and *farrant* (FARE). OED *unfaring*]

unfeary &c [ʌn'fɪrɪ] *adj* inactive, incapable of exertion; weak, infirm, uncertain in one's gait *16-e19*. [only Sc; see *feerie* (FERE¹). OED *unfeirie*]

unfeel &c [ʌn'fil] *adj* unpleasant, disagreeable, dirty, filthy; rough; uncomfortable *19-, S.* [*cf* Eng (now dial) *unfele*]

unfierdy &c; **unferdie** *la16* [ʌn'fɪrdɪ, *?-'ferdɪ] *adj* **1** clumsy, awkward *la16-*. **2** overgrown, unwieldy, not in proper trim *19-, now Sh.* [only Sc; see *ferdy* (FAIRD). OED *unfeirdy*]

unfilit &c [*ʌn'fəilɪt] *adj* undefiled; unfouled *16*. [ME *unfiled.* OED *unfiled*]

unfordersome; **unfurthersome &c** [ʌn'fordərsʌm, &c] *adj* slow, causing delay or hindrance *19-e20, only Sc.*

unforgiven &c *adj* **1** without any remission *15-e17, only Sc.* **2** = unforgiven.

unforlatit [*ʌnfor'letɪt] *adj* not drawn off from one container into another *e16*. [only Sc. MDu *verlaeten* draw off, rack (wine)]

unforleit [ʌnfor'lit] *adj* not abandoned, not given up *e16*. [only Sc. *cf* OE *unforlǣten* not left. OED *unforlet*]

unformal *adj* not in proper form, not properly drawn up *la17-18*. [var of *informal*]

unfrayit *e16*, **unfraid** *la17* [*ʌn'freɪt, *-'fre:d] *adj* undaunted. [only Sc. OED *unfrayed*]

unfree &c *adj* **1** = unfree *la17-*. **2** not having the rights of a freeman or burgess in a BURGH, not being a member of a GUILD or INCORPORATION *15-18*.

~**man** an UNFREE (*adj* 2) person *15-19*.

unfreely &c *19-, chf N;* **unfrely** *la15-16* [ʌn'frilɪ] *adj* **1** not beautiful *la15-16*. **2** heavy, weighty, unwieldy *19-, now Bnf.* [nME *unfreli*]

unfriend &c *17-;* **unfreind &c** *15-e17* [ʌn'frin(d)] *n* one who is not a friend, an enemy, *freq* be ~ of *or* to *15-e20*.

~**fully** unfriendly *e16*.

~**ship** enmity, ill-will *19-, now Sh.* [ME *onfreond; cf* MDu *onvrient*]

unfulʒeit [*ʌn'fəljɪt, &c] *adj* not exhausted *e16*. [only Sc. OED *unfulyeit*]

unfurthersome *see* UNFORDERSOME

unfynit [*ʌn'fəinɪt] *adj* unrefined, unpurified *la15*. [OED *unfined*]

unganand [*ʌn'genand] *adj* inappropriate, unbecoming, unsuitable *la15-16*. [nME *ungainand.* OED *ungainand*]

ungane *see* UNGONE

ungang *see* UMGANG

ungone *la17;* **ungane** *la15* [*'ʌn'gon, *-'gen] *adj* not (yet) gone or departed *la15*.

keep ~ keep from going *la17, only Sc.*

ungrate &c *adj* **1** = ungrate, unpleasant *e17*. **2** ungrateful *16-e19*.

unhabite *adj* uninhabited *la16*. [only Sc. OED *unhabit*]

unhalesome &c [ʌn'helsʌm] *adj* **1** = unwholesome *la19-*. **2** ugly, repulsive *la15*. [only Sc. OED *unwholesome*]

unhantit *adj* not practised or used *e16*. [only Sc. OED *unhaunted*]

unhanty &c [*ʌn'hantɪ] *adj* clumsy in figure, movement or action *la18-19*. [only Sc; *cf* HANTY and Eng *unhandy*]

unhap *vi* bring misfortune *la16, only Sc.* [eModEng, ME *unhap* (*n*) misfortune]

unhappily &c *adv* **1** = unhappily *la14-*. **2** unsuccessfully *e16, e19.*

unhappin [*ʌn'hapən] *adj, of a crime* miserable, wretched *e16*. [ME *unhappen.* OED *unhappen*]

unharnessed &c *adj* **1** not ornamented or trimmed *la15, only Sc.* **2** = unharnessed.

unheartsome &c *adj* cheerless, melancholy, dismal *17-e20*.

unhearty &c *adj* **1** = unhearty, not hearty or cordial *17*. **2** listless, dispirited; melancholy; in poor condition; rather uncomfortable *la17-, now Sh, only Sc.*

unhed, unhevd- [*ʌn'hid, *-'hivəd, &c] *vt* behead (a person) *la14*. [earlier in Sc. OED *unhead*]

unhine &c [*ʌn'həin] *adj* excessive, beyond moderation *19, N.* [ME *unheind, unhend* rough, discourteous]

unhonest &c *adj* dishonest *15-, now local.*

unhool [*ʌn'høl, &c] *vt* ~ **someone's saul** frighten the life out of someone *18-e19*. [see HUIL]

unhovin &c [*ʌn'hovən] *adj* unbaptized *la14-15*. [only Sc. OED *unhoven*]

unicorn &c [*'ønɪkorn] *n* **1** = unicorn. **2** *heraldry* one of the supporters of the royal arms of Scotland until 1603, now incorporated in the present royal arms of Great Britain as displayed in Scotland *la15-*. **3** one of the Scottish PURSUIVANTS *15-, only Sc.* **4** a gold coin, valued at 18 shillings SCOTS *la15-16*.

~ **weicht** a weight equivalent to about an eighth of an ounce *16, only Sc.*

uning *see* UNE²

union [*'ønɪən] *n* **1** = union *la16-*. **2** *law* the uniting into one tenantry of lands or TENEMENTS not lying contiguous, *latterly (la18-e19) chf* **charter** *or* **clause of** ~ *16-e19*.

unirkit &c [*ʌn'ɪrkɪt] *adj* (*adv*) not irked, not wearied (**of**) *e16, only Sc.*

unit [*'ønɪt, *ø'nəit] *ptp* united *la15-e17, only Sc.* [sometimes direct f L *ūnītus*, sometimes as ptp of UNE²]

united *adj* **1** = united *17-*. **2** *freq* in titles of Presbyterian churches which united or reunited after schisms and separations *17-*.

Continuing U~ Free Church *etc see U~ Free Church.* **U~ Associate Synod** (**of the Secession Church**) name taken by the *New Light* (LICHT¹) parties in the *Burgher* (BURGH) and ANTIBURGHER branches of the *Original Seceders* (SECEDE) on their reunion in 1820, *e19; cf U~ Presbyterian Church.* **U~ Free** (**Church** *or* **Kirk**), **U.F. 1** (1) the church formed by the union in 1900 of the majority of the members of the *Free Church of Scotland* (FREE) with the *U~ Presbyterian Church*, the majority of whose members later (1929) joined the Church of Scotland *e20*. (2) *also* **Continuing U~ Free Church** *e20* the minority group of members of the *U~ Free Church* who did not rejoin the Church of Scotland in 1929, *20-*. **2 U.F.** a member of 1 (1) or (2), *20-*. **U~ Presbyterian Church, U.P. 1** the church formed in 1847 by the union of the *U~ Associate Synod* and the *Relief Church* (RELIEF) *19-*. **2 U.P.** a member of that church *la19-*. **U~ Secession Church** = *U~ Associate Synod 19*. [see also DISRUPTION]

universal &c *adj* **1** = universal *16-*. **2** *law* (1) *of an heir* taking over the total rights, obligations etc of his predecessor, *chf* ~ **successor** *la17-*. (2) *of an executor* taking custody of all the effects of a deceased *18-19*.

in ~ entirely, wholly *e17*.

universitas [junɪ'vɛrsɪtas] *n, law* the whole property, of every kind, of a deceased person *la18-19, only Sc.* [L = the totality]

unjustice &c *n* = injustice *19-20*.

unk *see* THINK¹

unken; oonken *la19-e20, NE* [ʌn'kɛn; *NE also* un-] *vt* not to know, fail to recognize, be ignorant of *e19*.

~**nand** *la14*, ~**ning** *la18-, now Sh* unknowing, ignorant. ~(**n**)**ed &c** *la14-*, ~**t** *la18-*, **onkent**

&c *19-* [*adj* (*attrib*) 'ʌn'kɛnd, -'kɛnt, 'on-; *ptp* ʌn'kɛnt, on-] **1** *also* ~**t by** unknown, unfamiliar, strange (to) *la14-*. **2** *also* ~**t to** (1) untouched or unvisited (by); inexperienced (in), unfamiliar (with) *la18-19*. (2) unnoticed, unobserved (by) *la18-, N.*

unkin *see* UNCO

unlach *see* UNLAW

unlamyt [*ʌn'lemɪt] *adj* unharmed *la15*. [OED *unlamed*]

unland [*'ʌn'land] *n* non-arable land *la16-e17, only Sc.*

unlaw &c [*n* *?'ʌnlɑ; *v* *?ʌn'lɑ] *n* **1** *also* **unlach** *e17* [*'ʌnlɑx] an illegal act *14-15, e17*. **2** a fine, penalty *15-e18, only Sc; cf* UNLAY.

vt **1** fine (*chf* **for** an offence **in** a sum) *15-e18, only Sc.* **2** *vi* pay a fine *la17, only Sc.*

not worth the King's ~ *of a destitute person, when challenging his reliability as a witness* worthless *18, only Sc.* [ME; OE *unlagu* (*n*), ON *úlǫg*]

unlay [*?'ʌnle] *n* = UNLAW *n* 2, *e16, only Sc.* [un- + Eng *lay* (the imposition of) a tax]

unleeze [ʌn'liz] *vt* disentangle *la19-, wLoth local SW.* [LEASE¹]

unlefsum *see* UNLEISUM

unlegittimate *adj* not legitimated *e16*. [only Sc; *cf* eModEng *unlegitimate* (*v*) make illegitimate *e17*. OED *unlegitimate*]

unleifit [*ʌn'livɪt] *adj* not furnished with leaves *e16*. [OED *unleaved* (*adj*²)]

unleifsum *see* UNLEISUM

unless, onless &c *la19-e20, latterly N,* **onles &c** *la16;* **unles &c** *la16 conj* = unless *la16-. prep* except, but (**for**) *la19-, local.*

unlikely; unlikly &c *la14-19* [ʌn'ləiklɪ, *-'lɪklɪ] *adj* **1** not likely to occur or come to pass, improbable *la14-*. **2** = unlikely. **3** unattractive, unacceptable, disagreeable, objectionable *la15-e18*. **4** unpromising; poor in quality or condition *la16*.

unlucky *adj* **1** = unlucky. **2** *esp* **foul** ~ slatternly, slovenly *20-, Abd.*

unmaculat [*ʌn'makølat] *adj* immaculate *16-e17, only Sc.*

unmade &c *adj* **1** = unmade *la14-*. **2** *with complement, la15, only Sc:* 'quhat chancet on Pasche day..suld not be unmaid mentioune of'.

unmainnerfu *adj* (*adv*) rude, discourteous, unmannerly *la19-, now Sh Abd.*

unmoderly &c [*ʌn'mødərlɪ, &c] *adv* unkindly *15*. [only Sc. OED *unmotherly*]

unmovit &c [*ʌn'møvɪt] *adj, lit and fig* unmoved *la14-*. [earlier in Sc. OED *unmoved*]

unnatural *adj* **1** = unnatural. **2** abnormal, monstrous; simple-minded *16-e19, only Sc.*

unner *see* UNDER

unoorament *adj* uncomfortable, unpleasant *19-, now Cai.* [obscure]

unpay [*ʌn'pe, *-'pəi] *vt* leave unpaid; not pay *16*.

unpayment non-payment *la16, only Sc.* [earlier in Sc]

unprisit *see* ONPRISIT

unproven &c [ʌnˈprovn, *also* -ˈpruvn] *adj, adv* **1** = unproven. **2** *law* with a verdict of *not proven* (PRUIVE) *la19-, only Sc.*

unprovidedly *adv* unexpectedly, without warning *la16-17.* [*only* Sc; *cf* L *improviso*; Eng *unprovided* not provided *16-*]

unprovisit [*ʌnproˈvaɪzɪt] *adj* unforeseen, unconsidered *la15-16.* [*only* Sc. OED *unprovised*]

unquarrelable [*ʌnkwarəˈlebl, *-ˈkwarələbl] *adj, law* indisputable, unchallenged, incontrovertible *la17-e18, only Sc.*

unquented *adj* unfamiliar *la16.* [*only* Sc. OED *unquainted*]

unquietatioun *n* a disturbance *e17, Abd, only Sc.*

unreason &c; unressoun *16* [*ʌnˈrizun, &c*] *n* **1** unreasonable action or intention; injustice, impropriety *16-e17.* **2** = unreason, absence of reason.

unreconsiliat [*ʌnrɛkənˈsɪliat] *adj* unreconciled *la16.* [*only* Sc. OED *unreconciliate*]

unreduced *adj* **1** not annulled or repealed *la16-e17, only Sc.* **2** = unreduced.

unremedable &c [*ʌnrɛməˈdebl, *ʌnrɛˈmidəbl] *adj* = unremediable, irremediable *la15-e16.* [*only* Sc. OED *unremediable*]

unremembrand *adj* forgetful *e16.* [earlier in Sc. OED *unremembering*]

unresponsall [*ʌnrɪˈsponsəl] *adj* unresponsible, lacking substance or standing *la16, only Sc.*

unressoun *see* UNREASON

unrest *n* = unrest *16-.*
~**y** unrestful, ill at ease *19-, now Cai.* [see also WANREST]

unricht &c [ˈʌnˈrɪxt, ˈon-] *adj* not right, unjust; dishonest, improper *la19-, now Fif SW.*

unrockit &c *adj, fig* unrocked, in a state of excitement, *chf* ~ **ȝe** *etc* **raif** *la15-16.* [*only* Sc. OED *unrocked*]

unrove *see* UNRUFE

unrude [*ʌnˈrød] *adj* violent, rough; dreadful, outrageous *e16, e19.* [ME, var of ME *unride*, OE *ungerȳde* severe, violent]

unrufe; unrove *la16* [*ʌnˈrøv] *n* unrest, disquiet *la15-16.* [*only* Sc; var of ME *unro*]

unruleful [*ʌnˈrjulfʌl] *adj* unruly, rebellious *la15-17.* [also in ModEng dial]

unscathed *see* UNSKAITHED

unscaumit [ʌnˈskɑmɪt] *adj* not burned or scorched, unscathed *la19-, Sh Abd.*

unschait *see* UNSKAITHED

unscrapit &c [*ʌnˈskrepɪt] *adj, chf* ~ **tongue** abusive or uncivil speech *18-19, only Sc.*

unseely &c *19*; **unseilly &c** *e16*, **unsely** *e16* [*ʌnˈsili] *adj* **1** = unseely, unfortunate *e16.* **2** *of conditions etc* causing or involving misfortune, unhappiness or danger *e16, 19 (Abd).*

unsell &c, unsel &c [*ʌnˈsil, *-ˈsɛl, *ˈʌnsl] *adj* unlucky, wretched; wicked *la14-e17, only Sc.*
adv wickedly, vilely *la16, only Sc.*

n a wicked worthless person, wretch; a troublesome person *la16-e19.* [var of ME *unsele* (*adj*), f ME *noun* = mischance, OE *unsǣl* unhappiness]

unsely *see* UNSEELY

unsensible *adj* lacking sense or reasoning power *la17-e20.* [*cf* Eng *unsensible*, var of *insensible*]

unserved; one servit *la15* [*ˈʌnˈsɛrvɪt, *ˈon-, &c*] *adj* **1** = unserved, not attended to *la16-.* **2** not returned as heir *la15, only Sc.*

unset [*ʌnˈsɛt] *adj* **1** *of time or place* not previously appointed or arranged *la16.* **2** *of land, property etc* unlet; not allocated (**to** someone) *15-18.* **3** not seated at table *la15, only Sc.*

unsichtfull [*ʌnˈsɪxtfʌl] *adj* invisible *la14.* [*only* Sc. OED *unsightful*]

unsinnand &c *adj* unsinful *la14.* [*cf* Eng *unsinning* (*17-*). OED *unsinning*]

unskaithed *la16-e20,* **unscathed &c** *15-*; **unschait** *la14* [ʌnˈskeðɪt, &c; *-ˈskeɪt, &c*] *adj* unhurt, unharmed *la14-.* [ON *úskaðaðr*; adopted by Eng *19*]

unskilful &c *adj* **1** = unskilful. **2** uncouth *la15.* [*only* Sc. OED *unskilful*]

unsmart *adj, of a bow* slack *la15, only Sc.*

unsonsie &c, unsonsy [*ʌnˈsonsɪ] *adj* **1** luckless, hapless, unfortunate *la16-e19.* **2** bringing bad luck, ill-omened, associated with evil powers: (1) *of persons or animals, 19;* (2) *of things and places, 18-19.* **3** *specif of a blow, weapon etc* severe, harmful, causing death or injury *18-e19.* **4** unpleasant, treacherous, troublesome, mischievous *18-19.* **5** plain, unattractive; slovenly, untidy *19; cf* UNLUCKY.

unspoken &c *adj* **1** = unspoken. **2** not spoken of *la14.* **3** (1) without having spoken, in silence *la16.* (2) *chf folk-medicine, of a curative substance* not spoken over, gathered or handled in silence *19.*

unstable &c *adj* **1** = unstable *la15-.* **2** *of movement* unsteady, irregular *e16, only Sc.*

unsufficient *adj* **1** = unsufficient, insufficient *e16.* **2** *of a building* unsound, insecure *18.*

untauld; untald [ʌnˈtɑld] *adj* **1** *with pl nouns* in large numbers, countless *la15-.* **2** = untold *la19-e20.* [OED *untold*]

untellin *19-, now Lnk Slk;* **untelland** *e16* [ʌnˈtɛlən] *adj* past reckoning, impossible to tell, beyond words. [nME *untelland* innumerable]

unthirl [*ˈʌnˈθɪrl] *vt, only* ~**ed** **1** unsubjugated *e16.* **2** not bound by *thirlage* (THIRL²) to a particular mill *e18, Rox.*
n land outside the SUCKEN¹ or THIRL² of a particular mill; the dues paid to a mill for the grinding of corn grown on land not ASTRICTED to it *la18, Rox.*

unthochtful [ʌnˈθoxtfu, -fə] *adj* **1** not taking thought, unheeding **of** *la15.* **2** = unthoughtful *e20.* [OED *unthoughtful*]

unthrift *n* **1** = unthrift, an unthrifty person, a prodigal *la14.* **2** lack of thrift, extravagance; lack of success *18-e19.* [*cf* WANTHRIFT]

unthrive [*ʌn'θraɪv] *vi* = unthrive, fail to thrive *e17*.

unthriven, unthriving [*ʌn'θrɪvən] *of living things* unhealthy *18-19*.

until &c, ontil &c *la15-e20* [ʌn'tɪl, 'ʌntɪl, 'on-] *prep* **1** = until *16-*. **2** to, unto, as far as, towards *la15-e19*. **3** in contact with, against *16-e19*. **4** into *la18-20, now Abd, only Sc*.
conj = until *la15-*. [in OSc chf before vowels and *h*-; *cf* ONTO and TILL[1]]

unto *see* ONTO

untowtherly &c; untodderly &c [ʌn'tʌuðərlɪ, -'toðər-, -'todər-] *adj* **1** big, clumsy and unwieldy, ill-shaped *20-, NE*. **2** slovenly in dress or figure, unkempt, dishevelled *20-, NE*. [see SND]

untreuthfull *adj* unbelieving, infidel *la14-15*. [only Sc. OED *untruthful*]

untrowit &c [*ʌn'truɪt, *-'tru:d] *adj* unbelieved *la16-17*. [laME *untrowed*. OED *untrowed*]

untymis [*ʌn'təiməs] *adj* untimely *la15*. [prob var of Eng *untimeous*. OED *untime*]

unvisitly &c [*ʌn'vaizɪtlɪ] *adv* imprudently *la15*. [only Sc. OED *unvisedly*]

unwashen &c [ʌn'waʃn, &c] *adj* unwashed *19-, now Sh Abd*. [now arch in Eng]

unwaukit [ʌn'wɑkɪt] *adj, of cloth* not shrunk or fulled *la19-, now Sh*.

unweel &c, unwell; unweill &c *17* [ʌn'wil] *adj* not in good health, ill (suggesting a more serious illness than in Eng); sickly, ailing *17-*.
~ness bad health, illness *17-, now NE*.

unweildable [*ʌn'wildəbl] *adj* unwieldy *e16*. [only Sc. OED *unwieldable*]

unweill *see* UNWEEL

unweirdit [*ʌn'wirdɪt] *adj* subject to adverse fate, ill-fated *la16*. [only Sc. OED *unweirded*]

unwell *see* UNWEEL

unwenandly [*ʌn'winandlɪ] *adv* unexpectedly *la14*. [only Sc. OED *unweeningly*]

unwillis [*ʌn'wɪlz] *adv* against one's will, unwillingly *la14*. [eME *unwilles*, OE *unwillan*. OED *unwill*]

unwiselike [ʌn'wəisləik] *adj* indiscreet, imprudent, foolish *19-, now N*.

unwittand *see* UNWITTING

unwitten *adj* unknown *la15, only Sc*.

unwitting; unwittand &c *la14-e16* [ʌn'wɪtən, &c] *adj* **1** = unwitting *la14-*. **2** *with direct object, e15*: '*unwittand þar purposyng*'. **3** without the knowledge **of** (a person) *e16*. [*cf* UNWITTINS]

unwittins &c [ʌn'wɪtənz] *adv* (*adj*) unwittingly, inadvertently *la18-, now literary*. [UNWITTING + -*s*]

unwollit [*ʌn'wuɪt] *adj* lacking wool, shorn *e16, Abd*. [only Sc. OED *unwoolled*]

unworth &c [*'ʌn'wʌrθ] *adj* unworthy, worthless *la16-18*. [ME; OE *unweorþ. cf* WANWORTH]

unʒement *n* = oignement, ointment *e16*. [*cf* EYNTMENT]

up; upe *la14-16*, **oup &c** *16-e20*, **uppe** *la14* [ʌp, *also rare* up] *adv* **1** = up *la14-*. **2** into the state of being open, as **open, push, bang** *etc* ~ *la14-19*: '*he gert all wyde set up the ʒet*'. **3** *of a river* in flood *18-, N-Per WC, only Sc*. **4** *of persons* in a state of excitement or irritation *19-, now NE Ags*. **5** *also* ~ **in life,** ~ **in years** (1) *of a child growing up* adult, advanced in years; (2) *of an adult* advanced in years, elderly *19-*. **6** *of a chimney* on fire *la20-, local Ork-Per*.
prep = up *16-*.

oopie stiffie, oopsie doopsie *interj* encouraging a child to get to its feet *20-, NE Ags WC* [*cf* HOOPS and Eng *upsadaisy*]. ~**line** upwards *19-, now Sh Abd*.

neither ~ **nor doun 1** nowhere *20-, Sh Ork Abd*. **2** *esp of feelings etc* unaffected by events, the same as before *19-, Sh-Per*. ~ **about** somewhere in or near *20-, local Sh-Per, only Sc*. ~ **the country** in or from the upland or interior part of a district *19-, now NE, Ags*. ~ **and doun 1** = up and down *16-*. **2** from every angle, in every aspect, thoroughly *la19-, Ork N*. ~ **or doun** *in negative* neither one way nor the other, neither here nor there *19-, now Abd*. ~ **hill and doun dale** *esp of someone pursuing another with abuse etc* relentlessly, without restraint *la19-, Sh-Per*. ~ **the house** into the interior of a house, from the door inwards *18-, now Sh Ork Ags*. **upthrow and dounthrow** upwards and downwards through a space *la15-17*. ~ **wi 1** on an equality with, as good as; equal to, fit for, capable of *la18-, now Cai Ags*. **2** even with, quits with *19-, now Sh Ags*. ~ **wi't** *in song* hurrah!, bravo! *la18-*.

U.P. *see* UNITED

upaland *see* UPONLAND

upart *see* UPWART

upbiggit [ʌp'bɪgɪt] *adj* built up *15-, now Abd*. [only Sc. OED *upbigged*]

upbeild [*ʌp'bild] *vt* build, construct *16*. [*cf* ModEng *upbuild*. OED *upbuild*]

upbraid *vt* **1** = upbraid *16-*. **2** cast, pull, set up *15*.

upbrak ['ʌp'brak] *n* breaking up, *specif:* **1** the dispersal (of a gathering) *20-, now Sh*; **2** the beginning (of a thaw) *e20*. [var of obs Eng *upbreak* eruption, dissolution]

upbring ['ʌp'brɪŋ] *vt* **1** = upbring, bring up, rear *la14-*. **2** raise up, exalt *e16, only Sc*.
n training, education, maintenance during childhood *la19-, Sh NE Fif Dnbt, only Sc*.
~**ing 1** rearing, nurture, early training *la16-*. **2** the action of building *la15, only Sc*.

upby ['ʌp'bai] *adv* up there, up the way, up at or to a place, *esp* somewhere thought of as being more exalted than where the speaker is, *eg* Heaven or a mansion-house; upstairs *la18-*. [*cf doonby* (DOON[1]), INBY, OUTBY]

upcast &c *vt* [*v* 'ʌp'kast, ʌp'kast; *n* 'ʌp'kast] **1** = upcast, cast up. **2** throw or force open (a gate) *15-16, only Sc.* **3** taunt, reproach, bring up against someone, allege as a fault *19-, local Sh-WC.*

n **1** a taunt, reproach, ground or occasion for criticism *17-, now Sh-N Fif Lnk.* **2** an upset, a state of being overturned *19-, now Sh.* **3** *mining* (1) a fault in a seam of coal which forces it upwards *la18-*; (2) *also* ~ **shaft** the shaft by which the ventilating current returns to the surface *19-, now Fif.*

~**in**(**g**) a gathering of clouds, a cloud formation *19-, now Sh NE, only Sc.*

upcome &c ['ʌp'kʌm] *n* **1** *rare* an ascent, way up *la14, la19, only Sc.* **2** outward appearance, *esp* as being an indication for the future; promising aspect *e17, e19, only Sc: 'if all be good that is upcome'.* **3** a comment, saying, turn of phrase *la19-, N, only Sc.* **4** the final or decisive point, the result, outcome *19-, now Sh Per, only Sc.*

upcomin(**g**), **upcumming** *la14* **1** *lit and fig* an ascent, rise *la14-19.* **2** one's upbringing, development from childhood to adulthood *la19-, now Sh.*

upe *see* UP

uper *see* UPPER

upfesh; upfess- ['ʌp'fɛʃ, -'fɛs] *vt* ~**in &c** upbringing, the rearing and training of young people *la19-, chf NE.*

upgae ['ʌp'ge] *n, mining* a rise or ascent in the stratum of a coal-seam *la17, 20- (Fif).* [only Sc. OED *upgo*]

upgang &c [***'ʌp'gaŋ] *n* an act of ascending; an ascent *la14-e19.*

upget [***'ʌp'gɛt] *vti* get up, rise; put together *la19, only Sc.*

upgie *e20,* **upgive &c;** **upgif &c** *15-17* [***'ʌp'gi, &c] *vt, chf law* give up, deliver up, resign *15-e19.*

upgiver &c a person who provides information or particulars (**of** something) *la16-e17.* **upgiving &c 1** *chf law* surrender, abandonment *15-17.* **2** *law* a declaration, a statement on oath *la16-e18.* [only Sc]

uphald *see* UPHAUD

uphalie; uphelly- *la16:* **uphali**(**e**)**day &c,** ~**mes** *16* [***'ʌp'helɪ'de, ***-'helɪ'mɛs, ***-'halɪde] the festival of Epiphany as the end of Christmastide *la15-18.* [only Sc; UP over, finished + HALIE; *cf* Sh *uphellya*]

uphaud &c *la18-,* **uphold** *la15-;* **uphald &c** *la14-e20* [ʌp'had, -'hald] *v, pt, ptp* **upheld** *la15-,* **upheeld &c** *e16, la19- (NE), ptp also* ~**en** *15-19* **1** *vti* = uphold *15-.* **2** *vt* keep in a state of good repair, maintain, look after *16-, now local Sh-WC.* **3** provide or perform regularly *15-e16.* **4** maintain in argument, warrant, guarantee *la18-.* **5** raise, lift up *la15-, local.* **6** *vi* **upple &c,** *pt, ptp* **upp**(**a**)**led, uppelt &c** *chf of rain or snow, freq with* DEVAL stop falling, clear *19-e20, chf N.*

n ['ʌphad] **1** a person who upholds another, a

support *la14-e20.* **2** the support or maintenance of a person, estate etc; the upkeep of property *15-, now Sh-Cai.*

~**ing 1** sustenance *la14-16.* **2** maintenance in regular use or proper condition *14-15.* **3** the action of raising or holding up *la16.*

upheeze &c; upheis *e16* [ʌp'hiz] *vt* lift up, raise; exalt, elate *e16, 19-, now Lnk.* [UP + HEEZE]

uphei- *see* UP HIE

upheld *see* UPHAUD

uphelly- *see* UPHALIE

up hie; uphei- &c [***ʌp'hi] *vt* exalt, raise up *la15-16.* [ME. OED *uphigh*]

uphint [***ʌp'hint] *ptp* caught up; raised *e16.* [ME. OED *uphend*]

uphold *see* UPHAUD

upland &c [***'ʌpland] *adj* living out in the country; rustic, rural *e15.*

~**is** [***'ʌplandz, ***?-landɪs] = *adj, 15-16.* [ME, OE *uppeland* rural districts; *cf* UPONLAND]

uplift [ʌp'lɪft] *vt* **1** = uplift. **2** collect, draw, take possession of (money, rents, taxes etc) *15-, only Sc.* **3** dig up, harvest (potatoes and other root crops) *la19-, now local, only Sc.* **4** pick up, *eg* take on (passengers), collect (tickets, parcels) *20-.* **5** *freq in ptp* elated, in high spirits, proud *19-.*

~**er 1** collector (of rents etc) *la16-e17, only Sc.* **2** a person who raises or elevates someone or something *la17.*

uplook *n* a respite, let-up *la19-, Ags.*

upmade *see* UPMAK

upmaist, upmost *adj* **1** = upmost, uppermost *17-.* **2** = UMOST 2, *la16-e17, only Sc.*

upmak &c ['ʌp'mak] *vt, only Sc* **1** make up for (a defect, lack); supply, fill up where there is a deficiency *la15-e16.* **2** construct, build *e16, Abd.*

n, only Sc **1** invention, composition, a made-up story, song, plan etc *19-, Sh NE.* **2** compensation, reparation *la19-, now Sh Ork.*

upmade pleased, elated *20-, S.* ~(**k**)**er** a storyteller, composer *20-, Sh NE.* ~**ing &c** *n* **1** the act of making up or preparing something, *now specif* the assembly of lines of type into pages for printing *16-20.* **2** compensation *la16, e18, only Sc.* **3** = *n* 1, *la19-, Sh NE, only Sc. adj* compensating *la17-19, only Sc.* [OED *upmake*]

upmost *see* UPMAIST

upon &c, apon &c *la14-16, la19 (Sh)* **upo** *e15 la18-e20,* **apo** *la19-e20, Sh* [ə'po(n)] *prep* **1** *also unstressed* '**po** *la19-e20, Sh-N* = upon *la14-.* **2** *freq used where Eng (now) has different preps (cf* ON): (1) on *la14-;* (2) (*esp* remember, think *etc*) about, concerning *la14-e20;* (3) *of time* during, in the course of, on the occasion of *la14-, now Sh Ork NE: 'sleep upon the day';* (4) *of place or manner* in *la14-: 'meet one upon the street';* (5) at *la16-, freq* ~ **the heid o** *la18-, now Sh Abd;* (6) (be married *etc*) to, with *la15-.*

uponland &c *15*, **upaland** *16* [*'ʌponland, *'ʌpəland] *adv* = uponland, in the country as opposed to the town.

~**is** = UPLANDIS *la15-16, only Sc.* [UP + ON + LAND¹; *cf* UPLAND]

uppaled *see* UPHAUD

uppe *see* UP

uppelt *see* UPHAUD

upper; uper *la16, e18 adj* **1** = upper *la15-*. **2** *freq in farm-name combs, eg* **Upperton**, *freq applied to* the higher section of a divided estate *18-*: 'Bracco's Uper and Neither Guishaughs'.

~**mair &c** *adv* higher up, further up *16-e18*. [*cf* UVER]

uppie *n, hand-ba* (HAND): a member of the team playing towards the upward goal, the UPPIES *usu* coming from the upper part of the town *20-*, *now Ork S*; *cf* doonie (DOON).

uppit, up-put ['ʌp'pɪt, *-'pʌt, *St* -'put] *n* the ability to deceive *la17, only Sc.*

~**tar** a person who raises or erects *la16-18, only Sc.* ~(**t**)**ing 1** the action of erection, building, setting up *16-17, only Sc.* **2** lodging, accommodation *19-*, *now Loth.* **3** a business establishment, a domestic establishment or home; a (servant's) place or situation *19-e20, only Sc.*

upple *see* UPHAUD

up-put *see* UPPIT

upracht [*ʌp'rɑxt] *ptp* drawn up, raised *la14*. [UP + *ptp of* reach. OED *upraught*]

upredd [*v* ʌp'rɛd; *n* 'ʌp'rɛd] *vt* tidy, put in order *19-*, *now Sh.*

n the act of clearing away, a cleaning, tidying *20-, local.*

~**in** a scolding *la19-*, *now Sh Fif wLoth Dmf.* [UP + REDD¹]

upricht, upright ['ʌp'rɪxt, ʌp'rɪxt] *adj* **1** = upright *16-*. **2** vertically upward *la17*: 'his course should be upward and upright'. **3** *of an heir* true; undoubted; rightful *la15, only Sc.*

vt make reparation to (someone) or for (something), compensate *la15, Abd, only Sc.*

uproll [*ʌp'rol] *vt* **1** impel upwards by rolling *e16*. **2** roll or wind up *e17, only Sc.*

upsail *n* a hoisted sail *e17, only Sc.*

upseed-time [*?'ʌp'sid'təim] *n* harvest *la17-e18, only Sc.*

upset [*v, adj* ʌp'sɛt, 'ʌp'sɛt; *n* 'ʌp'sɛt] *vti* **1** = upset *16-*. **2** *vt* establish *la16, only Sc.* **3** make good, make up for; get over, recover from (a loss etc) *16-e19, only Sc.*

n **1** insurrection, revolt *e15, only Sc.* **2** (1) the act of setting up in business on one's own or of becoming a freeman in a particular trade *16-e18*. (2) the sum paid to a particular INCORPORATION when so doing *17-e19*. **3** *mining* a working place driven upwards following the course of the seam *18-*, *now Fif.* **4** = upset price (adj 2).

upset *adj* **1** set up, raised, erected *16-*. **2** [*chf* 'ʌp'sɛt] *specif of a price at an auction* which will be acceptable to the seller; *latterly also of a price of property* below which bids will not be accepted *la18-*.

upsetter 1 a person who sets up as a master workman, a person who starts in business *16-e18, only Sc.* **2** a person who posts up a placard *la16, only Sc.* **3** a founder *la16, only Sc.* **4** a support, prop *e17, only Sc.* **upsetting &c** *n* **1** (1) = upsetting, setting up *e16*. (2) *specif* the act of raising to or establishing in position or power *la15-e18, only Sc.* **2** arrogance, an unwarranted assumption of superiority *e19*. **3** a woman's first receiving of visitors after giving birth *e16*; *cf* Eng *upsitting*. *adj* haughty, presumptuously ambitious, giving oneself airs *19-*, *now local NE Dmf.*

upsides [ʌp'səidz] *adv* **be** ~ **wi, be** ~ **doun wi** (*la19-, Cai Abd*) be even with, have one's revenge on *18-*.

upsilly *see* UPSLAAG

upsitten *adj* indifferent, inactive *la17-e18, only Sc.* [see SND]

upsitting *n* indifference, lethargy *la17-e18, only Sc.* [*cf* Eng and prec]

upslaag &c *Sh*; **upslay** *Abd Kcdn*, **upsilly** *Abd Kcdn* ['ʌpslag, -sle, -sɪlɪ] *n* a change in weather, *esp* from hard frost to milder conditions, *eg* rain and a south wind *la19-*. [Norw dial *uppslag* breaking up, thaw]

upstand; upstan &c *la19-* [ʌp'stan(d), -'stan(d)] *vi* = upstand *16-*.

~**ing, upstannin** *la19- adj* **1** = upstanding, erect *17-*. **2** *of wages* regular, fixed, basic *la19-, WC, S. n*, *usu of foodstuffs* substance, solidity *la19-, NE*. **be upstanding** stand up, rise to one's feet, *specif* ceremonially to drink a toast, for a prayer etc *la19-*: 'Will you please be upstanding for the benediction'.

upstart [*v* *ʌp'start &c; *n* 'ʌp'start] *vi* = upstart *16-18*.

n **1** an upward start or spring *e17, only Sc.* **2** *building* an upright or vertically set jamb- or reveal-stone in a door or window-case *la18-, only Sc.*

upsteer *20-*; **upsteir** *la16*, **upstir** *17-* [ʌp'stir, -'stɪr] *vt* stir up, throw into turmoil etc; stimulate, encourage *la16-e20*.

upstirring *n* stimulation, encouragement *17-*. *adj* exciting, stimulating *la18-e19, only Sc.*

upstick &c [*ʌp'stɪk] *v* **upsticken &c** priggish, snobbish *la19*. [*cf* Eng *stuck up*]

upstir *see* UPSTEER

upstraucht [ʌp'strɑxt] *vir* straighten oneself up *e16, la19- (Abd).*

upsun *n* **with** (**the**) ~ at dawn, at sunrise *17-e18*. [ME *with up son*]

uptail ['ʌp'tel] **be** ~ **and awa** leave in haste, flee at once *20-, Ork-C.*

uptak, uptake *vt* [ʌp'tak; *sEC* -'tek; *-'te] **1** take possession of, occupy *15-16, only Sc.* **2**

obtain, exact by way of tax contribution or payment; levy *la14-18, only Sc.* **3** understand, comprehend *19-, now Sh.*

n ['ʌp'tak, -'tek] **1** the capacity for understanding, power of comprehension, intelligence, *freq* **gleg, slow** *etc* **in, of** *etc* **the** ~ *19-*. **2** dealings, involvement, relationship *20-, Sh Ags Per.* **3** the lifting or gathering of a crop, *esp* a root-crop *20-, Sh NE, only Sc.*

uptaker 1 a person who collects taxes etc *la16, only Sc.* **2** a PRECENTOR *17, la19 (NE), only Sc.*

uptaking [ʌp'takɪn, &c; 'ʌp'takɪn, &c] **1** (1) raising, picking or lifting up *la15-e17, la19, only Sc.* (2) taking up (of DITTAY) *e17, only Sc.* **2** the collection, levying (of rents etc) *la15-17, only Sc.* **3** the levying (of men) *la16, only Sc.* **4** ? drawing together, gathering (of cloth) *e16.* **5** the action of *precenting* (PRECENT) *la16-e17, only Sc.* **6** one's comprehension, conception, understanding *17-e18, only Sc.* **to someone's uptaking** as far as someone can understand, in someone's opinion *e18.* [chf Sc]

upthrou &c; upthrough ['ʌp'θru, -'θrʌu] *adv* in the upper part of the country, in or from the uplands, in the *Highlands* (HIELAND), inland from the sea *19-, local Sh-NE.*

adj UPLAND; inland *19-, chf Abd.*

upthrow &c ['ʌp'θro] *vt* throw or cast upwards *17-19.*

n, geol and mining an upward dislocation of a stratum or seam *19-, now Fif Loth Ayr.*

upwark *n* cessation of work *16, N, only Sc.*

upwart; upart *15, only Sc* [*'ʌpwərt, &c; *'ʌpərt] *adv (la14-e16), adj (e19)* = upward. [OED *upward*]

upweir *vt* defend *la16, only Sc.* [OED *up-*]

upwith ['ʌp'wɪθ] *adv* upwards *16-, now Abd.*

prep up along the course of *e16, only Sc.*

adj having an upward course; rising ground *16-e19.*

urban *adj* **1** = urban *17-.* **2** *law, of a lease etc* relating to a building, as opposed to land (whether in town or country) *la17-; cf* RURAL.

ure¹ &c; yower &c [jur] *n* the udder, *esp* of a cow or ewe *la18-, Dmf Rox.* [ME *ȝowre,* ON *júgr*]

ure² &c [ur] *n* **1** a damp mist; fine rain, drizzle *19-e20.* **2** an atmospheric haze, *esp* when radiated by sunbeams *19-, now Loth.* [ON *úr* drizzle]

ure³ &c [ør; *NE* ir] *n* **1** = ore *la15-e19.* **2** clay containing iron, barren ferruginous soil, red gravelly earth *18-, now Sh.* **3** an iron stain on linen *20-, NE; cf iron-eer* (IRON).

ure⁴ [*ør] *n* the point of a weapon *e15, only Sc.* [appar representing OE *ōr* beginning, front, taken in the sense of *ord* point, front]

ure⁵ [*ør, *?er-] *n* the monetary value of an ounce of silver.

~ **(of land)** *16-19, Sh Ork,* **urisland** *la15-, Sh Ork, now hist,* **eyrisland** *18-e20, Ork, hist* a measure of land, *orig* assessed at the monetary value

of an ounce of silver, *prob* corresponding to the Celtic DAVACH; *cf ounceland* (OUNCE), TIRUNG, *pennyland* (PENNY). [ON *eyrir* an ounce of silver, *eyrisland* land yielding rent of this value]

urison *see* ORISOUN

urlar ['urlər] *n, piping, in a* PIBROCH: the basic theme of the tune *20-.* [Gael = a floor; *also = n; cf ground* (GRUND)]

urn *see* ERN

urse *n* **1** *in pl* **the ursis** the Great and Little Bear constellations *e16.* **2** a bear *e17.* [only Sc; f L *ursa* (fem), *ursus* (masc) a bear; *cf* Eng *ursa*]

us; ous &c *la18-e20,* **wis** *19-e20,* **wiz** *la19-, now Sh,* **iz &c** *la19-e20, Sh Cai S,* **uz** *20-, now C; stressed* **hiz** *la19-,* **his** *e16, la19-20,* **huz &c** *la18-e20, chf S; unstressed* **s, z** *la19-e20* [ʌs, ʌz, ɪs, ɪz; *Sh also* wɪz; *us; unstressed* (ə)s, (ə)z; *stressed* hɪz, hʌz] *pronoun* **1** = us *la14-.* **2** = we: (1) *before sing personal name, e15, only Sc: 'vs Robert Steward';* (2) *in apposition to a plural noun subject 20-: 'us Varsity girls..'.* **3** *as non-emphatic substitute for me la19-: 'I tell'd him a lee..he jist felled iz like a herrin'.*

~ **anes,** ~ **yins** *etc (subject or object)* we, those of our group, party etc *la19-.* [*cf* WE]

us, usar *see* USE

uscova *see* USQUEBAE

use &c, oise &c *la14-16,* **yeese** *20-, Cai Mry,* **eese &c** *18-, N;* **us &c** *now Sh,* **yuise &c** *la19-e20 n, also* **yis(s) &c** *la19-e20* [n: *Sh S øs; NE* (j)is; *C, S* jøs, jɪs] **1** = use *la14-.* **2** accustomed manner or lifestyle *15, only Sc.* **3** need, occasion, reason **for** *or* **to** *la18-, now Sh-Ags.* **4** a part of a sermon etc devoted to the practical application of a doctrine, a specific precept drawn from a general theological principle *e19.*

vti, also **yaise &c** *20-* [v: *Sh S* øz; *NE* (j)iz; *C, S* jøz, jez; *pt, ptp N* (j)izd, (j)izt, ist; *C* jezd; &c; **used to** *C* 'jɪstɪ] **1** = use *la14-.* **2** *chf* **used wi, eest wi** made familiar with, habituated to, accustomed to *la14-.* **3** *vi* be or become inured or accustomed (**to**) *la14-e20.* **4** *vt* follow or pursue (a lifestyle etc) *la16-e19.*

eesage = usage *la18-e20, Abd.* **usar** *law* a person who enforced or executed a WRIT *la16-e17, only Sc.* ~**less** *adj* **1** = useless *19-.* **2** indisposed in health; incapacitated by illness or exhaustion *20-, Sh-N. adv, also* **ees(e)less** *la19-, NE* exceedingly, so much as to be ineffectual, far too *la19-, now local: 'the maid has put on useless many coals'.*

as ~ **is** as is customary *15-e18.* **be in (the)** ~ **to do** *or* **of doing** be in the habit of doing *la16-e19.* ~ **and wont** the usual practice and procedure *16-.* **used &c and wont** that is customary or usual, according to use and custom *16-e19.*

ush *vt* usher, walk before (a person of rank), escort, guide *19.* [back-formation f Eng *usher*]

ush *see* ISH

ushaw *see* ISCHEW

usher &c, **ischear** &c *la15-e17, only Sc n =* usher *la15-*.

Hereditary *or* Heritable **Usher** an officer of the Crown who directed Court ceremonial, including the opening of Parliament *17-18*. **Usher of the Green Rod** the official master of ceremonies in the *Order of the Thistle* (THRISSEL) *18-*.

usquebae &c *la17-e20*, **usquebaugh** *18-19*, **uscova** *e17*; **iskie bae** *la16, only Sc*, **usque** &c *18* ['uskə'be, 'uskɪ-; *'ɪskɪ-, *-'ba; *'uskɪ] *n* = WHISKY. [Sc and IrGael *uisge beatha* water of life, whisky]

usual, eeswal *la19-e20, NE*; **uswal** &c *18-e20* [*Sh Ork* 'øzwəl; *NE* 'izwəl; *C, S* 'jøzjəl, 'jez-, &c] *adj* = usual *la14-*.

~ **fruit** = usufruct *la16*. **one's** (**auld**) ~ one's usual state of health, frame of mind; one's old self *la18-*: '*he's in his usual*'.

usurp *v* **1** = usurp *la14-*. **2** practise or inflict (cruelty etc) *la15*.

uswal *see* USUAL

utensel *see* OUTAINSELL

uter *see* UTTER

uterance &c [*'ʌtərans] *n* = utterance, immoderate force, excess etc *la16*.

at the ~ to the utmost **of** (one's power) *e16, only Sc*. [OED *utterance²*]

uth [*øθ] *n* harmony *la15, only Sc*. [f ON óð-r poetry, melody. OED *uthe*]

uther *see* UDDER, ITHER

utland *see* OUTLAND

utlaw *see* OUTLAW

utmaist *see* OUTMOST

utouth *see* OUTWITH

Utrik *see* UTTRECHT

utrique *see* OUTREIK

uts *interj* = hoots (HOOT), tut! *la19-, only Sc*.

utter; uter *16-, now Sh* ['ʌtər] *adj* (*adv*) **1** = utter *la15-*. **2** outer, that is farther out than another, outward etc *la15-, now Sh*.

~**fine** *adj, of metals* superfine *la16-e17, only Sc*. [*cf* OUTER¹]

utter *see* OUTER²

Uttrecht &c *la15*; **Utrik** &c *la15-e17* [*'utrɛx(t), *'ʌt-, *-rɪk] *n* **1** a Utrecht gulden *la15, only Sc*. **2** *attrib, of coins* coined in Utrecht *la15-e17*. [OED *Utrecht*]

utwarde, utware *see* OUTWARE

utwith *see* OUTWITH

uver &c *la14-e19*, **over** &c [*'ʌvər; *St* 'ovər] *adj, latterly chf* **over 1** *freq in place-names* upper, higher, *eg* the upper or higher of two farms of the same name *la14-; cf* NETHER². **2** *in gen* upper, higher *la15-*. **3** *in a building* upper; upstairs *la15-17*. [ME *ufere, ouer* &c, OE *ufer(r)a*, which fell in with *over-* (*adv*) in combs in ME (*cf* OWER); cf also UPPER and IVER. SND also *ower*]

uz *see* US

V

vaarious *see* VARIOUS

vacance &c; vagans *e20, S* ['vekəns; *S also* 'veg-] *n* **1** a vacation, holiday, period of suspension of business etc *16-e20*. **2** *specif* a cessation or suspension (of laws) *e16, only Sc.* **3** a vacancy, an unfilled post; the fact of becoming vacant, the vacation (of a post) *16-18, only Sc.* **4** a vacant period, *eg* an interregnum *e16, only Sc.* [prob F *vacance* a holiday, or L *vacantia* vacation > Eng *vacancy*]

vacancy &c ['vekənsɪ; *Ags Per* *'vɑkənsɪ] *n* **1** a vacation, holiday *la16-19*. **2** = vacancy *17-*.

vacand &c; vakand &c *15-16*, **vacane** *e17* [*'vekən(d)] *adj* = vacant *15-e17*.
n **1** a person who is free to take a mate *e16*. **2** a vacant office, a vacancy *la16*. [only Sc, ? presp of VAIK or L *vacant-* (> Eng *vacant*)]

vacant [*'vekənt] *adj* = vacant.
n a vacant estate *la15, only Sc.*

vacation &c *n* **1** = vacation *15-*. **2** freedom or respite from work; time of rest *e15*. **3** a cessation (from business etc) *e17*.

vag- *see* VAIG

vagabond &c; vagabound &c *16*, **vagabon &c** *19-*, *now Uls*, **vaigabon &c** *19* ['vegəbon(d), -bən; *Mry* *'weg-] *n* = vagabond *16-*.
adj **1** = vagabond, wandering, nomadic *16-*. **2** *of laws* irregular *la15, only Sc* [*cf* OSc, ME *extravagant &c* irregular, unusual].

vagans *see* VACANCE

vagring [*'vegrən] *adj* vagrant, wandering; nomadic *e17, only Sc.* [f as Eng *vagrant* with substitution of Eng *-ing* for *-ant*]

vaig *la16-*, **vague** *17-*; **vag-** *15-18*, **vyaug &c** *e20, NE* [veg; *NE* v(j)ɑg] *vi* wander about idly, roam aimlessly; gad about *15-*, *now local Ork-Ayr.*
n **1** a vagrant, vagabond, tramp *19-*, *now Uls.* **2** *specif* (1) a rough-living disreputable person, a rascal, rogue *la19-*, *now Kcdn Ags*; (2) *of a woman* a gadabout, a coarse, disreputable, gossipy person *la19-*, *now Ags.*
wagand [*'vegən(d)] *n* a vagrant *e17*. *adj* wandering *e17*. **~er** an idle stroller, a footloose person, a gadabout *16-e20, only Sc.* **~in(g)** *n* idle rambling, wandering *la16-19*. *adj* roaming, vagrant, straying *17-*, *now chf literary.* [F *vaguer*, L *vagāri* roam; *n* perh reduced f *vaigabon(e)* (VAGABOND). OED *wagand*]

vaigabon *see* VAGABON

vaige *la15-*, *now Sh*, **voyage &c** *15-*; **viage &c** *la14-e16*, **vayage &c** *15-16*, **veyage &c** *la16*, **veage &c** *16-e17*, *20-*, *now Edb, only Sc*, **vo(d)ge &c** *la16, la19* ['veɪdʒ, -ədʒ, vedʒ; 'voedʒ; *vodʒ; *'vaɪedʒ; *'vi-] *n* **1** = voyage *la14-*. **2** *not* **voyage** a journey; a trip, outing, expedition *la14-*, *now Sh Edb.*
vi = voyage *19-*.
ill vage to ye bad luck to you *20-*, *now Sh.*
[Norman F *veage &c*, central OF *voiage &c*]

vaik &c, **vake &c** *vi* **1** fall vacant; remain vacant, unfilled: (1) *of an (esp ecclesiastical) office or position*, *15-e18*; (2) *of a* TACK[2] *or tenancy*, *la15-e16*. **2** *of persons* (1) ~ **for**, (**up**)**on**, **to** be free, have time or leisure for; be busy with *la15-e17*. (2) be at leisure, be free **from** (some occupation or business) *la15-e17*. [eModEng (once) = *n* **1** (1); F *vaquer*, L *vacāre*]

vailable &c; valabill &c *la15-16*, **valiable &c** *la16-e17, only Sc* [*'vel(j)əbl] *adj* **1** = vailable, legally valid *la16*. **2** morally profitable or allowable *la15, only Sc.* **3** of sufficient means, solvent *e17, only Sc.*

vailey *la19-*, *now Sh Loth Slk*; **valé &c** *la14-15, only Sc*, **valay** *la14-16* ['velɪ; *vɑ'li, &c] *n* = valley. [OED *valley*]

vaill &c [*vel] *n* **1** = vail, advantage, benefit *la15*. **2** value, worth; account, estimation *la15-16*.
v, also **va(i)lʒe &c** *la14-16* [*'velji] **1** = vail, be of use, avail *la15-e16*. **2** *of persons* be worth, in respect of means or wealth *la16, only Sc.*
~ **que** *or* **quod** ~ whatever may or might happen *16*. **of** (**na** *etc*) ~ of (no etc) value *la15-e16*. [OED *vail*]

vailleant *see* VALIANT

vaillie, vailye *see* VALUE

vailʒe *see* VAILL

vaincur *see* VANQUER

vainish *la19-*, *now Sh Abd, only Sc*, **wainish &c** *19-e20, only Sc*, **vanish** *16-*; **vanis &c** *la14-16* ['venɪʃ, 'wenɪʃ, 'wəi-; *-ɪs] *vi* = vanish *la14-*.
wainisht &c shrunken-looking, emaciated *19-e20*.

vainquis *see* VANQUISH

vainity *la19-*, *now Sh Ork*, **vanité &c** *e16* ['venɪtɪ] *n* = vanity.

vakand *see* VACAND

vake *see* VAIK

valabill *see* VAILABLE

valairie &c [və'lerɪ] *n* common valerian *la19-*, *Arg Uls.* [reduced f or dim of Eng *valerian*]

valay, valé *see* VAILEY

vale *see* VEAL

valent ['velənt] *n, law* the value of an estate or piece of land, *chf* ~ **clause** the clause in a RETOUR or *special service* (SERVICE) in which the *auld* and *new extent* (EXTENT) of the lands were specified *la18-19*. [only Sc; L *valent* are worth, 3 pers pl pres indicative of *valēre*, orig accompanying the list of items of land on a RETOUR]

Valentine; valentin &c *16-e19* *n* **1** = Valentine *17-*. **2** a sealed letter from the Crown to landholders for the apprehension of law-breakers *la16, only Sc.*
Valentine's deal(ing), dealing o the ~s a custom observed on St Valentine's eve of drawing by lot the name of one's sweetheart for the following year *la18-19*.

valentyne &c [*'valəntəin] *n, collective* birds, fowls *la15*. [ME *vilentyne &c*, altered f OF *volatile &c*. OED *volentine*]

valiable *see* VAILABLE

valiant &c *16-*; **vailleant** *la16*, **valӡant &c** *la15-16*, **valieӡeant &c** *16* ['valɪənt, 'veljənt] *adj* **1** = valiant *la15-*. **2** valid, effective, decisive *e17, only Sc.*
n value, worth *e17.*

validat [*'valɪdat] *adj* valid *la16*. [only Sc; MedL *validat-*, ptp stem of *validare*]

valieӡeant *see* VALIANT

value &c; wal(l)ow *17-e18, only Sc*, **vaillie &c** *la19-*, now Per Fif Loth, **vailye &c** *la19-*, chf NE ['valjɪ; NE also 'veljɪ; EC, S 'velɪ] *n* (*la14-*), *v* (*17-*) = value.
~**d rent** a valuation of land made in 1667 for the purpose of computing the land-tax and the apportionment for public and parochial expenditure, superseding the *auld* and *new extents* (EXTENT) *18-19.*

valӡant *see* VALIANT

valӡe *see* VAILL

vandgard *see* VANGAIRD

vane¹ &c [*ven] *n* **1** = vein *la14-16*. **2** *fig* a sap-vessel in a plant *e16*. **3** a slender stripe of a different colour or material on a garment *e16, only Sc.*
vt **1** = vein. **2** *also* **veyne &c** *e16* [*ven] ornament (a garment etc) with narrow stripes of some suitable material *16-17, only Sc.* [OED *vein*]

vane² &c *interj* call to a horse in harness to turn to the left *19-*, now C. [obscure; *cf* WYND², YAIN]

vangaird &c *16*, **vandgard &c** *la14, la16* [*'van'gerd] *n* = vanguard, the foremost division of an army. [OED *vanguard*]

vangel &c *la14-16*; **vangyle &c** *e15* [*'vandӡəl] *n* gospel. [ME, aphetic f Eng *evangel*]

vangelist [*'vandӡəlɪst] *n* an evangelist *la14-16*. [ME, aphetic f Eng *evangelist*]

vangyle *see* VANGEL

vanis, vanish *see* VAINISH

vanité *see* VAINITY

vanquer *la16*; **vaincur** *la15* [*'veŋkur, *-ər] *n* a conqueror. [F *vainqueur*. OED *vanquer, vainquer*]

vanquish &c *16-*; **vencus &c** *la14-16*, **vincus &c** *la14-16*, **vanquis &c** *la16*, **venques &c** *la15-16*, **vainquis** *16*, **vinkish &c** *la19-*, now Dmf ['vɪŋkʌs, -ɪʃ, 'vɪn-; St 'vaŋkwɪʃ, 'van-; *'vɪŋkwɪʃ, *'veŋkʌs, *-k(w)ɪs, *'veŋkwɪs, &c] *vt, ptp also* **vinqueist &c** *la16-e17*, **vincus** *la16* **1** = vanquish *la14-*. **2** excel, surpass *e16, only Sc.*
n a disease in sheep caused by cobalt deficiency *19-*, now SW.

vincust *adj* **1** *also* **vencust** *la15*, **vanquest** *la16* defeated, overcome, subdued *la15-16*. **2** exhausted, tired out *e20, Ags.*

vara *see* VERA

vardour *see* VERDOUR

variabil *see* VARY

variorum [varɪ'orəm] *n* **1** a change, novelty; a constant variation *la18-19*. **2** a decoration (in furniture, handwriting etc), an ornament, trinket *la19-*, now Sh Ork nEC SW. [L genitive pl masc of *varius* various]

various; vaarious *e20, Abd Fif*, **vawrious &c** *la19*, NE Loth ['varɪəs] *adj* = various.

varité *see* VERITY

varnage &c [*'vɛrnedӡ, *'varn-] *n* = vernage, a strong sweet white Italian wine *la15, only Sc.*

varneis *see* VERNISH

varra, varray *see* VERA

vary &c ['verɪ; *'varɪ] *v* **1** = vary *16-*. **2** *vi, only Sc* (1) wander in the mind, rave *16*. (2) show the first symptoms of delirium *19-e20, S.*
variabil &c **1** = variable *la15-16*. **2** *of weather, seasons etc* changeable *la15*. ~**and** **1** = varying, that varies, tending to vary or change *la15-16*. **2** varied in colour, variegated *la15, only Sc.*
varrit = varied *la16.*

vase; vawse &c *e20, Gsw Loth* [vez, vaz] *n* = vase.

vasquine &c; vaskene &c *n* a petticoat *16*. [only Sc; F]

vassal &c *n* **1** = vassal *la16-*. **2** *law* a person who holds HERITABLE property in FEU from a SUPERIOR *la15-*, only Sc.
~**age, waslage** *la14, only Sc* ['vasəledӡ; *'was(ə)ledӡ] **1** = vassalage, action befitting a good vassal, prowess in battle etc *la14-16*. **2** a brave or chivalrous act; a gallant exploit *la14-17.*

vast *n* a large number, quantity or amount, a great deal *la18-*, now Sh-N Bwk local SW. [*cf* adj in Eng and noun (= an immense space)]

vaticinar *n* a vaticinator, prophet *e16*. [only Sc; f L *vāticinārī* prophesy]

vaticinatress *n* a female vaticinator, prophetess *la17, only Sc.*

Vatland streit [*'watlɪn 'strit, *'wad-, *-lən] = Watling Street, the Milky Way *e16*. [OED *Watling Street*]

vaudie &c *adj* proud, vain, ostentatious, showing off; elated; frisky, merry *18-e20*. [only Sc; perh altered f VAUNTIE, infl by GAUDY]

vauntie &c ['vɑntɪ, 'vantɪ, 'van(d)ɪ] *adj, chf of persons, occas of things, esp dress* proud, boastful, vain; proud-looking, ostentatious, jaunty; pleased, elated *18-*, now chf literary. [f Eng *vaunt* boast]

vaut *see* VOWT

vawcum *n* = vacuum *la19-.*

vawrious *see* VARIOUS

vawse *see* VASE

vayage, veage *see* VAIGE

veal &c; veil &c *16-e18*, **vale &c** *20-*, now Ork [vil, vel] *n* **1** a calf, *esp* one killed for food or reared for this purpose *16-*, now Ork. **2** = veal.

veeand &c [*'viən(d)] *adj* lacking common sense; in one's dotage *19-e20, S.* [see VEED]

veecious &c *la19-e20*, **vicious** &c ['vɪʃ(ɪ)əs; 'vɪʃəs] *adj* **1** = vicious *16-*. **2** *also adv, of weather* severe, inclement *la19-*; see also *vitious intromission* and *intromitter* (INTROMIT).

veed &c [viːd] *adj* lacking understanding; in one's dotage, senile *la19-e20*, *S*. [this and VEE-AND *appar* ppl adjs of **vee (v) appar* be foolish, witless]

veelage *n* = village *20-*, *now Ork Ags*.

veeper &c *n* = viper *19-e20*.

vees &c [*viz] *n* = vives, hard swellings on the glands of a horse *la16-e17*, *only Sc*.

veesit &c *la19-*, *now Ork N*, **visit** *16-*; **vesit** &c *15-16* ['vizɪt, 'viz-] *vt, pt also* **vissit** &c *e15* = visit.

veet *n* = vet, veterinary surgeon *20-*, *Cai Abd*.

veeve *see* VIEVE

veeze *see* VISE

vehement *adj, also* **viement** *la16, only Sc* ['viːmənt] = vehement *16-*.
adv = vehemently *16, only Sc*.

veil *see* VEAL

veillane [*vɪ'len, *'vɪlen, *'vil-] *n* = villain *e16*. [OED *villain*]

velanous [*'vilənus, *-ʌs] *adj* = villainous *la16*. [OED *villainous*]

velany &c *la14-16*, **vilne** *la14, only Sc* [*'vilənɪ, 'vɪl(ə)nɪ] *n* = villainy. [OED *villainy*]

vellous &c; **velvous** &c [*'vel(v)us] *n, adj* velvet *la15-16*. [only Sc; OF *velous*]

venace *see* VENDACE

venal *see* VENNEL

venamus(e) *see* VENOME

vencus, vencust *see* VANQUISH

vendace *la19-*; **vendiss** &c *19*, **venace** *e18* ['vendes, -is; *'venes] *n* a species of char found in Britain only at Lochmaben, *Dmf*. [ScL *vandesius la17*; appar OF *vendoise, vendese* a dace]

vendicatife &c *adj* = vindicative, vindictive *e16*. [only Sc. OED *vindicative*]

vendiss *see* VENDACE

venenous &c [*'venənus] *adj* poisonous, venomous *e15*. [earlier in Sc]

venge; veng &c [vendʒ] *vt* = venge, avenge *la14-15*.

vengeable *adj, of persons and animals* inclined to take vengeance, cruel, destructive *la17, e19*. [ME]

vengeance &c *n* **1** = vengeance *la14-*. **2** *in imprecations, la16-*: '*what the vengeance ..*'

vennel &c; **venal** &c *15-18* ['venəl] *n* a narrow alley or lane between houses *15-*, *Gen except Sh Ork, almost obs NE*. [still freq in street-names; OF *venelle* a small street, MedL *venella*, f L *vēna* vein]

venome &c, **vennome** &c *la15-16, only Sc, vinam** *la16, only Sc* ['venəm] *n* = venom *la14-16*.
~(o)us &c *la15-e17*, **venamus(e)** *la14-e15* **1** = venomous. **2** of or like venom *15-*. [OED *venom*]

venques *see* VANQUISH

vent &c *n* **1** = vent *16-*. **2** the flue of a chimney; the duct used to convey smoke out of a room *18-*. **3** the opening of a fireplace *20-*, *now Sh NE*. **4** a chimney head or stack *18-*, *now local*. **5** a flaw in a mould *e16, only Sc*. **6** a hint or whisper (of something) *e17, only Sc*.
vti **1** put (money etc) into circulation or currency *17-e19*. **2** *of a chimney, room etc* discharge or emit smoke, allow smoke to pass through or from it *la18-*, *now local Sh-Lnk, only Sc*. **3** *vi, of smoke, foul air etc* find a way out, (have room to) pass away *17-19*.
take ~ *of coin* pass into circulation *e17, only Sc*.

ventilation; ventulacioun *la15* [ventɪ'leʃən; *ventɪ'lesɪun] *n* **1** a motion of the air, a current of air *la15*. **2** = ventilation.

ventur &c ['ventər] *n* = venture *18-*.

veol *see* VIOL

vera *la18-*, **wery** *18-e20*, **very; verr(a)y** &c *la14-16*, **verra** *la14-e20*, **varray** &c *16*, **var(r)a** *19-e20* ['verə, 'varə; *Mry* 'werɪ; *'vere, *'vare] = very *adj* (*la14-*), *adv* (*15-*), *n* (*la16*).

verbene *n* = verbena *e16*.

verdour &c; **vardour** &c *only Sc n* = verdour, verdure *la15-16*.

vergens ad inopiam ['verdʒenz ad ɪn'opɪam, *also* 'verdʒəns] *law* in the state preceding bankruptcy, approaching insolvency *18-*. [L = on the verge of insolvency]

verification &c *n* **1** *law* a formal assertion of truth *16*. **2** = verification.

verilies [verɪlɪz] *adv* = verily *20-*, *Ork NE*.

verisimilarie *adj* verisimilar, having the appearance of truth or reality *la17*. [only Sc. OED *verisimilary*]

verity; verité &c *la14-16*, **varité** *16* ['verɪtɪ; *'var-] *n* = verity *la14-*.
of ~ *only Sc* **1** *predic, freq law* true *16-19*: '*yet true it is and of verity ..*'. **2** *as adv* with emphatic force, *la16*: '*Johne fastit without meit or drink of veritie xxxij dayes*'.

vermeloun *e16*; **vermeling** *16, only Sc* [*'vermilun, *-ən] *n* = vermilion *16*.
adj, only **vermillion** *e17* [ver'mɪljən] painted with vermilion, rouged *e17, only Sc*. [OED *vermilion*]

vermin *n* **1** = vermin *la16-*. **2** *pejorative* a large quantity, swarm, crowd *18-*, *now Cai Bnf Ags*.

vernaculary *adj* = vernacular, indigenous *la17, only Sc*.

verneis *see* VERNISH

verngreis &c [*'verngris, *'varn-] *n* = verdigris *e16*. [only Sc. OED *verdigris*]

vernish &c *la16-*, *now Ork Ags*; **verneis** *16*, **varneis** &c *16* ['vernɪʃ; *'vernis, *-ɪs, *'varn-] *n, vt* = varnish. [OED *varnish*]

verra, verray, verry *see* VERA

version *n* **1** = version. **2** (1) the translation of a passage of English prose into Latin *chf* as a school exercise; the passage so translated *18-*,

NE Ags Loth. (2) *specif* one associated with the *bursary competition* (BURSARY) in Aberdeen University *18-19*.

vert *vt* turn up, root up (the ground) *la16*. [only Sc; L *vertere* turn, overturn]

verter, vertew *see* VIRTUE

vertie &c, verty *adj* 1 cautious, prudent *la14-18*. 2 energetic, active, up early and at work, early-rising *19-, now Bnf Abd*. [aphetic f rare OSc and ME *averty*, OF *averti*]

vertise &c *19-, Sh;* **verteis** *e16* ['vɛrtɪz; *'vɛrtɪs, *-ɪs] *vt* warn. [only Sc; aphetic f *averteis* and *advertise* (ADVERTEESE)]

vertu, vertusly *see* VIRTUE

verty *see* VERTIE

very *see* VERA

vesar *see* VYSAR

veseit *see* VIZZY

veshel &c, vessel; weshell &c *18-e20*, **veschail &c** *la14-e17* ['vɛʃl; *Mry Bnf* 'wɛʃl] *n* 1 = vessel *la14-*. 2 the udder (of a cow etc) *20-, Cai Per WC, SW, only Sc.*

vesit *see* VEESIT, VIZZY

vessel *see* VESHEL

vessit *see* VIZZY

vest *vti* 1 = vest, place (something) **in** (someone's possession) *15-*. 2 place, establish (a person) in full or legal possession or occupation of something *la14-, orig only* **vest** (*la16*) *or* ~**it** (*la14-16*) **and sesit** (**in**).

vesy *see* VIZZY

vesyne *see* VISION

vesynes [*?'vizɪnɛs] *n* caution, foresight, prudence *e15*. [only Sc; f *vesy*, aphetic f OSc, ME *avisé* cautious. OED *vesyness*]

vetite [*'vɛtɪt] *adj* forbidden *la15*. [only Sc; L *vetit-*, ptp stem of *vetāre* forbid]

veto *n* = veto *17-*.
V~ **Act** an act passed by the *General Assembly* (GENERAL) in 1834, providing that no MINISTER should be PRESENTED to a parish against the wish of the congregation; the precipitating cause of the DISRUPTION *19*.

veveres *see* VIVERS

veyage *see* VAIGE

veyne *see* VANE[1]

vex *vt, ptp also* **vext** *la18-* 1 = vex *la16-*. 2 cause (a person) mental agitation or trouble, make anxious or depressed, distress seriously *15-*.
n a source of regret, sorrow or annoyance *19-, only Sc.*
~**some** sorrowful, full of vexation *19-, now Lnk.*
be vexed for be sorry for (a person) *la19-, Sh-Cai Ags Per WC.*

veyra [*?'virə] meaning unknown *e16*: 'the *marynalis .. cryit thir vordis as eftir follouis, veyra, veyra ..*' [*?cf* eModEng *vera* a sailors' command]

veyton *n* = whitten, the water elder etc *e16*. [OED *whitten*]

viadant *n* a wayfarer, traveller *e17*. [only Sc; Span, Port, Ital *viandante*]

viage *see* VAIGE

vibrant *adj* 1 agitated with anger or emotion *la16, only Sc.* 2 = vibrant.

vicar &c; vicare *la14-16* ['vɪkar; *'vɪ'ker] *n* 1 = vicar *la14-*. 2 (1) a layman who claimed the title of the *vicarage teinds* (TEIND) after the Reformation *e18, Sh.* (2) the church PRECENTOR, who was given the *vicarage teinds* as his salary *19, Peebles.*

vicarage &c *n* 1 = vicarage, benefice, living or residence of a vicar *16-*. 2 a benefice attached to a parsonage *e16, only Sc.* 3 the lesser TEINDS, reserved for the actual incumbent of a parish, and exacted only by custom, not by law *la16-; cf* PARSONAGE and see SND.

vice[1] *n* 1 the place, position, stead (of another) *17-*. 2 (1) one's turn in a rota; one of the recurrent periods in a continuous series *17-e19, only Sc.* (2) *specif* applied to the right to PRESENT a MINISTER to a parish where the patronage was shared by two or more HERITORS who exercised their right in turn *18-e19*. [eModEng, L *vice*, ablative of *vicis* (genitive sing) change, turn, stead]

vice[2]; vis &c *la14-15* [vəis] *n* = vice, corruption of morals *la14-*.

vice[3] &c *vt* treat arrogantly or oppressively *15*. [only Sc; appar OF *vicier*, L *vitiāre* spoil]

vice *see* VOICE

vice-chancellor;   vice-chancellair &c *la16-17* *n* 1 a deputy or subordinate of a state official entitled *chancellor*, *la16-17*. 2 = vice-chancellor.

vicennial *adj, law* ~ **prescription** a twenty-year period of *prescription* (PRESCRIBE) applied to RETOURS (making them unchallengeable) and to holograph bonds (making them unenforceable) *17-e19*. [only Sc; *adj* f L *vicennium* a period of 20 years]

vicious *see* VEECIOUS

victaill *see* VICTUAL

victogall *n* a collector of tribute *e16*. [L *vectīgālis*, f *vectīgal* tribute. OED *vectigal*]

victor[1] *n* 1 = victor *16-*. 2 the DUX of a school *la17-e18, only Sc.*

victor[2]; victore &c *16* [*'vɪktor, *-ur] *n* victory *la14-e16*. [chf Sc; ME, OF *victore, victoire*]

victual *la16-;* **vittal &c** *la14-e20*, **vittail &c** *la14-e18*, **vittel &c** *la15-19*, **vitale &c** *la14-19*, **victaill &c** *la14-15* ['vɪtl] *n* 1 = victual *la14-*. 2 corn, grain, *latterly occas also* leguminous crops; a crop before or after harvesting *la15-, now local Kcdn-Loth, only Sc.*
vt = victual *la14-*.
~**house** a granary, *esp* the grain-store of an estate *la16-e18*. ~ **stipend** that part of a MINISTER's *stipend* (STEEPEND) formerly paid in grain or the cash equivalent thereof *19-e20; see* TEIND.

vidimus [*'vaɪdɪmʌs] *n* 1 = vidimus, an authenticated copy of a document *la16*. 2 an examination or inspection (*esp* of accounts or documents) *19, only Sc.*

viement *see* VEHEMENT

vieve &c, **vive**; **veeve** &c *la19-, now Sh* [viv] *adj* **1** = vive, (making a) vivid (impression) *e17*. **2** alive *la16*. **3** *of pictures, images* lifelike, closely resembling the original *la16-, now Sh NE Edb*. **4** bright, clear, vivid, distinct: (1) *of colours, la16-*; (2) *of sights, sounds, impressions, memories etc, la18-, now Sh*. ~**ly** &c **1** = vively, in a lively way *la16*. **2** clearly, distinctly, vividly *la16-, now Sh*. **3** sharply, to the quick *la16, only Sc*.

vievers *see* VIVERS

view; vyow &c *la19-, NE* [vju; *NE* vjʌu] *n* = view *17-*.

vild *see* WILE²

vilipensioun &c [*vɪlɪ'pɛnsɪun, &c] *n* the action or fact of despising *la15-17*. [OF *vilipension* or MedL *vīlipensio* (*n*), f *vīlipendere* (> Eng *vilipend*). OED *vilipension*]

vilne *see* VELANY

vinam *see* VENOME

vincus *see* VANQUISH

vindicable [*'vɪndɪkəbl] *adj* vengeful, vindictive *e17*. [only Sc; *cf* Eng]

vindicate *vt, ptp also* **vindicate** *la16* **1** = vindicate *17-*. **2** exercise (wrath) in revenge *e16, only Sc*.

vinkish, vinqueist *see* VANQUISH

viol; veol ['vaɪəl; *'vɪəl] *n* = viol *la16*.

violer a player of the viol; a fiddler *la16-e19*.

violent &c *adj* **1** = violent *la16-*. **2** *of natural forces* possessed of or operating with great force or strength, moving strongly and impetuously *la14-*.

vt treat with violence, use coercion on, ride roughshod over the wishes of (a person) *17-18*. ~ **profits** *law* penal damages due from a tenant when he refuses to vacate premises after termination of his lease etc *la16-, only Sc*. **lay** ~ **hands on** *etc* attack, seize with violence *la14-*.

viral *see* VIRL

Virgilian *adj* characteristic of the poet Virgil, suggestive of his style *16-*. [earlier in Sc]

Virginia *n* ~ **trade** the tobacco trade between Glasgow and Virginia *18*. [the US state]

virgult [*'vɪrgʌlt] *n* a bush, a shrub; a branch *e16*. [earlier in Sc; L *virgulta* (*pl*) bush, thicket]

virgus &c [*?'vɪrdʒøs] *n* = verjuice, sour fruit-juice *19-e20*.

virideer [*'vɪrɪdər] *n* a verderer, officer of royal forests *e17*. [only Sc; MedL *viridarius*]

virl &c; **virrel** &c *16-e20*, **viral** &c *la15-e16*, **virol** &c *la16-18* ['vɪr(ə)l] *n* a ferrule, a band of metal, wood, bone etc fitted around a rod, cane, or pipe etc to prevent splitting or fraying *la15-*.

~**ed** having a ferrule; clasped round as by a ferrule *19-, now Ork Per*. [ME *vyroll*, OF *virol(e)*, MedL *virola*, L *viriola*, dim of *viriae* bracelets; *cf* later Eng *ferrule*]

virr &c *n* vigour, energy, force, impetuosity *la16-, now local Ork-Loth*. [echoic]

virrel *see* VIRL

virtue; vertew *la14-e17*, **vertu** &c *la14-e16 n* **1** = virtue *la14-*. **2** industry, diligence *16-19*. **3** *also* **verter** *attrib, of a well, spring etc* medicinal *19, chf SE, S*.

vertusly *adv* with great skill or excellence *e15*. **house of** ~ ? a work-house *e17*.

vis *see* VICE²

vise; veeze &c [viz; *vaɪz] *n, mining* the line of fracture of a fault in a coal-seam, *usu* marked by a deposit of earth etc *la17-*. [uncertain]

visie, visied *see* VIZZY

vision; vesyne *16, only Sc*, **weeshan** &c *la19-, Abd* ['vɪʒən; *Abd* 'wɪʒən, 'wɪʃən] *n* **1** = vision *16-*. **2** a puny, emaciated person or animal, one who is wasting away; *transf* an insignificant characterless person *19-, now Sh Ork Stlg Dmf*.

visit *see* VEESIT

vis major ['vɪs 'medʒər] *law* a circumstance, *eg* a natural disaster, which cannot be reasonably expected or prevented, an act of God, a DAMNUM FATALE, which excludes responsibility for loss, damage or the non-performance of a contract *la19-*. [L = superior force]

visnet *n* a trial by jury *15*. [only Sc; OF *visnet*; see OED]

visnomy [*'vɪsnomɪ, *'vɪz-] *n* = physiognomy *19*.

vissie, vissier *see* VIZZY

vissit *see* VEESIT, VIZZY

vitale *see* VICTUAL

vitiat &c [*'vɪsɪat] *adj, law* rendered null or void; interfered with *la16-17*. [only Sc; *cf* Eng *vitiate* (*adj*). OED *vitiate*]

vitious intromission *see* INTROMIT

vitta(i)l, vittel *see* VICTUAL

vive *see* VIEVE

vivers *la16-e20*; **veveres** &c *16*, **vievers** &c *17-19* ['vɪvərz; *'vaɪvərz] *n* food, provisions, victuals. [chf Sc; OF *vivres*, pl of *vivre* food, substance, f *v* = live]

vizzy &c *18-*, **vizy** *18-e19*; **visie** &c *la14-e19*, **vesy** &c *la14-e20*, **vissie** &c *16* ['vɪzɪ, 'vizɪ] *v*, *pt* **veseit** *la15-e16*, **vissit** *la16-e18*, **vizzied** *la19-e20*; *ptp* **ves(s)it** &c *la16*, **visied** *la16* ['vɪzɪd; *'vɪz(ɪ)ɪt, *'vɪs(ɪ)ɪt] **1** *vt* go to see, visit (1) (a person) *la14-e17*; (2) (a place) *e16*. **2** (1) look at attentively, inspect, examine, squint at *la15-, now Sh*. (2) *vi* look, gaze *e16*. **3** take aim (with a gun etc), aim **at** (something) *la16-, now Sh*. **4** *vt* afflict (a person) **with** (sickness etc) *la15-, now Sh*. **5** punish (a sin etc) *la16*.

n **1** a look, glimpse, scrutiny, survey *18-, now Sh*. **2** a view, prospect *18-e20*. **3** an aim (with a weapon), *usu* **take a** ~ *18-, now Sh*. **4** *chf in combs, also* **vizé** *e17* ['vɪzɪ] the sight on the barrel of a gun *17-*.

vissier an inspector *la16*. [only Sc; northern OF *viseer*, L *visitare* visit; perh also later confusion w F *viser*, *visee* aim, laL *vīsāre*]

vlgare *see* VULGAR

vlgat &c [*'vʌlgat, *-et] *adj* = vulgate, commonly known *e16*. [only Sc. OED *vulgate*]

vlte *see* VULT

vocation &c *n* **1** = vocation *la16-*. **2** the summoning of an assembly or its members *la15*.

voce *see* VOICE

voche &c [*vutʃ] *vt* = vouch, assert a claim to *la15*. [only Sc. OED *vouch*]

vociferation &c *e15* [vosıfə'reʃn, *-'resıun] *n* **1** a clamour, an outcry *e15*. **2** = vociferation.

vocky *see* VOKE

vod(e) *see* VOID

vodge *see* VAIGE

vodur *see* VOIDER

voge *see* VAIGE

vogie *see* VOKE

voice; voce &c *la14-e17*, **vos(s)** *19-e20*, **vice** *19-e20* [vois; *N nEC, WC* vəis; *vos; *Fif also* *vʌus] *n* **1** = voice *la14-*. **2** the fame or renown **of** (something) *la15*.
vti = voice *17-*.
~**er** a person who votes or has the right to do so *17, only Sc*. **in ane** ~ unanimously *la16-e17, only Sc*.

void [void; *Sh* vod; *vəid; *Fif* *vʌud] *adj* (*also* **vode** *e16* [*vod]), *v* (*also* **vod** &c *la15*, **voud** *16, e19* [*vod, *vʌud]) = void *la14-*.

voidour; vydour *la15*, **vodur** *e16* [*'voidur, *-ər, *'vəid-, *'vod-] *n* **1** = voider, a basket etc for clearing dirty dishes, food-fragments etc during or after a meal *e16*. **2** an empty barrel, cask etc *la15-e17, only Sc*. **3** packing or wrappers removed from a bale, bundle of goods etc *e16, Edb, only Sc*. [OED *voider*]

voite *see* VOTE

voke *n* arrogance, vanity, conceit *la15*.
vogie &c *18-e20*, **voky** *16-18*, **vocky** &c *18*, **vougy** &c *18-e19* ['vogı; *Cai* 'wʌugı; *'vokı, *'vʌugı; *Abd also* *'vjokı, *'vʌukı] **1** (1) *of persons* proud, elated, vain *la16-e20*. (2) *of things* imposing, ostentatious *18-e20*. **2** merry, lighthearted, happy *18-20*. [only Sc; obscure; *-g*-forms poss w infl f Eng *vogue* popularity, public success etc *la16-*, of which the earliest examples are Sc]

volage &c; **fallauge** &c *19-e20*, *Abd* [*Abd* fə'ladʒ; *'voledʒ, *-ıʃ, *və'ladʒ, &c] *adj* **1** = volage, giddy, thoughtless *16-19*. **2** lavish, profuse, prodigal with money *19-e20*, *Abd, only Sc*.
~**ous** [*və'ledʒ(ı)ʌs, *və'ladʒ-] = *adj* 1, *la14-19, only Sc*.

vollum *see* VOLUME

volt *see* VOWT, VULT

volume *16-*; **vol(l)um** &c *15-e20* ['volʌm; *vo'ləm] *n* = volume.

volumen *n* a volume, book *e16*. [only Sc; L]

voluntar ['volʌntər] *adj* = voluntary *la16-20*, *chf NE*.
~**ly** = voluntarily *la16-e17*. [only Sc]

volve &c *vi* turn over, roll *la15*. [only Sc; L *volvere* turn etc, or F *volver*; *cf* obs Eng = turn over (pages) etc]

vomit &c *vti* **1** = vomit *la16-*. **2** *vi* issue with force or violence, rush **out** *e17*.
vomiter &c = vomitory, an emetic *la17-18*.

voo &c *la19-e20*, **vow** &c [vu] *n* = vow *la15-*.
vti **1** = vow *la15-*. **2** *vi* curse, swear *la20-, Ork Abd*.

vorax *adj* voracious, ravenous *e16*. [L = devouring]

vos(s) *see* VOICE

vost *see* VOUST

vote; vot(t) *la16-e20*, **voite** &c *la16-e18* [vot] *n* **1** a vow, a solemn promise or undertaking *16*. **2** a formal expression of opinion by a member of a deliberative assembly on a matter under discussion; a decision, verdict *16, only Sc*. **3** an indication whether one approves or disapproves, accepts or rejects a proposal, candidate etc *la15-*. **4** = vote *la16-*.
vtir **1** = vote *16-*. **2** vow (to do something) *e16, only Sc*. **3** declare one's opinion *la16, only Sc*. **4** submit (a matter) to a vote, vote upon *la16, only Sc*.
voter &c a person who has a right to vote, *esp* an elector *la16-*.
in ane ~ of one accord, unanimously *16, only Sc*. **put to the** ~ submit to the decision of the meeting *la16-*. [chf Sc *16*]

vouch sauf *la15*, **wouch(s)aiv** &c *la16-e17*, **witsaufe** *15-16*, **wit(s)chaif** &c *15-16, only Sc*, **wischeaf** *la16* [*'vutʃ'saf, *'wutʃ'sev, *wu'tʃef, *-'tʃev, *wıtʃ'sef, *wı'tʃef, *'-tʃaf, &c] *vt* = vouchsafe. [OED *vouchsafe*]

voud *see* VOID

vougy *see* VOKE

voult *see* VOWT

voust; vous *e15*, **vost** *16-e17* [vʌust, vust; *vost] *vi* boast, brag *16-, now Sh*.
n a boast *15-19*.
~**er** a braggart *16-17*. ~**y 1** ? puffed up *la14*. **2** boastful(ly), proud(ly) *la16-e20*. [only Sc; perh connected w Eng *boast*]

vow &c [*vʌu] *interj* expressing pleasure, admiration, surprise *18-19*. [*cf* WOW[2]; phonology rules out connection w Eng VOO]

vow *see* VOO

vowt &c *now Edb*; **vaut** *la16-e20*, **volt** *15-e17*, **voult** *la16-e17* [vʌut, vat; *Sh* vult] *n*, *vt* = vault. [OED *vault*]

voyage *see* VAIGE

vrack *see* WRACK[1]

vraith *see* WREATH

vrang *see* WRANG[1]

vratch *see* WRATCH

vreet *see* WRITE

vricht *see* WRICHT

vring *see* WRING

vrutten *see* WRITE

vulgar *la16-*; **vlgare** &c *e16, only Sc* ['vʌlgər] *adj* = vulgar.

vult *15-16*; **vlt(e)** *la14-e16*, **wout** *la15*, **volt** *e17*

[*vut] *n* a face, countenance; *esp* expression of the features, bearing. [chf Sc; OF *vult*, L *vultus* face]

vyaug *see* VAIG

vydour *see* VOIDER

vyow *see* VIEW

vyre *vti* **1** whirl, throw *la14, only Sc.* **2** turn; wind about *la15*. [OF *virer* turn. OED *vire*]

vysar &c, vesar &c ['vaɪzər; *'viz-] *n* = visor *la15-16*. [OED *visor*]

vyse &c [*vaɪz] *vr* bethink oneself (**well** *etc*) *la14-16*.

vysing advice *la14, only Sc.* [ME *vise*; see OED. OED *vise*]

W

wa¹ &c *la15-*, **wall** &c; **wae** *el7* [wɑ; *wal] *n* **1** = wall *la14-*. **2** *in pl* a roofless building, ruins *18-*, *chf SW*.
vt = wall *la14-*.
~ **bag** a bag hung on the wall, for holding odds and ends *la17-19*. ~ **coal** the middle section of coal in a seam *19-*, *now Fif*. ~ **drap 1** rainwater dripping from the eaves *20-*, *Cai Fif wLoth*. **2** a puny or insignificant person *20-*, *Cai*. ~ **heid** &c **1** the top of a wall *16-*. **2** *specif* the space between this and the roof-beams, used for storage *19-*. **3** *transf*, *chf in pl* the horizon, skyline *la19-*, *chf SW*. ~ **iron** a crowbar *la20-*, *NE*. ~ **rase** a wall-plate *el6*. ~ **stade** the foundation of a wall *la17-*, *now Sh*. ~ **toun** a walled or fortified town *la15*.
wa² &c, **way** *la16-* [wɑ, we] *adv* **1** = AWA *17-*. **2** *lit and expressing disbelief, impatience etc*, *freq* (**gae**) ~ (**wi ye**) go away *19-*, *local Sh-Lnk*.
~-**cast** something of little value *19-*, *Sh-Ags*. ~**coming** *n* coming away *la17*. ~-**gang** &c **1** departure, leave-taking *18-*, *now NE*. **2** a lingering taste or flavour; an after-taste *la18-*, *now Sh NE Ags*. **3** an outflow of water, *specif* from a millwheel, the tail-race *18-*, *now Sh*. ~-**gaun** &c *n*, *also* ~-**ganging** *la15-19* **1** departure, the action of going away *17-*, *now local N-SW*. **2** *specif* the departure of a farmer from his tenancy, *freq* ~-**gaun crop** *19*, ~-**going sale** *20-*, *N, EC Wgt*. *adj* departing, going away, *freq* ~-**going tenant** *19-*. ~-**pit** *v* (*n*), *freq transf* put(ting) away *16-*, *now Sh*. ~-**takin** removal, carrying off, *esp* by theft or violence *la15-*. [aphetic]
wa *see* WAE¹, WAE², WAW², WEY¹
waal *see* WALL
waar *see* WARE¹
wab *19-*, **web** *18-*; **wob** &c, **wub** *la19-*, *local Sh-Wgt* [wab, wob; *Per-Fif* wʌb; *Bnf Abd also* wʌub] *n* **1** = web *la15-*. **2** *mining* the extent of a face of coal, *esp* in thickness *la18-19*. **3** the omentum of animals *19-*, *Sh Cai Wgt*.
wobby covered with cobwebs *la20-*, *Bnf Abd Fif*.
~ **gless** &c a magnifying glass for examining a web of cloth *la19-*, *Fif*.
gie in the ~ assist a weaver to thread his loom by handing him the threads *la19-e20*, *C*. **have one's** ~ **oot** have one's piece of cloth completed and off the loom *la20*, *Ags Ayr*.
wabbit &c ['wabɪt; *also* 'wʌbɪt] *adj* exhausted, feeble *la19-*, *Gen except Sh Ork*.
~ **out** = prec *20-*, *chf C*. [see SND]
wabble &c *19-*; **wauble** &c *la18-20*, **waible** *19-e20* *vi* **1** = wobble, *specif* walk unsteadily, totter, waddle *la18-*. **2** wriggle about *20-*, *now Sh Ags*.
n wishy-washy, tasteless drink or liquid food *la19-*, *chf Abd*.
wabbie wishy-washy, thin *20-*, *local NE-Wgt*.
wabster *la16-*, **webster** &c; **wobster** &c

15-e20 ['wabstər; *NE Loth* 'wob-, *nEC* 'wʌb-] *n* **1** a weaver *la14-20*. **2** *transf* a spider *la18-*, *nEC, WC*. [obs Eng *webster*; *cf* WAB]
wach *see* WATCH
wacht [*wax] *n* = wough, a wall of a house *15*. [OED *wough* (*n*¹)]
wacht *see* WAUCHT, WECHT¹
wack &c, **waᴋ** [*wak] *adj* moist, damp *16-19*. *n* moisture *la15*.
~**nes** = *n*, *16*. [only Sc; ON, Icel *vǫkr*, MDu *wak* moist]
wack *see* WAULK
wad¹ &c *15-*, **wed** &c [wad, wɛd] *vt* **1** wager, bet *la16-*, *now local Sh-Wgt*. **2** = wed, marry *la14-*.
n **1** *also fig* a pledge, something deposited as security *la14-*, *now Sh Wgt*. **2** a stake, bet *la14-*, *now local*. **3** *in pl*, *only* **wads** &c name for various games in which forfeits are demanded *la18-*, *now Sh*.
waddin braws wedding clothes *19-*. **waddin fowk** the wedding party *19-*.
~ **fee** a wager, prize in a contest *16-el7*. ~ **man,** ~ **wife** a man or woman who kept a kind of servants' registry *el8*, *Edb*. **wad shooting** a challenge shooting match for staked prizes *18-19*, *chf Ags*.
be in (**a**) **wad** &c be liable to a forfeit in a game *19-e20*. **in** *or* **a** ~ (**of**) as a pledge or security (for) *la15-el9*. **lie in** ~ be in pawn *la15-el9*.
wad² [wad] *n* black lead, graphite; *hence* a mine of black lead; a lead pencil *la18-*, *now Kcb Dmf*. [nEng *dial*]
wad³ [*wad] *n* wadding, cotton wool *20*. [Eng *wad* a bundle of hay etc]
wad *see* WADE, WILL¹
wadder *see* WEATHER, WEDDER
waddin *see* WIELD
wade &c; **wed** &c *19-*, *Sh Ork*, **wad** &c *la19-*, *local*, **wide** &c *la18-*, *now NE Bwk* [wed; *Ork WC, SW Uls* wad, wad; *N, EC* wəid] *v*, *pt also* 'woid &c *16* [*wød]. *ptp also* **widden** *la19-20*, *NE* *1 vi* = wade, *chf* through water etc *la14-*. **2** *vt*, *also fig* cross by wading *la14-*. **3** *vi*, *of the moon or sun* move through cloud or mist *18-*, *now local*.
n the act of wading; a distance covered by wading *la19-*, *now N Per*.
wadeable &c fordable, that can be crossed on foot *la17-19*.
Wadensday *see* WEDNESDAY
wadge &c *N-S*, **wedge** [wadʒ] *n* **1** = wedge *16-*. **2** a thick slice (of bread, cheese etc) *20-*, *now Stlg wLoth Lnk*.
vt = wedge *16-*.
wadge *see* WAGE
wadna *see* WILL¹
Wadnesday *see* WEDNESDAY
wadset; wedset &c, **wodset** &c ['wadsɛt,

*'wɛd-, *'wʌd-] *vt*, *chf law* pledge (land or other HERITABLE property) in security, mortgage *la14-18*.
n **1** a mortgage of property, with a conditional right of redemption *15-18*. **2** *in gen* a pledge or thing pledged *la18-e19*, *SW*.
~**ter** the creditor or holder of a WADSET 1 *17-18*; cf *reverser* (REVERSE). [ME *wedsette* (v) pledge, f WAD¹ + Eng *set*]
wae¹ &c *15-*; **wa** *la14-16*, **way** *la14-16* [we] *interj* (adv), *n* = woe *la14-*.
adj, *comparative* **waer &c** *la15-19*; *superlative* **wa(e)st &c** *la15-e19* grieved, wretched, sorrowful *la14-*.
waebegane woebegone *19-*, *now Sh Cai*.
waefu &c woeful *18-*, *Gen except Ork*.
waesome sorrowful; causing sorrow *19-*, *Gen except Ork*. **waesuck(s) &c** alas! *la18-20*.
~ (**be**) **to** a curse upon, may sorrow befall *18-19*. ~'s **me** *la14-*, *Gen except Sh Ork*, ~'s (**my**) **heart** *la18-*, *now Cai Ags* alas! ~ **worth** a curse upon *la14-e20*. [OED *woe*]
wae² &c *19-e20*, *SW*, *S*; **wa &c** *la17-19* [wɑ, we; *S* *wəi] *used where Eng has* well! [see SND]
wae *see* WA¹, WI
waer *see* WAE¹
wa'er *see* WATER
waest, waesuck(s) *see* WAE¹
waff¹ &c; **wauff &c** *19-e20* [waf] *vti* **1** wave, move to and fro, flap *16-*, *now local Sh-SW*. **2** (1) *vt* set (air etc) in motion; fan *19-*, *now Sh NE*, *C*. (2) *vi*, *of wind etc* blow, waft *19-*, *chf C*. **3** *vti*, *in gen* move *19-*, *now Sh*.
n **1** (1) a flapping, waving movement *la17-*, *now local Sh-SW*. (2) a signal made by waving; a flag *17-*, *now Ork*. **2** (1) a puff, blast (of air etc) *17-*, *now Sh-C*. (2) a puff, flurry (of snow, smoke etc) *la19-*, *now Sh Abd*. **3** *transf*, *of something just perceptible* a slight odour, sound, glimpse, blow, illness, agreeable experience *la18-*, *now local*. **4** an apparition, ghost *18-e19*.
[nME *waffe* (v) wave, blow, var of Eng *wave*]
waff² &c *18-*, **waif &c** *17-*; **wauf &c** *19-e20* [waf, wef; *wɑf] *n* **1** = waif *la18-*. **2** a worthless person *la19-*, *now Cai*.
adj **1** (1) *of animals* strayed, wandering ownerless *17-e20*. (2) *of persons* vagrant, homeless *la18-e19*. (3) *of persons*, *places etc* solitary, lonely *18-e20*. **2** *of persons* vagabond-like, good-for-nothing; *freq of appearance* scruffy *la18-*, *now Cai nEC Wgt*. **3** (1) *of persons* feeble in body or mind *19-*, *local EC-S*; (2) *of things*, *qualities etc* lacking strength or substance, shoddy, of little account *19-*, *now Sh*.
~**er** a good-for-nothing *20-*, *local Fif-Rox*. ~**ie** *adj* = *adj* 2, *la19-*, *local Cai-Fif*. *n* = *n* 2; a vagabond *19-*, *now Fif*. ~**ish** *la19-e20*, ~ **like** *19-* = *adj* 2, 3 (1).
~**-looking** = *prec*, *esp of appearance 19-*, *Bwk Lnk S*.
waffer &c *n*, *mining* some kind of engineering work; ? a fan *la16*. [? deriv of WAFF¹]

waffinger &c *19-e20*, *literary*; **wavengeour &c** *la15-e16* [*'wafɪndʒər; *'wev-; &c] *n* a vagabond; a good-for-nothing. [appar f WAFF² w ending as Eng *messenger* etc. OED *wavenger*]
waffle &c; **wuffle** *la19-e20* ['wafl; *'wʌfl] *vti* **1** wave about, flap *19-*, *now Ork-SW*. **2** *vi*, *fig* waver, vacillate, hesitate *19-*, *C*, *S*. **3** stagger, totter *la20-*, *Sh Wgt*. **4** *vt* crease, wrinkle; tangle *19-*, *now Sh*.
n a feeble, silly person *la19-*, *now Loth S*.
adj **1** supple, pliant *19-*, *now Cai*. **2** inert, limp, feeble, sluggish *19-*, *now local Cai-Fif*.
waffle &c limp from weakness or exhaustion *la18-*, *now Loth*. **waffly &c** **1** = *prec*; feeble *la19-*, *local Sh-Fif*. **2** volatile, easily blown about, shaky *20-*, *Ork NE*. [frequentative of WAFF¹]
waft &c *la17-*, *now local Sh-Dmf*; **weft**; **woft** *17-*, *now Slk* [waft, woft, wʌft] *n* = weft, the woof or cross-threads of a web of cloth *17-*.
v **1** *vi* = weft, form a web *la18-*. **2** *vt* trounce, out-manoeuvre *e20*, *chf Abd*.
waft clew a hank or ball of yarn, *freq fig* in expressions of restlessness or impatience *18-*, *now Abd*.
wag¹ &c *vti* **1** = wag *la15-*. **2** *vi*, *of a leaf*, *plant etc* wave to and fro, shake in the wind *la16-*. **3** *vt* cause to shake; brandish (a weapon) *19-*. **4** *vi*, *also* ~ **about, awa** *or* **on** carry on, proceed *19-*, *local Sh-Dmf*. **5** (1) *vt* beckon, signal to *18-*, *local*. (2) *vi*, *freq* ~ **at** *or* **on** wave to (a person) *la19-*, *local*.
n a signal made with the hand *19-*, *NE-WC*.
waggie *la19-*, *Fif-S*, **waggitie** *20-*, *Ags Per* the pied wagtail.
wag-at-the-wa 1 a household goblin *e19*, *S*. **2** *also* **waggity-wa &c** an unencased pendulum clock *19-*.
wag² &c *n* name for the remains of iron-age houses in Cai *la18-*. [bookish adaptation of Gael *uamhag*, dim of *uamh* a cave]
wagand *see* VAIG
wage; **wag &c** *la14-16*, **wadge &c** *la15-e20*, **waig &c** *15-16*, **waidge** *la16-e17*, *e20*, **wauge &c** *la19-e20*, **wodge** *la19-20*, *Bnf* [wedʒ; *NE* wadʒ] *n* **1** = wage *la14-*. **2** *in pl* school fees *17-19*, *chf SW*.
vt **1** pledge *la16-18*. **2** = wage *la15-*. **3** wager, bet *19-*, *Cai EC*, *WC*. **4** wield (an implement), brandish or hurl (a weapon) *19-*, *NE Ags Fif*.
wager &c a mercenary soldier *la14-16*, *only Sc*. **lay in** ~ give as security *e16*.
wager; **wauger** *19-20*, **wu(d)ger** *e20*, **weeger** *la19*, *Kcb* ['wadʒər, 'wedʒər; *WC*, *SW* *'wʌdʒər] *vti*, *more colloq than in Eng* = wager *18-*.
n = wager *16-*.
waggitie *see* WAG¹
waggle &c; **waigle &c** *18-e20* *vti* = waggle *18-*.
n **1** = waggle *la19-*. **2** a marsh, bog, pool *la18-e19*, *N*.

waghorn &c [*'wag'horn] *n* a character in fable, the greatest of all liars; the Devil himself *la17-e20*. [presum Eng *wag* + *horn*; cf *hornie* (HORN)]

waible *see* WABBLE

waicht *see* WECHT¹, WECHT²

waid &c *n* = woad *la15-17*. [OED *woad*]

waidge *see* WAGE

waif¹ &c [*wef] *n* **1** ? a convolution, coil *e16*. **2** a small flag used as a signal *e16*. [? ON *veif* something waving or flapping; *cf* WAFF¹]

waif² [*wev] *vti* = wave, move to and fro *15-16*. [OED *waive* (*v²*)]

waif *see* WAFF²

waig *see* WAGE

waigle *see* WAGGLE

waik &c; **wyke** &c *la19-*, *Abd* [wek; *Abd* wəik] *adj* = weak *la14-*.
vt = weak, weaken *16*. [OED *weak*]

waile *see* WYLE

waill *see* WAUL¹

wain &c *n* a waggon, a large open two- or four-wheeled cart *la14-*, *now Fif*.
vt = wain, transport in a carriage etc *17-e19*.
~**gate** a cart-track *la16-17*. ~ **weight** ? a waggon-load *16*.

waingle *see* WINGLE

wainish *see* VAINISH

wainscot &c *la16-*; **wanskoth** *15*, **wynscott** *16* ['wenskot; *-ʃot] *n* = wainscot.

waint &c *v* = vaunt *la16*. [prob misspelling of *want, vant* (see OED *vaunt*)]

wair *adj* ? wild, stormy *la15*, *only Sc*.

wair *see* WEIR¹

waird *see* WARD, WEIRD

wairdour &c *n* a person in custody, a prisoner *la16-e17*. [only Sc; OED *warder*]

wairn *see* WARN¹

wairsh *see* WERSH

waist; west *16* [west; *wɛst] *n* = waist, middle of the trunk etc *la15-*.
~**less** having no waist or the appearance of no waist *e16*.

waist *see* WASTE

wait¹, **wat** *la14-16*; **wyte** &c *la16-*, *NE* [wet; *NE* wəit] *v* **1** *vt* watch with hostile intent, spy upon, lie in wait for *la14-16*. **2** await, remain in expectation of *la14-*, *now N nEC Rox*. **3** *vti* = wait *la14-*. **4** *vi* lodge, make one's temporary home *la20-*, *C*.
n **1** = wait *16-*. **2** ambush *16-18*.
waiter 1 = waiter *la16-*. **2** a watchman at the gates of Edinburgh *la17-e18*.
at (**the**) ~ on the watch *la15-e16*. **lie** ~ lie in wait *la16*. **take under** ~ capture or surprise by an ambush *e16*. ~ **of** call on, pay one's respects to; attend (the summons of) *la17-18*. ~ **on 1** *vt* (1) = prec *la16-19*. (2) wait for, await *la18-*. (3) attend to, look after (*esp* a sick or dying person) *la19-*, *now Cai*. **2** *vi* (1) linger, remain in attendance, stay on *18-*, *now NE Per*.

(2) *specif* be on the point of death *19-*, *now Cai*. (3) take care **that** .. *la16*. ~ **or** &c wait until *19-*. ~ (**the**) **table** wait at table, serve a meal *la19-*.

wait² *vt* treat (a person) **with** (unkindness etc) *la15-16*. [ME; ON *veita* show (kindness etc)]

wait *see* WEET¹

waiter *see* WATER

waith¹ &c *15-19*, **weth** *e17* [*weθ] *n* a piece of property which is found ownerless, *chf* **wrack and** ~ flotsam and jetsam *15-19*, *chf Sh Ork*.
adj, *of an animal* strayed, roaming loose *15-19*. [only Sc; altered f *waif* (WAFF²)]

waith² &c [*weθ] *n* cloth, *esp* when made up into garments *17-18*. [only Sc; ON *váð* cloth, cognate w Eng *weed*]

waith³ &c [*weθ] *n* **1** the action or practice of hunting or fishing (*chf* unlawfully) *15-e18*. **2** game; *in gen* spoil, booty *la15*.
~**ing** fishing; a catch of fish *la15-16*, *only Sc*.
~**man** a hunter, *esp* a forest outlaw *15-16*, *only Sc*. [nME; ON *veiðr* hunting, fishing]

waith⁴ &c [*weθ] *n* = wothe, danger, harm *la14-15*. [OED *wothe*]

waitter *see* WATER

waizel *see* WEASEL

wak *see* WACK, WAUK, WAULK

wake *see* WAUK

waken *see* WAUKEN

wakerife *see* WAUK

wakne *see* WAUKEN

waks *see* WAX¹

walawa &c, **wellaway** &c; **willy-** &c *la18-19* [*'walawa, *'walawe, *'walɪ-, *'wala-, *'wɪlɪ-, &c] *interj*, *also* **willawins** *la18-19* = wellaway!, alas! *la15-19*.
n = wellaway, a lamentation *la16-19*.
vi make lamentation; screech, yell *19*.

welcome *la19-*, **welcome** &c; **wylcome** &c *16*, *e20* ['walkʌm; *'wɪl-] *n* (*17-*), *v*, *adj*, *interj* = welcome *la14-*.
welcome-hame &c **1** a celebration in a bride's new house *e19*. **2** a celebration for the coming of new ploughmen to a farm *la19*.

wald¹ [*wald] *n* = wold, a hill, a piece of open country *la14-16*. [only Sc. OED *wold*]

wald² &c [*?wald, *?wald] *n* dyer's rocket, the plant; the yellow dye obtained from it *15-e19*. [only Sc; *cf* Eng *weld*. OED *weld*]

wald *see* WIELD, WILL¹

waldin heat *see* WALL

wale &c; **weil** &c *la16-19*, **wile** &c *la17-*, *now NE nEC*, **waul** &c *19-20* [wel; *Ork also* wal; *NE nEC* wəil; *Renfr Gall Uls* wal] *n* **1** choice, the act of choosing, scope for choice *la15-*, *now Sh NE*, *C*. **2 the** pick, **the** choice, the thing chosen as the best *16-*, *now local Sh-SW*.
vt **1** choose, select, pick out *la15-*, *now local*. **2** arrange, separate into lots, sort *20-*, *local*.
waled (carefully) chosen, choice *la15-*. **ill** **weel waled** badly or well chosen *18-*. **walin**

&c 1 the act or process of choosing *e17, 20-, NE Ags.* **2** the pick, the best *la19-, local Abd-Rox.* **3** the leavings, refuse *la20-, now Stlg Lnk SW.*
~ amang &c choose between *la19-, Sh NE Ags.* **~ for** choose carefully, look out for *la18-, now Sh Abd Ags.* **~ out** pick out after selection, choose from a particular group *18-, now Sh.* **will and ~** free choice *la15, 18-e19.* **wile warst** the very worst *la20-, Abd Kcdn;* cf *the weel warst* (WEEL[1]). **~ wight men** *ballad* the best and bravest men *la18-e20.* **~ yer** *etc* **feet, way** *etc* pick your etc way, step forward cautiously *la18-, now Sh Ags.* [nME; ON *val* choice, selection]

walgan &c ['walgən] *n* **1** a leather wool-sack, a bag *19-20, NE Ags.* **2** a large clumsy overgrown person or thing *la20-, now Abd.* [Gael *bhalgan,* f *balgan* a little bag, wallet]

walipen *see* WALLIPEND

walise &c [*?wa'liz, *?wə'liz] *n* = valise, a suitcase, saddle-bags *18-e19.*

walk[1] &c; wauk &c *18-, now Cai* [wɑk; *walk] *vti* **1** = walk *la15-.* **2** *vi* go from place to place, journey *e16.* **3** *of things* move about, be in motion *19-, now Cai.*
n **1** (1) = walk. (2) travel, wandering *la15.* **2** a ceremonial procession *la19-, local.* **3** a pasture for cattle *19-, now Ags Lnk.* **4** a passageway in a cowshed *20-, now Sh Ork Cai.*

walk[2] [*walk, *wɑk] *n* a cloud, clouds *16.* [only Sc; OE *wolc*]

walk *see* WAUK, WAULK

walkne, walkyn *see* WAUKEN

wall &c *la15-, in place-names la14-,* **well; woll** *16-e17,* **waal** *la19-e20* [wɑl, wal] *n* **1** (1) a natural spring of water which forms a pool or stream *la15-, Gen except Sh Ork.* (2) *freq in placenames* a mineral spring reputed to have medicinal qualities *la16, la19-e20.* **2** = well *16-.* **3** (1) a drinking fountain *la16-, now local, chf Sc.* (2) a water stand-pump *19-, local N-WC.* (3) a cold-water tap at a sink *20-, local NE-WC.*
vti **1** *lit and fig* boil (**up**) *la14-15, e19.* **2** *vi* well up as a spring of water *20-, now NE.* **3** *vt* (1) weld, join (metals) by means of heat *16-, now local Ork-SW.* (2) *fig* unite (people etc), join *la16, la19-e20.*
wallie a small well *la19-20, Mry Abd Ags.* **pee a wallie** *freq in imperative to coax a child* urinate *la20-, N.* **~in heat,** *also* **waldin-, welland- 1** the degree of heat necessary for welding metals *19-, local.* **2** *fig* fever pitch, the heights of passion *19-e20.*
~ e(y)e 1 a place in a bog from which a spring rises *e16, la18-e20.* **2** a spring, a well *19-, local N-S.* **~ grass &c** *la17-,* **~ girse kail** *19-* cress *now Abd.* **~heid** a spring which feeds a boggy piece of ground *19.* **~ink** brooklime, the plant *19-, now Dmf.* **~ kerse &c** = **~ grass,** *la16-e19.* **wall raik** weeds which grow round

a spring *20-, Abd.* **well strand** a streamlet from a spring *19.* **wall-wesher** a water-spider *20-, SW, S.*

wall *see* WA[1], WAW[2], WAW[3]

wallack *see* WALLOCH[2]

wallan &c; wallant &c ['walən(t)] *adj, of flowers* withered, faded, drooping *la19-20, Bnf Abd.* [reduced f *wallowand* (WALLOW)]

waller &c ['walər] *vi, lit and fig* toss or thrash about; surge, heave *19.*
n a confused crowd of living things, *esp* when in motion *19-e20, S.* [appar var of Eng *wallow*]

wallet &c ['walət] *n* **1** = wallet, a travelling bag, a pedlar's pack *16-.* **2** a fund of stories or poems *19-e20.*

wallicoat *see* WYLIECOAT

wallie &c, wally *18-;* **waly &c** *18-e20* ['walı, 'walɪ] *adj* **1** fine, pleasant, beautiful *16-, now Ork.* **2** *of persons and animals* big and strong, thriving, sturdy, plump *18-, now Sh Ork.* **3** *of the fist or grip* big, strong *la18-e20.* **4** *of things* (1) large, strong, imposing *18-, now Sh Ork;* (2) decorative, ornamental, *chf* **~ dugs** ornamental porcelain dogs displayed in pairs on mantelpieces *20-, C, S;* (3) made of porcelain, china, glazed *20-, C, S.*
adv finely, splendidly *18-e19.* *interj, expressing admiration, chf* **o** *or* **a ~** goodness!, my! *la18-19.*
n **1** *in sing* an ornament, trinket, toy; *in pl* fine clothes, finery *18-19.* **2** *in pl* the (male) genitals *la17-e19.* **3** the common daisy *la18-e19, SW, S.* **4** (1) porcelain, glazed earthenware or tiling; a dish or ornament made of such *la19-, C, S.* (2) *in pl* (a) broken pieces of china used as toys *20-, C.* (b) a set of false teeth *20-, C.*
~ close a tiled CLOSE[2] (*n* 4) considered a sign of social superiority *20-, WC.* **wally gowdy** *term of endearment* lovely jewel *e16.* **wally money** broken pieces of china used as toy money *20-, Per Stlg WC.*
~ fa good luck to *e16, e19.* [only Sc; obscure]

wallied *see* WALLOW

wallipend &c; walipen &c [*'walıpɛn(d), *'walə-] *vt* despise, abuse *19-e20, chf NE.* [Eng *vilipend;* cf VILIPENSIOUN]

wallit *see* WALLOW

walloch[1] &c ['waləx] *vi* **1** make violent heavy movements, *esp* in water or mud, move clumsily, flounder *la18-, now N.* **2** dance, skip, romp noisily *19, Bnf.*
n **1** the act of wallowing or of walking with difficulty; a floundering movement *19-, now Abd.* **2** a Highland dance (HIELAND) , the *Highland fling* (HIELAND) *la18-19.* [only Sc; frequentative of WALLOP[1]]

walloch[2] &c; wallack &c *Mry Bnf* ['waləx; *Mry Bnf also* 'walək] *vi* cry, shriek, howl *19-, now Abd.*
n **1** a scream, howl, wail *la19-, now Mry Abd.* **2** the lapwing *19-, now Mry.* [only Sc; perh deriv of WAUL[1]]

wallop[1] &c ['waləp] *v* **1** *vi* gallop *la14-e20.* **2**

move clumsily at great speed *18-*, *now Abd Ags Per*. **3** make violent struggling or convulsive movements, thrash about, flounder *la18-*. **4** *of the heart* throb, beat violently *la18-*, *now Sh-Per*, *only Sc*. **5** move to and fro, dangle, swing, flap *19-*, *now Sh-Per*. **6** = wallop.

n **1** a violent jerky movement, a floundering *19-*, *now Sh NE Ags*. **2** a leap, bound or figure in a lively dance *19-*, *now Stlg Lnk*. **3** a constant motion to and fro, a wagging (of the tongue) *la19-*, *Sh Abd*. **4** a strong beat of the heart or pulse, a throb *la18-*, *now Sh Per, only Sc*. **5** a fluttering rag, a piece of ragged clothing *18-*, *now Abd Ags*. **6** a gangling loose-limbed person or animal *la19-*, *now Ags*. **7** = wallop.

gae ~ go thump, move very suddenly *la19-*, *now Sh-Per*. **play** ~ thrash about, tumble over *19-*, *now Ags Per*. ~ **at** put all one's energies into *la18-*, *now Sh Cai*.

wallop² ['walǝp] *n, chf* ~**ie** the lapwing *la19-*, *Inv NE*.

~**ieweet &c** = *n*, *19-*, *Ork Inv Abd*. [only Sc; imit of the bird's call, perh w infl f WALLOP¹; *cf* WALLOCH² *n* 2]

wallow &c ['walǝ; *local C* 'walı] *vi, ptp, adj also* **wallied** *la19*, **wallit &c** *la18-20* wither, fade, waste away *15-*, *now local Cai-Lnk*. [ME *welowe*; OE *wealwian*]

wallow *see* VALUE

wally &c [*'walı] *n* a valet, a personal servant *19*.

wally *see* WALLIE, WAW²

wallydrag &c; warridrag &c *20-*, *Bnf Abd* ['walı'drag, 'walı'dreg, *NE also* 'warı-] *n* **1** a good-for-nothing, a slut *e16*, *la18-*, *now NE*. **2** an undersized person or animal *19-*, *now Bnf Abd*. **3** the smallest, weakest or youngest bird in the nest *la18-e19*.

wallydraigle &c *18-*, *local C* **wallydraggle** *la18-19*, **warydraggel &c** *la18-*, *now Bnf* = *n*. [uncertain]

wally-dye &c [*'walǝ'de, *'wel-, &c*] *interj*, *expressing sorrow, literary or arch* alas! *18-e20*. [Eng *well-a-day*]

walow *see* VALUE

walsh &c *19-e20*; **welsh &c** *16-17*, *19-e20* [*walʃ, *wɛlʃ] *adj* insipid, tasteless; nauseous. [also nEng dial; uncertain; *cf* WERSH]

walt¹ &c *16-*; **wat(t) &c** *16-e19*, **waut** *la15-e16*, *19-e20* [*NE Lnk SW, S* walt; *Ayr* wɑt] *n* = welt (of a shoe, garment etc) *16-*, *now local*. *vt* = welt *la15-e16*, *la18-19*.

~**ing &c** an edging, hem, selvedge *17-e19*. **waltened &c** bordered, edged, having a welt or selvedge *la18-19*. [OED *welt*]

walt² &c *e16*, *e20*, **welt** *e16* [*walt, *wɛlt] *v* **1** *vt* = welt, cast or throw **down** *e16*. **2** *vi* be on the point of falling; roll or tumble over *e16*, *e20*.

walt³ *n* ? beaten clay *la15*, *only Sc*.

waltam &c; wull-tam &c ['wal'tam, 'wʌl-] *n*, *in pl* = NICKIE-TAMS *20-*, *NE*, *nEC*. [only Sc; WALT¹ + TOME]

waltened *see* WALT¹

walter¹ &c; wolter *16* ['waltǝr; *Sh* 'wɑltǝr] *v* **1** roll to and fro, toss about (1) *vi*, *la15-*, *now Sh*; (2) *vt*, *la16*. **2** *vi* swing to and fro *la16*, *la19*. **3** *vt* overturn, overthrow *la16*.

n an upset, upheaval, overthrow *la16*. [ME *waltre*; frequentative of WALT²]

walter² *vt* be without, lack *la15*, *only Sc*. [prob misreading of WANT]

walter *see* WATER

walth &c *la16-*, *now Ags Ayr*, **wealth** *la18-*; **welth** *la14-e19* [walθ] *n* **1** = wealth *la15-*. **2** abundance, plenty, profusion *la16-*, *now Ags Ayr*.

~**y &c 1** = wealthy *la16-*. **2** *of a person, life etc* happy, prosperous; comfortable *la14-16*.

walx *see* WAX¹, WAX²

walxin *see* WAX²

waly &c [*'walı, *'welı] *interj*, *expressing sorrow* oh dear!, alas! *18-19*.

~ **fa &c** woe betide .., devil take .. etc *la18-e19*. [only Sc; prob reduced f WALAWA]

waly *see* WALLIE

wam *see* WAUM

wambe *see* WAME

wamble *see* WAMMLE

wame &c; wambe &c *16-e19*, **wime &c** *18-e20* [wem; *Sh Cai NE, nEC* wǝim] *n* **1** the belly *15-*. **2** *also* **womb** *e17* the belly-piece of a fur-skin *la14-e17*. **3** = womb *15-*, *now Cai*. **4** the seat of the passions or thoughts, the heart, the mind *19-e20*. **5** tripe etc used as food *18-*. *vr* fill oneself with food *19*.

-**wamed** having a belly of a specified kind, *eg* great, big, black etc *15-e20*. ~**fu &c** *16-*, *now Ags*, **wombfull** *e17* a bellyful. **wamie** big-bellied *19-*, *now Ags Fif*.

~ **ill** an illness affecting the stomach *16*.

wamfle &c ['wamfl] *vi* flap, flutter, wave about *19-e20*.

adj limp, weak, flexible *la19-*, *now Bnf Abd*. [only Sc; nasalized var of WAFFLE]

wamfler &c [*'wamflǝr] *n* ? a dandy, gallant *16*. [only Sc; perh f prec]

wammle &c *la15*, *18-*, **wamble &c** *la15-*; **waumle &c** *la19-20*, **wummle &c** *la19-20* ['waml, 'wɑml, 'wʌml] *v* **1** *vi* = wamble, feel nausea, be squeamish *la15*. **2** *of the stomach or its contents* stir uneasily, rumble queasily *la18-*, *now Bnf Abd Fif*. **3** *of persons and animals* roll about, wriggle, writhe *18-*, *now local Sh-SW*. **4** *of things* roll, toss, twist and turn *18-*, *now local Ork-SW*. **5** stagger, move with a weak, unsteady gait *17-*, *now local Sh-Lnk*. **6** move unsteadily to and fro in the air, sway, flap, dangle *17-e20*. **7** *of thoughts* creep into someone's mind, go round and round in someone's head *18-20*. **8** *vt* roll, turn over and over; tangle; wind, coil *la19-*, *now Ork Ags*.

n **1** a churning of the stomach, a feeling of sickness *la19-*, *NE Ags Fif*. **2** a rolling or unsteady motion, a wriggle *19-*, *now Ork NE*.

adv with a writhing or undulating motion *la19-, NE.*

wammily &c tottery, weak, feeble *la19-, now local NE-WC.*

womle &c brees a dish of the same ingredients as HAGGIS but of a liquid consistency *19-e20, Abd Kcdn.*

wampish &c [*'wampɪʃ] *v* **1** *vi* move to and fro, wave, flap about *19-20.* **2** *vt* wave, flourish, brandish *19.* [only Sc; based on WIMPLE, WAMPLE, WAMFLE]

wamplate *n* ? an ornamental plate on harness put below a horse's belly *e16.* [only Sc; WAME + Eng *plate*]

wample ['wampl] *vi* **1** wriggle, writhe *19-, SW.* **2** *of a stream* meander, flow gently *19-e20.* [only Sc; altered f WIMPLE, perh conflated w *wamble* (WAMMLE)]

wan[1] [wan] *numeral, pronoun, n* = one *17-, chf WC, SW.* [appar Sc representation (? via Ireland) of laME (? orig SW Eng dial) *won*, eME *won*, ModEng [wʌn], midl and sME *on(e)*, corresponding to nME *an(e)* > ANE[1]]

wan[2] [wan] *n, freq suffixed to noun* (in) the direction of..; -wards *19-20:* 'eastwan'; 'gaein to Aberdeenwan'. [see SND]

wan[3] *e16, e19,* **wane** *la14-e17* [*wan, *wen] *n* = wane, lack, defect *la14.*
adj **1** lacking, deficient, misshapen; *of the moon* not fully formed *la15-e16, e19.* **2** insufficient, (too) small *e17.*

wan[4] [*wan] *n* a dark-coloured mark produced by a blow, a bruise *16.* [only Sc; *cf* Eng *wen*]

wan[5] **&c** *19-, Sh Ork Cai;* **wane &c** *la14-16, 19-e20 (Sh Ork)* [wan; *Ork also* wen] *n* **1** hope, expectation; *latterly* liking *la14-16, 19-, now Sh Ork Cai.* **2** = wone, resources *la15.* [OED *wone*]

wan- [wan] *prefix* = UN- *la14-, latterly chf with adjs.* [ME, OE *wan &c;* in Sh Ork f ON *van;* f as WAN[3]]

wan *see* WAND, WIN[1], WIN[2], WIND[2]

wance *see* AINCE

wand &c; **wan &c** *la15, la18-e20,* **waun &c** *19,* **whaun &c** *19-e20* [wan(d); *C also* *wɑn] *n* **1** = wand *la15-.* **2** a slender pliant stick, *esp* one cut from a young tree *la15-20.* **3** a young shoot of willow used in making baskets *18-, now local NE-WC.* **4** a rod or stick used for punishment, a switch *16-19.* **5** a staff used as a symbol in various legal transactions *e15, la18.* **6** a fishing rod *16-, now Sh-Per.* **7** a pole or stout stick, *esp* a punting pole *19-e20.* **8** an animal's penis *la16-e18, la20- (Kcb).*
vt **1** interweave, plait *la15.* **2** beat with a wand or switch *la16.*

wand basket, chair *etc* a wickerwork basket, chair etc *la15-e19, only Sc.* **wan bane** the smaller bone of the forearm *la15.* **wand hand** the hand that holds the WAND or whip *17, only Sc.*

wand of peace &c *law* a baton carried by the king's messenger and used to touch an outlaw to show his restoration to the king's peace; *also* ceremonially broken by the messenger to indicate obstruction in the course of his duty *15-18, only Sc.* **under the wand of** under the rule of *la15-e17, only Sc.*

wand *see* WIND[2]

wander &c;   **wanner &c**   *la18-e20,* **waun(n)er** *la19-20* ['wan(d)ər; *N, C* 'wɑnər] *vti* **1** = wander *la14-.* **2** *vi* lose one's way, get lost *la19-, now local Sh-Ayr.* **3** *vt* lead astray, cause (someone) to lose his way *la19-, now Ags Per.* **4** *fig* confuse, perplex, bewilder *la19-, now Ags Per.*
~t &c **1** lost, uncertain of one's whereabouts *18-, now Sh N, WC.* **2** confused, bewildered; mentally disordered *la19-, now local Sh-Gsw.*
~ing folk beggars, gipsies, tramps *la19-, now Cai Per.*
wander the road be a vagrant, have no home *la19-, now Cai Per.*

wander *see* WANDRETH

wandis &c [*'wendɪs] *vi* retreat, give way *la14.* [only Sc; OF *wandiss-,* stem of *wandir*]

wandle [*'wandl] *vi* walk wearily or unsteadily *la17.* [uncertain]

wando *see* WINNOW

wandocht; **wandought** [*'wan'doxt] *n* **1** a feeble, weak person; a silly, sluggish, worthless person *18-19.* **2** lack of strength, feebleness *18-e19.*
adj feeble, puny, inert; contemptible, worthless *la18-e20, latterly literary.* [only Sc; *cf* UNDOCHT]

wandreth &c *16-17;* **wander** *16, only Sc* [*'wandrəð, *'wandər] *n* misery, hardship, poverty. [ME]

wane &c [*wen] *n* a dwelling, a house *la14-16, e19 (ballad).* [eME; *cf* WONE]

wane *see* WAN[3], WAN[5], WEAN

wanease &c [*'wan-] *n* uneasiness *16-18, only Sc.* [WAN- + Eng *ease*]

wanfortune [*'wan-] *n* misfortune *16-e18.* [only Sc; WAN- + Eng *fortune*]

wangrace[1] [*'wan-] *n* lack of grace, bad behaviour *16-e18.* [only Sc; WAN- + Eng *grace*]

wangrace[2] **&c** ['wan'gres, -'grɪs, *-'grɛs] *n* a kind of thin gruel sweetened with fresh butter and honey etc, and given to invalids *18-e20.* [only Sc; obscure]

wanhap &c [*'wan'hap] *n* misfortune *16.*
wanhappy &c unfortunate *la16.* [only Sc; WAN- + Eng *hap*]

wanhew &c [*'wan'hju] *vt* stain *e15.* [only Sc; WAN- + Eng *hue.* OED *wanhue*]

wankish &c *vt* twist, interlace, entwine *e19, Dmf Rox.* [only Sc; obscure]

wanlas &c *la15;* **wanles &c** *15-16* [*'wanləs] *n, hunting* = wanlace, a circuit made to intercept game *e15.*
at the *or* **a ~** in an ambush *la15-16.* [OED *wanlace*]

wanluck &c [*'wan-] *n* bad luck, misfortune *la16-, now Sh.* [only Sc; WAN- + Eng *luck*]

wanner *see* WANDER

wannle &c [*'wanl] *adj* supple, agile; active *19-e20, S.* [only Sc; prob f WAND]

wanpa [*'vampɪ] *n* a vamp of a shoe *e16.* [only Sc; var of eModEng *vampey*]

wanrest &c [*'wan-] *n* **1** unrest, a state of uneasiness or trouble *la16-, now Sh.* **2** the pendulum of a clock *17-e19.*

~**fu** *la18-e20,* ~**ie** *20-, now Sh* restless, unsettled. [only Sc; WAN- + Eng *rest*]

wanrufe [*'wan'røv] *n* disquiet, unrest *la15.* [only Sc; WAN- + *rufe,* var of obs Eng *ro* rest, peace]

wanshapen [*'wan-] *adj* misshapen, deformed *la16.* [WAN- + obs Eng *shapen*]

wanskoth *see* WAINSCOT

wansonsy &c [*'wan-] *adj, literary* mischievous, unpleasant, treacherous *17-19.* [only Sc; WAN- + *sonsie* 1 (SONSE); *cf* UNSONSIE]

want &c; wint *la19-, Bnf Abd Kcdn,* **wunt** *la19-, Abd* [want; *Nai-Buchan* wʌnt; *Bnf Abd Kcdn* wɪnt; *EC, S* want] *vti* **1** = want *la15-.* **2** *vi* be lacking or deficient *la14-e20.* **3** lack the basic necessities of life *la18-, now Sh Cai Ags Ayr.* **4** *vt* lack, be without, be free from *la14-.* **5** *freq with negative* unable to do or go without, unable to spare *la16-, now Sh-Per.* **6** *with omission of verb of motion* wish to go or come (in, home etc) *19-: 'the dog wants out'.*

n **1** = want *la15-.* **2** a defect, a missing or defective part of something; *specif* (1) *mining* a NIP (*n* 3), *la19-, now Fif;* (2) *fishing* a defective or damaged part of a net or line *la19-, now Kcdn Bwk.*

wanter &c an unmarried man or woman, a widow(er) *18-, now Ork.* **wantin 1** not having, without *18-.* **2** simple, mentally defective *20-.* **dae wantin** do without *la19-e20.*

hae a want *19-,* **want a feather in the wing, want a bit** *etc, 19-e20* be simple, be mentally defective.

wanthrift &c ['wan-] *n* **1** extravagance, lack of thrift *e16, 19-, now Sh.* **2** a thriftless person *16.* [only Sc; WAN- + Eng *thrift*]

wanthrifty [*'wan-] *adj* = WANTHRIVEN *la16, la19.*

wanthriven &c [*'wan-] *adj* stunted, in a state of decline, weakly *16, 19-, now Sh.* [only Sc; WAN- + Eng *thriven; cf* UNTHRIVE]

wanton &c [*'wantən] *adj* **1** = wanton *15-.* **2** insolent in triumph or prosperity *e16.* **3** jovial, jolly, waggish, free from care *la16.*

wanweird *la16-e17, 19;* **wanwerd &c** *16* [*'wan'wird] *n, chf literary* an unhappy fate. [only Sc; WAN- + WEIRD]

wanwit &c [*'wan-] *n* foolishness, lack of wit *15-e16.*

wanwitty foolish, stupid *e16.* [chf Sc; WAN- + Eng *wit*]

wanwordy &c [*'wan'wʌrdɪ] *adj, latterly literary* unworthy, worthless *la16, la18-e20.* [only Sc; WAN- + *wordy,* var of WORTH[1]; *cf* next]

wanworth &c [*'wan'wʌrθ] *n* **1** a very low price for an article, a bargain *19-e20.* **2** (1) a thing of little value, something worthless *20-, now Sh.* (2) a worthless person, a good-for-nothing *19-, now Sh.*

adj unworthy, worthless *19-e20.*

at *or* **for a** ~ at a bargain price, excessively cheaply *18-, now Sh.* [only Sc; WAN- + WORTH[1]; *cf* UNWORTH]

wap[1] &c; whap &c *19-e20,* **waup &c** *e20* [wap, wɑp, hwap, hwɑp] *v* **1** *vt, also fig* throw violently, thrust, fling *la14-, now Sh Ork NE Ags.* **2** cast (a fishing-line); fish (a river) *la19-, now Dnbt.* **3** (1) flap, wave, shake *19-, local Sh-WC.* (2) *vi* move to and fro, flap, move jerkily *19-, now Sh N Per.* **4** *vt* strike, thrash, hit *19-, now Ork.*

n **1** a blow, a thump *la16, 19-, now Ork NE.* **2** a sweeping or swinging movement, a flap, wave, shake *la18-, now Sh NE.* **3** a puff or gust of wind *19-, now Sh Abd.* **4** a disturbance, brawl, din, quarrel *19-, now NE Per Dmf.*

wapper something exceptionally large or fine of its kind, a whopper *19-e20.* **wappin(g) &c** large, whopping *18-e20.* [ME]

wap[2], wep *la14;* **wop &c** *la19-e20* [wap, wɑp] *vt* **1** wrap, fold, envelop *la14-e20.* **2** bind, tie, join, *esp* by splicing; whip with cord *18-, now Ork.*

n **1** a tie, a splicing or joining by means of a cord or twine tied round, a turn of string etc round something *19.* **2** a bundle of hay or straw *19-20.* [eModEng; *cf* WUP[1]]

wap *see* WASP

wapinschaw *see* WAPPENSHAW

wappen &c *la14-e20;* **wapon &c** *la14-, now Sh* ['wapn; *'wɑp-, *'wep-, *'wip-] *n* = weapon. [OED *weapon*]

wappenshaw &c; weaponshaw &c *la16, 18-e20* ['wapn'ʃa; *'wepn-; literary 'wɛpn-] *n* **1** a periodical muster or review of the men under arms in a particular lordship or district *16-, now hist.* **2** *chf* **wapinschaw** a rifle-shooting competition organized by volunteers, private rifle clubs etc *la19-, now Bnf.*

~**ing** = *n* 1, *15-, now hist.* [only Sc; WAPPEN + SHAW[1]. OED *wappens(c)haw*]

waps *see* WASP

war [*war] *n* = warre, a knot in timber *e16.* [OED *warre*]

war *see* BE, WARE[2], WAUR, WEAR, WEIR[1]

warander &c [*'warn(d)ər] *n* = warrener, a person in charge of a rabbit-warren *la15-16.* [OED *warrener*]

warba [*Cai* 'warbu; *Nai Mry Bnf* *'warbə] *n, freq* ~ **blade** waybread, the greater plantain *19-, now Cai.* [*cf* Eng *waybread* and WAYBURN LEAF]

warback *see* WARBLE[2]

warble¹ &c ['warbl; *'wɛrbl] *n, also* **wrable** *e16, only Sc,* **wrible** *e16, only Sc* = warble *16-.*
vti = warble, sing with trills etc.
warbler *piping* a group of grace notes, amounting to five or more *19-e20.* [OED *warble* (*n¹*), *wrable, wrible*]
warble² &c ['warbl; *'wʌrbl] *n* a warble, an abscess on the backs of cattle, deer etc *la16, 19-, now Sh-Cai Per.*

warback &c ['war'bak, 'warbɪ; *Ork* 'warbu] the warble- or gadfly, any of the flies of the family *Oestridae* which breed under the skin of cattle etc *19-, now Cai Per.* [*cf* Eng = a small lump on a horse's back]
warble *see* WURBLE
warcodling *see* WARE¹
ward &c; waird &c *16-e19* [ward; *werd] *n* **1** = ward *la14-.* **2** an appointed station or post (for a body of soldiers) *la14.* **3** custody, imprisonment; jail *la15-19, latterly literary.* **4** a (formerly administrative) division of a shire *15, 18-, now chf hist.* **5** a part or division of a forest *15-e16, only Sc.* **6** an enclosed piece of land, *chf* for pasture *la15-19, now in place-names.* **7** *law* the oldest form of feudal land tenure, *ie* by military service, with various rights and obligations, *esp* that of the SUPERIOR to uphold and draw the rents of the lands of a deceased VASSAL while the heir was not INFEFT or was a minor, as recompense for the loss of military services during this period *16-18.*
vt **1** = ward *la15-.* **2** keep (a person) in custody, imprison, confine *la15-, chf Sc, now hist.*
wardater &c [*'wardətər] *law* the person given by the original SUPERIOR the enjoyment of lands held in WARD (*n* 7) while the heir was a minor *16-18, only Sc.* **warded** detained in WARD (*n* 3), imprisoned *e17, only Sc.* **warding** imprisonment *la15-e20, latterly hist.* **warding place** a jail, prison *la16-18.* **act** *etc* **of warding** *law* a warrant for imprisonment for debt issued by magistrates in a *royal burgh* (ROYAL) *18.*
watching and ~ing one of the duties of a burgess in a *royal burgh, namely* taking one's turn to patrol the streets and help suppress disturbances *la16-18.*
~ dyke a wall enclosing grazing land *la16-e17.*
ward guard &c a protective covering or receptacle for clothes *la16, only Sc.* **ward-holding** *law* the tenure of land by WARD *n* 7, *la17-e18, only Sc.* **~ house** a guard-house for prisoners *la16-e17, only Sc.* **ward lands** lands held in WARD (*n* 7) *16-19, latterly hist.* **ward vassal** *law* a VASSAL who holds his land in WARD (*n* 7) *la17-e18, only Sc.*
hold ward *law, of a vassal* hold lands by WARD (*n* 7); *of lands* be held under WARD (*n* 7) *16-18.* **simple ward** *law* = *n* 7, *18*; cf *taxed ward* (TAX). **ward and warsel** ['warsl] security, pledge *17-e19, Abd.*
ward *see* BE, WARE³
wardatar *see* WARD

wardle *see* WARLD
wardon &c [*wɛr'dun, *war'dun] *n* a reward, a recompense *la14.* [only *Sc;* OF *werdon,* dial var of *guerredon; cf* Eng *guerdon*]
ware¹ &c; waar &c *19-e20,* **waur** *20* [wer; *Sh* war; *Cai Abd also* wɑr] *n* **1** a kind of seaweed, *chf* for use as manure *la15-, now Sh Ork EC, WC.* **2** *law* the right of gathering seaweed *la15-e17.*
vti manure with seaweed *18-20.*
wary &c covered with, living among or generally pertaining to seaweed *19-, now Sh Abd.*
warry codlin &c a young inshore cod *20-, Sh NE.*
ware barley *la18-e19,* **ware bear** *la18-e20, Abd* barley manured with seaweed.
warcodling = *warry codlin, e16.* **ware goose** the brent goose *la19-e20.* [OE *war*]
ware² &c *la14, la18-;* **war &c** *la14-18,* **waur &c** *19-20* [wer; *war] adj* **1** = ware, alert, cunning *la14-e17.* **2** aware, conscious, cautious of *la14, la16-, now Sh Ork.*
v **1** *vi* = ware *e16.* **2** *vt* be apprehensive or careful for *e15.*
wary &c beware, be on one's guard *la15, 18-19.*
ware³ &c; waur *la19-20* [wer; *Sh-nEC also* war] *v, pt also* **ward** *la15, 18-e20* **1** *vti* spend, lay out, dispose of (money, goods etc) *la14-, now local Abd-Stlg.* **2** *vt* (1) spend, employ, waste (one's time, life, efforts etc) *la15-e20.* (2) *specif* expend or waste (words) *19-20.*
ill &c ~ed ill-spent, wasted, out of place *16-, now Sh NE Fif.* **well ~ed** well-spent or bestowed, well deserved, worthwhile *la16-, now Sh NE Stlg.* **weel ~ed on** *etc him etc* it served him etc right *la19-e20.*
~ out spend, lay out (money) *16-e19.* [ME]
ware⁴ &c [wer; *war] *n* **1** = ware, goods *la14-.* **2** money, cash *la18-19.*
~ almery *la15,* **~sta &c** *16, only Sc* a cupboard for storing goods.
ware⁵ &c [*wer, *war] *n* spring, springtime *la14-19.*
~ day the first day of spring *la19-e20.* **~ quarter** the season of spring, the months of February to April *18-19.* **~ time** spring *19.* [ON *vár*]
ware *see* BE, WEAR
wargeld *see* WERGELT
wark¹ &c (*chf n*), **wirk &c** (*chf v*), **work** *16-;* **werk** *la14-e20* (*chf n*), **wurk** *la16* (*chf n*), *19-* [*n* wark, wark; *Cai-Mry Uls also* wɪrk; *EC, S also* wɑrk; *wɛrk; v wʌrk; Sh-Kcdn* wɪrk; *Sh Uls also* wark; *Uls also* wɪrk] *n* **1** = work *la14-.* **2** a building, *esp* a public or imposing one *la14, 18-, now hist.* **3** a building operation *la14-e15.* **4** a business, fuss; goings-on; trouble, outcry *la16-, now Sh-WC Dmf.* **5** a religious revival; *specif* the evangelical campaign at Cambuslang in 1742, *18-19.*
v, pt also **wrocht &c, wrought &c** *la14, 18-19,* **wraucht** *e15, e20. ptp also* **wrocht** now *Ags,*

wrought &c *la14, 17-e20* [(w)roxt] **1** *vti* = work *la14-*. **2** *vt* look after, herd (animals) *20-*, *now Ags Per midLoth*. **3** purge, act as a laxative on *20-*, *now local Sh-Per*. **4** affect physically or mentally, *esp* for the worse; trouble, annoy *la18-*. **5** sprain *19-*, *now Abd*. **6** *vi*, ~ **(up)on** operate on, have an influence on, affect *la14-*. **7** act in a specified way *la14, 19-*, *now Abd*.

warklike industrious *la19-*, *now Sh*.

~**lume &c 1** *chf in pl* tools, implements, instruments *la15-*, *now Sh*. **2** the penis; *in pl* the male genitals *18*. ~**man 1** = workman *la14-*. **2** a porter *la16-18*.

hae, haud *or* **mak a wark about** *etc* make a great fuss over, make a song-and-dance about *la18-*, *now Sh-Per*. **like a day's wark** with great vigour, for all one is worth *la19-*, *N nEC, SW*. ~ **for** deserve, earn (punishment or retribution) *la19-*, *now local Sh-Per*. **wirk one's** *etc* **wark** do (one's) work, perform what one etc is employed to do *18-*, *now Sh Ork NE*. **wirk wi** employ, use *la19-*, *local Sh-Per*.

wark²; werk [*wark, *wɛrk] *vi* ache, throb *la15-16*. [ME, ultimately f as WARK¹]

warld &c *only Sc*, **world** *la16-*; **wardle &c** *16-20, only Sc*, **wordle &c** *la16-e20*, **warle &c** *la18-*, *now NE, only Sc*, **worl &c** *la19-*, *now Uls* [warl(d), wɑrl(d); *N also* 'wardl, 'wardl, 'wordl; *C also* wɑrl(d); *C, S also* world, worlt; *Uls also* worl; *Fif also* *warlt*] *n* **1** = world *la14-*. **2** *in pl* things in general, one's circumstances *19-e20, Bnf Abd*. **3** worldly wealth, riches *la19-20, local Sh-Abd*.

~**like** normal in appearance, like everyone else *19-20*. **weel** *or* **wise and** ~**-like** *or* ~**(-like)** **and wise-like** *chf of a new-born baby* normal physically and mentally *19-*, *now local*. ~**lin &c** a worldling; a mean, grasping person *17-*, *now Abd*. ~**ly &c 1** = worldly *la15-*. **2** greedy *la18-e20*.

warld's gear worldly goods *la18-19*. **world wide** as wide as the world *e17*. ~**'s wonder &c** a person whose conduct is notorious and surprising *18-*, *now Ork NE nEC*. **warldis wrack 1** *contemptuous* worldly goods, gear, pelf *la15-16*. **2** the troubles and hardships of life *la18*.

like the ~ like everyone else, normal *la18-e20*.

warlock &c *la16-*; **warlo &c** *la14-e18, only Sc*, **warloch &c** *16* ['warlok, 'warlǝk; *'warlʌu, *'warlo] *n* **1** = warlock, a wicked person *la14-16*. **2** a savage or monstrous creature *la16*. **3** (1) a man thought to be in league with the powers of darkness and to have supernatural knowledge and means of bewitching and harming others, the male equivalent of a witch; *occas* used of women *la16-*. (2) a wizard, magician *18-*. **4** *term of abuse* an old, ugly or misanthropic man; a mischievous or troublesome man *la16,19-e20*.

adj bewitched, magical, supernatural; malevolent, mischievous *la16-e20*. [for *-ock* forms *cf* ELBUCK, WINNOCK]

warm &c [warm] *adj*, *n* = warm *la15-*. *vti* **1** = warm *la16-*. **2** *vt* beat, thrash, hit *19-*. ~**er** *of a person, used in admiration or disapproval* an extreme example of his or her kind, 'a right one' *20-, C, S*. ~**ly** *adj* full of warmth *e17*. ~**-hearted** generous and affectionate *16-*.

warn¹ &c; wairn &c *la16-e20* [warn, wern] *vt* **1** = warn, give advance notice to *la14-*. **2** (1) summon *la16, 19-*, *now Ork Cai*. (2) *specif* invite, as to a funeral *la19*. **3** *of a clock, chf* ~ **(for) nine, ten** *etc* make a clicking or whirring noise before striking *19-*, *now Ork Abd Per*; *cf* WARNISH *v* 2.

~**ing &c 1** = warning *la14-*. **2** a premonition, a portent *la19-*, *now Sh Ork Cai Ags*. **mak warning** warn *la14, only Sc*.

warn² &c [*warn, *wern] *vt* **1** = warn, refuse *la14-15*. **2** stop the way of, oppose (someone) *la14*.

~**er** ? a miser *e16, only Sc*.

warnish &c; warnice *la19* ['warnɪs, 'warnɪʃ] *v* **1** *vt* warn, caution, advise *la19-e20*. **2** *vti, of a clock* = WARN¹ *v* 3, *la19*.

warnisin warning *19-*, *now Kcdn Ags*. ~**ment &c** advice *19-*, *now Kcdn Ags*. [ME *warnis-*; OF *warniss-*, stem of *warnir* warn]

warp &c; werp *16-19*, **worp** *la16, e20* [warp; *C, S also* werp; *wɛrp] *v* **1** *vt* = warp, arrange threads in a warp; surround, twist *16-*. **2** cast, throw, fling *la14-e16*. **3** thrust one's hand **forth**, strike *la14*. **4** utter, pronounce (a word, speech etc); talk, speak **of** *15-e16*. **5** fling open (a gate etc) *e16*. **6** run (a ship) aground, *esp* on a sandbank *e16*. **7** ? swing round, whirl *e16*. **8** *vi, of a door* open **wide** etc *e16*. **9** *vt* plunge (a person) suddenly or roughly **into** (distress etc) *la16*. **10** *vi* move in an oblique direction; move to and fro, swing round *19*. **11** weave, contrive, devise *la17*. **12** *vti* (1) weave; plait; knit, cast **on** (stitches) *la18-e20*. (2) interlace the cross or horizontal ropes in the thatching of a cornstack *la20-, Per Fif Loth*.

n = warp *15-*.

warping &c 1 = warping, the preparation of a warp for weaving. **2** (1) = warping, something twisted or distorted. (2) *carpentry* a strut or struts, a brace or angle-piece *e16, 19-e20*. ~**ing ale** *or* **dinner** a drink of ale or some food given to the weaver after setting up a warp of homespun wool *la17-e18*. **warping fatt** a tub or trough in which the clews of yarn are laid for warping *la16-e18*. **warpin staik** one of the set of wooden uprights round which the yarn is wound in warping *17-e18*. **warple &c** ['warpl] *only Sc* **1** *vt* intertwine, twist, entangle; *fig* confuse *la18-, NE, local C*. **2** *vi* wrestle, tumble, wriggle *la18-e20*. **3** stagger, go in a zigzag course; *fig* struggle through *la19-e20*.

warpiss [*'warpɪs] *vt* cast or throw off, put aside *la14-e15*. [only Sc; OF *werpiss-*, stem of *werpir* quit, abandon]

warrand &c *la14-e19*, **warrant &c** *17-*; **warran &c** *la15-*, *now NE*, **werrand** *la15*, **waurn &c** *19-e20*, **quarrente** *17* ['war(ə)n(d), 'war(ə)nt] *n* **1** = warrant *la14-*. **2** a protector, defender *la14-e19*. **3** security or safety from one's enemies; a place of refuge *la14-16*. **4** a guarantor; surety, bail *la15-e17*, *only Sc*.
vt **1** = warrant *la14-*. **2** vouch for the truth of (an opinion) *la14*. **3** be surety for (someone) *la15-e17*.
warranty &c 1 = warranty. **2** *now chf with regard to the sale of livestock* a guarantee, assurance *19-*, *local Ork-Dmf*.
I'se warran &c I'll bet, I'll be bound *la18-*, *now local Sh-WC*.

warrandice &c *la15-*; **warrandise &c** *la14-e16*, *la18-19*, **werrandis** *la14-15* ['warəndɪs] *n* **1** a guarantee, an undertaking to protect another *la14-e20*. **2** *law* the undertaking by a granter or seller to indemnify a grantee or buyer of *esp* HERITABLE property threatened with eviction through defect of title *la14-*. **3** authorization, authority, warrant *in gen*; a document conferring such *19*. [chf Sc; *cf* Eng *warrantise*; AF *warandise*, var of OF *warentise*, f northern OF *warantir* (*v*) warrant, guarantee]

warrant *see* WARRAND

warren &c [*'warən] *adj* ~ **tre** a hard oak *e16*. [only Sc; perh f obs Eng *warre* a knot in wood]

warridrag *see* WALLYDRAG

warrior &c *18-*; **werriour &c** *la14-e16* [*'wɛrɪər; St 'wɔrɪər] *n* **1** = warrior *la14-*. **2** *freq* **a great** ~ joc or affectionate term for a lively, spirited person, *freq* a child *18-*. **3** *in pl* **the W~s** nickname for various football teams, *specif* Stenhousemuir and *occas* Third Lanark (*cf* HI HI) and Dumbarton (cf *Sons of the Rock* (SIN[1])) *la20-*.

warroch &c ['warəx] *n* **1** a knotty stick; a knot in wood *e19*. **2** a stunted, feeble, ill-grown person or plant *19*. **3** *chf* **a weary** ~ a good-for-nothing, ne'er-do-well *19-e20*. [only Sc; WAR + *-och*. OED *warre*]

warry codlin *see* WARE[1]

warse &c, worse &c; wers *e16* [wars, wʌrs; *'wɛrs] *adj, n, adv, chf literary, superlative also* **warst &c** *18-*, **werst** *la14-16* [warst; *'wɛrst; *midLoth* *warst] = worse *la14-*.
vt, only **warst** = worst.
worsing deterioration *la16, only Sc*.
the worse of drink the worse for drink, having drunk too much alcohol *18-, local*. [*cf* WAUR]

warset &c, wersslete *e15* *n* a hunting dog, a hound *13-e15*. [altered f ME *bercelet &c*]

warsh *see* WERSH

warsle &c *16-*, **worsle &c** *16-e17*, **wrestle; wrastle &c** *now Sh*, **wirstle &c** *15-19*,

werstle &c *15-16*, *e19* ['warsl, '(w)rasl; *'wɛrs(t)l, *'wɪrs(t)l, *'wʌrsl] *v* **1** *vi* = wrestle *15-*. **2** wrestle in prayer, pray earnestly *19-e20*. **3** *vt* drive or force (someone) **out of** (something) as by wrestling *17-19*. **4** wrestle with, engage in a bout with, overcome *la18-*, *now local Sh-WC*. **5** get by striving, achieve (an end) by great effort *la18-*, *now NE, WC*. **6** *vi* labour, try hard, exert oneself physically and mentally *19-, local Sh-WC*. **7** (1) move in a struggling, laborious way, wriggle, sprawl about, as in an effort to rise or free oneself *la18-*. (2) make one's way through life with much toil and difficulty, scrape along *19-, now local*.
n **1** a wrestling match, a physical tussle; a struggle, effort *19-, now local Sh-Per*. **2** a mental or moral struggle, a fight against circumstances or hardship *la18-, now local Sh-Per*.
warslin &c struggling; energetic, hardworking *la19-e20*.

warsle *or* **get warsled through** scrape through, get by *la19-, local*.

warst *see* WARSE

wart *see* WRITE

warth *see* WORTH[1], WRAITH[1]

warwolf &c *15-17*; **warwoof &c, werwoif** *16, pl* **-woolfes** *16*, **-woophs** *17* [*'wɛr'wʌlf, *'-wuf, *'war-] *n* = werewolf. [OED *werewolf*]

wary &c [*?'wɛrɪ, *?'wɪrɪ, *?'warɪ] *vti* **1** = wary, curse *la14-e17*. **2** *vt, of God, the Church etc* pronounce a formal curse against *la14-16*.
weriour = warier, a person who curses *e16*.

wary *see* WARE[1], WARE[2]

warydraggel *see* WALLYDRAG

warʒeld [*'war'jild] *n* a requital, recompense *la14*. [only Sc; uncertain. OED *waryeld*]

was *see* BE

wase &c *19-*; **wease &c** *17-20* [wez, wiz; *Sh Ork Cai also* waz] *n* **1** a bundle of straw, *esp* for thatching *la18-, now Kcdn*. **2** a circular band of straw (1) worn to relieve the pressure when carrying heavy burdens on the head *19-, now Kcdn*; (2) used to protect the hands, *eg* when knocking the husks from the ears of barley *19-e20*. **3** a bundle of twigs, straw etc placed against a cottage door as a windbreak or draught-excluder *19-e20*. **4** a bushy, unkempt shock of hair, whiskers etc *20-, now Sh*.
wassock &c ['wazok, -ək, 'wʌz-] = *n*, *19-, now Abd*. **weasie** an ox-collar *17*. [nME = a bundle of straw used as a torch; *cf* MDu *wase*, NFrisian *waas* a horse-collar pad]

wash &c *16-*; **wesh &c** *la14-e20*, **wish &c** *la15, la19-20*, **wass** *16* [waʃ; *Sh* wɪʃ; *SW, S* wɛʃ] *v, pt* **wecht** *15*, **woucht** *e16*, **woushe** *la16*, **woosh** *18-20*, **wuish &c** *18-*, *now wLoth*, **weesh &c** *18-, now NE*, **washt** *20-* [wøʃ, wɪʃ, wʌʃ; *N* wiʃ; *EC also* wuʃ; waʃt]. *ptp* **weshin &c** *e15*, *e20*, **wechst &c** *16*, **weschin &c** *16*, *e20*, **washen &c** *e15, la17-, now NE*, **wuishen &c** *19-, now Fif*, **weeshen &c** *la19-e20*, **wishen**

&c *e15, la19-e20*, **washt** *20-* ['waʃn, 'wøʃn; *sEC, S, SW also* 'wɛʃn; *Sh C also* 'wɪʃn; waʃt] *vti* **1** = wash *la15-*. **2** *vt, chf* ~ **down** *or* **off** cut to a slope or bevel *19-, now WC*.

n **1** = wash. **2** urine, *esp* when stale and used as a cleansing agent *la15-, now EC Lnk S*. **3** a bevelled edge or slope on a board, stone etc *la20, Abd Fif*.

~**er &c 1** = washer *16-*. **2** a person who scrubs and cleans fish after gutting, in preparation for curing *19-, Sh NE*. **washer-wife 1** a washer-woman, laundress *18-, local Ork-Ayr*. **2** a water-spider *20-, Mry Abd Ags Lnk*. ~**ing &c** = washing *la14-*. ~**ing board** skirting-board *la18-19*. **washing boyne &c** a (portable) wash-tub *19-e20*. **washing house** a wash-house *18-*.

wash bine &c = *washing boyne, la19-, now WC*. ~ **board** = *washing board, 19-, NE Fif SW*.

wash an apron celebrate the arrival of a new apprentice or an apprentice becoming a journeyman with an initiation ceremony which included the washing of his apron and a drinking party *18-e20*. **wash its face** *of a commercial enterprise* pay its way, break even *la20-*.

wasie &c [*?'wezɪ] *adj* wise, clever, quick-witted *19, Bnf Ags*. [only Sc; obscure]

waslage *see* VASSAL

wasna *see* BE

wasp &c; waps *20-*, **wap** *20, child's word* [wasp, wɔps] *n* **1** = wasp *la14-*. **2** *in pl* **the Wasps** nickname for Alloa Athletic football team *20* [from their yellow-and-black-striped jerseys].

~ **bike** a wasps' nest *19-, now local NE-WC*.

wasp *see* WISP

wasper *see* WAWSPER

wass *see* WASH

wassand *see* WIZZEN

wassock *see* WASE

wast &c *la15-*, **west &c** [wast] *adv* = west; *also less specifically directional* away from the speaker or the person addressed *la15-; cf* EAST *adv* 2. *adj* = west *la14-*. *n* = west *la15-*. *prep* above, along, across, over, to the west, on the west side of *la16-, now NE nEC*. *vi, of the wind* veer or back to the west *la19-, now Ork Stlg Loth*.

~**en &c** western *e16, la20-, now Sh*. ~**er** lying towards the west, western, *freq* contrasted with *easter* (EAST) *la14-, freq in place-names, chf Sc*. **westermar &c** farther west *la15, only Sc*. **the Western Isles** *see* ILE. ~**ert** = westward *18-, now NE*. **Wastie** familiar contraction of a farm name containing WAST or *waster*, applied to the tenant or owner *la19-, NE; cf Eastie* (EAST). **westie** = *West Highland* 2, *la20-*. ~**le** westward, to the west *19-e20*. ~**lin** western, from

or in the west, westerly *18-e20*. ~**lins** westward, to or in the west *18-, now Sh*. ~**most** westernmost, most westerly *la15-, now local Sh-Per, chf Sc*.

~**-by** westward, in a westerly direction *la18-, now Ags Per*. ~**-ender** an inhabitant of the west end of Hawick *20-, Rox*. **West Highland** *adj* originating in the west *Highlands* (HIE-LAND), *specif as noun* **1** a hardy breed of beef cattle *la18-e20*. **2** a small white rough-haired breed of terrier *20-*. ~ **land** *n* the west (*freq Highlands*) of Scotland *la15-16, 19*. *adj* coming or situated in the west of Scotland, western; *of the wind* westerly, blowing from the west *la15-, now Stlg Fif Ayr*. **westlander** an inhabitant of the west of Scotland *la17-e19*.

~ **about** *la16, la19*, ~ **awa** *19-, now Stlg Lnk* in or to the west. ~ **ower** (**bye**) westwards, to or in the west *19-, now Sh Kcdn*.

wast *see* WAE[1], WASTE

wastcoat *see* WESKIT

waste &c; wast *la14-18*, **waist** *15-e20*, **west** *la16, la18*, **wyste** *la19-20* [west; *NE Ags* wəist] *n* = waste *la14-*. *vti* **1** = waste *la14-*. **2** *vt* spoil by ill-usage or misuse *20-, now Cai nEC Gsw*. **3** spoil, pamper (a child, pet etc) *20-, C*. *adj* **1** = waste *la14-*. **2** void, destitute **of** *15-16, only Sc*. **3** *of buildings* ruined; unoccupied, empty *la14, 18-e19*. *adv* in vain, to no purpose *la16*. **wastage &c 1** = wastage. **2** a piece of waste ground; a ruin *la17-19*. **waster** *n* **1** = waster *la14-*. **2** an idler, a squanderer, good-for-nothing *la16*. **3** something on the wick of a candle causing it to gutter *la18-, now Ags wLoth*. **4** a person, animal or object of no further use, due to decrepitude, disease etc *la19-, local*. *adj* idle, wasteful, good-for-nothing *la16-e18*. **wasterful &c** *NE-SW*, **wastrife &c** ['~rɪf] *now NE-S, adj* wasteful, extravagant *19-*. **wastry &c** *n* **1** reckless extravagance, *esp* in living; wastefulness *la16-19*. **2** a waste **of** *19*. *adj* = *wasterful, la18-, now Rox*. **wasty** desolate, uninhabited *la14-16*. **wasty wanes &c** a stripped or emptied house *15-e16*.

waste one's wind waste one's breath, argue or plead in vain *19-, now NE*.

wastel &c ['wasl] *n* a kind of bread, SCONE or cake baked with the finest flour; a large SCONE made of oatmeal and wholemeal flour *la14-15, 18-, now Mry*. [ME]

waster &c [*'wastər] *n* a fishing spear with several prongs *19-e20*.

~**ing** the action of taking a fish with a WASTER *la16-e17, la19*. [only Sc; conflation of WAW-SPER and LEISTER. OED *wastering*]

wastrife, wastry *see* WASTE

wat &c *la14-e20*; **wate &c** *la14-e19*, **wite &c** *la19-, NE Ags* [wat; *NE Ags* wəit; *wet] *vti* = wot, know *la14-, now NE Ags*.

I ~ *19-, NE Ags*, **I** ~ **ye** *la19-, now Abd*, **weel**

&c I *or* **a** ~ *18-e20* indeed, I must say, I can tell you: '*well I wat that's true*'. [*cf* WEET² and WIT. OED *wot*]

wat *see* WAIT¹, WALT¹, WATCH, WEET¹

watch &c *la15-*; **wach &c** *la14-16 n, also* **wat** *la16* [watʃ] **1** = watch *la14-*. **2** a spy, look-out man *la14-15*.

vti, also **wauch** *la14* [*?*watʃ] **1** = watch *la14-*. **2** *vi* be on the look out *la14-*. **3** fulfil the duty of a watchman, sentinel or guard *la14-15*. **4** *vr* (1) ~ **one with** guard oneself against *la14*. (2) look after oneself, be on one's guard, watch out *la19-*.

~**ie** a watchmaker *la18-, now NE Ags*.

~ **knowe** a hill high enough to serve as a look-out station *17-e20, S, freq in place-names*.

wate *see* WAT, WYTE

water &c; watter &c *now local,* **walter** *16, e19,* **wait(t)er &c** *la18-, now sEC, S,* **wa'er** *la19-* ['watǝr, 'watǝr; *sEC, S* 'wetǝr, ***'wɛtǝr] *n* **1** = water *la14-*. **2** a stream, a river, *latterly usu* a small one *la14-, freq in river names, as* **A** ~ *or* ~ **of A**. **3** a river valley, the area and its inhabitants bordering a river *19-, now S*. **4** *in pl* the seas and oceans belonging to a particular nation or in a specified area of the globe *la17*. **5** dropsy; a disease of sheep *la19-e20*.

vti **1** = water *16-*. **2** *vt* produce a wavy lustrous finish on (silk etc) by moistening and pressing *la15*. **3** cover (one metal) **with** a film of another metal in a thin solution, wash *17-e18*.

watered &c 1 = watered. **2** soaked or steeped in water *la17*. **3** *of a coal-mine* subject to flooding *la19-20*. ~**ing &c 1** = watering. **2** *law* the right to take water from one piece of land for use on another *la17*. **3** *now chf in pl* a trough, pool in a stream etc where farm animals go to drink *la18-, now Ork Abd*. **4** the annual playing of *handball* (HAND) in the rivers Jed, Ale or Teviot *e20, Rox*. **watering bridle** a bridle with a snaffle-bit, *chf* used when taking a horse to be watered *e16*. **watering stone &c** a stone horse-trough *la18-e20*. ~**y &c** *n* **1** the pied wagtail *la19-, Bnf Abd Ags*. **2** a W.C. *20-, local Ork-Fif*. ~**y-nebbit &c** pale and sickly; starved looking; having a drip at the end of one's nose *la19-, Bnf Abd Ags*. ~**y pox** chicken-pox *la19-20, Ags Fif*. ~**y wagtail** = *watery* 1; the yellow wagtail *la19-20*.

~ **bailie 1** a water-bailiff employed to prevent poaching in rivers *la15, la19-, now N*. **2** a magistrate of Leith and Edinburgh and of Glasgow who had local jurisdiction over maritime cases in the Forth and Clyde respectively *la16-e20, latterly hist*. **3** one of the water-bug family, *esp* the water-strider *20-, Mry Abd*. **water bailliery** the jurisdiction of a *water bailie* 2, *la16, only Sc*. **water barge &c** a stone or wooden ledge on the edge of a roof etc for protection from rain *la16-18*. **water blackbird &c** *la19-, now Bwk,* **water bobbie &c** *la19-, now*

Kcdn Ags Per the dipper. **water brash** heartburn *19-*. **water brae &c** a slope beside a river *e17*. **water break** a sudden rush of water, a flood *e16*. **water broo &c** *19-, now Fif Loth,* **water brose** *la18-, now N* oatmeal mixed with boiling water. **water burn** a name for the phosphorescence seen on the sea *19-, now Mry Kcdn*. **water clearer** one of the small insects that skim over the surface of water and in doing so are said to clean it *la20-, local Ags-Lnk*. **water cock(ie)** = *water blackbird, 19-, now Mry*. ~ **corn &c** the grain paid by tenant-farmers for the upkeep of the dams and races of the estate mill *17-e19*. **water court** a court dealing with issues relating to a particular river or canal *la15*. **water cow &c** *Celtic folklore* a mythical amphibious beast supposed to live in lakes *la18-e19*. **water craw** = *water blackbird, la18-, now nEC Edb Lnk*. **water dog 1** = water dog *16-*. **2** the water-rat or water-vole *la18-, now Bnf*. **water dyke &c** a flood wall or embankment *e13, e20*. ~ **fall &c 1** = waterfall. **2** a slope of the ground sufficient to enable the fall or drainage of water *16-e17*. ~ **fast** watertight *16, only Sc*. **water firlot** a larger FIRLOT used for goods sold on board ship *la17; cf water met*. **water fit &c** the mouth of a river *18-, now in place-names*. **water-fur** *n* a drainage furrow to carry off surface water *la18-, now Ork Stlg Loth*. *vt* provide (land) with drainage furrows *18-19*. ~ **gang 1** a watercourse, channel, *esp* an artificial one *15-19*. **2** *law* the right of conveying water through a piece of SERVIENT ground for use on the adjoining dominant ground *la17; cf* DOMINANT TENEMENT. ~ **gate &c 1** = n 3, *la19-, S*. **2** a road and its branches which serve a valley *18-e20, S*. **3** a fence or grating suspended over a stream to prevent animals from straying or floating rubbish from entering a *mill-lade* (MILL) *20-, now Inv C*. **watergaw** an imperfect or fragmentary rainbow *la19-, now Sh nEC Gall*. ~ **glass** a glass container for water *e17*. **water heid &c** the source of a river, the upper end of a valley *20-, now local Ags-S*. **water hole 1** a hole or pit in which water collects, a well or pool *la18-, now Sh N Per*. **2** a detention cell under the old Guard-house in the High Street of Edinburgh, so called because there was always water in it *la18-e19*. **water horse** *chf Celtic folklore* a mythical spirit in the form of a horse which frequents lakes and rivers *19-e20*. **water kail &c** BROTH made without meat *la15-16, 19*. ~ **keeping &c** the guarding of a stretch of water against poachers *e15*. **water kelpie** = *water horse, la18-e20*. **water kit** a large wooden bucket narrower at the top than the bottom with a fixed cross-piece of wood as a handle *19-, now Sh*. ~ **kyle &c** meadow land possessed by tenants of an estate in annual rotation *la18-e19*. **water lead** = *mill lade* (MILL) *e17*. **water lip** the brink of a stream *19-, Ayr*.

~ **mail &c 1** a rent charged for fishing a stretch of water *la14-e18*. **2** a kind of fur *la15-e16*. **water mark &c 1** = watermark. **2** a boundary mark indicating the line of separation between the waters of rivers owned by different proprietors *e17, only Sc*. **water meggie** = *water blackbird, 20-, now midLoth Lnk*. ~ **met &c** a larger measure used for goods sold on board ship *16*. **water money** *mining* extra payment for working in wet conditions *20*. **water mouse** = *water dog* 2, *la18-e19*. ~ **mouth &c** the mouth of a river *la16-, now NE Ags Loth, only Sc*. **water neb** = prec, *specif* the confluence of the Cart and the Clyde *19*. **water pig** a container for water, a pitcher *la16, la18-, now Sh Ags*. **water purpie &c** the brooklime *17-e20*. **water pyot &c** = *water blackbird, 19-, now Per Ayr*. **water run &c** a runnel of water, a surface drain or gutter for carrying off water, a streamlet *19*. **water sand** freshwater sand as opposed to sand at the sea *la17*. **water serjant** one of the constables or officers of the court of the *water bailie* (2) in Glasgow *17-e18*. ~ **side &c** the side or brink of water, the bank of a river etc *la14, 18-e20*. ~ **sponge &c** a sponge for washing oneself *la15-e17*. **water stand** a water barrel, *esp* one standing on end *la16*. **water stank** a pond, a pool of water *la15, e18*. ~ **stowp &c** a wooden bucket *17-, now nEC, WC*. **watter strype** a strip of water, a stream *e17*. **water trip** the annual inspection of the waterworks, an occasion for a social outing for the Councillors *20-*. **water water** river water *19-, S*. ~ **wrack &c** weeds, leaves, sticks etc carried down by a river *la17-, now local Abd-S*. **water wraith &c** *folk-lore* a water spirit, a goblin which haunted streams and lakes *la18-19*. **water yett** = *water gate* 3, *la16, 20-, local C, S*. **take one's water off** make a fool of, take a rise out of *la19-, now Per*. **Water of Ayr stone** a kind of stone found on the banks of the Ayr used for making whetstones and in polishing *19-, now WC*.

Waterloo &c ['watər'lu] *marbles* a soft, brittle, clay marble *la20-, Per Stlg wLoth*.

wather *see* WEATHER, WEDDER

watlin *see* WATTLE

Watsonian [*St* wɔt'sonɪən] a pupil or former pupil of George Watson's Boys' or Ladies' Colleges in Edinburgh, which amalgamated 1974-5 to form George Watson's College; a member of the *Watsonian Club*, since 1980 open to former pupils of these schools and of John Watson's School, and to past and present members of staff *la19-*.

Women Watsonians name of the former pupils' club of George Watson's Ladies' College *20*. [f George Watson, whose educational endowment established the boys' school in 1741 and the girls' in 1870]

watt *see* WALT[1]

watter *see* WATER

Wattie &c ['watɪ, 'watɪ] pet form of Walter. **look like** ~ **to the worm** look disgusted or reluctant, look with loathing *la18-e20*.

wattins *n* ? = waddings, padding in clothing *la17*. [only Sc; *cf* F *ouate*]

wattle &c ['watl] *n* **1** a pliant rod, twig or wand *la17-19*. **2** *in pl, thatching* the interwoven twigs on which the turf or thatch was laid; also *orig* used to form the walls of buildings *la16-, now Per*. **3** *fig* a tangle, mix-up, confused mess *20-, Cai*. =
vt = wattle, interlace (twigs etc), *chf* **wat(t)lin &c** twigs etc which have been or can be plaited to form wattle-work *14, 17-19*.

wauble *see* WABBLE

wauch *la18-, now Bnf Abd Ags*; **waugh** *19-, now Abd*, **wauf &c** *19-e20* [wɑx; *S* wɑf] *adj* **1** *of a taste or smell* unpleasant, stale, unappetising *la18-, now Bnf Abd Ags*. **2** *of food, cooking etc* tasteless, unappetising; not nourishing *19-, now Abd Ags*. **3** unwell, faint, weary *19-e20*. **4** good-for-nothing, worthless, feeble *19-e20*. [*chf* Sc; OE *wealh* lukewarm, insipid > Eng *wallow*; *cf* Eng dial *waff*]

wauch *see* WATCH, WAUCHT

wauchie ['wɑxɪ] *adj* swampy, boggy *19-e20*. [presum f WACK, but confusion of form w WAUCH *adj*]

wauchle &c *la18-, now Ork-C Wgt*; **wochle** *la19-, now Sh-C* ['wɑxl] *v* **1** *vi* walk or make one's way laboriously or with difficulty, walk in a clumsy, ungainly way, stumble with fatigue etc *19-, now Sh-C*. **2** plod on amid difficulties, struggle with a situation or task *19-, now NE, C*. **3** *vt* last out (a period of time) in a weary, listless way; make (one's way) with difficulty *la18-, now Ork Ags*. **4** *chf* ~**d &c** perplexed, bewildered, muddle-headed *19-, now Ags*. =
n **1** a struggle, laborious effort *19-, now Sh NE Ags Wgt*. **2** a staggering ungainly movement, a wobble *la19-, now Fif Loth Fif*. [only Sc; prob altered f Eng *waggle*; *cf* SPRAUCHLE, TRAUCHLE]

wauch spear *see* WAWSPER

waucht *e16, 19-, now Fif*, **waught** *17-19*; **wacht &c** *la16, la20*, **wauch** *19* [wɑxt, wɑx] *vti, freq* ~ **out, ower, up** drink deeply, take large draughts (of), drain *16-, now Fif*. =
n **1** a draught of liquid, a swig or gulp of a drink *18-, now NE nEC, WC*. **2** a deep breath of air, a full inhalation *19-, now Abd*. [only Sc; see SND]

waucht *see* WECHT[1]

wauf *see* WAFF[2], WAUCH

wauff *see* WAFF[1]

wauge *see* WAGE

wauger *see* WAGER

waugh *see* WAUCH

waught *see* WAUCHT

wauk &c *18-*, **wake &c**; **walk** *la14-16*, **wak &c** *la14, 18-e19* [wɑk; wek] *v, pt also* **woik &c**

la14-e16, **wouk** &c *la15-e16* [*wøk] **1** *vti* = wake *la14-*. **2** *vi* be or stay awake, be sleepless or have wakened from sleep *la14-*. **3** *vt* (1) guard, watch over (places, livestock etc), *esp* during the night *la14-e20*. (2) stay up all night with, watch over (a sick person or corpse) *la14, la18-e20*.

n **1** = wake, abstinence from sleep; *latterly* a vigil over a corpse *la14-*. **2** (1) *in pl* a small band of musicians, maintained by a town to play in the streets, *usu* at Christmas and New Year *la19*. (2) a serenade, a midnight concert *e19*.

~**rife** &c ['~rɪf] **1** disinclined or unable to sleep; able to do with little sleep; watchful, vigilant *la15-*. **2** easily awakened, lightly sleeping *19-*, *now Ork Abd Ags*. ~**rifeness** sleeplessness, insomnia; vigilance *17-19*.

wide waukin wide-awake *19-*, *now Ork*. [*cf* WAUKEN]

wauk *see* WALK[1], WAULK

wauken &c *la18-*, **waken** &c; **walkyn** &c *la14-17*, **wa(1)kne** *la16-e17* ['wakən; *Cai-Mry sEC Kcb Dmf S Uls* 'wekən] *vti* **1** = waken *la14-*. **2** *vtr* arouse (oneself or another) from sleep, wake *la14-*. **3** *vt* watch (over), keep an eye on *e16*, *only Sc*. **4** *law* revive (a legal process) in which no action has been taken for a year *la16-*; *cf* SLEEP. **5** *vi* lose one's temper with someone, break out **on** someone *19-*, *now Ork N*.

waukened awake *20-*, *local Sh-Wgt*.

~**er** &c **1** = wakener, a person or thing that wakens *16-17*. **2** an alarm attached to a clock *la16*. **waukenin 1** = wakening *la17-*. **2** a severe reproof, a dressing down *19-*, *local Sh-SW*. **minute** *or* **summons of wakening** the document which WAKENS (*v* 4) a case *18-*. [*cf* WAUK]

waul[1] &c *la15-e16, 19-*, *now S*; **waill** *e16 vi* **1** of the eyes roll wildly *la15-e16, 19-20*. **2** roll the eyes, look **at** *or* **on** (someone) with wide rolling eyes in a stupid, surprised, or aggressive way *e16, 19-*, *now S*. [*cf* ME *wawil-eyed*, ModEng *wall-eyed* having very pale or staring eyes. OED *wall* (*v*[4])]

waul[2] *adj* supple, nimble, agile *19-e20*, *Pbls Dmf*. [only Sc; *appar* altered f YAULD, possibly by confusion w WALLIE]

waul *see* WALE

waulk *18-*, *now Sh C*, **walk** &c *14-e18*; **wa(c)k** *la17-e18*, **wauk** &c *18-e20* [wɑk] *v* **1** *vt* full (cloth), make (cloth) thick and felted by a process of soaking, beating and shrinking *la16-20*. **2** *vi, also* ~ **in** *of cloth* shrink as a result of being wetted *19-20*.

waukit &c *of skin, wool etc* matted, hardened, roughened; calloused *la17, 19-*, *now Sh C*. ~**er** &c *14-e19*, **walkster** *la16-e18* a fuller of cloth.

waulking song any suitably rhythmic GAELIC song *formerly* sung by a team of women engaged in *waulking* cloth in the Hebrides *la19-*.

~ **mill** &c a fulling mill *15-*, *now NE Per WC*.

waum *e20*, **wam** &c *la16 n* a scar, blemish. [only Sc; OE *wam(m)* &c, ON *vamm* spot, blemish; *cf* WAN[4]]

waumish *adj* faint and sick, out of sorts, dizzy *la19*, *Ags Fif*. [only Sc; *see* SND]

waumle *see* WAMMLE

waun *see* WAND

waunner *see* WANDER

waup *see* WAP[1]

waur *la18-*, **war** &c *16-e20*; **wer** &c *la14-15, la19* [wɑr; *Sh Ork also* wɛr; *war, *wør] *adj, adv, comparative* ~**er** *now joc, 18-*, *local* = worse *la14-*. *vt* get the better of, worst, overcome, outdo *la15-*, *now local Sh-Ayr*.

n the worse, that which is inferior or less desirable *18-*.

~**-faured** more ill-favoured, uglier *la18-*, *now Ork NE Ags*.

come by *or* **win the waur** come off worst, get the worst of something *la18-*, *now Sh Cai*. **get the war** get the worst of it *la14-16*. **ten waurs** ten times worse *la19-*, *now NE*. **(the) waur o(f)** (the) worse for *19-*. [*cf* WARSE]

waur *see* WARE[1], WARE[2], WARE[3]

waurn *see* WARRAND

waut *see* WALT[1]

wauther *see* WEATHER

wave &c *vti* **1** = wave *la14-*. **2** *vt* ~ **on** attract the attention of (someone) with a wave of the hand *la20-*, *Sh N Per*.

wavel &c *16-*, **weavle** *la17* ['wevl; *Sh* 'wɑvl] **1** *vi* rock unsteadily, sway to and fro, stagger *la17-*, *now Sh*. **2** *vti* flutter, waver, wag to and fro *e16, 20-*, *now Sh*. **3** *vt* twist (the mouth) *la17*.

wavengeour *see* WAFFINGER

waver &c *vti* **1** = waver *la14-*. **2** *vi, of water, waves* surge *e15*, *only Sc*. **3** stray **from** *la15-e17*, *only Sc*.

~**and 1** = wavering *la14-*. **2** wandering, vagrant *la14*. **3** (1) *of fortune, affairs etc* variable, fluctuating *e16*. (2) *of a person* having a doubtful or uncertain title *e15*. **4** of changing intensity, fitful, unsteady *la15-e16*.

waverin leaf *see* WAYBURN LEAF

waw[1] &c [wɑ; *Buchan* wɒv] *vi, of cats (and children)* mew piteously, caterwaul, wail *la18-*, *now Ork NE*.

n the sound made by a cat or child in distress *19-*, *now NE*. [imit; *cf* WOW[1]]

waw[2] *la14-e19*, **wall** *la15-e20*; **wa** *17-19* [wɑ] *n* a wave (of the sea) *la14-19*.

wally &c [*literary* 'wɑlɪ, 'wɑlɪ; *'wɒɪ] *verse, of the sea* tempestuous, wave-tossed, swelling *16-e20*. [ME *waȝe, wawe*]

waw[3] *15-e16*; **wall** *la15-e16* [*wɒ] *n* a measure of weight, *usu* of twelve stone. [MLowGer and MDu *wage*, corresponding to OE *wǣg* a standard of dry goods weight]

wawsper &c *e16, la19*; **wasper** *la15*, **wauch**

&c spear *e17* [*'wɑspər] *n* a (salmon-)fishing spear. [only Sc; perh ME *waw, waȝien* to shake, wave to and fro + Eng *spear; cf* WASTER]

wax[1] **&c; walx** *la15-17,* **waks** *e16* [waks, wɑks] *n* = wax *la14-*.

wexin = waxen, made of wax *e17*.

~ **cayme** a honeycomb *la14*. **wax cloth** *usu* canvas cloth coated with wax used *esp* for floor and table coverings: oilcloth; linoleum *19-*.

wax[2] **&c** *la14-*; **walx** *16* [waks] *vi, pt also* **woux** *la14-15,* **wox** *la14-e15,* **wolx** *e16* [*wɛks, *wuks, *wøks]. *ptp also* **walxin** *16* [*'waksən] = wax, increase.

way [we] *interj* **1** = way, a call to a horse to stop *la19-, now Lnk; cf* WO. **2** a call to a sheepdog to make a detour or move away from the sheep *20-* [prob reduced f Eng *away*].

way *see* WA[2], WAE[1], WEY[1]

wayburn &c leaf *17-19;* **waverin &c leaf** *19-, now Sh Ork* [*Sh Ork* 'wev(ə)rən, 'wɑv-; *'webrən] *n* waybread, the plant. [*cf* Eng *waybread-leaf.* OED *waybread*]

waynd &c *vi* = wonde, flinch; hesitate; refrain *15-e16.* [OED *wonde*]

wayre [*ver] *adj* varied or variegated in colour *e15.* [only Sc; OF *vair,* L *varium.* OED *vair*]

Waysiders nickname for Airdrieonians football team *20-.* [f the name *Wayside Club* given to the Club by one of its players; *cf the Diamonds* (DIAMOND)]

waywart &c *adj* = wayward *19-e20.*

wazzin *see* WIZZEN

we &c, oo &c *la19-, now S* [wi; *unstressed also* wɪ, wə; *sEC-S also* u; *S also* wəi] *personal pronoun* **1** = we *la14-.* **2 we** *la19-, now Ork nEC,* **oo** *20-, S, used as object* = us.

ool &c we will *la19-e20.* **we's &c** we shall *la18-e20.* [*cf* US]

we *see* WEE, WI

wealth *see* WALTH

wean *la18-, C;* **wyne** *e17,* **we'an &c** *18-19,* **wane &c** *la18-e20* [*C* wen; *N nEC* *wiən] *n* a child, *esp* a young one *17-, now C.*

weanish childish *20-, local C.* **weanly** = prec; weak, puny *19-, local C.*

gran(d) wean a grandchild *20-.* **laddie** *etc* **wean** a boy etc *19-.* [chf Sc; reduced f WEE + ANE[1]]

weaponshaw *see* WAPPENSHAW

wear *17-;* **wer &c** *la14-16,* **weir &c** *15-e20, only Sc* [wir; *Sh-Mry nEC* wer] *v, pt also* **war** *la15, only Sc,* **wour** *la14-15,* **woir** *15-16, only Sc,* **ware &c** *la15-18,* **wure &c** *la18-, now Sh* [wør; *wer], **weer &c** *la18-19* [*Cai NE* wir]; **weared &c** *18-e20* [wird; *'wɪrɪt]. *ptp also* **wurn** *la19-e20,* **wore** *19* **1** *vti* = wear *la14-.* **2** *vi* go, proceed, *chf* slowly and cautiously *la15, la18-, now Sh Ork nEC.* **3** *vt* cause to fly or flutter **out** *la15, only Sc.*

wearin(g) *n* **1** = wearing *la15-.* **2** a wasting

away from disease, a decline *la17. adj, of clothes* for everyday use, *esp* outside working hours *la19-, now local Sh-Dmf.*

wear awa &c 1 make off quietly, slip away *19-, now NE.* **2** pass away, die *19-.* **wear doun** (**the brae**) grow old *19-, now Ork Abd.* **wear intil &c** *or* **into** proceed slowly towards; approach (a time of the day etc) *19-, now Uls.* **wear on 1** = prec *la19-, now Ork.* **2** be advancing in age, grow older *20-, now Ork Ags.* **wear out of** pass from, leave (a friendship) behind *18-, now Abd.* **wear ower 1** *of time* grow late *la19-, now NE nEC.* **2** *of persons* = wear on 2, *la20-, Sh Abd.* **wear roun** walk slowly round; prevail on, get round (someone) *19-, now Sh Ork.* ~ **throu 1** get through a task by degrees *20-, Ork N.* **2** waste, consume *la19-, NE Per.* **wear to** *of weather* turn to, show signs of changing to *20-, now NE.* **wear one's wa(s)** make one's way, make off *la18-19, Bnf Abd.* ~ **up** grow, advance in time, age or amount *la18-, now Sh NE.*

weary &c *adj* **1** = weary *la14-.* **2** *of persons and objects* sickly, puny, weak, paltry *la14-19.* **3** *of persons* sad, miserable *18.* **4** depressing, dispiriting *18-, now NE.* **5** annoying, troublesome *18-e20.*

vti **1** = weary *la15-.* **2** *vi* become bored or listless *la18-.*

wearifu &c *of persons or animals* troublesome, annoying; sad, woeful *18-, now NE.*

~ **fa** *used to express exasperation* damn!, the devil take .. *19-, now Uls.* ~ **for** long for (*esp* something or someone missed for some time) *19-.* ~ **on,** ~ **tak** *etc* = ~ **fa,** *19.*

wease *see* WASE

weasel *la19-;* **quhasill** *la15,* **weazel &c** *e19,* **waizel &c** *17-e19,* **wheasel &c** *19-, now EC, WC, S* ['wizl, 'hwizl; *Slk Rox also* 'wezl; *Bwk Rox also* 'hwezl] *n* **1** = weasel *la15-.* **2** a sharp, restless, prying, sneaky person *la19.*

weasel-blawn *of an animal* affected by an unexplained ailment, supposed to be caused by the breath or hiss of a weasel; *of a person* unpleasant-looking; ill-natured *19.*

weason *see* WIZZEN

weather &c *la16-;* **wather** *la16-20,* **wether &c** *la16,* **wauther** *la19,* **wither** *la19-, now NE,* **wedder &c** *la14-e20,* **wadder** *16-, now Sh,* **widder** *la15, 20-, Abd,* **wo-** *16-, e20* ['wɪðər; *NE also* 'wɪdər; *C, S also* 'waðər; *Sh* 'wadər] *n* **1** = weather *la14-.* **2** *specif* (1) weather suitable for a particular purpose, favourable or seasonable weather *20-, now NE.* (2) wet stormy weather, rain or snow with blustery winds, rain *19.*

w(e)atherfu &c stormy, wet and windy *19-e20.*

weather gaw &c 1 = weather gall, an atmospheric appearance regarded as a portent of bad weather *18-, now local Sh-Uls.* **2** a bright calm spell between two periods of bad weather

thought to forewarn of snow *19-*, *now NE*.
weather glim &c 1 twilight; a band of clear
sky above the horizon often visible at this time
19-e20. **2** a place much exposed to the elements *la19-*, *now Bnf*.
this ~ &c just now, at the moment *20-*, *C*, *S*.

weave &c *16-*; **weff** *15-16*, **wyve** *la17-*, *NE*
[wiv; *NE* wəiv; *Sh nEC* wev] *vti*, *pt also* **wuive**
la19-20, *S* [wøv]; **weave &c** *la18-*, *NE* [wiv];
wyved, weivt *20*, *NE* [wəivd, wəivt]; *ptp also*
weif *15-16*, **weffin** *16*, **wiffen** *16*, **woifen** *16*,
wolvin *16*, **wuven** *la19-e20*, **wivven &c** *la19-*,
Abd; **weyvt** *la19-*, *now NE Ags* ['wovən; *NE*
'wivən; *S* 'wøvən; *NE Ags* wəivt; ***'wiv(ən)] **1**
= weave *15-*. **2** knit (*chf* stockings) *la17-*, *now
NE Ags*. **3** make or construct the mesh work of
(a herring net) *la20-*, *NE Ags*.
weaver &c, wyver *19-*, *NE* **1** = weaver *16-*. **2**
a spider *19-*, *local NE-Wgt*. **weaver-kneed 1**
knock-kneed *20-*, *C*. **2** having sensitive or ticklish knees *la20-*, *WC*. **weavin &c** knitting; a
piece of knitted wool *la18-*, *now NE Ags*. **in a
weavin &c** in a moment, in a jiffy *18-e19*, *N*.

weavle *see* WAVEL
weazel *see* WEASEL
web *see* WAB
webster *see* WABSTER
wechst *see* WASH
wecht[1], **weight &c**; **wycht &c** *15-19*,
waicht &c *16*, *e20*, **weiht** *e16*, **wacht &c**
19-, *Bnf Abd*, **waucht** *la19* [wɛxt, wixt; *S*
wəi(x)t; ***wɑxt] *n* **1** = weight *la14-*. **2** physical
force, impetus, *eg* in propelling a *curling-stone*
(CURL) *la18-*. **3** *in pl* a pair of scales *19-*. **4** *fig*
a large amount, a great number (of things)
la19-, *now local Cai-nEC*.
vt **1** = weigh *18-*, *local Sh-Wgt*. **2** oppress (the
mind) *17-e18*, *only Sc*. **3** add weight to,
increase the burden of, press down by weight
la19-e20.
~ie &c 1 = weighty *la16-*. **2** *of persons or animals* physically heavy and solidly corpulent *19-*,
now NE.
of ~ of full or standard weight *16*, *only Sc*.

wecht[2]; **weicht &c** *18-e20*, **waicht &c** *la19*
[wɛxt] *n* a wooden hoop, about two to three feet
in diameter, with skin or canvas stretched over
it, *orig* used for winnowing corn, *now usu* for carrying grain or potatoes *la16-*, *now Sh N Kcb*.
wechtfu &c the amount contained in a
WECHT[2], *freq* used as a measure *19*.
winding wecht &c = *n*, *18-e19*. [perh a
specif usage of WECHT[1] *n*, *orig* denoting a
container made to hold a certain weight of
grain; ME *weght, wehit*. OED *weight* (*n*[2])]
wecht *see* WASH
wed *see* WAD[1], WADE, WEED[1], WEED[2]
wedder &c, **wether** *17-*; **wodder** *la16*,
wadder &c *la16-e19*, **wather** *la17-e20*
['wɛdər; *NE Fif* 'widər; *sEC*, *WC*, *S* 'wadər;
WC, *S* *'waðər] *n* = wether *la14-*, *now local
NE-S*.

wedder bouk the carcass of a wether *16*, *only
Sc*. **wether gammond** a leg of mutton *la18*.
wedder gang a pasture or right of pasturage
for wethers *la16-e17*, *only Sc*. **wedder lamb** a
castrated male lamb *19-20*. **wadder silver**
money in lieu of a wether paid as a customary
rent or tax *la16*, *only Sc*.
wedder *see* WEATHER
Weddinsday *see* WEDNESDAY
wede [*wid] *vi* **1** = wede, be or become mad
la14-15. **2** *of waves, pestilence* rage, be furious
e15.
wedand raging, raving *la14-15*. [*cf* WUID[2]]
wede *see* WEED[1]
wedge *see* WADGE
Wednesday &c *la15*, *la18-*; **Woden(i)sday**
la14-e20, **Wendsday** *la16-e18*, **Weddinsday &c** *15-e18*, **Wadensday** *18-*, *local Cai-
Rox*, **Wadnesday &c** *la16-e20*, **Wensday**
18-, *now NE* ['wadnzde, -dɪ, 'wɛdnz-; *NE*
'wɪdnz-; *Per* 'wʌdnz-; *WC* *'wanz-; **?*'wodnz-]
n **1** = Wednesday *la14-*. **2** each of five winter
(cattle-)markets held on a Wednesday, *now only*
Big Wednesday the main market of the winter
held at MARTINMAS *la18-*, *now midLoth*.
gude Wednisday the Wednesday before
Easter *la15*.
wedonypha *see* WEIDINONFA
wedow *see* WIDOW
wedset *see* WADSET
wee *16-*; **we** *la14-18*, **wie** *16-e19* [wi; *S* *wəi] *n* **a
little ~** *la14-16*, **a ~** *la16-* a small measure,
quantity or degree of some thing or of time,
distance etc.
adj **1** small, tiny, little, restricted in size, *freq* ~
~, **little ~,** **~ sma** *etc la15-*. **2** as intensifier
with nouns signifying a small amount *eg* **a ~
bit** *noun phrase* a very small amount (of); *used as
adj* tiny; *used as adv* somewhat, to a small extent
la17-. **3** *football* used to describe the reserve
team *la20-*: '*wee Celtic*'; *cf the W~ Rangers*.
wee ane &c a young child, a little one *la17-e19*;
cf WEAN. **wee-boukit** of small size, physically
small *la19-*, *now midLoth*. **wee coal** a shal-
low-seam coal *19-e20*. **wee hauf** a nip of spirits, a small WHISKY, *orig* less than half an
imperial gill, *now usu* one-fifth *la19-*. **~ heavy**
a type of strong beer, *usu* sold in small bottles of
$\frac{1}{3}$ pint (approx. 0.2 litre) *20-*. **wee house** an
earth-closet, an outside toilet *20-*, *Gen except Sh
Ork S*. **wee man 1** an odd-job man *20-*, *Lnk
Dmf*. **2** the devil, *chf* **in the name o the wee
man!** *20-*, *local*. **wee pawn** an unlicensed
pawn-broker, often one engaged in illicit dealings *19*. **the Wee Rangers** occasional nickname for Berwick Rangers football team *la20-*;
cf adj 3. **wee school &c** the infant department in a school *la19-*, *local*. **wee thing** a
small child *la18-*. **wee yins &c** younger children *20-*, *local*. [nME *wei*; OE *wēg, wǣg* a
weight]
wee *see* WEY[2]

weeack &c ['wiək] *vi* chirp, whine, speak or sing in a thin squeaky voice, utter a shrill high-pitched sound *18-, NE.*
n a squeak, high-pitched utterance of a person or animal *19-, now Abd.* [imit; *cf* WHEEK and Eng *week (interj)*]
weebie &c *n, chf in pl* the common ragwort *19-20, nEC.* [obscure]
weed[1] **&c** [wid; *NE, Fif also* wəid] *n* = weed *15-.*
vti, pt, ptp also **wed** *18-, now Abd,* **wede** *19-e20* [wɛd, wid] = weed *16-.*
weeding iron a tool for removing weeds *la17.*
weedock &c a small weed *la18.*
weidheuk *la15,* **weedick** *e19,* **weedock** *la20* ['widək; *wid'hjuk] a weed-hook, an implement for cutting weeds.
wede awa(y) *literary* carry off, remove, *esp* by death *la18-.*
weed[2] **&c; wed &c** *14* [wid] *n* = weed, a garment; armour; a shroud *la14-.*
weed[3] **&c** [wid; *Abd also* *wəid] *n* **1** a high fever, a sudden feverish attack; *specif* puerperal fever *la18-, now N Fif Dmf.* **2** an attack of ague, a chill with trembling and chattering teeth *19-e20.* **3** *of farm animals* a feverish ailment thought to have been caused by a chill; *specif, of female animals* mastitis *19-, Gen except Sh.* [reduced f WEIDINONFA]
weeg *see* WIG[1]
weeger *see* WAGER
weegle &c ['wigl] *v, n* = wiggle *19-e20.*
wigglety-wagglety &c ['wiglti'waglti, &c] *adj (adv)* very unstable, tottery; unsteadily *19-, NE-S.*
week *18-e20;* **weik &c** *16-e18* [wik] *n* = wick (of a candle etc). [OED *wick (n*[1]*)*]
week *see* OUK, WICK[1]
weel[1] **&c, well &c** *adv* **1** = well *la14-.* **2** *as intensifier* very, quite, much *la14-e20.*
adj **1** = well *16-.* **2** *chf attrib* healthy *20-, local;* cf *no* ~. **3** *of food* fully cooked, ready to eat *19-e20.*
interj, freq ~ ~ = well!, well well! *la15-.*
weelness &c good health *la17-e20.*
~ **baken** well-baked *e16, only Sc.* ~ **biknaw** well-known *e16, only Sc.* **weel come &c 1** arriving at an opportune moment, welcome *la19-, now NE.* **2** *of persons* of good lineage, of honourable parentage *la18-, now Abd Dmf.* **weel-daein &c** well-to-do, prosperous *19-.* **weel-farrant &c** of pleasant appearance or behaviour *la14, la19.* **weel-faured &c** *of persons* **1** = well-favoured, good looking *16-.* **2** decent, respectable *19-e20.* **weel-faurdly &c** in a decent, proper or pleasant way *la18-19.* **weel-hained &c 1** *of persons* well preserved, in good shape *18-19.* **2** *chf literary* used sparingly or economically, saved to good purpose *la18-19.* **weel-handit &c** good with one's hands, deft; energetic in small matters *19-20.* **weel-happit** well covered up, well-protected *19-, now NE.* **weel-hertit &c 1** courageous, valiant

17-18. **2** good-hearted, generous, liberal *la18-19.* **weel-lookit** good-looking, handsome *18-19.* **weel-lookit tae &c** well-looked-after, blessed by fortune *la19-, now NE.* **weill menyt** kindly disposed *la15, only Sc.* **weel-natured** good-natured, kindly and amiable *la18-19.* **weel-peyd &c 1** = well-paid, well-satisfied *la17-.* **2** thoroughly beaten *19.* **weel seen 1** = well seen, evident *18-.* **2** well-versed, proficient, very knowledgeable **in** *la17-19.* **well set** well-disposed *17, only Sc.* ~ **usit** well practised or exercised *la15, only Sc.* **weel-willed &c** well-disposed, favourable; enthusiastic *la15-19.* **weel-willie &c** = well willy, kindly disposed, ready, willing *la14, la18-e20.* ~ **willing &c 1** = well-willing *la14-16.* **2** ready or keen (to do something) *la6.*
it's very weel *e19,* **it's weel and weel enuch** *19-, now NE* it's all very well. **no &c** *or* **nae** *(N)* **weel** unwell, in poor health *la17-.* **weel at anesel** in good physical condition, plump, stout *la18-e20.* ~ **a** *etc* **wat** *see* WAT. ~ **a** ~ **&c** very well, all right *la18-.* ~ **beit, wele be it** *interj* all right!, good! *15-e16.* **weel-hauden-in** saved to good purpose *la19-, now Abd.* **weel's me (on)** *18-e19,* **weel is on** *19* happy am I (because of), blessings on. **weel lo'es me o** blessings on, good luck to *la18.* **weel-pit(ten)-on** well-dressed, neatly-tailored *19-.* **weel-redd-up** tidy, well-in-order *19-.* **weel to be seen** having a good appearance, very presentable *20-, Sh NE Kcb.* **weel to live** in comfortable circumstances, well-off; tipsy *19.* **weel to pass (in the warld)** well-off, affluent, prosperous *19.* **wi than &c** all right then *19.* **weel upon't** = *weel to live, la19-, Abd.* **the weel warst &c** the very worst, the worst of the lot *la16-, now NE.*
weel[2] **&c** *la14-19;* **wel &c** *la14-16* [wil] *n* = weal, welfare. [cognate w WEEL[1]. OED *weal (n*[1]*)*]
weel[3] **&c** *vi* = well, boil, swell up, overflow *e19.* [phonol obscure; perh confused w SWEEL[1] or WEEL[4]; *cf* WALL]
weel[4] **&c** *n* a deep pool; an eddy, a whirlpool *16-, freq in place-names.* [nME; OE *wǣl*]
weel *see* WIELD
weelfare &c *la14-19,* **welfare** *la14- n* = welfare.
weem *n* **1** *also in place-names* a cave, a natural cavity in the ground, in a rock etc *18-19.* **2** an Iron Age underground storehouse, *chf* in the form of a curved slab-lined passageway *18-, chf Sh Abd Ags, now hist.* [only Sc; Gael *uaimh,* early Gael or MIr *uaim* a cave]
weemen *see* WOMAN
ween &c [win] *v, pt* **wend &c** *la14-16,* **whende** *14,* **wo(u)nt** *16,* **wint** *16* [*winıt, *wind, *wint, *wʌnt] *vt* **1** = ween *la14-, now arch or verse.* **2** surmise, guess, imagine *la14-19, latterly literary.*

n = ween *la14-15*.

but ~ *la14-16*, **forouten** ~ *la14* without doubt.

ween *see* WIND¹

weeng *see* WING

weenth *n* = width *20-*, *WC, SW*. [only Sc; w infl f LENTH, STRENTH; *cf* BRENTH]

weeper *n* a small cross-wall between the sleeper-walls in the foundation of a house, constructed so as to direct the ventilation through the foundations and dry out condensation *la20-*, *EC Wgt*. [only Sc; f Eng *weep* exude moisture]

weer *la18-*, *NE*, **were &c** *la14-e19*; **wer &c** *la14-15* [wir] *n* **1** = were, danger, fear *la14-e16*. **2** *latterly chf in pl* doubt, uncertainty, apprehension *la14-e19*.

werefull doubtful *la15, only Sc*.

but ~ *la14-16*, **forouten** ~ *la14-15*, *only Sc* without doubt. **the weers o**, *freq* **in** *or* **on** **(the) weers o** + *gerund* in danger of, on the brink of, just about to *19-*, *NE*.

weer *see* WEAR, OUR

weer *see* WIRE

weese *see* WEEZE

weesh &c *interj* a call to a horse in harness to turn right *19-*, *local Sh-Per*.

weesh *see* WASH, WISS¹

weeshen *see* VISION, WASH

weeshie-washie *see* WISHY-WASHY

weest &c [wizt] *adj* depressed, doleful; anxious, fidgety *19-e20*, *Abd*. [obscure]

weet¹ &c, **wat &c** *now C, S*, **wet**; **wait &c** *la14-e16* [wit; *sEC-Rox Uls* wat; *Per Fif also* wat; *Dmf* wʌt; **wet*] *adj* = wet *la14-*.

n **1** = wet *la15-*. **2** rain, drizzle, dew *16-*. **3** a drink *18-19*.

v, pt also **wat** *16-e20* [wat], **weetit** *19-*. *ptp also* **wat** *la18-e20* [wat], **weetit** *19-*, **wutten** *la19-*, *now Abd vt* **1** = wet *la14-*. **2** celebrate with a drink, drink to the success of (a bargain etc) *la19-*.

weetie &c wet, damp, rainy *la17-*, *now Sh NE*, *EC*. **weetin** a quantity of liquor, a drinking party *19-*, *now Stlg Fif Loth*.

watshod 1 = wet-shod *la19-*. **2** *of the eyes* wet with tears *la18-*, *now Ayr*.

cast off the wat take off one's wet clothes *la18-e20*. **weet the bairn's heid &c** toast the health of a newborn baby *20-*. **wat** (**a cup o**) **tea** make (a cup of) tea *20-*, *WC*. **weet-my-fit &c** the landrail or corncrake (from its cry) *19-e20*.

weet² *vti* know *19-e20*. [ME *wēten*, chf northern var of OE *witan*; *cf* WAT and WIT]

weeze &c, **weese**; **wheese** *e17* [wiz] *vi* ooze, drip, exude *17-e20*. [ME *wese*]

weezened *see* WIZEN

weff, weffin *see* WEAVE

weft *see* WAFT

weicht *see* WECHT²

weidheuk *see* WEED¹

weidinonfa &c *la18-e19*; **wedonypha** *16*

[**'widən'onfɑ; NE *'wəidən-, *'wəitən-*] *n* puerperal fever; any fever. [only Sc; OE *weden* mad, delirious + ONFA; *cf* WIND² and WEED³. OED *wedenonfa*]

weif *see* WEAVE

weigh *see* WEY²

weight, weiht *see* WECHT¹

weik *see* WEEK

weil *see* WALE

weilycott *see* WYLIECOAT

weind *see* WEND

weing *see* WING

weir¹ &c *la14-e20*, **war** *la15-*; **wer** *la14-16*, **wair &c** *16-17* [wir] *n, v* = war *la14-*.

pass in werefare go to war *e16, only Sc*. ~**lie** **&c 1** = warly, warlike *la15-16*. **2** *of actions, things* martial, warlike *16, only Sc*. ~**like &c** *la15-*, **wirlyk** *e15* = warlike.

weirman &c 1 a fighting man, warrior, soldier *la15-e16, chf Sc*. **2** a man-of-war, warship *e16, only Sc*.

weir² &c *la15-*, **were** *la14*; **wer** *la14-15* [wir] *v*, *pt also* **wor** *la15*. *ptp also* **worn** *19 vt* **1** guard, defend, protect from attack etc *la14-e20*. **2** stand guard over, keep a watch on, hold (an entrance etc); *latterly specif, of a sheepdog* stand in front of (a group of sheep) to prevent them breaking loose *la15-*, *now S*. **3** *freq* ~ **aff** keep off, ward off, hold at bay *la15-e20*. **4** *also fig* drive (animals or persons) gradually in a desired direction, shepherd *18-*, *Gen except Sh Ork*.

n = weir, a river dam *la18-*.

~**er** *n* a dog which is skilful in herding animals *20-*, *now Dmf*.

~ **wall** a rampart *la15-e16*. [OE *werian* (*v*) defend; *n* also f OE *wer* a river barrier, f the same stem]

weir *see* WEAR, WIRE

weird &c; werd *la14-16*, **waird** *16, 19* [wird] *n* **1** *now chf literary* fate, fortune, destiny; one's own particular fate *la14-*; *cf dree one's ain weird* (DREE¹). **2** *in pl* the Fates, the three goddesses of destiny *16-e19*. **3** an event destined to happen; predetermined events *la15-e16*. **4** a decree (of a god) *15-e16*. **5** an omen of a future event *e16*. **6** a prophecy, prediction; a mysterious saying *la18-19*. **7** someone with supernatural skill or knowledge *la17-e20*.

adj **1** having the power to control the destiny of men *15-17*. **2** troublesome, mischievous, harmful *19*. **3** = weird, strange, uncanny *19-*.

vt **1** ordain by fate, destine; assign a specific fate or fortune **to** *la16-e20*. **2** prophesy (someone's fate); warn ominously *la18-19*.

weirdfu fateful, fraught with the supernatural *la19-e20*. ~**less** *chf of persons* unfortunate; inept, incapable *la18-*, *now local Abd-Loth*. ~**lessness** thriftlessness, mismanagement of one's life and affairs *19*. **weirdly 1** lucky, prosperous *19*. **2** magical, eerie, dismal, sinister *19-e20*.

weird wife a prophetess, fortune-teller *la18-e20*. [OE *wyrd*; ModEng *adj* (also *adj* 3) due to misunderstanding or extension of meaning f Shakespeare's *Macbeth*; see SND]

weirdie &c ['wɪrdɪ, 'werdɪ] *n* the smallest or least thriving of a brood of animals, *esp* pigs or birds *19-*, *nEC*. [see SND]

weise *see* WISE

weist *see* WIT

weit *see* WYTE

weivt *see* WEAVE

wekit *see* WICKED

wel *see* WEEL[2]

welcome *see* WALCOME

welfare *see* WEELFARE

well *see* WALL, WEEL[1]

wellaway *see* WALAWA

wellie *n*, *chf in pl* = wellington boots *20-*.
~ **boot** = *n*, *20-*, *C*.

welsh *see* WALSH

welt *see* WALT[2]

welter &c *vti* **1** *now verse* = welter *la14-*. **2** *vi* roll down in a stream, flow *la14-e16*. **3** flutter *la15*. **4** *of a ship* roll to and fro (on the waves) *e15*. **5** *vti*, *of a vehicle* sway, rock, overthrow, overturn *la14-e19*, *chf Sc*. **6** *vi* reel, stagger, stumble, flounder *19-*, *now Cai*.
n = welter *la16*. [*cf* WALTER[1]]

welth *see* WALTH

wench &c; winch &c *16-* [wɪnʃ; *S* wʌnʃ] *n* = wench, *latterly freq* a little girl *la14-*, *now local N-S*.
vti, *only* **winch** court; keep company with someone of the opposite sex, *orig* of a man with a girl *la18-*: 'are ye winchin?'

wend &c; weind *la14-15* [wend; *wind] *vi*, *ptp* also **wynt** *16* [*?wɪnt] **1** = wend *la14-*. **2** *of things* pass away, disappear, perish *la15-16*.

wend *see* WEEN

Wendsday, Wensday *see* WEDNESDAY

went &c *19-*, *now NE*; **wint** *19-e20*, *Abd* [wɪnt; *Cai* wəint] *n* a quick or passing view, a short transient glimpse *19-*, *now NE*. [uncertain]

went *see* GAE

wep *see* WAP[2]

wer *see* WAUR, WEAR, WEER, WEIR[1], WEIR[2], OUR

werche *see* WRATCH

werd *see* WEIRD, WORD

were *see* WEER, WEIR[2]

wergelt &c *17*; **weregeheld** *13*, **wargeld** *la13-15* [*'wer'geld, *-'gelt, *-'gɪlt, *'wir-, *'war-] *n*, *law* the sum paid by way of compensation or fine to the victim or his family mainly in cases of homicide, to free the offender from further obligation or punishment. [OE *wergeld*, *wergield*, f *wer* man + *geld* yield; *cf* CRO[1], *assythement* (ASSYTH). OED *wergeld*]

weriour *see* WARY

werk *see* WARK[1], WARK[2]

werp *see* WARP

werrand *see* WARRAND

werrandis *see* WARRANDICE

werriour *see* WARRIOR

werrock &c *19-e20*; **wirrok &c** *e16* ['werək; *Cai* 'warəg; *'wɪrək] *n* a corn, bunion etc on the foot. [only Sc; see SND. OED *wirrock*]

wers *see* WARSE

wersh &c *la17-*, *Gen except Sh Ork*; **warsh &c** *la15-19*, **wairsh &c** *la16*, *la19-*, *now Rox* [werʃ; *Sh Ork Cai* wers, wars; *sEC Lnk S* werʃ; *Sh Ork N* also *warʃ] *adj* **1** *of food or drink* tasteless, insipid, unpalatable; cooked without salt; *of beer* flat *la16-*, *Gen except Sh Ork*; *cf* 7. **2** *fig*, *of a discourse or piece of writing* dull, tame, uninspiring *18-e20*. **3** *of land* of poor quality, exhausted, lacking fertility *18-e20*. **4** *of life, feelings, activity* dull, humdrum, lacking zest *la18-20*. **5** *of the stomach or appetite* disinclined towards food; faint from hunger, squeamish *la18-*, *now Abd Kcdn*. **6** *of persons* sickly, feeble in appearance; spiritless, depressed *la15-e20*. **7** bitter, harsh in taste, sour *20-*, *Cai C*, *S*; *cf* 1. **8** *of weather* raw, cold and damp *19-20*.

wershly &c insipidly, without cordiality *17*.

wersh crap &c *latterly hist* the third and last crop taken from the OUTFIELD before the fallow period *18-19*. [chf Sc; reduced f ME *werische* insipid; sickly]

wersslete *see* WARSET

werst *see* WARSE

werstle *see* WARSLE

werwoif, werwoolfes, werwoophs *see* WARWOLF

wery *see* VERA

wes *see* BE

wesch- *see* WITCH

weschin *see* WASH

weser [*'wizər] *n* = wizard *la16*. [only Sc. OED *wizard*]

wesh *see* WASH

weshell *see* VESHEL

weshin *see* WASH

weskit &c *18-20*; **wastcoat &c** *la19-e20*, **wystcoat &c** *la19-e20* ['weskɪt, 'waskot, &c; *NE* 'wəiskot, -kɪt, -kwəit] *n* = waistcoat.

westerne *n* a desert, wilderness *la14*. [ONorthumb *wæstern*, var of OE *wæsten*, *wēsten*. OED *western*]

wesle *see* WISSEL

west *see* WAIST, WAST, WASTE

wet *see* WEET[1]

weth *see* WAITH[1]

wether *see* WEATHER, WEDDER

weuch &c *15*, **wocht** *15* [*wjux, *wøx] *n*, *adj* = wough, wrong, evil. [OED *wough*]

wexin *see* WAX[1]

wey[1] *e16*, *la19-*, **way; wa** *la14*, *la18-19*, **wye &c** *19-* [*Ork C*, *S* wəi; *Sh N* wai; *wa*, *pl* *waz and Sh pl* wɪz, *chf in* **come**, **gae** *etc* one's ~(s)] *n* **1** = way *la14-*. **2** one's circumstances, way of life, business *la19-e20*.

weys &c used as a suffix -wise, in the manner specified *19-*: 'says he, affhand weys'.

way-flude &c the outflow of water from a

mill-wheel, the tail-race; a water channel *la18-*, now *Bnf Abd*. **waygate &c 1** a passageway, a thoroughfare; room, space *19-e20*. **2** speed, progress; push, drive, energy *19-*, now *Rox Lnk*. **way-lead &c** = *way-flude*, *la16*, only *Sc*.
a'wey &c everywhere *la19-*. **ae wey** one way *19-*, now *Ork Per*. **all weys** in every way or respect *20-*. **by his** *etc* ~ **o't** according to him etc, by his etc account *la19-*, local *Sh-Ayr*. **by way of** by the action of (a person or persons) *la15*, only *Sc*. **by way of deid** *law* by means of violence *16*. **come, gae** *etc* **one's** ~ *or (chf)* ~**s** come, go etc away or on one's way *la14*, *la18-*, local *Sh-Dnbt*. **hald one's way** *fig* continue a course of action, 'keep going' *la14*. **in a (dreedfu** *etc***) way** in a state of great distress, worried and upset **about** *la19-*, local *Sh-Ayr*. **be in the way o** have a habit of *18-*, now *local*. **naewey** nowhere *la19-*. **nae weys** in no way, by no manner of means *19*. **say ae wye** agree, concur *la19-*, now *Ork NE Per*. **somewey 1** somehow *19-*. **2** somewhere *19-*, now *Sh NE*. **some ither wey** somewhere else *la19-*, now *NE*. **that wey** in that manner, so; in that respect *la19-*, now *NE Per*. **the wey &c 1** *freq* **the wey that** because of the way or manner in which, from the way (that) *la19-*. **2** because *la19-*, now *Stlg Ayr*. **the wey at** the reason why *la20-*, *Sh-Per*. **the wey o** in the direction of *la19-*, *Sh Ork N, EC*. **wey o daein 1** a means of livelihood, a job *19-*, now *Ork NE-S*. **2** also **wey-dain** a fuss; a disturbance, uproar; a celebration *la19-*, *chf Ags*. **what wey 1** how, in what manner *15-*. **2** why, for what reason *18-*.
wey[2] **&c** now *local*, **weigh &c** *16-*; **wee** *la18-*, now *sEC Slk*, **wye** *la18-e20* [*Sh Ork N* wɑɪ; *nEC, SW, S* wəɪ; *sEC, WC* wi; *SW also* wi] *vti* **1** = weigh *la14-*. **2** *vt, fig* dispense or administer (justice) impartially *la16*. **3** *vi* ~ **up** *or* **down** *of the scale of a balance* rise or sink according to the weight it is holding *la14*. **4** pay heed or deference **to** *15*, only *Sc*.
n **1** *in pl* a (public) weighing-machine; a steelyard, beam and scales; the weights used with scales *15-*, now *Cai C, S*. **2** a measure of weight varying according to the district and the commodity *la14*, *18-e20*.
weigh bauk &c the beam of a pair of scales; *freq in pl* the scales themselves *la16-*, now *local Ork-Gall*. **weigh brods** *chf in pl* the boards used on a large pair of scales for weighing a heavy object *16-e20*. **wey butter, wey cheese** a game in which two people stand back to back with arms linked and lift one another alternately until one gives in *19-*, *local now Ork-SW*. ~ **wecht** the weights used with scales; *in pl* the scales themselves *la19-*, now *Ags nEC Ayr*.
weygilt &c [*'wiˈgɪlt] *n* a payment for weighing *la15*. [only *Sc*; after Du *waaggeld*, Ger *wagegeld*, *wäge-*. OED *weigh* (*v*[1])]
weynd *see* WIND[2]
weyvt *see* WEAVE

wha &c now *local*, only *Sc*, **who &c** *15-*, **fa** *18-*, now *Abd*; **quha &c** *la14-18*, only *Sc*, **quhay &c** *la14-16*, only *Sc*, **qua &c** *la14-16*, only *Sc*, **quho &c** *15-17*, only *Sc*, **whae** *17-*, now *local sEC-S*, only *Sc*, **whee &c** *la19-e20* [hwɑ; *N* fɑ; *sEC, S* hwe] *pronoun, accusative* **quham &c** *la14-17*, **quhoum &c** *la14-16*, **quhome &c** *14-18*, **quhem &c** *16*, **wham** *la17-19*, **whom** *la16-* [hwam; *hwʌm, *NE* *fʌm], *genitive* **quhais &c** *la14-18*, **whase &c** *15-*, now *local C*, **quhose &c** *la15-17*, **whose &c** *la16-*, **whaus &c** *la19-e20* [hwɑz; *N* fɑz; *sEC, S* hwez] **1** (1) *interrog* = who? *la14-*. (2) *relative, only literary or formal anglicized usage* = who *la14-*; *cf* THAT. **2** *accusative, relative and interrog, with prep immediately following, often written as one word* of, to etc whom *la14-e17*, *chf Sc*: 'It specifyit nocht quham fra the gudis .. wes takin.'
quha-sum-ever &c 1 *pronoun* = whomsoever, whoever *la14-16*. **2** *adj* whichever, whatever (person or persons) *15-16*.
~ **but he &c** a paragon, the 'cock of the walk' *17-*, now *NE Ags Loth*. **wha daur meddle wi me** free translation of the national motto *nemo me impune lacessit*. **wha deil** who the devil? *18-*, now *Sh Ork*. **wha (i)s aucht &c?** who is the owner, parent etc of? *19-*, now *Ags Per*. **wha like(s)** whoever (it may be), no matter who *la18-*, now *Sh Ork*.
wha *see* WHAT[1]
whaak &c [hwɑk] *vi* quack like a duck *19-*, now *Sh Ork*. [*cf* Norw dial *kvaka* (*v*) twitter, gabble, *kvakk* a croak]
whaal *19-*, now *Sh Abd Fif*, **whale** *17-*, **faal &c** *20-*, *NE*; **quhaill &c** *15-16*, **quhell** *15-16*, **whaul &c** *19-e20* [hwɑl, *NE* fɑl] *n* = whale *15-*.
whaal-bubble &c the jellyfish *e20*. **quhaill horne** whalebone *la16*. **whale schote** spermaceti *e17*.
whaap *see* WHAUP[1]
whack &c; whauk &c *18-* [hwak, hwɑk; *EC* *hwɛk] *vt* **1** = whack *17-*. **2** slash, cut severely with a sharp instrument *la18-19*.
n **1** a sharp, heavy stroke or blow, a thump, smack *18-*. **2** a cut, incision *la18-*, now *N Per*. **3** a great number, a large quantity *la19-*, now *local Sh-WC*.
get one's whacks be punished, get one's just deserts *18-*, local *N-Kcb*. [var of eModEng *thwack*; Sc form adopted into colloq Eng *18*]
whae *see* WHA
wha-hup [hwɑ-, hwɑ-ˈhʌp] *interj* a call to a horse to move off *20-*, *EC, S*. [*cf* HUP]
whair *see* WHAR
whaisk &c *vi* wheeze, breathe with difficulty, as with a heavy cold, gasp for breath *19-*, now *Rox*. [only *Sc*; conflation of Eng *wheeze* w HASK]
whaizle *see* WHEEZE[3]
whale *see* WHAAL
whalp &c *la18-*, *local*, **folp &c** *17-*, *N*; **quelpe &c** *14-15*, **quilpe &c** *14*, **quhelpe** *14-17*,

quhalp *16*, **quholpe** *la16* [hwalp, hwɑlp, hwʌlp, folp] *n* **1** = whelp *14-*. **2** *fig* term of abuse for a person *la18-, local*.

vti = whelp *14-*. [OED *whelp*]

wham[1] **&c** *la18-*; **quhawm** *la16* [hwam; *hwɑm] *n* **1** *freq in place-names* a dale or valley, a broad hollow among hills through which a stream runs *la16-, now Sh*. **2** a hollow piece of ground in a field etc, a depression, *esp* a marshy one *19-, now Sh*. [also in nEng place-names; ON *hvammr* a short valley surrounded by high ground; *cf* Norw dial *kvam* a nook, recess, hollow surrounded by high banks; cognate w OE *hwamm* a corner, angle]

wham[2] **&c** [hwam] *n* **1** a blow *18-, local*. **2** a thud, a dull sound *la20-, local*.

interj with a quick smart sound, smack *20-, C*. [earlier in Sc; onomat]

wham *see* WHA

whammle *see* WHUMMLE

whan &c *15-, Gen except N*, **when** *la16-*, **fan &c** *18-e20, N*; **quhen(e) &c** *la14-17*, **quhane &c** *la14-17*, **qwen &c** *la14-16*, **quhon(e)** *la15-16*, **whun** *19-e20* [hwan, hwʌn; *N* fan, *unstressed* fɪn, fən; *EC, S also* hwɑn] *adv, conj* = when *la14-*.

~ever &c 1 = whenever *la14-*. **2** as soon as, at the very moment when *18-*. **quhensa &c 1** on or after the occasion on which, as soon as *la14-16*. **2** = whenso, whenever *la15*.

whang &c *la16-*; **whing &c** *18-, now S*, **whank &c** *19-, local EC-S n* **1** (1) *also* **thwang &c** *16-, now local*, **thwayng &c** *15-17*, **thang** *la14-, now nEC Ayr Rox*, **quhang &c** *16, e19*, **fang &c** *18-, N* [θwaŋ; *N* faŋ; *nEC Ayr Rox also* θaŋ; *WC, SW* hweŋ] = thong *15-*. (2) a strip of dried (eel- or sheep-)skin, used as a hinge for a flail *la18-, now Sh*. (3) *also* **thwang &c** a leather bootlace; any kind of shoe-tie *18-, now Sh Ork C, S*. (4) a thong for whipping; a whiplash *18-e20, C Slk*. **2** a long stretch of rather narrow road, *specif* **the Lang Whang** the old Edinburgh to Lanark road, *esp* between Balerno and Carnwath *19-*. **3** (1) *also* **fang** a large thick slice of food, *esp* of cheese *18-*. (2) *in gen* a large amount or number, a chunk, large slice *19-, now WC*. **4** *only* **fang** a rascal, disagreeable person *la19-, NE*. **5** a stroke, blow; a cut with a whip *19-, now local Sh-SW*.

vti **1** (1) cut in chunks or sizeable portions, slice *18-, now EC Rox*. (2) *vt* cut with a slicing movement, slash, chop, snip *19-e20*. **2** move with sudden force, push, pull etc with a jerk *la19-e20, Kcb Rox*. **3** beat, lash (as) with a whip; beat, defeat *la18-, now Kinr Fif Rox*.

whanker a large or impressive specimen of its kind *19-, local Fif-Rox*. **the Whangie** a split rock through which a path runs in the Kilpatrick Hills, Dnbt *20-*. **whankie** a sickle-blade mounted on a long handle, for cutting down thistles, inaccessible twigs etc *19-, Loth Bwk S*.

whing-hole an eyelet for a lace in a boot or shoe *20-, C, S*. [OED *thong*]

whap *see* WAP[1], WHAUP[1]

whar *15-, Gen except N, though now freq literary in N instead of next form*, **far &c** *19-, N*, **where &c** *la16-*; **quhare &c** *la14-17*, **qware &c** *la14-15*, **quhere &c** *la16-17*, **for** *e16, NE*, **fair** *la16, NE*, **whair &c** *la16-e20*, **whaur** *19-, now local Sh-WC* [hwar; *N* far; *ɪEC, S* hwer; *St* hwer,hwɛr] *adv, conj* = where *la14-*.

~anent *chf law* concerning which, on account of which *la16-e18*. **~awa(y)** away in or to what place, where on earth, whither *16-, now Ags Per Ayr*. **quharever &c** *la14-17*, **whaurever &c** *19-e20* **1** = wherever *la14-e20*. **2** *in special contexts with reference to persons* whomever *la15*. **~ frae &c 1** *interrog* from what place, when? *16-e17, chf Sc*. **2** *relative* from which (place, action etc) *la14-, now Sh, chf Sc*. **quhareintill &c** wherein *16-17, only Sc*. **quhare-into &c 1** = whereinto, (in)to which *la16-*. **2** in which *16-e17*. **~ to &c 1** = whereto *15-*. **2** for what purpose, why *la15-, now Sh Ork*.

whase *see* WHA

what[1] **&c, fat &c** *la17-, N*; **quhat &c** *la14-e18*, **quat &c** *la14-15, la20 (Sh)*, **quhaitt &c** *16-e17*, **whit** *19-, chf C*, **whut** *20*, **wha** *20-*, **fit** *la20-, N* [hwat, hwɪt, hwʌt, hwɑ, hwɔ?; *N* fat, fɪt, fʌt; *Sh also* kwat] *pronoun* **1** *interrog* (1) = what? *la14-*. (2) *after verb indicating disbelief or disparagement* indeed *20-, Ork N, C*: 'I worked it aa out in ten minutes.—Did ye what?' **2** *relative* (1) = what *la14-*. (2) that amount which, that number which *16-17*.

adj **1** *interrog* (1) = what? *la14-*. (2) (a) what amount, degree or number of ? *la14-17*. (b) *with abstract nouns* = Eng how + *adj, la20-*: 'what age are you?' (3) *as exclam* (a) *with noun* how much!, how great! *la14-e17*: 'quhat loss quhat honour quhat renoun/Was spokin of him'. (b) *with indef art* + *pl noun* how many!, what a lot of! *la19-*: 'what a houses'. (4) which? *la19-, now Sh Ork Cai*. **2** *relative* = what *15-*.

adv **1** = what *la14-*. **2** *as exclam, with adj* how!, how very! *la19, now N-S*: 'what pretty it is!' **3** *interrog* why?, in what way?, how? *19-, now Sh*. **4** *relative, after* **than** *or as* where Eng has nothing, *19-, now Sh-Per*: 'I think I laughed heartier then than what I do now'.

conj **1** = what *la14-*. **2** *after negative verbs of saying, thinking, doubting etc* that *la18-*: 'I dinna think but what it'll be rain'. **3** to the utmost that; as much, as far or as hard etc as *19-, local*: 'she cried what she could cry'. **4** whether .. **or** .. *la16, only Sc*: 'my deputis quhat thay be greit or small'.

~ever &c 1 *pronoun, adj* = whatever *la14-*. **2** *adv* in any case, however, nevertheless, under any circumstances *la19-, now Ork NE, also (literary) Highl*. **quhatkin &c** *adj* **1** *interrog* what sort of?, what kind of? *la14-16*; *cf* WHATTEN. **2** *relative* no matter what or which (thing) *la14-e15.* ~**somever &c 1** *pronoun, adj =* whatsomever, whatever *la14-e17.* **2** *adj* whatever, any (person or thing) at all, no matter what or which (person or thing) *la15-,* now *local Sh-Pbls.* **quhatsumevery &c** any (person or thing) that, whatever (person or thing) *16, only Sc.*

what .. at why? *la19-.* **what be** what about .. ?, how about ..? *20-,* now *Sh Ork.* ~ **for 1** what kind of **a**? *17-,* now *Ork.* **2** why?, for what reason? *la18-.* **what for no** *la18-,* **fat for no** *la19-e20, Cai Mry* why not? **fat ither** what else?, of course *19-, Bnf Abd Ags.* ~ **like 1** what sort of?, resembling what in appearance, nature etc?, how? *18-.* **2** *only* **fat like** how are you? *la20-, NE.* **what o'clock is it?** a popular name for the dandelion from the children's practice of using the seeded head of the flower as a clock *la19-, local Ork-Lnk.* **quhat-time &c** *la14-16,* **fat time** *20-, NE Ags* when, whenever, as soon as. ~ **way &c 1** *also* **quhat wys** *e16* how?, in what manner? *15-.* **2** why?, for what reason? *18-.*

what² &c *la18-, local Per-Dmf;* **quhete** *15,* **quhit-** *e16* [hwat] *vt =* whet *15-.* **whatstick** a hone or emery-board with a wooden handle used by cobblers *20-, local Abd-Rox.* [OED *whet*]

whatten &c *la17-;* **quhattin &c** *16,* **fat(t)en &c** *la19-e20, N* ['hwatn, 'hwɪtn; *N* 'fatn, 'fɪtn] *adj, also with indef art* **whatna &c** *19-e20* ['hwatnə &c] **1** *chf with indef art =* quhatkin 1 (WHAT¹) *16-,* now *Sh Ork C, S.* **2** *relative and interrog, only* **whatten** what *la18-,* now *Ork Cai C, S.* **3** *exclam* what! *la16-,* now *local Sh-Lnk.* **4** *only* **whatten** which, of two or more *la18-,* now *local.* [reduced f *quhatkin* (WHAT¹)]

whattie see WHEET¹

whauk see WHACK

whauky &c *n* WHISKY *la18-e19.* [joc conflation of ACKWA w WHISKY]

whaul see WHAAL

whaun see WAND

whaup¹ *la18-,* **faap** *20-,* now *Cai,* **faup** *la19-e20, N;* **quha(i)p** *e16,* **wha(a)p** *la17-e20* [hwɑp; *N* fɑp] *n* **1** the curlew *16-.* **2** term of abuse for a person *la19-, local* [perh partly f WHAUP² in some areas]. *vi* whistle shrilly like a curlew *la20-, Bwk Dnbt SW, S.*

whaup-nebbit &c having a long beaky nose *18-,* now *Per.*

whaup i(n) the nest *freq proverb* something, *usu* annoying or unpleasant, likely to make its presence felt, something brewing or afoot *la18-e19; cf* WHAUP³. [var of OE *hwilpe* a kind of sea-bird, possibly cognate w Eng *whelp* a puppy, *ie* a whiner]

whaup² &c [hwɑp; *Bnf* *fɑp] *n* **1** the seed-pod of a leguminous vegetable, *esp* one before the peas etc have begun to develop or after they have

been shelled *19-,* now *Abd Loth.* **2** *chf* **lang (teem)** ~ a tall scrawny person *la19-, Abd Stlg Wgt.* [*cf* WHAUP¹ 2; see SND]

whaup³ &c *n* **whaup in the raip** see RAIP. [prob altered f WAP² w infl f *whaup in the nest* (WHAUP¹)]

whaup⁴ &c *n* a shrill noise, yelp, screech, outcry *la19-e20.* [onomat; perh w infl f WHAUP¹]

whaur see WHAR

whaus see WHA

whauze, whazzle see WHEEZE³

wheasel see WEASEL

whee see WHA

wheeber &c ['hwibər(t)] *vi* **1** whistle *20-, Bnf Abd Per.* **2** walk with hurried ungainly steps, scurry *la19-,* now *Abd.* *n* **1** a whistle *20-,* now *Per.* **2** [*also* 'hwɑbərt] (1) a lean, tall, ungainly person *e20, Bnf Abd.* (2) a person with disagreeable manners *la19-e20, Bnf Abd.* [see SND]

wheech¹ &c *19-,* now *N, C;* **wheek** *la19-, local Fif-Dmf* [hwix, hwik] *v* **1** *vi* move through the air, rush, dash with a whizzing sound *19-, N, C.* **2** *vt* remove (something) with a speedy, sweeping, forcible movement, snatch or whisk away *la19-,* now *N, C.* **3** beat, whack, hit *la19-,* now *local Ags-Ayr.* *n* **1** a soft whizzing sound *19-, NE Loth.* **2** (1) a blow delivered with a whizzing sound *la19-,* now *local Kcdn-WC;* (2) *usu in pl* strokes with the tawse (TAW¹), a belting at school *la20-, Fif Loth Lnk.* **3** a sudden sweeping motion, a whisk *la20-, NE Ags.* ~**er 1** something big or outstanding of its kind, something of top quality or excellence *20-,* now *Lnk Kcb Dmf.* **2** (**coal-**)~**er** a coal-carter, coalman *la19-e20, Loth.* **wheeky-whacky day** a day at school in which the *tawse* (TAW¹) is much in use *la20-, Fif Loth Lnk.* [only Sc; onomat]

wheech² [hwix] *n* a stench *20-, Cai Fif Loth.* [imit of the exclamation of disgust produced; *cf* FEECH¹]

wheedle &c *19-;* **whe(e)gle &c** *la18-,* now *local Stlg-Rox,* **wheetle** *19-e20* *n, vti =* wheedle.

wheef see WHEICH, WHIFF

wheefle &c *19-,* now *Lnk Ayr,* **whiffle** *la17-e20* *vti =* whiffle.

wheegee &c ['hwi:'dʒi] *n* a whim; a humming and hawing, prevarication *19.* [reduplicated formation based on GEE and perh FIDGE]

wheegle see WHEEDLE

wheek &c *19-,* now *Ags Per;* **quhaik** *e16* [hwik; *hwek] *vi* squeak, whine, whistle at intervals; complain peevishly. [onomat; *cf* WEEACK. OED *wheak*]

wheek see WHEECH¹

wheel *la17-;* **quhel** *la14,* **quheil &c** *la14-17,* **whele &c** *16,* **while** *16* [hwil] *n =* wheel *la14-.* *vti* **1** *=* wheel *la17-.* **2** whirl round in dancing, swing (one's partner) round, pirouette, reel *19-,* now *Sh Abd Per.* **3** *vi* make a bid at an auction for the purpose of raising the price *la19-20, Bnf Abd.*

~**er 1** = wheeler *la17-.* **2** *mining* the person who operates the *wheel-brae, la20-, Fif Loth.*

wheelin(**g**) *spinning* a coarse thick type of worsted yarn, *orig* from uncombed wool spun on the *muckle wheel* (MUCKLE) *17-.*

~**-band &c** *spinning* the driving belt of a spinning wheel, *usu* made of dried animal gut *la16-,* now *Sh Ork Cai.* ~**-brae** *mining* a COWSY *la19-,* now *Fif.* **quheill sled** a sledge moving on wheels *la16.* ~**sman** *mining* = *wheeler, la19-, Fif.* ~ **tree** *mining* the wooden post or pivot on which the wheel of a *wheel-brae* turns *la19-, C.*

~ **a brae** operate the haulage system on a ~*-brae, la20-, Fif Loth.*

wheelie-oe &c *n* the willow warbler *20-, Ayr.* [imit of the last notes of the bird's call; *cf* WHEET[1]]

wheem *n* = whim *la19-, local.*

wheen &c *la18-;* **quhe**(**y**)**n**(**e**) **&c** *la14-16,* **qwhayne** *15,* **whine &c** *la18* [hwɪn] *n* **1** (1) **a** ~ (**o**) a (good) few, a small number, several *la14-.* (2) *also as adj* few, not many *la14-16.* **2** *chf in pl* a separate or distinct number (of persons etc), a group, some as opposed to others *la18-e20.*

a bonnie, gey *etc* ~ a considerable amount *la18-,* now *Cai WC.* **a** ~ *as adv* a bit, somewhat *la19-e20.* [OE *hwēne* (*adv*) to some extent, instrumental case of *hwōn* (*n, adj*) (a) few; *cf* QUHON(E)]

wheenge *see* WHINGE

wheep &c *vi* **1** make a sharp shrill noise with pursed lips, whistle, *esp* to call a dog or attract attention; pipe shrilly like a bird, *esp* the lapwing *19-, local NE-S.* **2** make a shrill noise, squeak, emit a high-pitched buzz etc *19-,* now *NE.*

n a sharp cry or whistle *la19-,* now *N-Per.*

wheeple &c *v* **1** *vi* (1) *of a bird, and transf of the wind* whistle shrilly or with a long drawn-out note *19-,* now *Ags Per WC.* (2) *of persons* whistle, *esp* tunelessly or ineffectually *19-,* now *NE Ags.* **2** *vt* whistle (a tune) *20-,* now *NE Ags.* **3** *vi* whine, whimper *19-,* now *Ags.* *n* **1** the shrill call or whistle of a bird, *esp* the curlew *la18-,* now *local Ork-Ayr.* **2** a tuneless, unmusical whistling or playing on a whistle *19-20.* [onomat]

wheep *see* WHIP

wheeriorum &c ['hwɪrɪ'orəm] *n* a trifle, toy; a thingumajig *la19-, N.* [conflation of next w VARIORUM]

wheerum &c *n* a trifle, something insignificant; a toy *19-e20.* [see SND]

wheese *see* WEEZE

wheesh *see* WHISHT, WHUSH

wheesht *see* WHISHT

wheesk &c *n* a light creaking sound *19-e20.* [onomat]

wheet[1] **&c** [hwit] *chf in deriv forms* ~**ie &c** *19-,* now *S,* **whattie &c** *la19-e20* ['hwatɪ], ~**le** *19-,* now *Stlg Lnk interj, chf* ~**ie** a call to ducks, *19-,* now *Stlg Lnk S.*

n **1** *chf* ~**le**(**-wheetie**) a young bird, *esp* a duckling or chicken *19.* **2** *chf* **wheetie &c** the whitethroat *19-e20.*

vi **1** *chf* ~**le**(**-**~**le**) *of birds* twitter, chirp *19-,* now *EC, WC.* **2** *chf* ~**le** *of persons* whistle, warble, *usu* tunelessly *la19-,* now *Ork Per.*

~**ie whitebeard &c** ['hwitɪ 'hwəi(t)'bɪrd, *-'berd; Rox* 'hwatɪ'hwi('bɪrd); *&c*] the whitethroat; the willow-warbler *19-e20.* [onomat]

wheet[2] *19-, local; quh(e)it 16* [hwit] *n* = whit. [OED *whit*]

wheetie &c *adj* mean, stingy, shabby; underhand, shifty, evasive *19-, NE.* [see SND]

wheetle *see* WHEEDLE, WHEET[1]

wheety-whattie *see* WHITTIE-WHATTIE

wheeze[1] **&c** *n, v* = whizz *19.*

wheeze[2] **&c** *vti* flatter, coax, cajole *la18-e19, C.* [uncertain]

wheeze[3] **&c, foze** *la19-, NE;* **whauze** *la19-, NE* [hwiz, hwaz; *NE* foz] *n, v* = wheeze *19-.* **wheezle &c** *18-,* **fozle &c** *la19-e20, NE,* **huizle &c** *19-, S;* **whaizle &c** *la18-19,* **whazzle &c** *19-20,* **whosle &c** *la18-e19* ['hwizl, 'hwazl, 'hwezl; *NE* 'fozl; ***'hwozl] *vi* wheeze, breathe with a rasping sound as with asthma or catarrh, pant *la18-.* *n* **1** a wheeze, hard rough breathing *18-,* now *SW, NE.* **2** the **wheezles &c** asthma; bronchitis *la19-, local Ork-Wgt.*

whegle *see* WHEEDLE

wheich &c *la19-;* **wheuch** *la19-e20,* **wheef** *e20* [hwix; *S also* hwif, hwjux] *n* liquor, 'booze'; WHISKY *la19-,* now *Per Fif.* [perh extended usage of WHEECH[1], WHEECH[2]; *cf* Eng *whiff* a draught of liquor]

whele *see* WHEEL

when *see* WHAN

whende *see* WEEN

where *see* WHAR

wherry &c *n* **1** = wherry, a light boat. **2** a kind of sailing barge with one sail, and a mast stepped forward *la18-,* now *Loth Ayr.*

whether *la19-,* **fither &c** *la19-, NE Ags;* **quhethir &c** *14-17,* **quhedir &c** *14-17,* **quheythir** *14-17,* **quhither** *15-16,* **quhidder &c** *15-17,* **quither** *la16-17,* **whidder** *16, la19,* **whither &c** *la16, e20,* **wheyther** *la17,* **whuther** *la19-e20* ['hwɛðər, 'hwɪðər; *NE Ags* 'fɪðər, 'fɪdər; *St* 'hwɛðər] *conj, pronoun* = whether *14-.*

~**-or-no** uncertain, indecisive, dithering *la19-, EC Lnk Dmf.*

wheuch *see* WHEICH

whey *18-,* **fey &c** *19-, N;* **fy** *la18-,* now *NE,* **quhaye &c** *16* [hwəi; *N* faɪ; *nEC* hwaɪ] *n* = whey *16-.*

fy brose *20-,* now *NE,* **whey brose** *la19-,* now

Ork Abd: BROSE made with whey instead of water. **whey parritch** porridge made thus *la19-e20*.

wheyther *see* WHETHER

which *see* WHILK[2]

whick *vi, freq* ~**er** &c *of a child* whimper intermittently in a subdued way; titter, giggle *19-e20*. [onomat]

whid[1] &c *18-*; **quhyd** *16* [hwɪd] *n* **1** *also* **fud** *la18-*, *now Ags* a squall, (sudden) gust of wind *16-*, *now Sh Ork*. **2** *freq of a hare* a rapid, noiseless movement, a gambol, spurt *la18-e20*.
vi **1** *of or like wind* sweep in gusts *19-*, *now Sh Ork*. **2** *freq of a hare* move quickly and noiselessly, *esp* in a jerky or zigzag way; whisk, scamper, run *18-e20*.
in *or* **wi a whid** *literary* in a moment *18-e19*. [only Sc; see SND]

whid[2] *la18-*; **whud** *la18-e20 n* a lie, exaggeration, fib *la18-*, *now local Stlg-Kcb*.
vi lie, tell fibs *19-*, *now local Stlg-Kcb*. [obscure; *cf* Eng thieves' cant *whid* a word]

whidder &c *la16-*, *now Sh*, **whither** *18-e20*, **fudder** *16-*, *now Abd*; **whudder** *19-e20*, **whuther** *la18-e20*, **quhidder** &c *15-16*, **quhedir** &c *la14-15*, **quhethir** *15*, **futher** &c *18-*, *now Ags* ['hwɪdər, 'hwɪðər, 'hwʌdər, 'hwʌðər; *NE Ags* 'fʌðər; *NE* 'fʌdər] *v* **1** *vi* move with force or impetus, rush about; hum or whizz through the air, bluster or rage like the wind *la14-*, *now Abd*. **2** *of the wind* bluster, blow fiercely in gusts *19-*, *now Sh*. **3** *chf literary* run nimbly; *of a bird* dart, flutter *19*. **4** *vt* beat, hit; *fig* floor *19-e20*. **5** *vi, only* **fudder, futher** potter, trifle in a bustling way *la19-*, *now Abd Ags*.
n **1** a sudden or loud gust of wind; a whirlwind; a blowing, spurt of water etc *la15-*, *now Sh*. **2** an impetuous rush, a flurry; a scurry *16-*, *now Bnf*. **3** a blow, smart stroke *la18-e19*.
whitherspale a small whizzing toy; *fig* something very light *19-e20*. [frequentative of WHID[1]]

whidder *see* WHETHER

whiff &c; **whuff** *19-e20*, **wheef** &c *la19-e20* [*C, S* hwɪf, hwʌf; *Sh Ork* hwif] *n* **1** = whiff *la17-*. **2** *of illness, mood etc* a slight attack, a 'touch' *19-*, *local*. *vti* **1** = whiff *17-*. **2** *vt* drive or carry by blowing; blow out (a candle etc) *19-e20*.
in a ~ in a jiffy *la19-*, *local*.

whiffle *see* WHEEFLE

whig[1] &c *n* applied to various products resulting from the souring of milk, *specif* whey, buttermilk *la18-e20*. [eModEng; perh connected w WHEY]

whig[2] &c *v* **1** *vt* spur, urge (a horse) on *la17*. **2** *vi, freq* ~ **alang, awa** *etc* go quickly, move at an easy, steady pace, jog *la17-19*. [prob chf imit; *cf* WHEECH[1]]

whig[3] &c *n* **1** nickname for an adherent of the National Covenant of 1638 and hence of Presbyterianism in the 17th century, later applied

to the *Covenanters* (COVENANT) of South-West Scotland who rose in arms in the reigns of Charles II and James II, *17-*, *now hist*; *see* SND. **2** = Whig *18-*.
whig(g)ing playing the part of a WHIG[3], adhering to Presbyterian and anti-Jacobite principles *la17-e19*.

whig *see* WIG[3]

whiggamore &c *17-*; **whiggamaire** *e17*, **whigimyre** *la17*, **whigmuir** *la17*, **whiggammer** *la17* ['hwɪgamor; *hwɪg(ə)mer, &c] *n* a *Covenanter* (COVENANT), *orig* one who participated in the Whiggamore Raid of 1648, a Presbyterian of the 17th century, a WHIG[3] *now hist*. [see SND]

whigmaleerie &c, figmaleerie &c *now Abd Fif*, **feelimageery** &c *la19-e20* [hwɪgmə'liɪrɪ, fɪg-; fɪlɪmə'gɪrɪ, &c] *n* **1** *sometimes derog* a decorative object, a piece of ornamentation in dress, stonework etc, a fantastic contrivance or contraption *la18-*. **2** a whim, fanciful notion, fad *18-*, *now local N-Dmf*. [perh FYKE + fanciful ending *-maleerie*; *cf* KICKMALEERIE]

whigmuir *see* WHIGGAMORE

while &c *la16-*, **file** &c *la18-e20*, *N*; **whill** &c *14-e20*, **quhile** &c *14-17*, **quhill** &c *la14-e17*, **qwyl** &c *la14-16*, **quhel** *15* [hwəil; *N* fəil; *conj also* *hwɪl] *n* = while *14-*.
conj **1** = while *la14-*. **2** *orig also* ~ **that** until, up to the time that *la14-*, *now local Ork-Per*, *latterly literary*.
adv **1** = while, at times *la14-16*. **2** for a or the time, temporarily; at the same time *la15-e16*.
prep until *15-e18*.
whilie &c *19-*, *local*, **whil(e)ock** &c *19-e20* a little while.
a ~ **back** some time ago, in the past *20-*, *local*.
a ~'**s time** some time, a period of time *19-*, *now Ork Abd Per*. **a** ~ **syne** a certain time ago, for some time past *19-*. **this** ~ (**back** *etc*) for some time past, for the past days, weeks etc *la15, la18-*.

while *see* WHEEL

whiles &c *la17-*, **files** *19-e20*, *N*; **quhilis** &c *la14-16* [hwəilz; *N* fəilz] *adv* **1** formerly, once *la14-16*, *only Sc*. **2** *also* **fyllies** ['fəilɪz] *la20-*, *NE* sometimes, at times, occasionally *la14-*, *Gen except Sh Ork*, *chf Sc*.
conj while, whilst *la14-19*.
~ **..** ~ **..** at one time **..** at another **..** *la15-e20*.
[OE *hwīles* adverbial genitive of *hwīl* (> WHILE); *cf* Eng]

whilk[1] &c *vi, chf* **whilking** lively, playful as a kitten *19*. [perh altered f WHIG[2]]

whilk[2] &c, **filk** &c *19-*, *N*, **which** &c *la16-*; **quhilk** &c *la14-17*, **qwilke** &c *la14-17*, **quhelk** *15-17*, **wich** &c *la15-e17*, **qu(h)ich** &c *15-17*, **qhiche** &c *17* [hwɪlk, hwʌlk; *N* fɪlk, fʌlk] *pronoun* **1** *relative:* (1) *sometimes inflected when pl, la14-e18* = which *la14-*; (2) *before* **that** or **at** *15*; (3) *in accounts, introducing a clause which* anticipates the antecedent, e16: 'Giffin to Andro Aytoun quhilk was deliverit to him be Schir Hari Schaw..' **2** *interrog* = which? *la14-*.

adj **1** *relative, sometimes inflected when with pl noun*, *la14-17* = which *la14-*: '*in witnes of the whilkis thingis*'. **2** *interrog* = which? *la14-*.

whill *see* WHILE

whillilu &c ['hwɪlɪlu] *n* an uproar, a commotion *la18-e20*. [imit of an outcry]

whilly &c *vt* cheat, trick, *esp* by means of wheedling, cajole *18-e20*. [reduced f next]

whillywha &c ['hwɪlɪ'hwɑ] *vt* wheedle, coax, cajole (a person for something or a thing from a person) *19-20*.
n **1** a flatterer, a person who deceives by wheedling *la17-e20*. **2** flattery, cajolery *19-20*.
adj flattering, glib, deceitful, unreliable *19*. [only Sc; prob chf imit of equivocation; *cf* Eng *shilly-shally, dilly-dally*]

whilom &c *la14-e20*; **quhilom &c** *la14-16*, **qwylum** *15* [*'hwəiləm] *adv* **1** *freq* ~(i)s sometimes, at times *la16-20, latterly literary*. **2** = whilom, formerly, once, at some past time *la14-e15*.
adj former, one-time; deceased *la14-e19, chf Sc*.
this ~ for some time past *e17*.

whilter &c *n, draughts* a game characterized by a certain opening exchange of moves *la19*. [uncertain]

whiltie-whaltie [*'hwɪltɪ'hwaltɪ] *n*, *chf* **play** (**a**) ~ **of the heart** beat rapidly, palpitate *la18-e19*. [reduplicated formation, prob based on WALT², with *wh*- f WHILLYWHA etc]

whimper &c *19-*, **fumper** *la18-e20*, *N*; **quhymper** *16, only Sc* ['hwɪmpər; *N* 'fʌmpər] *vi* = whimper *16-*.
n **1** = whimper. **2** a rumour, a whisper *la19-*, *local Cai-Rox*.

whin¹ &c *la17-*, **fun** *la19-*, *now NE*; **quhyn &c** *16*, **whun** *la18-e20* [hwɪn, hwʌn; *NE* fʌn] *n* **1** one of several hard crystalline igneous rocks, *eg* basalt, flint or diorite; any hard stone used as road stone *16-*. **2** a piece of WHIN¹, a boulder, slab or stone *19-*, *local C*.
~ **boul** a hard nodule of WHIN¹ embedded in sandstone *la18-20, Ags*. ~ **dust:** *whinstone* dust or small rubble *la20-*, *EC-Wgt*. **whin-float** an intrusion or surface overflow of igneous rock *la19-e20*. **whin rock** = *n*, *la17-e19*. **whin-stone &c** *n* = *n*, *16-*, *now in StEng as a geol term*.
adj hard-hearted, inflexible; solid *la18-e20*. [nME *quin*; obscure]

whin² &c *17-*, *Gen except NE*, **fun** *19-*, *now NE*; **quyin** *16*, **quhinne &c** *16-17*, **whun** *la18-20* [hwɪn, hwʌn; *NE* fʌn] *n* the common furze or gorse; *in pl* a clump or area of furze *16-*.
whinnie &c composed of or overgrown with furze *18-*.
~-**bush &c** a furze bush *18-*, *N-S*.
~-**chacker(t) &c** the whinchat *la19-*, *local Cai-Wgt*. **whin-cow &c** a tuft or branch of furze *18-*, *now Per*. ~ **dyke** a fence consisting of

furze bushes *19-*, *now Cai nEC Loth*. ~-**howe &c** a mattock for uprooting furze bushes *19-*, *now Gall*. ~-**lintie 1** = *whin-chacker(t)*, *19-*, *now Ags Rox*. **2** the linnet *19-*, *now NE, SW*. ~-**mill &c** a kind of mill for crushing furze as fodder *la18-e20, latterly* hist. **whin-sparrow** the hedge-sparrow *19-*, *local Kcdn-Wgt*.

come, gie *or* **tak** (**someone**) **through the** ~**s** (cause a person to) come through an unpleasant or painful experience; give (someone) a dressing-down *19-*, *local EC-S*. [see SND]

whine *see* WHEEN

whing *see* WHANG

whinge &c *18-*, *now local NE-S*; **quhinge &c** *16*, **wheenge** *la19-20* [hwɪn(d)ʒ, hwin(d)ʒ] *vi*, *of a dog, child etc* whine, whimper, fret whiningly *16-*, *now NE-WC, S*.
n a whine, whimper, querulous complaint *16-*, *now local Ags-Ayr*.
whinger a person who whines or complains *la18-*, *local Stlg-S*. [northern eME *hwinsian*, deriv of *hwīnan* (*v*) whine]

whinger &c *la17-e20, latterly* hist; **quhingar &c** *16*, **quhinʒear** *16* [*'hwɪnjər, *'hwɪnʒər, *'hwɪnjər, *'hwɪnʒər] *n* a short stabbing sword, *usu* hung from the belt. [chf Sc; ME *whinyard*; obscure]

whink &c *vi*, *of dogs* bark in a sharp, suppressed way, yelp as when chasing game *19-*, *now Slk*.
n a sharp, suppressed bark or yelp from a dog; a child's sharp cry, a whimper *19-*, *now Slk*. [see SND]

whinner &c *17-*, *now Sh Ork*; **whunner &c** *19-e20 v* **1** *vi* whizz, whistle through the air; move quickly *19-e20*. **2** go **at** with all one's strength, hammer **at** *19-*, *now Sh*. **3** *vt* hit, strike (a person) *e17*.
n **1** a whizzing sound, the noise made by rapid flight or motion *e19*. **2** a crash, clatter; (the sound of) a heavy fall *19-*, *now Sh Ork*. **3** a resounding blow, a whack, wallop *19-*, *now Sh Ork*. [frequentative of Eng *whine*]

whip &c *la17-*, **fup** *la18-*, *now NE*; **quhip &c** *15-17*, **wheep** *18-*, *now NE*, **whup** *la18-*, *local Ork-Wgt* [*Sh-N* hwip; *C, S* hwʌp; *NE also* fʌp] *n* **1** = whip *15-*. **2** *also fig* a blow with a whip; *in pl* a whipping, *chf* **get, gie** *or* **hae ane's** ~**s** *15-*, *now EC Rox*. **3** a sudden quick movement: (1) *in gen* a start, jerk, swirl, gust *la16-e20*; (2) a crack, shot, go **at** *la19-*, *now local Ork-Lnk*. **4** *chf in pl* plenty, lots *la19-*, *now Cai*. **5** *weaving* a thread separate from the basic warp and weft which is introduced into the weave to form a pattern *19*. **6** a bandage *e16*, *only Sc*. **7** a wreath, garland *e16*, *only Sc*.
vt **1** = whip *16-*. **2** twine, bind about, twist, coil *16-e20*.
adv with a quick or sudden movement, like a shot, in a jiffy *19-*, *now Sh Abd Per*.

whipper &c-in a school attendance-officer *19-*, *Gen except Sh Ork*. **whippert** hasty and sharp in manner or behaviour *19-e20*. **whippie &c**

n **1** term of abuse for a girl, a hussy *19*. **2** a rope of twisted straw *20-, EC, S*. *adj* quick or brisk in movement, nimble, agile *19-, now Fif Wgt*.

whiplicker a carter; *specif in St Andrews* a member of the *Incorporated* (INCORPORATE) Society of Whiplickers or Carters *19-e20, Fif*.

whipman a carter; a member of one of the several societies of carters and ploughmen, *now only* in West Linton, where the local society celebrates an annual festival *la18-, now Pbls*. **lick a** *or the* **~shaft** kiss the rod, suffer humiliation or defeat *18-e19*.

at a(e) *or* **in a** ~ at one stroke or swoop, suddenly *19-, now local Ork-Wgt*. **eddy fup** a wind whipping round a corner *20-, NE*. **fup a haud o** seize in one's grip *e20, Bnf Abd*. **~ o dearth** an unexpected hardship, a time of need or emergency, 'a rainy day' *la19-e20*. **~ the cat** *chf of a tailor* go from house to house practising one's trade *19-, now hist*.

whippitie- &c; whuppity- &c *n* **Whuppity Scoorie** a traditional custom among young people in Lanark celebrated on 1 Mar *20-, Lnk; see* SND. **W~ Stourie** ['~ 'sturɪ] **1** name for a kind of household fairy or *brownie* (BROON) *19-e20*. **2** ~ **stourie** a light-footed nimble person *20-, now Fif Dnbt*. [only Sc; appar a dim or deriv of WHIP; for the second elements see SCOUR[2] *n* 1, 2 and STOUR *n* 6, *v* 1]

whirken &c; whurken *vt* choke, suffocate *19-e20, S*. [ME]

whirl &c, furl &c *la18-, now NE Ags*; **quhirll &c** *15-16*, **quherle** *e16*, **whurl &c** *la19-* [hwɪrl, hwʌrl; *NE Ags* fʌrl] *vti* **1** = whirl *15-*. **2** *vt* propel on wheels, trundle, cart; drive on *16-, now local Cai-SW*.

n = whirl *15-*.

~ie &c *n* **1** = HUTCH *n* 2, *19-, now Lnk*. **2** a chimney-cowl *la20-, Kcdn Lnk Rox*. *adj* = whirly. **~y** (**bed**) a bed on castors which can be rolled under another bed when not in use *la19-e20*. **~y-gate** *20-, now local Fif-Ayr*, **furlin yett** *la19-e20, Mry Bnf* a turnstile.

furl o birse the ace of spades, so called because of the intricate, flowery ornamentation *usu* found on this card *e20, Bnf Abd*.

whirligig &c *la18-*; **whirligigum &c** *la18-e20* ['hwɪrlɪgɪg(əm), 'hwʌrlɪ, -dʒɪg-] *n* **1** (1) = whirligig, a rotating contrivance *la19-*. (2) *specif* a revolving chimney cowl *la19-, C, S*. **2** a spiral or fancy ornament; a piece of unnecessary finery; an intricate symbol, design or diagram *la18-*.

whirliwha &c ['hwɪrlɪhwɑ] *n* a piece of fanciful ornamentation *19-e20*.

vt flatter, deceive by flattery, trick *19*. [conflation of *whirlie* (WHIRL) and WHILLYWHA]

whirr &c *19-*; **quirre** *15*, **quhir &c** *16*, **whurr** *19* [hwɪr, hwʌr] *vi* **1** = whirr *15-*. **2** use a strongly burred or uvular *r* in one's speech *la19-, now Lnk Wgt*.

n **1** = whirr. **2** commotion, rush, hurrying about *e16, la19-, now Bnf*. **3** a burr in speech, the use of the uvular *r la20-, Lnk SW*.

whirry &c *vt* carry off, drive away or out *18-e19*. [eModEng; perh conflation of prec w Eng *hurry*]

whishie &c; whusky &c ['hwɪʃɪ, 'hwʌʃɪ, 'hwʌskɪ] *n*, *also* **~-whey-beard** the whitethroat *la19*. [var of *wheetle* (WHEET[1]) altered to imitate the bird's song]

whisht; whist &c, wisht &c *19-*, **wheesht &c** *19-*, **wheesh &c** *20-*, **whush** *la19-e20* [hwɪʃ(t), hwiʃ(t), hwɪst, hwist, hwuʃ(t), wɪʃt, wiʃt, wuʃt] *interj* be quiet!, shut up! *18-*.

v **1** *vi* utter the interj *wheesht!*, call for silence *20-, Sh Cai EC, WC*. **2** *vt* silence, cause to be quiet, quieten *19-, now Sh Cai EC, WC*. **3** *vi* be quiet, remain silent *la18-*.

n, *also* **~ie** *chf in negative* the slightest sound, the least whisper; the faintest rumour or report *la18-, now local Sh-Loth*.

adj quiet, silent, hushed *18-*.

haud *or* **keep one's** ~ be quiet, keep silent, hold one's tongue *la18-*. [eModEng]

whisk *la17-*, **wisk &c** *only Sc*; **quhisk** *15-16*, *only Sc*, **whusk** *la19 vti* **1** = whisk *la15-*. **2** *vt* beat, whip (a person) *la18-e19*. **3** *vi, of the heart* flutter, palpitate *e19*.

n **1** a brief rapid sweeping movement (of a weapon etc); a sudden light stroke etc; a light stroke of a brush etc *la14-*. **2** a blow, swipe *19-e20*. **3** *chf in pl* a pair of small reels used to facilitate the winding of yarn onto a bobbin *19*. **4** *only* **wisk** a bunch, a tangled mass (of threads etc) *20-, Sh Ork Bnf Abd*.

wisker &c 1 a bunch of feathers, short straws etc whipped at one end to form a kind of handbrush *19-, NE*. **2** a bunch, *usu* of straw, used as a sheath for knitting needles at a woman's waist *19-, NE*. **~it &c** *of a horse* with a switched tail *18-19*.

with a ~ in an instant, in a flash *la14-16*. [earlier in Sc; prob Scand; *cf* ON *visk*]

whisky &c, fuskie &c *19-e20, NE*; **whusky &c** *19-*, **whisk** *la18-e19 n* a spirit distilled from malted barley in a pot still (**malt** ~ (MAUT)), or with the addition of unmalted grain spirit (*usu* maize) made in a patent still (**blended** ~) *18-*.

whiskied *19-e20*, **whiskified &c** *19* affected by WHISKY, tipsy.

~-house *la18-e19*. **~-pig** an earthenware jar for holding WHISKY *19-, now Sh Ork*. **~-tacket** a pimple on the face ascribed to too much WHISKY-drinking *19-, now local NE-Lnk*. [var of *usque* (USQUEBAE)]

whissille *see* WHISTLE

whissle *see* WISSEL

whist *see* WHISHT

whistle *19-*, **fussle &c** *19-, now NE*; **quhistle &c** *la14-e17*, **quyschile** *la14*, **qwistle** *15-16*,

whissille *la16-17*, **whustle &c** *19-*, *local*
['hwɪsl, 'hwʌsl; *Abd* 'fʌsl; *'hwɪʃl] *n* **1** = whistle *la14-*. **2** a wallop, swipe, swingeing blow
19-, *now Bnf Abd*.
vti **1** = whistle *la14-*. **2** *only* **fussle** beat
sharply, cuff *la19-20, NE*.
whistler &c 1 = whistler *16-*. **2** nickname
for an inhabitant of Fife *la19-*, *Per Fif* [a pun on
Eng *fifer*]. **3** a big specimen of anything *la20-*,
Cai Per Stlg. **whistlin** *or* **fusslin Sunday** the
fast day (FAST) (*usu* a Thursday) before Communion on which whistling was permitted *la19-*,
now Kcdn.
fusslebare *of land* poor, hilly, exposed *la19-*,
Abd. **~-binkie** a person who attended a *penny
wedding* (PENNY) without paying and had no
right to share in the entertainment; a mere
spectator (who sometimes whistled for his own
amusement) *e19*. **~-kirk** a church with an
organ, *freq specif* an Episcopalian Church since
they favoured the use of church organs in contrast to the Presbyterians *19*. **~-wood &c** any
tree with a slippery bark so that twigs can be
used to make a whistle *19-*, *now Dmf*.
no to gie a ~ not to give a damn, have nothing
but contempt for *la19-*, *now local Sh-Per*. ~
(on) one's thoum do nothing useful, twiddle
one's thumbs, be nonplussed after some snub
etc *18-*, *now local Sh-Per*.
whit *see* WHAT[1]
white[1] **&c** *16-*, **fite &c** *la19-*, *NE*; **quhit &c**
la14-e17, **quhite &c** *15-17*, **whit &c** *la16-e18*
[hwəit; *NE* fəit] *adj* **1** = white *la14-*. **2** *of coins*
silver *18-*, *now local Sh-Loth*. **3** *freq in place-
names*: (1) *of arable land* fallow, unploughed
la18-, *now Cai*; (2) *of hill-land* covered with
coarse bent or natural grass instead of heather,
bracken or scrub *19-*, *local Ags-SW*. **4** flattering, fair-seeming, *usu* implying an intention to
deceive *la15-e19*.
n (*la15-*), *vti* (*la16-*) = white.
fiteichtie ['fəitɪxtɪ] rather white, whitish *20-*,
NE. **whitie &c** the whiting *la19-*, *now Dnbt
Ayr*. **whitie-broon &c** *19-*, *now Ork Ags Fif*,
fitit- &c *e20, Bnf Abd or* **whited-broon &c**
la18-e20, Abd: *n*, (*adj*) applied to linen thread in
which the brown colour of the flax has been
lightened by washing but not bleaching.
whiting flattery *18-e19*. **~ly &c** pale, whitish, delicate-looking *la15-e20*.
~-bonnet &c a person at an auction sale
engaged by the seller to raise the bidding *la18-*.
~ **breid &c** white bread etc as opposed to *oat*
(AIT) or barley cakes *19-*. **white cockade** the
rosette worn by Jacobites to represent the *white
rose* as an emblem of the Stewart cause *18*. ~
cow remains of heather, WHIN[2] and broom
bleached by sun and rain after the annual
burning *la19-*, *now Ags*. **White Craw** nickname for a native of Carnwath, Lnk *la20-*, *Lnk*.
~-faced *of a sheep* applied to a breed with a
white face *la18-*, *now Cai*. **white hare** the

Alpine, Scottish mountain or blue hare, *esp* in
its white winter coat *19-*, *now N Ags Per*. ~
hause &c an oatmeal *pudding* (PUDDIN *n* 2)
cooked in a sheep's gullet *e16, e19*. **white
head** a white head-dress *la16*. ~ **herring**
herring which is cured by salting only *18-e19*.
~ **hoolet** the barn owl *la19-*, *local Stlg-Ayr*. ~
house a house built with stone and lime as
opposed to a *black-house* (BLACK) *la19-20, Cai
Hebrides Highl*. ~ **ice** *curling* (CURL) the ice up
the middle of the rink, whitened and roughened
by the friction of the stones *19-*, *now Per Ayr*.
~ **iron &c** tin-plate, tinned iron *la15-*, *now NE
Ags Per*. **fite-iron gentry** social upstarts; people who make a pretence of gentility *la19-e20*,
NE. **~-iron man** a tin-plate worker, a tinsmith *18*. **fite-iron wife** a female tinker *20-*,
NE. ~ **meal** oatmeal as distinct from barley
meal *18-*, *now Cai Fif Ayr*. ~ **meat** the flesh of
poultry or game *18-*. ~ **peat** a kind of sphag-
num moss found under the surface layer of vegetation *la18-*, *now Per*. ~ **puddin &c** a kind of
pudding (PUDDIN *n* 2) or sausage stuffed with
oatmeal, suet, salt, pepper and onions *17-*. ~
room a room in a textile factory where cloth is
inspected and prepared for despatch after finishing *20-*, *Dnbt Ayr*. **white rose** the emblem
of royalism and legitimacy, adopted in Scotland as the symbol of adherence to Jacobitism
and the Stewart cause *19-*, *hist*; cf *white cockade*.
~ **seam** plain needlework *18-19*. ~ **shower**
a shower of snow *19-*, *Sh NE*. ~ **siller** silver
money as opposed to coppers, cash in silver *19-*,
Sh-WC. ~ **sookie** *chf in pl* white clover *la19-*,
now local Ags-Lnk. ~ **victual** cereal or grain
crops as opposed to green crops *la18-*, *Per Stlg
Ayr*.
the ~ **o the pot** the last run of the wash in the
(illegal) distillation of WHISKY *la20-*, *WC*.
white[2] **&c** *18-*, *now local Ags-S*, **fite &c** *la19-*,
NE; **quhite** *16*, **twit &c** *20-*, *Sh Ork* [hwəit;
Sh Ork twit; *Cai* twəit; *Sh also* hwit, twɪt; *NE also*
fəit] *vt* cut with a knife, pare, whittle *18-*, *now
local NE-S*.
fite the (**idle**) **pin** fritter away time *la19-e20*,
Bnf Abd. [OE *þwitan*]
white[3] **&c** *la19-e20*, *NE*; **quhete &c** *la14-17*,
qwet *la14-15*, **quhite** *16* [hwit; *NE* hwəit;
NE also *fəit] *n* = wheat. [OED *wheat*]
whiteret *see* WHITRAT
whither *la17-*; **quhether &c** *15-e16*, **quhidder** *la15-e17* *adv, interrog and relative* = whither.
whither *see* WHETHER, WHIDDER
whitherspale *see* WHIDDER
whitin &c *18-19*, **fitin &c** *la19-*, *NE*; **quhiting** *17*, **quhittine** *17* ['hwəitɪn; *NE* 'fəit-] *n* **1**
= whiting *18-*, *now NE*. **2** an immature sea
trout *la18-e19*; *cf* next.
whitling &c *n* an immature sea trout at the
stage of development equivalent to the GRILSE
of the salmon *18-*, *now EC Ayr Rox*. [northern

eModEng *whiddelynge*, perh related to OE
hwītling the whiting, f *hwīt* white + dim suffix
-ling; *cf* prec]

whitrat &c *la18-*, now Sh Ross C, S, **futrat &c**
la19-, N, **whitret** *17-e20*; **quhitrat &c**
15-16, **quhitred &c** *15-16*, **quhitret**
la15-16, **fittret** *16*, **whitred** *la17-e19*, **whitterick &c** *17-e20*, C, S, **whiteret &c** *19-e20*
['hwɪtrət, 'hwʌt-, -(ə)rɪk; N 'fʌt-; *'fɪt-, *-rəd] *n*
1 an animal of the genus *Mustela*, *chf* the weasel
or stoat *15-*, *local*. **2** a thin, small, hatchet-
faced person of an active, ferrety disposition
19-, *local Sh-Dmf*. [ME *whitratt, whytrate*, orig a
compound of *white* and *rat*]

Whitsun &c *19-*; **quysson** *15* ['hwɪtsʌn,
'hwɪsən, 'hwʌsən; *'wɪtsʌn] *n* = Whitsun.
~ **Term** the third or summer term in the Universities of St Andrews and Glasgow *20-*.

Whitsunday *la17-*; **qw(h)yssonday &c**
la14-e15, **Wossonday &c** *la14*, **Witsounday &c** *la14-16*, **Whussenday &c**
la19-e20 ['hwʌtsʌnde, 'hwɪs(ə)ndɪ, 'hwʌs(ə)ndɪ;
NE 'wɪts(ə)ndɪ, 'wʌt-; *'wɪsəndɪ] *n* **1** = Whitsunday *la14-*. **2** 15 May, a Scottish quarter
day, one of the *term days* (TERM), though the date
for removals and for the employment of servants was changed in 1886 to 28 May) *la14-*.

whitter[1] *n* a small or insignificant object; a trifle
la18-, now Edb. [perh dim or frequentative of
Eng *whit* the least amount]

whitter[2] *vt* diminish by taking away small portions; whittle *19-*, now *Ork Ags Lnk*. [var of
Eng *whittle* pare]

whitter[3] *&c n* a drink of liquor; liquor *la18-*, now
Stlg. [see SND]

whitter[4] *&c* *la16*, *19-*, **quitter** *e16*;
qu(h)ittour *la16* *vti* **1** *of birds* twitter, warble,
chirp *e16*, *19-*, now *Wgt*. **2** *of persons* whisper,
mutter, *freq* rapidly *19-e20*. **3** *vi* flutter,
scamper, scurry, patter; flicker, quiver *e16*,
19-e20.
n chatter, prattle; a talkative person *la16*,
19-e20. [imit]

whitterick *n* the curlew *la19-*, local *Fif-Rox*.
[perh f its cry, with the form infl by *whitterick*
(WHITRAT)]

whitterick *see* WHITRAT

whittie-whattie &c *la17-*; **whytie-whatie
&c** *la17-e19*, **wheety-whattie &c** *la18-e20*
['hwɪtɪ'hwatɪ] *n* frivolous excuses, circumlocutions intended to conceal the truth; indecision
la17-20.
vi talk frivolously, shilly-shally; make frivolous
excuses *19-*, now *Sh*. [based on WHEET[2] and
WHEETIE]

whittle[1] *&c* *18-*, **futtle** *18-*, N; **quhittil** *la16*,
whuttle *19-e20 n* **1** *also* **thewtill** *la15* a knife
in gen, *la15-*, now *local*. **2** *specif* a harvest-hook,
sickle, scythe; a hedge-bill *18-*, now *Lnk Ayr*. **3**
a whetstone, *specif* one for sharpening scythes
19-, now *Sh WC*. **4** *only* **futtle** an inefficient or
useless instrument or tool *e20*, *Cai*.

vt = whittle *19-*. [OED *whittle, thwittle*]
whittle[2] **&c, futley &c** *la19-*, NE ['hwʌtl; NE
'fʌtlɪ] *n* = whitlow *la16-*.
~ **beal(in) &c** = *n*, *la19-*, now *local Sh-Ayr*.
[reduced form]

who *see* WHA
whoast *see* HOAST
whole *see* HAIL[1]
whom *see* WHA
whommle *see* WHUMMLE
whoo *see* HOO[1]
whoogh *see* HOOCH
whoom [hwum] *n* a blaze; a roaring sound *e20*,
Kcdn. [onomat]
whooper &c *n* nickname for certain natives of
Ayton, Bwk *la19*, *Bwk*. [perh for *hooper*, ie a
cooper in the local barrel-factory]
whope *see* HOPE[1]
whore *see* HURE
whorn *see* HORN
whose *see* WHA
whosle *see* WHEEZE[3]
whow [hwʌu] *interj* expressing astonishment or
surprise, *usu* with regret or weariness *19-*, now
EC Rox. [onomat]
whow *see* HOO[1]
whryne *la16*; **quhryne** *e16* [*hwrəin] *vi* whine,
squeak *16*.
n whining, a querulous cry *e16*. [only Sc; ON
hrína. OED *whrine*]
whud *see* WHID[2]
whudder *see* WHIDDER
whuff *see* WHIFF
whult &c *n* anything large of its kind, a whopper *19-e20*.
~**er** = *n*, *19-*, now *Stlg*. [imit]
whumart *see* FOUMART
whummle &c *la18-*, **fummle &c** *18-20*, NE;
quhemle *16*, **quhomle** *16*, **whommle &c**
18-e20, **whumble** *la18-19*, **whammle &c**
19-, **fommle &c** *19-20*, NE *vti* **1** capsize,
overturn *16-*, now *Sh C-S*. **2** *vt, of water* overwhelm, drown *la16-19*. **3** (1) turn (a
container etc) upside down, invert *18-*, now *Sh
C-S*; (2) *fig* overthrow, throw into ruin or confusion *19-20*. **4** empty (a container) by tilting it,
turn or pour out (the contents of a container
etc) *18-*, now *Sh Stlg Wgt*. **5** cover or conceal
(something) by inverting a hollow container
over it *19-*, now *Sh Ork*. **6** cause to turn or
revolve, turn inside out, stir or toss round and
round *19-*, now *EC Lnk SW*. **7** *vi* roll, revolve,
whirl; toss and turn, rock to and fro *la18-*, now
Ags Per. **8** go head over heels, fall, tumble or
sprawl suddenly; move unsteadily, stumble
la18-, now *local Sh-SW*. **9** *vt* knock down, push
or bowl over; propel or thrust forcibly *19-e20*.
10 overpower, defeat, get the better of; astonish
la19-, now *Fif*.
n **1** a capsizing, overturning, upset *19-*, *Sh, local
Stlg-Wgt*. **2** a turning, a whirling round; a

rocking, tossing or rolling from side to side *19*. **3** a tumble, fall, avalanche; *fig* a downfall, reversal of good fortune *19-*, *now Ags Per Dmf*. **dish** *etc* **o whammle** (*now Dmf*) *or* **whamlin(s)** &c (*now Lnk Kcb*) *joc* no food, nothing to eat or drink *20-*; *cf* DISH. [metath f ME *quelm*, *w(h)elm* > ModEng *overwhelm*. OED *whemmel*]

whun *see* WHAN, WHIN[1], WHIN[2]

whunner *see* WHINNER

whup *vt* **whupper** = whopper *la19-*, *now Ork Cai*.

whup *see* WHIP

whuppity *see* WHIPPITIE

whurken *see* WHIRKEN

whurl &c *19-20*, **forl** &c *e16*, *19-20*, *NE*; **thorl** &c *19-e20*; **quhorle** *e16* *n* **1** = whorl, the small perforated stone flywheel of a spindle; any perforated stone thought to have been used by the fairies *e16*, *19-e20*. **2** *also* **horl** &c a (small) wheel, pulley etc, *eg* on a child's toy cart, in the winding gear at a pithead *la18-*, *now Fif*.
~ **bane** the hip-bone or joint; a vertebra *19*. [OED *whorl*]

whurl *see* WHIRL

whurr *see* WHIRR

whush *19-*, *now Ork C*, **wheesh** *20-*, *now local NE-Wgt* *n*, *only* **whush** = whish, a rushing noise; a stir, commotion *19-*, *now Ork C*.
vi make a rushing sound, *chf* **wheesher** anything large of its kind, a whopper *la19-*, *now NE, local Stlg-Wgt*.
quhisch *interj* representing the sound of something moving rapidly through the air *e16*. [OED *whish*]

whush *see* WHISHT

whusk *see* WHISK

whusky *see* WHISHIE, WHISKY

whusper *19-e20*; **quhisper** *16* *n, v* = whisper. [OED *whisper*]

Whussenday *see* WHITSUNDAY

whustle *see* WHISTLE

whut *see* WHAT[1]

whuther *see* WHETHER, WHIDDER

whuttle *see* WHITTLE[1]

why *la16-*; **quhy** &c *la14-16* *adv* = why *la14-*.
~ **for** (**no**) why (not)? *19-*, *now local Sh-Lnk*.

whytie-whatie *see* WHITTIE-WHATTIE

wi *18-*, **with** &c; **wygh** &c *15*, **we** *18-e19*, **wae** *e20* [wɪ, wə, w; wi; *St* wɪθ] *prep* **1** = with *la14-*. **2** by: (1) *after passive verb* by means of, by the action of *la14-*: '*eaten with the mice*'. (2) *now followed by gerund* by reason of, through *la14-*: '*wi being ill he couldna come*'. (3) *referring to procreation* by (one or other parent) *la16-*, *now Sh-N*: '*a woman with whom he had four children*'. (4) by the conveyance of (bus, train etc) *20-*. **3** *with negative* in consequence of; on account of *19-*: '*they coudna fecht wi cauld*'. **4** in ownership of, as owner of; in possession of *15*.
dee ~ **die** of *19-*. **gude nicht** *etc* ~ good night etc to *19-*, *Gen except Ork*. **marry** ~ marry, be

married to *18-*. **be used** *etc* ~ be used to *la19-*. ~ **the mair** and more, and something over *la15-e16*. ~ **his** *etc* **tale** according to *him*, or so *he* says *19-*, *local*. **will** *or* **winna dae** *etc* ~ **me** *etc* can or cannot be done by me *19-*, *now Sh Cai Abd*: '*that buik winna read wi me*'.

wice *see* WISE

wich *see* WHILK[2]

wicht[1] &c, **wight** [wɪxt; *Ork also* wəit] *n* **1** *freq with contempt or pity* = wight, a human being, person *la14-20*. **2** a supernatural being; a being with supernatural powers *la18-e20*.

wicht[2], **wight** *la16-* [wɪxt] *adj, only verse, 18-* **1** valiant, courageous (1) *of persons, esp warriors, la14-e20*; (2) *of actions or attributes, la14-16*. (1) *of persons or animals, also fig* strong, vigorous *15-19*. (2) *of things* strongly constructed, stout *15-19*. **3** active, agile *la14-19*.
n a valiant man *la14*.
adv swiftly, nimbly *la16-18*. [arch and dial in Eng; eME *wiht* brave, ON *vígt*, neuter of *vígr* of fighting age]

wick[1]; week &c *n* **1** a corner of the mouth *18-*, *local*. **2** the corner of the eye *19-e20*. **3** *curling* (CURL), *bowls* a cannon of one stone etc off another towards the TEE[1] *19-*. **4** a cleft in the face of a hill, *specif* the **Wicks o Baiglie** on the edge of the Ochil Hills on the old Kinross to Perth road *19-*.
vti, curling (CURL) cannon one stone off another *la18-*.
hing by the ~s of the mouth hang on with grim determination for as long as possible *17-19*. [ME *wyke* = *n* 1; ON *vik* in *munnvik* corner of the mouth, *vikja* turn, deflect]

wick[2] *n* a wicked person, *now specif* a naughty child *la14*, *20-* (*Abd EC Ayr*). [ME *wikke*; OE *wicca* a wizard]

wick *see* OUK

wicked; wickit &c, **wicket** &c *19-e20*, *chf NE*, **wekit** &c *la14-e16* ['wɪkɪt; *'wikɪt] *adj* **1** = wicked *la14-*. **2** *of persons or animals or their actions* bad-tempered, ill-natured, viciously angry *16-*.

wicker[1] &c *n* **1** = wicker *16-*. **2** wickers collectively, wickerwork *14-*.

wicker[2] *vi, n, of the lip or eyelid* twitch, flicker *19-e20*. [prob frequentative of WICK[1], w infl f Eng *flicker*]

wicket *n* **1** a small opening or unglazed window in a wall *17-19*. **2** = wicket.

wicket, wickit *see* WICKED

Wiclefit [*'wɪklɪfɪt] *n* = Wycliffite, a follower of Wycliffe *la16*. [OED *Wycliffite*]

wictorag [*'vɪktəredʒ] *n* victory *la14*. [only Sc; VICTOR[1] + -*age*. OED *victorage*]

wid *see* WILL[1]

widd *see* WUID[1], WUID[2]

widden *see* WADE

widder *see* WEATHER

widderlok *see* WITHERLOCK

widdershins, widdersones *see* WITHERSHINS

widderwise *see* WITHERWYS

widdie &c *la15-*, **widdy &c** *16-20, chf Sc*, **withy &c** *e15, 19*; **woodie &c** *18-e20*, **wuddie &c** *19-e20 n* **1** a twig or wand of willow or other tough but flexible wood; several such intertwined to form a rope (1) *in gen, 15-*; (2) used for halters and harness *18-e20*; (3) made into a container for carrying things over the shoulder *19*. **2** the gallows rope *la15-e20*. **3** = withy, willow *la19-*. **4** a certain quantity of iron *15-e17*.

~fu &c ['~fu, '~fə] *n* a gallowsbird, scoundrel; *now chf joc* a rogue, scamp *16-20, only Sc.* **~ neck** a gallowsbird *la15-16, only Sc.* **in(to) the ~necks** at loggerheads, in a violent altercation *e20, Abd*.

cheat the ~ *v* escape hanging *19-, now Per. n* a rogue *19-, local*.

widdle¹ &c *vt* **1** invoke or inflict a curse on *la16*. **2** beguile, lead astray *la17*. [only Sc; obscure]

widdle² &c *vi* **1** move slowly and unsteadily, stagger, waddle *la18-, now Sh Ork Stlg*. **2** progress slowly and laboriously, struggle **on** *la18-, now Rox*.

n **1** *freq fig* a struggle *la18-e20*. **2** a bustle, tumult *e19*. [eModEng *widdle-waddle* unsteadily; altered f Eng *waddle*]

widdy *see* WIDDIE

wide &c *adj* **1** = wide *la14-*. **2** great (in non-physical sense) *la16*. **3** *of speech* unrestrained, violent *la16*.

adv = wide *la14-*.

~-gab the angler fish *19-e20*.

gae *or* **keep ~** *of a sheepdog* go ahead but well away from the sheep *la19-, now Cai Per Ayr*. **haud ~ o** keep clear of, avoid *20-, now Cai Per*. **~ to the wa** *of a door* wide open *19-, now Sh Ork NE*.

wide *see* WADE

widna *see* WILL¹

widow *la16-*; **wedow &c** ['widə, 'widɪ, 'wɪdə, wɪdɪ] *n* **1** *also freq attrib* = widow, a wife bereaved of her husband *la14-*: '*widow-woman*'. **2** *also attrib* a widower, a husband bereaved of his wife *la14-*.

widowity &c [*wɪ'd(j)uɪtɪ] widowhood *la16-18, only Sc* [altered f Eng *viduity*].

wie *see* WEE

wield &c, wald &c *now Ork*; **weel &c** *19-20, chf Abd* [wil(d); *Ork also* wald] *vti* **1** = wield *la14-*. **2** *vt* possess; obtain *la14-18*. **3** execute, perform *e16*. **4** direct, control (one's body, limbs etc) *la15-e19*.

n control, possession *la16*.

wielder &c **1** = wielder. **2** the author or cause **of** *la16*. **waldin** *15-e16*, **waddin &c** *19-e20* ['wadən, 'wadən; *'wald-, *'wald-] supple, vigorous; young, active. **hae the weelins o** have control or full use of (one's body, limbs etc) *20, Abd*.

wife &c *n, pl also* **wifes &c** [wəifs] **1** *now chf disparaging* a woman *in gen, now only* a middle-aged or older woman *la14-*. **2** = wife, a married woman *la14-*. **3** a kept mistress, concubine *e15*. **4** affectionate term for a female friend *e17*.

wifie &c *19-*, **wifock &c** *19-e20*, **wifockie &c** *la18-, chf N* ['wəif-] = *n* **1**; *also* **wife-carl** a man who occupies himself with women's affairs; a little girl *16-e19*.

wiffen *see* WEAVE

wiffer-waffer ['wɪfər'wafər] *n* a nonentity, a useless, ineffectual person *20-, Abd Kcdn*.

wifferty-wafferty ineffectual, doddering *la20-, Kcdn Ags*. [reduplicated f WAFF²]

wifie, wifock(ie) *see* WIFE

wig¹ &c; **weeg &c** *la17-19* [wɪg; *Ork-Mry, EC* wig] *n* = wig, artificial hair.

wig² &c *n* **frae ~ to wa** back and forward *17-e20, chf NE*. [ON *veggr* a wall]

wig³ &c *la18-e20*; **whig** *19-e20 n* a kind of small oblong currant bun. [ME *wigg* a kind of cake, MDu *wigge* a wedge, wedge-shaped cake]

wigglety-wagglety *see* WEEGLE

wight *see* WICHT¹, WICHT²

wi'in *see* WITHIN

wild; **wuld &c** *e15, 19-e20*, **wile &c** *la16, la19-, now Arg Wgt*, **will &c** *19-*, **wull &c** *19-* [wəil(d), wɪl, wʌl; *Per also* wald] *adj* **1** = wild *la14-*. **2** *of vocal sounds* loud and unrestrained *16-*. **3** strong-tasting, rank *la19-, local Sh-nEC*. **4** nickname for the extreme Evangelical party in the *Church of Scotland* (CHURCH) *la18-19*.

adv extremely, very *19-, local*.

wild cat &c *la15-*, **will cat &c** *la16-*, **wullcat &c** *19-* = wild cat. **tummle** *etc* **the, one's** *or* **ower one's wullcat(s)**, **wilkies &c** tumble head over heels, somersault *19-, chf WC*; cf *tummle or turn the cat* (TUMMLE, TURN). **~ coal** poor quality coal *19, WC*. **~fire 1** = wildfire *18-*. **2** summer lightning, lightning without thunder *la18-, now Ork-Per*. **3** *mining* fire-damp *la19-, now Fif*. **4** name of various wild flowers *19-, now Ags*. **~ kail** the wild radish; the charlock *19-, SW*. **~ parrot** an inferior kind of soft coal *20-, Fif sEC, WC*. **~ rhubarb &c** the common butterbur *la19-, Per-S*.

~ and .. = *adv, 20-, chf Stlg Arg*: '*the weather's wild an cold*'; cf Eng *good and ..*

wile¹ &c *vt* **1** deceive by a wile, beguile *la14, la19-e20, only Sc*. **2** get or bring by a wile (a person or animal to or from a place, or a thing from a person) *la15-, now local Sh-Per*.

n, also **quhile** *la14* [wəil] = wile, guile, a trick *la14-*.

wylie &c clever, sagacious, wise *la18-, now Sh Ags*.

wile² &c *la14-e20*, **vild &c** *la16-, now Sh* [wəil; *Sh* vəild] *adj* = vile.

wile *see* WALE, WILD

wilful *see* WILL²

wilk *see* WULK

wilkies *see* WILD

will¹ &c, wull *19-* *v, pres, with 2 pers sing pronoun*

wiltu &c *18-e20*, **wilter** &c *18-19; with negative* **winna** *18-*, **wunna** *19-e20* ['wɪnə, -nɪ, 'wʌnə, -nɪ]. *pt also* **wald** *la14-e19*, **wad** *la16-, now literary*, **wud** *19-, now C*, **wid** *la19-* [wad, wʌd, wɪd; *wald]; *with negative* **wadna** *la18-e20*, **wudna** *la19-, C*, **widna** *la19- vti* **1** = will *la14-.* **2** (1) *pres* = shall, *esp expressing the future in 1 pers, and stronger intention in 2 and 3 pers, 16-; cf* SALL. (2) *pt* = should, *in certain usages, la15-.* **wad** &c **1** = would *la14-.* **2** *with omission of 'have', 16-: 'But I wud not latt'n them say't'.* **twad** it would *la18-, now NE Ags Per.* **willin(g)** *16-*, **wullint** &c *19-, now Kcdn C, S* **1** = willing. **2** *of things* yielding, pliant *16-.* **3** eager, deliberately intending *e20.* **willingly** &c **1** = willingly *la16-.* **2** *only* **willintly** &c intentionally *19-, now Ags.*

it *etc* ~ **be** .. I think or expect it is .., it is approximately .. *17-.*

will² &c; **wull** *18- n* **1** = will, wish, intent *la14-.* **2** a request, command *16-e19.* **3** *law* a clause in a summons expressing a royal command, *chf* **the** ~ **of the summons** *la17-e20.* **willed**, **willy** wilful, headstrong *19.* **wilful** &c **1** = wilful *la14-.* **2** purposing, intending (to do something) *la14-e19.* **wilful empire** absolute sovereignty, autocracy *e16, only Sc.*

at one's ain ~ of one's own free will, as one wishes *la19-, Cai C.* **at all** ~ as much as one could wish for; *ironic* in all conscience *19-, local Sh-Ags.* **come in someone's** ~ submit oneself to someone's decision or wishes *la15-e19.* **get, hae** *or* **take one's will(s)** o get one's way with, do what one likes with, have at one's disposal or mercy *la18-, now local.* **hae** o *freq in negative* take no pleasure in, have no liking for *17-, now NE.* **I** *etc* **hinna** ~ **that** I etc hope that .. not *la19-, NE.* **if your willes is** *etc* if you will, wish, please etc *la14-15.* **in** ~ intending or purposing (to do something) *la14-e16.* **of** ~ **1** = prec *la14.* **2** spontaneously, of one's own accord *la14-19.* **put something in someone's** ~ leave something to someone's discretion *la18.* **what's your** ~ **1** formula used by (1) a servant in answering a summons *18-19;* (2) a shopkeeper to a customer *la19-e20;* **2** pardon? *(when asking someone to repeat something) e16, 19-e20.* **wi one's** ~ with one's consent or approval *16-, now Sh-N.*

will³ &c; **wull** *19- adj* **1** going or gone astray, wandering *15-, now Ork NE Ags.* **2** *fig* (1) misguided, erring, wayward *la14-e20;* (2) bewildered, perplexed, at a loss *la15-, now NE.* **3** *of a place* out of the way, desolate *e16, 19-20, latterly Abd.*

~-**like** in a perplexity; *freq of appearance* having a dazed look *la19-, NE.* **wilsome** &c *la15-*, **wulsome** &c *19-e20 adj* **1** *freq ballad, of a path etc* leading through wild or featureless country, confusing; *of a place* desolate, wild, dreary *la15-, now Sh Ork.* **2** *of persons* lost, wandering; forlorn *la15-e19.*

go ~ lose one's way, go astray *15-, now Ork NE Ags.* **walk** ~ (**of one's way**) go astray, lose oneself *la15, only Sc.* ~ **of rede** = *adj* 2 (2), *la14-e16.* ~ **of wane** = *adj* 1; homeless *la14-e16.* [ME; ON *villr* bewildered, astray]

will *see* WILD

willawins *see* WALAWA

William and Mary *n* the lungwort *la20, Bnf-Ags.* [male-and-female name from the impression of a two-colour flower as pinkish buds turn to blue flowers]

willie &c *la15-e20*, **willow** *17- n* = willow *la15-.*

willow earth compost made of rotten willow branches *la17.* **willie-muff** *or* -**muftie** the willow-warbler *19-e20.*

Willie &c; **Wullie** &c *19-* ~ **Cossar** *or* **Wull o Cossar** a long thick pin used *esp* for fastening shawls etc *19-20* [f the name of the maker, *appar* a pack-merchant in Rox]. **willie** &c **goo** &c **1** the herring gull *la19-, now Kcdn.* **2** a lost- or stupid-looking person *la19-, Abd Kcdn Ags.* **willie** &c **wagtail** &c the pied wagtail *19-, Gen except Sh Ork.* ~ **Wassle** &c a children's game *similar to Eng* Tom Tiddler's Ground *19-, sEC Dnbt.* ~ **Winkie** a nursery character supposed to send children to sleep, the sandman *19-.*

Sir Willie('s picture) a bank-note of the Edinburgh banking house Messrs Coutts (later Forbes, Hunter and Co.), bearing the portrait of its chairman, Sir William Forbes of Pitsligo (1739-1806) *e19.* ~ **and the wisp** the will-o'-the-wisp *la18-e19.* **willie-rin** &c-**hedge** the goosegrass *la19-, now Bnf Lnk.* ~-**whip-the-wind** the kestrel *19-, Ags.*

willie-waught &c ['wɪlɪ'wɑxt; *'wʌlɪ-] n* a hearty swig, *usu* of ale or other liquor *19-e20.* [f wrong division of the words in Burns *Auld Lang Syne;* see *guidwillie* (GUID) and WAUCHT]

willintly *see* WILL¹

willow *see* WILLIE

willsome &c *adj, arch or literary* wilful *19-e20.* [perh f WILL² + -SOME]

willyart &c *la18-;* **wilʒart** *la16* ['wɪl(j)ərt, -(j)ərd, 'wʌl-] *adj* **1** *of animals* wild; *of persons* awkward, shy; backward, dull *la16-, now Wgt.* **2** bewildered; undisciplined, wayward *19-, now Wgt.* **3** wilful, obstinate; *of an animal* unmanageable *la18-, now Wgt.* [appar f WILL³, w later infl f WILL² and perh f Eng *wayward*]

willywa(y) *see* WALAWA

wilrone &c *la16;* **wolroun** &c *e16* [*'wɪlrun, *'wʌl-] *n, chf as a term of abuse* a savage creature. [only Sc; WILD or WILL³ + OSc abusive suffix -*roun; cf* LAIDRON]

wilsome *see* WILL³

wilter, wiltu *see* WILL¹

wilʒart *see* WILLYART

wimble *see* WUMMLE

wime *see* WAME

wimple &c *16-;* **womple** &c *15-e16, only Sc,*

wumple &c *la16-e20, only Sc* ['wɪmpl, 'wʌmpl; *'hw-] *n* **1** = wimple *15-*. **2** *of a road or stream* a twist, turn, winding or meandering; a twisting movement, a ripple *16-, now local Sh-Loth*. **3** a tangle of material objects; *fig* a complication, intricacy; a wile, piece of trickery *17-, now N, only Sc.*

v **1** *vt* enfold, enwrap, entangle *16-, now NE*. **2** *vi* wriggle, writhe; whirl; curl *18-, now Sh*. **3** *of a river etc, freq also signifying the sound* meander, twist, turn, ripple *18-, now local Sh-WC*. **4** complicate; bewilder, perplex; tell a story in an involved deceitful way *18-19*.

win¹ &c; won &c *17-e20*, **wun** *la18-20* [wɪn, wʌn] *v, pt also* **wan &c** *now Sh NE, WC* [wan]. *ptp also* **wonnin &c** *la14-15*, **winin &c** *15*, **wun** *la16-*, **win** *16-19* [wʌn; *wɪn, *'wʌnən, *'wɪnən] *vti* **1** = win *la14-*. **2** *vt* beat, defeat, overpower *la14-, now N*. **3** earn, gain by labour *15-, now local Sh-WC*. **4** (1) gather in (crops etc), harvest *la14-, now local Sh-WC*. (2) *mining* extract (coal etc) by mining or quarrying; sink a pit or shaft to (a coal seam) *la15-20*. **5** deliver, drive home (a stroke, blow etc) *19-e20, S*. **6** *freq with prep or adv* (1) *vi* make or find one's way, proceed, succeed in arriving at some destination, *freq* with the idea of surmounting obstacles on the way *la14-*. (2) *vt* reach (a place, state etc), arrive at, come to *la16-e20*. **7** *vi, absol* manage to make a journey or attend a place despite difficulties; be permitted to go *18-, now local Sh-EC*. **8** ~ **to do** *etc* succeed in doing etc, manage or contrive to do *la16-, now Sh Ork NE*.

n **1** = win. **2** earnings, livelihood, profit, wealth *la15-19*. **3** the quantity of standing corn cut by a team of reapers while moving in one direction, *usu* one or two RIGS¹ taken together *19-, now Cai*.

win &c *la15-*, **winning &c** *e15* **1** = won *15-*. **2** *of stone etc* worked, quarried *e17*.

winner &c **1** = winner *la14-*. **2** *curling* (CURL) the stone played nearest the TEE¹ *la18-19*. **winnie &c** *marbles* a game in which the winner keeps his gains *la19-, local Ags-Kcb*; *cf* FUNNY. **winning &c 1** = winning *la15-*. **2** profit, gain, earnings *la14-e19*. **3** *mining* a pit and its fittings and machinery, a seam, a working or extraction of coal *la18-, now Fif*.

evill &c win ill-gotten *la15-16, only Sc.* ~ **abune &c** get over, overcome, recover from (an illness etc) *la18-, now Sh NE Ags.* ~ **aff &c** get away, escape; 'get off' *18-, now local Sh-Ags.* ~ **afore** get ahead of, outrun, anticipate *19-, now NE Ags.* ~ **asleep** get to sleep *20-, local Sh-Per.* ~ **at** reach, get at or to *18-, Sh-C.* ~ **awa &c 1** leave; escape, be permitted or find it possible to go *la14-, now local Sh-Ags.* **2** die, pass away, *esp* after great suffering *17-, Gen except Sh Ork.* ~ **by**(**e**) get past; avoid *19-, now local Sh-Ags.* ~ **farrer &c ben** be admitted to greater grace or favour *la20-, Sh Ork Ags.* ~

frae &c be allowed to leave, escape from *18-, now Sh Ork.* ~ **free** become free, escape, be released *19-, now Sh-Per.* ~ **in** obtain entry, get in *18-, now local Sh-Ags.* ~ **in about** get near or close to *la20-, NE.* ~ **in ahin** get the better of, outsmart *20-, NE.* ~ **in wi** find favour with *la20-.* ~ **on** get on (horseback etc), mount *la14-, Sh-Per.* ~ **on for** *or* **tae** secure election or appointment as *la20-, NE Ags Per.* ~ **out 1** get out, escape *18-.* **2** *mining* widen out a working *la19-, now Fif.* ~ **ower &c 1** (be allowed to) cross, pass over *la19-, now local Sh-Per.* **2** recover from, overcome *18-, now local Sh-SW.* ~ **redd o** escape from, get rid of *la19-, NE Ags.* ~ **tae &c 1** arrive at, reach *la15-, now Sh Ork NE, EC.* **2** (1) come near or within reach *la18-, now Ags Per.* (2) take a seat at table, begin eating *e19.* **3** ~ **tae &c wi** overtake, make up on; be even with *la19-, Abd.* ~ **to** (**the**) **fit** get to one's feet *la18-, now Sh Ork.* ~ **tae the road** *lit and fig* get a start *la19-, Sh Abd.* ~ **through &c** *vti* get through, accomplish *17-19.* ~ **till** = win tae *19-, now Sh N.* ~ **up 1** rise to one's feet, stand up *19-, now N Per.* **2** ~ **up tae** *or* **wi** get as far as, catch up on, overtake *19-, now NE.*

win² &c; wun *19-e20* *vti, pt* **wan** *la19-e20* [wan]. *ptp* **won** *la16-e20* [wʌn], **win &c** *18-* **1** *of cut corn, hay,* PEATS¹ *etc* dry and make or become ready for storage by exposure to air and sun *la16-.* **2** dry out, season (wood, cheese etc) *18-.* [f WIN¹ *v* 4 (1), w infl f WIND¹]

win³ &c *vi* dwell, live, reside *la14-19.* [var of WON, poss partly confused w WIN¹]

win *see* WIND¹

wincey &c ['wɪnsɪ] *n* a cloth with a woollen weft and a linen or cotton warp *la18-.* [f the second element of LINSEY-WINSEY]

winch &c [*wɪn(t)ʃ] *v* **1** *vi* wince, start back, flinch *la15-e19.* **2** *vti* kick, prance *19-e20.* [see SND]

winch *see* WENCH

wind¹ &c; wound *16-e17*, **win** *18-, now NE, WC*, **wund** *19-20*, **wun** *19-, now WC*, **ween** *la19-, Bnf Abd* [wɪnd; C, S wʌnd; NE, WC wɪn; WC, SW wʌn; Bnf Abd wɪn] *n* **1** = wind *la14-.* **2** breath, the air breathed *la14-.* **3** breath as used for speaking: (1) talk, speech, what one has to say *18-19*; (2) a boast, brag; a boaster, braggart *18-, now Sh.*

v **1** *vt* winnow *16-, now Ork.* **2** *vi* exaggerate, boast *19-20, Bnf Abd Ags.*

~**y &c 1** = windy *la16-.* **2** proud, conceited; boastful *16-, now Per.* ~**y wallets** a person who talks in a boastful exaggerated way *19-, now Rox.*

~**-bill** a bill of exchange drawn as a means to raise credit, a bill which negotiates a loan of money *la18-19.* ~**-blawn** *of a horse* broken-winded *20-, now Cai Fif.* **win-casten &c** *lit and fig* blown down by the wind *20-, Sh NE, WC.* **oon-egg** a wind-egg, an egg laid without a shell *19-*, *now Per.* ~**flaucht** with the force or speed of wind *e16.* **win-mull** = windmill; *fig* a notion, fancy *20-*, *NE.* ~**-raw &c** a row or line into which mown hay is raked or in which small piles of cut PEATS¹ are set to dry *la18-*, *now WC.* ~**skew &c** a smoke-deflector in a chimney, a chimney cowl *la16-*, *now Ork.* **brak the** ~ *of a medicine* relieve flatulence *la20-*, *Sh Cai Abd.* **keep** *or* **save one's** ~ **to cool one's kail** hold one's tongue, be quiet *la19-*, *now local Sh-Per.* **let the** ~ **in** (**amang**) **it** *or* **intil't** squander one's money or resources *20-*, *NE.* ~ **and watertight** *chf of a house, esp in leases* secure against wind and rain or flood *la19-*.

wind² &c; weynd &c *e16*, **wund** *e20*, **wun** *la20-*, *NE* [wɪn(d), wʌn(d), wəin(d)] *v, pt also* **wand** *la14-19*, **winned &c** *16-e19, only Sc*; **wan** *19-*, *now Abd* [wan(d), wɪn(d), wɪnt]. *ptp also* **woundit** *e15*, **wunded** *19-e20, only Sc* [wʌn(d), 'wɪndɪt, 'wʌndɪt]. *vti* **1** = wind, turn etc *15-*. **2** *vt* wrap (a corpse) in a shroud *la14-e19.* **3** draw (coal) to the pithead by means of a winding-engine *la18-*, *now Fif.*

~**er &c 1** = winder. **2** a windlass operator *15-e16.* **windle &c** ['wɪnl] *usu in pl, weaving* a device for winding yarn or thread on to bobbins *la16-20.*

~ **band &c** an iron hoop or band put round a wooden bar etc to strengthen it and prevent splintering *la15-20.* ~ **the** *or* **a** (**blue**) **clue** *specif* wind a ball of worsted in a kiln at *Hallow-een* (HALLOW²) in order to divine the name of one's future spouse *19-e20.*

wind *see* WYNT

winda, windae *see* WINDOW

windass &c; windois *16, only Sc* ['wɪn(d)əs] *n* **1** = windas, a windlass, *latterly specif* one used for taking up water from the shaft of a coalmine *16-*, *now Fif.* **2** a fan for winnowing grain *18-e20.*

~ **cord** a rope on a WINDASS *n* 1, *e16.* ~ **man** a windlass operator *17-18.* [OED *windas*]

winder *see* WUNNER

windick *see* WINNOCK

windie *see* WINDOW

windle &c *16-*; **winle &c** *18-e20*, **wunnle &c** *19-e20* ['wɪn(d)l, 'wʌnl] *n* a bundle of straw *la17-19.*

v **1** *vi* whirl, turn over and over *la14.* **2** *vt* wind (thread) *la16.* **3** make up (straw or hay) into bundles *la18-e20.*

windlin(**g**) **&c** a bundle of straw, *usu* as much as a man can carry in the crook of his arm *17-*, *now Sh Ork N, only Sc.*

~**strae &c** *n* **1** a tall, thin, withered stalk of grass *16-*, *now local N-S.* **2** *specif* applied to various kinds of natural grass with long thin stalks, *eg* the crested dogstail grass, the meadow soft grass etc *18-*, *local N-S.* **3** *fig* (1) *of something light or trifling* an atom, a mere fragment, a jot *17-e20.* (2) *contemptuous* a weapon, dagger

etc *19.* (3) *contemptuous* a thin or lanky person; a person who is weak in health or character *19-*, *now NE Ags WC. adj* easily blown about; weak, thin, delicate *19-e20.* [frequentative of WIND²; *cf* MDu *windelen* swathe, swaddle]

windle *see* WIND²

windock *see* WINNOCK

windois *see* WINDASS

window &c; wondow *la16*, **windie &c** *18-*, *now Fif WC*, **wundow &c** *19-e20*, **winda** *19-*, *now NE, WC*, **wundy &c** *la19-e20*, **windae** *20-*, *now sEC* ['wɪndə, 'wʌndə; *C* 'wɪndɪ; *C, S* 'wʌndɪ] *n* = window *la14-*.

~**-band** the hinge of a window *la16.* ~**-bole** an opening in the outer wall of a house, the lower half *freq* being unglazed, with wooden shutters *19-*, *now Abd Per.* ~**-brod &c** *or* **-board** a window-shutter *la16-*, *now Abd Per.* ~**-cheek** the side of a window *20-*, *NE.* ~**-chess** a window-sash *20-*, *now local Sh-Lnk.* ~**-sneck** a window catch *20-*, *Sh Ork NE, WC.* ~**-sole** a window-sill *18-.* **wunda-swalla** the house-martin *20-*, *now Fif Loth.* [*cf* WINNOCK]

window *see* WINNOW

wine &c *n* **1** = wine *la14-.* **2** *in urban areas* cheap fortified red wine or sherry *la20-*, *chf Gsw*; *cf red biddy* (REID¹).

~ **shop** a public house which serves cheap wine *la20-*, *Gsw.* ~ **slide** a coaster for a wine bottle or decanter which can be slid along a table *20-.*

wing *la16-*; **weing &c** *la14-e16*, **weeng** *la19-e20, Abd Ags Fif* [wɪŋ; *Abd Ags Fif* wiŋ] *n* **1** = wing *la14-.* **2** a detachable board which can be added to the side of a cart to increase its capacity *20-*, *now Cai Fif.*

wingle &c; waingle *19* ['wɪŋl, 'wiŋl; *Sh* 'wɪŋgl; *Ork also* 'wɪŋkl] *vi* **1** walk unsteadily, reel, stagger *19-*, *now Sh.* **2** twist, wriggle; *of a stream etc* meander *19-*, *now Sh Cai.* **3** hang loosely, dangle; flap, wag *19-*, *now Sh.*

n a winding object, something which bends or twists *la18-20.* [see SND]

winin *see* WIN¹

wink &c *v* **1** *vi* = wink *la14-.* **2** *vt* shut one's eyes to (an offence, fault etc) *la16.*

n = wink *la14-.*

~**er** *chf in pl* the eyelids, eyelashes *19-e20.* ~**ie** **1** a lamp, light, *esp* an unsteady or flickering one *19-e20.* **2** *specif* the lighted buoy marking the end of a line of herring nets *la20-*, *NE-WC.*

wink *see* WINNOCK

winklot *n* a wench *la15.* [only Sc; obscure]

winle *see* WINDLE

winna *see* WILL¹

winned *see* WIND²

winnel-skewed &c *adj* suffering from an optical illusion; squint-eyed; askew *19.* [appar f *windle* (WIND²) + SKEW²]

winner *see* WUNNER

winnerstan *see* UNDERSTAND

winnie, winning see WIN[1]

winnock &c *la16-*; **windock &c** *la15-e20*, **wink** *la16*, **windick &c** *la17-e19* ['wɪnək, 'wʌn-; *nEC* 'wɪndək, 'wʌnd-] *n* a window *la15-*, now *NE-WC*.
~**-bole** = *window-bole* (WINDOW) *19-e20*. ~ **brod &c** *e19*, ~ **bred** *e16* = *window-brod* (WINDOW). ~**-bunker** a window-seat *la18-e19*. ~**-neuk** a window-corner *la18-19*. ~**-sole** = *window-sole* (WINDOW) *la18-e20*. [only Sc; var of WINDOW; *cf* ELBUCK and WARLOCK]

winnow &c *la17-*; **wonnow** *15-16, only Sc*, **wando** *e16*, **window &c** *16-*, now *Sh Ork* ['wɪnə; *NE* 'wɪnɪ] *vt* = winnow *15-*.
~**ster &c 1** a person engaged in winnowing *16-e17*. **2** a machine for winnowing corn; the fanning apparatus on a threshing machine *19-*, now *NE*.

winsome &c *adj, chf of persons* attractive in appearance, manner or nature, charming *18-*. [ME *wunsum &c* pleasant, OE *wynsum* gracious; merciful]

wint see WANT, WEEN, WENT, WONT

winter[1] **&c** ['wɪntər; *C, S also* 'wʌntər] *n* **1** = winter *la14-*. **2** the last load of grain to be brought to the stackyard in harvest *la18-*, now *NE*. **3** the feast held to celebrate the end of harvest *19*. **4** the person who removed the last of the grain from the field to the stackyard *la19*. **5** the last person to turn up for work on HOGMANAY *la20-*, now *WC*.
vti = winter.
~**er 1** = winterer. **2** a farm animal kept for fattening over winter *la18-*, *Gen except S*. ~**in(g) &c 1** = wintering. **2** a winter pasture, winter keep for animals *la18-*, *Gen except Sh Ork*. **3** an animal which is kept over the winter *18-*, now *Cai Mry*. ~**ing money** money paid for the winter keep of animals *18-*, now *Per*. **weel-** *or* **ill-wintert** *of an animal* well- or ill-fed, (un)healthy *la19-*, *local Ork-Wgt*.
~**-dyke** *chf in pl* a clotheshorse *18-*, now *EC, WC Kcb* [f its resemblance, when covered with (white) clothes, to a snow-filled wall]. ~ **green** = *prec 20-*, now *WC*. ~ **town** the arable part of a farm as opposed to the summer pasture *la18-*, now *Ayr*.
get, hae, mak, tak *etc* ~ have reached the end of the harvest, have brought the crops in *19-e20*. **he** *etc* **never died o** *or* **a** ~ **yet** he etc survived, pulled through all difficulties or hardships *la19-*, *local Ork-Ayr*.

winter[2] *n* an iron or rack which hangs on the bars of a fire-grate to support a kettle or pot; a trivet *18-*, now *Per*. [see SND]

wintle; wuntle *19-e20 v* **1** *vi* stagger, rock from side to side, roll about *la18-e19*. **2** *vti, freq* ~ **ower** tumble, upset, go headlong *19-e20*. [only Sc; MDu *wintelen, wentelen* roll]

winze *n* a curse, imprecation *la18-e19*. [only Sc; MDu *wens(ch)* a wish; an imprecation, *wens(ch)en* wish evil to]

wi'oot see WITHOUT

wip see WUP[1]

wipe &c *vt* **1** = wipe *la14-*. **2** strike, beat, attack *la17-e20*.
n = wipe *la16-*.

wipp see WUP[1]

wir see OUR

wird see WORD

wirdy see WORTH[1]

wire &c *16-*; **weir &c** *la15-e20*, **weer &c** *18-*, now *NE* [wəir; *Sh nEC* wer; *N Wgt* wir] *n* **1** = wire *la15-*. **2** a knitting needle; *in pl* a set of knitting needles *la18-*. **3** a thin metal glazing- and frame-bar in a church- or similar window *18-e19*.
gold wyrin of gold wire *e16, only Sc*.

wirk see WARK

wirl &c; wurl *19-e20*, **wrow &c** *19-e20* [wɪrl, wʌrl; *NE* vrʌu; &c] *n* **1** a puny malformed person, animal or plant, a stunted or deformed creature, a dwarf *19-*, now *Fif*. **2** *applied to a mischievous child* a young scamp, a wicked creature *la19-*, *Fif Slk*.
~**ie &c** puny, stunted, undersized; *of persons* wrinkled, with wizened features *19-e20*. [perh reduced f Eng *werewolf*, poss w infl f next]

wirling &c *16-e19*; **worlin** *la16-19* [*'wɪrlɪn, *'wʌrlɪn] *n* a puny or stunted person or animal, a dwarf. [ME *wryling* a wretch]

wirlyk see WEIR[1]

wirm see WORM

wirr &c; wurr *la19-20 vi, of a dog etc or joc of a person* growl, snarl *la18-*, *NE Ags Per*.
n **1** the growl of a dog *la18-*, *NE Ags*. **2** a fit of bad temper *la19*. [onomat]

wirricow see WORRICOW

wirrok see WERROCK

wirry see WORRY

wirship see WORSHIP

wirsit see WORSET

wirstle see WARSLE

wirsum see WURSOM

wirt *16-e20*, **wort** *n, brewing* = wort *la15-*.
~ **dish** *la17-e18*, ~ **fatt** *la16* a vessel for holding wort, a fermentation vat. ~ **stane** a stone used in making wort, for keeping the barrel steady *16-*, now *Ork*. ~**troch** *la17*, ~ **tube** *la16* = wirt dish.

wirt see WORTH[1], WRIT

wirth see WORTH[1], WORTH[3]

wis see BE, US, WISS[2]

wisch- see WITCH

wische see WISS[2]

wischeaf see VOUCH SAUF

wise &c; wyss &c *la14-e20*, **weise &c** *19-e20*, **wice &c** *19-* [wəis] *adj* **1** = wise *la14-*. **2** clever, knowing, well-informed *la14-*, now *local Ork-Per*. **3** in one's right mind, sane, rational, *freq* **no** ~ *18-*, *local Ork-Per*. **4** skilled in magic, possessing powers of witchcraft, *chf* ~ **wife** *or* **woman** a witch, sorceress *17-*, now *Ork*. **5** as *adv* wisely *la14*.

v [wəiz; waɪz] **1** *vt* advise, direct *la14*. **2** guide, direct, show (a person) **to** (a place etc) (1) *in gen*, *19-e20*; (2) *specif, of a shepherd or his dog* direct, lead (sheep) *19-e20*; (3) lead, conduct (water) in a channel *19*. **3** coax, induce, entice, lead round by advice *la18-e20*. **4** aim, propel, shoot (a missile) *18-e20*. **5** work, manoeuvre, ease or cause to move gradually in a certain direction *18-e20*. **6** *vi* make one's way, go; *of an object* work itself, slip or slide in a certain direction *18-e20*. **7** *vti* contrive, obtain by guile *19*. **8** expend, use up, while **away** (time); dispose of (money, property) *19*.

~like *adj* **1** *also as adv* prudent, sensible, reasonable *19-*, *now local Sh-Per*. **2** *also as adv* respectable, proper, decent *19-*, *now Cai C*. **3** *of persons or things* of good appearance, handsome, pretty *19-*, *now Cai Kcdn eLoth*. **4** suitable, fitting, appropriate *19-e20*.

~-lookin handsome, good-looking *19-*, *now local Sh-Per*. **~-saying** a proverb *20-*, *now Sh*. **~-spoken** wise, sensible in speech *la19-*, *now local Sh-Per*.

no ~ eneuch &c off one's head, insane *la18-*, *NE*.

wisgan ['wɪzgən] *n, term of abuse* a stunted, useless, feckless person or creature *la19-*, *Bnf Ags*. [perh f Gael *ùruisgean*, dim of *ùruisg* a *brownie* (BROON), hobgoblin]

wish *see* WASH, WISS[1]

wishen *see* WASH

wisht *see* WHISHT

wishy-washy &c;   weeshie-washie &c *la19-* [-'waʃɪ] *adj* = wishy-washy *la17-*. *n* **1** thin watery drink, *eg* weak tea *19-*, *now Ork Ags Ayr*. **2** *in pl* circumlocutions, procrastination, humming and hawing *la18-*, *now Ags*.

wisk *see* WHISK

wisp &c *16-*; **wosp** *la15-e16*, **wasp** *15-16*, **wusp** *la18-e20* [wɪsp, wʌsp] *n* **1** = wisp, a handful, small bundle (of hay etc) *15-*. **2** a bundle or parcel containing a definite quantity of a commodity, *orig* tied up with a wisp of straw etc, *specif* (1) *of steel*, *la15-e17*; (2) *of fish*, *16-e20*, *Mry*.

vt **1** = wisp *la16-*. **2** put warmed straw into (boots, shoes etc) as an insole in cold weather *19-*, *now Stlg Dmf*.

wiss[1] **&c** *la15-*, *now local Sh-Fif*, **wish &c** *la16-*; **wosse** *e17*, **wuss** *19-e20*, **wush** *19-20*, **weesh &c** *la19-20* [*Sh Ork N* wɪs; *C, S* wʌs, wʌʃ; *Sh N also* wʌs; *WC Uls also* wɪʃ] *vti* **1** = wish *16-*. **2** *vt, with direct object* want, desire, wish for *la15-*: '*Do you wish any more?*' **3** *with object clause* hope, trust *17-e20*: '*I wish I binna fou*'.

n = wish *la15-*.

to a (very) ~ just as one would wish, to one's complete satisfaction *la18-e20*.

wiss[2]**, wis &c;** **wische** *e16* *vt* show, point out, direct *la14-e16*, *19-*, *now Sh*. [ME; OE *wissian*]

wissel &c;   wesle *la14*, **quhissel** *la16*,

whissle &c *18-e19* ['wɪsl; ***'hwɪsl] *vt* **1** (1) exchange, barter *la14-*, *now Cai*. (2) *specif* exchange (words) **with** (a person) *la16-e19*. **2** change (money), give out (change); spend (money) *la15-e19*.

n a building in which merchants assemble for the transaction of business *la15*.

in wisselling &c in exchange *la14-e17*.

get the ~ of one's groat *etc, fig* be paid in one's own coin, get one's just deserts *18-e19*. [chf Sc; MDu, MLowGer *wissel(en)* exchange]

wissen *see* WIZEN

wit &c; wott &c *la16*, **wut** *19-e20* [wɪt, wʌt] *n* **1** = wit *la14-*. **2** sanity, reason, one's senses *la14-e15*, *18-*, *now Sh-Per*. **3** intelligence, wisdom, common sense *la14-*. **4** knowledge, information *la14-19*. **5** a person of great mental ability *la15-16*.

v, pt also **wittit** *la14*, *e19*, **weist** *la16* [***wɪst]. *ptp also* **wittin(g)** *15-16* **1** *vti* = wit *la14-*. **2** *vt* know as a fact *la14-e20*. **3** *vi* become aware, realize, be conscious *la14-e20*.

wittandly &c 1 = wittingly *15-e16*. **2** wisely, skilfully *la14*.

get *or* **tak wit** learn, find out, become aware (**of**) *la14-16*, *19-*, *now NE-EC*. **let wit 1** let (a person) know something, inform of *18-*, *now local NE-Kcb*. **2** *law, in imperative* let it be known that, take notice that *18*. **out o one's wit** out of one's senses *18-19*. [*cf* WAT and WEET[2]]

witch &c; wesch- *la14*, **wisch-** *la14*, **wutch** *19-e20* [wɪtʃ, wʌtʃ; ***wɪtʃ] *n* **1** = witch *la14-*. **2** *transf, used of various animals, insects and objects associated with witches* (1) (a) a moth *la19-*, *now Kcdn Ags*; (b) a tortoise-shell butterfly *la19-*, *Bwk S*; (2) the pole flounder or dab *la19-*; (3) a red clay marble, *usu* one considered effective in winning games, a 'wizard' *la19-e20*.

vt = witch, affect by witchcraft *la14-*.

~ bird *la17*, **~ carline** *e16*, *e19* a witch.

witches' paps the foxglove *20-*, *Arg Ayr*.

witch(es')-thimbles = prec, *esp* its flowers *19-*, *Cai Mry C, S*.

witchaif *see* VOUCH SAUF

wite *see* WAT, WYTE

with *see* WI

witha *la18-e19*, **withal &c** *la14-*; **with aw** *la15* [***wɪθ'ɑ, ***-'al] *adv* = withal, as well.

wi than *see* WEEL[1]

with aw *see* WITHA

withdraw *vti* = withdraw *la14-*.

~er 1 = withdrawer. **2** *church* a person who did not conform to the established church *17*.

wither &c ['wɪðər; *Bwk Rox* 'wʌðər] *vti* **1** = wither. **2** *vt* wash the starch out of (summer garments) and put them away for winter unironed *la20*, *C*.

~ed &c 1 = withered *la15-*. **2** worn out, ragged *la15*.

wither *see* WEATHER

witherlins &c ['wɪðərlɪnz] *adv* = WITHERSHINS 2, *19-e20, chf Abd.* [obs Eng *wither-*, backwards, in a contrary direction + *-lins* manner, degree]

witherlock *19-*, *now Cai;* **widderlok** *la15* ['wɪðərlok; *'wɪdər-] *n* the tuft of a horse's mane above his withers. [Eng *withers* top of a horse's shoulders + *lock* a tuft of hair]

withershins *18-;* **widdershins &c** *16-20,* **-sones &c** *16,* **wodershins &c** *la16* ['wɪðərʃɪnz, 'wɪdər-] *adv* **1** *freq* ~ **about** in a direction opposite to the usual, the wrong way round *16-*, *now Ork.* **2** *specif* anti-clockwise, in a direction contrary to the apparent course of the sun, *usu* with the implication of bad luck or disaster *16-*, *now Sh C; cf* DEASIL. [chf Sc; MDu *wedersins*, MLowGer *weddersinnes* contrariwise]

witherwardis; woder- [*'wɪðərwardz, *'wɪdər-] *adv* = WITHERSHINS *e17.* [only Sc; obs Eng *wither-*, in a contrary direction + *-wards.* OED *witherwards*]

wither weicht &c *la18-20;* **wodderweght** *e17* ['wɪðər'wext; *'wɪdər-] *n* a weight put on one side of a pair of scales, a counterweight. [obs Eng *wither-*, counterbalance + WECHT[1]. OED *wither- (prefix[1])*]

witherwys *e17;* **widderwise** *la19-*, *Sh* ['wɪdərwaɪz; *'wɪðər-] *adv* = WITHERSHINS 2, *17-19.*

adj, of a person contrary, stubborn *20-*, *Sh.* [only Sc; obs Eng *wither-*, in a contrary direction + *-wise.* SND *wither-.* OED *wither (prefix[1])*]

withgang[1] [*'wɪθgaŋ] *n* success; advantage, profit *la15-e16.* [only Sc; ON *viðgangr* increase]

withgang[2] [*'wɪθgaŋ] *n* (*vt*) (give) unlimited permission, (give) licence *e16.* [only Sc; ON *viðganga* access, admission]

withgate &c [*?'wɪθget] *n* permission, free passage *la16-e18.* [only Sc; later var of prec, with GATE[1] *n* 1 for *-gang*]

with-haud *la19-;* **withhald** *la14-e16* [wɪθ'had; *-'hald, &c] *vti* **1** = withhold *la14-.* **2** *vt* hold *e16.*

within &c; wi'in *e20* [wɪ'θɪn, wɪ'(?)ɪn] *adv, prep* = within *la14-.*

within itself *etc, of a house:* not shared in its accommodation, self-contained (SEL[1]) *la18-*, *now NE: 'a lodging, within itself'.* [*cf* ATHIN]

without &c; withouten &c *la14-e20, latterly literary,* **wi'oot &c** *la19-*, *now sEC* [wɪ'θut, wɪ'θutən, wɪ'(?)ut] *adv, prep* = without *la14-.*

conj **without** (**that**) unless *la15-*, *now C.* [*cf* ATHOOT]

withy *see* WIDDIE

witness &c *n, vti* = witness *la14-.*

stand in ~ act as a witness *e16, only Sc.*

witnessman *n* a witness *la14-15.* [ON *vitnismaðr*]

witsaufe, witschaif *see* VOUCH SAUF

Witsounday *see* WHITSUNDAY

witter[1] &c *vt* inform, guide, direct *la14-e20.*

n **1** a sign, mark, token *16-e19.* **2** *curling* (CURL): the TEE[1] *la18-e20.*

~**ing** information; a hint, sign *la14-e20.*

~**-hole** a mark or depression made in a *witter-stone,* *17-e19, latterly hist.* ~**-stone** a boundary stone *17.* [ON *vitra* reveal, make to know; *cf* Norw *vitr(ing)* a warning sign]

witter[2] &c; wutter &c *e20 n* **1** the barb of a fish-hook, gaff etc *la18-*, *now Sh Ork N.* **2** *in pl, fig* the teeth *la18-19.*

~**(e)d &c 1** barbed, jagged *19-*, *now Sh Kcdn.* **2** intertwined, twisted, entangled *la18-*, *now Sh.*

be in *or* **flee in** (**someone's**) ~**s** start a quarrel with, fly at *la18-19.* [see SND]

witter[3] &c *la19-*, *now NE Ags;* **wutter** *la19-20 n* a sharp, active, restless, impatient, *freq* disagreeable person *20-*, *now NE Ags.*

vi **1** be restless with impatience, fret; grumble; mutter **on** about nothing *20-.* **2** struggle, carry on with difficulty, earn one's living precariously *19-20, NE* [perh a different word].

~**ous &c** of a CRABBIT, stubborn nature, venomous in temper *la19-, NE.* [uncertain]

wittin &c, witting &c *n* **1** the fact of knowing or being aware of something, knowledge *la14-*, *now Abd.* **2** *latterly chf in pl* knowledge imparted, information, intelligence, news *la14-e20.*

get ~(**s**) obtain information *la14, 19-*, *now Sh Ork N.* [partly f ON *vitand* consciousness, knowledge, f *vita* know, but later treated as the verbal noun of WIT]

wittin *see* WIT

witting *see* WIT, WITTIN

wittit *see* WIT

wivven *see* WEAVE

wiz *see* US

wizen &c *la18-;* **wissen &c** *16-e20* ['wɪzən] *vti, ptp also* **weezened &c** *19-e20,* **wuzzened &c** *19-e20, of any kind of tissue etc* (cause to) shrivel, shrink, wither *16-.*

~**ed &c** dried up, shrivelled, shrunken *16-.* [ME *wisen*, OE *wisnian* dry up, wither]

wiznan *see* BE

wizzen &c *18-e20;* **wassand &c** *la14-15,* **wyson** *18-e19,* **weason** *la18-e20,* **wazzin &c** *la18-*, *now Sh Ork Cai* ['wɪz(ə)n, 'waz(ə)n, 'wɪz(ə)n; *Sh Ork Cai Fif Uls* 'waz(ə)n] *n* **1** the gullet *la14-*, *now local Sh-Per.* **2** (1) the windpipe; *hence* the breath, life itself *18-*, *now local Sh-Abd.* (2) the throat as the source of the voice *la18-e20.*

weet one's ~ have a drink *18-e19.* [see SND. OED *weasand*]

wizzy *n, child's word* **do a** ~ urinate *20-, Edb.* [onomat]

wo &c *interj* = wo, a call to a horse to stop *la19-.*

~**-back** a call to a horse to stop or go backwards *la19-*, *Ork-Per.* ~**-hie** a call to a horse to turn left *20-*, *now Cai Per.* ~**-hup** a call to a horse to turn right *20-*, *now Cai Per.*

wob *see* WAB

wobat *see* OOBIT
wobster *see* WABSTER
wochle *see* WAUCHLE
wocht *see* WEUCH
wodder *see* WEATHER, WEDDER
wodderweght *see* WUID[1], WUID[2]
wode *see* WUID[1], WUID[2]
Wodenisday, Wodensday *see* WEDNESDAY
wodershins *see* WITHERSHINS
woderwardis *see* WITHERWARDIS
wodge *see* WAGE
wodset *see* WADSET
woft *see* WAFT
woid *see* WADE
woifen *see* WEAVE
woik *see* WAUK
woir *see* WEAR
wok *see* OUK
wolf *see* OOF
wolk *see* OUK
woll *see* OO[1], WALL
wolroun *see* WILRONE
wolter *see* WALTER[1]
wolvin *see* WEAVE
wolx *see* WAX[2]
woman &c; wumman &c *la19-*, **oman**
la18-e20, Abd, **umman** *20, Mry Abd* ['wʌmən;
NE 'ʌmən; *Fif also* 'umən] *n, pl* **weemen &c** *18-*
['wimən] **1** = woman *la14-.* **2** familiar,
though not necessarily derog or joc, form of
address, *occas* applied to a little girl *la18-20.* **3** a
wife *la18-e20.*
~ **bairn &c** a female child, a girl *la16-19.*
~**-body** a woman *19-.* **women &c-folk**
women *la19-.* ~**-grown** grown to womanhood,
adult *la18-, now Sh Per.* ~**-house** the laundry
of a mansion house *la16-e19.* ~**-length** =
~*-grown, 20-, Sh Ags Loth.* ~ **lowpar** a
whoremonger *la16.* ~**-muckle** = ~*-grown,
19-, now Cai Stlg Lnk.*
on ~**-wayis** after the manner of a woman or
women *la16.*
womb *see* WAME
women *see* WOMAN
woment [*?'womənt] *vti* = wayment, lament
la15-e16. [OED *wayment*]
womill *see* WUMMLE
womle brees *see* WAMMLE
womple *see* WIMPLE
won &c; wone &c [*wʌn] *vi* **1** *latterly arch* dwell,
live, stay habitually *la14-e20.* **2** = won,
remain in a certain state *la15.* [*cf* WONE]
won *see* WIN[1], WIN[2]
wonder *see* WUNNER
wondow *see* WINDOW
wone &c *n, literary* = wone, a dwelling, an
abode *e16, e19.* [either f WON or a literary borrowing f Eng *wone*]
wone *see* WON
wonner *see* WUNNER
wonnin *see* WIN[1]
wonnow *see* WINNOW

wont &c; wount *la14-e18,* **wunt** *19-e20,* **wint**
la19-, now Sh Ork [wʌnt; wɪnt] *adj* **1** = wont,
accustomed to *la14-.* **2** ~ **wi** accustomed or
used to, familiar with *la15-, now Sh Ork.*
vi be in the habit of, be used to *la16-, now Ork.*
n = wont *16-.*
wontsumnes custom, habit *e15.*
wont *see* WEEN
woo *see* OO[1]
wood *see* WUID[1], WUID[2]
woodie *see* WIDDIE
wool, woon *see* OO[1]
woosh *see* WASH
wooster &c [*'wu(:)stər] *n, literary* a wooer *19.*
[Eng *woo* + *-ster*]
wop *see* WAP[2], WUP[1]
wor *see* WEIR[2]
worble *see* WURBLE
word &c; wourd &c *la14-16,* **werd** *16-18,*
wird *16-e20* [*Sh-Per* wɪrd; *C, S* wʌrd; *Bwk also*
wɪrd] *n* **1** = word *la14-.* **2** *extended usages of Eng:*
(1) something said, an utterance or remark
la14-, now Sh N-Per; (2) *chf* **mason** *etc* ~ the
secret watchword of an initiated craftsman
18-19; (3) common talk, conversation among
the population at large *la14, la19- (Sh N-Per);*
(4) reputation, character *18-, now Ork N Lnk
Wgt.* **3** *freq in pl* prayers *la18-e20.* **4** the
faculty of speech; the sound of one's voice by
which one is recognized *la15-, now Sh-N, SW.*
vti = word.
get (a) ~ **o** converse with, talk to *18-, now Sh.*
pass the ~ **to** talk or converse with *la19-, Sh
Cai.* **put up a** ~ say a prayer *la19-, local Sh-C.*
put ~**s on** *or* **to** describe, express adequately
la19-, now Sh Ork. **speak a** ~ **to** rebuke,
admonish, advise *la19-, now Sh Cai.* ~ **of**
mouth an oral communication, a word *la19-,
now Sh Ork Cai.*
word, wordine *see* WORTH[3]
wordle *see* WARLD
wordy *see* WORTH[1]
wore *see* WEAR
work *see* WARK[1]
worl, world *see* WARLD
worlin *see* WIRLING
worm &c; wirm &c *15-, now Sh* [wʌrm; *chf Sh*
wɪrm] *n* **1** = worm *la15-.* **2** *fig* applied to a
person, expressing tenderness, playfulness or
commiseration *la19-, Sh Ags; cf* contemptuous
use in Eng. **3** *also* ~ **i(n) the, thy** *etc* **cheek**
la16, e20 toothache *17-, now Ork, only Sc.* **4**
colic; acidity in the stomach *16-19.*
vti = worm.
~**-eaten 1** = worm-eaten. **2** *fig* discontented;
decrepit *17-, now Ork.* ~ **month** the month of
July, or late July and early August, when cater-
pillars etc are most numerous *19-20.* ~ **web**
&c a spider's web, a cobweb; *fig* flimsy clothing
18-e19.
wormit &c ['wʌrmət] *n* wormwood *18-e20.*
[altered f ME *wermod, wormod*]

worn *see* WEIR[2]

worp *see* WARP

worricow &c *la18-19*; **wirricow &c** *18-e20* ['wʌrɪkʌu, 'wɪrɪ-] *n* **1** a hobgoblin, demon; a frightening- or repulsive-looking person *18-*, *now Lnk SW Rox.* **2** the Devil himself; an imp of Satan; a mischievous person *18-19.* [only Sc; perh f Eng *worry* harass, pester + COW[3]]

worry &c *16-*; **wirry &c** *now Sh* ['wʌrɪ, 'wɪrɪ; *'wɪrɪ] *vti* **1** = worry *la14-.* **2** *vt* strangle *la14-*, *now Sh Ork.* **3** *vti* choke (**on** a mouthful of food), suffocate *15-*, *now local Sh-Per.* **4** *vt*, *of smoke etc* stifle, suffocate *18-19.* **5** devour, gobble **up** *18-*, *now Abd Ags.*

n **1** = worry. **2** a dispute, wrangle, argument *la19-*, *now Ags.*

~**-carl(e) 1** a snarling, ill-natured person *19-e20, Bwk S.* **2** a large coarse winter pear *e19, Rox.*

eat the cow and ~ on the tail fail or lack success because of one small thing; be a stickler for trivialities *18-.*

worse *see* WARSE

worset &c *la14-*; **wirsit &c** *la14, la19-e20* ['wʌrsət, 'wɪrsət; *Sh* 'wɪrsɪd; *Cai* 'wʌrsad] *n* = worsted. [OED *worsted*]

worship &c; wirship &c *la14-16*, **wourship** *16* ['wʌrʃɪp; *'wɪrʃɪp] *n* **1** = worship *la14-.* **2** valour *la14-e15.* **3** a funeral ceremony *la14.* **4** family prayers *la19-20.*

vti = worship *la14-.*

worsle *see* WARSLE

worsum *see* WURSOM

wort [*wort, *wʌrt] *n* the snout of a pig *e16.*

vt, *of swine* root or dig **up** (ground) *16.* [only Sc; metath f ME *wrot*, eModEng *wroot*]

wort *see* WIRT

worth¹ &c; wirth *18-20*, **wirt** *la19-20, Sh Ork*, **warth** *la19* [wʌrθ; *NE Ags* wɪrθ; *Sh Ork* wɪrt; *'warθ] *n* = worth *la14-.*

adj **1** (1) = worth *la14-.* (2) *with* **the** + *verbal noun*, *20-*, *local Sh-Ayr*: 'somethin wirth the fryin'. **2** of use or service (for some purpose) *19-*, *local Sh-Per.*

~**y &c**, **wordy &c** *la14-e20*, **wirdy &c** *la16* ['wʌrθɪ, 'wʌrðɪ, 'wardɪ; *Sh* 'wɪrdɪ] *adj* **1** = worthy *la14-.* **2** worth (so much), of the value of *18-e19. adv, n* = worthy *la15.*

little ~ worthless, of small value *19-*, *chf Sh Ork.* **no ~ 1** a worthless piece, (something) of no use or value *la20-, Ork Cai Per.* **2** *as adv* hardly, scarcely; not even *19-*, *chf Sh Ork.*

worth² &c [wʌrθ, wʌθ; *'wɪrθ] *adv*: **gae etc (aa) ~** go to pot, become spoilt or useless, go to ruin *18-*, *now NE.* [orig prob f *aworth*, var of AWALD¹, later construed as *aa worth*]

worth³ *see* *la15-e20*; **word** *la14-17* [wʌrθ; *wɪrθ, *wʌrd] *v*, *pres also* **wourdis** *15* [*wʌrdz].

pres subjunctive **wirth** *e16.* *pt also* **word &c** *15-e19* [wʌrd; *Slk also* *urd], **worthit** *la14*, **wourthit** *la15* [*'wʌrθɪt]. *ptp* **wordine** *e16*,

word &c *17-e19* [*'wʌrdən, *wʌrd, *wʌrt] *vi* **1** = worth, come to be, become, befall *la14-e19.* **2** need, be necessary *la14-15*, *only Sc.*

wae *or* **weel ~** *literary, latterly arch* may ill *or* good betide *la15, 18-e20.*

wosp *see* WISP

wosse *see* WISS[1]

Wossenday *see* WHITSUNDAY

wott *see* WIT

woubit *see* OOBIT

wouchaiv, wouchsaiv *see* VOUCH SAUF

woucht *see* WASH

woud *see* WUID[1]

wouk *see* OUK

wouk *see* WAUK

woulk *see* OUK

wound &c *la14-*, **oun &c** *20-, S*; **woun** *19-e20* [wun(d); *Ayr, S* un] *n, vt* = wound.

wound *see* WIND[1]

woundit *see* WIND[2]

wount *see* WEEN

wount *see* WONT

woup *see* WUP[1]

wour *see* WEAR

wourd *see* WORD

wourdis *see* WORTH[3]

wourship *see* WORSHIP

wourthit *see* WORTH[3]

woushe *see* WASH

wout *see* VULT

woux *see* WAX[2]

wow¹ &c [wʌu] *n* a howl, deep-throated call or cry, bark *la18-*, *local Sh-Loth.*

vi howl, bark, bay *19-*, *Sh NE.* [imit]

wow² [wʌu] *interj* expressing admiration, astonishment or surprise; *occas, esp latterly* (by confusion with WAE¹) expressing regret *la15-20.* [chf Sc; *cf* vow]

wow *see* OO[1]

wowar [*'vuər] *n* a guardian, patron *la15.* [only Sc; *cf* Eng *vow* acknowledge. OED *vower*]

wowbar *see* OOBIT

wowf &c [wʌuf] *adj* touched, mad, violently agitated or excited *19-e20.* [only Sc; obscure]

wowf *see* OOF

wowff &c [wʌuf] *n* a low-pitched bark *la18-.*

vi, *of a dog* bark in a suppressed way *19-.*

adv with a dull thudding noise, thump! *20-*, *now NE.* [imit; *cf* Eng *woof*]

wox *see* WAX[2]

wra [*wre] *n* = wro, a nook, corner; a sheltered spot *la14-e16.* [OED *wro*]

wrable *see* WARBLE[1]

wrach *see* WRATCH

wrack¹ &c, **wreck** *la16-*, **wrake &c** *la14-17*, **wreak** *la16-*; **vrack &c** *19-e20, NE*, **rack** *la19-20 n* **1** = wrack, a shipwreck, destruction etc *15-.* **2** *only* **wrake** = wrake, suffering, punishment, vengeance *la14-16.* **3** *only* **wreak** = wreak, vengeance *la16-e17.* **4** *only* **wrake** a wrecked edifice *la16*, *only Sc.* **5** (1) fresh-or salt-

water weed, river or marine algae *16-, now Abd Fif Loth*. (2) seaweed and miscellaneous flotsam washed up by the sea *18-, Gen except Sh Ork*. **6** (1) field weeds, vegetable rubbish *18-20*. (2) *specif* (the roots of) the couch grass etc *la18-, NE-S*.
vti **1** *only* **wrake, wrack** = wreck, ruin, cause the destruction of *la16-*. **2** *only* **wrack, wrake** = wrack, cause the downfall of, undergo ruin *la16-*. **3** *vtr, chf* **weik** *la14-16*, **wryke &c** *15*, *ptp* **wrockin &c** *16*, **wrok** *16* = wreak, injure; avenge. **4** *vt, only* **wrack** = wreak, give vent to (feelings of rage or vengeance) *la18-19*.
adj, only **wrack &c** = wrack, damaged *la16*.
wraikful &c 1 vengeful *la15*. **2** destructive *e17, only Sc*.
wrack or **wreck goods** *law* goods driven ashore from a wreck *la17-e19*. **wrack ship** a wrecked ship *la17-, now Sh*. **wrack wid &c** driftwood *19-, now Ork*.
in wrake of in revenge or punishment for *la14-e16, only Sc*. [this entry covers several related words, corresponding to Eng *wrack, wrake, wreck, wreak*, all ultimately f Teutonic **wrek-*]
wrack² *17-e18*, **wrake &c** *la16-e17 vt* examine (goods etc) with a view to rejecting those which are faulty. [only Sc; MLowGer *wracken* reject, refuse]
wraikful *see* WRACK¹
wraing *see* WRANG²
wrait *see* WRITE
wraith¹ &c; **wrath** *16-e18*, **warth** *la18-19* [(w)reθ; **wraθ, *warθ] n **1** an apparition of a living person, *usu* taken as an omen of his death; any warning sign of danger or misfortune *16-*. **2** a ghost, the apparition of a dead person *16-, Gen except Sh Ork*. **3** any kind of fantastic image or apparition *19-e20*. [orig and chf Sc; obscure]
wraith² &c *la15-e20*; **wrath &c** *la14-16*, **wreth &c** *16* [(w)reθ] *adj* = wroth, angry. [OED *wroth*]
wraith *see* WRATH
wraitten *see* WRITE
wrake *see* WRACK¹, WRACK²
wrakling &c *n, esp* shipbuilding a large nail *la15*. [only Sc; MLowGer *wrakelinge*, MDu *wrakelinc*]
wramp *n, also fig* a wrench, twist, sprain *la17-18*. *vt, latterly arch* wrench, twist, sprain *la18-19*. [see SND]
wran &c *n* **1** *also* **wrannie &c** *la18-e20* = wren *la15-, now local Sh-SW*. **2** term of endearment (*esp* to a child) *19-e20*. [OED *wren*]
wranch &c *20-, local Sh-Dnbt*, **runch** *19-, now Cai WC, SW* [ranʃ, rʌnʃ, rɪnʃ; *Rox also* renʃ] *n* **1** = wrench, a twist. **2** a spanner or wrench for tightening bolts etc *19-, now local Sh-SW*.
vti, only **runch** = wrench *la19-, now Dnbt Kcb*.
wrang¹ &c, **wrong** *la16-*; **vrang** *19-20, chf NE adj* **1** = wrong *la15-*. **2** *of a person, limb etc*

crooked, deformed, out of joint *19-, now Abd*. **3** deranged, insane, 'touched' *19-, now NE*. **4** on the left side *e16*.
n **1** = wrong *la14-*. **2** *law* violation, transgression or infringement of law *14, e17, orig Sc*. **3** physical or material harm, damage *la18-19*.
vti **1** = wrong *la14-*. **2** *vt* cause physical harm or injury to, damage, hurt; spoil *18-, now local Ork-Lnk*.
adv = wrong *la15-*.
~ous &c *adj* **1** = wrongous *15-*. **2** *law, now only* **wrongous** contrary to law, illegal, wrongful *la17-*. **3** unjust, injurious; ill-gotten *15-e20, only Sc*. **4** inaccurate, incorrect, mistaken, badly aimed *la18-19*. *adv, also* **~ously 1** = wrongously *la14-e17*. **2** incorrectly *la16*. **3** improperly, illegally *18-e20*. **~ous imprisonment** *law* false imprisonment, imprisonment without the due form of law *18-*.
~ways incorrectly, the wrong way round *19-, now Sh NE*.
not come ~ (**to**) not come amiss (to), not be unwelcome (for), not disconcert *la19-, local Sh-Lnk*. **fa ~** (**to** or **till**) *of a woman* lose her virginity, be seduced (by) *la19-, SW*. **gae ~** *of food etc* go 'off', decompose *la19-, Sh NE-Per*. **rise aff one's ~ side** get up in a bad temper *la19-, now local Sh-Per*. **not say a ~ word** not use harsh, unjust or improper language *la20-, Sh-Per*. **~ in the heid** or **mind** = adj 3, *18-*. **~ one's pechan** or **stamack** make oneself sick with eating too much or the wrong food *19-e20*. **on the ~ side o the blanket** out of wedlock *la18-*.
wrang², wraing &c *n* = wrong, a rib of a ship *16*. [only Sc. OED *wrong* (*n¹*)]
wrang *see* WRING
wranglesome [ʼ(w)raŋlsʌm] *adj* quarrelsome, contentious *la19-, now Sh Ork Abd*. [Eng *wrangle* + *-SOME*]
wrap *vt* = wrap.
~per 1 a loose robe or gown worn as a dressing-gown or bed-jacket *19-, now NE*. **2** a woman's household overall, a smock *19-, now Ork N, C*. **3** a boot of thin leather, fastened by wrapping the upper part around the leg *la18-e19*.
wrastle *see* WARSLE
wrat &c *17-, now C, S*; **wrett** *e17* [(w)rat; **wret] n* = wart. [OED *wart*]
wrat *see* WRITE
wratch &c *la16-, now local Sh-Lnk*, **wretch &c** *la15-*; **wreche &c** *la14-e16*, **werche** *15*, **wrach &c** *la15-16*, **vratch &c** *la18-, now NE* [(w)ratʃ, (w)retʃ; **wertʃ] n* **1** = wretch *la15-*. **2** a miser, niggardly person *16-17, la19*.
vti become mean or niggardly; cheat, stint *la16-20, only Sc*.
~edly &c 1 = wretchedly *la14-*. **2** in a miserly or niggardly way *e16, only Sc*.
~edness &c 1 = wretchedness *la14-*. **2** miserliness, niggardliness *la15-e16, only Sc*.

wrath &c *18-*; **wreth** *la14-15, 19-, now Sh,* **wraith** &c *la15-19* [(w)rɛθ; *NE* vraθ; *wreθ] *n* = wrath *la14-*.
vt = wrath, make (a person) angry *la15*.

wrath *see* WRAITH[1], WRAITH[2]

wraucht *see* WARK[1]

wraw *vi* wail like a cat, mew *la17*. [eModEng; MDu *wrauwen,* imit]

wrax *see* RAX

wray[1] &c *la16-e19,* **wry; wre** *la14,* **wrey** &c *la16, e19* [(w)raɪ; *wri] *vti* **1** = wry, wriggle, turn away *la14-17*. **2** twist or distort (the face); make a wry face, grimace *16-e19*.
adj = wry *la16-*.
on *or* **upon wry** awry, crookedly *la14-e16*.

wray[2] &c *16*; **wre** *15* [*wre, *wri] *vt* = wray, reveal, disclose.

wre *see* WRAY[1], WRAY[2]

wreak *see* WRACK[1]

wreat(en) *see* WRITE

wreath &c; **wreth** *15,* **wride** *19-e20,* **vraith** &c *la19-20, NE* [*n* (w)riθ; *NE* also vreθ, vrəiθ; *wrəid; *nEC* *(w)red; *v* rið, riθ; *(w)reð] *n* **1** = wreath *la14-*. **2** a bank or drift of snow, *prob orig* an accumulation of swirls of snow *18-, Gen except Sh Ork.*
v **1** *vt* = wreathe *la16-*. **2** *only fig* tie (a yoke) round the neck of a draught-ox *la17-e19*. **3** *vti, of snow* accumulate into drifts; cover or bury *la18-, now SW, only Sc.*

wreche *see* WRATCH

wrecht *see* WRICHT

wreck *see* WRACK[1]

wreckling *see* RICKLING

wregling *see* RIGLEN

wreicht *see* WRICHT

wreik *see* WRACK[1]

wreist *see* WREST[1]

wreit *see* WRITE

wreitten *see* WRITE

wrele *vi* struggle, writhe *e16*. [only *Sc;* perh imit]

wrenk *la15;* **wrink** &c *la15-e16* *n* = wrench, a cunning action, trick, *freq used with* **wile.**

wrest[1]; **wreist** &c *16-e18,* **wriest** *la17,* **wrist** *la16-e20* (w)rist, (w)rɪst; *Sh Ork* (w)rest] *vti* **1** = wrest *la16-*. **2** *vt* sprain or wrench (a muscle or joint) *la16-, now Sh, chf Sc.*
n **1** = wrest, a twist, wrench *e16*. **2** a sprain, a wrenching or spraining of the muscles *17-, now Sh, only Sc.*

wrest[2] *n* = REEST[3] *la18-, now local C.* [var of REEST[3] w infl f prec]

wrestle *see* WARSLE

wret *see* WRITE

wretch *see* WRATCH

wreth *see* WRAITH[2], WRATH, WREATH

wrett *see* WRAT, WRITE

wrettin *see* WRITE

wrey *see* WRAY[1]

wrible *see* WARBLE[1]

wricht &c, **wright** *la16-19;* **wrecht** *15,*

wreicht *16,* **vricht** *la19-20, NE* [(w)rɪxt; *S* (w)rəi(x)t] *n* **1** = wright, a craftsman *la14-*. **2** a woodwright, a carpenter *la14-*.
vi follow the occupation of a wright, work as a carpenter or joiner *la19-, NE Ags.*
~-work &c carpentry, joinery *la16-18*.

wride *see* WREATH

wriest *see* WREST[1]

wright *see* WRICHT

wring &c *16-;* **wrink-** *16,* **vring** *la19-e20* *vt,* *pt also* **wrang** &c *la18-e20* = wring.

wringe *n* = wrench, a trick *e17, only Sc.*

wrink *see* WRENK

wrink- *see* WRING

wrinkle *see* WRUNKLE

wrist &c [rɪst; *(w)rist] *n* = wrist.
wristikin *19,* **~ie** *la20, Sh* a woollen muff for the wrist. **~y** a throw in the game of *knifie* (KNIFE) in which the wrist had to be touched before the throw was made *la20, Ags Loth.*

wrist *see* WREST[1]

writ &c; **wirt** *15,* **wryte** *15* *n* **1** = writ *la14-*. **2** writing, handwriting; a piece of writing, anything written *la14-20*. **3** a formal or legal document or writing, a deed (used *more gen* than in Eng where it is now *usu* restricted to written orders of a court) *la16-*.
in ~ in writing *la14-17*. [*cf* next]

write &c *la15-;* **writ** &c *la14-e18,* **wreit** &c *la16-17, la19,* **wreat** *16-e20,* **wrait** &c *la16-17,* **wret(t)** *la16-19,* **vreet** &c *la19-e20, Bnf Abd* [(w)rəit; *Sh nEC* also (w)ret, *NE* also vrit; *wrɪt, *wrɛt] *v,* *pt also* **wrait** &c now local *NE-Rox,* **wart** *e15,* **wrat** &c *la14-15, la19-e20,* **wreit** &c *16-17,* **wrett** &c *16-19,* **writ** &c *16-e20,* **wreat** *17-e18* [(w)ret, (w)rɪt; *NE Per* (v)rat; *wrɛt, *wart]. *ptp* **wrettin** &c *la14-17,* **wreitten** *la16-17,* **wraitten** *e17,* **wreat** *17,* **wreaten** *la17,* **vrutten** *la19-e20, NE* ['(w)rɪt(ən), '(w)rotən; *Sh* ret; *NE* 'vrʌtən; *'wɪrtən, *'writ(ən), *'wrɛt(ən), &c] *vtir* = write *la14-*.
n **1** = write, sacred writings *la14-16*. **2** handwriting, *esp* in ink; the art or style of writing, penmanship *17-, now NE, only Sc.* **3** writing, as opposed to speech, 'black and white' *la15-*. **4** a written record or document of any transaction, *esp* of a legal or formal nature *la15-e20*.
writer &c, *also* **writer chiel** *etc* **1** = writer *16-*. **2** a lawyer, notary, solicitor, attorney *16-e20, only Sc.* **writer to the Signet** (**W.S.**) a member of a society of solicitors in Edinburgh, *orig* the clerks by whom SIGNET WRITS (see SIGNET and WRIT) were prepared, *latterly* having the exclusive privilege of signing all SIGNET WRITS and drawing up crown WRITS, charters etc *la15-*. **writing** &c **1** = writing *16-*. **2** the occupation of a *writer 2, la16-17.* **writing buith** &c *la16-e17,* **writing chamber(s)** &c *17-e19* a lawyer's office.
~ book a (school) writing- or exercise-book *18-, now Ork.*

in ~ in writing, in 'black and white' *16-e19*. [*cf* prec]

writhe &c *vti* **1** = writhe *la14-*. **2** *vt, literary* twist about, turn or wrench round, wring *16-19*. **3** surround, wreathe *e16*.
n = writhe *e16*.

wrocht *see* WARK[1]

wrockin, wrok *see* WRACK[1]

wroke &c *n* active ill-will; spite, malice *la15-e16*. [only Sc; MLowGer *wrok, wruk* enmity, hatred, spite]

wrong *see* WRANG[1]

wrought *see* WARK[1]

wrow *see* WIRL

wrunkle &c *la19-*, **wrinkle &c** *n* (*16-*), *v* (*la19-*) = wrinkle.
    wrunklie crumpled *la20-, Ork NE, C.* [*cf* RUNKLE]

wry *see* WRAY[1]

wryke *see* WRACK[1]

wryte *see* WRIT

W.S. *see* WRITER

wub *see* WAB

wud *see* WILL[1], WUID[1], WUID[2]

wudd *see* WUID[1], WUID[2]

wuddie *see* WIDDIE

wude *see* WUID[2]

wudger *see* WAGER

wudna *see* WILL[1]

wuffle *see* WAFFLE

wuger *see* WAGER

wuid[1] &c *la18-*, **wood** *17-*; **woud &c** *la14*, **wode &c** *la14-17*, **widd &c** *la15-*, *now NE*, **wud(d)** *la18-e20* [wɪd; *Cai Abd C, S also* wʌd; *wød] n **1** = wood *la14-*. **2** an inferior type of small coal *la17-e19*.
vti = wood.
    ~**en breeks** *19-*, *now Per Ayr*, ~**en jeckit** *20-*, *now Ags Ayr*, ~**en overcoat** *la20-*, *WC* a coffin. **wooding** a planting of trees; the trees themselves; a copse or wood *la18-e20*.
~ **forester &c** a forester, a person in charge of the woods on an estate *18-19, only Sc.* ~ **fre** entitled to take wood without payment *la16*. ~**-ill** a disease of cattle *la18-e19*. ~**laid** floored with wood *20-, Cai Abd Loth*. ~**-lark** the tree-pipit *la18-e20*. ~ **leave &c** permission given to the tenants of an estate to cut growing timber *16-18*. ~ **man 1** = woodman. **2** an inhabitant of the woods, a wild man, savage *e15*. ~**-pecker 1** the tree-creeper *la19-e20*. **2** = woodpecker. ~ **rise** *verse* a small branch *la15*.

wuid[2] &c *16-*, **wood &c** *la14-e20*; **wode &c** *la14-e20*, **widd &c** *la16-e20*, **wud(d)** *la18-*, **wude** *19-e20* [wʌd, wɪd, wød] *adj* **1** (1) *of persons* mad, insane, demented *la14-*, *Gen except Sh Ork*. (2) *of animals* rabid, mad *16-e20*. **2** fierce, violent, wild *la15-e20*. **3** (1) furiously angry, beside oneself with rage *la16-*, *now local*

NE-Dmf. (2) *of wind, water etc* furious, raging *la15-e19*. **4** ~ **for, o** *or* **to** eager, desperately keen to *19-*, *now Stlg*.
adv crazily, in a daft or demented way; *freq as intensifier* absolutely, 'clean' *16-19*: '*the bodie's gane wood crazy*'.
in a ~**en dream** with a sudden frantic motion or effort, like fury *la18-e20*. ~**ness &c** *also fig* mad rage, a paroxysm affecting the brain *la14-e19*.
~**drim &c** ['~rɪm, '~rəm] *now literary* a dazed state, a great mental confusion as in waking from a dream; a brainstorm *19-e20*.
aince ~ **and aye (the) waur** getting madder and madder: daft once, daft always *18-e20*. **red** ~ stark, raving mad *la18-e19*. **rin** ~ go clean off one's head, behave wildly and recklessly *la18-e20*. [ME *wo(o)de*, OE *wōd* mad]

wuish, wuishen *see* WASH

wuive *see* WEAVE

wuld *see* WILD

wulk &c *la19-*; **wilk &c** *now Ork Cai*, **wylk** *20-*, *Sh* [wʌlk, wɪlk; *Sh* wəilk] *n* **1** = whelk, the BUCKIE[1] *16-*. **2** the periwinkle mollusc and shell *18-*. **3** *joc* the nose, *esp* **pick one's** ~ *la20-, Ags Fif Dnbt*.
as fou as a ~ very drunk *la19-, local NE-Ayr*. [OED *whelk*]

wull *see* WILD, WILL[1], WILL[2], WILL[3]

Wull, Wullie *see* WILLIE

wullint *see* WILL[1]

wull-tam *see* WALTAM

wulsome *see* WILL[3]

wumble *see* WUMMLE

wumman *see* WOMAN

wummle &c *la18-*, **wimble** *la17-e20*; **womill &c** *18-e20*, **wumble** *la18-19* ['wʌml, 'wɪml] *n* **1** an auger, gimlet *la17-*, *now Sh-Per Slk*. **2** a drill for boring through soil and rock for coal, water etc *18-19*.
~**-bore 1** an auger-hole *18-*, *now NE Per Fif*. **2** a cleft palate *19-*, *now nEC*.
heat a ~ a game with a young child held on the knee *19-e20*. [obs or dial in Eng]

wummle *see* WAMMLE

wumple *see* WIMPLE

wun *see* WIN[1], WIN[2], WIND[1], WIND[2]

wund *see* WIND[1], WIND[2]

wundae, wunda-swalla, wundow, wundy *see* WINDOW

wunna *see* WILL[1]

wunner *la19-*, **wonder &c**; **winder &c** *16-*, *now Sh Cai, only Sc*, **wonner &c** *la18-e20*, **winner** *la19-*, *NE* ['wʌnər; *Sh-Fif chf* 'wɪn(d)ər; *Fif also* 'wun(d)ər] *n* **1** = wonder *la14-*. **2** contemptuous term for a nasty, unpleasant or insignificant person *la18-*, *now N*.
vi = wonder *la16-*.
adv, literary wondrously, surprisingly *la14-19*.
~**ing** an object of wonder, a marvel *e16*. ~**some** wonderfully, remarkably *20-, WC, SW*.

I *etc* **widna** ~ **but what** I etc shouldn't be surprised if *20-*, *Sh Ork NE, WC*.

wunnle *see* WINDLE

wunt *see* WANT, WONT

wuntle *see* WINTLE

wup[1] **&c** *la19-*, **woup &c** *16-20*; **wop** *16*, **wip(p) &c** *16-20* [wʌp; *Sh also* wup; *Ork NE Ags also* wɪp] *v* **1** *vt* bind together by wrapping string, tape etc round and round a joint, splice, whip *16-*, *now Sh-nEC*. **2** wind (a cord etc) round an object tightly *la19-*, *now Ork N*. **3** tie, join by tying, lash *19-*, *now Ork*. **4** coil, become entangled or involved *20-*, *now Ork NE Ags*.
n **1** (1) a bandage *e16*. (2) a splice, a tying or binding with coils of string etc *19-*, *now NE*. **2** a ring; a finger ring without stones; an ear-ring *16-20*.
wuppit &c tied round and round *la16-*. [only Sc; see SND]

wup[2] *n* = whip, a driver of horses *e20, Abd*.

wuppen *see* OPEN

wur *see* BE, OUR

wurble &c *la18-e20*, **worble** *la16*; **warble** *17-19* ['wʌrbl; *'warbl, *'wrabl] *vi* move forward in a twisting, sinuous way, wriggle, crawl. [prob cognate w Du *wervelen* turn round, Ger *wirbeln* whirl, twist, spin]

wure *see* WEAR

wurf &c [(w)ʌrf] *n* a puny, ill-grown person, *esp* a child *19-e20*. [see SND]

wurk *see* WARK[1]

wurl *see* WIRL

wurn *vi, literary* be peevish and querulous, be constantly complaining *19-e20*. [perh onomat, based on YIRN[2]]

wurn *see* WEAR

wurp *see* ORP

wurpie *see* ORPIE

wurr *see* WIRR

wursom &c *18-*, *now Sh Ork Cai*, **worsum &c** *16-17*; **wirsum &c** *la16, e20* ['wʌrsʌm, 'wɪr-] *n* pus, the discharge from a festering sore. [ME *worsum*, OE *worsm*]

wus *see* BE

wush *see* WISS[1]

wusp *see* WISP

wuss &c [wʌs, wɪs] *n* juice, the liquid obtained from boiling or squeezing vegetable substances *19-*, *now Sh*. [ME *wus, wose* juice, sap, OE *wōs* moisture, exuded liquid; *cf* WEEZE]

wuss *see* WISS[1]

wut *see* WIT

wutch *see* WITCH

wutten *see* WEET[1]

wutter *see* WITTER[2], WITTER[3]

wuven *see* WEAVE

wuzzened *see* WIZEN

wy *see* WYE

wycht *see* WECHT[1]

wye; wy *n* **1** a fighting man, warrior, soldier *la15-e16*. **2** (1) a man of good strong character; a man, a person *in gen*, *la15-16*. (2) applied to God *la16*. **3** *transf* a woman, a lady *la16*. [ME; OE *wiga*]

wye *see* WEY[1], WEY[2]

wygh *see* WI

wyght *see* WYTE

wyke *see* WAIK

wylcome *see* WALCOME

wyle &c *19-20, sEC, SW, S*; **waile** *e16* *n, also* **wylie** *19-e20, sEC, SW, S* an instrument for twisting ropes from straw, a *thrawcruik* (THRAW). [reduced f *wavel* (WAVE), f the twisting motion of the instrument]

wylie *see* WILE[1], WYLE

wyliecoat &c; **wyle cot &c** *la15-16*, **weilycott &c** *17-e18*, **wallicoat &c** *17-19* ['wəɪlɪ'kot; *'walɪ-; *NE also *-'kwəɪt] *n* **1** a long under-waistcoat or short undercoat with sleeves, *usu* of flannel, worn by men for extra warmth *la15-*, *now Loth Bwk*. **2** *latterly literary* a woman's under-petticoat *16-e20*. **3** a kind of frock worn by children as an outer or under garment *la16-e20*. **4** a woman's sleeved nightdress *17-18*. [the origin of the first element is obscure]

wylk *see* WULK

wynd[1] **&c** *la13-*, *now chf in street names*; **wyne &c** *la16, la19-20* [wəɪn(d)] *n* a narrow, *freq* winding street, lane etc leading off a main thoroughfare in a town *la13-*.
~-head &c the top end of a WYND *16-18*. [ultimately f as WIND[2]; *cf* OE *gewind* a winding ascent and next]

wynd[2] **&c** *18-*, *now SW*; **wyne &c** *18-19* [wəɪn(d)] *vti* (command (draught-animals) to) turn to the left *19*.
interj a call to a yoked animal to turn to the left *19-*, *now SW*.
~er &c the leading ox on the right-hand side, which took the first steps to the left on the command to WYND *la18-19*. **~in &c** *freq in pl* **1** a long, awkwardly-shaped or steep piece of land, *orig* ploughed in only one direction by the plough turning left after each furrow *18-20*. **2** a group of RIGS[1] in a field which is divided into an upper and lower *wyndin* for convenience of ploughing *la18-*, *NE Loth*. [ultimately f as WIND[2]; *cf* prec]

wynd[3] **&c** [wəɪn(d)] **frae end to** ~ from end to end, completely *19-20, WC Uls*. [prob altered f *from eyn to eyn* from end to end; poss associated w WIND[2] or WYND[2]]

wyne *see* WEAN, WYND[1], WYND[2]

wynscott *see* WAINSCOT

wynt &c *19-*; **wind** *la18-e19* [wəɪnt, wɛnt, wɪn(d)] *vti, chf* **~ed &c** *of food or drink* allowed to spoil, soured, *orig* by exposure to the air *la16-*, *local*. [f WIND[1]; see SND]

wynt *see* WEND

wyrin *see* WIRE

wyson *see* WIZZEN

wyss *see* WISE
wystcoat *see* WESKIT
wyste *see* WASTE
wyte &c *la15-*, **wite &c** *15-20*; **wyt &c**
la14-e19, **weit &c** *e16*, **wyght &c** *la16, e20*,
quhyt *la16* [wəit] *vt, pt also* **wytt** *la14* [*wəit].
ptp also **wate** *17* [*wet] **1** blame, impute blame
or guilt to (a person or thing), accuse a (person) of responsibility for something *la14-, now
local.* **2** ~ **someone for, o** *or* **wi** blame someone for (something), accuse someone of (something) *16-e20*.

n **1** blame, reproach, responsibility for some
error or mischief *15-.* **2** the person or thing to
blame, the source of blame *16-e19, only Sc.* **3**
one's *etc* ~ one's fault, one's being to blame
19-.
~**less** blameless, innocent *la16-e18.*
to ~ to blame, at fault *la15-, now NE.* [ME
wite blame, offence, OE *wīte* penalty, *wītan* (*v*)
blame]
wyte *see* WAIT¹
wytt *see* WYTE
wyve *see* WEAVE

Y

ya *see* AE, YEA

yaag &c [jɑg] *vi, n* gossip, chatter *la19-, NE.*
[aphetic f *lyaag* (LAIG)]

yaave [jɑv] *n* one of the spokes or paddles on the
fanner of a winnowing machine or on the vane
of a corn-reaper or -binder *20, NE.* [var of
AWE[1]]

yaavin *see* YAWIN

yabb &c *vi* harp on a subject, talk incessantly
19-, now Sh-Ags.

yabble &c, yabber *la19-, now EC vi* **1** talk volubly or excitedly, chatter, gossip *la19-.* **2**
scold, be querulous *19-, chf Loth.* **3** *of animals,
birds* chatter, bark etc excitedly *la19-, now Ork
Abd Ags.*

n **1** a noisy clamour of voices *19-, NE-WC.* **2** a
garrulous person, a chatterbox *la19-, now Abd
Ags.* [only Sc; orig prob chf onomat; *cf* YAP[1]]

yable *see* ABLE

yachis &c ['jaxɪz, -ɪs, 'jex-] *n* the noise produced
by a dull blow or fall, a thump, thud, grunt
19-20, NE. [prob onomat; *cf* HAICHES]

yacht *see* AUCHT[3]

yack &c *n, occas contemptuous* an Eskimo *la19-, now
local Sh-Ags.*

~ie &c = *n, la19-20.* [appar orig a whalers'
word, perh f Du *Jak* Jack, a man, or imit of
Eskimo speech]

yad(e) *see* YAUD[1]

yae *see* AE

yaes *see* YE

yaff; yauff &c *19-e20 vi* **1** bark, yelp *19-, local
EC-Rox.* **2** chatter, talk pertly *19-, now Lnk.*
3 chide, scold, criticize *19-e20.*

n a chatterbox, a pert person; *contemptuous* a
peevish insignificant person *la19-, now local
Loth-S.* [onomat; also nEng dial; *cf* NYAFF,
YOWF]

yafu *see* AWFU

yagiment &c ['jagɪmənt] *n* a state of excitement, a flurry, agitation *19-20, Abd.* [only Sc;
altered f Eng *argument*]

yaik *see* YAWK

yain &c *interj* a call to a horse in harness to turn
left *20-, Stlg Lnk Ayr.* [? altered f VANE[2]]

yair &c; zair &c *la17-e19* [jer] *n* a fish-trap
across a river or bay in the form of an enclosure
or barrier of stone, wood or *formerly* of wicker,
and often also with a net *la14-, now Gall; cf*
CRUIVE *n* 1. [ScL *ihara* (*la12-e13*), nME *yare*,
OE *-gear* in *mylengear* an enclosure on a
millstream]

yaird[1] &c *la15-,* **yard &c; yeard &c** *la16-18,
only Sc* [jerd] *n* **1** = yard *la14-.* **2** a garden,
now *esp* a cottage- or kitchen-garden *15-.* **3**
also **yird** *la19-e20, only Sc* [by confusion w YIRD]
a churchyard *18-, now Ork NE, C.* **4** *chf in pl,
only Sc* a school playground, *specif* at the original
site of the High School, Edinburgh *la18-,* and
at the Edinburgh Academy *19-.*

~ dyke a garden wall *la16-, now Ork N, C.* **~
end** *e16,* **~ fit** *19-, now Loth Wgt* the foot of a
garden.

yaird[2] *18-;* **yeard** *la19-e20* [jerd; *sEC, S* jɪrd] *n*
= yard, the measure. [the SCOTS yard was
slightly longer than the Imperial yard]

yairn &c *18-, now Ork Cai C, S;* **yarn** *19-,*
yearn *18* [jern; *nEC, WC* jɛrn, *Bwk Rox* jɪrn] *n*
= yarn *18-.*

yarlins *la18-e20, NE,* **~ winnles &c** *19* a
yarn-reel for winding yarn into skeins.

yaise *see* USE

yak *n, orig and chf gipsy* the eye *20-, Rox.* [San-
skrit *akçi*]

yak *see* YAWK

yake *see* LAIK

yaldie, yaldrin *see* YOLDRIN

yall &c *20-;* **yawl &c** *la17-19* [jɑl] *vti* yell,
scream, howl *la17-, now Sh N.*

n a shout, cry, howl *19-, now N.* [ME ʒaule (v)
yell, var of YOWL; *cf* LowGer *jaulen* (v) howl,
Norw dial *jala* (v)]

yall *see* YEA, YOLE

yalla, yallochie, yallock, yallow *see* YELLA

yalmer *see* YAMMER

yalp *see* YELP

yam *n* **1** = yam. **2** a coarse variety of potato
la18-19.

yammer *16-;* **ʒamer &c** *la15-16, only Sc,*
yaumer &c *16-e20,* **yamour** *la18-e19, only
Sc,* **yalmer &c** *la16-e17, only Sc* ['jamər;
*'jɑmər] *vi* **1** howl, lament, cry out in distress;
whine, whimper; grumble, complain *la15-.* **2**
make a loud noise, raise a din; talk volubly or
incoherently; harp on, keep insisting *16-.* **3** *of
a bird or animal* utter repeated cries, chatter
la19-, now Per, only Sc.

n **1** lamentation, wailing, whining, a cry, whimper *16-, now only Sh.* **2** a great outcry, clamour, incessant talk *16-, now Ork, NE-S.* [ME
yamer (v), MDu, MLowGer *jammer(en)*]

yamp *see* YAUP

yamph &c *vi* bark, yap, yelp *18-19.*

n a dog's bark *19-e20.* [var of YAFF]

yane *see* ANE[1]

yank[1] *v* **1** *vt* (1) pull vigorously with a sharp sudden movement, jerk, twitch *la18-.* (2) *lit and
fig* drive or force on energetically *19-e20.* **2** *vi*
move quickly and vigorously *19-, now Stlg Ayr
Wgt.*

n **1** a sudden jerk or pull *20-.* **2** a sudden
severe blow, *esp* with the hand *la18-19.*

~er a smart agile person *19-e20.* [perh
onomat]

yank[2] *n, chf in pl* NICKIE-TAMS *la19-e20, Ags Kcdn.*
[ModEng dial *yanks* gaiters, leggings]

yap[1] &c *20-;* **yaup &c** *la18-e20 vi* **1** = yap,
bark. **2** cry shrilly, scream; whimper; chirp
plaintively *la18-, now Sh Cai, only Sc.* **3** chatter,
nag, speak querulously, harp on *la19-e20.* **4**

applied esp to English speakers or to Scots who ape them speak in an affected way la19-, local Abd-S, only Sc.
n **1** = yap, a bark *20-*. **2** a yelping dog *la20-*, *N-WC*. **3** the call of a bird in distress; the plaintive chirping of chickens *19-*, *Wgt, only Sc*. **4** incessant talking, *usu* implying nagging *19-*, *only Sc*. **5** a chatterbox; a windbag *la20-*, *only Sc*.

yap² *n, child's word* an apple *la19-*, *Edb*. [orig Heriot's Hospital slang; see SND]

yap(e) *see* YAUP

yard *see* YAIRD¹

yare &c *adj* **1** ready, prepared *la14, 19-e20 (literary)*. **2** eager, agile *19-e20*.
adv **1** quickly, promptly *la14-16, 19*. **2** = yare, well, thoroughly *la15-e16*. [ME; OE *gearu*]

yark *see* YERK

yarlin *see* YOLDRIN

yarlins, yarn *see* YAIRN

yarp &c *vi* grumble *19-*, *now Sh*. [orig chf onomat; *cf* YIRP]

yarr¹ &c *n* corn-spurrey *la18-*, *N, C*. [obscure]

yarr² &c *vi* snarl or growl as or like a dog *la17-18*. [ME; onomat]

yat *la19-, Sh*, **yet &c** *la14-19 v* **1** *vt* pour *la14-17*. **2** shed (tears, light) *e16*. **3** pour forth, cause to flow in a flood *e16, la19- (Sh), only Sc*. **4** *vi* gush *e16, la19- (Sh)*. **5** *vt* found, cast (metal) *15-e16, e20 (Sh)*. **6** set or fix (*eg* iron in stone) by means of molten lead *la16-e19*.

yetlin &c, yetling &c *n* **1** an article made of cast-iron: (1) a small cannon *la16, only Sc*; (2) a (three-legged) pot or kettle *la14-20*. **2** cast-iron *la18-, now Sh. adj* made of cast-iron *16-19*. [ME *ȝet &c*, OE *gēotan* pour]

yate *see* YETT

yatt &c [jat] *n* = yacht *20-*, *WC*.

yatter &c *v* **1** *vi* nag, harp on querulously, scold *19-*, *local*. **2** chatter, ramble on, talk interminably *19-*. **3** *vti, of a person speaking incoherently or in a foreign language* gabble; *of an animal* yelp *19-*. **4** *vi, of teeth* rattle, chatter, *eg* from fear *20-*, *now Ags*.
n **1** (continual) scolding, grumbling *19-*, *now Ork Ags*. **2** continuous chatter, rambling and persistent talk *19-*. **3** the confused noise of many people talking loudly all together, clamour, unintelligible speech *19-*, *local Sh-Per*. **4** an incessant talker; a gossip *19-*.
~**in**, ~**y** fretful, querulous, scolding *19-*, *now Sh*. [only Sc; onomat; *cf* Eng *chatter*, NATTER, Norw dial *jaddre* jabber]

yaucht *see* AUCHT³

yaud¹ &c; yad &c *16-e20*, **yade &c** *16-19* [jɑd; *jald; *?jed] *n* **1** an old mare or horse, *esp* a worn-out horse *16-*, *now S*. **2** a whore *e16*. **3** *contemptuous* a woman, *freq* a slovenly or dissolute one *la18-19*. **4** *of yarn* a thread that has not gone properly round the reel but is left hanging between the spokes *e19, only Sc*.

adj, of a horse worn-out *e16, only Sc*. [ME *ȝald* a whore, ON *jalda* a mare; also some infl f the etymologically unconnected Eng *jade* (*cf* JAUD)]

yaud² *interj far* ~ a call to a sheep-dog to drive sheep at a distance *e19, S*. [perh var of YONT]

yauff *see* YAFF

yauld &c; yaul &c *adj* active, alert, vigorous, healthy *la18-, now Bwk, WC-S*. [unknown]

yaumer *see* YAMMER

yaup &c *19-, only Sc*, **yap &c** *18-*; **yape &c** *la14-e19 adj* **1** clever, cunning; shrewd; active *la14-19*. **2** eager, ready *la15-19, only Sc*. **3** also **yamp** *e20, Abd* having a keen appetite, hungry *la18-, now Lnk, only Sc*.
vi gape with hunger, be hungry *18-20, only Sc*.
n a fool, oaf, yokel *la19-, Ags Fif S, only Sc* [poss a different word].
~**ish** = *adj* 3, *la18-, now Renfr Lnk, only Sc*. [nME *ȝape* eager, active, OE *gēap* var of *gēap* wide open, crafty > ME *yepe* cunning, alert]

yaup *see* YAP¹

yaval *see* AWALD¹, AWALD²

yavin *see* YAWIN

yaw &c *vi* mew, caterwaul; squeal *19*. [only Sc; onomat]

yaw *see* AWE²

yawin &c; ya(a)vin &c *20-, N*, **yewn &c** *19-*, *now Ross n, usu in pl* = awns, the beard or bristle of barley or oats.

yawk &c *19-*; **ya(i)k &c** *16, e19* [jɑk; *EC, S *jek] *vi* = ache *16-, now nEC, WC*.
~**in** perplexed; very eager *19-e20*. [OED *ache*]

yawl *see* YALL

yawn &c *n* a long sea-inlet or gully *20-, freq in place-names on Kcdn coast*. [only Sc; extension of Eng *yawn* a chasm]

yconquest [*ɪ'kɒnkwɛst] *adj* acquired *e16, only Sc*.

yd(d)ir &c [*'θɪdər] *adv* = thither *la14, only Sc*. [OED *thither*]

yden *see* EIDENT

ydir *see* YDDIR

ye &c, you &c [*sing and pl*: nominative, accusative and dative ji; *unstressed* jɪ; *accusative and dative also* ju, *S* jʌu; *emphatic and vocative* ju, *S* jʌu] *pronoun, pl also* **ye(e)z, yiz, yaes, youz(e) &c** *20-, C, only Sc* [jiz, jɪz, juz] **1** = ye, you *la14-*; in dials where THOU &c survives, **ye** and **you** are used deferentially *eg* by an inferior to a superior in rank. **2** *with imperative* with friendly or deferential force *la18-, only Sc*: 'haste ye back'. [see also E and *cf* THOU]

yea &c *la15-*, **ya &c** *la19-, now Sh Ork*, **ȝa &c** *la14-16*, **ȝe** *la15-16*, **ȝey** *la14*, **ȝie** *16* [je; *Sh Ork* jɑ; *ji] adv* **1** *answering a question etc* yes, indeed *la14-, now Sh Ork Ags*. **2** *expressing surprise, disbelief, vague assent or opposition* really, indeed *la15-, now NE*: 'Yea, d'ye think sae, Tammas?'. **3** *chf* ~ ~ *used derisively expressing contempt, 20-, now Abd Ags*. **4** *used before a repeated verb* again, over and over *la19-, NE, only Sc*: 'he tried and yea tried'.

yall &c *17-19, only Sc*, **yeltie &c** *la18-e20, only*

Sc [*jal, *jel, *'jaltə, *'jɛltɪ, *-tu, &c] = you would, would you; be careful; that's enough, now [contracted f *yea wilt thou* or *will ye*]. [ME *ye*, nME *ya* &c, OE *gēa, geā*; the Mod *ya* is prob f Norw or Du *ja*]

yeal *see* ALE

yealin(g)s *see* EILD

yean *vti, of a ewe* give birth to (a lamb) *la18-19*. [ME *eanen*, OE *eānian*; *cf* EENIE, INGY]

year &c, **'ear** *la19-* *n* **1** = year *la14-*. **2** *uninflected in pl after numerals etc, la14-*: '*fifty year*'.
~**aul(d)** &c ['(j)irɑl(d), -ɑlt, '(j)irl(d), '(j)irlt] *n* a yearling *19-*. *adj* year-old *la19-*. ~**tak** a year's lease *e16, Gsw, only Sc*.
monie a year and day for a very long time *la19-, NE Ags*. **up in** ~**s** on in years, elderly *19-, local Bnf-Kcb*. ~ **of God** a particular year of the Christian era, denoted by a number following *la15-16, only Sc*.

yeard *see* YAIRD[1], YAIRD[2], YIRD

yearn; yirn *vti* = earn (wages etc) *la19-e20, only Sc*.

yearn *see* YAIRN, YIRN[1], YIRN[2]

yearth *see* YIRD

yed *n, verse* strife, wrangling; struggle *18-19*. [eME *ʒedde*, OE *gyd* a song, poem, riddle]

yee *see* AE

yeel *see* YELD, YULE

yeese *see* USE

yeez *see* YE

yeild *see* EILD

yeird *see* YIRD

yeit *see* YET

yeld &c *15-*, **eild** &c *18-*; **yield** &c *16-*, now *Sh*, **yeel** &c *la17-19*, **yell** *18-*, now *Uls*, **yule** &c *19*, **eel** &c *19-e20* [jɛl(d), jil(d))] *adj* **1** *of animals* barren, not bearing young because of age or accident *la15-*, now *local Sh-C*. **2** *of birds* without a mate *16-19, only Sc*. **3** *of cows etc* not yielding milk because of age or being in calf *la17-*. **4** *of things* sterile, unproductive, unprofitable *15-e20*.
n, only **yeld** &c a barren cow, ewe etc *la19-*, now *Ork*. [ME; OE *gelde* barren; *cf* GELD]

yeldrick, yeldrin *see* YOLDRIN

yell *see* ALE, YELD

yella *20-*, **yellow** *la18-*; **yallow** &c *la14-20*, **yalla** *la19-*, now *Sh NE, WC, S*, **yelly** *e20* ['jɛlə, -ɪ, 'jalə, -ɪ] *adj* = yellow *la14-*.
yallochie ['jaləxɪ] yellowish, slightly yellow *la19-, Abd Ags, only Sc*. **yallock** &c the yellowhammer *la19-*, now *Mry, only Sc*.
~ **fin** the young of the sea-trout *19-*, now *Abd Dmf, only Sc*. ~ **fish** smoked (*now also* dyed *la20-*) fish, *esp* haddock *la19-*, now *local Ork-Dmf, only Sc*. ~ **gowan** the common buttercup *e19*.
~ **haddie**, ~ **haddock** = ~ *fish, la19-, NE, EC, only Sc*; *cf Finnan haddock* (FINNAN). ~ **lintie** the yellowhammer *20-, Abd Ags Ayr*.
~**-neb lintie** the twite *la19-*, now *Wgt, only Sc*.
~ **plover** the golden plover *la19-*, now *Mry Ags*

Fif, only Sc. ~ **wagtail** the grey wagtail *la19-*, now *Per, only Sc*. ~ **yite** *see* YITE. ~ **yoldrin** *see* YOLDRIN.
the religion *etc* **of the yellow stick** enforced Presbyterianism on the island of Rhum *18-e19* [see SND].

yelloch &c ['jɛləx] *vi* scream, shriek, yell *la18-19*. *n* a yell, shriek, scream *16-19*. [only *Sc*; Eng *yell* + *-och*]

yellow, yelly *see* YELLA

yellyhoo [*'jɛlɪ'hu] *v, only* ~**ing** shouting and screaming, yelling *19, local WC, SW*. [only *Sc*; poss an invention of Galt f Eng *yell* or YELLOCH + HOO[2]]

yelp &c; **yalp** *la19-*, now *Ork* [jɛlp; *Ork Ags* jalp] *n* a sharp shrill bark *16-*.
vi = yelp *16-*.

yeltie *see* YEA

yer *see* YOUR

yerb &c; **yirb** *19-e20* *n* = herb *la18-*, now *Ags Dmf*.

yerd *see* YIRD

yere *see* YOUR

yerk &c *17-*; **yark** *18-, Sh Ork N*, **yirk** *la19-20* *v* **1** *vt* bind tightly, tie firmly together (*eg* shoeleather in shoemaking or a woman's bodice lacing) *19-*, now *local Sh-Kcb*. **2** (1) *vti, lit and fig* beat, whip, strike; break by striking; hammer *18-*, now *local Sh-SW*. (2) *vi* crack down (**on**), make a sharp sound by striking etc *la18-, chf Abd*. (3) nag, find fault *19-*, now *Sh* [in *Sh* prob altered f *yarg* talk incessantly, carp]. (4) throb, ache, tingle *19-, local NE-Dmf*. **3** move suddenly: (1) *vt* snatch, tug, wrench, pull *19-*, now *local Sh-Per*; (2) throw, toss, pitch; jerk, slam *19-*, now *Sh Mry*; (3) *vi* move jerkily *la19-*, now *Sh Ork*. **4** (1) *vt* drive hard, put pressure on, stir to activity *la18-*, now *local Sh-midLoth*. (2) *vi* go **at** (a task), set **to**, exert oneself, press **on** *la19-*, now *Sh NE*. (3) *vt, freq* ~ **aff, out** or **up** rattle off (a speech *etc*), strike up (a tune), perform in a smart or lively way *18-e20*.
n **1** (1) a blow, a hard knock, a slap *17-*, now *Sh NE Ags*. (2) the sound of a blow or collision *la19-*, now *NE Ags*. **2** a jerk, tug, twitch *19-*. **3** a throb of pain; an ache *la20-, Abd Ags, only Sc*.
~**er** anything very large of its kind *19-*, now *Abd Lnk*. ~**in** **1** the side seam in a boot or shoe *19-*, now *Sh*. **2** a beating, a blow *19-e20, Bwk Rox*.
come (a) ~ **against** *etc* come against, collide with *la19-*, now *Sh NE*. **hae a** ~ **at** make a vigorous attempt at, have a go at *20-, Sh NE*. [eModEng]

yerl *see* EARL

Yerlston fever *ironic* a fit of laziness, a lazy mood *la20-, Bwk S*. [the people of Earlston, Bwk being thought lazy by their neighbours]

yerm *see* YIRM

yern-blit(t)er *see* EARN-BLEATER

yerp *see* YIRP

yertland *n* = yardland, a measure of land *la15*, *only Sc*. [OED *yardland*]

yesk &c *18-*, **yex** *la17*, **esk &c** *17-*, *N*; **yisk &c** *16-19*, **isk** *20-*, *Cai* [(j)ɛsk, (j)ısk; *jɛks] *vti* **1** hiccup, belch, vomit *16-19*. **2** *vi, only* **isk** sob *20-*, *Cai*.

n a hiccup, belch *17-20*. [ME *yexen* (*v*) belch, OE *giscian, geocsian* (*v*) sob, *gesca* a belch]

yestreen &c *16-*; **yistrene &c** *la14-16*, **the streen &c** *la16-*, *now Ork N*, **estreen &c** *19-*, *now Abd* [jɛ'strin; jı-, ðı-, ðə-] *adv* yesterday evening; last night; *latterly* yesterday *la14-*.

n yesterday evening *la18-*. [reduced f obs or dial Eng *yestereven*]

yet &c; yit &c, yeit &c *la14-19* [jɛt, jıt; *jit] *adv* (*conj*) **1** = yet *la14-*. **2** up to now, now as before, at the present time, still *la14-*. **3** *exclam* as a cheer or rallying cry hurrah **for** ..!, .. for ever! *la18-19, only Sc*: 'Haddington yet!'

yet *see* YAT

yether &c *n* **1** a long rod or withy *e19*. **2** a severe blow with *eg* a cane or the hand *19-e20*, *SW, S*. **3** the mark left by such a blow or by tight binding with cord etc, a weal, bruise *la19-e20, SW, S*.

vt **1** tie very firmly, *esp* so as to leave a pressure mark on what has been bound *19, SW, S*. **2** beat or lash severely, bruise with a cane *19, S*. [extension of *ether* (EDDER)]

yetlin(g) *see* YAT

yett &c; yate &c *la14-e20* [jɛt, jıt, jet] *n* **1** = gate *la14-*. **2** *archaeol* a kind of door made of interlacing iron bars *la19-*. **3** a natural pass between hills *19-*, *chf in place-names*: 'Yetts o Muckart'.

~ cheek &c the side-post of a gate *16-17*.

as daft as a ~ in a windy day scatter-brained, flighty, crazy *la19-, C*.

yett *see* AIT

yeuk &c *la18-*, **yuke &c** *18-*; **ʒuke &c** *15-16*, **youk &c** *18-*, **yuck &c** *19-*, **yock &c** *la19-*, *Abd*, **euk &c** *19-e20* [*Sh Ork nEC, WC* jʌk; *Cai-Bnf* hjuk; *NE Fif* juk; *sEC, SW, S* juk; *jøk] *v* **1** *vi*, of a part of the body itch, feel ticklish or itchy; *fig* be keen or eager; have a strong urge (to do something) *15-*. **2** *vti* scratch (a part of one-self) *la20-, Sh Ork NE*.

n **1** *also* **heuk** *20-, Cai Mry* itching, the itch; an itchiness *la16-*. **2** something disgusting or revolting, something of very poor quality *la20-, C*.

~ie &c 1 *also* **heukie &c** *la19-, Cai Bnf*, *of a part of the body* itching, itchy *18-*. **2** (1) excitedly eager, impatiently waiting to do something *18-*, *now local Sh-Stlg*; (2) sexually excited *la20-, NE Per Ayr*. **3** *derog* (1) *in gen* mean, shabby, rough, filthy *20-, local Fif-S*; (2) *of work* rough and careless, badly finished *20-, now Fif Ayr*.

(gar someone) claw *or* **scart where it's no ~ie** *19-* or **where he** *etc or* **it disna ~** *18-19*

freq in threats (make someone) smart or regret what he etc has done. **his** *etc* **neck is ~in** he etc is heading for the gallows *18-e20*.

yeul(l) *see* YULE

yewn *see* YAWIN

yex *see* YESK

yez *see* YE

yferis [*'ı'firz] *adv* = yfere, together *e16, only Sc*. [OED *yfere*]

yibble *see* ABLE

yibbles *see* ABLES

yickie-yawkie &c *n*, *shoemaking* a wooden tool used to polish the soles of shoes *19, SW*. [ono-mat f the sound made by the tool scraping across the leather]

yield &c *16-*; **ʒelde &c** *la14-e17*, **ʒald &c** *la14-e16* [jild; *jald] *vti, pt also* **ʒeild &c** *la16-e17*, **ʒald &c** *la14-16* [*jild, *jald]. *ptp also* **ʒoldin &c** *la14-16*, **ʒowdin** *e16*, **yowden &c** *18-* ['jʌudən; *'joldən] = yield *la14-*.

n **1** = yield *15-*. **2** payment for loss or injury, compensation *la15*.

ʒoldin *e16*, **yowden &c** *18-e20* soft, limp; tired out.

yield *see* YELD

yiff-yaff *n* **1** a small, insignificant, chattery per-son *19-, local Fif-S*. **2** chatter *20-*, *now Loth Stlg*.

yik *see* AIK

yill *see* ALE

yim¹ &c *n* a very small particle (**of** something) *19-e20, chf SW, S*. [prob aphetic f *nyim* (NIMP) by wrong division of *a nyim*]

yim² &c *n* a thin film or coating on a surface, a scum, a layer of dust, condensed vapour etc *la19-20, Bnf Abd*.

vti cover or become covered with a YIM² *la19-20, Bnf Abd*. [see SND]

yin *see* ANE¹, YON

yince, yinst *see* AINCE

ying *see* YOUNG

yip *n*, *esp of a child* a cheeky, pert person, an imp *20-, chf Rox*. [prob altered f Eng *ape*]

yirb *see* YERB

yird &c, yeard &c *la16-18, only Sc*; **yerd &c** *la14-19*, **yeird** *16*, **yearth &c** *19*, **yirth** *la18-* [jırd, jërd; *sEC, S* jırθ, jërθ; *jɛrd, *jɛrθ] *n* **1** = earth *la14-*. **2** *specif* the grave *19*. **3** *ploughing* the depth of a furrow; the angle at which the plough-sock is set to achieve this *18-*. **4** a heap of large boulders forming a den or small cave *19-, Gall*.

vt **1** = ERD *v*, *16-*, *now Sh Abd*. **2** press or cause to sink into the ground *19-*, *now Sh Ork*. **3** bring violently to the ground; strike with force *19-, NE*. **4** drive (a hunted animal) to earth *e19*.

~en earthen; of the world *19*. **~ie** (**bee**) a miner bee *19-*, *now Pbls WC*. **~ie tam** a mound of earth and weeds, a compost heap *18-*, *NE*. **~it 1** buried *la16-*. **2** bogged down *20-*, *Sh Abd*.

~ din thunder *19-*, *now NE*; cf *erd-dyn* (ERD).
~ drift drifting snow *19-*, *now NE*. **~ fast** *adj* = *erd fast* (ERD) *la16-*, *now NE Rox*. *n* a stone firmly embedded in the earth *19-*, *now Mry Bnf*. **~ hunger** a strong desire to possess land *18-19*. **~ meel &c** grave-mould, the dust of the churchyard *18-e19*, *Abd*. **~ pig**, **~ swine** = *erd hun* (ERD) *la19-*, *NE*. **yerd-silver** payment for burial ground *e16*. **~ taid &c** the common toad *19*.
~ the cogie *children's game* a rhythmic chant and quick stamping (to warm the feet) *la20-*, *Abd*. [Sc and Eng dial var of ERD]

yird *see* YAIRD[1]

yirk *see* YERK

yirl *see* EARL

yirlin *see* YOLDRIN

yirm; yerm &c *vi* **1** *of an animal* whine, wail; *of a person* complain, whine, harp on *19-*, *now S*. **2** *of a bird or insect* chirp, cry, sing *19-e20*. [ME *yarme* howl, OE *ȝyrman* lament]

yirn[1] &c, earn &c *18-*; **yearn &c** *la18-e20* [jɪrn, jern; *nEC* ern] *vti* (cause to) coagulate or curdle; *of milk* form curds with rennet and heat *16-*, *now Sh-N*.
~ed milk curds; junket *19-*, *local*. **~in &c 1** the act of *~ing*, *19-*. **2** rennet *la16-*, *now local Sh-Lnk*. **3** the stomach of an unweaned calf etc used in making rennet *la18-*, *now Sh-Cai*. **4** the human stomach *la19-*, *now Kcdn*. **~in bag** = *~in* 3, *la18-e20*. [ME *ernen, eornen*, metath f OE *rinnan* run and *rennan* cause to run)]

yirn[2]; yearn &c *19-e20* [jɪrn; *Rox* jern; *WC, SW* jʌrn] *vi*, *of a dog* whine; whimper; *of a person* wail, whine, complain *19-*, *now Wgt*.
n a complaint, whine *la19-*, *now Wgt*. [conflation of YIRM w GIRN[1]]

yirn *see* EARN, YEARN

yirp; yerp *vi* **1** *of a very young bird* chirp *la19-e20*. **2** *of persons* harp on something, wrangle, make a fuss or complaint *la19-*, *local Sh-Lnk*. [onomat, after Eng *chirp*, YAP[1] etc]

yirr &c *vi* **1** *of or as a dog* snarl, growl *19-*, *now Sh*. **2** make an outcry, keep complaining *19-*, *now Sh*.
n the snarl or growl of a dog *la19-*, *now Sh*. [prob onomat; *cf* ME *yerr*, OE *ȝyrran* growl]

yirran(t) *see* EERANT

yirth *see* YIRD

yis *see* USE

yisk *see* YESK

yiss *see* ACE, USE

yistrene *see* YESTREEN

yit *see* AIT, YET

yite[1]; yowt &c *la19-e20*, *local*, **yoit** *la19-*, *local* [jəit; *SW Uls* joit; *local Ross-Stlg WC also* joit; *nEC Dmf Uls also* jaut] **1** the yellowhammer, *freq* **yella ~** *19-*, *Gen except Sh Ork*. **2** a small person; contemptuous term for a person *la19-*, *local Per-Wgt*. [imit of the bird's call]

yite[2] *vi* play truant *20-*, *Ags Per Fif*. [perh verbal usage of prec, = be absent hunting YITES[1]]

yite[3] *interj* **~ hub**, **~ hup**, **~ wo** calls to a horse in harness *la19*. [unknown]

yitter *vi*, *of a person or bird* chatter *20-*, *local Stlg-Rox*. [onomat]

yivver *see* AIVER[2]

yiz *see* YE

ymangis [*ˈɪ'manȝ] *prep* = ymong, among *la15*. [only Sc; *cf amangis* (AMANG)]

yo *adv*, *a strong affirmative contradicting another's 'no'*: but yes *la20-*, *Sh-Per*; *cf* F *si*, Norw, Dan *jo*. [alteration of YEA after Eng *no*; *cf* SOT[2]]

yoam *see* OAM

yochel &c [ˈjoxl] *n* = yokel *la19-*, *now Ags Per*.

yock *see* YEUK, YOKE

yod *interj*, *as an oath* = God *19-20*, *Abd*. [euphemistic alteration]

yoit *see* YITE[1]

yoke &c *16-*; **ȝolk** *16*, *only Sc*, **yock &c** *la14-20*, *latterly chf Sh* [jok] *n* **1** (1) = yoke *la14-*. (2) the harness of a plough, cart etc; *specif* the main swingle-tree of a plough *20-*, *now Cai Abd*. **2** a horse and cart, horse and carriage etc, attached in full harness *20-*, *now Ags Per*. **3** (1) = *yokin* 3, *la18-20*. (2) = *yokin* 4, *19-e20*.
vti, *ptp also* **ȝakkit** *la14*, *only Sc*, **yolk** *16*, *only Sc* **1** = yoke *la14-*. **2** *vt* attach (a plough or cart) *la16-18*. **3** *vti* (1) link, join, unite *16-*, *now Sh*. (2) *specif* in marriage, *la16-*, *now local Ork-Ayr*. **4** (1) *vi*, *freq* **~ tae** *etc* start on some activity, set to, go about something (vigorously) *la16-*, *only Sc*. (2) *vt* start up (an activity) *la18-19*. (3) set (a person) to do something, start (a person) to work *19-*, *now Abd Ags Per*; *cf* LOWSE *v* 3. **5** *vi* deal **with**, have to do **with** (a person or persons) *la18-e20*. **6** (1) join battle **with**; start a dispute or quarrel **with** *16-19*, *only Sc*. (2) **~ on, to &c** set on (a person), attack with words or blows *19-*, *only Sc*. **7** *vt* burden, oppress *la18-19*.
yokin &c 1 = yoking (horses etc). **2** the starting of a spell of work, *freq* **yokin time** *la19-*. **3** (1) the period during which a team of horses or oxen is in harness at one stretch, *usu* half a day's work *16-20*. (2) *in gen* a spell of work, a stint, shift *19-*, *local N-S*. **4** a spell, bout of some leisure activity, a stretch *18-*, *local N-S*. **5** (1) a fight, contest, scuffle *la16-*, *now NE*. (2) a rough handling, a severe dressing down *19-*, *now NE*. **6** a measure of land, *prob orig* the amount ploughed in one *yoking* 3 (1), *la17-e18*. **yokit &c tuillie &c** [ˈjokɪt ˈtøli, ˈjokəˈtøli] a string of squatting skaters, each pulled along by clinging to the one in front *19-*, *Rox*. **ill-yokit** ill-matched in marriage *la18-*, *now NE*.
a-~, **in(to) the ~** in(to) harness *la19*, *NE*.

yoldrin &c *19-e20*, **yorlin &c** *la18-*, *now local N-Uls*; **yaldrin &c** *19*, **yeldrin** *e19*, **yirlin &c** *la19-*, *local*, **yarlin &c** *la19-20* [ˈjorlɪn; *Ork N nEC Uls* ˈjarlɪn; *NE sEC Lnk* ˈjɪrlɪn; *Abd also* 'jɛrlɪn; *C Uls also* 'jɛldrɪn; *WC Uls also* 'jaldrɪn; *Uls also* 'joldrɪn; *Rox also* *'jʌudrɪn] *n* the yellowhammer, *freq* **yella~** *la18-*.

yeldrick &c *19* [*'jɛldrɪk], **yaldie &c** *la19-*, *NE* ['jaldɪ] = *n*. [var of eModEng and ModEng dial *yowlring &c*, f *youlow* yellow + *ring*]

yole &c *18-*; **yoll &c, yowl &c** *18-e20*, **yall** *la17* [jol, jʌul] *n* a kind of small, undecked, two-masted fishing boat *la16-*, *now Sh-N*. [*cf* Eng *yawl*. OED *yawl*]

yolk &c; yowk &c *18-e20* [jok; *Bwk S* jʌuk] *n* **1** = yolk. **2** *fig* the best part *17-19*. **3** a hard nodule in a softer rock etc *18-e19*. **4** a kind of soft, free, good-burning coal *la18-e20*. **5** an opaque part of window glass *19-e20*.

yolk *see* YOKE

yoll *see* YOLE

yoller *vi* speak loudly, excitedly, angrily or incoherently, shout, bawl *19-*, *now Dmf*. [frequentative of ME *yoll* cry, howl]

yomf *see* YOWFF

yon &c; yin *e20*, *Ork Cai*, **yun** *20*, *Sh* adj, *pronoun* that (one), those over there, *usu (except Sh)* indicating a person or thing further away than THAT etc *la14-*.
adv **1** over there, YONDER *la15-*, *now Sh N*. **2** to that place over there *e20*, *C* [perh reduced f YONT].
ȝongat [*'jon'get] in that way *la14*. **~ kind** *euphemistic* used to describe persons or things in a poor state or persons who are uncomfortably embarrassed *20-*, *Sh N*. [ME *ȝone &c*, OE *geon*; *cf* THON]

yond *see* YONT

yonder &c; yonner &c *19-* ['jon(d)ər; *Sh* 'jʌndər] *adv* in that place, over there, indicating a person or thing at some distance *la14-*.
adj that (over there), distant, far *la15-*, *now Ags*.
~-abouts in that district, there or thereabouts *19-*, *now Sh Per*. **~ awa** *19-*, **yondru &c** *20-*, *Sh Ork* ['jondər ə'wɑ; *Sh Ork* 'jʌndru, 'jʌndrə] over there, in that place. **~maist &c** farthest, most distant *16-*, *now NE*.
far frae a' ~, nae (near) a' ~ half-witted, not all there *la19-*, *NE*. [ME *ȝonder; cf* THONDER]

yont &c *16-*, **yond &c** *la14-19 adv* **1** farther away or along, onwards, beyond, aside, apart *16-*, *now Abd EC Dmf*. **2** yonder, over there, on or to the other side *19-*, *now EC WC*.
prep **1** beyond, on or to the other side of *18-*, *now C, S*. **2** along, further along, onwards through or over *la18-*, *now Ags*.
adj far, distant *la14-19*.
~most &c farthest, most distant *17-e20*.
~ by over YONDER, across *19*, *Ags*. [ME *ȝond &c*; OE *geond (prep)*]

yopindaill &c *e16-*, **yowpindail &c** *la16* [*'jopɪn'del, *'jʌup-] *n* a 16th century silver coin of varying value from 15 to 20 shillings SCOTS. [*see* OED *yokindale*]

york *n*, *in pl* NICKIE-TAMS *la20-*, *local C*. [prob YANK[2] conflated w YERK *v*]

yorlin *see* YOLDRIN

you *see* YE

youch &c [jʌux] *vi*, *of a dog* bark *la19-e20*, *Kcb Uls*. [only Sc; onomat; *cf* YOWF]

youdith *see* YOUTH

youk *see* YEUK

young &c; ying &c *la14-17 adj* **1** = young *la14-*. **2** *in titles* prefixed to the name of a *Highland* (HIELAND) *chieftain* (CHIFTANE) or his estate to indicate his eldest son and heir *18-*.
~er &c 1 = younger *la16-*. **2** used after a person's name to distinguish him from an older person of the same name, *freq* title for the heir-apparent of a person with a territorial designation as part of his surname or with the style of a Scottish CHIEF, *esp* **A, younger of B,** *or (and now officially preferred)* **A of B (the) younger** *la14-*: '*Malcolm MacGregor of MacGregor, younger*'; *cf* MAISTER[1].
~ communicant a person intending to become a communicant member of a Presbyterian Church, who *usu* attends an instruction class *18-*. **~ folk** a newly-married couple, irrespective of age *19-*, *now local Ork-Ayr*. **~ laird &c** the heir-apparent of a landowner below peerage rank *la15-*. **~ man 1** = young man *15-*. **2** the eldest son and heir *17-18*. **3** the best man at a wedding *19-*, *Ork NE*. **4** an unmarried man *18-*, *now Ork*.

younker &c ['jʌŋkər] *n* **1** = younker, a young nobleman *e16*. **2** a youngster, a young lad or girl, a youth *16-*, *now N, EC Ayr*. **3** a young bird, a nestling *20-*, *now local Cai-Lnk*.
younk = *n* 3, *20-*, *now Per*.

youp &c [jup, jʌup] *n* a scream; a howling, wailing, as of a dog *la18-e20*, *Ork NE*. [onomat]

your &c; eer *20-*, *now S; chf unstressed* **yer &c** *19-*, **yere &c** *la18-e20* [jur, jir; *Mry S* ir; *unstressed* jɪr] *possessive adj* = your *la14-*.
~sel(l) &c, ersel *la19-*, *Loth Rox* **1** = yourself. **2** *referring to more than one person* yourselves *la16-18*. **3** *emphatic, esp representing Highl speech* you: '*och, it's yoursell*'.

youth &c *n* = youth *la14-*.
~heid &c, youdith &c *18-e20*, *chf literary* [*'juθhid, *'juɪt, *'judɪθ] **1** youth, the state or time of youth *la14-*, *now literary*. **2** young people *la16-e19*. **~ie &c** young, youthful, *esp* looking younger than one is *la18-*, *now Ork*.

youz(e) *see* YE

yove *vi, n* talk in a rambling way, rambling talk *e19*. [*see* SND]

yowden *see* YIELD

yowdendrift &c *19-*, **ewin-drift &c** *17-18* ['jʌudən'drɪft; *'jʌuən-] *n*, *chf literary* snow driven by the wind. [*see* SND]

yowder &c *19-e20*; **yowther** *19-e20*, **ewder &c** *18-e19*, **euther &c** *la18-e19* [*'jʌudər,

*'jʌuðər, *ʔ'judər, *ʔ'juðər] *n* **1** a very unpleasant smell of fumes from burning *18-e20*. **2** steam, smoke, vapour *e19*. **3** the fluff or dust of flax *19-e20*. [perh var of Eng *odour*]

yowe &c, ewe &c *18-* [jʌu] *n* **1** = ewe *la15-*. **2** a stupid, weak-willed person *la19*, *NE*. **3** *freq* **yowie** a fir cone *la19-*, *NE Ags*.
~ **bucht &c** a pen for ewes at milking- or weaning-time *18-*, *now Per*. **ewe gowan** the common daisy *19*. ~ **hog &c** a female HOG *la20-*. ~ **lammie** a little ewe lamb *la19-*. ~ **milk** ewe's milk *16-19*. ~(s) **trummle &c** a cold spell in early summer, about the time of sheep-shearing *20-*, *now nEC*, *S*.

yower *see* URE[1]

yowf &c [jʌuf] *vi*, *of a dog* bark *la17-*, *Sh*, *N-S*.
n a bark, barking sound *19-*, *Sh*, *N-S*. [onomat; cf YAFF and YOUCH]

yowff &c [jʌuf; *Sh N* juf] *n*, *also* **yomf &c** *19*, *SW* a sharp blow, a swipe, thump *19-*, *now Bnf Abd*.
vt knock, strike, swipe *18-e20*. [onomat]

yowk *see* YOLK

yowl &c *la16-*; **ʒoule &c** *la14-16* [jʌul; *Rox also* jul] *vi*, *of dogs or other animals* bark, howl, yell; *of persons* bawl, wail; complain, whine *la14-*.
n a howl, whine, mournful cry of a dog or other animal; a yell, wail, shriek of a person *la15-*. [ME *ʒoule &c*]

yowl *see* YOLE

yowpindail *see* YOPINDAILL

yowt &c; ʒewt *la16* [jʌut; *Rox also* jut] *vi*, *of persons or animals* cry, roar, shout, howl, hoot *la15-*, *now Per Stlg Rox*.
n a shout, roar, yell, cry *la16-*, *now Per Stlg Rox*. [see SND]

yowt *see* YITE[1]

yowther *see* YOWDER

ypir [*ʔipər, *ʔəipər] *n*, *appar* cloth from Ypres *e16*. [only Sc; Flem *Yper* the town in Flanders]

yplet *see* PLET

yrle [*ɪrl] *n* a dwarfish person *e16*. [only Sc; *cf* WIRLING, WIRL, YURLIN]

ythen *see* EIDENT

yuchle &c ['jʌxl] *n* a gob of sputum *la20-*, *wLoth Dnbt Renfr*. [onomat]

yuck &c *n* a stone, pebble *20-*, *EC*, *WC*, *S*. [orig schoolboy slang; perh reduced f *dyuck* (DEUK) as in *play ducks and drakes*]

yuck *see* YEUK

yuffie &c *n* **1** a W.C., *esp* one on a TENEMENT stair *20-*, *local EC*, *S*. **2** a dry closet *20-*, *midLoth*. [*cf* DUFFIE]

yuil *see* YULE

yuill *see* ALE, YULE

yuise *see* USE

yuke *see* YEUK

Yule &c, eel &c *la18-e20*, *N*; **ʒoil(1) &c** *la14-e16*, **yuil(1) &c** *la15-e18*, **yeul(1) &c** *17-19*, **yeel &c** *la18-*, *N* [jøl, jɪl; *NE* (j)il] *n* **1** Christmas; the day itself; the festive season associated with it, *freq* beginning before Christmas day and (*esp Sh*) continuing until after New Year *16-*, *now chf literary*. **2** the entertainment provided at Christmas, Christmas cheer *la19-*, *now Sh*.
vi keep Christmas *17*.
~ **bannock 1** *freq in pl*: oatcakes (AIT) specially baked on Christmas Eve both for one's own family and for children going from door to door *19-20*. **2** a gratuity of oatmeal paid at Christmas by tenants of a *barony* (BARON) to the *baron court* (BARON) officer *18*. ~ **bread &c** a richly-seasoned oat-bread baked for Christmas *19*. ~ **candle** a large long-burning Christmas candle *19*. ~ **day** Christmas day *la14-e20*. ~ **e'en**, ~ **even &c** Christmas eve *la14-e20*, *only Sc*. ~ **feast** a Christmas dinner *18-*, *now Sh*. ~ **girth &c** a time of immunity granted at Christmas *16*. **brak Yeel's gird** disturb the peace of Christmas by weeping on Christmas day, and so incur bad luck for the following year *la19*, *NE*. ~ **mart** an ox slaughtered and salted for Christmas and the winter *19-e20*. ~ **pins** *19-*, *now Sh*, ~ **preens** *19*, *NE* pins used as stakes in a Christmas game. ~ **shard** = ~'s yaud *20-*, *Abd*. ~ **sowans &c** SOWANS specially made for Christmas into which the usual objects of divination of marriage (*eg* a ring, button etc) were stirred before distribution among the company *la18-e20*. ~ **stok** ? a Yule log *la15*. ~ **strae &c** the supply of straw needed on a farm over Christmas and the New Year *la19-e20*, *NE*. ~ **tide &c** *la15-*, ~ **time** *la18-*, *now Sh* the season of YULE. ~ **vacance &c** the Christmas holidays or recess *17-19*. ~'s **yaud &c** *abusive* a person ill-prepared for YULE, *eg* one who leaves work unfinished before Christmas or the New Year, or who has nothing new to wear for the festivities *la15-e20*, *latterly chf N*.
Auld ~ Christmas day (Old Style): **1** 5 Jan *la18*; **2** 6 Jan *19*; **3** 7 Jan *20-*, *Sh NE*.

yule *see* YELD

yun *see* YON

yunk[1] *n*, *marbles* a stake marble *la20-*, *Loth Lnk Ayr*. [see SND]

yunk[2] *vi*, *of a horse* rear and plunge, buck *la20-*, *Fif Loth*. [see SND *v*[1] and *v*[2]]

yurlin &c *n* a puny stunted creature *la19*. [perh aphetic f *nyirlin (*cf nirlie* (NIRL)), but *cf* YRLE, WIRLING]

ʒ *letter* This letter-form was the one most commonly used in Middle Scots MSS and prints to represent the sound [j]. In Early Scots it varied with *y*, *ʒh* and (then the most common form) *yh*. In Middle Scots it predominated over its chief alternative *y*. It was indistinguishable in form from the (much less commonly used) letter-form *z*, used to represent the sound [z]. In MSS and black-letter prints (predominant in *e16*), a 'tailed' form of *ʒ/z* was used, but this gave way to the 'modern' more or less tail-less *z* in *la16* prints in roman and italic types. In *17* the regular use of *ʒ/z* for the sound [j] was given up in favour of the alternative practice of using *y*, which of course agreed with English usage, except for fossilized occurrences in a limited number of words such as CAPERCAILZIE, GABERLUNZIE, *tailzie* (TAILYIE) and the names *Menzies*, *Mackenzie* and (see below) ZETLAND. In many cases the latter spellings gave rise to new spelling-pronunciations with [z] where the 'etymological' pronunciation was with [j], some of these, such as that of *Mackenzie*, being now the only surviving pronunciations.

ʒa *see* YEA

ʒakkit *see* YOKE

ʒald *see* YIELD

ʒamer *see* YAMMER

ʒarne¹ &c [jɛrn, *jarn, *jern] *v* **1** *vi* = yearn *la14-15*. **2** *vt* desire earnestly *la14-16*. [OED *yearn*]

ʒarne² &c; ʒerne *e16* [*jɛrn, *jarn, *jern] *adj, adv* **1** eager(ly), earnest(ly) *la14-e16*. **2** = yern, quick(ly) *la14*. [OED *yern*]

ʒe *see* YEA

ʒeid *see* GAE

ʒeild, ʒelde *see* YIELD

ʒeman &c [*'jiman, *?'jʌman] *n* = yeoman *la14-16*.

~ man = *n*, *specif* in contrast with the nobility *la14-16*, *only Sc.* [OED *yeoman*]

ʒeme &c [*jim] *vt* take care of; have charge of; keep, observe *la14-16*.

ʒemsel &c [*'jɛmsəl, *jɛm'sil, *jim-] keeping, care, charge *la14-e15*. [ME; OE *gīeman* care for, guard, ON *geyma* heed, *geymsla* guardianship. OED *yeme, yemsel*]

ʒerne *see* ʒARNE²

ʒewt *see* YOWT

ʒey *see* YEA

ʒhus *adv* = yes *la14*. [OED *yes*]

ʒie *see* YEA

ʒoil(1) *see* YULE

ʒoldin *see* YIELD

ʒolk *see* YOKE

ʒongat *see* YON

ʒong frow &c [*'jʌŋfrʌu] *n*, *nautical* ? a dead-eye *la15-e17*. [see OED *yuffrouw*]

ʒoule *see* YOWL

ʒowdin *see* YIELD

ʒude *see* GAE

ʒuke *see* YEUK

Z

z *see* US

zair *see* YAIR

zeendi &c ['zɪndɪ, 'zendɪ, 'zɪntɪ, &c] *numeral, sheep-counting and children's rhymes* one *e20.* [usu ascribed to Welsh infl in SW Scotland; *cf* Welsh *un* [in] one, and EENDY, TEENTY, TETHERY, MUNDHERI, TICKERIE, BAOMBE, HECTURI, LECTURI, SEATER, OVER, DAOVER, DEK]

zeill &c [zil] *n* = zeal *16.*

    gude ~ good intent, kindly disposition *16, chf Sc.* [OED *zeal*]

Zetland &c *16-* ['zɛtland; *'jɛtland; *see etymology*] = Shetland, used as the official name of the county until 1975, and as a peerage title. [ON *Hjaltland*, which developed (1) into *Sj-* &c in some Norw dials (> SHETLAND) and *Sh-* &c in Sc and Eng (*lal3*-); (2) into *I-* or *Ih-* [j] in other Norw dials (*el3*), written in Sc as *Yh-* or *3-* [j], the latter having the same form in Sc MSS and prints as *Z-* (see **3** *letter*). The spelling-pronunciation [zɛt-] in place of the etymological [jɛt-] was established among the gentry and the professional classes by *e19,* and still survives alongside [ʃɛt-] (SHETLAND)]

zickety the first word in a children's counting-out rhyme, *poss* = one *19, Edb.* [*cf* ZEENDI]

zulu *n, also* **Z**~ name for a type of fishing-boat common *esp* in the Moray and Clyde Firths *c* 1880-1905, some of which were later fitted with engines. [named after the *Zulu War*]

SCOTTISH CURRENCY, WEIGHTS AND MEASURES

MONEY

The Scots currency was roughly equivalent in value to that of England till the later 14th century, when it began to depreciate by stages till at the time of the Act of Union in 1707, by the terms of which the Scots currency was abolished, the following values obtained:

SCOTS	STERLING	DECIMAL
1 PENNY	$\frac{1}{12}$ penny	—
2 pennies = 1 BODLE	$\frac{1}{6}$ penny	—
2 bodles = 1 PLACK	$\frac{1}{3}$ penny	—
3 bodles = 1 BAWBEE	1 halfpenny	—
2 bawbees = 1 SHILLING	1 penny	·42 penny
13 shillings 4 pence = 1 MERK	1s. 1$\frac{1}{2}$d.	5$\frac{1}{2}$ pence
20 shillings = 1 pound	1s. 8d.	8 pence

1826 Galt *The Last of the Lairds* ii: For on that day [Union of 1707] the pound stirling came in among our natural coin, and, like Moses' rod, swallow't up at ae gawpe, plack, bodle, mark, and bawbie.

WEIGHTS AND MEASURES

There was much confusion and diversity in early Scottish weights and measures and a succession of enactments from the 15th century failed to improve matters till in 1661 a commission was set up by Parliament which recommended the setting up of national standards, the exemplars of which were to be kept in the custody of certain burghs, the *ell* for lineal measure to be kept by Edinburgh, the *jug* for liquid capacity by Stirling, the *firlot* for dry measure by Linlithgow, and the *troy stone* for weight by Lanark. These recommendations in the main prevailed throughout Scotland, though there was some irregularity between commodities in dry measure; a further recommendation that *tron* weight should be entirely abolished was ignored and this measure fluctuated within fairly wide limits as between 22 and 28 ounces per pound. By Act 5 Geo. IV. c.74, 1824 uniformity of weights and measures was statutorily established and gradually this was conformed to although the names of the older measures like FIRLOT, FORPET, LIPPIE were transferred to fractions of the Imperial hundred-weight and are still sometimes heard.

WEIGHTS

1. According to the standard of LANARK, for TROY weight:

SCOTS	AVOIRDUPOIS	METRIC WEIGHT
1 drop (see DRAP)	1·093 drams	1·921 grammes
16 drops = 1 ounce	1 oz. 1·5 drams	31 grammes
16 ounces = 1 pound	1 lb. 1 oz. 8 dr.	496 grammes
16 pounds = 1 stone	17 lbs. 8 oz.	7·936 kilogrammes

2. According to the standard of Edinburgh for TRON weight:

SCOTS	AVOIRDUPOIS	METRIC WEIGHT
1 drop	1·378 drams	2·4404 grammes
16 drops = 1 ounce	1 oz. 6 drams	39·04 grammes
16 ounces = 1 pound	1 lb. 6 oz. 1 dram	624·74 grammes
16 pounds = 1 stone	1 stone 8 lbs. 1 oz.	9·996 kilogrammes

CAPACITY

Liquid measure according to the standard of Stirling. See JOUG.

SCOTS	IMPERIAL	METRIC
1 gill	·749 gill	·053 litres
4 gills = 1 MUTCHKIN	2·996 gills	·212 litres
2 mutchkins = 1 CHOPIN	1 pint 1·992 gills	·848 litres
2 chopins = 1 PINT	2 pints 3·984 gills	1·696 litres
8 pints = 1 gallon	3 gallons ·25 gills	13·638 litres
1 pint = 104·2034 Imp. cub. ins.	1 pint = 34·659 Imp. cub. ins.	1 litre = 61·027 cub. ins.

1731 *Two Students* (Dickinson 1952) lxvi: Each Bursar hath for breakfast the thrid part of a Scon & a mutckine of ale.

Dry measure according to the standard of LINLITHGOW.

1. For wheat, peas, beans, meal, etc.

1 LIPPIE (or FORPET)	·499 gallons	2·268 litres
4 lippies = 1 PECK	1·996 gallons	9·072 litres
4 pecks = 1 FIRLOT	3 pecks 1·986 gallons	36·286 litres
4 firlots = 1 BOLL	3 bushels 3 pecks 1·944 galls.	145·145 litres
16 bolls = 1 CHALDER	7 quarters 7 bushels 3 pecks 1·07 galls	2322·324 litres
1 firlot = 2214·322 cub. ins.	1 gallon = 277·274 cub. ins.	1 litre = 61·027 cub. ins.

1887 P. McNeill *Blawearie* 161: It's no jist so easy now ... to run off wi' a sheep or a firlot o' tatties.

2. For barley, oats, malt.

1 lippie (or forpet)	·728 gallons	3·037 litres
4 lippies = 1 peck	1 peck ·912 gallons	13·229 litres
4 pecks = 1 firlot	1 bushel 1 peck 1·650 gallons	52·916 litres
4 firlots = 1 boll	5 bushels 3 pecks ·600 gallons	211·664 litres
16 bolls = 1 chalder	11 quarters 5 bushels 1·615 gallons	3386·624 litres
1 firlot = 3230·305 cub. ins.		

1894 P. H. Hunter *James Inwick* 171: A faur-seein chiel, wha kent hoo mony lippies gae to the peck.

LINEAR AND SQUARE MEASURES

According to the standard ELL of Edinburgh.

Linear

1 inch	1·0016 inches	2·54 centimetres
8·88 inches = 1 SCOTS link	8·8942 inches	22·55 centimetres
12 inches = 1 foot	12·0192 inches	30·5287 centimetres
$3\frac{1}{12}$ feet = 1 ELL	37·0598 inches ($1\frac{1}{37}$ yards)	94·1318 centimetres
6 ells = 1 fall (FA)	6·1766 yards (1·123 poles)	5·6479 metres
4 falls = 1 chain	24·7064 yards (1·123 chains)	22·5916 metres
10 chains = 1 furlong	247·064 yards (1·123 furlongs)	225·916 metres
8 furlongs = 1 mile	1976·522 yards (1·123 miles)	1·8073 kilometres

Square

1 sq. inch	1·0256 sq. inch	6·4516 sq. centimetre
1 sq. ell	1·059 sq. yards	·8853 sq. metre
36 sq. ells = 1 sq. fall	38·125 sq. yards	31·87 sq. metres
	(1 pole 7·9 sq. yards)	
40 falls = 1 sq. rood	1525 sq. yards	12·7483 ares
	(1 rood 10 poles 13 sq. yards)	
4 roods = 1 sq. acre	6100 sq. yards (1·26 acres)	·5099 hectare

1845 *Second Statistical Account* I. 196: The extent of the glebe is 10 acres, 3 roods, 17 falls, 4 ells, Scotch measure.

YARN MEASURE

1 CUT = 300 yards
1 HEERE = 2 cuts or 600 yards
1 HEID = 2 heeres or 1200 yards
1 HANK or hesp = 3 heids or 3600 yards
1 SPINLE = 4 hanks or 14400 yards

The above applies to linen and handspun woollen yarn in the early 19th century. Earlier the measure was considerably shorter, and varied considerably with the kind of yarn spun.

1748 *Aberdeen Journal* (6 Sept.): 54 Hesps of Thread were stole from the Bleaching at Marnoch Kirk, they consisted some of 3, some 6, some 7, and some of 8 Cuts in the Hesp.

For Coal Measure see METT.

CHURCHES IN SCOTLAND

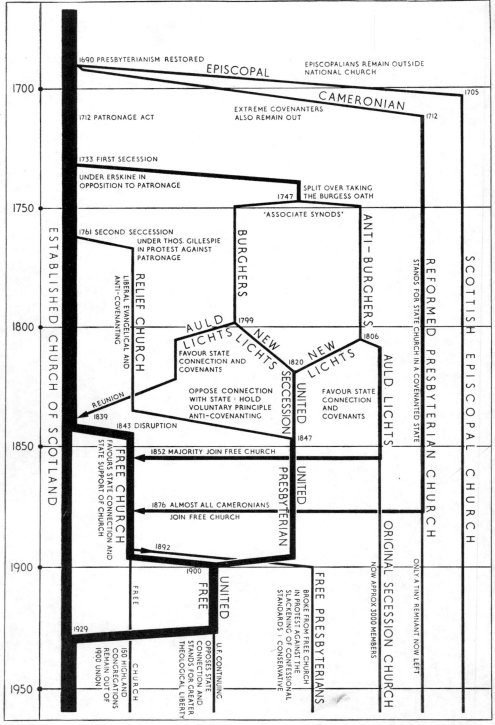

Churches in Scotland (reproduced from J. H. S. Burleigh *A Church History of Scotland*, 1960, by permission of J. K. Burleigh, Mrs Anne Macrae and the Hope Trust)